Peter,

I hope that this is of some
use. Please accept it
with my very best wishes.

Peter

November 2007

Scammell and Densham's Law of Agricultural Holdings

Ninth edition

Peter R Williams BA, FCIArb
Solicitor of the Supreme Court

Michael N Cardwell MA(Oxon)
Professor of Agricultural Law,
School of Law, University of Leeds

Vivienne Williams BA
Solicitor of the Supreme Court

LexisNexis®
Butterworths

Members of the LexisNexis Group worldwide

United Kingdom	LexisNexis Butterworths, a Division of Reed Elsevier (UK) Ltd, Halsbury House, 35 Chancery Lane, London, WC2A 1EL, and RSH, 1–3 Baxter's Place, Leith Walk Edinburgh EH1 3AF
Argentina	LexisNexis Argentina, Buenos Aires
Australia	LexisNexis Butterworths, Chatswood, New South Wales
Austria	LexisNexis Verlag ARD Orac GmbH & Co KG, Vienna
Benelux	LexisNexis Benelux, Amsterdam
Canada	LexisNexis Canada, Markham, Ontario
Chile	LexisNexis Chile Ltda, Santiago
China	LexisNexis China, Beijing and Shanghai
France	LexisNexis SA, Paris
Germany	LexisNexis Deutschland GmbH, Munster
Hong Kong	LexisNexis Hong Kong, Hong Kong
India	LexisNexis India, New Delhi
Italy	Giuffrè Editore, Milan
Japan	LexisNexis Japan, Tokyo
Malaysia	Malayan Law Journal Sdn Bhd, Kuala Lumpur
Mexico	LexisNexis Mexico, Mexico
New Zealand	LexisNexis NZ Ltd, Wellington
Poland	Wydawnictwo Prawnicze LexisNexis Sp, Warsaw
Singapore	LexisNexis Singapore, Singapore
South Africa	LexisNexis Butterworths, Durban
USA	LexisNexis, Dayton, Ohio

© Reed Elsevier (UK) Ltd 2007

Published by LexisNexis Butterworths

A CIP Catalogue record for this book is available from the British Library.

ISBN 13: 978 1 405 717 977

Typeset by Letterpart Ltd, Reigate, Surrey

Printed and bound in Great Britain by William Clowes Ltd, Beccles, Suffolk

Visit LexisNexis Butterworths at www.lexisnexis.co.uk

ISBN 978-1-4057-1797-7

9 781405 717977

Preface

Despite numerous previous writing commitments, including a substantial part of Halsbury's Laws (Agriculture Volume), nothing had prepared me (or my family) for what was involved in taking on the sole editorship of *Scammell and Densham*. Although a contributor to the last two editions, the mantle of sole editor brings with it not only responsibility to maintain the high standards set by my predecessors, Andrew Densham and Della Evans, but an opportunity to bring something new to such a well established textbook.

In particular, the text relating to the Agricultural Holdings Act 1986 has its origins in the complete overhaul which Andrew Densham applied to the 6th edition of the book when he took over editorship in 1978. Looking now at what he did, it was an extraordinary achievement. In the 9th edition, hopefully by way of evolution rather than revolution, I have sought to update the text and expand it into several new areas.

In relation to the section of the book concerning the Agricultural Tenancies Act 1995, my task has been more straightforward. The text first appeared in the last edition of the book, written by Della Evans. Since 1996 there have been some changes, notably the package contained in the Regulatory Reform (Agricultural Tenancies) (England and Wales) Order 2006. However, the extent to which the text has lent itself to development has been less than in the case of that relating to the 1986 Act.

Mr W S Scammell first established *Scammell's Law of Agricultural Holdings* as one of the leading textbooks. In chapter 1, dealing with the historical introduction to the law of agricultural holdings, I make reference to some of Mr Scammell's writing. What is consistent between that and what then followed, under first Andrew Densham and subsequently Andrew and Della Evans, is the sheer enjoyment for the subject. It is self-evident. Andrew brought enthusiasm and fun to the practice of the law of agricultural holdings. In Della he acquired a worthy sparring partner and an outstanding lawyer. Both Andrew and Della are now retired and are sorely missed.

It was entirely appropriate that Mr William Waldegrave, the then Minister at MAFF, when introducing the Agricultural Tenancies Bill for the final reading debate in the House of Commons on 19 April 1995, expressly thanked Andrew Densham and his team for the help given and the advice provided during the passage of the Bill. As two of the amendments introduced in that final reading debate were initiated by that team, the Minister's remarks had substance. Andrew has been awarded a CBE for his contribution to the agriculture industry.

I hope that in the 9th edition I have been true to the cause established by the previous editors. *Scammell and Densham* is first and foremost a practitioner's book. It was suggested to me when I started work on this last year that I should cease to have references to County Court decisions and indeed those of the Agricultural Land Tribunal. I have decided to maintain such references in the 9th edition. That is because, although they are not legal precedent, reference to decisions of the County Court and the ALT help practitioners understand how certain issues have been dealt with in practice, albeit that there is no guarantee that another court or tribunal would treat the issues in the same manner. Reference to such decisions also help in identifying issues which have emerged, where often there is no authority from the High Court or a higher court of appeal.

Nevertheless, I have paid regard to the need to move on. Some practitioners who are familiar with earlier editions of the book will, for example, mourn the passing of the 'Seven Deadly Sins' and their replacement as 'Special Cases'.

Other changes include:

- The historical introduction in chapter 1
- The separation of interests protected under the 1986 Act from those not protected
- The extension of the section on mixed user
- Dealing with the inter-relationship between the 1986 Act and other statutory codes
- Extending the text relating to partnerships
- The extension of the section dealing with repairs
- The introduction of standard leasehold covenants
- A new chapter on distress for the non-payment of rent
- A table of actions relating to different remedies in chapter 27
- A new chapter dealing with notices to quit part, joint interests and sub-tenancies
- Revising the text in relation to notices to quit, in particular the Special Cases
- A new chapter dealing with possession of land for non-agricultural use
- The treatment of tenant right
- A section dealing with compensation for compulsory purchase
- A detailed treatment of service of notices and the computation of time
- A new chapter dealing with remedies
- An overhaul of the dispute resolution chapters
- A new chapter on milk quota
- A new chapter on milk quota arbitrations

- A new chapter on the Mid-term Review of the Common Agricultural Policy.

I have a number of thank yous to people without whom it would not have been possible for me to produce this book.

I start first with Professor Michael Cardwell and Vivienne Williams. Michael was, in the mid-1980s, my articled clerk. We did *Puncknowle Farms Limited v Kane* together. Michael has since pursued an academic career and has become Professor of Law at Leeds University. His book on Milk Quota is an unrivalled publication. Nobody is better at making a difficult subject accessible. Michael has brought his considerable gifts to bear upon the Mid-term Review of the Common Agricultural Policy in chapter 52. He has done so with the same success as he achieved in his book on Milk Quota. I am very grateful to him.

Viv (no relation, as she puts it) is one of my partners. She is the 'rising star' and a worthy successor to the agriculture practice. Viv overhauled all of the dispute resolution chapters (46 to 48) and the connected precedents, which had previously been part of my contribution to the 8th edition of the book. They are vastly improved as a result of Viv's work. Viv has been a great support to me, not only during the writing of the book, but generally over the last eight years.

The next thank you is to Nicola Horrocks, who has worked with me for some eighteen years. Without Nicola's efforts, I simply would never have got anywhere near the publisher's deadline. Nicola not only updated all of the precedents for me, but also collated a huge amount of information to enable me to bring the law up to date since the last edition. Nicola has also updated the case references in the text of the 1995 Act.

Simon Leach has worked with me for some nineteen years. He has recently decided to set up a new practice. He will be greatly missed. Simon assisted me in relation to the book by updating the case references in relation to the text of the 1986 Act.

A number of friends and colleagues have been kind enough to read various parts of the text for me and provide comments. Those who have helped are Nicola Horrocks (the entirety of the text under the 1995 Act), Viv Williams (numerous sections), James Buxton (rent review under the 1986 Act and succession), Della Evans (partnerships and chapters 3 and 9, including writing part of those two chapters), Michael Cardwell (milk quota and chapter 19), Simon Leach (repairs under the 1986 Act), William Neville (chapter 31), Richard Bedford (chapter 45), Ben Sharples (chapter 42), Tony Collins, the Secretary of the ALT in Bristol (chapter 46), Mark Sanders of Carver Knowles, the RICS representative on TRIG and Derek Wood QC of Falcon Chambers (both chapter 9). Patrick Robinson assisted in relation to compulsory purchase. Michael Johnstone provided some input to succession. Ben Sharples helped in collating material for me in connection with the service of notices, preparing the table at paragraph 42.27, and liaising with Michael Cardwell, commenting on the chapter concerning the Mid-term Review of the Common Agricultural Policy. Alastair Morrison provided input in relation to the Land Registration Act 2002. The improvements to the text are theirs. The remaining errors are mine.

I owe a particular debt of gratitude to Falcon Chambers. Derek Wood QC was in part responsible for my decision to practice in this area of law. Derek's fingerprints are also on part of this edition of the book. His advice in relation to retrospectivity and the allied issues of eligibility for succession underpins the chapter on lifetime succession. Likewise, I have borrowed heavily from advice Derek has given to me in the past concerning mortgages of agricultural land.

Others at Falcon Chambers from whom I have learnt over the years, and who I have been lucky enough to count as friends, are David Neuberger, Kim Lewison, Paul Morgan, Jonathan Gaunt, Nick Dowding, Guy Fetherston-haugh, Tim Fancourt, Martin Rodger, Stephen Jourdan and Caroline Shea. Two others deserve special mention. First, Jonathan Brock who, aside from doing some of the most difficult cases which I have had with me, also shared in the disappointment in failing to get *Hoveringham v Scholey* reported very early in our careers. Tragically Jonathan died earlier this year. He has been a special friend. The other is the late Christopher Priday QC: simply one of the best people one could ever work with.

Lastly, the two most important thank yous: secretaries and family. As to secretaries, it is not only the lawyers who have made up my team over the past 27 years.

For almost 26 of those 27 years, Jenny Howell has been my secretary. The fact that she now continues, beyond retirement age, is a testament to her commitment. I would have been lost without her support. In the mid-1980s, as my output developed, Jenny was joined by a second secretary, Sophie Harding, another outstanding secretary. After 17 years Sophie retired, and she was replaced by Toni Mead, who has been a marvellous addition to the team. That team has lastly been supplemented, since I started work on the book, by my department's secretarial coordinator, Paula Marlton. Paula has undertaken the vast majority of the typing necessary for the book. That has allowed Jenny and Toni to continue with the rest of my work. Paula has done an outstanding job. I shall forever be grateful to her and indeed all of the secretaries who have served me so well during my career.

Last, but not least, my wife, Anne, and my three sons, Tom, Harry, and Ed. They are used to a workaholic husband/father, but the extent of my absentee-ism over the course of the last year or so has reached new levels. They have put up with that and been a marvellous support for me. I am lucky and grateful.

I have endeavoured to state the law as at 1 July 2007.

P R Williams

September 2007

viii

Contents

Contents

x

Table of Statutes

Paragraph references printed in **bold** type indicate where the Statute is set out in part or in full.

Table of Statutes

Table of Statutes

Table of Statutes

Table of Statutory Instruments

Paragraph references printed in **bold** type indicate where the Statutory Instrument is set out in part or in full.

Table of European Legislation

Paragraph references printed in **bold** type indicate where the Legislation is set out in part or in full.

Table of Cases

A

PARA

Table of Cases

Table of Cases

PARA

Table of Cases

PARA

Table of Cases

PARA

Table of Cases

c

Q

R

PARA

Table of Cases

Table of Cases

PARA

U

PARA

V

W

Table of Cases

Table of Cases

Section 1

HISTORY OF THE LAW OF AGRICULTURAL HOLDINGS

Section 1

HISTORY OF THE LAW OF AGRICULTURAL HOLDINGS

Contents

Chapter 1

PROTECTION OF AGRICULTURAL HOLDINGS TENANTS – HISTORICAL INTRODUCTION

FARMING IN THE NINETEENTH CENTURY

1.1 The period from 1770 to 1815 was one of great prosperity for agriculture in Great Britain. That ended abruptly with the conclusion of the Napoleonic wars. There then followed a period of deep depression which lasted for some 20 years. During this time large areas of agricultural land were abandoned altogether, remaining uncultivated. Many landlords and tenants were ruined.

By 1836 prosperity started to return, but the long period of depression had shown up the deficiencies of the landlord and tenant system in the provision of necessary funding for the running of a capital-intensive industry. This marked the start of the distinction between the improvements which fell to be funded by landlords and those were which the tenant would be responsible.

At this time, the law of landlord and tenant applicable to all other forms of property applied equally to agricultural land. With minor exceptions, such as provisions for emblements, customs of the country and implied conditions[1], there were no special provisions relating to the law of agricultural holdings.

Until 1875, as a general rule, the landlord and tenant relationships in respect of agricultural holdings were subject only to such terms as agreed between the parties themselves, as supplemented by limited common law provisions. Implied terms had evolved over the years to include an obligation on a tenant 'to manage and cultivate the land in a good and husband like manner'[2] and to 'keep the premises wind and water tight'[3]. However, these obligations were minimal.

The ancient doctrine of emblements had developed by custom enabling a tenant to have regress for harvesting corn or certain other annual crops which is sown. Of more practical consequence was the development of 'customs of the country' in some areas. These gave rise to entitlements for outgoing tenants to receive compensation on quitting for what came to be known as tenant right, even though there was no contractual entitlement to such a claim. Some counties had well developed customs, notably Lincolnshire and Norfolk. Others were less well developed. Some had no provisions at all.

1.1 *Protection of agricultural holdings tenants – historical introduction*

1 See para 1.4.
2 *Powley v Walker* (1793) 5 Term Rep 373. Also see, *Wedd v Porter* [1916] 2 KB 91, CA; *Warren v Keen* [1954] 1 QB 15, CA.
3 *Auworth v Johnson* (1832) 5 C & P 239.

1.2 Such legislation as existed in relation to agriculture focused on the rights of the landlord. For example, the Landlord and Tenant Act 1730 had been introduced to enable landlords to charge double rent against a tenant who wilfully remained in possession after the expiry of a notice to quit.

In 1848 a parliamentary committee was set up to inquire into the question of a standardised system for providing for tenant rights. In 1849 a Bill was introduced to implement the recommendations of the committee. That Bill failed to become law, as did subsequent attempts until 1875.

Even the repeal of the Corn Laws in 1846[1], which steadied prices, did not immediately damage the renewed agricultural prosperity. As a consequence, the impetus to reform the landlord and tenant relationship and, in particular, provide for the division of funding for investment in tenanted farms, was lost.

The desire not to interfere with the landlord and tenant system relating to agricultural holdings was consistent with the political philosophy at the time. The origins of what is known as the 'let alone' doctrine are somewhat elusive. Usually, it is taken as a common eighteenth century understanding of *laissez-faire*, associated most perhaps with Adam Smith, Bernard Mandeville and the Physiocrats. Regardless of its origin, the doctrine developed through the new utilitarianism of John Stuart Mill, which established a primary concern for self-development. Mill's understanding of the relation between authority and free inquiry, and his persistent eclectic desire to promote agreement, had all led by the early 1840s to an unambiguous conception of the conditions necessary for free individual agency.

This political philosophy was echoed in the speech of Lord Simon in one of the leading agricultural holdings cases, *Johnson v Moreton*[2], in 1980:

'Human felicity, it was argued, was best promoted by leaving to every person to seek his own advantage in competition with his fellows. A free market would ensure that the individual's effort was directed to anticipating and satisfying with maximum efficiency the wants of his fellows. The most powerful motive force – mans pursuit of his own interest – would thus be harnessed to drive a whole society forward. "Mans selfishness is God's providence" they said'.

This political creed was reflected in judicial decisions at the time, for example, Jessel MR in *Printing and Numerical Registering Co v Sampson*[3]:

'... if there is one thing which more than another public policy requires it is that men of full age and competent understanding shall have the utmost liberty of contracting, and that their contracts when entered into freely and voluntarily shall be held sacred and shall be enforced by Courts of Law'.

1 The repeal of the Corn Laws is a misnomer. Although agricultural tariffs were substantially reduced in 1846, it was not until the enactment of the Customs and Excise Warehousing Act 1869 that they were finally abolished.

²   [1980] AC 37, HL.
³   (1875) LR 19 Eq 462.

1.3 There were two significant developments in the last quarter of the nineteenth century which were fundamentally to disadvantage British agriculture. First, following the end of the American Civil War in 1865, by 1875 the development of farming in North America had been established with mass production of cereals. New machinery, a railway system and steamers crossing the Atlantic enabled large quantities of American produced cereals to swamp the British market and depress prices. A succession of bad harvests exacerbated the problem. By the end of the nineteenth century, corn production had fallen by some 2 million acres in Britain. Second, and arguably even more damaging, was the development by 1891 of reliable refrigeration systems enabling frozen meat to be transported from Australia, New Zealand and South America. As a result, cattle and sheep production fell in line with British cereal prices. These two developments provided the background against which it was imperative for British agriculture to receive support and protection. To put this into context, by 1890, it is believed that approximately 90% of all agricultural land in cultivation[1] was farmed by tenants. As a consequence, in the last quarter of the nineteenth century, attention returned to the landlord and tenant system in relation to agricultural holdings.

¹   Lord Northfield, Report of the Committee of Inquiry into the Acquisition and Occupancy of Agricultural Land (Cmnd 7599, 1979).

THE AGRICULTURAL HOLDINGS (ENGLAND) ACT 1875

1.4 Against the above backcloth, the Agricultural Holdings (England) Act 1875 was enacted. For the current editor, a Welshman, the title of the Act is curious as it applied not only to England, but also Wales, but not Scotland or Ireland. The 1875 Act was the first in a long line of Agricultural Holdings Acts spanning more than one hundred years and developing significant protection for tenants of agricultural holdings, before coming to an abrupt stop with the enactment of the Agricultural Tenancies Act 1995.

The 1875 Act applied the Lincolnshire custom for providing compensation for outgoing tenants to all tenants. It also gave tenants the rights to remove fixtures which they had provided. It extended the period of notice to quit required to be given to annual tenants from the common law period of six months to twelve months, terminating on the annual term date of the tenancy. It also introduced a specialist disputes procedure.

On the face of it this represented a very significant development in the protection afforded to agricultural tenants but, consistent with the political philosophy at the time, the 1875 Act contained a flaw. It did not prohibit contracting out. As a consequence, landlords who did not take kindly to the imposition of obligations on them exercised their right to contract out.

AGRICULTURAL HOLDINGS ACTS 1883 TO 1923

1.5 The lacuna in the 1875 Act was filled by the Agricultural Holdings (England) Act 1883. It too applied to England and Wales. The 1883 Act prohibited contracting out, unless the parties had agreed an alternative measure of compensation which was as valuable or better for the tenant. This statutory restriction on the parties' freedom of contract represented a watershed in the development of agricultural holdings legislation.

Further Agricultural Holdings Acts were passed in 1900 and 1906. The Agricultural Holdings Act 1900 substituted specialist arbitration in place of references to referees and an umpire as the means for specialist dispute resolution.

The Agricultural Holdings Act 1906 introduced:

(a)   freedom of cropping of arable land, except in the last year of the tenancy;

(b)   compensation for disturbance on quitting unless the tenancy was terminated for bad farming;

(c)   compensation for damage by game for which the tenant had no right to kill; and

(d)   a prohibition on the landlords charging penal rents, except for breaking up permanent pasture or felling or damaging trees.

By 1908, the law had been sufficiently and extensively varied in relation to agricultural holdings and it was necessary for a new consolidating statute. That was enacted as the Agricultural Holdings Act 1908.

Further Agricultural Holdings Acts were passed in 1914 and two in 1920. One of the 1920 Acts fixed compensation for disturbance at one year's rent with a second year's rent on proof of loss.

The law of agricultural holdings was again consolidated and developed by the Agricultural Holdings Act 1923. By then, the modern law provided for compensation on quitting and developed to that which continues to apply today under the Agricultural Holdings Act 1986. Many of the restrictions on landlords which continued to feature in the 1986 Act were developed by the 1923, with the significant exception of conferring security of tenure. Later additions to the list of heads of claim for compensation emerged as farming circumstances developed, for example, sod values, hefting of sheep and (much later) milk quota.

AGRICULTURE ACT 1947

1.6 The passing of the Agriculture Act 1947 in August 1947 represented not only a further development in relation to the law of agricultural holdings, but the birth of this book. On the passing of the 1947 Act, W S Scammell wrote a lengthy Memorandum on that Act at the invitation of the Chartered Auctioneers and Estate Agents Institute. On the passing of the Agricultural Holdings

Act 1948, the Royal Institution of Chartered Surveyors (RICS) joined with the Chartered Auctioneers and Estate Agents Institute to commission Mr W S Scammell to write the first edition of The Law of Agricultural Holdings.

The purpose of the 1947 Act was described in its preamble to be 'to make further provision for agriculture'. It contained five separate parts:

- Part I: Guaranteed prices and assured markets;
- Part II: Good estate management and good husbandry;
- Part III: Agricultural holdings;
- Part IV: Small holdings;
- Part V: Administrative and general.

The 1947 Act was not complete in itself. It amended the 1923 Act in many respects. After 1 March 1948, when Part III of the 1947 Act came into force, the law as to agricultural holdings was then to be found in Part III of the 1947 Act, combined with the 1923 Act, as amended by it. In the first edition of this book the provisions were united and cited together as 'the Agricultural Holdings Acts, 1923 to 1947'.

This potential for confusion did not last long. With what Mr W S Scammell described as 'commendable promptitude', the consolidation Act, the Agricultural Holdings Act 1948, received Royal Assent on 30 July 1948. The purpose of the 1948 Act was again reflected in its Preamble as 'An Act to consolidate the Agricultural Holdings Act 1923, Part III of the Agriculture Act, 1947, and certain other enactments relating to Agricultural Holdings, save, with respect to rights to Compensation, in their application to certain cases determined by reference to past events'. As Mr W S Scammell described it:

> '[it] gobbled up the whole of the 1923 Act and Part III of the 1947 Act, and a few very scattered provisions in other Statutes, and after due process of digestion and assimilation it produced in full statute the finished article of a Statute setting out the law of Agricultural Holdings'.

However, as Mr W S Scammell continued:

> '... in spite of its width, scope and completeness, the 1948 Act is not so proud and self-centred as to ignore completely its immediate ancestor, namely, the 1947 Act, whose Parts I, II, IV and V, with their respectively relevant Schedules it had not repealed, nor, with a few quite minor exceptions, affected. On the contrary, it fully recognises the continued existence of those Parts and Schedules of the 1947 Act and in a few instances it relies on the law therein declared (eg on Good Estate Management and Good Husbandry) and the procedure thereby established (eg the Agricultural Land Tribunals)'.

As the first edition of this book records:

> 'In this state of affairs it is not surprising to find that the principles underlying the 1947 and 1948 Acts are similar and those principles were and are Stability and Efficiency. "Stability" means that farmers shall be assured of prices and markets for their agricultural produce, and of security of tenure of their holding. "Efficiency" means that in return for stability the Agricultural industry, consisting as it does of owner-occupiers, landlords, tenant-farmers and small holders, must reach an efficient standard in their several capacity.

Stability, in regard to prices and markets, is provided for in the case of agricultural products listed in the First Schedule to the 1947 Act and, in security of tenure, it is provided for by a series of restrictions on the operation of Notices to Quit by Landlords to their Tenants. Efficiency is to be achieved by:

1 The creation and maintenance of a standard of Good Estate Management by Landlords and Owner-Occupiers, and Good Husbandry by Tenants or Owner-Occupier.

2 The infliction of control by means of Supervision Orders and Directions, and in the last resort Dispossession of those who fail to come up to the required standards'.

All of this reflected the way in which both the law and politics developed during this period. The rationale for this fundamental change in the relationship between landlords and tenants has been described in the speech of Lord Salmon in *Johnson v Moreton*[1] as follows:

'During the last War, the submarine menace was such that it would have been virtually impossible to import into this country any more goods vital for our survival and we, in fact, did. Accordingly it is extremely doubtful whether we could have survived had it not been for the food produced from our own farms ... It must have been clear to all that it was then and always would be a vital importance, both to the national economy and security, that the level of production and the efficiency of our farms should be maintained and improved. This could only be achieved by the skill and hard work of our farmers and the amount of their earnings, which they were prepared to plough back into the land from which these earnings had been derived ... The security of tenure which tenant farmers were accorded by the Act of 1947 was not only for their own protection as an important section of the public, nor only for the protection of the weak against the strong; it was for the protection of the nation itself'.

[1] [1980] AC 37, HL.

1.7 Another previous editor of this book, Mr Andrew Densham, observed that:

'So security of tenure was introduced for public policy reasons which transcended the narrow interests of the parties and was said to have included national security, staple food production social engineering. But by the time of *Johnson v Moreton*[1] in 1980, the country had joined the Common Market, and the whole European Community was already suffering from overproduction in nearly all sectors (with butter mountains and milk lakes and the like, as they were called). Some of Lord Salmon's speech sounded strangely inconsistent with the experience of the industry, in particular, the assumption that "It must have been clear to all that it ... always (sic) would be of vital importance ... that the level of production ... should be maintained and improved" '[2].

Significantly, Lord Simon in *Johnson v Moreton*[3], expressed the rationale for conferring security of tenure rather more philosophically:

'In short, it was held, the constriction of the market and the inequality of bargaining power enabled the landlord to dictate contractual terms which did not necessarily operate to the general benefit of society. It was to counteract this descried constriction of the market and to redress this descried inequality of bargaining power that the law – specifically, in the shape of legislation – came to intervene repeatedly to modify freedom of contract between landlord and tenant ... The Agricultural Holdings Act 1948 exemplifies such legislation activity specifically where the tenancy is of agricultural land'.

The method of conferring security of tenure was quite different from that relating to the Rent Acts or subsequently providing security to other forms of business tenants under the Landlord and Tenant Act 1954, Pt II.

The framework for security of tenure under the 1947 and 1948 Acts started with the definition of agriculture. 'Agriculture' was defined to include a range of traditional farming activities, but not exclusively so, surprisingly, it did not expressly include corn production. 'Agricultural holdings' included all agricultural land comprised in a contract of tenancy which was let for a trade or business. All short-term tenancies, and even licences, were converted into fully protected tenancies, with limited exceptions, most notably grazing agreements. Critically, the 1947 and 1948 Acts prohibited contracting out.

1   [1980] AC 37, HL.
2   H A C Densham, Agricultural Tenancies: Past and Present in Susan Bright (ed), *Landlord and Tenant Law: Past, Present and Future* (2006) Falcon Chambers, Hart Publishing.
3   [1980] AC 37, HL.

1.8   As a consequence of the law enacted in the 1948 Act, although a landlord wishing to secure possession could give a notice to quit, the tenant was entitled to serve a counter-notice within one month. That counter-notice rendered the landlord's notice of 'no effect' unless the consent of the Agricultural Land Tribunal was obtained to the operation of the notice to quit. The grounds on which the Agricultural Land Tribunal could consent was subject to an overriding provision that the Tribunal also had to be satisfied that a 'fair and reasonable landlord would [in] all the circumstances ... insist on possession'[1].

An alternative form of statutorily prescribed notice to quit could be given if the tenant had allegedly committed one of the 'Seven Deadly Sins', as they were characterised in previous editions of this book. To counter such a notice, a different form of counter-notice, demanding arbitration, had to be given in most such cases[2]. The giving of the wrong form of counter-notice was fatal. Landlords and tenants alike could be statute barred from defending by the most technical of defaults. The Agricultural Land Tribunal, specialist agricultural arbitration and the courts all had their own jurisdiction for designated types of notices to quit. The result of this regime was that tenants of agricultural holdings had far greater security of tenure than has ever been enjoyed by any other form of business tenant. In most cases, annual tenancies continued until the death of the tenant, with landlords unable to secure possession any earlier.

1   See para 30.16.
2   See para 30.1.

1.9   The prohibition upon contracting out applied not only to security of tenure, but also the compensation provisions of the new legislation. The current editor cannot put it better than Mr W S Scammell:

'The position can perhaps be illustrated by a mental picture of a piece of land in which are growing some stumps of plants above the surface. In the 1923 Act state of affairs the Act comes along as a tractor and actually uproots the stumps which offend it – they are "avoided". In the 1947 and 1948 Acts the effect of the Act-Tractor is not to uproot, but, by statutory magic, to push them below the surface and out of the way of the statutory rights of Compensation. One wondered whether they might not later on sprout again in some unexpected directions, not having been killed or avoided in the process of pushing them under the surface.

In the first edition of this book it was said that time and decisions of the courts would perhaps elucidate this position. The decision in *Coates v Diment* is now an authoritative answer on the point. Shortly stated, it was held that s 65 of the 1948 Act produces exactly the same position as did s 50 of the 1923 Act. A clause which offends the sanctity of a Tenant's rights under the Act to compensation is void for all purposes ...

We can, therefore, now with confidence press forward with the study of the 1948 Act, imbued with the principle that any provisions of an Agreement attempting to contract-out of the Act as regards Compensation legislated for in the Act, and not expressly permitted by its provisions, must quail and fail as regards restriction or denial of Compensation and also for all other purposes'.

Since the law enacted in the 1948 Act caused tenancies to endure, it became necessary to introduce other provisions. A rent review was introduced to enable rent to be revised at three-yearly intervals in accordance with a statutory formula[1] .This was merely described as 'the rent properly payable'. This soon fell far behind what was considered to be the market rent. As a consequence, the rental formula was then revised to the open market rental by the Agricultural Holdings Act 1958. A further revision of this formula was an essential feature of the Agricultural Holdings Act 1984.

Another change which was heralded by the legislation of the late 1940s was the introduction of 'model clauses'. A model form of maintenance, repairing and ensuring provision was introduced by Statutory Instrument[2]. Not only did this provide for model clauses in the absence of express contractual provision between the parties, but it also enabled the parties to apply to an arbitrator to introduce the model clauses to override the existing contractual provisions[3].

[1] See para 25.10.
[2] See para 23.8.
[3] See para 23.21.

AGRICULTURE (MISCELLANEOUS PROVISIONS) ACTS 1949 TO 1972

1.10 Inevitably, with such a radical change in the law, a number of unintended problems emerged which needed correcting. A useful vehicle for such regular, minor adjustments was available in the form of the annual Agriculture (Miscellaneous Provisions) Acts. These were required to give effect to the deficiency payment system which was required under the payment support provisions applicable to farm prices before the United Kingdom signed the Treaty of Rome and became a member of the EEC. Under this system, each year negotiations between the Ministry of Agriculture and the National

Farmers Union determined the support prices to be paid for each form of agricultural product. This was then enacted in the annual Agriculture (Miscellaneous Provisions) Act. Additionally, this was used for minor changes to the Agricultural Holdings Act 1948. With the exception of the Agriculture Act 1958, this was the means by which amendments were made by way of Agriculture (Miscellaneous Provisions) Acts 1949, 1954, 1963, 1968 and 1972. 1972 was the last year before the United Kingdom joined the Common Market. The need for annual Agriculture (Miscellaneous Provisions) Act ceased, except for the very important Act of 1976. That Act was intended initially merely to abolish the Sugar and Hop Boards but was used at a very late stage in the passing of the Bill to introduce what proved to be another fundamental change to the Law of Agricultural Holdings.

AGRICULTURE (MISCELLANEOUS PROVISIONS) ACT 1976

1.11 The year 1976 provided another major landmark which was almost as far reaching in its consequence as the 1947/48 legislation. The Agriculture (Miscellaneous Provisions) Act 1976 introduced the right to apply for a new tenancy in succession on the death of a sitting tenant for a limited class of close relations of the sitting tenant. This extended to up to two further generations of tenant. As a consequence the value to the tenant of his tenancy was significantly increased, as was the loss to the landlord in the value of his freehold.

To qualify as a potential successor, a party had to show that he was eligible and suitable. Each of those criteria was subject to sub-tests. To be eligible, the applicant had to be closely related to the tenant who had just died; he had to have derived his principal source of livelihood from farming that land for at least five of the preceding seven years; and he was required not to have secure rights of occupation over another commercially viable farm: the so-called 'commercial unit' test. As regards suitability, the tests were directed to ensuring that the potential new tenant was competent to farm, having regard to his 'age, health and financial standing'. Although the landlord is entitled to oppose an application for succession, the landlord's position was not unlike that applying in relation to notice to quit. In practice, the landlord would rarely achieve success in opposing an application for succession, just as it would be very rare for a landlord to succeed in obtaining consent from the Agricultural Land Tribunal for the operation of a notice to quit on grounds that a 'fair and reasonable landlord would [in] all the circumstances ... insist on possession'[1].

The law of succession to agricultural holdings was never part of the policy of either the Labour or Conservative parties. It arose because it was the price demanded by Plaid Cymru for their support of the Callaghan minority administration in 1976 during the period inaccurately known as the Lib/Lab Pact.

The law of succession, as introduced in 1976, needed substantial refinement and improvement. This came about primarily in the Agricultural Holdings Act 1984, when succession was extended to apply to retirement, as an alternative to the death of the tenant.

¹ See para 30.16.

AGRICULTURAL HOLDINGS ACT 1984

1.12 As a consequence of the security of tenure introduced by the Agriculture Act 1947, then consolidated in the 1948 Act, landowners developed all sorts of schemes to avoid full security of tenure applying to lettings of agricultural land. By 1960, the statutory lacuna had been established whereby it was possible to enter into a letting for a fixed term of between one and two years without conferring security of tenure[1]. Another mechanism much used by landowners, particularly those who wished to participate in some way in relation to the farming of their land, was to use a farming partnership, particularly after it was established in 1964 that a licence conferred in relation to a farming partnership was not statutorily converted by what became known as the 'statutory magic' of s 2 of the 1948 Act into a fully protected tenancy under the Act[2].

[1] See para 20.13.
[2] See para 20.5.

1.13 As a result of the introduction of succession in 1976, there was a further growth in schemes to avoid security of tenure being granted. In particular, arrangements were entered into taking advantage of the absence of security of tenure conferred upon sub-tenants[1].It was as a consequence that in the 1980s there was a growth in the number of cases which came before the courts considering whether arrangements entered into between a landowner and the occupier of the farm were, for example, contrary to public policy[2].

When the Callaghan Government fell in 1979, many anticipated that the repeal of the succession provisions contained in the 1976 Act would be an early victim of the Thatcher administration. That did not happen. Instead, Mr Peter Walker, the then Minister of Agriculture, let it be known that if the Country Landowners Association (CLA) (on behalf of landlords) and the National Farmers Union (NFU) (on behalf of tenants) could reach an agreement as to what changes were required in respect of Agricultural Holdings legislation, he would secure the necessary parliamentary time for its enactment.

By way of background, in June 1977, Mr John Silkin, the then Minister of Agriculture, asked Lord Northfield to chair a committee, the remit of which was, ostensibly, to consider the apparently widespread acquisition of the best farmland in Britain by both foreign buyers and institutions, and further to consider recent trends in occupancy as this might affect the structure of the agricultural industry. In the event, the Northfield Committee considered the landlord and tenant system in detail and it formed a major part of their report.

In the meantime, the NFU and CLA had started discussions to try to achieve a consensus, primarily driven by disquiet about rents. Even before the publication of the Northfield Committee's report, in April 1979 the Ministry set up another small group of CLA, NFU and RICS members to consider technical amendments to the agricultural holdings legislation.

In July 1979 the Northfield Committee's report was published, contributing to the continuing discussions between the NFU and the CLA.

[1] See para 29.17.
[2] See para 19.50.

1.14 The result of the NFU/CLA discussions was finally published by way of a press release on 21 May 1981. It became generally known as 'the Package'. After introductory comment about the achievement of a consensus and appeal to both the Government and opposition to ensure the early introduction and passing of the necessary legislation, the press release commented in detail on five main areas:

(a) a new rent formula;
(b) the landlord and tenant system;
(c) a general review of agricultural holdings legislation;
(d) help for new entrants;
(e) farm partnerships.

The CLA/NFU Package did not tackle the fundamental issue of security of tenure. Instead, the political compromise was that, although succession was introduced upon the retirement of tenants, henceforth no newly created tenancies would carry with them succession rights.

The rent formula was amended with the intention moving away from the open market formula to one which reflected 'the productive capacity and the related earning capacity' of the holding. The 1984 Act also contained a large number of miscellaneous amendments to a range of provisions contained in the 1948 Act. The changes included in the published Bill were the result of a detailed study within the Ministry's Working Party. The 1979 sessions looked in detail at 171 possible amendments. In the event, some 90 amendments appeared in the Bill of which it was considered at the time that 41 were substantial, 25 were technically important and 24 were classed as clarifying.

The Ministry's Working Party also considered the issue of new entrants and whether it might be possible to amend the working of the ministerial discretion under the provisions of s 2 of the 1948 Act which enable the Minister to give approval for a letting of up to two years without conferring security of tenure[1]. The CLA/NFU Package sought two particular extensions to the use of the ministerial discretion:

(i) for the purpose of a trial period before concluding a full tenancy; and
(ii) where there was a definite intention that the landowner's son or daughter should farm the land within a relatively short time.

15

1.14   *Protection of agricultural holdings tenants – historical introduction*

In July 1979 the Northfield Committee's report was published, informing the continuing discussions between the NFU and the CLA.

In accordance with their earlier promise, the Government published a Bill based upon the NFU/CLA Package on 28 October 1983. Many amendments were made to the Bill during its passage through Parliament. Finally, on 9 July 1984, it was approved. As an initial Bill, it comprised 33 pages. By the time that it received Royal Assent on 12 July 1984, it was an Act of 56 pages.

[1]   See para 18.6.

AGRICULTURE ACT 1986: MILK QUOTA

1.15 In April 1984[1] milk quota was introduced into the United Kingdom arising from quantitative controls imposed on the production of milk and other dairy products under the Common Agricultural Policy of the European Economic Community, now the European Community (EC). Initially, the quota system, introduced on 2 April 1984, operated for five years. It has subsequently been amended and extended, particularly in 1992[2]. The milk quota system continues, notwithstanding the Mid-term Review of the Common Agricultural Policy[3].

The notable thing about milk quota is that it was the first time that EC legislation directly affected the landlord and tenant relationship applying in respect of agricultural holdings. Between 1984 and the mid-1990s, milk quota increased in value very substantially. As a consequence, a significant value attributed to an agricultural holding was regarded as having passed to the separate asset of milk quota. The question as to whether milk quota 'attached' to land and how it was to be dealt with between the landlord and the tenant exercised practitioners after 1984.

It was as a consequence that in 1986 the Agriculture Act 1986 (AHA 1986) was enacted to ensure that on the termination of a tenancy, the tenant should share in such part of the value of the quota as was attributable to the quota attached to the agricultural holding being vacated[4].

Because in recent times the value of milk quota has fallen, it is now much less of an issue both between landlords and tenants and, indeed, mortgagors and mortgagees. Nevertheless, it represents the first significant incursion of EC law into the law of agricultural holdings. That has since been followed as a consequence of the Mid-term Review of the Common Agricultural Policy and the introduction of Entitlements[5]. Again, both Entitlements and the right to the Single Payment income represent significant issues for landlords and tenants in respect of agricultural holdings, including lettings under the Agricultural Tenancies Act 1995 (ATA 1995).

[1]   See para 49.1.
[2]   See para 49.1.
[3]   See para 52.18.
[4]   See para 49.28.
[5]   See para 52.1.

THE AGRICULTURAL TENANCIES ACT 1995

1.16 The need for deregulation was perceived following the dramatic decline in let land[1] and the increasing use of devices to avoid granting security of tenure under the AHA 1986, either utilising exceptions or loopholes in the AHA 1986 (grazing agreements or *Gladstone v Bower* agreements[2]) or avoiding the landlord and tenant relationship altogether by the use of partnership, contracting or share farming arrangements.

In February 1991, the Ministry of Agriculture, Fisheries and Food (MAFF) published a Consultation Paper advocating the deregulation and simplification of the agricultural landlord and tenant relationship. Its aim was to encourage the letting of land and to provide a framework of legislation which would endure to accommodate change within the industry. In the outline proposals contained in the 1991 Consultation Paper there was to be virtually no regulation and almost complete freedom of contract: no provision was to be made for rent review and statutory compensation for improvements was only envisaged as a fall-back in the absence of express provisions in the tenancy agreement. There was to be no security of tenure and no interference with the common law rules on the length of notices to quit.

Following the 1991 document, MAFF produced a detailed proposals paper in September 1992[3]. It had already become clear that in order to satisfy the various industry groups and to obtain industry support for any legislation, more of a compromise was required. The detailed proposals paper envisaged extended periods for notices to quit; compulsory compensation for tenant's improvements and the right to a rent review on an open market basis in the absence of anything to the contrary in the tenancy agreement.

Negotiations within the industry continued and in December 1993 a short statement (known as the Joint Industry Statement) was issued by the National Farmers' Union, the Country Landowners' Association, the Tenant Farmers' Association and the National Federation of Young Farmers' Clubs setting out proposals which the various sectors had agreed to put to Ministers for the reform of agricultural tenancy law. The Joint Industry Statement formed the basis of the ATA 1995 which was announced in the Queen's Speech in November 1994.

As the Agricultural Tenancies Bill completed its Report Stage and Third Reading in the House of Commons on 19 April 1995, MAFF issued a press release quoting the Minister, William Waldegrave. He said:

'This Bill ... will give a major boost to the rented sector in agriculture. It will bring hope for many young people who want to farm on their own account but those plans have been frustrated by the desperate shortage of tenancies on offer'.

The press release referred to a survey carried out in the summer of 1994 by the Royal Institution of Chartered Surveyors indicating that almost a million acres (400,000 hectares) of new lettings could be expected once the Bill was in force. The Bill received Royal Assent on 9 May 1995. That followed the recommendations of the Tenancy Reform Industry Group (TRIG1).

1   In 1910, 90% of agricultural land was tenanted. This had fallen to 36% by 1991: see
    MAFF Consultation Paper on the Reform of Agricultural Tenancy Law (February 1991).
2   *Gladstone v Bower* [1960] 2 QB 384. See para 20.13.
3   Reform of Agricultural Holdings Legislation: Detailed Proposals (MAFF, September 1992).

1.17 As a consequence, the ATA 1995 applies to most tenancies of agricultural land beginning[1] on or after 1 September 1995[2].

As indicated above, in 1994, the RICS survey[3] of its members (managing 3.26 million acres) predicted that an extra one million acres would be available for letting under the new regime. The Central Association of Agricultural Valuers (CAAV) Annual Tenanted Farms Survey for 1995, which covered just the first two months of the new legislation, showed that 1,179 new farm business tenancies covering 130,934 acres of land in England and Wales were entered into. The average size of unit let was 111 acres, with 20% being larger than 200 acres and the average length of tenancy (understood by taking annual periodic tenancies as being for one year) was three years and 10.2 months with 115 farm business tenancies for lets of ten years or more and 1,018 for five years or less.

1   See para 2.1.
2   See para 1.16.
3   Farm Business Tenancies, New Farms and Land 1995 to 1997 (RICS, October 1994).

1.18 In outline, the main features of the ATA 1995 are as follows:

(a)   No minimum term.
(b)   Minimal security of tenure, being only an extension of the common law notice period for notices to quit annual tenancies; a requirement for fixed-term tenancies of more than two years to be terminated by a prescribed period of notice and a control over the length of notice required to exercise contractual break provisions in certain fixed-term contracts.
(c)   The ability to allow substantial diversification away from agriculture without losing the status of the tenancy as a farm business tenancy.
(d)   Limited freedom over rent review. The parties can choose to have no reviews or one of the statutory options but otherwise the rent will be reviewed on an open market basis. Timing and frequency of reviews are a matter of contract, with a fall-back provision to allow reviews every three years.
(e)   Almost complete freedom for the tenant to remove tenant's fixtures.
(f)   A compulsory statutory scheme for the compensation of tenant's improvements, but otherwise compensation is left to the bargain between the parties.
(g)   The emphasis for dispute resolution is on ADR (alternative dispute resolution) with a fall-back of arbitration under the Arbitration Act 1996.
(h)   All other terms are a matter for the parties.

The ATA 1995 reformed only the law of landlord and tenant. It did not offer any structural support for farming nor, other than the intended encouragement to landowners to let land, did it purport to be the answer to the problem of encouraging new entrants into farming. It was opposed by the Labour Party, and this and certain tax disadvantages for landowners who let land were perceived, at the time, as being insurmountable problems to the success of the Act. If the Labour Party were to be returned to power in the next general election, would landowners find themselves with farm business tenants who had suddenly acquired enhanced security of tenure?

In September 1994, the Labour Party had produced a policy statement confirming its commitment to returning to a legislative regime based upon the AHA 1986, but removing the lacuna by which security of tenure could be avoided. This was also the position adopted by the Labour's then shadow Minister, Mr Gavin Strang, during debates relating to the Bill. The Labour Party finally gave a commitment not to introduce legislation which would retrospectively confer security on farm business tenants. Ten years on, the Labour Government has not returned to its previous policy position. The ATA 1995 continues to govern new lettings.

1.19 As far as taxation is concerned, s 155 of the Finance Act 1995 introduced an amendment to s 116 of the Inheritance Tax Act 1984 to allow landowners 100% agricultural property relief in respect of the agricultural value of let land where the tenancy began on or after 1 September 1995.

In order to test the aims of the ATA 1995 – to slow the decline in let land and revitalise the tenanted sector – the CAAV carried out its Annual Tenanted Farms Survey in 1999[1]. It showed a marked increase in the net inflow of new land into the tenanted sector in 1999. With 77,000 previously unlet acres being let on farm business tenancies, the net increase (allowing for losses of land to the tenanted sector) is 61,000 acres. 75% of land in AHA 1986 tenancies which terminated were re-let on farm business tenancies. Prior to the coming into force of the ATA 1995, the CAAV surveys showed losses to the tenanted sector of 50,000–70,000 acres a year. At least part of the increase in the period concerned by the survey is the decision by some to cease their own farming operation and let out their land in response to the current agricultural recession, matched by others seeking to expand their enterprises for the same reason. The 1999 CAAV survey recorded the average length of farm business tenancies to be four years and one month, but for holdings with buildings and a house to be eleven years.

In 2002, Lord Whitty and Mr Alun Michael MP invited Mr Julian Sayers to chair the newly constituted Tenancy Reform Industry Group (TRIG2). TRIG2 met for the first time on 11 November 2002.

TRIG2 came into being at a time of economic pressure on farming, particularly in the wake of the 2001 outbreak of foot and mouth disease. The forerunner to TRIG2 was the report of the Policy Commission on Food and Farming under the chairmanship of Sir Don Curry, which included recommendations relating to the importance of the tenanted sector. As a consequence of the Curry Report, the Department for Environment, Food and Rural Affairs (DEFRA – the successor to MAFF) commissioned the University of Plymouth to undertake an economic evaluation of the ATA 1995.

¹ Available from the Central Association of Agricultural Valuers, Market Chambers, 35 Market Place, Coleford, Gloucester GL16 8AA.

1.20 It was the recommendations of the University of Plymouth's Report which were in turn considered by TRIG2. The remit of TRIG2 identified four key principles:

(a)   Tenancy legislation can directly affect, positively as well as negatively, the availability of land to let and the operation of the tenanted sector.

(b)   Where possible, non-legislative measures should be used to maintain confidence in the framework of the legislation taking into account the long-term nature of rural land management.

(c)   The long-term view requires the need to provide flexibility for circumstances as yet unforeseen which are generally best delivered by greater freedom of contract with appropriate legislative safeguards.

(d)   There should be a level playing field between tenancies and other means for delivering land management and the tax system should treat them equally so that decisions can be taken on practical and not artificial grounds.

TRIG2 reported in May 2003, presenting its Report on 3 June 2003 to DEFRA. The key recommendations of TRIG2 were as follows:

(i)   Greater flexibility for landlords and tenants to agree the rent review provisions for a farm business tenancy, whilst retaining the exclusion on upwards only review clauses. The present legislation imposes certain restrictions on the parties which can fetter and sometimes frustrate practical negotiations that could otherwise lead to new tenancies being granted.

(ii)   An option for the end-of-tenancy compensation payable by a landlord to a tenant for improvements carried out under the provisions of the ATA 1995 to be capped at the outset. This will remove a barrier to consent being given for such works as presently the liability to pay compensation cannot be quantified by a landlord until the tenancy comes to an end.

(iii) Clarifying the circumstances whereby land, including buildings, can be added to a holding let under the provisions of the AHA 1986 without removing the tenant's rights under that Act. This will ensure flexibility where AHA 1986 tenancies are concerned, ease estate management and bring certainty to what in practice has proved a difficult matter. This should not be a means to increase the rate of agricultural property relief from inheritance tax.

(iv)   Removing the upper limit of 24 months for the notice period required to terminate a farm business tenancy. This will allow the creation of longer term 'rolling' tenancies with the associated flexibility.

(v)   Amending the livelihood 'test' for succession to a tenancy under the AHA 1986 so that non-farming income derived from a holding where landlord's consent has been granted for diversification can be taken into account. This will aid rather than count against an applicant.

(vi) Removing the specific arbitration provisions of the AHA 1986 and relying directly on the provisions of the Arbitration Act 1996 which already applies to disputes concerning other businesses and letting regimes, including the ATA 1995 and affords greater flexibility to the parties.

(vii) Providing the industry with 'model' clauses for the key issues that can be used to 'mirror' the terms of an AHA 1986 tenancy within an agreement under the ATA 1995 to help tenants transfer between holdings in certain circumstances.

Allied to the recommendations set out above, TRIG2 also supported wide-ranging fiscal measures.

In December 2003, DEFRA produced its response to TRIG2, supporting the proposals for tenancy reform. The Government agreed to use the Regulatory Reform Act 2001 to make a Regulatory Reform Order to introduce the necessary changes to the law. It did so when the Regulatory Reform (Agricultural Tenancies) (England and Wales) Order 2006[1] (RRO 2006) was made on 18 October 2006, coming into force the following day[2].

The fiscal reforms recommended by TRIG2 have not been adopted.

[1]   SI 2006/2805.
[2]   Article 1(1).

1.21 DEFRA's press release of 31 March 2006 summarised the effect of the (then proposed) RRO 2006 would be to:

(a)   remove the requirement for a potential successor to a tenancy to earn a living primarily from agricultural work on the holding;

(b)   enable landlords and tenants to reach their own agreements on rent reviews and end-of-tenancy compensation;

(c)   make it easier for landlords and tenants to restructure holdings held under an AHA 1986 tenancy;

(d)   remove the need for unnecessary applications to the Agricultural Land Tribunal where a landlord agrees on the successor to a tenancy;

(e)   enable landlords and tenants to agree a notice period to terminate a tenancy to suit their particular circumstances, providing it is longer than the minimum period of 12 months.

Part of the terms of reference of TRIG2 was to enable tenant farmers to 'diversify where this will improve the viability of their business' and 'take steps to enhance and protect the environment', in both cases 'without fear of losing their tenancy or jeopardising succession rights'.

As a consequence, TRIG2 made the following recommendations.

(i)   The matter of diversification within farm tenancies should be handled by the formulation of a Code of Good Practice.

(ii)   To ensure that the Code of Good Practice has authority it should be backed by an Ombudsman scheme, free at the point of use, to which disputes can be referred when they cannot be settled between the parties. The Ombudsman should have authority to adjudicate on the reasonableness of the proposal or objections, giving a non-binding decision to the parties. It will be primarily evidence from the Ombudsman that will be used to determine whether or not the Code of Good Practice is delivering the required change in attitude.

(iii) Ministers should give a very clear and unambiguous commitment to consider legislation if the Code of Good Practice does not provide an adequate mechanism for resolving potential disputes between landlords and tenants when considering proposals for farm diversification. If, after a period of years, it can be shown that tenants have a legitimate problem with landlords who consistently thwart reasonable diversification plans or impose unrealistic conditions then legislation should be considered to extend the tenant's statutory right to appeal against a landlord's unreasonable refusal to grant consent for the diversified activity.

The recommendation of TRIG2 that there should be a Code of Good Practice has been adopted. The 'Code of good practice for agri-environment schemes and diversification projects within agricultural tenancies' was published in 2005 by DEFRA. The following organisations were involved in the preparation of, and signed up to, the Code of Good Practice: Agricultural Law Association, Association of Chief Estates Surveyors and Property Managers in Local Government, Central Association of Agricultural Valuers, Country Land and Business Association, Farmers Union of Wales, Local Government Association, National Farmers Union, National Federation of Young Farmers Clubs, Royal Institution of Chartered Surveyors and the Tenant Farmers Association.

The Code leads the parties through five steps which propose:

(1)   early consultation between the parties once a project starts to be planned;
(2)   agreeing a timetable during which the landlord and tenant will seek to agree terms;
(3)   preparation of detailed proposals with a guide as to information which might be relevant depending on the nature and scale of the project;
(4)   issues to be addressed in considering the proposals and the need for a written response;
(5)   preparation of a formal written agreement between the parties.

The Code includes details of an adjudication scheme to consider cases where landlords and tenants are unable to reach agreement. Copies of the Code may be obtained through DEFRA[1]. Originally funding for the scheme was to be provided by DEFRA for a period of four years. In December 2006 it was announced that funding by DEFRA had been withdrawn after no-one applied to use the scheme in the first year of its operation.

The ATA 1995 has now been in force for over 12 years. There is still no significant guidance or case authority on any of the specific provisions of the ATA 1995 and there have been very few arbitrations under the provisions of the Act. Experience shows that, along with rent review clauses and clauses concerned with improvements, much of the advice sought continues to be on the question of the interface between the AHA 1986 and the ATA 1995 and the impact that the latter has on the ability of the AHA 1986 landlords and tenants to manage the AHA 1986 land effectively, not only to manage the land, but also to resolve disputes between them (eg relating to succession or the existence or otherwise of an AHA 1986 tenancy) by means of the grant of a farm business tenancy. This is much more of a compromise than no tenancy or a tenancy with full security of tenure – an all or nothing situation which produced much litigation. The editor does not consider that the RRO 2006 will have a significant impact in this regard.

Empirical evidence would suggest that farm business tenancies are proving rather a conduit to land consolidation, with those operating on a smaller scale being squeezed out by economic pressures[2].

[1] See para 2.7 below.
[2] Central Association of Agricultural Valuers, the Central Association of Agricultural Valuers Annual Tenanted Farms Survey 2004 (Coleford, Central Association of Agricultural Valuers, 2005).

THE MID-TERM REVIEW AND THE FUTURE

1.22 Although freedom of contract has continued to be the touchstone for agricultural tenancies in the United Kingdom, it has to be considered within the broader constraints that operate both at EC and world trade levels.

It may be argued that the Mid-term Review of the Common Agricultural Policy[1] has unshackled farmers from the detailed rules of earlier, more specific subsidy regimes, in that the Single Payment embraces most of those regimes and is not dependant upon any particular form of production or production at all[2]. Conversely, the reforms have been characterised as 'decoupling with strings attached'[3].

Although for the purposes of Council Regulation (EC) 1782/2003, governing the introduction of the Mid-term Review of the Common Agricultural Policy, 'agricultural activity' is defined as 'the production, rearing or growing of agricultural products including harvesting, milking, breeding animals for farming purposes, or maintaining the land in good agricultural and environmental condition'[4], what is clear is that, for the purpose of the cross-compliance obligations imposed by Council Regulation (EC) 1782/2003, the farmers obligations are to comprise first, statutory management requirements and, second, a requirement to maintain all agricultural land in good agricultural and environmental condition[5]. This represents a considerable departure from the role of agriculture as described by Lord Salmon in *Johnson v Moreton*[6]. Indeed, as Mrs Margaret Beckett, the then Minister at DEFRA, put it at the Labour Party Conference in September 2005, farmers must redirect their activities from food production to land management[7].

1 See Ch 52.
2 See 2003 Horizontal Regulation [2003] OJ L270/1, Annex VI, as amended.
3 For instance, see: Centre for World Food Studies, Amsterdam, and Netherlands Bureau for Economic Policy Analysis, the Hague, The CAP-reform Proposal of the Mid-Term Review: Decoupling with Strings Attached (Brussels, European Commission, 2002).
4 See para 52.19.
5 In respect of this obligation, a European Community framework is set out in Annex VI to the 2003 Horizontal Regulation [2003] OJ L270/1.
6 [1980] AC 37, HL.
7 The editor is grateful to HAC Densham and MN Cardwell for permission to use material from their essays in Susan Bright (ed), *Landlord and Tenant Law: Past, Present and Future* (2006) Falcon Chambers, Hart Publishing.

AGRICULTURAL TENANCIES ACT 1995

Part I

INTRODUCTION

Contents

Chapter 2
FARM BUSINESS TENANCIES UNDER THE AGRICULTURAL TENANCIES ACT 1995

THE ENACTMENT OF THE AGRICULTURAL TENANCIES ACT 1995

2.1 The Agricultural Tenancies Act 1995 (ATA 1995) applies to most tenancies of agricultural land beginning[1] on or after 1 September 1995[2], subject only to the exceptions set out in s 4 of the Act[3].

The ATA 1995 substantially deregulated the agricultural landlord and tenant relationship, leaving more to be determined by the parties, and also recognised the growing need for tenants to be free to increase their income from diversification activities. The need for deregulation was perceived following the dramatic decline in let land[4] and the increasing use of devices to avoid granting security of tenure under the Agricultural Holdings Act 1986 (AHA 1986), either utilising exceptions or loopholes in the AHA 1986 (grazing agreements[5] or *Gladstone v Bower* agreements[6]) or avoiding the landlord and tenant relationship altogether by the use of partnership, contracting or share farming arrangements.

The background to the legislative process is covered in Chapter 1.

[1] Within the meaning of ATA 1995, s 38(4).
[2] A tenancy commencing before 1 September 1995 cannot be a farm business tenancy under the ATA 1995: s 2(1)(a).
[3] See para 3.4ff.
[4] In 1910, 90% of agricultural land was tenanted. This had fallen to 36% by 1991. See MAFF Consultation Paper on the Reform of Agricultural Tenancy Law (February 1991) and 'Agriculture Land Tenure in England and Wales' Winter, Richardson Short and Watkins, Centre for Rural Studies, Cirencester (1990) RICS.
[5] See para 21.2.
[6] See para 20.13.

2.2 The Agricultural Tenancies Bill received Royal Assent on 9 May 1995. That followed the recommendations of the Tenancy Reform Industry Group (TRIG1).

This section of the book will look in detail at the provisions of the ATA 1995, but will go beyond that. As more is left to the bargain reached by the parties, those advising them need to have a greater awareness of the general law of landlord and tenant, particularly in relation to the drafting and interpretation of tenancy agreements and the remedies available for default. An outline of the more important provisions is also therefore given. This section of the book will consider:

(a)   the formation of a farm business tenancy;
(b)   the terms of a farm business tenancy;
(c)   termination of a farm business tenancy;
(d)   fixtures and compensation for improvements; and
(e)   various miscellaneous matters, including the rules on service of notices.

MAIN FEATURES OF THE AGRICULTURAL TENANCIES ACT 1995

2.3 As seen in Chapter 1 above, in outline, the main features introduced by the AHA 1995 were as follows:

(a)   No minimum term.
(b)   Minimal security of tenure, being only an extension of the common law notice period for notices to quit annual tenancies; a requirement for fixed-term tenancies of more than two years to be terminated by a prescribed period of notice and a control over the length of notice required to exercise contractual break provisions in certain fixed-term contracts.
(c)   The ability to allow substantial diversification away from agriculture without losing the status of the tenancy as a farm business tenancy.
(d)   Limited freedom over rent review. The parties can choose to have no reviews or one of the statutory options but otherwise the rent will be reviewed on an open market basis. Timing and frequency of reviews are a matter of contract, with a fall-back provision to allow reviews every three years.
(e)   Almost complete freedom for the tenant to remove tenant's fixtures.
(f)   A compulsory statutory scheme for the compensation of tenant's improvements, but otherwise compensation is left to the bargain between the parties.
(g)   The emphasis for dispute resolution is on ADR (alternative dispute resolution) with a fall-back of arbitration under the Arbitration Act 1996.
(h)   All other terms are a matter for the parties.

TENANCY REFORM INDUSTRY GROUP

2.4 In 2002 Lord Whitty and Mr Alun Michael MP set up the newly constituted Tenancy Reform Industry Group (TRIG2). TRIG2 reported in May 2003, presenting its report on 3 June 2003 to DEFRA. The key recommendations of TRIG2 are set out in Ch 1[1].

The opportunity was not taken in TRIG2 to deal with all of the wide range of lacuna existing in relation to the law applying to agricultural holdings. For example, the issue which subsequently arose in the Agricultural Land Tribunal case of *Crabtree v Shirley*[2]. Nevertheless, a number of problem areas have been resolved as a consequence of the legislative changes introduced.

In December 2003, DEFRA produced its response to TRIG2, supporting the proposals for tenancy reform. The Government agreed to use the Regulatory Reform Act 2001 to make a Regulatory Reform Order to introduce the necessary changes to the law. It did so when the Regulatory Reform (Agricultural Tenancies) (England and Wales) Order 2006[3] (RRO 2006) was made on 18 October 2006, coming into force the following day[4].

[1] See para 1.20 above.
[2] [2007] EWHC 1532 (Admin); see para 36.20.
[3] SI 2006/2805.
[4] Article 1(1).

REGULATORY REFORM ORDER 2006

2.5 DEFRA's press release of 31 March 2006 summarised the effect of the (then proposed) RRO 2006 would be to:

(a)   remove the requirement for a potential successor to a tenancy to earn a living primarily from agricultural work on the holding;

(b)   enable landlords and tenants to reach their own agreements on rent reviews and end of tenancy compensation;

(c)   make it easier for landlords and tenants to restructure holdings held under a 1986 Act tenancy;

(d)   remove the need for unnecessary applications to the Agricultural Land Tribunal where a landlord agrees on the successor to a tenancy;

(e)   enable landlords and tenants to agree a notice period to terminate a tenancy to suit their particular circumstances, providing it is longer than the minimum period of 12 months.

CODE OF GOOD PRACTICE

2.6 Part of the terms of reference of TRIG2 was to enable tenant farmers to 'diversify where this will improve the viability of their business' and 'take steps to enhance and protect the environment', in both cases 'without fear of losing their tenancy or jeopardising succession rights'.

As a consequence, TRIG2 made the following recommendations.

(a)   The matter of diversification within farm tenancies should be handled by the formulation of a Code of Good Practice.

(b)   To ensure that the Code of Good Practice has authority it should be backed by an Ombudsman scheme, free at the point of use, to which disputes can be referred when they cannot be settled between the parties. The Ombudsman should have authority to adjudicate on the reasonableness of the proposal or objections, giving a non-binding decision to the parties. It will be primarily evidence from the Ombudsman that will be used to determine whether or not the Code of Good Practice is delivering the required change in attitude.

(c)   Ministers should give a very clear and unambiguous commitment to consider legislation if the Code of Good Practice does not provide an adequate mechanism for resolving potential disputes between landlords and tenants when considering proposals for farm diversification. If, after a period of years, it can be shown that tenants have a legitimate problem with landlords who consistently thwart reasonable diversification plans or impose unrealistic conditions then legislation should be considered to extend the tenant's statutory right to appeal against a landlord's unreasonable refusal to grant consent for the diversified activity.

2.7 The recommendation of TRIG 2 that there should be a Code of Good Practice has been adopted. The 'Code of good practice for agri-environment schemes and diversification projects within agricultural tenancies' was published in 2005 by DEFRA. The following organisations were involved in the preparation of and signed up to the Code of Good Practice: Agricultural Law Association, Association of Chief Estates Surveyors and Property Managers in Local Government, Central Association of Agricultural Valuers, Country Land and Business Association, Farmers Union of Wales, Local Government Association, National Farmers Union, National Federation of Young Farmers Clubs, Royal Institution of Chartered Surveyors, Tenant Farmers Association.

The Code leads the parties through five steps which propose:

(a)   Early consultation between the parties once a project starts to be planned.
(b)   Agreeing a timetable during which the landlord and tenant will seek to agree terms.
(c)   Preparation of detailed proposals with a guide as to information which might be relevant depending on the nature and scale of the project.
(d)   Issues to be addressed in considering the proposals and the need for a written response.
(e)   Preparation of a formal written agreement between the parties.

The Code includes details of an adjudication scheme to consider cases where landlords and tenants are unable to reach agreement. Copies of the Code may be obtained through DEFRA, Area 2D, Ergon House, Horseferry Road, London SW1P 2AL. Tel 020 7238 6811. Originally funding for the scheme was to be provided by DEFRA for a period of four years. In December 2006 it was announced that funding by DEFRA had been withdrawn after no-one applied to use the scheme in the first year of its operation.

Part II

FORMATION OF A FARM BUSINESS TENANCY

Contents

Chapter 3

FORMATION OF A FARM BUSINESS TENANCY

INTRODUCTION

3.1 A farm business tenancy is a tenancy which:

(a) complies with the conditions and definition in s 1 of the Agricultural Tenancies Act 1995 (ATA 1995);

(b) is not excluded by s 2 of the ATA 1995 by reason of the fact that it is a tenancy which begins before 1 September 1995; and

(c) is not a tenancy excluded by s 2 of the Act because it is a tenancy to which the Agricultural Holdings Act 1986 (AHA 1986) applies by reason of one of the exceptions contained in s 4 of the ATA 1995.

Whether a tenancy is a farm business tenancy is not, therefore, a matter of choice for the parties: they cannot opt into the regime (for example to avoid the security of tenure of Pt II of the Landlord and Tenant Act 1954 for commercial lettings) nor can they opt out of it (for example, by contracting back into the AHA 1986).

The definition of a farm business tenancy is set out in s 1. As one of the aims of the ATA 1995 is to allow tenants to diversify into non-agricultural activities, the definition had to allow for this whilst at the same time ensuring that the regime was available only to businesses which were, at least at the outset, agricultural businesses. The solution is a definition which requires a minimum of primary agricultural use at the outset but which allows the parties to choose to stay in the farm business tenancy regime thereafter, even if there is then substantial diversification, for so long as there is some farming activity on the holding[1]. The diversification of agricultural businesses is thereby catered for without allowing the ATA 1995 to be used by landlords in connection with other commercial enterprises properly governed by Pt II of the Landlord and Tenant Act 1954 (LTA 1954) where the tenant may have greater security of tenure[2].

The ATA 1995 came into force on 1 September 1995 and is not retrospective. Most lettings of land for the carrying on of agricultural businesses beginning on or after 1 September 1995 will be farm business tenancies. The ATA 1995 was amended by the RRO 2006[3], following the recommendations of TRIG2[4], most, but not all, of those amendments apply only to tenancies granted on or after 19 October 2006 (when the RRO 2006 came into force) or to variations or consents to existing tenancies made on or after that date.

1   ATA 1995, s 1.
2   Under the LTA 1954, save where the parties have agreed to exclude security of tenure by an agreement (LTA 1954, s 38(A)), tenancies continue unless brought to an end in accordance with the procedures set out in the Act – by a landlord's notice under s 25 or a tenant's request for a new tenancy under s 26. In either case, the tenant can apply to the court for a new tenancy which can only be resisted by the landlord on one of the grounds set out in s 30 of the Act. The grounds include failure of the tenant to comply with repairing obligations; persistent failure to pay rent; substantial breaches of covenant by the tenant; landlord prepared to provide suitable alternative accommodation at reasonable cost; where, in certain circumstances, the landlord wishes to terminate a letting of part; landlord intends to demolish, reconstruct or carry out major works and needs possession to do so; or, in certain circumstances, that the landlord wishes to occupy himself.
3   Regulatory Reform (Agricultural Tenancies) (England and Wales) Order 2006, SI 2006/2805. See para 2.5.
4   Tenancy Reform Industry Group (2002).

WHAT IS A FARM BUSINESS TENANCY?

3.2 As can be seen from the Introduction to this Part, there are two questions to be asked:

(a)   when does the tenancy 'begin'; and
(b)   does the tenancy comply with the conditions set out in s 1 of the ATA 1995?

When does the tenancy begin?

3.3 The ATA 1995 came into force on 1 September 1995 and is not retrospective. Section 2(1) provides that a tenancy cannot be a farm business tenancy if it 'begins' before 1 September 1995. All agricultural tenancies which began before that date will therefore continue to be governed by the AHA 1986 and the two systems (agricultural holdings under the AHA 1986 and farm business tenancies under the ATA 1995) will continue to run side by side until such time as all of the AHA 1986 tenancies have come to an end. Most tenancies which begin on or after 1 September 1995 will be farm business tenancies, although s 4 of the ATA 1995 does provide exceptions where the AHA 1986 will apply to certain lettings beginning on or after that date.

Where a contractual licence arrangement which would have been converted under s 2 of the AHA 1986 begins on or after 1 September 1995, it will not fall to be converted under the AHA 1986 and, not being a tenancy, it will not fall within the farm business tenancy regime[1].

In establishing which Act governs a particular tenancy care needs to be taken with the word 'begin'. It is given a special meaning by s 38(4) of the ATA 1995 and it will not necessarily mean the date upon which the tenancy agreement is signed or the date upon which the term is stated to commence in the body of the tenancy agreement. For the purposes of the ATA 1995, a tenancy begins on the date upon which the tenant is entitled to possession under the terms of the tenancy. So, for example, a tenancy which is agreed on 31 August 1995, but which does not entitle the tenant to go into possession until Michaelmas, would be a farm business tenancy[2]. Conversely, an agreement made on 31 August 1995 to let on a long fixed-term lease where the tenant is entitled to immediate possession but where the necessary deed was not drawn up until the following month would fall under the AHA 1986 regime[3].

[1] ATA 1995, s 4(1).
[2] Subject to any s 4 exception applying.
[3] Note that a contract for a tenancy is a tenancy for the purposes of the ATA 1995: s 38(1). If the contract allows the tenant into possession before the actual tenancy is drawn up, then, for the purposes of the ATA 1995, the tenancy has begun. Furthermore, the tenancy subsequently granted pursuant to the contract is taken, for the purposes of the Act, to have been granted when the contract was entered into: s 38(3).

The section 4 exceptions

3.4 Section 4 of the ATA 1995 provides that certain tenancies beginning on or after 1 September 1995 will be governed by the AHA 1986 by way of exception to the general rule. Otherwise than in relation to these exceptions, the AHA 1986 will not apply to any tenancies beginning on or after 1 September 1995. The s 4 exceptions are to ensure that the ATA 1995 has no retrospective effect whatsoever, either in relation to existing lettings or in relation to new lettings where the tenant might be said to have a legitimate expectation of security. The exceptions are very limited. The idea of the ATA 1995 is to bring an end to AHA 1986 security as quickly as possible. The parties are unable to choose to contract back into the AHA 1986[1]. If the situation does not fall within one of the exceptions in s 4, they have no option but to let on a farm business tenancy. The s 4 exceptions are set out below.

As a consequence of the reforms recommended by TRIG2 and contained within the RRO 2006, amendments to s 4 have clarified problem areas which have become apparent since 1995 and have widened the circumstances in which AHA 1986 status can be maintained. It should be noted that these amendments arising from the RRO 2006 apply only to tenancies granted on or after 19 October 2006 and to variations or consents to existing tenancies made on or after that date[2].

[1] Although this did appear in s 4, almost certainly inadvertently in an earlier draft of the Bill prior to amendments introduced at Report Stage in the House of Lords on 23 January 1995. Before that amendment, clause 4(1)(d) read, 'is granted by a written contract of tenancy indicating (in whatever terms) that Part IV of the AHA 1986 is to apply in relation to the tenancy'. This wording would have allowed parties to choose to contract back into the AHA 1986 security.
[2] SI 2006/2805, art 1.

The window of opportunity

3.5 Section 4(1)(a) of the ATA 1995 was introduced at Committee Stage in the House of Commons. It provides that where tenancies beginning on or after

3.5 *Formation of a farm business tenancy*

1 September 1995 are granted pursuant to a written contract of tenancy entered into before that date which indicates (in whatever terms) that the AHA 1986 is to apply to the tenancy, the AHA 1986 will apply. The stated reason for the introduction of the amendment was to ensure that, where it was clear by their contract that the parties intended the AHA 1986 to apply, the amendment was necessary to ensure that the Act did not have a retrospective effect on existing contracts (as opposed to existing tenancies). However, the exception generally provided a window of opportunity for landowners in the run up to 1 September 1995 to reorganise estates or otherwise arrange new tenancies or surrenders and re-grants without actually having to move the tenants before that date, possibly at an inconvenient time of the year, and yet still preserve or grant AHA 1986 security. Without the exception, because the tenants would not be entitled to possession under the new tenancy until on or after 1 September 1995, the tenancies would 'begin' after the coming into force of the Act and thus be farm business tenancies.

Succession tenancies

3.6 Section 4(1)(b) to (d) contain further exceptions in relation to succession tenancies. A tenant occupying under an AHA 1986 tenancy which carries succession rights has a legitimate expectation that his successor will enjoy similar security of tenure. This group of exceptions ensures that succession tenancies beginning on or after 1 September 1995 continue to fall to be governed by the AHA 1986. Succession tenancies are protected whether they come about as a result of a direction of an Agricultural Land Tribunal (ALT) (whether on the death of or following the retirement of the previous tenant)[1]; or as a result of the grant of a tenancy by the landlord to the new tenant following a direction in the new tenant's favour[2], or where they are granted on an agreed succession[3].

An agreed succession is defined by s 4(2) of the ATA 1995 in such a way as to ensure that only genuine succession tenancies will continue to be governed by the AHA 1986 and that s 4(1)(d) cannot be used to contract back into the AHA 1986 by the simple expedient of calling any new tenancy an 'agreed succession'.

The RRO 2006 amends the definition of an agreed succession, rendering it less complex than the original wording of the ATA 1995 and to clarifying the original draftsmanship[4]. The amendments apply only to tenancies granted on or after 19 October 2006 or to variations and consents to existing tenancies made on or after that date[5]. Should any question arise concerning the status of a tenancy entered into before 19 October 2006 and whether it is an agreed succession, the original wording of agreed succession will apply.

Consequential upon the amendments contained in the RRO 2006, a tenancy is an agreed succession if, and only if:

38

(a)   the previous tenancy of the holding or a related holding was a tenancy to which Pt IV of the AHA 1986 applied. In other words, the old tenancy, to which the new tenant is succeeding, has to be one which carried succession rights[6]; and

(b)   the tenancy is granted to a tenant who would be defined as a 'close relative' of the previous tenant had the previous tenant died immediately before the grant[7]; and either

(c)   the tenant had become the sole or sole remaining applicant for a direction of the ALT for the new tenancy; or

(d)   the tenancy is granted as a result of an agreement between the landlord and the previous tenant and is granted and begins before the date of any retirement notice[8] by the previous tenant or, if no retirement notice is given, before the date of the death of the previous tenant.

The new wording introduced to the ATA 1995 by the RRO 2006 in relation to agreed succession makes it clear that an agreed retirement succession can be an agreed succession for the purposes of s 4(1)(d) of the ATA 1995. Under the original wording, this was not clear. The cautious were able, where the original tenant fulfilled the conditions for serving a retirement notice, to apply to the ALT for a direction, but in the absence of such direction, the status of an agreed retirement succession before 19 October 2006 remains unclear. The new wording will cover agreed retirement successions regardless of whether or not the outgoing tenant would have been able to serve a retirement notice.

Where the status of a tenancy which was granted before 19 October 2006 is in question, the old s 4(2) of the ATA 1995 applies. The need for the old tenancy to which the new tenant is succeeding to carry succession rights under the AHA 1986 is the same. The new tenancy, whose status is in question, is then tested by reference to whether (were it an AHA 1986 tenancy) it would have counted as one of the two succession 'occasions' under s 37(1)(a) or (b) of the AHA 1986. It is in the testing of the new tenancy by reference to this hypothesis (if it were granted under the AHA 1986, would it have counted as a succession under s 37 of the AHA 1986) that the perceived problem with retirement successions occurred[9].

Section 37(1)(a) refers to directions of the ALT or grants following a direction. Section 37(1)(b) refers only to the new tenancy being granted to a close relative of a tenant who has *died*. There is no direct reference in s 37 to the retirement of a tenant. Section 51 of the AHA 1986 states that s 37 will apply to exclude further retirement successions subject to modifications, including references to the date of death being read as references to the date of the giving of a retirement notice. However, s 51 does not operate so as to amend or extend s 37 itself, but merely to state that its terms will apply with modifications to retirement successions. As s 4(2) of the ATA 1995 refers only to s 37 of the AHA 1986 in defining agreed succession for the purposes of the ATA 1995, and not to s 51, there is some doubt whether, technically, retirement successions agreed between landlord and tenant can be agreed successions and hence continue to be protected under the AHA 1986.

[1]   ATA 1995, s 4(1)(b).
[2]   ATA 1995, s 4(1)(c) and AHA 1986, s 45(6) and see Ch 35 and Ch 36.

3.6 Formation of a farm business tenancy

3   ATA 1995, s 4(1)(d). Agreed succession is defined, for the purposes of the ATA 1995, in s 4(2), as amended by the RRO 2006 in respect of tenancies granted on or after 19 October 2006: see RRO 2006, SI 2006/2805, art 12(12).
4   See A1.214.
5   RRO 2006, SI 2006/2805, art 1(1).
6   ATA 1995, s 4(2)(a).
7   ATA 1995, s 4(3)(b): 'close relative' has the meaning given by s 35(2) of the AHA 1986.
8   RRO 2006, SI 2006/2805, art 12(11)(c) where 'retirement notice' is defined by reference to s 49(3) of the AHA 1986.
9   Section 4(2) of the ATA 1995 tests the new tenancy by reference to whether or not it would count as a succession tenancy under the AHA 1986 ie would count as one of the two succession 'occasions' under s 37(1)(a) or (b) such as would prevent further successions.

The Evesham Custom

3.7 Section 4(1)(e) of the ATA 1995 contains an exception in relation to the Evesham Custom. The Evesham Custom, given statutory force by s 80(3) to (5) of the AHA 1986, is detailed in Chapter 40. In brief, it encourages investment in market gardening by ensuring that, in certain circumstances when the tenant quits the holding, the new incoming tenant, and not the landlord, pays the outgoing tenant for the improvements. Additional rights are given to the tenant to effect certain improvements[1]. If the tenant subsequently becomes insolvent or serves notice to quit, he will not obtain compensation for the improvements from the landlord unless he produces an offer from a new tenant to take a new tenancy on the same terms and conditions and to pay compensation for the improvements to the old tenant. The landlord can then accept that offer or choose to pay the compensation.

If the new tenant were not given AHA 1986 security, it is unlikely that one could be found who was prepared to pay for the improvements. Hence the outgoing tenant would be left in a position where he could not fulfil the condition (producing an offer from a new tenant) to obtain compensation. Accordingly, this exception is, once again, to protect the legitimate expectations of those tenants who have effected improvements on a market garden pursuant to s 79(2) to (5) of the AHA 1986 and who expected to be able thereafter to fulfil the condition for compensation. It provides that where the new tenancy is created by the acceptance of a tenant of a new tenancy on the same terms and conditions as the old in accordance with the Evesham Custom, the new tenancy will be an AHA 1986 tenancy.

1   AHA 1986, s 79(2)–(5).

Surrender and re-grant

3.8 If the parties to an AHA 1986 tenancy purport to vary the terms of that tenancy, it is possible that, as a matter of law, they will actually effect a surrender and re-grant. Without the exception contained in s 4(1)(f) and (g), the re-grant (being a tenancy beginning on or after 1 September 1995) would be a farm business tenancy.

For the efficient management of AHA 1986 tenancies, it was important that this should not happen, particularly if a surrender would be effected by implication of law in the relatively common situation of adding further land to an existing tenancy[1].

In general, a surrender by implication of law is only going to arise where further land or premises are added to the tenancy or the term is extended[2]. An extension of the term of a lease can only take effect by surrender and re-grant[3]. The addition of a new tenant is not necessarily a surrender and re-grant[4]. Whether other changes to the terms amount to a surrender and re-grant is a matter of the intention of the parties[5]. The question to be asked if whether the variation is so fundamental that it goes to the root of the tenancy or is inconsistent with the continuation of the tenancy.

Section 4(1)(f) was designed to ensure that the tenant did not lose his AHA 1986 protection by an inadvertent surrender and re-grant. Section 4(1)(f) has been amended by the RRO 2006, which also has added s 4(1)(g). These amendments apply only to tenancies granted on or after 19 October 2006 or to variations and consents to existing tenancies on or after that date[6]. The original wording of s 4(1)(f) will continue to apply to determine the status of tenancies granted or variations made before that date.

[1] *Friends' Provident Life Office v British Railways Board* [1995] EGCS 140, CA. Cf *Fredco Estates Ltd v Bryant* [1961] 1 WLR 76, CA.
[2] *Friends' Provident Life Office v British Railways Board* (1995) EGCS 140. In this case, an increase in rent and a relaxation of the prohibition against assignment was held to be a variation only.
[3] *Re Savile* [1931] 2 Ch 210; *Baker v Merckel* [1960] 1 QB 657, CA; *Jenkin R Lewis & Son v Kerman* [1971] Ch 477; *J W Childers Trustees v Anker* [1996] 1 EGLR 6; *Friends Provident Life Office v British Railways Board* [1995] EGCS 140, CA.
[4] *Saunders v Ralph* [1993] 2 EGLR 1, [1993] 28 EG 127.
[5] *Take Harvest Ltd v Liu* [1993] AC 552, PC.
[6] SI 2006/2805, art 1(1).

Tenancies granted and variations made before 19 October 2006

3.9 Section 4(1)(f), as originally enacted, protected the AHA 1986 status of the new tenancy where it comes about:

'... merely because a purported variation of the previous tenancy (not being an agreement expressed to take effect as a new tenancy between the parties) has effect as an implied surrender followed by the grant of the tenancy'.

The following points should be noted for tenancies granted or variations made before 19 October 2006:

(a) Section 4(1)(f) only provides protection where the new tenancy is granted to the same tenant. If the re-grant is not to the tenant but, for example, to the tenant and another, it will not fall within s 4(1)(f). It may, depending upon the circumstances, fall within the exception for succession tenancies[1].

(b) The re-grant must be to the person who was the tenant of '... the holding or of any agricultural holding which comprised the whole or a substantial part of the land comprised in the new holding under the re-grant'. Where new premises or land are added to the demise, it will almost always be by surrender and re-grant[2]. Provided that a substantial part of the new holding was also in the old tenancy, s 4(1)(f) is capable of operating. What is substantial will be a matter of fact in each and every case, but it does not necessarily mean that the additional land must amount to only a small percentage of the new holding: the wording is *a* substantial part, not *the* substantial part. There is no further guidance in the original wording as to whether a substantial part must refer only to acreage or area of the new holding. This can be contrasted with the amendment in the RRO 2006 for tenancies granted or variations made on or after 19 October 2006 where it is made clear that a substantial part can be determined by reference either to area or value[3].

[1]   ATA 1995, s 4(1)(b)–(d).
[2]   *Friends' Provident Life Office v British Railways Board* (1995) EGCS 140. Cf *Fredco Estates Ltd v Bryant* [1961] 1 WLR 76.
[3]   See para 3.14.

3.10 Since the enactment of s 4(1)(f), there has been an issue as to whether the intention of the parties in purporting only to vary the existing tenancy should be judged objectively or subjectively. This became an issue in part because of amendments to the Inheritance Tax Act 1984, designed to encourage landlords to enter into new tenancies. Section 155 of the Finance Act 1995 introduced an amendment to s 116 of the Inheritance Tax Act 1984 so that property let on a tenancy beginning on or after 1 September 1995 is capable of attracting 100% agricultural property relief and not the 50% relief available to a landlord with land let before that date. It should be noted that there is no requirement for the new tenancy to be a farm business tenancy. While designed to encourage new lettings, an opportunity was perceived for landlords with existing tenants to move those tenants onto new tenancies and accordingly take advantage of the better inheritance tax relief. Tenants were reluctant to lose their AHA 1986 security in order to facilitate this.

Some tenants were persuaded to move to new farm business tenancies on terms which, as far as possible, mirrored the express terms and statutory provisions applying to their existing AHA 1986 tenancies. Another approach was to attempt to utilise s 4(1)(f) to ensure that the new letting was still an AHA 1986 tenancy. This involved bringing about a surrender and re-grant, for example by adding land to the existing tenancy, knowing (and needing for inheritance tax purposes) that this amounted to a surrender and re-grant and a new tenancy, but calling the arrangement a variation to bring it into operation s 4(1)(f) so that the re-grant was an AHA 1986 tenancy and not a 1995 Act tenancy.

There are two possible results from such a scheme:

(a)   The 'purported variation' took effect as a surrender and re-grant and, because on the face of the document recording the 'variation', there was no mention of the grant of a new tenancy, the new tenancy falls within

42

s 4(1)(f). The tenant then held his tenancy under a new AHA 1986 letting, beginning on or after 1 September 1995 and the landlord gained his inheritance tax advantage.

(b)   The fact that the parties intended there to be a surrender and re-grant, and that the variation was not inadvertent, prevented it from being 'purported' and/or means that the new tenancy was not granted '... merely because ...' of the purported variation but because the parties wanted and intended that result. If that analysis is correct, there would be a new tenancy and the landlord would obtain the inheritance tax advantage. However, the new tenancy would not fall within s 4(1)(f). It would be a farm business tenancy, and possibly an annual periodic tenancy (unless the 'variation' is an extension of the term by the grant of a fixed term of years).

One question was whether the statutory language allowed the intention of the parties to be considered. It would appear that the intention of Parliament was that it would be relevant. Lord Howe at Report Stage in the House of Lords[1] accepted that it would be inequitable, in the case of implied surrender and re-grant, for the new tenancy not to have 1986 Act protection '... when the parties had not intended that to happen ...'. The word 'purported' itself could be interpreted to allow an investigation into the intention of the parties as could the words 'merely because'[2].

From this analysis it can be seen that the risks of the scheme failing were much greater for the tenant. Caution had to be exercised by advisers before embarking upon such a scheme. Even if it was possible by contractual provisions in the document recording the 'variation', to ensure that the new tenancy, even if not an AHA 1986 tenancy, gave the tenant as near as possible equivalent protection, the more the document looks, on its face, like a new tenancy agreement, the greater the chance that the agreement would be found to be one which is '... expressed to take effect as a new tenancy ...' or at least does not look like a 'purported variation'. The issues created by this have been addressed by the RRO 2006[3].

The above passage of this book was referred to in the judgment in *Well Barn Farming Ltd v Backhouse*[4]. The judge expressed no opinion as to whether the above observations are right or wrong. He did state that even if s 4(1)(f) could not be manipulated in the way described, and even if that involved an approach that breaches the normal rule that the parties' intentions are to be judged objectively, he did not see any sufficient reason to extrapolate from that particular instance so as to admit the subjective intentions of the parties when applying s 4(1)(f) in the *Well Barn* case.

[1]   23 January 1995.
[2]   See Sydenham 'Country Landowner' February 1996, p 22; *Farm Tax Brief*, Vol 11, No 6, June 1996.
[3]   See para 3.12. As a consequence of the introduction of ATA 1995, s 4(1)(g), it is submitted that it is now possible for a landlord and a tenant to achieve the tax advantage referred to in this paragraph by means of an express surrender and re-grant, provided that the conditions contained in s 4(1)(g) are complied with: see para 3.14.
[4]   [2005] EWHC 1520 (Ch), [2005] 3 EGLR 109 at para 116K.

3.11 *Formation of a farm business tenancy*

3.11 Section 4(1)(f) was considered in the case of *Well Barn Farming Ltd v Backhouse*[1]. The issue in that case was whether the owners were entitled to possession of a small copse. The tenants argued that a licence to occupy the copse had been converted by the operation of s 2 of the AHA 1986 into an AHA 1986 tenancy[2]. Or, in the alternative, that a later 1996 rent review memorandum had added the copse to the land let and that the result was a surrender and re-grant which fell within s 4(1)(f). The case was decided on the first basis, but the judge went on to consider the alternative submission.

The 1996 rent review memorandum was not expressed to have effect as a new tenancy. The judge concluded that whether the creation of a new tenancy is deliberate or inadvertent was to be judged objectively (in accordance with the normal approach to construing documents) and that in the ordinary case the reference in s 4(1)(f) to a purported variation should not involve an inquiry into the subjective states of mind of the parties, but should merely differentiate the case from one where there is an express grant of a new tenancy.

On the face of the 1996 memorandum, judged objectively, there was a purported variation of the original tenancy by adding land. Section 4(1)(f) would apply. If *Well Barn* is correct, then the intention of the parties is irrelevant in determining whether a deliberate surrender and re-grant can be a purported variation, but the case was not dealing with a situation where the parties had deliberately set out to use s 4(1)(f) to gain a fiscal advantage. Indeed, the judge was careful to refer to the discussion of the issue in the last edition of this book[3] and to express no opinion as to whether the argument in that edition was right or wrong. An argument was put forward that the word 'purported' and the phrase 'merely because' would prevent the successful manipulation of s 4(1)(f) to gain the fiscal advantage. In other words, that the intention of the parties would be relevant to the application of s 4(1)(f) to that situation. It is still not known therefore whether any such schemes which were entered into for the purpose of securing 100% agricultural property relief for the landlord have or have not resulted in the tenant moving on to a new AHA 1986 tenancy as a result of the operation of s 4(1)(f).

As will be seen from the following section in this book, dealing with tenancies granted or variations made on or after 19 October 2006, significant amendments to s 4(1)(f) and the new s 4(1)(g), will mean that it is much more straightforward for landlords and tenants to manage AHA 1986 tenancies without the risk of the loss of AHA 1986 protection.

[1] [2005] 3 EGLR 109.
[2] See para 20.5.
[3] See p 908 of the eighth edition.

Tenancies granted and variations made on or after 19 October 2006

3.12 TRIG2[1] acknowledged that the operation of s 4(1)(f) of the ATA 1995 and the doctrine of implied surrender and re-grant had caused confusion to landlords and tenants alike, and their professional advisers. As a consequence, TRIG2 made the following recommendations:

44

(a)   An additional provision to be included within s 4(1)(f) enabling existing parties to an AHA 1986 tenancy, by mutual consent, to include additional land and buildings within their holding resulting in the 'new' holding being governed by the AHA 1986 and on the same terms (mutatis mutandis) as the original tenancy.

(b)   It should no longer be necessary for the 'original' holding to form a substantial part of the 'new' holding either by area or value (whichever is the more significant).

DEFRA accepted the recommendations of TRIG2 and put forward proposals for reform contained in the RRO 2006[2]. As set out in DEFRA's Explanatory Note[3]:

(i)   The proposal would amend s 4(1)(f) of the ATA 1995 with the effect that the AHA 1986 will apply to the tenancy in the cases where:
   •   the parties come to an agreement (eg to add land to the holding) but which, without their knowledge or intention that it should do so, has effect as a surrender and re-grant; and
   •   the parties come to such an agreement and *are* aware that it will have effect as a surrender and re-grant.

(ii)   In both the above cases the original holding must be the whole or a substantial part of the new holding.

(iii)   The proposal would add a new s 4(1)(g) which would provide that the AHA 1986 will apply where there is a written contract of tenancy which states that the AHA 1986 is to apply, and the tenant previously held an AHA 1986 tenancy of all or a substantial part of the holding.

(iv)   The proposal would introduce an anti-avoidance provision (new s 4(2B)), to stop parties from using the amended s 4(1)(f) or new s 4(1)(g) to add land incrementally to a holding and so get around the 'whole or substantial part' requirement. The proposal would also define 'substantial' in s 4(1)(g) as meaning either substantial in area or substantial in value, widening the cases in which the new s 4(1)(g) could apply to a proposed restructuring of a holding.

The proposals have been enacted in the RRO 2006[4] with effect from 19 October 2006.

(A)   For the words:

   '("the previous tenancy") and is so granted merely because a purported variation of the previous tenancy (not being an agreement expressed to take effect as a new tenancy between the parties) has effect as an implied surrender followed by the grant of the tenancy',
   there has been substituted:

   ', and is so granted because an agreement between the parties (not being an agreement expressed to take effect as a new tenancy between the parties) has effect as an implied surrender followed by the grant of the tenant, or'[5].

(B)   A new s 4(1)(g) has been inserted[6]:

   '(g) is granted to a person who, immediately before the grant of the tenancy, was the tenant of the holding, or of any agricultural holding which comprised the whole or a substantial part of the land compromised in the holding, under a tenancy in relation to which the AHA 1986 applied, and is so granted by a written contract of tenancy indicating (in whatever terms) that the AHA 1986 is to apply in relation to the tenancy'.

As a consequence of the amendments, the parties to an existing 1986 Act tenancy are able to apply the AHA 1986 to a new tenancy by express provision in the contract of tenancy, provided that the tenant previously held an AHA 1986 tenancy of all or a substantial part of the holding[7].

The significant amendments to s 4(1)(f); a new s 4(1)(g) and an anti-avoidance provision contained in s 4(2) of the ATA 1995, have made it easier for landlords and tenants of AHA 1986 tenancies to add land and make other changes without the risk of losing AHA 1986 security, while ensuring that this section cannot be manipulated beyond what was intended by repeated surrenders and re-grants leading to incremental changes in the land let.

[1]   See para 1.19.
[2]   SI 2006/2805.
[3]   Explanatory Document: The Regulatory Reform (Agricultural Tenancies) (England and Wales) Order 2006: Statement by the Department for the Environment, Food and Rural Affairs, March 2006.
[4]   SI 2006/2805.
[5]   SI 2006/2805, art 12(4).
[6]   SI 2006/2805, art 12(5).
[7]   As to a substantial part of the holding, see the AHA 1986, ss 69(1A) and 73(1A).

Section 4(1)(f) as amended by the RRO 2006

3.13   As regards s 4(1)(f), two requirements remain the same as they were prior to the RRO 2006 coming into force on 19 October 2006[1]. The first is that the re-grant must be to the same tenant. The second is that the land in the original holding must form a substantial part of the land in the new holding under the re-grant.

While art 12(10) of the RRO 2006 inserts a new s 4(2C) into the ATA 1995, which defines a substantial part to mean a substantial part determined by reference to either area or value, that definition applies only to the use of the phrase in s 4(1)(g) and s 4(2B)[2] and not to s 4(1)(f)[3] where the phrase remains undefined.

The amended section requires that:

(a)   there be an agreement between the parties;
(b)   the agreement is not expressed to take effect as a new tenancy between the parties; and
(c)   the re-grant comes about because that agreement has the effect of an implied surrender followed by the grant of a new tenancy.

When looked at together with s 4(1)(g) below, it is clear that this provision is intended to deal with the inadvertent or implied surrender and re-grant, but the removal of the phrases 'merely because' and 'purported variation', which gave rise to problems and confusion in the original s 4(1)(f) makes the test clear and objective: the new tenancy will be AHA 1986 protected if it is not expressed to take effect as a new tenancy. This is consistent with the interpretation of the original s 4(1)(f) in the *Well Barn* decision[4].

¹ SI 2006/2805, art 1(1).
² See para 3.15.
³ Also see the amendments to ss 34, 35 and 49 of the AHA 1986.
⁴ See para 3.11.

Section 4(1)(g)

3.14 Section 4(1)(g) was introduced into the ATA 1995 by art 12(5) of the RRO 2006. This new provision allows the parties to surrender an AHA 1986 tenancy and enter into a new tenancy on or after 19 October 2006 where the new tenancy will take effect as a tenancy under the AHA 1986 provided that it meets certain requirements contained in s 4(1)(g) and the new s 4(2B).

The requirements are:

(a)   the tenant must be the same;
(b)   the land in the original holding must form a substantial part of the land in the new holding;
(c)   the original holding must itself have been protected by the AHA 1986;
(d)   the new tenancy must be granted by a written contract of tenancy; and
(e)   the written contract of tenancy must indicate (in whatever terms) that the AHA 1986 is to apply to it.

The following points should be noted in relation to the operation of s 4(1)(g):

(i)   for the purposes of s 4(1)(g)[1] a substantial part of the holding is defined by s 4(2C)[2] to mean 'a substantial part determined by reference to either area or value'. It may be that an area relatively small in terms of the total acreage under the new tenancy, but highly valuable when considered against the other land in the new tenancy, is all that remains of the original holding. That may be enough for the new tenancy to obtain AHA 1986 protection;
(ii)   s 4(1)(g) only applies where the new letting is contained in a written contract of tenancy. Any oral arrangements fall to be considered under s 4(1)(f);
(iii)   any subsequent alterations in relation to the new tenancy will need to be considered in the context of the anti-avoidance provisions contained in s 4(2B).

¹ And s 4(2B) introduced by RRO 2006, SI 2006/2805, art 12(9).
² RRO 2006, SI 2006/2805, art 12(10).

Anti-avoidance

3.15 Additionally, the RRO 2006 enacted the insertion of three new subsections to s 4(2) of the ATA 1995:

'(2A) The conditions referred to in subsection (2)(c) above are:

(a)   the current tenancy is granted to a person (alone or jointly with other persons) who was or had become the sole or sole remaining applicant for a direction of an Agricultural Land Tribunal for a tenancy, and

(b)   the current tenancy—

(i)   is granted as a result of an agreement between the landlord and the previous tenant, and

(ii)   is granted, and begins, before the date of the giving of any retirement notice by the previous tenant, or if no retirement notice is given, before the date of death of the previous tenant.[1]

(2B) AHA 1986 shall not apply by virtue of subsection (1)(f) or (g) above in relation to the tenancy of an agricultural holding ('the current holding') where—

(a)   the whole or a substantial part of the land comprised in the current holding was comprised in an agricultural holding ('the previous holding') which was subject to a tenancy granted after the commencement of this subsection in relation to which the AHA 1986 applied by virtue of subsection (1)(f) or (g) above;

(b)   the whole or a substantial part of the land comprised in the previous holding was comprised in an agricultural holding ('the original holding') which was at the commencement of this subsection subject to a tenancy in relation to which the AHA 1986 applied; and

(c)   the land comprised in the original holding does not, on the date of the grant of the tenancy of the current holding, comprise the whole or a substantial part of the land comprised in the current holding.[2]

(2C) The references in subsections (1)(g) and (2B) above to a substantial part of the land comprised in the holding mean a substantial part determined by reference to either area or value'[3].

The purpose of the amendments to s 4(2) of the ATA 1995 is to prevent parties from using sub-ss (1)(f) and (1)(g) of s 4 incrementally to avoid the 'whole or substantial part' requirement of those subsections.

[1]   The RRO 2006, SI 2006/2805, art 12(8).
[2]   RRO 2006, SI 2006/2805, art 12(9).
[3]   RRO 2006, SI 2006/2805, art 12(10).

3.16 Section 4(2B) restricts the parties' ability to maintain AHA 1986 protection. It is designed to ensure that a series of surrenders and re-grants, resulting in a substantially different holding to that which existed at the commencement of the series of agreements, cannot be used to ensure AHA 1986 protection for a tenant who has essentially moved from one holding to another.

Section 4(2B) is not retrospective. It only applies in relation to changes occurring after the commencement of the RRO 2006 on 19 October 2006[1].

In order to understand the way in which s 4(2B) operates, it is necessary to consider the definitions used in the section for the various holdings in the series:

(a)   'the original holding': an agricultural holding which was subject to an AHA 1986 tenancy on 19 October 2006;

(b)   'the previous holding': the land which was, immediately before the tenancy under review, subject to a tenancy granted on or after 19 October 2006 and to which the AHA 1986 applied by reason of s 4(1)(f) or (g);

(c)   'the current holding': the land with the tenancy whose status is being tested by s 4(2B).

Section 4(2B) provides that the AHA 1986 shall not apply to the current holding where the whole or a substantial part of that land was comprised in the previous holding and the whole or substantial part of the previous holding was comprised in the original holding but where the land comprised in the original holding does not form the whole or a substantial part of the current holding. In other words, where the incremental changes brought about by a series of surrenders and re-grants means that the holding achieved by that series of agreements does not contain a substantial part of the land that was in the AHA 1986 holding as it stood on 19 October 2006. Changes prior to the RRO 2006 coming into force on 19 October 2006 are irrelevant.

The definition of a substantial part is governed by the new s 4(2C) and is determined by reference to either area or value. This is consistent with the definition applying to s 4(1)(g), but while the definition does not apply in the application or s 4(1)(f) to the tenancy, it will apply to any tenancy under s 4(1)(f) when it comes to the application of the anti-avoidance provision.

[1]   RRO 2006, SI 2006/2805, art 1(1).

The definition of a farm business tenancy

3.17 Section 1(1) of the ATA 1995 provides that a tenancy will be a farm business tenancy if it meets the business conditions together with either the agriculture condition or the notice conditions. Proof of compliance with these conditions, which are set out in s 1(2) to (4), is assisted by a presumption in favour of compliance[1] and a disregard for uses not permitted by the tenancy agreement[2].

From this definition it can be seen that all farm business tenancies must comply with the business conditions. The parties then have a choice, which they exercise at the beginning of a tenancy, either to comply, in addition, with the notice conditions or with the agriculture condition. If the parties decide not to serve notices in compliance with the notice conditions, the tenancy must, at the relevant time, comply with the agriculture condition. The agriculture condition can be seen, therefore, as a fall-back. As we shall see, it is the combination of the business conditions and the notice conditions which allow for major diversification into non-agricultural activities: the business conditions require only minimal farming throughout the life of the tenancy and the notice conditions require primary agricultural use only at the beginning of the tenancy. If the parties rely on the agriculture condition and do not serve notices, however, the tenancy must be primarily agricultural at any time that the status of the tenancy as a farm business tenancy is challenged.

[1] ATA 1995, s 1(7).
[2] ATA 1995, s 1(8).

Must be a tenancy

3.18 The first point of difference between the ATA 1995 and the AHA 1986 is that the ATA 1995 only applies to tenancies. If the arrangement between the parties amounts to a licence only[1], it falls outside the Act: there is no 'magical conversion' of licences into tenancies as there is under the AHA 1986. There would be little point in such a provision. The security of tenure offered by the ATA 1995 is minimal[2] and, therefore, there is little or no advantage to the occupier of conversion. Furthermore, a landlord who knows exactly when he will get his land back (as he will under the farm business tenancy regime) is less likely to seek to avoid a tenancy. Not only will this mean fewer licences, but partnerships; contracting agreements and share farming arrangements previously chosen by landowners to avoid letting their land with security of tenure will now be arrangements used only to satisfy other commercial and fiscal requirements.

As the provisions of s 2 of the AHA 1986 only operate to convert licences conferring exclusive possession on the occupier[3] and only those supported by consideration[4], the distinction between arrangements which will be tenancies and therefore fall within the ATA 1995 and arrangements which would be convertible licences under the AHA 1986 is limited. The hallmark of a tenancy is the granting of exclusive possession[5] and, whilst the tenant must be providing some benefit to the landlord or suffering some detriment there is no requirement that a tenancy be supported by the payment of a monetary rent rather than by any other form of consideration.

While the ATA 1995 only applies to tenancies, it does not impose any restrictions on duration[6] or a statutory minimum term nor does the Act require that all farm business tenancies must be in writing[7] – both suggestions put forward but dismissed during the passage of the Bill. A farm business tenancy can, therefore, be periodic or fixed-term; if periodic, for any period (monthly; quarterly, annual); if fixed-term, for any duration (1 day; 1 year, 99 years). It is, therefore, an extremely flexible method of letting land and, as farm business tenancies of two years or less expire by effluxion of time[8], is capable of replacing the one crop agreements; grazing agreements for a grazing season and *Gladstone v Bower* agreements all used to avoid security of tenure under the AHA 1986 regime, without leaving the landlord in any worse a position than he was under that Act[9].

It is possible, of course, not to use the ATA 1995 at all and to continue to use licences, for example, for grazing. If, however, the arrangement confers exclusive possession on the occupier, it will almost certainly be held to be a tenancy.

'Tenancy' has an extended meaning under the ATA 1995. It is defined in s 38(1) to include a sub-tenancy and an agreement for a tenancy or a sub-tenancy, but to exclude a tenancy at will[10]. As contracts for tenancies can be farm business tenancies, it is possible, where the tenant is entitled to go into possession pursuant to the contract, for all of the provisions of the ATA 1995 to apply from the date of the contract. Furthermore, s 38(3) provides that a tenancy granted pursuant to a contract shall be taken for the purposes of the Act to have been granted when the contract was entered into.

1   For the distinction, see *Street v Mountford* [1985] AC 809. See also the House of Lords decision in *Bruton v London & Quadrant Housing Trust* [2000] 1 AC 406.
2   See ATA 1995, ss 5–7 and Ch 12.
3   *Bahamas International Trust Co Ltd v Threadgold* [1974] 3 All ER 881.
4   See Ch 18.
5   While exclusive possession is necessary to a tenancy, not all occupiers granted rights of exclusive possession are tenants (*Street v Mountford* [1985] AC 809); their rights may be attributable to some other legal status (*Errington v Errington and Woods* [1952] 1 KB 290, CA). See also *Onyx (UK) Ltd v Beard* [1996] EGCS 55.
6   Although the term must be of a certain maximum duration, see Ch 6.
7   Although there may be formal requirements, see Ch 4.
8   ATA 1995, ss 5 and 6 and see Ch 12.
9   See Ch 18 and Ch 19.
10 Cf the AHA 1986 where a tenancy at will, being for an interest less than a tenancy from year to year, is converted by s 2 of the AHA 1986 into a fully protected annual tenancy: *Keen v Holland* [1984] 1 All ER 75.

The business conditions

INTRODUCTION

3.19 Failure to comply with the business conditions means that the tenancy cannot be a farm business tenancy. The conditions are set out in s 1(2) of the ATA 1995. They are:

'(a)   that all or part of the land comprised in the tenancy is farmed for the purposes of a trade or business; and
(b)   that, since the beginning of the tenancy, all or part of the land so comprised has been so farmed'.

The essence of the business conditions is, therefore, that commercial farming must take place on some part of the holding throughout the duration of the tenancy.

BEGINNING OF THE TENANCY

3.20 Compliance must start at the 'beginning' of the tenancy. The beginning of the tenancy is defined by s 38(4) of the ATA 1995 as being the date upon which the tenant is entitled under the terms of the tenancy to possession of the holding. It would clearly be impossible for the tenant to comply with the business conditions before he was entitled to possession, even though there is no requirement in the Act for the farming to be conducted personally by the tenant.

NO BREAK IN COMPLIANCE

3.21 There must be no break in compliance from the beginning of the tenancy right up to the date when the status of the tenancy is challenged. By this date is meant the date by reference to which its status is in issue and not necessarily the later date when that issue is raised in proceedings. If, at any stage during the tenancy there is no commercial farming being conducted on the holding, for however short a period and for whatever reason, the tenancy will have lost its status as a farm business tenancy. It is not possible for the tenancy to regain that status if the tenant restarts commercial farming[1] at a later date: once the status is lost, it is lost for ever. However, the party seeking to show that the tenancy is a farm business tenancy is helped by a presumption relating to historical non-compliance.

Section 1(7) of the ATA 1995 provides that where in any proceedings any question as to whether a tenancy is a farm business tenancy at any time arises then, provided that the relevant party can prove that the land or part of it was farmed for the purposes of a trade or business at that time, compliance since the beginning of the tenancy shall be presumed. This does not stop a landlord or tenant from rebutting that presumption by proving historical non-compliance. If he is able to do so, the tenancy will not be a farm business tenancy and will have lost its status on the first day that there was no longer any commercial farming on the holding. The presumption only operates 'unless the contrary is proved'. However, it is nevertheless valuable, particularly where it is the landlord who wishes to establish that the tenancy is a farm business tenancy. It may be difficult if not impossible for him to prove that the tenant has farmed commercially throughout the tenancy, with no breaks whatsoever. What amounts to a cessation of commercial farming will be a question of fact in every case.

Challenge to the status of the tenancy may be during the term (as, for example, in response to a tenant's application for arbitrator's approval to the provision of a tenant's improvement under s 19 of the ATA 1995[2]) or at the end of the term, for example, where the tenant seeks to make a compensation claim for tenant's improvements under the Act. It may, of course, be either party who is seeking to establish non-compliance with the business conditions. If there is no other commercial activity on the holding at the time of challenge, the landlord may wish to show historical non-compliance so that the tenancy becomes a common law tenancy, protected by no code; determinable (if periodic) by the common law notice period and without the benefit of, for example, the compensation provisions in the ATA 1995. If there is other commercial activity on the holding, it may be the tenant who is trying to show that the tenancy is no longer a farm business tenancy but that it has become a tenancy governed by Pt II of the Landlord and Tenant Act 1954 which will give him greater security of tenure[3] and the ability, in many cases, to acquire a new tenancy at the end of his existing term.

---

[1]   Cf non-compliance with the agriculture condition.
[2]   See Ch 16.
[3]   For a brief outline of the security offered by Pt II of the Landlord and Tenant Act 1954, see
      para 3.22.

MONITORING COMPLIANCE

3.22 In most cases, a landlord will be keen to ensure compliance with the business conditions, unless there is no longer any commercial activity of any sort on the holding. The danger he will most want to guard against is the tenant obtaining security of tenure under Pt II of the Landlord and Tenant Act 1954 (LTA 1954). The LTA 1954 applies to tenancies where the demised premises includes premises occupied by the tenant for the purposes of a business carried on by him or for business and other purposes[1]. Certain tenancies, including agricultural holdings under the AHA 1986 and farm business tenancies under the ATA 1995 are excluded from the LTA 1954[2]. Under the LTA 1954, tenancies continue when brought to an end by either a landlord's notice under s 25 or a tenant's request for a new tenancy under s 26. Following either type of notice, the tenant can apply to the court for a new tenancy. The landlord has only limited grounds set out in s 30 of the LTA 1954 upon which he can oppose the grant of a new tenancy and it is this which provides the tenant with security[3].

Apart from physically monitoring what the tenant is doing, how can a landlord protect himself? He is helped substantially by s 1(8) of the ATA 1995 which is similar in terms to s 1(3) of the AHA 1986. Section 1(8) prevents the tenant from unilaterally removing himself from the farm business tenancy regime by conducting himself in such a way as to be in breach of the terms of his tenancy. It provides that any use of the land in breach of the terms of the tenancy; any commercial activities carried on in breach and the cessation of any activities in the light of a positive obligation to carry on those activities are to be disregarded in determining whether the tenancy complies with the business conditions or, indeed, with the agriculture condition. The disregard does not apply where the landlord or his predecessor in title has consented to the breach or acquiesced in the breach, but will otherwise ensure that a tenant will be deemed to be complying with the business conditions even where there is no commercial farming but where he is obliged to farm for the purposes of a trade or business by the terms of this tenancy.

In the light of s 1(8) of the ATA 1995, the landlord can, in most cases, ensure compliance through the terms of the tenancy itself. Appropriately drawn user covenants, restricting use to agriculture or to a particular type of agricultural activity or, where the landlord is prepared to allow diversification, a simple obligation which mirrors the business conditions – at all times to farm part of the holding for the purposes of a trade or business – may suffice[4].

In cases where the letting is for a fixed term, and particularly where it is unclear as to whether the proposed use of the holding is 'farming' or not, it may be possible for the parties to exclude the security of tenure provisions of the LTA 1954. If it is not a farm business tenancy, the tenancy will still, in all other respects, be an LTA 1954 tenancy. Formerly it was necessary for the parties to apply to the court to exclude the provisions of the LTA 1954. Since 1 June 2004, it is achieved by the serving of a prescribed declaration of a statutory declaration[5].

[1] LTA 1954, s 23.

² LTA 1954, s 43 as amended by para 10 of the Sch to the ATA 1995.
³ In outline the s 30 grounds are the failing of the tenant to comply with repairing
   obligations; persistent delay by the tenant in paying the rent; substantial breaches of
   covenant by the tenant; where the landlord is prepared to provide suitable alternative
   accommodation at reasonable cost; where, in certain circumstances, the landlord wishes to
   terminate a letting of part; where the landlord intends to demolish, reconstruct or carry out
   major construction works to the premises and needs possession to do so; or, in certain
   cases, where the landlord wishes to occupy himself.
⁴ See Ch 7.
⁵ LTA 1954, s 38(A); Regulatory Reform (Business Tenancies) (England and Wales)
   Order 2003, SI 2003/3096.

FARMED

3.23 The requirement is that all or part of the land comprised in the tenancy
must be farmed for the purpose of a trade or business. Minimal commercial
farming will, therefore, suffice, although, as will be seen, the character of the
tenancy has to be primarily or wholly agricultural at the outset, whether the
parties choose to serve notices or not[1]. Diversification within the farm
business tenancy regime is only possible for those businesses which were
primarily agricultural at the beginning of the tenancy. However, for the
business conditions, there is no requirement that the part farmed should be
substantial, that it should be a self-sufficient business or that the business it
supports should itself be agricultural. Further, there is no requirement that the
part of the holding which is farmed should be the same throughout the
tenancy.

The condition is that part of the land should be *farmed*, not that it should be
used for agriculture. This can be compared with the notice conditions and the
agriculture condition which both refer to 'agriculture' and not 'farming'. No
definition of farming is given, although s 38(2) of the ATA 1995 provides that
references to farming the land include the carrying on in relation to land of
any agricultural activity. It can be assumed, therefore, that farming may go
beyond agricultural activity and include activities which do not fall within the
definition of agriculture.

'Agriculture' is defined in s 38(1) of the ATA 1995. It is the same definition as
appears in the AHA 1986[2]. The definition includes livestock breeding and
keeping, but the definition of livestock, also in s 38, is not the same as the
AHA 1986. The AHA 1986 definition, but not the ATA 1995 definition,
includes any creature kept for the purpose of carrying on in relation to land of
any agricultural activity but it is arguable that such words were in any event
superfluous.

When will an activity be 'farming' which will not be 'agricultural'? In part, the
choice of the word 'farmed' is to cater for future changes in the industry which
cannot yet be foreseen. However, certain activities which have been held not
to be agricultural can be seen as farming. For example, the growing of crops
for the testing of pesticides[3] or the breeding of livestock for research purposes.
Whilst such activities may satisfy the business conditions they will not satisfy
the agriculture condition which requires primary agricultural use at the time

54

of challenge, nor the notice conditions which requires the tenancy to be primarily agricultural at the outset. The non-agricultural-farming activities are, therefore, regarded as diversification activities. If the intention at the outset is for the entire or a substantial part of the holding to be used for such purposes, the tenancy will not be a farm business tenancy.

Whilst the tenant must act in accordance with his obligations under the tenancy, it is not a requirement of the business conditions that the tenant personally farm the holding.

In determining whether the tenancy is being farmed for the purposes of the ATA 1995, it is necessary to disregard commercial use being carried out in breach of the user covenant or a cessation of activities defined in the user covenant[4].

[1] See the notice conditions (ATA 1995, s 1(4)) and the agriculture condition (ATA 1995, s 1(3)).
[2] See Ch 18.
[3] *Dow Agrochemicals v Lane (EA) (North Lynn)* (1965) 192 Estates Gazette 737.
[4] ATA 1995, s 1(8), discussed in relation to the business conditions.

TRADE OR BUSINESS

3.24 The farming must be for the purposes of a trade or business. This is familiar territory. Under the AHA 1986, 'agricultural land' means land used for agriculture which is so used for the purposes of a trade or business[1] and the cases decided under that section and its predecessors will be helpful. The farming of land for hobby or recreational purposes or where the predominant purpose is to use the produce for home consumption (even if the surplus is sold) will not be farming sufficient to support the business conditions[2].

The trade or business supported by the farming need not itself be agricultural: for example, rearing livestock for a medical research business; grazing horses for a riding school business; running a farm as a tourist attraction will all comply with the business conditions. Whether or not the tenancy is a farm business tenancy will then depend upon compliance with either the agriculture condition or the notice conditions.

The running of a community farm, which was a non-profit making enterprise, will not fall within the definition of trade or business[3].

[1] AHA 1986, s 1(4).
[2] See Ch 18 and the case of *Hickson & Welch v Cann* (1977) 40 P & CR 218n.
[3] *Secretary of State for Transport v Jenkins, Jenkins, Spence and Taylor* (2000) 79 P& CR 118, (1997) 73 P & CR 118, CA.

HORSES

3.25 The position in relation to horses requires special mention. As it often raises questions concerned with the trade or business requirement, it will be considered in this section although reference will also need to be made to the sections on the notice and agriculture conditions. The position is similar to that under the AHA 1986[1].

Horses, unless kept for consumption or in connection with the farming of the land, are not livestock with the meaning given in s 38(1) of the ATA 1995[2]. Grazing[3] is, however, as it is under the AHA 1986, an independent agricultural activity[4], regardless of the type of animal which grazes the land, and is hence farming. The security of tenure (though not other) provisions of the LTA 1954 should be excluded[5].

If the grazing is supporting a trade or business, whatever that trade or business may be, the business conditions have been complied with. If, on the other hand, the tenancy is for grazing horses kept for recreational purposes, the business conditions will not have been complied with. The tenancy will be governed only by common law.

If the grazing supports a trade or business, whether or not the tenancy is a farm business tenancy depends upon whether at the time of challenge (for the agriculture condition) or at the beginning of the tenancy (for the notice conditions) the tenancy is primarily or wholly agricultural in nature. If the grazing supports a non-agricultural business, such as a stud farm or a riding school, which is off the holding so that the *only* activity conducted on the tenanted land is grazing, the tenancy will be primarily or wholly agricultural. If the supported non-agricultural business is on the holding, the position is as follows.

(a) If notices were served to comply with the notice conditions[6], the position depends upon when the non-agricultural trade or business started. If it was contemplated at the beginning of the tenancy, the question is whether it can be said that the tenancy was primarily agricultural at the beginning (see the note in relation to (ii) below). If the business started later, the grazing will be farming for the business conditions and it does not matter that the primary use of the holding is now in connection with the non-agricultural business.

(b) If notices were not served so that the status of the tenancy as a farm business tenancy depends upon compliance with the business conditions together with the agriculture condition, the question is whether, at the time of challenge, the character of the tenancy is primarily agricultural. If the use of the land is as a stud farm; livery stables or riding school with ancillary grazing, the tenancy will not be primarily agricultural. As it is, however, commercial in nature, it will fall within Pt II of the LTA 1954 and the tenant will have the greater security of tenure of that Act.

---

1 See Ch 18 and Ch 19.
2 As to livestock and user, note the decision in *Field v Bryant* [2003] EWCA Civ 1957, [2004] PLSCS 22, where a user covenant in a farm business tenancy requiring the tenant to use the holding for 'permanent pasture for livestock only' was to be read against the material background of known to the parties at the time that the terms of the tenancy were agreed. In that context, they were found to permit the tenant to continue to carry on his milk and dairy business from the holding. Also see, *Cooke v Horne* [2006] PLSCS 18, where the claimant's fish were held not to be kept for production of food as this was not the predominant purpose for which they were kept.

3   As to rights of common grazing, see *Bettison v Langton* [2001] UKHL 24, [2002] 1 AC 27, [2001] 3 All ER 417.
4   ATA 1995, s 38(1).
5   See para 3.22.
6   ATA 1995, s 1(4).

The agriculture condition

3.26 In addition to the business conditions, a tenancy must comply with either the agriculture condition or the notice conditions to be a farm business tenancy. Compliance with the notice conditions requires action by the parties at the beginning of the tenancy[1] and, therefore, is a matter of choice for the parties. As seen above[2], it is the combination of the business conditions (requiring only minimal farming) and the notice conditions (looking only at the beginning of the tenancy) which allows for substantial diversification away from agriculture during the tenancy without the danger of falling outside the farm business tenancy regime and into Pt II of the LTA 1954. If there is any danger of diversification, the landlord is likely to insist on notices being exchanged and, therefore, the agriculture condition is only likely to be relevant where:

(a)   the tenancy was set up without professional advice and notices have not been exchanged;

(b)   the tenancy is relatively short term with tight user covenants limiting use to agriculture, and so the parties have decided that there is no danger of lawful diversification[3] and therefore no need to exchange notices. A short-term grazing tenancy limiting use to grazing and/or mowing only might fall into this category;

(c)   notices have been served but are in some way defective or there has been defective service.

The agriculture condition does not allow for substantial diversification away from agriculture. The condition is set out in s 1(3) and is that, having regard to:

(i)   the terms of the tenancy;

(ii)   the use of the land comprised in the tenancy;

(iii)   the nature of any commercial activities carried on on that land; and

(iv)   any other relevant circumstances,

the character of the tenancy is primarily or wholly agricultural.

1   ATA 1995, s 1(4).
2   See the introduction to this Section at para 3.22.
3   Unlawful uses can be disregarded: see the ATA 1995, s 1(8), discussed in relation to the business conditions.

3.27 The use must be primarily or wholly agricultural. Unlike the business conditions, there is no use of the word 'farmed'. If, therefore, the holding is primarily used for a type of farming which is not an agricultural activity, the agriculture condition will not be met. Agriculture is defined in s 38(1) of the ATA 1995 in the same way as it is defined under the AHA 1986 save for a small change in the definition of livestock[1].

The business conditions require unbroken compliance from the beginning of the tenancy and any period of non-compliance will take the tenancy outside the ATA 1995. The agriculture condition is only really relevant at the time when the status of the tenancy needs to be established. If, at that time, the tenancy complies with the agriculture condition, it will be a farm business tenancy regardless of any historical non-compliance. In other words, if the character of the tenancy ceases to be primarily agricultural at any stage, it will fall outside the ATA 1995. If it later becomes primarily agricultural again, it will come back into the ATA 1995 provided that, at all times, there has been some commercial farming on the holding.

Section 1(8) of the ATA 1995 applies to compliance with the agriculture condition as well as to compliance with the business conditions. This means that uses in breach of the terms of the tenancy or the cessation of any activities in breach of an obligation to carry them out can be disregarded provided that the landlord has not consented to or acquiesced in the breach. Again, therefore, just as with compliance with the business conditions, the landlord can achieve a measure of control through the user covenants in a tenancy[2]. Where the length of the tenancy is such that the danger of acquiescence by the landlord in any breaches is low and the restrictive user covenants are acceptable in terms of the rent achievable, the parties may be content to rely on controls through the user covenants to keep the tenancy within the farm business tenancy regime rather than go to the trouble of exchanging notices.

At the time of testing, the character of the tenancy must be 'primarily or wholly agricultural' having regard to the factors set out in the subsection. The phrase 'primarily or wholly agricultural' is not one used under the AHA 1986 and, therefore, further assistance in its meaning will have to await decided cases. However, the phrase is similar in concept to the definition of an agricultural tenancy under the AHA 1986 where it is provided that a contract of tenancy will be for an agricultural tenancy where the whole of the land subject to such exceptions as do not substantially affect the character of the tenancy is let for use as agricultural land[3]. The cases decided under the AHA 1986 may be of some use, but caution should be exercised: the phrase is a new one and the problems of anticipated mixed user, where it is intended at the outset that some non-agricultural activities will take place on the holding, will have to be worked out through the cases. In cases of doubt, the landlord should seek the tenant's agreement to exclude security of tenure under the LTA 1954[4].

No guidance is given as to the particular weight to be attached to those factors specified in s 1(3) and each case will turn on its own facts. However, the amount of land used for agricultural and non-agricultural activities; the income generated by and the profitability of each activity; the amount of time and labour each activity takes up will all be relevant. As the requirement, at its lowest, is only that the tenancy should be 'primarily' agricultural, some non-agricultural activity (perhaps farming of some other sort) can be carried out.

As with the AHA 1986, the tenancy either will be a farm business tenancy, being primarily agricultural in character, or it will not. One tenancy cannot fall as to part under one regime and as to part under another. If it is primarily agricultural, all of the land, whether used for agriculture or not, will fall within the farm business tenancy.

Because the agriculture condition is relevant only at the time of testing, it is the actual use of the holding then which must be considered. Whilst the terms of the tenancy are relevant[5], a tenancy could fail the agriculture condition test in circumstances where the agricultural activity has been reduced, even though such a reduction would not have amounted to abandonment to take the tenancy outside of the AHA 1986[6]. A comparison with the previous position under the tenancy is not what is required.

1   See business conditions, para 3.19ff.
2   See business conditions, para 3.19.
3   AHA 1986, s 1(2) and see Ch 2.
4   See the notes in relation to the business conditions at para 3.19ff.
5   ATA 1995, s 1(3).
6   See Ch 18.

The notice conditions

INTRODUCTION

3.28 As seen above, the combination of the business conditions and the notice conditions allows for major diversification away from agriculture without the danger that the tenancy will come out of the farm business tenancy regime[1]. This is because the business conditions require only minimal farming activity on the holding[2] and the notice conditions, whilst requiring the tenancy to be primarily agricultural, look only at the position at the beginning of the tenancy[3].

1   See para 3.23.
2   See para 3.19.
3   ATA 1995, s 38(4). The beginning of the tenancy is the date upon which, under the terms of the tenancy, the tenant is entitled to possession.

THE CONDITIONS

3.29 There are two notice conditions. They are set out in s 1(4) of the ATA 1995 and are that:

(a)   on or before the relevant day, the landlord and the tenant each gave the other a written notice. The notice must identify the land to be comprised in the tenancy and contain a statement 'to the effect' that the person giving the notice intends that the tenancy is to be and *is to remain* a farm business tenancy; and

(b)   at the beginning of the tenancy (and therefore at the time when the tenant is entitled to go into possession[1]), the character of the tenancy, having regard to its terms and any other relevant circumstances, is primarily or wholly agricultural.

In looking at the agriculture and notice conditions, and assuming the business conditions to be fulfilled, it can be seen that whenever the character of the tenancy is primarily or wholly agricultural, there will be a farm business tenancy. The purpose in serving the notices is to confine the need for the character of the tenancy to be primarily agricultural to the beginning of the tenancy and not a requirement that it be so on each and every occasion of challenge[2]. It is a snapshot of what the position is at the outset. If the diversification on the holding is then such that non-agricultural activities dominate, then provided that there is still minimal commercial farming so as to comply with the business conditions, the tenancy will retain its status as a farm business tenancy provided that the parties validly served the notices referred to above. The exchange of notices is a safeguard for the landlord against the tenancy moving into the LTA 1954, Pt II in circumstances where diversification is anticipated or allowed or where there is, because of the length of the tenancy, a danger that the landlord could acquiesce in non-agricultural activities in breach of the terms of the tenancy[3]: without the notices, reliance would have to be placed on the agriculture condition.

Notices must be served on or before the relevant day. The relevant day is defined in s 1(5) to mean the *earlier* of either the day on which the parties enter into any instrument creating the tenancy (other than a contract for a tenancy at a later date) or the beginning of the tenancy, ie the date upon which the tenant is entitled to go into possession[4]. It can be seen that if the tenancy is oral, and not, therefore, created by instrument, the relevant day is always going to be the date upon which the tenant is entitled to go into possession. If the parties entered into a contract for a tenancy which does not allow the tenant into possession before the completion of formalities, the position is that, whilst the contract will fall within the definition of tenancy in s 38(1) (because of the wording of s 1(5)), the relevant day will not be the date of the contract, but the date the tenant is entitled to possession. Conversely, however, if he is entitled to go into possession before the formalities have been completed, then because of the extended definition of tenancy to cover contracts for tenancies, the notices must be served on or before the date upon which, under the terms of the *contract*, the tenant is entitled to possession[5].

There is no requirement that the notices must be exchanged first on the relevant day, before the tenancy is entered into and the tenant is entitled to possession, although the wording of s 4(1)(a) seems to assume that the notices will be exchanged first. It would be wise, therefore, to exchange notices first and preferably before the relevant day to avoid argument[6].

If notices are not served on or before the relevant day or if, although served, they do not contain the prescribed information, or are not properly served[7], the tenancy may still be a farm business tenancy if the agriculture condition is complied with.

There is no prescribed form for the notice[8] although it must be in writing, regardless of whether or not the tenancy itself is in writing, and must contain the information prescribed by s 1(4)(a)(i) and (ii) – it must describe the land and state that the party giving the notice intends the tenancy to be and to remain a farm business tenancy. It would be advisable to use the same description of the land and the same plan in both the tenancy agreement itself and the notice. Whilst there is no requirement that the notices be signed, it would be good practice for each notice to be dated and signed by the party giving the notice and for the notice to require an acknowledgment of receipt by the other party. Prescribed methods of service are set out in s 36 of the ATA 1995[9].

[1] ATA 1995, s 38(4).
[2] Cf agriculture condition – see the ATA 1995, s 1(3).
[3] ATA 1995, s 1(8) provides that, in the absence of consent or acquiescence, unlawful uses can be disregarded in assessing compliance with the business and agriculture condition.
[4] ATA 1995, s 38(4).
[5] A tenancy does not begin until it has been created: see *Bradshaw v Pawley* [1979] 3 All ER 273; *Keen v Holland* [1984] 1 All ER 75, CA; *Pahl v Trevor* [1992] 1 EGLR 22, CA.
[6] If there is an issue as to which came first on the relevant day and notices are to be exchanged on the same day as the tenancy agreement is entered into, evidence of a witness should be obtained as to which happened first. In the absence of evidence, it would not be assumed that notices came first: *Bedfordshire County Council v Clarke* (1974) 230 Estates Gazette 1587.
[7] NB: For service of all documents under the Act see ATA 1995, s 36 and see Ch 17.
[8] See Form Al.
[9] See Ch 17.

3.30 The ATA 1995 requires an exchange of notices – one from landlord to the tenant and one from tenant to the landlord. It is not enough, for example, for the tenant to acknowledge receipt of the landlord's notice and to agree with its contents. He must serve his own notice.

The notice must not be contained in the tenancy agreement itself, but must be a separate document[1]. It is considered more likely that the notice will be seen, read and understood if it is not simply one more clause in a long tenancy agreement[2].

The phrase 'primarily or wholly agricultural' has been considered in the context of the agriculture condition[3]. Here the agricultural nature of the tenancy is being considered at the beginning of the tenancy only[4]. It is a snapshot of the character of the tenancy at that date. At that stage, unless the tenant has already been in occupation of the holding under an earlier tenancy, there will be no use of the land or commercial activities to consider and perforce the terms of the tenancy will assume a far greater importance. It may be the only indication of the intention of the parties, although the court is entitled to consider both the terms of the tenancy and any other relevant circumstances.

According to the provisions of s 1(4) of the ATA 1995, the notice conditions must be complied with on or before the relevant day for each farm business tenancy, regardless of whether or not the tenancy is in favour of the same tenant, on the same terms and in respect of the same holding. This could cause problems in two situations. First, it is anticipated that, at least during the early years of the ATA 1995, land owners may be reluctant to let on long fixed-term tenancies. If therefore, they let on a series of shorter terms[5], the notice conditions would have to be complied with at the beginning of each new tenancy or (if earlier) the date when the new tenancy is entered into. Second, the notice conditions would have to be complied with where there is an implied surrender and re-grant following what the parties thought would be a variation only[6]. Since the parties would not have anticipated a surrender and re-grant, they certainly would not have considered compliance with the notice conditions. This may not be fatal if the new tenancy is primarily or wholly agricultural and, therefore, will be a farm business tenancy as a result of compliance with the agriculture condition, but what of diversified estates?

[1]   ATA 1995, s 1(6).
[2]   Similar provisions existed in relation to notices for assured shorthold tenancies under the Housing Act 1988.
[3]   See para 3.27.
[4]   As defined in the ATA 1995, s 38(4).
[5]   Whilst it is open to the parties, where the term is for more than two years, simply to let it run on as an annual periodic tenancy (see ATA 1995, s 5 and Ch 12), this may not be sufficient security for the tenant as the landlord can then terminate on giving 12 months' notice (see ATA 1995, s 6 and Ch 12).
[6]   As to what will lead to an implied surrender and re-grant, see the commentary on the ATA 1995, s 4(1)(f) at para 3.8.

3.31 In both of the circumstances set out above, it would be impossible to comply with the notice conditions where the estate has diversified to such an extent that the tenancy is no longer primarily or wholly agricultural in character. It is not simply a matter of serving fresh notices: both notice conditions must be complied with. Furthermore, because of the diversification, compliance with the agriculture condition will not be possible and the parties would not, therefore, be able to relet on a farm business tenancy.

Section 3 of the ATA 1995 goes some way towards dealing with these problems, although it is limited in its scope. The section provides that, in certain circumstances, the new tenancy will be taken to meet the notice conditions in s 1(4). In those cases which fall within s 3, there will be no need to serve fresh notices and no need to show that the character of the new tenancy is primarily or wholly agricultural at the beginning.

The following conditions must be met before a new tenancy will fall within s 3:

(a)   the tenant under the new tenancy must, immediately before the grant of a new tenancy, have been a tenant under a farm business tenancy which met the notice conditions[1]; and

(b)   the terms of the new tenancy must be substantially the same as the terms of the old save for the matters which are mentioned in s 3(2) and (3) and matters consequential on them[2]; and either

(c)   the land in the new tenancy is the same as the land in the old apart from changes which are small in relation to the size of the holding and do not affect the character of the holding (the s 3(2) condition); or

(d)   the old and the new tenancies are both fixed-term tenancies, but the term date under the new is earlier than the term date under the old (the s 3(3) condition).

While s 3 of the ATA 1995 is headed 'compliance with notice conditions in cases of surrender and re-grant' it is clearly wide enough (through the s 3(2) condition) to cover some situations where a fixed-term tenancy comes to an end and a new tenancy is granted to the same tenant of the same holding on essentially the same terms.

¹ ATA 1995, s 3(1)(a).
² ATA 1995, s 3(1)(b).

Miscellaneous

3.32 Farm business tenancies are excluded from the definition of allotments[1]. They are also excluded from rights to compensation in relation to smallholdings[2]. There are no special rules relating to farm business tenancies in respect of distress for the non-payment of rent[3].

As in relation to the AHA 1986, the ATA 1995 is excluded from compensation for business tenants under the Landlord and Tenant Act 1927[4] and the provisions relating to disrepair in the Leasehold Property (Repairs) Act 1938[5].

¹ ATA 1995, Sch para 3 excludes the Allotments Act 1922. This includes excluding the rights to compensation.
² ATA 1995, Sch para 1, excluding the Smallholdings and Allotments Act 1908.
³ See Ch 29.
⁴ ATA 1995, Sch para 5.
⁵ ATA 1995, para 8.

FORMALITIES

Introduction

3.33 The emphasis in the ATA 1995 is away from statutory imposed security of tenure to security of tenure stemming from the bargain agreed between the parties[1].

This will inevitably lead to a far greater number of fixed-term tenancies being granted and a move away from annual periodic tenancies which, under the ATA 1995, would offer the tenant little or no security. In many cases, the degree of formality required to grant a legal term of years and the conveyancing requirements will be much greater than was the case under the AHA 1986 where the grant of an annual periodic tenancy was the norm.

Before looking at the formalities, it is worth saying that there is no legal distinction between a lease and a tenancy: the terms are interchangeable and are so used in this part of the book. It is common, however, to find the word 'lease' used more frequently to describe longer fixed-term lettings and 'tenancy' used to describe periodic or shorter fixed-term lettings.

¹ The view is expressed in Muir Watt and Moss, *Agricultural Holdings* (14th edn, 1998) Sweet & Maxwell, p 21 that this view of the width of s 3 is too optimistic and that its terms and confined to cases of surrender and re-grant. It appears that the learned authors

accept that s 3 would be available where a fixed-term tenancy of more than two years has continued as a result of the operation of s 5 and that the section is only unavailable in respect of a series of fixed-term tenancies which expire by effluxion of time.

Formalities

A contract

3.34 All lettings of land involve a contract between the parties. As such, the agreement between the parties on the basic terms must be sufficiently certain. In the context of letting land this means that the agreement must be clear on the following basic matters:

(a)   parties;
(b)   the extent of the land demised;
(c)   the payment or consideration for the occupation;
(d)   the term[1].

In addition there are particular formal requirements which relate only to contracts for the sale or other disposition of an interest in land which the parties and their advisers need to be aware of. All contracts for the sale or other disposition of an interest in land (and hence including a tenancy or lease) concluded on or after 27 September 1989 must, in accordance with the Law of Property (Miscellaneous Provisions) Act 1989 (LP(MP)A 1989), be in writing and incorporate all the terms which the parties have expressly agreed in one document or, where contracts are exchanged, in each[2]. That document must be signed by, or on behalf of, each party to the contract. If there is an exchange of contracts, each party must sign the document, but not necessarily the same one[3]. Any contract which does not comply with the requirements of the LP(MP)A 1989 is void and ineffective unless it falls within one of the very limited exceptions in the Act. Two exceptions of relevance may be mentioned:

(a)   short leases such as fall within s 54(2) of the Law of Property Act 1925 (LPA 1925) (see below);
(b)   contracts made in the course of a public auction.

Whilst the Act requires the terms to be contained in one document, s 2(2) allows that one document to incorporate terms by reference to some other document rather than to set them out verbatim[4].

It has not been common in the past for the contract for the tenancy and the grant of the tenancy itself to form separate transactions. If there is no preliminary contract, the actual tenancy will be the contract and must (subject to the exceptions for short leases) comply with both the LP(MP)A 1989 and the formal requirements of the LPA 1925. With the increase in fixed-term tenancies, the additional searches and enquiries which a tenant may wish to conduct, and in many cases the need for a deed, a separate contract leading to completion (as with sales of freeholds) may become more common. In which case, the contract must comply with the LP(MP)A 1989 and the disposition itself with the LPA 1925.

1   In the absence of a specified date for the commencement of a lease, it may be construed by the court: *Liverpool City Council v Walton Group plc* [2002] 1 EGLR 149.
2   LP(MP)A 1989, s 2(1). An arrangement which fails to comply with s 2(1) may be saved by s 2(5) which expressly preserves the creation and operation of constructive trusts. Such a trust which arises in relation to an agreement, arrangement or understanding is closely akin to, if not indistinguishable from, proprietary estoppel. See *Yaxley v Gott* [2000] Ch 162, [1999] 2 EGLR 181, CA. Cf *James v Evans* [2000] ECGS 95 where proprietary estoppel can operate through a constructive trust, s 2(5) may help to save oral agreements or incomplete contracts. See *McCauseland v Duncan Lawrie Ltd* [1997] 1 WLR 38, CA: agreements to vary the contract must likewise comply with s 2.
3   LP(MP)A 1989, s 2(3).
4   *Record v Bell* [1991] 1 WLR 853; *Tootal Clothing Ltd v Guinea Properties Ltd* (1992) 64 P & CR 452; *Commission for New Towns v Cooper* [1995] Ch 259, [1995] 2 All ER 929; *Firstpost Homes Ltd v Johnson* [1995] 4 All ER 355, CA.

Requirement for a deed

3.35 As a result of the interaction of several provisions of the Law of Property Act 1925, all fixed-term tenancies for a term exceeding three years must be created by deed. Most which are for three years or less can be made without a deed – orally or simply in writing. The provisions are as follows:

(a)   s 52(1) of the LPA 1925 requires all conveyances of land or of any interest in land to be by deed. If there is no deed, a conveyance of the legal estate is void;
(b)   s 52(2) provides, however, that no deed is required in respect of leases and tenancies not required by law to be made in writing;
(c)   s 54(2) provides that leases which take effect in possession for a term not exceeding three years at the best rent which can reasonably be obtained without taking a fine can be made orally.

There are several points to note as follows:

(i)   To take advantage of the exception in s 54(2), the short lease must take effect in possession and must be at the best rent. These additional requirements need to be borne in mind. In establishing best rent, s 33 of the ATA 1995 provides that it shall not be necessary to take account against the tenant of any increase in the value of the land arising from tenant's improvements.
(ii)   A term not exceeding three years will include a letting for three years or less where the tenant has an option to renew or extend the term, but will not include a term of more than three years simply because one or both of the parties can break the term within the first three years[1].
(iii)   A periodic tenancy is for a term not exceeding three years even though it is capable of lasting for longer than three years and, therefore, can be created orally or in writing. A deed is not required[2].
(iv)   The exception in s 54(2) applies only to the creation of tenancies. Any assignment of an existing tenancy, however long the term is for, must be by deed in accordance with s 52(1) of the LPA 1925[3].

1   *Kushner v Law Society* [1952] 1 KB 264.
2   *Re Knight, ex parte Voisey* (1882) 21 Ch D 442, CA; *Hammond v Farrow* [1904] 2 KB 332.

3.35 *Formation of a farm business tenancy*

3   See *Parc Battersea Ltd v Hutchinson* [1999] 2 EGLR 33: assignments which are by operation of law as where a sub-tenancy is granted which must last longer than the head tenancy and this operates as an assignment by the head tenant of his interest.

Preparation and execution of deeds

3.36 The law relating to deeds was changed by the LP(MP)A 1989 for deeds executed on or after 31 July 1990. The position is now as follows:

(a)   An instrument cannot be a deed unless it is clear on the face of the document that it is intended to be a deed[1]. This indication could be by way of an express reference at the beginning of the document to the fact that it is a deed or it could be indirect, for example, because the document expresses itself to be *executed* as a deed.

(b)   An instrument cannot be a deed unless it is validly executed as a deed. Valid execution requires, signature and delivery[2]. A seal is no longer required for individuals[3]. For companies, the company seal is not required but is one way of executing the deed. The alternative is for a director and secretary of the company or two directors to sign, provided that it is clear in the deed that the execution is by the company and not by the officers personally.

(c)   Signatures must be witnessed or attested. If the party, whose deed it is, is unable to sign, the deed must be signed at his direction and in his presence and in the presence of two attesting witnesses[4].

Delivery does not necessarily require physical delivery of the document to the other side. It simply requires an act or statement by the relevant party that shows that he intends irrevocably to be bound by the deed. Section 1(5) of the LP(MP)A 1989 provides that a solicitor or licensed conveyancer instructed in connection with a transaction involving (amongst other things) the creation of an interest in land is conclusively presumed in favour of a purchaser to have the authority of the relevant party to deliver the deed. If a land agent is dealing with the transaction (as to which see below), his authority to deliver the deed must be proved. A written authority from the party for whom he is acting will suffice: it is no longer necessary for such an authority itself to be by deed[5]. Solicitors and licensed conveyancers also need to be aware that the conclusive presumption in their favour only operates in favour of a purchaser, although 'purchaser' is defined by s 1(6) of the LP(MP)A 1989 by reference to s 205 of the Law of Property Act 1925 which includes a tenant for valuable consideration.

The Solicitors Act 1974 makes it a criminal offence for an 'unqualified person' to draw or prepare instruments relating to real or personal estate if done in expectation of fee, gain or reward[6]. There is an exception for short leases (those of three years duration or less) and contracts for such leases. Unqualified persons included, before the coming into force of the ATA 1995, land agents. However, s 25 of the ATA 1995 amends the Solicitors Act 1974 to ensure that certain accredited land agents are now able to prepare deeds which lead to creation of a farm business tenancy or which vary such a tenancy. Land agents have traditionally been involved in drafting agricultural tenancies

66

and it was felt that the move to longer fixed-term tenancies should not exclude them from continuing that involvement. Accordingly, full members of the CAAV; Associates or Fellows of the ISVA; and Associates or Fellows of the RICS are able to prepare deeds which create, or which they reasonably believe will create, a farm business tenancy or which relate to an existing tenancy which they reasonably believe to be a farm business tenancy. The conveyancing and other formal requirements which attend such longer leases also need to be considered however, and any land agent who intends to draft such deeds needs to be aware of, and comply with, those requirements. Furthermore, given the comparative lack of regulation in the ATA 1995, an awareness of the common law of landlord and tenant is also required.

1   LP(MP)A 1989, s 1(2).
2   LP(MP)A 1989, s 1(3).
3   LP(MP)A 1989, s 1(1)(b).
4   LP(MP)A 1989, s 1(2)(a).
5   LP(MP)A 1989, s 1(a).
6   Solicitors Act 1974, s 22.

Conveyancing requirements and formalities

3.37 It is beyond the scope of this book to set out in full the conveyancing requirements and formalities for long leases or to consider in detail the good practice of investigating the landlord's title. However, the following points can be made:

(a)   The longer the term, the more important it is that the tenant investigates the landlord's title, just as he would were he buying the freehold. Why is it more important? The tenant under a long fixed-term tenancy does not, in the absence of an appropriate break clause, have the ability as he would under the AHA 1986 to bring the tenancy to an end. He is a tenant until the end of the term and it is, therefore, vital that he knows exactly what he is getting. If the tenant's landlord is not the freeholder, it may also be necessary to investigate the freeholder's title. The sort of things the tenant will be looking for are that the correct legal owner is granting the tenancy (often important where the land is owned by a family trust but effectively managed by one member of the family); that there are no covenants and restrictions on the freehold title that would prevent the tenant's use of the property; that the position in respect of rights of way, wayleaves, etc, is understood and that the landlord is free to grant a farm business tenancy and is not, for example, restricted by a post-31 August 1995 mortgage from doing so in such a way as to bind his mortgagee[1].

(b)   In addition to investigating the landlord's title, tenants would be advised to conduct the usual searches and inquiries. If a tenant is taking the land for a long time he must be in a position to understand planning permissions; pipelines; access; highways; the environmental position on the holding and the position relating to services.

(c)   Prior to the completion of the deed, it may be wise to register the contract to grant the lease[2]. Following the execution of the deed,

3.37 *Formation of a farm business tenancy*

> registration may be necessary (in compliance with the terms of the Land Registration Act 2002)[3] and stamp duty and land tax[4] will have to be dealt with.

1   ATA 1995, s 31 and LPA 1925, s 99.
2   As an estate contract (unregistered land) or as a caution on the register of the freehold title if registered land.
3   See para 3.38.
4   See para 3.38.

Land Registration Act 2002

3.38 Following the commencement of the Land Registration Act 2002 (LRA 2002) on 13 October 2003, the general rule is that a lease or sub-lease for more than seven years granted out of either an unregistered title or a registered title is itself registerable as a new leasehold interest at the Land Registry.

If a lease is granted out of an unregistered freehold title or out of an unregistered leasehold title with more than seven years to run at the date of grant, the lease is registerable if it is either:

(a)   for a term of more than seven years from the date of grant and granted for valuable or other consideration by way of gift or pursuant to a Court Order[1]; or

(b)   a lease of any term which takes effect in possession more than three months from the date of grant[2].

The unregistered title out of which the lease or sublease is granted does not itself have to be registered as a result of the grant of the lease or sublease. However, unless the superior title is properly deduced by the grantor the Land Registry is likely to grant good leasehold title, which is less acceptable to mortgagees of the lease than absolute leasehold title.

If a lease is granted out of registered freehold or leasehold title the lease is registerable if the lease is for a term of more than seven years from the date of grant or it takes effect in possession more than three months after the date of grant[3].

The granting of a lease may become known to third parties in various ways:

(i)   Once the lease has been registered, it becomes a public document in accordance with s 6 of the LRA 2002 and third parties can request copies from the Land Registry. Although some clauses can be excluded from publication in some circumstances, it is not possible to exclude the names of the various parties.

(ii)   If the lease is granted out of registered land, then if a restriction appears on the register for that superior title stating that no disposition of the land can be made without the consent of the mortgagee, then the Land Registry will reject the application for registration of the lease unless that consent can be produced.

(iii)   If a lease (of whatever length) contains an option to renew that lease, the option will need to be protected by a notice on the superior title at the Land Registry.

Failure to register a lease granted out of an unregistered title within two months from the date of the grant makes the lease void as regards the legal estate, but the lease will take effect as a contract for valuable consideration to grant the lease. The grantee can still apply for registration of the lease and there is no financial penalty on late registration, but until the lease is registered he will be vulnerable to transfers of the freehold interest being made without notice of the grantees equitable interest. Parties entering into a lease falling within paragraph (iii) above will need to decide whether to register the lease and trigger notification to the mortgagee.

Failure to register a lease granted out of registered title within the priority period given by the official search risks the grantee's interest being postponed to later dispositions which have been registered or protected by there own priority search.

A further issue for the parties is that in order for the Land Registry to register the lease, Stamp Duty Land Tax (SDLT) must be paid on the rent and on any premium charged and the appropriate certificate obtained from HM Revenue & Customs. If the parties do not pay SDLT within 30 days of the date of grant, then there are penalties[4].

[1]   LRA 2002, s 4(1)(c).
[2]   LRA 2002, s 4(1)(d).
[3]   LRA 2002, s 27(2)(b).
[4]   The penalty is £100 which rises to £200 if the SDLT is paid more than three months late, plus interest. If the Land Transaction Return is more than a year late, a further penalty can be levied which may be equal to the tax that may be due. Failure to submit an SDLT return is also a criminal offence.

Failure to comply with formalities

3.39 If a lease for a term exceeding three years is granted other than by deed, s 52 of the LPA 1925 provides that such a grant is void for the purpose of conveying or creating a legal estate. That does not necessarily mean that the tenant is without any rights.

The informal grant will be a valid contract to grant a lease provided that it complies with the requirements of the LP(MP)A 1989[1]. Such a contract is a tenancy for the purposes of the ATA 1995[2] and hence can create a farm business tenancy between the landlord and tenant which will 'begin' for the purposes of the ATA 1995 when the tenant is entitled under the terms of the contract to enter into possession[3] and will be taken to have been granted when the contract was entered into.[4]

[1]   Generally see, *Grossman v Hooper* [2001] EWCA Civ 615, [2001] 2 EGLR 82, [2001] 27 EG 135.
[2]   ATA 1995, s 38 (1).
[3]   ATA 1995, s 38(4).
[4]   ATA 1995, s 38(3).

3.40 While specific performance is a discretionary remedy[1], it is usually granted where the contract is for the disposition of an interest in land. If the parties are entitled to a decree of specific performance, the equitable maxim 'equity treats as done that which ought to be done' and the principle in the case of *Walsh v Lonsdale*[2] means that, in equity, the tenant is the rightful occupant of the land, but only under an equitable lease, albeit on the same terms and conditions as the intended lease. He can also call for the grant of the lease by deed.

If, in the above circumstances, the tenant has gone into possession and paid rent, he may have acquired a legal periodic tenancy, the period being referable to the frequency of the rental payments[3], This may improve the tenant's position vis-à-vis third parties whilst, against the landlord, he is still entitled to rely upon the equitable rights in the contract including, therefore, any agreement to a fixed term of years and is not, vis-à-vis the landlord forced to rely on the legal periodic tenancy[4].

Legal interests bind the whole world. More needs to be done to protect an equitable interest against third parties. An equitable lease may not bind a later purchaser (including a later tenant) of the legal estate even if he is aware of the letting[5] unless:

(a) if the land is unregistered, the contract for the lease has been registered as an estate contract[6];

(b) if the land is registered, it is protected by a notice on the register of the superior title[7];

(c) if the land is registered and the tenant is in occupation, that occupation will protect his equitable rights provided that the purchaser does not make inquiries of the tenant who fails then to disclose his interest[8].

The position in relation to registered land and the failure to register a lease of more than seven years or a lease to take effect in possession after the end of the period of three months from the grant[9], is dealt with in para 3.38 above. It should be noted that there is a discretion to extend the time limit[10].

[1] See para 45.23.
[2] (1882) 21 Ch D 9.
[3] *Martin v Smith* (1874) LR 9 Exch 50; *Inntrepreneuer Estates Ltd v Mason* [1993] 2 EGLR 189, [1993] 45 EG 130; *Long v Tower Hamlets London Borough Council* [1998] Ch 197.
[4] *Walsh v Lonsdale* (1882) 21 Ch D 9. As to the application of this principle to agricultural tenancies, see *Padgham v Rochelle* [2002] PLSCS 197.
[5] *Midland Bank Trust Co Ltd v Green* [1981] AC 513, HL; *Lloyds Bank plc v Carrick* [1996] 4 All ER 630.
[6] Land Charges Act 1972, ss 2 and 4.
[7] LRA 2002, ss 32–39.
[8] LRA 2002, ss 11, 12 and Sch 1 para 2.
[9] LRA 2002, s 27(2)(b).
[10] LRA 2002, s 6(5).

Part III

THE TENANCY AGREEMENT

Contents

Chapter 4

THE TENANCY AGREEMENT

INTRODUCTION

4.1 The mutual rights and obligations of the parties to a farm business tenancy derive, as they do in respect of agricultural holdings under the Agricultural Holdings Act 1986 (AHA 1986), from three sources:

(a)   the contract of tenancy;
(b)   common law and custom; and
(c)   statutory provisions contained in the Agricultural Tenancies Act 1995 (ATA 1995).

Under the ATA 1995, very much more is left to the agreement reached by the parties in the contract of tenancy and very much less to regulation by statutory provision. Statutory intervention is limited to the following matters:

  (i)   for annual tenancies, a requirement that notices to quit must be of at least 12 months' duration[1];
 (ii)   fixed-term tenancies of more than two years require notice as in (a) above to bring them to an end, otherwise they continue as annual periodic tenancies[2];
(iii)   break clauses in fixed-term tenancies of more than two years can only be exercised by 12 months' notice[3];
 (iv)   providing for the removal of fixtures[4];
  (v)   rent review[5];
 (vi)   compensation for tenant's improvements[6]; and
(vii)   arbitration for disputes as a fall-back[7].

[1]   ATA 1995, s 6 and see Ch 12.
[2]   ATA 1995, s 5 and see Ch 12.
[3]   ATA 1995, s 7 and see Ch 12.
[4]   ATA 1995, s 8 and see Ch 12.
[5]   ATA 1995, ss 9–14 and see Ch 9.
[6]   ATA 1995, ss 15–27 and see Ch 16.
[7]   ATA 1995, s 28 and see Ch 16.

4.2 Unlike the AHA 1986, the ATA 1995 does not:

(a)   provide machinery for a written tenancy agreement on standard terms;

(b)   impose repairing obligations in the absence of agreements to the contrary;

(c)   allow for the tenant to apply for the provision of fixed equipment by the landlord;

(d)   interfere with the common law of distress;

(e)   contain *any* farming provisions relating to cultivation of the land, disposal of produce, good husbandry or good estate management;

(f)   provide for compensation on quitting, save in respect of tenant's improvements[1].

The difference in the degree of regulation is reflected in the relative lengths of the two Acts. The AHA 1986 comprises some 102 sections and 15 Schedules whereas the ATA 1995 runs only to 41 sections and one Schedule containing consequential amendments.

This part of this book does not contain a complete exposition of the general law of landlord and tenant. That law, and the case law that has developed in relation to common terms in leases of non-agricultural commercial properties, will be of direct relevance to farm business tenancies which will be regulated predominantly by the express terms agreed between the parties. This part will consider the more important terms which are likely to feature in a farm business tenancy and provide an outline of the general law relating to such terms. It will also consider the extent to which, in the absence of statutory regulation or express agreements, the common law will imply terms into the contract of tenancy. More extensive treatment will be given to the general law in this section of the book than in relation to the 1986 Act where much of the general law is overridden or varied by the statutory provisions.

References to the Minister are references to:

(i)   the Secretary of State for the Department for the Environment, Food and Rural Affairs (DEFRA) in England[2]; and

(ii)   the National Assembly for Wales (NAW) in Wales[3].

[1]   As defined in the ATA 1995, s 15. See Ch 19.
[2]   The Ministry of Agriculture, Fisheries and Food (Dissolution) Order 2002, SI 2002/794.
[3]   The National Assembly for Wales (Transfer of Functions) Order 1999, SI 1999/672.

Chapter 5
IMPLIED TERMS AND USUAL COVENANTS

GENERALLY

5.1 In the absence of express agreement between the parties[1], certain terms will be implied by common law. They are minimal and are no substitute for a well-drawn tenancy agreement. Certain terms will be implied into every lease where the parties have failed to make provision. Others will be implied on the basis that the implication is necessary to make the lease workable or give it business efficacy[2]. Implied covenants will not apply where the tenancy agreement already makes express provision[3].

[1]   *Miller v Emcer Products Ltd* [1956] Ch 304, CA.
[2]   *Liverpool City Council v Irwin* [1977] AC 239, HL. The courts are generally reluctant to imply terms: see *Smith v Harwich Corpn* (1857) 2 CBNS 651; *Duke of Westminster v Guild* [1985] QB 688, CA.
[3]   *Miller v Emcer Products Ltd* [1956] Ch 304, CA.

IMPLIED COVENANTS BY THE LANDLORD

5.2 In every lease there will be an implied covenant by the landlord for quiet enjoyment[1]. This gives the tenant the right to be in possession of the land without suffering any physical interference or disturbance from the landlord or those claiming under him[2]. Harassment of the tenant; attempting to drive him from the holding; changing locks or cutting off services[3]; blocking his access to the holding[4]; removing the tenant's livestock or machinery from the holding may all amount to a breach of the covenant for quiet enjoyment. It will include the situation where the landlord purports to let the property without having possession of it[5]. It will not place the landlord under an obligation to repair where he is not otherwise obliged to do so[6].

Where a tenancy agreement contains a provision to enter onto the holding to carry out repairs, the obligation must be construed to be consistent with the covenant (express or implied) for quiet enjoyment. Accordingly, the threshold for disturbance by repairs requires the landlord to take all reasonable precautions, rather than all possible precautions[7].

The landlord is also liable for the acts of those claiming under him, for example, his other tenants. In some cases, the tenant may have a direct right of action as where the act is tortious and gives rise to a claim for damages in nuisance, negligence or under the principle in *Rylands v Fletcher*[8].

1   The word 'covenant' will be used throughout this part of the book in its non-technical sense to mean contractual obligation. Technically there can be no covenant unless the lease is by deed.
2   *Hudson v Cripps* [1896] 1 Ch 265; *Jaeger v Mansions Consolidated Ltd* (1903) 87 LT 690, CA; *Budd-Scott v Daniell* [1902] 2 KB 351; *McCall v Abelesz* [1976] QB 585, CA.
3   *Perera v Vandiyar* [1953] 1 WLR 672, CA.
4   *Hilton v James Smith & Sons (Norwood) Ltd* [1979] 2 EGLR 44.
5   *Stranks v St John* (1867) LR 2 CP 376.
6   *Duke of Westminster v Guild* [1985] QB 688, CA; *Southwark London Borough Council v Mills* [2001] Ch 1, [1998] 3 EGLR 46, CA.
7   *Goldmile Properties Ltd v Lechouritis* [2003] EWCA Civ 49, [2003] 1 EGLR 60, [2003] 15 EG 143.
8   (1868) LR 3 HL 330.

5.3 In those cases, there will be no breach of the covenant for quiet enjoyment. The landlord is only liable where the acts of those claiming under him are not wrongful. An example can be seen in the case of *Sanderson v Berwick-upon-Tweed Corpn*[1]. A tenant farmer suffered damage from the overflow of drains from two adjoining farms. All of the farms belonged to the same landlord and all were let. The landlord was held liable under his covenant for quiet enjoyment in respect of one farm where the damage was caused by the use of drains which were defective, but not in respect of the other farm where the problem was caused by the tenant's excessive use of drains which were not defective.

The other implied obligation of the landlord is not to derogate from his grant[2]. There is an overlap between this obligation and the covenant for quiet enjoyment. However, the two are not identical. The essence of non-derogation from grant is that the landlord (and those claiming under him) must not do anything to render the holding substantially less fit for the purpose for which it was let or to frustrate that purpose. For example, this will apply where the landlord prevents the airflow to the tenant's drying sheds[3].

There is no implied obligation on the landlord in connection with the state of the premises or the fitness of the holding[4] although he may be liable under statute[5].

1   (1884) 13 QBD 547.
2   *Birmingham Dudley and District Banking Co v Ross* (1888) 38 Ch D 295; *Molton Builders Ltd v City of Westminster London Borough Council* (1975) 30 P & CR 182, CA.
3   *Aldin v Latimer Clark, Muirhead & Co* [1894] 2 Ch 437.
4   Although covenants may be implied to make the lease workable or give it business efficacy or to make sense of an express covenant: *Liverpool City Council v Irwin* [1977] AC 239, HL; *Barrett v Lounova (1982) Ltd* [1990] 1 QB 348, CA.
5   See, for example, the Defective Premises Act 1972, s 4.

IMPLIED COVENANTS BY THE TENANT

5.4 In the absence of express agreement, in all tenancies there will be an implied covenant by the tenant to pay the rent, rates and all other charges relating to the property.

There is an implied covenant by the tenant not to derogate from the reservations of the landlord[1].

While the tenant is under no implied obligation to repair, as such, he is under an obligation not to commit the tort of waste. The extent of that obligation depends upon the type of tenancy. The tort of waste is designed to prevent the use of the land by the tenant in such a way as to damage the landlord's reversion. It will be committed by any act which changes the nature of the land. Waste may be 'permissive' (an omission by the tenant to do what he ought to do[2]) or 'voluntary' (requiring a positive act by the tenant).

A tenant under a fixed-term tenancy is liable for both voluntary and permissive waste. This is generally thought to mean that even where the tenancy agreement makes no provision for repairs, the tenant is obliged to repair to the extent necessary to prevent him from committing waste and to maintain the property in the condition in which he took it[3]. This will obviously, to some extent, render the tenant liable for acts of husbandry which result in waste.

[1]   *Johnston & Sons Ltd v Holland* [1988] 1 EGLR 264, CA.
[2]   Although not the failure to cultivate land: see *Hutton v Warren* (1836) 1 M & W 466.
[3]   Megarry & Wade, *The Law of Real Property* (5th edn, 1984), p 702; Gray, *Elements of Land Law*, 2nd edn, p 801, but see Denning LJ (as he then was) in *Warren v Keen* [1954] 1 QB 15 at 20, CA, where he suggested that even a tenant under a fixed-term tenancy had no obligation to carry out repairs.

5.5   The annual tenant will be liable for permissive waste in so far as it stems from a failure to keep the holding wind and water tight[1], but not so far as it results from fair wear and tear.

Under a periodic tenancy, the tenant is obliged to use the property in a 'tenantlike' manner[2]. In terms of a tenant under a farm business tenancy, this requirement translates itself into a limited implication in relation to good husbandry: to use and cultivate the land in a good and husbandlike manner and according to the custom of the country[3]. There is no corresponding obligation relating to estate management. In *Wedd v Porter*[4], the obligation on the tenant to farm in a good and husbandlike manner was described as follows:

> 'A tenant from year to year of a farm and buildings at a fixed rent, who has not entered into any other express covenant with the landlord then as to the amount of rent, is under an obligation implied by law to use and cultivate the lands in a husbandlike manner according to the custom of the country ... and to keep the buildings wind and watertight'.

It can be seen that this obligation is minimal. It is important that express husbandry clauses are included in all farm business tenancies.

The tenant is not under a duty to 'sustain and uphold the premises'[5]. There is no obligation to deliver the farm up in a proper condition at the termination of the tenancy. Indeed, if the land was in very good condition at the grant of the tenancy, there is no obligation on the tenant to maintain it as such. It is sufficient that he farms the land properly.

A 'custom of the country' may be implied. The custom of the country must be reasonable. It will apply if it is universally applicable in that part of the country where the farm is situated. It need not have been practised since time immemorial. It is sufficient that it has subsisted for a reasonable length of time[6]. It can be expressly excluded from the terms of a written tenancy[7].

The landlord's remedy for a breach of the implied covenant in relation to the 'custom of the country' is damages to recover the sum equivalent to the impact on the reversion[8].

[1] *Wedd v Porter* [1916] 2 KB 91, CA.
[2] See the explanation of this phrase in *Warren v Keen* [1954] 1 QB 15, CA.
[3] *Powley v Walker* (1793) 5 Term Rep 373.
[4] [1916] 2 KB 91, CA.
[5] *Anworth v Johnson* (1832) 5 C & P 239.
[6] *Tucker v Linger* (1882) 21 Ch D 18, CA.
[7] *Hutton v Warren* (1836) 1 M & W 466; *Senior v Armytage* (1816) Holt NP 197.
[8] *Williams v Lewis* [1915] 3 KB 493. See para 10.12.

FREEDOM OF CROPPING

5.6 Under the Agricultural Tenancies Act 1995 (ATA 1995), there is no restriction on the inclusion of terms restricting the tenant's freedom of cropping or the right to dispose of the produce of the holding[1]. Further, there is no restriction on the inclusion of terms preventing the ploughing of permanent pasture[2]. Under the Agricultural Holdings Act 1986 (AHA 1986), the tenant's freedom of cropping is guaranteed[3]. Any restriction upon the ploughing of permanent pasture can be modified through arbitration under the AHA 1986 if it is in the interests of 'full and efficient farming' of the holding[4]. There are no like provisions in the ATA 1995. The parties have complete freedom of contract to agree the farming system to be practised on the holding and to make provision for it in the tenancy agreement. A farm business tenancy can restrict the farming of certain areas of the holding, for example conservation sites or for sporting rights. The tenant has no redress under the ATA 1995 to challenge any contractual restriction upon his freedom of cropping.

The ATA 1995 makes no statutory provision for a record of the condition of the holding to be made at the commencement of the tenancy[5]. The parties may consider that it is sensible to have such a record, but it is a matter for them to agree. Further, there is no provision for compensation to be paid to the tenant for damage caused by game[6]. Again, it is a matter for the parties to agree, if the tenant wishes to protect against game damage where the sporting rights are reserved to the landlord.

[1] AHA 1986, s 15. See para 24.9.
[2] AHA 1986, s 14. See para 24.8.
[3] AHA 1986, s 15.
[4] AHA 1986, s 14.

5 Compare the provision in the AHA 1986, s 22. See para 24.13.
6 AHA 1986, s 20. See para 24.11.

GOOD HUSBANDRY

5.7 Sections 10 and 11 of the Agriculture Act 1947 contained rules of good husbandry and good estate management. The sanctions for breach of the rules were repealed by the Agriculture Act 1958[1]. The rules of good estate management, set out the 1947 Act, are unenforceable by a tenant against a landlord unless they are expressly incorporated into the tenancy agreement. Under the AHA 1986, the rules of good husbandry (despite the repeal enacted by the Agriculture Act 1958) have maintained their relevance because of the ability of a landlord to rely upon them in connection with the enforcement of obligations in the recovery of possession under the statutory framework contained in the AHA 1986[2]. The ATA 1995 does not incorporate the rules of good husbandry into a farm business tenancy. Further, in the absence of a statutory framework such as that contained in the AHA 1986 Act, the rules of good husbandry have no indirect relevance under the ATA 1995. If the parties want to incorporate the rules of good husbandry, as a means to assess the tenant's farming, it is necessary to do so expressly in the tenancy agreement.

The ability of the Minister to serve a notice on an occupier to deal with injurious weeds should be noted[3].

1 Agriculture Act 1958, s 10(1) and Sch 2.
2 See paras 24.4 and 30.7.
3 Weeds Act 1959. See para 24.7.

THE USUAL COVENANTS

5.8 The 'usual covenants' are only relevant where either the parties expressly agree that the lease is on the usual covenants or where the grant of a lease is preceded by an agreement to grant it (ie a contract for a lease being itself an equitable lease under the principle enunciated in *Walsh v Lonsdale*[1]) which is silent on the terms to be included in the lease. In those circumstances, the contract will contain an implied term that the lease will be granted on the 'usual covenants'.

The usual covenants are[2]:

(a) by the landlord, for quiet enjoyment;
(b) by the tenant to pay rent and rates; to keep in repair and deliver up in repair; to permit the landlord to enter and view (if landlord is under an obligation to repair);
(c) a forfeiture provision for non-payment of rent;
(d) covenants which are 'usual' for leases of that nature in that area. This is a question of fact and may involve evidence from practitioners as to what is usual[3]. It may mean that the lease will, for example, contain a prohibition on making alterations or a right of re-entry for breach of any covenant[4].

5.8   Implied terms and usual covenants

1   (1882) 21 Ch D 9, CA.
2   *Hampshire v Wickens* (1878) 7 Ch D 555. Also see, *Woodfall: Landlord and Tenant* (Looseleaf edition, 1994) Sweet & Maxwell).
3   *Flexman v Corbett* [1930] 1 Ch 672, where Maughan J suggested that if it could be shown that a particular covenant was found in nine out of ten leases of the particular type in the particular locality the court would find that it was 'usual'.
4   *Chester v Buckingham Travel Ltd* [1981] 1 All ER 386.

Chapter 6

TERM

GENERALLY

6.1 Despite pressure from, in particular, the Labour Party[1] and the Farmers Union of Wales, the Agricultural Tenancies Act 1995 (ATA 1995) does not contain any requirements as to the minimum term for which land can be let on a farm business tenancy. In the absence of statutory intervention, the term can be of any length from one day to 999 years or can be a periodic tenancy of any period – weekly, monthly, quarterly or annual – and is entirely a matter for negotiation between the parties. Apart from a length of notice requirement in connection with some tenancies[2], a farm business tenancy carries no security of tenure beyond the term granted. In order to be valid at law the maximum duration of the term must be ascertainable at the outset. If it is not the term granted will be void[3].

An example of an uncertain term can be seen in the case of *Prudential Assurance Co Ltd v London Residuary Body*[4], where it was held by the House of Lords[5] that a letting of a strip of land fronting a highway at a yearly rent of £30 to continue until the land was required for the widening of the highway was void. Its maximum duration could not be ascertained at the outset even though the position would be clear at the time of termination. Because of the occupation by the tenant and the payment of an annual rent, the House of Lords was able to find an implied annual periodic tenancy determinable, at common law, by six months' notice to quit. The position would be more difficult where the lease did not provide for a periodic monetary payment.

The length of a term is calculated from the date the tenancy is entered into and not any earlier date when the term is expressed to begin in the body of the agreement[6].

[1] See para 1.18.
[2] See ATA 1995, ss 5–7 and see also Ch 12.
[3] See *Lace v Chantler* [1944] KB 368, CA; *Prudential Assurance Co Ltd v London Residuary Body* [1992] 2 AC 386, HL.
[4] [1992] 2 AC 386, HL.
[5] On the basis that *Ashburn Anstalt v Arnold* [1989] Ch 1, CA had been wrongly decided. The lease there was held to be valid where it was for an indefinite rent-free period but subject to the landlord's ability to determine on three months' notice – because the

83

termination was in the hands of the parties. Periodic tenancies are for a term certain because, in the words of Lord Templeman in the *Prudential Assurance* case: '... each party has power by notice to determine at the end of any year. The term continues until determined as if both parties made a new agreement at the end of each year for a new term for the ensuing year'.

6   *Keen v Holland* [1984] 1 All ER 75, CA; *Roberts v Church Comrs for England* [1972] 1 QB 278, CA.

6.2 The term commences on that date. This was of considerable importance under the Agricultural Holdings Act 1986 (AHA 1986) when looking at whether a particular letting was a *Gladstone v Bower* letting of more than 12 but less than 24 months' duration, and hence outside the security of tenure provisions of the 1986 Act[1]. It may also be of importance in the case of a farm business tenancy if the tenant believes that he is being granted a term of more than two years (which will give him, amongst other things, the right to 12 months' notice to quit[2]) but where, for example, the agreement is signed at a time when there is less than two years left to run. The earlier date in the body of the tenancy agreement expressed to be the commencement of the term exists as a reference date from which periods of time or events can be calculated, for example, the expiration of the term and the period for the exercise of any break options or rent review provisions. It may also signify an intention by the parties to create obligations from the earlier date, although nothing done before the execution of the lease can constitute a breach of covenant[3].

Whether the parties to a farm business tenancy choose a fixed-term or a periodic tenancy will depend upon the circumstances in every case. The following factors may be relevant:

(a)   The length of the term granted should not be looked at in isolation so far as the extent of the parties' obligations are concerned. Two other factors will be relevant: first, whether the tenancy will allow the tenant to assign or sub-let[4]; and second, whether the tenancy is to contain any break provisions[5].

(b)   A longer fixed term obviously provides greater security to the tenant which may enable him to raise finance more easily and may encourage greater capital investment in the holding.

(c)   In the absence of break clauses or the ability to assign, the tenant is tied in for the entire fixed term. The position is very different to that under the AHA 1986 where, although the tenant has effectively lifetime security of tenure, he can serve 12 months' notice to determine the tenancy at any time. Even death will not determine a fixed term. The remainder of the term will simply vest in the tenant's estate. With the possibility that the rent will be reviewed (in accordance with the open market formula in s 13 of the ATA 1995[6]) to levels which are uneconomic, the tenant may be left with an estate in land which he can neither dispose of nor determine.

So far as the landlord is concerned, he will consider his ability to get the land back should he want it, for example, for development or for his own purposes. He will also consider his ability to control or rid himself of a defaulting tenant and his willingness or otherwise to have improvements made to the land which will result in him paying compensation under section 16 of the Act on the termination of the tenancy when the tenant quits the holding[7]. All of these factors will need to be balanced against the fact that a tenant with the greater security of tenure of a longer fixed term may be prepared to pay a higher rent.

[1] See para 20.13.
[2] See ATA 1995, s 5.
[3] *Bradshaw v Pawley* [1980] 1 WLR 10.
[4] See Ch 8.
[5] See Ch 11.
[6] See Ch 9.
[7] See Ch 16.

ISSUES FOR THE LANDLORD

6.3 The landlord will need to consider the following.

(a)   If he lets for a term in excess of two years, he will have to serve notice in accordance with ATA 1995, s 5[1] of at least 12 months' notice to bring the tenancy to an end. If he does not, it will continue as an annual periodic tenancy.

(b)   If he lets for a term of more than two years, with break clauses in his favour, he still has to give at least 12 months' notice to operate the break provision[2]. If he requires the land back quickly, because of some change in the tax regime or because of a development opportunity, he may not be able to get it back in the absence of the co-operation of the tenant to a surrender.

(c)   If the tenant is in default, the landlord, if he can, will have to rely on forfeiture to oust the tenant from the holding. Forfeiture is dealt with in Chapter 13. It is a remedy which, in most cases, has to be pursued through the courts and where the tenant can apply for relief from forfeiture, making the outcome uncertain for the landlord.

(d)   By controlling the length of lettings, the landlord can avoid any rent reviews and the costs associated with reviews. At the start of a new letting, he is free to set the initial rent as he wishes.

(e)   The longer the letting, the greater will be the diminution in the value of the landlord's reversionary interest.

(f)   The shorter the term, the less likely an arbitrator might be to approve substantial physical improvements to the holding. If, in the absence of landlord's consent, the arbitrator does approve an improvement, the landlord has no option but to pay compensation to the tenant upon the termination of the tenancy on the tenant quitting the holding in accordance with the right contained in ATA 1995, s 16[3].

[1] See para 12.3.
[2] See ATA 1995, s 7; see also, para 12.7.
[3] See 16.11.

6.4 An issue which sometimes arises in practice is where the tenant goes into possession and pays a rent or alternatively holds over. In deciding whether a new tenancy has been granted it is necessary to ask the question: 'Is it right and proper to infer from all of the circumstances that the parties have reached an agreement for a new tenancy?' There must be two 'assenting minds'[1] reaching an agreement, applying the ordinary principles relating to the formation of a contract: offer, acceptance and agreement as to terms[2]. The old common law presumption of the creation of a tenancy from the payment and acceptance of rent no longer applies. This issue is dealt with in greater detail in relation to the 1986 Act[3].

[1] *Maconochie Bros Ltd v Brand* [1946] 2 All ER 778.
[2] This issue has generated a great deal of case law, see *Doe d Cheny v Batten* (1775) 1 Cowp 243; *Clarke v Grant* [1950] 1 KB 104; *Hollington Bros Ltd v Rhodes* [1951] 2 TLR 691; *Sidney Bolsom Investment Trust v E Karmios & Co (London)* [1956] 1 QB 529, CA; *Leveson v Parfum Marcel Rochas (England) Ltd* (1966) 200 Estates Gazette 407; *Longrigg Burrough and Trounson v Smith* [1979] 2 EGLR 42, CA; *Cardiothoracic Institute v Shrewdcrest* [1986] 1 WLR 368; *Morrison-Low v Paterson* 1985 SLT 255; *Sector Properties v Meah* (1973) 229 Estates Gazette 1097; *Land v Sykes* [1991] 1 EGLR 18; *Javad v Aqil* [1991] 1 All ER 243; and *Hackney London Borough Council v Otchere* [2001] EWCA Crim 1850.
[3] See para 21.19ff.

Chapter 7

USER COVENANTS

GENERALLY

7.1 There is nothing in the Agricultural Tenancies Act 1995 (ATA 1995) that impinges upon the parties' freedom to reach whatever agreement they wish in respect of the use to which the holding may be put.

Section 1(8) of the ATA 1995 provides that, for the purposes of compliance with the business conditions or the agriculture condition, any use of the land in breach of a term of the tenancy or any cessation of use in breach of the terms of the tenancy shall be disregarded when the landlord has consented to or acquiesced in the breach[1].

In certain circumstances where the landlord refuses consent to a tenant's improvement, the tenant can apply instead for the approval of an arbitrator. In deciding whether or not to approve the provision of the improvement, the arbitrator will take into account, inter alia, the terms of the tenancy agreement[2]. It would only be in the most unusual circumstances that an arbitrator would consent to the provision of an improvement for a use not permitted by the tenancy agreement.

Restrictions on use may impact adversely on a rent review where the review is on the basis of the statutory open market formula[3].

By compliance with the business conditions and the notice conditions, a high degree of diversification away from agriculture may be allowed without any danger that the tenancy will no longer be a farm business tenancy[4].

[1] See para 3.27.
[2] See para 16.13ff.
[3] See para 9.5.
[4] See para 3.19ff.

OPTIONS

7.2 In broad terms, the options for user covenants in a farm business tenancy include the following:

7.2   User covenants

(a)   Restricting use to a particular agricultural use or uses only[1].

(b)   Restricting use to 'agriculture'.

(c)   Restricting use to agriculture and some specified diversification activities already in the contemplation of the tenant provided that the extent of the *intended* diversification activities do not impact so much on the character of the tenancy that it could not be said to be primarily or wholly agricultural at the outset and hence will fall outside the ATA 1995.

(d)   Restricting use only to the extent necessary to ensure compliance with the business conditions by placing an obligation on the tenant always to conduct some commercial farming on the holding[2]. So long as the landlord does not consent to or acquiesce in the breach of this covenant, the user covenant and the disregard in s 1(8) of the ATA 1995 for unlawful uses will ensure that the tenancy remains a farm business tenancy regardless of whether or not there is actually any commercial farming being conducted on the holding. The decision in *Montross Associated Investments SA v Moussaieff*[3] shows that careful drafting is necessary to impose an obligation on the tenant to use premises in a particular way. The wording may be interpreted only as an emphatic way of prohibiting other uses. In that case, at first instance[4], it was held that a user covenant that the tenant 'will use' the premises for certain stated businesses did not impose an obligation on the tenant to use for those businesses but simply identified prohibited and permitted uses[5].

Beyond the considerations which particularly relate to provisions in the ATA 1995, all of the usual factors will be taken into account in deciding upon the extent of restrictions to be placed on the tenant. For example, the degree of control the landlord requires over the holding; the prohibition of uses which may reduce the value of the holding; the need for particular activities to be carried on or for particular restrictions to apply to preserve quotas or to comply with environmental designations or licences will all feature in the decision.

In the absence of any restriction on use, the tenant will be entitled to use the holding for any lawful purpose[6]. If that purpose is commercial (but not agricultural), such that s 23 of the Landlord and Tenant Act 1954 (LTA 1954), Pt II applies, the tenant will have the greater security of tenure afforded by the 1954 Act regime[7].

1   *Jewell v McGowan* [2002] EWCA Civ 145, [2002] 3 EGLR 87.
2   ATA 1995, s 1(2) which sets out the business conditions. See para 3.30.
3   (1990) 61 P & CR 437.
4   For the Court of Appeal, see (1991) 63 P & CR 31.
5   Conversely, see *Basildon Development Corpn v Mactro* [1986] 1 EGLR 137, CA; *Creery v Summersell and Flowerdew & Co* [1949] Ch 751.
6   But not so as to commit waste.
7   The landlord may also be worse off for other reasons. For example, if the parties have been content to say nothing about rent review but to leave it to the ATA 1995 provisions, the landlord may be left with a tenant, protected under the LTA 1954 and with no ability to review the rent.

ABSOLUTE V QUALIFIED

7.3 Restrictions on use may be absolute or qualified (ie requiring the landlord's consent). If qualified, the lease may specify that the landlord's consent is not to be unreasonably withheld[1]. Whether or not consent has been unreasonably withheld will probably be decided upon the same principles as apply in the case of assignment[2]. If the landlord gives consent 'in principle', that cannot be subsequently qualified[3].

In *Jewell v McGowan*[4], the tenant covenanted to use the holding 'for agricultural purposes only'. The tenant wished to encourage members of the public to visit the farm by creating a route-marked trail and access to look at crops and animals. Rides on trailers pulled by tractors were also part of the attraction. The majority of the facilities, such as a shop, tea room, etc, were sited on freehold land owned by the tenant adjacent to the holding. The Court of Appeal decided (reversing the judge in the county court) that the proposed activities were in breach of the terms of the tenancy. The tenant was proposing an open farm activity for the purpose of an enterprise that was distinct in character and purpose from his agricultural enterprise. The proposed activity would constitute a distinct activity for non-agricultural purposes. This was not permitted by the use of the word 'only' in the user clause. This is an important restriction upon a tenant's desire to diversify without the consent of the landlord.

In *Field v Bryant*[5], the farmers owned a 71-acre farm, upon which they operated a dairy herd and a flock of sheep. They entered into an agreement to sell the land to B, conditional upon the grant of planning permission for residential development. The agreement provided that, upon completion, B would grant a farm business tenancy to the farmers. Planning permission was obtained and the sale was completed. The parties entered into a farm business tenancy, restricting the use to 'agricultural purposes' and 'permanent pasture for livestock only'. At the termination of the tenancy there was a dispute. The judge at first instance determined that the tenancy did not permit the carrying on of a milking and dairy enterprise. The decision was overruled by the Court of Appeal. The court decided that the true construction of the tenancy agreement needed to be read against the material background facts, the most important of which was that, immediately before the grant of the tenancy, the farmers had been carrying on a milking and dairy business. There was no positive indication that it was within the contemplation of the parties that such business would cease.

[1] In the absence of such a clause in the lease, there will be no implied term that the landlord will not unreasonably withhold his consent and hence the landlord may act entirely capriciously (*Guardian Assurance Co Ltd v Gants Hill Holdings Ltd* [1983] 2 EGLR 36). Note also that s 19(3) of the Landlord and Tenant Act 1927 (LTA 1927) – which prevents the landlord from making his consent subject to the payment of a fine or sum of money in the nature of a fine in certain cases – does not apply to farm business tenancies (ATA 1995, Sch para 6, amending s 19(4) of the LTA 1927).

[2] See *Woodfall: Landlord and Tenant* (Looseleaf edn, 1994) Sweet & Maxwell, para 11.195. A landlord is entitled to have regard to any impact of the change of use on any business of his own and whether or not the business of the landlord existed at the date of the lease.

[3] *Aubergine Enterprises Ltd v Lakewood International Ltd* [2001] 3 EGLR 71, [2001] 39 EG 141.

⁴   [2002] EWCA Civ 145, [2002] 3 EGLR 87.
⁵   [2003] EWCA Civ 1957, [2003] PLSCS 22.

Chapter 8
ASSIGNMENT AND SUB-LETTING

GENERALLY

8.1 Farm business tenancies are freely alienable in the absence of any restrictions in the tenancy agreement. Furthermore, there is no requirement that the tenant be personally involved in farming the holding.

For long fixed-term tenancies, giving the tenant controlled rights to assign or sub-let may be an alternative to break clauses to mitigate the potential problems for the tenant of being tied into the tenancy for the full length of the term. This alternative is more beneficial to the tenant since the Landlord and Tenant (Covenants) Act 1995 came into force[1]. This Act is considered at 8.5 below.

It is usual for the Agricultural Holdings Act 1986 (AHA 1986) tenancies to contain an absolute prohibition on assignment, sub-letting or parting with possession of the holding[2]. For this reason, farm business tenancies may continue to include such absolute prohibitions. However, the prohibitions found in the AHA 1986 tenancies are more easily accepted by a tenant (who may, in any event, serve 12 months' notice to quit to determine the tenancy) and more legitimately required by a landlord (who, with the security of tenure offered by the AHA 1986, could be left in a position where the land is tied up for a considerably longer period of time than it would have been had the original tenant not assigned – particularly if, for example, the assignment is to a company). Advisers need to consider the needs of the relationship between the prospective landlord and tenant.

A prohibition against assignment may be absolute or qualified, ie made subject to landlord's consent[3]. If qualified, it may place an obligation on the landlord not to withhold consent unreasonably. This type of covenant is known as a 'fully qualified' covenant. A qualified prohibition subject to a reasonableness test gives the landlord a degree of control over the assignment and the identity of the proposed assignee and, therefore, represents a compromise between complete freedom and complete prohibition[4].

---

[1]   For lettings after 31 December 1995.
[2]   See para 24.18 and see also AHA 1986, s 6.

91

8.1 *Assignment and sub-letting*

3   LTA 1927, s 19, which imposes an obligation on landlords not to withhold consent
     unreasonably, does not apply to qualified covenants in farm business tenancies (s 19(4),
     inserted by the Agricultural Tenancies Act 1995, Sch para 6). Note that a consent 'subject
     to licence' may be immediately effective: *Prudential Assurance Co Ltd v Mount Eden Land
     Ltd* [1997] 1 EGLR 37, CA; *Next plc v NFU Mutual Insurance Co Ltd* [1997] EGCS 181.
     Also, if the landlord gives consent 'in principle', that cannot be subsequently qualified:
     Aubergine Enterprises Ltd v Lakewood International Ltd [2001] 3 ELGR 71, [2001]
     39 EG 141.
4   What is a reasonable refusal will depend on the circumstances, but see para 8.4 below.

8.2 As a prohibition against assignment does not invalidate the assignment itself[1], in order to be fully effective, a right of forfeiture for breach of covenant is also needed. In those circumstances, the tenancy may be brought to an end if the covenant against assignment is broken[2].

An absolute prohibition on assignment in a tenancy to joint tenants will prohibit an assignment by all joint tenants to only one or some of their number. The prohibition may be avoided by the use of a deed of release by the outgoing joint tenants to the remaining tenant or tenants of their interest in the tenancy but there is a significant risk that this would still be held to an assignment[3].

The extent of the prohibition will depend upon the degree of control the landlord wants and the tenant will accept. It may also depend upon the nature of any diversification activities the tenant intends to carry out and whether he will undertake them himself. A prohibition may be against assignment only or may extend to all or any of the sub-letting; parting with possession or sharing possession of all or any part of the holding.

A prohibition against assignment will not prevent sub-letting, unless the sub-lease is for the same term or longer than the head lease, in which case it is effectively a conveyance of the tenant's existing interest[4]. All assignments must be by deed[5]. Any attempt to assign other than by deed will not be a breach of the covenant.

A covenant 'not to assign' or 'not to sub-let' prevents assignments or sub-lettings of the whole only[6]. A prohibition against assignments or sub-letting of any part of the premises also prohibits assignments or sub-lettings of the whole[7].

A covenant against parting with possession will prohibit assignments and sub-lettings[8]. Such a covenant will not prevent a tenant from sharing posses-sion. So, for example, a tenant who farms in partnership where the partner-ship is granted a licence to farm the holding would not be in breach of such a prohibition. Neither would it prevent the tenant from, for example, employing contractors to farm the holding for him. 'Parting with possession' means parting with the right to legal possession of the premises, not simply allowing somebody else into occupation[9].

A covenant against sharing possession has been interpreted to prohibit the sharing of the use of the premises, rather than anything more technical[10].

In *Wallace v C Brian Barrett & Son Ltd*[11], the use by a family company tenant of contractors as its agents to farm a holding consisting of arable land with no dwellings or buildings was held not to be a sharing of occupation by the tenant in breach of an agreement 'not to assign, under let, part with or share possession or occupation of the whole or any part of the holding'. The Court of Appeal pointed out that as the company was only capable of acting through agents, the occupation of an agent, carrying out farming operations on behalf of the tenant, was the occupation of the principal/tenant.

1   *Old Grovebury Manor Farm Ltd v W Seymour Plant Sales and Hire Ltd (No 2)* [1979] 3 All ER 504.
2   Provided that no estoppel operates: *Troop v Gibson* [1986] 1 EGLR 1, CA.
3   See *Burton v Camden London Borough Council* [2000] 2 AC 399, HL, where the majority held that this would not work in the context of a statutory bar on assignment in s 91 of the Housing Act 1985 as there was no indication that the word 'assign' in s 91 was not wide enough to cover the situation where a joint tenant 'dropped out'. However, see the strong dissenting speech of Lord Millett.
4   *Langford v Selmes* (1857) 3 K & J 220.
5   *Crago v Julian* [1992] 1 WLR 372, CA.
6   *Wilson v Rosenthal* (1906) 22 TLR 233.
7   *Field v Barkworth* [1986] 1 WLR 137.
8   *Marks v Warren* [1979] 1 All ER 29.
9   *Chaplin v Smith* [1926] 1 KB 198, CA; *Stening v Abrahams* [1931] 1 Ch 470; *Lam Kee Ying Sdn Bhd v Lam Shes Tong* [1975] AC 247, PC.
10 *Tulapam Properties Ltd v De Almeida* (1981) 260 Estates Gazette 919.
11 [1997] 2 EGLR 1, CA.

8.3 It has been held, in relation to commercial premises, that there is no precise test of the meaning of 'sharing occupation'. The starting point is to consider the nature of the permitted use. The fact that the tenant remained 'exclusively responsible for everything concerned with the property' indicated that the premises had not been shared[1].

In *Akici v L R Butlin Ltd*[2], Neuberger LJ (as he then was) acknowledged that the difference between possession and occupation can be elusive, but it is a difference which is recognised and should be adhered to. Where the owner had unrestricted access to the property, on the facts in *Akici*[3], it was found that there had been no parting with possession.

What was also noteworthy about the *Akici*[4] decision is that the judge limited the impact of the *Scala House and District Property Co Ltd v Forbes*[5] decision to cases where a legal interest had either been created or transferred. Where, as in the *Akici* case, the tenant had allowed a company in which the tenant had no formal interest to operate a business from the premises, if such an act was in breach of covenant it was remediable.

1   *Mean Fiddler Holdings Ltd v Islington London Borough Council* [2003] EWCA Civ 160, [2003] 2 EGLR 7 at 10H.
2   [2005] EWCA Civ 1296, [2006] 1 ELGR 36, [2006] 07 EG 136, overruling *Tulapam Properties Ltd v De Almeida* (1981) 260 Estates Gazette 919.
3   [2005] EWCA Civ 1296, [2006] 1 ELGR 36, [2006] 07 EG 136.
4   [2005] EWCA Civ 1296, [2006] 1 ELGR 36, [2006] 07 EG 136.
5   [1974] QB 575, [1973] 3 All ER 308, [1973] 3 WLR 14, 117 Sol Jo 467, 227 Estates Gazette 1161.

FULLY QUALIFIED COVENANTS

8.4 If the prohibition against alienation is fully qualified, the landlord is under statutory duties in connection with the exercise of his discretion. These duties are contained in the Landlord and Tenant Act 1988 (LTA 1988) and breach may result in a damages claim against him[1].

The LTA 1988 provides that where the landlord receives a written request from the tenant for consent to a disposition, he must, within a reasonable time, give consent, unless it is not reasonable for him to do so, and serve written notice of his decision on the tenant specifying any conditions attached to the consent or, if he is refusing consent, specifying the reasons for the refusal.

While the LTA 1988 shifts the burden of showing reasonableness onto the landlord[2], it does not interfere with the common law as to what will, and what will not, amount to an unreasonable refusal of consent. In the context of non-agricultural commercial lettings, it is usual to have a qualified prohibition. There is extensive case law as to whether or not a landlord has acted reasonably. The extent to which these cases easily translate into the agricultural setting remains to be established, but the following indications from the case law may be useful.

(a)   The landlord is required to act reasonably. It does not matter that there may be other landlords who would not have reached the same conclusion. It is a question of whether a reasonable landlord could have refused consent in these circumstances.

(b)   It is not a question of whether the landlord's concerns can be justified, but simply whether he acted reasonably[3].

(c)   The reason for refusal may be to do with the assignor, rather than the assignee. For example, if the assignor is in breach of covenant and the landlord reasonably suspects that he will not put it right or that the assignee will not put it right, he may be justified in refusing consent if the breach is serious[4].

(d)   It may be reasonable to refuse consent for reasons to do with the personal and financial attributes of the assignee, particularly if the concern is whether or not the assignee will be able to pay the rent and perform the covenants. Unsatisfactory references procured by the landlord may be sufficient reason to refuse consent[5]. Further, in the context of farm business tenancies, it may be legitimate for the landlord to consider the training and practical experience of farming of the proposed assignee and require references as to his husbandry skills. Potential damage to the landlord's reversion by poor farming techniques may be a reason for refusing consent. Personal considerations of race, sex, age, sexual orientation or disability as reasons for refusing consent will not be reasonable in view of the fact that discrimination on such grounds is unlawful in most cases under the Race Relations Act 1976, the Sex Discrimination Act 1975, the Employment Equality (Age) Regulations 2006[6], the Civil Partnerships Act 2004 and the Disability Discrimination Acts 1995 and 2005.

(e)   Can the landlord refuse consent for considerations of sound estate management? It was held in *International Drilling Fluids v Louisville Investments (Uxbridge) Ltd*[7] that the refusal of the landlord must have something to do with the particular landlord and tenant relationship. Conversely, it has been held in *Re Town Investments Underlease*[8] that the landlord is entitled to take into account the effect of the assignment on his entire estate. The landlord is not allowed to refuse consent to force the tenant to surrender so as to achieve the collateral advantage of getting the holding back in hand[9]. The answer must depend on the particular facts of the case, but to refuse consent to an assignment where the assignee intends to use the holding for a use which is within the user covenant (and which, therefore, the original tenant himself could have carried out) because it does not fit with the farming pattern on the estate as a whole may not be reasonable[10].

(f)   Refusing consent where the intended use would be in breach of the user covenant (and hence where consent would amount to a waiver by the landlord in relation to the breach) is likely to be reasonable[11].

[1]   Landlord and Tenant Act 1988, s 4.
[2]   At common law, the burden is on the tenant to show that the landlord was acting unreasonably: *Shanly v Ward* (1913) 29 TLR 714.
[3]   *Air India v Balabel* [1993] 2 EGLR 66, CA; *Beale v Worth* [1993] EGCS 135, CA.
[4]   *Goldstein v Sanders* [1915] 1 Ch 549; *Orlando Investments v Grosvenor Estate Belgravia* (1989) 59 P & CR 21, [1989] 2 EGLR 74, CA.
[5]   *Shanly v Ward* (1913) 29 TLR 714.
[6]   SI 2006/1031.
[7]   [1986] Ch 513, CA.
[8]   [1954] Ch 301.
[9]   *Bromley Park Garden Estates Ltd v Moss* [1982] 1 WLR 1019, CA.
[10]   Although see *Bates v Donaldson* [1896] 2 QB 241, CA.
[11]   *Killick v Second Covent Garden Property Co Ltd* [1973] 1 WLR 658, CA and cf *Bates v Donaldson* (ante). See also *Ashworth Frazer Ltd v Gloucester City Council* (1999) 80 P & CR 11, [2000] 1 EGLR 44, CA.

LANDLORD AND TENANT (COVENANTS) ACT 1995

8.5   This Act came into force on 1 January 1996. Some of its provisions apply to all existing leases[1] and some only to leases entered into after 31 December 1995 ('new leases')[2]. It abolishes privity of contract between landlord and tenant[3] to new leases so that, on assignment, the tenant is released from his obligations, including that of paying rent[4]. The landlord is also released from his covenants[5]. For leases entered into before 1 January 1996, privity of contract still applies and the original tenant remains liable under the tenancy throughout the term even after he has assigned, leaving the tenant vulnerable to actions on the covenants where the assignee defaults.

While the tenant under a new lease is better off, the landlord is clearly worse off[6] and the Landlord and Tenant (Covenants) Act 1995 makes some provision to compensate by the provision in s 16 that a landlord may, as a condition of consent to assignment where there is a qualified prohibition, require the original tenant to enter into an authorised guarantee agreement

8.5 *Assignment and sub-letting*

(AGA) whereby he guarantees the performance of the tenant covenants by his immediate assignee, although there are strict controls over what can be contained in such an agreement[7].

1   The Agricultural Tenancies Act 1995 (ATA 1995), ss 17–20. As to the relevance of the Landlord and Tenant (Covenants) Act 1995 to remedies, see Ch 45.
2   As defined in the ATA 1995, s 1(3). It should be noted that delivery of the lease in escrow is not the relevant date: *Dyment v Boyden* [2004] EWCA Civ 1586, [2005] 1 EGLR 19, [2005] 06 EG 142.
3   ATA 1995, s 5.
4   Provided that the assignment is not in breach of covenant or results from, for example, the tenant's bankruptcy. In these cases, the tenant continues to be bound until the next assignment.
5   ATA 1995, s 2.
6   *Scottish & Newcastle plc v Raguz* [2006] EWHC 821 (Ch), [2006] 4 All ER 524; affd [2007] EWCA Civ 150, [2007] 2 All ER 871.
7   For the creation of a valid AGA, see the requirements set out in the ATA 1995, s 16.

PROTECTION FOR SUB-TENANTS

8.6 If the landlord terminated the head tenancy under the ATA 1995, any sub-tenancy will likewise be terminated by reason of the common law[1]. The ATA 1995 provides no protection for a sub-tenant[2].

If the head tenant seeks to terminate the interest of the sub-tenant, if the sub-tenancy fulfils the qualifying criteria for protection as a farm business tenancy, then the sub-tenant's rights will be the same as a head tenant under the ATA 1995[3].

1   *Bendall v McWhirter* [1952] 2 QB 466, CA.
2   For an analysis of the more complicated position relating to the AHA 1986 and the position of sub-tenants generally, see Ch 29.
3   See Ch 29.

Chapter 9
RENT AND RENT REVIEW

INTRODUCTION

9.1 The Agricultural Tenancies Act 1995 (ATA 1995) contains detailed provisions dealing with rent review[1]. This part of the Act was initially the starkest example of the compromise between freedom of contract and statutory regulation of the landlord and tenant relationship. In the initial Ministry of Agriculture, Fisheries and Food (MAFF) consultation paper in relation to the reform of agricultural tenancy law[2], the emphasis was very much on freedom of contract and, after stressing the complexity of the Agricultural Holdings Act 1986 (AHA 1986) rent review provisions, it was proposed that the parties should be left entirely free to make their own arrangements in respect of rent and rent review. The new Act would contain no regulation whatsoever. By September 1992, and the publication of the detailed proposals paper[3], it was envisaged that the new Act would need to contain fall-back provisions: first, to preserve the right to a rent review for tenancies other than those of a fixed term of less than five years, and second, to provide a mechanism and formula for review, but only in the absence of express agreement between the parties. The emphasis was still very much on freedom of contract with the provisions of the Act only having any role in circumstances where the parties had failed to address their minds to the issue.

By the time the Agricultural Tenancies Bill had been introduced into Parliament, the concept of fall-back provisions had been compromised[4]. When the ATA 1995 came into being while the parties were still free to agree anything they wanted in relation to rent review, neither party was bound to follow through his contractual promise save in very limited circumstances. Each party had an opportunity, save in those limited circumstances, at each and every review to ignore the express rent review agreement and opt back into the statutory formula. That required the rent to be reviewed on an open market basis. That would be determined by arbitration, in the absence of agreement. The ATA 1995 was unusual in giving parties two chances to decide whether or not to use the statutory formula, rather than the usual formula of forbidding contracting out of statutory regulation altogether.

[1]   ATA 1995, Pt II, ss 9–14.

97

9.1 *Rent and rent review*

2 MAFF, 'Agricultural Tenancy Law – Proposals for Reform – A Consultation Paper' (February 1991).
3 Reform of Agricultural Holdings Legislation; Detailed Proposals (September 1992).
4 There were very few changes to the rent review provisions from the time of the introduction of the Bill to the final Act.

9.2 In brief, the position relating to rent review under the ATA 1995 was as follows:

(a)   The parties were free to decide what to do about rent review. They could agree to have no reviews or they could agree any rent review formula they wished and they could decide on the dates and frequency of those reviews.

(b)   If the parties did not agree provisions for rent review, or were content to let the ATA 1995 statutory mechanism apply, the provisions of Pt II of the ATA 1995 ensured a three-yearly review on an open market basis.

(c)   If the parties agreed the date and timing of reviews, each would be kept to his contractual bargain[1].

(d)   If the parties specified in a written tenancy agreement one of the options for review set out in s 9 of the ATA 1995, each would be kept to his contractual bargain and would not be able to opt back into the statutory open market formula[2].

(e)   If the parties chose any other rent review formula[3], either could decide at each and every review whether to follow through the express formula or whether to opt back into the statutory open market formula[4].

1 ATA 1995, s 10(4).
2 The choice of a section 9 option disapplies the rest of Pt II of the ATA 1995.
3 Or choose a section 9 option but do not embody that agreement in a written tenancy as s 9 requires.
4 This conclusion is reached because of the mechanism for the appointment of an arbitrator in ATA 1995, s 12.

9.3 TRIG2[1] agreed that the provisions of the ATA 1995, as originally enacted, were unnecessary in principle and led to needless complication in some cases. The parties should be given greater flexibility to agree their own arrangements.

There was a political expedient leading to the dismantling of the previous compromise. TRIG2 noted that a relaxation in the rules governing rent review provisions would remove a major reason why some AHA 1986 tenants would not consider surrendering their 'protected' tenancies in exchange for better holdings let on farm business tenancies. Under the original rent review provisions under the ATA 1995, TRIG2 observed that a 1995 Act rent could not easily be reviewed adopting the 1986 Act formula.

TRIG2 also considered it appropriate that the arbitrator (including any other person appointed to determine the rent) should be entitled to fix the rent by reference to all provisions within the tenancy agreement including those by reference to which the rent is to be determined. The ATA 1995 prohibited the arbitrator from considering rent review criteria previously agreed between the parties[2].

TRIG2 recommended that:

(a)   section 9 of the ATA 1995 should be modified to apply Pt II in every case, except where the parties agree otherwise in writing, provided that no such agreement be permitted which would result in an upwards-only rent review provision;

(b)   the parties to an ATA 1995 tenancy should be precluded from proceeding to arbitration under the statutory rules in cases where the tenancy agreement itself provides another mechanism for settling disputes as to the amount of the rent;

(c)   it should be open to an arbitrator to fix the rent by reference to all provisions of a tenancy agreement, including those by reference to which the rent is to be determined.

These recommendations have been adopted and implemented by the Regulatory Reform (Agricultural Tenancies) (England and Wales) Order 2006 (RRO 2006)[3] coming into force on 19 October 2006[4].

Accordingly, the RRO 2006 now enables the parties to reach a *binding* to review the rent on any basis they choose (including reference to the AHA 1986 rent review formula) provided that certain conditions are satisfied[5].

Article 14 of the RRO 2006, which introduced these amendments, provides that the amendments will only apply 'where the provision in the instrument creating the tenancy referred to in the new section 9(c)' is made on or after 19 October 2006. This does not confine the amendment to tenancies granted on or after that date. The parties can agree to vary the rent review mechanism in any existing tenancy.

The original options under s 9 are still available after 19 October 2006 and, if the parties choose to adopt them, will continue to attract the same issues which existed before the amendments introduced by the RRO 2006. It is unlikely that, save in very limited circumstances, any post-RRO 2006 tenancy considering a rent review other than on the statutory open market basis would do anything other than rely upon s 9(c)[6].

This represents a move away from the rent review compromise originally contained in the ATA 1995 to almost total freedom of contract for the parties. It is in part in recognition of the problems of managing AHA 1986 tenancies. The vast majority of issues which have arisen since the ATA 1995 came into force in relation to rent review have not been with farm business tenancies, but the resultant lack of flexibility for landlords and tenants in connection with AHA 1986 protected tenancies. The changes introduced by the RRO 2006, whether in relation to surrender and re-grant (where the risk to a tenant of losing AHA 1986 security has been reduced) or in relation to rent review (where the amendments have removed one of the major hurdles to moving AHA 1986 tenants onto farm business tenancies) have greatly eased the management of AHA 1986 tenancies.

1 Tenancy Reform Industry Group (2002), see para 1.19.
2 ATA 1995, s 13(2), as originally enacted. See para 9.16ff.
3 SI 2006/2805.
4 SI 2006/2805, art 1(1).
5 See para 9.13.
6 See para 9.14.

INITIAL RENT

9.4 The ATA 1995 is silent in relation to initial rent. As with the AHA 1986, the parties are free to negotiate and agree the initial rent. As the parties are also free to decide on the length of the farm business tenancy term[1], and as the tenant does not have security of tenure, an alternative to rent review would be for a landlord to grant a three- or five-year farm business tenancy leaving him free to negotiate a new rent for a new letting with the tenant at the end of the fixed-term period[2].

There is nothing in the ATA 1995 which prevents the parties agreeing that the tenant should pay a premium[3]. Although s 19(3) of the Landlord and Tenant Act 1927 prohibits the taking of a premium as a condition of change of use, this section does not apply to the ATA 1995[4]. It is submitted that there is nothing to prevent the parties agreeing that a premium be paid[5]. Further, they may agree that it should be paid by way of instalments, in effect as an extra rent[6].

1 See Ch 6.
2 This cannot be looked at in isolation. A land owner would need to consider all other factors including the impact on rent; the tenant's willingness to invest; the ability of the tenant to raise finance etc.
3 Also known as a fine.
4 Landlord and Tenant Act 1927, s 17(1), as amended by the ATA 1995, Sch para 5(1).
5 *Hill v Booth* [1930] 1 KB 381, CA.
6 *Regor Estates v Wright* [1951] 1 KB 689, CA. Cf *Barclays Bank plc v Bean* [2004] 3 EGLR 71, [2004] 41 EG 152.

RENT REVIEW FORMULA – EXPRESS TERMS

General

9.5 The parties are free to choose any basis for rent review that they wish or to choose not to have a review at all. There may be many reasons why a straight open market review is not appropriate to the particular holding or parties concerned. Examples would be as follows:

(a) A letting for five years where the parties may decide that the cost of a review is not justified and therefore prefer to have a higher initial rent and no review.

(b) Where the parties prefer to have the certainty at the outset of knowing exactly what is going to happen to the rent throughout the term and therefore prefer a stepped rent, particularly where the length of the term is such that there would otherwise only be one rent review.

(c)   A landlord may wish to persuade an AHA 1986 protected tenant to move to a different farm (and therefore on to a farm business tenancy) and the tenant may only be prepared to do so if the landlord agrees to a rent review formula equivalent to the basis set out in the AHA 1986.

(d)   The parties may want the rent to be tied to turnover or to the price of a particular commodity because they want there to be a stronger relationship between the earning capacity of the holding and the rental level than there would be if the rent were reviewed on an open market basis.

If the basis for review which best suits the parties fulfils the requirements of s 9 of the ATA 1995, the parties will be bound by it. If not, the parties can opt back into the statutory rent review formula at each and every review.

Section 9 options

General

9.6 Section 9 of the ATA 1995 provides that the remaining provisions of Part II of the ATA 1995 (dealing with rent review) would apply unless the conditions in that section are met. Part II deals with, not only the statutory rent review on an open market basis, but also the mechanics relevant to the review. Section 9 provides that Pt II will apply unless:

(a)   the tenancy was created by an instrument[1] and either;
(b)   the tenancy agreement expressly stated that the rent was not to be reviewed during the tenancy[2]; or
(c)   the tenancy agreement provided for the rent to be varied at specified times during the tenancy:
   (i)   by or to a specified amount; or
   (ii)   in accordance with a specified formula which does not preclude a reduction and which does not require or permit the exercise by any person of any judgment or discretion in relation to the determination of the rent of the holding,
but (in the case of (i) or (ii) was otherwise to remain fixed[3];
(d)   the tenancy agreement was created by an instrument and contains a provision made on or after 19 October 2006 which:
   (i)   does not preclude a reduction in the rent during the tenancy; and either
   (ii)   expressly excludes Pt II of the ATA 1995; or
   (iii)   makes provision for the reference of rent reviews to an independent expert whose decision is final[4].

---

[1]   ATA 1995, s 9.
[2]   ATA 1995, s 9(a).
[3]   ATA 1995, s 9(b).
[4]   ATA 1995, s 9(c), introduced by the RRO 2006, art 14(1).

9.7 Before looking at the options (which, for the sake of brevity, will be called collectively the 'section 9 options') in greater detail, the following points should be noted.

To exclude the remaining provisions of the ATA 1995 in relation to rent review, the section 9 option must be contained in a tenancy created by an 'instrument'. 'Instrument' is not defined in the ATA 1995, but it is clear that the section 9 option must be contained in a written tenancy agreement[1]. This restriction avoids the evidential problems there would otherwise be of proving an oral agreement for a section 9 option. A section 9 option, as part of an oral agreement, will be treated as an express choice not within s 9 and the parties would be able to avoid it on each and every review[2].

If the parties choose one of the options in s 9(b), the written tenancy agreement must contain an express statement that, other than in respect of the variations in line with the section 9 option chosen, the rent is to remain fixed. If that statement is not expressly made, even if the parties' intentions are clear by implication, they will not have fulfilled the requirements of s 9(b).

Section 9 of the ATA 1995 operates so as to exclude the remaining provisions of Pt II of the ATA 1995. This includes the statutory provisions as to timing and frequency of rent reviews and the provisions in s 10 of the ATA 1995 for the service of the statutory trigger notice (known as the statutory review notice). It is important that the parties consider, inter alia, the trigger mechanism to start the review process; the review date, the date from which the rent is to be reviewed; the frequency of reviews and the definition of a review in order to ensure certainty as to the correct timing of the next review[3].

If the chosen option is found not to fall within the provisions of s 9, the parties may still be bound by their contractual bargain in relation to dates, timing and frequency of reviews[4]. If the dates, timing and frequency are not suitable to the application of the statutory open market formula, it should be made clear in the tenancy agreement that the express provisions are only applicable in the event that the chosen option falls within s 9.

---

[1] The definition of 'instrument' in the Law of Property Act 1925, s 205(1)(viii) simply excludes a statute unless the statute creates a settlement.

[2] See para 9.13. Express rent review provisions are not within s 9 of the ATA 1995.

[3] There is authority that if the machinery (as opposed to the substance) of a rent review breaks down, the court can and should supplement it where the proper construction of the lease is that there should be a rent review for each of the rental periods: see *Royal Bank of Scotland plc v Jennings* [1997] 1 EGLR 101, where the court found that on a true construction of the lease there was an agreement for a rent review for each period. The lease provided for the landlord only to serve notice, but the court would not allow the landlord to frustrate the rent review by refusing to operate the machinery of rent review. (They upheld the decision of the judge at first instance who imposed a mandatory order on the landlord to serve the requisite notice.) See also *Adding v Secretary of State for the Environment* [1997] 1 EGLR 99, [1997] 14 EG 132.

[4] ATA 1995, s 10(4) and (5).

9.8 Section 9 excludes Pt II of the ATA 1995 if the rent review option chosen meets the conditions of s 9. It excludes the specific statutory arbitration for rent contained in ss 12 and 13 of the ATA 1995. An arbitrator appointed under s 12 can only review on an open-market basis. Accordingly, in relation to any dispute under s 9, it will be dealt with as follows:

(a)   For provisions made prior to 19 October 2006, ss 28 and 29 (the general dispute resolution sections)[1] will apply in the unlikely event of a dispute arising under the limited options then available under s 9(a) or (b).

(b)   For provisions made on or after 19 October 2006, ss 28 and 29 will apply unless the rent review provisions fulfil the conditions set out in s 9(c)(ii). This applies to a written tenancy agreement where the rent review formula does not preclude a reduction and where the parties have agreed for rent reviews to be referred to an independent expert whose decision will be binding. In those circumstances, the parties will not be able to opt back into a s 28 arbitration but will be bound by their agreement[2]. Where there has been no such agreement regarding the appointment of an expert, ss 28 and 29 will apply.

It is not clear whether a rent review provision which could be triggered by the landlord alone would fall within s 9. The trigger mechanism is a matter of agreement between the parties[3], but a trigger which can be exercised by the landlord alone would have the effect of making any formula chosen in accordance with s 9(b)(ii) upwards only. Upwards-only reviews are not permitted by s 9.

[1]   See para 47.3ff.
[2]   ATA 1995, s 28(5)(d), introduced by the RRO 2006, SI 2006/2805, art 14(2).
[3]   The statutory trigger (the statutory review notice) in s 10 will not apply to a section 9 option.

Section 9(a) – no review

9.9 Examples of where this option could be used are:

(a)   the farm business tenancy is for a fixed term of longer than three years but the length is not such as to justify the expense of a rent review; or

(b)   in any case where the parties require certainty as to their obligations throughout the term.

If the parties do not want the rent to be reviewed during the tenancy, they must expressly say so in a written tenancy agreement. It is not enough to state in a fixed-term agreement that the rent shall be, for example, £x per annum throughout the term. While from that statement it can easily be implied that the parties do not anticipate a rent review, the wording of the ATA 1995 clearly envisages an express statement that the rent is not to be reviewed during the tenancy. This emphatic and specific requirement fits with the requirement, in relation to the other section 9 options, that the tenancy agreement has to state that the rent is, apart from variations in accordance with the section 9 option, to remain fixed.

While s 9(a) makes it clear that this option is only available where the tenancy states that there is to be no review at all during the tenancy, the ability of the parties to choose the dates, timings and frequency of reviews[1] gives a greater flexibility outside the ambit of s 9. The parties may not want reviews in the early years, perhaps because of a high initial rent or because of work which a tenant is to do on the holding or equipment he is to provide, but would wish there to be reviews in the latter years of the tenancy. As the parties are free to choose, for example, their first review date, there can effectively be a review-free period at the beginning of the tenancy with, say, three-yearly reviews thereafter.

Reference should be made to the general notes to s 9 above for other restrictions on the use of this option.

1   ATA 1995, s 10(4) and (5).

Section 9(b)(i) – variations by or to a specified amount

9.10 This option survives TRIG2[1] and the RRO 2006[2], but it remains likely to be of limited appeal, particularly in fixed-term tenancies of any length when neither party is likely to want to predict the market.

Examples of where this option could be used are:

(a)   where the length of the tenancy is such that the parties only envisage one review; or

(b)   where a higher than usual initial rent is taken by way of a rentalised premium at the outset and the parties want to reduce the rent at a specified date in the term; or

(c)   where the tenant is being offered a rent-free or low rent initial period to reflect equipment he is obliged to provide or the state of the holding which he is taking,

and other than that one adjustment, the parties are content that there should be no reviews.

Reference should be made to the general notes on s 9 above for other restrictions on the use of this option[3].

1   See para 1.19.
2   SI 2006/2805. See para 2.5.
3   See para 9.9ff.

Section 9(b)(ii) – the objective formula

9.11 The purpose of the option contained in s 9(b)(ii) was that there should be no room for dispute between the parties as to the application of the chosen formula in reviewing the rent. With the introduction of the options in s 9(c) for provisions made on or after 19 October 2006, s 9(b)(ii) is likely to be of limited application.

The chosen formula must not permit the use of judgment or discretion by any person 'in relation to the determination of the rent of the holding'. Rent review formulae which fall within s 9(b)(ii), therefore, are likely to be one of the following:

(a)   indexation of some kind;
(b)   a turnover linked rent; or
(c)   linking the rent to the price of a particular commodity or basket of
        commodities.

Extreme care needed to be taken when drafting such a formula to ensure that
there was no element of judgment or discretion and to ensure that the formula
was appropriate to review the rent of a farm business tenancy.

The Retail Price Index has often been used as a basis for reviewing the rents of
commercial premises. It is unlikely to be an appropriate indicator of farm
profitability or movement in farm rents. Even with indexation of this sort,
there were problems with drafting the formula to fall within the strictures of
s 9(b)(ii). In longer fixed-term commercial leases, it is usual to provide for the
possibility that an index may cease to be published. The eventuality is often
covered by the inclusion in the rent review clause of a provision allowing for
the appointment of the third party to determine the replacement for the
chosen index. Such a provision in a farm business tenancy would be fatal to
the whole rent review provision from the outset because it would introduce an
element of judgment or discretion by the third party in the choice of the
replacement index. Either party could thus ignore the express formula on any
review and opt back into the open market formula if that were a pre-
19 October 2006 provision[1]. After the amendments made by the RRO 2006
came into operation, the option could well fall within s 9(c).

[1]   ATA 1995, s 12.

9.12 A particular problem which has arisen since 1 September 1995 relates to
the movement of AHA 1986 protected tenants onto farm business tenancies.
There are many reasons why a landlord may wish to move a tenant onto a
farm business tenancy even where he is not concerned about security of
tenure. For example, the landlord may wish to move the tenant to a larger or
better farm on the estate or there may be changes made to the tenancy which
amount to a surrender and re-grant in circumstances which do not fall within
s 4(1)(f) or (g) of the ATA 1995[1]. There may be the added advantage to the
landlord of 100% agricultural property relief on the new letting[2].

As TRIG2 noted[3], what frequently held up such re-arrangements was the
inability of the landlord to guarantee to the tenant that he would continue to
pay rent at the level he would have paid under the AHA 1986 tenancy. In
order to provide such a guarantee, a way would have to be found of fitting a
formula which produced a rental equivalent to that which would be payable
under an AHA 1986 tenancy into the mechanical formula required by
s 9(b)(ii). That is not possible: the AHA 1986 rent review involves judgment
and discretion and, therefore, would not fall within s 9(b)(ii). The tenant
would be left vulnerable because the landlord could, at each and every review,
opt back into the statutory formula[4].

An express option of, say, market rent less a stated percentage designed to
attempt to bring the rental level into line with AHA 1986 lettings was not a

formula within s 9, even though the only factor additional to market rent to be taken into account was itself mechanical – a percentage.

One possibility identified in the last edition of this book, was to state that the rent would be reviewed so as to be the same as the rent on another comparable holding which was let under the AHA 1986. That involved no judgment or discretion in relation to the determination of the rent of the subject holding, but was likely to be less than satisfactory in most cases.

For provisions made on or after 19 October 2005, replicating the AHA 1986 rent review formula is not a problem under s 9(c)[5]. As the RRO 2006 applies to provisions made after it came into force (and not only to tenancies entered into after that date), an appropriate s 9(c) option should now be considered for those existing farm business tenancies where the parties wish to link the rent review formula to that operating under the AHA 1986.

[1] See Ch 3.
[2] For lettings beginning on or after 1 September 1995, 100% agricultural property relief (APR) from inheritance tax has been available to the landowner: Inheritance Tax Act 1984, s 116, as amended by the Finance Act 1995.
[3] See para 1.19.
[4] See para 9.11.
[5] See para 9.13.

Section 9(c)

9.13 Section 9(c) of the ATA 1995 was introduced by art 14(1) of the RRO 2006 and applies only to provisions made on or after 19 October 2006, whether or not the tenancy agreement which contains the rent review provision pre-dates or post-dates the RRO 2006 coming into force.

Section 9(c) disapplies Pt II of the ATA 1995 whenever, in respect of a written tenancy agreement, the parties have an agreement which either:

(a)   expressly excludes Pt II of the ATA 1995; or
(b)   which makes provision for the reference of rent review to an independent expert whose decision is final,

and which, in either case, does not preclude the reduction of rent during the tenancy.

This means that the parties are free, on or after 19 October 2006, to agree any rent review formula they wish, provided that they comply with the requirement of s 9(c). That would include the ability to have rent reviews determined by reference to the statutory rent review formula contained in the AHA 1986.

If Pt II of the ATA 1995 is expressly excluded, but the parties have not made provision for the reference of rent reviews to an independent expert in accordance with s 9(c)(ii), any rent review will be dealt with by arbitration under ss 28 and 29 of the ATA 1995[1]. If the parties provide for expert determination, then the arbitration provisions under the ATA 1995 are excluded[2].

¹   See para 47.3ff.
²   ATA 1995, ss 9(c)(ii) and 28(5)(d).

Express rent review provisions not within section 9

9.14 Given the almost total freedom of contract in the amended s 9, it is unlikely that there will be many rent review provisions made on or after 19 October 2006 which do not fall within its ambit. There will remain issues in respect of pre-19 October 2006 express rent review agreements which fall outside the amended s 9. The parties may amend those express rent review agreements so as to bring the amended s 9 into operation.

The comments which follow in this section apply to:

(a)   pre-19 October 2006 express rent review provisions which have not been varied so as to introduce the amended s 9; and

(b)   in the unusual event that there are express provisions in respect of an agreement entered into on or after 19 October 2006 which do not comply with the provisions of s 9.

While at first sight it may appear that the application of a statutory rent review formula is mandatory in the absence of an express option within s 9, that is not the case. Arbitration in relation to the statutory formula is a last resort. Section 12(b) recognises that parties may wish to follow through an option which they have agreed for rent review but which is not within s 9. If the parties choose to do so, they are permitted to do so. However, at each and every review the parties will have the option of following through their non-section 9 contractual rent review provision or opting back into the statutory formula.

The rationale for this approach in the ATA 1995 is a recognition that parties have always been able to settle their rent reviews. There is no reason to make the arbitration mandatory. The ATA 1995 simply allows the parties to think about settlement in advance and put a settlement mechanism (ie the rent review formula) into the tenancy agreement. The ATA 1995 then permits the parties to follow through that settlement mechanism should they wish to do so by appointing a third party under s 12(b) to assist in the settlement process.

The only constraint upon the parties¹ is that they may not appoint any person as *arbitrator* to determine the rent on any basis other than the open-market formula set out in s 13. If they require the assistance of a third party, it has to be in some other capacity, the most obvious being as an independent expert. There is no express statement to this effect in the Act. The authority is found obliquely in s 12 which deals with the appointment of the arbitrator to deal with the statutory rent review.

The effect of s 12 of the ATA 1995 is to prohibit the parties from applying to the President of the Royal Institution of Chartered Surveyors (RICS) for the appointment of an arbitrator to determine the rent on an open-market basis where either the parties have already appointed the arbitrator by agreement or where the parties have appointed a person (not acting as an arbitrator) to determine the rent 'on a basis agreed by the parties' following the service of a statutory review notice[2]. It is only at the stage of the appointment of the third party that the parties are bound to follow through their non-section 9 agreed rent review provision or, more accurately, are not permitted to apply to the President of the RICS for the appointment of an arbitrator following the service of the statutory review notice.

[1] ATA 1995, ss 12(b) and 13(1).
[2] ATA 1995, s 10 (for the definition of a statutory review notice) and s 12.

9.15 The other requirement of s 12 of the ATA 1995 is that the third party must have been appointed under an agreement reached between the parties since the service of a statutory review notice. Two points need to be noted as follows:

(a) A party is unable to rely on s 12(b) as preventing an application for the appointment of an arbitrator on the basis of an expert named and agreed in the tenancy agreement. If that were possible, one could have effectively rendered mandatory an express option not within s 9 simply by agreeing the identity of the third party expert at the outset.

(b) The review process has to be started by the service of a statutory review notice as defined in s 10 which, peculiarly in this context, must require the question of the rent to be payable to be referred to arbitration. If a statutory review notice is not served before the appointment of the third party, s 12(b) does not prevent either party from applying for the appointment of an arbitrator to review on the open market basis. If a determination is made by the third party, that determination will trigger the three-year statutory rent review cycle.

THE STATUTORY RENT REVIEW FORMULA

The formula

9.16 The task of the arbitrator is set out in s 13 of the ATA 1995[1]. Section 13 provides that the arbitrator shall:

'... determine the rent properly payable in respect of the holding at the review date and accordingly shall, with effect from that date, increase or reduce the rent previously payable or direct that it shall continue unchanged'.

The review date is defined in s 10(2) of the ATA 1995 as a date which is specified in the statutory review notice and which complies with the provisions of s 10(3) to (6)[2]. In specifying the review date as both the date from which the new rent is payable and the date at which the new rent is to be determined, the ATA 1995 differs from the AHA 1986. In the AHA 1986, the new rent is payable as from the next termination date[3] but the date for determining the level of rent properly payable is the date of the appointment of the arbitrator, which is generally earlier[4].

[1] See para 9.17.
[2] As to which see para 9.22.

3   AHA 1986, s 12(1) and (4).
4   AHA 1986, s 12(2).

The rent properly payable in respect of the holding

Introduction

9.17 This wording is familiar from Sch 2 to the AHA 1986. Like the AHA 1986, s 13 of the ATA 1995 sets out what the rent properly payable is; what the arbitrator must have regard to; and to determine the ambit of his inquiry by imposing disregards.

Section 13(2) provides that the rent properly payable in respect of the holding is:

> '... the rent at which the holding might reasonably be expected to be let on the open market by a willing landlord to a willing tenant taking into account (subject to subsections (3) and (4) below) all relevant factors, including (in every case) the terms of the tenancy (including those which are relevant for the purposes of section 10(4) to (6) of this Act, but not those which (apart from this section) preclude a reduction in the rent during the tenancy)'[1].

From this definition, it can be seen that, save in so far as it impacts upon the determination of the open market rent, the arbitrator does not have to have regard to the productive capacity or related earning capacity of the holding. It is clear that in many cases the earning capacity of the holding will have an impact on demand and therefore on the rent which the market is willing to pay. Neither, in contrast to the AHA 1986, is the arbitrator *directed* to consider the rent of comparable holdings[2] or the character and situation of the holding and, while he has to assume that the parties are willing, he does not have to assume that they are prudent[3].

The review of rents on an open-market basis does reflect the move away from security of tenure to freedom of contract. Supply and demand governs the level of rents payable. On review, it is supply and demand for the particular letting and, therefore, the terms of the tenancy must be taken into account by the arbitrator. Some terms will have more impact that others. User covenants which restrict the tenant's ability to develop and diversify, while assisting the protection of the tenancy's status as a farm business tenancy, may depress the rent. Conversely, user covenants which allow for significant diversification may increase the rent, even though that tenant is not actually diversifying, the potential non-agricultural income from diversification is a matter which will be taken into account.

Full repairing leases may at first seem attractive to a landlord of a dilapidated estate, but will undoubtedly have an impact on review. The length of the term will be important as will be the tenant's ability to escape his obligations by utilising break provisions or by assigning the remainder of the term. The frequency of reviews and whether rent is payable in advance of arrears will also have an impact. The arbitrator is specifically directed to consider these factors.

Prior to the RRO 2006, when an arbitrator was determining the open market rent under s 13(2) of the ATA 1995, he was not permitted to take into account any terms in the tenancy agreement relating to the criteria by reference to which any new rent was to be determined. As seen above, this restriction no longer applies. The only term which the arbitrator is now to ignore is any provision which would preclude a reduction in the rent. This amendment applies to all tenancies or rent review provisions under the ATA 1995, whenever entered into, and it is not limited to tenancies granted on or after 19 October 2006 when the RRO 2006 came into force[4].

1   ATA 1995, s 13(2), as amended by the RRO 2006, SI 2006/2805, arts 11 and 15.
2   And note the restriction on his considering other arbitrator's awards: *Land Securities plc v Westminster City Council* [1992] 2 EGLR 15.
3   Cf Sch 2 to the AHA 1986.
4   ATA 1995, s 13(2), as amended by the RRO 2006, SI 2006/2805, arts 11 and 15.

The basis of valuation

9.18   The concept of the open market is familiar, not only in connection with sales, but also through the express rent review provisions in commercial leases where it is often the starting point for the determination of the new rent. Guidance on its meaning can be taken from RICS Appraisal and Valuation Manual. The definition of the open market value of a sale assumes:

(a)   a willing seller;
(b)   that, prior to the date of valuation, there had been a reasonable period (having regard to the nature of the property and the state of the market) for the proper marketing of the interest, for the agreement of the price and terms and for the completion of the sale;
(c)   that the state of the market, level of values and other circumstances were, on any earlier assumed date of exchange of contracts, the same as on the date of valuation;
(d)   that no account is taken of any additional bid by a prospective purchaser with a special interest; and
(e)   that both parties to the transaction had acted knowledgeably, prudently and without compulsion.

While not specifically directed at rent review, this does offer some guidance on the nature of the inquiry to be made.

The arbitrator is able to take account of a wide range of factors which may impact on the rent other than the terms of the tenancy agreement. The scarcity value of the holding (demand and supply) and marriage value (ie the value to an established farmer of being able to take the subject holding and farm in conjunction with his other land) are factors which it is clear that the arbitrator should consider[1].

In broad terms, the arbitrator must assume that the holding is being offered on the market on the terms of the particular tenancy agreement between the landlord and the tenant. The best rent offered will be the market rent. 'Open' merely ensures that the arbitrator is to assume that there is to be no restriction on the person or class of persons who may bid but otherwise makes no difference[2]. Slightly more problematic is the use of the word 'reasonably' as in '... the rent at which the holding might *reasonably* be let on the open market ...'. It is clear that the wording is not intended to ensure a rent which is reasonable as between the particular landlord and the particular tenant and this would not fit with the open market formula. It is likely that what is intended is that exceptional or unusual or freak circumstances which would produce a particular rent in the market at that time should be ignored[3].

It is beyond the scope of this book to discuss all aspects of rent review. There is a considerable volume of law which has been built up in connection with commercial rent review[4].

[1] Cf the position under the AHA 1986 following the decision of the Court of Appeal in *J W Childers Trustees v Anker* [1996] 1 EGLR 1, [1996] 01 EG 102. See para 25.18.
[2] *Sterling Land Office Developments v Lloyds Bank plc* [1984] 2 EGLR 135.
[3] See Lord Fraser in *Ponsford v HMS Aerosols Ltd* [1979] AC 63; Megarry J in *Cuff v J & F Stone Property Co Ltd* [1979] AC 87n, [1978] 2 All ER 833, Ch D. In considering the meaning of a reasonable rent, Meggary J held that the word 'reasonable' required the valuer to ignore a rent which, although it was obtainable in the market because of special circumstances exceeded the rent for the premises which was right and fair – in a valuation rather than a moral sense.
[4] See *Woodfall: Landlord and Tenant* (Looseleaf edn, 1994) Sweet & Maxwell, para 8.001ff.

9.19 A rent review clause contemplates the assessment of the rent which would be achieved on a hypothetical letting. This exercise, involving a hypothetical transaction, contains four stages in the arbitrator's analysis:

(a)   the hypothetical landlord and tenant;
(b)   the property to be valued;
(c)   the duration of the hypothetical letting; and
(d)   the terms of the hypothetical letting.

The hypothetical willing landlord and willing tenant have been the subject of judicial scrutiny in the context of contractual provisions in commercial leases. From the case of *F R Evans (Leeds) Ltd v English Electric Co Ltd*[1], it is worth noting the explanation of the willing landlord and the willing tenant given by Donaldson J where he clarifies the extent of the hypothesis. He makes it clear that the willing party is an abstraction and a hypothetical person so that circumstances personal to the particular party should not be taken into account. The landlord is not affected by personal ills such as a cash flow crisis but neither is he to be taken to be willing to wait to let. The assumption is that he is willing, though not desperate, to let at the review date. Similarly, the willing tenant is to be taken to be actively seeking premises but unaffected by liquidity problems. However, the parties are not to be taken to be totally isolated from the real world. In the words of Donaldson J, they are not to be taken to be negotiating in a vacuum. Those real factors that would have an impact on every landlord or tenant negotiating the hypothetical letting, such as the availability of other land, the rent on comparable holdings, etc, should be taken into account.

The property to be valued is the demised property let by the farm business tenancy. It is necessary for the arbitrator to consider the physical subject matter of the property to be valued as it stands at the date of valuation[2]. The exercise in valuing the property to be valued is not as straightforward as it first appears. First, it is subject to the statutory disregards which are contained in ss 13(3) and 4(b)[3]. Second, there are other factors which have a bearing on the assumed physical subject matter. In the context of commercial leases, this has given rise to a number of issues such as the valuation of property in an assumed state[4]. The issue of an assumed state is not one which may have exercised values of agricultural property in the past, but with increasing diversification, issues about assumed state may have greater prominence. For example, an assumption that the property is fully fitted out and equipped for occupation does not require the rentalisation of equipment which is not fixed to the property[5].

As to the duration of the hypothetical letting, this is a difficult point in the case of farm business tenancies, which are typically quite short and often periodic. In commercial rent review cases, there is a strong assumption that the duration of the hypothetical letting is equal to the unexpired term of the actual lease. In the case of AHA 1986 tenancies, it has never been a live issue because the tenant had security of tenure and the rent review would be triennial.

There is no guidance in s 13 of the ATA 1995 as to the notional term of the hypothetical new letting. In commercial leases, with express rent review provisions, the notional term is often expressly stated. The parties to farm business tenancies do not have the freedom to add to the s 13 formula[6]. The question is whether the arbitrator is to assume a new letting for the unexpired term of the old or is to assume a new letting for the same original term as the subject tenancy or for some other term.

In the absence of guidance in s 13 of the ATA 1995 as to the length of the new hypothetical letting, the common law position must be relied upon. The position is that the arbitrator should value the unexpired residue of the term as at the review date. This accords with the case law on commercial lettings[7]. A 12-year term with three years left to run will, therefore, be looked at as a three-year term for the purposes of review, but as a letting on the terms of the original tenancy which may, of course, be wholly inappropriate or unduly onerous against the assumption of a letting for three years.

Lastly, the arbitrator is required by s 13(1)(a) of the ATA 1995 to take into account the terms of the hypothetical letting, including those relating to the review of rent. These will include restrictions on user and repairing[8] and similar obligations[9].

1 (1977) 36 P & CR 185, CA.
2 *Ponsford v HMS Aerosols Ltd* [1979] AC 63, HL.
3 See para 9.20.
4 See *Woodfall: Landlord and Tenant* (Looseleaf edn, 1994) Sweet & Maxwell, para 8.032.
5 *Ocean Accident and Guarantee Corpn v Next* [1996] 2 EGLR 84.
6 Other than adopting it as an express review.
7 *R & A Millett (Shops) Ltd v Legal & General Assurance Society Ltd* [1985] 1 EGLR 103; *Norwich Union Life Assurance Society v Trustee Savings Bank Central Board* [1986] 1 EGLR 136 and *Ritz Hotel (London) Ltd v Ritz Casino Ltd* [1989] 2 EGLR 135.

Disregards

9.20 Section 13(3) of the ATA 1995 sets out the extent of the disregard for tenant's improvements. Tenant's improvements are for the purposes of this subsection, defined by reference to the definition set out in s 15 of the ATA 1995. In brief, it encompasses physical improvements and those intangible advantages which become attached to the holding, in each case where the improvement has been provided by the tenant by his own effort or wholly or partly at his own expense[1]. While for the purposes of obtaining compensation on quitting for a tenant's improvement, the consent of the landlord or, in many cases, of an arbitrator is required[2], it is important to note that this is not a necessary element for the increase in rental value due to the improvement to be disregarded on a rent review. Improvements carried out without consent or approval also fall to be disregarded.

The arbitrator must disregard any increase in the rental value due to a tenant's improvement in all cases other than those set out below:

(a)   Where the improvement is provided under an obligation imposed on the tenant by the terms of his tenancy or any previous tenancy and which arose on or before the beginning of the tenancy in question, it will on the face of it be taken into account on a review. If the improvement is provided by way of a premium by the tenant, the arbitrator will no doubt have regard to this when taking into account all of the terms of the tenancy. It should be noted that the improvement will only be taken into account where the obligation to provide it is contained in the relevant tenancy agreement from the outset and not where it comes about through some later variation following from a conditional consent of the landlord to the provision of the improvement. This disposes of one problem which arose under the AHA 1986 equivalent provision[3] where the position of subsequent variations is unclear.

(b)   The arbitrator is able to take account of tenant's improvements to the extent that the tenant has received any allowance or benefit from the landlord in consideration of the provision of the improvement. The benefit or allowance need not be equivalent[4], but falls to be valued. It is not clear how this provision works. In many cases, the allowance or benefit allowed to the tenant will not be a direct percentage contribution to the cost of the improvement in question. If it is not, then there must first be a valuation of that benefit. That value must then be compared with the cost of providing the improvement and be taken as a percentage. The increase in rental value of the holding due to the improvement should then be taken into account on review to the value of that percentage only. It should also be noted that the disregard is limited only by reference to benefits made or given by the landlord and that any grant-aided element of a tenant's improvement still falls to be disregarded. The grant is regarded as being for the benefit of the tenant.

113

(c)   A tenant's improvement will be taken into account where the tenant has
        already received compensation for it from the landlord, for example, on
        the termination of an earlier tenancy. Again, it is not clear how the
        section works. The subsection refers to the improvement being taken
        into account 'to the extent that the tenant has received compensation
        …'. In this case, it is the editor's view that if the compensation is
        compensation on quitting for the improvement, then the increase in
        rental value of the holding due to the improvement is to be borne by the
        tenant entirely, even though the compensation may not be anywhere
        near the cost of the improvement.

In addition to disregards for tenant's improvements, there are two further
disregards. First, the arbitrator is not entitled to take into account any effect
on the rent of the fact that the tenant is in occupation of the holding. This is
also disregarded under the AHA 1986[5] and the rationale for it is to ensure
that the landlord does not benefit from the fact that the actual tenant in
occupation would probably pay a higher rent than anyone else simply to avoid
business disruption[6]. Second, again as is the case under the AHA 1986, the
arbitrator is to disregard any dilapidation deterioration or damage to buildings or land caused or permitted by the tenant[7].

[1]   See Ch 16.
[2]   See Ch 16.
[3]   ATA 1995, s 7 and see Ch 12.
[4]   Cf the AHA 1986.
[5]   See Ch 26.
[6]   See *Harewood Hotels Ltd v Harris* [1958] 1 All ER 104 and, in particular, the judgment of
      Lord Evershed in respect of similar wording in s 34 of the Landlord and Tenant Act 1954.
[7]   For a commentary on a comparable provision, see *Metropolitan Properties Co Ltd v
      Wooldridge* (1968) 20 P & CR 64. There is no disregard for other breaches of contract
      and, it should be noted, landlord's dilapidations are not disregarded and could, therefore,
      lead to a decrease in the rental value of the holding.

DATES AND FREQUENCY OF REVIEW

9.21 Section 10 of the ATA 1995 provides that a rent review on the statutory
formula is to review the rent as from the review date. The review date is the
date contained in the statutory review notice and either agreed in writing by
the parties or as defined in s 10(6).

Provided that they record their agreement in writing, the parties can agree:

(a)   when reviews are to commence;
(b)   the interval between reviews; and
(c)   the actual review date.

It is only in the absence of agreement in writing (not necessarily contained in
the tenancy agreement itself) that s 10 of the ATA 1995 defines the review date
and determines the frequency of reviews. This freedom of contract, when
combined with the section 9 options, gives great flexibility to the parties, for

example, to delay the start of reviews to reflect a high initial rent or because of onerous obligations on the tenant in the early years of the tenancy[1].

[1]   See para 9.13.

9.22 In the absence of agreement, s 10 of the ATA 1995 provides, in essence, for a three-yearly review to take place on the anniversary of the beginning of the tenancy[1]. As the parties could choose the date and interval of reviews; the date but not the interval; or the interval but not the date, there is considerable scope for interplay between the contractual and statutory provisions. For example, the parties may be content with three-yearly reviews, but may wish the reviews to take place on one of the usual rent days. Because of the definition of the beginning of the tenancy (as being the date when the tenant was entitled to go into possession and not necessarily the date of the tenancy agreement[2]), they may need to make express provision.

Section 10 of the ATA 1995 provides that, in the absence of written agreement:

(a)   the review date must be on the anniversary of the beginning of the tenancy; and

(b)   must not fall before the end of the period of three years beginning with the latest of the following dates:

   (i)   the beginning of the tenancy (so that the first review takes place three years after the tenant is first entitled to go into possession under the terms of the tenancy);

   (ii)   any previous direction of the arbitrator as to the amount of rent;

   (iii)   any previous determination by a third party appointed by the parties as to the amount of rent (and therefore ensuring no review for three years following the determination of a third party expert or an express rent review provision);

   (iv)   any previous agreement *in writing* between the parties entered into since the grant of the tenancy as to the amount of rent.

Section 10 gives equal validity to a settlement reached between the parties (provided that it is recorded in writing); the determination of an expert and the direction of an arbitrator: each will start time running for rent review purposes and each will do so regardless of whether the rent was reviewed upwards or downwards or remained the same. This can be compared with the AHA 1986 where only an arbitrator's decision that the rent remain unchanged will trigger the start of another three-year period. An agreement between the parties to that effect does not[3].

Importantly, the three-year period will be triggered whether or not the review is comprehensive or results from, for example, the surrender of a small parcel of land or a cottage. This is the same as the position under the AHA 1986[4]. However, the problem is not as difficult to solve as it is under the AHA 1986. Following such a surrender, it is always open to the parties to agree that the consequent adjustment to the rent will not count as a review. They are simply thereby agreeing a variation on the frequency of their rent reviews as s 10 envisages they can do[5].

1   As defined by the ATA 1995, s 38(4).
2   ATA 1995, s 38(4).
3   See Ch 25.
4   *Mann v Gardner* (1990) 61 P & CR 1; *Secretary of State for Defence v Spencer* [2003] 1 WLR 2701.
5   This is important because the ATA 1995 does not contain an equivalent to the provisions of Sch 2, para 4(2) which allows certain minor changes in the rent to be disregarded when assessing whether or not the three-year period has been triggered which are, in any event, specific to the provisions of the AHA 1986.

SEVERED REVERSIONS

9.23 The problems of the service of rent review trigger notices following the severance of the landlord's reversionary interest arise also in connection with AHA 1986 tenancies[1]. Following the severance of the reversion, where the original tenancy remains, the severance does not itself create separate tenancies[2]. If that is all that has happened, the severance has no impact on rent review at all, save to make it more difficult for one landlord to review the rent without the concurrence of the other[3]. However, separate tenancies of each severed part will arise if either:

(1)   there is an express agreement with the tenant to enter into new tenancies; or

(2)   the tenant is a party to the deed of severance and agrees to apportion the rent between the severed parts.

It may be in the interest of the landlords to seek agreement in relation to new tenancies to get around the problem of the service of notices. Where they do so, then provided that the rent payable under each new tenancy is merely the apportioned part of that payable under the old tenancy, the rent review cycle will continue through to the new tenancy[4]. If, for example, the rent had been reviewed under the old tenancy two years previously, and assuming three-yearly reviews, the first review under the new tenancy will be one year after the severance.

1   See para 25.6ff.
2   Cf *Jelley v Buckman* [1974] QB 488.
3   *Stiles v Farrow* (1977) 241 Estates Gazette 623.
4   ATA 1995, s 11.

PROCEDURE AND THE ARBITRATION

Triggering the rent review procedure

9.24 The trigger mechanism necessary to commence the review procedure depends upon whether the rent review formula is one which falls within s 9 of the ATA 1995 or not. If the parties are seeking to review the rent by reference to a section 9 option, it may be that no trigger is necessary. If the choices are mechanical (ie one of the original section 9(a) or (b) options), the parties may have chosen to make the review automatic rather than provide for it to be instigated by one of the parties[1]. If the parties do require there to be a trigger, they will have to provide for it specifically. A trigger is likely for a section 9(c) option. If there is a trigger, such provision should make clear:

(a)   who is entitled to trigger the review[2];
(b)   when the trigger notice can be served;
(c)   the form of the notice and whether writing is required;
(d)   service requirements – as the trigger will not be a notice or document required or authorised to be served under the ATA 1995, the provisions of s 36 will not apply;
(e)   whether the notice needs to set out the amount of rent required by the landlord; and
(f)   whether time is to be of the essence[3].

One issue which can arise is the relevant date for the rent review. In *Bisichi Mining Ltd v Bass Holdings Ltd*[4], the High Court held that where the lease entitled the landlord to give notice seeking a review during the first six weeks of certain specified years of 'the said term', this meant the term commencing on the execution of the lease and the first rent payment and not, as the arbitrator had decided, the term date specified in the lease.

[1] Although in the commercial sector see the case of *Stylo Shoes Ltd v Wetherall Bond Street W1 Ltd* (1974) 237 Estates Gazette 343 where it was held that if the lease did not expressly require the service of a trigger notice, one would be implied. The implication could only be necessary in relation to the section 9 option which is the application of a mechanical formula and will depend upon the wording of the review formula. See, on the other hand, *Edwin Woodhouse Trustee Co Ltd v Sheffield Brick Co plc* [1984] 1 EGLR 130.

[2] *First Property Growth Partnership LP v Royal & Sun Alliance Property Services Ltd* [2002] EWHC 305 (Ch), [2002] 2 EGLR 11, [2002] 22 EG 140, affd [2002] EWCA Civ 1687, [2003] 1 All ER 533.

[3] It will not be unless the clause expressly so provides or it is implied by other terms of the lease (*United Scientific Holdings Ltd v Burnley Borough Council* [1978] AC 904). A deeming provision – which provides that a tenant will be deemed to have agreed to a rent level proposed by the landlord in the absence of the service of a counter notice with a set time – will not of itself make time of the essence *Starmark Enterprises Ltd v CPL Distribution Ltd* [2001] EWCA Civ 1252, [2002] Ch 306, [2002] 4 All ER 264, following *Mecca Leisure Ltd v Renown Investments (Holdings) Ltd* [1984] 2 EGLR 137. Also see, *McDonald's Property Co Ltd v HSBC Bank plc* [2001] 3 EGLR 19, [2001] 36 EG 181.

[4] [2002] EWHC 375 (Ch), [2002] 2 EGLR 4, (2002) 18 EG 159. Also see *Riverside Housing Association Ltd v White* [2005] EWCA Civ 1385, [2006] 1 EGLR 45.

9.25 The parties cannot rely on the provisions in s 10(1) of the ATA 1995 in relation to the service of a statutory review notice because s 9 expressly provides that the remaining provisions of Pt II of the Act (including s 10) do not apply where a section 9 option has been chosen. In all other cases, including where the parties are following through an express choice not within s 9, the trigger is the statutory review notice referred to in s 10(1)[1]. If the parties wishing to follow through an express formula not within s 9 do not start the procedure with the service of a statutory review notice, the subsequent appointment of the third party expert will not have the effect of preventing one or other party from applying for the appointment of an arbitrator to review on the statutory open market basis[2]. While the service of a notice specifically stating that the serving party wishes to refer the question of rent to arbitration is counter-intuitive where the parties have no intention of going to arbitration and could, if served without warning, antagonise the other party who is expecting a reference on the contractual formula, neverthe-less the ATA 1995 effectively requires it. This is likely to be less of a problem as a consequence of the extension of the section 9 options.

The statutory review notice has no prescribed form but must comply with the provisions of s 10(1) of the ATA 1995. It must:

(a)   be in writing;
(b)   be given to the other party[3];
(c)   require that the rent payable in respect of the holding as from the review date be referred to arbitration in accordance with the ATA 1995; and
(d)   specify the review date.

The statutory review notice can be given either by the landlord or the tenant[4] and, being similar in concept to the equivalent notice under s 12 of the AHA 1986, it is likely that a court would find that, once served, it could not be unilaterally withdrawn by the serving party[5].

As the statutory review notice is a notice which is '... required or authorised to be given ...' under the AA 1996, it must be served in accordance with the provisions of s 36 of the ATA 1995[6] which requires it to be 'given' to the other party as that word is defined in s 36.

The review date specified in the notice must be a date upon which the rent can be reviewed in accordance with the agreement reached between the parties and/or the statute. It must also be a date which is at least 12 months after the date on which the statutory review notice is given. In other words, not less than 12 months' notice is to be given of the review.

[1]   See para 9.22.
[2]   ATA 1995, s 12(b).
[3]   ATA 1995, s 36.
[4]   ATA 1995, s 10(11).
[5]   In relation to the AHA 1986, see *Buckinghamshire County Council v Gordon* [1986] 2 EGLR 8, 279 Estates Gazette 853.
[6]   See Ch 17.

Resolution of the dispute

9.26 Following the service of the statutory review notice, the parties can either:

(a)   appoint an arbitrator by agreement to review the rent on the statutory open market basis[1];
(b)   appoint a third party to act otherwise than as arbitrator (undoubtedly usually as an expert) to determine the rent on a basis agreed by the parties outside of s 9[2]. That agreed basis could be contained in the tenancy agreement as an express rent review formula[3] or could be agreed subsequently between the parties. It should be noted that the third party expert cannot be chosen and identified in the tenancy

agreement. Section 12(b) of the ATA 1995 makes it clear that the third party must be appointed following the service of a statutory review notice.

Where either of the above has happened, the parties are unable then, pursuant to that statutory review notice, to apply to the President of the RICS for the appointment of an arbitrator. It is at the stage of the appointment of the third party, therefore, that the parties' agreed basis for review outside of s 9 becomes the only way of reviewing the rent on the back of that particular statutory review notice. Whether the parties then have to follow through the appointment and accept the reviewed rent is a matter of construction of the agreement between them. If they are, it will be a review for the purposes of s 10 of the ATA 1995 and will, therefore, trigger time. If they are not, there is nothing to stop either party from serving a new statutory review notice and the consequence, in that case, is therefore one of delay only. A new statutory review notice can be served, but the delay could be considerable given the requirement for not less than 12 months' notice.

If the parties are unable to agree the appointment of an arbitrator or a third party, either party may, during the six months ending with the review date, apply to the President of the RICS for the appointment of an arbitrator by him. Such application need not be made by the party who originally served the notice.

The application must be made in writing and accompanied by '... such reasonable fee as the President may determine in respect of the costs of making the appointment'[4]. It should be noted that, in appointing the arbitrator, the President is acting in an administrative and not a judicial capacity[5] and any complaints about the arbitrator's credentials or suitability to act must therefore be addressed to the arbitrator himself.

Pursuant to the provisions of s 30 of the ATA 1995, all arbitrations conducted under the Act are to be conducted by a sole arbitrator.

[1]   ATA 1995, s 12(a).
[2]   ATA 1995, s 12(b).
[3]   This is less likely after 18 October 2006 as most expressly agreed rent formulae will be within s 9.
[4]   ATA 1995, s 30(2).
[5]   *Ramsay v McLaren* 1936 SLT 35, Ct of Sess.

Determination by an expert

9.27 If the rent review is being conducted by an expert appointed by the parties (either as a result of utilising s 9(c)(i) or as a consequence of an agreement between the parties), his role is very different from that of an arbitrator[1]. He is not constrained by the evidence or the arguments of the parties and can rely on his own expertise. He owes a duty of care to the parties[2]. He will be in breach of that duty of care if he fails to take into account matters which he should[3].

The status of the decision of an expert has also been the subject of judicial scrutiny, most recently, Lightman J in *British Shipbuilders v VSEL Consortium plc*[4], who, considering earlier authorities[5], set out his view of the status of the expert's decision. In particular, he made it clear that the role of the expert and the ambit of his remit were essentially a matter of construction of the agreement between the parties and the expert. If the expert alone is entitled to determine the issue exclusively, the court may only intervene if he has failed to comply with the agreement and may then set aside his decision. However, the court may be asked, in advance of the expert's decision, to determine questions as to the limits of his remit. It will seldom do so, however, because the nature of the question is at that stage hypothetical[6].

1 See Ch 47.
2 Confirmed in the Court of Appeal decision in *Zubaida v Hargreaves* [1995] 1 EGLR 127.
3 *Belvedere Motors Ltd v King* [1981] 2 EGLR 131.
4 [1997] 1 Lloyd's Rep 106, ChD.
5 Including the House of Lords in *Mercury Communications Ltd v Director General of Telecommunications* [1996] 1 All ER 575 and whether that case had or had not overruled *Jones v Sherwood Computer Services plc* [1992] 2 All ER 170 and *Norwich Union Life Assurance Society v P & O Property Holdings Ltd* [1993] 1 EGLR 164 (see *Woodfall: Landlord and Tenant* (Looseleaf edn, 1994) Sweet & Maxwell, Vol 1, para 8.030).
6 *Top Shop Estates Ltd v Danino* [1985] 1 EGLR 9; *Fox v PG Wellfair Ltd* [1981] 2 Lloyd's Rep 514.

Determination by an arbitrator

9.28 The role of an arbitrator is discussed in Chapter 47. Unlike the expert, the arbitrator is not entitled to go beyond the evidence adduced by the parties in determining the rent[1], although he can use his own expertise on his evaluation and assessment of the evidence adduced. Unlike the expert, the arbitrator cannot be pursued for negligence by the parties as he acts in a quasi-judicial capacity[2].

1 See also *National Grid v M25 Group* [1998] 32 EG 90. Generally, see Ch 48.
2 *Sirros v Moore* [1975] QB 118.

Evidence

9.29 Evidence of the open market rent is going to come primarily from evidence of comparable lettings. A comparable is any other property which has any evidential contribution to make in the assessment of the rent of the property in question. The weight to be attached to the comparable may, because of differences in material characteristics between the holdings, be limited but that does not prevent it from being a comparable. Likewise, incomplete information will not prevent a property from being a comparable although, again, the weight to be attached to such evidence could be limited as a result[1].

Land Securities v Westminster City Council (No 2)[2] is authority for the proposition that another arbitrator's award is not evidence of the market value of the property.

In *Spath Holme Ltd v Greater Manchester and Lancashire Rent Assessment Committee*[3] it was suggested that lettings under a different code cannot be rejected as inadmissible as comparables simply because of that fact. However, the effect on the rent of different levels of security and the different terms of the letting must be evaluated and taken into account[4]. The problem of comparables and the hearsay rule has disappeared following the abolition of the hearsay rule in civil cases[5]. Nevertheless, the case of *Land Securities v Westminster City Council*[6] still presents a problem so far as the use of a previous arbitration award to provide evidence of market value is concerned. It is an award of a tribunal as a matter of fact and is inadmissible to prove any fact before another tribunal[7].

[1] See *Living Waters Christian Centres Ltd v Fetherstonhaugh* [1999] 2 EGLR 1.
[2] [1993] 1 WLR 286.
[3] [1995] 2 EGLR 80. See also *Curtis v Chairman of the London Rent Assessment Committee* [1998] 1 EGLR 79, [1998] 15 EG 120, CA affirming and clarifying the *Spath Homes* decision; *Minja Properties Ltd v Cussins Property Group plc* [1998] 2 EGLR 52.
[4] See also Ch 25 in relation to AHA 1986 lettings.
[5] Civil Evidence Act 1995.
[6] [1993] 1 WLR 286.
[7] See *Woodfall: Landlord and Tenant* (Looseleaf edn, 1994) Sweet & Maxwell, para 8.050, fn 1 for possible ways around the problem.

DISTRESS

9.30 The use of distress as a remedy for non-payment of rent is discussed in Chapter 26 in connection with the AHA 1986[1]. Unlike the AHA 1986, there are no special rules or restrictions relating to the landlord's ability to distrain against the goods of a farm business tenant. So, for example, distress is not limited to one year's unpaid rent but can be levied for up to six years' arrears under the general provisions of s 19 of the Limitation Act 1980.

[1] Also note the proposals for reform, see para 26.13.

Chapter 10

REPAIRS

INTRODUCTION

10.1 Chapter 5 has already considered the limited extent to which repairing obligations are implied into contracts of tenancy in the absence of any agreement between the parties. The Agricultural Tenancies Act 1995 (ATA 1995) makes no provision whatsoever in respect of repairs or dilapidations claims. It is left to the parties to make whatever bargain they want. This is in contrast to the position under the Agricultural Holdings Act 1986 (AHA 1986)[1]. The parties are there free to reach agreement on repairs, but the AHA 1986 ensures that each and every item is the responsibility of either the landlord or the tenant through the 'model clauses'[2]. The model clauses are deemed to be incorporated into every tenancy agreement, save to the extent that the parties have made provision placing the particular repairing obligation on the other party. The clauses are more than a mere fall-back. While the section is not much used, s 8 of the AHA 1986 allows a party to apply to arbitration to have the model clauses written into the tenancy agreement and hence override the parties' express agreement in relation to repairs.

The model clauses are very familiar to those advising landlords and tenants of agricultural land. There is evidence that many farm business tenancies have been prepared incorporating the model clauses. There is nothing to prevent the parties from doing this. It is always possible to incorporate terms into a contract by reference to another document, whether that other document is a standard form contract used in the particular industry or whether it is an item of legislation. Careful drafting is, however, required. Incorporating terms by reference in this way will incorporate those terms as they stood at the date of incorporation. In the context of the model clauses, this means incorporating the Agriculture (Maintenance, Repair and Insurance of Fixed Equipment) Regulations 1973[3]. It is a convenient shorthand alternative to setting out the clauses in full in the tenancy agreement. Later changes or amendments will not, without specific provision, form part of the contract between the parties.

One issue which fell away as a consequence of the RRO 2006[4] is the relevance of the arbitration provisions. Part III of SI 1973/1473 provides for arbitration in the case of dispute. As a result of the provisions of ss 28 and 29 of the ATA

1995, the parties are able to reach their own arbitration agreement, but the arbitration would be conducted under the Arbitration Act 1996 and not under the discrete AHA 1986 code. Since the 2006 Order, that discrete code no longer applies[5].

1   See Ch 23.
2   The name given in the AHA 1986 to the regulations currently contained is the Agriculture (Maintenance, Repair and Insurance of Fixed Equipment) Regulations 1973, SI 1973/1473, as amended by the Agriculture (Maintenance, Repair and Insurance of Fixed Equipment) (Amendment) Regulations 1988, SI 1988/281.
3   SI 1973/1473, as amended by SI 1988/281.
4   The Regulatory Reform (Agricultural Tenancies) (England and Wales) Order 2006, SI 2006/2805.
5   See para 47.13.

10.2 While it is tempting for advisers to go for the familiar, incorporating the model clauses into farm business tenancies, thought ought to be given as to whether this is appropriate in all cases. The division of responsibility for repairs between landlord and tenant in the model clauses has been applied on the basis of an annual periodic tenancy, albeit with potentially lifetime security. It may not be appropriate for the landlord to retain such a high burden of responsibility where the land is being let for a long fixed term. It also needs to be noted that the harsher the repairing obligations on the tenant, the greater will be the impact on rent review. For example, a full repairing lease for the tenant to keep the holding in repair, where the buildings are traditional and dilapidated, would have a severe impact, not only at rent review, but on the initial rent attainable for the holding. What may actually be required, depending upon the nature of the particular holding, is different repairing obligations for different parts of the holding. For example, greater obligations may be placed on the tenant in relation to the modern buildings than in relation to the traditional buildings.

Like all express provisions in tenancy agreements, repairing obligations are construed by reference to the intention of the parties to be construed by reference to the tenancy agreement as a whole. However, again mostly in the commercial sector, case law has developed to provide guidance as to the meaning of many common types of repairing clauses. This chapter will give brief consideration to those. It should be emphasised that the cases are decisions relating to the construction of particular clauses in particular leases of particular types of property and can provide guidance only.

First the concept of disrepair and repair must be looked at. A party can only be in breach of the covenant to repair if there is disrepair in the first place.

DISREPAIR AND REPAIR

10.3 Whatever the extent of a party's obligations to repair, the holding must be in disrepair before the obligation arises. Disrepair arises from a deterioration of the subject matter, causing damage. Inherent defects in the item or inadequacy for its purpose cannot be disrepair[1]. There has been no deterioration as it has always, since construction of the premises, been in that state. It should be noted that whether or not there is disrepair is decided by a comparison of the condition of the subject matter at the date of *construction* and not at the date of the tenancy agreement[2]. Whether or not the tenant is obliged to put right the disrepair may depend on the state of the subject matter at the date of the lease, but that is a separate issue.

Damp cases illustrate the problem in this area. It is insufficient for a party to allege and prove the existence of damp. It is necessary to establish a duty to investigate the dampness and that requires establishing that the damp was caused by physical damage to the structure or the exterior[3].

Virtually all remedial work requires an amount of renewal, but an obligation to repair does not include an obligation to renew the subject matter or improve the holding[4] however difficult it may be on any particular occasion to draw the line. Where repair stops and renewal begins is a question of fact and degree and, most importantly, of the parties' intentions at the time of entering into the covenant[5] and whether the work required to remedy the disrepair would have been contemplated by them. In the words of Sachs LJ in *Brew Bros Ltd v Snax (Ross) Ltd*[6]:

'... the correct approach is to look at the state which it is in at the date of the lease, to look at the precise terms of the lease and then come to a conclusion as to whether, on a fair interpretation of those terms in relation to that state, the requisite work can fairly be termed "repair" '.

In *Lurcott v Wakely and Wheeler*[7], Fletcher Moulton LJ stated:

'The word "repair" refers to an operation to which the tenants find themselves to have recourse. For my own part, when the word repair is applied to a complex matter like a house, I have no doubt that the repair includes the replacement of parts. Of course, if a house is tumble-down or was down, the word repair could not be used to cover rebuilding'[8].

In the same case, Buckley J (as he then was) stated:

'Repair and renew are not words expressive of clear contrast. Repair always involves renewal; renewal of part; of a subordinate part ... repairs, restoration by renewal, or replacement of subsidiary parts of a whole. Renewal, as distinguished from repair, is reconstruction of the entirety, meaning by the entirety not necessarily the whole, but substantially the whole subject matter under discussion'[9].

Where the renewal is of subsidiary parts of the whole only, the work may be said to be repair[10]. Where renewal is of substantially the whole of the item in disrepair, for example rebuilding a barn, it goes beyond 'repair' and is unlikely to have been contemplated by the parties[11]. The tenant is under no obligation to give back to the landlord something substantially different in kind from that which was let to him at the outset, taking into account the terms of the lease and the age of the subject matter of repair[12]. This may be particularly important in the context of traditional farm buildings where the costs of maintenance are likely to be particularly high against the value of the buildings[13]. The cost of disputed works has in some cases had an effect in determining whether there has been a breach of an obligation to repair[14].

[1] *Quick v Taff-Ely Borough Council* [1986] QB 809, CA; *Post Office v Aquarius Properties Ltd* [1987] 1 All ER 1055, CA. If, however, that defect causes damage and, therefore, disrepair, the disrepair must be put right and this may, in certain circumstances, lead to an obligation to put right the defect as well (*Quick v Taff-Ely Borough Council* per Dillon LJ) even though this may amount to an improvement to the holding.

[2] See Dowding and Reynolds *Dilapidations: The Modern Law and Practice* (3rd edn, 1995) Sweet & Maxwell, p 112 and *Post Office v Aquarius Properties Ltd* [1987] 1 All ER 1055, CA.

[3] *Southwark London Borough Council v McIntosh* [2002] 1 EGLR 25, [2002] 08 EG 164.

[4] *Lister v Lane* [1893] 2 QB 212, CA; *Wright v Lawson* (1903) 19 TLR 510, CA; *BHP Petroleum Great Britain Ltd v Chesterfield Properties Ltd* [2001] EWCA Civ 1797, [2002] 2 EGLR 121; *Gibson Investments Ltd v Chesterton plc* [2002] EWHC 19 (Ch), [2003] 1 EGLR 142.

[5] *Lurcott v Wakely and Wheeler* [1911] 1 KB 905, CA.

[6] [1970] 1 QB 612, CA.

[7] *Lurcott v Wakely and Wheeler* [1911] 1 KB 905, CA.

[8] *Lurcott v Wakely and Wheeler* [1911] 1 KB 905 at 918, CA.

[9] *Lurcott v Wakely and Wheeler* [1911] 1 KB 905 at 923, CA.

[10] *Roper v Prudential Assurance Co Ltd* [1992] 1 EGLR 5.

[11] *Collins v Flynn* [1963] 2 All ER 1068; *Ravenseft Properties Ltd v Davstone (Holdings) Ltd* [1980] QB 12; *Riverside Property Investments Ltd v Blackhawk Automotive* [2004] EWHC 3052 (TCC), [2005] 1 EGLR 114,

[12] *Lister v Lane and Nesham* [1893] 2 QB 212, CA.

[13] A comparison of the cost of the repairs as against the unrepaired value of the buildings and the effect of the repairs on the value and lifespan of the buildings may be looked at: *Holding and Management v Property Holding and Investment Trust* [1990] 1 EGLR 65, CA.

[14] *Ravenseft Properties Ltd v Davstone (Holdings) Ltd* [1980] QB 12; *Quick v Taff-Ely Borough Council* [1986] QB 809, CA; *Elite Investments v T I Bainbridge Silencers Ltd* [1986] 2 EGLR 43; *Halliard Property Co Ltd v Nicholas Clarke Investments Ltd* [1984] 1 EGLR 45; *Elmcroft Developments Ltd v Tankersley-Sawyer* [1984] 1 EGLR 47.

PARTICULAR COVENANTS AND THE STANDARD OF REPAIRS

10.4 The wording of the particular covenant, the surrounding circumstances and the age and state of the demised premises will indicate the standard of repair required to satisfy the covenant. While each case will depend upon the intention of the parties, guidance from previously decided cases may be helpful.

To repair

10.5 A covenant to repair requires that the holding be kept in substantial and not a perfect state of repair[1]. Very minor or trivial defects unlikely to lead to significant damage may, depending on the circumstances, be ignored.

In many cases, the addition of the words 'good', 'substantial', 'tenantable' or 'habitable' to the word 'repair' may add little to the general obligation[2]. It should be stressed that the particular covenant must be construed. It is possible that the same phrase in a short lease and a long lease will not be construed in the same way. Nor would it necessarily be construed in the same way for a different type of holding in a different place. In the context of a residential letting, in *Proudfoot v Hart*[3], it was said that 'good tenantable repair' in the context of a three-year tenancy meant '... such repair, as having

125

regard to the age, character and locality of the house, would make it reasonably fit for the occupation of a reasonably minded tenant of the class who would be likely to take it'. In the same case it was said that 'good repair' meant much the same thing as 'tenantable repair'. One factor of particular importance in ascertaining the standard of repair required by the covenant will be the age of the subject matter. Traditional farm buildings, for example, would be required, by a covenant to repair, to be kept in repair to a standard appropriate to the age of the building in question[4] and this may not be the same standard as would be required by a covenant to repair new buildings.

Another factor of importance is the general state of the premises when the lease is taken[5] simply because it will provide guidance as to the likely intention of the parties of the standard contemplated by the repairing obligation. That is not to say that every item to be repaired will be in repair to the standard required at the date of the demise[6]. A schedule of condition as at the date of the lease will be invaluable. In the absence of any evidence, the holding will be assumed to have been in tenantable repair[7].

The duration of the obligation to repair may also be an issue. In *British Glass Manufacturers' Confederation v University of Sheffield*[8], it was held that, on the proper construction of the lease, the parties had not intended that the tenant should be obliged to keep in repair for 1,000 years the very same building that had originally been erected.

---

1   *Harris v Jones* (1832) 1 Mood & R 173.
2   In *Anstruther-Gough-Calthorpe v McOscar* [1924] 1 KB 716, CA, Bankes LJ, commenting on the expression 'well and sufficiently to repair, support and uphold', said: 'I attach no importance to the particular form of words used in the covenant. The effect is the same, in my opinion, whatever words the parties used, provided that they plainly expressed their intention that the premises are to be repaired, kept in repair and yielded up in repair'.
3   (1890) 25 QBD 42, CA.
4   *Payne v Haine* (1847) 16 M & W 541; *Proudfoot v Hart* (1890) 25 QBD 42, CA.
5   Note the interpretation of a covenant to keep in repair which shows that a party may be under an obligation to put into repair premises which are below the standard required by the repairing covenant: *Proudfoot v Hart* (1890) 25 QBD 42, CA.
6   *Proudfoot v Hart* (1890) 25 QBD 42, CA.
7   *Brown v Trumper* (1858) 26 Beav 11.
8   [2003] EWHC 3108 (Ch), [2004] 1 EGLR 40.

To keep in repair

10.6 An obligation to keep in repair includes an obligation to put premises into repair[1] where they are dilapidated at the beginning of the term. The general state of the premises, even in the light of such an obligation, is still of relevance in providing guidance as to the standard of repair contemplated by the parties, even though there may be specific items requiring repair immediately upon commencement of the tenancy. To keep in repair generally means to keep in repair at all times. Hence there will be a breach of the repairing obligation as soon as a defect occurs[2]. Where the obligation is on the landlord to repair, his obligation only arises when he has knowledge of the defect or of facts which would put a reasonable landlord on inquiry. Such a limitation is implied into the contract of tenancy[3].

1   *Proudfoot v Hart* (1890) 25 QBD 42, CA. Note that the *Proudfoot* test may not apply in
    longer leases: *Anstruther-Gough-Calthorpe v McOscar* [1924] 1 KB 716, CA (a lease of 95
    years).
2   *British Telecommunications plc v Sun Life Assurance Society plc* [1996] Ch 69, CA.
3   *Makin v Watkinson* (1870) LR 6 Exch 25.

The 'fact and degree' test

10.7 In addition to the test applied in *Proudfoot v Hart*[1], to qualify as a work
of repair, the work must also satisfy the 'fact and degree' test. This returns to
the distinction between repair and disrepair[2]. The 'fact and degree' test has as
its touchstone the fact that 'repair' is an ordinary English word[3]. The
following statement by Nicholls LJ in *Holding and Management Ltd v
Property Holding and Investment Trust*[4] characterises the requirements:

> 'The exercise involves considering the context in which the word "repair"
> appears in a particular lease and also the defect and the remedial works
> proposed. Accordingly the circumstances to be taken into account in a
> particular case under one or other of these heads will include some or all of the
> following: the nature of the building; the terms of the lease; the state of the
> building at the date of the lease; the nature and extent of the defect sought to be
> remedied; the nature, extent and cost of the proposed remedial works; at whose
> expense the proposed remedial works are to be done, the value of the building
> and its expected lifespan; the effect of the works on such value and lifespan;
> current building practice; the likelihood of recurrence if one method rather than
> another is adopted; and the comparative cost of alternative remedial works and
> their impact on the use and enjoyment of the building by the occupants. The
> weight to be attached to these circumstances will vary from case to case'.

To similar effect is the statement of Mustill LJ in *McDougall v Eastington
District Council*[5]:

> 'Three different tests may be discerned, which may be applied separately or
> concurrently as the circumstances of the individual case may demand, but all to
> be approached in the light of the nature and age of the premises, their condition
> when the tenant went into occupation and the other express terms of the
> tenancy:
> * whether the alterations went to the whole of substantially the whole of
>   the structure or only a subsidiary part;
> * whether the effect of the alterations was to produce a building of a
>   wholly different character from that which had been let;
> * what was the cost of the works in relation to the previous value of the
>   building and what was their effect on the value and lifespan of the
>   building'.

1   (1890) 25 QBD 42, CA.
2   See para 10.3.
3   Per Hoffman J in *Post Office v Aquarius Properties* [1987] 1 All ER 1055, CA.
4   [1989] 1 WLR 1313, CA.
5   (1989) 58 P & CR 201, CA.

To keep in proper working order

10.8 As regards installations, the obligation often imposed upon one of the
parties will be to keep the installations in 'proper working order'. This

requires that the design of the installations is, in the first instance, capable of working properly. The installations must then operate under the conditions that it is reasonable to anticipate would prevail[1].

[1]   *O'Connor v Old Etonian Housing Association Ltd* [2002] EWCA Civ 150, [2002] Ch 295, [2005] 2 All ER 1015.

To leave in repair/to yield up in repair

10.9 If the only covenant given by a tenant is to leave or yield up the holding in repair, the landlord has no dilapidations claim until the tenancy has terminated. However, such a clause is usually combined with an obligation to keep the demise in repair.

To keep wind and water tight

10.10 There is no clear authority on what it means to keep premises wind and water tight. The only discussion has occurred in cases considering the extent of a tenant's liability in the tort of waste[1]. There, it was suggested that the obligation goes no further than a tenant's obligation to use the premises in a tenantlike manner[2]. Of course, if such an obligation is inserted as an express obligation in a lease, it shall be construed accordingly, and the intention of the parties considered.

[1]   See Denning LJ (as he then was) in *Warren v Keen* [1954] 1 QB 15, CA.
[2]   See Dowding & Reynolds, *Dilapidations: The Modern Law and Practice* (1995) Sweet & Maxwell, pp 354–356.

Fair wear and tear

10.11 Where an obligation to repair is placed upon a tenant, it is often (particularly for short lets) subject to an exception for disrepair caused by fair wear and tear. This releases the tenant from liability for disrepair caused by his reasonable use of the premises for the purpose for which they were let and by time and the elements[1].

[1]   *Terrell v Murray* (1901) 17 TLR 570; *Haskell v Marlow* [1928] 2 KB 45; *Regis Property Co Ltd v Dudley* [1959] AC 370, HL; *British Glass Manufacturers' Confederaton v University of Sheffield* [2003] EWHC 3108 (Ch), [2004] 1 EGLR 40.

REMEDIES

The landlord's remedies

10.12 The landlord may have four options:

(a)   to sue for damages;
(b)   to enter, carry out the repairs and sue for debt;
(c)   to forfeit the lease;[1]
(d)   apply for specific performance.

Until recently it was thought that a landlord could not obtain a decree of specific performance against the tenant[2]. However, it would seem that, on the authority of *Rainbow Estates Ltd v Tokenhold Ltd*[3], a decree may be available in appropriate circumstances. In the *Rainbow* case, there was no power for the landlord to enter to carry out repairs, nor was there a valid forfeiture clause. These factors were considerations in the court's decision to grant specific performance.

The Leasehold Property (Repairs) Act 1938, which requires a landlord to obtain the leave of the court before suing for damages for forfeiting for breach of a repairing covenant during the term of certain leases, does not apply to farm business tenancies[4].

The amount of damages recoverable, whether during the term or at the end, is circumscribed by s 18(1) of the Landlord and Tenant Act 1927 (LTA 1927). The LTA 1927 provides that the landlord's damages are in no case to exceed the amount by which the value of the reversion is diminished by reason of the breach[5]. From this it can be seen that, the earlier during a term a landlord brings an action, the less will be the damage to the reversion in most cases and the lower the ceiling on the damages. Towards the end of the term, particularly where, as with farm business tenancies, there is no security of tenure, the more likely it is that the breach of covenant will lead to a substantial diminution in the value of the landlord's interest. It is important to note that s 18(1) does not affect the measure of damages at all, but simply places a cap on recovery.

It has long been established that generally, where the landlord intends to carry out the repairs or he has carried them out, the measure of damages will be the cost of the repairs[6].

1   See Ch 13.
2   *Hill v Barclay* (1810) 16 Ves 402; *Jeune v Queen's Cross Properties Ltd* [1974] Ch 97.
3   [1999] Ch 64.
4   ATA 1995, Sch para 8.
5   LTA 1927, s 18(1).
6   *Jones v Herxheimer* [1950] 2 KB 106, CA. Also see *Mason v Totalfinaelf UK Ltd* [2003] EWHC 1604 (Ch), [2003] 3 EGLR 91, where *Crewe Services & Investment Corpn* was not cited; *Latimer v Carney* [2006] EWCA Civ 1417, [2007] 1 P & CR 213.

10.13 In *Crewe Services & Investment Corpn v Silk*[1], the letting was of an AHA1986 tenancy. The landlord sued for damages for disrepair during the term of the tenancy. At first instance, referring to *Jones v Herxheimer*[2], the judge assessed damages at £15,940. The Court of Appeal allowed the appeal. The court confirmed that the test at common law for assessing damages for breach of a repairing covenant during a continuing tenancy is the diminution in the value of the freehold reversion. The judge was found to have relied too much on the general principle stated in *Jones v Herxheimer*[3] that the cost of repairs may represent the damage to the value of the reversion. The permissible heads of damage and the measure of damages must in principle be arrived at by an objective test. At the end of a tenancy, the cost of repairs, or that cost only slightly discounted, may be the best evidence of the diminution of the value of the freehold reversion if the tenant fails to establish, by leading evidence, that the diminution is less. However, it was wrong to treat the undiscounted costs of repairs as a safe guide to the damage to the value of the reversion where the landlord owned the farm subject to a continuing, protected tenancy of an unpredictable duration, and where there was no evidence that the landlord intended to undertake the repairs. The judge would have been assisted by evidence of the effect of the disrepair caused by the tenant's breaches of covenant on the value of the freehold reversion if it had been put on the market, subject to and with the benefit of the tenancy, at the date of the hearing. In the absence of such evidence, the judge was not bound to award nominal damages. The cost of repairs was discounted by almost three-quarters to take account of the uncertainties.

Once the amount of damages has been assessed, it must be compared with the diminution in the value of the landlord's reversion. This is done by looking at the value of the reversion with the premises in their actual state and the value it would be had there been no breach of covenant.

If an action is brought for damages at the end of the term (the landlord's dilapidations claim) the same limitation applies. Further, LTA 1927, s 18(1) provides that no damages will be payable if it can be shown that the premises, in whatever state of repair, are going to be demolished. This may be the case where, for example, the land is to be acquired under a CPO or where the landlord is intending to redevelop.

A well drawn tenancy agreement will reserve to the landlord the right to enter the holding and to carry out repairs which the tenant has failed to execute[4]. It will usually go on to provide that the repairs executed by the landlord will be at the tenant's expense. The sums expended by the landlord are recoverable as a debt from the tenant and not as damages[5]. The balance of authority seems to suggest that, in such circumstances, the ceiling on damages in s 18(1) of the LTA 1927 would not apply[6].

Forfeiture is the only remedy available to a landlord with a tenant in breach of repairing covenant which gets the holding back in hand, subject to the tenant's right to apply for relief. Forfeiture is dealt with in detail in Chapter 13.

[1] (1997) 79 P & CR 500, [1988] 2 EGLR 1. Also see, *Latimer v Carney* [2006] EWCA Civ 1417, [2007] 1 P & CR 213.
[2] [1950] 2 KB 106, CA.
[3] [1950] 2 KB 106, CA.
[4] The landlord has no implied right of entry to carry out the tenant's repairing obligations, although he does to carry out his own.
[5] This is important for commercial lettings as a way of avoiding the strictures of the Leasehold Property (Repairs) Act 1938 which applies to damages claims only – see, inter alia, *Colchester Estates (Cardiff) Ltd v Carlton Industries plc* [1986] Ch 80; *Elite Investments Ltd v T I Bainbridge Silencers Ltd* [1986] 2 EGLR 43.
[6] See the cases at fn 1 above.

The tenant's remedies

10.14 The tenant may:

(a)   sue for damages;

(b)   apply for specific performance; and

(c)   in certain circumstances, set off the cost of repairs against the rent[1].

As regards damages, there is no ceiling equivalent to that contained in s 18(1) of the LTA 1927. A tenant is entitled to the usual contract measure of damages: to put him in the position he would have been in had the landlord properly performed his repairing obligation. Each case will depend upon its own facts. If, for example, the tenant has been unable to use storage facilities on the holding it may be the cost to him of the alternative storage facilities off the holding and the costs of transportation to and from that alternative facility.

A tenant may in appropriate circumstances be granted a decree of specific performance to force the landlord to perform his repairing covenants[2]. Specific performance is a discretionary remedy. It will only be granted where damages would not be an adequate remedy and where it is just in all the circumstances[3]. Damages are unlikely to be adequate during the term of a tenancy where the continuing failure to repair will interfere with the tenant's occupation. A decree of specific performance will only be available if the court is convinced that it can control compliance with the decree and this will require a fully particularised schedule of what needs to be done.

Finally, the tenant may be able to set off against rent his claim for damages for breach of the landlord's repairing covenant[4], although such a right may be excluded by the terms of the lease itself[5]. It is not necessary for the tenant to have expended money on executing repairs before he can exercise his right to set off[6]. In equity, he can set off an estimated sum[7].

[1]   As to remedies generally, see Ch 45.

[2]   *Jeune v Queen's Cross Properties* [1974] Ch 97; *Joyce v Liverpool City Council* [1996] QB 252, CA.

[3]   See para 45.23.

[4]   *British Anzani (Felixstowe) Ltd v International Marine (UK) Ltd* [1980] QB 137, [1979] 2 All ER 1063; *Lee-Parker v Izzet* [1971] 1 WLR 1688; *Asco Developments and Newman v Lowes Lewis and Graham* (1978) 248 Estates Gazette 683.

[5]   An obligation to pay rent 'without any deduction' is not sufficient to exclude the right to set off. See *Connaught Restaurants v Indoor Leisure* [1993] 2 EGLR 108. See also *Electricity Supply Nominees Ltd v IAF Group Ltd* [1993] 2 EGLR 95.

[6]   *Melville v Grapelodge Developments Ltd* (1978) 39 P & CR 179.

[7]   Cf the position of the tenant under the AHA 1986 faced with a notice to pay. See para 31.32.

10.15   Where the landlord is owed rent for a particular period and, at the end of that period, with the rent still owing, he assigns the reversion to A, if A claims that rent against the tenant, then the tenant is entitled to set-off his claim for damages against the original landlord for breach of a repairing covenant[1].

If the landlord assigns the reversion to A, and A claims rent for a subsequent period, then the tenant cannot set-off his claim for damages against the original landlord for breach of a repairing obligation in defending against A's claim[2].

10.15 *Repairs*

1   *Muscat v Smith* [2003] EWCA Civ 962, [2003] 1 WLR 2853, [2003] 3 EGLR 11.
2   *Edlington Properties Ltd v JH Fenner & Co Ltd* [2005] EWHC 2158 (QB), [2006]
    1 EGLR 29, [2006] 05 EG 274.

Dilapidations protocol

10.16 In 1998, the Civil Procedure Rules introduced the concept of pre-action protocols. The aim was to reduce litigation. Since June 2000, the Property Litigation Association has sought to promote a dilapidations protocol for commercial landlords and tenants[1]. So far it has not been implemented and currently it has no relevance to the agricultural sector.

1   See an article in the Estates Gazette, 11 November 2006, 'Further debate needed by all
    parties', P Stell.

Chapter 11
OTHER TERMS

SERVICE OF NOTICES

11.1 Section 36 of the Agricultural Tenancies Act 1995 (ATA 1995) sets out methods of service for any notices or documents required or authorised to be given under the Act[1]. A notice or document is duly given to a recipient if (inter alia) it is given to him in a manner authorised by a written agreement made before the giving of the notice[2]. While an express agreement does not, seemingly, oust the other effective methods of service, it may be in the parties' interests to agree additional methods of service, including the possibility of service by facsimile or other electronic means, otherwise not deemed good service by s 36[3].

---

[1] See Ch 17.
[2] ATA 1995, s 36(2)(c).
[3] ATA 1995, s 36(3).

FIXTURES AND IMPROVEMENTS

11.2 The following provisions of the ATA 1995 impinge upon the freedom of contract of a landlord and a tenant in relation to a farm business tenancy.

(a)   In relation to fixtures, ATA 1995, s 8 gives the tenant a right to remove in most circumstances[1] and the parties are unable to contract out[2]. Furthermore, no additional rights given to the tenant to remove fixtures, whether by common law or by agreement, are enforceable by him[3].

(b)   There are compulsory provisions for compensation for 'tenant's improvements' (as defined by s 15) under Pt III of the ATA 1995[4]. As with fixtures, contracting out is not permitted where the Act provides for compensation and neither are the parties entitled to enforce any additional rights[5]. For items not within the definition of tenant's improvements, the parties are free, should they wish, to make their own arrangements for compensation.

---

[1] See Ch 15.
[2] ATA 1995, s 8(6).
[3] ATA 1995, s 8(7).

11.2 *Other terms*

⁴ See Ch 16.
⁵ ATA 1995, s 26(1).

ALTERATIONS

11.3 There are no direct restrictions in the ATA 1995 to prevent the parties from agreeing absolute or qualified prohibitions on the making of alterations and/or improvements. In the absence of such restrictions, the tenant is entitled to alter the holding, unless such an alteration would amount to waste or would be in breach of a repairing obligation, and to make improvements. If the alteration amounts to an improvement (within the meaning of the 1995 Act)[1], effective control is usually maintained because the tenant will not obtain compensation for the improvement in the absence of landlord's written consent or, in some cases, the approval of an arbitrator[2] and is, therefore, unlikely to embark upon the provision of the improvement in the absence of consent or approval[3]. Absolute or qualified prohibitions may nevertheless be an appropriate additional safeguard against a tenant who improves or alters the holding without seeking the consent necessary to enable him to make a compensation claim if the landlord's reason for the prohibition is to enable him to maintain control.

[1] See para 16.2.
[2] ATA 1995, ss 20–22. See Ch 16.
[3] Even where the landlord's refusal takes the shape of a prohibition in the tenancy agreement, an application to the arbitrator can be made, although the prohibition will be a factor which the arbitrator takes into account.

REINSTATEMENT CLAUSES

11.4 There is nothing in the ATA 1995 directly to prevent the parties from agreeing a reinstatement provision in the tenancy agreement, placing an obligation on the tenant to reinstate the holding at the end of the term. Such a provision may be found to be a contracting out of the compensation provisions for tenant's improvements by virtue of s 26(1) of the Act, if its effect is to ensure that the application of the compensation formula to the improvements which the tenant is obliged to reinstate results in no payment being due to the tenant. Such reinstatement obligations placed on a tenant have been used under the Landlord and Tenant Act 1927 for tenancies protected by the Land and Tenant Act 1954, Pt II on the basis that the obligation to reinstate removes any benefit to the landlord of the improvement.

EARLY RESUMPTION OR BREAK CLAUSES

11.5 There is nothing in the ATA 1995 to prevent the parties agreeing an early resumption clause or option to break a fixed-term tenancy before its term date[1]. For fixed-term leases of over two years there is a requirement that any notice necessary to exercise the option must be of at least 12 months' duration[2]. Such a requirement will override any shorter notice provision in the lease.

For longer fixed-term tenancies, break clauses will be important to the tenant, who might otherwise be locked in for the entire fixed term with a rent he can no longer afford and if he is unable to assign[3]. It may be important for the landlord where changes in fiscal policy, personal circumstances or redevelopment opportunities may lead to a change in priorities for the land.

An option to break can be exercisable by the landlord or the tenant or by both. It can be limited to the happening of specific events or to specific times (perhaps to coincide with rent review) or can be unrestricted. Where there are no conditions which need to be met (either events or time), the motive of the person exercising the option is irrelevant[4]. While the courts are astute to ensure that break clauses based on the default of the tenant are properly interpreted as forfeiture clauses (thus allowing the tenant to apply for relief)[5], it is not possible to look at the motive of a landlord exercising an open option to break.

Options to break will be strictly construed both in relation to any conditions which must be met before exercise[6] and, subject to s 7 of the ATA 1995, any time limits which are laid down. Time is of the essence[7].

The impact of a break clause on, for example, the rent; the ability of the tenant to raise finance and the willingness of the tenant to invest in the holding, will depend upon the circumstances in which the option can be exercised and how frequently it can be exercised. If the parties are concerned, and particularly if the purpose of the break is to enable a landlord to take advantage of possible development opportunities, it may be possible to grant a separate, periodic, or short fixed-term tenancy of part of the holding. Such a split may have an impact at rent review. Furthermore, depending upon the intended use of the holding, it could mean that part of the letting is not then 'primarily or wholly agricultural' so as to comply with the notice conditions[8] or the agriculture condition[9]. In the alternative, for a fixed-term tenancy, the parties may agree that the tenancy of the part, which is not primarily or wholly agricultural, to be excluded from the security of tenure provisions of Pt II of the Landlord and Tenant Act 1954, if protection under that Act would otherwise arise[10].

---

[1]   See Ch 12.
[2]   ATA 1995, s 7.
[3]   Cf the Agricultural Holdings Act 1986 where the tenant can always serve a 12-month notice to quit. See para 28.10.
[4]   *Batty v Vincent and City of London Real Property Co* (1921) 90 LJ Ch 302; *Re Knight and Hubbard's Underlease* [1923] 1 Ch 130.
[5]   See Ch 13.
[6]   *George Francis (Provinces) Ltd v Ruxdra Investments Ltd* (1960) 176 Estates Gazette 871, CA.
[7]   *United Scientific Holdings Ltd v Burnley Borough Council* [1978] AC 904, HL.
[8]   ATA 1995, s 1(4).
[9]   ATA 1995, s 1(3).

RIGHTS OF RE-ENTRY/FORFEITURE CLAUSES

11.6 In the absence of an express forfeiture clause in the lease, a landlord will almost never be able to forfeit[1]. All well drawn leases will contain a right of re-entry for the landlord upon the happening of certain events. If a fixed-term lease does not contain a forfeiture clause, a landlord will not be able to determine the lease where the tenant is in default or insolvent[2]. Whether a landlord is able to forfeit will depend upon the construction of the particular clause. Commonly, the landlord will reserve a right of re-entry upon non-payment of rent; the breach of any other covenant by the tenant or upon the tenant's insolvency or upon execution being levied against the tenant's interest or upon distress being levied against the tenant's goods.

Under the 1986 Act, it was held in *Parry v Million Pigs Ltd*[3] that a forfeiture clause which entitled the landlord to re-enter without giving the tenant sufficient time to make the compensation claims which have to be made before the termination of the tenancy was void. There are no such claims to be made by the tenant under a farm business tenancy. Section 8 provides that a tenant only has the right to remove tenant's fixtures during the continuance of the tenancy or whilst he remains on the holding as tenant. It is arguable that the landlord must give the tenant a reasonable time to remove fixtures before re-entering. It is submitted that the better view is that there is no such requirement. The common law position in relation to the removal of fixtures is that they should be removed before or on termination. Failure to remove before a forfeiture simply means that the right to remove is lost[4].

1 See Ch 13.
2 He may be able to exercise an open break clause where his motive for exercise is irrelevant. See para 12.7.
3 (1980) 260 Estates Gazette 281.
4 *Pugh v Arton* (1869) LR 8 Eq 626. Also see, *Re Palmiero* [1999] 3 EGLR 27. For greater detail, see Ch 13.

INSURANCE

11.7 There is nothing in the ATA 1995 dealing with insurance. The parties are free to negotiate and provision should be made in the tenancy agreement. There is no fall-back. In the absence of express provision, neither party will be under any obligation to insure. This can be compared with the position under the Agricultural Holdings Act 1986 (AHA 1986) where the 'model clauses'[1] apply to all oral tenancies and to written tenancies where no express provision is made placing the obligation on one party or the other for the insurance of fixed equipment[2].

The parties will need to consider who is to insure and with whom; who is to bear the cost of insuring; in whose name the policy is to be taken; the risks to be covered and whether or not insurance moneys are to be expended in the reinstatement of the property. Where a covenant exists obliging the landlord or the tenant to insure, the proceeds of the insurance claim must be spent on reinstatement of the insured property[3].

1   The provisions of the Agriculture (Maintenance, Repair and Insurance of Fixed Equipment) Regulations 1973, SI 1973/1473 as amended.
2   Subject to the tenant's ability to apply under AHA 1986, s 8 to have the model clauses incorporated.
3   The Fires Prevention (Metropolis) Act 1774, s 83.

FARMING PROVISIONS

11.8 Unlike the AHA 1986, the ATA 1995 contains no regulation of the farming of the holding. Apart from an implied obligation on the tenant to use and cultivate the land in a good and husbandlike manner and according to the custom of the country[1], the parties must reach express agreement on the extent of the tenant's obligations. Thought should be given not only to the rules of good husbandry but also, for example, to whether the landlord wishes to restrict the tenant's freedom of cropping; whether there are environmental or conservation issues which impact upon the use of the holding and whether tenant-right matters not falling within the definition of routine improvements[2] need to be dealt with.

1   *Powley v Walker* (1793) 5 Term Rep 373. See para 5.5.
2   ATA 1995, s 19(1).

FARMHOUSE RESIDENCE

11.9 Most modern agricultural tenancy agreements contain a provision requiring the tenant to reside in the farmhouse. The ATA 1995 does not have any such requirement. Most landlords will want to have such a covenant in a farm business tenancy in order to ensure the tenant's personal involvement in the farming of the holding and to create an obligation on the tenant to supervise personally the performance of all of the tenant's obligations, particularly those relating to good husbandry[1]. The obligation does not require unbroken residence at the farmhouse. The suspension of personal occupation for a reasonable period was expressly found to be permitted where it arose consequential upon the death of the tenant[2] and will clearly allow a tenant to take a holiday. Absence for more than a temporary period, for example, where the tenant is in prison, will represent a breach of the farmhouse residence covenant[3]. A breach of a farmhouse residence clause is remediable.

1   *Sumnal v Statt* (1984) 49 P & CR 367, CA; *Lloyds Bank Ltd v Jones* [1955] 2 QB 298, CA.
2   *Lloyds Bank Ltd v Jones* [1955] 2 QB 298, CA at 324 per Jenkins LJ.
3   *Sumnal v Statt* (1984) 49 P & CR 367, CA; *Amoah v London Borough of Barking and Dagenham* (2001) 82 P & CR DG6.

137

QUOTA CLAUSES

11.10 The freedom of contract philosophy underpinning the 1995 Act applies in relation to quotas and entitlements/Single Payments. The ATA 1995 makes no provision for the landlord's protection in relation to these 'assets'. It requires the parties to agree whatever terms they wish to deal with quotas and entitlements/Single Payments[1]. In particular, the parties need to consider the following questions:

(a)   Is the quota/entitlements to remain 'attached' to the holding upon the termination of the tenancy?

(b)   Is the tenant to deal with the quota/entitlements in a particular manner during the term of the tenancy, for example, is leasing out permitted?

(c)   What compensation (if any) should be paid to the landlord if the tenant can dispose of the quota/entitlements during the course of the tenancy?

(d)   What compensation (if any) should be paid to the tenant if the quota/entitlements is to remain with the holding at the termination of the tenancy?

[1]   As to the issues arising in relation to these 'assets', see the discussion of them in relation to the AHA 1986 at para 23.25 et seq.

AGRI-ENVIRONMENT SCHEMES/CONSERVATION

11.11 The ATA 1995 makes no provision relating to agri-environment schemes or conservation. Although technically the tenant's adoption of conservation, objectives could put him in breach of the rules of good husbandry[1], this does not carry with it the potentially draconian consequences which apply under the AHA 1986[2]. The parties may nevertheless wish to deal with conservation expressly in the farm business tenancy agreement.

There is a wide range of agri-environment schemes. Schemes vary as to their requirements in relation to the landlord's participation of express consent. A landlord may wish to include a covenant that he is to be consulted and that his consent is required before the tenant can enter into any such scheme. This issue is more important as a consequence of the minimal farming requirements imposed by the Mid-term Review of the Common Agricultural Policy[3].

[1]   See para 23.4.
[2]   See para 30.7.
[3]   See para 52.26.

Part IV

TERMINATION OF A FARM BUSINESS TENANCY

Contents

Chapter 12

STATUTORY SECURITY OF TENURE UNDER THE AGRICULTURAL TENANCIES ACT 1995

INTRODUCTION TO TERMINATION OF A FARM BUSINESS TENANCY

12.1 One of the features of the Agricultural Tenancies Act 1995 (ATA 1995) is that the tenant has virtually no security of tenure other than that bargained for with the landlord. Unlike the position under the Agricultural Holdings Act 1986 (AHA 1986)[1], there is little interference with the parties' common law rights to bring their tenancy to an end or with the general law on termination. Attempts in 1995 to persuade the Conservative Government to allow some security of tenure by the imposition of a statutory minimum term[2] for which the holding could be let on a farm business tenancy failed. The Government's attitude was that the imposition of such a statutory minimum term would, as had lifetime security of tenure under the AHA 1986, discourage landowners from letting land and that, if the decline in let land were to be halted, freedom of contract and the functioning of a free market were necessary to do it[3]. This was intended to be a feature of the new legislation from the outset. It reflects the guiding principles of the initial proposals: to deregulate the agricultural landlord and tenant system and to encourage the letting of land. The Government's approach was that if the landlord is certain as to when he can get the holding back in hand, and can cater for unforeseen changes in personal circumstances, he may be more inclined to enter into a landlord and tenant relationship[4].

Sections 5 to 7 of the ATA 1995 contain the only security for the tenant. They impose a requirement that, in certain cases, a particular length of notice must be given if the tenancy is to terminate. If the correct length of notice is given, and if the notice is served correctly in accordance with s 36 of the 1995 Act[5], the tenant has no answer to the notice. The effectiveness of the notice is not dependent upon any default by the tenant or limited by the landlord having to have particular reasons for requiring the land back. The parties are left free, in this respect at least, to make their own bargain. The extent of the tenant's security stems from that bargain: from the length of term granted and the nature and frequency of any break provisions in the landlord's favour. The only respect in which the tenant's behaviour can lead to the termination of a fixed-term tenancy during the term is if the landlord is able to and chooses to forfeit for the tenant's default[6].

This part of this book will look at the rules for terminating fixed-term tenancies (including by the exercise of an option to break); periodic tenancies and the termination of a fixed term by forfeiture. Where a notice to quit is required, the length of that notice may be regulated by the ATA 1995, but otherwise the common law rules will apply.

1   See Part III of Section 3 of this book.
2   By, amongst others, the Farmers' Union of Wales.
3   See *Hansard* House of Lords Vol 559 Col 1 526 and the comments of Lord Howe in the Second Reading Debate.
4   See MAFF Consultation Paper 'Agricultural Tenancy Law – Proposals for Reform' (February 1991); 'Reform of Agricultural Holdings Legislations: Detailed Proposals' (September 1992).
5   See para 17.1.
6   See Ch 13.

FIXED-TERM TENANCIES

12.2 At common law, a fixed-term tenancy simply expires by 'effluxion of time' at the end of the fixed term. In other words, the tenancy automatically ends on that day without the need for any action at all on the part of the landlord or tenant, without any need for a notice to quit and generally without the need for court proceedings[1].

1   Where premises are 'let as a dwelling', the landlord cannot simply re-enter to enforce his right to possession but must take court proceedings: Protection from Eviction Act 1977 (PEA 1977), s 3(1) (as amended by Housing Act 1988, s 30). However, s 3 does not apply to 'statutorily protected tenancies' as defined in PEA 1977, s 8. By para 29 of the Schedule to the ATA 1995, a farm business tenancy is a statutorily protected tenancy and, therefore, s 3 does not apply. In any event, under the AHA 1986 it has been held by the Court of Appeal that an agricultural holding which includes a dwelling house does not amount to 'premises let as a dwelling' for the purpose of PEA 1977, s 5. The same result would follow for farm business tenancies and, therefore, it will be unnecessary in notices to quit ATA 1995 tenancies to include in the notice the prescribed information contained in s 5 of the PEA 1977: *National Trust for Places of Historic Interest or Natural Beauty v Knipe* [1997] 2 EGLR 9; *Phaik Seang Tan v Sitkowski* [2007] EWCA Civ 30, Times, 15 February.

Lettings of more than two years

12.3 Section 5 of the ATA 1995 interferes with the common law position for farm business tenancies for a fixed term of more than two years by providing the following:

(a)   a farm business tenancy which is for a fixed term of more than two years will not automatically terminate by effluxion of time on its term date[1];
(b)   if a landlord or a tenant wants to end the tenancy on the term date, he must take positive action to do so by serving a written notice on the other party of his intention to terminate the tenancy on that date[2];

(c)   the notice must be served[3] at least 12 months[4] before the term date. There is no prescribed form for the notice[5], but prescribed methods of service are set out in ATA 1995, s 36.

[1]   ATA 1995, s 5(1). 'Term date' is defined in s 5(2) as meaning the date fixed for the expiry of the term. If there is any doubt as to the need to serve a notice (arising, for example, in connection with the validity of the tenancy or the length of the grant, a notice may be served 'without prejudice' to any contention by the landlord as to the existence or length of term: *Grammer v Lane* [2000] 1 EGLR 1, CA.
[2]   ATA 1995, s 5(1).
[3]   Or 'given' in the words of the ATA 1995. For service methods, see ATA 1995, s 36 and see also Ch 17.
[4]   Until 19 October 2006, the notice also had to be of less than 24 months' duration. That upper limit was removed by the Regulatory Reform (Agricultural Tenancies) (England and Wales) Order 2006, SI 2006/2805 (RRO 2006), art 13.
[5]   For a precedent, see Form C1.

12.4 If no notice is served by either party, the tenancy will continue after the term date as an annual periodic tenancy on the same terms and conditions (so far as applicable) as the original term[1].

There is no contracting out of the provisions of s 5[2], although that does not prevent the parties from agreeing a surrender of the tenancy. It will prevent the operation of a provision in the tenancy agreement for no notice or for a period of notice shorter than the statutory period. If an agreement to surrender is, in reality, a contracting out of the requirement for 12 months' notice, it may also be void. Once the term date has passed, and the tenancy becomes an annual periodic tenancy, it is terminated by notice to quit in the same way as those tenancies which have been annual periodic tenancies from the outset[3].

The nature of the continuation tenancy, after the expiry of the fixed term, is not clear: is it contractual or statutory in nature? If contractual, the tenant will continue to hold an estate in land and be subject to the benefit and burdens of the covenants. If statutory, the tenant will have a personal right to occupy only. While the wording is different in respect of the continuation tenancy under the Landlord and Tenant Act 1954, Pt II, where s 24 provides that the tenancy '... shall not come to an end when terminated in accordance with ... [the provisions of the Act]', it has been held that the continuation tenancy is an extension of the contractual term with a variation as to the method of termination[4]. It is likely that the same conclusion would be reached in relation to a farm business tenancy. Section 5 of the ATA 1995 provides that the tenancy '... shall continue ... on the terms of the original tenancy so far as applicable'.

If neither party to a fixed-term tenancy of more than two years wants the tenant to vacate the holding, they have two options. They can either do nothing and let the tenancy continue as an annual periodic tenancy under s 5, or they can agree to relet the holding to the tenant on a new fixed-term tenancy. What suits the parties will depend upon the circumstances in every case, but care needs to be taken where the tenant has diversified to a significant extent away from agriculture so that it could not be said, at the beginning of any new tenancy, that the character of the tenancy is primarily or wholly agricultural. In those circumstances, save where s 3 of the ATA 1995 will assist[5], it will not be possible to relet under the farm business tenancy regime and the parties may, if they want to stay within the ATA 1995, have no choice but to let the existing tenancy continue under the provisions of s 5 of the Act.

1   ATA 1995, s 5(1).
2   ATA 1995, s 5(4).
3   See ATA 1995, s 6. Section 6(2) deals with the situation where notice is given during the fixed-term tenancy to expire on the first anniversary of the term date, which would not be a notice under s 5 and which would not otherwise be a notice under s 6 which applies to notices served in respect of an annual tenancy.
4   See, for example, *Weinbergs Weatherproofs v Radcliffe Paper Mill Co* [1958] Ch 437; *City of London Corpn v Fell* [1993] QB 589, CA; affd [1994] 1 AC 458, HL.
5   See Ch 3.

Lettings of two years or less

12.5 In respect of lettings for a fixed term of two years or less, there is nothing in the ATA 1995 to interfere with the common law position. Such lettings will expire on the term date by effluxion of time. In practical terms, such lettings have replaced the grazing agreements and *Gladstone v Bower*[1] agreements under the AHA 1986 where there is a genuine need for a short-term agreement. A landlord letting under such a farm business tenancy is no worse off than he would have been under the AHA 1986 where a grazing agreement for a specified period of the year or a *Gladstone v Bower* agreement of more than 12 but less than 24 months' duration expired by effluxion of time[2].

Other than to avoid the requirement of 12 months' notice to quit, there may be good reason to let for two years or less. Options to break (or early resumption clauses) in tenancies of more than two years require 12 months' notice. If resumption of the whole or part is, or may be, required more quickly, a shorter fixed term or a periodic tenancy may be appropriate.

A tenant, who is expecting a fixed term of more than two years (and hence 12 months' notice to quit or the continuation of the tenancy as an annual periodic tenancy, and possibly 12 months' notice of an option to break being exercised) should bear in mind the cases of *Roberts v Church Comrs for England*[3] and *Keen v Holland*[4]. Those cases make it clear that, for the purposes of ascertaining its length, the term cannot commence before the agreement is entered into, regardless of what is stated to be the commencement date in the body of the agreement. A delay in signing and dating the agreement could lead to the tenant having a term of two years or less rather than the longer term he was expecting to receive[5].

1   *Gladstone v Bower* [1960] 2 QB 384.
2   See Ch 18 and Ch 19.
3   [1972] 1 QB 278, CA.
4   [1984] 1 All ER 75, CA.
5   From the landlord's point of view, if there is a dispute, a notice could be served 'without prejudice' to his contention that it is not needed: see *Grammer v Lane* [2000] 1 EGLR 1, CA.

Leases for life

12.6 Fixed-term tenancies continue until their term date[1] regardless of whether or not the parties are alive. If the tenant dies, the term becomes vested in his personal representatives. It is possible to provide that the fixed term will determine upon the happening of some stated event, including the death of one of the parties[2]. At common law, a tenancy which is made so determinable comes to an end automatically on the happening of the specified event. By section 149(6) of the Law of Property Act 1925, leases made determinable upon death or marriage are converted to 90-year terms, determinable upon the death or marriage by one month's notice in writing expiring on a quarter day. While the ATA 1995 imposes a requirement for 12 months' notice where notice is given in pursuance of an option to break a fixed term[3], there is a specific saving for those lettings which fall within s 149(6) so that the notice requirements of s 149(6) continue to apply. Where s 149(6) does not apply to a determinable fixed term, the common law continues to apply. The lease will determine automatically upon the happening of the relevant event[4].

[1]   And beyond if ATA 1995, s 5 applies.
[2]   The maximum duration of the term must, however, be certain. See Ch 27 and the House of Lords' decision in *Prudential Assurance Co Ltd v London Residuary Body* [1992] 2 AC 386 even if that maximum duration is capable of ending early on the happening of the determining event.
[3]   ATA 1995, s 7 and see Ch 12.
[4]   Save where ATA 1995, s 7 applies.

Options to break/early resumption clauses

12.7   As seen in Chapter 11, it is common for fixed-term tenancies to contain 'break clauses' allowing one or other or both of the parties to serve a notice to determine the tenancy before its term date[1]. Such clauses may be event-based[2], allowing a party to terminate on the happening of a particular event, may give the right to break only at specific times, for example to coincide with rent reviews or after a specified number of years have elapsed, or may be available at any time during the term of the lease. It may be in favour of the landlord only. The tenant only or both and it may entitle the party in whose favour it is granted to determine the lease in respect of the whole only or in respect of any part of the holding. A lease containing an option to break or early resumption provision should be compared to a determinable lease where, save where s 149(6) of the Law of Property Act 1925 applies, the lease will automatically come to an end on the happening of certain events[3]. It should be noted that a break clause will pass on assignment as it 'touches and concerns' the land[4].

Section 7 of the ATA 1995 overrides or supplements the agreement between the parties where a tenancy is for a fixed term of more than two years and contains an option to break[5]. It provides that any 'notice to quit' of the whole or part of a holding served in pursuance of a term of the tenancy shall be invalid unless it is:

(a)   in writing; and
(b)   given at least 12 months[6] before the date upon which it is to take effect.
   For all options to break in fixed-term tenancies of more than two years

at least 12 months' notice is therefore required before the option can be exercised. This may be too long for a landlord wanting to take advantage of a development opportunity and, in some cases, the landlord is worse off than he would be under the AHA 1986. Under that Act, a notice given pursuant to a contractual provision authorising resumption for a specified purpose other than agriculture will be valid if in accordance with the tenancy agreement and provided that it allows the tenant sufficient time to make his compensation claims[7]. Where a landlord anticipates requiring possession more quickly than s 7 will allow, consideration should be given to letting for a fixed term of two years or less where there is no statutory control of break provisions or letting on a periodic tenancy of an appropriate period to enable him to determine the tenancy by notice to quit[8].

[1] Or even in some circumstances for the lease to determine without any notice at all, as to which see para 12.6 above.
[2] Although if the specified events are the default of the tenant, the clause will be construed as a forfeiture provision: *Richard Clarke & Co Ltd v Widnall* [1976] 3 All ER 301, CA.
[3] If based on the default of the tenant and, therefore, in reality a forfeiture provision, it shall be construed as such: *Richard Clarke & Co Ltd v Widnall* [1976] 3 All ER 301, CA.
[4] *Harbour Estates Ltd v HSBC Bank plc* [2004] EWHC 1714 (Ch), [2005] Ch 194, [2005] 1 EGLR 107.
[5] The section does not, despite a saving for s 149(6), apply to determinable leases. It clearly only applies where the tenancy requires a notice to be served to determine the term: see ATA 1995, s 7(1).
[6] Until 19 October 2006, the notice also had to be of less than 24 months' duration. That upper limit was removed by the RRO 2006, SI 2006/2805, art 13.
[7] AHA 1986, s 21(2) and *Re Disraeli's Agreement* [1939] Ch 382; *Coates v Diment* [1951] 1 All ER 890. See para 28.14.
[8] If there is any doubt over the length of the term, the landlord should consider the service of a notice in compliance with ATA 1995, s 7 'without prejudice' to his position that the term is for two years or less: *Grammer v Lane* [2000] 1 EGLR 1, CA.

12.8 It should be noted that there is no requirement that the notice under s 7 of the ATA 1995 should expire on an anniversary day, although that could be an additional requirement of the particular option and, if so, it must be strictly complied with.

Other time limits in a break clause, for example, giving specified times during the term when an option can be exercised, must also be strictly complied with. In that event time will be computed from the notional date in the body of the lease from which the term is said to run and not the date on which the lease was executed[1]. Following the House of Lords decision in *Mannai Investment Co Ltd v Eagle Star Life Assurance Co Ltd*[2], the more rigid rule previously applicable to break notices has gone. The validity or otherwise of a break clause is now tested by the 'standard of commercial construction'. Would a reasonable recipient of the notice in question be left in no reasonable doubt as to what was intended by the notice? In other words, it is the same test as applies to the validity of a notice to quit. The minor error in *Mannai* (specifying the anniversary date of the lease as the 12th rather than the 13th) was not enough to perplex the reasonable recipient[3]: it must also have been served, in accordance with the terms of the break clause, at a time or following an event which entitled the relevant party to serve the notice. If the notice is in relation to a tenant's break clause, all joint tenants must join in the giving of the notice. The break clause cannot be exercised by one joint tenant acting unilaterally[4].

Section 7 of the ATA 1995 applies 'notwithstanding any provision to the contrary in the tenancy agreement'. Two things should be noted:

(a)   the wording of s 7 is such that it clearly only applies where the break provision in the tenancy agreement actually calls for a notice to be served. It does not apply to determinable leases where the happening of an event automatically determines the lease[5];

(b)   s 7(1) makes it clear that it is the *notice* exercising the option which is invalid if it does not comply with s 7(1).

While contracting out is prohibited, it is likely that any provision in an option agreement for shorter notice will simply be overridden by the requirements of s 7. The option to break itself will continue, subject to those overriding requirements, to have contractual force. Any notice served in accordance with the contractual provision will not operate to bring the term to an end.

---

1   See, for example, *Trane (UK) Ltd v Provident Mutual Life Assurance* [1995] 1 EGLR 33.
2   [1997] AC 749, [1997] 1 EGLR 57. *Hanley v Clavering* [1942] 2 KB 326, CA was overruled by the House of Lords. See also para 28.3ff.
3   Cf *Lemmerbell Ltd v Britannia LAS Direct Ltd* [1998] 3 EGLR 67, CA where confusion over the identity of the tenant was sufficient to render the notice invalid. See also *Havant International Holdings Ltd v Lionsgate (H) Investment Ltd* [1999] EGCS 144; *Procter & Gamble Technical Centres Ltd v Brixton Estates plc* [2002] EWHC 2835 (Ch), [2003] 2 EGLR 24, [2003] 32 EG 69; *Peer Freeholds Ltd v Clean Wash International Ltd* [2005] EWHC 179 (Ch), [2005] 1 EGLR 47, [2005] 17 EG 124.
4   *Hammersmith and Fulham London Borough Council v Monk* [1992] 1 AC 478, [1992] 1 All ER 1, HL; *Hounslow London Borough Council v Pilling* (1993) 25 HLR 305, CA.
5   Save in respect of leases for life or until marriage converted into 90-year terms determinable by notice after the determining event: Law of Property Act 1925, s 149(6). See para 12.6.

12.9 A break clause is in some cases dependent upon the tenant having complied with all of the tenant's obligations under the tenancy. It has been held that a provision requiring 'material compliance', this did not require strict compliance. A breach was only material if it was fair and reasonable to refuse the tenant the privilege of termination granted by the tenancy[1].

---

1   *Fitzroy House Epworth Street (No 1) Ltd v Financial Times Ltd* [2005] EWHC 2391 (TCC), [2006] 1 EGLR 19, [2006] 02 EG 112.

Death of the tenant

12.10 Where a fixed-term tenancy is entered into the parties should consider including a break clause arising on the tenant's death. In the absence of express agreement, the tenancy will continue in the tenant's personal representatives until its termination date or further agreement.

By reason of s 7 of the ATA 1995, any break clause arising upon the tenant's death would require 12 months' notice. The only exception arises under s 149(6) of the Law of Property Act 1925. That provision converts a tenancy for life or for a term of years terminable with the life or lives of the tenant(s) or on marriage into a fixed-term tenancy of 90 years. After the tenant's death or marriage (whichever applies), either party is entitled to terminate the tenancy by giving one month's written notice ending on a quarter day applicable to the tenancy[1]. The operation of s 149(6) is unaffected by the ATA 1995[2], although such tenancies are rare in practice.

[1]   If there is no quarter day applicable to the tenancy, a usual quarter day will apply.
[2]   ATA 1995, s 7(3).

PERIODIC TENANCIES

12.11 Section 6 of the ATA 1995 applies to annual periodic tenancies, whether such tenancies were from year to year at the outset or are from year to year as a result of the operation of s 5 of the 1995 Act. A notice to quit in respect of an annual periodic tenancy is invalid unless:

(a)   it is in writing;
(b)   it is to take effect at the end of a year of the tenancy[1]; and
(c)   it is given (within the meaning of s 36 of the Act) at least 12 months[2] before the date upon which it is to take effect.

Section 6 of the ATA 1995 overrides the common law, which provides that annual tenancies can be terminated upon six months' notice ending on a term date. The Act gives an extended period of notice. As with s 5, there is no contracting out of the provisions of s 6[3], although the parties can always agree to surrender. Either party may give the notice. For the common law requirements for notices to quit, reference should be made to the commentary under the AHA 1986[4].

Other periodic tenancies continue to be governed by the common law rules. In other words, they are terminated by one full period's notice to quit unless the parties agree to some other period of notice[5]. The service requirements for notices to quit periodic tenancies other than annual are *not* within s 36 of the ATA 1995 and reference should be made to the common law[6].

[1]   *Sidebotham v Holland* [1895] 1 QB 378; *Yeandle v Reigate and Banstead Borough Council* [1996] 1 EGLR 20, CA. If the anniversary date is 29 September, a notice expiring on either 28 or 29 September will satisfy this requirement.
[2]   Until 19 October 2006, the notice also had to be of less than 24 months' duration. That upper ceiling was removed by the RRO 2006, SI 2006/2805, art 13.
[3]   ATA 1995, s 6(1).
[4]   See para 28.2ff.
[5]   *Re Threlfall* (1880) 16 Ch D 274, CA and subject to the statutory interference of s 5 of the Protection from Eviction Act 1977 requiring written notice of at least four weeks' duration where property is 'let as a dwelling'. As to which, see *Wolfe v Hogan* [1949] 2 KB 194; *Ponder v Hillman* [1969] 3 All ER 694; *Phaik Seang Tan v Sitkowski* [2007] EWCA Civ 30, Times, 15 February.
[6]   In the absence of evidence to the contrary, a notice is deemed to have been served if posted in the ordinary course of the post (Interpretation Act 1978, s 7). Notices need not be served personally on a tenant but can be left at his dwellinghouse with his wife or servant (*Smith v Clark* (1840) 9 Dowl 202) but not simply left without any evidence that the tenant ever received it (subject to the statutory presumption in favour of posting). If it can

be shown that the tenant received it, service is effected (*Alford v Vickery* (1842) Car & M 280). Notices to quit can be oral at common law, but not where s 5 of the Protection from Eviction Act 1977 applies.

Chapter 13

FORFEITURE

INTRODUCTION

13.1 During the term of a lease or a tenancy, and other than by the operation of a break clause in his favour[1], the landlord's only method of ending the lease is by forfeiture for breach of a covenant in the tenancy agreement or upon breach of a condition of the lease[2].

Under the Agricultural Tenancies Act 1995 (ATA 1995), this is an extremely important remedy for the landlord. Lettings are generally for a fixed term to give the tenant some degree of security and encourage capital investment in the holding. If the landlord cannot forfeit the lease during the fixed term then, other than in very limited circumstances, the lease will continue with a defaulting tenant – possibly not paying his rent or with the holding in disrepair – until the end of the term.

Forfeiture is a remedy available to a landlord with a tenant holding under an Agricultural Holdings Act 1986 (AHA 1986) tenancy. Historically the remedy is little used under that Act (and its statutory predecessor) because, in most cases, other than possibly Case D where the procedural requirements are many and complex[3], the notice to quit route is more certain. A tenant under the AHA 1986 who does not pay his rent on time, and who does not comply with a notice to pay, will face a notice to quit to which he has no defence, regardless of any extenuating circumstances[4]. If a tenancy is forfeited by the landlord for non-payment of rent, the tenant can apply for relief from forfeiture and, in almost all cases, he will succeed. To that extent, landlords letting on fixed terms under the ATA 1995 regime are worse off than landlords under the AHA 1986 where the tenant is in default.

[1] A break clause based upon allowing the landlord to terminate the lease upon the default of the tenant will be treated by the courts as a forfeiture clause: *Richard Clarke & Co Ltd v Widnall* [1976] 3 All ER 301, CA. To do otherwise would be to deprive the tenant of the protection of an application for relief.

[2] Landlord includes an equitable assignee of the reversionary interest: *Scribes West Ltd v Relsa Anstalt* [2004] EWCA Civ 1744, [2005] 1 EGLR 22, [2005] 09 EG 190.

[3] See Ch 31.

[4] See Ch 31.

13.2 It may not always be in the interests of the landlord to forfeit the lease. Every case should be the subject of careful consideration, taking into account, for example, the ease with which the holding could be relet; the likelihood of other remedies succeeding in controlling the tenant; and whether or not any new tenancy is likely to be on terms as favourable to the landlord as the terms of the current tenancy. In addition, the costs of forfeiting may be high and the tenant may well obtain relief from forfeiture even after the end of any necessary court proceedings. During the time that it takes any proceedings to come to court, the landlord may not be receiving an income from the holding[1]; the tenant cannot be put out of physical occupation and yet will not be liable, for example, for breach of his covenants after the date of the forfeiture which may result in the eventual return to the landlord of a holding in a dilapidated state with the only remedy being in the tort of waste[2]. While the landlord would have personal remedies against the tenant, they are only as good as the ability of the tenant to pay. Furthermore, even after the landlord has obtained his order for possession, the tenant may be able to apply for relief from forfeiture. If he obtains relief, it is as if the lease were never forfeit. This leaves the landlord with the difficulty of knowing whether or not he should relet the holding within the time during which the tenant can make his application for relief. Accordingly, the landlord must think carefully before deciding to forfeit, particularly as, once he has re-entered, whether physically or by the issue of court proceedings, he cannot unilaterally withdraw his forfeiture[3].

For the tenant, the position is much improved from the position under the AHA 1986. This can be seen as something of a quid pro quo for the lack of security of tenure under a farm business tenancy. The security comes from the fixed term. It should not be too easy for the landlord to determine the tenant's estate. In every case where the tenant is entitled to apply for relief from forfeiture following his default, the court will be able to take account of the particular circumstances which led to the default; the previous behaviour of the tenant; and any relevant personal circumstances. None of these factors can be taken into account following the service of an incontestable notice to quit under the AHA 1986[4]. Moreover, whether to forfeit or not is a matter of choice for the landlord, but if he waives the right to forfeit (which he may do unintentionally by treating the lease as continuing), the tenant cannot be deprived of his tenancy for that breach.

The law in relation to forfeiture, particularly the jurisdiction of the courts to grant relief to the tenant, is complex and depends upon the nature of the default (non-payment of rent or other) and the court (High Court or county court) in which any proceedings for possession are brought. It is beyond the scope of this book to give a detailed analysis but, given the importance of the remedy to landlords, an outline of the right to forfeit; how to forfeit; the effect of forfeiture and relief from forfeiture is set out below[5].

[1] Although he may be able to make an application to the court for an interim payment in respect of the tenant's use and occupation of the property (RSC Ord 29, r 10).
[2] As to which see Ch 5 and the case of *Associated Deliveries Ltd v Harrison* [1984] 2 EGLR 76, CA.
[3] *GS Fashions Ltd v B & Q plc* [1995] 1 WLR 1088.
[4] See Ch 28.
[5] For a full treatment, see Woodfall, *Landlord and Tenant* (Looseleaf edn, 1994) Sweet & Maxwell, Vol 1, Ch 17; Pawlowski, *The Forfeiture of Leases* (1993) Sweet & Maxwell.

13.3 *Forfeiture*

THE RIGHT TO FORFEIT

13.3 The first point to be made is that if the landlord effects a re-entry onto a holding where he has no right to forfeit, he will be committing a trespass[1].

In most cases, an express and valid reservation in the tenancy agreement allowing the landlord to re-enter for breach of covenant or upon breach of condition will be necessary to give the landlord the right to forfeit. A right of re-entry cannot generally be implied[2]. The only circumstances where such an express reservation is not necessary are as follows:

(a) where the tenant has denied the landlord's title – this may be a positive averment in his defence to the landlord's claim for possession[3] or where the tenant has intentionally, deliberately and unequivocally set up a title adverse to that of his landlord[4];

(b) where the tenant's obligation, rather than being a covenant, is actually a condition of the lease – if the lease is conditional upon the tenant doing or not doing something, the failure of the tenant to fulfil the condition entitles the landlord to forfeit even in the absence of an express forfeiture clause. Breach of a condition renders the lease voidable at the option of the landlord[5]. The breach of the condition need not be a default by the tenant but it may be. A letting to a tenant 'for so long as he resides in the farmhouse'; or 'on condition that he keeps the holding in repair' may fall into this category. Whether or not a particular term of the tenancy agreement is a covenant or a condition is a matter of interpreting the intention of the parties from a construction of the tenancy agreement as a whole.

If breach of a condition entitles the landlord to forfeit even in the absence of an express forfeiture clause, why not make all tenant's obligations conditions? The disadvantage with conditions (as opposed to covenants) is that while they may entitle the landlord to forfeit in the absence of an express condition of re-entry, they do not entitle him to damages. The tenant is not in breach of contractual obligation as he would be with a covenant where he has promised to do or refrain from doing something. The best solution for a landlord is to deal with obligations by way of covenant and have a well drafted and wide-ranging forfeiture clause in the tenancy agreement[6].

---

[1] *Yelloly v Morley* (1910) 27 TLR 20.

[2] Although a right of re-entry for non-payment of rent is a 'usual covenant' which will be implied into a contract for a lease, if the contract is silent on the terms of the lease: *Hodgkinson v Crowe* (1875) 10 Ch App 622.

[3] Although not by a general denial of allegations, which merely puts the landlord to proof of his title (*Warner v Sampson* [1959] 1 QB 297, CA) and not where the denial is as to part of the land only because that would not show an intention to deny the landlord and tenant relationship (*WG Clark (Properties) Ltd v Dupre Properties Ltd* [1992] Ch 297).

[4] *Wisbech St Mary Parish Council v Lilley* [1956] 1 All ER 301, CA. For a thorough treatment, see Pawlowski, *The Forfeiture of Leases*, (1st edn, 1993) Sweet & Maxwell, pp 48–57.

[5] *Doe d Bryan v Bancks* (1821) 4 B & Ald 401; *Roberts v Davey* (1833) 4 B & Ad 664; *Doe d Lockwood v Clarke* (1807) 8 East 185, 103 ER 313.

[6] It is possible for a term to be both a covenant and a condition but it would seem that, in that case, the only remedy is forfeiture: *Bashir v Crown Lands Comr* [1960] AC 44, PC.

13.4 In all other cases, an express reservation in the tenancy agreement is necessary if the landlord is to be able to forfeit. There is no equivalent for lettings under the ATA 1995 to s 6 and Sch 1 to the AHA 1986, which would allow the landlord to an AHA 1986 tenancy to apply to an arbitrator for provision to be made in a written tenancy agreement for forfeiture where the parties' agreement (whether written or oral) makes no such provision[1].

An express forfeiture clause will generally reserve to the landlord a right of re-entry[2] to the holding upon the failure of the tenant to pay rent; upon breach by the tenant of any covenants or upon the tenant's insolvency. It will usually specify the period of days after default when the re-entry can take place.

Before the landlord can forfeit, he must ensure that his forfeiture clause is valid and that an event has happened which, on a proper construction of the clause, (and of the covenant the tenant is accused of breaking), gives a right of re-entry, otherwise he will be trespassing[3].

While forfeiture is not popular under the AHA 1986, it is not unknown and many tenancies contain forfeiture clauses. However, many of those clauses are not valid. In *Parry v Million Pigs Ltd*[4] it was held that where a forfeiture clause was so drafted that it gave insufficient time for the tenant to give the one month's notice required before the termination of the tenancy for certain compensation claims under the AHA 1986, it was void. Under the ATA 1995, the only statutory compensation is in relation to tenant's improvements and the claim does not need to be made until the tenancy has terminated[5].

Under s 8 of the ATA 1995, the tenant has the right to remove tenant's fixtures '... at any time during the continuance of the tenancy or at any time after the termination of the tenancy when he remains in possession as tenant (whether or not under a new tenancy)...'[6] . It is arguable that a forfeiture clause which did not allow the tenant sufficient time to remove his fixtures would be void. However, at common law, a tenant has a similar right to remove fixtures during the term or so long as he holds the premises under a right still to consider himself as tenant[7]. If a tenant does not remove fixtures before the tenancy is forfeited, the right to remove is lost[8]. Upon a physical re-entry, the right to remove is lost upon re-entry[9]. Where the forfeiture is by court proceedings, it is submitted that the tenant retains the right to remove up until judgment for possession is given.

[1] See Ch 23.
[2] The right of re-entry is not merely a contractual right but a proprietary interest: see Law of Property Act 1925, s 1(2)(e).
[3] *Yelloly v Morley* (1910) 27 TLR 20.
[4] (1980) 260 Estates Gazette 281.
[5] ATA 1995, s 22.
[6] ATA 1995, s 8(1).
[7] *Weeton v Woodcock* (1840) 7 M & W 14.
[8] *Pugh v Arton* (1869) LR 8 EQ 626.
[9] *Re Palmiero* [1999] 3 EGLR 27.

13.5 In considering whether there has been a breach of the obligation to pay rent, s 48 of the Landlord and Tenant Act 1987 should be considered. This section will apply to farm business tenancies which include a dwellinghouse[1]. It requires the landlord to provide the tenant with written advice of an address in England and Wales at which notices (for example of court proceedings) may be served[2]. Until the tenant is so notified, no rent or service charge can be treated as due[3].

In many cases, the fact that the name and address of the landlord is in the lease will suffice[4], although more may need to be done where the landlord is non-resident[5]. Care also needs to be taken on a change of landlord to ensure that s 48 is complied with.

A right of re-entry is only exercisable for 12 years from the accrual of the right[6] although it is almost certain that the landlord will have waived the right long before the expiration of the 12-year period.

1   *Dallhold Estates (UK) Property Ltd v Lindsey Trading Properties Inc* [1994] 1 EGLR 93, CA.
2   Landlord and Tenant Act 1987, s 48(1). See *Rogan v Woodfield Building Services Ltd* [1995] 1 EGLR 72, CA.
3   Landlord and Tenant Act 1987, s 48(2).
4   *Rogan v Woodfield Building Services Ltd* [1995] 1 EGLR 72, CA.
5   *Dallhold Estates (UK) Property Ltd v Lindsey Trading Properties Inc* [1994] 1 EGLR 93, CA.
6   Limitation Act 1980, s 15(1).

WAIVER OF THE RIGHT TO FORFEIT

13.6 Even where the landlord has a right to forfeit, he may, by waiver, deprive himself of it. When an event occurs which allows the landlord to forfeit, he can choose either to exercise his right of re-entry or to allow the lease to continue. If, knowing of the breach of covenant or other event, the landlord subsequently does any act which unequivocally recognises the continued existence of the lease, whether or not he intended to waive his rights[1], he is taken to have elected for the continuance of the lease and waived his right to forfeit for that particular breach. This is of particular importance in the context of agricultural tenancies, where holdings are often managed by agents, because the knowledge of the landlord's agent of the breach will constitute knowledge of the landlord. Knowledge of facts which give rise to a right to forfeit will suffice. It is not necessary to appreciate the legal significance of those facts[2]. Once the forfeiture has occurred (whether by re-entry or the service of court proceedings), the landlord has made his choice. No subsequent acts by him will operate as a waiver[3].

In addition to waiver, it is necessary to consider whether the landlord's conduct has amounted to an assent sufficient to cause the landlord to be estopped from insisting on strict compliance with the terms of the tenancy[4].

1   See *Central Estates (Belgravia) Ltd v Woolgar (No 2)* [1972] 3 All ER 610, CA where it was made clear that the test is objective.
2   But see *Chrisdell Ltd v Johnson & Tickner* (1987) 54 P & CR 257, CA; *David Blackstone Ltd v Burnetts (West End) Ltd* [1973] 1 WLR 1487. The onus is on the tenant to show that the landlord had knowledge of the relevant facts: *Matthews v Smallwood* [1910] 1 Ch 777.

³   *Civil Service Co-operative Society v McGrigor's Trustee* [1923] 2 Ch 347; the acceptance
    of rent following a forfeiture may, however, be evidence of a new tenancy (*Evans v Wyatt*
    (1880) 43 LT 176; *Land v Sykes* [1991] 1 EGLR 18, CA).
⁴   *Hazel v Akhtar* [2001] EWCA Civ 1883, [2002] 2 P & CR 17. As to proprietary estoppel
    generally, see para 21.24.

Acts amounting to waiver

13.7 Most problems in relation to waiver arise from the demand for, or
acceptance of, rent following a breach of covenant or condition. Either will be
a waiver of the landlord's right to forfeit for an existing breach as amounting
to an act recognising the continued existence of the lease. Increasingly,
landlords or their agents make use of systems for the collection of rent which
rely upon automatic demands being sent out to tenants or rely on clerks to
deal with the rent demands who may have no direct knowledge of circumstances on the holding. As the intention of the landlord is irrelevant to the
question of whether or not the breach has been waived, the fact that a rent
demand may have been sent out in error is equally irrelevant. The landlord
will have been taken to have waived the breach[1]. It is important that the
landlord or his agent managing an estate has a system in place for stopping
demands being made for rent once a breach is known or until such time as the
landlord has decided what to do.

The following points arise in relation to demands for and acceptance of rent:

(a)   The demand for rent accruing after the breach or acceptance of rent
      'under protest' or 'without prejudice' will still result in a waiver[2].
(b)   Waiver will not arise where the rent which is demanded or accepted
      accrued due before the facts giving rise to the right to forfeit[3].
(c)   A demand for rent is not treated as having been made for these
      purposes if it is not received by the tenant[4].
(d)   Where the tenant pays rent, as a matter of course, into the landlord's
      bank account, it may amount to a waiver even if the bank has been
      instructed by the landlord not to accept it[5]. In *John Lewis Proper-
      ties plc v Viscount Chelsea*[6], it was stated that had there been a breach
      of covenant in that case, the receipt of rent by the landlord's bank
      would not have amounted to a waiver because the landlord had made it
      clear, in writing, that it was not accepting or demanding rent following
      the alleged breach and, when rent was received, it was returned to the
      tenant.
(e)   Where the rent is payable in advance, the demand or acceptance of rent
      will waive the right to forfeit in respect of breaches before the demand
      or acceptance and those which continue beyond the demand but which
      the landlord knew about at the time and knew would continue through
      the period covered by the rent[7]. Demand or acceptance will not waive
      for future breaches which may arise during the period covered by the
      rent but about which the landlord had no knowledge at the date of
      demand or acceptance.
(f)   A landlord who distrains for rent, whether accruing before or after the
      breach, will waive the right to forfeit[8].

13.7   Forfeiture

1   *Central Estates (Belgravia) Ltd v Woolgar (No 2)* [1972] 3 All ER 610, CA.
2   *Davenport v R* (1877) 3 App Cas 115, PC; *Segal Securities Ltd v Thoseby* [1963] 1 QB 887; *Windmill Investments (London) Ltd v Milano Restaurants Ltd* [1962] 2 QB 373.
3   *Price v Worwood* (1859) 4 H & N 512; *Re a Debtor (No 13 A 10 of 1995)* [1995] EGCS 58. As to appropriation of rent in the case of a voluntary arrangement by the tenant, see *Thomas v Ken Thomas Ltd* [2006] EWCA Civ 1504, [2007] 01 EG 94.
4   *Henry Smith's Charity Trustees v Willson* [1983] QB 316, CA.
5   *Pierson v Harvey* (1885) 1 TLR 430.
6   [1993] 2 EGLR 77.
7   *Segal Securities Ltd v Thoseby* [1963] 1 QB 887.
8   *Green's Case* (1582) Cro Eliz 3, 78 ER 269.

13.8 Other acts by the landlord which may, depending on the circumstances, constitute waiver would be:

(a)   serving a rent review notice;
(b)   serving a notice to quit;
(c)   granting a licence, for example, to sub-let;
(d)   complying with repairing obligations;
(e)   seeking an injunction to restrain a breach of covenant[1].

In all cases other than the demand for or the acceptance of the rent, the court is entitled to consider all the circumstances of the case in order to decide whether the act is an unequivocal acceptance of the existence of the tenancy[2].

Entering into negotiations on a without prejudice basis will not, of itself, constitute an unequivocal acceptance of the continued existence of the lease[3].

1   *Calabar Properties Ltd v Seagull Autos Ltd* [1969] 1 Ch 451.
2   *Expert Clothing Service and Sales Ltd v Hillgate House Ltd* [1986] Ch 340, CA. See also *Yorkshire Metropolitan Properties Ltd v Co-operative Retail Services Ltd* [1997] EGCS 57.
3   *Re National Jazz Centre Ltd* [1988] 2 EGLR 57; *Expert Clothing Services and Sales Ltd v Hillgate House Ltd* [1986] Ch 340, CA – a deed of variation of the lease sent in the course of negotiations would not necessarily amount to waiver.

Effect of waiver

13.9 What is waived is the right of the landlord to forfeit for a breach which has occurred and which he knows about. How devastating that waiver is depends upon the nature of the breach: is it continuing or once and for all? If it is continuing there is, as it were, a fresh breach every day that the tenant remains in breach and, whilst the landlord may have waived previous breaches, he can subsequently forfeit. Waiver in respect of a continuing breach is not generally of as much concern as in the case of a once and for all breach where waiver is fatal to the landlord's right to forfeit.

Even with a once and for all breach waiver will only operate to prevent the landlord forfeiting in respect of the particular breach. The landlord will be able to forfeit for later breaches of the same covenant. So, for example, a landlord may have waived the non-payment of rent for a particular quarter, but he will be able for forfeit in respect of the following quarter's rent if the tenant fails to pay again.

There is no single test which can be applied to establish whether a particular breach is continuing or once and for all. The distinction lies in whether the covenant imposes continuing obligations on the tenant or requires him to do, or refrain from doing, a particular act[1]. The following have been held to be continuing breaches:

(a)   failure to repair[2];
(b)   breach of a user covenant[3];
(c)   breach of a covenant to insure[4].

Examples of once and for all breaches are:

(i)   breach of a covenant against assignment or sub-letting[5] but not parting with possession[6];
(ii)   failure to pay insurance monies towards reinstatement[7];
(iii) failure to pay rent (although the failure to make the next payment will give rise to a fresh right to forfeit)[8];
(iv) unauthorised alterations[9];
(v)   the insolvency of the tenant[10].

Waiver of the landlord's right to forfeiture does not operate as a waiver of the landlord's right to damages for a breach of covenant[11] or an injunction.

1   *Farimani v Gates* [1984] 2 EGLR 66, CA. The fact that the tenant can remedy the breach of the obligation does not make it a continuing breach.
2   *Doe d Baker v Jones* (1850) 5 Exch 498, 155 ER 218; *Coward v Gregory* (1866) LR 2 CP 153.
3   *Doe d Ambler v Woodbridge* (1829) 9 B & C 376, 109 ER 140; *Segal Securities Ltd v Thoseby* [1963] 1 QB 887; *Marsden v Edward Heyes Ltd* [1927] 2 KB 1, CA.
4   *Doe d Muston v Gladwin* (1845) 6 QB 953.
5   *Walrond v Hawkins* (1875) LR 10 CP 342; *Scala House and District Property Co Ltd v Forbes* [1974] QB 575, [1973] 3 All ER 308, 227 Estates Gazette 1161. See para 8.1ff.
6   *Akici v L R Butlin Ltd* [2005] EWCA Civ 1296, [2006] 1 EGLR 34, [2006] 07 EG 136.
7   *Farimani v Gates* [1984] 2 EGLR 66, CA.
8   *London and County (A & D) Ltd v W Sportsman Ltd* [1971] Ch 764, CA.
9   *Iperion Investments Corpn v Broadwalk House Residents Ltd* [1992] 2 EGLR 235.
10 *Doe d Gatehouse v Reese* (1838) 4 Bing NC 384, 132 ER 835.
11 *Stephens v Junior Army & Navy Stores Ltd* [1914] 2 Ch 516, CA.

HOW TO FORFEIT

Re-entry

13.10 Forfeiture occurs upon the exercise by the landlord of his right of re-entry. That re-entry may be physical[1] or by the service of court proceedings[2]. The vast majority of forfeiture occurs by the service of court proceedings for the following reasons:

(a)   Physical re-entry onto premises is not permitted where there is somebody lawfully residing on the premises or any part of them where the premises are let as a dwelling[3].
(b)   Even after physical re-entry, the tenant is entitled to apply for relief from forfeiture and there is no guarantee that prolonged court proceedings will be avoided. There is no more certainty for the landlord following re-entry[4].

(c)   The re-entry must be peaceable. If there is any violence or threat of violence to person or property, the landlord leaves himself open to criminal prosecution under s 6 of the Criminal Law Act 1977 where there is, to the knowledge of the landlord, someone on the premises who is opposed to the re-entry.

(d)   The landlord will have the problem of dealing with the tenant's goods. This may include livestock and in respect of which the landlord will have bailor's obligations[5]. There is no guarantee that a tenant whose lease is forfeited by court proceedings would not have, eventually, to be evicted when the problem with his goods would be the same unless there is also a judgment for unpaid rent or otherwise.

(e)   The problem of re-entry itself and of securing the land. Most well-drafted forfeiture clauses will allow the landlord to re-enter part of the land in the name of the whole. If this is the case, re-entering part of the holding may be sufficient.

In appropriate cases, where there is little chance of an application for relief; where the holding consists of bare land only; and where re-entry can be effected without the presence of the tenant, peaceable re-entry may be a cheaper and quicker option. The re-entry should be unequivocal, clear and for the purpose of forfeiting the lease. It is usual to change the locks on commercial premises. For farmland, this may not be appropriate although locks on gates can be changed; gates can be chained and clear notices placed around the land stating that the landlord has re-entered.

To exercise his election to treat the lease as forfeited by court proceedings, the landlord must commence proceedings. Under the Civil Procedure Rules, proceedings commence upon the issue by the court of the claim form (whether the action is commenced in High Court or county court).

[1]   Or, more accurately, actual, as re-entry can occur, for example, by the landlord reletting premises to a sub-tenant who is already in occupation: *London and County (A & D) Ltd v Wilfred Sportsman Ltd* [1971] Ch 764, CA; *Ashton v Sobelman* [1987] 1 All ER 755. As to peaceable re-entry prior to the purchaser of the reversion becoming the registered proprietor of the land, see *Rother District Investments Ltd v Corke* [2004] EWHC 14 (Ch), (2004) 2 P & CR 311.

[2]   In the Law Commission Report Number 142 'Report on Forfeiture of Tenancies', these two methods were called 'actual re-entry' and 'constructive re-entry'. Note that the proceedings should be brought in the name of the correct landlord: *Mountcook Land Ltd v The Media Centre (Properties) Ltd* [2006] PLSCS 189.

[3]   Protection from Eviction Act 1977, s 2. As to whether premises are let as a dwelling, see *Wolfe v Hogan* [1949] 2 KB 194; *Ponder v Hillman* [1969] 3 All ER 694; *Patel v Pirabakaran* [2006] EWCA Civ 685, [2006] 1 WLR 3112. Note also the restrictions upon forfeiting a long lease introduced by the Commonhold and Leasehold Reform Act 2002.

[4]   *Billson v Residential Apartments Ltd* [1992] 1 AC 494.

[5]   Torts (Interference with Goods) Act 1977.

Preliminaries

13.11 Depending upon the nature of the breach, the landlord may have to go through certain preliminaries before he can re-enter. The main distinction to be drawn is between forfeiture for non-payment of rent and forfeiture for breach of any other covenant or condition.

Non-payment of rent

13.12 Before forfeiting, the landlord must have made a formal demand for the rent unless there is a provision in the lease exempting him from making such a demand. The requirements of making an effective formal demand are such that all well drawn leases will exempt the landlord from doing so by providing that the lease may be forfeited if the rent is x days in arrears 'whether formally demanded or not'.

In certain cases, where forfeiture is to be by court proceedings, even in the absence of an express exemption in the lease, the landlord is exempt from making a formal demand. Section 210 of the Common Law Procedure Act 1852 provides that a formal demand need not be made where half a year's rent is in arrear at the date of the service of proceedings and there are insufficient goods found on the premises available for distress to satisfy all of the arrears due.

If a formal demand is necessary:

> '... the landlord or his authorised agent must demand the exact sum due on the day when it falls due at such convenient hour before sunset as will give time to count out the money, the demand being made upon the demised premises and continuing until sunset'[1].

[1] Megarry & Wade, *The Law of Real Property* (5th edn, 1984), p 675 (Stevens).

Other breaches

13.13 The preliminary requirements in respect of forfeiture for breaches other than non-payment of rent are statutory and contained in s 146 of the Law of Property Act 1925[1].

Section 146 requires the landlord, in cases of forfeiture (whether the forfeiture is to be effected by physical re-entry or court proceedings[2]) other than for non-payment of rent, to serve a preliminary notice in the statutory form on the tenant[3]. Failure to comply means that the right of re-entry is unenforceable[4].

The section 146 notice must:

(a)   specify the breach complained of; and
(b)   if the breach is capable of remedy[5], require the tenant to remedy the breach; and
(c)   in any case, require the tenant to make compensation in money for the breach[6].

[1] The Leasehold Property (Repairs) Act 1938 which contains special provisions relating to the breach of repairing obligations does not apply to lettings under the ATA 1995: ATA 1995, Sch para 8.
[2] *Re Riggs, ex p Lovell* [1901] 2 KB 16.
[3] The provisions for the service of notices under s 196 of the Law of Property Act 1925 should be followed. This is not a document or notice required or authorised to be served by the ATA 1995. Section 36 of the ATA 1995 does not apply. See para 17.1.
[4] Law of Property Act 1925, s 146(1).

5   As to whether a particular breach is remediable or irremediable, see para 13.14.
6   But only if the landlord wants it: *Lock v Pearce* [1893] 2 Ch 271, CA.

13.14 The landlord can proceed to forfeit after the expiry of a reasonable time from the date of the service of the notice. What is a reasonable time will depend on the facts of each case and, where the breach is remediable, on what is a reasonable time to remedy all of the breaches complained of[1]. What is reasonable, particularly in the context of repairing obligations, will very much depend upon the facts of the case, but landlords should err on the side of generosity[2].

If the breach is irremediable, sufficient time should be given to allow the defendant to consider his position; whether or not he should admit the breach; whether he should offer any compensation and whether or not he ought to apply for relief from forfeiture[3]. Even in cases of irremediable breach, what is a reasonable time will depend upon the facts. In *Horsey Estate Ltd v Steiger*[4], two days was insufficient, but in *Civil Service Co-operative Society v McGrigor's Trustee*[5], 14 days was held to be sufficient.

The notice must contain sufficient details of the breach to enable the tenant to know what is required of him[6]. In the case of breaches of a repairing covenant it will be insufficient to state that the tenant has not repaired. The particular item in disrepair should be mentioned. The landlord does not need to inform the tenant what he needs to do to remedy the breach[7].

The notice must require the tenant to remedy the breach if it is capable of remedy. Accordingly, the distinction between remediable and irremediable breaches is of importance.

Examples of remediable breaches are:

(a)   non-payment of rent;
(b)   failure to repair;
(c)   failure to carry out works on time[8];
(d)   unauthorised alterations;
(e)   unauthorised use[9].

Examples of irremediable breaches are:

(i)   unauthorised assignment, sub-letting on parting with possession[10];
(ii)   bankruptcy or liquidation[11];
(iii) illegal or immoral user[12].

Section 146(9) of the Law of Property Act 1925 provides that a s 146 notice is not required where the forfeiture is for the tenant's bankruptcy[13] if the forfeiture clause is contained in certain types of lease. One type of lease is a lease of agricultural or pastoral land. What this means is that for cases falling within s 146(9), the tenant has no right to relief against forfeiture[14]. If a particular case does not fall within s 146(9), a s 146 notice will be required and relief will be available when forfeiting for bankruptcy or liquidation if the tenant's interest is sold within one year of the bankruptcy or liquidation on the taking of that interest in execution, but otherwise will apply only for the first year[15].

1   *Kent v Conniff* [1953] 1 QB 361, CA.
2   Some cases suggest that, in normal circumstances, three months will generally be sufficient, but it would be dangerous to rely on this rather than seek to estimate a genuine reasonable time: *Gulliver Investments Ltd v Abbott* [1966] EGD 299; *Bhojwani v Kingsley Investment Trust Ltd* [1992] 2 EGLR 70.
3   See Lord Russell LJ in *Horsey Estate Ltd v Steiger* [1899] 2 QB 79 at 91, CA.
4   [1899] 2 QB 79, CA.
5   [1923] 2 Ch 347.
6   *Fox v Jolly* [1916] 1 AC 1, HL; *Cardigan Properties Ltd v Consolidated Property Investments Ltd* [1991] 1 EGLR 64; *Adagio Properties Ltd v Ansari* [1998] 2 EGLR 69.
7   *Fox v Jolly* [1916] 1 AC 1, HL; *John Lewis Properties plc v Viscount Chelsea* [1993] 2 EGLR 77.
8   *Expert Clothing Services and Sales Ltd v Hillgate House Ltd* [1986] Ch 340, CA.
9   See eg *Cooper v Henderson* (1982) 263 Estates Gazette 592, CA; although not where the user has a stigma attached to it where the taint will linger even after the user has ceased – see para 7.1ff.
10 *Scala House and District Property Co Ltd v Forbes* [1974] QB 575, CA. Cf *Akici v L R Butlin Ltd* [2005] EWCA Civ 1296, [2006] 1 EGLR 34, [2006] 07 EG 136. See para 8.3.
11 *Civil Service Co-operative Society Ltd v McGrigor's Trustee* [1923] 2 Ch 347.
12 Where the taint will remain even after the user has ceased: *Rugby School v Tannahill* [1935] 1 KB 87, CA.
13 This includes liquidation: *Horsey Estate Ltd v Steiger* [1899] 2 QB 79, CA.
14 Either under the statutory provisions or otherwise: *Official Custodian for Charities v Parway Estates Development Ltd* [1985] Ch 151, CA.
15 Law of Property Act 1925, s 146(1).

EFFECT OF FORFEITURE

13.15 Forfeiture terminates the lease. Forfeiture takes effect upon re-entry. Re-entry by court proceedings occurs when the claim form is issued by the court. If a possession order is made, the forfeiture dates back to the date of the service of proceedings, but if the tenant obtains relief from forfeiture, it is as if the forfeiture never happened[1].

After the issue of the claim form, but before a possession order is made, the lease is in what one judge has described as the 'twilight period'[2]. The exact status of the lease during this period is unclear, but the following points can be made:

(a)   Generally speaking, the landlord cannot rely on the covenants in the lease following the service of proceedings. Although the landlord himself may be bound, at least for the purposes of applying for a mandatory injunction, where the tenant had taken the decision to apply for relief[3]. This means, for example, that damages for breach of a repairing covenant by a tenant are assessed at the date of the issue of the claim form and not when the landlord gets his possession order[4].

(b)   After forfeiture, the tenant is no longer liable to pay rent, although he will be liable for mesne profits[5] and the landlord may be able to obtain an interim payment for the tenant's use and occupation.

13.15 *Forfeiture*

Where the tenant applies for relief, and the court proceedings take a considerable amount of time to be heard, the landlord is in a difficult position, particularly as, in some cases, the tenant can still apply for relief *after* the possession order has been granted. If the tenant obtains relief, it is as if the forfeiture never happened and all covenants are enforceable for the entire period[6].

It should be noted that if the parties enter into a consent order for possession it will only be in exceptional circumstances that the court will interfere with such order[7].

1   *Liverpool Properties Ltd v Oldbridge Investments Ltd* [1985] 2 EGLR 111, CA.
2   See Sir Robert Megarry VC in *Meadows v Clerical, Medical and General Life Assurance Society* [1981] Ch 70. See also, *Maryland Estates Ltd v Joseph* [1999] 1 WLR 83, CA.
3   *Peninsula Maritime Ltd v Padseal Ltd* [1981] 2 EGLR 43, CA.
4   *Associated Deliveries Ltd v Harrison* [1984] 2 EGLR 76, CA.
5   *Capital and City Holdings Ltd v Dean Warburg Ltd* [1989] 1 EGLR 90, CA.
6   If the proceedings are discontinued, the lease is treated as not having been forfeited: *Ivory Gale Ltd v Spetale* [1998] 2 EGLR 43, CA.
7   *Fivecourts Ltd v J R Leisure Development Co Ltd* (2000) 81 P & CR 292.

RELIEF FROM FORFEITURE

Introduction

13.16 The jurisdiction to grant relief from forfeiture is complex and depends upon the nature of the covenant broken (rent or others); the method of forfeiture (actual re-entry or court proceedings); and, if by court proceedings, which court the landlord has chosen (High Court or county court). The ability to apply for relief is a right of the tenant which cannot be avoided, whether by direct contracting out or indirectly by re-casting a forfeiture provision as a break clause[1].

1   *Richard Clarke & Co Ltd v Widnall* [1976] 1 WLR 845, CA.

Jurisdiction and time limits

Non-payment of rent

13.17 The jurisdiction to allow relief from forfeiture for non-payment of rent is equitable, but supplemented or modified by statute in certain circumstances.

ISSUE OF PROCEEDINGS IN THE HIGH COURT

13.18 The court has an equitable jurisdiction to grant relief from forfeiture. However, if a tenant being at least six months' rent in arrears[1] pays all of the arrears of rent and costs before judgment, he is entitled to have the proceedings stayed by virtue of s 212 of the Common Law Procedure Act 1852. If payment is not made before judgment, s 210 of the 1852 Act limits the discretion of the High Court to a period of six months following the execution of the order for possession where the tenant owes six months' rent. If during that time the arrears and costs are paid, it is almost certain that the tenant would obtain relief. If the tenant does not apply during that six-month period[2] and his rent is at least six months in arrears, he is banned from all remedy.

It would appear that where the tenant owes less than six months' rent, he may apply, under the inherent equitable jurisdiction at any time, although delay in applying will be a relevant factor in deciding whether or not to grant relief[3].

1   *Standard Pattern Co Ltd v Ivey* [1962] Ch 432.
2   Supreme Court Act 1981, s 38.
3   *Thatcher v C H Pearce & Sons (Contractors)* [1968] 1 WLR 748.

ISSUE OF PROCEEDINGS IN THE COUNTY COURT

13.19 Under section 138(2) of the County Courts Act 1984, where a tenant pays into court or to the landlord, not less than five clear days before the return date for the hearing of the possession summons, all of the arrears of rent and the costs, the landlord's action will be stayed.

Further, the county court must postpone the making of a possession order for 28 days if the tenant seeks relief at trial. If, within that period, the tenant pays the arrears and costs, he is automatically entitled to relief[1]. After the end of that period, the tenant has to rely on the court exercising its discretion. The county court may exercise its discretion to grant relief on an application by the tenant within six months after the recovery of possession by the landlord.

1   County Courts Act 1984, s 138(3) and (4).

PEACEABLE RE-ENTRY

13.20 In the High Court, the tenant must rely on the equitable jurisdiction of the court. In the county court, the tenant can apply for relief within six months of the re-entry under s 139(2) of the County Courts Act 1984. The jurisdiction of the court to grant relief within that period is the same as the High Court.

Other breaches of covenant

13.21 In all cases, whether re-entry is actual[1] or by the issue of proceedings in the High Court or county court, the jurisdiction for granting relief is entirely statutory and is to be found in s 146(2) of the Law of Property Act 1925. The tenant can apply for relief as soon as the s 146 notice has been served on him[2], although he does not have to. The tenant's right to apply for relief is exhausted once a landlord, who has forfeited by the issue of court proceedings, has obtained an order for possession and has executed that order by entering into possession[3]. At that stage, it cannot be said that the landlord is any longer 'proceeding, by action or otherwise, to enforce his right of re-entry on forfeiture' as s 146(2) of the Law of Property Act 1925 requires. This situation can be compared with the position where the forfeiture is for non-payment of rent where, in most cases, the tenant has six months following the execution of the order for possession to apply for relief.

Where the landlord has forfeited by peaceable re-entry, there is no executed judgment to act as a cut-off point for the application for relief and hence it is a matter for the discretion of the court[4]. The longer the delay the less likely it is that the tenant will obtain relief.

1   *Billson v Residential Apartments Ltd* [1992] 1 AC 494.
2   *Billson v Residential Apartments Ltd* [1992] 1 AC 494.
3   *Billson v Residential Apartments Ltd* [1992] 1 AC 494.
4   *Billson v Residential Apartments Ltd* [1992] 1 AC 494.

Relief for persons other than the tenant

13.22 Independent rights to apply for relief are granted to mortgagees of the tenant and to sub-tenants in certain circumstances[1] and depending upon whether the breach is for the non-payment of rent or otherwise. Relief is on such terms as the court thinks fit. For sub-tenants, their right to relief is found only in s 146(4) of the Law of Property Act 1925. For mortgagees, it is under s 146(4)[2], save where the forfeiture relates to non-payment of rent, where it has additional rights to apply under the Common Law Procedure Act 1852 (if proceedings are in the High Court) or the County Courts Act 1984 (if proceedings are in the county court). Under s 146(4), the relief is the grant of a new tenancy to the sub-tenant or mortgagee before the landlord has taken possession. Relief is also available to an equitable assignee of the tenancy[3].

1   Law of Property Act 1925, s 146(4). Also see, *Duarte v Mount Cook Land Ltd* [2001] 33 EG 87(CS).
2   The mortgagee by charge or by way of legal mortgage having the same right to apply for relief as if he had a sub-lease (Law of Property Act 1925, s 8(1)): *Abbey National Building Society v Maybeech Ltd* [1985] Ch 190. An equitable chargee has a right to relief: *Bland v Ingram's Estates Ltd* [2001] 2 EGLR 23, [2001] 24 EG 163, CA; *Bland v Ingram's Estates Ltd (No 2)* [2001] EWCA Civ 1088, [2001] 2 EGLR 34, [2001] 50 EG 92.
3   *Test Valley Borough Council v Minilec Engineering Ltd* [2005] 2 EGLR 113.

Section 147 of the Law of Property Act 1925

13.23 This section applies to forfeiture based on a failure by the tenant to deal with internal decorative repairs. It gives the court additional powers to grant relief. The court can grant relief from the forfeiture *and* from the need to do the repairs, where it is satisfied that the s 146 notice is unreasonable. Section 147 will not apply:

(a)   where the liability arises under an express agreement to put the property into a decorative state of repair and the tenant has never performed the covenant;
(b)   where the matters specified are necessary for putting or keeping the property in a sanitary condition or necessary for the maintenance or preservation of the structure;

(c)   to any statutory liability to keep the house reasonably fit for human habitation;

(d)   to any covenant to yield up the premises in a specified state of repairs at the end of the term.

Guidelines for the grant of relief from forfeiture

13.24 The jurisdiction in relation to the non-payment of rent derives from the equitable jurisdiction to grant relief whenever it is just and equitable so to do. Under s 146(2), the court is directed to have regard to the proceedings and conduct of the parties and to all other circumstances and may grant relief on such terms (including as to costs; expenses; damages; compensation penalty and otherwise including the grant of an injunction to restrain future breaches) as it thinks fit.

For non-payment of rent, the payment by the tenant of all arrears and costs will usually result in his obtaining relief from forfeiture, even where there have been problems in the past with the payment of rent or historical breaches of covenants. This is because, historically, a forfeiture provision, so far as it relates to the non-payment of rent, was seen only as a security for the payment of rent, and it is possible to put the landlord back in the position he was in before the breach[1].

For other breaches, the Court of Appeal in *Rose v Hyman*[2] laid down guidelines as follows[3]:

(a)   the applicant must generally remedy those breaches capable of remedy and pay reasonable compensation for those that are not[4]

(b)   if the breach is of a negative covenant, the applicant must undertake to observe the covenant in the future or, at least, must not intend to repeat the breach;

(c)   if the act complained of is such that the court would have restrained it during the lease on the ground of waste, the applicant must, if it is possible to do so, undertake to make good the waste;

(d)   if the act complained of is one where substantial damages might be paid in an action on the covenant the applicant must undertake not to repeat the wrongful act or be guilty of a continuing breach.

Other factors which may influence the court are:

(i)   the seriousness of the breach[5];

(ii)   whether or not the breach was wilful[6];

(iii)   whether or not the landlord has relet to a third party[7];

(iv)   the personal and financial positions of each of the parties[8];

(v)   the fact that the tenant has remedied the breach or that it occurred without his knowledge or consent[9].

Even in the case of a deliberate and wilful breach or breaches resulting from the 'sloppy practice' of the tenant, the test of whether the tenant is granted relief is still an issue of proportionality[10].

1   *Ladup Ltd v Williams & Glyn's Bank plc* [1985] 1 WLR 851 and the comments of
    Lord Wilberforce at 860. Note that 'all rent in arrears' for the purposes of relief under
    section 138 County Courts Act 1984 means the total rent in arrears at the time the court
    makes it order not just that in arrears at the date of commencement of proceedings:
    Maryland Estates Ltd v Bar Joseph [1998] 2 EGLR 47, CA. Note *Inntrepreneur Pub Co
    (CPC) v Langton* [2000] 1 EGLR 34, where the tenant's ability to pay the arrears of rent
    was dependant upon the success of a damages claim against a third party and relief was
    not granted.
2   [1911] 2 KB 234.
3   The House of Lords in *Rose v Hyman* [1912] AC 623 warned against rigid rules but the
    guidelines are nevertheless useful.
4   The court may grant relief upon conditions to be fulfilled within a set period of time.
    Although extensions to that timetable may be granted, the court could run out of patience
    and order delivery up of the holding to the landlord: *Crawford v Clarke* [2000] EGCS 33,
    where the tenant's application for a third extension of time to complete repairs – required
    because the builders had left the site following the tenant's failure to pay them – was
    refused even though the works were nearly complete.
5   Particular regard being had to the difference between the value of the property and the
    extent of the damage caused.
6   *Southern Depot Co Ltd v British Railways Board* [1990] 2 EGLR 39.
7   *Fuller v Judy Properties Ltd* (1991) 64 P & CR 176, CA where relief was granted, but
    subject to the new tenant's interest. See also, *Stanhope v Haworth* (1886) 3 TLR 34, CA;
    Silverman v AFCO (UK) Ltd (1988) 56 P & CR 185, CA.
8   See *Earl Bathurst v Fine* [1974] 1 WLR 905, CA, where it was held that it was legitimate
    to take into account the personal qualifications of the tenant where they were important
    for the preservation of the value or character of the property let. Also see, *Barrett v
    Morgan* [2000] 2 AC 264, [2000] 06 EG 165, HL.
9   *Glass v Kencakes Ltd* [1966] 1 QB 611.
10 *Mount Cook Land Ltd v Hantley* [2000] EGCS 26.

Reform

13.25 At the beginning of 1994, the Termination of Tenancies Bill was
ordered to be printed by the House of Commons[1]. If the Bill had become law,
a landlord would no longer have a right of forfeiture but would be able to
bring 'termination order' proceedings in the court unless the lease specifically
excludes his right to do so. There would be no need for preliminary notices,
save in the case of a breach of a repairing obligation. The tenancy would
terminate on the date the court orders it should end: either by an 'absolute
order' that it should end on a particular day or by a 'remedial order' which
will end the lease after a specified period if certain remedial action is not taken
by the tenant. The remedial order effectively replaces the tenant's application
to apply for relief.

The Termination of Tenancies Bill was designed to remove most of the
inherent complexities in the law of forfeiture. The Bill did not proceed to
become law.

In 2004, the Law Commission published a consultation paper on termination
of tenancies for tenant default[2]. There was strong support for reform. In 2006,
the Law Commission published its final report[3], setting out its recommendations for the reform of the law and includes a draft Bill[4]. At the time of
writing, the timetable for this to be laid before Parliament remains to be
established. The proposals reflect the earlier Termination of Tenancies Bill.

1 Which will affect agricultural property, see Law Commission No 221.
2 Law Commission No 174.
3 Law Commission No 303.
4 See 'A dinosaur close to extinction', Stuart Bridge, EG 4 November 2006.

Chapter 14

OTHER METHODS
OF TERMINATION

Which will affect agricultural property see Law Commission No 22
law (Commission No 134)
Law Commission No 50)
A discussion close to exhaustion, situ.

SURRENDER

14.1 The Agricultural Tenancies Act 1995 (ATA 1995) does not prevent the termination of the tenancy by surrender[1]. Sections 5 to 7 of the ATA 1995 govern one method of termination and, while contracting out of these sections is not permitted, it does not prevent the parties from choosing to terminate in some other way.

If a tenancy is to be surrendered, it must be by all of the tenants. One cannot act unilaterally[2]. An express surrender must, to be effective at law, be by deed[3] and must be accompanied by the tenant giving up possession. There must also be conduct by the landlord accepting that the tenancy is at an end[4]. An agreement to give up possession at some date in the future is not a surrender. An agreement to surrender may also be void if it is in reality an attempt to contract out of the notice requirements of ss 5 to 7 of the ATA 1995.

Surrender may be implied by operation of law. It may, but need not, result from the tenant actually delivering up possession of the holding in an unequivocal way such as returning all keys to the landlord and vacating the holding[5], although ultimately it is a matter of the intention of the parties to be established from their conduct[6]. Other circumstances in which a surrender will be implied have been discussed in relation to ss 3 and 4 of the ATA 1995[7] and include, for example, the extension of a term date[8] or the addition of land[9] or the grant of a new lease of the same land[10]. Note that a surrender does not prejudice the rights of sub-tenants or mortgagees[11].

---

[1]   As to surrender under the Agricultural Holdings Act 1986, see Ch 33.
[2]   *Greenwich London Borough Council v McGrady* (1982) 46 P & CR 223, CA; *Hammersmith and Fulham London Borough Council v Monk* [1992] 1 AC 478, HL.
[3]   Law of Property Act 1925, s 52(1).
[4]   *Bellcourt Estates Ltd v Adisina* [2005] EWCA Civ 208, [2005] 2 EGLR 33, [2005] 18 EG 150.
[5]   *John Laing Construction Ltd v Amber Pass Ltd* [2004] 2 EGLR 128.
[6]   For examples, see *Proudreed Ltd v Microgen Holdings plc* (1995) 72 P & CR 388; *Filering v Taylor Commercials Ltd* [1996] EGCS 95, CA; *Borakat v Ealing London Borough Council* [1996] EGCS 67.
[7]   See paras 3.10ff.

8   *Re Savile Settled Estates* [1931] 2 Ch 210; *Friends' Provident Life Office v British Railways Board* (1995) 73 P & CR 9, CA.
9   *Jenkin R Lewis & Son Ltd v Kerman* [1971] Ch 477; *Friends' Provident Life Office v British Railways Board* (1995) 73 P & CR 9, CA; *Well Barn Farming Ltd v Backhouse* [2005] EWHC 1520 (Ch), [2005] 3 EGLR 109.
10 *Jenkin R Lewis & Son Ltd v Kerman* [1971] Ch 477.
11 *Mellor v Watkins* (1874) LR 9 QB 400.

MERGER

14.2 If the landlord acquires the tenant's title or the tenant the landlord's, the freehold and leasehold estates will merge and the lease is, subject to any contrary intention, extinguished.

MERGER/DENIAL OF TITLE

14.3 Other methods of termination of a tenancy at common law, such as merger, apply without special provision under the ATA 1995.

The denial of the landlord's title by the tenant allows the landlord to forfeit the lease even in the absence of an express forfeiture provision[1].

1   See Ch 13.

DISCLAIMER

14.4 Disclaimer may arise on the insolvency of the tenant[1]. A liquidator of a company may disclaim any leasehold property held by the company[2] provided that the lease is 'onerous' which will catch all leases where there is an obligation to pay rent. A trustee in bankruptcy of an individual may also disclaim in the same circumstances[3].

1   See para 45.60ff.
2   Insolvency Act 1986, s 178.
3   Insolvency Act 1986, ss 315–321.

Part V

FIXTURES AND COMPENSATION FOR IMPROVEMENTS

Contents

Chapter 15

FIXTURES AND BUILDINGS

INTRODUCTION TO FIXTURES AND COMPENSATION FOR IMPROVEMENTS

15.1 Fixtures and compensation for improvements are dealt with together because both are concerned, in most cases, with adjustments at the end of the tenancy. Both allow the tenant, by removal or by compensation, some payment for his investment in or on the landlord's land.

The relationship between fixtures and improvements under the Agricultural Tenancies Act 1995 (ATA 1995) is very different from that under the Agricultural Holdings Act 1986 (AHA 1986). Under the ATA 1995, if an item fulfils the definition of a fixture[1], and is also a tenant's improvement within s 15[2], the tenant will, in most cases, have a choice either to remove or claim compensation. Two restrictions on this choice under the AHA 1986 do not exist under the ATA 1995, namely the inability of the tenant to remove as fixtures, buildings which are also improvements and the landlord's ability to elect to take to a fixture[3]. This makes the tenant's position more straightforward under the ATA 1995.

Whether a particular item is a fixture or a chattel, and the common law position in relation to the removal of fixtures, is dealt with in the context of the AHA 1986[4]. This section will deal only with the tenant's right to remove fixtures and buildings under the provisions of s 8 of the ATA 1995.

[1]   See para 15.2.
[2]   See Ch 16.
[3]   See Ch 16.
[4]   See Ch 23.

RIGHT TO REMOVE

15.2 Subject to restrictions in s 8(2) to (4) of the ATA 1995, a tenant under a farm business tenancy is entitled to remove:

(a)   any fixtures affixed to the holding, whether affixed by the tenant under a farm business tenancy or acquired by him, for example from a previous tenant; and

(b)   any building erected by him or acquired by him from a previous tenant[1].

The ability of the tenant to take inherited or purchased fixtures is important. It is unlikely that such items, not having been provided by the tenant himself, would fall to be compensated under the statutory compensation scheme[2]. Compensation would only be available if the tenant reached express agreement with the landlord.

The distinction drawn in s 8(1) between fixtures and buildings follows the AHA 1986[3], where the treatment of buildings is slightly different. They are still capable of being fixtures, but the tenant there has no right to remove a building which is also an improvement and must instead take his compensation. The right to remove extends to fixtures 'of whatever description'. It is not confined to general agricultural fixtures. This is important in the context of an Act which anticipates non-agricultural activities. Fixtures affixed for some other commercial enterprise on the holding or, indeed, for domestic or ornamental purposes, may also be removed under the provisions of s 8[4].

1   ATA 1995, ss 8(1)(a), (b) and 8(5).
2   See the definition of tenant's improvement: ATA 1995, s 15.
3   See Ch 23.
4   As to what is a fixture as opposed to a tenant's chattel and the interrelationship of the tests directed to the degree of annexation and the purpose for which it has been affixed, see *Botham v TSB Bank plc* (1996) 73 P & CR D1, [1996] EGCS 149, CA.

15.3   The parties are unable to contract out of the provisions of s 8[1] save to the limited extent provided by s 8(2)(d). The tenant is always entitled to remove fixtures, regardless of the terms of the tenancy agreement. By virtue of s 8(7), the only right the tenant has to remove fixtures is that set out in s 8. Section 8(7) provides that the tenant under a farm business tenancy is not entitled to rely on any other right to remove, such as, for example, the common law right to remove trade fixtures. This can be compared with the position under the AHA 1986, where the tenant is still entitled to exercise his common law rights, but where the statutory ability to remove is more circumscribed.

A landlord who wishes to keep control over fixtures has only one option: he must refuse consent in the tenancy agreement to the erection of tenant's fixtures. Giving specific consent in the tenancy agreement to the erection of fixtures will, in any event, very often be consent to the erection of the fixture as an improvement for the purposes of the compensation provisions and may be something which the landlord would want to avoid. When the tenant seeks consent, as he must do to preserve his ability to claim compensation for the item as an improvement at the end of the tenancy, the landlord is able to grant consent conditionally. The condition can be that the tenant must not remove the item as a fixture[2]. The implication of s 8(2)(d), which provides that such a conditional consent will override the tenant's right to remove, is that such a condition would be acceptable as falling within s 17(3) and (4) of the ATA 1995, which allows the landlord to give consent to an improvement condition-ally so long as the condition imposed relates to the improvement in question. The alternative is for the landlord to grant consent to certain types of improvement in the tenancy agreement, conditional upon them not being removed as fixtures.

1   ATA 1995, s 8(6).
2   ATA 1995, s 8(2)(d).

RESTRICTIONS

Timing

15.4 Section 8(1) of the ATA 1995 provides that fixtures may be removed by the tenant '... at any time during the continuance of the tenancy or at any time after the termination of the tenancy when he remains in possession as tenant (whether or not under a new tenancy)'. Under the AHA 1986, by comparison, the tenant is given a period of two months after the termination of the tenancy to remove his fixtures[1].

1   See Ch 23. A proposed amendment at Committee Stage in the House of Lords to allow the same period of removal for farm business tenancies was rejected on the basis that the long notice period required to end most farm business tenancies (under ss 5 to 7) would mean that the tenant would have sufficient notice to be able to comply with rules requiring removal whilst he remained the tenant. This ignores the position following forfeiture.

15.5 'The tenancy' referred to in s 8(1) must be the tenancy in existence at the time that the fixture in question was affixed or acquired by the tenant seeking to remove. The tenant who continues to occupy under a series of farm business tenancies or, indeed, who changes from a farm business tenancy to a commercial tenancy under the Landlord and Tenant Act 1954, Pt II, will be in possession 'as tenant' and his right to remove is preserved[1]. A tenant holding over with landlord's permission may be in possession 'as tenant'. The fact that he may be a tenant at will and that such a tenancy cannot be a farm business tenancy[2] is irrelevant. A tenant who remains in possession at the end of a fixed-term farm business tenancy of more than two years, where neither party has served a notice to terminate the tenancy, remains in possession as tenant from year to year[3]. A tenant who remains on the holding without permission following the expiry of a notice to quit or the forfeiture of the tenancy will not be in possession as a tenant but as a trespasser and will no longer have any right to remove fixtures.

Section 38(5) of the ATA 1995 provides that the designations of landlord and tenant continue to apply until the conclusion of any proceedings taken in respect of compensation for improvements. It is not thought that this 'description' extends the time for the removal of fixtures. The designation is unlikely to mean that the tenant is still 'in possession' as tenant, but is likely to ease matters so far as the language of the Act is concerned where the words 'landlord' and 'tenant' are used even in respect of claims following termina-tion.

15.5 Fixtures and buildings

If it were to be found that s 38(5) did extend the tenant's right to remove fixtures until the conclusion of the compensation proceedings, it would have the logic of ensuring that the tenant's choice was exercisable at the time when he was in full possession of all information to enable him to decide whether it is better to remove the item as a fixture or to take the compensation offered. He is then able to remove fixtures save where he has actually *obtained* compensation.

The ATA 1995 does not provide for the problem of a tenancy which is forfeited. The position of a tenant where forfeiture proceedings have begun is difficult[4]. If the forfeiture is confirmed at the end of court proceedings, and the tenant has not obtained relief, the tenancy is taken to have been terminated by the forfeiture from the time of the service of the court proceedings. The tenant will have been trespassing from that date and will not, at the end of the proceedings, when he knows he will not obtain relief, be in possession as a tenant such as to enable him to remove his fixtures.

[1] Tenants will need to be aware that they may be forced into removing if this occurs and may not be able to claim compensation. Section 23 of the ATA 1995 provides for roll over of compensation claims from one farm business tenancy to another, but s 16 prevents the tenant from insisting on taking his compensation at the end of a farm business tenancy unless he is also quitting the holding.

[2] ATA 1995, s 38(1).

[3] ATA 1995, s 5(1).

[4] See Ch 13.

15.6 This raises the question of the application of the principle in *Parry v Million Pigs Ltd*[1] to forfeiture clauses in farm business tenancies to deal with the problem of the removal of fixtures. In *Parry v Million Pigs Ltd* it was held that a forfeiture clause in a tenancy agreement governed by the AHA 1986 was void because it allowed the landlord to resume possession after no notice or notice which gave the tenant insufficient time to give notice of his compensation claim. In the AHA 1986 there are specific statutory time limits within which certain claims had to be made. At common law, the right to remove fixtures is confined to the period when the tenant occupies during his term or so long as he continues to occupy with a right still to consider himself as tenant[2]. Following the termination of the lease by a forfeiture, the tenant simply loses his right to remove fixtures[3], although it is thought that he would be entitled to remove them during any court action for possession. If forfeiture is by re-entry, the tenant would simply lose his right to remove upon the re-entry being effected[4]. It is considered likely that a court would follow the common law position in connection with the removal of fixtures under s 8 and that forfeiture clauses which do not give the tenant any time to remove fixtures will still be valid, the loss of the right to remove being the price the tenant pays for being in a position which leads to a forfeiture from which the court has concluded he is not deserving of relief[5].

If this conclusion is not correct, the drafting of a successful forfeiture clause which is practical is difficult. What is a reasonable or sufficient time for the tenant to remove his fixtures? Must the tenant be put in a position of having to remove his fixtures (and thus suffer substantial interference with his farming) in case the forfeiture succeeds and his application for relief is unsuccessful or should the reasonable time for removal extend beyond the determination of the court proceedings? The problem is of vital importance. Forfeiture is going to be the main weapon in the landlord's armoury to force compliance by tenants on fixed-term farm business tenancies. A practical valuable forfeiture clause is essential but one that is void would be of no use at all.

1   (1980) 260 Estates Gazette 281.
2   *Weeton v Woodcock* (1840) 7 M & W 14.
3   *Pugh v Arton* (1869) LR 8 Eq 626.
4   See *Woodfall: Landlord and Tenant* (Looseleaf edn) Sweet & Maxwell, Vol 1, para 13.157.
     See also *Re Palmiero* [1999] 3 EGLR 27.
5   See Ch 13.

Obligation

15.7 If the fixture or building has been affixed or erected pursuant to some obligation, the tenant is not entitled to remove it under s 8[1] and would not be entitled to rely on any right in the tenancy agreement to remove it[2]. The obligation referred to in s 8(2)(a) need not be a term of the tenancy agreement, but could equally be a statutory requirement, for example in relation to pollution control measures where it would be extremely inconvenient for the landlord if it were to be removed.

1   ATA 1995, s 8(2)(a).
2   ATA 1995, s 8(7).

15.8 The fact that the fixture has been erected pursuant to an obligation does not mean that the tenant is without remedy. If consent has been given to its provision, which it necessarily will have been if the obligation was imposed by the landlord, the tenant is still entitled to compensation for the item as an improvement under Pt III of the ATA 1995, if it falls within the definition of tenant's improvement in s 15[1].

1   See para 16.2.

Replacement for landlord's fixture

15.9 Where the fixture or building replaces one which belonged to the landlord, the tenant is not entitled to remove it[1]. The tenant may be entitled to compensation for the item as an improvement[2].

1   ATA 1995, s 8(2)(b).
2   ATA 1995, Pt III and see Ch 16.

Improvements

15.10 The tenant has virtually a free choice where the item provided is both a fixture and an improvement, either to remove it or to take his compensation. There are two restrictions, as follows:

(a)   If the tenant has already obtained compensation for the item, then clearly he cannot remove it[1]. This is regardless of whether the compensation is statutory compensation under s 16 of the ATA 1995 or agreed compensation in respect of an item which does not fall within the definition of tenant's improvement in s 15[2].

(b)   Section 17 of the ATA 1995 requires a tenant to obtain landlord's consent[3] to the provision of an improvement before the tenant is entitled to compensation. The consent can be conditional upon the tenant agreeing to a variation in the terms of his tenancy provided that the variation relates to the improvement[4]. The landlord may impose a condition that the tenant must not remove the improvement and, if so, s 8(2)(d) provides that the tenant may not remove the item as a fixture.

These are the only restrictions, making the position of the tenant, compared with the AHA 1986, relatively straightforward. There is no requirement that the tenant must show that he has complied with all the terms of his tenancy agreement and is not in breach, which is an onerous provision in the AHA 1986. This makes the landlord's position worse under the ATA 1995. He cannot easily prevent removal, even though the tenant may be in default. He will have to rely on other remedies. The tenant does not have to serve any notice on the landlord of his intention to remove or, indeed, inform him of the removal. Further, the landlord does not have any right to elect to take the fixture to prevent removal, although the ability to give conditional consent to an improvement referred to above avoids the need for this to the extent that the landlord is able to forecast what he will want to do at the end of the tenancy.

[1]   ATA 1995, s 8(2)(c).
[2]   In respect of which the parties can reach their own agreement: ATA 1995, s 26.
[3]   Or, in substitute in most cases, the approval of an arbitrator.
[4]   ATA 1995, s 17(3) and (4).

DAMAGE

15.11 In removing a fixture or a building, the tenant must not do any avoidable damage to the holding[1] and is under an obligation to make good all damage caused, whether avoidable or not, immediately after removal[2]. This means to restore the property to the condition in which it was in immediately before the damage, and not that pecuniary compensation be paid[3]. Failure to comply with these obligations may expose the tenant to an action in damages.

[1]   ATA 1995, s 8(3).
[2]   ATA 1995, s 8(4).
[3]   *Wells v Ody* (1836) 5 LJ Ex 199; *Crofts v Haldane* (1867) LR 2 QB 194.

OWNERSHIP

15.12 At common law, regardless of the fact that the tenant may have certain rights to remove fixtures, the ownership of the fixture passes to the landlord immediately it becomes affixed. It becomes part of the land to which it attaches. As in the case of the AHA 1986[1], the ATA 1995 alters the common law position. It provides that for as long as the tenant has the right to remove the fixture under s 8, it remains his property[2]. This has consequences. If the fixture is the property of the tenant, it is vulnerable to enforcement proceedings by third parties pursuing the tenant. Moreover, it means that third parties with better title to the item than the tenant do not lose the right, when the item becomes affixed, of pursuing the item rather than being left with personal remedies only in the tort of conversion.

[1] AHA 1986, s 10(1).
[2] ATA 1995, s 8(1).

Chapter 16

COMPENSATION FOR IMPROVEMENTS

INTRODUCTION

16.1 The only termination claim provided for in the Agricultural Tenancies Act 1995 (ATA 1995) is compensation for the tenant in respect of tenant's improvements, as defined by s 15 of the ATA 1995. All other claims are a matter of contract between the parties. Compensation for tenant's improvements is dealt with in Pt III of the ATA 1995 which, running from ss 15 to 27 inclusive, makes Pt III the largest part of the Act. This is not because the provisions are particularly complex, but because of the fact that planning permission obtained by the tenant, which is capable of being a tenant's improvement, requires different treatment from other improvements.

Section 15 of the ATA 1995 sets out the definition of a tenant's improvement. The definition represents a new approach to that contained in previous agricultural holdings legislation. Rather than the detailed lists of the Agricultural Holdings Act 1986 (AHA 1986)[1], which it was thought would quickly become out of date, the ATA 1995 contains a wide definition capable of dealing with non-agricultural activities and of allowing for changes in the agricultural industry. A tenant's improvement may be a physical improvement, which would include some tenant-right matters, or fall into a new category called 'intangible advantages'. Intangible advantages are essentially things which cannot be seen with the eye[2] and are a recognition, to a large extent, of increasing regulation of the agricultural industry. The more matters are regulated, the more value attaches to what might broadly be called 'permission'. The category of intangible advantages recognises that fact and also that there may be other matters which add value to a holding but which are not physical.

Compensation is only payable if landlord's consent to the improvement has been obtained or, save in the case of planning permission, in the absence of such consent, an arbitrator's approval[3] and the amount payable is, in essence, the capitalised increase in the rental value of the holding arising from the provision of the improvement. Where an improvement falls within the definition of a tenant's improvement, there is no contracting out of the provisions of the ATA 1995 to avoid the payment of compensation altogether[4].

Under the ATA 1995 as originally enacted, it was not possible for the parties to substitute a measure of compensation of their own choosing. As a consequence of the RRO 2006[5], the parties now have the option of agreeing an upper limit to the amount of compensation payable[6].

The combination of the ability of the tenant in most cases to apply to an arbitrator for approval and the anti-avoidance provisions have caused landlords considerable concern about being forced into a position of paying a tenant compensation for an improvement which they did not want on the holding. This may itself have an impact on the length of farm business tenancies which landowners are prepared to grant and the extent to which they are prepared to allow freedom of use: the shorter the term and the greater the restrictions on use, the less likely it may be that an arbitrator will override a landlord's refusal of consent or, indeed, that a tenant would be prepared to invest the time and expense of an application to an arbitrator for approval.

This chapter will look in detail at the definition of tenant's improvements; the conditions for claiming compensation; the amount of compensation; compensation other than under Pt III of the ATA 1995 and the rules applicable to compensation where the tenant is quitting only part of the holding.

[1]   See Ch 38.
[2]   Whilst it is accepted that certain physical improvements cannot be seen with the eye, for example, the improvement resulting from fertilising or liming, it is in each case an improvement to the land itself rather than, in the case of an intangible advantage, to the use to which the land can be put or to the value which attaches to a particular use.
[3]   ATA 1995, ss 17–19.
[4]   ATA 1995, s 26.
[5]   The Regulatory Reform (Agricultural Tenancies) (England and Wales) Order 2006, SI 2006/2805.
[6]   See para 16.28.

TENANT'S IMPROVEMENTS

16.2 Section 15 of the ATA 1995 sets out the definition of a tenant's improvement. Any item which is not within this definition will not attract compensation under the ATA 1995. Such an item may be removable by the tenant as a fixture under the provisions of s 8[1] or may be the subject of an express compensation agreement in the tenancy agreement itself[2].

The definition of a tenant's improvement in s 15 breaks improvements down into two main categories:

(a)   physical improvements made on the holding by the tenant by his own effort or wholly or partly at his own expense[3]; and

(b)   intangible advantages obtained for the holding by the tenant by his own effort or wholly or partly at his own expense and which become attached to the holding[4].

Section 16 of the ATA 1995 makes it clear that compensation is only payable where the physical improvement is not removed and where the intangible advantage remains attached to the holding when the tenant's entitlement to claim (upon the termination of the tenancy and upon quitting the holding) arises.

1   See Ch 15.
2   ATA 1995, s 26 only restricts the parties from reaching their own agreement on compensation for items which are compensatable as tenant's improvements under the Act: see para 16.1.
3   ATA 1995, s 15(a).
4   ATA 1995, s 15(b).

16.3 There is a sub-category of physical improvements called routine improvements[1]. The only relevance of separating routine improvements into a sub-category is because of the timing of an application to an arbitrator for approval to the improvement in the absence of an acceptable consent from the landlord. Intangible advantages are divided into 'planning permissions' and 'others' with separate treatment for planning permissions in connection with eligibility for compensation and the compensation formula itself.

In the case of all improvements the following conditions apply:

(a)   The improvement must have been provided, effected or obtained for the holding by the tenant who is making the claim for compensation. Any improvement which the tenant has acquired, for example by purchase from a previous tenant or which he provided himself under an earlier AHA 1986 tenancy, will not fall within the s 15 definition. In these cases, the ability of the tenant to remove physical improvements as fixtures is important[2]. In cases where this is not helpful, the tenant will need the express agreement of the landlord to pay compensation.

(a)   The improvement must have been provided by the tenant making the claim by his own effort or wholly or partly at his own expense. This means that where the landlord provides materials and the tenant provides the labour, or where the landlord shares the costs of providing the improvement, the tenant will still have a compensation claim, although the value of that claim may be reduced by the amount of the landlord's input[3].

Where the tenant is a member of a partnership farming the land and the partnership has provided the improvement or where the tenant farms through the medium of a farming company or where the improvement has been effected by a sub-tenant, there may be difficulties in sustaining a claim. In the case of a general partnership, the tenant will be able to say that the improvement has been provided partly at his expense since he is a part-owner of the business, but has the improvement been made or obtained by the tenant? Where the tenant farms through the medium of a farming company, the position is even more difficult because of the separate legal personality of the company. In all cases, since the question of alienation to the person or body farming the land would almost invariably have to be addressed with the landlord, it may be as well to reach express agreement on compensation at the same time.

1   ATA 1995, s 19(10).
2   ATA 1995, s 8.

³ See ATA 1995, s 20(2), but only where the landlord's input is the subject of an agreement in writing.

Physical improvements and routine improvements

16.4 For the most part, the concept of a physical improvement causes no problems. It connotes the provision by the tenant of some physical item or works carried out on the holding. Whether or not such an improvement adds value (ie improved), the land itself goes to the question of compensation. Some examples are obvious: the provision of buildings or fixed equipment; drainage; pollution control systems; or the addition of gates and hedges. Some examples are less obvious but nevertheless will fall within the category of physical improvements. These are matters which would, under the AHA 1986, have made up some, but not all, of the tenant's tenant-right claim[1]. This type of physical improvement is specifically identified in s 19(10) of the ATA 1995 and called a 'routine improvement'. Routine improvements are treated separately from other physical improvements for the purpose only of the timing of any application to an arbitrator for consent to their provision.

Throughout the passage of the Bill through Parliament, concern had been expressed that compensation for tenant right was not specifically to be dealt with in the Act and was to be left to negotiation between the parties. This was not strictly the case: in so far as tenant-right matters fell within the definition of a 'physical improvement', provision was made for compensation, although many considered that the valuation formula in s 20 was wholly inappropriate.

Even to the extent that tenant-right matters fell within the definition of a physical improvement, it was felt that for such routine farming operations, the requirement to obtain the landlord's written consent with a fallback of arbitrator's approval *only* if application were made before the tenant began to provide the improvement[2] was unduly onerous and would interfere far too much with the day-to-day farming. In effect, the position would be that a tenant would end up not being compensated for physical routine farming operations if a landlord were ultimately to refuse consent as the tenant would be unlikely to have addressed his mind to applying to an arbitrator before beginning the improvement. Even if a tenant had addressed his mind to it, in the face of an unco-operative landlord, making such an application for each act of husbandry would be prohibitively expensive and practically unworkable. In many cases, where the improvement was short-lived, consent would only have to be obtained in the final year of the tenancy and, in many cases, consent could have been given in the tenancy agreement itself either directly or impliedly through the user covenant or good husbandry obligations. Nevertheless, concern remained, particularly in relation to growing crops and particularly because a farm business tenancy will, in many cases, be capable of being brought to an end during the term by forfeiture.

Accordingly, right at the very last moment, some concession in respect of tenant-right was made. On 19 April 1995, at Report Stage of the Bill in the House of Commons, an amendment was introduced by Michael Jack, the then

Minister of State, to ensure that arbitrator's approval for a 'routine improvement' could be sought retrospectively after the improvement had been provided. In effect, this meant one application, should it prove necessary, at the end of the tenancy when the tenant will know which items continue to have a value and which will be the subject of a claim for compensation.

[1]   AHA 1986, Sch 8 Pt II.
[2]   As is the case with all other physical improvements – ATA 1995, s 19.

16.5   Routine improvements are defined in ATA 1995, s 19(1) as:

(a)   physical improvements made in the normal course of farming the holding or any part of the holding;
(b)   which do not consist of the provision of fixed equipment or of an improvement to fixed equipment; and
(c)   which are not prohibited by the terms of the tenancy.

Fixed equipment is also defined in s 19(1) of the ATA 1995. The definition is very similar, though not identical, to that contained in s 96 of the AHA 1986. It has the effect of excluding from the definition of routine improvements buildings; structures; works constructed on, in, over or under the land and anything grown on the land for a purpose other than use after severance; consumption or amenity.

Routine improvements must be made in the normal course of farming the holding. While farming may cover a wider range of activities than agriculture[1], it is not intended that routine improvements could result from non-farming commercial activities. Therefore, the types of activity likely to lead to a routine improvement are growing crops, fertilising, liming, irrigation and cultivations. It is unlikely to extend to cover hefted sheep as the acclimatisation of sheep is not an improvement to the land. It certainly will not cover other tenant-right matters such as severed crops or hay, straw or silage which are no longer part of the land. As these items will fall outside of the definition of a tenant's improvements for the purposes of ATA 1995, s 15, it is open to the parties to reach their own agreement as to whether such items are to remain and, if so, the basis upon which the outgoing tenant is to be compensated[2]. It is important that these matters are addressed by the parties at the outset in the negotiations for the tenancy agreement. Indeed, given the difficulty of applying the compensation formula in ATA 1995, s 20 to most routine improvements, the greater the number of tenant-right matters left to negotiation between the parties, the better.

Improvements cannot be routine improvements if their provision is actually prohibited by the terms of the tenancy either directly or, presumably, because the improvement is in breach of the general restrictions imposed by the user covenant. This is not to say that the parties are free to negotiate their own compensation provisions by the simple expedient of prohibiting all routine improvements in the tenancy agreement. Apart from the fact that such a prohibition is likely to be in conflict with the user covenant and the general consent that that will imply, the prohibition merely means that the improvement will not be 'routine', not that it is not a physical improvement within the definition of a tenant's improvement in s 15 of the Act and hence within the compensation provisions of the ATA 1995. A general prohibition against the making of routine improvements may affect only the ability of the tenant to apply for the approval of the arbitrator to the improvement *after* the improvement has begun[3].

1   ATA 1995, s 38(2) and see Ch 3.
2   ATA 1995, s 26(2). If a particular item is not a tenant's improvement within the meaning of the Act, the parties are free to reach their own agreement.
3   ATA 1995, s 19(10).

Intangible advantages

16.6 The concept of the intangible advantage is new: it is a recognition that value can be added to a holding by things other than physical improvements and, in particular, that increasing regulation and restrictions with resultant permissions, designations and licences can have a significant impact on the use to which land can be put and on its profitability.

Only those intangible advantages which, upon provision by the tenant, become attached to the holding and which remain attached to the holding at the termination of the tenancy upon the tenant quitting the holding will attract compensation[1]. The only assistance to be gleaned from the ATA 1995 itself as to what these might be comes indirectly from other provisions within the ATA 1995.

1   ATA 1995, ss 15(b) and 16.

Planning permission

16.7 Sections 18 and 21 of the ATA 1995 deal exclusively with compensation for planning permission. Provided that the permission granted is not personal to the tenant[1], planning permissions will be intangible advantages and will fall to be compensated provided that the conditions for compensation set out in s 18 are fulfilled[2].

1   Town and Country Planning Act 1990, s 72.
2   See para 16.11.

Milk quota

16.8 Whether milk quota is an intangible advantage raises two issues. First, the nature of milk quota itself and whether it 'becomes attached to the holding'. Second, whether it was intended that milk quota should be dealt with under the provisions of the Act rather than be left as a matter for negotiation between the parties. If milk quota does attach to the holding, it is the type of asset which the phrase 'intangible advantage' is designed to catch. It adds value, not by improving the land, but by effectively enabling the land to be put to a particular use. Milk quota has been referred to as an 'advantage' in the European Court[1].

16.8 *Compensation for improvements*

Section 16(3) of the ATA 1995, which sets out the basic right to compensation, specifically excludes the application of s 13 of and Sch 1 to the Agriculture Act 1986 (AgA 1986) in relation to a farm business tenancy. This means that a tenant moving from an AHA 1986 protected tenancy on to a farm business tenancy cannot 'rollover' his compensation claim under the AgA 1986 at the end of the AHA 1986 tenancy. He can agree to a delayed payment. However, the exclusion of the AgA 1986 provisions is at least an indication that one statutory compensation scheme is to be replaced with another.

1   *R v Ministry of Agriculture Fisheries and Food, ex p Bostock* C-2/92 [1994] ECR I-955, ECJ.

16.9 The second assistance comes from Lord Howe and the then Minister of Agriculture, Fisheries and Food, Mr William Waldegrave during the parliamentary debates in relation to the Agricultural Tenancies Bill. Lord Howe stated specifically that:

> '... milk quota will count as an intangible advantage if supplied by the tenant. So he will be eligible for compensation under the Bill for any such quota that the tenant provided during the farm business tenancy which obviously remains attached to the holding at the end'[1].

When he opened the Second Reading Debate of the Bill in the House of Commons on 6 February 1995[2], William Waldegrave said of intangible advantages:

> 'Milk quotas are an extremely good example, since milk quotas – as opposed to other quotas – are attached to the land that might have been obtained by the tenant, which would be for the benefit of a holding. Therefore a tenant would have a right to compensation at the market rent for the milk quotas at the time of the ending of the tenancy'.

It was clearly envisaged that milk quota provided by the tenant would be compensated under the provisions of the Act and not otherwise. Any expressly agreed compensation provisions and any provisions which directly or indirectly amount to a contracting-out of the rights to the statutory compensation provisions in the tenancy agreement will not apply if milk quota falls to be compensated as a tenant's improvement within the meaning of s 15 of the ATA 1995.

As to the nature of milk quota itself, this has been the subject of judicial scrutiny[3].

1   *Hansard* House of Lords Cols 1213–1214, Dec 1994.
2   *Hansard* Vol 254 Col 27.
3   See para 49.16.

Others

16.10 Apart from planning permissions and milk quota, there is no indication in the ATA 1995 as to any other matters which may be intangible advantages. Having regard to the definition in s 15, the following may qualify:

(a)   environmental designations and licences;
(b)   abstraction licences;
(c)   goodwill, if it can be said to remain for the benefit of the holding and not be personal to the tenant.

Other subsidies and premium schemes such as sheep annual premium and suckler cow premium were personal to the farmer and cannot be said to attach to the land. They have been superseded by entitlements and single payments, which likewise do not attach to the land[1]. With the continuing intervention in agriculture and increasing regulation of land use and farming methods, this category of tenant's improvement may become extremely important. In the meantime, in so far as there is any difficulty in establishing the status as an intangible advantage of any particular matter, the parties should consider providing a back-up mechanism for compensation in the tenancy itself, to apply if the particular item is not an intangible advantage.

[1] See para 52.14.

ENTITLEMENT TO COMPENSATION

16.11 Section 16 of the ATA 1995 sets out the tenant's entitlement to compensation for tenant's improvements within the meaning of the ATA 1995. Section 16(1) sets out the conditions the tenant must meet, as follows:

(a)   The tenant must comply with the provisions of Pt III of the ATA 1995. In brief, this requires the tenant to have obtained the landlord's consent to the improvement in respect of which he is claiming compensation[1]. In all cases other than planning permission the tenant may be able to apply to an arbitrator for approval if he cannot obtain consent[2].
(b)   The tenant's entitlement arises when two things coincide:
   (i)   a farm business tenancy has terminated; and
   (ii)   the tenant has quit the holding.

In other words, the tenant is not entitled to compensation in the following circumstances:

 (i)   Where the tenant has left the holding, but the tenancy continues. For example, a fixed-term tenancy with no break clause does not entitle the tenant to serve notice to quit. The tenant remains subject to all of the obligations of the tenancy agreement throughout the term[3] and cannot make his compensation claims.
 (ii)   The tenancy has terminated but the tenant remains in possession. This is regardless of whether the tenant's continuing occupation of the holding is as a trespasser; holding over with the permission of the landlord or as the result of a new tenancy – whether a farm business tenancy or a commercial letting under Part II of the Landlord and Tenant Act 1954 or simply a common law letting.
 (iii)   At the termination of the tenancy, the letting is not a farm business tenancy. This could happen either as a result of non-compliance with the business conditions at any time during the tenancy or because the

187

tenancy does not comply with the agriculture condition at termination and notices were not served at the outset[4].

1   ATA 1995, ss 17 and 18.
2   ATA 1995, s 19.
3   Save where he assigns and the provisions of the Landlord and Tenant (Covenants) Act 1995 apply.
4   See Ch 3.

16.12 In considering a tenant's entitlement to claim, the interaction of three statutory provisions needs to be considered:

(a)   Section 16 which sets out the basic entitlement.
(b)   Section 22 which contains, inter alia, the timetable within which the tenant must make his claim.
(c)   Section 23 which provides for compensation where the tenant has been in possession under a series of farm business tenancies.

The position is as follows:

(i)   Section 16 provides that the entitlement to compensation arises on termination of the tenancy upon the tenant quitting the holding.
(ii)   If the tenant does not quit the holding, but remains in possession, his entitlement to compensation does not arise.
(iii) Section 22 provides that any claim for compensation must be made within two months of the termination of the tenancy.
(iv)   Without more, if the tenant does not quit the holding within the two months following termination, for whatever reason, he has no entitlement to claim and, when he does quit, he will be out of time for claiming.
(v)   Two provisions exist in the ATA 1995 to assist the tenant to some extent:
  (a)   Section 22(5) of the ATA 1995 which extends the period for a tenant who lawfully remains in occupation of part of the holding after termination. It provides that, in the case of a claim relating to that part of the holding, the time periods are to run from the termination of that occupation. This will clearly cover the situation where, for example, the tenant is holding over in the buildings, but it is far from clear that it would assist a tenant who remained in occupation of the entire holding under a new tenancy not within the ATA 1995. It should also be noted that s 22(5) only applies where the tenant lawfully remains in occupation. If the tenant remains in occupation because he believes that the landlord has incorrectly exercised an option to break, he must protect himself. The advice is the same as it has always been under the AHA 1986. A tenant in such circumstances should serve his notice without prejudice to his contention that the tenancy is continuing.
  (b)   In certain cases where the tenant does not quit the holding, his right to claim compensation is preserved during subsequent tenancies. Section 23 of the ATA 1995 provides that if the tenant under a farm business tenancy has remained in the holding

188

during two or more such tenancies, his right to compensation shall be rolled over through the tenancies until he actually quits the holding. At that stage he claims his compensation and it does not matter that the improvement in respect of which he is claiming was not provided during the tenancy at the termination of which he quits the holding.

The latter provision is clearly important, particularly if a pattern is established of letting to the same tenant on a series of relatively short farm business tenancies. However, certain problems remain for the tenant. Rollover of compensation through successive farm business tenancies is not an option for the tenant. He has no choice. If he can persuade the landlord to agree, s 23(2) allows the parties to agree that the tenant should take the compensation at the termination of the tenancy even though at that termination the tenant remains on the holding under a new tenancy. Reaching agreement with the landlord could be important in three circumstances.

It is clear from the wording of s 23(1) and s 16(1) of the ATA 1995 that the ability to roll over only applies where the later tenancies are farm business tenancies. If the tenant remains on the holding under, for example, a letting under Pt II of the Landlord and Tenant Act 1954, his right to compensation for tenant's improvements under the ATA 1995 may be lost. If the move from one type of tenancy to another is conscious, the tenant should insist on the landlord's agreement under s 23(2) to take his compensation at the end of the farm business tenancy. This will not help in two situations:

(A)   Where the parties believed that the new letting would be a farm business tenancy but where, for example, because the primary use was no longer agriculture, the new letting was a commercial letting under the Landlord and Tenant Act 1954.
(B)   Where on a highly diversified estate there has been an inadvertent surrender and re-grant, and where the agricultural use of the holding was too limited on the re-grant to make the tenancy a farm business tenancy and where s 3 of the ATA 1995[1] does not assist.

Section 23(1) of the ATA 1995 provides for roll over where the tenant has remained in 'the holding' during two or more farm business tenancies. 'Holding' is defined in s 38 of the ATA 1995 as meaning '… the aggregate of the land comprised in the tenancy'. It is possible to interpret this to mean that the roll-over provisions are only available where the land in the new and the old farm business tenancies are the same. While there are provisions in the ATA 1995 to deal with the situation where the landlord has resumed possession of part[2], both in relation to improvements on the part and on the remaining land, those provisions seem to assume the continuance of the old farm business tenancy. They do not deal with the situation where a new farm business tenancy contains less or more land than the old. Unless s 23(1) can be interpreted to mean that the farm business tenant remains on part of the holding under a new tenancy, rights to compensation may be lost. He has not quit the entire holding, but he is not in possession of the entire holding either.

189

16.12 *Compensation for improvements*

There may be circumstances, other than those where the right to compensation might otherwise be lost, where the tenant would be advised to seek his landlord's agreement to take his compensation early under s 23(2). An improvement which has cost a considerable amount of money, and which may be worth a lot to the tenant at the end of one farm business tenancy, may be worthless in terms of compensation at the end of a subsequent farm business tenancy. The tenant may prefer to take his compensation earlier. Two things need to be considered. First, if the landlord can clearly see that the improvement will be worthless at the end of the new farm business tenancy, he may not agree to pay. Second, the tenant needs to take into account the impact of having received compensation on the initial rent for the new letting and on any subsequent rent review when that improvement will not be a disregard.

1   See Ch 3.
2   See para 16.34ff.

CONSENT OF THE LANDLORD

16.13 As a condition of claiming compensation in respect of an improvement, the tenant must have obtained the landlord's consent to the provision of the improvement. This is so even in the case of routine improvements, such as liming, fertilising or growing crops. In the case of routine improvements, provided that such activities are not in breach of his tenancy agreement, in many cases where the improvement or added value is short-lived, the tenant may decide to obtain consent only in the last year of the tenancy when his compensation claim will be made. In all cases other than planning permission, the approval of an arbitrator may be substituted if the landlord does not consent, but consent must have been sought first[1]. If the tenancy agreement contains a blanket refusal the tenant should still apply for consent. Time will not start to run under s 19(1)(b) of the ATA 1995 until he does so.

The landlord's consent must be in writing. It can be in the tenancy agreement but need not be[2]. In the case of improvements other than planning permission the consent must be to the 'provision of the tenant's improvement'. In the case of planning permission, it must be to the 'making of the application for planning permission'[3].

Consent may be given in the tenancy agreement to a particular improvement or to a class of improvements. For example, the parties may agree to give blanket consent to all routine improvements consistent with the use by the tenant of the holding in accordance with the user provisions in the tenancy agreement.

1   ATA 1995, s 19(1).
2   ATA 1995, s 17(2).
3   ATA 1995, ss 17(1) and 18(1)(a) respectively.

16.14 It may be possible to give consent indirectly in the tenancy agreement through the obligations which are placed upon the tenant. Placing an obligation upon the tenant to farm in a particular manner or in accordance with certain husbandry requirements must impliedly give consent to do all

190

matters necessary to fulfil these obligations. A permission for a particular use as opposed to an obligation, may not amount to consent, although each case will turn on its facts. For example, a user covenant which permitted the use of the holding only as a dairy farm and where no quota has been provided by the landlord may be taken as an indirect consent to the tenant to bring milk quota onto the holding. In all cases, however, the tenant would be far safer obtaining a separate and specific written consent from the landlord.

There is no requirement that the tenant should obtain the landlord's consent before he has begun to provide the improvement. If he does not, he has worsened his position in respect of all improvements other than planning permission and routine improvements. For all other improvements, the alternative of obtaining the approval of the arbitrator should the landlord refuse consent is only available before the tenant has begun to provide the improvement[1]. Once he has started, it is too late. While he can then seek his landlord's consent which, if given, will enable him to claim compensation, he has no recourse to arbitration should the landlord refuse. That inevitably puts the tenant in a weak bargaining position. For planning permission, the alternative of arbitration is not available[2]. For routine improvements, the tenant can apply to an arbitrator even after the improvement has been provided[3].

The problem highlighted above is particularly acute in relation to the improvement to the holding by the provision of milk quota where the tenant might easily begin to provide the improvement inadvertently. The moment that the tenant, relying on his own milk quota, begins to use the holding for milk production, he has begun to provide the improvement. The Dairy Produce Quotas Regulations 2005[4] will require an apportionment of the milk quota across all of the land used by the tenant in his milk production on the termination of the tenancy and this will inevitably lead to an apportionment in favour of the holding[5]. Any tenant taking a farm business tenancy where the holding is to be used at all for milk production needs to ensure that consent is given in the tenancy agreement and before the beginning of the tenancy for the provision of milk quota as an improvement[6].

1   ATA 1995, s 19(2).
2   ATA 1995, ss 17(5) and 19(1)(a).
3   ATA 1995, s 19(2).
4   SI 2005/465.
5   *Puncknowle Farms Ltd v Kane* [1985] 2 EGLR 8, (1985) 275 Estates Gazette 1283 for the meaning of this phrase.
6   See the section on contracting-out at para 16.32 for the status of the usual milk quota indemnity clauses.

16.15 The landlord may give consent upon condition that the tenant agrees to a specified variation in the terms of the tenancy[1]. In the case of improvements other than planning permission, such a variation must relate to the improvement itself. In the case of planning permission it must relate to the physical improvement or change of use in respect of which planning permission is to be sought[2]. Permitted variations would be things such as:

(a)   repairing obligations relating to the improvement;

16.15 *Compensation for improvements*

(b) insurance provisions relating to the improvement;
(c) specific requirements as to the structure, materials and siting of a physical improvement;
(d) a condition that the tenant shall not remove the improvement at the end of the tenancy as a fixture[3]; and
(e) the use to which the improvement might be put.

The conditions cannot relate to compensation as this would be contrary to the anti-avoidance provisions in s 26(1)[4] and neither, it is submitted, can they provide for an increase in rent.

In relation to consent for an application for planning permission under s 18 of the ATA 1995, the consent must be expressed to be given for the purpose of either:

(i) enabling a specified physical improvement such as would fall within the definition in s 15(a) to be provided lawfully by the tenant; or
(ii) enabling the tenant lawfully to effect a specified change of use[5].

The purpose of the compensation provisions relating to planning permissions is not to provide the tenant with a windfall benefit. He is only entitled to consent where the purpose of obtaining the planning permission is to carry out a particular development or obtain authorisation for an anticipated change of use and not simply to improve the value of the land. If the physical improvement has been completed or change of use effected by the date of the termination of the tenancy, the tenant is not entitled to compensation in respect of the planning permission. The amount of compensation in respect of any resulting physical improvement will reflect the fact that it was authorised by a planning permission[6] but no separate payment will be due. Section 18(1)(c) makes it clear that compensation is only payable in respect of a planning permission where the physical improvement or change of use specified in the consent has not been completed or effected as the case may be. This is likely to happen where the tenancy is brought to an end early, for example by forfeiture or the operation of a break clause or where unforeseen circumstances prevent the tenant from completing the works. It is to obtain compensation in these circumstances that a tenant, when seeking consent to a physical improvement or change of use, should also seek consent to the application for planning permission itself.

The tenant should always seek the consent of the landlord by a request in writing. In cases other than consent to planning permission, this is to start time running for the purposes of s 19(1)(b) should the landlord not respond and should the tenant wish to proceed to arbitration[7].

1 ATA 1995, ss 17(3) and 18(2).
2 ATA 1995, ss 17(4) and 18(3).
3 ATA 1995, s 8(2)(d) envisages such a condition.
4 See para 16.32ff.
5 ATA 1995, s 18(1)(b)(i) and (ii).
6 ATA 1995, s 20(3).
7 See para 16.17.

REFUSAL OF CONSENT

16.16 This convenient shorthand is used to cover three situations:

(a)   the landlord refuses consent to the improvement;

(b)   the landlord does not respond to a tenant's written request for consent within two months;

(c)   the landlord gives consent but subject to conditions which the tenant does not wish to accept.

For the purposes of this section, it is necessary to consider separately physical improvements (other than routine) and intangible advantages (other than planning permissions); routine improvements and planning permissions.

Improvements other than routine improvements or planning permissions

16.17 If the tenant has begun to provide the improvement, he can still seek the landlord's consent, but should it be refused, should his request go unanswered for two months, or should the landlord wish to impose onerous conditions, the tenant will be unable to give notice to refer the matter to arbitration[1]. It is essential that the tenant should establish the landlord's reaction, and request his consent, before he has begun the improvement. If he does not, at the very best he may have to accept onerous conditions from a landlord who realises he is in a weak bargaining position. At worst the landlord may refuse consent and the improvement will go uncompensated[2]. If, in these circumstances, the landlord does seek to impose onerous conditions, it should be remembered that he is only entitled to do so if the resultant variation in the terms of the tenancy relates to the improvement in question. It is unclear what the tenant could do if the conditions were unrelated in circumstances, where he was not in a position to apply to an arbitrator under s 19 of the ATA 1995. It may be possible, theoretically, for the tenant to seek arbitration in relation to the issue of whether the conditions did relate to the improvement under the general arbitration provisions in s 28 of the ATA 1995[3]. It may be possible in these circumstances for the landlord simply to withdraw his conditional consent, not accepted by the tenant, and leave the tenant without remedy.

Assuming that the tenant has not begun to provide the improvement, s 19(1) of the ATA 1995 provides that if the tenant is 'aggrieved' by:

(a)   the refusal of the landlord to grant consent; or

(b)   the landlord's failure to grant consent within two months of a written request by the tenant; or

(c)   the variations in the tenancy which the landlord requires as a condition of granting consent,

he can apply to arbitration.

---

[1]   ATA 1995, s 19(2).

[2]   If the improvement is a fixture, the tenant may be able to remove it under s 8 of the ATA 1995.

[3]   See para 47.3.

16.18 To avoid delay and to start time running under (b) in 16.17 above, the tenant should make all requests for consent in writing in the first instance.

As far as the conditions imposed by the landlord are concerned, the tenant will be able to demand arbitration where either he believes that the conditions do not relate to the improvement in question or where the conditions do relate to the improvement in question but the tenant regards them, for whatever reason, as unreasonable or unacceptable. The imposition of such conditions on consent by the landlord is a gamble because of the combination of the limited jurisdiction of the arbitrator and s 19(8) of the ATA 1995[1].

The tenant must give notice in writing to the landlord demanding that the question (the issue in respect of which he is 'aggrieved') be referred to arbitration. There are no provisions as to the form of such notice or as to its contents. The service requirements in ATA 1995, s 36 will apply[2].

The tenant has a limited time within which to serve his notice. If his complaint is the refusal of consent by the landlord or the imposition of unacceptable conditions, his notice must be 'given' (as defined in s 36(2)) within two months of being given notice of the refusal or conditional consent[3]. If the application is because of the landlord's failure to respond, the tenant has two months to serve his notice following the expiry of two months from the written request made by the tenant. In other words, the notice must be served within four months of the written request but cannot be served until the landlord has failed to respond for two months[4].

If the tenant fails to serve his demand for arbitration on time, he cannot proceed to arbitration based upon that refusal; failure; or conditional consent. There is nothing in the ATA 1995 to prevent the tenant from reiterating his request for consent and then applying to an arbitrator.

[1]   See para 16.21ff.
[2]   See para 17.2.
[3]   ATA 1995, s 19(3)(a).
[4]   ATA 1995, s 19(1)(b) and (3)(b).

Routine improvements

16.19 The position in respect of routine improvements is exactly the same as for other improvements (other than planning permission) save in one respect. The tenant is entitled to demand arbitration even after he has begun to provide or has provided the improvement in question[1]. This distinction was introduced very late during the final stages of the Bill in the House of Commons and is a recognition of the impossible task a tenant would have were he to have to seek consent in respect of every act of husbandry in the absence of a blanket consent in the tenancy agreement itself. As a result of the fact that he can apply to an arbitrator after he has provided the improvement, the tenant need, in effect, do nothing until the tenancy is to terminate. He can then assess those routine improvements which are likely to result in a compensation payment as likely at the time of termination to lead to an increase in value of the holding as land comprised in a tenancy;[2] seek consent

194

in respect of those items and, if it is not forthcoming, demand arbitration. This is clearly what is envisaged. Section 22 of the ATA 1995, which provides for arbitration as to the amount of compensation, envisages that the arbitration as to consent to routine improvements and as to the amount payable at the termination of the tenancy in respect of those improvements, may take place at the same time. Section 22(4) of the ATA 1995 provides that in such circumstances, upon an application, the President of the Royal Institution of Chartered Surveyors (RICS) shall appoint the same person on both applications and for one fee.

[1]   ATA 1995, s 19(2).
[2]   See the compensation formula in the ATA 1995, s 20(1).

Planning permissions

16.20 Section 19(1) of the ATA 1995 provides for the aggrieved tenant to demand arbitration in respect of consents sought under s 17 of the ATA 1995. Subsection (5) provides that s 17 does not apply where the tenant's improvement consists of planning permission. Hence, subject to what was said at para 16.17 above regarding the tenant's ability to apply for a general arbitration under section 28 in respect of the imposition of conditions not related to the improvement or change of use, the tenant has no fall-back of arbitration. In many instances, a tenant who wishes to effect, for example, a physical improvement will require planning permission and will require the consent of the landlord both to the planning permission and to the improvement itself. Consent to the planning permission is sought only in case the tenant is unable, for whatever reason, to implement it. It is only in those circumstances that a separate compensation payment will be made[1].

If the landlord refuses consent to the application for permission and to the provision of the physical improvement, there is nothing to stop the tenant from applying for planning permission and proceeding to arbitration for consent to the physical improvement. Indeed, if he is to go to the expense of an arbitration on the improvement, it may be as well to ensure that planning permission is forthcoming first. The risk for the tenant is that if he obtains the arbitrator's approval to the physical improvement, but does not complete it before the end of the tenancy, there will be no compensation in respect of the unimplemented permission. Before taking any decisions, the tenant will therefore consider the length of term remaining; the ability of the landlord to break the tenancy early (either by break options or by forfeiture) and the likelihood, within those confines, of his implementing the permission.

[1]   ATA 1995, s 18(1)(c).

THE CONSENT ARBITRATION

16.21 Once the tenant has served notice demanding arbitration, the position is as follows:

16.21 *Compensation for improvements*

(a) If no arbitrator has been appointed by an agreement made since the notice demanding arbitration was given, either party may apply to the President of the RICS for the appointment of an arbitrator by him.

(b) To prevent an application to the President of the RICS, any agreement to appoint must be reached after the service of the notice demanding arbitration and cannot be agreed in advance, for example, in the tenancy agreement.

(c) The application to the RICS must be made in writing and accompanied by such reasonable fee as the President determines[1].

(d) The arbitration will be conducted by a sole arbitrator[2] and, if consent is being sought in respect of routine improvements at the same time as an application in respect of compensation for these improvements, the same arbitrator will be appointed to determine both issues.

There is no time limit within which the application must be made to the President of the RICS. There are sufficient controls to ensure that an application is made, should the tenant wish to proceed, within s 19(9) which applies in all cases, save in respect of routine improvements. Section 19(9) effectively stops the arbitration process should the tenant begin to provide the improvement at any stage after the service of his demand for arbitration but before approval of the arbitrator has been made. The tenant cannot 'jump the gun'. If he does so, the arbitration will be terminated and the tenant will then be unable to obtain compensation for the improvement. He cannot start the arbitration process again following a further request of the landlord because he will have begun to provide the improvement.

The provisions of s 19(9) of the ATA 1995 are as follows:

(i) If the tenant begins to provide the improvement following the service of his demand for arbitration, no application can then be made to the President for the appointment of an arbitrator.

(ii) If the tenant begins to provide the improvement following an application to the President of the RICS but before the appointment of the arbitrator, the application is treated as being ineffective.

(iii) If an arbitrator has already been appointed at the time that the tenant begins to provide the improvement, whether that appointment was following an agreement between the parties or an application to the President of the RICS, his jurisdiction becomes limited to an award in respect of the costs of the reference and the award. He cannot make any award regarding his approval or otherwise to the improvement in question.

1 ATA 1995, s 30(2).
2 ATA 1995, s 30(1).

16.22 The arbitrator's task, once appointed, is set out in s 19(5) of the ATA 1995. He is to:

'... consider whether, having regard to the terms of the tenancy and any other relevant circumstances (including the circumstances of the tenant and the landlord), it is reasonable for the tenant to provide the tenant's improvement'.

The things which are likely to have a particular impact on the decision of the arbitrator are as follows:

(a)   The length of the unexpired term of the tenancy. If the tenancy is a long fixed-term tenancy with a good number of years remaining, the tenant is more likely to obtain approval. With a periodic tenancy; a fixed-term tenancy with break clauses allowing the landlord to break on a short cycle; or a fixed-term nearing its expiry, the tenant is less likely to obtain consent when the factors listed below are taken into account. Indeed, it is less likely that the tenant would apply in those circumstances, particularly if he has any expectation of a new tenancy from the landlord.

(b)   The anticipated life of the improvement when compared with the unexpired term. In other words, how likely it is that the landlord will have to pay compensation[1].

(c)   The suitability of the proposed improvement to the size, location, and nature of the holding and whether it is likely to be of use/interest to the landlord or next tenant.

(d)   How the improvement fits with any restrictions in the tenancy agreement, for example, in the user covenants. It would only be in the most unusual circumstance that a tenant would obtain the approval of an arbitrator to an improvement which could only be used in connection with an activity prohibited by the terms of the tenancy[2].

(e)   Whether the refusal of consent was to a specific request of the tenant only or whether it mirrored a restriction in the tenancy agreement. While it is clear that the tenant is able to apply to the arbitrator, even in the light of a prohibition in the tenancy agreement against the provision of improvements, that prohibition will be a factor that the arbitrator will take into account. It is difficult to predict what weight the arbitrator will attach to it. It can be seen as simply a refusal of consent at an earlier stage. Alternatively, it is a prohibition which the tenant was aware of at the outset and which was part of the bargain he reached. It is something which he agreed to rather than had imposed on him after agreement and would have been a factor in determining, for example, the amount of rent he was prepared to pay and whether he was prepared to enter into the tenancy. There will be circumstances when an arbitrator would be prepared to override such a prohibition. For example, perhaps where the improvement was necessary to comply with new statutory or regulatory requirements or where circumstances or farming methods have so changed since the commencement of the lease that the provision of the improvement is reasonable.

(f)   The arbitrator is specifically directed to take into account the circumstances of the tenant and the landlord. For the tenant, this must include his ability to continue to farm without the improvements; the profitability of the farm; and his exposure to criminal liability for breach of any statutory or regulatory requirements. For the landlord it could include what he intends to do with the holding at the end of the tenancy; his financial circumstances; and whether he would be in a position to be able to afford to pay the statutory compensation to the tenant.

(g)   If the landlord has given consent subject to the tenant agreeing to a specified variation in the terms of the tenancy, the arbitrator will be

197

able to take the reasonableness or otherwise of those conditions into account. If they are unreasonable, he can give consent to the improvement. If they are reasonable, the correct course would be for him to refuse consent knowing that the tenant can then go back and rely on the conditional consent[3].

(h) An offer by the landlord to provide the improvement will be another factor which will be taken into account. The landlord may prefer to do this and get his return through a rent increase at the next rent review, rather than to have the uncertainty of a compensation claim. How far it weighs with the arbitrator will depend on the circumstances. For example, the cost to the tenant of providing the improvement compared to the likely increase in rent should the landlord provide it, will be something to consider and weigh against, inter alia, the personal financial circumstances of the parties.

Having considered all relevant factors, the arbitrator must determine whether or not it is *reasonable* for the tenant to provide the improvement. It is an exercise in balancing competing interests. The tenant does not need to show that the improvement is necessary. If the arbitrator concludes that it is reasonable to provide the improvement, he must unconditionally approve the provision of the improvement. If not, he must withhold his approval. Unlike the landlord, the arbitrator may not give his approval subject to any conditions, nor can he seek to vary conditions imposed by the landlord[4]. A decision by a landlord to grant conditional consent is, therefore, something of a gamble: it is not such a great gamble for the tenant. If the conditions imposed are too harsh and the tenant proceeds to arbitration, the landlord may well end up with an improvement over which he has no control in terms of siting, materials, construction, timing, etc because the arbitrator's approval will be without any conditions whatsoever. If the tenant fails at arbitration and the arbitrator withholds his approval, the tenant can return to and accept the conditional consent. Section 19(8) of the ATA 1995 provides that the withholding of approval by the arbitrator in these circumstances '... shall not affect the validity of the landlord's consent or of the condition subject to which it was given'.

If the arbitrator gives his approval to the provision of the improvement, s 19(7) provides that approval shall have effect as if it were the consent of the landlord, both for the purposes of Pt III of the ATA 1995 and for the purposes of the terms of the farm business tenancy. In respect of the latter, it means that a tenant who implements an arbitrator's approval in the light of a prohibition in the tenancy agreement will not put himself in breach of covenant.

---

[1] See the valuation formula in the ATA 1995, s 20(1).
[2] See Ch 7 for considerations in drafting user covenants.
[3] ATA 1995, s 19(8).
[4] ATA 1995, s 19(6).

AMOUNT OF COMPENSATION – IMPROVEMENTS OTHER THAN PLANNING PERMISSION

The statutory formula

16.23 Section 20 of the ATA 1995 contains the formula for the amount of compensation due in respect of all tenant's improvements other than those consisting of planning permissions. The idea behind the formula is not unique. It is similar in concept to the formula for long-term improvements under the AHA 1986, as set out in s 66(1) of the Act. It is not related to the cost to the tenant in providing the improvement. It is designed to ensure that it is the tenant, rather than the landlord, who takes the benefit of the improvement for its entire life. In other words, it is restitutionary in nature and prevents the potential unjust enrichment of the landlord at the tenant's expense. It assumes that after the termination of the tenancy the improvement will produce an income for the landlord and diverts that income, through a capitalised lump sum, to the tenant.

Section 20(1) of the ATA 1995 provides that the compensation payable to the tenant shall be '… an amount equal to the increase attributable to the improvement in the value of the holding at the termination of the tenancy as land comprised in a tenancy'. The question to be asked is whether the improvement in question would lead to the payment of a higher rent by a tenant. What is the rent which the holding could command without the improvement and what is the rent which the holding could command with the improvement? If the latter is higher, the difference is capitalised by reference to the anticipated remaining life of the improvement at the end of the tenancy and that sum represents the compensation payable to the tenant.

The assumption in the valuation formula is that the land will continue to be let but with the benefit of the improvement. No guidance is given as to the nature of the letting. It is the increase in the value of the holding as land comprised in *a* tenancy, not *the* tenancy under which the claimant tenant has been holding and not, it would seem, necessarily a farm business tenancy. This position can be compared with the AHA 1986 where it is made clear in s 66(1) of the AHA 1986 that the assumption is that the land will continue to be let on a fully protected AHA 1986 tenancy[1].

Without the effectively lifetime security of tenure of the AHA 1986, the next question is what assumption is to be made about the length of the tenancy? Once again there is no guidance but, in order to make sense of what s 20 of the ATA 1995 is trying to achieve, the assumption must be that the land is let for at least as long as the anticipated remaining life of the improvement in question in order to ensure that the landlord pays the tenant in respect of the entire time during which he could exploit the improvement, by gaining an increased return from the holding as a result of it.

[1]   See Ch 37.

16.24 While one is to assume that the land is to continue to be let, the assumption is not that a tenant could be found who would want or need the improvement. That is part of the investigation into whether the improvement would result in an increased rent being attainable. If the improvement is particularly esoteric or of a particularly specialised nature so that any tenant is unlikely to use it, it may actually result in a decrease in the rent to compensate the tenant for maintenance obligations. In these circumstances, no compensation would be payable.

There is no guidance on the terms of the assumed letting. If, for example, a tenant has accepted a conditional consent from the landlord on condition that he agrees to particularly onerous repairing obligations in respect of the improvement, is one to assume that those obligations are in the hypothetical letting?

Whether or not the improvement will increase the letting value of the land is determined at the termination of the tenancy upon the tenant quitting the holding. All of the risk is on the tenant. Changes in technology, fashion or regulatory controls may all mean that an improvement with an otherwise long anticipated remaining life does not add any value to the holding as land comprised in a tenancy at the end of the term. Indeed, the investigation into the anticipated remaining life of the improvement, which will determine the years' purchase to be applied to capitalise the rental increase, will take into account the likelihood of such changes after the termination of the tenancy. For example, the uncertainty surrounding the future of milk quota may well mean that a relatively low year's purchase could be justified. Combine that with the application of the section 20(1) formula and a tenant may find that the statutory compensation for milk quota (assuming that it is an intangible advantage and falls to be compensated under the ATA 1995) is less than its capital value were it to be sold on the open market.

The same valuation formula is applicable to all improvements[1] whether that improvement is a building or an act of husbandry such as fertilising or growing crops. Industry attempts to persuade DEFRA to provide a different basis of valuation for routine improvements, possibly based on the value to an incoming tenant, failed. Accordingly, the compensation for growing crops, fertilising, liming, cultivations, unexhausted and residual manual values, etc is the capitalised increased rent which a tenant would be prepared to pay as a result of these improvements. The calculation could be difficult, and more difficult than the sums would often justify given the relatively minor nature of some of the works and the fact that many such improvements will be relatively short-lived. In response to concerns expressed along these lines, the only comfort offered was a statement by Michael Jack (the then Minister of State at the Ministry of Agriculture Fisheries and Food) in the House of Commons as follows:

> 'Some concern has been expressed that [the valuation formula] could result in routine improvements, which may have a small value relative to the overall value of the holding, being overlooked. However, the same principles of valuation will apply for small and routine improvements as for large ones. If they add value, they should be compensated accordingly'[2].

The need is for an agreed professional practice will establish itself amongst land agents and valuers, either informally or through the guidance of the professional bodies[3].

1   Save for planning permissions, as to which, see paras 16.20 and 16.29ff.
2   *Hansard* 19 April 1995, Col 245.
3   See CAAV Publication No 166, 'Commentary on the Valuation of Improvements under the Agricultural Tenancies Act 1995' December 1995.

16.25 The assumption in the valuation formula in s 20(1) of the ATA 1995 is that each improvement should be identified and its impact on the value of the holding assessed separately. Where each improvement is looked at, it should be remembered that the comparison is with the holding without that improvement but with all of the other improvements in place. The base rent should be identified accordingly. The circularity and double counting that this could lead to is unfortunate. This could result, in appropriate cases, in an agreement between valuers to take a more global view of the overall impact of the improvements in question[1].

Planning permissions may attract compensation in their own right. Such compensation is only payable where the specified physical improvement has not been completed or the change of use effected[2]. Section 20(4) of the ATA 1995 makes it clear that this restriction on separate compensation does not mean that no account is to be taken of implemented planning permissions. Where a physical improvement or intangible advantage (resulting from a change of use) adds more value to the holding because it was authorised by planning permission, this is something which can be taken into account when determining the amount of compensation payable in respect of the physical improvement or intangible advantage.

Once the amount of compensation payable in respect of the improvement has been determined in accordance with the section 20(1) formula, the next stage is to establish whether there are any deductions to be made from that base sum. Subsections (2) and (3) of s 20 contain provisions for reducing the amount payable in respect of benefits provided by the landlord and grants obtained by the tenant.

1   The advice of the CAAV to its members (see their 'Commentary on the Valuation of Improvements under the Agricultural Tenancies Act 1995', Publication No 166) is that valuers should consider each improvement separately but should recognise that a claim which would unjustly enrich the tenant may not be upheld.
2   ATA 1995, s 18(1)(c).

Benefits provided by the landlord

16.26 A benefit given or allowed to the tenant will reduce the amount of compensation payable in respect of the relevant improvement where:

(a)   the agreement to give or allow the benefit is in writing, whether contained in the tenancy agreement or otherwise; and

(b)   the benefit given or allowed is in consideration of the provision of the tenant's improvement in question.

16.26 *Compensation for improvements*

The benefit need not be directly related to the improvement. In other words, it does not need to be a contribution by the landlord to the cost of providing the improvement or the provision of labour or materials to assist in its construction. The *reason* for the provision of the benefit must be the corresponding provision by the tenant of the tenant's improvement. So, for example, benefits as diverse as a rent reduction; a lower initial rent; a delayed rent review; an agreement to bring a son or daughter onto the tenancy; a relaxation of an alienation provision to allow sub-letting; or the provision by the landlord of other fixed equipment could all count if the reason for providing the benefit is entirely as a quid pro quo for the tenant providing the improvement. Once again, the restitutionary nature of the compensation provisions is illustrated. The tenant is only to be compensated for what might be called the net value of that which he has provided.

If such a benefit is provided, the amount of compensation is reduced by '... the proportion which the value of the benefit bears to the amount of the total cost of providing the improvement'. This can be compared with the position under s 66(3) of the AHA 1986 where benefits provided in consideration of a tenant carrying out an improvement within Pt I of Sch 8 to that Act (short-term improvements begun on or after 1 March 1948 to which no consent is required) are simply to be 'taken into account' in assessing compensation.

The exercise to be carried out under the ATA 1995 is as follows.

(a) Value the benefit given or allowed by the landlord. It is not clear from s 20(2) whether the value of the benefit is to be taken as the cost of providing it to the landlord or of its value to the tenant. It is submitted that it is the value to the tenant which must be looked at. What has he already had by way of return for his investment in providing the improvement? Valuation may be straightforward – as in the case of rent reduction or lower initial rents – or difficult – as in the case of a relaxation in other terms of the tenancy.

(b) Determine the total cost of providing the improvement. This will not only be the cost of materials but also labour costs, even if the tenant has effected the improvement by the use of his own labour.

(c) Compare the value of the benefit and the cost of providing the improvement. If the value of the benefit is, for example, 20% of the cost of providing the improvement, the compensation payable to the tenant in respect of the improvement is reduced by 20%.

(d) Establish the compensation payable in accordance with the formula in s 20(1) of the ATA 1995.

(e) Reduce the compensation figure found in (d) by the relevant percentage found in (c) above.

Grants out of public money

16.27 If a grant has been, or will be, made to the tenant out of public money in respect of an improvement, the compensation payable for that improvement will be reduced by the proportion which the amount of the grant bears to the amount of the total cost of providing the improvement. The exercise is exactly the same as that set out above in relation to benefits provided by the landlord.

It should be noted that there is no obligation on the tenant to apply for such a grant. If he chooses not to do so, his compensation will not be reduced. An obligation on the tenant in the tenancy agreement to apply for all available grants is, therefore, advisable for those advising landlords. If the tenant then fails to claim, the landlord will have an action for damages for breach of covenant and the loss will be the additional compensation he has to pay the tenant in respect of the improvement as a result of the tenant's failure to apply for the grant.

The contractual formula

16.28 Until the RRO 2006[1], it was not possible to contract out of the statutory provisions relating to compensation under the ATA 1995. Those provisions created a problem in practice. Landlords who agreed to permit tenants to make improvements had no way of determining in advance what the compensation payable at the termination of the tenancy would be.

TRIG2[2] recommended amending the ATA 1995 to allow the level of compensation for tenant's improvements to be capped at the amount of the tenant's investment in making that improvement. As a consequence, s 20 of the ATA 1995 has been amended to introduce a new subsection 29(4A)[3]. The effect of the new provision is to allow the landlord and the tenant the option of agreeing an upper limit to the amount of compensation payable. Where they agree that there should be a limit, but are unable to agree on the amount of the limit, the amount is the cost to the tenant of making the improvements.

[1]   The Regulatory Reform (Agricultural Tenancies) (England and Wales) Order 2006, SI 2006/2805, effective from 19 October 2006.
[2]   Tenancy Reform Industry Group (2002), see para 1.19.
[3]   RRO 2006, SI 2006/2805, art 16.

AMOUNT OF COMPENSATION – IMPROVEMENTS CONSISTING OF PLANNING PERMISSIONS

16.29 The valuation formula set out in s 21(2) of the ATA 1995 is similar to that for other improvements. It is the amount equal to:

> '... the income attributable to the fact that the relevant development is authorised by the planning permission in the value of the holding at the termination of the tenancy as land comprised in a tenancy'.

The 'relevant development' is defined in s 21(2) as being the physical improvement or change of use specified in the landlord's consent to the application for planning permission[1].

The planning permission actually obtained by the tenant may permit a much wider range of developments than the use to which the tenant intends to put it and may unlock all sorts of potential developments, adding significantly to the value of the land. The definition of the 'relevant development' limits the tenant's ability to share in that. Furthermore, as the valuation formula refers to increases in the value of the land as land comprised in a tenancy, the potentially significant increases in the freehold value of the land are the landlord's alone.

As for other improvements, the compensation payable to the tenant will be reduced where a benefit has been given or allowed by the landlord[2]. The exercise is exactly the same as that set out above[3], with the comparison here being between the value of the benefit and the total cost of obtaining the planning permission.

[1] The requirement for the consent to be expressed to be for the purpose of enabling a specified physical improvement or change of use to be effected is set out in s 18(1)(b).
[2] ATA 1995, s 21(3).
[3] See para 16.26.

SETTLEMENT OF COMPENSATION CLAIMS

16.30 As with the AHA 1986, the tenant has a limited time within which to make his claim and, thereafter, if necessary, to appoint the arbitrator.

The tenant must give notice in writing to his landlord of his intention to make a claim and of the nature of the claim before the end of the period of two months starting with the date of the termination of the tenancy[1]. This is likely to be interpreted in the same way as such requirements under the AHA 1986 have been interpreted so that a notice served before the termination of the tenancy would be valid[2]. As considered above, this creates the potential problems for a tenant whose tenancy has terminated; who has not quit the holding, but whose continued occupation is not under a farm business tenancy[3]. Section 16 of the ATA 1995 provides that he has no claim until he has quit the holding. Section 23 of the ATA 1995 provides for roll over only when the new occupation is under a farm business tenancy and yet he has only two months from the termination of the tenancy to make his claim and four months to commence the arbitration, unless s 22(5) assists to extend that timetable.

There is no prescribed form for the notice and the only prescribed information is that referred to in s 22(2) of the ATA 1995. While s 22(2) requires the notice to specify the nature of the claim, it does not go on, as does the AHA 1986, to give an example of the type of description that will suffice. The definition of 'given' in ATA 1995, s 36 and the permitted service methods should be borne in mind.

To pursue the claim, either party can apply to the President of the RICS for the appointment of an arbitrator by him. They can do so provided that:

(a) no agreement in writing has been reached between the parties to settle the claim; and

(b)   no arbitrator has been appointed under an agreement reached since the tenant served his notice; and

(c)   a period of four months beginning with the date of the termination of the tenancy (or the termination of the occupation if s 22(5) applies) has elapsed.

In brief:

(i)   the appointment by agreement must have been made in writing[4];

(ii)   the arbitrator must have accepted the appointment although this may be done before the formal act of appointment[5];

(iii)   the arbitrator must have received notice of appointment;

(iv)   the parties must themselves have received notice.

1   ATA 1995, s 22(2).
2   *Lady Hallinan v Jones* [1984] 2 EGLR 20, 272 Estates Gazette 1081: see para 41.3ff.
3   See pp 1032–1035.
4   *F R Evans (Leeds) Ltd v Webster* (1962) 112 L Jo 703.
5   *Sclater v Horton* [1954] 2 QB 1, CA; *Tradax Export SA v Volkswagenwerk AG* [1970] 1 QB 537, CA.

16.31 As with the AHA 1986[1], there is no time limit following the expiration of the statutory period (four months under the ATA 1995; eight months under the AHA 1986) within which the arbitrator must be appointed. Undue delay could lead to a successful defence based on estoppel or laches.

If an application is made to the President of the RICS for the appointment of an arbitrator, it must be in writing and accompanied by such reasonable fee as the President may determine in respect of the costs of making the appointment[2]. The arbitration will be conducted by a sole arbitrator[3]. If the application is being made in respect, wholly or partly, of compensation for routine improvements and is made at the same time as an application for consent to the provision of those routine improvements, the President is directed by s 22(4) to appoint the same arbitrator on both applications and, if the applications are by the same party, to charge only one fee.

The arbitration will be an arbitration under the Arbitration Act 1996, as to the conduct of which see further Part V. Unlike with the arbitration on rent review and the general arbitrations under s 28 of the ATA 1995, any alternative dispute resolution chosen by the parties in connection with the determination of the tenant's claim for compensation will not take the parties out of the arbitration process unless an agreement in writing has been reached[4].

1   AHA 1986, s 83(4).
2   ATA 1995, s 30(2).
3   ATA 1995, s 30(1).
4   See ATA 1995, s 12 (rent review) and ss 28 and 29 (general dispute resolution) for a comparison.

CONTRACTING-OUT

16.32 To the extent that Pt III of the ATA 1995 provides for compensation, the tenant is entitled to that compensation only but is so entitled regardless of any agreement to the contrary[1]. However, to the extent that the ATA 1995 does not provide for compensation, any agreement the tenant has reached with the landlord is valid or enforceable[2].

Section 26(1) prevents contracting-out where the provisions of Pt III of the ATA 1995 'provide for compensation'. This must mean that contracting-out is prohibited for all improvements which fall within the definition of tenant's improvement in s 15 of the ATA 1995 rather than only those improvements in respect of which consent is obtained; the preliminary notice given on time etc. A landlord is unlikely to escape the application of the valuation formula by refusing consent to improvements in the tenancy agreement but having an express valuation formula for improvements provided or by an agreement with the tenant not to serve his notice in time in return for compensation calculated on some other basis.

Consent to an improvement can be given on condition that the tenant does not remove it as a fixture[3], but consent given on the basis that it is removed as a fixture may be regarded as contracting-out and contrary to s 26(1) of the ATA 1995.

[1] ATA 1995, s 26(1).
[2] ATA 1995, s 26(2).
[3] ATA 1995, s 8(2)(d).

16.33 In respect of lettings within Pt II of the Landlord and Tenant Act 1954, compensation for improvements is payable under the provisions of the Landlord and Tenant Act 1927, subject to the fulfilment of certain conditions[1]. However, a practice has grown up in commercial leases of including a provision in the lease requiring the tenant to reinstate all alterations, additions and improvements made to the premises during the term as a way of avoiding the payment of statutory compensation. It is not clear whether such a clause would be effective to prevent the tenant from obtaining compensation under the ATA 1995. In any event, such a clause would not cover all items which would fall within the definition of a tenant's improvement in s 15. How would such a reinstatement provision work? One argument is that it removes any benefit to the landlord in having the improvement; another is that it works simply on the practical level of ensuring that in most cases the landlord and tenant simply agree that the landlord will not enforce the covenant if the tenant does not pursue his claim for compensation, or they agree – the tenant being in breach of the covenant to reinstate that their respective claims are equal in value and cancel each other out.

Payments of compensation will be reduced by the proportion which the value of any benefit given by the landlord in consideration for the improvement bears to the amount of the total cost of providing the improvement. At the time that a claim is being made by the tenant, the parties may agree that the value of the benefit given is equal to the total cost of providing the improvement. Such an agreement reached in advance, however, might be regarded as contracting-out.

Assuming milk quota is an intangible advantage within the meaning of s 15 of the ATA 1995, traditional quota clauses may well amount to contracting out of the compensation provisions of the ATA 1995, if they require or permit, for example, the tenant to take the quota with him at the end of the tenancy in lieu of taking statutory compensation.

For matters which are clearly not covered by the ATA 1995, there will be no compensation unless the parties have reached specific agreement in the tenancy agreement. Those items of tenant right which do not fall within the definition of routine improvements but are chattels which the tenant can take with him when he leaves will need to be thought about. If the landlord wants the tenant to leave a clamp of silage or hay or straw at the end of the tenancy, he will have to place the tenant under an obligation to do so in the tenancy agreement and the parties will have to agree the method of valuation for such chattels as are left behind.

[1]   See the Landlord and Tenant Act 1927, ss 1–3, as amended by the Landlord and Tenant Act 1954, Pt III.

MISCELLANEOUS

Resumption of possession of part of a holding

16.34 Section 24 of the ATA 1995 contains similar provisions to those contained in s 74 of the AHA 1986[1]. It safeguards the tenant's right to compensation by providing that where part of a holding held under a farm business tenancy is repossessed, that part is treated as a separate holding for the purposes of the tenant's compensation claim. His compensation claim in relation to that part then arises at the time that that part is repossessed. The section applies whether it is a simple case of a landlord resuming possession of part by virtue of a provision in the tenancy allowing him to do so or where a person entitled to a severed part of a reversionary estate serves a notice under s 140 of the Law of Property Act 1925.

At the time of the repossession of the part in question, compensation is payable, in respect of improvements other than planning permission, for the tenant's improvements which were 'provided for' that part[2]. The improvement need not, therefore, be on the land repossessed: it could be an adjoining land but service only the part taken back, as could happen, for example, in the case of drainage or storage facilities. It will still be compensatable at the time of the repossession of the part.

For improvements consisting of planning permissions, the permission must actually relate to the part taken back[3].

16.34 *Compensation for improvements*

There is obviously scope for distortion in the compensation payable, both at the time of the resumption of part and, so far as the remaining improvements are concerned, at the termination of the tenancy upon the tenant quitting the remainder of the holding. For example, if the improvement on the part consists of the storage facilities for the grain off the entire holding and the part is to be looked at as a separate holding for the compensation claim, the storage facilities will clearly be excessive for that separate holding. Similarly, if a large block of arable land is repossessed and the grain storage is on the land remaining in the tenancy, those facilities will be excessive for that remaining land and could impact on the compensation payable.

1 See Ch 41.
2 ATA 1995, s 24(2).
3 ATA 1995, s 24(3).

16.35 Section 24 of the ATA 1995 contains anti-distortion provisions to deal with both of these situations. The section is designed to ensure that the tenant's overall compensation for improvements is no different than it would have been had the entire original holding been repossessed at the same time. It does it as follows:

(a) The compensation payable in respect of improvements (other than planning permission) provided for the relevant part is an amount equal to the increase attributable to the improvement in the value of the *original holding as* land comprised in a tenancy[1].

(b) For planning permissions, the provision is similar: it is the increase, attributable to the fact that the relevant development (that authorised by the landlord's consent) is authorised by the permission, in the value of the original holding as land comprised in a tenancy[2].

(c) When it comes to the termination of the tenancy itself, the compensation claim for the remaining improvements is once again settled by reference to the increase in value of the original holding[3].

(d) The 'original holding' may mean different things for different improvements. The idea behind the section is to meet the parties' expectations so far as compensation is concerned. Those expectations, as to the value of the improvement, will be fixed by reference to the land in the tenancy at the time that the improvement is sanctioned. Hence, s 24(5) provides that the original holding means the land comprised in the farm business tenancy on the date the landlord gave his consent to the improvement or, if sanctioned by an arbitrator, on the date of the arbitrator's approval.

Where the parties have, in accordance with s 20(4A) of the ATA 1995[4] agreed to a compensation limit in relation to end of tenancy claims, if the tenant has received some compensation in respect of the improvement at the time that he gave up the part, and the tenant is entitled to further compensation in relation to the improvement at the end of the tenancy, the total amount of compensation he receives does not exceed the compensation limit[5].

1 ATA 1995, s 24(2).
2 ATA 1995, s 24(3).
3 ATA 1995, s 24(4).
4 See para 16.28.

Severance of the reversionary estate

16.36 Section 25 of the ATA 1995 mirrors s 75 of the AHA 1986 to safeguard a tenant's claim[1]. Where the reversionary estate in a holding comprised in a farm business tenancy is vested in more than one person, the tenant is entitled, at his election, on quitting the entire holding, to have his compensation assessed as if the reversion were not severed. If he does so elect, the arbitrator has jurisdiction then to apportion the compensation awarded between all those persons who together constitute the landlord[2].

This is an enabling provision. It is not compulsory for the tenant to elect. In many cases, the outcome will be the same whether the tenant elects or not. If s 24 of the ATA 1995 applies, the assessment of compensation for each improvement will, in any event, be by reference to the original holding. Section 24 is limited in its application to cases where the landlord has instigated the resumption of possession of part, and for cases outside s 24, the tenant may find it financially advantageous not to elect under s 25 of the ATA 1995.

1   See Ch 41.
2   ATA 1995, s 25(2).

209

Part VI

MISCELLANEOUS

Contents

Chapter 17
MISCELLANEOUS PROVISIONS

SERVICE OF NOTICES OR DOCUMENTS

17.1 Section 36 of the Agricultural Tenancies Act 1995 (ATA 1995) makes specific provision for the service of all notices or documents 'required or authorised to be given' under the Act[1]. This includes:

(a) the notices exchanged in order to comply with the notice conditions under section 1(4);

(b) the notice required to terminate a fixed-term tenancy of more than two years under s 5;

(c) a notice to quit given pursuant to s 6;

(d) a notice to activate a break provision under s 7[2];

(e) the statutory rent review notice under s 10, but not any contractual trigger notices for express rent review options within s 9[3];

(f) a demand for arbitration by the tenant who is aggrieved, inter alia, by the landlord's refusal to consent to an improvement under s 19[4];

(g) a tenant's written notice of his intention to make a compensation claim for tenant's improvements given pursuant to s 22(2)[5];

(h) a demand for arbitration pursuant to s 28(2)[6]; and

(j) a notice pursuant to s 29(1)(b)(ii)[7].

---

[1]   ATA 1995, s 36(1).
[2]   Although it is arguable that this notice and the notice to quit an annual periodic tenancy under s 6 are not notices required or authorised under the ATA 1995 but are required by common law or by the lease respectively. It is submitted, however, that both notices are intended to be caught by s 36 as both are only valid if in compliance with the provisions in the Act as to writing, length of notice, etc.
[3]   See Ch 9.
[4]   See Ch 15.
[5]   See Ch 15.
[6]   See Ch 16.
[7]   See Ch 16.

17.2 Throughout the ATA 1995, the reference to notices and documents is to them having been 'given' or requiring them to be 'given'. Section 36 defines 'given'. A document is duly given to an intended recipient if:

(a)   it is delivered to him; or if

(b)   it is left at his proper address; or if
(c)   it is given to him in a manner which is authorised by a written agreement between the parties to the notice[1]. Such an agreement need not be contained in the tenancy agreement but it must be made before the notice in question is given: it cannot retrospectively validate a notice already given[2]. An agreement as to a particular method of service for the preliminary notices necessary to comply with the notice conditions[3] cannot be contained in the tenancy agreement and must be the subject of an earlier separate written agreement.

[1]   ATA 1995, s 36(2).
[2]   ATA 1995, s 36(2)(c).
[3]   ATA 1995, s 1(4).

Posting

17.3 While it is not absolutely clear from the wording of s 36(2), it is not thought that personal service is required by the words 'delivered to him' or 'left' at his proper address. Postal service should be sufficient[1]. As to the issues concerning registered post and recorded delivery, see Ch 42.

[1]   The Agricultural Holdings Act 1986 (AHA 1986), s 93 provides that notices are given if delivered; left at the recipient's proper address; or sent by post in a registered letter or by recorded delivery service. It is clear that ordinary post has been considered sufficient under that section. As to the rules on service by post, see Ch 44.

Agreed methods of service

17.4 The parties can specify in the tenancy agreement[1] the methods of service they require. It would seem, however, that even where they do so, the other statutory methods will still be valid[2].

[1]   Or an earlier written agreement if the notices are to comply with the notice conditions in the ATA 1995, s 1(4).
[2]   See the wording of the ATA 1995, s 36(2).

Service by facsimile or other electronic methods

17.5 It should be noted that a specific agreement in accordance with s 36(2)(c) is needed before service by facsimile or other electronic means (for example, an e-mail) will suffice. In the absence of such an agreement, s 36(3) provides that service is not effected. Electronic methods such as facsimile or e-mail may be particularly useful where service is to be effected by an agent or on an agent in accordance with s 36(5), although it would be sensible for evidential safeguards to be built into the notice provisions to ensure that receipt is acknowledged within a specified timescale.

Service by Document Exchange

17.6 Service by the Document Exchange system is not authorised by s 36(2)(a) or (b) and will not suffice unless either a specific agreement for service by that method exists or where, following delivery, receipt can be proved when the document will have been 'delivered to him'[1].

[1]   See Ch 42 and para 42.17.

Physical delivery

17.7   Physical delivery to the intended recipient will clearly suffice. Reference should be made to cases under the AHA 1986[1].

[1]   See Ch 42 and para 42.19.

Service on joint tenants/previous tenants

17.8   The position is the same as under the AHA 1986[1].

[1]   See paras 42.20 and 42.21. Also see Ch 29.

Proper address

17.9   A recipient's 'proper address' is defined as being the last known address of the person in question, unless service is on the secretary or clerk of a body corporate when the proper address is the registered or principal office of that body[1].

[1]   ATA 1995, s 36(2)(b). Service on a body corporate is duly given if given to the secretary or clerk of the body corporate – see ATA 1995, s 36(4). Also see para 42.26.

Agents

17.10   Service upon agents or servants of the landlord or tenant may be effective depending on the circumstances of the particular case:

(a)   service on an agent or servant of the landlord is effective if the agent or servant is '... responsible for the control of the management of the holding ...'[1];

(b)   service on an agent or servant of the tenant will suffice if the agent or servant is '... responsible for the carrying on of a business on the holding'[2]; and

(c)   service on an authorised agent (whether express or implied) will not be good service following the death of the principal[3].

[1]   ATA 1995, s 36(5)(a).
[2]   ATA 1995, s 36(5)(b). See also (in the context of s 196(3) of the Law of Property Act 1925) *Kinch v Bullard* [1999] 1 WLR 423. Also see para 42.22.
[3]   *Lodgepower Ltd v Taylor* [2004] EWCA Civ 1367, [2005] 1 EGLR 1, [2005] 08 EG 192.

17.11   In both cases, of course, one of the prescribed service methods in ATA 1995, s 36 must be used. To avoid concerns about whether a particular agent or servant fulfils the requirements of being in control of management or responsible for carrying on a business on the holding as the case may be, the parties could agree the identity of such a person at the outset, to be reviewed as and when appropriate.

Change of landlord

17.12   The tenant is entitled to serve notices on a particular landlord unless or until he receives notice that that landlord has ceased to be entitled to receive the rents and profits from the holding and has been given the name and address of his successor[1]. There is no requirement that the notice of the successor should be in writing but it is obviously preferable, from an evidential point of view, that it should be[2]. As with s 93 of the AHA 1986, there is no corresponding provision the other way. If a tenant can, and does, assign without notifying the landlord, it would seem that service on the previous tenant would not be good service[3].

[1]   ATA 1995, s 36(7).
[2]   See Ch 42 and para 42.25.
[3]   Note that ss 47 and 48 of the Landlord and Tenant Act 1987 apply to agricultural holdings.

COMPUTATION OF TIME

17.13   For the purpose of calculating time limits under the ATA 1995 the 'corresponding day' rule applies[1]. If an act is authorised to be performed within one month, then one month elapses on the corresponding day of the next month, provided that the day of the act itself is excluded from the computation. Where a notice was given on 30 September, to expire one month later, time began to run from when the clock struck midnight on 30 September and expired one month later when the clock struck midnight on 30 October[2]: 31 October would be out of time. The position is unaffected by the fact that the relevant month is February, April, June, September or November.

In notices generally the following interpretations apply to deadlines using 25 March as the trigger date:

(a)   'by': a notice can be served up until midnight on 25 March;
(b)   'from': the date specified will generally be excluded. If the term of the tenancy is stated to run from 25 March, it will commence immediately after midnight on 26 March;
(c)   'not less than': the first and last days are excluded. A notice served not less than three days after 25 March must be served on or after 29 March. Not less equates to 'at least';
(d)   'at the end of': means the same as 'after the end of'[3];
(e)   'within one month': the calendar month is used[4]. A notice to be served within one month of 31 March must be served before midnight on 30 April. Within one month of 25 March is before midnight on 25 April;

(f)   'within one year': the calendar year is used. A notice to be served within one year of 25 March 2007 must be served before midnight on 25 March 2008.

1   *Dodds v Walker* [1981] 2 All ER 609, [1981] 1 WLR 1027, HL; *E J Riley Investments Ltd v Eurostile Holdings Ltd* [1985] 3 All ER 181, CA. Cf *Trafford Metropolitan Borough Council v Total Fitness UK Ltd* [2002] EWCA Civ 1513, [2002] PLSCS 220.
2   *Lester v Garland* (1808) 15 Ves 248.
3   *Notting Hill Housing Trust v Roomus* [2006] EWCA Civ 407, [2006] 1 WLR 1375. Cf *Fernandez v McDonald* [2003] EWCA Civ 1219, [2004] 1 WLR 1027.
4   *Dodds v Walker* [1981] 2 All ER 609, [1981] 1 WLR 1027, HL. See para 42.27.

POWERS OF LIMITED OWNERS

17.14 Section 32 of the ATA 1995 is similar to s 88 of the AHA 1986 in defining the powers of owners with a limited interest in the land in connection with farm business tenancies[1]. It provides that a landlord of a farm business tenancy, whatever his estate or interest in the land, may give any consents and enter into any agreements or have any act done to him as if he were the owner in fee simple or, if he has an interest in the leasehold estate, as if he were absolutely entitled to that leasehold interest[2].

Section 33 of the ATA 1995 deals with the payment of capital monies under existing strict settlements[3]. Similar provisions exist in s 89 of the AHA 1986[4], although certain problems associated with s 89 of the AHA 1986 have been eliminated in the ATA 1995. The provisions in s 73 of the Settled Land Act 1925 dealing with the payment of capital moneys are designed to hold the correct balance between the tenant for life, entitled to the income of the holding, and the remaindermen entitled to the capital value. Under the AHA 1986, because of the fact that repairs to fixed equipment were included in Sch 7 to the AHA 1986 and hence, by s 89, could be paid out of capital money, that balance was upset: those entitled to capital ended up paying for repairs[5]. The ATA 1995 puts this right in respect of farm business tenancies.

1   See Ch 44 for a commentary on s 88 of the AHA 1986.
2   As to consent, see *Aubergine Enterprises Ltd v Lakewood International Ltd* [2001] 39 EG 141.
3   ATA 1995, s 33 is amended by the Trusts of Land and Appointment of Trustees Act 1996 so that applies as originally enacted or in relation to trusts of land.
4   See Ch 44 for a commentary.
5   See Ch 44.

17.15 Capital moneys may be paid for the purposes specified in s 73 including defraying the expenses of any improvement mentioned in Pt I of Sch 3 to the Settled Land Act 1925[1]. Section 33 of the ATA 1995 extends s 73 to include payments:

(a)   in respect of the expenses incurred by a landlord under a farm business tenancy in connection with the making of any physical improvements in the holding;

(b)   in respect of the payment of compensation for tenant's improvements under s 16 of the ATA 1995[2];

217

(c)   in respect of the payment of costs, charges or other expenses incurred by a landlord or a reference to arbitration for consent to an improvement or for compensation for a tenant's improvement,

and gives the trustee for sale or tenant for life the right to require all sums which he has paid out in respect of compensation for tenant's improvements (including costs and expenses) to be paid back to him out of capital money[3].

Reference should be made to ss 83 to 89 and Sch 3 to the Settled Land Act 1925 for the rules relating to the repayment out of income and any sums paid out of capital.

[1]   The Settled Land Act 1925, s 73(1)(xiii).
[2]   A sum paid under s 16 of the ATA 1995 can be raised by mortgage. See ATA 1995, s 33(2) and the Settled Land Act 1925, s 71.
[3]   This avoids the problem highlighted in the case of *Duke of Wellington's Parliamentary Estates* [1972] Ch 374 which arises under s 89 of the AHA 1986 – that that section does not allow for a tenant for life or trustee for life to obtain recompense from the settlement if he has paid out compensation or expenses himself.

ESTIMATION OF BEST RENT

17.16   In many instances where power is given by statute to grant a lease, it is on condition that the best rent is reserved. For example as follows:

(1)   Section 42 of the Settled Land Act 1925 confers powers on a tenant for life (and, by s 28 of the Law of Property Act 1925 on a trustee for sale) to grant leases provided that they reserve the best rent.
(2)   Section 54 of the Law of Property Act 1925 allows leases not exceeding three years to be created orally provided that they are at the best rent.
(3)   Section 99 of the Law of Property Act 1925 (as amended by ATA 1995, s 31) allows a mortgagor to grant certain leases binding upon his mortgagee provided that they reserve the best rent.

Section 34 of the ATA 1995 provides that in estimating the best rent of land comprised in a farm business tenancy, any increase in the value of the land arising from tenant's improvements shall not be taken into account.

CROWN LAND

17.17   Land in which the Crown, the Duchy of Cornwall, the Duchy of Lancaster or a Government Department (whether held on trust for Her Majesty for the purposes of a Government Department or where that Department has management of the land) is all covered by the ATA 1995[1].

Section 37 also ensures that compensation payable for tenant's improvements may be raised and paid, in respect of the Duchy of Lancaster, under s 25 of the Duchy of Lancaster Act 1817 and in respect of the Duchy of Cornwall under s 8 of the Duchy of Cornwall Management Act 1863.

[1]   ATA 1995, s 37.

LETTINGS BY MORTGAGORS OF AGRICULTURAL LAND

17.18 The issues relating to the letting by mortgagors of agricultural land providing security by way of a mortgage are dealt with extensively in Ch 43. The extent to which this was a problem for mortgagees of agricultural land was ameliorated by the ATA 1995.

By 1995 the political climate that had seen it as desirable to prevent mortgagees from being able to restrict the ability to let agricultural land had changed. Rations had been replaced by butter mountains and milk lakes. The statutorily prescribed and enforced husbandry provisions of the Agriculture Act 1947 gave way to the Common Agricultural Policy. As a consequence, despite the fact that the Tenancy Reform Industry Group (TRIG)[1] had not considered this issue, the banking lobby was able to have s 31 of the ATA 1995 introduced during the final reading debate in the House of Commons.

[1]   See para 1.16.

17.19 Section 31 of the ATA 1995 repealed Sch 14 para 12 of the AHA 1986[1] with regard to mortgages of agricultural land created on or after 1 September 1995. As a consequence, since 1 September 1995, if a mortgage of agricultural land is entered into, the mortgagee is able to introduce the standard contractual requirement restricting the mortgagor's ability to grant any tenancy in relation to the mortgaged land without the mortgagee's consent[2].

[1]   See para 43.3.
[2]   The Law of Property Act 1925, s 99(13). See para 43.3.

17.20 It should be noted that s 31 of the ATA 1995 is not retrospective and only applies to mortgages of agricultural land created on or after 1 September 1995. Many mortgages of agricultural land still in force were entered into before 1 September 1995. The issues considered in Ch 44 continue to apply to such mortgages. If a tenancy has been created in relation to such a mortgage before 1 September 1995, it will be necessary to consider whether the tenancy attracts statutory protection under the AHA 1986. If a tenancy is created on or after 1 September 1995, the tenancy will be governed by the ATA 1995 as a farm business tenancy.

In *Barclays Bank plc v Bean*[1], there were the two separate payments reserved by the farm business tenancy. One was the open market rent (subject to a rent review provision) and the other was a premium paid over the course of the term of the tenancy. The Deputy Judge in the High Court held that both satisfied the statutory definition of rent in s 205(1)(xxiii) of the Law of Property Act 1925. Accordingly, both the market rent and the premium payments fell within the statutory rent review formula of s 13 of the ATA 1995. As a consequence, an arbitrator would reduce the totality of the payments agreed to be made to a single market rent. This caused the transaction as a whole to be one at an undervalue, set aside under s 423 of the Insolvency Act 1986[2].

The legal basis for the mortgagee's challenge was removed upon the amendment being made to s 9 of the ATA 1995 pursuant to the Regulatory Reform (Agricultural Tenancies) (England and Wales) Order 2006[3]. The parties are now free to contract out of the statutory rent review provision[4]. Accordingly, the position will revert to that which applied prior to *Barclays Bank plc v Bean*, namely that it will be necessary to consider in each case (by reference to expert evidence) whether the rent reserved by the s 99 tenancy is sufficient to reflect the marriage or ransom value. If it does, then (based upon the decision in *National Westminster Bank plc v Jones)[5]*, the tenancy will be binding upon the mortgagee[6].

1   [2004] 3 EGLR 71, [2004] 41 EG 152.
2   The case was settled before hearing in the Court of Appeal.
3   SI 2006/2805, effective from 19 October 2006.
4   See para 9.3.
5   [2001] 1 BCLC 98, [2000] EGCS 82; affd [2001] EWCA Civ 1541, [2002] 1 P & CR D12.
6   See para 43.17.

Section 3

AGRICULTURAL HOLDINGS ACT 1986

Part I

SECURITY OF TENURE

Contents

Chapter 18

EXTENT OF THE AGRICULTURAL HOLDINGS ACT 1986 CODE

THE SCOPE OF THE LEGISLATION

18.1 The agricultural holdings legislation[1] applies only to agricultural holdings as defined by s 1 of the Agricultural Holdings Act 1986 (AHA 1986)[2]. This section of the book contains a commentary upon those forms of arrangement entered into between landowners and farmers for the occupation of land which constitute, either expressly or by statutory conversion, agricultural holdings, and their relationship with other bases for occupation which did not confer security of tenure under the AHA 1986.

The AHA 1986 applies only to an agreement entered into before 1 September 1995. Any tenancy created on or after 1 September 1995 will be a farm business tenancy governed by the Agricultural Tenancies Act 1995 (ATA 1995)[3].

Although tenancies granted after 1 September 1995 will be governed by the ATA 1995, the AHA 1986 will continue to provide protection for tenants for a considerable period. Aside from the fact that tenancies of agricultural holdings protected under the AHA 1986 enjoy long-term security of tenure, many also benefit from the statutory rights to succession. Succession tenancies granted after 1 September 1995 will remain within the AHA 1986. Also, because of the marked contrast between the long-term security of tenure available under the AHA 1986 and the freedom of contract provisions which apply under the ATA 1995, the body of case law which has been built up under the AHA 1986 as to whether security of tenure applies is likely to continue to generate consideration of arrangements entered into between a land owner and occupier prior to 1 September 1995.

[1] The term 'agricultural holdings legislation' is used to mean (a) the Agricultural Holdings Act 1986 – the consolidating statute which repealed and re-enacted the Agricultural Holdings Act 1948 – and all the subsequent amending statutes (in particular the Agricultural Holdings Act 1984); and (b) the subordinate statutory instruments and regulations passed under the AHA 1986 or (where still extant) under the previous legislation; and (c) any amending or supplemental legislation, eg the Agriculture Act 1986 in so far as it affects agricultural holdings.

[2] There is a possible exception to this general rule in the case of a tenancy for more than one but less than two years: see *Gladstone v Bower* [1960] 2 QB 384, [1960] 3 All ER 353 CA, and the commentary para 20.13, but see *EWP Ltd v Moore* [1992] QB 460, CA.

227

18.1 *Extent of the Agricultural Holdings Act 1986 Code*

3   There are limited exceptions to this general rule where an agreement which is entered into on or after 1 September 1995 can remain a tenancy protected under the AHA 1986. This is consequential upon the saving provisions contained in s 4 of the ATA 1995, for example, the surrender and re-grant of an existing tenancy or a tenancy granted by way of succession to an agricultural holding: see para 3.8.

THE STATUTORY SCHEME

18.2 The way in which the agricultural holdings legislation operates is to provide a statutory superstructure upon the common law.

The main features of the agricultural holdings legislation are that they affect the relationship of landlord and tenant in the following ways:

(a)   by conferring security of tenure on the tenant (by imposing restrictions upon any notice to quit given by the landlord);

(b)   by regulating the terms of the tenancy (particularly as to rent) and, in some instances, varying or overriding them;

(c)   by giving rights of succession on the death or retirement of the tenant to certain close relations;

(d)   by providing for compensation on the termination of the tenancy; and

(e)   in a variety of different miscellaneous matters.

CATEGORISATION OF AGRICULTURAL HOLDINGS AND OTHER ARRANGEMENTS

18.3 Not all arrangements for the occupation of agricultural land made between a landowner and a farmer involved, directly or indirectly, the formation of an agricultural holding. Many arrangements which were not intended to result in the creation of such a tenancy are statutorily converted.

It is necessary at the outset to categorise and distinguish a variety of different forms of agreement commonly entered into between landowners and farmers for the occupation of agricultural land prior to the ATA 1995 coming into force on 1 September 1995.

WHAT IS AN AGRICULTURAL HOLDING?

Security of tenure

18.4 This primary category comprises those arrangements where the parties, either intentionally or unintentionally, created the tenancy of an agricultural holding with the owner becoming the landlord and the farmer/occupier becoming the tenant. Most usually these are annual periodic tenancies. Not least because of extent of the security of tenure which is provided to a tenant under the AHA 1986, prior to the ATA 1995 coming into force, a great deal of case law evolved as to whether or not the parties had achieved the creation of a protected tenancy.

Within this category it is necessary to distinguish between:

(a)　those agricultural holdings which attract all the incidents of the agricultural holdings legislation, including security of tenure, succession, compensation on quitting, rent control, etc; and

(b)　those which either involve no security of tenure, or other arrangements which avoid some aspects of the agricultural holdings legislation (other than security of tenure).

No security of tenure

Gladstone v Bower tenancies

18.5　These were tenancies granted before 1 September 1995 for a fixed term for more than one but less than two years[1]. In *Gladstone v Bower*[2], the Court of Appeal determined that such tenancies did not confer security of tenure under the AHA 1986.

It has been suggested that such tenancies, while attracting no security of tenure, also fell wholly outside the definition of an agricultural holding. It is submitted that that view is mistaken[3].

[1]　These tenancies are of mostly historic significance as it has not been possible to grant one since 1 September 1995: see para 3.3.
[2]　[1960] 2 QB 384, [1960] 3 All ER 353, CA. See 20.13.
[3]　*EWP Ltd v Moore* [1992] QB 460, CA.

Ministry consent tenancies (two to five years)

18.6　Tenancies or licences granted pursuant to certain forms of consent by the Minister of Agriculture, Fisheries and Food[1], carry with them no security of tenure[2]. Licences[3] granted in this way do not involve the creation of an agricultural holding at all, nor do tenancies for less than a year[4]. However, the definition of agricultural holding is wide enough to encompass a lease or tenancy[5], subject to prior Ministry consent, created for between two and five years. It is outside the statutory provisions relating to security of tenure but attracts all the other statutory provisions applicable to agricultural holdings.

[1]　Now the Department for the Environment, Food and Rural Affairs (DEFRA) or the National Assembly for Wales: see para 4.2.
[2]　See the AHA 1986, s 5 which provides the exception to the general rule contained in s 3 that all tenancies for two years or upwards shall, on the expiration of the fixed term, continue as tenancies from year to year: see 20.15.
[3]　See AHA 1986, s 2(1), read in conjunction with s 2(2)(b).
[4]　See AHA 1986, s 2(1), read in conjunction with s 2(2)(a) and the statutory definition of an agricultural holding which requires a contract of tenancy which, in turn, is defined by s 1(5) so as to exclude such a tenancy.
[5]　This is because of the statutory definition of a contract of tenancy in the AHA 1986, s 1(5), which includes a letting for a term of years but excludes a letting for less than a year.

Sub-tenancies

18.7   Section 29 and Sch 4 to the AHA 1986 authorise the Lord Chancellor to make regulations to protect sub-tenants[1]. Although this power has existed since the Agricultural Holdings Act 1948, no regulations have ever been made.

Sub-tenants of tenants of agricultural holdings under the AHA 1986 will, if the statutory requirements are satisfied, be occupying agricultural holdings, which may confer security of tenure and provide the other incidents of the AHA 1986 as between the sub-tenant and the immediate landlord, the head tenant. However, their security of tenure can, in certain circumstances, be circumvented or destroyed by the destruction by the head landlord of the head tenancy[2].

The widespread use of sub-tenancies by head landlords, letting to closely connected persons so that they could sub-let with a view to avoiding security for the sub-tenant against the head landlord, has been held by the Court of Appeal to be ineffective[3].

[1]   Originally contained in the Agricultural Holdings Act 1948, s 26(2)(d): see 29.17.
[2]   See para 29.20ff.
[3]   *Gisborne v Burton* [1989] QB 390, [1988] 3 All ER 760, [1988] 2 EGLR 9, CA.

Lettings to farm partnerships

18.8   A possible fourth example of a letting which attracted no, or at least limited, security under the AHA 1986 was a letting by a landlord to himself and others, often with a view to the landlord (in his capacity as tenant) and his co-tenants then farming together in partnership. Such lettings gave rise to particular difficulties and are considered in detail in Chapter 19.

Other arrangements

Post-1984 tenancies

18.9   Leases or tenancies created after 12 July 1984[1] and/or 12 September 1984[2] attract special consideration and treatment under the agricultural holdings legislation, notably:

(a)   all rights to succession to such tenancies are expressly excluded[3]; and
(b)   there are special provisions as to termination in the event of the death of the tenant during the currency of the fixed term[4].

In all other respects such tenancies or leases attract the same provisions of the agricultural holdings legislation as leases or tenancies created before July/September 1984.

[1]   The date of the passing of the Agricultural Holdings Act 1984 (AHA 1984).
[2]   The date when most of the provisions of the AHA 1984 came into effect.
[3]   See AHA 1986, s 34(1)(a).
[4]   See AHA 1986, s 4.

Statutory smallholdings

18.10 Statutory smallholdings are smallholdings within the meaning of Pt III of the Agriculture Act 1970, held of a smallholdings authority or the Minister[1]. These are agricultural holdings within the meaning of the AHA 1986. They are excluded from succession by s 38(4) of the AHA 1986 and if granted after 12 September 1984 can, in certain circumstances, be terminated on the tenant attaining the age of 65[2]. The freedom of cropping provided by s 15 of the AHA 1986 does not apply to such smallholdings[3]. Other special provisions contained in the smallholdings legislation apply to such tenancies, though in most other respects they enjoy the rights, obligations and special provisions contained in the agricultural holdings legislation generally.

[1] Now DEFRA.
[2] For a fuller commentary, see 20.19.
[3] See AHA 1986, s 82.

Market gardens

18.11 A market garden also comes within the definition of an agricultural holding. It enjoys special provisions as to compensation and as to the nomination of a new tenant in place of the existing tenant on termination of the existing tenancy[1].

[1] For a commentary upon market gardens, see 20.21.

Fixed-term tenancies

18.12 Fixed-term tenancies[1] involve the creation of agricultural holdings and fall to be treated in all respects as annual tenancies except:

(a)   rent review – the statutory machinery is inoperative during the currency of the lease;
(b)   a Case G notice to quit on the death of a tenant cannot be given except in very limited circumstances[2].

[1] For a commentary upon such tenancies, see 20.7.
[2] See para 20.8(b).

WHAT IS NOT AN AGRICULTURAL HOLDING?

18.13 Certain forms of arrangement for the occupation of agricultural land are expressly excluded from statutory conversion into agricultural holdings. Others have been found by judicial construction of the statutory provisions not to be converted and, therefore, to fall wholly outside the scope of the agricultural holdings legislation.

It is necessary to distinguish between:

(a)   express exclusions, ie those arrangements which are specifically and expressly excluded;

231

(b)   implied exclusions, ie those arrangements which have been held by judicial authority not to be converted into tenancies of agricultural holdings.

Express exclusions

Grazing and/or mowing agreements

18.14 Section 2(3) of the AHA 1986 provides for the statutory conversion into annual tenancies of a large variety of short-term tenancies and also licences of any duration. It expressly excludes licences or tenancies which are:

(a)   for a specified period of the year; and
(b)   limit the occupants' rights of use of the land to grazing and/or mowing only.

Such agreements are commonly encountered in practice and have given rise to much litigation[1].

[1]   For a full commentary on grazing and/or mowing agreements, see 21.2.

Ministry consent licences and short-term tenancies

18.15 It has already been noted[1] that the Minister had the power, pursuant to s 5 of the AHA 1986, to give consent to the parties to enter into a lease or tenancy of between two and five years which then fell wholly outside the provisions relating to security of tenure[2].

By virtue of s 2(1) of the AHA 1986, the Minister alternatively had the power to grant consent to the creation either of a licence of any duration, or a tenancy for a term certain of less than a year. In either event, such licence or tenancy granted pursuant to such Ministry consent would not be converted into a tenancy from year to year and would fall wholly outside the definition of an agricultural holding altogether[3].

The consequence has been that both a tenancy for two to five years, subject to prior Ministry consent, and a tenancy for less than a year, subject to such consent, avoid security of tenure. The former was a tenancy of an agricultural holding but the latter was not. A Ministry consent licence was not a tenancy at all[4].

[1]   See para 18.6.
[2]   See para 20.15.
[3]   These arrangements are now of historic significance as it has not been possible to grant a Ministry consent tenancy or licence since 1 September 1995.
[4]   See para 21.9.

Tenancies or licences for non-commercial purposes

18.16 Tenancies or licences to persons for occupation of land for hobby user, for example for grazing by the occupant's own horses kept for recreational purposes, fall outside the definition of an agricultural holding which requires the letting to be for a trade or business[1].

1   See para 21.10.

Tenancies or licences granted to employees

18.17 The definition of an agricultural holding expressly excludes lettings or licences granted to employees which continue during the employee/tenant's employment under the landlord[1].

1   See para 21.13.

Implied exclusions

Gratuitous licences

18.18 By virtue of s 2 of the AHA 1986, a licence to occupy land for use as agricultural land falls to be converted into a tenancy from year to year. Section 2 does not apply to a purely gratuitous licence[1]. Before an agreement can be converted there must first be a contract supported by valuable consideration.

1   See *Goldsack v Shore* [1950] 1 KB 708, [1950] 1 All ER 276: see para 21.15.

Non-exclusive licences

18.19 The Court of Appeal[1] (in the context of a farming partnership) and the House of Lords[2] (in the context of a home-made licence) both held that a licence had to confer the right to exclusive possession for agricultural purposes in order to be converted into a tenancy from year to year, and brought within the definition of an agricultural holding and confer security under s 2 of the AHA 1986[3]. A licence to share occupation or a licence whereby the land-owner preserves full rights of occupation for himself is not so converted.

This important exception to the general principle of statutory conversion provided for by s 2 of the AHA 1986 is considered in detail in the context of those forms of arrangement most commonly encountered in practice and which seek to avoid exclusive possession, namely:

(a)   farm partnerships[4];
(b)   'share cropping agreements'[5];
(c)   contractor agreements[6]; and
(d)   manager agreements[7].

In this context the hybrid arrangement of a letting by a landlord to himself and others with a view to the landlord and his co-tenants then farming in partnership is also considered. Such arrangements involving conflicts between the landowner's rights as landlord and his duties as partner and joint tenant give rise to particular difficulty.

1 *Harrison-Broadley v Smith* [1963] 3 All ER 586, [1963] 1 WLR 1262.
2 *Bahamas International Trust Co Ltd v Threadgold* [1974] 3 All ER 881, [1974] 1 WLR 1514.
3 See 20.5.
4 See 19.31.
5 See 19.34.
6 See 21.13.
7 See 21.13.

CONTRACTING-OUT

18.20 Many of the features of the agricultural holdings legislation (especially security of tenure) were so unattractive to landowners that a variety of means were adopted to circumvent the application of the AHA 1986 by agreement with the potential tenant. This practice is often described by the convenient, but not entirely accurate, shorthand term, contracting-out. It has received close judicial consideration from the House of Lords[1] and the Court of Appeal[2].

In brief, the general rule of law would now appear to be that the parties may agree never to contract into a landlord and tenant relationship either expressly or in such a way as to give rise to statutory conversion[3]. If, however, they entered into an agreement which either overtly or by statutory conversion gave rise to the formation of a contract of tenancy of an agricultural holding, then the following propositions apply:

(a) They could not contract out of security of tenure by directly or indirectly fettering the right of the tenant to invoke or implement the statutory scheme for conferring such security of tenure. To do so is contrary to public policy.
(b) On parity of reasoning, public policy would probably prohibit some forms of attempt to contract out of existing established right to succession (particularly where those rights affect infants).
(c) Where there are no overriding considerations of public policy, and the statute itself does not prohibit contracting-out, the parties were free, if they wished, to contract out, for example, probably by varying or eliminating the statutory rent review procedures and formula[4].

Consideration is also given to the separate concepts of sham and mislabelling of documents and their related consequences – contracting-out, sham and mislabelling all involve different legal concepts which are often confused.

Where the parties did agree to enter into an agreement to contract-out, in order to avoid security of tenure arising under the AHA 1986, then if they did not act on that agreement, so that it was a sham, the court can look behind that agreement and construe by reference to the true agreement between the parties[5].

1 *Johnson v Moreton* [1980] AC 37, [1978] 3 All ER 37.
2 *Elsden v Pick* [1980] 3 All ER 235, [1980] 1 WLR 898; *Featherstone v Staples* [1986] 2 All ER 461, [1986] 1 WLR 861, CA; *Gisborne v Burton* [1989] QB 390, [1988] 3 All ER 760, CA.
3 Eg they may enter into a form of shared occupation agreement.

4   But there is as yet no authority on this important possibility.
5   *Snook v London and West Riding Investments Ltd* [1967] 2 QB 786, [1967] 1 All ER 518, CA. Also see, *National Westminster Bank plc v Jones* [2000] EGCS 82, [2001] 1 BCLC 98; affd [2001] EWCA Civ 1541, [2002] 1 BCLC 55.

Chapter 19

WHAT IS AN AGRICULTURAL HOLDING?

AGRICULTURAL HOLDING: DEFINITIONS

Commencement

19.1 All agricultural holdings must have been created by agreements commenced[1] before 1 September 1995, subject only to the exceptions provided for by s 4 of the Agricultural Tenancies Act 1995 (ATA 1995)[2]. No new agricultural holdings can be created except in the limited circumstances provided by s 4 of the ATA 1995. Existing agricultural holdings continue otherwise unaffected by the 1995 legislation. Many, especially succession tenancies, are likely to endure for several decades to come and even be newly created in the case of tenancies to which s 4 of the ATA 1995 applies.

[1] A tenancy begins on the day on which, under the terms of the tenancy, the tenant is entitled to possession under that tenancy Section 38(4) of the ATA 1995 fixes the commencement date for farm business tenancies.
[2] For these exceptions, see para 3.44ff.

Agricultural holding

19.2 An 'agricultural holding' means more than simply a letting of agricultural land. It must satisfy the requirements of s 1 of the Agricultural Holdings Act 1986 (AHA 1986) to obtain protection under that Act.

An agricultural holding was defined by s 1 of the Agricultural Holdings Act 1948 (AHA 1948). The definition gave rise to extensive litigation. As a consequence, the Agricultural Holdings Act 1984 (AHA 1984) sought to re-define 'agricultural holding' to reflect the case law. The result was a new definition, now contained in the consolidating statute, the AHA 1986. Accordingly, it is necessary to approach all case authority pre-dating the AHA 1984[1] with caution as the definition of agricultural holding under consideration is not that which now applies.

[1] The definition of agricultural holding in the AHA 1984 came into force on 12 September 1984.

236

19.3 Section 1 of the AHA 1986 defines an 'agricultural holding' as follows:

'**1.** (1) In this Act 'agricultural holding' means the aggregate of the land (whether agricultural land or not) comprised in a contract of tenancy which is a contract for an agricultural tenancy not being a contract under which the land is let to the tenant during his continuance in any office, appointment or employment held under the landlord.

(2) For the purposes of this section, a contract of tenancy relating to any land is a contract for an agricultural tenancy if, having regard to:

  the terms of the tenancy,
  the actual or contemplated use of the land at the time of the conclusion of the
    contract and subsequently, and
  any other relevant circumstances,

the whole of the land comprised in the contract, subject to such exceptions only as do not substantially affect the character of the tenancy, is let for use as agricultural land.

(3) A change in user of the land concerned subsequent to the conclusion of a contract of tenancy which involves any breach of the terms of the tenancy shall be disregarded for the purpose of determining whether a contract which was not originally a contract for an agricultural tenancy has subsequently become one unless it is effected with the landlord's permission, consent or acquiescence.

(4) In this Act 'agricultural land' means:

  land used for agriculture which is so used for the purposes of a trade or business, and
  any other land which, by virtue of a designation under s 109(1) of the Agriculture
    Act 1947, is agricultural land within the meaning of that Act.

(5) In this Act 'contract of tenancy' means a letting of land, or agreement for letting land, for a term of years or from year to year; and for the purposes of this definition a letting of land, or an agreement for letting land, which, by virtue of subsection (6) of section 149 of the Law of Property Act 1925, takes effect as such a letting of land or agreement for letting land as is mentioned in that subsection shall be deemed to be a letting of land, or as the case may be, an agreement for letting land, for a term of years.'

The effect of this extensive definition is that an 'agricultural holding' must satisfy the following requirements:

(a) there must be land which must be *agricultural land*;
(b) it must be used for a *trade or business*;
(c) it must be included in a '*contract of tenancy*';
(d) the tenancy must be an agricultural tenancy expressly or impliedly[1] by operation of s 2 of the AHA 1986; and
(e) the tenancy must not be one where land is let to the tenant during the continuation of the tenant's *office, appointment or employment* held under the landlord.

Further, the AHA 1986 defines 'agricultural tenancy'[2]; 'change in user'[3]; 'agricultural land'[4]; 'contract of tenancy'[5]; 'agriculture' 'landlord' and 'tenant'[6].

---

[1] Impliedly means where a licence is statutorily converted inot a tenancy by s 2 of the AHA 1986.
[2] AHA 1986, s 1(2).

19.3 What is an agricultural holding?

3 AHA 1986, s 1(3).
4 AHA 1986, s 1(4).
5 AHA 1986, s 1(5).
6 AHA 1986, s 96.

Agricultural land

19.4 The definition of 'agricultural land' contains the following elements:

(a) land; and
(b) use for agriculture; or
(c) designation by the Minister; and
(d) aggregation with non-agricultural land.

Land

19.5 The statutory definition refers to land. The judicial construction of what constitutes land is as follows:

(a) land includes buildings on the land[1];
(b) a building without any land, except for the site upon which it is built, can be 'land' for the purpose of the definition[2];
(c) there is no minimum size. A half-acre allotment used to produce vegetables for sale was held to be an agricultural holding[3].

1 In *Blackmore v Butler* [1954] 2 QB 171, CA, a cottage and its curtilage was let to a farmer for occupation by the tenant's farmer worker. It was held that as between the farmer and landlord the cottage comprised an agricultural holding. Also see, *Lester v Ridd* [1990] 2 QB 430, CA where it was held that, following severance of the leasehold interest without the consent of the landlord, a dwellinghouse occupied without land remained part of an agricultural holding. Cf *Godfrey v Waite* (1951) 157 Estates Gazette 582, just because a cottage is required by an agricultural worker does not make it into agricultural land. Also see, *Tyack v Secretary of State for the Environment* [1989] 1 WLR 1392, HL.
2 *Blackmore v Butler* [1954] 2 QB 171, CA; *Godfrey v Waite* (1951) 157 Estates Gazette 582; *Adsetts v Heath* (1951) unreported, cited in 95 Sol Jo 620; and *Hasell v McAulay* [1952] 2 All ER 825. For a rating case, see *Corser (Valuation Officer) and Gloucestershire Marketing Society Ltd* (1981) 79 LGR 393, CA concerning an auction hall forming part of a fruit and vegetable market.
3 *Stevens v Sedgeman* [1951] 2 KB 434, [1951] 2 All ER 33, CA.

Used for agriculture

19.6 The following features of the definition of 'agriculture' contained in s 96(1) of the AHA 1986[1] should be noted:

(a) The definition is not exhaustive. Any activity falling within the ordinary meaning of agriculture is included, the most obvious example being cereal production which does not appear in the list of activities referred to in s 96(1)[2].
(b) A dictionary definition of 'agriculture' is quoted by Viscount Dilhorne in *Normanton v Giles*[3]: 'the science and art of cultivation of the soil; including the allied pursuits of gathering in the crops and rearing

238

livestock'[4]. In the same case, Lord Wilberforce added that 'agriculture, however wide that activity has become, does not include everything that goes on in the country'[5].

(c)   The definition includes 'livestock breeding and keeping' and the 'use of land as grazing land'. This raises a number of difficulties in the context of land used for horses[6].

(d)   Horticulture is included. Property consisting of part of a river and its adjacent channels let for growing watercress may be an agricultural holding[7].

(e)   The definition of 'livestock' in s 96(1) of the AHA 1986 is not exhaustive. A dictionary definition of livestock was quoted by Viscount Dilhorne in *Normanton v Giles*[8]: 'domestic animals generally; animals of any kind kept or dealt in for use or profit'[9]. This is not the definition used in s 96(1) which provides that livestock 'includes any creature kept for the production of food, wool, skins, or fur or for the purpose of its use in the farming of land or the carrying on in relation to land or any agricultural activity'.

(f)   The definition of 'livestock' in s 96(1) includes birds[10], fish[11], and even bees in certain circumstances. Horses are only livestock if 'kept for the production of food', etc (a rare situation) or used in the farming of land, ie cart horses[12]. A trout farm has been held not to be an agricultural holding[13].

(g)   The use of land for agriculture must be a lawful use[14]. If the lawful agricultural use ceases, then the holding may cease to be an agricultural holding, even though the cessation is unilateral[15] and even though s 1(3) requires the use to be considered at the time of the grant. Conversely, if a tenant unilaterally and unlawfully uses land for agriculture in breach, that does not bring the holding within the definition of an agricultural holding[16].

(h)   It should be noted that long use in breach of covenant with the landlord's knowledge will be held to imply that the landlord has acquiesced in its variation[17]. No precise period can be laid down for such use, but a short period will be insufficient. Breach of a user covenant is a continuing breach, so that if the landlord accepts rent, even with full knowledge of the breach, he will normally be found to have merely waived his right to forfeit for past breaches, without prejudicing his rights in the future. An actual waiver of the benefit of a covenant does not extend to any further breach of the same covenant[18]. Acquiescence for periods of 18 years[19] and 30 years[20] have been held to render covenants no longer enforceable. Conversely, acquiescence for a period of 50 years has been held to remove the landlord's right to forfeit for those particular breaches, but otherwise leaving the covenant enforceable in relation to future breaches[21]. The cases in this regard are difficult to reconcile.

(i)   The effect of the decisions of the court under the AHA 1948 definition[22] has now been statutorily incorporated in s 1(3) of the AHA 1986. This was intended to give statutory effect to the rule of law which emerged from the earlier decisions[23].

19.6 *What is an agricultural holding?*

(j)   As to whether land is used for agriculture, 'the enquiry is a matter of degree and a question for the trial judge prima facie to determine as a matter of fact in each particular case'[24].

(k)   An attempt to widen the definition of 'agriculture' to reflect diversification failed in *Jewell v McGowan*[25].

[1]   It should be noted that most features of the definition derive from cases under the AHA 1948. There has been little case authority directly on the AHA 1986 definition, introduced by the AHA 1984.

[2]   'Although I have referred to it as such, that is not a definition in the exclusive sense. It does not in terms include the commonest form of agriculture, namely the growing of corn': per Stamp LJ in *McClinton v McFall* (1974) 232 Estates Gazette 707, CA.

[3]   [1980] 1 All ER 106, [1980] 1 WLR 28, HL: a case considering protection under the Rent (Agriculture) Act 1976 and accordingly a different definition of agriculture.

[4]   *Normanton v Giles* [1980] 1 All ER 106, [1980] 1 WLR 28 at 35.

[5]   *Normanton v Giles* [1980] 1 All ER 106, [1980] 1 WLR 28 at 33. Also see the judgment of Lord Scarman in *Lord Glendyne v Rapley* [1978] 1 WLR 601 at 603, CA, another case under the Rent (Agriculture) Act 1976. For a case considering 'agriculture' in the context of the Town and Country Planning Act 1990, see *Millington v Secretary of State for the Environment, Transport and the Regions* [1999] EGCS 95, [2000] JPL 297, CA concerning winemaking as ancillary use of land used for a vineyard.

[6]   See para 19.10.

[7]   Cf *Dow Agrochemicals Ltd v E A Lane (North Lynn) Ltd* [1965] EGD 195, CCA where growing crops and weeds for testing weed killers held not to be 'agriculture': see the earlier authority cited therein and distinguished.

[8]   [1980] 1 All ER 106, [1980] 1 WLR 28, HL: a case considering protection under the Rent (Agriculture) Act 1976.

[9]   *Normanton v Giles* [1980] 1 All ER 106, [1980] 1 WLR 28 at 35.

[10] Keeping and breeding pheasants for shooting is not 'agriculture': see (in the context of the Rent (Agriculture) Act 1976) *Lord Glendyne v Rapley* [1978] 2 All ER 110, [1978] 1 WLR 601, CA; *Reeve v Atterby* [1978] CLY 73; *Normanton v Giles* [1980] 1 All ER 106, [1980] 1 WLR 28.

[11] *Jones v Bateman* (1974) 232 Estates Gazette 1392, CA (a rating case). Cf *Wallace v Perth and Kinross Assessor* 1975 SLT 118, and *Gunter v Newtown Oyster Fishery Co Ltd* (1977) 244 Estates Gazette 140. Note the definition of agriculture for rating purposes in s 26 of the General Rate Act 1967. Fish are 'creatures' within the meaning of s 96(1) of the AHA 1986 even if not 'mammals or birds' for the purposes of the General Rate Act 1967. See *Cresswell v British Oxygen Co Ltd* [1980] 3 All ER 443, [1980] 1 WLR 1556, CA.

[12] See para 19.10.

[13] *Cook v Horne* [2006] PLSCS 18.

[14] *Iredell v Brocklehurst* (1950) 155 Estates Gazette 268, CA; *Kempe v Dillon-Trenchard* [1951] EGD 13.

[15] *Hickson & Welch Ltd v Cann* (1977) 40 P & CR 218n, CA; *Wetherall v Smith* [1980] 2 All ER 530, [1980] 1 WLR 1290, CA; *Russell v Booker* (1982) 5 HLR 10, [1982] 2 EGLR 86, CA. Note the changed wording introduced by the AHA 1984 after these decisions on the wording of the AHA 1948. Also see, *Short v Greeves* [1988] 1 EGLR 1 [1988] 08 EG 109, CA.

[16] See para 19.17.

[17] *Ashcombe v Mitchell* (1895) 12 TLR 17, CA.

[18] Law of Property Act 1925, s 148.

[19] *Rogers v Great Northern Rly Co* (1889) 53 JP 484.

[20] *Re Summerson, Downie v Summerson* [1900] 1 Ch 112n.

[21] *Chelsea Estates Ltd v Kadri* [1970] EGD 425.

[22] See para 19.13ff.

[23] See para 19.14.

[24] Per Evershed MR in *Godfrey v Waite* (1951) 157 Estates Gazette 582, CA. Also see, *Adsetts v Heath* (1951) County Court, unreported cited in 95 Sol Jo 620; *Hassell v MacAulay* [1952] 2 All ER 825; *Blackmore v Butler* [1954] 2 QB 171, CA.

[25] [2002] EWCA Civ 145, [2002] 3 EGLR 87.

Designation by the Minister

19.7 The Minister[1] is empowered by s 109(1) of the Agriculture Act 1947 to designate as agricultural land, certain land which would not otherwise be within the definition. There are restrictions. He may not designate pleasure grounds, private gardens or allotment gardens, or land kept or preserved mainly or exclusively for sport, or recreation, unless the Minister is satisfied that its use for agriculture would not be inconsistent with its use for sport or recreation.

[1] See para 4.2.

19.8 Although the definition of agricultural land includes land so designated the Minister has not ever made any designation pursuant to the powers granted to him by the Agriculture Act 1947. This is therefore now a spent provision since new agricultural holdings of such land cannot be created after 1 September 1995[1].

[1] Cf designation by the Minister, see para 19.7, where the use does not have to be commercial. However, since the Minister has never in fact designated any land as agricultural land within the meaning of s 109(1) of the Agriculture Act 1947, that distinction is of no practical consequence.

Trade or business

Commercial use

19.9 The use must be essentially commercial in character[1]. A paddock of land used for amenity or pleasure, such as for horses or ponies for hunting or polo, etc, or a cow or goats to provide milk for the house[2], would not be within the meaning of the term. A community free farm, carried on in the spirit of public benevolence, has been held not to be a trade or business giving rise to protection under the AHA 1986[3]. An allotment used by way of trade or business, not being an 'allotment garden', may well be 'agricultural land'[4].

The requirement that the land must be 'used for the purpose of a trade or business' is a continuous requirement. This is clear from the wording of s 1(2)(b) of the AHA 1986 which requires the 'actual or contemplated' use of the land at the time of the conclusion of the contract *and subsequently* to be established if the land is to be comprised within an 'agricultural tenancy' as therein defined.

It was decided under the wording of s 1 of the AHA 1948 in *Wetherall v Smith*[5], and applied to the AHA 1986 in *Short v Greeves*[6], that if commercial use is abandoned altogether, the holding will cease to be an agricultural holding[7].

The cases show that the tenancy is not to be regarded as alternating between being within and outside the AHA 1948 (now the AHA 1986) as minor changes of use take place, and that, when the tenancy is clearly an agricultural one to start with, strong evidence is needed to show that the agricultural use has been abandoned.

A related but different problem is where the user remains commercial throughout (ie the land is used for a trade or business) but non-agricultural commercial activities are introduced or intensified at the expense of the agricultural user. The effect of these changes in the character of the tenancy upon its continued compliance with the definition of an agricultural holding is considered later in this chapter[8].

1   In *Iredell v Brocklehurst* [1950] 155 Estates Gazette 268, CA, a cottage used for agricultural workers let with 12 acres of pasture was held to comprise an agricultural holding despite a covenant against use for trade or business because the covenant was construed as meaning 'other than the business of agriculture'. Cf *R v Agricultural Land Tribunal (South Eastern Province), ex p Palmer* (1954) 163 Estates Gazette 106, where land was let subject to a covenant that the premises were to be used for private occupation only and that the tenant should not carry on any trade or business except the keeping of fowls and the like. This case can be explained by the fact that the tenant had, in fact, used the land agriculturally and had himself invoked the AHA 1948 when his landlord served a notice to quit upon him. He later contended that the tribunal had no jurisdiction because the land was not an agricultural holding. The Court of Appeal rejected this contention and held in the circumstances the holding was an agricultural holding within the meaning of the Act, in spite of the covenant, and made an order of mandamus to the Agricultural Land Tribunal (ALT) requiring it to hear and dispose of the case on that footing. See also *Blackmore v Butler* [1954] 2 QB 171, [1954] 2 All ER 403, where an agricultural cottage was let to a tenant farmer of an adjoining holding who took the cottage for housing one of his agricultural workers. This letting was held to be a letting of agricultural land and comprised an agricultural holding. See also *Godfrey v Waite* [1951] EGD 9, but cf *Hickson & Welch Ltd v Cann* (1977) 40 P & CR 218n, CA and *Russell v Booker* (1982) 5 HLR 10, [1982] 2 EGLR 86, CA.

2   See the remarks of Bridge LJ in *Hickson & Welch Ltd v Cann* (1977) 40 P & CR 218n, CA: 'There is all the difference in the world between what hundreds and hundreds of people all over the country do, namely, add a small income to their earnings by buying or selling animals of one sort or another, and the carrying on of a trade or business of an agricultural nature': Cf *Rutherford v Maurer* [1962] 1 QB 16, [1961] 2 All ER 775, CA. See also *Russell v Booker* (1982) 5 HLR 10, [1982] 2 EGLR 86, CA and see para 19.18ff. For a case of hobby user (not involving 'livestock') see *Gurton v Parrott* [1991] 1 EGLR 98, CA. Also see *Secretary of State for Transport v Jenkins* (1997) 79 P & CR 118, CA.

3   *Secretary of State for Transport v Jenkins* (1997) 79 P & CR 118, CA. As to use for motorcycling activities, in the context of alleged breaches of planning, see *Hart District Council v Benford* [2006] EWHC 240 (QB), [2006] 09 EG 185 (CS).

4   An 'allotment garden' can never be an agricultural holding because of the definition (s 22 of the Allotments Act 1922 and s 109(3) of the Agriculture Act 1947); it must be used for producing vegetables or fruit for the allotment holder or his family. Allotments generally may, in addition to being agricultural holdings, come within the Allotment Acts 1908 to 1950.

5   [1980] 2 All ER 530 at 537G, CA.

6   [1988] 1 EGLR 1, [1988] 08 EG 109, CA.

7   See para 19.16.

8   See para 19.11.

Horses

19.10 The requirement for commerciality can best be illustrated by land used for horses. The trade or business does not itself need to be agricultural so long as the user is[1]. Land let for grazing (an agricultural use) by animals which are not agricultural (because it is outside the definition of 'livestock') in connection with a non-agricultural business (for example, a riding school) will fall within the definition of an agricultural holding if the other requirements of the definition of an agricultural holding are met as well.

The use of land for horses frequently has given rise to problems in practice. The result of a series of cases upon the effect of the letting of land for use by horses is as follows:

(a)   Horses are not 'livestock' unless used in the farming of land or for the carrying on in relation to land of any agricultural activity (for example cart horses). This is because they are not kept 'for the production of food, wool, skins or fur' (except in the rare instance of horses destined for dog food or the continental meat trade). Therefore, land used for keeping horses rather than grazing by horses is not land used for agriculture within the meaning of s 96(1)[2].

(b)   If the land is let for grazing, then even though the animals which graze the land are not 'livestock', the land is agricultural land within the meaning of AHA 1986, ss 1(4) and 96(1). The definition of 'agriculture' includes the use of land as grazing land without restriction on the animals that graze.

(c)   If the land is used not merely for grazing by horses but also for a trade or business (for example for the grazing of horses forming part of a commercial riding school), then the holding will be an agricultural holding if the requirements of that definition are met. This is because the trade or business need not necessarily be an agricultural trade or business. If the land is let for grazing by horses for non-commercial purposes, for example, a pony paddock let for the tenant's personal hunters, hacks or show jumpers or those of his children, then the land will not constitute an agricultural holding[3].

---

[1]   *Rutherford v Maurer* [1962] 1 QB 16, [1961] 2 All ER 775, CA.

[2]   *Belmont Farm Ltd v Ministry of Housing and Local Government* (1962) 13 P & CR 417 and see *South Oxfordshire District Council v Secretary of State for the Environment* [1981] 1 All ER 954, [1981] 1 WLR 1092. Note that for the purposes of the Town and Country Planning Acts there is a similar but not identical definition of agriculture. Accordingly, the keeping and breeding of horses on agricultural land constitutes a change of use and requires planning consent which, if obtained, might entitle a landlord to serve notice to quit under s 26 and Sch 3, Case B, on the basis that the land was required for a use other than agriculture for which planning consent had been obtained, as to which see para 31.20.

[3]   See *McClinton v McFall* (1974) 232 Estates Gazette 707, CA. Compare the position with that which applies to, for example, rating: see *Hemens v Whitsbury Farm and Stud Ltd* [1987] QB 390, [1987] 1 All ER 430, (1987) 281 Estates Gazette 1065.

MIXED USER: AGGREGATE OF AGRICULTURAL LAND

19.11 The statutory definition of an agricultural holding includes in s 1(1) of the AHA 1986 the phrase that it comprises 'the aggregate of the land (whether agricultural land or not)'[1]. This issue is increasingly important in the context of diversification. On first reading this would suggest that it was merely the parcels of land which were to be aggregated in determining the extent of the agricultural holding.

19.11 *What is an agricultural holding?*

The multiplicity of decisions under s 1 of the AHA 1948 made it clear that it was also the land *uses* which fell to be aggregated, in addition to the parcels themselves, albeit that some of the decisions themselves are difficult to reconcile. In relation to the AHA 1948 definition, the following cases found that protection did arise under the AHA 1948:

(a) *Dunn v Fidoe*[2]: a letting of an inn, outbuildings and 12 acres of land where the inn and the garden occupied 0.381 acres. The landlord purchased the property for £5,500, of which £600 was attributable to the value of the land. The inn was fully licensed and did a substantial trade. The tenant also made significant profits from selling fruit from the land. The house was not a farmhouse. It was held by the Court of Appeal that the inn buildings were used in connection with the agricultural trade of the tenant, and as the test for ascertaining whether premises were an agricultural holding was no longer the dominant or main user, the whole premises, including the inn, constituted an agricultural holding. It is submitted that this case is difficult to reconcile with subsequent decisions.

(b) *Howkins v Jardine*[3]: in the Court of Appeal, Jenkins LJ held that: 'One must look at the substance of the matter and see whether as a matter of substance the land comprised in this tenancy, taken as a whole, is an agricultural holding. If it is, then the whole of it is entitled to the protection of the [1948] Act. If it is not then none of it is so entitled'[4]. Applying that test, the court held that seven acres of agricultural land, let with three cottages occupied by persons not employed in agriculture, were protected under the AHA 1948.

(c) *Adsetts v Heath*[5]: the letting of a smithy with an orchard and garden where the court held that there was a substantial benefit derived from the sale of fruit and vegetables and the keeping of hens.

(d) *Iredell v Brocklehurst*[6]: the letting of a farmhouse with 15 acres of agricultural land, notwithstanding the inclusion in the lease of a prohibition against carrying on 'a profession, trade or business'.

(e) *R v Agricultural Land Tribunal (South East Province), ex p Palmer*[7]: the letting of a house with three acres. It should be noted that this may be regarded as a special case because of the tenant's conduct.

(f) *McClinton v McFall*[8]: a letting of 56 acres 'as a stud farm for all aspects of horse trade, including breeding, training and schooling and showing', where the court held that the predominant user was grazing and the production of hay[9].

[1] Contrast the wording of s 1 of the AHA 1948 which reads 'the aggregate of the agricultural land let'.
[2] [1950] 2 All ER 685.
[3] [1951] 1 KB 614, [1951] 1 All ER 320.
[4] *Howkins v Jardine* [1951] 1 KB 614, [1951] 1 All ER 320 at 628.
[5] (1951) County Court, unreported, cited in 95 Sol Jo 620.
[6] (1950) 155 Estates Gazette 268, CA.
[7] (1954) 163 Estates Gazette 106.
[8] (1974) 232 Estates Gazette 707.
[9] Cf the position in Scotland: see *McGhie v Laing* (1952) 102 L Jo 365; *McNeill v Duke of Hamilton's Trustees* 1918 SC 221, Ct of Sess.

19.12 Conversely, the courts have held that protection under the AHA 1948 did not arise in the following cases:

(a)   *Godfrey v Waite*[1]: the letting of a former farmhouse separately from, but occupied with, some 32 acres of agricultural land.

(b)   *Kempe v Dillon-Trenchard*[2]: the letting of a house and nine acres of land used for keeping poultry and cattle, where the lease prohibited use otherwise than as a private dwellinghouse.

(c)   *Lord Monson v Bound*[3]: the letting of a retail florist's shop with a stock garden of one-third of an acre where some one-sixth of the produce sold was grown on the let premises.

(d)   *Deith v Brown*[4]: the letting of a riding school comprising stables, a cottage and 12 acres, on part of which agricultural activities were carried on.

(e)   *Price v Vaughan*[5]: a tenancy granted to a blacksmith in relation to the smithy together with 1.5 acres, part of which was used for agricultural purposes.

[1]   [1951] EGD 9, CA.
[2]   [1951] EGD 13.
[3]   [1954] 3 All ER 228, [1954] 1 WLR 1321.
[4]   (1956) 167 Estates Gazette 513.
[5]   (1958) 172 Estates Gazette 161.

19.13 The decisions referred to above, relating to the different wording of s 1 of the AHA 1948, made it clear that if the tenancy as a whole was in substance[1] a tenancy of agricultural land, then the aggregate of all the land let, including the non-agricultural land, would together constitute one single holding to which the agricultural holdings legislation would apply. There could be no mixed tenancy falling partly within the agricultural holdings legislation and partly within other legislation, giving security of tenure, or indeed falling outside protective legislation altogether[2].

[1]   Cf *Howkins v Jardine* [1951] 1 KB 614, [1951] 1 All ER 320; *Lord Monson v Bound* [1954] 3 All ER 228, [1954] 1 WLR 1321; *Deith v Brown* (1956) 167 Estates Gazette 513; *Darby v Williams* (1974) 232 Estates Gazette 579, CA.
[2]   As to the relationship between agricultural holdings legislation and the Rent Acts/Housing Acts and the Landlord and Tenant Act 1954, see paras 19.26, 19.28 and 19.22.

19.14 The words of the definition in s 1(1) of the AHA 1986[1] have now been supplemented by s 1(2). Section 1(1) provides expressly that the parcels of land fall to be aggregated whether the individual parcels are agricultural or not. Section 1(2) provides that a contract of tenancy relating to any land is a contract for an agricultural tenancy if, having regard to:

(1)   the terms of the tenancy;
(2)   the actual or contemplated use of the land at the time of the conclusion of the contract and subsequently; and
(3)   any other relevant circumstances,

the whole of the land comprised in the contract, subject to such exceptions only as do not substantially affect the character of the tenancy, is let for use as agricultural land.

The letting must comprise a single contract of tenancy[2]. Where, for example, a cottage and agricultural land were let on different terms, at different rents, albeit at the same time and conditionally one upon the other, it was held that the two properties were not to be aggregated so as to comprise a single letting comprising an agricultural holding[3].

As stated above, the statutory definition of an agricultural holding, and in particular the phrase 'the aggregate of the land (whether agricultural land or not)' contained in the AHA 1986, was first enacted by the AHA 1984. That definition was intended to reflect the case law applying to the AHA 1948 definition. Analysing the relevant cases[4], it is submitted that the following propositions of law may be identified:

(a)   The first and primary task is to determine what the substantial purpose was for which the premises were let.

(b)   If, as a matter of substance, the land comprised in the tenancy agreement, taken as a whole, was an agricultural holding, then the whole of the holding is entitled to protection under the agricultural holdings legislation whereas, if it was not, then none of the holding is so entitled.

(c)   In determining what the substantial purpose was, the terms of the tenancy granted must be considered, in as much as if those terms provided for or contemplated the use of the premises for a particular purpose then, subject to (e) below, that purpose is the essential factor in deciding whether or not the premises were let as an agricultural holding so as to be entitled to protection under the agricultural holdings legislation.

(d)   Where the original tenancy provided for or contemplated the use of the premises for some particular purpose but, by the time possession proceedings are commenced, their use is wholly or substantially abandoned (in support of which strong evidence is needed), then the tenant ceases to be entitled to the statutory protection (if any) to which use for that purpose would have entitled him[5].

(e)   Where the original tenancy agreement provided for or contemplated the use of the premises for some particular purpose but, by the time when possession proceedings are commenced, that agreement has been superseded by a subsequent contract providing for a different user, the subsequent contract may be considered in deciding whether the tenancy is entitled to statutory protection.

(f)   If a tenant changes the use of the premises, and the fact of the change of use is fully known to and accepted by the landlord, it may be possible for the court to infer a subsequent contract to let those premises for such changed purpose, although this would be a contract different in essentials to the original tenancy agreement.

(g)   Unless such a contract referred to in paragraph (f) can be established, a mere unilateral change of user will not enable a tenant to claim the protection under a particular Act in a case where the terms of the tenancy agreement itself provide for and contemplate the user of the premises for some particular purpose which does not attract the protection of that Act.

(h)   Where the tenancy agreement itself does not provide for or contemplate the use of the premises for any particular purpose, actual subsequent user has to be looked at in determining whether the premises are let so as to come under the system of protection of one Act rather than of another.

1   Note that the AHA 1986 definition represents a development from the AHA 1948 definition as a consequence of the amendments made by the AHA 1984.
2   *Blackmore v Butler* [1954] 2 QB 171, CA; *Darby v Williams* (1974) 232 Estates Gazette 579, CA; *Jenkins R Lewis & Son Ltd v Kerman* [1971] Ch 477. Also see, *J W Childers Trustees v Anker* [1996] 1 EGLR 1, [1996] 01 EG 102, CA.
3   *Darby v Williams* (1974) 232 Estates Gazette 579, CA. Cf *Dodson Bull Carpet Co Ltd v City of London Corpn* [1975] 2 All ER 497, [1975] 1 WLR 781.
4   *Wolfe v Hogan* [1949] 2 KB 194, CA; *Whitty v Scott-Russell* [1950] 2 KB 32, CA; *Howkins v Jardine* [1951] 1 KB 614, [1951] 1 All ER 320, CA; *Wetherall v Smith* [1980] 2 All ER 530, [1980] 1 WLR 1290; *Russell v Booker* (1982) 5 HLR 10, [1982] 2 EGLR 86, CA; *British Land Co Ltd v Herbert Silver (Menswear) Ltd* [1958] 1 QB 530; *Berry v Berry* [1929] 2 KB 316; *South West Water Authority v Palmer* (1983) 268 Estates Gazette 357; *Centrovincial Estates plc v Merchants Investors Assurance Co Ltd* (1983), Times, 8 March.
5   See para 19.18.

19.15   Since the enactment of the AHA 1984, and its subsequent consolidation in the AHA 1986, the issue of mixed user has been considered by the courts.

In *Short v Greeves*[1], the issue was not what statutory protection applied at the outset of the tenancy, but what was the effect of a change in the user during the course of the letting. Initially the tenancy was protected as an agricultural holding where a garden centre was let with some six acres of agricultural land which provided all of the produce for the garden centre. Subsequent developments led to some 60% of the garden centre's produce being bought in. Nevertheless, the court held that this was insufficient to deprive the tenancy of its 1986 Act protection[2].

In *Gold v Jacques Amand Ltd*[3], the primary issue was whether a licence to occupy agricultural land gave rise to protection under the AHA 1986. In finding that it did, the court also determined that such protection was unaffected by the fact that no retail sales in relation to a business of buying and selling bulbs was to be carried out from the land and the holding only provided some 15–20% of the production for the business. Further, it was relevant that there was a wholesale bulb business.

It is submitted that the principles set out in para 19.14 have been affected by the amendment to the statutory definition by the AHA 1984, now consolidated in the AHA 1986. Whereas under the AHA 1948, the terms of the tenancy (if any) was the dominant factor in determining whether protection arose under that Act, s 1(2) of the AHA 1986 provides that this is just one of three matters to have regard to[4]. It is likely that the court would have regard to implied as well as express terms. This would be consistent with the way in which the court has construed the word 'contemplation' when dealing with cases under s 2 of the AHA 1986 (and its statutory predecessor)[5]. It is nevertheless submitted that the court is still governed by express terms in the tenancy agreement unless sham is alleged[6]. If the tenancy agreement is silent, then the court is entitled to look at other matters relevant to the contemplation of the parties[7].

19.15   *What is an agricultural holding?*

Accordingly, it appears that the combined effect of the pre-AHA 1984 case law, the AHA 1986 statutory definition and the post-AHA 1984 decisions establish that:

(a)   If, as a matter of substance, the land comprised in the tenancy agreement, taken as a whole, was an agricultural holding and its commencement, then the whole of the holding is entitled to the protection of the AHA 1986. If it was not, then none of the holding is so entitled.

(b)   In determining what the substantial purpose was, the terms of the tenancy granted must be considered, if those terms provided for or contemplated the use of the premises for a particular purpose. Then, subject to any subsequent agreement, that purpose is the essential factor in deciding whether or not the holding was let as an agricultural holding so as to be entitled to the protection of the AHA 1986[8].

In carrying out its assessment, in the absence of clear contractual agreement as to the use of the premises, the court may consider a number of factors, including:

(i)   the contribution made to the income or profits of the tenant[9];
(ii)   whether the use is continuous or intermittent[10];
(iii)   the proportion of the land used for various purposes[11];
(iv)   evidence as to the paramount purpose of the letting[12].

1   [1988] 1 EGLR 1 [1988] 08 EG 108, CA. Also see *Lester v Ridd* [1990] 2 QB 430, [1989] 1 All ER 1111, CA.
2   Note *Lord Monson v Bound* [1954] 3 All ER 228, where only 10% of agricultural production was generated on the holding and protection under the AHA 1948 was not found to apply.
3   (1991) 63 P & CR 1.
4   See para 19.14.
5   See *Scene Estates Ltd v Amos* [1957] 2 QB 205 at 211, CA.
6   See para 19.54.
7   See *Scene Estates Ltd v Amos* [1957] 2 QB 205 at 213, CA.
8   See *Tan v Sitkowski* [2007] EWCA Civ 30, (2007) Times, 15 February, [2007] 06 EG 165 (CS); *Jewell v McGowan* [2002] EWCA Civ 145, [2002] 3 EGLR 87, CA, where the court appeared to place much weight on the fact that the tendancy agreement obliged the tenant to use the lead for agricultural purposes only. Also see para 32.12.
9   *Lord Monson v Bound* [1954] 3 All ER 228; *Deith v Brown* (1956) 167 Estates Gazette 513.
10   *McClinton v McFall* (1974) 232 Estates Gazette 707, CA.
11   *McClinton v McFall* (1974) 232 Estates Gazette 707, CA.
12   *Howkins v Jardine* [1951] 1 KB 614, [1951] 1 All ER 320, CA.

CHANGE OF STATUS

Abandonment of agricultural use

19.16   If the agricultural use is wholly or substantially discontinued the holding will cease to be an agricultural holding. This applies even if the abandonment is in breach of covenant or without landlord's consent[1]. The time for deciding whether the holding remains an agricultural holding is when its status is called into question.

[1]   *Wetherall v Smith* [1980] 2 All ER 530, [1980] 1 WLR 1290.

Unlawful agricultural use

19.17 The use prescribed in the tenancy agreement will apply, and thereby define the statutory code to apply. Any departure from it requires a new contract of tenancy or a variation of the existing contract. 'Nothing short of a new contract or variation of contract will suffice'[1]. Section 1(3) of the AHA 1986 makes it clear that a holding cannot become an agricultural holding if the agricultural use is in breach of contract unless that breach was with the permission, consent or acquiescence of the landlord[2].

[1]   *Court v Robinson* [1951] 2 KB 60, per Asquith LJ at 70.
[2]   See para 19.6(g).

Implied variation

19.18 If the tenant changes the use of the holding, and this is fact is fully known and accepted by the landlord, it may be possible for the court to infer a subsequent contract to let the holding for the new purpose, even though this would be a contract different in essentials to the original tenancy. Constructive knowledge of the change of use is not sufficient for this purpose[1]. Long use in breach of covenant, with the landlord's knowledge, can be held to imply that the landlord has acquiesced in its variation[2]. Mere acceptance of rent, with knowledge of the changed use, will have no effect 'unless it can be inferred, as a matter of fact, that the landlord has affirmatively assented to the change of user'[3].

[1]   *Russell v Booker* (1982) 5 HLR 10, [1982] 2 EGLR 86, CA.
[2]   See para 19.6(h).
[3]   *Wolfe v Hogan* [1949] 2 KB 194, per Denning LJ at 206.

Unilateral change of user

19.19 Unless a subsequent contract can be established, a mere unilateral change of user will not enable the tenant to claim the protection of the AHA 1986 in a case where the terms of the tenancy agreement itself provides for and contemplates the use of the holding for some other purpose[1]. This has been reinforced by the Court of Appeal decision in *Tan v Sitkowski*[2]. In that case premises were let for a business with protection under the Landlord and Tenant Act 1954. The tenant ceased his business use, retaining the first-floor living accommodation and using the remainder of the premises for storage. The tenant claimed protection under the Rent Act 1977. The claim was rejected.

19.19   *What is an agricultural holding?*

1   *Russell v Booker* (1982) 5 HLR 10, [1982] 2 EGLR 86, CA; *Tomkins v Basildon District Council* [2002] EWCA Civ 876, [2002] 3 EGLR 33.
2   [2007] EWCA Civ 30, [2007] 06 EG 165 (CS).

Reduction of agricultural use and increase of non-agricultural use

19.20   A more difficult problem is where a holding was undoubtedly an agricultural holding at its inception but due to the adoption, for example, of a diversification scheme then a non-agricultural use has been introduced or intensified so as to affect the character of the holding and the tenancy. In such circumstances, will the holding cease to be an agricultural holding only possibly to return to being one again when the balance changes and reverts to the original position?

The present law following the passing of the AHA 1984 and AHA 1986 was extensively considered and applied in *Short v Greeves*[1]. The test applied in *Wetherall v Smith*[2] was held to apply:

> 'The cases show that the tenancy is not to be regarded as alternating between being within and outside the Agricultural Holdings Act 1948 [now the AHA 1986] as minor changes of use take place, and that, when the tenancy is clearly an agricultural one to start with strong evidence is needed to show that the agricultural use has been abandoned'.

This can mean that a holding whose current use is predominantly non-agricultural may still be an agricultural holding if it was one at the outset and the agricultural use has not been abandoned but merely reduced.

1   [1988] 1 EGLR 1 [1988] 08 EG 109, CA. The wording from *Wetherall v Smith* was quoted in *Short v Greeves*.
2   [1980] 2 All ER 530, [1980] 1 WLR 1290.

THE RELATIONSHIP BETWEEN THE AHA 1986 AND OTHER PROTECTIVE CODES

Single contract of tenancy

19.21   It should be noted that, particularly in the context of separate lettings of residential accommodation, if, for example, a cottage is let separately from agricultural land by a different tenancy agreement, then the two agreements will fall to be considered individually. This is despite the fact that the two lettings may be linked or even conditional, one upon the other[1].

1   *Darby v Williams* (1974) 232 Estates Gazette 579, CA.

The Landlord and Tenant Act 1954 and agricultural land

19.22   As noted above in relation to businesses involving the keeping of horses[1], in some cases issues arise as to whether a tenancy is protected under the AHA 1986 (or, since 1 September 1995, the ATA 1995) or whether it is a business tenancy within the Landlord and Tenant Act 1954, Pt II (LTA 1954).

Section 43(1)(a) of the LTA 1954[2] excludes from protection given to business tenancies all tenancies of agricultural holdings, including those tenancies (such as grazing agreements) which are not technically tenancies of agricultural holdings because they come outside the scope of s 2 of the AHA 1986.

Conversely, neither the AHA 1986 nor the ATA 1995 exclude from their respective statutory codes a tenancy which would otherwise qualify as a business letting within the LTA 1954. It is submitted that this is not a statutory lacuna. The effect is that if a tenancy were to qualify under both the business tenancy code and the agricultural holdings/tenancies code, then the latter would prevail in order to provide protection for the tenant.

The question as to whether a letting entered into before 1 September 1995 was protected under the AHA 1986 or under the LTA 1954 does have a number of important consequences, including in relation to:

(a)   the protection afforded to licences and tenancies at will;
(b)   recovering possession;
(c)   the payment of compensation for improvements and disturbance.

1   See para 19.10.
2   As amended, initially by the Agriculture Act 1958 and subsequently by the ATA 1995, Sch para 10.

Licences/tenancies at will

19.23   Neither a licence nor a tenancy at will of business premises is protected by the LTA 1954[1]. Conversely, a licence conferring exclusive possession of an agricultural holding entered into before 1 September 1995 is statutorily protected under the AHA 1986 by way of the statutory conversion contained in s 2 of the AHA 1986[2]. Likewise, a tenancy at will of agricultural land is a letting 'for an interest less than a tenancy from year to year' and therefore if granted before 1 September 1995, it too is protected by s 2 of the AHA 1986.

1   As to tenancies at will, see *Cardiothoracic Institute v Shrewdcrest Ltd* [1986] 1 WLR 368; *Uzun v Ramadan* [1986] 2 EGLR 255. As to licences, see the LTA 1954, s 23.
2   See para 20.5. It should be noted that neither a licence nor a tenancy at will entered into on or after 1 September 1995 will be protected as a farm business tenancy under the ATA 1995: ATA 1995, s 38.

Recovering possession

19.24   It is easier for a landlord to recover possession of business premises under the LTA 1954 than it is under the AHA 1986. In particular, under the LTA 1954, the landlord is able to rely upon s 30(1)(f) and (g), which enables the landlord to recover possession where the landlord wishes to carry out works of reconstruction or demolition or alternatively to occupy the premises for himself for business purposes.

19.25   *What is an agricultural holding?*

Compensation for improvements and disturbance

19.25 If a tenancy of business premises is protected under the LTA 1954, compensation for improvements is governed by the Landlord and Tenant Act 1927, Pt I (LTA 1927). The LTA 1927 expressly excludes agricultural holdings and farm business tenancies[1].

There are a number of differences between the statutory code for recovering compensation under the AHA 1986 (and indeed the ATA 1995) and the LTA 1927. For example, there are different procedures for obtaining consent and for making a claim at the termination of the tenancy under the LTA 1927. Under the LTA 1927, the tenant is able to apply to the court for permission to carry out an improvement if it is refused by the landlord[2]. As to making a claim, under the LTA 1954, a tenant has three months from the service of a statutory notice of termination of the tenancy in order to make a claim[3].

The provisions for making a claim for compensation for disturbance also differ between the two statutory codes. In the case of a business tenancy, compensation is referable to the rateable value rather than the annual rent[4].

A further point to note in respect of the relationship between the AHA 1986 and the LTA 1954 is that if there has been abandonment of agricultural use in relation to a tenancy which was at its outset protected under the AHA 1986, even though it may be still a letting for business purposes, it does not follow that it will be automatically protected under the LTA 1954. The LTA 1954 requires occupation 'for the purpose of a business', but, unlike the AHA 1986, the business use must be substantial[5].

[1]   LTA 1927, s 17.
[2]   LTA 1927, s 3.
[3]   LTA 1954, s 47.
[4]   LTA 1954, s 37. Also note that no claim for compensation for disturbance may be made on the termination of a farm business tenancy under the ATA 1995.
[5]   LTA 1954, s 23.

The Rent Acts and agricultural land

19.26 It is beyond the scope of this book to deal in any detail with residential lettings, whether of agricultural tied accommodation (ie the provision of accommodation to agricultural workers) or residential lettings generally in relation to farmhouses and cottages on agricultural holdings[1].

It should nevertheless be noted that residential lettings entered into before 15 January 1989 are governed by the Rent Act 1977 (RA 1977) in respect of non tied accommodation and the Rent (Agriculture) Act 1976 (R(A)A 1976) in respect of tied agricultural accommodation. Lettings of residential premises, whether in respect of tied accommodation or otherwise, entered into on or after 15 January 1989 are governed by the Housing Act 1988 (HA 1988).

Section 10 of the RA 1977 provides that a tenancy is not a protected tenancy under the RA 1977 if the dwellinghouse is comprised in an agricultural

252

holding (within the meaning of the AHA 1986) and is occupied by the person responsible for the control (whether as tenant or as servant or agent of the tenant) of the farming of the holding[2].

It should also be noted that tenancies comprising a dwellinghouse with agricultural land exceeding two acres are also expressly excluded from the RA 1977 protection[3].

The definition of agricultural land, for the purposes of the provisions contained in the RA 1977, is a different definition to that for agricultural land contained in the AHA 1986.

The definition of agricultural land is any land used as arable, meadow or pasture ground only, land used for a plantation or a wood or for the growth of saleable underwood, land exceeding one-quarter of an acre used for the purpose of poultry farming, cottage gardens exceeding one-quarter of an acre, market gardens, nursery grounds, orchards or allotments, including allotment gardens within the meaning of the Allotments Act 1922. A cottage garden is a garden attached to a house occupied as a dwelling by a person of (what the statute describes as) the 'labouring classes'. Agricultural land does not include land occupied together with a house as a park, gardens (other than as mentioned above), pleasure grounds all land kept or preserved mainly or exclusively for the purposes of sport or recreation, or land used as a racecourse[4].

In the context of mixed user[5], the following cases should be noted:

(a) *Stanhope v Bashford*[6]: a letting of a house and four acres of meadow which the tenant covenanted to keep in good heart and condition. The tenant kept it as a park or land for sport or recreation, including maintaining three young racing colts. The court held that this was not agricultural land.

(b) *Hill v Morgan*[7]: a letting of a house and 2.5 acres of land of which 1.5 acres was meadow and the rest was garden. Held not to be agricultural land.

(c) *Chubb v Foord*[8]: a letting of a cottage with three plots of land. Two plots were agricultural land amounting to less than two acres and the third plot was a garden planted with fruit trees and vegetables. Again, the court found that the plot of land on which the house stood was planted with fruit trees and vegetables and that this clearly came within the definition of agricultural land. Accordingly, the letting did not have protection under the Rent Restrictions Acts then in force[9].

The position is more complicated where an AHA 1986 tenant sublets the farmhouse or a cottage either to an agricultural employee or a third party. If the letting is to an agricultural employee, at a low rent, any letting which was entered into before 15 January 1989 will be protected by the R(A)A 1976. If the letting is to a non-agricultural employee, it is governed by the RA 1977.

It should be noted that the application of the R(A)A 1976 or the RA 1977 only operates as between the AHA 1986 protected tenant and his sub-tenant.

19.26 *What is an agricultural holding?*

If the AHA 1986 tenancy were to be terminated then, at common law, the sub-tenancy would also be determined unless the termination was by way of surrender[10].

The statutory codes of both the R(A)A 1976 and the RA 1977 extend to provide protection for sub-tenants. Section 9(3) of the R(A)A 1976 provides protection where the superior 'premises' comprise an agricultural holding and part of it is let as tied accommodation. Section 9(3) of the R(A)A 1976 provides that, from the coming to an end of the superior tenancy, the R(A)A 1976 shall apply in relation to the dwellinghouse as if, in lieu of the superior tenancy, there had been separate tenancies of the dwellinghouse and the remainder of the premises, for the like purposes as under the superior tenancy and at rents equal to the just proportion of the rent under the superior tenancy. As a consequence, there is a notional head lease of the dwelling and the remainder of the holding. The sub-tenant becomes the tenant of the head landlord on the same terms as if his statutorily protected tenancy had continued held from the tenant under the AHA 1986. It should be noted that this protection only arises if the sub-tenancy is lawful and the head tenancy is a 'statutorily protected tenancy', ie a tenancy protected by the AHA 1986[11].

It should be noted that the protection afforded to sub-tenants only applies to lawful sub-tenants[12].

1   As to issues which have arisen in relation to residential property and agricultural land, see *National Trust v Knipe* [1997] 4 All ER 17, [1997] 1 WLR 230 (whether a farmhouse was let as a dwelling for the Protection from Eviction Act 1977).
2   See *Lester v Ridd* [1990] 2 QB 430, [1989] 1 All ER 1111, CA.
3   RA 1977, ss 6 and 26.
4   RA 1977, s 26(2); General Rate Act 1967, s 26(3)(a).
5   See para 19.11.
6   [1942] EGD 134.
7   [1946] EGD 198.
8   (1947) 150 Estates Gazette 304.
9   Also see *Smith v Richmond* [1899] AC 448, HL; *Umberslade Estates v Miller* (1943) 143 Estates Gazette 19; *Parry v Anglesey Assessment Committee* [1949] 1 KB 246; *Bradshaw v Smith* [1980] 2 EGLR 89, (1980) 255 Estates Gazette 699, CA.
10   *Bendall v McWhirter* [1952] 2 QB 466, CA. Also see *Pennell v Payne* [1995] QB 192, [1995] 2 All ER 592.
11   R(A)A 1976, s 9(4). See para 19.6(g).
12   See *Parker v Jones* [1910] 2 KB 32; *Factors (Sundries) Ltd v Miller* [1952] 2 All ER 630, CA. Also, in relation to relief against forfeiture, see Law of Property Act 1925, s 146(4).

19.27 A similar provision applies in relation to the operation of the RA 1977, contained in s 137(3) of the RA 1977. Section 137(3) of that Act provides like protection for a lawful sub-tenant[1] as that provided for a farm worker by the R(A)A 1976[2].

In 1975, in *Maunsell v Olins*[3], it was held by the House of Lords that the phrase 'premises' in s 137(3), referring to the head tenancy, did not include an agricultural holding. This statutory lacuna was in part reversed by the enactment of the R(A)A 1976, which added an express proviso to s 137(3) that 'premises' includes an agricultural holding protected by the AHA 1986. Further, it provided that protection would only arise for the sub-tenant 'if the sub-tenancy in question is a protected or statutory tenancy to which section 99 of the Rent Act 1977 applies'. Accordingly, a sub-tenant will only be protected if he is an agricultural worker and he would have protection under the R(A)A 1976 but for the fact that it is not a letting at a low rent[4].

1   See para 19.6(g).
2   It should be noted that s 137(3) of the RA 1977 reversed the earlier Court of Appeal decision in *Cow v Casey* [1949] 1 KB 474.
3   [1975] AC 373, HL.
4   RA 1977, s 99.

The Housing Act 1988 and agricultural land

19.28 Lettings of dwellinghouses, whether as tied accommodation or otherwise, entered into on or after 15 January 1989, are governed by the HA 1988, superseding the statutory codes contained in the RA 1977 and the R(A)A 1976.

Section 2 of the HA 1988 provides that if a dwellinghouse is let together with other land then for so long as the main purpose of the letting is the provision of a home to the tenant (or joint tenants), then other land shall be treated as part of the dwellinghouse and that shall be the main purpose of the letting. Such tenancies will be protected as either assured tenancies (in relation to non-tied accommodation) or assured agricultural occupancies (in respect of tied accommodation)[1].

Where the dwellinghouse is comprised in an agricultural holding and is occupied by the person responsible for the control (whether as tenant, or as a servant or agent of the tenant) of the farming of the holding, then HA 1988 protection is excluded[2].

Tenancies which cannot be assured tenancies or assured agricultural occupancies under the HA 1988 include a tenancy under which agricultural land, exceeding two acres, is let together with the dwellinghouse[3]. The definition of agricultural land is the same as that which applies to the RA 1977[4].

1   Unless the letting is an assured shorthold tenancy under the HA 1988.
2   HA 1988, Sch 1 para 6.
3   HA 1988, Sch 1 para 6.
4   HA 1988, Sch 1 para 6(2); General Rate Act 1967, s 26(3)(a). See para 19.26.

19.29 Where a lawful sub-tenancy[1] is created in relation to a dwellinghouse forming part of an agricultural holding on or after 15 January 1989, the provisions of the HA 1988 will apply to that letting.

Section 18(1) of the HA 1988 protects a sub-tenant whose interest, as between himself and his immediate landlord, constitutes an assured tenancy, as defined by the HA 1988. This includes an assured agricultural occupancy, protecting tied accommodation.

The protection afforded to the sub-tenant by s 18(1) of the HA 1988 applies if a dwellinghouse is lawfully let on an assured tenancy and the immediate landlord is himself a tenant under a superior tenancy which comes to an end. In those circumstances the assured tenancy will continue as a tenancy held of 'the person whose interest would, apart from the continuance of the assured tenancy, entitle him to actual possession of the dwellinghouse at that time'.

The protection provided by s 18(1) of the HA 1988 applies if the head tenancy is protected by the AHA 1986, the ATA 1995 or the LTA 1954[2].

¹   See para 19.6(g).
²   *Pittalis v Grant* [1989] QB 605, [1989] 2 All ER 622, CA.

JOINT VENTURES AND PARTNERSHIPS

Introduction

19.30 The background to this section is that partnerships or other joint venture agreements have been widely used as trading vehicles in relation to agricultural holdings. Family farming businesses have been generally partnerships. It has been relatively rare for such businesses to be conducted through the medium of limited companies. Limited liability partnerships did not exist on 1 September 1995, when the AHA 1986 regime was generally superseded by the ATA 1995[1].

Until the ATA 1995 came into force[2], landowners who wished to farm their land in conjunction with a non-landowning, active farmer have also used partnerships, or alternatively share farming agreements, as a means to seek to avoid the active farmer acquiring security under the AHA 1986.

Practitioners are often asked to advise in relation to a re-organisation of a family farming partnership or in respect of a breakdown in relations between either family members of such a partnership or a landowner and the active farmer.

This section considers:

(a)   the distinction between general partnership, limited partnership and share farming;
(b)   the different ways in which a partnership may occupy land;
(c)   the issues which arise in relation to security of tenure under the AHA 1986;
(d)   some of the principles of partnership law which arise in practice in relation to disputes concerning agricultural holdings[3].

¹   See para 3.3.
²   On 1 September 1995: see para 3.3.
³   It is beyond the scope of this book to consider the law relating to partnership disputes in general. Reference should be made to Blackett-Ord, *Partnership* (2nd edn, 2002) Butterworths, and *Lindley and Banks on Partnership* (18th edn, 2002) Sweet & Maxwell.

General partnership

19.31 Partnership is defined as 'the relation which subsists between persons carrying on a business in common with a view to profit'[1]. Partners may occupy land either pursuant to:

(a)   a tenancy held outside the partnership; or
(b)   a tenancy held as an asset of the partnership; or
(c)   a licence (express or implied).

In the case of a tenancy granted by the landowner to himself and another or others, there has been a longstanding issue as to whether, as a matter of property law, this is possible[2].

Licences under the AHA 1986 are converted by the 'statutory magic' of s 2 of the AHA 1986 into fully protected tenancies[3]. In the case of partnerships, it was found by the Court of Appeal in *Harrison-Broadley v Smith*[4] that a licence was capable of being a 'non-exclusive' licence, ie one not conferring exclusive possession, and as such the 'statutory magic' would not apply. The 'non-exclusive' licence would not obtain protection under the AHA 1986[5].

The Court of Appeal's decision in *Harrison-Broadley v Smith*[6] was followed by the House of Lords in *Bahamas International Trust Co Ltd v Threadgold*[7]. As a consequence of those decisions, partnerships have been widely used by landowners as a means of avoiding security of tenure under the AHA 1986[8].

If the licence to occupy is to be found to be a non-exclusive licence, and not subject to statutory conversion, not only must the form of the agreement itself show that the parties intended to enter into a non-exclusive licence, but also it must be shown that, in fact, the licence granted was non-exclusive[9]. This might be shown by the licensor being a member of the partnership and retaining rights to carry on, in common with his partners, the agricultural activities on the holding and retaining the right whether or not it has been exercised to continue to occupy the holding. If the right to continue to occupy the holding is not exercised, there may be a degree of sham[10].

---

[1]   Partnership Act 1890, s 1(1). Also see, *Stackel v Ellice* [1973] 1 WLR 191.
[2]   See para 19.36ff.
[3]   See para 20.5.
[4]   [1964] 1 All ER 867, [1964] 1 WLR 456, CA. A different perspective as to the position of a non-landowning partner should be noted from the unreported High Court decision of Forbes J in *Brooks v Brown* (1986): see para 21.18.
[5]   Or its statutory predecessor, the AHA 1948.
[6]   [1964] 1 All ER 867, [1964] 1 WLR 456, CA.
[7]   [1974] 3 All ER 881, [1974] 1 WLR 1514.
[8]   As to licences and the AHA 1986 generally, see para 21.15ff.
[9]   See para 21.16.
[10]   See para 19.54.

Limited partnership

19.32 Where the landowner/licensor is only a limited partner in a limited partnership he may not, if he is to retain his limited liability, take part in the day-to-day business activities of the partnership[1]. Because of this, doubts have been expressed as to the nature of any licence that he (as opposed to a general partner) may grant to the partners to carry on the partnership business on and from the land. However, a limited partner is not excluded from exercising rights of occupation over the land, despite the prohibition upon his taking part in the business activities. Furthermore, he is still entitled (by virtue of his limited capital) to claim that the stock and crops on the land belong to him as well as to his general partners. Nevertheless, his retained rights of occupation are little more than nominal and there are severe doubts as to whether any licence granted before 1 September 1995 by a mere limited partner to his general partners and still subsisting would have escaped statutory conversion by s 2 of the AHA 1986.

[1] Limited Partnerships Act 1907.

Limited companies and limited liability partnership

19.33 Generally in commercial business (but not professional business), the limited liability company has been the preferred vehicle for trading. This has not generally been the case in farming businesses. Farmers have forsaken limited liability, possibly having regard to the disadvantages of corporate status, namely:

(a) the formalities of Companies House, including the need for annual returns; and
(b) public access to accounts.

It should be noted that the new legal entity of limited liability partnerships was not created until the Limited Liability Partnerships Act 2000 came into force[1].

[1] The Act was enacted on 20 July 2000 and came into effect, pursuant to the Limited Liability Partnerships Regulations 2001, SI 2001/1090, on 6 April 2001.

Share farming agreement

19.34 The expression 'share farming'[1] is not a term of art but has been frequently used to define an arrangement between a landowner and a farmer for the farming of the land. The objectives of share farming agreements are to avoid the arrangement being characterised either as a partnership or a letting. A share farming arrangement is generally distinguished from a partnership on the basis that it is an agreement to share gross receipts and for net profits. The cautious landowner prefers sharing only grass profits. Although the term is wholly undefined and is used in different contexts by different people to mean different things, normally a share farming agreement involves an arrangement entered into between two or more persons to make available from their separate businesses assets or services for the carrying out of specified farming operations, the gross receipts from which are to be divided between and paid to the separate businesses in agreed proportions. Rights to occupy land for the purposes of this sort of venture will not have involved either the grant of a tenancy or an exclusive licence if, upon its true construction, the arrangement made did not give the non-landowning party rights of exclusive possession[2].

A great many share farming agreements may be found on their true construction to be general partnerships or lettings. Where such an agreement is found to be a joint venture[3] which is not a general partnership, any licence granted by one party to the other to occupy agricultural land must have been carefully constructed and carefully scrutinised to ensure that the rights granted to the non-landowning party did not amount to an exclusive licence with the licensor receiving a fluctuating return[4].

1   See Cardwell, 'Arable Farming in the Short Term' (1993), The Conveyancer, 138.
2   See *McCarthy v Bence* [1990] 1 EGLR 1, for a case in which a 'share milking' agreement was considered by the Court of Appeal. Also see, *Lam Kee Ying Sdn Bhd v Lam Shes Tong (t/a Lian Joe Co)* [1975] AC 247, PC; *Tulapam Properties Ltd v De Almeida* (1981) 260 Estates Gazette 919; *Akici v L R Butlin Ltd* [2005] EWCA Civ 1296, [2006] 2 All ER 872.
3   Also see, *Rowan v Dann* [1991] EGCS 19; affd (1991) 64 P & CR 202. See para 19.52.
4   Turnover leases for public houses in the licensed victuallers trade are well known. The fact that the rent is a fluctuating sum does not detract from the fact that there is a grant of a tenancy. For a case of an agricultural holding with a fluctuating rent, see *Bolesworth Estate Co Ltd v Cook* (1966) 116 NLJ 1318.

19.35 In the decided cases[1], the test has been whether the landowner had preserved rights which, both in substance as well as form, prevented the licence from being exclusive. Commonly in share farming agreements, the ownership of the stock or crops remained with the landowner until sale or severance, with the non-landowning party being granted only such rights of access to the holding as were required to enable him to fulfil his obligations to the joint venture. An agreement was not prevented from being a joint venture other than a partnership by reason of the fact that the stock or crops were owned jointly by the parties. Provisions indicating that the stock or crops on the land belonged to the non-landowning party were likely to result in statutory conversion of the agreement to a tenancy from year to year if entered into before 1 September 1995.

If the landowning party sold the standing crop to the non-landowning party it is probable that from that time the non-landowning share-farmer would be found to have been in exclusive possession of the land in question. It is submitted that, in such circumstances, s 2 of the AHA 1986 would have, in some cases, operated to convert the licence into a tenancy from year to year[2].

Very frequently complex documents were prepared to give effect to the proposed share farming agreement but the parties, in fact, operated the farming of the holding in a way inconsistent with the documents prepared. In such circumstances, if the documents were not mere shams and, therefore, of no legal effect, there will probably be found to have been a novation with the new agreement being determined by the parties' conduct and the consequent agreement expressly or impliedly founded upon that[3].

Share farming agreements are still being entered into after 1 September 1995 where for fiscal, operational or other reasons, a tenancy is not considered desirable.

19.35 What is an agricultural holding?

1   See para 21.6.
2   *Harrison-Broadley v Smith* [1963] 3 All ER 586, [1963] 1 WLR 1262 and especially the doubts expressed by the Court of Appeal as to the correctness of the decision in *Wyatt v King* (1951) 157 Estates Gazette 124, CA.
3   For useful precedents, see Encyclopaedia of Forms and Precedents, Vol 2(1), Agriculture.

Lettings by a landowner to himself and his partners

19.36 Sometimes a landowner, instead of merely allowing his partners to share occupation of the land with him[1], purports to let the land to himself and his partners.

The first problem to which they give rise is whether a person can let to himself and another and covenant with himself as both landlord and tenant. The point is one of some difficulty.

1   Such an arrangement would not give rise to a protected tenancy under the AHA 1986, see *Harrison-Broadley v Smith* [1964] 1 All ER 867, [1964] 1 WLR 456.

19.37 The matter was considered by the House of Lords in the case of *Rye v Rye*[1]. It is far from clear that the dicta of the five Law Lords in deciding *Rye v Rye* supports the contention that a landowner can let to himself and others. There is no other decision of the court specifically on the point but it has been widely assumed to be possible since *Rye v Rye*[2].

At common law a person could not let to himself, nor to himself and another or others, nor could two or more persons let to themselves[3]. *Rye v Rye* was concerned with the problem as to whether ss 72 and 82 of the Law of Property Act 1925 had changed that rule of law. The House of Lords, in *Rye v Rye*, decided that an owner of land could not let it to himself, nor could two or more owners let to themselves jointly. However, the court did not determine whether it was possible for a person to let land to himself and others[4].

Lord Radcliffe thought that it was possible for a person, in certain circumstances, to let land to himself or for two persons to let land to themselves, but such a transaction had to be carried into effect by a 'conveyance' within the special meaning given to that word by s 205(1)(ii) of the Law of Property Act 1925. Lord Radcliffe stated that a conveyance, while not necessarily made under seal, had to be in writing. This view was supported by four out of the five Law Lords in the House of Lords. The result is that it would appear from the House of Lords' decision in *Rye v Rye* that it is not possible for a person orally to let land to himself and others, nor can two or more owners orally let to themselves and others[5]. Indeed, lettings involving one or more of the landlords also being one of the tenants are so common that there seems to be a general assumption that their legality is axiomatic.

If it is possible for a landowner to grant a tenancy to himself and another, and if such agreement was entered into before 1 September 1995[6], the further problem arises as to the protection afforded to the non-landowning tenant. If the tenancy so created falls within the definition contained in s 1 of the AHA 1986, then the tenancy will be protected by that Act.

1   [1962] AC 496, [1962] 1 All ER 146. Lord Denning, who was himself a member of the House of Lords, stated in *Joseph v Joseph* [1967] Ch 78, [1966] 3 All ER 486, CA; 'That agreement by A and B to grant a lease to A, B and C was perfectly good, see *Rye v Rye*.'

2   *Rye v Rye* has been referred to in two further Scottish cases: *Pinkerton v Pinkerton* 1986 SLT 672, Ct of Sess and *Clydesdale Bank plc v Davidson* 1998 SLT 522, HL. The latter distinguished the former. *Rye v Rye* was also referred to in the House of Lords again in *Ingram v IRC* [2000] 1 AC 293. It was observed that: 'A lease requires a lessor and a lessee, so Lady Ingram could not have granted a lease to herself: see *Rye v Rye*'. None of these cases provide definitive assistance.

3   See *Faulkner v Lowe* (1848) 2 Exch 595 at 597 and the maxim '*nemo potest esse tenens et dominus*' (nobody can be both tenant and landlord).

4   It should also be noted that *Rye v Rye* was not referred to by the Court of Appeal in *Harrison-Broadley v Smith* [1964] 1 All ER 867, [1964] 1 WLR 456 because on the facts of that case the owner simply let his partner into possession without purporting to grant a tenancy. However, in their respective judgments in the Court of Appeal, Harman LJ and Davies LJ were less than complimentary about the notion that it was possible for a landowner to let to himself and others, describing it as 'bizarre' and 'absurd'. This has given rise to an interesting academic argument as to whether it is possible for the House of Lords to overturn the decision in *Harrison-Broadley v Smith* on the basis that the Court of Appeal started from a false premise as to the effect of the House of Lords' own decision in *Rye v Rye*. It is submitted that the correct approach is that the Court of Appeal's decision in *Harrison-Broadley v Smith* is not reviewable as the ability of a landowner to let to himself and others was not the critical factor in that case.

5   The position is further complicated by the suggestion of Lord Denning that ss 72(4) and 82(1) of the Law of Property Act 1925 'only apply where one of the persons, at any rate, is not on both sides'; *Rye v Rye* [1962] AC 496 at 514.

6   It is noteworthy that the proposition was not questioned in the cases of *Sykes v Land* [1984] 2 EGLR 8, CA; *Featherstone v Staples* [1986] 2 All ER 461, [1986] 1 WLR 861. It now seems to be generally assumed that it is possible despite the absence of any specific and direct authority on the point.

Protection under the AHA 1986

19.38   That protection may be more illusory than real. The question arises as to whether an owner can be compelled to concur in the serving on himself of the necessary notices or counter-notices which are an essential element in many of the rights under agricultural holdings legislation. This gives rise to a number of issues which are dealt with in this section in relation to their relevance to partnerships.

The issues relate to who can give a valid notice to quit and who can give a valid counter-notice under the AHA 1986. These matters are considered generally in Chapter 29 in relation to joint interests but are dealt with in this section in relation to their relevance to partnerships.

The first is whether a landlord can give a notice to quit to his fellow tenant or whether his rights are fettered by his position as landlord and tenant or as fellow partners. That was considered in the case of *Brenner v Rose*[1] where it was decided that there was no limitation upon the landlord's ability to serve a notice to quit[2].

The next problem is whether the non-landowning tenant is able to give a valid counter-notice to the notice to quit under agricultural holdings legislation. It is now well established that any counter-notice to a notice to quit under agricultural holdings legislation must be given by *all* tenants where there are joint tenants[3]. The phrase 'the tenant' in the context of s 26(1)(b) of the AHA 1986[4] in the case of any joint tenancy, means 'the joint tenants' and not 'the joint tenants or any one or more of them'[5]. If a counter-notice is signed by only one of two joint tenants it is ineffective[6].

The exception to that rule arises where the one joint tenant giving the counter-notice has either implied or express authority to do so. Such authority may be implied as a consequence of a partnership or it may be express, for example, where a court order gives power to the joint tenant to conduct the farming business[7].

1   [1973] 2 All ER 535, [1973] 1 WLR 443. Also see *Harrison v Wing* [1988] 2 EGLR 4, [1988] 29 EG 101, CA.
2   Per Brightman J, as he then was: 'In my judgment the right of a landlord in such circumstances either to have possession or to recover the rent is not to be whittled away by the mere fact that he is one of the partners and is a purchaser of the reversion expectant on the underlease. I do not see that the defendant's fiduciary capacity as a member of a partnership which includes the benefit and burden of the underlease raises any sort of equity which should be allowed to prevent him from exercising his rights as landlord that he would have had if he were a stranger to the partnership': *Brenner v Rose* [1973] 2 All ER 535 at 539. This needs to be considered in the context of the fiduciary duties which may exist: see para 29.16.
3   *Newman v Keedwell* (1977) 244 Estates Gazette 469 and *Featherstone v Staples* [1985] 1 EGLR 1, 278 Estates Gazette 867. This principle is wholly consistent with the situation where relief is sought against forfeiture under s 146 of the Law of Property Act 1925. In the case of a joint tenancy it is well established that all the joint tenants must join in the application for relief: see *TM Fairclough & Sons Ltd v Berliner* [1931] 1 Ch 60.
4   Formerly s 2(1)(b) of the Agricultural Holdings (Notices to Quit) Act 1977.
5   See *Jacobs v Chaudhuri* [1968] 2 QB 470, [1968] 2 All ER 124, CA; *Turley v Panton* (1975) 29 P & CR 397; *Newman v Keedwell* (1977) 244 Estates Gazette 469; and *Featherstone v Staples* [1985] 1 EGLR 1, 278 Estates Gazette 867. There have been two cases in which the courts have construed the phrase 'the tenant' as meaning 'the joint tenants or any one of them'. The first was *Howson v Buxton* (1928) 97 LJKB 749, CA. That case concerned the notice provisions for the payment of compensation under s 12 of the Agricultural Holdings Act 1923. The case has since been distinguished by Winn LJ in *Jacobs v Chaudhuri* [1968] 2 QB 470 at 476, CA, and by Fox J in *Newman v Keedwell* (1977) 244 Estates Gazette 469 at 472. The relevance of *Howson v Buxton* in the context of the termination of a tenancy protected by the AHA 1986 was finally disposed of by Slade LJ in *Featherstone v Staples* [1985] 1 EGLR 1 at 871. The second case was *Lloyd v Sadler* [1978] QB 774, [1978] 2 All ER 529, CA. That case related to a claim for protection under the Rent Act 1968 and was relied upon in the judgment of Nourse J at first instance in *Featherstone v Staples* (1984) 273 Estates Gazette 193. In the Court of Appeal, however, Slade LJ, whilst accepting that 'there is no immutable doctrine that the phrase 'the tenant', when appearing in a statute, must always be construed as referring to all the joint tenants in any case where a joint tenancy is involved' (*Featherstone v Staples* [1985] 1 EGLR 1, 278 Estates Gazette 867 at 871), preferred to place reliance upon what Megaw LJ in *Lloyd v Sadler* [1978] QB 774, [1978] 2 All ER 529 at 783 described as 'the ordinary law as to joint tenancy, as it affects rights of property' and then upheld the decision of Fox J in *Newman v Keedwell* (1977) 244 Estates Gazette 469 as to the meaning of the phrase 'the tenant' in relation to the provisions to terminate a tenancy protected by the AHA 1986. See para 29.9ff for the principles which emerge from these cases in their general application.
6   Per Slade LJ in *Featherstone v Staples* [1985] 1 EGLR 1, 278 Estates Gazette 867 at 875.
7   *Combey v Gumbrill* [1990] 2 EGLR 7. For further discussion and criticism, see (1986) EG (Muir Watt) and (1986) 50 Conv 429 (Rodgers). Also see, (1983) 47 Conv 194 (Webb).

19.39   The non-landowning tenant is not wholly without a remedy where the landlord (in his capacity as one of the tenants) refuses to join in the giving of a counter-notice. It is open to the non-landowning tenant to seek a court order to compel the co-operation of his co-tenants[1], or an award of damages representing the non-landowning tenant's share in the tenancy as a partnership asset[2]. It was accepted by Slade LJ in *Harris v Black*[3] that a joint tenancy of the landlord and the non-landowning tenant created a statutory trust for sale defined in the Law of Property Act 1925. It was also accepted by Slade LJ in argument that the property under the trust includes not only the tenancy itself but statutory rights of continuation.

In the last two editions of this book, it was submitted that, in an appropriate case, the court would make an order compelling the landlord to join his co-trustee (the non-landowning tenant) to sign a counter-notice[4]. The court did make such an order in *Cork v Cork*[5]. It should be noted that trusts for sale are now trusts of land governed by the Trusts of Land and Appointment of Trustees Act 1996.

Notwithstanding the issues of statutory construction, the position of the non-landowning tenant has been enhanced by the Court of Appeal's decision in *Featherstone v Staples*[6]. The court placed full reliance upon the House of Lords' decision in *Johnson v Moreton*[7] and decided that if a landowner chooses to grant a tenancy of agricultural land to other persons (whether or not including himself as a tenant), public policy requires that the non-landowning tenant(s) should have authority to serve counter-notice under s 26(1)(b) of the AHA 1986[8].

That is not the end of the matter. An agricultural tenancy protected by the AHA 1986 may not only be terminated by a notice to quit served by the landlord upon the tenant, but also by a notice to quit served by the tenant upon the landlord[9]. A number of problems arise:

(a)   A notice to quit signed by one of several joint tenants on behalf of the others is sufficient to determine a tenancy from year to year[10].

(b)   A joint tenant can give notice to quit without the concurrence of his joint tenant in his capacity as landlord[11].

(c)   The courts have also held that it is not necessary to the validity of a notice to quit that it be served by all joint tenants or with the concurrence of all joint tenants unless the terms of the tenancy provide otherwise[12].

(d)   If this analysis is correct then it is possible for the landlord to give a notice to quit in his capacity as tenant. That step does not bring into operation any counter-notice provisions and, therefore, prima facie, the tenancy would be duly terminated[13].

1   *Harris v Black* (1983) 46 P & CR 366, CA; *Sykes v Land* (1984) 271 Estates Gazette 1264.
2   Cf *Crawley Borough Council v Ure* [1996] QB 13, [1996] 1 All ER 724, CA.
3   *Harris v Black* (1983) 46 P & CR 366 at 372, CA.
4   On the facts, no such order was made by the court in *Harris v Black*, which was an interlocutory appeal, but an order was made in *Sykes v Land* (1984) 271 Estates Gazette 1264. However, where the court does not make an order it is as well for the landlord's advisers to note the warning given by Slade LJ in *Harris v Black* (1983) 46 P & CR 366 at 374: 'There is nothing in any judgment which this court may now deliver which precludes the plaintiff from prosecuting and maybe establishing that claim. If he does establish it, it

is, I suppose, possible that the defendant could find himself liable to make heavy pecuniary compensation to the plaintiff.' As to fiduciary duties generally, see para 29.16.

5   [1997] 1 EGLR 5, [1997] 16 EG 430.
6   [1985] 1 EGLR 1, 278 EG 867
7   [1980] AC 37, [1978] 3 All ER 37.
8   Per Slade LJ in *Featherstone v Staples* [1985] 2 All ER 461 at 467.
9   See, eg, *Featherstone v Staples* [1986] 2 All ER 461 at 467 and the cases cited there.
10 *Doe d Aslin v Summersett* (1830) 1 B & Ad 135. Also see, *Doe d Kindersley v Hughes* (1840) 7 M & W 139.
11 *Parsons v Parsons* [1983] 1 WLR 1390.
12 *Greenwich London Borough Council v McGrady* (1982) 267 Estates Gazette 515, 81 LGR 288, CA, followed in *Parsons v Parsons* [1983] 1 WLR 1390; *Hammersmith and Fulham London Borough Council v Monk* [1992] 1 AC 478, [1992] 1 All ER 1, HL; *Crawley Borough Council v Ure* [1996] QB 13, [1996] 1 All ER 724, CA; *Notting Hill Housing Trust v Brackley* [2001] EWCA Civ 601, [2001] 3 EGLR 11, [2001] 35 EG 106. Cf one of two joint tenants cannot operate a break clause (*Hounslow London Borough Council v Pilling* [1994] 1 All ER 432, CA) or effect a surrender (*Leek and Moorlands Building Society v Clark* [1952] 2 QB 788, CA) without the concurrence of his joint tenant(s).
13 This must be open to attack following the public policy approach adopted in *Featherstone v Staples* [1986] 2 All ER 461; *Gisborne v Burton* [1989] QB 390, [1988] 2 EGLR 9, CA; and *Sykes v Land* (1984) 271 Estates Gazette 1264.

Partnership property

19.40 The termination of an agricultural tenancy protected by the AHA 1986 is made more complicated where the landowner has granted a tenancy to himself and another and the landowner and the non-landowning party farm in partnership. A number of issues need to be considered.

The first issue which arises is to ensure that the property being considered is partnership property. The Partnership Act 1890 contains only a basic definition. Section 20(1) provides:

'All property and rights and interests in property originally brought into the partnership stock or acquired, whether by purchase or otherwise, on account of the firm or for the purposes and in the course of the partnership business, are called in this Act partnership property, and must be held and applied by partners exclusively for the purposes of the partnership and in accordance with the partnership agreement'.

There are two distinct features: first, the existence of partnership property and, second, establishing the nature of a partner's interest in the property. It is beyond the scope of this book to consider these issues in depth. It should, however, be noted that a partner holds partnership property as agent 'for the purposes' of the partnership[1], and land upon trust for it[2].

Section 20(2) of the Partnership Act 1890 provides that land:

'which belongs to the partnership shall devolve according to the nature and tenure thereof, and the general rules thereto applicable, but in trust, so far as necessary, for the persons beneficially interested in the land under this section'.

Because a partnership (as distinct from its members) lacks a corporate identity, no land (including any lease) can be vested in it as such[3]. Any lease or freehold reversion that belongs to the partnership should be vest in trustees for the partnership. There may be no more than four trustees[4].

It should be noted that it is not unusual in farming partnerships to find that a partnership agreement has been drafted but not completed. When a joint business commences, but the partnership agreement is never finalised, a partnership will have come into existence, but it will not be governed by the terms of the draft agreement[5] unless the agreement has been acted on[6]. In such a case, the duration of the partnership will be one at will[7]. Such a partnership may be dissolved by notice with immediate effect or in the future[8].

[1] *Burdick v Garrick* (1870) 5 Ch App 233; *Brown v IRC* [1965] AC 244, HL.
[2] Partnership Act 1890, s 20(2).
[3] *Jarrott v Ackerley* (1915) 85 LJ Ch 135.
[4] Law of Property Act 1925 ss 34 and 36.
[5] *Popat v Shonchhrata* [1995] 1 WLR 908, CA. Also see *Re Vanderplank* (1841) 2 Mont D & De G 339.
[6] *Baxter v West* (1860) 1 Drew & Son 173.
[7] *Firth v Amslake* (1964) 108 Sol Jo 198.
[8] Partnership Act 1890, s 32(c). *Peacock v Peacock* (1809) 16 Ves 49; *Miles v Thomas* (1839) 9 Sim 606; *Firth v Amslake* (1964) 108 Sol Jo 198.

19.41 Partnership property can either be brought into the firm or acquired on account of the firm. Property brought in as capital is partnership property. Subsequent acquisitions may also be included. If the property is itemised in the accounts or recorded in the partnership agreement as partnership property, there is little difficulty. In other cases the court may be asked to infer an implied agreement that the property was brought in or acquired as partnership property from the surrounding circumstances.

It should be noted that the courts have appeared to be loathe to imply that an asset has become partnership property, in the absence of clear evidence as to the agreement between the partners[1]. In *Miles v Clarke*[2], Miles and Clarke were partners at will in a photography business. Clarke owned the lease. Miles was a well known photographer. Both partners contributed to the stock in trade. There was no formal agreement as to the assets of the partnership. On dissolution the court declined to imply any terms as to change of ownership so that Clarke retained the lease.

If a dispute relates to property which was subsequently bought with partnership profits, two other sections of the Partnership Act 1890 may apply. Section 21 provides:

'Unless the contrary intention appears, property bought with money belonging to the firm is deemed to have been bought on account of the firm'.

Thus property so acquired is not automatically partnership property. It is also true that an asset acquired at the expense of an individual partner may still be a partnership asset. What Section 21 does is raise a presumption which needs to be rebutted[3].

The other section in the Partnership Act 1890 which applies to subsequent acquisitions is s 20(3). This provides:

19.41   *What is an agricultural holding?*

'Where co-owners of an estate or interest in any land … not being itself partnership property, are partners as to profits made by the use of that land or estate, and purchase other land or estate out of the profits to be used in like manner, the land or estate so purchased belongs to them, in the absence of an agreement to the contrary, not as partners but as co-owners for the same respective estates and interests as are held by them in the land or estate first mentioned at the time of the purchase'.

Under the Partnership Act 1890, co-ownership of land does not of itself make that land a partnership asset even though the profits from it are shared by the co-owners as partners. Section 20(3) applies to property bought out of those profits and used 'in like manner' to the original land[4].

[1]   As to the position in relation to milk quota as partnership property, see *Faulks v Faulks* [1992] 1 EGLR 9, [1992] 15 EG 82.
[2]   [1953] 1 All ER 779.
[3]   *Jones v Jones* (1870) 4 SALR 12.
[4]   *Davis v Davis* [1894] 1 Ch 393.

Dissolution of a partnership

19.42   On dissolution of a partnership it is therefore necessary to consider the general rules which apply in relation to:

(a)   a tenancy (one or more of the partners being tenants) which is partnership property or held on trust for the partnership; and
(b)   a tenancy which is not partnership property and which is not held on trust for the partnership.

In the case of (a) above, one or more of the outgoing partners (or in the case of death, their executors) can insist on realisation of the value of the tenancy by sale either by virtue of s 39 of the Partnership Act 1890 or by insisting on the execution of any trust for sale involved. The latter, however, needs to be considered in the context of the Trusts of Land and Appointment of Trustees Act 1996 (TLATA 1996)[1].

It is beyond the scope of this book to consider the applicaton of TLATA 1996 in detail[2], nevertheless it should be noted that in relation to a property which is the subject of either a trust of land[3] or a trust of sale of proceeds of land[4], the court has a discretion to make such order as it thinks fit in relation to:

(i)   the exercise by trustees of their functions[5]; and
(ii)   the nature or extent of a person's interest in property which is subject to the trust[6].

In exercising its discretion, the matters to which the court is required to have regard include:

(A)   the intentions of the person or persons (if any) who created the trust;
(B)   the purpose for which the property subject to the trust is held;
(C)   the interests of any minor who occupies or might reasonably be expected to occupy the land which is subject to the trust as his home; and

(D) the interests of any secured creditor of the beneficiary[7].

All beneficiaries have the right to apply to the court under TLATA 1996 for an order to resolve disputes in relation to trust property[8]. In exercising its discretion, the court may order sale; the payment of an occupation rent; exclusion from occupation of one or more of the beneficiaries; or partition[9].

Dissolution needs to be contrasted with retirement. It is beyond the scope of this book to consider and compare the two concepts in detail[10]. It should be noted that retirement only arises where there is provision for this in the partnership agreement or it arises with the consent of all of the partners[11]. The Partnership Act 1890 contains no rules governing the retirement of a partner. The court will enforce any retirement arrangement agreed between the partners.

[1] As to authorities prior to the Trusts of Land and Appointments of Trustees Act 1996, see *Re Mayo* [1943] Ch 302, [1943] 2 All ER 440, and *Thompson's Trustee in Bankruptcy v Heaton* [1974] 1 All ER 1239, [1974] 1 WLR 605, as to the extent of the fiduciary duties.
[2] See Charles Harpum, *Megarry and Wade: The Law of Real Property* (6th edn, 2000) Sweet & Maxwell, Chs 8 and 9.
[3] TLATA 1996, s 14(1).
[4] TLATA 1996, s 17(2).
[5] TLATA 1996, s 14(2)(a).
[6] TLATA 1996, s 14(2)(b).
[7] TLATA 1996, s 15(1).
[8] TLATA 1996, s 14(1).
[9] TLATA 1996, ss 12–14.
[10] Reference should be made to Blackett-Ord, *Partnership* (2nd edn, 2002) Butterworths and *Lindley and Banks on Partnership* (18th edn, 2002) Sweet & Maxwell.
[11] It can be unclear as to whether an agreement is one of retirement or dissolution: see *Sobell v Boston* [1975] 2 All ER 282, [1975] 1 WLR 1587. Also see generally *Mullins v Laughton* [2002] EWHC 2761 (Ch), [2003] Ch 250.

19.43 The general rule is that, upon dissolution, a partner may insist upon all partnership assets being sold:

'In the absence of a special agreement to the contrary, the general rule is that on the dissolution of a partnership all of the property belonging to the partnership shall be converted into money by a sale, even though a sale may not be necessary for the payment of debts'[1].

The court does have a discretion not to order sale, for example, in the case of a small minority share[2].

Partners may not insist upon their 'share' in the partnership business remaining unsold for them[3]. Also, critically, a partition of partnership land will not be ordered unless all the partners agree a partition[4].

When a solvent partnership's assets are being sold by the order of the court, it is the usual practice to allow any partner to bid for them[5]. Often, particularly following dissolution, a partner will seek the appointment of a receiver by the court to deal with the realisation of property in the winding up of the partnership[6]. Such an appointment is not automatic[7].

19.43 *What is an agricultural holding?*

If none of the partners insists on an immediate sale or realisation of value, and the named tenants continue to farm the holding after the dissolution of the partnership, then s 42 of the Partnership Act 1890 applies. This entitles an outgoing partner to such share of the profits made since the dissolution as the court may find to be attribute to the use of his share of the partnership assets or to interest at the rate of 5% per annum on the amount of his share of the partnership assets[8]. This does not affect the right of sale[9].

If a tenancy which was used by a partnership is not partnership property and is not held on trust for the partnership, then on dissolution the named tenants are entitled to continue as tenants. If one partner holds a tenancy on trust for the partnership, then the tenancy is held on trust for the partners, but for the purposes of the partnership[10].

1   *Hugh Stevenson & Sons Ltd v AG für Cartonnagen-Industrie* [1917] 1 KB 842, CA; affd [1918] AC 239, HL.
2   *Syers v Syers* (1876) 1 App Cas 174, HL.
3   *Darby v Darby* (1856) 3 Drew 495.
4   *Redwood v Redwood* (1908) 28 NZLR 260.
5   *Choudri v Palta* [1994] 1 BCLC 184, CA.
6   Supreme Court Act 1981, s 37; Civil Procedure Rules Pt 69. *Skip v Harwood* (1747) 3 AtK 564; *Re Prytherch, Prytherch v Williams* (1889) 42 Ch D 590; *Foxwell v Van Grutten* [1897] 1 Ch 64, CA; *John v John* [1898] 2 Ch 573, CA; *Toker v Akgul* (2 November 1995, unreported), CA; *Wilton-Davies v Turk* [1998] 1 BCLC 274.
7   *Toker v Akgul* (2 November 1995, unreported), CA; *Wilton-Davies v Turk* [1998] 1 BCLC 274.
8   Also see *Popat v Shonchhrata* [1997] 1 WLR 1367; *Sandhu v Gill* [2005] EWCA Civ 1297, [2006] 2 WLR 8. As to dealing with assets pending the concluding of the winding up of a partnership and accounting for funds realised, see *Richardson v Bank of England* (1838) 4 My and Cr 165, CA and *Gratton Hughes v Lloyd Ellis* (1991, unreported), CA.
9   *Barclays Bank Trust Co Ltd v Bluff* [1982] Ch 172.
10   *Ashworth v Munn* (1880) 15 Ch D 363, CA. Also see, *Faulks v Faulks* [1992] 1 EGLR 9, [1992] 15 EG 82.

19.44 Equity recognises no right of survivorship as regards partnership property[1]. Therefore, the legal estate in the land vested in the partners forming part of partnership property[2] is held by the partners as joint tenants upon trust of land[3], but the beneficial interest in the property is held as tenants in common for the purpose of the partnership and in accordance with the partnership agreement[4].

It follows that, upon the dissolution of the partnership upon the death or retirement of a partner or otherwise[5], the undivided share in the partnership property of that partner should not be used further in the partnership business without express or implied authority[6].

1   This has been expressed by the maxim '*jus accrescendi inter mercatores locum non habet*' (the right of survivorship does not apply among businessmen): see Co Litt 182a.
2   Land may be vested at law in one partner only and also be partnership property: see *Re Rayleigh Weir Stadium* [1954] 2 All ER 283, [1954] 1 WLR 786. Where this arises it appears that the other partner has an equitable right to his share and thus a right to have a share of the proceeds of sale of the land. However, in *Eardley v Broad* (1970) 215 Estates Gazette 823, where a partnership agreement between a father and son stated that the partnership capital was to consist of the stock, machinery and other assets of the business of a farmer carried on by the father as an agricultural holding, but it did not specifically refer to the farm lease it was held that although the rent had been paid by the partnership

and that the holding was indispensable to the farming business, there were no grounds for inferring any assignment of the lease to the partnership.

3   *Re Fuller's Contract* [1933] Ch 652; Trusts of Land and Appointment of Trustees Act 1996.
4   Partnership Act 1890, s 20(1) and (2).
5   It is noteworthy that where no fixed term has been agreed upon for the duration of the partnership, any partner may determine it at any time on giving notice of his intention to do so to all of his fellow partners; see Partnership Act 1890, s 26(1). Also, whilst there may be an implied agreement to continue the partnership for a definite period (see *Crawshay v Maule* (1818) 1 Swan 495), the fact that the partners agree to enter into a lease for a fixed period is not in itself necessarily sufficient evidence of such an implied agreement; see *Syers v Syers* (1876) 1 App Cas 174 and *Pocock v Carter* [1912] 1 Ch 663.
6   *Crawshay v Collins* (1808) 15 Ves 218.

19.45 It is clear from *Popat v Shonchhatra*[1] that a distinction must be drawn between the capital and profit sharing entitlements of the partners and the assets of the partnership. Nourse LJ states this, referring to the 1983 decision of *Reed v Young*[2], where he himself had said:

'The capital of a partnership is the aggregate of the contributions made by the parties, either in cash or in kind, for the purpose of commencing or carrying on the partnership business and intended to be risked by them therein. Each contribution must be of a fixed amount. If it is in cash it speaks for itself. If it is in kind, it must be valued at a stated amount. It is important to distinguish between the capital of a partnership, a fixed sum, on the one hand and its assets which may vary from day to day and include everything belonging to the firm ...'

In *Popat v Shonchhatra*[3], Nourse LJ made it clear that:

'... while each partner has a proprietary interest in each and every asset, he has no entitlement to any specific asset and, in consequence, no right without the consent of the other partners or partner, to require the whole or even a share of any particular asset to be vested in him'[4].

Nourse LJ also considered the size of a partner's share in the assets of the partnership during the currency of the partnership (as opposed to his share in the capital or in the profits). He concludes that 'subject to any agreement, all the partners are entitled to share equally in the partnership property'[5].

In reaching his conclusion, Nourse LJ found no answer in s 24 of the Partnership Act 1890, which deals only with 'the capital and profits of the business'. Agreements between the parties relating to capital and profit sharing ratios are, therefore, irrelevant. *Popat v Shonchhatra*[6] makes it clear that:

(a)   the fact that one partner introduced the assets (and hence any capital value it has resides in his capital account) is irrelevant; and
(b)   the agreements relating to capital and profits are irrelevant.

Where no agreement has been reached in a partnership as to how the parties would share the assets of the partnership, in accordance with the well established rule referred to by Nourse LJ, they must share equally. During the currency of the partnership no one partner has any greater rights than the others in relation to the assets.

1   [1997] 1 WLR 1367.
2   (1983) 59 TC 196 at 215.
3   [1997] 1 WLR 1367.
4   At 1372.
5   At 1372G.
6   [1997] 1 WLR 1367.

Non-assignable tenancies

19.46 Upon the dissolution of the partnership, the non-landowning tenant, as partner, is entitled to his due proportion of the realisable equity in the value of the tenancy which, being protected by the AHA 1986 and assignable in the absence of an express covenant against assignment, may have considerable value[1]. The tenancy, as an asset of the partnership, may be sold in the winding up of the partnership. The non-landowning tenant will not be allowed to bid for the tenancy, unless authorised by the terms of the partnership or with the agreement of his partners. Further, if the partnership assets are administered by the court, the court may be asked to direct an assignment to the non-landowning tenant beneficially at a price to be fixed by the court on the basis of independent valuation advice.

A problem arises where the tenancy is non-assignable. This may arise from an express provision in the partnership agreement or an ancillary tenancy agreement. Alternatively, the landlord, or his personal representatives, may serve a notice under s 6 of the AHA 1986[2], thereby introducing a prohibition upon assignment[3].

Where there is an express covenant against assignment it is submitted, in the absence of any authority on the point, that the correct approach is to value the tenancy as a partnership asset on the basis that it is non-assignable[4]. That value would be credited to the partnership account for distribution upon dissolution[5].

It is beyond the scope of this book to consider the position of a farming partnership dissolution in respect of jointly owned land which is the subject of a tenancy in favour of the partnership. It is submitted that the principles set out above are of equal application where they arise. Regard must also be had to the fiduciary duties of a joint trustee[6] and the rights of a beneficial co-owner who is excluded from occupation to receive an occupation rent[7]; and the provisions of the Trusts of Land and Appointment of Trustees Act 1996[8].

1   Unless the partnership agreement provides otherwise.
2   AHA 1986, s 6(5) provides for the immediate imposition of a conditional prohibition upon assignment, sub-letting or parting with possession of the holding. See para 23.3.
3   It has to be considered whether the service of s 6 notice at the time of the dissolution of a partnership may constitute a breach of trust by the landlord: see *Harris v Black* (1983) 46 P & CR 366, especially per Slade LJ at 374.
4   A task often undertaken for Revenue purposes. As to valuation, see: *Layzell v Smith Morton & Long* [1992] 1 EGLR 169, [1992] 13 EG 118; *Baird's Executors v IRC* 1991 SLT (Lands Tr) 9; *IRC v Gray* [1994] STC 360, CA; *Walton's Executors v IRC* [1996] 1 EGLR 159, [1996] 21 EG 144, CA; *Greenbank v Pickles* [2001] 1 EGLR 1, [2001] 09 EG 230, CA.

⁵ *Sobell v Boston* [1975] 2 All ER 282.
⁶ *Regal (Hastings) Ltd v Gulliver (1942)* [1967] 2 AC 134n, [1967] 1 All ER 378, HL.
⁷ *Re Pavlou* [1993] 3 All ER 955.
⁸ See para 19.42.

Distribution on dissolution

19.47 When the rights in relation to partnership property are resolved, s 44 of the Partnership Act 1890 provides that, in settling accounts between the partners after a dissolution of a partnership, the following rules shall (subject to any contrary agreement) be observed.

(a) Losses (including losses and deficiencies of capital) shall be paid first out of profits, next out of capital and lastly (if necessary) by the partners individually in the proportion which they are entitled to share in profits.

(b) The assets of the partnership, including the sums (if any) contributed by the partners to make up losses of deficiencies of capital, shall be applied in the following manner and order:
  (i) in paying the debts and liabilities of the partnership to persons who are not partners in it;
  (ii) in paying to each partner rateably what is due from the partnership to him for advances, as distinguished from capital;
  (iii) in paying to each partner rateably what is due from the partnership to him in respect of capital; and
  (iv) the ultimate residue (if any) shall be divided among the partners in the proportion in which the profits are divisible.

Tax

19.48 It is likewise beyond the scope of this book to consider the tax implications of a farming partnership dissolution or tax generally. The following points may assist practitioners before they consult specialist tax publications:

(a) an AHA 1986 tenancy is an asset for the purposes of capital gains tax (CGT)[1];
(b) the extinction of an asset is a disposal for CGT purposes[2];
(c) the receipt of a capital sum by way of compensation for the loss, destruction or dissipation of an asset is a disposal for CGT purposes[3];
(d) in addition to standard reliefs, the incidence of CGT on a partnership dissolution may be ameliorated by the application of the extra statutory concession D26.

If a farm is partnership property and sold upon the dissolution of a farming partnership, it will be a chargeable transfer for the purposes of stamp duty and land tax (SDLT). If the farm is transferred to one of the partners in its entirety, then SDLT may often be avoided, particularly if the parties are 'connected'[4].

19.48 *What is an agricultural holding?*

For a farming partnership, agricultural property relief (APR) will have considerable significance in relation to inheritance tax (IHT). Section 116 of the Inheritance Tax Act 1984 (ITA 1984) contains the relief from the charge to IHT. Relief is provided for 'the value transferred where that value is attributable to the agricultural value of agricultural property'.

The amount of the relief is either 100% or 50%. The former applies where the transferor can recover possession within 24 months or where he satisfies the pre-1981 full-time working farmer relief provisions[5]. In all other cases, it is 50%. APR takes precedence over business property relief. It should be noted that, by contrast, if the tenancy commenced on or after 1 September 1995, then 100% APR is available to the landowner[6].

Agricultural property means:

'... agricultural land or pasture including woodland and any buildings used in conjunction with livestock if the woodland or building is occupied with agricultural land or pasture and the occupation is ancillary to that of the agricultural land or pasture; and also includes such cottages, farm buildings and farmhouses, together with the land occupied with them, as are of a character appropriate to the property'[7].

Section 116 of the ITA 1984 does not apply to any agricultural property unless:

(a)   it was occupied by the transferor for the purposes of agriculture throughout the period of two years ending with the date of the transfer; or

(b)   it was owned by him throughout the period of seven years ending with that date and was throughout that period occupied (by him or another) for the purposes of agriculture[8].

The issue which has emerged from these definitions is whether the house lived in by the farmer is a farmhouse attracting APR or whether it stands separately as a residential unit attracting IHT[9]. To be a farmhouse it must be 'a dwelling for the farmer from which the farm is managed' and is occupied by 'the farmer of the land [who] is the person who farms it on a day-to-day basis'[10].

---

1   The Taxation of Chargeable Gains Act 1992 (TCGA 1992), s 21 which provides that 'all forms of property shall be assets for the purposes of this Act'.
2   TCGA 1992, s 24.
3   TCGA 1992, s 22.
4   See Finance Act 2003, Sch 15 para 18, as amended by the Finance Act 2006.
5   See ITA 1984, s 116(2)(b).
6   Finance Act 1995, s 155.
7   ITA 1984, s 115. See *Starke v IRC* [1994] STC 295, affd [1996] 1 All ER 622.
8   ITA 1984, s 117.
9   See *Lloyds TSB Private Banking plc (Personal Representative of Antrobus, Deceased) v IRC* [2002] STC (SCD) 468; *Lloyds TSB Private Banking plc v Twiddy* [2006] 1 EGLR 157; *Arnander (Executors of McKenna, Deceased) v IRC* [2006] STC (SCD) 800.
10   *Arnander (Executors of McKenna, Deceased) v IRC* [2006] STC (SCD) 800.

CONTRACTING-OUT, SHAM AND MISLABELLING

Introduction

19.49 There was no express prohibition in the AHA 1986 (nor was there in any of its predecessors) preventing the parties from contracting-out of the agricultural holdings legislation altogether. Certain individual sections expressly prohibited contracting-out[1], others expressly permitted it[2] and a third category were silent one way or the other[3]. The courts have applied public policy considerations in order to uphold security of tenure[4].

Since 1 September 1995, no new agreement between a landowner and a farmer will be affected by these considerations. Nevertheless, consideration will have to be given to the matters referred to below in respect of agreements which are still extant and which began before 1 September 1995.

The agricultural holdings legislation generally was very unpopular with many landowners who, though anxious to grant tenancies, were equally anxious to avoid the whole, or certain parts, of the agricultural holdings legislation, particularly those which conferred security of tenure upon the tenants. As a consequence, numerous attempts were made either to contract out of the agricultural holdings legislation altogether, or to avoid certain unpopular features of the legislation, while enjoying the benefit of other features.

The many decisions of the courts upon the efficacy of such attempts are now considered in three sections.

(a)   *Contracting-out*: By this inaccurate but convenient shorthand turn of phrase, consideration is given as to whether the parties were entitled by the terms of their agreement to exclude the whole or those parts of the agricultural holdings legislation.

(b)   *Sham*: It is frequently alleged that certain forms of agreement designed to circumvent provisions of the agricultural holdings legislation or, alternatively, to take advantage of others, fell to be overridden as shams. The many judicial decisions upon such claims and contentions are analysed and applied in the context of the agricultural holdings legislation.

(c)   *Mislabelling*: A separate and different legal concept is involved in the case of documents in which the relationship between the parties is described in one way, though the substance of the document upon its true legal construction is to different effect. In such circumstances, the documents are here described as having been 'mislabelled' and the various decisions upon that phenomenon are further considered.

---

[1]   Eg, s 25 (length of notice to quit).
[2]   Eg, s 7 (model clause repairing liabilities).
[3]   Eg, s 12 (rent review).
[4]   *Johnson v Moreton* [1980] AC 37, HL; *Featherstone v Staples* [1986] 2 All ER 461, [1986] 1 WLR 861, [1986] 1 EGLR 6, CA; *Gisborne v Burton* [1989] QB 390, [1988] 3 All ER 760, [1988] 2 EGLR 9, CA.

Public policy

19.50 The decisions reached in respect of agreements beginning before 1 September 1995 when the ATA 1995 came into effect were founded upon public policy as it was perceived to be during the period from 1947 (the passing of the Agriculture Act 1947) until 1995 (the passing of the ATA 1995). During that time the public policy was to confer security of tenure and other privileges upon farmers to enable them to maximise production from the land and to farm for the long-term benefit of the community as well as to protect those in a weaker bargaining position (the farmer) as against the landowner. Since the United Kingdom joined the European Community, almost all forms of agricultural production have been in surplus. It has been the policy of the Community to limit production by the introduction of quotas, set-aside and the like. Although surpluses are now increasingly under control (and indeed it has been indicated that set-aside may be abolished), the policy was reflected in the provisions of the ATA 1995 in respect of all new tenancies and other arrangements for the farming of land beginning on or after 1 September 1995. Nevertheless, the former public policy still applies to agreements entered into before that date. The provisions set out below apply to such agreements.

Contracting-out

19.51 The decisions of the House of Lords in *Johnson v Moreton*[1] and the Court of Appeal in *Featherstone v Staples*[2], *Elsden v Pick*[3] and *Gisborne v Burton*[4], together with the other relevant decisions, give rise to a number of propositions.

First, the parties were free to arrange their affairs so that the agreement that they reached never came within the provisions of the agricultural holdings legislation at all. They could have agreed that the farmer should be granted a licence to share occupation with the landowner. Such form of licence would not have been converted into a tenancy from year to year, nor would it have involved the creation of an agricultural holding, or have been affected in any way by the agricultural holdings legislation[5].

Although the primary motive of the landowning partner in insisting upon a particular form of arrangement for the occupation of the land may have been to avoid security of tenure (or the other consequences of the statutory regulation of the parties affairs contained in the AHA 1986), that had no relevance in determining whether or not the agreement entered into between the parties upon its true construction created an agricultural holding in the first place or not[6].

If the parties had agreed upon an arrangement which either expressly, or by necessary implication, or by statutory conversion, involved the creation of a tenancy of an agricultural holding, then whether or not the parties were free to contract out of any of the express provisions of the AHA 1986 or the subordinate legislation depended upon consideration of the following matters:

(a)   If the section or sections desired to be avoided expressly prohibit contracting out, then any agreement in contravention of that provision would be illegal and null and void[7].

(b)   By contrast, where the legislation expressly permitted variation by agreement, the parties were free so to do[8].

(c)   Where the statute was silent as to whether its terms could be varied by agreement, prima facie the parties were entitled to agree to exclude the statutory provisions unless public policy dictated that the statute should override the agreement of the parties[9].

(d)   If the agreement was a 'sham'[10], the courts have not taken judicial notice of the desire of the landowners to exclude statutory protection[11].

(e)   Until 1 September 1995 public policy dictated that any agreement entered into between the parties which precluded, however obliquely and indirectly, and whether in the tenancy agreement itself[12] or in a collateral agreement[13], the right of the tenant to invoke the provisions giving him statutory security of tenure would be contrary to public policy and therefore invalid. It is now possible that in the changed political climate following the passing of the ATA 1995 that that principle will be extended even for agreements entered into before 1 September 1995.

In *Persey v Bazley*[14], a conveyance to a nominee of the landlord upon a severance of his reversionary interest, so as to entitle that nominee to give notice to quit part in reliance upon s 140 of the Law of Property Act 1925, where the nominee was expressed on the face of the conveyance to be a mere nominee, was held to be ineffective to entitle the landlord of the severed part to give notice to quit relying upon s 140 of the Law of Property Act 1925.

1   [1980] AC 37, [1978] 3 All ER 37.
2   [1986] 2 All ER 461, [1986] 1 WLR 861.
3   [1980] 3 All ER 235, [1980] 1 WLR 898.
4   [1989] QB 390, [1988] 2 EGLR 9.
5   *Harrison-Broadley v Smith* [1964] 1 All ER 867, [1964] 1 WLR 456, CA and *Bahamas International Trust Co Ltd v Threadgold* [1974] 3 All ER 881, [1974] 1 WLR 1514, HL.
6   *Shell-Mex and BP Ltd v Manchester Garages Ltd* [1971] 1 All ER 841, [1971] 1 WLR 612, CA when a scheme designed to avoid the Landlord and Tenant Act 1954, Pt II was considered. 'One cannot take that into account in the process of construing such a document to find out what the true nature of the transaction is' per Buckley LJ at 619 and per Lawton LJ in *O'Malley v Seymour* (1978) 250 Estates Gazette 1083 at 1088: 'A property owner is entitled to arrange his affairs so as not to get his property enmeshed in the Rent Acts', nor, it is submitted, in the AHA 1986, as the case may be.
7   Eg s 15 (freedom of cropping), s 78 (statutory right to compensation of landlord and tenant), and many of the individual compensation provisions. As to, by analogy, the contracting out provisions of the Law of Property Act 1925, see *Aribasala v St James (Grosvenor Dock) Ltd* [2007] EWHC 1694 (Ch), [2007] 37 EG 234.
8   See, eg, the model clauses for repairs, s 7, and certain of the provisions for establishing the measure of compensation for improvements.
9   *Johnson v Moreton* [1980] AC 37, [1978] 3 All ER 37, HL; *Featherstone v Staples* [1986] 2 All ER 461, [1986] 1 WLR 861, CA.
10   See para 19.54.
11   *Aslan v Murphy (No 2)* [1990] 1 WLR 766, CA.
12   *Johnson v Moreton* [1980] AC 37, [1978] 3 All ER 37, HL.
13   *Featherstone v Staples* [1986] 2 All ER 461, [1986] 1 WLR 861.
14   (1983) 267 Estates Gazette 519, CA.

19.52 In *Featherstone v Staples*[1], it was held that where the landlord let to his alter ego (who was not a professional farmer) and others (who were professional farmers), and there was a provision in the partnership agreement entered into between the tenants that the partners would not give counter-notice to any notice to quit that might be given by the landlord, this prevented the landlord enforcing a notice to quit in reliance upon the fact that the nominee/alter ego of the landlord, who was also one of the tenants, had vetoed the giving of a counter-notice.

In *Sykes v Land*[2], the landowner let the holding to a partnership of himself and another. The court accepted that any counter-notice had to be served by both joint tenants, but exercised an equitable jurisdiction to cause the landowner to join in giving the counter-notice in order to protect the main trust asset.

It has now been held that the principle in *Johnson v Moreton*[3], as applied in *Featherstone v Staples*, also applied to a letting to a nominee (whether expressed as such or not) with a view to the nominee sub-letting to the person selected for the farming of the holding (see *Gisborne v Burton*[4]). The head landlord on seeking possession gave notice to quit to the head tenant in reliance upon the head tenant not giving a counter-notice. The head landlord then contended that the sub-tenant was precluded from giving a counter-notice or invoking security of tenure. The Court of Appeal held that the sub-tenant had full security of tenure as against the head landlord.

The rule of law can be expressed quite simply in this way. The parties were free never to enter into the relationship of landlord and tenant at all and instead to share occupation, for example, as partners or in some other way. If, however, they decided to become landlord and tenant respectively (or if the agreement, even unintentionally, had that effect or was converted into a tenancy by s 2 of the AHA 1986) then, no matter what arrangement or arrangements (even contained in several documents) the parties may have made to ensure that the landlord could unilaterally recover possession at his own behest in due course, such an arrangement was contrary to public policy. Public policy demanded that such arrangements are invalid if their effect, directly or indirectly, would be to prevent the tenant from claiming the security of tenure which Parliament had determined should be available to him or implementing the statutory procedure for enforcing such security.

It should be noted that the right to security of tenure is a right and not an obligation and there is nothing to prevent the tenant from forgoing that right if he wishes. Any agreement, on the other hand, that he must do so is unenforceable at the instance of the landlord.

1   *Featherstone v Staples* [1986] 2 All ER 461, [1986] 1 WLR 861.
2   [1984] 2 EGLR 8, 271 Estates Gazette 1264.
3   [1980] AC 37, [1978] 3 All ER 37.
4   [1989] QB 390, [1988] 2 EGLR 9, CA, holding that an earlier unreported decision of French J of *Bayer v Mitcham* was wrongly decided.

19.53 An agreement to surrender before the date upon which a notice to quit could take effect is enforceable and does not involve contracting out of security of tenure[1]. This is because the parties are not obliged to remain landlord and tenant respectively when both have agreed otherwise. However, there is as yet no authority as to the question of whether an agreement to surrender some years hence would be enforceable by the landlord if the tenant sought to claim security and to renege upon the agreement. An agreement to surrender at a future date as a condition of the grant of the tenancy would almost certainly be found to be unenforceable by virtue of the principle in *Johnson v Moreton*[2] and *Featherstone v Staples*[3].

An agreement to assign when called upon to do so at some future date to a third party, if that third party was a nominee of the landlord, would, it is submitted, be held to be unenforceable as contrary to public policy if it could be shown that the purpose of the assignment was to effect a surrender and to circumvent security of tenure. This would be so particularly if the grant of the tenancy was subject to the tenant first agreeing to enter into an agreement to assign in due course to the landlord's nominee.

Although agreements which directly or indirectly fetter the right of the tenant to claim security of tenure are avoided as being contrary to public policy, it is less clear as to whether public policy considerations would also render unenforceable agreements to avoid other provisions of the agricultural holdings legislation, for example rent review. Whether the provisions as to the revision of rent can be the subject of lawful variations by agreement is considered in Chapter 25[4].

A case decided upon trust law and equitable principles which is difficult to reconcile with these public policy principles is *Rowan v Dann*[5]. In that case three people were negotiating a joint venture for the farming of land. While the negotiations were in progress one granted a formal tenancy to one of the other two. The court held that the landlord was entitled to recover possession when the negotiations for the joint venture failed and, since the tenant held the tenancy upon a resulting trust for the landlord, the court ordered that the tenant had to give up possession to the landlord.

[1] *Elsden v Pick* [1980] 3 All ER 235, [1980] 1 WLR 898.
[2] [1980] AC 37, [1978] 3 All ER 37.
[3] *Featherstone v Staples* [1986] 2 All ER 461, [1986] 1 WLR 861.
[4] See para 25.46. Note that it is probably not contrary to public policy to vary the rent review provisions.
[5] [1991] EGCS 19; affd (1991) 64 P & CR 202, CA. Also see, *Kilcarne Holdings Ltd v Targetfollow (Birmingham) Ltd* [2005] EWCA Civ 1355, (2006) 1 P & CR D55.

Sham

19.54 Agreements between landowners and farmers which, upon their true construction, avoid the formation of an agricultural holding, are frequently challenged on the basis that they are mere shams, particularly in the context of grazing agreements[1]. Similar considerations apply in the case of somewhat artificial farm partnership agreements and contractor agreements and share cropping agreements, many of which were self-evidently and unashamedly attempts to enter into a relationship as close as possible to that of the relationship of landlord and tenant but to avoid actually creating a tenancy of an agricultural holding and thereby becoming 'enmeshed'[2] in the agricultural holdings legislation generally. In such circumstances, when attempts are made by the landowner to recover possession, a contention frequently made on behalf of the farmer/occupier is that the agreement was colourable and a mere sham and that the true agreement between the parties was for the grant of a tenancy, albeit by another name.

Sham involves a different legal concept, from both contracting-out and mislabelling. If the parties agree that there should be a letting, or a licence of such a nature and kind as is converted into a letting, and in either case the letting would be of an agricultural holding, then they may not by their documentation reflect the agreement reached. The purpose of the documentation is to give the appearance of an agreement of a different nature and kind. The agreement will take effect in accordance with its true terms as negotiated, and not as represented in the document. Such a document will be disregarded as a sham.

Whether it is a sham is a question of fact in each case to be proved by the party seeking to impugn the document that it is a sham. The term was judicially defined in *Snook v London and West Riding Investments Ltd* by Diplock LJ[3] in the following terms:

> 'It is I think necessary to consider what (if any) legal concept is involved in the use of this popular and pejorative word. I apprehend that if it has any meaning in law, it means acts done or documents executed by the parties to the sham which are intended by them to give to third parties or to the court the appearance of creating between the parties legal rights and obligations between them different from the actual legal rights and obligations (if any) which the parties intend to create. But one thing I think is clear in legal principle, morality and authorities (see *Yorkshire Railway Wagon Co v Maclure* (1882) 21 Ch D 309 and *Stoneleigh Finance Ltd v Phillips* [1965] 2 QB 537, [1965] 1 All ER 513) that for acts or documents to be a "sham" with whatever legal consequences follow from this, all the parties thereto must have a common intention that the acts or documents are not to create the legal rights and obligations which they give the appearance of creating. No unexpressed intentions of a "shammer" affects the legal rights of a party whom he deceived'.

[1]   As to which, see *Boyce v Rendells* (1983) 268 Estates Gazette 268, CA; *Scene Estate Ltd v Amos* [1957] 2 QB 205, [1957] 2 All ER 325, CA, and *Short Bros (Plant) Ltd v Edwards* (1978) 249 Estates Gazette 539, CA. See para 21.2ff.

[2]   Adopting the description of Lawton LJ in *O'Malley v Seymour* (1978) 250 Estates Gazette 1083 at 1088, CA.

[3]   [1967] 2 QB 786, [1967] 1 All ER 518 at 802, CA.

19.55 The concept of sham has been considered by the courts in relation to grazing agreement disputes. In *Boyce v Rendells*[1], where the parties entered into a grazing agreement and the farmer intended all the time to use the land for corn growing and did so, it was held that the document was not a sham, notwithstanding the fact that there was reference to barley etc, on the plan which accompanied the document because the landowner (who was resident in America at the time) always intended the agreement to be a grazing agreement. If the landowner had been resident locally and had witnessed without comment the corn growing and renewed the 'grazing agreement' with the land in stubble or planted to corn, it would have been difficult for the court to have avoided the conclusion that the document was a sham.

Parliament seems to have contemplated the use of the grazing agreement in circumstances where it would be a mere sham: hence the reference to 'whether or not the agreement expressly so provides' in s 2(3)(a) of the AHA 1986.

The expectation, even though mutual (if not expressed), that an agreement entered into for a specified period of the year, will be renewed, is not sufficient to render the document a sham[2].

In the context of agricultural property, sham has been considered extensively by Neuberger J (as he then was) in *National Westminster Bank plc v Jones*[3].

Sham has arisen in the context of the Rent Acts on numerous occasions[4].

[1]   (1983) 268 Estates Gazette 268, CA.
[2]   But note that that does not entitle either party to claim sham in the absence of being able to prove mutual contemplation that the agreement should not operate in accordance with its terms. See *Scene Estate Ltd v Amos* [1957] 2 QB 205, [1957] 2 All ER 325, CA.
[3]   [2000] EGCS 82, [2001] 1 BCLC 98; affd [2001] EWCA Civ 1541, [2002] 1 BCLC 55. Also generally see, *Belvedere Court Management Ltd v Frogmore Developments Ltd* [1997] QB 858, [1996] 1 EGLR 59, CA.
[4]   See *Somma v Hazlehurst* [1978] 2 All ER 1011, [1978] 1 WLR 1014, CA (now overruled by *Street v Mountford* [1985] AC 809 (HL), but not on this point); *Walsh v Griffiths-Jones* [1978] 2 All ER 1002; *Aldrington Garages Ltd v Fielder* (1978) 37 P & CR 461; *Demuren v Seal Estates Ltd* (1978) 249 Estates Gazette 440; *O'Malley v Seymour* (1978) 250 Estates Gazette 1083; *Buchmann v May* [1978] 2 All ER 993; *A G Securites v Vaughan and Antoniades v Villiers* [1990] 1 AC 417; *Aslan v Murphy (Nos 1 and 2)* [1990] 1 WLR 766; *Duke v Wynne* [1989] 3 All ER 130, [1990] 1 WLR 766; *Uratemp Ventures Ltd v Collins* [2001] UKHL 43, [2002] 1 AC 301; *Pankhania v Hackney London Borough Council* [2004] EWHC 323 (Ch), [2004] 1 EGLR 135.

Mislabelling

19.56 It not infrequently happens that the parties enter into an agreement which is described as, say, a licence but which upon its true construction in fact creates a tenancy. Thus, where, for example, the landowner was given consent by the Minister pursuant to s 2[1] of the AHA 1986 to grant a licence for the occupation of agricultural land falling outside the statutory conversion by s 2 into a tenancy from year to year and pursuant to such consent the parties entered into an agreement which was in substance a tenancy agreement, albeit that the labels had been changed; such agreement will take effect as a tenancy and not as a licence. In such cases the landlord may have been described as the licensor and the tenant as the licensee, the rent as the licence fee etc[2], but all the hallmarks of a tenancy are present. The parties, in such circumstances, will have been held to have misconstrued their own document and legal effect will be given to the substance rather than the nomenclature of the document.

No such agreements can have been entered into on or after 1 September 1995 when Ministry licences or consents ceased to be available upon the coming into effect of the ATA 1995.

19.56 *What is an agricultural holding?*

Whether a document falls to be disregarded as a sham is a question of fact. Whether a document is mislabelled is a question of law, founded upon the true construction of the document in question, without looking outside the document, save in so far as that is permitted by the canons of construction.

1   Note: it may have proved in practice to be impossible to have structured an agreement between a landowner and a farmer, if it was to be of any duration, in circumstances where it would operate as a licence properly so called and, therefore, within the terms of the Ministry consent, because a licence giving exclusive possession is not a licence at all: see *Street v Mountford* [1985] AC 809 (HL), except in the rarest of circumstances which are unlikely to apply. A licence not giving exclusive possession would not have been converted anyway, regardless of the Minister's consent. It is apprehended that most 'licences' granted pursuant to Ministry consent were, in fact, converted into tenancies from year to year, whether the parties realised it or not, for these reasons.

2   *Addiscombe Garden Estates Ltd v Crabbe* [1958] 1 QB 513, [1957] 3 All ER 563, CA.

Chapter 20

INTERESTS PROTECTED BY THE AGRICULTURAL HOLDINGS ACT 1986

CONTRACT OF TENANCY

20.1 Section 1(1) of the Agricultural Holdings Act 1986 (AHA 1986) provides that for agricultural land to comprise an agricultural holding the land must be included in a 'contract of tenancy' which is also a contract for an 'agricultural tenancy'[1].

Section 1(5) of the AHA 1986 defines a contract of tenancy as a tenancy which is either:

(a)   a tenancy from year to year (to include lettings deemed to be from year to year and converted into such lettings by virtue of s 2); or

(b)   for a term of years (to include a letting converted by s 149 of the Law of Property Act 1925 into a letting for 99 years).

Such a contract of tenancy, if it begins on or after 1 September 1995[2], cannot create an agricultural holding unless it falls within one of the exceptions provided for in s 4 of the Agricultural Tenancies Act 1995[3].

[1]   AHA 1986, s 1(2).
[2]   A tenancy begins on the day on which, under the terms of the tenancy, the tenant is entitled to possession under that tenancy: the Agricultural Tenancies Act 1995 (ATA 1995), s 38(4).
[3]   See para 3.4. They can be briefly summarised as to: (a) pre-1 September 1995 agreements taking effect after that date (ATA 1995, s 4(1)(a)); (b) succession tenancies (s 4(1)(b)–(d)); (c) Evesham custom tenancies (s 4(1)(e)); (d) tenancies created by surrenders and re-grants (s 4(1)(f), (g)). A 'succession tenancy' is not a term of art but is used here to mean a tenancy created in favour of a close relative of a deceased or retired former tenant within Pt IV of the AHA 1986, ss 34–59.

20.2 It should be noted that the above definition created a problem in the case of tenancy for a term certain of more than one but less than two years[1]. Such a letting fell outside the statutory conversion provisions contained in ss 2 and 3 and never, therefore, became a tenancy from year to year, but was it nevertheless an agricultural holding? If so, the other provisions of the AHA 1986 would have applied to it. After a period of some doubt the matter was finally resolved by the Court of Appeal in *EWP Ltd v Moore*[2]. A *Gladstone v Bower* tenancy was a tenancy of an agricultural holding albeit excluded from the security of tenure and succession provisions. Therefore, for example, the compensation on quitting, freedom of cropping provisions etc, applied.

It should also be noted that there must be a single contract of tenancy for the formation of a single agricultural holding. If there are two or more contracts of tenancy, even between the same landlord and the same tenant, these will create separate agricultural holdings and the contracts of tenancy will not be aggregated, nor will separate concurrent agreements between the same parties be read together as a single agreement for the purposes of conferring security of tenure[3]. If, therefore, a grazing agreement was entered into in respect of the grassland and a *Gladstone v Bower* (18-month) tenancy agreement was entered into in respect of the arable land comprised within the same farm, the two will not be read together to be converted into a tenancy of a single agricultural holding.

Where land is 'added' to an existing holding and a single rent is agreed upon without apportionment, then the doctrine of termination and regrant will apply so that all the land will then be comprised in one single contract of tenancy[4]. However, where there are two separate lettings of two blocks of land to the same tenant and later a single unapportioned rent is agreed upon on review for all the land together, the doctrine of surrender and regrant will not be invoked and the two holdings will remain two separate agricultural holdings[5].

[1] This is popularly known as a *Gladstone v Bower* tenancy by reason of the decision of the Court of Appeal in that name: [1960] 2 QB 384, [1960] 3 All ER 353. For a commentary on such lettings generally, see para 20.13.
[2] [1992] QB 460.
[3] *Darby v Williams* (1974) 232 Estates Gazette 579, CA.
[4] See *Jenkins R Lewis & Son Ltd v Kerman* [1971] Ch 477, [1970] 1 All ER 833.
[5] *Trustees of J W Childers v Anker* [1996] 1 EGLR 1. As to surrender and re-grant generally, see para 33.5ff.

A letting from year to year

20.3 Until the ATA 1995 came into effect on 1 September 1995, by virtue of s 2 of the AHA 1986, a letting of agricultural land for an interest less than a tenancy from year to year or a licence[1] to occupy land as agricultural land of any duration were both[2] converted by s 2 into lettings from year to year. That is subject to statutory exceptions which are considered in detail in Chapter 21. In outline the exceptions are where:

(a)   the Minister[3] (in practice, the Divisional Surveyor) had approved the agreement before the agreement was entered into – 'Ministry consent licences and short-term tenancies';
(b)   the agreement for the letting of the land, or the granting of a licence was made:
    (i)   in contemplation of the use of the land only for grazing and/or mowing; and
    (ii)   during some specified period of the year – 'grazing/mowing agreement'; or

(iii)   the licence or tenancy was granted by a person 'whose interest in the land is less than a tenancy from year to year'[4];

(iv)   a further exception, contained in para 1 of Sch 12 of the AHA 1986, that s 2 of the AHA 1986 should not apply to an agreement made before 1 March 1948 preserved an exception to s 2 of the 1948 Act. This only applied to periodic tenancies which were less than from year to year created before 1 March 1948. It is doubtful whether any such are still subsisting[5].

The effect of s 2 of the AHA 1986 is that many informal agreements which were never intended to create agricultural holdings when entered into[6], and agreements which were expressly intended to fall outside the agricultural holdings legislation[7], were converted by s 2[8] into agricultural holdings, with all the consequent security of tenure, compensation and other provisions.

[1]   This means a licence supported by valuable consideration and not a mere gratuitous licence; see Ch 21, and a licence conferring rights of exclusive possession; see *Bahamas International Trust Co Ltd v Threadgold* [1974] 3 All ER 881, [1974] 1 WLR 1514, HL.

[2]   In the case of licences, the 'circumstances' must be 'such' that if the interest were a tenancy from year to year, the holder would be a tenant of an agricultural holding.

[3]   See para 4.2.

[4]   There has been no case law on this obscure provision since persons with an interest less than that of tenants from year to year, whose interests have not been converted into tenancies from year to year itself, are very rare.

[5]   See *Land Settlement Association Ltd v Carr* [1944] KB 657, [1944] 2 All ER 126, CA, a decision under the Agricultural Holdings Act 1923 which gave rise to the creation of periodic tenancies of unusual terms and hence the statutory conversion for all such created after 1 March 1948.

[6]   Eg *Verrall v Fames* [1966] 2 All ER 808, [1966] 1 WLR 1254; *Holder v Holder* [1968] Ch 353, [1968] 1 All ER 665, CA; *Mitton v Farrow* [1980] 2 EGLR 1, CA and *James v Lock* (1977) 246 Estates Gazette 395, CA.

[7]   Eg *Lory v London Borough of Brent* [1971] 1 All ER 1042, [1971] 1 WLR 823, *Bedfordshire County Council v Clarke* (1974) 230 Estates Gazette 1587 and *Short Bros (Plant) Ltd v Edwards* (1978) 249 Estates Gazette 539. CA.

[8]   The process of conversion was described in earlier editions of this book by the evocative phrase 'statutory magic'.

Tenancies of one year and tenancies at will

20.4   Apart from the express provisions of AHA 1986, s 2 dealing with short-term tenancies or licences which are converted into tenancies from year to year, the effect of the decisions reached upon the wording of s 2 has been that the following forms of agreement attract the operation of the statute:

(a)   a tenancy for one year exactly has been held by the Court of Appeal to amount to a letting 'for an interest less than a tenancy from year to year' and thus be converted into a tenancy from year to year by s 2[1];

(b)   tenancies at will are lettings 'for an interest less than a tenancy from year to year', again converted by s 2;

(c)   licences[2].

[1]   *Bernays v Prosser* [1963] 2 QB 592, [1963] 2 All ER 321 and see *Rutherford v Maurer* [1962] 1 QB 16, [1961] 2 All ER 775 and *Lower v Sorrell* [1963] 1 QB 959, [1962] 3 All ER 1074, cf a tenancy for more than one but less than two years, *Gladstone v Bower* [1960] 1 QB 170, [1960] 3 All ER 353, CA.

2   As to whether an occupier entered land as a tenant at will or as a licensee, and the nature
     of a tenancy at will, see *Ramnarace v Lutchman* [2001] UKPC 25, [2001] 1 WLR 1651,
     [2002] 1 P & CR 371.

Licences

20.5 Licences to occupy land, even of an informal nature, were converted
into tenancies from year to year by AHA 1986, s 2, provided that the
circumstances were such that if the occupier's interest were a tenancy he
would in respect of that land be a tenant of an agricultural holding. The
licence to occupy must have been a licence to occupy land and not merely to
take its produce[1]. The licence to occupy must have given exclusive rights of
occupation to the farmer/occupant and not, for example, have involved a
sharing of the land with the landowner[2]. When the licence was converted into
a tenancy all the agreed terms remained, except the label. Gratuitous licences
were not converted[3].

The licence may have been of any duration. Section 2 expressly converted
short-term tenancies into tenancies from year to year, but not tenancies for a
term of more than a year[4]. However, a licence may have been converted into a
tenancy from year to year even though it was to be of uncertain duration[5], or
for more than one year but less than two years, or indeed for more than two
years.

The statutory conversion of licences gave rise to particular problems for
tenants who incorporated their farming businesses and then continued farming through the medium of the company. In such circumstances, if no specific
agreement was reached expressly with the company, which may be the alter
ego of the tenant, then, if the company farmed the holding, paid the rent,
complied with the tenant's covenants and occupied the holding, the tenant
may well, inadvertently at the least, have granted a licence to the company
which was converted into a sub-tenancy as occurred in *Snell v Snell*[6].

1   *Wyatt v King* (1951) 157 Estates Gazette 124, CA (doubted in *Harrison-Broadley v Smith*
     [1963] 3 All ER 586, [1963] 1 WLR 1262, CA); and see *Finbow v Air Ministry* [1963]
     2 All ER 647, [1963] 1 WLR 697. Also see, Cardwell, 'Arable Farming in the Short Term',
     The Conveyancer, 1990, 138.
2   *Harrison-Broadley v Smith* [1963] 3 All ER 586, [1963] 1 WLR 1262, CA and *Bahamas
     International Trust Co Ltd v Threadgold* [1974] 3 All ER 881, [1974] 1 WLR 1514, HL.
     For a fuller commentary, see para 21.16.
3   See para 21.15.
4   *Gladstone v Bower* [1960] 2 QB 384, [1960] 3 All ER 353, CA, but note section 3: see
     para 20.7ff.
5   Eg, for life: see *Snell v Snell* (1964) 191 Estates Gazette 361, CA.
6   (1964) 191 Estates Gazette 361, CA. Cf *Chaplin v Smith* [1926] 1 KB 198, CA.

20.6 This may also result in a breach by the tenant of the prohibition upon
sub-letting which is irremediable[1]. Whether such a sub-letting may be capable
of being relied upon to support a Case E notice to quit will depend upon
whether there has been material prejudice to the landlord[2].

A right of hold-over whereby a tenant is permitted to remain in occupation after termination of the tenancy gave rise to the inadvertent creation of a new tenancy by virtue of the statutory conversion of that licence into a tenancy from year to year[3].

It is probable that following the sale of a standing crop the necessary licence granted to the purchaser to enter and harvest the crop would also have given rise to the operation of the statutory conversion into a protected tenancy for the purchaser by reason of s 2 of the AHA 1986. However, problems can no longer arise for new hold-overs or other licences if granted to operate on or after 1 September 1995.

Where a 'licence' entered into so as to give effect to a consent under s 5 of the AHA 1986[4] it was held to create a tenancy and therefore confer security[5]. Likewise, where a prospective purchaser was allowed into possession, there was an implied contractual licence granted for value which was converted by s 2 of the AHA 1986 into an annual tenancy[6]. Conversely, where a tenant of an agricultural holding exercised an option to purchase the freehold – stopped paying rent and received notice to quit for non-compliance with a notice to pay – he then failed to complete the purchase. It was held that his continued occupation was unlawful[7].

[1] *Troop v Gibson* [1986] 1 EGLR 1, 277 Estates Gazette 1134, CA and *Scala House and District Property Co Ltd v Forbes* [1974] QB 575, [1973] 3 All ER 308, CA.
[2] *Pennell v Payne* [1995] QB 192, [1995] 2 All ER 592, CA, and para 21.21.
[3] *Milton (Peterborough) Estates Co v Harris* [1989] 2 EGLR 229, HC, but note that on the facts of that case it was held that no right of hold-over was in fact granted.
[4] See para 20.15.
[5] *Ashdale Land & Property Co Ltd v Manners* [1992] 2 EGLR 5, [1992] 34 EG 76.
[6] *Gold v Jacques Amand Ltd* (1991) 63 P & CR 1.
[7] *Dockerill v Fitzpatrick* [1989] 1 EGLR 1, CA. Cf *Walters v Roberts* (1980) 41 P & CR 210.

A letting for two years or more

20.7 Section 3 of the AHA 1986 converts into annual tenancies at the end of the fixed term any lease or tenancy for a period of two years or more[1]. This still applies to fixed-term leases which began before 1 September 1995 which expire after that date. This is achieved by providing that such a tenancy shall, instead of terminating 'on the expiration of the term for which it was granted', continue 'as from the expiration of the tenancy' from year to year[2].

[1] For the position regarding a tenancy of more than one but less than two years, see para 20.13.
[2] Section 3 of the Agricultural Holdings Act 1948 (AHA 1948) (which s 3 of the AHA 1986 very closely follows) contained an express prohibition upon contracting out (see AHA 1948, s 3(4)). Section 3 of the AHA 1986 contains no such express prohibition. This is because agreements entered into after 12 September 1984 are subject to the special provisions excluding succession: see para 35.8.

20.8 The circumstances in which the statutory conversion of fixed-term leases into tenancies from year to year do not apply are as follows:

20.8 *Interests protected by the Agricultural Holdings Act 1986*

(a) Where not less than one nor more than two years before the term date either party has given to the other a notice of his intention to terminate the tenancy and such notice is effective. A tenant who receives such a notice from his landlord is entitled to give a counter-notice, unless the notice is given on one of the special 'incontestable' grounds for possession contained in Cases A to H of Sch 3 to the AHA 1986[1]. This is because s 3(2) of the AHA 1986 provides that such a notice is deemed to be a notice to quit. In most such cases[2], a tenant in receipt of such a notice to quit can, however, give a demand for arbitration although not a counter-notice[3].

(b) The statutory conversion into an annual tenancy does not apply where the lease was granted on or after 12 September 1984[4] and the conditions of s 4 of the AHA 1986 apply. Section 4 provides that if the tenant died during the currency of the lease, the tenancy would automatically expire by effluxion of time on the term date specified in the lease. An exception to this rule is that if the tenant dies during the last year of the lease or tenancy, the lease will then continue for one further year. No notice is required to be given by the landlord. The expiration of the lease in each case will take place by effluxion of time, though for the purposes of assessing compensation the lease will have been deemed to have been terminated by notice to quit given by the landlord[5].

(c) The statutory conversion by s 3 does not apply to a lease for a life or lives which is converted by s 149(6) of the Law of Property Act 1925 into a lease for 90 years.

(d) Section 3 does not apply to any subsisting tenancy granted before 1 January 1921. Such a tenancy, if created for a fixed term which expires, will not be converted into a tenancy from year to year. It is one of the few remaining examples of a tenancy created before 1 September 1995 which expires by effluxion of time.

(e) Section 3 does not apply to a tenancy granted after 1 September 1995 because of the exclusion of these tenancies created after that date from the AHA 1986 except in the limited circumstances set out in s 4 of the ATA 1995[6].

[1] For a commentary upon such provisions, see Ch 31.
[2] Ie Cases B, D and E.
[3] For a commentary on Cases A–H, see Ch 31.
[4] When the Agricultural Holdings Act 1984 came into force.
[5] The automatic termination at the expiration of the fixed term in the event of the death of the tenant during the currency of the tenancy, applies where the original tenant dies. If the original tenant has assigned the tenancy during the currency of the lease, the assignee's tenancy will come to an end on the expiration of the fixed term because of the death of the original tenant. This brings such leases into line with the old law (pre-1976) provided by s 24(2)(g) of the AHA 1948 as applies to annual tenancies (though not fixed-term leases) by reason of the old decisions of *Clarke v Hall* [1961] 2 QB 331, [1961] 2 All ER 365 and *Costagliola v Bunting* [1958] 1 All ER 846, [1958] 1 WLR 580.
[6] For a commentary on s 4 of the ATA 1995, see para 3.4ff.

Extension of tenancies on death of landlord: emblements

20.9 In the rare case of a tenancy which is held of a landlord entitled for life, or any other uncertain interest, the common law provided that a tenant dispossessed by reason of the cesser of the landlord's interest was only entitled to a claim for emblements. This entitled such tenants merely to hold over and harvest that year's annual crops subject to complex rules of entitlement[1]. Section 21 of the AHA 1986 (like s 4 of the AHA 1948 which it replaced[2]) substituted for the common law claim for emblements an entitlement to 12 months' notice to quit expiring on the annual term date of the tenancy. Further, the tenant is able to serve a counter-notice invoking the security of tenure provisions contained in Pt III of the AHA 1986.

Since the Settled Land Act 1925, a tenant for life of settled land enjoys powers of leasing which are not terminable on the death of the life tenant/landlord. It is unlikely that s 21 will, therefore, any longer have any practical importance. The example of *Stephens v Balls*[3] of a tenancy granted by an incumbent in respect of glebe land will not now be repeated since incumbents no longer enjoy powers of leasing ecclesiastical glebe.

[1] For a commentary on the unsatisfactory nature of a claim for emblements, see the Historical Introduction in Ch 1 at para 1.1.
[2] And earlier sections going back to 1851.
[3] (1957) 107 L Jo 764, CC. Note also the abolition of the special rules as to ecclesiastical land which were contained in the AHA 1948, as to which see Ch 42.

AGRICULTURAL TENANCY

20.10 For a 'contract of tenancy' to have created an 'agricultural holding', it must also have satisfied the definition of an 'agricultural tenancy'[1].

An agricultural tenancy is one by which 'the whole of the land comprised in the contract' must have been 'let for use as agricultural land'[2]. That stringent requirement is subject 'to such exceptions only as do not substantially affect the character of the tenancy'.

Whether the contract of tenancy is or is not an agricultural tenancy is first determined by the terms of the tenancy[3]. Only if the terms of the tenancy are inconclusive will the court consider:

(a)   the actual or contemplated use of the land at the time of the conclusion of the contract and subsequently; and
(b)   any other relevant circumstances.

The issue of mixed use is dealt with extensively in Chapter 19[4].

[1] AHA 1986, s 1(2).
[2] AHA 1986, s 1.
[3] See para 19.2ff.
[4] See para 19.11ff.

DISPUTES PROCEDURES

20.11 Despite the provisions of s 2(4) of the AHA 1986, a dispute between the parties as to whether an agreement relating to agricultural land involves the formation of an agricultural holding is not compulsorily referable to arbitration. The Court of Appeal decided that such a dispute fell within the jurisdiction of the courts but a dispute as to how s 2 should be operated (for example, as to what necessary modifications had to be made to the agreement) must be referred to arbitration[1].

1   *Goldsack v Shore* [1950] 1 KB 708, [1950] 1 All ER 276.

AGRICULTURAL HOLDINGS WITH NO SECURITY OF TENURE

20.12 In this important category of agricultural holding there are certain forms of tenancy which are tenancies of agricultural holdings in the fullest sense of the term, but which, for a variety of reasons, either attract no security of tenure at all, or else very limited security. They are of finite and diminishing importance because as they fall they cannot be created anew since 1 September 1995 following the ATA 1995 coming into force. They fall to be distinguished from those forms of arrangement which do not involve the creation of an agricultural holding in the first place. The former category attracts all the other incidents of a tenancy of an agricultural holding, for example compensation on quitting, freedom of cropping and so forth, whereas arrangements which never constitute tenancies of agricultural holdings are subject to no such statutory control or regularisation. The terms of the parties' agreement are not varied, supplemented, overridden or altered in any way by any of the provisions of the agricultural holdings legislation.

The agreements which constituted agricultural holdings, but without security of tenure, were as follows:

(a)   lettings for more than one year but less than two years created before 1 September 1995 ('*Gladstone v Bower* agreements')[1];
(b)   Ministry consent tenancies created before 1 September 1995 by virtue of s 5 of the AHA 1986;
(c)   sub-tenancies beginning before 1 September 1995.

There is a fourth category of arrangement to consider in this context: joint ventures and partnerships. These give rise to a number of issues which require separate consideration[2].

1   [1960] 2 QB 384, [1960] 3 All ER 353, CA.
2   See para 19.30ff.

Gladstone v Bower agreements

20.13 By reason of what was thought to be a lacuna, or even an oversight, on the part of the parliamentary draftsman of the AHA 1948, a tenancy for a term certain of more than one but less than two years was held by the Court of Appeal not to be converted into a tenancy from year to year either by operation of s 2 or s 3 of what was then the 1948 Act and is now the AHA 1986. Such a tenancy, which in the case of *Gladstone v Bower*[1] itself was for a period of 18 months, is not for a period which is less than a year, nor is it for a period of two years or upwards. It is for a period which attracts statutory conversion neither by s 2 nor s 3 of the AHA 1986 (nor of the AHA 1948 before it). Accordingly, on the expiration of the fixed term the tenancy expired by effluxion of time and the landlord was entitled to recover possession.

The expectation of many, following the decision in *Gladstone v Bower*[2], was that an amending statute would soon be enacted as there seemed no possible logical reason for Parliament having intended to confer security of tenure on short-term lettings, lettings from year to year and lettings for two years and upwards, but not lettings for so curious and anomalous a period as more than one but less than two years. The decision in *Gladstone v Bower*[3] was reached in 1959. There were numerous opportunities for Parliament to remedy the drafting error (if such it ever was). No amending statute was introduced. What is more, first in 1976[4] and, then, in 1984[5] and 1986[6] statutory support for the correctness of the decision in *Gladstone v Bower* was given in that such agreements are expressly excluded from succession[7]. The exclusion of such tenancies from security of tenure is now accepted.

[1] [1960] 2 QB 384, [1960] 3 All ER 353.
[2] [1960] 2 QB 384, [1960] 3 All ER 353.
[3] [1960] 2 QB 384, [1960] 3 All ER 353.
[4] See the Agriculture (Miscellaneous Provisions) Act 1976.
[5] See AHA 1984.
[6] See AHA 1986.
[7] AHA 1986, s 36(2)(b) (succession on death). Succession on retirement only applies to a tenancy from year to year.

20.14 Following the enactment of the ATA 1995, *Gladstone v Bower* agreements are likely to be of limited or no relevance. Nevertheless, the following points should be noted:

(a) A *Gladstone v Bower*[1] agreement could not be 'back-dated'[2]. The tenancy took effect from the date of execution and completion of the tenancy agreement for the purpose of assessing the duration of the term. If a tenancy, expressed to run from, say, 25 March, for a term of, say, 18 months, was not executed and completed until a date during the last year of the term created, ie after 25 September, the tenancy would have been converted into a tenancy from year to year by operation of s 2 of the AHA 1986.

(b) It is submitted that if the true agreement between the parties was that there should be a series of *Gladstone v Bower* agreements, each one restricted to a period of more than one but less than two years, that the true agreement between the parties would be found to have been for the aggregate of such term which, if it exceeded two years, would have been converted into a tenancy from year to year by s 3 of the AHA 1986[3]. Thus, people holding over after the expiration of the last of a line of *Gladstone v Bower* agreements may still be able to maintain that they have AHA 1986 security beginning before 1 September 1995.

(c) It has been held by the Court of Appeal in *EWP Ltd v Moore*[4] that although a tenancy for more than one but less than two years was not converted into an annual tenancy by either s 2 or s 3 of the 1948 Act (as it then was), nevertheless the tenancy fell within the definition of a 'contract of tenancy' and within the definition of an 'agricultural holding'. It did not attract security of tenure under the Landlord and Tenant Act 1954, Pt II[5], but did attract compensation on quitting and all the other incidents (apart from security of tenure, and now succession) of an agricultural holding.

1   [1960] 2 QB 384, [1960] 3 All ER 353, CA.
2   *Keen v Holland* [1984] 1 All ER 75, [1984] 1 WLR 251, CA following *Bradshaw v Pawley* [1979] 3 All ER 273, [1980] 1 WLR 10 and *Hoveringham Group Ltd v Scholey* (1982) unreported – a case of a letting for a year and a day accepted just after the start of the term.
3   There is no authority directly upon this proposition but the comparable decisions in the context of agreements for a succession of grazing licences or tenancies would appear to apply equally to a succession of *Gladstone v Bower* agreements. See *Short Bros (Plant) Ltd v Edwards* (1978) 249 Estates Gazette 539, CA; *Scene Estate Ltd v Amos* [1957] 2 QB 205, [1957] 2 All ER 325, CA; *Rutherford v Maurer* [1962] 1 QB 16, [1961] 2 All ER 775, CA.
4   [1992] QB 460.
5   Section 43(1)(a) of the Landlord and Tenant Act 1954, Pt II, was amended by s 8 of the Agriculture Act 1958, and Sch 1 para 29, to exclude from the 1954 Act grazing agreements and agreements subject to prior Ministry consent, but not (understandably since *Gladstone v Bower* was decided in 1960) tenancies for more than one but less than two years.

Ministry consent tenancies created

20.15   By virtue of s 5 of the AHA 1986, the Minister[1] was empowered to give prior consent to the grant of a tenancy of an agricultural holding for a term of not less than two and not more than five years, which will then not attract the statutory conversion provided for by s 3 if the Ministry consent was complied with and the lease or tenancy agreement confirmed the necessary reference to the statutory exclusion. Upon the expiration of the fixed term, such a lease or tenancy will not be converted into a tenancy from year to year and thereby confer security of tenure upon the tenant. It will, nevertheless, come within the definition of an agricultural holding and will attract all the other provisions of the agricultural holdings legislation, for example, as to compensation on quitting.

1   AHA 1986, s 96(1). See para 4.2.

20.16   This should be contrasted with the parallel power for the Minister contained in s 2 of the AHA 1986 to give similar consent in respect of a tenancy for less than a year, or a licence of any duration. That latter category of tenancy or licence falls outside the definition of an agricultural holding[1].

As in the case of *Gladstone v Bower* agreements, following the enactment of the ATA 1995, Ministry tenancies are likely to be of limited or no relevance. Nevertheless, the following points should be noted:

(a)   The consent of the Minister must have been obtained before the grant of a tenancy[2].

(b)   The contract of tenancy entered into pursuant to the consent must be in writing and must have a statement endorsed upon it indicating '(in whatever terms) that s 3 does not apply to the tenancy'[3]. There is no equivalent provision in respect of a Ministry consent tenancy granted pursuant to s 2.

(c)   At one time Ministry consents were very difficult to obtain except by government departments (eg Ministry of Defence) or nationalised industries (eg the Coal Board). In later years, before the passing of the ATA 1995 they were readily granted when both parties applied[4]. They are no longer available since 1 September 1995.

(d)   As to back-dating, in *Pahl v Trevor*[5] it was re-affirmed that, following *Keen v Holland*[6], it was not possible to grant a tenancy to comply with the Minister's consent for a term starting before the lease or tenancy is completed but where the Minister grants approval for a 'period' starting on a specified date, that could pre-date completion of the documents and therefore the formal grant of the tenancy. An argument that the Minister could not impose terms at all, but merely grant or refuse consent, unconditionally failed.

1   As to which see para 18.15.
2   In *Bedfordshire County Council v Clarke* (1974) 230 Estates Gazette 1587 (a decision under the predecessor to s 2 of the AHA 1986) where the Minister's consent and the tenancy both bore the same date and the landlord was unable to prove that the Minister's consent was obtained prior to the consent, the statutory conversion into a tenancy from year to year was held not to have been excluded.
3   AHA 1986, s 5(3).
4   The Minister's statements dated 19 August 1984 and 10 August 1989.
5   [1992] 1 EGLR 22, [1992] 25 EG 130, CA.
6   [1984] 1 All ER 75, [1984] 1 WLR 251, CA.

Sub-tenancies

20.17 Where a tenant is granted a tenancy which falls within the definition of an agricultural holding, but which is granted by a person who is not himself the freeholder but is a tenant, such tenancy constitutes a sub-tenancy. The sub-tenant enjoys all the same security as against his landlord (the head tenant) as he would if his landlord were the freeholder[1]. However, if the superior tenancy is itself terminated by the unilateral action of the head tenant, the sub-tenancy carved out of the head tenancy will thereby be terminated by operation of law, whether or not the head tenant gives notice to quit to the sub-tenant[2]. It is inaccurate to refer to such tenancies as not attracting security of tenure, save in that one very important instance of termination of the head tenancy as above.

The use of this rule of law so as to enable a landlord with the concurrence of a 'tame' intermediary to whom a head tenancy is granted so that he can forthwith sub-let to the selected farmer of the holding had been widely used. The intention was to deny such farmer security of tenure. The Court of Appeal in *Gisborne v Burton*[3] decided that such sub-tenancies are fully protected as against the head landlord.

1   *Brown v Wilson* (1949) 208 LT 144, *Mellor v Watkins* (1874) LR 9 QB 400 and *Pennell v Payne* [1995] QB 192, [1995] 2 All ER 592, [1995] 1 EGLR 6, CA and the commentary on sub-tenants generally, see para 29.17ff.
2   *Pennell v Payne* [1995] QB 192, [1995] 2 All ER 592, [1995] 1 EGLR 6, CA.
3   [1989] QB 390, [1988] 2 EGLR 9. For a fuller commentary, see para 29.24.

AGRICULTURAL HOLDINGS – OTHER SPECIAL FEATURES

Tenancies created between 12 July 1984 and 1 September 1995

20.18 Tenancies created after 12 July 1984[1] but beginning before 1 September 1995, though 'agricultural tenancies', are excluded from the provisions relating to succession either on death or retirement[2] unless the tenancy comes within one of the exceptions contained in s 34(1)(b) of the AHA 1986[3]. Nevertheless, such holdings are agricultural holdings properly so called and all the remaining provisions of the agricultural holdings legislation apply to them.

In the case of a tenancy of an agricultural holding granted after 12 September 1984[4] but before 1 September 1995 for a term of two years or upwards, such tenancies will expire by effluxion of time in the event of the original grantee of the tenancy dying during the currency of the fixed term[5].

The two-stage implementation of the AHA 1984 creates a curious lacuna in respect of tenancies or leases for fixed terms of two years or upwards granted after 12 July 1984 (in which case no rights of succession apply), but before 12 September 1984. The former do not expire by effluxion of time on the death of the tenant during the currency of the fixed-term tenancy, but have to be terminated by notice to quit. Such a notice cannot be given pursuant to Case G if the death occurs and the landlord receives written notice of the death more than two years and three months before the expiration of the fixed term.

[1] The date when the AHA 1984 was enacted and part of that Act came into effect.
[2] AHA 1986, s 34(1)(a).
[3] As to which, see para 35.2ff.
[4] The date on which the remainder of the AHA 1984 became law. Note the lacuna between 12 July and 12 September 1984.
[5] For a fuller commentary upon the provisions of s 4, see para 3.4.

Statutory smallholdings

20.19 Tenants of statutory smallholdings[1], far from attracting, as one might expect, particular protection, are the most under-protected tenants of agricultural holdings. The following applies:

(a) They are excluded from the provisions relating to succession[2].
(b) Tenancies of such holdings created after 12 September 1984[3], but beginning before 1 September 1995, can be the subject of a valid and incontestable notice to quit under Case G to take effect after the tenant has attained the age of 65 in certain circumstances[4].
(c) They are subject to the special provisions contained in the Agriculture Act 1970 (AA 1970) which apply to smallholdings.
(d) They are more vulnerable to notice to quit for irremediable breach under Case E because of the special provisions set out in AHA 1986, Sch 3, Pt II, para 11[5].
(e) Even the peculiar rules relating to servicemen exclude notices to quit given under Case A, ie to certain forms of statutory smallholders[6].

Nevertheless, such holdings, in addition to being smallholdings within the meaning of the Agriculture Act 1970, are also agricultural holdings within the meaning of the agricultural holdings legislation and, subject to the exceptions referred to above, attract all the other rights and obligations imposed by the AHA 1986 created before 1 September 1995.

The reason for the exclusion of so many rights enjoyed by other tenants from smallholders would appear to be that statutory smallholdings are designed to be 'starter units', giving tenants a place on 'the first rung of the farming ladder'. In practice, such tenants usually find that, in the absence of new lettings generally at affordable rents and with the high cost of agricultural land, there are now no further 'rungs' available on the 'farming ladder' and their sons and other close relations are even denied a statutory right to the 'first rung' for themselves.

[1]   Ie a smallholding let by a smallholdings authority, or the Minister in pursuance of Pt III of the Agriculture Act 1970.
[2]   See the AHA 1986, s 38(4) (succession on death) and s 51 (succession on retirement) and see also paras 25.12 and 36.13.
[3]   Being the date when the relevant provisions of the AHA 1984 came into effect.
[4]   See para 31.13.
[5]   See para 31.76ff.
[6]   See para 31.18.

20.20 There are a number of features of smallholdings which should be noted:

(a)   A smallholding can only be let to the person who will farm it. He must either qualify by reason of his agricultural experience or the authority must be satisfied that he will become eligible to be so regarded within a reasonably short time[1].

(b)   Land can be let to two or more farmers, as one or more smallholdings, if they are proposing to farm the land together on a co-operative basis[2].

(c)   Smallholding authorities have general powers in relation to the management of land held by them for the purposes of smallholdings. This includes the power to purchase or hire machinery and equipment, stock, fertilizer, seeds and other requisites, and to sell or let them to smallholders so as to assist in the conduct of farming of smallholdings held by the authority[3].

(d)   When fixing the rent at which a smallholding is initially to be let, the smallholdings authority must have regard to the rent which it might reasonably be expected to achieve if it were already let as an agricultural holding under the AHA 1986[4]. The authority must assume the terms of that letting to be the same as those on which they propose to let, and that the level of rent payable for the smallholding has been determined by arbitration under the AHA 1986[5].

(e)   The authority has power to equip smallholdings by providing, improving and repairing fixed equipment and carrying out other improvements for the benefit of the land[6]. The authority and the smallholder are free to agree the terms on which such improvements and/or fixed equipment are carried out.

(f)   The freedom of cropping and disposal of produce provisions contained in the AHA 1986, s 15 are excluded in relation to lettings of smallholdings[7].

1   AA 1970, s 44(2).
2   AA 1970, s 44(3).
3   AA 1970, s 47(2), (3).
4   AA 1970, s 45.
5   AA 1970, s 45(1).
6   AA 1970, s 46 (2).
7   AHA 1986, s 82 and see para 24.9.

Fixed-term leases commencing before 1 September 1995

20.21 In addition to providing protection for tenancies from year to year, the definition of 'agricultural holding' includes leases for a term of years. Fixed term leases attract all the incidents of an agricultural holding with the exception of the following.

Rent review: The statutory machinery for reviewing the rent[1] is governed by the date on which the tenancy could be terminated by notice to quit. In such circumstances leases for more than three years cannot be subject to the statutory trienniel rent review provision unless the lease contains a contractual rent review formula and machinery. The rent otherwise remains fixed throughout the duration of the lease[2].

Death of the tenant: With the exception of such leases granted after 12 September 1984, in the event of the death of the tenant during the currency of the fixed-term lease, the lease will not usually be terminable by a Case G notice to quit[3].

1   See para 25.4ff.
2   For a commentary on rent review generally, see Ch 25.
3   Unless the death occurs and notice is given of it not later than two years and three months before the expiration of the fixed term: see para 35.8.

Market gardens

20.22 Market gardens are agricultural holdings within the AHA 1986 if created before 1 September 1995. If the tenancy agreement expressly provides that the holding shall be let as, or treated as, a market garden, or if the landlord subsequently consents, or if the Agricultural Land Tribunal so directs, they will attract additional rights and privileges, notably:

(a)   the incorporation of the Evesham Custom, whereby, in certain circumstances, the tenant can produce a 'substantial and otherwise suitable person' to accept the tenancy of the holding after termination of the existing tenancy in lieu of compensation[1]; and
(b)   receive special compensation on quitting[2].

1   AHA 1986, s 80(3) and (4). For a commentary on the Evesham Custom, see para 38.99.
2   AHA 1986, ss 79 and 80 and Sch 10. See also para 38.90 ff.

Chapter 21

INTERESTS NOT PROTECTED BY THE AGRICULTURAL HOLDINGS ACT 1986

GENERAL STATEMENT

21.1 After considering the agreements entered into before 1 September 1995, which either expressly or by statutory conversion resulted in the formation of 'agricultural holdings' it is necessary to consider those other forms of arrangement which did not result in the creation of an 'agricultural tenancy' of 'an agricultural holding'.

The consequences of the creation of a tenancy protected by the Agricultural Holdings Act 1986 (AHA 1986), particularly the very substantial devaluation of the agricultural land if so let, had resulted in many landowners going to great lengths to try to ensure that the agreements they reached with the farmers did not attract the provisions of the agricultural holdings legislation. The scarcity of agricultural land, coupled with an ever-increasing demand, had resulted in landowners being able in the main to dictate to farmers the terms upon which the land should be occupied. Frequently the objective was to enter into an agreement which was intended to come as close to being a tenancy as was legally permissible, without falling within the scope of the agricultural holdings legislation.

Following the enactment of the Agricultural Tenancies Act 1995 (ATA 1995), it is no longer possible either intentionally or inadvertently to create a tenancy with security of tenure for the tenant, except as provided in s 4 of the ATA 1995[1]. The 'old law' remains relevant and important for agreements beginning before 1 September 1995.

These arrangements are considered in two categories:

(a)   those specifically and expressly excluded by the agricultural holdings legislation itself; and

(b)   those which have been held by judicial authority not to be brought within the statutory provisions[2].

---

[1]   For a commentary on s 4 of the ATA 1995 and the circumstances in which tenancies of agricultural holdings falling within the AHA 1986 can be created beginning on or after 1 September 1995, see Ch 2.

[2]   See Cardwell, 'Arable Farming in the Short Term', [1993] The Conveyancer, 138–150.

EXPRESS STATUTORY EXCEPTIONS

Grazing and/or mowing agreements

21.2 Section 2(3) of the AHA 1986[1] expressly excluded the statutory conversion into a tenancy from year to year of any licence or tenancy which was both:

(a) 'made ... in contemplation of the use of the land only for grazing or mowing (or both)'; and

(b) 'during some specified period of the year'.

In both cases the exclusion from statutory conversion applied 'whether or not' the agreement 'expressly so provides'[2].

These provisions have been the subject of extensive litigation. However, they are now of limited or no relevance as they only apply to agreements entered into before the ATA 1995 came into force on 1 September 1995. There may still be cases where it is necessary to consider whether an agreement commenced before 1 September 1995 conferred security of tenure under the AHA 1986. In that event, the following applies.

[1] Formerly the proviso to s 2(1) of the Agricultural Holdings Act 1948 (AHA 1948).
[2] AHA 1986, s 2.

The agreement must be for grazing and/or mowing only

21.3 If the tenant or licensee was required or entitled to use the land for arable cropping, the statutory conversion will apply[1]. However, if the tenant is entitled, or even obliged, to carry out cultivations for the purpose of promoting and fostering the growth of grass, this will not result in the statutory conversion of the agreement into a tenancy from year to year. Similarly, an obligation on the tenant or licensee to fertilise, spray, cut thistles, fence against his stock, etc will not be inconsistent with a grazing or mowing agreement[2].

An agreement whereby the farmer's rights are restricted to grazing or mowing only will not be converted if the farmer in fact ploughs and grows corn in breach of his agreement unless the agreement is a sham[3].

The words of s 2(1) of the AHA 1948 referred to 'grazing or mowing only'. This was amended by the Agricultural Holdings Act 1984 (AHA 1984). Section 2(3) of the AHA 1986 provides for grazing or mowing (or both). It is permissible for an agreement to provide for the farmer to mow the standing crop of grass and then graze the land (provided the duration of the agreement falls within the time limitation of a specified period of the year)[4].

[1] *Lory v London Borough of Brent* [1971] 1 All ER 1042, [1971] 1 WLR 823.
[2] *Lory v London Borough of Brent* [1971] 1 All ER 1042, [1971] 1 WLR 823.
[3] See para 19.54.
[4] See para 21.5.

21.4 Although the inclusion of buildings with the land may in some circumstances be strong evidence of an intention that the land should be used for more than grazing or mowing only, a large parcel of land let with ancillary buildings will not necessarily be converted into a tenancy from year to year[1].

A grazing or mowing agreement cannot be made in respect of any form of farming enterprise not involving the growing of grass. There is a popular fallacy that short-term specialist agreements, for example, for the growing of carrots which cannot be grown for successive seasons on the same land, or potatoes, would not have involved the creation of an agricultural holding. Although, in practice, the grower may not have claimed security, it was available to him if he wished and if he satisfied the other requirements of the definition of an agricultural holding[2].

A grazing agreement should be distinguished from a contract of agistment where animals are taken on to the holding to be fed without any parcel of land being allocated to the animals in question[3].

A grazing agreement will fall within s 2(3) of the AHA 1986 even if the animals which graze the land are not within the definition of livestock[4], for example, horses.

If a grazing agreement was entered into and, upon its expiration, the grazier was permitted to remain in occupation paying the same sum as in the previous season without any express new agreement being entered into, the implication was that a new agreement was entered into upon the same terms as the expired agreement and, therefore, no tenancy from year to year was thereby created[5]. Since 1 September 1995, any new agreement whether express or implied cannot, except in the very limited circumstances set out in s 4 of the ATA 1995, be converted into a protected tenancy of an agricultural holding under the AHA 1986.

The exclusion of the statutory conversion under s 2 of the AHA 1986 applies only where the term is for 'some specified period of the year'[6]. The period does not have to have an agricultural significance, such as hay-making, taking cuts of silage or summer or winter grazing[7].

'Specified period of the year' means 'specified part of the year'[8]. An agreement for 364 days is for a specified period of the year[9]. An agreement 'from 1 April to 31 March' will constitute a 365-day letting and be converted into a tenancy from year to year[10]. Similarly, a letting of land for grazing for a year, but on condition that livestock was not to be grazed during March and April when daffodils were in bloom, was not restricted to a specified period of the year and was statutorily converted[11].

---

[1] *Avon County Council v Clothier* (1977) 242 Estates Gazette 1048. Note the use of the buildings was pursuant to a gratuitous licence and the decision was primarily founded upon that fact.

[2] Cf an agreement merely to enter on land to harvest a crop, eg where a crop of standing corn is sold. See *Wyatt v King* (1951) 157 Estates Gazette 124, CA: note the doubts expressed upon it by the Court of Appeal in *Harrison-Broadley v Smith* [1963] 3 All ER 586, [1963] 1 WLR 1262.

3   *Richards v Davies* [1921] 1 Ch 90.
4   *Rutherford v Maurer* [1962] 1 QB 16, [1961] 2 All ER 775, CA; *McClinton v McFall* (1974) 232 Estates Gazette 707, CA.
5   *Reid v Dawson* [1955] 1 QB 214, [1954] 3 All ER 498, CA.
6   AHA 1986, s 2(3).
7   *Reid v Dawson* [1955] 1 QB 214, [1954] 3 All ER 498, CA.
8   *Reid v Dawson* [1955] 1 QB 214, [1954] 3 All ER 498, CA.
9   *Reid v Dawson* [1955] 1 QB 214, [1954] 3 All ER 498, CA, but for the danger of 364-day agreements, see *Cox v Husk* (1976) 239 Estates Gazette 123 where, inadvertently, the 365th day was included, though no tenancy from year to year was, in fact, created. Also see, *Brown v Teirnan* [1993] 1 EGLR 11, [1993] 18 EG 134. Cf *Barnes v Hadley Court* (1981) unreported, CA where an agreement 'from' a specified date was held to include that date and thereby to include the whole year and to be converted.
10 *Cox v Husk* (1976) 239 Estates Gazette 123.
11 *Brown v Tiernan* [1993] 1 EGLR 11.

The term of the agreement must be restricted to a specified period of the year

21.5 A letting of 'six months' periods' has been held to imply a minimum of two such periods and, therefore, a minimum of a whole year and thus converted into a tenancy from year to year[1]. A specified period of the year can be specified in the most oblique terms, for example summer grass keeping, or a seasonal let[2].

An agreement for a full year, whereby the grazier was entitled to graze only during the grazing season, with the land being under water and unusable during the rest of the year, was held to come within the grazing or mowing exception[3].

There is no requirement that the land should be vacated at the expiration of the grazing period before a new agreement comes into effect. Thus each of 20 or more successive agreements, resulting in continuous occupation without breaks between each successive agreement, have been held by the Court of Appeal not to be converted into a tenancy from year to year[4]. However, in a case on similar facts, where the parties expressly agreed to renewals, the statutory conversion did apply[5].

1   *Rutherford v Maurer* [1962] 1 QB 16, [1961] 2 All ER 775.
2   *Chaloner v Bower* [1984] 1 EGLR 4. Also see, *Butterfield v Burniston* (1961) 111 L Jo 696; *Mackenzie v Laird* 1959 SC 266, 1959 SLT 268, Ct of Sess; *Luton v Tinsey* (1978) 249 Estates Gazette 239; *Somerset County Council v Pearse* [1977] CLY 53 and *Watts v Yeend* [1987] 1 All ER 744, [1987] 1 WLR 323, CA.
3   *Stone v Whitcombe* (1980) 257 Estates Gazette 929, CA.
4   *Scene Estate Ltd v Amos* [1957] 2 QB 205, [1957] 2 All ER 325.
5   *Short Bros (Plant) Ltd v Edwards* (1978) 249 Estates Gazette 539.

Contemplation of the parties

21.6 The contemplation of the parties must be mutual between the landlord and the tenant at the time of the agreement or, if there is a series of agreements, at the time of the relevant agreement. This is an objective test, in accordance with the ordinary rules applying to the formation of contracts[1]. If

298

the landlord cannot establish the mutual contemplation, the agreement will be converted into a tenancy from year to year under s 2 of the AHA 1986.

If the express terms of the agreement as to user and duration are clear, it is not possible to consider extrinsic evidence, other than to seek to establish that the agreement was a sham[2]. If the express terms are absent in relation to either user or duration, it is possible to consider extrinsic evidence[3].

It is not what the farmer does on the land which is the relevant consideration, but what it was agreed that he should do or was permitted to do. Thus even though the farmer may have ploughed and grown corn crops for successive seasons, that does not bring the agreement outside the definition of a grazing and/or mowing agreement, unless the farmer can show that the mutual intention of the parties was that he should do so[4].

[1]   *Chaloner v Bower* [1984] 1 EGLR 4.
[2]   *Scene Estate Ltd v Amos* [1957] 2 QB 205, [1957] 2 All ER 325, CA; *Short Bros (Plant Ltd v Edwards* (1978) 249 Estates Gazette 539 and *Boyce v Rendells* (1983) 268 Estates Gazette 268. As to sham, see para 19.54.
[3]   *Scene Estate Ltd v Amos* [1957] 2 QB 205, [1957] 2 All ER 325, CA.
[4]   *Boyce v Rendells* (1983) 268 Estates Gazette 268.

21.7 If the farmer can show that despite the fact that the agreement specified that it was for a six-month period only, an oral agreement had been entered into that there would be a succession of such agreements for six-monthly periods, then the agreement is converted[1].

There must be an agreement, although it may be implied[2]. The burden of proof in establishing that the statutory conversion does not apply because of the grazing or mowing exception rests with the landowner[3].

A gentleman's agreement is not an agreement at all[4], nor is a gratuitous agreement[5], but consideration may take the form of an obligation to put the land into good heart without any periodic payment being necessary[6].

[1]   *Short Bros (Plant Ltd v Edwards* (1978) 249 Estates Gazette 539.
[2]   *Chaloner v Bower* (1983) 269 EG 725. The judge at first instance held that there was no consensus. The Court of Appeal held that the parties must have been deemed to have entered into an agreement but that the terms of that agreement were that the farmer's occupation should be limited to grazing or mowing only during some specified period of the year, even though no specific period had been agreed upon.
[3]   *Scene Estate Ltd v Amos* [1957] 2 QB 205, [1957] 2 All ER 325, CA; *James v Lock* (1977) 246 Estates Gazette 395, CA.
[4]   *Rhodes v Dalby* [1971] 2 All ER 1144, [1971] 1 WLR 1325.
[5]   *Goldsack v Shore* [1950] 1 KB 708, [1950] 1 All ER 276, CA.
[6]   *Mitton v Farrow* [1980] 2 EGLR 1; *Verrall v Farnes* [1966] 2 All ER 808, [1966] 1 WLR 1254.

General points

21.8 The possibility of a grazing agreement falling outside the definition of an agricultural holding, but being caught by the Landlord and Tenant Act 1954,

Pt II, in the case of a tenancy for grazing or mowing only was expressly excluded by para 29 of Sch 1 to the Agriculture Act 1958.

Although a full tenancy enjoying security of tenure can be surrendered by operation of law in consideration of the grant of a grazing agreement[1], clear evidence that the transaction is genuine is required[2]: once a sham always a sham[3].

Grazing agreements are quite separate from rights of common grazing and pasturage[4].

1   *Foster v Robinson* [1951] 1 KB 149, CA (a Rent Act case).
2   *Somerset County Council v Pearse* [1977] CLY 53; *Short Bros (Plant) Ltd v Edwards* (1978) 249 Estates Gazette 539, CA.
3   *Short Bros (Plant Ltd v Edwards* (1978) 249 Estates Gazette 539; cf *Foster v Robinson* [1951] 1 KB 149.
4   As to whether registration of rights of common grazing are capable of transforming non-severable rights of pasturage into severable rights, see *Bettison v Langton* [2001] UKHL 24, [2002] 1 AC 27, [2001] 3 All ER 417.

Ministry consent licences and short-term tenancies

21.9   It has already been noted that the Minister[1] had power, by virtue of s 5 of the AHA 1986, to give consent for the grant of a lease or tenancy for a term of not less than two and not more than five years, which would attract no security of tenure. The Minister also had power, pursuant to s 2 of the AHA 1986 to consent to the granting of a tenancy of lesser duration than a year or a licence of any duration. Such a tenancy or licence would not have constituted an agricultural holding at all since it fell outside the definition of a 'contract of tenancy'.

By definition, no tenancies of less than a year can be extant after 31 August 1996 because the Minister's powers were spent on 1 September 1995. However, in theory a licence granted pursuant to the Minister's consent before 1 September 1995 could still subsist.

A licence is not a licence merely because it is described as such[2]. If it was not to be a tenancy by another name, and therefore outside the scope of the Ministry consent, it must have imposed no tenant-like obligations on the licensee nor conferred upon him rights of exclusive possession (except in exceptional circumstances)[3]. Following the decision in *Street v Mountford*[4] it is difficult to see how it is possible to draft an agreement for the farming of land which is a licence and not a tenancy[5]. It follows that it is difficult to see how the Minister may have granted consent for a licence as opposed to a short-term tenancy[6]. If the Minister granted consent for a licence, but the parties, albeit inadvertently, entered into an agreement which upon its true construction involved the creation of a tenancy, then the Ministry consent did not operate, since it was not consent for the grant of a tenancy but consent for the grant of a licence. If no exclusive possession was given so as to avoid the 'licence' being a tenancy by another name the Minister's consent was otiose because the licence did not fall to be converted regardless of the Minister's consent[7].

1 AHA 1986, s 96(1). See para 4.2.
2 *Street v Mountford* [1985] AC 809, [1985] 2 All ER 289, HL. Also see para 21.16.
3 *Street v Mountford* [1985] AC 809, [1985] 2 All ER 289, HL.
4 *Street v Mountford* [1985] AC 809, [1985] 2 All ER 289, HL.
5 In the context of agriculture, see *McCarthy v Bence* [1990] 1 EGLR 1, CA for a case concerning a 'share milking' agreement. Also see para 19.34 ff.
6 See para 18.15.
7 *Harrison-Broadley v Smith* [1964] 1 All ER 867, [1964] 1 WLR 456, CA.

Tenancies or licences granted for non-commercial purposes

21.10 Tenancies or licences granted for purposes other than for 'a trade or business', for example, hobby user, fall outside the definition of an agricultural holding. The definition of an agricultural holding requires the land to be 'agricultural land' which is defined by s 1(4) of the AHA 1986 as land which is 'so used for the purposes of a trade or business'. If land which is agricultural was let for some non-commercial purpose (for example, for the tenant to graze by horses for the tenant's own enjoyment rather than as part of a commercial or business enterprise), such a letting did not constitute a letting of an agricultural holding[1]. Although the land is 'agricultural' in the ordinary sense of the word, it is not agricultural land within the meaning of s 1(4).

1 *Secretary of State for Transport v Jenkins* (1997) 79 P & CR 118. Also see para 19.9.

Agreements made before 1 March 1948

21.11 Section 2(1) of the AHA 1986 only operates to convert lettings into annual periodic tenancies where they were created on or after 1 March 1948. Conversely, fixed term lettings granted before 1 March 1948 are protected by s 3 of the AHA 1986 provided that they were entered into on or after 1 January 1921[1].

1 AHA 1986, Sch 12 para 2.

Agreements by persons with limited interests

21.12 Section 2 of the AHA 1986 expressly excludes from its operation any short-term letting or licence granted by a person whose interest in the land which is the subject of the agreement is itself less than a tenancy from year to year and which has not itself been statutorily converted into an annual periodic tenancy[1]. This will rarely be encountered in practice.

1 AHA 1986, s 2(3)(b).

OFFICE, APPOINTMENT OR EMPLOYMENT

21.13 Section 1(1) of the AHA 1986 excludes from the definition of agricultural holding land let to a tenant during his 'continuance in any office, appointment or employment held under the landlord'. Thus, a farm manager or bailiff who is let land by his employer during the period of his employment will not be in possession of an agricultural holding and his tenancy will not be 'an agricultural holding'.

The effect of the exclusion is also to exclude 'tied cottages'. These are subject to statutory protection in certain circumstances under the Rent (Agriculture) Act 1976 in relation to agreements before 15 January 1989 and after that under the Housing Act 1988.

Land and a cottage rented by a farmer from a third party for use and occupation by one of the farmer's agricultural workers will constitute an agricultural holding since the contract of employment is not as between the landlord and the tenant but between the tenant and his employee[1].

An informal arrangement between a landowner and a farmer, whereby the farmer was allowed into possession for a probationary period on unusual terms, was held not to be an appointment within the meaning of section 1(1)[2].

The employment of a contractor will also not give rise to security of tenure under the AHA 1986 under this provision, although, in practice, contractors' agreements are sometimes mislabelled and are in fact share farming agreements[3].

[1] *Blackmore v Butler* [1954] 2 QB 171, [1954] 2 All ER 403, CA.
[2] *Verrall v Farnes* [1966] 2 All ER 808, [1966] 1 WLR 1254.
[3] See para 19.34.

IMPLIED EXCLUSIONS

21.14 Implied exclusions are those arrangements which have been held by the courts not to be converted into tenancies of agricultural holdings. As with all the commentary in this part of this book, this only applies to such arrangements beginning before 1 September 1995.

Gratuitous and non-contractual licences

21.15 Before there can be any contract of tenancy, there must first be a contract. That means that there must be an agreement supported by valuable consideration or under seal. A purely gratuitous licence, as an act of kindness between neighbours has been held not to constitute a contractual licence and not to be converted into a tenancy from year to year[1].

The fact that no periodic payment is demanded, or payable, does not mean that the arrangement is purely gratuitous. Consideration can take other forms, for example, an obligation on the part of the farmer to bring the land into good heart[2]. The occupier's agreement to reseed the land farmed after he had harvested his crop was sufficient consideration to support the agreement as a legal contract[3]. An agreement whereby the farmer was allowed to occupy rent free during a probationary period, before a decision as to him having a full tenancy, was held not to be a gratuitous licence[4]. A non-contractual licence, even though it may confer exclusive possession upon the licensee, will not be converted if there was no intention to create legal relations because, for example, the arrangements were made between closely related members of the same family[5]. Conversely, a letting by a mother to her son, at a very concessionary rent was held to have involved an intention to create legal relations giving rise to protection[6].

1 *Verrall v Farnes* [1966] 2 All ER 808, [1966] 1 WLR 1254.
2 *Mitton v Farrow* [1980] 2 EGLR 1. Also see, *Secretary of State for Social Services v Beavington* (1981) 262 Estates Gazette 551; *Ashburn Anstalt v Arnold* [1989] Ch 1, CA; *Davies v Davies* [2002] EWCA Civ 1791, [2003] 01 EG 65 (CS); *Well Barn Farming Ltd v Backhouse* [2005] EWHC 1520 (Ch), [2005] 3 EGLR 109.
3 *Davies v Davies* [2002] EWCA Civ 1791, [2003] 01 EG 65 (CS).
4 *Verrall v Farnes* [1966] 2 All ER 808, [1966] 1 WLR 1254.
5 *Holder v Holder* [1968] Ch 353, [1966] 2 All ER 116, CA; *Nunn v Dalrymple* (1990) 59 P & CR 231, CA; *Padgham v Rochelle* [2002] PLSCS 197.
6 *Collier v Hollinshead* (1984) 272 Estates Gazette 941.

Non-exclusive licences

21.16 A very important category of licence which was not converted into a tenancy from year to year, and did not therefore attract security of tenure, is a non-exclusive licence. Indeed, the great majority of arrangements made before 1 September 1995 between landowners who do not farm for active farmers to occupy and farm their land without creating tenancies and security of tenure, relied upon the general rule of law as specified in *Harrison-Broadley v Smith*[1] and *Bahamas International Trust Co Ltd v Threadgold*[2], that for the statutory conversion of s 2 to have operated, the licence must, upon its true construction, have conferred upon the licensee rights of exclusive possession.

It is now clear from the decision of the House of Lords in *Street v Mountford*[3] that a licence granted for valuable consideration, conferring exclusive possession[4] upon the licensee necessarily involves the creation of a tenancy at common law without regard to the provisions of s 2 of the AHA 1986, so that no statutory conversion is involved.

In the last edition of this book, it was submitted that, in these circumstances, it was difficult to see how the statutory conversion of a licence, as provided by s 2 of the AHA 1986, can have operated at all. If a non-exclusive licence is not converted[5] and an exclusive licence for consideration is not a licence at all but a tenancy under another name[6], and a gratuitous or non-contractual licence is not converted either[7], it is unclear as to what form of licence Parliament can have intended to be capable of creation and then conversion by the statutory operation of s 2.

1 [1964] 1 All ER 867, [1964] 1 WLR 456, CA.

2 [1974] 3 All ER 881, [1974] 1 WLR 1514, HL. Also see, *McCarthy v Bence* [1990] 1 EGLR 1, CA.

3 [1985] AC 809, [1985] 2 All ER 289. For an excellent analysis of the impact of *Street v Mountford*, see 'Street v Mountford Revisited', an essay by Professor Susan Bright in *Land and Tenant Law: Past, Present and Future* (2006) Hart Publishing/Falcon Chambers.

4 As to the issue of sharing occupation of possession, see *Akici v L R Butlin Ltd* [2005] EWCA Civ 1296, [2006] 1 EGLR 34, [2006] 07 EG 136.

5 Which it clearly is not: see *Harrison-Broadley v Smith* [1964] 1 All ER 867, [1964] 1 WLR 456, CA and *Bahamas International Trust Co Ltd v Threadgold* [1974] 3 All ER 881, [1974] 1 WLR 1514, HL.

6 *Street v Mountford* [1985] AC 809, [1985] 2 All ER 289, HL.

7 *Goldsack v Shore* [1950] 1 KB 708, [1950] 1 All ER 276, CA.

21.17 The decision in *Street v Mountford*[1] may be seen as confirmatory of the requirement which already existed in the law of agricultural holdings, namely that s 2(2)(b) of the AHA 1986 operates only in relation to licences which confer exclusive possession.

What is clear is that the principles established in *Street v Mountford*[2] apply to lettings of agricultural land[3]. This raises the interesting point that although a tenancy of a fixed term of between one and two years does not confer security of tenure under the AHA 1986[4], a licence for the same period, conferring exclusive possession, would fall within s 2 of the AHA 1986.

In *McCarthy v Bence*[5], it was suggested that the residual effect of s 2(2)(b) may be in relation to licences for grazing and/or mowing which are not excluded from s 2 by sub-s (3) because they are not limited to some specified period of the year.

Non-exclusive licences should be distinguished from arrangements which, although they reserve certain rights in favour of the landowner, grant to the licensee exclusively other rights which in themselves were sufficient to constitute an exclusive licence to occupy the land. The latter give rise to protection under s 2 of the AHA 1986[6].

For a licence to be non-exclusive, the right of occupation granted must be enjoyed in common by the parties[7]. An important (but not conclusive) right in the case of agricultural land is the right to carry out on the land agricultural operations[8] and to participate generally in the farming business being carried on there. This is an important consideration particularly in the context of share farming agreements[9].

1 [1985] AC 809, [1985] 2 All ER 289, HL.

2 *Street v Mountford* [1985] AC 809, [1985] 2 All ER 289, HL.

3 *Colchester Borough Council v Smith* [1991] Ch 448; *Ashdale Land Property Co v Mannus* [1992] 2 EGLR 5.

4 *Gladstone v Bower* [1960] 2 QB 384, [1960] 3 All ER 353. See para 20.13.

5 [1990] 1 EGLR 1, [1990] 17 EG 78.

6 *Lampard v Barker* (1984) 272 Estates Gazette 783, CA.

7 Note that a licence with contractual rights of access is not entitled to legal possession: *Countryside Residential (North Thames) Ltd v Tugwell* [2000] 2 EGLR 59, [2000] 34 EG 87. Also see, *National Car Parks Ltd v Trinity Development Co (Banbury) Ltd* [2001] 2 EGLR 43, [2001] 28 EG 144; *Clear Channel UK Ltd v Manchester City Council* [2005]

EWCA Civ 1304, [2006] 1 P & CR D49; and para 31.84. Sometimes the exercise of establishing exclusivity can prove to be beyond the court; see *Gibbons v Pickard* [2002] EWCA Civ 1780, [2002] PLSCS 247.
8   See the definition of farming in s 109 of the Agriculture Act 1947 (as amended), see para 24.5.
9   See para 19.34.

21.18 It should be noted that the courts have not always been content to characterise an occupier as a mere licensee with no security of tenure, particularly in the context of a family farming partnership. In *Brooks v Brown*[1], Forbes J held that, partly by reason of s 38 of the Partnership Act 1890:

'A farming partner who is on the land is ... there (particularly if he is a family farming partner) not as a mere licensee or as a licensee only, he has rights and duties if he is the working partner which mean that he has more security of tenure than a mere licensee. His position will protected ... in the Chancery Division as a partner in the operations he wants to carry out on the land ... This is a situation which it seems to me gives him some security of tenure, using that expression with a very wide meaning as I am sure Lord Russell intended to use it ... As long as it can be shown that the occupier occupies because he is either the working farmer or one of the working farmers in a family farming partnership it really ... cannot within any sense of reality be said that he is there in occupation as a licensee only. His position ... his rights deriving from occupation as a working farmer will be protected in a way that they could not be ... if he was a licensee only. The position of the respondent, as the only family farmer left farming the land in the new family partnership ... means that his occupation of the land carries with it a greater security of tenure ... than that possessed by a licensee only'.

This decision was in the context of considering an application for succession on death. The court was considering whether the applicant for succession had occupied agricultural land as a licensee only for the purposes of s 18(2)(c) of the Agriculture (Miscellaneous Provisions) Act 1976[2].

1   (1986) unreported.
2   Now see the AHA 1986, s 36.

HOLDOVER/EARLY ENTRY

21.19 Issues as to the rights arising from the payment and acceptance of rent are commonplace in relation to the law of agricultural holdings and in landlord and tenant generally. There are three common situations where issues arise:

(a)   when a new occupier is allowed into occupation of premises pending the conclusion of negotiations or the formal grant of an interest in the land, whether a tenancy or indeed the acquisition of the freehold. This is commonly known as 'early entry';

(b)   where an existing licence or tenancy has come to an end and the tenant or licensee remains in occupation. This is commonly known as 'holdover';

(c)   the third area where it arises is where a tenant has committed a breach
        or breaches of the terms of his tenancy and the landlord is in a position
        to forfeit. The impact of the payment and acceptance of rent after the
        landlord has knowledge of a breach is critical in relation to whether the
        landlord is then found to have waived the breach[1].

1   This issue is dealt with Ch 13.

Early entry

21.20 The grant of exclusive possession of an agricultural holding for a term
or a period at a rent prima facie creates a tenancy, whether or not the payment
is characterised as rent[1]. The overriding consideration is whether the parties
intended to create a legal relationship[2]. As seen in relation to the issue of
licences[3], even the most informal relationship may give rise to security of
tenure under the AHA 1986[4].

In addition to arguments as to whether early entry gives rise to tenanted
rights, the occupier may claim that an oral agreement, which would not
comply with the provisions of the Law of Property (Miscellaneous Provisions)
Act 1989[5], has given rise to rights by reason of a constructive trust[6] or
proprietary estoppel[7].

1   *Street v Mountford* [1985] AC 809, HL.
2   *Verrall v Farnes* [1966] 1 WLR 1254; *McCarthy v Bence* [1990] 1 EGLR 1, CA.
3   See para 21.55ff.
4   See, generally, *Dockerill v Fitzpatrick* [1989] 1 EGLR 1, CA; *Javad v Aqil* [1991] 1 WLR
      1007, CA; *V G Fraulo & Co Ltd v Papa* [1993] 39 EG 127, CA; *Taylor v Inntrepreneur
      Estates (CPC) Ltd* [2001] PLSCS 33. Also, in relation to vendor and purchaser, see *Walters
      v Roberts* (1980) 258 Estates Gazette 965.
5   See para 3.39. Also see, *Grossman v Hooper* [2001] EWCA Civ 615, [2001] 2 EGLR 82,
      [2001] 27 EG 135.
6   *Yaxley v Gotts* [2000] Ch 162, [2000] 1 All ER 711, [1999] 2 EGLR 181, CA; *Edwin
      Shirley Productions Ltd v Workspace Management Ltd* [2001] 2 EGLR 16, [2001] 23 EG
      158; *Rowan v Dann* [1991] EGCS 19; affd (1991) 64 P & CR 202, CA. See para 21.26.
7   *James v Evans* [2000] 3 EGLR 1, [2000] 42 EG 173, CA; *Edwin Shirley Productions Ltd
      v Workspace Management Ltd* [2001] 2 EGLR 16, [2001] 23 EG 158. See para 21.24.

Holdover

21.21 As to holdover, the first thing to note is that the payment and
acceptance of rent will not operate to waive a landlord's right to rely upon a
notice to quit during the currency of that notice to quit[1].

In *Doe d Cheny v Batten*[2], Lord Mansfield held that:

> 'The question ... is, quo animo the rent was received, and what the real
> intention of both parties was? If the truth of the case is that both parties
> intended the tenancy should continue, there is an end of the Plaintiff's title; if
> not, the landlord is not barred of his remedy of ejectment ...'.

For a tenant to acquire a new tenancy as a consequence of holding over and
then paying rent to the landlord, which the landlord accepts, there must be
'two assenting minds'[3].

1 *Sidney Bolsom Investment Trust v E Karmios & Co (London)* [1956] 1 QB 529, CA.
2 (1775) 1 Cowp 243.
3 Per Henn Collins J in *Maconochie Bros Ltd v Brand* [1946] 2 All ER 778.

21.22 In deciding whether the parties have reached an agreement for a new tenancy, the ordinary principles relating to the formation of contracts apply. There must be a consensus as to the terms of the proposed tenancy. There must be an offer, express or implied, by the landlord to grant a tenancy on those terms. There must be acceptance by the tenant, express or implied, to take the tenancy on the terms offered. There is certainly no presumption that a new tenancy will be created by the payment and acceptance of a sum in the nature of rent[1]. In all of those cases no new tenancy was found to have come into existence. For a case where a tenancy was found to exist, see the Scottish case of *Morrison-Low v Paterson*[2].

The type of problems which have arisen in practice are illustrated by the following cases:

(a) In *Walters v Roberts*[3], a purchaser entered into a contract to buy a sheep farm with vacant possession for £100,000. There was a discrepancy in relation to the area described in the contract as 3,156 acres. On admeasurement it was found to be 1,515 acres. A further contract was entered into and the purchaser was allowed into possession. Problems arose and the sale was never completed. It was held by the High Court that the occupier's rights:

> 'resulted from the second contract and the Agricultural Holdings Act 1948 did not extend to the rights of a person who had contracted to purchase the land and was let into occupation pursuant only to that contract and whose occupation was never intended to survive its extinction and that accordingly the Plaintiffs were entitled to a decree of specific performance'.

Nourse J continued:

> 'If a licence for a purchaser to occupy pending completion of the purchase were to be transformed into a tenancy from year to year ... it would be the transformation of a licence of a special and subordinate character liable to be determined without notice and with no existence independent of the purchaser's equitable interest in the land into an agreement for a tenancy ... with an independent existence of its own. In my judgement that must be a most remarkable state of affairs if the 1948 Act did catch an arrangement of this kind and afforded a protection which was clearly never intended'.

(b) In *Dockerill v Fitzpatrick*[4], a tenant of an agricultural holding had an option to purchase at a price to be agreed or determined by arbitration. The tenant exercised the option to purchase as to part only of the holding and ceased paying rent. He maintained that he was in occupation as a prospective purchaser of part and as tenant of the balance and that he had no need to pay rent until the rent had been apportioned. The landlord served a notice to pay, which was not complied with, followed by a notice to quit. The notice to pay related to the rent of the entirety of the holding, including the land over which the option had been exercised. The Court of Appeal held that a tenant who remains in

occupation of land pending the conveyance of land to him in performance of an agreement to buy it is entitled to occupy only as tenant and
not as a potential purchaser. Accordingly, he remains obliged to pay
rent until such time as the contract for the purchase is completed. The
notice to quit was upheld.

(c) In *Gold v Jacques Amand Ltd*[5], the owner of 6 acres of land negotiated
for the sale of the property to a prospective purchaser. The purchaser
undertook to erect an agricultural building on the land at its own
expense and to pay £40 per week for use and occupation. Negotiations
broke down, resulting in the owner seeking an order for possession.
The High Court held that the negotiations which had led to an
agreement in principle did not give rise to an enforceable contract
because there was uncertainty as to a number of elements. However, the
prospective purchaser was allowed into possession in anticipation that
the negotiations would be successful and on terms that the agricultural
building would be erected. After the company had entered onto the
land and had started to build, it was under an obligation to complete
the building. The court inferred the existence of an implied contractual
licence granted for value. The licence was to occupy the land for
agricultural purposes. Accordingly, the licence was converted into a
tenancy from year to year by s 2 of the AHA 1986.

(d) In *Javad v Aqil*[6], a prospective tenant was allowed to enter into
possession and thereafter he paid periodic payments of rent while
negotiations proceeded as to the terms of a tenancy to be granted to
him. It was inferred, in the absence of any other material factors, that
the parties intended to create a tenancy at will rather than a periodic
tenancy pending the outcome of the negotiations. As the land in
question was not agricultural land, the tenancy at will did not give the
occupier any protection. The owner was entitled to possession upon
terminating the tenancy at will.

(e) In *V G Fraulo & Co Ltd v Papa*[7], without the owner's authority, the
owner's surveyor gave the occupier a key to the property and the
occupier moved in. The owner's solicitor wrote two letters to the
occupier. In the first, an open letter, the solicitor stated that the
occupation was unlawful and that possession was required. The second,
marked without prejudice, offered a tenancy which would be back-
dated. In a telephone conversation the occupier confirmed that she
would enter into the agreement. The occupier did not sign any tenancy
agreement did not pay rent. In proceedings for possession, the County
Court Judge decided that the without prejudice letter and telephone
conversation were admissible and dismissed the claim for possession.
The Court of Appeal allowed an appeal. The court held that the
without prejudice letter constituted an offer upon conditions which
were never satisfied. The reference within to any tenancy relating back
did not make the defendant's occupation lawful. It was not possible to
impute a licence resulting from acquiescence in the defendant's occupation. There was never a concluded agreement between the parties and
therefore it was not possible to look at the without prejudice letter.

[1] See *Clarke v Grant* [1950] 1 KB 104, CA; *Sector Properties v Meah* (1973) 229 Estates
Gazette 1097, CA; *Longrigg Burrough Trounson v Smith* [1979] 2 EGLR 42,(1979) 251
Estates Gazette 847, CA; *Cardiothoracic Institute v Shrewdcrest* [1986] 1 WLR 368; *Land*

v Sykes [1991] 1 EGLR 18; affd [1992] 3 EG 115, CA; *Bennett Properties v H & S Engineering* [1998] CLY 3683; *Stirling v Leadenhall Residential 2 Ltd* [2001] EWCA Civ 1011, [2001] 3 All ER 645.
2   1985 SLT 255, HL.
3   (1980) 258 Estates Gazette 965.
4   (1989) 1 EGLR 1, CA.
5   (1992) 63 P & CR 1.
6   [1991] 1 WLR 1007, CA.
7   (1993) 39 EG 127, CA.

ADVERSE POSSESSION

21.23 It is beyond the scope of this book to consider the issue of adverse possession. Reference should be made to the leading textbook: Jourdan, *Adverse Possession*[1].

1   (2003) Butterworths. Also see cases relating to agricultural land: *J A Pye (Oxford) Ltd v Graham* [2000] Ch 676, [2000] 2 EGLR 137, affirmed by the House of Lords [2002] UKHL 30, [2003] 1 AC 419, [2002] 3 All ER 865; *Lambeth London Borough Council v Blackburn* [2001] EWCA Civ 912, 82 P & CR 494; *King (t/a Oakland Services UK) v Job* [2002] EWCA Civ 181, [2002] 2 P & CR DG7; *Purbrick v Hackney London Borough Council* [2003] EWHC 1871 (Ch), [2004] 1 P & CR 553; *J A Pye (Oxford) Ltd v United Kingdom* [2005] 3 EGLR 1, ECtHR; *Beaulane Properties Ltd v Palmer* [2005] EWHC 1071 (Ch), [2006] Ch 79, [2005] 3 EGLR 85; *Tower Hamlets London Borough Council v Barrett* [2005] EWCA Civ 923, [2006] 1 P & CR 132; *Tennant v Adamczyk* [2005] EWCA Civ 1239, [2006] 1 P & CR 485; *Batt v Adams* [2001] 2 EGLR 92, [2001] 32 EG 90; *Williams v Jones* [2002] EWCA Civ 1097, [2002] 3 EGLR 69.

PROPRIETARY ESTOPPEL

21.24 It is also beyond the scope of this book to consider the doctrine of proprietary estoppel. Nevertheless, it should be noted that, in a rare case, it is possible for a tenant, with full protection under the AHA 1986, to lose that protection by reason of his conduct giving rise to a claim for possession by his landlord based upon the doctrine of proprietary estoppel[1]. It may also be relevant to the landlord's ability to enforce the terms of the tenancy agreement[2].

In short, pursuant to the doctrine of proprietary estoppel, an equity arises where:

(a)   the owner of land (O) induces, encourages or allows the claimant (C) to believe that he has or will enjoy some right or benefit over O's property;
(b)   in reliance upon this belief, C acts to his detriment to the knowledge of O; and
(c)   O then seeks to take unconscionable advantage of C by denying him the right or benefit which he expected to receive[3].

The classic formulation of the doctrine is contained in the speech of Lord Kingsdown in *Ramsden v Dyson*[4]:

'These factors ordinarily are considered to be an expectation created or encouraged by the owner of the land that a person will have a certain interest in it, that person then taking no occupation, and upon the faith of the expectation, with the knowledge of the owner of the land and without objection, lays out money upon the land'[5].

1   *J S Bloor (Measham) Ltd v Calcott* [2002] 1 EGLR 1, [2002] 09 EG 222.
2   *Hazel v Akhtar* [2001] EWCA Civ 1883, [2002] 2 P & CR 17.
3   See Charles Harpum, *Megarry & Wade: The Law of Real Property* (6th edn, 2000) Sweet & Maxwell, para 13–001ff.
4   (1866) LR 1 HL 129. Also see, *Gillett v Holt* [2001] Ch 210, CA.
5   Also see, *Sutcliffe v Lloyd* [2007] EWCA Civ 153, [2007] 22 EG 162.

21.25 The practice of the landlord to renew tenancies does not found proprietary estoppel[1]. But it may be relevant where there has been a failure to conclude a tenancy[2].

Cause of action or issue estoppel may also be relevant to a party's ability to enforce contractual rights[3].

1   *Keelwalk Properties Ltd v Walker* [2002] EWCA Civ 1076, [2002] 3 EGLR 79, [2002] 48 EG 142.
2   *James v Evans* [2000] 42 EG 173, CA; *Charlton v Hawking* [2003] EWHC 570 of 2002 (Ch) Leeds, unreported.
3   *Thoday v Thoday* [1964] P 181, [1964] 1 All ER 341, CA; *Arnold v National Westminster Bank plc* [1991] 2 AC 93, [1991] 3 All ER 41, HL; *Meretz Investments NV v ACP Ltd* [2006] EWHC 74 (Ch), [2007] Ch 197.

CONSTRUCTIVE TRUST

21.26 It is likewise beyond the scope of this book to consider the law of constructive and resulting trusts, although these concepts may be relevant to a claim for a tenancy.

There is no accepted definition of a constructive trust. It is 'a judicial remedy giving rise to an enforceable equitable obligation'[1]. A constructive trustee may be personally liable to account for any improper gain which he has made or for any loss which his acts or omissions have caused, or in appropriate circumstances, he may hold specific property in his hands on trust[2].

Where the court found that negotiations for a joint venture failed, it decided that the tenant held the tenancy on a resulting trust for the landlord. The court ordered that the tenant had to give up possession to the landlord[3].

In *Charlton v Hawking*[4], where the court rejected claims to a tenancy protected under the AHA 1986 and found that there was no implied agreement giving rise to a constructive trust, it decided that the application of the doctrine of proprietary estoppel should provide the occupier with a licence for so long as the occupier wished to carry on her business.

1   *Westdeutsche Landesbank Girozentrale v Islington London Borough Council* [1996] AC 669 at 714, HL, per Lord Browne-Wilkinson.
2   *Megarry and Wade: 'The Law of Real Property* (6th edn, 1999), Sweet & Maxwell, para 10–017ff.

3   *Rowan v Dann* [1991] EGCS 19; affd (1991) 64 P & CR 202, CA. Also see, *Kilcarne Holdings Ltd v Targetfellow (Birmingham) Ltd* [2005] EWCA Civ 1355, [2006] 1 P & CR D55; *Lalani v Crump Holdings Ltd* [2007] EWHC 47 (Ch), [2007] 08 EG 136 (CS).

4   [2003] EWHC 370 of 2002 Leeds, unreported. Also see, *Stack v Dowden* [2007] UKHL 17, [2007] 2 All ER 929.

Part II

THE TENANCY AGREEMENT

Contents

Chapter 24 Farming: Good Husbandry and Standard Leasehold Covenants 350

Chapter 25 Rent Review 370

Chapter 22

INTRODUCTION: THE TENANCY AGREEMENT

INTRODUCTION

22.1 As with all other provisions in this section of the book, the following provisions only apply to agricultural holdings falling within the provisions of the Agricultural Holdings Act 1986 (AHA 1986).

Unlike the freedom of contract applying under the Agricultural Tenancies Act 1995 (ATA 1995), the mutual rights and obligations of landlords and tenants of agricultural holdings during the currency of the tenancy derive from four sources:

(a)   the contract of tenancy;
(b)   supplemental provisions derived from common law and custom[1];
(c)   'model clauses' as to repair and maintenance of fixed equipment implied by the AHA 1986[2]; and
(d)   standards of good husbandry and sound estate management applying under statute[3].

The statutory provisions have the effect of supplementing, varying or overriding the terms of the agreement reached between the landlord and tenant whether oral or written.

The obligations arising in relation to the AHA 1986 tenancies have their origin in the political agenda following the Second World War, namely to increase productivity and to ensure that agricultural land was farmed[4]. The freedom of contract contained in the ATA 1995 reflected the change in priorities. The Mid-term Review of the Common Agricultural Policy moved the process on again by releasing the obligations imposed upon farmers in relation to farming[5].

Under the AHA 1986, the tenancy agreement need not be in writing, but three points should be noted:

 (i)   either the landlord or the tenant may require the other to agree that certain statutorily prescribed terms are reduced into writing[6];

317

(ii)   a tenancy for a fixed term of three years or more must be made by deed if it is to create a legal lease[7];

(iii) the lease must comply with the requirements of the Land Registration Act 2002[8].

It should also be noted that:

(A)   no formality is required for the creation of a lease which takes effect in possession for a term not exceeding three years, at the best rent obtainable without taking a fine[9];

(B)   a contract to grant a lease taking effect in possession for a term not exceeding three years is exempt from the requirements of the Law of Property (Miscellaneous Provisions) Act 1989 as to the formalities necessary for the creation of land contracts[10]. Such contracts can therefore be made orally.

[1]   The common law provisions for supplementing tenancy agreements which did not contain minimal provisions, eg an implied obligation to farm in a good and tenantlike manner, the doctrine of emblements and an implied obligation to maintain premises in a good and tenantlike manner, have now, since the passing of the agricultural holdings legislation, been largely superseded by the statutory provisions.
[2]   AHA 1986, ss 6–24.
[3]   Agriculture Act 1947, ss 10 and 11.
[4]   See the speech of Viscount Simon in *Johnson v Moreton* [1980] AC 37, HL.
[5]   See Ch 52.
[6]   AHA 1986, s 6: see para 22.2 below.
[7]   Law of Property Act 1925, s 52(1) and (2).
[8]   See para 3.38 et seq.
[9]   Law of Property Act 1925, s 54(1).
[10] Law of Property (Miscellaneous Provisions) Act 1989, s 2(1) and (5)(a).

WRITTEN TENANCY AGREEMENTS AND FIXED EQUIPMENT

22.2 Section 6 of the AHA 1986 contains provision for a written tenancy agreement where there is either no such agreement existing or, if there is, it makes no provision for any one or more of the matters listed in Sch 1 to the Act[1].

Section 7 of the AHA 1986[2] (together with the regulations passed under it[3]) provide a code of maintenance, repair and insurance obligations which are automatically applied to the contract of tenancy, if and in so far as the written tenancy agreement does not provide to the contrary[4]. If a written tenancy agreement substantially departs from such code, either party may require that the agreement be modified so as to conform to the code[5].

Section 9 of the AHA 1986 provides for compensation to be payable where the terms of a tenancy agreement are varied by the implementation of s 6 and/or s 7.

[1]   See para 23.2.
[2]   Or its predecessor, s 6 of the Agricultural Holdings Act 1948 (AHA 1948).
[3]   These are the Agriculture (Maintenance, Repair and Insurance of Fixed Equipment) Regulations 1948, SI 1948/184, now superseded and substituted by the 1973 Regulations, SI 1973/1473, as amended by SI 1988/281.

4   A clause in the tenancy agreement relieving a party of a liability, which by the regulations
    he would otherwise have imposed upon him, is effective and may create a lacuna: *Burden
    v Hannaford* [1956] 1 QB 142, [1955] 3 All ER 401, CA.
5   AHA 1986, s 8.

TENANT'S RIGHT TO REMOVE FIXTURES AND BUILDINGS

22.3 Section 10 of the AHA 1986 provides that a limited right is given to the
tenant to remove fixtures and buildings on the holding, provided certain
preconditions are satisfied by the tenant, notably the obligation to comply
with all the terms of the tenancy and the giving of the relevant notice.

PROVISION OF FIXED EQUIPMENT

22.4 Section 4 of the Agriculture Act 1958[1] introduced a new right for a
tenant to apply to the Agricultural Land Tribunal for a direction that the
landlord carries out within a specified period such work for the provision or
alteration, or repair of fixed equipment, as would enable the tenant to comply
with his statutory obligations. Section 4 of the Agriculture Act 1958 was
repealed and now is re-enacted as s 11 of the AHA 1986. It should be noted
that s 11 imposes so many restrictions upon the right of the tenant that, in
practice, very few tenants have been able to satisfy the statutory preconditions
of entitlement to such a direction. Section 11 applications to overcome
pollution control problems have become quite common.

1   AHA 1986, s 11.

RENT REVIEW AND DISTRESS

22.5 Sections 12 and 13 and Sch 2 to the AHA 1986 provide machinery for
the variation of the rent payable under the tenancy agreement. Section 12
provides for a general rent review at intervals of not more than once every
three years. Its predecessor, s 8 of the AHA 1948 was very heavily revised and
amended, first by s 2 of the Agriculture Act 1958, and then by s 1 of the
Agricultural Holdings Act 1984.

Section 13 of the AHA 1986 entitles a landlord to increase the rent of the
holding where he has carried out improvements in certain circumstances.

The common law of distress for the non-payment of rent, as a remedy for
recovering rent, applies to agricultural holdings as to other forms of property.
There are certain specific amendments, variations and special provisions,
contained in ss 16 to 19 of the AHA 1986.

FARMING PROVISIONS

22.6 There are a number of statutory provisions which affect the cultivation
of the land, the disposal of produce from the land, good husbandry and good
estate management. Briefly, these are to:

(a)   enable a tenant to seek a variation of the terms of the agreement relating to permanent pasture (AHA 1986, s 14);

(b)   give a tenant freedom to dispose of his produce and from restrictions upon any system of cropping arable land (AHA 1986, s 15);

(c)   prohibit the removal of manure, roots and so forth during the last year of the tenancy (AHA 1986, s 15(3)); and

(d)   indirectly impose obligations, or at least sanctions if the 'obligations' are not complied with, to farm the land in accordance with the rules of good husbandry and similar guidance to landlords as to what constitutes good estate management (Agriculture Act 1947, ss 10 and 11).

The Agriculture Act 1947 established a Code of Practice designed to ensure the full and efficient use of agricultural land during the immediate post-war period. The Code operated to impose restrictions and limitations on owners and occupiers respectively of agricultural land. That part of the 1947 Act has now been repealed except for the statutory definition of the rules of good estate management (s 10) and the rules of good husbandry (s 11). Neither of the unrepealed parts of that Act, nor the AHA 1986 itself, expressly provide that landlords and tenants respectively are under an implied obligation to comply with either set of rules. In the AHA 1986 there are a number of references particularly to the rules of good husbandry, which themselves make reference to rules of good estate management[1]. The result is that neither party is, in the absence of any express contractual provision, under any statutory obligation to comply with the rules, but sanctions are imposed in the event of non-compliance. The rules appear, therefore, to be guides to practice and interpretation of the expressions used from time to time in the legislation[2]. Many contracts of tenancy do not expressly impose such an obligation upon a tenant and yet, if he nevertheless fails to comply with such 'obligation', certain sanctions and consequences apply. These may result in the termination of the tenancy and the right to compensation for the landlord on quitting.

[1]   See, in particular, Case C of Sch 3 and s 27 of the AHA 1986 and also see AHA 1986, ss 11, 71(1) and 64(1).

[2]   They are incorporated into the AHA 1986 by the definition section: s 96.

MISCELLANEOUS

22.7 Sections 20 and 22 to 24 of the AHA 1986 contain a miscellaneous collection of provisions regulating the relationship of landlord and tenant as follows:

(a)   by giving a tenant a right to compensation for damage by game where the landlord has reserved sporting rights (AHA 1986, s 20);

(b)   by giving both landlord and tenant a right to require the making of a record of condition of the holding from time to time (AHA 1986, s 22);

(c)   by giving power to the landlord who has not expressly reserved the right, to enter and view the holding in certain circumstances (AHA 1986, s 23); and

(d)   by preventing a landlord from claiming penal damages in excess of his actual loss under the terms of the tenancy agreement for breach of it (AHA 1986, s 24).

SERVICE OF NOTICES

22.8 Throughout the AHA 1986 there is provision made for the service of notices, counter-notices, demands for arbitration and other similar documents. The rules relating to the service of such documents are contained in s 93 of the AHA 1986 and are of paramount importance. Full commentary on the methods of effecting service sanctioned by s 93 is contained in Chapter 42.

Chapter 23

WRITTEN TENANCY AGREEMENT AND FIXED EQUIPMENT

WRITTEN TENANCY AGREEMENT

Section 6 notice

23.1 Section 6 of the Agricultural Holdings Act 1986 (AHA 1986)[1] contains provisions for either landlord or tenant to refer to arbitration the provision of a written 'agreement' containing the rights and obligations of the parties. The right to do so arises either when the tenancy agreement is purely oral or when it is in writing, but provision is not made in the written agreement for all the terms agreed between the parties or for one or more of the matters specified in Sch 1 to the AHA 1986[2].

In order to activate the provisions of s 6, there must first be a request by either landlord or tenant to the other to enter into a written agreement containing these provisions. The request does not need to be in writing, but it must demand the inclusion of all of the terms contained in Sch 1 of the AHA 1986 and not just some of them. Where the request is made by the landlord, the tenant may not, without the landlord's written consent, assign, sub-let or part with possession of the holding or any part of it between the date on which the landlord's request was served on the tenant and either an agreement is concluded between landlord and tenant or the award of an arbitrator appointed under s 6 takes effect[3]. Any such transaction is statutorily rendered void[4]. Therefore, if a tenant after such a request assigns his tenancy, a landlord cannot give a valid notice to quit under Case E[5].

It should be noted that it is only if the demand under s 6 is made by the landlord that the tenant's right to assign is postponed until after the arbitration. A tenant's demand does not have that consequence.

There is no time limit prescribed by the AHA 1986 for the parties to enter into an agreement after the service of a request under s 6. In the event of no agreement being concluded between the landlord and the tenant following the request, the matter will be determined by arbitration. Only the party who has made the request under s 6 can refer the terms of the tenancy to arbitration[6]. In the absence of agreement as to the appointment of the arbitrator, the party that made the s 6 request may apply to the President of the Royal Institution of Chartered Surveyors (RICS) for an appointment.

1   Formerly the Agricultural Holdings Act 1948 (AHA 1948), s 5(1).
2   AHA 1986, s 6(1). The request to enter into an agreement need not necessarily be made in writing, although for evidential purposes this is advisable. The request may be made at any time during the subsistence of the tenancy and is a condition precedent to arbitration.
3   Unless restricted by the terms of the lease, the tenant may freely assign or sub-let without the landlord's permission: *Church v Brown* (1808) 15 Ves 258.
4   AHA 1986, s 6(5) and (6). These provisions were first introduced by Sch 3, para 3(3) to the Agricultural Holdings Act 1984, with the object of preventing a pre-emptive assignment or other disposition of the tenancy by the tenant between the request to enter into the agreement in writing and the arbitrator's award. The use of the word 'void' eliminates any argument to the effect that although the disposition was unlawful it nevertheless was effective to vest the tenancy in the assignee: see *Old Grovebury Manor Farm Ltd v Seymour Plant Sales and Hire Ltd (No 2)* [1979] 3 All ER 504, [1977] 1 WLR 1397, CA.
5   This conclusion was reached in *Wilson v Hereford and Worcester County Council* (1991) County Court, unreported. Also see para 23.3.
6   AHA 1986, s 6(1).

Schedule 1 terms

23.2 The terms contained in Sch 1 are[1]:

(a)   the names of the parties;
(b)   a description of the holding;
(c)   the duration of the tenancy;
(d)   the rent (and details of when payable);
(e)   the incidence of rates including drainage rates;
(f)   reinstatement provisions by the tenant in respect of harvested crops;
(g)   insurance provisions by the tenant in respect of dead stock and harvested crops;
(h)   a forfeiture clause[2];
(i)   prohibition against assigning, sub-letting or parting with possession ('alienation') of the holding or any part of it without the landlord's written consent[3].

It should be noted that the arbitrator is not obliged to write into the agreement all the provisions contained in Sch 1 and could refuse to do so if he felt that it would not be 'reasonable and just' so to do, for example, if the parties had expressly agreed to the contrary.

1   It should be noted that the list in Sch 1 to the AHA 1986 differs from the list in Sch 1 of the AHA 1948, as amended. The repairing obligations are omitted. This is because s 7 (see para 23.4) fills this gap by incorporating the 'model clauses' in every case unless there is a written agreement to contrary effect (AHA 1986, s 7(3)).
2   Care should be taken by arbitrators in drafting the form of forfeiture clause to ensure it complies with the decision in *Parry v Million Pigs Ltd* (1980) 260 Estates Gazette 281. See para 24.26.
3   The Landlord and Tenant Act 1927, s 19 provides that generally covenants in leases which prohibit assignment, underletting, charging or parting with possession without the landlord's consent, are deemed to be subject to the proviso that such consent is not to be unreasonably withheld. This does not apply to agricultural holdings. For the full text of Sch 1 see para A1.190. For the text of s 6 see para A1.93. The above précis is an abbreviation.

Arbitration under section 6

23.3 The arbitrator's jurisdiction is expressly limited by s 6(2) of the AHA 1986 so that his award can only deal with three matters:

(a)   It must specify the existing terms of the tenancy, subject to variations agreed between the landlord and the tenants.

(b)   In so far as the existing terms (as varied or otherwise) neither makes provision for the matters specified in Sch 1 nor makes provision inconsistent with the matters contained in Sch 1, the award must make provision for all those matters having such effect as may be agreed between the parties or, in default of agreement, as appears to the arbitrator to be 'reasonable and just between them'.

(c)   The award can also include any further provisions relating to the tenancy which may be agreed between the landlord and the tenant.

It should be noted that Sch 1 matters will only be included in the tenancy agreement pursuant to the arbitrator's award if either the tenancy is silent or it makes no inconsistent provision. If the arbitrator determines that the tenancy agreement makes contrary provision to the Sch 1 matters, then the agreement prevails. The arbitrator cannot impose Sch 1 provisions for those previously agreed between the parties. If the tenancy agreement expressly permitted sub-letting, then the arbitrator's award will permit sub-letting. The arbitrator can only incorporate Sch 1 matters where he determines that it is 'reasonable and just' to do so. That will be an issue of fact between the parties.

The arbitrator is given no general power to rewrite the tenancy agreement so as to bring it up to date. His task is to determine the existing terms of the tenancy and then only add to or vary those terms in accordance with the express provisions of the legislation.

If it appears to the arbitrator that, by reason of any provision which he is required to include in his award, it is equitable that the rent of the holding should be varied, he may vary the rent accordingly[1].

The incorporation of a prohibition against alienation is of major importance to landlords, particularly following the change in the wording of notices to quit given by reason of death[2]. It should be noted that assignment in the face of a prohibition constitutes an irremediable breach of the term of the tenancy giving rise to the possibility of a notice to quit under Case E[3]. But an assignment following a section 6 notice before such a prohibition is agreed upon or imposed does not[4].

Section 19 of the Landlord and Tenant Act 1927, requiring a landlord's consent to an assignment not to be unreasonably withheld, does not apply to agricultural holdings[5]. The landlord's consent to assignment can therefore be withheld for any reason. It is not subject to the requirements of reasonableness. Where the statutory covenant in Sch 1 is included, the tenancy becomes non-assignable as the statutory covenant does not include any provision relating to reasonableness[6].

The procedure under s 6 is as follows:

(a) The landlord or tenant who wishes to have a written agreement established must first request the other to enter into such an agreement.

(b) If the request is not accepted, the party making the request may then demand arbitration and, in default of agreement, apply to the President[7] for an arbitrator to be appointed.

(c) The arbitrator appointed, following the arbitration hearing, must make an award specifying the existing terms of the tenancy, subject to agreed variations or additions and such of the Sch 1 items, whether agreed or not, which the arbitrator considers are reasonable and just to be included, unless they would be inconsistent with the terms otherwise agreed[8]. There is no need to convert the award into a formal tenancy agreement since the award is effective as an agreement. If such a conversion is made there is a potential liability to stamp duty which otherwise would be avoided. Moreover, the unco-operative party may well refuse to execute such an 'agreement' which is in reality not an agreement at all. The terms and provision in the arbitrator's award take effect by way of variation of the tenancy agreement previously in force, either from the date of the award or such later date specified in the award. The making of an award does not affect an existing notice to quit served by the landlord or any notice served by the tenant.

A problem, in relation to which there is as yet no authority, is whether a notice given under s 6 which is not further activated for many years will eventually lapse or otherwise be rendered ineffective[9].

---

[1] AHA 1986, s 6(3). Any such variation is to be disregarded for the purpose of applying the three-year rent cycle; AHA 1986, Sch 2, para 4(2)(a). Note also that this does not permit a general rent review by reference to changed economic circumstances. It is only a revision of rent to take account of the revised terms which is provided for.

[2] See the AHA 1948, s 24(2)(g) as amended by s 16 of the 1976 Act – now repealed and re-enacted in Sch 3 of the AHA 1986 as Case G. For a commentary on assignments and their interrelationship with succession, see 35.18ff.

[3] As to which, see 31.76ff.

[4] *Wilson v Hereford and Worcester County Council* (1991) unreported. Also see para 31.88ff.

[5] Landlord and Tenant Act 1927, s 19(4).

[6] This could give rise to a case where, exceptionally, the arbitrator applies the 'reasonable and just' requirement so as to introduce the concept of reasonableness and the criteria approved in *International Drilling Fluids Ltd v Louisville Investments (Uxbridge) Ltd* [1986] Ch 513, CA.

[7] As with all references in this book to 'the President' this means the President of the Royal Institution of Chartered Surveyors.

[8] AHA 1986, s 6(4) provides that the arbitrator's award shall take effect 'by way of variation of the agreement previously in force in respect of the tenancy'. These words were originally added by Sch 3, para 4 of the Agricultural Holdings Act 1984 in order to make clear that an arbitrator's award does not create a fresh tenancy. The decision in *Hollings v Swindle* (1950) 155 EG 269 is thereby inapplicable since 1984.

[9] See the Limitation Act 1980, ss 5, 34 and especially 34(6). Note the distinction between statutory and contractual arbitrations in the context of delay: *Bremer Vulkan Schiffbau und Maschinenfabrik v South India Shipping Corpn Ltd* [1981] AC 909 at 962, HL.

REPAIR, MAINTENANCE AND REMOVAL OF FIXED EQUIPMENT

23.4 The AHA 1986 contains three provisions governing the rights and liabilities of a landlord and a tenant under an AHA 1986 tenancy in relation to the provision, repair, maintenance and removal of fixed equipment[1]. The three provisions are as follows:

(a)   Section 7 of the AHA 1986 empowers the Minister[2], after consultation with such bodies of persons 'as appear to him to represent the interests of landlords and tenants of agricultural holdings' to make regulations prescribing terms as to the maintenance, repair and insurance of fixed equipment. These are known as the 'model clauses'. These model clauses are incorporated into every tenancy agreement (with limited exceptions)[3].

(b)   A tenant is given the right to apply to the Agricultural Land Tribunal in limited circumstances for an order directing he landlord to provide fixed equipment[4].

(c)   Section 10 of the AHA 1986 provides for the removal of fixtures and buildings provided by the tenant at the end of the tenancy[5].

'Fixed equipment' is defined to include 'any building or structure affixed to land and any works on, in, over or under land, and also includes anything grown on land for a purpose other than use after severance from the land, consumption of the thing grown or of its produce, or amenity'[6].

[1]   As to the definition of 'fixed equipment', see para 23.4.
[2]   See para 4.2.
[3]   See para 23.6.
[4]   As to the definition of 'fixed equipment', see para 23.4.
[5]   See para 23.23.
[6]   AHA 1986, s 96(1).

MAINTENANCE, REPAIR AND INSURANCE OBLIGATIONS

Contractual obligations

23.5 The landlord and tenant are free to agree whatever terms they wish as to who should be responsible for maintaining, repairing or insuring the buildings and other fixed equipment[1] on the holding and, if both are to be responsible, in what proportions and to what extent[2].

The following points should be noted:

(a)   At common law, there are limited implied terms. As to the landlord, there is no implied term to repair. A tenant has an implied obligation to use the premises in a tenant like manner and to manage and cultivate the land in a good and husbandlike manner according to the custom of the country[3].

(b)   Section 4 of the Defective Premises Act 1972 applies where premises are let under a tenancy which imposes on the landlord an obligation for the maintenance and repair of the premises[4]. In such a case, a landlord owes a duty to all persons who might reasonably be affected by defects in the state of the premises, including the tenant, to take such care as is reasonable in all of the circumstances to ensure that they are reasonably safe from personal injury or damage to the property caused by a relevant defect[5].

(c)   Section 11 of the Landlord and Tenant Act 1985, which imposes statutorily implied repairing obligations on a landlord in relation to tenancies of a dwellinghouse, does not apply to the agricultural holding[6].

(d)   It is usual to see express obligations in a tenancy agreement requiring a tenant to farm in accordance with the rules of good husbandry[7].

An analysis of repair/disrepair; particular standards of repair; and common law remedies is contained in Chapter 10.

Where model clauses[8] are incorporated into a tenancy agreement, if there is an inconsistency between the model clauses and other obligations in the tenancy agreement, the express terms of the written contract will prevail[9].

[1]   See para 23.4.
[2]   As to the operation of contractual repairing obligations, see the commentary under the Agricultural Tenancies Act 1995: see also Ch 10.
[3]   *Wedd v Porter* [1916] 2 KB 91, CA. See para 24.3.
[4]   The letting must include a dwellinghouse, but has been held to apply to business and other premises: *Smith v Bradford Metropolitan Council* (1982) 44 P & CR 171, CA.
[5]   For a detailed consideration of the Defective Premises Act 1972, see Dowding and Reynolds, *Dilapidations: The Modern Law and Practice* (3rd edn, 2004) Sweet & Maxwell.
[6]   The Landlord and Tenant Act 1985, s 14(3).
[7]   See para 24.4.
[8]   See para 23.6.
[9]   *Burden v Hannaford* [1956] 1 QB 142, CA; *Roper v Prudential Assurance co Ltd* [1992] 1 EGLR 5, [1992] 09 EG 141. See para 23.7.

Incorporation of model clauses

23.6   The AHA 1986 imposes standard terms as to the repair, maintenance and insurance of fixed equipment[1] (including buildings) which apply unless the parties have otherwise agreed. Pursuant to the authority vested in the Minister to consult[2], the Minister has made regulations under s 7(1) of the AHA 1986 which are known as 'the model clauses'. The regulations currently in force are the Agriculture (Maintenance, Repair and Insurance of Fixed Equipment) Regulations 1973[3], as amended by the Agriculture (Maintenance, Repair and Insurance of Fixed Equipment) (Amendment) Regulations 1988[4].

By section 7(3) of the AHA 1986, the regulations are to be deemed to be incorporated in all tenancy agreements 'except in so far as they would impose on one of the parties to an agreement in writing a liability which under the agreement is imposed on the other'[5]. The combined effect of s 7 and SI 1973/1473 (as amended) is that the obligations of landlord and tenant set out in the regulations are incorporated in every tenancy agreement wherever the agreement is silent on the matter in question and by this means the statutory obligations are inserted to complete the agreement in respect of those items.

1 For the definition of 'Fixed Equipment', see para 23.4.
2 See para 23.4.
3 SI 1973/1473. Those previously in force were SI 1948/184.
4 SI 1988/281, effective from 24 March 1988.
5 *Re Sutherland Settlement Trusts* [1953] Ch 792 at 804 per Harman J: '… under the Act of 1948 as I understand it, the Minister has produced a code in the form of a statutory instrument putting all those liabilities on one side of the line or the other, so that they are either the landlord's or the tenant's liability'.

23.7 Section 7(3) of the AHA 1986 provides that the model clauses are to be incorporated into every contract of tenancy of an agricultural holding 'except insofar as they would impose on one of the parties to an agreement in writing a liability which under the agreement is imposed on the other'. Accordingly, the model clauses will apply where the tenancy agreement is oral. The proviso to section 7(3) of the AHA 1986 reserves the principle of freedom of contract by excluding the model clauses where the tenancy agreement makes contrary provision.

The AHA 1986 nevertheless seeks to promote standardisation of repairing obligations by providing in s 8 that where the terms of a tenancy agreement substantially modify the operation of the model clauses, either party can request a variation so as to bring the tenancy into conformity with the latter. If the parties are unable to reach agreement, the terms are referred to arbitration under the AHA 1986[1]. Section 8(3) of the AHA 1986 imposes upon the arbitrator a duty to consider whether the terms concerned are justified, having regard to the circumstances of the holding and the circumstances of both the landlord and the tenant (but not the rent). If the arbitrator is satisfied that the terms concerned are not justifiable, he can vary them 'in such a manner as appears to him to be reasonable and just as between the landlord and tenant'[2]. This might involve varying the tenancy agreement to bring it into conformity with the model clauses, or varying its terms in a way which reflects the special circumstances of the holding or the parties. In doing so, the arbitrator can vary the rent, if appropriate[3]. Where an award has been made, no further reference under s 8 can be made for three years from the date of the award[4].

Where an arbitration (or agreement) pursuant to s 6 or s 8 of the AHA 1986 transfers the liability for repair or maintenance from one party to the other, s 9 of the Act enables any dispute as to prior failure to carry out repairing obligations to be decided at the date of the variation of the tenancy (and not later on termination) by arbitration[5]. Where a variation is effected by the issue of new regulations, s 9(4) of the AHA 1986 empowers an arbitrator, for a prescribed period, to disregard the variation when settling the terms of the tenancy on a reference under s 6 of the AHA 1986[6].

The Court of Appeal considered the proviso to s 7(3) of the AHA 1986 in *Burden v Hannaford*[7]. The court considered the exclusion of the model clauses where 'they would impose on one of the parties to an agreement in writing a liability which under the agreement is imposed on the other'. The tenancy agreement expressly relieved the tenant of the liability to repair hedges and fences, an obligation which would have been imposed upon the tenant under the model clauses. The court decided that where there was any inconsistency between the tenancy agreement and the model clauses, this had to be resolved by giving effect to the contractual terms and not the model clauses. The model clauses were incorporated, as there was no positive obligation in the tenancy agreement to fence which was at variance with the regulations, but in construing the contract of tenancy and the model clauses together, the former prevailed. The consequence was that neither party was liable to repair the hedges and fences.

The effect of the court's decision in *Burden v Hannaford* is that there may be cases in which no liability to repair items of fixed equipment exists, as a consequence of the tenancy agreement relieving one party of an obligation, without imposing it on the other. Conversely, it is possible to impose on one party an obligation which is placed on the other by model clauses. This occurred in *Roper v Prudential Assurance Co Ltd*[8], where the tenant's express repairing obligations extended to electrical wiring in the context of a general obligation to repair and maintain the farmhouse, cottages and buildings on the holding. Repair in this case was held to include replacing the existing electrical wiring and installations in the farmhouse, an obligation which the model clauses placed on the landlord where the wiring was in need to replacement due to age (and not the neglect of the tenant). Liability therefore was imposed on the tenant, reversing the model clause liability for replacement which would have fallen on the landlord.

[1] This important right for tenants to request an arbitration is frequently overlooked and rarely invoked. If shortly after the grant of the tenancy the tenant demands arbitration so as to have the 'model clauses' substituted for full repairing obligations, the liability for dilapidations is not likely to be great because of the rule in *Evans v Jones* [1955] 2 QB 58, [1955] 2 All ER 118, CA, as to which see para 39.7.

[2] AHA 1986, s 8(3).

[3] AHA 1986, s 8(4).

[4] AHA 1986, s 8(6).

[5] AHA 1986, ss 9(2) and 71.

[6] By virtue of the Agriculture (Time Limit) Regulations 1988, SI 1988/2821, the prescribed period during which an arbitrator could ignore the amendments made to the model clauses by SI 1988/281 was the three months following their commencement on 24 March 1988. Clearly, s 9(4) of the AHA 1986 is of sporadic importance, remaining dormant in the intervals between the issue of fresh regulations, which itself is an infrequent occurrence.

[7] [1956] 1 QB 142, [1955] 3 All ER 401, CA.

[8] [1992] 1 EGLR 5, [1992] 09 EG 141.

MODEL CLAUSES

23.8 The Schedule to the Agriculture (Maintenance, Repair and Insurance of Fixed Equipment) Regulations 1973 (as amended), which superseded the 1948 Regulations and came into effect on 29 September 1974[1], is in three parts:

(a) Part I – model clauses specifying the rights and liabilities of the landlord;

(b) Part II – the rights and liabilities of tenants;

(c) Part III – general provisions dealing with redundant equipment[2].

It has now been amended by the Agriculture (Maintenance Repair and Insurance of Fixed Equipment) (Amendment) Regulations 1988[3]. These regulations have made very minor amendments to SI 1973/1473.

1   The old regulations, ie SI 1948/184, still apply where the tenancy agreement specifically incorporates the regulations without any saving words, eg 'for any statutory modification or re-enactment of the same' or 'such other regulations as may from time to time be in force'. As to the interrelationship between the 1948 and 1973 Regulations, see an article by J Muir Watt at (1973) 227 Estates Gazette 1767.
2   For a judicial consideration of the 1948 Regulations see *Evans v Jones* [1955] 2 QB 58, [1955] 2 All ER 118, CA.
3   SI 1988/281.

Part I: Rights and liabilities of the landlord

Obligations of the landlord

23.9 The landlord's obligation is to execute all repairs and replacements to the main structure of the buildings, ie to the main walls and the exterior walls (however constructed) of the farmhouses, cottages and farm buildings, including roofs, chimneys, eaves, gutters and downpipes, walls and fences of open or covered yards, and garden walls, together with such interior repairs or decoration as are made necessary by structural defects.

The landlord is also liable for such internal structural items of the farmhouse and cottages as floors, floor joists[1], ceiling joists and timbers, exterior staircases, fixed ladders (including banisters and hand rails) and doors, windows[2] and skylights, including the frames of such doors, windows and skylights (but excepting glass or glass substitute, sashcords, locks and fastenings)[3].

The landlord is liable as often as may be necessary in order to prevent deterioration, and in any case at intervals of not more than five years, properly to paint with at least two coats of a suitable quality or properly and adequately to gas-tar, creosote or otherwise effectively treat as a preservative material:

(a)   all outside wood and ironwork of all external outward opening doors and windows of farm buildings (but not the farmhouse or cottages);
(b)   the interior structural steelwork of open-sided farm buildings which have been previously painted, gas-tarred, creosoted or otherwise treated with preservative material or which is necessary in order to prevent deterioration of the same so as to paint, gas-tar, creosote or treat with preservative material[4].

The landlord is liable to replace those items which the tenant is liable to repair under para 5(1) of the Schedule[5], but which have become beyond repair, except when that has happened because of the wilful act or negligence of the tenant, any member of his household, or his employees, or because of the tenant's failure to carry out his repairing liabilities[6]. This liability frequently arises in the context of electrical wiring which due to age is not capable of repair but requires replacement[7].

Apart from the buildings, the landlord is responsible for repairs and replacements to underground water supplies, wells, boreholes and reservoirs and also to sewage disposal systems, including septic tanks, filtering media and cesspools (but excluding covers and tops)[8]. In addition to these repairing and redecorating obligations, the regulations impose upon the landlord an obligation to insure the farmhouse, cottages and buildings to their full value, and to make good damage caused by fire, unless this was caused by a wilful act or negligence of the tenant[9].

[1] SI 1973/1473 makes express provision for floor joists. This is consistent with the common law where floor joists have been found to be part of the 'main structure' of a building: *Marlborough Park Services Ltd v Rowe* [2006] EWCA Civ 436, [2006] 2 EGLR 27, [2006] 23 EG 166.
[2] Under the earlier regulations contained in SI 1948/184 the landlord's liability extended to glass substitute and sash-cords for doors, windows and skylights from which he is now exempt.
[3] SI 1973/1473, Sch para 1(1). The additional items of landlord's liability under the 1973 regulations, which were not imposed upon by SI 1948/184, are chimney pots; chimney stacks; fences of open and covered yards (cf walls); floor joists and timbers; exterior and interior staircases and fixed ladders of the farmhouse and cottages; doors and frames of doors, windows and skylights.
[4] SI 1973/1473, Sch para 3(1).
[5] See para 23.16ff.
[6] SI 1973/1473, Sch para 1(3). Cf the position under SI 1948/184.
[7] *Roper v Prudential Assurance Co Ltd* [1992] 1 EGLR 5, [1992] 09 EG 141.
[8] SI 1973/1473, Sch para 1(2). Certain difficulties under the previous regulations, SI 1948/184, have been removed.
[9] SI 1973/1473, Sch para 2.

Limitations on the landlord's obligations

23.10 Subject to the landlord's obligation to make good damage caused by fire[1], the landlord is under no liability to execute repairs or replacements rendered necessary by the wilful act or negligence of the tenant or any members of his household or his employees[2]. What constitutes a wilful act or negligence can give rise to problems in practice.

The landlord (and also the tenant) is not liable to execute any work if and in so far as the execution of it is rendered impossible (except at prohibitive or unreasonable expense) by reason of subsidence of any land or the blocking of outfalls which are not under the control of the landlord or the tenant[3].

The landlord's obligation to repair is qualified in relation to the renewal of all broken or cracked tiles or slates and the replacement of slipped tiles or slates. The tenant is obliged to deal with these, up to a cost of £100 in any one year of the tenancy[4].

The landlord is under no liability to execute repairs or replacements or to insure buildings or fixtures which are the property of the tenant[5].

[1] SI 1973/1473, Sch para 2.
[2] SI 1973/1473, Sch para 4(1)(b).
[3] SI 1973/1473, Sch para 14(2).
[4] SI 1973/1473, Sch paras 1(3) and 8.
[5] SI 1973/1473, Sch para 4(1)(a).

Contributions to the landlord's liability

23.11 Where the landlord is required to carry out repairs or replacements to floorboards, interior staircases and fixed ladders (including banisters or handrails), doors and windows and opening skylights (including frames), eaves-guttering and downpipes, other than where the damage is caused by fire[1], the landlord may recover one-half of the reasonable costs of such works from the tenant[2].

Where the landlord is required to paint or otherwise treat doors, windows, eaves-guttering and downpipes, the landlord may recover one-half of the reasonable cost of such works from the tenant. If any such works are completed before the commencement of the fifth year of the tenancy, the sum which the landlord may recover from the tenant is restricted to an amount equal to the aggregate of one-tenth of such reasonable cost in respect of each year that has elapsed between the commencement of the tenancy and the completion of such work[3].

The first point to note is that provisions contained in the model clauses themselves to deal with a failure by the landlord to comply with his obligations do not include dealing with the landlord's failure to insure. This lacuna is presumably intentional as subsequent legislative opportunities to deal with it have not been taken.

1   SI 1973/1473, Sch para 2(2).
2   SI 1973/1473, Sch para 1(1). The additional half-cost items, not previously included in SI 1948/184, are interior staircases, fixed ladders and open skylights and frames.
3   SI 1973/1473, Sch para 3(1).

Sanctions

23.12 The express sanction contained in the 'model clauses' themselves for default by the landlord in complying with the obligations imposed on him is that the tenant may serve notice on the landlord who fails to carry out his repairing or replacement obligations, and in default of the landlord complying with the notice within generally three months[1], the tenant may then do the work himself and (subject to the landlord's right to arbitration) recover the reasonable cost from the landlord.

A new provision was introduced by the amending regulations of 1988[2] enabling tenants to make repairs to underground waterpipes for which the landlord is responsible[3] one week after informing the landlord of the damage instead of the three months otherwise applicable. This provision is unsatisfactory because at the expiry of one week the tenant will not know whether the landlord intends to contest his liability. The landlord does not have to serve a counter-notice to contest his liability until up to one month of service of the tenant's notice[4]. The tenant's right to recover the reasonable cost of the repairs specified does not arise until the liability is determined by the arbitrator. It therefore arises from the termination of the arbitration[5].

This is subject to a restriction (in the case of replacements, but not repairs)[6] that the amount shall not in any one year exceed £2,000[7], or one year's rent, whichever is the less. This is not a very satisfactory remedy in practice because the tenant is obliged to carry out the work and pay for it before recovering the cost from the landlord. Furthermore, the debt carries no interest with it and is recoverable usually (unless the amount is small) only by deduction from rent and therefore by instalments possibly over a long, or even a very long, period.

[1] SI 1973/1473, Sch para 12(3).
[2] SI 1988/281.
[3] Note that this provision does not apply where, under the terms of paragraphs 1–4 of the model clauses, the tenant is liable to contribute to the cost of the works: SI 1973/1473, Sch para 12(2).
[4] SI 1973/1473, Sch para 12(5)(a).
[5] SI 1973/1473, Sch para 12(5)(c).
[6] The contrast between repairs and replacements is a troublesome one because most repairs necessarily involve an element of replacement and the two words do not denote contradistinction: see *Lurcott v Wakely and Wheeler* [1911] 1 KB 905 at 918, CA: 'I have no doubt that repair includes the replacement of parts. Of course, if a house was tumble down or was down, the word repair could not be used to cover rebuilding', per Fletcher Moulton LJ and see Buckley LJ on the distinction (or lack of it) between repairs and renewals.
[7] The figure of £2,000 was substituted for £500 by SI 1988/281. The regulations make a distinction between repairs (see para 12(1)) and replacements (see para 12(2)). Since the £2,000 limit is only expressed to apply to replacements, the tenant will be able to recover sums in excess of this where he has executed repairs, provided the expenses are 'reasonable'. For the difference between repairs and replacements, see 10.3ff.

23.13 If a landlord wishes to contest his liability to execute any repairs or replacements he can serve a counter-notice within one month and refer the matter to arbitration under the AHA 1986 for determination[1]. After the landlord has served the counter-notice, the operation of the tenant's notice is suspended pending the outcome of the arbitration. The tenant's notice will subsequently be reinstated if, consequent upon the decision of the arbitrator, the landlord's objection is not upheld. The obligation arises on the termination of the arbitration which is the date on which the arbitrator's award is delivered to the landlord[2].

Time is of the essence in relation to the landlord's counter-notice[3]. If the landlord fails to serve an effective counter-notice, he cannot deny liability for the matters specified in the tenant's notice[4]. This has been found to apply whether the tenant seeks to enforce the model clauses or whether he seeks specific performance and damages for breach[5].

[1] It should be noted that under the AHA 1948 model clauses there is no provision for the landlord to serve a counter-notice. If the landlord fails to carry out repairs within three months of the tenant's written request, the tenant may execute the repairs and recover the reasonable cost of the repairs from the landlord forthwith: SI 1948/184, Sch para 13.
[2] SI 1973/1473, Sch para 12(5)(d).
[3] *Hammond v Allen* [1994] 1 All ER 307.
[4] *Hammond v Allen* [1994] 1 All ER 307.
[5] *Hammond v Allen* [1994] 1 All ER 307.

Alternative sanctions

23.14 In view of the unsatisfactory and inadequate nature of these provisions for tenants seeking to enforce the landlord's obligations to repair, some tenants have sought alternative remedies, for example, applications to the court for specific performance by the landlord of his repairing obligations.

In *Grayless v Watkinson*[1], a case on complicated facts, the main issue was whether and to what extent and how a tenant could enforce 'model clauses' repairing obligations against his landlord. It was held that:

> 'Where a tenant is subject to the model clauses, ie the Agricultural Holdings (Maintenance, Repair and Insurance of Fixed Equipment) Regulations 1973, SI 1473/1973, as amended, the tenant's sole right' is "derived from paragraph 12(2) and he is bound by the restriction imposed by the proviso" ' (per Dillon LJ)

and

> 'The true position as I see it is that paragraph 12(2) is the sole source of the tenant's right to recover the cost of replacing the barn roof from the landlord and the tenant must accept paragraph 12(2) as a whole, including the proviso' (per Stuart Smith LJ).

In *Grayless v Watkinson*[2], the Court of Appeal decided:

(a)   the limitation of £2,000 does not restrict the tenant to a single sum in that amount. The tenant can recover that amount during each year of the tenancy until the cost of the works is recovered in full. It should be noted that there is no provision for the payment of interest;

(b)   the tenant is not entitled to disregard the £2,000 limit by suing for damages for breach of contract or breach of statutory duty, and thereby asserting that the proper measure of damages is the full cost of the works.

The above principles deriving from *Grayless v Watkinson*[3] apply:

(i)   where the tenancy agreement contains no provision for repairs and the model clauses are accordingly incorporated, and

(ii)   where the model clauses are expressly incorporated.

If the tenancy agreement provides that the repairing obligations are to be in accordance with the model clauses, but the monetary limitation is not expressly incorporated, it is submitted that the tenant can sue for damages for breach of contract. Such damages would include the reasonable cost of the works of replacement carried out by the tenant as a consequence of the landlord's default[4].

In *Hammond v Allen*[5], the tenant served notice under reg 12 of the Agriculture (Maintenance, Repair and Insurance of Fixed Equipment) Regulations 1973. The landlord failed to serve counter-notice requiring arbitration as to his liability. The tenant then sought an order for specific performance of the landlord's repairing obligations in accordance with the general principle in *Jeune v Queen's Cross Properties*[6]. It was held that the tenant was entitled to claim specific performance and claim for damages.

[1]   [1990] 1 EGLR 6, CA.
[2]   [1990] 1 EGLR 6, CA.
[3]   [1990] 1 EGLR 6, CA.

4   [1990] 1 EGLR 6, CA, per Ralph Gibson LJ at B.
5   [1994] 1 All ER 307.
6   [1974] Ch 97.

23.15 By contrast, in *Tustian v Johnston*[1], the High Court refused specific performance and held:

> 'There should be compulsory arbitration on the issues of the extent of a repairing obligation and the existence of a breach of those obligations. It would in my view be hopelessly unsatisfactory to allow simultaneous court proceedings for specific performance with arbitration on the question of whether the obligation has been breached'[2].

On appeal, the Court of Appeal[3] lifted the stay imposed by the High Court in order to allow the tenant to apply for summary judgment but not for any other reason and without determining the merits. The Court of Appeal considered that the test was essentially the same where there is an application for summary judgment and an application to lift a stay in arbitration proceedings. It would appear that the court's attitude is that, if the matters in dispute are such that a summary judgment application would succeed, then the tenant should not be forced to go through the arbitration procedure. This may arise where the differences are minimal or where the disrepair is such that it is plain that the covenanting party is in breach[4].

The effect of these decisions is that, if the landlord challenges liability by giving notice under the regulations, usually a two-stage process applies before the court can order specific performance. First, the liability (or its extent) must be established at arbitration. The court will stay proceedings until the arbitrator makes his award. Only then will the court consider a claim for specific performance and damages. The exception to this two-stage process will be where the differences are such that the tenant should succeed before the court in a summary judgment application.

1   [1993] 2 All ER 673.
2   [1993] 2 All ER 673, Knox J at 681.
3   [1993] 3 All ER 534n.
4   [1993] 3 All ER 534n.

Part II: Rights and liabilities of the tenant

Obligations of the tenant

23.16 The tenant's maintenance and repairing obligations in respect of the farmhouse, cottages and buildings does not include those items which fall to be undertaken by the landlord[1].

The liabilities of the tenant are set out in paras 5 to 11 of the Schedule to SI 1973/1473. The tenant's liabilities are as follows:

(a)   The tenant is liable to repair and to keep and leave clean and in good tenantable repair, order and condition the farmhouse, cottages and farm buildings together with the following which are in or upon the holding, or which during the tenancy may be erected or provided thereon:

  (i)   all fixtures and fittings;
  (ii) boilers, ranges and grates;
  (iii) drains, sewers, gulleys, grease-traps, man-holes and inspection chambers;
  (iv) electrical supply systems and fittings[2];
  (v)   water supply systems and fittings in so far as they are situated above ground, including pipes, tanks, cisterns, sanitary fittings, drinking troughs and pumping equipment, hydraulic rams (whether situated above or below ground);
  (vi) fences, hedges[3], field walls, stiles, gates and posts;
  (vii) cattle grids, bridges;
  (viii) culverts, ponds, watercourses, sluices, ditches;
  (ix) roads and yards[4].

(b) The tenant is liable to repair or replace all removable covers to manholes, to inspection chambers and to sewage disposal systems[5].

(c) The tenant is liable to keep clean and in good working order all roof valleys, eaves-guttering and downpipes, wells, septic tanks, cesspools and sewage disposal systems[6].

(d) The tenant is liable to use items carefully so as to protect from wilful, reckless or negligent damage all items for the repair or replacement of which the landlord is responsible under model clauses[7].

(e) The tenant is liable to report in writing immediately to the landlord any damage, however caused, to items for the repair or replacement of which the landlord is responsible[8].

(f) The tenant is liable to replace or repair, and upon replacement or repair, adequately to paint, gas-tar, creosote or otherwise treat with effective preservative material as may be proper, all items of fixed equipment, and to do any work, where such replacement, repair or work is rendered necessary by the wilful act or negligence of the tenant or any members of his household or his employees; however, this liability is subject to the landlord's liability to make good damage by fire[9].

(g) The tenant is liable to replace anything mentioned in paragraph 5(1) of the model clauses[10] which has worn out or otherwise become incapable of repair if its condition has been brought about by, or is substantially due to, the tenant's failure to repair it[11].

(h) The tenant is liable, as often as may be necessary, and in any case at intervals of not more than seven years, properly to clean, colour, whiten, paper, paint, limewash or otherwise treat with materials of suitable quality the inside of the farmhouse, cottages and farm buildings, including the interior of outward opening doors and windows of the farmhouse and cottages, which have been previously so treated and in the last year of the tenancy to limewash the inside of all buildings which previously have been limewashed[12].

(i) Notwithstanding the general liability of the landlord for repairs and replacements, the tenant is liable to renew all broken or cracked tiles or slates and to replace all slipped tiles or slates from time to time as the damage occurs, but so that the cost shall not exceed £100 in any one year of the tenancy[13].

(j)   The tenant is liable to cut, trim or lay a proper proportion of the hedges in each year of the tenancy so as to maintain them in good and sound condition[14].

(k)   The tenant is liable to dig out, scour and cleanse all ponds, water-courses, ditches and grips, as may be necessary to maintain them at sufficient width and depth, and to keep clear from obstruction all field drains and their outlets[15].

(l)   If the last year of the tenancy is not a year in which such cleaning, colouring, whitening, papering, painting, limewashing or other treat-ment required in paragraph (h) above is due to be carried out, the tenant is liable to pay to the landlord at the end of such last year either the estimated reasonable cost thereof or a sum equal to the aggregate of one-seventh part of that cost in respect of each year that has elapsed since such last cleaning, colouring, whitening, papering, painting, limewashing or other treatment as aforesaid, was completed, whichever is the less[16]. In the assessment of any compensation payable by the tenant on the termination of the tenancy in respect of dilapidation, any accrued liability under para 11(1) or 11(2) shall be taken into account[17].

(m)   If the last year of the tenancy is not a year in which the landlord is liable, under paragraph 3 of the model clauses[18] to paint, gas-tar, creosote or otherwise treat the doors, windows, eaves-guttering and downpipes of buildings, the tenant is liable to pay to the landlord at the end of such last year either one-half of the estimated reasonable cost thereof or a sum equal to the aggregate of one-tenth part of that cost in respect of each year that has elapsed since the last such painting, gas-tarring, creosoting or other treatment as aforesaid, was completed, whichever is the less[19].

The tenant is not liable to execute any work if and so far as the execution of such work is impossible (except at prohibitive or unreasonable expense) by reason of subsidence of any land or the blocking of outfalls which are not under the control of either the landlord or the tenant[20].

The tenant's obligation to repair and to keep and leave clean and in good tenantable repair, order and condition the items set out above is not merely to keep and leave them as clean and in as good repair as they happened to be at the beginning of the tenancy. In determining whether the obligation has been complied with in relation to any particular item, regard should be had to its age and character and its general condition at the commencement of the tenancy. Regard should also be had to the length of the tenancy and the time the tenant had to do that which he was called upon to carry out[21].

---

[1]   See para 23.9ff.
[2]   If the electrical systems need replacing by rewiring because the existing wiring is beyond repair the liability rests with the landlord: *Roper v Prudential Assurance Ltd* [1992] 1 EGLR 5, [1992] 09 EG 141.
[3]   For an interesting article on tenant's liability for boundaries see the Estates Gazette (1982) 10 June, 26 June and 10 July.

4   SI 1973/1473, Sch para 5(1).
5   SI 1973/1473, Sch para 5(2).
6   SI 1973/1473, Sch para 5(3).
7   SI 1973/1473, Sch para 5(4).
8   SI 1973/1473, Sch para 5(4).
9   SI 1973/1473, Sch para 6(1).
10 See para 23.16(a).
11 SI 1973/1473, Sch para 6(2).
12 SI 1973/1473, Sch para 7.
13 SI 1973/1473, Sch para 8(1).
14 SI 1973/1473, Sch para 9. Cf SI 1948/184 where the obligation was limited to 'cut and lay'.
15 SI 1973/1473, Sch para 10.
16 SI 1973/1473, Sch para 11(1).
17 SI 1973/1473, Sch para 11(2).
18 See para 23.9.
19 SI 1973/1473, Sch para 11(2).
20 SI 1973/1473, Sch para 14(2).
21 *Evans v Jones* [1955] 2 QB 58 at 66.

Sanctions where the tenant fails to comply with his obligations

23.17 The sanction under the regulations imposed on a tenant who fails to carry out his repairing liabilities is for the landlord to serve a written notice[1] on him requiring him to do so. If the work is not started within two months, and completed within three months, of receiving the notice, the landlord can enter and execute the work himself and recover the reasonable costs of doing so from the tenant.

In the event of the tenant disputing his liability to execute repairs specified by the landlord in his notice, the tenant must within one month of receipt of the landlord's notice serve a counter-notice on the landlord requiring the issue to be referred to arbitration under the AHA 1986.

If the tenant serves a counter-notice on the landlord, the operation of the landlord's notice is suspended in relation to items set out in the counter-notice, until the termination of the arbitration[2]. In this case, the model clauses do not define termination[3]. By parity of reasoning as to the position where a landlord serves a counter-notice, the termination of the arbitration will be either when the arbitrator's award is delivered to the tenant or, possibly, the date of publication of the award for the purposes of the arbitration provisions under the AHA 1986[4].

Although the model clauses do not make express provision, it is submitted that failure by the tenant to serve a counter-notice should have the same effect as where a landlord fails to do so[5].

By parity of reasoning, it would appear that the model clauses do not exclude the landlord's ability to pursue other remedies[6].

1   The notice need not be a formal 'notice to remedy' in the prescribed form under the AHA 1986, as to which see para 31.51ff, and note the different sanctions. Those sanctions are much more severe, so a formal notice to remedy will usually be the preferred sanction of the landlord.

2   SI 1973/1473, Sch para 4(3)(b).
3   Cf the position in relation to a landlord's counter-notice: see para 23.13.
4   See para 47.3ff.
5   See para 23.13ff.
6   See *Hammond v Allen* [1994] 1 All ER 307 and see para 23.14ff. Also see, *Crewe Services & Investment Corpn v Silk* [1998] 2 EGLR 1, CA, for a case considering the measure of damages for a tenant's breach of a repairing obligation during the term of the tenancy: see para 10.13.

23.18 In practice the landlord may well decide to rely upon a notice to remedy, or make an application for a certificate of bad husbandry, since these remedies are likely to be much more effective in their operation than the sanction contained in the regulations which is rarely employed[1].

The tenant's limited liability to maintain and repair extends to buildings and other fixtures provided by the tenant himself. The regulations make it clear that the liability of the landlord in respect, for example, of structural repairs, does not extend to buildings or fixtures which are 'the property of the tenant'[2].

At common law any building or fixture becomes the property of the landlord on annexure to the freehold. However, s 10 of the AHA 1986 provides that the property in such building or fixture remains vested in the tenant[3]. This only applies to fixtures and not improvements. Therefore, the anomalous position exists where it would appear that the landlord is liable to repair tenant's compensatable improvements, but not fixtures.

1   *Halliday v Fergusson (Wm) & Sons* 1961 SC 24, 1961 SLT 176, Ct of Sess.
2   SI 1973/1473, Sch para 4(1)(a).
3   AHA 1986, s 10(1).

Part III: General provisions: obsolete and redundant buildings

23.19 Part III, para 13 of the 1973 Regulations contains the obligations of the parties in relation to items of fixed equipment redundant to the farming of the holding. Either a landlord or a tenant who is of the opinion that any item of fixed equipment is redundant (or was so before it was damaged or destroyed by fire) is entitled to give two months' notice in writing to the other requiring the question of redundancy to be determined in default of agreement by arbitration. The arbitrator must then determine whether or not the item of fixed equipment is (or was before damage or destruction by fire) 'redundant to the farming of the holding'[1].

When deciding the issue of redundancy, the arbitrator must consider whether repair or replacement of the item is reasonable having regard to:

(a)   the landlord's responsibility to manage the holding in accordance with the rules of good estate management; and

(b)   the period for which the holding may reasonably be expected to remain a separate holding; and

(c)   the character and situation of the holding and the average requirements of a tenant reasonably skilled in husbandry[2].

23.19   *Written tenancy agreement and fixed equipment*

It is noted that these provisions are phrased in the negative, ie the arbitrator is not to determine the item as redundant in his award unless he is satisfied that the repair or replacement of the item is not reasonably required, having regard to these criteria. In practice, the general provisions are of little assistance to an arbitrator in determining whether or not an item is redundant. It is submitted that the word 'redundant' has its normal dictionary meaning and is not synonymous with obsolete. Accordingly, the arbitration procedure referred to above is available only in the case of redundant fixed equipment that is surplus to the needs of the holding. Correspondingly, arbitration is not available where the fixed equipment is merely 'obsolete' or obsolescent, ie where old buildings which are expensive to maintain and repair exist on the holding and would be better replaced with modern buildings, but until then are still needed for the purpose of farming the holding efficiently. Accordingly, the parties are only relieved from their obligations in respect of obsolete fixed equipment if they have agreed in writing that the item of fixed equipment is obsolete.

The effect of agreement as to redundancy or obsolescence or an arbitrator's award that an item is redundant is that both parties are then relieved of any further liability to maintain or repair the item in question[3]. Furthermore, the landlord is entitled to remove the redundant item[4].

In deciding whether to agree that an item of fixed equipment is redundant the parties should bear in mind that the consequence will often be more than merely a relieving of contractual repairing obligations. The planning consequences and the possibility of a Case B notice to quit and the possible loss by removal of the building should also be taken into account before agreement is reached as to redundancy. Consideration should also be given to consequent insuring liability, especially for personal injury to third parties from falling masonry.

As stated above, in addition to redundant and obsolete buildings, there is a third category of items of repair, maintenance, etc from which the parties are or can be relieved. This is any item of work which is 'rendered impossible (except at prohibitive or unreasonable expense) by reason of subsidence of any land or the blocking of outfalls which are not under the control of either the landlord or the tenant'[5].

Unreasonable or prohibitive expense does not relieve liability if it is occasioned by any other failure, for example, cracked or blocked field drains, although it might well assist a tenant if the field drains had become out of alignment over the course of time consequent upon the occurrence of subsidence.

[1]   SI 1973/1473, Sch para 13(1).
[2]   SI 1973/1473, Sch para 13(2).
[3]   SI 1973/1473, Sch paras 13(1) and 14.
[4]   SI 1973/1473, Sch para 13(1).
[5]   SI 1973/1473, Sch para 14(2).

Arbitration under the model clauses

23.20 If any claim, question or difference arises between the landlord and the tenant under the provisions of the model clauses, not being a matter which, otherwise than under the model clauses, is required by, or by virtue of, the AHA 1986 or regulations or orders made under the AHA 1986 to be determined by arbitration under the AHA 1986, such claim, question or difference shall be determined, in default of agreement, by arbitration under the AHA 1986[1].

[1]   SI 1973/1473, Sch para 15. As to the inter-relationship between the arbitration provisions and the jurisdiction of the courts, see para 23.14ff.

ARBITRATION TO REVISE TENANCY TERMS INCONSISTENT WITH THE MODEL CLAUSES

23.21 Where the terms of the written tenancy agreement are inconsistent with the model clauses, s 8 of the AHA 1986 provides that, if those inconsistencies effect 'substantial modifications in the operation of the regulations'[1], either party may seek a variation of the tenancy so as to bring it into line with the model clauses. This provision, which has particular value to a tenant holding under terms imposing full repairing and insuring obligations upon him, has been rarely employed in practice.

Although the AHA 1986 provides for either the landlord or the tenant to make a request to vary the terms of the tenancy, the AHA 1986 does not provide that such a request should be in writing[2]. Clearly it is advisable for a party to make such a request in writing.

The AHA 1986 does not provide a timetable for the appointment of the arbitrator in relation to a s 8 arbitration. The general provisions as to arbitration under the AHA 1986 will apply[3].

An arbitrator's award pursuant to a s 8 arbitration has effect as if the terms and provisions specified and made in the award were contained in the tenancy agreement and have effect as from the date of the making of the award or such other date specified by the arbitrator, by way of variation of the tenancy agreement previously in force[4].

Where there has been a s 8 arbitration, no further reference to arbitration under s 8 may be made before the expiry of three years from the previous award coming into effect[5].

Upon any variation, the arbitrator varying the terms of the tenancy may also award a variation in the rent of the holding, if it is considered by him equitable to do so by reason of 'any provision included in his award'[6]. This inevitably will mean that a tenant who seeks and obtains relief from the full repairing obligations imposed upon him by agreement will 'trigger' a rent increase, but not a comprehensive rent increase taking into account economic circumstances generally. It will be limited to an increase in rent by reason of the transfer in responsibility for maintenance and repair.

There is no obligation upon the arbitrator in every case to vary the terms of the tenancy so as to incorporate the model clauses. The arbitrator has a discretion. The arbitrator must only order such variations as he considers 'justifiable having regard to the circumstances of the holding and of the landlord and the tenant'. The variation must be such as he considers to be 'reasonable and just'[7].

The provisions of s 8 of the AHA 1986 should be read in conjunction with s 9 of the Act. Section 9 provides for compensation payable upon any variation in terms of the tenancy. It follows that if a tenant, subject to full repairing and insuring liability, wishes to relieve himself of that obligation, he may have to pay not merely an increased rent to take into account that fact, but also compensation in the form of what in effect is an accumulated dilapidation claim for any breaches committed by him during the currency of the tenancy before variation. If the tenancy has endured for only a short time before arbitration, the accumulated dilapidations and the consequent compensation may be modest[8].

1 SI 1973/1473.
2 AHA 1986, s 8(1) and (2).
3 See Ch 47.
4 AHA 1986, s 8(5). Cf *Hollings v Swindle* (1950) 155 Estates Gazette 269.
5 AHA 1986, s 8(6).
6 AHA 1986, s 8(4).
7 AHA 1986, s 8(3).
8 See *Evans v Jones* [1955] 2 QB 58, [1955] 2 All ER 118, CA.

CONSEQUENTIAL COMPENSATION

23.22 Compensation under s 9 of the AHA 1986 has wider application than in relation to s 8 arbitrations. If either the landlord or the tenant obtains some variation in the contractual terms of the tenancy agreement by virtue of an arbitration under ss 6, 7 or 8 of the AHA 1986, and the contractual liability of the parties in respect of their maintenance or repairing obligations in respect of fixed equipment is then varied, compensation may be awarded under s 9 to the party to whom the obligation is transferred[1] for existing breaches by the other party.

Any claim by the landlord or the tenant to compensation under s 9 of the AHA 1986 must be made within one month of the effective transfer of the liability[2].

The power of the arbitrator to vary the rental in consequence of any such transfer of liability only arises under s 8 arbitrations[3].

Where the terms of a tenancy are varied by new model clauses relating to maintenance, repair and insurance, then if there is a subsequent reference to arbitration under s 6[4], and the reference is made within three months of the new model clauses coming into force, the arbitrator must disregard the variation made by the new model clauses[5].

1   AHA 1986, s 9(1).
2   The Agriculture (Miscellaneous Time-Limits) Regulations 1959, SI 1959/171, reg 2(2) and (3).
3   See para 23.21.
4   See para 23.3.
5   AHA 1986, s 9(4); the Agriculture (Time-Limit) Regulations 1988, SI 1988/282, reg 2.

TENANT'S RIGHT TO REMOVE FIXTURES AND BUILDINGS

23.23 Section 10 of the AHA 1986 varies the general common law rule that anything fixed to the freehold becomes part of the freehold, and thus the property of the landlord.

Section 10 has no application to chattels that are not firmly fastened to the ground: these may be removed without restriction[1]. There is sometimes uncertainty as to whether the items are chattels, for example, bulk milk tanks[2].

1   *Wansbrough v Maton* (1836) 4 Ad & El 884.
2   See *Dean v Andrews* (1985) 135 NLJ 728 (July 15); *Botham v TSB Bank plc* (1996) 73 P & CR D1, [1996] EGCS 149, CA.

23.24 Although the common law rule was relaxed to allow trade fixtures to be removed in the absence of any agreement to the contrary, this exception was not extended by the courts to agricultural fixtures[1]. Market gardeners and nurserymen were held to be entitled to remove fixtures such as greenhouses and hot-houses erected by way of business, and also shrubs and trees planted to sell[2]. Section 22 of the Agricultural Holdings Act 1923, as amended by the Agriculture Act 1947, gave agricultural tenants a statutory right to remove fixtures and buildings either during, or before the expiration of two months from the termination of, the tenancy. The modern law is now contained in s 10 of the AHA 1986[3].

The following provisions of s 10 should be noted:

(a)   The section applies to fixtures 'of whatever description' affixed[4] to an agricultural holding by the tenant whether for the purpose of agriculture or not[5]. The reference to 'any engine, machinery, fencing or other fixtures' in the text of the Act merely provides examples of such fixtures.

(b)   As to what is a fixture as opposed to a tenant's chattel and the interrelationship of the tests directed to the degree of annexation on the one hand and the purpose for which the item has been affixed on the other, see *Botham v TSB Bank plc* (and the cases cited in it)[6].

(c)   In the case of buildings, the right is only given if the tenant is not entitled to compensation under the Act or otherwise in respect thereof, for example, because the building was an improvement erected with the landlord's consent.

(d)   The right to remove a fixture only applies in the following circumstances:

(i)   the tenant must have given, at least one month before the
exercise of the right and termination of the tenancy, notice in
writing[7] of his intention to remove the fixture or building;

(ii)   the tenant must have paid all rent owing by him and 'performed
or satisfied all his other obligations to the landlord in respect of
the holding'. This latter requirement is impossible to perform if
strictly construed, since it is in the nature of farming that weeds
constantly grow and cannot be totally eliminated and buildings
decay and are constantly in need of attention. The application of
the de minimis rule would not appear to be sufficient in most
cases to alleviate the tenant from the harsh requirements of
s 10(3)(a)[8];

(iii) the fixture must not have been affixed pursuant to an obligation
imposed on the tenant or in substitution for some other fixture
or building belonging to the landlord;

(iv)   the tenant's right to remove the fixture must be exercised not
later than two months after termination of the tenancy[9];

(v)   the tenant may remove fixtures if the right to do so exists
independently of s 10 and in these circumstances a failure to
comply with the provisions of s 10 would not prejudice the
exercise of such a right[10]. This might apply if there was an
express provision to that effect in the tenancy agreement.

(e)   The right to remove fixtures is lost if, before the notice given by the
tenant of his intention to remove the fixture has expired, the landlord
gives a counter-notice[11], but in that case he is liable to pay the tenant
the 'fair value' of the fixture to an incoming tenant of the holding. Any
dispute between the landlord and the tenant as to the amount of
compensation payable by the landlord is to be determined by arbitration under the AHA 1986[12].

(f)   In removing the fixture the tenant must not cause avoidable damage to
any other building or other part of the holding, and immediately after
the removal he is obliged to make good all damage so caused[13].

(g)   The right does not apply to any fixture or building provided before
1 January 1884, although it is highly improbable that such a tenancy
would still be subsisting or if it was that any such fixture or building
would be worth removing[14].

1   *Elwes v Maw* (1802) 3 East 38.
2   *Penton v Robart* (1801) 2 East 88 and 90, and *Mears v Callender* [1901] 2 Ch 388.
3   Formerly s 13 of the AHA1948. Although it was assumed to be permissible to contract out
of the provisions of the section (see *Premier Dairies Ltd v Garlick* [1920] 2 Ch 17) doubts
as to the correctness of this view were expressed in *Johnson v Moreton* [1980] AC 37,
[1978] 3 All ER 37, HL by Lord Hailsham.
4   More than mere contact with the ground is required, the particular fixture being let into or
united with the land, or a substance previously connected to it: *Palser v Grinling* [1948]
AC 291, [1948] 1 All ER 1, HL; and see *Dean v Andrews* (1985) 135 NLJ 728 (July 15).
5   These words contained in s 10(1)(a) of the AHA 1986 were originally introduced by Sch 3,
para 6(2) of the Agricultural Holdings Act 1984 in order to negative the *ejusdem generis*
interpretation of the phrase 'engine, machinery, fencing or other fixture'.
6   (1996) 73 P & CR D1, [1996] EGCS 149, CA.

7 AHA 1986, s 10(3)(b). Both conditions must be satisfied, ie the notice must be given at least one month before the removal and one month before termination. If both these conditions are not satisfied, and the fixture is nevertheless removed, it is open to the landlord to sue for conversion and damages.

8 For cases where the courts have construed a similar requirement strictly in the context of the exercise of an option to renew a tenancy, see *Bass Holdings Ltd v Morton Music Ltd* [1988] Ch 493; *Bairstow Eves (Securities) Ltd v Ripley* [1992] 2 EGLR 47, [1992] 32 EG 52, CA.

9 AHA 1986, s 10(1)(b). This provision varies the common law rule whereby the right of removal generally ceases when the tenancy expires.

10 AHA 1986, s 10(8), introduced by Sch 3 para 6(3) of the Agricultural Holdings Act 1984.

11 AHA 1986, s 10(4).

12 AHA 1986, s 10(6). The revised wording of this subsection (originally introduced by Sch 3, para 6(3) of the Agricultural Holdings Act 1984) makes it clear that a dispute as to fair value occurring during or on termination of the tenancy can be referred to arbitration.

13 AHA 1986, s 10(5). A failure on the part of the tenant to comply with this requirement would expose him to an action for damages, or compensation if the claim arose on the termination of the tenancy.

14 AHA 1986, s 10(3)(d).

PROVISION OF FIXED EQUIPMENT

23.25 It frequently occurs that an agricultural holding is deficient of suitable or adequate fixed equipment for the farming of the holding either because the existing fixed equipment becomes outdated[1], or because there simply is no suitable fixed equipment to enable the holding to be farmed to best advantage[2].

1 Eg labour intensive compartmentalised buildings with small apertures which cannot readily be adapted for use by modern machinery.
2 Eg a shortage of covered accommodation for the winter on a dairy farm.

23.26 A tenant confronted with this problem has a number of courses of action available to him:

(a) Under the 'model clauses'[1], he may serve notice on his landlord requiring the landlord to carry out works of repair for which the landlord is responsible and thereafter, in default by the landlord, do the work himself and charge the landlord[2]. This remedy relates only to repair of fixed equipment and not to alteration of existing equipment, nor the provision of new fixed equipment. What is more, it is unsatisfactory to the tenant who has to expend his own money and then seek to recover as much as he can from the landlord[3].

(b) The tenant may provide items of fixed equipment at his own expense with the landlord's prior written consent and he will then be entitled to recover compensation for those improvements at the end of the tenancy[4] and have the improvements disregarded upon a rent review.

(c) If the landlord refuses to give written consent to the carrying out of the improvement[5] or consents only on unacceptable terms, the tenant may apply to the Agricultural Land Tribunal for approval of the carrying out of the improvement under s 67(3) of the AHA 1986[6].

(d) The tenant may erect the building, even without the landlord's consent (unless there is an express prohibition in the contract of tenancy on doing so) in which event the building will fall to be treated as a tenant's fixture. Provided the provisions of s 10 of the AHA 1986 are complied with[7], the tenant would then be entitled to remove the fixture on due notice.

(e)   The tenant could apply to the Agricultural Land Tribunal under s 11 of the AHA 1986[8] for a direction compelling the landlord himself to provide, alter or repair fixed equipment on the holding to enable the tenant to comply with certain statutory requirements. This is the re-enactment of the old, unsatisfactory and, until recently, rarely employed provision of s 4 of the Agriculture Act 1958.

1   The Agriculture (Maintenance, Repair and Insurance of Fixed Equipment) Regulations 1973, SI 1973/1473.
2   SI 1973/1473, Sch para 12.
3   For a fuller commentary see 23.12ff.
4   AHA 1986, Pt II of Sch 7 and ss 64–69.
5   AHA 1986, s 67(1).
6   For a commentary on this provision see 38.18, and note the terms and conditions applicable to s 67 of the AHA 1986.
7   As to which, see 23.23.
8   Replacing the Agriculture Act 1958, s 4. The 1958 Act has been repealed.

TENANT'S APPLICATION TO THE AGRICULTURAL LAND TRIBUNAL

Conditions for a direction of the Agricultural Land Tribunal to the landlord

23.27 If the tenant is successfully to obtain a direction from the Agricultural Land Tribunal (ALT) under section 11 of the AHA 1986 requiring the landlord to carry out 'within a period specified in the direction, such work for the provision or, as the case may be, the alteration or repair' of the particular piece of 'fixed equipment', the following requirements are to be satisfied:

(a)   The ALT must be satisfied 'that it is reasonable, having regard to the tenant's responsibilities to farm the holding in accordance with the rules of good husbandry, that he should carry on on the holding an agricultural activity specified in the application to the extent and in the manner specified therein'[1].

(b)   The tenant will contravene statutory requirements unless either fixed equipment is provided on the holding[2], or existing fixed equipment is altered or repaired[3]. This is the condition which, until recently, the tenant would rarely have satisfied, thereby rendering the remedy more notional than real.

(c)   If the tenant's 'agricultural activity' specified in his application had not been carried on on the holding continuously[4] for at least three years immediately preceding his application, the ALT may not give the direction unless the activity does not, or will not, involve a substantial alteration to the type of farming[5].

(d)   The ALT must be satisfied that it is reasonable to direct the landlord to carry out the work, having regard to the landlord's responsibility to manage the land in accordance with the rules of good estate management and also having regard to the period for which the holding may be expected to remain a separate holding, and to any other material consideration[6].

(e)   The tenant must have requested the landlord in writing to carry out the work and the landlord have either refused to do so or not agreed to do so within a reasonable time of being asked[7].

(f)   The ALT may not give a direction where the tenancy or any other agreement provides for either the landlord or the tenant to carry out the work. Nor may it make the direction if there is a statutory duty on the landlord to carry out the work in question or either the landlord or the tenant is contractually obliged to do the work[8].

The burden of proof is on the tenant.

[1]   AHA 1986, s 11(1).
[2]   AHA 1986, s 11(1)(a). There are very few such requirements, but see eg the Milk and Dairies (General) Regulations 1959, SI 1959/277 and the Agriculture (Safety, Health and Welfare Provisions) Act 1956 and more particularly and of current application, s 85 of the Water Resources Act 1991 and the Control of Pollution (Silage, Slurry and Agricultural Fuel Oil) Regulations 1991, SI 1991/324.
[3]   AHA 1986, s 11(1)(b).
[4]   The word 'continuously' was originally inserted into the former s 4 of the Agriculture Act 1958 by Sch 3 para 30 of the Agricultural Holdings Act 1984 as an additional precondition. It clarified a possible ambiguity in s 4 of the Agriculture Act 1958 Act.
[5]   AHA 1986, s 11(2). Note that the wording is in the negative.
[6]   AHA 1986, s 11(3)(a). This precondition gives the Tribunal a wide discretion to refuse a direction. The reference to the period for which the holding may be expected to remain a separate holding presumably refers to at least a provisional intention on the part of the landlord to amalgamate different holdings on an estate, thereby rendering the provision, alteration or repair of the fixed equipment superfluous. It is to be noted that this precondition is also phrased in the negative. It is an open question whether the phrase 'material consideration' is subjective or objective.
[7]   AHA 1986, s 11(3)(b).
[8]   AHA 1986, s 11(4).

Pollution

23.28 With the substantially increased regulation of environmental protection in recent years, a number of statutory requirements to avoid pollution particularly of rivers and watercourses have been enacted, eg s 85 of the Water Resources Act 1991. Many livestock farmers, particularly dairy farmers, have therefore been threatened with prosecution by the Environment Agency (formerly the National Rivers Authority) and other statutory bodies. In these circumstances, applications by tenants to the ALT for directions under s 11 of the AHA 1986 against their landlords, have greater significance.

Procedure

23.29 If the landlord refuses to carry out the work on being requested in writing to do so by the tenant, or refuses to do so within a reasonable time of being so requested[1], the next stage is for the tenant to make an application to the ALT in the prescribed form, or a form substantially to the like effect[2].

The landlord, if he wishes to oppose the application, must serve a reply within one month[3].

23.29 *Written tenancy agreement and fixed equipment*

The tenant's application must specify the 'agricultural activity' which the tenant proposes to carry on.

The procedure before the ALT is discussed later in this book[4].

1   AHA 1986, s 11(3)(b).
2   Ie Form 5 – see the Appendix to Sch 1 to the Agricultural Land Tribunals (Rules) Order 1978, SI 1978/259.
3   See Form 5R.
4   See Ch 46.

Effect of direction

23.30 If the ALT is satisfied as to all the requirements of s 11 of the AHA 1986 it may direct the landlord to carry out such work for the provision, alteration or repair of fixed equipment as is necessary to enable the tenant to comply with his statutory obligations within the time specified in the direction. The ALT has power to grant successive extensions of time if it is satisfied that the period hitherto allowed will not allow a sufficient time for the preliminary arrangements and the carrying out of the work[1]. The preliminary arrangements envisaged may include the determination of an application for Government grant aid to help the landlord get the necessary work done[2], or planning consent in some instances.

1   AHA 1986, s 11(7).
2   This possibility is specifically referred to in the AHA 1986, s 11(7), but grants are now few and modest because of over-production throughout the European Union.

23.31 If the landlord defaults in complying with the ALT's directions, the tenant's remedies are the same as if the landlord had been bound by the contract of tenancy to carry out the work in question and within the time directed by the ALT[1]. This means that the tenant would have an action for damages against his landlord for breach of contract and additionally it is provided that, notwithstanding any provisions in the actual contract of tenancy to the contrary, the tenant shall have the right to carry out the work in question himself and recover from the landlord the reasonable cost[2].

The basis of damages for breach of contract would only support a supplementary claim by the tenant for any special loss he might have suffered from any period of delay and default of the landlord[3]. There is no provision in the section for arbitration or other means to determine what is the 'reasonable cost'. Therefore, the courts will have to determine what is, and what is not, a reasonable cost of the work in question, if and when the tenant sues his landlord under these provisions to recover such cost.

The amount of any Government grant received by the tenant must in any case be deducted from the amount to be recovered by the tenant from his landlord[4]. The work which a landlord does under directions under this section qualify as an improvement for which he can seek an increase in rent[5]. The same is true where the tenant has done the work on the landlord's default, provided the tenant has duly recovered the cost thereof from the landlord.

1   AHA 1986, s 11(5).
2   AHA 1986, s 11(6).
3   An amendment proposed in Parliament to give an express right to the tenant for damages in this connection was negatived because the words already in the section were adequate to confer that right.
4   AHA 1986, s 11(8).
5   AHA 1986, s 13(2)(b).

Sub-tenants

23.32 Where work has been done by a head tenant under a direction made by the ALT on the application of a sub-tenant, the head tenant may claim compensation for the improvement from his landlord at the end of the head tenancy[1]. If the head tenant has failed to comply with the ALT's direction, and the sub-tenant carries out the work, the head tenant can claim against the head landlord for compensation at the end of the tenancy since the sub-tenant has a right to recover the reasonable cost of the work from the head tenant[2]. In such circumstances any grant out of public money paid to the sub-tenant is treated for the purpose of calculating compensation as if it had been made to the head tenant[3]. Where the whole or any part of an agricultural holding has been sub-let, every landlord, tenant and sub-tenant is deemed to be a party to the proceedings before an ALT with respect to the holding and is entitled to be heard by the ALT[4].

1   AHA 1986, s 68(2).
2   AHA 1986, s 68(2)(b).
3   This provision was not included in the Agriculture Act1958 and derives from para 2 of the Appendix to the Report of the Law Commission on the Agricultural Holdings Bill (Cmnd 9665).
4   SI 1978/259, r 13 – for the text, see para A1.524.

Chapter 24

FARMING: GOOD HUSBANDRY AND STANDARD
LEASEHOLD COVENANTS

INTRODUCTION

24.1 The common law imposes minimal obligations upon tenants of agricultural holdings as to cultivation, including a duty to farm according to the custom of the country in a good and husbandlike manner[1]. Following the Second World War, as a consequence of the emphasis upon producing food as efficiently as possible and utilising all agricultural land to best effect, the Agriculture Act 1947 (AA 1947) was introduced. That Act introduced statutory standards of good husbandry and estate management.

The United Kingdom joining the European Community and, in particular, participating in the Common Agricultural Policy, has significantly changed the requirements of farming. The requirements of a farmer to qualify for the payment of Single Payments, consequential upon the Mid-term Review of the Common Agricultural Policy[2], provides a quite different regime to that which has applied to agricultural holdings governed by the AHA 1986 and, indeed, farm business tenancies governed by the Agricultural Tenancies Act 1995 (ATA 1995)[3].

[1] See Ch 5 and para 24.3.
[2] As to the impact of the Mid-term Review of the Common Agricultural Policy, see Ch 52.
[3] Note that the rules of good husbandry and estate management provided by the Agriculture Act 1947 do not apply to farm business tenancies under the ATA 1995, unless incorporated by agreement into the tenancy.

24.2 In addition to the common law and the statutory standards of good husbandry and good estate management, introduced by the AA 1947, the AHA 1986 contains three provisions enabling a tenant to take advantage of a statutory variation in terms otherwise agreed in a contract of tenancy. The three statutory variations apply to:

(a)   permanent pasture[1];
(b)   freedom of cropping and disposal of produce[2];
(c)   removal of manure[3].

[1] AHA 1986, s 14.
[2] AHA 1986, s 15.
[3] AHA 1986, s 15(3).

350

GOOD HUSBANDRY AND GOOD ESTATE MANAGEMENT

Common law

24.3 At common law there has never been any implied obligation on a landlord to manage his estate in accordance with the rules of good estate management[1], or any common law equivalent. At least since 1793[2], a tenant has been under an implied covenant to use and cultivate the land in a good and husbandlike manner according to the custom of the country and to keep the buildings windproof and watertight[3]. The phrase 'custom of the country' refers to the obligation (either express or implied) requiring the tenant to farm the land in a particular manner consistent with the usage generally adopted in the particular part of the country in which the farm is situated. It has been said that the custom must have subsisted for a reasonable length of time and be adequately proved, not by what witnesses say they think the custom is, but what has publicly gone on throughout the district[4]. If the custom is proved to exist, it will apply unless express terms of the tenancy agreement are inconsistent with it negativing the intention of the parties that it should apply[5].

The common law obligation on the tenant is thus minimal and results in the tenant being under no obligation to deliver up the land on the termination of the tenancy in a clean and proper condition, nor to leave the land in as good a condition on quitting as when he came into possession. At common law the tenant has no obligation to improve land which, at the commencement of the tenancy, is in poor condition or to maintain land farmed to a high standard prior to the commencement of the tenancy in that condition[6]. The extent of the common law obligation and the nature of the custom of the country prevailing in different parts of the country are now of little practical consequence in view of the more clearly defined obligations contained in ss 10 and 11 of the AA 1947[7].

It remains to be seen whether under the ATA 1995, reliance upon custom of the country, in the absence of express contractual obligations as to husbandry, may re-emerge. Sections 10 and 11 of the AA 1947 do not apply to a farm business tenancy under the ATA 1995[8].

---

[1] Note: the rules are rules of 'good estate management'. The AHA 1986, s 27(3)(b) (formerly s 3(3)(b) of the Agricultural Holdings (Notices to Quit) Act 1977) refers to 'sound management of the estate'. These expressions are not synonymous. See para 24.5ff.

[2] See *Powley v Walker* (1793) 5 Term Rep 373.

[3] Per Swinfen Eady LJ in *Wedd v Porter* [1916] 2 KB 91 at 100, CA. See also *Powley v Walker* (1793) 5 Term Rep 373.

[4] *Tucker v Linger* (1882) 21 Ch D 18 and 34, CA, per Jessel MR.

[5] *Hutton v Warren* (1836) 1 M & W 466. 'The relations of landlord and tenant have long been regulated upon the supposition that all customary obligations, not altered by the contract, are to remain in force', per Parke B at 475.

[6] *Williams v Lewis* [1915] 3 KB 493, per Bray J.

[7] Sections 10 and 11 of the AA 1947 are not so much definition sections as explanatory.

[8] See para 5.7.

Statutory

24.4 Part II of the AA 1947 contains definitions of good estate management (s 10) and good husbandry (s 11). It also contained a series of statutory sanctions to be imposed upon owners and occupiers of agricultural land and agricultural units respectively, enforceable by the Minister in the event of non-compliance.

As indicated in the Introduction at 24.1 above, the purpose of Pt II of the AA 1947 was to legislate for the maintenance of efficiency in agriculture following the end of the Second World War, complementing the provisions in Pt I of the Act designed to achieve stability in markets and prices and security of tenure conferred by Pt III of the Act. With this object in view, the AA 1947 provided a statement of the rules of good estate management and good husbandry and established a series of sanctions or penalties for those owners, owner-occupiers and tenants who failed to comply with the rules[1]. The system included provisions for the supervision of defaulters, directions to them to carry out certain duties, and, ultimately, dispossession.

All of Pt II of the AA 1947 has now been repealed[2], with the exception of the definitions contained in ss 10 and 11, respectively relating to 'good estate management' and 'good husbandry'. The definitions exist in limbo and no obligation or implied covenant to comply with either set of rules was imposed either by the AHA 1948 or the AHA 1986 or by any other statutory provisions.

Nevertheless, throughout the AHA 1948, reference was made to both sets of rules, and sanctions imposed upon tenants for non-compliance[3]. This has been continued in the AHA 1986[4]. Clearly, if the contract of tenancy provides that the tenant shall comply with the rules of good husbandry, he is under a contractual obligation to do so, but in the absence of any express contractual obligation, there is no obligation implied either by contract or statute merely because the tenant is a tenant of an agricultural holding.

The consequence appears to be that although a tenant who fails to comply with the rules of good husbandry may still have sanctions[5] imposed upon him (for example, the grant of a certificate of bad husbandry issued by the Agricultural Land Tribunal and, thereafter, notice to quit[6]) or be rendered liable for dilapidations under s 71 etc of the AHA 1986, there is no further remedy available to a landlord. It follows that a landlord may *not* give notice to remedy on the basis that the breach by the tenant is a breach of compliance with the rules of good husbandry[7], nor may he, during the currency of the tenancy, recover damages under the principle in *Kent v Conniff*[8] or otherwise.

It is possible that the failure by Parliament to provide for such an obligation to be implied in every contract of tenancy of an agricultural holding was an oversight, since references to the tenant's obligations to comply with the rules of good husbandry are made in circumstances which suggest that such an implied obligation exists[9].

It is to be noted that there are no sanctions imposed or enforcement procedures available against a landlord for a breach of the rules of good estate management by him.

1   Note: the rules refer to owners and occupiers, not to landlords and tenants, and are, therefore, more far-reaching, not being confined to the landlord and tenant system: for the definition of an occupier, see AA 1947, s 109.
2   By the Agriculture Act 1958 (AA 1958), ss 1, 10(1) and Sch 2, Pt I.
3   See the former ss 24(2)(c) and 27 of the AHA 1948 (repealed and now re-enacted in the AHA 1986, Sch 3(1) Pt 1, Case C and Sch 3, Pt 2, para 9(1)) and the former s 47(1)(b) and s 57(1) of the AHA 1948 (now repealed and re-enacted in the AHA 1986, s 65(2)(b) and s 71(1)). See also the former s 4 of the AA 1958, repealed by the AHA 1986, Sch 15, Pt I.
4   AHA 1986, s 10. The Opencast Coal Act 1958, s 14(1) provides a further example of the statutory use of the phrase 'good husbandry': a tenant will not be taken to have failed to fulfil his good husbandry responsibilities by reason of his activities on the land connected with authorised opencast coal production.
5   Although these sanctions will not be derived from the AA 1947.
6   See the AHA 1986, Sch 3, Pt I, Case C.
7   Unless there is an express term in the contract of tenancy to that effect.
8   [1953] 1 QB 361, [1953] 1 All ER 155, CA. See para 39.11.
9   See the rules themselves and AHA 1986, Sch 3, Pt I, Cases D and E, as well as the other sections referred to.

The rules of good estate management

24.5   Section 10 of the AA 1947 explains rather than defines what is meant by the rules of good estate management. The management must be such as to be reasonably adequate, having regard to the character and situation of the holding and 'other relevant circumstances', to enable an occupier reasonably skilled in husbandry to maintain efficient production as regards both the kind of produce and the quantity and quality of produce. This does not mean that the landlord must provide ancillary services for the tenant on the landlord's estate generally, such as carpenter's yards and workshops, drying-plants, artificial insemination centres, etc. These may have been provided by the landlord, though they are very unlikely to be available in recent times.

The landlord must provide such 'fixed equipment' as is necessary to enable a reasonably skilled occupier to maintain efficient production. The rules also require that the landlord must carry out his legal obligations in relation to the maintenance and repair of fixed equipment provided by him. The landlord's obligations in respect of the fixed equipment will be governed by the terms of the tenancy agreement or the 'model clauses' contained in the Agriculture (Maintenance, Repair and Insurance of Fixed Equipment) Regulations 1973[1].

'Fixed equipment' is a wide term. It was defined, first, by s 109 of the AA 1947. It is now defined in s 96 of the AHA 1986[2], as including not only buildings but also other items which are not so obvious, such as land drainage works, ditches and hedges and belts of woodland and bushes for shelter of stock[3]. The landlord's duties do not end with the provision of the fixed equipment. He must also discharge his duties to improve, maintain and repair, so far as is necessary to sustain efficient production. The extent of the landlord's duties will be governed by the terms of the tenancy agreement and the provisions of the model clauses[4], where appropriate.

There is no mention in s 10 of the AA 1947 of any duty on the landlord to provide materials for repairs which a tenant is liable to carry out. This was quite a common practice in the past, but where a tenant is liable to do repairs he must, in the absence of an express liability on the landlord under a written agreement, provide the necessary materials at his own expense. Provision of materials is not any part of the landlord's duties under the rules of good estate management.

Section 10 of the AA 1947 also requires that the landlord should efficiently manage any other land within his management outside the particular holding in question so far as it would affect the holding[5].

1 SI 1973/1473: see para 23.6.
2 Formerly s 94 of the AHA 1948.
3 For the definition in s 96(1), see para 23.4.
4 See para 23.16ff.
5 For the definition of agricultural land, see s 1 of the AHA 1986: see para 19.4. Note the definition of 'relevant circumstances' in s 109 of the AA 1947 as including 'all circumstances affecting management or farming other than the personal circumstances of the owner or occupier'.

The rules of good husbandry

24.6 An occupier of an agricultural unit is considered to be farming it in accordance with the rules of good husbandry if he is maintaining a reasonable standard of efficient production, having regard to the character and situation of the holding, the owner's standards of management and other 'relevant circumstances'. The obligation is applied to the kind of produce, its quality and quantity. It extends to enabling this standard of production to be maintained in the future.

In deciding whether or not the unit is being farmed according to the rules of good husbandry, the matters set out in s 11(2) of the AA 1947 must be considered[1]. These deal with the condition of permanent pasture, cropping of arable land, cleanliness of the land, stocking of the land, protection and preservation of harvested crops and livestock, including from disease and infestation, and works of maintenance and repair.

It would seem clear that the duty imposed by s 11 of the AA 1947 is substantially more onerous than the tenant's common law duty already referred to[2]. At common law the tenant is not under an obligation to leave the land in good heart and condition on termination of the tenancy. Breaches of the rules of good husbandry may enable the landlord to make a successful application to the Agricultural Land Tribunal for a certificate of bad husbandry. Where notice to quit is served following the grant of such a certificate, disturbance compensation is not payable[3].

Now that the European Union and consequent English domestic legislation is providing incentives to occupiers of agricultural land to reduce or even abandon agricultural production, it is difficult to reconcile the ability of a landlord to dispossess a tenant for non-compliance with the rules of good husbandry, resulting in the granting by an Agricultural Land Tribunal of a certificate of bad husbandry, with compliance with, say, the rules arising from the mid-term review of the Common Agricultural Policy.

Most disputes in relation to the interpretation of the obligations imposed on a tenant consequential upon s 11 of the AA 1947 do not reach the higher courts. In one county court decision, where the court had to consider a contractual obligation contained in the tenancy agreement 'to farm ... in a husbandlike manner', the court decided that this did not incorporate a contractual obligation to comply with the rules of good husbandry contained in s 11 of the AA 1947, but it did require the tenant to protect milk quota so that it remained 'attached' to the holding[4].

[1] For the text of s 11(2) of the AA 1947, see A1.1.
[2] See para 24.3.
[3] See the AHA 1986, Sch 3 Pt I, Case C and s 61.
[4] *Wilson v Hereford and Worcester County Council* (1991) unreported. For a Scottish case in which the rules of good husbandry were extensively considered, see *Cambusmore Estate Trustees v Little* 1991 SLT (Land Ct) 33.

Weeds Act 1959

24.7 Although there is no longer any power in the State to discipline a tenant for breaches of the rules of good husbandry under the agricultural holdings legislation, there is a residual provision under the Weeds Act 1959 (WA 1959) in respect of certain weeds.

The WA 1959 empowers the Minister, where he is satisfied that injurious weeds[1] are growing on any land, to serve a notice on the occupier requiring him, within a specified time, to take such action as may be necessary to prevent the weeds from spreading[2]. The Act confers powers on the Minister to enter onto the land in default[3], and to delegate his powers to the local authority[4]. The Act prescribes penalties for failure to comply with a notice[5].

[1] The Act applies to spear thistle, creeping or field thistle, curled dock, broad-leaved dock and ragwort: WA 1959, s 1(2).
[2] WA 1959, s 1(1).
[3] WA 1959, s 4.
[4] WA 1959, s 5.
[5] WA 1959, s 2.

VARIATION OF TERMS OF TENANCY AS TO PERMANENT PASTURE

24.8 Section 14[1] of the AHA 1986 gives both the landlord and the tenant power to serve notice on the other demanding a reference to arbitration where the tenancy agreement[2] contains a provision that specified land, or a specified proportion of the holding, be maintained as permanent pasture and one party wishes to reduce the extent of the pasture.

'Permanent pasture' is not defined in the AHA 1986 (neither was it in the AHA 1948). There are numerous and conflicting decisions on the meaning attributable to the phrase, the earliest being *Atkins v Temple*[3], and the remainder being eighteenth- and nineteenth-century cases. A combination of factors will normally determine the matter, for example, age, the nature of the herbage and the terms of the tenancy agreement itself.

The question to be determined by arbitration, following such a notice in writing, is 'whether it is expedient in order to secure the full and efficient farming of the holding that the amount of land required to be maintained as permanent pasture should be reduced'[4]. The arbitrator to whom the reference is made may, by his award, direct modifications[5] of the provision in the tenancy agreement as to the land which is to be maintained as permanent pasture or treated as arable, and as to cropping. The tenancy agreement shall then have effect subject to such modifications.

In addition, if the arbitrator directs a reduction in the land to be maintained as permanent pasture, he may order a variation to the provisions in the tenancy agreement. He may provide that on termination of the tenancy the tenant should leave as permanent pasture, or as temporary pasture, with such seeds mixture as may be specified, such additional area of land as he may specify[6]. The area of land to which such an order relates will be additional to the permanent pasture required under the tenancy but must not exceed in area the amount by which the permanent pasture was reduced by the direction contained in the award[7]. Apart from a variation as to permanent pasture being effected by the award of an arbitrator following a reference to arbitration, the parties may, under s 78(2) of the AHA 1986, agree in writing that there should be a variation, such as could be made by direction or order under s 14 of the AHA 1986. Such an agreement may provide for the exclusion of compensation.

[1]   The section originates from s 10 of the AHA 1948 as amended by s 8 and para 6 of Sch 1 to the AA 1958 which was substituted for s 10 of the AHA 1948. It is to be noted that the amendment did not affect the validity of anything done before 1 August 1958, the date of the passing of the AA 1958, in pursuance of an order under the old s 10: see AA 1958, Sch 4 para 1.
[2]   This applies to tenancies whenever granted if within the Agricultural Holdings regime.
[3]   (1626) 1 Rep Ch 13.
[4]   AHA 1986, s 14(2).
[5]   Despite the use of the word 'modifications' in s 14(3), the arbitrator's jurisdiction is confined to considering whether or not there should be a reduction in permanent pasture.
[6]   AHA 1986, s 14(4).
[7]   AHA 1986, s 14(5).

FREEDOM OF CROPPING

24.9 Section 15(1) of the AHA 1986 contains provisions overriding both the tenancy agreement and any custom of the country relating to the disposal of produce (other than manure) and also to the method of cropping arable land[1]. The tenant has general freedom of cropping and disposal of produce, subject to the following restrictions:

(a)   The tenant must, either before 'or as soon as possible' after exercising his rights, make suitable and adequate provision to return to the holding the full equivalent manurial value of all crops sold off or removed from the holding in contravention of any custom, contract or agreement and, in the case of an exercise of the right to practise any system of cropping, to protect the holding from injury or deterioration[2].

(b)   The right to freedom of cropping only applies to 'arable land', but the absence of any restriction on disposing of produce relates to all land, including, for example, hay from land scheduled as pasture[3].

(c)   The rights granted by s 15(1) do not apply:

    (i)   in the case of a tenancy from year to year as respects the year before the tenant quits the holding or any period after he has given or received notice to quit which results in his quitting the holding; or

    (ii)   in the case of any other tenancy, as respects the year before its termination[4].

(d)   Section 15(5) provides specific and exclusive sanctions[5] for a tenant who exercises his rights under s 15(1) in such a way as to be likely to 'injure or deteriorate the holding'. These include an injunction during the currency of the tenancy and damages after termination. It is further provided that for the purpose of the injunction proceedings, the question of injury or deterioration to the holding shall be determined by arbitration under the AHA 1986 and that the award of the arbitrator shall, for the purpose of any of the proceedings brought under s 15(5), including the landlord's claim for damages after the tenant has quit the holding, be conclusive proof of the facts stated in the award[6]. The consequence of these provisions is that the landlord is placed in a very disadvantaged position. Before he can seek an injunction he must obtain an arbitrator's award that injury or deterioration is occurring.

[1]   AHA 1986, s 15(1) is excluded from applying to smallholdings by s 82: see *Williams v Minister of Agriculture, Fisheries and Food* (1986) Times, 17 October, HL as to the duties of the Minister in relation to the organisation of smallholdings.

[2]   AHA 1986, s 15(4).

[3]   In the Scottish case of *Taylor v Steele Maitland* 1913 SC 562, Ct of Sess, arable land was held not to include market gardens.

[4]   AHA 1986, s 15(2). The effect of s 15(2) is probably to exclude the rights granted by s 15(1) in any case during the 12 months preceding the termination of the tenancy (ie irrespective of the length of the notice actually given) and in the case of a longer notice to quit than 12 months, during that longer period.

[5]   An action for damages based on the principle in *Kent v Conniff* [1953] 1 QB 361, [1953] 1 All ER 155, CA, for example, would be excluded.

[6]   AHA 1986, s 15(6). An arbitrator's award is, therefore, a prerequisite for injunction proceedings. It is undecided whether damages could be awarded in lieu of an injunction, or whether damages are available as a remedy at any time prior to the tenant quitting the holding.

PROHIBITION OF REMOVAL OF MANURE

24.10 Unless the landlord and tenant agree otherwise in writing, the tenant is prohibited by s 15(3) of the AHA 1986 at any time after he has given or received notice to quit the holding, from selling or removing from the holding any manure or compost, or any hay or straw or roots[1] grown in the last year of the tenancy, without the landlord's prior written consent.

'Roots' are defined as any root crop[2] of a kind normally grown for consumption on the holding[3]. The AHA 1986 does not provide sanctions for tenants who breach the provisions of s 15(3), but if the landlord were to claim under s 71(1) (in the absence of an express agreement within s 15(3)) for dilapidations on termination, he would be entitled to recover subject to the limitation contained in the subsection to the extent that he suffered loss from the tenant's breach.

¹   *Thomas v National Farmers' Union Mutual Insurance Society Ltd* [1961] 1 All ER 363, [1961] 1 WLR 386, where it was held that the combined effect of s 12(1) and s 47(1) of the AHA 1948 was to pass the property in crops left on the holding to the landlord on termination of the tenancy, thereby rendering him liable to insure. The tenant was then entitled to compensation.
²   For example, mangolds, turnips, sugarbeet, carrots or potatoes.
³   AHA 1986, s 15(9).

STATUTORY RIGHTS

Compensation for damage by game

24.11 Section 20(1) of the AHA 1986 sets out provisions which entitle a tenant to recover damages where his crops have sustained damage from any wild animals or birds, where the sporting rights are vested in the landlord or anyone (other than the tenant himself) to whom the landlord has granted the sporting rights¹. This right does not apply to damage by animals or birds where the tenant himself has permission in writing from the landlord to kill the animals or game in question².

There is as yet no authority on two problems of construction. First, does the adjective 'wild' qualify both animals and birds? It is submitted that it does, in the same way as 'farm labourers' was held to qualify both 'cottages and other houses' in *Paddock Investments Ltd v Lory*³. Second, if so, are hand-reared pheasants which after release exhibit tendencies of tameness really 'wild birds'? It is submitted that once released into the wild, they are then 'wild birds' despite their origins and propensities.

The right gives a remedy to recover damages from the landlord⁴, even though the landlord may have let the shooting rights elsewhere.

The right to recover compensation⁵ is excluded unless the following applies:

(a)   The tenant gives notice in writing to the landlord of the occurrence of the damage within one month after he first became, or ought reasonably to have become, aware of it⁶.
(b)   The tenant gives the landlord a reasonable opportunity to inspect the damage before the crop in question is harvested, if the damage is to a growing crop, or before the crop is removed from the land, if the damage in question is to a crop already harvested⁷. Seed once sown is treated as a growing crop whether or not it has germinated⁸.
(c)   Written notice of the claim, together with particulars of it, must be given to the landlord within one month after the expiry of the year in which the claim is made⁹. It is to be noted that 'year' in this context means any period of 12 months ending, in any year, with 29 September

or such other date as may by agreement between the landlord and the tenant be substituted for that date[10].

1   The revised wording contained in the AHA 1986 protects the tenant's position and enables him to make a claim if the landlord enjoys the sporting rights following a sub-letting by the tenant to him, rather than by means of a reservation.

2   By the former s 14 of the AHA 1948, the right to compensation was restricted to game which by s 14(4) was defined as meaning 'deer, pheasants, partridges, grouse and black game'. These restrictions on the right to compensation were removed by the AHA 1984, Sch 3 para 7.

3   [1975] 2 EGLR 5, 236 Estates Gazette 803.

4   AHA 1986, s 20(1).

5   Contracting out is prohibited: AHA 1986, s 78(1).

6   AHA 1986, s 20(2)(a).

7   AHA 1986, s 20(2)(b). The notice under s 20(2)(a) and (c) and the giving to the landlord of a reasonable opportunity to inspect the damage under s 20(2)(b) are essential prerequisites to the recovery of compensation. The question of whether or not reasonable opportunity has been given to the landlord will depend on all the circumstances.

8   AHA 1986, s 20(3)(a). This provision removes a doubt previously existing as to whether ungerminated seed amounted to a growing crop. The provision was first introduced by the AHA 1984, Sch 3 para 7(2)(c). It is very important because pheasant damage to seed corn is more detrimental normally than any damage caused by the birds just before harvest.

9   AHA 1986, s 20(2)(c).

10   AHA 1986, s 20(3)(b). The provision as enacted in s 14(1)(b) of the AHA 1948 provided for notice of the claim to be given to the landlord within one month after the expiration of the calendar year, or such other period of 12 months as may have been substituted by agreement between landlord and tenant.

24.12 The corresponding provision in the AHA 1948 created problems, especially in relation to damage caused by game to autumn drilled corn shortly after germination, when the extent of the damage, if any, was impossible to assess. The current provisions revise the timetable in relation to the making of a claim by a tenant to take into account this difficulty. They were originally introduced by the AHA 1984[1]. Flexibility has been retained in that the parties can, if they agree, opt for a different date[2].

The amount of compensation payable to the tenant is determined by arbitration under the AHA 1986 and is now unlimited[3]. Although the claim for compensation is against the landlord, he has a specific right to an indemnity from his shooting tenant or licensee, any question arising under this right being determined by arbitration[4].

A tenant can obtain a charge on the holding for game damage compensation[5]. The provisions contained in the AHA 1986 do not interfere with the tenant's rights to kill ground game, ie hares and rabbits, under the Ground Game Act 1880, as amended by the Ground Game (Amendment) Act 1906. This can give rise to problems in practice when a tenant exercises these rights shortly before the landlord's game shoot thereby resulting in the conserved game birds flying off and being available in reduced numbers on the landlord's shoot days.

1   AHA 1984, Sch 3 para 7.

2   AHA 1986, s 20(3)(b).

3   AHA 1948, s 14(1) imposed a limitation of 12p per hectare which over the years had become wholly inadequate. In assessing damages, the arbitrator will be obliged to exclude damage caused by wild animals or birds not satisfying the s 14(1) requirements.

Frequently, there is therefore argument as to the extent of the damage attributable to, eg pigeons and rabbits as opposed to pheasants or other game birds.

4   AHA 1986, s 20(5). This subsection does not refer to the landlord's right to an indemnity as against the tenant or licensee in respect of costs and, accordingly, the landlord is likely to be best protected if, in the absence of an agreement as to the compensation payable to the agricultural tenant, that question and the landlord's rights of indemnity against the shooting tenant or licensee are dealt with simultaneously in one arbitration.

5   AHA 1986, s 85(2).

Record of condition

24.13 Section 22 of the AHA 1986 gives both the landlord and tenant a right at any time during the tenancy to require the making of a record of the condition of the fixed equipment[1] on the holding and of the general condition of the holding itself, including any parts not under cultivation[2]. Moreover, the tenant (but not the landlord) may require the making of a record of any fixtures or buildings which, under s 10 of the AHA 1986[3], he is entitled to remove and of existing improvements executed by him or in respect of the execution of which, with the written consent of the landlord, he paid compensation to an outgoing tenant[4].

In the absence of agreement between landlord and tenant, the record is made by a person appointed by the President of the Royal Institution of Chartered Surveyors[5] and any person thus appointed may, on production of evidence of his appointment, enter the holding at all reasonable times for the purpose of making the record[6]. In default of agreement, the cost of making the record is borne by the landlord and tenant equally.

The record does not in any way restrict the tenant's liability to repair[7]. The mere fact that the holding was in poor condition at the start of the tenancy does not override the general common law rule that a tenant's obligation to keep the holding in repair carries with it an obligation to put into repair in so far as the land and premises were not in repair at the outset[8]. In determining whether a repairing obligation has been complied with as regards any particular item, the arbitrator must have regard to its age and character and its condition at the beginning of the tenancy and of the length of the tenancy[9]. If the tenancy has continued for some years it will be difficult for the tenant to escape liability for repairs, cultivations and condition of hedges and ditches, etc which, as a good husbandman, he should have managed to restore to order[10].

A record of condition prepared, in default of agreement by the parties, by a person appointed by the President of the Royal Institution of Chartered Surveyors, is a precondition to a compensation claim for 'high farming' under s 70 of the AHA 1986[11].

1   AHA 1986, s 96: see 23.4.
2   AHA 1948, s 16 from which s 22 of the AHA 1986 is derived, specifically referred to a record of the condition of the buildings, fences, gates, roads, drains and ditches on, and the cultivation of, the holding and did not make it clear that the record was to cover every aspect of the holding. By amendments originally introduced by Sch 3 para 8(a) to the AHA 1984 the scope of the record had been widened as indicated in the text.
3   See para 23.23.

4   AHA 1986, s 22(1)(b).
5   AHA 1986, s 22(3). The prescribed fee is now £115 payable on application. No value
    added tax is payable. An application unaccompanied by the fee is invalid.
6   AHA 1986, s 22(2). The former s 16(2) of the AHA 1948 did not expressly provide a
    power of entry to the person appointed for the purpose of making the record. This defect
    has now been cured by the additional wording to be found in s 22(2) of the AHA 1986,
    originally introduced by Sch 3 para 8(b) to the AHA 1984.
7   *Evans v Jones* [1955] 2 QB 58, [1955] 2 All ER 118, CA; cf *Proudfoot v Hart* (1890) 25
    QBD 42, CA.
8   *Proudfoot v Hart* (1890) 25 QBD 42.
9   See fn 7 above.
10 *Williams v Lewis* [1915] 3 KB 493.
11 AHA 1986, s 70(3).

Landlord's power of entry

24.14 Section 23 of the AHA 1986[1] should be read in conjunction with
para 4(2) of the Schedule to the Agriculture (Maintenance, Repair and
Insurance of Fixed Equipment) Regulations 1973[2]. The combined effect of
these provisions is to give a landlord a right of entry on to the holding,
notwithstanding the implied covenant for quiet enjoyment, for the purposes
of:

(a)   viewing the state of the holding;
(b)   fulfilling the landlord's responsibilities to manage the holding in accord-
      ance with the rules of good estate management;
(c)   providing or improving fixed equipment on the holding otherwise than
      in fulfilment of the landlord's responsibilities; and
(d)   carrying out repairs if the tenant has not started work on them within
      two months, or has not completed them within three months, of
      receiving written notice from the landlord[3].

The right of entry extends to any person authorised by the landlord and by
s 22 of the AHA 1986 to any person appointed to make a record of condition
of the holding. The landlord or any person authorised by him is not obliged to
seek permission from the tenant or make an appointment. The only restriction
is that the exercise of the right must be at 'reasonable times'.

A tenancy agreement will often reserve a right of entry for the landlord for
other purposes, for example, to take game.

1   Section 23 of the AHA 1986 derives from s 17 of the AHA 1948 which in turn derives
    from s 28 of the Agricultural Holdings Act 1923 (restricting the landlord's power of entry
    to viewing the state and condition of the holding) and s 43 of the AA 1947 (extending the
    landlord's powers of entry for the purposes indicated in (b) and (c) in the text).
2   SI 1973/1473, as amended by SI 1988/281.
3   See para 4(2) of SI 1973/1473.

Penal rents and liquidated damages

24.15 Section 24 of the AHA 1986 provides that a landlord may recover not
more than his actual loss or damage resulting from a breach of a term of a
tenancy, notwithstanding the fact that the tenancy agreement itself may

provide for more substantial or 'penal' damages. At one time it was quite common for agricultural tenancy agreements to include a stipulation that additional rent at a penal level should be paid (though inflation in time made them appear very modest) where the tenant was in breach of covenant, for example, ploughing up pasture, converting land into tillage, removing produce from the premises, taking more than the specified number of successive crops, etc. Section 24 of the AHA 1986, together with s 71(5) of the AHA 1986[1] and s 18(1) of the Landlord and Tenant Act 1927, which deals with repairing covenants, ensures that the landlord's right to recover damages is restricted to actual loss[2]. Section 24 is wider in its application than s 18(1) of the Landlord and Tenant Act 1927. It applies to all breaches (not confined to repairs) by the tenant of the terms of the tenancy agreement.

[1] This provision limits the landlord's claim for dilapidation, deterioration or damage to the holding to the loss in the value of the freehold reversion: see Ch 9.
[2] It is submitted that the interrelationship between s 24 and s 71(5) in respect of claims made under AHA 1986, ss 71(1) and 72 have the effect of cutting down the landlord's entitlement to damages to the diminution in the value of the freehold.

STANDARD LEASEHOLD COVENANTS

24.16 There are a number of standard leasehold covenants which are encountered in practice and which have given rise to issues in relation to tenancies of agricultural holdings protected by the AHA 1986.

Short notice

24.17 Case B of Sch 3 of the AHA 1986 entitles a landlord to possess a holding (or part of it) where land is required for a non-agricultural use for which planning permission has been obtained or where planning permission is not necessary. In such a case, in the absence of an express covenant providing to the contrary in the tenancy agreement, it is necessary for the landlord to give a minimum of 12 months' notice to quit, having established the ability to rely upon Case B, terminating on the term date of the tenancy[1]. Section 25(2)(b) of the AHA 1986 allows the landlord to serve a notice to quit which is less than the statutory minimum period, but only if the notice is given in pursuance of a provision in the contract of tenancy authorising the resumption of possession of the holding for a specified non-agricultural use. A 'specified' non-agricultural use has been held to include a power to repossess for all non-agricultural purposes[2].

A short notice clause is typically of either two or three months' duration. It must allow for at least one month's notice of repossession. This is because a tenant has a statutory right to claim compensation for disturbance[3] and high farming[4], as well as for improvements[5]. The claims for disturbance and high farming are subject to a prerequisite that the tenant must serve a notice of intention to make a claim at least one month prior to the termination of the tenancy. A short notice clause which enables the landlord to resume possession without giving at least one month's notice to the tenant will be void. It prevents the tenant from serving notice to claim compensation and accordingly infringes the rule against 'contracting out' of compensation under the AHA 1986[6].

1   AHA 1986, s 25(1).
2   *Dow Agrochemicals Ltd v E A Lane (North Lynn) Ltd* (1965) 192 Estates Gazette 737; *Paddock Investments Ltd v Lory* [1975] 2 EGLR 5, 236 Estates Gazette 803.
3   See para 38.47.
4   See para 38.87.
5   See para 38.1ff.
6   *Coates v Diment* [1951] 1 All ER 890; *Re Disraeli's Agreement* [1939] Ch 382. As to 'contracting out', see *Johnson v Moreton* [1980] AC 37, [1978] 3 All ER 37, HL and see also para 40.11.

Alienation

24.18 The combined effect of s 6 and Sch 1 to the AHA 1986 enables a landlord to introduce a covenant against alienation into a tenancy agreement if none exists[1]. The form of covenant contained in the AHA 1986 prevents the tenant from assigning, subletting or parting with possession of the whole or any part of the holding.

Incorporation of a prohibition against alienation is of major importance to landlords, particularly following the change in the wording of notices to quit given by reason of death[2]. It should also be noted that assignment in the face of a prohibition against alienation constitutes an irremediable breach of the term of the tenancy giving rise to the possibility of a notice to quit under Case E[3]. It should be noted that the landlord can be estopped by convention from being able to rely upon the covenant against alienation. This occurred in *Troop v Gibson*[4]. In that case the landlord sought to rely upon the clause prohibiting alienation, despite the fact that, during a lengthy period when the tenancy agreement was lost, the parties acted on the common assumption that there was no restriction on assignment and they engaged in rent arbitration proceedings on that basis. Conversely, a tenant will be estopped from denying the existence of a contract of sale or assignment if he allows the assignee to act to his detriment in reliance upon his representation as to the existence of a contract of sale or assignment (for example, by the assignee selling his own farm), even if the contract was entered into by an agent acting without authority[5].

Section 19 of the Landlord and Tenant Act 1927, requiring a landlord's consent to an assignment not to be unreasonably withheld, does not apply to agricultural holdings[6]. The landlord's consent to assignment can therefore be withheld for any reason. It is not subject to the requirements of reasonableness. Where it has been given 'in principle', it cannot be subsequently qualified[7]. Where a standard prohibition or the statutory covenant contained in Sch 1 to the AHA 1986 is included, the tenancy becomes non-assignable because the statutory covenant does not include any provision relating to reasonableness. If a tenant wishes to introduce a provision relating to reasonableness, there must be an express covenant to that effect[8].

1   See para 23.3.

24.18 *Farming: good husbandry and standard leasehold covenants*

2   See AHA 1948, s 24(2)(g), as amended by s 16 of the Agriculture (Miscellaneous Provisions) Act 1976 – now repealed and re-enacted in Sch 3 to the AHA 1986 as Case G. For a commentary on assignments and their interrelationship with succession, see 35.18.
3   As to which, see para 31.76ff. Also see, *Scala House and District Property Co Ltd v Forbes* [1974] QB 575, CA; *Troop v Gibson* [1986] 1 EGLR 1, CA.
4   [1986] 1 EGLR 1, CA.
5   *Worboys v Carter* [1987] 2 EGLR 1, CA.
6   Landlord and Tenant Act 1927, s 19(4).
7   *Aubergine Enterprises Ltd v Lakewood International Ltd* [2001] 3 EGLR 71, (2001) 39 EG 141.
8   If the tenancy agreement does provide for the application of the concept of reasonableness, the criteria approved in *International Drilling Fluids Ltd v Louisville Investments (Uxbridge) Ltd* [1986] Ch 513, CA, will be applied.

24.19 The question as to whether there has been a parting with or sharing of possession sometimes arises in practice. In *Akici v L R Butlin Ltd*[1], Neuberger LJ (as he then was) acknowledged that the difference between possession and occupation can be elusive, but it is a difference which is recognised and should be adhered to. Where the owner had unrestricted access to the property, on the facts in *Akici* it was found that there had been no parting with possession.

What was also noteworthy about the *Akici* decision is that the judge limited the impact of the *Scala House and District Property Co Ltd v Forbes*[2] decision to cases where a legal interest had either been created or transferred. In *Scala House*, the court had held that a breach of a covenant against assignment, subletting or parting with possession is an irremediable breach of covenant. Where, as in *Akici*, the tenant had allowed a company in which the tenant had no formal interest to operate business from the premises, if such an act was in breach of covenant it was remediable.

1   [2005] EWCA Civ 1296, [2006] 1 EGLR 34, [2006] 07 EG 136, overruling *Tulapam Properties Ltd v De Almeida* (1981) 260 Estates Gazette 919.
2   [1974] QB 575, [1973] 3 All ER 308, CA.

Farmhouse residence

24.20 Many tenancy agreements in relation to agricultural holdings protected by the AHA 1986 include a covenant requiring the tenant to reside constantly at the farmhouse on the holding. It creates an obligation to make the farmhouse the usual place of residence of the tenant and for the tenant to have to supervise personally the performance of all of the tenant's obligations, particularly those relating to good husbandry[1]. The obligation does not require unbroken residence at the farmhouse. The suspension of personal occupation for a reasonable period was expressly found to be permitted where it arose consequential upon the death of the tenant[2] and will clearly allow a tenant to take a holiday. Absence for more than a temporary period will constitute a breach of the farmhouse residence covenant, for example, where the tenant is in prison[3]. A breach of a farmhouse residence clause is remediable. Accordingly, a landlord's remedy, within the statutory framework of the AHA 1986, is by way of service of a Case D notice to quit and not a Case E notice to quit[4].

1   *Sumnal v Statt* (1984) 49 P & CR 367, CA; *Lloyds Bank Ltd v Jones* [1955] 2 QB 298, CA.
2   *Lloyds Bank Ltd v Jones* [1955] 2 QB 298 at 324, CA, per Jenkins LJ.
3   *Sumnal v Statt* (1984) 49 P & CR 367; *Amoah v London Borough of Barking and Dagenham* (2001) 82 P & CR DG6.
4   *Sumnal v Statt* (1984) 49 P & CR 367 at 377 per Cummin-Bruce LJ.

User

24.21 A standard provision in a tenancy agreement of an agricultural holding under the AHA 1986 restricts the use of the holding to farming[1]. Sometimes the user covenant is more specific, for example, requiring the holding to be used as a dairy farm. As in the case of a farmhouse residence clause, a breach of the user covenant is remediable. As such a landlord relying upon the statutory framework of the AHA 1986 to recover possession must serve a Case D notice to quit and not a Case E notice to quit.

In the absence of a covenant to the contrary, at common law the tenant is entitled to use the premises demised to him for any lawful purpose. He cannot use them for an illegal purpose[2]. In order to qualify for protection under the AHA 1986, the use of the agricultural holding must be prescribed to be substantially agricultural use[3].

Restrictions as to use have become more an issue as a consequence of greater diversification in agriculture. In *Jewell v McGowan*[4], the Court of Appeal considered the impact of a restriction contained in the tenancy agreement of an agricultural holding limiting the use of the holding 'for agricultural purposes only'. The tenant owned a small area of land adjoining the tenanted land. The tenant wished to encourage members of the public to visit the holding. The tenant proposed to carry out activities which involved the creation of a new farm access, parking for visitors' vehicle, a route-marked trail, an access for visitors to roam, look at crops and animals and to be given rides on trailers pulled by tractors. The bulk of the facilities, such as the shop, tea room, school room, museum and lavatories were intended to be sited on the land owned by the tenant. The Court of Appeal held that the proposed activities would breach the terms of the tenancy agreement. The court held that the proposed commercial enterprise was different in character and purpose from the prescribed agricultural activity and as a consequence, having regard to the use of the word 'only' and the user covenant, would be in breach of the tenancy agreement.

1   Also see Ch 7.
2   *Gas Light and Coke Co v Turner* (1840) 6 Bing NC 324. Note that there is no implied term prohibiting the tenant from using the premises for immoral purposes, see *Burfort Financial Investments v Chotard* [1976] 2 EGLR 53.
3   AHA 1986, s 1(1). See *Howkins v Jardine* [1951] 1 KB 614, CA and para 19.11ff.
4   [2002] EWCA Civ 145, [2002] 3 EGLR 87.

Good husbandry

24.22 It is commonplace to see a covenant contained in a tenancy agreement of an agricultural holding under the AHA 1986 requiring the tenant to observe the rules of good husbandry set out in s 11 of the Agriculture Act 1947[1]. The inclusion of such a covenant makes it a term of the tenancy. This is important because the statutory sanctions formerly contained in the Agriculture Act 1947 have been repealed[2]. By incorporating the statutory obligation to observe the rules of good husbandry into the tenancy agreement enables a landlord to be able to rely upon Case D should it become necessary for the landlord to take steps to enforce this obligation under the terms of the statutory framework contained in the AHA 1986.

[1] See para 24.4.
[2] See para 24.4.

Conservation

24.23 A covenant which is not regularly seen in tenancy agreements of agricultural holdings protected by the AHA 1986 is one relating to conservation. However, clearly the pursuit of conservation objectives could operate contrary to a tenant's obligations to farm in accordance with the rules of good husbandry[1]. The AHA 1986 provides protection to a tenant by reason of Sch 3 para 9(2). This provides that a tenant will be protected in proceedings brought by the landlord before the Agricultural Land Tribunal for a certificate of bad husbandry if the practice complained of is adopted pursuant to a provision in the tenancy, or any other agreement with the landlord, which indicates (in whatever form) that its object is the furtherance of one or more stated conservation objectives, namely the conservation of flora or fauna, the protection of buildings of archaeological/historical interest, and the conservation or enhancement of the natural beauty of the countryside. The ALT must disregard the practice alleged only if it is permitted by a provision in the tenancy or some other written agreement with the landlord (for example, a management agreement to which the landlord is a party). Often such provisions are contained in separate management agreements, for example, if the holding has been notified a Site of Special Scientific Interest under the Wildlife and Countryside Act 1981 or it is in an Environmentally Sensitive Area designated under the Agriculture Act 1986. It is submitted that if the rules of good husbandry have been incorporated as a term of the tenancy agreement, then the inclusion of a conservation covenant should remove the possibility of a landlord seeking to pursue a complaint against the tenant under, for example, Case D.

[1] See para 24.4.

Repair

24.24 As seen in Chapter 23, section 7(3) of the AHA 1986, the Agriculture (Maintenance, Repair and Insurance of Fixed Equipment) Regulations 1973[1], are deemed to be incorporated in all tenancy agreements 'except insofar as they would impose on one of the parties to an agreement in writing a liability which under the agreement is imposed on the other'. The combined effect of s 7 and SI 1973/1473 (as amended) is that the obligations of landlord and tenant set out in the regulations are incorporated in every tenancy agreement wherever the agreement is silent on the matter in question and by this means the statutory obligations are inserted to complete the agreement in respect of those items[2].

The effect of case authority in relation to consideration of the 'model clauses' is that it is possible that if the tenancy agreement expressly relieves the tenant of a liability which would otherwise be imposed upon the tenant under the 'model clauses', a lacuna may emerge where neither party is responsible for a particular obligation[3].

Conversely, it is possible to impose on one party an obligation which is placed on the other by model clauses. This occurred in *Roper v Prudential Assurance Co Ltd*[4] where the tenant's express repairing obligations extended to electrical wiring in the context of a general obligation to repair and maintain the farmhouse, cottages and buildings on the holding. Repair in this case was held to include replacing the existing electrical wiring and installations in the farmhouse, an obligation which the model clauses placed on the landlord where the wiring was in need of replacement due to age (and not the neglect of the tenant). Liability therefore was imposed on the tenant, reversing the model clause liability for replacement which would have fallen on the landlord.

[1] SI 1973/1473, as amended by the Agriculture (Maintenance, Repair and Insurance of Fixed Equipment) (Amendment) Regulations 1988, SI 1988/281, effective from 24 March 1988. The regulations previously in force were SI 1948/184.
[2] See 23.6.
[3] *Burden v Hannaford* [1956] 1 QB 142, [1955] 3 All ER 401, CA.
[4] [1992] 1 EGLR 5, [1992] 09 EG 141.

Quota protection

24.25 The introduction of milk quota[1] in April 1984, consequential upon the Dairy Produce Quotas Regulations 1984[2], introduced a new issue. Milk quota has been determined to be referable to 'areas of land used for dairy production' within a holding[3] and to be 'attached' to the holding[4]. The Agricultural Holdings Act 1948 was amended by the Agriculture Act 1986 in order to introduce compensation payable to tenants in relation to milk quota upon the termination of a tenancy protected under the AHA 1948. The provisions are now consolidated in the AHA 1986. However, a question arose as to whether the tenant was free to be able to deal with the milk quota prior to the termination of the tenancy and accordingly enjoy the full value of the quota.

It was not unusual for pre-milk quota tenancy agreements of agricultural holdings protected by the AHA 1986 to include a covenant relating to quotas. This practice arose in relation to landlords seeking to protect themselves in relation to, for example, potato marketing schemes. In *Lee v Heaton*[5], it was held that a covenant 'not to dispose of the whole or any part of any basic quota under a marketing scheme' did not apply to prevent a disposition of milk quota.

24.25   *Farming: good husbandry and standard leasehold covenants*

Notwithstanding the inability of a landlord to be able to rely upon a covenant referable to basic quota under a marketing scheme in order to protect his interests in respect of milk quota allocated to an agricultural holding following its introduction in April 1984, in practice the landlord's position was protected during the term of the tenancy provided that the tenancy contained an anti-alienation provision. Even if it did not, the landlord was able to introduce one by the expedient of serving a notice pursuant to s 6 of the AHA 1986[6]. The reason for this is that, save in exceptional cases[7], the Dairy Produce Quotas Regulations, in force from time to time after 1984[8], provided for the transfer and re-registration of ownership of milk quota pursuant to a change of occupation of a holding (or part of it) pursuant to an agreement granting rights of occupation of a minimum of ten months. As a consequence, a tenant was unable to transfer milk quota in the face of an anti-alienation provision without running the risk of a landlord being able to serve a Case E notice to quit in relation to any irremediable breach of covenant.

The position with regard to the disposal of milk quota changed when the Dairy Produce Quotas Regulations 2000[9] came into force. The 2000 Regulations broke the linkage between a transfer of milk quota and the grant of an interest in the holding or part of it of a minimum of ten months. Accordingly, the landlord's ability to restrict a tenant dealing with milk quota prior to the termination of a tenancy can no longer rely upon the anti-alienation provision. The landlord therefore requires an express quota protection clause to be included in an AHA 1986 tenancy agreement[10].

Milk quotas have survived the Mid-term Review of the Common Agricultural Policy. That Review has, with effect from May 2005, introduced new 'quota' rights in the form of 'entitlements'. It is 'entitlements' which give rise to a farmer's right to 'Single Payments' under the reformed Common Agricultural Policy[11]. Unlike milk quota, entitlements do not 'attach' to the holding. Accordingly, if the landlord and tenant under an AHA 1986 tenancy wish to regulate their agreement in respect of entitlements and the consequential Single Payment income stream, they must provide for this by way of an express covenant in the tenancy agreement.

The parties may wish to consider, when revising terms of an AHA 1986 tenancy, the following questions.

(a)   Is the quota/entitlements to remain 'attached' to the holding upon the termination of the tenancy?

(b)   Is the tenant to deal with the quota/entitlements in a particular manner during the term of the tenancy, for example, is leasing out permitted?

(c)   What compensation (if any) should be paid to the landlord if the tenant can dispose of the quota/entitlements during the course of the tenancy?

(d)   What compensation (if any)[12] should be paid to the tenant if the quota/entitlements is to remain with the holding at the termination of the tenancy?

---

1   For the leading analysis of the law relating to milk quotas, see M N Cardwell, *Milk Quotas: European Community and United Kingdom Law* (1996) Oxford University Press.
2   SI 1984/1047.
3   *Puncknowle Farms Ltd v Kane* [1985] 2 EGLR 8, 275 Estates Gazette 1283.

4   *Faulks v Faulks* [1992] 1 EGLR 9, [1992] 15 EG 82; *Harries v Barclays Bank plc* [1997]
    2 EGLR 15; *Davies v H & R Ecroyd Ltd* [1996] 30 EG 97. Cf *Swift v Dairywise
    Farms Ltd* [2000] 1 All ER 320 , CA and *Cottle v Caldicott* [1995] STC (SCD) 239.
5   [1987] 2 EGLR 12.
6   See para 23.1.
7   The position changed in 1992 with the introduction of transfers without land: See para
    49.29.
8   This applied in each set of the Dairy Produce Quotas Regulations from 1984 up to and
    including those of 1997: SI 1997/733.
9   The relevant legislation is now contained in the Dairy Produce Quotas Regulations 2005,
    SI 2005/465, reg 13.
10 See para 49.32.
11 See Ch 52.
12 Outside the terms of the Agriculture Act 1986, see Ch 50.

Forfeiture

24.26 A landlord has a wide range of statutory rights under the AHA 1986 in
respect of which he may, in the circumstances specified, give a notice to quit to
the tenant for the purpose of seeking to terminate the tenancy. Cases D and E
provide grounds for a landlord to be able to give a notice to quit in the event
of a breach of covenant on the part of the tenant. Case F enables the landlord
to be able to give notice to quit in the event of the insolvency of the tenant. In
addition to these rights, the landlord can rely upon the general law of
forfeiture[1].

In order to be able to forfeit a tenancy of an agricultural holding under the
AHA 1986, it is first necessary for the tenancy agreement to include a
forfeiture clause, otherwise known as a proviso for re-entry. Where the
tenancy is oral or it is written, but does not include a forfeiture clause, the
landlord can seek the introduction of a forfeiture clause into the tenancy
consequential upon the landlord serving a notice pursuant to s 6 of the AHA
1986, activating the statutory procedure for reducing the tenancy into writing
to cover the matters contained in Sch 1 to the AHA 1986[2]. One of the
clauses contained in Sch 1 of the AHA 1986 is a proviso for re-entry.

Where there is a forfeiture clause in a tenancy of an agricultural holding under
the AHA 1986, in order for it to be valid, it is necessary for it to fulfil another
criterion. It must include the provision for the right to forfeit to be exercisable
on the expiry of some period of notice exceeding one month. In *Parry v
Million Pigs Ltd*[3], it was held that a forfeiture clause which provided for no
notice of re-entry, or notice of less than one month, will be void as it would
prevent the tenant from serving notice to claim compensation under ss 60(6)
and 70(2) (for disturbance and high farming) under the AHA 1986. It would
infringe the rule against 'contracting out'[4].

1   See para 33.8 and Ch 13.
2   See para 23.2.
3   (1980) 260 Estates Gazette 281.
4   AHA 1986, s 78(1). See *Coates v Diment* [1951] 1 All ER 890; *Re Disraeli's Agreement*
    [1939] Ch 382. Also see para 40.11.

Chapter 25

RENT REVIEW

GENERAL RENT REVIEW

Introduction

General

25.1 A consequence of the long-term security of tenure provided by the Agricultural Holdings Act 1986 (AHA 1986), removing or varying the normal common law contractual rights of termination, is that either party should be free at appropriate intervals during the currency of the tenancy to have the rent payable reviewed by reference to current financial conditions prevailing from time to time. Before the passing of the Agricultural Holdings Act 1984 (AHA 1984), that invariably meant that the rent fell to be increased on review. After 1984, rent arbitrations at the instigation of the tenant seeking a reduction in rent became commonplace before rents started to rise again in the mid-1990s.

In addition to rent reviews referable to current economic circumstances, the rent can be revised because of a change in what has been provided by the landlord. Landlord's additional fixed equipment, the erection of buildings, the provision of drainage or irrigation, etc can result in a rent increase.

Rent reviews by reason of both changed economic circumstances (under AHA 1986, s 12 and Sch 2), and the provision by the landlord of improvements (under s 13) are considered in detail in this chapter.

Rent assessment on review is essentially an exercise in valuation rather than strict application of legally defined principles. The role of the courts in rent reviews was described by Forbes J in *Estates Projects Ltd v Greenwich London Borough*[1] as follows:

> 'Now this court is not a valuer. All I can do is to say whether there is an error of law if a method of valuation is adopted which clearly does not follow the intention of [Parliament]. I can say therefore whether a method of valuation is wrong but not necessarily what method of valuation is right'.

The uncertainty, unpredictability and range of 'right' answers that can therefore be produced is exacerbated, particularly since 1984 (when the current rent formula was introduced) by the formula itself. As will be seen, it requires the 'rent properly payable' to be assessed. It is explicit as to what must be taken into account, but wholly silent as to whether the resultant rent 'properly payable' is to be governed primarily by current market levels or what a prospective tenant could afford to pay from his earnings derived from the holding (an 'economic' or 'sustainable' rent) or some other criteria.

[1] [1979] 2 EGLR 85, 251 Estates Gazette 851.

Historical

25.2 The rent review procedure was first introduced in the Agricultural Holdings Act 1948 (AHA 1948), which provided for reviews to take place by means of a very informal procedure[1] whereby the matter could be referred to an arbitrator. The arbitrator had power to increase or reduce the rent or direct that it should remain unchanged. The AHA 1948, as originally enacted, merely directed the arbitrator to determine the rent that he was to assess should be 'the rent properly payable'. There was no guidance to him as to how that rent was to be arrived at.

From an early stage there was a very wide variation in the level of rents fixed by arbitration. Some arbitrators sought to ensure that the rent was kept in line with current open market rents. Others preferred to determine the rent properly payable by apportioning between landlord and tenant the notional income which would be derived from the holding, the apportionment varying from one arbitrator to another. For many years some valuers even stoutly maintained that the two approaches were the same.

Section 2 of the Agriculture Act 1958 (AA 1958) was enacted with a view to standardising rents. Section 2 of the AA 1958 required that the 'rent properly payable' was to be the rent at which, having regard to specified factors, 'the holding might reasonably be expected to be let in the open market by a willing landlord to a willing tenant'. There were various factors which fell to be disregarded with a view to ensuring that the open market rent to be assessed did not, for example, require the tenant to pay any additional rent by reason of improvements effected by the tenant himself.

The then Minister of Agriculture, Sir John Hare, when introducing the Agriculture Bill which became the Act of 1958, said:

> 'Surely the existing tenant of a farm can reasonably be asked to pay the rent which a new tenant coming into the farm would pay. The existing tenant rightly enjoys security of tenure but most people will agree I think that security should not mean the right to farm at a rent below the market level'.

Thereafter, for a variety of reasons, landowners became increasingly more reluctant to let or relet their land on a basis providing the tenant with security of tenure and preferred either to take land in hand and farm it themselves or to make some other arrangements for the farming of the holding not involving the grant of a tenancy carrying with it security of tenure.

1   See s 8 of the AHA 1948 (as originally enacted). Cf the Landlord and Tenant Act 1954, Pt II, and the Rent Acts for different forms of machinery for rent revision as an incident of security of tenure.

25.3 The consequence of this in terms of rentals was that, on the rare occasions when farms came onto the open market for letting, the demand was very substantial. Many established farmers, wishing to increase their acreage, were prepared to tender (and many landlords were prepared to accept) rents substantially in excess of the rent which could be justified by reference to the income which would be generated from farming the holding. Many tenderers for new farms were even prepared to tender a rent which would show that the farm would have to be farmed at a loss in the hope that the effects of inflation on the value of farm input would reduce the rent in real terms to a more economic figure and that the arbitrator, at the first rent review, would be reluctant to maintain the rent at the figure tendered, whether or not, technically, it represented 'open market' value.

Potential tenants, who already occupied other land, could justify a high tender rent by averaging the rental cost applicable to the new letting over the whole of their agricultural unit. Many bidders were prepared to wait for inflation to reduce in real terms the rent being paid by them. This was a phenomenon of the 1960s and 1970s. Landlords reacted to this by claiming against their sitting-tenants that tender rents were the best, if not the only, evidence of market value for the purposes of successive rent reviews under s 8 of the AHA 1948, and began to seek high figures which many protected tenants could not afford to pay.

The Northfield Report[1] recommended that amendments to the existing Agricultural Holdings legislation (then contained in the AHA 1948, as amended by a series of subsequent Acts) should be agreed between government and the organisations involved in the agriculture industry, notably the National Farmers' Union (NFU) (representing the interests of tenants) and the Country Landowners' Association (CLA) (representing the interests of landlords). The AHA 1984 was based on a series of measures agreed by the NFU and the CLA. It also incorporated a large number of technical amendments, implementing many of the Northfield Report's recommendations. The AHA 1984 received Royal Assent on 12 July 1984 and came into force on 12 September 1984. One of these was a revision of the rental formula designed to ensure that the rent properly payable was closely related to the rent which a competent tenant farming the holding could reasonably afford to pay in the agricultural economic climate viewed at the time of the rent review.

To give effect to this intention, s 1 of the AHA 1984 contained a substantial redefinition of the 'rent properly payable', together with a number of other refinements of the factors to be disregarded[2]. It now seems doubtful that the intention of the NFU/CLA package was achieved by the formula enacted in what is now Sch 2 to the AHA 1986 in view of the obiter dicta in *J W Childers Trustees v Anker*[3].

The 1948 Act and its amending statutes, including the AHA 1984, were all repealed and re-enacted in the current consolidating statute – the Agricultural Holdings Act 1986 – in which all the statutory procedures relating to rent reviews are now contained.

1   In 1977, prompted by growing concern about large financial institutions purchasing agricultural land, a Committee of Inquiry was set up under Lord Northfield to examine trends in the Acquisition and Occupancy of Agricultural Land. The Northfield Report was published in 1979.
2   For a practitioner's guide to the AHA 1984, see Troup DAG, 'Agricultural Holdings Act 1984', Royal Institution of Chartered Surveyors.
3   [1996] 1 EGLR 1, [1996] 01 EG 102, CA. See para 25.18.

Outline of the current law

25.4 Section 12 and Sch 2 to the AHA 1986 set up a procedural code which is generally informal, but contains a number of technicalities which need careful consideration.

In outline, the rent review procedure commences when either the landlord or the tenant may demand arbitration as to the rent properly payable. The new rent then takes effect from the earliest date on which the tenancy could next have been terminated by notice to quit, ie the first annual term date of the tenancy not earlier than 12 months following the date of the demand. Subject to specified exceptions, such reviews can take place not more than once every three years.

Where the AHA 1986 applies to a new tenancy by virtue of the operation of s 4(1)(g) of the Agricultural Tenancies Act 1995 (ATA 1995), and the rent is unchanged from the rent payable under the previous tenancy, disregarding any changes resulting from adjustments to the boundary of the holding, the three-year rent review cycle is uninterrupted[1].

The arbitrator must determine the rent properly payable in accordance with the statutory rental formula. The rent property payable in respect of a holding is the rent at which the holding might reasonably be expected to be let by a prudent and willing landlord to a prudent and willing tenant[2], taking into account all relevant factors, including (in every case):

(a)   the terms of the tenancy (including those relating to rent)[3];
(b)   the character and situation of the holding (including the locality in which it is situated)[4];
(c)   the productive capacity of the holding[5] and its related earning capacity[6]; and
(d)   the current levels of rents for comparable lettings[7].

He is required to disregard factors such as tenant's improvements, tenant's fixtures, the grant-aided element of landlord's improvements, 'high farming', the fact that the tenant is in occupation, any tenant's dilapidations and the like[8].

The arbitrator is expressly directed to disregard certain matters.

25.4 *Rent review*

The arbitrator must determine whether the rent should be increased, reduced or remain the same and must award the appropriate rent in consequence.

Both The Royal Institution of Chartered Surveyors and The Central Association of Agricultural Valuers publish excellent Guidance Notes for valuers acting in relation to valuations under the AHA 1986[9].

The tenancy continues with the arbitrator's awarded rent substituted for the rent previously payable. The parties can, of course (and usually will) agree the rent rather than go through the entire statutory arbitration procedure.

[1]   AHA 1986, Sch 2 para 7, inserted by the Regulatory Reform (Agricultural Tenancies) (England and Wales) Order 2006 (RRO 2006), SI 2006/2805, art 8.
[2]   AHA 1986, Sch 2 para 1(1).
[3]   AHA 1986, Sch 2 para 1(1). The arbitrator must take account of the existing rent: *Enfield London Borough Council v Pott* [1990] 2 EGLR 7, [1990] 34 EG 60.
[4]   AHA 1986, Sch 2 para 1(1). See para 25.20.
[5]   AHA 1986, Sch 2 paras 1(1) and (2)(a). See para 25.21.
[6]   AHA 1986, Sch 2 paras 1(1) and (2)(b). See para 25.21.
[7]   AHA 1986, Sch 2 para 1(1). See para 25.30ff.
[8]   AHA 1986, Sch 2 paras 1(3) and 2(1), (2). See para 25.36ff.
[9]   Available respectively from Surveyor Court, Westwood Business Park, Coventry CV4 8JE and Market Chambers, 35 Market Place, Coleford, Gloucestershire GL16 8AA.

Procedure

25.5 As with the exercise of all rights granted by the agricultural holdings legislation, strict compliance with the statutory procedures for the exercise of such rights is essential if the rights are not to be lost or statute barred. Rent reviews are no exception to this general proposition and indeed have procedural complications of their own which must be most carefully followed.

In brief, these are as follows:

(a)   the party wishing to seek the review must give a demand for arbitration which is the notice which triggers the whole arbitration procedure;
(b)   then, if the notice is not to lapse and become statute barred, either an arbitrator must have been appointed or an application to the President of the Royal Institution of Chartered Surveyors must have been made before the next date on which the tenancy could have been terminated at the date when the trigger notice was given;
(c)   thereafter, once the arbitrator has been appointed the general provisions applicable to all arbitrations under the AHA 1986 apply[1].

In general, statutory rent reviews cannot take place more than once every three years. There are further jurisdictional and procedural matters to be considered which are dealt with below.

[1]   See Ch 47.

The trigger notice

25.6 By virtue of s 12(1) of the AHA 1986 the right to instigate a rent review is given both to the landlord and the tenant. The party wishing to revise the rent must give a demand for arbitration in writing. Such a demand must require the rent payable to be referred to arbitration 'as from the next termination date'. By virtue of s 12(4) of the AHA 1986 the next termination date is defined by reference to the earliest date at which the tenancy could have been terminated by notice to quit. That normally means the first term date not less than 12 months after the giving of the demand for arbitration. Thus, if the annual term date of the tenancy is 29 September and a landlord or tenant wishes to refer the rent to arbitration and thereby to effect a review of the rent, he must give his demand for arbitration before, say, 29 September 2006 if the rent is to be revised with effect from 29 September 2007. In those circumstances, if on the facts of the particular case, the tenancy could be terminated on the 28th or 29th September in the year following, the 'next' termination date would be the 28th and not the 29th September[1].

A problem met in recent years has been as to whether a party, having given a demand for arbitration, who then decides that he does not wish to have the rent revised (for example because he is the landlord and rents are going down), can withdraw the notice. It has been held in one county court case that a demand for arbitration is a trigger notice which once given cannot be 'ungiven'. The recipient is as entitled as the giver of the notice to rely upon it and to pursue the arbitration[2]. It is submitted that that decision is clearly right, particularly if the recipient of the notice has taken some step to his detriment in reliance upon it, or has forgone a right, for example to give notice himself.

[1] *Yeandle v Reigate and Banstead Borough Council* [1996] 1 EGLR 20, [1996] 14 EG 90, CA.
[2] *Buckinghamshire County Council v Gordon* [1986] 2 EGLR 8, 279 Estates Gazette 853.

Appointment of arbitrator

25.7 The notice once given will not endure for ever. The parties must either agree upon the appointment of an arbitrator before the 'next termination date', or else one or other party must apply to the President of the Royal Institution of Chartered Surveyors (RICS) for the appointment of an arbitrator[1]. There was no statutorily prescribed time limit of this sort before the passing of the AHA 1984, though the Court of Appeal had decided that in effect such a time limit was implied[2].

The 'next termination date' is the next date on which the tenancy could have been terminated by notice to quit. If, as in most cases, there are two alternative such dates, it is this earlier date which is the 'next'. The appointment of the arbitrator or the application to the RICS must in either case have been effected *before* and not on the *next* termination date[3].

An arbitrator is appointed by the President at the time that the President executes the appointment itself[4], but he is not appointed by agreement until he has accepted the appointment and all the parties have been notified[5]. It is vital that if the parties agree as to who the arbitrator should be, they should perfect the appointment before the term date. What is more, once having agreed who the arbitrator should be, there is no procedure available for applying to the President for an arbitrator, since the President of the RICS's jurisdiction is to appoint an arbitrator only in default of agreement[6]. Difficulties can be experienced in practice if discussion regarding the identity of the arbitrator is left to a late stage before the term date from which the new rent is to take effect. If an arbitrator is then agreed upon, but the procedures for appointing him, notifying him and obtaining his acceptance, etc, are not completed, the right to apply to the President of the RICS will be lost if the application to the RICS is not made by the next term date.

[1] AHA 1986, s 12(3). Also see, *Bradley v Thompson* (2006) Birmingham County Court, Lawtel, 15 January 2007: para 42.16.
[2] *Sclater v Horton* [1954] 2 QB 1, [1954] 1 All ER 712; *University College, Oxford v Durdy* [1982] Ch 413, [1982] 1 All ER 1108.
[3] See the commentary on the trigger notices, para 25.6 and, in particular, *Yeandle v Reigate and Banstead Borough Council* (1996) 14 EG 90.
[4] See the AHA 1986, Sch 11 para 31.
[5] For a county court case to this effect, see *Richards v Allinson* (1978) 249 Estates Gazette 59 and note the cases cited in it. Also see *Robinson v Moody* [1994] 2 EGLR 16, [1994] 37 EG 154, CA and *Hannaford v Smallacombe* [1994] 1 EGLR 9, CA.
[6] AHA 1986, Sch 11 para 1(1).

25.8 No application may be made to the President of the RICS earlier than four months before the date from which the new rent is to take effect. In the case of the example, therefore, of the notice given before 29 September 2007 to take effect on 29 September 2008, no application could be made to the President of the RICS for the appointment of an arbitrator until 29 May 2008[1] or possibly 28 May 2008.

It was the case that the date of appointment of the arbitrator was of importance in determining the level of rent properly payable. This was because the arbitrator did not have to fix the rent by reference to current rent conditions applying at the date from which the new rent runs (in the example given, 29 September 2008) but by reference to conditions applying at the date of his appointment which, normally, was earlier than the date from which the new rent comes into effect. There was no statutory direction to this effect, but the matter was determined by the Court of Appeal[2].

This issue has been resolved by the RRO 2006. Section 12(2) of the AHA 1986 has been amended. No longer is it the case that the arbitrator now determines the rent properly payable at the next termination date[3] following the date of the demand for arbitration: 29 September 2008 in the example[4].

All the other matters relating to the appointment of an arbitrator referred to in the chapter on arbitration should also be taken into account[5]. Although an arbitrator has to be appointed before the term date, if the arbitrator appointed dies or is incapable of acting or refuses to act after notice, a new arbitrator appointed, even though appointed after the term date, is deemed to be appointed in time[6].

1   AHA 1986, Sch 11 para 1(3).
2   *Sclater v Horton* [1954] 2 QB 1, [1954] 1 All ER 712. It could be later if the application for the appointment was before 29 September 2007 but the actual appointment was later (in the given example).
3   AHA 1986, s 12(4).
4   The RRO 2006, SI 2006/2805, art 3.
5   See Ch 47.
6   AHA 1986, Sch 2 para 3 giving statutory effect to the county court decision in *Pennington-Ramsden v McWilliam* [1982] CLY 28.

Subsequent procedures

25.9 The procedures for assessing the rent after the arbitrator has been appointed are the same as for all other arbitrations[1]. A hearing will be convened; evidence adduced etc, before the arbitrator ultimately makes his award. The prescribed time limits must be strictly complied with. An arbitrator is not a valuer appointed to fix the rent, but the equivalent of a judge appointed to adjudicate between two conflicting points of view and sets of evidence[2].

1   See para Ch 47.
2   *Fox v P G Wellfair Ltd* (1981) 263 Estates Gazette 589, CA.

Frequency of rent reviews

25.10 The general rule (subject to exceptions) is that the rent of an agricultural holding can only be reviewed once every three years. If a demand for arbitration is given to take effect earlier than three years from the last rent review, or from the start of the tenancy, the demand for arbitration is ineffective. The demand itself can, and invariably will, be given before the expiration of three years from the last rent review because not less than 12 months' notice must be given. It is the date from which the notice takes effect which is the relevant date in determining whether the notice is premature by reference to the three-year rule and not the date of service.

The AHA 1986[1] provides that the dates from which the rent is fixed for three years are as follows:

(a)   the commencement of the tenancy; or
(b)   the date on which the last variation in the rent occurred[2]; or
(c)   the date on which an arbitrator awarded that there should be no variation in the rent.

Paragraph 4(2) of Sch 2 to the AHA 1986 sets out certain circumstances in which alterations in rent are specifically provided for in the AHA 1986, and which are to 'be disregarded for the purposes' of para 4(1)(b). One of those is boundary changes[3].

There are a number of exceptions to this general rule.

First, where there has been a variation in the rent because of an arbitrator's award specifying the terms of a written tenancy agreement. In such circumstances if the existing terms of the tenancy are varied, there is a consequential variation in the rent. This will not involve a comprehensive review of the rent by reference to current economic circumstances and, therefore, will not result in the three-year rent review cycle being triggered[4].

Second, a rent review where an arbitrator has made an award bringing the terms of the tenancy in line with the model clauses[5]. This can occur where the terms of the tenancy as to repairs are inconsistent with the statutorily prescribed model clauses. In those circumstances the tenant may demand arbitration under s 8 of the AHA 1986, in which event the terms of the tenancy will be revised to bring them in line with the terms of the model clauses. This may well have an effect on the rent; either to increase it, if the tenant is being relieved of liability, or to reduce it, if the tenant is undertaking liability. That will not involve a comprehensive review of the overall rent by reference to current economic circumstances – hence the statutory exception to such a provision triggering time for the three-year rent review cycle[6].

An increase in rent by reason only of improvements carried out by the landlord pursuant to s 13 of the AHA 1986 or a reduction in consequence of any change in the fixed equipment provided on the holding will not disturb the three-year rent review cycle[7]. This exception has the same justification as the exceptions referred to above[8].

[1] AHA 1986, Sch 2 para 4(1).
[2] Whether by agreement or arbitration and whether up or down. But an agreed standstill is not relevant. Cf an arbitrator's award of no change. Also see para 25.4
[3] AHA 1986, Sch 2 para 6. See para 25.12.
[4] AHA 1986, s 6(3) and Sch 2 para 4(2)(a).
[5] AHA 1986, s 8(4) and Sch 2 para 4(2)(a).
[6] See para 27.4ff.
[7] AHA 1986, s 13(1), (3) and Sch 2 para 4(2)(b).
[8] This provision has been extensively considered in *Mann v Gardner* (1990) 61 P & CR 1, [1991] 1 EGLR 9, CA, and in *Secretary of State for Defence v Spencer* [2002] EWHC 2116 (Ch), [2003] 1 WLR 75; affd [2003] EWCA Civ 784, [2003] 1 WLR 2701 (see para 25.13). It should be noted that in the *Secretary of State for Defence v Spencer* case, the Court of Appeal decided that the conclusion (but not the reasoning) of the Court of Appeal in *Mann v Gardner* was per incuriam: see para 25.12ff.

25.11 If there is a reduction in rent as the result of the landlord recovering possession of part of the holding under s 33 of the AHA 1986, or under a provision to that effect in the tenancy agreement, such a reduction will not cause the recommencement of the three-year rent review cycle. This too is for the same reason as the earlier exceptions. Paragraph 4(2)(c) of Sch 2 to the AHA 1986 reproduces the wording of s 8(3)(iii) of the AHA 1948.

The severance of the landlord's reversion does not itself create new tenancies of the severed parts, neither does partition of the tenant's leasehold interest[1]. Following severance, the tenant may enter into new contracts of tenancy with the owners of the severed portions of the reversionary interest. In order to prevent this from triggering the three-year rent review cycle, para 5 of Sch 2 to the AHA 1986 provides that the period of review shall be calculated by reference to the commencement date of the original tenancy and its subsequent rent reviews, but only when the rent payable in respect of the new holding represents merely the 'appropriate portion of the rent payable in respect of the original holding'. The appropriate portion is not defined. It needs to be determined by reference to the size of the new holding, compared with the old holding, and its relative productive capacity, compared to that of the original holding.

It has been held that a rent formula contained in a tenancy agreement which resulted in a fluctuating rent does not perpetually preclude a rent review because there was no increase or reduction in the rent each time the formula was operated until the formula itself was changed[2]. Although this decision clearly provided a just and equitable result on the facts of the particular case, it is doubtful whether it can strictly be reconciled with the statutory wording.

1   *Jelley v Buckman* [1974] QB 488, CA; *Lester v Ridd* [1990] 2 QB 430, [1989] 1 All ER 1111; *John v George and Watton* (1995) 71 P & CR 375, CA.
2   *Bolesworth Estate Co Ltd v Cook* (1966) 116 NLJ 1318, CC, where the rent was linked to the price of milk.

Boundary changes

25.12 Boundary changes have given rise to problems in practice in relation to the operation of the three-year rent review cycle. Paragraph 6 of Sch 2 to the AHA 1986 provides:

> 'Where under an agreement between the landlord and the tenant of the holding (not being an agreement expressed to take effect as a new contract of tenancy between the parties) provision is made for adjustment of the boundaries of the holding or for any other variation of the terms of the tenancy, exclusive of those relating to rent, then, unless the agreement otherwise provides (a) that provision shall for the purposes of sub-paragraph (1) of paragraph 4 above be treated as not operating to terminate the tenancy, and accordingly as not resulting in the commencement of a new contract of tenancy between the parties, and (b) any increase or reduction of rent solely attributable to any such adjustment or variation as aforesaid shall be disregarded for the purposes of paragraph (b) of that sub-paragraph'.

In *Mann v Gardner*[1], during the three-year cycle the tenant surrendered a surplus farmhouse and curtilage. The rent was reduced by £100 per annum. The tenant demanded arbitration to secure a rent reduction. The landlord also demanded arbitration for a rent increase. The landlord did not pursue his demand. The tenant obtained an appointment of an arbitrator. The landlord put in a statement of case seeking a rent increase (later abandoned). The tenant sought a reduction. At the hearing the landlord raised a jurisdictional issue. The tenant in reply argued:

(a)   the surrender of a farmhouse, plus the reduction pro rata in the rent, constituted a reduction of rent in consequence of the change in the fixed equipment provided on the holding by the landlord;[2]

(b)   the rent variation was because of a boundary change, ie the removal of the house and its curtilage[3].

It was held by the Court of Appeal that:

(i)   there was not a change in fixed equipment. That only applied to the removal of, say, the bricks and mortar of a building, not the land, even if the land is merely the site of the building. The surrender of a farmhouse, being part of the holding, constitute a change in the holding itself;

(ii) there was not a boundary change, even though the boundaries were thereafter in fact changed.

Accordingly, the three-year rent review cycle had been triggered by the surrender of the farmhouse. The landlord succeeded.

¹   (1990) 61 P & CR 1, CA.
²   AHA 1986, Sch 2 para 4(2)(b).
³   AHA 1986, Sch 2 para 6.

25.13 The issues arising in respect of boundary changes were again considered by the Court of Appeal in *Secretary of State for Defence v Spencer*¹. The facts were that an area of 1.156 acres was added to the tenancy. The tenant argued that this had the effect of shielding him from having a rent review for a period of three years from the date when a formal agreement was entered into confirming the addition of the land. This replicated an alternative argument raised by the tenants in *Mann v Gardner*², namely that the agreement by which the cottage in that case was surrendered was one by which 'provision [was] made for adjustment of the boundaries of the holding' within para 6 of Sch 2 to the AHA 1986.

In *Mann v Gardner*³ Nourse LJ said:

'a surrender of part of the holding to the landlord which is not an arrangement, putting in order harmonisation or adoption (those are the dictionary meanings 'adjustment') of the boundaries between the holding and some other property cannot fall within paragraph 6. It is impossible to describe the surrender which took place here as having been any of those things. On the facts of this case the point is put beyond argument by the location of [the cottage], not on the boundary of the holding, but at its centre. Even if it has been on the boundary, my conclusion would have been the same. If [the tenant's counsel's] argument were correct, it would not only defy the natural and ordinary meaning of the expression which has to be applied. It would enable paragraph 6 to be used as a wholesale means of escaping from the effects of paragraph 4 as I have construed it'.

Glidewell LJ agreed with that reasoning. So did Purchas LJ, where he said that the reference in para 6 to the adjustment of boundaries was 'clearly directed towards minor adjustments in boundaries without any substantial alteration in the extent of the holding involved'. No consideration was given by the Court of Appeal as to whether the surrender of the cottage was within the words 'any other variation of the terms of the tenancy', contained within para 6 of Sch 2 to the AHA 1986.

In *Secretary of State for Defence v Spencer*⁴, the primary contention on behalf of the landlord was that any variation to the property comprised in an agricultural tenancy which results in the boundaries being altered is one which makes 'provision ... for adjustment of the boundaries of the holding' in accordance with para 6 of Sch 2 to the AHA 1986. That submission was rejected, adopting the same reasoning of the Court of Appeal in *Mann v Gardner*⁵.

¹ [2002] EWHC 2116 (Ch), [2003] 1 WLR 75; affd [2003] EWCA Civ 784, [2003] 1 WLR 2701.
² (1990) 61 P & CR 1, CA.
³ (1990) 61 P & CR 1, CA.
⁴ [2002] EWHC 2116 (Ch), (2002) PLSCS 254; affirmed [2003] 1 WLR 2701.
⁵ (1990) 61 P & CR 1, CA.

25.14 In *Secretary of State for Defence v Spencer*¹, a different argument was raised by the landlord, not apparently considered by the Court of Appeal in *Mann v Gardner*². The landlord's second point was that the arrangement which was entered into between the landlord and the tenant, adding the further land, amounted to a 'provision ... for any other variation of the terms of the tenancy'. The court decided that, construing the expression 'the terms of the tenancy' in the context of para 6 of Sch 2 to the AHA 1986, it would seem that the legislature envisaged the property comprised in the tenancy as being within the expression. That is because 'the terms of the tenancy' are immediately preceded by the words 'any other variation of', and the word 'other' refers back to the immediately preceding phrase, 'adjustment of the boundaries of the holding'. It follows that an adjustment of the boundaries of the holding is treated as being a 'variation of the terms of the tenancy'. Since an adjustment of the boundaries must, by definition, involve adding and/or subtracting land from the tenancy, the concept of removing, adding, land from, or to, the tenancy could well have been seen by the draftsman as a variation of the terms of the tenancy. Paragraph 6(a) of Sch 2 to the AHA 1986 is only concerned with arrangements which the parties intend to take effect as a variation, and not as a surrender and re-grant (because of the bracketed words in para 6), but which nonetheless take effect as a matter of law as a surrender and re-grant. The only types of arrangement which would fall within that category are those which involve extending the terms of the tenancy or extending the property comprised in the tenancy³. Accordingly, the court held in favour of the landlord, reaching the conclusion that rendered the conclusion (but not the reasoning) of the Court of Appeal in *Mann v Gardner*⁴ per incuriam.

This conclusion is consistent with the thrust and purpose of the arbitration provisions of the AHA 1986. The parties of an agricultural tenancy are to be entitled to a rent review every three years, and the purpose of para 4(1) of Sch 2 to the AHA 1986 is to ensure that they do not have a rent review more frequently. However, the legislature recognised that, in certain circumstances, the provisions of para 4(1) could work an injustice, which para 6 was enacted to prevent. A variation in the rent which was solely attributable to a variation in the tenancy (irrespective of whether that variation was treated in law as effecting a surrender and re-grant) as not to be treated as an event which started the three-year period running afresh. Thus, if the parties agreed a substantial relaxation of certain of the tenant's covenants (for example, with regard to alienation and repair), that might justify a substantial increase in the rent, but if that increase was simply limited to the annualised value of the benefit to the tenant of the relaxation of his covenants, then it would not be treated as falling within para 4(1) of Sch 2. On that basis, the subtraction from, or addition to, the tenancy of a piece of land, particularly if it is a small amount of land, which leads to a decrease or an increase in the rent which merely reflects the value of that piece of land, should not engage para 4(1).

Accordingly, if there is a significant change in the composition of the holding, for example, where a block of land is added to the existing holding and a new rent is agreed, unapportioned between the original holding and the additional land, the saving provision does not apply[5].

1   [2002] EWHC 2116 (Ch), [2003] 1 WLR 75; affd [2003] EWCA Civ 784, [2003] 1 WLR 2701.
2   (1990) 61 P & CR 1, CA.
3   *Jenkin R Lewis & Son Ltd v Kerman* [1971] Ch 477; *Friends' Provident Life Office v British Railways Board* [1996] 1 All ER 336, CA; *Well Barn Farming Ltd v Backhouse* [2005] EWHC 1520 (Ch), [2005] 3 EGLR 109.
4   (1990) 61 P & CR 1, CA.
5   *Secretary of State for Defence v Spencer* [2002] EWHC 2116 (Ch), [2003] 1 WLR 75; affd [2003] EWCA Civ 784, [2003] 1 WLR 2701; *Family Management v Gray* [1980] 1 EGLR 46, 253 Estates Gazette 369; *Harmsworth Pension Funds Trustees Ltd v Charringtons Industrial Holdings Ltd* [1985] 1 EGLR 97, 274 Estates Gazette 588.

25.15 It is submitted that if the parties agree a rent formula whereby there will be a 'stepped' increase of £X in year one, say, £XX in year two and £XXX in year three, it will not be possible to revise the rent for a further three years after year three, ie six years from the start of operation of the agreed formula, because the rent will have been increased in each of the previous three years. It is difficult to see any variation in principle between such a situation and a fluctuating rent formula linked to commodity values[1]. Per contra, an agreed rent increase of £XXX, with an abatement in years one and two, may well not result in inadvertent triggering of the three-year rule.

The problem which frequently arises is whether landlords of a severed reversion can act independently and give separate notices, and indeed reach separate agreements as to their separate reversionary interests. As indicated above, it was held by the Court of Appeal[2] that severance of the reversion, whether or not accompanied by an apportionment of the rent, did not operate to create new tenancies. It was, therefore, held in one county court case[3] that the several landlords of the severed reversion would have to act in concert and give one single notice and that if several notices were given by the landlords of the severed parts in respect of their own reversionary interest, each notice would be invalid. However, in another county court case[4] it was held that where each of the landlords concurrently gave notices which could then be read together and which collectively covered all the land contained in the contract of tenancy, such notices were thereby valid. There is as yet no higher authority. It is submitted that if one of the landlords was actively to veto the giving of a s 12 notice, even though the motive for such veto was that the landlord had a close interest in the welfare of the tenant (for example, because she was his wife), that would effectively frustrate the statutory rent review procedures. The safer course to follow for landlords acting in concert is to give one single notice in respect of the whole holding jointly and collectively. It is submitted that it is probable that several notices, provided they cover all the land, will be valid, despite the decision in *Stiles v Farrow*[5].

1   *Bolesworth Estate Co Ltd v Cook* (1966) 116 NLJ 1318.
2   *Jelley v Buckman* [1974] QB 488.
3   *Stiles v Farrow* (1977) 241 Estates Gazette 623.
4   *Greenway v Tempest* (1983) unreported, in which *Stiles v Farrow* was cited but not followed.
5   (1977) 241 Estates Gazette 623.

Extent of the jurisdiction of the arbitrator

25.16 Frequently an arbitrator, appointed to determine the rent, will find that there is a variety of other disputes between the landlord and the tenant which do not directly relate to the rent. In such circumstances, although the arbitrator's jurisdiction is confined to determination of the rent, all relevant ancillary matters which must first be determined before the rent can be assessed (for example, as to the extent of the holding, as to the terms of the tenancy, or as to the pedigree of improvements) before the arbitrator can then determine the rent. Such matters do not fall outside the scope of his jurisdiction, even though his jurisdiction will be limited by the terms of his appointment to determining the rent[1].

1   *Kirby v Robinson* [1965] EGD 236, CA.

The valuation formula: the amount of the rent properly payable

25.17 The 'rent properly payable' for the purposes of s 12 of the AHA 1986 is defined in para 1 of Sch 2 to the AHA 1986. These provisions are, in certain respects, somewhat obscure and oblique. Nevertheless, as seen above[1], the rent properly payable in respect of a holding is the rent at which the holding might reasonably be expected to be let by a prudent and willing landlord to a prudent and willing tenant, taking into account all relevant factors[2] and disregarding certain matters specified in the AHA 1986[3].

The rent is first defined in terms very similar to the provisions of s 2 of the Agriculture Act 1958 (with only minor semantic distinctions) as follows:

> 'The rent properly payable in respect of a holding shall be the rent at which the holding might reasonably be expected to be let by a prudent and willing landlord to a prudent and willing tenant, taking into account (subject to sub-paragraph (3) and paragraphs 2 and 3 below) all relevant factors, including (in every case) the terms of the tenancy (including those relating to rent), the character and situation of the holding (including the locality in which it is situated), the productive capacity of the holding and its related earning capacity and the current level of rents for comparable lettings as determined in accordance with sub-paragraph (3) below ...'.

It will be noted that the primary formula closely follows the conventional definition of an open market rent contained in the Agriculture Act 1958 (AA

1958). The words 'open market', which appeared in s 2 of the AA 1958 have been omitted. The landlord and tenant are now to be not only 'willing' (as before) but also 'prudent'. However, the statute does not stipulate a 'reasonable' rent – the word 'reasonable' qualifying 'expected', not 'let' or 'landlord'.

Furthermore, the rent 'properly payable' of itself sets no standard unlike, say, a rent assessed by determining financial output in accordance with a formula the sum arrived at by reference to the earning potential of the farm. The formula is explicit as to what must be taken into account but not as to how this is to be done, in particular as to the weight to be given to the different parts of the formula. When the demand for farms outstrips supply, many open market rents are set at levels far higher than could be justified from the production of the holding in question. Rents assessed by 'farming at the margins' cannot be sustained except by the few who make up the open market.

1   See para 25.4.
2   See para 25.4.
3   See para 25.4.

25.18 In the leading case of *J W Childers Trustees v Anker*[1], the Court of Appeal had to consider the statutory formula for the level of rent and the statutory disregards. The court provided the following assistance:

(a)   The rent envisaged by the statutory formula is not 'the open market rent' – 'Section 12(2) and Schedule 2 ... provide a complete statutory code to fix a rent and that code should be applied without addition or subtraction;'[2]. Schedule 2 does envisage the rent being set at a market rent level, but the assumptions made (eg as to what the market would know or not know about the holding in an open market rental valuation) would not apply when the statutory formula was being given effect to[3].

(b)   All relevant information that the arbitrator required (even if confidential to the tenant) was admissible and must be supplied to enable the arbitrator to determine the rent properly payable. This would normally include quota details, Single Farm Payment information, information relating to grants, etc.

(c)   Where a holding was subject to any management agreement that had been or could be expected to be obtained, any payments under such an agreement fell to be taken into account not as part of the productive capacity of the holding, but as another 'relevant factor'.

(d)   Marriage value (ie the special value to an established farmer in the district in being able to take on the subject holding and farm in conjunction with his other land as one single enlarged agricultural unit) did not fall to be disregarded, but to be included in the rent properly payable.

As to scarcity value, although the correct treatment of scarcity value was not in issue in *Childers v Anker*[4], there were strong indications in the judgment of Morritt LJ that if that matter had been put in issue, the court would have determined that scarcity value does not fall to be disregarded.

The existing rent can be one relevant factor to be taken into account[5], but the existence of a preferential rent will not prejudice the application of the Sch 2 rent formula.

There is no obligation on either party to activate a rent review every three years. Failure to do so is irrelevant in determining the new rent at arbitration.

Non-farming income generally is a relevant factor in fixing the rent under Sch 2, particularly given the increased extent of diversification: for example, farm shops and caravan sites. It nevertheless remains unclear as to what extent income generating potential from non-agricultural sources can be taken into account. Productive capacity expressly includes the situation in which the tenant has permission to diversify into non-agricultural land uses. The user covenant is clearly relevant in relation to this issue[6].

One area which gives rise to difficulties is the treatment of dwellinghouses, for example, the treatment of bed and breakfast income derived from such use of the farmhouse and rental income from cottages. Each case falls to be considered on its individual facts. It should nevertheless not be assumed that rental income derived from a lawful sub-letting of a cottage should be passed in full to the landlord of the agricultural holding. For example, the repairing obligations between the head landlord and the head tenant are unlikely to reflect the obligations between the tenant and the sub-tenant. Also, the valuer of the AHA 1986 tenant may seek to factor into the assessment of the rent management charges[7].

[1]   [1996] 1 EGLR 1, [1996] 01 EG 102. See also, *Enfield London Borough Council v Potts* [1990] 2 EGLR 7, [1990] 34 EG 60.
[2]   *J W Childers Trustees v Anker* [1996] 1 EGLR 1, per His Honour Judge Bromley, approved in the Court of Appeal.
[3]   *J W Childers Trustees v Anker* [1996] 1 EGLR 1, per Morritt LJ in the Court of Appeal.
[4]   *J W Childers Trustees v Anker* [1996] 1 EGLR 1.
[5]   *Enfield London Borough Council v Pott* [1990] 2 EGLR 7, [1990] 34 EG 60.
[6]   See the county court case of *Tummon v Barclays Bank Trust Co Ltd* (1979) 250 Estates Gazette 980, in which it was decided that the holding fell to be valued *rebus sic stantibus*, ie as it stands. If the holding had potential for enhanced value use which was not realised by the tenant, then that latent value did not fall to be assessed and added to the rent. It may be that now the arbitrator is directed to take into account 'the productive capacity' of the holding which suggests the potential rather than realised capacity that the county court case is no longer applicable in that respect. Furthermore, potential non-agricultural income available to the tenant who is permitted by his tenancy agreement to 'diversify' would be relevant as an 'other relevant matter'. Note further that the *Tummon* case was decided before the substantial changes in the provisions of the rent formula were introduced by the AHA 1984. Also see, *Jewell v McGowan* [2002] EWCA Cuv 145, [2002] 3 EGLR 87: see para 24.21.
[7]   For further discussion of these issues, see the Guidance Notes issued by the RICS and the CAAV: see fn 2 of para 25.3.

The valuation formula: factors to be taken into account

25.19 The arbitrator is directed in every case to take into account the terms of the tenancy. It should be noted that the terms of the tenancy that the arbitrator is required to take into account include those relating to rent[1]. By contrast, s 2 of the AA 1958 required the arbitrator to disregard the terms of the tenancy relating to rent[2]. This would suggest that if, for example, the tenant was obliged to pay his rent in advance, whereas most agricultural holdings are let on terms whereby the tenant pays the rent in arrears, or the tenant had agreed to pay interest on any arrears of rent, those matters could be taken into account in assessing the rent properly payable. Likewise, if rent is suspended while repairs are carried out, this is to be taken into account[3].

[1]   Including the existing rent: *Enfield London Borough Council v Pott* [1990] 2 EGLR 7; [1990] 34 EG 60.
[2]   '[H]aving regard to the terms of the tenancy (other than those relating to rent)': AA 1958, s 2.
[3]   *Burton v Timmis* [1987] 1 EGLR 1, CA.

The character and situation of the holding

25.20 The arbitrator is also expressly required to take into account in every case 'the character and situation of the holding (including the locality in which it is situated)'.

Productive capacity and related earning capacity: generally

25.21 Schedule 2 paras 1(1) and 1(2) of the AHA 1986 provide that the arbitrator must in every case take into account the productive capacity and related earning capacity of the holding. This gives statutory effect to what in many, indeed most, rental arbitration cases, even before the new provisions were enacted, were treated as central features of the rental valuation process.

The productive capacity of the holding is defined in Sch 2 para 1(2)(a) as follows:

> ' "Productive capacity" means the productive capacity of the holding (taking into account fixed equipment and any other available facilities of the holding) on the assumption that it is in the occupation of a competent tenant practising a system of farming suitable to the holding'.

The productive capacity of the holding requires the arbitrator to determine how the farm would be farmed if farmed under competent management and what enterprises should be assumed to be carried out on the holding – whether cereals should be grown: what break crops should be selected: what livestock should be kept and so forth. This underlines the hypothetical nature of the exercise. It is submitted that, if the holding is capable, in the hands of a competent tenant, of sustaining a number of different suitable systems, the arbitrator should evaluate all of them.

Having determined what system or systems of farming should be carried on on the holding, and what the holding would produce in consequence, the arbitrator must then determine 'the related earning capacity'. Schedule 2 para 1(2)(b) defines this as meaning:

'The extent to which in the light of that productive capacity a competent tenant practising such a system of farming could reasonably be expected to profit from the farming of the holding'.

This exercise envisages determination by budgets, costings and other similar methods, as to what notional profit before rent could be achieved from the holding. Once the arbitrator has arrived at the appropriate figure, it then becomes one of the factors which must be taken into account by him in determining the rent properly payable.

The definition of related earning capacity, although linked to that of productive capacity, is clearly subsidiary. As a consequence, in respect of related earning capacity, the arbitrator must consider only that level of income and profits which would be generated by agricultural production. Income from non-agricultural activities (for example, a farm shop or caravan site), together with any other payments not directly connected to agricultural production, would not affect rental value by reason of the arbitrator's consideration of related earning capacity. This limitation would apply in respect of grants paid to the tenant which are not directly connected to agricultural production. Further, marketing quotas would not fall under this head. However, these would be 'relevant factors' for consideration under the definition in Sch 2 para 1(1), if these factors affect the potential profitability of the farming of the holding as a whole. It follows that the existence of a management agreement, and the income generated by it, is not to be considered by the arbitrator as part of the related earning capacity of the holding, but will be taken into account as one of the relevant factors for the purpose of Sch 2 para 1(1)[1].

Experience has shown that some valuers have drawn the inference from the inclusion of productive capacity and related-earning capacity that Parliament has decided that farms are to be valued simply according to a profits method. As a consequence, they determine the rent properly payable by apportioning the notional net profit on a conventional percentage basis between the landlord and tenant. There is no statutory basis for such an approach. It is clearly inapplicable in the case of a holding which is not capable of making a commercial profit from farming, or can make only a low profit, but nevertheless may possess a high rental value for other reasons. In certain circumstances, an apportionment of prospective profits might determine what rent a prudent and willing landlord and tenant might agree upon, perhaps because a consideration of the other relevant factors pointed to the same or similar conclusion.

Productive capacity and related earning capacity are only two of a lengthy series of factors each of which has to be given its appropriate weight by the arbitrator according to the circumstances of each case, including the terms of the tenancy (including as to rent), the character and situation of the holding (including the locality in which it is situated) and the current level of rents for comparable holdings[2].

[1] *J W Childers Trustees v Anker* [1996] 1 EGLR 1 at 5: 'it will be a matter for the arbitrator to determine the weight if any to be attached to the management agreement. As the matter to be determined is the equivalent of actual earning capacity not how the market would

have seen it the fact ... that the management agreement and the details it contains are normally confidential is immaterial', per Morritt LJ.
2   See para 25.4.

Productive capacity and related earning capacity: milk quota

25.22 In the case of dairy farms, the imposition of milk quotas[1] since 2 April 1984 has restricted the ability of some milk producers to dispose (at a profit) of the entire quantity of milk which their holding is capable of producing. Accordingly, although the theoretical 'productive capacity' of a dairy farm remains unaffected, the 'related earning capacity' of the holding may be restricted by the quota allocated to the holding and registered in the name of the tenant and the rent properly payable under s 12 and Sch 2 to the AHA 1986 is correspondingly affected and restricted.

1   In the European Community legislation, what has come to be known in the UK as 'milk quotas' are referred to as 'reference quantities'. For a comprehensive commentary on milk quotas, see Cardwell M, *Milk Quotas: European Community and United Kingdom Law* (1996) Oxford University Press.

25.23 There are a number of matters to be borne in mind when determining the earning capacity of the holding for the purpose of assessing the rent taking into account milk quota.

Where the subject holding, ie the agricultural holding, is part of a larger 'holding'[1] (often called an 'Euro holding'), there is provision for apportionments in accordance with the Dairy Produce Quotas Regulations 2005[2]. This is the first exercise which must be undertaken to determine how much of the registered quota is applicable to the subject agricultural holding. Thereafter the following matters fall for consideration.

1   A 'holding' within the meaning of the Dairy Produce Quotas Regulations 2005, SI 2005/465: see Agriculture Act 1986, s 15(3). See para 49.6.
2   This apportionment will be in accordance with the Dairy Produce Quotas Regulations 2005 as interpreted in *Puncknowle Farms Ltd v Kane* [1985] 2 EGLR 8, 275 Estates Gazette 1283. For a fuller commentary on such apportionments which have also to be made for the purpose of determining relevant quota when compensation to an outgoing tenant on quitting is assessed, see para 49.28.

Transferred quota

25.24 Section 15 of the Agriculture Act 1986[1] provides that where there is a reference to arbitration of land which comprises a holding[2] in respect of which quota is registered under the Dairy Produce Quotas Regulations 2005[3] which was transferred to the tenant by virtue of a transaction the cost of which was borne wholly or partly by the tenant, the arbitrator must disregard any increase in the rental value of the land which is due to that quota. Where the tenant has only partly paid for the transferred quota, it is the 'corresponding part', ie the part he has paid for, which falls to be disregarded, and not the whole of the quota transferred.

Section 15(2) of the Agriculture Act 1986 provides that in determining whether quota was transferred to a tenant by virtue of a transaction the cost of which was borne wholly or partly by the tenant:

(a)   any payment made by the tenant in consideration for the grant or assignment to him of the tenancy or any previous tenancy of any land comprised in the holding falls to be disregarded;

(b)   any person who would be treated under paras 2, 3 or 4 of Sch 1 to the Agriculture Act 1986 (being the former tenant on death or retirement) as having had quota transferred to him or having paid the whole or part of the cost of any transaction for the purposes of a claim under Sch 1 shall be so treated for the purposes of s 15(2) of the Agriculture Act 1986;

(c)   any person who would be so treated under para 4 of Sch 1 to the Agriculture Act 1986 (being a sub-tenant) if the sub-tenancy to which the tenancy is subject had terminated shall be so treated for the purposes of s 15(2) of the Agriculture Act 1986.

There is to be no such disregard in relation to transferred quota if the landlord and tenant have agreed otherwise[4].

[1]   Not to be confused with the Agricultural Holdings Act 1986.
[2]   A 'holding' within the meaning of the Dairy Produce Quotas Regulations 2005, SI 2005/465: see Agriculture Act 1986, s 15(3). See para 49.6.
[3]   SI 2005/465.
[4]   The Agriculture Act 1986, s 15(1).

Agricultural holding with inadequate quota

25.25 The allocation of quota to an agricultural holding was determined in the main by the level of production of milk on that holding during 1983 (less 9%) with further subsequent reductions. The level of production on the holding during 1983 was, therefore, crucial.

The problem then arises as to whether a landlord, whose tenant or his predecessor was achieving during the relevant period a level of production lower than that which the holding (if competently farmed) might have achieved, is entitled to have the rent assessed not by reference to the quota actually registered, but by reference to the higher quota which would have been registered if an adequate quantity of milk had been produced. In such circumstances, does the landlord fall to be penalised by a reduced assessment of rent?

It is submitted that the answer to that question is yes. The rent has to be assessed by reference to the productive capacity and the related earning capacity of the agricultural holding. This, in turn, must mean the earning capacity lawfully achievable in the hands of a hypothetical competent tenant. A competent tenant can only produce milk and, therefore, earnings for the holding within the restraints of the quotas historically imposed. Further, even if the quota is reduced by reason of a breach of obligation on the part of the tenant, the landlord cannot, it is submitted, pray in aid para 3(b) of Sch 2 to the AHA 1986 because although the arbitrator is there required to disregard dilapidations to land and buildings, this does not apply to other breaches of covenant or defaults on the part of the sitting tenant. The 'prudent and willing' tenant will not have available more than the quota found to be 'attached to' the holding.

Agricultural holdings with excess quotas

25.26 A tenant in possession who was farming in 1983 to a very high standard and producing milk, possibly well in excess of the level of production which could have been expected of the hypothetical competent tenant, will, therefore, have acquired a correspondingly high allocation of quota. In such circumstances, does the rent fall to be assessed by reference to the level of production and corresponding earning capacity which would have been achieved if his quota allocation had been at the lower figure which the merely competent tenant would have achieved? It is submitted that the answer to that question will depend upon the facts of each particular case. If the increased quota was obtained by reason of the adoption by the tenant of a system of farming more beneficial to the holding than required by the tenancy agreement or normal practice, for example, where the tenant adopted a system of unusually high inputs of concentrates or three times a day milking then, under the provisions of para 2(4) of Sch 2, it is arguable that the excess quota falls to be disregarded as an improvement executed by the tenant at his expense.

In most cases those with higher levels of quota allocated to them will not be able to have the surplus level disregarded by application of para 2(4). In a county court case[1], it was held that where a tenant with a substantial quantity of milk quota registered in his name a substantial quantity of milk quota, as a consequence of production in 1983 from land held on seasonal grazing agreements, he was not entitled to have any part of the quota disregarded. It did not fall to be treated as a 'tenant's improvement' nor as 'high farming'. Since Parliament provided that only transferred quota fell to be disregarded by s 15 of the Agriculture Act 1986, it was held not to be permissible to substitute the amount of quota one would reasonably have expected to have been available for the amount of quota actually registered when assessing the rent properly payable.

[1]   *Marshall v Hughes* (1992) unreported, Newport (Gwent) County Court.

Milk quota leasing

25.27 A problem which has arisen as a result of milk quota leasing[1] is whether, and if so how, that income (actual or potential) can be taken into account. Frequently it has been demonstrated that a dairy farmer would be able to generate more income, and therefore potentially the holding would command a higher rent, if dairy farming was discontinued and a lower value farming activity substituted with the milk quota being leased out. Alternatively, sometimes a tenant may discontinue milk production and lease out the quota because the landlord's failure to repair fixed equipment, provide pollution control measures or the like resulting in it being impossible to continue in dairy production. Alternatively the tenant may prefer a less labour and capital intensive farming system which yields a high reward from quota leasing.

1. Referred to in both the UK statutory instruments and the EU Community Regulations as 'temporary transfer', see Council Regulation (EEC) 3950/92 and the Dairy Produce Quota Regulations 2005, SI 2005/465. See also Cardwell M, *Milk Quotas: European Community and United Kingdom Law* (1996) Oxford University Press.

25.28 Although there remains no authority for these propositions, the following is submitted.

(a)   If the 'system of farming suitable to the holding' is for the holding to be used for milk production, then the rent should be set at the level appropriate for a holding being used for milk production without leasing the quota to a third party. This is because the arbitrator must in every case take into account the 'productive capacity' of the holding and that in turn obliges the arbitrator to proceed on the basis that the holding is occupied by a tenant 'practising a system of farming suitable to the holding'. If that is dairying, the quota will not be available for leasing out. The fact that the actual tenant rather than the 'prudent and willing' tenant is in fact leasing out the quota is in that event irrelevant.

(b)   Similarly, if the holding can only not be so used by reason of some breach by the landlord of his repairing or other obligations, the rent should be assessed as for an actual dairy farm. The landlord cannot secure a higher rent than would be payable if he were not in breach of his obligations to the tenant. It is submitted that to do so would offend the principle that the landlord may not profit from his own breach of covenant.

Productive capacity and related earning capacity: entitlements

25.29 As seen in Chapter 52, entitlements allocated to farmers under Mid-term Review of the Common Agricultural Policy only give rise to income to the farmer in the form of Single Payment[1] when matched against land in the region. Nevertheless, entitlements are not attached to the land. They are assets belonging to the farmer.

As the rent review formula under the AHA 1986 assumes a hypothetical tenant when assessing the rent payable, it is submitted that the entitlements registered in the name of the farmer fall to be disregarded, unless the parties make express provision for them to be taken into account in the tenancy agreement.

As seen above, one of the factors that an arbitrator must take into account is the terms of the tenancy agreement. A quota provision which restricts or regulates the use and disposal of entitlements, affecting the income that can be generated by the tenant, will be a relevant consideration. Likewise, if the user covenant imposes upon the tenant an obligation to farm the holding in a manner which precludes him from just keeping the land in good agricultural and environmental condition, in accordance with the restrictions imposed by the European Regulations, then that will also be a relevant consideration.

The Single Farm Payment is expressly decoupled from production. Logically it cannot form part of the productive capacity or related earnings capacity of the holding. However, it will be a 'relevant factor', in a similar manner to income derived from management agreements[2].

It is submitted that entitlements do not fall to be disregarded on the basis of them falling within the definition of tenant's improvements or fixed equipment[3].

1   Known as the Single Farm Payment.
2   *J W Childers Trustees v Anker* [1996] 1 EGLR 1, CA.
3   See para 52.31. For further commentary on the impact of entitlements and Single Payments in relation to rent review, see 'Mid-Term Review, A Valuer's Interim Guide' (2004) Central Association of Agricultural Valuers and Moody J and Neville W, *Mid-Term Review, A Practical Guide* (2004) Burges Salmon LLP.

Comparables

25.30 Schedule 2 para 1(3) of the AHA 1986 directs the arbitrator to have regard to any available evidence of rents which are, or (in view of rents currently being tendered) are likely to become, payable in respect of tenancies of comparable agricultural holdings on terms (other than terms fixing the rent payable) similar to the tenancy being the subject of the rent review. The arbitrator can consider rents arrived at either by agreement or as a consequence of arbitration, as well as current tenders for rent payable in respect of comparable holdings[1].

When assessing comparable holdings, Sch 2 para 1(3) of the AHA 1986 goes on to direct the arbitrator to disregard three factors in his assessment as to a true comparison with the subject holding. The three factors are:

(a)   'any element of the rents in question which is due to an appreciable scarcity of comparable holdings available for letting on such terms, compared with the number of persons seeking to become tenants of such holdings on such terms' (referred to henceforth as 'scarcity value');

(b)   'any element of those rents which is due to the fact that the tenant of or a person tendering for any comparable holding is in occupation of other land in the vicinity of that holding that may conveniently be occupied together with that holding' (referred to henceforth as 'marriage value'); and

(c)   'any effect on those rents which is due to any allowances or reductions made in consideration of the charging of premiums' (referred to henceforth as 'premium value').

1   These include those 'whether fixed by agreement or by arbitration' and even includes those which '(in view of rents currently being tendered) are likely to become payable'. Therefore the decision in the case of a commercial arbitration of *Land Securities plc v Westminster City Council* [1992] 2 EGLR 15 has no application to AHA 1986 rent arbitrations.

Scarcity value

25.31 Since the widely recognised factors which in the past had given rise to the high level of open market rents were the high level of demand for agricultural holdings and the low level of supply, it soon became clear that if scarcity value had to be valued out of the comparable holdings this would involve a substantial adjustment in most cases. The first and most fundamental question that the AHA 1986 formula asks is whether, if the arbitrator has to value out scarcity from comparables, he is also obliged to eliminate scarcity value from the rent properly payable in respect of the subject holding.

Perhaps surprisingly, although Sch 2 para 1(3)(a) requires scarcity value to be valued out of the rent of comparable holdings, the provision is silent as to whether it is to be disregarded in relation to the subject holding itself. It might be argued that if the intention of the legislature was that the scarcity value of the subject holding itself had to be disregarded, then it was surprising that this most important factor was not expressly mentioned in Sch 2. It is submitted that scarcity value should be disregarded in the subject holding, despite the fact that this is not expressly required by the AHA 1986. That conclusion is consistent with an analysis of the NFU/CLA package which resulted in the amendment of the rent review formula in the Agricultural Holdings Act 1984[1]. However, that view was challenged in *J W Childers Trustees v Anker*[2]. In that case the tenant placed reliance upon the decision in *99 Bishopsgate Ltd v Prudential Assurance Co Ltd*[3].

In *99 Bishopsgate Ltd v Prudential Assurance Co Ltd*, a building in the City of London had to be valued by reference to the rental values of comparable property 'let with vacant possession'. Lloyd J described as 'irresistible' an argument that 'there could be no conceivable point' in directing the arbitrator to have regard to comparable lettings with vacant possession if the subject premises were to be valued subject to existing occupational leases. The decision of Lloyd J was upheld by the Court of Appeal[4].

The same argument might be thought to apply to Sch 2 para 1(3)(a) of the AHA 1986. In *J W Childers v Anker*[5], the tenant argued that both scarcity value and marriage value must be valued out of the rental of comparable holdings, on the basis that the objective was to arrive at an undistorted rental value for the subject holding. The Court of Appeal rejected this argument in relation to marriage value, deciding that marriage value in the subject holding is relevant and to be taken into account. The fact that it was to be disregarded in valuing comparables did not mean that it should be disregarded in respect of the subject holding. However, the Court of Appeal expressly left open to question whether the same analysis should be applied in relation to scarcity value. The court stated:

> 'This case is not concerned with whether scarcity (whether of demand or supply) is to be considered or excluded in the assessment of the rent for the subject holding, that question must await determination in a case in which it is raised'[6].

The Court of Appeal declined to determine the issue of scarcity value notwithstanding the fact that it was invited to do so. It was argued that,

393

following the principle in *Pepper v Hart*[7], the court could have regard to Hansard, where in Parliament clear indications were given that scarcity value was to be excluded from the subject holding. Indeed, such a conclusion was critical to the whole basis of the NFU/CLA package[8] upon which the rent review formula in the AHA 1986 was founded. If scarcity value were allowed in respect of the subject holding it would undermine the central aim of the Sch 2 rental formula to link rent to productive capacity and related earning capacity, breaking the link with inflated tenders on the first lettings. The point remains to be resolved before the courts.

1   See para 25.2.
2   [1996] 1 EGLR 1, [1996] 01 EG 102, CA.
3   [1985] 1 EGLR 72, 273 Estates Gazette 984.
4   (1984) 270 EG 950; [1985] 1 EGLR 72. As to a Scottish case in relation to the equivalent wording of the Scottish Act, see *Aberdeen Endowments Trust v Wills* 1985 SLT (Land Ct) 23.
5   [1996] 1 EGLR 1, [1996] 01 EG 102, CA.
6   *J W Childers Trustees v Anker* [1996] 1 EGLR 1, per Morritt LJ, CA.
7   [1993] AC 593.
8   See para 25.2.

Marriage value

25.32 After a period of doubt and controversy it has now been held authoritatively by the Court of Appeal in *J W Childers Trustees v Anker*[1] that although marriage value falls to be disregarded in the case of comparables, it does not for the subject holding. Therefore when assessing the rent of an agricultural holding (though not the comparable), any value the holding may have for farmers in the district with established and often equipped holdings to take on the subject holding to be farmed with the prospective tenant's existing established land holdings as part of an enlarged single agricultural unit, must be taken into account.

This does not mean that in every case, particularly where the actual tenant happens to farm other land as well, that some premium or additional rent is payable over and above the rent that would otherwise be payable. It does mean by contrast that the tenant cannot argue that the subject holding must be assessed as if it was farmed in isolation without other available land held by other prospective tenants in the district.

1   [1996] 1 EGLR 1, [1996] 01 EG 102, CA.

Premium value

25.33 The premium referred to is the premium charged as a capital sum for the grant of the tenancy. Clearly this has to be valued out of the comparable letting because it distorts the amount of the rent which would otherwise be charged. Likewise, the subject holding falls to be assessed upon the assumption that no premium is charged[1].

[1]   Premium value creates little problem. Premiums for the grant of tenancies of agricultural holdings are rarely met with in practice, because of the level of tax payable upon such consideration. For a commentary in support of this view, see Muir Watt's annotation of the Agricultural Holdings Act 1986 – Current Law Statutes Annotated Reprints, pp 5–131.

Types of comparable

25.34 The statutory definition of the comparables which have to be taken into account in every case is contained in Sch 2 para 1(3) of the AHA 1986. As indicated above, such comparables are not confined to open market lettings, by tender or otherwise, but include rents fixed by agreement between parties, rents fixed by arbitration under existing tenancies, and rents which are 'likely to become payable in respect of tenancies of comparable agricultural holdings'.

Under the general law, evidence of an arbitrator's award in another arbitration that determined the rent of a property on review is inadmissible as a comparable on a subsequent rent review[1]. However, under the AHA 1986, the arbitrator is expressly required to have regard to the current level of rents for comparable holdings and rent awards made by arbitrators in relation to such holdings[2].

The issue which follows from the statutory definition in the AHA 1986 as to what the arbitrator is to take into account in assessing the rent of an agricultural holding under the AHA 1986 is whether he can have regard to rents paid for farm business tenancies under the Agricultural Tenancies Act 1995. In practice, such rents under the Agricultural Tenancies Act 1995 (ATA 1995) have been significantly higher than those for comparable lettings of agricultural holdings under the AHA 1986.

Two cases concerning the basis of valuing a 'fair' rent for residential dwellings under the Rent Act 1977 provide support for the argument that the arbitrator under the AHA 1986 should be allowed to take into account rents payable in respect of lettings under the ATA 1995[3]. In *Curtis v London Rent Assessment Committee*[4], the court held that the starting point when valuing a 'fair' rent was the market rent. For the purposes of the Rent Act 1977, that market rent was then to be discounted to eliminate any element of scarcity value. It should be noted that it was accepted in *Spath Holme v Chairman of the Greater Manchester and Lancashire Rent Assessment Committee*[5] (and confirmed in *Curtis v London Rent Assessment Committee*[6]) that if there is in fact no scarcity, then in theory the fair rent should equate to the market rent. The Court of Appeal held in *Curtis v London Rent Assessment Committee*[7] that the best evidence of market values was evidence of comparable rents for assured tenancies let under the Housing Act 1988. The court directed that these should be used instead of the diminishing number of registered fair rent comparables available under the Rent Act 1977.

It is submitted that the position relating to the interrelationship of rents payable under the AHA 1986 and those payable under the ATA 1995 is different to the relationship applying between the Rent Act 1977 and the

Housing Act 1988. Schedule 2 para 1(3) of the AHA 1986 specifically directs the arbitrator consider the current level of rents payable or currently being tendered in respect of tenancies of *comparable agricultural holdings* [emphasis added]. This limits the comparison to agricultural holdings within the definition contained in the AHA 1986[8]. Further, the formula to be adopted under the AHA 1986 is quite different to that which applies under the Rent Act 1977 where there is no requirement on the part of the rent assessment committee in determining the fair rent to consider factors such as the productive capacity and the related earning capacity.

If lettings under a different code are preferred as comparables, eg farm business tenancies created under the ATA 1995, it would appear on parity of reasoning with the *Spath Holme* case that they cannot be rejected as inadmissible on that account alone. However, the difficulty arises as to whether a new letting of a farm business tenancy falls within the definition of an 'agricultural holding' within the meaning of para 1(3) of Sch 2 to the AHA 1986 since it refers to '… tenancies of comparable *agricultural holdings* on terms …'. It is submitted that the effect on rent of the different levels of security and the difference in the terms of the letting must be evaluated and taken into account when undertaking the valuation exercise.

[1]   *Land Securities plc v Westminster City Council (No 2)* [1995] 1 EGLR 245.
[2]   AHA 1986, Sch 2 para 1(1) and (3).
[3]   *Spath Holme v Chairman of the Greater Manchester and Lancashire Rent Assessment Committee* [1995] 2 EGLR 80; *Curtis v London Rent Assessment Committee* [1999] QB 92, [1997] 4 All ER 842. Also, see *BTE Ltd v Merseyside and Cheshire Rent Assessment Committee* (1991) 24 HLR 514.
[4]   [1999] QB 92, [1997] 4 All ER 842.
[5]   [1995] 2 EGLR 80.
[6]   [1997] 4 All ER 842.
[7]   [1997] 4 All ER 842.
[8]   AHA 1986, ss 1(1) and 96(1).

25.35 It is submitted that the arbitrator under the AHA 1986 cannot have regard to rents payable under farm business tenancies governed by the ATA 1995 when determining the rent payable in relation to an agricultural holding under the AHA 1986. There is also an important provision that those comparables to be taken into account are comparables where the holdings in question are or will be let 'on terms other than the terms fixing the rent payable, similar to those of the tenancy under consideration'. The statutory wording suggests that comparable holdings which are not let on similar terms do not fall to be taken into account. It is not sufficient for the arbitrator merely to identify the incomparable features of the proposed 'comparable' holding, for example, that the holding which is comparable in terms of size, soil type, fixed equipment and the like is let on incomparable terms (such as full repairing and insuring rather than model clause repairing liabilities).

The valuation formula: factors to be disregarded

25.36 A number of factors are required to be disregarded by the arbitrator in determining the rent payable. The expression previously employed in s 8(2) of the AHA 1948 was that the arbitrator should not 'take into account' those factors. This expression was found to be ambiguous on the basis that it could mean that the arbitrator should ignore them altogether or it could mean that he should attribute a rental value to the item and then deduct that rental value from the rent of the holding as seen.

It was held in *Guthe v Broatch*[1], in relation to the corresponding Scottish provision, that the arbitrator had to make the necessary adjustments to ensure that the rent awarded involved the valuing out of these factors. The definition contained in Sch 2 para 2(1) of the AHA 1986 makes it clear that these factors must be valued out and must not be ignored.

The factors which are to be disregarded in all cases (and not just when assessing comparables) when determining the rent payable in relation to an agricultural holding under the AHA 1986 are:

(a) tenant's improvements;
(b) tenant's fixed equipment;
(c) landlord's improvements;
(d) high farming;
(e) the tenant's occupation;
(f) tenant's dilapidations.

[1] 1956 SC 132, Ct of Sess.

Tenant's improvements

25.37 Schedule 2 para 2(1)(a) requires the arbitrator to disregard any tenant's improvements or fixed equipment, other than equipment provided pursuant to an obligation imposed on the tenant by the contract of tenancy. Tenant's improvements are defined to mean:

> '... any improvements which have been executed on the holding, in so far as they were executed wholly or partly at the expense of the tenant (whether or not that expense has been or will be reimbursed by a grant out of money provided by Parliament or local government funds) without any equivalent allowance or benefit made or given by the landlord in consideration for their execution'[1].

It is unclear as to how the valuation exercise giving effect to the statutory injunction should be carried out. One possible approach is to adopt 'the black patch' and simply value the holding as if the matter to be disregarded did not exist and the holding was still in its unimproved condition. Such an approach does not meet the objection that the statutory direction is to disregard the rental value attributable to the improvement in question and not to disregard the improvement itself[2]. In some cases that may amount to the same thing. In many it will not, especially if latent value is released by the improvements having been carried out, nor will the 'black patch' approach necessarily take into account any deterioration in the improvement.

An alternative approach which more closely follows the statutory wording is for the holding to be valued in its improved condition and for the proportion of that rental attributable to the tenant's improvement to be assessed and then deducted from the rental which would otherwise have been payable in arriving at the rent to be awarded. This figure to be deducted will rarely, if ever, be arrived at by taking the current capital value of the improvement (still less its historical cost) and then applying an interest charge to it, any more than the rent of the holding itself might be arrived at in that way.

1   AHA 1986, Sch 2 para 2(2)(a).
2   *GREA Real Property Investments Ltd v Williams* (1979) 250 Estates Gazette 651. However, the ultimate conclusion of Forbes J that the way to ensure that one was disregarding the rental value of the improvement rather than disregarding the improvement itself suggests that there may in fact, in some instances, be no difference between the two approaches. He suggested that the rent of comparable holdings with and without the improvements should be determined. The resultant exercise is likely to produce the same result as the 'black patch' approach. See also *Tummon v Barclays Trust Co Bank Ltd* (1979) 250 Estates Gazette 980.

25.38 A closely related problem is the extent to which any latent value in the holding, which either has not been realised or else has only been realised by the expenditure by the tenant of his own money on improvements or fixtures, should be taken into account when the rent properly payable to the landlord is determined. The only guidance available is derived from a county court case[1] decided under the earlier, and different, provisions of the AHA 1948 (now repealed). In that case it was held that the holding fell to be valued as it stands. Therefore, if the latent value had not been realised, no account could be taken of it, but if it had, even if that resulted from tenant's improvements, the rent properly payable should reflect from the benefit of the landlord the latent value as released. However, the allowance to be made to the tenant for realising that latent value would probably be less than its full enhancement in the value of the holding which results from the improvement.

It is important not to confuse cost and value[2] so a valuation method involving the application of an interest charge to the current or historic cost will rarely be valid as a matter of valuation principle.

As indicated above, the statutory disregard does not apply to those tenant's improvements (or fixed equipment) which were provided or executed under an obligation imposed on the tenant by the terms of the contract of tenancy. Where the tenancy agreement itself expressly provided at the time it was entered into that the tenant would carry out improvements, no problem of statutory construction arises. The rationale for the provision would appear to be that the rent and the terms of the tenancy generally were fixed by reference to this obligation imposed upon the tenant.

It not infrequently happens that a tenant carries out improvements with the landlord's consent in writing (which is necessary to enable the tenant to obtain compensation on quitting) and the terms of the consent are contained in a memorandum which is said to be supplemental to the terms of the tenancy agreement itself. It could be argued in those circumstances that if the tenant agreed to carry out the improvements with the landlord's consent, and the landlord agreed to pay compensation written off over a period by reference to the anticipated life of the improvements in question, that the tenant had taken upon himself an obligation to carry out the improvement in an agreement which supplemented the tenancy agreement itself. Therefore, the improvement would not fall to be disregarded for rental purposes. It is submitted that this is a wrong construction of the provision. It is only those improvements which the tenant was obliged to carry out as a condition of the grant of the tenancy and where the obligation was contained in the tenancy agreement itself which do not fall to be disregarded. Improvements carried out by the tenant subsequently by agreement with the landlord as a condition of the landlord's consent (and the landlord undertaking the obligation to pay compensation) do not fall to be rentalised and valued as part of the holding, even though the tenant took on an obligation to carry them out in an agreement supplemental to the original tenancy agreement.

1   *Tummon v Barclays Trust Co Bank Ltd* (1979) 250 EG 980.
2   *GREA Real Property Investments Ltd v Williams* (1979) 250 Estates Gazette 651.

25.39 As regards the definition of tenant's improvements, the following points should be noted:

(a)   Any grant obtained by the tenant for the carrying out of the improve-ment is for the benefit of the tenant in that the tenant obtains credit, not merely for that element of the improvement for which he paid out of his own resources, but also that element paid for out of parliamentary or local government funds.

(b)   An 'equivalent allowance' by the landlord will negative the disregard provision. For example, if the landlord agreed upon the improvement in consideration of the tenant being allowed to assign the tenancy to himself and his son, this might, on the facts of an individual case, be found to be an equivalent allowance. The allowance must be 'equiva-lent' to the value of the improvement. The provision that the landlord will pay compensation (which he is statutorily obliged to do anyway if his consent in writing is obtained) will be an allowance that would, as a matter of valuation, probably not be found to be nearly sufficient to constitute an equivalent allowance. Similarly, some minor benefit passing from the landlord to the tenant which was not equivalent in value to the improvement would be insufficient to negative the require-ment that such an improvement should be disregarded.

(c)   The improvements must be carried out at the expense of the tenant. An improvement carried out by a third party (even if closely connected to the tenant) would appear not to fall to be disregarded. A problem arises in the case of improvements carried out by sub-tenants as to whether they too fall to be disregarded. It is submitted that the extended definition of tenant contained in s 96 of the AHA 1986 (including persons deriving title from the tenant) is sufficiently wide and all-embracing to include a sub-tenant[1].

(d)   In the case of a tenant who has held a tenancy of the agricultural holding under a series of tenancies, improvements carried out under a previous tenancy fall to be disregarded[2]. It should be noted that it is only a series of tenancies in favour of the same tenant which carry with them the rollover provision. If, for example, the tenant acquired his tenancy by succession, improvements carried out during the currency of, for example, his father's tenancy do not fall to be disregarded, unless special provision was made for this at the time of the grant of the succession tenancy. This is because the tenant in question had not held under a previous tenancy of the holding. The previous tenancy had been held by his deceased or retired close relation[3].

(e) The disregard provision does not apply if the tenant had received compensation on termination of the previous tenancy.

(f) Improvements carried out in anticipation of the grant of a tenancy fall to be disregarded[4].

(g) A problem can arise where the tenant carries out improvements for the benefit of the holding on adjoining land and not, therefore, physically on the holding itself. This would occur where the tenant builds a road to provide access to the holding for milk lorries. Such improvements are not 'executed on the holding' if a restricted or narrow construction of para 2(2)(a) of Sch 2 to the AHA 1986 is applied. It is submitted that nevertheless they fall to be valued out and the benefit of them falls to be credited to the tenant in arriving at the rent properly payable. A wider construction is likely to be favoured – 'on' meaning in connection with rather than merely physically within[5]. By contrast, tenant's buildings on an adjoining holding which are used to service both the tenant's own land and the subject holding do not fall to be disregarded for the purpose of rent reviews on the subject holding.

1   Note the *ejusdem generis* rule and the genus of persons within the statutory definition, namely, 'executors, administrators, assigns or trustee in bankruptcy of tenant'; a list of persons all of whom derive title laterally from the tenant rather than subordinately.

2   AHA 1986, Sch 2 para 2(3)(a). This provision was introduced to correct an injustice highlighted under the previous law by the decision in *East Coast Amusement Co Ltd v British Transport Board* [1965] AC 58, [1963] 2 WLR 1426, HL, and *Ponsford v HMS Aerosols Ltd* [1979] AC 63, 38 P & CR 270, HL. See also *GREA Real Property Investments Ltd v Williams* (1979) 250 EG 651, and, in the context of fixtures, *New Zealand Government Property Corpn v HM & S Ltd* [1981] 1 All ER 759, [1981] 1 WLR 870.

3   AHA 1986, Sch 2 para 2(3).

4   *Hambros Bank Executor and Trustee Co Ltd v Superdrug Stores Ltd* [1985] 1 EGLR 99, 274 Estates Gazette 590; *Scottish and Newcastle Breweries plc v Sir Richard Sutton's Settled Estates* [1985] 2 EGLR 130, 276 Estates Gazette 77.

5   A similar construction is normally applied to agricultural work 'on the holding' which includes going to market to buy or sell produce when determining an applicant for succession's principal source of livelihood.

Tenant's fixed equipment

25.40 Similar considerations apply to tenant's fixed equipment. In practice, the distinction between tenant's improvements and fixed equipment is that tenant's fixed equipment is capable of being removed from the holding on quitting, provided the requirements of s 10 of the AHA 1986 are complied with, whereas tenant's improvements must be left on the holding, with the tenant receiving statutory or substituted compensation for them. An item such as a new building would constitute an improvement, if subject to landlord's written consent, but otherwise would be treated as tenant's fixed equipment.

Both titles are misleading since any item of improvement or fixed equipment annexed to the freehold belongs to the freeholder and the property in it passes to the landlord. At common law such items as buildings erected by the tenant never become the property of the tenant[1]. However, the statutory rights to compensation or removal are given to the tenant who erects buildings or other items of fixed equipment on the holding.

The same provisions apply for the purposes of disregarding tenant's fixed equipment as for tenant's improvements[2].

[1] In the case of an agricultural holding, the common law is displaced by s 10(1)(a) of the AHA 1986 which provides that a tenant's fixture which is to 'remain his property' so long as he retains the right to remove it. See also AHA 1986, s 10(7) and the model clauses, SI 1973/1473, Schedule para 4(1)(a). The matter is dealt with differently in the definition of tenant's fixture in the AHA 1986, Sch 2 para 2(2)(b).
[2] AHA 1986, Sch 2 para 2(1). As to the relevant provisions, see para 25.37ff.

Landlord's improvements

25.41 To give effect to the principle that the tenant and not the landlord should have the benefit of any grant-aid for the provision of improvements or fixed equipment when the rent is to be assessed, Sch 2 para 2(1)(b) of the AHA 1986 provides that the arbitrator shall also disregard any grants received by the landlord out of money provided by Parliament or local government in respect of the execution of any improvements by the landlord. It should be noted that, although there is a rollover provision in Sch 2 para 2(3) of the AHA 1986 in the case of tenant's improvements and fixed equipment carried out under a previous tenancy, there is no equivalent provision for the grant-aided element of landlord's improvements.

High farming

25.42

'The continuous adoption by the tenant of a system of farming more beneficial to the holding:
(a)   than the system of farming required by the contract of tenancy; or
(b)   in so far as no system is so required, than the system of farming normally practised on comparable agricultural holdings,
shall be treated as an improvement executed at his expense'[1].

This is known as high farming and has long been a feature of the agricultural holdings legislation. High farming is treated as an improvement for the purposes of compensation on quitting by s 70 of the AHA 1986[2]. The conditions relating to it are such that very rarely is such a claim sustainable in practice. High farming falls to be treated as a tenant's improvement for the purposes of assessing the rent and, as such, to be disregarded[3].

[1] AHA 1986, Sch 2 para 2(4).
[2] Formerly s 56 of the AHA 1948.
[3] AHA 1986, Sch 2 para 2(2)(a) and (4).

25.43 It should be noted that the requirements of Sch 2 para 2(4) to the AHA 1986 are significantly different from those of s 70. High farming is more likely to be encountered in the context of rent reviews. Further, this provision should also be borne in mind when considering the milk quota allocated to an agricultural holding in the case of a dairy farm[1]. If the system of farming which resulted in an unusually high level of production, and a higher than normal allocation of quota was responsible for this, then this disregard may be applicable. However, if it was not the system of farming as such, but the skill of the farmer which was responsible, then the 'high farming' disregard has no application.

[1]   See para 25.22ff.

Tenant's occupation of the holding

25.44 A further factor to be disregarded is 'any effect on the rent of the fact that the tenant who is a party to the arbitration is in occupation of the holding'[1]. This direction eliminates any extra rent that the actual tenant might be shown to be prepared to pay because of the importance to him of retaining his occupation of the holding. In such circumstances a landlord might otherwise be able to show that the actual tenant in occupation would be prepared to pay more rent to avoid the upheaval of removal or because the holding is of some special or particular value to him. These factors have to be disregarded. The rent is assessed objectively by reference to the attributes of the holding and not subjectively by reference to the requirements or circumstances of the particular parties[2].

In *J W Childers Trustees v Anker*[3], it was held that this 'disregard' did not entitle the arbitrator to treat the sitting tenant as not being available as one of the potential tenants envisaged as 'prudent and willing'.

It is submitted that it follows, by reference to this disregard, that any enhancement of rental value arising from the good husbandry (falling short of high farming) should be disregarded.

[1]   AHA 1986, Sch 2 para 3(a).
[2]   For a commentary on the similar words applied in the case of business premises under s 34 of the Landlord and Tenant Act 1954, see *Harewood Hotels Ltd v Harris* [1958] 1 All ER 104, [1958] 1 WLR 108, CA and in particular the judgment of Lord Evershed MR.
[3]   [1996] 1 EGLR 1, [1996] 01 EG 102, CA.

Tenant's dilapidations

25.45 The arbitrator is required to assess the holding as if there were no tenant's dilapidations[1] to land or buildings caused or permitted by the tenant[2]. Other breaches of contract are not to be disregarded.

It should be noted that landlord's dilapidations do not fall to be disregarded. Therefore, any reduction in the value of the holding because of the failure by the landlord to carry out his obligations must be taken into account in assessing the rental value of the holding. The reason for this inconsistent treatment would appear to be that tenants have very few and very ineffective sanctions to apply against landlords. They may have to suffer the burden of farming the holding with fixed equipment in want of repair, whereas landlords have very effective sanctions for breaches by the tenant, ultimately involving the giving of notice to quit to tenants who default in their obligations.

1   For a commentary on a comparable provision, see *Metropolitan Properties Co Ltd v Wooldridge* (1968) 20 P & CR 64.
2   AHA 1986, Sch 2 para 3(b).

Contracting-out and contracting-in

25.46 The statutory formula for revising the rent is extensive and makes no mention of whether the statutory procedures, or the rental formula, or any other matter prescribed by s 12 or Sch 2 to the AHA 1986 can be revised or varied by agreement or can be abandoned altogether. This could occur on the basis that the parties agreed there should be no rent review at all during the currency of the tenancy or that rent reviews should be carried out in accordance with the parties' own contractual formula. In *Johnson v Moreton*[1], Lord Russell remarked upon the absence of any statutory provision either authorising or prohibiting contracting-out, but as the matter was not directly in issue, came to no conclusion as to whether public policy demanded that the statutory procedures should override any agreement reached between the parties in the same way as the parties are precluded from contracting-out of the provisions protecting tenants in relation to notices to quit[2].

In *Goldsworthy v Brickell*[3], the Court of Appeal considered the matter in the context of a case where a fixed rent was agreed at the outset to apply for the lifetime of the landlord. The court came to no conclusion as the tenancy was set aside, having been procured by undue influence.

The problem is one of considerable practical importance. It is surprising that there is no authority on the point. The following is submitted.

(a)   There is no overriding consideration of public policy which would preclude the parties from agreeing their own particular machinery for revising the rent. Indeed, the statutory rental formula can only operate at all during the currency of a periodic tenancy, or during the last two years (to take effect at the expiration) of a fixed-term lease. In the case of a fixed-term lease for, say, 21 years, it would be very remarkable indeed if it could be said to be contrary to public policy for the parties to agree their own rent review machinery so as to provide for periodic rent reviews during the currency of the lease. If it is not contrary to public policy for the parties to agree their own formula in the case of a fixed-term lease, it is difficult to see what public policy considerations would apply differently in the case of a periodic tenancy. What is more difficult to predict is whether it would be perceived by the courts to be contrary to public policy for the rent formula, as opposed to the review machinery, to be varied by agreement.

(b)   In the absence of any overriding consideration of public policy, parties are always entitled to vary by agreement or contract-out altogether of statutory rights and restrictions[4]. Further, it will be noted that although there is a statutory procedure for revising any contractual provisions relating to repairs which are not consistent with the model clauses, and substituting the model clauses by arbitration[5], there is no equivalent provision for substituting the statutory rental formula for any contractual formula that the parties may otherwise agree upon.

For the reasons indicated earlier in the introduction to this chapter, the rent formula introduced by the AHA 1984 was a central feature of that Act and was the primary ingredient of the so-called 'NFU/CLA package'[6]. A contractual formula which caused the rent to be fixed by reference to current open market levels of rental could in practice amount indirectly to contracting-out of security of tenure which is arguably contrary to public policy. *Johnson v Moreton*[7] was decided on such wide and general principles that it is possible that it would be held, on parity of reasoning, that a rental formula which resulted in an uneconomic or 'penal' rent would be overridden as contrary to public policy. However, in the light of obiter dicta of Morritt LJ in *J W Childers Trustees v Anker*[8], it is now doubtful as to whether there is any equivalent public policy consideration requiring adherence to the rent review provisions contained in the AHA 1986.

[1]   [1980] AC 37, [1978] 3 All ER 37.
[2]   Now the AHA 1986, s 26(1).
[3]   [1987] Ch 378, [1987] 1 All ER 853.
[4]   See *Johnson v Moreton* [1980] AC 37, [1978] 3 All ER 37 and the cases cited.
[5]   AHA 1986, s 8.
[6]   See para 25.2.
[7]   [1980] AC 37, [1978] 3 All ER 37.
[8]   [1996] 1 EGLR 1, [1996] 01 EG 102, CA.

25.47 A related issue arises where the parties agree the rent payable in respect of an agricultural holding under the AHA 1986 on the understanding that there will be no increase of rent sought for an agreed period. The issue is then whether such an agreement can exclude either party's right to a rent review under s 12 of the AHA 1986 at three-yearly intervals. In *Plumb Bros v Dolmac (Agriculture) Ltd*[1], the Court of Appeal held that a collateral agreement not to increase rent will be binding, even where such agreement was not under seal, provided that the tenancy agreement and the agreement as to rent are part of a single composite transaction. In those circumstances, consideration supporting, for example, the landlord's undertaking not to seek a rent increase may be found in the tenant's promise to perform the obligations in the tenancy agreement. It should be noted that if a promise to defer any rent increase is unsupported by consideration, it will be unenforceable if it is not contained in a deed.

It is submitted that there is no public policy reason for the parties not to be able to contract out of the statutory rent formula under the AHA 1986, notwithstanding the fact that this was one of the central planks of the 'NFU/CLA Package'[2], which gave rise to the rent review formula in the Agricultural Holdings Act 1984[3].

1   (1984) 271 Estates Gazette 373.
2   National Farmers Union/Country Landowners Association.
3   See para 25.2.

RENT VARIATIONS FOR IMPROVEMENTS

Introduction

25.48 Section 13 of the AHA 1986 entitles a landlord who has carried out improvements to an agricultural holding to obtain an increase in rent by reason of the improvement in certain circumstances. He must first give notice within six months of completion of the improvement. The amount of the rent increase will be an amount equal to the increase in the rental value of the holding attributable to the carrying out of the improvement. The increase takes effect from completion of the improvement. The tenant receives the benefit of any grant (if any). There is no increase in rent for the grant-aided element of the improvement. There is a provision for arbitration in the event of the parties not being able to agree the amount of the increase[1].

Section 13 applies to the following improvements:

(a)   An improvement carried out at the request of or in agreement with the tenant[2]. This in practice is the most common form of improvement which carries with it an entitlement to a rent increase for the landlord. It should be noted that even where there is agreement to carry out the improvement, the landlord must still give six months' notice[3] before he can obtain an increase in rent.

(b)   The improvement was carried out by the landlord under a direction from the Agricultural Land Tribunal (ALT) under s 11 of the AHA 1986[4].

(c)   The landlord, having refused the tenant consent to the carrying out of the improvement, is subject to a direction from the ALT that the consent has been unreasonably withheld. In such circumstances the landlord may himself carry out the improvement and charge rent by virtue of the provisions of s 67(5) of the AHA 1986. Such an improvement entitles the landlord to an increase in rent under s 13[5].

(d)   The improvement is carried out by the landlord in compliance with a direction given by the Minister under powers conferred on him by or under any enactment[6]. An example of such an enactment is s 95 of the Agriculture Act 1947, though such directions are very rarely met in practice.

(e)   The works were executed on the holding for the purpose of complying with the requirements of a notice under s 3 of the Agriculture (Safety, Health and Welfare Provisions) Act 1956 (provision of sanitary conveniences and washing facilities)[7]. Such notices are also rarely, if ever, met with in practice.

(f)   An improvement carried out in compliance with an improvement notice served or an undertaking accepted under Pt VII of the Housing Act 1985 or Pt VIII of the Housing Act 1974[8].

405

No increase of rent is permitted under s 13(1) of the AHA 1986 in relation to an improvement falling within sub-paragraphs (a), (b) or (f) above if, within six months from the completion of the improvement, the landlord and tenant agree on any increase of rent or other benefit to the landlord in respect of the improvement[9].

Section 13(1) of the AHA 1986 provides that the amount of the increase in rent is 'an amount equal to the increase in the rental value of the holding attributable to the carrying out of the improvement'[10].

Section 13 also applies to an improvement whether or not it is one in respect of which compensation is payable under Pt V or VI of the AHA 1986[11].

[1] AHA 1986, s 13(7).
[2] AHA 1986, s 13(1) and (2).
[3] AHA 1986, s 13(1).
[4] AHA 1986, s 13(2)(b), previously Agriculture Act 1947. As to the provision of s 11 of the AHA 1986, see para 23.25.
[5] AHA 1986, s 13(2)(c).
[6] AHA 1986, s 13(2)(d).
[7] AHA 1986, s 13(2)(e).
[8] AHA 1986, s 13(2)(f). It is surprising that the reference to Pt VIII of the Housing Act 1974 should have survived the repeal of that provision by the Housing (Consequential Provisions) Act 1985, s 3 and Sch 1. It is now a spent provision – the relevant provisions of Pt VII are ss 214, 215 and 231.
[9] AHA 1986, s 13(3).
[10] AHA 1986, s 13(1).
[11] AHA 1986, s 13(8).

The amount of the increase

25.49 The increase in rent permitted by s 13(1) of the AHA 1986 shall be reduced proportionately as follows:

(a)   In the case of an improvement carried out in compliance with a direction given by the ALT under s 11 of the AHA 1986, where a grant has been made to the landlord in respect of the improvement out of money provided by parliament[1].

(b)   In the case of an improvement within paragraphs (a), (c), (d), (e) and (f) of para 25.48 above, where a grant has been made to the landlord in respect of the improvement out of money provided by parliament or local government funds[2].

(c)   In the case of an improvement carried out in compliance with an improvement notice served or an undertaking accepted under Pt VII of the Housing Act 1988 or Pt VIII of the Housing Act 1974, where the tenant has contributed to the cost incurred by his landlord in carrying out the improvement[3].

If the landlord fails to carry out an improvement in compliance with a direction given by the ALT under s 11 of the AHA 1986, and the tenant has himself carried out the improvement, then the improvement is treated as having been carried out by the landlord and as if any grant made to the tenant in respect of the improvement out of money provided by Parliament had been made to the landlord[4].

However, no increase in the rent shall take effect in these circumstances until the tenant has recovered from the landlord the reasonable cost of the improvement, reduced by the amount of any grant made to the tenant in respect of the improvement out of money provided by Parliament[5].

Any dispute arising between the landlord and the tenant of the holding under s 13 of the AHA 1986 shall be determined by arbitration under the AHA 1986[6].

[1]   AHA 1986, s 13(4)(a).
[2]   AHA 1986, s 13(4)(b).
[3]   AHA 1986, s 13(4)(c).
[4]   AHA 1986, s 13(5).
[5]   AHA 1986, s 13(6).
[6]   AHA 1986, s 13(7).

Procedural requirements

25.50 To obtain an increase in rent the landlord must give notice in writing to the tenant within six months of the completion of the improvement[1]. If he fails to do so, having first agreed with the tenant that interest shall be payable on the improvement, he does not forgo that interest but merely cannot claim it as rent. The practical consequences of this are that the landlord can neither levy distress nor give a two months' notice to pay under Case D nor enjoy any other of the special benefits which apply to rent in respect of that amount[2]. The money is payable by the tenant but not as rent. If it is payable by reason of an agreement supplemental to the tenancy agreement, then a notice to remedy in Form 3 can be given and can thereafter found a notice to quit in the event of non-compliance[3].

If the landlord agrees an increase in rent with the tenant without going through the statutory notice procedures under s 13 of the AHA 1986, he will start the three-year rent review cycle and may thereby delay an overall rent review.

If the landlord fails to implement the provisions of s 13 and fails to agree as a condition precedent for the carrying out of the improvement, that interest shall be charged at a specified rate, he does not irrevocably lose any benefit from that improvement, but must wait until the next rent review under s 12 of the AHA 1986 before any income in respect of the improvement is recoverable by him. The improvement then, being part of the fixed equipment of the holding, is part of the holding for which the notional open market rent, as adjusted, must be assessed and awarded.

[1]   AHA 1986, s 13(1).
[2]   This is supported by a county court case, *Busk v Hallett* (1969) unreported.
[3]   See *Official Solicitor v Thomas* [1986] 2 EGLR 1, 279 Estates Gazette 407, CA.

Chapter 26

DISTRESS FOR NON-PAYMENT OF RENT

GENERAL

26.1 The Shorter Oxford English Dictionary defines 'distress' as, amongst other things, anguish. It certainly can be anguish for the tenant. Distress is an ancient[1] common law form of self-help available to a landlord where rent or a money payment reserved as rent[2] is due and unpaid[3]. It does not need to be specifically referred to in the tenancy agreement and, while it originally was limited to a power to seize and detain chattels, a power of sale was conferred by the Distress for Rent Act 1689.

It is beyond the scope of this book to consider distress in detail[4]. It is a highly technical remedy. Briefly, it enables a landlord to instruct a certificated bailiff to enter onto the holding and seize goods and chattels of the tenant. The bailiff may subsequently sell the goods and chattels to satisfy the unpaid rent. There are a number of provisions contained in ss 16 to 19 of the AHA 1986[5] modifying the application of the remedy of distress in relation to agricultural holdings protected under the Agricultural Holdings Act 1986 (AHA 1986).

---

[1]   It is founded upon the origins of the landlord and tenant system. Rent was considered as more than mere money and the obligation to pay it was, therefore, considered to be very much greater than the obligation to discharge a debt (even a secured debt). In consequence the draconian and anachronistic remedy of seizing the tenant's property was given to landlords. It is unlikely that this remedy will endure much longer. The Law Commission has actively considered its total abolition – see the Law Commission Working Paper No 97 'The Law Commission provisionally recommends abolition' and see also para 26.13.

[2]   Or a money payment reserved as rent.

[3]   This is in addition to the other remedies available to a landlord, eg notice to pay, forfeiture, recovery by action through the court or the service of a statutory demand as a preliminary to bankrupt an individual tenant or put a corporate tenant into compulsory liquidation.

[4]   See Woodfall: Landlord and Tenant (Looseleaf edn, 1994) Sweet & Maxwell and Tanney and Travers, Distress for Rent (1st edn, 2000) Jordans.

[5]   Formerly, the Agricultural Holdings Act 1948, ss 18–22.

Who may distrain?

26.2 Apart from the landlord, the power to distrain is also available to a receiver of a landlord appointed under the Law of Property Act 1925 (LPA

1925)[1]. However, when a receiver of a landlord is appointed under the LPA 1925 by a mortgagee, then any subsequent distress levied by the mortgagor landlord is illegal[2]. A joint tenant may distrain against his co-tenants[3].

[1]   LPA 1925, s 109(3).
[2]   *Woolston v Ross* [1900] 1 Ch 788.
[3]   *Robinson v Hoffman* (1828) 4 Bing 562.

When available?

26.3 Distress is available when four conditions are satisfied:

(a)   the relationship of landlord and tenant must exist when the rent accrues and when the distress is levied. If there is more than one holding farmed by the tenant, the landlord can only distrain against goods on the holding in respect of which there are rent arrears. Each holding stands independently;

(b)   there must be arrears of rent. Although at common law, six years' arrears of rent may be recovered by distress, under the AHA 1986, the landlord is not entitled to distrain for rent due more than one year before the distress is levied[1]. The only exception applies where in the ordinary course of dealing between the landlord and the tenant, the payment of rent has been deferred until a quarter or half year after the date on which the rent legally became due[2]. If the tenant is adjudicated bankrupt, only six months' arrears of rent can be distrained for[3];

(c)   the rent must be certain (or capable of being made certain) when payment is due; and

(d)   the reversion of the tenancy agreement must be vested in the party seeking to distrain.

[1]   AHA 1986, s 16(1).
[2]   AHA 1986, s 16(2). Note: rent becomes due on the morning of the day for payment specified in the contract of tenancy. It does not become in arrears until after midnight: *Re: Aspinall, Aspinall v Aspinall* [1961] Ch 526, [1961] 2 All ER 751.
[3]   Insolvency Act 1985, s 180.

What can be seized?

26.4 Subject to certain exceptions, the landlord can seize all the goods and chattels found on the demised premises whether they belong to the tenant or to a third party.

Generally, at common law and under statute, there are certain types of goods which are exempt from distress, for example:

(a)   goods which have already been taken in execution[1];
(b)   goods in actual use[2];
(c)   perishable goods[3];
(d)   loose money; and
(e)   the tools and implements of the tenant's trade to a total value of £150[4].

26.4 *Distress for non-payment of rent*

The AHA 1986 does provide some measure of protection against distress for property on agricultural holdings:

(i) Section 18(1)(a) prohibits distress on a third party's machinery which is subject to an agreement for its hire or use in the conduct of the tenant's business. This would appear to include not merely hired equipment, but machinery being purchased under a hire purchase or conditional sale agreement[5]. It does not cover equipment which is being borrowed from a neighbouring farmer.

(ii) Section 18(1)(b) prohibits distress on a third party's livestock which is on the holding solely for breeding purposes.

Further, even if the goods are not exempt, they may be 'conditionally exempt', ie only liable to distress if there is no other sufficient distress on the holding.

The AHA 1986[6] provides a category of conditionally exempt assets in the form of agisted stock[7]. Provided that the agistment agreement is not gratuitous[8], if there is insufficient distress levied on other goods, distress against the agisted stock is limited to the amount agreed to be paid for the agistment or any unpaid balance. The AHA 1986 also contains provisions enabling the owner of the stock to recover it by discharging his indebtedness to the tenant[9].

---

1 Co.Lit. 47(a); *R v Cotton* (1751) Park 112.
2 Co.Lit. 47(a); *Field v Adames* (1840) 12 Ad & El 649.
3 *Wilson v Ducket* (1675) 2 Mod Rep 61.
4 Or such other amount that may be prescribed from time to time by order of the Lord Chancellor: Administration of Justice Act 1956, s 37. The present limit was set by the Protection from Eviction (Prescribed Value) Order 1980, SI 1980/26.
5 Although the point is not free from doubt.
6 AHA 1986, s 18(2)–(5).
7 Agistment is a contract of bailment where the land owner takes in another's stock and feeds it for a fixed price: see *Masters v Green* (1888) 20 QBD 807.
8 Payment can be in kind: see *London and Yorkshire Bank v Belton* (1885) 15 QBD 457.
9 AHA 1986, s 18(3).

26.5 Other categories of conditionally exempt assets include:

(a) beasts which 'gain' the tenant's land, for example, beasts of the plough[1];
(b) sheep belonging to the tenant[2]; and
(c) Sheep of a sub-tenant belonging to the sub-tenant or a third party[3].

Notwithstanding the various exceptions and conditional exemptions, a wide range of agricultural assets can be distrained against including the following:

(i) Growing crops – at common growing crops were exempt from distress. By statute the landlord may distrain on all sorts of corn, grass, hops, roots, fruits, pulse and other products whatsoever growing upon any part of the demised premises[4]. The landlord may cut, gather, make, cure, carry and lay up the crops, when ripe, in the barns or other proper place on the premises[5]. If there is no such place on the premises, he may store them in any other barn or proper place which he hires or otherwise procures for that purpose, as near as may be to the premises. In convenient time the landlord may appraise, sell, or otherwise dispose of the same, towards satisfaction of the rent, and of the charges of such distress, appraisement (sic) and sale[6].

(ii) Harvested crops – at common law, corn in sheaves or stocks was exempt from distress[7]. By statute a landlord may distrain on any sheaves or cocks of corn, or corn loose, or in the straw, or hay upon any part of the land (charged with the rent), and lock up or detain the same in the place where it is found, but it must not be removed from such a place to the damage of the owner[8]. It also appears that the landlord must sell at the expiry of five days if the corn is not 'replevied' (recovered by replevin)[9].

(iii) Beef and dairy cattle[10] – although the landlord or bailiff must feed livestock which are impounded.

(iv) There is a limited common law right to distrain against beasts which come onto the tenant's land through the negligence or default of their owner[11].

(v) A landlord may distrain against cattle which are driven off the holding by the tenant[12].

(vi) Generally, wild animals cannot be distrained because there is no right of property. However, if an animal has been tamed or captured, then it may be distrained. Thus if deer are kept in a private enclosure (not being apart) for the purpose of sale or profit, then they may be distrained for rent[13].

[1]   Save that if the only other assets available for distress are growing crops, not yet ripe, the landlord can distrain on the beasts of the plough: see *Jenner v Yolland* (1818) 6 Price 3.
[2]   *Davies v Aston* (1845) 1 CB 746.
[3]   *Keen v Priest* (1859) 4 H & N 236.
[4]   Distress for Rent Act 1689, s 2.
[5]   Distress for Rent Act 1689, s 2.
[6]   Distress for Rent Act 1689, s 2.
[7]   *Griffin v Scott* (1762) 1 Barn KB 3.
[8]   Distress for Rent Act 1689, s 2.
[9]   *Piggott v Birtles* (1836) 1 M & W 441.
[10] *Keen v Priest* (1859) 4 H & N 236.
[11] Co.Lit. 47(a).
[12] Co.Lit. 161(a).
[13] *Davies v Powell* (1737) Willes 46.

Third party goods

26.6 In addition to the restrictions imposed by the AHA 1986 itself in relation to the levy of distress by the landlord against the goods of a third party[1], the landlord cannot distrain on goods of a third party if:

(a)   the landlord himself brought the goods onto the premises[2];
(b)   the third party brought them onto the land with the landlord's consent[3];
(c)   the third party occupies as the landlord's agent or with his permission[4]; and
(d)   the landlord has agreed not to distrain on the third party's goods[5].

Further protection is provided for a third party by the Law of Distress Amendment Act 1901. Subject to certain exceptions, this Act protects from distress:

(i)   the goods of a sub-tenant who pays his rent by equal instalments quarterly or at more frequent intervals and whose rent is the full annual value of the premises or any part of it which is comprised in his tenancy;

(ii) the goods of any lodger; and

(iii) the goods of any person, not being a tenant of the premises or any part of it and not having any beneficial interests in any tenancy of the premises or any part of it[6]. As the Law of Distress Amendment Act 1908 interferes with the landlord's rights of common law, it is construed strictly and in the landlord's favour[7].

1   See para 26.4.
2   *Paton v Carter* (1883) Cab & El 183.
3   *Fowkes v Joyce* (1689) 2 Vern 129.
4   *Wheeler v Stevenson* (1860) 6 H & N 155.
5   *Welsh v Rose* (1830) 6 Bing 638.
6   Law of Distress Amendment Act 1908, s 1.
7   Law of Distress Amendment Act 1908, s 9.

When, where and for how much?

26.7 The right to distrain can be exercised as soon as the rent in question is due. The landlord of an agricultural holding is not entitled to distrain for rent which became due in respect of that holding more than one year before the making of the distress[1]. This is only modified where rent is payable a quarter or half year after it was due. Where the ordinary course of dealings between the parties indicates that such deferred payment has been the normal practice, then the rent shall be deemed to have become due at the expiry of that quarter or half year as the case may be[2]. Unpaid rent which is irrecoverable by distress may be pursued by court proceedings subject to the six-year limitation period[3].

In general, the right to distress is limited to goods found on the demised premises[4]. The landlord can distrain for unpaid rent and for the costs of levying the distress. Nevertheless, importantly the right to distress is lost by:

(a)   judgment for the rent in proceedings;
(b)   forfeiture;
(c)   payment or lawful tender of the rent due[5]; and
(d)   agreement, ie the waiver of the right to distrain.

1   AHA 1986, s 16(1).
2   AHA 1986, s 16(2).
3   Limitation Act 1980.
4   Except in the case of fraudulent removal of cattle feeding on common land appurtenant to the holding, see the Distress for Rent Act 1737, s 8.
5   *Branscombe v Bridges* (1823) 1 B & C 145.

26.8 In the case of a compulsory liquidation of a tenant company, if the landlord distrains before a winding-up petition is presented, and the distress is not completed before the petition is presented, the company, any creditor or contributory can apply to the court to stay the distress[1]. After the winding-up order has been made by the court, the landlord will have to apply to the court to continue the levy of distress. The landlord will need the leave of the court to sell the goods distrained on[2]. If the landlord distrains after the winding-up petition is presented, but before a winding-up order is made, the distress if void[3]. A landlord who wishes to levy distress after the presentation of a petition, should wait until the winding-up order is made and then make an application for leave to distrain under s 130 of the Insolvency Act 1986.

In the case of a voluntary liquidation of a company, there is no restriction on the landlord's right to distrain. The liquidator of the company or any contributory or creditor can apply to the court to impose a stay on any distress[4]. As with compulsory liquidation, leave will probably be given to complete a distress commenced before the liquidation, but not if the distress was commenced after the presentation of the winding-up petition in relation to rent which was due before the liquidation[5].

Where the tenant is an individual and is made bankrupt, the landlord can still distrain, but not for arrears that are more than six months before the bankruptcy order is made. If the landlord distrains after a petition has been presented, but before the order is made, any monies recovered which are in excess of the six months' rent are to be held for the bankrupt estate[6]. The landlord can distrain for all rent due after bankruptcy if the trustee in bankruptcy remains in possession and renders himself liable by not disclaiming the lease[7].

Distress cannot be levied against a company in administration except with the leave of the court or, following the administration order, with the leave of the court or the consent of the administrator[8]. The same applies in relation to an administration of an insolvent partnership[9].

[1] Insolvency Act 1986 (IA 1986), s 126.
[2] IA 1986, s 130.
[3] IA 1986, s 128.
[4] IA 1986, s 112.
[5] *Re Margot Bywaters Ltd* [1942] Ch 121.
[6] IA 1986, s 347(2).
[7] *Re Binns, ex p Hale* (1875) 1 Ch D 285.
[8] IA 1986, ss 10 and 11.
[9] Insolvent Partnerships Order 1994, SI 1994/2421.

Set off

26.9 If a tenant is entitled to compensation from the landlord under the AHA 1986 or otherwise, the amount of that compensation must be set off against the rent due[1]. However, it is unlikely that during a subsisting tenancy any compensation will be due[2].

[1] AHA 1986, s 17 uses the words 'may be set off', but does not entitle the landlord to distrain for more than the balance.
[2] Save perhaps for game damage, see the AHA 1986, s 20. This may apply, for example, to game damage compensation under s 20 although compensation had been 'ascertained' by agreement or the award of an arbitrator. At one time it was frequently stated that a tenant could not set off an unliquidated debt from his landlord against a claim for rent and in any event in answer to a distress. No doubt s 22 of the Agricultural Holdings Act 1948 (the

forerunner of s 17) was enacted to give a tenant some relief against this rule. However, the current view is that a tenant may generally set off such a claim against a claim for rent – see *Lee-Parker v Izzet* [1971] 3 All ER 1099, [1971] 1 WLR 1688. It is arguable whether this general provision extends to agricultural tenancies and distress. See also, *British Anzani (Felixstowe) Ltd v International Marine Management (UK) Ltd* [1980] QB 137, [1979] 2 All ER 1063 and see *The Conveyancer*, May/June 1981, p 199: 'Repairs and Deductions from Rent'.

How?

26.10 The landlord may distrain personally or through a certificated bailiff. In view of the myriad of rules governing distress, and the physical nature of seizure, it is a brave, and perhaps unwise, landlord who opts for the former course. The certificated bailiff may enter the holding in any way short of breaking in and once he is in, he must seize the goods.

Disputes

26.11 The ancient remedy of replevin enabled the tenant to prove that the distress was wrongful and to obtain the return of the goods[1]. In the case of agricultural holdings, s 19 of the AHA 1986 provides for any dispute relating to distress to be settled by the county court or the magistrates' court.

[1]   See *Woodfall: Landlord and Tenant*, (Looseleaf edn, 1994) Sweet & Maxell, para 1–0989.

Sub-tenants

26.12 Section 6 of the Law of Distress Amendment Act 1908 enables the landlord to bypass a defaulting tenant and levy distress against the sub-tenant or require the sub-tenant to pay his rent to the landlord until the defaulting tenant's arrears are paid off. Payments made by the sub-tenant to the head landlord under this provision are credited against his liability to his immediate landlord[1]. The appointment of a receiver by the mortgagee of the defaulting tenant will not affect the ability of the landlord to claim rent from a sub-tenant under s 6 of the 1908 Act. The landlord will have priority over a chargee of book debts and/or rent[2].

[1]   Law of Distress Amendment Act 1908, s 3.
[2]   *Rhodes v Allied Dunbar (Pension Services) Ltd* [1989] 1 All ER 1161.

The future

26.13 On 25 July 2006 the draft of the Tribunals, Courts and Enforcement Bill was published. It proposes to abolish the right for a landlord of commercial premises to distrain against the tenant's goods for rent arrears. Distress will be replaced by a procedure described as commercial rent arrears recovery. Whether this proposal will be introduced, and whether the existing law relating to distress in respect of agricultural premises will be affected, remains to be established.

Part III

TERMINATION OF AN AGRICULTURAL HOLDINGS ACT 1986 TENANCY

Contents

Chapter 27

INTRODUCTION: THE STATUTORY SCHEME AND SECURITY OF TENURE

GENERAL

27.1 Security of tenure is granted to tenants of agricultural holdings by the imposition of restrictions upon notices to quit given by landlords. This is quite unlike the scheme for giving security of tenure under the Housing Act 1988 or the Landlord and Tenant Act 1954, Pt II, where instead the statutory mode of termination is prescribed. The AHA 1986 has its own unique code. The policy of the legislation is supplemented by ss 2 and 3 of the AHA 1986 which have the combined effect of preventing tenancies of agricultural holdings from expiring by effluxion of time[1].

The common law rules relating to other methods of termination of tenancies, for example, by surrender, merger or forfeiture, remain largely unaffected.

The provisions of the AHA 1986, giving security of tenure, are contained in ss 25 to 33 and Schs 3, 4 and 5, and the regulations passed under them.

This part of this book contains a commentary upon those statutory provisions together with those common law rules which remain unaffected.

The table at the end of this chapter attempts to summarise the landlord's remedies and the tenant's means of challenging the landlord under the AHA 1986 and the general law of forfeiture.

[1] See para 20.3 ff.

RESTRICTIONS ON NOTICES TO QUIT UNDER THE AHA 1986

27.2 The statutory scheme under the AHA 1986 has two limbs interfering with the common law provisions relating to notice to quit. First, subject to exceptions[1], the AHA 1986 extends the common law period of notice. The common law rule is that six months' notice expiring on the annual term date of the tenancy is sufficient to terminate an annual tenancy. Subject to exceptions[2], the statutory requirement is for a minimum of 12 months' notice expiring on the term day.

1   For the exceptions, see para 28.13.
2   See para 28.23 and para 28.13.

27.3 Section 25(2) of the AHA 1986 specifies that an express provision in the contract may provide for a lesser period of notice in certain limited circumstances. However, it has been held that if the period of notice provided for by the tenancy agreement is too short to enable the tenant to give the necessary notices before quitting to entitle him to recover certain forms of statutory compensation, the contractual provision will be ineffective[1] and the whole clause void.

The second limb is to distinguish between two classes of notice to quit.

(a)   For the first type of notice to quit to be valid it does not need to state any reason for why it is given. Its effectiveness is subject to the tenant's ability to give a counter-notice within one month under s 26(1) of the AHA 1986. If the tenant does so, the notice to quit will only be effective if the landlord then makes an application to the Agricultural Land Tribunal (ALT) for consent to the operation of the notice to quit. The ALT will only give consent in limited circumstances[2].

(b)   The second type of notice to quit is one given for a specified reason[3]. Schedule 3 to the AHA 1986 contains eight special grounds (Cases A to H) where the counter-notice procedure does not apply. These Special Cases have their own statutorily prescribed scheme for regulation and determining whether a notice to quit given for one or more of the reasons stated shall be valid and effective[4].

1   *Re Disraeli's Agreement* [1939] Ch 382, [1938] 4 All ER 658; *Coates v Diment* [1951] 1 All ER 890; *Parry v Million Pigs Ltd* (1980) 260 Estates Gazette 281.
2   See para 30.6 ff.
3   In previous editions of this book these reasons were known as the 'seven deadly sins'.
4   See para Ch 31.

REQUIREMENTS FOR A VALID NOTICE TO QUIT

27.4 For a notice to quit an agricultural holding protected by the AHA 1986 to be valid and effective, it must comply with three requirements:

(a)   it must be valid at common law[1];
(b)   it must comply with any further contractual requirements contained in the tenancy agreement[2]; and
(c)   it must comply with all relevant statutory requirements[3].

1   See para 28.2.
2   See para 28.9.
3   See para 28.10.

RESTRICTIONS ON NOTICES TO QUIT PART UNDER THE AHA 1986

27.5 At common law a notice to quit part is invalid[1]. The AHA 1986 modifies the common law in the following cases:

(a)   section 31 of the AHA 1986 authorises the landlord to give notice to quit in respect of part only of the holding, in certain limited circumstances as listed in that section[2].

(b)   the tenancy agreement may itself expressly permit such a notice. The contractual right to provide for notice to quit part in the tenancy agreement is expanded by s 25(2) of the AHA 1986 to a right to give a shorter period of notice than would otherwise be permissible[3].

[1]   The common law rule is that the notice to quit must relate to the whole holding: *Re Bebington's Tenancy* [1921] 1 Ch 559; *Woodward v Earl of Dudley* [1954] Ch 283, [1954] 1 All ER 559.
[2]   See Ch 31.
[3]   See para 28.9.

27.6 Additionally, s 140 of the Law of Property Act 1925 (LPA 1925) entitles a landlord of part of a holding in which the reversion has been severed, i e divided between two or more separate landlords, to give notice in respect of the whole of that part which is vested in the landlord giving the notice[1].

[1]   The applicability of s 140 of the LPA 1925 to agricultural holdings is implicit in s 32(1)(b) of the AHA 1986 and has been expressly so held in *Persey v Bazley* (1983) 47 P & CR 37, CA and *John v George* [1995] 1 EGLR 9, [1995] 22 EG 146, CA.

DISPUTES PROCEDURE

27.7 The way in which the validity or effectiveness of a notice to quit can be disputed depends upon the nature and type of the notice to quit given. The AHA 1986 divides jurisdiction to determine such disputes between:

(a)   arbitrators;
(b)   the ALT; and
(c)   the courts.

Each forum has exclusive jurisdiction in respect of the particular type of notice to quit which can be given[1]. To invoke the jurisdiction of the appropriate forum, either a counter-notice, or a demand for arbitration, or an application to the court must be made. In the case of a counter-notice and demand for arbitration, a time limit of one month is imposed. Failure to take the appropriate step to counter or dispute the notice to quit, or the reasons stated in it, is fatal to the tenant's ability to protect his tenancy and to challenge the landlord's notice to quit upon its merits subsequently[2].

[1]   Reference should also be made to the table below at 27.19.
[2]   *Magdalen College, Oxford v Heritage* [1974] 1 All ER 1065, [1974] 1 WLR 441, CA; *Morris v Muirhead* 1969 SLT 70; *Harding v Marshall* (1983) 267 Estates Gazette 161. Cf *Rous v Mitchell* [1991] 1 All ER 676, CA.

27.8 In the case of a notice to quit to which a demand for arbitration has been given, the tenant must within a further three months either agree the appointment of an arbitrator or apply to the President of the Royal Institution of Chartered Surveyors for one to be appointed. If he fails to do so his notice will be rendered ineffective[1].

27.8 *Introduction: the statutory scheme and security of tenure*

Where a notice to quit has been challenged by a counter-notice under s 26 of the AHA 1986, the landlord must apply to the ALT for consent to the operation of the notice to quit within one month. In default, the landlord's notice to quit is ineffective.[1]

A landlord giving the wrong form of notice to quit for the grounds upon which he is relying cannot subsequently amend it. In certain circumstances he may even lose an opportunity to give a new notice to quit altogether[2].

It is essential that both landlords and tenants should adhere closely to the procedural requirements for establishing or disputing (as the case may be) forms of notice given, as well as be familiar with the substantive law relating to the rights and duties of the parties in respect of those notices.

Briefly, the disputes procedures are as follows:

(a)   If the landlord's notice to quit contains no reason or ground upon which it is given, or if it is given for one of the reasons stated in s 27(3) of the AHA 1986, then a counter-notice requiring the provisions of s 26(1) to apply *must* be given, otherwise the notice to quit becomes incontestable and will terminate the tenancy, even if no good reason is available for doing so[3].

(b)   If the landlord's notice to quit is stated to have been given for one of the reasons stated in Cases A (certain statutory smallholdings), B (non-agricultural development and planning consent), D (non-compliance with notice to pay rent or notice to remedy) or E (irremediable breach), then a demand for arbitration must be made within one month of service of the notice to quit[4].

(c)   If the landlord's notice to quit is stated to have been given under Cases C, F, G or H, and the tenant wishes to contest the reason stated in the notice to quit, then no counter-notice is appropriate[5], nor is any demand for arbitration[6]. The tenant may either seek a declaration of the court as to the validity of the notice to quit given at that stage, or else wait until the landlord claims possession and then raise the issue in his defence in the court proceedings[7].

---

[1]   See the Agricultural Holdings (Arbitration on Notices) Order 1987, SI 1987/710, reg 10.

[2]   Eg in the case of the death of a tenant, an incontestable notice to quit can be given within three months of certain events following death: see Case G. If such a notice is not given within that time, the tenancy, having vested in the personal representatives of the deceased tenant, will continue and the landlord's right to terminate the tenancy on that ground will be lost for all time.

[3]   The only available ground of contest in those circumstances would be the common law validity of the notice to quit: see *Magdalen College, Oxford v Heritage* [1974] 1 All ER 1065, [1974] 1 WLR 441, CA or fraud as in *Rous v Mitchell* [1991] 1 All ER 676, CA.

[4]   See the Agricultural Holdings (Arbitration on Notices) Order 1987 and *Magdalen College, Oxford v Heritage* [1974] 1 All ER 1065, [1974] 1 WLR 441, CA.

[5]   *Cowan v Wrayford* [1953] 2 All ER 1138, [1953] 1 WLR 1340, CA.

[6]   See the Agricultural Holdings (Arbitration on Notices) Order 1987, SI 1987/710, reg 9.

[7]   For the preservation of its inherent jurisdiction, see in particular s 97 of the AHA 1986 and *Paddock Investments Ltd v Lory* [1975] 2 EGLR 5, 236 Estates Gazette 803.

SPECIAL CLASSES OF TENANT

Servicemen

27.9 The wartime origins of the Agricultural Holdings Act 1948 (AHA 1948) have lived on in s 30 and Sch 5 to the AHA 1986. Tenants of agricultural holdings who are also servicemen in the Reserve or Auxiliary Armed Forces, and whose holdings include a dwellinghouse occupied by a person responsible for the control of the farming of the holding, are given power to give a counter-notice in respect of a notice to quit requiring the ALT's consent to the operation of such a notice. A provision for a third party to serve protective notices on his behalf during his absence is also incorporated.

Sub-tenants

27.10 The AHA 1986 does not provide direct protection for sub-tenants. The common law rules still apply. These are very harsh in their effect and in most circumstances deprive sub-tenants of security of tenure if the head landlord terminates the head tenancy unilaterally or if the head tenant gives notice to quit to the head landlord[1].

Parliament foresaw these problems and, by virtue first of s 26(1)(d) of the 1948 Act[2], later by se 5(1)(d) of the Agricultural Holdings (Notice to Quit) Act 1977, and now Sch 4 para 7 to the AHA 1986, gave the Lord Chancellor power to make regulations to protect sub-tenants. No such regulations have been made. It is doubtful whether they ever will be.

Detailed consideration is given in this part of the book to the nature and extent of the security of tenure enjoyed by tenants whose immediate landlords are not themselves the freeholders but merely tenants under a superior landlord. The use of the sub-tenancy as a device to circumvent security of tenure is also considered.

[1]   *Pennell v Payne* [1995] 1 EGLR 6, [1995] 06 EG 152.
[2]   In the substituted form provided by the Agriculture Act 1958, s 8, Sch 1 para 10.

OTHER METHODS OF TERMINATION

27.11 Apart from notice to quit, at common law a tenancy can be terminated in a number of ways.

Effluxion of time

27.12 Termination by effluxion of time has effectively been superseded by the effect of ss 2 and 3 of the AHA 1986 which convert term tenancies into tenancies from year to year on the expiration of the fixed term[1].

[1]   For a commentary on these provisions, see Ch 20.

Surrender

27.13 Surrender can be effected at common law either expressly by a deed or following a surrender agreement or impliedly or by operation of law. The common law rules relating to surrender remain largely unaffected by the agricultural holdings legislation[1].

1   See para 33.4 ff.

Forfeiture

27.14 Where there is a forfeiture clause or a term is made a condition in the tenancy agreement, subject to the provisions of s 146 of the Law of Property Act 1925, the landlord may forfeit the tenancy for a breach, subject to the tenant's right to seek relief[1]. It has been held that the common law provisions as to forfeiture are effected, in the context of agricultural holdings, by a rule that a clause in the tenancy agreement, permitting termination of the tenancy without providing the tenant with adequate time to serve the necessary notices to entitle him to compensation, is invalid[2].

1   In the case of forfeiture of leases of 'agricultural or pastoral' land, no relief is obtainable under s 146 of the Law of Property Act 1925 if forfeiture is by reason of bankruptcy or liquidation of the tenant.
2   *Parry v Million Pigs Ltd* (1980) 260 Estates Gazette 281; *Re Disraeli's Agreement* [1939] Ch 382, [1938] 4 All ER 658.

Disclaimer

27.15 On the bankruptcy or liquidation of a tenant, the tenancy may be brought to an end by notice to quit given by the landlord under Case F, or by forfeiture, or by disclaimer by the trustee in bankruptcy or liquidator on behalf of the tenant[1]. Here the common law rules and the general provisions of the Insolvency Act 1986 apply in the same way as for any other class of tenant, save that the right to obtain relief from forfeiture is excluded[2].

1   The Insolvency Act 1986, ss 315–320 (bankruptcy) and 178–182 (liquidation). See Ch 45.
2   The Law of Property Act 1925, s 146(8).

CONTRACTING-OUT

27.16 The agricultural holdings legislation contains no express prohibition upon any agreement or device whereby a tenant is denied the opportunity to take advantage of the right to give a counter-notice, or in any other way invoke the security of tenure provisions contained in the legislation[1]. The House of Lords has authoritatively decided that any scheme whereby a tenant is deprived of his right to invoke the provisions relating to security of tenure is contrary to public policy and unenforceable[2]. Accordingly, it is not open to a tenant to agree in advance to give up the right to serve a counter-notice. This has been extended by the Court of Appeal to impose a positive obligation upon a landlord's alter ego, who was one of several joint tenants, to concur in the giving of a counter-notice so as to preserve the tenancy following the landlord's notice to quit[3]. It has further been extended to protect sub-tenants where the head landlord negotiated the sub-tenancy with an intermediate head tenant/mesne landlord selected with a view to denying the sub-tenant security of tenure[4]. After a tenant has given a counter-notice in response to a notice to quit from the landlord, if the dispute is then settled on terms that the tenant will deliver up possession of the holding, then it is submitted that those terms of settlement are binding on the tenant[5].

[1]   For a commentary on contracting out of the agricultural holdings legislation generally, see para 19.49 ff.
[2]   *Johnson v Moreton* [1980] AC 37, [1978] 3 All ER 37.
[3]   *Featherstone v Staples* [1986] 2 All ER 461, [1986] 1 WLR 861.
[4]   *Gisborne v Burton* [1989] QB 390, [1988] 3 All ER 760, CA.
[5]   *Kildrummy (Hersey) v Calder* 1994 SLT 888, Ct of Sess, in relation to like provisions contained in the Agricultural Holdings (Scotland) Act 1991, ss 21(1) and 22(1).

SERVICE OF NOTICES

27.17 The commentary upon the methods of service of notices to quit and all other forms of 'notice, request or other instrument' given in respect of an agricultural holding appears in Chapter 42.

EFFECT OF AGREEMENT FOR SALE ON NOTICE TO QUIT

27.18 An anomalous provision, dating back to 1919, that if a landlord contracted to sell his interest in the whole or part of an agricultural holding which was subject to notice to quit, that rendered the notice to quit ineffective, has been repealed. The many problems to which the provision of s 7 of the Agricultural Holdings (Notice to Quit) Act 1977 and its predecessor, s 30 of the AHA 1948, gave rise have been removed by its repeal in the Agricultural Holdings Act 1984 and the omission of the provision from the AHA 1986.

TABLE OF LANDLORD'S REMEDIES AND TENANT'S MEANS OF CHALLENGING THE LANDLORD UNDER THE AHA 1986 AND THE LAW OF FORFEITURE

27.19 This table appears on the following pages.

Landlord's remedies	AHA 1986 provision	Tenant's challenges						Forfeiture	
		Counter-notice[19]	ALT	Fair and reasonable landlord test[20]	Arbitration[21]	Court	Available[22]	S146 notice[23]	Relief[24]
Smallholdings tenant[1]	Case A	✗	✗	✗	✓	✓	✗	✗	✗
Planning permission for non-agricultural use[2]	Case B	✗	✗	✗	✓	✓	✗	✗	✗
Certificate of bad husbandry[3]	Case C	✗	✗	✗	✗	✓	✓	✓	✓
Unpaid rent[4]	Case D	✗	✓	✗	✓	✓	✓	✗	✓
Failure to remedy (work required)[5]	Case D	✓	✗	✓	✓	✓	✓	✗	✗
Failure to remedy (no work required)[6]	Case D	✗	✗	✗	✓	✓	✓	✗	✗
Irremediable breach[7]	Case E	✗	✗	✗	✓	✓	✓	✓	✗
Insolvent tenant[8]	Case F	✗	✗	✗	✓	✓	✓	✗	✓
Death of tenant	Case G	✗	✗	✗	✓	✓	✓	✗	✓
Succession application made[9]		✗	✗	✓	✗	✗	✗	✗	✗

× ×× ✓×× ×××

× ×× ✓×× ×××

× ×× ✓×× ×××

✓ ✓✓ ✓✓✓ ✓✓✓ ✓

× ×× ×××××× ×××

× ×× ✓✓✓ ✓✓✓

× ×× ✓✓✓ ✓✓✓

× ×× ✓✓✓ ✓✓✓

× ×× ✓✓✓ ✓✓✓

Case H

s27(3)(a)

s27(3)(b)

s27(3)(c)

s27(3)(d)

s27(3)(e)

s27(3)(f)

No successful application[10]

No succession rights[11]

Ministry amalgamations[12]

Good husbandry[13]

Sound estate management[14]

Agricultural research/smallholdings[15]

Allotments[16]

Greater hardship[17]

Non-agricultural use authorised by planning legislation[18]

1   Arbitration is available in relation to whether the case is established and suitable accommodation: see para 31.18 ff.
2   Cf non-agricultural use authorised by planning legislation. Generally see para 32.10 ff.
3   See para 31.21 ff.
4   Under the AHA 1986 a preliminary notice to pay must be served in the statutorily prescribed form. Arbitration is available in relation to the notice to pay and any subsequent notice to quit: see para 31.28 ff.
5   Under the AHA 1986 Act a preliminary notice to do work must be served in the statutorily prescribed form (Form 2). Arbitration is available in relation to the notice to do work and any subsequent notice to quit. Uniquely under the AHA 1986, after the notice to quit the tenant may serve a counter-notice. If the counter-notice is valid, the notice to quit will not have effect unless the consent of the Agricultural Land Tribunal is given in response to an application by the landlord: see s 28(2) of the AHA 1986. Generally see para 31.51 ff.
6   Under the AHA 1986, where the tenant is in breach of covenant which can be remedied without work then a notice to remedy in the statutorily prescribed form (Form 3) must be served. The tenant has no right to demand arbitration in relation to the notice to remedy, but can demand arbitration in relation to the subsequent notice to quit. The tenant has no right to issue a counter-notice. Generally, see para 31.70 ff.
7   See para 31.76 ff.
8   'Insolvent' is statutorily defined: see AHA 1986, s 96. Generally, see para 31.88 ff.
9   Where the tenancy was granted before 12 July 1984. If the application is successful, the landlord may apply to the Agricultural Land Tribunal for consent to the notice to quit. Generally, see para 31.90 ff.
10 Or no application made. Generally, see para 31.98 ff.
11 Tenancies granted on or after 12 July 1984. Generally, see para 35.2 ff.
12 See para 31.102 ff.
13 Cf a certificate of bad husbandry. Generally, see para 35.2 ff.
14 See para 30.6 ff.
15 See para 30.10.
16 See para 30.11.
17 See para 30.12.
18 Cf Case B: planning permission for non-agricultural use. Generally, see para 32.10 ff.
19 The counter-notice must be served on the landlord 'not later than one month from the giving of the notice to quit': see AHA 1986, s 26(1)(b). One month is a calendar month: see Law of Property Act 1925, s 61. If a valid counter-notice is given, the landlord must:
    (a)apply to the ALT for consent to the operation of the notice to quit;
    (b)establish the ground for consent on which he relies; and
    (c)satisfy the ALT that the 'fair and reasonable landlord' would require possession.

20 See para 30.16.
21 The tenant's demand for arbitration must be served on the landlord 'within one month' of service of the relevant notice or notices to quit: see art 9 of the Agricultural Holdings (Arbitration on Notices) Order 1987, SI 1987/710. In addition, the demand for arbitration will cease to be valid unless within three months of the service of the demand for arbitration an arbitrator has been appointed by the parties or an application has been made to the President of the RICS for the appointment of an arbitrator in default of agreement between the parties: see art 10 of the Agricultural Holdings (Arbitration on Notices) Order 1987. Generally, see para 31.11 ff.
22 Forfeiture is only available where there is an express and valid proviso for re-entry in the tenancy agreement: see para 13.3.
23 See para 13.3.
24 See para 13.16 ff. Note – relief is not available in relation to a notice to quit: see para 13.16.

Chapter 28

NOTICES TO QUIT: GENERAL RULES

INTRODUCTION

28.1 It is beyond the scope of this book to set out the common law requirement of notices to quit in detail. The following points listed are not exhaustive and the standard textbooks on landlord and tenant should be consulted[1].

For a notice to quit of an agricultural holding protected by the AHA 1986 to be valid and effective, it must comply with three requirements:

(a)   it must be valid at common law;
(b)   it must comply with any further contractual requirements contained in the tenancy agreement; and
(c)   it must comply with all relevant statutory requirements.

[1]   See *Woodfall: Landlord and Tenant* (Looseleaf edition, 1994) Sweet & Maxwell.

COMMON LAW REQUIREMENTS

28.2 In the usual case[1], a tenancy of an agricultural holding will be an annual periodic tenancy either by reason of express grant or as a consequence of the operation of ss 2 and 3 of the AHA 1986.

The common law lays down various requirements as to the validity of a notice to quit in relation to a tenancy from year to year including its form and contents, the persons who may give and receive the notice, the length of the notice, the date of expiry and provisions in relation to service[2].

Where a landlord serves a notice to quit in reliance on certain grounds where the landlord does not at the date of the service of the notice have an honest belief that the grounds exist, a notice is bad at common law[3].

[1]   Note the special case where a notice to quit is required by s 3(1) of the AHA 1986 to prevent a fixed-term tenancy from continuing after the term date as a tenancy from year to year.
[2]   As to provisions relating to the service of a notice to quit, see Ch 42.

3   *Rous v Mitchell* [1991] 1 All ER 676, CA; *Luttenberger v North Thoresby Farms Ltd* [1992] 1 EGLR 261, CA; *Omnivale Ltd v Boldan* [1994] EGCS 63, CA. For a commentary, see para 31.15.

Accuracy

28.3   The notice must be clear and precise. It must leave the tenant in no doubt as to when he is required to quit. It must provide that the tenancy will terminate on a specified date mentioned in so many words in the notice, or at least on a date which the wording of the notice indicates clearly enough to a person of ordinary intelligence[1]. The notice to quit must leave the recipient in no reasonable doubt as to what it means, when the tenancy is to terminate, and if a special reason for the giving of the notice needs to be, and is, stated, it must also be clear and fairly state what that reason is so that the recipient may know what is alleged against him[2].

The law relating to the validity and effectiveness of notices to quit has been extensively reviewed by the House of Lords in *Mannai Investments Co Ltd v Eagle Star Life Assurance Co Ltd*[3]. Until then the courts had been inconsistent in their approach to the need for accuracy in notices to quit. The House of Lords overruled the decision in *Hankey v Clavering*[4] and decided that the real question that fell to be answered in individual cases was: 'Is the notice quite clear to a reasonable tenant reading it? Is it plain that he cannot be misled by it?'. In the *Mannai* case itself the tenant had served a break clause in a lease and inadvertently had specified the wrong date. He was one day out. It was held that this was not misleading and his intention was clear and therefore the notice was valid.

A notice to quit is a technical document and besides being clear and unambiguous, it should be accurate, but an inconsequential inaccuracy will not render the notice invalid[5]. The general rule is that a gap or ambiguity can and generally will be resolved in favour of validity and a misstatement on a minor point will be overlooked if a recipient of ordinary intelligence will be likely to have understood it correctly[6].

1   Per Lopes LJ in *Bury v Thompson* [1895] 1 QB 696, CA: 'a notice to quit is a good notice if it be so expressed that a person of ordinary capacity receiving the notice cannot well mistake its nature; it must be clear and unambiguous'.
2   *Cowan v Wrayford* [1953] 2 All ER 1138, [1953] 1 WLR 1340, CA; *Mills v Edwards* [1971] 1 QB 379, [1971] 1 All ER 922, CA; *Hammon v Fairbrother* [1956] 2 All ER 108, [1956] 1 WLR 490.
3   [1997] AC 749, [1997] 1 EGLR 57.
4   [1942] 2 KB 326.
5   *Mannai Investments Co Ltd v Eagle Star Life Assurance Co Ltd* [1997] AC 749, [1997] 1 EGLR 57, overruling *Hankey v Clavering* [1942] 2 KB 326. Also see *Price v Mann* [1942] 1 All ER 453, CA; *Carradine Properties Ltd v Aslam* [1976] 1 All ER 573, [1976] 1 WLR 442; *Germax Securities Ltd v Spiegal* (1978) 37 P & CR 204, CA; *Ravenseft Properties Ltd v Hall* [2001] EWCA Civ 2034, [2002] 1 EGLR 9, [2002] 11 EG 156.
6   *Mannai Investments Co Ltd v Eagle Star Assurance Co Ltd* [1997] AC 749, [1997] 1 EGLR 57.

28.4   An illustration of the court's approach can be found in *Peaceform Ltd v Cussens*[1]. In that case, the lease conferred on the tenant an option to purchase the freehold exercisable at any time before 6 February 2004 by giving not less than[2] three months' notice. A letter from the tenant's solicitor dated 27 August 2003 purported to give notice to exercise the option stating that 'you are entitled to not less than 3 months' notice and accordingly I confirm that this notice may be deemed to expire on 7 November 2003'. The landlords argued that, by giving a date for expiry that was less than three months from the date of service, the tenant had failed to serve a valid notice of the exercise of the option. Before *Mannai*[3] a notice containing this type of error would have been invalid. In this case, the court held in favour of the landlords, but not because of the wrong date. The deputy judge accepted that the wrong date did not invalidate the notice. The real issue was whether the letter would leave a reasonable recipient, with knowledge of the terms of the option, in any doubt as to how and when it was being exercised. Here (unusually) the notice period was not less than three months expiring no later than 6 February 2004. The expiry date in the letter purporting to give notice was neither clearly defined nor obvious from the context. Even assuming that a reasonable recipient would have realised that the tenant had intended to give a valid notice and that there had been a mere slip, the recipient would still not have known what the expiry date was intended to be.

The development of the application of the rules of construction to notices to quit and other notices to like effect given under the Landlord and Tenant Act 1954, Pt II, is that there has been a growing tendency of the courts to apply liberal rules of construction and to overlook even such matters as specifying an impossible term date[4], but there are limits to the courts' benevolence[5].

A court will treat a notice as invalid if it concludes that a reasonable recipient would not have understood its intention[6]. Also, a failure to provide core information required by legislation has also rendered a notice ineffective[7]. Likewise, a failure to reflect accurately the precise terms of a break clause may render a notice invalid[8], or not specifying the date correctly in relation to a rent review[9].

1   [2006] EWHC 2657 (Ch), [2006] 47 EG 182.
2   See para 42.27.
3   *Mannai Investments Co Ltd v Eagle Star Assurance Co Ltd* [1997] AC 749, [1997] 1 EGLR 57.
4   *Carradine Properties Ltd v Aslam* [1976] 1 All ER 573, [1976] 1 WLR 442.
5   *Morrow v Nadeem* [1986] 2EGLR 73, 279 Estates Gazette 1083, wrongly identified landlord – notice bad. Cf *Parsons v Parsons* [1983] 1 WLR 1390 and *Frankland v Capstick* [1959] 1 All ER 209, [1959] 1 WLR 205. Also see *Pearson v Alyo* [1990] 1 EGLR 114, CA, following *Morrow v Nadeem*, a notice under the Landlord and Tenant Act 1954 naming the husband alone as landlord when the husband and his wife were joint landlords, was held to be invalid even though the husband was the sole equitable owner. Cf *Divall v Harrison* [1991] 1 EGLR 17: where a notice to quit an agricultural holding given by solicitors on behalf of equitable owners (beneficiaries under a will) and not on behalf of legal owners was held to be valid – tenants not likely to be misled. *Combey v Gumbrill* [1990] 2 EGLR 7: where a counter-notice demanding arbitration given by one of two joint tenants was held to be valid because authority to serve on behalf of both given by the courts to the wife-tenant in certain matrimonial orders. Also see *Hammersmith and Fulham London Borough Council v Monk* [1992] 1 AC 478, [1992] 1 All ER 1, HL in which a joint tenancy was validly determined by one of two joint tenants without the knowledge or consent of the other.
6   *Barclays Bank plc v Bee* [2001] EWCA Civ 1126, [2001] 3 EGLR 41, [2001] 37 EG 153.

28.4 Notices to quit: general rules

7 *Speedwell Estates Ltd v Dalziel* [2001] EWCA Civ 1277, [2002] 1 EGLR 55, [2002] 02 EG 104.
8 *Peer Freeholds Ltd v Clean Wash International* [2005] EWCA 179 (Ch), [2005] 1 EGLR 47, [2005] 17 EG 124.
9 *Riverside Housing Association Ltd v White* [2007] UKHL 20, [2007] 18 EG 152 (CS).

Who can give a notice to quit?

28.5 In the case of joint owners[1], a notice to quit given by one of several joint owners is effective[2] and one of several joint tenants can give notice to quit without the concurrence of his joint tenants[3]. This is because the tenancy endures so long as each and every tenant (or landlord as the case may be) wishes it. Service of the notice addressed to all the joint tenants[4] upon any one of them is good[5].

Notice may be given by an agent[6].

1 See, generally, Ch 30.
2 *Parsons v Parsons* [1983] 1 WLR 1390.
3 *Newman v Keedwell* (1977) 35 P & CR 393.
4 *Jones v Lewis* (1973) 25 P & CR 375, CA.
5 See *Woodfall: Landlord and Tenant* (Looseleaf edn, 1994) Sweet & Maxwell. Cf the position on forfeiture in *Blewett v Blewett* [1936] 2 All ER 188, CA.
6 As to the position of agents giving notices to quit on behalf of a landlord, see *Frankland v Capstick* [1959] 1 All ER 209, [1959] 1 WLR 205; *Pickard v Bishop*, (1975) 31 P & CR 108; *LCC v Agricultural Food Products Ltd* [1955] 2 QB 218, [1955] 2 All ER 22, CA; *Germax Securities Ltd v Spiegal* (1978) 37 P & CR 204.

The date of expiry

28.6 The notice to quit must direct termination of the tenancy at the end of a periodic term, ie at the end of the year of the tenancy. That must be the actual anniversary date of the commencement without distinction as to whether the tenancy began 'on' or 'from' any specified date[1].

A notice to a tenant to quit 'on or before' a fixed date is valid. It operates to give notice to determine the tenancy on the date named and, secondly, to give the tenant an option to terminate the tenancy on any earlier date of the tenant's choice[2]. Likewise, a notice seeking possession 'at the end of the period of your tenancy' has been held to mean the same as 'after the end of the period of your tenancy' and was a normal use of language in a temporal context[3].

A 'running notice', ie a notice which calls upon the tenant to quit on a certain date, or at the expiration of the year of his tenancy which should expire next after the end of 12 months from the service of the notice, is good[4]. It is a wise precaution for a notice to contain the 'running words' if there is any doubt as to when the annual term date of the tenancy falls.

1 *Bathavon RDC v Carlile* [1958] 1 QB 461, [1958] 1 All ER 801, CA, and the cases cited therein, namely *Sidebotham v Holland* [1895] 1 QB 378, CA; *Queen's Club Gardens Estates Ltd v Bignell* [1924] 1 KB 117; *Crate v Miller* [1947] KB 946, [1947] 2 All ER

45, CA; and *Lemon v Lardeur* [1946] KB 613, [1946] 2 All ER 329, CA. As to the term date in the case of a tenancy starting 'from the ...', see *Ladyman v Wirral Estates Ltd* [1968] 2 All ER 197.

2   *Dagger v Shepherd* [1946] KB 215, [1946] 1 All ER 133, CA; *Micrografix v Woking 8 Ltd* [1995] 2 EGLR 32, [1995] 37 EG 179; *Mannai Investments Co Ltd v Eagle Star Life Assurance Co Ltd* [1997] AC 749, [1997] 1 EGLR 57, HL.

3   *Notting Hill Housing Trust v Roomus* [2006] EWCA Civ 407, [2006] 1 WLR 1375. Cf *Fernandez v McDonald* [2003] EWCA Civ 1219, [2004] 1 WLR 1027.

4   *Addis v Burrows* [1948] 1 KB 444, [1948] 1 All ER 177, CA.

The effect of a further notice

28.7 If a landlord is in doubt as to the validity of the notice he has given, he does not prejudice its effect if it does after all prove to be valid by giving a second notice to quit, unless coupled with other evidence it is clear that in so doing he intends to be thereby creating or in any way recognising a new tenancy[1]. Similarly, if the landlord gives a notice to quit and simultaneously gives another notice inconsistent with the notice to quit, for example, a rent review notice under s 12 of the AHA 1986, it is a wise precaution to make it clear in the notice or in the covering letter that the rent review notice is intended to take effect only if the notice to quit is inoperative.

1   *Loewenthal v Vanhoute* [1947] KB 342, [1947] 1 All ER 116. Cf *Lower v Sorrell* [1963] 1 QB 959, [1962] 3 All ER 1074, CA. See *Grammer v Lane* [2000] 04 EG 135. See also para 28.16.

The length of the notice

28.8 At common law, the parties are free to specify any length of notice they wish, but in the absence of any agreed period in the case of an annual tenancy, not less than six months' notice to quit must be given to terminate on the annual term date of the tenancy.

CONTRACTUAL REQUIREMENTS

28.9 The terms of the tenancy may impose further restrictions on the ability of a party to give a notice to quit[1]. Alternatively, the terms may seek to relax the common law requirements. The validity of any relaxation will depend on whether they conflict with an overriding statutory requirement. In the case of agricultural holdings, it is common to find a provision in the tenancy agreement that the landlord may give short notice to quit where the landlord intends to use the land for certain non-agricultural purposes[2]. Such provisions will be invalid if they provide for the landlord to give such period of notice that would prevent the tenant from making an effective claim to all relevant compensation under the AHA 1986[3].

1   *Datnow v Jones* [1985] 2 EGLR 1, CA; *Prudential Assurance Co Ltd v London Residuary Body* [1992] 2 AC 286, HL.

2   *Coates v Diment* [1951] 1 All ER 890; *Paddock Investments Ltd v Lory* (1975) 236 Estates Gazette 803; *Rugby Joint Waterboard v Foottit* [1973] AC 202, HL; *Floyer-Ackland v Osmond* (2000) 80 P & CR 229, CA.

28.9 *Notices to quit: general rules*

3   *Re Disraeli's Agreement* [1939] Ch 382; *Coates v Diment* [1951] 1 All ER 890; *Parry v Million Pigs Ltd* (1980) 260 Estates Gazette 281. See also para 24.26.

STATUTORY REQUIREMENTS

28.10 In the case of a tenancy of an agricultural holding protected by the AHA 1986, the common law requirements as to the length of notice and the ability to serve a counter-notice or demand for arbitration are modified by the provisions of the AHA 1986.

Where the property let includes a dwellinghouse as part of an agricultural holding protected under the AHA 1986, the premises are not 'let as a dwelling'. Accordingly, a notice to quit such premises does not need to comply with the provisions of s 5 of the Protection from Eviction Act 1977[1].

1   *National Trust v Knipe* [1997] 2 EGLR 9, [1997] 40 EG 151.

Accuracy

28.11 Strict rules of construction have been applied to the preliminary notices given under the agricultural holdings legislation[1]. They have been construed by reference to the similar rules which apply to forfeiture notices. Strict rules of construction have been applied to forfeiture notices, notices to pay and notices to remedy, but more liberal rules of construction have been applied to notices to quit which have been treated as commercial documents to which effect is to be given unless to do so would offend the canons of construction[2]. It is still undecided as to whether strict or more liberal rules of construction are applied to errors contained in notices to quit relying on the Special Cases[3]. It is submitted that they do not fall to be strictly construed. Also, a distinction should be drawn between the requirement of a landlord to comply strictly with the provisions of the Special Cases before he can validly give a notice founded upon them and the requirement that the notices themselves must be free from error. The requirement for strictness applies to satisfying the provisions of the statute, but not necessarily to the form of the notice to quit then given.

In one case, a notice to quit which was stated to be given 'In order to go to arbitration for rent', when in fact a rent review notice should have been given, was held to be a valid notice to quit, notwithstanding the very misleading covering letter[4].

In *Ravenseft Properties Ltd v Hall*[5], the issues concerned the validity of notices served under s 20 of the Housing Act 1988 and whether each notice was in a form substantially to the same effect as that prescribed by the Assured Tenancies and Agricultural Occupancies (Forms) Regulations 1988[6]. In that case a notice mis-stated the commencement date of the tenancy and the prescribed guidance notes. The Court of Appeal decided that the notice was valid, applying the approach to construction laid down in *Mannai Investment Co Ltd v Eagle Star Assurance Co Ltd*[7].

1   The reason for strict rules being applied to notices to remedy and notices to pay rent is 'where a provision enabled landlords to forfeit a tenant's interest and security of tenure, notices leading to such a result must be strictly construed', per Lord Denning MR in *Pickard v Bishop* (1975) 31 P & CR 108.

2   In the light of the authoritative ruling of the House of Lords in *Mannai Investments Co Ltd v Eagle Star Assurance Co Ltd* [1997] AC 749, [1997] 1 EGLR 57 (overruling [1942] 2 KB 326), *Carradine Properties Ltd v Aslam* [1976] 1 All ER 573, [1976] 1 WLR 442 and *Germax Securities Ltd v Spiegal* (1978) 37 P7CR 204, CA, correctly state the law as it now is. See also *Ravenseft Properties Ltd v Hall* [2001] EWCA Civ 2034, [2002] 1 EGLR 9, [2002] 11 EG 156.

3   Cases A to H of AHA 1986, Sch 3.

4   *Roberts v Magor* [1953] EGD 18. *Sed quaere* in the light of the dicta of Lord Denning MR in *Pickard v Bishop* (1975) 31 P & CR 108 and *Cowan v Wrayford* [1953] 2 All ER 1138, [1953] 1 WLR 1340.

5   [2001] EWCA Civ 2034, [2002] 1 EGLR 9, [2002] 11 EG 156.

6   SI 1988/2203.

7   [1997] AC 749, [1997] 1 EGLR 57.

The length of the notice

28.12   Agricultural holdings are subject to special statutory exceptions to the common law rule. Section 25(1) of the AHA 1986 provides that 'notwithstanding any provision to the contrary in the contract of tenancy of the holding' any notice to quit[1] shall be invalid if it purports to terminate the tenancy before[2] the expiration of 12 months from the end of the then current year of the tenancy prevails[3].

1   A notice exercising an option to determine a lease before its expiration by effluxion of time, is a notice to quit within the AHA 1986, s 25: see *Edell v Dulieu* [1924] AC 38, HL. The same applies to a notice to quit given by a tenant to a landlord: *Flather v Hood* (1928) 44 TLR 698. Cf *Elsden v Pick* [1980] 3 All ER 235, CA, where the recipient may waive a defect in the notice given. The notice cannot be given before the start of the tenancy: *Lower v Sorrell* [1963] 1 QB 959, [1962] 3 All ER 1074, CA.

2   If the tenancy agreement provides for longer notice than 12 months the tenancy agreement

3   AHA 1986, s 25(5); *Re Midland Rly Co's Agreement* [1971] Ch 725, [1971] 1 All ER 1007, CA.

28.13   The exceptions to the general rule stated at 28.12 above are to be found in s 25 itself and arts 7 and 14 of the Agricultural Holdings (Arbitration on Notices) Order 1987[1]. They are as follows:

(a)   Where the tenant is insolvent[2].

(b)   Where a notice to quit is given pursuant to a provision in the contract of tenancy authorising resumption of possession of the holding or some part thereof for some specified purpose[3] other than agricultural use. The minimum duration of such a notice is not specified in the AHA 1986 but it has been held[4] that the provision in the contract will be wholly invalid if it does not provide sufficient time to enable the tenant to make compensation claims within the time specified by the AHA 1986[5].

(c)   A notice given by a tenant to a sub-tenant[6].

(d)   In the case of a lease for life or lives, which, by virtue of s 149(6) of the Law of Property Act 1925, now takes effect as a lease for a term of 90 years determinable as mentioned in that section (one month's notice terminating on a quarter day)[7].

(e)   Where an arbitrator has specified a date for the termination of a tenancy on the tenant's failure to do work under a notice to remedy or where there has been an extension of time under a notice to remedy after notice to quit[8].

(f)   if, after a rent review, the arbitrator awards an increased rent, the tenant may serve not less than six months' notice to terminate the tenancy at the end of the first year of the tenancy following the increase[9]. This modest benefit for a tenant confronted with an unacceptable rent rise merely saves him one year of occupation.

(g)   When the ALT has granted a certificate of bad husbandry it can specify in its certificate a minimum period of not less than two months'[10] notice instead of 12 months[11]. The landlord must be careful to ensure that his consequent notice to quit is given pursuant to the ALT's direction. This provision brings to a speedy conclusion any continuing deterioration to a holding.

[1]   SI 1987/710
[2]   AHA 1986, s 25(2)(a). 'Insolvent' is defined in s 96(2) as follows:

'For the purposes of this Act, a tenant is insolvent if:

(a) he has been adjudged bankrupt or has made a composition or arrangement with his creditors, or

(b) where the tenant is a body corporate, a winding-up order has been made with respect to it or a resolution for voluntary winding-up has been passed with respect to it (other than a resolution passed solely for the purposes of its reconstruction or of its amalgamation with another body corporate)'.

A receiving order in bankruptcy is not, therefore, sufficient. Adjudication is necessary when the tenant is an individual (rather than a company).

[3]   For the purposes of this exception a provision in the contract authorising the resumption of possession for any non-agricultural purposes is a 'specified purpose': see *Paddock Investments Ltd v Lory* [1975] 2 EGLR 5, 236 Estates Gazette 803, specified does not mean 'specific'. An unspecific purpose such as 'any non-agricultural development' can be a specified purpose.

[4]   *Re Disraeli's Agreement* [1939] Ch 382, [1938] 4 All ER 658; *Coates v Diment* [1951] 1 All ER 890; *Parry v Million Pigs Ltd* (1980) 260 Estates Gazette 281. See para 24.26.

[5]   For example, the one month's notice required under s 70 for high farming or ss 60(6)(a) and 62 for additional compensation for disturbance.

[6]   AHA 1986, s 25(3)(c). This exception is not confined to the case where the tenant (intermediate landlord) has himself received a notice to quit and is giving notice to the sub-tenant on that account.

[7]   By virtue of s 3(3) of the AHA 1986 it will be seen that such tenancies are also excluded from the provisions of that section. Although, therefore, s 3 of the AHA 1986 does not require a notice to quit to terminate such a term of 90 years, and although s 25 excludes any necessity for 12 months' notice to quit in respect of it, nevertheless the Law of Property Act 1925 itself does require at least one month's notice to terminate on a quarter day applicable to the tenancy. It could be argued that this one-month period suggests that the reasoning which resulted in the decision of the line of cases, including *Coates v Diment* [1951] 1 All ER 890, is capable of challenge.

[8]   The Agricultural Holdings (Arbitration on Notices) Order 1987, SI 1987/710, arts 7 and 14.

[9]   AHA 1986, s 25(3).

[10]   The statutory requirement of not less than two months would appear to be an indirect recognition of the correctness of the decision in *Coates v Diment* [1951] 1 All ER 890 and *Parry v Million Pigs Ltd* (1980) 260 EG 281.

[11]   AHA 1986, s 25(4).

28.14 The special provisions, formerly contained in s 1(2)(d) of the Agricultural Holdings (Notice to Quit) Act 1977, relating to certain tenancies created pre-25 March 1947, are now set out at length in para 4 of Sch 12 to the AHA 1986[1]. These relate to certain special forms of agricultural tenancies created now more than 40 years ago by certain public bodies, for example, the Secretary of State concerning land required for military purposes, a corporation carrying on on a railway, dock, canal water or other undertaking including Associated British Ports, British Railways Board, British Waterways Board and London Regional Transport and subsidiaries.

Although in these cases 12 months' notice to quit is not required by s 25 of the AHA 1986, there is still the question as to what length of notice should be given[2]. If not otherwise provided in the tenancy agreement, the common law rule will require six months' notice to end a yearly tenancy on the anniversary of its commencement. Any provisions in the tenancy agreement permitting resumption of possession will be subject to the principle that a clause will be void if it purports to allow resumption without notice or by a notice which would leave the tenant insufficient time in which to give the one-month preliminary notice of intention to claim compensation for disturbance under ss 60 to 62 or for adoption of a special system of farming under s 70 of the AHA 1986 or to remove fixtures under s 10 of the AHA 1986[3].

[1] The text of which is reproduced at para A1.202 ff.
[2] The period is specified in the case of a notice following a rent review or certificate of bad husbandry: see para 28.13.
[3] *Re Disraeli's Agreement* [1939] 1 Ch 382; *Coates v Diment* [1951] 1 All ER 890; *Beckett v Birmingham Corpn* (1956) 6 P & CR 352; *Parry v Million Pigs Limited* (1980) 260 Estates Gazette 281.

28.15 The requirement to receive 12 months' notice can be waived by the recipient of the notice. When a tenant gave notice to quit of less than 12 months' duration which the landlord accepted, the landlord was able to obtain an order for possession when the tenant sought to plead the invalidity of his own notice[1]. Waiver by the recipient is not contrary to public policy, but it is submitted that an agreement in advance to accept short notice would probably be unenforceable as being contrary to public policy[2].

It is submitted that if there is an express provision that 12 months' notice must be given to terminate the tenancy, then even though, for example, the tenant becomes insolvent[3], the landlord could not give a six months' notice. This is because section 25(2)(a) overrides the general provision that 12 months' notice must be given notwithstanding any lesser period provided for in the tenancy agreement. It does not override a contractual extension of the common law period of six months rule to twelve months.

[1] *Elsden v Pick* [1980] 3 All ER 235, [1980] 1 WLR 898, CA.
[2] See para 19.50.
[3] AHA 1986, s 25(2)(a).

Can a notice to quit be given without prejudice?

28.16 In *Grammer v Lane*[1], there was a dispute as to whether or not a landowner had created a tenancy. The landlord gave notice to revise the rent under s 12 'without prejudice' to his contention that there was no existing tenancy at all. He similarly gave a notice to remedy breaches. Thereafter he sought the appointment of an arbitrator in each case. Concurrently the 'tenant' had issued proceedings for a declaration that he held a tenancy.

It was held that there was 'no reason in principle why a freeholder could not serve a notice or take relevant arbitrarial steps pending the resolution of an outstanding dispute as to whether any tenancy existed at all'. The scheme of the AHA 1986 was not 'flouted'.

¹   [2000] 04 EG 135.

SERVICE OF NOTICES TO QUIT

28.17 The special rules relating to service of notices to quit and all other forms of 'notice, request, demand or other instrument' given in respect of an agricultural holding are contained in s 93 of the AHA 1986. These rules are of the utmost practical importance and strict compliance with one or more of the methods of service specified in s 93 is essential if due service is to be proved.

There is no general or statutory requirement that a notice to quit should be signed or witnessed. The notice does not have to be given by the landlord or tenant, it can be given by an agent¹. The agent must have the necessary authority when giving the notice². It is not sufficient if he obtains that authority subsequently. Further, the notice must be authenticated so that the recipient can rely upon it³.

¹   See para 28.5.
²   *Harmond Properties Ltd v Gajdzis* [1968] 3 All ER 263, [1968] 1 WLR 1858 and *LCC v Agricultural Food Products Ltd* [1955] 2 QB 218, [1955] 2 All ER 229; cf *Frankland v Capstick* [1959] 1 All ER 209, [1959] 1 WLR 205; *Pickard v Bishop* (1975) 31 P & CR 108; *Germax Securities Ltd v Spiegal* (1978) 37 P & CR 204.
³   See Ch 42.

Chapter 29

NOTICES TO QUIT PART, JOINT INTERESTS AND SUB-TENANCIES

NOTICE TO QUIT PART

The common law

29.1 At common law a notice can only be given in respect of the whole of the land comprised in the contract of tenancy[1]. Notice to quit part of an agricultural holding is invalid at common law, subject to three exceptions[2].

If different pieces of land are let at different times, by separate tenancy agreements, to the same tenant by the same landlord, then, unless these agreements have been 'consolidated'[3], they will continue to be separate tenancies of separate agricultural holdings and a notice to quit in respect of any one of them would not be a notice to quit part.

[1] *Re Bebington's Tenancy* [1921] 1 Ch 559; *Woodward v Earl of Dudley* [1954] Ch 283, [1954] 1 All ER 559.
[2] See para 29.2.
[3] *Jenkin R Lewis & Son Ltd v Kerman* [1971] Ch 477, [1970] 1 All ER 833 and the doctrine of surrender and re-grant generally. Note 'consolidation' in this way is a matter of intention. Where two holdings were let by the same landlord to the same tenant and one single rent was fixed for all the land unapportioned at a rent review, the two holdings remained two separate holdings and the doctrine of surrender and re-grant did not apply: see *J W Childers Trustees v Anker* [1996] 1 EGLR 1, [1996] 01 EG 102, CA. See para 33.4.

The exceptions

29.2 The exceptions when a valid notice to quit part of an agricultural holding can be given are as follows:

(a)   express provision in tenancy agreement;
(b)   a statutory exception – s 31 of the Agricultural Holdings Act 1986 (AHA 1986);
(c)   severance of the landlord's reversion.

Express provision in tenancy agreement

29.3 Where there is an express provision in the tenancy agreement authorising the landlord to terminate the tenancy as to part only of the holding, then a notice to quit given in reliance upon such a provision will be valid: the contractual provision will be effective. A notice to quit given pursuant to such a provision must still be a full 12 months' notice to expire on the annual term date of the tenancy and the provisions of s 26(1) of the AHA 1986 (requiring the landlord to obtain the consent of the ALT to the operation of the notice to quit) will apply, unless the circumstances provided for by s 25(2)(b) are applicable.

Section 25(2)(b) of the AHA 1986 provides that a notice given pursuant to a provision in the contract of tenancy authorising the resumption of possession of the holding or some part thereof for some specified non-agricultural purpose is valid even though the provision in the tenancy agreement authorises less than the full 12 months' notice[1]. It should be noted that the period specified in the short notice clause contained in the tenancy agreement must be sufficient to enable the tenant to give certain forms of counter-notice claiming compensation on quitting[2].

[1]   See para 32.2 ff.
[2]   *Coates v Diment* [1951] 1 All ER 890 and see the commentary generally at para 24.26.

Statutory exception

29.4 Section 31 of the AHA 1986 authorises the landlord to give notice to quit in respect of part only of a holding in certain limited circumstances listed in the section. Section 31 contains a collection of objects, formerly contained in s 31 of the AHA 1948, whose origins date back to the first Agricultural Holdings (England) Act of 1875[1]. Their common denominator seems to be that (by reference to the standards of 1875) they contain a collection of socially desirable objects for which a landlord should be entitled to resume possession of part only of the holding. These objects and purposes are as follows:

(a)   adjusting boundaries between agricultural units or amalgamating agricultural units or parts thereof;

(b)   the erection of cottages or other houses for farm labourers, whether with or without gardens[2];

(c)   the provision of gardens for cottages or other houses for farm labourers;

(d)   the provision of allotments;

(e)   the letting of land (with or without other land) as a smallholding under Pt II of the Agriculture Act 1970[3];

(f)   the planting of trees[4];

(g)   the opening or working of a deposit of coal or other specified minerals, quarries, gravel pits, or the construction of ancillary works or buildings;

(h)   the making of a watercourse or reservoir;

(i)   the making of a road, railway, tramroad, siding, canal or basin, wharf, pier, or other work connected therewith.

1   The Agricultural Holdings (England) Act 1875, s 52.
2   The wording of s 31 of the AHA 1948 was ambiguous. The new wording gives statutory
    effect to the decision of the Court of Appeal in *Paddock Investments Ltd v Lory* [1975]
    2 EGLR 5, 236 Estates Gazette 803.
3   Cf the wording of s 31 of the AHA 1948 which referred to smallholdings 'as defined by'
    the various statutes mentioned in full in the section. Note also that s 31(2)(d) of the AHA
    1948 related to 'the provision of smallholdings', whereas the wording of s 31 of the AHA
    1986 is the letting of land (with or without other land) as a smallholding. Section 31 of the
    AHA 1986 does not apply unless there is to be a letting.
4   For a case involving such a notice, see *Secretary of State for Wales v Pugh* [1969] CLY 45,
    120 NLJ 357 (CC).

29.5 Although s 31 of the AHA 1986 permits the giving of a notice to quit
part in the cases listed, this does not mean that the remaining statutory
provisions for the giving of security of tenure do not apply. A tenant
confronted with a notice under s 31 of the AHA 1986 can give counter-notice
and thereby invoke the security of tenure provisions contained in ss 26 and 27
of the AHA 1986. For the notice to quit to be effective, the landlord must be
able to establish ground for possession under the Special Cases[1] or alternatively under s 27(3) of the AHA 1986[2].

In practice, this will usually mean a Case B[3] ground where the landlord has
first obtained planning consent, for example, for gravel working. The fact that
planning consent has been obtained in respect of part of the holding for
non-agricultural development will not enable the landlord to give notice to
quit that part of the holding which is the subject of planning consent, unless
that purpose falls within s 31 of the AHA 1986. This problem most frequently
arises in the case of general residential development. It is only the erection of
cottages or other houses for farm labourers which is specified in s 31. A notice
to quit must state that it is given for the specified purpose or with a view to
the specified use if the Case B ground is to be relied upon as well as s 31.

1   See Ch 31.
2   See Ch 30.
3   See Ch 32.

Severance of the landlord's reversion

29.6 Until 1925, if a landlord conveyed part of the freehold[1] (ie thereby
severing the reversion), the various landlords of the various severed parts
could not give notice to quit in respect of the individual part which each
owned without joining in concert and giving notice to quit the whole holding[2].
Section 140 of the Law of Property Act 1925 (LPA 1925), as amended by the
Law of Property (Amendment) Act 1926, remedied this difficulty[3].

Severance of the landlord's interest only applies where the reversion is divided
up between two or more landlords. A disposal of the freehold to two
landlords, for example, a husband and wife, who purchase the whole holding
jointly, does not operate as a severance of the reversion. Conversely, if each
were to take separate conveyances of separate defined parts, that would
constitute a severance. Severance can be effected otherwise than by sale, for
example, by gift.

29.6 *Notices to quit part, joint interests and sub-tenancies*

Severance of the freehold reversion does not operate to create two or more new tenancies, whether or not accompanied by a legal apportionment of the rent[4]. If the landlord of the newly created severed part is a mere nominee or bare trustee of the landlord of the remaining part and, although not a sham, was a device to enable the service of a notice to quit part of the holding, it has been held that the severance is ineffective. The nominee landlord of the severed part will not be able to implement the provisions of s 140 of the LPA 1925[5].

1   Severance of the reversion can also apply where the landlord's reversionary interest is not that of a freeholder, eg because he is the head tenant.
2   *Re Bebington's Tenancy* [1921] 1 Ch 559; *Smith v Kinsey* [1936] 3 All ER 73.
3   The combined effect of the LPA 1925, the Law of Property (Amendment) Act 1926 and s 12 of the Agricultural Holdings Act 1923 were described in early editions as 'a nightmare to construe'.
4   *Jelley v Buckman* [1974] QB 488, [1973] 3 All ER 853; *Stiles v Farrow* (1977) 241 Estates Gazette 623. Cf *Paul v Caldwell* (1960) 176 Estates Gazette 743.
5   *Persey v Bazley* (1983) 267 Estates Gazette 519. This decision has been criticised. It is consistent with other decisions under s 140: *Re Clayton's Deed Poll* [1980] Ch 99; *Nevill Long & Co (Boards) Ltd v Firmenich & Co* (1983) 47 P & CR 59.

Enlargement of notice to quit part

29.7 Section 32 of the AHA 1986 entitles a tenant who has had a notice to quit part of the holding to enlarge that notice to quit so that it will terminate the tenancy of the whole holding:

(a)   where the notice to quit was given pursuant to s 31 of the AHA 1986; or

(b)   where the notice was given by the landlord of a severed part of the freehold.

The right to enlarge the notice to quit of part to the entire holding does not apply if the notice to quit was given pursuant to a provision in the contract of tenancy authorising the landlord to terminate the tenancy of part only of the holding.

In order to rely upon s 32 of the AHA 1986, the tenant must serve a counter-notice within 28 days after receipt of the notice to quit, or where the operation of the notice depends on any proceedings 'under the preceding provisions of this Act', after the time at which it is determined that the notice shall take effect. The counter-notice must provide that the tenant accepts the notice to quit as a notice to quit the entire holding.

Where a notice to quit is enlarged so as to operate as a notice to quit the entire holding, disturbance compensation will be payable in respect of the whole holding, unless excluded under s 63(3) of the AHA 1986[1]. This right to compensation for disturbance after enlargement of the notice to quit does not apply, except to the land the subject of the original notice before enlargement, if the amount of land to be taken is less than a quarter of the entire holding and the holding as diminished is reasonably capable of being farmed as a separate holding.

Where a tenant who has enlarged the notice to quit under s 32 of the AHA 1986 serves a notice to quit on his sub-tenant on the grounds that a notice to quit has been served on him (the head tenant) by the head landlord, then the sub-tenant cannot give counter-notice under s 26(1) of the AHA 1986. This rule applies whether the tenant serves on the sub-tenant a notice to quit in respect of the whole or part of the land subject to the sub-tenancy. If the head landlord's notice to quit is effective, the sub-tenancy will perish on the expiration of the head tenancy[2].

1   See para 38.47 ff.
2   See para 29.17 ff.

Reduction of rent after notice to quit part

29.8 Section 33 of the AHA 1986 provides for a reduction in the rent after notice to quit part of the holding has been given:

(a)   where notice to quit has been given pursuant to s 31 of the AHA 1986; or

(b)   where it has been given pursuant to a provision in the contract of tenancy.

Section 33 does not apply where the tenant surrenders part of the holding, although the contract of tenancy itself may provide for a rent reduction.

If a rent reduction is made it will not amount to a 'reduction of rent' under para 4(2)(a) of Sch 2 to the AHA 1986 and thereby start the three-year period between rent reviews afresh[1]. It will not be exempt under para 4(2)(c) because it will not be a rent reduction under s 33 of the AHA 1986[2].

Section 33 provides for arbitration. It does not do so 'in default of agreement', although this may be regarded as axiomatic. It is arguable, therefore, that a rental variation by agreement, even under threat of arbitration, would fall outside the provisions of para 4(2)(c) of Sch 2 to the AHA 1986.

As seen in para 29.7, the severance of the landlord's reversion does not create separate tenancies of the severed parts[3]. The rent may have been apportioned between the reversioners pursuant to the contract creating the severance. Section 140 of the LPA 1925 apportions contractual rights between the reversioners of the severed parts, but this does not impact on rent review. Rent review is a statutory right enjoyed by the landlord as a consequence of the AHA 1986. Accordingly, all of the reversionary owners must act jointly to obtain a rent review under the AHA 1986. Separate demands for arbitration by the reversionary owners will be invalid[4].

If the parties agree that there is a new letting consequential on the severance (which would not be the case in the absence of express agreement), para 5 of Sch 2 to the AHA 1986 will operate so as to provide a further exception to the provisions which would otherwise apply so as to trigger time for the three-year rule.

The amount of the reduction to be determined under s 33 of the AHA 1986 is to be proportionate to the part resumed and must take into account any consequent depreciation in the value of the residue of the holding to the tenant[5].

Even though the rent may have been agreed upon at £x per acre, the rent reduction formula in s 33 of the AHA 1986 will usually result in a reduction which differs from a mere rateable reduction calculated by reference to the acreage lost to the tenant. The quality of the land contained in the tenancy will usually vary and the depreciation in the value of the residue of the holding will usually differ from the amount arrived at by a straightforward rateable reduction calculated by reference to area.

The amount is to be settled by arbitration under the AHA 1986[6]. Where notice to quit part is served under a resumption clause in the tenancy agreement, the arbitrator must take into account any benefit or relief afforded to the tenant under the tenancy agreement in respect of the part resumed[7]. The arbitrator must also take into account in all cases the use to be made of the part severed, ie the part the landlord has taken back[8]. This does not mean that if the landlord puts the part recovered by him to a high value use this entitles the tenant to a greater reduction in rent. It means instead that it is the effect of the use to be made of the part severed upon the remainder of the holding which must be assessed and valued in determining the depreciation to the tenant of that remainder which is retained by him.

1   *Mann v Gardner* (1990) 61 P & CR 1, CA. Also see para 25.10 ff.
2   See para 25.11.
3   *Jelley v Buckman* [1974] QB 488, [1973] 3 All ER 853, CA.
4   *Stiles v Farrow* (1977) 241 Estates Gazette 623.
5   AHA 1986, s 33(1).
6   AHA 1986, s 33(3).
7   AHA 1986, s 33(3).
8   AHA 1986, s 33(1).

JOINT TENANCIES

29.9 Most agricultural tenancies are annual periodic tenancies. It is, therefore, necessary to consider the position where the property has been let to joint tenants, or the reversionary estate is held by joint tenants under a trust of land[1], and the effect of the common law rules of joint tenancy.

The doctrine of joint tenancy was stated by Lord Tenterden CJ in *Doe d Aslin v Summersett*[2] as follows:

> 'Upon a joint demise by Joint Tenants, upon a joint tenancy from year to year, the true character of the tenancy is this ... that [each tenant] holds the whole of all so long as he and each shall please, and as soon as any one of the joint tenants give a notice to quit he effectively puts an end to that tenancy'.

At common law, a periodic agricultural tenancy can only be continued into the next period if all holders of a joint interest in the reversion or in the tenancy agree. If one joint tenant does not agree, he can unilaterally determine the tenancy[3]. It is also necessary to consider the common law position in the context of the statutory overlay of the AHA 1986 and the principles applying to breach of trust.

[1] *Re Fuller's Contract* [1933] Ch 652; Trusts of Land and Appointment of Trustees Act 1996.
[2] (1830) 1 B & Ad 135. Also see, *Doe d Kindersley v Hughes* (1840) 7 M & W 139; *Leek and Moorlands Building Society v Clark* [1952] 2 QB 788, CA.
[3] *Doe d Aslin v Summersett* (1830) 1 B & Ad 135.

Notice to quit by landlord

29.10 Where the freehold reversion is held by joint tenants on a trust of land, a notice to quit served by one such joint tenant is effective to terminate the tenancy[1]. The principle was stated by Brightman J (as he then was) in *Brenner v Rose*[2] as follows:

> 'In my judgment the right of a landlord in such circumstances either to have possession or to recover the rent is not to be whittled away by the mere fact that he is one of the partners and is a purchaser of the reversion expectant on the underlease. I do not see that the defendant's fiduciary capacity as a member of a partnership which includes the benefit and burden of the underlease raises any sort of equity which should be allowed to prevent him from exercising his rights as landlord that he would have had if he were a stranger to the partnership'.

If service of a notice to quit by one of several joint trustees causes expense which is greater than the benefit accruing, the trustee responsible may be liable for breach of trust[3].

At common law, it is equally clear that a notice to quit given to one of several joint tenants is sufficient for all unless the tenancy agreement on its true construction requires all to be served[4].

It has also been held that service by the landlord on one of the joint tenants of the property is effective provided it is addressed to all[5].

There are arguments that all of the joint tenants of an agricultural holding must be served with a notice to quit for that notice to be valid.

First, in *Jones v Lewis*[6], Denning MR stated:

> 'If work has to be done by two joint tenants to avoid forfeiture or to avoid losing their farm it is important that both should have notice of it'.

It might be argued that all tenants must be given the opportunity to challenge a notice to quit by being served with a copy of it. Support for this view may be derived from the fact that a valid counter-notice under s 26(1) of the AHA 1986 may only be served by all joint tenants acting together[7].

Second, in relation to a notice claiming compensation under the provisions of the Agricultural Holdings Act 1923, it was held that a notice claiming compensation by one only of joint tenants, being the one who actually suffered loss, was a sufficient notice for the purposes of the compensation provisions[8]. If only one of a number of joint tenants can make a valid claim for compensation, then arguably each of the joint tenants must be given the opportunity to make such a claim.

[1]   *Brenner v Rose* [1973] 2 All ER 535; *Parsons v Parsons* [1983] 1 WLR 1390; *Bevan v Webb* [1905] 1 Ch 620.
[2]   *Brenner v Rose* [1973] 2 All ER 535, at 539.
[3]   See para 29.16.
[4]   *Doe d Bradford v Watkins* (1806) 7 East 551; *Quartermains v Selby* (1889) 5 TLR 223, CA.
[5]   *Jones v Lewis* (1973) 25 P & CR 375, 117 Sol Jo 373, CA.
[6]   *Jones v Lewis* (1973) 25 P & CR 375, 117 Sol Jo 373, CA.
[7]   *Newman v Keedwell* (1977) 35 P&CR 393; *Featherstone v Staples* [1986] 1 WLR 861. See para 29.13 ff.
[8]   *Howson v Buxton* [1928] 97 LJKB 749. This decision has been doubted: see para 29.14.

Notice to quit by tenant

29.11   A notice to quit which is signed by one of several joint tenants on behalf of the others is sufficient to terminate a tenancy from year to year[1]. The courts have also held that it is not necessary for the validity of a notice to quit that it is served by all joint tenants or with the concurrence of all joint tenants unless the terms of the tenancy provide otherwise[2]. It follows that the concurrence of all joint tenants is required to exercise a break clause in relation to a fixed term tenancy[3]. Provided that the tenant can establish that he was not limited in his ability to serve a notice to quit by the terms of the tenancy agreement, he will not be acting in breach of trust[4]. The position needs to be compared with that of a joint tenant failing to serve a counter-notice following a notice to quit from the landlord[5].

[1]   *Doe d Aslin v Summersett* (1830) 1 B & Ad 135; *Doe d Kindersley v Hughes* (1840) 7 McW 139; *Greenwich London Borough Council v McGrady* (1982) 81 LGR 288; *Hammersmith and Fulham London Borough Council v Monk* [1992] 1 AC 478, [1992] 1 All ER 1, HL; *Crawley Borough Council v Ure* [1996] QB 13, [1996] 1 All ER 734, CA; *Notting Hill Housing Trust v Brackley* [2001] EWCA Civ 601, [2001] 3 EGLR 11, [2001] 35 EG 106. Also see, *Smith v Grayton Estates Ltd* 1960 SC 349.
[2]   *Greenwich London Borough Council v McGrady* (1982) 81 LGR 288; *Parsons v Parsons* [1983] 1 WLR 1390; *Hammersmith and Fulham London Borough Council v Monk* [1992] 1 AC 478, [1992] 1 All ER 1, HL; *Crawley Borough Council v Ure* [1996] QB 13, [1995] 3 WLR 92, [1996] 1 All ER 734; *Notting Hill Housing Trust v Brackley* [2001] 3 EGLR 11, (2001) 35 EG 106.
[3]   *Hammersmith and Fulham London Borough Council v Monk* [1992] 1 AC 478, [1992] 1 All ER 1, HL.
[4]   *Crawley Borough Council v Ure* [1996] QB 13, [1995] 3 WLR 92, [1996] 1 All ER 734.
[5]   See para 29.10.

Surrender of tenancy

29.12   All joint tenants must concur in order to surrender a tenancy before its expiry date. Accordingly, a single joint tenant cannot validly surrender the tenancy before the contractual term date[1].

[1]   *Leek and Moorlands Building Society v Clark* [1952] 2 QB 788, CA; *Greenwich London Borough Council v McGrady* (1982) 81 LGR 288.

Tenant's counter-notice

29.13 Section 26(1) of the AHA 1986 requires that a counter-notice claiming reference of the landlord's notice to quit to an agricultural land tribunal must be served by 'the tenant'. The phrase 'the tenant', in the context of s 26(1)(b) of the AHA 1986[1], in the case of any joint tenancy, means 'the joint tenants' and not 'the joint tenants or any one of them'[2]. Accordingly, any counter-notice to a notice to quit under the AHA 1986 must be given by all tenants where there are joint tenants[3].

[1] Formerly s 2(1)(b) of the Agricultural Holdings (Notices to Quit) Act 1977.
[2] *Jacobs v Chaudhuri* [1968] 2 QB 470, [1968] 2 All ER 127, CA; *Turley v Panton* (1975) 29 P & CR 397; *Newman v Keedwell* (1977) 244 Estates Gazette 469; *Featherstone v Staples* [1986] 2 All ER 461, [1986] 1 WLR 861, CA.
[3] *Newman v Keedwell* (1977) 244 EG 469; *Featherstone v Staples* [1986] 2 All ER 461, [1986] 1 WLR 861. This principle is consistent with the position where relief is sought against forfeiture under s 146 of the Law of Property Act 1925. In the case of a joint tenancy, it is well established that all joint tenants must join in the application for relief: *TM Fairclough & Sons Ltd v Berliner* [1931] 1 Ch 60.

29.14 There have been two cases in which the courts have construed the phrase 'the tenant' as meaning 'the joint tenants or any of them'. The first was *Howson v Buxton*[1]. That case concerned the notice provisions for the payment of compensation under s 12 of the Agricultural Holdings Act 1923. The case has since been distinguished in *Jacobs v Chaudhuri*[2] and *Newman v Keedwell*[3]. The relevance of *Howson v Buxton* in the context of the termination of a tenancy protected under the AHA 1986 was also commented on by the Court of Appeal in *Featherstone v Staples*[4].

The second case was *Lloyd v Sadler*[5]. That case related to a claim for protection under the Rent Act 1968 and was relied upon in the judgment of Nourse J at first instance in *Featherstone v Staples*[6]. In the Court of Appeal in *Featherstone v Staples*[7], Slade LJ, while accepting that 'there is no immutable doctrine that the phrase 'the tenant', when appearing in a statute, must always be construed as referring to all the joint tenants in any case where a joint tenancy is involved', preferred to place reliance upon what Megaw LJ described in *Lloyd v Sadler*[8] as 'the ordinary law as to joint tenancy, as it affects rights of property'. The Court of Appeal upheld the decision of Fox J in *Newman v Keedwell*[9] as to the meaning of the phrase 'the tenant' in relation to the provisions to terminate a tenancy protected by the AHA 1986.

[1] (1928) 97 LJKB 749, CA.
[2] [1968] 2 QB 470 at 476, CA.
[3] (1977) 244 Estates Gazette 469 at 472.
[4] [1986] 1 WLR 861 at 871.
[5] [1978] QB 774, [1978] 2 All ER 529.
[6] (1984) 49 P & CR 273, [1985] 1 EGLR 1, CA.
[7] (1985) 278 Estates Gazette 867 at 871.
[8] *Lloyd v Sadler* [1978] QB 744, [1978] 2 All ER 529 at 783.
[9] (1977) 244 EG 469.

29.15 If a counter-notice is signed by only one of two joint tenants, it is ineffective[1]. The exception to that rule arises where the one joint tenant giving a counter-notice has either implied or express authority to do so. Such authority may be implied as a consequence of a partnership or it may be express, for example, where a court order gives power to the joint tenant to conduct the farming business[2].

[1] Per Slade LJ in *Featherstone v Staples* (1985) 278 EG 867 at 875. Also see *Sykes v Land* [1984] 2 EGLR 8, CA.

[2] *Combey v Gumbrill* [1990] 2 EGLR 7. For further discussion and criticism, see (1986) EG (Muir Watt) and (1986) 50 Conv 429 (Rodgers). Also see (1983) 47 Conv 194 (Webb). Also see, *Cork v Cork* [1997] 1 EGLR 5, [1997] 16 EG 430.

Breach of trust

29.16 The obligations arising in relation to the giving of notices to quit and counter-notices also result in difficult issues of breach of trust. This has already been seen in respect of the interrelationship between security of tenure and partnerships[1].

The courts have been prepared to exercise their equitable jurisdiction to compel a landlord to join in with his co-tenant in serving a counter-notice in order to preserve the tenancy where, for example, it was being held for third party beneficiaries[2]. In *Featherstone v Staples*[3], the land was let to a partnership comprising the tenants and a company controlled by the landlord. It was the tenants who undertook the farming. In the partnership agreement it provided that no partners would serve a counter-notice without the consent of the nominee company tenant. The landlord subsequently served a notice to quit. The Court of Appeal held that the phrase 'the tenant' in s 26(1) of the AHA 1986, in relation to any joint tenancy, must mean 'the joint tenants' and not 'the joint tenants or any one or more of them'. However, in *Featherstone v Staples*, the Court of Appeal applied public policy considerations, adopting the wider rationale of *Johnson v Moreton*[4], deciding that the concurrence of the nominee company tenant was unnecessary to the security of tenure of the other joint tenant. Where such compliance is dispensed with altogether, no issue of breach of trust can arise.

In *Harris v Black*[5], the Court of Appeal held that where joint lessees hold the tenancy for themselves alone, then the equitable jurisdiction will not normally be exercised so as to compel a reluctant tenant to assume continuing obligations. In *Sykes v Land*[6], the farm was let by the landlord to a partnership of himself and a joint tenant. The partnership agreement provided that on dissolution of the partnership, the joint tenant should have the right to purchase the landlord's share of the partnership assets. The Court of Appeal accepted that, on the facts, any counter-notice would have to be served by both joint tenants, but exercised as equitable jurisdiction to compel the landlord to join in with the joint tenant in serving a counter-notice so as to preserve the tenancy.

In *Cork v Cork*[7], the court granted an interlocutory injunction to compel one joint tenant to join in the service of a counter-notice. In this case the reluctant joint tenant had entered into an arrangement which he had agreed to leave his beneficial interest intact. The court considered that this was sufficient evidence to enable the court to exercise its equitable jurisdiction to compel the service of a counter-notice and preserve the trust assets.

1 See para 19.38.
2 *Re Biss* [1903] 2 Ch 40.
3 (1985) 278 EG 867.
4 [1980] AC 37, HL.
5 (1983) 46 P & CR 366.
6 [1984] 2 EGLR 8.
7 [1997] 1 EGLR 5.

SUB-TENANTS

Introduction

29.17 The AHA 1986 (and indeed previous agricultural holdings legislation) does not provide direct protection for sub-tenants. The common law rules still apply. These are very harsh in their effect and, in most circumstances, deprive sub-tenants of security of tenure if the head landlord terminates the head tenancy unilaterally or if the head tenant gives notice to quit to the head landlord[1].

Parliament foresaw these problems and, by virtue first of s 26(1)(d) of the AHA 1948, and later by s 5(1)(d) of the Agricultural Holdings (Notices to Quit) Act 1977, and now s 29 and Sch 4 paras 6 and 7 of the AHA 1986, gave the Lord Chancellor power to make regulations to protect sub-tenants. No such regulations have been made. It is doubtful whether they will ever be.

With the exception of the absence of security of tenure, the relationship between the head tenant and the sub-tenant in respect of an agricultural holding is otherwise exactly the same as that which applies between a landlord and a tenant in the normal way governed by the AHA 1986. All of the provisions in respect of compensation, implied terms, rent review and succession remain the same.

This section deals primarily with the position of a sub-tenant of an agricultural holding where the head tenancy is terminated. Where it is the tenant himself who seeks to determine the sub-tenancy, the ordinary rules about notices to quit served by a landlord or a tenant apply between the tenant and the sub-tenant.

It should also be noted that different considerations apply where there are concurrent tenancies. If a landlord grants a tenancy of an agricultural holding, and then grants a concurrent tenancy (usually called a tenancy of the reversion), a notice to quit terminating the tenancy of the reversion leaves the first tenancy unaffected.

1 *Pennell v Payne* [1995] QB 192, [1995] 1 EGLR 6, CA.

29.18 *Notices to quit part, joint interests and sub-tenancies*

Common law position

29.18 The common law position is that where a head tenancy is terminated by forfeiture, the expiry of a fixed term or notice to quit given by the landlord, any sub-tenancy automatically terminates when the head tenancy ends. This is regardless of whether the tenant has given notice to the sub-tenant or not.

Where there is a surrender of the head tenancy, or a merger of the head tenancy with the freehold reversion, the position is different. In those cases the sub-tenancy is directly binding upon the head landlord. The common law position was enacted by s 139 of the Law of Property Act 1925.

The rule relating to what happens in the event of a surrender of the head tenancy applies even where the sub-tenancy has been granted in breach of the terms of the head tenancy[1].

[1] *Parker v Jones* [1910] 2 KB 32.

Agricultural Land Tribunal

29.19 In proceedings before the Agricultural Land Tribunal (ALT) between the head landlord and head tenant, the sub-tenant is entitled to be heard. However, this will not assist him if the head tenant has not given counter-notice to a notice to quit given by the landlord as there will be no proceedings before the ALT in that case[1].

[1] Agricultural Land Tribunals (Rules) Order 1978, SI 1978/259, r 12.

Notice to quit

29.20 If the head landlord unilaterally terminates the tenancy of the head tenant by giving a notice to quit, then under the AHA 1986, the sub-tenancy will also automatically terminate. This is because the head tenancy is 'carved out' of the head tenancy and if the head tenancy no longer exists, there is no legal estate to support the sub-tenancy. The common law position accordingly prevails.

It was thought that, if the head landlord and the head tenant 'colluded', so that, for example, the head landlord gave a notice to quit at the invitation of the head tenant so as to destroy the sub-tenancy, the sub-tenancy would survive, being treated as the equivalent of an agreement to surrender. That analysis has now been rejected by the House of Lords in *Barrett v Morgan*[1]. If a head landlord gives a notice to quit to a head tenant, whether at his invitation or not, it will have the effect of terminating the sub-tenancy.

Applying the like analysis as to 'collusive' notices to quit, it was thought that if the head tenant gave a notice to quit to his head landlord, then that again would not destroy the sub-tenancy[2]. The reasoning was again that this should be treated as a case where the tenant was in breach of his covenants as to title implied in the sub-tenancy agreement and as such the arrangement should be regarded as being similar to an agreement to surrender. That analysis has been rejected by the Court of Appeal in *Pennell v Payne*[3]. The court held that if the head tenant gives notice to quit to the head landlord, the sub-tenancy was not preserved.

If the head tenant is also one of several head landlords, a notice to quit given by the head landlords which terminates the head tenancy will also destroy any sub-tenancy[4].

[1] [2000] 2 AC 264, [2000] 1 All ER 481. Cf *Cowen v Tanner* [1900] 2 QB 609, a decision unlikely to be followed as a consequence of *Barrett v Morgan*.
[2] *Mellor v Watkins* (1874) LR 9 QB 400; *Brown v Wilson* (1949) 208 LT 144.
[3] [1995] 1 EGLR 6, (1995) 06 EG 152, CA. Also see, *PW & Co v Milton Gate Investments Ltd* [2003] EWHC 1994 (Ch), [2004] 3 EGLR 103.
[4] *Harrison v Wing* [1988] 2 EGLR 4 [1988] 29 EG 101.

29.21 If the head tenant gives the sub-tenant notice to quit where the head tenant himself has not received a notice to quit, the sub-tenant is in the same position as any other tenant of an agricultural holding. The sub-tenant may give a counter-notice or a demand for arbitration, in appropriate cases, or otherwise contest the validity and effectiveness of the notice to quit on any grounds available to him in the same way as the head tenant would be able to in response to a notice to quit from the head landlord.

If the head tenant gives the sub-tenant notice to quit where the head tenant has himself received a notice to quit from the head landlord, and the head tenant states that fact in the notice given to the sub-tenant, then the sub-tenant has no right to give a counter-notice under s 26(1) of the AHA 1986[1].

Conversely, if the head tenant gives the sub-tenant notice to quit where the head tenant has himself received notice to quit from the head landlord and states that fact in the notice given to the sub-tenant, if for some reason the head landlord's notice to quit is, or becomes, ineffective, then even though the sub-tenant has not given a counter-notice (because he is precluded from doing so), his sub-tenancy will nevertheless survive[2].

If the head tenant gives the sub-tenant notice to quit where the head landlord has given notice to quit to the head tenant, and the head tenant then gives notice to quit to the sub-tenant, but fails to state in his notice to the sub-tenant that it is given by reason of a head landlord having given him notice to quit, then the sub-tenant's right to serve a counter-notice under s 26(1) of the AHA 1986 is not precluded. In that case, the head tenant would, if his notice to quit was not to be rendered ineffective, have to apply to the ALT for consent to the operation of a notice to quit. This is despite the fact that the head landlord would be entitled to rely upon the unilateral destruction by the head landlord of the head tenancy to terminate the sub-tenant's sub-tenancy by operation of law[3]. As a consequence, the head landlord will be entitled to possession in any event.

[1] The Agricultural Holdings (Arbitration on Notices) Order 1987, SI 1987/710, art 16.
[2] Article 16 of SI 1987/710.
[3] *Sherwood v Moody* [1952] 1 All ER 389.

Length of notice

29.22 The general rule that it is necessary to give 12 months' notice to quit under the AHA 1986, expiring on the annual term date of the tenancy does not apply to a notice to quit given by a tenant to a sub-tenant[1]. The normal common law period of notice will apply between the head tenant and the sub-tenant unless the sub-tenancy agreement provides to the contrary. Accordingly, if the sub-tenancy is an annual periodic tenancy, it may be terminated on six months' notice expiring on the annual term date of the annual tenancy. This applies regardless of whether the head tenant has himself been given notice to quit.

[1]   AHA 1986, s 25(2)(c).

Public policy

29.23 As seen above, the position of sub-tenants is perilous. They enjoy all the benefits of the provisions of the AHA 1986, including a security of tenure as against the head tenant, but subject to the fatal flaw that the termination of a head tenancy destroys the sub-tenancy.

Before the decisions of the House of Lords in *Barrett v Morgan*[1] and the Court of Appeal in *Pennell v Payne*[2], the practice developed where landlords arranged lettings to persons closely connected with them with a view to such tenants immediately sub-letting to the person selected for the actual farming of the holding with a view to the selected farmer becoming merely a sub-tenant. The head letting and the sub-letting are all part of the overall transaction. The object was to enable the head landlord to recover possession by the simple expedient of giving notice to quit to his head tenant and relying upon the head tenant not to give counter-notice.

In the sixth edition of this book, severe misgivings were expressed as to whether such a scheme, if challenged, would be judicially upheld. A scheme to this effect was first challenged in the High Court. It was held by French J to be effective[3]. In the later case of *Gisborne v Burton*[4], the Court of Appeal ruled that such a scheme was contrary to public policy. The court held that, on the termination of the head tenancy in whatever manner selected by the head landlord, the sub-tenancy continued. The sub-tenant became the direct tenant of the head landlord.

[1]   [2000] 1 All ER 481; [2000] 2 WLR 284.
[2]   [1995] 1 EGLR 6, (1995) 06 EG 152.
[3]   *Bayer v Mitcham*, High Court (24 February 1983, unreported).
[4]   [1988] 3 All ER 760 [1988] 38 EG 129.

29.24 The decision in *Gisborne v Burton*[1] is consistent with that in *Featherstone v Staples*[2], considered in the context of the requirements in relation to the giving of a counter-notice to a notice to quit[3]. Both decisions are difficult to reconcile with the Court of Appeal's decisions in *Shell-Mex and BP Ltd v Manchester Garages Ltd*[4] and *Sparkes v Smart*[5]. The first case involved a different scheme designed to avoid security of tenure under the Landlord and

Tenant Act 1954. In *Sparkes v Smart*, a tenant who had sub-let inadvertently was offered the freehold. He arranged for a close relation to buy and for the new freeholder to give him, as head tenant, a notice to quit. The head tenant did not give a counter-notice and the head landlord then claimed possession against the sub-tenant. The Court of Appeal held that the notice to quit was ineffective to destroy the sub-tenancy and that the sub-tenant became the direct tenant of the freeholder. These cases are difficult to reconcile with the subsequent decisions of the House of Lords in *Barrett v Morgan*[6] and the Court of Appeal in *Pennell v Payne*[7].

New sub-tenancies since 1 September 1995 will normally come within the Agricultural Tenancies Act 1995 as farm business tenancies.

[1]   [1988] 3 All ER 760 (1988) 38 EG 129.
[2]   [1986] 2 All ER 461 [1986] 1 WLR 861.
[3]   See para 29.14.
[4]   [1971] 1 All ER 841 [1971] 1 WLR 612.
[5]   [1990] 2 EGLR 245.
[6]   [2000] 1 All ER 481; [2000] 2 WLR 284.
[7]   [1995] 1 EGLR 6, (1995) 06 EG 152, CA.

Reversionary leases

29.25 If a landlord of an existing tenancy grants a lease of his reversionary interest so as to transform the existing tenant into a sub-tenant, then it is probable that on termination of the reversionary lease, the sub-tenancy would be held to have survived. This is because the sub-tenancy is not 'carved out' of the head tenancy but is a concurrent tenancy with the head tenancy, notwithstanding the fact that the head tenant is the sub-tenant's immediate landlord, if the head tenancy is of longer duration than the sub-tenancy.

In the case of succession following the grant of a reversionary tenancy, the new tenancy falls to be granted not by the reversionary tenant, but by the direct successor to the person who granted the original tenancy[1]. It follows that where a tenant of an agricultural holding dies in circumstances where there were extant reversionary tenancies, the successor to the tenant of the holding becomes a direct tenant of the freeholder and does not become a sub-tenant of the reversionary tenant. This provision was enacted to overcome a loophole in the earlier legislation demonstrated by *Chesshire v Colesbourne Estate Co*[2].

[1]   AHA 1986, s 45(3).
[2]   (1979) ALT, South Western Area.

Compensation

29.26 A problem for sub-tenants whose tenancies were terminated by operation of law which existed prior to the passing of the Agricultural Holdings Act 1984 was that since their tenancies were not terminated by notice to quit, they would not be entitled to compensation for disturbance. Sub-tenants are now entitled to compensation for disturbance whether their tenancies are terminated by notice to quit or by operation of law[1]. The head tenant is entitled to claim similar compensation from the head landlord by virtue of s 63(2) of the AHA 1986[2].

[1] AHA 1986, s 33(1).
[2] For a commentary on compensation and disturbance generally, see para 38.47.

SERVICEMEN

29.27 An anachronistic relic of the wartime origins of the Agricultural Holdings Act 1948 and its successors has been preserved by s 30 and Sch 5 to the AHA 1986. The origins of these provisions are to be found in ss 21 and 22 of the Reserve and Auxiliary Forces (Protection of Civil Interests) Act 1951, as amended by the Agriculture Act 1958, s 8 and Sch 1 paras 23 and 24, as further amended by s 117(2) and Sch 15, Pt 2 of the Rent Act 1968 and s 10 of the Rent Act 1977. It was designed principally to deal with agricultural tenants who were called up to do National Service.

Conditions for qualification

29.28 For a tenant to qualify for the special provisions contained in Sch 5 to the AHA 1986, the following conditions must be fulfilled:

(a) the tenant must be performing 'a period of relevant service other than a short period of training'. This does not apply to members of the regular Armed Forces and most of the forms of relevant service contained in the Reserve and Auxiliary Forces (Protection of Civil Interests) Act 1951 have been abolished;

(b) the tenant must be the tenant of an agricultural holding which comprises a dwellinghouse occupied by the person responsible for the control of the farming of the holding or, alternatively, any part of an agricultural holding which consists of or comprises such a dwellinghouse;

(c) the tenant must have received notice to quit the whole or part of the holding during the period of 'relevant service' or a further four months thereafter.

Provided these conditions are fulfilled, the following privileges are enjoyed by the tenant who is also such a serviceman.

Special privileges

29.29 If the tenant who satisfies the conditions described above receives notice to quit, he may serve a counter-notice under s 26(1) of the AHA 1986 notwithstanding 'the existence of any such circumstances as are mentioned in Cases B to G', ie the notice to quit will be treated as a contestable notice to quit which has to be referred to the ALT and not an incontestable one. This general rule is subject to the proviso that if the landlord then applies to the ALT for consent to the operation of the notice to quit, he does not have to make out one of the grounds specified in s 26(3) of the AHA 1986, but may instead satisfy the ALT that one of the Case B to G grounds is available[1]. In that case, the ALT has to determine 'to what extent (if at all) the existence of those circumstances is directly or indirectly attributable to the serviceman performing or having performed the period of service in question'.

[1]   For a commentary on such cases, see Ch 31.

29.30 Whether the landlord makes out a ground under s 27(3) or Cases B to G inclusive, or not, the ALT must:

> 'consider to what extent (if at all) the giving of such consent at a time during the period of protection would cause special hardship in view of circumstances, directly or indirectly, attributable to the serviceman performing or having performed that period of service'[1].

In either case the ALT must withhold their consent to the operation of a notice to quit unless 'in all the circumstances they consider it reasonable to give their consent thereto'[2].

There are special provisions where the notice to quit and counter-notice are given before the tenant qualifies as a serviceman but before the ALT has made its decision the tenant starts the 'period of residence protection'[3]. In those circumstances the special serviceman's privileges apply to the tenant, notwithstanding the fact that at the date of the giving of the notice and of the counter-notice he did not qualify.

There are further special provisions enabling the Lord Chancellor to make regulations. The regulations currently in force are still the Reserve and Auxiliary Forces (Agriculture Tenants) Regulations 1959[4]. These regulations, as well as supplementing the statutory provisions referred to above, also provide that where the serviceman is serving abroad and is unable to serve a counter-notice under s 26(1) of the AHA 1986, or to take some necessary step in subsequent proceedings and has not authorised anyone to do so on his behalf, the chairman of the ALT may authorise a suitable person to do so instead.

[1]   AHA 1986, Sch 5 para 3(2).
[2]   The wording differs slightly from the wording of s 27(2) of the AHA 1986. The ALT only has to consider whether it is reasonable to give their consent and not whether a fair and reasonable landlord would insist upon possession.
[3]   Ie starts his period of service other than a short period of training.
[4]   SI 1959/84

EFFECT OF AGREEMENT FOR SALE ON NOTICE TO QUIT

29.31 A rule dating back to the Agricultural Land Sales (Restriction of Notices to Quit) Act 1919, which was retained in all the subsequent Agricultural Holdings Acts[1], was finally abolished and repealed by Sch 4 to the Agricultural Holdings Act 1984. This rule was that, except in limited circumstances, a notice to quit was rendered ineffective if the landlord entered into a contract for sale of his interest during the currency of the notice. The purpose of the original provision was to discourage landlords from giving notice to quit with a view instantly to realising the vacant possession premium because when inflation was first experienced in modern times many landlords, believing their assets had been enhanced in value in real terms, gave notice to their tenants so as to sell. This was considered very undesirable. The 1919 Act was never effective for the purpose intended but created major problems for practitioners, many of whom overlooked it with serious consequences when it came to completion of the sale of the freehold 'with vacant possession'.

That problem has now been wholly eliminated. Any sale by the landlord of the freehold reversion during the currency of the notice to quit has no effect upon the enforceability of the notice. The purchaser can, in due course, enforce the notice to quit in the same way as the giver of the notice could have done had he retained his interest in reversion.

1   The Agricultural Holdings Act 1923; s 32 of the Agriculture Act 1947; s 30 of the Agricultural Holdings Act 1948 and s 7 of the Agricultural Holdings (Notices to Quit) Act 1977.

Chapter 30

THE STATUTORY RESTRICTIONS ON NOTICES TO QUIT: COUNTER-NOTICE

GENERAL

30.1 Under the AHA 1986, a notice to quit (if valid at common law) is, prima facie, effective to terminate the tenancy[1]. That general rule is subject to the ability of the tenant to serve on the landlord a counter-notice in writing requiring that s 26(1) of the AHA 1986 shall apply to the notice to quit. Such counter-notice must be served within one month of service of the notice to quit. This restriction on the operation of a notice to quit an agricultural holding applies equally to a notice to quit part given by a landlord to a tenant[2].

The notice to quit may be unqualified, ie state no reason for its being given[3], or contain one or more of the reasons contained in s 27(3) of the AHA 1986 or contain one or more of the reasons contained in Sch 3 to the AHA 1986 (the 'Special Cases')[4]. If it relies on one of the Special Cases, then there is *no* power to give a counter-notice[5].

Practitioners need to be aware that a notice may be given relying on one or more of the Special Cases and then state that it is given in the alternative as an unqualified notice[6]. In such a case, the tenant must serve counter-notice.

If a counter-notice is given and is appropriate, the notice to quit is thereby rendered ineffective unless and until the Agricultural Land Tribunal (ALT) for the area[7] in which the holding is situate consents to the operation of the notice to quit on one of the limited grounds specified in s 27(3) of the AHA 1986. Statutory rules have been made for the obtaining of the consent of the ALT[8].

---

[1] Subject to the extended period of notice required, as to which see para 28.10 ff.
[2] AHA 1986, s 26(1)(a).
[3] It is rarely advisable to give such a notice to quit. If a ground as specified in s 27(3) is available, and that fact is not stated in the notice to quit, increased compensation on quitting for disturbance will be payable.
[4] In previous editions of this book these were known as the 'seven deadly sins'. They are also often, inappropriately, described as 'incontestable' notices to quit. They are not strictly 'incontestable' but different rules apply.
[5] See para 31.1 in relation to so-called incontestable notices and note that a demand for arbitration may be necessary instead.

6   Such a notice must be very carefully worded and make the position perfectly clear to the
      tenant: *Cowan v Wrayford* [1953] 2 All ER 1138, [1953] 1 WLR 1340.
7   For details showing the areas covered by each tribunal, see para 46.3.
8   The current rules are the Agricultural Land Tribunals (Rules) Order 1978, SI 1978/259.

30.2 Such consent of the ALT must be sought by the landlord on an application made within one month of service of the counter-notice[1]. The application must be in the prescribed form[2].

Contracting out of the right to give a counter-notice, though not prohibited expressly by the AHA 1986, has been held by the House of Lords to be contrary to public policy and ineffective[3].

The general rule that a counter-notice is required does not apply in the case of a notice which sets out one of the Special Cases of Sch 3 to the AHA 1986[4].

There is no prescribed form for the counter-notice. All that is required is that the notice (which can be very informal, eg in the form of a letter) should be in writing and should specify in terms that it requires s 26(1) of the AHA 1986 to apply[5].

Care needs to be taken to ensure that the counter-notice is served on the correct landlord, particularly following a severance of the freehold reversion[6].

As to the calculation of the period of one month, the 'corresponding day' rule applies. One month from 1 February expires on 1 March regardless of whether February happens to fall in a leap year or not[7].

Until the passing of the AHA 1986, the equivalent provisions were contained in s 24(1) of the Agricultural Holdings Act 1948 (AHA 1948) and then in s 2(1) of the Agricultural Holdings (Notice to Quit) Act 1977. By virtue of s 99 of the AHA 1986, a counter-notice invoking s 24(1) of the AHA 1948 or 2(1) of the 1977 Act (though these are now repealed) will probably be valid and effective[8].

The one-month requirement is rigid and inflexible. There is no power to extend the period. But where the notice to quit is a dual one, relying on one of the Special Cases and stating that, in the alternative, it is to be treated as an unqualified notice, then in that case if the tenant goes to arbitration as to the reason stated in the notice to quit and fails, he may serve his counter-notice within one month from the termination of the arbitration[9]. Indeed, he *must* do so otherwise the notice to quit will take effect.

1   The Agricultural Land Tribunals (Rules) Order 1978, SI 1978/259, r 2.
2   The Agricultural Land Tribunals (Rules) Order 1978, the Schedule. Note the saving
      provision 'or substantially to the like effect': art 1(4)(b).
3   *Johnson v Moreton* [1980] AC 37, [1978] 3 All ER 37.
4   See para 31.1.
5   In *Mountford v Hodkinson* [1956] 2 All ER 17, [1956] 1 WLR 422, CA, a tenant wrote an
      angry letter to the landlord saying, 'I don't intend to go. I shall appeal against it and take
      the matter up with' the County Agricultural Executive Committee (at that time the
      appropriate body), the Agricultural Land Tribunal at that time being an appellate body.
      This was before the passing of the Agriculture Act 1958. It was held that the language of

the letter was insufficient to constitute an intention to invoke the provisions of s 24(1) of the AHA 1948 (now s 26(1) of the AHA 1986) and the letter did not operate as a counter-notice. For a more modern case in which the requirements of a valid counter-notice were judicially considered, see *Edlingham v MFI Furniture Centres Ltd* [1981] 2 EGLR 97, 259 Estates Gazette 421; and *Price v Mann* [1942] 1 All ER 453 and *Glofield Property Ltd v Morley* [1988] 1 EGLR 113, [1988] 02 EG 62. For a case in which the decision in *Mountford v Hodgkinson* (above) was reconsidered and applied to an agricultural holding, see *Rous v Mitchell* [1991] 1 All ER 676.

6   See para 32.6.
7   *Dodds v Walker* [1981] 2 All ER 609, [1981] 1 WLR 1027, HL. See also *Schnabel v Allard* [1967] 1 QB 627, [1966] 3 All ER 816. See para 40.27 ff.
8   For a similar situation, after the repeal of the equivalent provisions in the 1947 Act and their re-enactment in the AHA 1948, see *Ward v Scott* [1950] WN 76.
9   The Agricultural Holdings (Arbitration on Notices) Order 1987, SI 1987/710, art 10 and *Cowan v Wrayford* [1953] 2 All ER 1138, [1953] 1 WLR 1340.

30.3 A landlord who has received a counter-notice must, within one month of receipt, apply in the prescribed form to the appropriate ALT for consent to the operation of his notice to quit[1]. If he does not, his notice to quit is rendered ineffective by the counter-notice. However, unlike the one month available to the tenant, which is a statutory and inflexible time limit, the one month available to the landlord is provided not by the statute itself but by the Agricultural Land Tribunal (Rules) Order 1978. It is non-statutory and can be extended with the leave of the chairman of the ALT[2].

The power to give or withhold consent exercised by the ALT was, until 26 January 1959, exercised by the Minister through the County Agricultural Executive Committee, with the right of appeal to the ALT. From 26 January 1959, by virtue of para 8 of Sch 1 to the Agriculture Act 1958, the ALT became the tribunal at first instance, and the right of appeal was lost. The equivalent of an appeal from the ALT is by way of case stated to the High Court[3].

In the case of a tenant who is performing a period of service with the Armed Forces of the Crown, and who may be disabled or prejudiced in serving the counter-notice, there are powers to authorise some suitable person to do it and other necessary acts or conduct any proceedings on his behalf[4].

1   The form of application to the ALT, see Form 1 in the Appendix to the Agricultural Land Tribunals (Rules) Order 1987, SI 1978/259.
2   The Agricultural Land Tribunals (Rules) Order 1978, rr 2 and 37 and see *Kellett v Alexander* (1980) 257 Estates Gazette 494.
3   See para 46.17.
4   See the Reserve and Auxiliary Forces (Agriculture Tenants) Regulations 1959, SI 1959/84, and see also para A1.505.

APPLICATION FOR THE ALT'S CONSENT TO NOTICE TO QUIT

30.4 Section 27 of the AHA 1986 provides six grounds pursuant to which the ALT may give consent to the operation of the landlord's notice to quit. There is a direction[1] that even if such a ground has been made out, the ALT must withhold consent if satisfied that 'in all the circumstances it appears to them that a fair and reasonable landlord would not insist on possession'[2].

¹   It appeared as a proviso to s 25 of the AHA 1948 which was repealed and re-enacted as s 3 of the Agricultural Holdings (Notice to Quit) Act 1977. It now appears not as a proviso but as a separate direction to the ALT, see the AHA 1986, s 27(2).
²   AHA 1986, s 27(2). Cf the position before the Agriculture Act 1958 where the application had to be made to the Minister with a right to appeal to the ALT and where the Minister had an unqualified discretion to refuse consent even where a ground had been made out.

30.5 The application to the ALT must be made in the prescribed form, or in a form substantially to the like effect¹. Non-compliance with the time limit renders the application invalid unless the chairman consents to an extension of time for making the application. This contrasts with the statutory inflexible time limit for giving a counter-notice. The time limit for applying to the ALT is non-statutory and contained in the regulations².

If the ALT consents to the operation of a notice to quit it may, either of its own motion or on the tenant's application³, postpone the termination of the tenancy by the notice to quit for any period not exceeding 12 months if the notice would otherwise have come into operation on or within six months after the giving of the ALT's consent⁴.

¹   The Agricultural Land Tribunals (Rules) Order 1978, rr 2 and 1(4)(b) and Form 1 in its Appendix.
²   The Agricultural Land Tribunals (Rules) Order 1978, rr 2 and 37; *Kellett v Alexander* (1980) 257 Estates Gazette 494.
³   This must be made not later than 14 days after the giving of the consent. See the Agricultural Holdings (Arbitration on Notices) Order 1987, SI 1987/710, art 13.
⁴   Similar provisions apply where an arbitrator awards under Cases A, B, D or E that the reason stated in one of those notices to quit has been made out.

GROUNDS FOR CONSENT

30.6 Where an application has been made to the ALT for consent to the operation of a notice to quit, the ALT must first decide whether the landlord has made out any one or more of the six grounds available to him. Then, before consenting to the operation of the notice to quit, the ALT must, as a separate exercise, consider the fair and reasonable landlord requirement¹. If satisfied that such a landlord would not insist on possession, then they must withhold their consent². It should be noted that s 27(1) of the AHA 1986 requires that the ground upon which consent is sought must be 'specified by the landlord in his application for their consent'. That is a statutory requirement and not merely a requirement of the Agricultural Land Tribunals (Rules) Order 1978.

The grounds are as follows:

(a)   good husbandry;
(b)   sound management of the estate;
(c)   agricultural research, education, experiment or demonstration, or for the purpose of enactments relating to smallholdings;
(d)   a purpose desirable for enactments relating to allotments;
(e)   greater hardship would be cause by withholding than by giving consent;

(f)   the landlord proposes to terminate the tenancy for the purpose of the land being used other than for agriculture, not falling with Case B[3].

[1]   *R v Agricultural Land Tribunal for Eastern Province of England, ex p Grant* [1956] 3 All ER 321, [1956] 1 WLR 1240; *Evans v Roper* [1960] 2 All ER 507, [1960] 1 WLR 814.
[2]   This is an obligation upon them; they do not merely have a discretion on the matter.
[3]   AHA 1986, s 27(3). As to Case B, see para 32.10.

Ground (a): Good husbandry

30.7   Ground (a) is:

'... the carrying out of the purpose for which the landlord proposes to terminate the tenancy is desirable in the interests of good husbandry[1] as respects the land to which the notices relates, treated as a separate unit'[2].

It is not sufficient for the landlord to show that the farm is being badly farmed at present. He must show that the land would be better farmed under the proposed new regime. The good husbandry ground envisages a comparison between the present system of husbandry and the proposed new system[3].

It is not permissible under this ground for the landlord to seek to show that the holding would be better farmed if amalgamated with other land[4]. If this is the landlord's case, it falls to be considered under ground (b), sound estate management.

It is submitted that this does not mean that the ALT may not consider any land farmed by the proposed new occupant, be he the landlord or a new proposed tenant, in deciding whether or not he is likely to farm the land better than the existing tenant. The ALT may not consider that land in terms of its being farmed jointly with the land the subject of the application.

Historically it has been assumed that it is in the interests of good husbandry that greater productivity should be achieved from all land in agricultural use. Now that many agricultural commodities are over-produced, and there are statutory restraints and quotas which restrict productivity, good husbandry and higher productivity are no longer synonymous. It may be in the interests of good husbandry to farm in such a way as not necessarily to achieve maximum output[5].

A landlord who wishes to obtain possession to sell can (almost by definition) not make out this ground for possession because he will not be able to show how the land will be farmed in future. He may in special circumstances be able to make out a greater hardship case.

It may be possible for a landlord to present a case under ground (a) (ie good husbandry) and ground (b) (ie sound estate management). Some facts and evidence may be relevant to both grounds. Nevertheless, the ALT should consider each ground and the evidence relevant to each separately.

Although there are very many cases where various ALTs have considered applications by landlords for consent to the operation of their notices to quit on the good husbandry ground, consideration of them in detail is of little or no assistance. Each case turns on its own facts. Just because in a given set of circumstances one particular ALT found either in favour of the landlord or against him, as the case may be, is of limited assistance and gives little guidance to the likely outcome of any other subsequent case even on apparently similar facts.

1   For the rules of good husbandry, see para 24.3.
2   AHA 1986, s 27(3)(a).
3   Note the remarks of the Chairman of the ALT in *Graham v Harman* (1949) 154 Estates Gazette 132.
4   *R v Agricultural Land Tribunal for the Wales and Monmouth Area, ex p Davies* [1953] 1 All ER 1182, [1953] 1 WLR 722, and *R v Agricultural Land Tribunal for Eastern Province of England, ex p Grant* [1956] 3 All ER 321, [1956] 1 WLR 1240. Note that these decisions were pre-1958, from which the present wording stems. Also, see *Davies v Price* [1958] 1 All ER 671, [1958] 1 WLR 434.
5   For an opinion to that effect, see the remarks of the Chairman (Mr Wilson Mellor, QC) of the West Midlands ALT quoted as a footnote in *Jackson v Barlow* (1978) unreported when considering what constituted a suitable tenant; see para 35.74.

Ground (b): Sound estate management

30.8   Ground (b) is:

'... the carrying out thereof is desirable in the interests of sound management[1] of the estate of which the land to which the notice relates forms part or which the land constitutes'[2].

This ground, like the good husbandry ground, involves a comparison between the existing system of farming carried on by the tenant and the proposed new system, but subject this time to the proviso that the ALT must consider not merely the land the subject of the notice to quit but also the remainder of the landlord's estate.

There is no definition of 'estate'. Technically the land which is the subject of the notice to quit may be the only land under consideration. Usually that will not be the case. It is not necessary for the landlord to show that the holding is being badly farmed. It is sufficient for the landlord to show that to combine the holding with other land will improve estate management of all of the land.

The classic example of sound estate management in the past has been the case where the landlord is able to show that by recovering possession of the land let, and by amalgamating it with other land, he is able to convert two uneconomic units into a single economic and efficient farm or unit. In the current agricultural economic climate the considerations specified in para 30.7 in relation to good husbandry apply equally to this ground.

The definition in s 10 of the Agriculture Act 1947 is of 'good' estate management and not 'sound' management of the estate, which is the expression which appears in s 27(3)(b) of the AHA 1986. It may be that there is more than a semantic difference between the two words in their respective contexts. The definition of 'good' estate management seems to be directed to the farming of the land in question. 'Sound' estate management seems to embrace a wider conception: the possible use of the land for other purposes altogether. Sound estate management envisages looking at the whole estate in the physical sense and considering what effect it would have on the management of the estate. The mere personal financial interest of the landlord in isolation is not sufficient, for example, where he merely wishes to alter financial terms of the tenancy[3].

As stated above, there is no statutory definition of an 'estate' in this context. The mere fact that the landlord may happen to own a number of scattered parcels in different parts of the country will not necessarily constitute those parcels an estate. The notion that an estate comprises all the assets of a landlord, as would apply when considering the distribution of the assets on death and the administration of his estate in that sense would not appear to be apposite in the context of sound estate management. That suggests a substantial block of land with some cohesive identity. In classic form, this would comprise a mansion house, some parkland, a home farm and some let farms. It is doubtful that the term 'estate' is as narrowly confined as that. There is no authority on the point.

A well thought-out scheme in detail is required, but this could be established by a proposal to sell off parts of the holding, including worn-out buildings, and applying the proceeds to improving the fixed equipment on the remainder of the holding[4]. A landlord who has persistently been in breach of his repairing obligations will normally have considerable difficulty in persuading an ALT to give consent to the dispossession of a tenant so that the landlord can sell at the enhanced vacant possession price and use the proceeds of sale to remedy the landlord's own breaches of covenant.

This ground does not enable a landlord to improve on the terms of the tenancy agreement by terminating the old tenancy subject to an undertaking to relet on terms more favourable to him[5]. It is possible that a landlord who has obtained planning permission to develop part only of the holding may be able to establish, if he is not empowered to serve a notice to quit part[6], that it would be sound estate management to give notice to quit the whole holding. If he is 'fair and reasonable', this may involve his offering to relet the balance of the holding to the existing tenant[7].

The ALT may not consider such matters as hardship to the tenant when considering whether the ground has been made out, but must take these factors into consideration when applying the fair and reasonable landlord requirement[8].

---

1 For the text of the rules of 'good' estate management, see para 24.5.
2 AHA 1986, s 27(3)(b).
3 *National Coal Board v Naylor* [1972] 1 All ER 1153, [1972] 1 WLR 908.
4 *Lewis v Moss* (1961) 181 Estates Gazette 685. For examples of what does not constitute sound estate management, see *Burnett v Smith* (1951) 159 Estates Gazette 3. Cf *Trustees of A Merchant v Sterry* (1954) 163 Estates Gazette 655; *Copeland v Ingram* (1956) Scottish Journal of the RICS, April, p 105; *Greeves v Mitchell* (1971) 222 Estates Gazette 1395.
5 *National Coal Board v Naylor* [1972] 1 All ER 1153, [1972] 1 WLR 908.

6   See Ch 29, as to notices to quit part generally.
7   But see the dicta of the Lord Chief Justice in *National Coal Board v Naylor* [1972] 1 All ER 1153, [1972] 1 WLR 908. In the circumstances quoted the landlord would probably be better advised to sever the freehold reversion so that the new owner of the severed part with development potential can then give a notice to quit in respect of the whole of that part of the holding vested in him – see para 29.6.
8   *Evans v Roper* [1960] 2 All ER 507, [1960] 1 WLR 814.

30.9 Agricultural land has for many years been substantially more valuable if available with vacant possession than if tenanted, however good or bad the tenant may be. It is submitted that it cannot be that the statutory ground for possession merely requires the landlord to establish that his assets (ie estate in that sense) would be enhanced substantially in value by the recovery of vacant possession.

As with the good husbandry ground, each case turns on its own facts, and consideration of previous apparently similar cases which have been heard by individual ALTs is unlikely to be of any significant assistance.

Ground (c): Agricultural research etc, or smallholdings

30.10 Ground (c) is:

'... the carrying out thereof is desirable for the purposes of agricultural research, education, experiment or demonstration, or for the purposes of the enactments relating to smallholdings'[1].

This composite ground covers agricultural[2] research[3], or education or experiment, or demonstration, or smallholdings.

In contrast to the normal purpose of amalgamations constituting sound estate management, the second part of s 27(3)(c) of the AHA 1986 appears to envisage fragmentation for certain very limited, but socially desirable purposes specified in that paragraph of the subsection.

1   AHA 1986, s 27(3)(c).
2   The adjective 'agricultural' would appear to govern all the following nouns. For a similar decision on the wording of what is now s 31(2)(a) of the AHA 1986, see *Paddock Investments Ltd v Lory* [1975] 2 EGLR 5, 236 Estates Gazette 803.
3   For the judicial consideration of agricultural research etc, see *Wilts County Council v Habershon* (1952) 159 Estates Gazette 157; *Wood v East Sussex County Council* (1954) 164 Estates Gazette 402.

Ground (d): Allotments

30.11 Ground (d) is:

'... the carrying out of the purpose is desirable for the purposes of the enactments relating to allotments'[1].

Allotments take two possible forms: allotments properly so called and allotment gardens. The special provisions relating to allotments are contained in the Allotments Acts 1908 to 1950. They are small agricultural holdings statutorily established for special purposes, for example, to rehabilitate retiring Great War Veterans and to provide to every man an acre, a cow, etc – 'a land fit for heroes to live in'. An allotment garden is a small parcel of land used for producing vegetables or fruit for the allotment holder or his family[2]; they can never be agricultural holdings because they are required to be used for the production of vegetables for consumption by the allotment holder and his family and not for the purpose of a trade or business.

Since many county councils are disposing of their allotments and allotments are thought by many to be anachronistic, it is unlikely that s 27(3)(d) will be evoked in practice.

[1]   AHA 1986, s 27(3)(d).
[2]   The Allotments Act 1922, s 22 and the Agriculture Act 1947, s 109(3).

Ground (e): Greater hardship

30.12 Ground (e) is:

'... greater hardship would be caused by withholding than by giving consent to the operation of the notice'[1].

Section 27(3)(e) of the AHA 1986[2] merely requires the landlord to show that greater hardship would be caused to him by the ALT's withholding its consent than would be caused to the tenant by the giving of consent to the operation of the notice to quit.

Since all landlords must satisfy the 'fair and reasonable' landlord requirement, it follows that in nearly every case consideration of relative hardship is at the forefront of all applications. Greater hardship and the 'fair and reasonable' landlord requirement usually, but not necessarily always, traverse very similar ground[3].

[1]   AHA 1986, s 27(3)(e).
[2]   It re-enacts s 25(2)(d) of the AHA 1948 and s 3(3)(d) of the Agricultural Holdings (Notice to Quit) Act 1977.
[3]   But see para 30.17 and *Jones v Burgoyne* (1963) 188 Estates Gazette 497.

30.13 The matters which the ALT may be called upon to consider in this connection are diverse[1]. The assessment of greater hardship is inevitably subjective. The published, though unreported, decisions of different ALTs have continued to reveal a marked divergence as to what different ALTs, and indeed differently constituted ALTs even in the same area, consider turn the scales one way or the other on the issue of greater hardship. Inevitably, there will always be heart-searchings and disappointments for litigants and anxiety for ALTs on this point.

The financial result for the respective parties estimated to flow from the granting or withholding of consent may sometimes prove to be the largest single deciding factor[2] of the problem, but it can by no means be the only one. Other important factors are the tenant's chances of earning his living and obtaining a residence for himself and his family elsewhere. Conversely, the landlord's position on similar points has to be considered if consent to the operation of the notice to quit is withheld. Hardship there is bound to be whatever decision is given, but the ALT has the difficult task of deciding where the greater hardship lies.

Cases in relation to ground (e) will often involve assessing the financial positions of the parties. The landlord can submit that he intends to sell the holding with vacant possession in order to relieve his financial position[3]. The landlord can argue that he wishes to replace a poor farmer with a better one to improve his overall financial position[4].

The matters constituting greater hardship must arise from the grant or refusal of consent. It involves a utilitarian balance sheet comparing hardship to each party[5].

Hardship to third parties will be taken into account but only in so far as hardship to those third parties is hardship to the landlord or tenant respectively. The principle set out by Asquith LJ in *Harte v Frampton*[6] has been applied to agricultural holdings cases by the Court of Appeal[7]:

> 'To attempt to define classes, hardship to whom and to whom alone (apart from the parties) can be taken into account (whether as an element entering into the parties' hardship or on its own account) appears to us an unhelpful line of approach to the construction of the proviso. The true view we think is that the county court judge [and the Agricultural Land Tribunal] should take into account hardship to all who may be affected by the grant or refusal of an order for possession – relatives, dependants, lodgers, guests and the stranger within the gates – but should weigh such hardship with due regard to the status of the person affected and their 'proximity' to the tenant or landlord and the extent to which consequently hardship to them would be hardship to him. The inability to take in a guest for the weekend would no doubt be assessed by the judge at nil. The extrusion of a loved and trusted relation whether dependent or not would weigh heavily in the scales'.

[1]   But they must relate to the giving or withholding of consent to the notice to quit; see *Cooke v Talbot* (1977) 243 EG 831.
[2]   *Purser v Bailey* [1967] 2 QB 500, [1967] 2 All ER 189, CA.
[3]   *Purser v Bailey* [1967] 2 QB 500, [1967] 2 All ER 189, CA.
[4]   *R v Agricultural Land Tribunal for the South Eastern Area, ex p Parslow* [1979] 2 EGLR 1.
[5]   *Cooke v Talbot* (1977) 243 Estates Gazette 831.
[6]   [1948] 1 KB 73, [1947] 2 All ER 604, CA.
[7]   *Purser v Bailey* [1967] 2 QB 500, [1967] 2 All ER 189, CA.

30.14   Applying those principles, it has been held that hardship to nephews or nieces of the landlord, after the landlord's death, was too remote, but note that this case was rather special on its facts[1].

Although it is very rare for a landlord to succeed before the ALT on the greater hardship test, there has been a case where the landlord has done so, but then failed on the 'fair and reasonable landlord' proviso[2].

Although the hardship, to be relevant, must bear a causal relationship with the grant or refusal of consent to the operation of the notice to quit, any hardship which is not so attributable may be taken into account when applying the fair and reasonable landlord proviso. In relation to the fair and reasonable landlord test, the ALT has a wide discretion to take into account all issues of hardship to either party[3].

There have been Rent Act cases in which relative hardship has been considered[4]. The agricultural holdings legislation exists primarily in the interests of promoting productivity in the national interest from agricultural land as explained by the House of Lords in *Johnson v Moreton*[5], although (like the Rent Acts) there is also a social engineering element to the policy which gave rise to the AHA 1986 and its predecessors.

1   *Raine's Trustees v Raine* (1985) 275 Estates Gazette 374.
2   *Jones v Burgoyne* (1963) 188 Estates Gazette 497.
3   *Cooke v Talbot* (1977) 243 EG 831, per Widgery LCJ in which the ALT wrongly took into account the conduct of one of the parties' legal advisers, which was wrongly considered to be improper.
4   Eg *Rhodes v Cornford* [1947] 2 All ER 601, CA; *Sims v Wilson* [1946] 2 All ER 261, CA; *Thomas v Fryer* [1970] 2 All ER 1, [1970] 1 WLR 845, CA; *Harte v Frampton* [1948] 1 KB 73, [1947] 2 All ER 604, CA.
5   [1980] AC 37, [1978] 3 All ER 37.

Ground (f): Non-agricultural use

30.15 Ground (f) is:

'... that the landlord proposes to terminate the tenancy for the purpose of the land's being used for a use, other than for agriculture, not falling within Case B'[1].

Normally a landlord who wishes to terminate the tenancy, so as to use the holding for some non-agricultural purpose, will require planning consent and will fall within Case B[2].

Ground (f) requires the landlord to seek and obtain the consent of the ALT to the operation of his notice to quit if the non-agricultural use to which he proposes to put the holding is one which by virtue of the Town and Country Planning Acts themselves does not require planning consent, for example, private forestry[3]. As to the distinction between Case B and ground (f), see Chapter 32.

1   AHA 1986, s 27(3)(f). Formerly s 25(1)(e) of the AHA 1948 and s 3(3)(e) of the Agricultural Holdings (Notice to Quit) Act 1977.
2   See para 32.10.
3   *Ministry of Agriculture, Fisheries and Food v Jenkins* [1963] 2 QB 317, [1963] 2 All ER 147, CA. Cf *Bell v McCubbin* [1990] 1 QB 976, CA. Note the Agricultural Holdings (Amendment) Act 1990. See para 32.10.

'FAIR AND REASONABLE LANDLORD' REQUIREMENT

30.16 Grounds (a) to (f) are subject to the further proviso:

'Even if they are satisfied as mentioned in subsection (1) above, the ALT shall withhold consent under section 26 [of the AHA 1986] to the operation of the notice to quit if in all the circumstances it appears to them that a fair and reasonable landlord would not insist on possession'[1].

Even though the ALT may be satisfied that the landlord has established his case under s 27(3) of the AHA 1986, it must nevertheless withhold its consent to the operation of the notice to quit if in all the circumstances it appears to the ALT that a fair and reasonable landlord[2] would not insist on possession. Formerly this proviso appeared at the end of s 25(1) of the AHA 1948, but in the 1977 statute (and now the AHA 1986), it is re-enacted, not as a proviso, but as a separate subsection preceding the grounds set out in s 27(3) upon which the ALT is entitled to be satisfied that the landlord has made out his case.

1   AHA 1986, s 27(2).
2   Note that the landlord has to satisfy a double standard, ie both fair and reasonable.

30.17 Although ostensibly the fair and reasonable landlord requirement imposes an objective test[1], thereby restricting the discretion of the ALT, inevitably the application of the requirement is subjective. Experience reveals that conduct which certain ALTs would treat as not that of a fair and reasonable landlord is not so treated by others. There can, of course, be no definition of reasonableness in the abstract. What is reasonable to one reasonable person may be unreasonable to another equally reasonable person. Furthermore, the fair and reasonable proviso involves wider considerations than relative hardship[2].

In *Evans v Roper*[3], the court held that the ALT was not entitled to take into account, when considering the sound estate management ground, whether the tenant of a farm from which 54 acres was to be taken would suffer hardship, but they could decide that point under the fair and reasonable landlord proviso.

In *Jones v Burgoyne*[4], the ALT found in favour of the landlord on the grounds of greater hardship, but consent to the notice to quit was refused under the fair and reasonable landlord proviso. The landlord had no experience of farming except assisting on farms in his spare time, nor had he any experience of farm management. His son, who was to help him run the farm, was more experienced but even his experience was somewhat limited. The ALT decided that because of this lack of practical farming experience on the part of the landlord and his son, a reasonable landlord would not insist on recovering possession to manage the farm himself, when it could be managed better, and no doubt more profitably, by the sitting tenant.

In *Collins v Spurway*[5], it was decided that the ALT was entitled to consider a financial inducement which the landlord had offered and the tenant rejected when determining whether a fair and reasonable landlord would insist upon possession.

1   For example, most of the greater hardship cases are equally applicable to the fair and reasonable landlord test.

2   See the remarks of Widgery LCJ in *Cooke v Talbot* (1977) 243 EG 831.
3   [1960] 2 All ER 507, [1960] 1 WLR 814.
4   (1963) 188 Estates Gazette 497.
5   (1967) 204 Estates Gazette 801.

IMPOSITION OF CONDITIONS BY THE AGRICULTURAL LAND TRIBUNAL WHEN CONSENTING TO NOTICES TO QUIT

30.18 Section 27(4) of the AHA 1986 empowers an ALT, when giving consent to the operation of a notice to quit, to:

'impose such conditions as appear to the ALT requisite for securing that the land to which the notice relates will be used for the purpose for which the landlord proposes to terminate the tenancy'.

Section 27(5) enables the ALT to vary or revoke any such condition on the landlord's application where they are satisfied that a change of circumstances justifies this course.

The ALT's power to impose conditions is limited. They must be 'requisite for securing that the land will be used ...'. The ALT cannot, for example, impose a condition that the landlord should relet to the tenant a part of the holding, for example, the farmhouse and a small acreage, even though such a course would, in the opinion of the ALT, be just and equitable. It may, in that event, withhold consent to the operation of a notice to quit altogether under the fair and reasonable landlord provision of s 27(2) unless the landlord makes such an offer to the tenant.

The provisions of s 27(4) are ineffective to prevent a landlord subsequently changing his mind if, having implemented his intention and complied with the ALT's conditions, he then revises his plans[1]. In such a case, the landlord may apply to the ALT for variation or revocation[2] of the condition[3]. A breach of the condition does not entitle the outgoing tenant to remain in possession, or to have the notice to quit[4] discharged, except possibly in the case of fraud[5].

The statutory sanction is to be found in s 27(6)[6] which gives an ALT power to impose on a landlord a fine of up to the equivalent of two years' rent of the holding in question and to order him to pay the costs. Enforcement of this order involves forfeiting the moneys to the Crown and not to the outgoing tenant[7]. An order for the imposition of a penalty or for the payment of costs is enforceable in the same manner as a judgment or order of the county court to the like effect[8].

By reason of the very limited and unsatisfactory powers given to the ALT for imposing conditions they have rarely arisen since the early cases under the AHA 1948 were decided. It is submitted that if the ALT is in sufficient doubt, as to the bona fides of the landlord or as to whether he genuinely intends to do what he contends, it would probably be more appropriate for that consent to be withheld rather than granted on terms.

30.18　The statutory restrictions on notices to quit: counter-notice

1　*R v Agricultural Land Tribunal (South Eastern Area), ex p Boucher* (1952) 159 Estates Gazette 192, where the ALT's decision was quashed on judicial review by the Divisional Court.
2　As to variation or revocation of conditions, see *Jones v West Midlands Agricultural Land Tribunal* (1962) 184 Estates Gazette 78.
3　AHA 1986, s 27(5).
4　*Martin-Smith v Smale* [1954] 1 All ER 237, [1954] 1 WLR 247, CA, where the ALT's consent was given, subject to a condition that the landlord should appoint a bailiff approved by the County Agricultural Executive Committee before taking possession; the landlord appointed a bailiff but the committee did not report favourably upon him and the tenant was not entitled to dispute the effectiveness of the notice to quit. It was held that even if the condition attached to the notice to quit was not complied with, it was a matter to be enforced by the Minister and not one of which the tenant could take advantage.
5　See para 31.15.
6　Formerly s 29 of the AHA 1948, as amended and substituted by the Agriculture Act 1958 and later re-enacted as s 6 of the Agricultural Holdings (Notice to Quit) Act 1977.
7　AHA 1986, s 27(8).
8　AHA 1986, s 27(9).

Chapter 31

THE STATUTORY RESTRICTIONS ON NOTICES TO QUIT: CASES A TO H

GENERAL PRINCIPLES

The statutory scheme

31.1 As seen in Chapters 27, 28 and 30, the way in which the Agricultural Holdings Act 1986 (AHA 1986) confers security of tenure is by restricting the operation of notices to quit given by the landlord. Generally, this is by way of the tenant being able to serve a counter-notice and the landlord having to apply to the Agricultural Land Tribunal (ALT)[1] for consent to the operation of the notice to quit. Section 26 of the AHA 1986 excludes the tenant's ability to serve a counter-notice in a number of 'Cases' contained in Sch 3 to the AHA 1986 ('Special Case notices to quit')[2]. These Special Cases have their own rules, the common features of which are that:

(a)   the ALT has no jurisdiction in relation to a notice to quit which expressly specifies that it is given for one of the reasons set out in Cases A to H of Sch 3; and

(b)   whereas standard s 26 notices to quit do not require a landlord to state any reason for them, Special Case notices to quit must state the reason in the notice itself[3].

In earlier editions of this book, the Special Case notices to quit were described as the 'deadly sins'[4]. They have often been described elsewhere as 'incontestable' notices to quit. As pointed out in the last edition of this book, this is misleading because they may be contested and the statutory procedure in relation to several of the cases expressly anticipates a challenge by the tenant. The only extent to which they are 'incontestable' is that they may not be contested before the ALT.

The Special Cases where a tenant's right to serve counter-notice is expressly excluded consist of the following:

(a)   Case A – retirement: statutory smallholdings
(b)   Case B – planning consent: non-agricultural use
(c)   Case C – certificate of bad husbandry
(d)   Case D – non-compliance with a notice to pay rent or notice to remedy

(e)   Case E – irremediable breach
(f)   Case F – insolvency
(g)   Case G – death of tenant
(h)   Case H – Ministry amalgamations

1   See Ch 30.
2   For the origins of Sch 3, see s 24(2) of the Agricultural Holdings Act 1948 (AHA 1948), as
     amended and s 2(3) of the Agricultural Holdings (Notice to Quit) Act 1977.
3   See Glidewell LJ in *Rous v Mitchell* [1991] 1 All ER 676, [1991] 1 WLR 469, CA.
4   A footnote to the eighth edition of this book provided: 'The reference to seven deadly sins,
     which was always difficult mathematically because Case D involves two alternative sins, is
     now even more inappropriate since Cases A to H add up to eight. Theologically, it is
     difficult too. Cases A and B involve no 'sin' on the part of the tenant and Case G involves
     'sin' only in the sense that 'the wages of sin is death'. The expression is … a convenient and
     evocative shorthand description of the notices in question'.

31.2 It is vital for a tenant who has received a notice under Cases A, B, D or
E, if he wishes to dispute the reason stated for the giving of the notice, to do
so by demanding arbitration within one month of receipt by him of the notice
to quit[1]. If he fails to do so he is statute barred from raising any issue as to the
reasons stated later, for example, when proceedings are taken for possession
even where the reason stated for the giving of the notice to quit cannot be
validly made out[2]. Further, the tenant must, within three months of giving a
valid demand for arbitration, apply to the RICS for the appointment of an
arbitrator or obtain the appointment of an arbitrator, otherwise the demand
for arbitration will be rendered ineffective[3].

Special Case notices to quit do not have to be in a statutorily prescribed form
or to draw the recipient's attention to the need to give a demand for
arbitration.

The time limits and procedures are mandatory and inflexible. There is no
power for any arbitrator or court to relax or extend them[4].

Given the inflexibility in relation to the time limits and procedures, this is
balanced by more stringent rules applied to the landlord's adherence with the
requirements of s 26(2) and Sch 3 to the AHA 1986[5]. The principles as to
certainty and avoiding ambiguity which apply to notices to quit generally[6]
have had a more stringent code applied by the courts to Special Case notices
to quit[7]. It is submitted that, notwithstanding the commonsense approach
adopted by the House of Lords in *Mannai Investments Co Ltd v Eagle Star
Life Assurance Co Ltd*[8], the more rigorous approach applied by the courts in
relation to Special Case notices to quit will continue.

1   See Chs 44 and 47.
2   *Magdalen College, Oxford v Heritage* [1974] 1 All ER 1065, [1974] 1 WLR 441, CA;
     Harding v Marshall (1983) 267 Estates Gazette 161. Note that the notice to quit may be
     successfully challenged in these circumstances if fraud is established: *Rous v Mitchell*
     [1991] 1 All ER 676, [1991] 1 WLR 469, [1991] 1 EGLR 1, CA.
3   The Agricultural Holdings (Arbitration on Notices) Order 1987, SI 1987/710, art 10. See
     para 31.11.

4   Cf time limits specified in regulations such as the Agricultural Land Tribunals (Rules) Order 1978, SI 1978/259, which unlike the Agricultural Holdings (Arbitration on Notices) Order 1987, SI 1987/710, contains powers entitling the Chairman or Tribunal to extend time. See *Kellett v Alexander* (1980) 257 Estates Gazette 494; *Harding v Marshall* (1983) 267 Estates Gazette 161.
5   *Pickard v Bishop* (1975) 31 P & CR 108.
6   See para 28.11.
7   This is not surprising given that Cases A to H represent what Professor Rodgers has described as 'a species of statutory forfeiture': Agricultural Law, C P Rodgers (2nd edn, 1998), Butterworths, at para 7.38.
8   [1997] AC 749, [1997] 1 EGLR 57. See para 24.3 ff.

Certainty as to the type of notice

31.3 If the landlord is relying upon one of the Special Cases, then although no prescribed form of words is specifically required, he must make it clear as to which Special Case he is relying. If he employs ambiguous language[1], then his notice to quit will be invalid[2]. In *Budge v Hicks*[3], it was unclear as to whether the landlord was relying upon breaches which were remediable or irremediable. As a consequence, the notice was held to be ineffective.

This problem is often encountered when a landlord gives notice to quit in reliance upon a short notice clause in the tenancy agreement authorising the resumption of possession of the whole or part of the holding for non-agricultural purposes. Care must be taken when giving notice to quit in such circumstances to ensure that there is no ambiguity as to whether the landlord is also relying upon Case B or s 27(3)(f) or neither.

1   Described as a 'calculated obscurity' in *Macnabb v Anderson* 1957 SC 213, 1958 SLT 8. Also see *Hammon v Fairbrother* [1956] 2 All ER 108, [1956] 1 WLR 490.
2   *Budge v Hicks* [1951] 2 KB 335, [1951] 2 All ER 245, CA.
3   *Budge v Hicks* [1951] 2 KB 335, [1951] 2 All ER 245, CA.

31.4 In each of the eight Special Cases, the reason for the notice must not only accord with the particular Special Case in question, but the reason for the notice must be stated in the notice itself. Indeed, each Special Case (except Case H) specifically states the ground and then goes on to say 'and the fact is stated in the notice' (per Cases B and C) or 'and it is stated in the notice to quit that it is given by reason of the said matter' (Cases A, D, E and F) or 'it is stated in the notice to quit that it is given by reason of that person's death' (Case G). All require the statement to be in the notice itself. Stating the reason in an accompanying letter is not good practice and may be rejected by the court applying the strict rules of compliance under s 26(2) and Sch 3[1].

The terms of the notice to quit must be such that no reasonable tenant would be left in any reasonable doubt as to whether the notice was served for one of the reasons contained in Special Cases or for some other reason[2]. If it fails to make it clear, it will be invalid.

If the notice to quit is given under one of Special Cases, but the landlord fails to establish the ground relied on, the notice will not take effect as an unqualified notice under s 26(1) of the AHA 1986[3].

31.4 *The statutory restrictions on notices to quit: Cases A to H*

A landlord may give an unqualified notice to quit under s 26(1) but include in it reasons. This may be done to avoid a claim for additional compensation for disturbance[4]. However, the landlord must ensure that there is no possibility of the reasons stated in the notice to quit being any of the reasons falling within the Special Cases. If there is any confusion, the notice to quit will be invalid[5].

[1]   In Scotland letters have been accepted: *Graham v Lamont* 1971 SC 170 and *Copeland v McQuaker* 1973 SLT 186. If it is necessary to argue reliance on a letter, see *Turton v Turnbull* [1934] 2 KB 197, CA. Also see *Re Digby and Penny* [1932] 2 KB 491, CA; *Sherwood v Moody* [1952] 1 All ER 389; *Riggs v Lawford* (1951) unreported (cited in earlier editions of this book).
[2]   *Mills v Edwards* [1971] 1 QB 379, [1971] 1 All ER 922, CA. Also see *Nunes v Davies Laing & Dick Ltd* (1985) 51 P & CR 310.
[3]   *Cowan v Wrayford* [1953] 2 All ER 1138.
[4]   See para 38.47 ff.
[5]   *Hammon v Fairbrother* [1956] 2 All ER 108. Also see *Harley v Moss* (1962) 181 Estates Gazette 707, doubted in *Mills v Edwards* [1971] 1 QB 379, [1971] 1 All ER 922, CA.

Certainty as to the obligations breached

31.5   The preliminary requirements contained in Sch 3 applying to the Special Cases must be strictly complied with. This is particularly so in relation to Cases D and E relating to the non-payment of rent or breach of covenant. Failure to meet the statutory requirements will cause the notice to quit to be invalid[1].

In relation to notices to pay[2], for example, the preliminary notice must:

(a)   be in the statutorily prescribed form[3];
(b)   correctly record the identity of the landlord[4]; and
(c)   set out the exact figure for the alleged arrears of rent[5].

Both any preliminary notice and the subsequent notice to quit must be addressed to all joint tenants if there are more than one, notwithstanding the fact that service on one alone is sufficient[6].

It is submitted that, notwithstanding the House of Lords decision in *Mannai Investments Co Ltd v Eagle Star Assurance Co Ltd*[7], the courts are likely to continue to construe strictly preliminary notices and the precise identification of the obligations allegedly breached giving rise to a notice to quit given pursuant to Special Cases[8]. The court may permit an error which is de minimis and would not have misled the reasonable tenant[9].

[1]   *Pickard v Bishop* (1975) 31 P & CR 108, CA.
[2]   See para 31.28 ff.
[3]   See para 31.28.
[4]   *Pickard v Bishop* (1975) 31 P & CR 108, CA.
[5]   *Dickinson v Boucher* [1984] 1 EGLR 12, CA.
[6]   *Jones v Lewis* (1973) 25 P & CR 375, CA. See para 29.10.
[7]   [1997] AC 749, [1997] 1 EGLR 57. See para 28.3.
[8]   *Speedwell Estates Ltd v Dalziel* [2002] EWCA Civ 1277, [2002] 02 EG 104.
[9]   In *Official Solicitor v Thomas* [1986] 2 EGLR 1, 279 Estates Gazette 407, the notice to quit was not invalidated where the notice described supplemental agreements in the singular and not the plural.

Certainty as to the ground for possession relied on

31.6 It is not necessary to refer expressly to Sch 3 to the AHA 1986 or one of the Special Cases referred to in it in the notice to quit. However, the notice to quit needs to make it clear which Special Case the landlord is relying on. Any ambiguity is construed against the landlord making the notice to quit invalid[1].

[1] *Budge v Hicks* [1951] 2 KB 335, [1951] 2 All ER 245, CA.

Contesting a notice to quit given under Cases A, B, D and E

31.7 When notice to quit is given upon one or more of the grounds set out in Cases A, B, D and E, and this is expressly stated in the notice, then if the tenant wishes to dispute the reasons stated for the giving of the notice to quit, he can only do so if he first demands arbitration and gives that demand within one month of the date of service upon him of the notice to quit[1].

This form of demand for arbitration is sometimes referred to as a counter-notice, though it is preferable to describe it as a demand for arbitration so as not to confuse it with a counter-notice invoking the provisions of s 26(1) of the AHA 1986. The right to give the latter form of counter-notice is expressly excluded where the tenant receives a notice to quit relying upon any of the Special Cases.

In *Rous v Mitchell*[2], a tenant gave a counter-notice under s 26(1) following a notice to quit relying on Case D. It was argued that this was sufficient to constitute a demand for arbitration since the tenant had made it clear that he wished to dispute the validity of the notice to quit. The Court of Appeal rejected that argument although, on the facts of the case, the notice to quit was found to be void because it was fraudulent.

There is provision for the tenant to give a demand for arbitration in Cases A, B, D and E, but not in Cases C, F, G or H. In those latter cases, if the tenant wishes to dispute the validity of the reasons stated for the giving of the notice to quit, no form of counter-notice or demand for arbitration may be given. If the tenant wishes to contest a notice to quit under Cases C, F, G or H, he must wait until proceedings for possession are commenced and then defend them on the basis that the reasons stated cannot be established. Alternatively, he may apply to the court to seek a declaration as to the validity of the notice.

[1] The Agricultural Holdings (Arbitration on Notices) Order 1987, SI 1987/710, art 10.
[2] [1991] 1 All ER 676.

31.8 In Cases A, B, D and E, if the tenant fails to give a demand for arbitration within one month, he is statute barred from raising those issues at all, even where, as in the case of *Magdalen College, Oxford v Heritage*[1], the landlord had to acknowledge that the notice to pay upon which the notice to quit was founded was invalid.

The Court of Appeal reaffirmed its decision in *Magdalen College, Oxford v Heritage*[2] in the later cases of *Parrish v Kinsey*[3] and *Harding v Marshall*[4]. As a result of that latter case, prescribed forms of notice to pay were introduced.

As indicated above[5], following the giving of the demand for arbitration, the tenant must also ensure either that an arbitrator is appointed by agreement or that an application has been made to the President of the RICS for the appointment of an arbitrator within the further period of three months from the giving of the demand for arbitration[6]. Failure by the tenant to comply with that mandatory requirement also renders him statute barred from raising any issue as to the validity of the reason stated for the giving of the notice to quit.

These draconian consequences for the tenant should be contrasted with the position following the giving of a counter-notice under s 26(1) of the AHA 1986 in the case of a notice to quit which does not specify one of the Special Cases as the reason for the notice. A tenant who is entitled to and who does give a counter-notice under s 26(1) of the AHA 1986 has to take no further immediate steps to protect himself. The initiative lies with the landlord, who must within one month apply to the ALT for consent. Otherwise the notice to quit is rendered ineffective.

The sanction in the case of a demand for arbitration is not that the notice to quit is rendered ineffective if no arbitrator is appointed within three months of the date of service of the demand for arbitration, but the reverse. The demand for arbitration itself is rendered ineffective and the reason stated in the notice to quit then becomes incontestable, even though the landlord cannot make out the ground for the giving of the notice[7]. The manifest injustice of this rule of law caused the Court of Appeal in *Magdalen College, Oxford v Heritage*[8] to grant leave to defend following High Court proceedings for summary judgement. Although leave to defend was given, when the defence itself was considered by the Court of Appeal, it was found by the court (differently constituted) that the obligation to give a demand for arbitration was mandatory and not permissive.

There is no statutorily prescribed form of demand for arbitration. An informal letter will suffice, but it must make it clear that the tenant disputes the validity of the reasons stated for the giving of the notice to quit. It is insufficient that he should merely telephone the landlord to negotiate[9]. It is not necessary in the demand to specify all or any of the issues the tenant wishes to raise[10].

1 [1974] 1 All ER 1065, [1974] 1 WLR 441.
2 [1974] 1 All ER 1065, [1974] 1 WLR 441. See para 31.15.
3 [1983] 2 EGLR 13, 268 Estates Gazette 1113.
4 (1983) 267 Estates Gazette 161, CA.
5 See para 31.2.
6 The Agricultural Holdings (Arbitration on Notices) Order 1987, SI 1987/710, art 10.
7 Unless ground is established: see *Rous v Mitchell* [1991] 1 All ER 676, CA. See para 31.7.
8 [1974] 1 All ER 1065, [1974] 1 WLR 441. Also see *Crown Estate Comrs v Allingham* (1972) 226 Estates Gazette 2153.
9 For a hard case of an invalid counter-notice, see *Mountford v Hodkinson* [1956] 2 All ER 17, [1956] 1 WLR 422. Also see *Rous v Mitchell* [1991] 1 All ER 676, CA. As to what constitutes an effective counter-notice, see *Edlingham Ltd v MFI Furniture Centres Ltd* [1981] 2 EGLR 97, 259 Estates Gazette 421.

10   There is no authority for this proposition which was followed in *Thomas v Wildem* (1980) unreported, Swindon County Court.

31.9 It should be noted that, in the case of a joint tenancy, it is necessary for all joint tenants to join in the giving of a demand for arbitration[1].

There is nothing invalid in a provision in a tenancy agreement which requires the landlord to give more than the statutory minimum period of notice of which imposes an additional restriction upon the landlord[2]. Further, a landlord may, in appropriate circumstances, be estopped from serving a notice to quit at all[3].

The combined effect of art 9 of the Agricultural Holdings (Arbitration on Notices) Order 1987 and the decision in *Magdalen College Oxford v Heritage*[4] (and the other cases cited at 31.8 above) is that it is only 'the reason stated for the giving of the notice to quit' in question which has to be referred to arbitration. If the tenant wishes to challenge any other aspect of the notice to quit, for example, as to whether it relates to the whole of the holding or is invalid as a notice to quit part only or as to whether the notice was duly served or generally in relation to the common law validity of the notice, then there is no requirement that the tenant should give a notice demanding arbitration. The tenant is entitled to raise his defence when the landlord seeks an order for possession or seek a declaration as to the validity of the notice given. The tenant is not restricted from raising such matters not falling within the meaning of 'the reasons stated for the giving of the notice to quit'.

In Cases A, B, D and E, where the arbitration provisions apply, arbitration is the only means by which the tenant can contest the facts on which the notice to quit is based[5]. It should again be noted that, however harsh or unfair the consequences, if the tenant fails to demand arbitration within one month of service of the notice to quit or appoint an arbitrator within three months of service of the demand for arbitration, then the court has no residual power to grant relief to the tenant[6]. Other than in the case of fraud[7], the notice to quit will take effect.

1   *Newman v Keedwell* (1977) 35 P & CR 393. See para 29.10.
2   *Re Midland Railway Co's Agreement, Charles Clay & Sons Ltd v British Railways Board* [1971] Ch 725, CA.
3   *Datnow v Jones* (1985) 275 Estates Gazette 145; *John v George* [1996] 1 EGLR 7.
4   [1974] 1 All ER 1065, [1974] 1 WLR 441.
5   *Harding v Marshall* (1983) 267 Estates Gazette 161; *Parrish v Kinsey* [1983] 2 EGLR 13.
6   *Milton (Peterborough) Estates Co v Harris* [1989] 2 EGLR 229; *Parrish v Kinsey* (1983) 268 EG 1113. See paras 31.2 and 13.16.
7   *Rous v Mitchell* [1991] 1 All ER 676, CA. See para 31.15.

31.10 What is less clear is the extent of the arbitrator's jurisdiction to determine matters not confined simply to the reasons stated. It is submitted that, on parity of reasoning with the decision of the Court of Appeal in *Kirkby v Robinson*[1], the test is whether the matter being raised is inextricably a part of the reasons stated so that the arbitrator must or would find it desirable to determine such matter in order to discharge his duties to determine the validity of the reasons stated.

In *Cawley v Pratt*[2], a tenant failed to demand arbitration, but challenged a Case B notice because it allegedly related to part only of the holding. The Court of Appeal decided that, on its true construction, the notice related to the whole holding. Therefore it was valid, even though only part was required for non-agricultural purposes.

A formal, or indeed an informal, letter which makes it clear that the tenant wishes to dispute the validity of the reasons stated for the giving of a notice must also say that he demands arbitration. It is insufficient merely to make it clear that the tenant challenges the landlord's notice to quit[3].

¹   (1965) 195 Estates Gazette 363.
²   [1988] 2 EGLR 6, CA.
³   *Rous v Mitchell* [1991] 1 All ER 676, CA.

Lapse of demand for arbitration

31.11 As already noted, a demand for arbitration will cease to be effective three months after the date of its service unless, within that period, either:

(a)   an arbitrator has been appointed by agreement; or (in default)
(b)   an application has been made to the President of the RICS for the appointment of an arbitrator[1].

If the tenant fails to appoint the arbitrator by one of these methods within the prescribed three months, then the notice to quit will take effect. The demand for arbitration shall be treated as void[2].

It should be noted that the arbitrator's appointment takes effect from when he accepts the appointment and not when he notifies the parties that he has done so[3].

¹   The Agricultural Holdings (Arbitration on Notices) Order 1987, SI 1987/710, art 10.
²   *Cawley v Pratt* [1988] 2 EGLR 6, CA; *Land v Sykes* [1992] 1 EGLR 1.
³   *Robinson v Moody* [1988] 2 EGLR 6. As to when an appointment by the President of the Royal Institution of Chartered Surveyors (RICS) takes effect, see para 47.17.

Notice to quit in the alternative

31.12 When a landlord serves a notice to quit which is capable of taking effect both under s 26(1)[1] and under s 26(2)[2] of the AHA 1986[3], then the first stage in dealing with such a notice to quit is by way of arbitration (following a demand for arbitration and compliance with art 10 of the Agricultural Holdings (Arbitration on Notices) Order 1987[4]). If the landlord fails at the arbitration to establish the ground for possession under one of the Special Cases, then the notice to quit then falls to be considered as an unqualified notice to quit under s 26(1) of the AHA 1986.

In these cases, the time limit for serving a counter-notice under s 26(1) is extended to one month from the termination of the arbitration[5].

There is a potential pitfall. Often, in response to a dual notice to quit, the tenant's adviser will serve both a demand for arbitration and a counter-notice. It is good practice to do so. If the notice to quit then falls to be considered at an arbitration and the landlord fails, the tenant must serve a further counter-notice within one month of the termination of the arbitration[6] in order to rely upon the protection afforded by the service of a valid counter-notice, namely that the landlord must apply to the ALT for consent to the operation of the notice to quit[7].

[1]   See para 30.1.
[2]   Cases A to H. See para 31.1.
[3]   As often happens in relation to attempts to recover possession for non-agricultural use. See Ch 32.
[4]   SI 1987/701.
[5]   SI 1987/701, art 11.
[6]   SI 1987/701, art 11.
[7]   See para 30.1.

Postponement of notice to quit

31.13 As seen, a tenant may invoke art 9 of the Agricultural Holdings (Arbitration on Notices) Order 1987[1] requiring any question arising out of a notice to quit to be determined by arbitration, the operation of the notice to quit is suspended:

(a)   in all cases, for the three-month period allowed by art 10 for an application for the appointment of an arbitrator; and

(b)   if an appointment, or an application for such to the RICS, is made within that period, the notice to quit is further postponed until the termination of the subsequent arbitration.

If the arbitrator upholds the notice to quit, and the latter would come into effect within six months of the termination of the arbitration, the arbitrator can further postpone the operation of the notice to quit. Termination of the tenancy can be postponed in this way for a period not exceeding 12 months[2]. The postponement can be made by the arbitrator on his own motion, or on the application of the tenant, which latter must be made within 14 days after service on the tenant of the arbitrator's award.

[1]   SI 1987/710.
[2]   SI 1987/710, art 13(1).

Arbitration on notice to remedy

31.14 In the case of a notice to remedy to do work under Case D[1], arbitration can be invoked in response to that notice, before a subsequent notice to quit[2].

[1]   As to notices to remedy, see para 31.44. Note that arbitration prior to a notice to quit is not available in relation to a notice to remedy not requiring the doing of work, see para 31.72.
[2]   See para 31.60.

Fraudulent notices to quit

31.15 In *Rous v Mitchell*[1], a notice to quit which was found to contain false representations was held to be invalid, even though the tenant had not demanded arbitration following the giving of the notice to quit. It was void ab initio. The landlord had alleged that the tenant had sub-let cottages in breach of a prohibition on sub-letting. In each case (except one), the landlord knew, or did not care, that the statements in the notice were not true. The notice was given to put the tenant under pressure. The Court of Appeal held that fraud was present when a false representation was made knowingly or without belief in its truth or recklessly careless whether it be true or false. It was irrelevant whether the false statement must have actually deceived, or at least be capable of deceiving, the person to whom it was addressed. Where fraud is established, the notice to quit is a nullity.

In *Omnivale Ltd v Boldan*[2], the landlord gave notice to quit in respect of land required for development and alleged he had planning consent in respect of the land. In fact the planning consent did not extend to all the land subject to the notice to quit. It was held that the notice had been carelessly given, but it was not sufficiently reckless as to amount to fraud.

[1]   [1991] 1 All ER 676, [1991] 1 WLR 469. Also see the Fraud Act 2006: and see para 45.71.
[2]   [1994] EGCS 63.

No relief against notice to quit

31.16 In a number of cases, the Court of Appeal has considered whether there is any power to grant relief to a tenant who has received an incontestable notice to quit in circumstances which create great hardship to the tenant[1]. It was finally decided in *Parrish v Kinsey*[2] that the statutory provisions are 'precise and ... absolute in their operation'. Even if the tenant is very elderly (as in *Parrish v Kinsey*), and incapable of understanding the consequences of the notice served upon him, if the statutory requirements are satisfied the court cannot grant any relief or stay any proceedings taken thereafter for possession.

[1]   *Shepherd v Lomas* [1963] 2 All ER 902, [1963] 1 WLR 962; *Stoneman v Brown* [1973] 2 All ER 225, [1973] 1 WLR 459; *Pickard v Bishop* (1975) 31 P & CR 108.
[2]   [1983] 2 EGLR 13, 268 Estates Gazette 1113.

Servicemen

31.17 Where the tenant is serving as a reservist with the Armed Forces of the Crown, the landlord does not have an absolute right under the Special Cases to possession but must obtain the ALT's consent[1]. Since the abolition of National Service, it is unlikely that such circumstances will arise.

[1]   AHA 1986, s 30 and Sch 5. See para 27.9.

CASE A – SMALLHOLDINGS

31.18 Case A provides:

'The holding is let as a smallholding by a smallholdings authority or the Minister in pursuance of Part II of the Agriculture Act 1970 and was so let on or after 12 September 1984, and:
 (a)   the tenant has attained the age of 65; and
 (b)   if the result of the notice to quit taking effect would be to deprive the tenant of living accommodation occupied by him under the tenancy, suitable alternative accommodation is available for him, or will be available for him when the notice takes effect; and
 (c)   the instrument under which the tenancy was granted contains an acknowledgment signed by the tenant that the tenancy is subject to the provisions of this Case (or to those of Case I in section 2(3) of the Agricultural Holdings (Notices to Quit) Act 1977),
and it is stated in the notice to quit that it is given by reason of the said matter'.

This new case was introduced by the Agricultural Holdings Act 1984 (AHA 1984). It was initially inserted as Case I in s 2(3) of the Agricultural Holdings (Notices to Quit) Act 1977. Upon the consolidation of the legislation in the AHA 1986, it was moved to Case A. The former Case A applied where a notice to quit was given and the ALT had already consented to its operation on one of more of the grounds set out in s 3(3) of the 1977 Act. By 1984 this was recognised to be a 'dead letter'[1]. It was consequentially repealed by the AHA 1984[2].

Until the Court of Appeal decision in *Saul v Norfolk County Council*[3], there was doubt as to whether tenancies of statutory smallholdings[4] granted before the enactment of the Agriculture Act 1970 were subject to the statutory succession regime. The court decided that they were. The decision was in effect reversed by the AHA 1984, which amended s 18(4)(f) of the Agricultural Holdings (Notices to Quit) Act 1977 Act[5]. The AHA 1984 ensured that succession did not apply to smallholdings.

The enactment of the new Case A in the AHA 1984 arose following considerable debate in the House of Lords. It was recognised that smallholdings were not effective as providing 'starter units' and that few farmers moved up the ladder to larger farms. The present provision[6] was intended to address this issue.

It should be noted that there is no equivalent power for any other landlord to dispossess his tenant who has attained the age of 65 on the provision of suitable alternative living accommodation. On the contrary, such tenants will normally be able to invoke the succession provisions[7].

There are four requirements of Case A:

(a)   the tenancy must have commenced after the AHA 1984 came into force[8];
(b)   the tenant must be 65 or older at the date of the giving of the notice to quit;

483

(c)   the tenancy agreement must contain a provision that the landlord may rely upon Case A;

(d)   where the tenant lives in the farmhouse, then the landlord must provide suitable alternative accommodation at the date of the expiry of the notice to quit.

There are extensive provisions set out in Pt II, paras 1 to 7 of Sch 3 to the AHA 1986 for determining whether suitable alternative accommodation is, or will be, available for the tenant[9]. These have to be complied with if the landlord is to give an effective notice to quit denying the tenant his right to give counter-notice.

1   J Muir Watt, Estate Gazettes Law Reports, 12 November 1983.
2   AHA 1984 Act, s 6(2) and Sch 4.
3   [1984] QB 559, [1984] 2 All ER 489.
4   See para 20.19.
5   AHA 1984 Act, Sch 1 para 2(b).
6   Introduced in the Third Reading debate in the House of Lords by Lord Northfield.
7   See Chs 34–36.
8   12 September 1984: AHA 1984, s 11.
9   These are modelled on the provisions of the Rent Act 1977, Sch 15.

31.19 The burden of proof, to establish the availability of suitable alternative accommodation, is on the landlord. The landlord must discharge that burden of proof as at the date of the order for possession, as opposed to the date on which the notice to quit is given[1].

The landlord can establish the availability of suitable alternative accommodation through two alternative routes as follows.

(a)   The first is to obtain a certificate from the local housing authority certifying that the authority will provide suitable alternative accommodation by a specified date. This is conclusive evidence that suitable alternative accommodation will be available on that date[2].

(b)   If no local housing authority certificate is obtained, the accommodation is considered to be suitable for the purposes of Case A if the premises concerned are such that the letting will be an assured tenancy under the Housing Act 1988. Alternatively, the premises must be available to let to the tenant on terms that will afford him security of tenure 'reasonably equivalent' to that of a protected tenancy under the Rent Act 1977 or an assured tenancy under the Housing Act 1988[3]. If a local housing authority certificate is not available, the accommodation must, in addition, be reasonably suitable to the needs of the tenant's family as regards proximity to place of work, and either similar as regards rental or accommodation to other accommodation provided by the housing authority to tenants with similar needs, or reasonably suitable to the means of the tenant and the needs of him and his family as regards extent and character[4].

A tenant in receipt of notice to quit specifying the Case A ground, who wishes to challenge the reason stated for giving the notice to quit, must within one month demand arbitration. This is the only method of challenge available to the tenant as to any question arising under Case A[5]. The procedures and consequences of not giving a demand for arbitration are the same as for notices to quit given under Cases B, D or E[6]. The arbitrator may not consider the merits of the landlord's claims for possession, but merely whether he has satisfied all the requirements of Case A.

If a landlord achieves vacant possession under Case A, basic compensation is payable to the tenant for disturbance, but not additional compensation[7].

1   *Selwyn v Hamill* [1948] 1 All ER 70.
2   AHA 1986, Sch 3 para 2.
3   Housing Act 1988, Sch 17 para 69.
4   AHA 1986, Sch 3 Pt II para 3.
5   *Magdalen College, Oxford v Heritage* [1974] 1 All ER 1065, [1974] 1 WLR 441.
6   See para 31.8.
7   AHA 1986, s 61(2). See para 38.55.

CASE B – PLANNING CONSENT: NON-AGRICULTURAL USE

31.20 Case B provides:

'The notice to quit is given on the ground that the land is required for a use, other than for agriculture:
(a)   for which permission has been granted on an application made under the enactments relating to town and country planning;
(b)   for which permission under those enactments is granted by a general development order by reason only of the fact that the use is authorised by:
         (i)   a private or local Act;
         (ii)   an order approved by both Houses of Parliament; or
         (iii)   an order made under section 14 or 16 of the Harbours Act 1964;
(c)   for which any provision that:
         (i)   is contained in an Act; but
         (ii)   does not form part of the enactments relating to town and country planning, deems permission under those enactments to have been granted;
(d)   which any such provisions deems not to constitute development for the purposes of those enactments; or
(e)   for which permission is not required under the enactments relating to town and country planning by reason only of Crown immunity, and that fact is stated in the notice'.

The wording of paragraphs (b) to (e) above was introduced following the decision of the Court of Appeal in *Bell v McCubbin*[1] by the Agricultural Holdings (Amendment) Act 1990.

Case B is dealt with in Chapter 32[2].

1   [1990] 1 QB 976.
2   See para 32.10.

CASE C – CERTIFICATE OF BAD HUSBANDRY

31.21 Case C provides:

'Not more than six months before the giving of the notice to quit, the Tribunal granted a certificate under paragraph 9 of Part II of this Schedule that the tenant of the holding was not fulfilling his responsibilities to farm in accordance with the rules of good husbandry, and that fact is stated in the notice'.

The AHA 1984 introduced further provisions relating to a certificate of bad husbandry[1] as follows:

'(1)   For the purposes of Case C the landlord of an agricultural holding may apply to the Tribunal for a certificate that the tenant is not fulfilling his responsibilities to farm in accordance with the rules of good husbandry; and the Tribunal, if satisfied that the tenant is not fulfilling his said responsibilities, shall grant such a certificate.

(2)   In determining whether to grant a certificate under this paragraph the Tribunal shall disregard any practice adopted by the tenant in pursuance of any provision of the contract of tenancy, or of any other agreement with the landlord, which indicates (in whatever terms) that its object is the furtherance of one or more of the following purposes, namely:

(a)   the conservation of flora or fauna or of geological or physiographical features of special interest;

(b)   the protection of buildings or other objects of archaeological, architectural or historic interest;

(c)   the conservation or enhancement of the natural beauty or amenity of the countryside or the promotion of its enjoyment by the public'.

[1]   AHA 1986, Sch 3 Pt II para 9(1) and (2).

31.22   Further, the AHA 1986 provides that in determining whether to grant a certificate of bad husbandry, the ALT shall disregard any practice adopted by the tenant in compliance with any obligation accepted or imposed on the tenant under s 94 or 95 of the Water Resources Act 1991[1].

Moreover, it should be noted that the tenant is not in breach of his responsibilities under the rules of good husbandry if he permits occupation for authorised coal working or facilitating the use of land for such purposes[2].

[1]   AHA 1986, Sch 3 Part II para 9(3).
[2]   Opencast Coal Act 1958, s 14(3), as substituted by the Housing and Planning Act 1986, Sch 8 para 5.

Good husbandry

31.23   The text of the rules of good husbandry are set out later in this book[1]. It should be noted that the rules of good husbandry were a product of policy immediately after the Second World War aimed at increasing output and efficiency. Their relevance, in the context of modern day farming is considered elsewhere in this book[2]. It is unclear as to what extent modern environmental practices are considered to be consistent with good husbandry. In construing these provisions, regard may be had to the parallel rules in Scotland[3].

Where a tenant elects to 'set aside' arable land in accordance with EC Regulations, the land so set aside is frequently neglected. Weeds are allowed to become established and to seed and the holding may deteriorate. In such circumstances, is a landlord entitled to obtain a certificate of bad husbandry and to dispossess the tenant under Case C? Invariably each case of this type turns on its own facts.

1   See para A1.2.
2   See para 24.4.
3   Agricultural Holdings (Scotland) 1948, s 28. See para 24.6.

The notice to quit

31.24 The notice to quit must be given not later than six months after the obtaining of the certificate of bad husbandry. This contrasts with the previous requirement prior to the enactment of the AHA 1984 that the notice to quit had to be given not later than six months following the application for the certificate[1]. That provided major problems in practice with the certificate being frustrated from time to time[2].

1   The Agricultural Holdings (Notices to Quit) Act 1977, s 2(3), Case C and s 24(2)(c) of the AHA 1948, amended by the AHA 1984, s 6(3).
2   *Cooke v Talbot* (1977) 243 Estates Gazette 831.

A certificate from the Agricultural Land Tribunal

31.25 When granting a certificate, the ALT may specify (in the certificate itself) a minimum period of notice for termination of the tenancy. This is to prevent the holding deteriorating still further because of what could otherwise be between 12 and 24 months of notice. The period specified must be not less than two months and it does not need to expire on a term date of the tenancy[1].

There has in the past been considerable reluctance on the part of ALTs to grant certificates of bad husbandry. In previous editions of this book, it was observed that such certificates obtained some notoriety, particularly during the wartime era, when they were widely believed to have been abused by certain wartime Agricultural Executive Committees whose members then acquired the right to farm the land in question. Thereafter, landlords most frequently relied upon the notice to remedy procedures specified now in Case D[2]. However, since considerable restrictions were imposed, particularly by the Agriculture (Miscellaneous Provisions) Act 1976 upon the landlord's right to recover possession for breach of a term or condition of the tenancy involving the doing of work of maintenance, repair or replacement, notices to remedy have been more sparingly used since then and an application for a certificate of bad husbandry in the case of a neglected holding can now prove to be a more effective, expeditious and less expensive remedy for a landlord anxious to protect his holding from further deterioration and to recover possession.

In the Scottish Land Court it was held:

(a)   the Scottish Land Court (in England, the equivalent forum is the Agricultural Land Tribunal) had no discretion on equitable grounds to

487

withhold their consent and had, therefore, to grant a certificate of bad husbandry when the grounds were proved;

(d) temporary breaches of the rules of good husbandry, for example where a tenant was suffering from a physical or mental disability, would not be likely to establish a breach; but

(c) the phrase 'other relevant circumstances' in s 11(1) of the Agriculture Act 1947 is restricted to circumstances relating to the unit itself and its production and not to mitigating factors relating to the tenant's personal circumstances[3].

In *Goodwin v Clarke*[4], where a landlord had applied for a certificate of bad husbandry and before the hearing, on inspection, he had discovered that the breaches committed previously by the tenant had been remedied, it was held that since the landlord did not withdraw his application for a certificate, by continuing with the litigation he was then guilty of 'vexatious, frivolous or oppressive' behaviour and as such was liable for the costs of the tenant from that time onwards[5].

[1] AHA 1986, s 25(4).
[2] See para 31.44.
[3] *Cambusmore Estate Trustees v Little* 1991 SLT (Land Ct) 33.
[4] Decision of the Eastern Area ALT [1992] EA 605. For a similar decision of an ALT (Yorkshire and Humberside) in the case of a succession case, see *Clappison v Marr Trustees*.
[5] As to the power to award costs, see para 46.14.

Challenging a notice to quit

31.26 A tenant in receipt of a notice to quit alleging that it is founded upon a certificate of bad husbandry is not entitled to demand arbitration as to the reasons stated[1]. His only remedy, in these circumstances, if he disputes the validity of the reasons stated (for example, because the certificate was obtained more than six months prior to the service of the notice to quit upon him) is either to seek a declaration of the court as to the validity of the notice at common law or to defend proceedings taken for possession upon the expiration of the notice to quit.

The court has no inherent jurisdiction or equitable power which would entitle it to prevent the landlord enforcing a notice to quit on the grounds of unfairness or hardship for the tenant[2].

If a landlord achieves vacant possession under Case C, neither basic nor additional compensation for disturbance is payable to the tenant upon quitting on the termination of the tenancy[3].

[1] Cf the position where the notice is founded upon Cases A, B, D or E.
[2] *Shepherd v Lomas* [1963] 2 All ER 902, [1963] 1 WLR 962; *Stoneman v Brown* [1973] 2 All ER 225, [1973] 1 WLR 459; *Pickard v Bishop* (1975) 31 P & CR 108; *Parrish v Kinsey* [1983] 2 EGLR 13, 268 Estates Gazette 1113.
[3] AHA 1986, s 61(1). See para 38.47 ff.

CASE D – NON-COMPLIANCE WITH NOTICE TO PAY RENT, OR NOTICE TO REMEDY A BREACH OF THE TENANCY: THE STATUTORY FRAMEWORK

31.27 Case D provides:

'At the date of the giving of the notice to quit the tenant had failed to comply with a notice in writing served on him by the landlord being either:

(a) a notice requiring him within two months from the service of the notice to pay any rent due in respect of the agricultural holding to which the notices to quit relates; or

(b) a notice requiring him within a reasonable period specified in the notice to remedy any breach by the tenant that was capable of being remedied of any term or condition of the tenancy which was not inconsistent with the fulfilment of his responsibilities to farm in accordance with the rules of good husbandry',

and it is stated in the notice to quit that it is given by reason of the said matter.

Case D contains two alternative grounds for giving a notice to quit to which a counter-notice cannot be given[1]. The first is for non-payment of rent after notice to pay and the second for any other remediable breach of the tenancy after notice to remedy. Notices to remedy breaches are now subject to substantial statutory restrictions[2].

There are two types of notice to remedy – notices to do work and those not requiring work to be undertaken – each with different available disputes procedures.

[1]   Both have their origins in s 24(2)(d) of the AHA 1948.
[2]   These were provided first by s 19 of the Agriculture (Miscellaneous Provisions) Act 1963, and latterly by ss 11 and 12 of the Agriculture (Miscellaneous Provisions) Act 1976. These were then repealed and re-enacted in the 1977 consolidating Act. They were further amended in the Agricultural Holdings Act 1984. All have now been repealed and re-enacted in the current consolidating statute – the AHA 1986, s 28 and Sch 3 Pt II para 10.

CASE D – NON-PAYMENT OF RENT AFTER NOTICE TO PAY

Introduction

31.28 Case D, paragraph (a) entitles a landlord to give a notice to quit if, at the date of the giving of the notice, the tenant has failed to comply with a notice in writing (in the currently prescribed form) served on him by the landlord requiring him within two months of the service of the notice to pay any rent due in respect of the agricultural holding to which the notice to quit relates.

A notice to pay must be in the statutorily prescribed form (Form 1) contained in the Agricultural Holdings (Forms of Notice to Pay Rent or to Remedy) Regulations 1987[1]. This form is significantly different from its predecessor[2]. It has given prominence to a warning as to the consequences of non-compliance.

It is not the continued existence of arrears of rent but the tenant's default in complying with the statutory form of notice served upon him requiring him to pay the rent which entitles the landlord to give a Case D notice to quit[3].

1 SI 1987/711.
2 The reference to the earlier regulations of the same name, SI 1984/1308, which were introduced following the remarks of the Court of Appeal in *Dickinson v Boucher* (1983) 269 Estates Gazette 1159. Note there is no provision for the notice to be given in a form substantially to the like effect. Cf *Morris v Patel* (1986) 281 Estates Gazette 419 a case not involving a penal notice.
3 *Luttenberger v North Thoresby Farms Ltd* [1993] 1 EGLR 3. See para 31.88.

Extra-statutory requirements

31.29 Part VI of the Landlord and Tenant Act 1987 applies to agricultural holdings which include a dwelling[1]. Section 47 provides that the landlord must serve written notice on his part specifying:

(a)   the name and address of the landlord; and
(b)   if that address is not in England and Wales, an address in England and Wales at which notices (including notices in proceedings) may be served on the landlord by the tenant.

This information must be contained in any written demand the landlord makes for rent or other sums payable to the landlord under the terms of the tenancy[2].

The penalty for non-compliance with s 47 is that the part of the amount demanded which consists of a 'service charge' is deemed not to be due[3]. 'Service charge' is widely defined to include any variable payments made directly 'or indirectly for services, repairs, maintenance or insurance'[4]. This will rarely apply to agricultural holdings. Normally where the 'model clauses' apply, the rent is not variable 'according to the relevant costs'[5].

Non-compliance with s 47 will almost certainly invalidate any notice to pay rent served by the landlord.

More importantly in relation to agricultural holdings, s 48 of the Landlord and Tenant Act 1987 (LTA 1987) must also be complied with. Section 48 provides that the rent otherwise due from the tenant is not payable until notice of an address in England and Wales at which notices (including notices in proceedings) may be served on the landlord is given to the tenant. Section 48 is of wider application than s 47. It applies even where there is no 'service charge' payable. When s 48 applies, and not s 47, the notice only needs to be given once and not in every demand 'for rent or other sums payable to the landlord under the terms of the tenancy'[6].

1 The Act is not primarily directed towards agricultural holdings. Part VI applies 'to premises which consist of or include a dwelling and are not held under a tenancy to which Part II of the Landlord and Tenant Act 1954 applies': LTA 1987, s 46(1).
2 LTA 1987, s 47(2).
3 LTA 1987, s 47(2) and (3). See also *Mannai Investments Co Ltd v Eagle Star Life Assurance Co Ltd* [1997] AC 749, [1997] 1 EGLR 57. See para 28.3.

4   LTA 1987, s 46(2) and the Landlord and Tenant Act 1985 (LTA 1985), s 18(1).
5   LTA 1985, s 18(1).
6   *Dallhold Estates (UK) Property Ltd v Lindsey Trading Properties Inc* [1994] 1 EGLR 93.
    Cf *Rogan v Woodfield Building Services Ltd* [1995] 1 EGLR 72. The notice can take the
    form of the landlord's name and address being set out in the tenancy agreement itself.

Rent due

31.30 In order for a landlord to utilise the notice to pay procedure he must
first establish the 'rent due[1]. This involves two stages: first, identifying what is
rent; and second, that it is due.

The terms of the tenancy will usually govern the amount of the rent and when
and (in some cases) how it is to be paid. The rent may be varied in accordance
with the statutory provisions contained in the AHA 1986[2]. The amount of
rent due may also be affected by the general law applying to set-off[3].

A notice to pay rent should not include a claim for any other money due from
the tenant. If interest on unpaid rent is contractually due to the landlord, it
cannot be included in the notice to pay, unless it is expressly reserved as rent in
the tenancy agreement. As the landlord must strictly comply with the statutory
requirements applying to a notice to pay, he should err on the side of caution
when inserting the amount of rent due in a notice to pay. A notice to pay must
not include, for example, interest on improvements or an insurance premium.

1   In an unreported county court case, *Busk v Hallett* (1969) unreported, it was held that, not
    only must the amount claimed be due, but it must be as 'rent'.
2   See Ch 25. Under the Housing Act 1988 it has been held that if the tenant counterclaims
    for damages, extinguishing the liability for rent by set-off, rent is not lawfully due. In such
    a case the court has no jurisdiction to make an order for possession where the ground for
    possession is rent arrears: *Baygreen Properties Ltd v Gil* [2002] EWCA Civ 1340, [2002]
    3 EGLR 42, [2002] 49 EG 126.
3   See para 31.32 ff.

31.31 The rent must be due and owing at the date of service of the notice to
pay[1]. A notice given before midnight on the day the rent falls due is not
sufficient.

If a tenant owes money, which is not rent – for example, interest on
improvements – and if that money is due and owing pursuant to a term or
condition of the tenancy or an agreement supplemental to it, the landlord may
give a notice to remedy in Form 3 (non-work notice) demanding payment
within two months of that money and then give notice to quit for non-
compliance with that notice to remedy[2].

1   *Urwick v Taylor* [1969] EGD 1106. Cf *Sharpley v Manby* [1942] 1 KB 217, [1942]
    1 All ER 66, CA (a case decided under the different wording of the 1923 Act); *Hayward v
    Lloyds Bank* (1972) unreported. See also, *Busk v Hallett* (1969) unreported (CC); *Pickard
    v Bishop* (1975) 31 P & CR 108, CA. Cf *Hayward v Lloyds Bank* (1972) unreported (CC).
    Also see, *T & E Homes Ltd v Robinson* [1979] 2 All ER 522, [1979] 1 WLR 452; *Official
    Solicitor v Thomas* (1986) 279 Estates Gazette 407.
2   *Official Solicitor v Thomas* (1986) 279 Estates Gazette 407.

Set-off

31.32   If the tenant has a valid claim to set-off, the rent otherwise payable will be reduced or extinguished. The existence of an arguable claim first creates a problem from the landlord who is required to state the precise amount of the arrears of rent in the notice to pay[1].

Whether an equitable set-off can be claimed against rent demanded in a notice to pay is open to doubt[2]. What is clear is that an equitable set-off cannot arise from a contingent liability on the part of the landlord[3]. In *Sloan Stanley Estate Trustees v Baribal*[4], the tenant sought to set-off against rent demanded in the notice to pay the landlord's part of the drainage rate. The rate was payable by the tenant, as occupier of the land, but recoverable against the landlord under the Land Drainage Act 1991. The Court of Appeal held that no set-off arose because the tenant had not paid the drainage rate to the authority before the service of the notice to pay. As a consequence, the notice to pay and subsequent notice to quit were found to be valid.

1   See para 31.35.
2   *Hanak v Green* [1958] 2 QB 9, CA.
3   *Sloan Stanley Estate Trustees v Baribal* [1994] 2 EGLR 8, [1994] 44 EG 237.
4   [1994] 2 EGLR 8, [1994] 44 EG 237.

31.33   It frequently happens that the landlord is in breach of his obligations under the terms of the tenancy, for example, because he has failed to carry out repairs after due notice from the tenant[1]. At one time it was thought that the tenant had no right of set-off against the rent by reason of the landlord's breach. However, the modern law is that the tenant is entitled to counter-claim and to set-off against rent monies due by way of damages, whether liquidated or unliquidated, for breach by the landlord of his repairing obligations[2]. In the last edition of this book, it was submitted that it was probable, although there was no authority on this point, that in these circumstances a tenant who has defaulted on receipt of a notice to pay, and who can show that the landlord is himself in breach of his repairing or any other obligations, after having had due notice from the tenant, can thereby establish that the whole of the monies claimed to be due and owing as rent are not due and owing because of his entitlement to set-off against that rental payment the unliquidated damages due to him for breach by the landlord of his repairing obligations. This approach has been followed since in Scotland in relation to the like provisions of the Agricultural Holdings (Scotland) Act 1991[3].

In *Sloan Stanley Estate Trustees v Barribal*[4], the Court of Appeal left open the question as to whether the equitable set-off might be available against rent demanded affecting the validity of a notice to pay. Nevertheless, given the draconian consequences for a tenant failing to pay rent due in response to a valid notice to pay, the advice to a tenant must be 'pay under protest' and pursue the tenant's claims for equitable set-off separately.

The decision in *Muscat v Smith*[5] should also be noted. The case involved a statutory tenancy of a dwellinghouse. Following service of a repairs notice under the Housing Act 1985, the then landlord, W, carried out remedial work, which caused major disruption and inconvenience. The tenant withheld rent. The freehold was assigned with the right to recover the arrears of rent. At first instance, the court held that the tenant's claim against W could not be set off against the arrears of rent. The Court of Appeal overturned that decision. It accepted that the general principle of set-off did not assist the tenant because, inter alia, the breaches of contract were those of W. However, on the application of principles that differed from those of general equitable set-off, the tenant had been entitled to set-off against the successor landlord's claim for arrears of rent any damages due to him for W's breach of his repairing obligations. That was because the debt was a chose in action, vested in the successor landlord as assignee subject to all equities which were available to the tenant against W.

Conversely, if the landlord assigns the reversion to A, and A claims rent for a subsequent period, then the tenant cannot set-off his claim for damages against the original landlord for breach of a repairing obligation in defending against A's claim[6].

1   See para 23.17 ff.
2   *British Anzani (Felixstowe) Ltd v International Marine Management (UK) Ltd* [1980] QB 137, [1979] 2 All ER 1063; *Melville v Grapelodge Developments Ltd* (1978) 39 P & CR 179; *Calabar Properties Ltd v Stitcher* [1983] 3 All ER 759, [1984] 1 WLR 287, CA. *Fuller v Happy Shopper Markets Ltd* [2001] 2 EGLR 32, [2001] 25 EG 159; *Baygreen Properties Ltd v Gil* [2002] 3 EGLR 42, (2002) 49 EG 126; *Maunder Taylor v Blaquiere* [2002] EWCA Civ 1633, [2003] 1 WLR 379.
3   *Alexander v Royal Hotel (Caithness) Ltd* [2001] 1 EGLR 6, [2001] 16 EG 148.
4   *Sloan Stanley Estate Trustees v Baribal* [1994] 2 EGLR 8, [1994] 44 EG 237.
5   [2003] EWCA Civ 962, [2003] 1 WLR 2853, [2003] 3 EGLR 11.
6   *Edlington Properties Ltd v J H Fenner & Co Ltd* [2005] EWHC 2158 (QB), [2006] 1 EGLR 29, [2006] 05 EG 274.

Form of notice to pay rent

31.34 A notice to pay must be in the statutorily prescribed form[1]. It should be noted that the prescribed form was first introduced by the AHA 1984[2]. Cases before 1984 relating to notices to pay need to be considered in that context.

The landlord may use a form 'substantially to the same effect' as the prescribed form[3]. The notice should include the notes which form part of the notice[4]. The notice to pay must expressly demand payment within two months. The notice to pay must be given by or on behalf of the landlord[5]. It must be given to the tenant and, if there is more than one tenant, it must be addressed to all of them and served on all of them[6].

In *Pickard v Bishop*[7], a notice to pay was invalid where the landlord had transferred his reversionary interest to trustees under a discretionary trust but gave the notice in his own name.

1   AHA 1986, Sch 3 Pt II para 10(1)(a); the Agricultural Holdings (Forms of Notice to Pay Rent or to Remedy) Regulations 1984, SI 1984/1308, reg 3, Form 1. For the precedent, see A2.40.
2   AHA 1984, s 6(4).

3   The Agricultural Holdings (Forms of Notice to Pay Rent or to Remedy) Regulations 1984, SI 1984/1308, reg 2(2). Also see *Ravenseft Properties Ltd v Hall* [2001] EWCA Civ 2034, [2002] 1 EGLR 9, [2002] 11 EG 156 and para 28.11.
4   *Bolton (House Furnishers) Ltd v Oppenheim* [1959] 1 WLR 913, CA.
5   *Pickard v Bishop* (1975) 31 P & CR 108, CA.
6   *Jones v Lewis* (1973) 25 P & CR 375, CA. See para 29.10.
7   (1975) 31 P & CR 108, CA.

31.35 If the notice to pay demands a sum in excess of the rent due and owing at the date of the notice to pay, then the notice to pay is invalid, whether or not the tenant was misled[1]. An inconsequential error in the form of the notice (but not the amount of rent) will not invalidate it[2].

The notice to pay must correctly state the amount of the rent due. Where a notice to pay stated that the arrears of rent amounted to £650, but were in fact £625, it was found to be invalid[3].

If the notice is despatched before the date on which the rent is due, but received, and therefore served, after it has become due, the notice is valid[4]. It should be noted that s 23 of the AHA 1986 provides that a notice may be sent by pre-paid registered post, which includes recorded delivery post. It is then deemed to be served when it would ordinarily be delivered in the normal course of post[5].

Service of a notice by leaving a notice at the farmhouse, where it slipped under the linoleum and remained undetected, was held to be sufficient[6].

In *Dockerill v Fitzpatrick*[7], a tenant who had exercised an option to purchase, but where the option had not been completed, was found still to be in occupation as tenant and required to comply with a notice to pay.

1   *Dickinson v Boucher* (1983) 269 Estates Gazette 1159, CA; *Busk v Hallett* (1969) unreported; *Pickard v Bishop* (1975) 31 P & CR 108, CA.
2   *Waller v Legh* (1955) 161 Estates Gazette 201; *Official Solicitor v Thomas* (1986) 279 Estates Gazette 407. Cf *Pickard v Bishop* (1975) 31 P & CR 108, CA.
3   *Dickinson v Boucher* (1983) 269 Estates Gazette 1159. Also see, *Dallhold Estates (UK) Property Ltd v Lindsey Trading Properties Inc* [1994] 1 EGLR 93; *Official Solicitor v Thomas* (1986) 279 Estates Gazette 407.
4   *French v Elliott* [1959] 3 All ER 866, [1960] 1 WLR 40. Cf *Beavers v Mason* (1979) 37 P & CR 42, CA.
5   The Interpretation Act 1978, s 7. For the position as to service of notices generally, see para 42.13 ff.
6   *Lord Newborough v Jones* [1975] Ch 90.
7   (1989) 1 EGLR 1.

Compliance

31.36 The general common law rule is that rent must be paid in cash before the end of the two-month period. Where the landlord and tenant have, by course of dealing between them, shown that the landlord has been willing to accept payment by cheque posted on or before the due date, then even though the cheque is received later, payment in that manner will suffice. Subject to due honouring of the cheque on presentation, the rent is deemed to have been paid from the moment of posting[1].

In *Beevers v Mason*[2], the cheque was posted shortly before the end of the two-month period in circumstances where it would not in the ordinary course of post (and, in fact, did not) arrive within the two-month period. Nevertheless, it was held that the notice to pay had been validly complied with and the notice to quit was invalid.

1   *Norman v Ricketts* (1886) 3 TLR 182, CA; *Beevers v Mason* (1979) 37 P & CR 42, CA.
2   (1979) 37 P & CR 42.

Method of payment

31.37 The notice to pay must be strictly complied with and all the rent demanded must have been paid before the expiration of two months[1]. Substantial compliance is insufficient, unless the shortfall is de minimis[2]. In *Luttenberger v North Thoresby Farms Ltd*[3], the tenant failed to pay the sum of £458.40 in relation to a notice to pay for £15,264. That was found to be de minimis.

1   *Flint v Fox* (1956) 106 L Jo 828; *Stoneman v Brown* [1973] 2 All ER 225, [1973] 1 WLR 459; *Pickard v Bishop* (1975) 31 P & CR 108.
2   *Price v Romilly* [1960] 3 All ER 429, [1960] 1 WLR 1360.
3   [1993] 1 EGLR 3.

31.38 In *Luttenberger v North Thoresby Farms Ltd*[1], the usual rule that payment is deemed to be made when the cheque is posted did not apply where the paying bank is not bound to honour the cheque. That happened in this case where the cheque only had one signature on it where two were required. The cheque was backdated to when the second signature was added which was outside the two-month period.

In *Hannacombe v Smallacombe*[2], the usual rule again did not apply where the cheque was returned marked 'refer to drawer, please re-present'.

Payment of rent by leaving a cheque for the landlord in the dairy was held to be insufficient compliance with the notice to pay[3].

Although a cheque sent by post is usually despatched at the tenant's risk, such risk passes to the landlord if he has impliedly accepted this method of payment. Accordingly, payment will be deemed to have been made even if the cheque is lost in the post[4].

1   [1993] 1 EGLR 3.
2   (1993) 69 P & CR 399, [1994] 1 EGLR 9, CA. also see, *Oakley v Young* (1970), an unreported decision of Judge Bulger in the Cheltenham County Court referred to in J Muir Watt, *Agricultural Holdings* (13th edn), Sweet & Maxwell.
3   *Flint v Fox* (1956) 106 L Jo 928.
4   *Luttges v Sherwood* (1895) 11 TLR 233; *Pennington v Crossley & Son* (1897) 13 TLR 513.

Tender

31.39 At common law, tender of payment by cheque, even if unconditional, does not discharge a debt. It does provide a tenant with a defence to possession proceedings, if the tenant can establish that he made the tender and is still able to make payment[1].

Technically, payment by cheque is conditional. The debt is only satisfied if the cheque is honoured. If it is dishonoured, the debt is not met and a notice to pay would not be satisfied leading to a notice to quit[2]. The fact that the cheque is subsequently met does interfere with the landlord's right to determine the tenancy by a Case D, paragraph (a) notice to quit[3].

The defence of tender is only available if the landlord refuses to accept payment. It does not apply if the landlord asks for a new cheque and one is not supplied[4].

1   *Dixon v Clark* (1848) 5 CB 365.
2   *Milton (Peterborough) Estates Co v Harris* [1989] 2 EGLR 229.
3   *Hannaford v Smallacombe* [1994] 1 EGLR 9.
4   *Official Solicitor v Thomas* (1986) 279 Estates Gazette 407.

Appropriation

31.40 In the case of several instalments of rent being unpaid, the subsequent appropriation of payments made by the tenant may be of critical importance in relation to compliance with a notice to pay.

At common law, when a tenant pays rent he is entitled to appropriate it to debts as he chooses. If he fails to do so, the landlord may choose[1]. He may do so expressly or impliedly[2]. Where recovery is statute barred by the Limitation Act 1980, payments are impliedly appropriated to debts not statute barred[3].

A stark example of appropriation arose in *Official Solicitor v Thomas*[4]. The landlord was held to have appropriated payments to unpaid rent where distress could not be levied, leaving a notice to pay not satisfied.

1   *The Mecca* [1897] AC 286, HL.
2   *Leeson v Leeson* [1936] 2 KB 156, CA; *Official Solicitor v Thomas* (1986) 279 Estates Gazette 407.
3   *Nash v Hodgson* (1855) 6 De GM & G 474.
4   (1986) 279 Estates Gazette 407.

Failure to comply

31.41 If the tenant fails to pay within two months of service of a notice to pay, the landlord is entitled to serve a notice to quit. That entitlement is unaffected by the subsequent payment of the rent due by the tenant[1]. The relevant time for determining whether the tenant made the payment of rent due within the two-month period is when the subsequent notice to quit is served on the tenant and not when it is despatched[2].

In *French v Elliott*[3], the notice to pay was found to expire at midnight on the last day of the two-month period. Before the expiry of that deadline, the landlord sent the notice to quit to the tenant by post. It was received after the deadline. It was found to be a valid notice to quit.

¹   *Stoneman v Brown* [1973] 2 All ER 225, CA; *A-G (Duchy of Lancaster) v Simcock* [1966] Ch 1.
²   *French v Elliott* [1959] 3 All ER 866, [1960] 1 WLR 40.
³   [1959] 3 All ER 866, [1960] 1 WLR 40.

Challenging a notice to pay

31.42   There is no power for a tenant to dispute the validity of a notice to pay on receipt of the notice itself. There is no equivalent of the arbitration procedures available within one month of receipt by the tenant of a notice to remedy in Form 2 (a work notice)[1]. The tenant is in much the same position as a tenant in receipt of a notice to remedy in Form 3 (a non-work notice). He must either comply with the notice or run the risk of a notice to quit, knowing that if he is unable to establish that the notice to pay was invalid when subsequently challenging the notice to quit, he will have no defence to the notice to quit.

A tenant in these circumstances would be well advised to make the payment under protest, thereby preserving for himself the right to recover any excess payments[2].

Although the tenant could apply to the court for a declaration as to the validity of the notice to pay, this remedy is impractical because no such declaration is likely to be obtained in practice within the period of only two months allowed by the notice.

¹   See para 31.51.
²   Recovery of a payment paid under protest cannot be guaranteed as a right. If the landlord refuses to pay and court action is taken to recover the sum, the court has to determine whether the payment was voluntarily made or made in circumstances of sufficient pressure genuinely to warrant the payment under protest. Cf *William Whiteley Ltd v R* (1909) 26 TLR 19; *Twyford v Manchester Corpn* [1946] Ch 236, [1946] 1 All ER 621.

Challenging the notice to quit

31.43   A tenant in receipt of a notice to quit alleging non-compliance with a notice to pay *must*, if he wishes to put in issue the reasons stated for the notice to quit, give a demand for arbitration within one month[1]. Failure to give a demand for arbitration within the prescribed period of one month is fatal. The tenant is then statute barred and cannot put in issue the reasons stated for the notice[2]. He can only challenge the common law validity of the notice itself[3].

There is no prescribed form of demand for arbitration, unlike the prescribed form for the notice to pay itself. A counter-notice invoking the provisions of s 26(1) of the AHA 1986 instead of a demand for arbitration is a nullity[4].

31.43 *The statutory restrictions on notices to quit: Cases A to H*

Following the giving of the demand for arbitration, the tenant must then either secure the appointment of an arbitrator by agreement or ensure that an application for an appointment by the President of the RICS is made within three months of the date of service of the demand for arbitration[5]. The procedures are the same as for notice to quit under Cases A, B and E.

1   The Agricultural Holdings (Arbitration on Notices) Order 1987, SI 1987/710, art 9.
2   *Magdalen College, Oxford v Heritage* [1974] 1 All ER 1065, [1974] 1 WLR 441. See para 31.8.
3   For example, on grounds of ambiguity or fraud: *Rous v Mitchell* [1991] 1 All ER 676, [1991] 1 WLR 469, [1991] 1 EGLR 1. See para 31.15.
4   In Scotland, in *Morris v Muirhead* 1969 SLT 70, a negligence claim against a solicitor proceeded upon the assumption that the counter-notice was a nullity. For more recent cases when a more benign approach to construction of counter-notices has been adopted by the courts, see *Glofield Properties Ltd v Morley* [1988] 1 EGLR 113, [1988] 02 EG 62 and the cases cited in it and *Rous v Mitchell* [1991] 1 All ER 676, [1991] 1 WLR 469, [1991] 1 EGLR 1, CA.
5   See para 31.11.

CASE D – FAILURE TO REMEDY A BREACH OTHER THAN THE NON-PAYMENT OF RENT

Historical evolution of the current law

31.44 Section 24(2)(d) of the AHA 1948[1], as originally enacted, provided a simple procedure whereby if the tenant was in breach of any of the terms or conditions of his tenancy, which were 'not inconsistent with the fulfilment of his responsibilities to farm in accordance with the rules of good husbandry', the landlord could give a notice in writing requiring the tenant 'within such reasonable period as was specified in a notice' to remedy the breach complained of. Then, if the tenant failed to comply with the notice to remedy, the landlord was entitled to give a notice to quit and to state in the notice to quit that it was given 'by reason of the matter aforesaid'. The tenant was precluded from serving a counter-notice and thereby invoking the statutory security of tenure procedures operated by the ALT.

The obligation upon the tenant to comply with the notice to remedy was (and still is) strictly construed[2]. The tenant was not given a second chance if he had failed to comply with the notice to remedy, even when the tenant's failure was comparatively minor in the context of the whole holding[3].

As a consequence, the notice to remedy was thought to have been used as a trap to catch the unwary, rather than as a means of ensuring that the holding was properly farmed and that a tenant who had committed serious breaches was brought up to the mark and only dispossessed if the breaches were still not remedied. In an endeavour to overcome and counter the way in which tenants were in some cases being dispossessed, and were suffering 'a forfeiture' from which 'there was no relief'[4] for breaches which might be by no means serious, s 19 of the Agriculture (Miscellaneous Provisions) Act 1963 provided a number of restrictions upon the landlord's right to give notice to remedy and thereafter to dispossess the tenant. A second set of restrictions on the notice to remedy were later imposed by the Agriculture (Miscellaneous Provisions) Act 1976[5].

Section 24(2)(d) of the AHA 1948, s 19 of the Agriculture (Miscellaneous Provisions) Act 1963 and ss 11 and 12 of the Agriculture (Miscellaneous Provisions) Act 1976 were then repealed and re-enacted in the Agricultural Holdings (Notices to Quit) Act 1977[6]. The substantive law was then further amended by the Agricultural Holdings Act 1984 (AHA 1984). The provisions (as amended by the AHA 1984) has now been repealed and re-enacted in the AHA 1986.

[1] The provision was later heavily amended and then repealed and re-enacted as Case D of Sch 3 to the AHA 1986.
[2] *Price v Romilly* [1960] 3 All ER 429, [1960] 1 WLR 1360. See para 28.11.
[3] There is a legal maxim, *de minimis non curat lex*, the law does not care for the smallest things. This was applied, for example, in *Luttenberger v North Thoresway Farms Ltd* [1993] 1 EGLR 3, where a failure to pay £458.40 in relation to a notice to pay rent of £15,264 was described as de minimis.
[4] See the remarks of Lord Denning MR in *Pickard v Bishop* (1975) 31 P & CR 108, but cf *Parrish v Kinsey* [1983] 2 EGLR 13, 268 Estates Gazette 1113, in which the reference to 'forfeiture' was held to be inaccurate and misleading.
[5] The Agriculture (Miscellaneous Provisions) Act 1976, ss 11 and 12.
[6] In the case of ss 11 and 12, the repeal took effect before the sections had been implemented. They did not of themselves change the law but merely gave power to the Lord Chancellor to make regulations, which power was not exercised before the repeal and re-enactment. The power was then exercised under the Agricultural Holdings (Notices to Quit) Act 1977: see Agricultural Holdings (Arbitration on Notices) Order 1978, SI 1978/257.

31.45 A landlord who, after 1986, gives a notice to remedy (particularly a notice to remedy requiring the doing of work of repair, maintenance or replacement) may inadvertently set off a chain reaction which is difficult to control and may result in protracted and costly litigation.

This is because of the right of the tenant to demand arbitration within one month of the notice to remedy[1] which will have the effect of extending the time for doing the work until the arbitration is completed. Then, if the tenant fails to comply and the landlord gives notice to quit within one month under art 9 of the the Agricultural Holdings (Arbitration on Notices) Order 1986, the tenant may demand arbitration again. If the arbitration extends the time, and the tenant still fails to comply, there could then be a third arbitration. If this goes against the tenant, he may then serve a counter-notice and invoke the jurisdiction of the ALT, where a further hearing will be necessary. This multiplicity of arbitrations and an ALT hearing are cumbersome and costly. The evil which the 1976 and 1977 Acts were designed to overcome has been replaced by another.

[1] See the Agricultural Holdings (Arbitration on Notices) Order 1986, SI 1986/710, art 5.

The present law

The statutory provisions

31.46 Schedule 3, Case D of the AHA 1986 provides that a tenant is prevented[1] from giving a counter-notice, invoking the jurisdiction of the ALT, if he receives a notice to quit which states that it is given by reason of the tenant's failure to:

'... comply with a notice in writing served on him by the landlord ... requiring him within a reasonable period specified in the notice to remedy any breach by the tenant that was capable of being remedied of any term or condition of his tenancy which was not inconsistent with the fulfilment of his responsibilities to farm in accordance with the rules of good husbandry'[2].

There are four additional requirements contained in para 10 of Pt II of Sch 3 to the AHA 1986:

'(1) For the purposes of Case D—

(a)   a notice such as that mentioned in paragraph (a) or (b) of that Case[3] must be in the prescribed form[4];

(b)   where such a notice in the prescribed form requires the doing of any work of repair, maintenance or replacement, any further notice requiring the doing of any such work which is served on the tenant less than 12 months after the earlier notice shall be disregarded unless the earlier notice was withdrawn with his agreement in writing[5];

(c)   a period of less than six months shall not be treated as a reasonable period within which to do any such work[6]; and

(d)   any provision such as is mentioned in paragraph 9(2)[7] above shall (if it would not otherwise be so regarded) be regarded as a term or condition of the tenancy which is not inconsistent with the tenant's responsibilities to farm in accordance with the rules of good husbandry[8].

(2)   Different forms may be prescribed for the purpose of paragraph (b) of Case D in relation to different circumstances'.

1   But see the exceptions to this general rule in the AHA 1986, s 28. See para 31.1.
2   The text of Case D, para (b), is identical to s 24(2)(d) of the AHA 1948, though the addition of the right now to serve counter-notice under s 28 of the AHA 1986, thereby invoking the jurisdiction of the ALT under that section, makes the opening words to s 26 somewhat misleading.
3   Ie a notice to do work (or, more accurately), a notice requiring the doing of any work of repair, maintenance or replacement.
4   The current prescribed forms are contained in the Agricultural Holdings (Forms of Notice to Pay Rent or to Remedy) Regulations 1987, SI 1987/710, replacing SI 1984/1308. A notice requiring the doing of work of repair, maintenance or replacement must be in Form 2. A non-work notice must be in Form 3.
5   As to whether a number of Form 2 notices to remedy can be given simultaneously, specifying different times, for different items, it was held in *Lovell v Winchester College* (1974) unreported, Basingstoke Count Court, that that was irregular. In *Wykes v Davis* [1975] QB 843, [1975] 1 All ER 399, Buckley LJ indicated (obiter) otherwise. As to withdrawal of an earlier notice, see *Mercantile and General Re-Insurance Co Ltd v Groves* [1974] QB 43, [1973] 3 All ER 330, CA.
6   Less than six months can be reasonable for a non-work notice to remedy: see para 31.54.
7   The text of para 9(2) of Pt II of Sch 3 to the AHA 1986 is as follows:

'(2) In the determining whether to grant a certificate under this paragraph the Tribunal shall disregard any practice adopted by the tenant in pursuance of any provision of the contract of tenancy, or of any other agreement with the landlord, which indicates (in whatever terms) that its object is the furtherance of one or more of the following purposes, namely—

(a) the conservation of flora or fauna or of geological or physiographical features of special interest;
(b) the protection of buildings or other objects of archaeological, architectural or historic interest;

(c) the conservation or enhancement of the natural beauty or amenity of the countryside or the promotion of its enjoyment by the public'.

8 See para 24.3 ff.

31.47 Other statutory provisions relating to notices to remedy are contained in s 28 of the AHA 1986. Section 28 provides that, in the case of a notice to quit the whole or part of an agricultural holding containing a statement in accordance with Case D to the effect that it is given by reason of the tenant's failure to comply with the notice to do work[1], certain additional restrictions on the operation of the landlord's notice to quit are to apply.

A tenant may, instead of demanding arbitration on the basis that he has complied with the notice to remedy or that the notice was invalid in some way, give a counter-notice invoking the jurisdiction of the ALT. In that event, the ALT has to determine whether it would be fair and reasonable for the landlord to insist upon possession.

Alternatively, the tenant can demand arbitration and then, if he fails in the arbitration, and the notice is upheld by the arbitrator's award, within one month after the arbitrator's award, he can give a counter-notice and invoke the jurisdiction of the ALT.

1 Case D notices to quit invariably state, as Case D itself requires, that the tenant has failed to comply with a notice to remedy without specifying what form of notice to remedy that is. If Parliament intended s 28(1)(b) of the AHA 1986 to apply to notices to quit given under Case D, where the preliminary notice was, in fact, a notice to do work, whether or not that fact is stated in the notice to quit, it is curious that the form of words is as prescribed.

31.48 If the tenant gives both a demand for arbitration and a counter-notice, the counter-notice is rendered null and void. The arbitration proceeds. If the tenant loses at the arbitration, he has a right to give a counter-notice, again within one month of the arbitrator's award, and invoke the jurisdiction of the ALT[1]. In addition, s 29 and Sch 4 to the AHA 1986 provide for the making of regulations[2]. In the main these regulations provide for arbitration both at notice to remedy stage, in the case of a Form 2 notice (a notice to do work) and notice to quit stage (in either case). In addition, they postpone the operation of the notice to remedy and the subsequent notice to quit. They give the arbitrator a power to extend the time for the notice to remedy, or the notice to quit, as the case may be, and also give the arbitrator wide powers to modify or vary a notice to remedy.

1 See para 31.67.
2 For the text of the statutory provisions, see Sch 4 to the AHA 1986. For the Regulations themselves which have been passed pursuant to those powers, see para A1.546 ff.

The application of the statutory provisions

31.49 Case D, paragraph (b) accordingly allows a landlord to serve a notice to quit on the tenant where the tenant has failed to comply with a notice requiring him, within a reasonable period, to remedy any breach of term or condition of the tenancy which is capable of being remedied.

This requires two distinctions to be drawn: first, between remediable[1] and irremediable[2] breaches; second, between these remediable breaches of a term of condition of the tenancy which requires work and those which do not.

[1]   To which Case D applies.
[2]   To which Case E applies: see para 31.76 ff.

Breach of a term or condition of tenancy

31.50 The term or condition of the tenancy must be one which is not inconsistent with the tenant's responsibilities to farm in accordance with the rules of good husbandy[1]. It is not inconsistent with the tenant's responsibilities to farm in accordance with the rules of good husbandry if the tenant is acting in the furtherance of one or more of the following purposes:

(a)   the conservation of flora or fauna or of geological or physiographical features of special interest;

(d)   the protection of buildings or other objects of archaeological, architectural of historic interest;

(c)   the conservation or enhancement of the natural beauty or amenity of the countryside or the promotion of its enjoyment by the public[2].

It should also be noted that compliance with any obligation which is accepted by or imposed on the tenant under the Water Resources Act 1993 is not capable of constituting a breach by the tenant of the terms or conditions of his tenancy[3].

[1]   AHA 1986, Sch 3 Pt I, Case D.
[2]   AHA 1986, Sch 3 Pt II para 10(1)(d).
[3]   AHA 1986, Sch 3 Pt II para 10(3).

Notice to do work: Form 2

General points

31.51 If the tenant fails to keep the holding in good repair (in accordance with the contractual or statutory obligations imposed on him) or if he fails to farm in accordance with the rules of good husbandry, then the landlord must first serve a notice to do work in Form 2[1]. The notice must be in the prescribed form or be 'in a form substantially to the same effect'[2].

The notice must set out the works of repair, maintenance or replacement required to be carried out in order to remedy the breach alleged. The notice must give a reasonable period for the tenant to carry out the work. The period cannot be less than six months[3].

After the service of a notice to do works, the landlord cannot serve another notice to do works for a period of 12 months after the service of the earlier notice. Any later notice served within the 12-month period shall be disregarded, unless the earlier notice has been withdrawn. Withdrawal requires the written agreement of the tenant[4].

1   Agricultural Holdings (Forms of Notice to Pay Rent or to Remedy) Regulations 1987, SI 1987/711. For a precedent, see para A2.41.
2   SI 1987/711, art 2(2). Also see, *Waller v Legh* [1955] EGD 201, CC; *Ravenseft Properties Ltd v Hall* [2001] EWCA Civ 2034, [2002] 1 EGLR 9, [2002] 11 EG 156 and para 28.11.
3   AHA 1986, Sch 3 Pt II para 10(3)(c).
4   AHA 1986, Sch 3 Pt II para 10(1)(b).

31.52 Subject to the rule *de minimis non curat lex* (the law does not care for the small things)[1], failure to remedy any breaches specified in a notice to do works will be sufficient to found the subsequent service of a Case D, paragraph (b) notice to quit. Substantial compliance will not be enough[2].

A change in the identity of the landlord between the service of the notice to do works and the service of the subsequent Case D, paragraph (b) notice to quit will not invalidate the latter[3].

The same requirements that apply to a notice to pay in relation to service by the landlord and service on the tenant(s) apply to notices to do works[4].

1   See para 31.44 fn 3.
2   *Price v Romilly* [1960] 3 All ER 429, [1960] 1 WLR 1360.
3   For example, when the freehold reversion has been sold: *Farrow v Orttewell* [1933] Ch 480, CA. See para 42.25.
4   See para 31.35.

Remediable and irremediable breaches

31.53 There is no exhaustive list of which breaches are remediable or irremediable. The following examples are taken from decided authorities:

(a)   remediable breaches:
   (i)   a covenant to use as a private residence only[1];
   (ii)   a covenant to reside in the farmhouse[2];
   (iii) a covenant to pay water rates or insurance premiums, or other money (rent is treated separately)[3];
   (iv)   failure to keep the property adequately insured or to reinstate after a fire[4];
   (v)   filling up a ditch in breach of a covenant not to obstruct it[5];
   (vi)   failure to reinstate by a particular date even after the date had passed[6];
   (vii) to share possession[7];
(b)   irremediable breaches:
   (i)   breach of prohibition on assigning and sub-letting[8];
   (ii)   a breach of covenant to farm in accordance with the rules of good husbandry will usually be capable of remedy unless the state of affairs is such that the remedy would take an excessive

> time to complete. For example, continuous cropping with succes-
> sive white straw crops without adequate return of manure,
> ie cross-cropping and breaches of proper rotation[9];
>
> (iii) cutting down a tree in breach of a covenant not to do so[10];
>
> (iv) probably failure to give notice of the death of the tenant
> pursuant to an obligation to that effect in the tenancy agreement
> but since the change in the provisions for giving notice to quit on
> death, it is doubtful whether that would prejudice the landlord.

[1]   *Segal Securities Ltd v Thoseby* [1963] 1 QB 887, [1963] 1 All ER 500.
[2]   *Lloyds Bank Ltd v Jones* [1955] 2 QB 298, [1955] 2 All ER 409, CA; *Sumnal v Statt* (1984) 271 Estates Gazette 628.
[3]   *Official Solicitor v Thomas* (1986) 279 Estates Gazette 407.
[4]   *Farimani v Gates* (1984) 271 Estates Gazette 887.
[5]   *Sumnal v Statt* (1984) 271 Estates Gazette 628.
[6]   *Expert Clothing Service & Sales Ltd v Hillgate House Ltd* [1986] Ch 340, [1985] 2 All ER 998.
[7]   *Akici v L R Butlin Ltd* [2005] EWCA Civ 1296, [2006] 07 EG 136. See para 31.84.
[8]   *Scala House and District Property Co Ltd v Forbes* [1974] QB 575, [1973] 3 All ER 308; *Troop v Gibson* (1985) 277 Estates Gazette 1134; *Pennell v Payne* [1995] QB 192, [1995] 2 All ER 592, [1995] 1 EGLR 6. Cf *Akici v L R Butlin Ltd* [2005] EWCA Civ 1296, [2006] 07 EG 136: see para 31.84.
[9]   *Peach v Partridge* (1953) unreported. Note that in that case it was found that it would take a period of at least four years to restore the land to proper fertility and condition. The case was decided many years ago. It is doubtful whether a similar decision would be reached today when continuous white straw cropping is an accepted system of husbandry. In a sense, given unlimited time, nearly all breaches are ultimately remediable but it is submitted that they are not remediable in the sense used in Case D if the time is inordinate but there is no judicial guidance as to how long that would be. See also, *Savva v Hussein* (1996) 73 P & CR 150, CA.
[10]   *Sumnal v Statt* (1984) 271 Estates Gazette 628.

The period for remedying the breach

31.54   Case D, paragraph (b) requires the period to remedy the breach to be both reasonable and specified in the notice. The prescribed forms require the period to be specifically stated. If a number of items are included in the notice to remedy, the time must be reasonable for all the breaches to be remedied collectively. If the time is unreasonable for any one breach viewed in isolation, the whole notice is invalid[1].

As seen above, where the notice to remedy is a notice to do works of repairs, maintenance or replacement, the reasonable period to carry out those works cannot be less than six months[2].

What is not clear (and there is as yet no authority on the point) is whether, if there are a large number of breaches specified, and the tenant challenges his liability, and the arbitrator upholds the challenge as to some items which are then deleted, the time must have been reasonable for complying with the notice as drawn or as reduced.

Similarly, if the arbitrator modifies the work required of the tenant, it is not clear whether he may thereby render valid a notice which would otherwise have been invalid. It is submitted that the time falls to be considered at the outset. A notice which is invalid *ab initio*, because too much work is specified, cannot be rendered valid by reducing the requirements after a challenge by the tenant. The tenant must be able to act upon the notice to remedy and determine for himself whether it is valid or not when it is served.

The tenant's personal circumstances may be relevant to calculating the reasonableness of the period. It was, for example, where the landlord sought to enforce the farmhouse residence clause where the tenant was in prison[3].

It has been suggested that it may be possible to draft a notice to remedy specifying different periods for different breaches[4].

If, subsequent to the service of the notice to remedy, there are supervening events which cause the period for compliance to be unreasonable, the tenant may raise the matter. The tenant may do so at an arbitration at the notice to do work stage. If the arbitrator finds that the period allowed was reasonable, the arbitrator may nevertheless extend the period to compensate for the time taken to resolve the issue by way of arbitration. The arbitrator cannot extend time which was unreasonable at the time that the notice to remedy was first served.

If supervening events make the time, as extended by the arbitrator, unreasonable, the tenant may raise that issue at the arbitration in respect of the notice to quit. The tenant can only do so as a consequence of supervening events.

1 *Wykes v Davis* [1975] QB 843, [1975] 1 All ER 399. Also see, *Parry v Million Pigs Ltd* (1980) 260 Estates Gazette 281.
2 See para 31.51.
3 *Sumnal v Statt* (1984) 271 EG 628.
4 *Wykes v Davis* [1975] QB 843, [1975] 1 All ER 399 at 860E. The court did not express a view as to whether this would be effective.

Multiple breaches

31.55 Subject to the proviso that the time given must be reasonable to remedy all breaches[1], the notice to remedy would appear to be severable[2]. Indeed, the fact that the tenant may demand arbitration as to his liability to comply with certain items specified in the notice and not others makes it clear that Parliament intended an arbitrator to be able to uphold the notice in part, or to vary it in part. As a notice to remedy containing several items of work is severable, if any one or more is not complied with or otherwise remedied, when it should have been within the reasonable time specified or allowed, such notice should be upheld and effective for the purpose of Case D. This principle accords with the decisions on notices under s 146 of the Law of Property Act 1925[3].

A notice to quit alleging several breaches will be void if the landlord acts fraudulently in relation to any of the alleged breaches[4].

If a notice to quit is given for more than one reason and one of the reasons stated can be made out, but not the other, the notice is valid[5].

1   See para 31.54.
2   *Shepherd v Lomas* [1963] 2 All ER 902, [1963] 1 WLR 962; *French v Elliott* [1959] 3 All ER 866, [1960] 1 WLR 40, per Paull J: 'If a notice to quit has to give a good reason and gives that good reason, I cannot see that it becomes a bad notice to quit because it gives in addition a bad reason'. Cf *Wykes v Davis* [1975] QB 843, [1975] 1 All ER 399.
3   *Pannell v City of London Brewery Co* [1900] 1 Ch 496; *Fox v Jolly* [1916] 1 AC 1, HL (especially Lord Buckmaster's speech); *Silvester v Ostrowska* [1959] 3 All ER 642, [1959] 1 WLR 1060.
4   *Rous v Mitchell* [1991] 1 All ER 676, [1991] 1 WLR 469, [1991] 1 EGLR 1: see para 31.15.
5   *French v Elliott* [1959] 3 All ER 866, [1960] 1 WLR 40. Also see the Court of Appeal judgment in *Burrell v Ninnis* [1964] EGD 293, where the tenant was held to be reasonably able to know which of two previous notices to remedy previously served upon him was the one referred to in the subsequent notice to quit based thereon under this case. There was no ambiguity and the notice to quit was valid. *Sed quaere* in the light of the judgment, in particular of Lord Denning, in *Pickard v Bishop* (1975) 31 P & CR 108, and the requirement of strict construction of notices given under Cases A to H.

Work or non-work

31.56   It is not clear whether work of weed control is work of maintenance, repair and replacement. The definition in art 3 of the Agricultural Holdings (Arbitration on Notices) Order 1987[1] of 'notice to do work' is not explicit. Not all work is necessarily work of maintenance, repair or replacement. The wording of the rules of good husbandry, and the decision in another context in *Hereford and Worcester County Council v Newman*[2], support the view that weed control comes within the definition as work of maintenance.

1   SI 1987/710.
2   [1975] 2 All ER 673, [1975] 1 WLR 901. Also see *Haydon v Kent County Council* [1978] QB 343, [1978] 2 All ER 97.

Waiver

31.57   If, subsequent to the notice to remedy, the landlord takes some action which indicates his intention to waive the notice to remedy, for example, by signing a new tenancy agreement, or demanding arbitration as to the terms of the tenancy, then his right subsequently to rely upon a notice to remedy may thereby be waived[1]. It should be noted that waiver does not apply after the service of a notice to quit[2].

As an alternative to waiver, the tenant may argue that the actions of the landlord give rise to estoppel, discharging the tenant of his obligation to comply with a notice to remedy[3].

1   *Shepton Mallet Transport Ltd v Clark* [1953] CPL 343.
2   *Sidney Bolsom Investment Trust v E Karmies & Co (London) Ltd* [1956] 1 QB 529.
3   Such an argument failed on the facts in *Taylor v Lancashire County Council* [2001] EWCA Civ 174, 82 P & CR D10. On a separate point this case returned to the Court of Appeal: [2005] EWCA Civ 284, [2005] 1 WLR 2668.

Undisputed work

31.58 If there is any work specified in the notice to do work which the tenant does not dispute, he should carry out that work, rather than await the outcome of the arbitration in respect of matters which he disputes. If the tenant does not carry out undisputed work, the landlord may serve a notice for non-compliance[1]. It should also be noted that the Agricultural Holdings (Arbitration on Notices) Order 1987[2] contains provisions to enable a tenant to recover the cost of work which the tenant has carried out, although it is subsequently established that he is under no obligation to do so[3].

1   *Ladds Radio and Television Service Ltd v Docker* (1973) 226 Estates Gazette 1565.
2   SI 1987/710.
3   SI 1987/710, art 8.

Landlord's breaches

31.59 The fact that a landlord may himself be in breach of his obligations does not preclude him from serving notice to remedy on his tenant or subsequently enforcing a notice to quit[1]. If the landlord's breach goes to the heart of whether the tenant is in breach, then the position will be otherwise[2].

1   *Wilson-Clarke v Graham* 1963 SLT 2.
2   *Shepherd v Lomas* [1963] 2 All ER 902, [1963] 1 WLR 962, where the landlord was obliged to provide materials and failed to do so after a request from the tenant. See also, *Chatwood Safe and Engineering Co Ltd v Frank* [1952] CPL 532.

Challenging the validity of a notice to do work

31.60 The ability of the tenant to challenge the notice to remedy served upon him varies, depending upon whether a Form 2 notice (to do work) or a Form 3 notice (non-work) has been given[1].

In the case of a notice to remedy in Form 2 (notice to do work), the tenant has a number of opportunities to challenge the landlord.

The first opportunity which the tenant has to challenge a notice in Form 2 is by serving written notice requiring the matter specified in it to be referred to arbitration under the AHA 1986. If the tenant wishes to:

(a)   contest his liability to do the work, or any part of the work, required by the notice to do work; and/or

(b)   request the deletion from the notice of any item of work on the ground that it is unnecessary or unjustified; and/or

(c)   request the substitution, in the case of any item of work, of a different method or material for the method or material required to be used by the notice,

then he must, within one month after service of the notice to do work, serve written notice on the landlord requiring the questions identified by him to be referred to arbitration[2].

This is the only opportunity which the tenant has to challenge these three matters. If the tenant fails to do so, he is precluded from raising them again at the notice to quit stage.

The tenant's demand for arbitration does not need to be in a prescribed form[3]. It must set out clearly those items in respect of which the tenant denies liabilities; those items which he claims are unnecessary or unjustified; and also any method or material in respect of which he desires a substitution to be made[4]. If any of these matters are referred to arbitration, the tenant is not obliged to carry out the work which is the subject of the reference to arbitration until the arbitrator decides that he is liable to do it. He must carry out any other work which is undisputed[5].

[1]   See para 31.56.
[2]   The Agricultural Holdings (Arbitration on Notices) Order, SI 1987/710, art 3(1) and (2).
[3]   For a precedent, see para A2.53.
[4]   SI 1987/710, art 3(3).
[5]   *Ladds Radio and Television Service Ltd v Docker* (1973) 226 Estates Gazette 1565. See para 31.58.

31.61 If the tenant decides to refer any of the three matters referred to at 31.60 above to arbitration, he must also at the same time refer to arbitration any other question arising under the notice to do work which he wishes to dispute[1]. For example, if the tenant wishes to challenge the reasonableness of the period allowed to carry out the work, he must do so at the same arbitration.

If the tenant does not at the notice to remedy stage wish to challenge any of the three matters referred to above, but he has other matters which he wishes to put in issue, he has a choice. He may either do it by way of arbitration at the notice to remedy stage or subsequently following the service of the notice to quit[2]. If the tenant wishes to challenge any aspect of the notice to remedy by way of arbitration in response to the notice to remedy, he must again serve a written notice on the landlord, within one month after service of the notice to do work, requiring arbitration under the AHA 1986 in respect of the issues which he has identified in his written notice[3].

[1]   SI 1987/710, art 4(1).
[2]   SI 1987/710, art 4(2).
[3]   SI 1987/710, art 3.

Powers of the arbitrator at the notice to remedy arbitration

31.62 The arbitrator has wide powers to modify the notice to remedy so as to delete any items of work which he considers unnecessary or unjustified. The arbitrator must have regard to the overriding interests of good husbandry and of sound management of the estate[1]. The arbitrator may determine that the tenant is under no obligation to do the work required. In that event the notice to remedy is found to be ineffective.

If the tenant refers the methods and/or materials to be used to carry out the work to arbitration when challenging the notice to remedy, the arbitrator can modify the notice to substitute different methods or materials, provided that he is satisfied that those specified in the notice to remedy itself would involve undue difficulty or expense. The materials or methods substituted must be as effective for the purpose of carrying out the works as those originally specified in the notice to remedy[2]. The time within which to carry out the work is suspended until the determination of the arbitrator[3]. The time stipulated in the notice to remedy is not extended in relation to undisputed work[4]. If the tenant does not carry out that work within the time allowed, the landlord may serve a notice to quit for non-compliance.

[1]   SI 1987/710, art 5(a).
[2]   SI 1987/710, art 5(b).
[3]   SI 1987/710, art 6(1).
[4]   *Ladds Radio and Television Service Ltd v Docker* (1973) 226 Estates Gazette 1565.

31.63   If the tenant disputes his liability to do the work referred to in the notice to remedy, then notwithstanding the fact that he has demanded arbitration and pursues an arbitration, he may wish to carry out some of the work which is the subject of the reference to arbitration without awaiting the arbitrator's award. If he does so, and the arbitrator subsequently determines that he has carried out work where it was not his obligation to do so, then the arbitrator can determine the reasonable cost of the work that has been carried out and award that this be recoverable from the landlord[1].

Where the arbitrator determines that the tenant is liable to comply with a notice to do work, or part of it, he can further extend the time for carrying out that work by such period as he thinks fit[2]. Where the arbitrator allows such an extension of time, he may, either on his own motion or on an application made by the landlord not less than 14 days after the end of the arbitration, set a fixed date for the termination of the tenancy if the tenant fails to comply with a notice within the extended period[3]. The date fixed by the arbitrator for the termination of the tenancy cannot be earlier than the date on which the tenancy could have been terminated by notice to quit served on the expiration of the time originally specified in the notice to do work, or six months after the end of the extended period for compliance, whichever is the later[4]. If the landlord applies for the fixing of a termination date, he must give notice of the application to the tenant. The tenant is entitled to be heard on the landlord's application. If the tenant fails to do the work requested within the extended period, the landlord must serve his notice to quit within one month after the expiry of the extended time. If the landlord does so, the notice to quit will be valid, even though it does not expire on a term date of the tenancy and is of less than 12 months' duration. It will expire on the date for termination fixed by the arbitrator[5].

[1]   SI 1987/710, art 8.
[2]   SI 1987/710, art 6(2).
[3]   SI 1987/710, art 7(1).
[4]   SI 1987/710, art 7(2).
[5]   SI 1987/710, art 7(4).

31.64   If the time specified in the notice to remedy is unreasonable from the outset in respect of all or any of the items, then the arbitrator has no power to extend the time. He must hold that the whole notice is invalid[1]. If the time allowed was reasonable from the outset, but ceased to be so by reason of some event which occurred after the notice to remedy, for example, unusually unfavourable weather conditions, injury or incapacity of the tenant, or some other extraneous unforeseen factor, then the arbitrator has power to extend the time for the doing of the work.

[1]   See para 31.54.

Challenging the notice to quit

31.65   If the tenant fails to comply with a notice to do work, the landlord can serve a Case D notice to quit. At this stage it is too late for the tenant to contest his liability to do the work; or the necessity or justification for any work; or the methods or materials specified in the notice to do work. Moreover, the tenant cannot challenge other matters previously raised in an arbitration relating to the notice to do work, other than the time allowed for compliance.

The tenant may wish to contest other issues. For example, the tenant may wish to contend that he has carried out the work which was required. Alternatively, the tenant may wish to contend that supervening events have caused the time originally allowed in the notice to be unreasonable. If the tenant wishes to raise such matters, the tenant must serve a written notice on the landlord within one month of the notice to quit, requiring the notice to be referred to arbitration under the AHA 1986[1]. As in the case of an arbitration under the notice to do work, the operation of the notice to quit is suspended until the termination of the arbitration[2].

If, at an arbitration in response to the notice to quit, the tenant alleges that the time specified in the notice to do work, while originally reasonable, has become unreasonable by reason of supervening events, the arbitrator has power to extend the period allowed for the work to be done. The arbitrator's powers are similar to those available at the notice to do work stage. He can extend the period allowed for the work to be completed by such period as he considers reasonable, having regard to the length of time which has elapsed since the original service of the notice to do work[3]. Where the arbitrator makes such determination, he has similar powers to those available in relation to a notice to do work arbitration to fix a termination date for the tenancy in the event of non-compliance by the tenant within the extended period[4].

If the tenant does not complete the work within the extended period ordered by the arbitrator, the landlord must then serve a second notice to quit within one month of the expiration of the extended term. The second notice to quit will be valid, even though it is of less than 12 months' duration and expires on a date other than the term date of the tenancy[5]. The second notice to quit cannot take effect if the tenant serves a counter-notice to that second notice to quit within one month of service, unless the ALT then consents to the operation of the second notice to quit. On an application by the landlord for consent to the operation of his second notice to quit, the ALT must consent, unless it appears to them that a fair and reasonable landlord would not insist on possession. In making that determination, the ALT must have regard to the extent to which the tenant has failed to comply with the notice to do work, the consequences of that failure and the circumstances surrounding it[6].

Where the notice to quit has effect following an arbitration (or because the ALT has consented to its operation[7]), the tenant can apply to the arbitrator for a postponement of the termination of the tenancy. If the notice to quit would come into operation within six months of the termination of the arbitration or the granting of the ALT consent, the tenant can within 14 days of the termination of the arbitration or the giving of consent by the ALT apply to the arbitrator for a postponement. The arbitrator has power to postpone the termination of the tenancy for a period not exceeding 12 months[8]. Where the tenant applies to the arbitrator of the ALT for such a postponement, he must at the same time give written notice of the application to the landlord (except where the application is made at the arbitration hearing itself or at the hearing before the ALT) and the landlord shall be entitled to be heard on the application[9].

[1]   SI 1987/710, art 9.
[2]   SI 1987/710, art 12.
[3]   SI 1987/710, art 14.
[4]   SI 1987/710, art 15.
[5]   SI 1987/710, art 15(4).
[6]   SI 1987/710, art 15(6).
[7]   See para 31.67.
[8]   SI 1987/710, art 13(1).
[9]   SI 1987/710, art 13(2).

31.66 It should be noted that, following any demand for arbitration made by the tenant, he must either secure the appointment of an arbitrator or apply to the President of the RICS, in either case within three months of service of the demand for arbitration. In default his demand is rendered ineffective and his challenge to the reason stated for the giving of the notice to quit is statute barred[1].

[1]   SI 1987/710, art 10.

Consent of the Agricultural Land Tribunal

31.67 Where a landlord seeks possession of an agricultural holding following service of a Form 2 notice to do works and a subsequent notice to quit, there is a final stage before he can succeed in recovering possession. Section 28 of the AHA 1986 enables the tenant to refer the landlord's notice to quit to the ALT. The tenant may do this if he has been unsuccessful in challenging the reasons stated in the notice to do works or if he has not challenged the notice at all. In either case, the tenant is required to serve a counter-notice within one month of the service of the notice to quit[1] or (where the tenant has required an arbitration as to the validity of the reason stated in the notice to quit) within one month of the date on which the arbitrator's award is delivered to the tenant[2]. If the tenant does so, then the notice to quit will not be effective until the landlord obtains the ALT's consent to its operation. The procedure is available to the tenant either instead of, or in addition to, demanding arbitration on the notice to quit.

If the tenant makes a valid demand for arbitration, as to the reason stated in the notice to quit, and also serves a counter-notice, the counter-notice is thereby rendered invalid[3]. The demand for arbitration takes precedence.

As noted above, if the arbitration takes place and the award is unfavourable to the tenant, then the tenant may then give counter-notice, in which case the notice to quit is rendered ineffective unless the ALT consents to its operation[4].

After service by the tenant of a valid counter-notice, the landlord must within one month apply to the ALT for consent to the operation of his notice to quit. In default, the notice to quit is rendered ineffective[5].

1 AHA 1986, s 28(3).
2 AHA 1986, s 28(4). This provision does not apply where the demand for arbitration and the counter-notice are served at the same time: *William Smith (Wakefield) Ltd v Parisride Ltd* [2005] EWHC 462 (Admin), [2005] 2 EGLR 22, [2005] 24 EG 180.
3 AHA 1986, s 28(2), (4). The wording of s 28 is clear. There are two alternative forms of counter-notice which can be given: under s 28(2) if no demand is made for arbitration and under s 28(4) if there has been such a demand which resulted in an award against the tenant. If the wrong form of counter-notice is given, it would appear that it will be a nullity: see *Morris v Muirhead* 1969 SLT 70 and *Rous v Mitchell* [1991] 1 All ER 676, [1991] 1 WLR 469, [1991] 1 EGLR 1, following *Mountford v Hodgkinson* [1956] 2 All ER 17, [1956] 1 WLR 422.
4 AHA 1986, s 28(4)(a). This procedure was brought in by the Agricultural Holdings (Notices to Quit) Act 1977 to govern cases based on notices to do work. A notice to quit may be given for a specified reason (being one of the cases set out in Sch 3 to the AHA 1986) and state in the alternative that it is also to be treated as a general notice. In such a case it seems that a notice requiring arbitration should be given if the reason stated falls within Cases A, B, D or E and also a counter-notice under s 26(1) of the AHA 1986 in respect of the alternative (see *Paddock Investments Ltd v Lory* (1975) 236 Estates Gazette 803) though that counter-notice need not be given until after termination of the arbitration.
5 AHA 1986, s 28(2).

31.68 Upon an application to the ALT, the powers of the ALT are governed by s 28(5) of the AHA 1986. That provides:

'The Tribunal shall consent under subsection (2) above to the operation of the notice to quit unless it appears to them, having regard—
(a) to the extent to which the tenant has failed to comply with the notice to do work;
(b) to the consequences of his failure to comply with it in any respect; and
(c) to the circumstances surrounding any such failure;
that a fair and reasonable landlord would not insist on possession.

In the section, 'notice to do work' means a notice served on a tenant of an agricultural holding for the purposes of paragraph (b) of Case D, being a notice requiring the doing of any work of repair, maintenance or replacement'.

The effect of s 28(5) of the AHA 1986 is to restrict the ALT's discretion in relation to its consent to the operation of the notice to quit. Prima facie, the ALT is not entitled to consider greater hardship. It is submitted that the discretion of the ALT is not as restricted as would first appear to be the case. The factors applying to 'circumstances surrounding any such failure' would appear to give the ALT at least a residual discretion. The current provisions contained in s 28(5) of the AHA 1986 were introduced by the 1984 Act[1]. It is submitted that the ALT is entitled to look at, for example, substantial compliance and that this may result in a refusal on the part of the ALT to give consent to the operation of the notice to quit.

In *William Smith (Wakefield) Ltd v Parisride Ltd*[2], after the landlord had served a notice to do works, an arbitrator decided that the tenant was required to carry out the works and that they were to be completed within 12 months. The landlord subsequently served a Case D notice to quit, claiming that the works had not been carried out during the specified period. The tenant served a counter-notice and a separate demand for arbitration in reliance upon s 28(5) of the AHA 1986. The landlord initiated an application to the ALT. the tenant took no further steps in relation to the arbitration. The landlord contended before the ALT that the AHA 1986 did not allow the tenant to pursue two routes to context the notice to quit and that the decision to arbitrate rendered the counter-notice ineffective. The ALT found against the landlord, deciding that the counter-notice was valid. It also refused consent to the operation of the notice to quit.

The landlord applied to the High Court for a direction that the ALT state a case as to the validity of the counter-notice and the merits of the substantive decision to refuse consent to the operation of the notice to quit. The application failed. The court held that the test for whether the ALT should be directed to state a case was whether there was a fairly arguable point of law. In this case there was not, for two reasons:

(a) the counter-notice was not invalid because of the concurrent demand for arbitration. Neither notice initiated proceedings. The counter-notice required an application to the ALT by the landlord. The demand for arbitration required either party to initiate the appointment of an arbitrator;

(b) the ALT was entitled to take into account all of the circumstances that it had relied upon in reaching its decision on the substantive issues that a fair and reasonable landlord would not insist on possession. The ALT had found that the tenant had complied to a substantial extent with the obligations imposed by the notice to do works; any failure to comply had not damaged the holding in any way; and account had to be had of the size and nature of the holding.

---

[1] AHA 1984 Act, s 7, amending the Agricultural Holdings (Notices to Quit) Act 1977, s 4(4). The new provision was intended to overrule the decision in *Clegg v Fraser* (1982) 264 Estates Gazette 144.

[2] [2005] EWHC 462 (Admin), [2005] 2 EGLR 22, [2005] 24 EG 180.

Conclusion

31.69 The previous edition of this book concluded that with such a multiplicity and complexity of challenges available to a tenant, first, by arbitration at notice to remedy stage, then, at notice to quit stage and, finally, by counter-notice, it is perhaps not surprising that notices to remedy in Form 2 are now very sparingly used. They can set off a chain reaction which is very costly and difficult to control so that for the landlord the last state is worse than the first. It is also a serious indictment of the notice to remedy procedures that many cases are determined, not on their merits, but by reason of one or other party failing to take the correct procedural step within the short time limits permitted. It is difficult to fault that conclusion.

Notice to remedy not involving works: Form 3

General points

31.70 If the tenant commits a remediable[1] breach of a term or condition of his tenancy which is not a breach which involves the doing of works of repair, maintenance or replacement or failure to farm in accordance with the rules of good husbandry[2], then the landlord must first serve a notice to remedy in Form 3[3]. The notice must be in the prescribed form or be 'in a form substantially to the same effect'[4].

1   For an irremediable breach the landlord must use Case E: see para 31.76. As to the difference between remediable and irremediable breaches, see para 31.53.
2   For such breaches the landlord must use Form 2, see para 31.51 ff.
3   Agricultural Holdings (Forms of Notice to Pay Rent or to Remedy) Regulations 1987, SI 1987/711. For a precedent, see para A2.42.
4   SI 1987/711, art 2(2). Also see, *Walker v Legh* [1955] EGD 201, CC; *Ravenseft Properties Ltd v Hall* [2001] EWCA Civ 2034, [2002] 1 EGLR 9, [2002] 11 EG 156 and para 28.11.

31.71 The notice must set out clearly the breaches required to be remedied. The notice must give a reasonable period for the tenant to remedy the breaches[1]. There is no minimum period prescribed and, unlike Form 2, there are no restrictions on the service of subsequent notices[2].

The provisions relating to a change of landlord[3] and service on tenants[4] are the same as those which apply to Form 2.

1   AHA 1986, Sch 3 Pt I Case D. Also see, *Sumnal v Statt* (1984) 271 EG 628 and para 31.54.
2   See para 31.54 ff.
3   See para 31.52 and 42.25.
4   See para 31.35 and 31.52.

Challenging the notice to remedy

31.72 In the case of a Form 3 notice (non-work), as is expressly stated in the prescribed form, the tenant is precluded from referring to arbitration his liability to comply with the notice to remedy at that stage. He is entitled to do so at notice to quit stage, if a notice to quit is given on the ground that the tenant has failed to comply with the notice to remedy.

A tenant in receipt of a notice to remedy in Form 3 (non-work) is very much at risk because once the notice has expired he has no opportunity of complying with the notice and avoiding a notice to quit. If he denies his liability to comply with the notice, he must either comply with it so as to preserve his tenancy, or else apply to the court for a declaration as to the validity of the notice (if he has time).

Challenging the notice to quit

31.73 If the landlord proceeds to serve a notice to quit, if he contends that the tenant has failed to comply with a notice to remedy (other than to do works), the tenant may challenge the notice to quit by demanding arbitration. The tenant must serve a written demand for arbitration on the landlord within one month of service of notice to quit[1]. This is the tenant's only opportunity to challenge either the matters relied upon in the notice to remedy or any other issues raised by the landlord in connection with the landlord's pursuit of the recovery of possession following service of a notice in Form 3[2].

It should again be noted that, following any demand for arbitration made by the tenant, he must either secure the appointment of an arbitrator or apply to the President of the RICS, in either case within three months of service of the demand for arbitration. In default, his demand is rendered ineffective and his challenge for the reasons stated for the giving of the notice to quit is statute barred[3].

For the duration of the arbitration, the notice to quit is suspended[4]. If the arbitrator upholds the notice to quit, and if it would come into effect on or within six months after the termination of the arbitration, the tenant has 14 days after the delivery of the arbitrator's award in which to apply for a postponement in the operation of the notice to quit[5]. The arbitrator may, on his own motion or on the application of the tenant, postpone the termination of the tenancy for a period not exceeding 12 months[6]. Where the tenant applies to the arbitrator, he is required at the same time to give written notice of the application to the landlord and the landlord shall be entitled to be heard on the application[7].

[1] The Agricultural Holdings (Arbitration on Notices) Order 1987, SI 1987/710, art 9.
[2] The tenant may challenge either the notice to remedy in Form 3 or the notice to quit before the court, for example, in cases of ambiguity, fraud, etc: see paras 28.11 and 31.15.
[3] SI 1987/710, art 10.
[4] SI 1987/710, art 12.
[5] SI 1987/710, art 13(1).
[6] SI 1987/710, art 13(1).
[7] SI 1987/710, art 13(2).

31.74 If the notice to remedy allowed a reasonable period for compliance, but that period subsequently becomes unreasonable because of supervening events, the arbitrator has power to extend the time by such period as he considers reasonable[1]. The arbitrator has power to specify a date for the termination of the tenancy in the event of non-compliance by the tenant within the extended period[2].

If the tenant fails to succeed in his challenge to the notice to quit by arbitration, unlike Form 2, there is no residual jurisdiction vested in the ALT. The landlord is not required to go to the ALT for consent to the operation of his notice to quit.

The differences in treatment between the two different types of notice to remedy does not contravene any provision of the Human Rights Act 1998[3].

1   SI 1987/710, art 14.
2   SI 1987/710, art 15.
3   *Lancashire County Council v Taylor* [2005] EWCA Civ 284, [2005] 1 WLR 2668, [2005] 2 EGLR 17.

Compensation for disturbance

31.75 Neither basic nor additional compensation is payable to the tenant on quitting as a consequence of a notice to quit given pursuant to Case D[1].

1   AHA 1986, s 61(1).

CASE E – IRREMEDIABLE BREACH

31.76 Case E provides:

'At the date of the giving of the notice to quit, the interest of the landlord in the agricultural holding had been materially prejudiced by the commission by the tenant of a breach which was not capable of being remedied, of any term or condition of the tenancy that was not inconsistent with the tenant's responsibilities to farm in accordance with the rules of good husbandry, and it is stated in the notice that it is given by reason of the said matter'[1].

There are two additional provisions relating to Case E notices to quit[2] as follows:

'(1)   Where—
(a)   the landlord is a smallholdings authority; or
(b)   the landlord is the Minister and the holding is on land held by him for the purposes of smallholdings,
then, in considering whether the interest of the landlord has been materially prejudiced as mentioned in Case E, regard shall be had to the effect of the breach in question not only on the holding itself but also on the carrying out of the arrangements made by the smallholdings authority or the Minister (as the case may be) for the letting and conduct of smallholdings.
(2)   For the purposes of Case E any provision such as is mentioned in paragraph 9(2) of Schedule 3 of the AHA 1986[3] shall (if it would not otherwise be so regarded) be regarded as a term or condition of the tenancy which is not inconsistent with the tenant's responsibilities to farm in accordance with the rules of good husbandry'.

1   AHA 1986, Sch 3 Pt I, Case E.
2   AHA 1986, Sch 3 Pt II para 11.
3   See para 24.3 ff.

The application of Case E

31.77 Case E accordingly entitles the landlord to give notice to quit where: (a) his interest has been materially prejudiced by (b) the commission by the tenant of a breach which was not capable of being remedied of any term or condition of the tenancy which (c) was not inconsistent with the fulfilment by the tenant of his responsibilities to farm in accordance with the rules of good husbandry.

Good husbandry

31.78 The first requirement of Case E is that the breach of the term or condition of the tenancy must not be inconsistent with the tenant's obligations to farm in accordance with the rules of good husbandry[1]. The rules in this regard are the same as those which apply to Case D[2], including in relation to responsibilities arising under the Water Resources Act 1991[3].

A conservation covenant is not considered to be inconsistent with the tenant's responsibility to farm in accordance with the rules of good husbandry[4].

[1]   As to rules of good husbandry, see para 24.3.
[2]   See para 31.50.
[3]   See para 31.50.
[4]   AHA 1986, Sch 3 Pt II para 11(2).

Irremediable breach

31.79 The second requirement of Case E is that the breach of term or condition of the tenancy must be irremediable[1]. If it is remediable, Case D applies.

[1]   As to what constitutes an irremediable breach, see para 31.53.

Material prejudice

31.80 The third requirement of Case E is that the irremediable breach of term or condition of the tenancy must cause material prejudice to the landlord. This is a very important safeguard in relation to the tenant's interest. It stops the landlord being able to terminate the tenancy by reason of a minor, technical irremediable breach. It is essential because there is no general power given to the court to grant relief to a tenant faced with an effective Case E notice to quit[1].

There is no case authority deciding when the material prejudice must exist. It is submitted that it should be assessed at the date that the notice to quit is given[2].

There is also no general guidance in either the AHA 1986 or case authority as to what precisely constitutes material prejudice. The only guidance applies

517

where the landlord is a smallholdings authority or the Minister and the holding is on land held by him for use as smallholdings. In such cases, when considering whether there has been material prejudice, regard must be had to the effect of the breach in question not only on the holding itself but also on the carrying out of the arrangements made by the smallholdings authority or the Minister for the letting and conduct of smallholdings[3].

The guidance given in relation to smallholdings does not assist as to what constitutes material prejudice. It is submitted that material prejudice is material adverse impact on the landlord's reversionary interest.

It should be noted that a term or condition of the tenancy which gives rise to an irremediable breach, but which is void for being contrary to public policy, cannot found a successful Case E notice to quit[4].

1   *Parrish v Kinsey* (1983) 268 Estates Gazette 1113.
2   See *Pennell v Payne* [1995] QB 192, [1995] 1 EGLR 6, CA.
3   AHA 1986, Sch 3 Pt II para 11(1).
4   *Johnson v Moreton* [1980] AC 37, HL.

The Case E notice to quit

31.81   There is no preliminary notice required in relation to a Case E notice to quit[1]. There is also no statutorily prescribed form for a Case E notice to quit, but it should be clear on the face of it that it is given pursuant to Case E and not, for example, Case D. It should not be drafted in a manner to constitute a 'calculated obscurity'[2]. It should expressly refer to the reasons stated in Case E[3]. It needs to be clear on the face of the notice to quit that it is not one to which s 26(1) of the AHA 1986 applies, enabling the tenant to serve a counter-notice, resulting in an application to the ALT[4].

If the Case E notice to quit contains statements which the landlord knows are false, or which are made recklessly as to their truth, the notice will be a nullity[5]. Mere carelessness will not render the notice to quit effective[6].

1   Cf the requirement to give a notice under s 146 of the Law of Property Act 1925 prior to forfeiture for an irremediable breach of covenant.
2   *Macnab of Macnab v Anderson* 1958 SLT 8, Ct of Sess.
3   See para 31.76.
4   See para 30.1.
5   *Rous v Mitchell* [1991] 1 All ER 676: see para 31.15.
6   *Omnivale Ltd v Boldan* [1994] EGCS 63.

Anti-alienation provisions

31.82   The most common use of a Case E notice to quit is in relation to breaches of a term of the tenancy prohibiting sub-letting, parting with possession or occupation or assignment[1].

In the case of an oral tenancy, or one in writing but not covering all of the terms set out in Sch 1 to the AHA 1986, the landlord may introduce a prohibition upon assignment, sub-letting or parting with possession[2] of the holding without the landlord's written consent by service of a s 6 notice[3].

It has been held that if the parties have agreed that 'the usual covenants' shall apply to the tenancy, this does not include a prohibition on alienation[4]. Most cases will nevertheless turn on their own facts in respect of the evidence as to what has been agreed. If, for example, the agreement relates to the 'usual covenants' imposed by the AHA 1986 where there has been a s 6 notice, that would include an anti-alienation provision.

1   *Troop v Gibson* [1986] 1 EGLR 1, 277 Estates Gazette 1134. As to the distinction between sharing occupation and sharing possession, see *Akici v L R Butlin Ltd* [2005] EWCA Civ 1296, [2006] 1 EGLR 34, (2006) 07 EG 136. See para 31.84.
2   But not sharing occupation.
3   See para 23.1.
4   *Chester v Buckingham Travel Ltd* [1981] 1 All ER 386, [1981] 1 WLR 96.

31.83 Until the passing of the Agriculture (Miscellaneous Provisions) Act 1976, assignments of agricultural holdings were very rarely encountered in practice. This was because a landlord could serve notice to quit under s 24(2)(g) of the AHA 1948 (the predecessor of Case G contained in Sch 3 to the AHA 1986) on the death of the tenant 'with whom the contract of tenancy was made'. This was held to mean, where there had been an assignment, that it was on the death of the original tenant that the landlord could give notice to quit[1]. Very little was achieved if an elderly tenant wished to benefit his son, or remoter issue, by assigning the tenancy to such relation or to a company formed for the purpose etc. The new tenant (the assignee) was liable to be dispossessed upon the death of the assignor.

In 1976, with the introduction of succession to agricultural holdings, it was necessary for the right to give notice to quit on death to be revised so as to ensure that it was the death of the tenant in possession whose death gave rise to the notice to quit and to the right to apply for succession. Accordingly, the wording of s 24(2)(g) of the AHA 1948 was amended to provide for notice to quit on the death of the tenant 'under the contract of tenancy'. This is the wording which applies now[2]. As a consequence, if a tenant were to assign his tenancy to a child or remoter offspring, or, still more, to a company formed for the purpose, he could thereby ensure that the landlord would either never have the right to give a Case G notice to quit or, alternatively, that right would be postponed for possibly a very protracted period.

It soon became well known that a tenant possessed either of a 'defective' tenancy agreement, in that it contained no prohibition upon assignment, or a tenant who held under oral terms where neither party had turned his mind to such considerations, still less agreed upon them, was possessed of a very valuable asset which could either be transmitted for the benefit of his family or sold on the open market by assignment to a third party. Assignments, hitherto rare, suddenly became popular.

A tenant who proceeded to assign in breach of a prohibition upon assignment, was liable to be dispossessed pursuant to a notice to quit given under Case E of Sch 3 to the AHA 1986, on the grounds that the breach committed was irremediable[3]. There has been a number of cases of tenants who, anxious to secure the tenancy for a period extending beyond their own lifetimes, have assigned but the assignee has immediately been confronted with a Case E notice. As a result, far from prolonging the life of the tenancy beyond the lifetime of the original tenant, the assignee has been dispossessed on 12 months' notice.

The following points in relation to prohibitions upon assignment should also be noted:

(a)   A prohibition upon parting with possession precludes assignment[4], even if the prohibition merely restrain parting with possession of any part of the holding.

(b)   It is probable that a prohibition upon sub-letting alone does not restrain assignment[5].

(c)   If the tenancy agreement containing a prohibition upon assignment has been lost and both parties have proceeded upon the assumption that there is no prohibition on assignment because there are no special terms affecting the parties, and have agreed to revise the rent from time to time upon that commonly assumed basis, then the doctrine of estoppel by convention will apply. The landlord will be precluded from re-establishing the prohibition upon assignment without first giving notice to the tenant[6].

(d)   An assignment, even in breach of a prohibition upon assignment, nevertheless is valid and effective to convey the legal estate. The notice to quit should be given to the assignee rather than the assignor[7].

[1]   *Clarke v Hall* [1961] 2 QB 331, [1961] 2 All ER 365.
[2]   AHA 1986, Sch 3, Case G.
[3]   *Scala House and District Property Co Ltd v Forbes* [1974] QB 575, [1973] 3 All ER 308 (a case decided in the context of forfeiture); *Troop v Gibson* [1986] 1 EGLR 1, 277 Estates Gazette 1134. Cf *Akici v L R Butlin Ltd* [2005] EWCA Civ 1296, [2006] 07 EG 136: see para 31.84.
[4]   *Marks v Warren* [1979] 1 All ER 29 per Brown Wilkinson J; *Troop v Gibson* [1986] 1 EGLR 1, 277 Estates Gazette 1134.
[5]   *Lovell v Ireland* (1980) unreported – a decision of HH Judge Pennant in Dorchester County Court. Cf *Woodfall: Landlord and Tenant*, Vol 28, Sweet & Maxwell.
[6]   *Troop v Gibson* [1986] 1 EGLR 1, 277 Estates Gazette 1134.
[7]   *Old Grovebury Manor Farm Ltd v W Seymour Plant Sales and Hire Ltd (No 2)* [1979] 3 All ER 504, [1979] 1 WLR 1397.

31.84   The question as to whether there has been a parting with or sharing of possessions sometimes arises in practice. In *Akici v L R Butlin Ltd*[1], Neuberger LJ (as he then was) acknowledged that the difference between possession and occupation can be elusive, but it is a difference which is recognised and should be adhered to[2]. Where the owner had unrestricted access to the property, on the facts in *Akici*[3], it was found that there had been no parting with possession.

What is also noteworthy about the *Akici*[4] decision is that the judge limited the impact of the *Scala House and District Property Co Ltd v Forbes*[5] decision to cases where a legal interest had either been created or transferred. Where, as in this case, the tenant had allowed a company in which the tenant had no formal interest to operate a business from the premises, if such an act was in breach of covenant it was remediable.

1   [2005] ECWA Civ 1296, [2006] 07 EG 136.
2   Overruling *Tulapam Properties Ltd v De Almeida* (1981) 260 Estates Gazette 919.
3   *Akici v L R Butlin Ltd* [2005] ECWA Civ 1296, [2006] 07 EG 136.
4   *Akici v L R Butlin Ltd* [2005] ECWA Civ 1296, [2006] 07 EG 136.
5   [1974] QB 575, [1973] 3 All ER 308.

31.85 In *Wallace v C Brian Barratt & Son Ltd*[1], it was held that where a company tenant farmed through the agency of a partnership, there was no parting or sharing of possession or occupation.

Sub-letting will not necessarily constitute material prejudice to the landlord because the landlord is not forced into a direct relationship with the sub-tenant[2]. Further, the sub-tenant does not acquire security of tenure against the head landlord as a consequence of the Lord Chancellor's failure to make regulations to protect the interest of the sub tenant[3].

In *Pennell v Payne*[4], the landlord was unable to establish material prejudice where the tenancy was sub-let to a limited company. It is submitted that there probably would be material prejudice if the tenancy was assigned to a limited company.

If the landlord cannot establish material prejudice as a consequence of sub-letting in breach of a prohibition in the tenancy agreement or as a consequence of a s 6 notice[5], he is not without a remedy. If the landlord has not waived the breach[6], he may forfeit the tenancy[7], provided that there is a valid forfeiture clause[8].

1   [1997] 2 EGLR 1.
2   As regards relief against forfeiture, see the Law of Property Act 1925, s 146(4); *Duarte v Mount Cook Land Ltd* [2001] 33 EG 87 (CS). Also, see para 13.21 ff.
3   See para 29.17.
4   [1995] QB 192, [1995] 1 EGLR 6, CA.
5   See para 23.1.
6   See para 13.6.
7   See para 33.8.
8   *Parry v Million Pigs Ltd* (1980) 260 Estates Gazette 281. See para 24.26.

Challenging a Case E notice to quit

31.86 If a tenant wishes to contest any question arising from a Case E notice to quit, he must serve a written demand for arbitration on the landlord within one month of service of the notice to quit[1]. Other than demanding arbitration, the only method available to the tenant to challenge the Case E notice to quit is by an application to the court in cases of common law invalidity[2].

It should again be noted that, following any demand for arbitration made by the tenant, he must either secure the appointment of an arbitrator or apply to the President of the RICS, in either case within three months of service of the demand for arbitration. In default, his demand is rendered ineffective and his challenge to the reasons stated for the giving of the notice to quit is statute barred[3].

1   The Agricultural Holdings (Arbitration on Notices) Order 1987, SI 1987/710, art 9.
2   See Ch 28.
3   SI 1987/710, art 10.

Compensation for disturbance

31.87 Neither basic nor additional compensation is payable to the tenant on quitting as a consequence of a notice to quit given pursuant to Case E[1].

1   AHA 1986, s 61(1). See para 38.47 ff.

CASE F – INSOLVENCY

31.88 Case F provides:

> 'At the date of the giving of the notice to quit the tenant was a person who had become insolvent, and it is stated in the notice that it is given by reason of the said matter'.

The term 'insolvent' is statutorily defined as follows:

> 'For the purposes of this Act, a tenant is insolvent if—
> (a)   he has been adjudged bankrupt or has made a composition or arrangement with his creditors; or
> (b)   where the tenant is a body corporate, a winding-up-order has been made with respect to it or a resolution for voluntary winding-up has been passed with respect to it (other than a resolution passed solely for the purposes of its reconstruction or of its amalgamation with another body corporate)'[1].

The revised wording of Case F, which was introduced by the AHA 1984, has dealt with some anomalies which applied previously. In particular:

(a)   there is a statutory recognition of the fact that some tenants are companies and not individuals. The previous wording, referring only to bankruptcy or composition with creditors, was inapplicable to insolvent companies;

(b)   the wording of Case F is now consistent with the wording of s 25(2)(a), which entitles a landlord to give less than 12 months' notice to quit on the insolvency of the tenant. Previously Case F only referred to the tenant becoming bankrupt[2].

There is as yet no authority as to the ability of a landlord to give notice to quit to a tenant who:

(i)   having been adjudicated bankrupt then obtained his discharge before the notice to quit was given; or

(ii)   who had been, but was no longer, subject to a voluntary arrangement in favour of his creditors.

522

On first reading, it would appear that in either case, the tenant 'had become' insolvent even though he no longer was. However, on parity of reason with *Rous v Mitchell*[3], it is likely that the contrary view will be found to prevail. In that case it was held, inter alia, that a tenant who, having sub-let one of several cottages, had recovered possession before notice to quit, was not, in respect of that cottage, in breach within the meaning of the similar wording in Case E even though such breach was incapable of remedy.

[1]   AHA 1986, s 96(2).
[2]   The predecessor of s 25 of the AHA 1986 (ie s 23 of AHA 1948) referred to a receiving order in bankruptcy being made.
[3]   [1991] 1 All ER 676, [1991] 1 WLR 469, CA.

31.89 There is no preliminary notice required in relation to a Case F notice to quit[1]. There is no statutorily prescribed form for a Case F notice to quit, but it should be clear on the face of it that it is given pursuant to Case F. It should expressly refer to the reasons stated in Case F[2]. It needs to be clear on the face of the notice to quit that it is not one to which s 26(1) of the AHA 1986 applies, enabling the tenant to serve a counter-notice, resulting in an application to the ALT[3].

Section 25(2)(a) of the AHA 1986 provides that the statutory requirement that a notice to quit an agricultural holding must not terminate the tenancy before the expiry of 12 months ending on the term date does not apply where the tenant is insolvent. Accordingly, the period of notice required in respect of a Case F notice to quit will depend upon the term of the tenancy. In the case of an annual periodic tenancy, the common law requirement will be a notice to quit of six months' duration.

There are two cases where the landlord may consider relying upon the general law of forfeiture to recover possession of an agricultural holding in the event of the insolvency of the tenant:

(a)   if the landlord wishes to seek to recover possession sooner than, for example, the six-month period of a notice to quit arising in relation to an annual periodic tenancy; or

(b)   if the tenancy is of a fixed term and the fixed term has not yet expired. In this case, Case F has no relevance.

The landlord's ability to rely upon the general law of forfeiture is dependent upon two factors:

(i)   he must not have waived the once and for all breach represented by the tenant's insolvency, for example, by accepting rent after knowledge that the tenant has become insolvent[4]; and

(ii)   the tenancy agreement must contain a valid forfeiture clause permitting the landlord to forfeit in the event of the tenant's insolvency[5].

There is no arbitration provision available to the tenant to challenge a Case F notice to quit. The only remedy available to the tenant is to either seek a declaration from the court or to defend subsequent possession proceedings[6]. The tenant may do so, for example, if he alleges that Case F does not apply, because he was not insolvent, or because the notice to quit may otherwise be challenged, for example, by reason of ambiguity, fraud, etc[7].

Neither basic nor additional compensation is payable to the tenant on quitting as a consequence of a notice to quit given pursuant to Case F[8].

1   Cf the requirement to give a notice under s 146 of the Law of Property Act 1925 prior to forfeiture by reason of the insolvency of the tenant.
2   See para 31.3.
3   See para 30.1.
4   See para 31.88.
5   *Parry v Million Pigs Ltd* (1980) 260 Estates Gazette 281. See para 24.26.
6   See para 27.8.
7   See paras 28.11 and 31.15.
8   AHA 1986, s 61(1).

CASE G – THE DEATH OF THE TENANT

31.90 Case G provides:

'The notice is given—
(a)   following the death of a person who immediately before his death was the sole (or sole surviving) tenant under the contract of tenancy, and
(b)   not later than the end of the period of three months beginning with the date of any relevant notice,
and it is stated in the notice to quit that it is given by reason of that person's death'[1].

There is an additional provision relating to Case G:

'For the purposes of Case G—
(a)   'tenant' does not include an executor, administrator, trustee in bankruptcy or other person deriving title from a tenant by operation of law, and
(b)   the reference to the date of any relevant notice shall be construed as a reference—
　　(i)   to the date on which a notice in writing was served on the landlord by or on behalf of an executor or administrator of the tenant's estate informing the landlord of the tenant's death or the date on which the landlord was given notice by virtue of section 40(5) of this Act of any application with respect to the holding under section 39 or 41, or
　　(ii)   where both of those events occur, to the date of whichever of them occurs first'[2].

1   AHA 1986, Sch 3 Pt I, Case G.
2   AHA 1986, Sch 3 Pt II para 12.

The operation of Case G

Effect of death on the tenancy

31.91 Although, by virtue of the AHA 1986[1], on the death of the tenant certain members of a very restricted class of close relations may apply to the

ALT for a direction that a new tenancy be granted to them, this does not mean that the old tenancy will automatically terminate on the death of the tenant[2]. At common law such a tenancy automatically vests by operation of law in the personal representatives of the deceased tenant and continues as before until duly terminated.

[1] Previously the Agriculture (Miscellaneous Provisions) Act 1976, see Ch 35.
[2] If an application to the ALT is successful and no notice to quit has been given, the old tenancy is automatically terminated by operation of law; AHA 1986, s 45(5).

Time for giving a Case G notice to quit

31.92 Case G[1] entitles a landlord to give a notice to quit within three months of his receiving written notice of the death of the tenant for the time being[2] or notice of an application for succession, whichever first happens. The written notice should be served on the landlord by or on behalf of an executor or administrator of the tenant's estate.

The period of three months used to run from the date of death, with no obligation upon anybody to give the landlord notice of the death of the tenant. This produced injustice to an absentee landlord. The three-month period now runs from the date on which the landlord receives either written notice of the death or written notice of an application for succession[3]. If he receives both, the earlier notice starts time running.

Problems have arisen in practice where the landlord and tenant are very well known to each other, indeed are even close relations. In such circumstances, where the tenant's personal representatives know full well that the landlord is fully aware of the death of the tenant (for example, because he attends the funeral), frequently the personal representatives will not go through the process of giving formal notice. They inadvertently extend the time for the landlord to give a Case G notice to quit. The test is not whether the landlord knew of the tenant's death, but whether he had written notice[4]. Any written notice must have been given by the personal representative of the late tenant to start time running.

[1] Formerly s 24(2)(g) of the AHA 1948, as subsequently amended by s 16 of the Agriculture (Miscellaneous Provisions) Act 1976.
[2] AHA 1986, Sch 3 Pt II para 12.
[3] AHA 1986, Sch 3 Pt II para 12(b).
[4] *BSC Pension Fund Trustees Ltd v Downing* [1990] 1 EGLR 4.

Notice to the landlord

31.93 The following principles apply:

(a)   Notice in a newspaper or obituary column is not sufficient. It is not given by the personal representatives.
(b)   In the case of an intestacy, where there are no personal representatives before a grant of letters of administration, written notice of the death does not start time running because it has not been given on behalf of the personal representatives[1].

(c)   A cheque for rent sent by the executors, drawn on the executors' bank account was insufficient notice of the death[2].

If no executor has been appointed, or letters of administration obtained, no notice can be given to the landlord[3].

1   *BSC Pension Fund Trustees Ltd v Downing* [1990] 1 EGLR 4. Also see, *Land v Sykes* [1992] 1 EGLR 1, [1993] 03 EG 115; *Amalgamated Estates Ltde v Joystretch Manufacturing Ltd* (1980) 257 Estates Gazette 489.
2   *Lees v Tatchell* [1990] 1 EGLR 10.
3   AHA 1986, Sch 3 Pt II para 12.

Joint tenants

31.94   A Case G notice to quit can only be given on 'the death of the sole (or sole surviving) tenant'[1]. Where the tenancy is vested in joint tenants, Case G only arises on the death of the last surviving tenant.

Under the AHA 1948 the position was different. Notice could be given on the death of the tenant 'with whom the contract of tenancy was made'. In 1961 this was held to mean the original tenant, even if he had subsequently assigned his tenancy[2]. This was amended to the present law by the Agriculture (Miscellaneous Provisions) Act 1976[3].

If a joint tenancy includes a company, the right to serve a Case G notice to quit never arises.

1   AHA 1986, Sch 3 Pt I, Case G, para (a).
2   *Clarke v Hall* [1961] 2 QB 331, [1961] 2 All ER 365.
3   Section 16. For an article discussing the interpretation of these provisions, see 'Conveyancer and Property Lawyer' (1977) Vol 41, No 4, p 273.

Definition of tenant

31.95   The definition of 'tenant' in Case G expressly excludes 'an executor, administrator, trustee in bankruptcy or other person deriving title from a tenant by operation of law'[1]. The death of such a person does not permit the service of a Case G notice to quit. Accordingly, if the landlord fails to serve a notice to quit within three months of a relevant notice, the tenancy will remain vested in the personal representatives and their subsequent deaths will not give rise to the right to serve a Case G notice to quit[2].

1   AHA 1986, Sch 3 Pt II para 12(a).
2   Cf *Costagliola v Bunting* [1958] 1 All ER 846, in respect of the pre-1976 Act law.

The notice to quit

31.96   There is no statutorily prescribed form for a Case G notice to quit, but it should be clear on the face of it that it is given pursuant to Case G on the death of the sole (or sole surviving) tenant[1].

It is not necessary for the landlord to wait until he has received notice of the tenant's death or a succession application before he can serve a Case G notice to quit. In practice, a landlord will often wait to establish whether there is going to be an application for succession before serving a Case G notice to quit. An application for succession must be made within three months of the date of death. The three-month period starts to run on the day after the death[2].

The Case G notice to quit should be served on the personal representatives of the tenant if they have obtained a grant of probate. Additionally, or alternatively (if it appears that no grant has been taken out), service is effective on the person responsible for the control or management of the holding[3]. In the event of doubt, the notice to quit should be served on the Public Trustee[4].

The notice for the Public Trustee should be sent to the Public Trustee Office, PO Box 3010, London WC2B 6JS. It should be noted that service on the Public Trustee alone is insufficient if the tenant died testate and executors prove the will[5].

1 See para 31.3.
2 AHA 1986, s 39(1).
3 AHA 1986, s 93(3).
4 Practice Direction [1995] 3 All ER 192. For the form of application to the Public Trustee for registration of a notice to quit where the Public Trustee (Notices Affecting Land) (Title on Death) Regulations 1995, SI 1995/1330, apply, see para A1.579E.
5 *Thorlby v Olivant* [1960] EGD 257.

Effect of an application to the Agricultural Land Tribunal

31.97 If a landlord fails to give notice to quit under Case G, but nevertheless an application is made to the ALT by a close relation for succession, if that application is unsuccessful, the tenancy still continues, but is vested in the personal representatives rather than in the applicant. If the applicant is successful, then the making of the direction of itself destroys the previous tenancy, even though no notice to quit has been given[1].

1 AHA 1986, s 45(5).

31.98 A Case G notice to quit does not become effective unless:

(a)   no application for succession is made; or
(b)   one or more such applications are made but:
      (i)   none of the applications succeed; or
      (ii) the ALT consent to the operation of the notice to quit in relation to the whole of part of the holding[1].

Where the ALT consents to the operation of a Case G notice to quit in relation to part only of the holding, the notice has effect as a notice to quit that part and is not invalid by reason that it relates only to part[2].

1 AHA 1986, s 43(1).
2 AHA 1986, s 43(2).

31.99 A landlord with written notice of the death of the tenant who fails to give a Case G notice to quit within three months, on the basis that a son or other close relation of the tenant will undoubtedly succeed in any application he might choose to make for the grant of a new tenancy, will have severely prejudiced his position if the potential successor abandons his application, relying on the continuance of the old tenancy for the following reasons:

(a)   he will have denied himself the right to have a rent review on the transmission from deceased tenant to successor;

(b)   there will be no opportunity to obtain a variation of the terms of the tenancy by arbitration following the direction of the ALT;

(c)   if the applicant abandons his application, and relies upon the subsisting tenancy agreement vested in the executors, who do not assent to the vesting of it in beneficiaries, then such tenancy will not be terminable even on the death of the potential applicant, nor will there have been a first succession;

(d)   on a transmission of a tenancy by succession, all fixtures and improvements pass to the landlord for the purposes of assessing future rent, subject to the landlord's obligation to pay what is usually a written-down value for them, subject to the ruling of the arbitrator, if arbitration as to the terms of the new tenancy takes place. The opportunity for the landlord of obtaining an increased rental for farm fixtures or improvements for the future will be lost.

Disputing the validity of the notice

31.100 Arbitration is not available in relation to a Case G notice to quit. The tenant's only means of challenge is before the court, either seeking a declaration as to the validity and effectiveness of the notice or defending possession proceedings. If the landlord himself anticipates a dispute, he too may seek a declaration from the court, thereby using the 'dead time' pending the expiry of the notice to quit[1].

[1]   See para 27.8.

Compensation for disturbance

31.101 Neither basic nor additional compensation is payable to the tenant on quitting as a consequence of a notice to quit given pursuant to Case G[1].

[1]   AHA 1986, s 61(1).

CASE H – MINISTRY AMALGAMATIONS

31.102 Case H provides:

'The notice to quit is given by the Minister and—

(a)   the Minister[1] certifies in writing that the notice to quit is given in order to enable him to use or dispose of the land for the purpose of effecting any amalgamation (within the meaning of section 26(1) of the Agriculture Act 1967) or the reshaping of any agricultural unit; and

(b)   the instrument under which the tenancy was granted contains an acknowledgment signed by the tenant that the tenancy is subject to the provisions of this Case (or to those of Case H in section 2(3) of the Agricultural Holdings (Notices to Quit) Act 1977 or of section 29 of the Agriculture Act 1967)'[2].

For a Case H notice to be effective, the following requirements must be satisfied:

(a)   the notice to quit must be given by the Minister in order to enable him to use or dispose of the land for the purpose of effecting an amalgamation[3], or the reshaping of any agricultural unit;

(b)   the Minister must certify in writing that the notice to quit is given for that purpose; and

(c)   the instrument under which the tenancy was granted must contain an acknowledgment signed by the tenant that the tenancy is subject to the provisions of Case H (or to those of s 29 of the Agriculture Act 1967).

1   AHA 1986, s 96(1).
2   AHA 1986, Sch 3 Pt I Case H.
3   For the definition of the word 'amalgamation' in this context, see the Agriculture Act 1967, s 26(1).

31.103 Case H does not require that the certificate is set out in or annexed to the Case H notice to quit nor that the Case H notice to quit is given by reason of any such matter.

Arbitration is not available to challenge a Case H notice to quit. As in the case of a Case G notice to quit, the only forum for dispute is the court[1].

Neither basic nor additional compensation is payable to the tenant on quitting as a consequence of a notice to quit given to pursuant to Case H[2].

1   See para 27.8.
2   AHA 1986, s 61(1).

Chapter 32

RECOVERY OF POSSESSION FOR NON-AGRICULTURAL USE

INTRODUCTION

32.1 One issue which practitioners are often asked to consider is the ability of a landlord to recover possession under the Agricultural Holdings Act 1986 (AHA 1986) where he seeks to do so because he requires the holding, or often part of it, for the purposes of development or other non-agricultural use. Likewise practitioners are often asked to advise a tenant in defending such a claim.

The issues which arise may involve having to consider a range of matters dealt with elsewhere in this book, for example: notice to quit part[1], the operation of s 31 of the AHA 1986[2], severance of the freehold reversion[3], notice to quit for non-agricultural use[4], Case B[5] and compensation for disturbance, and more generally[6]. The aim of this chapter is to draw these various strands together in one place in order to assist the practitioner in analysing the issues which may arise. As a consequence, some parts of this chapter are necessarily repetitious of other sections of this book. Case B is dealt with substantively in this chapter[7].

[1] See para 29.1.
[2] See para 29.4.
[3] See para 29.6.
[4] See para 30.15.
[5] See para 31.20. Case B is dealt with substantively at para 32.10 ff.
[6] See para 30.47 and Chs 38 and 40 generally.
[7] See para 32.10.

NOTICE TO QUIT

Length of notice

32.2 The starting point is that if an AHA 1986 tenancy is terminated under the statutory framework, then it requires the service of a valid notice to quit. As seen in Chapters 27 and 28, there is no prescribed form of notice to quit. Nevertheless, aside from having to comply with the normal common law requirements as to clarity, a notice to quit must fulfil the statutory requirements contained in s 25(1) of the AHA 1986 which provides that:

'A notice to quit of an agricultural holding or part of an agricultural holding shall (notwithstanding any provision to the contrary in the contract of tenancy of the holding) be invalid if it purports to terminate the tenancy before the expiry of twelve months from the end of the then current year of tenancy'.

This effectively imposes a requirement of a *minimum* 12 months' notice in relation to all agricultural tenancies under the AHA 1986 (apart from a very small number of closely defined exceptions)[1]. This statutory requirement expressly overrides any contractual stipulation providing for a shorter period of notice. It also overrides the common law period of six months' notice implied in the case of other annual periodic tenancies. Further, any notice to quit which is served must terminate on the term date of the tenancy. If the tenancy concerned is a Michaelmas tenancy, ie 29 September, the landlord's notice to quit must expire on either 28 or 29 September to be valid[2].

Also, although s 25(1) of the AHA 1986 expressly invalidates any agreement between the parties whereby they undertake in advance to accept any lesser period of notice, if during the currency of the tenancy one party serves a 'short' notice to quit on the other, who agrees to accept it, and thus to waive his statutory right to the full 12 months expiring on the term date, such a waiver may be binding and the notice, if otherwise valid, will be effective to terminate the tenancy[3].

There are a small number of exceptions to the rule that a minimum of 12 months' notice is required pursuant to s 25(1) of the AHA 1986. The exceptions are now set out in s 25(2), (3) and (4) of the AHA 1986[4]. For example, a 'short' notice is permitted in the case of the insolvency of the tenant. It is however relevant to note that 'short' notice is permitted where the notice to quit is given pursuant to a provision in the tenancy agreement which authorises the resumption of possession of the holding or part of it for a specified non-agricultural purpose[5]. This includes any non-agricultural purpose so long as it is expressly provided for in the tenancy[6]. There is no specified minimum period of notice in the AHA 1986 for such cases, but the period of notice must be sufficient to enable the tenant to make any appropriate claims for compensation upon the termination of the tenancy and as such it must be more than one month[7].

[1] See para 28.13.
[2] *Sidebottom v Holland* [1895] 1 QB 378, CA.
[3] *Elsden v Pick* [1980] 3 All ER 235, CA. See para 28.12.
[4] See para 28.13.
[5] AHA 1986, s 25(2)(b).
[6] *Paddock Investments Ltd v Lory* [1975] 2 EGLR 5, 236 EG 803.
[7] *Re Disraeli's Agreement* [1939] Ch 382.

Notice to quit part

32.3 At common, law a notice to quit part only of the property let by a tenancy is invalid[1]. The notice can only apply to the entirety of the premises[2].

32.3 *Recovery of possession for non-agricultural use*

However, in the case of agricultural holdings protected under the AHA 1986, there are three cases where the notice to quit part may be given:

(a)   those covered by s 31 of the AHA 1986[3];
(b)   those where express provision is made in the tenancy agreement for the notice to quit part to be given[4];
(c)   those covered by s 140 of the Law of Property Act 1925 (LPA 1925) (severance of the reversion)[5].

The impact of ss 32 and 33 of the AHA 1986 should also be noted:

(i)   Section 32 gives the tenant the right to treat a notice to quit part validated by either s 31 of the AHA 1986 or by s 140 of the LPA 1925 as a notice to quit the entire holding. This is sometimes referred to as the right of 'enlargement'.
(ii)   Section 33 provides that where the landlord resumes possession of part of the holding, either by reason of s 31 of the AHA 1986 or by reason of a provision in the tenancy agreement, then the tenant will be entitled to a proportionately reduced rent which should also reflect any depreciation in the value of his retained land caused by the severance which the landlord has achieved or by the use intended for the severed land.

[1]   See para 29.1.
[2]   *Re: Bebington's Tenancy* [1921] 1 Ch 559.
[3]   See para 32.4.
[4]   See para 32.5.
[5]   See para 32.6.

32.4 Section 31 provides that a notice to quit part of an agricultural holding under the AHA 1986 given by the landlord will not be invalid if it is for one of the purposes specified in the section and the notice to quit itself states this fact. The approved purposes are:

(a)   adjusting the boundaries between the agricultural units or amalgamating units[1],
(b)   the public interest purposes:
       (i)   the erection of cottages or other homes for farm labourers, with or without gardens;
       (ii)   the provision of gardens for cottages or other houses for farm labourers;
       (iii) the provision of allotments;
       (iv)   the letting of land as a smallholding;
       (v)   the planting of trees;
       (vi)   the opening or working of a deposit of coal, etc;
       (vii) the making of a watercourse or reservoir;
       (viii) the making of a road, railway, a tram road, siding, canal or basin or connected works[2].

Although s 31 provides the landlord with the ability to give notice to quit as to part, it remains subject to the overriding provision of s 25(1) as to the length of the notice to quit. The exception applying to the resumption of possession for a specified non-agricultural purpose depends upon there being a provision in the tenancy agreement to that effect and not upon the landlord being able to rely upon s 31 of the AHA 1986.

The 'double negative' contained in s 31 provides that a notice to quit will be valid if (amongst other reasons) it is given for the purpose of 'making ... a road [and/or] railway'. The following points should be noted:

(1) Such a notice to quit does not require the severance of the freehold reversion[3].

(2) In the absence of an early resumption clause, such notice to quit must be of a minimum of 12 months' duration terminating on the term date of the tenancy[4].

(3) All that s 31 of the AHA 1986 does is validate a notice to quit in respect of part of an agricultural holding where one of the public interest provisions apply or the adjustment in the boundaries applies. A tenant faced with such a notice to quit can still challenge it by giving a counter-notice and invoking the security of tenure provisions contained in ss 26 and 27 of the AHA 1986. Many of the s 31 objects require planning permission. Accordingly, for the landlord to succeed in relation to a notice to quit part of an agricultural holding, for example, for the making of a road and/or railway, the landlord must establish, in the case of such development, its entitlement to possession under Case B This means that planning consent must first be obtained.

[1] AHA 1986, s 31(1)(a).
[2] AHA 1986, s 31(2).
[3] See para 32.6.
[4] See para 32.2.

The contractual entitlement to give notice to quit part

32.5 Notice to quit part can be given if there is an express contractual provision in the tenancy agreement itself. In such cases the same period of notice and other common law and statutory requirements apply to notices to quit part of the holding as apply to notices to quit the whole. The 12 months' minimum notice will be required unless the situation is one of the specified exceptions. The most usual exception is where the tenancy expressly provides the landlord to resume possession of part of the holding for a specified non-agricultural purpose[1]. The tenant is not able to enlarge a notice to quit part given pursuant to a contractual provision in the tenancy agreement.

It should be noted that there are provisions contained in the AHA 1986 dealing with rent reduction where the landlord resumes possession of part only of the original agricultural holding under the AHA 1986[2].

It should also be noted that until 1984 the agricultural holdings legislation included a provision to the effect that a contract to sale or part with the landlord's interest concluded during the currency of a notice to quit the agricultural holding would render the notice of no effect. That was repealed by Sch 4 to the Agricultural Holdings Act 1984 (now consolidated in the AHA

1986). Accordingly, any sale of the landlord's interest can now go ahead without prejudicing any current notice to quit[3].

1 AHA 1986, s 25(2)(b).
2 See paras 29.8 and 32.7.
3 See para 29.31.

Severance of the freehold reversion

32.6 Section 140 of the Law of Property Act 1925 provides that where the freehold reversion is severed, the landlord of any severed part may give an independent notice to quit in relation to that part. Thus if the original landlord of the entire holding sells or gives up his interest in a defined part of the land to a third party, that person will be entitled to serve on the tenant notice to quit in respect of the severed part which he now owns.

Any severance which is relied on as validating a notice to quit part must be a genuine transfer of a part of the reversion and not merely a device designed to enable such a notice to be given. The courts have been prepared to look at the substance of the transaction rather than its mere form. For example, where a transfer of part of the reversionary estate to bare trustees was seen in substance to be merely a transfer to agents for the purposes of serving a notice to quit part, the court intervened finding that it was not a true severance and the notice to quit was invalid[1].

Severance of the freehold reversion does not of itself create two tenancies. The tenant continues to hold under one single lease, whether or not there has been any apportionment of the rent[2].

Section 140(2) of the LPA 1925 gives the tenant who is served with a notice to quit part of the premises the right to serve a counter-notice on the owner of the remainder of the reversionary estate which terminates the tenancy of the entire holding. Such counter-notice must be served within one month of the notice to quit and must expire at the same time as that notice. The counter-notice operates as a notice to quit by the tenant and s 140(2) effectively gives the tenant the right to enlarge the notice to quit part into a notice to quit the whole. In the case of agricultural holdings under the AHA 1986, a tenant wishing to exercise his right will do so under s 32 of the AHA 1986 rather than s 140(2) because the latter would disentitle the tenant to the payment of compensation for disturbance, which is available if the enlargement takes place under s 32 of the AHA 1986.

1 *Persey v Bazley* (1983) 267 Estates Gazette 519.
2 *Jelley v Buckman* [1974] QB 488, CA.

Reduction of rent

32.7 Section 33(1) of the AHA 1986 provides for a 'proportionate' reduction of rent where the landlord 'resumes possession' of part of the holding either in reliance on s 31 or an early resumption clause in the tenancy agreement. A 'proportionate' reduction of rent is a matter of valuation rather than arithmetic based on acreage. Also, the tenant is entitled to have taken into account in the reduction 'any depreciation of the value to him of the residue of the holding caused by the severance or by the use to be made of the part severed'[1].

Where the tenancy agreement provides that the tenant is to be entitled to some benefit or relief if the landlord exercises his contractual right to resume possession of the part, the arbitrator, if there is a dispute referred to arbitration in respect of the rent, is to take this into account in assessing the amount of the reduction. The amount of the reduction under s 33 may be settled by agreement between the parties after the landlord resumes possession of the part, but in default of agreement, it is to be determined by arbitration under the AHA 1986[2].

Section 33 does not contain a reference to the apportionment of rent on the severance of the reversion. That is because it is not purely a matter between the landlord and the tenant because it involves the rights of two or more owners of the freehold and the rights of the tenant. Accordingly, the arbitration procedure under the AHA 1986 does not apply. Legal apportionment of rent on the severance of the reversion requires the consent of all of the parties concerned or judicial process. There are some cases where statute may intervene, for example, s 20 of the Landlord and Tenant Act 1927.

[1]   AHA 1986, s 33(1). See para 29.8.
[2]   See para 29.8.

Summary

32.8 If the landlord relies upon a provision in the tenancy agreement authorising the notice to quit to be given in respect of part of the holding, the following propositions apply:

(a)   the tenancy agreement must clearly authorise the giving of notice to quit as to part;

(b)   if the resumption is for a non-agricultural use of the land, then the landlord does not need to give the statutory period of notice, but can give a lesser period of notice as specified in the tenancy agreement;

(c)   such early resumption clause must nevertheless allow the tenant sufficient time to make a claim for compensation and therefore the period of the notice to quit must be more than one month[1].

If the landlord seeks possession for non-agricultural use, the landlord must still fulfil the Case B criteria (as to which, see 32.10 below), unless Case B does not apply because, for example, no planning permission is required.

[1]   *Parry v Million Pigs Ltd* (1980) 260 Estates Gazette 281. See para 24.26.

UNQUALIFIED NOTICE TO QUIT FOR NON-AGRICULTURAL USE

32.9 There are two separate provisions in the AHA 1986 governing the landlord's ability to recover possession of an agricultural holding where possession of the holding is sought for a use other than for agriculture. In cases where planning permission is required, Case B applies[1]. In those cases where planning permission is not required, the landlord's ability to obtain vacant possession is governed by s 27(3)(f) of the AHA 1986[2]. This covers cases where, for example, the development is permitted by reason of the General Development Order[3]. Perhaps the most common change of use which is covered by this provision is a change to forestry, as this is not expressly development within the town and country planning legislation and therefore does not require planning permission.

In cases where s 27(3)(f) of the AHA 1986 applies, it is necessary for the landlord to serve a notice to quit and then apply to the Agricultural Land Tribunal (ALT) for 'consent' to the operation of the notice to quit. The ALT will consider not only whether the case falls within s 27(3)(f), but also whether in all the circumstances it appears to the ALT that a fair and reasonable landlord would not insist on possession. In practice, this is often an insurmountable hurdle for the landlord[4].

1 See para 32.10.
2 See para 30.15.
3 The condition contained in this ground for giving a notice to quit is not satisfied if the non-agricultural use is in relation to 'permitted activities' in respect of opencast coal production: Opencast Coal Act 1958, s 14(6), as substituted by the Housing and Planning Act 1986, Sch 8 para 5.
4 See para 30.16.

CASE B

Case B generally

32.10 Case B covers the position where a landlord is entitled to serve a notice to quit and recover possession where he requires the agricultural holding for a non-agricultural use without having to obtain the consent of the ALT to the operation of the notice to quit in accordance with s 27(3)(f) of the AHA 1986.

Case B provides:

'The notice to quit is given on the ground that the land is required for a use, other than for agriculture—
(a) for which permission has been granted on an application made under the enactments relating to town and country planning,
(b) for which permission under those enactments is granted by a general development order by reason only of the fact that the use is authorised by—
(i) a private or local Act,
(ii) an order approved by both Houses of Parliament, or
(iii) an order made under s 14 or 16 of the Harbours Act 1964,
(c) for which any provision that—
(i) is contained in an Act, but
(ii) does not form part of the enactments relating to town and country planning,
deems permission under those enactments to have been granted,

(d)   which any such provisions deems not to constitute development for the purposes of those enactments, or

(e)   for which permission is not required under the enactments relating to town and country planning by reason only of Crown immunity,

and that fact is stated in the notice'.

The wording of paragraphs (b) to (e) of Case B was introduced upon the enactment of a Private Member's Bill, supported by the Government in 1990, the Agricultural Holdings (Amendment) Act 1990[1]. This followed the Court of Appeal case of *Bell v McCubbin*[2]. The decision in this case defied what had previously been the conventional wisdom.

Prior to the enactment of the Agricultural Holdings (Amendment) Act 1990, the planning condition applying to non-agricultural use was simpler. It was one:

(a)   for which permission has been granted on an application made under the enactments relating to town and country planning[3]; or

(b)   for which, otherwise than by virtue of any provision of those enactments, such permission is not required[4].

[1]   The Act came into force on 29 July 1990, applying to notices to quit given on or after that date.
[2]   [1990] 1 QB 976, [1989] 2 EGLR 3.
[3]   This was not defined until the Agricultural Holdings (Amendment) Act 1990.
[4]   This was held to apply where no planning permission was required by way of Crown immunity: *Ministry of Agriculture, Fisheries and Food v Jenkins* [1963] 2 QB 317.

Bell v McCubbin

32.11 In *Bell v McCubbin*[1], the tenancy agreement provided for the recovery of any part of the holding (not exceeding 5 acres) for a non-agricultural purpose. The tenant was not required to use the farmhouse and, in fact, let it for residential (non-agricultural) purposes. The landlord sought possession under Case B. The Court of Appeal overturned the county court judge. The Court of Appeal held that the farmhouse was required for a use other than agriculture in accordance with a provision in the tenancy agreement. The use was one for which, 'otherwise than by virtue of any provision in the planning enactments, permission was not required'. The Case B notice was effective.

The *Bell v McCubbin* decision caused uproar. The conventional wisdom was reinstated by the Agricultural Holdings (Amendment) Act 1990. The result is that the present position is that Case B basically covers two situations. First, the situation where planning permission has already been obtained by the date of the service of the notice to quit. Second, those cases where planning permission is not required for the reasons set out in Case B, paragraphs (b) to (e).

[1]   [1990] 1 QB 976, [1989] 2 EGLR 3.

32.12   *Recovery of possession for non-agricultural use*

Examples of non-agricultural use

32.12 Examples of situations where non-agricultural use has resulted in a successful Case B notice to quit are:

(a)   use as a sports ground[1];
(b)   forestry not ancillary to farming[2];
(c)   use of land for testing chemicals on weeds[3];
(d)   use for a reservoir[4];
(e)   quarrying[5];
(f)   use for gardens[6];
(g)   residential use not ancillary to farming[7];
(h)   mineral extraction[8].

It should be noted that polytunnels do represent development requiring planning permission and are not permitted development within Class A of Pt 4 of Sch 2 to the Town and Country Planning (General Permitted Development) Order 1995[9]. This grants permission for certain temporary buildings and uses in connection with, and for the duration of, operations carried out on, in, under or over the land in question[10].

1   *Jones v Gates* [1954] 1 All ER 158, CA.
2   *Ministry of Agriculture, Fisheries and Food v Jenkins* [1963] 2 QB 317.
3   *Dow Agrochemicals Ltd v E A Lane (North Lynn) Ltd* (1965) 192 Estates Gazette 737.
4   *Dow Agrochemicals Ltd v E A Lane (North Lynn) Ltd* (1965) 192 Estates Gazette 737.
5   *Rugby Joint Water Board v Foottit* [1973] AC 202, HL.
6   *Paddock Investments Ltd v Lory* [1975] 2 EGLR 5, 236 EG 803.
7   *Bell v McCubbin* [1990] 1 QB 976, [1989] 2 EGLR 3.
8   *Floyer-Acland v Osmond* [2000] 2 EGLR 1, [2000] 22 EG 134.
9   SI 1995/418.
10   *Hall Hunter Partnership v First Secretary of State* [2006] EWHC 3482 (Admin), [2007] 2 P & CR 73, applying the test in *Cardiff Rating Authority v Guest Keen Baldwin's Iron and Steel Co Ltd* [1949] 1 KB 385.

Key issues

32.13 There are five key issues to be addressed in relation to the operation of Case B.

(1)   What does 'required' mean?
(2)   Whether all of the land must be 'required'?
(3)   Does the requirement have to be for use by the landlord himself?
(4)   What sort of planning permission is required?
(5)   What is the effect of a failure to implement the scheme?

Required for non-agricultural use

32.14 For Case B to be applicable, the land must be 'required' for non-agricultural use. The landlord must establish that there is a *present* intention to develop the land. A future intention, for example where the landlord intends to sell to a non-identified prospective developer, will not suffice[1]. The language of Case B suggests that the land must be required at the date of the giving of the notice to quit. It has been suggested that the requirement must be for use on the expiry of the notice to quit or a relatively short time thereafter[2]. This point has not been determined by the courts.

1 *Jones v Gates* [1954] 1 All ER 158, CA; *Paddock Investments Ltd v Lory* [1975] 2 EGLR 5, 236 EG 803.
2 Muir Watt and Moss, *Agricultural Holdings*, (14th edn, 1998), Sweet & Maxwell at para 12.50.1.

The extent of planning permission

32.15 The better view is that all of the land which is the subject of the notice to quit must be required for the purpose specified in Case B. It is not sufficient if merely a substantial part of the land has the benefit of planning[1].

1 *Public Trustee v Randag* [1966] Ch 649, [1965] 3 All ER 88. Cf *Fernandez v Walding* [1968] 2 QB 606, [1968] 1 All ER 994, CA. Also see, *Heath v Telford Corpn* (1988) unreported (CC); *Cawley v Pratt* [1988] 2 EGLR 6, CA; *Omnivale v Bolden Ltd* [1994] EGCS 63, CA.

Required for use by the landlord

32.16 The land does not have to be 'required' for the use of the landlord himself. The requirement of any person obtaining planning permission is included, whether that person is the landlord, a prospective purchaser of the landlord's reversion or a body intending to compulsorily purchase the landlord's interest[1]. If the landlord is intending to sell to a third-party developer, the latter must be identified and establish a bona fide intention to develop the land with a reasonable prospect of doing so[2].

1 *Rugby Joint Water Board v Foottit* [1973] AC 202.
2 *Paddock Investments Ltd v Lory* [1975] 2 EGLR 5, 236 EG 803.

Planning permission

32.17 Where Case B is relied upon to facilitate re-development, the planning permission must have been obtained after the tenancy was granted[1]. Also, the planning permission must have been obtained. It is not sufficient if the proposed user is sanctioned by the implied permission of the General Development Order or by the Use Classes Order[2].

Case B does give the landlord considerable power to remove a tenant where planning permission has been obtained. The tenant is entitled to make representations to the planning authority in relation to the planning application. The fact that he is the tenant and may lose his livelihood is only one factor to be considered[3].

1 *Paddock Investments Ltd v Lory* (1975) 236 EG 803, (1975) EGD 37.
2 *Ministry of Agriculture, Fisheries and Food v Jenkins* [1963] 2 QB 317.
3 *Fowler v Secretary of State for the Environment and North Wiltshire District Council* [1993] JPL 365.

32.18 In *Bell v McCubbin*[1], the problem for the tenant in relation to the landlord's Case B notice in respect of the farmhouse was that the landlord was proposing to use the farmhouse for letting it himself. There was no change in the non-agricultural use of the property. Therefore, planning permission was not required. Since the Agricultural Holdings (Amendment) Act 1990, if the landlord wishes to repossess, in order to continue a non-agricultural use which is already being carried on by the tenant (as in *Bell v McCubbin*), he will no longer be able to use Case B. Instead he will have to serve an unqualified notice to quit and seek the consent of the ALT to its operation[2].

In addition to the landlord's ability to rely upon Case B where planning permission has been granted, the re-modelled Case B enables a landlord to serve a notice to quit in four other cases:

(a) where land is required for a non-agricultural use for which planning permission is granted by a general development order, by reason only of the fact that the use is authorised by either a private or local Act, an order approved by both Houses of Parliament, or an order made under s 14 or 16 of the Harbours Act 1964. Under the current General Permitted Development Order, permission does not authorise any building works, or the formation of means of access, unless the prior approval of detailed plans and specifications by the local planning authority has been obtained. The approval required is limited to the siting of the development and the design and/or the external appearance of buildings and other structures;

(b) where land is required for a non-agricultural use which is deemed to have planning permission by any provision contained in an Act of Parliament, but which does not form part of the enactments relating to town and country planning;

(c) where land is required for a non-agricultural purpose which an Act, other than one forming part of the town and country planning legislation, deems what is proposed not to constitute 'development' and, as a consequence, does not require planning permission;

(d) where land is required for a non-agricultural use for which permission is not required under the town and country planning legislation, 'by reason only of Crown immunity'.

---

1 [1990] 1 QB 976, [1989] 2 EGLR 3.
2 *Quaere*: what happens if the landlord obtains planning permission to knock down the farmhouse and replace it with another? Also, note the tenant's vulnerability to the landlord seeking and obtaining planning permission for the conversion of agricultural buildings to a dwelling: see *Sanderson v Preston City Council*, 12 June 2006: decision of the Planning Inspector, unreported.

32.19 In *Floyer-Acland v Osmond*[1], a landlord who had obtained planning permission to extract sand and gravel from part of a holding gave a notice to quit under Case B. The tenancy agreement excepted and reserved to the landlords the sand and gravel, with liberty to search and remove on giving three months' notice. The tenancy agreement also made it lawful for the landlords, on giving not less than three months' notice, to resume possession of any part or parts of the holding not exceeding one-tenth of the total area 'for any purpose or purposes not being the use of land for agriculture'[2]. The Court of Appeal held:

(a)   clause 43 did not limit the purposes so as to exclude mineral working;

(b)   the landlords were not precluded from using clause 43 where they required possession for mineral workings and subsequent works of restoration and aftercare, even though, subsequent to those works, the land would be used for agriculture; and

(c)   works of restoration and aftercare did not involve the use of the land for agriculture. Accordingly, possession was required for Case B.

The court rejected the tenant's argument that, because the landlords could work the minerals under the exceptions and reservations, the land was not 'required'. Restoration rights went beyond the exceptions and reservations.

Where the operation of Case B requires planning permission, it has been held that an outline permission will be sufficient[3]. The decision was that of the county court, subsequently cited with approval by the Court of Appeal[4]. Although outline permission has been found to be sufficient to enable a landlord to be able to rely upon Case B, in any substantial development there are likely to be matters within the planning permission which are reserved. These issues may impact upon the landlord's ability to rely upon Case B or, more usually, the timetable for being able to rely upon Case B. It may be argued by a tenant that if there are matters which are reserved, then that will go both to the question of the settled intention to proceed with the development and the ability to proceed with the development. Each case will clearly turn upon its own facts, but it may be that the landlord's ability to rely upon Case B is postponed until matters reserved within a planning permission are resolved.

[1]   [2000] 2 EGLR 1, (2000) 22 EG 134.
[2]   Clause 43.
[3]   *Dow Agrochemicals Ltd v E A Lane (North Lynn) Ltd* (1965) 192 Estates Gazette 737.
[4]   *Paddock Investments Ltd v Lory* [1975] 2 EGLR 5, 236 EG 803.

32.20 The courts have introduced an important check on the landlord's ability to rely upon Case B where they consider it to be inequitable for the landlord to do so by reason of estoppel[1]. Where the tenant supported an application for planning consent to convert farm buildings, as part of a renovation scheme under which his dairy parlour was to be re-located to new premises, the landlord was subsequently estopped from relying upon the planning consent to give notice to quit under Case B because the scheme had not been fully carried out as agreed between the landlord and the tenant.

It should also be noted that a Case B notice to quit will fail if the planning permission upon which it relies is subsequently quashed. This occurred in *R v Vale of Glamorgan District Council, ex p Adams*[2]. The freehold owners obtained planning permission to convert three barns into residential use. They served a notice to quit in relation to that part of the farm. The barns were essential to the continued use of the farm for its existing dairy business. The local authority applied the Planning Policy Guidance (PPG) and received the tenant's representations. The planning sub-committee granted permission following the planning officer's advice. The court held that the sub-committee had mis-directed itself in relation to the PPG as a consequence of the advice received. The permission was quashed and, as a result, the notice to quit failed.

1   *John v George* [1996] 1 EGLR 7, CA.
2   [2001] JPL 93, HC.

LANDSCAPING

32.21 Depending on what it consists of, landscaping will not normally be an agricultural use. If it is parkland which will be grazed, for example, by sheep or is open land which will be let off to a grazier, perhaps whilst building takes place on the remainder of the land, the grazing areas are likely to be construed as being used for an agricultural purpose, which will be fatal to a Case B notice to quit if such grazing areas are included within the notice to quit.

Further, in relation to landscaping involving trees, it is necessary to focus upon the relationship between Case B and s 27(3)(f). For example, it may be necessary to take land for private forestry (which does not need planning permission) by an application to the ALT in order to comply with requirements imposed by the planning authority which would not otherwise authorise yet further land to be the subject of a planning permission. This would introduce the potentially hazardous hurdle of having to persuade the ALT that a fair and reasonable landlord would insist on possession of that part of the land to be taken for private forestry. Such an application would clearly be strengthened on behalf of the landlord if it is intended to supplement a development falling within Case B. Should this arise, there can be no guarantee that the ALT would give consent to the operation of a notice to quit in respect of the part required for forestry.

RECOVERY OF POSSESSION UNDER CASE B

32.22 Even in the case where the recovery of possession by the landlord under Case B is considered to have an excellent prospect of success, the tenant's ability to delay and upset the timetable should not be underestimated.

A Case B notice to quit is vulnerable to challenge as follows.

(a)   A notice to quit under Case B may be challenged by the tenant demanding arbitration. This is the only means by which the tenant may contest a notice to quit given under Case B[1]. The tenant can challenge the notice to quit for 'appropriate issues' which are defined as 'any other reasons' stated in the notice[2]. The 'reasons' stated in the notice are subject to the exclusive jurisdiction of arbitration[3].

(b)   A tenant must serve a notice demanding arbitration on the landlord within one month after service of the relevant notice to quit. This time limit is inflexible and if the tenant seeks to demand arbitration out of time, he cannot[4].

(c)   The notice requiring arbitration will cease to be effective three months after the date of the service of that notice unless before the expiry of those three months either an arbitrator has been appointed by agreement between the parties or an application has been made to the President of the Royal Institution of Chartered Surveyors (RICS) for the appointment of an arbitrator in default of agreement between the parties[5].

(d)   The tenant's request for arbitration suspends the landlord's notice to quit[6]. The postponement will take effect until the arbitration is determined.

(e)   Under Sch 11 to the AHA 1986, although the arbitrator was required to issue his award within 56 days of his appointment[7], the President of the RICS was entitled to enlarge that time period whether it has expired or not[8]. If the case involved a point of law, a case stated to the county court may have followed[9]. Following the Regulatory Reform (Agricultural Tenancies) (England and Wales) Order 2006[10] coming into force, the arbitration procedure is governed by the Arbitration Act 1996[11].

(f)   Even if the landlord is successful under Case B, possession will still have to be obtained by court proceedings if the tenant refuses to go.

(g)   Whenever a valid incontestable notice to quit is served pursuant to Case B, and the landlord makes out the facts within Case B against the tenant and there is no other reason to impugn the notice, possession will ultimately be ordered. The court has no residual jurisdiction to grant relief[12].

(h)   All notices to quit may be challenged before the courts on the grounds of invalidity at common law, whether for ambiguity, inadequate period of notice or whatever. A tenant wishing to make a challenge on these general grounds may wait until the notice to quit has expired. The landlord brings possession proceedings to evict and the tenant can then challenge the notice. If the tenant is able to establish a genuine ground to impugn the effectiveness of the notice, the landlord has to start again which, in the context of the minimum of a 12-month period which applies generally to notices to quit under the AHA 1986, is obviously of major significance.

Cumulatively it can be seen that the tenant has some opportunity for creating delay within the legitimate workings of the procedures available to him.

[1] *Magdalen College, Oxford v Heritage* [1974] 1 WLR 441, CA, unless the tenant can establish fraud: *Rous v Michell* [1991] 1 All ER 676, CA – see para 31.15.
[2] The Agricultural Holdings (Arbitration on Notices) Order 1978, SI 1978/257, art 9.
[3] *Harding v Marshall* (1983) 267 Estates Gazette 161.
[4] SI 1978/257, art 9.
[5] SI 1978/257, added by the Agricultural Holdings (Arbitration on Notices) (Variation) Order 1984, SI 1984/1300.
[6] SI 1978/257, art 11.
[7] AHA 1986, Sch 11 para 14(1).
[8] AHA 1986, Sch 11 para 14(2).
[9] AHA 1986, Sch 11 para 26.
[10] SI 2006/2805.
[11] See Ch 47.
[12] *Parrish v Kinsey* [1983] 2 EGLR 13, 268 Estates Gazette 1113, CA.

32.23 Both basic and additional compensation for disturbance is payable to the tenant upon the tenant quitting the holding on the termination of the tenancy consequential upon the service of a Case B notice to quit[1].

[1] AHA 1986, ss 60 and 61. See para 38.47.

Chapter 33

OTHER METHODS
OF TERMINATION

GENERAL

33.1 The Agricultural Holdings Act 1986 (AHA 1986) grants security of tenure to tenants by imposing restrictions upon notices to quit given by landlords. It imposes no restrictions directly upon other methods of termination of tenancies[1] except for termination by effluxion of time, which normally is overridden by s 3 of the Act[2].

Indirectly these other methods of termination are effected, for example:

(a) where to implement them would preclude a tenant from claiming statutory compensation[3]; or
(b) where to implement them (possibly) might infringe public policy[4].

Every tenancy will end by effluxion of time, unless it is either prematurely terminated or continued by virtue of the provisions of the AHA 1986 or some other statutory provision. There are many ways to terminate a tenancy prematurely. They include:

(i)   service of a notice to quit;
(ii)   exercising a break clause;
(iii) forfeiture;
(iv)   disclaimer on behalf of an insolvent party;
(v)   merger;
(vi)   surrender.

In relation to some of these there are special provisions of issues which require consideration in relation to tenancies governed by the AHA 1986.

---

[1] Cf the position under the Rent Acts and the Landlord and Tenant Act 1954, Pt II.
[2] See para 20.7 and 33.2.
[3] *Coates v Diment* [1951] 1 All ER 890 and *Parry v Million Pigs Ltd* (1980) 260 Estates Gazette 281. See para 24.26.
[4] See para 19.50.

EFFLUXION OF TIME

33.2 At common law, a tenancy granted for a fixed period, whether one year, five years, or whatever period, is automatically terminated on the expiration of that period by 'effluxion of time'. Although the 'cesser of contract of tenancy by reason of effluxion of time' is included in the definition of termination in s 96(1) of the AHA 1986, this should be read in the context of the provisions of s 3 of the AHA 1986, in the case of a tenancy for two years or upwards, and s 2 of the AHA 1986 in respect of a tenancy which is for less than 'from year to year'[1].

[1]   This includes a tenancy for one year certain; see *Bernays v Prosser* [1963] 2 QB 592, [1963] 2 All ER 321, CA.

33.3 The exceptions to the general rule that a tenancy of an agricultural holding will not expire by effluxion of time, but will be made artificially to continue as a tenancy from year to year by operation of s 2 or 3 of the AHA 1986, are as follows:

(a)   A tenancy for more than one and less than two years[1] – this is known as a *Gladstone v Bower* tenancy. Such agreements are now spent. No such agreement can be created on or after 1 September 1995. Any such letting would be a farm business tenancy and being less than two years would terminate automatically without notice[2].

(b)   A tenancy for less than a year subject to prior approval of the Minister of Agriculture, Fisheries and Food under the AHA 1986, s 2[3] – such a tenancy falls outside the definition of an agricultural holding altogether. Again, this is now a spent provision.

(c)   A tenancy for a term certain of not less than two nor more than five years subject to prior approval of the Minister under the AHA 1986, s 5[4] – this provision is also spent.

(d)   A tenancy granted after 12 September 1984 for a term of two years or more when the tenant dies one year or more before the term date and the provisions of AHA 1986, s 4 apply[5].

The following exceptions are not true exceptions:

(i)   A lease for life or lives which is converted by s 149(6) of the Law of Property Act 1925 into a lease for 99 years determinable after the death of the tenant by a month's notice[6].

(ii)   A licence of any duration which is not converted into a tenancy from year to year because the Minister of Agriculture, Fisheries and Food gives his prior written consent under s 2 of the AHA 1986[7].

[1]   *Gladstone v Bower* [1960] 2 QB 384, [1960] 3 All ER 353, CA. For a discussion of such tenancies, see para 20.13.
[2]   See para 20.14.
[3]   For a discussion on such tenancies, see paras 18.15 and 20.16.
[4]   For a discussion on such tenancies, see para 20.15.
[5]   For a discussion on such tenancies, see paras 20.8, 20.18 and 20.20.
[6]   See para 20.8.
[7]   Such a licence expires by effluxion of time but is not an exception to the general rule because it never becomes a tenancy and the land never became an agricultural holding within the meaning of s 1 of the AHA 1986. In practice, it too is likely to be spent.

SURRENDER

Introduction

33.4 A surrender involves the yielding up of the tenancy by the tenant to his immediate landlord, with the consent of the immediate landlord, during the original term of the tenancy or any statutory continuation of it. It results in the absorption[1] of the tenant's leasehold interest in the landlord's freehold reversion, such that the lease is extinguished by operation of law[2]. The surrender operates solely between the tenant and his immediate landlord. It has no effect on any sub-tenancy or superior interest[3]. The surrender may be either express or implied by operation of law.

[1]   Per Lord Millett in *Barrett v Morgan* [2000] 2 AC 264, HL.
[2]   *Allen v Rochdale Borough Council* [2000] Ch 221, CA.
[3]   *Leek and Moorlands Building Society v Clark* [1952] 2 QB 788, CA.

Agreement to surrender

33.5 An agreement between a landlord and a tenant of an agricultural holding protected by the AHA 1986 for the tenant to surrender his tenancy to the landlord is enforceable at common law. The AHA 1986 does not expressly impose any restrictions upon the freedom of the parties to contract to surrender and to effect a surrender by deed or operation of law. Following the decision of the House of Lords in *Johnson v Moreton*[1], doubts have been expressed as to whether an agreement to surrender in the future (as opposed to an immediate surrender) would be enforceable or whether it would be held to be unenforceable as being contrary to public policy[2].

In *Elsden v Pick*[3], the Court of Appeal decided that defect in a notice to quit could be waived by the recipient. It was commented, strictly obiter, by Buckley LJ, that an agreement to surrender within one year would be enforceable. It is open to question as to whether an executory agreement to surrender would be enforced if the tenant sought to resile from it before completion[4]. It is submitted that an agreement to surrender, entered into at the time of the grant of the tenancy governed by the AHA 1986, would almost certainly be found to be contrary to public policy[5].

[1]   [1980] AC 37.
[2]   See para 19.50.
[3]   [1980] 3 All ER 235. [1981] WLR 898.
[4]   Also see, *Short Bros (Plant) Ltd v Edwards* (1978) 249 Estates Gazette 539, where the Court of Appeal expressed doubts as to the enforceability of an agreement to surrender under the Agricultural Holdings Act 1948.
[5]   Applying the principles specified in *Johnson v Moreton* [1980] AC 37.

Surrender by operation of law

33.6 An express surrender must, to be effective at law, be by deed[1] and accompanied by the tenant giving up possession. The basis of surrender by operation of law is estoppel. It arises where the tenant deliberately does some act which is inconsistent with the continuation of the tenancy and the landlord concurs or acquiesces. In those circumstances, it would be inequitable for the parties to rely upon the argument that there had been no surrender by deed in order to assert that the term of the tenancy was still continuing.

Surrender by operation of law will take place irrespective of the actual intentions of the parties[2] and despite the absence of any form of documentation. There is no requirement for the tenant actually to deliver up vacant possession of the holding. It is established that the following acts will give rise to a surrender by operation of law:

(a)   the tenant vacating the premises and handing back the keys to the landlord who accepts them unconditionally and not by mistake[3];

(b)   the grant by the landlord, and the acceptance by the tenant, of a new tenancy of the premises, provided that it is a valid tenancy; it commences during the term of the old tenancy and it is not granted subject to the old tenancy;

(c)   the variation of the tenancy by an increase of the premises demised[4] or the increase of the length of the contractual term[5];

(d)   the variation of the tenancy by the insertion of a tenant's option to extend the original contractual term[6].

[1]   Law of Property Act 1925, s 52(1).
[2]   'This does not depend on the intention of parties but upon the impossibility of the two demises co-existing', per Buckley J in *Jenkin R Lewis & Son Ltd v Kerman* [1971] Ch 477.
[3]   *John Laing Construction Ltd v Amber Pass Ltd* [2004] 2 EGLR 128; *Bellcourt Estates Ltd v Adesina* [2005] EWCA Civ 208, [2005] 2 EGLR 33, [2005] 18 EG 150.
[4]   *Jenkin R Lewis & Son Ltd v Kerman* [1971] Ch 477; *Well Barn Farming Ltd v Backhouse* [2005] EWHC 1520 (Ch), [2005] 3 EGLR 109.
[5]   *Re Savile Settled Estates* [1931] 2 Ch 210.
[6]   *Re Savile Settled Estates* [1931] 2 Ch 210, *Baker v Merckel* [1960] 1 QB 657, CA; *Friends Provident Life Office v British Railways Board* (1995) 73 P & CR 9, CA.

33.7 If the increase in the extent of the demised premises gives rise to a surrender and re-grant, it raises the question as to the impact of a reduction in the extent of the holding. This may come about in two distinct ways. First, by the parties entering into a surrender of part of the holding. Second, by the parties varying the demise by a deed of variation. A surrender of part, whether or not accompanied by a consequential reduction in rent, will not give rise to an implied surrender of the whole of the lease and the grant of a new tenancy of the retained portion. The doctrine of implied surrender and re-grant is founded on the essential inconsistency between the intended variation and the continuation of the original tenancy. There is no inconsistency between a surrender of part and the continuation of the original tenancy, albeit without the part which has been surrendered.

It has been suggested that the case of *Jones v Bridgman*[1] is authority for the proposition that a surrender of part can give rise to an implied surrender and re-grant. It is submitted that this is a misconstruction, notwithstanding the fact that there is a statement in support of the proposition in *Re Savile Settled Estates*[2], where Maugham J expressed the view, albeit obiter, that 'giving up' a part of the premises, in conjunction with a reduction in the rent paid, could cause a surrender by operation of law. However, this runs contrary to the more detailed consideration given to the issue by Buckley J in *Jenkin R Lewis & Son Ltd v Kerman*[3], where the distinction between a surrender of part and a variation which causes a reduction of the demise is drawn.

Following termination of a tenancy under the AHA 1986 by surrender (or otherwise), s 83 will apply to the tenant's claim for compensation and the landlord's claim for dilapidation[4]. The tenant will not be able to claim compensation for disturbance, his tenancy not having been terminated by a notice to quit[5].

A surrender does not prejudice the rights of sub-tenants or mortgagees[6].

1   (1878) 39 LT 500.
2   [1931] 2 Ch 210. Also see *Holme v Brunskill* (1878) 3 QBD 495, CA; *Saunders v Ralph* (1993) 66 P & CR 335. See para 35.16. See also Bignall and Dollar, 'Landlord and Tenant Review' (2006) Vol 10, Issue 2.
3   [1971] Ch 477.
4   AHA 1986, s 83. See para 41.3 ff.
5   AHA 1986, ss 60 and 63. See para 38.47.
6   *Mellor v Watkins* (1874) LR 9 QB 400.

FORFEITURE

33.8 The agricultural holdings legislation imposes no express restriction on the landlord's right to forfeit or to sue for damages for breach of covenant during the term[1]. Accordingly, with one qualification, a landlord is free to sue for forfeiture for non-payment of rent or other breach of covenant condition. It is an essential pre-requisite that there is a valid forfeiture clause.

The qualification to the general proposition that a landlord of an agricultural holding may pursue the common law right to seek forfeiture of the tenancy for breach is that the forfeiture clause in the tenancy agreement must provide for the landlord to give sufficient prior notice of his intention to exercise his right of forfeiture to enable the tenant to give notice of his intention to claim compensation on quitting. Certain forms of claim for compensation require the tenant to give notice not less than one month prior to termination of the tenancy of his intention to claim[2].

The view was expressed, rather tentatively, in the seventh edition of this book, that it would be prudent to provide in a forfeiture clause in a lease or tenancy agreement that the right to re-enter should only be exercised by the landlord after giving a minimum of, say, six weeks' prior notice. It has now been held that not merely would it be prudent to provide that the right to forfeit should be exercisable on the expiry of such notice given by the landlord, but that it is essential if the forfeiture clause is to be relied upon as being a valid and enforceable clause[3].

If there is a valid forfeiture clause, the landlord must comply with the provisions of the general law and serve a notice under s 146 of the Law of Property Act 1925 for a breach other than the non-payment of rent. The tenant will have all the usual remedies available to tenants, such as the right to seek relief from forfeiture, available to him[4].

If a tenant fails to pay his rent or commits some other breach of covenant, the landlord can elect whether to exercise his right to forfeit or his right to give notice to quit based on the tenant's failure[5]. If he has given a notice to quit which is going to take effect under the AHA 1986 he may decide not to wait until its expiry if the rent remains unpaid or the breach, if it is a continuing one, remains unremedied. He may commence proceedings for forfeiture in the hope of obtaining earlier possession.

Historically, forfeiture has been sparingly used by landlords of agricultural holdings, particularly in relation to the non-payment of rent, because of the harsher remedy available of the giving of a notice to quit pursuant to Case D of Sch 3 to the AHA 1986 following the giving of a prior notice to remedy or, in particular, notice to pay rent.

Moreover, forfeiture involves (in most cases) the exercise of the court's discretion to reinstate a tenancy, in contrast to the position applying in relation to a notice to quit[6]. Forfeiture is the only available remedy for a landlord in the case of a fixed-term lease which still has some time to run because notice to quit cannot be given more than two years before the expiration of the fixed term due to the restriction imposed by s 3 of the AHA 1986.

[1]   *Kent v Conniff* [1952] 2 TLR 209; affd [1953] 1 QB 361, [1953] 1 All ER 155, CA.
[2]   Eg for 'high farming' under s 70 of the AHA 1986 and the removal of tenant's fixtures under s 10.
[3]   *Parry v Million Pigs Ltd* (1980) 260 Estates Gazette 281 founded upon the earlier decisions of *Re Disraeli's Agreement* [1939] Ch 382, [1938] 4 All ER 658 and *Coates v Diment* [1951] 1 All ER 890 which related to notices to quit.
[4]   See Ch 13 for a more detailed analysis of forfeiture.
[5]   Provided the necessary preliminary notice has been given.
[6]   See Ch 13.

33.9 In the case of forfeiture for bankruptcy of the tenant, or the taking in execution of the tenant's interest, s 146 of the Law of Property Act 1925 does not apply[1].

A forfeiture disguised as a surrender is nevertheless a forfeiture in respect of which due notice under s 146 must be given and against which a claim for relief is available[2].

[1]   The Law of Property Act 1925, s 146(9). This is because the personality of the tenant of an agricultural holding is important. See *Earl Bathurst v Fine* [1974] 2 All ER 1160, [1974] 1 WLR 905, CA. Note, in the case of bankruptcy the tenant's trustee in bankruptcy may, alternatively, disclaim the tenancy. See also para 13.24.
[2]   See *Plymouth Corporation v Harvey* [1971] 1 All ER 623, [1971] 1 WLR 549, in which a deed of surrender was delivered in escrow to an independent solicitor on terms that he should deliver it to the landlord if he was not satisfied that by a certain date certain breaches of the tenant's covenants had been remedied. It was held that this was a device to circumvent the security granted by s 146 of the Law of Property Act 1925 and as such was ineffective.

MERGER, DENIAL OF TITLE AND DISCLAIMER

33.10 The other methods of termination of the tenancy at common law apply without special provision applicable to agricultural holdings in the same way as under the Agricultural Tenancies Act 1995. Likewise, disclaimer may arise on the insolvency of the tenant[1].

The denial of the landlord's title by the tenant allows the landlord to forfeit the lease even in the absence of an express forfeiture provision[2].

[1] See para 14.3 ff.
[2] See Ch 13.

Part IV

SUCCESSION ON DEATH OR RETIREMENT OF TENANT

Contents

Chapter 34

INTRODUCTION TO SUCCESSION

GENERAL

34.1 Until 14 November 1976, there was no statutory entitlement for anybody on the death of the tenant to apply for the grant of a new tenancy in succession to the previous tenant as of right. The effect of the death of the tenant upon his tenancy was that the tenancy could be terminated by the landlord by giving notice to quit for the reason stated in what was then s 24(2)(g) of the Agricultural Holdings Act 1948 (AHA 1948) (now Case G of Sch 3 of the Agricultural Holdings Act 1986 (AHA 1986))[1]. Provided the landlord stated in the notice to quit that it was given by reason of the death of the tenant, and provided the notice to quit was given within three months of the date of the death of the tenant 'with whom the contract of tenancy was made'[2], the tenancy was automatically terminated on the expiration of the notice. The right of the personal representatives of the deceased tenant to give a counter-notice was excluded and there was no right for any member of the deceased tenant's family to retain security of tenure.

If no such notice to quit was given within the three-month period, the right to give a notice under Case G was lost for all time since the tenancy then vested in the personal representatives of the deceased tenant, who were not the tenant 'with whom the contract of tenancy was made'[3]. If the tenant had assigned his tenancy, whether or not in breach of the terms of the tenancy agreement, the assignee could be dispossessed by notice given on the death of the original tenant[4], even though the tenant in occupation was still alive.

Succession provisions are now contained in the AHA 1986. Part IV of the Act entitles certain close relatives of tenant farmers whose tenancies are protected by the AHA 1986 to obtain by way of statutory succession a new protected tenancy of the holding on the death or retirement of the original tenant. The qualifications which a close relative must possess in order to claim the benefit of the succession provisions, and the circumstances in which a claim can be successfully made, are narrowly defined. In order to understand the present law it is necessary to explain its historical context.

[1] See para 31.90.
[2] AHA 1948, s 24(2)(g).

3   *Costagliola v Bunting* [1958] 1 All ER 846, [1958] 1 WLR 580.
4   *Clarke v Hall* [1961] 2 QB 331, [1961] 2 All ER 365, in which s 24(2)(b) of the AHA 1948
    was interpreted to produce this anomalous result, even though the tenancy might have
    been assigned many years before and might have been subject to intermediate assignments.
    The effect of the decision was that the security of tenure of the sitting tenant in these
    circumstances was dependent on the event with which he was wholly disconnected,
    namely, the death of a stranger.

THE AGRICULTURE (MISCELLANEOUS PROVISIONS) ACT 1976

34.2 The Agriculture (Miscellaneous Provisions) Act 1976 (A(MP)A 1976)
introduced succession on death (but not on retirement) and provided the
scheme for succession which, subject to amendment, particularly to the
commercial unit occupation test of eligibility provided by the Agricultural
Holdings Act 1984 (AHA 1984), is otherwise very largely the scheme as
re-enacted in the consolidating AHA 1986.

The A(MP)A 1976 changed the wording of section 24(2)(g) of the AHA 1948.
Section 16 of the A(MP)A 1976 provided that the right to give notice to quit
on death accrued *not* on the death of the tenant (or the sole surviving tenant
where there had been joint tenants) 'with whom the contract of tenancy was
made' and provided for the right to arise on the death of the tenant for the
time being, ie 'the tenant under the contract of tenancy'. Additionally, the
definition of 'tenant' in the case of a notice to quit on death was changed so as
to exclude executors and other persons deriving title by operation of law[1].
Therefore, the decision in *Costagliola v Bunting*[2] would still apply, albeit for
different reasons under the revised law, in the event of failure to give notice to
quit on death and in consequence the tenancy devolving on the personal
representatives of the deceased tenant.

Although following the A(MP)A 1976 the landlord still had his incontestable
right to terminate the deceased tenant's tenancy, provisions were introduced
for any one or more of a limited class of close relations of the deceased tenant,
who satisfied the eligibility tests laid down in the 1976 Act, to make
application to the Agricultural Land Tribunal (ALT) for the area in which the
holding was situated for a new tenancy to take effect on termination of the old
tenancy[3].

The eligibility tests to be satisfied by the successful applicant can be summarised as:

(a)   close relationship to the deceased tenant, as defined in the A(MP)A
      1976; and
(b)   derivation of principal source of livelihood from the holding for at least
      five of the seven years preceding death; and
(c)   the commercial unit occupation test, intended to ensure that the
      applicant does not occupy sufficient other agricultural land to enable
      him to make a living without the subject holding.

Apart from considering whether the applicant had satisfied the eligibility tests,
the ALT had also to decide if the applicant was suitable. If so, the ALT was

obliged to direct that the applicant should be granted a new tenancy unless it granted consent to the landlord for the operation of the notice to quit served following death.

The A(MP)A 1976 made provision for the possibility of there being several applicants and the basis on which the ALT should treat such applications. It also made provision for the landlord, where notice to quit had been given by him, to apply for consent to the operation of his notice to quit, as if the notice to quit was one of the class which did not specify an incontestable ground[4].

The A(MP)A 1976 also introduced provisions for arbitration as to the rent and the terms of the new tenancy and for destroying the old tenancy in the event of there being no (or no effective) notice to quit given by the landlord.

Regulations were passed pursuant to the A(MP)A 1976 setting out procedures which had to be adopted by applicants and by the landlord to implement the provisions of the A(MP)A 1976.

1   Cf the definition in AHA 1986, s 96 of 'tenant' for all other purposes.
2   [1958] 1 All ER 846, [1958] 1 WLR 580.
3   These were contained in Pt II of the A(MP)A 1976.
4   For a commentary on such notices to quit, see Chs 30 and 31.

THE AGRICULTURAL HOLDINGS ACT 1984

34.3 The AHA 1984 came about after the Northfield Report[1] recommended that the Government and the organisations involved in the agricultural industry should collaborate to promote amendments to the AHA 1948. This resulted in the so-called NFU/CLA package[2].

The early experience of the working of the A(MP)A 1976 showed that the eligibility tests in particular were failing to eliminate applicants who were never intended to qualify for statutory succession, particularly those who were already adequately provided with land of their own, but who were nevertheless able to satisfy the commercial unit occupation test of eligibility. Additionally, there were numerous applicants who were disqualified by reason of their failure to satisfy the commercial unit occupation test who were inadequately provided with land, independently of the subject holding. As a consequence, the AHA 1984 substantially altered the commercial unit occupation test. The principal source of livelihood test was also found to operate unsatisfactorily and harshly, particularly in the case of widows. It too was revised by the AHA 1984.

Most radically, the AHA 1984 introduced provisions for the tenant to serve a retirement notice to take effect on or after his attaining the age of 65, or in the event of his being permanently incapacitated. This notice was required to nominate his successor who might then apply to the ALT for the new tenancy as if the tenant had died. The provisions relating to retirement notices included the important proviso that if the applicant failed in his application, the retiring tenant nevertheless retained the tenancy until his death.

34.3 *Introduction to succession*

The AHA 1984 was passed by Parliament on 12 July 1984 and came into force for the most part on 12 September 1984, although part was 'deemed' to have come into force on 1 March 1984[3].

1   See para 1.13.
2   See para 1.14.
3   AHA 1984, s 11(2).

THE AGRICULTURAL HOLDINGS ACT 1986

34.4 The rules relating to succession, both on death and retirement, are now complex, but they are of major importance to both landlords and tenants alike.

All the provisions of the A(MP)A 1976 and the AHA 1984 were repealed and re-enacted in the current agricultural holdings statute, the AHA 1986.

THE AGRICULTURAL TENANCIES ACT 1995

34.5 Although protected tenancies being tenancies of agricultural holdings as defined by the AHA 1986 can generally no longer come into existence after 1 September 1995, exceptions are provided in s 4 of the Agricultural Tenancies Act 1995. These include succession tenancies. The succession legislation contained in Pt IV of the AHA 1986 is preserved and remains applicable to those tenancies falling within the AHA 1986 which carry with them succession rights.

Chapter 35

SUCCESSION ON DEATH

APPLICATION OF SUCCESSION RIGHTS

35.1 The general rule is that all tenancies of agricultural holdings carry with them succession rights and that, on the death or retirement of the tenant, an eligible person may apply for succession. The exceptions to that general rule are contained in ss 34, 36(2), 37 and 38 of the Agricultural Holdings Act 1986 (AHA 1986).

Tenancies granted after 12 July 1984

35.2 Section 34(1) of the AHA 1986 provides that tenancies granted on or after 12 July 1984 do not carry with them any rights of succession, subject to the following exceptions where succession rights are available as for tenancies granted before 12 July 1984.

If the tenancy was granted as the result of a direction by the Agricultural Land Tribunal

35.3 This exception was introduced to preserve the rule that there were to be two possible generations entitled to succession[1]. If the original tenancy was granted before 12 July 1984, but after that date a tenant acquired a tenancy as a first succession tenancy following the direction of the Agricultural Land Tribunal (ALT), then his successors could apply on his death for a second succession tenancy, notwithstanding the fact that the first succession tenancy was granted after 12 July 1984[2].

---

[1] See para 35.14.
[2] See AHA 1986, ss 34(1)(b)(i), 39 and 53 which provide for such directions by the ALT. Note, also, AHA 1986, 37(2) and the deeming provisions where no direction has been obtained.

Where the tenancy was granted after a direction of the ALT by agreement between landlord and tenant and before the ALT direction took effect

35.4 This exception deals with the situation where the landlord and tenant agree upon the grant of a new tenancy which is not strictly in accordance with the direction that was made by the ALT resulting in the tenant taking his tenancy by a direct grant from the landlord in accordance with s 45(6) of the AHA 1986. The ALT's direction must provide for the new tenancy to start on the date on which the landlord's Case G notice to quit takes effect, or, if no such notice has been given, on the first anniversary of the tenancy, not less than 12 months after the death of the former tenant. However, on some occasions, the landlord and the new successor tenant agree that the new tenancy shall come into effect before that date and enter into a new tenancy agreement. Such an agreement is not strictly in accordance with the direction of the ALT and would not fall within s 34(1)(b)(i) of the AHA 1986[1]. This second exception therefore protects the successor tenant from inadvertently destroying the rights of his successor to a second succession[2].

[1] See paras 35.3 and 35.5.
[2] AHA 1986, s 34(1)(b)(ii).

Where the parties contract into succession

35.5 Provisions in tenancies created before 12 July 1984, which purported to exclude succession, were likely to be found to be contrary to public policy in accordance with the rule in *Johnson v Moreton*[1]. However, tenancies created between 12 July 1984 and 1 September 1995, when the Agricultural Tenancies Act 1995 (ATA 1995) came into force, were, and are, prima facie without rights to succession[2]. Section 34(1)(b)(iii) of the AHA 1986 enabled the parties to contract into succession expressly if they wished to do so provided that the tenancy was granted by a written contract indicating (in whatever terms) that the succession provisions of the AHA 1986 were to apply. A written contract of tenancy indicating (in whatever terms) that s 2(1) of the Agricultural Holdings Act 1984 (AHA 1984) is not to apply is to be taken to be within s 34(1)(b)(iii) of the AHA 1986[3].

There is a parallel provision in s 4(1) of the ATA 1995 to the effect that the AHA 1986 shall not apply in relation to any tenancy beginning on or after 1 September 1995 unless (among other things) it is granted by a written contract of tenancy entered into before that date which indicates (in whatever terms) that the AHA 1986 should apply to it. In these two respects Parliament is expressly authorising the parties to contract-into the AHA 1986 or the relevant part of it according to their own wishes.

Whether parties can contract-in or contract-out otherwise is uncertain and highly doubtful. The well-known decision of the House of Lords in *Johnson v Moreton*[4] established that the parties to an agricultural tenancy cannot, on public interest grounds, contract-out of statutory security of tenure. This decision was followed by the Court of Appeal in *Featherstone v Staples*[5] where a landowner had granted a tenancy to himself and his farming partner.

A clause in the partnership agreement entitling the landowning-partner to block an attempt to claim security of tenure was held to be unlawful.

It is submitted that the strict rules relating to statutory succession fall within the same broad ambit of public interest. For example, as regards any attempt at widening or narrowing of the meaning of 'close relative', it is submitted that this cannot be achieved in any proceedings which end up before the ALT. The ALT must exercise its jurisdiction according to the terms of the AHA 1986. If it is presented with someone who is not a close relative, for example a grandchild who has never been treated by a deceased tenant as a child of the family in relation to his or her marriage, the ALT could not make a declaration in that person's favour. Similarly, if a would-be applicant had agreed with the landlord at some time in the past that he or she was not, for example, a child of the deceased it is submitted that such person would not be prevented in due course from claiming before the ALT that he or she is the deceased's child.

Correspondingly, there is a certain danger for landlords if they enter into a voluntary agreement under s 37(2) of the AHA 1986 with an outgoing tenant and someone whom everyone believes to be a close relative but who later turns out not to be. It might be argued in those circumstances that the new tenant to whom a new tenancy is granted or the current tenancy is assigned is estopped from asserting that he or she was not a close relative. Here the particular circumstances would be relevant. It might be possible that one party or the other might be entitled to set the agreement aside on the ground of fundamental mistake of fact.

Similarly, there may be concerns in relation to agreements between the parties which might vary the test of eligibility, except in so far as those agreements are authorised under the The Regulatory Reform (Agricultural Tenancies) (England and Wales) Order 2006 (RRO 2006)[6], How parties might arrive at these bargains is a matter for them, and might depend upon their different aspirations. Whether they can enforce agreements which the legislation does not expressly permit is extremely doubtful.

[1]   [1980] AC 37, HL. See para 19.50.
[2]   AHA 1986, s 38(1)(b)(iii).
[3]   AHA 1986, Sch 13 para 1(2).
[4]   [1980] AC 37, HL.
[5]   [1986] 1 WLR 861.
[6]   SI 2006/2805.

If the new tenancy was granted to an existing tenant of the holding or a substantial part of it

35.6 This exception protects the position of a tenant whose tenancy was granted prior to 12 July 1984 but who, for example, agrees to additional land being included in the tenancy which, as a consequence of the operation of law, results in a surrender and re-grant[1]. Such a new tenancy, if created after

12 July 1984, would have destroyed the pre-existing rights of succession in the absence of this exception. Accumulated rights of succession are therefore preserved in such circumstances.

[1] *Jenkin R Lewis & Son Ltd v Kerman* [1971] Ch 477, [1970] 1 All ER 833, CA. See para 33.4 ff in relation to surrender and re-grant generally.

35.7 The exception only applies where the tenant was a tenant of the holding or of any agricultural holding which comprised the whole or a substantial part of the land comprised in the holding[1].

As a consequence of the enactment of s 4(1)(g) of the ATA 1995[2], an express surrender and re-grant, on or after 19 October 2006, will not result in loss of AHA 1986 protection. If the tenancy in question for succession arose as a consequence of the operation of s 4(1)(g) of the ATA 1995, then a substantial part of the land comprised in the holding means a substantial part determined by reference to either area or value[3].

The addition or removal of land gives rise to issues. The boundaries of farms are always changing. Land is added. Land is taken back. In relation to tenancies which do not fall within paras (a), (b) or (c) of s 37(8) of the AHA 1986, a new tenancy granted or obtained under s 37(1) or (2) will count as a succession whether or not it 'relates to' the whole of the land held by the previous tenant[4]. It is submitted that this means that the new tenant can take part only of the land held by the previous tenant and still be counted as a successor. However, where the tenancy includes land additional to that held by the previous tenant the result may be different. Both subsections (1) and (2) are concerned with new tenancies 'of the holding or of a related holding'. The expression 'related holding' means 'any agricultural holding comprising the whole or a substantial part of the land comprised in the holding'[5]. The word 'comprising' in this context may mean 'consisting of'. On that basis it would not include a letting of additional land. But in s 37(4)(a) of the AHA 1986 the language is more flexible. A tenancy will certainly 'relate to' the whole of the land held by the previous tenant if it comprises that land and no more. Likewise it will 'relate to' part of that land, if it comprises merely some part of it. If the tenancy includes the whole or part of the land held by the previous tenant plus additional land which the previous tenant did not hold, it is submitted that it is on a fine balance that it may still be said to 'relate to' the whole or part of the land held by the previous tenant. Otherwise, the addition of the smallest extra piece of land to the new tenancy would prevent it from counting as a succession. It is suggested that a court could be easily persuaded that this was the intention of Parliament. It is too technical an interpretation.

As to the meaning of the word 'substantial' in this context, some assistance is provided in *Thomson v Church Comrs for England*[6] where a deputy judge of the High Court had to consider whether an ALT had made an error of law in deciding that an applicant for a tenancy by way of succession following the death of her brother had not satisfied the principal source of livelihood condition 'to a material extent' for the purposes of s 41(1)(b) of the AHA 1986. In para 17 of his judgment the deputy judge held that:

'Whether the livelihood condition is satisfied to a material extent is a question of assessment, judgment and appreciation for the ALT'.

It is suggested that exactly the same approach is to be adopted to the word 'substantial'. There is some jurisprudence under the Rent Acts which illuminate the way in which the courts should approach the word 'substantial'. Section 2 of the Rent Act 1968 (following earlier Rent Acts) excluded from statutory protection any tenancy under which the rent included payments in respect of (among other things) the use of furniture of the amount of rent fairly attributable to the use of furniture 'forms a substantial part of the whole rent'. In *Palser v Grinling; Property Holding Co Ltd v Mischeff*[7], it was held by Viscount Simon in the House of Lords that the meaning of the word 'substantial' must be left to the discretion of the Judge 'to decide as best he can according to the circumstances in each case ...'. He suggested that one of the primary meanings of the word is equivalent to 'considerable, solid or big'. This decision was followed by the Court of Appeal in *Woodward v Docherty*[8], where Scarman LJ stressed that the matter should be governed by commonsense consideration. No particular percentage is of any assistance. Whether part of a holding forms a substantial part of it must be judged as a question of fact on a case-by-case basis.

[1]   AHA 1986, s 34(1)(b)(iv).
[2]   See para 3.14.
[3]   AHA 1986, s 34(3), inserted by the RRO 2006, SI 2006/2805, art 4(1).
[4]   AHA 1986, s 37(4).
[5]   AHA 1986, s 35(2).
[6]   [2006] EWHC 1773 (Admin), (2006) 43 EG 180.
[7]   [1948] AC 291, HL.
[8]   [1974] 1 WLR 966.

Fixed-term tenancies of two years or more

35.8 If the tenant, at the date of his death, held under the terms of a lease or tenancy agreement for a fixed term of years, of which more than 27 months remained unexpired at the date of death, then no application for succession may be made[1]. No notice to quit can be given by the landlord either in that case. The tenancy will vest in the personal representatives of the deceased tenant and will terminate either on the original expiry dates or on the first anniversary of that date[2].

The period of 27 months is arrived at by virtue of the fact that s 3 of the AHA 1986 prevents a landlord from giving notice to quit more than two years before the term date (ie 24 months) and the further three months is the three months provided for by Case G of Sch 3 to the AHA 1986 in which the landlord can give such a notice to quit.

There is a slight inconsistency here as the three-month period provided for in Case G runs not from the date of death but from the date on which either a written notice of the tenant's death is given or notice of an application for succession is given to the landlord, whichever is the earlier event[3]. That, in practice, would add up to more than 27 months. Nevertheless, the exclusion from succession is expressed to apply only to a tenancy with more than 27 months of the term remaining unexpired at the date of death.

A lease or tenancy created after 1 September 1995 is wholly outside the AHA 1986 altogether[4].

[1] AHA 1986, s 36(2)(a).
[2] AHA 1986, s4. There is a limited need for s 36(2)(a) of the AHA 1986 in that s4 applies only to tenancies granted on or after 12 September 1984, whereas s 36(2)(a) applies to tenancies granted after 12 July 1984.
[3] See para 31.90 ff.
[4] Unless s 4 of the ATA 1995 otherwise provides, see para 3.4 ff.

Fixed-term tenancies of between one and two years

35.9 A tenancy for a fixed term of more than one, but less than two years, known as a *Gladstone v Bower* tenancy, has always fallen outside the security of tenure provisions of the Agricultural Holdings Act 1948 and subsequently the AHA 1986[1]. Such a tenancy did not have rights to succession[2].

[1] *Gladstone v Bower* [1960] 2 QB 384, [1960] 3 All ER 353, and for a commentary on so called '*Gladstone v Bower* tenancies', see para 20.13.
[2] AHA 1986, s 36(2)(b). *Gladstone v Bower* tenancies have not been capable of being granted since the ATA 1995 came into force on 1 September 1995.

Tenancies subject to pre-death notice to quit

35.10 If, before the death of the tenant whose tenancy is potentially subject to an application for succession, the landlord had given notice to quit, and the various disputes procedures available had either been gone through or had been forgone, so that the notice to quit had become 'final', then even though it had not come into effect at the date of death of the tenant and the old tenancy was still subsisting, no application may be made for succession[1].

[1] AHA 1986, s 38.

35.11 The ways in which a notice to quit can become 'final' are contained in s 38(1) to (3) inclusive of the AHA 1986:

(a) In the case of a notice to quit to which Sch 3 to the AHA 1986 does not apply[1], notice to quit, either the month for giving a counter-notice under s 26(1) of the AHA 1986 has expired or, if a counter-notice has been given, the ALT has consented to the operation of the notice to quit[2].

(b) In the case of notices to quit given on the grounds specified in Cases B, D or E[3] of Sch 3 to the AHA 1986, either the time in which to give a demand for arbitration has expired, with no such demand having been given, or, if the demand has been given, the arbitrator has upheld the validity of the notice to quit and has made his award, or in some other way (for example, by agreement) the notice has been upheld. In the case of a notice to quit following a notice to remedy requiring the doing of work, if the matter has been referred to the ALT, then the ALT must have consented to the operation of the notice before the right to apply for succession is denied[4].

(c) In the case of notices to quit given on the grounds specified in Cases C or F[5], because there is no procedure for either giving a counter-notice or a demand for arbitration, the statutory exclusion applies if the notice in question is simply a valid notice to quit. This cannot be tested by counter-notice or demand for arbitration but will be determined by the ALT as a preliminary issue following an application after such a notice[6].

It should be noted that in the case of succession on retirement, the provisions excluding succession following notice to quit are different and more restrictive[7].

[1] Ie Special Cases: see para 31.1.
[2] AHA 1986, s 38(1)(a) and (b).
[3] Case A is omitted because smallholdings are excluded from succession, see para 31.18.
[4] AHA 1986, s 38(3).
[5] For a commentary on notices to quit given under Case C and F, see paras 31.21 and 31.88.
[6] AHA 1986, s 38(2).
[7] AHA 1986, s 51. See Ch 36.

Smallholdings

35.12 The Agriculture (Miscellaneous Provisions) Act 1976 provided that certain forms of smallholding should not be subject to rights of succession. The Court of Appeal held in *Saul v Norfolk County Council*[1], that since this exception only applied to tenancies of smallholdings granted 'pursuant to Part III' of the Agriculture Act 1970 and that it did not apply to smallholdings created before 1970. That anomaly has now been corrected by s 38(4) of the AHA 1986 which provides that any agricultural holding held by a tenant from a smallholdings authority or the Minister for the purposes of smallholdings within the meaning of Pt III of the Agriculture Act 1970 is to be excluded, whether the tenancy was granted before or after the commencement of Part III of the 1970 Act.

A smallholding which does not fall within that definition and is not a statutory smallholding carries with it succession rights as for any other form of agricultural holding[2].

[1] [1984] QB 559, [1984] 2 All ER 489.
[2] See para 20.19.

Certain charitable trusts

35.13 A tenancy granted by trustees, in whom the land is vested on charitable trusts, 'the sole or principal object of which is the settlement or employment in agriculture of persons who have served in any of Her Majesty's naval, military or air forces' is excluded from succession[1]. Such charitable trusts are now extremely rare. They are a relic of the desire to resettle returning World War veterans to a 'land fit for heroes ...' and are a further example of the war-time origins of the agricultural holdings legislation generally. It should be noted that land which is held of landlords who are charitable trustees, but whose charitable trusts do not have such sole or principal objects, still carry rights of succession[2].

1   AHA 1986, s 38(5).
2   AHA 1986, s 38(5).

Two previous successions

35.14 The issue which generally creates greatest difficulty in relation to whether succession rights are available at all is the two previous successions rule. The Agriculture (Miscellaneous Provisions) Act 1976 provided that there were to be two potential succession tenancies, ie on the death of the original tenant a first succession tenancy could be obtained by direction of the ALT, and on the death of that tenant, a second succession tenancy could be obtained similarly. On the death of the second successor, no further rights of succession were available to the close relations of the second successor tenant[1].

The statutory scheme under the AHA 1986 continues to allow for two successions of the tenancy. This principle is contained in s 37 of the AHA 1986. The terms of s 37 of the AHA 1986 are not straightforward, but provide that no application for succession can be made if, on each of the last two occasions when a sole surviving tenant of the holding died:

(a)   either a tenancy of the holding (or a related holding) was obtained by a direction of the ALT; or
(b)   a tenancy of the holding was granted by the landlord to a close relative of the deceased who had become the sole remaining applicant for a direction of the ALT. An ALT application must have been made if the tenancy is to count as one succession under the AHA 1986, and the successor must be the only, or sole remaining, applicant for a direction[2].

It should be noted that the provision contained in s 37 of the AHA 1986 applies also to a 'related holding'. A related holding is defined as 'any agricultural holding comprising the whole or a substantial part of the land comprised in the holding'[3]. The purpose of this provision was to prevent any problem arising as a consequence of any minor variation in the size and composition of the holding from time to time.

In order to encourage agreed successions, the Agricultural Holdings Act 1984 (AHA 1984) introduced amendments enabling the grant of new tenancies which could count as one succession under the statutory scheme. Where, on any occasion prior to the date of the tenant's death, as a result of an agreement between the landlord and the tenant for the time being of the holding or of a related holding, the holding or a related holding was let under a tenancy granted by the landlord or by virtue of an assignment of the current tenancy to a person who, if the tenant had died immediately before the grant or assignment would have been his close relative, that occasion is deemed to be a succession under the statutory scheme[4]. A 'close relative' of a deceased tenant means the wife, husband, brother, sister or child of the deceased or any person who, in the case of any marriage to which the deceased was at any time a party, was treated by the deceased as a child of the family in relation to that marriage[5].

Difficulties can arise in practice in determining whether previous transactions are to be treated as a succession or not. From the landlord's perspective, if it is proposed to add a family member to the tenancy, it is particularly important to ensure that the transaction falls within the agreed succession provisions and therefore counts as a statutory succession. If it does not, the transaction will not use up one of the tenant's two statutory successions.

[1] Agriculture (Miscellaneous Provisions) Act 1976, s 18(4)(e).
[2] AHA 1986, s 37(1).
[3] AHA 1986, s 35(2). Where the AHA 1986 applies in relation to a tenancy by virtue of s 4(1)(g) of the ATA 1995 (see para 3.14), the reference to a substantial part of the land comprised in the holding means a substantial part determined by reference to either area or value: the AHA 1986, s 35(3), inserted by the RRO 2006, SI 2006/2805, art 4(2).
[4] AHA 1986, s 37(2).
[5] AHA 1986, s 35(2).

35.15 The rules for determining what does or does not count as a succession are contained in s 37 of the AHA 1986. It should be noted that this Act is a consolidating Act. Part IV of the AHA 1986 consolidates the provisions of Pt II of the Agriculture (Miscellaneous Provisions) Act 1976 (A(MP)A 1976), as amended by Schs 1 and 2 to the AHA 1984. The A(MP)A 1976 came into force on 14 November 1976 and the AHA 1984 on 12 September 1984[1].

The limited circumstances in which a consolidating Act can be construed by reference to earlier legislation are well-known. A consolidating Act must, in general, be interpreted in accordance with its own terms as any other Act of Parliament, with recourse to such aids to interpretation as are generally available. It must be understood in its context, and some reference may be made to earlier law to understand the context. The earlier legislation that is consolidated into a consolidating Act may also be referred to resolve ambiguities[2]. The A(MP)A 1976 and the AHA 1984 provide a historical context for the AHA 1986; but in general they are not helpful in resolving the many ambiguities in the AHA 1986. They are the genesis of them.

Part IV off the AHA 1986 applies to tenancies of agricultural holdings granted before 12 July 1984[3], and to four categories only of tenancies granted on or after that date. Previously, as a result of the A(MP)A 1976, rights of succession were conferred on the close relatives of tenant farmers, irrespective of whether their predecessor's tenancy was granted before or after the provisions for succession came into force under the A(MP)A 1976.

The AHA 1984 contained a variety of measures intended to encourage the letting of farms: it reformed the system of rent review, allowed succession to be claimed on the retirement as well as on death, and generally prevented any succession rights from attaching to new tenancies granted in the future. Accordingly, with regard to the future, the only tenancies to which Pt IV would apply were those which were obtained under the succession machinery itself, those to which it was agreed between landlord and tenant that Pt IV should apply, and tenancies granted to tenants who, immediately before 12 July 1984, were tenants of the same holding, or of any agricultural holding which comprised the whole or a substantial part of the land comprised in that holding. These provisions are all set out in s 34 of the AHA 1986.

Sections 36 to 48 inclusive of the AHA 1986 provide for succession on the death of the tenant. The framework enables a person who can bring himself or herself within the definition of 'close relative' of the deceased tenant under s 35(2)(a)–(d) to apply to the ALT on the death of the previous tenant for a direction entitling him or her to a new tenancy. A new tenancy will be directed if but only if the applicant can prove that he or she is both 'eligible' as defined by s 36 and is in he opinion of the ALT 'a suitable person to become the tenant of the holding'[4]. An application must be made within three months beginning with the day after the date of death[5]. There are provisions which enable the ALT to choose between competing applicants if both or all of them are eligible and suitable[6]. The ALT may, with the consent of the landlord, give a direction specifying that any two, three or four eligible and suitable applicants shall be entitled to a joint tenancy of the holding[7].

The provisions for succession on retirement are contained in ss 49 to 58 inclusive of the AHA 1986. They entitle an eligible person who is named in a notice given by the retiring tenant to apply to the ALT for a direction entitling him or her to a tenancy of the holding. In this case only one person may be nominated by the retiring tenant for succession. The tests which a nominated successor has to satisfy with regard to his or her close relationship with the retiring tenant, eligibility and suitability are the same as those set out for would-be successors on death[8].

[1]   The editor wishes to acknowledge the contribution of Mr Derek Wood QC to this section of this chapter.
[2]   *Farrell v Alexander* [1977] AC 59, per Lord Wilberforce at 73B, Lord Simon at 84G085A and Lord Edmund-Davies at 97A–97D, and the earlier dicta of the House of Lords in *Maunsell v Olins* [1975] AC 373, at 392–393.
[3]   When the 1984 Act came into force in relation to these provisions.
[4]   AHA 1986, s 39(2). See para 35.22.
[5]   AHA 1986, s 39(1).
[6]   AHA 1986, s 39(3)–(6).
[7]   AHA 1986, s 39(6) and (9).
[8]   See Ch 36.

35.16 The policy of the AHA 1986 is to exclude any further statutory succession after two successions have already occurred. The relevant rules are set out in s 37 of the AHA 1986, which on their face apply only to cases of retirement on death; but the combined effect of ss 37(6), 50(1) and 53(7) is that a succession under the retirement provisions also counts as one of the two permissible statutory successions.

Under s 37 the following events count as one statutory succession under the express terms of s 37 supplemented by other express provisions of Pt IV:

(a)   the grant of a tenancy to a single applicant obtained under a direction of the ALT;

(b)   the grant of a tenancy to two, three or four applicants jointly obtained under a direction of the ALT if the landlord agrees;

(c)   the grant of a tenancy by the landlord to a close relative who had become the sole or sole remaining application for a direction;

(d)   the grant of a tenancy prior to the date of the tenant's death, as a result of an agreement between the landlord and the tenant, to a person who would have been a close relative of the tenant if he had died immediately before the grant;

(e)   in relation to any time on or after 12 September 1984 the assignment of a tenancy, with the agreement of the landlord and tenant for the time being, to a person who, if the tenant had died immediately before the assignment, would have been his close relative. Except in the case of tenancies which were granted before 12 September 1984, or were obtained by virtue of a direction made by the Tribunal following an application made before 12 September 1984, or were granted (following such a direction) in circumstances falling within s 23(6) of the A(MP)A 1976, three further cases arise;

(f)   the grant or obtaining of a tenancy of part only of the land held by the previous tenant;

(g)   the grant of a joint tenancy by the landlord to persons only one of whom is or would have been a close relative;

(h)   an assignment to joint tenants only one of whom is or would have been a close relative.

Some aspects of these provisions were considered by Jowitt J in his decision in *Trustees of Saunders v Ralph*[1].

In *Saunders v Ralph*, the respondent's grandfather, Gilbert Ralph, had been granted a tenancy of the relevant holding on 9 June 1943. In 1957 the original landlord's trustees entered into a memorandum of agreement with Gilbert Ralph and his son Victor which provided that, with effect from 10 October 1957, Victor 'shall become joint tenant of the said holding and the said Gilbert James Ralph and Victor James Ralph shall jointly and severally become responsible for the due performance of all the agreements on the part of the Tenant' contained in the tenancy agreement. In 1988 Victor retired and his son, the respondent, applied to and obtained from the ALT a direction that he was entitled to a tenancy of the holding as Victor's nominated successor. The question between the parties was whether that was a first or second succession. The answer to that question depended upon whether the 1957 transaction was a first succession.

The judge held that it was not. The landlord's argument was that it took effect as a letting of the holding made, as a result of an agreement between the landlord and the tenant for the time being, under a new tenancy granted by the landlord to a person who, if the tenant had died immediately before the grant, would have been his close relative[2]. The judge dismissed that argument on the basis that the 1957 transaction was not a grant of a tenancy at all. It was merely a variation of the existing tenancy, adding an additional tenant to the previous sole tenant. An alternative analysis would have been that it took effect as an assignment of the tenancy by the father to the father and son jointly. Either way, it would not have been a 'grant' and, since it occurred before 12 September 1984, could not have fallen within s 37(2). This part of the judge's decision is correct.

The judge then considered a further argument advanced by the tenant. He held that, even if the 1957 transaction had taken effect as a surrender of the old tenancy and the grant of a new tenancy, it still would not have fallen within the terms of s 37(2). His starting point was the predecessor of s 37(2), ie s 18(5) of the A(MP)A 1976. Under that section he held that 'the statutory reference to a new tenancy granted to a person who would have been a close relative of the outgoing tenant is not apt to include a tenancy granted to that person and another who is not a close relative'. He then noted that the scope of s 18(5) had been enlarged by provisions in the AHA 1984 which are now s 37(4)(b) of the AHA 1986; but that this enlargement did not apply to tenancies falling within what is now subsection (8). The editor agrees with this conclusion, although it may have been reached by starting with s 37 of the AHA 1986 itself.

The judge further held that he would have reached the same conclusion if the transaction had taken effect as an assignment. In reaching this conclusion he was influenced by the provisions of s 37(5) which expressly capture assignments to joint tenants of whom only one is a close relative, and subsection (8) which excludes from subsection (5) any tenancy granted before 12 September 1984. Finally, the judge dealt with an argument advanced by the respondent's counsel in these terms.

'Retrospectivity

For the sake of completeness I deal with the issue of retrospectivity raised by Mr Denbin for the respondent. He submits that in any event a succession falling within subsection (2) of section 37 cannot be one which occurred before the passing of the 1976 Act. The submission, in my judgment, is misconceived. Before the passing of that Act there were no rights of succession. The Act created such rights and subsection (2), just as subsection (1) of what is now section 37, merely placed time limits upon the availability of those rights'.

This conclusion is not easily analysed or understood. Counsel appeared to be arguing that no transaction entered into before the succession provisions came onto the statute-book under the A(MP)A 1976 on 14 November 1976 could count as a succession because, on a proper interpretation of the A(MP)A 1976, it was not the intention of Parliament to treat as first (and possibly second) successions agreements between landlords, outgoing tenants and close relatives of outgoing tenants which had taken place many years and many times before 1976. The argument as formulated by the judge appears to be misconceived but the point is not straightforward and is discussed further below.

¹   (1993) 66 P & CR 335 [1993] 2 EGLR 1.
²   AHA 1986, s 37(2), as amended by s 37(7).

Succession following death of tenant

35.17 In relation to transactions occurring after the tenant's death, the issue of retrospectivity discussed Jowitt J in *Saunders v Ralph*[1] cannot arise.

Case 1:	Tenant dies.	Close relative applies to ALT.	Direction made entitling close relative to a new tenancy.	The grant of the new tenancy will count as a succession[2]. It will not matter if the grant of the tenancy is advanced before the date upon which the old tenancy will come to an end under s 46[3].
Case 2:	Tenant dies.	Close relatives apply to ALT.	ALT decides that more than one close relative is eligible and suitable. Landlord agrees to direction for joint tenancy.	The grant of the new joint tenancy will count as a succession[4].
Case 3:	Tenant dies.	Close relative applies to ALT.	Landlord grants tenancy before application heard.	A tenancy granted by way of compromise of proceedings before the Tribunal in these circumstances will count as a succession[5].

Case 4:   Tenant dies.   Landlord grants tenancy to close relative before close relative applies to the Tribunal.

It is not clear whether this would count as a succession. Section 37(1)(b) refers to a voluntary grant by the landlord to an 'applicant' which, read literally, would mean someone who has already made an application. A close relative has three months after the date of death in which to apply for a direction. It is conceivable that the landlord and that person would agree on a new tenancy without wishing to incur any legal costs. In the editor's opinion the court would take a sympathetic view of the landlord's position, construing the word 'applicant' more broadly, perhaps as 'candidate', or 'applicant to the landlord'. The well-advised landlord should always insist on the making of a formal application.

Case 5:	Tenant dies.	A sole close relative or two or more close relatives apply to the ALT.	Either in response to a direction under 37(1)(a) or otherwise under 37(1)(b), landlord grants a joint tenancy to persons not all of whom are close relatives.

Section 37(4)(b) provides (among other things) that s 37(1) applies where a joint tenancy is granted by the landlord to persons one of whom is a close relative. But this extension of s 37(1) does not apply in relation to 'any tenancy' if it was granted before 12 September 1984 or was obtained by virtue of a direction given by an ALT under the A(MP)A 1976 arising out of an application made before 12 September 1984, or was granted (following such a direction) in circumstances falling within s 23(6) of the A(MP)A 1976: see s 37(8). Section 23(6) of the A(MP)A 1976 is the equivalent of what is now s 45(6) of the AHA 1986 which is concerned with tenancies granted before the statutory expiry of the old tenancy: see Case 1 above. The expression any tenancy' in subsection (8) in the editor's opinion means what it says: both an original tenancy and any tenancy granted by way of succession. The policy behind s 37(8) is difficult to follow. There is no assistance from looking at its predecessor (AHA 1984, s 2(7), amending the A(MP)A 1976). The wording of the AHA 1986 is nevertheless clear enough. The grant of any tenancy falling within any of the three categories set out in subsection (8) to joint tenants of whom one or more is not a close relative will not count as a succession. In the case of other joint tenancies it will.

1   (1993) 66 P & CR 335 [1993] 2 EGLR 1.
2   AHA 1986, s 37(1)(a).
3   AHA 1986, s 45(6).
4   AHA 1986, ss 37(1)(a) and 39(9).
5   AHA 1986, s 37(1)(b).

Succession before the death of the tenant

35.18 Section 37(2) deems certain transactions occurring before the death of a tenant to be successions for the purposes of s 37(1). This section is confined to transactions occurring after 14 November 1976, when the succession provisions first came into force. Transactions occurring before that date are dealt with separately below.

Case 6:	Tenant surren- ders.	Landlord grants new tenancy to close relative.	This is a succession[1].

Case 7:	Tenant surrenders.	Landlord grants new tenancy to close relative and tenant jointly. Alternatively, landlord grants a new tenancy to close relative and someone who is not a close relative.	This is one of the points decided in *Saunders v Ralph*[2]. It would count as a succession under subsection (4)(b) unless the tenancy fell within any of the three categories set out in subsection (8). This Case parallels Case 5 above.
Case 8:	Tenant surrenders.	Landlord grants new tenancy to more than one close relative jointly.	It is submitted that this transaction will fall within s 37(2) on the simple basis that the reference to 'a person' and 'close relative' can include the plural 'persons' and 'close relatives'. The result would be the same whether or not subsection (2) had to read as amended by subsection (7), depending upon the time at which the transaction took place.
Case 9:	Tenant assigns to close relative with landlord's consent.		This transaction will count as a succession if it took place at any time on or after 12 September 1984[3].
Case 10:	Tenant assigns tenancy to close relative and himself (or a third party) with the landlord's consent.		

The combined effect of s 37(2) and (5) is that an assignment of a tenancy to a person who is a close relative or to joint tenants one of whom is a close relative counts as a succession if the transaction took place at any time on or after 12 September 1984[4]. It cannot make a difference that one of the joint assignees is the outgoing tenant. In his judgment in *Saunders v Ralph*[5], Jowitt J did not address the distinction between the grant of a new tenancy (or an assignment by the outgoing tenant) to the close relative and a third party on the one hand and a grant or assignment to the close relative and the outgoing tenant himself on the other. It is submitted that there is no valid distinction.

[1]   AHA 1986, s 37(2)(a).
[2]   (1993) 66 P & CR 335 [1993] 2 EGLR 1.
[3]   AHA 1986, s 37(2), as amended by subsection (7).
[4]   AHA 1986, s 37(7).
[5]   (1993) 66 P & CR 335 [1993] 2 EGLR 1.

Retrospectivity

35.19 The preceding paragraphs made the assumption, when considering Cases 6 to 10 inclusive, that the transactions under consideration had all occurred since 14 November 1976 when the A(MP)A 1976 came into force. The effect of s 37(7) of the AHA 1986 is that an assignment of a tenancy by the original tenant to a close relative with or without others cannot count as a succession if it took place at any time before 12 September 1984. However, that leaves open the question as to how far back in time it is permissible to enquire into a grant of a new tenancy falling within s 37(2).

Ignoring subsections (7) and (8), which have special provisions concerning dates, s 37 taken at its face value would appear to apply only to successions occurring after the AHA 1986 came into force. However, it is clear that successions occurring under the A(MP)A 1976, as amended by the AHA 1984, also count by virtue of the transitional provisions contained in para 1(1) of Sch 13 to the Act:

> 'Any reference, whether express or implied, in any enactment, instrument or document (including this Act and any enactment amended by Schedule 14 to this Act) to, or to things done or falling to be done under or for the purposes of, any provision of this Act shall, if in so far as the nature of the reference permits, be construed as including, in relation to the times, circumstances or purposes in relation to which the corresponding provision repealed by this Act has or has had effect, a reference to, or as the case may be, to things done or falling to be done under or for the purposes of, that corresponding provision'.

The unsurprising result of this is that, for example, a tenancy obtained by a direction of the ALT under the A(MP)A 1976 counts as a succession just as much as if it were obtained after the 1976 Act had been replaced by the AHA 1986. It is submitted that the same would apply to a voluntary surrender and new grant falling within s 37(2) made at an earlier time when the corresponding provisions of s 18(5) of the A(MP)A 1976 were in force.

The next question is: what about similar voluntary transactions which were entered into before the A(MP)A 1976 came into force? This is the question which appears to have been raised by counsel for the respondent in *Saunders v Ralph*[1] and which the judge did not properly answer.

The transaction under scrutiny in that case had occurred in 1957, some 19 years before statutory succession was introduced. As a matter of impression it would be very surprising if Parliament intended that landlords could exhume the past in this way. The purpose of s 18(5) of the A(MP)A 1976 and its replacement is to allow the parties to come to a voluntary arrangement over succession without having to wait for the original tenant to die. But that is all within the framework of the statutory scheme.

If any voluntary arrangement of the description, whenever made, counts as a first succession, the possible extent of retrospectivity is limitless. It would be possible for the owner of a traditionally managed estate to point to a succession of handovers from one family member to another stretching back over decades. In *Saunders v Ralph*[2], it is submitted that had Gilbert Ralph taken over the tenancy from his father, who had retired on the grounds of old age or disability in 1943, no statutory succession occurred either then or subsequently in 1957, as both events took place before the introduction of statutory succession.

To solve this problem it is submitted that it is legitimate to go back to s 18(5) of the A(MP)A 1976[3]. The voluntary surrender by the outgoing tenant of his tenancy followed by the letting of the holding under a new tenancy fell under subsection (5) if the new tenant was:

'a person who, if the outgoing tenant had died immediately before the grant, would have fallen within paragraphs (a) to (d) of subsection (1) above ...'.

Section 18(1) of the A(MP)A 1976 provided:

'Where after the passing of this Act the sole (or sole surviving) tenant of an agricultural holding dies and is survived by any of the following persons (a) ... (d) ... the following sections of this Part of this Act ... shall apply ...'.

It would also seem that the succession provisions contained in Pt II of the A(MP)A 1976 are wholly governed by those opening words 'Where after the passing of this Act ...'. The editor does not consider that a person who had taken a new tenancy of a holding, with the agreement of the outgoing tenant, before the Act was passed could have been a person who, if the outgoing tenant had died immediately before the grant, would have 'fallen' within paragraphs (a) to (d), since the Act was not in force. To put it another way, if the date of the grant of the new tenancy, and therefore the date on which the outgoing tenant hypothetically died, occurred before the passing of the Act the new tenant could not at that date have fallen within paragraphs (a) to (d) of the Act, because sub-s (1) did not, and could not, at that time, have applied to him.

Applying this analysis, it is not possible to agree with the judgment of Jowitt J in *Saunders v Ralph*[4] on this point. The judge's remarks on this point are plainly obiter. He deals with the argument 'for the sake of completeness', having already decided the case in favour of the respondent on the two major points previously discussed. It is submitted that this part of his judgment would not be followed in a case in which the point had to be fully argued and decided.

[1]   (1993) 66 P & CR 335 [1993] 2 EGLR 1.
[2]   (1993) 66 P & CR 335 [1993] 2 EGLR 1.
[3]   AHA 1986, Sch 13 para 1(1).
[4]   (1993) 66 P & CR 335 [1993] 2 EGLR 1.

35.20 As indicated above, succession by assignment can be effected even when succession by surrender and re-grant is not possible. This is because an assignment succession can operate for a tenancy granted to joint tenants where only one satisfies the requirements of s 37(2) of the AHA 1986 as being a close relative of the previous tenant[1]. Furthermore, such assignee does not need to have satisfied the other tests of eligibility or of suitability. The close relationship test alone has to have been satisfied[2]. Moreover, it should be remembered that between 1976 with the passing of the A(MP)A 1976 and 12 September 1984, succession could only be effected by the grant of a new tenancy and not by assignment.

35.20 *Succession on death*

A tenancy obtained pursuant to the provisions of s 37 of the AHA 1986, following the retirement of the tenant, counts as one succession for the purposes of the statutory scheme applying both on both death and retirement of the tenant[3].

1 AHA 1986, s 37(5).
2 AHA 1986, s 37(1)(b).
3 AHA 1986, s 37(6).

Agricultural Tenancies Act 1995, s 4(1)(d)

35.21 Section 4(1)(d) of the ATA 1995 excludes from the operation of the AHA 1986 any tenancy beginning on or after 1 September 1995 unless it falls within one of the various categories set out in that subsection. It provides that one of the types of tenancy to which the AHA 1986 will still apply is a tenancy 'granted on an agreed succession by a written contract of tenancy indicating (in whatever terms) that Pt IV of the AHA 1986 is to apply in relation to the tenancy'.

In its original form, s 4(2) of the ATA 1995 provided that a tenancy would be regarded as having been granted 'on an agreed succession' if (a) the previous tenancy of the holding or a related holding was a tenancy to which Pt IV of the AHA 1986 applied and:

'(b)   the current tenancy is granted otherwise than as mentioned in paragraph (b) or (c) of subsection (1) above but in such circumstances that if—

   (i)   Part IV of the AHA 1986 applied in relation to the current tenancy, and

   (ii)   a sole (or sole surviving) tenant under the current tenancy were to die and be survived by a close relative of his,

the occasion on which the current tenancy is granted would for the purposes of subsection (1) of section 37 of the AHA 1986 be taken to be an occasion falling within paragraph (a) or (b) of that subsection'.

The language of s 4(2)(b) of the ATA 1995 is extremely convoluted. It is submitted that it is intended to convey the following meaning. If: (i) the previous tenant was protected by the AHA 1986; (ii) the current tenancy was granted in circumstances which fell within Pt IV of the AHA 1986; and (iii) the new tenant himself were to die and be survived by a close relative, then the grant of the current tenancy would count as an agreed succession for the purposes of s 4(1)(d) of the ATA 1995, and the AHA 1986 would apply to it. The subsection ends by referring to subsection (1) of s 37. It may be suggested that the grant of the current tenancy would, for that reason, only count if it were obtained as a result of, or in the course of, ALT proceedings. That is a bad point. Section 4(2) of the ATA 1995 is defining an 'agreed succession' for the purposes of s 4(1)(d). Section 4(2) is a deeming provision. If the current tenancy fits the description set out in s 4(2)(a) and (b) it is an 'agreed succession' if the occasion on which it is granted 'would be taken to be an occasion falling within paragraph (a) or (b) of s 37(1) of the AHA 1986.' One of the occasions on which it 'would be taken' to fall within s 37(1)(a) or (b) would be an occasion falling within s 37(2), because that is what s 37(2) says.

578

However, s 4(2) of the ATA 1995 has been amended by the RRO 2006[1]. For a tenancy to fall within s 4(1)(d) of the ATA 1995 now it must satisfy these conditions;

(a)   (as before) the previous tenancy must have been protected by the AHA 1986; and

(b)   It must have been granted to a person who 'if the tenant under [the] previous tenancy ... had died immediately before the grant, would have been his close relative'.

This suggests that an 'agreed succession' is an inter vivos arrangement, as one would expect. But in addition 'either of the conditions specified in subsection (2A)' must also be satisfied.

Subsection (2A) divides into '(a) and (b)' linked by the word 'and'. They are, however, alternatives. That is clear from the use of the word 'either' above. The first alternative (a) is that the current tenancy is granted to a person 'who was or had become the sole or sole remaining applicant for a direction of an [ALT] for a tenancy'. It is difficult to reconcile this provision with s 4(2)(b). That is concerned with inter vivos successions, not succession on death. But alternatively, (2A)(a) appears to be dealing with a situation in which the previous tenant has died and the close relative has proceedings under way following death. The proceedings may, of course, also be proceedings by a nominated successor under the retirement provisions; but the words 'sole or sole remaining applicant' more naturally refer to an application made on death.

The other alternative is that the current tenancy was granted with the agreement of the previous tenant (which is now familiar territory) and:

> '(ii)   is granted and begins before the date of the giving of any retirement notice by the previous tenant, or if no retirement notice is given before the date of death of the previous tenant'.

Section 4(2A)(b)(ii) of the ATA 1995 does not apply to a grant made after a retirement notice. Once the retirement notice has been served then the prospective tenant must apply to the ALT.

[1]   SI 2006/2805.

QUALIFICATIONS FOR SUCCESSION

35.22 Before an applicant for succession can obtain a direction of the ALT compelling the landlord to grant him a new tenancy of the agricultural holding in question, he[1] must satisfy the ALT that:

(a)   he is *eligible* to be granted a new tenancy[2];

(b)   he is *suitable*[3];

(c)   *consent* to the operation of the landlord's notice to quit, if applied for, *should not be granted*[4].

If there is more than one applicant for succession, the ALT must determine which of the candidates is the most suitable and, in default of the landlord agreeing to a joint tenancy, must make the direction in favour of the most suitable applicant[5].

1   Succession applies to men and women and reference to the applicant as 'he' is for convenience only.
2   AHA 1986, s 35(3).
3   AHA 1986, s 39(2) and (8).
4   AHA 1986, s 44.
5   See para 35.86.

ELIGIBLE PERSONS

35.23 The underlying policy of the AHA 1986 (arising from the NFU/CLA package incorporated into the 1984 Act)[1] is that it is only in the most deserving cases that the ALT should make a direction against an unwilling landlord compelling him to take the successful applicant as his tenant.

1   See para 1.16.

35.24 To give effect to that policy, three tests of eligibility have been statutorily devised. They are designed to ensure that the successful applicant:

(a)   is closely related to the deceased tenant;
(b)   has a real commitment to the holding and has worked on it and been primarily dependent upon it for his living for at least five of the previous seven years; and
(c)   does not occupy sufficient other agricultural land to enable him to make a living without the subject holding.

These eligibility tests have been found in practice to produce many anomalies. Apart from a limited discretion to the ALT in the case of the principal source of livelihood test, they allow for no flexibility on the part of the ALT. Nevertheless, they have the advantage that the outcome of the application of the tests in each individual case is capable of being predicted by the applicant or his professional advisers with considerable accuracy.

In contrast, the application of the suitability tests should give rise to no such anomalies or injustice, but they are subjective in their application and less predictable in their outcome. The three eligibility tests are:

(a)   the close relationship test;
(b)   the principal source of livelihood test; and
(c)   the commercial unit occupation test.

Time for determining eligibility

35.25 After a period of some doubt, it was established by the House of Lords in *Jackson v Hall*[1] that although the close relationship test and the principal source of livelihood test must clearly have been satisfied by the date of death, the commercial unit occupation test has to be satisfied not merely on the date of death, but also on the date of the applicant's application to the ALT and on the date of the hearing of that application. It is submitted that (although it was not decided specifically in *Jackson v Hall*) the applicant must also satisfy the test at all intervening times. As a consequence, he could not, for example, acquire a commercial unit between the date of the application and hearing (possibly by inheritance from the deceased tenant) and divest himself of it as well before the date of the hearing so as to maintain his status of eligibility which was existing at the date of the application[2].

1   [1980] AC 854, [1980] 1 All ER 177.
2   AHA 1986, s 39(2).

The close relationship test

35.26 Section 35(2) of the AHA 1986 provides that only the following persons satisfy the close relationship test:

(a)   the wife or husband (including the civil partner) of the deceased tenant (spouse);
(b)   the brother or sister of the deceased (sibling);
(c)   a child of the deceased (child); or
(d)   any person (not within (b) or (c) above) who in the case of any marriage or civil partnership to which the deceased was at any time a party was treated by the deceased as a child of the family in relation to that marriage or civil partnership (treated child)[1].

1   AHA 1986, s 35(2), as amended by the Civil Partnership Act 2004, s 81 and Sch 8.

Children-in-law

35.27 It should be noted that children do not include children-in-law. If, for example, the daughter of a tenant marries a farmer who farms in partnership with his father-in-law, the son-in-law will not be eligible to apply for succession and the daughter may have difficulty in satisfying the principal source of livelihood test (because of her dependence on her husband's income) and/or in establishing her suitability[1].

1   As to which, see para 35.69.

Joint tenants

35.28 Particular problems also apply in the case of joint tenants. For example, if two brothers are joint tenants of an agricultural holding, one with eligible children and the other with none, the eligible children will satisfy the test if their uncle predeceases their father. If the father predeceases his brother (their uncle) then none is eligible since each is the nephew of the sole surviving tenant and merely the son of the predeceasing tenant. Nephews fall outside the category of close relations specified in s 35(2) of the AHA 1986[1].

[1] This problem can be overcome usually by a judicious use of the retirement procedures, as to which see para Ch 36.

Bachelor tenant

35.29 The treated child provisions have created problems in practice. A child who was not adopted, but was brought up by his bachelor uncle from the age of three and was 'treated as a son' of the deceased tenant, nevertheless failed to satisfy the test because 'the absence of any marriage to which the deceased was a party' resulted in the application being dismissed[1].

[1] *Berridge v Fitzroy Newdegate* (1980) ALT, West Midland; *Duthrie v Marquess of Northampton* (1984) ALT, Eastern Area (a case of an unsuccessful attempt at last-minute adoption before the applicant's eighteenth birthday by his widowed great uncle).

Grandchildren

35.30 The class of close relations involve transmissions sideways or downwards one generation at a time. If a tenant retired in favour of his son, who then predeceased the father, the father (the former tenant) could not apply for succession. He would be outside the limited class of eligible applicants. Similarly, succession cannot 'jump' a generation. A grandchild cannot apply on the death of his grandfather, even though his father predeceased him. Similarly, an orphaned grandchild would not qualify if brought up by his grandparents, unless it could be shown that he was treated not as an orphaned grandchild as such, but as a child of the marriage of the grandparents themselves: an unlikely situation.

Civil partners

35.31 The AHA 1986 has been amended to enable civil partners to fall within the definition of close relative[1].

[1] Civil Partnership Act 2004, s 81 and Sch 8.

Treated as a child of the family

35.32 This category has given rise to difficulties. The ALT has accepted a distant cousin[1] and a stepson[2] who have lived with the deceased tenant and his wife as member of their family. However, where the nephew of a deceased tenant lived with him, but the deceased tenant was single, the ALT determined that the nephew was ineligible[3]. The ALT's approach may be affected by the introduction of civil partners as eligible successors.

[1] *Williams v Lady Douglas* (1980) ALT, Wales Area.
[2] *Ashby v Holiday* (1983) ALT, Yorks and Lancs Area.
[3] *Berridge v Fitzroy* (1980) ALT, West Midlands Area. Also see, *Varley v Marquess of Northampton* (1984) ALT, East Midlands Area.

The principal source of livelihood test

35.33 The provisions governing the principal source of livelihood test are contained in ss 36(3)(a) and 41 and Sch 6 para 2 to the AHA 1986. For an applicant to satisfy this test he must prove that he is either fully eligible[1] or that he should be treated as eligible[2].

1   AHA 1986, s 36(3)(a).
2   AHA 1986, s 41.

Applicant fully eligible

THE TEST

35.34 For the applicant to satisfy the principal source of livelihood test, he must establish that 'in the seven years ending with the date of death' of the former tenant 'his', ie the applicant's, 'only or principal source of livelihood throughout a continuous period of not less than five years, or two or more discontinuous periods together amounting to not less than five years, derived from his agricultural work on the holding or on an agricultural unit of which the holding forms part': AHA 1986, s 36(3)(a)[1].

1   AHA 1986, s 36(3)(a). Note that s 36(3)(a) also refers to the need to satisfy the commercial unit test: see para 35.55.

35.35 An agricultural unit is defined in s 109(2) of the Agriculture Act 1947[1]. The definition is as follows:

> 'In this Act the expression "agricultural unit" means land which is occupied as a unit for agricultural purposes, including—
> (a)   any dwellinghouse or other building occupied by the same person for the purpose of farming the land; and
> (b)   any other land falling within the definition in this Act of the expression "agricultural land" which is in the occupation of the same person, being land as to which the Minister is satisfied that having regard to the character and situation thereof and other relevant circumstances it ought in the interests of full and efficient production to be farmed in conjunction with the agricultural unit, and directs accordingly.
>
> Provided that the Minister shall not give a direction under this subsection as respects any land unless it is for the time being not in use for any purpose which appears to him to be substantial having regard to the use to which it might be put for agriculture'.

The test is subject to an exception in the case of an applicant who is the widow of the former tenant as follows:

> 'In the case of the deceased's wife, the reference in subsection (3)(a) of section 36 of the AHA 1986 "to the relative's agricultural work" shall be read as a reference to agricultural work carried out by either the wife or the deceased (or both of them)'[2].

1   That definition is incorporated into the AHA 1986 by s 96(1).
2   AHA 1986, s 36(4).

583

35.36 A further proviso is contained in para 2 of Sch 6 to the AHA 1986:

'For the purposes of the livelihood condition any period during which a close relative of the deceased was, in the period of seven years mentioned in that condition, attending a full-time course at a university, college or other establishment of further education shall be treated as a period throughout which his only or principal source of livelihood derived from his agricultural work on the holding; but not more than three years in all shall be so treated by virtue of this paragraph'.

The principal source of livelihood test, though simple to state, has given rise to numerous problems of construction and of application in relation to:

(a)   agricultural work;
(b)   establishing livelihood;
(c)   sources of livelihood;
(d)   the agricultural unit;
(e)   entitlements or drawings;
(f)   the treatment of losses;
(g)   work on the holding;
(h)   the relevant period;
(i)   further education.

AGRICULTURAL WORK

35.37 The AHA 1986 makes it clear that the applicant's principal source of livelihood must not merely have been derived from his work upon the holding in question or a larger agricultural unit of which it forms a part but that it must have been 'agricultural' work[1].

There is no consensus of opinion amongst ALTs as to what is meant by the term 'agricultural work'. As yet there are no appellate decisions. The first instance constructions put upon the term 'agricultural work' fall into three categories:

(a)   those where agricultural work has been equated to manual work[2];
(b)   cases containing definitions which, whilst including some non-manual work within the definition of agricultural work, did so only to a limited extent[3];
(c)   cases where manual work was held not to be an essential ingredient at all[4].

The problem in the context of widows has now been largely, if not wholly, removed by the provisions of s 36(4) which require the widow to have derived her principal source of livelihood either from her own agricultural work or her husband's or both. However, difficulties still arise in the context of married daughters who do not come within the provisions of s 36(4) of the AHA 1986 and who still have to satisfy the ALT that their own principal source of livelihood has come from their own agricultural work rather than from their husband's agricultural work[5].

It is submitted that the proper approach is that the adjective 'agricultural' must qualify and restrict the 'work' carried on upon the holding or larger agricultural unit etc, which qualifies the applicant for eligibility. Accordingly, any form of work upon the holding, whether it be manual, managerial, administrative or otherwise, which contributes to the farming business and which assists in the production of the farming income, is agricultural work. It is a misconstruction of the section to seek to draw a distinction between physical or manual work and secretarial or managerial work. The decision of the Court of Appeal in *Casswell v Welby*[6], though not directed to this issue, suggests that the court will approach this problem in a purposeful manner and reject arguments attempting to define restrictively what work in and about the promotion of the farm business in question can be said to be 'agricultural work'.

[1]   AHA 1986, s 36(3)(a).
[2]   See *Morris v Morris* (1980) ALT, Wales: When the applicant admitted in evidence, she had done hardly anything by way of outside manual work on the farm during the last three years, a basic requirement of what was then s 18(2)(b) of the A(MP)A 1976 'was missing'; *Heal v Sidcot School* (1978) ALT, South West: '[The applicant] did undoubtedly do some work that might be categorised as agricultural work, but much of the work was secretarial of a type which was equally applicable to any type of business and not to be classed as agricultural work'.
[3]   See *Wright v Crown Estate Comrs* (1979) ALT, Yorks/Lancs: 'Work, such as telephoning, writing letters, seeing visitors at the farm and general wifely duties did not constitute 'agricultural work' and, therefore, in the present case the applicant should be declared ineligible'; *Firth v Barraclough* (1977) ALT, Yorks/Lancs in which the ALT considered by analogy a doctor and his wife: 'The doctor sees his patients; the wife answers the telephone, addresses letters and, in addition, brings up the children and cooks the dinner. Without the wife's work the husband could not carry on his practice nearly as effectively, but is the work that the wife does (even the answering the telephone and sticking stamps on letters) in any way to be regarded as medical work? The answer is clearly, no. It is in part the ordinary work of a housewife and in part, the work of a receptionist but it is not the work of a doctor'; *Colson v Midwood Trustees* (1979) ALT, Eastern Area: ' "Agricultural work" is not confined to outdoor manual work. It follows that *some* office or secretarial work can be covered – no hard and fast dividing lines can be laid down'.
[4]   *Dagg v Lovett* (1979) 251 Estates Gazette 75, where the Northern Area ALT held: 'This tribunal takes the view that it is right within the context to include not only physical labour but also managerial or supervisory functions and record-keeping'. In that case the applicant was found not to have been 'involved to any significant extent in actual physical agricultural work' but nevertheless the applicant was held to have been engaged in agricultural work and to have derived her principal source of livelihood from that agricultural work to a material extent.
[5]   Note in *Littlewood v Rolfe* [1981] 2 All ER 51, the Divisional Court held: 'I do not think one can approach the question of source of livelihood of husband and wife in two separate compartments. Husbands and wives usually pool their income', per Judge Fay QC. Also see, *Thomson v Church Comrs for England* [2006] EWHC 1773 (Admin), [2006] 43 EG 180.
[6]   (1995) 71 P & CR 137.

35.38   Agricultural work which is closely connected with, but not actually upon the holding causes problems, for example contract work on nearby holdings[1], cattle haulage with farm wagons and cattle dealing. Such work is typically connected with the holding because farm machinery and other equipment is kept on the subject holding and used for the contracting.

The distinction between farming on the holding or the larger unit and dealing in livestock unconnected with the holding is extremely difficult to determine in practice. At the one extreme, an applicant who purchases livestock at markets for the benefit of customers and sells them on without their visiting the holding at all, would probably, to the extent that that income contributed to his livelihood, not have been deriving it from agricultural work on the holding. Alternatively, an applicant who purchases livestock, fattens the animals on the holding and then sells them out finished or as stores, would appear to be engaged in agricultural work to the extent to which the profit is derived from the fattening activity. It is not easy to draw a distinction between those two activities where there is a rapid turnover in livestock which have visited the holding perhaps on little more than a 'bed and breakfast' basis.

As to whether income derived from quota leasing, where a dairy farming enterprise had been discontinued and both the milk quota and sheep quota was leased out, was qualifying income, it has been decided that 'the source of the quota rents was immaterial. The proper consideration was how the applicant had access to them. Once they had gone into the partnership account the only reason he was able to draw on them was because what he drew was in recognition of his agricultural work on the unit of which the holding formed part. He was economically dependent on that unit. His agricultural work on that unit was the source of almost the whole of his livelihood, certainly well over 50%'[2].

1   For a case in which the ALT has decided that work undertaken by an applicant as a contractor on land away from the holding, nevertheless fell to be treated as qualifying agricultural work on the holding, see *Sandercock v Sandercock* (2000) ALT, Midlands Area.
2   *Sandercock v Sandercock* (2000) ALT, Midlands Area.

LIVELIHOOD

35.39 There is a general consensus amongst ALTs that 'livelihood' is a term wider in its implication than mere income and that it covers not merely benefits which are measurable directly in cash terms, such as wages, but also benefits in kind[1]. Therefore, if the applicant has enjoyed rent and rate free living accommodation, with electricity, oil and other services paid for through the farm account and free, or subsidised, motoring, meals and the like, provided those benefits have been granted to the applicant by reason of his agricultural work upon the subject holding, or the larger agricultural unit of which it forms part, then they fall to be evaluated and added to the income received by the applicant in determining the applicant's principal source of livelihood. The first instance ALT decision was upheld by the Divisional Court[2].

1   *Judge v Umpleby Trustees* (1978) ALT, Yorks/Lancs Area.
2   *Littlewood v Rolfe* [1981] 2 All ER 51.

SOURCES OF LIVELIHOOD

35.40 If the applicant has other sources of livelihood, apart from his agricultural work or other work upon or from[1] the subject holding or the larger agricultural unit of which it forms part, then they have to be evaluated and set against the sources of livelihood derived from the applicant's agricultural work etc, in determining the applicant's principal source of livelihood. Principal in this context means more than 50%[2].

Sources of livelihood derived from agriculture, but not from agricultural work or other work on or from[3] the holding or larger agricultural unit of which the holding forms part, constitute outside sources of livelihood for this purpose.

In *Casswell v Welby* [4], the Court of Appeal held that the proper test is not where the sums spent by the applicant come from, but why he had access to them. The court applied a test of 'economic dependence': was the applicant economically dependent for his livelihood on his work on the holding? If net profits from the business were insufficient to pay the son's drawings, it was irrelevant that they were funded by increased family loans and overdraft facilities, provided that they were in payment for his work on the farm. Section 36(3)(a) requires the applicant to establish his economic dependence on the holding. In *Casswell v Welby*[5], the applicant's work on the holding was the sole source of his livelihood. Where net profits were insufficient, it was irrelevant how his living expenses were funded.

[1]   *Littlewood v Rolfe* [1981] 2 All ER 51.
[2]   *Littlewood v Rolfe* [1981] 2 All ER 51.
[3]   See para 35.41.
[4]   (1995) 71 P & CR 137.
[5]   (1995) 71 P & CR 137.

35.41 In the last edition of this book, it was submitted that agricultural work on the holding or on the larger agricultural unit is likely to be liberally construed to mean that agricultural work in promotion of the farm business carried on from the holding is sufficient to constitute compliance[1]. Since the last edition of this book, the position has been affected by the RRO 2006[2]. TRIG2[3] recognised the importance of diversification to the agricultural and rural sector. It considered that it would be inconsistent and illogical if greater access to diversification on a holding prejudiced applications to succeed to the tenancy of that holding. Although TRIG2 accepted that the 'commercial unit' test under the AHA 1986 is inextricably linked to the 'livelihood' test, it concluded that no amendment was necessary to the former. It did recommend an amendment to the 'livelihood' test. It proposed that income from other (non-agricultural) work carried out on the holding should be included within the test provided that the landlord had provided consent to such diversification[4].

The proposal of the Tenancy Reform Industry Group (2002) (TRIG2) was accepted by the Department for Environment, Food and Rural Affairs (DEFRA) and, as a consequence, a new subsection (6) has been inserted into s 36 of the AHA 1986[5] as follows:

'(6)   The reference in subsection (3)(a) above to agricultural work carried out by a person on the holding or on an agricultural unit of which the holding forms part includes—
   (a)   agricultural work carried out by him from the holding or an agricultural unit of which the holding forms part, and

(b)   other work carried out by him on or from the holding or an agricultural unit of which the holding forms part,

which is of a description approved in writing by the landlord after the commencement of this subsection'.

The same amendment has been made in relation to succession upon retirement by the insertion of a new s 59(4) into the AHA 1986, adopting the same words used in s 36(1) of the AHA 1986[6].

1   See *Casswell v Welby* [1995] 2 EGLR 1.
2   SI 2006/2805.
3   See para 1.19.
4   TRIG2 also recommended a Code of Good Practice in relation to agri-environment issues and diversification: see para 1.21.
5   Effective since 19 October 2006: SI 2006/2805, art 1(1).
6   SI 2006/2805, art 1(1).

35.42 In its Explanatory Note[1], DEFRA observed that the proposal, since adopted in the RRO 2006, would amend the criteria in ss 36 and 50 of the AHA 1986 for eligibility for succession to a tenancy to allow income from:

(a)   agricultural work carried out from the holding approved in writing by the landlord; and

(b)   other work carried out on or from the holding approved in writing by the landlord,

to count towards the principal source of livelihood for the purposes of meeting the livelihood test for succession to a tenancy, as well as income from agricultural work on the holding. The landlord's approval for the agricultural work from the holding and the non-agricultural work would have to be given after the entry into force of the RRO 2006, so the amendment would not apply retrospectively.

Additionally, the Explanatory Note observed:

(i)   the proposal would remove a burden from prospective successors to a tenancy by no longer requiring them to derive their principal income from agricultural work on the holding in order to be eligible for statutory succession. It would also remove a restriction on the ability of the tenant and landlord to decide what work should be counted for succession purposes and what would not;

(ii)   the proposal would impose a minor new burden on tenants and landlords, as agricultural work carried out from the holding and non-agricultural work carried out on or from the holding would need to be approved in writing by the landlord to count towards the livelihood test.

Prior to the RRO 2006 coming into effect[2], the problem of diversification was well illustrated by the ALT decision in *Keene v Trustees for Guy's and St Thomas' Charity*[3]. In that case the AHA 1986 tenancy was of some 800 acres. There was some additional rented land and a small block of freehold land owned by the tenant on which a farm shop had been built. The farm was operated by five partners. It was very diversified: arable, livestock, vegetables, soft fruit, pick your own fruit (PYO), firewood sales, some 750 free range chickens and the farm shop. The applicant for succession operated the mainstream farming side of the business. Other partners were responsible for the PYO and farm shop. The shop had started selling produce predominantly from the farm, but as time passed had grown to a substantial enterprise with a turnover close to £1m, an in-house bakery and franchised butchery. It still sourced produce from the farm where it could, but perhaps less than 50%.

There was no argument about suitability, but the landlords contended that:

(1) the PYO business based on one of the other blocks of rented land did not form part of the same agricultural unit and thus that income was to be ruled out of account;

(2) the farm shop similarly did not form part of the same agricultural unit and so that income did not fall to be taken into account;

(3) the PYO business was another commercial unit occupied by the applicant and disqualified him.

The ALT determined that there was a clear overlap and integration between the PYO business and the wider farming, and whilst one partner had particular responsibility for that part of the business, it was all part and parcel of the same business and was clearly agricultural. It fell within the definition of the wider 'agricultural unit'. The ALT's conclusion in relation to the second issue was the reverse; simply because it was satisfied that the nature of that business was too far removed from agriculture for it to form part of the agricultural unit.

The arguments on the part of the applicant did not stop there. He pursued two alternative routes to include the income he was receiving from the partnership:

(A) First, he argued that all his work was agricultural and so the only basis upon which he received any payment from the partnership was due to his agricultural work on the agricultural unit (whether that includes the farm shop or not) and thus it did not matter where the income might be derived from. As far as he was concerned, it was all attributed to his agricultural work. The ALT did not accept this argument.

(B) As an alternative, the applicant argued that he should at least be allowed to count that proportion of the farm shop profits derived from produce supplied by the farm. The ALT again rejected that submission. The farm shop notionally paid the farm for the produce it purchased from it and the profits shown by the farm shop were the mark up it achieved over and above the price paid to the farm. Thus again there was a separation in the income streams and all that the applicant could include was the direct income attributable to the farm business.

---

1 Explanatory Document: The Regulatory Reform (Agricultural Tenancies) (England and Wales) Order 2006: Statement by the Department for Environment, Food and Rural Affairs, March 2006.

2 19 October 2006: SI 2006/2805, art 1(1).

3 (2005) ALT, South Western.

35.43 The amendments introduced by the RRO 2006 have two component parts:

(a) 'agricultural work ... *from* the holding or an agricultural unit of which the holding forms part'[1]; and

(b) the inclusion of '*other work* carried out by him *on or from* the holding or an agricultural unit of which the holding forms part'.

Limb (a) of the amended definition of qualifying livelihood would include the PYO operation in *Keene v Trustees for Guy's and St Thomas' Charity*[2] and agricultural contracting. Limb (b) would include the farm shop.

The real issue concerning the amendments to the livelihood test focuses upon the requirement for the written approval of the landlord obtained after the amendment came into operation on 19 October 2006. Pre-existing consents will not be sufficient.

Why would the landlord wish to give consent so as to widen the scope of eligibility for succession? The only obvious answer to that question is if the landlord considers that such consent would result in a significant rent increase. There is certainly no encouragement for the landlord to repeat an earlier consent, for example permitting part of the holding to be used as a livery business, because there will be no benefit to the landlord in doing so. The RRO 2006 does not contain any provision enabling a tenant to apply to an independent third party for permission to extend the use, similar to the provisions applying to improvements[3].

[1] Note that an earlier draft of the RRO 2006 did not include the wider agricultural unit.
[2] (2005) ALT, South Western.
[3] See para 16.6 ff.

ENTITLEMENT OR DRAWINGS

35.44 The expression 'source of livelihood' was considered by the Divisional Court in *Trinity College, Cambridge v Caines*[1]. The court held that that source of livelihood meant:

> 'what the applicant spends or consumes on her ordinary living expenses from time to time in money and/or kind and ... does not include money that she has available to spend but does not in fact spend for that purpose'[2].

If the applicant is entitled to more than he receives for his agricultural work on the holding, but leaves it undrawn, then this will not 'count' for the purpose of calculating his 'source of livelihood'. This needs to be contrasted with benefits enjoyed by the applicant which need to be evaluated and taken into account in determining livelihood.

[1] (1983) 272 Estates Gazette 1287.
[2] *Trinity College, Cambridge v Caines* (1983) 272 EG 1287 at 1292.

LOSSES

35.45 A problem which frequently arises is whether a partner in a farming business which makes losses or fails to make sufficient profits to cover the partner/applicant's drawings can then be said to be deriving his principal source of livelihood or indeed any part of his livelihood for his agricultural work. During such times it could be argued that the applicant's endeavours do not contribute to the discharge of his living expenses if the drawings are funded by an increased overdraft with the bank or injections of capital into the business from outside sources. It has been decided by the Court of Appeal[1] that in such circumstances the applicant is deriving his livelihood from his agricultural work etc. Without such work he would not have received the moneys from which he drew. The source of the funds is immaterial.

[1]   *Casswell v Welby* (1995) 71 P & CR 137, *sub nom Welby v Casswell* [1995] 2 EGLR 1, reversing (on this point) *Bailey v Sitwell* [1986] 2 EGLR 7.

WORK ON THE HOLDING

35.46 Where a farm business derives its income from farming an agricultural holding and other land as one unit, and also supplemental income is derived from related activities not confined to agricultural work on the holding itself, eg agricultural contracting for neighbours, cattle haulage etc, the qualification of such supplemental income may be called into question. It was submitted in the last edition of this book that, on parity of reasoning with the decision in *Casswell v Welby*[1], the income of the farm business does not fall to be analysed and apportioned between that earned narrowly by agricultural work on the holding or its larger unit and that derived from wider related activities. It was suggested that the test would appear to be whether the business is in essence a farm business and the applicant's primary contribution is in farm work on the holding or larger agricultural unit of which it forms part. Section 36(3)(a) of the AHA 1986 required that the applicant for a tenancy had to establish his economic dependence on the holding. In *Casswell v Welby*[2], the applicant's work on the holding was the sole source of his livelihood and where the net profits were insufficient, it was irrelevant how his living expenses were funded. The treatment of supplemental income may not be as straightforward as previously submitted. Nevertheless, the position now needs to be considered in the context of the diversification permitted by the RRO 2006[3].

[1]   *Casswell v Welby* (1995) 71 P & CR 137, *sub nom Welby v Casswell* [1995] 2 EGLR 1, reversing (on this point) *Bailey v Sitwell* [1986] 2 EGLR 7.
[2]   [1995] 2 EGLR 1.
[3]   See para 35.41.

THE AGRICULTURAL UNIT

35.47 It was held by the Divisional Court in *Trinity College, Cambridge v Caines*[1] that the agricultural unit of which the holding had to form part must be established at the date of death. If the unit had changed in its constitution, and land which formerly, during the seven-year period, formed part of the unit, had been disposed of, or other land had been acquired, the ALT has to determine the extent of the unit at the date of death. If and in so far as the applicant's livelihood was derived from agricultural work upon land which was part of the unit at the date in question, but has ceased to be so by the date of death, that source of livelihood was deemed to be a source of livelihood derived not from the applicant's agricultural work upon the unit in question. Therefore, it fell to be aggregated with the applicant's other sources of livelihood in determining what was his principal source of livelihood.

Considerable difficulties have been experienced, despite the statutory definition in s 109(2) of the Agriculture Act 1947, in determining what constitutes an agricultural unit at any one time. It is unclear, for example, as to whether land the subject of a seasonal grazing agreement can thereby constitute part of the agricultural unit. It is probable that such land would be excluded[2].

1   (1983) 272 Estates Gazette 1287.
2   *Keene v Trustees for Guy's and St Thomas' Charity* (2005) ALT, South Western.

THE RELEVANT PERIOD

35.48 For the purposes of satisfying the full eligibility test, the applicant must show that his principal source of livelihood was derived from his agricultural work etc, during five of the seven years ending with the date of death. Although the wording of the statute speaks of continuous and discontinuous periods, it is clear that any five out of the seven years ending with the date of death will suffice. Whether this is confined to selecting five individual years or not was expressly left open by the Divisional Court and the Court of Appeal in *Welby v Casswell*[1].

1   [1995] 2 EGLR 1.

FURTHER EDUCATION

35.49 The AHA 1986 provides that a period not exceeding three out of the seven years, ending with the date of death during which the applicant was engaged on 'a full-time course at a university, college or other establishment of further education', is to count towards the five-year minimum period of principal source of livelihood[1].

That does not cover every form of post-school education. In *Littlewood v Rolfe*[2], the applicant had spent three years as a pupil nurse in a training hospital. The ALT decided that:

> 'The mere fact that educational training is conducted in an establishment does not of itself make that establishment another "establishment of further education". The words must be construed *ejusdem generis* with university or college'.

That case was the subject of an appeal to the Divisional Court but the ALT's ruling on that matter was not in issue in the higher court.

1   AHA 1986, Sch 6 para 2.
2   [1981] 2 All ER 51, 258 Estates Gazette 168.

35.50 The course at university attended by the applicant need not be agriculturally related. By contrast, work as a student on another farm will not count, since the other farm is not a university, college or other establishment of further education. Similarly, time spent abroad in, for example, Australia or Canada acquiring foreign farming experience is not deemed to be time spent deriving livelihood from the holding. Time spent teaching at university rather than learning has been held not to qualify[1].

1   *Clark v Barnard* (1980) ALT, South East.

Applicant treated as eligible

35.51 An applicant, who is not fully eligible so far as the principal source of livelihood test is concerned, may apply to be treated as eligible pursuant to the provisions of s 41 of the AHA 1986. He may do so if:

(a)   he is in all other respects an eligible person;

(b)   the principal source of livelihood test, 'though not fully satisfied', is satisfied 'to a material extent';

(c)   it would be fair and reasonable for him to be treated as fully eligible[1].

An application to be treated as eligible must, like the primary application itself, be made within three months beginning with the day after the date of death[2]. If the application is not made within that three-month period, the ALT may not subsequently entertain such an application[3]. An applicant who believes that he is fully eligible and proceeds upon that basis, only to discover later that for one reason or another he does not satisfy the primary test fully, cannot at the hearing invite the ALT nevertheless to treat him as fully eligible. If there is any doubt as to eligibility, it is wise to draft the applicant to the ALT in the alternative[4].

The primary test must have been satisfied 'to a material extent'. The problem of how one can satisfy the principal source of livelihood test to a material extent has been considered in *Littlewood v Rolfe*[5], *Wilson v Earl Spencer's Settlement Trustees*[6] and *Thomson v Church Comrs for England*[7]. The combined effect of these three cases is that for the full test to be satisfied to a material extent, the contribution to the applicant's livelihood derived from his agricultural work must be 'substantial in terms of time and important in terms of value'. A shortfall of as much as 50% from compliance with the full test can, in a proper case, amount to compliance with the full test to a 'material extent'. Conversely, it is not sufficient for the applicant merely to show that his agricultural work upon the unit or holding in question made an important contribution towards his livelihood. That is to view the matter the wrong way round. The ALT must determine the amount of the shortfall and then see whether the extent of compliance is sufficient[8].

1   AHA 1986, s 41(1)(b).
2   AHA 1986, s 41(2).
3   *Kellett v Cady* (1980) 257 Estates Gazette 494.
4   See para 35.86 ff.
5   [1981] 2 All ER 51, 258 Estates Gazette 168.
6   (1985) 274 Estates Gazette 1254.

7   [2006] EWHC 1773 (Admin), [2006] 43 EG 180.
8   *Littlewood v Rolfe* [1981] 2 All ER 51, (1981) 258 EG 168; *Thomson v Church Comrs for England* [2006] EWHC 1773 (Admin), [2006] 43 EG 180. Also see the discussion at para 35.37.

35.52 The AHA 1986 itself gives an example of how an applicant, though not fully eligible, might be treated as eligible. Section 41(6) provides that an applicant can be treated as eligible if the contribution that his agricultural work on the holding in question fell short of providing him with his principal source of livelihood because the holding was too small[1]. If the tenant had other farms or land, the applicant may also be assisted by the direction that the ALT may take into account income derived from work on 'a unit of which the holding forms part'[2].

Section 41 also provides assistance to the applicant where the applicant has worked on the holding, or a unit of which the holding forms part, for less than the five years required by the required by the livelihood test. The issue was considered in *Raine's Trustee v Raine*[3] where the applicant had only worked on the holding for three years in the seven years prior to the tenant's death. The court, applying the guidance in *Littlewood v Rolfe*[4], directed that the correct test in these circumstances was whether the time spent working on the holding was a 'substantial' satisfaction of the five years required. Applying that test, an applicant with as little as two and a half years' work on the holding could qualify for eligibility. In each case it is a question of fact for the ALT.

1   This was considered in *Wilson v Earl Spencer's Settlement Trustees* (1985) 274 Estates Gazette 1254.
2   AHA 1986, s 36(3).
3   (1985) 275 EG 374.
4   [1981] 2 All ER 51.

DUAL APPLICATIONS

35.53 An applicant may apply on the basis that he is fully eligible and may also apply in the alternative to be treated as eligible[1]. As indicated above, this is a very sensible course for an applicant to take in the event of there being any doubt at all as to whether he is fully eligible. Applicants can fail the full eligibility tests on the most technical of bases, for example:

(a)   in the case of a married daughter, because of the contribution of her husband to her livelihood; or
(b)   because of some closely related agricultural activity which does not strictly constitute agricultural work upon the holding, such as cattle dealing, a retail milk round, agricultural machinery repairing or even possibly agricultural contracting.

In those circumstances, it is a wise precaution to make an application to be treated as eligible without prejudice to the applicant's primary contention that he is in any event fully eligible.

1   AHA 1986, s 41(5).

THE FAIR AND REASONABLE TEST

35.54 It is not sufficient for the applicant to show that he has satisfied the full eligibility test to a material extent and assert that he should be treated as eligible. The applicant must go on and satisfy the ALT that in all circumstances it would be fair and reasonable for the applicant to be able to apply under s 39 of the AHA 1986 for a direction entitling him to a tenancy of the holding. This requires a wide-ranging inquiry and the ALT might, for example, determine that it would not be fair and reasonable for the applicant to be treated as fully eligible if there were substantial land holdings available to him, which did not disqualify him under the commercial unit occupation test because he had so arranged his affairs that he was not a disqualifying occupier, though he had available to him the use of that land. The provision is essentially directed to whether the applicant can satisfy the test, not to initiating a general investigation of the merits of the application. Therefore, consideration of the effect on the beneficiaries of the trustee landlords is not relevant[1].

[1]   *James Raine's Trustee v Raine* (1985) 275 Estates Gazette 374.

Commercial unit occupation test

35.55 The third test which the applicant must satisfy if he is to establish eligibility before the ALT is that 'he is not the occupier of a commercial unit of agricultural land'[1].

This test emanates from the Agriculture (Miscellaneous Provisions) Act 1976. It has been the subject of very substantial amendment in the AHA 1984, now incorporated in Pt I of Sch 6 to the AHA 1986 which contains:

(a)   the definition of commercial unit of agricultural land; and
(b)   extensive definitions of what constitutes occupation and deemed occupation and also as to how joint occupation falls to be treated.

[1]   AHA 1986, s 36(3)(b).

Commercial unit of agricultural land

35.56 A commercial unit is defined as 'a unit of agricultural land which is capable when farmed under competent management of producing a net annual income of an amount not less than the aggregate of the average annual earning of two full-time male agricultural workers, aged 20 or over'[1].

The Minister[2] has power to prescribe by order Units of Production Regulations by which the productive capacity of a unit of agricultural land falls to be assessed[3]. These Agricultural Holdings (Units of Production) Regulations apply for any period of 12 months, as specified in the regulations. They are the subject of annual review. The first such set of regulations made were entitled the Agriculture (Miscellaneous Provisions) Act 1976 (Units of Production) Order 1984[4]. These have been revoked and replaced every 12 months[5].

35.56 *Succession on death*

The procedure for applying the regulations to the land (which is, or may be, a commercial unit) which falls for consideration in the context of the application is for the Secretary of the ALT, or any close relation of the deceased, or the landlord, to request the Minister to determine, by reference to the provisions of the order in force at the time, the net annual income which in his view the land is capable of producing. The Minister, in practice, delegates this function to the local divisional surveyor for the area where the land is situated. The Minister is required to issue a written statement of his view and the reasons for it to the person making the request[6]. The reason is that, before making a direction in favour of the applicant, the ALT is required to determine that the applicant was an eligible person at the date of death, and no eligibility includes the requirement that the applicant is not the occupier of a commercial unit of agricultural land, the ALT must satisfy itself the applicant satisfies this latter requirement[7].

If before the hearing of the application, a subsequent order is made which will have affected any matter on which the Minister's determination was based, then a revised determination has to be made[8].

At the hearing the Minister's assessment is to be taken as evidence, but not as conclusive evidence, of whether or not the land which is the subject of the determination is a commercial unit[9].

[1]   AHA 1986, Sch 6 Pt I para 3(1).
[2]   See para 4.2.
[3]   AHA 1986, Sch 6 Pt I para 4.
[4]   SI 1984/1309.
[5]   New regulations have come into effect in September of each year since 1984. The current regulations are the Agricultural Holdings (Units of Production) (England) Order 2006, SI 2006/2628. Following the enactment of the Government of Wales Act 1998 and the consequent devolution of certain central government functions to an elected Assembly of Wales, it is probable that a new set of concurrent Units of Production Order applicable only to Wales will be made. Currently, no such Order of equivalent provision has been made and for the time being the current regulations applicable to England will also apply to Wales.
[6]   AHA 1986, Sch 6 Pt I para 5(1).
[7]   See *Keene v Trustees for Guy's and St Thomas' Charity* (2005) ALT, South Western, albeit that this case related to a retirement notice.
[8]   AHA 1986, Sch 6 Pt I para 5(3).
[9]   This contrasts with the provisions contained formerly in s 18(6) of the A(MP)A 1976, which provided that the Minister's determination was conclusive on the matter. Now the Minister's determination is open to challenge.

Agricultural Holdings (Units of Production) Regulations

35.57 The Units of Production Regulations make no allowance for land quality, stock holding capacity or otherwise. Livestock enterprises are determined by reference to the number of stock capable of being carried on the relevant land. This is regardless of whether the whole or a substantial part of the feedstuffs can be grown on the holding, so as to render the livestock enterprise self-sufficient, or whether they have to be bought in. It is also regardless of whether or not in establishing, say, an intensive livestock enterprise, the applicant has had to embark upon substantial borrowings. It follows that applicants can fall to be disqualified because they own or rent a small block of land on which an intensive livestock enterprise is established which is wholly dependent upon the subject holding for the supply of feedstuffs. This is notwithstanding the fact that the disqualifying commercial unit is a wholly uneconomic unit which could not be self-sufficient. If it can be shown that the unit, considered in isolation, would continue as an intensive livestock farm reliant upon bought-in feedstuffs, then it is a disqualifying commercial unit.

It is not the actual stocking or cropping of the land which is the subject of the commercial unit assessment that is the determining feature, but the notional stocking or cropping of that land when 'farmed under competent management'. An adjustment may need to be made in individual cases so as to vary the stocking or cropping appropriately. Once that adjustment has been made, the units of production figures have to be applied, even though the current economic climate or the limitations of the holding or its fixed equipment are such that in reality the notional income would be unlikely to be achievable.

The mere fact that there is fixed equipment which could support the enterprise subject to alteration and improvement, but such an enterprise would not normally be carried on upon that holding, does not require the Tribunal to attribute a notional income to those buildings by reference to the Units of Production Regulations. The test is whether under competent management such an enterprise would be established upon the land in question by reason of current economic or other conditions. Therefore, for example, a redundant range of traditional piggeries will not necessarily be treated as capable of carrying the appropriate number of livestock for commercial unit assessment purposes just because the buildings are still there on the land.

Although the Minister is required by order to prescribe units of production so as to determine the notional income and productive capacity of the land, there is no corresponding provision for the Minister to prescribe the aggregate of the average annual earnings of two full-time male agricultural workers aged 20 or over. Thus, the Ministry press release in which the Minister states that, because he has determined the Unit of Production Regulations by averaging statistical information gained over the previous three years, the aggregate of the average annual earnings should, similarly, be determined by averaging the previous three years earnings, is of no binding effect. It is submitted that the Minister has misapplied the statutory provisions contained in para 3(1) of Sch 6 and that the *current* average annual earnings should be considered and not the historic earnings. This is because the income needed to pay two full-time male agricultural workers aged 20 or over requires them to be paid at the current level of wages and not at any historic level[1].

In the case of most cattle enterprises, there is provision in the Regulations[2] for a pro-rata adjustment in the published figures to be made where the livestock are kept on the land in question for less than 12 months. There is no such provision for other livestock, eg sheep, which are over-wintered on the land. The result is inconsistent and produces further distortion in the practical application of the Regulations.

597

With the changes made to the Common Agricultural Policy, the Minister has changed his method of calculating the notional income and productive capacity of land. CAP payments are taken into account[3].

With fluctuating farming profitability, the commercial unit test becomes arbitrary. The date of death may be critical in the cycle of profitability.

The practice of the Minister had been to publish statistical average evidence of the 'the aggregate of the average annual earnings of full-time male agricultural workers aged 20 or over' quarterly[4]. These figures have been widely used by ALTs as the relevant figures to be compared with the figures produced by the Agricultural Holdings (Units of Production) Order figures in determining the notational income available from the holding. This practice has now been discontinued. In the absence of available statistical information, considerable difficulties are presented to individual litigants and ALTs, in determining which set of statistics should be used and whether, for example, overtime should be included and, if so, to what extent.

[1] For decisions of ALTs to this effect, see *York v Little Houghton Estate* (1986) ALT, Eastern Area. *Tripp v Partridge* (1987) ALT, South Western Area and *Lemon v Butler* (1988) ALT, South Western Area.
[2] The Agricultural Holdings (Units of Production) (England) Order 2006, SI 2006/2628.
[3] SI 2006/2628.
[4] This wording mirrors AHA 1986, Sch 6 para 3(1).

Exceptions to the commercial unit occupation test

35.58 It is not all forms of occupation of a commercial unit which disqualify an applicant. There are a number of exceptions to the general rule that an applicant who occupies a commercial unit is disqualified. Conversely, even though the applicant may not technically occupy (for example, because occupation is by his spouse or company), there he may be deemed to be in occupation.

NON-DISQUALIFYING OCCUPATION

35.59 The common feature of all forms of non-disqualifying occupation are that in each case the applicant enjoys no security of tenure or greater interest in respect of the land in question. There is a further non-disqualifying form of occupation where the applicant is a joint occupier and his interest is less than a commercial interest in the land in question. In detail these exceptions are contained in paras 6 and 7 of Sch 6 to the AHA 1986 and are discussed below[1].

[1] The exceptions listed in para 35.60 are all now spent because of the enactment of the Agricultural Tenancies Act 1995.

35.60 *Tenancy approved by Minister:* If the applicant occupied under a short-term tenancy approved by the Minister under s 2(1) of the AHA 1986, then he is not disqualified[1]. This covered the short-term tenancy of less than a year with no security, because the Minister's approval was granted before the tenancy was created[2]. No such new tenancies can be created since 1 September 1995 after the ATA 1995 came into force and, accordingly, this provision is in practice no longer applicable.

A tenancy for between two and five years, subject to Minister's prior consent: Such a tenancy[3], again, affords no security to the applicant. Such tenancies can no longer be created since 1 September 1995[4].

Grazing agreement: A grazing agreement could constitute either a licence[5] or a tenancy and for some specified period of the year, where the land was being used for grazing or mowing only[6]. Such a tenant enjoyed no security of tenure and was not disqualified from succession[7]. This exception has no application after 1 September 1995 as a short-term grazing tenancy is now merely a species of farm business tenancy under the ATA 1995 with no special attributes because of the grazing restriction.

Gladstone v Bower agreement: A tenancy for more than one but less than two years, called a *Gladstone v Bower* tenancy, fell outside security of tenure under the AHA 1986[8]. The tenancy itself could not be the subject of succession rights, and a tenant of such a tenancy disqualified from applying for succession to the deceased's annual tenancy of another subject holding by reason of such a tenancy. Although no such tenancies can now be created, a short-term farm business tenancy would come within this exception[9].

A tenancy falling outside the definition of a contract of tenancy within the meaning of the AHA 1986: Since 1 September 1995 it is difficult to determine what sort of tenancies falling outside such definition are covered by this exception[10].

A licensee: This exception was contained in s 18(2)(c) of the 1976 Act[11]. Nearly all forms of licence were converted by s 2 of the AHA 1986 to tenancies from year to year unless they were grazing or mowing licences for a specified period of the year[12]. Licences which were not converted included licences to share occupation with the landowner, whether pursuant to a partnership agreement[13], or by reason of some other shared occupation arrangement[14]. However, it should be noted that the occupation by the licensee applicant must be occupation as licensee 'only' if the licensed land is to be disregarded for the purpose of applying the commercial unit occupation test[15].

1   AHA 1986, Sch 6 para 6(1)(a).
2   See paras 18.15 and 20.16.
3   AHA 1986, s 5.
4   AHA 1986, Sch 6 para 6(1)(d).
5   In which case the applicant was not disqualified anyway, see para 21.2 and 21.14.
6   See para 21.2.
7   AHA 1986, Sch 6 Pt I para 6(1)(a).
8   See para 20.13.
9   AHA 1986, Sch 6 para 6(1)(b).
10 AHA 1986, Sch 6 para 6(1)(c).
11 It is now contained in AHA 1986, Sch 6 Pt I para 6(1)(e).
12 See para 21.2 and 21.14 ff.

13 *Harrison-Broadley v Smith* [1964] 1 All ER 867, [1964] 1 WLR 456.
14 As, for example, occurred in *Bahamas International Trust Co Ltd v Threadgold* [1974] 3 All ER 881, [1974] 1 WLR 1514.
15 See para 35.61.

35.61 In *Brooks v Brown*[1], the applicant had farmed three holdings in partnership with his father who had been the tenant of all three, held from different landlords. The tenancies were not partnership property. After his father's death, the applicant established a new partnership with his mother and his sister, who had both been granted letters of administration in respect of his father's estate. The applicant was the only working farmer in the newly formed partnership. The landlords contested the applicant's eligibility on the basis that he did not occupy as a 'licensee *only*' [emphasis added]. The ALT decided in favour of the applicant's eligibility stating:

> 'As at the date of death and as at the date of hearing the applicant had no security of tenure in relation to [the unit] ... our conclusion is that the term 'occupies as a licenses only' means that he does not occupy by virtue of being the owner, a tenant or a licensee whose licence would be converted into a letting from year to year by virtue of s 2 of the Agricultural Holdings Act 1986. In our judgment the applicant occupied [the unit] as a licensee only'.

On appeal, in the Divisional Court, Forbes J adopted a more restrictive interpretation in favour of the landlords, holding that the applicant's occupation was not merely that of a 'licensee only'. His partnership rights gave him a degree of security beyond that which could be disregarded. In his judgment, Forbes J held that, by reference to s 38 of the Partnership Act 1890:

> 'a farming partner who is on the land is ... there (particularly if he is a family farming partner) not as a mere licensee or as a licensee only, he has rights and duties if he is the working partner which means that he has more security of tenure than a mere licensee. His position will be protected ... in the Chancery Division as a partner in the operations he wants to carry out on the land ... This is a situation which it seems to me gives him some security of tenure, using that expression with a very wide meaning ... As long as it can be shown that the occupier occupies because he is either the working farmer or one of the working farmers in a family farming partnership it really ... cannot with any sense of reality be said that he is there in occupation as a licensee only. His position ... his rights deriving from occupation as a working farming will be protected in a way that they could not be ... if he was a licensee only. The position of the [applicant], as the only family farmer left farming the land in the new family partnership ... means that his occupation of the land carries with it a greater security of tenure ... than that possessed by a licensee only'.

It is submitted that, although this decision is binding upon all ALTs, it does not sit comfortably with the decision of the Court of Appeal in *Harrison-Broadley v Smith*[2].

1 (1986) unreported, HC. See the 'Conveyancer and Property Lawyer', Vol 50 (1986), p 327 and see an article by Slatter M at p 320 – ' "Only". A Four-Letter Word?'.
2 [1964] 1 All ER 867, [1964] 1 WLR 456.

35.61A *Occupation as an executor, administrator, trustee in bankruptcy or person otherwise deriving title from another person by operation of law:* It should be noted that the wording of para 6(1) of Sch 6 to the AHA 1986 is that such occupation defined in that Schedule does not disqualify the applicant if he occupies 'only' in one of those restricted capacities. If the applicant occupied as, say, as executor, but was also entitled as a beneficiary and merely had not assented to the vesting of the holding in himself, so as to become the occupier as unrestricted owner, then it is arguable that his occupation is not that of executor 'only'. Difficulties attaching to the word 'only' were referred to by Lord Russell in *Jackson v Hall*[1] when considering the expression 'licensee only'[2].

Farm business tenancies: A farm business tenancy 'for less than five years (including a farm business tenancy which is a periodic tenancy)'[3], is occupation which does not disqualify the applicant. The words used are not for a fixed term of which less than five years remain unexpired. Therefore, where the applicant occupies under a farm business tenancy which was granted for a term of five years or more, but less than five years remain unexpired, then the farm business tenancy does not fall to be disregarded and the applicant's occupation must be taken into account in determining whether he falls to be rendered ineligible as the occupier of a commercial unit.

[1]   [1980] AC 854, [1980] 1 All ER 177.
[2]   [1980] AC 854, [1980] 1 All ER 177, 'The applicant asserts that ... his occupation of the unit has been as licensee only; I suppose as licensee of his brother. I do not find it obvious that this is so. The brothers farmed the unit in partnership with the tenancy relevantly the sole partnership asset. The partnership presumably continued unaffected by the assignment with, for example, any growing crops or dairy herd or dead stock thereon as assets of the partnership and the applicant would supposedly have some rights as co-partner in respect of entry on the land. The respondent applicant in this case to this House states that after the assignment he continued to occupy the unit jointly with his brother as his partner. However, no point was suggested on these lines and I say no more about it.' It should be noted that Forbes J considered this passage in *Brooks v Brown* (1986) unreported, HC.
[3]   AHA 1986, Sch 6 Pt I para 6(1)(dd).

JOINT OCCUPATION

35.62 It was decided by the House of Lords in *Williamson v Thompson*[1], under the A(MP)A 1976, that joint occupiers fell to be disqualified in the same way as sole occupiers, regardless of how many joint occupiers there were. Thus, a parcel of land might be a commercial unit by a narrow margin and be occupied by three or four brothers. In such circumstances, the land could not possibly provide a living for all of them and yet each was disqualified from succession. That injustice has been remedied. Where there is joint occupation by two or more persons as beneficial joint tenants, tenants in common, joint tenants under a tenancy, or joint licensees, although the applicant is treated as occupying all the land in question, the ALT must determine the appropriate share of the net annual income[2]. If an applicant is one of three joint equal owners, the unit in question will have to be a commercial unit three times over before the applicant is disqualified. In the case of tenants in common, since they may hold in unequal shares, the notional income attributable to the applicant is to be determined by apportioning to him the proportion of the income that his undivided share in the land bears to the whole. If two brothers jointly own a parcel of land, and the applicant brother is a tenant in common whose undivided share is 25% of the proceeds of sale of the land in question, then that block of land will have to be a commercial unit four times over before that applicant is disqualified by reason of his occupation of it.

¹   [1980] AC 854, [1980] 1 All ER 177.
²   AHA 1986, Sch 6 Pt I para 7.

DEEMED OCCUPATION: GENERALLY

35.63 *Following an ALT direction:* There have never been any restrictions on the number of holdings to which an applicant may apply for succession. However, if he applies for a direction entitling him to the grant of a new tenancy in succession to the late tenant, when a direction has been made by the ALT to a successful applicant entitling him to the grant of a new tenancy of any one holding or part of a holding, the applicant is deemed then to be in occupation of that holding or part holding¹.

For the purposes of applying the commercial unit occupation test, that land (together with any other land that he occupies) falls to be assessed in determining whether he is disqualified as the occupier of sufficient land to constitute a commercial unit. In the case of multiple applications, the applicant may determine the order in which the applications fall to be heard and determined by the ALT². That is subject to the proviso that where there are two or more applicants, then their joint election determines the order, but if they have not been able to agree between themselves, the Chairman of the ALT must then determine the order of hearing³. The Chairman's determination must be by reference to the size of the holdings, with the largest being heard first⁴. Individual applicants are unlikely to elect for the hearings to take place in that order, since the larger unit may well disqualify the applicant from proceeding with the hearing in respect of the smaller units.

¹   AHA 1986, Sch 6 Pt I para 8.
²   AHA 1986, s 42(2)(a).
³   AHA 1986, s 42(2)(b).
⁴   AHA 1986, s 42(3).

35.64 There is nothing in the AHA 1986 to preclude the applicant from first choosing sufficient holdings to amount to a little under a commercial unit's worth of land for determination, and for the largest holding to be selected immediately next. In this way the applicant is able to maximise succession in relation to the holdings.

DEEMED OCCUPATION BY SPOUSE OR CIVIL PARTNER

35.65 Before the passing of the AHA 1984, following the introduction of the A(MP)A 1976, many applicants, or potential applicants, anxious to avoid disqualification, vested disqualifying units of agricultural land in their spouses so that they could then demonstrate that they themselves did not occupy a commercial unit of land in order to satisfy the commercial unit occupation test. Any land occupied by a spouse or civil partner of the applicant is deemed to be occupied by the applicant[1]. It is no longer possible for an applicant to vest land in his spouse and thereby satisfy the commercial unit occupation test. There is no equivalent deemed occupation provision for other closely connected persons.

1   AHA 1986, Sch 6 Pt I para 9(1)(a), as amended by the Civil Partnerships Act 2004, s 81 and Sch 8 para 39(5).

DEEMED OCCUPATION BY CONTROLLED COMPANY

35.66 Similarly, before the passing of the AHA 1984, many applicants were able to satisfy the commercial unit occupation test, notwithstanding the fact that they and/or their spouses owned the whole or a substantial part of the shareholding in a company which, in turn, occupied a commercial unit of agricultural land. The applicant was then able to succeed in the argument that he himself did not occupy any land – he was a mere director and shareholder of the company which, being a separate legal person, occupied separately. Any land occupied by a company which is controlled by the applicant, or by the applicant's spouse or civil partner, or by their combined shareholding (or control otherwise exercised) will, if it in turn occupies a commercial unit of agricultural land, disqualify the applicant. Land occupied by such a company falls to be aggregated with any other land the applicant may occupy for determining whether or not the applicant is the occupier of a commercial unit[1].

1   AHA 1986, Sch 6 Pt I para 9(1)(b).

35.67 Similarly, if such a spouse, civil partner or company let land to an applicant, which the applicant would not be deemed to occupy by virtue of para 6 of Sch 6 to the AHA 1986 because he did not have rights of occupation carrying security of tenure, the applicant will not be saved by the disregarding provisions of para 6, since he himself will be deemed to be the occupier by virtue of para 9 and the express provisions of para 6(2) of Sch 6 and para 10 will apply. On the other hand, if the applicant's interest in the company falls short of a controlling interest, the company's occupational rights in any land is disregarded altogether. The position is different in the case of joint occupation.

DEEMED OCCUPATION BY LANDLORD/GRANTOR IN SOME CIRCUMSTANCES

35.68 It has already been noted that what used to be *Gladstone v Bower* agreements or other short-term tenancies or licences are not disqualifying land occupations[1]. Conversely, persons who grant such short-term arrangements, with very limited security, are themselves deemed to remain in occupation, notwithstanding such grants[2]. This covers all of the forms of non-disqualifying tenancies and licences specified in parag 6(1)(a) to (e) of Sch 6[3]. It is not possible, therefore, for an occupant of a commercial unit to divest himself by such a short-term arrangement so as to acquire a direction in respect of the subject holding and then resume occupation of his otherwise disqualifying commercial unit after succession.

1   See para 35.60.
2   AHA 1986, Sch 6 Pt I para 10.
3   See para 35.59 ff.

SUITABLE PERSONS

35.69 Whereas the tests of eligibility are highly technical and often produce arbitrary results, the tests of suitability are not technical, leaving wide discretion to the ALT members to use their common sense and knowledge of agriculture as to the general overall competence and ability of the applicant. The ALT is given a very wide discretion to make its determination. It must merely have regard to 'all relevant matters' in determining whether, in its opinion, a particular applicant is 'suitable' to be granted a tenancy in succession to the deceased tenant[1]. This has the advantage that cases are decided on their merits within the spirit and intention of the law, but the disadvantage that the standards applied vary greatly from Tribunal to Tribunal.

1   AHA 1986, s 39(2).

35.70 By virtue of s 39(8) of the AHA 1986, the term 'all relevant matters' includes the following specific matters:

'(a)   The extent to which the applicant or each of [the] applicants has been trained in or has had practical experience of agriculture.

(b)   The age, physical health and financial standing of the applicant or each of [the] applicants.

(c)   The views (if any) stated by the landlord on the suitability of the applicant or any of [the] applicants'.

Training or practical experience

35.71 It should be noted that the statutory requirement is in the alternative. The applicant does not have to show that he has had both training and experience. Either will suffice. Moreover, the applicant may be found to be suitable even though the agricultural work will be principally performed by a close relative[1].

1   *White v de Pelet* (1993) ALT, South Western Area, where the applicant was found to be suitable although his grandson would undertake the principal work on the farm.

Age, health and financial standing

35.72 Here, too, it should be noted that these are relevant factors, no one of which is itself necessarily a determining factor. Thus the fact that the applicant may be beyond the age of retirement or still very young and inexperienced will not necessarily mean that the applicant is unsuitable, although in some cases this may be (particularly when coupled with other considerations) sufficient for the ALT to find the applicant unsuitable.

So far as the applicant's financial standing is concerned, it is not necessary for the applicant to have to show that he himself owns all the live and deadstock and has all the working capital and is the sole proprietor of the farming business. If he, with the assistance of other members of the family, is adequately capitalised and if the other members of the family are prepared to make the necessary long-term financial commitment to satisfy the ALT that the farm business is adequately financed, and the landlord is not subject to unacceptable risks from an under-capitalised tenant, then the applicant will have satisfied that aspect of the suitability tests.

Landlord's view of suitability

35.73 This third set of provisions which the ALT has to take into account does not raise any new points but merely acknowledges that the landlord's views have to be taken into account. The landlord's observations are limited to his views on the suitability of the applicant which, in turn, means that it is merely the landlord's views on all relevant matters, including those specified in s 39(8)(a) and (b) of the AHA 1986, which have to be considered (ie training or practical experience and age, physical health and financial standing).

Burden of proof

35.74 The onus of proof is upon the applicant to prove that he is suitable[1]. The applicant must adduce all necessary evidence as to his suitability. This, in practice, will normally involve production of the farm accounts, a medical certificate, his birth certificate, a full statement of his assets, documents evidencing borrowing arrangements and all other necessary documentary evidence to support and corroborate his oral evidence. Witnesses will need to be called to corroborate matters in issue.

The majority of ALTs consider that the standard by which the applicant falls to be judged is that of the reasonable or prudent landlord. The applicant will need to show that he can achieve more than mere survival[2].

[1]   *Dagg v Lovett* (1980) 256 Estates Gazette 491.
[2]   See a decision to that effect from the West Midlands ALT in *Jackson v Barlow* (1978): 'Suitable ... sets its own unqualified standard and we see no reason to superimpose any elaborate qualifications upon it when Parliament has furnished us with a test couched in familiar language to apply. We approach our task in an objective way, aware of the importance of the landlord of seeing that his rent is paid, the performance of his covenants is reasonably assured and his farm is kept in good heart, well stocked and farmed efficiently. We are aware too that fair and reasonable landlords set some store by the standing of a tenant amongst his neighbouring farmers by family connections which may be a source of strength in a difficult agricultural or climatic situation and in continuity of policy is contrasted with farming for quick or excessive returns by pressing stock or land too hard but at the end of the day we have to ask the simple question – Is he suitable to be tenant of this holding?'. When considering the standard by which an applicant's suitability is to be assessed, a further difficulty has been introduced by the steep decline in farming profitability due to the reduction in the value, or at least the prices paid, for most forms of farm production. For an example of an applicant who was a casualty of declining farming profitability, see *R W Cant v British Steel plc* (1998) EA 861, 12 November.

REDUCING THE NUMBER OF APPLICATIONS

35.75 If the ALT has determined that each of a number of the applicants is eligible and suitable, it must then reduce the number of applications to one. The procedure adopted by the ALT is dealt with below[1]. In practice, it is extremely rare to find competing applicants. It is quite common to find a number of applications made by, for example, a son or sons and a widow of the applicant, not because they are in competition – all being equally happy with any one as tenant – but so as to safeguard the possibility of any one being disqualified as ineligible or being found unsuitable, thereby losing occupation of the holding for all.

[1]   See para 35.79.

THE LANDLORD'S NOTICE TO QUIT

35.76 In the case of a single applicant, or when in the case of multiple applications the ALT has determined who should be the single applicant, the next step for the ALT to take before making a direction upon the application for succession is to consider any application the landlord may make for consent to the operation of his notice to quit.

The landlord can, and in practice invariably will, serve a notice to quit[1] on the personal representatives of the deceased tenant under Case G[2]. Although that notice to quit is incontestable, and although the old tenancy will terminate in any event (regardless of the fate of any application made for succession – assuming the notice was valid and effective and duly served), the landlord is entitled to apply for consent to the operation of the notice to quit[3].

Consent to the operation of the notice to quit is a somewhat misleading description. What in effect is provided for by the AHA 1986 is not consent to the operation of the notice to quit at all, but the imposition of a bar on the making of a direction in favour of an applicant who is both eligible and suitable on the basis that the landlord can make out one of the grounds which are specified in s 27(3) of the AHA 1986 against the applicant, as if the applicant was a sitting tenant.

The procedure is for an application to be made by the landlord to the ALT within four months after service upon him of an application for succession, unless there are two or more applications for succession, in which case he has the extended time of not later than one month following the reduction of the number of applications to one (or such earlier date as the chairman may specify). The Secretary of the ALT is required to notify the landlord of the start of the relevant period of four months, or one month, as the case may be. Thereafter, the applicant has one month following service upon him of the landlord's application for service of a reply[4].

[1]   AHA 1986, s 26, Sch 3 Pt I.

2   If the landlord fails to serve such a notice after due notice of the death or application for succession his right to give a notice to quit is then lost and the applicant for succession could safely abandon his application in favour of the existing tenancy vested in the personal representatives of the deceased former tenant. For a commentary on Case G notices generally, see para 31.90.

3   AHA 1986, s 27.

4   For the procedures generally, see para 35.79.

35.77   The seven grounds under which the landlord can seek the consent of the ALT to the operation of his notice to quit are:

(a)   'the carrying out of the purpose for which the landlord proposes to terminate the tenancy is desirable in the interests of good husbandry as respects the land to which the notice relates, treated as a separate unit';

(b)   'the carry out of the purposes desirable in the interests of sound management of the estate of which the land to which the notice relates forms part or which that land constitutes';

(c)   'the carrying out of the purposes desirable for the purposes of agricultural research, education, experiment or demonstration, or for the purposes of the enactments relating to smallholdings';

(d)   'the carrying out of the purpose is desirable for the purposes of the enactments relating to allotments';

(e)   'greater hardship would be caused by withholding than by giving consent to the operation of the notice';

(f)   'the landlord proposes to terminate the tenancy for the purpose of the land's being used for a use, other than for agriculture, not falling within Case B'[1].

It will be seen from the above list of grounds upon which the landlord can seek the ALT's consent to the notice to quit that, with the exception of greater hardship, it would only be in an unusual case that one of the other six grounds would apply. This is reinforced by the fact that, as a necessary pre-condition of the ALT giving consent to the operation of the landlord's notice to quit, the ALT must be satisfied that 'in all the circumstances' it appears to the ALT that 'a fair and reasonable landlord' would insist on possession[2].

1   AHA 1986, s 27(3). See Ch 30.

2   AHA 1986, s 27(2).

35.78   An applicant who is eligible and who has shown a major commitment to the holding from which he has derived his principal source of livelihood, and who does not occupy a commercial unit of his own and has been found to be suitable, is very unlikely to be denied a direction entitling him to a tenancy of the holding on the grounds of greater hardship to the landlord. The sort of instance where such a situation could occur is where the landlord himself had a son who had been to agricultural college and had worked on another farm and was now ready to take on the farm himself. In those circumstances, if the landlord had no other land available for his own son, the ALT might well consider, that faced with the competing claims of the applicant's own son and the deceased tenant's son, that, as it was described in one case, one of the few remaining advantages of agricultural land ownership is that a landlord in those circumstances should at least be entitled to prefer the claims of his own son[1].

Many landlords make applications for consent to the operation of the notice to quit regardless of the circumstances, in the belief that they may damage their cause if they do not take advantage of the opportunity afforded to them by the statute to do so. It is submitted that such a view is mistaken and may often lead to undesirable consequences for the landlord. For example, if the landlord pleads hardship in inappropriate circumstances, he may, and probably will, be obliged to disclose full details of his own personal circumstances and those of any persons whom he claims will suffer hardship if possession is not given. This may involve his being obliged to disclose considerable amounts of information which he may consider confidential and inappropriate for disclosure to the ALT, the applicant and, through them (possibly), to the world at large.

[1] For a case to that effect, see *Holloway v Wingfield* (1977) ALT, West Midlands. On the
    facts of that case no consent was in fact given.

PROCEDURE

35.79 As with all features of the agricultural holdings legislation, it is vital for applicants and landlords alike to follow very strictly the procedures laid down both in the AHA 1986 itself and in the regulations passed under it. These are currently the Agricultural Land Tribunals (Succession to Agricultural Tenancies) Order 1984, SI 1984/1301 ('the 1984 Succession Order'), and the Agricultural Land Tribunals (Rules) Order 1978, SI 1978/259 ('the 1978 Rules Order')[1]. The replacement Agricultural Land Tribunals (Rules) Order was expected to be made in 2007.

Those time limits and procedures which are statutorily prescribed are mandatory and inflexible. Failure to comply with them is fatal to the defaulting party. Those time limits and procedures which are prescribed in the regulations passed under the statute are subject to variation by the Chairman of the Agricultural Land Tribunal under rule 37 of the 1978 Rules Order as to time and rule 38 contains a further saving provision.

[1] New Orders following the passing of the AHA 1986 have been awaited but they remain to
    be made: see para 46.20.

35.80 The interrelationship between the statutory requirements and the requirements of the regulations was considered extensively by the Divisional Court[1]. The principal statutory requirement, which must be strictly complied with if the applicant is not to become statute barred, is the time limit of three months of the day following the date of death of the original tenant. During this time the applicant must make his application to the ALT.

The commentary set out below does not cover each and every one of the regulations. It is no substitute for detailed consideration of the regulations themselves. It merely highlights those points most frequently met with in practice[2].

[1] *Kellett v Alexander* (1980) 257 Estates Gazette 494.
[2] See also the commentary in Ch 46.

Application by potential new tenant

35.81 Any eligible person wishing to apply for a new tenancy must make his application within three months of the date following the date of death of the deceased tenant in accordance with Form 1 (Succession on Death) which appears in the Appendix to the 1984 Succession Order, or in a form 'substantially to the like effect'[1].

The application must relate to the whole holding. There is no provision for applying for succession in respect of part only[2].

The three-month time limit is expressed to be 'the period of three months beginning with the day after the date of death'[3]. The corresponding day rule applies[4].

If the applicant is not fully eligible, but wishes to apply under s 41 of the AHA 1986 to be treated as eligible, that application must be made within the same three-month period. The prescribed form for an application under s 41 contains a part (Part B) dealing with a person who is not fully eligible but who wishes to be treated as if he was. If there is doubt as to whether the applicant is fully eligible or not, that part of the form can be completed without prejudice to the applicant's primary contention that he is fully eligible. If he does not complete that part of the form in the belief that he is fully eligible, and he is found not to be fully eligible, he is not then able to apply at that stage to be treated as eligible: his failure to complete the form in the first place being then fatal.

1   See r 3 read with art 1(3)(b) of the 1984 Succession Order. But see also *Morris v Patel* (1986) 281 Estates Gazette 419 where an out-of-date prescribed form was used. It was nevertheless held to be substantially to the like effect as the current form despite material differences. Note that ALTs use forms referring to the AHA 1986 notwithstanding the fact that the 1984 Succession Order refers to the Agricultural Holdings (Notice to Quit) Act 1977.
2   For the provisions relating to the making of a direction in respect of part only, see para 35.93.
3   AHA 1986, s 39(1).
4   *Dodds v Walker* [1981] 2 All ER 609, [1981] 1 WLR 1027, HL. See para 42.27.

35.82 The time limit of three months for applying to be treated as eligible is statutorily prescribed and is, therefore, mandatory and inflexible. Neither the chairman nor the ALT has any power to extend the time.

At the same time as making an application to the ALT, the applicant must give notice of his application to the landlord in Form 3 (Succession on Death)[1]. However, failure to serve notice of the application upon the landlord is not fatal to the applicant, provided the landlord is not prejudiced[2].

The application must be accompanied by various documents, as listed in art 16(4) of the Agricultural Land Tribunals (Rules) Order 1978. These include all documents on which the party making the application intends to rely in support of his case. This rule has been more honoured in the breach than in the observance. In practice, documents are often produced by the parties after the application has been made.

Normally an applicant will need to produce the following documents to establish his eligibility and suitability to be granted a new tenancy in succession to the deceased former tenant:

(a) the deceased tenant's death certificate, so as to establish the fact and date of death;

(b) the applicant's birth certificate – full, not shortened form – so as to establish the close relationship;

(c) the applicant's marriage certificate – in the case of a widow or married daughter applicant;

(d) farm partnership agreement or contract of employment (if applicable);

(e) the farm accounts for the relevant five years, ending with the date of death. It is a wise precaution to produce seven years' accounts so that selection of the five years can be made by discarding any two where losses or problems of eligibility arise;

(f) a statement of the applicant's wages (if applicable);

(g) a statement setting out any outside sources of livelihood, whether agriculturally related (for example, contracting, cattle dealing, cattle haulage, share farming, etc) or non-agricultural (for example, dividend income from stock exchange investments);

(h) a copy of any tenancy agreement or other agreement relating to any other land occupied by the applicant;

(i) copies of certificates relating to any relevant academic qualifications of the applicant (for example, HND, City & Guilds certificates, etc);

(j) a medical certificate stating the applicant's state of health;

(k) a full statement of the applicant's own capital and any other capital available to be used to finance the farming in the event of the applicant being successful (for example, capital belonging to members of the applicant's family, with an appropriate statement as to the arrangements made or to be made with the financier concerned);

(l) if an overdraft or other form of borrowing is to be relied upon, a letter from the bank or lending house specifying the facility available and the term or terms of the loan;

(m) if any changes are to be made in the farming system, a statement of those changes and a forward farm budget and cash flow projection showing how the farm is to be farmed henceforth;

(n) the deceased tenant's will, probate and Inland Revenue account – if the applicant is relying upon any inherited monies;

(o) a map of the subject holding to the scale of 6' to one mile or 1/10.000, or larger;

(p) a similar map or plan of any other land comprised in the agricultural unit of which the holding forms part and any other land occupied by the applicant;

(q) the notice to quit given (if any);

(r) the tenancy agreement of the subject holding.

This list is not exhaustive, but is indicative of the type of documents that a successful applicant is likely to have to adduce and which should accompany his application. If any document is unavailable at the time the application is made, it can be provided subsequently. An applicant should not delay the lodging of his application on account of unavailability of documents.

1   See the forms contained in the Schedule to SI 1984/1301 at para A1.550.
2   *Kellett v Alexander* (1980) 257 EG 494.

The landlord's reply

35.83 If the landlord wishes to oppose the whole or any part of the applicant's application, he must complete Form 1R (Succession on Death)[1] and return this within one month from the date on which the copy of the application by the applicant was served by the ALT on the landlord.

1   See the Schedule to SI 1984/1301. Note Form 1A.

35.84 Frequently, the landlord will find that the applicant has not provided sufficient information to enable the landlord to determine whether the applicant is prima facie eligible and/or suitable. The landlord will require further information and the supply of further documents to make such an assessment. In those circumstances it is normal for the landlord to put the applicant to proof, while at the same time seeking through the ALT the supply of further information and the delivery of documents in support.

If the landlord fails to reply within the prescribed period of one month, or such further period as the Chairman shall allow by the exercise of his discretion provided by r 36[1], then the landlord is not entitled to dispute any matter alleged by the applicant in his application[2].

1   The Agricultural Land Tribunals (Rules) Order 1978, SI 1978/259.
2   The Agricultural Land Tribunals (Succession to Agricultural Tenancies) Order 1984, SI 1984/1301, Schedule r 15(1).

Landlord's application for consent to operation of the notice to quit

35.85 A landlord who has given notice to quit pursuant to Case G of Pt I of Sch 3 to the AHA 1986 may apply for consent to the operation of the notice to quit[1]. The time limit for the making of an application by the landlord for consent to the operation of the notice to quit is as follows:

(a)   Where only one application for the grant of a new tenancy is made, at any time after the landlord receives notice of the application until the expiration of four months after a copy of the application itself has been served upon him. The Secretary of the ALT is required to inform the landlord at the start of the period of four months[2].
(b)   If two or more applications for succession are made then the four-month period is extended until one month after the date on which the number of applications which are pending is reduced to one, or within one month of such earlier date as the ALT may direct[3].

Many landlords make applications for consent to the operation of the notice to quit almost as a matter of course, though very rarely are they well advised to do so[4]. Any application by the landlord must also be accompanied by all documents on which the landlord relies (as for the applicant's application)[5]. The landlord should also give all necessary particulars of hardship and the like, if a greater hardship ground is relied upon. Even if it is not, he should do so to satisfy the fair and reasonable landlord proviso.

1   For the commentary on this provision, see para 31.90 and note that even if no application for consent is made the notice to quit will still take effect regardless of the success of the application. The effect of consent is not to render a notice which would otherwise be inoperative effective but to preclude an applicant who is eligible and suitable from obtaining a direction for succession. AHA 1986, s 44.
2   SI 1984/1301, Schedule r 4.
3   SI 1984/1301, Schedule r 4(4).
4   See para 35.78.
5   See para 35.82.

Multiple applications

35.86 If more than one application is received by the ALT within the relevant period of three months from the date of death of the tenant, then the procedures to be followed by the ALT are set out in the AHA 1986.

If one of the applicants is a person 'validly designated by the deceased in his will as the person he wishes to succeed him as tenant of the holding', the ALT must first determine whether that person is both eligible and suitable. The ALT may only consider any other applicant if the ALT determines that the person designated in the will is not an eligible and/or suitable person to become the tenant of the holding[1]. It is a wise precaution for a tenant to nominate his successor in his will or codicil[2].

1   AHA 1986, s 39(4).
2   See para 35.89.

35.87 If no person is designated by the will, or if the person so designated is found by the ALT to be ineligible and/or unsuitable, then the ALT must consider each of the other applicants and determine whether each is both eligible and suitable[1].

1   AHA 1986, s 39(6).

35.88 If the landlord consents, the ALT may give a direction specifying any two, three or four applicants as being entitled to a joint tenancy of the holding[1]. If the landlord objects to a joint tenancy, or indeed to any one of the applicants being the subject of a direction entitling him to a tenancy of the holding, then the ALT must, subject to affording the landlord an opportunity of stating his views on the suitability of that applicant[2], determine which, in the ALT's opinion, is the most suitable person to be the subject of a direction entitling him to the tenancy of the holding[3].

1   AHA 1986, s 39(9).

2   AHA 1986, s 39(7).
3   AHA 1986, s 39(8).

35.89 It very frequently happens that multiple applications are made not because the applicants are in competition for the holding, but so as to safeguard the tenancy being lost by some technical disqualification of a sole applicant. For example, a widow and son might apply in circumstances where both wish the son to be successful but the widow's application was made in case the son might be found too inexperienced or not to have satisfied the principal source of livelihood test fully. In those circumstances, a wise precaution for the tenant to take during his lifetime is to nominate his son in his will so that the widow's application can be left in abeyance pending determination of the son's. If there is no such nomination, the ALT must hear both applications together and determine which applicant is the more suitable. If the widow is then successful, despite the views of both applicants that the son should be treated as the favoured candidate, one of the two potential rights of succession will have been 'used up'.

Where two or more applications are made, each applicant may, if he wishes to oppose any of the other applicants, file a reply to the other applications in Form 4 (Succession on Death) and, if he wishes to do so, must file the reply with the ALT within one month of the expiry of the relevant period[1].

If the applicants are not in competition, but wish to apply for a joint tenancy, the form, suitably adapted, must be completed within the same period of one month so as to constitute the application for a joint tenancy[2].

1   SI 1984/1301, Schedule r 8(1).
2   SI 1984/1301, Schedule r 8(2).

Interlocutory matters

35.90 Once the exchange of applications and replies has been concluded, the Secretary of the ALT is required 'as soon as practicable' to fix a date, time and place for the hearing of the application and to give at least 14 days' notice of the hearing[1].

Frequently, documents will not have been supplied by either the applicant in support of his application for a direction, or the landlord in support of his application for consent to the operation of the notice to quit, in which event the aggrieved party may apply under r 19[2], in writing, for any directions on any matter which the Chairman has power to determine, including a request for the provision of documents or other information[3].

Before making a determination in the case of any applicant, the ALT must give the landlord an opportunity to state his views as to the suitability of the applicant[4].

1   SI 1984/1301, Schedule r 29.
2   The 1978 Rules Order, SI 1978/259.

3   For the provisions regarding interlocutory matters generally, see Ch 46.
4   AHA 1986, s 39(7).

The hearing

A *single applicant*

35.91 If there is only one application for succession, then the applicant must open his case. If the landlord has sought consent to the operation of his notice to quit, that is treated as a counter-claim. The procedure is the same as for civil proceedings in the High Court[1].

1   SI 1984/1301, Schedule r 16.

Multiple applications

35.92 As to the procedure as to multiple applications[1], if the ALT determines that one or more of several applicants is both eligible and suitable, but no application has been made by the landlord for consent to the operation of his notice to quit, before making any direction in favour of the applicant in question, the proceedings must first be adjourned to enable the landlord within one month thereafter to make an application if he wishes for consent to the operation of his notice to quit[2].

1   See para 35.86.
2   SI 1984/1301, r 13.

DIRECTION OF THE AGRICULTURAL LAND TRIBUNAL

Succession to part only

35.93 Under the original scheme devised by the A(MP)A 1976, there was no power for the ALT to grant a direction in respect of part only of the holding. A limited power was given to the ALT by the AHA 1984 to make a direction in respect of part[1]. This has now been repealed and re-enacted in the AHA 1986[2].

Section 39(10) of the AHA 1986 provides that any person or persons who would otherwise be entitled to a direction in respect of the whole holding may accept (in lieu) a direction given by the ALT in respect of part only of the holding. In those circumstances, the ALT may make a direction in respect of that part. It should be noted that this only applies if the applicant or applicants themselves consent. There is no power for the ALT to compel an applicant to accept a direction in respect of part only. If the ALT feels that, for example, the justice of the case requires that the applicant should succeed on part, but that the landlord should be entitled to recover part, but the parties do not agree, the ALT cannot make any direction to that effect. It must determine instead whether the applicant is entitled to a direction in respect of the whole and, if so, make such a direction and, if not, withhold the direction in respect of the entire holding. This prevents the ALT descending into the arena and becoming involved in negotiating what the members of the ALT might perceive to be a just and equitable settlement.

Section 44(5) of the AHA 1986 entitles the ALT to give consent to the operation of the notice to quit given by the landlord in respect of part only. Here too the ALT's power is restricted to those cases where, by agreement between the landlord and the applicant, consent from the ALT is sought in respect of part only.

It should be noted that this procedure contrasts with the procedure as to succession on retirement, where there is no power for the ALT to make a direction in respect of part only. There is no equivalent of s 39(10) of the AHA 1986 under, for example, s 53, which is the equivalent provision to s 39 applying to a retirement application.

¹   AHA 1984, Sch 1 para 3.
²   AHA 1986, ss 39(1) and 44(5).

Effect of direction

35.94 If an applicant satisfies the ALT that he is both eligible and suitable, then unless the landlord obtains consent to the operation of his notice to quit, the ALT must make a direction entitling the applicant to the grant of a new tenancy in respect of the whole holding[1].

Section 45 of the AHA 1986 provides that a new tenancy (or joint tenancy) is to be deemed to be granted by the landlord to, and accepted by, the successful applicant with effect from the 'relevant time'. That is:

(a)   Where a Case G notice to quit was given by reason of the death, and has not yet expired, the date upon which the notice to quit takes effect.

(b)   Where a Case G notice to quit has been given, but the ALT does not make its direction until after the notice has expired, or would have expired were it not for s 43 of the AHA 1986, then s 43 postpones the operation of a notice to quit given by ensuring that such a notice shall not take effect unless either no application has been made for succession or each application made has been dismissed. Until such time as the determination by the ALT of the application for succession has been made, the Case G notice does not take effect.

(c)   Where no Case G notice to quit was given, then the new tenancy is to take effect at the end of the 12 months immediately following the end of the year of the tenancy in which the deceased tenant died. This will usually be the date on which any notice to quit which could have been given would have taken effect, but it could be earlier.

(d)   If the direction is made before the expiration of the relevant time, then the ALT may, if the tenant applies, specify in its direction as the relevant time any time within the period of three months following the expiration of the original relevant time, as the ALT thinks fit.

(e)   If the ALT gives its direction after the expiration of the original relevant time, then the ALT must specify a new relevant time within the period of three months following the date of the giving of the direction[2]. If the ALT fails to do so, the direction will be invalid because the obligation is statutorily prescribed. It is not merely an obligation provided for in regulations.

These time limits are of major importance and must be closely monitored by applicants and landlords alike because, in the case of a successful application, they affect the subsequent arbitration provisions as to rent and the terms of the new tenancy[3].

In the case of an unsuccessful application, there is no power to extend the period for the operation of the notice to quit. If the landlord has not given a notice to quit pursuant to Case G or, alternatively, has given an invalid notice, then, although the applicant will not obtain a new tenancy, the old tenancy will endure, vested in the personal representatives. Even on their death the landlord will not be able to recover possession, since they will not come within the relevant definition of a 'tenant' for the purposes of Case G. They hold in a fiduciary capacity. They may be required to vest the tenancy in the beneficiary or beneficiaries under the deceased's will[4].

[1]   As to the position regarding succession of part only, see para 35.93.
[2]   AHA 1986, s 46(2).
[3]   See para 35.96.
[4]   See para 31.95.

Terms of new tenancy

35.95   The terms of the new tenancy will be the same as the terms of the old tenancy unless the terms are:

(a)   varied by agreement; or
(b)   varied by arbitration under s 48 of the AHA 1986[1].

[1]   AHA 1986, s 47.

35.96   This is subject to two provisos:

(a)   where the deceased held a fixed-term lease[1]. In such a case, the new tenancy is converted into an annual tenancy;
(b)   if there was no prohibition upon assigning, sub-letting or parting with possession in the deceased tenant's tenancy agreement, then the terms of the new tenancy to which the successful applicant is entitled is deemed to include such a covenant[2].

The provisions as to arbitration are contained in s 48 of the AHA 1986. They entitle either the landlord or the tenant to apply for arbitration on one or other or both of two questions:

(i)   What variations in the terms of the tenancy which the deceased tenant held are justifiable having regard to the circumstances of the holding and the length of time since the holding was let on those terms?

(ii) What rent should be, or should have been, properly payable in respect of the holding at the relevant time?

As always with the agricultural holdings legislation, time limits are prescribed which are inflexible, mandatory and, if missed, preclude the arbitration from proceeding. The time for demanding arbitration is within the 'prescribed period' which is defined as being the period between the giving of the direction and the end of three months immediately following the relevant time[3]. If the direction is made after the end of the relevant time, the prescribed period expires on the expiration of three months from the date of the giving of the direction.

The terms of the new tenancy will include a covenant against assigning, sub-letting or parting with possession, whether or not the old tenancy contains such provision[4]. The arbitrator may, if he considers it equitable, vary the rent, even though only the terms of the tenancy have been referred to arbitration and not the rent itself. This power is limited to a variation in rental by reason of the variation of the terms and does not enable a comprehensive rent review to take place if the rent itself has not been referred to arbitration.

The rent that the arbitrator has to determine, if the rent has been referred to arbitration, is the rent properly payable in accordance with the provisions of s 12 of the AHA 1986, so that there is no difference between the rent to be assessed following a succession and the rent to be assessed for a sitting tenant[5].

[1] AHA 1986, s 47(2). Such a lease normally would preclude any claim for succession unless the lease had less than 27 months of its term unexpired: AHA 1986, see s 36(2)(a). See para 35.8.
[2] AHA 1986, s 47(3).
[3] AHA 1986, s 48(2). As has been seen earlier, the relevant time is normally the time when the notice to quit would have expired, but for the exceptions: see para 35.94.
[4] AHA 1986, s 45(2).
[5] AHA 1986, s 48(9) and Sch 2 para 1.

35.97 It should be remembered that the old tenancy will have been determined and a new tenancy will be being granted by the operation of the succession provisions. Accordingly, the landlord will be entitled to claim dilapidations and the personal representatives of the deceased tenant will be entitled to claim tenant right, compensation for improvements and the like. The arbitrator appointed under s 48, even though he is not appointed to deal with the normal claims and counter-claims on termination of a tenancy which are dealt with under s 83, may include in his award provision for:

(a) the landlord to recover from the incoming tenant the payments that he would otherwise be obliged to make to the outgoing tenant for tenant right, compensation for improvements and the like; and
(b) the incoming tenant to recover from the landlord an ingoing payment for dilapidations[1].

In practice, it is normal for the landlord, the outgoing tenant and the incoming tenant to treat the claims and counter-claims as 'rolled over'. There is little purpose in dealing with dilapidations against the personal representatives of the deceased tenant if an allowance is to be made to the applicant of a similar amount, particularly since the applicant and the personal representatives of the deceased tenant are very often one and the same person, albeit in different capacities.

A problem frequently encountered in practice is how tenant's improvements which may have been written down to a fraction of their full value pursuant to an agreed formula for assessing compensation fall to be dealt with on the transmission of the tenancy on succession. In many cases it would be inequitable for an incoming tenant who may himself have helped to fund and provide the improvements to pay a rent assessed without any allowance for those improvements and for the outgoing tenant to be paid what may be little more than nominal compensation for improvements which may be of substantial value to the holding. In such a case, if the arbitrator appointed were to consider it appropriate, he could direct that the incoming tenant (the successful applicant) should pay the compensation and take over the improvements and have the benefit of them for future rent assessment purposes. The AHA 1986 makes express provision for such an award[2].

There is no authority on the extent of the arbitrator's powers if, for example, the landlord was anxious to pay the outgoing tenant modest compensation, without recovery from the incoming tenant, so as to enhance (at moderate cost to himself) the landlord's future rental from the holding.

There is also provision for the arbitrator to include in his award any agreed matters over and above those statutorily referred to arbitration[3].

If the arbitrator's award made under s 48 is made before the 'relevant time' then the new tenancy granted as a consequence of a direction of the ALT shall be on the same terms on which the holding was let immediately before it ceased to be let under the contract of tenancy under which it was let at the date of the deceased tenant's death, subject to such variations or terms contained in the arbitrator's award[4].

The 'relevant time' has the meaning given by s 46(1), (2) of the AHA 1986. Except where s 46(2) applies, the relevant time means the end of the 12 months immediately following the end of the year of the tenancy in which the deceased died, or if a notice to quit the holding was given to the tenant by reason of the death of the deceased, being a notice falling within Case G which, apart from s 43 of the AHA 1986, would have terminated the tenancy at a time after the end of those 12 months, means that time. Where the ALT gives a direction under s 39(5), (6) or (9), in relation to the holding at any time after the period of three months ending with the relevant time apart from the operation of s 46(2), then:

(i)   if the direction is given within that period, the ALT may, on the application of the tenant, specify in the direction, as the relevant time for the purposes of ss 46 and 48, such a time falling within the period of three months immediately following the original relevant time as they think fit; or

(ii)   if the direction is given at any time after the original relevant period, the ALT shall specify in the direction, as the relevant time for those purposes, such a time falling within the period of three months immediately following the date of the giving of the direction as they think fit.

If the award of the arbitrator made under s 48 of the AHA 1986 is made after the 'relevant time'[5], it shall have effect as if the terms of the award were contained in an agreement in writing entered into by the landlord and the tenant and having effect as from the relevant time[6].

[1]   AHA 1986, s 48(5) and (8).
[2]   AHA 1986, s 48(5)(b).
[3]   AHA 1986, s 48(10).
[4]   AHA 1986, s 48(11).
[5]   AHA 1986, s 47(1).
[6]   AHA 1986, s 48(12).

MISCELLANEOUS

Death of applicant

35.98 The AHA 1986 itself does not provide for the situation which would arise in the event of an applicant himself dying after having made an application. Section 45(8) entitles the Lord Chancellor to make regulations to rectify this omission. This is a re-enactment of the provision originally contained in s 23(8) of the A(MP)A 1976 pursuant to which the Lord Chancellor made the Agriculture (Miscellaneous Provisions) Act 1976 (Application of Provisions) Regulations 1977 ('the 1977 Regulations')[1].

The 1977 Regulations provide that, if no direction has been made and the applicant was a sole applicant, his application dies with him and none of his close relations is able to apply for succession. This is because he was not himself tenant at the date of his death. Alternatively, if the applicant had obtained a direction at the date of his death then he is deemed to be the tenant and his eligible close relations can apply for succession. If he was one of several joint applicants and he died before the making of the direction, the other applications proceed and if the death occurred after the making of the direction, the joint tenancy granted vests then in them.

[1]   SI 1977/1215.

Sub-tenancies and concurrent interests

35.99 A concurrent tenant in possession enjoys full security of tenure. If a tenancy was granted and subsequently the freeholder granted a concurrent tenancy to a third party, even though that third party would then become the landlord of the original tenant, entitled to rent, etc, the original tenant would not enjoy any less security and termination of the concurrent tenancy in reversion would not destroy his tenancy.

Sub-tenants have no statutory security of tenure[1]. As a consequence a difficulty arises if the landlord introduces a concurrent tenancy to a third party (a mesne tenancy) after the grant of the deceased's interest. In this event, the grant of a new tenancy by way of succession could turn the successor into a sub-tenant, his interest arising after that of the mesne tenant. The effect would be to destroy any security of tenure, placing him in the position of a standard sub-tenant[2].

To remedy this anomaly, s 3 of the AHA 1984 was enacted. This has now been repealed and re-enacted in the AHA 1986. Where the deceased's tenancy was not derived from the interest held by his immediate landlord at the date of death, the tenancy to be granted to the successful applicant is to be deemed to be granted by the original landlord or his successor in title and not the intervening head tenant[3]. The AHA 1986 contains a wide definition of the 'supervening interests'[4]. It means 'any interest in the land comprised in the deceased's tenancy, being an interest created subsequently to that tenancy and derived (whether immediately or otherwise) from the interest from which that tenancy was derived and still subsisting at the relevant time'.

Although this ensures that the use of the concurrent head tenancy device to circumvent the security which would otherwise be enjoyed by a successful applicant is ineffective, it does not in any way affect existing sub-tenancies which were carved out of head tenancies. A successor to such a sub-tenant will enjoy no greater security than the deceased tenant enjoyed in respect of his tenancy during his lifetime.

[1]   SI 1977/1215.
[2]   For a commentary, see para 29.20.
[3]   *Chesshire v Colesbourne Estate Co* (1979) ALT, South Western.
[4]   AHA 1986, s 45(2)–(4).
[5]   AHA 1986, s 45(3).

Chapter 36

SUCCESSION ON RETIREMENT

INTRODUCTION

Historical

36.1 When succession on death was introduced in 1976, there was no provision for a tenant who was elderly or sick to retire and activate the succession provisions enacted by the Agriculture (Miscellaneous Provisions) Act 1976 (A(MP)A 1976). Section 18(5) of the A(MP)A 1976 provided for a voluntary transmission which would rank as a first succession for the purposes of the two succession rule where the landlord agreed that the tenant could retire and be replaced by a successor. There was no provision for a potential successor to obtain a tenancy without the concurrence of the landlord.

As part of the NFU/CLA package[1], the Agricultural Holdings Act 1984 (AHA 1984) introduced provisions for a tenant, on attaining the age of 65 or upon becoming permanently incapacitated, to serve a retirement notice nominating an eligible person as his potential successor. If the landlord was not prepared to agree to the grant of a new tenancy to the nominated successor, then the nominated successor could apply to the Agricultural Land Tribunal (ALT) for the grant of a new tenancy. In such a case, the procedures followed very closely the procedures which would have applied had the retiring tenant died.

Critically, under the new scheme introduced by the Agricultural Holdings Act 1984 (AHA 1984), if the applicant was refused a direction by the ALT, then he was precluded from making any further application[2]. However, if he withdrew his application[3], then the applicant was to be treated as if the application had never been made. The tenant could re-nominate the applicant, who could apply again. This enabled an applicant to address any potentially disqualifying feature of his application. This important and far-reaching set of provisions was introduced by s 4 and Sch 2 to the AHA 1984.

The whole of the AHA 1984 has now been repealed and re-enacted in the consolidating statute, the AHA 1986, in which the law relating to succession on retirement is now to be found in ss 34 and 49 to 59 and Sch 6.

621

1   See para 1.14.
2   Whether on death or retirement of the sitting-tenant. There is a possible exception to this
     general rule in the case of an applicant found to be ineligible.
3   Eg, because it became clear there he would be likely to fail.

Scheme of the statutory provisions

36.2 Sections 49 to 58 of the AHA 1986 mirror very closely the equivalent provisions for succession on death contained in ss 35 to 48 of the AHA 1986. Sections 34 and 59 apply to succession both on death and retirement. Schedule 6, containing the provisions as to eligibility of an applicant, is common to both succession on death or retirement. Part II of Sch 6 contains those modifications necessary for the purposes of applying the eligibility rules on retirement rather than death.

There are three important differences between succession on death and retirement:

(a)   there is no provision for succession to part of a holding on retirement, unlike succession on death[1];

(b)   there is no provision for the applicant to choose the order in which several concurrent applications fall to be heard in the case of succession on retirement, unlike succession on death[2];

(c)   there is no provision for an applicant who is not fully eligible to apply to be treated as eligible on retirement[3].

Since the provisions which apply to succession on retirement are so similar to those which apply on death, to avoid repetition in this chapter, wherever possible, reference is made to the commentary on succession on death.

1   See para 35.93.
2   See paras 35.86 and 35.92.
3   See para 35.51.

TENANCIES WITH AND WITHOUT SUCCESSION RIGHTS

36.3 As in the case of succession on death, it is not all tenancies which carry with them rights to succession, enabling a retirement notice to be served, as certain forms of tenancy carry with them no succession rights. These are as discussed below.

Post-July 1984 tenancies

36.4 Section 34 of the AHA 1986 provides that (with certain exceptions) any tenancy of an agricultural holding granted on or after 12 July 1984 does not carry with it any succession rights and any such tenant, therefore, is not entitled to serve a retirement notice and nominate a successor.

The exceptions to that general rule have already been commented upon[1], and s 34 of the AHA 1986 applies equally to succession on death or retirement[2]. In the case of a tenancy arising as a consequence of the operation of s 4(1)(g) of the AHA 1986[3], a substantial part of the land comprised in the holding means a substantial part determined by reference to either area of value[4].

1　See para 35.2 ff.
2　AHA 1986, s 49.
3　See para 3.14.
4　AHA 1986, s 49(4), inserted by the Regulatory Reform (Agricultural Tenancies) (England and Wales) Order 2006, SI 2006/2805, art 4(3).

Two previous successions

36.5 As upon the death of the tenant, on retirement two successions only are permissible.

Whether a lifetime succession arising before the A(MP)A 1976 could operate as a first succession is not straightforwardly answered[1]. The relevant analysis is in Chapter 35[2].

1　See *Trustees of Saunders v Ralph* (1993) 66 P & CR 335, [1993] 2 EGLR 1.
2　See para 35.14 ff.

Tenant under notice to quit

36.6 If the tenant is already subject to notice to quit given by his landlord, and either the disputes procedures have been gone through or, alternatively, the time limits for disputing the notice to quit in question (whether by counter-notice, demand for arbitration or otherwise) have expired with no issue raised, then the tenant is precluded from serving a retirement notice[1].

If the existing tenancy is the subject of a notice to quit, but the time for challenging it is either still current, or an arbitrator or the ALT (as the case may be) has yet to rule upon the notice, then the position is rather more complex than in the case of a tenant who died while under notice to quit.

1　AHA 1986, s 52, applying s 38 of the AHA 1986 to succession on retirement. See para 35.10.

Notice to quit before retirement notice

36.7 If the sitting-tenant has had notice to quit and has disputed the validity of the notice by demanding arbitration (in the case of a notice given under Cases A[1], B, D or E), and if the procedures for determining the validity of the notice to quit are in the course of being determined at the time that the tenant serves a retirement notice, then the operation of the retirement notice is suspended until either:

(a)　the arbitrator awards that the notice to quit is invalid; or
(b)　the ALT has withheld consent to the operation of the notice to quit.

In those circumstances, the nominated successor has one month following service of the arbitrator's award, or the ALT's decision, in which to apply to the ALT for a direction entitling him to a tenancy of the holding[2].

This process of suspension of the time for the nominated successor to apply for a direction entitling him to the grant of a new tenancy in succession to the retiring tenant only applies to notices to quit given under Case B, D or E[3]. There is no provision for suspension in the case of a notice challenged by counter-notice under s 26(1) of the AHA 1986.

[1]   Although Case A is included by definition, such a tenancy, being a smallholding, and therefore outside succession altogether, will not carry succession rights, so the fact that notice to quit is given under Case A is irrelevant.
[2]   AHA 1986, s 51(4), (5) and (6).
[3]   AHA 1986, s 51(4).

36.8 If the notice to quit is served before the retirement notice, then the ALT has no jurisdiction in the following cases:

(a)   If the notice to quit is given under Case C[1] (because the landlord had already obtained a certificate of bad husbandry) or is given on the ground contained in Case F[2] (insolvency of the tenant), the retirement notice is rendered ineffective[3]. No further proceedings can be taken upon it. The application by the nominated successor is then treated as if it had never been made. The retiring tenant retains the tenancy until the notice to quit takes effect. This arises because such notices to quit cannot be challenged by arbitration or through the ALT.

(b)   If the notice to quit is given pursuant to Case B (because the land is required for non-agricultural use for which planning permission has been obtained) or Case D (following non-compliance with a notice to pay o notice to remedy) or Case E (following an irremediable breach of covenant) and either:
   (i)   the month allowed for reference to arbitration on the notice to quit has expired; or
   (ii)   the notice to quit has been referred to arbitration and upheld; or
   (iii)   (where applicable) the ALT has consented to the operation of the notice to quit.

(c)   If the tenancy is subject to a valid notice to quit given pursuant to s 26 of the AHA 1986 and either:
   (i)   the month allowed for the tenant to give a counter-notice has expired; or
   (ii)   the ALT has consented to the notice to quit[4].

[1]   AHA 1986, s 52(1)(a).
[2]   AHA 1986, s 52(1)(b).
[3]   AHA 1986, s 52(1).
[4]   AHA 1986, s 51(1), applying s 38(1), (3).

Notice to quit given on or after retirement notice

36.9 If a notice to quit is served on or after the retirement notice under Case C (because the landlord has already obtained a certificate of bad husbandry) or Case D (following non-compliance with a notice to pay or notice to remedy), the notice to quit will only be effective if the certificate of bad husbandry was applied for, or the notice to pay or notice to remedy was applied for, or the notice to pay or notice to remedy was given, before the service of the retirement notice[1].

Where a valid notice to quit was given before the retirement notice, but before the ALT has commenced hearing the application of the nominated successor, again different rules apply depending upon the basis upon which the notice to quit was given.

If the notice to quit was given pursuant to Case B (because land is required for non-agricultural use for which planning permission has been obtained) or Case D (following non-compliance with a notice to pay or notice to remedy), then the retirement notice is suspended until either:

(a)   it is determined by arbitration that the notice to quit is ineffective; or

(b)   in respect of Case D in relation to a notice to do work, the tenant has served a counter-notice[2] and either:

   (i)   the ALT has withheld consent to the operation of the notice to quit; or

   (ii)   the landlord fails to apply for consent to the operation of the notice to quit[3].

Where a notice to quit is revived in these cases, the tenant has one month from the date of the arbitration's award, the date of the ALT's decision or the expiry of the period for the landlord to apply for consent, to apply for a direction from the ALT entitling him to the grant of a tenancy[4].

1   AHA 1986, s 52(1)(a) and (2)(b).
2   See para 31.67.
3   AHA 1986, s 52(2) and (3).
4   AHA 1986, s 52(4).

36.10 If a notice to quit is given on or after the retirement notice under Case C (because the landlord had already obtained a certificate of bad husbandry) or Case F (insolvency of the tenant), the retirement notice is rendered ineffective in the same manner as if such notice to quit pre-dated the retirement notice[1].

If an application by a nominated successor is invalidated by the operation of a notice to quit for any of the reasons set out in paras 36.8–36.10, it is treated as if it has never been made. The result is that, if the tenant defeats the notice to quit and retains the tenancy, he is able to make a fresh application for succession on retirement at a later date[2].

1   AHA 1986, s 52(1). See para 36.8(a).
2   AHA 1986, s 52(1)(a) and (2)(b).

36.10A If the retirement notice, having been suspended, is then revived by either of those events, the tenant then has one month from the date of delivery of the arbitrator's award, or the date of the ALT's decision to refuse consent, or the expiration of the time for applying for consent (as the case may be) in which to apply for a direction entitling him to the grant of a new tenancy[1].

If an application by the nominated successor is invalidated by the operation of the provisions set out in paras 36.18 and 36.19, it is treated as if it had never been made. The result is that, if the tenant retains the tenancy (despite the notice to quit), he is able to serve a fresh retirement notice at a later date[2].

It would appear that a notice to quit served by the landlord on or after the date of a retirement notice under Cases C or D will only be effective if the certificate of bad husbandry was applied for, or the notice to pay or remedy was served, before the retirement notice[3].

[1] AHA 1986, s 52(4).
[2] AHA 1986, s 52(5).
[3] AHA 1986, ss 52(1)(a) and 52(2)(b).

NOTICE TO QUIT GIVEN CASE G OR NO CASE

36.11 Case G (notice to quit on death) is dealt with indirectly elsewhere by s 57 of the AHA 1986. That section provides that, where the tenant of the holding dies after giving a retirement notice, but before any application for succession has been finally disposed of, then the retirement notice is rendered ineffective and the applicant must re-apply via the succession on death provisions.

There is no provision for suspending the operation of a retirement notice where the landlord gives notice to quit, not relying upon any of the Special Cases[1] but, for example, on the grounds of good husbandry, sound estate management or greater hardship, or any of the other grounds contained in s 27 of the AHA 1986. This is because a landlord has a limited power on hardship grounds only to oppose an application for succession in his reply[2].

A tenant who gives notice to quit, and later gives a retirement notice, would not appear to have invalidated his later retirement notice by his earlier notice to quit.

[1] See Ch 31.
[2] See para 36.27.

OTHER EXCLUDED CASES

36.12 The other excluded cases specified in ss 37 and 38 apply equally to preclude succession by retirement, for example, fixed-term tenancies with 27 months' unexpired, the former *Gladstone v Bower* tenancies, statutory smallholdings, tenancies created by landlords holding under certain charitable trusts, etc[1]. The important addition to this list, following the ATA 1995 coming into force, is a farm business tenancy for less than five years[2].

The definition of 'tenant' excludes an executor, administrator, trustee in bankruptcy or other person deriving title from a tenant by operation of law[3]. Any person holding in one of those capacities is not able to serve a retirement notice.

[1] AHA 1986, s 51. See para 35.8 ff.
[2] AHA 1986, Sch 6 para 6(1)(dd).
[3] AHA 1986, ss 49(2) and 34(2).

Landlord's notice to quit

36.13 Any notice to quit given by a landlord, whether before or after the giving of a retirement notice, not covered by paras 36.8–36.12, is suspended and treated as if no effect:

(a)   during the one-month period for making an application for succession; or

(b)   during the course of succession proceedings in an application is made.

If the ALT grants a direction in favour of the nominated successor, the notice to quit is of no effect[1]. This will apply to a notice to quit to which s 26(1) applies and where such notice to quit was given and the period for making an application for consent to the operation of the notice to quit has not expired[2].

[1] AHA 1986, s 54.
[2] Cf para 36.8(c).

QUALIFICATION FOR SUCCESSION GENERALLY

36.14 The eligibility rules mirror those applicable to succession on death. The major difference is that there is no provision enabling a nominated successor to be treated as eligible[1].

In order to be eligible, the nominated successor must:

(a)   be a 'close relative' of the retiring tenant[2];
(b)   satisfy the 'livelihood condition'[3]; and
(c)   not be an occupier of a commercial unit of agricultural land, or if he is, he must occupy as a licensee only[4].

The nominated successor must be eligible at the date of the giving of the retirement notice and must continue to be eligible up to the determination of the application by the ALT[5]. If he occupies a commercial unit (other than as a licensee), he must divest himself of that interest before the retirement notice is given.

The qualifications for succession on retirement require:

(i)   the retiring tenant to satisfy certain preconditions before he can give his retirement notice; and

(ii)   the applicant to satisfy further and different preconditions before he can successfully obtain a direction entitling him to the grant of a new tenancy.

1   See para 35.51.
2   AHA 1986, s 49(3). The definition of 'close relative' of the retiring tenant is now amended at s 49(3)(a) and (d) so as to include a civil partner: Civil Partnerships Act 2004, s 81 and Sch 8 para 36(2) and (3).
3   AHA 1986, s 50(2)(a).
4   AHA 1986, s 50(2)(b).
5   AHA 1986, s 53(5)(a) and (b).

THE RETIRING TENANT'S QUALIFICATION FOR SUCCESSION

Single tenant

36.15 Where there is only one tenant of the holding who wishes to serve a retirement notice, then he must either have attained the age of 65 at the date when the notice takes effect, or else be permanently physically or mentally incapacitated at that date[1].

The retiring tenant does not have to have attained the retirement age or be incapacitated at the date on which the notice itself is given, but must have attained that qualification by the date on which the retirement notice will take effect[2]. That is the first annual term date of the tenancy not less than 12 months following the service of the notice, ie the same date on which the would-be retiring tenant could have given notice to quit[3].

The tenant can give a retirement notice in anticipation of his 65th birthday, provided it falls before the date on which the retirement notice takes effect. Similarly, the tenant can give notice in anticipation of his becoming physically or mentally incapacitated.

It is not all forms of physical or mental incapacity which entitle the tenant to give a retirement notice. Such physical or mental incapacity must also be:

(a)   likely to be permanent[4]; and
(b)   such as to render the tenant incapable of conducting the farming of the holding in such a way as to secure the fulfilment by him of his responsibilities to farm in accordance with the rules of good husbandry[5].

1   AHA 1986, s 51(3).
2   AHA 1986.
3   AHA 1986, s 51(3), read against the definition of the retirement date contained in s 49(3) and also see s 49(1)(b).
4   AHA 1986, s 51(3)(b).
5   AHA 1986, s 51(3)(a).

Joint tenancies

36.16 In the case of joint tenancies, all the retiring, or would-be retiring, tenants must have acquired the age or health qualification, ie all must by the date on which the retirement notice takes effect either be over the age of 65 or physically or mentally incapacitated to such an extent as to be incapable of farming the holding in accordance with the rules of good husbandry. The qualification of one or more is insufficient. The qualification must be satisfied by all[1].

1   AHA 1986, ss 49(3) and 51(3)(a).

Incapacity

36.17 If a tenant under the age of 65[1] gives a retirement notice in reliance upon his physical or mental incapacity and the extent of his incapacity is disputed, the ALT must first determine whether he is sufficiently incapacitated as a preliminary issue[2].

The ALT must be satisfied that:

(a)   the retiring tenant or (as the case may be) each of the retiring tenants either is, or will at the retirement date be, incapable, by reason of bodily or mental infirmity, of conducting the farming of the holding in such a way as to secure the fulfilment of the responsibilities of the tenant to farm in accordance with the rules of good husbandry; and

(b)   any such incapacity is likely to be permanent[3].

If the ALT is not so satisfied, the application fails at that stage. If the ALT dispose of the nominated successor's application, otherwise than by giving a direction that the nominated successor is a suitable person to become the tenant of the holding[4], the retirement notice shall have no effect[5]. The applicant is not precluded from reapplying for succession on the death of the tenant.

For a case in which the ALT considered how incapacitated a tenant had to be to be able to give a retirement notice, see *Wyatt v Lord Wraxall*[6]. It is probable that different standards apply to different types of holding and their different forms of physical labour requirements.

1   AHA 1986, s 51(3). A person attains a particular age expressed in years at the commencement of the relevant anniversary of the date of his birth: see the Family Law Reform Act 1969, s 9.
2   AHA 1986, s 53(4).
3   AHA 1986.
4   AHA 1986, s 53(7).
5   AHA 1986, s 53(9). This is stated to be without prejudice to s 51(2).
6   (1992) ALT, South Western

THE APPLICANT'S QUALIFICATION FOR SUCCESSION

36.18 The nominated successor must be both eligible and suitable for succession. These qualifications follow very closely the equivalent eligibility and suitability qualifications applicable to an application following the death of the tenant[1]. The important distinctions are highlighted below. In all other respects the qualifications are merely summarised.

36.18 *Succession on retirement*

The ALT has to be satisfied that the nominated successor has the following qualifications:

(a)   eligibility:
     (i)   close relative
     (ii)   principal source of livelihood;
     (iii) commercial unit occupation test;
(b)   suitability.

The ALT must be further satisfied that, in granting a direction in favour of the nominated successor, it is not causing greater hardship to the landlord[2].

1   See para 35.22.
2   See para 36.27.

Eligibility

Close relative

36.19 The category of close relatives applicable for succession on retirement is the same as those applicable on death, ie spouse (including civil partner), sibling, child, or treated child[1].

There is an important qualification in the context of succession on retirement, namely that the applicant need only be sufficiently closely related to one of the joint tenants in the case of a joint tenancy[2]. This is of great importance in the case, for example, of joint tenants who are brothers (a not unusual arrangement). If one brother/tenant has a son who is a potential successor, and the other has no close relative, then if no retirement notice is given, the prospective qualifying son will be very greatly at risk. If his father predeceases his uncle who is the joint tenant, then no application for succession can be made because his father was not the sole or sole surviving tenant at the date of his death, his uncle becomes such. On the death of his uncle, he cannot apply either because he is not a close enough relation.

This problem can be overcome by the two joint tenants, on attaining the age of 65 or upon becoming physically or mentally incapacitated, giving a retirement notice nominating the son of one of them so that the uncertainties as to the order of death can be avoided.

1   See para 35.23 ff.
2   AHA 1986, s 49(1)(b) and (3).

Principal source of livelihood test

36.20 As in relation to succession on death, in succession on retirement, the nominated successor must show that during five of the last seven years his only or principal source of livelihood was derived from his agricultural work on the holding in question or an agricultural unit of which the holding forms part[1]. This is the same test which applies on death and the cases and difficulties relating to the principal source of livelihood test set out in Chapter

35[2] apply equally to the application of this test on retirement as on death. The following points, however, should be noted.

[1]   AHA 1986, s 50(2)(a).
[2]   See para 35.33.

APPLICANT NOT FULLY ELIGIBLE

36.21 As indicated above, whereas on an application on death an applicant who was not fully eligible could apply to be treated as eligible, there is no such provision in the case of an applicant applying on the retirement of the sitting-tenant. The applicant must satisfy the full eligibility test in the event of a retirement notice being given, otherwise he is disqualified.

WIVES OR CIVIL PARTNERS

36.22 As in succession on death, the widow or civil partner need not satisfy the principal source of livelihood test by reason of her or his own work[1]. On the retirement of the tenant, the agricultural work carried on upon the holding (or the larger agricultural unit) must be that of either the wife or civil partner or the retiring tenant or both of them[2].

[1]   It is sufficient if she and/or her husband have derived their principal source of livelihood in the manner prescribed.
[2]   AHA 1986, s 50(3), as amended by the Civil Partnerships Act 2004, s 81 and Sch 8 para 36(1).

TIME AT COLLEGE

36.23 Any period, up to a maximum of three years, during which time the applicant was engaged in full-time education at a university, college or other establishment of further education, is treated as time during which he has derived his principal source of livelihood from his agricultural work on the holding or the larger agricultural unit of which the holding forms part[1].

[1]   AHA 1986, Sch 6 para 2. See also *Littlewood v Rolfe* [1981] 2 All ER 51 as to the application of that provision in the context of a hospital which was held not to be a university, college or other establishment of further education. See para 35.49.

TIME FOR SATISFYING THE TEST

36.24 Section 50(2)(a) of the AHA 1986 refers to the principal source of livelihood test in 'the last seven years'. It does not specify whether the seven-year period expires on the date of the retirement notice, on the date of the application or the date on which the retirement notice is to take effect (ie more than a year after the date of the retirement notice). In the previous edition of this book and the draft of this edition, it was submitted that, as the retirement notice must nominate a 'single eligible person'[1], the applicant must be possessed of the qualifications of eligibility at the date on which the retirement notice is given. That would support the conclusion that the seven-year period expires on the date of the retirement notice and not at any later date[2]. Section 53(5) of the AHA 1986 reinforces this view by requiring the ALT to be satisfied in due course that the applicant was 'an eligible person at the date of the giving of the retirement notice'. The contrary argument was that the principal livelihood test had to be satisfied at all times during a period from the date of service of the retirement notice until the consideration of the issue by the ALT[3]. The view expressed in this book was adopted by the ALT in *Shirley v Crabtree*[4]. The ALT stated a case for the High Court which upheld the decision of the ALT[5].

[1] See AHA 1986, s 49(1)(b).
[2] This would also be consistent with the decision of the House of Lords in *Jackson v Hall* [1980] AC 854, [1980] 1 All ER 177, where it was held that the commercial unit occupation test had to be satisfied at the date of death and continuing thereafter.
[3] This view is expressed by the editor of *Woodfall: Landlord and Tenant* (Looseleaf edn, 1994) Sweet & Maxwell, at para 21.195.
[4] (2006) ALT, Midlands.
[5] [2007] EWHC 1532 (Admin), [2007] All ER (D) 332 (Jun).

Commercial unit occupation test

36.25 The nominated successor must not be 'the occupier of a commercial unit of agricultural land'[1]. Most of the same rules which apply to succession on death apply equally to succession on retirement, for example:

(a) occupation only as licensee, or any of the other capacities referred to in para 6(1) of Pt I of Sch 6 including the important addition of occupation as a farm business tenant for a term of less than five years, do not render the applicant ineligible[2];

(b) the definition of a commercial unit, and the method of assessment contained in paras 3, 4 and 5 of Pt I of Sch 6 of the AHA 1986, apply equally to succession on retirement as they do on death[3];

(c) joint occupation, occupation by a spouse or a controlled company and deemed occupation by reason of a tenancy or licence granted by a close relative, spouse or controlled company, all apply equally to succession on retirement as they do to succession on death[4].

By contrast, in relation to succession on retirement, there is no provision for determining the order in which applications fall to be heard equivalent to s 42 of the AHA 1986 which applies only to applications for succession on death. If a retiring tenant serves several retirement notices, because he holds several holdings, and the nominated successor makes several applications for succession, there is no procedure laid down for determining in which order they should be heard. This is of particular significance in the context of the application of the commercial unit occupation test[5].

The provisions relating to 'deemed occupation in case of Tribunal Direction' apply to an application on retirement as much as to an application on death[6].

A commercial unit occupied by the retiring tenant, for example, as owner, but not occupied by the nominated successor (except in some non-disqualifying capacity, for example, as licensee only), will not disqualify the nominated successor. This is a useful exception for the benefit of the retiring tenant and nominated successor because if the nominated successor might otherwise inherit the commercial unit under the terms of the retiring tenant's will, he would thereby be disqualified on an application for succession following the death of the retiring tenant. He would not be ineligible on a lifetime application for succession.

1   AHA 1986, s 50(2)(b).
2   See para 35.60.
3   See para 35.55 ff.
4   See para 35.62 ff.
5   See paras 35.86 and 35.89.
6   AHA 1986, Sch 6 Pt 2 para 16.

Suitability

36.26 In relation to an application for succession on retirement, as regards the qualifying criteria, the AHA 1986 only provides for the applicant being required to be an 'eligible person'[1]. It does not specify that the applicant must also be suitable to be granted a tenancy. However, although a valid retirement notice can be given nominating a person who is merely eligible, without being suitable, a nominated successor will not obtain any direction from the ALT entitling him to the grant of a new tenancy unless he can also satisfy the ALT that he is suitable to be granted a tenancy in succession to the retiring tenant[2].

The requirements of suitability are the same whether the application arises by reason of the death or the retirement of the tenant, ie the ALT must have regard to 'all relevant matters'. These include:

(a)   the extent to which the nominated successor has been trained in or has had practical experience of agriculture;
(b)   his age, physical health and financial standing;
(c)   the views (if any) stated by the landlord on his suitability[3].

All the requirements set out in Chapter 35[4] relating to the suitability of the applicant for succession on death apply equally on retirement. It is for the applicant to discharge the onus of proof, which is upon him, that he is a suitable person to be granted a new tenancy.

1   AHA 1986, ss 49(1)(b) and 50(1).
2   AHA 1986, s 53(5).
3   AHA 1986, s 53(6).
4   See para 35.69.

Hardship to landlord

36.27 Where a nominated successor applies to the ALT and satisfies the ALT that he is both eligible and suitable, he is in principle entitled as of right to a direction for a new tenancy. The landlord can only challenge the applicant's assertions as to his eligibility and suitability after the ALT has determined whether the applicant is eligible and suitable[1]. The nominated successor's right to be granted a direction is subject to the landlord establishing at that stage of the proceedings that greater hardship would be caused by giving the direction than by refusing the application[2].

Unlike succession on death, where the landlord can apply to defeat the applicant on the grounds of good husbandry, sound estate management, or any of the other grounds in the case of succession on retirement, the landlord has the limited ground of greater hardship alone[3]. This distinction is more nominal than real because, in the case of an application for succession on death, if the landlord seeks consent to the operation of his notice to quit on any of the grounds specified in s 27(3), he must also satisfy the fair and reasonable landlord proviso. In practice this involves consideration of comparative hardship. Nevertheless, it is only consideration of comparative hardship which can be made in the case of an application for succession on retirement.

[1]   AHA 1986, s 53(5) and (7).
[2]   AHA 1986, s 53(8). Also see, *Jones v Burgoyne* (1963) 188 Estates Gazette 497.
[3]   Ie the equivalent of s 27(3)(e) of the AHA 1986: s 53(8). See para 30.12.

36.28 To defeat an applicant who has been found to be both eligible and suitable, the landlord must satisfy the ALT that greater hardship would be caused by giving the direction than by refusing the nominated successor's application. Although the wording is slightly different from the wording of s 27(3)(e) of the AHA 1986 (because of the context in which relative hardship falls to be considered), it is submitted that exactly the same considerations apply. Therefore, the commentary on greater hardship[1] applies equally to an application for succession on retirement, with the applicant being in the equivalent position of the tenant where a notice to quit has been served on him.

Many landlords, aggrieved by an application for succession on retirement having been made (with the consequent devaluing effect upon the holding of a further generation of tenant), having hoped or anticipated that possession would be recovered shortly, oppose applications for succession and automatically make allegations of greater hardship in circumstances where there is little or no prospect of success. Landlords would be well advised to consider carefully whether it is sensible to make such an application, bearing in mind that they may later be subjected to a claim for further and better particulars and for full discovery of documents relating to their personal circumstances, income and the like, which they may be reluctant to disclose. In such circumstances, it may be better never to have made the application than having done so to withdraw when pressed for full disclosure.

[1]   See para 30.12

PROCEDURE

36.29 As with nearly all features of the agricultural holdings legislation, the procedural requirements relating to an application for succession on retirement must be most strictly complied with. Failure to satisfy the statutory time limits and procedures is fatal to the applicant's and/or landlord's case. The time limits are short.

Although there is limited power for the chairman or the ALT itself to relieve an applicant or landlord from non-compliance with the regulations[1], there is no such power if the failure is to comply with a statutory time limit. The procedural requirements, therefore, must be most closely studied and followed. They are as follows.

[1]   See the Agricultural Land Tribunal (Rules) Order 1978, SI 1978/259, r 37.

Retirement notice

36.30 The procedural trigger for succession on retirement is the retirement notice[1] to be given by the tenant of the holding (or in the case of a joint tenancy, all the tenants)[2]. There is no prescribed form for a retirement notice. All that is required is that the tenant (or if there is a joint tenancy, all the tenants) must give notice to the landlord, in whatever terms, that he or they 'wish a single eligible person named in the notice to succeed him or them as tenant of the holding as from a date specified in the notice'[3]. That date has to be a date on which the tenancy could have been terminated by notice to quit falling not less than one nor more than two years from the date of the notice, ie the annual term date between one and two years after the date of the notice[4].

The tenant who can give a retirement notice does not include any person who is holding the tenancy in a fiduciary capacity, ie as executor, administrator, committee of the estate, trustee in bankruptcy or other person deriving title from a tenant by operation of law. This is because the definition of tenant for the purposes of the giving of a retirement notice is the same as the definition of a tenant whose death can give rise to a Case G notice to quit[5].

The retiring tenant (or each of them, if there is more than one) must have attained the age of 65 or be permanently incapacitated[6].

The AHA 1986 does not specify that the notice must be in writing. It is implied. The retirement notice has to accompany the application to be made by the nominated successor[7]. Unless the notice is in writing, that requirement cannot be satisfied.

Where the ALT considers the nominated successor's application and refuses to make a direction, the unsuccessful nominated successor is barred from applying for succession on the tenant's later death[8]. This will be the case even where a significant period has elapsed between the ALT's refusal of succession pursuant to a retirement notice and the tenant's later death, during which the unsuccessful nominated successor may have overcome the earlier obstacles to him establishing both eligibility and suitability.

If the ALT rejects the nominated successor's application, the tenancy remains vested in the retiring tenant. The retirement notice is of no effect[9]. This is described in the AHA 1986 as being without prejudice to the operation of s 51(2), as a result of which this retirement notice, even though it has become

635

abortive by the dismissal of the application by the ALT, will have excluded any further application pursuant to a retirement notice given by the tenant[10].

It is clear that a second retirement notice cannot be given, nominating as a successor somebody who has already applied and failed to obtain a direction from the ALT because he was found to be unsuitable or because the landlord succeeded on greater hardship grounds. In the last edition of this book it was suggested that an applicant who is found to be ineligible might, upon acquiring the eligibility requirements, be able to reapply pursuant to a second retirement notice. This is because the definition of a retirement notice is a notice specifying an eligible person[11]. There remains no authority in relation to this point.

If an application for retirement succession is withdrawn or abandoned, it is treated as if it had never been made. A further retirement notice can be given[12]. This is an important safeguard for an applicant who discovers a flaw in his application at some stage up to the time when the ALT hearing takes place. Such an applicant can always withdraw, but the application must be withdrawn prior to the hearing[13]. The procedures can be gone through afresh with a new retirement notice and a fresh application then being made. Time will be lost in the process, but the applicant will not then stand to lose the opportunity to become tenant of the farm for all time.

[1]   AHA 1986, s 49(3).
[2]   AHA 1986.
[3]   AHA 1986, s 49(1)(b).
[4]   AHA 1986.
[5]   AHA 1986, ss 49(2) and 34(2). See para 31.95.
[6]   AHA 1986, s 51(3). See para 36.15 ff.
[7]   AHA 1986, s 53(3)(a).
[8]   AHA 1986, s 57(4).
[9]   AHA 1986, s 53(9).
[10] AHA 1986.
[11] AHA 1986, ss 49(1)(b), 49(3), 51(2) and 53.
[12] AHA 1986, s 53(10).
[13] Agricultural Land Tribunals (Rules) Order 1978, SI 1978/259, r 18(1).

36.31 Although an application for succession on death can be signed by a duly authorised agent for the applicant, it has been held by ALT that the obligation on the retiring tenant to sign the retirement notice by the retiring tenant, and to make the application to the ALT signed by the retiring tenant and the applicant for succession, precludes signature by an agent[1] .

[1]   AHA 1986, s 53(3)(b). Also see *White v de Pelet* (1993) ALT South Western Area.

Application for succession

36.32 Once a retirement notice has been given, then the nominated successor must within one month apply to the ALT on Form 5[1] for the grant of a new tenancy. The time limit of one month runs from the day after the date of the giving of the retirement notice. It is a statutorily prescribed time limit which is mandatory and inflexible[2]. The application must be signed by both the retiring tenant and the nominated successor[3]. It must be accompanied by the retirement notice. These requirements are also statutory requirements[4].

The Agricultural Land Tribunals (Rules) Order 1978 requires that the application should also be accompanied by any plan[5] or other document[6] which the party making the application intends to adduce in support of his case. This provision is non-statutory. The chairman may dispense with these requirements[7]. For a commentary on the documents which should accompany the application, see para 35.82.

At the same time as the applicant applies to the ALT for the grant of a new tenancy in succession to the retiring tenant, the applicant must give notice of the application to the landlord in Form 6[8]. This requirement is not a statutory requirement and, if not satisfied, does not invalidate the application[9].

[1] Form 5 in the Appendix to the Agricultural Land Tribunals (Succession) Rules 1984 contained in the Agricultural Land Tribunals (Succession to Agricultural Tenancies) Order 1984, SI 1984/1301: see para A1.550.
[2] AHA 1986, s 53(2). See *Kellett v Alexander* (1980) 257 Estates Gazette 494. For the corresponding day rule and the calculation of the one-month period, see *Dodds v Walker* [1981] 2 All ER 609, [1981] 1 WLR 1027.
[3] Signature by an agent has been found to be insufficient: see *White v de Pelet* (1993) ALT, South Western Area.
[4] AHA 1986, s 53(3).
[5] SI 1978/259, Sch 1 r 16(3).
[6] SI 1978/259, Sch 1 r 16(4).
[7] SI 1978/259, Sch 1 r 16(6).
[8] The Agricultural Land Tribunals (Succession to Agricultural Tenancies) Order 1984, SI 1984/1301, Schedule r 24.
[9] See *Kellett v Alexander* (1980) 257 Estates Gazette 494.

Landlord's reply

36.33 A landlord who intends to oppose the whole or any part of the application made by the nominated successor must, within one month of the service of the application upon him, serve a reply in Form 5R[1]. The requirement of the landlord to file a reply within one month is not a statutory requirement. The landlord may apply to the chairman for an extension of time, which the chairman may grant on such terms and conditions, if any, as appear to him just[2].

If the landlord wishes to allege that greater hardship would be caused to him by the ALT giving the direction than would be caused to the applicant by refusing his application, he must specify such allegation in the reply and set out the reasons for the claim[3].

[1] The Agricultural Land Tribunals (Succession to Agricultural Tenancies) Order 1984, SI 1984/1301, Schedule, r 25.
[2] The Agricultural Land Tribunals (Rules) Order 1978, SI 1978/259, r 37.
[3] SI 1984/1301, Schedule r 4(2).

Interlocutory matters

36.34 The same interlocutory procedures as apply in the case of an application for succession on death apply in the case of an application for succession on retirement. Thus the provisions for seeking and obtaining a commercial unit assessment by the Divisional Surveyor, for obtaining discovery, further and better particulars and so forth all apply in the same way as for an application for succession on death[1].

[1] For the commentary on the provisions relating to interlocutory matters in the context of an application for succession on death, see para 35.90. For a commentary on the Agricultural Land Tribunals Rules generally, see Ch 46.

Hearing

36.35 If the retirement notice specifies that the retiring tenant (or tenants) are mentally or physically incapacitated, rather than that they have attained the age of 65, the ALT must first satisfy itself as to whether or not the retiring tenant or tenants are indeed physically or mentally incapacitated, and whether such incapacity is likely to be permanent before proceeding further with the application[1].

If the ALT is satisfied that the retirement notice relates to a qualifying tenant, it must then proceed to satisfy itself as to whether the nominated successor was an eligible person at the date of the giving of the retirement notice and, if so, whether he has ceased to be eligible[2].

This statutory provision gives effect to the House of Lords decision in *Jackson v Hall*[3]. A tenant who satisfies the close relationship test is bound to retain that qualification throughout (except in the case of a spouse or civil partner who is divorced in the interim). Similarly, the principal source of livelihood qualification is measured by reference to the applicant's sources of livelihood during the seven years ending with the retirement notice. That qualification, once acquired, cannot be lost. The statute would appear to be directed to the possibility of the applicant becoming disqualified by reason of his having acquired a disqualifying interest in a commercial unit or sufficient land to increase his existing land holdings to that of a commercial unit.

[1] AHA 1986, s 53(4).
[2] AHA 1986, s 53(5).
[3] [1980] AC 854, [1980] 1 All ER 177.

36.36 Once the ALT has determined whether or not the applicant is an eligible person, it must then determine whether or not the applicant is suitable[1].

If the landlord has included in his reply an allegation of hardship, the next step for the ALT to take, assuming eligibility and suitability have been established, is to determine whether or not greater hardship would be caused to the landlord. If no such allegation is made, or if the allegation is not substantiated before the ALT, then the ALT must finally make a direction in favour of the applicant, entitling him to the grant of a new tenancy in succession to the retiring tenant. The ALT does not have discretion in the matter. The provision is mandatory[2].

The procedure follows very closely the procedure on an application for succession on death[3]. The following points should be noted:

(a)   Whereas there is provision for the ALT to grant a direction in respect of part only by consent in the case of an application for succession on the death of a tenant, there is no such provision in the case of an application for succession on retirement[4]. This presents major practical procedural difficulties where the landlord and applicant negotiate, agree terms for possession of part to be given, and a direction to be given in respect of the remainder of the holding. The landlord may wish in such a case to have the direction of the ALT so as to ensure that the new tenancy operates as a first or second succession (as the case may be) and to reduce prospective inheritance tax and equally the applicant may want to have the direction so as to reduce the chances of there being a charge to inheritance tax in due course or to avoid the inadvertent creation of an unprotected farm business tenancy.

(b)   On an application for succession on death, there is provision for determining the order in which the applications fall to be decided[5]. There is no equivalent provision in the case of several applications for succession on retirement.

1   AHA 1986, s 53(5) and (6).
2   AHA 1986, s 53(7).
3   AHA 1986, s 39 and para 35.79.
4   AHA 1986, ss 39(10) and 44(5).
5   AHA 1986, s 42.

EFFECT OF A DIRECTION

The terms of the new tenancy

36.37 If the ALT makes a direction entitling the nominated successor to the grant of a new tenancy of the holding, he is then entitled to a tenancy of the holding as from the retirement date specified in the retirement notice[1]. The new tenancy will be on the same terms as those on which the holding was let at the date on which the retirement notice took effect, subject to any variations that may be agreed upon between the parties, or may be determined by arbitration[2].

The new tenancy is deemed to be granted by the landlord, and accepted by the nominated successor, with effect from that date[3]. The retiring tenant's tenancy will then automatically be terminated by operation of law with effect from the date of the grant of the new tenancy[4]. It is treated as if it had been terminated by a valid notice to quit given by the tenant himself rather than by the retirement notice which he will have given. This of itself does not terminate his tenancy. The new successor tenant is not entitled to assign the right to the grant of a new tenancy[5], nor will he be entitled to assign the new tenancy that is granted to him without the landlord's consent in writing, even though the old tenancy may have contained no prohibition upon assignment. This is because the AHA 1986 provides that a covenant by the tenant not to assign, sub-let or part with possession of the holding or any part of it, without the landlord's consent in writing, is to be included in the new tenancy[6].

There may be problems regarding the changeover from the retiring tenant to the successor if the ALT's direction is not made until a very late stage during the life of the retirement notice. In those circumstances:

(a)   If the ALT's direction is given within three months before the retirement date, the ALT may, on the application of the tenant, specify a later date within the period of three months following the retirement date as the ALT thinks fit. This is an important provision for the purpose of the giving of notices necessary to preserve rights of compensation etc, on quitting by the retiring tenant[7].

(b)   If the ALT's direction is given at any time after the retirement date, the ALT must specify in the direction a date within the period of three months following the direction from which the new tenancy is to run[8].

[1]   This will be the same date as the date on which a notice to quit could have taken effect given by the tenant at the date of the retirement notice, ie the next annual term date not earlier than 12 months or later than two years following the retirement notice: AHA 1986, s 56(1).
[2]   See para 36.38.
[3]   AHA 1986, s 55(1).
[4]   AHA 1986, s 55(5).
[5]   AHA 1986, s 55(6).
[6]   AHA 1986, s 56(2).
[7]   AHA 1986, s 55(8).
[8]   AHA 1986, s 55(8).

Arbitration

36.38 Either the landlord or the tenant may demand arbitration in respect of either or both of the same two questions as apply on a death succession case, namely:

(a)   what variations in the terms of the tenancy which the tenant is entitled to or has obtained by virtue of the direction are justifiable having regard to the circumstances of the holding and the length of time since the holding was first let on those terms; and

(b)   what rent should be or should have been properly payable in respect of the holding at the relevant time[1].

The provision is the same and the procedures are the same as for succession on death[2].

The same time limits apply with the demand for arbitration having to be given within three months from the date on which the new tenancy takes effect (called the 'relevant time') subject to the extension of time referred to in para 35.94[3].

It should be noted that it is important to both the retiring tenant and the nominated successor for the former to serve notice under s 83 of the AHA 1986 so as to preserve his claim for compensation for improvements, tenant-right, etc, since such claims will not be 'rolled over' in the absence of their having been preserved by such notice. In default, the outgoing tenant will lose all claims to compensation and the incoming tenant will have to pay rent by reference to the holding in its improved condition, notwithstanding the fact that the improvements were carried out by the nominated successor himself during the currency of the retiring tenant's tenancy. Such notice must be served within two months of the termination of the tenancy[4].

The provisions of s 69 of the AHA 1986, safeguarding the right to compensation for tenant's improvements on successive tenancies, do not apply because there is a change of tenant. Conversely, the incoming tenant may be liable for the outgoing tenant's dilapidations, either expressly or because of the obligation to keep the holding in repair under the Agriculture (Maintenance, Repair and Insurance of Fixed Equipment) Regulations 1973[5] where appropriate.

[1] AHA 1986, s 56(3), which incorporates the provisions of the AHA 1986, s 48(3)–(12).
[2] For a commentary on those provisions, see para 35.95. Note, in particular, the problems relating to the 'rollover' of improvements.
[3] AHA 1986, s 56(4).
[4] AHA 1986, s 83(2).
[5] SI 1973/1473 (as amended): see para 23.4 ff. See also, *Proudfoot v Hart* (1890) 25 QBD 42, CA: the construction of the word 'keep' meaning 'put' and 'keep where appropriate': see para 10.5.

Death of retiring tenant or nominated successor

Retiring tenant

36.39 If the retiring tenant dies after serving his retirement notice, but before the nominated successor's application has been finally disposed of by the ALT, then the retirement notice is rendered ineffective[1]. The nominated successor may then apply again within three months of the date of death in accordance with the provisions which apply for succession on death[2]. Any proceedings which have been started following service of the retirement notice have to be discontinued and the whole procedure will be gone through again.

If the retiring tenant dies after the ALT has made its direction, but before the date when the new tenancy comes into effect, then the matter proceeds regardless of the death of the retiring tenant. No further application for succession following the death of the tenant has to be made[3].

[1] AHA 1986, s 57(1) and (2).
[2] See para 35.81.
[3] AHA 1986, s 57(1) and (3).

36.40 Where the tenant dies after an application has been made, and the application is abandoned or discontinued, then the nominated successor may apply again by reason of the death of the tenant. This is because an application which is withdrawn or abandoned is treated as if it had never been made[1]. If the nominated successor had applied, and the ALT had dismissed his application, then he may not apply again on the death of the retiring death as an applicant for succession on death[2].

1   AHA 1986, s 53(10).
2   AHA 1986, s 57(4). See para 36.44.

Death of nominated successor

36.41 There is provision for the Lord Chancellor to make regulations providing for the eventuality that if, instead of the retiring tenant dying, the nominated successor were to die before the application had been disposed of[1]. Such regulations were made under the A(MP)A 1976 for the death of an applicant for succession on death[2]. In brief, these provided that if the applicant was one of two or more successful joint applicants, the direction proceeded in favour of the survivor or survivors alone, but if the applicant was the sole successful applicant, or the sole survivor of two or more, then he was to be treated as if he was the tenant at the date of his death for the purpose of further applications arising out of his death. No such regulations have yet been made pursuant to the power conferred upon the Lord Chancellor under the AHA 1986.

1   AHA 1986, s 55(7).
2   See Agriculture (Miscellaneous Provisions) Act 1976 (Application of Provisions) Regulations 1977, SI 1977/1215.

Multiple applications

36.42 If the retiring tenant is the tenant of several holdings, retirement notices can be given in respect of each of the holdings. Subsequent applications for succession by the nominated successor can be made in respect of each such holding. However, if the ALT makes a direction in respect of any such holding, the applicant is then deemed to be the occupier for the purposes of applying the commercial unit occupation test of eligibility. If the holding in respect of which the applicant has obtained a direction is a commercial unit, or if that holding, together with any other land occupied by the applicant, is sufficient to constitute a commercial unit, then the applicant is disqualified from pursuing his application in respect of any other holding[1]. Note the absence of any provisions for determining the order in which multiple applications on retirement fall to be considered[2].

1   AHA 1986, s 58, Sch 6 paras 8 and 16.
2   See paras 35.86 and 35.92.

Sub-tenancies/concurrent tenancies

36.43 A provision was introduced in the context of succession on death, which applies equally to succession on retirement, entitling the successful applicant for succession to the grant of a new tenancy from the landlord from whom the retiring tenant's tenancy was derived[1]. This provision was designed to avoid the problem which arose in *Chesshire v Colesbourne Estate Co*[2] in which a landlord, during the currency of the tenancy created in favour of the subsequently deceased tenant, granted a concurrent tenancy in reversion. The reversionary tenant became the landlord of the existing tenant and on the existing tenant's death it was the reversionary tenant who was the immediate landlord against whom the direction for succession fell to be made. Accordingly, the tenant entitled to the grant of a new tenancy in succession became a sub-tenant, with all the consequent insecurity applicable to sub-tenancies[3]. The AHA 1986 now ensures that the nominated successor obtains a tenancy with the same measure of security as the retiring tenant enjoyed during the subsistence of his tenancy.

[1]   AHA 1986, s 55(2) and (3).
[2]   (1979) ALT, South Western Area.
[3]   See para 28.17.

EFFECT OF FAILURE TO OBTAIN DIRECTION

36.44 If the application for succession by the nominated successor is heard by the ALT, and the ALT determines that the applicant is ineligible or unsuitable, or that greater hardship would be suffered by the landlord than by the nominated successor if a direction was made, and accordingly the ALT refuses to make the direction, then the application fails, but the retiring tenant's tenancy continues, until it can be determined. The way in which this operates is that the retirement notice becomes of no effect[1].

In those circumstances, no further application can be made for retirement succession, though it is arguable that if the applicant was found to be ineligible (as opposed to unsuitable), a further application could be made since the retirement notice in those circumstances would not be a retirement notice within the meaning of the AHA 1986[2]. It should also be noted that the statutory provision is not limited to a further application for retirement succession by the unsuccessful applicant. It excludes any further such application for succession by anyone.

If the application by the nominated successor is withdrawn or abandoned, then a further retirement notice can be given and a further application can be made by the applicant if he wishes[3]. An unsuccessful applicant falls to be disqualified if the application is not withdrawn or abandoned before the ALT hearing.

The golden rule for potential successors is that it is imperative that, if there is any danger of their application being dismissed, the application should be withdrawn or abandoned before the ALT hearing, so that there is an opportunity of endeavouring to acquire the necessary qualifications afresh.

[1]   AHA 1986, s 53(9).
[2]   See para 36.30.
[3]   AHA 1986, s 53(10). See para 36.30.

ALTERNATIVES TO LIFETIME SUCCESSION

Assignment generally

36.45 A tenant wishing to secure the tenancy for the next generation (or for any other person) may, as an alternative to succession, secure the position by means of assignment (unless the tenancy contains a prohibition on assignment). Such a situation might arise if the tenant held his tenancy under the terms of an oral agreement which contained no prohibition upon assignment, either because neither party turned his mind to the possibility of assignment, or because each overlooked the possibility. It also sometimes happens, particularly with the older form of tenancy agreement, that no prohibition was included even in the written agreement, though such cases are becoming rarer.

Alternatively, a qualified prohibition on assignment may have been agreed upon, for example, that the assignment should not take place without the landlord's written consent, 'such consent not to be unreasonably withheld'[1].

[1] For a commentary in relation to the effect of this type of covenant, see 24.18.

36.46 A qualified prohibition on assignment, requiring the landlord's prior written consent, is not subject to the further implied provision that such consent shall not be unreasonably withheld because s 19 of the Landlord and Tenant Act 1927 does not apply to agricultural holdings.

Tenants of agricultural holdings, and their potential successors, would be well advised, before planning for succession, or making applications for succession, to give careful consideration to the possibility of assignment as an alternative to succession by way of a direction from the ALT. Assignment may provide a speedier, cheaper and simpler means of securing the tenancy for the next generation or, if the assignment is to a company, for an indefinite period.

Assignment with consent of the landlord

36.47 An alternative course, in the case of a tenancy subject to a qualified prohibition upon assignment, or indeed even subject to an absolute prohibition, is to seek the landlord's consent to assignment. If the landlord consents, the tenant can avoid having to serve a retirement notice and the nominated successor does not have to apply thereafter for the grant of a new tenancy by succession. The 'succession' can be dealt with by assignment with the landlord's consent.

Such an assignment can operate as a first succession for the purposes of applying the two succession rule[1]. It will only do so if the assignee was a close relation of the assignor, within the meaning of the close relationship test of eligibility.

[1] This was provided for originally by s 18(5) of the A(MP)A 1976, which has now been repealed and re-enacted as s 37(2)(b) and s 51 of the AHA 1986.

Assignment without consent or knowledge of the landlord

36.48 If the tenancy agreement contains no prohibition upon assignment, not only is no consent required by the landlord to the assignment, but the landlord does not even need to be informed of the assignment. All that is required is for a deed of assignment to be executed and completed and the legal estate in the tenancy is then vested in the assignee.

There are disadvantages to tenants who wish to secure the tenancy for the next generation in that way, and these are discussed below.

Irremediable breach

36.49 A tenant who assigns in breach of a prohibition against assignment, not merely fails to secure the tenancy, but renders it liable to be the subject of a Case E notice to quit for irremediable breach[1], if the interest of the landlord has been materially prejudiced[2] or forfeiture[3].

A prohibition upon assignment may have been incorporated referentially in circumstances overlooked by the tenant. For example, where the oral agreement was that the tenant should be granted a tenancy on the estate's standard terms, or on the same terms as his father, or on the Estates Gazette standard form or some other similar form which contains a prohibition on assignment.

A prohibition on parting with possession of any part of an agricultural holding restrains assignment[4] but the landlord may be estopped from relying on such a prohibition if by the convention of the parties the rent has been revised upon the assumption that there is no ascertainable written tenancy agreement[5].

[1]   *Scala House and District Property Co Ltd v Forbes* [1974] QB 575, [1973] 3 All ER 308, CA and *Troop v Gibson* (1985) 277 Estates Gazette 1134, CA. Cf *Akici v L R Butlin Ltd* [2005] EWCA Civ 1296, [2006] 1 EGLR 34, [2006] 07 EG 136. See para 31.84.
[2]   As to Case E, see para 31.80.
[3]   As to forfeiture, see paras 33.8 and Ch 13.
[4]   *Troop v Gibson* (1985) 277 EG 1134.
[5]   *Troop v Gibson* (1985) 277 EG 1134.

Service of a notice under section 6

36.50 An assignment following service of a notice under s 6 of the AHA 1986 will be rendered void and of no effect by virtue of s 6[1]. Such an assignment cannot therefore give rise to a valid Case E notice to quit.

[1]   See para 23.3.

Taxation

36.51 It is beyond the scope of this book to deal with matters of taxation generally, including the taxation consequences of any assignment or other

transaction. As with all transactions involving valuable assets, the tax considerations applicable at the time of the assignment should be carefully reviewed.

SUCCESSION PLANNING: DEATH OR RETIREMENT

36.52 Sitting-tenants and potential successors, when planning for succession,
will frequently need to consider whether it is more desirable to plan for
succession by retirement or to await the death of the sitting-tenant, with a
view to an application then being made for succession following the death.

The ability to abandon a retirement notice

36.53 If the parties wait until the death of the tenant, before the potential
applicant for succession makes his application, there will be no opportunity, in
the event of a flaw in the applicant's case being discovered, for the application
to be abandoned and for a fresh application to be made. This is because the
three-month rule provides that the application must be made within three
months of the date of death and no further application can be made after that
time[1]. This is to be compared with the provision on retirement where an
application can be abandoned or withdrawn by the applicant, in which event
the application is treated as if it had never been made[2].

[1] See para 35.81.
[2] See paras 36.40 and 36.44.

Joint tenants

36.54 In the case of joint tenants, a potential applicant for succession, who
might be eligible in the event of his close relation being the surviving tenant,
may wish to proceed by a retirement succession. This may arise, for example,
if the potential applicant's father is the joint tenant with his uncle, if with the
risk that his father might die first with no succession application being
possible on his uncle's death. The only way in those circumstances for the
potential successor to safeguard his position is for both of the joint tenants to
serve a retirement notice nominating the potential successor after both of the
joint tenants have attained the age of 65 or have become permanently
incapacitated[1].

[1] See para 36.15.

Commercial unit occupation

36.55 Commercial unit occupation is another issue. It not infrequently
happens that the sitting-tenant owns land constituting a commercial unit and
which is destined in due course for inheritance by the potential nominated
successor. In those circumstances, if the tenant dies, the applicant will be
disqualified by reason of the inheritance of such land. If before the death of
the tenant, a retirement notice is given when the applicant is not the occupier

(except in some non-disqualifying capacity) of the land in question, the applicant will be eligible during the retiring tenant's lifetime and therefore in a position to obtain the land subsequent to the tenancy which would not have been possible on the tenant's death.

Principal source of livelihood

36.56 Principal source of livelihood is a further issue in relation to potential loss. With the difficult economic climate for agriculture, tenants and their potential successors frequently have to supplement their agricultural income from outside sources. For example, contracting, cattle dealing, the exploitation of leisure activities (caravans on the holding and the like), which are not sources of livelihood derived from agricultural work upon the holding or a larger unit of which the holding forms part. An applicant who is fully eligible may lose that eligibility qualification if the outside source of livelihood is developed until it exceeds the source of livelihood derived from the agricultural work of the applicant upon the unit in question. In these circumstances, the retiring tenant would be well advised to serve a retirement notice, before the eligibility qualification of the applicant is lost, since otherwise the applicant may be forced to take unattractive commercial decisions and deny himself the supplement to his income lest he might otherwise lose his eligibility qualifications.

Principal source of livelihood is also an issue in relation to being treated as eligible. An applicant who is not fully eligible may not apply to be treated as eligible following the service of a retirement notice, whereas he can on death. In those circumstances, the potential retiring tenant and potential nominated successor would be ill advised to pursue the retirement route to succession. The applicant would be better advised to await the death of the tenant unless he previously obtains the full eligibility qualification[1].

[1]   As to the impact of the Tenancy Reform Industry Group (TRIG2) reforms, see para 35.42 in relation to the effect of diversification.

Taxation consequences

36.57 Capital taxation is subject to regular and often radical review. The taxation consequences of a succession applicable at the date of the transaction should be carefully considered.

Long-living tenants

36.58 It frequently happens that tenants live to a very great age by which time the next generation of potential tenant is already beyond the age of normal retirement or has predeceased. In such circumstances, if succession is delayed too long, there is a danger that the potential applicant for succession will himself be found to be unsuitable by reason of his age already beyond the age of normal retirement by the time of his application. A generation cannot be missed in those circumstances[1]. An application cannot be made by a grandchild, he being ineligible for succession on the death or retirement of the grandfather.

[1]   See para 35.40. See *White v de Pelet* (1993) ALT, South Western Area.

Farmhouse residence clauses

36.59 Many tenancy agreements require the tenant to reside in the farmhouse. Following succession, the new tenant will be the nominated successor, who will then be required to satisfy the farmhouse residence clause. This fact should be considered when reviewing the effect of retirement succession on the tenant's domestic arrangements.

Rollover of improvements

36.60 If the tenant has undertaken a substantial number of improvements with an entitlement to compensation written down to nominal values, the consequence of a succession, and therefore change of tenant and the ability to have the improvements disregarded at future rent reviews should be carefully considered. In default of agreement with the landlord, the outcome of an arbitration following the change of tenancy will be unknown until after the parties are committed to the change of tenancy and after the direction has been made by the ALT[1].

[1]   See paras 36.38.

Part V

COMPENSATION ON QUITTING

Contents

Chapter 37

GENERAL INTRODUCTION TO COMPENSATION ON QUITTING

INTRODUCTION

37.1 At common law, no compensation was payable to the agricultural tenant on quitting the holding on termination of the tenancy. A tenant who did more for the holding than fulfil his implied duty[1], and thereby enhanced the value of the landlord's interest, had no right to recover compensation for this from his landlord. Conversely, at the end of the tenancy, the landlord was entitled at common law to claim damages for breach of the tenant's obligations under the tenancy agreement, including obligations in relation to maintenance and repair of the premises, commonly called 'dilapidations'. In addition, the landlord could claim for waste[2].

The rights of the tenant to compensation on quitting were limited to his rights under the tenancy agreement, which were usually very restricted, and under the custom of the country where this applied[3]. The agricultural holdings legislation was passed initially with the almost exclusive objective of providing compensation to tenants on quitting. The main features of the present code of entitlement were developed at an early stage in the history of the legislation[4].

[1] See para 24.1.
[2] For more detailed observations on the position of tenants historically, see Ch 1. Note the very recent development of tenant's claims against landlords for dilapidations.
[3] *Wigglesworth v Dallison* (1779) 1 Doug KB 201. In many areas of the country customary rights to compensation arose whereby the tenant was entitled by custom to claim the cost of seed and labour expended in the last year of the tenancy and the cost of the manure applied in the last year. See para 1.1.
[4] The only significant variations in the established code of tenant's claims in recent years have been first, the introduction (originally by ss 9 and 10 of the Agriculture (Miscellaneous Provisions) Act 1968) of substantial increases in compensation for disturbance in certain circumstances and the introduction of special rules where the tenant's interest has been compulsorily purchased by the Land Compensation Act 1973; and second, the introduction of compensation for milk quota contained in the Agriculture Act 1986.

37.2 The AHA 1986 contains a comprehensive code of compensation rights for both a landlord and a tenant. 'Customary' rights only have a minor, residual relevance. The AHA 1986 provides that neither a landlord or a tenant of an agricultural holding shall be entitled to any compensation under custom

653

for any improvement or tenant right claim other than for 'old improvements', ie those commenced before 1 March 1948[1].

The AHA 1986 (like the AHA 1948 before it) contains substantially more extensive provisions in relation to tenant's claims than landlord's claims. Traditionally, the landlord's claims have been called 'the landlord's counter-claim', although more recently landlord's dilapidation claims, even where the farm in question is not necessarily particularly badly farmed, have tended to exceed the tenant's claims, sometimes by very substantial amounts.

[1] AHA 1986, s 77. As to 'old improvements', see para 38.1.

37.3 The rights given to a tenant by the AHA 1986 are provided by a comprehensive list of improvements for which compensation is payable. These are contained in Schs 7 and 8[1]. These are almost entirely agricultural improvements. Compensation is measured as the increased rental value of the holding as an agricultural enterprise. No regard is had under the AHA 1986 to diversification.

A separate code for milk quota compensation payable to a tenant on the termination of a tenancy of an agricultural holding is contained in the Agriculture Act 1986[2]. It should be noted that the Agriculture Act 1986 was not part of the consolidation of agricultural holdings legislation contained in the AHA 1986.

[1] See Ch 38.
[2] See Ch 50.

37.4 The rights to compensation discussed in this section of this book only relate to tenancies protected by the AHA 1986. The Agricultural Tenancies Act 1995 (ATA 1995) departs from its underlying concept of freedom of contract to replicate the concerns of earlier agricultural holdings legislation to provide a statutory code for compensation. It should be noted that the ATA 1995 provides a tenant with wider rights to compensation than the AHA 1986, for example in relation to non-agricultural improvements[1].

It should be noted that, with limited exceptions, 'contracting out' of the compensation provisions of the AHA 1986 is not permitted[2].

[1] See Ch 16.
[2] See AHA 1986, s 78(1). See also para 40.11.

37.5 A brief introduction to the scheme of the AHA 1986 is set out in this chapter so that the various claims and counter-claims available to the parties can be readily ascertained. Details of the nature and extent of the claims and procedures to be followed in pursuing these are set out in Chapters 38–41.

TENANT'S CLAIMS

Improvements

37.6 A tenant's claim for compensation for improvements has been divided in the AHA 1986 into the following categories:

(a)   old improvements begun before 1 March 1948[1]; and

(b)   new improvements begun on or after 1 March 1948 for which compensation is payable[2].

These are sub-divided into:

(i)   those requiring the landlord's consent[3]; and

(ii)   those requiring the consent of the landlord or the approval of the Agricultural Land Tribunal[4].

These are further sub-divided into:

(1)   long-term improvements[5]; and

(2)   short-term improvements[6].

[1]   AHA 1986, ss 64 and 79 and Sch 9 Pts I and II. The types of old improvement for which compensation is payable have been reduced in number and now comprise improvements of a type likely to be still relevant today.

[2]   AHA 1986, ss 64–69 and Sch 7 Pts I and II and Sch 8 Pt I. See para 38.17, 38.19 and 38.23.

[3]   AHA 1986, Sch 7 Pt I.

[4]   AHA 1986, Sch 7 Pt II. The AHA 1986 has retained, subject to certain exclusions, what were formerly Pts 1 and II of Sch 2 to the AHA 1948.

[5]   AHA 1986, Sch 7 Pts I and II.

[6]   AHA 1986, Sch 8 Pt I.

Tenant-right

37.7 'Tenant-right'[1] is the residual element of compensation payable to a tenant of an agricultural holding under custom, originally not recoverable under agricultural holdings legislation. These matters are listed in Sch 8 Pt II[2]. They are matters for which the tenant is entitled to be compensated (in effect usually reimbursed)[3] for his expenditure on materials and labour in respect of various farming activities carried on by him for which he does not reap the full benefit during his period of occupation. Those improvements to the holdings, which are more permanent in their effect, are in the main treated as improvements.

Tenant-right claims arise automatically on the termination of tenancies of agricultural holdings protected by the AHA 1986 entered into after 1 March 1948[4]. A tenant of a tenancy entered into after 1 March 1948 may elect to fall within the statutory compensation provisions[5].

[1]   The expression 'tenant-right' (though not appearing in the AHA 1948) is referred to in the AHA 1986 both in the marginal note to s 65 and in the heading to Sch 8 Pt II. There is no statutory definition. It is the term used to express the right of a tenant to take or receive,

after the termination of his tenancy, the benefit of labour and capital spent by him in cleaning, tilling and sowing the land during his tenancy, which he would otherwise lose as a result of the termination of the tenancy.
2   AHA 1986, s 65 and Sch 8 Pt II. See para 38.35.
3   Because of the measure of compensation so provided, although there are exceptions, eg tenant's pastures are paid for at face value.
4   AHA 1986, s 65 and Sch 8 Pt I.
5   AHA 1986, Sch 12 para 6.

Disturbance

37.8 Compensation for disturbance[1] is payable by the landlord where the tenancy terminates following a landlord's notice to quit in relation to the entire holding or after a tenant's counter-notice enlarging the landlord's notice to quit as to part[2].

Basic compensation is calculated by reference to the rent payable immediately before the tenancy terminated[3]. The amount is one year's rent as of right, and up to two years' rent if additional loss can be proved[4].

Additional compensation may also be payable[5]. This is again calculated by reference to the rent payable immediately before the tenancy terminated. The amount is four years' rent[6].

Compensation is also payable where the tenant's interest has been compulsorily acquired, or notice to quit has been given by a landlord possessing compulsory purchase powers[7].

1   AHA 1986, s 60(1).
2   Ie under the AHA 1986, s 32. See para 29.7.
3   AHA 1986, s 69(2)(a). See para 38.47.
4   AHA 1986, s 60(3).
5   AHA 1986, s 69(2)(b). See para 38.55.
6   AHA 1986, s 60(4).
7   Land Compensation Act 1973, s 48.

High farming

37.9 'High farming' is the continuous adoption of a special system of farming[1]. It is a provision rarely met with in practice. A tenant is entitled to special additional compensation if he shows that he has adopted continuously a system of farming more beneficial to the holding than his contractual obligation, or the local norm, requires[2].

1   AHA 1986, s 70(1).
2   AHA 1986, s 70(1).

Fixtures and fittings

37.10 Tenant's fixtures and fittings are subject to the statutory right of removal[1]. The landlord can elect to purchase the building and/or fixtures[2].

1   AHA 1986, s 10(1). See para 23.23 ff.
2   AHA 1986, s 10(4). See para 23.23.

Landlord's dilapidations

37.11 Until the 1980s, it was virtually unheard of for a tenant to claim damages for breach of the landlord's obligations. The possibility of such a claim has always existed at common law. Cases decided in the context of the general law of landlord and tenant show that such claims are sustainable and substantial damages are recoverable in appropriate cases[1].

1   See *Calabar Properties Ltd v Stitcher* [1983] 3 All ER 759, [1984] 1 WLR 287; *McGreal v Wake* [1984] 1 EGLR 42; *Bradley v Chorley Borough Council* (1985) 17 HLR 305; *Taylor v Knowsley Borough Council* (1985) 17 HLR 376; *Lubren v London Borough of Lambeth* (1987) 20 HLR 165 and articles in the Law Society Gazette 'Damages for Disrepair' (1984) Legal Action May 51; 'Tenants' Remedies for Disrepair' (1984) 9 May 1269 and 'Damages for Breach of Repairing Obligations' (1988) 20 July 17. Problems arising from the interrelationship between common law remedies and the 'model clauses' have resulted in extensive recent litigation: See para 23.14 ff.

Early resumption clauses

37.12 Where a tenant quits a tenancy of an agricultural holding protected under the AHA 1986 as a consequence of an early resumption clause where the landlord requires possession for a non-agricultural use, additional compensation is payable to the tenant[1].

1   AHA 1986, s 62.

Notice to quit part

37.13 If the landlord is entitled to recover possession of part of an agricultural holding protected by the AHA 1986[1], the tenant can claim compensation[2].

1   As to the circumstances when this entitlement arises, see para 29.7.
2   AHA 1986, s 74.

Milk quota

37.14 A new head of claim for a compensation payable to a tenant who qualifies was introduced by the Agriculture Act 1986 (not to be confused with the Agricultural Holdings Act 1986). This head of claim is of some complexity[1].

1   See Ch 50.

Damage by game

37.15 A tenant has a statutory right to claim game damage compensation from his landlord[1].

[1] See para 24.11.

Market gardens

37.15A Market gardens[1] are a form of agricultural holding to which special rules apply when assessing compensation on quitting[2]. In all other respects, market gardens are treated in the same way as any other form of agricultural holding[3].

Sections 79 and 80 of the AHA 1986, together with Sch 10, make special provisions as to compensation for market gardens unless, by agreement, a fair and reasonable measure of compensation or the 'Evesham Custom' is substituted[4].

[1] There is no statutory definition.
[2] For an agricultural holding to attract the compensation provisions afforded to market gardens, the holding must (a) be a market garden in fact and (b) be subject to landlord's written approval or Agricultural Land Tribunal consent in lieu: AHA 1986, s 80.
[3] See para 38.90 ff.
[4] AHA 1986, s 81(2).

THE LANDLORD'S CLAIMS

37.16 The common law right of the landlord to claim damages for breach of the tenant's obligations under his contract of tenancy has been preserved by the AHA 1986[1]. On termination of a tenancy of an agricultural holding protected by the AHA 1986, the landlord may have a claim for compensation for disrepair and dilapidations.

It should be noted that the landlord's remedies for breach of a tenant's repairing obligation may also be pursued during the term of the tenancy[2].

The common law rights of a landlord have been supplemented in two important respects by the AHA 1986:

(a)   By giving a landlord an alternative right to claim compensation for 'the dilapidation or deterioration of or damage to any part of the holding … caused by the failure of the tenant to farm in accordance with the rules of good husbandry'[3]. The AHA 1986 substitutes a statutory measure of damages for the common law measure[4]. This right is subject to the limitation that the amount of compensation must not exceed the amount (if any) by which the value of the landlord's reversion in the holding is diminished owing to the dilapidation, deterioration or damage in question[5].

(b)   By giving a landlord an additional right to recover compensation where the value of the holding has been reduced as a result of general deterioration, if and in so far as the measure of damages referred to in sub-paragraph (a) above is insufficient to compensate him[6].

[1]   AHA 1986, s 71(3).
[2]   *Kent v Conniff* [1953] 1 QB 361, [1953] 1 All ER 155. See para 39.9.
[3]   AHA 1986, s 71(1). See para 39.3.
[4]   AHA 1986, s 71(2).
[5]   AHA 1986, s 71(5). See para 39.15.
[6]   AHA 1986, s 72. See para 39.12.

MISCELLANEOUS PROVISIONS

Generally

37.17 Sections 69, 73, 76, 77 and 87 contain consequential amendments to the general common law rules:

(a)   accumulation (sometimes called 'rollover') both of the landlord's and tenant's claims where there has been a series of tenancies[1];
(b)   improvements paid for on entry[2];
(c)   exclusion of compensation for work which the tenant was compelled by the AHA 1986 to undertake[3];
(d)   the abolition of compensation based on custom[4];
(e)   the position relating to charges under the AHA 1986[5].

[1]   AHA 1986, ss 69(1) and 73. See Ch 40.
[2]   AHA 1986, s 69(2) and (3). See Ch 40.
[3]   AHA 1986, s 76(1). See para 40.9.
[4]   AHA 1986, s 77. See para 40.10.
[5]   AHA 1986, s 87(6). See para 40.13.

Severance of the reversion

37.18 Where the reversionary interest has been severed, and is vested in more than one person, the tenant is entitled to require that compensation payable under the AHA 1986 is calculated as if the reversion had not been severed[1].

[1]   AHA 1986, s 75(1). As to severance generally, see para 29.6. Also see para 40.8.

PROCEDURAL REQUIREMENTS

37.19 Before considering the substantive provisions of the legislation affecting compensation, it is essential to note that, as with all features of the agricultural holdings legislation, strict compliance with the procedural requirements for establishing a claim is essential if that claim is not to be irrevocably lost. Certain claims must, to be enforceable at all, have been preceded by a notice given before termination of the tenancy. These are listed below.

Tenant's claims

37.20

Category of claim	Statutory requirement
(1) Additional compensation for disturbance[1]	Notice in writing to the landlord not less than one month before the termination of the tenancy[2]
(2) Right to remove fixtures[3]	Notice in writing to the landlord not less than one month before the exercise of the right and the termination of the tenancy[4]
(3) Claim for 'high farming'[5]	Notice in writing to the landlord not less than one month before the termination of the tenancy[6]
(4) Claim for tenant-right under statute where tenant entered the holding before 1 March 1948[7]	Notice in writing to the landlord before termination[8]
(5) Claim for 'acclimatisation, hefting or settlement of hill sheep on hill land' under statute where tenant entered the holding after 1 March 1948 but before 31 December 1951[9]	Notice in writing to the landlord before termination[10]

1   AHA 1986, s 60(3)(b).
2   AHA 1986, s 60(6)(a).
3   AHA 1986, s 10(1).
4   Note that the removal must be not later than two months after termination of the tenancy: see para 23.24. AHA 1986, s 10(3)(b).
5   AHA 1986, s 70(1).
6   AHA 1986, s 70(2)(a).
7   AHA 1986, s 65(3).
8   AHA 1986, Sch 12 para 6(1).
9   AHA 1986, s 65 (1).
10 AHA 1986, Sch 12 para 7(2).

Landlord's claims

37.21

Category of claim	Statutory requirement
Compensation for general deterioration of the holding[1]	Notice in writing to the tenant not less than one month before termination of the tenancy[2]

1   AHA 1986, s 72(1).
2   AHA 1986, s 72(4).

Mandatory time limits after preliminary notices

37.22 Whether or not a claim subject of a preliminary notice given before termination, all claims by either party become statute barred and unenforceable unless within two months after termination notice of intention to make the claim is given to the other party[1].

There are further time limits to be observed, all of which are inflexible and cannot, except in rare circumstances, be extended[2].

[1] AHA 1986, s 83(2).
[2] For a detailed commentary on disputes procedures, time limits and notices applicable to compensation claims on quitting, see Ch 41.

SERVICE OF NOTICES

37.23 The rules relating to the service of notices and other documents under the agricultural holdings legislation are of paramount importance. They are contained in s 93 of the AHA 1986. A commentary upon them is to be found in Chapter 42.

Chapter 38

THE TENANT'S CLAIMS ON QUITTING: GENERAL

COMPENSATION FOR OLD IMPROVEMENTS

38.1 As stated in Chapter 37, the Agricultural Holdings Act 1986 (AHA 1986) contains a comprehensive code for claims for compensation by a tenant upon the termination of a tenancy of an agricultural holding protected by the AHA 1986. The statutory provisions include improvements, tenant right and disturbance.

The first head of claim is for relevant improvements. These break down into old and new improvements. They sub-divide into:

(a)   those requiring the landlord's consent; and
(b)   those requiring either the landlord's consent or the approval of the Agricultural Land Tribunal (ALT).

They further divide into long-term and short-term improvements[1]. Each is dealt with in turn in this chapter.

[1]   See para 37.6.

38.2 A tenant has a statutory right on the termination of his tenancy and upon quitting the agricultural holding to obtain from his landlord compensation for specified improvements carried on on the holding and begun before 1 March 1948. Such improvements are termed 'old improvements'[1].

[1]   AHA 1986, s 64(4), Sch 9 Pt I para 1(2).

Rules for entitlement

38.3 The tenant does not have a right to compensation in respect of old improvements where the contract of tenancy was made before 1 January 1921 and the improvement was one which he was required to carry out by the terms of his tenancy[1]. Further, the old improvement must have been one made on land which, at the time when the improvement was begun, was either a holding within the meaning of the Agricultural Holdings Act 1923 (AHA 1923) (as originally enacted)[2], or fell to be treated as such[3].

'Fell to be treated as such' means treated as such by virtue of the AHA 1923, s 33, which provided that where land comprised in a contract of tenancy was not a holding within the meaning of the AHA 1923 by reason only of the fact that the land so comprised included land (called 'non-statutory land'), which, owing to the nature of the buildings on it or the use to which it was put, would not, if it had been separately let, be a holding within the meaning of the AHA 1923, the provisions of the AHA 1923 relating to compensation and disturbance should, unless otherwise agreed in writing, apply to the part of the land exclusive of the non-statutory land as if that part were a separate holding. This did not apply to contracts of tenancy made before 1 January 1921.

[1] AHA 1986, Sch 9 Pt I para 1(3); *Huckell v Saintey* [1923] 1 KB 150, CA.
[2] A 'holding' for the purposes of the AHA 1923 was any parcel of land held by a tenant which was either wholly agricultural or wholly pastoral, or in part agricultural and as to the residue pastoral, or in whole or in part cultivated as a market garden, and was let or agreed to be let for a term of years, or for lives, or for lives and years, or from year to year, and not let to a tenant during his continuance in any office, appointment, or employment held under the landlord, but it did not include any allotment garden or any land cultivated as a garden unless it was cultivated wholly or mainly for the purposes of the trade or business of market gardening: AHA 1923, s 57(1). See *Re Lancaster and Macnamara* [1918] 2 KB 472, CA; *Howatson v M'Clymont* 1914 51 ScLR 153; *Re Russell and Harding* (1922) 128 LT 476, CA; *Re Joel's Lease, Berwick v Baird* [1930] 2 Ch 359; and *Land Settlement Association Ltd v Carr* [1944] KB 657, CA.
[3] AHA 1986, Sch 9 Pt I para 1(5).

38.4 In lieu of statutory compensation, a tenant may claim compensation under custom, agreement or otherwise, if he is so entitled[1].

[1] AHA 1986, Sch 9 Pt I para 1(4).

38.5 Subject to certain exclusions, the AHA 1986 has retained what were formerly Pts I and II of Sch 2 to the Agricultural Holdings Act 1948 (AHA 1948). In the revised list[1], laying down of permanent pasture, protecting young fruit trees and, in the case of arable land, the removal of bracken, gorse, tree roots, boulders or other like obstructions to cultivation have been deleted from the list of improvements formerly contained in Sch 2 to the AHA 1948, for which compensation was payable if the consent of the landlord was obtained to their execution. Pt III of Sch 3 to the AHA 1948, covering improvements of a short-term nature, has been deleted altogether because any claim under this head will now be spent.

[1] AHA 1986, Sch 9 Pt II.

38.6 The right to compensation applies whether or not the tenant was under an obligation to carry out the improvement, except in a case where the tenant was required to carry out the improvement by the terms of a tenancy agreement made before 1 January 1921[1].

38.6 *The tenant's claims on quitting: general*

1 AHA 1986, Sch 9 Pt I para 1(3). Few will now be of any practical consequence, though some may still have considerable value, eg Dutch barns where 'open-ended' consent was given by the landlord.

38.7 The landlord must have consented in writing (whether unconditionally or upon terms as to compensation or otherwise agreed between him and the tenant) to the execution of the improvement[1].

Compensation is not payable for an old improvement consisting of drainage[2] unless the tenant gave to the landlord, not more than three nor less than two months before beginning to execute the improvement, notice in writing under s 3 of the AHA 1923 of his intention to execute the improvement, and of the manner in which he proposed to execute it, and the landlord and tenant agreed on the terms on which the improvement was to be executed or, if no agreement was reached, and the tenant did not withdraw the notice, the landlord failed to exercise the right conferred on him by s 3 of the AHA 1923 to execute the improvement himself within a reasonable time[3]. This provision does not have effect if the landlord and tenant agreed, by the contract of tenancy or otherwise, to dispense with the notice under s 3 of the AHA 1923. An agreement to dispense with notice need not be in writing.

1 AHA 1986, Sch 9 Pt I para 3(1). The consent may be signified in the contract of tenancy itself, provided it is specific: *Mears v Callender* [1901] 2 Ch 388; *Gardner v Beck* (1947) 150 Estates Gazette 458; *Re Morse and Dixon* (1917) 87 LJKB 1, CA.
2 AHA 1986, Sch 9 Pt II para 16.
3 AHA 1986, Sch 9 Pt I para 4(1).

The categories of old improvements where compensation is payable

38.8 Old improvements for which compensation is payable are as follows:

(a) erection, alteration or enlargement of buildings;
(b) formation of silos;
(c) making and planting of osier beds;
(d) making of water meadows or works or irrigation;
(e) making of gardens;
(f) making or improvement of roads or bridges;
(g) making or improvement of water courses, ponds, wells or reservoirs or of works for the application of water power or for the supply of water for agricultural or domestic purposes;
(h) making or removal of permanent fences;
(i) planting of hops;
(j) planting of orchards or fruit bushes;
(k) reclaiming of waste land;
(l) warping or weiring of land;
(m) embankments and sluices against floods;
(n) erection of wire work in hop gardens;
(o) provision of permanent sheep-dipping accommodation;
(p) drainage[1].

1 AHA 1986, s 64(4), Sch 9 Pt II.

38.9 Until the Agricultural Holdings Act 1984 (AHA 1984) was enacted[1], there was a category of improvements for which no notice or consent was required for a claim for compensation[2].

1 The AHA 1984 received royal assent on 12 July 1984 and came into force on 12 September 1984: AHA 1984, s 11(2).
2 Ie improvements specified in the AHA 1948, Sch 2 Pt II (now repealed). These improvements were chalking of land; clay-burning; claying of land or spreading blaes [soft slate] upon the land; liming of land; marling of land; application to land of purchased artificial or other purchased manure; consumption on the holding by cattle, sheep, pigs or by horses other than those regularly employed on the holding; of corn, cake or other feeding-stuff not produced on the holding; consumption in the same manner of corn proved to have been produced and consumed on the holding; laying down temporary pasture with clover, grass, lucerne, sainfoin, or other seeds, sown more than two years prior to the termination of the tenancy, in so far as the value of the temporary pasture on the holding at the time of quitting exceeds the value of the temporary pasture on the holding at the commencement of the tenancy for which the tenant did not pay compensation; repairs to buildings, being buildings necessary for the proper cultivation or working of the holding, other than repairs which the tenant himself was under an obligation to execute. This provision was repealed as spent by the AHA 1984, s 10(1), Sch 3 para 27(a).

38.10 It will be seen from the list of old improvements that these, in the main, involve substantial works on the part of the tenant, for example, the erection of buildings or major works to the holding itself[1]. The landlord's consent may be unconditional or on terms as to the compensation 'or otherwise'[2] although it has been held that a condition that no compensation at all should be paid is invalid[3]. The correctness of that decision has been questioned[4].

It is to be noted that there was no procedure for ALT consent in the alternative to the consent of the landlord himself.

1 *Hamilton Ogilvy v Elliot* (1904) 7 F 1115.
2 AHA 1986, Sch 9 Pt I para 3(1).
3 *Mears v Callender* [1901] 2 Ch 388.
4 *Turnbull v Millar* 1942 SC 521, Ct of Sess, and see also *Johnson v Moreton* [1980] AC 37, [1978] 3 All ER 37.

Amount of compensation

38.11 The measure of compensation shall be an amount equal to the increase attributable to the improvement in the value of the agricultural holding as a holding, having regard to the character and situation of the holding and the average requirements of tenants reasonably skilled in husbandry[1].

In ascertaining the amount of the statutory compensation, a deduction has to be made in respect of any benefit given or allowed by the landlord in consideration of the tenant executing the improvement, whether it is expressly stated in the contract of tenancy that it is so given or allowed or not[2].

Where the landlord gave consent to an old improvement the rights of a tenant to claim compensation to which he may be entitled under custom or agreement, or otherwise instead of compensation provided by the AHA 1986, are not prejudiced[3].

38.11 *The tenant's claims on quitting: general*

Where the consent of the landlord was given upon agreed terms as to compensation, such compensation payable under the agreement is substituted for compensation payable under the AHA 1986[4].

Where the landlord and tenant agreed on terms as to compensation (whether after notice was given under the AHA 1923, s 3, or by an agreement to dispense with notice under that section), such compensation payable under the agreement is substituted for compensation payable under the AHA 1986[5].

[1] AHA 1986, s 64(4), Sch 9 Pt I para 2(1). It should be noted that by the AHA 1948, s 37, the measure of compensation for old improvements was 'such sum as fairly represents the value of the improvement to an incoming tenant'. The revised measure of compensation was introduced by the AHA 1984, Sch 3 para 10. It brings the measure of compensation into line with what is now s 66(1) of the AHA 1986, ie the compensation payable for new improvements and tenant-right matters.

[2] AHA 1986, Sch 9 Pt 1 para 1(4).

[3] AHA 1986, Sch 9 Pt 1 para 3(2).

[4] AHA 1986, Sch 9 Pt 1 para 4(3).

[5] AHA 1986, Sch 9 Pt 1 para 2(2). Note that the benefit must have been given or allowed in consideration of the improvement: in many cases (but not all) this will consist of a reduction in rent.

Miscellaneous

38.12 There are two important miscellaneous provisions relating to old improvements:

1 Successive tenancies:

Even though the tenant who is quitting may have carried out the improvements under a former tenancy, which is not the one now being terminated, he is entitled to 'rollover' the improvements[1].

2 Recovery of compensation paid:

An incoming tenant who has paid compensation to the previous outgoing tenant with the landlord's written consent[2] is entitled to recover that compensation for himself when he is the outgoing tenant[3]. In other words, there is a similar rollover provision where there has been a change in the identity of the tenant. It should be noted that this provision does not apply to market garden improvements.

[1] AHA 1986, Sch 9 Pt I para 5(1). This may occur, eg, where there is a technical surrender and regrant: see *Jenkin R Lewis & Son Ltd v Kerman* [1971] Ch 477, [1970] 1 All ER 833, CA. If this provision is to apply there must not be a material change in the identity of the holding. See para 33.4 ff.

[2] AHA 1986, Sch 9 Pt I para 5(2). There is no substitute for the landlord's written consent which is a prerequisite to the tenant relying upon this section.

[3] AHA 1986, Sch 9 Pt I para 5(2).

38.13 If the incoming tenant agrees to pay on entry such sum as shall be found to be due as compensation from the landlord, the liability to pay arises at, and the period of limitation runs from, the date at which the amount due has been ascertained[1]. An agreement between the incoming tenant and the outgoing tenant relating to compensation for old improvements does not affect the landlord's rights if he is not a party to the agreement[2]. An agreement between the landlord and the outgoing tenant that the landlord will only seek compensation against the incoming tenant for old improvements will be void[3].

[1]   *Cheshire County Council v Hopley* (1923) 130 LT 123, 21 LGR 524.
[2]   *Petri v Daniel* (1804) 1 Smith KB 199.
[3]   This is by virtue of the AHA 1986, s 78. Cf *Greenshields v Roger* 1922 SC (HL) 140.

COMPENSATION FOR NEW IMPROVEMENTS

38.14 A tenant of an agricultural holding is entitled (subject to certain exceptions)[1], on quitting the holding on the termination of the tenancy, to obtain from his landlord compensation for relevant improvements carried out by the tenant[2]. Relevant improvements are those specified in the AHA 1986[3] and begun on or after 1 March 1948[4]. These are known as 'new improvements'. The list of new improvements contained in the AHA 1986 significantly varies and extends those contained in the AHA 1948[5].

The Minister[6] has power to vary by order the provisions which specify relevant improvements after consultation with such bodies as appear to him to represent the interests of landlords and tenants of agricultural holdings[7]. Orders are of no effect unless approved by Parliament[8].

[1]   See para 40.9.
[2]   AHA 1986, s 64 and Schs 7 and 8 Pt I.
[3]   AHA 1986, Schs 7 and 8 Pt I.
[4]   AHA 1986, s 64(1).
[5]   AHA 1948, Schs 3 and 4 Pt I.
[6]   AHA 1986, s 96(1): see para 4.2.
[7]   AHA 1986, s 91(1). An order under this section may make such provision as to the operation of the AHA 1986 in relation to tenancies current when the order takes effect as appears to the Minister to be just having regard to the variation of the Schedules affected by the order: AHA 1986, s 91(2). The power to vary extends beyond Schs 7 and 8 to Sch 10 (market garden improvements).
[8]   AHA 1986, s 94(4).

38.15 New improvements, by virtue of s 64 of the AHA 1986, comprise those begun on or after 1 March 1948 which are specified in Sch 7 or in Pt I of Sch 8. Although the list of old and new improvements are similar, the specified new improvements are more numerous. The list of new improvements contained in Sch 7 Pts I and II of the AHA 1986 significantly varies and extends those contained in Sch 3 and Pt I of Sch 4 to the AHA 1948[1].

The test for determining whether an improvement is an old or a new improvement is the date when the improvement itself was begun, not the date on which the tenant went into occupation[2]. If the improvement was begun before 1 March 1948, then it is an old improvement. If it was begun on or after 1 March 1948, then it is a new improvement. Accordingly, a tenant who entered into occupation before 1 March 1948, but continued in occupation thereafter, may well have a claim for some old improvements and some new improvements, depending on when each was begun.

38.15 *The tenant's claims on quitting: general*

[1] The changes were originally introduced under the AHA 1984, Sch 3 para 25.
[2] AHA 1986, s 64(3).

Rules for entitlement

38.16 Relevant improvements for which compensation is payable under the AHA 1986 are either long-term improvements[1] or short-term improvements for which no consent is required[2] carried out on the holding by the tenant on or after 1 March 1948[3].

[1] AHA 1986, s 64, Sch 7.
[2] AHA 1986, s 64, Sch 8 Pt I.
[3] AHA 1986, s 64(1) and (2).

Long-term improvements requiring landlord's consent

38.17 The long-term improvements for which the consent of the landlord is required are as follows:

(a)   making or planting of osier beds;
(b)   making of water meadows;
(c)   making of watercress beds;
(d)   planting of hops;
(e)   planting of orchards or fruit bushes;
(f)   warping or weiring of land;
(g)   making of gardens;
(h)   provision of underground tanks[1].

The list formerly contained in Sch 3 Pt I of the AHA 1948 has been amended as follows:

(i)   'works or irrigation' has been omitted from item 2 in Sch 7 Pt I; and
(ii)   'provision of underground tanks' now forms part of Sch 7 Pt I, having been added as item 8.

As to orchards and fruit bushes, it should be noted that special rules apply in the context of market gardens[2], but that otherwise written consent of the landlord is required as a mere prerequisite to obtaining compensation.

There is no substitute for the landlord's consent which is an essential precondition. If it is withheld, that is fatal to a claim for compensation by the tenant, no matter how unreasonable the landlord was in withholding his consent[3].

[1] AHA 1986, Sch 7 Pt I.
[2] See para 38.90.
[3] The AHA 1984, s 64. In some cases the tenant may be able to treat these items as fixtures instead where he has failed to obtain the required consent and then remove them if all necessary conditions for removal are satisfied.

38.18 The consent may be conditional or given upon such terms as to compensation or otherwise as may be agreed upon in writing between the landlord and the tenant[1]. Any such agreement concerning compensation will override the statutory measure of compensation laid down in the AHA 1986[2].

The landlord's consent may be contained in the tenancy agreement itself[3].

The landlord's consent in writing does not need to be given before the improvement is executed[4].

[1] AHA 1986, s 67(2).
[2] AHA 1986, s 67(2). As to whether an agreement that no compensation at all will be payable, see para 38.10. Also see, *Mears v Callender* [1901] 2 Ch 388, but note the criticism of that decision, particularly in the argument in *Johnson v Moreton* [1980] AC 37, HL.
[3] *Gardner v Beck* [1947] EGD 169.
[4] Cf the requirements in the case of old improvements under Sch 9 Pt I para 3(1). In practice, a tenant who carries out the improvement without having obtained the landlord's consent 'before the execution thereof' is very ill-advised and has little or no negotiating position with his landlord in attempting to persuade him subsequently to consent in writing. In practice, landlords often give their written consent by counter-signing an application for grant aid.

Long-term improvements requiring either the landlord's consent or approval of the Agricultural Land Tribunal[1]

38.19 The improvements which require either the consent of the landlord or the approval of the ALT are as follows:

(a)   erection, alteration or enlargement of buildings, and making or improvement of permanent yards;
(b)   carrying out works in compliance with an improvement notice served, or an undertaking accepted, under certain housing legislation[2];
(c)   erection or construction of loading platforms, ramps, hardstandings for vehicles or other similar facilities;
(d)   construction of silos;
(e)   claying of land;
(f)   marling of land;
(g)   making or improvement of roads or bridges;
(h)   making or improvement of water courses, culverts, ponds, wells or reservoirs, or of works for the application of water power for agricultural or domestic purposes or of works for the supply, distribution or use of water for such purposes (including the erection or installation of any structures or equipment which form part of or are to be used for or in connection with operating any such works);
(i)   making or removal of permanent fences;
(j)   reclaiming of wasteland;
(k)   making or improvement of embankments or sluices;
(l)   erection of wire work for hop gardens;
(m)   provision of permanent sheep-dipping accommodation;
(n)   removal of bracken, gorse, tree roots of boulders or other like obstructions to cultivation;
(o)   land drainage (other than improvements relating to mole drainage)[3];
(p)   provision or laying-on of electric light or power;

(q) provision of facilities for the storage or disposal of sewage or farm waste;
(r) repairs to fixed equipment, being equipment reasonably required for the proper farming of the holding, other than repairs which the tenant is under an obligation to carry out;
(s) the grubbing up of orchards or fruit bushes;
(t) planting trees otherwise than as an orchard and bushes other than fruit bushes[4].

1 Originally, the AHA 1948 provided for the approval to be obtained from the Minister. Section 50 of the Agriculture Act 1958 substituted the ALT for the Minister, but failed to direct this substitution in the headings of the Sch 3 to the AHA 1948. This omission has now been corrected in the headings to Sch 7 Pt II to the AHA 1986.
2 The Housing Act 1985, Pt VII (ss 209–238) or the Housing Act 1974, Pt VIII (repealed).
3 Ie falling within the AHA 1986, Sch 8 Pt I para 1.
4 AHA 1986, Sch 7 Pt II.

38.20 The list of long-term improvements originally contained in Pt II of Sch 3 to the AHA 1948 has been varied as follows:

(a) 'Carrying out works in compliance with an improvement notice served, or an undertaking accepted, under Part VII of the Housing Act 1985 or Part VIII of the Housing Act 1974' has been inserted as item 10.
(b) 'The erection or construction of loading platforms, ramps, hard standings for vehicles or other similar facilities' has been inserted as item 11.
(c) The former item 13 has been replaced by a more comprehensive formula relating to water installations being 'the making or improvement of watercourses, culverts, ponds, wells or reservoirs, or of works for the application of water power for agricultural or domestic purposes or of works for the supply, distribution or use of water for such purposes (including the erection or installation of any structures or equipment which form part of or are to be used for or in connection with operating any such works)'.
(d) Item 25 now reads 'Provision of facilities for the storage or disposal of sewage or farm waste'.
(e) 'The grubbing up of orchards or fruit bushes' has been inserted as item 27.
(f) 'Planting trees otherwise than as an orchard and bushes other than fruit bushes' has been inserted as item 28.
(g) The growing of herbage crops for commercial seed production has been transferred to Sch 8.

The provisions relating to consents set out at paras 38.17 to 38.19 apply equally here.

If the landlord either refuses his consent, or grants consent subject to conditions unacceptable to the tenant, the tenant may apply to the ALT for its approval in place of that of the landlord[1].

1 AHA 1986, s 67(3).

38.21 The ALT may give consent conditionally, or unconditionally, or refuse consent altogether. The conditions may relate to compensation and may reduce the amount of compensation, though it would appear that the compensation cannot be increased.

If the ALT gives consent, the landlord may serve notice in writing on the ALT and the tenant that the landlord proposes to carry out the improvement himself[1]. If no such notice is given, or if it is given and the ALT decides, following the tenant's application, that the landlord has failed to carry out the improvement within a reasonable time, then the ALT's approval operates as if it was the landlord's consent[2].

1   Service is required within one month from receiving notification of the Tribunal's decision: see r 7(2) of the Agricultural Land Tribunals (Rules) Order 1978, SI 1978/259: see AHA 1986, s 67(5).
2   AHA 1986, s 67(6).

38.22 In *Barton v Lincolnshire Trust for Nature Conservancy*[1], the ALT considered and granted consent for an improvement, without any restriction being imposed upon the compensation payable, where the landlord had only been prepared to give consent subject to a write-off for compensation. In that case, it was agreed that the construction of an eight million gallon irrigation reservoir to catch winter rainfall on tenanted land in Lincolnshire was desirable, but the landlord argued that it needed to be able to establish its accumulated liability for compensation. The landlord proposed a write-off over 20 years and agreed that this was necessary to avoid criticism by the Charity Commission. The ALT decided that any condition or write-off would not be justified. It directed that compensation should be payable in accordance with the statutory formula under the AHA 1986, particularly since the value of the improvement at the end of the tenancy 'cannot be guessed before that time comes'.

If the landlord carries out the improvement, he will qualify for an increase of rent under s 13 of the AHA 1986. Conversely, if the tenant does the work, he will be entitled to compensation for the improvement on the termination of the tenancy and to have the improvement disregarded for rent review purposes[2].

1   (1997) ALT, Eastern Area.
2   AHA 1986, s 13(6).

Short-term improvements

38.23 The relevant improvements in respect of which compensation is payable to a tenant of an agricultural holding (subject to certain exceptions)[1], on quitting the holding on the termination of the tenancy, includes short-term improvements[2].

Short-term improvements begun on or after 1 March 1948 for which compensation is payable are as follows:

(a)   mole drainage and works carried out to secure its efficient functioning;
(b)   protection of fruit trees against animals[3];
(c)   clay burning;
(d)   liming (including chalking) of land;
(e)   application to land of purchased manure and fertiliser, whether organic or inorganic;
(f)   consumption on the holding of corn (whether produced on the holding or not), or of cake or other feeding-stuff not produced on the holding, by horses, cattle, sheep, pigs or poultry[4].

The landlord's consent or approval is not a prerequisite to a tenant's claim for statutory compensation in respect of short-term improvements[5].

A tenant is not entitled to statutory compensation for mole drainage and works carried out to secure its efficient functioning unless, not later than one month before the improvement was commenced, the tenant gave notice in writing to the landlord of his intention to carry out the improvement[6].

There is no power to contract out of the statutory compensation in respect of the items mentioned in Pt I of Sch 8 of the AHA 1986.

1   See para 40.9.
2   AHA 1986, s 64 and Sch 8 Pt I.
3   See *Gardner v Beck* (1947) 150 Estates Gazette 458.
4   See *Gardner v Beck* (1947) 150 Estates Gazette 458. These are identical to the improvements listed in AHA 1948, Sch 4 Pt I.
5   AHA 1986, s 65 Sch 8 Pt II.
6   AHA 1986, s 68(1). The reason for this notice or what purpose it serves, or what the landlord can do if given such a notice, is not clear. He can check that the work is being done. It may not be apparent from inspection later. Cf the position in the case of old improvements under Pt II of Sch 9 which relates to all forms of drainage.

Amount of compensation

Long-term improvements

38.24   The amount of compensation in respect of a long-term improvement is the increased value of the holding as a holding, having regard to the character and situation of the holding and the average requirements of tenants reasonably skilled in husbandry[1]. This definition suggests that the proper approach is to assess the extent to which the improvements enable the landlord to let the holding at an increased rent and to capitalise such increase. A common method is to take the notional increase and the rental value of the holding resulting from the improvement and to multiply this by an appropriate number of years' purchase in order to arrive at the increase in the value of the holding. The number of years' purchase will depend upon the probable period of life and usefulness of the type of improvements concerned[2]. In this connection, regard has to be had to 'the character and situation of the holding and the average requirements of tenants reasonably skilled in husbandry'[3]. There are no regulations prescribed to determine the method of calculating the compensation[4].

1 AHA 1986, s 66(1). Note the provisions of s 66(5) which provides that where a grant out of money provided by Parliament or local government funds has been, or will be, made to the tenant of an agricultural holding in respect of a relevant improvement, the grant shall be taken into account in assessing the compensation for the improvement. The inclusion of local government funds in the subsection originates from the AHA 1984, Sch 3 para 11.
2 Eg the installation of a water supply will surely endure usefully longer and need less maintenance than, say, an overhead electricity supply or an engine to pump water to a certain height and pressure.
3 This provision makes clear that the test is objective.
4 Cf Sch 8 improvements and tenant-right matters.

Short-term improvements

38.25 Since short-term improvements are less permanent than long-term improvements, the measure of compensation is specified as 'the value of the improvement or matter to an incoming tenant calculated in accordance with such method, if any, as may be prescribed'[1].

The regulations currently in force are the Agriculture (Calculation of Value for Compensation) Regulations 1978[2], the Agriculture (Calculation of Value for Compensation) (Amendment) Regulations 1981[3] and the Agriculture (Calculation of Value for Compensation) (Amendment) Regulations 1983[4].

Contracting-out is prohibited[5] but consideration must be given to any benefit given to the tenant by a landlord in any agreement in writing between them in assessing compensation for a short-term improvement.

1 AHA 1986, s 66(2).
2 SI 1978/809.
3 SI 1981/822.
4 SI 1983/1475.
5 AHA 1986, s 78.

38.26 Where the tenant of an agricultural holding has remained on the holding during two or more tenancies, he is not to be deprived of his right to compensation under the AHA 1986 in respect of relevant improvements because the improvements were made during a tenancy other than the one at the termination of which he is quitting the holding[1].

Where, with the written consent of the landlord[2], on going into occupation of an agricultural holding, the tenant paid to an outgoing tenant any compensation payable by the landlord[3] in respect of the whole or any part of a relevant improvement, or has paid to the landlord himself the amount of any such compensation payable to an outgoing tenant, the tenant is entitled (on quitting the holding) to claim compensation in respect of the relevant improvement as the outgoing would have been entitled if the outgoing tenant had remained tenant of the holding and quitted at the same time as the tenant himself quits[4].

The provision contained in s 69 of the AHA 1986 to protect the tenant's right to compensation in relation to successive tenancies also applies where the tenancy comprises the substantial part of the land comprised in the original letting[5].

1   AHA 1986, s 69(1), as amended by the Regulatory Reform (Agricultural Tenancies) (England and Wales) Order 2006 (RRO 2006), SI 2006/2805, art 6.
2   The consent may be contained in the contract of tenancy. An alleged custom that the outgoing tenant should seek payment from the incoming tenant rather than the landlord for compensation has been held to be bad: see *Bradburn v Foley* (1878) 3 CPD 129.
3   Ie under the AHA 1986 or the AHA 1948 or the Agriculture Act 1947, Pt III.
4   AHA 1986, s 69(2). The tenant only has rights commensurate with those of his predecessor. As to the enforcement of an agreement by the incoming tenant to pay compensation to the outgoing tenant, see *Cheshire County Council v Hopley* (1923) 130 LT 123.
5   AHA 1986, s 69(1), as amended by the RRO 2006, SI 2006/2805, art 6. See para 40.3.

38.27 In cases not falling within the above provisions, a tenant who, in going into occupation of the holding, paid to his landlord any amount in respect of the whole or part of a relevant improvement, is entitled on quitting the holding (subject to any written agreement between himself and the landlord) to claim compensation in respect of that relevant improvement, as he would have been entitled if he had been the tenant of the holding at the time when the improvement was carried out and the improvement or part had been carried out by him[1].

1   AHA 1986, s 69(3).

TENANT-RIGHT

Introduction

38.28 'Tenant-right' is a term used to express the right of the tenant to take or receive after the termination of his tenancy the benefit of the labour and capital expended by him in cleaning, tilling and sowing the land during the tenancy, which he would otherwise lose by the termination of the tenancy[1].

In the AHA 1986, the expression 'tenant-right matters' is used to describe specified items[2] for which compensation may be payable under the AHA 1986, except in the case of a tenant who entered into occupation of the holding before 1 March 1948 and who does not elect that the AHA 1986 provision should apply to him[3]. Such a tenant is excluded from the general prohibition on the payment of compensation by custom where the matter in question is covered by statute[4].

As seen below[5], if the tenant entered into occupation on or after 1 March 1948, the provisions of the AHA 1986 apply to compensation for tenant-right matters, without any option for the tenant to claim under custom or the agreement[6]. It should also be noted that a claim for compensation based upon custom is excluded under the AHA 1986[7].

1   Tenant-right did not usually include permanent improvements as these were not the subject of compensation by the custom of the country with certain exceptions, for example, in Lincolnshire. It included such things as growing or severed crops or produce left on the farm by the outgoing tenant, for example, hay, straw, sometimes farmyard manure, and seeds sown, tillages, cultivations or acts of husbandry carried out by the outgoer, the benefit of which would fall to his successor.
2   Ie specified in the AHA 1986, s 65 and Sch 8 Pt II. See para 38.35.

3   AHA 1986, Sch 12 para 6. As to election by the tenant, see para 38.38.
4   AHA 1986, ss 77 and 78(3). Also see paras 40.10 and 40.12.
5   See para 38.37.
6   AHA 1986, s 65(3).
7   AHA 1986, s 77. See para 40.10.

38.29 An assignment by a tenant of an agricultural holding of all of his goods and effects on the holding and 'all his estate and interest thereon and therein' includes the tenant-right or tillages on the holding[1]. An assignment by the tenant of all of his goods and effects etc, and 'all his tenant-right and interest yet to come and unexpired in and to the farms and premises' passes the tenant's interest in crops grown in future years, including away-going crops[2]. Tenant-right, including prospective tenant-right, constitutes an 'other agricultural asset' for the purposes of the Agricultural Credits Act 1928[3].

Tillages are the expenses and acts of husbandry in general, such as seeds and labour, fallows and unapplied manure[4]. If the landlord accepts tillage and manure, an agreement by him to pay for it will be implied[5].

1   *Cary v Cary* (1862) 10 WR 669.
2   *Petch v Tutin* (1846) 15 M & W 110, following *Grantham v Hawley* (1616) Hob 132, on the point that goods to come into existence at a future time are assignable by deed.
3   Agricultural Credits Act 1928, s 5(7), as amended by the AHA 1986, s 100, Sch 14 para 16.
4   *Martin v Coulman* (1834) 4 LJKB 37.
5   *Dalby v Hirst* (1819) 1 Brod & Bing 224; *Martin v Coulman* (1834) 4 LJKB 37; *Hutton v Warren* (1836) 1 M & W 466. Where a tenant becomes an annual period tenant on such of the terms of a written agreement as are applicable for a yearly tenancy, these terms will include a stipulation for payment for tillages: *Brocklington v Saunders* (1864) 13 WR 46. An alternative method is for the incoming tenant to enter to plough and sow during the last year of the expiring tenancy: see *Milner v Jordan* (1846) 8 QB 615.

38.30 The rights between the parties in respect of tillages are not prejudiced by the provisions of the AHA 1986[1]. Tillages are tenant-right matters for which compensation is payable under the AHA 1986, except in the case of a tenant who entered into occupation before 1 March 1948 and who does not elect that the provisions of the AHA 1986 should apply to him[2].

Where the landlord is liable to pay an outgoing tenant for tillages etc, the liability attaches to the landlord's interest in the land. That devolves upon the person who, when the payment becomes due, is then in receipt, or entitled to receipt, of the rent[3].

A vendor, who after the contract for sale, but before completion, pays the outgoing tenant's valuation, is entitled, in the absence of a stipulation to the contrary, to be reimbursed by the purchaser[4]. A purchaser of land subject to the terms of an existing tenancy is deemed to have notice of the tenant's claim to compensation under the AHA 1986[5]. The outgoing tenant's valuation means such sum as is found to be payable by the landlord to the tenant after balancing any payment due by the tenant to the landlord for dilapidations and any payment due from the landlord to the tenant in respect of tenant-right etc[6].

1   AHA 1986, s 97.

2 AHA 1986, s 65 and Sch 8 Pt II para 8.
3 *Mansel v Norton* (1883) 22 Ch D 769, CA; *Faviell v Gaskoin* (1852) 7 Exch 273; *Womersley v Dally* (1857) 26 LJ Ex 219. These cases deal with customary compensation. In cases of compensation under the AHA 1986, the same result follows on the definition of 'landlord' in s 96(1).
4 *Bennett v Stone* [1902] 1 Ch 226, CA.
5 *Re Earl of Derby and Fergusson's Contracts* [1912] 1 Ch 479. Also see *Dale v Hatfield Chase Corpn* [1922] 2 KB 282, CA. These cases were decided under corresponding provisions of the AHA 1948. As to the tenant's right to continue to serve documents on the vendor, until he has noticed of the sale, see the AHA 1986, s 93(5).
6 *Oades v Spafford* [1948] 2 KB 74n, applying *Dalton v Pickard* (1911) [1926] 2 KB 545, CA.

38.31 An alleged custom that the outgoing tenant should look to the incoming tenant, to the exclusion of the landlord's liability, for payment of seeds, tillages, etc is unreasonable and cannot be supported[1]. The incoming tenant may become liable, however, to the outgoing tenant by express or tacit agreement[2].

A tenant is not entitled to be paid for tillages etc, if he quits the holding before the due termination of the tenancy[3]. If a contract of tenancy for a term of years is terminable by notice at the expiry of a lesser period, the tenant's rights are preserved on his quitting after due notice at the earlier date[4]. The trustee of a bankrupt tenant, who disclaims, is not entitled to compensation for tenant-right[5].

1 *Bradburn v Foley* (1878) 3 CPD 129.
2 *Bradburn v Foley* (1878) 3 CPD 129; *Codd v Brown* (1867) 15 LT 536; *Stafford v Gardner* (1872) LR 7 CP 242. Such an agreement does not affect any existing rights of the landlord: see *Petrie v Daniel* (1804) 1 Smith KB 199.
3 *Whittaker v Barker* (1832) 1 Cr & M 113; *England v Shearburn* (1884) 52 LT 22. Also see, *Marquis of Breadalbane v Stewart* [1904] AC 217, HL.
4 *Bevan v Chambers* (1896) 12 TLR 417, CA.
5 *Re Wadsley, Bettinson's Representative v Trustee* (1925) 94 LJ Ch 215. As to disclaimer generally, see para 45.60 ff.

38.32 The tenant may also, either by custom or agreement[1], have the right to the benefit of work which has been done, but has not become productive during the last year of the term. He may have the right to sell the away-going crops himself[2]. Apart from such custom or agreement, the tenant must at the end of the term give up possession of the farm with all growing crops[3]. A custom as to any of these matters is excluded by express agreement which is inconsistent with it[4]. Where a Lady Day tenancy is prematurely determined by a judicial proceeding (such as the award of an arbitrator), the custom that the tenant should have an away-going crop is inoperative[5].

1 Rights to away-going crops are not prejudiced by the AHA 1986, s 97. Crops or produce which the tenant has a right to sell or remove are not the subject of a claim for compensation under the AHA 1986, s 67 and Sch 8 Pt II para 7. Also see para 38.28 generally.
2 *Wigglesworth v Dallison* (1779) 1 Doug KB 201.
3 *Caldecott v Smythies* (1837) 7 C & P 808.
4 A custom for the tenant to have away-going crops is excluded by an agreement as to such crops: *Boraston v Green* (1812) 16 East 71; and see *Clarke v Roystone* (1842) 13 M & W 752 as to the custom to pay for manure.

⁵   *Thorpe v Eyre* (1834) 1 Ad & El 926; and see *Re Wadsley, Bettinson's Representative v Trustee* (1925) 94 LJ Ch 215.

38.33 A clause in a tenancy agreement entitling the tenant to take an away-going crop does not entitle the tenant to retain possession of any part of the holding against the landlord after the termination of the tenancy. It does import a licence to the tenant to enter the land for purpose of taking the crop[1]. Where the tenant is entitled by custom to the away-going crop, and is bound to repair fences, he may be entitled also to actual possession of the land on which the crop is growing until the crop is carried away[2]. By custom, a tenant may also be entitled to leave his away-going crop in the barn of the farm after he has quit the holding[3]. The landlord or the incoming tenant cannot pursue a claim for trespass against the outgoing tenant for taking an away-going crop according to the custom of the country, even though the outgoing tenant has committed a breach of covenant in cropping too much of the land and not manuring it[4].

¹   *Strickland v Maxwell* (1834) 2 Cr & M 539.
²   *Griffiths v Puleston* (1844) 13 M & W 358. This does not prevent recovery of possession of the part of the holding to which the privilege does not extend: *Doe d Waters v Houghton* (1827) 1 Man & Ry KB 208.
³   *Beavan v Delahay* (1788) 1 Hy Bl 5; *Lewis v Harris* (1778) 1 Hy Bl 7n.
⁴   *Boraston v Green* (1812) 16 East 71. Also see *Griffiths v Tombs* (1833) 7 C & P 810, where the overcropping was an oral permission from the landlord.

38.34 The tenant of an agricultural holding who has no right to sell or remove from the holding crops or produce grown on the holding in the last year of the tenancy may be entitled to claim statutory compensation for them from his landlord[1].

At common law[2], a tenant holding for an uncertain interest[3], whose interest terminates otherwise than as a consequence of his own act[4], has the right, under the name of emblements, to enter onto the land after the termination of the tenancy to cut and carry away those crops[5] that normally repay within the year[6] the labour from which they are produced[7].

¹   AHA 1986, s 65(1), Sch 8 Pt II para 7. Also see, *Thomas v National Farmers' Union Mutual Insurance Society Ltd* [1961] 1 All ER 363, [1961] 1 WLR 386.
²   As to the statutory right to an extended tenancy in place of emblements conferred by the AHA 1986, s 21, see para 20.9. Note that the AHA 1986, s 97 preserves the common law right in cases to which s 21 does not apply.
³   This includes a tenancy from year to year: *Kingsbury v Collins and Elmes* (1827) 4 Bing 202: *Graves v Weld* (1833) 5 B & Ad 105.
⁴   For example, by forfeiture for breach of covenant: *Bulwer v Bulwer* (1819) 2 B & Ald 470. No right to emblements arises where a tenancy at will is terminated by the tenant: Co Litt 68 cited in *Kingsbury v Collins and Elmes* (1827) 4 Bing 202.
⁵   For example, grain crops, roots, clover, potatoes and hops; Co Litt 55b: *Latham v Atwood* (1638) Cro Car 515; *Evans v Roberts* (1826) 5 B&C 829; *Graves v Weld* (1833) 5 B & Ad 105.
⁶   *Graves v Weld* (1833) 5 B & Ad 105.
⁷   *Hayling v Okey* (1853) 8 Exch 531; *Kingsbury v Collins and Elmes* (1827) 4 Bing 202. The right to emblements is personal property and not an interest in land: Co Litt 55b; *Hallen v Runder* (1834) 1 Cr M & R 266, citing *Mayfield v Wadsley* (1824) 3 B & C 357.

The application of the AHA 1986

38.35   On quitting the holding on the termination of the tenancy, a tenant of an agricultural holding is entitled (subject to certain exceptions)[1] to obtain from his landlord compensation for tenant-right matters[2].

Statutory tenant-right matters are as follows:

(a)   Growing crops and severed or harvested crops and produce, being in either case crops or produce grown on the holding in the last year of the tenancy, but not including crops or produce which the tenant has a right to sell or remove from the holding[3].

(b)   Seeds sown and cultivations, fallows and acts of husbandry performed on the holding at the expense of the tenant (including the growing of herbage crops for commercial seed production)[4].

(c)   Pasture laid down with clover, grass, lucerne, sainfoin or other seeds, being either pasture laid down at the expense of the tenant, otherwise in compliance with an obligation imposed on him by an agreement in writing to lay it down to replace temporary pasture comprised in the holding when the tenant entered on the holding which was not paid for by him, or pasture paid for by the tenant on entering on the holding[5].

(d)   Acclimatisation, hefting or settlement of hill sheep[6] on hill land[7].

(e)   In areas of the country where arable crops can be grown[8] in an unbroken series of not less than six years, and it is reasonable that they should be grown on the holding or part of it, the residual fertility value of the sod of the excess qualifying leys[9] on the holding, if any[10].

1   See para 40.9.
2   AHA 1986, s 65(1).
3   AHA 1986, s 65(1) and Sch 8 Pt II para 7.
4   AHA 1986, Sch 8 Pt II para 8.
5   AHA 1986, Sch 8 Pt II para 9.
6   'Hill sheep' means sheep which: (a) have been reared and managed on a particular hill or mountain; (b) have developed an instinct not to stray from the hill or mountains; (c) are able to withstand the climatic conditions typical of the hill or mountain; and (d) have developed resistance to diseases which are likely to occur in the area in which the hill or mountain is situated: AHA 1986, Sch 8 Pt II para 10(2).
7   AHA 1986, Sch 8 Pt II para 10(1). 'Hill land' means any hill or mountain where only hill sheep are likely to thrive throughout the year: Sch 8 Pt II para 10(2).
8   For the purpose of this provision: (a) the growing of an arable crop includes the growing of clover, grass, lucerne, sanfoin or other seeds grown for a period of less than one year but does not include the laying down of a ley continuously maintained as such for more than one year; (b) the qualifying leys comprising the excess qualifying leys are those indicated to be such by the tenant; and (c) qualifying leys laid down at the expense of the landlord without reimbursement by the tenant or any previous tenant of the holding or laid down by and at the expense of the tenant pursuant to agreement by him with the landlord for the establishment of a specified area of leys on the holding as a condition of the landlord giving consent to the ploughing or other destruction of permanent pasture or pursuant to a direction given by an arbitrator on a reference under s 14(2) of the AHA 1986 (see para 24.8) are not included in the excess qualifying leys: AHA 1986, Sch 8 Pt II para 11(2).
9   'Leys' means laid down with clover, grass, lucerne, sainfoin or other seeds, but does not include permanent pasture. 'Qualifying leys' means leys continuously maintained as such for a period of three or more growing seasons since being laid down, and arable land which within the three growing seasons immediately preceding the termination of the tenancy was ley continuously maintained before being destroyed by ploughing or some other means for the production of a tillage crop or crops: AHA 1986, Sch 8 Pt II para 11(3).
10   AHA 1986, Sch 8 Pt II para 11(1).

Entry into occupation before 1 March 1948

38.36 If the tenant entered into occupation of the holding before 1 March 1948, compensation for tenant-right will not be payable under the AHA 1986, unless before the termination of the tenancy the tenant gives notice in writing to the landlord electing that those provisions shall apply to him[1]. If he does not serve such a notice of election, compensation for tenant-right will be payable under the custom of the district and the provisions (if any) of the tenancy agreement[2].

[1] AHA 1986, Sch 12 para 6(1).
[2] Section 77 of the AHA 1986 provides that, as a general rule, no claims can be made for compensation for improvement or tenant-right under custom. Tenant-right claims in the case of tenants who went into occupation before 1 March 1948 are an exception to this rule: AHA 1986, Sch 12 para 8(1)(b).

Entry into occupation on or after 1 March 1948

38.37 If the tenant entered into occupation on or after 1 March 1948, the provisions of the AHA 1986 apply to compensation for tenant-right matters, without any option for the tenant to claim under custom or the agreement[1].

[1] AHA 1986, s 65(3).

Rules for entitlement

38.38 If the tenant went into occupation before 1 March 1948, then he must, if he is to claim the statutory compensation, have made his election to have the AHA 1986 provisions apply to the tenancy before the termination of the tenancy[1].

If the tenancy is being terminated by a notice to quit, the landlord may force the tenant to make his election by serving notice on him requiring him to do so[2]. The tenant must then, within a month of the landlord's notice, give notice of his election, unless the landlord's notice to quit is one which has been challenged and depends upon the outcome of proceedings under s 26 or s 27 of the AHA 1986, or arbitration proceedings. In those cases the election must be made within one month of the termination of those proceedings. If the tenant fails to elect within the one-month period, he will be debarred from electing for the statutory basis. The election is required to be total rather than partial. Accordingly, the tenant cannot select those items which suit him best under the tenancy agreement or custom and those items for which he prefers the statutory measure of compensation to apply.

Special rules continue to apply to 'acclimatisation, hefting or settlement of hill sheep on hill land'[3]. Following the passing of the AHA 1948, this head of tenant-right claim was added by the Agricultural Holdings Act (Variation of Schedule 4) Order 1951[4]. In the case of a tenant in occupation before 1 March 1948 who had made an election in favour of the statutory measure of compensation before the statutory instrument came into force (31 December

1951), it was necessary to make a new election under s 47(1)(c) of the AHA 1948 relating specifically to this one item in order to maintain a claim in respect of it. Correspondingly, a tenant who entered into occupation after 1 March 1948, but before 31 December 1951, is required to make an election that s 47(1)(c) of the AHA 1948 should apply to him in order to maintain a claim. It should be noted that a failure to do so may still enable a tenant in such a situation to claim customary compensation, if a customary claim can be established, notwithstanding the general abolition of customary compensation by s 77 of the AHA 1986.

No consent of the landlord or approval of the ALT is required as a condition precedent for compensation[5].

1   AHA 1986, Sch 12 para 6.
2   AHA 1986, Sch 12 para 6(2).
3   AHA 1986, Sch 12 para 7. For the statutory power of the Minister to vary Schs 7, 8 and 10 to the AHA 1986 and, therefore, Sch 8 Pt II: see s 91. See para 40.15. By Sch 12 para 9, the Minister is also given power to revoke or vary the provisions of paras 6–8 of the Schedule so far as they relate to the matters specified in para 10 of Pt II of Sch 8, namely, acclimatisation, hefting, or settlement of hill sheep on hill land.
4   SI 1951/2168. The reason for this head of claim is to reflect the fact that over the course of time a hill flock develops immunity from disease and an ability to remain within the confines of a particular hill or mountain without the need for fencing: the outgoing tenant (assuming that the flock he leaves behind at the termination of his tenancy belonged to him) is entitled to be paid this additional value, as opposed to the ordinary market value of the stock in question. 'Hill sheep' and 'hill land' are now defined in Sch 8 Pt II, para 10 of the AHA 1986. See paras 38.35 and 38.43.
5   AHA 1986, s 65 and Sch 8 Pt II.

38.39 The tenant is not entitled to compensation under the AHA 1986 (nor indeed under custom or agreement), if the item relates to work done pursuant to an order included in an arbitrator's award under s 14(4) of the AHA 1986 which modifies the terms of the tenancy relating to permanent pasture[1].

No compensation is payable for crops or produce grown, seeds sown, cultivations, fallows or acts of husbandry performed or pastures laid down in contravention of the terms of the written contract of tenancy, unless this was reasonably necessary in consequence of a direction given under the Agriculture Act 1947[2], or the tenant shows that the term of the contract contravened was itself inconsistent with his obligations to farm in accordance with the rules of good husbandry[3].

In the case of a tenancy agreement entered into before 1 January 1921, no compensation is payable if the tenant was required to carry out the tenant-right item by the terms of his tenancy agreement[4].

The provisions relating to a change of tenancy or tenant in relation to relevant improvements apply equally to statutory compensation under the AHA 1986 in relation to tenant-right[5].

1   AHA 1986, s 76(1)(a).
2   Agriculture Act 1947, s 95.
3   AHA 1986, s 65(2).

4   AHA 1986, Sch 12 para 5.
5   AHA 1986, s 69(1). See para 38.26.

Amount of compensation generally

38.40 Under the AHA 1986, compensation for tenant-right is calculated in the same manner as to short-term improvements. The general rule is that the amount of compensation is 'the value to an incoming tenant' calculated in accordance with the regulations for the time being in force[1].

This general rule is subject to two exceptions:

(a)   Unlike the position relating to short-term improvements, the parties may, in their written tenancy agreement, substitute an alternative measure of compensation for statutory tenant right. The express agreement will prevail[2].

(b)   As in the case of short-term improvements, the parties may agree that compensation will be payable for items not covered by the AHA 1986. Any such agreement must be in writing[3].

As in the case of relevant improvements, statutory tenant-right matters, set out in the AHA 1986, may be varied by the Minister[4], after consultation with representative bodies who appear to the Minister to represent the interest of the landlords and tenants of agricultural holdings[5]. Under the corresponding provision in the AHA 1948, the Agricultural Holdings Act (Variation of Schedule 4) Order 1951[6] was brought into force relating to acclimatisation, hefting or settlement of hill sheep on hill land[7], together with the Agricultural Holdings Act 1948 (Variation of Schedule 4) Order 1978[8] and the Agricultural Holdings Act 1948 (Variation of Schedule 4) Order 1985[9], the latter two statutory instruments relating to residual soil fertility for which all tenants are now eligible[10].

1   AHA 1986, s 66(2). For details of the regulations currently in force, see para 38.25. It is to be noted that the actual method of calculation for improvements within Sch 7 is not prescribed, the usual method being to capitalise the increased rental value due to the improvement.
2   AHA 1986, s 66(4).
3   AHA 1986, s 66(3).
4   AHA 1986, s 96(1). See para 4.2.
5   AHA 1986 s 91(1). See para 40.15.
6   SI 1951/2168.
7   See para 38.43.
8   SI 1978/742.
9   SI 1985/1947.
10   It was originally provided that tenants entering into occupation between 1 March 1948 and 30 June 1978 had to elect for this item – Agricultural Holdings Act 1948 (Variation of Schedule 4) Order 1978, SI 1978/742. By the Agricultural Holdings Act 1948 (Variation of Schedule 4) Order 1985, SI 1985/1947, the 1978 Order was revoked and accordingly all tenants are now eligible. These Orders have both now been revoked by Sch 15 Pt II of the AHA 1986.

38.41 The Agriculture (Calculation of Value for Compensation) Regulations 1978[1] gave effect to the amendments to the Sch 4 Pts I and II, of the AHA 1948[2] and together with the Agriculture (Calculation of Value for

Compensation) (Amendment) Regulations 1981[3] and the Agriculture (Calculation of Value for Compensation) (Amendment) Regulations 1983[4] which amended the 1978 Regulations consolidate the present position. In outline, this is as follows.

[1] SI 1978/809.
[2] Now Sch 8 of the AHA 1986.
[3] SI 1981/822.
[4] SI 1983/1475.

Unexhausted manurial value of feeding stuffs

38.42 The Agriculture (Calculation of Value for Compensation) Regulations 1978[1] contained nine tables to be used for the purpose of this valuation. It was considered that this number of tables was cumbersome and in some cases could lead to misinterpretation. Accordingly, the tables have now been reduced to two, together with an additional table which sets out appropriate adjustments, depending upon the method of preparation and storage of manure. Table 5(a) shows the unexhausted manurial value of feeding stuffs fed to cattle, sheep and pigs where the manure is preserved as open slurry, produced and stored under average conditions. Table 5(b) gives the unexhausted manurial value of feeding stuffs fed to poultry, where the manure is kept as open slurry, produced and stored under average conditions. Table 6 sets out the percentage adjustments to the values assessed under Table 5(a) in order to indicate to valuers three adjustments to be made in arriving at compensation reasonably payable for different forms of manure stored under varying conditions. Table 6 also deals with the position where feeding stuffs are fed directly on the land.

[1] SI 1978/809.

Acclimatisation, hefting or settlement of hill sheep on hill land

38.43 An acclimatised flock has an additional value to an incoming tenant[1]. In order to compensate the outgoer for this additional value a payment by the landlord (or in practice the incoming tenant), known in various parts of the country as acclimatisation, hefting or settlement value has been made for many years. Latterly the compensation has been provided for in the Agriculture (Calculation of Value for Compensation) Regulations 1978 (as amended)[2]. The present basis of compensation comprises a fixed monetary figure representing the extra shepherding associated with hefting and a percentage figure (10%) based on the market value of the hill ewe representing disease and stress factors. It should be noted that the figures of compensation set out in the statutory instrument are maximum figures. Accordingly, the facts relating to each case need to be closely examined in order to determine whether or not a full or a reduced payment should be made. In this connection relevant factors include the height, severity and accessibility of terrain, the type and breed of sheep and whether the flock is disease free.

[1] See para 38.35.
[2] SI 1978/809, as amended by SI 1983/1475.

Enhancement value

38.44 The regulations made following the passing of the AHA 1948 directed that the compensation payable to an outgoing tenant of a holding for growing crops was to be restricted to the actual costs of the seed sown and the cost of cultivations carried out in the establishment of the crop. It became obvious that this method of valuation was inequitable, being frequently unfair to the outgoer. For example, the outgoer who quitted his holding in the spring would receive only limited compensation in respect of autumn-sown corn, although at the end of the tenancy he had left a well-established crop. There was no incentive to an outgoer to sow autumn corn crops, as would have occurred had the tenancy not been terminated. In order to rectify this inequity, the Agriculture (Calculation of Value for Compensation) Regulations 1978[1] provided that extra compensation should be paid by the incomer for the 'enhanced' value to him of these established crops. The rules to be applied in the assessment of 'enhancement value' are set out in the Agriculture (Calculation of Value for Compensation) Regulations 1978.

[1] SI 1978/809, amended by SI 1983/1475.

38.45 The effect of these rules is as follows:

(a) Enhancement value is only to be paid for autumn-sown crops in cases in which the land is held under a spring tenancy, subject to the exception that grass and clover seeds sown on land held under either a spring or autumn tenancy in which no crop has been taken before the end of the tenancy qualify for the payment of enhancement value. For this purpose the regulations define a spring tenancy as one which has a term date between 1 January and 30 June and an autumn tenancy as having a term date between 1 September and 31 December.

(b) The enhancement value must not exceed one year's rent of the ground sown to the crop. In practice the value may well be less, since it is not to exceed the value to an incoming tenant. Conversely, it may well be more, but the compensation is limited.

(c) The annual rental value is assessed for the ground sown to the crop. The criteria for the assessment of rent is that contained in s 8 of the AHA 1948 (sic), as amended by the Agriculture Act 1958. There has as yet been no revised statutory instrument to take account of the amendments introduced by the AHA 1984 now contained in s 12 and Sch 2 of the AHA 1986.

(d) Enhancement value is only payable for an area of land which normally would be expected to be sown to the crop. In assessing the extent of this area, regard must be had to the character and type of the holding and the terms of the tenancy agreement.

It should be noted that enhancement value payable is added to the cost of cultivations and seeds sown, in order to arrive at the total compensation for the growing crops. There is no reimbursement for the rent actually paid during the period since the crop was sown nor interest on the capital employed by the tenant in establishing the crop.

Residual sod fertility value

38.46 This head of claim was first introduced by the Agriculture (Calculation of Value for Compensation) Regulations 1978[1], although previously tenant's pasture value as a head of claim was available representing the value of the face or surface of the ley. However, additionally a ley produces a root system under the surface of the ground which may store nitrogen and improve soil structure, both assets being available to the occupier when he wishes to benefit from them, for example, by ploughing up and growing corn crops. The introduction of the Agriculture (Calculation of Value for Compensation) Regulations 1978 reflected the fact that if an outgoing tenant leaves the leys for the landlord, the landlord has available to him assets which he may exploit. A prerequisite to this head of claim is that the land in question must be capable of growing arable crops for an unbroken series of not less than six years, and it is considered reasonable that those crops could be grown on the land in question.

It should be noted that compensation is paid only on 'excess qualifying leys'. That is on 'qualifying leys' over and above a certain basic percentage, known as the 'accepted proportion'. The 'accepted proportion' is the area of leys or new seeds reasonably required to be left at the end of the tenancy for the fertility and proper management of the holding, bearing in mind the area of the holding excluding any permanent pasture. It is to be noted that the tenancy agreement may stipulate a higher proportion than otherwise would be assessed by a valuer, in which event that higher proportion must be used. A 'qualifying ley' on termination of the tenancy is the established ley being three or more growing seasons old, or a former established ley being one which was three or four growing seasons old, prior to being ploughed or cropped.

Section 92 of the AHA 1986 requires the Minister[2] to appoint a committee of experts on valuation to advise him as to the provisions to be included in the regulations governing the calculation of compensation.

[1] SI 1978/809, as amended by SI 1983/1475.
[2] AHA 1986, s 96(1). See para 4.2.

COMPENSATION FOR DISTURBANCE UNDER THE AHA 1986

38.47 The tenant's entitlement to compensation for disturbance arises only:

(a) where the tenancy is terminated by a landlord's notice to quit or tenant's counter-notice enlarging the landlord's notice to quit part[1] and, in either case only, in limited circumstances; or

(b) where the tenant's interest is compulsorily acquired[2].

This section of this book deals point (a) above.

The AHA 1986 provides a right to receive basic compensation[3] and, in certain circumstances, additional compensation[4].

[1] See para 29.7.
[2] See para 38.63 ff.

³   AHA 1986, s 60. Formerly 'compensation for disturbance' under s 34 of the AHA 1948.
⁴   AHA 1986, s 60. Formerly 'a sum to assist in the reorganisation of the tenant's affairs'
    under ss 9 and 10 of the Agricultural Holdings Act 1968.

Rules for entitlement generally

38.48   The tenancy must have terminated, either by notice to quit the holding given by the landlord[1] or by the tenant 'enlarging' a notice to quit part of the holding by a counter-notice to the notice to quit given under s 32 of the AHA 1986[2].

No compensation is payable if the landlord's notice to quit is given for one of the reasons stated in Cases C, D, E, F or G[3], but compensation is payable in the case of all other landlord's notices whether stating a reason or not.

Further, additional compensation is not payable where a notice to quit is given pursuant to Cases A and H[4]. Notices to quit given under Case B attract basic and additional compensation for disturbance.

In the case of notice to quit part, if a tenant enlarges the notice by a counter-notice and the landlord's notice relates to less than one-quarter of the original holding and the balance of the holding (less the part the subject of the landlord's notice) is 'reasonably capable of being farmed as a separate holding', then no compensation for disturbance is payable, except in respect of the part covered by the landlord's notice to quit[5].

The tenant must 'quit the holding in consequence of' the notice to quit or counter-notice. The tenant must establish the causal connection between the notice to quit and his departure. A tenant who quits as a consequence of an invalid notice to quit, believing it to be valid, is entitled to compensation[6]. No compensation is payable for disturbance if, for example, the tenancy is terminated by reason of forfeiture[7]. If compensation is being negotiated and agreed between the parties, care needs to be taken in the drafting to ensure that the agreement avoids the implication that a surrender has taken place[8].

1   For the definition of 'landlord', see the AHA 1986, s 96(1). The right subsists even if the landlord at the date of quitting is not the landlord who gave the notice: see *Dale v Hatfield Chase Corpn* [1922] 2 KB 282, but note that only a legal owner, and not an equitable owner, can give a valid notice to quit.
2   For the circumstances where such a counter-notice may be given, and for a commentary on s 32 of the AHA 1986, see para 29.7.
3   AHA 1986, s 61(1). This applies following a certificate of bad husbandry (Case C), a notice to remedy or notice to pay (Case D); an irremediable breach (Case E); insolvency (Case F) or death (Case G).
4   AHA 1986, s 61(2).
5   AHA 1986, s 63(3). Nevertheless the enlarged notice to quit still terminates the tenancy of the whole holding.
6   See para 38.50.
7   See para 33.8 and Ch 13.
8   As to surrender generally, see para 33.4.

Amount of basic compensation

38.49 The amount of compensation payable is:

(a) an amount equal to one year's rent[1] of the holding, at the rate at which rent was payable immediately before the termination of the tenancy in any event, without proof of loss[2]; or

(b) a greater amount equal either to the amount of the tenant's actual loss or two years' rent of the holding whichever is the smaller[3].

In order to qualify for the greater sum referred to in (b) above, the tenant must establish:

(i) the tenant's loss or expenditure directly attributable to the quitting of the holding is unavoidably incurred by the tenant upon or in connection with the sale or removal of his household goods, implements of husbandry, fixtures, farm produce or farm stock, on or used in connection with the holding, including any expenses reasonably incurred by him in the preparation of his claim for basic compensation, excluding the costs involved in an arbitration under s 60 or s 61 required to establish the liability for compensation[4]; and[5]

(ii) the landlord has been given a reasonable opportunity before the sale to make a valuation of any such goods, implements, fixtures, produce or stock; and[6]

(iii) notice in writing of the tenant's intention[7] to claim the additional compensation has been given to the landlord not less than one month before termination of the tenancy.

[1]   AHA 1986, s 60(3). The one year's rent formula is applied to the rent payable immediately before termination. If, therefore, a rent review has taken place which would have come into effect simultaneously with the expiry of the notice to quit, the old rent is applied.
[2]   AHA 1986, s 60(2)(a), (3)(a).
[3]   AHA 1986, s 60(3)(b).
[4]   AHA 1986, s 60(5).
[5]   Note that all conditions must be satisfied.
[6]   As fn 5 above.
[7]   The decision in *Howson v Buxton* (1928) 97 LJKB 749, CA to the effect that notice by one only of joint tenants (the one who suffered the loss) is sufficient probably remains good law in view of the decisions in *Lloyd v Sadler* [1978] QB 774, [1978] 2 All ER 529. See the discussion at paras 19.50 ff and 29.14. Also see *Tilling v Whiteman* [1980] AC 1, [1979] 1 All ER 737, HL; and, most importantly *Featherstone v Staples* [1986] 2 All ER 461, [1986] 1 WLR 861, CA. However, it would clearly be prudent for all joint tenants to join in the notice under s 60(6)(a). Note that a forfeiture clause in a tenancy agreement is void if it does not allow the tenant to give the one month's notice required by s 60(6)(a) of the AHA 1986 to make a claim for compensation: *Re Disraeli Agreement* [1939] Ch 382, [1938] 4 All ER 658; *Coates v Diment* [1951] 1 All ER 890; *Parry v Million Pigs Ltd* (1980) 260 Estates Gazette 281. See para 24.26.

38.50 The tenant needs to be able to show a causal link between the notice to quit and his departure[1]. Where the tenant holds over, after the expiration of the notice, and subsequently vacates the land, after a judgment for possession or on being ejected or otherwise, it is a question to be decided on the facts of the case whether or not the tenant quitted in consequence of the notice to quit[2]. A tenant who quits in consequence of a notice to quit which is in fact invalid, but which he accepts as valid, is entitled to claim compensation for disturbance[3]. The right subsists even where there is a change of landlord between the date of the notice to quit and the date of quitting[4]. The notice to quit must have been given by the landlord within the definition in the AHA 1986[5]. Accordingly, an equitable owner has no standing[6].

[1] This may also be of considerable importance for tax purposes: see para 38.62.
[2] *Preston v Norfolk County Council* [1947] KB 775, [1947] 2 All ER 124, CA, following *Mills v Rose* (1923) 68 Sol Jo 420, CA, distinguishing *Cave v Page* (1923) 67 Sol Jo 659, CA (a case under the Agricultural Holdings Act 1908, s 11), and disagreeing with *Hendry v Walker* 1927 SLT 333, Ct of Sess. Also see *Gulliver v Catt* [1952] 2 QB 308, [1952] 1 All ER 929, CA.
[3] *Westlake v Page* [1926] 1 KB 299, CA; *Kestell v Langmaid* [1950] 1 KB 233, [1949] 2 All ER 749, CA.
[4] *Dale v Hatfield Chase Corpn* [1922] 2 KB 282, CA.
[5] AHA 1986, s 96(1).
[6] *Bradshaw v Bird* [1920] 3 KB 144, CA; *Farrow v Orttewell* [1933] Ch 480, CA.

38.51 Although it has been held that if the landlord's notice to quit is invalid either because of, for example, ambiguity or uncertainty[1], or because or its failure to meet statutory requirements[2], so that in both cases if the tenant has relied upon it, the tenant is entitled to compensation for disturbance, there is no authority in relation to the position where a notice to quit does not comply with the statutory minimum notice of 12 months. It is submitted that although such a notice would be invalid[3], if the tenant relies upon it, the tenant will again be entitled to compensation for disturbance.

[1] *Westlake v Page* [1926] 1 KB 299, CA.
[2] *Kestell v Langmaid* [1950] 1 KB 233, [1949] 2 All ER 749, CA.
[3] AHA 1986, s 25(1).

38.52 Although the costs of an arbitration to determine liability for compensation are not recoverable as basic compensation, it should be noted that the losses incurred on the forced sale of stock and implements are recoverable, together with the valuers' fees incurred in preparing a claim for compensation. The valuers' fees are recoverable provided that they are reasonably incurred by the tenant in the preparation of his claim, even if the claim for compensation is not subsequently made[1]. Whether a loss is too remote to be considered to be 'directly attributable' to the tenant's quitting the holding is a question of fact, to be determined by the arbitrator in the event of dispute. Valuers' fees for the valuation of stock prior to the sale are not an unavoidable expense of the sale and are not recoverable[2].

It is perhaps hardly surprising that the claim for the second year's rent under the AHA 1986 can rarely in practice be substantiated[3].

[1] *Re Agricultural Holdings Act 1923, Dunstan v Benney* [1938] 2 KB 1, CA.
[2] *Re Evans and Glamorgan County Council's Arbitration* (1912) 76 JP 468.
[3] Note that in assessing compensation, no credit has to be allowed for improvements or tenant-right or other matters since the disturbance compensation is payable in addition to any other compensation: see the AHA 1986, s 60(7).

38.53 Where a fixed-term tenancy of two years or more has been granted after 12 September 1984[1], and it terminates as a consequence of the landlord's

Case G notice to quit following the tenant's death, the AHA 1986 preserves the tenant's right to compensation for disturbance[2].

[1] The date on which the Agricultural Holdings Act 1984 came into force in relation to this provision.
[2] AHA 1986, s 4(3).

38.54 It is not possible to contract out of the tenant's entitlement to statutory compensation for disturbance under the AHA 1986[1].

[1] AHA 1986, s 78(1).

Additional compensation

Rules for entitlement

38.55 A tenant eligible for basic compensation under the AHA 1986 may also be eligible for additional compensation for disturbance[1], equivalent to a further four years' rent.

In the case of the termination of a tenancy of part of a holding, the amount will be equivalent to four times the appropriate portion of the annual rent[2]. The object of the provision is to provide additional compensation in cases in which the tenancy is terminated in order to enable the land to be used for development, forestry or some other non-agricultural purpose. It is, however, of wider application.

It is to be noted that the right to additional compensation is excluded in the following cases:

(a)   where the notice to quit is given under Case A or H[3];
(b)   where there is no entitlement to basic compensation: for example, because the notice to quit was given on grounds C, D, E, F or G[4];
(c)   where the notice to quit contains a statement either that the carrying out of the purpose for which the landlord proposes to terminate the tenancy is desirable on any of the grounds contained in sub-paras (a) to (c) of s 27(3) of the AHA 1986[5] or that the landlord will suffer hardship unless the notice has effect and an application for consent to the operation of the notice is made to the ALT which then consents to its operation stating in its reasons for the decision that it is satisfied as to any of these matters[6].

[1] AHA 1986, s 69(2)(b). This species of compensation derives from s 9 of the Agriculture (Miscellaneous Provisions) Act 1968 and is there referred to as 'the sum to assist in the reorganisation of the tenant's affairs'.
[2] AHA 1986, s 74.
[3] AHA 1986, s 61(2). Case A relates to notices to quit to smallholding tenants on attaining the age of 65 years and Case H to notices to quit by the Minister for the purpose of amalgamations or the reshaping of agricultural units. Cf the position in relation to basic compensation for disturbance: see para 38.48.
[4] See para 38.47.
[5] Ie good husbandry, sound management of the estate, agricultural research, etc or enactments relating to allotments.
[6] AHA 1986, s 61(3).

38.56 Additional compensation is not excluded where the ALT consents to the operation of the notice either on the ground that a non-agricultural use (not falling within Case B of Sch 3) has been established[1], or where the application to the ALT under s 61(3)(b) relies exclusively upon sound management of the estate[2] (and not upon use for a non-agricultural purpose not falling within Case B of Sch 3[3]) and the ALT, while being satisfied on this ground, would also have been satisfied on the other ground (ie use for a non-agricultural purpose not falling within Case B of Sch 3) had that been specified in the notice, and the ALT includes a statement to that effect in its decision[4].

The tenant is entitled to additional compensation without proof of actual loss. It follows that a landlord who serves notice to quit with the object of recovering the land for an agricultural purpose will be liable to pay the additional compensation unless he drafts his notice to quit so as to qualify for exemption in accordance with paragraph 38.55(c) above[5]. It follows that a landlord would be well advised not to serve a plain common law notice to quit with no reason stated in it for the giving of it in these circumstances, but to serve a notice to quit relying upon the provisions in s 61(3) of the AHA 1986[6].

[1]   AHA 1986, s 61(4)(a).
[2]   AHA 1986, s 27(3)(b).
[3]   AHA 1986, s 27(3)(f).
[4]   AHA 1986, s 61(5). This subsection might operate, for example, where the landlord relied upon greater hardship and promoted his application to the tribunal on the basis of his requiring possession of the land for a development project involving a non-agricultural use.
[5]   AHA 1986, s 61(3).
[6]   See para 38.55(c).

Amount of additional compensation

38.57 In addition to the one or two years' rent payable in respect of basic compensation, a further four years' rent[1], making a total of five (or in some cases six) times the annual rent is payable at the date of termination of the tenancy[2].

[1]   Ie four times the rent payable at the date of quitting. The combined total equals five to six years' rent, as the case may be. Tenants on a low rent whose landlords are seeking, and are likely to obtain, planning consent for non-agricultural development, may sometimes be well advised to demand arbitration under s 12 of the AHA 1986 as to the rent properly payable, with a view to getting the rent increased and thereby directly increasing their compensation for disturbance.
[2]   Note that the rent must be payable at the time of quitting. If the rent has been reviewed, but the new rent only becomes payable from the term date when the tenancy is actually terminated, the old rent and not the new rent is the factor to be multiplied.

Recovery of compensation for disturbance

38.58 In addition, the tenant must give a further preliminary notice, one month before the termination of the tenancy, where a further year's rent is claimed as part of the basic compensation for disburbance[1].

As with all compensation payable on quitting, in order to claim compensation for disturbance the tenant must give a notice under s 83 of the AHA 1986 within two months after the date of termination[2].

1 AHA 1986, s 60(6)(a).
2 It is questionable whether one notice would satisfy both s 60(6)(a) and s 83(2): see the county court decision in *Lady Hallinan v Jones* [1984] 2 EGLR 20, 272 Estates Gazette 1081. The safe course is to serve two notices. For an interesting article on compensation for disturbance generally by N E Mustoe, see (1969) EG, 4 January, p 37. For a detailed analysis of this issue, see para 41.3 ff.

Compensation for early resumption

38.59 Section 62 of the AHA 1986 makes provision for those cases where a tenant quits an agricultural holding for a non-agricultural purpose at short notice under a clause authorising such notice in the tenancy agreement. The purpose of this provision is to ensure that the tenant in such a case will be compensated for the loss of the additional benefit he would have received if his tenancy had been terminated on the usual statutory 12 months' notice to quit[1]. In the case of a fixed-term tenancy of a duration of two years or more, the relevant period for assessment is the date on which it could have been terminated if it was a normal annual tenancy[2].

The additional compensation by virtue of s 62(2) that the tenant is entitled to is the 'value of additional benefit (if any)' he would have been able to receive if a full 12 months' notice to quit had been given. This may be a substantial sum if the tenant's farming is severely disrupted by, for example, the loss of buildings on short notice at a critical time in the winter months.

The procedures for recovery are the same as for the rest of the compensation for disturbance under s 60 of the AHA 1986[3].

Contracting out of s 62 is prohibited[4].

Where the tenant has sub-let the holding and in consequence of a notice to quit given by his landlord becomes liable to pay compensation under s 62 to the sub-tenant, the tenant is not debarred from recovering compensation by reason only of the fact that, because he was not personally in occupation of the holding, he did not quit the holding on termination[5].

1 AHA 1986, s 62(2).
2 AHA 1986, s 62(3).
3 See para 41.8.
4 AHA 1986, s 78(1)(2).
5 AHA 1986, s 63(2). This provision overcomes the previous difficulty whereby the head tenant who paid compensation to his sub-tenant could be said not to have quitted the holding.

Agreed compensation

38.60 Although the parties cannot contract out of the tenant's right to claim compensation for disturbance under the AHA 1986[1], they are able to agree that additional compensation should be paid in excess of the statutory calculation. This may be provided for in the contract of tenancy itself or in a supplemental agreement. Care needs to be taken in the drafting of such a provision. Where a tenancy agreement gave the tenant the right to claim compensation for 'any loss or damage he may sustain through ... disturbance', the court was prepared to construe that provision as going beyond the statutory calculation to provide a greater measure of compensation. The court was prepared to allow the tenant to claim loss of profit[2].

1   AHA 1986, s 78.
2   *Dean v Secretary of State for War* [1950] 1 All ER 344, CA.

Miscellaneous provisions

38.61   In the context of compensation payable for disturbance, regard should be had to:

(a)   notice to quit part of an agricultural holding generally[1];
(b)   severance of the freehold reversion[2];
(c)   the provisions relating to permanent pasture[3].

1   AHA 1986, s 74. See para 29.1 ff.
2   AHA 1986, s 75(1). See para 29.6.
3   AHA 1986, s 14, s 76(1)(b). See para 24.8.

Taxation

38.62   It is beyond the scope of this book to consider taxation which in any case is regularly and often radically subject to revision. The commentary below is intended to highlight potential issues, but should be checked against the Finance Acts and the like provisions introduced from time to time.

Sums paid to the tenant as compensation for disturbance under the AHA 1986 are not liable to capital gains tax[1]. The amount paid to the tenant under these statutory provisions is a sum of money given to compensate him for loss or expense which is unavoidably incurred and as such does not represent a gain to the taxpayer[2].

Furthermore, it is not a capital sum derived from the disposal of an asset (the tenancy) nor a capital sum received for the surrender of rights[3].

Sums paid for statutorily prescribed compensation for disturbance under the AHA 1986 must be carefully distinguished from all other sums which may be paid by a landlord to a tenant on termination of the tenancy and on quitting, whether or not a valid notice to quit has been served[4]. Other payments may be subject to the payment of tax.

1   *Davis v Powell* [1977] 1 All ER 471, [1977] STC 32, followed in *Drummond (Inspector of Taxes) v Austin Brown* [1985] Ch 52, [1984] STC 321, CA. See also, *Davis v Henderson* [1995] STC (SCD) 308 and *Pritchard v Purves* [1995] STC (SCD) 316 where payments were made by a landlord to his tenant under a surrender agreement following the service of a notice to quit and where the tenant vacated prior to the expiry of the notice period. In

these circumstances HMRC does not consider that the part of the landlord's payment that represents statutory compensation is chargeable to capital gains tax.

2   *Davis v Powell* [1977] 1 All ER 471, [1977] STC 32 at 260, per Templeman J (as he then was). It is to be noted that the judgment in *Davis v Powell* proceeded on the assumption, expressly made by Templeman J, that the sum in question was paid by way of compensation for disturbance under what was then s 34 of the Agricultural Holdings Act 1948. See also Walton J in *Drummond (Inspector of Taxes) v Austin Brown* [1985] Ch 52, [1984] STC 321, CA. This case concerned statutory provisions for compensation contained in Pt II of the Landlord and Tenant Act 1954 '... It would be onerous in the extreme if a gain were held to be made out of a sum of money given to compensate for loss or expense without proper provision being made for deduction of such loss or expense actually suffered and, no such provision being made in the statute, I am not prepared to assume that the legislature has enacted anything so monstrously unjust or perverse', per Walton J at 515.

3   *Davis v Powell* [1977] 1 All ER 471, [1977] STC 32 at 260.

4   The tax treatment of any other sums so paid must be carefully considered in the light of their nature and purpose. They could either attract capital gains tax or even be taxable under the Income Tax (Trading and Other Income) Act 2005, s 5 (or Schedule D under the Income and Corporation Taxes Act 1988 in the case of companies) as an income profit of the taxpayer's trade.

COMPENSATION FOR DISTURBANCE: COMPULSORY PURCHASE

The historical position

38.63 The measure of compensation payable to tenants of agricultural holdings, whose interest in the land was compulsorily purchased, has altered with recent years. It was held in *Rugby Joint Water Board v Foottit*[1] that because a landlord was entitled[2] to give notice to quit where the land was required not only by the landlord but, in the alternative, by an authority possessing compulsory purchase powers, the tenancy was unprotected and compensation should be assessed on the basis that the landlord was entitled to obtain vacant possession of the land on the expiry of such a notice to quit.

1   [1973] AC 202, [1972] 1 All ER 1057, HL.
2   Under the predecessor of Sch 3, Case B to the AHA 1986.

The Agriculture (Miscellaneous Provisions) Act 1968

38.64 The harshness of this decision was ameliorated by ss 12 and 13 of the Agriculture (Miscellaneous Provisions) Act 1968 (A(MP)A 1968), which have not been repealed by the AHA 1986. The Agricultural Holdings Act 1968 Act introduced 'additional payments' to be paid by an acquiring authority upon compulsory purchase.

Where as a consequence of any enactment requiring the acquisition or taking of possession[1] of land compulsorily, an acquiring authority[2] acquires the interest in an agricultural holding[3] (or any part of it) of the tenant[4], or takes possession of such holding (or any part of it), then (subject to the provisions of the A(MP)A 1968) provisions for the payment of additional compensation for disturbance[5] apply as if the acquiring authority was the landlord and on the date of acquisition or taking of possession the tenancy had been terminated pursuant to a notice to quit or a counter-notice treating a notice to quit part of a holding as notice to quit the entire holding, and the tenanted had quitted the holding (or the part of it)[6].

1   'Possession' means actual possession: A(MP)A 1968, s 17(1).
2   An 'acquiring authority' is any person authorised by any enactment to acquire or take possession of land compulsorily, A(MP)A 1968, ss 12(1), 17(1).
3   A(MP)A 1968, s 17(1). Expressions used in the A(MP)A 1968 and the AHA 1986 have the meanings assigned to them by the AHA 1986, unless the context otherwise requires.
4   See fn 3 above. For the purposes of the A(MP)A 1968, s 12(1) a tenant of an agricultural holding is treated as not being a tenant of it in so far as, immediately before the acquiring of the interest or the taking of possession, he was neither in possession nor entitled to take possession of any land comprised in the holding. In determining whether a tenant was so entitled, any agreement under the AHA 1986 which relates to the land and has not taken effect as an agreement for a tenancy from year to year must be disregarded: the A(MP)A 1968, s 13(1) (as amended by the AHA 1986, Sch 14 para 45).
5   AHA 1986, s 60. See para 38.47 ff.
6   A(MP)A 1968, s 12(1) (amended by the AHA 1986, Sch 14 para 44).

38.65 Additional payments in relation to the compulsory acquisition or taking of possession of an agricultural holding do not arise unless the date on which the acquisition or taking of possession occurs is later than 3 July 1968[1] and in two other cases as follows.

(a)   In respect of an agricultural holding held on a tenancy for a term of two years or more, except in a case where the amount of compensation payable to the tenant of the holding by the acquiring authority as a result of the acquisition or taking of possession is exceeded by the aggregate of the amounts which, if the tenancy had been from year to year, would have been so payable by way of compensation, and in any such case the sum payable by virtue of those provisions as a consequence of the acquisition or taking of possession in question is, subject to contrary determination by the Lands Tribunal, to be an amount equal to the excess[2].

(b)   Where the acquiring authority requires the land comprised in the agricultural holding or part of it for the purposes of agricultural research or experiment or for demonstrating agricultural methods or for the purposes of the enactments relating to smallholdings, nor where the Minister[3] acquires the land to ensure full and efficient use of it[4].

1   Ie the date of commencement of the A(MP)A 1968.
2   A(MP)A 1968, s 12(2).
3   A(MP)A 1968, s 50(1).
4   Ie under the Agriculture Act 1947, s 84(1)(c). Also see The Town and Country Planning Act 1990, ss 226 and 230; A(MP)A 1968, s 13(2).

38.66 Formerly, where a tenant's interest was compulsorily acquired by an acquiring authority under statutory powers, any provision in the contract of tenancy which authorised the resumption of possession of the holding at short notice for non-agricultural purposes was to be treated as though it authorised resumption on the usual 12 months' notice to quit. Where a tenant was compulsorily dispossessed by an acquiring authority, the resumption clause was to be disregarded for the purpose of calculating the payment of additional compensation under the A(MP)A 1968[1]. That provision has been repealed, except in relating to compensation falling to be assessed by reference to prices current before 23 May 1973 and except for certain purposes for the Land Compensation Act 1973[2].

1   A(MP)A 1968, s 15(1).
2   Land Compensation Act 1973, s 48(4).

The Land Compensation Act 1973

Entitlement to farm loss payment

38.67 Where a person in occupation of land constituting or included in an agricultural unit[1] has an owner's interest[2] then if:

(a)   as a consequence of compulsory acquisition of his interest in the whole of the land ('the land acquired'), he is displaced[3] from the whole of that land on or after 17 October 1972[4]; and

(b)   not more than three years after the date of displacement he begins to farm another agricultural unit ('the new unit') elsewhere in Great Britain,

he is entitled to receive a payment known as 'a farm loss payment' from the acquiring authority[5].

The farm loss payments scheme which was introduced by the Land Compensation Act 1973 (LCA 1973) was replaced from 31 October 2004 by a scheme of loss payments governed by the Planning and Compulsory Purchase Act 2004[6]. The new scheme does not apply to acquisitions before 31 October 2004. Since that date, the scheme of payments is governed by ss 33A to 33C of the LCA 1973[7].

1   'Agricultural unit' has the meaning given in the Town and Country Planning Act 1990, s 171(1): LCA 1973, s 87(1) (amended by the Planning (Consequential Provisions) Act 1990, s 4, Sch 2 para 29(11)).
2   'Owner's interest' means a freehold interest or a tenancy granted or extended for a term of years certain of which not less than three years remain unexpired at the date of displacement: LCA 1973, s 34(2).
3   A person is displaced from land as a consequence of compulsory acquisition of his interest if, and only if, he gives up possession on being required to do so by the acquiring authority; on completion of the acquisition; or where the acquiring authority permits him to remain in possession of the land under a tenancy or licence of a kind not making him a tenant as defined in the Agricultural Holdings Act 1986 on the expiration of that tenancy or licence. References to the date of displacement are references to the date on which the person concerned gives up possession: LCA 1973, s 34(3) (amended by the AHA 1986, s 100, Sch 14 para 52).
4   LCA 1973, s 34(8); and the Planning and Compulsory Purchase Act 2004.
5   LCA 1973, s 34(1). 'Acquiring authority' has the same meaning as in the Land Compensation Act 1961, s 39(1), namely 'in relation to an interest in land, [it] means the person or body of persons by whom the interest is, or is proposed to be, acquired': LCA 1973, s 87(1).
6   For a more detailed analysis of compulsory purchase generally, see G Soloman and G Messent, *Property Transactions: Planning and Environment* (1st edn, 2007) Sweet & Maxwell.
7   See para 38.66.

38.68 No farm loss payment may be made:

(a)   To any person unless on the date on which he begins to farm the new unit he is in occupation of the whole of that unit by reason of a freehold or tenanted interest, not having been entitled to any such interest before the date on which the acquiring authority was authorised to acquire his interest in the land acquired[1].

(b)   By virtue of the displacement of a person from any land if he is entitled to a payment under the A(MP)A 1968[2] as a consequence of the acquisition of an interest in, or the taking of possession of, that land[3].

(c)   To any person displaced from land as a consequence of the compulsory acquisition of his interest if the acquisition of his interest in the whole or any part of that land is pursuant to the service by him of a blight notice[4] or a notice under the New Towns Act 1965[5].

(d)   Except on a claim made by a person entitled to it before the expiration of the period of one year beginning with the date on which the requirement in (a) is complied with, and any such claim must be in writing and must be accompanied or supplemented by such particulars as the acquiring authority may reasonably require to enable it to determine whether that person is entitled to a payment and, if so, the amount of the payment[6].

[1]   LCA 1973, s 34(4) and s 33B in relation to post-31 October 2004 acquisitions.
[2]   Ie under the A(MP)A 1968, s 12(1): see para 38.62.
[3]   LCA 1973, s 34(5).
[4]   Ie a blight notice under the Town and Country Planning Act 1990, s 149.
[5]   LCA 1973, s 35(6) (amended by the Planning (Consequential Provisions) Act 1990, Sch 2 para 29(5)). The reference to the New Towns Act 1965 is a reference to s 11 of that Act, which has been repealed, except in relation to notices served before 23 May 1973.
[6]   LCA 1973, s 36(1).

38.69 Where the agricultural unit containing the land acquired is occupied for the purposes of a farming partnership, the provisions as to entitlement and the amount of farm loss payment are payable to the partnership and not the partners individually. Any interest of a partner in land acquired is treated as an interest in the partnership. The requirements as to the new unit are treated as being complied with in relation to the partnership as soon as they are complied with by any one of the partners[1].

[1]   LCA 1973, s 36(2).

Amount of farm loss payment

38.70 The amount of any farm loss payment must be equal to the average annual profit derived from the use for agricultural purposes of the agricultural land comprised in the land acquired. That profit is calculated by reference to the profits to the three years ending with the date of displacement or, if the person concerned has been in occupation for a shorter period, that shorter period ('the standard measure of compensation')[1]. The standard measure of compensation has effect where accounts have been made up in respect of the profits of the person concerned for a period or consecutive periods of 12 months and that period, or the last of them, ends not more than one year after the date of displacement, as if the date on which that period or the last of those periods ends were the date of displacement[2].

[1] LCA 1973, s 35(1).
[2] LCA 1973, s 35(2).

38.71 Where the acquiring authority has permitted the occupier to remain in possession of the land under a tenancy or licence of a kind not making him a tenant as defined in the AHA 1986[1], the date of displacement is determined accordingly, and the person concerned has on that date been in occupation for more than three years, he may elect that the average annual profit, instead of being calculated by reference to the standard measure of compensation, be calculated by reference to profits for:

(a)   any three consecutive periods of 12 months for which accounts in respect of his profits have been made up, being periods for which he has been in occupation and the last of which ends on or after the date of completion of the acquisition; or

(b)   if there are no such periods, any three consecutive years for which he has been in occupation and the last of which ends on or after the date of completion of the acquisition[2].

[1] LCA 1973, s 34(3)(c).
[2] LCA 1973, s 35(3).

38.72 In calculating the profits for the standard measure of compensation, there must be deducted a sum equal to the rent that might reasonably be expected to be payable in relation to the agricultural land comprised in the land acquired if it were let for agricultural purposes to a tenant responsible for rates, repair and other outgoings. That deduction must be made whether or not the land is in fact let and, if it is, must be made to the exclusion of any deduction for the rent actually payable[1]. There must also be left out of account profits from any activity if a sum in respect of loss of profits from that activity would fall to be included in the compensation, so far as attributable to disturbance, for the acquisition of the interest in the land acquired[2].

[1] LCA 1973, s 35(4).
[2] LCA 1973, s 35(5).

38.73 Where the value of the agricultural land comprised in the land acquired exceeds the value of the agricultural land comprised in the new unit, the amount of the farm loss payment must be proportionately reduced[1]. The amount of farm loss payment must not be greater than the amount, if any, by which that payment[2], together with compensation for the acquisition of the interest in the land acquired assessed on certain statutory assumptions[3], exceeds the compensation actually payable for the acquisition of that interest[4]. The value of land must be assessed:

(a)   on the basis of its value as land used solely for agriculture and as for a freehold interest with vacant possession;

(b)   by reference to the condition of the land and surroundings and to prices current on the date of displacement of the land acquired or on the date on which the new unit begins to be farmed;

(c)   in accordance with s 5 of the Land Compensation Act 1961[5]; and

(d)   without regard to the principal dwelling (if any) on the same agricultural unit as that land[6].

1   LCA 1973, s 35(6).
2   Calculated apart from s 35(18) of the LCA 1973.
3   Ie the assumption set out in LCA 1973, s 5(2)–(4).
4   LCA 1973, s 35(8).
5   It is beyond the scope of this book to deal with these provisions. Reference should be made to *Halsburys Laws*, Compulsory Acquisition.
6   LCA 1973, s 35(7).

38.74 Any dispute as to the amount of a farm loss payment must be referred to and determined by the Lands Tribunal[1].

1   LCA 1973, s 35(9).

Compensation in respect of agricultural holdings

38.75 Special rules apply to the assessment of compensation where, as a consequence of any enactment providing for the acquisition or taking of possession compulsorily, an acquiring authority[1] either acquires the interest of the landlord in an agricultural holding or any part of it, or acquires the interest of the tenant in, or takes possession of, an agricultural holding or any part of it[2].

1   See para 38.64 fn 2.
2   LCA 1973, s 48(1).

38.76 In the case of a payment by the acquiring authority to the landlord, in assessing the compensation, there must be disregarded any right of the landlord to serve a notice to quit, and any notice to quit already served by the landlord, which would not be or would not have been effective if:

(a)   in Case B[1] the reference to the land being required did not include a reference to it being required by an acquiring authority; and

(b)   the reference in the AHA 1986[2] in relation to the landlord's proposal to terminate the tenancy for use other than agriculture, not falling within Case B, did not include a reference to its being used by an acquiring authority.

If the tenant has quitted the holding (or any part of it) by reason of a notice to quit which is to be so disregarded, it must be assumed that he has not done so for the purposes of assessing the compensation[3].

1   AHA 1986, s 26(2), Sch 3 Pt I Case B: land required for non-agricultural use for which planning permission has been granted, etc: see para 32.10.
2   AHA 1986, s 27(3)(f). This is one of the matters as to which the ALT must be satisfied before giving consent to a notice to quit: see para 30.15.
3   LCA 1973, s 48(2), as amended by the AHA 1986, s 100, Sch 14 para 53(2).

38.77 In the case of a payment by an acquiring authority to a tenant, in assessing the tenant's compensation, there must be disregarded any right of the landlord to serve a notice to quit, and any notice to quit already served by the landlord, which would not be or would not have been effective if Case B and the related reference[1] were not construed as above[2]. The tenant's compensation must be reduced by an amount equal to any payment which the acquiring authority is liable to make to him, in respect of the acquisition or taking of possession in question, under the provisions relating to additional payments[3]. If the tenant's compensation, so calculated, is less than it would have been had the above provision not been enacted, it must be increased to the amount of the difficiency[4]. Further, in assessing the tenant's compensation, no account is to be taken of any benefit which might accrue to the tenant by virtue of the additional compensation provisions contained in the AHA 1986[5].

[1]   Ie the AHA 1986, Sch 3 Pt I, Case B: see paras 32.10 and 38.76.
[2]   LCA 1973, s 48(3), as amended by the AHA 1986, s 100 Sch 14 para 53(3).
[3]   LCA 1973, s 48(5). The provisions relating to additional payments on compulsory acquisition or taking of possession are contained in the A(MP)A 1968, s 12: see para 38.64.
[4]   LCA 1973, s 48(6).
[5]   LCA 1973, s 48(6A) (added by the AHA 1986, Sch 14 para 53(4)). The additional compensation provisions in this context mean s 60(2)(b) of the AHA 1986, but not including that provision as applied by the A(MP)A 1968, s 12: LCA 1973, s 48(6A).

Notice to treat in respect of part of agricultural land

38.78 Where an acquiring authority serves notice to treat in respect of any agricultural land on a person, whether in occupation or not, who has a greater interest in the land than as tenant for a year or from year to year, and that person has such an interest in other agricultural land comprised in the same agricultural unit, that person (the claimant) may, within two months beginning on the date of service of the notice to treat, serve a counter-notice[1] on the acquiring authority claiming that the other land is not reasonably capable of being farmed, either by itself or in conjunction with other relevant land[2], as a separate agricultural unit, and requiring the acquiring authority to purchase his interest in the whole of the other land[3].

[1]   Where a counter-notice is served, the claimant must, within the same period of two months, serve a copy on any other person who has an interest in the land to which the requirement in the counter-notice relates. Failure to do so does not invalidate the counter-notice: LCA 1973, s 53(2).
[2]   'Other relevant land' means: (1) land comprised in the same agricultural unit as the land to which the notice to treat relates, being land in which the claimant does not have an interest greater than as a tenant for a year or from year to year; and (2) land comprised in any other agricultural unit occupied by him on the date of service of the notice to treat, being land in respect of which he is entitled to a greater interest than as a tenant for a year or from year to year: LCA 1973, s 53(3). Where an acquiring authority has served a notice to treat in respect of land in the holding other than that to which the notice relates, or in respect of other relevant land, or such a notice is deemed to have been served by virtue of the Town and Country Planning Act 1990, ss 137–144 (purchase notices), then, unless and until the notice to treat is withdrawn, the provisions of this paragraph have effect as if that land did not form part of the other agricultural land in the holding or did not constitute other relevant land: LCA 1973, s 53(4) (amended by the Planning (Consequential Provisions) Act 1990, s 4, Sch 2 para 29(9)).
[3]   LCA 1973, s 53(1).

38.79 If within two months beginning with the date of service of the counter-notice, the acquiring authority does not agree in writing to accept the counter-notice as valid, the claimant or the acquiring authority may in the two months after that period refer the issue to the Lands Tribunal. The Lands Tribunal must determine whether the claim in the counter-notice is justified and make a declaration as to its validity[1]. Where the counter-notice is declared valid, the acquiring authority is deemed to be authorised to acquire compulsorily the land to which the claim relates and to have served a notice to treat in respect of it on the date of the original notice to treat[2]. A counter-notice may be withdrawn by the claimant at any time before the Lands Tribunal has determined compensation or during the six weeks beginning with the date of such determination[3]. The compensation payable pursuant to a notice to treat which is deemed to have been served by the acquiring authority must be assessed on certain statutory assumptions relating to planning permission[4].

[1] LCA 1973, s 54(1).
[2] LCA 1973, s 54(2).
[3] LCA 1973, s 54(3). Where a counter-notice is withdrawn, any notice to treat deemed to have been served as a consequence of a counter-notice is also deemed to be withdrawn: LCA 1973, s 54(3). The general power to withdraw a notice to treat pursuant to s 31 of the Land Compensation Act 1961 is not exercisable in the case of a notice to treat which is deemed to have been served as a consequence of a counter-notice under s 54 of the LCA 1973: see *Halsburys Laws*, Compulsory Acquisition.
[4] LCA 1973, s 54(5).

38.80 Where, as a consequence of a counter-notice requiring an acquiring authority to purchase the whole of a claimant's interest in land[1], the acquiring authority becomes entitled to a lease of any land, but not to the interest of the landlord, the acquiring authority must offer to surrender the lease to the landlord on such terms as the acquiring authority considers reasonable[2]. If the landlord refuses to accept any sum offered, or refuses or fails to make out his title to the acquiring authority's satisfactory, the acquiring authority may pay the sum payable to the landlord into court[3]. Where an acquiring authority which becomes entitled to the lease of any land in these circumstances is a corporate body or does so under any enactment, the corporate powers of the acquiring authority include (if they would not otherwise do so) power to farm the land[4].

[1] Ie a counter-notice under ss 53 and 54 of the LCA 1973.
[2] LCA 1973, s 54(6)(a). The question of what terms are reasonable may be referred by the acquiring authority or the landlord to the Lands Tribunal. If the issue has not been resolved by agreement between the acquiring authority and the landlord at the end of three months after the offer of surrender, the reference to the Lands Tribunal is compulsory: LCA 1973, s 54(6)(b),(c).
[3] LCA 1973, s 54(7).
[4] LCA 1973, s 54(8).

Notice of entry in respect of part of an agricultural holding

38.81 Where the acquiring authority serves a notice of entry[1] on the person in occupation of an agricultural holding, being a person with no greater interest than as a tenant for a year or from year to year, and the notice relates to part only of that holding, then that person (the claimant) may, within two months beginning on the date of service of the notice of entry, serve on the acquiring authority a counter-notice claiming that the remainder of the holding is not reasonably capable of being farmed, either by itself or in conjunction with other relevant land[2], as a separate agricultural unit, and electing to treat the notice of entry as a notice relating to the entire holding[3]. The claimant must also serve a copy of a counter-notice on the landlord of the holding, but failure to do so does not invalidate the counter-notice[4].

[1] Ie notice of entry under the Compulsory Purchase Act 1965, s 11(1); LCA 1973, s 55.
[2] 'Other relevant land' means land comprised in the same agricultural unit as the agricultural holding and land comprised in any other agricultural unit occupied by the claimant on the date of service of the notice of entry, being land in respect of which he is then entitled to a greater interest than as a tenant for a year or from year to year: LCA 1973, s 55(3). Where an authority has served a notice to treat in respect of land in the holding, other than that to which the notice of entry relates or in respect of other relevant land, then unless and until the notice to treat is withdrawn, the provisions of this paragraph have effect as if that land did not form part of a holding or did not constitute 'other relevant land' as the case may be: LCA 1973, s 55(4).
[3] LCA 1973, s 56(1).
[4] LCA 1973, s 55(2).

38.82 If within the period of two months from service of the counter-notice, the acquiring authority does not accept the validity of the counter-notice in writing, the claimant or the acquiring authority may, within the two months after the end of that period, refer the counter-notice to the Lands Tribunal. The Lands Tribunal must determine whether the claim in the counter-notice is justified and make a declaration as to its validity[1]. Where the counter-notice is accepted or declared valid by the Lands Tribunal, if before the end of 12 months after such acceptance or declaration, the tenant has given up to the acquiring authority possession of every part of the holding, then the notice of entry is deemed to have extended to the part of the holding to which it did not relate. The acquiring authority is deemed to have taken possession of that part pursuant to the notice of entry on the day before the expiration of the year of the tenancy which is current at the date of acceptance or declaration[2].

[1] LCA 1973, s 56(1).
[2] LCA 1973, s 56(2).

38.83 Where the claimant gives up possession of a holding to the acquiring authority, but the acquiring authority has not been authorised to acquire the landlord's interest in the land not subject to compulsory purchase[1], then:

(a) neither the claimant nor the acquiring authority is liable to the landlord by reason of the claimant giving up possession or the acquiring authority taking possession of the land not subject to the compulsory purchase[2];

(b) immediately after the date on which the acquiring authority takes possession of that land, it must give up possession of it to the landlord[3];

(c) the tenancy is treated as terminated on the date on which the tenant gives up possession of the holding[4];

(d) any rights and liabilities of the tenant in relation to the landlord arising under sub-paragraph (c)[5] are transferred to the acquiring authority, and any question as to payments in respect of such rights and liabilities must be determined by the Lands Tribunal in the absence of agreement[6]; and

(e) any increase in value of the land, not subject to the compulsory purchase, which is attributable to the landlord taking possession under (b) above must be deducted from the compensation payable in respect of the acquisition of his interest in the remainder of the holding[7].

[1] 'The land not subject to compulsory purchase' is the part of the holding to which the notice of entry does not relate: LCA 1973, s 56(3).
[2] LCA 1973, s 56(3)(a).
[3] LCA 1973, s 56(3)(b).
[4] LCA 1973, s 56(3)(c). If a claimant gives up different parts of the holding at different times, the tenancy is treated as terminated on the date of the claimant giving up the last part. The provisions relating to the date on which the tenancy is to be treated as terminated are without prejudice to any rights or liabilities of the landlord or the claimant accruing before that date: LCA 1973, s 56(3)(c). As to the application of s 72 of the AHA 1986 (compensation payable to the landlord for deterioration of the holding), to a tenancy terminated under this provision, see s 56(4) of the LCA 1973 (amended by the AHA 1986, s 100, Sch 14 para 54(3)). As to the AHA 1986, s 72, see para 39.12.
[5] Ie rights under the contract of tenancy, the AHA 1986 or otherwise.
[6] LCA 1973, s 56(3)(d) (amended by the AHA 1986, s 100, Sch 14 para 54(2)).
[7] LCA 1973, s 56(3)(e).

Loss payments under the Planning and Compulsory Purchase Act 2004

38.84 Under s 33A of the LCA 1973[1], a person who has a qualifying interest in land[2] acquired compulsorily is entitled to a basic loss payment. If the land acquired is agricultural, the person is additionally entitled to an occupier's loss payment for agricultural land[3]. Payment will not be made if notice has been served under various statutes as a consequence of the condition of the land requiring remedial works to be carried out[4].

The basic loss payment is calculated by reference to the owner's claim for compensation for the value of the land acquired on compulsory purchase. The payment is calculated as the lower of 7.5% of the value of the claimant's property acquired or £75,000[5].

The occupier's loss payment for agricultural land is similarly calculated by reference to the overall compensation claim for the land acquired or by reference to one of two other sums defined in the legislation as the 'land amount'[6] and the 'building amount'[7]. The greatest of these three sums is payable as the occupier's loss payment, subject to a maximum of £25,000.

All of the amounts and percentages referred to above are capable of change by statutory instrument[8].

Claims should be made in writing and supported by sufficient information to enable the claim to be calculated[9]. Provision is made for claims arising on the insolvency or death of the claimant[10].

Where there is a dual entitlement to payment under s 33B of the LCA 1973 and s 12(1) of the A(MP)A 1968, then there is only one payment but at the greater amount arising under the respective statutory codes[11].

[1] As to periods of occupation required to qualify for these payments, see LCA 1973, s 33A(4).
[2] LCA 1973, s 33A.
[3] LCA 1973, s 33B.
[4] LCA 1973, s 33D(4).
[5] LCA 1973, s 33A(2).
[6] LCA 1973, s 33B(8).
[7] LCA 1973, s 33B(9).
[8] LCA 1973, s 33K.
[9] LCA 1973, s 33E.
[10] LCA 1973, ss 33F and 33G.
[11] LCA 1973, s 33H.

Open cast coal mining

38.85 Where the British Coal Corporation[1] compulsorily acquires temporary rights of occupation and use of agricultural land for the purposes of open cast coal mining by means of a compulsory rights order[2], the occupier is entitled to receive from the Corporation annual compensation based on the annual value of the land, adjusted by reference to expected profit or loss, and also compensation for the cost of removal and in relation to forced sales of property[3].

[1] Formerly the National Coal Board: see the Coal Industry Act 1987, s 1.
[2] Ie a compulsory rights order made under the Opencast Coal Act 1958, Pt I, ss 4, 5, 7–12 and 14–16.
[3] Open Cast Coal Act 1958, ss 17–20, 27 Sch 3.

38.86 On the termination of the occupation by the British Coal Corporation, the occupier is entitled to compensation by way of payment of the cost of works for restoring the land and compensation for diminution in the value of the holding. There may be additional compensation payable upon re-occupation[1]. Where the land subject to the compulsory rights order consists of, or includes, land which constitutes or forms part of an agricultural holding, provision is made for modifying the right of the tenant to receive compensation from his landlord in respect of long-term improvements and the adoption of a special farming system, ie high farming[2]. Compensation is payable by the Corporation to a tenant in respect of short-term improvements and tenant-right matters and in relation to market garden improvements[3].

[1] The Open Cast Coal Act 1958, ss 21–23 and 23A (added by the Coal Industry Act 1975, s 6(1)).
[2] Open Cast Coal Act 1958, ss 24, 25, 37 and Sch 7 Pt I. As to long term improvements and high farming, see paras 38.17 and 38.87 respectively.
[3] Open Cast Coal Act 1958, ss 26, 28 and Sch 4.

HIGH FARMING

38.87 Section 70 of the AHA 1986[1] enables a tenant on quitting the holding on termination of the tenancy to claim compensation for 'high farming'[2]. That is, the continuous adoption of a system of farming more beneficial to the holding either than the system of farming required by the contract of tenancy or, in so far as no system of farming is required, the system of farming normally practised on comparable agricultural holdings. The value to the holding as a holding must have thus increased during the tenancy at the end of which the compensation is claimed[3].

¹ Formerly s 56 of the AHA 1948.
² 'High farming' is not a statutory expression.
³ Ie the tenant cannot base his claim on occupation during any earlier tenancy.

38.88 To make a successful claim for high farming, two conditions must be met[1]:

(a)   not later than one month before the termination of the tenancy, the tenant must give his landlord notice in writing[2] stating his intention to claim this type of compensation[3];

(b)   a record must have been made of the condition of the fixed equipment on the holding and of the general condition of the holding, as provided for by s 22 of the AHA 1986[4]. Compensation for high farming cannot be paid in respect of any matter arising before the date on which the record was made or, if more than one such record has been made, the first of them[5].

The amount of compensation for high farming is the 'increase in value of the holding as a holding'[6] having regard to the character and situation of the holding and the average requirements of tenants reasonably skilled in husbandry[7].

To prevent the tenant getting a double-credit, it is provided that a tenant who has obtained compensation for improvements, or tenant-right, will not qualify for compensation for high farming in respect of items for which he has already been compensated under those heads[8]. Also, a tenant cannot claim compensation for high farming in respect of improvements and tenant-right matters to which he would not be entitled to claim directly under the provisions of the AHA 1986 which apply to them[9], for example, because he had failed to obtain the landlord's consent to an improvement which requires consent. These difficulties have in practice prevented a successful claim for 'high farming' in most cases[10].

¹ AHA 1986, s 70(2).
² It is questionable, in the light of *Lady Hallinan v Jones* [1984] 2 EGLR 20, 272 Estates Gazette 1081, whether a separate notice under s 83(2) is strictly required, although undoubtedly the safe course is to serve one: see para 41.3 ff. The notice under s 83(2) should follow the statutory wording rather than refer to 'high farming'.
³ This was one of the justifications, in the cases of *Coates v Diment* [1951] 1 All ER 890, following *Re Disraeli Agreement* [1939] Ch 382, [1938] 4 All ER 658 for the court holding that a clause in a tenancy agreement purporting to allow resumption of possession without notice, or on notice of one month or less, is void, because it would prejudice the tenant's claim for compensation under this section as well as the provisions of s 60 for the second year's rent as disturbance compensation. Also see, *Beckett v Birmingham Corpn* (1956) 6 P & CR 352, and *Parry v Million Pigs Ltd* (1980) 260 Estates Gazette 281.
⁴ Under s 56(1)(b)(ii) of the AHA 1948, the record required to be made under s 16 of that Act was confined to the condition of the buildings, fences, gates, roads, drains and ditches on, and the cultivation of, the holding. The scope of the record has now been extended to

cover all fixed equipment and the general condition of the holding: this amendment was
originally contained in the AHA 1984, Sch 3 para 12.
5   AHA 1986, s 70(3).
6   AHA 1986, s 66(1): the measure is identical to that of a relevant improvement under Sch 7.
7   AHA 1986, s 70(1).
8   AHA 1986, s 70(4). There are obvious practical difficulties in identifying those improve-
    ments to which the claim for 'high farming' relates and those which are the subject of other
    claims.
9   AHA 1986, s 70(5).
10 The claim was described in previous editions as 'virtually a dead letter'. *Sed quaere* the
    ability of the tenant of a dairy farm to which has been allocated a milk quota substantially
    in excess of standard quota to maintain a successful claim.

LANDLORD'S DILAPIDATIONS

38.89 It not infrequently happens that a landlord is, and has for many years
been, in breach of his repairing obligations during the currency of the tenancy.
All landlords, unless the written agreement provides to the contrary, are liable
to comply with the model clauses[1]. In many cases the buildings on the holding
are traditional and expensive to maintain, and have therefore been neglected
for many years. In such cases, frequently tenants have been unable or
unwilling to persuade the landlord to comply with his repairing obligations
and have found that the sanction for non-compliance upon the landlord
contained in the model clauses themselves have proved to be unsatisfactory
and ineffective. Frequently also landlords have maintained the rent of the
holding at a low level so as to appease the aggrieved tenant in the hope that no
claim would then be made by the tenant for damages.

If the tenant has suffered loss during the currency of the tenancy, then subject
to statute barring due to delay, there is no reason in principle why the tenant
should not sustain a claim for damages for breach of contract by the landlord
in compliance with his repairing obligations in much the same way as a
landlord can claim dilapidations against the tenant. The tenant's loss will be
confined to past losses since the tenant on quitting, by definition, is vacating
the holding. The tenant will also have to show that the landlord's breaches
occurred after due notice. Particular problems arise where the repairing
obligations of both parties were those set out in the model clauses[2].

1   SI 1973/1473 (as amended), as to which see para 23.8 ff.
2   For a commentary on the enforceability of the landlord's obligations by the tenant, see
    para 23.12 ff.

MARKET GARDENS

38.90 Sections 79 to 81 of the AHA 1986[1] contain special rules relating to
the compensation payable to the tenants of market gardens, conferring on
them rights to compensation additional to those applicable to other agricultural holdings, although in all other respects market gardens are treated as
ordinary agricultural holdings.

1   Formerly ss 67–69 of the AHA 1948.

Definition of market garden

38.91 The AHA 1986 does not define the expression 'market garden' and neither did its predecessors, the AHA 1948 and the Agriculture Act 1947. Although the expression was defined in the Agricultural Holdings Act 1923[1], that definition was repealed by the 1947 Act and not re-enacted[2]. In a case decided under the Agricultural Holdings Act 1923, the expression was held to include any trade or business which produces a class of goods characteristic of a greengrocer's shop and which in the ordinary course reaches that shop via the early morning market where such goods are disposed of wholesale[3].

In order to fall within the AHA 1986 the market gardening must be carried on as a trade or business[4]. Whereas the occasional sale of a crop from a garden used mainly for domestic purposes would be insufficient[5], land used exclusively or predominantly for fruit or vegetable growing has been held to qualify[6].

[1]   The Agricultural Holdings Act 1923, s 57(1).
[2]   'It looked as though the legislature had given up in despair the attempt to define the term': per Dankwerts J in *Hood Barrs v Howard* (1967) 201 Estates Gazette 768. For cases before the Agricultural Holdings Act 1923, see *Re Wallis, ex p Sully* (1885) 14 QBD 950 and *Re Morse and Dixon* (1917) 87 LJKB 1, CA.
[3]   *Watters v Hunter* 1927 SC 310, Ct of Sess.
[4]   AHA 1986, s 1(4)(a).
[5]   *Bickerdike v Lucy* [1920] 1 KB 707 and *Re Wallis, ex p Sully* (1885) 14 QBD 950.
[6]   See *Purser v Worthing Local Board of Health* (1887) 18 QBD 818; *Smith v Richmond* [1899] AC 448, HL; and *Lowther v Clifford* [1927] 1 KB 130, CA.

Qualifications for compensation

38.92 In order that a valid claim for additional compensation can be made, it is necessary not only for the holding to constitute a market garden as a matter of law, but also as a matter of fact. Further, it must fulfil one of the three specific preconditions contained in the AHA 1986. These are as follows:

(a)   it may be a tenancy in existence as a market garden prior to 1 January 1896;

(b)   there may be an agreement in writing between the parties to treat it as a market garden;

(c)   there may have been a direction of the ALT.

Tenancy in existence on 1 January 1896

38.93 In the unusual case in which the tenancy of an agricultural holding was in existence on 1 January 1896, and as of that date was in actual cultivation as a market garden with the knowledge of the landlord, it will qualify for the special compensation provisions applicable to market gardens if the tenant had by that date executed on the holding (without having received before the execution a written notice of dissent by the landlord) an improvement of a type specified in Sch 10 of the AHA 1986[1].

[1]   AHA 1986, Sch 12 para 10(2), reproducing Sch 5 to the AHA 1948.

Agreement in writing

38.94 The special compensation provisions apply in the case of an agricultural holding in respect of which it is agreed in writing[1] that the holding shall be let or treated as a market garden[2] provided that the agreement was made on or after 1 January 1896[3]. The fact that the agreement contains only a permissive right to cultivate as a market garden does not prevent the provisions applying[4]. If the land to which the agreement relates comprises only part of the holding (for example, if a specified part of the land is identified in the tenancy agreement for use as a market garden) the compensation provisions apply as if that part was a separate holding[5]. It is nevertheless possible for the part in question to vary in accordance with the terms of the tenancy agreement[6]. The burden of proof that the land is let as a market garden is on the tenant[7].

[1] The agreement in writing need not be comprised in the tenancy agreement. A contractual agreement requires to be proved and mere de facto use of the holding as a market garden is insufficient. For an analogous principle applied in relation to the permissive occupation of other agricultural land, see *Chaloner v Bower* (1983) 269 Estates Gazette 725.
[2] In *Saunders-Jacob v Yates* [1933] 1 KB 392, CA it was held that the expression 'let as a market garden' means let for the purpose of a market garden.
[3] AHA 1986, s 79(1) and Sch 12 para 10(4).
[4] *Re Morse and Dixon* (1917) 87 LJKB 1, CA.
[5] AHA 1986, s 79.
[6] *Taylor v Steel Maitland* (1913) 50 SLR 395, Ct of Sess.
[7] *Bickerdike v Lucy* [1920] 1 KB 707.

Direction by the ALT

38.95 A tenant may apply to the ALT for a direction that the holding (or part of it) be treated as a market garden. It is a pre-condition to the ALT having jurisdiction that there has been a refusal by the landlord that the holding should be treated as a market garden or a failure on his part to agree within a reasonable time[1]. If the ALT is satisfied that the holding (or part of it) is suitable for the purposes of market gardening, it may direct that the special compensation provisions contained in s 79(2) to (5) of the AHA 1986 apply to the holding or that part of it found suitable, either in respect of all the Sch 10 improvements or only some of them[2].

A direction under s 80(2) of the AHA 1986 may be given subject to such conditions for the protection of the landlord as the ALT thinks fit[3]. On the application of the landlord, the direction may be given subject to the condition that it shall become operative only in the event of the tenant consenting to the division of the holding into two parts, one being that to which the direction relates (to be held at a rent settled by arbitration in the absence of agreement, but otherwise on the same terms and conditions (so far as applicable) as those on which the balance of the holding is held)[4]. It should be noted that such a tenancy is deemed not to be a new tenancy for the purposes of Sch 2 to the AHA 1986[5]. Accordingly, the three-year rent cycle is not reactivated following the giving of the direction. The special compensation provisions will apply in respect of any improvements executed after that date on any part of the holding which the tribunal has designated as a market garden.

If these conditions are fulfilled, the right to special compensation for improvements applies as much to improvements carried out after 1 January 1986, as to those carried out before that date. There is no requirement for a written agreement between the parties. The provisions may apply to part of a holding[6].

1 AHA 1986, s 80(1). The fact that the contract of tenancy prohibits use as a market garden does not prevent the jurisdiction being invoked, although this rarely occurs in practice.
2 AHA 1986, s 80(2).
3 AHA 1986, s 80(6).
4 AHA 1986, s 80(7).
5 AHA 1986, s 80(8).
6 AHA 1986, Sch 12 para 10(4).

Provisions as to compensation

38.96 Section 79(2) of the AHA 1986 provides that improvements as specified in Sch 10 of the AHA 1986, begun on or after 1 March 1948, are included among the short-term new improvements (to which no consent is required) specified in Pt I of Sch 8 to the AHA 1986[1], and those begun before 1 March 1948, consisting of the erection or enlargement of buildings for the purpose of the trade or business of a market gardener, are included among the old improvements specified in Pt II of Sch 9 to the AHA 1986[2].

1 Compensation for Sch 10 market garden improvements has lapsed in respect of such improvements begun before 1 March 1948, apart from Item 5: this still qualified if begun before 1 March 1948 but only in relation to the erection or enlargement of buildings (not their alteration).
2 AHA 1986, s 79(2).

38.97 The five categories of market garden improvements are as follows:

(a) planting of standard or other fruit trees permanently set out;
(b) planting of fruit bushes permanently set out;
(c) planting of strawberry plants;
(d) planting of asparagus, rhubarb and other vegetable crops which continue productive for two or more years;
(e) erection, alteration or enlargement of buildings for the purpose of the trade or business of a market gardener[1].

It should be noted in relation to the fifth category at (e) above that the alteration of a building not constituting an enlargement of it does not qualify[2].

Two specific privileges are accorded to the market garden tenant concerning the removal of buildings on termination of the tenancy:

(i) in relation to any building erected by him on the holding, or acquired by him for the purposes of his trade or business as a market gardener, his right of removal is not excluded because he is entitled to compensation[3];
(ii) his right to remove a building acquired by him applies irrespective of when the building was erected[4].

Additionally, the tenant can remove all fruit trees and fruit bushes planted by him on the holding, and not permanently set out, although if he does not remove them before the termination of his tenancy, they remain the property of the landlord, and the tenant is not entitled to any compensation in respect of them[5]. Moreover, the tenant can claim compensation for an improvement which he has purchased as an incomer even though his landlord did not consent in writing to the purchase[6].

1   AHA 1986, Sch 7 para 9.
2   AHA 1986, s 79(2).
3   AHA 1986, s 79(3)(a).
4   AHA 1986, s 79(3)(b).
5   AHA 1986, s 79(4).
6   AHA 1986, s 79(5). Note that an ordinary agricultural tenant must obtain consent under s 69(2).

Contracting out

38.98 Subject to certain limitations, the parties are able to contract out of the statutory provisions relating to compensation in respect of market gardens. They cannot contract out of the general compensation provisions of the AHA 1986 relating to improvements, tenant-right and disturbance[1]. The limitations are contained in s 81 of the AHA 1986. The parties can only contract out:

(a)   where they agree to do so in writing; and
(b)   where the agreement provides for the tenant 'fair and reasonable compensation' for improvements for which compensation would other-wise be payable under ss 79 and 80 of the AHA 1986. This is a question of fact to be determined in each case.

1   AHA 1986, s 78.

The Evesham Custom

38.99 Where the holding qualified as a market garden by virtue of a direction of the ALT[1], compensation for any improvement specified in the direction and executed after its date will be subject to the 'Evesham Custom'. The 'Evesham Custom' is incorporated and given statutory effect by s 80(3) to (5) of the AHA 1986[2].

The Evesham Custom provides that where the ALT has given a direction and the tenancy is subsequently terminated by the tenant[3] giving notice to quit or becoming insolvent[4], he shall not be entitled to compensation in respect of the improvement specified in the direction unless certain conditions are satisfied. These conditions are that not later than one month after the date on which the notice to quit is given, or the date of the insolvency, the tenant produces to the landlord a written offer by a substantial and otherwise suitable person (being an offer which is to hold good for three months from the date it is produced) to accept the tenancy of the holding from the termination of the existing tenancy on the pre-existing terms in so far as they are applicable, and to pay to the outgoing tenant all compensation payable either pursuant to the AHA 1986 or the tenancy agreement.

1   AHA 1986, s 80(2).
2   The principle underlying the 'Evesham Custom' is to ensure that the landlord is not subject to the substantial financial liability involved in the payment of market garden compensation in circumstances in which the tenant has changed the nature of the holding and thereby caused such compensation to become payable.
3   Note that the notice to quit must be given by the tenant, rather than the landlord.
4   By the AHA 1986, s 80(9), applying s 96(2)(a) and (b). 'Insolvent' in relation to the tenant means being adjudged bankrupt or compounding or making arrangement with his creditors or, if the tenant is a body corporate, a winding-up order being made or a resolution for voluntary winding up being passed with respect to it, other than a resolution passed solely for the purposes of its reconstruction or its amalgamation with another body corporate. The relevant date is that on which the event occurred.

38.100 If the landlord accepts the outgoing tenant's offer, the nominated incoming tenant is liable to pay the landlord on demand all sums payable by the outgoing tenant in respect of rent or breach of contract 'or otherwise'[1] in respect of the holding and by agreement between the incoming and outgoing tenants, there may be a set-off in respect of the sum payable by the incoming tenant to the landlord and to the outgoing tenant. If the landlord fails to accept the outgoing tenant's offer within three months after it has been made, the outgoing tenant is entitled to the statutory compensation. Further, if the outgoing tenant fails to find a suitable alternative tenant, he loses his right to compensation altogether, apart from the general compensation due to an outgoing tenant of an agricultural holding[2].

A new tenancy created by the landlord accepting the tenant proposed to him by the outgoing tenant is not a new tenancy for rent review purposes[3].

Although the 'Evesham Custom' normally only applies where there has been a direction by the ALT designating the holding (or part of it) as a market garden, the parties can agree to substitute its provisions for compensation where they agree that the holding (or part of it) is to be a market garden pursuant to a written agreement[4].

1   This is presumably a reference to dilapidations or deterioration to the holding under ss 71 and 72 of the AHA 1986.
2   AHA 1986, s 80(4)(b).
3   AHA 1986, s 80(8).
4   AHA 1986, s 81(2).

Amount of compensation

38.101 The amount of compensation is the value of the improvements to an incoming tenant. Apart from being able to substitute the 'Evesham Custom' for the compensation provisions that otherwise would be applicable, the parties may by agreement in writing substitute fair and reasonable compensation for the statutory compensation, having regard to the circumstances existing when the agreement was made[1].

38.101   *The tenant's claims on quitting: general*

A new tenancy created under the 'Evesham Custom' after 1 September 1995 is one of the exceptional cases of a tenancy of an agricultural holding subject to the AHA 1986 and not a farm business tenancy subject to the ATA 1995.

1   AHA 1986, s 81(1).

Chapter 39

THE LANDLORD'S CLAIMS ON QUITTING

INTRODUCTION

39.1 On the termination of a tenancy of an agricultural holding, the landlord may have claims for disrepair and dilapidations[1]. The Agricultural Holdings Act 1986 (AHA 1986) itself provides for such claims.

[1] The landlord may, in addition, pursue a claim in relation to the tenant's breach of his repairing obligation during the currency of the tenancy: *Kent v Coniff* [1953] 1 QB 361, CA.

General

39.2 In contrast to the tenant's claims, which are the subject of the detailed statutory code contained in ss 64 to 69 and Schs 7 to 10 to the AHA 1986, the landlord's claims are dealt with very briefly in ss 71 to 73. They are based either on the terms of the agreement reached between the parties, as supplemented by the terms implied by statute[1], or alternatively upon the statutory regulations and the rules of good husbandry.

The landlord's claims are subject to procedural restrictions laid down by the AHA 1986. It is beyond the scope of this book to give a full commentary on the general principles relating to construction of express contractual repairing obligations, the standard of repair which is implied by such obligations, and the common law measure of damages[2]. Those common law principles which apply to agricultural holdings are considered in summary[3].

[1] AHA 1986, s 7 and the Agriculture (Maintenance and Insurance of Fixed Equipment) Regulations 1973, SI 1973/1473. For commentary on the regulations, see para 23.4 ff.
[2] Reference should be made to Dowding and Reynolds, *Dilapidations: The Modern Law and Practice* (3rd edn, 1995) Sweet & Maxwell. Also see Ch 10.
[3] Care should be taken when relating general landlord and tenant law to agricultural holdings because many of the statutory provisions expressly exclude agricultural holdings, e g the Leasehold Property (Repairs) Act 1938 and the Housing Act 1961: see para 24.24.

The statutory provisions

39.3   Section 71(1) of the AHA 1986 provides that the landlord may recover compensation on the tenant quitting the holding on the termination of the tenancy in respect of any dilapidation, deterioration or damage to the holding if the tenant has failed to fulfil his responsibilities to farm in accordance with the rules of good husbandry[1]. The amount of compensation payable is the cost of making good the dilapidation, deterioration or damage[2].

It should be noted that s 71 refers to the rules of good husbandry. An arbitrator, determining compensation payable under s 71, must take account of the terms of the tenancy agreement and the model clauses[3].

[1]   The Agriculture Act 1947, s 11. This continues to have statutory effect in relation to its operation under s 71(1) of the AHA 1986.
[2]   AHA 1986, s 71(2).
[3]   *Barrow Green Estate Co v Walker's Executors* [1954] 1 All ER 204, CA. As to the model clauses, see para 24.3 ff.

39.4   Section 71(3) of the AHA 1986 entitles the landlord to claim for breaches of the written tenancy agreement[1].

Additionally, s 72 of the AHA 1986 enables the landlord to claim for general deterioration of the holding, subject to certain pre-conditions and limitations, if and in so far as his claim under s 71 does not adequately compensate him. Section 72 applies to 'a general depreciation of his farm as a whole'[2]. Again, a claim under s 72 only arises on the termination of the tenancy. Any sum payable in relation to a claim under s 71 is to be taken into account when assessing compensation under s 72. The landlord cannot recover twice.

The landlord's claims must be the subject of a s 83 notice given within two months after termination of the tenancy[3]. The procedural requirements of s 83, especially the time limits, must be strictly complied with[4]. In the case of a general deterioration claim under s 72, a preliminary notice must be given in addition, not later than one month *before* termination[5].

If there is a dispute as to termination, for example, because the tenant challenges the validity of the landlord's notice to quit, the landlord should nevertheless give notice under s 83 within two months[6] of the date on which the landlord contends the tenancy terminated in order that the tenant may enforce his termination claims if the landlord's contention is upheld[7].

[1]   See para 39.11 ff.
[2]   *Evans v Jones* [1955] 2 QB 58, [1955] 2 All ER 118.
[3]   The notice is given pursuant to the AHA 1986, s 78(3). This applies to claims both under s 71 and s 72, but see *Lady Hallinan v Jones* [1984] 2 EGLR 20, 272 Estates Gazette 1081: See para 41.3 ff.
[4]   See para 41.3 ff.
[5]   AHA 1986, s 72(4).
[6]   The landlord should also serve notice pursuant to s 72 if he intends to pursue a claim for general deterioration.
[7]   The tenant in such circumstances should also serve notice, albeit without prejudice to his contention that the tenancy has not been validly terminated.

TENANT'S LIABILITY

Extent of tenant's liability to repair

39.5 The variations between the repairing obligations contained in different tenancy agreements are myriad. It is beyond the scope of this book to consider the scope and effect of repairing obligations in detail. It should be noted that:

(a) at common law, there are limited implied terms[1];

(b) the express obligations in the tenancy agreement are paramount. Where the model clauses[2] are incorporated into the agreement, if there is an inconsistency between the model clauses and other obligations in the tenancy agreement, the express terms in the written contract will prevail[3];

(c) the AHA 1986 imposes standards of repair, maintenance and insurance of fixed equipment through the model clauses unless the parties have otherwise agreed[4];

(d) where the terms of the written tenancy agreement are inconsistent with the model clauses, s 8 of the AHA 1986 provides that if those inconsistencies cause 'substantial modifications in the operation of the regulations'[5], either party may seek a variation in the tenancy so as to bring it into line with the model clause[6]. This may be obtained through arbitration, in default of agreement[7];

(e) the AHA 1986 applies modifications to other statutory provisions relevant to repairing obligations including the Leasehold Property (Repairs) Act 1938[8], the Defective Premises Act 1972[9], and the Landlord and Tenant Act 1985[10].

1   See para 24.1.
2   AHA 1986, s 7 and the Agriculture (Maintenance, Repair and Insurance of Fixed Equipment) Regulations 1973, SI 1973/1473, as amended. See para 23.4 ff.
3   See para 23.5.
4   See para 23.6.
5   See para 23.7 and 23.21.
6   See para 23.21.
7   See para 23.21.
8   AHA 1986, s 99 and Sch 13 para 17 disapply the provisions of the Leasehold Property (Repairs) Act 1938 to AHA 1986 tenancies.
9   See para 23.5.
10 See para 23.5.

Tenant's repairing obligations

39.6 Aside from the obligations imposed on a tenant by the model clauses[1], in relation to express repairing obligations contained in a tenancy agreement, it is necessary to consider the obligations through a number of stages:

(a) what is meant by repair: the distinction between repair and disrepair[2];

(b) the fact and degree test[3];

(c) the meaning of an obligation 'to keep in proper working obligation'[4];

(d) the meaning of 'to keep in repair'[5];

(e) the meaning of 'to keep wind and water tight'[6];

(f) what is permitted by 'fair wear and tear'[7];

(g)   the meaning of the obligation to 'leave in repair'[8].

All of these issues are considered in Chapter 10 in relation to repairing obligations arising in relation to farm business tenancies under the Agricultural Tenancies Act 1995 (ATA 1995)[9].

1   See para 23.4 ff.
2   See para 10.3.
3   See para 10.7.
4   See para 10.8.
5   See para 10.6.
6   See para 10.10.
7   See para 10.11.
8   See para 10.9.
9   For a detailed analysis of these issues, see Dowding and Reynolds, *Dilapidations: The Modern Law and Practice*, (3rd edn, 1995) Sweet & Maxwell.

The duration of the term of the tenancy

39.7 In *Evans v Jones*[1], a case involving an agricultural holding, it was held that regard must be had to the length of the tenancy. If the tenancy had been in existence for a short time, and the tenant could not reasonably have been expected during the continuance of the tenancy to put the premises in repair (having regard to their condition at the outset), this factor must be taken into account when assessing the landlord's entitlement to dilapidations.

1   [1955] 2 QB 58, [1955] 2 All ER 118, CA.

Standard of repair

39.8 The standard of repair required of the tenant will depend upon the precise wording of the repairing covenant, the condition of the premises at the commencement of the tenancy, their character and age and 'the class of tenant' likely to occupy them[1], the length of the term granted[2] and any other factors that may be relevant. Repairing covenants contained in a head tenancy and in a sub-tenancy which are identical in form may impose differing standards of repair, since each will be interpreted according to the state of the premises subsisting at its commencement.

1   *Anstruther-Gough-Calthorpe v McOscar* [1924] 1 KB 716, CA.
2   See para 10.6 for the position where the tenant is required to 'repair, keep and leave' the premises in as good repair as at the time he took his tenancy or where the premises are out of repair at the commencement of the tenancy and the tenant is required to 'put' the tenancies in repair, ie remedy any disrepair which then exists.

LANDLORD'S REMEDIES DURING THE SUBSISTENCE OF THE TENANCY

39.9 Although this chapter relates only to claims arising on termination, it should be noted that it has been held by the Court of Appeal in *Kent v Conniff*[1] that the wording of the predecessor of s 71(3) and (4) of the AHA 1986[2] is not so restrictive as to prevent the landlord from claiming damages during the currency of the tenancy. It should be noted that, in that case the landlord claimed damages for breach of the repairing provisions contained in SI 1948/184. The current Regulations SI 1973/1473[3] contain a mandatory reference to arbitration. The relationship between the sanctions contained in SI 1973/1473 and the court's jurisdiction has been the subject of extensive litigation[4].

The landlord also has a number of other remedies for enforcing repairing covenants, notably the power to give notice to quit either following the obtaining of a certificate of bad husbandry, or following the tenant's failure to comply with a notice to remedy[5].

1   [1953] 1 QB 361, [1953] 1 All ER 155, CA.
2   The Agricultural Holdings Act 1948 (AHA 1948), s 57(3).
3   Agriculture (Maintenance, Repair and Insurance of Fixed Equipment) Regulations 1973, SI 1973/1473.
4   See para 23.12 ff.
5   AHA 1986, Sch 3, Cases C and D. There are also a number of remedies contained in SI 1973/1473 together with the common law remedies of forfeiture and damages for common law waste; see Ch 23.

LANDLORD'S REMEDIES AFTER TERMINATION

The statutory claim

39.10   A landlord has a statutory right to recover compensation for dilapidations, deterioration and other damage from the tenant, on the termination of the tenancy[1] either under s 71(1), or under s 71(3), but not both[2]. Additionally, the landlord may claim compensation for general deterioration of the holding under s 72[3].

The terms 'dilapidation' and 'deterioration' are not defined in the AHA 1986. A dilapidations claim will generally be made for items such as failure to repair gates, fences, drains, buildings, roads, ditches, etc, in breach of the terms of the tenancy agreement or of the statutory repairing clauses. A deterioration claim would be made in respect of the kind of damage which could not readily be put right, for example, where the tenant has allowed a serious loss of soil fertility to occur and it would take a long time as well as skill and money to restore the condition of the soil. A further example might be where the tenant, who covenanted to use his holding primarily as a dairy holding, ceased dairy production without his landlord's consent before 2 April 1984, thereby causing no milk quota to be allocated to the holding.

In *Evans v Jones*[4], the Court of Appeal considered the right to compensation in relation to both dilapidations and deterioration. The court held that in the case of allegations of not properly feeding or fertilising pastures, a landlord was entitled (under the predecessor to the present s 71 of the AHA 1986)[5] to compensation for the cost of bringing those fields back into a proper state of health and might also very well be entitled to further compensation (under the predecessor to the present s 72 of the AHA 1986)[6] if he could prove 'a general depreciation of his farm'.

39.10   *The landlord's claims on quitting*

In *Barrow Green Estate Co v Walker's Executors*[7], the Court of Appeal held, in determining a claim under the predecessor to the present s 71 of the AHA 1986[8], that the arbitrator was bound to take into account the terms of the contract of tenancy[9], together with the terms of any other agreement affecting the holding and the statutory regulations as to repair[10]. It is clear that the landlord cannot maintain an argument to the effect that the terms of the tenancy agreement must be disregarded altogether. Accordingly, a provision in the agreement that the landlord should provide materials, or should put certain items in repair before the start of the tenancy, must be taken into account in assessing the liability of the tenant[11].

In order to activate the statutory claim, the notice requirements of s 83 of the AHA 1986 need to be strictly complied with[12]. Further, in the event of dispute in relation to the pursuit of the statutory claim, any issue falls to be determined by arbitration[13].

1   The statutory claim cannot be pursued whilst the tenancy is subsisting.
2   See para 39.2 ff.
3   See para 39.4.
4   [1955] 2 QB 58, [1955] 2 All ER 118.
5   AHA 1948, s 57.
6   AHA 1948, s 58.
7   [1954] 1 All ER 204, [1954] 1 WLR 231.
8   AHA 1948, s 57.
9   Though, it is submitted, only for restricting the claim and not of increasing it beyond the statutory maximum.
10 The current Regulations are the Agriculture (Maintenance, Repair and Insurance of Fixed Equipment) Regulations 1973, SI 1973/1473, as amended.
11 *Robertson-Ackerman v George* (1953) 103 L Jo 496.
12 See para 41.3 ff.
13 AHA 1986, s 83(1).

The contractual claim

39.11   As an alternative to the statutory claim under s 71(1) of the AHA 1986, the landlord may claim under s 71(3) in respect of any matter relating to dilapidations or deterioration of, or damage to, any part of the holding etc, in accordance with the written contract of tenancy[1].

It should be noted that such a claim is 'in lieu of' a claim under s 71(1). Accordingly, it is necessary for the landlord to make an election[2]. A claim for breach of repairing obligations by the tenant contained in the tenancy agreement is independent of s 71(3). A landlord may sue separately in the courts[3] and he is not precluded from suing for forfeiture and/or damages during the currency of the tenancy[4]. The claim under s 71(3) only arises on the termination of the tenancy.

Although it has been held to be permissible to claim in the alternative, and to defer electing between the statutory and the contractual basis of claim until the hearing of the arbitration[5], the landlord must ultimately opt for one or other basis of compensation exclusively.

716

The alternative contractual claim under s 71(3) of the AHA 1986 enables the landlord to impose on the tenant an obligation to repair and in relation to good husbandry beyond those imposed by statute and to recover compensation accordingly.

Like the statutory claim under s 71(1), the contractual claim pursuant to s 71(3) of the AHA 1986 must (in the absence of agreement) be determined by arbitration[6]. Further, the requirements of s 83 as to the giving of notices must be strictly complied with[7].

[1]   This is the construction of the phrase 'in respect of matters specified therein' contained in the former s 57(3) of the AHA 1948, per Morris LJ in *Kent v Conniff* [1953] 1 QB 361, [1953] 1 All ER 155, CA. Apart from the application of the transitional arrangements where liability in respect of fixed equipment is transferred under s 9 of the AHA 1986, the contractual claim under s 71(3) can only be pursued at the end of the tenancy, although it may be that a common law action for damages can be brought during the subsistence of the tenancy in reliance on the principle in *Kent v Conniff* [1953] 1 QB 361: see para 39.9.

[2]   The landlord may give notice of his claim in the alternative under s 83 and then elect at, or before, the arbitration hearing: *Boyd v Wilton* [1957] 2 QB 277, [1957] 2 All ER 102, CA.

[3]   *Gulliver v Catt* [1952] 2 QB 308, [1952] 1 All ER 929, CA.

[4]   *Kent v Conniff* [1953] 1 QB 361, [1953] 1 All ER 155, CA.

[5]   *Boyd v Wilton* [1957] 2 QB 277, [1957] 2 All ER 102, CA, in which the claims were framed in the alternative, but at the hearing the landlord elected to rely exclusively on the contractual claim.

[6]   AHA 1986, s 83(1).

[7]   See para 41.3 ff.

General deterioration

39.12   Section 72 of the AHA 1986 gives an additional remedy to a landlord to claim for general deterioration to the holding, in so far as his claim for specific dilapidations under s 71(1) or (3) does not effectively compensate him for the reduction in value of the holding due to the tenant's failure to farm in accordance with the rules of good husbandry[1].

At first sight, ss 71 and 72 would appear to overlap. Section 71 expressly entitles a landlord to claim for deterioration to the holding, in addition to dilapidation of it. Section 72 entitles a landlord to claim for dilapidation, deterioration or damage to the holding, if 'the landlord shows that the value of the holding generally has been reduced' by such dilapidation etc, 'or otherwise by non-fulfilment by the tenant of his responsibility to farm in accordance with the rules of good husbandry'.

In *Evans v Jones*[2], the Court of Appeal determined that the difference between the predecessors to the present ss 71 and 72[3] was that the former section entitled the landlord to claim for specific failures by the tenant, whereas the latter section entitled the landlord to recover further compensation where he can 'also prove a general depreciation of the farm as a whole'.

The claim under s 72 is subject to the limitation, specified in s 72(2), that the amount claimed and recovered under s 71 has to be brought into account when assessing the s 72 claim, in order to prevent a double credit arising.

1   The claim may be made in conjunction or independently of s 71.
2   [1955] 2 QB 58, [1955] 2 All ER 118.
3   AHA 1948, ss 57 and 58.

39.13 The most common example of a s 72 claim is where a landlord is entitled to claim under s 71 for the cost of remedying specific defects, but under s 72 for the loss of rental value during the time it will take for the defects to be remedied[1].

1   For example, the costs of spray treatment to wild oats, which would be recoverable under s 71, and the loss of rental whilst the wild oats were eradicated, or at least brought under control, recoverable under s 72.

Time limits

39.14 Section 72 claims are subject to the condition that, not later than one month before termination of the tenancy, the landlord must give notice of his intention to claim compensation under that section. If he fails to do so, he cannot claim. It has been held that a combined notice may be served under ss 72 and 83 not later than a month before the termination of the tenancy, thereby precluding the necessity for the service of a notice under s 83 after the termination of the tenancy but before the expiry of two months thereafter[1].

1   *Lady Hallinan v Jones* [1984] 2 EGLR 20, 272 Estates Gazette 1081. See para 41.3 ff for an analysis of the obligations in relation to the service of notices.

AMOUNT OF THE CLAIM

The statutory claim

39.15 The measure of compensation payable on a claim by a landlord under s 71(1) is defined by sub-s (2) as 'the cost, as at the date of the tenant's quitting the holding, of making good the dilapidation, deterioration or damage'. This is subject to the limitation that the amount of compensation recoverable 'shall in no case exceed the amount (if any) by which the value of the landlord's reversion in the holding is diminished owing to the dilapidation, deterioration or damage in question'[1].

The combined effect of s 71(2) and s 71(5) provides a ceiling for the landlord's statutory claim. It also provides the measure of compensation where the contractual claim, based on the tenancy agreement, is pursued pursuant to s 71(3). The basic test is the difference in the value of the reversion at the end of the tenancy between the property in its then state of disrepair and the state it would have been in if the repairing obligations had been fulfilled[2]. The issue is the extent to which the market value of the landlord's interest diminished at the end of the lease by reason of the tenant's failure to comply with his obligations.

In limited circumstances it is possible to take into consideration the impact of future events in relation to the calculation of compensation. For example, if it is the settled intention of the landlord to demolish buildings at the end of the tenancy, rendering repairs by the tenant as worthless, this will reduce the amount of the compensation payable to the landlord. However, strong evidence is required as to the landlord's intention at the date of the termination of the tenancy[3].

Where repairs have been undertaken by the landlord (or are going to be undertaken), the cost of executing those repairs will provide strong evidence as to the damage to the freehold reversion[4]. The starting point for the measure of damages will be the sum reasonably expended to put the property into the state of repair in which the tenant ought to have left it in compliance with his repairing obligation or his statutory duty[5]. The measure of damages is not affected by the landlord subsequently having let the property and being no worse off than he would have been if the tenant's covenant had not been performed[6].

Where the landlord does not intend to carry out the repairs himself, the proper basis for valuing the adverse impact upon the freehold reversion will be by reference to the rent which the property would be likely to produce immediately following the termination of the tenancy[7]. Where the holding is re-let, the injury to the freehold reversion will be quantifiable by reference to the diminution in the rent obtained by the landlord on re-letting, or the allowance that he has to make to an incoming tenant to reflect the state of disrepair of the holding[8].

As will be seen below[9], s 18(1) of the Landlord and Tenant Act 1927 operates to restrict the landlord's claim for damages in relation to his contractual claim under s 71(3) of the AHA 1986 as a consequence of the tenant's breach of covenant 'to keep or put premises in repair'. Although this provision does not apply directly to the landlord's claim under s 71(1) in relation to the tenant's failure to comply with his obligations in relation to good husbandry, it is submitted that the arbitrator, in determining a landlord's claim under s 71(1) of the AHA 1986, will have regard to the statutory ceiling imposed by s 18(1) of the Landlord and Tenant Act 1927 where the arbitrator is asked to consider the tenant's breach of his repairing obligation as part of his overall assessment of the tenant's breach of the rules of good husbandry[10].

[1] AHA 1986, s 71(5).
[2] *Smiley v Townshend* [1950] 2 KB 311, CA; *Hanson v Newman* [1934] Ch 298.
[3] *Family Management v Gray* [1980] 1 EGLR 46, CA.
[4] *Jones v Herxheimer* [1950] 2 KB 106. Cf *Crewe Services & Investment Corpn v Silk* [1998] 2 EGLR 1, (1997) 70 P & CR 500, as to the court's approach where the claim is brought during the subsistence of the tenancy. Also see *Latimer v Carney* [2006] EWCA Civ 1417, [2007] 1 P & CR 213.
[5] *Ebbetts v Conquest* [1895] 2 Ch 377, CA. Also see *Williams v Lewis* [1915] 3 KB 493. For a case in which the diminution principle was considered in juxtaposition to the cost of reinstatement, see *CR Taylor (Wholesale) Ltd v Hepworths Ltd* [1977] 2 All ER 784, [1977] 1 WLR 659.
[6] *Joyner v Weeks* [1891] 2 QB 31, CA.
[7] *Family Management v Gray* [1980] 1 EGLR 46, CA. Also see, *Crewe Services & Investment Corpn v Silk* [1998] 2 EGLR 1, (1997) 70 P & CR 500. See para 10.13.
[8] *Williams v Lewis* [1915] 3 KB 493.
[9] See para 39.16.

¹⁰   *Eyre v Rea* [1947] KB 567, [1947] 1 All ER 415; *Duke of Westminster v Swinton* [1948]
1 KB 524, [1948] 1 All ER 248.

The contractual claim

39.16 Where a contractual claim is made under s 71(3) of the AHA 1986, the
measure of damages is governed by the ordinary rules applicable to breaches
of contract. The common law, for measure of damages for failure to repair
was the amount by which the reversion was depreciated in its marketable
value by the property being out of repair. The cost of putting the property into
repair, as in relation to the statutory claim, provides prima facie evidence of
the damage to the reversion¹.

The amount of damages recoverable pursuant to a claim under s 71(3) of the
AHA 1986 is subject to two limitations:

(a)   the first is that the amount of compensation must in no case exceed the
      diminution (if any) of the value of the reversion²;
(b)   the second limitation arises from the operation of s 18(1) of the
      Landlord and Tenant Act 1927. This provision applies in relation to
      damages claimed for breach of covenant 'to keep or put premises in
      repair'. Section 18(1) refers to 'premises'. It is arguable that it is limited
      to its application to buildings or fixed equipment. The editor considers
      that the better view is that it applies to the entirety of the holding.
      Section 18(1) restricts the claim to 'the amount (if any) by which the
      value of the reversion (whether immediate or not) in the premises is
      diminished'.

Applying the provisions of s 18(1) of the Landlord and Tenant Act 1927, the
courts have decided that a landlord's claim failed where the building was
going to be pulled down at or shortly after the termination of the tenancy³. If
the landlord is proposing, at the end of the tenancy, to convert any part of the
holding to non-agricultural use, involving the demolition of premises or
radical rebuilding, this will impact to reduce the landlord's claim for compensation. In such cases, it will be necessary for the arbitrator to consider the
extent of the settled intention of the landlord to proceed with a proposed
scheme⁴.

It should also be noted, in relation to considering a landlord's contractual
claim under s 71(3) of the AHA 1986, the impact of s 24 of the AHA 1986.
Section 24 prevents a landlord from recovering more than the amount of the
actual damage suffered by him, in consequence of the tenant's breach of
contract, notwithstanding a provision for penal rent or other liquidated
damages.

¹   *Joyner v Weeks* [1891] 2 QB 31; *Jones v Herxheimer* [1950] 2 KB 106. Cf *Crewe Services
    & Investment Corpn v Silk* [1998] 2 EGLR 1, (1997) 70 P & CR 500.
²   AHA 1986, s 71(5). This applies equally to the contractual claim and the statutory claim.
³   *Salisbury v Gilmore* [1942] 2 KB 38, [1942] 1 All ER 457, CA.
⁴   *Cunliffe v Goodman* [1950] 2 KB 237, [1950] 1 All ER 720, CA.

Quantum generally

39.17 Section 71(5) of the AHA 1986 provides that in all cases the amount of damages will not exceed the diminution in value of the landlord's reversion. Accordingly, if the diminution in value of the landlord's reversionary interest is less than the cost of making good, only the lesser sum is recoverable. It is submitted that it is an essential prerequisite under sub-ss (1) or (3) of s 71 that the landlord should prove that he has suffered actual damage or loss as is implicit in the terms 'compensation' and 'cost'[1].

It should also be noted that, in practice, it is only in exceptional cases, for example, where the land is taken out of agriculture, that the application of the statutory measure of damage under s 71(2) and the contractual common law measure of damage of 'diminution in value of the reversion' will produce different figures[2].

[1]   Note that in *Robertson-Aikerman v George* (1953) 103 L Jo 496, cost was held to mean 'ascertained cost'. For cases on the meaning of these words, see, as to 'compensation', *Great Western Railway Co v Helps* [1918] AC 141 at 141, CA; *Skinners' Co v Knight* [1891] 2 QB 542 at 544, CA. As to 'cost', see *Associated Portland Cement Manufacturers (1900) Ltd v Great Northern Rly Co* [1916] 2 KB 262, CA; *Litherland UDC v Liverpool Corpn* [1958] 2 All ER 489, [1958] 1 WLR 913; and *Ferrier v Scottish Milk Marketing Board* [1937] AC 126, [1936] 2 All ER 1131, HL. For cases where the diminution in value of the reversion was judicially considered, see *Hanson v Newman* [1934] Ch 298, CA; *Salisbury v Gilmore* [1942] 2 KB 38, [1942] 1 All ER 457, CA; *Portman v Latta* [1942] WN 97; *Landeau v Marchbank* [1949] 2 All ER 172; *Jones v Herxheimer* [1950] 2 KB 106, CA; *Smiley v Townshend* [1949] 2 All ER 817, CA; *CR Taylor (Wholesale) Ltd v Hepworths Ltd* [1977] 2 All ER 784, [1977] 1 WLR 659; *Crewe Services & Investment Corpn v Silk* [1998] 2 EGLR 1, (1997) 70 P & CR 500.
[2]   See *Jones v Herzheimer* [1950] 2 KB 106; cf *Salisbury v Gilmore* [1942] 2 KB 38, [1942] 1 All ER 457.

The deterioration claim

39.18 Compensation for loss of value arising from general deterioration of the holding by reason of dilapidations or the tenant's failure to repair, or otherwise by the non-fulfilment by the tenant of his responsibilities to farm in accordance with the rules of good husbandry, provide a different head of compensation under s 72 of the AHA 1986. Such compensation is recoverable in addition to compensation under s 71(1) and (3). However, as noted above, any compensation recoverable under s 71 must be brought into account in a claim under s 72 so as to avoid double payment.

The measure of damages recoverable under s 72 of the AHA 1986 is an amount equal to the decrease, attributable to the matters in question, in the value of the holding as a holding, having regard to the character and situation of the holding and the average requirements of tenants reasonably skilled in husbandry[1]. The decrease in the value of the holding will, prima facie, be the difference between the value of the holding in the condition in which the tenant left it and the value of the holding had the buildings, fixtures and fittings been left in good repair, and the land left clean and in good heart[2].

39.18 *The landlord's claims on quitting*

1   AHA 1986, s 72(3).
2   *Evans v Jones* [1955] 2 QB 58, [1955] 2 All ER 118.

CHANGES IN IDENTITY OF THE LANDLORD

39.19 It was decided in the case of *Re King, Robinson v Gray*[1] that after the landlord had sold his reversionary interest in the freehold, the purchaser alone was entitled to recover from damages the tenant for breaches of a covenant to repair[2]. This applied whether the breaches were occasioned during the purchaser's period of ownership or during the previous owner's ownership. It also applies whether a claim is at common law or under statute.

It should be noted that if the landlord sells his interest after termination of the tenancy and while the procedures under s 83 are still pending, he will not thereby forgo his entitlement to claim[3].

1   [1963] Ch 459, [1963] 1 All ER 781, CA.
2   In *London and County Ltd v W Sportsman Ltd* [1971] Ch 764, CA, it was held that an assignee of the reversion may sue and re-enter for rent in arrears at the date of the assignment. This followed the obiter dictum of Lord Denning MR in *Re King, Robinson v Gray* [1963] Ch 459, [1963] 1 All ER 781, when considering the effect of s 141 of the Law of Property Act 1925 not being followed. The court followed *Rickett v Green* [1910] 1 KB 253, and rejected *Flight v Bentley* (1835) 7 Sim 149.
3   *Re Lyne-Stephens and Scott-Miller's Contract* [1920] 1 Ch 472, CA.

TERMINATION OF TENANCY OF PART OF THE HOLDING

39.20 Section 74(1) of the AHA 1986 provides that where the landlord of an agricultural holding resumes possession of part of the holding by virtue of s 31[1] or s 43(2)[2] of the AHA 1986, the provisions of the AHA 1986 in relation to compensation shall apply to that part of the holding as if it were a separate holding which the tenant had quitted as a consequence of a notice to quit.

Likewise, where the landlord of an agricultural holding resumes possession of part of an agricultural holding pursuant to an early resumption clause[3] in a tenancy agreement, the provisions of the AHA 1986 in relation to compensation shall apply to that part of the holding as if it were a separate holding which the tenant had quitted as a consequence of a notice to quit[4]. In such a case, in assessing the amount of compensation payable, the arbitrator shall take into consideration any benefit or relief allowed to the tenant under the tenancy agreement in respect of the part of the holding in relation to which the landlord resumes possession[5].

Where a person entitled to a severed part of the reversionary estate[6] in an agricultural holding resumes possession of part of the holding by reason of a notice to quit that part given to the tenant by virtue of s 140 of the Law of Property Act 1925, the provisions of the AHA 1986 in relation to compensation shall apply to that part of the holding as if:

(a)   it were a separate holding which the tenant has quitted as a conse-
       quence of a notice to quit; and

(b)   the person resuming possession were the landlord of that separate
       holding[7].

If the tenant enlarged the notice to quit by virtue of the provisions contained
in s 32 of the AHA 1986, then a claim for compensation under the AHA 1986
would arise as the termination would then be that of the entire holding. It
would not be necessary to rely upon the provisions of s 74 of the AHA 1986.

[1]   Notice to quit part as a consequence of socially desirable objectives: see para 29.4.
[2]   Consent to the notice to quit part given by the ALT on the death of a tenant following a
       Case G notice to quit: see para 35.76.
[3]   See para 24.17 and 32.5 ff.
[4]   AHA 1986, s 74(2)(a).
[5]   AHA 1986, s 74(2)(b).
[6]   As to severance, see para 29.6.
[7]   AHA 1986, s 74(3).

CONTRACTING OUT

39.21 Section 78(1) of the AHA 1986 provides that, save as expressly
provided in the AHA 1986 itself, the only case in which the provisions of the
AHA 1986 provide for compensation, a tenant or landlord shall be entitled to
compensation in accordance with the statutory provisions 'and not otherwise'.
The tenant or the landlord shall be entitled notwithstanding any agreement to
the contrary. Accordingly, the parties cannot contract out of the landlord's
claims under the AHA 1986[1].

[1]   See para 40.11.

Chapter 40
SUPPLEMENTARY AND MISCELLANEOUS PROVISIONS

40.1 During the course of the commentary in Chapters 38 and 39 relating to claims for compensation by landlords and tenants of agricultural holdings on quitting, a number of miscellaneous and supplementary provisions have been referred to. This chapter is concerned with the miscellany of supplementary provisions contained primarily in ss 69, 73, 74, 78 and 87(6) of the Agricultural Holdings Act 1986 (AHA 1986). The provisions relating to settlement of claims on quitting are contained in Chapter 41.

SERIES OF TENANCIES

40.2 Sections 69 and 73 of the AHA 1986 safeguard the rights of tenants and landlords in respect of their claims for compensation where there has been a series of tenancies. This situation may arise, for example, where a tenant by agreement surrenders his tenancy and is granted a new one, as might happen where the old tenancy agreement was outdated in form and contained provisions relating to outmoded methods of farming[1] and is replaced by a new tenancy agreement containing modern provisions and incorporating the modern statutory regulations[2]. In those circumstances, claims should be made by the landlord under ss 71 and 72 and the tenant under ss 60 to 68, but since the parties agree that there is to be a continuing contractual relationship between them, little would be gained by the expense and burden of a quantification of cross-claims and cross-allowances. The purposes of ss 69 and 73 is to ensure that, in those circumstances, the fact that no such claims were made would not prevent the parties from preserving their rights *inter se*, so that these can be quantified, settled and enforced upon the termination of the landlord and tenant relationship.

Section 69 provides that where the tenant of an agricultural holding has remained in the holding for two or more successive tenancies, he shall not be deprived of his right to compensation under the AHA 1986 in respect of relevant improvements[3] by reason only that the improvements were made during a tenancy other than the one at the termination of which he quits the holding.

724

Section 73 provides that where the tenant of an agricultural holding has remained on the holding during two or more tenancies, his landlord shall not be deprived of his right to compensation under ss 71[4] and 72[5] in respect of any dilapidation, deterioration or damage by reason only that the tenancy during which the act or omission of the tenant arose, resulting in the dilapidation, deterioration or damage, was a tenancy other than the tenancy at the termination of which the tenant quits the holding.

[1]   Eg provision of thatch, the strict compliance with the Norfolk four-course shift and an obligation upon the landlord to provide materials in the rough at the nearest canal head or rail terminus.
[2]   Ie currently Agriculture (Maintenance, Repair and Insurance of Fixed Equipment) Regulations 1973, SI 1973/1473 (as amended). See para 24.4 ff.
[3]   Relevant improvements are those specified in Sch 7 and Sch 8 Pt I of the AHA 1986. See paras 38.17, 38.19, 38.23 and 38.35.
[4]   See para 39.3.
[5]   See para 39.12.

40.3 The provisions of ss 69 and 73 did not apply where there had been a change either in the parties or in the holding itself (other than de minimis boundary changes). If, for example, on termination of the old tenancy, a new succession tenancy is granted to the former tenant's son, ss 69 and 73 would have no application[1]. If these circumstances apply, the landlord's claims for compensation may be substantially reduced[2] and the tenant's claims in respect of fixtures and fittings under s 10 may be lost, together with the claim for improvements which by then would be annexed to, and form part of, the freehold and become the free property of the landlord. Equally, time would start to run again for the purpose of the three-year rent cycle[3].

Sections 69 and 73 of the AHA 1986[4] have been amended by the RRO 2006[5]. The amendments provide that the two sections also apply where the earlier tenancy was of a holding which comprised the whole or a substantial part of the land comprised in the holding[6]. The amendments do not apply in relation to compensation payable on the termination of a tenancy where that tenancy was granted before the amending provision came into force[7].

[1]   Note that Sch 2 para 5 to the AHA 1986 provides that an agreement for the adjustment of the boundaries of the holding or for any variation in the terms of the tenancy (apart from those relating to rent) shall be treated as not operating to terminate the tenancy, unless the parties agree otherwise, and thus for the purpose of triggering the rent cycle, not operating as the commencement of a new tenancy. However, these provisions are expressed to relate to rent only and it should be borne in mind that for the purpose of the operation of ss 69 and 73 an adjustment of boundaries may result in the original tenancy losing its identity and these sections, therefore, being inapplicable: see *Jenkin R Lewis & Son Ltd v Kerman* [1971] Ch 477, [1970] 1 All ER 833: see paras 25.12 and 33.4 ff. As to the reluctance of the Court of Appeal to apply the doctrine of surrender and re-grant and the legal fiction which that entails, see *JW Childers Trustees v Anker* [1996] 1 EGLR 1, [1996] 01 EG 102, CA. See paras 25.18 and 33.4 ff.
[2]   *Evans v Jones* [1955] 2 QB 58, [1955] 2 All ER 118, CA.
[3]   As to which, see Ch 25.
[4]   The amendments also apply to Sch 9 para 5 to the AHA 1986 in relation to old improvements.
[5]   The Regulatory Reform (Agricultural Tenancies) (England and Wales) Order 2006, SI 2006/2805.
[6]   SI 2006/2805, art 6. Article 6 also makes amendments consequential on the insertion of s 4(1)(g) of the Agricultural Tenancies Act 1995.

7   SI 2006/2805, art 6(8). The RRO 2006 came into operation on 19 October 2006: SI 2006/2805, art 1(1).

TENANT'S RIGHT TO COMPENSATION FOR IMPROVEMENTS PAID FOR ON ENTRY

40.4 Section 69(2)(a) of the AHA 1986 gives to the tenant a right to claim compensation in respect of the whole or part of a relevant improvement[1] for which, with the consent in writing of the landlord[2], he paid his predecessor as outgoing tenant. Section 69(2)(b) provides the tenant with a similar claim where he paid to the landlord the amount of compensation payable to an outgoing tenant. The right is granted by means of the tenant being placed in a position precisely equivalent to that of his predecessor (had the predecessor remained in possession), except that the improvements fall to be treated as if they were the tenant's own improvements[3]. Provision is made to protect the tenant's position in the situation in which a payment is made to the landlord either where there is no outgoing tenant or because the outgoing tenant is not eligible to receive compensation[4].

1   Relevant improvements are those specified in Sch 7 and Sch 8 Pt I of the AHA 1986. See paras 39.17, 38.19, 38.23 and 38.35.
2   The landlord's consent (which may be embodied in the tenancy agreement) in writing is a prerequisite to recover under s 69(2)(a). It is not required in the case of a market garden tenant: AHA 1986, s 79(5).
3   AHA 1986, s 69(2).
4   AHA 1986, s 69(3).

ISSUES RELATING TO PART OF THE HOLDING

Early resumption clauses

40.5 Section 62 of the AHA 1986 applies special rules where the tenancy agreement contains an early resumption clause enabling the landlord to repossess the holding for some specified use other than agriculture, on giving less than the statutory minimum notice to quit[1]. Where the tenant quits in these circumstances, the landlord is liable to pay an additional sum of compensation, equal to the value of the additional benefit (if any) which would have accrued to the tenant had the tenancy been terminated (as would otherwise be the case) by 12 months' notice ending on a term date[2]. The tenant's claim for compensation purposes is treated as the same as if he had been given the normal statutory notice to quit of a minimum of 12 months' duration.

1   AHA 1986, s 25(2)(b).
2   AHA 1986, s 62(2).

Notice to quit part of the holding

40.6 Section 74 of the AHA 1986 provides that, where the landlord resumes possession of part of a holding in any one of three alternative ways, the tenant can claim compensation under the AHA 1986, as if it were a separate holding which he had quitted as a consequence of the notice to quit. The three cases in which this applies are:

(a)   where notice to quit part is given pursuant to s 31 of the AHA 1986, ie for one of the purposes specified in s 31, such as the planting of trees[1]; or

(b)   where possession of part is resumed partial to an early resumption clause in the tenancy agreement itself[2]. Any payment due to the tenant, as consideration for the exercise of the early resumption clause, must be taken into consideration by the arbitrator when calculating compensation, but only if the payment or benefit is contained in the contract of tenancy itself[3]; or

(c)   where the owner of a severed portion of the reversionary estate serves notice to quit part in reliance on the right to do so under s 140 of the Law of Property Act 1925[4]. Special rules apply for compensation for disturbance where the tenant exercises his statutory right to enlarge the notice into a notice to quit the whole of the holding[5].

[1]   AHA 1986, s 74(1).
[2]   AHA 1986, s 74(2).
[3]   AHA 1986, s 74(2)(b).
[4]   See para 40.8.
[5]   See para 38.48.

40.7 A defect in the former s 60 of the AHA 1948 was that it did not provide for the situation in which notice to quit part was given by a landlord who had purchased part of the reversionary estate[1]. It is now provided by s 74(3) of the AHA 1986[2] that where a person entitled to a severed part of the reversionary estate resumes part of a holding by virtue of a notice to quit[3], the tenant can claim compensation as if the severed part repossessed was a separate holding of which the reversioner is landlord.

[1]   Under the former provisions a tenant served with notice to quit part could not obtain compensation in respect of that part only, his only option if he was to claim compensation being to enlarge the notice to quit to cover the entire holding.
[2]   This provision was introduced by the Agricultural Holdings Act 1984, Sch 3 para 14.
[3]   Served pursuant to the power vested in the reversionary owner by the Law of Property Act 1925, s 140: see para 29.6 and 40.8.

Severance of the reversion

40.8 Section 75(1) of the AHA 1986 provides that, where the reversionary estate has been severed, and is for the time being vested in more than one person in several parts, the tenant of the entirety is entitled to require that the compensation payable under the AHA 1986 be determined as if the reversion had not been severed. The tenant cannot be compelled to have the compensation calculated in this manner. Where the tenant elects to have compensation calculated as if no severance has occurred, the arbitrator is directed to apportion the amount awarded between the persons who for the purposes of the AHA 1986 together constitute the landlord of the holding[1]. The AHA 1986 does not contain any guidance as to the basis of the apportionment to be applied by the arbitrator.

[1] AHA 1986, s 75(2).

COMPENSATION NOT PAYABLE FOR THINGS DONE IN COMPLIANCE WITH THE AHA 1986

40.9 Section 76[1] lists a number of circumstances to which the tenant's right to compensation does not apply. They are as follows:

(a)   If an arbitrator's award is made varying the terms of the tenancy as to permanent pasture, and this award includes an order under s 14(4) of the AHA 1986 requiring that, on quitting the holding, the tenant shall leave land as permanent pasture, or as temporary pasture, sown with seeds mixture of such kinds as the arbitrator may specify, the tenant is not entitled to compensation for complying with that order.

(b)   Where land has been ploughed up pursuant to a direction given by an arbitrator under s 14(4) of the AHA 1986, the amount of compensation for the pasture[2] laid down by the tenant to restore the pasture area shall not exceed the average value per hectare of the whole of the tenant's pasture. The purpose of this provision is to prevent the tenant from treating the least valuable pasture as that laid down to comply with the order and claiming compensation for new pasture on the most valuable pieces[3].

(c)   It has already been noted under s 15 of the AHA 1986[4] that tenants are given certain rights to dispose of produce and the general right of cropping of arable land. If under s 15(4) the tenant exercises his rights to dispose of produce and in consideration of that right reinstates the full equivalent manurial value of the holding, s 76(3) prevents him from obtaining a double credit in respect of the introduction of those manurial values.

[1]   Contracting out of s 76 is specifically forbidden: AHA 1986, s 76(1).
[2]   Ie the pasture which he can claim for, excluding the pasture the subject of the arbitrator's award under the AHA 1986, s 14(4).
[3]   Note that AHA 1986, s 78(2) contains an exception to the general rule, prohibiting contracting out from statutory compensation where parties by agreement, without going to arbitration, modify a pasture clause.
[4]   See para 24.9.

GENERAL PROHIBITION ON CLAIMING COMPENSATION FOR IMPROVEMENTS BASED ON CUSTOM

40.10 Section 77 of the AHA 1986 contains a general prohibition against either landlord or tenant claiming compensation based on custom, apart from compensation for improvements of the kind specified in Sch 7 or Pt I of Sch 8 to the AHA 1986 begun before 1 March 1948[1].

[1]   See para 38.36.

CONTRACTING-OUT AND CONTRACTING-IN

40.11 Section 78(1) of the AHA 1986 contains a general prohibition on contracting out of the provisions in the AHA 1986 relating to compensation, except where contracting-out is expressly permitted by the AHA 1986[1].

As a consequence, the commonly encountered agreement for surrender where both parties agree to forgo their claims to tenant-right and improvements (for the tenant) and dilapidations (for the landlord) are probably unlawful. However, the parties are free to compromise their claims and to set them off the one against the other. In such cases it would be wiser when negotiating a surrender agreement to seek to agree the extinguishment of the claims and counter-claims by set-off rather than by purporting to contract out unlawfully of the entitlement to claim at all.

Agreements purporting to oust the compensation provisions have been held to be void whether the ousting is directly or indirectly achieved[2].

Section 78(2) of the AHA 1986 enables a landlord and a tenant to enter into an agreement in writing for a variation of the terms of the tenancy agreement relating to permanent pasture as could be effected under s 14 of the AHA 1986 by a direction or award of an arbitrator. Such an agreement may include provision for the exclusion of compensation, in the same way as s 76(1)(a) of the AHA 1986 facilitates the exclusion of compensation where the variation is made pursuant to an award.

[1] In addition to the sections of the AHA 1986 referred to in s 78, those which permit contracting out are AHA 1986 ss 66(4), 67(2), 71(3), 81(1), Sch 9 paras 1(4) and 3(2).
[2] For example, *Mears v Callender* [1901] 2 Ch 388, but note the House of Lords doubted the correctness of this decision in *Johnson v Moreton* [1980] AC 37; *Gardner v Beck* [1947] EGD 169; *Re Disraeli Agreement* [1939] Ch 382, [1938] 4 All ER 658; *Coates v Diment* [1951] 1 All ER 890; and *Parry v Million Pigs Ltd* (1980) 260 Estates Gazette 281. Also this has not been followed in the Scottish courts: see *Turnbull v Miller* 1942 SC 521, CT of Sess.

40.12 Section 78(3) of the AHA 1986 provides that there is nothing to prevent a landlord and tenant from agreeing on payment of compensation for matters in respect of which the AHA 1986 makes no provision for compensation to be paid, provided such an agreement is in writing. This is subject to the exception that if the tenant has not elected for the statutory basis of tenant-right compensation (either wholly, or in respect of the 'acclimatisation, hefting or settlement of hill sheep on hill land') he may instead rely upon customary rights[1].

In the context of contracting out, it should be noted that s 24 of the AHA 1986 prevents a landlord from recovering a higher rent or other liquidated damages in the event of a breach of non-fulfilment of a term or condition of the contract of tenancy by the tenant, in excess of the damage actually suffered by him as a consequence of the breach or non-fulfilment by the tenant.

[1] AHA 1986, Sch 12 para 8.

40.13 *Supplementary and miscellaneous provisions*

TENANT'S COMPENSATION AGAINST CERTAIN MORTGAGEES

40.13 Section 74 of the Agricultural Holdings Act 1948 (AHA 1948) provided that a mortgagee of an agricultural holding should not be liable personally to pay any sums due to a tenant under s 66 of that Act by way of compensation or costs, but that such sums could be set off against rent or other sums due from the tenant. If the sum is not set off, the occupier is entitled to obtain from the Minister an order charging the holding with the payment of the sum[1].

Section 87(6) of the AHA 1986 provides that a charge created under s 85 of the AHA 1986 (or under s 74 of the AHA 1948) should take priority over any other charge however and whenever created and arising, the charges as between themselves ranking in order of their creation[2].

It should be noted that the statutory power of a mortgagor in possession to create a lease of agricultural land binding on the mortgagee is exercisable in the case of mortgages of agricultural land made after 1 March 1948, notwithstanding any contrary intention that may be expressed in the mortgage deed, or otherwise, in writing[3].

[1] Sections 74 and 76 of the AHA 1948 were repealed by the Agricultural Holdings Act 1984, Sch 4. The reference to s 74 in s 87(6) of the AHA 1986 is intended to cover changes already existing at the date of repeal.
[2] See para 42.6.
[3] See the Law of Property Act 1925, s 99 and the AHA 1986, s 100 and Sch 14 para 12 which excludes the application of sub-s (13) of s 99 of the Law of Property Act 1925 in relation to mortgages of agricultural land made after 1 March 1948 and is to be construed as one with s 99 of the 1925 Act. Note the repeal of this provision in the Agricultural Tenancies Act 1995 in respect of mortgages created after 1 September 1995. See Ch 43.

PARTIES TO A DISPUTE RELATING TO COMPENSATION

40.14 Section 96(6) of the AHA 1986 provides that the designations of 'landlord' and 'tenant' should continue to apply to the parties until the conclusion of proceedings taken under or pursuant to the AHA 1986 in relation to compensation.

VARIATIONS IN PROVISIONS RELATING TO IMPROVEMENTS

40.15 The Minister[1] has power to vary by order the provisions which specify relevant improvements and tenant-right matters[2] after consultation with such bodies as appears to him to represent the interests of landlords and tenants of agricultural holdings[3].

[1] AHA 1986, s 96(1). See para 4.2.
[2] Ie improvements set out in AHA 1986, Schs 7 and 8.
[3] AHA 1986, s 91(1).

Chapter 41

SETTLEMENT OF CLAIMS MADE ON QUITTING

DISPUTES PROCEDURE

41.1 This chapter deals only with the settlement of claims arising 'on or out of the termination of the tenancy' relating to compensation. It does not cover disputes arising in respect of agricultural holdings generally[1].

All end of tenancy claims are compulsorily referable to arbitration under the Agricultural Holdings Act 1986 (AHA 1986)[2]. This is the exclusive method of resolution, in the absence of agreement[3]. The court does not have jurisdiction. Strict compliance with the procedures laid down by the AHA 1986[4] is essential as is strict compliance with the short and inflexible statutory time limits.

[1] For the commentary on the various different methods of resolving disputes under the AHA 1986 generally, see Chapters 44, 46, 47 and 48.
[2] AHA 1986, s 84, Sch 11, as amended by the Regulatory Reform (Agricultural Tenancies) (England and Wales) Order 2006, SI 2006/2805: see Chapter 47.
[3] Certain matters preliminary to the determination of a claim (for example, the validity of a notice to quit) may be decided by the court: see *Paddock Investments Ltd v Lory* [1975] 2 EGLR 5, 236 Estates Gazette 803. It has also been held that an arbitrator has power to determine such preliminary matters: see *Kirby v Robinson* [1965] EGD 236, CA.
[4] AHA 1986, s 83.

41.2 It is only claims arising 'on or out of the termination of the tenancy' which are compulsorily referable to arbitration under the AHA 1986. Other claims which might arise during a tenancy, eg claims for damages by a tenant arising from the felling or removing of timber by the landlord, or claims arising from the landlord's exercise of mineral rights[1], are not compulsorily referable to arbitration.

There is nothing to prevent the parties resolving their disputes by agreement. Arbitration is merely a fall back for resolution in default of agreement[2].

[1] Other examples include claims on the landlord's part for breaches of agreement other than breaches of the rules of good husbandry (see *Kent v Conniff* [1953] 1 QB 361, [1953] 1 All ER 155, CA), or claims arising from the tenant's exercise of his rights to freedom of cropping or disposal of produce, not being breaches of the rules of good husbandry. But claims for damages for breach of the model clauses are compulsorily referable to

arbitration by reason of the provisions of the model clauses themselves. However, note *Tustian v Johnston* [1993] 2 EGLR 8, [1993] 47 EG 189, CA and the commentary at para 23.15.

2   It is rare for a case to be settled without arbitration procedures at least having been set in motion, if not actually completed, unless as commonly occurs, the agreed basis of compensation is that the termination claims on either side will not be pursued. Failure to set the procedures in motion, on the basis that the parties will in due course reach agreement, is fatal. The party who lets a time limit expire destroys his negotiating position and the professional adviser who does so, whilst acting on his behalf, risks a claim in negligence: see para 41.8 fn 1.

STATUTORY PROCEDURES

Preliminary notice of intention to claim

41.3   Section 83(2) of the AHA 1986[1] provides that a claim for compensation made either by the landlord or the tenant under the AHA 1986, or any custom or agreement arising on or out of the termination of the tenancy, will not be enforceable unless the claimant has served on the other party a notice of his intention to make a claim. Such notices must be served not later than two months after the date of termination of the tenancy[2].

There is no power for the arbitrator or any other third party to waive, vary, extend or dispense with the essential prerequisite of a preliminary notice.

It has been held in a county court case, *Lady Hallinan v Jones*[3], that a notice served under s 72(4) of the AHA 1986[4] not later than a month before the termination of the tenancy, satisfied the requirements of ss 72(4) and 83(2). Accordingly, there was no need to serve a further notice under s 83(2) after the tenancy had actually terminated[5].

1   Formerly s 70(2) of the Agricultural Holdings Act 1948 (AHA 1948).
2   It was held in Scotland that the two-month period dates from the termination of the tenancy and not from the date on which the tenant actually gives possession, eg by exercising his limited rights in connection with an away going crop; see *Coutts v Barclay-Harvey* 1956 SLT Sh Ct 54. It is essential for the other party to receive the preliminary notice within the two-month period.
3   [1984] 2 EGLR 20, 272 Estates Gazette 1081.
4   AHA 1986, s 72(4) requires notice of a claim for compensation for general deterioration of a holding to be given not later than one month before termination.
5   Notwithstanding the decision in *Lady Hallinan v Jones* [1984] 2 EGLR 20, 272 Estates Gazette 1081 ra, it would be wise to serve a notice (even if a further notice) within the two-month period following termination. Note that this case is also authority for the proposition that a notice of intention to serve a notice of intention to claim does not itself constitute sufficient notice.

41.4   There are two issues facing a landlord who is seeking to rely upon a notice given under s 72 as an effective notice for the purposes of s 83. The first is whether, if the notice makes no reference to s 83, it is ineffective by reason of misdescription. The second is timing.

It is submitted that a misdescription in a notice, such as calling it a 's 72 notice', where it is intended to be a notice embracing s 83, would not invalidate it if the meaning of the notice is so plain that the recipient cannot mistake what is meant[1]. This approach to the notice is consistent with the general common law test which is now applied following the House of Lords decision in *Mannai Investment Co Ltd v Eagle Star Life Assurance Co Ltd* [2]. The test is whether the notice is sufficiently clear and unambiguous to leave a reasonable recipient in no reasonable doubt as to how and when the notice is intended to operate. It is submitted that a court would construe a notice which was served as being sufficient for the purposes of s 83 if it indicates an intention on the part of the landlord to pursue a claim.

The second question is whether a notice which is served before the termination of the tenancy can be valid and effective for the purposes of s 83. Section 83(2) provides that any claim by a landlord of an agricultural holding under the provisions of the AHA 1986 shall only be enforceable if 'before the expiry of two months from the termination of the tenancy the [landlord] has served notice in writing on his [tenant] … of his intention to make a claim'. What is clear from that wording is that a notice served after the expiry of two months from the termination of the tenancy is too late. However, the section itself does not give an obvious answer to the question as to whether the preliminary notice under s 83 can be given before the termination of the tenancy.

In *Lady Hallinan v Jones*[3], a decision of Mr Peter Langdon-Davies, sitting as an assistant recorder in the Aberystwyth county court, the judge considered the provisions of ss 58 and 70 of the AHA 1948, the wording of which is identical to what are now ss 72 and 83 of the AHA 1986. The judge had to consider two notices which had been served by the landlord. One was a formal notice, purporting to be under s 58 (now s 72). The other was a letter indicating that a schedule was going to be prepared and that it was the intention of the landlord to serve a notice under s 70 (now s 83). This second notice was found not to be good notice under s 70 because it was merely a statement that a schedule of dilapidations was going to be drawn up. It was not notice of an intention to make a claim. It was a statement of the intention to give notice of intention.

[1] *Frankland v Capstick* [1959] 1 All ER 209, [1959] 1 WLR 205, CA; *Mountford v Hodgkinson* [1956] 2 All ER 17, [1956] 1 WLR 422, CA; *Pickard v Bishop* (1975) 31 P & CR 108 (1975) 235 Estates Gazette 133; *Walker v Crocker* [1992] 1 EGLR 29, [1992] 23 EG 123.
[2] [1996] 1 All ER 55, [1995] 1 WLR 1508.
[3] [1984] 2 EGLR 20, 272 Estates Gazette 1081.

41.5 The first notice stated:

'We hereby give you Notice of our intention, on your quitting the holding, on the termination of your tenancy, to claim compensation under section 58 of the above Act for general deterioration of the holding as therein mentioned'.

In that case, the tenancy terminated on 29 September 1982. The notice had been sent by post on 25 August 1982. It was argued on behalf of the tenant that the notice was defective because it was given before the termination of the tenancy. The judge held that, by parity of reasoning with the more stringent wording applying to the timetable for objections to licensing sex establishments under the Local Government (Miscellaneous Provisions) Act 1982, service of the preliminary notice before the termination of the tenancy satisfied the provisions of s 70. The judge relied upon the Court of Appeal decision in *R v Preston Borough Council, ex p Quietlynn Ltd*[1]. The judge decided that the service of the notice before the termination of the tenancy was still more than two months before the expiry of the period of two months after the termination of the tenancy. Accordingly, the notice was valid and effective.

In the *Hallinan*[2] case, it was also argued for the tenant that if it was possible to serve the preliminary notice before the termination of the tenancy then in theory it could be served at any time. The judge answered that by saying that this issue did not in his view 'throw ... light on the construction of section 70(2)'. The judge decided that the notice which had been served was in his view 'a notice of the landlord's intention to make a claim and it sufficiently specifies the nature of the claim by reference to the statutory provision under which it is made'. It therefore complied 'perfectly with the requirements of section 70(2)'.

In the same case, a further argument was raised by the tenant. That was that the notice referred to s 58 and that the AHA 1948 required that two Notices should be served, one being a preliminary notice satisfying s 70(2) and one satisfying s 58. In this submission, the tenant relied upon a passage in *Woodfall's Law on Landlord and Tenant*[3]. The 28th edition had been published in 1978 and suggested that two separate notices were required. The judge disagreed with that proposition. He decided that:

> 'Once it is established that a valid notice under section 70 can be served before the termination of the tenancy it follows, in my judgment, that a valid notice under section 58 contains all of the ingredients required of a section 70 notice and as far as a claim under section 58 is concerned no second notice is required'.

The current edition of *Woodfall*[4] provides:

> 'This notice of intention to claim [under section 83] applies to all claims under the [1986] Act. It does not take the place of and is not displaced by the necessity of giving other and additional notices of intention to claim specified in other sections of the [1986] Act, eg claim for disturbance under section 60(6), claim for compensation for continuous adoption of special system of farming under section 70(2) and claim by landlord for compensation for deterioration of holding under section 72(4); in such cases the [1986] Act makes two notices necessary and one without the other is not sufficient'.

In a separate footnote the Editor of *Woodfall* adds that this statement has been questioned in the county court in the *Hallinan*[5] case and observes:

> 'The statement is plainly correct if the notice under section 83(2) is served after the termination of the tenancy since the other notices must be served before that event. However, if, as would seem possible, the notice under section 83(2) is served before termination, the two notices may be combined in one notice, if carefully drawn'.

In the eighth edition of this book, it was suggested that it would be wise to serve a second notice under s 83 within the two-month period following the termination of the tenancy in order to avoid any dispute as to whether a s 83 notice served before the termination of the tenancy is ineffective. The current editor of this book reinforces that advice. Notwithstanding the decision in the *Hallinan* case, it is clearly arguable that s 83 anticipated a notice given in the two-month period after termination of the tenancy. The opportunity to resolve this issue was not taken in the RRO 2006[6].

1   (1984) 83 LGR 308.
2   *Lady Hallinan v Jones* [1984] 2 EGLR 20, 272 Estates Gazette 1081.
3   *Woodfall's Law on Landlord and Tenant* (28th edn, 1978) Sweet & Maxwell.
4   *Woodfall: Landlord and Tenant* (Looseleaf edn, 1994) Sweet & Maxwell.
5   *Lady Hallinan v Jones* [1984] 2 EGLR 20, 272 Estates Gazette 1081.
6   Regulatory Reform (Agricultural Tenancies) (England and Wales) Act 2006, SI 2006/2805.

41.6 As to the form and contents of the preliminary notice, s 83(3) merely states that the notice 'shall specify the nature of the claim'. It goes on to provide an example of sufficient specification, ie that it shall be sufficient 'if the notice refers to the statutory provision, custom or term of an agreement under which the claim is made'. This does not mean that the method has to be employed, but merely that that will be a sufficient specification[1]. It would appear that the reason for the preliminary notice is to enable the party receiving it to know, at least in general terms, the nature of the claim that he has to meet so that he can collect or retain the relevant evidence[2].

It has been held in relation to the statement of case to be delivered following service of the preliminary notice and following the appointment of an arbitrator that an arbitrator was ordinarily required to give leave to amend if after the amendment the respondent would know sufficiently the particulars of the case he had to meet and if he would be no worse off than if the statement of case had been properly drafted when originally delivered. If there are any consequential costs, these can be ordered in the opposite party's favour[3].

1   See *Newborough v Davies* (1966) 116 NLJ 1291, where a landlord served a written notice of claim headed 'Notice under section 70 of the Agricultural Holdings Act 1948'. This was supported by a schedule of details of the work necessary and the cost involved. It was held that the notice sufficiently specified the nature of the claim since it referred to s 70 of the Act and the schedule obviously gave effect to s 70(2). See also, *Hewetson v Pennington-Ramsden* (1966) 116 NLJ 613, in which it was held that the following letter from a tenant was a valid notice: 'I hereby give notice to my landlord via his agent that as per the instructions of s 70 of the 1948 Agriculture Act, that it is necessary to give notice only of the general nature of the claim within two months of the termination of the tenancy, my claim will be for tenant-right, improvements, painting and under clause quiet enjoyment'. See *ED & AD Cooke Bourne (Farms) Ltd v Mellows* [1983] QB 104, [1982] 2 All ER 208, CA for a comparison between the preliminary notice of intention to claim (now under s 83(2) of the AHA 1986) and the subsequent statement of case to be delivered to the arbitrator.
2   For the cases under the Agricultural Holdings Act 1923, see *Spreckley v Leicestershire County Council* [1934] 1 KB 366, CA, and *Re O'Connor and Brewin's Arbitration* [1933] 1 KB 20. Note the 1923 Act was differently worded: see s 16(2) of that Act. Reference to a clause number in a tenancy agreement may be insufficient. In two county court cases under the AHA 1986 informal letters written 'without prejudice' were held to constitute

sufficient notice: *Walker v Crocker* [1992] 1 EGLR 29, (1992) 23 EG 123 and *Sawbridge v Fricker* (1992), adopting the reasoning in *Nunes v Davies Laing & Dick Ltd* (1985) 51 P & CR 310.
3   *ED & AD Cooke Bourne (Farms) Ltd v Mellows* [1983] QB 104, [1982] 2 All ER 208.

41.7 It frequently happens that there is a dispute between landlord and tenant as to whether or not the tenancy has in fact been terminated, and that dispute takes considerably longer than two months after the date of termination to resolve[1], during which period the tenant remains in possession and continues to farm. In those circumstances, the parties to the dispute must give their s 83 notices, in the event that the tenancy might be found to have terminated, since a failure to do so would cause the claims arising on termination to be statute barred[2]. In order to obviate the possibility that the giving of the notices is construed as an acknowledgment of termination, the tenant disputing the landlord's claim that the tenancy had terminated would be well advised to make clear that his notice is given without prejudice to his contention that the tenancy is still subsisting[3].

The two-month period is extended by s 83(6) of the AHA 1986 if the tenant lawfully remains in occupation after the termination of the tenancy. However, that extension of time does not apply where the tenant remains in occupation because he denies the validity of what is in fact a valid notice to quit.

1   Eg where an incontestable notice to quit is given and the reason stated is not compulsorily referable to arbitration as, for example, a notice to quit under Case A, B, D or E would be if contested.
2   The claims would not be saved under the AHA 1986, s 83.
3   *Lowenthal v Vanhoute* [1947] KB 342, [1947] 1 All ER 116. Also see para 28.16.

Subsequent steps for enforcement of claims

41.8 Having given the s 83 notice within two months of termination[1], the landlord and tenant are then allowed by s 83(4) a period of eight months from the termination of the tenancy[2] within which to settle 'by agreement in writing'[3]. If by the time this period has expired, the claim has not been settled, it is then determined by arbitration[4].

It should be noted that section 83(4) does not impose any time limit, following the expiry of the eight-month period, for the appointment of an arbitrator, although undue delay in effecting the appointment of an arbitrator could result in a successful argument to the effect that the application of the equitable doctrines of laches or estoppel, should preclude the claim being pursued if the facts supported this.

A problem which often arises in practice is as to whether the parties are obliged to wait the full eight-month period specified in s 83 before an application can be made for the appointment of an arbitrator. The problem has often been particularly acute in the context of milk quota compensation claims where there may have been substantial sums at issue. The landlord will have had the whole of the milk quota (including the transferred quota) transferred to him on termination of the tenancy. The tenant will receive no compensation unless and until agreement has been reached between the parties or an arbitrator's award has been made.

Further, the arbitrator's award only carries interest from the date specified by the arbitrator, which must be after the date of the award[5].

Section 83(1) of the AHA 1986 provides a mandatory requirement for any dispute to be determined by arbitration. Section 83(4) provides that the parties may, within eight months from the termination of the tenancy, settle by agreement. Section 83(5) provides that there must be determination by arbitration after the expiration of the eight-month period. There is nothing to prevent either party seeking the appointment of an arbitrator before the eight-month period has expired. The parties are not obliged to await the expiration of the eight-month period before an application can be made for the appointment of an arbitrator. The paying party may not therefore postpone his liability to pay without interest or cost penalties.

1   Solicitors or valuers acting for a party whose claim becomes statute barred in this way are virtually defenceless against a claim for negligence, rendering themselves personally liable to reimburse their client for the monies he would have recovered from the other party. Note also that a solicitor or valuer who, without the authority of his client, fails to take advantage of the missed time limit by his opponent may well find himself liable in negligence in consequence of having helped out an opponent and thereby denied his own client a complete defence to the claim.
2   In practice, this period will be less than eight months after the giving of the notice, unless the notice is given before termination: see *Lady Hallinan v Jones* [1984] 2 EGLR 20, 272 Estates Gazette 1081.
3   Under the AHA 1948, s 70(3), the initial period was four months from termination of the tenancy, although the parties could apply to the Minister for up to two extensions of two months. The procedure for application to be made to the Minister for extensions of time has now been abolished.
4   AHA 1986, s 83(5).
5   AHA 1986, s 84, as amended by the RRO 2006, SI 2006/2805, art 7.

Occupation of part following termination of tenancy

41.9 Section 83(6) of the AHA 1986 provides that where a tenant lawfully remains in occupation of part of an agricultural holding after the termination of a tenancy, the references in s 83(2) and (4) to the termination of the tenancy must be construed as references to the termination of that occupation. These provisions relate to the situation in which the tenant is permitted to hold over for a limited period after termination of the tenancy. It is to be noted that:

(a)   It has been held that where parts of one farm are held under one tenancy agreement, providing for different dates for the termination of different parts of the tenanted land, the tenancy does not terminate until the latest of such dates[1].

(b)   The holding over must be lawful. Section 83(6) does not apply where a tenant refuses to vacate after notice to quit has expired, if the notice validly and effectively terminated the tenancy.

(c)   Until 1 September 1995 and the passing of the Agricultural Tenancies Act 1995 (ATA 1995), landlords were very reluctant to allow tenants to 'hold over' for fear of inadvertently creating a new fully protected tenancy[2]. That danger has now been eliminated by the ATA 1995 and the consequent removal of the statutory conversion of informal licences into fully protected tenancies by s 2 of the AHA 1986.

1   *Swinburne v Andrews* [1923] 2 KB 483, CA. Cf *Coutts v Barclay-Harvey* 1956 SLT (Sh Ct) 54.
2   *Milton (Peterborough) Estates Co v Harris* [1989] 2 EGLR 229.

Part VI

MISCELLANEOUS

Contents

Chapter 42

MISCELLANEOUS PROVISIONS

INTRODUCTION

42.1 Sections 85 to 102 and Schs 13 and 14 to the Agricultural Holdings Act 1986 (AHA 1986) contain a miscellaneous set of provisions which are mostly consequential upon the main provisions set out in the previous parts of this book.

Sections 85 to 87 provide machinery for recovering (if needs be obtaining a charging order on the holding) monies due under the AHA 1986.

Owners with limited powers are subject to certain special provisions under the AHA 1986 relating to the giving of consents and the application of capital moneys. The relevant provisions are contained in AHA 1986, ss 88 and 89.

Sections 86(4) and 95 of the AHA 1986 provide special rules relating to these special category of landowners. The special provisions relating to ecclesiastical land, previously contained in the Agricultural Holdings Act 1948 (AHA 1948), have now been repealed.

A critical element of the AHA 1986, contained in this miscellaneous section, is the rules relating to the method of service of notices under the AHA 1986. These are contained in s 93 of the AHA 1986, which also includes guidance as to the computation of time, in particular in relation to notices to quit: see para 42.13.

Sections 97 to 99 and Schs 12 and 13 to the AHA 1986 contain transitional provisions to ensure that, as the AHA 1986 is a consolidating statute which is not innovative, it does not affect the validity of matters which were either current on the passing of the statute, or could have been dealt with under previous legislation repealed by the AHA 1986 in the consolidation.

One particular provision which has generated analysis and dispute is the unusual power given to a mortgagor farmer to enter into leases without the mortgagee's consent[1].

---

[1] See Ch 43.

ENFORCEMENT AND RECOVERY OF SUMS DUE

42.2 There are two methods of enforcing payment of sums due under the AHA 1986:

(a)   by action; and
(b)   by charging order.

By action

42.3 Section 85(1) of the AHA 1986[1] provides that a sum agreed or awarded under the AHA 1986 to be paid for compensation, costs, or otherwise by a landlord or tenant of an agricultural holding[2], if not paid within 14 days from the date due, may be recovered under order made by the county court in the same way as any other money may be ordered to be paid under the court's ordinary jurisdiction[3]. 'Agreed' is defined in s 96 as 'an agreement arrived at by means of valuation or otherwise'. Section 85(1) is made subject to s 85(3) which expressly relieves a person entitled to receive the rents and profits of the holding (otherwise than for his own benefit, for example a trustee-landlord) from personal liability[4].

[1]   This section is derived from the AHA 1948, s 71 and the Agricultural Holdings Act 1923, s 19.
[2]   All forms of compensation are included within this wide provision including sums payable following death or retirement under AHA 1986, s 48(5) and s 56(3), as well as rent increased as the result of a rental arbitration: see *Grundy v Hewson* [1933] 1 KB 787.
[3]   It was held in *Horrell v St John of Bletso* [1928] 2 KB 616 that there is nothing to prevent a High Court writ being issued for a sum due, if the amount is in excess of the amount ordinarily recoverable under the county court's jurisdiction. This decision was questioned by Megaw J in *Jones v Pembrokeshire County Council* [1967] 1 QB 181, [1966] 1 All ER 1027 as being inconsistent with the principle in *Re Jones and Carter's Arbitration* [1922] 2 Ch 599, CA.
[4]   Section 85(3) is derived from s 73 of the AHA 1948. See the article by E H Scammell, 'The Special Position of Limited Owners of Agricultural Land' (1951) 15 Conv (NS) 415 as to the question of whether tenant-for-life of settled land is within s 85(3). There would be nothing to prevent a landlord within s 85(3) paying the sum due and thereafter obtaining a charge under s 86(1).

42.4 The procedure for recovery in the county court is laid down in the Civil Procedure Rules (CPR) at CPR 70.5 and a supplemental practice direction. CPR 70.5(4)–(7) provide for an application for an enforcement order to be made without notice by filing an application notice in Practice Form N322A. The application notice must state the name and address of the person against whom it is sought to enforce the award and how much of the award remains unpaid. A copy of the award, order or agreement under which the sum is payable (or a duplicate) must be filed with the application notice[1]. Unless otherwise provided, the application must be made to the court for the district in which the person by whom the sum is payable resides and carries on business[2]. The application may be dealt with by a court either without a hearing or heard and determined by the District Judge[3].

A different procedure in the county court applies when proceedings are taken for the enforcement of an order under s 27(6) of the AHA 1986[4]. By

Order 44, rule 4 of the County Court Rules 1981 (CCR), the party in whose favour the order was made is required to file a certified copy of the order together with an affidavit verifying the amount due under the order and stating whether any previous proceedings have been taken for its enforcement and, if so, the nature of the proceedings and their result[5].

Where it is desired to enforce the order by a warrant of execution, the proceedings may be taken in the district in which execution is to be levied[6].

[1] CPR 70.5(6). It is to be noted that the proceedings to enforce an award derive from the failure to comply with its terms and, therefore, comprise a separate course of action. For limitation purposes the period runs from the date of non-compliance rather than the date from which the original cause of action accrued: see *Agromet Matoimport Ltd v Maulden Engineering Co (Beds) Ltd* [1985] 2 All ER 436, [1985] 1 WLR 762.

[2] CPR 70.4(4)(b). The sub-rule contemplates that the arbitrator or the county court itself may direct that the application is made to another court.

[3] CPR 70.5(7).

[4] Ie a penalty not exceeding two years' rent imposed by the tribunal which on giving consent to the operation of a notice to quit under s 26 had imposed a condition on the landlord which has been contravened or not complied with.

[5] CCR Ord 44, r 4(1).

[6] CCR Ord 44, r 4(2). Note that if a method other than warrant of execution is selected for enforcement of an order made under s 27(6) of the AHA 1986, it is enforceable in the same manner as a judgment or order of the county court, ie in the court for the district in which the holding or the larger part of the holding is situate.

By charging order

42.5 The tenant is given the right to obtain from the Minister[1] an order charging the holding with payment of the amount due in two circumstances following default in payment one month from the due date:

(a) by s 85(2) of the AHA 1986[2] in respect of compensation[3] due to him from the landlord. A charging order will include all costs properly incurred in obtaining the charge[4];

(b) by s 85(3) of the AHA 1986 in respect of any sum agreed or awarded under the AHA 1986, payable by the landlord to the tenant, where the landlord is not entitled to the rents and profits for his own benefit, for example, a trustee-landlord.

[1] AHA 1986, s 96; see para 4.2.

[2] Note that only 'compensation' is included under s 85(2), to be contrasted with the wider expressions in s 85(1) ('compensation, costs or otherwise') and s 85(3)(a) ('any sum agreed or awarded under this Act').

[3] This section is derived from s 72 of the AHA 1948.

[4] AHA 1986, Sch 9.

42.6 Under s 86 of the AHA 1986, a landlord is entitled to a charging order on the holding where he has paid the tenant amounts due under the AHA 1986, custom or agreement, or otherwise, in respect of compensation for old improvements[1], new improvements[2], tenant-right[3], or disturbance, or if he has borne the cost of executing an improvement of a kind specified in Sch 7 Pt II to the AHA 1986, having elected to do so following a tenant's application for consent under s 67(5) of the AHA 1986[4]. In such a case, an arbitrator may certify the amount to be so charged on the holding and the time for which the charge may endure[5].

These provisions are likely to be of use principally to a trustee-landlord, or to a landlord whose interest is limited to his life (or some lesser period of time), so as to enable him or his representatives to recover the amount due to him from the succeeding owner. The detailed provisions as to charging orders are to be found in s 87 of the AHA 1986 under which the Minister makes the order for the sums due, plus the costs properly incurred in obtaining it[6]. The order will make provision for payment of interest and the principal sum by instalments, and for other directions the Minister thinks fit for giving effect to the charge[7].

A charge under s 86 of the AHA 1986 will bind the landlord's successors, but if the landlord himself is a leaseholder, the charge will not extend beyond the interest of the landlord, his executors, administrators and assigns[8]. Equally, where the landlord is not an absolute owner for his own benefit (for example, if he is a trustee), the order made by the Minister is required to be restricted to the extent that no instalment or interest is payable after the time when the improvement, in respect of which the compensation is paid, has become exhausted[9].

A charge created by a tenant under s 85(2) of the AHA 1986 or a landlord under s 86 of the AHA 1986 will not give rise to the determination or forfeiture of the estate or interest in question, notwithstanding any provision to the contrary[10].

Charges thus created in favour of the tenant against his landlord under s 85[11] take priority over any and every other charge, howsoever and whenever created or arising, and as between themselves rank in the order of their creation and not in the order of their registration under the Land Charges Act 1972[12]. They also bind the Crown[13]. The results are far-reaching in that the tenant's charge takes priority, for example, over any charge for tax, such as inheritance tax. It is important to remember to register charges in favour of a landlord under s 86 of the AHA 1986 under the Land Charges Act 1972 if the holding is part of unregistered land or the Land Registration Act 2002 if the title is registered.

[1]   AHA 1986, Schs 7 and 8 Pt 1.
[2]   AHA 1986, Sch 8 Pt II.
[3]   See para 38.28. Note that compensation in respect of game damage is excluded.
[4]   AHA 1986, s 86(1).
[5]   AHA 1986, s 86(2).
[6]   AHA 1986, s 87(1).
[7]   AHA 1986, s 87(2).
[8]   AHA 1986, s 87(3).
[9]   AHA 1986, s 87(4).
[10] AHA 1986, s 87(5).
[11] Or under its predecessor, the AHA 1948, s 74.
[12] AHA 1986, s 87(6). Note that s 74 of the AHA 1948 was repealed by the Agricultural Holdings Act 1984, Sch 4.
[13] AHA 1986, s 87(8).

42.7 A charge in favour of the landlord under s 86 does not take priority over other charges and such a charge will rank in the ordinary way according to the date of registration under the Land Registration Act 2002 (if registered land) or the Land Charges Act 1925 (if unregistered land). This point was not perhaps entirely clear under the pre-1948 Act legislation, but it is reinforced by the clear wording of s 87(6) of the AHA 1986.

By s 87(7) of the AHA 1986 a company incorporated by Parliament[1] and having the power to advance money for the improvement of land may take an assignment of a charge created under s 85(2) or 86(1) of the AHA 1986, on terms agreed between the company and the person entitled to the charge, and may further assign the charge.

1   This section originally derived from s 40 of the Agricultural Holdings Act 1923, as materially amended by the Agriculture Act 1947, Sch 7 para 11. Subsequently it was enacted in s 80 of the AHA 1948.

POWERS OF LIMITED OWNERS

42.8 Section 88 of the AHA 1986[1] provides that a landlord of an agricultural holding may give any consent or enter into any agreement which he could have done as freeholder, or where he was entitled to an interest as a leaseholder, even though he has a more limited interest in the land.

Section 89 of the AHA 1986 provides that improvements specified in Sch 7 to the AHA 1986[2] are deemed to be improvements authorised by Pt 1 of Sch 3 to the Settled Land Act 1925[3]. Where capital moneys are applied under that Act, or the Law of Property Act 1925, to such improvements, capital moneys so expended will not have to be repaid out of income[4].

As to the application of capital moneys to expenditure incurred on repairs to fixed equipment, in *Re Duke of Northumberland, Halifax v Northumberland*[5], it was held in that case that:

(a)   a tenant for life of settled land satisfies the definition of landlord under the former AHA 1948 as being a person for the time being entitled to receive the rents and profits of the land in question;

(b)   it is not necessary for the purposes of the Settled Land Act 1925 that the settled land should be within the definition of an 'agricultural holding' under the AHA 1948;

(c)   in pursuance of the above principles it follows that a tenant for life could require a trustee of a settlement to apply capital money within the settlement to reimburse him for such expenditure, including any incurred since some reasonable past date (in that case five years previously), on repairs to fixed equipment within para 26 of Pt II of Sch 7 to the AHA 1986; and that this is so both in respect of holdings let to ordinary agricultural tenants and also other parts of the settled land not so let, for example, cottages etc, occupied by estate workmen, notwithstanding that the latter are excluded from 'agricultural holdings' as defined for the purposes of the AHA 1986;

(d)   the trustees should nevertheless not act automatically on the request of the tenant for life for reimbursement but should take the proper professional advice of lawyers or surveyors (or both) to ascertain that the work in question was fairly within the type and scope of both the Settled Land Act 1925 and the AHA 1986, and presumably also that it was reasonably required and properly executed and at reasonable cost.

Where capital monies are applied under the Universities and College Estates Act 1925 for payment of improvements specified in Sch 7 to the AHA 1986, those monies will not have to be repaid out of income, unless the Minister so requires under s 26(5) of the Universities and College Estates Act 1925, or in certain cases where the university or college thinks it necessary to do so under the Universities and College Estates Act 1964[6]. The relevant provisions of the Settled Land Act 1925 are ss 73(1)(iv) and 75(2); and of the AHA 1986, s 1(1) (definition of 'agricultural holdings'), s 89(1), s 96(1) (definition of 'landlord'), Sch 13 para 1(1) (substitution of the Schedules of the AHA 1986 for the purposes of the Settled Land Act or any other Acts).

[1]   This section originally derived from s 42 of the Agriculture Act 1947, as amended by s 4 and Pt 1 of Sch 3 to the Universities and College Estates Act 1964. Subsequently, it was enacted in s 81 of the AHA 1948.
[2]   Long-term improvements begun on or after 1 March 1948 for which compensation is payable.
[3]   See further 48 Halsbury's Statutes (4th edn) 443, notes to Sch 3 to the Settled Land Act 1925; also the Hill Farming Act 1946, s 11; SI 1951/1816; and the Agriculture Act 1970, s 30.
[4]   AHA 1986, s 89(2).
[5]   [1951] Ch 202, [1950] 2 All ER 1181.
[6]   *Re Duke of Wellington's Parliamentary Estates* [1972] Ch 374, [1971] 2 All ER 1140.

42.9   A tenant for life cannot be repaid out of capital monies sums which he has paid to agricultural tenants on the settled estate for compensation for improvements, although the tenant for life can obtain a charge under s 86 of the AHA 1986 and the trustees of the settled land can redeem the charge out of the capital moneys in accordance with s 73(1)(ii) of the Settled Land Act 1925[1].

A tenant for life is entitled to have the cost of repairs to fixed equipment on an agricultural holding or other parts of a settled estate consisting of agricultural land paid out of capital, irrespective of whether or not he was liable as landlord to carry out those repairs. The same principle will apply even if he is not in receipt of the rents and profits of the settled land, provided he is a person having the statutory powers of a tenant for life of settled land. There is some doubt as to whether the cost of repairs to fixed equipment can be met out of capital monies where the tenant of agricultural land is liable to do those repairs.

A tenant for life must act in accordance with his responsibilities as a trustee for the remainder. He is not obliged to account to the trustees for income tax allowance and reliefs, even though the cost of repairs on which those allowances and reliefs were founded was paid out of capital.

Sections 86(1) and 87(4) of the AHA 1986 provide for the decision of an arbitrator or the Minister as to how much of the expenditure incurred for an improvement by a landlord shall be chargeable on the holding and for what period of time instalments shall be payable, having regard to the period during which the particular improvement will endure before becoming exhausted. It is likely to be in the financial interests of a tenant for life of settled land to carry out, or to agree with the tenant to bear the cost of, the necessary work, and then to claim payment or repayment of the cost of repairs out of the capital of the settlement, if available[2]. By these means the tenant for life is likely to obtain reimbursement for his outlay sooner than would occur if the tenant of the holding undertakes the work on his own initiative or, alternatively, obliges the tenant for life as landlord to undertake it and thereafter takes a charge on the holding under ss 86 and 87 of the AHA 1986.

Limited owners, such as a tenant for life, are sometimes required by an Act[3], deed or other instrument authorising a tenancy to be made, to ensure that they obtain the best rent. In the case of an agricultural holding let under the AHA 1986, in establishing rent, or a reservation in the nature of rent, it is not necessary to take into account against the tenant any increase in the value of the holding arising from any improvements made or paid for by him[4].

[1]   Namely, *Re Duke of Northumberland, Halifax v Northumberland* [1951] Ch 202, [1951] 2 All ER 1181; *Re Sutherland's Settlement Trusts* [1953] Ch 792, [1953] 2 All ER 27; *Re Lord Brougham and Vaux's Settled Estates* [1954] Ch 24, [1953] 2 All ER 655; *Re Wynn* [1955] 2 All ER 865, [1955] 1 WLR 940; *Re Lord Boston's Will Trusts* [1956] Ch 395, [1956] 1 All ER 593; and *Re Pelly* [1957] Ch 1, [1956] 2 All ER 326, CA.
[2]   This section is derived from ss 43–45 of the Agricultural Holdings Act 1923, as amended by s 46(2) of and para 13 of Sch 7 to the Agriculture Act 1947 and s 87 of the AHA 1948.
[3]   For example, under the Settled Land Act 1925, ss 29(2) and 42.
[4]   AHA 1986, s 90.

CROWN LAND, ECCLESIASTICAL AND CHARITABLE LAND

Crown land

42.10 Section 95 of the AHA 1986 provides that, with the exception of s 11 of the AHA 1986[1], it shall apply to land belonging to the Crown[2], including where the land is held on behalf of the Crown for the purposes of any government department, subject to modifications that may be prescribed by statutory instrument[3]. The Monarch's own personal estates (for example, Sandringham or Windsor) are wholly excluded from the agricultural holdings legislation. Compensation payable by the Chancellor of the Duchy of Lancaster for long-term improvements[4] must be raised and paid as an expense incurred in improvement of land belonging to the Monarch in right of the Duchy[5], whereas compensation under s 60(2)(b)[6] or 62 of the AHA 1986[7] may be thus paid[8]. Compensation payable for short-term improvements and tenant-right matters[9] must be paid out of the annual revenues of the Duchy. Special provisions also apply in relation to compensation payable by the Duke of Cornwall, or other possessor for the time being of the Duchy of Cornwall. Compensation for long-term improvements must, and compensation under s 60(2)(b) or s 62 may, be paid and advances made for this purpose in the manner and subject to the provisions of s 8 of the Duchy of Cornwall Management Act 1863[10].

1. Provision of fixed equipment necessary to comply with statutory requirements.
2. The Monarch in right of the Crown or the Duchy of Lancaster or the Duchy of Cornwall.
3. AHA 1986, s 95(3). No regulations have yet been made. Since the passing of the Crown Estate Act 1956, the Commissioners of Crown land were reconstituted and are now the Crown Estate Commissioners and have full powers of management of the Crown Estates.
4. Long-term improvements are defined as meaning relevant improvements specified in Sch 7 to the AHA 1986, improvements falling within s 64(4) and improvements specified in Sch 10.
5. Within the Duchy of Lancaster Act 1817, s 25.
6. Additional compensation on termination of tenancy: see para 38.47.
7. Compensation on the termination of a tenancy in pursuance of an early resumption clause: see para 38.59.
8. AHA 1986, s 95(4).
9. Short-term improvements and tenant-right matters are defined by s 95(7) of the AHA 1986 as meaning relevant improvements specified in Pt 1 of Sch 8 to the AHA 1986 and such matters as are specified in Pt II of that Schedule.
10. AHA 1986, s 95(4).

Ecclesiastical land

42.11 Section 88 of the AHA 1948[1] provided that in the case of ecclesiastical land, the landlord's right to obtain a charging order was required to be exercised with specified consents. Following the repeal of the AHA 1948 by the AHA 1986[2], this section has not been re-enacted.

1. This section was derived from s 46 of the Agricultural Holdings Act 1923.
2. AHA 1986, Sch 15 Pt 1.

Charitable land

42.12 Section 86(4) of the AHA 1986 provides that the rights to obtain charging orders where land is vested in trustees for ecclesiastical or charitable purposes can only be exercised with consent in writing of the Charity Commissioners.

SERVICE OF NOTICES

42.13 The provisions relating to the method of service of notices are contained in s 93 of the AHA 1986 and are of the utmost practical importance.

Section 93(1) provides that any notice, request, demand or other instrument under the AHA 1986[1] shall be duly given to or served on the person to or on whom it is to be given or served if it is delivered to him, or left at his proper address, or sent to him by post in a registered letter or by the recorded delivery service. The effect of this section, and the numerous decisions under it, can be summarised as follows.

1. Ie all notices served under the provisions of the AHA 1986.

Service by post: ordinary post

42.14 If any notice, request, demand, or other instrument is sent by ordinary post, there is a rebuttable presumption that the notice was duly served in the ordinary course of post[1]. If it can be shown that the addressee in fact received a notice by those means, good service is effected[2].

1   This means, where first-class post is used, the second working day after posting and, where second-class post is used, the fourth day after posting: see *Practice Direction* [1985] 1 All ER 889. The Practice Direction provides that unless the contrary is shown, service by post will be deemed to have been effected by second-class post. Proof that the letter has been properly addressed, prepaid and posted to the proper address of the person to be served and not returned by the Post Office affords prima facie evidence that it has been delivered in the ordinary course of post: Interpretation Act 1978, s 7. It has been held that service of a document was regular and deemed to have been duly effected being posted to the correct address of the party to whom it was sent, despite the fact that he was temporarily absent and did not know of the arrival of the document until after the relevant event occurred: *Cooper v Scott-Farnell* [1969] 1 All ER 178, [1969] 1 WLR 120, CA. However, in *R v County of London Quarter Sessions Appeal Committee, ex p Rossi* [1956] 1 QB 682, [1956] 1 All ER 670, it was held that there was no presumption that a letter had been duly served that had been returned through the post undelivered to the addressee, although properly addressed, prepaid and posted to the proper address of the person to be served. Equally, a document sent through the post and returned through the post marked 'Gone away' is not deemed to have been served at any particular time and the service of a document is not effected if it is posted to an address which at the time of posting is not the residence or place of business of the party sought to be served and which does not, in fact, reach him: see notes to CPR 6.5. It has been held that the sending of a writ by post for the purposes of service under CPR Pt 6 did not refer merely to the initial dispatch of the claim but connoted the whole process of despatch, transmission and delivery to the receiver and that accordingly service had been validly effected where delivery (despite the incorrect address) had, in fact, been effected by the Post Office: *Austin Rover Group Ltd v Crouch Butler Savage Associates* [1986] 3 All ER 50, CA. But note the rules for service of documents contained in the CPR and those which apply to other forms of proceedings are not the same as those laid down by s 93 of the AHA 1986. It is erroneous therefore to assume that cases decided by reference to those other procedures provide reliable guidance in the context of a case decided under s 93 of the AHA 1986.
2   See *Sharpley v Manby* [1942] 1 KB 217, CA, but note that decision was under s 53 of the AHA 1923. See also, *Re Poyser and Mills' Arbitration* [1964] 2 QB 467, [1963] 1 All ER 612, and *Hemington v Walter* (1950) 100 L Jo 51. For a similar decision under the Landlord and Tenant Act 1927, s 23(1) (as applied by s 66(4) of the Landlord and Tenant Act 1954), see *Stylo Shoes Ltd v Prices Tailors Ltd* [1960] Ch 396, [1959] 3 All ER 901.

Service by post: registered post and recorded delivery

42.15 Section 93(1) of the AHA 1986 expressly authorises service by registered post or by recorded delivery[1]. If a notice, request, demand or other instrument under the AHA 1986 is 'sent' by registered post or recorded delivery, again due service (ie service in the ordinary course of post) is presumed, unless the contrary is proved. The practical advantage of sending notices and other formal communications in this way is that the sender does not need to rely upon the rebuttable presumption of due service in the ordinary course of post. If the recorded service is used, the sender should be able to prove due service positively[2]. If a notice is served by recorded delivery post, but the addressee refuses to accept the document and it is then returned through the 'dead letter post' system, it is submitted that due service has not been effected[3].

¹   AHA 1986, s 93(1) is derived from the AHA 1984, Sch 2 para 1(7), Sch 3 para 21, and AHA 1948, s 92. Although the Recorded Delivery Service Act 1962, ss 1 and 2, clearly applied to the service of notices under s 92 of the AHA 1948, the matter has now been put beyond doubt by s 93 of the AHA 1986 which extends the former s 92 by specifically referring to the recorded delivery service.

²   For cases in which notices were held not to have been served although the registered or recorded delivery postal service were used, see *Beer v Davies* [1958] 2 QB 187, [1958] 2 All ER 255; *Layton v Shires* [1960] 2 QB 294, [1959] 3 All ER 587; *Hosier v Goodall* [1962] 2 QB 401, [1962] 1 All ER 30; and *R v County of London Quarter Sessions Appeal Committee, ex p Rossi* [1956] 1 QB 682, [1956] 1 All ER 670, CA. NB: this was because the contrary of due service was proved.

³   For a decision to contrary effect, see *Van Grutten v Trevenen* [1902] 2 KB 82, CA, but note that this was a decision under the 1883 Act, ie an Act passed before the Interpretation Act 1889. Note the wording of s 26 of the Interpretation Act 1889 which negatives the presumption in s 93(1) where the contrary to due service is proved. See also, *French v Elliott* [1959] 3 All ER 866, [1960] 1 WLR 40.

42.16   In *C A Webber (Transport) Ltd v Railtrack Ltd*¹, the tenancies were lettings of business premises. The landlord sent notices on a Friday to the tenant terminating the tenancies and stating that it would oppose any application to the court for new tenancies. The tenant had an arrangement with the Post Office not to receive post on a Saturday. It received the notices on the Monday or Tuesday. The tenant commenced proceedings contending that the notices were invalid because they were served less than six months before the termination of the tenancies. This argument would not have been available had the notices been received on the Saturday. The county court judge held that the service of the notices was governed by s 23 of the Landlord and Tenant Act 1927 and not s 7 of the Interpretation Act 1972. She also found that had s 7 applied, then service would have been effected on the Saturday. The tenant appealed contending:

(a)   The date of receipt was governed by s 7 of the Interpretation Act 1972.

(b)   Alternatively, on its proper construction, s 23 of the Landlord and Tenant Act 1927, meant that the notices had been served at the time of the attempt to deliver or on actual delivery.

(c)   Alternatively, s 3 of the Human Rights Act 1998 required the court to give effect to s 23 in a manner which was compatible with rights under the European Convention of Human Rights: art 6(1) and art 1 of the First Protocol.

The Court of Appeal dismissed the appeal². It held that where a notice is served by a primary method authorised by s 23 of the Landlord and Tenant Act 1927, for example, by recorded delivery, it is immaterial whether the notice is received. Section 7 of the Interpretation Act 1978 has no application and the risk of non-receipt lies with the intended recipient. The date of service is the date on which the server puts the notice in the post³.

In *WX Investments Ltd v Begg*⁴, a tenancy of business premises incorporated the provisions as to service of notices contained in s 196(4) of the Law of Property Act 1925⁵, by virtue of which notices under the lease were sufficiently served if sent by the recorded delivery service. The tenant had the right to serve a counter-notice within 14 days of the receipt of a rent notice specifying the rent that she was willing to pay. If no counter-notice was served, the rent was fixed at that in the rent notice. On 22 September the landlord sent a rent notice. The tenant's agent posted a counter-notice by first-class recorded delivery. Unsuccessful attempts were made to deliver it on 25 September and 30 September. On the second occasion, a card was left informing the landlord's agent that the Post Office was holding an item of mail. By the time that the counter-notice was collected, the 14-day period had expired. The Court of Appeal, in dismissing the landlord's appeal, held that s 196(4) of the Law of Property Act 1925 did not merely provide for service by recorded delivery at the time at which delivery was actually effected but by using the words 'and that service shall be deemed' introduced a presumed date of delivery regardless of when, or if, delivery actually took place. Service of the counter-notice was deemed to have occurred on the first occasion on which the Post Office attempted to deliver it notwithstanding the fact that it was not received until much later.

In a county court case it was found that the deemed service provisions of s 23 of the Landlord and Tenant Act 1927 do not apply to a letting of an agricultural holding under the AHA 1986 because s 93 of the AHA 1986 is subject to the provisions of the Interpretation Act 1978. Accordingly, there is deemed service in the ordinary course of post and not when the notice is committed to the postal system[6].

1   [2003] EWCA Civ 1167, [2004] 1 P & CR 307, [2004] 1 EGLR 490.
2   It also decided that *Lex Services plc v Johns* (1989) 59 P & CR 427, [1990] 1 EGLR 92 was decided per incuriam.
3   Cf *WX Investments Ltd v Begg* [2002] EWHC 925 (Ch), [2002] 1 WLR 2849.
4   [2002] EWHC 925 (Ch), [2002] 1 WLR 2849. Also see, *Holwell Securities Ltd v Hughes* [1974] 1 WLR 155, CA; *Godwin v Swindon Borough Council* [2001] EWCA Civ 1478, [2002] 1 WLR 997; *Wilderbrook Ltd v Olowu* [2005] EWCA Civ 1361, [2006] 1 P & CR 54.
5   As adapted by the Recorded Delivery Service Act 1962, s 1(1).
6   *Thompson v Bradley* (2006), Birmingham County Court. Lawtel 15 January 2007.

Service by the Document Exchange

42.17 Although Document Exchange service is approved for service of documents in accordance with CPR Pt 6 and the Family Proceedings Rules 1991, r 10(2), it should be noted that this method of service is not authorised by s 93 of the AHA 1986. Nevertheless, if it is used, and due receipt can be proved, then good service will have been effected by the 'physical delivery' method.

Service by facsimile and e-mail

42.18 Service by email or other comparable modern electronic transmission presents a greater problem for the party seeking to rely upon such transmission as constituting due service. An e-mail communication which is available, but not taken up, or even one which is read from a screen with no hard copy taken, can hardly be said to have been delivered to the recipient or 'left at his proper address'.

42.18 *Miscellaneous provisions*

In some areas of law, provision has been made for service by electronic means of communication[1]. No provisions have been introduced applying such means to the AHA 1986.

The Agricultural Tenancies Act 1995 (ATA 1995) specifically provides that in the case of farm business tenancies, text transmitted by 'facsimile or other electronic means' is not to constitute due service unless service in that way is authorised 'by written agreement made at any time before the giving of the Notice'[2].

1   See, for example, Companies Act 1985 (Electronic Communications) Order 2000, SI 2000/3373. Also see, *PNC Telecom plc v Thomas* [2002] EWHC 2848 (Ch), [2004] 1 BCLC 88.
2   ATA 1995, s 36(2) and (3). See para 17.2. Note that the application of *Hastie and Jenkinson v McMahon* [1991] 1 All ER 255, [1990] 1 WLR 1575, CA, should not be relied upon as being necessarily applicable to the service of notices under the AHA 1986.

Physical delivery

42.19 Section 93(1) of the AHA 1986 provides, as an alternative to postal service, physical delivery to the address of the tenant. The Court of Appeal has held that physical delivery at the farmhouse was sufficient even though the document in that case was slipped under the door and said to have been concealed from view under the linoleum flooring, where it lay undetected until after the period for a counter-notice had expired[1]. It should be noted that Russell LJ stated that the notice must be left in a proper way, that is to say, in a manner which a reasonable person would adopt in order to bring the document to the attention of the person to whom it was addressed[2].

1   *Lord Newborough v Jones* [1975] Ch 90, [1974] 3 All ER 17.
2   *Lord Newborough v Jones* [1975] Ch 90, [1974] 3 All ER 17. Also, in *Datnow v Jones* [1985] 2 EGLR 1, 275 Estates Gazette 145 good service was held to have been effected in a case in which a notice was put through a letter box at the back of the farmhouse though not actually received by the tenant.

Previous tenants

42.20 Under the Landlord and Tenant Act 1954, a notice to terminate the tenancy addressed to a person who had long ceased to be the tenant has been held by the Court of Appeal not to be valid[1].

1   *R (on the application of Morris) v London Rent Assessment Committee* [2002] EWCA Civ 276, [2002] 2 EGLR 13, [2002] 24 EG 149.

Joint tenants

42.21 In the case of joint tenants, the common law rule is that a notice or other document addressed to all of the joint tenants served on any one of them, on behalf of them all, constitutes good service[1]. It has also been held that service of a notice addressed to a firm is good service on the partners[2].

1   *Doe d Lord Doe d Macartney v Crick* (1805) 5 Esp 196. It is nevertheless safer to serve
    notices on all the joint tenants. See *Jones v Lewis* (1973) 226 Estates Gazette 805 for a case
    in which the notice was bad because it was only addressed to one of two joint tenants and
    the statutorily prescribed form had strictly to be complied with. See also *Blewett v Blewett*
    [1936] 2 All ER 188, CA in the context of forfeiture.
2   *Carpenter v Phelps Bros* (1979) unreported. *Sed quaere* especially in the case of a 'penal
    notice' such as a notice to remedy or a notice to pay. But for a case in which service on a
    partnership of High Court proceedings was considered, see *Marsden v Kingswell Watts*
    [1992] 2 All ER 239, CA.

Service on agent or servant

42.22 The effect of s 93(3) of the AHA 1986 is that service on an agent is due
service, provided the agent was authorised to receive such notice on behalf of
his principal[1]. The person responsible for the control of the management or
farming, as the case may be, of the agricultural holding, is deemed to be agent
for the tenant[2].

Generally a landlord's statutory notice can be served on the duly authorised
agent of the tenant[3]. The agency does not survive the death of the principal[4].

1   *Hemington v Walter* (1950) 100 L Jo 51, CC; *Tanham v Nicholson* (1872) LR 5 HL 561;
    and *Wilbraham v Coclough* [1952] 1 All ER 979.
2   *Egerton v Rutter* [1951] 1 KB 472, where son of deceased intestate tenant in possession of
    and running the holding, was held to be deemed to be agent for the President of the Family
    Division (now the Public Trustee). Also see, *Earl Harrowby v Snelson* [1951] 1 All ER 140.
3   *Galinski v McHugh* (1988) 57 P & CR 359, [1989] 1 EGLR 109, CA; *Yenula
    Properties Ltd v Naidu* [2002] EWCA Civ 719, [2002] 3 EGLR 28, [2002] 42 EG 162.
4   *Lodgepower Ltd v Taylor* [2004] EWCA Civ 1367, [2005] 1 EGLR 1, [2005] 08 EG 192.

Service of notice to quit on death

42.23 The combined effect of s 93 and the decisions under the former s 92 of
the AHA 1948 is as follows:

(a)   If the deceased died leaving a will, service on his executors is good
      service, even though they have not taken out a grant of probate[1].
      Alternatively, service on the person having the control of the manage-
      ment of farming will be good service, he being deemed to be agent for
      the executors[2].
(b)   If the tenant leaves no will and therefore dies intestate, or leaves a will
      appointing no executors, or none who survives the tenant, service must
      be effected on The Public Trustee, PO Box 3010, London WC2A 1AX
      (Tel: 020 7911 7027). A prescribed form must be used, accompanied by
      a fee payable to 'The Public Trustee[3]. Service on the person in control of
      the management of farming of the holding will be good service, he
      being deemed to be agent for the Probate Judge[4].
(c)   Frequently, the landlord may not know whether the tenant died testate
      or intestate, or who the executors were if testate, or whether they
      intend to renounce probate. There is also a problem that a later will
      may be found. In those circumstances, the safest course is to serve
      notices addressed to the personal representatives on the President, the

farmhouse, the person in control of the management or farming of the holding and any solicitors or agents thought to be acting. Duplication of the notice will not invalidate the notice, particularly if it is explained that the duplicated service is being effected out of an abundance of caution. In this way, with the minimum of additional effort at an early stage, the right to serve a notice to quit on death under Sch 3 Pt I to the AHA 1986 will be assured[5].

Many of the problems are now alleviated by the provision that the three-month time limit for serving notice to quit on death does not run until after notice in writing of the death from the personal representatives has been received or an application for succession has been made. In that event, service on the person giving notice to the landlord will normally suffice.

[1]   The grant, when obtained, operates from death; *sed quaere* if probate is renounced.
[2]   See para 42.22.
[3]   See *Practice Direction* [1995] 1 WLR 1120. Cf, previous *Practice Direction* [1985] 1 WLR 360 which required service to be on the President of the Family Division of the High Court, c/o The Treasury Solicitor, Queen Anne's Chambers, 28 Broadway, London SW1H 9JS. That latter address is no longer applicable. Also see, *Thorlby v Olivant* [1960] EGD 257. The fee is currently £40.
[4]   See para 42.22.
[5]   In other words, when in doubt serve all possible recipients rather than confine service to the most probable candidate for having the tenancy vested in him by operation of law following death.

Companies

42.24   If a company is the tenant, s 93(2) of the AHA 1986 authorises service on the secretary or clerk of the company or body. Section 93(4) provides that the proper address in the case of service on the secretary or clerk of an incorporated company or body is the registered or principal office of the company or body.

Changes in identity of the landlord

42.25   Section 93(5) of the AHA 1986 provides that, if the identity of the landlord changes without the tenant having received notice[1] of the identity of the new landlord, any notice served by the tenant on the original landlord is good service[2].

There is no corresponding provision the other way. If, therefore, a tenant who is not subject to a term of his tenancy prohibiting assignment proceeds to assign, service of notice on the original tenant by the landlord, even though he has had no notice of the assignment, would appear not to be good service[3].

[1]   A notice given of the change of landlord is not stated as having to be in writing. Also note the provisions of the Landlord and Tenant Act 1987: see para 31.29.
[2]   As to service on an agent, see para 42.22.
[3]   *Old Grovebury Manor Farm Ltd v W Seymour Plant Sales and Hire Ltd (No 2)* (1979) 38 P & CR 374, CA.

Address for service

42.26 Apart from service of notice to quit on death, or on companies, the proper address of any person to, or on, whom service is to be effected is the last known address of the person in question[1].

In a case concerning business premises, the Court of Appeal held that a counter-notice had not been served in accordance with the terms of a lease where the tenant served it at the address contained in the lease after the landlord had notified the solicitor acting for the tenant, by letter, of his change of address. The solicitor's knowledge was imputed to the tenant[2].

[1] AHA 1986, s 93(4).
[2] *Arundel Corpn v Khokher* [2003] EWCA Civ 1784, [2003] PLSCS 23.

COMPUTATION OF TIME

42.27 For the purpose of calculating time limits under the AHA 1986 the 'corresponding day' rule applies[1]. If an act is authorised to be performed within one month, then one month elapses on the corresponding day of the next month, provided that the day of the act itself is excluded from the computation. Where a notice was given on 30 September, to expire one month later, time began to run from when the clock struck midnight on 30 September and expired one month later when the clock struck midnight on 30 October[2]. 31 October would be out of time. The position is unaffected by the fact that the relevant month is February, April, June, September or November.

In notices generally the following interpretations apply to deadlines using 25 March as the trigger date:

(a) 'by': a notice can be served up until midnight on 25 March;
(b) 'from': the date specified will generally be excluded. If the term of the tenancy is stated to run from 25 March, it will commence immediately after midnight on 26 March;
(c) 'not less than': the first and last days are excluded. A notice served not less than three days after 25 March must be served on or after 29 March. Not less than equates to 'at least';
(d) 'at the end of': means the same as 'after the end of'[3];
(e) 'within one month': the calendar month is used[4]. A notice to be served within one month of 31 March must be served before midnight on 30 April. Within one month of 25 March is before midnight on 25 April;
(f) 'within one year': the calendar year is used. A notice to be served within one year of 25 March 2007 must be served before midnight on 25 March 2008.

The following table is provided to assist in the calculation of periods of notice required under the AHA 1986. The table shows the various time limits that apply using the 25 March as the 'trigger date'.

Section of AHA 1986	Wording of AHA 1986	Interpretation	Action/Expiry date
s 10(1)	'before the expiry of 2 months from'	Exclude the day on which the tenancy terminates	Midnight on 25 May
s 10(3)	'at least one month before'	Exclude either the day of service of the notice or the day on which the tenancy terminates	24/25 February is the last day on which the notice can be served for a 24/25 March termination date
s 11(2)	'at least 3 years immediately preceding'		The period of 3 years ending at midnight on the day that the application was made to the tribunal
s 13(3)	'within 6 months from'	Exclude the day of completion of the improvement	25 September
s 20(c)	'within 1 month after the expiry of the year in respect of which the claim is made'		25 April
s 25(1) s 62(2)	'before the expiry of 12 months from the end of the then current year of tenancy'	Exclude the day on which the tenancy terminates	Notice may be served up to midnight on 25 March in the year before the termination date
25(3)	'at least 6 months before'	Exclude the day on which the tenancy terminates	25 September
s 26(1)(b) s 28(3)	'not later than one month from'	Exclude the day on which the tenancy terminates	25 April
s 32(2)(a)	'within 28 days after'	Period begins at midnight on 25 March	22 April

s 39 s 41(2) s 44(7)	'3 months beginning with the day after the date of death'	Assuming that the date of death is 24 March, include the day after the date of death	24 June
s 41(1)	'7 years ending with'		Go back 7 years from the date of death
s 44(6) s 46(2) s 55(8)	'3 months ending with'		Period starts on 25 December
s 49	'not less than one year but not more than 2 years after'		Notice can be served in the year before 25 March to expire at midnight on the 25 March following
s 51(6) s 52(4)	'1 month beginning with'	Include the day on which the arbitrator's award is delivered	Midnight on 24 April
s 53(2) s 54(3)	'1 month beginning with'	Include the day after the date of the giving of the retirement notice served on 24 March	24 June
s 68(1) s 70(2) s 72(4)	'not later than 1 month before the improvement was began'	Exclude the day on which the improvement was began	Notice must be served on 24 February
s 80(4)	'not later than 1 month after'	Exclude the day on which the event occurs	25 April

---

1   *Dodds v Walker* [1981] 2 All ER 609, [1981] 1 WLR 1027, HL; *E J Riley Investments Ltd v Eurostile Holdings Ltd* [1985] 3 All ER 181, CA. Cf *Trafford Metropolitan Borough Council v Total Fitness UK Ltd* [2002] EWCA Civ 1513, [2003] 2 P & CR 8.
2   *Lester v Garland* (1808) 15 Ves 248.
3   *Notting Hill Housing Trust v Roomus* [2006] EWCA Civ 407, [2006]1 WLR 1375. Cf *Fernandez v McDonald* [2003] EWCA Civ 1219, [2004] 1 WLR 1027.
4   *Dodds v Walker* [1981] 2 All ER 609, [1981] 1 WLR 1027, HL.

DEFINITIONS: INTERPRETATION

42.28 Section 96 of the AHA 1986 is the definitions section of the AHA 1986. Its terms have been considered as and when the expressions appear throughout this book. Only the definition of an 'agricultural holding' is contained elsewhere[1].

[1]   AHA 1986, s 1.

AMENDMENTS OF OTHER ACTS

42.29 The AHA 1986 was a consolidating Act and the consequential amendments contained in Sch 14 to the AHA 1986 are part of that consolidation[1].

[1]   AHA 1986, Sch 14 contains consequential amendments to the following Acts: the Small Holdings and Allotments Act 1908; the Law of Distress Amendment Act 1908; the Chequers Estate Act 1917; the Land Settlement (Facilities) Act 1919; the Allotments Act 1922; the Settled Land Act 1925; the Law of Property Act 1925; the Universities and College Estates Act 1925; the Landlord and Tenant Act 1927; the Agricultural Credits Act 1928; the Leasehold Property (Repairs) Act 1938; the Agriculture Act 1947; the Reserve and Auxiliary Forces (Protection of Civil Interests) Act 1951; the Landlord and Tenant Act 1954; the Agriculture (Safety, Health and Welfare Provisions) Act 1956; the Coal Mining (Subsidence) Act 1957; the Opencast Coal Act 1958; the Chevening Estate Act 1959; the Horticulture Act 1960; the Agriculture (Miscellaneous Provisions) Act 1963; the Agriculture Act 1967; the Leasehold Reform Act 1967; the Agriculture (Miscellaneous Provisions) Act 1968; the Tribunals and Inquiries Act 1971; the Town and Country Planning Act 1971; the Land Charges Act 1972; the Land Compensation Act 1973; the Rent (Agriculture) Act 1976; the Rent Act 1977; the Protection from Eviction Act 1977; the Cycle Tracks Act 1984; the Housing Act 1985; and the Landlord and Tenant Act 1985.

TRANSITIONAL PROVISIONS AND GENERAL SAVINGS

42.30 Section 97 of the AHA 1986 provides that subject to s 15(5)[1] and s 83(1)[2], in particular, and to any other provision which otherwise expressly provides, nothing in the Act shall prejudicially affect any power, right or remedy of a landlord, tenant or other person exercisable by him by virtue of any other Act or law or under any custom of the country or otherwise, in respect of a contract of tenancy or other contract, or of any improvements, deteriorations, waste, emblements, tillages, away-going crops, fixtures, tax, rate, tithe rent-charge, rent or other thing. The jurisdiction of the courts is thus preserved in respect of all matters, apart from where the legislation otherwise provides[3].

Section 98(1) of the AHA 1986 provides that, subject to ss 4[4], 34[5] and Sch 12[6], and 'any other provision to the contrary', the AHA 1986 applies irrespective of the date of the tenancy agreement or other act giving rise to the applicability of the Act. By s 98(2) of the AHA 1986, it applies subject to the modifications contained in Sch 12 already referred to. By s 98(3) of the AHA 1986, it provides that paras 6 to 9 of Sch 12 shall apply. These paragraphs provide for compensation for tenant-right matters for tenants who entered into occupation prior to 31 December 1951.

1   AHA 1986, s 15(5) enables a landlord to obtain against his tenant who in accordance with s 15(1) exercises his rights to dispose of the produce of the holding (other than manure produced on the holding) and/or practises any system of cropping on the arable land on the holding to obtain an injunction during the currency of the tenancy, or to recover damages on the termination of the tenancy for deterioration to the holding, if in consequence of the exercise of these rights injury or deterioration to the holding is thereby caused.

2   AHA 1986, s 83(1) provides that claims arising on or out of the termination of the tenancy or part of it must be determined by arbitration.

3   *Kent v Conniff* [1953] 1 QB 361, [1953] 1 All ER 155, CA is authority for the proposition that the landlord may bring an action for damages during the currency of the tenancy for breach of contract, to include claims for dilapidations (ie to buildings and other fixed equipment) and for breaches which affect the land itself: see para 39.9.

4   AHA 1986, s 4(1) provides for the termination of a fixed-term tenancy of two years or more granted on or after 12 September 1984 where the tenant (or surviving joint tenant) dies before the termination date and no effective notice to terminate the tenancy had been given in accordance with s 3(1)(a). The effect of the provision is that in the event of the death occurring more than one year before the contractual term date, the tenancy terminates on that date, whereas if the death occurs less than one year before the contractual term date, the tenancy continues for one year from that date.

5   AHA 1986, s 34(1) specifies the circumstances in which the succession provisions apply.

6   AHA 1986, Sch 12 contains modifications to the Act applicable to tenancies granted on specified dates prior to 1 March 1948.

42.31 It is provided by s 99 that Sch 13 to the AHA 1986 shall have effect: this Schedule contains transitional provisions and savings and exempts from the operation of the Act certain cases current on 18 June 1986, the date of commencement of the Act.

It should also be noted that the AHA 1986 was merely a consolidating statute. If a notice is given pursuant to any provision contained in an earlier repealed statute which could have been given under the AHA 1986 the notice will be good. The mere fact that reference is made in error to the earlier repealed provision when it should have been made to the current AHA 1986 provision will not invalidate the notice[1]. What is more, a number of prescribed forms referring to repealed provisions of the pre-1986 Act statutes have survived for some time after the passing of the AHA 1986. New prescribed forms are still to be made. It remains correct to give notices in the unamended prescribed forms referring to statutory provisions which have, in fact, been repealed[2].

1   For a case where notice was given under the repealed provision of the Agriculture Act 1947, when it should have been given specifying its equivalent provision in the AHA 1948, and the notice was held to be good, see *Ward v Scott* [1950] WN 76. See also *Price v Mann* [1942] 1 All ER 453, CA.

2   For a case where an out-of-date prescribed form was used (in the context of the Landlord and Tenant Act 1954, Part II) and the notice was nevertheless held to be good, see *Morris v Patel* [1987] 1 EGLR 75, 281 Estates Gazette 419, CA.

LETTINGS BY A MORTGAGOR OF AGRICULTURAL LAND

GENERAL

43.1 Lettings by a mortgagor of agricultural land requires consideration of s 99 of the Law of Property Act 1925 (LPA 1925).

It should be noted that, since 1 September 1995, s 99 of the LPA 1925 has been amended by the introduction of s 99(13A) so as to dis-apply the impact of s 99 in relation to mortgages of agricultural land made either before 1 March 1948 or after 1 September 1995[1].

[1]   Agricultural Tenancies Act 1995, s 31. See para 17.18 ff.

THE STATUTORY POWER

43.2 Section 99(1) of the LPA 1925 gives mortgagors the power to make such leases of mortgaged land as are authorised by the section. Leases authorised by the section include:

> 'agricultural or occupation leases for any term not exceeding twenty-one years, or, in the case of a mortgage made after the commencement of this Act, fifty years …'[1].

In order to bind the mortgagee, such leases must satisfy the following additional requirements of sub-ss (5) to (7) inclusive:

(a)   they must be made to take effect in possession not later than 12 months after the date of creation[2];

(b)   they must reserve 'the best rent that can reasonably be obtained, regard being had to the circumstances of the case, but without any fine being taken'[3];

(c)   they must contain a covenant by the tenant for payment of the rent, and a condition for re-entry if the rent is unpaid for a period not exceeding 30 days[4];

(d)   a counterpart must be made and delivered by the tenant[5];

760

(e)   in the case of a lease by a mortgagor, a counterpart must be delivered to the mortgagee within one month after the date of execution 'but the lessee shall not be concerned to see that this provision is complied with'[6].

Section 99(17) of the LPA 1925 provides that the provisions of s 99 'referring to a lease shall be construed to extend and apply, as far as circumstances admit, to any letting, and to an agreement, whether in writing or not, for leasing or letting'.

1   LPA 1925, s 99(3)(i).
2   LPA 1925, s 99(5).
3   LPA 1925, s 99(6).
4   LPA 1925, s 99(7).
5   LPA 1925, s 99(8).
6   LPA 1925, s 99(11).

EXCLUSION OF THE POWER

43.3   In general, the power of the mortgagor to grant such leases and other lettings, so as to make them binding on the mortgagee, can be excluded by the terms of a mortgage document[1]. It is standard practice in institutional mortgages and charge documents, including those used by banks relating to agricultural land, to insert a covenant on the part of the mortgagor not to grant any such leases without the consent of the mortgagee. There is no implication of law that consent will not be unreasonably withheld. A lease or other tenancy granted in breach will not bind the mortgagee. The breach will normally entitle the mortgagee to exercise the usual remedies, including the power of sale.

This general restriction on the power of a mortgagor to grant a tenancy without the consent of the mortgagee has never applied 'in relation to a mortgage made after 1 March 1948 of agricultural land within the meaning of the Agriculture Act 1947'[2]. The fact that the statutory regime operated so as to avoid any restriction upon the letting of agricultural land in the aftermath of the First and Second World Wars is not surprising and is consistent with other provisions applying to agricultural land[3].

For the period from 1 March 1948 until 1 September 1995, in order to establish whether an 'agricultural or occupation lease', granted in breach of a covenant in the mortgage document, is valid, it is necessary first to inquire whether the mortgaged land is 'agricultural land' within the meaning of the Agriculture Act 1947 (AA 1947).

Section 109(1) of the AA 1947 defines 'agricultural land' as:

'... the land used for agriculture which is used for the purposes of a trade or business or which is designated by the Minister for the purposes of this subsection ...'.

No land has been designated by the Minister for this purpose.

43.3 Lettings by a mortgagor of agricultural land

1 LPA 1925, s 99(13).
2 The Agricultural Holdings Act 1986 (AHA 1986), Sch 14 para 12 (consolidating earlier legislation contained in the Agricultural Holdings Act 1948 (AHA 1948) applicable to such mortgages until 1 September 1995.
3 See para 24.1 ff.

43.4 Section 109(3) of the AA 1947 provides that for the purposes of that Act:

'..."agriculture" includes horticulture, fruit growing, seed growing, dairy farming and livestock breeding and keeping the use of land as grazing land, meadow land, osier land, market gardens and nursery ground and the use of land for woodland where that use is ancillary for the farming of land for other agricultural purposes ...'

'Livestock' includes 'any creature kept for the production of food, wool, skins or fur, or for the purposes of its use in the farming of land'[1].

This definition[2] is wide enough to embrace land with agricultural buildings and dwellings, such as a farmhouse and workers' cottages, as well as bare land. Difficult questions may arise where the land is used for agricultural and other purposes, such as the keeping of horses (which are not 'livestock'), sporting activities, the non-agricultural but commercial use of farm buildings, the sub-letting of cottages to non-workers and the like. It is submitted that such land would qualify as agricultural land within the definition provided that its predominant and most important use was agricultural, and the non-agricultural uses were of no great significance. The introduction of a significant non-agricultural use (even if it were the secondary use) would take the land outside the definition.

The other potentially difficult question relates to the time at which the statutory test has been applied. Must the land be 'agricultural land' at the date of the mortgage, the date of the grant of the lease, or at the date when the mortgagee seeks to exercise its rights against the lessee? It is submitted that the statutory power of leasing, and its preservation by the AHA 1986, represent a type of incumbrance on the land, subject to which the mortgagee entered into the mortgage with the mortgagor. It is important that mortgagees should know where they stand when they take a mortgage of land. Does it at that date carry a statutory power of leasing, which cannot be overridden by contractual terms, or does it not? Clearly it would be intolerable if, by a significant change of use, land which was not agricultural at the date of the mortgage could become agricultural, and the mortgagor could thereby acquire a power of leasing which the mortgagee had been unwilling to grant. It is submitted that the land must be 'agricultural land' at least at the date of the mortgage. It is also strongly arguable that the land must also continue to be agricultural land at the date when the lease or tenancy is granted.

1 AA 1947, s 109(3).
2 Note that the definition is the same as that in the AHA 1986.

43.5 This approach is consistent with the decision in *Rhodes v Dalby*[1]. In that case the mortgagor had mortgaged his farm and buildings by legal charge to the lender. Clause 5(b) of the charge contained a covenant not to grant a lease or tenancy in respect of the property without the lender's consent. Subsequently, he allowed a schoolteacher to live in a bungalow on the property under an oral agreement without consent. The lender alleged that the transaction amounted to an unauthorised letting. The judge held, on the facts, that no tenancy had been created; but on the footing that there might have been, the judge considered the effect of LPA 1925, s 99(13) on clause 5(b), and the effect of the provision of para 2 of Sch 7 to the AHA 1948 (which corresponded to Sch 14 para 12 of the AHA 1986 on s 99(13).

In *Rhodes v Dalby*[2], the court considered the argument that the mortgaged property was not 'agricultural land' within the meaning of the AA 1947, apparently because the bungalow was not used in connection with the farming. The judge, after reciting the description of the land contained in the conveyance to the mortgagor, said: 'Those premises appear to me to be, in their entirety, quite clearly an agricultural holding (sic)'[3].

[1]   [1971] 2 All ER 1144.
[2]   [1971] 2 All ER 1144.
[3]   [1971] 2 All ER 1144 at 1146b.

43.6 The judge must have meant 'agricultural land'. Later in his judgment, Goff J (as he then was) again made it clear that he was looking at the property as a whole in relation to LPA 1925, s 99(13) and the exempting provisions of the AHA 1948:

> 'It is said that para 2 does not apply because the tenancy alleged to have been granted by the borrower was exclusively one of non-agricultural land – as indeed it was, the subject matter being a bungalow on the demised premises, and because the person who took it did not require it for agricultural purposes. In my judgment, however, that is not the point.
>
> Paragraph 2 of Sch 7 to the AHA 1948 is concerned with what is comprised in the mortgage, not what part of the premises may be subsequently let. There are, as I see it, no words of severance or limited application. The provision is that section 99(13) shall not have effect in relation to a mortgage, made after the relevant date, of agricultural land ...'[1].

The mixed use of the property clearly did not count against it.

Rhodes v Dalby[2] did not, however, raise the point discussed in para 43.2 above, concerning the time at which the question has to be answered.

[1]   [1971] 2 All ER 1144 at 1147.
[2]   [1971] 2 All ER 1144.

Characteristics of a valid lease

43.7 The decision in *Rhodes v Dalby*[1] also emphasises that a restrictive clause, such as clause 5(b), is overridden by the Agricultural Holdings Acts only in so far as the lease or tenancy granted by the mortgagor complies with all the requirements of LPA 1925, s 99, other than s 99(13).

¹ [1971] 2 All ER 1144.

Agricultural or occupation lease

43.8 Ignoring 'building leases'¹, the only leases authorised by LPA 1925, s 99 are 'agricultural or occupation' leases. The words 'agricultural' and 'occupation' are not defined and must be interpreted according to their ordinary and natural meaning. It is submitted that an 'agricultural lease' is a lease of land which is to be used by the tenant for agricultural purposes. The ordinary and natural meaning of that word 'agricultural', as it is found in s 99, would exclude any of the agricultural activities comprised within the definition of 'agriculture' in the AA 1947. The comments made in para 43.6 above about mixed uses would also apply here.

It is submitted that an 'occupation lease' is a lease granted for the purpose of enabling the tenant to have physical use and occupation of the premises when the lease is executed. It is to be contrasted with a reversionary lease or a 'building lease'. Whether a lease which gives the tenant a right to sub-let is an 'occupation lease' is an open question. The transaction in *Rhodes v Dalby*², if it had amounted to a letting, would have qualified as an 'occupation lease'. It was clearly not an 'agricultural lease'. It is submitted that the word 'occupation' is not restricted to residential occupation. Occupation by the tenant for any purpose is sufficient.

¹ LPA 1925, s 99(3)(iii).
² [1971] 2 All ER 1144.

Term of years and commencement

43.9 The requirements that the term granted must not exceed 50 years¹ and that the lease must be made to take effect in possession not later than 12 months after its date² are self-explanatory.

¹ LPA 1925, s 99(3)(i).
² LPA 1925, s 99(5).

Best rent

43.10 The lease must reserve 'the best rent that can reasonably be obtained, regard being had to the circumstances of the case'¹. This is a clear direction that the landlord must obtain the best rent reasonably obtainable in the open market, not the best rent which it would be reasonable for the chosen tenant to pay the landlord. The best rent reasonably obtainable will be that which a prudent landlord would reserve after taking all reasonable steps to offer the property in the market for letting by tender, auction or private treaty, whichever is appropriate. The best method of marketing will depend upon circumstances of time and place. If the mortgagor intends to let to a favoured individual or company without offering the property on the market, the highest rent reasonably obtainable must be reserved, if the letting is to be immune from attack by the mortgagee. In seeking to set aside a tenancy created by the mortgagor, it might be possible for the mortgagee to argue that the only way of achieving the best rent reasonably obtainable is to carry out a real, competitive marketing exercise: see, for example, *Tomkins v Commission for the New Towns*[2].

In an appropriate case, and certainly in a case where the subject-matter of the letting is a farm business tenancy governed by the Agricultural Tenancies Act 1995, the terms of the letting should provide for rent review. An inadequate reservation of rent could not be cured by s 152 of the LPA 1925[3].

1   LPA 1925, s 99(6).
2   [1989] 1 EGLR 24, CA.
3   See para 44.11.

Covenant to pay rent and proviso for re-entry

43.11 In the case of leases or agreements in writing, there must be both a covenant to pay rent and a proviso for re-entry, entitling the landlord to forfeit the tenancy if the rent remains unpaid for a period not exceeding 30 days[1]. Where the letting is a letting of an agricultural holding, the proviso, in order to be valid for the purposes of the AHA 1986, must also have a built-in delay mechanism, giving the tenant who is threatened with forfeiture sufficient time to make his claim for compensation[2].

In *Pawson v Revell*[3], Jenkins LJ expressed the view, obiter, that an oral letting might have to contain such a covenant and proviso (which in the latter case would, presumably, also have to satisfy the test laid down in the *Million Pigs* case). However, the defect in that case was cured by recourse to s 152(1) and (6) of the LPA 1925 which provides that:

> '(1)   Where in the intended exercise of any power of leasing, whether conferred by an Act of Parliament or any other instrument, a lease (in this section referred to as an invalid lease) is granted which by reason of any failure to comply with the terms of the power is invalid, then – (a) as against the person entitled after the determination of the interest of the grantor to the reversion; or (b) as against any other person, who, subject to any lease properly granted under the power, would have been entitled to the land comprised in the lease; the lease, if it was made in good faith, and the lessee has entered thereunder, shall take effect in equity as a contract for the grant, at the request of the lessee, of a valid lease under the power, of like effect as the invalid lease, subject to such variations as may be necessary in order to comply with the terms of the power ...
>
> ...
>
> (6)   Where a valid power of leasing is vested in or may be exercised by a person who grants a lease which by reason of the determination of the interest of the grantor or otherwise, cannot have effect and continuance according to the terms thereof independently of the power, the lease

> shall for the purposes of this section be deemed to have been granted in the intended exercise of the power although the power is not referred to in the lease'.

1   The LPA 1925, s 99(7).
2   *Parry v Million Pigs Ltd* (1980) 260 Estates Gazette 281. See para 24.26.
3   [1958] 2 QB 360, CA.

43.12 The same point was considered by Goff J in *Rhodes v Dalby*[1] where the judge preferred the view expressed by the editors of *Wolstenholme and Cherry's Conveyancing Statutes*[2] to that tentatively expressed by Jenkins LJ, and he decided the point in favour of the mortgagor.

Where the tenancy granted by the mortgagor is a contract of letting of an agricultural holding under the AHA 1986, it may also be possible to cure any defect in the agreement by recourse to arbitration under s 6 and Sch 1 to the AHA 1986[3]. Schedule 1, paras 3 and 4 empower an arbitrator to make provision for the payment of rent, which should include a covenant or agreement to pay it. Paragraph 8 empowers the arbitrator to insert a proviso for re-entry (a forfeiture clause).

1   [1971] 2 All ER 1144.
2   Vol 1 (12th edn, 1932) Sweet & Maxwell, p 400.
3   See para 23.1 ff.

Delivery of counterpart

43.13 Section 99(8) of the LPA 1925 requires the delivery of a counterpart by the lessee to the lessor, and s 99(11) requires the mortgagor, within one month after making the lease, to deliver it to the mortgagee. Failure to deliver the counterpart would appear to be a breach of this statutory obligation, but it is unlikely to be breach of obligation under the terms of the legal charge, because the charge instrument is unlikely to contain such a requirement. If it does, that breach will activate the mortgagee's various remedies.

The failure of the mortgagor to deliver a counterpart to the mortgagee does not affect the validity of the lease as between lessee and mortgagee, because s 99(11) specifically provides that 'the lessee shall not be concerned to see that this provision is complied with'[1].

In *Rhodes v Dalby*[2], Goff J held that the provisions of s 99(8) and (11) of the LPA 1925 should stand or fall together in their application to oral tenancies. He held that, since there was no counterpart to be delivered to the lessor by the lessee under s 99(8), there was no obligation on the mortgagor to deliver anything in writing to the mortgagee under s 99(11).

1   *Public Trustee v Lawrence* [1912] 1 Ch 789.
2   [1971] 2 All ER 1144 at 1180.

LICENCES CONVERTED INTO TENANCIES BY SECTION 2 OF THE AHA 1986

43.14 Licences of agricultural land, whether they are granted in writing or orally are (with certain exceptions) automatically converted into tenancies from year to year[1]. When s 99 of the LPA 1925 was passed, there was no such provision in the statute book. It was first introduced by s 2 of the AHA 1948.

It is submitted that a licence which (whatever the parties may have intended) takes effect, by virtue of the statute, as a tenancy falls with the meaning of the expression 'any letting' in LPA 1925, s 99(17). It follows, therefore, that it will be authorised in so far as it otherwise complies with the requirements of s 99, including in particular the requirement that the best rent should be reserved. Formal defects such as a failure to include a covenant to pay rent and a proviso for re-entry may, again, be cured by recourse to s 152 of the LPA 1925, or the arbitration machinery in s 6 of and Sch 1 to the AHA 1986. If it does not comply with the requirements of s 99, it will not be binding on the mortgagee, and the grant may amount to a breach of the terms of the mortgage entitling the mortgagee to exercise the usual remedies.

[1]   AHA 1986, s 2.

IMPEACHING A LEASE OR TENANCY GRANTED BY A MORTGAGOR

43.15 Lenders who have lent money to farmers secured by a charge over agricultural land valued for mortgage purposes on the basis of an unincumbered freehold are understandably dismayed to find that, when they come to enforce their security, the property is burdened by a lease or tenancy which has been granted to a third party apparently in full conformity with the provisions of LPA 1925, s 99. In such a case, the lender cannot sell with vacant possession, and the tenanted value of the land is often substantially less than the outstanding amount of the loan. Three different cases have to be considered:

(a)   a lease or tenancy (or licence taking effect as a tenancy pursuant to the AHA 1986) granted in the ordinary course of dealing to a third party who is at arm's length from the mortgagor;

(b)   a lease or tenancy (or licence taking effect as a tenancy pursuant to the AHA 1986) granted in the ordinary course of business to a third party who, although a 'connected party' (for example, a farmer granting a tenancy to his sons/daughters who are to continue farming in partnership), is at arm's length from the mortgagor and is not set up with the purpose of defeating a creditor's claim;

(c)   a lease or tenancy granted by the mortgagor to a company wholly controlled by him, with or without other members of his family, or to a family partnership, or to some other person close to the mortgagor.

In case (c) above, the grant may be made at various times: immediately upon the execution of the mortgage; at sometime thereafter when the mortgagor's finances are still reasonably sound; or when financial trouble is imminent. In the last instance, and perhaps in the others also, the grant is made deliberately in order to protect the mortgagor and his family and their business from eviction if the mortgagee were to attempt to exercise its power of sale.

A number of lines of argument have been advanced by mortgagees to overcome this problem. The starting point is the statutory power of leasing which should be regarded as a type of incumbrance subject to which the land is mortgaged. When agricultural land was offered as security for a loan between 1 March 1948 and 1 September 1995, the lender should have appreciated that the security is, by reason of LPA 1925, s 99, capable of being leased or let, notwithstanding any agreement to the contrary. Thus, when the power of leasing is exercised, it is not a case of the mortgagor 'taking back' something which he has 'given' to the mortgagee. To put it more formally, it is not a case of derogation by the mortgagor from his grant. The existence of the statutory power is something which lenders should bear in mind when they are deciding upon the value to be attached to the security.

For that reason, it is submitted that there should not be any general ground upon which leases or tenancies falling within case (a) above could be attacked. Likewise, unless the mortgagee can establish evidentially that the arrangement under consideration in case (b) above is akin to that in case (c), for example, because it was set up with the intention to defeat the claims of creditors[1], then it would fall to be dealt with as in case (a).

[1] See Insolvency Act 1986, s 423.

Section 423 of the Insolvency Act 1986

43.16 Since the purpose of grants falling within case (c) (at 43.15 above) will almost invariably be to improve the position of the mortgagor or his family or associates against the mortgagee, lenders instinctively raise the question whether the transaction is a fraud on creditors under s 423 of the Insolvency Act 1986 (IA 1986).

This section confers upon the court wide powers to set aside 'transactions entered into at an undervalue', or otherwise to protect the interests of creditors or potential creditors, if the court is satisfied that the transaction was entered into for the purpose of putting assets beyond their reach, or of otherwise prejudicing their interests.

Section 423(2) sets out the scope of these provisions:

'This section relates to transactions entered into at an undervalue; and a person enters into such a transaction with another person if:
(a)   he makes a gift to the other person or he otherwise enters into a transaction on terms that provide for him to receive no consideration;
(b)   he enters into a transaction with the other in consideration of marriage; or
(c)   he enters into a transaction with the other for a consideration the value of which, in money or money's worth, is significantly less than the value, in money or money's worth, of the consideration provided by himself'.

Section 99 and section 423 appear to be mutually exclusive. In order to comply with the requirements of LPA 1925, s 99, the lease or tenancy must be granted 'at the best rent that can reasonably be obtained'. That would seem to preclude the possibility that the grant could at the same time be regarded as a transaction 'entered into at an undervalue' for the purposes of s 423(1). For these purposes, it is not necessary to come to a conclusion as to whether paras (a) (b) and (c) in s 423(1) are intended to stand as an exhaustive definition of the expression 'transactions entered into at an undervalue' or whether they are merely examples. It is, however, to be observed that the test of validity under s 99 is more stringent than the test of 'undervalue' under s 423(1)(c)[1]. Section 99 requires a reservation of the best rent that can reasonably be obtained. If the rent falls below that amount then, subject only to a de minimis rule, the lease will not be authorised. But the grant will not have been made at an undervalue under s 423(1)(c), unless the rent was 'significantly less' than the letting value.

This issue was considered in the *Agricultural Mortgage Corpn plc v Woodward*[2]. The facts were that the mortgagor farmed as a freehold landowner. On 18 April 1989, the mortgagor granted a legal mortgage over his farm to the Agricultural Mortgage Corporation (AMC). The mortgagor fell into arrears and shortly before a deadline set by the AMC to clear those arrears, on 16 April 1992 the mortgagor granted a tenancy of the farm to his wife. It was an annual tenancy terminable upon 12 months notice. The tenancy was protected by the AHA 1986. The annual rent reserved was agreed to represent the full market rent. The AMC sought to set aside the tenancy pursuant to s 423 of the IA 1986.

[1] See *Re M C Bacon Ltd* [1990] BCLC 324. Cf *Hill v Spread Trustee Co Ltd* [2006] EWCA Civ 542, [2007] 1 All ER 1106.
[2] (1994) 70 P & CR 53, [1995] 1 EGLR 1, CA.

43.17 The High Court decided that as the tenancy reserved the full market rent, and this was sufficient for it to satisfy the 'best rent' provision in s 99(6) of the LPA 1925, the tenancy was not one at an undervalue, and accordingly could not be set aside pursuant to s 423 of the IA 1986.

The AMC successfully appealed to the Court of Appeal. The Court of Appeal decided that the tenancy granted to the mortgagor's wife had three intended consequences, additional to any benefit which she received from the tenancy, namely:

(a)   safeguarding the family home;
(b)   the acquisition by the mortgagor's wife of the farming business free from its previous creditors; and
(c)   the benefit of the tenancy surrender value which was of particular importance given that the property was mortgaged.

The Court of Appeal decided that the purpose of the tenancy was to ensure that the AMC did not get vacant possession of the farm and that this was prejudicial to the interests of the AMC. By granting the tenancy, the mortgagor's wife had acquired the benefit of the surrender value which placed her in a 'ransom position' in any future dealings with the mortgagee. If the tenancy was effective, the AMC would have to negotiate with the mortgagor's wife and pay a high price to her before it could obtain vacant possession of the farm and sell it pursuant to the enforcement of its security in order to repay the debt owed to it by the mortgagor.

Some commentators have suggested that the decision of the Court of Appeal in *Agricultural Mortgage Corpn v Woodward*[1] was wrong and that, on the same facts, the House of Lords might reverse the decision, upholding the analysis of the High Court Judge in that case. This view is reinforced by consideration of authorities relating to s 423 outside the particular sphere of its operation in relation to agricultural tenancies[2].

Thus far no case has been pursued, on similar facts, to the House of Lords. That is no doubt in part due to the subsequent decision in *National Westminster Bank plc v Jones*[3]. In that case, the Court of Appeal upheld the High Court, finding on the facts that the rent reserved had failed to reflect sufficiently the marriage or ransom value of the tenancy.

The facts in *National Westminster Bank plc v Jones* are that the mortgagors farmed and owned the freehold of Neuadd Goch Farm. On 31 January 1990, the mortgagors granted a legal mortgage to the bank. In December 1998 a creditor commenced bankruptcy proceedings against one of the mortgagors. On 12 March 1999, the bank made a formal demand of the mortgagors. It was not satisfied. On 12 April 1999, Neuadd Goch Farm Limited (NGFL) was incorporated. The mortgagors were the sole directors and shareholders. The bank was then informed that the mortgagors would be granting a tenancy of the farm to NGFL and transferring the farming assets to NGFL. The bank declined to consent to the transaction. Subsequently, on 27 April 1999, a tenancy and asset sale agreement was entered into between the mortgagors and NGFL. The tenancy was for a term of 20 years from 27 April 1999 requiring the payment of £1,000 per year for the first five years, rising to £4,276 a year for the remaining 15 years (described as the base rent). A further rent was payable at the rate of £17,420 a year to be reviewed to the market rent as at 1 June 2004, 2009 and 2014. NGFL was put under full repairing and insuring obligations. The mortgagors also transferred their agricultural assets to NGFL for the sum of £341,880, payable by 20 equal instalments. The bank sent a letter before action on 12 July 1999. On 17 September 1999 the bank served a further formal demand and four days later appointed receivers. The bank commenced proceedings on 28 September 1999, seeking an order under s 423 of the IA 1986 to set aside the tenancy and the asset sale agreement.

1 (1994) 70 P & CR 53, [1995] 1 EGLR 1, CA.
2 *Phillips v Brewin Dolphin Bell Lawrie Ltd* [2001] UKHL 2, [2001] 1 WLR 143.
3 [2001] 1 BCLC 98, [2000] EGCS 82; affd [2001] EWCA Civ 1541, [2002] 1 P & CR D20.

43.18 The exhaustive judgment of Neuberger J (as he then was) in the High Court in *National Westminster Bank plc v Jones*[1] was followed by the Court of Appeal. The judgment recognised that, provided that the rent reserved by the s 99 tenancy was sufficient to reflect the full marriage or ransom value of the tenancy, the tenancy would be binding on the mortgagee.

It was as a consequence of the decision in *National Westminster Bank v Jones* that another bank sought to establish that the statutory rent review provisions of the Agricultural Tenancies Act 1995 (ATA 1995) made it impossible for the mortgagor to grant a tenancy for a term beyond three years which could sufficiently reflect the full marriage or ransom value. That is the point which was taken in *Barclays Bank plc v Bean*[2].

In *Barclays Bank plc v Bean*, there were the two separate payments reserved by the farm business tenancy. One was the open market rent (subject to a rent review provision) and the other was a premium paid over the course of the terms of the tenancy. The Deputy Judge in the High Court held that both satisfied the statutory definition of rent in s 205(1)(xxiii) of the Law of Property Act 1925. Accordingly, both the market rent and the premium payments fell within the statutory rent review formula of s 13 of the ATA 1995. As a consequence, an arbitrator would reduce the totality of the payments agreed to be made to a single market rent. This caused the transaction as a whole to be one at an undervalue, set aside under s 423[3].

The legal basis for the bank's challenge was removed upon the amendment being made to s 9 of the ATA 1995 pursuant to the RRO 2006[4]. The parties are now free to contract out of the statutory rent review provision[5]. Accordingly, the position will revert to that which applied prior to *Barclays Bank plc v Bean*, namely that it will be necessary to consider in each case (by reference to expert evidence) whether the rent reserved by the s 99 tenancy is sufficient to reflect the marriage or ransom value. If it does, then (based upon the decision in *National Westminster Bank plc v Jones*[6]) the tenancy will be binding upon the mortgagee.

There appears to be a predilection on the part of the courts to favour the mortgagee against the mortgagor in these type of cases[7]. This is reflected by another decision of the Court of Appeal in *Department for Environment, Food and Rural Affairs v Feakins*[8], where the Court of Appeal was prepared to uphold the decision of the High Court setting aside the disposal of the freehold of a farm by a bank pursuant to s 423 of the IA 1986, where the effect of the transaction was to prejudice DEFRA as a creditor with the benefit of a charging order granted by the court.

There remains open the possibility of a challenge to the Court of Appeal decision in *Agricultural Mortgage Corpn v Woodward*[9], in order to establish that it is unnecessary for the rent to reflect sufficiently the marriage or surrender value. It is enough for the rent to be 'the best rent that can reasonably be obtained, regard being had to the circumstances of the case', in accordance with the statutory definition contained in s 99(6) of the LPA 1925.

1   [2001] 1 BCLC 98, [2000] EGCS 82; affd [2001] EWCA Civ 1541, [2002] 1 P & CR D20.
2   [2004] 3 EGLR 71, [2004] 41 EG 152.
3   The case was settled before hearing in the Court of Appeal.
4   Regulatory Reform (Agricultural Tenancies) (England and Wales) Order 2006, SI 2006/2805, effective from 19 October 2006.

[5] See para 9.3 ff.
[6] (2000) EGCS 82, [2001] 1 BCLC 98; affd [2001] EWCA Civ 1541, (2002) 1 P&CR DG 12.
[7] See, for example, *Barclays Bank plc v Eustice* [1995] 1 WLR 1238, CA.
[8] [2005] EWCA Civ 1513, [2005] All ER (D) 153 (Dec).
[9] (1994) 70 P & CR 53, [1995] 1 EGLR 1, CA.

Sham or device

43.19 Any apparently valid legal transaction can be set aside by the courts on the ground that it is a sham. A transaction is a sham if it is designed to give the appearance to the outside world that the parties to it have entered into legal rights and obligations which are different to the legal rights and obligations which they have really undertaken: see the classic definition by Diplock LJ in *Snook v London and West Riding Investments Ltd*[1]. One of the most frequently encountered types of sham in the field of property transactions is the creation of a document which appears to suggest that parties have entered into a licence to occupy a house or flat, whereas in substance what the parties really intended to create was a tenancy[2].

The court may also be prepared to refuse to give effect to the apparent exercise of a legal power if it appears that the power is being exploited for an ulterior purpose[3]. In *Quennell v Maltby*[4], the plaintiff's husband was the mortgagor of a house let to a statutory tenant whose tenancy had been granted in breach of the terms of the mortgage deed. The husband wanted the tenant evicted, and invited the mortgagee bank to exercise its power of sale. The bank refused, and the husband and the bank transferred the mortgage to the plaintiff who then took possession proceedings against the tenant on the ground that the tenancy was not binding upon her. It was held that the court was entitled to, and would, look behind the formal legal relationship of the parties, because a mortgagee would not be granted possession unless it was sought bona fide and reasonably, for the purpose of enforcing the security. Here the mortgagee was acting with the ulterior motive of assisting her husband in obtaining vacant possession and defeating the protection afforded to the tenant by the Rent Acts. In those circumstances she was to be treated as her husband's agent, and the action failed.

[1] [1967] 2 QB 786, CA.
[2] See *Street v Mountford* [1985] AC 809, [1985] 2 All ER 289, HL.
[3] See *Quennell v Maltby* [1979] 1 All ER 568, CA.
[4] [1979] 1 All ER 568, CA.

43.20 Even in the absence of any intention to deceive, or of any ulterior motive, the court will always look at the substance of any legal document, and construe it according to its real effect in law, irrespective of the label which the parties may have attached to it, or the language in which they seek to describe what they have achieved. In *Addiscombe Garden Estates Ltd v Crabbe*[1] where a document which purported to be a grant by a 'licensor' to a 'licensee' or a 'licence' of land was held on a true interpretation to amount to a lease.

Assuming the lease to be genuine, it is submitted that it would be difficult for the mortgagee to argue that the grant is an illegitimate abuse of the statutory power. The case is not at all like that of *Quennell v Maltby*[2]. The view taken by the Court of Appeal in that case was that the right of the mortgagee to take possession and sell is specifically granted for the purpose of enforcing the security, but it was being exploited in that case for reasons wholly unconnected with the enforcement of those rights. By contrast, the statutory power of leasing is given to the mortgagor in the most general terms, and it is submitted it would not be plausible to argue that it was only intended to be exercised in favour of a third party who had no connection with the mortgagor, whatever that may mean. To argue that there are some tenants in whose favour s 99 of the LPA 1925 can operate but others in whose favour it cannot would give rise to the construction of definitions and boundaries which cannot be deduced from the statutory language, and would be impossible to implement in practice.

[1]   [1958] 1 QB 513, [1957] 3 All ER 563.
[2]   [1979] 1 All ER 568, CA.

43.21 The issue of sham was considered by Neuberger J in *National Westminster Bank v Jones*[1] in considerable detail. The court decided that while the admitted artificiality of the lease could be taken into account in deciding whether it was a sham, the mortgagors had not done anything which was intended to give to third parties or the court the appearance of creating legal rights and obligations different from those they actually intended to create. Although subsequent in action on the part of the mortgagors and NGFL could be adduced as evidence of their state of mind when granting the lease, the bank had failed to establish that they were engaged in the necessary pretence[2]. The fact that the mortgagors and NGFL had simply not given thought to their future rights and obligations did not mean that they had no intention of going through with the leasing transactions.

[1]   [2001] 1 BCLC 98, [2000] EGCS 82; affd [2001] EWCA Civ 1541, [2002] 1 P & CR D20.
[2]   See per Sir Thomas Bingham MR in *Belvedere Court Management Ltd v Frogmore Developments Ltd* [1997] QB 858 at 876, CA.

Piercing the veil of incorporation

43.22 A variant upon this argument is to suggest that, where the tenant is a company wholly or predominantly owned or controlled by the mortgagor, the court should pierce the veil of incorporation, and treat the company and the mortgagor as one and the same. It is submitted that as the company is in law a separate entity, and the tenancy granted to it is a genuine lease, there would be no legal ground for disregarding the tenant's separate corporate status.

Again, this issue was considered by Neuberger J in *National Westminster Bank v Jones*[1]. The court held that the fact that NGFL was owned and controlled by the mortgagors afforded no reason for disregarding its separate legal existence. There was no case for piercing the corporate veil[2]. Secondly, even if the mortgagors had taken the farm as joint lessees, their interest would have been quite different from the respective interest in the freehold reversions.

¹   [2001] 1 BCLC 98, [2000] EGCS 82; affd [2001] EWCA Civ 1541, [2002] 1 P & CR D20.
²   See *Ingram v IRC* [2000] 1 AC 293, [1999] 1 All ER 297, HL.

Re-ordering the priorities

43.23 The decisions of the Court of Appeal in *Bristol and West Building Society v Henning*¹ and *Equity and Law Home Loans Ltd v Prestige*² concerned a building society mortgagee's claim for possession of a house which had been mortgaged by a man holding himself out to be the sole legal and beneficial owner. In fact, each of the men lived with a woman partner who, as against the mortgagor, had a beneficial interest in the property. When the building society claimed possession, the partner in each case resisted the claim on the ground that her beneficial interest was binding upon the building society. In each case the Court of Appeal held that the mortgagee's claim took priority, because each partner knew or must be taken to have known of the existence of the mortgage, and must have had the actual or imputed intention that her interest should not take priority over the mortgagee.

It is submitted that it would be difficult to argue that those cases should apply by analogy to the type of lease or tenancy being considered here. The actual intention of both mortgagor and lessee in this type of case is to grant an interest which is fully binding on the mortgagee by force of LPA 1925, s 99 and it would be entirely artificial for the court to hold that, notwithstanding the actual facts, those parties must be taken to have intended otherwise.

¹   [1985] 2 All ER 606.
²   [1992] 1 All ER 909.

Estoppel or trust

43.24 Another way in which the case might be put against the mortgagee and the tenant is that an estoppel operates to prevent them from setting up the tenancy. It is tempting to construct an argument on these lines. When the mortgagor first approached the mortgagee for finance, the whole question of the value to be attributed to the security would have been gone into, and it would have been represented to the mortgagee by conduct if not by actual words that the land was being mortgaged with vacant possession free of incumbrances. Further, the mortgagee might have secured a promise from the mortgagor that he would do nothing in the future to depreciate the value of the security. Alternatively, some promise to that effect might be constructed from his conduct. Therefore, it is argued that, if a tenancy is subsequently granted, the mortgagor at least is estopped from setting it up against the mortgagee.

At this point the argument breaks down. In view of the fact that the relevant provisions of the AHA 1986 override the ability of the mortgagee under s 99(13) of the LPA 1925 to exclude the power of leasing under the terms of the mortgage deed itself, it is submitted that a collateral promise by the mortgagor, outside the terms of the document, cannot have any greater effect. Further, it is difficult to see how the tenant might be estopped, not having been a party to the original promise and having no nexus with the mortgagee. The same analysis applies to the argument that the mortgagor holds the property under an implied trust not to grant leases. The implication of such a trust would seem to be inconsistent with, and the declaration of an express trust overridden by, the AHA 1986.

Conspiracy to defraud or injure

43.25 Fraud unravels everything. If it could be shown that a tenancy purportedly granted under LPA 1925, s 99 resulted from a fraudulent conspiracy by the mortgagor and the tenant, the court would set it aside. It is submitted that such a case could not be made out.

In *Lonrho plc v Fayed*[1] the House of Lords considered the ingredients of the tort of conspiracy. They are set out in the speech of Lord Bridge[2] as follows:

> 'where conspirators act with the predominant purpose of injuring the plaintiff and inflict damage on him, but do not nothing which would have been actionable if done by an individual acting alone, it is in the fact of their concerted action for that illegitimate purpose that the law, however anomalous it may now seem, finds a sufficient ground to condemn their action as illegal and tortious. But when conspirators intentionally injure the plaintiff and use unlawful means to do so, it is no defence for them to show that their primary purpose was to further or protect their own interests; it is sufficient to make their action tortious that the means used were unlawful'.

The granting of a tenancy by a mortgagor does not involve the use of unlawful means to injure the mortgagee. If for any reason the tenancy granted is unlawful (in other words granted outside the scope of the statutory powers), it will be of no effect anyway, and the tort of conspiracy does not arise. The worst that could be said is that the mortgagor and the tenant have, by lawful means, injured the mortgagee. But it is submitted that this would not have been their 'predominant purpose'. Their predominant purpose will have been to secure the position of the mortgagor, and the damage correspondingly suffered by the mortgagee is simply the by-product of that. This is a situation which constantly arises in commercial life. Where business interests conflict, the advancement of the interests of one party is bound to have a detrimental effect upon the interest of the other; but none of that is sufficient to amount to the tort of conspiracy.

[1] [1991] 3 All ER 303.
[2] *Lonrho plc v Fayed* [1991] 3 All ER 303 at 309J.

43.26 Much less is there a criminal conspiracy. At the root of the crime of conspiracy to defraud is an intention 'by dishonesty to deprive a person of something which is his or to which he would be or might be entitled ...'[1].

First, it is submitted that the conduct in question could not be described as dishonest. The test of 'dishonesty' for the purposes of the criminal law was laid down by the Court of Appeal (Criminal Division) in *R v Ghosh*[2]. A jury can convict a defendant of dishonesty but only if it is satisfied that:

(1) the conduct in question would be regarded by reasonable persons as dishonest; and

(2) the defendant was aware of that fact.

It is submitted that the valid exercise of a statutory power cannot be characterised as dishonest simply because it was being exploited to further the interests of one party to a commercial arrangement against the interest of the other.

Second, and in any event, when a mortgagor is validly exercising his statutory power of leasing he is not depriving the mortgagee 'of something which is his or to which he is or would be or might be entitled ...' The subject of the mortgage, being agricultural land, is land which, by virtue of LPA 1925, s 99, is capable of being burdened by a lease or tenancy binding on the mortgagee from the moment it is mortgaged. The mortgagee cannot therefore argue that he has an entrenched right to vacant possession which is being unlawfully infringed.

¹   *Scott v Metropolitan Police Comr* [1975] AC 819, per Viscount Dilhorne at 1039.
²   [1982] QB 1053. Also see *Meretz Invetments NV v ACP Ltd* [2006] EWHC 74 (Ch), [2007] Ch 197.

Want of registration

43.27 A further question is whether an agreement for leasing or letting might be void against the mortgagee on the ground that it has not been registered. Under s 99(17) of the LPA 1925 agreements for lease or letting are put on the same footing as leases themselves. It is submitted that the question of registration does not arise, save for the statutory overlay of the Land Registration Act 2002 (LRA 2002)¹. Subject to the LRA 2002, the doctrine of registration is applicable to cases where there are competing interests to property which have been granted at different times. In certain circumstances, the interest granted earlier in time will only prevail against the later interest if it is registered as a charge or other interest in whichever register is appropriate, depending upon whether the land is registered or unregistered land. That doctrine has no relevance here. What is being considered here is an interest granted subsequent to the mortgage. Leases or tenancies granted in exercise of the statutory power after the date of the mortgage are as much binding on mortgagee as leases or tenancies granted with their express consent and approval. They are an incumbrance on the land which the mortgagee has authorised or is to be taken as having authorised.

The legal analysis of the position may have its origin in the days when mortgages took effect by way of demise, so that the grant of a lease by the mortgagor became a sub-demise made by the mortgagor as agent for the mortgagee. Similarly, the mortgagee is entitled, by virtue of LPA 1925, s 99, to grant leases which bind the mortgagor. Historically, that too may date back to the time when the mortgagee had an estate in the land. The modern system of mortgage by way of legal charge possesses by analogy all the legal attributes of mortgage by way of demise. The doctrines of notice and registration have no part to play in this relationship.

[1]   See paras 43.28 and 3.38 ff.

Land Registration Act 2002

43.28 Following the commencement of the LRA 2002 on 13 October 2003, the general rule is that a lease or sub-lease granted for more than seven years granted out of either an unregistered or registered title is itself registerable as a new leasehold interest at the Land Registry[1].

[1]   See para 3.38 ff.

43.29 A further issue for the parties in relation is that in order for the Land Registry to register the lease, stamp duty and land tax (SDLT) must be paid on the rent and the appropriate certificate obtained from HM Revenue and Customs. If the parties delay in registering the lease, and do not pay SDLT within three months of the date of grant, then there is a penalty[1].

[1]   The penalty is £100 which rises to £200 if the SDLT paid is more than three months late, plus interest. It the Land Transaction Return is more than a year late a penalty may be levied which may be equal to the tax that may be due. Failure to submit an SDLT return is also a criminal offence.

Appointment of a receiver

43.30 Section 99(19) of the LPA 1925 provides that the statutory power of leasing given to the mortgagor shall become exercisable 'after a receiver of the income of the mortgaged property or any part thereof has been appointed by a mortgagee under his statutory power', by the mortgagee in place of the mortgagor. The statutory power to appoint a receiver arises under s 101(1) of the LPA 1925[1]:

'A mortgagee, where the mortgage is made by deed, shall, by virtue of this Act, have the following powers ...:

...

(iii)   a power, when the mortgage money has become due, to appoint a receiver of the income of the mortgaged property, or any part thereof'.

Accordingly, if the mortgagee appoints a receiver, the mortgagor loses the power to grant a tenancy which would be binding on the mortgagee.

[1]   See also s 109(1) of the LPA 1925 which postpones the statutory right to appoint a receiver until the time when the power of sale has arisen.

Section 4

DISPUTE RESOLUTION

Section 4

DISPUTE RESOLUTION

Contents

Chapter 44

GENERAL INTRODUCTION TO DISPUTE RESOLUTION

THE AGRICULTURAL TENANCIES ACT 1995

44.1 This section of the book is concerned with the remedies under the Agricultural Tenancies Act 1995 (ATA 1995) and the Agricultural Holdings Act 1986 (AHA 1986) available to the landlord or tenant for breaches of the tenancy agreement and the dispute resolution procedures under both Acts.

It covers the landlord's remedies in the event of non-payment of rent and the remedies available to either the landlord or the tenant for breach of a repairing covenant.

During a farm business tenancy, other than by the operation of a break clause in his favour, the landlord's only method of ending the lease is by forfeiture for a breach of covenant in the lease or upon breach of a condition in the lease. Although peaceable re-entry is an option for the landlord[1], the courts will be the usual venue for resolving issues as to the landlord's right to forfeit and the tenant's right to relief[2].

The courts also provide the forum for other disputes relating to the enforcement of covenants contained in a farm business tenancy whether, for example, it is a party seeking specific performance of an obligation or a party requiring an injunction to restrain a breach of covenant[3]. Alternatively, the landlord might employ a straightforward rent action in the court to recover unpaid rent[4].

Some disputes might be resolved by a form of 'self-help'. For example, the lease might reserve to the landlord the right to enter the holding and to carry out repairs which the tenant has failed to execute[5]. The most likely area of 'self-help' to arise in practice will be where the landlord relies upon the ancient remedy of the law of distress to levy distraint upon the tenant's assets to recover unpaid rent lawfully due[6].

Resolving other disputes under the ATA 1995 is something of a minefield. It was said of the Housing Act 1988, when it introduced wholesale reform of the residential landlord and tenant sector, that: 'in thickets such as these, unaided, few sheep will safely graze'[7]. The main problem for the sheep in relation to dispute resolution under the ATA 1995 is that, when faced with the multi-limbed fingerpost, it is difficult for them to find the grazing.

[1]   See Ch 13.
[2]   See Ch 13.
[3]   See Ch 13.
[4]   See Ch 45.
[5]   See Ch 45.
[6]   See Ch 45.
[7]   Megarry RE and Arden A, *The Rent Acts*, Vol 3 (11th edn, 1989) Sweet & Maxwell, Preface.

44.2 The ATA 1995 provides two methods for determining disputes: arbitration and alternative dispute resolution. The Act contains limited provisions relating to arbitration. It employs the code generally used in arbitrations now contained in the Arbitration Act 1996 and previously in the Arbitration Acts 1950 to 1979[1]. The Arbitration Act 1996 (AA 1996) provides a restatement and improvement of the law relating to arbitration pursuant to an arbitration agreement[2] repealing and, where appropriate, re-enacting the Arbitration Acts 1950 to 1979.

The provisions of Pt I of the AA 1996[3] governing arbitrations pursuant to arbitration agreements apply to every arbitration under an enactment (a 'statutory arbitration'), whether the enactment was passed or made before or after the commencement of the AA 1996[4], subject to certain adaptations and exclusions[5], if and to the extent that the provisions of Pt I of the AA 1996 are not inconsistent with the provisions of the enactment or with any rules or procedure authorised or recognised by it or are excluded by any other enactment[6].

The general law of arbitration is based upon a combination of statute[7] and substantial case law. It is beyond the scope of this chapter to analyse the evolution of the AA 1996 and its relationship with existing case authority[8]. It is the differences in the procedures which apply under the ATA 1995 and the AA 1996 that are highlighted in this section of the book.

[1]   Pt I of the Arbitration Act 1950 and the entirety of the Arbitration Act 1979 are repealed by the Arbitration Act 1996.
[2]   An 'arbitration agreement' means an agreement to submit to arbitration present or future disputes (whether they are contractual or not): see the AA 1996, s 6(1).
[3]   Sections 1–84.
[4]   The AA 1996 commenced on 31 January 1997.
[5]   AA 1996, ss 95–98.
[6]   AA 1996, s 94(1) and (2).
[7]   The Arbitration Acts 1950 to 1979 until the repeal of Pt I of the Arbitration Act 1950 and the entirety of the Arbitration Act 1979 upon the enactment of the AA 1996 on 13 June 1996.
[8]   For analysis of the AA 1996, see Robert Merkin, *Arbitration Act 1996*, (3rd edn, 2005) LLP.

44.3 The second statutorily prescribed method for resolving disputes contained in the ATA 1995 is alternative dispute resolution provisions which allow the parties to employ whatever mechanism they agree upon to determine any dispute between them[1].

1   ATA 1995, s 29, save in the case of improvements arbitrations and compensation arbitrations, see para 47.4.

THE AGRICULTURAL HOLDINGS ACT 1986

Resolving disputes

44.4 This section of the book examines the remedies available to a landlord or a tenant and the dispute resolution procedures under the AHA 1986. The Act provides three methods of resolving disputes between landlords and tenants, namely:

(a)   the Agricultural Land Tribunal;
(b)   arbitration; and
(c)   the courts.

Practitioners should beware. It is of paramount importance both that the appropriate forum for resolution of the dispute is selected and the machinery specified for pursuing the claim is strictly followed. The selection of the wrong forum is usually fatal to the ability of the landlord or tenant to bring the claim or defend it.

The AHA 1986 does not provide for alternative dispute resolution. There is nothing to stop a landlord or tenant trying to settle disputes through without prejudice negotiations or agreeing in their tenancy agreement to refer disputes to an expert[1] where they are not compulsorily referable to arbitration by the terms of the AHA 1986.

1   For expert determination, see 48.6.

Agricultural Land Tribunals (ALT)

44.5 The ALTs were created by the Agriculture Act 1958 and are not to be confused with the Lands Tribunal. Their spheres of activity extend beyond landlord and tenant matters to include drainage disputes between neighbours under the Land Drainage Act 1991[1].

The most important matters for which the ALTs have jurisdiction are:

(a)   the giving or withholding consent to the operation of a notice to quit[2];
(b)   certificates of bad husbandry;
(c)   determining applications for succession to tenancies on death or retirement[3];
(d)   determining whether a holding is a market garden[4];
(e)   approving long-term improvements where the landlord refuses to do so or directing the landlord to carry out improvements[5];
(f)   directing a landlord to provide or repair fixed equipment[6].

1   These provisions fall outside the scope of this book.
2   Excluding notices to quit to which AHA 1986, s 26(2) and (3) and Sch 3 apply.
3   Under Pt IV of the AHA 1986.
4   See para 20.21.

789

Arbitration

44.6 Most disputes, particularly those governed by practical agricultural considerations, are compulsorily referable to arbitration under the AHA 1986.

These disputes in the main¹ comprise the following:

(a)   disputes as to the operation of s 2 in relation to any agreement;
(b)   securing a written tenancy agreement under s 6;
(c)   varying or modifying repairing obligations under ss 7 to 9;
(d)   revising the rent under ss 12 and 13;
(e)   game damage under s 20;
(f)   notice to remedy and notices to quit under Cases A, B, D or E of Sch 3;
(g)   all the claims arising on or out of the termination of the tenancy under s 83.

Arbitrations under the AHA 1986 have been fundamentally altered by the changes implemented by the Regulatory Reform (Agricultural Tenancies) (England and Wales) Order 2006 (RRO 2006)². Prior to the commencement of the RRO 2006³, arbitrations were conducted in accordance with the statutory code set out in Sch 11 to the AHA 1986. The RRO 2006 repealed Sch 11 and with the exception of two procedural points contained in the AHA 1986⁴, arbitrations under that Act are now⁵ conducted in accordance with the AA 1996, replicating the provisions of arbitrations under the ATA 1995.

Where the arbitrator was appointed before 19 October 2006, the arbitration continues to be conducted under the former Sch 11 code⁶.

¹   See also, the AHA 1986, ss 14 and 15.
²   SI 2006/2805.
³   Commencement date – 19 October 2006: SI 2006/2805, art 1(1).
⁴   See para 47.14ff.
⁵   With effect from 19 October 2006.
⁶   SI 2006/2805, art 10. Reference should be made to the eighth edition of this book for commentary in relation to the former Sch 11 code.

The courts

44.7 In all cases, except where the AHA 1986 expressly provides for a dispute to be governed by the ALT or by arbitration, the jurisdiction of the courts is preserved.

The courts have guarded their inherent jurisdiction¹, but reliance upon it, where it has been ousted by statute, is fatal². Clear and express provisions ousting the court's jurisdiction are necessary to have that effect³.

The following disputes are determined by the courts:

(a)   the issue as to whether the AHA 1986 applies to a tenancy;

(b)   issues of construction on the terms of the tenancy agreement;
(c)   assessment of damages for breach of a repairing covenant in a tenancy agreement;
(d)   determining the validity of a notice to quit, for example where fraud is alleged;
(e)   forfeiture proceedings; and
(f)   other possession proceedings.

In addition to this list, the courts have jurisdiction over all other claims where jurisdiction is not expressly allocated by the AHA 1986[4].

1   See for example *Goldsack v Shore* [1950] 1 KB 708, [1950] 1 All ER 276; *Paddock Investments Ltd v Lory* (1975) 236 Estates Gazette 803; *Rous v Mitchell* [1991] 1 All ER 676, [1991] 1 WLR 469. Cf *Jones v Pembrokeshire County Council* [1967] 1 QB 181, [1966] 1 All ER 1027 and *Kirby v Robinson* [1965] EGD 236.
2   See *Magdalen College, Oxford v Heritage* [1974] 1 All ER 1065, [1974] 1 WLR 441 and *Harding v Marshall* (1983) 267 Estates Gazette 161, CA.
3   *Goldsack v Shore* [1950] 1 KB 708, [1950] 1 All ER 276.
4   AHA 1986, s 97.

Chapter 45
REMEDIES

INTRODUCTION

45.1 The purpose of this chapter is to provide a guide to the remedies available to a landlord in relation to the non-payment of rent or breach of other term or condition of the tenancy by the tenant and to a tenant for breach by the landlord of a term or condition of the tenancy under both the Agricultural Holdings Act 1986 (AHA 1986) and the Agricultural Tenancies Act 1995 (ATA 1995). The aim is not to provide a detailed analysis of the remedies themselves. Where, in relation to the operation of the AHA 1986 or the ATA 1995, it has been necessary to consider a remedy in detail (such as notices to quit under the AHA 1986[1]), that has already been dealt with earlier in this book.

[1] See Ch 27ff.

NON-PAYMENT OF RENT

Generally

45.2 The remedies which a landlord may consider include:

(a) suing the tenant for payment;
(b) suing people other than the present tenant;
(c) demanding rent from any sub-tenant;
(d) threatening bankruptcy if the tenant is an individual;
(e) threatening winding-up if the tenant is a company;
(f) forfeiture; and
(g) levying distress.

Additionally, in the case of the AHA 1986, the landlord may serve a notice to pay, as a preliminary step to a Case D(a) notice to quit, if the tenant does not pay rent within two months of the service of a notice to pay[1].

There are a number of points which the landlord may wish to consider in choosing the appropriate remedy. These include the following:

(i) Does the landlord want possession?
(ii) Could the holding easily be re-let?
(iii) If the holding could easily be re-let, would it be to a better covenant, would it be on better rent or would the other terms be as favourable to the landlord?
(iv) The physical state of the premises, as well as the current market, may be a relevant factor.
(v) Does the landlord want to retain the current tenant?
(vi) Are there any previous tenants to be sued?
(vii) Are there are any sureties to be sued?
(viii) Is the holding or any part of it sub-let? If so, has the tenant been receiving rent from the sub-tenant and not paying it to the landlord?
(ix) Is the right to forfeit available? For example, is there a valid forfeiture clause and has the landlord waived the breach?
(x) Are there goods on the holding enabling the landlord to levy distress?
(xi) Is there a danger that there will be insufficient goods to levy distress, thereby losing the landlord the right to forfeit?
(xii) In relation to the AHA 1986, is the notice to pay route the obvious answer?
(xiii) Is there is a set-off issue?
(xiv) Is any remedy affected by, or likely to be affected by, the impact of an insolvency procedure?

[1]   See para 31.28.

The present tenant or other people?

45.3 In commercial leases, the matrix of liability between the present tenant, the original tenant, assignees and sureties is often much more relevant than in relation to agricultural holdings and tenancies[1]. As a consequence, it is beyond the scope of this book to consider that matrix in detail.

[1]   See *Woodfall: Landlord and Tenant* (Looseleaf edn, 1994) Sweet & Maxwell.

The original tenant

45.4 An original tenant is prima facie liable under the terms of the tenancy for the entirety of the term[1], regardless of whether he later assigns the tenancy to a third party.

Even if the tenant does not expressly covenant 'for himself and his successors in title', this will be implied by s 79 of the Law of Property Act 1925[2].

In some cases, the original tenant may be released from liability upon assignment, either because of an agreement with the landlord or by reason of statute.

[1]   *Walker's Case* (1587) 3 Co Rep 22a.
[2]   Save in relation to tenancies to which the Landlord and Tenant (Covenants) Act 1995 applies, see para 45.5.

45.5   The original tenant will usually benefit from a statutory release if the tenancy was one granted after 1 January 1996, when the Landlord and Tenant (Covenants) Act 1995 (LT(C)A 1995) came into force. The exceptions are:

(a)   where the tenancy is granted pursuant to an agreement or an option (including a right of pre-emption) entered into before 1 January 1996; or

(b)   where it is granted pursuant to a court order made before 1 January 1996; or

(c)   where it is an overriding lease granted pursuant to s 19 of the Landlord LT(C)A 1995 in relation to a tenancy which is not a tenancy protected under the LT(C)A 1995[1].

It should be noted that the LT(C)A 1995 may apply in relation to a tenancy where a variation of an existing tenancy is such so as to cause an implied surrender and re-grant[2].

The original tenant's liability will include an obligation to pay interest on late payments, but only if the tenancy agreement reserves the right to charge interest. The landlord may claim interest on late payment under s 35A of the Supreme Court Act 1981, but the court is only likely to award interest against the original tenant from the date on which it is claimed from the original tenant by the landlord and not from when the rent became due[3].

As to the effect of the death of the original tenant, generally, if a contracting party dies, he is not discharged from contractual obligations which continue to affect his estate[4]. Accordingly, if the original tenant has died, his estate is probably liable by privity of contract for the duration of the term of the tenancy agreement[5]. The general rule may be excluded by an express provision in the tenancy agreement[6].

[1]   LT(C)A 1995, ss 5, 11.
[2]   LT(C)A 1995, s 1(5). As to surrender and re-grant, see para 33.5ff.
[3]   *Estates Gazette Ltd v Benjamin Restaurants Ltd* [1995] 1 All ER 129.
[4]   Law Reform (Miscellaneous Provisions) Act 1934.
[5]   *Youngmin v Heath* [1974] 1 All ER 461.
[6]   *Kennewell v Dye* [1949] Ch 517.

45.6   As to the bankruptcy of the original tenant, the law is not entirely clear as to whether this discharges the original tenant from liability. It is considered that the original tenant's liability should be the subject of a proof of debt in his bankruptcy (as a contingent liability) and that if the landlord fails to prove in the bankruptcy, the debt is discharged[1].

The original tenant's obligations will be limited to those applying to the terms of the original contract. The original tenant will not be liable for variations agreed between the landlord and a subsequent assignee[2].

Upon a disclaimer of the tenancy by a liquidator or a trustee in bankruptcy[3] for an assignee, the original tenant will remain liable, but is entitled to seek an order vesting the tenancy in him or some other party, for example, a sub-tenant or mortgagee[4].

¹   *Hardy v Fothergill* (1888) 13 App Cas 351, HL; *James Smith & Sons (Norwood) Ltd v Goodman* [1936] Ch 216, CA.

²   *Friends Provident Life Office v British Railways Board* [1995] 2 EGLR 55. Cf *Selous Street Properties Ltd v Oronel Fabrics Ltd* (1984) 270 Estates Gazette 643; *GUS Property Management Ltd v Texas Homecare Ltd* [1993] 27 EG 130.

³   See para 45.60ff.

⁴   See para 45.64.

Assignees

45.7 The general rule is that an assignee is only directly liable to the landlord during the period of the assignee's 'ownership' of the tenancy[1]. The reason for this rule is that the assignee did not contract with the landlord and accordingly there is no 'privity of contract', merely 'privity of estate'.

Although an assignee is not directly liable for breaches of the terms of the tenancy committed by a previous tenant[2], the position is complicated where the breach is a continuing breach, such as disrepair or unlawful user. The assignee will be liable to the landlord, even though the breach first occurred prior to the assignee's ownership[3].

In relation to tenancies entered into before the LT(C)A 1995 came into force on 1 January 1996, in the absence of a contract imposing a greater liability, an assignee will not be liable in relation to all of the terms of the tenancy. This is because liability depends upon 'privity of estate' and accordingly the assignee is only liable upon the terms in the tenancy which relate to that estate or which are said to 'touch and concern' the land[4].

In relation to tenancies created after 1 January 1996, the assignee will normally be bound by all of the tenant's covenants in the tenancy without making any distinction between those which 'touch and concern' the land and those which do not[5].

Although it may rarely be relevant in the context of agricultural holdings and agricultural tenancies, the right to pursue an intermediate tenant, in respect of arrears of rent, is subject to the requirement that he should be served with a statutory notice within six months of the sums becoming due[6].

¹   *Valliant v Dodemede* (1742) 2 Atk 546. Also see *Avonridge Property Co Ltd v Mashru* [2005] UKHL 70, [2006] 01 EG 100 and *Edlington Properties Ltd v J H Taylor & Co Ltd* [2006] EWCA Civ 403, 2006] 22 EG 178.

²   LT(C)A 1995, s 23(1).

³   *Middlegate Properties Ltd v Bilbao (Caroline Construction Co Ltd)* (1972) 24 P & CR 329. Note the principle that an assignee's damages are capped to those of an assignor: see *Dawson v Great Northern and City Railway Co* [1905] 1 KB 260; *Bizspace (NE) Ltd v Baird Corporatewear Ltd* [2007] 17 EG 174.

⁴   *Spencer's Case* (1583) 5 Co Rep 16a.

⁵   LT(C)A 1995, s 3.

⁶   LT(C)A 1995, s 17.

45.8 *Remedies*

Sureties

45.8 A surety has been characterised as a 'quasi-tenant'[1]. The liability of a surety will depend upon the terms of the contract. There is a distinction between a contract of 'guarantee' and one of 'indemnity'. The latter is described as a 'primary' liability, whereas the former is a 'secondary' liability. In practice, surety covenants are often drafted as a hybrid, the obligation initially being that of a guarantee, but taking effect as an indemnity in the event that the tenant is discharged of liability[2]. The distinction is probably of no practical significance while the tenancy continues[3].

Usually the following rules apply in respect of sureties:

(a)   a surety is liable for rent as reviewed;

(b)   the liability of the surety continues for the period of any statutory continuation of a tenancy after the expiry of the original term[4];

(c)   the liability ceases upon forfeiture[5];

(d)   the surety's contract is with the landlord only and therefore he is not liable to the original tenant[6];

(e)   the liability of the surety continues if the landlord sells the freehold reversion[7];

(f)   whether the surety's obligations continue beyond the death of the surety depends upon the contractual terms[8];

(g)   if the surety becomes bankrupt, the landlord can prove in his bankruptcy[9]; and

(h)   if the tenancy is disclaimed by a liquidator or trustee in bankruptcy[10], the tenancy does not end entirely. It does so only to relieve the insolvent tenant from liability. The position of a guarantor (and a former tenant) is unaffected[11]. The surety may be required to take a new lease[12].

1   *P & A Swift Investments v Combined English Stores Group plc* [1989] AC 632, HL.
2   *General Produce Co v United Bank Ltd* [1979] 2 Lloyd's Rep 255.
3   *NRG Vision Ltd v Churchfield Leasing Ltd* [1988] BCLC 624.
4   *Junction Estates v Cope* (1974) 27 P & CR 482.
5   *Associated Dairies Ltd v Pierce* (1982) 43 P & CR 208; *Capital and City Holdings Ltd v Dean Warburg Ltd* (1988) 58 P & CR 346, CA.
6   This point is not without difficulty: see *Becton Dickinson UK Ltd v Zwebner* [1989] QB 208.
7   *P & A Swift Investments v Combined English Stores Group plc* [1989] AC 632, HL.
8   *Holme v Brunskill* (1878) 3 QBD 495, CA.
9   *Re Houlder* [1929] 1 Ch 205.
10   See para 45.60ff.
11   *Hindcastle Ltd v Barbara Attenborough Associates Ltd* [1995] QB 95, [1994] 4 All ER 129; *Basch v Stekel* (2001) 81 P & CR DG 1; *Scottish Widows plc v Tripipatkul* [2003] EWHC 1874 (Ch), [2004] 1 P & CR 461.
12   *Active Estates Ltd v Parness* [2002] EWHC 893 (Ch), [2002] 3 EGLR 13, [2002] 36 EG 147.

The present tenant

45.9 It should first be noted that rent is not 'due' until the tenant has been given written notice of the landlord's address for service of documents and notices, as required by s 48 of the Landlord and Tenant Act 1987[1].

The next question is to ensure that the rent is due. Most tenancy agreements provide for rent to be paid in advance, but if the tenancy agreement is silent, the rent is due in arrears.

The landlord also has to consider whether the tenant is entitled to make deductions from the rent and whether this explains non-payment[2]. Deductions may be made:

(a)   as authorised by the tenancy agreement;
(b)   as authorised by statute;
(c)   where the tenant has a claim to set off[3].

---

[1]   *Dallhold Estates (UK) Property Ltd v Lindsey Trading Properties Inc* [1994] 1 EGLR 93, CA. See para 31.29.
[2]   *Televantos v McCulloch* [1991] 1 EGLR 123, CA.
[3]   See para 45.10.

Set off

45.10 Originally, any deduction from rent by way of set off could only be in respect of a liquidated sum. The law has developed so that an unliquidated claim for damages for breach of covenant by the landlord can also be set off. For example, if the landlord has failed to fulfil his repairing obligations and the tenant has expended money undertaking the necessary work. The landlord's obligation to repair normally arises only on notice and therefore he should have been given notice of the disrepair. Importantly, unless the tenant relies on the equitable doctrine of set off[1], the tenant must have paid the sums that he seeks to set off[2].

As noted above, pursuant to the provisions of the LT(C)A 1995, a landlord is not able to recover any fixed charge (including rent) from a former tenant or his surety unless, within six months of the liability becoming due, he has served on that person a notice informing him that the liability is now due and that the landlord intends to recover that amount and any interest payable[3].

There is no right of set off if the tenant has not carried out and paid for the repairs but, in some circumstances, the tenant may be entitled to rely upon the doctrine of equitable set off, if he has a cross-claim for damages against the landlord. In *British Anzani (Felixstowe) Ltd v International Marine Management (UK) Ltd*[4], the tenant was able to set off £1m, following the landlord's failure to repair two warehouses, against £540,000 rent arrears, even though the landlord's obligation was not contained in the tenancy agreement, but in a prior agreement to construct the warehouses and lease them to the tenant. To rely upon this doctrine, the tenant must show the close connection between his counterclaim and the landlord's claim for rent.

Unless the tenant can show that the tenancy agreement has been frustrated[5], the tenant is not entitled to deduct rent simply because the premises have been damaged or are partially unusable. If the landlord's failure to comply with the

45.10 *Remedies*

covenants in the tenancy agreement are so serious so as to constitute a
repudiation of the tenancy agreement, then the tenant may rely upon the
equitable doctrine of set off[6].

1   See para 31.32.
2   *Lee-Parker v Izzet* [1971] 3 All ER 1099.
3   LT(C)A 1995, s 17. See *Scottish & Newcastle plc v Raguz* [2006] EWHC 821 (Ch), [2006]
     4 All ER 524.
4   [1980] QB 137, [1979] 2 All ER 1063.
5   *National Carriers Ltd v Panalpina (Northern) Ltd* [1981] AC 675, HL.
6   *Hussein v Mehlman* [1992] 32 EG 59. In that case, a failure by the landlord to comply
     with a repairing obligation was held to allow the tenant to vacate the property and return
     the keys to the landlord, bringing the tenancy to an end by the tenant's acceptance of the
     landlord's breach repudiating the tenancy. It is submitted that such cases would be rare,
     even more rare in relation to agricultural holdings.

45.11 A clause in the tenancy agreement may expressly prohibit any set off.
This is the case in relation to the standard Royal Institution of Chartered
Surveyors (RICS) precedent for a farm business tenancy. Such a clause will
prevent the tenant lawfully relying on a set off, although the tenant may still
have a counterclaim for the landlord's breach of covenant. Such a clause does
not operate contrary to the provisions of the Unfair Contract Terms Act 1977
and accordingly will be enforceable[1]. A provision in a tenancy agreement that
the rent should be paid 'without any deduction' was found not to be sufficient
to exclude by implication a tenant's equitable right of set off[2].

1   *Electricity Supply Nominees Ltd v IAF Group Ltd* [1993] 1 WLR 1059.
2   *Connaught Restaurants Ltd v Indoor Leisure Ltd* [1994] 1 WLR 501, CA. Cf *Famous
     Army Stores v Meehan* [1993] 1 EGLR 73, [1993] 09 EG 111.

Limitation

45.12 No action for arrears of rent may be brought six years after the date on
which the arrears fell due[1].

1   Limitation Act 1980, s 19. Also see para 45.10 in respect of the operation of s 17 of the
     LT(C)A 1995.

Court proceedings

45.13 It is beyond the scope of this book to provide details of the court
procedure arising in relation to a claim by a landlord for the recovery of rent
against either the present tenant or any other party liable to the landlord. It
should be noted that, since 1 July 1991, the county court has unlimited
jurisdiction and accordingly the landlord may elect between the county court
or the High Court. If the landlord decides to issue proceedings in the county
court, the claim may be commenced in any court, no matter where the tenant
resides or where the cause of action arose. The tenant may, however, apply to
transfer the action to another court and the court will subsequently give
consideration as to the appropriate trial venue.

798

An action for the recovery of rent through the court may be appropriate where:

(a)   distress[1] is unavailable;

(b)   there is a prospect of a dispute, causing the statutory demand route to be inappropriate[2];

(c)   there is no sub-tenancy and therefore no opportunity to recover rent from a sub-tenant[3];

(d)   forfeiture is unavailable or undesirable because the landlord does not wish to recover possession of the holding[4];

(e)   in the case of an AHA 1986 tenancy, the landlord does not wish to recover possession of the holding and accordingly the notice to pay route is inappropriate[5];

(f)   the landlord merely wishes to recover the rent through the range of enforcement methods available in the event that the landlord obtains a judgment in the High Court or the county court.

[1]   See Ch 26 and para 45.15.
[2]   See para 45.16ff.
[3]   See para 45.15.
[4]   See para 45.21.
[5]   See para 31.28ff.

Rent from a sub-tenant

45.14 Section 6 of the Law of Distress Amendment Act 1908 enables the landlord to serve a notice on a sub-tenant requiring payment of any rent due from the sub-tenant to be made direct to the landlord until the tenant's arrears are cleared. The service of the notice creates a relationship of landlord and tenant between the head landlord and the sub-tenant. Payments pursuant to such a notice are credited against the liability of the sub-tenant to his immediate landlord, the tenant[1].

Alternatively, s 6 of the Law of Distress Amendment Act 1908 enables the landlord to levy distress against the sub-tenant in relation to the defaulting tenant's arrears of rent.

The appointment of a receiver by the mortgagee of the defaulting tenant will not affect the ability of the landlord to claim rent from a sub-tenant under s 6 of the Law of Distress Amendment Act 1908. The landlord will have priority over a chargee of book debts and/or rent[2].

[1]   Law of Distress Amendment Act 1908, s 3.
[2]   *Rhodes v Allied Dunbar Pension Services Ltd* [1989] 1 All ER 1161, CA.

Distress

45.15 The landlord may decide to levy distress against the tenant's possessions in respect of the non-payment of rent. This subject has already been dealt with in this book in respect of the AHA 1986[1] and the ATA 1995[2].

Aside from the obvious impact which the levy of distress has, beyond the attempted recovery of the rent itself, on the landlord and tenant relationship, the other point to note is that the levy of distress represents an acknowledgement by the landlord of the continuation of the tenancy agreement. Accordingly, it will operate as a waiver for the general law of forfeiture[3].

There is no reason why a landlord should not levy distress and, if that is not wholly successful, follow it with a notice to pay in respect of a letting under the AHA 1986[4]. Waiver does not operate in this case.

1 See Chapter 26.
2 See para 9.30.
3 See para 13.6ff.
4 See para 31.28ff.

Bankruptcy/Liquidation

45.16 If there is a debt exceeding £750, the landlord may serve a statutory demand for payment on any person liable. If payment is not made within 21 days of service of the statutory demand, the landlord may proceed to issue either a bankruptcy or winding-up petition[1].

It is beyond the scope of this book to deal with this subject in detail, but the following is intended to assist the landlord in making his choice of remedy.

1 Insolvency Rules 1986, SI 1986/1925, Pts 4 and 6.

Liquidation

45.17 The most common ground for the court ordering the winding up (ie liquidation) of a company is that it is unable to pay its debts. The Insolvency Act 1986 (IA 1986) sets out the circumstances where a company is deemed unable to pay its debts[1]. A winding-up petition may be granted even though one of the deemed circumstances does not apply, if there is evidence before the court that the company is in fact unable to pay its debts[2].

The court will deem a company unable to pay its debts if, following service of a statutory demand in respect of an amount over £750, where the demand requires the company to pay the debt or to secure or compound it to the reasonable satisfaction of the creditor, the company fails to do so within 21 clear days[3].

The statutory demand must be in the prescribed form[4]. It must be in writing, dated and signed by the creditor or his authorised agent[5]. It must be served at the registered office of the company.

The tenant may challenge the demand by applying to the court for an injunction to restrain the presentation of a winding-up petition or, if the petition has been presented, to restrain its advertisement and any further proceedings[6]. Such an application must be made to the Companies Court. The tenant must show some prospect of defeating the claim and that it is solvent. If the tenant does not challenge the statutory demand, or a challenge fails, the court may proceed to order the liquidation of the company. The landlord will then deal with the liquidator in respect of the recovery of the debt due and the issue of possession of the holding[7].

1   IA 1986, s 123.
2   *Taylor's Industrial Flooring Ltd v M & H Plant Hire (Manchester) Ltd* [1990] BCC 44.
3   Excluding the day of service of the demand and the day of presentation of the winding-up petition. The court may extend the time for compliance: Insolvency Rules 1986, r 4.3.
4   Insolvency Rules 1986, Pt 4.
5   *Re Horne* [2000] 4 All ER 550, CA.
6   *Re a Company* [2006] EWHC 3436 (Ch), [2007] BPIR 1.
7   See para 45.44. Note the limited circumstances in which a director may be personally liable: see IA 1986, s 216; *First Independent Factors and Finance Ltd v Churchill* [2006] EWCA Civ 1623, [2007] BCC 45.

Bankruptcy

45.18 A creditor may present a bankruptcy petition against an individual tenant in respect of a debt which the debtor appears either to be unable to pay or to have no reasonable prospect of being able to pay[1]. The IA 1986 defines 'inability to pay' and provides that a debtor will be deemed unable to pay a debt if the debt is payable immediately and the creditor to whom the debt is owed has served on the debtor a statutory demand requiring him to pay the debt and the demand has not been complied with nor set aside[2].

The statutory demand must be in the prescribed form[3]. It must be in writing, dated and signed by the creditor or his authorised agent[4]. The debt must be for a liquidated sum of at least £750 and must be unsecured[5].

A secured creditor may petition for a bankruptcy order if either he relinquishes his security or he values the security and seeks to petition only in respect of the unsecured balance[6].

1   IA 1986, s 267(2)(c).
2   IA 1986, s 268.
3   Insolvency Rules 1986, Sch 4, Form 6.1 or, if a judgment has been obtained, Form 6.2.
4   *Re Horne* [2000] 4 All ER 550.
5   IA 1986, s 267.
6   *Re a Debtor (No 64 of 1992)* [1994] 2 All ER 177.

45.19 The demand may include interest if the debt is due pursuant to a written agreement (as will be the case in relation to a tenancy agreement) and is payable at a certain time[1]. Interest may be claimed for the period from that date to the date of the bankruptcy order[2].

An overstatement of the sum due will not invalidate the statutory demand, unless the amount actually due has been paid[3]. The court also has discretion to deal with formal deficiencies in relation to the demand[4].

The creditor must 'do all that is reasonable to bring the statutory demand to the debtor's attention and, if practicable, to cause personal service to be effected'[5]. In the case of agricultural property, this will invariably involve personal service on the tenant. If this is not possible, and the tenant is evading service, there is no process such as substituted service which would apply in court proceedings. Guidelines have been issued as to the steps which a landlord should take in these circumstances[6].

1. Judgments Act 1838, s 17.
2. Insolvency Rules 1986, r 6.113.
3. *Re a Debtor (No 490 – SD –1991)* [1992] 2 All ER 664.
4. *Re a Debtor (No 1 of 1987, Lancaster)* [1989] 2 All ER 46.
5. *Practice Note (No 4 of 1986)* [1987] 1 All ER 604.
6. *Practice Note (No 4 of 1986)* [1987] 1 All ER 604.

45.20 If the statutory demand is not complied with within 21 clear days of service, the creditor may issue a bankruptcy petition at the court. Unlike the position in relation to a statutory demand in respect of a company tenant, the individual tenant does not need to apply to the court for an injunction to restrain the presentation of the bankruptcy petition. Instead, there is a procedure whereby the debtor may, within 18 days of service of the statutory demand, apply to the court to set aside the demand on the following grounds:

(a) the debtor has a counterclaim, set off or cross-claim that equals or exceeds the debt specified in the statutory demand;
(b) the debt is disputed on substantial ground;
(c) the creditor holds some security in respect of the debt and either the demand does not state the nature of the security and the value of it, and claims only the balance that is unsecured, or the court is satisfied that the value of the security equals or exceeds the amount of the debt;
(d) the court is satisfied on other grounds that the demand should be set aside[1].

The court will not usually set aside a statutory demand:

(i) because it overstates the sum due or because part of the debt is disputed, unless the debtor has suffered prejudice or the actual sum due or the undisputed part of the debt is paid[2]; or
(ii) because of technical defects in the demand[3].

1. Insolvency Rules 1986, r 6.5(4).
2. *Re a Debtor (No 490 – SD –1991)* [1992] 2 All ER 664.
3. *Re a Debtor (No 1 of 1987, Lancaster)* [1989] 2 All ER 46.

Forfeiture

45.21 The general law of forfeiture has been dealt with in this book in some detail in relation to the ATA 1995[1] and also in respect of the AHA 1986[2].

In the context of the landlord's choice of remedies, the following points should be noted:

(a) Forfeiture is only available if there is a forfeiture clause relating to the breach of term or condition of the tenancy in issue[3].

(b)   In the case of an AHA 1986 tenancy, this is subject to the additional requirement that, for the forfeiture clause to be valid, it must be drafted in a manner which does not preclude the tenant's exercise of his statutory rights to compensation[4].

(c)   If (as in the case of rent), the breach complained of is a 'once and for all' breach[5], it is capable of being waived[6].

(d)   The acceptance of rent will operate as an act of waiver[7]. Rent cannot be accepted 'without prejudice'[8].

[1]   See Ch 13.
[2]   See para 33.8ff.
[3]   See para 13.3.
[4]   *Parry v Million Pigs Ltd* (1980) 260 Estates Gazette 281. See para 24.26.
[5]   See para 13.9.
[6]   See para 13.6ff.
[7]   See para 13.7.
[8]   *Segal Securities Ltd v Thoseby* [1963] 1 QB 887. See para 13.7. As to the appropriation of rent in the case of a voluntary arrangement of the tenant, see *Thomas v Ken Thomas Ltd* [2006] EWCA Civ 1504, [2007] 01 EG 94.

TENANT'S BREACH OF COVENANT OTHER THAN NON-PAYMENT OF RENT

Generally

45.22   The remedies which a landlord may consider include:

(a)   an injunction or specific performance;
(b)   suing for damages;
(c)   self help;
(d)   forfeiture.

Additionally, in the case of the AHA 1986, the landlord may serve:

(i)   a notice to remedy to do works followed by a Case D notice to quit[1]; or
(ii)   a notice to remedy not requiring the carrying out of works followed by a Case D notice to quit[2]; or
(iii)   a Case E notice to quit[3]; or
(iv)   a Case F notice to quit, in the case of the tenant's insolvency[4].

As in the case of a tenant's non-payment of rent, there are a number of factors which the landlord may wish to consider in choosing the appropriate remedy[5].

It is beyond the scope of this book to deal with the remedies of specific performance, injunction and damages in detail[6]. What follows is a summary of these remedies to assist the practitioner in choosing the appropriate remedy[7].

[1]   See para 31.44ff.
[2]   See para 31.70ff.
[3]   See para 31.76ff.
[4]   See para 31.88.
[5]   See para 45.2.

6   Reference should be made to the standard law of contract text books.
7   In relation to disrepair, reference should also be made to Ch 10.

Specific performance

45.23 Specific performance is a discretionary remedy, born of the Court of Chancery, to provide a remedy where the remedy at law is inadequate. It follows that where damages provide the injured party with full compensation, the court will not, as a general principle, order specific performance.

Conversely, the court will not automatically grant specific performance even where damages are insufficient. Specific performance is a discretionary remedy. It may be refused on grounds of laches[1], mistake or hardship which would arise to the defendant.

Until 1858 the court did not have power to award damages in lieu of specific performance. It was necessary for the aggrieved party to commence separate proceedings in a common law court. The Chancery Amendment Act 1858[2] provided that where the court had jurisdiction to grant an injunction or an order for specific performance, it could (if it thought fit) award damages 'either in addition to or in substitution for' the injunction or order for specific performance.

The current jurisdiction of the court to award damages is contained in s 50 of the Supreme Court Act 1981 which provides:

> 'Where the Court of Appeal or the High Court has jurisdiction to entertain an application for an injunction or specific performance, it may award damages in addition to, or in substitution for, an injunction of specific performance'.

Damages in substitution are not available if the court has no jurisdiction to specifically enforce the contract. Damages will not be awarded if there is a defence to specific performance. Damages may be awarded if specific performance is refused pursuant to the court's discretion, for example, due to laches.

One question which does arise in practice in relation to agricultural holdings is whether a landlord can obtain specific performance of a tenant's repairing obligation. Often the landlord will first consider relying upon the law of forfeiture[3] or (in the case of an AHA 1986 tenancy) a notice to remedy to do works[4]. Alternatively, if the tenancy agreement contains a provision allowing the landlord to enter and carry out works, the landlord may choose that route for enforcement. Nevertheless, in an exceptional case, the court will order specific performance of the tenant's repairing obligation[5]. In *Rainbow Estates Ltd v Tokenhold Ltd*, it was relevant to the court's exercise of its jurisdiction that the tenancy agreement did not contain a power for the landlord to enter to carry out works or a valid forfeiture clause[6].

1   Negligence or unreasonable delay in asserting or enforcing a right.
2   Better known as Lord Cairns' Act.
3   See para 45.21.
4   See para 31.44ff.

⁵   *Rainbow Estates Ltd v Tokenhold Ltd* [1999] Ch 64, [1998] 2 EGLR 34. Cf *Hill v Barclays* (1810) 16 Ves 402.
⁶   See para 10.12ff.

Injunction

45.24 An injunction is the usual remedy to enforce a breach of a negative prohibition in a tenancy agreement. It directs a party to do the specified act or, more usually, to refrain from doing it. There are prohibitory, mandatory, *quia timet* and interim injunctions:

(a)   a prohibitory injunction is an order not to do something[1];
(b)   a mandatory injunction is an order to do something[2];
(c)   a *quia timet* injunction can be ordered before any breach occurs on the basis that the claimant has a well founded fear of an imminent breach. This will usually be a prohibitory injunction, although it may be mandatory[3];
(d)   an interim injunction is granted in the early stages of proceedings before a final determination of the substantive issues by the court. The court will consider the balance of convenience[4].

¹   *Lumley v Wagner* (1852) 1 De GM & G 604; *Medina Housing Association Ltd v Case* [2002] EWCA Civ 2001, [2003] 1 All ER 1084.
²   *Esso Petroleum Co Ltd v Kingswood Motors (Addlestone) Ltd* [1974] QB 142; *Hemingway Securities v Dunraven* [1995] 1 EGLR 61. Cf *Law Debenture Trust Corpn v Ural Caspian Oil Corpn Ltd* [1995] Ch 152.
³   *Redland Bricks Ltd v Morris* [1970] AC 652, HL. Damages in lieu is available: *Leeds Industrial Co-operative Society v Slack* [1924] AC 851, HL; *Hooper v Rogers* [1975] Ch 43, CA.
⁴   *American Cyanamid Co v Ethicon Ltd* [1975] AC 396, [1975] 1 All ER 504.

45.25 As in the case of specific performance, it is a discretionary remedy. Again, laches (delay), mistake or hardship to the defendant may result in an injunction not being granted. The conduct of the parties will also be relevant. Maxims, such as the need for the party applying for the injunction to have 'clean hands' will be relevant. Also, estoppel may apply[1].

Also, as in the case of specific performance, the court may decline to order an injunction if damages is an adequate remedy. Section 50 of the Supreme Court Act 1981 applies equally to injunctions[2].

Generally a landlord may enforce his right to enter premises to carry out repairs by injunction[3].

When damages is an adequate remedy, an injunction may not be granted even where this operates to 'licence future wrongs'[4].

¹   *Hazel v Akhtar* [2001] EWCA Civ 1883, [2002] 2 P & CR 17.
²   See para 45.23.
³   *Jervis v Harris* [1996] Ch 195, [1996] 1 EGLR 78; *Janet Reger International Ltd v Tiree Ltd* [2006] EWHC 1743 (Ch), [2006] PLSCS 15. Cf *Creska Ltd v London Borough of Hammersmith and Fulham* [1998] 3 EGLR 35.
⁴   *Jaggard v Sawyer* [1995] 1 WLR 269 at 285. Also see, *Regan v Paul Properties Ltd* [2006] EWCA Civ 1391, [2007] Ch 135, [2006) 46 EG 210.

Damages in lieu

45.26 The court's exercise of its discretionary power to award damages in lieu of an injunction is guided by the decision of A L Smith LJ in *Shelfer v City of London Electric Lighting Co*[1]:

> '... it may be stated as a good working rule that—
> (1)   if the injury to the plaintiff's rights is small
> (2)   and is one which is capable of being estimated in money
> (3)   and is one which can be adequately compensated by a small money payment
> (4)   and the case is one in which it would be oppressive to the defendant to grant an injunction
> then damages in substitution for an injunction may be given'.

A key feature of the 'good working rule' is the oppressiveness test, which is applied at the date that the injunction is sought.

> 'The outcome of any particular case usually turns on the question: would it in all the circumstances be oppressive to the defendant to grant the injunction to which the plaintiff is prima facie entitled?[2]

In relation to breaches of leasehold covenants, the starting point for the measure of damages is the cost to the landlord of performing the covenant breached.

The court also has jurisdiction to award damages in lieu based upon 'lost opportunity'. This jurisdiction emerged in relation to restrictive covenant cases in respect of freehold land[3]. It may also be relevant in the case of landlord and tenant disputes.

In the context of damages in lieu, it may also be possible to recover quasi-restitutionary damages, ie a share in profits, based upon the House of Lords decision in *A-G v Blake*[4]. In that case, Lord Nicholls stated:

> 'The *Wrotham Park* case, therefore, still shines, rather as a solitary beacon, showing that in contract as well as tort damages are not always narrowly confined to recoupment of financial loss. In a suitable case damages for breach of contract may be measured by the benefit gained by the wrongdoer from the breach. The defendant must make a reasonable payment in respect of the benefit he has gained ...

> Circumstances do arise when the just response to a breach of contract is that the wrongdoer should not be permitted to retain any profit from the breach ...

> When, exceptionally, a just response to a breach of contract so requires, the court should be able to grant the discretionary remedy of requiring a defendant to account to the plaintiff for the benefits he has received from his breach of contract ...

> When the circumstances require, damages are measured by reference to the benefit obtained by the wrongdoer. This applies to interference with property rights. Recently, the like approach has been adopted to breach of contract.

> The court will have regard to all the circumstances, including the subject matter of the contract, the purpose of the contractual provision which has been breached, the circumstances in which the breach occurred, the consequences of

the breach circumstances in which relief is being sought. A useful general guide, although not exhaustive, is whether the plaintiff had a legitimate interest in preventing the defendant's profit-making activity and, hence, in depriving him of his profit'.

It is submitted that this approach to the measure of damages fits more naturally with damages in lieu of an injunction or specific performance, rather than damages or breach of contract.

It should also be noted that mitigation of loss does apply where a landlord is seeking damages for breach of contract[5].

1   [1895] 1 Ch 287 at 322. Also see *Lunn Poly Ltd v Liverpool & Lancashire Properties Ltd* [2006] EWCA Civ 430, [2006] 25 EG 210.
2   Per Millett LJ in *Jaggard v Sawyer* [1995] 1 WLR 269. Followed in *Midtown Ltd v City of London Rail Property Co Ltd* [2005] EWHC 33 (Ch), [2005] 1 EGLR 65.
3   *Wrotham Park Estate Co v Parkside Homes Ltd* [1974] 1 WLR 798; *Jaggard v Sawyer*, [1995] 1 WLR 269; *Bracewell v Appleby* [1975] Ch 408; *Gafford v Graham* (1998) 77 P & CR 73.
4   [2001] 1 AC 268. Also see *Amec Developments v Jury's Hotel Management* [2001] 1 EGLR 81; *Experience Hendrix LLC v PPX Enterprises Inc* [2003] EWCA Civ 323, [2003] 1 All ER (Comm) 830; *WWF v World Wrestling Federation* [2007] EWCA Civ 286, [2007] All ER (D) 13 (Apr).
5   *Reichman v Beveridge* [2006] EWCA Civ 1659, [2007] 08 EG 138.

Damages generally

45.27 The points made above in relation to damages in lieu of an injunction or specific performance apply generally in relation to a claim for damages for breach of contract arising from a breach of a term or condition of a tenancy agreement[1].

In relation to claims for disrepair, a landlord is circumscribed by the Landlord and Tenant Act 1927[2]. Section 18 restricts the landlord to damages not exceeding the amount by which the value of the freehold reversion is diminished by reason of the breach[3].

1   *Niazi Services Ltd v Van Der Loo* [2004] EWCA Civ 53, [2004] 1 WLR 1254, [2004] 1 EGLR 62.
2   Note that the provisions of the Leasehold Property (Repairs) Act 1938, requiring a landlord to obtain leave of the court before commencing proceedings does not apply to a farm business tenancy under the ATA 1995 (ATA 1995, Schedule para 8) or an agricultural holding under the AHA 1986 (AHA 1986, Sch 14 para 17).
3   See para 10.12ff. Also see *Eyre v Rea* [1947] KB 567.

Damages for trespass

45.28 An issue which arises in practice is the measure of damages recoverable by the landlord in relation to unlawful occupation, whether because the tenant unlawfully holds over or otherwise.

Trespass is actionable per se. A landowner may recover nominal damages for trespass even if no loss has been suffered. This will be the case where a landowner is wrongfully deprived of his land but suffers no direct loss[1]. Alternatively, damages may be substantial[2].

Mesne profits and damages for use and occupation are terms which are often used interchangeably[3]. There is a difference, as explained by Lloyd LJ in *Ministry of Defence v Ashman*:

> 'As to mesne profits they are, as I understand it, simply damages for trespass recoverable against a tenant who holds over after the lawful termination of the tenancy. A claim for mesne profits is thus to be distinguished from an action for use and occupation where the tenant holds over with the consent of his landlord. The former action is grounded in tort, the latter in quasi-contract'[4].

In *Ministry of Defence v Ashman*[5], the tenant had paid a subsidised rent. The landlord claimed market rent as the appropriate measure of damages, although there was no evidence that it would have let the property on the open market. The Court of Appeal found that the Ministry had elected for restitutionary damages, but determined that the market rent was not payable because it was not the value of the land to the trespasser. The value was limited to that sum which the defendant would have had to pay for suitable local authority housing.

In *A-G v Blake*[6], Lord Nicholls identified that, as a general rule:

> 'Damages are measured by the plaintiff's loss, not the defendant's gain. But the common law, pragmatic as ever, has long recognised that there are many commonplace situations where a strict application of this principle would not do justice between the parties. The compensation for the wrong done to the plaintiff is measured by a different yardstick. A trespasser who enters another's land may cause the land owner no financial loss. In such a case damages are measured by the benefit received by the trespasser, namely, by his use of the land'.

The assessment of the quantum of damages for trespass depends upon whether the landowner elects to claim damages for actual loss suffered or restitutionary damages. The election does not need to be made before bringing a claim, but before judgment[7].

The danger for a trespasser is that the court will assess the measure of damages to include a loss of opportunity (for example, to develop the holding) or, in an exceptional case, on account of profits[8].

---

1   *Swordheath Properties Ltd v Tabet* [1979] 1 WLR 285, CA.
2   As to the award of aggravated damages where the trespass is accompanied by high-handed, insulting or oppressive behaviour, see *Horsford v Bird* [2006] UKPC 3, [2006] 15 EG 136.
3   *Dean and Chapter of the Cathedral and Metropolitan Church of Christ Canterbury v Whitbread plc* [1995] 1 EGLR 82.
4   [1993] 2 EGLR 102 at 102. Also see *Phillips v Homfrey* (1871) 6 Ch App 770; *A-G v De Keyser's Royal Hotel Ltd* [1920] AC 508, HL; *Morris v Tarrant* [1971] 2 QB 143.
5   [1993] 2 EGLR 102. Followed in *Ministry of Defence v Thompson* [1993] 2 EGLR 107, CA. Also see, *Inverugie Investments Ltd v Hackett* [1995] 1 WLR 713, PC; *A-G v Blake* [2001] 1 AC 268.
6   [2001] 1 AC 268 at 279.
7   *Ministry of Defence v Ashman* [1993] 2 EGLR 102, CA.
8   *Experience Hendrix LLC v PPX Enterprises Inc* [2003] 1 All ER 830; *Severn Trent Water Ltd v Barnes* [2004] EWCA Civ 570, [2004] 2 EGLR 95.

Action for double rent

45.29 Section 1 of the Landlord and Tenant Act 1730 enables a landlord to recover double the yearly value of the premises from a tenant who holds over after the landlord has demanded possession in writing. Section 1 provides:

> 'For securing to lessors and landowners their just rights and to prevent frauds frequently committed by tenants, in case any tenant or tenants for any term for life, lives or years, or other person or persons, who are or shall come into possession of any lands, tenements, or hereditaments, by, or from or under, or by collusion with such tenant or tenants, shall wilfully hold over any lands, tenements, or hereditaments, after the determination of such term or terms, and thereof, by his or their landlords of lessors, or the person or persons to which the remainder or reversion of such lands, tenements, or hereditaments shall belong, his or their agent or agents thereto lawfully authorised; then and in such case such person or persons holding over shall, for and during the time he, or she, and [sic] they shall so hold over. Or keep the person or persons entitled out of possession of the said lands, tenements and hereditaments, as aforesaid, pay to the person or persons kept out of possession, their executors, administrators of assigns, at the rate of double the yearly value of the lands, tenements and hereditaments so determined, for so long time as the same are detailed, to be recovered in any of His Majesty's courts of record, by action of debt ...'.

An action is maintainable against 'any tenant or tenants for any term for life, lives or years'. It applies to a tenant for a fixed term, a tenancy from year to year but not to other periodic tenancies. The tenant must hold over wilfully. He must hold over in the absence of a genuine belief that he is justified in doing so. If a tenant holds over after a notice to quit has been given he does not hold over wilfully if he thinks the notice was bad. In *French v Elliott*[1] it was said:

> 'It has been held that "wilfully" means "contumaciously", but I can see no reason why the old English word "wilfully" does not exactly express the true meaning of the statute. The statute does not mean that a tenant is a contumacious tenant. It deals only with the moment of time when the tenancy comes to an end. At that moment of time a tenant may say: "I shall stay on. I think I have a right to do so". His staying on is not wilful. On the other hand, a tenant might say: "I will stay on, although I know I have no right to do so". That is wilful, and well illustrates the now sometimes forgotten distinction between "I shall" and the instant "I will".'

It is submitted that a valid notice to quit will be sufficient notice for the purposes of s 1 of the Landlord and Tenant Act 1730.

Where a tenant gives a notice to quit, an action for double rent may be maintained under s 18 of the Distress for Rent Act 1737 which provides:

> 'In case any tenant or tenants shall give notice of his, her or their intention to quit the premises by him, her or them holden, at a time mentioned in such notice, and shall not accordingly deliver up the possession thereof at the time in such notice contained, then the said tenant, tenants, his, her or their executors or administrators shall from thenceforward pay to the landlord or landlords, lessor or lessors, double the rent or sum which he, she or they should otherwise

have paid, to be levied, sued for or recovered; all such double rent or sum shall continue to be paid during all the times such tenant shall continue in possession aforesaid'.

The 1737 Act is of wider application than the 1730 Act because it applies to all types of tenancies. Together they provide a single code[2].

1   [1959] 3 All ER 866, [1960] 1 WLR 40.
2   *Oliver Ashworth (Holdings) Ltd v Ballard (Kent) Ltd* [2000] Ch 12, [1999] 2 All ER 791, CA.

Self-help

45.30   There is no common law entitlement for a landlord to be able to enter onto a holding to carry out works. An express reservation in the tenancy agreement is required[1].

There is an implied licence for the landlord to enter and repair where the landlord covenants to repair[2].

The costs of any works carried out by the landlord may be recovered as a debt[3]. The works must be repair and not improvements[4].

1   *Regional Properties Ltd v City of London Real Property Co Ltd* (1979) 257 Estates Gazette 64.
2   *Saner v Bilton* (1878) 7 Ch D 815. The right is also implied in relation to a weekly tenancy, although it is difficult to imagine where such a tenancy would arise in relation to an agricultural holding: *Mint v Good* [1957] 1 KB 517, CA.
3   *Hamilton v Mantell Securities Ltd* [1984] Ch 266, [1984] 1 All ER 665.
4   *Yeoman's Row Management Ltd v Bodentien-Meyrick* [2002] EWCA Civ 860, [2002] 2 EGLR 39, [2002] 34 EG 84.

Forfeiture

45.31   The general law of forfeiture has been dealt with in this book in some detail in relation to the ATA 1995[1] and also in respect of the AHA 1986[2].

In the context of the landlord's choice of remedies, the following points should be noted:

(a)   forfeiture is only available if there is a forfeiture clause relating to the breach of term or condition of the tenancy in issue[3];

(b)   in the case of an AHA 1986 tenancy, this is subject to the additional requirement that, for the forfeiture clause to be valid, it must be drafted in a manner which does not preclude the tenant's exercise of his statutory rights to compensation[4];

(c)   if (as in the case of rent), the breach complained of is a 'once and for all' breach[5], it is capable of being waived[6];

(d)   the acceptance of rent will operate as an act of waiver[7]. Rent cannot be accepted 'without prejudice'[8].

(e)   waiver of the right to forfeit does not operate as a waiver to a landlord's right to damages[9].

1   See Ch 13.
2   See para 33.8.
3   See para 13.3.
4   *Parry v Million Pigs Ltd* (1980) 260 Estates Gazette 281. See para 24.26.
5   See para 13.9.
6   See para 13.6ff.
7   See para 13.9.
8   *Segal Securities Ltd v Thoseby* [1963] 1 QB 887.
9   *Stephens v Junior Army and Navy Stores Ltd* [1914] 2 Ch 516, CA.

RECTIFICATION

45.32 It is beyond the scope of this book to consider in detail the remedy of rectification. It is sometimes relevant in respect of tenancy agreements and landlord and tenant relationships.

Rectification is an equitable remedy causing the correction of a written document if, by mistake, it does not correctly record the true agreement between the parties[1]. Critically, what is rectified is not a mistake in the transaction itself, but a mistake in the way in which that transaction has been expressed in writing[2].

Rectification is a remedy of last resort. A court will first try to establish the true construction of a document in order to seek to give it contractual effect. Alternatively, the court will consider assistance provided by a collateral contract. The latter does not apply in relation to a contract for the sale or disposition of land governed by the Law of Property (Miscellaneous Provisions) Act 1989[3].

In *Weeds v Blaney*[4] the court identified two kinds of rectification:

> 'There are two kinds of rectification. One is where both parties are under a common mistake – that is, both of them believe that the concluded instrument expresses their common intention in regard to a particular provision or aspect of the agreement – but both of them are mistaken in that the instrument on its proper construction does not carry out that common intention. Both contribute to the mistake. The one party who sends forward a draft containing the mistake. The other party who returns it without correcting it ... The other kind of rectification is where there is a unilateral mistake by one party which is known to the other party. Such as where a party puts forward a contract or instrument for signature, but himself makes a mistake in the drafting of it – maybe a negligent mistake: and the other party spots the mistake – and turns a blind eye to it. He sees that it will or may operate to his advantage and so says nothing about it, and signs the contract as it stands. Such conduct on his part savours of sharp practice: and the court will rectify the instrument so as to correct the mistake.
>
> In both those kinds of rectification there is a negligent mistake by the plaintiff or his solicitors, but that is no bar to rectification. It is indeed the very reason why rectification is granted'.

In general the court will not order rectification unless there has been a mistake in the written document which was common to all of the parties.

1 *Frederick E Rose (London) Ltd v William H Pim Jnr & Co Ltd* [1953] 2 QB 450, CA.
2 *Racal Group Services Ltd v Ashmore* [1995] STC 1151, CA.
3 *Wright v Robert Leonard Developments* [1994] EGCS 69, CA.
4 [1978] 2 EGLR 84 at 85.

TENANT'S REMEDIES

45.33 The remedies which a tenant may consider include:

(a) suing for damages;
(b) applying for an injunction or an order for specific performance;
(c) set off.

The principles which apply to injunctions, specific performance and damages in lieu are the same as those which apply where a landlord seeks the above remedies[1].

There are no statutory restrictions upon the usual contractual measure of damages[2].

As to set off, claims arising from the same contract may be set off[3]. There is no general rule that a tenant may withhold rent where the landlord is in breach of covenant. A tenant may execute repairs and recoup the sum from future payments of rent[4]. It is dangerous for the tenant to do so, particularly when faced with a notice to pay rent under the AHA 1986[5].

1 See paras 45.23, 45.24 and 45.26.
2 See para 10.12ff.
3 *British Anzani (Felixstowe) Ltd v International Marine Management (UK) Ltd* [1980] QB 137, [1979] 2 All ER 1063.
4 *Lee-Parker v Izzet* [1971] 1 WLR 1688; *Asco Developments and Newman v Lowes Lewis and Gordon* (1978) 248 Estates Gazette 683. Also see para 10.14.
5 See para 31.32ff.

THE EFFECT OF INSOLVENCY

Background

45.34 The law of insolvency was comprehensively reviewed by a committee chaired by Sir Kenneth Cork[1]. The Cork Report led to the amendment and consolidation of the law which is now contained in the IA 1986 and the Insolvency Rules 1986.

The first substantial changes to the Insolvency Act were incorporated in the Enterprise Act 2002 EnA 2002), which received royal assent on 7 November 2002 and, so far as the corporate insolvency provisions in Pt 10 of the EnA 2002 are concerned, came into force on 15 September 2003[2].

The EnA 2002 shifts the balance away from individual insolvency procedures and the protection of the rights of particular groups of creditors (in particular, the Crown), in favour of a standard form administration procedure and the treatment of all creditors as equally as possible. The EnA 2002 also substantially changed the provisions relating to bankruptcy. In particular, the period of bankruptcy was reduced from three years to one year[3].

As regards corporate insolvency, the EnA 2002:

(a) removes the ability of lenders to appoint administrative receivers, save in limited circumstances;

(b) provides for a prescribed part of floating charge assets to be made available to unsecured creditors;

(c) abolishes Crown preference;

(d) introduces a streamlined administration procedure (which also applies to partnership administrations); and

(e) requires liquidators to seek sanction from the court or the creditors' committee in order to commence proceedings for voidable transactions and wrongful trading.

[1]   The Cork Report 1982, Cmnd 8558.
[2]   See Dennis and Fox, 'The New Law of Insolvency', The Law Society, 2003.
[3]   EnA 2002, s 269.

Types of insolvency

Voluntary arrangements

45.35 Voluntary arrangements are a procedure enabling a company[1], partnership[2] or individual[3] to settle with their creditors without a formal liquidation, bankruptcy or administration order.

[1]   IA 1986, ss 1–7.
[2]   The Insolvent Partnerships Order 1994, SI 1994/2421.
[3]   IA 1986, ss 252–263.

Administrative receiver

45.36 Until the EnA 2002 came into force on 15 September 2003, floating charge holders of a company (secured by way of debenture) were entitled to appoint an administrative receiver to protect the assets charged to the lender. The administrative receiver is entitled to manage the business and, if necessary, to realise the assets.

Since 15 September 2003, a floating charge holder no longer has an unfettered right to appoint an administrative receiver. Instead, the provisions of the EnA 2002 require a holder of a 'qualifying floating charge' to pursue the route of administration.

Administration

45.37 Administration is a procedure whereby the court will make an order for administration, following the presentation of a petition by the company, its directors, a creditor or creditors, directing that the business and the property of the company[1] should be managed by an administrator for a specified period[2].

An administration order will only be granted if:

(a)   a company is, or is likely to become, unable to pay its debts as they fall due or the value of its assets is, or is likely to become, less than the amount of its liabilities, taking into account contingent and prospective liabilities; and

(b)   the court is satisfied that one or more of the statutorily prescribed purposes apply.

The statutorily prescribed purposes are:

(i)   the survival of the company as a going concern; or
(ii)   the approval of a voluntary arrangement; or
(iii)   the sanctioning under s 425 of the Companies Act 1985[3] of a compromise or arrangement between the company and any such persons mentioned in that section; or
(iv)   a more advantageous realisation of the company's assets than will be effected on a winding up.

[1]   The procedure is also available in the case of a partnership: see The Insolvent Partnerships Order 1994, SI 1994/2421.
[2]   IA 1986, ss 8–27.
[3]   To be re-enacted as Companies Act 2006, s 895 at a date to be appointed.

Liquidation

45.38 Compulsory liquidation of a company follows non-compliance with a statutory notice demanding payment within 21 days resulting in the presentation of a winding-up petition to the court and a subsequent order for liquidation[1].

Voluntary liquidation of a company may arise for a reason mentioned in s 84 of the IA 1986, for example, pursuant to an extraordinary resolution of the company to the effect that it cannot by reason of its liabilities continue its business[2].

In both compulsory and voluntary liquidations, a liquidator is appointed, although often, pending the appointment of an insolvency practitioner, the Official Receiver will first act[3].

[1]   IA 1986, Pt IV, Ch VI. Also see para 45.17.
[2]   IA 1986, Pt IV, Chas II–V.
[3]   IA 1986, Pt IV, Chs VII–X.

Bankruptcy

45.39 Bankruptcy of an individual follows non compliance with a statutory notice demanding payment of an unsecured debt within 21 days resulting in the presentation of a petition of a creditor and the subsequent bankruptcy order made by the court[1].

1   IA 1986, ss 264–387.

Receivership

45.40 Receivership is the appointment of an individual to protect the assets of a lender secured by way of a charge. If empowered to do so, the receiver may manage the business (if any). More usually the role of a receiver is to realise assets charged.

In relation to a company, such a receiver, in respect of floating charge assets, would be an administrative receiver, the appointment of which is now restricted as a consequence of the EnA 2002 coming into force[1].

The prohibition upon receivership appointments arising from the EnA 2002 does not apply to the appointment of non-administrative receivers under fixed charges (whether pre- or post-15 September 2003) nor to the appointment of receivers by the court[2].

More usually, in the context of agricultural holdings, a receiver will be an individual appointed by the holder of a legal charge or mortgage. The receiver is often described as a 'LPA receiver'. Such a receiver will have the powers and obligations conferred by the Law of Property Act 1925, but in the majority of cases such powers will be significantly extended by the contractual provisions contained in the legal charge or mortgage[3].

1   See para 45.36.
2   CPR Pt 69.
3   As to the relevance of receivers in the context of mortgages of agricultural land, see Ch 43.

The effect of insolvency on enforcement (other than distress)

Voluntary arrangements

45.41 A distinction needs to be drawn between an individual voluntary arrangement and a company voluntary arrangement. In the case of the former, a statutory moratorium can be imposed under an interim order so that no action can be commenced against the individual (or a partnership) without the leave of the court. In the latter case, a moratorium arises in cases of 'small companies'[1] or where an administration order has been made[2].

If a tenant is contemplating an individual voluntary arrangement, then the effect of obtaining an interim order[3] is:

45.41 *Remedies*

(a)   forfeiture is no longer available to the landlord without the permission of the court;
(b)   no other proceedings can be instituted without the leave of the court;
(c)   there can be no distraint for rent[4]; and
(d)   disclaimer is not available[5].

Where the tenant is a company entering into a company voluntary arrangement, unless the company is a 'small company' or an administration order has been made:

(i)   forfeiture (including peaceable re-entry) are available to the landlord;
(ii)   proceedings may be issued by the landlord; and
(iii)   the landlord may distrain for rent.

The interim order ceases to have effect after 28 days[6]. Once the proposals for the voluntary arrangement are approved by the court, following a vote by the creditors, it binds all interested parties[7]. A creditor whose interests have been unfairly prejudiced by the voluntary arrangement may challenge the order in the court[8].

[1]   Companies Act 1985, s 247. To be replaced by Companies Act 2006, ss 382 and 465 at a date to be appointed.
[2]   IA 1986, ss 5(2), 6.
[3]   An interim order requires an application to the court. It is not an automatic consequence of a voluntary arrangement.
[4]   See para 45.15.
[5]   See para 45.60.
[6]   IA 1986, s 260(4).
[7]   IA 1986, s 260(2).
[8]   IA 1986, s 262. *Re Naeem (a Bankrupt) (No 18 of 1988)* [1990] 1 WLR 48.

Administrative receiver

45.42 In the case of pre-EnA 2002 floating charges, where the charge holder appoints an administrative receiver[1], the duty of the administrative receiver is to look after the property for the benefit of all of those interested in it[2].

The appointment of an administrative receiver does not interfere with the rights of the landlord or any other creditor to pursue any remedies available to them against the tenant.

The administrative receiver is not obliged to pay the rent, if it is advantageous to allow forfeiture[3]. In the event of the landlord taking forfeiture proceedings, the administrative receiver may prompt the tenant to apply for relief against forfeiture. Alternatively, the administrative receiver may himself apply for relief against forfeiture on equitable grounds[4].

An administrative receiver continues to be entitled to receive the income from the sub-tenants of the tenant, and to discharge the current outgoings from such monies, between the date of forfeiture (by service of a claim form) and any order for possession[5].

It is not necessary for the administrative receiver to be named in the charge deed in order to enable him to sell the property[6].

1   As to the power to appoint an administrative receiver, see *Hart v Emelkirk Ltd* [1983] 3 All ER 15; *Evans v Clayhope Properties Ltd* [1988] 1 All ER 444, [1988] 1 EGLR 33.
2   *Knight v Lawrence* [1993] BCLC 215, [1991] 1 EGLR 143.
3   *Hand v Blow* [1901] 2 Ch 721.
4   Law of Property Act 1925, s 146(2).
5   *Official Custodian for Charities v Mackey* [1985] Ch 168, [1984] 3 All ER 689.
6   *Phoenix Properties Ltd v Wimpole Street Nominees Ltd* [1989] EGCS 167.

Administration

45.43 No proceedings nor execution nor other legal process may be commenced or continued against a company (or a partnership) or its property without the leave of the court, and subject to such conditions as the court may impose, after an administration order has been made[1]. Previously leave was not required for peaceable re-entry[2]. That position was reversed when the Insolvency Act 2000 (IA 2000) came into force[3]. It is now necessary for a landlord to obtain permission of the court or the administrator before being able to proceed with forfeiture either by way of proceedings or peaceable re-entry.

The administrator has a power of sale[4]. If a landlord or a mortgagee considers himself to be unfairly prejudiced by the acts of the administrator, there is a procedure to enable him to apply to the court, which can then grant such relief as it thinks fit[5].

The courts have decided that administrators have the power to pay administration expenses as they fall due[6]. There is little guidance as to whether ongoing rent is to be paid as an expense. However, the Insolvency (Amendment) Rules 2003 and 2005[7] introduced new provisions that deal with administration expenses. It is arguable that these rules (reflecting those applying to liquidations) validate the payment of ongoing rent as an expense[8].

It should be noted that where a company is in administration it has been held that business rates are an expense of the administration[9].

1   IA 1986, ss 10, 11. *Re Atlantic Computer Systems plc* [1992] Ch 505; *Metro Nominees (Wandsworth) (No 1) Ltd v K Rayment*, HC 16 October 2006 (2006 Westlaw 3933204).
2   *Re Lomax Leisure Ltd* [2000] Ch 502, [1999] 3 All ER 22; *Metro Nominees (Wandsworth) (No 1) Ltd v K Rayment* HC 16 October 2006 (2006 Westlaw 3933204).
3   IA 2000, s 9, with effect from 2 April 2001.
4   IA 2000, s 14 and Sch 1.
5   IA 2000, s 27.
6   *Re Salmet International Ltd (in administration)* [2001] BCC 796.
7   SI 2003/1730 and SI 2005/527.
8   See Levaggi and Marsden, 'Expensive Quandry', EG 10 March 2007.
9   *Exeter City Council v Bairstow* [2007] EWHC 400 (Ch), [2007] All ER (D) 45 (Mar).

45.44   *Remedies*

Liquidation

45.44 In the case of compulsory liquidation, a company or a creditor or a contributory may apply to the court to stay any proceedings after the presentation of the winding-up petition[1]. Once the winding-up order has been made, or a provisional liquidator appointed, no action can be commenced or proceeded with against the company without the leave of the court[2].

Unlike bankruptcy, the leave of the court will be required for an action for rent, damages, forfeiture or possession. However, the court has the power to make a possession order on a summons in the liquidation[3]. The application for leave and possession should be made simultaneously[4].

The court will usually grant leave to a landlord to forfeit in the case of rent arrears[5]. The liquidator is entitled to seek relief from forfeiture on the same terms as the tenant[6]. The liquidator seeks relief in the name of the company[7].

The court will normally grant leave to a landlord to sue for current rent where that rent is a proper expense of the liquidation, ie where the liquidator is retaining the property for use or to sell to best advantage[8].

In a voluntary liquidation, the liquidator can apply to the court to determine any question in the winding up. The court may exercise any powers available to it as if the winding up had been compulsory[9]. The court exercises an equitable discretion. It may not apply the same rules as would apply in a compulsory liquidation[10].

1   IA 1986, s 126(1).
2   IA 1986, s 130(2).
3   *Re Blue Jeans Sales Ltd* [1979] 1 All ER 641, [1979] 1 WLR 362.
4   *Re Brompton Securities Ltd* [1988] 2 EGLR 93, [1988] 49 EG 77.
5   *General Share and Trust Co v Wetley Brick and Pottery Co* (1882) 20 Ch D 260.
6   *Re Brompton Securities Ltd (No 2)* [1988] 3 All ER 677, [1988] BCLC 616, [1988] 2 EGLR 95.
7   *Official Custodian for Charities v Parway Estates Developments Ltd* [1985] Ch 151, [1984] 3 All ER 679.
8   *Re ABC Coupler and Engineering Co Ltd (No 3)* [1970] 1 All ER 650, [1970] 1 WLR 702; *Re Downer Enterprises Ltd* [1974] 2 All ER 1074, [1974] 1 WLR 1460.
9   IA 1986, s 112.
10 *Herbert Berry Associates Ltd v IRC* [1977] 1 WLR 1437, HL.

Bankruptcy

45.45 Proceedings cannot be commenced after a bankruptcy order has been made without the leave of the court. Further, the court has power to stay existing proceedings[1]. Leave is not required to commence forfeiture proceedings[2].

1   IA 1986, s 285.
2   *Ezekiel v Orakpo* [1977] QB 260.

Receivership

45.46 The rules applying to receiverships are the same as those which apply to administrative receivership[1].

1   See para 45.42.

The effect of insolvency on distress

Preferential creditors

45.47 Goods distrained within the three months prior to a bankruptcy order or winding-up order may be made subject to charges in favour of preferential creditors, so a distraining landlord may have to pay the proceeds recovered to preferential creditors before he can be paid himself[1].

1   IA 1986, ss 176 and 347.

Voluntary arrangements

45.48 Where the tenant is an individual seeking approval of an individual voluntary arrangement, s 252 of the IA 1986 provides that the interim order establishes a statutory moratorium so that no proceedings, execution or other legal process may be commenced or continued without the leave of the court. It has been held that a landlord's right to distrain is not affected by s 252[1]. By parity of reasoning, the same would apply in relation to a company voluntary arrangement.

1   *McMullen & Sons Ltd v Cerrone* (1993) 66 P & CR 351.

Administrative receivership/receivership

45.49 Where a receiver has been appointed, either as an administrative receiver or a receiver under some other form of charge, the rights of other creditors, including the landlord, are unaffected. The landlord may distrain against goods on the demised premises, notwithstanding the fact that the goods are subject to a floating charge[1].

1   *Re Roundwood Colliery Co* [1897] 1 Ch 373, CA; *New City Constitutional Club, ex p Purssell* (1887) 34 Ch D 646, CA.

Administration

45.50 No distress can be levied against a company or partnership which is the subject of an administration order without the leave of the court or the consent of the administrator[1]. The wording of the IA 1986 provides that leave is required:

'... and no other proceedings and no execution or other legal process may be commenced or continued, and no distress may be levied ... except with the consent of the administrator or the leave of the court'[2].

Unlike the position with regard to voluntary arrangements, express provision is made in relation to distress.

1   IA 1986, ss 10 and 11.
2   IA 1986.

Liquidation

45.51 Upon the compulsory liquidation of a company, following the making of a winding-up order, no action or proceedings can be proceeded with or commenced against a company or property of a company, except with the leave of the court[1]. For this purpose, the winding up is deemed to commence on the presentation of the petition[2].

Distress (or execution) after the compulsory winding-up order has been made is void[3]. The benefit of any execution against goods or land is lost by a creditor unless it is completed before the presentation of the petition, subject to the court's general discretion to override this[4].

The court will not usually restrain distress commenced before the winding up, but will restrain distress for rent due after liquidation (or after the presentation of the winding-up petition)[5].

Where a liquidator retains premises to sell them, or for some other purpose, he must pay the rent in full, which will be an expense of the liquidation. If he fails to do so, then he will be liable for distress[6].

Where a liquidator abstains from doing anything with a property, it will not give the landlord the right to distrain for rent subsequent to the winding up. The rent is merely a debt for which the landlord must prove in the liquidation[7]. The landlord shall be paid in full, or be allowed to distrain, if the liquidator is continuing to use the property[8].

Where a tenant is in liquidation, but has sub-tenants, under the Law of Distress Amendment Act 1908, the sub-tenant's goods are protected from seizure by the landlord, if the sub-tenant makes a declaration that the goods are not the property of the tenant in liquidation and if the sub-tenant undertakes to pay rent directly to the superior landlord until the arrears are paid in respect of which the levy is threatened. The sub-tenant becomes the immediate tenant of the landlord. It is necessary for the landlord to serve a notice on the sub-tenant pursuant to s 6 of the Law of Distress Amendment Act 1908[9].

Upon the voluntary liquidation of a company, the liquidator can ask the court to determine the validity of any distress levied[10]. The court can stay proceedings against the company, after the commencement of a voluntary winding up, and thereby restrain any distress. There is no automatic stay[11].

1   IA 1986, s 130.
2   IA 1986, s 129.
3   IA 1986, s 128.
4   IA 1986, s 183.
5   *Herbert Berry Associates Ltd v IRC* [1977] 1 WLR 1437, HL; *Re Roundwood Colliery Co* [1897] 1 Ch 373, CA.
6   *Re Downer Enterprises Ltd* [1974] 2 All ER 1074, [1974] 1 WLR 1460.
7   *Re ABC Coupler and Engineering Co Ltd (No 3)* [1970] 1 All ER 650, [1970] 1 WLR 702, (1970) 209 EG 1197.
8   *Re Atlantic Computer Systems Ltd* [1992] Ch 505.
9   *Re Offshore Ventilations Ltd* [1989] BCLC 318, 5 BCC 160, CA.
10   IA 1986, s 112.
11   IA 1986, ss 112(10) and 126(1).

Bankruptcy

45.52 The landlord may distrain for rent payable for six months only before the commencement of the bankruptcy. Any excess amount must be held for the bankrupt's estate[1]. The money recovered by the landlord stands charged for the benefit of the bankrupt's estate to the extent that the estate has insufficient funds to meet those debts[2]. The landlord assumes the role of a preferential creditor.

Following a bankruptcy order, the landlord cannot distrain for future rent[3]. The landlord cannot at any time after the discharge of the bankrupt distrain on any goods in the bankrupt's estate[4].

Any right to distrain is unaffected by the vesting of the assets of the bankrupt in his trustee in bankruptcy[5]. The landlord may always prove for the rent in the bankruptcy[6]. The landlord may distrain for rent due after the bankruptcy, if the trustee is in possession and the tenancy is not disclaimed. The restriction on the levy of distress arising upon bankruptcy only applies to rent due before the onset of bankruptcy. No leave is required to distrain for post-bankruptcy rent[7].

1   IA 1986, s 347(1) and (2).
2   IA 1986, s 347(3).
3   IA 1986, s 347(1), (2) and (6).
4   IA 1986, s 347(5).
5   IA 1986, s 347(9).
6   IA 1986, s 347(10).
7   *Re Binns, ex p Hale* (1875) 1 Ch D 285.

Insolvency and forfeiture

Right to forfeit

45.53 The terms of the tenancy agreement may permit forfeiture upon insolvency. This requires an express provision in the forfeiture clause. If there is no such provision, then forfeiture may be available to the landlord by reason of the non-payment of rent or a breach of some other term or condition of the tenancy[1].

Normally it will only be the bankruptcy of the current tenant which will permit forfeiture for the bankruptcy of the tenant[2]. Conversely, a right to forfeit, arising on the liquidation of a company tenant, gives a right to forfeit on a solvent liquidation for the purposes of reconstruction, unless the forfeiture clause expressly provides to the contrary[3].

1 See para 13.3.
2 *Smith v Gronow* [1891] 2 QB 394.
3 *Fryer v Ewart* [1902] AC 187, HL.

Waiver

45.54 A landlord does not waive his right to forfeit by reason of having constructive notice of liquidation through notification of the winding-up order in the London Gazette and acceptance of rent afterwards[1].

1 *Official Custodian for Charities v Parway Estates Developments Ltd* [1985] Ch 151, [1984] 3 All ER 679.

Section 146 notice?

45.55 Save in the case of the non-payment of rent, normally a necessary preliminary to the landlord forfeiting the tenancy is the service of a notice under s 146 of the Law of Property Act 1925[1]. Where the landlord is relying upon the bankruptcy or liquidation of the tenant as a ground for forfeiture, the position in respect of the service of a s 146 notice is governed by s 146(9) and (10) of the Law of Property Act 1925.

Section 146(9) of the Law of Property Act 1925 provides that no s 146 notice is required prior to forfeiture for bankruptcy or liquidation (but not any other insolvency event), where the lease is of:

(a)   agricultural or pastoral land;
(b)   mines or minerals;
(c)   a house used or intended to be used as a public house or beer shop;
(d)   a house let as a dwellinghouse with the use of furniture etc; and
(e)   any property where the personal qualifications of the tenant are of importance for the preservation of the value or character of the property or on the ground of neighbourhood to the landlord or any person holding under him.

1 See para 13.13.

45.56 In the case of leases other than those governed by s 146(9) of the Law of Property Act 1925, s 146(10) provides that where a condition of forfeiture on the bankruptcy or liquidation of the tenant or on taking in execution the tenant's interest then:

(a)   if the lease is sold within the first year of bankruptcy or liquidation, and the landlord is attempting to forfeit the lease in the hands of the assignee (whether within or outside the first year), then a s 146 notice must be served prior to forfeiture;

(b)   if the lease is not sold within the first year of bankruptcy or liquidation, and the landlord wishes to forfeit within that year, a s 146 notice must be served upon the tenant;

(c)   if the lease is not sold within the first year of the bankruptcy or liquidation, and the landlord wishes to forfeit after the expiry of the year, a s 146 notice need not be served upon the tenant or (if the lease has been sold after the first year) upon the assignee. Sold includes a contract of sale within the year[1].

1   *Re Henry Castle & Sons Ltd* (1906) 94 LT 396.

Is leave required?

45.57 Leave to proceed with forfeiture is not required in the case of voluntary liquidation, but any action for forfeiture may be stayed upon an application to the court[1].

In the case of compulsory liquidation, leave will be required for forfeiture by proceedings[2]. If forfeiture is sought by peaceable re-entry, leave of the court is not required[3].

Leave of the court is not required for forfeiture by proceedings in the case of bankruptcy[4].

Leave of the court or the consent of the administrator will be required for forfeiture by proceedings after an administration order[5]. Leave is not required for peaceable re-entry[6].

Leave of the court is not required for forfeiture in the case of administrative receivership, any other form of receivership or a voluntary arrangement[7].

1   See para 45.44.
2   IA 1986, s 130(2).
3   *Re Lomax Leisure Ltd* [1999] 3 All ER 22; this is a case on administration, but is a general application. Also see *Exchange Travel Agency Ltd v Triton Property Trust plc* [1991] 2 EGLR 50; *Razzaq v Pala* [1997] 2 EGLR 53; *Re a Debtor (No 13A of 1995)* [1996] 1 All ER 691.
4   *Ezekiel v Orakpo* [1977] QB 260; IA 1986, s 285(3).
5   IA 1986, ss 10 and 11.
6   *Re Lomax Leisure Ltd* [1999] 3 All ER 22.
7   *Re Naeem (a bankrupt) (No 18 of 1988)* [1990] 1 WLR 48; *R A Securities v Mercantile Credit* [1995] 3 All ER 581.

Relief from forfeiture

45.58 Under s 146(9) of the Law of Property Act 1925, there is no relief from forfeiture on the ground of the bankruptcy or liquidation of the tenant where the lease is in any of the categories referred to in para 45.56. In other cases of forfeiture for bankruptcy or liquidation, the tenant can only apply for relief within the first year of the bankruptcy or liquidation, although proceedings for relief commenced within the year may be continued thereafter[1].

It has been suggested that it may be difficult to obtain relief where forfeiture has been pursued following the making of a winding-up order. Nevertheless, if the liquidator has an assignee, and the assignee can pay the arrears of rent on the assignment, it is likely that relief will be granted[2]. A liquidator's claim for relief may be made on an application in the liquidation[3]. Not only can a liquidator or trustee in bankruptcy apply for relief, but the right to do so can be assigned to a third party[4].

The court has jurisdiction to grant relief against forfeiture as to part of the premises[5]. The tenant will probably not get relief where the premises have subsequently been re-let[6]. The effect of a consent order for possession should also be noted. This may operate as an implied surrender, losing the right to relief[7].

A sub-tenant or mortgagee has an independent right to relief from forfeiture[8]. The right applies even where the landlord has forfeited by peaceable re-entry after disclaimer[9]. The sub-tenant may not be entitled to possession until relief is granted[10]. Relief granted to a sub-tenant or mortgagee is by way of a vesting order, giving a new lease, normally on similar terms to the lease forfeited[11].

[1]   *Pearson v Gee* [1934] AC 272.
[2]   *General Share and Trust Co v Wetley Brick and Pottery Co* (1882) 20 Ch D 260.
[3]   *Re Brompton Securities Ltd (No 2)* [1988] 3 All ER 677, [1988] BCLC 616, [1988] 2 EGLR 95.
[4]   *Howard v Fanshawe* [1895] 2 Ch 581.
[5]   *GMS Syndicate Ltd v Gary Elliott Ltd* [1982] Ch 1, [1981] 1 All ER 619.
[6]   *Stanhope v Howorth* (1886) 3 TLR 34; *Silverman v AFCO (UK) Ltd* [1988] 1 EGLR 51.
[7]   *Howard v Central Board of Finance of the Church of England* (1977) 244 Estates Gazette 51.
[8]   Law of Property Act 1925, s 146(4).
[9]   *Barclays Bank plc v Prudential Life Assurance Co Ltd* [1998] 1 EGLR 44.
[10] *Pellicano v MEPC plc* [1994] 1 EGLR 104.
[11] *Hill v Griffin* [1987] 1 EGLR 81.

Case F

45.59 It should be noted that, in addition to a landlord's ability to forfeit upon the bankruptcy or liquidation of a tenant, under the AHA 1986 the landlord has an additional right to serve a Case F notice to quit[1].

[1]   See para 31.88.

Disclaimer

The jurisdiction to disclaim

45.60 Disclaimer is an important alternative method of termination of a tenancy in the case of insolvency of the tenant by reason of liquidation or bankruptcy. A liquidator (whether in a voluntary or compulsory liquidation) or a trustee in bankruptcy may disclaim the lease under the IA 1986[1]. No-one else, including, in particular, an administrator or receiver, can disclaim.

The liquidator or trustee may disclaim 'onerous' property. That means, in the case of leasehold property, the lease must be unsaleable or not readily saleable or may give rise to a liability to pay money or to perform any other onerous act[2].

The liquidator or trustee may disclaim notwithstanding the fact that he has taken possession of the property, tried to sell it, or otherwise exercised rights of ownership[3].

The liquidator and trustee no longer require leave of the court to disclaim. Further, an earlier provision imposing a 12-month time limit for disclaiming has been abolished. Similarly, the landlord's right to object to the disclaimer has effectively been removed. The landlord's remedy for loss resulting as a consequence of the operation of the disclaimer is to prove in the winding up or bankruptcy[4].

1   IA 1986, ss 178, and 170 (liquidation); ss 315–317 (bankruptcy).
2   IA 1986, s 178(3) (liquidation); s 315 (bankruptcy); *Eyre v Hall* [1986] 2 EGLR 95.
3   IA 1986, s 178(2) (liquidation); s 315(2) (bankruptcy).
4   IA 1986, s 178(6) (liquidation); s 315(6) (bankruptcy).

Time limit

45.61 There is no prescribed time limit for the liquidator or the trustee to disclaim onerous property, but a person interested in the property may impose a 28-day time limit upon the liquidator or the trustee, requiring him to elect to disclaim within that period[1]. The court has power to extend the time, but only in special circumstances, such as illness[2].

On bankruptcy of an individual, all of his property vests in his trustee in bankruptcy. Accordingly, unlike the liquidator, the trustee can incur a personal liability. If the trustee fails to disclaim, he will be personally liable. If the liquidator fails to disclaim, following notice to elect, it is likely that the liquidator continues to have no personal liability[3].

1   IA 1986, s 178(5) (liquidation); s 316 (bankruptcy).
2   *Re Jones* (1874) 9 Ch App 586.
3   *Graham v Edge* (1888) 20 QBD 683; *Stead, Hazel & Co v Cooper* [1933] 1 KB 840.

Notice of disclaimer

45.62 In order to disclaim, the liquidator or trustee must:

(a)   give notice of disclaimer to any person claiming to be a sub-tenant or mortgagee and notice to any occupier; and

(b)   ensure that no application has been made to the court by any person with an interest in the property or under a liability in respect of the property within 14 days of the service of the notice referred to in paragraph (a)[1].

45.62 *Remedies*

The liquidator or trustee must also file a prescribed notice of disclaimer in court[2].

1   IA 1986, s 179(1) (liquidation); s 317(1) (bankruptcy).
2   Insolvency Rules 1986, r 4.187.

Effect of disclaimer

45.63 Disclaimer:

> 'operates so as to determine from the date of the disclaimer, the rights, interests and liabilities of [the company/the bankrupt] in or in respect of the property disclaimed; but does not, except so far as is necessary for the purpose of releasing [the company/bankrupt] from liability, affect the rights or liabilities of any other person'[1].

In the case of leases granted after the LT(C)A 1995 came into force on 1 January 1996, if the original tenant is insolvent, disclaimer ends the lease, but not the liability of any surety for the original tenant[2]. If an assignee is insolvent, disclaimer does not end the liability of the original tenant or his surety[3]. It has been held that it does end the liability of the assignee's surety[4].

The disclaimer ends any sub-lease, but the sub-tenant retains the right to remain in possession for the residue of the sub-lease. The landlord retains rights of forfeiture and distress under the head lease[5]. However, it appears that the tenant is not otherwise liable under the covenants and may remain in possession until the landlord serves notice to elect in respect of a vesting order[6]. The position of a guarantor should be noted[7].

The landlord may put the sub-tenant or mortgagee to an election to have the lease vested in him or to be excluded from the property[8].

1   IA 1986, s 178 (liquidation); s 315 (bankruptcy).
2   *Hindcastle v Barbara Attenborough Associates Ltd* [1997] AC 70, [1996] 1 All ER 737, overruling *Stacey v Hill* [1901] 1 KB 660, HL.
3   *Hindcastle v Barbara Attenborough Associates Ltd* [1996] 1 All ER 737; *Warnford Investments Ltd v Duckworth* [1979] Ch 127.
4   *Murphy v Sawyer-Hoare* [1993] 2 EGLR 61.
5   *Re AE Realisations (1985) Ltd* [1987] 3 All ER 83, [1988] 1 WLR 200.
6   See para 45.64.
7   See para 45.8.
8   *Re Finley, ex p Clothworkers' Co* (1888) 21 QBD 475.

Vesting order

45.64 The disclaimer does not take effect unless either:

(a)   no application for the vesting of the lease in a third party is made within 14 days of service of the last copy of the disclaimer; or

(b)   where such an application has been made, the court directs that the disclaimer shall take effect[1].

Any person who 'claims an interest in the disclaimed property' or any person 'who is under any liability in respect of the disclaimed property, not being a liability discharged by the disclaimer' may apply to the court for a vesting order[2].

An application for a vesting order must be made within three months of the applicant becoming aware of the disclaimer[3], whether he becomes aware by receipt of the notice from the trustee or liquidator or otherwise. Even if the time limits are missed, it appears that in both bankruptcy and liquidation, time can be extended[4].

The court will not make a vesting order, except on terms that the person is subject to the same liabilities as the company/bankrupt was subject to at the commencement of the winding up or bankruptcy or the same liabilities as the person would have been subject to had they taken an assignment at the commencement of the winding up. The landlord is a person interested in the disclaimed property[5], but he cannot obtain a vesting order for the purpose of preserving sub-leases where the sub-tenants have declined to apply for a vesting order[6]. A person whose interest is discharged by the disclaimer cannot claim a vesting order, for example, a surety[7].

A vesting order can be made in respect of part only of the premises under the IA 1986[8], but on terms that the tenant of part will be subject to the same obligations as the original tenant was. If there is a disclaimer, and a person declines to accept a vesting order, that person shall be excluded from all interests in the property[9].

Unfortunately the sections in the IA 1986 do not make any clear provision for the apportionment of rent and other obligations upon the grant of a vesting order in respect of part of the premises. This may be of particular significance in the context of an agricultural holding.

1   IA 1986, s 179 (liquidation); s 317 (bankruptcy).
2   IA 1986, s 181 (liquidation); s 320 (bankruptcy).
3   Insolvency Rules 1986, rr 4.194 and 6.186. This extends to an equitable assignee: *Test Valley Borough Council v Minilec Engineeering Ltd (in liquidation)* [2005] 2 EGLR 113.
4   IA 1986, s 376.
5   *Re Cock, ex p Shilson* (1887) 20 QBD 343.
6   *Sterling Estates v Pickard UK Ltd* [1997] 2 EGLR 33.
7   *Re Yarmarine (IW) Ltd* [1992] BCLC 276.
8   IA 1986, s 182(2) (liquidation); s 321(2) (bankruptcy).
9   IA 1986, s 182(4) (liquidation); s 321(4) (bankruptcy); *Re AE Realisations (1985) Ltd* [1987] 3 All ER 83, [1988] 1 WLR 200.

Loss caused by disclaimer

45.65 In the case of the liquidation or bankruptcy of the original tenant, the lease ends. No future rents are due, but any person sustaining loss or damage as a consequence of the disclaimer is entitled to prove for that loss or damage as a debt in the liquidation or bankruptcy[1].

Where the landlord has recovered possession of the holding, as a result of the disclaimer, the measure of the injury will normally be the difference between the value of the property at the rent reserved by the tenancy agreement and the value of the property at the rent obtainable after the disclaimer, together with the cost of any repairs which the tenant should have carried out[2]. That will also be the normal measure of loss for a previous tenant proving for loss caused by the disclaimer[3]. A claim for future rent should however be discounted for early payment[4].

If a sub-tenant has to pay a higher rent reserved by the disclaimed head lease to avoid distress or forfeiture or on taking a vesting order, the sub-tenant will be able to prove for the increase in rent as damages resulting from the disclaimer in either the liquidation or the bankruptcy[5].

1   IA 1986, s 178(6) (liquidation); s 315(5) (bankruptcy).
2   *Re Hide, ex p Llynvi Coal and Iron Co* (1871) 7 Ch App 28; *Re McEwan, ex p Blake* (1879) 11 Ch D 572.
3   *Re Carruthers, ex p Tobit* (1895) 2 Mans 172.
4   *Re Park Air Services, Christopher Moran Holdings v Bairstow* [2000] 2 AC 172, [1999] 1 All ER 673, HL.
5   *Re Levy, ex p Walton* (1881) 17 Ch D 746, CA.

Effect of no disclaimer

45.66 If the liquidator does not disclaim the lease, the landlord may be able to claim the rent for the duration of the liquidation as an expense of the liquidation, but failure to disclaim does not make the liquidator personally liable upon the terms of the lease[1].

Upon the completion of the winding up, the company is dissolved[2]. The title to the lease will vest in the Crown as 'bona vicantia'[3].

The Crown will become liable under the terms of the lease, upon it vesting as 'bona vicantia'. The Crown has the option to disclaim the lease itself[4]. The Crown must do so within 12 months of the date on which the vesting in the Crown came to the Treasury Solicitor's notice or within three months of receipt of a notice from a person interested in the property requiring him to decide whether or not to disclaim. In the event that the Crown does disclaim, the lease is deemed not to have vested in the Crown. The lease is treated as if it had been disclaimed by the liquidator immediately before the dissolution of the company[5].

In the case of bankruptcy, if there is no disclaimer, the effect is that the trustee in bankruptcy will remain liable upon the terms of the tenancy by virtue of privity of estate. If the bankrupt tenant was the original tenant, he will remain liable by privity of contract. Liability for all rent accruing after the date of the bankruptcy order will continue, notwithstanding the discharge of the tenant from bankruptcy[6]. If the trustee in bankruptcy wishes to be released from the liability, it is necessary for him to disclaim the lease or to assign it to a third party.

1   *Stead, Hazel & Co v Cooper* [1933] 1 KB 840; *Graham v Edge* (1888) 20 QBD 683.

2   IA 1986, ss 201–202.
3   Companies Act 1985, s 654 (to be replaced by Companies Act 2006, s 1012 at a date to be appointed); *Re Wells* [1933] Ch 29.
4   Companies Act 1985, s 656 (to be replaced by Companies Act 2006, s 1013 at a date to be appointed).
5   IA 1986, ss 178(4), 179–182.
6   *Metropolis Estates Co Ltd v Wilde* [1940] 2 KB 536, CA.

Liability of the insolvency practitioner

Liquidation

45.67 The liquidator is not personally liable[1].

Rent due prior to the liquidation is an unsecured debt. Rent due after the liquidation will also be an unsecured debt, except where the liquidator uses the holding for the purposes of the liquidation. In that case the rent may be a liquidation expense, entitling the landlord to claim in full ahead of other creditors[2].

The Insolvency Rules 1986 provide that 'expenses properly chargeable or incurred by the official receiver or liquidator in preserving, realising or getting in any assets of the company' may be liquidation expenses[3]. Rent will probably an expense incurred in preserving the tenancy if the landlord would have forfeited it if the rent was not paid[4].

The Insolvency Rules 1986 also provide for the liquidator to be able to incur 'any necessary disbursements by the liquidator in the course of his administration'[5]. The Insolvency Rules 1986 are more extensive than the rules under the Companies Act 1948, which governed liquidation expenses until the IA 1986 came into force. 'Necessary disbursements' was included in the previous rules[6]. Under those rules it was held that the test was whether the rent was paid for the convenience of the liquidation or whether there is some other 'special equity' allowing rent to be given priority[7].

Where the rent is paid for the convenience of the liquidation was considered in detail in *Re ABC Coupler and Engineering Co (No 3) Ltd*[8]. From that case the following principles may be derived:

(a)   prima facie rent due after the commencement of liquidation is not payable in full, but only provable;
(b)   the onus of persuading the court to the contrary is on the applicant landlord;
(c)   the court has a discretion to allow payment in full (see now s 156 of the IA 1986);
(d)   rent will be payable in full if the liquidator retains possession for the convenience of the winding up, which depends on his purpose in retaining possession;
(e)   it is enough if the liquidator uses the property for carrying on the company's business, or keeps the property in order to sell it or to do the best he can with it;

829

(f) it is not enough if the liquidator keeps possession by arrangement with the landlord and for the landlord's benefit as well as for the benefit of the company and there is no agreement with the liquidator that he shall pay rent; or where the liquidator does no more than abstain from trying to get rid of the property;

(g) if the landlord threatens re-entry then rent will have to be paid in full to avoid the re-entry;

(h) there may be special circumstances rendering it inequitable for the rent not to be paid in full;

(i) it is not enough for the liquidator to leave existing plant and machinery on the premises, to have them valued, to deal with enquiries by third parties concerning a sale of the property, nor to fail to surrender the lease;

(j) it is enough if the liquidator retains the property for the purpose of carrying out advice which he receives as to the best method of selling the company's assets.

1   *Graham v Edge* (1888) 20 QBD 683.
2   IA 1986, ss 115 and 156; Insolvency Rules 1986, r 4.218(1)(a) and (m).
3   Insolvency Rules 1986, r 4.218(1)(a).
4   *Re Linda Marie Ltd (In Liquidation)* [1989] BCLC 46.
5   Insolvency Rules 1986, r 4.218(1)(m).
6   Companies (Winding Up) Rules 1949, SI 1949/330, r 195.
7   *Re Kentish Homes Ltd* [1993] BCLC 1375.
8   [1970] 1 All ER 650, [1970] 1 WLR 702.

Bankruptcy

45.68 In the case of bankruptcy, if there is no disclaimer, the effect is that the trustee in bankruptcy will remain liable upon the terms of the tenancy by virtue of privity of estate. If the bankrupt tenant was the original tenant, he will remain liable by privity of contract. Liability for all rent accruing after the date of the bankruptcy order will continue, notwithstanding the discharge of the tenant from bankruptcy[1]. If the trustee in bankruptcy wishes to be released from the liability, it is necessary for him to disclaim the lease or to assign it to a third party.

If the trustee in bankruptcy disclaims the tenancy, he is released from all liability. The landlord may prove for rent and other liabilities up to the date of the bankruptcy order and may also seek rent from the date of the bankruptcy order to the date of the disclaimer.

1   *Metropolis Estates Co Ltd v Wilde* [1940] 2 KB 536.

Administration

45.69 Like the liquidator, an administrator acts on behalf of the company or the partnership in respect of which he has been appointed. He has no personal liability.

The landlord must claim arrears of rent with the same priority as an ordinary unsecured creditor. The court has a discretion to order the administrator to pay rent for the period of the administration as a condition of refusing the landlord leave to forfeit or distrain[1] .

1 *Re Atlantic Computer Systems Ltd* [1992] Ch 505, CA.

Receivership

45.70 Receivership under a legal charge, a mortgage or a debenture does not affect the liability of the tenant to pay rent. The receiver acts as the agent of the tenant and does not become personally liable for the rent[1].

The position is different where there is a court appointed receiver. The court appointed receiver must pay rent due under any tenancy of the holding occupied by the tenant out of monies received by the receiver[2].

1 Law of Property Act 1925, s 109; IA 1986, s 44; *Liverpool Corpn v Hope* [1938] 1 KB 751, CA.
2 *Balfe v Blake* (1850) 1 I Ch R 365.

FRAUD ACT 2006

45.71 The Fraud Act 2006 came into force on 15 January 2007. It applies to England, Wales and Northern Ireland. It repeals the deception offences previously contained in the Theft Acts 1968 and 1979. It replaces those offences with a single offence of fraud.

The Fraud Act 2006 states that fraud can be committed in one of three ways:

(a) by false representation[1];
(b) by failure to disclose information when there is a legal duty to do so[2]; and
(c) by an abuse of position[3].

The Fraud Act 2006 widens the scope of events that can be classed as fraud. It provides that a maximum sentence of ten years' imprisonment can be imposed on a person found guilty under the Fraud Act 2006.

The Fraud Act 2006 may arise in relation to landlord and tenant relationships and to property related transactions more generally. For example, the Fraud Act 2006 may have relevance in relation to cases of the type of *Rous v Mitchell*[4], where the tenant relies upon the tort of deceit to set aside a landlord's notice to quit.

Under the Theft Acts 1968 and 1979, it was necessary for a party asserting reliance upon the deception offences to establish that a loss had been suffered. The Fraud Act 2006 provides that allegations of fraud can be investigated where no loss has been suffered and no gain made. Further, the representation or statement made, for the purposes of s 2 of the Fraud Act 2006, does not have to be untrue. It may be sufficient that it is merely misleading.

1   Fraud Act 2006, s 2.
2   Fraud Act 2006, s 3.
3   Fraud Act 2006, s 4.
4   [1989] 2 EGLR 5, [1989] 48 EG 59; affd [1991] 1 All ER 676, [1991] 1 WLR 469. See para 31.15.

Chapter 46

AGRICULTURAL LAND TRIBUNALS

INTRODUCTION

46.1 The Agricultural Land Tribunals ('the ALT') were set up by s 73 of the Agriculture Act 1947. Their original role was as an appellate court hearing appeals from decisions of the Minister or the County Agricultural Executive Committees.

Following the Agriculture Act 1958, the ALT now has a very important role to play as a court of first instance determining disputes under agricultural legislation, principally the Agricultural Holdings Act 1986 (AHA 1986). Indeed, following the enactment of the Agricultural Tenancies Act 1995 (ATA 1995), and the withering on the vine of the AHA 1986, it will increasingly be the case that practitioners dealing with matters under the AHA 1986 will find that it is the ALT which maintains its residual significance as tenants continue to seek succession tenancies[1].

[1] See Chs 34–36.

Current jurisdiction

46.2 The current jurisdiction of the ALT falls into three separate categories. First and foremost, the ALT deals with applications for succession to an existing AHA 1986 protected tenancy upon the death or retirement of the sitting tenant. This jurisdiction was introduced for succession upon death by the Agriculture (Miscellaneous Provisions) Act 1976, Pt II, which was extended for succession on retirement by the Agricultural Holdings Act 1984. It should be noted that although the 1984 Act extended succession to retirement of the sitting tenant, at the same time that Act withdrew succession on death in relation to tenancies granted on or after 12 July 1984 with limited exceptions[1].

In addition to its jurisdiction dealing with succession, the ALT has two other roles. First, it is the ALT which deals with applications under the Land Drainage Act 1991[2]. These provide a remedy for owners and occupiers of any land which has suffered injury or which has been prevented from being improved by drainage through a neighbour's neglect of ditches.

Second, the ALT has an additional jurisdiction in relation to agricultural holdings in eight cases:

(a)   Applications for consent to the operation of a notice to quit[3].

(b)   Applications for a certificate of bad husbandry as a precondition to a landlord being able to give a so-called incontestable notice to quit to the tenant under Case C of Sch 3 of the AHA 1986[4].

(c)   The variation or revocation of conditions imposed on consents by the ALT[5].

(d)   An application for a direction to provide, alter or repair fixed equipment[6].

(e)   Applications for approval, in default of consent from the landlord, for long term improvements to be carried out by the tenant[7].

(f)   An application dealing with a determination in relation to a landlord's failure to carry out improvements[8].

(g)   An application for a direction that an agricultural holding be treated as a market garden[9].

(h)   An application for a direction to avoid or relax a provision in a lease dealing with heather or grass burning[10].

---

[1]   See Chs 34–36.
[2]   Land Drainage Act 1991, ss 28 or 30.
[3]   AHA 1986, s 27(3).
[4]   AHA 1986, Sch 3 para 9(1).
[5]   AHA 1986, s 27(5).
[6]   AHA 1986, s 11(1).
[7]   AHA 1986, s 67(3).
[8]   AHA 1986, s 67(6)(b).
[9]   AHA 1986, s 80.
[10]   Hill Farming Act 1946, s 21 (as amended by the Agriculture Act 1958 (AA 1958)).

Constitution

46.3   England and Wales are served by eight ALTs with separate geographical jurisdictions[1]. The areas and addresses of ALTs are, since the making of the Agricultural Land Tribunals (Areas) Order 1982[2], as follows:

Area	Counties and London Boroughs	Address
Northern	Cleveland Cumbria Durham Northumberland Tyne & Wear	Defra Buildings Electra Way Crewe Cheshire CW1 6GJ Tel: 01270 754208 Fax: 01270 754260
Yorkshire and	Humberside	Crewe Office

Humberside	North Yorkshire South Yorkshire West Yorkshire	
Midlands	Derbyshire Hereford and Worcester Leicestershire Nottinghamshire Warwickshire West Midlands	Crewe Office
Western	Cheshire Greater Manchester Lancashire Merseyside Shropshire Staffordshire	Crewe Office
South Western	Avon (the former county of) Cornwall Devon Dorset Gloucestershire Somerset Wiltshire Isles of Scilly	Block 3 Government Buildings Burghill Road Westbury-on-Trym Bristol BS10 6NJ Tel: 0117 959 8684 Fax: 0117 959 8605
South Eastern	Berkshire Buckinghamshire East Sussex Hampshire Isle of Wight Kent Oxfordshire Surrey West Sussex London Boroughs South of the River Thames including Richmond upon Thames	Bristol Office
Eastern	Bedfordshire Cambridgeshire Essex Hertfordshire Lincolnshire Norfolk Northamptonshire Suffolk	Bristol Office

	London Boroughs north of the River Thames except Richmond upon Thames	
Welsh	Gwynedd	Government Buildings
	Clwyd	Spa Road East
	Dyfed	Llandrindod Wells
	Gwent	Powys LD1 5HA
	Powys	Tel: 01597 823777
	Mid/South/West	Fax: 01597 828385
	Glamorgan	

1   The constitution of individual ALTs is governed by the Agriculture Act 1947 (AA 1947), Sch 9 paras 13–16, as amended by the Agriculture Act 1958, Sch 1 para 5(1) and (2).
2   SI 1982/07.

46.4 Where an agricultural holding falls partly within the area of one tribunal and partly within the area of another, then the tribunal for the area in which the greater part is situated has jurisdiction[1].

Since the Agricultural Land Tribunals (Areas) Order 1982, the description of the areas within which each tribunal has jurisdiction has not been revised following local government re-organisation to accord with the new local authorities and no new statutory instrument has been made. However, since re-organisation of local authorities, some of the counties no longer exist, eg Avon, Humberside and some of the Welsh counties[2].

Each ALT consists of panels of suitable persons appointed for each area, including a chairman and deputy chairmen and members appointed by the Lord Chancellor. For the hearing of each individual case, the ALT will consist of three people. One will be the chairman (or a deputy chairman) together with a representative of the interests of owners of agricultural land and a representative of the interests of farmers. The chairman and deputy chairmen must be qualified lawyers, being a barrister or solicitor of at least seven years standing, appointed by the Lord Chancellor. In addition to the three usual members of the ALT, the chairman may also nominate two assessors to assist at the hearing, should he deem it necessary. The assessors are selected from a panel of surveyors nominated by the President of the Royal Institution of Chartered Surveyors.

A technical slip in the constitution of the ALT, or even the disqualification of a person sitting as a member, will not invalidate the decision[3]. Further, the decision of the ALT need not be unanimous.

1   See the Agricultural Land Tribunals (Rules) Order 1978, SI 1978/259, r 1(2) and AA 1947, s 75 (as amended by AA 1958, Sch 1 para 4) whereby the Lord Chancellor was given power to direct, on application, that the whole of the land should be treated as being in the area of one or other of the tribunals in an appropriate case.
2   For the earlier provisions, see Agricultural Land Tribunals (Areas) Order 1974, SI 1974/66, as amended by Agricultural Land Tribunals (Areas) (Amendment) Order 1976, SI 1976/208. The current order is the Agricultural Land Tribunals (Areas) Order 1982, SI 1982/97.

³ Agriculture Act 1947, Sch 9 para 20(2).
⁴ Cf *Brain v Minister of Pensions* [1947] KB 625, [1947] 1 All ER 892 and *Minister of Pensions v Horsey* [1949] 2 KB 526, [1949] 2 All ER 314; and the Agricultural Land Tribunals (Rules) Order 1978, SI 1978/259, r 31.

Time limits

46.5 As with many aspects of the AHA 1986, time limits are of critical importance. Reference should be made to chapters 34–36 dealing with the provisions in the AHA 1986 relating to succession. It is worth noting that there are two critical and inflexible time limits which must be complied with in connection with succession applications, namely:

(a) Following the death of a sitting tenant, an application for succession *must* be made within three months from the date of death[1].
(b) If the application for succession is given pursuant to a retirement notice by the sitting tenant, the application to the ALT for succession must be made within one month of such notice[2].

Secondly, the Agricultural Land Tribunals (Rules) Order 1978[3] lays down strict time limits in connection with applications to the ALT. These range from the service of all documents in connection with an application to, for example:

(i) A one-month time limit for applying for consent to the operation of a landlord's notice to quit, where appropriate[4].
(ii) A one-month time limit for replying to an application for consent or for succession.

The time limits must be complied with, but r 37[5] provides that the chairman may extend the time for any step in connection with ALT proceedings 'on such terms and conditions, if any, as appear to him just'. The chairman's discretion whether to allow, conditionally or unconditionally, or to refuse such an extension is absolute[6].

Any failure to comply with the provisions of the Agricultural Land Tribunals (Rules) Order 1978[7] does not render the proceedings, or any part of the proceedings, invalid unless the chairman or the ALT so direct[8].

¹ AHA 1986, s 39(1) and Agricultural Land Tribunals (Succession to Agricultural Tenancies) Order 1984, SI 1984/1301, art 3(3).
² AHA 1986, s 53(2) and the Agricultural Land Tribunals (Succession to Agricultural Tenancies) Order 1984, SI 1984/1301, art 23(2).
³ SI 1978/259.
⁴ Agricultural Land Tribunals (Rules) Order 1978, SI 1978/259, r 2.
⁵ Agricultural Land Tribunals (Rules) Order 1978, SI 1978/259.
⁶ *Moss v National Coal Board* (1982) 264 Estates Gazette 52. Also, see generally, *Kellett v Alexander* (1980) 257 Estates Gazette 494.
⁷ SI 1978/259.
⁸ Agricultural Land Tribunals (Rules) Order 1978, SI 1978/259, r 37. Also see *Purser v Bailey* [1967] 2 QB 500, CA.

ALT PROCEDURE

Application and reply

46.6 Any application to the ALT must be made in the prescribed form or a form 'substantially to the like effect'[1]. Practitioners will find that the forms appear deceptively straightforward, but in practice require very careful and detailed consideration, together with the supply of a considerable amount of information.

Each application should be accompanied by:

(a) two copies of a map of the land which is the subject of the application on a scale of 6 inches to 1 mile or 1/10,000, or larger;

(b) a similar map or plan in respect of any other land about which the party intends to give evidence; and

(c) two copies of any plan or other document which the party making the application or reply intends to adduce in support of the case[2].

Further, in connection with an application for succession, normally an applicant will need to produce the following documents to establish his eligibility and suitability to be granted a new tenancy in succession to the deceased former tenant:

(a) the deceased tenant's death certificate;

(b) the applicant's birth certificate;

(c) the applicant's marriage certificate in the case of a widow or married daughter applicant;

(d) any farm partnership agreement or contract of employment;

(e) farm accounts for the relevant five years, ending with the date of death. In practice it is wise to produce seven years' accounts;

(f) a statement of the applicant's wages (if any);

(g) a statement identifying any outside sources of livelihood, whether derived from agriculture or otherwise;

(h) a copy of any tenancy agreement or other agreement relating to any other land farmed by the applicant;

(i) copies of certificates relating to any relevant academic qualifications of the applicant;

(j) a medical certificate stating the applicant's state of health;

(k) a full statement of the applicant's capital resources and any other capital available to be used to finance the farming;

(l) documentation from the applicant's bank or other lender detailing any lending to the applicant and the terms of such lending;

(m) if changes are proposed in relation to the farming system, details of those changes together with a farm budget and cashflow projection;

(n) the deceased tenant's will, probate and Her Majesty's Revenue & Customs (HMRC) account if the applicant is relying upon any inherited funds;

(o) the notice to quit served by the landlord (if any);

(p) the tenancy agreement of the subject holding.

A proper preparation of the documents which are necessary to be supplied to the ALT cannot be overemphasised. Although, for example, it is possible to seek a direction from the chairman to dispense with the provision of a map, plan or any other document required to be provided[3], good practice dictates that this should be avoided.

It should be noted that every application and reply must be signed by the party making it, or by a person authorised to do so on his behalf, and should be delivered or sent in duplicate to the secretary of the ALT[4]. On receiving from any party an application, reply or other document referred to in the Agricultural Land Tribunals (Rules) Order 1978, the secretary shall forthwith serve one copy on every other party to the proceedings[5].

[1]   Agricultural Land Tribunals (Rules) Order 1978, SI 1978/259, art 1(4)(b). Also see, *Morris v Patel* [1987] 1 EGLR 75, (1986) 281 Estates Gazette 419, CA, where an out of date form was used. It was held to be 'substantially to the like effect' to the forms then in use so the application was not invalid.
[2]   SI 1978/259, r 6(4).
[3]   SI 1978/259, r 16(6), (7).
[4]   SI 1978/259, r 16(1).
[5]   SI 1978/259, r 17.

Service

46.7 Every application, reply or other document required or authorised by the rules governing the procedure before the ALT shall be deemed to have been duly served if it was delivered to him or left at his proper address or sent to him by registered post or recorded delivery[1].

[1]   Agricultural Land Tribunals (Rules) Order 1978, SI 1978/259, r 35(1).

Withdrawal of application or reply

46.8 A party may withdraw his application or reply by giving notice in writing to the secretary of the ALT at any time before the hearing. On receipt of such notice the secretary shall forthwith notify all other parties. Where a reply is withdrawn, the ALT may, except in a drainage case, decide to make an order in the terms of the application without a formal hearing. If, on the withdrawal of an application or reply, it appears to the chairman that the case is a proper one for the award of costs under power conferred by s 5 of the Agriculture (Miscellaneous Provisions) Act 1954, he shall cause the ALT to be convened for the purpose of determining whether costs should be awarded, and the secretary shall give all parties not less than seven days' notice of the date, time and place appointed for that purpose[1].

[1]   Agricultural Land Tribunals (Rules) Order 1978, SI 1978/259, r 18(1), (2) and (3). See para 46.14.

Interlocutory applications

46.9 There is no prescribed timetable or procedure affecting interlocutory applications to the ALT. Unless the chairman orders otherwise, an application for directions on any matter which the chairman has power to determine under the Agriculture Land Tribunals (Rules) Order 1978 is to be made in writing to the ALT stating the grounds of the application. It is to be delivered or sent to the secretary of the ALT together with a sufficient number of copies for service on all other parties[1].

The only other provision of general application in connection with the preparation for a hearing before the ALT applies to the disclosure of documents. A party is required to provide the secretary of the ALT on his request with any document or other information which the ALT may require and which is in the power of that party to provide. The party is also to give the other parties an opportunity to inspect such document or to provide a copy of such document. This provision is subject to a public interest exception[2].

The Agricultural Land Tribunals (Rules) Order 1978 provides for a report from the Minister[3] and for a summary determination in drainage cases[4].

Notwithstanding the absence of detailed provisions in connection with the preparation for hearing, the parties are well advised to treat this as a court hearing and prepare bundles of documents in an orderly manner as if this would be presented to the court or to an arbitrator.

[1]   Agricultural Land Tribunals (Rules) Order 1978, SI 1978/259, r 19.
[2]   SI 1978/259, r 20.
[3]   See para 4.2.
[4]   SI 1978/259, rr 21 and 22.

Notice of hearing

46.10 The fact that extensive interlocutory issues are not anticipated before the ALT, as soon as practicable after the receipt of the reply, or as the case may be, after the time for replying has expired, the chairman of the ALT is required to fix a date, time and place for the hearing of the application[1]. The chairman may alter the arrangements if it appears to him to be necessary or desirable to do so in order to avoid hardship to the parties or for other good cause. The secretary must give notice of the hearing in the prescribed form 14 clear days before the hearing is due to take place[2]. In practice, the parties to the dispute may be attempting to negotiate a settlement and, as the issues are often complex, much time can be taken in negotiations during which the parties might request that a hearing is deferred.

[1]   Agricultural Land Tribunals (Rules) Order 1978, SI 1978/259, r 23(1).
[2]   SI 1978/259, r 23(3) and (4).

Inspection

46.11 Practice differs from ALT to ALT as to whether inspection of the subject holding will take place immediately before the main hearing commences or whether the ALT convenes initially and then adjourns to carry out the inspection or whether the inspection takes place after the main hearing. An inspection of the holding is usually an important part of the hearing of any case, unless the issues have been narrowed to the extent that an inspection would not assist deliberations. The ALT is authorised to enter and inspect an agricultural holding owned or occupied by any party and to inspect fixed equipment, produce, livestock, etc. The members of the ALT panel may be accompanied by the parties, their representatives and expert witnesses, but, as in the case of arbitration, care should be taken not to treat the inspection as a quasi-hearing[1].

The ALT sits in public unless it appears to the members of the panel that there are exceptional reasons which make it desirable that the hearing or some part of it should take place in private[2].

Any party may appear or be heard in person or alternatively represented by a barrister, solicitor, surveyor or otherwise. In the case of a surveyor or other representative, the appointment must be made in writing[3].

At the hearing the party making the application shall begin and other parties shall be heard in such order as the ALT may determine[4]. Further, the flexibility employed is reflected in the provision that the procedure of the hearing shall be such as the ALT may direct[5]. The ALT may adjourn the hearing from time to time if for any reason it appears to it to be necessary or desirable to do so[6].

If a party fails to appear at the hearing at the time fixed, the ALT may (if it is satisfied that the party has been given adequate opportunity to attend) dismiss the application (where the party failing to appear is the applicant) or in any other case, proceed to determine the application in the absence of that party[7].

[1] Agricultural Land Tribunals (Rules) Order 1978, SI 1978/259, r 30.
[2] SI 1978/259, r 24. It should be noted that where a hearing or part of it takes place in private, a member of the Council on Tribunals is entitled to attend.
[3] SI 1978/259, r 25.
[4] SI 1978/259, r 26(1).
[5] SI 1978/259, r 26(2).
[6] SI 1978/259, r 26(3).
[7] SI 1978/259, r 27.

Evidence

46.12 The ALT may admit evidence notwithstanding that it would not be admissible in a court of law. Further, evidence may be given orally, on oath or on affirmation or otherwise; by affidavit, if the parties consent, or by means of written statements produced by the maker when giving evidence or, if the ALT consents, by another witness. At any stage of the proceedings, the ALT may, on its own motion or on an application by any party, order the personal attendance of the maker of a written statement for examination and cross-examination, or may admit any map, plan or other document in evidence[1].

The ALT will give every party an opportunity to call witnesses and to cross-examine any witness called by, or on behalf of, any other party and to re-examine his own witnesses after cross-examination. Further, a party may, if he so desires, give evidence as a witness on his own behalf. The ALT may call a witness itself who may, after giving evidence, be cross-examined by any party. The ALT may require any witness to give evidence on oath or affirmation[2].

The provisions of the Civil Procedure Rules as to the issuing of witness summonses, subject to such modifications as may be prescribed by such Rules, apply for the purposes of a hearing before the ALT as if it were a claim in the County Court. If a person who is summoned pursuant to the Civil Procedure Rules as a witness to the ALT hearing refuses or neglects, without sufficient cause, to appear or to produce any documents required by the summons to be produced or, having appeared, refuses to be sworn or to give evidence, that person shall forfeit such fine as the County Court may direct[3].

[1] Agricultural Land Tribunals (Rules) Order 1978, SI 1978/259, r 28.
[2] SI 1978/259, r 29(1)–(3).
[3] SI 1978/259, r 29(4).

Decision of the ALT

46.13 The decision of the ALT is given in writing together with a statement of the ALT's reasons for its decision. In the event of a disagreement between the members of the panel, the decision may be a majority one. The chairman is able to correct any clerical mistake in the written record of the ALT's decision. The secretary of the ALT sends a copy of the decision and the reasons to each of the parties together with a further copy to any party who, as the Rules describe it, 'appears reasonably to require it'[1].

[1] Agricultural Land Tribunals (Rules) Order 1978, SI 1978/259, r 31(1)–(4).

Costs

46.14 Originally, under the Agricultural Holdings Act 1948, the ALT had no power to make any costs order. Section 5 of the Agriculture (Miscellaneous Provisions) Act 1954 introduced a limited power for the ALT to award costs, but only against a party who had acted 'frivolously, vexatiously or oppressively'. A further extension was introduced by the Agriculture Act 1958. That gave the ALT power to order a 'reasonable contribution towards costs' against any party in proceedings relating to the enforcement of a condition attaching to the giving of consent to a notice to quit.

When the 1948 Act was repealed and re-enacted, the AHA 1986, s 27(7) included a power for the ALT, in proceedings under that section, to provide for the payment by any party of such sum as the ALT considers a reasonable contribution to costs. The width of this jurisdiction has been the subject of confusion and debate. In *Newall v Wright*[1], the ALT decided that this was not a general power to award costs against a landlord or a tenant in relation to any application for consent to the operation of a notice to quit. This is contrary to the view expressed in the previous (eighth) edition of this book[2].

Section 27(7) of the AHA 1986 provides that the ALT 'may, in proceedings under this section, by order provide for the payment of any party of such sum as the [ALT] consider a reasonable contribution towards costs'. In *Newall v Wright*, it was determined that an application by a landlord for consent to the operation of a notice to quit does not involve 'proceedings under this section'. A definitive answer to the issue from the courts is awaited.

Otherwise, in proceedings before the ALT, the power to award costs is limited to cases where the ALT determines that a party has acted 'frivolously, vexatiously or oppressively'.[3]

[1]   (2005) ALT, Eastern Area.
[2]   See *Scammell and Densham's Law of Agricultural Holdings* (8th edn, 1997), p 425, para (7).
[3]   Agriculture (Miscellaneous Provisions) Act 1954, s 5. It was not until the enactment of that section that the ALT had any power to award costs. The power was then extended in relation to certain cases involving consent to the operation of the landlord's notice to quit by the Agriculture Act 1958, Sch 1 para 13.

Date of postponement of operation of notice to quit

46.15 When the ALT consents to the operation of a notice to quit it has power either of its own motion or on the application of the tenant to postpone the termination of the tenancy for a period not exceeding 12 months if the notice to quit would otherwise become effective on or within six months after the giving of consent[1]. The tenant's application must be made within 14 days of the consent being given[2]. It is unclear as to whether the 12-month period commences on the date that consent is given or when the notice to quit would otherwise expire[3].

[1]   Agricultural Holdings (Arbitration Notices) Order 1987, SI 1987/710, art 13(1).
[2]   SI 1987/710, art 13(1).
[3]   SI 1987/710, art 13(1).

APPEALS AGAINST A DECISION OF THE ALT

Generally

46.16 There are two methods of challenging a decision of the ALT. First, either during the ALT proceedings or after their conclusion, a point of law may be referred to the High Court by way of case stated.

The second method of disputing a decision of the ALT is by way of an application for judicial review seeking a prerogative order from the High Court.

Appeal by way of case stated

46.17 Section 6 of the Agriculture (Miscellaneous Provisions) Act 1954 set up an appeal by way of case stated procedure. This is now supplemented by the

Agricultural Land Tribunals (Rules) Order 1978, rr 33 and 34[1]. This procedure of a case stated is in effect 'an appeal by way of case stated'[2]. The appeal lies only on a point of law and must be the subject of a request by either party[3]. The ALT cannot state a case of its own motion.

The method of appeal is by a case stated by the ALT which will be decided by the High Court[4].

Any party wishing to appeal from a decision of the ALT must make a request either at the hearing, or in writing to the secretary of the ALT, not later than 14 days from the date when the decision is 'sent' to the said party. 'Sent' would appear to mean dispatched rather than served upon, despite the inconvenience of this construction[5].

The appellant must also send to the secretary of the ALT sufficient copies of his request at the same time, to enable the secretary to serve a copy on every other party to the proceedings before the ALT[6].

If the ALT decides to refuse a request, the ALT must, within 14 days of receipt of it, give a notice in writing to that effect to all parties[7].

Where the ALT has refused a request to refer a question of law to the High Court, the appellant has a right to apply to the court for an order directing the ALT to state a case[8]. The method of application is by motion to the Administrative Court of the Queen's Bench Division. The procedure is that the appellant must, within seven days after receiving notice of the refusal, serve on the secretary a notice in writing (with sufficient copies as above) of his intended application[9].

The appellant also has to file his notice of motion within 21 days of his receipt of the ALT's refusal of his request to them[10].

The notice of motion should be filed in the Crown Office and copies must also (within the same 21-day period) be served on all other parties to the proceedings and the secretary of the ALT. It is also necessary in cases of applications of s 11 of the AHA 1986 (the provision of fixed equipment, etc) that the notice of motion and case stated should be served on the authority having power to enforce the statutory requirement specified in the application. The authority has the right to be heard.

It is submitted that the test which the court should apply in deciding whether to require the ALT to state a case is whether the court is satisfied that there is a fairly arguable point of law which would justify ordering the ALT to refer it to the High Court for decision[11].

1   SI 1978/259.
2   *Davies v Price* [1958] 1 All ER 671, [1958] 1 WLR 434, per Parker LJ.
3   Cf the arbitrator's position, where the case stated lies only before the making of the award and where the arbitrator may state a case of his own motion.
4   Agricultural Land Tribunals (Rules) Order 1978, SI 1978/259, r 33(1).

5   See *Tankexpress A/S v Compagnie Financière Belge des Pétroles SA* [1949] AC 76, HL, but
    cf Interpretation Act 1978, s 7 which relates only to statutory construction. A draft of new
    proposed regulations address this point, but at the time of writing the new regulations have
    not yet been made.
6   SI 1978/259, r 33(1).
7   SI 1978/259, r 33(1).
8   Agriculture (Miscellaneous Provisions) Act 1954, s 6(4).
9   SI 1978/259, r 33(2).
10 SI 1978/259, r 33(2).
11 *William Smith (Wakefield) Ltd v Parisride Ltd* [2005] 2 EGLR 22. Cf *Davies v
    Agricultural Land Tribunal (Wales)* [2007] EWHC 1395 (Admin); *Ross v Donaldson*
    [1982] SLT 26; *Maggs v Worsley* (1982) ALT, South Western Area.

46.18 The case stated is to set out the facts found by the ALT and the
questions of law to be referred to the High Court. It is to be signed by the
chairman of the ALT and delivered to the appellant within two months after
the date of his request for it or the date of the order of the High Court, as the
case may be[1]. It is normally most convenient for the parties to seek to agree
the form and contents of the case stated rather than to leave the matter to the
ALT[2].

The appellant, within ten days of the date of receipt of the case from the ALT,
must file it in the Crown Office. Copies for use by the judge should also be
lodged with the Crown Office. Further, within 14 days from the date, he must
also serve on all other parties to the proceedings before the ALT (and on the
Minister) a notice that the case be entered for hearing, together with a copy of
the case[3].

The Agricultural Land Tribunals (Rules) Order 1978 provides for modification of the ALT's decision after the High Court proceedings[4], including as to
the procedure for any further hearing that may be necessary by the ALT and
for the constitution of a new ALT if the further hearing 'cannot conveniently
take place before the ALT as originally constituted'[5].

1   Agricultural Land Tribunals (Rules) Order 1978, SI 1978/259, r 33(3).
2   See the remarks of Widgery LCJ in *Cooke v Talbot* (1977) 243 Estates Gazette 831. As to
    the method of formulating an appeal by way of case stated, see the remarks of Megaw LJ
    in *Camden London Borough v Civil Aviation Authority* (1980) 257 Estates Gazette 273 at
    277. See also *R v Agricultural Land Tribunal for the South Eastern Area, ex p Parslow*
    (1979) 251 Estates Gazette 667.
3   In *Cooke v Talbot* (1977) 243 EG 831 where the ALT refused to state a case when invited
    to do so by the tenant, the Lord Chief Justice said that it was desirable in such cases for the
    parties to seek to agree the statement of facts and the questions of law rather than leave
    this to the tribunal.
4   Agricultural Land Tribunals (Rules) Order 1978, SI 1978/259, r 34.
5   It was held in *Cooke v Talbot* (1977) 243 EG 831 that the Divisional Court had no power
    to compel the reconstitution of the ALT for the purposes of the further hearing, even if they
    felt it was desirable to do so. Also see *R v Agricultural Land Tribunal (Wales), ex p Hughes*
    (1980) 255 EG 703.

Judicial review

46.19 Until the passing of s 6 of the Agriculture (Miscellaneous Provisions)
Act 1954, the only right of appeal from the ALT lay by way of prerogative

order of certiorari, mandamus or prohibition. These orders have now been amalgamated in one form of prerogative order known as judicial review. This is a restricted remedy which will only rarely be appropriate. In principle, this is still available in order to challenge the decision of the ALT on the same grounds as that of an arbitrator[1].

The uniform procedure for the exercise by the High Court of its jurisdiction to supervise the proceedings of inferior courts, tribunals or arbitrations, was introduced by Order 53 of the Rules of the Supreme Court (as substituted by the Rules of the Supreme Court (Amendment No 3) 1977)[2]. There is a two-tier system for making the application. First, it is necessary to obtain leave to apply for a judicial review and, thereafter, the substantive application is heard. The relief sought may include one of the prerogative orders.

1   *Re Jones and Carter's Arbitration* [1922] 2 Ch 599; *Maxwell-Lefroy v Bracey* (1956) 167 Estates Gazette 147; and *Price v Romilly* [1960] 3 All ER 429, [1960] 1 WLR 1360; and see Tribunals and Inquiries Act 1958, s 11. See also, *Davies v Price* [1958] 1 All ER 671, [1958] 1 WLR 434.
2   SI 1977/1955. Now see CPR Pt 54. Reference should be made to the current edition of the Civil Procedure Rules as to the procedure to be adopted.

THE FUTURE

46.20 The publication of this edition of this book was delayed in the hope that it would be possible to incorporate the promised new rules applying to ALT procedure. Regrettably, at the end of August 2007, the timetable for finalising the new rules, laying them before Parliament and implementing them, remains uncertain.

In January 2007, DEFRA published a draft of the revised Agricultural Land Tribunals (Rules) Order for England and Wales for consultation. The new rules arose from the concern expressed by ALT chairmen that the current rules are outdated and hamper their ability to carry out their activities effectively and in the best interests of the parties. The existing rules do not reflect either modern civil procedure rules or the new 'Model Rules of Procedure for Tribunals', published by the Council on Tribunals in 2003.

The draft of the new rules was substantially revised as a consequence of the consultation process. By the end of August 2007, the final form of the new rules has not been settled and published. The new rules will be the subject of a supplement to this book following their publication and implementation.

Chapter 47

ARBITRATION

ARBITRATION UNDER THE AGRICULTURAL TENANCIES ACT 1995

Introduction

47.1 Section 28 of the Agricultural Tenancies Act 1995 (ATA 1995) provides that any dispute between the landlord and the tenant under a farm business tenancy, concerning their rights and obligations under the ATA 1995, under the terms of the farm business tenancy or any custom, shall be determined by arbitration[1] (a 'general arbitration').

The ATA 1995 also provides for three instances where there are specific statutory rights for the parties to a farm business tenancy to invoke the arbitration procedure under the ATA 1995. They are:

(a)   the determination of the rent pursuant to a statutory review notice[2] (a 'rent arbitration');

(b)   the landlord's refusal or failure to give consent to, or his imposition of an unreasonable condition upon, a proposed improvement to be carried out by the tenant[3] (an 'improvements arbitration'); and

(c)   any claim for compensation under Pt III of the ATA 1995[4] (a 'compensation arbitration').

The provisions set out in s 28 do not apply:

(i)   so as to oust the jurisdiction of the courts[5];

(ii)   to a rent arbitration, an improvements arbitration or a compensation arbitration[6]; and

(iii) where the parties have agreed alternative dispute resolution procedures[7].

In respect of rent arbitrations, an improvement or compensation arbitration, the ATA 1995 contains a statutory timetable[8] so that the provisions in s 28 do not apply. In an improvement or compensation arbitration any dispute between the landlord and the tenant is compulsorily referred to arbitration under the ATA 1995.

[1]   ATA 1995, s 28(1).

847

2   Ch 9 and ATA 1995, s 10(1).
3   Ch 9 and ATA 1995, s 19(1).
4   Ch 16 and ATA 1995, s 22(1).
5   ATA 1995, s 28(1) and (4).
6   ATA 1995, s 28(1) and (5).
7   ATA 1995, ss 28 and 29. This includes where the parties have agreed to refer a rent review
      to an independent expert in accordance with s 9(c)(ii).
8   See paras 47.6–47.11.

Stay of proceedings

47.2 In relation to the court's jurisdiction, regard must be had to s 9 of the Arbitration Act 1996 (AA 1996)[1], which gives the court power to stay proceedings before the court where the litigants are parties to a binding arbitration agreement[2].

The power given to the court by s 9 of the AA 1996 applies where:

(a)   a party to an arbitration agreement against whom legal proceedings are brought (whether by way of claim or counter-claim) in respect of a matter under which the agreement is to be referred to arbitration may (upon notice to the other parties to the proceedings) apply to the court in which the proceedings have been brought to stay the proceedings so far as they concern that matter[3]; and

(b)   the person applying to stay the proceedings has taken the appropriate procedural step (if any) to acknowledge the legal proceedings against him[4]; and

(c)   the person making the application to stay the legal proceedings has not taken any step in those proceedings to answer the substantive claim[5]; and

(d)   the court is satisfied that the arbitration agreement is not null and void, inoperative or incapable of being performed[6].

The courts upheld the validity of an arbitration agreement and stayed court proceedings in the face of a challenge that it contravened a party's right to have his case heard in court under art 6 of the European Convention on Human Rights 1950. The arbitration agreement constituted a waiver of the individual's rights under art 6(1)[7].

An application may be made to the court to stay proceedings notwithstanding that the matter is to be referred to arbitration only after the exhaustion of other dispute resolution procedures[8]. The arbitration procedure under the ATA 1995 is statutory. The power given to the court by s 9 of the AA 1996 to stay legal proceedings applies equally to statutory arbitrations[9].

1   It should not be forgotten that the court has an inherent jurisdiction to stay proceedings which can be used in circumstances outside those considered in s 9: see *Al-Naimi v Islamic Press Agency* [2000] 1 Lloyd's Rep 522.
2   The provision to stay legal proceedings was formerly contained in s 4 of the Arbitration Act 1950, which was specifically referred to in s 28(4) of the ATA 1995. See the House of Lords decision in *Inco Europe Ltd v First Choice Distributions* [2000] 1 WLR 586.
3   AA 1996, s 9(1).

4   AA 1996, s 9(3). *Capital Trust Investments Ltd v Radio Design TJ AB* [2002] EWCA Civ 135, [2002] 2 All ER 159.
5   AA 1996, s 9(3). An application to set aside default judgment, applying (unnecessarily) for leave to defend and applying for consequential directions do not amount to steps in the proceedings to answer the substantive claim.
6   AA 1996, s 9(4). If the court refuses to stay the legal proceedings, any provision that an award is a condition precedent to the bringing of legal proceedings in respect of any matter is of no effect in relation to those proceedings: AA 1996, s 9(5).
7   *Stretford v Football Association Ltd* [2006] EWHC 479 (Ch), [2006] All ER (D) 275 (Mar).
8   AA 1996, s 9(2).
9   AA 1996, s 9(4).

General arbitration

47.3 Where a dispute has arisen between the landlord and the tenant under a farm business tenancy, concerning their rights and obligations under the ATA 1995, under the terms of the farm business tenancy or any custom, such disputes shall be determined by arbitration under the ATA 1995[1]. The general arbitration provisions contained in the ATA 1995 are discrete and separate from those described below in relation to rent arbitrations, improvements arbitrations and compensation arbitrations[2]. In addition to the provisions set out in s 28, general arbitrations operate under the provisions of the AA 1996[3].

Where a dispute has arisen to which s 28 of the ATA 1995 applies, the procedure to activate the arbitration requires the landlord or the tenant to give notice in writing to the other specifying the dispute. The notice must also state that, unless before the end of the period of two months beginning with the day on which the notice is given the parties have appointed an arbitrator by agreement, the party giving notice proposes to apply to the President of the Royal Institution of Chartered Surveyors (RICS) for the appointment of an arbitrator by him[4].

Where such notice has been given by the landlord or the tenant, but no arbitrator has been appointed by agreement, either party may, after the end of the period of two months referred to in the preliminary notice, apply to the President of the RICS for the appointment of an arbitrator by him[5]. Either party may make the application to the President of the RICS. It is not necessary for the person who served the preliminary notice to do so.

There is no prescribed form of notice, although the prescribed information set out in s 28(2) of the ATA 1995 must be contained in the notice[6]. Although the ATA 1995 provides that no application may be made to the President of the RICS for the appointment of an arbitrator within the period of two months following the service of the preliminary notice, the ATA 1995 does not contain a deadline by which such application must be made.

The provisions set out in s 28 do not apply to a rent arbitration, an improvement or compensation arbitration or where the landlord and tenant have agreed an alternative dispute resolution procedure.

1   ATA 1995, s 28. As to the exceptions to this provision, see para 47.4.

47.3 *Arbitration*

See paras 47.6–47.11.
3 Repealing and re-enacting as necessary Pt I of the Arbitration Act 1950 and the Arbitration Act 1979.
4 ATA 1995, s 28(2).
5 ATA 1995, s 28(3).
6 See Form E2 at para A2.15.

Arbitrations in accordance with s 29 of the ATA 1995

47.4 Section 29 of the ATA 1995 applies where a written tenancy agreement provides for disputes to be resolved by anyone other than the landlord or tenant or a third party appointed by only one party without the consent of the other.

Section 29 applies where the tenancy agreement refers to a determination by an arbitrator[1] and the requirements of sub-s (1)(b) are satisfied.

Section 29(1)(b) requires that either the parties have jointly appointed the arbitrator or third party or one of the parties has referred the dispute to the arbitrator or third party and notified the other party of the reference. If after four weeks the other party has not served a notice under s 28(2) to bring the dispute back into the operation of s 28 as a general arbitration, the dispute will continue as a contractual arbitration or alternative dispute resolution (ADR) under s 29.

Section 29 does not apply to improvement arbitrations or compensation arbitrations. A landlord and tenant can agree in the tenancy agreement to resolve a dispute on rent using an independent expert[2].

The general provisions relating to arbitrations[3] under the ATA 1995 do not apply to contractual arbitrations under s 29. The mandatory provisions of the AA 1996 also apply and override any term in the tenancy agreement that is inconsistent. The terms of the tenancy agreement then apply and in the event that the parties have not agreed terms, ss 1 to 84 of the AA 1996 apply.

1 Section 29 also provides for expert determination or mediation where the tenancy agreement allows them to give a decision which is binding on both parties. For further discussion on alternate dispute resolution mechanisms, see Ch 48.
2 The tenancy agreement must not contain any provision which precludes a reduction in rent during the tenancy. These provisions only apply to tenancy agreements entered into on or after 19 October 2006, the commencement date of the Regulatory Reform (Agricultural Tenancies) (England and Wales) Order 2006, SI 2006/2805.
3 See para 47.5.

General provisions applying to arbitrations under the ATA 1995

47.5 The ATA 1995 contains three provisions which apply to arbitrations under the ATA 1995. The three provisions apply to rent, improvements, compensation and general arbitrations[1]. They are:

(a)   The determination of any issue referable to arbitration shall be by a sole arbitrator[2].

(b)   Any application made under the ATA 1995 to the President of the RICS for the appointment of an arbitrator by him must be made in writing and must be accompanied by such reasonable fee as the President may determine in respect of the costs of making the appointment[3].

(c)   Where an arbitrator appointed for the purposes of the ATA 1995 dies or is incapable of acting and no new arbitrator has been appointed by agreement, either party may apply to the President of the RICS for the appointment of a new arbitrator by him[4].

These provisions override the terms of the AA 1996, in so far as the ATA 1995 is inconsistent with the AA 1996.

[1]   The general provisions set out in s 30 apply only to matters required to be determined under the ATA 1995. They do not extend to arbitrations established under s 29. See para 47.4.

[2]   ATA 1995, s 30(1).

[3]   ATA 1995, s 30(2).

[4]   ATA 1995, s 30(3). The arbitrator is only incapable of acting of the disability is serious enough to put him out of action altogether in acting in the arbitration: see *Succula Ltd and Pomona Shipping Co Ltd v Harland and Wolff Ltd* [1980] 2 Lloyd's Rep 381 at 388.

Rent arbitration

47.6 The statutory rent review procedure under the ATA 1995[1] commences where the landlord or tenant under a farm business tenancy gives notice in writing to the other (the statutory review notice) requiring that the rent payable in respect of the holding as from the review date shall be referred to arbitration in accordance with the provisions of the ATA 1995[2].

It should be noted that it is not necessary for all rent review disputes under the ATA 1995 to be referred to arbitration. It is permissible for the parties to a farm business tenancy to agree their own dispute resolution mechanism whether by expert or otherwise (but not by arbitration) under the ATA 1995[3].

[1]   See Ch 9.

[2]   ATA 1995, s 10(1).

[3]   ATA 1995, s 9(c). See Ch 9. For alternative methods of dispute resolution, see Ch 48.

47.7 Where a statutory review notice has been given in relation to a farm business tenancy to commence the statutory rent review mechanism, then provided:

(a)   no arbitrator has been appointed under an agreement made since the notice was given[1]; and

(b)   no person has been appointed under such an agreement to determine the question of rent (otherwise than as an arbitrator) on a basis agreed by the parties[2],

either party may, at any time during the six months ending with the review date, apply to the President of the RICS for the appointment of an arbitrator by him[3].

It should be noted that the application to the President of the RICS for the appointment of an arbitrator *must* be made before the review date pursuant to the statutory review notice. The application need not be made by the person who served the statutory review notice.

The provisions in s 28 of the ATA 1995 which relate to the commencement of general arbitrations do not apply to rent arbitrations. Practitioners are reminded that s 30 applies to rent arbitrations[4]. As in the case of all arbitrations under the ATA 1995, the rent arbitration is governed by the AA 1996 in so far as it is not inconsistent with the provisions set out above.

[1]   ATA 1995, s 12(a).
[2]   ATA 1995, s 12(b).
[3]   ATA 1995, s 12.
[4]   See para 47.5.

Improvements arbitration

47.8 Where a tenant under a farm business tenancy seeks to carry out a tenant's improvement, and is aggrieved by:

(a)   the refusal of his landlord to give his consent under s 17(1) of the ATA 1995;[1]

(b)   the failure of his landlord to give such consent within two months of a written request by the tenant for such consent[2]; or

(c)   any variation in the terms of the tenancy required by the landlord as a condition of giving such consent[3],

the tenant may by notice in writing given to the landlord demand that the question shall be referred to arbitration under s 19 of the ATA 1995[4].

[1]   See Ch 16 and ATA 1995, s 19(1)(a).
[2]   See Ch 16 and ATA 1995, s 19(1)(b).
[3]   See Ch 16 and ATA 1995, s 19(1)(c).
[4]   ATA 1995, s 19(1).

47.9 The tenant cannot give notice to commence such an arbitration where:

(a)   The tenant has already provided or begun to provide the tenant's improvement[1], unless that improvement is a routine improvement[2].

(b)   After the end of the period of two months beginning with the day on which the notice of the refusal of the landlord to give his consent under s 17(1) of the ATA 1995 or any variation in the terms of the tenancy required by the landlord as a condition of giving such consent was given to the tenant[3].

(c)   After the end of the period of four months beginning with the day on which the written request was given to the landlord seeking consent to the carrying out of the tenant's improvement[4].

Where the tenant has given notice to the landlord demanding that the question relating to the landlord's refusal or failure to give consent or the imposition of a condition unacceptable to the tenant, but no arbitrator has been appointed under an agreement made since the notice was given, the tenant or the landlord may apply to the President of the RICS for the appointment of an arbitrator by him[5].

The landlord and tenant's ability to apply to the President of the RICS for the appointment of an arbitrator is restricted. Where, after notice has been given by the tenant in respect of the landlord's refusal or failure to give consent or the landlord's imposition of a condition unacceptable to the tenant, in relation to any tenant's improvement which is not a routine improvement, if the tenant begins to provide the improvement:

(i)   no application may be made to the President of the RICS for the appointment of an arbitrator after the tenant begins to provide the improvement[6];

(ii)   where such an application has been made, but no arbitrator has been appointed before that time, the application shall be ineffective[7];

(iii)   no award may be made by the arbitrator after the tenant begins to provide the improvement except as to the costs of the reference and award in a case where the arbitrator was appointed before that time[8].

Subject to those restrictions the arbitrator may unconditionally approve the provision of the tenant's improvement or may withhold his approval, but may not give his approval subject to any condition or vary any condition required by the landlord under s 17(3) of the ATA 1995[9].

If the arbitrator gives his approval, that approval shall have effect for the purposes of Pt I of the ATA 1995 and for the purposes of the farm business tenancy as if it were the consent of the landlord[10].

[1]   ATA 1995, s 19(2).
[2]   ATA 1995, s 19(2) and (10). For the definition of a routine improvement, see para 16.5.
[3]   ATA 1995, s 19(3)(a).
[4]   ATA 1995, s 19(3)(b).
[5]   ATA 1995, s 19(4).
[6]   ATA 1995, s 19(9)(a).
[7]   ATA 1995, s 19(9)(b).
[8]   ATA 1995, s 19(9)(c).
[9]   ATA 1995, s 19(6).
[10]   ATA 1995, s 19(7).

47.10 Where the landlord has sought to impose a variation in the terms of the tenancy as a condition of giving consent to the proposed tenant's improvement, the withholding by the arbitrator of his approval shall not affect the validity of the landlord's consent or of the condition subject to which it was given[1]. It should be noted that the ability of the tenant to refer the matter of consent to a tenant's improvement to arbitration is confined to the refusal to give consent under s 17 of the ATA 1995. Section 17 does not apply to planning permissions and therefore it is not possible to apply to an arbitrator to override a landlord's refusal to grant consent to obtain planning permission[2].

The provisions applying to general arbitrations governed by s 28 of the ATA 1995[3] do not apply to improvements arbitrations but the provisions set out in s 30 are applicable[4]. The alternative dispute resolution provisions contained in s 29 of the ATA 1995[5] are not available as an alternative to improvements arbitrations. As in the case of all arbitrations under the ATA 1995, an improvement arbitration is governed by the provisions of the AA 1996 in so far as they are not inconsistent with the terms set out above.

[1]   ATA 1995, s 19(8).
[2]   See Ch 16.
[3]   See para 47.3.
[4]   See para 47.5.
[5]   See para 47.4.

Compensation arbitration

47.11   Section 22 of the ATA 1995 provides that any claim by a tenant under a farm business tenancy for compensation under s 16 of the ATA 1995[1] shall, subject to the provisions of s 22, be determined by arbitration under the provisions of the section[2]. The provisions applying to general arbitrations contained in s 28 of the ATA 1995 do not apply to compensation arbitrations[3], however, s 30 is applicable[4]. The alternative dispute resolution provisions contained in s 29 are unavailable[5]. As with all arbitrations under the ATA 1995, a compensation arbitration is governed by the AA 1996 in so far as its terms are not inconsistent with the ATA 1995.

Before the tenant can rely upon the arbitration provisions contained in s 22 of the ATA 1995 for a compensation arbitration, it is necessary for the tenant to have given notice in writing to his landlord of his intention to make a claim for compensation at the termination of the tenancy and to give details of the nature of the claim[6]. Such preliminary notice must be given before the end of the period of two months beginning with the date of the termination of the tenancy and no claim for compensation shall be enforceable unless such notice is given[7].

[1]   See Ch 16.
[2]   ATA 1995, s 22(1).
[3]   ATA 1995, s 28(5).
[4]   See para 47.5.
[5]   ATA 1995, s 28(1).
[6]   ATA 1995, s 22(2).
[7]   ATA 1995, s 22(2).

47.12   Where the tenant has given a valid and effective preliminary notice indicating his intention to make a claim for compensation and the nature of the claim, if:

(a)   the landlord and the tenant have not settled the claim by agreement in writing[1], and

(b)   no arbitrator has been appointed under an agreement made since the preliminary notice given by the tenant indicating his intention to make the claim for compensation and the nature of the claim was given[2],

either party may, after the end of the period of four months beginning with the date of the termination of the tenancy, apply to the President of the RICS for the appointment of an arbitrator by him[3].

Accordingly, where the landlord and tenant of a farm business tenancy fail to agree the amount of compensation due to the tenant in respect of the claims indicated in his preliminary notice, the ATA 1995 provides for a mandatory reference to arbitration to assess the amount of compensation payable.

As in the case of the rent arbitration and the improvement arbitration, the compensation arbitration has a discrete timetable.

Unlike the improvement arbitration, which does not encompass planning permissions[4], the compensation arbitration applies to all tenant's improvements including routine improvements. However, where the application to the President of the RICS for the appointment of an arbitrator for the purposes of a compensation arbitration relates wholly or partly to compensation in respect of a routine improvement[5] which the tenant has provided or has begun to provide[6], and that application is made at the same time as an application under s 19(4) of the ATA 1995 relating to the provision of that improvement[7], the President shall appoint the same arbitrator on both applications and, if both applications are made by the same person, only one fee shall be payable in respect of them[8].

It should be noted that where a tenant lawfully remains in occupation of part of the holding after the termination of a farm business tenancy, references in s 22 to the termination of a tenancy, for the purposes of a compensation arbitration, shall, in a case of a claim relating to that part of the holding, be construed as references to the termination of the occupation[9]. This extends the period for claiming compensation in the event of the tenant holding over, for example, in the buildings until the sale of the grain or on the land to take a late harvested crop.

1   ATA 1995, s 22(3)(a).
2   ATA 1995, s 22(3)(b).
3   ATA 1995, s 22(3).
4   See para 47.10.
5   ATA 1995, s 19(10).
6   ATA 1995, s 22(4)(a).
7   ATA 1995, s 22(4)(b).
8   ATA 1995, ss 22(4) and 30(2).
9   ATA 1995, s 22(5).

ARBITRATION UNDER THE AGRICULTURAL HOLDINGS ACT 1986

Introduction

47.13 Arbitration is the primary method of dispute resolution under the Agricultural Holdings Act 1986 (AHA 1986). Throughout earlier parts of this book, frequent references have been made to disputes or other matters being compulsorily referable to arbitration. This does not mean, however, that disputes arising in respect of agricultural holdings cannot be settled by agreement where a dispute is compulsorily referable to arbitration – this is a fallback provision. Arbitration provides the machinery for resolving the dispute in default of agreement[1]. If the right to proceed to arbitration is to be preserved, care must be taken to comply with the procedures and time limits specified in the AHA 1986. This usually means taking steps concurrently with negotiating a possible settlement.

When the AHA 1986 came into force[2] it included its own arbitration code in Schedule 11. The code originated from the Agricultural Holdings Act 1948.

The arbitration procedures have been substantially reformed following the recommendations made by the Tenancy Reform Industry Group (TRIG2)[3] when they presented their final report to the Government in May 2003.

TRIG2 concluded that the procedures contained in Sch 11 were antiquated and often, though unintentionally, promoted delay in the resolution of disputes. TRIG proposed the complete removal of the arbitration provisions in the AHA 1986 so that disputes are covered by the more modern and flexible AA 1996. TRIG2 believed that the greater flexibility offered by the AA 1996 would enable the parties to an arbitration to be more in control of the process[4].

TRIG2's recommendations were implemented by the RRO 2006[5] which came into effect on 19 October 2006. Arbitrations commenced[6] before 19 October 2006 are conducted in accordance with the old rules under Sch 11[7]. Arbitrations commenced on or after 19 October 2006 are, subject to two exceptions[8], governed entirely by the AA 1996. This chapter provides a commentary on the procedures to be followed under the AHA 1986 and AA 1996.

The changes made by the RRO 2006 only affect the procedural steps after the arbitrator has been appointed. The RRO 2006 does not impact on the initial procedures for demanding arbitration and the time limits that apply for the service of a demand or the appointment of an arbitrator. These have been dealt with in the commentary on the substantive law relating to each dispute in question.

[1]   It is sometimes argued that, in the case of s 83 (post termination claims made on quitting) if the time limit for settling the dispute (eight months) has not achieved a settlement, any agreement reached after that time, which is not subsequently ratified by an arbitrator's award, is unenforceable. It is submitted that this view is wrong and any such agreement is enforceable in the usual way being an agreement supported by valuable consideration being the forbearance to obtain the appointment of an arbitrator and to incur the burden and expense of an arbitration.
[2]   On 18 June 1986.
[3]   See para 18.1.
[4]   Paragraph 4.32 of the TRIG Final Report, May 2003.
[5]   Regulatory Reform (Agricultural Tenancies) (England and Wales) Order 2006, SI 2006/2805.
[6]   The date the arbitrator is appointed.
[7]   For a commentary on Schedule 11 refer to the 8th Edition of this book.
[8]   See para 47.14.

General provisions applying to all arbitrations under the AHA 1986

47.14 Aside from the repeal of Sch 11, the RRO 2006 made two further changes to the AHA 1986 which relate to arbitration. The first relates to the timing of the appointment of an arbitrator appointed by the President of the RICS to determine a dispute over rent and has been dealt with earlier in the book[1]. The second relates to the number of arbitrators. The AA 1996 provides for the appointment of more than one arbitrator and the parties to a large commercial arbitration will often appoint more than one. This will not occur in the context of agricultural holdings since s 84 of the AHA 1986 requires a determination by a sole arbitrator.

1   See Ch 25.

The arbitration procedures

The preliminary notice

47.15 Most of the matters which are compulsorily referable to arbitration are subject to a requirement contained in the relevant section of the AHA 1986, or the appropriate regulations passed under it which specify arbitration as the disputes procedure, that a preliminary notice must be given setting the arbitration procedures in motion. The form and contents of such notices, the time limit for giving them, and the circumstances in which they can be given, vary, depending upon the dispute in question and are described in the commentary on the substantive law elsewhere in the text. They can be summarised as follows[1]:

(a)   *Rent reviews* – the same notice as for notice to quit must be given (namely, not less than 12 months' notice terminating on the next termination date of the tenancy) and such notices cannot be given to implement a rent review at intervals more frequent than every three years[2].

(b)   *Notices to quit (AHA 1986, Sch 3, Cases A, B, D and E)* – the demand for arbitration[3] must be given within one month of the date of service of the notice to quit which contains the reason stated in the notice which is to be challenged. Likewise, following a notice to remedy in Form 2[4], if the tenant wishes to dispute his liability to undertake the work in question, a demand for arbitration must be given within one month of the date of service of the notice to remedy[5].

(c)   *Claims arising on quitting* – s 83 provides that the preliminary notice, which is not a demand for arbitration but merely a notice of intention to claim, must be given within two months of the date of termination of the tenancy[6].

It is essential that, if any arbitrator subsequently appointed is to be given jurisdiction to determine the issue in dispute, any preliminary notice required should be valid and effective and duly served in accordance with the time limits set down in the sections or regulations which provide for arbitration. If no valid preliminary notice has been given, then any arbitrator purportedly appointed pursuant to such a notice has no jurisdiction, and any award he may make would be void, or at least voidable[7]. However, the general law as to waiver probably applies[8].

1   Examples of the provisions for giving preliminary notices are: s 2(4) where there is no express provision for a preliminary notice; s 8 requires a preliminary demand for arbitration but does not specify time limits, or the contents of the demand; s 12 requires at least one year's notice; s 9 and SI 1959/171 specifies the time limits of one year and one month respectively; s 13 requires notice given within six months from completion of the improvement; s 14 requires a preliminary notice but specifies no time limits; s 20 (damage by game) requires numerous preconditions and time limits to be complied with (see s 20(2)(a) and (b)).

2   See AHA 1986, s 12 and Sch 2 respectively, and note the exceptions to the general rule and the commentary at para 25.6.

3   Frequently referred to, misleadingly, as a counter-notice. A counter-notice is a counter-notice under s 26(1) invoking the jurisdiction of the Agricultural Land Tribunal (ALT). The so-called counter-notice to a notice to quit under Cases A, B, D or E of Sch 3 (see the Agricultural Holdings (Arbitration on Notices) Order 1987, SI 1987/710, art 9) is, if valid in its form, a demand for arbitration.

4   Ie a notice requiring the doing of any work of repair, maintenance or replacement. The form is prescribed by regulations: see the Agricultural Holdings (Forms of Notice to Pay Rent or to Remedy) Regulations 1987, SI 1987/711.

5   The Agricultural Holdings (Arbitration on Notices) Order 1987, arts 3, 4 and 9.

6   For a commentary on s 83 provisions, see Ch 41.

7   For the position where an arbitrator has no jurisdiction, see para 47.7. For an example of an arbitrator deprived of jurisdiction by an invalid demand for arbitration, see *Stiles v Farrow* (1977) 241 Estates Gazette 623.

8   *Kammins Ballrooms Co Ltd v Zenith Investments (Torquay) Ltd* [1971] AC 850, [1970] 2 All ER 871, HL.

The appointment of the arbitrator

47.16 Once a demand for arbitration or other preliminary notice has been given, the next stage is for an arbitrator to be appointed. In the case of disputes arising on quitting, s 83 sets out time limits after which the arbitrator must be appointed. In the case of rent review under s 12 and Sch 2, the arbitrator must be appointed before the next date following service of the s 12 notice when the tenancy would have been terminated by notice to quit. If no such appointment has been made, an application for appointment must be made before that date[1].

In the case of a notice to quit given for one of the reasons specified in Cases A, B, D or E, the arbitrator must be appointed within three months of the date of the demand for arbitration, otherwise the demand is rendered ineffective and the notice to quit takes effect regardless of whether the landlord could have made out the ground for giving the notice[2] or not. In other cases there are no such time limits[3].

An arbitrator under the AHA 1986 procedure may be appointed by agreement between the parties, or, if the parties cannot agree, by the President of the RICS on the application of either[4]. There is no condition that the parties should seek to agree before applying to the President of the RICS[5]. All that matters is that the parties should not, in fact, have agreed.

1   ATA 1995, s 12(3).

2   See Agricultural Holdings (Arbitration on Notices) Order 1987, SI 1987/710.

3   Though the equitable doctrines of waiver, estoppel (and even, possibly, laches, in very extreme cases, where no action is taken over a very protracted period) may cause the demand for arbitration to 'lapse' or be rendered unenforceable. There is no authority on such 'lapsing' of a demand for arbitration.

⁴ AHA 1986, s 84(2), as amended by the RRO 2006, SI 2006/2805, art 7(2). It is a courteous practice of many valuers not to apply ex p to the President but to seek the concurrence of the other party. This is not an essential prerequisite. In many cases where the parties are 'daggers drawn' it is not practical either. Note, also, that if the tenancy agreement provides for some other method of appointment, that must be followed.
⁵ *F R Evans (Leeds) Ltd v Webster* (1962) 112 L Jo 703.

47.17 Where the arbitrator is appointed by the parties they must meet the conditions under the AA 1996 to make a valid appointment[1]. The parties can agree to appoint anyone to act as arbitrator.

Where the parties have not discussed or failed to agree upon the appointment of the arbitrator, s 84 of the AHA 1986 provides for either party to apply to the President of the RICS for the appointment[2]. Following the changes implemented by the RRO 2006[3], the President is no longer restricted to making his appointment from a particular panel.

If the arbitrator dies or is incapable of acting, a new arbitrator may be appointed as if no arbitrator has been appointed[4].

No application may be made to the President of RICS for an arbitrator to be appointed by him unless the application is accompanied by such fee as may be prescribed as the fee for such application[5]. This is an important point where an application is made close to a deadline. *Thompson v Bradley*[6] has cast doubt on the assertion that the application is treated as not having been made until the fee is received by the President. The county court judge had to consider the validity of an application to the RICS made by fax on the last day before the rent review notice ceased to have effect, with the hard copy sent by recorded delivery with the cheque which arrived the following day. In this instance, the RICS had agreed that the application would be processed on the day the fax was received, with payment arriving the following day. The court held the payment provisions were directory and not mandatory and the RICS had, on the facts of this case, waived its entitlement to the fee on the day the application was made. Despite the landlord's success in this instance, practitioners should avoid last minute applications to the RICS.

Once the fee has been paid, no further fee is payable for any subsequent application for the appointment of a new arbitrator in relation to that arbitration[7].

1 See para 47.20.
2 AHA 1986, s 84(2).
3 SI 2006/2805.
4 AHA 1986, s 84(3).
5 AHA 1986, s 84(4). The fee is prescribed by the Minister and not by the President of the RICS: AHA 1986, ss 94(1) and 96(1). The current fee is £115: see the Agricultural Holdings (Fee) Regulations 1996, SI 1996/337, as amended.
6 (2006) Birmingham County Court, Lawtel 15 January 2007.
7 AHA 1986, s 84(4).

THE ARBITRAL PROCESS UNDER THE ARBITRATION ACT 1996

Introduction

47.18 The AA 1996 applies to:

(a) all arbitrations conducted under the AHA 1986 save that they must be conducted by a single arbitrator;

(b) all arbitrations under the ATA 1995 save that:
   (i) the general provisions set out at 47.5 et seq above override any parts of the AA 1996 that are inconsistent;
   (ii) separate provisions set out in the ATA 1995 apply to general arbitrations, rent arbitrations, improvement arbitrations and compensation arbitrations and the AA 1996 only applies when it is not inconsistent with these provisions.

Appointment of the arbitrator

Appointment by agreement

47.19 The AA 1996 provides a comprehensive code governing the arbitral tribunal including the procedure for the appointment of arbitrators and a failure of appointment procedure[1]. The provisions contained in the AA 1996 are, however, subject to the statutory requirements of the ATA 1995 and the AHA 1986 including a requirement that any dispute shall be determined by a sole arbitrator[2] and the procedure requiring an application to the President of the RICS for the appointment of an arbitrator in default of agreement.

There is no obligation upon the parties to seek to agree the appointment of the arbitrator. They may simply rely upon the statutory power of appointment.

[1] AA 1996, ss 15–29.
[2] ATA 1995, s 30(1) and the AHA 1986, s 84(1).

47.20 In order to perfect the appointment of an arbitrator by agreement between the parties it is necessary to comply with the following steps:

(a) the appointment should be made in writing[1];
(b) either before or after the appointment is made in writing between the parties, the arbitrator must have accepted the appointment[2]; and
(c) the arbitrator must have received notice of the appointment[3].

When those steps have been implemented, the appointment takes effect.

There is nothing to stop the parties to a tenancy agreement agreeing the identity of the arbitrator at the outset. In practice, this will be rare. Where the parties have agreed an arbitration procedure in the terms of the tenancy agreement including an agreement when the arbitration is to be regarded as commenced, the parties can rely and implement such terms where the ATA 1995 and the AHA 1986 do not specify that the dispute must be referred to arbitration and the statutory provisions govern.

1   Under the former provisions of the AHA 1986 (Sch 11, para 5), it was expressly provided that the appointment had to be in writing. Neither the ATA 1995 nor the AHA 1986 (now amended by the RRO 2006, SI 2006/2805) provide for the appointment to be in writing. This is one of a number of shortcomings in the new code.
2   *Sclater v Horton* [1954] 2 QB 1, CA; *Tradax Export SA v Volkswagenwerk AG* [1970] 1 QB 537, CA.
3   *Robinson v Moody* [1994] 37 EG 154; *Hannaford v Smallacombe* [1994] 15 EG 155.

Appointment by the President of the RICS

47.21   The appointment must be made in writing[1]. The application must be accompanied by such reasonable fee as the President of the RICS may determine in respect of the costs of making the appointment[2].

Where the application for the appointment of an arbitrator was sent to the RICS within time by fax, but the application form and fee followed by post and was received out of time, the application has been found by the county court to be valid. It was treated as having been made when the fax was received[3].

The President can only appoint an arbitrator in default of agreement. Therefore, once the parties have agreed who should act as arbitrator there is no recourse to the President of the RICS.

In making the appointment to the arbitrator, the President is acting in an administrative and not a judicial capacity[4]. Accordingly, if either party disputes the validity of the arbitrator's appointment, the matter should be raised with the arbitrator himself and not with the President of the RICS.

The AHA 1986 and the ATA 1995 do not specifically provide for the appointment of the arbitrator by the President to take effect from the date when the President executes the instrument of appointment[5].

1   ATA 1995, s 30(2).
2   ATA 1995, s 30(2); AHA 1986, s 84(3). See paras 47.5 and 47.17.
3   *Thompson v Bradley* (2006) Birmingham County Court, Lawtel 15 January 2007. See para 47.17.
4   *Ramsey v McLaren* 1936 SLT 35, Ct of Sess.
5   As to issues as to the timing of the appointment, see para 47.20.

Arbitrations in Wales

47.22   There is no requirement under the AHA 1986, the ATA 1995 or the AA 1996 for an arbitrator to possess a knowledge of Welsh agricultural conditions or a knowledge of the Welsh language in order to conduct an arbitration in Wales.

Extensions of time to begin the arbitration process

47.23   These provisions only apply where the parties have agreed to refer a dispute to arbitration and they are not compelled by statute to do so. If a tenancy agreement provides an arbitration clause, but includes a provision that the right to refer a matter to arbitration will be extinguished unless within a fixed time some step is taken to begin the arbitration or some other dispute resolution procedure, the court may extend the time for taking that step[1]. The court has a wide discretion to extend time for such period and on such terms as it thinks fit.

The right to apply for an extension of time does not apply to an arbitration under the AHA 1986 or ATA 1995 when a party has failed to serve a notice or commence arbitration within a statutory time limit. The application for an extension of time under s 12 of the AA 1996 only applies where the parties have agreed to refer matters to arbitration under s 29 of the ATA 1995 or where they are not compelled to arbitrate by the AHA 1986 to refer the dispute to arbitration.

[1]   AA 1996 Act, s 12.

Dispute as to jurisdiction

47.24 Previously, under the Arbitration Acts 1950 to 1979, an arbitrator could not determine his own jurisdiction[1], but the AA 1996 provides a procedure to deal with an objection to the substantive jurisdiction of the tribunal[2] and the parties cannot alter this procedure by agreement.

If a party objects to the arbitrator's substantive jurisdiction at the outset of the proceedings, that party must raise the issue not later than the time when he takes the first step in the proceedings to contest the merits of any matter in relation to which he challenges the arbitrator's jurisdiction[3]. A party is not precluded from raising such an objection by the fact that he has appointed or participated in the appointment of an arbitrator[4].

Any objection during the course of the arbitration that the arbitrator is exceeding his substantive jurisdiction must be made as soon as possible after the matter alleged to be beyond his jurisdiction is raised[5].

The arbitrator may admit an objection to his substantive jurisdiction at a later stage if he considers the delay justified[6].

When an objection is made to the arbitrator's substantive jurisdiction, the arbitrator has power to rule on his own jurisdiction and may:

(a)   rule on the matter in an award as to jurisdiction[7]; or
(b)   deal with the objection in his award on merits[8].

If the parties agree which of these courses the arbitrator should take, the arbitration shall proceed accordingly[9].

The arbitrator may in any case, and is required to if the parties so agree, stay the arbitration proceedings whilst an application is made to the court for a determination of a preliminary point of jurisdiction[10]. The court may, on the application of either party to an arbitration (upon notice to the other parties), determine any question as to the substantive jurisdiction of the tribunal[11]. The court will only consider an application to determine jurisdiction if:

(a)   it is made with the agreement in writing of all of the other parties to the proceedings[12]; or

(b)   it is made with the permission of the arbitrator and the court is satisfied that:

    (i)   the determination of the question is likely to produce substantial savings in costs;

    (ii)   the application was made without delay; and

    (iii)   there is a good reason why the matter should be decided by the court[13].

[1]   *Heyman v Darwins Ltd* [1942] AC 356, HL.
[2]   AA 1996, s 31.
[3]   AA 1996, s 31(1).
[4]   AA 1996, s 31(1).
[5]   AA 1996, s 31(2).
[6]   AA 1996, s 31(3).
[7]   AA 1996, s 31(4).
[8]   AA 1996, s 31(4)(b).
[9]   AA 1996, s 31(4).
[10]   AA 1996, ss 31(5) and 32.
[11]   AA 1996, s 32(1).
[12]   AA 1996, s 32(2)(a).
[13]   AA 1996, s 32(2)(b).

47.25   If an application is made to the court, unless it is made with the agreement of all of the other parties to the proceedings, it must state the grounds on which it is said that the matter shall be decided by the court[1]. Further, unless otherwise agreed by the parties to the arbitration, the arbitrator may continue the arbitration and make an award while an application to the court is pending[2].

No appeal lies from a decision of the court without leave of the court[3]. The decision of the court on the question of jurisdiction shall be treated as a judgment of the court for the purposes of an appeal[4]. No appeal lies without the leave of the court which shall not be given unless the court considers that the question involves a point of law which is one of general importance or is one which for some other special reason shall be considered by the Court of Appeal[5].

It should also be noted that a party may lose the right to object if he took part, or continues to take part, in an arbitration without raising an objection[6].

[1]   AA 1996, s 32(3).
[2]   AA 1996, s 32(4).
[3]   AA 1996, s 32(5).
[4]   AA 1996, s 32(6).
[5]   AA 1996, s 32(6).
[6]   AA 1996, s 73.

47.26 *Arbitration*

Death of a party

47.26 Unless otherwise agreed by the parties, an arbitration agreement is not discharged by the death of a party and may be enforced by or against the personal representatives of that party[1]. This will apply in cases where the parties have entered into their own arbitration agreement as their chosen method of alternative dispute resolution pursuant to s 29 of the ATA 1995[2] or under the AHA 1986 where the nature of the dispute means it is not compulsorily referable to arbitration. It will not apply to a rent arbitration, an improvements arbitration, a compensation arbitration or a general arbitration under the ATA 1995 because the general principle as to the effect of the death of a party to an arbitration agreement is subject to two exceptions:

(a)   it does not affect the operation of any enactment or rule of law by virtue of which a substantive right or obligation is extinguished by death[3]; and

(b)   it does not apply to a statutory arbitration[4].

1   AA 1996, s 8(1).
2   See para 47.4.
3   AA 1996, s 8(2).
4   AA 1996, s 97(a). As to the definition of 'statutory arbitration', see para 44.2. It includes a rent arbitration, an improvements arbitration, a compensation arbitration and a general arbitration under the ATA 1995.

Remuneration of the arbitrator

47.27 The AHA 1986 and the ATA 1995 are silent upon the issue of remuneration.

The remuneration of the arbitrator is comprehensively dealt with in the AA 1996. The following provisions should be noted:

(a)   The parties are jointly and severally liable to pay the arbitrator such reasonable fee and expenses (if any) as are appropriate in the circumstances[1].

(b)   Any party may apply to the court (upon notice to the other parties and to the arbitrator) which may order that the amount of the arbitrator's fees and expenses shall be considered and adjusted by such means and upon such terms as it may direct[2].

(c)   If the application is made after any amount has been paid to the arbitrator by way of fees or expenses, the court may order the repayment of such amount (if any) as is shown to be excessive, but shall not do so unless it is shown that it is reasonable in the circumstances to order repayment[3].

(d)   The statutory provisions contained in paragraphs (a) to (c) above do not affect any liability of a party to any other party to pay all or any of the costs of the arbitration or any contractual right of the arbitrator to payment of his fees and expenses[4]. Further, the arbitrator has power to refuse to deliver an award to the parties except upon full payment of the fees and expenses of the arbitrator in the arbitration[5]. As to the extent of the fees and expenses of the arbitrator, unless otherwise agreed by the parties, the recoverable costs shall include only such reasonable fees and expenses of the arbitrator as are appropriate in the circumstances[6].

The court has power to determine whether the fees and expenses of the arbitrator are reasonable[7].

If no agreement is reached between the parties as to the remuneration of the arbitrator, the arbitrator is entitled to reasonable remuneration[8].

[1]   AA 1996, s 28(1).
[2]   AA 1996, s 28(2).
[3]   AA 1996, s 28(3).
[4]   AA 1996, s 28(5).
[5]   AA 1996, s 56(1).
[6]   AA 1996, s 64(1).
[7]   AA 1996, s 64(2).
[8]   *Brown v Llandovery Terra Cotta Co Ltd* (1909) 25 TLR 625.

Immunity of arbitrator and the appointing body

47.28   An arbitrator is not liable for anything done by him or omitted to be done by him in the discharge or purported discharge of his functions as arbitrator unless the act or omission is shown to have been in bad faith[1]. Further, this immunity applies to an employee or agent of the arbitrator as it applies to the arbitrator himself[2], but it does not affect any liability incurred by an arbitrator by reason of his resignation[3].

Section 74 of the AA 1996 extends the immunity conferred upon arbitrators to the institutions who appointed them which may have acted negligently in the appointment or failed to exercise supervisory powers[4].

[1]   AA 1996, s 29(1).
[2]   AA 1996, s 29(2).
[3]   AA 1996, ss 29(3) and 25.
[4]   *Epoch Properties Ltd v British Home Stores (Jersey) Ltd* [2004] 3 EGLR 34, [2004] 48 EG 134.

Replacement of the arbitrator

Death or incapacity of the arbitrator

47.29   As seen above[1], one of the limited number of general provisions contained in the ATA 1995 and the AHA 1986 relating to arbitrations governs the position if the arbitrator dies or is incapable of acting. If no new arbitrator has been appointed by agreement, either party may apply to the President of the RICS for the appointment of a new arbitrator by him[2].

The AA 1996 provides that the authority of the arbitrator is personal and ceases on his death[3]. Further, the comprehensive code contained in the AA 1996 deals with the position where the person by whom an arbitrator was appointed dies. The AA 1996 provides that, unless otherwise agreed by the parties, the death of such person does not revoke the arbitrator's authority[4].

1   See ATA 1995, s 30(3) and AHA 1986, s 84(3). Also see paras 47.5 and 47.17.
2   ATA 1995, s 30(3).
3   AA 1996, s 26(1).
4   AA 1996, s 26(2).

Resignation of the arbitrator

47.30 If it is agreed between the parties that the arbitrator should cease to act, he may resign. The parties are free to agree with the arbitrator the consequences of such resignation as regards the arbitrator's entitlement (if any) to fees or expenses and any liability thereby incurred by him[1]. The court has no power to reopen any agreement made between the parties and the arbitrator.

If the arbitrator resigns, and there is no agreement between the arbitrator and the parties as to the consequences of his resignation, then the arbitrator may (upon notice to the parties) apply to the court:

(a)   to grant him relief from any liability incurred by him, and to make such order as the court thinks fit in relation to his entitlement (if any) to fees or expenses or the repayment of any fees and expenses already paid[2];
(b)   if the court is satisfied that, in all the circumstances, it was reasonable for the arbitrator to resign, it may grant such relief as is sought by the arbitrator on such terms as it thinks fit[3];
(c)   if either party wishes to appeal against the decision of the court in relation to the terms applying to the resignation of the arbitrator, leave of the court is required to pursue an appeal[4].

1   AA 1996, s 25(1).
2   AA 1996, s 25(2).
3   AA 1996, s 25(4).
4   AA 1996, s 25(5).

Removal of the arbitrator

47.31 A party to an arbitration may (upon notice to the other parties and to the arbitrator) apply to the court to remove an arbitrator on the following grounds:

(a)   that circumstances exist that give rise to justifiable doubts as to the arbitrator's impartiality[1];
(b)   that the arbitrator does not possess the qualifications required by the arbitration agreement[2];
(c)   that the arbitrator is physically or mentally incapable of conducting the proceedings or there are justifiable doubts as to his capacity to do so;
(d)   that the arbitrator has refused or failed:
    (i)   properly to conduct the proceedings; or
    (ii)   to use all reasonable despatch in conducting the proceedings or making an award,

and that substantial injustice has been or will be caused to the applicant[3].

Subject to the specific statutory provision contained in the ATA 1995 applying if the arbitrator dies or is incapable of acting[4], the provisions of the AA 1996 apply to the filling of the vacancy in the event of the arbitrator ceasing to act. Where the arbitrator ceases to hold office, the parties are free to agree:

(1)   whether and if so how the vacancy is to be filled;
(2)   whether and if so to what extent the previous proceedings should stand; and
(3)   what effect (if any) the arbitrator ceasing to hold office has on any appointment made by him[5].

Where the court removes an arbitrator, it may make such order as it thinks fit with respect to entitlement to fees and expenses, or the repayment of any fees and expenses[6]. Removal by the court does not automatically lead to disentitlement to fees and each case will turn on its facts[7]. Section 24 of the AA 1996 does not operate to allow a general action for damages against the arbitrator and any such action can only be brought where the arbitrator acts in bad faith[8].

The arbitrator is entitled to appear and be heard by the court before it makes any order under this section[9]. The leave of the court is required for any appeal from a decision of the court[10].

[1]   AA 1996, s 24(1)(a). See the guidance of the Court of Appeal in *Locabail (UK) Ltd v Bayfield Properties Ltd* [2000] QB 451 as to the issue of bias for judges. There must be a real likelihood of bias or grounds for reasonable suspicion. Note, also, the Human Rights Act 1998 (in force 2 October 2000) and the right to a fair trial contained in art 6. This may extend to compulsory (though not voluntary) references to arbitration. See, also, *Laker Airways v FLS Aerospace Ltd* [2000] 1 WLR 113 and *Andrews v Bradshaw* (1999) Times, 11 October, CA
[2]   There are no stated qualifications in the AHA 1986, ATA 1995 or AA 1996. AA 1996, s 24(1)(b) can only apply where there are specific criteria laid down in the tenancy or arbitration agreement or otherwise separately agreed.
[3]   *Norbrook Laboratories Ltd v Tank* [2006] EWHC 1055 (Comm), [2006] 2 Lloyd's Rep 485, where the arbitrator was removed for contacting witnesses direct but a number of other complaints were not upheld. The AA 1996, s 24 goes on to deal with the consequences of a successful application to the court to remove the arbitrator. This provision is not intended to allow the court to substitute its own view. The choice of a particular procedure, unless it breaches the duties imposed on arbitrators by s 33, should not justify the removal even if the court would not have done it that way.
[4]   See para 47.5.
[5]   AA 1996, s 27(1).
[6]   AA 1996, s 24(4).
[7]   *Wicketts and Sterndale v Brine Builders* [2001] CILL 1805.
[8]   AA 1996, s 29, see para 47.28.
[9]   AA 1996, s 24(5).
[10]   AA 1996, s 24(6).

General duty of the arbitrator

47.32   The AA 1996 imposes certain general duties upon the arbitrator. The arbitrator is obliged to act fairly and impartially as between the parties, giving each party a reasonable opportunity of putting his case and dealing with that of his opponent, and to adopt procedures suitable to the circumstances of the particular case, avoiding unnecessary delay or expense, so as to provide a fair means for the resolution of the matters falling to be determined[1]. The arbitrator must comply with those general duties in conducting the arbitration, in his decisions on matters of procedure and evidence and in the exercise of all other powers conferred upon him[2]. The duty is widely drafted and cannot be excluded by agreement of the parties.

Unlike the expert[3], the arbitrator is not entitled to go beyond the evidence adduced by the parties[4], nor can he be pursued for negligence if he acts in a quasi-judicial capacity[5]. If the arbitrator fails to comply with the duties set out in s 33 such that his actions cause substantial injustice, this will be a serious irregularity[6].

1   AA 1996, s 33(1). See also *Norbrook Laboratories Ltd v Tank* [2006] 2 Lloyd's Rep 485.
2   AA 1996, s 33(2).
3   See para 48.6.
4   *Fisher v PG Wellfair Ltd* [1981] 2 Lloyd's Rep 514, CA; *Top Shop Estates Ltd v Danino* [1985] 1 EGLR 9. See paras 47.33–47.35.
5   *Sirros v Moore* [1975] QB 118, CA.
6   See para 47.66.

Statement of case and particulars

47.33 The AA 1996 contains no provisions dealing with the delivery of a statement of case or its amendment. It provides freedom to the arbitrator to decide whether, for example, statements of case are required, and if so, whether their exchange should be mutual or sequential. The AA 1996 specifically provides that it shall be for the arbitrator to decide all procedural and evidential matters, subject to the right of the parties to agree any matter[1]. The procedural matters are defined to include what form of written statements of case are to be used, when these should be supplied and the extent to which such statements can later be amended[2]. Accordingly, the arbitrator may allow further particulars or the amendment of any pleading or statement of case in his discretion.

Failure on the part of either party to comply with the arbitrator's directions for the service of pleadings or statements of case does not have the automatic, draconian results that used to apply under the statutorily prescribed system in Sch 11 of the AHA 1986[3].

The arbitrator has no general power to make an award in favour of a party on the ground that the opposing party has failed to comply with the directions, but the defaulting party should have regard to costs, interest and the arbitrator proceeding to a hearing[4].

In addition, the parties are free to agree on the powers of the arbitrator in the case of a party's failure to do something necessary for the proper and expeditious conduct of the arbitration[5].

It should also be noted that the arbitrator, unless otherwise agreed by the parties, has a power to dismiss the claim[6]. Further, the parties must have regard to the general duties imposed upon them by the AA 1996[7], and the powers of the court to enforce a peremptory order of the arbitrator[8].

1 AA 1996, s 34(1).
2 AA 1996, s 34(2)(c).
3 Prior to its amendment by the Regulatory Reform (Agricultural Tenancies) (England and Wales) Order 2006, SI 2006/2805. For a commentary on Sch 11 of the AHA 1986, see the 8th edition of this book.
4 See the provisions of the AA 1996, s 41(4)–(7), and see also paras 47.38, 47.39 and 47.61.
5 AA 1996, s 41(1).
6 See para 47.40.
7 AA 1996, s 40 and see para 47.37.
8 AA 1996, s 42 and see para 47.39.

Interlocutory matters

47.34 The AA 1996 provides that it should be for the arbitrator to decide on all procedural and evidential matters, subject to the right of the parties to agree any matter[1].

The procedural and evidential matters include, in addition to the provision relating to statements of cases[2], the following:

(a) when and where any part of the proceedings is to be held;
(b) the language or languages to be used in the proceedings and whether translations of any relevant documents are to be supplied[3];
(c) whether any and if so which documents or classes of documents should be disclosed between and produced by the parties and at what stage[4];
(d) whether any and if so what questions should be put to and answered by the respective parties and when and in what form this should be done;
(e) whether to apply strict rules of evidence (or any other rules) as to the admissibility, relevance or weight of any material (oral, written or other) sought to be tendered on any matters of fact or opinion, and the time, manner and form in which such material should be exchanged and presented;
(f) whether and to what extent the arbitrator should take the initiative in ascertaining the facts and the law; and
(g) whether and to what extent there should be oral or written evidence or submissions[5].

The arbitrator may fix the time within which any directions given by him are to be complied with, and may if he thinks fit extend the time so fixed (whether or not it has expired)[6]. If the arbitrator departs from the agreed directions it may amount to serious irregularity[7].

1 AA 1996, s 34(1).
2 See para 47.33.
3 This provision might be relevant to arbitrations in Wales.
4 The rules that apply in court proceedings which prevent privileged communications being disclosed, also apply in relation to witness evidence.
5 AA 1996, s 34(2).

Hearings

47.35 There is no obligation on the arbitrator to determine the case at a hearing[1]. The arbitrator has the power to decide procedure and whether a hearing is appropriate.

If a hearing takes place, the arbitrator must consider how the evidence should be presented. He will need to decide whether there is any need for oral witness evidence or if it is sufficient to rely on witness statements[2]. If the arbitrator has allowed the parties to use expert evidence, the arbitrator will consider if oral evidence is required from the expert.

In the absence of an agreement to the contrary, the arbitrator is free to decide the procedure for the hearing. He can follow the usual court procedure, but there is no obligation to do so.

The party on whom the onus of proof lies (the equivalent of the claimant in a court action) should open his case. The opening address should merely outline the case. Being an address, it is not evidence and must not contain any factual allegations which are not subsequently supported by formal evidence.

Witnesses may then be called. If the onus of proof is to be discharged they must be called. The party defending may then cross-examine and the quasi-claimant may re-examine. Cross-examination, as long as it is not obviously irrelevant, should be unrestricted. Re-examination is only permissible on matters with which the witnesses' cross-examination has already dealt, except by the arbitrator's leave, which should be sparingly given. If new points are thereby introduced it means that the other party may well need the chance of further cross-examination, and so on. In this way proceedings can easily degenerate into an argument.

The defending party then, likewise, may call witnesses who are subjected to cross-examination, and then close. The final closing address is made by the party opening[3]. It is beyond the scope of this book to consider the rules of procedure in detail. The standard textbooks on this subject should be consulted.

¹   Cf the position that used to apply under Sch 11 of the AHA 1986.
²   AA 1996, s 34(2)(h).
³   He has the double advantage of opening the case and closing, thereby having the last word.

Inspection

47.36 Most arbitrators will wish to inspect the holding. When the issue between the parties is a money claim, or one involving practical considerations of agriculture, this may well be an essential and vital part of the whole procedure. Where the issue between the parties does not directly affect the state and condition of the holding, an inspection will not be necessary[1]. Considerable care should be taken to ensure that justice is seen to be done in the context of the inspection. Therefore, the arbitrator should never inspect with one party only[2]. He should beware of attaching too much importance to matters he notices on his inspection which have not been the subject of evidence at the hearing[3].

[1] Eg where on a Case B arbitration the issue is as to whether a planning consent is valid or, on a Case D arbitration, whether the rent was, in fact, paid within two months of the notice to pay, etc.

[2] See *Hegarty v Winters* (1953) 162 Estates Gazette 89; *Re: O'Connor and Whitelaw's Arbitration* (1919) 88 LJKB 1242; and *Ellis v Lewin* (1963) 188 Estates Gazette 493 (the Court of Appeal set aside the award of an arbitrator who took an architect with him some two or three days after the hearing to examine a farmhouse without notifying the parties, or giving them any opportunity to exchange or cross-examine the architect). Also see, *Zermalt Holdings SA v Nu-Life Upholstery Repairs Ltd* [1985] 2 EGLR 14, 275 Estates Gazette 1134.

[3] See *Fairmount Investments Ltd v Secretary of State for the Environment* [1976] 2 All ER 865, [1976] 1 WLR 1255, HL where an inspector, following a Ministry inquiry, visited the site and inspected the foundations of an old building and made assumptions as to the state and condition, without having reconvened the hearing. The equivalent of his award (had he been an arbitrator) was set aside by the court in consequence.

General duty of the parties

47.37 The AA 1996 imposes a general duty upon the parties to do all things necessary for the proper and expeditious conduct of the arbitration[1]. This includes complying, without delay, with any determination of the arbitrator as to procedural and evidential matters, or with any order or directions of the arbitrator, and where appropriate, taking without delay any necessary steps to obtain a decision of the court on a preliminary question of jurisdiction or law[2].

[1] AA 1996, s 40(1).

[2] AA 1996, s 40(2). See also *Bremer Vulkan Schiffbau und Maschinenfabrik v South India Shipping Corpn Ltd* [1981] AC 909, [1981] 1 All ER 289, HL.

Failure of the parties to act properly and expeditiously

47.38 The parties are also free to agree upon the powers of the arbitrator in the case of a party's failure to do something necessary for the proper and expeditious conduct of the arbitration[1].

[1] AA 1996, s 41(1).

Enforcement of peremptory order/strike-out

47.39 In the event of a party failing to comply with a peremptory order made by the arbitrator (ie an order prescribing time for compliance)[1], an application can be made to the court for an order requiring compliance by the defaulting party[2].

An application to the court may be made:

(a)   by the arbitrator (upon notice to the parties);

(b)   by a party to the arbitration with the permission of the arbitrator (and upon notice to the other party); or

(c)   where the parties have agreed that the powers of the court to enforce peremptory orders shall be available[3].

The court may only make an order requiring compliance with the peremptory order of the arbitrator if it is satisfied that the applicant has exhausted any available arbitral process in respect of failure to comply with the arbitrator's order[4]. Further, the court will not make an order unless it is satisfied that the person to whom the arbitrator's order was directed has failed to comply with it within the time prescribed in the order or, if no time was prescribed, within a reasonable time[5].

1   AA 1996, ss 82 and 41(5).
2   AA 1996, s 42(1).
3   AA 1996, s 42(2).
4   AA 1996, s 42(3).
5   AA 1996, s 42(4). It should be noted that any appeal against the decision of the court under s 42 of the AA 1996 requires leave of the court.

47.40   Unless otherwise agreed by the parties, the arbitrator has power, if he is satisfied that there has been inordinate and inexcusable delay on the part of the claimant in pursuing his claim and that the delay:

(a)   gives rise, or was likely to give rise, to a substantial risk that it is not possible to have a fair resolution of the issues in that claim; or

(b)   has caused, or was likely to cause, serious prejudice to the respondent,

the arbitrator may make an award dismissing the claim[1]. In the event of an application being made to dismiss the claim, regard should be had to the detailed provisions of s 41(4) to (7) of the AA 1996. Those provisions enable the arbitrator to:

(i)   proceed in the absence of a party, including the making of an award, if a party fails to attend an oral hearing (notice of which has been given) or submit written evidence;

(ii)   make an order prescribing the time for compliance with such order;

(iii) make an award dismissing the claim if the claimant fails to comply with a peremptory order[2] of the arbitrator to provide security for costs.

Further, if a party fails to comply with any other kind of peremptory order of the arbitrator, the arbitrator may, as well as being able to rely upon the court's power to enforce such order[3]:

(A)   direct that the party in default shall not be entitled to rely upon any allegation or material which was the subject matter of the order;

(B)   draw such adverse inferences from the act of non-compliance as the circumstances justify;

(C)   proceed to an award on the basis of such materials as have been properly provided to it;

(D)   make such order as it thinks fit as to the payment of costs of the arbitration incurred in consequence of the non-compliance.

1   AA 1996, s 41(2), (3).
2   As to the definition of peremptory orders, see para 47.39.
3   See para 47.39.

General powers of the arbitrator

47.41 The parties are free to agree on the powers exercisable by the arbitrator for the purposes of and in relation to the proceedings[1]. Unless otherwise agreed by the parties, the arbitrator has power to:

(a)   order a claimant to provide security for costs[2]; and
(b)   give directions in relation to any property which is the subject matter of the proceedings dealing with, inter alia, inspection, photographing and the taking of samples[3];
(c)   direct that a party or a witness shall be examined on oath or affirmation and may for that purpose administer any necessary oath or take any necessary affirmation[4];
(d)   give directions to a party for the preservation for the purposes of the proceedings of any evidence in his custody or control[5].

It should be noted that, unless the parties agree, the arbitrator does not have power to make a provisional award[6] nor to order the consolidation of proceedings or concurrent hearings[7]. With the agreement of the parties, the arbitrator has such powers[8].

In the context of the general powers of the arbitrator, it is convenient to observe here that the arbitrator (and indeed the parties) should have regard to the guidance which the court decisions have provided in relation to the extent to which the arbitrator may rely upon his own expertise[9].

1   AA 1996, s 38(1).
2   AA 1996, s 38(3).
3   AA 1996, s 38(4).
4   AA 1996, s 38(5).
5   AA 1996, s 38(6).
6   AA 1996, s 39.
7   AA 1996, s 35.
8   AA 1996, ss 39 and 35.
9   See para 47.68.

Preliminary point of law

47.42 Unless otherwise agreed by the parties, the court may on the application of a party to the arbitration (upon notice to the other parties) determine any question of law arising in the course of the proceedings which the court is satisfied substantially affects the rights of one or more of the parties[1].

It should be noted that an agreement to dispense with reasons for the arbitrator's award shall be considered an agreement to exclude the court's jurisdiction to determine a preliminary point of law[2].

No application can be made to the court unless it is with the agreement of the parties or the permission of the arbitrator[3]. In the case of the latter, the court must also be sure that the determination of the point of law is likely to produce a substantial saving in costs and the application is made without delay[4]. Unless the parties agree otherwise, it is open to the arbitrator to continue with the arbitration and make an award while the application to the court is pending[5]. Once the court decides the question of law, no appeal lies without leave. Leave will not be given unless the court considers the question is of general importance or one which should be considered by the Court of Appeal.

[1]   AA 1996, s 45(1) and see the provisions of s 45 generally as to procedure and the effect upon the arbitrator's award.
[2]   AA 1996, s 45(1).
[3]   Any application is made pursuant to Part 62 of the Civil Procedure Rules (CPR).
[4]   AA 1996, s 45(2)(b).
[5]   AA 1996, s 45(4).

Procedural points

Securing attendance of witnesses

47.43 A party to an arbitration may use the same court procedures as are available in relation to legal proceedings to secure the attendance before the arbitrator of a witness in order to give oral testimony or to produce documents or other material evidence[1]. This may be done with the permission of the arbitrator or the agreement of the parties.

[1]   AA 1996, s 43(1). See CPR Pt 34 and CPR Pt 62.

Service of notices

47.44 The parties are free to agree on the manner of service of any notice or other documents required or authorised to be given or served in pursuance of the arbitration agreement or for the purposes of the arbitration proceedings[1].

If there is no such agreement between the parties, the AA 1996 provides rules relating to the service of notices or other documents[2]. In addition to providing that service may be 'by any effective means'[3], the AA 1996 provides that a notice will be treated as effectively served if addressed, prepaid and delivered by post:

(a)   to the addressee's last known principal residence or, if he is or has been carrying on a trade, professional business, his last known principal business address; or

(b)   where the addressee is a body corporate, to the body's registered or principal office[4].

These rules only apply where notices must be served under the AA 1996. Where notices are required under the AHA 1986[5] or the ATA 1995[6], the provisions applying in each of the Acts for the service of notices are relevant[7].

[1] AA 1996, s 76(1). As to service generally, see para 17.1 ff (in relation to the ATA 1995) and para 42.13 ff (in relation to the AHA 1986).
[2] AA 1996, s 76(2).
[3] AA 1996, s 76(3). This includes service by email: see *Bernuth Lines Ltd v High Seas Shipping Ltd* [2005] EWHC 3020 (Comm), [2006] 1 All ER (Comm) 359.
[4] AA 1996, s 76(4).
[5] For example, the service of a demand for arbitration, see para 42.13 ff.
[6] For example, a preliminary notice under s 28, see para 47.3.
[7] See paras 17.1 ff and 42.13 ff.

The court's power for substituted service

47.45 In the event of the above provisions in the AA 1996 relating to the service of a document or notice not being reasonably practicable, the court has power to order as it thinks fit for service in such a manner as the court may direct or for dispensing with service of a document[1]. There is no such provision under the AHA 1986 or the ATA 1995 relating to the service of notices under these statutes.

[1] AA 1996, s 77(1) and (2).

Reckoning of periods of time

47.46 The parties are free to agree on the method of reckoning periods of time for the purpose of any provision agreed by them[1]. Alternatively, the AA 1996 provides for the reckoning of periods of time[2].

It should be noted that, unless the parties otherwise agree, the court has power to extend any time limit agreed by the parties in relation to any matter relating to the arbitration[3] save where there are statutory time limits operating under the AHA 1986 and the ATA 1995. The court will not exercise this power unless it is satisfied that any available recourse to the arbitrator has been exhausted and a substantial injustice would otherwise be done.

[1] AA 1996, s 78(1).
[2] AA 1996, s 78(3)–(5). Where the act is required to be done within a specified period after or from a specified date, the period begins immediately after that date. Where the act is required to be done a specified number of clear days after a specified date, at least that number of days must intervene between the day on which the act is done and that date. Where the period is a period of seven days or less which would include a Saturday, Sunday or a public holiday in the place where anything which has to be done within the period falls to be done, that day shall be excluded. In relation to England and Wales or Northern Ireland, a 'public holiday' means Christmas Day, Good Friday or a day which under the Banking and Financial Dealings Act 1971 is a bank holiday.
[3] AA 1996, s 79(1) and see s 79 generally.

The court's powers in support of the arbitrator

47.47 Unless otherwise agreed by the parties, the court has the same powers that it has in relation to legal proceedings to support the arbitrator in connection with the arbitration including the taking of evidence of witnesses; the preservation of evidence; the making of orders in relation to property; and the granting of an interim injunction or the appointment of a receiver[1].

1   AA 1996, s 44(1) and (2).

Legal representation

47.48 Unless otherwise agreed by the parties, a party to an arbitration may be represented in the proceedings by a lawyer or other person chosen by him[1].

Unless otherwise agreed by the parties, the arbitrator may appoint experts or legal advisers to report to him and the parties, or appoint assessors to assist him on technical matters, and may allow any such expert, legal adviser or assessor to attend the proceedings[2]. The parties must be given a reasonable opportunity to comment on any information, opinion or advice offered by any such person[3].

The fees and expenses of an expert, legal adviser or assessor appointed by the arbitrator for which the arbitrator is liable are expenses of the arbitrator for the purposes of the AA 1996[4].

1   AA 1996, s 36.
2   AA 1996, s 37(1)(a).
3   AA 1996, s 37(1)(b).
4   AA 1996, s 37(2) and see para 47.63.

Expert evidence

47.49 Unless otherwise agreed by the parties, the arbitrator may appoint experts or legal advisers to report to him and the parties, or appoint assessors to assist him on technical matters, and may allow any such expert, legal adviser or assessor to attend the arbitration[1]. The parties must be given a reasonable opportunity to comment on any information, opinion or advice offered by such person to the arbitrator[2]. The arbitrator may also permit the parties to rely on expert evidence.

The fees and expenses of an expert, legal adviser or assessor appointed by the arbitrator for which the arbitrator is liable are expenses of the arbitrator for the purposes of the AA 1996[3]. This is a mandatory provision and the parties cannot agree otherwise and deprive experts of their fees and expenses. Such fees and expenses are costs of the arbitrator and recoverable as part of the costs of the arbitration under s 64(1).

As a matter of good practice, experts should consider the rules set out in CPR Pt 35. While not binding on arbitrations, it sets out the duties of the expert and the form and content of the expert's report. The issues are the same for experts who deal with property in the courts or before an arbitrator.

The expert's overriding duty is to the arbitrator, even if he has been appointed by one of the parties. An expert must be independent and must not do anything to compromise his independence or objectivity[4].

An expert has immunity from suit in respect of evidence given in court and statements made for the purposes of giving evidence but the immunity of an expert witness does not extend to disciplinary proceedings by the professional body of which he is a member[5]. It is submitted that the same analysis will apply to an expert acting in an arbitration.

[1] AA 1996, s 37(1)(a).
[2] AA 1996, s 37(1)(b).
[3] AA 1996, s 37(2).
[4] Any expert should also bear in mind any practice statements provided by his professional body, for example the RICS practice statement 'Surveyors Acting as Expert Witnesses' (3rd edn) and the Civil Justice Council's 'Protocol for the Instruction of Experts Giving Evidence in Civil Claims', and the accompanying Code of Practice for Experts, agreed jointly by the Academy of Experts and the Expert Witness Institute, Published June 2005.
[5] *Meadow v General Medical Council* [2006] EWCA Civ 1390, [2007] 1 All ER 1, [2006] 44 EG 196 (CS).

Issues relating to the arbitrator's award

Awards on different issues

47.50 Unless otherwise agreed by the parties, the arbitrator may make more than one award at different times on different aspects of the matters to be determined[1].

[1] AA 1996, s 47(1) and see s 47 generally.

Remedies

47.51 The parties are free to agree the powers exercisable by the arbitrator as regards remedies[1].

Unless otherwise agreed by the parties, the arbitrator will have power to make a declaration as to any matter to be determined in the proceedings; an order for the payment of a sum of money; and the same powers as the court to order a party to do or refrain from doing any act; to order specific performance of a contract (other than a contract relating to land); and to order rectification, setting aside or cancellation of a deed or other document[2].

[1] AA 1996, s 48(1).
[2] AA 1996, s 48(2)–(5).

Interest

47.52 The parties are free to agree on the powers of the arbitrator as regards the award of interest[1]. The AA 1996 provides a fall-back position in the widest terms permitting the arbitrator to award simple or compound interest from such date, at such rates and with such rests as he considers meets the justice of the case[2].

[1]   AA 1996, s 49(1).
[2]   AA 1996, s 49(2) and (3).

Extension of time for making award

47.53 The AA 1996 does not place any restriction upon the time for making an award[1]. The parties can impose a time limit if they wish. If the time for making the award is limited by agreement, then, unless otherwise agreed by the parties (who can exclude the jurisdiction of the court), the court may make an order extending time upon the application of the arbitrator (upon notice to the parties) or by any of the parties to the proceedings (upon notice to the arbitrator and the other parties), but only after the court is satisfied that the applicant has exhausted any available arbitral process for obtaining an extension of time and that a substantial injustice would be done if an extension of time were not granted[2].

The court can extend time retrospectively even though the time previously fixed has expired. The leave of the trial judge is required for any appeal from a decision of the court.

[1]   AA 1996, s 50(1).
[2]   AA 1996, s 50(1)–(3).

Settlement

47.54 The parties are able to agree provisions governing what happens in the event of a settlement being achieved in the arbitration before its determination by the arbitrator[1].

In the absence of specific agreement by the parties as to the provisions which would apply in the event of a settlement in advance of the arbitration hearing, the AA 1996 lays down rules governing the position. The arbitrator is required to terminate the substantive proceedings and, if requested by the parties and not objected to by the arbitrator himself, to record the settlement in the form of an agreed award[2].

[1]   AA 1996, s 51(1).
[2]   AA 1996, s 51(1) and (2).

The arbitrator's award

Form of award

47.55 The AA 1996 permits the parties freedom to agree on the form of the award[1]. Neither the AHA 1986 or the ATA 1995 place any restriction on the form of award.

If or to the extent that there is no agreement, the AA 1996 provides that the award must be in writing and signed by the arbitrator or all those assenting to the award[2]. The award must contain the reasons for the award unless it is an agreed award or the parties have agreed to dispense with reasons[3]. Accordingly, if the parties do not want the arbitrator to give reasons for his award, that should be agreed in advance of the delivery of the award.

The award must state the seat of the arbitration[4].

Unless otherwise agreed by the parties, the arbitrator will have power to make a declaration as to any matter to be determined in the arbitration; an order for the payment of a sum of money; the same powers as the court to order a party to do or refrain from any act; to order specific performance of a contract (other than a contract relating to land); and to other rectification, setting aside or the cancellation of a deed or other document[5].

[1] AA 1996, s 52(1).
[2] AA 1996, s 52(2) and (3).
[3] AA 1996, s 52(4). The arbitrator should refer to the facts found to be admitted or proved; whether and to what extent the submissions were convincing and the methods by which the valuations were arrived at: *Guppys Properties Ltd v Knott* (1977) 245 Estates Gazette 1023; *Re Poyser and Mills Arbitrations* [1964] 2 QB 467, [1963] 1 All ER 612.
[4] AA 1996, s 52(5). This provision is unfamiliar to agricultural arbitrators, but reflects the fact that the AA 1996 encompasses foreign jurisdiction. Unless otherwise agreed by the parties, where the seat of the arbitration is in England and Wales or Northern Ireland, any award in the proceedings shall be treated as made there, regardless of where it was signed, despatched or delivered to any of the parties: AA 1996, s 53. Every statutory arbitration is taken to have its seat in England and Wales or, as the case may be, Northern Ireland: AA 1996, s 95(3).
[5] AA 1996, s 48(2)–(5).

Date of award

47.56 Unless otherwise agreed by the parties, the arbitrator may decide what is to be taken to be the date on which the award was made[1].

In the absence of any such decision by the arbitrator, the date of the award shall be taken to be the date on which it is signed by the arbitrator[2].

[1] AA 1996, s 54(1).
[2] AA 1996, s 54(2).

Notification of award

47.57 The parties are free to agree on the requirements as to the notification of the award to the parties[1]. If there is no such agreement, the award shall be notified to the parties by service on them of copies of the award, which shall be done without delay after the award is made[2]. The provisions for the notification of the award are subject to the power of the arbitrator to withhold the award in the case of non-payment of his fees and expenses[3].

1   AA 1996, s 55(1).
2   AA 1996, s 55(2).
3   AA 1996, s 55(3). See para 47.58.

Power to withhold the award

47.58 The arbitrator may refuse to deliver an award to the parties except upon full payment of his fees and expenses[1]. The usual practice is for the arbitrator to notify the parties that the award is available for collection on payment of the amount specified. A party to the arbitration may (upon notice to the other parties and the arbitrator) apply to the court. The court may order, inter alia, that the arbitrator shall deliver the award on the payment into court by the applicant of the fees and expenses demanded, or such lesser amount as the court may specify[2]. No appeal may be brought against the court's decision without leave.

1   AA 1996, s 56(1).
2   AA 1996, s 56(2)(a) and see s 56 generally.

Correction/additional award

47.59 The parties are free to agree on the powers of the arbitrator to correct an award or make an additional award[1]. If or to the extent that there is no such agreement, the arbitrator may on his own initiative or on the application of a party:

(a)   correct an award so as to remove any clerical mistake or error arising from an accidental slip or omission or clarify or remove any ambiguity in the award; or

(b)   make an additional award in respect of any claim (including a claim for interest or costs) which was presented to the arbitrator but was not dealt with in the award[2]. These powers shall not be exercised without first giving the other parties a reasonable opportunity to make representations to the arbitrator[3].

Any application for the exercise of these powers must be made within 28 days of the date of the award or such longer period as the parties may agree[4]. Any correction of an award shall be made within 28 days of the date the application was received by the arbitrator or, where the correction is made by the arbitrator on his own initiative, within 28 days of the date of the award or, in either case, such longer period as the parties may agree[5]. Any correction of an award shall form part of the award[6].

Any additional award shall be made within 56 days of the date of the original award or such longer period as the parties may agree[7].

1   AA 1996, s 57(1).
2   AA 1996, s 57(2) and (3).
3   AA 1996, s 57(3).
4   AA 1996, s 57(4).
5   AA 1996, s 57(5).
6   AA 1996, s 57(7).
7   AA 1996, s 57(6). Applications under s 68 (see para 47.66) must be made within 28 days of the award. The trigger date for an application under s 68 is the date of the issue of the corrected award or the refusal to make a corrected award and not the date of the original award: *Al Hadha Trading Co v Tradigrain SA* [2002] 2 Lloyd's Rep 512.

Effect of award

47.60 Unless otherwise agreed by the parties, an award made by the arbitrator pursuant to an arbitration agreement is final and binding both on the parties or any persons claiming through or under them[1]. This does not affect the right of a person to challenge the award by any available process of appeal or review under the AA 1996[2]. An award remains a private matter between the parties and cannot directly affect the rights of third parties.

1   AA 1996, s 58(1). It should be noted that an arbitrator's decision on a point of law on, for example, a first rent review, will not create an issue estoppel which would settle the point of law for the remainder of the term of the tenancy. A dissatisfied party is able to apply to the court in construction proceedings for a determination of the issue by the court: *British Railways Board v Ringbest Ltd* [1996] 2 EGLR 82, [1996] 30 EG 94.
2   AA 1996, s 58(2).

Costs of the arbitration

47.61 The costs of the arbitration are defined in the AA 1996 as comprising the arbitrator's fees and expenses, the fees and expenses of any arbitral institution concerned, and the legal or other costs of the parties[1]. The costs include those costs of or incidental to any proceedings to determine the amount of the recoverable costs of the arbitration[2].

An agreement which has the effect that a party is to pay the whole or part of the costs of the arbitration in any event is only valid if made after the dispute in question has arisen[3].

Subject to any agreement between the parties, the arbitrator may make an award allocating the costs of the arbitration as between them[4]. Unless the parties otherwise agree, the arbitrator shall award costs on the general principle that costs should follow the event except where it appears to the arbitrator that in the circumstances this is not appropriate in relation to the whole or part of the costs[5]. If the arbitrator decides to do something other than award costs which follow the event, the award should explain the reasons for that. Although not bound by them, the arbitrator should consider the principles which apply in the courts when determining the issue of costs[6].

Unless the parties otherwise agree, any obligation under the agreement between them as to how the costs of the arbitration are to be borne, or under an award allocating the costs of the arbitration, extends only to such costs as are recoverable[7]. The parties are free to agree what costs of the arbitration are recoverable[8]. If or to the extent that there is no such agreement, the arbitrator may determine by award the recoverable costs of the arbitration on such basis as he thinks fit. If he does so, he must specify the basis on which he has acted and the items of recoverable costs and the amount referable to each[9].

[1]   AA 1996, s 59(1).
[2]   AA 1996, s 59(2), see also s 63.
[3]   AA 1996, s 60.
[4]   AA 1996, s 61(1).
[5]   AA 1996, s 61(2). For a more detailed guidance as to the principles applying in respect of the arbitrator's discretion as to costs, see Mustill and Boyd, *Commercial Arbitration* (2nd edn, 1989), Butterworths, Ch 26E and the 2000 companion volume.
[6]   The CPR Pt 44.
[7]   AA 1996, s 62.
[8]   AA 1996, s 63(1).
[9]   AA 1996, s 63(2) and (3).

47.62 If the arbitrator does not determine the recoverable costs of the arbitration, any party to the arbitration may apply to the court (upon notice to the other parties). The court may:

(a)   determine the recoverable costs of the arbitration on such basis as it thinks fit; or
(b)   order that they should be determined by such means and upon such terms as it may specify[1].

Unless the court determines otherwise the recoverable costs of the arbitration shall be determined on the basis that there shall be allowed a reasonable amount in respect of all costs reasonably incurred, and any doubt as to whether costs were reasonably incurred or were reasonable in amount shall be resolved in favour of the paying party[2].

The provisions relating to the costs of the arbitration are subject to the provisions contained in s 64 of the AA 1996 in respect of the recoverable fees and expenses of the arbitrator[3]. The recoverable costs of the arbitration shall include only such reasonable fees and expenses of the arbitrator as are appropriate in the circumstances.

Nothing contained in the AA 1996 dealing with the recoverability of costs of the arbitration affects any rights of the arbitrator, any expert, legal adviser or assessor appointed by the arbitrator, or any arbitral institution, to payment of their fees and expenses[4].

Unless otherwise agreed by the parties, the arbitrator may direct that the recoverable costs of the arbitration, or of any part of the arbitral proceedings, shall be limited to a specified amount[5]. Any direction in this regard may be made or varied at any stage of the arbitration, but it must be done sufficiently in advance of the incurring of costs to which it relates, or the taking of any steps in the proceedings which may be affected by it, for the limit to be taken into account[6].

Conditional fee agreements are permissible in arbitrations and can be allowed by arbitrators[7]. Costs of lay representatives acting in arbitrations have also been allowed[8]. The costs of lay representatives are not recoverable for any court application.

There is no express right of appeal against a court decision although it has been held that such right exists[9]. Permission to appeal can be given by the trial judge or the Court of Appeal.

1   AA 1996, s 63(4).
2   AA 1996, s 63(5). The procedure for determining the costs of the arbitration is therefore akin to a standard basis assessment before the court: see CPR Pt 47. The courts can also award costs on an indemnity basis. This means that any doubt as to whether costs were reasonably incurred or were reasonable in amount shall be resolved in favour of the receiving party. The AA 1996 does not rule out the possibility of indemnity costs but gives no guidance on when such an award would be appropriate. The arbitrator should consider the guidance set out in case law and must bear in mind that an unjustified departure from the standard basis may be considered to be a serious irregularity, see para 47.66.
3   AA 1996, ss 63(6) and 64. See para 47.63.
4   AA 1996, s 63(7).
5   AA 1996, s 65(1).
6   AA 1996, s 65(2).
7   *Bevan Ashford v Geoff Yeandle (Contractors) Ltd* [1999] Ch 239, [1998] 3 All ER 238.
8   *Piper Double Glazing Ltd v DC Contracts (1992) Ltd* [1994] 1 All ER 177.
9   *Inco Europe Ltd v First Choice Distribution* [2000] 1 Lloyd's Rep 467.

Recoverable fees and expenses of the arbitrator

47.63 Unless otherwise agreed by the parties, the recoverable costs of the arbitration[1] shall include in respect of the fees and expenses of the arbitrator only such reasonable fees and expenses as are appropriate in the circumstances[2].

If there is any question as to what reasonable fees and expenses are appropriate in the circumstances, and the matter is not already before the court on an application to determine the recoverable costs of the arbitration[3], the court may, on the application of any party (upon notice to the other parties), determine the matter, or order that it may be determined by such means and upon such terms as the court may specify[4].

Nothing in the AA 1996 governing the recoverability of fees and expenses of the arbitrator affects any right of the arbitrator to payment of his fees and expenses[5].

1   See para 47.61.
2   AA 1996, s 64(1). This subsection has effect subject to any order of the court as to the entitlement to fees or expenses in the case of the removal or resignation of the arbitrator pursuant to s 24(4) or s 25(3)(b) of the AA 1996. See paras 47.30 and 47.31.
3   AA 1996, s 63(4).
4   AA 1996, s 64(2).
5   AA 1996, s 64(4).

Enforcement of the award

47.64 An award made by the arbitrator pursuant to an arbitration agreement may, by leave of the court, be enforced in the same manner as a judgment or order of the court to the same effect[1]. Where leave is so given, judgment may be entered in terms of the award[2]. Leave to enforce an award shall not be given where, or to the extent that, the person against whom it is sought to be enforced shows that the arbitrator lacks substantive jurisdiction to make the award[3]. The right to raise such an objection may have been lost[4].

1   AA 1996, s 66(1).
2   AA 1996, s 66(2).
3   AA 1996, s 66(3).
4   AA 1996, s 73 and see para 47.75.

Challenging the award

Substantive jurisdiction

47.65 A party to an arbitration may (upon notice to the other parties and to the arbitrator) apply to the court:

(a)   challenging any award of the arbitrator as to its substantive juris-
       diction; or
(b)   for an order declaring an award made by the arbitrator on the merits to
       be of no effect, in whole or in part, because the arbitrator did not have
       substantive jurisdiction[1].

Challenges on this ground arise where the original agreement to refer to arbitration is invalid, there is some defect in the appointment process or some disagreement over what matters should have been submitted to arbitration[2]. Section 30 allows the arbitrator to determine his own jurisdiction. A challenge under s 67 will only arise if the arbitrator has determined his own jurisdiction under s 30 and a party has not appeared in an arbitration, or has appeared and then registered a prompt objection that the arbitrator has not resolved by an interim award[3]. A party is not precluded from objecting by the fact that he has appointed or participated in the appointment of the arbitrator[4].

A party may lose the right to object[5] and the right to apply is subject to statutory restrictions contained in the AA 1996[6].

On an application to challenge the award as to its substantive jurisdiction, the court has power to confirm the award, vary it or set it aside in whole or in part[7].

The arbitrator may continue the arbitration and make a further award while an application to the court in respect of his substantive jurisdiction is pending[8].

After the court has made the decision, no appeal lies against the court's decision without leave. Leave will not be given unless the court considered that the question of law involves a point which is of general importance or is one which for some other special reason should be considered by the Court of Appeal.

1   AA 1996, s 67(1).
2   AA 1996, s 30.
3   *Amec Civil Engineering Ltd v Secretary of State for Transport* [2005] EWCA Civ 291, [2005] 1 WLR 2339.
4   AA 1996, s 31(1).
5   AA 1996, s 73 and see para 47.75.
6   AA 1996, s 70(2) and (3) and see para 47.71.
7   AA 1996, s 67(3). The leave of the court is required for any appeal from a decision of the court: s 67(4).
8   AA 1996, s 67(2).

Serious irregularity

47.66 A party to an arbitration may (upon notice to the other parties and to the arbitrator) apply to the court challenging an award in the proceedings on the ground of serious irregularity affecting the arbitrator, the proceedings or the award[1]. A party may lose the right to object[2] and again is subject to statutory restrictions contained in the AA 1996[3].

The AA 1996 defines serious irregularity as an irregularity which the court considers has caused or will cause substantial injustice to the applicant. It means one or more of the following:

(a)   failure of the arbitrator to comply with his general duties contained in s 33 of the AA 1996[4];
(b)   the arbitrator exceeding his powers (otherwise than by exceeding his substantive jurisdiction)[5];
(c)   failure by the arbitrator to conduct the proceedings in accordance with the procedure agreed by the parties[6];
(d)   failure by the arbitrator to deal with all of the issues that were put to him[7];
(e)   any arbitral or other institution or person vested by the parties with powers in relation to the proceedings or the award exceeding its powers[8];
(f)   uncertainty or ambiguity as to the effect of the award;
(g)   the award being obtained by fraud or the award or the way in which it was procured being contrary to public policy;
(h)   failure to comply with the requirements as to the form of the award[9];
(i)   any irregularity in the conduct of the proceedings or in the award which is admitted by the arbitrator or by any arbitral or other institution or person vested by the parties with powers in relation to the proceedings or the award[10].

1   AA 1996, s 68(1).
2   AA 1996, s 73 and see para 47.75.
3   AA 1996, s 70(2) and (3) and see para 47.71.
4   See para 47.32. *Petroships Pte Ltd v Petec Trading and Investment Corpn, The Petro Ranger* [2001] 2 Lloyd's Rep 348.
5   AA 1996, s 67.

6   *Norbrook Laboratories Ltd v Tank* [2006] EWHC 1055 (Comm), [2006] 2 Lloyd's Rep 485 where the arbitrator contacted witnesses direct and failed to inform the parties.
7   This could include a deficiency of reasons in a reasoned award if the arbitrator fails to deal with all issues put to him, see *Margulead Ltd v Exide Technologies* [2004] EWHC 1019 (Comm), [2005] 1 Lloyd's Rep 324. See also *Torch Offshort LLC v Cable Shipping Inc* [[2004] EWHC 787 (Comm), [2004] 2 Lloyd's Rep 446.
8   In practice, in relation to agricultural arbitrations this is likely to be the RICS, although there is no reason why the arbitration agreement should not permit another institution to appoint the arbitrator, for example, the Central Association of Agricultural Valuers or the Law Society.
9   See para 47.55.
10 AA 1996, s 68(2).

47.67 The term 'substantial injustice' is not defined in the AA 1996[1]. The courts are reluctant to interfere and have set a high threshold[2].

If there is shown to be serious irregularity affecting the arbitrator, the proceedings or the award, the court may:

(a)   remit the award to the arbitrator, in whole or in part, for reconsideration;
(b)   set the award aside in whole or in part; or
(c)   declare the award to be of no effect, in whole or in part[3].

In order for the court to exercise its power to set aside the award or to declare it to be of no effect, in whole or in part, it must be satisfied that it would be inappropriate to remit the matters in question to the arbitrator for reconsideration[4]. The courts are reluctant to set aside awards and a successful application is more likely to end with an order for remittal.

1   Paragraph 280 of the Departmental Advisory Committee (DAC) report dated February 1996 that preceded the introduction of the AA 1996 stated 'the test of substantial injustice is intended to be applied by way of support for the arbitral process, not be way of interference with that process. Thus it is only in those cases where it can be said that what has happened is so far removed from what could reasonably be expected of the arbitral process that we would expect the court to take action … In short [s 68] is really designed as a long stop, only available in extreme cases where the tribunal has gone so wrong in its conduct of the arbitration that justice calls out for it to be corrected'.
2   *Groundshire v VHE Construction* [2001] BLR 395.
3   AA 1996, 68(3).
4   AA 1996, s 68(3). The leave of the court is required for any appeal from a decision of the court in respect of its determination in relation to such an application: s 68(4).

47.68 Since its enactment, many cases in relation to the AA 1996 have been mainly concerned with challenges brought under s 68 of that Act. The courts have been asked to examine whether a serious irregularity arose from the fact that the arbitrator relied on his own experience in making a determination[1] and whether an arbitrator could rely upon his own analysis of the figures presented by the parties[2]. In the case of *St George's Investment Co v Gemini Consulting Ltd*[3], the High Court provided some clarity and guidance. The following points can be drawn from the judgment:

(a)   The arbitrator is entitled to use his expert knowledge, provided that it is within a range of knowledge that would be reasonably expected of the arbitrator and that it is used to evaluate the evidence called. The arbitrator is not to introduce new and different evidence[4] or surprise the parties even if he has come up with his own figures which are correct[5]. As the deputy judge put it, 'an arbitrator does not have blanket permission to use his own expert knowledge to arrive at an award'.

(b)   The arbitrator is entitled to arrive at his award by deploying the evidence in a way that is materially different from the way that the parties deployed the evidence provided the matter is one that the parties have put up for discussion and they have an opportunity to comment. The award must, however, address a matter that has been put into the arena by the valuers and with which they have had an opportunity to deal[6].

(c)   The issue is not whether the arbitrator came to the right conclusion, but whether he committed a serious irregularity in reaching his conclusion.

(d)   The court should not decide what rent the arbitrator might have fixed if he had dealt with the case differently. The deputy judge explained:

'the court should try to assess how the aggrieved party would have conducted his case but for the irregularity. Only if the aggrieved party has suffered a substantial injustice because he was unable to present his case and so obtain a fair hearing of this case will the irregularity be treated as falling with section 68 …'.

A substantial increase in rent which a tenant might view as a substantial burden may not equate to a substantial injustice[7].

(e)   The test of 'substantial injustice' is intended to be applied by way of support of the arbitral process and not constitute an interference with the process. The deputy judge added:

'it is only in those cases where it can be said that what has happened was so far removed from what could reasonably be expected of the arbitral process that the court will interfere. Section 68 is a long stop which is only available in extreme cases where the arbitrator has gone so wrong in his conduct of the arbitration that justice calls out for it to be corrected. It is not a soft alternative to an application for leave to appeal …'.

(f)   The court must accord a reasonably generous margin of leeway to arbitrators in the discharge of their functions. Finally, the arbitrator must not make an award based on arguments and evidence not presented to him or on a basis that is contrary to the common assumption of the parties as represented to him[8].

[1]   *Checkpoint Ltd v Strathclyde Pension Fund* [2003] EWCA Civ 84, [2003] 1 EGLR 1.
[2]   *Warborough Investments Ltd v S Robinson & Sons (Holdings) Ltd* [2003] EWCA Civ 751, [2003] 2 EGLR 149.
[3]   [2004] EWHC 2353 (Ch), [2005] 1 EGLR 5.
[4]   *Checkpoint Ltd v Strathclyde Pension Fund* [2003] 1 EGLR 1.
[5]   *Handley v Nationwide Anglia Building Society* [1992] 2 EGLR 114.
[6]   *Warborough Investments Ltd v S Robinson & Sons (Holdings) Ltd* [2003] 2 EGLR 149.
[7]   *Checkpoint Ltd v Strathclyde Pension Fund* [2003] 1 EGLR 1.
[8]   *Zermalt Holdings SA v Nu-Life Upholstery Repairs Ltd* [1985] 2 EGLR 14.

Appeal on a point of law

47.69   Unless otherwise agreed by the parties, a party to an arbitration may (upon notice to the other parties and to the arbitrator) appeal to the court on a question of law arising out of an award made in the proceedings[1].

An agreement to dispense with reasons for the arbitrator's award shall be considered an agreement to exclude the court's jurisdiction to hear an appeal on a question of law arising out of the award[2].

An appeal to the court can only be made with the agreement of all of the other parties to the proceedings or with the leave of the court[3]. The right of appeal is also subject to the statutory restrictions contained in the AA 1996[4].

Leave to appeal will only be given by the court if it is satisfied that:

(a) the determination of the question will substantially affect the rights of one or more of the parties;

(b) the question is one which the arbitrator was asked to determine[5];

(c) on the basis of the findings of fact in the award:

   (i)   the decision of the arbitrator on the question is obviously wrong; or

   (ii) the question is one of general public importance and the decision of the arbitrator is at least open to serious doubt; and

(d) despite the agreement of the parties to resolve the matter by arbitration, it is just and proper in all the circumstances for the court to determine the question[6].

If an application is made to the court for leave to appeal on a point of law, the applicant must identify the question of law to be determined and state the grounds on which it is alleged that leave to appeal should be granted[7]. The court will decide whether leave should be given without convening a hearing unless the court considers that a hearing is required[8].

On an appeal on a point of law, the court may by order confirm the award, vary it, remit it to the arbitrator, in whole or in part, for reconsideration in the light of the court's determination, or set aside the award in whole or in part[9].

---

[1] AA 1996, s 69(1). An arbitration clause which excludes an appeal to a court on a point of law under s 69 is not in breach of the right to a fair trial under art 6 of the European Convention of Human Rights: see *Sumakan Ltd v Commonwealth Secretariat* [2007] EWCA Civ 243, [2007] 3 All ER 342.

[2] AA 1996, s 69(1).

[3] AA 1996, s 69(2).

[4] AA 1996, s 70(2) and (3) and see para 47.71.

[5] *Historic Buildings and Monuments Commission for England v Isambard Estates Ltd* [2005] All ER (D) 151 (Jun). It is not necessary to establish that the question had been raised in the arbitration in the same form as it is raised on appeal: *Safeway Stores v Legal & General Assurance Society Ltd* [2004] EWHC 415 (Ch), [2005] 1 P & CR 9.

[6] AA 1996, s 69(3).

[7] AA 1996, s 69(4).

[8] AA 1996, s 69(5). The leave of the court is required for any appeal from a decision of the court in respect of its decision to grant or refuse leave to appeal: s 69(6).

[9] AA 1996, s 69(7). The courts are loath to interfere. Where a decision was no more than an error of law, the court will not quash the decision of the arbitrator or remit it on the grounds that it represents an 'excess of power': *Lesotho Highlands Development Authority v Impregilo SpA* [2005] UKHL 43, [2006] 1 AC 221. For the principles to be applied by the court to an arbitrator's award, see *Kershaw Mechanical Services Ltd v Kendrick Construction Ltd* [2006] EWHC 727 (TCC), [2006] 4 All ER 79.

47.70 The court shall not exercise its power to set aside an award, in whole or in part, unless it is satisfied that it would be inappropriate to remit the matters in question to the arbitrator for reconsideration[1].

No further appeal can be pursued without leave of the trial judge which shall not be given unless the court considers the question is one of general importance or is one which for some other special reason should be considered by the Court of Appeal[2]. The Court of Appeal cannot grant permission where this has not been given by the trial judge[3].

1   AA 1996, s 69(7). The decision of the court on an appeal on a point of law shall be treated as a judgment of the court for the purpose of a further appeal. No such further appeal can be pursued without the leave of the court which shall not be given unless the court considers that the question is one of general importance or is one which for some other special reason should be considered by the Court of Appeal: s 69(8).
2   AA 1996, s 69(8).
3   *Henry Boot Construction (UK) Ltd v Malmaison Hotel (Manchester) Ltd* [2001] QB 388, [2001] 1 All ER 257; *Athletic Union of Constantinople v National Basketball Association* [2002] EWCA Civ 830, [2002] 2 All ER (Comm) 385.

Statutory restrictions under the AA 1996

47.71 An application or appeal based upon the substantive jurisdiction of the arbitrator, a serious irregularity or a point of law is subject to statutory restrictions contained in the AA 1996[1].

An application or appeal may not be brought in respect of a challenge to the award by reason of its substantive jurisdiction or serious irregularity or in respect of a point of law unless the applicant or appellant has first exhausted any available arbitral process of appeal or review, and any available recourse by way of the correction of the award or an additional award[2].

Further, any application or appeal must be brought within 28 days of the date of the award or, if there has been any arbitral process of appeal or review, within 28 days of the date when the applicant or appellant was notified of the result of that process[3].

If on an application or appeal it appears to the court that the award does not contain the arbitrator's reasons or does not set them out in sufficient detail to enable the court properly to consider the application or appeal, the court may order the arbitrator to state the reasons for his award in sufficient detail for that purpose[4]. Deficiency of reasoning in an award is therefore the subject of a specific remedy under the AA 1996, making it very difficult to argue that the failure to give reasons amounts to a serious irregularity under s 68[5].

1   AA 1996, s 70.
2   AA 1996, ss 70(2) and 57: see para 47.59.
3   AA 1996, s 70(3).
4   AA 1996, s 70(4) and see generally s 70(5)–(8).
5   *Margulead Ltd v Exide Technologies* [2004] EWHC 1019 (Comm), [2005] 1 Lloyd's Rep 324.

Effect of the order of the court

47.72   Where the court makes an order upon an application challenging the award by reason of its substantive jurisdiction, a serious irregularity or a point of law, and the award is varied by the court, the variation has effect as part of the arbitrator's award[1].

Where the award is remitted to the arbitrator, in whole or in part, for reconsideration, the arbitrator shall make a fresh award in respect of the matters remitted to him within three months of the date for remission or such longer or shorter period as the court may direct[2].

[1]   AA 1996, s 71(1) and (2).
[2]   AA 1996, s 71(3).

47.73   Where the award is set aside or declared to be of no effect, in whole or in part, the court may also order that any provision that an award is a condition precedent to the bringing of legal proceedings in respect of a matter to which the arbitration agreement applies, is of no effect as regards the subject matter of the award or, as the case may be, the relevant part of the award[1].

[1]   AA 1996, s 71(4). This provision does not apply to a statutory arbitration: AA 1996, s 97(c).

The rights of third parties

47.74   A person alleged to be a party to an arbitration, but who takes no part in the proceedings, may question whether there is a valid arbitration agreement, whether the arbitration tribunal is properly constituted, or what matters have been submitted to arbitration in accordance with the arbitration agreement. Such person may question those issues by way of proceedings in the court for a declaration or injunction or other appropriate relief[1].

Such person also has the same right as a party to the arbitration to challenge the award either on the basis of a lack of substantive jurisdiction[2] or on the ground of serious irregularity[3]. It should be noted that the obligation upon a party to the arbitration to exhaust arbitral procedures[4] does not apply in this case[5].

[1]   AA 1996, s 72(1).
[2]   See para 47.65.
[3]   See para 47.66.
[4]   AA 1996, s 70(2) and see para 47.71.
[5]   AA 1996, s 72(2).

Loss of the right to object

47.75   If a party to an arbitration takes part, or continues to take part, in the proceedings without making, either forthwith or within such time as is allowed by the arbitration agreement or by the arbitrator or by any provision contained in the AA 1996, any objection that the arbitrator lacks substantive jurisdiction, the proceedings have been improperly conducted or that there has been a failure to comply with the arbitration agreement or any provision contained in the AA 1996, or there has been any other irregularity affecting the arbitrator or the proceedings, he may not raise that objection later, before the arbitrator or the court, unless he shows that, at the time that he took part or continued to take part in the proceedings, he did not know and could not with reasonable diligence have discovered the grounds for the objection[1].

1   AA 1996, s 73(1) and see s 73(2) dealing with the position where the arbitrator has ruled that he has substantive jurisdiction.

Chapter 48

EXPERT DETERMINATION AND THE COURTS

ALTERNATIVE DISPUTE RESOLUTION UNDER THE AGRICULTURAL TENANCIES ACT 1995

General

48.1 The Agricultural Tenancies Act 1995 (ATA 1995) provides for an alternative dispute resolution (ADR) mechanism[1]. The ATA 1995 envisages that the parties to a farm business tenancy may agree contractual arrangements for dispute resolution and that the arbitration provisions under s 28 of the ATA 1995 will only provide a fallback.

It should first be noted that the ADR procedure contained in s 29 of the ATA 1995 only applies to oust the arbitration mechanism under s 28 of the ATA 1995 applying to general arbitrations[2]. It does not oust the specific arbitration provisions relating to rent arbitrations[3], improvement arbitrations[4] or compensation arbitrations[5].

So far as improvement arbitrations and compensation arbitrations are concerned, their arbitration codes are mandatory and cannot be replaced by the ADR procedure[6]. A reading of ss 28 and 29 of the ATA 1995 would indicate that the same conclusion should apply to rent arbitrations. However, whilst the statutory ADR provisions do not apply to statutory rent reviews under the ATA 1995, the parties may provide for their own rent review procedure, outside the statutory mechanism, by employing a third party (other than an arbitrator) to determine the rent review under the farm business tenancy[7].

Unlike the contractual alternative to the statutory rent review provision, which is limited to situations where the parties have appointed a person by agreement to determine the question of rent (otherwise than as an arbitrator)[8], there is nothing in s 29 of the ATA 1995 to preclude the parties from entering into an arbitration agreement in order to provide their own discrete code for determining matters in dispute between them arising from the farm business tenancy. Many of the provisions contained in the Arbitration Act 1996 (AA 1996) governing arbitrations arising under the ATA 1995, are subject to the proviso 'unless otherwise agreed by the parties'. The parties might decide that they wished to preclude some or all of the general provisions of the AA 1996 and/or that they would prefer the appointor of the arbitrator to be an institution, body or person other than the Royal Institution of Chartered Surveyors (RICS).

1   ATA 1995, s 29.
2   The Arbitration Act 1996, s 29(1). As to 'general arbitrations', see para 47.3.
3   See para 47.6.
4   See para 47.8.
5   See para 47.11.
6   See para 47.8 and 47.11.
7   ATA 1995, ss 9(c) and 12(b) where the tenancy agreement provides for the reference of rent reviews to an independent expert whose decision is final it must not contain any provision which precludes a reduction in rent during the tenancy.
8   ATA 1995, s 9(c).

ADR provisions in the Agricultural Tenancies Act 1995

48.2 The ADR provisions in the ATA 1995 only apply if:

(a)   the tenancy is created by an instrument which includes provision for disputes to be resolved by a person other than:
  (i)   the landlord or the tenant; or
  (ii)   a third party appointed by either of them without the consent or concurrence of the other; and
(b)   either of the following has occurred:
  (i)   the landlord and the tenant have jointly referred the dispute to the third party under the provision; or
  (ii)   the landlord or the tenant has referred the dispute to the third party under the provision and notified the other in writing of the making of the reference[1].

After the notification referred to in paragraph (b)(ii) above, a period of four weeks must have elapsed, starting on the date of the notification, before the general arbitration provisions of s 28 of the ATA 1995 are disapplied and the parties are committed to the agreed ADR procedure[2], subject to an opt-out provision[3].

If the farm business tenancy contains an ADR provision, it should require all disputes to be referable to ADR[4]. The parties must understand that there is nothing to stop either the landlord or the tenant deciding to override the ADR mechanism in the event of a dispute. The party wishing to override the ADR mechanism must invoke the general arbitration provisions of s 28 of the ATA 1995 by serving notice under s 28(2) of the ATA 1995, within the 28-day period following notification of the activation of the ADR procedure, specifying the matter in dispute and requiring the appointment of an arbitrator by the President of the RICS after two months[5]. There is no such 'opt-out' if the parties have jointly referred the dispute under their agreed procedure to a third party for determination[6].

The parties to a farm business tenancy may agree to refer a dispute to ADR notwithstanding the absence of an ADR provision in the tenancy agreement itself. In that event the statutory timetable described above would not apply.

1   AA 1996, s 29(1).
2   AA 1996, s 29(1).
3   AA 1996, s 29(2).
4   AA 1996, s 29(1)(a).
5   AA 1996, s 28(2).
6   AA 1996, s 29(1)(b)(i).

Resolution of disputes binding in law

48.3 In addition to the initial opportunity provided for the parties to opt out of the ADR procedure[1], the ATA 1995 provides that the determination of disputes by a third party under s 29 of the ATA 1995 by ADR is limited to disputes where the third party (whether or not acting as an arbitrator) is able, under the terms of the tenancy, to give a decision which is binding in law on both parties.

Where the third party cannot give a decision which is binding in law then, notwithstanding the fact that the dispute was jointly referred to the third party under the ADR mechanism[1], or the fact that the party who did not activate the ADR procedure failed to give a counter-notice within 28 days of notification that the procedure was to be commenced[2], the dispute is not one which can be 'resolved' for the purposes of s 29(1) of the ATA 1995[3]. This situation may apply where the parties elect for mediation or some other form of ADR where there is no decision binding in law.

Whether the parties to ADR can abandon the ADR mechanism before an award or determination has been made will depend upon the contractual terms of the reference to ADR itself. Where the parties do so they will, however, be left in some difficulty in the resolution of the dispute because they are unable to opt back into the general arbitration procedure of s 28 of the ATA 1995 once their agreed third party has been appointed[4].

1   AA 1996, s 29(1)(b)(i).
2   AA 1996, s 29(1)(b)(ii).
3   AA 1996, s 29(2).
4   AA 1996, s 29(1)(b)(i).

Form of ADR

48.4 The ATA 1995 provides the parties with complete freedom of contract as to the method of ADR to be employed. It might be by way of a tailored arbitration agreement or, at the other end of the spectrum, mediation or some other form of ADR. Most usually it will be a determination by an expert.

ALTERNATIVE DISPUTE RESOLUTION UNDER THE AGRICULTURAL HOLDINGS ACT 1986

48.5 By contrast with the ATA 1995, the Agricultural Holdings Act 1986 (AHA 1986) does not provide for ADR. It is important to note that there is nothing to stop the parties to a tenancy agreement governed by the AHA 1986 resolving their dispute through formal or informal ADR or without prejudice negotiations. The parties may choose to include provisions in their tenancy agreement or otherwise to refer a dispute, for example, to an expert for determination.

If a settlement is reached it is important to ensure it is properly documented to ensure it is legally binding on the parties.

If the dispute is not governed by arbitration and does not fall within the ambit of the Agricultural Land Tribunal (ALT), the parties may resort to the courts.

METHODS OF DISPUTE RESOLUTION

Determination by an expert

48.6 The following points should be noted.

(a) The words appointing an expert should be clear and unambiguous to avoid any dispute as to whether an expert or an arbitrator is intended to be appointed[1].

(b) The role of an expert is to decide upon an issue of mutual interest to the parties in order to avoid a dispute. This is in contra- distinction to the role of the arbitrator who determines the outcome of a dispute[2].

(c) The expert's role is not to perform a judicial function. That is the role of an arbitrator. The expert's duties are to investigate and to reach a decision by his own inquiries and expertise[3]. The expert could come to a decision without receiving any evidence or argument from the parties.

(d) The provisions in the ATA 1995 and the AA 1996 relating to the appointment of arbitrators do not apply to experts. The parties must ensure that the contractual provisions for appointment and determination are clear and cannot be frustrated[4].

(e) As to the role of the President of the RICS in relation to the appointment of an expert pursuant to the terms of a lease and the question of the expert's relevant experience, see *Epoch Properties Ltd v British Home Stores Ltd* [5].

(f) The expert may receive written representations from the parties, but he is not required to do so, unless provision is made in the terms of his appointment, and he need not take such representations into account in reaching a decision.

(g) Unlike an arbitrator[6], the expert may act entirely on his own evidence and opinion[7]. However, the expert does owe a duty of care to the parties[8] which he will be in breach of if he fails to take into account matters which he should not[9].

(h) The parties cannot require a hearing, unless provision is made in the terms of the expert's appointment. If a hearing does take place, the rules of evidence do not apply, evidence is not given on oath, and there is no provision for discovery, interrogatories or notices to admit.

(i) Unless bound to do so by the terms of his appointment, there is no requirement that the expert's decision should contain his reasons.

48.6 *Expert determination and the courts*

(j)   The expert's powers as to costs and his remuneration derive exclusively from the terms of his appointment and cannot be determined or assessed by the court.

(k)   Although an expert's decision will usually be stated to be final and binding, the courts have been prepared to impugn an expert's decision. The position is summarised in the decision of Nourse J in *Burgess v Purchase & Sons (Farms) Ltd*[10].

'In my judgment the present state of the law can be summarised as follows. The question whether a valuation made by an expert on a fundamentally erroneous basis can be impugned or not depends on the terms expressed or to be implied in the contract pursuant to which it is made. A non-speaking valuation made of the right property by the right man and in good faith cannot be impugned, although it may still be possible, in the case of an uncompleted transaction, for equitable relief (as opposed to damages) to be refused to the party who wishes to sustain the valuation. On the other hand, there are at least three decisions at first instance to the effect that a speaking valuation which demonstrates that it has been made on a fundamentally erroneous basis can be impugned. In such a case the completion of the transaction does not necessarily defeat the party who wishes to impugn the valuation'[11].

The status of the decision of an expert has been considered more recently by Lightman J in *British Shipbuilders v VSEL Consortium plc*[12], who, considering earlier authorities[13] set out his view of the status of the expert's decision. In particular, he made it clear that the role of the expert and the ambit of his remit were essentially a matter of construction of the agreement between the parties and the expert. If the expert alone is entitled to determine the issue exclusively, the court may only intervene if he has failed to comply with the agreement and may then set aside his decision. However, the court may be asked, in advance of the expert's decision, to determine questions as to the limits of his remit. It will seldom do so, however, because the nature of the question is at that stage hypothetical[14].

1   *Langham House Developments Ltd v Brompton Securities Ltd* (1980) 256 Estates Gazette 719; *Safeway Food Stores Ltd v Banderway Ltd* (1983) 267 Estates Gazette 850.
2   *Sutcliffe v Thackrah* [1974] AC 727, HL; *Arenson v Casson Beckman Rutley & Co* [1977] AC 405, HL. Cf *Leigh v English Property Corpn Ltd* [1976] 2 Lloyd's Rep 298.
3   *Sutcliffe v Thackrah* [1974] AC 727, HL.
4   In the event of a dispute the court may assist: see *Sudbrook Trading Estate Ltd v Eggleton* [1983] 1 AC 444, 265 EG 215, HL.
5   [2004] 3 EGLR 34.
6   *Fox v P G Wellfair Ltd* [1981] 2 Lloyd's Rep 514, CA.
7   *Belvedere Motors Ltd v King* [1981] 2 EGLR 131.
8   *Zubaida v Hargreaves* [1995] 1 EGLR 127, CA.
9   *Belvedere Motors Ltd v King* [1981] 2 EGLR 131.
10 [1983] Ch 216, [1983] 2 All ER 4.
11 *Burgess v Purchase & Sons (Farms) Ltd* [1983] 2 All ER 4, at p 11. Also see: *Baber v Kenwood Manufacturing Co Ltd* [1978] 1 Lloyd's Rep 175; *Heyes v Earl of Derby* (1984) 272 Estates Gazette 935; *Quietfield Ltd v Vascroft Contractors Ltd* [2006] EWHC 174 (TCC), 109 Con LR 29, upheld at [2006] EWCA Civ 1737, [2007] BLR 67.
12 [1997] 1 Lloyd's Rep 106.
13 Including the House of Lords in *Mercury Communications Ltd v Director General of Telecommunications* [1996] 1 All ER 575 and whether that case had or had not overruled *Jones v Sherwood Computer Services plc* [1992] 2 All ER 170, CA and *Norwich Union Life Assurance Society v P & O Property Holdings Ltd* (1994) 68 P & CR 261, HL (see *Woodfall: Landlord and Tenant*, Vol 1 (Looseleaf edn) Sweet & Maxwell at para 8.048).

[14] See *National Grid Co plc v M25 Group Ltd* [1998] 32 EG 90 where the extent of the expert's remit was looked at in the context of a rent review: it was held that where an expert was appointed to determine the rent, matters of construction relating to the rent review provision were not necessarily within the 'exclusive remit' of the expert and could, therefore, be challenged in the courts or the subject of a preliminary hearing in the court.

Mediation

48.7 Mediation is a negotiation facilitated by a third party ('the mediator'). The mediator does not make any judgment about the parties' cases, but helps facilitate an agreement.

Mediation is confidential and can produce settlements and use remedies that are not available through the courts. All discussions are usually agreed to be without prejudice and cannot (save in exceptional circumstances) be referred to in court proceedings.

Mediation is not subject to any binding procedures. It may not be suitable where:

(a)   the parties need a determination from the court on the key issue[1];
(b)   the suggestion of mediation may have come too early or too late to be realistic;
(c)   other settlement methods have been tried and failed; or
(d)   the costs will be disproportionately high.

Mediators can have a range of expertise and do not need to be lawyers. A mediator will focus attention on the commercial aspects of the dispute rather than the legal ones. The parties do not need legal representation at a mediation.

If agreement is reached, it is important that the terms are properly documented to ensure that it is binding on the parties.

[1]   *McCook v Lobo* [2002] EWCA Civ 1760, [2003] ICR 89.

THE COURTS

The Agricultural Holdings Act 1986

48.8 Litigation remains the most common form of dispute resolution. This is despite the introduction of the Civil Procedure Rules (CPR) which have encouraged parties to consider ADR. The courts have penalised parties in costs at the end of a hearing for failing to address ADR procedures[1].

Under the AHA 1986, the jurisdiction of the courts is preserved by s 97 of that Act. The jurisdiction of the court is applied mainly to matters of dispute arising as to rights other than those expressly created by the agricultural holdings legislation itself and thereby referred to arbitration or the Agricultural Land Tribunal (ALT). The section is not as wide as might at first appear in its operation.

The principle enshrined in s 97 of the AHA 1986 is not made expressly subservient to:

(a)   the provisions of s 15(4) and (5) of the AHA 1986 which restrict a landlord's rights during the tenancy, in the case of an alleged abuse of a tenant's freedom of disposal of produce and cropping of his arable land, to the remedy of an injunction (no damages, except on quitting). The question as to whether the tenant has exercised his right so as to injure or deteriorate the holding has to be decided by arbitration (AHA 1986, s 15(6));

(b)   the provisions of s 83 of the AHA 1986, which sets out the compulsory reference to arbitration under that Act of all claims between landlord and tenant arising under the Act, custom or agreement, and 'on or out of the termination of the tenancy of the holding or any part thereof';

(c)   the other provisions of the AHA 1986 'which otherwise expressly' so provide.

These may be illustrated by the express provisions against contracting-out of the AHA 1986[2] and the provisions of s 15(1). Since the decision in *Kent v Conniff*[3], it can no longer be said, as was at one time thought, that there is, on the true construction of s 71 of the AHA 1986, any denial of a landlord's rights to claim damages during the tenancy for breaches of a tenant's obligations of any type under the tenancy agreement.

On the affirmative side, the effect of s 97 of the AHA 1986 is to preserve custom, in so far as it is permissible expressly by s 77 of the Act, as a basis for compensation claims, and so such customs as those for pre-entry or hold-over for certain purposes are saved by this section. So also are customs as to compensation for a tenant who entered on the holding before 1 March 1948 and who has not elected by notice under s 64(1) and Sch 12 para 6 to invoke the relevant provisions of this Act regarding items of tenant-right compensation which are itemised in Pt II of Sch 8 to the AHA 1986. It must be noted that it is only in respect of such items and in such circumstances that custom is preserved.

---

1   *Dunnett v Railtrack plc* [2002] EWCA Civ 303, [2002] 1 WLR 2434; *Cowl v Plymouth City Council* [2001] EWCA Civ 1935, [2002] 1 WLR 803; *Halsey v Milton Keynes NHS Trust* [2004] EWCA Civ 576, [2004] 1 WLR 3002.

2   For example, AHA1986, s 3.

3   [1953] 1 QB 361, [1953] 1 All ER 155, CA. But note this case was decided before the making of the Agriculture (Maintenance, Repair and Insurance of Fixed Equipment) Regulations 1973, SI 1973/1473 (as amended) which expressly provides now for arbitration in the case of such disputes.

48.9 In summary, the following disputes under the AHA 1986 are determined by the courts:

(a)   the issue as to whether the AHA 1986 applies to the tenancy;

(b)   issues of construction relating to the tenancy agreement;

(c)   damages for breach of a repairing covenant during the tenancy;

(d)   the enforcement of a covenant to pay outgoings;

(e)   determining the validity of a notice to quit (for example, where fraud is alleged)[1];

(f)   forfeiture proceedings;

(g)   other possession proceedings;

(h)   all other claims where jurisdiction is not expressly allocated by the AHA 1986[2].

[1]   For a case where a notice to quit was given under Case B and a demand for arbitration followed by the landlord sought declaratory relief without proceeding before the arbitrator and the Court of Appeal accepted jurisdiction, albeit where there was no argument or issue taken as to jurisdiction, see *Paddock Investments Ltd v Lory* [1975] 2 EGLR 5.

[2]   AHA 1986, s 97.

The Agricultural Tenancies Act 1995

48.10 By contrast, the ATA 1995 does not provide for disputes to be resolved through the courts, it provides two methods for determining disputes: arbitration and alternative dispute resolution.

The appellate jurisdiction of the court from arbitrators appointed to determine disputes under the ATA 1995 or the AHA 1986 (by way of an appeal) on substantive jurisdiction, serious irregularity or a point of law to the High Court, thence to the Court of Appeal and the House of Lords, is preserved[1]. Likewise, the appellate procedure from the Agricultural Land Tribunal to the High Court by way of case stated and thence to the Court of Appeal and the House of Lords[2] is likewise preserved.

The majority of agricultural holdings cases determined by the higher courts emanate by way of appeal from an arbitrator or the ALT or from the first instance jurisdiction of the county court or High Court where appropriate[3] on a claim for possession, following the expiration of a notice to quit, or forfeiture or otherwise[4].

[1]   See para 47.65–47.70.

[2]   See para Ch 46.

[3]   See CPR 55.3.

[4]   See, eg, *Elsden v Pick* [1980] 3 All ER 235, [1980] 1 WLR 898, CA and *Parry v Million Pigs Ltd* (1980) 260 Estates Gazette 281.

Section 5

MILK QUOTA AND THE MID-TERM REVIEW OF THE COMMON AGRICULTURAL POLICY

Section 5

MILK QUOTA AND THE MID-TERM REVIEW OF THE COMMON AGRICULTURAL POLICY

Contents

Chapter 49

MILK QUOTA

OVERVIEW OF THE SYSTEM OF MILK QUOTA

Introduction of milk quota

49.1 Milk production quotas were introduced on 2 April 1984 arising from quantitative controls imposed on the production of milk and other dairy products under the Common Agricultural Policy of the European Economic Community, now the European Community (EC)[1]. Initially the quota system, introduced on 2 April 1984, operated for five years. It has subsequently been amended and extended, particularly in 1992. Currently it has been extended until 31 March 2015[2].

In the United Kingdom milk quotas were first introduced by the Dairy Produce Quota Regulations 1984[3]. Occupiers of holdings identified as dairy holdings had registered against their holding an amount called a 'reference quantity' or 'quota'. The effect of the registration was to set a maximum quantity of milk production or other dairy products so that if the producer exceeds that level in any quota year, a levy may be imposed on the excess.

At one time quota was a valuable asset. More recently quota prices have fallen.

[1]   It is beyond the scope of this book to consider the scope of the European milk quota scheme. For the definitive analysis, see Cardwell, *Milk Quotas: European and UK Law* (1996) OUP. Also see, Usher, *Legal Aspects of Agriculture in the European Community* (1988) Clarendon; Snyder, *The Law of the Common Agricultural Policy* (1986); and Wood, Priday, Carter and Moss, *Milk Quotas: Law and Practice* (1986) Farmgate Communications Limited.
[2]   Council Regulation (EC) 1788/2003 (OJ 2003 L 270/123).
[3]   SI 1984/1047. In this chapter, the Dairy Produce Quota Regulations for the time being in force are referred to as DPQR.

Reference quantity

49.2 Under Council Regulation (EEC) 804/68, as amended, each Member State was entitled to produce milk and dairy products to a specified ceiling described as 'a reference quantity'. If the reference quantity is exceeded, then levy becomes payable to the EC in relation to the over-production of the Member State. The system is convoluted because the levy is generally recovered[1] from the individual producers by reference to their own individually allocated milk quota, but the levy is collected by purchasers of milk (ie the dairies) in the case of wholesale deliveries or from the producer in the case of direct sales[2].

1   The collection of levy was the responsibility of the Intervention Board for England and Wales until 2002. It has since been collected by the Rural Payments Agency (RPA), as agent for the Department of Environment, Food and Rural Affairs (DEFRA) in England and the National Assembly for Wales.
2   Until the Dairy Produce Quotas Regulations 2005, SI 2005/465 (DPQR 2005) came into force on 31 March 2005, the RPA could not (other than in exceptional circumstances) collect levy direct from a producer: see *Intervention Board for Agricultural Produce for England and Wales v Penycoed Farming Partnership* Case C-230/01, [2004] ECR I-937, ECJ. This lacuna was dealt with by the DPQR 2005 to enable the RPA to collect direct from producers: SI 2005/465, reg 31. This amendment to the regulations followed an unreported county court decision, in *Duckworth v Department for Environment and Rural Affairs* (2005) Barrow-in-Furness County Court.

Direct sales and wholesale quota

49.3 The two main categories of quota are direct sales and wholesale[1]. Direct sales quota is the quantity of dairy produce which may be sold by direct sale from a holding in a quota year without the seller being liable to pay levy. Wholesale quota is the quantity of dairy produce which may be delivered by wholesale delivery to a purchaser from a holding in a quota year without the producer in occupation of that holding being liable to pay levy. Wholesale quota represents the major part of quota allocated in the UK.

The RPA is required to keep a direct sales and a wholesale register, in which are entered details of each individual producers quota, identification of the holding for which it is registered and, in the case of the wholesale register, details of the relevant wholesale purchaser. The RPA must also keep a register of purchasers' notices, in which there must be set out the name of each purchaser, a description of its undertaking, its purchaser quota and its purchaser special quota[2].

1   For other categories of quota: see para 49.4ff.
2   See para 49.5.

Other forms of quota

49.4 There have been three other categories of quota since the introduction of milk quota in 1984:

(a)   purchaser quota;
(b)   purchaser special quota; and
(c)   'special' quota, normally known as 'SLOM' quota.

908

Purchaser quota is the quantity of dairy produce which can be delivered by wholesale delivery to a purchaser during a quota year without that purchaser being liable to pay levy[1].

Purchaser special quota was the quantity of dairy produce which could be delivered by wholesale delivery against a producer's special quota to a purchaser during a quota year without the purchaser being liable to pay levy[2]. The DPQR 2005 no longer makes specific reference to this type of quota. Accordingly, it is subsumed into quotas generally.

The Dairy Produce Quotas (Amendment) Regulations 1990[3] made special provision for the implementation of EC legislation to enable qualifying producers who participated in the non-marketing of milk or dairy herd conversion schemes to apply for the allocation of 'special' quota[4]. This is usually referred to as 'SLOM' quota.

Special allocations of quota were required for producers who participated in the EC non-marketing and conversion schemes and who had reduced or ceased their dairy output in their country's reference year: 1983 in the UK. As a result of litigation before the European Court in the cases of *Mulder I*[5] and *Von Deetzen I*[6], it was determined that such producers had been treated inequitably and accordingly special quota should be allocated to them.

There were three rounds of SLOM quota allocations following the decisions in *Mulder I* and *Von Deetzen I*. The first SLOM quota was provided for in Council Regulation EEC 764/89. It was allocated subject to various conditions, one of which restricted a producer's right to receive special quota limited to 60% of the amount of milk delivered during the 12 months preceding the month in which the application to participate in the non-marketing or conversion scheme was made. This limitation was ruled to be unlawful by the European Court[7]. This resulted in a second round of SLOM allocations under Council Regulation EEC 1639/91. That in turn was challenged[8]. As a consequence, a third round of SLOM quota was allocated pursuant to Council Regulation EEC 2055/93. As in the case of purchaser special quota, the DPQR 2005 no longer makes specific reference to this type of quota. Accordingly, it is subsumed into quotas generally.

1   DPQR 2005, SI 2005/465, reg 2(1).
2   Dairy Produce Quotas Regulations 2002, SI 2002/457.
3   SI 1990/132.
4   Council Regulation (EC) 3950/92, art 4(3) and Council Regulation (EEC) 2055/93, art 1(1).
5   C-104/89: [1989] 2 CMLR 1.
6   C-170/86: [1989] 2 CMLR 327.
7   *Spagl v Hauptzollamt Rosenheim* C-189/89 [1990] ECR I-4539; *Pastätter v Hauptzollamt Bad Reichenhall* C-217/89 [1990] ECR I-4585.
8   In *Wehrs v Hauptzollamt Lüneberg* C-264/90 [1992] ECR I-6285 a producer took over a holding subject to a non-marketing or conversion undertaking, but was barred from the SLOM allocation by reason of having obtained a reference quantity under other provisions of the milk quota scheme. Also see *Twijnstra v Minister van Landbouw, Natuurbeheer en Visserij* C-81/91 [1993] ECR I-2455.

49.5   Milk quota

Purchasers/producers

49.5 In the UK any levy which arises as a result of the Member States production exceeding the reference quantity for the 12 months concerned (where the quota year runs from 1 April to 31 March in each year) is payable by the 'purchaser' on milk delivered to it by 'producers'[1]. The purchaser is then under a duty to recover the levy from producers proportionately to their contributions to the reference quantity being exceeded. The system is administered by the RPA[2]. In the case of direct sales, the producer processor pays the RPA direct any levy payable.

The purchasers are purchasing dairies which have operated since the deregulation of the milk market by the Agriculture Act 1993. Each purchaser has a quota, which is the quantity of dairy produce which may be delivered by wholesale deliveries to that purchaser from holdings in a region during a quota year without the purchaser being liable to pay levy. It is the ability of producers to trade their quota and transfer it which has not only given milk quota an economic value, but also has resulted in disputes in relation to transfers and matters relating to transfers.

[1]   See fn 1 at para 49.2 above. As to the definition of producers, see para 49.7.
[2]   Formerly the Intervention Board for Agricultural Produce.

Holding

49.6 Quota is registered in relation to a producer's 'holding', often known as the Euro Holding. The holding is defined as 'all of the production units managed by a farmer situated within the territory of the same Member State'[1]. The holding, therefore, may include both freehold and leasehold land. Importantly, it is not an 'agricultural holding' within the definition contained in the Agricultural Holdings Act 1986 (AHA 1986).

[1]   DPQR 2005, SI 2005/465, reg 2(1) and Council Regulation (EC) 1788/2003, art 2(d) (OJ 2003 L 270/123) which cross refers to Council Regulation (EC) 1782/32003 (OJ 2003 L 270/1). Note that 'a farm is perfectly capable of being a holding even if the cows have all gone', per McCowan LJ in *WE & RA Holdcroft v Staffordshire County Council* [1994] 2 EGLR 1, [1994] 28 EG 131 at 134.

Farmer/producer

49.7 A 'farmer' means 'a natural or legal person or group of natural or legal persons whatever legal status is granted to the group and its members by national law whose holding is situate within Community Territory and who exercise an agricultural activity'[1].

A 'producer' means 'a farmer with a holding in the territory of a Member State who produces and markets milk or who [is] preparing to do so in the very near future'[2].

The definition of producer is not limited to individuals, but extends to farming companies and partnerships. In the case of *R v Dairy Produce Quota Tribunal for England and Wales, ex p Atkinson*[3], two brothers, one on his own and one jointly with his wife, lodged claims before the prescribed date for a share in their region's reserved quota under the exceptional hardship provisions in the Dairy Produce Quotas Regulations 1984. In each case the applicants had purchased the farms in 1984, but were not producing milk on those farms during the year ending 31 March 1985. However, at all material times the two brothers had been in partnership with their father in relation to another farm which was an active dairy farm to which a primary quota attached. The Quota Tribunal rejected the applicants' claim on the ground that no actual dairy farming was being carried out in the year ending 31 March 1985 on either of the newly purchased farms. As such neither of the applicants were 'producers'. It was argued that the applicants were producers as they were part of a partnership on their father's farm where the main occupation was dairy farming. Accordingly, the decision of the Quota Tribunal was quashed and the case remitted for fresh consideration by a differently constituted Tribunal.

[1]   Council Regulation (EC) 1788/2003, art 2(c) (OJ 2003 L 270/123) which cross refers to the definition of farmer in Council Regulation (EC) 1782/2003 (OJ 2003 L 270/1).
[2]   Council Regulation (EC) 1788/2003.
[3]   (1985) 276 Estates Gazette 1158.

Leasing

49.8 It is permissible for one producer to agree with another to make a temporary transfer of the entirety or part of a producer's unused quota which is registered with him as permanently held by him for a period of one quota year to that other producer, commonly known as 'leasing'[1]. This is not a permanent transfer of quota to which the arbitration provisions contained in the DPQR 2005 apply[2].

[1]   Council Regulation (EC) 1788/2003 (OJ 2003 L 270/123), art 16.
[2]   See DPQR 2005, SI 2005/465, reg. 15.

Transfers

49.9 Whenever there is a sale, lease or transfer by inheritance of a holding, all or part of the corresponding reference quantity (ie the quota) must be transferred to the purchaser, tenant or heir according to procedures which the European Community provide it should be laid down by individual Member States[1]. This relates to the general rule where quota is transferred with land. As seen below[2], transfers without land are authorised for the purposes of improving the structure of milk production[3]. It should be noted that in order to transfer quota with land it is necessary for the transferor and the transferee to enter into a tenancy of a minimum of ten months duration[4].

In the UK, changes to the occupation of an entire holding which have registered quota carry a transfer of the entire quota with them. Changes in occupation of part of holdings require an apportionment[5]. In default of agreement between the parties, such apportionment is made by arbitration[6].

1   Council Regulation (EC) 1788/2003 (OJ 2003 L 270/123), art 17.
2   See para 49.29.
3   Council Regulation (EC) 1788/2003 (OJ 2003 L 270/123), art 18(1)(e); DPQR 2005, SI 2005/465, reg 13.
4   DPQR 2005, SI 2005/465, reg 16. See para 49.14.
5   SI 2005/465, reg 10.
6   SI 2005/465, reg 10(2) and Sch 1.

49.10 The arbitration rules for the apportionment of milk quota are contained in regs 9 to 12 and 39 and Sch 1 to the DPQR 2005[1]. The Arbitration Act 1996 does not apply to arbitrations under the DPQR 2005 which has its own unique arbitration code based upon the now defunct provisions of Sch 11 to the AHA 1986.

1   SI 2005/465. For arbitrations in Wales, see Dairy Produce Quotas (Wales) Regulations 2005, SI 2005/537.

End of tenancy claims

49.11 Where the tenant is a registered producer in respect of a milk quota holding which consists entirely of land comprised in the tenancy, then the entire quota belonging to the quota reverts to the landlord at the end of the tenancy. There is no question of apportionment. A tenant has a right under para 13 of Sch 1 to the Agriculture Act 1986 to receive compensation for such part of the quota as, in broad terms is attributable to efficient farming practices or fixed equipment introduced by the tenant or has been purchased by the tenant[1].

Claims for compensation under the Agriculture Act 1986 are settled either at the end of the tenancy, or before, by arbitration. The procedures laid down in the AHA 1986 apply, now adopting the terms of the Arbitration Act 1996[2].

In some cases the position will be complicated. The tenant may occupy land let to one landlord and other land let to another landlord or owned by the farmer. Upon quitting part of the milk quota holding there would be an apportionment of milk quota which must first be settled by arbitration under the DPQR 2005 and claims for compensation then have to be settled under the Agriculture Act 1986.

As regards tenancies under the AHA 1986 ending after 31 March 2005, where:

(a)   a tenant of any land in a holding[3] has quota registered as available to him;

(b)   the quota is so registered by virtue of a transfer referred to in reg 13 of the DPQR 2005[4], the cost of which was not borne by the tenant's landlord;

(c)   the tenancy of the land in question expires without any possibility of renewal in similar terms;

(d)   the tenant and his landlord have not agreed that, after the expiry of the tenancy, the quota should no longer be available to the tenant; and

(e)   the tenant continues to be a producer after the expiry of the tenancy in relation to:

   (i)   another holding; or
   (ii)   another part of the holding of which the land formed part,

the tenant may submit a notice to the Secretary of State[5] that the quota is to be available to him by virtue of his occupation of that holding or that other part of the holding of which the land formed part[6].

The notice referred to above must:

(i)   be in such form as the Secretary of State may reasonably require;
(ii)   reach the Secretary of State no later than 31 March in the quota year in which the tenancy expires; and
(iii)   include a statement by the tenant that:

   (a)   he and his landlord have not agreed that, after the expiry of the tenancy, the quota should be registered in relation to the holding which then comprises or, as the case may be, includes, the land stating the amounts of used and unused quota[7] involved; and

   (b)   he continues to be a producer[8].

---

[1]   The complex provisions relating to the calculation of compensation are dealt with in detail in Ch 50.
[2]   Agriculture Act 1986, Sch 1 paras 10 and 11.
[3]   DPQR 2005, SI 2005/465, reg 2(1). Note that this is the definition of 'holding' for milk quota ('the Euro Holding') and not for the purposes of the AHA 1986. See para 49.6.
[4]   See para 49.29.
[5]   Secretary of State for Environment, Food and Rural Affairs: SI 2005/465, reg 2(1).
[6]   SI 2005/465, reg 14(2).
[7]   SI 2005/465, reg 2(1): ' "unused quota" means quota remaining unused after direct sales or deliveries have been taken into account' and ' "used quota" shall be construed accordingly'.
[8]   SI 2005/465, reg 14(3).

LEGISLATION GOVERNING THE QUOTA SYSTEM

49.12 In the UK the milk quota system was initially governed by the Dairy Produce Quotas Regulations 1984, but following a series of amending and consolidating regulations, the quota system is now the subject of the DPQR 2005[1], as amended[2]. Formerly the milk quota regime for England and Wales was the same, contained in the Dairy Produce Quotas Regulations 1997. Now the DPQR 2005 apply to England and the Dairy Produce Quotas (Wales) Regulations 2005[3] apply to Wales. Despite the separation, the rules applying in Wales are basically the same as in England.

---

[1]   SI 2005/465. Also see the Dairy Produce Quotas (General Provisions) (Amendment) Regulations 2005, SI 2005/466.
[2]   The Dairy Produce Quotas (Amendment) Regulations 2006, SI 2006/120 and the Dairy Produce Quotas (Amendment) Regulations 2007, SI 2007/106.
[3]   SI 2005/537.

THE BACKGROUND TO THE ARBITRAL PROCESS

The mechanics of transfer

49.13   Save in limited circumstances[1], in the case of a transfer of the whole or part of a 'holding', the transferee[2] must submit to the RPA a notice of transfer in such form as may reasonably be required by Secretary of State, in the case of transfers with land on or before 31 March in the quota year[3] in which the transfer takes place, regardless of whether or not by lease[4].

Such notice shall, include a statement from the transferor[5] and transferee specifying the amounts of used and unused quota transferred.

[1]   Retention of quotas at the end of a tenancy or leasing: see DPQR 2005, SI 2005/465, regs 14 and 15.
[2]   Transferee means '(a) where quota is transferred with a holding or part of a holding, a person who replaces another as occupier of that holding or part of a holding; and (b) in any other case, the person to whom quota is transferred': SI 2005/465, reg 2(1).
[3]   The quota year means any of the periods of 12 months referred to in art 1(1) of Council Regulation (EC) 1788/2003 as commencing on 1 April in any year.
[4]   SI 2007/106, reg 9. Note that under the DPQR 2005 a distinction was drawn between leases entered into before and after 1 March in any quota year.
[5]   Transferor means '(a) where quota is transferred with a holding or part of a holding, a person who is replaced by another occupier of that holding or part of a holding; and (b) in any other case, the person from whom quota is transferred': SI 2005/465, reg 2(1).

49.14   In the case of a transfer of the whole holding, the notice must include a consent or sole interest notice provided by the transferor in respect of the holding[1]. Where the transferor is a tenant, the landlord must sign the consent notice before the tenant can transfer.

Where there is a transfer of part of a holding, the DPQR 2005 require that:

(a)   an apportionment of the quota relating to the holding must either be agreed between the transferee and the transferor and contained in the notice required to be lodged with the RPA or, in the absence of such agreement, determined by arbitration in accordance with Sch 1 to the DPQR 2005 in England; *and*

(b)   any dairy produce which has been sold by direct sale or delivered by wholesale delivery from the holding during the quota year in which the change of occupation takes place and prior to that transfer shall be deemed, for the purposes of any levy calculation, to have been sold or delivered from each part of the holding in proportion to that apportionment, unless the parties agree otherwise and notify the RPA of the agreement in such form as the RPA may reasonably require, at the time of the submission of the notice or other information pursuant to reg 9 of the DPQR 2005[2].

There are limited circumstances in which there is no transfer of quota upon the transfer of the whole or part of a holding. This is in the case of the grant or termination of either a licence to occupy land or a tenancy or lease of a holding for a period of less than ten months (where the holding is in

England)[3]. Accordingly, a transfer of quota with land must be pursuant to a tenancy of the whole or part of the Euro Holding for a period of not less than ten months[4].

1 DPQR, SI 2005/465, reg 9(5)(c).
2 SI 2005/465, reg 10.
3 SI 2005/465, reg 16. There are like provisions in Wales, see Dairy Produce Quotas (Wales) Regulations 2005, SI 2005/537.
4 SI 2005/465, reg 16(1)(b).

The arbitral code

49.15 Milk quota arbitrations are conducted in accordance with their own self contained rules which is set out in Sch 1 to the DPQR 2005[1].

Paragraph 3 of Sch 1 requires an arbitrator to base his award on findings made by him as to the areas used for milk production[2] in the five years during which milk production took place preceding the change of occupation or in the case of a prospective apportionment, preceding his appointment as arbitrator.

Arbitrators appointed under the DPQR 2005 are appointed either by agreement or by the President of the RICS. Prior to the TRIG[3] reforms resulting in the RRO 2006[4], the President had to appoint a member of the panel drawn up by the Lord Chancellor for the purpose of conducting arbitrations under the AHA 1986. The panel will be scrapped and so this is no longer the case.

1 See Ch 51.
2 As to areas used for milk production, see *Puncknowle Farms Ltd v Kane* [1985] 2 EGLR 8, 275 Estates Gazette 1283. See para 49.28.
3 Tenancy Reform Industry Group.
4 The Regulatory Reform (Agricultural Tenancies) (England and Wales) Order 2006, SI 2006/2805.

KEY LEGAL ISSUES

The nature of a milk quota transfer

49.16 Since the introduction of milk quotas in 1984, the trading in milk quota that has arisen has been underpinned by agreements by transferors and transferees to transfer the entirety or part of the milk quota attaching to a holding.

The typical transaction, where the parties intend to transfer milk quota without a permanent transfer of land, is the grant of a tenancy of a minimum of ten months by the transferee in respect of the whole or part of his holding. Upon the change of occupation occasioned by the grant of the tenancy, an agreed amount of milk quota is transferred to the transferee and becomes immediately registerable in the transferee's name. As part of the transaction, the transferee agrees that for the period of the tenancy he will not use any part of the land comprised in the tenancy for milk production, so that it is no longer an 'area used for milk production'. Accordingly, the land ceases to form part of the holding (often known as the Euro-Holding) of either party. At the termination of the tenancy, because the land has ceased to be part of any parties holding during the period of the tenancy, there is no change of occupation in respect of a holding. As a consequence, there is no re-transfer of the quota which has been registered in the name of the transferee.

The extent of the holding

49.17 A holding under the European Community legislation extends to 'all of the production units managed by a farmer situated within the territory of the same Member State'[1].

It has been determined by the European Court that the definition of a holding is a broad one and, in particular, the definition is wide enough to include tenanted land, even where the production units at the date of the grant have neither dairy cows nor the necessary facilities for milk production, and the agreement imposes no obligation to engage in milk production[2].

In the UK, it has been held that land which the occupier was obliged by contract not to use for milk production could not be regarded as part of a holding[3].

---

[1]   DPQR 2005, SI 2005/465, reg 2(1) and Council Regulation (EC) 1788/2003, art 2(d). Originally a holding extended to all such production units within the Community. The definition was changed in Council Regulation (EEC) 1560/93 (OJ 1993 L 154/30).

[2]   See *Wachauf v Germany* Case C-5/88, [1989] ECR 2609, [1991] 1 CMLR 328.

[3]   *Carson v Cornwall County Council* [1993] 1 EGLR 21, [1993] 03 EG 119. Cf *WE & RA Holdcroft v Staffordshire County Council* [1994] 2 EGLR 1.

Definition of the producer

49.18 As seen above[1], a 'producer' is defined as 'a farmer with a holding in the territory of a Member State who produces and markets milk or who are preparing to do so in the very near future'[2]. Production units have not been defined in the European legislation.

'Producer' covers both farmers making direct sales and those more usually involved in wholesale deliveries to purchasers. It embraces tenants and freehold owners[3]. It extends to business structures, including partnerships and companies. This gives rise to two issues. First, the legal status of the producer; and second, the extent to which a producer must be actively engaged in milk production.

As to the legal status of the producer, in the case of partnerships the general practice has been to register the milk quota in the name of the partnership rather than in the name of the individual partners[4]. In the UK it was held that it was sufficient to qualify as a producer if an individual was a member of a partnership engaged in dairy farming[5]. It is now established that this means actively engaged in milk production[6].

¹ See para 49.7.
² Council Regulation (EC) 1788/2003, art 2(c). As to the definition of 'farmer', see para 49.7.
³ *Ballmann v Hauptzollamt Osnabru CK* Case C-341/89, [1991] ECR I-25.
⁴ See *Herbrink v Minister van Landbouw, Natuurbeheer en Visserij* Case C-98/91, [1994] ECR I-223, [1994] 3 CMLR 645; *R v Ministry of Agriculture, Fisheries and Food, ex p Dent* Case C-84/90 [1992] ECR I-2009, [1992] 2 CMLR 597.
⁵ *R v Dairy Produce Quota Tribunal for England and Wales, ex p Atkinson* (1985) 276 Estates Gazette 1158.
⁶ See para 49.30.

Transfer/change of occupation

49.19 Save in the case of a limited category of transfers excluded from the operation of the transferors by the DPQR 2005[1], any transaction which involves both a 'transfer' and a 'change of occupation' of a holding, or part of it, will require a re-registration of quota. There must therefore be a transfer of a holding or part of it. As a consequence, there must also be a change of occupation. The courts have not sought to break down the transaction into the component parts. The courts have considered the transaction as a whole[2]. In *WE & RA Holdcroft v Staffordshire County Council*, McCowan LJ observed: 'It is plain ..., in my judgment, that when the regulations talk about 'transfer' they are talking in terms of occupation and not legal title'[3].

As has been seen above[4], the concept of transfer is defined by reference to 'transferor' and 'transferee' in the DPQR 2005. The definitions are however imprecise. The 'occupier' of a holding is defined as including the person entitled to grant occupation of that land to another[5]. The concept of change of occupation has given rise to a number of difficulties including whether physical occupation is required. It appears that the absence of physical occupation consequential upon the grant of a tenancy with the attendant right to occupy will be insufficient to give rise to a change of occupation causing the transfer of milk quota. It has also been suggested that de minimis physical occupation will be insufficient. In *R v Ministry of Agriculture, Fisheries and Food, ex p Cox*[6], the vendor sold milk quota using a grazing agreement. Subsequently, when it became apparent that the purchaser had failed to graze stock on the land during the term of the agreement, the vendor applied for the re-registration of the quota in his name. It was held that the effect of Council Regulation (EC) 1371/84 (as amended) was to require actual occupation of the land, and not the acquisition of a mere right to occupy.

¹ See para 49.9ff.
² See, for example, *WE & RA Holdcroft v Staffordshire County Council* [1994] 2 EGLR 1.
³ [1994] 2 EGLR 1 at 134.
⁴ See para 49.9.
⁵ DPQR 2005, SI 2005/465, reg 2(1).
⁶ [1993] 1 EGLR 17, [1993] 22 EG 111.

The nature of milk quota

Interest in land: the statutory provisions

49.20 Disputes between partners as to their entitlement in respect of milk quota, together with litigation between lenders and borrowers[1] has given rise to consideration of the juridical nature of milk quota.

917

49.20 *Milk quota*

The starting point is that milk quota is said to attach to the land and passes with the land to which it relates[2]. It raises the question as to whether it is an interest in land.

Section 2 of the Law of Property (Miscellaneous Provisions) Act 1989 provides that a contract for the sale or other disposition of an interest in land can only be made in writing and only by incorporating all the terms which the parties have expressly agreed in one document or, where contracts are being exchanged, in each document. 'Interest in land' is defined as 'any estate, interest or charge in or over land'[3]. The Law of Property (Miscellaneous Provisions) Act 1989 further provides that 'nothing in this section [s 2] affects the creation or operation of resulting, implied or constructive trusts'[4].

Section 53 of the Law of Property Act 1925 provides that no interest in land can be created or disposed of except by signed writing, and that a declaration of trust in respect of any land or any interest in land must be proved by signed writing. As with the Law of Property (Miscellaneous Provisions) Act 1989, the Law of Property Act 1925 does not affect the creation or operation of resulting, implied or constructive trusts.

Section 205(1)(ix) of the Law of Property Act 1925 defines 'land' widely, as including a rent, other incorporeal hereditaments, and an easement, right, privilege, or benefit in, over, or derived from the land. An interest in land has been described as a right which has 'the quality of being capable of enduring through different ownership of the land, according to normal conceptions of title to real property'[5]. An interest in the proceeds of sale of land has been held to be an interest in land[6]. In this analysis, it should be noted that the Trusts of Land and Appointment of Trustees Act 1996 removed trusts for sale and the doctrine of conversion.

[1] See para 49.21.
[2] See *Wachauf v Bundesamt fur Ernahrung und Forstwirtschaft* Case C-5/88, [1989] ECR 2609, [1991] 1 CMLR 328.
[3] Law of Property (Miscellaneous Provisions) Act 1989, s 2(6).
[4] Law of Property (Miscellaneous Provisions) Act 1989, s 2(5).
[5] *Nurdin & Peacock plc v DB Ramsden & Co Ltd* [1999] 1 EGLR 119 at 124K–124L.
[6] *Cooper v Critchley* [1955] Ch 431.

Is milk quota an interest in land?

49.21 Milk quota was allocated to a 'producer', being a farmer supplying milk in respect of a 'holding'. The quota then attached to the holding and passed with it. On a sale of part, it was apportioned. In *Faulks v Faulks*[1], Chadwick J held that quota was not an asset capable of being enjoyed, or transferred, independently of the land in respect of which it is registered:

'The fact that the transfer of a potential liability is likely to be matched by a payment to the person assuming that liability may enable it to be said that the quota transferred has an intrinsic economic value, but that does not of itself lead to the conclusion that quota is an asset separate and distinct from the holding in relation to which it was, or becomes, registered'.

That decision was followed by Blackburne J in *Davies and H & R Ecroyd Ltd*[2]:

> '... while it is well recognised that in certain circumstances, milk quota may become severed from the land with which it would otherwise run, the fundamental principle is that milk quota attaches to and passes with the land to which it relates'[3].

In *Harries v Barclays Bank plc*[4], the Court of Appeal held that a bank which held a charge over a farm, but not over the farmer's quota, was entitled to retain the proceeds of sale of the farm which were attributable to the value of the quota, and also the proceeds of leasing the quota. The proceeds of sale attributable to the value of the quota were not capable of separate treatment from that attributable to the value of the land. The proceeds from the quota leasing were an incident of possession of the farm to which the bank had become entitled under the charge. The proceeds formed part of the rents and profits of the land to which the bank was entitled as one of the products of its possession of the mortgaged property.

The European Court of Justice has affirmed a number of times the fundamental principle that milk quota attaches to and follows the land in respect of which it is registered. In *EARL de Kerlast*[5], the Court said, at para 17:

> 'The Court has consistently held that the entire system of reference quantities is based on the general principle laid down by Article 7 of Regulation No 857/84 and Article 7 of Regulation No 1546/88, that a reference quantity is allocated in relation to land and must therefore be transferred with that land ...'.

It should also be noted that Preamble (18) of Council Regulation (EC) 1788/2003[6] refers to milk quota being 'tied to farms'. The European Community legislation does grant certain options for the tie to be broken[7], including what appears as a total break of the link with land with the phrase 'centralise and supervise transfers of reference quantities without land'[8]. The UK has not chosen to follow this route[9].

It is submitted that milk quota is an interest in land. It is allocated in relation to land. It is transferred with land. The fact that in certain circumstances it may be detached from the land does not prevent it from having the essential characteristics of an interest in land until it is so detached. A fixture is land until it is severed, as are minerals and timber. Milk quota is attached to land, unless there are specific policy reasons to detach it.

In *Cottle v Coldicott*[10], the Special Commissioners held that, in computing capital gains tax on the sale of quota, no part of the acquisition cost of the land could be taken into account as forming the consideration 'given by him ... wholly and exclusively for the consideration of the asset'. It was not argued that quota was an interest in land. The Commissioners' decision was solely addressed to the capital gains tax legislation. It was reached principally because of the difficulty of allocating the acquisition cost of any particular part of the holding to the sale of quota. Part of the reasoning in that decision is inconsistent with *Faulks v Faulks*[11]; *Davies and H&R Eckroyd Limited*[12];

and *Harries v Barclays Bank plc*[13]. If the decision was correct, it is submitted that it is only so in the context of capital gains tax legislation.

1   [1992] 1 EGLR 9.
2   [1996] 2 EGLR 5.
3   *Davies and H & R Ecroyd Limited* [1996] 2 EGLR 5 at 8F.
4   [1997] 2 EGLR 15.
5   [1997] ECR I-1961.
6   (OJ 2003 L 270/123).
7   (EC) 1788/2003, Recital (18) and art 18.
8   (EC) 1788/2003, art 18(1)(c). Also note, *Demand v Hauptzollamt Trier* Case C-186/96, [1998] ECR I-8529 at I-8541. See fn 16 at para 52.14.
9   See para 49.22.
10 [1995] STC 239.
11 [1992] 1 EGLR 9.
12 *Davies and H & R Ecroyd Limited* [1996] 2 EGLR 5.
13 [1997] 2 EGLR 15.

49.22 In *Foxton v Revenue and Customs Comr*[1], the Special Commissioners followed *Cottle v Coldicott*[2]. They rejected an argument that quota was land. They said that:

> 'While milk quota is related to holdings of land that does not mean that it is the same asset as the holding because it can be dealt with separately by the method adopted in this case of granting a short sub-tenancy, which is not itself a disposal of the land'.

It is submitted that the decision was either wrong, or correct for capital gains tax purposes only.

There is no doubt that a land owner can act so as to be subject to a constructive trust of his land, obliging him to deal with the land in such a way as to transfer the benefit of quota allocated to the land[3].

It should be noted that s 4(1) of the Law of Property Act 1925 provides:

> 'Interests in land validly created or arising after the commencement of this Act, which are not capable of subsisting as legal estates, shall take effect as equitable interests, and, save as otherwise expressly provided by statute, interests in land which under the Statute of Uses or otherwise could before the commencement of this Act have been created as legal interests, shall be capable of being created as equitable interests: Provided that, after the commencement of this Act (and save as hereinafter expressly enacted), an equitable interest in land shall only be capable of being validly created in any case in which an equivalent equitable interest in property real or personal could have been validly created before such commencement'.

Section 4(1) of the Law of Property Act 1925 has not been judicially considered in any reported case. It was not referred to in Megarry and Wade: *The Law of Real Property* (5th edn) at all. The current edition deals with it at paras 4-090-91, and speculates that it was intended to preclude the creation of novel forms of equitable interests. Wolstenholme and Cherry: *Conveyancing Statutes* (13th edn) takes a different view. Cheshire and Burn's *Modern Law of Real Property* (16th edn) does not deal with the subsection at all.

Section 4(1) of the Law of Property Act 1925 may well prevent parties from creating novel forms of interest in land and making them capable of binding or benefiting the land. This does not prevent Parliament, or the European Community, authorised by the European Communities Act 1972, from creating a novel right which runs with land and so is an interest in land. It is submitted that milk quota is such a right. Further, if milk quota had been introduced before 1926, it would have been a validly created interest in land then.

It should be noted that, in January 2004, DEFRA issued an 'Explanatory Statement' in relation to the then DPQR including the following:

'In the light of the responses to the consultation [in relation to the DPQR 2002] and the provisions of the new European Council regulation on milk quota ... we have decided not to introduce new regulations breaking the link between quota and land entirely'.

1   [2005] SWTI 1481.
2   [1995] STC 239.
3   See, for example, *Swift v Dairywise Farms Ltd* [2001] EWCA Civ 145, [2001] 3 EGLR 101.

Milk quota and partnerships

49.23 The creation or termination of a partnership gives rise to particular problems not least because an excluded category of transfer is a licence and many partnerships proceed on the basis of the partnership being granted a licence to occupy the holding farmed by the partnership. It has been decided by the High Court in *Faulks v Faulks* that milk quota is not itself a partnership asset[1].

In *Faulks*, two brothers farmed an agricultural holding pursuant to a tenancy granted to one brother alone. The partnership deed provided that the brother who was tenant stood possessed of the tenancy in trust for the partnership. The quota passed with the tenancy, which was held on trust only for the duration of the partnership. The issue which arose was whether the milk quota was an asset of the partnership upon its dissolution. It was held that milk quota is attached to the land. Although the quota has an intrinsic economic value, that does not lead to the conclusion that the quota is an asset separate and distinct from the holding in relation to which it is registered. Accordingly, the milk quota formerly registered in the name of the partnership, prior to its dissolution, could not properly be regarded as property and as an asset of the partnership.

In *Davies v H & R Ecroyd Ltd* [2], the parties entered into a farming partnership agreement on 1 February 1983 in relation to a dairy holding. It was agreed that the holding itself, which was owned by one of the parties, was not a partnership asset. Milk quota was subsequently allocated to the holding in April 1984. The partnership was dissolved in February 1998. The non-land owning party claimed that the milk quota was an asset of the partnership. The milk quota was introduced after the parties entered into the partnership. It was impossible to attribute to the partners any intention other than the milk quota should be treated in the same way as the holding. The milk quota allocated to the holding in 1984 was not an asset of the partnership.

1 [1992] 1 EGLR 9, [1992] 15 EG 82.
2 [1996] 2 EGLR 5, [1996] 30 EG 97.

49.24 In *Carson v Cornwall County Council*[1], an arbitrator ruled that there were sufficient doubts about the legality of the UK milk quota transfer system that it was unsafe to determine the value of milk quota for the purposes of the Agriculture Act 1986 compensation by reference to quota transfers which were taking place on the open market. Accordingly, alternative methods of valuation would have to be applied, including assessing the appropriate years purchased to the monies realised by quota leasing and comparisons of transactions involving land with and without quota attached.

For the purposes of a milk quota security scheme, milk quota has been treated as an independent asset. In *Swift v Dairywise Farms Ltd*[2], the facts were complicated involving two sister companies trading in milk quota and the extent to which such quota could be treated as security for a loan. In short, loans were made by Dairywise Limited to farmers whose milk quota was transferred to Dairywise Farms Limited as security for the loan. After Dairywise Limited went into liquidation, its liquidators brought proceedings against Dairywise Farms Limited contending that Dairywise Farms Limited held the milk quota for the benefit of Dairywise Limited. The decision at first instance of Jacob J considered the juridical nature of milk quota. The judge held that milk quota constituted property within the definition of s 436 of the Insolvency Act 1986 and was capable of forming the subject matter of a trust between Dairywise Limited and Dairywise Farms Limited.

The decision at first instance was the subject of an appeal to the Court of Appeal. The Court of Appeal[3] did not adopt the analysis or reasoning of Jacob J, in short determining the issues as an interlocutory matter based upon the contractual arrangements between Dairywise Limited and Dairywise Farms Limited. The court held that borrowers had an equitable right to require the re-transfer of quota.

1 [1993] 1 EGLR 21.
2 [2000] 1 All ER 320.
3 [2001] EWCA Civ 145, [2001] 3 EGLR 101. The Court of Appeal included Chadwick LJ, the judge in *Faulks v Faulks* [1992] 1 EGLR 9, [1992] 15 EG 82.

Surrender of a lease

49.25 Both the European Court[1] and the Court of Appeal in the UK[2] have held that the surrender of a lease is a transaction of comparable legal effect for the purposes of occasioning a transfer of milk quota.

In *WE & RA Holdcroft v Staffordshire County Council*[3], the tenant of a dairy farm with wholesale milk quota gave a notice to quit to the landlord effective on 25 March 1990. The farm was farmed in partnership with the tenant's son and wife. The tenant's son formed a new partnership with his own wife and bought another farm. The dairy herd was removed to that new farm on 1 March 1990. The original farming partnership was dissolved and possession of the tenanted farm was given up to the landlord on 25 March 1990. This gave rise to two issues. First, was the surrender a transfer entitling the landlord to a claim in relation to the quota? Second, was the re-arrangement of occupation under the partnership which took place on 1 March 1990 a transfer of comparable legal effect justifying an arbitration and the apportionment of the milk quota? It was held that the surrender of a tenancy amounts to a transaction having 'comparable legal effect' to a transfer by sale, lease or inheritance. It therefore entitled the landlord to a share of the quota. Further, the transfer of occupation which took place on the earlier dissolution of the first partnership on 1 March 1990 was also a transfer and could trigger arbitration proceedings and a possible apportionment of the milk quota pursuant to the DPQR.

¹ In *Wachauf v Germany* Case C-5/88, [1989] ECR 2609, [1991] 1 CMLR 328.
² *WE and RA Holdcroft v Staffordshire County Council* [1994] 2 EGLR 1, [1994] 28 EG 131.
³ [1994] 2 EGLR 1, (1994) 28 EG 131.

Mortgagee enforcement

49.26 Where a mortgagee exercises its right to possession of mortgaged farm land, it has been held that repossession and subsequent sale by the mortgagee is a change of occupation for the purposes of the DPQR. In *Harries v Barclays Bank plc*¹, a farmer granted a legal charge to the bank over his agricultural holding to secure his debt. Subsequently, in April 1984 a substantial milk quota was allocated to the holding. Following the appointment of a receiver by the bank, the dairy herd was sold in February 1988. The bank then took possession of the holding under the terms of its charge and had the milk quota registered in its name. Between April 1988 and April 1994, the bank entered into leases of the milk quota. The holding was sold by the bank in April 1994. The farmer claimed that the bank was not entitled to retain the proceeds from the leasing of the milk quota. The farmer's claim failed. The milk quota was attached to the land which was in the possession of the bank. The bank was entitled to retain the rents as one of the products of its possession of the mortgaged property and that included the milk quota leasing income.

In *Huish v Ellis*², following the appointment of receivers, a bank sold a farm charged to it together with the milk quota attaching to the holding. The farmer subsequently argued that the land and the quota should have been sold separately in order to maximise the value of the asset. The farmer's claim was dismissed on the basis that it had no cause of action. The High Court held that the bank had no power or right to deal separately with the milk quota. Accordingly it had adopted the proper course by selling the land with the quota. It should be noted that the receivers were dealing with the land charged to the bank by legal mortgage. There was no suggestion that the milk quota itself was separately charged³.

¹ [1997] 2 EGLR 15, [1997] 45 EG 145. Also see, *Swift v Dairywise Farms Ltd* [2001] EWCA Civ 145, [2001] 3 EGLR 101.

² [1995] BCC 462.
³ *Sed quaere*, had there been a separate charge taken in relation to the milk quota; a practice adopted in many cases by the bank which lent in the *Huish* case. Note that milk quota is not an asset forming part of 'farming stock and other agricultural assets' capable of being charged by way of an agricultural charge under the Agricultural Credits Act 1928.

Sham/failure to implement the DPQR

49.27 Difficulties can arise both in respect of the amount of milk quota transferred and the nature of the transaction. First, the RPA (and its predecessor) have sought to prevent the transfer of an unjustifiable amount of milk quota per hectare or acre (commonly known as 'quota loading'). In guidance notes issued by the RPA, it has been indicated that an apportionment of over 20,000 litres per hectare or 8,094 litres per acre would give rise to closer investigation[1]. It should be noted that in determining an apportionment an arbitrator is required to base his award on findings made by him as to areas used for milk production in the last five years during which production took place before the change of occupation in relation to the standard milk quota transfer[2].

As to the nature of the transaction, this may involve two considerations. First, whether the arrangements between the parties is a 'sham', ie where the parties to the agreement are intending to give to third parties or to the court the appearance of creating between them legal rights and obligations different from the actual legal rights and obligations (if any) which the parties intend to create[3]. Alternatively, the arrangements entered into between the parties may be capable of being impugned on the basis that they do not constitute a transfer (for example, because it is a licence) or because there is no change of occupation (for example, because there is no physical occupation)[4].

¹ Also see Hansard (HL) Vol 458, Col 777.
² DPQR 2005, SI 2005/465, Sch 1 para. 3(1).
³ For the classic enunciation of the doctrine of sham, see *Snook v London and West Riding Investments Ltd* [1967] 2 QB 786, [1967] 1 All ER 51, CA. Also see *National Westminster Bank plc v Jones* [2000] EGCS 82, [2001] 1 BCLC 98, affd [2001] EWCA Civ 1541, [2002] 1 BCLC 55.
⁴ *R v Ministry of Agriculture, Fisheries and Food, ex p Cox* [1993] 1 EGLR 17, [1993] 22 EG 111: see para 49.19.

Areas used for milk production

49.28 Milk quota attaches to such land that falls within the definition of 'areas used for milk production in the last five-year period during which production took place before the change of occupation, or, in the case of a prospective apportionment, in the last five-year period during which production took place before the appointment of the arbitrator'[1]. The definition of areas used for milk production was considered in the case of *Puncknowle Farms Limited v Kane*[2]. The High Court adopted the definition of areas used for milk production applied by the arbitrator as comprising:

'the forage areas used by the dairy herd and to support the dairy herd by the growing of grass and any fodder crops for the milking dairy herd, dry cows and all dairy following female young stock (and homebred dairy or dual purpose bulls for use on the premises, if applicable), if bred to enter the production herd and not for sale. In this case, maize, silage, hay and grass were the fodder crops, but consideration would have been given to corn crops, or part of corn crops, grown for consumption by the dairy herd or young stock, including the use of straw, had agreed evidence been produced'.

The phrase was to be given a wide meaning.

An unresolved issue is whether an area used for milk production which is occupied pursuant to an agreement which itself would not constitute a transfer for the purposes of the DPQR 2005[3] is an area which will be taken into account by the arbitrator in determining the apportionment of milk quota over the five-year period upon which he has to base his award.

In *Posthumus v Oosterwoud*[4], the European Court of Justice determined a case concerning the objective criteria to be applied by Member States when introducing legislation as to quota apportionment. The Advocate General's opinion[5] was that only a mathematical apportionment fell to be carried out unless a Member State had laid down its own objective criteria for some different approach to the appointment. It is not an objective criterion to leave the parties free to negotiate and agree their own apportionment. Member States should not 'leave the matter to the discretion of the parties. That would be contrary both to the terms of the legislation and especially the notion of 'objective criteria' and contrary also to what must be assumed to be the purpose of the legislation, namely to avoid manipulation of the quota system and to prevent trading in quotas'. The Advocate General's opinion continued, where parties do reach agreement, Member States must take measures to see that the community legislation has been satisfied and that those measures 'might also include the scrutiny of the terms of compensation agreed in order to ensure that such agreements do not amount to a disguised form of trading quotas'.

The European Court itself emphasised the fact that Member States had the option to lay down objective criteria in relation to the assessment of areas used for milk production. Where a Member State had not laid down such objective criteria, apportionment was to be strictly in accordance with areas used for milk production. No account could be taken of the extent to which the different areas contributed to total milk production[6].

1 DPQR 2005, SI 2005/465, Sch 1 para 3(1).
2 [1985] 2 EGLR 8, 275 Estates Gazette 1283.
3 For example, occupied pursuant to a licence.
4 [1991] ECR I-5833, [1992] 2 CMLR 336.
5 Advocate General Jacobs.
6 The 'artistic' approach preferred by the Irish High Court was not embraced: *Lawlor v Minister for Agriculture* [1990] 1 IR 356, [1988] 3 CMLR 22.

Transfer of quota without transfer of land

49.29 Notwithstanding the basic principle that quota attaches to, and follows, the land used for dairy production, a limited concession was introduced in 1992, allowing transfers of quota separate from and without a transfer of the corresponding land. This concession was extended and previously required undertakings were removed in 2002[1]. It has been suggested that the Court of Appeal has now determined that the transfer system as practiced by a short-term grazing licence is valid and effective[2]. This may be overstating the position. The Court of Appeal recognised the existence of the practice: a practice described in the same case at first instance by Rattee J as 'artificial'[3].

A transferee must submit a notice of transfer without land by no later than 31 March in the quota year of the transfer and must include confirmation from the transferor and transferee if the amounts of used and unused quota transferred, a consent or sole interest notice given by the transferor in respect of the holding from which the quota is to be transferred and a statement from the transferee that he is a producer[4].

[1] Council Regulation (EC) 1788/2003, art 18 (OJ 2003 L 270/123). The implementation of the domestic legislation is now contained in DPQR 2005, SI 2005/465, reg 13.
[2] *Harries v Barclays Bank plc* [1997] 2 EGLR 15 at 18.
[3] [1995] NPC 201, [1997] BPIR 204.
[4] SI 2005/465, reg 13.

Non-producer producers

49.30 A question regularly raised between the introduction of milk quota in 1984 and 2002 was whether milk quota could be safely retained (and leased out) by a farmer who was registered as a producer but who was not engaged in milk production. From the outset, the DPQR contained confiscation provisions for non-use[1]. However, so-called 'non-producer producers' avoided confiscation by leasing out their quota on an annual basis.

In 2002 the European Court of Justice held that those holding milk quota should be genuine producers[2].

[1] See DPQR 2005, SI 2005/465, reg 38.
[2] Case C-401/99 *Thomsen v Amt für Ländliche Räume Husum* [2002] ECR I-5775. Also see, Case C-275/05 *Kibler v Land Baden-Württemburg* [2006] All ER (D) 323 (Oct). Note that in *Harries v Barclays Bank plc* [1997] 2 EGLR 15, the Court of Appeal did not deal with how the mortgagee in possession (as opposed to a receiver appointed by the mortgagee) could be a producer. Also cf the enduring nature of a 'holding': see para 49.6.

The legality of the UK milk quota transfer system

49.31 The range of key legal issues identified above indicate why, in the last edition of this book, the legality of the UK milk quota transfer system was scrutinised. This also reflects the evolution of the case law since the introduction of milk quota in 1984[1]. In *Harries v Barclays Bank plc*, the Court of Appeal has recognised the existence of the UK milk quota transfer system, as practised by way of a short-term grazing tenancy[2]. As indicated above, the nature and legal status of milk quota was extensively considered by the courts in the 1990s. However, the combined effect of the fall in value in milk quota and the introduction of the ability to transfer milk quota without a concurrent transaction in land[3] has resulted in there being less litigation concerning milk quota generally.

[1]   In particular, *Posthumus v Oosterwoud* [1991] ECR I-5833, [1992] 2 CMLR 336: see para 49.28.
[2]   [1997] 2 EGLR 15. See comments in para 49.21.
[3]   A practice first authorised by the Dairy Produce Quotas Regulations 1994, SI 1994/672, reg 13.

Milk quota 'theft'

49.32 An issue which has arisen in practice is whether a tenant can avoid the impact of the compensation provisions contained in the Agriculture Act 1986[1] and acquire for himself the full value of the milk quota (whether transferred quota[2] or otherwise) by disposing of all milk quota registered in his name before the termination of the tenancy. In the absence of an effective quota protection clause[3], it is submitted that it may be possible for the tenant to engage in what is inelegantly and inappropriately sometimes described as quota 'theft' and/or quota 'massage'.

Quota 'massage' arises where the tenant engages in a course of use of an agricultural holding protected by the AHA 1986[4] whereby he ceases using that part of his Euro Holding[5] which comprises tenanted land. As the tenanted land will then cease to be 'areas of milk production'[6], over a period of five years[7], the quota will cease to attach to the tenanted land upon an apportionment of quota arising at the end of the tenancy. In the absence of express provision in the tenancy agreement, there is nothing to stop a tenant engaging in this quota 'massage'.

[1]   See Ch 50.
[2]   See para 50.7.
[3]   See para 24.25.
[4]   Technically the same may apply to a farm business tenancy under the Agricultural Tenancies Act 1995 (ATA 1995), although in practice it is less likely to arise.
[5]   See para 49.6.
[6]   See para 49.28.
[7]   See para 49.28.

49.33 In the absence of a milk quota protection clause[1], a tenant under a tenancy within either the AHA 1986 or the ATA 1995 may dispose of quota registered in his name by way of permanent transfer[2]. Until the relaxation in transfer without land, the landlord had an indirect means of ensuring that quota remained 'attached' to the holding. Because of the need to transfer quota within land by use of a tenancy, as almost all tenancies contain anti-alienation provisions, the landlord would refuse consent for the grant of a sub-tenancy. If the tenant acted in breach of the prohibition against sub-letting, he would face forfeiture[3] or, in the case of the AHA 1986, alternatively a Case E notice to quit[4].

In addition to reliance upon anti-alienation provisions, under AHA 1986 tenancies landlords have considered that because of the provisions relating to compensation[5], which pre-suppose that the milk quota remains with the holding for the benefit of the landlord, the tenant is not entitled to remove the quota. That is incorrect. Unless the tenancy agreement contains an effective prohibition upon the tenant disposing of the quota, he is free to do so.

In the case of transfers without land, there is arguably one hurdle for the tenant. As seen above[6], to complete a transfer of milk, the tenant must lodge a notice with the Secretary of State at DEFRA[7] by 31 March in the relevant quota year. The notice must include:

(a)   statements by the transferor and transferee that they have agreed to the transfer of quota, stating the amounts used and unused quota transferred;

(b)   a consent or sole interest notice given by the transferor in respect of the holding from which the quota is to be transferred; and

(c)   a statement by the transferee that he is a producer[8].

'A consent or sole interest notice' is not defined. 'Interest' is defined. The DPQR 2005 provides that interest 'includes a licence to occupy land and the interest of a mortgagee and a trustee, but does not include the interest of a beneficiary under a trust or settlement'[9].

Assuming that a landlord has an interest in the land and is not a signatory to the notice required by reg 13 of the DPQR 2005, it may not assist him. In the absence of a milk quota protection clause, the recourse of a landlord under the DPQR 2005 in relation to a transfer of quota with land is limited to requiring an arbitration in order to establish the apportionment of the milk quota[10]. Transfers without land do not provide for the apportionment of quota. Further, the restrictions imposed on quota transfers contained in reg 16 of the DPQR 2005[11] do not apply to transfers without land and do not impact upon the tenant's ability to transfer milk quota without the landlord's consent.

It remains to be seen how a court would deal with this situation. It would be argued on behalf of the landlord that, without a completed consent notice, there should be no valid transfer.

[1]   See para 24.25. Note that a general quota protection has been found not to apply to milk quota: *Lee v Heaton* [1987] 2 EGLR 12, 283 Estates Gazette 1076.
[2]   See para 49.9.
[3]   Under the ATA 1995, see Ch 13. Under the AHA 1986, see Ch 33.
[4]   See para 31.76ff.
[5]   See Ch 51.
[6]   See para 49.11.
[7]   In practice this is dealt with by the RPA.
[8]   The DPQR 2005, SI 2005/465, reg 13.
[9]   SI 2005/465, reg 2(1).
[10] SI 2005/465, regs 10–12 and Sch 1.
[11] See para 49.14.

Chapter 50

THE TENANT'S CLAIMS ON QUITTING: MILK QUOTA

INTRODUCTION

50.1 Because of the restriction on production caused by the introduction of the quota system, milk quota acquired a substantial capital value. The Agriculture Act 1986 (AgA 1986) was enacted to ensure that on the termination of a tenancy, the tenant should share in such part of the value as is attributable to the quota attached to the agricultural holding being vacated. The amount of that share is intended to reflect the extent to which the tenant had, by efficient farming or the provision of fixed equipment, increased the amount of quota registered in respect of the agricultural holding.

Apart from providing for compensation for efficient farming, the AgA 1986 also provides that a tenant should receive compensation for quota, the cost of which he had financed wholly or in part by buying in quota from another milk producer. The statutory provisions enabling compensation to be awarded to a tenant in these circumstances are contained in the AgA 1986, s 13[1] and Sch 1 and the Milk Quota (Calculation of Standard Quota) Order 1992[2], which supplements the AgA 1986[3].

Regrettably, but perhaps inevitably, the calculations necessary to arrive at the compensation payable are exceedingly complex and have given rise to many disputes[4]. In order to make these calculations, it is necessary to understand the terminology employed in the AgA 1986 and its subordinate legislation, in particular the meaning of 'holding'[5], 'relevant quota'[6], 'allocated quota'[7], 'transferred quota'[8], 'standard quota'[9], 'the relevant number of hectares'[10], 'the prescribed quota per hectare'[11] and 'the tenant's fraction'[12] and many other terms of art[13].

The AgA 1986 came into effect on 25 September 1986 and only applied to tenancies which terminated on or after 25 July 1986. Accordingly, there was no provision for compensation payable to tenants who quit their holdings at any time after 2 April 1984 (the date on which milk quotas were introduced) and before 25 July 1986.

Bostock was such a farmer who, together with others, applied for judicial review of the decision of the Minister to introduce legislation providing for compensation, but excluding tenants who quit during the period prior to the coming into effect of the AHA 1986[14]. The case went to the European Court where the court followed its earlier decision in *Wachauf v Germany*[15]. It held that Member States were not obliged to introduce compensation schemes for tenants on quitting.

The AgA 1986 introduced limited compensation for tenants holding under 1986 Act tenancies who satisfied the statutory criteria. Farm business tenants holding under the Agricultural Tenancies Act 1995 (ATA 1995) will only be entitled to compensation, if at all, for 'intangible benefits' or otherwise by agreement[16]. Accordingly, what follows in this chapter only relates to AHA 1986 tenancies.

[1] Section 13 of the AgA 1986 was brought into force on 25 September 1986 by the Agriculture Act (Commencement) (No 1) Order 1986, SI 1986/1484.
[2] SI 1992/1225.
[3] Section 15 of the AgA 1986 also contains provisions as to the effect of milk quota on rent – for a full commentary on those provisions, see para 25.22ff.
[4] For a surveyor's guide to milk quota compensation calculations, see Edwards, *Milk Quotas Explained* (1995) RICS.
[5] A 'holding' in this context is not the same as an 'agricultural holding'. It is often known as a 'Euro holding', see para 49.6].
[6] See para 50.5.
[7] See para 50.3.
[8] See para 50.7.
[9] See para 50.8.
[10] See para 50.8.
[11] See para 50.9.
[12] See para 50.12.
[13] For example, 'dairy cows', 'feeding of dairy cows', 'the reasonable amount', 'prescribed average yield','dairy improvement', 'dairy fixed equipment', etc.
[14] *R v Minister of Agriculture, Fisheries and Food, ex p Bostock* [1991] 2 EGLR 1. The case proceeded to the European Court of Justice by way of a reference for a preliminary ruling in the course of an application to the English High Court for judicial review: C-2/92 [1994] ECR I-955, [1994] 3 CMLR 547.
[15] [1989] ECR 2609.
[16] See para 16.6ff.

ENTITLEMENT TO COMPENSATION

Pre-requisites for entitlement

50.2 In order to be entitled to claim compensation, the tenant must satisfy a number of preliminary requirements.

First, the tenancy in respect of which the tenant makes the claim must be:

(a) a tenancy from year to year (or be treated as such by the operation of s 2 of the AHA 1986); or

(b) a fixed-term tenancy of two years or more to which s 3 of the AHA 1986 applies; or

(c) a tenancy which would give rise to security but for the fact that prior Ministry consent or approval under s 2 or s 5 of the AHA 1986 was obtained[1].

Accordingly, a *Gladstone v Bower* tenancy agreement[2] or a letting or licence for grazing or mowing (or both) during some specified period of the year[3] were outside the definition[4].

Secondly, the tenancy of the land must have terminated[5]. In most cases this will have occurred by surrender or notice to quit.

Thirdly, the tenant[6] must have the quota registered 'as his'[7] in relation to a holding[8] consisting of or including the land comprised in the tenancy.

1 AgA 1986, Sch 1 para 18(1).
2 [1960] 2 QB 384, [1960] 3 All ER 353. A tenancy for a term of between one and two years.
3 AHA 1986, s 2(3)(a).
4 It has not been possible to create either type of agreement since 1 September 1995: see paras 18.5 and 18.6.
5 AgA 1986, Sch 1 Pt I para 1(1).
6 For the special rules which apply to succession tenants, sub-tenants and assignees, see para 50.17ff.
7 See para 50.3.
8 By the Dairy Produce Quotas Regulations 2005, SI 2005/465, 'holding' has the meaning assigned to it by art 2(b) of Council Regulation (EC) 1782/2003. See para 49.6. The definition is not to be confused with the definition of 'agricultural holding' contained in the AHA 1986.

50.3 Fourthly, either:

(a) the quota must have been allocated directly to the tenant by the Minister. This species of quota is termed 'allocated quota', being statutorily defined as that part of the relevant quota which consists of quota allocated to the tenant in relation to the land comprised in the holding[1]; or

(b) the tenant must have been in occupation on 2 April 1984 and subsequently acquired quota and borne the cost of the transaction, wholly or partly, himself[2]. This species of quota is termed 'transferred quota', being statutorily defined as quota transferred to the tenant by virtue of a transfer to him of the whole or part of a holding[3].

In almost all cases, those milk producers who received allocated quota must have been in occupation of their holdings on 2 April 1984 when quotas were introduced and must have been allocated a primary quota based on their level of production during 'the relevant period' which, for wholesale producers, was normally 1983[4].

Additional to the primary quota allocation, such producers may also have had secondary or exceptional hardship quota awarded to them by the Dairy Produce Quota Tribunal. This also ranks as 'allocated quota'. Although in most cases the tenant must have been in occupation of the holding and producing milk from it on 2 April 1984, tenants who were committed to starting milk production prior to 2 April 1984, but did not actually move on to the land until after that date, may subsequently have been allocated quota pursuant to exceptional hardship awards from the Dairy Produce Quota Tribunal. This will also rank as allocated quota.

50.3 *The tenant's claims on quitting: milk quota*

1   AgA 1986, Sch 1 para 1(1)(a). The ascertainment of the allocated quota where the deeming provisions apply (ie in the cases of succession, assignment or sub-letting) is in accordance with AgA 1986, Sch 1 paras 2, 3 and 4. See para 50.17ff.
2   AgA 1986, Sch 1 para 1(1)(b).
3   AgA 1986, Sch 1 Pt I para 1(2). The ascertainment of the transferred quota where the deeming provisions apply (see fn 1 above) are in accordance with AgA 1986, Sch 1 paras 2–4.
4   'Relevant period' is defined in para 8 of Sch 1 to the AgA 1986. It means 'the period in relation to which the allocated quota was determined'. This will normally have been the calendar year 1983. In some cases a different period, eg 1981 or 1982, may have been selected, in which case those years will apply. Paragraph 8(b) of Sch 1 to the AgA 1986 deals with the problem where more than one period was used for determining allocated quota. 1983 will not be the 'relevant period' where a successful base year revision claim was made or in some cases of hardship allocation.

50.4 The requirement that a tenant must have the quota registered 'as his' gives rise to problems. No difficulty as to entitlement will arise if the tenant is the registered producer. If a farm partnership is the registered producer, and the tenant is a partner, although he is not the sole registered producer, it is submitted that the partnership will qualify for compensation. The compensation will be distributed in accordance with the partnership terms[1]. It is further submitted that the tenant, as an individual, would not be entitled to claim if a farming company is the registered producer, rather than the tenant[2]. The status of the producer has to be determined as at the date of termination of the tenancy. Therefore, if the identity of the registered producer is retrospectively changed after the tenancy is terminated, in order to correspond with the identity of the tenant, such a procedure would not resolve any issues which arise. It should also be noted that the quitting tenant has to have quota 'allocated to him' in most instances of a sustainable claim[3].

A tenant may have acquired transferred quota either because he did not receive any allocated quota (for example, because he was not in milk production on 2 April 1984 and thereafter failed to obtain an exceptional hardship award from the Dairy Produce Quota Tribunal) or, alternatively, because the allocated quota was insufficient for his needs and he bought in quota in order to supplement the allocated quota.

It should be noted that, in the case of a farming partnership, after the tenant's entitlement to compensation is assessed under the AgA 1986, it may be necessary to consider the impact of the provisions of the partnership as to the rights between the partners[4].

1   *Faulks v Faulks* [1992] 1 EGLR 9, [1992] 15 EG 82; *Davies v H & R Ecroyd Ltd* [1996] 2 EGLR 5. Cf *Cottle v Coldicott* [1995] STC (SCD) 239. See para 49.21ff.
2   *Woolfson v Strathclyde Regional Council* (1978) 38 P & CR 521, HL; *Snell v Snell* (1964) 191 Estates Gazette 361, CA. Cf *DHN Food Distributors Ltd v Tower Hamlets London Borough Council* [1976] 3 All ER 462, [1976] 1 WLR 852, CA.
3   AgA 1986, Sch 1 para 1(1)(a).
4   *Faulks v Faulks* [1992] 1 EGLR 9, [1992] 15 EG 82 and *Davies v H & R Ecroyd Ltd* [1996] 2 EGLR 5. Note also the possibility of the partners who are not tenants claiming some entitlement to the compensation under the principles in *Pawsey v Armstrong* (1831) 18 Ch D 698 and *Miles v Clarke* [1953] 1 WLR 537.

Relevant quota

50.5 The first stage in the determination of the compensation to which an outgoing tenant is entitled is to identify that part of the 'registered quota' (being allocated and/or transferred quota) which is 'relevant quota'. Relevant quota is either the quota registered exclusively in relation to the land in respect of which the tenancy has terminated (ie the subject agricultural holding) or the proportion of the quota that falls to be apportioned to that land, if the registered quota extends to other land[1]. The statutory objective is to ensure that the tenant only receives compensation for quota which 'attaches to' land covered by the tenancy in question[2].

If the holding to which the registered quota attaches consists only of the tenanted land, the whole of that quota will be relevant quota[3]. If not, the quota will have to be apportioned between the tenanted land and the other land in order that the quantum of quota for compensation purposes can be determined[4]. It would seem that in cases in which arbitration is necessary in order to determine the tenant's compensation for quota, the first duty of the arbitrator, where the quota is registered in respect of land in addition to the tenanted land, will be to make a determination as to how the quota is to be apportioned between the different areas of land. The AgA 1986 does not contain any direction as to how such an apportionment should be undertaken, but it is submitted that the apportionment should be in accordance with the Dairy Produce Quotas Regulations 2005 (DPQR 2005)[5].

[1] AgA 1986, Sch 1 Pt I para 1(2). The quota register maintained originally by the Milk Marketing Board, later the Intervention Board for England and Wales and now by the Rural Payments Agency (RPA) will only show a single quota figure for each producer, relating to the entirety of the land that he occupies, ie the holding as defined for milk quota purposes. The holding is often referred to colloquially as the 'Euro holding'.
[2] As to whether quota attaches to land at all, cf *Faulks v Faulks* [1992] 1 EGLR 9, [1992] 15 EG 82 and *Cottle v Coldicott* [1995] STC (SCD) 239.
[3] AgA 1986, Sch 1 Pt I para 1(2)(a).
[4] AgA 1986, Sch 1 Pt I para 1(2)(b) and see *Puncknowle Farms Ltd v Kane* [1985] 3 All ER 79, [1985] 2 EGLR 8.
[5] SI 2005/465. By Sch 1, para 3(1) of the DPQR 2005 the apportionment, if undertaken by the arbitration process, is 'based on findings made by the arbitrator as to areas used for milk production' in the five years preceding the change of occupation. It is to be noted that this provision is different from those contained in the Dairy Produce Quotas Regulations 1984, SI 1984/1047, reg 5(6) and Sch 2 para 6(3)(e). The meaning of 'areas used for milk production' was considered by the High Court in *Puncknowle Farms Ltd v Kane* [1985] 3 All ER 79, [1985] 2 EGLR 8. After a period of some doubt, it now is clear that in the absence of prescribed objective criteria for making the apportionment, a strictly mathematical apportionment by reference to the areas used for milk production must be employed regardless acre for acre of the relative value and productive capacity of the land in question: see the European Court decisions in C-121/90: *Posthumus v Oosterwoud* [1991] ECR I-5833 and C-79/91: *Knüfer v Buchmann* [1992] ECR I-6895.

ASSESSMENT OF COMPENSATION

The statutory scheme

50.6 The provisions in the AgA 1986 covering calculation of compensation are intended to provide the outgoing tenant with compensation for the direct and indirect contributions that he made to the build up of the allocated quota through his managerial skills as a producer and the cash investments he has made in the form of dairy improvements and fixed equipment to the holding. Additionally, the provisions enable the tenant to recover the proportion of the cost of any transferred quota that he financed.

The tenant is thus eligible to receive compensation under three heads:

(a)   if the tenant has acquired transferred quota, he is entitled to compensation to the extent to which he has financed the transaction[1] – 'transferred quota';

(b)   if the allocated quota in respect of the tenanted land[2] exceeds the standard quota[3] the tenant is entitled to compensation in respect of the excess – 'excess over standard quota'[4];

(c)   the tenant is entitled to receive compensation which is computed by reference to investments made by the tenant in dairy improvements and dairy fixed equipment[5] – 'the tenant's fraction'[6].

[1]   Note that the compensation to which the tenant will be entitled is the value of that part of the transferred quota in respect of which he bore the cost of the transaction.
[2]   See para 50.5 as to the meaning of relevant quota and the need for apportionment in all cases except those in which the milk quota was allocated exclusively to the land comprised in the tenancy.
[3]   Details of the standard quota are contained in the Milk Quota (Calculation of Standard Quota) Order 1992, SI 1992/1225.
[4]   See para 50.8ff.
[5]   See para 50.8ff.
[6]   See para 50.12.

Transferred quota

50.7 'Transferred quota' is defined as meaning milk quota transferred to the tenant by virtue of the transfer to him of the whole or part of a holding[1]. Transferred quota in most cases will consist of quota which the tenant has purchased on the open market by means of his being granted some interest such as a short-term grazing tenancy[2] by the vendor of the quota on terms that give effect to the transfer of the quota to the purchaser's holding[3]. The amount of the payment to which the tenant is entitled in respect of transferred quota depends upon whether he bore the whole or only part of the cost[4].

In a case where the tenant bore the whole cost of the transaction by virtue of which the quota was transferred to him, he is entitled to compensation amounting to the value of the transferred quota[5]. If the tenant bore only part of the cost, he is entitled to compensation in respect of the value of the corresponding part of the transferred quota[6]. It should be noted that transferred quota does not enter into the calculation for the purpose of assessing the amounts due under the next two heads of claim – 'excess over standard quota' and the 'tenant's fraction'.

[1]   AgA 1986, Sch 1 Pt I para 1(2).
[2]   A licence was not sufficient to effect a transfer of quota and the tenancy had to be for not less than ten months. This is no longer the case since the relaxation in the transfer of quota without land: see the Dairy Quotas Produce Regulations 2005, SI 2005/465, reg 10.

3   Transactions of this type are now common. Despite the very large number of such transactions, and the amount of milk quota transferred in this way, there is as yet no final and definitive authority as to the legal efficacy of such quota transfer transactions. It is possible that the whole quota transfer system, prior to the relaxation in transfers of quota without land, was fundamentally flawed. However, it is submitted that this is not the case see *Faulks v Faulks* [1992] 1 EGLR 9, [1992] 15 EG 82 and *Cottle v Coldicott* [1995] STC (SCD) 239. See also the European cases of *Wachauf v Germany* C-5/88, [1989] ECR 2609, [1991] 1 CMLR 328 and *R v Minister of Agriculture, Fisheries and Food, ex p Bostock* C-2/92, [1994] ECR I-955, [1994] 3 CMLR 547, at first instance, [1991] 2 EGLR 1.
4   It would appear that the tenant is not entitled to compensation at all if he did not bear any part of the cost, directly or possibly indirectly (for example, if the cost was borne by a farming company). Care should be taken when structuring a transaction for the purchase of transferred quota to avoid difficulties of this kind.
5   AgA 1986, Sch 1 Pt II para 5(3)(a).
6   AgA 1986, Sch 1 Pt II para 5(3)(b).

Excess over standard quota

The 'normal case'

50.8 In order to ascertain whether compensation is due to the tenant in respect of excess of allocated quota over standard quota, it is necessary to calculate the standard quota by reference to the statutory instrument[1] and the provisions of the AgA 1986. In the case of composite holdings[2], an apportionment of the quota (being either allocated and/or transferred quota) will by this stage have already been made in order to determine the proportion of the total quota allocated to the tenant which is referable to the subject agricultural holding.

It is then necessary to apportion the relevant hectares from the remaining hectares which together constitute the subject agricultural holding in order to determine 'the relevant number of hectares'. For this purpose, 'the relevant number of hectares' is defined as 'the average number of hectares of the agricultural holding used during the relevant period[3] for the feeding of dairy cows kept on the land[4] or, if different[5], the average number of hectares of the land which could reasonably be expected to have been so used (having regard to the number of grazing animals other than dairy cows kept on the land during that period)'[6]. This definition is supplemented by it being provided that references to land used for the feeding of dairy cows kept on the land do not include land used for growing cereal crops for feeding to dairy cows in the form[7] of loose grain[8]. Also, references to dairy cows are to cows kept for dairy production. These include cows, calved heifers and in-calf cows temporarily dry but part of a milking herd, but does not include in-calf heifers or followers[9]. It should be noted that the basis of assessment of the number of hectares relevant for computing standard quota is narrower than the phrase 'areas used for milk production' contained in the DPQR and widely interpreted (in the context of the Dairy Produce Quotas Regulations 1984) in *Puncknowle Farms Ltd v Kane*[10].

It is the 'average' and not the total number of hectares used for the feeding of dairy cows kept on the land, etc, which is relevant. Even though a time apportionment between the animals kept on the land, eg cows in summer and sheep in winter, might reduce the 'average number of hectares' substantially, it is submitted that would not be a correct method of giving effect to the statutory averaging exercise. It would be more appropriate to apportion the relevant hectares between feeding dairy cows and other animals on the basis of their relative consumption from the land. This could be achieved by a livestock unit calculation[11].

1 Milk Quota (Calculation of Standard Quota) Order 1992, SI 1992/1225.
2 See para 50.5. Composite holding means in this case a holding which includes land additional to the subject agricultural holding itself.
3 'The relevant period' means the period in relation to which the allocated quota was determined or, where it was determined in relation to more than one period, the period in relation to which the majority was determined or, if equal amounts were determined in relation to different periods, the latter of those periods: AgA 1986, Sch 1 Pt II para 8. For wholesale producers the relevant period will normally be from 1 January 1983 to 31 December 1983. Special provision is made for the situation in which the relevant period (ie the period or periods during which the allocated quota was determined) is less than or greater than 12 months, or if rent was only payable by the tenant in respect of part of the relevant period. In these circumstances, the rent payable is annualised: AgA 1986, Sch 1 Pt II para 7(3).
4 It seems probable that the reference to 'hectares ... used ... for the feeding of dairy cows kept on the land' is both the land on which the dairy cows were physically placed and land from which they were supported during the relevant period (eg land used for hay or silage making) subject only to the exclusion of land used for growing cereal crops for 'feeding in the form of loose grain'. This phrase (contained in para 6(5) of Sch 1 of the AgA 1986) has given rise to problems in practice since grain fed to dairy cows is usually processed through a mill and mix machine and is rarely, if ever, fed 'in the form of loose grain' (see *Grounds v A-G of the Duchy of Lancaster* [1989] 1 EGLR 6, CA). Land used for growing barley when the straw is fed to the dairy cows or the whole crop is ensiled would appear not to be excluded.
5 A problem arises as to whether the alternative or 'if different' calculation requires a subjective or objective test to be applied. The reference to the other 'grazing animals ... kept on the land' makes it clear that in part at least the alternative calculation must have regard to the actual grazing system employed by the tenant during the relevant period. On the other hand, if the fixed equipment could have supported a larger number of dairy cows than were in fact kept because the tenant grew corn on the land which might reasonably have been expected to have been used to feed dairy cows, the 'if different' calculation should be applied. If the land was used for grazing sheep or beef animals or dairy followers, etc, the 'if different' calculation should not be applied. This partially subjective and partially objective test appears arbitrary.
6 AgA 1986, Sch 1 Pt II para 6(1)(a). This provision suggests that in some cases a determination should be made as to areas that might reasonably be expected to have been used for the feeding of dairy cows kept on the land, as compared with the areas actually used – as to which see post 'if different'.
7 Note the expression 'loose grain'. If the grain was crushed and compounded through a mill and mix system it is doubtful whether it was thus fed as loose grain.
8 AgA 1986, Sch 1 Pt II para 6(5)(a).
9 AgA 1986, Sch 1 Pt II para 6(5)(b).
10 [1985] 2 EGLR 8, 275 Estates Gazette 1283.
11 Milk Quota (Calculation of Standard Quota) Order 1992, SI 1992/1225.

50.9 Calculation of the standard quota is made by multiplying the 'relevant number of hectares' by the prescribed quota per hectare and thereby ascertaining whether the allocated quota exceeds the standard quota[1]. The prescribed quota per hectare is laid down in the statutory instrument[2]. This includes a Schedule which itself prescribes in columns 2(a), 3(a) and 4(a) varying quota per hectare, dependent upon the quality of the land and the type of dairy cows carried on the land. It should be noted that the tenant is only entitled to compensation under this head if the allocated quota is greater than the standard quota[3]. If allocated quota and standard quota are equal, no compensation is payable under this head[4], and if the allocated quota is less than the standard quota, not only will the tenant receive no compensation under this head but also the tenant's compensation (if any) due in respect of the tenant's fraction will be adversely affected[5].

The calculation of standard quota is such that even where the allocated quota is less than the prescribed quota the standard quota may be adjusted downwards, thereby ensuring that some excess quota is available to the tenant for the purposes of assessing his entitlement to compensation. The intention of the statute would appear to be to ensure that in most cases a tenant whose performance was below average will still receive some compensation for excess over standard quota unless his performance was very poor indeed.

[1]   AgA 1986, Sch 1 Pt II para 6(1). This method of calculation does not apply where the circumstances set out in Sch 1 Pt II para 6(2) exist, in which case an alternative method of calculation is applicable. The latter method of calculation is likely to be applicable in many cases.
[2]   The Milk Quota (Calculation of Standard Quota) Order 1986, SI 1986/1530, as amended by the Milk Quota (Calculation of Standard Quota) (Amendment) Order 1987, SI 1987/626 and later annual amendments to SI 1992/1225 made pursuant to the AgA 1986, Sch 1 Pt II para 6. The Minister is enabled to make different provision for different cases in such an Order: AgA 1986, Sch 1 para 6(6).
[3]   AgA 1986, Sch 1 Pt II,para 5(2)(a)(ii).
[4]   AgA 1986, Sch 1 Pt II para 5(2)(b).
[5]   AgA 1986, Sch 1 Pt II para 5(2)(c). As to compensation in respect of the tenant's fraction, see para 50.8ff.

Special situations: the 'reasonable amount'

50.10 Schedule 1 para 6(2) of the AgA 1986 applies a different calculation in substitution for the normal calculation of standard quota[1]. This applies when by virtue of the quality of the land in question, or climatic conditions in the area[2], the amount of milk that could reasonably be expected to have been produced from[3] one hectare of land[4] during the relevant period[5] (termed 'the reasonable amount') was either greater or less than the prescribed average yield per hectare. The prescribed average yield per hectare[6] is also laid down in the statutory instrument[7] which in columns 2(b), 3(b) and 4(b) prescribes varying average yields per hectare, dependent on the quality of the land and the type of stock carried on the land[8].

It follows that in many cases the calculation of standard quota will be by reference to this formula rather than 'prescribed quota'. If these circumstances apply, the standard quota is calculated by multiplying the relevant number of hectares[9] by such proportion of the prescribed quota per hectare[10] as the reasonable amount bears to the prescribed average yield per hectare. The first amending statutory instrument, SI 1987/626 (and no doubt all subsequent amending statutory instruments), has been made to give effect to EC cut-backs in registered quota from time to time.

These provisions have been considered by the Court of Appeal in *Grounds v A-G of the Duchy of Lancaster*[11]. It was held in *Grounds v A-G of the Duchy of Lancaster* that the arbitrator, when determining the standard quota, must take into account the practice of reasonably skilled and successful farmers. This would normally include feeding bought-in concentrate. Furthermore, the expression 'land used for growing cereals for feeding to dairy cows in the form of loose grain' encompasses grain which has been processed, e g through a mill and mix machine. Cows cannot digest unprocessed loose grain.

In *Surrey County Council v Main*[12], a county court judge considered the circumstances in which the 'reasonable' calculation fell to be made.

Paragraph 6(2) of Sch 1 to the AgA 1986 provides that for the purposes of assessing standard quota the relevant number of hectares fall to be multiplied by the prescribed quota per hectare. However, an alternative calculation (the 'reasonable amount') falls to be undertaken:

> '… where, by virtue of the quality of the land in question, or climatic conditions in the area, the amount of milk which could reasonably be expected to have been produced from one hectare of the land during the relevant period, is greater or less than the prescribed average yield per acre'.

1   See para 50.8ff.
2   Note 'the reasonable' amount calculation only applies when the difference between the land in question and its productive capacity and the average is attributable to either 'the quality of the land' or 'climatic conditions'. Other considerations, such as the quality of the buildings, cannot give rise to this calculation.
3   'Milk … produced from … land' – another arcane expression. Land does not produce milk – cows do. It was held by the Court of Appeal that the production of milk does not have to be confined to home-grown grass and forage crops and exclude bought-in feedstuffs. See, *Grounds v A-G of the Duchy of Lancaster* [1989] 1 EGLR 6.
4   It is wholly unclear as to what 'one hectare of land' means. If it requires each of the relevant hectares to be considered separately and individually that creates anomalies and difficulties (e g the absence of buildings which are not usually on the land used simply for the feeding of dairy cows). On the other hand, it may mean each of the hectares being quitted by the tenant. In that case, that would include the buildings being used for milking as well as the land used for feeding but would also include other land used for other systems of farming. That too will distort the resultant figures. The precise meaning of the 'one hectare' provision is unclear.
5   See para 50.8.
6   Note the difference in terminology between 'the prescribed quota per hectare' and 'the prescribed average yield per hectare'.
7   Milk Quota (Calculation of Standard Quota) Order 1992, SI 1992/1225.
8   Note that in each case the figures are higher than those used for the normal calculation of standard quota set out in Columns 2(a), 3(a) and 4(a) of the Schedule.
9   See para 50.8.
10 Ie as set out in columns 2(a), (b) and (c) of the Schedule to SI 1992/1225.
11 [1989] 1 EGLR 6, CA.
12 [1992] 1 EGLR 26, [1992] 06 EG 159.

50.11 The argument mounted on behalf of the landlord in *Surrey County Council v Main*[1] was that this required, in every case, the arbitrator to carry out the 'reasonable amount' calculation, to which a fraction then had to be applied, with the resultant figure being compared to the standard quota calculated by reference to the para 6(1) calculation. It was held by the county court judge that this was not correct and that the arbitrator was entitled to approach the matter in the way that he had done in that case, i e to consider, first, the quality of the land in question and, second, the climatic conditions so as to determine whether there was anything exceptional in either, and if they were neither better nor worse than average during the relevant period (in that case, 1983), then the para 6(1) calculation had to be used so that the 'reasonable amount' calculation only fell to be undertaken in exceptional cases.

Paragraph 6(3) of Sch 1 to the AgA 1986[2] requires an adjustment to the calculation of the standard quota to be made in cases in which the quota actually allocated to the tenant in pursuance of an award of quota made by the Dairy Produce Quota Tribunal was less than the Tribunal's award. In such circumstances the standard quota is reduced by the amount by which the quota actually allocated in pursuance of the Tribunal's award falls short of the amount awarded[3].

Paragraph 6(3) is to be read together with para 6(4), the latter sub-paragraph requiring similar adjustments to be made to the computation of allocated quota where there have been subsequent allocations of milk quota. These are to be taken into account in making the adjustment described in para 6(3).

[1]   [1992] 1 EGLR 26, (1992) 06 EG 159.
[2]   The situation to which para 6(3) relates applies particularly in the case of wholesale development quota.
[3]   These figures have now been amended by SI 1987/626 and will no doubt be amended again from time to time as further EU cut-backs are made to registered quota.

The tenant's fraction

50.12 The tenant's fraction consists of that part of the standard quota, or the allocated quota (if this is equal to or less than the standard quota) which is credited to the tenant in order to reflect his direct contribution to the quota on the holding through dairy improvements and the provision of fixed equipment. The fraction is applied either to the standard quota or to the allocated quota (if it is less) for the purpose of ascertaining the proportion in respect of which the applicant is to be paid compensation.

Where the allocated quota is less than the standard quota, the tenant's fraction has to be reduced by a further calculation. The tenant's fraction must be applied after a proportionate reduction to the allocated quota. The proportion is that which the allocated quota bears to the standard quota[1].

[1]   AgA 1986, Sch 1 para 5(2)(c).

The numerator

50.13 The tenant's fraction consists of a numerator equivalent to the annual rental value at the end of the relevant period of the tenant's dairy improvements and fixed equipment[1]. The amount in question comprises the sum referable to those improvements and items of fixed equipment which would fall to be disregarded under para 2(1) of Sch 2 to the AHA 1986 on a rent arbitration under s 12 of that Act[2] which are also 'dairy' improvements or fixed equipment. The further qualification 'dairy' means those tenant's improvements to, or items of tenant's fixed equipment on, land which is used for the feeding, accommodation or milking of dairy cows kept on the land in question[3]. However, this is subject to certain modifications necessary because the historic position during the relevant period, rather than the current position, is relevant for calculation of compensation purposes.

First, any allowance made or benefit given by the landlord after the end of the relevant period[4] in consideration of the execution of improvements wholly or partly at the expense of the tenant is to be disregarded[5]. Second, any compensation received by the tenant after the end of the relevant period[6] in respect of any improvement or fixed equipment is to be disregarded[7]. The effect of this provision is that tenant's improvements bought out by the landlord after the end of the relevant period are still to be treated as tenant's improvements for quota compensation purposes. Third, in relation to succession tenancies, tenant's improvements and tenant's fixed equipment made by the earlier tenant are treated as if they had been made by the new tenant[8].

If the rent passing was lower than might be expected that does not reduce the rental value of the tenant's dairy fixtures and dairy improvements[9].

1   AgA 1986, Sch 1 Pt II para 7(1)(a).
2   There are some rather surprising improvements within the definition including, eg, a particularly beneficial system such as a very high input/high output system, see para 2(4) of Sch 2 to the AHA 1986.
3   AgA 1986, Sch 1 Pt I para 7(2). It should be noted that the fixed equipment in respect of which an annual rental value is to be assessed is closely defined. There is no guidance as to the approach to be adopted in the case of tenant's fixed equipment used partly for dairying purposes and partly for other purposes. Note also the distinction between tenant's fixtures and tenant's chattels. Many items provided on dairy holdings by tenants which are loosely called 'tenant's fixtures' are, on legal analysis, really chattels, eg milking equipment. For recent cases in which the distinction between fixtures and chattels was judicially considered, see *Dean v Andrews* (1985) 135 NLJ 728 and *Young v Dalgety plc* (1986) 281 Estates Gazette 427, CA. Note also that annexure alone is not the test. The reason for annexure is the determining factor. See also, *TSB Bank plc v Botham* [1996] EGCS 149, *sub nom Botham v TSB Bank plc* (1996) 73 P & CR D1.
4   AgA 1986, Sch 1 Pt II para 8.
5   AgA 1986, Sch 1 Pt II para 7(4)(a). Note that the AHA 1986, Sch 2 para 2(2)(a) defines 'tenant's improvements' as any improvements which have been executed on the holding, in so far as they were executed wholly or partly at the expense of the tenant (whether or not that expense has been or will be reimbursed by a grant out of money provided by Parliament or local government funds), without any equivalent allowance or benefit made or given by the landlord in consideration of their execution. See para 25.37 for a commentary on this provision.
6   See fn 3 at para 50.11.
7   AgA 1986, Sch 1 Pt II para 7(4)(b).
8   AgA 1986, Sch 1 Pt II para 7(4)(c). Note that under the AHA 1986, Sch 2 para 2(3), tenant's improvements and tenant's fixed equipment undertaken during the previous tenancy are not disregarded if 'the tenant received any compensation on the termination of that (or any other) tenancy'.
9   *Creear v Fearon* [1994] 2 EGLR 12, [1994] 46 EG 202. In that case the tenant's fraction was severely distorted as a consequence.

The denominator

50.14 The denominator of the tenant's fraction consists of the numerator (see above) and such part of the rent payable by the tenant in respect of the relevant period as is attributable to the land used in that period for the feeding, accommodation or milking[1] of dairy cows kept on the land[2]. If the relevant period is less than, or greater than, 12 months, or if the rent was only payable by the tenant in respect of part of the relevant period, the average rent payable in respect of one month during the relevant period, or that part of the relevant period, is determined in order to compute the corresponding annual amount[3]. No provision is made to cover the eventuality of an alteration of rent occurring during the relevant period[4].

In *Creear v Fearon*[5], the rent actually passing in 1983 was only £400 per annum for 101 acres. The tenant's dairy improvements consisted merely of a second-hand milking bail, yet application of the fraction gave the tenant a very substantial proportion of the standard quota for a very low value improvement.

[1]   It is not clear as to what land that covers. It is submitted that houses, even if occupied by cowmen, have to be excluded. They are not used for the feeding, accommodating or milking of dairy cows but rather dairy men.

[2]   AgA 1986, Sch 1 Pt II para 7(1)(b). It is to be noted that this definition is different from 'areas used for milk production' (see the Dairy Produce Quotas Regulations 2005, Sch 1 para 3(1)) and 'land used during the relevant period for the feeding of dairy cows kept on the land' (see AgA 1986, Sch 1 Pt II para 6(1)(a)). Note, also, it is the total number of hectares used for the feeding accommodation or milking which has to be considered; cf the 'relevant hectares' which are confined to the *average* number of hectares.

[3]   AgA 1986, Sch 1 Pt II para 7(3).

[4]   In such a case it would appear clear that it is the whole of the relevant rent which was actually payable within the period. Note that the rental value of the dairy improvements and fixed equipment is assessed at the end of the relevant period. On the other hand, the rent of the dairy land for the denominator in the tenant's fraction is the rent payable during the relevant period, normally the calendar year 1983. If there had been a rent review during that year, this can significantly distort the fraction.

[5]   [1994] 2 EGLR 12, [1994] 46 EG 202.

Calculating the tenant's fraction

50.15 For the purposes of calculating compensation, the tenant's fraction is applied as follows:

(a)   to the standard quota, if this is exceeded by the allocated quota[1];

(b)   to the allocated quota, if this is equal to the standard quota[2]; and

(c)   proportionately to the allocated quota, if this is less than the standard quota, the proportionate reduction corresponding with the proportion that the allocated quota bears to the standard quota[3].

In order to avoid uncertainty, and potential dispute as to the identity of tenant's dairy improvements and items of fixed equipment on the holding during the relevant period[4], and also as to the land used for dairy production as defined[5], it is essential that both landlords and tenants make appropriate records without delay.

[1]   AgA 1986, Sch 1 Pt II para 5(2)(a)(i).

[2]   AgA 1986, Sch 1 Pt II para 5(2)(b).

[3]   AgA 1986, Sch 1 Pt II para 5(2)(c).

[4]   See para 50.2ff.

[5]   AgA 1986, Sch 1 Pt II para 6(1)(a).

VALUATION OF THE CLAIM

50.16 The payment which the tenant is entitled to obtain from his landlord on quitting the tenanted land[1] is by reference to the value of the milk quota for which compensation is payable[2]. For this purpose, the value of the quota to be applied is the value at the time of the termination of the tenancy in question. In determining that value on termination, all available evidence is to be taken into account including evidence as to the differential in market price paid for land where milk quota is registered and where it is not registered[3]. This may well produce a substantially lower figure than the price paid for milk quota when sold independently, rather than attached to the freehold itself.

The value to be attributed to the litreage of compensatable milk quota has given rise to many of the most difficult problems of milk quota compensation.

Since 1984, a market in milk quota developed with the quota originally being transferred by means of a short-term change of occupation of the land to which the quota is 'attached' (as it is called) and subsequently without land, as the restrictions imposed by the DPQR were relaxed. Two problems arise over the application of the sums realised in that way to the milk quota compensation valuation exercise, namely:

(a)   the legality of the transactions whereby the milk quota is detached from the holding in respect of which it was originally allocated; and

(b)   the accuracy of valuing the milk quota allocated to a holding by reference to comparatively small quantities of quota acquired by milk producers so as to secure marginal increases in their production of milk.

The legality of transactions whereby milk quota has been transferred from the land to which it was originally allocated has been considered in Chapter 49[4].

Assuming that the UK quota sale system is and has been lawful, it is arguable whether, as a matter of valuation rather than law, the prices realised have reflected the overall value of milk quota for the purposes of para 9 of Sch 1 to the AgA 1986. It could be argued that the price paid by a dairy farmer, fearing payment of the levy, so as to 'top up' his available quota, does not truly reflect the value of the underlying quota attached to the holding. Valuing 'at the margin' and applying that value 'across the board' involves a distortion. However, that argument would apply to any commodity, even eg rent, when supply and demand are out of balance.

[1]   AgA 1986, Sch 1 Pt I para 1.
[2]   AgA 1986, Sch 1 Pt II para 5.
[3]   AgA 1986, Sch 1 Pt II para 9. It would seem that in most cases evidence will be adduced as to the market price of quota sold 'independently' of land at the date of termination. In practice, that is substantially greater than the enhanced value of the land sold with the quota still attached to it. However, the legal efficacy of quota transfer by tenants of short-term grazing tenancies has still to be tested. An arbitrator must take into account all relevant evidence, including both forms of valuation, and make his award accordingly. He may not ignore one set of values and rely exclusively on the other.
[4]   See para 49.31.

PROCEDURAL MATTERS

Succession

50.17 In the case of a statutory succession to a tenancy[1] taking place on land to which milk quota is attached, compensation is not payable to the deceased tenant's estate, or to the retiring tenant. Instead the right to compensation conferred by Sch 1 to the AgA 1986 is passed to the new tenant[2].

For 'transferred quota' claim purposes the new tenant is treated as if he had paid a sum equivalent to that paid by the former tenant as the cost of acquiring the transferred quota[3].

For excess quota and tenant's fraction claim purposes, the new tenant is deemed to have been in occupation of the land on 2 April 1984, or is treated as having been in occupation on that date, if the former tenant could have satisfied those conditions[4].

If the statutory succession took place before the AHA 1986 came into force[5] the position in relation to the claim for compensation is identical[6]. The effect of these provisions is that in most cases succession will result in the new tenant merely stepping into the shoes of the deceased or retiring tenant and acquiring his accumulated right to compensation with no payment being made until the new tenancy is terminated.

[1]   AgA 1986, Sch 1 Pt I para 2(1) lists the four different statutory bases under which statutory succession could have taken place, namely: (i) a direction under the AHA 1986, s 39; (ii) a direction under the AHA 1986, s 53; (iii) a direction has been made and a new tenancy agreement is entered into not strictly in accordance with the direction; and (iv) no direction being made by the Agricultural Land Tribunal (ALT) but the grant of a new tenancy or an assignment of the old tenancy to a close relative eligible to obtain such a tenancy if he had applied for one, the AHA 1986, s 37(1)(b) and (2) applying.
[2]   AgA 1986, Sch 1 Pt I para 2(2): It is 'rolled over' to the succession tenant.
[3]   AgA 1986, Sch 1 Pt I para 2(2)(b)(i).
[4]   AgA 1986, Sch 1 Pt I para 2(2)(b)(ii).
[5]   Ie under the Agriculture (Miscellaneous Provisions) Act 1976, as amended by the AHA 1984. The AHA 1986 came into force on 12 June 1986.
[6]   AgA 1986, Sch 1 Pt I para 2(3).

Assignments

50.18 Where a tenancy has been assigned, whether by deed or operation of law on any date after 2 April 1984[1], the right to compensation under Sch 1, para 1 is passed to the assignee[2]. For this purpose the assignee is treated as having paid so much of the cost of acquiring transferred quota as was borne by the assignor[3] and equally the assignee is treated as having been in occupation on that date or is to be treated as if he was in occupation[4]. By this means the assignee is treated similarly to a new tenant by succession. However, the assignee, not having been in possession on 1 April 1984, will not receive compensation for transferred quota which he, rather than the assignor, acquired.

[1]   The date on which milk quotas were introduced into the United Kingdom.

2   AgA 1986, Sch 1 Pt I para 3(a).
3   AgA 1986, Sch 1 Pt II para 3(b)(i).
4   AgA 1986, Sch 1 Pt I para 3(b)(ii).

Sub-tenancies

50.19 A sub-tenant who has been in occupation of the land since 2 April 1984, or who is treated as having been in occupation on that date, is eligible for compensation on the termination of his sub-tenancy because of the wide definition of 'tenancy'[1]. Paragraph 4 of Sch 1 to the AgA 1986 contains provisions which enable the head tenant to recover from his landlord (the head landlord) a sum equivalent to the compensation paid to the sub-tenant. This will be deferred until actual quitting if the sub-landlord/head tenant occupies the holding on termination of the sub-tenancy[2].

1   See AgA 1986, Sch 1 Pt III para 18.
2   AgA 1986, Sch 1 Pt I para 4(c).

Termination of tenancy of part

50.20 Reference to the termination of the tenancy of any land[1] is supplemented by provisions which enable compensation to be claimed by a tenant where there is a resumption of possession of part of the tenanted land by the landlord in specified circumstances[2]. In order that effect can be given to these provisions it may be necessary for there to be an apportionment of the quota as between the subject agricultural holding and any other land owned or occupied by the tenant which together constitute 'the holding' as well as an apportionment between the land vacated and the land retained by the tenant.

1   AgA 1986, Sch 1 Pt I para 1(1).
2   AgA 1986, Sch 1 Pt III para 13. The circumstances are: (a) a notice to quit part given by the landlord under the AHA 1986, s 31 or s 43(2); (b) the landlord resuming possession in pursuance of a provision in the tenancy agreement; or (c) a notice to quit part given by a person entitled to a severed part of the reversionary estate in the land by virtue of the Law of Property Act 1925, s 140.

Severance of reversionary estate

50.21 Where the reversionary estate in the tenanted land is vested in more than one person in several parts, the tenant may require that the assessment of compensation payable to him is determined as if the reversionary estate had not been severed[1]. The tenant may thus be able to take advantage of a higher value being attributable to the quota when assessed as a block, rather than in separate parcels. The arbitrator must where necessary apportion the sum awarded between the various owners of the reversionary estate and any additional costs of his award caused by this apportionment must be paid by them in such proportions as may be determined by the arbitrator[2].

1   AgA 1986, Sch 1 Pt III para 14(1).
2   AgA 1986, Sch 1 Pt III para 14(2).

Settlement of tenant's claim on termination

50.22 In order to claim compensation under Sch 1 Pt I to the AgA 1986, the tenant must serve notice in writing on the landlord of his intention to make the claim within two months of the termination of the tenancy. A failure to serve such a notice renders the claim unenforceable[1]. This is the same procedure as applies to all outgoing tenant's claims on quitting to which s 83 of the AHA 1986 applies[2].

This general rule is subject to the exception that if, on the termination of the tenancy, a new tenancy of the land or part of it is granted to a new tenant by virtue of the direction being given by the ALT for a succession tenancy[3], the notice of intention to claim compensation must be served within the 'relevant time' as defined in the succession provisions[4]. If the tenant lawfully remains in occupation of part of the tenanted land subject to the tenancy[5] after termination of the tenancy or after the time substituted for the termination of the tenancy by reason of the succession provisions applying, the period of two months during which notice of the claim must be served commences from the date of termination of that occupation[6].

Following the termination of the tenancy the landlord and tenant may within eight months settle the claim by agreement, but if the claim has not been settled during that period, it is determined by arbitration under the AHA 1986[7]. In cases in which the tenant lawfully remains in occupation of part of the land after the termination of the tenancy or the commencement of the period during which notice of intention to claim is artificially prolonged[8], the eight months' period commences from that time[9]. These provisions are almost identical to the provisions for enforcing all other outgoing tenants' claims, for example, tenant-right and compensation for improvements on quitting[10], with slight variations in the case of succession tenancies.

1   AgA 1986, Sch 1 Pt III para 11(1).
2   As to which, see Ch 41. Note that a notice of intention may be given very informally as in *Walker v Crocker* [1992] 1 EGLR 29, [1992] 23 EG 123. See para 41.3ff.
3   Ie under the AHA 1986, s 39.
4   AgA 1986, Sch 1 Pt III para 11(3).
5   Eg under a grazing licence or an unprotected agricultural tenancy or farm business tenancy.
6   AgA 1986, Sch 1 Pt III para 11(4).
7   AgA 1986, Sch 1 Pt III para 11(2). This provision is identical to that contained in the AHA 1986, s 83(4) relating to the settlement of other claims as between landlord and tenant arising on termination.
8   Under AgA 1986, Sch 1 Pt III para 11(3).
9   AgA 1986, Sch 1 Pt III para 11(4).
10   AHA 1986, s 83. See para 41.3ff.

Arbitration

50.23 Section 84 of the AHA 1986, which lays down the general rules for arbitrations under that Act, applies to the tenant's claim under the AgA 1986 on termination of the tenancy. The only variation is that the arbitrator must fix the date for payment of compensation, costs or otherwise not later than three months after the date of the award[1]. The arbitrator's powers are severely curtailed either if the landlord and the tenant have agreed in writing the amount of the standard quota or the tenant's fraction, or the value of the quota, for the purpose of calculating the compensation payable, or if the standard quota or the tenant's fraction has been determined respectively[2].

1   AgA 1986, Sch 1 Pt III para 11(5).
2   For prospective determination by arbitration, see para 50.27.

Enforcement

50.24   Section 85 of the AHA 1986, which relates to the enforcement of sums due by a landlord or a tenant, together with s 86(1), (3) and (4) of the AHA 1986, which relates to the power of a landlord to obtain a charge on the holding, apply to enforcement of payment of any sum which is due to a tenant under Sch 1 of the AgA 1986[1].

1   AgA 1986, Sch 1 Pt III para 12. For a commentary, see Ch 41.

Service of notices

50.25   The provisions relating to the service of any notice under the AgA 1986 are identical to those applicable to the service of notices under the AHA 1986[1].

1   AgA 1986, Sch 1 Pt III para 16 and see the AHA 1986, s 93. For a commentary, see Ch 42.

Crown land

50.26   The provisions relating to tenant's compensation for quota apply to land which belongs to Her Majesty in right of the Crown or to the Duchy of Lancaster, the Duchy of Cornwall, or a Government Department, or which is held in trust for Her Majesty for the purposes of a Government Department, subject in each case to such modifications as the Minister may prescribe in regulations[1]. For the purposes of Sch 1 of the AgA 1986, the person or body of persons deemed to be the landlord are specifically identified[2].

1   AgA 1986, Sch 1 Pt III para 17(1).
2   AgA 1986, Sch 1 Pt III para 17(2). It would seem that in the event of this point being disputed by the landlord, it would have to be decided as a preliminary point by the arbitrator.

PROSPECTIVE DETERMINATION OF STANDARD QUOTA OR TENANT'S FRACTION

50.27   Where the tenant may be entitled to payment of compensation for quota, either the landlord or the tenant may, at any time before the termination of the tenancy, by notice in writing served on the other, demand that the determination of the standard quota for the land, or the tenant's fraction, be referred to arbitration[1].

The landlord may wish to take this course in order to ascertain his prospective financial liability on the termination of the tenancy. Correspondingly, the tenant may wish to ascertain his prospective entitlement before reaching a decision as to whether to terminate the tenancy. It should be noted that para 10(1) of Sch 1 to the AgA 1986 refers to determination of the standard quota or the tenant's fraction, not both. In cases where determination is required of both the standard quota and the tenant's fraction, it will presumably be necessary for two notices to be served. In most cases the parties will no doubt agree that both determinations should be made in the same arbitration. Alternatively, it may be found that since the statutory right is exercised in respect of one or other head of claim it is spent and there is no further right to obtain a prospective apportionment on the other head of claim. On exercising the one right, the tenant's entitlement is spent.

Upon the issue being referred to arbitration, the arbitrator must determine the standard quota or the tenant's fraction for the land, in so far as the tenant's fraction is determinable, as at the date of the reference[2]. The arbitration is to be conducted in accordance with the provisions of s 84 of the AHA 1986[3].

It should be noted that an arbitrator appointed to determine the tenant's claim following termination of the tenancy is obliged to award payment in accordance with any determination made in advance of the tenancy terminating[4] unless it appears to him that any circumstances relevant to the determination were materially different at the time of the termination of the tenancy from those at the time that the determination was made. If a material difference can be identified, the arbitrator must disregard so much of the determination as appears to him to be affected by the change in circumstances[5].

[1]   AgA 1986, Sch 1 Pt III para 10(1).
[2]   AgA 1986, Sch 1 Pt III para 10(2).
[3]   AgA 1986, Sch 1 Pt III para 10(3).
[4]   AgA 1986, Sch 1 Pt III para 11(6).
[5]   AgA 1986, Sch 1 Pt III para 11(7). The difference between prospective apportionment of quota under the Dairy Produce Quotas Regulations 2005, SI 2005/465, Sch 1 para (3(1), and the determination of the standard quota or the tenant's fraction before the end of the tenancy should be noted. Whereas a prospective apportionment of quota under the regulations only lasts for six months and may be revoked earlier, a determination of the standard quota or tenant's fraction continues to apply throughout the currency of the tenancy and subject to Sch 1 Pt III para 11(7) of the AgA 1986, will be binding on the arbitrator appointed to assess the tenant's claims on termination. In practice, a prospective determination may be of considerable assistance to landlord or tenant (or both) in planning future farming policy or whether to give notice to quit.

AGREEMENT AS TO STANDARD QUOTA OR TENANT'S FRACTION OR VALUE OF QUOTA

50.28   At any time before the termination of the tenancy the landlord and the tenant may, instead of going to arbitration, agree in writing the amount of the standard quota for the land comprised in the tenancy or the tenant's fraction, or the value of quota which is to be used for the purpose of calculating the payment due to the tenant on quitting[1]. The arbitrator must award payment in accordance with the written agreement[2] unless it appears to him that any circumstances relevant to the agreement were materially different at the time of the termination of the tenancy from those applying at the time the agreement was made, in which case he must disregard so much of the agreement as appears to him to be affected by the change in circumstances[3].

1   AgA 1986, Sch 1 Pt III para 11(6)(a).
2   AgA 1986, Sch 1 Pt III para 11(6).
3   AgA 1986, Sch 1 Pt III para 11(7).

Chapter 51

DISPUTE RESOLUTION: MILK QUOTA

THE ARBITRAL PROCESS

51.1 The Tenancy Reform Industry Group (TRIG2) reforms[1] have not imposed the provisions of the Arbitration Act 1996 on the arbitral process under the Dairy Produce Quotas Regulations 2005[2], (DPQR 2005). The DPQR 2005 continues to have its own unique and self-contained arbitral scheme[3]. Paragraph 34 of Sch 1 to the DPQR 2005 states that the Arbitration Act 1996 (AA 1996) does not apply to an arbitration determined in accordance with the Schedule.

[1] See para 1.19.
[2] SI 2005/465.
[3] The Regulatory Reform (Agricultural Tenancies) (England and Wales) Order 2006, SI 2006/2805 (RRO 2006), amended paras 1(2), 4(2) and repealed para 7 of Sch 1.

The method of determination

51.2 The apportionment of milk quota may, and generally will, be concluded by agreement between the parties or their respective agents. In the absence of agreement, the DPQR 2005 provide for apportionment to be resolved by statutory arbitration[1].

Apportionment by arbitration must occur if there has been a transfer of part of a holding and the Rural Payments Agency (RPA) have reasonable grounds for believing that the areas used for milk production are not as specified in the notice or those areas were not taken fully into account at the time of apportionment. If those circumstances arise, the RPA can decide that the apportionment must be referred to arbitration[2].

Notwithstanding any agreement to the contrary as to the method of determination, any apportionment arising under the DPQR 2005 must be determined (in the absence of agreement) by arbitration pursuant to the unique code of statutory arbitration contained in the DPQR 2005[3]. That unique code requires a determination by a single arbitrator according to the provisions of Sch 1 to the DPQR 2005[4].

¹   DPQR 2005, SI 2005/465, reg 10(2).
²   SI 2005/465, reg 12.
³   SI 2005/465, Sch 1.
⁴   SI 2005/465, Sch 1 para 1(1).

Timing and appointment of arbitrator

51.3 As seen in Chapter 49¹, the transferor and the transferee have a period in which to lodge with the RPA a notice containing an agreed apportionment of milk quota. In any case where an apportionment is to be carried out by arbitration, an arbitrator shall be appointed by agreement between the transferor and the transferee². The transferee shall give notice of the appointment of the arbitrator to the RPA of the appointment³. Formerly this was required to be done within 14 days under the DPQR 1997. That is no longer the case.

The transferor or the transferee may at any time within the relevant period make an application to the President to the Royal Institution of Chartered Surveyors ('the President') for the appointment of an arbitrator⁴. The person who makes an application to the President shall give notice of that fact to the RPA⁵.

If an arbitrator has not been appointed by agreement between the transferor and the transferee and no application has been made to the President for an appointment from the members of the panel, the RPA shall make an application to the President for the appointment of an arbitrator⁶.

¹   See para 49.9 ff.
²   DPQR 2005, SI 2005/465, Sch 1 para 1(1).
³   SI 2005/465, Sch 1 para 1(1).
⁴   SI 2005/465, Sch 1 para 1(2).
⁵   SI 2005/465, Sch 1 para 1(2).
⁶   SI 2005/465, Sch 1 para 1(3).

51.4 Where the RPA has reasonable grounds for believing that the areas used for milk production on a holding are not as specified in a notice or application agreed by the parties and submitted to the RPA within the relevant period or that the areas used for milk production on a holding were not as agreed between the parties at the time of the apportionment in a case where no notice or application has yet been submitted to the RPA, the RPA may give notice of this fact to the person who submitted the form to it or, if there is no such notice or application, to the transferee¹. In such cases, the RPA shall make an application to the President for the appointment of an arbitrator and the RPA shall be a party to the arbitration².

Upon an application by a producer for the restoration of milk quota which has been confiscated³, requiring an apportionment to be carried out by arbitration, the producer shall either appoint an arbitrator by agreement with all persons with an interest in the holding or make an application to the President for the appointment of an arbitrator from members of the panel⁴. No timetable is prescribed for such an appointment by the DPQR 2005.

There are two cases where a prospective apportionment is to be made by arbitration. The first is where the RPA has reasonable grounds for believing that either the areas used for milk production on a holding are not as specified in a notice where applications submitted by the parties to the RPA or that the areas used for milk production on a holding were not as agreed between the parties at the time of the apportionment in a case where no notice or application has yet been submitted[5]. In such cases, an arbitrator shall be appointed by the President. In any other case requiring a prospective apportionment to be made by arbitration, the arbitrator shall be appointed by agreement between the occupier of the relevant holding and any other interested party or, in default, by the President on the application on the occupier. In such cases, the occupier shall give notice to the RPA of the appointment of the arbitrator pursuant to the agreement, or of the application to the President for the appointment of the arbitrator[6].

[1] DPQR 2005, SI 2005/465, reg 12.
[2] SI 2005/465, Sch 1 para 1(4).
[3] In accordance with SI 2005/465, reg 39(4)(b).
[4] SI 2005/465, Sch 1 para 1(5).
[5] SI 2005/465, reg 12(1).
[6] SI 2005/465, Sch 1 para 2.

Appointments by the President of the Royal Institution of Chartered Surveyors

51.5 The President will only make an appointment upon an application for the appointment of an arbitrator if the application is accompanied by the prescribed fee, but once the fee has been paid in connection with any such application, no further fee shall be payable in connection with any subsequent application for the President to exercise any function exercisable by him in relation to the arbitration by virtue of Sch 1 to the DPQR 2005 (including an application for the appointment by him in an appropriate case of a new arbitrator)[1].

The prescribed fee shall be that which applies for the appointment of an arbitrator by the President in accordance with the Agricultural Holdings Act 1986 (AHA 1986)[2].

Where the RPA makes an application to the President for the appointment of an arbitrator, the fee payable to the President in respect of that application shall again be the fee prescribed for the appointment of an arbitrator in accordance with the provisions of the AHA 1986, but the fees shall be recoverable by the RPA as a debt due from the other parties to the arbitration jointly and severally[3]. Any application, appointment, notice or revocation must be in writing[4].

The President is required to make an appointment of an arbitrator upon an application to him as soon as possible after receiving the application[5].

An arbitrator appointed by the President shall be taken to have been so appointed at the time when the President executed the instrument of appointment in accordance with the law in force at the time of such execution[6].

Any instrument of appointment or other document purporting to be made in exercise of any function exercisable by the President under Sch 1 to the DPQR 2005 and to be signed by or on behalf of the President shall be taken to be such an instrument or document unless the contrary is shown[7].

1   DPQR 2005, SI 2005/465, Sch 1 para 4(1).
2   AHA 1986, s 84; SI 2005/465, Sch 1 para 4(2).
3   SI 2005/465, Sch 1 para 5.
4   SI 2005/465, Sch 1 para 10.
5   SI 2005/465, Sch 1 para 6.
6   SI 2005/465, Sch 1 para 32.
7   SI 2005/465, Sch 1 para 33.

Notices relating to the appointment of an arbitrator

51.6 Every appointment or application relating to the appointment of an arbitrator or any notice in respect of his appointment, including the revocation of his appointment, must be in writing[1].

1   DPQR 2002, SI 2002/457, Sch 1 para 10.

Dispute as to the jurisdiction of an arbitrator

51.7 If an arbitrator is appointed, whether by the President or by agreement, and there is a dispute as to his jurisdiction, either party may make an application for judicial review for an Order prohibiting him from acting[1]. Alternatively, the arbitrator may seek the opinion of the county court by way of case stated as to whether he has jurisdiction[2].

1   *R v London County Justices and LCC* [1894] 1 QB 453, CA; *Westwood v Barnett* 1925 SC 624, Ct of Sess; *R v Powell, ex p Marquis Camden* [1925] 1 KB 641; *R v Liverpool Justices, ex p Roberts* [1960] 2 All ER 384n, [1960] 1 WLR 585.
2   DPQR 2002, SI 2002/457, Sch 1 para 28. This is the same procedure which applied to the AHA 1986 before the RRO 2006, SI 2006/2805.

Remuneration of the arbitrator

51.8 The remuneration of the arbitrator appointed by agreement under the statutory procedure is such amount as may be agreed between the arbitrator and the parties or, in default of agreement, fixed by the District Judge of the county court (subject to an appeal to the judge) on an application made by the arbitrator or any party[1].

Where the arbitrator is appointed by the President, in default of agreement between the parties, the remuneration is such amount as may be agreed between the arbitrator and the parties or, in default of agreement, fixed by the President[2].

The arbitrator may recover his remuneration as a debt due to him from any parties to the arbitration who are jointly and severally liable[3].

Any amount paid in respect of the remuneration of the arbitrator by any party to the arbitration in excess of the amount (if any) directed by the arbitrator's award to be paid by him in respect of the costs of the award shall be recoverable from the other party or jointly from the other parties[4].

1   DPQR 2005, SI 2005/465, Sch 1 para 11(1)(a).
2   SI 2005/465, Sch 1 para 11(1)(b).
3   SI 2005/465, Sch 1 para 11(2).
4   SI 2005/465, Sch 1 para 31.

Replacement of an arbitrator

51.9 If an arbitrator dies or is incapable of acting, or for seven days after notice from any party requiring him to act fails to act, a new arbitrator may be appointed as if no arbitrator had been appointed[1]. Any notice given must be in writing[2].

No party to the arbitration shall have power to revoke the appointment of the arbitrator without the consent of any other party, nor is the arbitrator's appointment revoked by the death of any party[3]. Any consent must be in writing[4].

1   DPQR 2005, SI 2005/465, Sch 1 para 8. See also *Pennington-Ramsden v McWilliam* [1982] CLY 28, County Court.
2   SI 2005/465, Sch 1 para 10.
3   SI 2005/465, Sch 1 para 9.
4   SI 2005/465, Sch 1 para 10.

Requirements of the arbitrator

51.10 The arbitrator must conduct the arbitration in accordance with Sch 1 to the DPQR 2005[1]. Save where the arbitration relates to the restoration of milk quota following confiscation[2], the arbitrator is required to base his award as to the apportionment of milk quota on findings made by him as to areas used for milk production in the last five-year period during which production took place before the change of occupation giving rise to the apportionment of the milk quota, or in the case of a prospective apportionment in the last five-year period during which production took place before the appointment of the arbitrator[3].

Where the arbitrator is appointed to deal with the apportionment of milk quota upon its restoration following confiscation in accordance with reg 33(5) of the DPQR 2005, he is required to base his award on findings made by him as to the areas used for milk production in the last five-year period during which production took place[4].

In all arbitrations under Sch 1 to the DPQR, the arbitrator is required to base his award on findings made by him in accordance with the law in force at the time the event giving rise to an application for arbitration took place[5].

1   DPQR 2005, SI 2005/465, Sch 1 para 3(1).
2   As to which, see para 51.11.

3   SI 2005/465, Sch 1 para 3(1).
4   SI 2005/465, Sch 1 para 3(2).
5   SI 2005/465, Sch 1 para 3(3).

The parties to an arbitration

51.11 Where an arbitration takes place to deal with the apportionment of quota upon its restoration following confiscation[1], any person with an interest in the holding who has refused to sign a statement of the agreed apportionment of quota taking account of the areas used for milk production[2] is required to be a party to the arbitration[3].

Further, in any arbitration to which Sch 1 to the DPQR 2005 applies, the arbitrator may, in his absolute discretion join as a party to the arbitration any person having an interest in the holding, whether or not such person has applied to become a party to the arbitration, provided that such person consents to be joined[4].

1   See para 51.4.
2   Pursuant to DPQR 2002, SI 2002/457, reg 39(4)(b).
3   SI 2005/465, Sch 1 para 12(2).
4   SI 2005/465, Sch 1 para 12(1).

Statement of case and particulars

51.12 The parties are required to deliver a statement of their respective cases with all necessary particulars to the arbitrator within 35 days from his appointment[1], or such further period as the arbitrator may determine. Whilst there is no High Court authority, the majority of county court judges have decided that the failure of a party to deliver a Statement of Case within the 35 days or within such further time limit as the arbitrator decides means that a party is unable to produce any evidence in support of his claim. He may cross-examine his opponent's witnesses, but he may not call any evidence to support his own case[2]. There may be no amendment or addition to the Statements of Case or particulars after the expiry of the 35-day time limit except with the consent of the arbitrator[3]. Arbitrators should be liberal in consenting to amendments or additions provided that there is no injustice caused to the opposing party[4].

The formal contents of the Statement of Case are not statutorily prescribed. If the document delivered to the arbitrator does not constitute a Statement of Case, it is not possible to cure this defect by subsequent amendment[5].

1   DPQR 2005, SI 2005/465, Sch 1 para 13.
2   See *Collett v Deeley* (1949) 100 LJ 108, Oxford County Court. This was followed in *Langford v Quartley* (1952) unreported, Taunton County Court. Cf *Goulden v Agnew* (1956) unreported, Llandrindod Wells County Court, being a case running contrary to the other decisions.
3   SI 2005/465, Sch 1 para 13(a).
4   *ED & AD Cooke Bourne (Farms) Ltd v Mellows* [1983] QB 104, [1982] 2 All ER 208.
5   *Robertsons Trustees v Cunningham* 1951 SLT (Sh Ct) 89.

51.13 A party to the arbitration shall be confined at the hearing to the matters alleged in the Statement of Case and particulars delivered by him and any amendment or addition duly made[1].

There is nothing in the statutory arbitration procedure contained in the DPQR 2005 that requires either party to deliver a copy of a Statement of Case to the other nor for the arbitrator to deliver a duplicate of a copy sent to him to the other party, although the latter is the normal practice.

The process of simultaneous delivery of Statements of Case means that the party defending is unaware of the allegations made against him at the time of the delivery of the Statement of Case by the party bringing the claim. It is submitted that in these circumstances the arbitrator should liberally apply his discretion to permit amendments, alterations and additions[2].

[1]   DPQR 2005, SI 2005/465, Sch 1 para 13(b).
[2]   Note that it is only a claim and not a defence which needs to be pleaded in the Statement of Case. There are no rules for formulating a defence: see *Earl of Plymouth v Glamorgan County Council* (1974) 232 Estates Gazette 1235.

Interlocutory matters

51.14 Schedule 1 of the DPQR 2005 contains no express provision for interlocutory matters such as Orders for disclosure of documents. There is authority in relation to the like provisions contained under earlier agricultural holdings legislation prior to the Agricultural Holdings Act 1986 for the proposition that an arbitrator has jurisdiction to make appropriate interlocutory Orders[1].

[1]   See *Kursell v Timber Operators and Contractors Ltd* [1923] 2 KB 202; *Vasso v Vasso, The Vasso* [1983] 3 All ER 211, [1983] 1 WLR 838 and the cases cited in that decision.

Fixing the hearing

51.15 Although arbitrators appointed under the statutory procedure are not usually lawyers[1], arbitration is a judicial process. Accordingly, in advance of the hearing, the arbitrator should have no dealings with one party without the knowledge of the other. This principle of fairness to the parties should be applied equally to the arrangements for fixing the hearing. The arbitrator should have reasonable regard to the convenience of the parties in making the necessary arrangements notwithstanding the time constraints contained in Sch 1 to the DPQR 2005. Schedule 1 provides for an award to be delivered by the arbitrator within 56 days of the date of his appointment[2]. However, the President (whether the appointment of the arbitrator is by the President or by agreement) may extend the time limit for making the award, whether that time has expired or not[3]. There is no limit upon the number of extensions that may be made.

[1]   They may be if they are appointed by agreement rather than by the President from the Panel, see para 51.5.
[2]   DPQR 2005, SI 2005/465, Sch 1 para 21(1).
[3]   SI 2005/465, Sch 1 para 21(2).

The conduct of the hearing

51.16 The arbitrator should adopt the procedure used before the court[1]. Where general provisions are used before the court and those contained in Sch 1 to the DPQR 2005 conflict, the latter will prevail. The arbitrator may deal with preliminary points of law, but more usually will have such matters resolved by the case stated procedure[2]. If a party fails to attend the hearing, after due notice, the arbitrator may proceed in that party's absence[3].

[1] See para 47.35.
[2] See para 51.23.
[3] The arbitrator should only adopt this procedure in the most clear cut case to avoid the allegation that he is guilty of misconduct: see *Thomas v Official Solicitor* (1982) 265 Estates Gazette 601.

Witnesses

51.17 The parties to the arbitration and all persons claiming through them shall, subject to any legal objection, submit to be examined by the arbitrator, on oath or affirmation, in relation to the matters in dispute and shall, subject to any such objection, produce before the arbitrator all samples and documents within their possession or power which may be required or called for, and do such other things as the arbitrator reasonably may require for the purpose of the arbitration[1].

Any person having an interest in the holding to which the arbitration relates (regardless of whether they are a party) shall be entitled to make representations to the arbitrator[2].

Witnesses appearing at the arbitration shall, if the arbitrator thinks fit, be examined on oath or affirmation. The arbitrator shall have power to administer oaths to, or take the affirmation of, the parties and witnesses appearing[3].

The provisions of the Civil Procedure Rules as to the issuing of witness summonses, subject to such modifications as may be prescribed by such rules, apply for the purposes of the arbitration as if it were a claim in the county court[4].

If a person, who is summoned pursuant to the Civil Procedure Rules as a witness to the arbitration, refuses or neglects, without sufficient cause, to appear or to produce any documents required by the summons to be produced or, having appeared, refuses to be sworn or to give evidence, that person shall forfeit such fine as the judge of the county court may direct[5]. Powers are also provided to cause the attendance of a prisoner at the arbitration[6].

[1] DPQR 2005, SI 2005/465, Sch 1 para 14.
[2] SI 2005/465, Sch 1 para 15.
[3] SI 2005/465, Sch 1 para 16.
[4] SI 2005/465, Sch 1 para 17. See CPR Pts 34 and 62.
[5] SI 2005/465, Sch 1 para 18(1). As to the powers of the court in relation to the enforcement of this provision, see Sch 1 para 18.
[6] SI 2005/465, Sch 1 paras 19 and 20.

The arbitrator's award

51.18 The arbitrator must make and sign his award within 56 days of his appointment unless the period has been extended by the President, whether the time for making the award has expired or not[1].

Unlike the position in relation to an arbitration under the Agricultural Holdings Act 1986, there is no prescribed form for the award.

The award must fix a date not later than one month after the delivery of the award for the payment of any costs consequential upon the award[2].

The award shall be final and binding on the parties and any persons claiming under them[3]. The arbitrator shall have power to correct in the award any clerical mistake or error arising from an accidental slip or omission[4]. The arbitrator must notify the terms of his award to the RPA within 8 days of the delivery of the award[5].

1 DPQR 2005, SI 2005/465, Sch 1 para 21(1) and (2).
2 SI 2005/465, Sch 1 para 21(4).
3 SI 2005/465, Sch 1 para 22.
4 SI 2005/465, Sch 1 para 23.
5 SI 2005/465, Sch 1 para 21(3).

Statement of reasons

51.19 A statement of reason should include the facts found to be admitted or proved; whether and to what extent the submissions of the parties were convincing or not; and by what method or methods of valuation the determination was arrived at[1].

Where the arbitrator is requested by any party to the arbitration, on or before making the award (but not afterwards), to make a statement, either written or oral, of the reasons for the award, the arbitrator must furnish such a statement[2].

1 *Guppys Properties Ltd v Knott* (1977) 245 Estates Gazette 1023. Also see *Re Poyser and Mills Arbitrations* [1964] 2 QB 467, [1963] 1 All ER 612 and *R v Dairy Produce Quota Tribunal for England and Wales, ex p PA Cooper & Sons* [1993] 1 EGLR 13, [1993] 19 EG 138.
2 DPQR 2005, SI 2005/465, Sch 1 para. 24; Tribunals and Inquiries Act 1971, s 12.

Costs

51.20 The costs of, and incidental to, the arbitration and the award of the arbitrator shall be in the discretion of the arbitrator who may direct to and by whom and in what manner the costs, or any part of the costs, are to be paid[1]. Such costs shall include any fee paid to the President in respect of the appointment of an arbitrator and any sum paid to the RPA[2].

When awarding costs, the arbitrator must take into consideration:

(a)   the reasonableness or unreasonableness of the claim of any party, whether in respect of the amount or otherwise;

(b)   any unreasonable demand for particulars or refusal to supply particulars; and

(c)   generally all the circumstances of the case[3].

The arbitrator may disallow any costs which he considers to have been unnecessarily incurred, including the costs of any witness whom he considers to have been called unnecessarily[4].

The parties may before the arbitration make an agreement as to costs which will be valid and enforceable[5], subject to assessment in the county court. On the application of any party, any such costs shall be assessed in the county court according the Civil Procedure Rules as may be directed by the arbitrator or, in the absence of such direction, by the county court[6].

[1]   DPQR 2005, SI 2005/465, Sch 1 para 25.
[2]   SI 2005/465, Sch 1 para 25.
[3]   SI 2005/465, Sch 1 para 27.
[4]   SI 2005/465, Sch 1 para 27(2).
[5]   *Mansfield v Robinson* [1928] 2 KB 353.
[6]   SI 2005/465, Sch 1 para 26.

Interest on awards

51.21   There is no provision under Sch 1 to the DPQR 2005 for the payment of interest on any sum directed to be paid pursuant to the award.

Legal assistance for the arbitrator

51.22   It is submitted that legal assistance for the arbitrator is available even though there is no direct provision under the DPQR 2005. There are conflicting authorities as to the extent and circumstances in which an arbitrator may seek legal assistance. One thing can be said with certainty: and that is that if the arbitrator obtains the prior consent of all parties as to obtaining legal assistance (including, in particular, if the legal adviser is to sit with the arbitrator), then no difficulty arises. It follows that it is good practice for the arbitrator to seek such consent.

In the absence of agreement on the part of the parties, it appears that the arbitrator may obtain:

(a)   legal assistance in the drawing of his award[1];

(b)   advice concerning procedure and rules of evidence[2];

(c)   advice on the general principles of law which are relevant to the case[3];

(d)   advice on the interpretation of a document in dispute[4].

For those purposes the arbitrator may have a legal adviser to sit with him at the hearing[5]. However, without the consent of the parties, the arbitrator should not obtain legal assistance as to the actual issues of law in the arbitration[6]. Further, in the absence of the parties' consent, guidance may be obtained from the court by way of case stated[7].

1   *Threlfall v Fanshawe* (1851) 1 LM & P 340; *Galloway v Keyworth* (1854) 15 CB 228; *Re Underwood and Bedford and Cambridge Railway Co* (1861) 11 CBNS 442; *Re Collyer-Bristow & Co* [1901] 2 KB 839. It is submitted that legal assistance in the preparation of a special case is also permitted without the consent of the parties.
2   *Threlfall v Fanshawe* (1851) 1 LM & P 340; *Galloway v Keyworth* (1854) 15 CB 228; *Re Underwood and Bedford and Cambridge Railway Co* (1861) 11 CBNS 442; *Re Collyer-Bristow & Co* [1901] 2 KB 839.
3   *Louise Dreyfus & Co v Arunachala Ayya* (1931) LR 58 Ind App 381.
4   *Giacomo Costa Fu Andrea v British Italian Trading Co Ltd* [1963] 1 QB 201, [1962] 2 All ER 53, CA.
5   *Giacomo Costa Fu Andrea v British Italian Trading Co Ltd* [1963] 1 QB 201, [1962] 2 All ER 53, CA.
6   *Louis Dreyfus & Co v Arunachala Ayya* (1931) LR 58 Ind App 381.
7   See para 51.7.

CHALLENGING THE ARBITRATOR'S AWARD

Special case/case stated

51.23 The arbitrator may at any stage of the arbitration, and must if so directed by the judge of the county court upon an application made by any party, state in the form of a special case for the opinion of the county court any question of law arising in the course of the arbitration and any question as to the jurisdiction of the arbitrator[1]. This is commonly known as the 'case stated' procedure. The jurisdiction of the High Court is excluded in cases to which this procedure applies[2].

More than one case may be stated in the course of the arbitration[3]. The arbitrator cannot state a case after he has made his award[4].

An appeal against any direction to state a case or against the opinion of the county court on a case stated lies to the Court of Appeal. The opinion of the court is binding on the arbitrator and must be applied by him[5].

If the arbitrator is satisfied and confident that he is able to adjudicate upon an issue raised by the parties without recourse to stating a case, he may do so. Alternatively, before making his award, the arbitrator may advise the parties as to his opinion in relation to a legal issue and give the parties a limited period in which to invite him to state a case.

1   DPQR 2005, SI 2005/457, Sch 1 para 28.
2   *Jones v Pembrokeshire County Council* [1967] 1 QB 181, [1966] 1 All ER 1027.
3   *Public Trustee v Randag* [1966] Ch 649, [1965] 3 All ER 88.
4   *Tabernacle Permanent Building Society v Knight* [1892] AC 298, HL.
5   *Mitchell-Gill v Buchan* 1921 SC 390, Ct of Sess.

Setting aside the arbitrator's award and remission

51.24 Where the arbitrator has misconducted himself, or an arbitration or award has been improperly procured, or there is an error of law on the face of

51.24 *Dispute resolution: milk quota*

the award, the county court may set the award aside[1]. Where the arbitrator has misconducted himself, the county court may remove him[2].

The county court may from time to time remit the award, or any part of the award, to the arbitrator for reconsideration[3]. In any case where it appears to the county court that there is an error of law on the face of the award, the court may, instead of exercising its power of remission, vary the award by substituting for so much of it as is affected by the error such award as the court considers that it would have been proper for the arbitrator to make in the circumstances. The award shall have effect as so varied[4].

Where remission is ordered by the county court, the arbitrator shall, unless the order otherwise directs, make and sign his award within 30 days of the date of the order[5]. If the county court is satisfied that the time limited for making the award is for any good reason insufficient, the court may extend or further extend that time for such period as it thinks proper[6].

[1]   DPQR 2005, SI 2005/465, Sch 1 para 29(2).
[2]   SI 2005/465, Sch 1 para 29(1).
[3]   SI 2005/465, Sch 1 para 30(1).
[4]   SI 2005/465, Sch 1 para 30(2).
[5]   SI 2005/465, Sch 1 para 31(3).
[6]   SI 2005/465, Sch 1 para 30(4).

Chapter 52

MID-TERM REVIEW OF THE COMMON AGRICULTURAL POLICY

INTRODUCTION

52.1 On 10 July 2002 the European Commission issued their Communication, *Mid-term Review of the Common Agricultural Policy*, which heralded arguably the most substantial reform of the Common Agricultural Policy since its inception[1]. The original mandate for this initiative was to address specific matters left outstanding when the Agenda 2000 reforms were agreed at the Berlin Summit in March 1999[2]. Most notably, it was envisaged that a decision would be reached to phase out milk quotas by 2006[3]. In the event, however, the Mid-term Review gave rise to sweeping change and, in particular, root-and-branch recasting of the legislation which governs direct payments to farmers.

Without doubt, broad considerations drove this reform, at both European Community and international levels. For example, there was a clear determination to secure greater acceptance by society of support to farmers, on the basis that this support was provided in return for the provision of 'public goods', such as high standards of environmental protection and animal welfare[4]. Likewise, the new direct payment regime was intended to be largely compatible with world trade obligations[5]. In particular, it was intended that the vast majority of direct payments should be exempt from domestic support reduction commitments under the Uruguay Round Agreement on Agriculture, by virtue of their qualifying as 'de-coupled income support'[6].

While such broad considerations would seem far from the day-to-day operation of agricultural tenancies, they have nonetheless shaped the way in which land is to be farmed. Importantly, the receipt of direct payments is dependent upon compliance with obligations designed to ensure good farming practice (cross-compliance). Moreover, in purely economic terms, it has become demonstrably clear that access to European Community direct payments is essential to the profitability of most farming businesses[7]. The result is that it may now be regarded as essential to address European Community direct payment schemes in any treatment of the law of agricultural tenancies. This may be effected in three stages:

961

(a)   first, examination of the European Community framework as instituted by the Mid-term Review;

(b)   second, examination of the implementation of this European Community framework in England and Wales; and

(c)   third, a more detailed analysis of the landlord and tenant implications.

1   COM(2002)394. See, generally, eg, J Moody and W Neville *Mid Term Review: a Practical Guide* (2004) Burges Salmon, Bristol; Central Association of Agricultural Valuers, *Mid Term Review: a Valuer's Interim Guide* (2004) Central Association of Agricultural Valuers, Coleford; M Cardwell *The European Model of Agriculture* (2004) Oxford University Press, Oxford, pp 159–174; and Central Association of Agricultural Valuers *Mid Term Review: a Valuer's Second Interim Guide* (2005) Central Association of Agricultural Valuers, Coleford.

2   For the Communication which launched the Agenda 2000 Reforms see European Commission *Agenda 2000: For a Stronger and Wider Union* (*Bulletin of the European Union, Supplement 5/97*), COM(97)2000. For the agreement reached in Berlin, see European Commission, *Bulletin of the European Union, 3–1999*. See also, generally, eg R Ackrill *The Common Agricultural Policy* (2000) Sheffield Academic Press, Sheffield, pp 115–131; and M Cardwell *The European Model of Agriculture* (2004) Oxford University Press, Oxford, pp 57–129.

3   Council Regulation (EC) 1259/1999, OJ 1999 L 160/73, art 3.

4   See, eg, European Commission *Mid-term Review of the Common Agricultural Policy* COM(2002)394, 2 and 8–9; and European Commission *Report from the Commission to the Council on the Application of the System of Cross-compliance* COM(2007)147, 2.

5   European Commission *Mid-term Review of the Common Agricultural Policy* COM(2002)394, 20.

6   The criteria governing 'de-coupled income support' are set out in the Uruguay Round Agreement on Agriculture, Annex 2, para 6. In particular, no production is required in order to receive such support (on which aspect see the decision of the Appellate Body in *United States – Subsidies on Upland Cotton* (2005) WT/DS267/AB/R). On the Uruguay Round Agreement on Agriculture see, generally, eg, JA McMahon *The WTO Agreement on Agriculture: a Commentary* (2006) Oxford University Press, Oxford; and on the compatibility of European Community direct payments with world trade commitments see, eg, A Swinbank and R Tranter 'Decoupling EU Farm Support: Does the New Single Payment Scheme Fit within the Green Box?' (2005) 6 *Estey Centre Journal of International Law and Trade Policy* 47–61.

7   See, eg, Deloitte Press Releases, 'Farm Incomes Set for Roller Coaster Ride, Warns Deloitte', 14 October 2004; and 'Farmers Predicted to Produce Food at Loss', 3 November 2005.

EUROPEAN COMMUNITY LEGISLATION

Introduction

52.2 As indicated, the most significant feature of the Mid-term Review was reform of the legislation which governs direct payments to farmers. With limited exceptions, most direct payments have been channelled into the Single Payment Scheme, characterised in the European Community legislation as 'income support'[1]. In accordance with the general rule, the Single Payment Scheme has been implemented in the United Kingdom as from 1 January 2005[2]; and it is apprehended to permit farmers to refocus on producing for the market, free from any distortions created by the pre-existing plethora of support schemes. As highlighted in the policy documentation, since receipt is not dependent upon any particular form of production or, indeed, production at all, farmers should enjoy the flexibility to respond to consumer demands[3]. However, while the Single Payment Scheme formed the centre piece of the reforms, it is vital to note that they also introduced general rules (such as those on cross-compliance), which cover all direct payments, not just those under the umbrella of the Single Payment Scheme.

The European Community legislation considered will be that applicable in the fifteen 'old' Member States.

1   Council Regulation (EC) 1782/2003, OJ 2003 L 270/1, art 1. For the direct payments which remain outside the Single Payment Scheme see para 52.13.
2   Council Regulation (EC) 1782/2003, OJ 2003 L 270/1, art 156(2)(d). Member States were granted the option to delay implementation until either 1 January 2006 or 1 January 2007, but the United Kingdom did not avail itself of this option: art 71.
3   See, eg, European Commission *Mid-term Review of the Common Agricultural Policy* COM(2002)394, 19. It is this breaking of the link with production that gives rise to the expression 'de-coupled' support, as found, for example, in the Uruguay Round Agreement on Agriculture (Annex 2, para 6).

General rules: outline

52.3 Turning first to the general rules, four aspects may be examined, namely:

(a)   statutory definitions;
(b)   cross-compliance;
(c)   modulation; and
(d)   artificiality[1].

All have the capacity to impact materially upon the landlord and tenant relationship.

1   The European Community legislative framework also provides general rules to govern the integrated administration and control system: Council Regulation (EC) 1782/2003, OJ 2003 L 270/1, arts 17–27. For national implementation in the United Kingdom see the Common Agricultural Policy Single Payment and Support Schemes (Integrated Administration and Control System) Regulations 2005, SI 2005/218. These detailed rules are outside the scope of this work; but it may be noted that their application to cross-compliance has proved controversial: see, eg, European Commission *Report from the Commission to the Council on the Application of the System of Cross-compliance* COM(2007)147. See, generally, eg, J Moody and W Neville *Mid Term Review: a Practical Guide* (2004) Burges Salmon, Bristol, pp 106–112.

General rules: statutory definitions

52.4 For the purposes of implementing the European Community legislation on direct payments, Council Regulation (EC) 1782/2003 provides specific definitions of 'farmer', 'holding' and 'agricultural activity'; and their interaction with national definitions in the 1986 Act and the 1995 Act may, on occasion, prove difficult.

A 'farmer' is defined as 'a natural or legal person, or a group of natural or legal persons, whatever legal status is granted to the group and its members by national law, whose holding is situated within Community territory ... and who exercises an agricultural activity'[1].

In turn, a holding is defined as 'all the production units managed by a farmer situated within the territory of the same Member State'[2]; and 'agricultural activity' is defined as 'the production, rearing or growing of agricultural products including harvesting, milking, breeding animals and keeping animals for farming purposes, or maintaining the land in good agricultural and environmental condition'[3].

These definitions in the European Community legislation would seem to differ from agricultural holdings legislation in two material respects. First, art 2(b) of Council Regulation 1782/2003 makes reference to 'all the production units managed by a farmer situated within the territory of the same Member State'. Accordingly, it would seem clear that, where a farmer manages production units in one or more of England, Northern Ireland, Scotland and Wales, those production units comprise the same holding for the purposes of the European Community legislation (as has long been the case with milk quotas). However, it would be rare indeed if they were to comprise the same holding for the purposes of landlord and tenant legislation[4].

Second, it is very evident that the definition of 'agricultural activity' extends beyond the definition of 'agriculture' as found in s 96(1) of the Agricultural Holdings Act 1986 (AHA 1986) and s 38(1) of the Agricultural Tenancies Act 1995 (ATA 1995)[5]. Not least, it covers also the maintenance of land in good agricultural and environmental condition, without any obligation to engage in production[6].

[1]   Council Regulation (EC) 1782/2003, OJ 2003 L 270/1, art 2(a). The definition would seem apt, therefore, to include companies and partnerships.
[2]   Council Regulation (EC) 1782/2003, OJ 2003 L 270/1, art 2(b). This wording is not unlike that found earlier in the milk quota legislation: see, eg, prior to its repeal, Council Regulation (EEC) 3950/92, OJ 1992 L 405/1, art 9(d), as amended by Council Regulation (EEC) 1560/93, OJ 1993 L 154/30 (and, for interpretation of the term 'holding' by the European Court of Justice (ECJ) in the context of milk quotas, see, eg, Case 5/88 *Wachauf v Germany* [1989] ECR 2609). It is of interest that the term 'production unit' is retained notwithstanding that production is not required in order to receive the Single Farm Payment.
[3]   Council Regulation (EC) 1782/2003, OJ 2003 L 270/1, art 2(c).
[4]   For the position where a farming enterprise operates in more than one Member State see Case C-463/93 *Katholische Kirchengemeinde St Martinus Elten v Landwirtschaftskammer Rheinland* [1997] ECR I-255 (relating to milk quotas).
[5]   See paras 19.6 and 3.23.
[6]   On this aspect see, generally, eg L Bodiguel and M Cardwell 'Evolving Definitions of 'Agriculture' for an Evolving Agriculture?' [2005] *Conveyancer* 419–446; and see further para 52.26.

General rules: cross-compliance

52.5 In the case of all direct payments, receipt is dependent upon observance of cross-compliance obligations as stipulated in the European Community legislation. In consequence, there is great incentive for farmers to tailor their farming practices so as to meet this criterion for European Community support. The cross-compliance obligations comprise:

(a)   statutory management requirements;

(b)   a requirement to maintain all agricultural land in good agricultural and environmental condition; and

(c)   an obligation to maintain land under permanent pasture[1].

The statutory management requirements relate to: public, animal and plant health; the environment; and animal welfare. They have been phased in over three years, the final tranche becoming applicable as from 1 January 2007; and the detailed requirements are listed in Annex III to Council Regulation (EC) 1782/2003[2].

By contrast, the minimum requirements for good agricultural and environmental condition are defined by the Member States, at national or regional level, taking into account the specific characteristics of the areas concerned, including soil and climatic condition, existing farming systems, land use, crop rotation, farming practices and farm structures. Member States must, however, define these minimum requirements on the basis of a European Community framework, set out in Annex IV to Council Regulation (EC) 1782/2003. The framework covers four issues:

 (i)   soil erosion, with standards imposed in relation to minimum soil cover, minimum land management reflecting site-specific conditions and the retention of terraces;

 (ii)   soil organic matter, with standards imposed in relation to crop rotation, where applicable, and arable stubble management;

(iii)   soil structure, with standards imposed in relation to appropriate machinery use; and

(iv)   a minimum level of maintenance, with standards imposed in relation to minimum livestock stocking rates and/or appropriate regimes, the protection of permanent pasture, the retention of landscape features, including, where appropriate, the prohibition of the grubbing up of olive trees, the avoidance of encroachment of unwanted vegetation on agricultural land and the maintenance of olive groves in good vegetative condition[3].

The cross-compliance requirements are currently laid down in England by the Common Agricultural Policy Single Payment and Support Schemes (Cross-compliance) (England) Regulations 2005[4] and in Wales by the Common Agricultural Policy Single Payment and Support Schemes (Cross Compliance) (Wales) Regulations 2004[5]. A matter of some importance is that, more onerous obligations having been imposed in England than in the other regions of the United Kingdom, challenge has been initiated against the original English regulations, on the basis that they were discriminatory[6].

Additionally, in the case of old Member States, such as the United Kingdom, land which was under permanent pasture as at 15 May 2003 must be maintained under permanent pasture[7]. For the purposes of the legislation, 'permanent pasture' is defined as 'land used to grow grasses or other herbaceous forage naturally (self-seeded) or through cultivation (sown) and that is not included in the crop rotation of the holding for five years or longer'[8]. By way of exception, Member States can choose in duly justified circumstances to dispense with this obligation, provided that they take action

965

to prevent any significant decrease in their total permanent pasture area[9]. Under the detailed rules, this would mean a decrease of more than 10% as compared with the ratio of land under permanent pasture in 2003[10]. By way of further exception, the obligation to maintain land under permanent pasture does not apply where the land is to be afforested, so long as the afforestation is compatible with the environment (and, in this context, the afforestation must not be plantations of Christmas trees or fast-growing species cultivated in the short term)[11].

[1]   Council Regulation (EC) 1782/2003, OJ 2003 L 270/1, arts 3–9.
[2]   These detailed requirements are as follows:
      (1) Council Directive 79/409/EEC (Wild Birds Directive), OJ 1979 L 103/1, arts 3, 4(1), (2), (4), 5, 7 and 8);
      (2) Council Directive 80/68/EEC (protection against groundwater pollution), OJ 1980 L 20/43, arts 4 and 5;
      (3) Council Directive 86/278/EEC (use of sewage sludge in agriculture), OJ 1986 L 181/ 6, art 3;
      (4) Council Directive 91/676/EEC (Nitrates Directive), OJ 1991 L 375/1, arts 4 and 5;
      (5) Council Directive 92/43/EEC (Habitats Directive), OJ 1992 L 206/7, arts 6, 13, 15 and 22(b);
      (6) Council Directive 92/102/EEC (identification and registration of animals), OJ 1992 L 355/32, arts 3, 4 and 5;
      (7) Commission Regulation (EC) 2629/97 (identification and registration of bovine animals), OJ 1997 L 354/19, arts 6 and 8;
      (8) Regulation (EC) 1760/2000 of the European Parliament and of the Council (identification and registration of bovine animals and the labelling of beef and beef products), OJ 2000 L 204/1, arts 4 and 7;
      (9) Council Regulation (EC) 21/2004 (identification and registration of ovine and caprine animals), OJ 2004 L 5/8, arts 3, 4 and 5;
      (10) Council Directive 91/414/EEC (the placing of plant protection products on the market), OJ 1991 L 230/1, art 3;
      (11) Council Directive 96/22/EC (prohibition of the use in stockfarming of certain substances having a hormonal or thyrostatic action and of beta-agonists), OJ 1996 L 125/3, arts 3, 4, 5 and 7;
      (12) Regulation (EC) 178/2002 of the European Parliament and of the Council (Food Law Regulation), OJ 2002 L 131/1, arts 14, 15, 17(1), 18, 19 and 20;
      (13) Regulation (EC) 999/2001 of the European Parliament and of the Council (prevention, control and eradication of certain transmissible spongiform encephalopathies), OJ 2001 L 147/1, arts 7, 11, 12, 13 and 15;
      (14) Council Directive 85/511/EEC (control of foot-and-mouth disease), OJ 1985 L 315/11, art 3;
      (15) Council Directive 92/119/EEC (control of certain animal diseases together with specific measures relating to swine vesicular disease), OJ 1992 L 62/69, art 3;
      (16) Council Directive 2000/75/EC (control and eradication of bluetongue), OJ 2000 L 327/74, art 3;
      (17) Council Directive 91/629/EEC (minimum standards for the protection of calves), OJ 1991 L 340/28, arts 3 and 4;
      (18) Council Directive 91/630/EEC (minimum standards for the protection of pigs) OJ 1991 L 340/33, arts 3 and 4(1); and
      (19) Council Directive 98/58/EC (protection of animals kept for farming purposes), OJ 1998 L 221/23, art 4.

[3]   Council Regulation (EC) 1782/2003, OJ 2003 L 270/1, Annex IV (as amended by Council Regulation (EC) 864/2004, OJ 2004 L 161/48).
[4]   SI 2005/3459 (as amended by SI 2006/3254 and SI 2007/2003). See further para 52.19.
[5]   S 2004/3280 (W.284) (as amended by SI 2006/2831 (W.252) and SI 2007/970 (W.87)). See further para 52.19.
[6]   *R (on the application of Horvath) v Secretary of State for the Environment, Food and Rural Affairs* [2007] EWCA Civ 620, [2007] All ER (D) 355 (Jun) (for the English legislation concerned see the Common Agricultural Policy Single Payment and Support

Schemes (Cross Compliance) (England) Regulations 2004, SI 2004/3196, which were in all material aspects similar to the current legislation).
7   Council Regulation (EC) 1782/2003, OJ 2003 l 270/1, art 5(2) (as amended by Council Regulation (EC) 583/2004, OJ 2004 L 91/1).
8   Commission Regulation (EC) 796/2004, OJ 2004 L 141/18, art 2(2). See also Commission Regulation (EC) 795/2004, OJ 2004 L 141/1, art 2(e) (as amended by Commission Regulation (EC) 1974/2004, OJ 2004 L 345/85.
9   Council Regulation (EC) 1782/2003, OJ 2003 L 270/1, art 5(2).
10 Commission Regulation (EC) 796/2004, OJ 2004 L 141/18, art 3(2).
11 Council Regulation (EC) 1782/2003, OJ 2003 L 270/1, art 5(2).

General rules: modulation

52.6 Under the European Community legislation a proportion of all direct payments to farmers is to be compulsorily deducted each year, so as to increase the level of financing for rural development measures[1]. This transfer of resources, known as 'modulation', is intended to redress, at least partially, the disproportionately low percentage of overall Common Agricultural Policy expenditure devoted to rural development[2].

As a general rule, the deduction throughout the Member States commenced at 3% in 2005, rose to 4% in 2006 and will then remain at 5% for the period 2007 to 2012[3]. However, in the United Kingdom the position was somewhat complicated by the fact that, prior to the Mid-term Review, the decision had already been taken to implement voluntary modulation, and at rates higher than those which were compulsorily introduced under the Mid-term Review: a 4.5% rate was to be applicable for both 2005 and 2006[4]. To meet this difficulty, continued voluntary modulation was expressly sanctioned by European Community provision[5]; and in both England and Wales advantage was taken of this provision[6].

Notwithstanding these measures, the United Kingdom Government displayed further appetite for significant transfers of direct payments to fuel rural development[7]; and in 2007 it was agreed at European Community level that, where a Member State was already applying additional reductions, they could impose voluntary modulation up to a maximum of 20%[8]. Moreover, the rates could be regionally differentiated according to objective criteria if the Member State was operating the Single Payment Scheme on a regional basis, as has been the policy choice for the United Kingdom[9]. The detailed rules will be considered later[10]. For the time being, however, it may be noted that farmers in England will be subject to 14% voluntary modulation by 2009[11], this being in addition to compulsory modulation[12]. Accordingly, they will be subject in total to a 19% deduction, whereas, for example, a farmer in France will be subject to only a 5% deduction. This imbalance has the potential to create distortions in competition, as is evident on the face of the European Community legislation. For example, Member States applying voluntary modulation and the European Commission are to monitor closely the impact of the measures, 'in particular as regards the economic situation of the farms, taking into account the need to avoid unjustified unequal treatment between farmers'[13]. That said, for United Kingdom producers to show discrimination may be no easy task; and this will be especially so in circumstances where all producers within a Member State are subject to the same constraints on the basis of objective criteria[14]. Nonetheless, the extent of such reductions in direct payments cannot fail to impact heavily upon freehold owners and tenants alike.

1   Council Regulation (EC) 1782/2003, OJ 2003 L 270/1, art 10. For the legislation now governing rural development see Council Regulation (EC) 1698/2005, OJ 2005 L 277/1; and para 52.15.
2   Under the Agenda 2000 reforms it was projected that only 4,370 million Euros would be spent on rural development and ancillary measures by 2006, as opposed to 37,290 million Euros on other Common Agricultural Policy costs: European Commission, *Bulletin of the European Union, 3–1999*, at I.12.
3   Council Regulation (EC) 1782/2003, OJ 2003 L 270/1, art 10(1). An additional amount of aid has the effect of reimbursing farmers for any modulation on up to 5,000 Euros of direct payments: Council Regulation (EC) 1782/2003 L 270/1, art 12.
4   For the European Community legislation see Council Regulation (EC) 1259/1999, OJ 1999 L 160/113, arts 4–5. For the English legislation see the Common Agricultural Policy Support Schemes (Modulation) Regulations 2000, SI 2000/3127 (as amended by SI 2001/3686 and SI 2004/2330); and for the Welsh legislation see the Common Agricultural Policy Support Schemes (Modulation) (Wales) Regulations 2000, SI 2000/3294 (W.216) (as amended by SI 2001/3680 (W.301) and SI 2004/2662 (W.233)).
5   Commission Regulation (EC) 1655/2004, OJ 2004 L 298/3.
6   For the detailed rules as implemented in England and Wales see para 52.22; but it may be noted for the time being that in England the overall rate (combining both the compulsory and voluntary elements) amounted to 5% in 2005 and 10% in 2006.
7   Policy documentation had for some time favoured an increase in the rate of modulation to 20%: see, eg Policy Commission on the Future of Farming and Food, *Farming and Food: a Sustainable Future (Curry Report)* (2002) Cabinet Office, London, p 77.
8   Council Regulation (EC) 378/2007, OJ 2007 L 95/1. This option was also available where a Member State was granted a derogation (under art 70(4a) of Council Regulation (EC) 1698/2005, OJ 2005 L 277/1) from the requirement to co-finance European Community support.
9   Council Regulation (EC) 378/2007, OJ 2007 L 95/1, art 3(1). For operation of the Single Payment Scheme on a regional basis, see para 52.9.
10 See para 52.22.
11 Hansard (HC) 29 March 2007, Vol 458, Col 131WS (Written Statement: Secretary of State for Environment, Food and Rural Affairs).
12 Council Regulation (EC) 378/2007, OJ 2007 L 95/1, Preamble (1): '[r]eductions of direct payments applied in respect of voluntary modulation should be additional to those resulting from the application of compulsory modulation provided for in Article 10 of Regulation (EC) No 1782/2003'.
13 Council Regulation (EC) 378/2007, OJ 2007 L 95/1, art 5.
14 See, eg, Case C-292/97 *Karlsson* [2000] ECR I-2737.

General rules: artificiality

52.7 The European Community legislation provides that 'no payment shall be made in favour of beneficiaries for whom it is established that they artificially created the conditions required for obtaining such payments with a view to obtaining advantage contrary to the objectives of [the individual support scheme]'[1]. This provision reflects concern on the part of the European Community institutions that assets created under the umbrella of the Common Agricultural Policy should not become the subject of speculation. For example, in the context of milk quotas, the ECJ has emphasised that producers could not 'expect that a common organisation of the market would confer on them a commercial advantage which did not derive from their occupational activity'[2]. Likewise, it has also emphasised 'the need to prevent a reference quantity from being claimed for the sole purpose of deriving a purely financial advantage therefrom'[3].

More recently, the ECJ has generated judicial momentum in addressing 'abusive practices by economic operators'[4]. These may be characterised as 'transactions carried out not in the context of normal commercial operations, but solely for the purpose of wrongfully obtaining advantages provided for by Community law'[5]. To constitute an abusive practice, two elements must be satisfied[6]. First, notwithstanding formal observance of the legislative conditions, the transaction concerned must objectively result in the accrual of an advantage whose grant would be contrary to the purposes of European Community law: in other words, the commercial operation was not carried out for an economic purpose. Second, subjectively, there must be an intention to obtain such an advantage. With regard to this second element, it is the responsibility of the national court to determine the real substance and significance of the transactions concerned. In this regard, it may take account of their purely artificial nature and the links of a legal, economic and/or personal nature between the operators involved[7].

Accordingly, both landlords and tenants should ensure that their dealings are not tainted by any artificiality; and this imperative is only reinforced by the fact that the ECJ has shown a willingness to extend its jurisprudence on abusive practices from taxation to the receipt of European Community support by farmers.

1   Council Regulation (EC) 1782/2003, OJ 2003 L 270/1, art 29.
2   Case C-44/89 *Von Deetzen v Hauptzollamt Oldenburg* [1991] ECR I-5119 at I-5155.
3   Case C-236/90 *Maier v Freistaat Bayern* [1992] ECR I-4483 at I-4511 (again a milk quota case).
4   See, generally, eg, HL McCarthy 'Abuse of Rights: the Effect of the Doctrine on VAT Planning' [2007] *British Tax Review* 160–174. See also, in the national court, *WHA Ltd v Revenue and Customs Commissioners* [2007] EWCA Civ 728.
5   Case C-255/02 *Halifax plc v Customs and Excise Comrs* [2006] Ch 387, para 69 (a VAT case).
6   See, eg, Case C-110/99 *Emsland-Stärke GmbH v Hauptzollamt Hamburg-Jonas* [2000] ECR I-11569, at I-11612–11613; Case C-255/02 *Halifax plc v Customs and Excise Comrs* [2006] Ch 387, paras 74–75: and Case C-196/04 *Cadbury Schweppes plc v Revenue and Customs Comrs* [2007] Ch 30, para 64 (a corporate tax case).
7   Case C-255/02 *Halifax plc v Customs and Excise Comrs* [2006] Ch 387, para 81.

Single Farm Payment: introduction

52.8 While these general rules apply to all direct payments, their greatest impact is in relation to the Single Payment Scheme, unquestionably the greatest innovation of the Mid-term Review. As has been seen, this scheme is characterised as income support. It is also apprehended to be decoupled from production, with consequent benefits in terms of permitting farmers to produce for the market and in terms of exemption from domestic support reduction commitments under the Uruguay Round Agreement on Agriculture. In addition, it forms part of an overall drive to achieve simplification of European Community legislation[1].

52.8   *Mid-term Review of the Common Agricultural Policy*

Against this policy background, it may be emphasised that the Single Payment Scheme already replaces the vast majority of earlier support schemes; and the intention is that it should become even more all-embracing[2]. For the time being, however, the support schemes included are those listed in Annex VI to Council Regulation (EC) 1782/2003[3]. In the case of the United Kingdom, the most significant are direct payments in the following sectors: arable crops; beef and veal; milk and milk products (dairy premium and additional payments); sheep and goats; and sugar[4].

[1]   See, eg, European Commission *Mid-term Review of the Common Agricultural Policy* COM(2002)394, 2 and 10; and European Commission *Simplification and Better Regulation for the Common Agricultural Policy* COM(2005)509.

[2]   See, eg, European Commission *Mid-term Review of the Common Agricultural Policy* COM(2002)394, 19–20. By way of example, following reform of their regime, fruit and vegetables are also to be comprised in the Single Payment Scheme: IP/07/810, CAP *Reform: Fruit and Vegetable Reform Will Raise Competitiveness, Promote Consumption, Ease Market Crises and Improve Environmental Protection*, Brussels, 12 June 2007 (available at http://europa.eu/rapid).

[3]   OJ 2003 L 270/1 (as last amended by Council Regulation (EC) 2013/2006, OJ 2006 L 384/13).

[4]   As a general rule, the dairy premium and additional payments, as introduced by the Mid-term Review, have become comprised in the Single Payment Scheme as from 2007: Council Regulation (EC) 1782/2003, OJ 2003 L 270/1, art 50. (For the provisions implementing the dairy premium and additional payments see arts 95–97). However, where the Single Payment Scheme is implemented on a regional basis, then the decision could be taken to comprise them within the Single Payment Scheme ab initio: art 62. This course of action has been adopted in England and in Wales: the Common Agricultural Policy Single Payment and Support Schemes Regulations 2005, SI 2005/219, reg 7; and the Common Agricultural Policy Single Payment and Support Schemes (Wales) Regulations 2005, SI 2005/360 (W.29), reg 7 (and see further para 52.18). It may also be noted that, even though certain of the support schemes in principle became comprised within the Single Payment Scheme, the European Community legislation permitted Member States to retain varying levels of payment coupled to production. In particular, Member States could opt to retain coupled to production up to 25% of arable area payments, up to 50% of sheep and goat payments and up to 100% of suckler cow premiums: Council Regulation (EC) 1782/2003, OJ 2003 L 270/1, arts 64–68. This option has not been exercised in the United Kingdom. In addition, Member States were granted the option to retain up to 10% of national ceilings in any of the sectors comprised within the Single Payment Scheme so as to make additional payments for specific types of farming which are important for the protection or enhancement of the environment or for improving the quality and marketing of agricultural products: art 69. Again this option has not been exercised in England and Wales, but in Scotland it was exercised so as to introduce the Beef Calf Scheme: the Common Agricultural Policy Single Farm Payment and Support Schemes (Scotland) Regulations 2005, SI 2005/143, regs 19–25.

Single Farm Payment: allocation

52.9   Under the European Community legislation, allocation of the Single Farm Payment could be made either nationally on an historic basis or on a regional basis.

In the former case, the allocation was based upon the total amount of payments which the farmer had received under the Annex VI support schemes, averaged over a three-year reference period[1]. The reference period covered the calendar years 2000, 2001 and 2002[2]. Specific provisions conferred access to the payment entitlements where the farmer received the holding or part of the

970

holding by way of actual or anticipated inheritance[3]; or where the farmer received a payment entitlement from the national reserve or by transfer[4]. Further specific provisions addressed the position where a farmer had changed his legal status or denomination prior to the date by which application forms were to be lodged in the first year of the application of the Single Payment Scheme[5]; or where there had been a 'merger' or 'scission' prior to that date[6].

While, as a general rule, allocation would be made nationally on an historic basis, Member States could opt in the alternative to allocate the Single Farm Payment on a regional basis[7]. If this option was implemented, Member States enjoyed further discretion. They could permit the historic basis to apply; or, in duly justified cases and according to objective criteria, they could divide all, or some, of the Single Farm Payments falling within a particular regional ceiling between all the farmers whose holdings were located in that region[8]. Any such allocation was to be made by dividing the regional ceiling by the number of eligible hectares, established at regional level[9]; and, for this purpose, 'eligible hectare' was defined as 'any agricultural area of the holding taken up by arable land and permanent pasture except areas under permanent crops, forests or used for non agricultural activities'[10]. Accordingly, farmers would receive a flat-rate payment per eligible hectare.

In the United Kingdom allocation has been made on a regional basis. This aspect will be considered in greater detail later[11]. For the time being, however, it may be noted that in the case of Wales, historic entitlement was retained (under the general rule), whereas in the case of England, the decision was taken to opt for a flat-rate payment, with this being phased in over the period 2005–2012.

In addition, two distinct forms of payment were allocated within the Single Payment Scheme: payment entitlements subject to special conditions[12]; and set-aside entitlements[13].

The former are of relatively slight importance in the United Kingdom, in that they address the situation of farmers who were granted specified payments in the livestock sector, but who had no historic area in the reference period, or whose entitlement per hectare would be higher than 5,000 Euros[14]. In other words, they are primarily concerned with intensive livestock operations, such as the feed lots more commonly found in the United States.

Set-aside entitlements, by contrast, are of wider importance; and, while they fall under the Single Payment Scheme, they are subject to separate (yet similar) rules. Moreover, these rules vary depending upon whether the Single Payment Scheme is being operated on an historic or on a flat-rate basis[15]. If it is being operated on an historic basis, the total number of set-aside entitlements to be allocated to the farmer equalled the average number of hectares that he compulsorily set aside over the 2000–2002 reference period[16]. If the Single Payment Scheme is being operated on a flat-rate basis, the number of set-aside entitlements was established by multiplying the amount of eligible land declared by a farmer in the first year of the Single Payment Scheme by a set-aside rate. The set-aside rate was calculated by multiplying the basic 10%

compulsory set-aside rate by the proportion of eligible land in the region which received arable area payments in the reference period[17]. For the purposes of the rules governing set-aside, eligible land enjoys a separate definition, to be distinguished from that for 'eligible hectares' under the general rules governing the Single Payment Scheme[18]. By way of derogation from that general definition, a 'hectare eligible for set-aside entitlement' means 'any agricultural area of the holding taken up by arable land, except areas which at the date provided for the area aid applications for 2003 were under permanent crops, forests or used for non-agricultural activities or under permanent pasture'[19]. However, exceptions are made for land set aside under specified agri-environmental schemes or afforested as a result of an application made after 28 June 1995[20]. Accordingly, 'hectares eligible for set-aside entitlements' extend beyond areas that had been eligible for arable area payments, so as to include, for example, temporary grass and fodder crops. As shall be seen, the fact that more land has been brought within the set-aside scheme has resulted in a lower set-aside rate in England[21].

Where the Single Payment Scheme is being operated on a flat-rate basis, as in England, no allocation was made to farmers declaring less hectares eligible for set-aside entitlements than would have been required to produce 92 tonnes of cereals on the basis of regional yields in the year before the year of application of the Single Payment Scheme (as adjusted to take account of the lower set-aside rate)[22].

Land set aside must likewise be maintained in good agricultural and environmental condition[23]. However, although it may be subject to rotation, it shall not as a general rule be used for agricultural purposes and shall not produce any crop for commercial purposes[24]. That said, in this regard two major exemptions from the set-aside obligation apply:

(a) where the entire holding is managed organically for the totality of its production; and

(b) where the land set aside is used for the provision of materials for the manufacture within the European Community of products not primarily intended for human or animal consumption[25].

Energy crops can be grown on land set aside; but, if that course of action is adopted, an application cannot also be made for aid for energy crops[26].

---

[1] Council Regulation (EC) 1782/2003, OJ 2003 L 270/1, art 37(1). Where a farmer commenced an agricultural activity during the reference period, the average was based on the payments that he was granted in the calendar year or years during which he exercised the agricultural activity: art 37(2).

[2] Council Regulation (EC) 1782/2003, OJ 2003 L 270/1, art 38.

[3] Council Regulation (EC) 1782/2003, OJ 2003 L 270/1, art 33(1)(b).

[4] Council Regulation (EC) 1782/2003, OJ 2003 L 270/1, art 33(1)(c). For the operation of the national reserve, see art 42 (the national reserve could not amount to more than 3% of total allocations); and for transfers, see art 46 and para 52.12.

[5] Council Regulation (EC) 1782/2003, OJ 2003 L 270/1, art 33(2). The cut-off date was supplied by Commission Regulation (EC) 795/2004, OJ 2004 L 141/1, art 14(2).

[6] Council Regulation (EC) 1782/2003, OJ 2003 L 270/1, art 33(3) (and see, for the cut-off date, Commission Regulation (EC) 795/2004, OJ 2004 L 141/1, art 15(3)). A 'merger' is the merger of two or more separate farmers; and a 'scission' is the scission of one farmer

into at least two new separate farmers or the scission of one farmer into at least one new separate farmer (for the detailed rules see Commission Regulation (EC) 795/2004, OJ 2004 L 141/1, art 15(1) and (2)).

7   Council Regulation (EC) 1782/2003, OJ 2003 L 270/1, art 58.
8   Council Regulation (EC) 1782/2003, OJ 2003 L 270/1, art 59(1).
9   Council Regulation (EC) 1782/2003, OJ 2003 L 270/1, art 59(2).
10   Council Regulation (EC) 1782/2003, OJ 2003 L 270/1, art 44(2). For more detailed consideration of this definition see para 52.10.
11   See para 52.17.
12   Council Regulation (EC) 1782/2003, OJ 2003 L 270/1, arts 47–49.
13   Council Regulation (EC) 1782/2003, OJ 2003 L 270/1, arts 53–57. It may be noted that, in light of tightening supplies, it was proposed in July 2007 that a zero set-aside rate be applied to autumn 2007 and spring 2008 sowings: IP07/1101, *Cereals: Proposals to Set at Zero the Set-aside Rate for Autumn 2007 and Spring 2008 Sowings*, Brussels, 16 July 2007 (available at http://europa.eu/rapid).
14   Council Regulation (EC) 1782/2003, OJ 2003 L 270/1, art 48. The specified livestock payments are set out at art 47. They include, in particular: slaughter premium; beef special premium and suckler cow premium, where the farmer was exempted from the stocking rate requirement on the basis that he had not more than 15 livestock units (unless he had applied for extensification premium); and dairy premium and additional payments. For fuller consideration of payment entitlements subject to special conditions, and the difficulties that arise on their implementation in England, see, eg, J Moody and W Neville, *Mid Term Review: a Practical Guide* (2004) Burges Salmon, Bristol, pp 129–132.
15   The historic basis is applicable either under the general rule or, alternatively, where the Single Payment Scheme is operated regionally but no decision has been taken to implement the flat-rate basis of allocation (as in Wales). The flat-rate basis is applicable only where the Member State opts to implement the Single Payment Scheme regionally and to implement the flat-rate basis (as is being phased in in England).
16   Council Regulation (EC) 1782/2003, OJ 2003 L 270/1, art 53.
17   Council Regulation (EC) 1782/2003, OJ 2003 L 270/1, art 63(2).
18   For the general definition see Council Regulation (EC) 1782/2003, OJ 2003 L 270/1, art 44(2).
19   Council Regulation (EC) 1782/2003, OJ 2003 L 270/1, art 54(2).
20   For the agri-environmental and afforestation schemes in question see respectively Council Regulation (EC) 1257/1999, OJ 1999 L 160/80, arts 22–24 and art 31.
21   See para 52.20.
22   Council Regulation (EC) 1782/2003, OJ 2003 L 270/1, art 63(2).
23   Council Regulation (EC) 1782/2003, OJ 2003 L 270/1, art 56(1).
24   Council Regulation (EC) 1782/2003, OJ 2003 L 270/1, art 56(1) and (2).
25   Council Regulation (EC) 1782/2003, OJ 2003 L 270/1, art 55.
26   Council Regulation (EC) 1782/2003, OJ 2003 L 270/1, art 90; and see para 52.13.

Single Farm Payment: unlocking payment entitlements

52.10 Where a farmer has been allocated a payment entitlement under the Single Payment Scheme, it can only be unlocked when matched against 'eligible hectares'[1]. Accordingly, there is a 'link' to land, with landlord and tenant implications[2].

For this purpose, 'eligible hectares' is defined as 'any agricultural area of the holding taken up by arable land and permanent pasture except areas under permanent crops, forests or used for non-agricultural activities'[3].

In turn, 'arable land' is defined as 'land cultivated for crop production and land under set-aside, or maintained in good agricultural and environmental condition ... or land under greenhouses or under fixed or mobile cover'[4]; 'permanent pasture' is defined as 'land used to grow grasses or other herbaceous forage naturally (self-seeded) or through cultivation (sown) and that is not included in the crop rotation of the holding for five years or longer'[5]; and 'permanent crops' are defined as 'non-rotational crops other then permanent pasture that occupy the land for five years or longer and yield repeated harvests [including specified forms of nursery], with the exception of multiannual crops and the nurseries of such multiannual crops'[6]. Multiannual crops include artichokes, asparagus, raspberries, blackberries, short rotation coppice and miscanthus sinensis[7].

Accordingly, the definition of 'eligible hectares' is very broad indeed, apt to cover even land that is kept in good agricultural and environmental condition. Production, therefore, is not a pre-requisite.

Moreover, where land is in crop production, the range of crops which may render land eligible is also very broad; and two categories may be highlighted. First, it is possible to match payment entitlements against land used to grow certain energy crops, such as short rotation coppice and miscanthus sinensis. Second, in England (but not in Wales), it is possible to match payment entitlements against land used to grow a wide range of fruit, vegetables and potatoes (other than starch potatoes)[8]. The reason for this is that where, as in England, the Single Farm Payment Scheme is implemented regionally on a flat-rate basis, the Member State may, by way of derogation[9], also permit farmers to match payment entitlements against land used to grow fruit and vegetables as referred to in art 1(2) of Council Regulation (EC) 2200/96[10] and art 1(2) of Council Regulation (EC) 2201/96[11]; and against land used to grow potatoes (other than starch potatoes, which are dealt with outside the Single Payment Scheme)[12]. Fruits and vegetables which benefit from this derogation include tomatoes, lettuce and carrots. That said, permanent crops are excluded, unless they fall within the multiannual crop exemption already mentioned. Thus, for example, apples and pears would be excluded; but the multiannual exemption would permit raspberries and blackberries to qualify. Such cropping is, however, placed subject to limitations at the level of the region and at the level of the individual farmer. At the level of the region, a ceiling has been imposed by reference to the average number of hectares used to grow the specified fruit, vegetables and potatoes over the period 2000–2002[13]. At the level of the individual farmer, authorisations for such cropping cannot exceed the number of hectares that were used for their production in 2003 (together with any further hectares granted by reason of hardship or through the national reserve)[14]. These authorisations attach to payment entitlements within the region concerned[15]. They also have the potential to be of considerable financial advantage, in that they allow farmers in England (and Northern Ireland) to produce a wide range of fruit, vegetables and potatoes with the benefit of income support, whereas in Scotland and Wales farmers enjoy no such benefit[16].

In addition, for an eligible hectare to unlock payment, it must be at the disposal of the farmer for a period of at least ten months, except in case of force majeure or exceptional circumstances[17]. The commencement date of the ten-month period may be a single date fixed for all farmers by the Member State, not earlier than 1 September of the calendar year preceding the year of lodging the Single Farm Payment application and not later than 30 April of the following calendar year; or, alternatively, the Member State may allow each farmer to choose their own commencement date within this fixed period. However, by amendment in 2005, Member States may authorise farmers to fix two different dates, where specific agricultural conditions so warrant[18].

Finally, and importantly, set-aside entitlements may only be matched against hectares eligible for set-aside entitlements[19]; and they shall be claimed before any other entitlement[20].

[1] Council Regulation (EC) 1782/2003, OJ 2003 L 270/1, arts 36 and 44(1).
[2] See, in particular, Council Regulation (EC) 1782/2003, OJ 2003 L 270/1, Preamble (30): '[t]he overall amount to which a farm is entitled should be split into parts (payment entitlements) and linked to a certain number of eligible hectares to be defined, in order to facilitate transfer of the premium rights. To avoid speculative transfers leading to the accumulation of payment entitlements without a corresponding agricultural basis, in granting aid, it is appropriate to provide for a link between entitlements and a certain number of eligible hectares, as well as the possibility of limiting the transfer of entitlements within a region'. For the landlord and tenant implications see para 52.25.
[3] Council Regulation (EC) 1782/2003, OJ 2003 L 270/1, art 44(2) (as indicated, this definition should be distinguished from that applicable in the context of set-aside, as found at art 54(2)). It may also be noted that 'eligible hectares' also include 'areas planted with hops or being under a temporary resting obligation or planted with bananas, or areas under olive trees': art 44(2) (as last amended by Council Regulation (EC) 2013/2006, OJ 2006 L 384/13). For what amount to 'non-agricultural activities' see para 52.21.
[4] Commission Regulation (EC) 796/2004, OJ 2004 L 141/18, art 2(1). See also Commission Regulation (EC) 795/2004, OJ 2004 L 141/1, art 2(b) (as amended by Commission Regulation (EC) 1974/2004, OJ 2004 L 345/85).
[5] Commission Regulation (EC) 796/2004, OJ 2004 L 141/18, art 2(2). See also Commission Regulation (EC) 795/2004, OJ 2004 L 141/1, art 2(e) (as amended by Commission Regulation (EC) 1974/2004, OJ 2004 L 345/85).
[6] Commission Regulation (EC) 795/2004, OJ 2004 L 141/1, art 2(c). The specified forms of nursery are set out in Commission Decision 2000/115/EC, OJ 2000 L 38/1, Annex I, G/05. They include nurseries for fruit trees and for forest trees (except where grown within woodland for the requirements of the holding itself) and commercial forest-tree nurseries.
[7] Commission Regulation (EC) 795/2004, OJ 2004 L 141/1, art 2(d).
[8] Because under the general rule it is not possible to match land used to grow such crops against payment entitlements, they are frequently termed 'negative list crops'. However, as indicated, these fruit and vegetables are to be brought under the umbrella of the Single Payment Scheme; and this reform will remove them from the 'negative list': IP/07/810, *CAP Reform: Fruit and Vegetable Reform Will Raise Competitiveness, Promote Consumption, Ease Market Crises and Improve Environmental Protection*, Brussels, 12 June 2007 (available at http://europa.eu/rapid).
[9] Council Regulation (EC) 1782/2003, OJ 2003 L 270/1, art 60 (as amended by Council Regulation (EC) 2012/2006, OJ 2006 L 384/8).
[10] OJ 1996 L 297/1.
[11] OJ 1996 L 297/29.
[12] For the provisions governing aid for starch potatoes see Council Regulation (EC) 1782/2003, OJ 2003 L 270/1, arts 93–94.
[13] Council Regulation (EC) 1782/2003, OJ 2003 L 270/1, art 60(2).
[14] Council Regulation (EC) 1782/2003, OJ 2003 L 270/1, art 60(3). Any surplus remaining within the regional ceiling was then allocated according to detailed rules, with priority accorded to farmers who had undertaken such production in 2004: art 60(4).
[15] Council Regulation (EC) 1782/2003, OJ 2003 L 270/1, art 60(7).
[16] An argument might be advanced that this opens the door for distortions of competition. Indeed, in the Preamble to Council Regulation (EC) 1782/2003, it is expressly stated that 'in order to avoid distortions of competition some products should be excluded from production on eligible land' [including, as a general rule, fruit, vegetables and potatoes (other than starch potatoes)]: Preamble (28). In the case of fruit and vegetables, any such distortions should soon be ended, as and when they are incorporated within the Single Payment Scheme.

17   Council Regulation (EC) 1782/2003, OJ 2003 L 270/1, art 44(3). For qualification as land at the 'disposal' of the farmer see para 52.25.
18   Council Regulation (EC) 1782/2003, OJ 2003 L 270/1, art 44(3); and Commission Regulation (EC) 795/2004, OJ 2004 L 141/1, art 24(2) (as amended by Commission Regulation (EC) 606/2005, OJ 2005 L 100/15). For the commencement date as implemented in England and Wales see para 52.21.
19   Council Regulation (EC) 1782/2003, OJ 2003 L 270/1, art 54(1).
20   Council Regulation (EC) 1782/2003, OJ 2003 L 270/1, art 54(6). This can give rise to serious problems, since, if the set-aside entitlements are not validly claimed, the entire Single Payment Scheme application may be jeopardised. Where a farmer has insufficient hectares eligible for set-aside entitlements to meet his set-aside obligation, guidance indicates that he need only claim against the reduced (or nil) number of hectares: see, eg, Rural Payments Agency and Department for Environment, Food and Rural Affairs *Set-aside Handbook and Guidance for England: 2006 Edition* (Rural Payments Agency and Department for Environment, Food and Rural Affairs, London), para 46.

Single Farm Payment: non-use

52.11 Payment entitlements that have not been used for a period of three years are to revert to the national reserve, except in cases of force majeure and exceptional circumstances[1]. Force majeure or exceptional circumstances are for these purposes defined, non-exhaustively, to include: the death of the farmer; long-term professional incapacity of the farmer; a severe natural disaster gravely affecting the agricultural land of the holding; the accidental destruction of livestock buildings on the holding; and an epizootic affecting part or all of the livestock of the farmer[2]. Further, payment entitlements received from the national reserve must be used during each of the five years starting from their allocation; and failure to do so results in their reversion back to the national reserve[3].

The fact that payment entitlements are not lost for three years (unless received from the national reserve) may provide some comfort for tenants who lack security, since, in the event that their tenancy comes to end, they are granted a period of grace either to find new eligible hectares against which they may match their entitlements or to dispose of them[4].

1   Council Regulation (EC) 1782/2003, OJ 2003 L 270/1, art 45. Comparison may be drawn with the milk quota legislation: see now Council Regulation (EC) 1788/2003, OJ 2003 L 270/123, art 15.
2   Council Regulation (EC) 1782/2003, OJ 2003 L 270/1, art 40(4).
3   Council Regulation (EC) 1782/2003, OJ 2003 L 270/1, art 42(8). This requirement is relaxed where an award from the national reserve resulted in a 'top-up' element of more than 20%. In such circumstances, non-use leads to loss of only the 'top-up' element, the payment entitlement then assuming normal status: Commission Regulation (EC) 795/2004, OJ 2004 L 141/1, art 6(3) (as amended by Commission Regulation (EC) 1291/2006, OJ 2006 L 236/20). It should be noted that there is no reversion back to the national reserve where the 'top-up' was 20% or less: Commission Regulation (EC) 795/2004, OJ 2004 L 141/1, art 6(3) (as amended by Commission Regulation (EC) 1291/2006, OJ 2006 L 236/20).
4   See, eg, J Moody and W Neville *Mid Term Review: a Practical Guide* (2004) Burges Salmon, Bristol, p 118.

Single Farm Payment: transfers

52.12 Under the European Community legislation provision is made for the transfer of payment entitlements[1]. Such transfers may occur at any time in the year; and it is for the transferor to inform the competent authority of the Member State within a period established by the Member State[2]. However, transfer may only occur in favour of another farmer established within the same Member State, except in the case of transfer by actual or anticipated inheritance (and, even in this case, the payment entitlements may only be used within the same Member State)[3]. Further, Member States may decide that payment entitlements may only be transferred within the same region[4]. As indicated, a theme expressly underpinning these provisions is the need to avoid 'speculative transfers'[5]; and, in this context, it may also be emphasised that transfers may only be made in favour of 'farmers'. That said, it has been seen that the demands made of a 'farmer' in terms of 'agricultural activity' are not onerous, it being sufficient to maintain the land in good agricultural and environmental condition. Nonetheless, there may be dangers in discounting these provisions too lightly, in that the ECJ has shown an increasingly robust attitude towards the requirement that those holding milk quota should be genuine producers[6].

Payment entitlements may be transferred by sale or by any other definitive transfer, with or without land[7]. By contrast, where the transfer is effected by lease or similar types of transactions, then the payment entitlements transferred must be accompanied by the transfer of an equivalent number of eligible hectares. In addition, there is a more general restriction on the transfer of payment entitlements without land. Except in the case of force majeure or exceptional circumstances[8], a farmer may only transfer his payment entitlements without land after he has used at least 80% of them during at least one calendar year or after he has voluntarily surrendered to the national reserve all the payment entitlements that he has not used in the first year of application of the Single Payment Scheme[9].

In the case of a sale (but not a lease) of entitlements, whether or not with land, Member States could, acting in compliance with the general principles of European Community law, decide that part of the payment entitlements sold should revert to the national reserve or that their unit value should be reduced in favour of the national reserve[10]. In the United Kingdom this discretion has not been exercised. If it were exercised, then care would be required to ensure that there was compliance with the general principles of European Community law: for example, the measure must be proportionate[11].

Importantly, there are restrictions on the transfer of payment entitlements received from the national reserve. In principle, these cannot be transferred for a period of five years from their allocation[12]. However, ab initio, an exception was made in the case of transfer by actual or anticipated inheritance[13]; and, more recently, this exception has been extended to cases of merger and scission[14]. There are also restrictions on the transfer of payment entitlements subject to special conditions. If their full benefit is to be preserved, all such payment entitlements must be transferred to the transferee[15].

---

1   Council Regulation (EC) 1782/2003, OJ 2003 L 270/1, art 46.
2   Commission Regulation (EC) 795/2004, OJ 2004 L 141/1, art 25.
3   Council Regulation (EC) 1782/2003, OJ 2003 L 270/1, art 46(1). It is possible that guidance as to what constitutes 'inheritance' may be sought by analogy from milk quota cases: see, eg, Case C-44/89 *Von Deetzen v Hauptzollamt Oldenburg* [1991] ECR I-5119.

What would seem tolerably clear, in any event, is that the ECJ would be reluctant to give more than general guidance, leaving detailed consideration of particular instances to national courts: at I-5160. See also Commission Regulation (EC) 795/2004, OJ 2004 L 141/1, art 13(5).

4   Council Regulation (EC) 1782/2003, OJ 2003 L 270/1, art 46(1). Similarly, under the earlier sheep annual premium and suckler cow premium regimes, Member States could restrict the transfer of sheep and suckler cow quotas from sensitive zones or regions where sheep or beef and veal production were particularly important for the local economy. For implementation of such provisions in the United Kingdom see the Sheep Annual Premium and Suckler Cow Premium Quotas Regulations 2003, SI 2003/2261, regs 7 and 8.

5   Council Regulation (EC) 1782/2003, OJ 2003 L 270/1, Preamble (30).

6   See, eg, Case C-401/99 *Thomsen v Amt für Ländliche Räume Husum* [2002] ECR I-5775; and Case C-275/05 *Kibler v Land Baden-Württemburg* [2006] All ER (D) 323 (Oct).

7   Council Regulation (EC) 1782/2003, OJ 2003 L 270/1, art 46(2).

8   For force majeure or exceptional circumstances see para 52.11.

9   Council Regulation (EC) 1782/2003, OJ 2003 L 270/1, art 46(2). In the United Kingdom the first year of application of the Single Payment Scheme was 2005. An '80% rule' was earlier used on the allocation of SLOM quota (quota allocated to farmers who, by reason of their participation in non-marketing and conversion schemes, had no representative production during the reference year for milk quotas). Such allocations were originally made on a provisional basis and were not rendered definitive unless the farmer could show that in the previous 12 months direct sales/deliveries had reached 80% of the provisional allocation: Council Regulation (EEC) 857/84, OJ 1984 L 90/13, art 3(a) (as amended by Council Regulation (EEC) 764/89, OJ 1989 L 84/2).

10   Council Regulation (EC) 1782/2003, OJ 2003 L 270/1, art 46(3). Under the earlier sheep annual premium and suckler cow premium regimes, a similar 'siphon' was operated in the case of a transfer of rights without transfer of the holding. For its implementation at the full rate of 15% in the United Kingdom see the Sheep Annual Premium and Suckler Cow Premium Quotas Regulations 2003, SI 2003/2261, reg 5. A 'siphon' is also currently authorised under the milk quota regime (but not implemented in the United Kingdom): Council Regulation (EC) 1788/2003, OJ 2003 L 270/123, art 19.

11   See, eg, in the context of milk quotas, Case C-313/99 *Mulligan v Minister for Agriculture and Food* [2002] ECR I-5719.

12   Council Regulation (EC) 1782/2003, OJ 2003 L 270/1, art 42(8). For the operation of the national reserve see art 42; and, generally, eg J Moody and W Neville *Mid Term Review: a Practical Guide* (2004) Burges Salmon, Bristol, pp 71–83.

13   Council Regulation (EC) 1782/2003, OJ 2003 L 270/1, art 42(8).

14   Council Regulation (EC) 1782/2003, OJ 2003 L 270/1 (as amended by Council Regulation (EC) 2012/2006, OJ 2006 L 384/8). It may also be noted that the transfer restrictions only apply where the unit value of the payment entitlements has been 'topped-up' from the national reserve by more than 20%: Commission Regulation (EC) 795/2004, OJ 2004 L 141/1, art 6(3) (as amended by Commission Regulation (EC) 1291/2006, OJ 2006 L 236/20).

15   Council Regulation (EC) 1782/2003, OJ 2003 L 270/1, art 49(2).

Direct payments not within the Single Payment Scheme

52.13 As indicated, the Single Payment Scheme does not cover all direct payments to farmers, the Mid-term Review preserving a variety of crop-specific support. The rationale behind this decision was largely to maintain production in areas traditionally associated with such crops[1]. That said, there is a continuing drive to extend decoupling under the Single Payment Scheme[2]. Not least, this has advantages in terms of securing that the payments are world trade compatible.

Of the regimes where crop-specific support is made available, three are of particular relevance in the United Kingdom:

(a) dairy premiums and additional payments;
(b) protein crop supplement; and
(c) aid for energy crops[3].

As has been seen, the Mid-term Review instituted dairy premiums and additional payments for the period 2004–2007, to compensate for reductions in intervention prices for butter and skimmed milk powder[4]. Dairy premiums were granted by reference to the amount of milk quota held by a producer. By contrast, additional payments were granted through a 'national envelope', in the case of the United Kingdom amounting to 53.4 million Euros in 2004 and rising to 160.64 million Euros for 2006 and 2007[5]. As has also been seen, where the Single Payment Scheme is operated on a regional basis, both dairy premiums and additional payments could be comprised within it ab initio[6]; and this course of action has been adopted in both England and Wales[7]. Moreover, even where the regional basis is not operated, the Single Payment Scheme comprises dairy premiums and additional payments as from 2007[8].

A protein crop premium is available in the case of specified types of peas, field beans and sweet lupins[9]. The amount of the premium is 55.57 Euros per hectare of protein crops harvested after the stage of lactic ripeness[10]. A maximum guaranteed area of 1,400,000 hectares was established at European Community level for the fifteen 'old' Member States, with scaleback provisions if this maximum guaranteed area is exceeded[11].

Aid at the rate of 45 Euros per hectare is provided for energy crops[12]. Energy crops are defined as crops supplied essentially for the production of the following energy products: biofuels within the meaning of art 2(2) of Directive 2003/30/EC of the European Parliament and of the Council[13]; and electric and thermal energy produced from biomass. Indeed, energy crop aid is available for any agricultural raw material, provided that it is intended primarily for use in the production of such energy products[14]. As a rule, aid is only granted in respect of areas whose production is covered by a contract between the farmer and the processing industry, although exemption is conferred where the farmer himself undertakes the processing[15]. Originally, a maximum guaranteed area of 1,500,000 hectares was established at European Community level, again with scaleback provisions in the event of it being exceeded[16]. However, with the increased emphasis on biofuel production, this maximum guaranteed area has been raised to 2 million hectares[17]. Moreover, Member States are now authorised to pay national aid up to 50% of the costs associated with establishing permanent crops for the areas which have been subject to an application for energy crop aid[18]. As has been seen, where areas have been subject to an application for such aid, they cannot count as being set-aside[19]. That said, it is possible to grow energy crops on set-aside land; and, although energy crop aid is not available, Member States are authorised to pay national aid up to 50% of the costs associated with establishing permanent crops intended for biomass production[20].

1   European Commission *Mid-term Review of the Common Agricultural Policy* COM(2002)394, 20.
2   See, eg, Commissioner Fischer Boel, Speech/07/1, *A Vision for EU Agriculture and Opportunities for UK Farmers*, Oxford, 4 January 2007 (available at http://europa.eu/rapid).

3   Specific support which is of greater relevance outside the United Kingdom includes that for durum wheat, rice, nuts, hops, cotton, olive groves and tobacco.

4   Council Regulation (EC) 1782/2003, OJ 2003 L 270/1, arts 95–97.

5   Council Regulation (EC) 1782/2003, OJ 2003 L 270/1, art 96(2).

6   Council Regulation (EC) 1782/2003, OJ 2003 L 270/1, art 62; and see para 52.8.

7   The Common Agricultural Policy Single Payment and Support Schemes Regulations 2005, SI 2005/219, reg 7; and the Common Agricultural Policy Single Payment and Support Schemes (Wales) Regulations 2005, SI 2005/360 (W.29), reg 7.

8   Council Regulation (EC) 1782/2003, OJ 2003 L 270/1, Annex VI.

9   Council Regulation (EC) 1782/2003, OJ 2003 L 270/1, art 76.

10 Council Regulation (EC) 1782/2003, OJ 2003 L 270/1, art 77. A derogation is available where the crops do not reach lactic ripeness as a result of exceptional weather conditions: Council Regulation (EC) 1782/2003, OJ 2003 L 270/1, art 77; and a further derogation is available where protein crops are traditionally sown in a mixture with cereals, provided that the protein crops are predominant: Commission Regulation (EC) 1973/2004, OJ 2004 L 345/1, art 11.

11 Council Regulation (EC) 1782/2003, OJ 2003 L 270/1, art 78.

12 Council Regulation (EC) 1782/2003, OJ 2003 L 270/1, art 88.

13 OJ 2003 L123/42.

14 Commission Regulation (EC) 1973/2004, OJ 2004 L 345/1, art 24(1) (as amended by Commission Regulation (EC) 270/2007, OJ 2007 L 75/8). Originally sugar beet was excluded; but, consequent upon its incorporation into the Single Payment Scheme, this exclusion has been ended.

15 Council Regulation (EC) 1782/2003, OJ 2003 L 270/1, art 90; and for the detailed provisions, see Commission Regulation (EC) 1973/2004, OJ 2004 L 345/1, arts 23–44 (as amended by Commission Regulation (EC) 270/2007, OJ 2007 L 75/8).

16 Council Regulation (EC) 1782/2003, OJ 2003 L 270/1, art 89.

17 Council Regulation (EC) 1782/2003, OJ 2003 L 270/1, art 89 (as amended by Council Regulation (EC) 2012/2006, OJ 2006 L 384/8).

18 Council Regulation (EC) 1782/2003, OJ 2003 L 270/1, art 90a (as amended by Council Regulation (EC) 2012/2006, OJ 2006 L 384/8).

19 Council Regulation (EC) 1782/2003, OJ 2003 L 270/1, art 90.

20 Council Regulation (EC) 1782/2003, OJ 2003 L 270/1, art 56(4) (as amended by Council Regulation (EC) 2012/2006, OJ 2006 L 384/8).

The nature of the asset

52.14   Under Council Regulation (EC) 1782/2003, the Single Farm Payment is stated to be 'income support'[1]. This is consistent with the European Community objective that it should qualify as 'de-coupled income support' for the purposes of the Uruguay Round Agreement on Agriculture, so securing exemption from domestic support reduction commitments[2]. Other direct payments, such as the protein crop supplement, could likewise be characterised as income support (albeit coupled to production)[3].

Prioritising one of the objectives of the Common Agricultural Policy, the particular target of the income support schemes is to ensure a fair standard of living for the agricultural community[4]. The beneficiaries, therefore, are intended to be farmers; and the support is correspondingly linked to the producer. Indeed, the reforms effected by the Mid-term Review are expressly understood 'to complete the shift from production support to producer support'[5].

Accordingly, the Single Farm Payment and other forms of direct payment show considerable similarities to the earlier premiums in the sheep and goat and beef and veal sectors, which were also intended to offset lost income[6].

Significantly, the ECJ in *R v Minister of Agriculture, Fisheries and Food, ex p Country Landowners Association* unequivocally held that such premiums were 'linked to producers', as opposed to the holding[7]. The corollary of this should be that, in the landlord and tenant context, the Single Farm Payment and other forms of direct payment should, in principle, be the property of the tenant farmer, as opposed to the landlord.

That said, Council Regulation (EC) 1782/2003 does also seek to relate the Single Farm Payment to land, in that payment entitlements are 'linked to a certain number of eligible hectares'[8]. The basis for this is '[t]o avoid speculative transfers leading to the accumulation of payment entitlements without a corresponding agricultural basis'[9]. This terminology is similar to that which has been found in the milk quota legislation. For example, the Preamble to Council Regulation (EEC) 3950/92 referred to 'the principle linking reference quantities to holdings'[10]; and again the purpose was to prevent 'speculative operations'[11]. Under the current milk quota legislation slightly revised wording has been adopted, but the underlying rationale would seem to remain the same: the Preamble to Council Regulation (EC) 1788/2003 refers to 'the principle that reference quantities are tied to farms'[12]. Further, in the case of milk quotas the link to the holding has found its clearest expression in the general requirement for a land transaction to trigger their transfer[13]; and in the case of the Single Farm Payment it may be emphasised that a lease of payment entitlements or similar types of transactions will only be permitted if the payment entitlements transferred are accompanied by an equivalent number of eligible hectares[14].

Nonetheless, this link to a certain number of eligible hectares would not seem sufficient to render the Single Farm Payment an interest in land. Its function as income support for producers arguably outweighs any such link with land for the purposes of avoiding speculative transfers. Moreover, sale without land is permitted[15]; and there is no link with specific parcels of land: a farmer (including a tenant) can in principle match payment entitlements against any eligible hectares at his disposal for the requisite ten-month period[16].

Such an interpretation has also been adopted by HM Revenue and Customs[17]. They do not countenance that receipt of the Single Farm Payment may be regarded as income from land. Rather, in the usual case, it will be treated as income from farming (under Schedule D, Case 1 of the Income and Corporation Taxes Act 1988 or s 9 of the Income Tax (Trading and Other Income) Act 2005)[18]. Similarly, the payment entitlements themselves are considered separate chargeable assets for Capital Gains Tax purposes (although not wasting assets, since there is no clarity as to the future of the Single Payment Scheme after 2012)[19].

1 OJ 2003 L 270/1, art 1.
2 See para 52.1.
3 Council Regulation (EC) 1782/2003 expressly refers to the 'various income support schemes in the framework of the common agricultural policy': OJ 2003 L 270/1, Preamble (1).
4 Council Regulation (EC) 1782/2003, OJ 2003 L 270/1, Preamble (21). For the objectives of the Common Agricultural Policy, see EC Treaty, art 33(1). It has long been established that the European Community institutions may temporarily accord greater weight to one

of these objectives, in order to meet the demands of economic factors or conditions: see, eg, Case 5/73 *Balkan-Import-Export v Hauptzollamt Berlin-Packhof* [1973] ECR 1091; and Case C-280/93 *Germany v Council* [1994] ECR I-4973.

5   Council Regulation (EC) 1782/2003, OJ 2003 L 270/1, Preamble (24). See also, eg, European Commission *A Long-term Policy Perspective for Sustainable Agriculture* COM(2003)23, 3.

6   See, eg Council Regulation (EEC) 1837/80, OJ 1980 L 183/1, art 5(1).

7   Case C-38/94, [1995] ECR I-3875, at I-3906.

8   Council Regulation (EC) 1782/2003, OJ 2003 L 270/1, Preamble (30).

9   Council Regulation (EC) 1782/2003, OJ 2003 L 270/1, Preamble (30).

10 OJ 1992 L 405/1, Preamble (now repealed). For discussion of the attachment of milk quota to land, see also, eg, Case C-98/91 *Herbrink v Minister van Landbouw, Natuurbeheer en Visserij* [1994] ECR I-223.

11 See, eg, Case 5/88 *Wachauf v Germany* [1989] ECR 2609, at 2618 (written submission of the European Commission).

12 Council Regulation (EC) 1788/2003, OJ 2003 L 270/123, Preamble (18).

13 See now Council Regulation (EC) 1788/2003, OJ 2003 L 270/123, art 17.

14 Council Regulation (EC) 1782/2003, OJ 2003 L 270/1, art 46(2).

15 Council Regulation (EC) 1782/2003, OJ 2003 L 270/1, art 46(2). (It may be noted that, in the case of milk quotas, permanent transfer without land are only permitted by way of derogation: Council Regulation (EC) 1788/2003, OJ 2003 L 270/123, art 18.)

16 More generally, as indicated, it remains the case that milk quotas are tied to farms under Council Regulation (EC) 1788/2003, OJ 2003 L 270/123. Moreover, this principle has been consistently defended by the ECJ: see, eg, Case C-15/95 *EARL de Kerlast v Unicopa* [1997] ECR I-1961 and para 49.21. Yet, a matter of interest is that the attachment of milk quota to land has been so reduced over the years that it too may on occasion be viewed as a separate asset: see, eg, Case C-186/96 *Demand v Hauptzollamt Trier* [1998] ECR I-8529, at I-8540, where Advocate General Ruiz-Jarabo Colomer stated that 'the relaxation of the conditions governing the transfer of quotas reinforces the concept which traders legitimately have of the quota as an autonomous valuable asset. In those circumstances, and in spite of the great differences in regard to this matter between the individual national legal orders, I believe that milk quotas must currently be regarded as authentic intangible assets'.

17 HM Revenue and Customs, *Tax Bulletin: Special Edition – Single Payment Scheme* (June 2005).

18 HM Revenue and Customs, *Tax Bulletin: Special Edition – Single Payment Scheme* (June 2005), 4. The position may, however, be more complex. For example, as shall be seen, the level of activity may be considered insufficient to constitute the carrying on of a trade (as when the land is simply being maintained in good agricultural and environmental condition): see para 52.26. In such circumstances, status as trading income may be denied.

19 HM Revenue and Customs, *Tax Bulletin: Special Edition – Single Payment Scheme* (June 2005), 5. Comparison may be drawn with the treatment of milk quota as a separate asset for Capital Gains Tax purposes in *Cottle v Coldicott* [1995] STC (SCD) 239; and *Foxton v Revenue and Customs Comrs* [2005] STC (SCD) 661. See para 49.22.

Rural development

52.15 The Mid-term Review was primarily directed at recasting direct payments to farmers. In addition, however, it reinforced support for rural development by amendment to the framework regulation then in force, Council Regulation (EC) 1257/1999[1]. Three such amendments may be highlighted, all of which constitute a potentially significant source of finance for tenant farmers.

First, support was introduced to help farmers to meet demanding standards based on European Community legislation in the fields of: the environment; public, animal and plant health; animal welfare; and occupational safety[2].

Second, further support was introduced for agricultural production methods designed to improve the quality of agricultural products and for the promotion of those products[3].

Third, the regime providing support for agri-environmental commitments was extended so as to cover also animal welfare commitments (with the minimum period in either case being five years)[4].

Besides, the Mid-term Review did not mark a conclusion to reform of the legislation governing rural development. As from 1 January 2007 Council Regulation (EC) 1257/1999 has been replaced, as a general rule, by Council Regulation (EC) 1698/2005[5]. This was supplemented by Strategic Guidelines, adopted on 20 February 2006[6]. The new framework regulation in essence preserves the same range of rural development measures, but these are ordered under four heads or 'Axes':

(a)   Axis 1 addresses improving the competitiveness of the agricultural and forestry sector;
(b)   Axis 2 addresses improving the environment and the countryside;
(c)   Axis 3 addresses the quality of life in rural areas and diversification of the rural economy; and
(d)   Axis 4 addresses the leader initiative[7].

As between these Axes it was expressly provided that at least 10% of European Community funding must be spent on Axis 1 and Axis 3, at least 25% on Axis 2 and at least 5% on Axis 4[8].

The English and Welsh measures most likely to prove of relevance to tenants are as follows:

(i)   under Axis 1, measures to modernise agricultural holdings, measures to help farmers to adapt to demanding standards based on European Community legislation and measures to support farmers who participate in food quality schemes[9];
(ii)   under Axis 2, payments to farmers in areas with handicaps (other than mountain areas)[10], Natura 2000 payments[11], payments linked to the Water Framework Directive[12], agri-environmental payments and animal welfare payments[13]; and
(iii) under Axis 3, measures to support diversification into non-agricultural activities.

It may be emphasised that such rural development support should be clearly distinguished from direct payments under Council Regulation (EC) 1782/2003. Indeed, they fall under separate 'Pillars' of the Common Agricultural Policy (direct payments and market management measures constituting the 'First Pillar' and rural development the 'Second Pillar'). Of particular note is the fact that receipt of agri-environmental payments or animal welfare payments is dependent upon undertaking voluntary obligations which extend beyond the compulsory cross-compliance requirements as attached to the Single Farm Payment and other direct payments[14].

1   OJ 1999 L 160/80. For the detailed rules see Commission Regulation (EC) 445/2002, OJ 2002 L 74/1; and see, generally, eg, J Moody and W Neville, *Mid Term Review: a Practical Guide* (2004) Burges Salmon, Bristol, pp 176–179.
2   Council Regulation (EC) 1257/1999, OJ 1999 L160/80, art 21a–d (as amended by Council Regulation (EC) 1783/2003, OJ L2003 L270/70).
3   Council Regulation (EC) 1257/1999, OJ 1999 L160/80, art 24a–d (as amended by Council Regulation (EC) 1783/2003, OJ L2003 L270/70).
4   Council Regulation (EC) 1257/1999, OJ 1999 L160/80, arts 22–24 (as amended by Council Regulation (EC) 1783/2003, OJ L2003 L270/70).
5   OJ 2005 L 277/1. For the earlier proposed regulation see European Commission COM(2004)490; and for the transitional rules see Commission Regulation (EC) 1320/2006, OJ 2006 L 243/6.
6   Council Decision 2006/144/EC of 20 February 2006, OJ 2006 L 55/20.
7   'Leader' is the acronym for '*Liaison entre actions de développement de l'économie rurale*'; and its focus has been the promotion of local rural development action groups. The regime as enacted under Council Regulation (EC) 1698/2005 had been preceded by: Leader I (EC Commission notice at OJ 1991 C 73/33); Leader II (EC Commission notice at OJ 1994 C 180/48); and Leader+ (EC Commission notice (as amended) at OJ 2000 C 139/5).
8   Council Regulation (EC) 1698/2005, OJ 2005 L 277/1, art 17.
9   Accordingly, Axis 1 covers, inter alia, the meeting standards and food quality schemes as introduced by the Mid-term Review.
10 These payments will replace payments in respect of less-favoured areas and areas with natural restrictions which were implemented under Council Regulation (EC) 1257/1999, OJ 1999 L 160/80, arts 13–21 (as amended by Council Regulation (EC) 1783/2003, OJ L2003 L270/70). Introduction of the new regime under Council Regulation (EC) 1698/2005 has, however, proved problematic. In particular, the European Community institutions have been critical of the generous interpretation accorded to 'less-favoured areas' by some Member States: see, eg, Court of Auditors *Special Report No 4/2003 Concerning Rural Development Support for Less-favoured Areas* (2003). In order to resolve these difficulties of designation, the earlier less-favoured areas regime is to continue until 1 January 2010: Council Regulation (EC) 1698/2005, OJ 2005 L 277/1, art 93.
11 Natura 2000 payments are those made in order to advance the objectives of the Wild Birds Directive (Council Directive 79/409/EEC, OJ 1979 L 103/1) and the Habitats Directive (Council Directive 92/43/EEC, OJ 1992 L 206/7).
12 Directive 2000/60/EC of the European Parliament and of the Council, OJ 2000 L 327/1.
13 These payments are essentially the same as those provided for under the Mid-term Review.
14 Council Regulation (EC) 1698/2005, OJ 2005 L 277/1, arts 39(2) and (3) and 40(1) and (2).

IMPLEMENTATION IN ENGLAND AND WALES

Introduction

52.16 A key facet of the Mid-term Review was emphasis on appropriate sharing of responsibilities between the European Commission and the Member States[1]. The reforms were understood to provide an opportunity for the promotion of subsidiarity, bringing agricultural policy closer to consumers[2]. However, Commissioner Fischler fiercely resisted notions that this amounted to renationalisation of the Common Agricultural Policy[3]. Not least, the European Commission was concerned that different national implementation might lead to distortions of competition; and such concerns found expression in, for example, the requirement that Member States respect a framework at European Community level when implementing their cross-compliance obligations[4].

In the case of England and Wales, seven areas may be identified where the European Community legislation afforded particular discretion:

(a)   regional implementation;
(b)   dairy premium and additional payments;
(c)   cross-compliance;
(d)   set-aside;
(e)   the detailed rules with which a farmer must comply in order to unlock payment entitlements;
(f)   additional modulation; and
(g)   determination of the minimum size of holding that may qualify for payment entitlement.

1   See, eg, European Commission, *Mid-term Review of the Common Agricultural Policy* COM(2002)394, 2.
2   European Commission, *Mid-term Review of the Common Agricultural Policy* COM(2002)394, 3 and 10. On subsidiarity, generally, see, eg, A Estrella, *The EU Principle of Subsidiarity and its Critique* (2002) Oxford University Press, Oxford.
3   See, eg, Speech/03/356, *CAP Reform*, Brussels, 9 July 2003 (available at http://europa.eu/rapid).
4   Council Regulation (EC) 1782/2003, OJ 2003 L 270/1, art 5 and Annex IV; and see further para 52.5.

Regional implementation

52.17 As has been seen, the major choice for Member States was whether or not to implement the Single Payment Scheme on a regional basis[1]. In the case of the United Kingdom, the decision was taken to do so[2]. Northern Ireland, Scotland and Wales each became a separate region[3]; and England was divided into three separate regions: moorland; severely disadvantaged areas, excluding moorland; and all other land[4].

In turn, as has also been seen, regional implementation permitted the Member State, in duly justified cases and according to objective criteria, to opt for allocation of the Single Farm Payment on a flat-rate basis per eligible hectare within a particular region[5]. This option was exercised in respect of the three English regions. However, rather than imposing the flat-rate basis immediately as from 2005, it was also decided that there should be a phased transition from the historic basis over an eight-year period. It was apprehended that this graduated approach would prevent too swift a redistribution of support away from farmers with high historic entitlements; and that the industry would be able better to adapt to the market[6]. Accordingly, in 2005 the flat-rate element of support was only 10%, as opposed to an historic element of 90%; but annual increases in the flat-rate element will remove any historic element by 2012[7].

Year	Flate-rate element	Historic element
2005	10%	90%
2006	15%	85%
2007	30%	70%
2008	45%	55%
2009	60%	40%
2010	75%	25%
2011	90%	10%

2012	100%	0%

In Wales the historic basis was retained, as also in Scotland; but in Northern Ireland a 'hybrid static' model was adopted, with a fixed proportion of flat-rate and historic entitlements[8]. In consequence, there is a significant level of variation throughout the United Kingdom, which has the capacity to impact adversely on individual farmers, most particularly in border areas[9].

As indicated, where the flat-rate basis is adopted, the amount of entitlement enjoyed by a farmer is determined by multiplying the total flat-rate amount for the region by the number of 'eligible hectares'[10]. As a general rule, the number of eligible hectares is to be established using the number of hectares declared for the first year of application of the Single Payment Scheme[11]. Accordingly, for English (and Northern Irish) farmers their 2005 declarations are critical. Further, during the English 2005–2012 transition period, any historic element will be loaded onto those same eligible hectares. This land should be entered on the Rural Land Register, whose creation pre-dated the Mid-term Review.

1   Council Regulation (EC) 1782/2003, OJ 2003 L 270/1, art 58; and see further para 52.9.
2   By July 2003 it was already clear that regional implementation would be the policy choice: see, eg, Department for Environment, Food and Rural Affairs Press Release 301/03, *Government Presses Ahead With Consultation on Farm Reforms*, 22 July 2003.
3   For Northern Ireland see the Common Agricultural Policy Single Payment and Support Schemes Regulations (Northern Ireland) 2005, SR 2005/256, reg 3; for Scotland see the Common Agricultural Policy Single Farm Payment and Support Schemes (Scotland) Regulations 2005, SSI 2005/143, reg 3; and for Wales see the Common Agricultural Policy Single Payment and Support Schemes (Wales) Regulations 2005, SI 2005/360 (W.29), reg 3.
4   Hansard (HC) 22 April 2004, Vol 420, Cols 26–28WS (Written Statement: Secretary of State for Environment, Food and Rural Affairs); and the Common Agricultural Policy Single Payment and Support Schemes Regulations 2005, SI 2005/219, reg 3. Originally it had been proposed that there be two regions (severely disadvantaged areas and all other land): Announcement by the Secretary of State for Environment, Food and Rural Affairs, Hansard (HC) 12 February 2004, Vol 417, Col 1586.
5   Council Regulation (EC) 1782/2003, OJ 2003 L 270/1, art 59; and see further para 52.9.
6   Announcement by the Secretary of State for Environment, Food and Rural Affairs, Hansard (HC) 12 February 2004, Vol 417, Col 1586.
7   The Common Agricultural Policy Single Payment and Support Schemes Regulations 2005, SI 2005/219, reg 8 and Sch 1.
8   For the Northern Irish provisions see the Common Agricultural Policy Single Payment and Support Schemes Regulations (Northern Ireland) 2005, SR 2005/256, reg 8 and Sch 1.
9   Concern at potential distortion of competition was articulated from the moment that these decisions were announced: Hansard (HC) 12 February 2004, Vol 417, Col 1588 (Theresa May).
10   For the definition of 'eligible hectares', see Council Regulation (EC) 1782/2003, OJ 2003 L 270/1, art 44(2); and see paras 52.9 and 52.10.
11   Commission Regulation (EC) 795/2004, OJ 2004 L 141/1, art 38(1).

Dairy premium

52.18 As has been seen, a further important choice for Member States which opted for the regional basis of allocation was whether or not to incorporate the dairy premium and additional payments into the Single Payment Scheme ab initio (rather than, under the general rule, as from 2007)[1]. In both England

and Wales, this derogation was exercised[2]. For English dairy producers such decisions have not worked to their advantage. The dairy premium and additional payments were directed to compensate them specifically for reductions in the intervention price in the dairy sector; and yet those payments are to be subsumed within regional flat-rate payments which will benefit equally all farmers.

1   Council Regulation (EC) 1782/2003, OJ 2003 L 270/1, art 62; and see further para 52.13. It may be noted that, where a Member State opted for the regional basis of allocation, these payments could be incorporated into the Single Payment Scheme ab initio, whether or not payment entitlements were allocated within a particular region on an historic or on a flat-rate basis.
2   For England see the Common Agricultural Policy Single Payment and Support Schemes Regulations 2005, SI 2005/219, reg 7; and for Wales see the Common Agricultural Policy Single Payment and Support Schemes (Wales) Regulations 2005, SI 2005/360 (W.29), reg 7. Indeed, the same approach was adopted in both Northern Ireland and Scotland: see respectively the Common Agricultural Policy Single Payment and Support Schemes Regulations (Northern Ireland) 2005, SR 2005/256, reg 7; the Common Agricultural Policy Single Farm Payment and Support Schemes (Scotland) Regulations 2005, SSI 2005/143, reg 7.

Cross-compliance

52.19 As again indicated, under the Mid-term Review a wide range of cross-compliance obligations became applicable; and these affect all direct payments, not just the Single Farm Payment[1]. While Member States must respect the framework established at European Community level, it is expressly provided that they may take into account the specific characteristics of the areas concerned, including soil and climatic condition, existing farm systems, land use, crop rotation, farming practices and farm structures[2].

In the United Kingdom this discretion was reflected in the imposition of different cross-compliance obligations in England, Northern Ireland, Scotland and Wales[3]. However, as recognised by the European Commission, '[s]triking the appropriate balance between a common EU framework, on the one hand, and local specific situations, on the other, is one of the most important challenges faced by the system'[4]. Indeed, the variation between the English and other cross-compliance obligations has already given rise to challenge, on the basis of discrimination against English farmers[5]. More generally, however, the Government has been swift to affirm that the level of burden is 'relatively light ... representing a mixture of common-sense farming practice and support for existing legislation'[6]. In this may be detected an awareness of criticism that the United Kingdom has 'gold-plated' legislation emanating from Brussels.

The detailed cross-compliance measures applicable in England are currently set out in the Common Agricultural Policy Single Payment and Support Schemes (Cross-compliance) (England) Regulations 2005[7]; and those for Wales are set out in the Common Agricultural Policy Single Payment and Support Schemes (Cross Compliance) (Wales) Regulations 2004[8].

Many of the requirements are no more than might be expected as an integral part of good farming practice: for example, the provisions governing post-harvest management of land after combinable crops or the general prohibition of mechanical field operations on waterlogged soil. Likewise, other provisions do no more than reinforce existing legislation, for example, certain obligations under the Crop (Residues) Burning Regulations 1993[9] and the Hedgerows Regulations 1997[10]. This has led to criticism that the cross-compliance obligations in fact realise little public benefit[11]; and even the European Commission has acknowledged that the statutory management requirements do not create new obligations[12].

That said, there is novelty in some aspects of the requirement that farmers maintain all agricultural land in good agricultural and environmental condition. Importantly, as has been seen, land must be so maintained even if it is not in agricultural production; and in this regard both the English and Welsh implementing legislation impose specific rules. Thus, for example, a farmer must generally cut down any scrub or cut down or graze any rank vegetation at least once every five years[13]; and, with only limited exceptions, there must be no application of inorganic fertiliser[14]. In addition, whether or not the land is in agricultural production, more extensive protection is accorded to hedgerows and watercourses. Thus, as a general rule, in England a farmer must not cultivate or apply fertilisers or pesticides to land within two metres of the centre of a hedgerow, watercourse or field ditch and land which is within one metre of the top of the bank of a watercourse or field ditch[15]. Further, the penalties for breach of cross-compliance obligations are additional to those exacted under any of the European Community legislation which together comprises the statutory management requirements[16]. Accordingly, they constitute a further and strong incentive to reach the standard of good agricultural practice, not least because the penalties for their breach may, in an extreme case, lead to total exclusion from one or several aid schemes for one or more calendar years[17].

1   See para 52.5.
2   Council Regulation (EC) 1782/2003, OJ 2003 L 270/1, art 5(1).
3   See respectively the Common Agricultural Policy Single Payment and Support Schemes (Cross-compliance) (England) Regulations 2005, SI 2005/3459 (as amended by SI 2006/3254 and SI 2007/2003) (replacing the Common Agricultural Policy Single Payment and Support Schemes (Cross Compliance) (England) Regulations 2004, SI 2004/3196, as amended by SI 2005/918)); the Common Agricultural Policy Single Payment and Support Schemes (Cross Compliance) Regulations (Northern Ireland) 2005, SR 2005/6 (as amended by SR 2006/459); the Common Agricultural Policy Schemes (Cross-compliance) (Scotland) Regulations 2004, SSI 2004/518; and the Common Agricultural Policy Single Payment and Support Schemes (Cross Compliance) (Wales) Regulations 2004, SI 2004/3280 (W.284) (as amended by SI 2006/2831 (W.252) and SI 2007/970 (W.87)).
4   European Commission *Report form the Commission to the Council on the Application of the System of Cross-compliance* COM(2007)147, 3.
5   *(R (on the application of Horvath) v Secretary of State for Environment, Food and Rural Affairs* [2007] EWCA Civ 620 (challenging the Common Agricultural Policy Single Payment and Support Schemes (Cross Compliance) (England) Regulations 2004, SI 2004/3196). For example, only the English regulations imposed obligations in respect of public rights of way.
6   Hansard (HC) 22 July 2004, Vol 424, Col 69WS (Written Statement: Secretary of State for Environment, Food and Rural Affairs).
7   SI 2005/3459 (as amended by SI 2006/3254 and SI 2007/2003).
8   SI 2004/3280 (W.284) (as amended by SI 2006/2831 (W.252) and SI 2007/970 (W.87)).
9   SI 1993/1366.
10 SI 1997/1160 (as amended by SI 2003/2155).

11 See, eg, GFA-RACE Partners Limited in Association with IEEP, *Impacts of CAP Reform Agreement on Diverse Water Pollution from Agriculture* (Department for Environment, Food and Rural Affairs, London, 2004) (which concluded that the pressure to impose light cross-compliance obligations would preclude any major effect on nitrate pollution).
12 European Commission *Report form the Commission to the Council on the Application of the System of Cross-compliance* COM(2007)147, 3.
13 The Common Agricultural Policy Single Payment and Support Schemes (Cross-compliance) (England) Regulations 2005, SI 2005/3459, Schedule para 7(1)(a); and the Common Agricultural Policy Single Payment and Support Schemes (Cross Compliance) (Wales) Regulations 2004, SI 2004/3280 (W.284), Schedule para 7(1)(a).
14 The Common Agricultural Policy Single Payment and Support Schemes (Cross-compliance) (England) Regulations 2005, SI 2005/3459, Schedule para 7(1)(d); and the Common Agricultural Policy Single Payment and Support Schemes (Cross Compliance) (Wales) Regulations 2004, SI 2004/3280 (W.284), Schedule para 7(1)(d).
15 The Common Agricultural Policy Single Payment and Support Schemes (Cross-compliance) (England) Regulations 2005, SI 2005/3459, Schedule para 10. It was recognised by the Government ab initio that these measures would be controversial, but pointed out that there would be the benefit of 'double counting', in that their observance would also meet the requirements of the hedgerow management options for the purposes of Entry Level Stewardship, as was to be introduced under the Environmental Stewardship (England) Regulations 2005, SI 2005/621: Hansard (HC) 22 July 2004, Vol 424, Col 69WS (Written Statement: Secretary of State for Environment, Food and Rural Affairs).
16 See, eg, Council Regulation (EC) 1782/2003, OJ 2003 L 270/1, Preamble, Recital (2): '[i]f those basic standards are not met, Member States should withdraw direct aid in whole or in part on the basis of criteria that are proportionate, objective and graduated. Such withdrawal should be without prejudice to sanctions laid down now or in the future under other provisions of Community or national law'. For the statutory management requirements see Council Regulation (EC) 1782/2003, OJ 2003 L 270/1, Annex III; and para 52.5.
17 Council Regulation (EC) 1782/2003, OJ 2003 L 270/1, art 7.

Set-aside

52.20 Since the decision was taken in the case of England to implement the Single Payment Scheme on a flat-rate basis (albeit over a 2005–2012 transitional period), it became necessary to determine the set-aside rate under the detailed rules contained in Article 63(2) of Council Regulation (EC) 1782/2003, as opposed simply to applying under the general rule a three-year average over the 2000–2002 reference period[1].

The operation of these detailed rules resulted in there being no set-aside obligation for the moorland region, a 1.3% rate for the region comprising severely disadvantaged areas (excluding moorland) and an 8% rate for the region comprising all other land[2]. Thus, even the highest rate was lower than the general 10% rate. The reason for this was that a greater proportion of land has become subject to set-aside obligations, since, as has been seen, they now extend to, for example, temporary grass and fodder crops[3]. In consequence, the lower rates have secured the same overall volume of land set aside.

In addition, national legislation has provided detailed rules governing the management of land set aside. In England these rules are contained in the Common Agricultural Policy Single Payment Scheme (Set-aside) (England)

Regulations 2004[4]; and in Wales they are contained in the Common Agricultural Policy Single Payment Scheme (Set-aside) (Wales) Regulations 2005[5]. In large part they continue the obligations applicable under the earlier Arable Area Payments Scheme[6].

[1] Council Regulation (EC) 1782/2003, OJ 2003 L 270/1, art 63(2); and see para 52.9.
[2] Hansard (HC) 22 July 2004, Vol 424, Col 71WS (Written Statement: Secretary of State for Environment, Food and Rural Affairs).
[3] See para 52.9.
[4] SI 2004/3385 (as amended by SI 2005/3460 and SI 2007/633).
[5] SI 2005/45 (W.4).
[6] The Arable Area Payments Regulations 1996, SI 1996/3142 (as amended by SI 1997/2969, SI 1998/3169 and SI 1999/8).

Detailed rules for unlocking payment entitlements

52.21 The European Community rules which govern the unlocking of payment entitlements are relatively generous. As already seen, farmers can receive payment by matching their payment entitlements against 'eligible hectares'; and 'eligible hectares' are broadly defined[1]. Production is not a pre-requisite; but, if a farmer does undertake production, payment entitlements may be matched against, inter alia, land used to grow certain energy crops and, in England, land used to grow a wide range of fruit and vegetables, and potatoes (other than starch potatoes). In addition, Government guidance affirms that land grazed by horses may benefit from the Single Payment Scheme, even though the horses concerned are used for recreational as opposed to agricultural purposes[2]. Likewise, traditional orchards with the potential to be grazed are also understood to be eligible[3]. Further Government guidance clarifies which 'non-agricultural activities' will preclude eligibility[4]. Generally permitted activities would include, for example: walking, school or university nature or farm visits, fishing and non-commercial game shooting. Other activities are permitted up to a 28-day limit, for example: clay-pigeon shooting, car boot sales and motor sports. Activities inconsistent with the land being considered as remaining in agricultural use would include where the principal purpose of the land is recreational or other non-agricultural activities, such as golf courses, other permanent sports facilities, gallops or airports[5].

Over and above this broad definition of 'eligible hectares', Member States enjoy some latitude when implementing the detailed provisions on the unlocking of payment entitlements. As noted, payment entitlements cannot be unlocked unless the eligible hectare is at the disposal of the farmer for a period of at least ten months (except in case of force majeure or exceptional circumstances)[6]; and determination of the commencement date of this ten-month period is a matter for the Member States, within parameters set at European Community level. They may either fix a single date for all farmers, not earlier than 1 September of the calendar year preceding the year of lodging the Single Farm Payment application and not later than 30 April of the following calendar year; or, alternatively, that they may allow each farmer to choose their own commencement date within this fixed period. However, where agricultural conditions so warrant, Member States may authorise farmers to fix two different dates[7]. In England the decision has been taken to allow farmers to choose up to two commencement dates. These must be within the period beginning on 1 October of the calendar year preceding the year of lodging the Single Farm Payment application and ending on 30 April of the year of application[8]. Likewise, in Wales farmers may fix two commencement dates within that period[9].

1   Council Regulation (EC) 1782/2003, OJ 2003 L 270/1, art 44(2); and see para 52.10.
2   Department for Environment, Food and Rural Affairs News Release 439/04, *Land Grazed by Horses will Benefit from Common Agricultural Policy Single Payment*, 2 November 2004; and Department for Environment, Food and Rural Affairs News Release 441/04, *Rolling Out the Single Payment Scheme: Land Grazed by Horses; Orchards; National Reserve; and Two Metre Borders*, 2 November 2004.
3   Department for Environment, Food and Rural Affairs News Release 441/04, *Rolling Out the Single Payment Scheme: Land Grazed by Horses; Orchards; National Reserve; and Two Metre Borders*, 2 November 2004.
4   As has been seen, 'eligible hectares' are defined as 'any agricultural area of the holding taken up by arable land and permanent pasture except areas under permanent crops, forests or used for non-agricultural activities': Council Regulation (EC) 1782/2003, OJ 2003 L 270/1, art 44(2).
5   For the updated guidance see Department for Environment, Food and Rural Affairs News Release 201/05, *Single Payment: Updated Guidance on Non-agricultural Use*, 13 May 2005. It was emphasised that these restrictions only apply during the ten-month period when the farmer must have the land at his disposal.
6   Council Regulation (EC) 1782/2003, OJ 2003 L 270/1, art 44(3); and see para 52.10.
7   Council Regulation (EC) 1782/2003, OJ 2003 L 270/1, art 44(3); and Commission Regulation (EC) 795/2004, OJ 2004 L 141/1, art 24(2) (as amended by Commission Regulation (EC) 606/2005, OJ 2005 L 100/15).
8   The Common Agricultural Policy Single Payment and Support Schemes Regulations 2005, SI 2005/219, reg 6 (as amended by SI 2006/239). If the farmer makes no choice, the ten-month period commences on 1 February of the year of application.
9   The Common Agricultural Policy Single Payment and Support Schemes (Wales) Regulations 2005, SI 2005/360 (W.29), reg 6 (as amended by SI 2006/357 (W.45)).

Voluntary modulation

52.22 Under European Community rules a proportion of all direct payments are to be compulsorily deducted each year, so as to increase the level of financing for rural development measures[1]. The general rate of compulsory modulation commenced at the rate of 3% in 2005, rose to 4% in 2006, and will then remain at 5% for the period 2007 to 2012.

However, it may be re-emphasised that Member States have been granted the option to impose voluntary modulation, over and above these compulsory levels. Initially, such option was granted where Member States had already introduced voluntary modulation prior to the Mid-term Review[2]. The United Kingdom met this criterion and in England an additional 2% was transferred to finance rural development measures in 2005, the proportion being increased to 6% in 2006[3]. When combined with the compulsory rate, this led to an overall reduction of 5% in 2005 and 10% in 2006. In Wales voluntary modulation was likewise imposed, but the additional percentages were lower: 1.5% in 2005 and 0.5% in 2006[4].

More recently, as has again been seen, European Community legislation enacted in 2007 authorised far more extensive voluntary modulation, at rates of up to 20%, where the Member State was already applying additional reductions[5]. The European Community legislation also authorised Member States to differentiate rates between regions according to objective criteria rates if the Single Payment Scheme was being operated on a regional basis[6]. In the United Kingdom additional reductions were already being applied and the Single Payment Scheme is operated on a regional basis. Accordingly, there was the opportunity both to impose voluntary modulation and to differentiate rates between regions. In England an additional rate of 12% was introduced in 2007, rising to 13% in 2008 and then remaining at 14% from 2009 to 2012[7]. As justification for this decision, much weight was placed upon the need to secure funding for the Rural Development Programme for England 2007–2013 and, in particular, agri-environmental schemes[8]. In Wales the additional rates are again lower: 0% in 2007; 2.5% in 2008; 4.2% in 2009; 5.8% in 2010; and 6.5% in 2011 and 2012[9].

[1] Council Regulation (EC) 1782/2003, OJ 2003 L 270/1, art 10; and see para 52.6.
[2] Commission Regulation (EC) 1655/2004, OJ 2004 L 298/3; and see para 52.6.
[3] The Common Agricultural Policy Single Payment and Support Schemes Regulations 2005, SI 2005/219, reg 11.
[4] The Common Agricultural Policy Single Payment and Support Schemes (Wales) Regulations 2005, SI 2005/360 (W.29), reg 10.
[5] Council Regulation (EC) 378/2007, OJ 2007 L 95/1; and see para 52.6.
[6] Council Regulation (EC) 378/2007, OJ 2007 L 95/1, art 3(1). For operation of the Single Payment Scheme on a regional basis see para 52.9.
[7] Hansard (HC) 29 March 2007, Vol 458, Col 131WS (Written Statement: Secretary of State for Environment, Food and Rural Affairs).
[8] Hansard (HC) 29 March 2007, Vol 458, Col 131WS (Written Statement: Secretary of State for Environment, Food and Rural Affairs).
[9] Welsh Assembly Government Press Release, *6.5 Per Cent Voluntary Modulation for Wales, by 2011*, 12 June 2007.

Minimum size of holding

52.23 Under Commission Regulation (EC) 795/2004, Member States could decide to fix a minimum size per holding for which the establishment of payment entitlements might be requested, subject to the proviso that the minimum size was not to be higher than 0.3 of a hectare[1]. In both England and Wales the decision was taken to implement a minimum size of 0.3 of a hectare[2].

[1] OJ 2004 L 141/1, art 12(6). An exception was made in the case of payment entitlements subject to special conditions: art 12(7).
[2] See respectively the Common Agricultural Policy Single Payment and Support Schemes Regulations 2005, SI 2005/219, reg 5; and the Common Agricultural Policy Single Payment and Support Schemes (Wales) Regulations 2005, SI 2005/360 (W.29), reg 5. The same limit was imposed in Northern Ireland and in Scotland.

LANDLORD AND TENANT ISSUES

General

52.24 While the Mid-term Review had major impact on the way agricultural land is farmed and on the profitability of farming enterprises, landlord and tenant issues do not feature large in the legislative framework itself. For example, unlike in the case of the milk quota legislation, there is no specific provision dealing with the position of payment entitlements on the termination of tenancies[1]. This would seem consistent with the fact that the Single Farm Payment is characterised as 'income support' to the farmer[2]. Moreover, the ECJ has affirmed that, as a rule, landlord and tenant issues remain within the competence of the Member States[3].

That said, the European Community legislation does require that payment entitlements be matched against eligible hectares for their value to be unlocked[4]; and, as has been seen, in Council Regulation (EC) 1782/2003 express reference is made to their 'link' to such eligible hectares[5]. As a consequence, in the landlord and tenant context there is arguably the potential for a symbiotic relationship: the tenant, as the farmer exercising the agricultural activity[6], will be entitled to apply for the direct payments; and the landlord, owner of the eligible hectares[7], will be able to provide the land to unlock them. It is perhaps no coincidence, therefore, that a spirit of co-operation has been advocated. For example, the Tenancy Reform Industry Group stressed that 'the parties should treat each other fairly in these matters as the best way to unlock value to their mutual benefit'[8].

Accordingly, the direct payments regime as established under the Mid-term Review has the capacity materially to affect numerous aspects of the landlord and tenant relationship; and seven such aspects may be considered:

(a)   occupation of the land;
(b)   use of the land and user clauses;
(c)   termination of tenancies;
(d)   quota protection clauses;
(e)   rent review;
(f)   transfers; and
(g)   succession[9].

[1]   For the current provision governing the treatment of milk quotas on the termination of a tenancy see Council Regulation (EC) 1788/2003, OJ 2003 L 270/123, art 17(4): '[w]here there is no agreement between the parties, in the case of tenancies due to expire without any possibility of renewal on similar terms, or in situations involving comparable legal effects, the individual reference quantities in question shall be transferred in whole or in part to the producer taking them over, in accordance with such provisions adopted or to be adopted by the Member States, taking account of the legitimate interests of the parties'.
[2]   Council Regulation (EC) 1782/2003, OJ 2003 L 270/1, art 1.
[3]   See, eg, Case C-2/92 *R v Ministry of Agriculture, Fisheries and Food, ex p Bostock* [1994] ECR I-955 at I-985: 'legal relations between lessees and lessors, in particular on the expiry of a lease, are, as Community law now stands, still governed by the law of the Member States in question'.
[4]   Council Regulation (EC) 1782/2003, OJ 2003 L 270/1, arts 36 and 44(1); and see para 52.10. It may be reiterated that, in the case of set-aside entitlements, these must be matched against hectares eligible for set-aside entitlements: art 54(1).
[5]   Council Regulation (EC) 1782/2003, OJ 2003 L 270/1, Preamble (30); and see para 52.14.
[6]   For the definitions of 'farmer' and 'agricultural activity' see Council Regulation (EC) 1782/2003, OJ 2003 L 270/1, art 2(a) and (c); and see para 52.4.
[7]   For the definition of 'eligible hectares' see Council Regulation (EC) 1782/2003, OJ 2003 L 270/1, art 44(2); and para 52.10.
[8]   *Notes to Aid Tenants and Landlords on CAP Reform* (2004), para 35.
[9]   See generally, eg, J Moody and W Neville *Mid Term Review: a Practical Guide* (2004) Burges Salmon, Bristol, pp 196–213; Central Association of Agricultural Valuers *Mid Term Review: a Valuer's Interim Guide* (2004) Central Association of Agricultural Valuers,

Coleford, pp 97–99; and Central Association of Agricultural Valuers *Mid Term Review: a Valuer's Second Interim Guide* (Central Association of Agricultural Valuers (2005), pp 119–130 and 135–137.

Occupation of the land

52.25 Where a farmer is a tenant, whether under the AHA 1986 or the ATA 1995, in the usual course he will be seeking to match his payment entitlements against the land comprised within the tenancy so as to secure receipt of the Single Farm Payment. For this purpose, the land should be entered on the Rural Land Register[1].

In principle, his occupation of the land should meet the requirement that the eligible hectares be at his disposal for a period of at least ten months (except in case of force majeure or exceptional circumstances)[2]. However, care may be required in the case of short term tenancies, for example those for specialist cropping, in that there is the potential for both the landowner and the tenant mutually to exclude each other from meeting this criterion[3]. Thus, a six-month tenancy for the growing season from 1 March to 31 August would leave neither party with the requisite ten-month period. Some flexibility and comfort may be provided by the fact that European Community rules now make it possible to select up to two commencement dates for the ten-month period[4]. In both England and Wales, as has been seen, the decision was taken to allow farmers to choose two commencement dates within the period beginning on 1 October of the calendar year preceding the year of lodging the Single Farm Payment application and ending on 30 April of the year of application[5]. Care will also be required where milk quota attaches to the land. A tenancy for a term of at least ten months will ensure that the tenant has the land at his disposal for the purposes of the Single Farm Payment; but it will also be sufficient to trigger a transfer of milk quota[6].

The position may be more complex if there is an agreement or arrangement for less than a tenancy. As a preliminary matter, it will be necessary to determine whether, notwithstanding the label, the agreement is indeed a tenancy under the test established in *Street v Mountford*[7]. Many grazing 'licences' still being granted would seem vulnerable on this account[8]. Accordingly, where there is grazing land and the landowner wishes himself to claim the Single Farm Payment, a better course might be an agistment agreement. This should arguably preserve the land at his disposal.

Nonetheless, it must be recognised that the term 'disposal' is likely to prove an elusive concept at law, it giving no indication as to the degree of exclusivity required. However, logic dictates that, for a person to have the eligible hectares at their disposal, they should enjoy sufficient exclusivity to be able to meet the various cross-compliance obligations. Indeed, it would be wise for any agreement to be explicit as to which party is to undertake such obligations; and there would be danger of artificiality if the same party does not, on the basis that the eligible hectares are at their disposal, make the claim for direct payments. Conversely, if a landowner is seeking to prevent an occupier gaining exclusive possession for the purposes of the AHA 1986 and the ATA 1995, it would very probably be prejudicial to his position to impose on the occupier any cross-compliance obligations in respect of the Single Farm Payment or other direct payments.

Similar considerations would seem to arise in the case of share farming and contracting agreements[9]. As a rule, these are not intended to confer exclusive possession and, accordingly, a tenancy on the working farmer. Instinctively, therefore, the land should remain at the disposal of the landowner; and it would be for the landowner to claim the Single Farm Payment or other direct payments[10]. That said, the distinctions between a share farming agreement and a tenancy have been fine[11]; and much will depend on the manner in which the agreement is operated in practice, with the emphasis on substance rather than form. Like principles would seem to apply to contracting agreements. In the simple case, where the contractor undertakes operations at a fixed rate per hour, there should be sufficient control vested in the landowner to maintain the land at his disposal. This might be an appropriate solution, for example, where a landowner in England has the benefit of authorisations to grow fruit, vegetables and potatoes, but does not have all the requisite machinery or expertise[12]. By contrast, if the landowner has in effect handed over control of the farming operations to the contractor, then it would be hard to show that the land was not at the disposal of the contractor[13]. What is readily apparent, however, is that care and attention should be paid to ensuring that a clear decision is taken as to who will be matching payment entitlements against the eligible hectares; and then that the form and substance of any agreement determine with sufficient clarity that the land is at their disposal.

1   Land may be added to the Rural Land Register; but in England it was that registered for 2005 which fixed the total number of eligible hectares against which payment entitlements may be matched.
2   Council Regulation (EC) 1782/2003, OJ 2003 L 270/1, art 44(3); and see para 52.10.
3   The difficulties created by the ten-month rule have been recognised by the European Commission and its operation is being reviewed: European Commission *Report form the Commission to the Council on the Application of the System of Cross-compliance* COM(2007)147, 9.
4   Commission Regulation (EC) 795/2004, OJ 2004 L 141/1, art 24(2) (as amended by Commission Regulation (EC) 606/2005, OJ 2005 L 100/15).
5   Respectively the Common Agricultural Policy Single Payment and Support Schemes Regulations 2005, SI 2005/219, reg 6 (as amended by SI 2006/239); and the Common Agricultural Policy Single Payment and Support Schemes (Wales) Regulations 2005, SI 2005/360 (W.29), reg 6 (as amended by SI 2006/357 (W.45)).
6   See, in the case of England, the Dairy Produce Quotas Regulations 2005, SI 2005/465, reg 16; and, in the case of Wales, the Dairy Produce Quotas (Wales) Regulations 2005, SI 2005/537 (W.47), reg 16.
7   [1985] 1 AC 809. For a recent analysis of the decision and its importance see, eg, S Bright, '*Street v Mountford* Revisited', in S Bright (ed.) *Landlord and Tenant Law: Past, Present and Future* (2006) Hart Publishing, Oxford, pp 19–39.
8   See para 19.34 ff.
9   On share farming agreements, generally, see paras 19.34 and 19.35.
10 On this aspect see, eg P N di C Willan, 'Share Farming', in A A Lennon and R E O McKay *Agricultural Law, Tax and Finance* (looseleaf) Sweet & Maxwell, at D4.3.
11 See, eg *McCarthy v Bence* [1990] 1 EGLR 1.
12 For authorisations to grow fruit, vegetables and potatoes (other than starch potatoes) see para 52.10; and it may be reiterated that such authorisations are not found in Wales, since in Wales the Single Payment Scheme is operated on an historic basis.

¹³ For discussion of contract farming agreements in the context of Inheritance Tax see, eg, *Arnander, Lloyd and Villiers v Revenue and Customs Comrs* [2006] STC (SCD) 800: a farmhouse was held not to be occupied for the purposes of agriculture where the contractors undertook the day to day farming activities; and it may also be noted that it was the contractors who made the claim for arable area payments.

Use of the land and user clauses

52.26 Most tenancy agreements will contain a clause requiring the tenant to use the land for agricultural purposes only¹. Moreover, these clauses have been interpreted relatively strictly by the courts. For example, in *Jewell v McGowan* there was held to be breach where the tenant had diversified into open farm activities, which were estimated to contribute one third of the income of the farm². However, in this context there may be tensions between national law in England and Wales and the European Community legislation which governs the various direct payment regimes.

Perhaps most importantly, for a farmer to qualify for any direct payments (not just the Single Farm Payment), he must undertake 'agricultural activity'. As has been seen, this term is broadly defined as 'the production, rearing or growing of agricultural products including harvesting, milking, breeding animals and keeping animals for farming purposes, or maintaining the land in good agricultural and environmental condition'³. Accordingly, the definition extends beyond 'production agriculture' and the definition of 'agriculture' found in both the AHA 1986 and the ATA 1995⁴. More specifically, it includes maintaining the land in good agricultural and environmental condition, with the result that a farmer undertaking agricultural activity for the purposes of the European Community direct payment regimes may not qualify as an agricultural tenant under either the AHA 1986 or the ATA 1995⁵.

While this mismatch may be thought to give rise only to theoretical difficulties, it may be noted that in the Scottish landlord and tenant case of *Cambusmore Estate Trustees v Little* absence of production was found *prima facie* to amount to a breach of Rule 1 of the rules of good husbandry, which imposes on the occupier an obligation, inter alia, to maintain a reasonable standard of efficient production⁶. Against this background, perhaps surprisingly the Government declined to update the definition of 'agriculture' during the passage of the Agricultural Tenancies Bill through Parliament, so as to include, for example, crops for industrial and fuel uses and set-aside⁷. Further, although detailed tax considerations are beyond the scope of this work, a matter of some significance is that HM Revenue and Customs do not regard the simple maintenance of the land in good agricultural and environmental condition as a trade for income tax purposes⁸.

Nonetheless, in order to meet the business condition, which is a prerequisite for any farm business tenancy, it is sufficient that:

'(a)   that all or part of the land comprised in the tenancy is farmed for the purposes of a trade or business; and

(b)   that, since the beginning of the tenancy, all or part of the land so comprised has been so farmed'⁹.

Importantly, 'farming' is defined more broadly than 'agriculture':

> '[r]eferences in this Act to the farming of land includes references to the carrying on in relation to land of any agricultural activity'[10].

This might bring some comfort to tenants choosing simply to maintain the land in good agricultural and environmental condition, not least since that words 'agricultural activity' are found in both the national and European Community legislation. On the other hand, to qualify as a farm business tenancy, it is also necessary to satisfy either the agriculture condition or the notice condition[11]; and in each case reference is made to the character of the tenancy being primarily or wholly 'agricultural' (as opposed to any reference to 'farming')[12].

1   For a useful analysis of the contents of farm business tenancies see, eg, I Whitehead, A Errington, N Millard and T Felton *An Economic Evaluation of the Agricultural Tenancies Act 1995* (2002) University of Plymouth, Plymouth, pp 28–38.
2   [2002] EWCA Civ 145, CA; and see, generally, eg, W Barr 'Agricultural Law Update' (2002) 146 Sol.J. 657. Considerable weight was placed upon the fact that the clause was to use the land for agricultural purposes *only*.
3   Council Regulation (EC) 1782/2003, OJ 2003 L270/1, art 2(c); and see para 52.4.
4   Under both the AHA 1986 and the ATA 1995 'agriculture' is non-exhaustively defined so as to include 'horticulture, fruit growing, seed growing, dairy farming and livestock breeding and keeping, the use of land as grazing land, meadow land, osier land, market gardens and nursery grounds, and the use of land for woodlands where that use is ancillary to the farming of land for other agricultural purposes': AHA 1986, s 96(1); and ATA 1995, s 38(1). See further para 19.6 and para 3.23.
5   See, eg, L Bodiguel and M Cardwell 'Evolving Definitions of 'Agriculture' for an Evolving Agriculture?' [2005] *Conveyancer* 419–446.
6   1991 SLT (Land Ct) 33. The rules of good husbandry applicable in Scotland mirror those applicable in England and Wales: see respectively the Agriculture (Scotland) Act 1948, Sch 6; and the Agriculture Act 1947, s 11.
7   Such amendment was expressly advocated: Hansard (HC) 6 February 1995, Vol 254, Col 82 (Mr Clifton-Brown). Likewise, the Tenancy Reform Industry Group did not propose a change in the definition of 'agriculture', on the basis that no recognisable redefinition could include all forms of diversification: *Tenancy Reform Industry Group (TRIG): Final Report* (Department for Environment, Food and Rural Affairs, London, 2003), para 4.3.3.
8   HM Revenue and Customs *Tax Bulletin: Special Edition – Single Payment Scheme* (June 2005), 4.
9   ATA 1995, s 1(2). See further para 3.23.
10 ATA 1995, s 38(2).
11 ATA 1995, s 1(3) and (4). See further paras 3.23 and 3.28 ff.
12 In the case of the notice condition it may be emphasised that it is only necessary to show that the character of the tenancy was primarily or wholly agricultural at its commencement, leaving substantial scope for change of use.

52.27 In the context of land use, this is arguably not the only tension between national law governing agricultural tenancies and European Community law governing the single payment scheme. As has been seen, in order to unlock payment entitlements, they must be matched against 'eligible hectares'; and the European Community law definition of 'eligible hectares', as interpreted in national guidance, again extends to land that would not necessarily be considered agricultural for the purposes of the AHA 1986 and the ATA 1995. At a glance there is considerable coherence between the European Community law definition and what constitutes agriculture in English and Welsh law, since 'eligible hectares' are 'any agricultural area of the holding taken up by arable land and permanent pasture except areas under permanent crops, forests or used for non agricultural activities'[1]. However, on closer inspection differences may be detected.

First, the European Community law definition seems to address each area of the holding individually, whereas under the AHA 1986 it is established that an agricultural holding can include non-agricultural land, provided that the use is substantially agricultural[2]. Indeed, s 1(1) defines 'agricultural holding' as 'the aggregate of the land (whether agricultural land or not) comprised in a contract of tenancy ...'. Similarly, under the ATA 1995 the agriculture condition looks to whether the character of the tenancy is primarily or wholly agricultural, while the notice condition looks to whether it was so at the commencement of the tenancy[3].

Second, the European Community law definition excludes forests, whereas under both the AHA 1986 and the ATA 1995 woodlands are included if their use is ancillary to the farming of land for other agricultural purposes.

Third, national guidance on what constitutes 'eligible hectares' is somewhat at odds with what constitutes 'agriculture' under both the AHA 1986 and the ATA 1995. In particular, the national guidance states that it is not only traditional farmland grazed by horses that is potentially eligible. Rather, it is any land so grazed, provided that it is kept in good agricultural and environmental condition and is not used for a non-agricultural purpose[4]. This would seem to cover a broader range of circumstances than either the AHA 1986 or the ATA 1995. For example, there is no requirement for commercial use. Accordingly, paddocks used to graze ponies or horses for recreational purposes would qualify as 'eligible hectares'[5]; but they would not qualify as an agricultural holding or as land comprised in a farm business tenancy[6]. Further, national guidance on the extent of non-agricultural use permitted on eligible hectares may be more generous than case law under the AHA 1986. For example, school or university nature or farm visits are permitted without restriction[7]; but the tenant in *Jewell v McGowan* was in breach of the covenant to use the land for agricultural purposes only, notwithstanding that approximately half of those visiting the open farm activities were local schoolchildren[8]. On the other hand, in this context there is also considerable overlap between European Community and national legislation. Thus, race-horse gallops would fail to qualify both as 'eligible hectares' and as an agricultural holding[9]. Moreover, on occasion 'agriculture' for the purposes of both the AHA 1986 and the ATA 1995 would seem more extensive than for the purposes of the Single Payment Scheme. For example, it is apt to cover orchards; but these, as 'permanent crops', would be excluded from the definition of 'eligible hectares', unless dual use could be established by their concurrent grazing[10]. In consequence, where the land is tenanted no general assumption can be made that eligible hectares, against which payment entitlements can be matched, would necessarily fall within the agricultural holdings or farm business tenancy regimes: the example of a pony paddock may be reiterated. Likewise, there will be land comprised within agricultural holdings and farm business tenancies which does not qualify as an eligible hectare, such as where there is clear non-agricultural use of an individual parcel, but that does not preclude the overall use of the tenanted land remaining substantially or primarily agricultural.

1   Council Regulation (EC) 1782/2003, OJ 2003 L 270/1, art 44(2).
2   See, generally, paras 19.6.
3   Section 1(3) and (4).
4   Department for Environment, Food and Rural Affairs News Release 439/04, *Land Grazed by Horses will Benefit from Common Agricultural Policy Single Payment*, 2 November 2004; and Department for Environment, Food and Rural Affairs News Release 441/04, *Rolling Out the Single Payment Scheme: Land Grazed by Horses; Orchards; National Reserve; and Two Metre Borders*, 2 November 2004.
5   Indeed, the national guidance emphasises the recreational benefits of horses: see fn 4 above.
6   See paras 19.2 and paras 3.2 ff. It may be noted, however, that under the agricultural holdings legislation it is not necessary that the trade or business be agricultural, so long as there is a trade or business: see, eg, *Rutherford v Maurer* [1962] 1 QB 16 (where land used to graze horses for a riding school was held to be agricultural). Again, HM Revenue and Customs have indicated that, although land used for grazing horses or ponies for leisure purposes may unlock the Single Farm Payment, they do not regard such activity as a trade for income tax purposes: HM Revenue and Customs *Tax Bulletin: Special Edition – Single Payment Scheme* (June 2005), 4.
7   For the updated guidance see Department for Environment, Food and Rural Affairs News Release 201/05, *Single Payment: Updated Guidance on Non-agricultural Use*, 13 May 2005.
8   [2002] EWCA Civ 145, CA.
9   See Department for Environment, Food and Rural Affairs News Release 201/05, *Single Payment: Updated Guidance on Non-agricultural Use*, 13 May 2005; and *Bracey v Read* [1963] Ch 88; and *University of Reading v Johnson-Houghton* (1985) 276 Estates Gazette 1353.
10   Department for Environment, Food and Rural Affairs News Release 441/04, *Rolling Out the Single Payment Scheme: Land Grazed by Horses; Orchards; National Reserve; and Two Metre Borders*, 2 November 2004. That said, orchards may qualify for support in England under the Environmental Stewardship (England) Regulations 2005, SI 2005/621, Sch 2 Pt 3 para 3 (as an option under the Higher Level Schemes); and in Wales under the Tir Cynnal (Wales) Regulations 2006, SI 2006/41 (W.7).

Termination of tenancies

52.28 On the termination of tenancies it is necessary to ascertain whether, in principle, the payment entitlements and other forms of direct payment will revert with the land to the landowner or whether, as separate assets, they will remain at the disposal of the tenant. In this regard, much would seem to depend more generally upon how they are to be characterised in law.

As has been seen, the Single Farm Payment and other forms of direct payment are characterised in Council Regulation (EC) 1782/3003 as 'income support'[1]. It has also been seen that there are close analogies between them and the earlier premiums in the sheep and goat and beef and veal sectors; and that the ECJ in *R v Minister of Agriculture, Fisheries and Food, ex p Country Landowners Association* unequivocally held that these premiums were 'linked to producers', as opposed to the holding[2]. Moreover, specifically in the landlord and tenant context, it was confirmed in the same case that neither the regulatory framework nor any general principle of European Community law required Member States to provide a mechanism for compensating detriment caused to owners of agricultural land by the introduction of such a system of premium rights, even where premium rights were transferred by producers who did not own the land on which they farmed[3]. This would point to the conclusion that the producer-linked payment entitlements and other forms of direct payment will remain with the tenant on the termination of the tenancy, unless some contractual provision (and, more particularly, a quota clause) has provided otherwise.

However, it should be reiterated that Council Regulation (EC) 1782/2003 does also seek to link the Single Farm Payment to a certain number of eligible hectares, in order to avoid speculative transfers[4]. This finds perhaps clearest expression in the context of transfers; most notably, leases of payment entitlements or similar types of transactions must be accompanied by an equivalent number of eligible hectares[5].

That said, there would seem to be nothing in the legislation which would, in principle, preclude a tenant from retaining his payment entitlements at the termination of the tenancy. This may be contrasted with the position in the case of milk quotas, where it is expressly stipulated that:

> '[w]here there is no agreement between the parties, in the case of tenancies due to expire without any possibility of renewal on similar terms, or in situations involving comparable legal effects, the individual reference quantities in question shall be transferred in whole or in part to the producer taking them over, in accordance with provisions adopted or to be adopted by the Member States, taking account of the legitimate interests of the parties'[6].

Accordingly, on the termination of a tenancy, a tenant should, in principle, be free to match his payment entitlements against other eligible hectares at his disposal for the requisite ten-month period, since they are not associated with individual parcels of land or, in the terminology of milk quotas, 'tied to farms'[7]. Besides, such an interpretation would accord with the overriding objective of the legislation, namely to provide decoupled income support for producers.

[1] OJ 2003 L 270/1, Preamble (1) and art 1; and see further para 52.14.
[2] Case C-38/94, [1995] ECR I-3875 at I-3906.
[3] At I-3906.
[4] Council Regulation (EC) 1782/2003, OJ 2003 L 270/1, Preamble (30); and see further para 52.14.
[5] Council Regulation (EC) 1782/2003, OJ 2003 L 270/1, art 46(2).
[6] Council Regulation (EC) 1788/2003, OJ 2003 L 270/123, art 17(4).
[7] Council Regulation (EC) 1782/2003, OJ 2003 L 270/1, Preamble (18).

Quota protection clauses

52.29 In consequence, it would appear that, if a landlord wishes to take over the payment entitlements on the termination of the tenancy, he must rely on express contractual provision, as envisaged in respect of livestock quotas in *R v Minister of Agriculture, Fisheries and Food, ex p Country Landowners Association*[1]. However, if the tenancy agreement was negotiated and entered into before the announcement of the Mid-term Review on 10 July 2002, there is a distinct possibility that any quota protection clause will not cover payment entitlements. Indeed, the difficulty for the draftsman in anticipating future forms of support was expressly recognised in *R v Minister of Agriculture, Fisheries and Food, ex p Country Landowners Association* (where the ECJ highlighted that problems would be likely to arise if contractual relationships were already in existence when new forms of support were introduced)[2].

A further hurdle for the landlord is that the national court has shown itself relatively strict in construing quota protection clauses. For example, in *Lee v Heaton* a clause drafted by reference to 'any basic quota under a marketing scheme' was held insufficient to capture wholesale milk quota[3]. The milk quota system did not establish, or seek to establish, a scheme for regulating the marketing of milk. Rather, it imposed a levy on disposals of milk products. Since the Single Farm Payment is 'income support' and, moreover, income support decoupled from production, it too is unlikely to be captured by a quota protection clause framed by reference to a marketing scheme or, indeed, by reference to a quota. Further, for the reasons already considered[4], it is equally unlikely to be captured where such a clause is limited to rights that are attached to the land.

Nonetheless, there is perhaps greater scope for debate where the quota protection clause is expressed to cover 'successor' regimes, for example, if reference is made to any regime that replaces the Arable Area Payments Scheme. Since the Arable Area Payments Scheme is now comprised within the Single Payment Scheme, there is an argument that such a clause would be effective, the more so where implementation, as in Wales, is on a purely historic basis and the allocation of payment entitlements tracks earlier receipt of support[5].

Although such uncertainty is likely to persist, there is no doubt that much will depend upon the particular wording of the quota protection clause itself.

By contrast, in the case of the tenancy agreements negotiated and entered into after the announcement of the Mid-term Review, the draftsman will be able to proceed with greater certainty as to the nature of the rights to be covered by the quota protection clause. That said, care will need to be taken to ensure that the clause is sufficiently wide to cover not just the Single Farm Payment but all forms of direct payment under Council Regulation (EC) 1782/2003[6].

1   Case C-38/94, [1995] ECR I-3875.
2   Case C-38/94, [1995] ECR I-3875 at I-3907.
3   [1987] 2 EGLR 12, 283 Estates Gazette 1076.
4   See para 52.14.
5   In the context of the Uruguay Round Agreement on Agriculture, some guidance as to what constitutes a 'successor regime' may be found in the decision of the Appellate Body in *United States – Subsidies on Upland Cotton* (2005) WT/DS267/AB/R.
6   OJ 2003 L 270/1. For the full list of direct payments see Annex 1 (as amended by Council Regulation (EC) 319/2006, OJ 2006 L 58/32).

52.30 Where the landlord has made available the payment entitlements to the tenant, contractual provisions requiring the tenant to transfer them without compensation to the landlord on termination of the tenancy would seem unobjectionable[1]. However, where the payment entitlements have been generated by the efforts of the tenant, it is possible that such a provision could fall foul of European Community law. In the milk quota case of *Wachauf v Germany*, the ECJ stated that:

'... it must be observed that Community rules which, upon the expiry of the lease, had the effect of depriving the lessee, without compensation, of the fruits of his labours and of his investments in the tenanted holding, would be incompatible with the requirements of the protection of fundamental rights in the Community legal order'[2].

This statement would be particularly apposite where the Single Farm Payment is based upon historic production carried out by the tenant, as is the case in Wales (and, for the time being, at least partially in the case of England).

In this context, it is of importance to ascertain whether the payment entitlements have been received from the national reserve. As has been seen, any payment entitlements so received cannot be transferred for a period of five years from their allocation, except in the case of actual or anticipated inheritance, merger or scission[3]. Accordingly, there is the danger that, even if the payment entitlements are captured by the quota protection clause and there is an obligation to transfer them to the landlord, any such obligation would be defeated by European Community law.

Over and above provision for the destination of payment entitlements on the termination of the tenancy, it would be prudent for the landlord to oblige the tenant to use those entitlements annually. As has been seen, if they have not been used for a period of three years, they are to revert to the national reserve, except in cases of force majeure and exceptional circumstances[4]. Such a provision would be of particular importance where the landlord had made the payment entitlements available to the tenant at the commencement of the tenancy agreement.

[1]   In Case C-38/94 *R v Minister of Agriculture, Fisheries and Food, ex p Country Landowners Association* [1995] ECR I-3875, the ECJ appeared to accept that it was possible to determine the destination of livestock quotas by contractual arrangement: at I-3907. (It would be normal to record the number of payment entitlements made available in the tenancy agreement.)

[2]   Case 5/88, [1989] ECR 2609 at 2639. See also, eg, JHH Weiler and NJS Lockhart, ' "Taking Rights Seriously" Seriously: the European Court and its Fundamental Rights Jurisprudence' (1995) 32 *Common Market Law Review* 51–94 and 579–627.

[3]   Council Regulation (EC) 1782/2003, OJ 2003 L 270/1, art 42(8) (as amended by Council Regulation (EC) 2012/2006, OJ 2006 L 384/8); and see para 52.12.

[4]   Council Regulation (EC) 1782/2003, OJ 2003 L 270/1, art 45. As noted, if the payment entitlements were received from the national reserve, they must be used during each of the five years starting from their allocation: art 42(8).

Rent review

52.31 The Single Farm Payment and other direct payments have the capacity to improve the profitability of farms; and early evidence of the operation of the new regime in practice would tend to confirm this[1]. The effect may be most marked in England, where, as the flat-rate basis is phased in, relatively unproductive land where margins were tight will acquire the same rate of support per eligible hectare as land which had enjoyed high levels of historic support. Further, farmers will have the viable option of simply maintaining their land in good agricultural and environmental condition, so long as any cross-compliance costs are less than the amount of direct payments received[2]. However, as indicated, a tenant farmer will need to ensure that adopting this course will not breach any user clause[3].

With the profitability of farms at least partially dependent upon receipt of the Single Farm Payment and other direct payments, their treatment on rent review will inevitably be an important issue.

Under the AHA 1986, the rent properly payable in respect of a holding is to be the rent at which the holding might reasonably be expected to be let by a prudent and willing landlord to a prudent and willing tenant. All relevant factors are to be taken into account, including (in every case): the terms of the tenancy (including those relating to rent); the character and situation of the holding (including the locality in which it is situated); the productive capacity of the holding and its related earning capacity; and the current level of rents for comparable lettings[4]. In the case of payment entitlements, the terms of the tenancy may be relevant: for example, if they restrict the ability of the tenant to dispose of payment entitlements; or if there is a user clause which obliges the tenant to use the land for agricultural purposes only (which, as seen, may affect the ability of the tenant to pursue the option of simply maintaining the land in good agricultural and environmental condition)[5]. On the other hand, the productive capacity of the holding and its related earning capacity should arguably not be at issue in the case of the Single Farm Payment, a key objective of the Mid-term Review being to decouple such support from production.

Rather, the Single Farm Payment and, indeed, all other direct payments would most naturally fall to be dealt with as another 'relevant factor', by analogy with the treatment in *J W Childers Trustees v Anker* of compensation payments in respect of a Site of Special Scientific Interest[6]. The Court of Appeal had no hesitation in holding that the ability to restrict normal agricultural operations by virtue of a management agreement and the existence of compensation payments were both relevant factors. Although the analogy is not precise, since the Single Farm Payment is not characterised as compensation, but as income support paid in return for the observance of cross-compliance obligations, it would seem unlikely that a court would not adopt the same approach as in *Childers v Anker*. Moreover, the same reasoning would seem to apply to other forms of direct payment (such as protein crop premium) and payments made in England under the Environmental Stewardship (England) Regulations 2005 and in Wales under the Tir Cynnal (Wales) Regulations 2006[7].

In the case of farm business tenancies under the ATA 1995, on any reference in pursuance of a statutory review notice, the arbitrator is to determine the rent properly payable in respect of the holding[8]; and, for these purposes, the rent properly payable in respect of the holding is the rent at which the holding might reasonably be expected to be let on the open market by a willing landlord to a willing tenant[9]. Again, in principle, 'all relevant factors' are to be taken into account[10]. As with the AHA 1986, such provisions would seem apt to cover both the Single Farm Payment and other direct payments, together with agri-environmental payments.

[1]   See, eg, Deloitte Press Releases, 'Farm Incomes Set for Roller Coaster Ride, Warns Deloitte', 14 October 2005; and 'Farmers Predicted to Produce Food at Loss', 3 November 2004.

[2]   See, generally, eg, J Moody and W Neville, *Mid Term Review: a Practical Guide* (2004) Burges Salmon, Bristol, p 199.

[3]   See para 52.26.

[4]   The AHA 1986, Sch 2 para 1(1); and see further para 25.30 ff.

[5]   For the extent that maintaining the land in good agricultural and environmental condition constitutes 'agriculture' see para 52.26.

[6]   [1996] 1 EGLR 1, [1996] 01 EG 102. For a broad interpretation of relevant factors see, eg, *Enfield London Borough Council v Pott* [1990] 2 EGLR 7, [1990] 34 EG 60 (relating to a farm shop).

[7]   Respectively SI 2005/621 (as amended by SI 2005/2003, SI 2006/991 and SI 2006/2075); and SI 2006/41 (W.7).

[8]   ATA 1995, s 13(1). The rent review procedure under the ATA 1995 does not, however, apply in two circumstances. First, it is open to the parties to agree expressly in the tenancy agreement that the rent is not to be reviewed; and, second, the agreement can provide that the rent be varied, at a specified time or times during the tenancy, either (i) by or to a specified amount or (ii) in accordance with a specified formula which does not preclude a reduction and which does not require or permit the exercise by any person of any judgment or discretion in relation to the determination of the rent of the holding: ATA 1995, s 9. See further para 9.6 ff. It is possible to envisage that a specified formula could be employed to take account of, for example, a declining Single Farm Payment as a high historic element is replaced by the flat-rate element.

[9]   ATA 1995, s 13(2).

[10] This obligation to take into account all relevant factors is subject to exceptions: ATA 1995, s 13(3) and (4). For example, the arbitrator is to disregard any effect on the rent of the fact that the tenant is in occupation of the holding. See further paras tbc.

Transfer

52.32 It has been seen that payment entitlements may be transferred by sale or by any other definitive transfer, with or without land[1]. As a general rule, it would appear that tenants are freely able to effect transfers and that European Community law will not impose on Member States any obligation to compensate landlords[2]. As has been seen, such an interpretation would be consistent with the decision of the ECJ in *R v Minister of Agriculture, Fisheries and Food, ex p Country Landowners Association*[3]. Although the case related specifically to premium rights, they shared with the Single Farm Payment the characteristic of being linked to the producer as opposed to the holding; and the ECJ was clear that, in the context of transfer by the tenant, landlords could not look to either the regulations or any general principle of European Community law for compensation[4].

That said, it has also been seen that the ECJ in same case countenanced the use by landlords of express provision to restrict the ability of their tenants to effect transfers[5]. Further, if a land transaction accompanies or is otherwise required for transfer, the landlord will have a powerful lever to extract value from the tenant. In this context, reference may be made to milk quotas. Under that regime, a tenancy for a period of ten months or more is, in principle, required to effect permanent transfer; and such requirement has permitted landlords a significant degree of control[6]. Similarly, under the Single Payment Scheme, a land transaction is not only necessary in the simple case of a transfer by sale with land; it is also necessary on any transfer of payment entitlements by lease or similar types of transactions, since the payment entitlements transferred must be accompanied by the transfer of an equivalent number of eligible hectares[7].

A matter of considerable practical importance is that, when transferring payment entitlements, both landlords and tenants take care to ensure compliance with communication deadlines. In England, for transfers communicated after 23 April 2006, the transferor must communicate the transfer to the relevant competent authority no later than six weeks before the transfer is to take place and no later than six weeks before the last day for submission of the application for direct payments[8]. Since the last day for submission of the application for direct payments is 15 May in each year, the transferor must therefore ensure that any communication has taken place by 2 April. In Wales, it has always been the case that the transferor of payment entitlements must communicate the transfer to the National Assembly no later than six weeks before the last day for submission of the application for direct payments, but no earlier than six weeks before the transfer is to take place[9].

1   Council Regulation (EC) 1782/2003, OJ 2003 L 270/1, art 46(2); and see further para 52.12.
2   Importantly, however, express statutory provision requires that payment entitlements established in Wales may only be transferred within Wales: the Common Agricultural Policy Single Payment and Support Schemes (Wales) Regulations 2005, SI 2005/360 (W.29), reg 9(1). Likewise, in England it has throughout been affirmed that payment entitlements can only be used in the region where they are established: see, eg Rural Payments Agency and Department for Environment, Food and Rural Affairs *Single Payment Scheme: Handbook and Guidance for England 2005* (Rural Payments Agency and Department for Environment, Food and Rural Affairs, London), para 390.
3   Case C-38/94, [1995] ECR I-3875; and see further para 52.28.
4   It may be noted that one of the implementing regulations, Commission Regulation (EEC) 3567/92, provided that 'Member States may, if necessary, take appropriate transitional measures with a view to finding equitable solutions to problems which might arise in contractual relationships existing at the time this Regulation enters into force between producers who do not own all the land they farm, in the event of a transfer of premium rights or of other actions having equivalent effect. Such measures may only be taken in order to resolve the difficulties connected with the introduction of a premium rights system linked to the producer and must in any event respect the principles governing that link': OJ 1992 L 362/41, art 13. The ECJ did not feel that the provision extended to the introduction of a mechanism to compensate detriment to landlords; and, moreover, it was for Member States to assess the need for protective measures, having regard in particular to national arrangements for implementing the rules in question and national rules governing the legal relationship between landlord and tenant. It may also be noted that no such provision is found in the context of the Single Payment Scheme.
5   Case C-38/94, [1995] ECR I-3875 at I-3907; and see further para 52.30.
6   For the current legislation see, in the case of England, the Dairy Produce Quotas Regulations 2005, SI 2005/465, reg 16; and, in the case of Wales, the Dairy Produce Quotas (Wales) Regulations 2005, SI 2005/537 (W.47), reg 16.
7   Council Regulation (EC) 1782/2003, OJ 2003 L 270/1, art 46(2).
8   The Common Agricultural Policy Single Payment and Support Schemes Regulations 2005, SI 2005/219, reg 10 (as amended by SI 2006/989). For the (not immediately clear) European Community legislation see Commission Regulation (EC) 795/2004, OJ 2004 L 141/1, art 25(3): '[a] Member State may require that the transferor shall communicate the

transfer to the competent authority of the Member State where the transfer will operate, within a time period to be established by that Member State but not earlier than six weeks before the transfer shall take place and taking into account the last date for lodging an application under the single payment scheme'.

9   The Common Agricultural Policy Single Payment and Support Schemes (Wales) Regulations 2005, SI 2005/360 (W.29), reg 9(2). Guidance, however, has indicated that communication should occur at least six weeks before the trade is due to take place.

Succession

52.33 The Single Farm Payment and other direct payments have inevitably had a material impact upon succession. In particular, they are crucial to any assessment of net annual income for the purposes of determining whether the applicant meets the criterion that 'he is not the occupier of a commercial unit of agricultural land'[1]. As has been seen, a 'commercial unit of agricultural land' is 'a unit of agricultural land which is capable, when farmed under competent management, of producing a net annual income of an amount not less than the aggregate of the average annual earnings of two full-time, male agricultural workers aged twenty or over'[2]. Central to this calculation have been the units of production orders, issued annually, by reference to whose provisions the net annual income is ascertained[3].

For such purposes, the economic and financial importance of the Single Farm Payment and other direct payments was soon recognised. Indeed, in its 2005 consultation paper, the Department for Environment, Food and Rural Affairs stated that '[s]ubsidies as a percentage of net farm income typically range from between 25 to 125%'[4]. Moreover, it also affirmed that 'an assessment, which excluded [the Single Farm Payment], would not be meaningful'[5]. Following this consultation exercise, the Agricultural Holdings (Units of Production) (England) Order 2006, applicable from 7 November 2006 to 6 November 2007, includes values for eligible hectares under the Single Payment Scheme[6]. It also includes, for example, specific sums in respect of the protein crop premium for beans and dried peas[7]. This accords well with the current realities of farming. However, it may be observed that, in light of the nature and pace of diversity and change in the agricultural world, the Government is considering replacing units of production orders with a system under which it would be for the parties to seek agreement as to whether the commercial unit test was satisfied; and, failing agreement, the matter would fall to be dealt with before the Tribunal[8].

The Single Farm Payment and other direct payments may also generate complications when determining whether the applicant meets the principal source of livelihood test. In particular, for these purposes there may be doubt as to the consequences of the applicant having limited his activities to maintenance of the land in good agricultural and environmental condition.

Under the principal source of livelihood test, the applicant must show that, in the seven years ending with the date of death of the former tenant (in the case of succession on death) or in the previous seven years (in the case of succession on retirement), his only or principal source of livelihood throughout a continuous period of not less than five years (or two or more discontinuous periods together amounting to not less than five years) derived from his agricultural work on the holding or on an agricultural unit of which the holding forms part[9]. Under the Regulatory Reform (Agricultural Tenancies) (England and Wales) Order 2006 there has been expansion of what amounts to agricultural work carried out by a person on the holding or on an agricultural unit of which the holding forms part[10]. This now includes: (i) agricultural work carried out by him from the holding or an agricultural unit of which the holding forms part and (ii) other work carried out by him on or from the holding or an agricultural unit of which the holding forms part. In either case there must be approval in writing by the landlord after 19 October 2006.

As noted, it is far from clear that maintenance of the land in good agricultural and environmental condition qualifies as 'agriculture' for the purposes of the AHA 1986[11]. Accordingly, an applicant who restricts his operations in this way could fail the principal source of livelihood test, notwithstanding that he is conforming with European Community policy. On the other hand, it could be argued that maintaining the land in good agricultural and environmental condition amounts to 'other work carried out' by the applicant on the holding, so as to take advantage of the amendment effected by the Regulatory Reform (Agricultural Tenancies) (England and Wales) Order 2006. However, it must be reiterated that the applicant would need to show approval in writing by the landlord after 19 October 2006. The safer option must be to remain in production if there is any possibility of succession; and, indeed, there is some logic in preserving succession rights for those who engage in farming as their profession as opposed to those who meet relatively light cross-compliance obligations in return for European Community support.

[1] For the 'commercial unit test' see the AHA 1986, s 36(3)(b) (in the case of succession on death) and s 50(2)(b) (in the case of succession on retirement); and see further para 35.55 ff.

[2] AHA 1986, Sch 6 para 3(1).

[3] AHA 1986, Sch 6 paras 3(2) and 4.

[4] Department for Environment, Food and Rural Affairs, 'Consultation Paper on Proposed Changes to the Annual Agricultural Holdings (Units of Production) (England) Order Required Under Schedule 6 of the Agricultural Holdings Act 1986' (Department for Environment, Food and Rural Affairs, London, 2005), para 6.

[5] Department for Environment, Food and Rural Affairs, 'Consultation Paper on Proposed Changes to the Annual Agricultural Holdings (Units of Production) (England) Order Required Under Schedule 6 of the Agricultural Holdings Act 1986' (Department for Environment, Food and Rural Affairs, London, 2005), para 6.

[6] SI 2006/2628, Schedule para 6. Cf the Agricultural Holdings (Units of Production) (Wales) Order 2006, SI 2006/2796 (W.235).

[7] SI 2006/2628, Schedule para 2.

[8] Department for Environment, Food and Rural Affairs, 'Consultation Paper on Proposed Changes to the Annual Agricultural Holdings (Units of Production) (England) Order Required Under Schedule 6 of the Agricultural Holdings Act 1986' (Department for Environment, Food and Rural Affairs, London, 2005), paras 23–24.

[9] AHA 1986, s 36(3)(a) (in the case of succession on death) and s 50(2)(a) (in the case of succession on retirement); and see further para 35.33.

[10] SI 2006/2805.

[11] See para 52.26.

Appendix I
LEGISLATION

Part 1

STATUTES

Contents

Part 1
STATUTES

AGRICULTURE ACT 1947

(1947 C 48)

ARRANGEMENT OF SECTIONS

An Act to make further provision for agriculture

[6th August 1947]

Rules of good estate management and good husbandry

A1.1

10   Good estate management

(1)   For the purposes of this Act, an owner of agricultural land shall be deemed to fulfil his responsibilities to manage it in accordance with the rules of good estate management in so far as his management of the land and (so far as it affects the management of that land) of other land managed by him is such as to be reasonably adequate, having regard to the character and situation of the land and other relevant circumstances, to enable an occupier of the land reasonably skilled in husbandry to maintain efficient production as respects both the kind of produce and the quality and quantity thereof.

(2)   In determining whether the management of land is such as aforesaid, regard shall be had, but without prejudice to the generality of the provisions of the last foregoing subsection, to the extent to which the owner is providing, improving, maintaining and repairing fixed equipment on the land in so far as is necessary to enable an occupier of the land reasonably skilled in husbandry to maintain efficient production as aforesaid.

(3)   The responsibilities under the rules of good estate management of an owner of land in the occupation of another person shall not in relation to the maintenance and repair of fixed equipment include an obligation to do anything which that other person is under an obligation to do by virtue of any agreement.

NOTES

Initial Commencement

To be appointed.

Appointment

Appointment: 1 March 1948: see SI 1948/342, art 1.

Extent

This section does not extend to Scotland: see s 111(3).

Notes

For a commentary, see paras 24.4 and 24.5.

Definitions. For 'agricultural land', see s 109(1); for 'fixed equipment', 'produce' and 'relevant circumstances', see s 109(3); for 'occupier', see s 109(5).

A1.2

11   Good husbandry

(1)   For the purposes of this Act, the occupier of an agricultural unit shall be deemed to fulfil his responsibilities to farm it in accordance with the rules of good husbandry in so far as the extent to which and the manner in which the unit is being farmed (as respects both the kind of operations carried out and the way in which they are carried out) is such that, having regard to the character and situation of the unit, the standard of management thereof by the owner and other relevant circumstances, the occupier is maintaining a reasonable standard of efficient production, as respects both the kind of produce and the quality and quantity thereof, while keeping the unit in a condition to enable such a standard to be maintained in the future.

(2)   In determining whether the manner in which a unit is being farmed is such as aforesaid, regard shall be had, but without prejudice to the generality of the provisions of the last foregoing subsection, to the extent to which—

    (a)   permanent pasture is being properly mown or grazed and maintained in a good state of cultivation and fertility and in good condition;

    (b)   the manner in which arable land is being cropped is such as to maintain that land clean and in a good state of cultivation and fertility and in good condition;

    (c)   the unit is properly stocked where the system of farming practised requires the keeping of livestock, and an efficient standard of management of livestock is maintained where livestock are kept and of breeding where the breeding of livestock is carried out;

(d) the necessary steps are being taken to secure and maintain crops and livestock free from disease and from infestation by insects and other pests;

(e) the necessary steps are being taken for the protection and preservation of crops harvested or lifted, or in course of being harvested or lifted;

(f) the necessary work of maintenance and repair is being carried out.

(3) The responsibilities under the rules of good husbandry of an occupier of an agricultural unit which is not owned by him shall not include an obligation to carry out any work of maintenance or repair which the owner of the unit or any part thereof is under an obligation to carry out in order to fulfil his responsibilities to manage in accordance with the rules of good estate management.

NOTES

Initial Commencement

To be appointed.

Appointment

Appointment: 1 March 1948: see SI 1948/342, art 1.

Extent

This section does not extend to Scotland: see s 111(3).

Notes

For a commentary, see paras 24.4 and 24.6.

Definitions. For 'agricultural unit', see s 109(2); for 'fixed equipment', 'pasture', 'produce' and 'relevant circumstances', see s 109(3); for 'occupier' see s 109(5) (where there is also an interpretation of 'the farming of land').

Agricultural Land Tribunals

A1.3

73   Establishment, constitution and procedure of Agricultural Land Tribunals

(1) [For the purposes of this section the Lord Chancellor shall, after consulting the Chairman of the Agricultural Land Tribunals,] by order constitute such number of areas, together comprising the whole of England and Wales, as he may consider expedient, and for each area so constituted there shall be established an Agricultural Land Tribunal, which shall be charged with the duty of [hearing and determining references and applications made to them under any enactment].

(2) The provisions in that behalf of the Ninth Schedule to this Act shall have effect as to the constitution of Agricultural Land Tribunals and otherwise in relation thereto.

(3) [The Lord Chancellor] may by order make provision for the procedure of Agricultural Land Tribunals, and in particular—

[(aa) as to the manner in which applications are to be made to the Tribunals and the time within which they are to be made;]

(a) for the taking of evidence on oath, affirmation or otherwise, the cross-examination of witnesses, and for the summoning of witnesses in like manner as for the purposes of an arbitration under the [Agricultural Holdings Act 1986];

(b) for the recording and proof of the decisions of the Tribunals, and for enabling the Tribunals to decide by a majority;

(c) ...

(4) An order under the last foregoing subsection may make different provision for the procedure on different classes of reference [or application] to the Tribunals.

[(5) An Agricultural Land Tribunal may, for the purpose of hearing and determining applications and references made to them under any enactment, sit in two or more divisions, and, in relation to the hearing and determination of any such application or reference by such a division, that division shall be deemed to be the Tribunal.]

NOTES

Initial Commencement

To be appointed.

Appointment

Appointment: 1 October 1947: see SI 1947/1767, art 2.

Extent

This section does not extend to Scotland: see s 111(3).

Amendment

Sub-s (1): words from 'For the purposes' to 'Agricultural Land Tribunals,' in square brackets substituted by the Constitutional Reform Act 2005, s 15(1), Sch 4, Pt 1, paras 29, 30.

Date in force: 3 April 2006: see SI 2006/1014, art 2(a), Sch 1, paras 10, 11(d).

Sub-s (1): words 'hearing and determining references and applications made to them under any enactment' in square brackets substituted by the Agriculture Act 1958, s 8(1), Sch 1, Pt I, para 3.

Sub-s (3): first words in square brackets substituted, para (aa) inserted, and para (c) repealed, by the Agriculture Act 1958, ss 8(1), 10(1), Sch 1, Part I, para 3, Sch 3, Part I; words in square brackets in para (a) substituted by the Agricultural Holdings Act 1986, s 100, Sch 14, para 18.

Sub-s (4): words in square brackets inserted by the Agriculture Act 1958, ss 8(1), 10(1), Sch 1, Part I, para 3, Sch 3, Part I.

Sub-s (5): inserted by the Agriculture Act 1958, ss 8(1), 10(1), Sch 1, Part I, para 3, Sch 3, Part I.

See Further

See further: the Agriculture Act 1958, s 5 and the Agricultural Holdings Act 1986, s 53(11).

Subordinate Legislation

Agricultural Land Tribunals (Areas) Order 1982, SI 1982/97.

Agricultural Land Tribunals (Succession to Agricultural Tenancies) Order 1984, SI 1984/1301 (made under sub-ss (3), (4)).

Notes

For a commentary, see Ch 46.

Lord Chancellor. Ie the High Lord Chancellor of Great Britain; see the Interpretation Act 1978, s 5, Sch 1.

By order. Orders under this section must be laid before Parliament (s 108(1)).

Agricultural Land Tribunal. See Sch 9, paras 13–23. Generally, see also 1 Halsbury's Laws (4th edn, reissue) paras 971–975.

An Agricultural Land Tribunal is empowered by the Agriculture (Miscellaneous Provisions) Act 1954, s 5, to award costs but only against a person who is 'vexatious, frivolous or oppressive'; and by s 6 of that Act, it is empowered, or may be directed, to refer questions of law to the High Court, for which latter purpose the power to make orders under sub-s (3) above is extended (see the note 'Orders under this section' below). Procedure on references by Agricultural Land Tribunals is governed by RSC Ord 56, rr 7, 9–11 and Ord 94, r 7.

The functions conferred on the Minister of Agriculture, Fisheries and Food in relation to Agricultural Land Tribunals by this section are transferred to the Lord Chancellor, though the duty of providing the Tribunals with the necessary officers and servants and of paying salaries, fees and allowances (see paras 22(2) and 23(1), (2) of Sch 9 to this Act) remains with the Minister; see the Agriculture Act 1958, s 5.

As to the jurisdiction of an Agricultural Land Tribunal with respect to the cleansing of ditches, and its composition and incidental powers in relation to that jurisdiction, see the Land Drainage Act 1991, ss 28–31.

Agricultural Land Tribunals are under the direct supervision of the Council on Tribunals; see the Tribunals and Inquiries Act 1992, s 1, Sch 1, Pt I, para 1(a) (the Tribunals and Inquiries Act 1971, s 1, Sch 1, Pt I, para 1(a), are repealed by s 18(2) of, and Sch 4, Pt I to, the 1992 Act).

Orders under this section. The Agricultural Land Tribunals (Succession to Agricultural Tenancies) Order 1984, SI 1984/1301; the Agricultural Holdings (Arbitration on Notices) Order 1987, SI 1987/710; the Agricultural Land Tribunal (Rules) Order 1978, SI 1978/259, as amended by SI 1984/1301; the Agricultural Land Tribunals (Areas) Order 1982, SI 1982/97.

The Agricultural Holdings Act 1986, s 40(5), provides that provision is to be made by order requiring notice of applications under ss 39, 41 of the Act, to be given to the landlord and to other interested persons. Such provision is contained in r 5 in the Schedule to SI 1984/1301, noted above.

For a further extension of the power of the Lord Chancellor to make orders in relation to applications for directions, see the Agricultural Holdings Act 1986, s 53(11).

A1.4

109   Interpretation

(1)   In this Act the expression 'agricultural land' means land used for agriculture which is so used for the purposes of a trade or business, or which is designated by the Minister for the purposes of this subsection, and includes any land so designated as land which in the opinion of the Minister ought to be brought into use for agriculture:
    Provided that no designation under this subsection shall extend—

  (a)   to land used as pleasure grounds, private gardens or allotment gardens, or
  (b)   to land kept or preserved mainly or exclusively for the purposes of sport or recreation, except where the Minister is satisfied that its use for agriculture would not be inconsistent with its use for the said purposes and it is so stated in the designation.

(2)   In this Act the expression 'agricultural unit' means land which occupied as a unit for agricultural purposes, including—

  (a)   any dwelling-house or other building occupied by the same person for the purpose of farming the land, and
  (b)   any other land falling within the definition in this Act of the expression 'agricultural land' which is in the occupation of the same person, being land as to which the Minister is satisfied that having regard to the character and situation thereof and other relevant circumstances it ought in the interests of full and efficient production to be farmed in conjunction with the agricultural unit, and directs accordingly:
    Provided that the Minister shall not give a direction under this subsection as respects any land unless it is for the time being not in use for any purpose which appears to him to be substantial having regard to the use to which it might be put for agriculture.

(3)   In this Act the following expressions have the meanings hereby respectively assigned to them, that is to say:—

'agriculture' includes horticulture, fruit growing, seed growing, dairy farming and livestock breeding and keeping, the use of land as grazing land, meadow land, osier land, market gardens and nursery grounds, and the use of land for woodlands where that use is ancillary to the farming of land for other agricultural purposes, and 'agricultural' shall be construed accordingly;

'allotment garden' means an allotment not exceeding [0.10 hectare] in extent which is wholly or mainly cultivated by the occupier for the production of vegetables or fruit for consumption by himself or his family;

'fixed equipment' includes any building or structure affixed to land and any works on, in, over or under land, and also includes anything grown on land for a purpose other than use after severance from the land, consumption of the thing grown or of produce thereof, or amenity, and references to fixed equipment on land shall be construed accordingly;

'functions' includes powers and duties;

'livestock' includes any creature kept for the production of food, wool, skins or fur, or for the purpose of its use in the farming of land;

'pasture' includes meadow;

'prescribed' has the meaning assigned to it by the last foregoing section;

'produce' includes anything (whether live or dead) produced in the course of agriculture;

'relevant circumstances', in relation to an owner or occupier, includes all circumstances affecting management or farming other than the personal circumstances of the owner or occupier.

(4)   References in this Act to any enactment shall be construed, except where the context otherwise requires, as references to that enactment as amended by or under any other enactment, including this Act.

(5)   References in this Act to the farming of land include references to the carrying on in relation to the land of any agricultural activity; and in relation to any agricultural activity the person having the right to carry it on shall be deemed to be the occupier of the land.

(6)   References in this Act to the use of land for agriculture include, in relation to land forming part of an agricultural unit, references to any use of the land in connection with the farming of the unit.

NOTES

Initial Commencement

To be appointed.

Appointment

Appointment: 1 October 1947: see SI 1947/1767, art 2.

Extent

This section does not extend to Scotland: see s 111(3).

Amendment

Sub-s (3): in definition 'allotment garden' words in square brackets substituted by SI 1978/446.

Transfer of Functions

Transfer of Function: functions exercisable by the Minister transferred by virtue of the Transfer of Functions (Wales) (No 1) Order 1978, SI 1978/272, art 2, Sch 1.

Functions under this section, so far as exercisable in relation to Wales, transferred to the National Assembly for Wales, by the National Assembly for Wales (Transfer of Functions) Order 1999, SI 1999/672, art 2, Sch 1.

SCHEDULE 9
CONSTITUTION ETC OF COMMISSION, SUB-COMMISSION, COMMITTEES
AND TRIBUNALS

Sections 68, 71, 73

Agricultural Land Tribunals

A1.5

[13   (1)   The Lord Chancellor shall appoint a chairman for each Agricultural Land Tribunal, who shall be a [person who has a 7 year general qualification, within the meaning of section 71 of the Courts and Legal Services Act 1990].

(2)   [Subject to sub-paragraph (2A) of this paragraph,] the chairman shall hold office for [such period as may be specified in the terms of his appointment], and a chairman whose term of office expires shall be eligible to be re-appointed as chairman.

[(2A)   No appointment of a person to be the chairman shall be such as to extend beyond the day on which he attains the age of seventy years; but this sub-paragraph is subject to section 26(4) to (6) of the Judicial Pensions and Retirement Act 1993 (power to authorise continuance in office up to the age of seventy-five years).]

(3)   The chairman may resign his office by notice in writing to the Lord Chancellor.

(4)   If the Lord Chancellor [and Lord Chief Justice are both] satisfied that the chairman is incapacitated by infirmity of mind or body from discharging the duties of his office, or if the chairman is adjudged bankrupt or makes a composition or arrangement with his creditors, the Lord Chancellor may[, with the concurrence of the Lord Chief Justice,] revoke the appointment of the chairman.

14   [(1)]   The Lord Chancellor shall draw up for each Agricultural Land Tribunal and from time to time revise a panel of deputy-chairmen, who shall be [persons eligible for appointment under paragraph 13(1).]

[(2)   A member of the panel of deputy-chairmen shall vacate his office on the day on which he attains the age of seventy years; but this sub-paragraph is subject to section 26(4) to (6) of the Judicial Pensions and Retirement Act 1993 (power to authorise continuance in office up to the age of seventy-five years).]

15   (1)   The Lord Chancellor shall draw up for each Agricultural Land Tribunal and from time to time revise a panel of persons appearing to him to represent the interests of farmers and a panel of persons appearing to him to represent the interests of owners of agricultural land.

[(1A)   A member of either of the panels drawn up under sub-paragraph (1) of this paragraph shall vacate his office on the day on which he attains the age of seventy years; but this sub-paragraph is subject to section 26(4) to (6) of the Judicial Pensions and Retirement Act 1993 (power to authorise continuance in office up to the age of seventy-five years).]

(2)   Subject to the following sub-paragraph, the persons to be placed on either panel shall be selected by the Lord Chancellor from nominations made at his request by persons appearing to him to represent the interests of farmers or of owners of agricultural land, as the case may be.

(3)   The last foregoing sub-paragraph shall not prevent the Lord Chancellor from placing on either of the panels a person not nominated in accordance with that

sub-paragraph, if the persons requested to make the nominations for that purpose do not make the required number of nominations, or the nominations they make do not include enough persons who appear to the Lord Chancellor to be suitable.

16   (1)   For each hearing by an Agricultural Land Tribunal of an application or reference thereto the members of the Tribunal shall be—

(a)   the chairman, or a person nominated by the chairman either from the panel of deputy-chairmen (whether for that Tribunal or for any other Agricultural Land Tribunal) or from among the chairmen of other Agricultural Land Tribunals, and

(b)   one person nominated by the chairman from each of the panels for that Tribunal drawn up under the last foregoing paragraph or from a corresponding panel for any other Agricultural Land Tribunal.

(2)   The chairman may, if it appears to him expedient so to do, nominate two assessors to be added to the Tribunal for the hearing of an application or reference thereto in order to assist the Tribunal in the hearing.

(3)   The assessors shall be selected by the chairman from a panel of persons nominated by the President of the Royal Institution of Chartered Surveyors.

16A   [(1)]   If the chairman of an Agricultural Land Tribunal is prevented by sickness or any other reason from making nominations under sub-paragraphs (1) and (2) of the last foregoing paragraph or from otherwise discharging the duties of his office, those duties may be discharged by a person appointed from the panel of deputy-chairmen for that Tribunal by the chairman or, if the chairman is unable to make the appointment, by the [Lord Chief Justice, after consulting the Lord Chancellor].

[(2)   The Lord Chief Justice may nominate a judicial office holder (as defined in section 109(4) of the Constitutional Reform Act 2005) to exercise his functions under sub-paragraph (1).]]

17   (1)   [The Lord Chancellor] may by order direct that the foregoing provisions of this Schedule as to the nominated members of Agricultural Land Tribunals shall have effect subject to such modification of the number of such members, and such additions to the classes of persons referred to in paragraph 15 of this Schedule, as may be specified in the order.

(2)   Any order under this paragraph shall be of no effect unless approved by resolution of each House of Parliament.

NOTES

Initial Commencement

To be appointed.

Appointment

Appointment: 1 October 1947: see SI 1947/1767, art 2.

Extent

This section does not extend to Scotland: see s 111(3).

Amendment

Para 13: substituted, together with paras 14–16, 16A, for paras 13–16 as originally enacted, by the Agriculture Act 1958, s 8(1), Sch 1, Pt I, para 5.

Para 13: in sub-para (1) words from 'person who has' to 'the Courts and Legal Services Act 1990' in square brackets substituted by the Courts and Legal Services Act 1990, s 71(2), Sch 10, para 6.

Para 13: in sub-para (2) words 'Subject to sub-paragraph (2A) of this paragraph,' in square brackets inserted by the Judicial Pensions and Retirement Act 1993, s 26(10), Sch 6, para 46(1), (2)(a); for savings see s 27, Sch 7 thereto.

Para 13: in sub-para (2) words 'such period as may be specified in the terms of his appointment' in square brackets substituted by the Judicial Pensions and Retirement Act 1993, s 26(10), Sch 6, para 46(1), (2)(b); for savings see s 27, Sch 7 thereto.

Para 13: sub-para (2A) inserted by the Judicial Pensions and Retirement Act 1993, s 26(10), Sch 6, para 46(1), (3); for savings see s 27, Sch 7 thereto.

Para 13: in sub-para (4) words 'and Lord Chief Justice are both' in square brackets substituted by the Constitutional Reform Act 2005, s 15(1), Sch 4, Pt 1, paras 29, 33(1), (2)(a).

Date in force: 3 April 2006: see SI 2006/1014, art 2(a), Sch 1, paras 10, 11(d).

Para 13: in sub-para (4) words ', with the concurrence of the Lord Chief Justice,' in square brackets inserted by the Constitutional Reform Act 2005, s 15(1), Sch 4, Pt 1, paras 29, 33(1), (2)(b).

Date in force: 3 April 2006: see SI 2006/1014, art 2(a), Sch 1, paras 10, 11(d).

Para 14: substituted together with paras 13, 15–16A for paras 13–16 as originally enacted, by the Agriculture Act 1958, s 8(1), Sch 1, Part I, para 5; sub-para (1) numbered as such with savings by the Judicial Pensions and Retirement Act 1993, s 26, Sch 6, para 46(4), for savings see s 27, Sch 7 thereof, words in square brackets substituted by the Courts and Legal Services Act 1990, s 71(2), Sch 10, para 6; sub-para (2) inserted with savings by the Judicial Pensions and Retirement Act 1993, s 26, Sch 6, para 46(4), for savings see s 27, Sch 7 thereof.

Para 15: substituted together with paras 13, 14, 16, 16A for paras 13–16 as originally enacted, by the Agriculture Act 1958, s 8(1), Sch 1, Part I, para 5; sub-para (1A) inserted with savings by the Judicial Pensions and Retirement Act 1993, s 26, Sch 6, para 46(5), for savings see s 27, Sch 7 thereof.

Paras 16, 16A: substituted, together with paras 13–15, for paras 13–16 as originally enacted, by the Agriculture Act 1958, s 8(1), Sch 1, Pt I, para 5.

Para 16A: sub-para (1) numbered as such by the Constitutional Reform Act 2005, s 15(1), Sch 4, Pt 1, paras 29, 33(1), (3)(a).

Date in force: 3 April 2006: see SI 2006/1014, art 2(a), Sch 1, paras 10, 11(d).

Para 16A: in sub-para (1) words 'Lord Chief Justice, after consulting with the Lord Chancellor' in square brackets substituted by the Constitutional Reform Act 2005, s 15(1), Sch 4, Pt 1, paras 29, 33(1), (3)(b).

Date in force: 3 April 2006: see SI 2006/1014, art 2(a), Sch 1, paras 10, 11(d).

Para 16A: sub-para (2) inserted by the Constitutional Reform Act 2005, s 15(1), Sch 4, Pt 1, paras 29, 33(1), (3)(c).

Date in force: 3 April 2006: see SI 2006/1014, art 2(a), Sch 1, paras 10, 11(d).

Para 17: in sub-para (1) words in square brackets substituted by the Agriculture Act 1958, s 8(1), Sch 1, Part I, para 5.

Transfer of Functions

Functions of the Minister, so far as exercisable in relation to Wales, transferred to the National Assembly for Wales, by the National Assembly for Wales (Transfer of Functions) Order 1999, SI 1999/672, art 2, Sch 1.

Notes

For a commentary, see Ch 46.

AGRICULTURE (MISCELLANEOUS PROVISIONS) ACT 1954

(1954 C 39)

ARRANGEMENT OF SECTIONS

An Act to continue the power to make grants or contributions in respect of field drainage, liming and other matters; to amend Part IV of the Agriculture Act 1947 with respect to the holdings to be treated as smallholdings, and to the contributions to losses of smallholdings authorities; to alter the manner of appointing nominated members of Agricultural Land Tribunals, and enable those Tribunals to award costs and to refer questions of law to the High Court; to amend the Agricultural Holdings Act 1948 with respect to the operation of certain notices to quit; to make further provision with respect to research and education in sugar beet growing, to the collection of waste for use as animal feedings stuffs, to preventing the spread of pests and diseases by imported bees and to the application of the Diseases of Animals Act 1950 to air transport; to amend the Seeds Act 1920 with respect to the consequences of contraventions of that Act, and to the delivery and effect of particulars given thereunder; to amend the law as to agricultural wages of holiday workers in Scotland; and to extend the Corn Returns Act 1882 to Scotland

[4th June 1954]

A1.6

1 ...

...

NOTES

Amendment

Repealed by the Statute Law (Repeals) Act 1993.

A1.7

2   ...

...

NOTES

Amendment

Repealed by the Statute Law (Repeals) Act 1986.

A1.8

3   ...

...

NOTES

Amendment

Repealed by the Statute Law (Repeals) Act 2004.

Date in force: 22 July 2004: (no specific commencement provision).

A1.9

4   ...

...

NOTES

Amendment

Repealed by the Agriculture Act 1958, s 10(1), Sch 2, Pt I.

A1.10

5   Power of Agricultural Land Tribunal to award costs

(1) An Agricultural Land Tribunal, where it appears to them that any person concerned in a reference [or application] to them (including any Minister of the Crown or Government department so concerned) has acted frivolously, vexatiously or oppressively in applying for or in connection with the reference [or application] may order that person to pay to any other person either a specified sum in respect of the costs incurred by him at or with a view to the hearing or the taxed amount of those costs; and an order may be made under this subsection whether or not the reference [or application] proceeds to a hearing.

(2) Any costs required by an order under this section to be taxed may be taxed in the county court according to such of the scales prescribed by county court rules for proceedings in the county court as may be directed by the order or, if the order gives no direction, by the county court.

(3) Any sum payable by virtue of an order of an Agricultural Land Tribunal under this section shall, if the county court so orders, be recoverable by execution issued from the county court or otherwise as if payable under an order of that court; and, subject to county court rules, an application for an order of the county court under this subsection may be made *ex parte*.

(4) The powers of the county court under this section may be exercised by the registrar.

NOTES

Initial Commencement

Royal Assent: 4 June 1954: (no specific commencement provision).

Amendment

Sub-s (1): words in square brackets inserted by the Agriculture Act 1958, s 8(1), Sch 1, Part I, para 26.

A1.11

6 **Power of Agricultural Land Tribunal to refer questions of Law to High Court**

(1) Any question of law arising in the course of proceedings before an Agricultural Land Tribunal may, at the request of any party to the proceedings, be referred by the Tribunal to the High Court for decision, whether before or after the Tribunal have given their decision in the proceedings.

(2) Subject to the following provisions of this section, if an Agricultural Land Tribunal, after giving their decision in any proceedings, refuse any such request to refer a question to the High Court under this section, any person aggrieved by the refusal may apply to the High Court for an order directing them to do so.

(3) ...

(4) Provision shall be made by order under subsection (3) of section seventy-three of the Agriculture Act 1947 (which relates to the procedure of Agricultural Land Tribunals), for limiting the time for requesting a Tribunal to refer a question to the High Court under this section, and for requiring notice to be given to a Tribunal within a time limited by the order of any intended application to the High Court under this section; and provision shall be made by rules of court for limiting the time for instituting proceedings in the High Court under subsection (2) of this section.

(5) Where, after an Agricultural Land Tribunal have given their decision in any proceedings, they refer a question to the High Court under this section, or receive notice of an intended application to the High Court for an order directing them to do so, effect shall not be given to the Tribunal's decision unless and until the Tribunal otherwise order after the proceedings in the High Court and any proceedings arising therefrom have been concluded (or the right to take or continue any such proceedings has lapsed); and any such order of the Tribunal shall, where necessary, modify their decision so as to give effect to the decision on any reference to the High Court and, in a case relating to a notice to quit, may postpone (or further postpone) the date at which the tenancy is to be terminated by the notice, if it has effect.

(6) [The Lord Chancellor] may, by order under subsection (3) of section seventy-three of the Agriculture Act 1947, make such provision as he thinks necessary or expedient for enabling the chairman of an Agricultural Land Tribunal to exercise all or any of the Tribunal's powers under the last foregoing subsection, and for regulating any proceedings before an Agricultural Land Tribunal which are consequent on the reference of any question to the High Court under this section or on the decision on such a reference, and enabling any such proceedings to be dealt with by an Agricultural Land Tribunal constituted for the purpose, where they cannot conveniently be dealt with by the Tribunal originally constituted for the purpose of the proceedings in the course of which the question arose.

(7) ...

NOTES

Initial Commencement

To be appointed: see sub-s (7) above.

Appointment

Appointment: 1 September 1954: see SI 1954/1137, art 3.

Amendment

Sub-s (3): repealed by the Agriculture Act 1958, ss 8(1), 10(1), Sch 1, Part I, para 27, Sch 2, Part I.

Sub-s (6): words in square brackets substituted by the Agriculture Act 1958, s 8(1), Sch 1, Part I, para 27.

Sub-s (7): repealed by the Statute Law (Repeals) Act 2004.

Date in force: 22 July 2004: (no specific commencement provision).

Subordinate Legislation

Agriculture (Miscellaneous Provisions) Act 1954 (Commencement) Order 1954, SI 1954/1137.

A1.12

7 ...

...

NOTES

Amendment

Repealed by the Agriculture (Miscellaneous Provisions) Act 1976, s 26(3), Sch 4, Pt II.

A1.13

8 ...

...

NOTES

Amendment

Repealed by the Sugar Act 1956, s 32(2).

A1.14

9   Collection of kitchen waste etc for animal feeding stuffs in England and Wales

(1)   A local authority in England or Wales may, whether in the discharge of their functions as to the removal of house or trade refuse or otherwise, collect kitchen or other waste in their area for use as animal feeding stuffs, with or without processing.

(2)   An authority collecting waste under this section may agree to pay for waste saved for collection by them, may process the waste they collect, and may sell it processed or unprocessed; and, if they process it, they may acquire other materials for processing with it, including kitchen or other waste collected by any other local authority or person.

(3)   ...

(4)   A local authority collecting waste under this section may provide receptacles in which the waste may be deposited for collection, and may place any receptacles so provided in any street or public place.

(5)   If a person wilfully deposits in any receptacle provided under the last foregoing subsection, or otherwise used for the deposit of waste to be collected under this section, anything which he knows or has reasonable cause to believe to be unsuitable for use as animal feeding stuffs, he shall be liable on summary conviction to a fine not exceeding [level 1 on the standard scale]; and if any person (other than a person employed in connection with the local authority's collection of the waste) removes the whole or part of the contents of any such receptacle when placed in a street or public place or set out for the purpose of its contents being removed under this section, he shall be liable on summary conviction to a fine not exceeding [level 1 on the standard scale].

(6)   A local authority may make bye-laws regulating in their area or any part of it the collection of kitchen or other waste for use as animal feeding stuffs and the carriage of waste so collected (whether there or elsewhere), and in particular for securing the use of suitable times, routes, vehicles and receptacles; and the fines which may be imposed by the bye-laws on persons offending against them may be of an amount not exceeding [level 1 on the standard scale or not exceeding a lesser amount], with, in the case of a continuing offence, a further sum not exceeding [£2] for each day during which the offence continues after conviction therefor.
    Bye-laws made under this subsection shall require confirmation of the [Secretary of State].

(7)   Proceedings in respect of an offence created by or under this section shall not be taken by any person other than the local authority in whose area the offence is alleged to have been committed, unless taken by or with the consent of the Director of Public Prosecutions:
    Provided that, where a local authority collects waste under this section outside their area, they may without the consent of the Director of Public Prosecutions take proceedings in respect of an offence under subsection (5) of this section alleged to have been committed at any place within the limits of their collection.

(8)   Nothing in this section shall be taken as authorising anything to be used unprocessed as animal feeding stuffs where processing is required by or under any other enactment.

(9)   In this section the expression "local authority" means the council of a borough, urban district or rural district or an authority which is a sanitary authority for the purposes of the Public Health (London) Act 1936.

(10) There shall be paid out of moneys provided by Parliament any increase attributable to this section in the sums so payable under Part I of the Local Government Act 1948, or under the Local Government (Financial Provisions) (Scotland) Act 1954.

NOTES

Initial Commencement

Royal Assent: 4 June 1954: (no specific commencement provision).

Amendment

Sub-s (3): repealed by the Local Government Act 1972, s 272(1), Sch 30.

Sub-s (5): first-mentioned maximum fine increased and converted to a level on the standard scale, other maximum fine increased and converted to a level on the standard scale with the enhanced penalty on a subsequent conviction being abolished, by the Criminal Justice Act 1982, ss 35, 37, 38, 46.

Sub-s (6): first-mentioned maximum fine increased and converted to a reference to the standard scale by the Criminal Justice Act 1982, ss 37, 46; second amendment in square brackets made by the Decimal Currency Act 1969, s 10(1); third amendment in square brackets made by virtue of SI 1970/1681, art 2(1).

Transfer of Functions

Secretary of State: functions under sub-s (6) in relation to Wales now exercisable by the Secretary of State for Wales by virtue of the Secretary of State for Wales and Minister of Land and Natural Resources Order 1965, SI 1965/319.

Functions of the Secretary of State referred to in sub-s (6) above, transferred to the National Assembly for Wales, by the National Assembly for Wales (Transfer of Functions) Order 1999, SI 1999/672, art 2, Sch 1.

A1.15

10 ...

...

NOTES

Amendment

Repealed by the Bees Act 1980, s 5(3).

A1.16

11 ...

...

NOTES

Amendment

Repealed by the Animal Health Act 1981, s 96, Sch 6.

A1.17

12 ...

...

NOTES

Amendment

Repealed by the Plant Varieties and Seeds Act 1964, s 31(1), Sch 6.

A1.18

13 ...

...

NOTES

Amendment

Repealed by the Statute Law (Repeals) Act 1973.

A1.19

14   Extension of Corn Returns Act 1882, to Scotland

(1) The Corn Returns Act 1882 (which provides for the making of returns of purchases of British corn and for the computation and publication of the average prices of each sort of British corn, and for purposes connected with the matters aforesaid), shall, subject to the modifications specified in the next following subsection, extend to Scotland.

(2) The modifications referred to in the foregoing subsection are—

   (a) for any reference to the Board of Trade or to the Minister of Agriculture and Fisheries there shall be substituted a reference to the Secretary of State;

   (b) for any reference to the London Gazette there shall be substituted a reference to the Edinburgh Gazette;

   (c) in section twelve for the words "shall be guilty of a misdemeanour" there shall be substituted the words "shall be guilty of an offence and shall be liable on summary conviction to a fine not exceeding twenty pounds"; ...

   (d) ...

(3) The expenses of the Secretary of State under the Corn Returns Act 1882, as extended by this section shall be paid out of moneys provided by Parliament.

NOTES

Initial Commencement

Royal Assent: 4 June 1954: (no specific commencement provision).

Extent

This section applies to Scotland only.

Amendment

Sub-s (2): para (d) and word omitted immediately preceding it repealed by the Statute Law (Repeals) Act 1993, s 1(1), Sch 1, Pt II.

A1.20

15   Construction of references to enactments

Any reference in this Act to any previous enactment shall, except in so far as the contrary intention appears, be construed as a reference to that enactment as amended, extended or applied by any subsequent enactment, including this Act.

NOTES

Initial Commencement

Royal Assent: 4 June 1954: (no specific commencement provision).

A1.21

16   Application to Northern Ireland

The provisions of this Act do not extend to Northern Ireland, ... , ...

NOTES

Initial Commencement

Royal Assent: 4 June 1954: (no specific commencement provision).

Amendment

First words omitted repealed by the Statute Law (Repeals) Act 1993; final words omitted repealed by the Northern Ireland Constitution Act 1973, s 41(1), Sch 6, Part I, and the Statute Law (Repeals) Act 1973.

A1.22

17   Short title and repeal

(1)   This Act may be cited as the Agriculture (Miscellaneous Provisions) Act 1954.

(2)   ...

NOTES

Initial Commencement

Royal Assent: 4 June 1954: (no specific commencement provision).

Amendment

Sub-s (2): repealed by the Statute Law (Repeals) Act 1973.

SCHEDULE 1

...

A1.23

...

NOTES

Amendment

Repealed by the Agriculture Act 1958, s 10(1), Sch 2, Pt I.

SCHEDULE 2

...

A1.24

...

NOTES

Amendment

Repealed by the Animal Health Act 1981, s 96, Sch 6.

SCHEDULE 3

...

...

A1.25

...

NOTES

Amendment

Repealed by the Statute Law (Repeals) Act 1973.

AGRICULTURE (MISCELLANEOUS PROVISIONS) ACT 1968

(1968 C 34)

ARRANGEMENT OF SECTIONS

A1.26 *Statutes*

SCHEDULE 3
Supplementary provisions with respect to payments under s 12(1) in England and Wales

SCHEDULE 4
...

SCHEDULE 5
...

SCHEDULE 6
...

SCHEDULE 7
...

SCHEDULE 8
Repeals

An Act to make further provision with respect to the welfare of livestock; to provide for additional payments for certain tenants of agricultural holdings who receive compensation for disturbance in respect of their holdings or whose land is acquired or taken possession of compulsorily or whose landlords resume possession of the land for non-agricultural purposes; to make further provision with respect to the termination of tenancies of agricultural holdings in Scotland acquired by succession; to make further provision for England and Wales with respect to drainage charges, drainage rates and grants and advances to drainage authorities; to provide for payments in respect of bacon and grants in respect of break crops and the supply of water to certain buildings; to make further provision with respect to the compensation of tenants of agricultural holdings whose land is acquired or taken possession of compulsorily; to amend section 3 of the Parks Regulation (Amendment) Act 1926, the Agricultural Wages Act 1948 and the Agricultural Wages (Scotland) Act 1949, the Restrictive Trade Practices Act 1956 in its application to agricultural marketing boards, section 53(2) of the Agricultural Marketing Act 1958, section 1 of the Agricultural and Forestry Associations Act 1962, the Plant Varieties and Seeds Act 1964 and section 49 of the Agriculture Act 1967; and for purposes connected with the matters aforesaid

[3rd July 1968]

PART I: WELFARE OF LIVESTOCK

NOTES
Amendment
Repealed by the Animal Welfare Act 2006, s 65, Sch 4.
Date in force (for certain purposes): 27 March 2007: see SI 2007/1030, art 2(1)(k), (m).
Date in force (for certain purposes): 6 April 2007: see SI 2007/499, art 2(2)(m).
Date in force (for remaining purposes): to be appointed: see the Animal Welfare Act 2006, s 68(3).

A1.26

1   ...

...

NOTES

Amendment

Repealed by the Animal Health and Welfare (Scotland) Act 2006, s 52, Sch 2, para 8(1) and the Animal Welfare Act 2006, s 65, Sch 4.

Date in force (in relation to Scotland): 6 October 2006: see SSI 2006/482, art 2.

Date in force (in relation to Wales): 27 March 2007: see SI 2007/1030, art 2(1)(k), (m).

Date in force (in relation to England): 6 April 2007: see SI 2007/499, art 2(2)(m).

A1.27

2   Regulations with respect to the welfare of livestock

(1)   The Ministers may, after consultation with such persons appearing to them to represent any interests concerned as the Ministers consider appropriate, by regulations make such provision with respect to the welfare of livestock for the time being situated on agricultural land as they think fit; and without prejudice to the generality of the foregoing provisions of this section the regulations may in particular include provision—

(a)   *with respect to the dimensions and layout of accommodation for livestock, the materials to be used in constructing any such accommodation and the facilities by way of lighting, heating, cooling, ventilation, drainage, water supply and otherwise to be provided in connection with any accommodation;*

(b)   *for ensuring the provision of balanced diets for livestock and for prohibiting or regulating the use of any substance as food for livestock and the importation and supply of any substance intended for use as food for livestock;*

(c)   *for prohibiting the bleeding of livestock and the mutilation of livestock in any manner specified in the regulations, and for prohibiting or regulating the use of any method of marking or restraining livestock or interfering with the capacity of livestock to smell, see, hear, emit sound or exercise any other faculty.*

(2)   Without prejudice to the generality of the powers conferred by subsection (1) of this section, regulations under this section may—

(a)   *provide that a person who contravenes or fails to comply with specified provisions of the regulations shall be guilty of an offence under this section;*

(b)   *provide for exemptions, either subject to conditions prescribed by the regulations or without conditions, from any provisions of the regulations; and*

(c)   *contain such incidental and supplemental provisions as the Ministers consider expedient for the purposes of the regulations.*

(3)   No regulations shall be made under this section unless a draft of the regulations has been approved by a resolution of each House of Parliament.

NOTES

Initial Commencement

Specified date: 3 September 1968: see s 54(2).

Amendment

Repealed by the Animal Health and Welfare (Scotland) Act 2006, s 52, Sch 2, para 8(1) and the Animal Welfare Act 2006, s 65, Sch 4.

Date in force (in relation to Scotland): 6 October 2006: see SSI 2006/482, art 2; for savings see art 4(3) thereof.

Date in force (in relation to England and Wales): to be appointed: see the Animal Welfare Act 2006, s 68(3).

Transfer of Functions

Functions of the Minister and the Ministers, so far as exercisable in relation to Wales, transferred to the National Assembly for Wales, by the National Assembly for Wales (Transfer of Functions) Order 1999, SI 1999/672, art 2, Sch 1.

Subordinate Legislation

UK

Welfare of Farmed Animals (England) Regulations 2000, SI 2000/1870.

Welfare of Farmed Animals (Wales) Regulations 2001, SI 2001/2682.

Welfare of Farmed Animals (England) (Amendment) Regulations 2002, SI 2002/1646.

Welfare of Farmed Animals (Wales) (Amendment) Regulations 2002, SI 2002/1898.

Welfare of Farmed Animals (England) (Amendment) Regulations 2003, SI 2003/299.

Welfare of Farmed Animals (Wales) (Amendment) Regulations 2003, SI 2003/1726.

Welfare of Animals (Miscellaneous Revocations) (Wales) Regulations 2007, SI 2007/1027.

Welfare of Animals (Miscellaneous Revocations) (England) Regulations 2007, SI 2007/1101.

Scotland

Welfare of Farmed Animals (Scotland) Regulations 2000, SSI 2000/442.

Welfare of Farmed Animals (Scotland) Amendment Regulations 2002, SSI 2002/334.

Welfare of Farmed Animals (Scotland) Amendment Regulations 2003, SSI 2003/488.

A1.28

3   Codes of recommendations for the welfare of livestock

(1)   The Ministers may from time to time, after consultation with such persons appearing to them to represent any interests concerned as the Ministers consider appropriate,—

>   *(a)   prepare codes containing such recommendations with respect to the welfare of livestock for the time being situated on agricultural land as they consider proper for the guidance of persons concerned with livestock; and*
>   *(b)   revise any such code by revoking, varying, amending or adding to the provisions of the code in such manner as the Ministers think fit.*

(2)   A code prepared in pursuance of this section and any alterations proposed to be made on a revision of such a code shall be laid before both Houses of Parliament forthwith after being prepared; and the code or revised code, as the case may be, shall not be issued until the code or the proposed alterations have been approved by both Houses.

(3)   Subject to subsection (2) of this section, the Ministers shall cause every code prepared or revised in pursuance of this section to be printed, and may cause copies of it to be put on sale to the public at such a price as the Ministers may determine.

(4)   A failure on the part of any person to observe a provision of a code for the time being issued under this section shall not of itself render that person liable to proceedings of any kind; but such a failure on the part of any person may, in

proceedings against him for an offence under section 1 of this Act, be relied upon by the prosecution as tending to establish the guilt of the accused unless it is shown that he cannot reasonably be expected to have observed the provision in question within the period which has elapsed since that provision was first included in a code issued under this section.

[(5) *In relation to the exercise by the Scottish Ministers of functions under this section, the references in subsection (2) of this section to both Houses of Parliament shall be read as references to the Scottish Parliament.*]

NOTES

Initial Commencement

Specified date: 3 September 1968: see s 54(2).

Amendment

Repealed by the Animal Health and Welfare (Scotland) Act 2006, s 52, Sch 2, para 8(1) and the Animal Welfare Act 2006, s 65, Sch 4.

Date in force (in relation to Scotland): 6 October 2006: see SSI 2006/482, art 2; for savings see art 4(2) thereof.

Date in force (in relation to England and Wales): to be appointed: see the Animal Welfare Act 2006, s 68(3).

Sub-s (5): inserted by SI 1999/1820, art 4, Sch 2, Pt I, para 46.

Date in force: 1 July 1999: see SI 1999/1820, art 1(2).

Transfer of Functions

Functions of the Minister and the Ministers, so far as exercisable in relation to Wales, transferred to the National Assembly for Wales, by the National Assembly for Wales (Transfer of Functions) Order 1999, SI 1999/672, art 2, Sch 1.

A1.29

4   Expenditure on free advice on the welfare of livestock

Without prejudice to the generality of his powers to incur expenditure under the enactments relating to the eradication and prevention of diseases of animals, the Minister may, with the approval of the Treasury, spend such sums as he thinks fit on the giving of advice, free of charge, to persons concerned with livestock on matters relating to the welfare of livestock.

NOTES

Initial Commencement

Specified date: 3 September 1968: see s 54(2).

Amendment

Repealed by the Animal Welfare Act 2006, s 65, Sch 4.

Date in force (in relation to Wales): 27 March 2007: see SI 2007/1030, art 2(1)(k), (m).

Date in force (in relation to England): 6 April 2007: see SI 2007/499, art 2(2)(m).

Date in force (in relation to Scotland): to be appointed: see the Animal Welfare Act 2006, s 68(3).

A1.30

5   Extension of classes of operations in which anaesthetics must be used

The Ministers may, after consultation with the Royal College of Veterinary Surgeons and with such persons appearing to the Ministers to represent any other interests concerned as the Ministers consider appropriate, by order provide that paragraphs 7 and 8 of Schedule 1 to the Protection of Animals (Anaesthetics) Act 1954 (which exempt certain minor operations from the requirement to use anaesthetics imposed by that Act) shall not permit the performance, either in any circumstances or in such circumstances as may be specified in the order, of such operations as may be so specified.

NOTES

Initial Commencement

Specified date: 3 September 1968: see s 54(2).

Amendment

Repealed by the Animal Welfare Act 2006, s 65, Sch 4.

Date in force (in relation to Wales): 27 March 2007: see SI 2007/1030, art 2(1)(k), (m).

Date in force (in relation to England): 6 April 2007: see SI 2007/499, art 2(2)(m).

Date in force (in relation to Scotland): to be appointed: see the Animal Welfare Act 2006, s 68(3).

Subordinate Legislation

Docking of Pigs (Use of Anaesthetics) Order 1974, SI 1974/798.

Removal of Antlers in Velvet (Anaesthetics) Order 1980, SI 1980/685.

A1.31

6   Powers of entry, etc

(1)   A person duly authorised in writing by the Minister may at any reasonable time enter upon any land, other than premises used wholly or mainly as a dwelling, for the purpose of ascertaining whether an offence under this Part of this Act has been committed on the land.

(2)   A person duly authorised in writing by a local authority may at any reasonable time enter upon any land, other than such premises as aforesaid, for the purpose of ascertaining whether an offence under this Part of this Act has been committed on the land, being an offence consisting of a contravention of or failure to comply with provisions of regulations made in pursuance of section 2(1)(b) of this Act.

(3)   A person authorised as mentioned in the foregoing provisions of this section to enter upon any land—

(a)   shall if so required produce evidence of his authority before entering and while present on the land; and

(b)   may take with him on to the land such other persons as he considers necessary.

(4)   Any person authorised as aforesaid may take for analysis a sample of any substance which he finds on the land and which appears to him to be intended for use as food for livestock; ....

(5) *Any veterinary surgeon or veterinary practitioner authorised as mentioned in subsection (1) of this section to enter upon any land may examine any livestock which he finds on the land and apply to and take from the livestock such tests and samples as he considers appropriate; and a person by whom a sample is taken from livestock in pursuance of this subsection shall, if before the sample is taken he is requested to do so by any person appearing to him to have the custody of the livestock, deliver a part of the sample or a similar sample to the person who made the request.*

(6) *If a person entitled to enter upon any land in pursuance of this section requests any person present on the land, being the occupier or a servant of the occupier of the land or a person having the custody of any livestock present on the land,—*

(a) *to indicate to the person so entitled the places on the land used for the accommodation of livestock or for the storage or treatment of any substance intended for use as food for livestock; or*

(b) *to facilitate the access of the person so entitled to any such place,*

it shall be the duty of the person to whom the request is addressed to comply with the request so far as he is able to do so.

(7) *A person who fails to perform his duty under subsection (6) of this section or otherwise wilfully obstructs a person entitled as aforesaid in the execution of that person's powers under this section shall be guilty of an offence under this section.*

NOTES

Initial Commencement

Specified date: 3 September 1968: see s 54(2).

Amendment

Repealed by the Animal Health and Welfare (Scotland) Act 2006, s 52, Sch 2, para 8(1) and the Animal Welfare Act 2006, s 65, Sch 4.

Date in force (in relation to Scotland): 6 October 2006: see SSI 2006/482, art 2; for savings see art 4(3) thereof.

Date in force (in relation to England and Wales): to be appointed: see the Animal Welfare Act 2006, s 68(3).

Sub-s (4): repealed by the Statute Law (Repeals) Act 2004.

Date in force: 22 July 2004: (no specific commencement provision).

Transfer of Functions

Functions of the Minister and the Ministers, so far as exercisable in relation to Wales, transferred to the National Assembly for Wales, by the National Assembly for Wales (Transfer of Functions) Order 1999, SI 1999/672, art 2, Sch 1.

A1.32

7 Punishment of offences under Part I

(1) *A person guilty of an offence under section 1 or section 2 of this Act shall be liable on summary conviction to imprisonment for a term not exceeding three months [51 weeks] or a fine not exceeding [level 4 on the standard scale].*

(2) *A person guilty of an offence under section 6 of this Act shall be liable on summary conviction to a fine not exceeding [level 3 on the standard scale].*

(3) *In England and Wales a local authority shall, without prejudice to the powers of any other person to institute proceedings for an offence under this Part of this Act, have power to institute proceedings for such an offence as is mentioned in section 6(2) of this Act which is alleged to have been committed in their area.*

NOTES

Initial Commencement

Specified date: 3 September 1968: see s 54(2).

Amendment

Repealed by the Animal Health and Welfare (Scotland) Act 2006, s 52, Sch 2, para 8(1) and the Animal Welfare Act 2006, s 65, Sch 4.

Date in force (in relation to Scotland): 6 October 2006: see SSI 2006/482, art 2; for savings see art 4(3) thereof.

Date in force (in relation to England and Wales): to be appointed: see the Animal Welfare Act 2006, s 68(3).

Sub-s (1): words 'three months' repealed and subsequent words in square brackets substituted by the Criminal Justice Act 2003, s 280(2), (3), Sch 26, para 21.

Date in force: to be appointed: see the Criminal Justice Act 2003, s 336(3).

Sub-s (1): maximum fine on any conviction increased by the Criminal Law Act 1977, s 31, Sch 6, and converted to a level on the standard scale by the Criminal Justice Act 1982, ss 37, 46.

Sub-s (2): maximum fine increased and converted to a level on the standard scale by the Criminal Justice Act 1982, ss 37, 39(2), 46, Sch 3.

A1.33

8   Interpretation etc of Part I

(1) *In this Part of this Act—*

'agricultural land' means land used for agriculture (within the meaning of the Agriculture Act 1947 or, in Scotland, the Agriculture (Scotland) Act 1948) which is so used for the purposes of a trade or business; and

'livestock' means any creature kept for the production of food, wool, skin or fur or for use in the farming of land or for such purpose as the Minister may by order specify.

(2) *Subsections (2) and (3) of [section 50 of the Animal Health Act 1981] (which define the expression 'local authority') shall have effect for the purposes of this Part of this Act as if for references to that Act there were substituted references to this Part of this Act and as if [paragraph (b)(ii) were omitted from subsection (2)]*

(3) *This Part of this Act applies to officers and servants of the Crown, and references to land in this Part of this Act include references to land belonging to Her Majesty in right of the Crown or the Duchy of Lancaster, land belonging to the Duchy of Cornwall and land held on behalf of Her Majesty for the purposes of any Government department; and in relation to any such land occupied by or on behalf of Her Majesty or the Duchy of Cornwall section 6 of this Act shall have effect as if subsection (2) were omitted.*

(4) *Without prejudice to the powers conferred on the Ministers, in relation to Great Britain, by sections 2 and 3 of this Act, the powers conferred on them by either of those sections may be exercised, in relation to England and Wales only, by the Minister*

of Agriculture, Fisheries and Food and, in relation to Scotland only, by the Secretary of State; and references in those sections to the Ministers shall be construed accordingly.

(5)   Nothing in this Part of this Act shall be construed as prejudicing any provision of the Protection of Animals Acts 1911 to 1964 or the Protection of Animals (Scotland) Acts 1912 to 1964.

NOTES

Initial Commencement

Specified date: 3 September 1968: see s 54(2).

Amendment

Repealed by the Animal Welfare Act 2006, s 65, Sch 4.

Date in force: to be appointed: see the Animal Welfare Act 2006, s 68(3).

Sub-s (1): definition 'agricultural land' repealed by the Animal Health and Welfare (Scotland) Act 2006, s 52, Sch 2, para 8(1)(c)(i).

Date in force: 6 October 2006: see SSI 2006/482, art 2; for savings see art 4(3) thereof.

Sub-s (2): repealed by the Animal Health and Welfare (Scotland) Act 2006, s 52, Sch 2, para 8(1).

Date in force: 6 October 2006: see SSI 2006/482, art 2; for savings see art 4(3) thereof.

Sub-s (2): amended by the Animal Health Act 1981, s 96, Sch 5, para 8.

Sub-s (3): repealed, for certain purposes, by the Animal Health and Welfare (Scotland) Act 2006, s 52, Sch 2, para 8(1)(c)(ii).

Date in force: 6 October 2006: see SSI 2006/482, art 2; for savings see art 4(3) thereof.

Sub-ss (4), (5): repealed by the Animal Health and Welfare (Scotland) Act 2006, s 52, Sch 2, para 8(1).

Date in force: 6 October 2006: see SSI 2006/482, art 2; for savings see art 4(3) thereof.

Transfer of Functions

Functions of the Minister and the Ministers, so far as exercisable in relation to Wales, transferred to the National Assembly for Wales, by the National Assembly for Wales (Transfer of Functions) Order 1999, SI 1999/672, art 2, Sch 1.

Subordinate Legislation

Welfare of Livestock (Deer) Order 1980, SI 1980/593 (made under sub-s (1)).

PART II: ADDITIONAL PAYMENTS TO TENANT FARMERS

A1.34

9   ...

...

NOTES

Amendment

Repealed by the Agricultural Holdings Act 1986, s 101(1), Sch 15, Pt I, and the Agricultural Holdings (Scotland) Act 1991, s 88(2), Sch 13.

A1.35

10 ...

...

NOTES

Amendment

Repealed by the Agricultural Holdings Act 1986, s 101(1), Sch 15, Pt I, and the Agricultural Holdings (Scotland) Act 1991, s 88(2), Sch 13.

A1.36

11 ...

...

NOTES

Amendment

Repealed by the Agricultural Holdings (Scotland) Act 1991, s 88(2), Sch 13.

A1.37

12   Additional payments in consequence of compulsory acquisition, etc of agricultural holdings

(1)   Where in pursuance of any enactment providing for the acquisition or taking of possession of land compulsorily by any person (hereafter in this Part of this Act referred to as an 'acquiring authority'), an acquiring authority acquire the interest in an agricultural holding or any part of it of the tenant of the holding or take possession of such a holding or any part of it, then, subject to the provisions of this Part of this Act, [subsection (2)(b) of section 60 of the Agricultural Holdings Act 1986 (additional compensation to tenant for disturbance) shall apply as if the acquiring authority were the landlord of the holding and on the date of the acquisition or taking of possession the tenancy of the holding or part of it had terminated, and the tenant had quitted the holding or part of it, in consequence of such a notice or counter-notice as is mentioned in subsection (1) of that section; and section 61 of that Act (exceptions to section 60) shall not apply in such a case.]

[(1A)   No sum shall be payable by virtue of subsection (1) of this section in respect of any land comprised in a farm business tenancy within the meaning of the Agricultural Tenancies Act 1995.]

(2)   No sum shall be payable by virtue of subsection (1) of this section in respect of any agricultural holding held on a tenancy for a term of two years or upwards except in a case where the amount of compensation payable to the tenant of the holding by the acquiring authority in consequence of the acquisition or taking of possession in question is exceeded by the aggregate of the amounts which, if the tenancy had been from year to year, would have been so payable by way of compensation and by virtue of that subsection; and in any such case the sum payable by virtue of that subsection in consequence of the acquisition or taking of possession in question shall, subject to sections 13(3) and 14(3) of this Act, be of an amount equal to the excess.

(3)   No sum shall be payable to the tenant of an agricultural holding by virtue of subsection (1) of this section in consequence of such an acquiring of an interest or

taking of possession as is there mentioned unless the date on which the acquisition or taking of possession occurs is later than the date of the passing of this Act and—

(a) in the case of such an acquisition, unless the date on which notice to treat in respect of the interest to be acquired is served or treated as served on the tenant by the acquiring authority is after the initial date; and

(b) where in the case of such a taking of possession prior notice of the taking of possession is by virtue of any enactment required to be served on the tenant by the acquiring authority, unless the date on which the notice is so served is after the initial date.

[(4) If a person is entitled in respect of the same interest in land to a payment both—

(a) by virtue of subsection (1), and

(b) under section 33B of the Land Compensation Act 1973 (additional loss payment for agricultural land),

section 33H of that Act (only one payment to be made if a person has dual entitlement) applies.]

NOTES

Initial Commencement

Royal Assent: 3 July 1968: (no specific commencement provision).

Amendment

Repealed in relation to Scotland by the Agricultural Holdings (Scotland) Act 1991, s 88, Sch 13, Part I.

Sub-s (1): words in square brackets substituted by the Agricultural Holdings Act 1986, s 100, Sch 14, para 44.

Sub-s (1A): inserted by the Agricultural Tenancies Act 1995, s 40, Schedule, para 23.

Sub-s (4): inserted by the Planning and Compulsory Purchase Act 2004, s 118(2), Sch 7, para 4.

Date in force: 31 October 2004: see SI 2004/2593, art 2(d).

A1.38

13   Provisions supplementary to s 12 in England and Wales

(1) For the purposes of subsection (1) of section 12 of this Act, a tenant of an agricultural holding shall be treated as not being a tenant of it in so far as, immediately before the acquiring of the interest or taking of possession mentioned in that subsection, he was neither in possession nor entitled to take possession of any land comprised in the holding; and in determining for those purposes whether a tenant was so entitled, any such agreement as is mentioned in [section 2(2) of the Agricultural Holdings Act 1986] which relates to the land and has not taken effect as an agreement for the letting of the land for a tenancy from year to year shall be disregarded.

(2) Section 12(1) of this Act shall not apply where the acquiring authority require the land comprised in the holding or part in question for the purposes of agricultural research or experiment or of demonstrating agricultural methods or for the purposes of the enactments relating to smallholdings, nor where the Minister acquires the land under section 84(1)(c) of the Agriculture Act 1947; but where an acquiring authority exercise in relation to any land any power to acquire or take possession of land compulsorily which is conferred on the authority by virtue of [section 226 or 230 of

the Town and Country Planning Act 1990] or [section 10 of the New Towns Act 1981] [...], the authority shall be deemed for the purposes of this subsection not to require the land for any of the purposes aforesaid.

(3) The provisions of Schedule 3 to this Act shall have effect for the purposes of section 12 of this Act in its application to England and Wales.

NOTES

Initial Commencement

Royal Assent: 3 July 1968: (no specific commencement provision).

Amendment

Repealed in relation to Scotland by the Agricultural Holdings (Scotland) Act 1991, s 88, Sch 13, Part I.

Sub-s (1): words in square brackets substituted by the Agricultural Holdings Act 1986, ss 99, 100, Sch 13, para 3, Sch 14, para 45.

Sub-s (2): words 'section 226 or 230 of the Town and Country Planning Act 1990' in square brackets inserted by the Planning (Consequential Provisions) Act 1990, s 4, Sch 2, para 19.

Sub-s (2): words 'section 10 of the New Towns Act 1981' in square brackets inserted by the New Towns Act 1981, s 81, Sch 12, para 4.

Sub-s (2): words omitted inserted by the Development of Rural Wales Act 1976, s 27, Sch 7, para 7, repealed by the Government of Wales Act 1998, s 152, Sch 18, Pt IV.

Date in force: 1 October 1998: see SI 1998/2244, art 4.

A1.39

14   ...

...

NOTES

Amendment

Repealed by the Agricultural Holdings (Scotland) Act 1991, s 88(2), Sch 13.

A1.40

15   **Effect of early resumption clauses on compensation**

(1)–(3)   ...

(4)   ... subsections (4) to (6) of section 11 of this Act shall apply to compensation claimed or payable under subsection (3) of this section, as if for references to sums claimed or payable in pursuance of section 9 of this Act there were substituted references to compensation claimed or payable under the said ... subsection (3), ... ; and section 12(3) of this Act shall apply to any increase of compensation in pursuance of subsection (1) of this section as it applies to a sum payable by virtue of section 12(1) of this Act as if for references to the said section 12(1) there were substituted references to subsection (1) of this section.

(5)   For the purposes of subsection (1) to (3) of this section, the current year of a tenancy for a term of two years or upwards is the year beginning with such day in the period of twelve months ending—

   (a) for the purposes of subsection (1) ... , with the date on which the notice mentioned in that subsection is served; and

   (b) for the purposes of subsection (3), with a date two months before the resumption mentioned in that subsection,

as corresponds to the day on which the term would expire by the effluxion of time.

(6) ...

NOTES

Initial Commencement

Royal Assent: 3 July 1968: (no specific commencement provision).

Amendment

Repealed in relation to Scotland by the Agricultural Holdings (Scotland) Act 1991, s 88, Sch 13, Part I.

Sub-s (1): repealed by the Land Compensation Act 1973, ss 48(4), (6), 86, 89(3), Sch 3.

Sub-s (2): repealed by the Agricultural Holdings Act 1986, s 101, Sch 15, Part I.

Sub-ss (4), (5): words omitted repealed by the Agricultural Holdings Act 1986, s 101, Sch 15, Part I.

Sub-ss (3), (6): apply to Scotland only.

A1.41

16   ...

...

NOTES

Amendment

Repealed by the Agricultural Holdings (Scotland) Act 1991, s 88(2), Sch 13.

A1.42

17   Interpretation etc of Part II

(1) In this Part of this Act—

   'acquiring authority' has the meaning assigned to it by section 12(1) of this Act;
   'the initial date' means 1st November 1967;
   'possession' means actual possession;
   ...
   'the principal Scottish Act' means the Agricultural Holdings (Scotland) Act 1949;

and unless the context otherwise requires expressions used in this Part of this Act and the [Agricultural Holdings Act 1986] or, as the case may be, the principal Scottish Act have the same meanings in this Part of this Act as in that Act.

(2) In this Part of this Act ... references to the acquisition of any property are references to the vesting of the property in the person acquiring it.

(3) [Section 95(1), (2) and (3) of the Agricultural Holdings Act 1986] and section 86(1) and (2) of the principal Scottish Act (Crown land) shall have effect as if references to that Act included references to this Part of this Act.

(4) References in this section to this Part of this Act include references to Schedules 1 to 4 to this Act.

(5) ...

NOTES

Initial Commencement

Royal Assent: 3 July 1968: (no specific commencement provision).

Amendment

Sub-s (5): repealed by virtue of the Agricultural Holdings (Scotland) Act 1991, s 88, Sch 13, Part I.

Repealed in relation to Scotland by the Agricultural Holdings (Scotland) Act 1991, s 88, Sch 13, Part I.

Sub-s (1): words omitted repealed and words in square brackets substituted by the Agricultural Holdings Act 1986, ss 100, 101, Sch 14, para 46, Sch 15, Part I.

Sub-s (2): words omitted repealed by the Agricultural Holdings Act 1986, s 101, Sch 15, Part I.

Sub-s (3): words in square brackets substituted by the Agricultural Holdings Act 1986, s 100, Sch 14, para 46.

PART III: ...

...

A1.43

18– 20 ...

...

NOTES

Amendment

Repealed by the Agricultural Holdings (Amendment) (Scotland) Act 1983, s 6, Sch 2.

PART IV: ...

A1.44

21– 37 ...

...

NOTES

Amendment

Repealed by the Land Drainage Act 1976, s 117(3), Sch 8.

PART V: MISCELLANEOUS AND GENERAL

Miscellaneous

A1.45

38– 40 ...

...

NOTES

Amendment

Repealed by the Statute Law (Repeals) Act 1986, s 1(1), Sch 1, Pt II.

A1.46

41   ...

...

NOTES

Amendment

Repealed by the Agriculture Act 1970, ss 29(6), 113(3), Sch 5, Pt I, and the Statute Law (Repeals) Act 1993, s 1(1), Sch 1, Pt II.

A1.47

42   ...

...

NOTES

Amendment

Repealed with savings by the Land Compensation Act 1973, ss 48(4), (6), 86, 89(3), Sch 3.

A1.48

43   ...

...

NOTES

Amendment

Repealed by the Plant Varieties Act 1997, s 52, Sch 4.

Date in force: 8 May 1998: see SI 1998/1028, art 2.

A1.49

44   ...

...

NOTES

Amendment

Repealed by the Restrictive Trade Practices Act 1976, s 44, Sch 6.

A1.50

45   ...

...

NOTES

Amendment

Repealed by SI 2000/311, art 8.

Date in force: 1 March 2000: see SI 2000/311, art 1.

A1.51

46   **Further functions of agricultural wages committees**

(1)   The Minister may by regulations—

   (a)   provide that the functions under the Agricultural Wages Act 1948 of agricultural wages committees established in pursuance of that Act shall include such further functions as the Minister considers appropriate for the purpose of enabling or requiring those committees to give effect to orders made or which may be made by the Agricultural Wages Board for England and Wales under that Act and (without prejudice to the generality of the foregoing provisions in this paragraph) to determine whether any person is a member of any special class of workers as defined in such an order;

   (b)   make provision with respect to the procedure to be followed in connection with the exercise of the further functions aforesaid and provide that section 15 of that Act (which relates to evidence of resolutions and orders) shall apply with such modifications as the Minister considers appropriate to decisions made in the exercise of those functions.

(2)   In this section 'functions' means powers and duties.

(3)   ...

NOTES

Initial Commencement

Royal Assent: 3 July 1968: (no specific commencement provision).

Amendment

Sub-s (3): repealed by the Agriculture (Miscellaneous Provisions) Act 1972, s 26(3), Sch 6.

Transfer of Functions

Functions of the Minister and the Ministers, so far as exercisable in relation to Wales, transferred to the National Assembly for Wales, by the National Assembly for Wales (Transfer of Functions) Order 1999, SI 1999/672, art 2, Sch 1.

Subordinate Legislation

Agricultural Wages Committees (Wages Structure) Regulations 1971, SI 1971/844 (made under sub-s (1)).

A1.52

47   Further exemptions of transfers of land from control of Rural Development Boards

...

NOTES

Initial Commencement

Royal Assent: 3 July 1968: (no specific commencement provision).

Extent

This section does not extend to Scotland: see s 54(3).

Amendment

Words omitted repealed in part by the Water Act 1989, s 190, Sch 27, Part I; remainder amend the Agriculture Act 1967, s 50(3).

A1.53

48   Extension of s 3 of Parks Regulation (Amendment) Act 1926

In section 3 of the Parks Regulation (Amendment) Act 1926 (under which, among other things, the Minister of Agriculture, Fisheries and Food has power to regulate the conduct of persons using the Royal Botanic Gardens at Kew), the second reference to the said Gardens shall include a reference to any park, garden, recreation ground, open space and other land for the time being vested in or under the control or management of the said Minister.

NOTES

Initial Commencement

Royal Assent: 3 July 1968: (no specific commencement provision).

Extent

This section does not extend to Scotland: see s 54(3).

A1.54

49 ...

...

NOTES

Amendment

Repealed by the Northern Ireland Constitution Act 1973, s 41(1), Sch 6, Pt I.

Supplemental

A1.55

50   Interpretation etc—general

(1)   Subject to subsection (7) of section 45 of this Act, in this Act—

'the Minister' means, except in the application of this Act to Scotland, the Minister of Agriculture, Fisheries and Food and, in the application of this Act to Scotland, the Secretary of State;

'the Ministers' means the Minister of Agriculture, Fisheries and Food and the Secretary of State acting jointly; and

'notice' means notice in writing.

(2)   ...

(3)   Any reference in this Act to any enactment is a reference to it as amended, and includes a reference to it as applied, by or under any other enactment including an enactment in this Act.

(4)   Where an offence under this Act committed by a body corporate is proved to have been committed with the consent or connivance of, or to be attributable to any neglect on the part of, any director, manager, secretary or other similar officer of the body corporate or any person who was purporting to act in any such capacity, he as well as the body corporate shall be guilty of that offence and shall be liable to be proceeded against and punished accordingly.

In this subsection 'director', in relation to a body corporate established by or under any enactment for the purpose of carrying on under national ownership any industry or undertaking or part of an industry or undertaking, being a body corporate whose affairs are managed by its members, means a member of that body corporate.

NOTES

Initial Commencement

Royal Assent: 3 July 1968: (no specific commencement provision).

Amendment

Sub-s (2): repealed by the Water Act 1973, s 40(3), Sch 9.

Transfer of Functions

Functions of the Minister and the Ministers, so far as exercisable in relation to Wales, transferred to the National Assembly for Wales, by the National Assembly for Wales (Transfer of Functions) Order 1999, SI 1999/672, art 2, Sch 1.

A1.56

51   Orders, regulations and schemes

(1)   Any power conferred by this Act to make regulations or a scheme or an order (other than an order under section 23(1)(a)) shall be exercisable by statutory instrument.

(2)   Any statutory instrument containing an order or regulations made under any provision of this Act, other than an order under section 23(1)(b) and regulations under section 2, shall be subject to annulment in pursuance of a resolution of either House of Parliament.

(3)   No scheme shall be made under this Act unless a draft of the scheme has been approved by each House of Parliament.

(4)   Any order or scheme made under any provision of this Act may be revoked or varied by a subsequent order or scheme made thereunder.

(5)   Any order, scheme or regulations under this Act may make different provision for different circumstances; and nothing in any other provision of this Act authorising the

making of different provision for such different cases as may be specified in that provision shall be construed as prejudicing the generality of the power conferred by this subsection.

NOTES

Initial Commencement

Royal Assent: 3 July 1968: (no specific commencement provision).

A1.57

52   Repeals

The enactments mentioned in Schedule 8 to this Act are hereby repealed to the extent specified in column 3 of that Schedule.

NOTES

Initial Commencement

Royal Assent: 3 July 1968: (no specific commencement provision).

A1.58

53   Financial provisions

There shall be defrayed out of moneys provided by Parliament—

(a)   any expenses incurred by virtue of this Act by any Minister or government department ... ; and

(b)   any increase attributable to the provisions of this Act in the sums payable out of such moneys under any other Act;

and any sums received by the Minister or the Ministers by virtue of this Act shall be paid into the Exchequer.

NOTES

Initial Commencement

Royal Assent: 3 July 1968: (no specific commencement provision).

Amendment

Words omitted repealed by the Post Office Act 1969, s 141, Sch 11, Part II.

A1.59

54   Short title, commencement and extent, etc

(1)   This Act may be cited as the Agriculture (Miscellaneous Provisions) Act 1968.

(2)   ...

(3)   This Act, except Part IV and sections 10, 13, 47 and 48, extends to Scotland, and sections 11, 14 and 16 and Part III of this Act extend to Scotland only.

(4)   This Part of this Act, except sections 41, 42 and 46 to 48, extends to Northern Ireland < ... >

A1.60 *Statutes*

NOTES

Initial Commencement

Royal Assent: 3 July 1968: (no specific commencement provision).

Amendment

Sub-s (2): repealed by the Statute Law (Repeals) Act 2004.

Date in force: 22 July 2004: (no specific commencement provision).

Sub-s (4): words omitted repealed by the Northern Ireland Constitution Act 1973, s 41(1), Sch 6, Part I.

Miscellaneous

Sub-s (2) stated that Pt I hereof would come into operation on the expiration of two months beginning with the date on which this Act is passed.

SCHEDULE 1
...

...

A1.60

...

NOTES

Amendment

Repealed by the Statute Law (Repeals) Act 1977, s 1(1), Sch 1, Pt XIX.

SCHEDULE 2
...

...

A1.61

...

NOTES

Amendment

Repealed by the Statute Law (Repeals) Act 1977, s 1(1), Sch 1, Pt XIX.

SCHEDULE 3
SUPPLEMENTARY PROVISIONS WITH RESPECT TO PAYMENTS UNDER S 12(1) IN
ENGLAND AND WALES

Section 13(3)

A1.62

1   Subject to paragraph 4 of this Schedule, any dispute with respect to any sum which may be or become payable by virtue of section 12(1) of this Act shall be referred to and determined by the Lands Tribunal.

2   If in any case the sum to be paid by virtue of the said section 12(1) to the tenant of an agricultural holding by an acquiring authority would, apart from this paragraph and paragraph 3 of this Schedule, fall to be ascertained in pursuance of [section 60(4) of the Agricultural Holdings Act 1986] by reference to the rent of the holding at a rate which was not determined by arbitration under [section 12 or section 13 of the Agricultural Holdings Act 1986] and which the authority consider is unduly high, the authority may make an application to the Lands Tribunal for the rent to be considered by the tribunal.

3   Where, on an application under paragraph 2 above, the tribunal are satisfied that—

(a)   the rent to which the application relates is not substantially higher than the rent which in their opinion would be determined for the holding in question on a reference to arbitration duly made in pursuance of [section 12 of the Agricultural Holdings Act 1986] on the date of the application (hereafter in this paragraph referred to as 'the appropriate rent'); or

(b)   the rent to which the application relates is substantially higher than the appropriate rent but was not fixed by the parties to the relevant contract of tenancy with a view to increasing the amount of any compensation payable, or of any sum to be paid by virtue of the said section 12(1), in consequence of the compulsory acquisition or taking of possession of any land included in the holding,

they shall dismiss the application; and if the tribunal do not dismiss the application in pursuance of the foregoing provisions of this paragraph they shall determine that, in the case to which the application relates, the sum to be paid by virtue of the said section 12(1) shall be ascertained in pursuance of the said [section 60(4)] by reference to the appropriate rent instead of by reference to the rent to which the application relates.

4   The enactments mentioned in paragraph 5 of this Schedule shall, subject to any necessary modifications, have effect in their application to such an acquiring of an interest or taking of possession as is mentioned in subsection (1) of section 12 of this Act (hereafter in this paragraph referred to as 'the relevant event')—

(a)   in so far as those enactments make provision for the doing, before the relevant event, of any thing connected with compensation (including in particular provision for determining the amount of or the liability to pay compensation or for the payment of it into court or otherwise), as if references to compensation, except compensation for damage or injurious affection, included references to any sum which will become payable by virtue of the said subsection (1) in consequence of the relevant event; and

(b)   subject to sub-paragraph (a) above, as if references to compensation (except as aforesaid) included references to sums payable or, as the context may require, to sums paid by virtue of the said subsection (1) in consequence of the relevant event.

5   The enactments aforesaid are—

(a)   Part I and section 32 of the Land Compensation Act 1961;

(b)   the following provisions of the Compulsory Purchase Act 1965, that is to say, sections 6, 9, 11, 12, 20(4) and (5), 22 (except subsection (4)) and 26; in Schedule 1, paragraphs 6 to 8 and 10; Schedule 2 and Schedule 3;

(c)   any provision of the Lands Clauses Acts or of any other enactment or any instrument having effect by virtue of an enactment, being a provision corresponding to a provision mentioned in sub-paragraph (b) of this paragraph.

A1.63 *Statutes*

NOTES
Initial Commencement
Royal Assent: 3 July 1968: (no specific commencement provision).

Amendment
Paras 2, 3: words in square brackets substituted by the Agricultural Holdings Act 1986, ss 99, 100, Sch 13, para 3, Sch 14, para 48.

SCHEDULE 4

...

A1.63

...

NOTES
Amendment
Repealed by the Agricultural Holdings (Scotland) Act 1991, s 88(2), Sch 13, Pt I.

SCHEDULE 5

...

...

A1.64

...

NOTES
Amendment
Repealed by the Agricultural Holdings (Scotland) Act 1991, s 88(2), Sch 13, Pt I.

SCHEDULE 6

...

...

A1.65

...

NOTES
Amendment
Repealed by the Land Drainage Act 1976, s 117(3), Sch 8.

SCHEDULE 7

...

...

A1.66

...

NOTES

Amendment

Repealed by the Plant Varieties Act 1997, s 52, Sch 4.

SCHEDULE 8
REPEALS

Section 52

A1.67

Chapter	Short Title	Extent of Repeal
1944 c 28	The Agriculture (Miscellaneous Provisions) Act 1944	Section 5, expect in its application to Scotland.
1958 c 47	The Agricultural Marketing Act 1958	In section 53(2), the words from 'as subserving' to 'them'.
1961 c 48	The Land Drainage Act 1961	Sections 1(2) and (3), 2 and 4(2) and (4).
		In section 6(2), the words from 'affixed' to 'and'.
		Section 7.
		In section 8, sub-paragraph (ii) of subsection (1)(c), subsection (2), and in subsection (3) the words 'or of the said subsection (2)' and the words 'owner and'.
		Section 9(4).
		In section 10(3), the words 'section 7 or'.
		Section 14.
		Section 22(3).
1963 c 25	The Finance Act 1963	In Schedule 12, sub-paragraphs (1) to (6) of paragraph 24.
1964 c 14	The Plant Varieties and Seeds Act 1964	Section 20(5).
		In section 21(1), the words 'but which is not in the Index'.

1053

		In Part II of Schedule 2, in paragraph 2(5), the words 'which having been' and the words from 'has been found' onwards.

NOTES

Initial Commencement

Royal Assent: 3 July 1968: (no specific commencement provision).

LAND COMPENSATION ACT 1973

(1973 C 26)

ARRANGEMENT OF SECTIONS

An Act to confer a new right to compensation for depreciation of the value of interests in land caused by the use of highways, aerodromes and other public works; to confer powers for mitigating the injurious effect of such works on their surroundings; to make new provision for the benefit of persons displaced from land by public authorities; to amend the law relating to compulsory purchase and planning blight; to amend section 35 of the Roads (Scotland) Act 1970; and for purposes connected with those matters

[23rd May 1973]

A1.68

34 ...

...

NOTES

Amendment

Repealed by the Planning and Compulsory Purchase Act 2004, ss 118(2), 120, Sch 7, para 7(1), (3), Sch 9.

Date in force: 31 October 2004 (except in relation to a compulsory purchase order made or made in draft before that date): see SI 2004/2593, art 2(d), (e)(i) and the Planning and Compulsory Purchase Act 2004, Sch 7, para 7(5).

Notes

For a commentary, see para 38.63 ff.

General Note. The somewhat similar disturbance payment under the Agricultural Holdings Act 1986, s 60 ff, is available to tenants of agricultural holdings only, and on a restricted basis to those whose tenancies are for a term of two years or upwards. There is thus only a small overlap between the scope of this section and the 1968 Act. Sub-s (5) above operates to prevent duplication of payments in that area.

Person. Unless the contrary intention appears this includes a body of persons corporate or unincorporate; see the Interpretation Act 1978, s 5, Sch 1. There seems to be nothing to exclude the application of this section to a company.

Great Britain. Ie England, Scotland and Wales; see the Union with Scotland Act 1706, preamble, Art I, as read with the Interpretation Act 1978, s 22(1), Sch 2, para (5)(a).

Term of years certain. See the note to s 2 of this Act (9 Halsbury's Statutes (4th edn, 1994 Reissue) 263).

17th October 1972. Cf the note 17th October 1969 to s 1 of this Act (9 Halsbury's Statutes (4th edn, 1994 Reissue) 262).

Further provisions. As to the amount of a farm loss payment, see s 35, and for supplementary provisions see s 36. Note that while land used for agriculture is excluded from eligibility for disturbance payments under s 37(7) there is no such exclusion in the cases of home loss payments (ss 29, 30, 32, 33) or the special old person's business disturbance payment under s 46.

Definitions. For 'agricultural unit', 'acquiring authority' and 'tenancy', see s 87(1).

Agricultural Holdings Act 1986. For the definition of 'tenant' in that Act, see s 96(1). As to tenancies not falling within that Act, see further 1 Halsbury's Laws (4th edn, reissue) para 301.

A1.69

35 ...

...

NOTES

Amendment

Repealed by the Planning and Compulsory Purchase Act 2004, ss 118(2), 120, Sch 7, para 7(1), (3), Sch 9.

Date in force: 31 October 2004 (except in relation to a compulsory purchase order made or made in draft before that date): see SI 2004/2593, art 2(d), (e)(i) and the Planning and Compulsory Purchase Act 2004, Sch 7, para 7(5).

Notes

For a commentary, see para 38.63 ff.

No reduction in respect of rehousing. See the note to s 30 of this Act (9 Halsbury's Statutes (4th edn, 1994 Reissue) 287).

A1.70 *Statutes*

Farm loss payment. For the circumstances in which this is payable, see s 34.

Person. See the note to s 34.

Land Tribunal. See the note to s 3 of this Act (9 Halsbury's Statutes (4th edn, 1994 Reissue) 265).

Definitions. For 'the land acquired', 'the new unit' and 'farm loss payment', see s 34(1); for 'date of displacement', see s 34(3); for 'agriculture', 'agricultural land', 'dwelling' and 'tenancy', see s 87(1).

A1.70

36 ...

...

NOTES

Amendment

Repealed by the Planning and Compulsory Purchase Act 2004, ss 118(2), 120, Sch 7, para 7(1), (3), Sch 9.

Date in force: 31 October 2004 (except in relation to a compulsory purchase order made or made in draft before that date): see SI 2004/2593, art 2(d), (e)(i) and the Planning and Compulsory Purchase Act 2004, Sch 7, para 7(5).

Notes

For a commentary, see para 38.63 ff.

Farm loss payment. For the circumstances in which this is payable, see s 34, and for its amount, see s 35.

Writing. See the note to s 15 of this Act (9 Halsbury's Statutes (4th edn, 1994 Reissue) 277).

Land Tribunal. See the note to s 3 of this Act (9 Halsbury's Statutes (4th edn, 1994 Reissue) 265).

Interest. As to payments on account of such interest, see the Planning and Compensation Act 1991, s 80(2), (3) and Sch 18, Pt II.

Rate ... prescribed. See the note to s 18 of this Act (9 Halsbury's Statutes (4th edn, 1994 Reissue) 278).

Passing of this Act. This Act was passed (ie received the Royal Assent) on 23 May 1973.

Definitions. For 'the land acquired', 'the new unit' and 'farm loss payment', see s 34(1); for 'acquiring authority' and 'authority possessing compulsory purchase powers', see s 87(1).

PART IV: COMPULSORY PURCHASE

Assessment of compensation

A1.71

48 Compensation in respect of agricultural holdings

(1) [Subject to subsection (1A) below] this section has effect where in pursuance of any enactment providing for the acquisition or taking of possession of land compulsorily an acquiring authority—

   (a) acquire the interest of the landlord in an agricultural holding or any part of it; or

   (b) acquire the interest of the tenant in, or take possession of, an agricultural holding or any part of it.

[(1A) This section does not have effect where the tenancy of the agricultural holding is a tenancy to which, by virtue of section 4 of the Agricultural Tenancies Act 1995, the Agricultural Holdings Act 1986 does not apply.]

(2) In assessing the compensation payable by the acquiring authority to the landlord in connection with any such acquisition of an interest as is mentioned in subsection (1)(a) above—

  (a) there shall be disregarded any right of the landlord to serve a notice to quit, and any notice to quit already served by the landlord, which would not be or would not have been effective if—
    (i) in [Case B in Part I of Schedule 3 to the Agricultural Holdings Act 1986] (land required for non-agricultural use for which planning permission has been granted etc) the reference to the land being required did not include a reference to its being required by an acquiring authority; and
    (ii) in [section 27(3)(f)] of that Act (proposed termination of tenancy for purpose of land's being used for non-agricultural use not falling within [the said Case B]) the reference to the land's being used did not include a reference to its being used by an acquiring authority; and
  (b) if the tenant has quitted the holding or any part of it by reason of a notice to quit which is to be so disregarded, it shall be assumed that he has not done so.

(3) In assessing the compensation payable by the acquiring authority to the tenant in connection with any such acquisition of an interest or taking of possession of land as is mentioned in subsection (1) (b) above (hereafter referred to as 'the tenant's compensation'), there shall be disregarded any right of the landlord to serve a notice to quit, and any notice to quit already served by the landlord, which would not be or would not have been effective if the said [Case B and section 27(3)(f)] were construed in accordance with subsection (2)(a)(i) and (ii) above.

(4) ...

(5) The tenant's compensation shall be reduced by an amount equal to any payment which the acquiring authority are liable to make to him, in respect of the acquisition or taking of possession in question, under section 12 of the said Act of 1968 (additional payments by acquiring authority in circumstances described in subsection (1)(b) above).

(6) If the tenant's compensation as determined in accordance with subsections (3) to (5) above is less than it would have been if those subsections had not been enacted, it shall be increased by the amount of the deficiency.

[(6A) In assessing the tenant's compensation no account shall be taken of any benefit which might accrue to the tenant by virtue of section 60(2)(b) of the Agricultural Holdings Act 1986 (additional payments by landlord for disturbance); and in this subsection the reference to the said section 60(2)(b) does not include a reference to it as applied by section 12 of the Agriculture (Miscellaneous Provisions) Act 1968.]

(7) ...

NOTES

Initial Commencement

Royal Assent: 23 May 1973: (no specific commencement provision).

Extent

In consequence of the amendment made by the Land Compensation (Scotland) Act 1973, s 81(1), Sch 2, Pt I, to s 89(4), this section does not extend to Scotland.

Amendment

Sub-s (6A): inserted by the Agricultural Holdings Act 1986, ss 99, 100, Sch 13, para 3, Sch 14, para 53.

Sub-s (7): repealed by the Land Compensation (Scotland) Act 1973, s 81(1), Sch 2, Part I.

Sub-s (1): words in square brackets inserted by the Agricultural Tenancies Act 1995, s 40, Schedule, para 24.

Sub-s (1A): inserted by the Agricultural Tenancies Act 1995, s 40, Schedule, para 24.

Sub-s (2): first and second words in square brackets substituted by the Agricultural Holdings Act 1986, ss 99, 100, Sch 13, para 3, Sch 14, para 53; final words in square brackets substituted by the Agricultural Holdings (Notices to Quit) Act 1977, s 13(1), Sch 1, para 6, continued in force by the Agricultural Holdings Act 1986, ss 99, 100, Sch 13, para 3, Sch 14, para 53.

Sub-s (3): words in square brackets substituted by the Agricultural Holdings Act 1986, ss 99, 100, Sch 13, para 3, Sch 14, para 53.

Sub-s (4): repeals the Agriculture (Miscellaneous Provisions) Act 1968, ss 15(1), 42.

Notes

For a commentary, see para 38.75 ff.

Said Act of 1968. Ie the Agriculture (Miscellaneous Provisions) Act 1968.

Definitions. For 'acquiring authority', 'agricultural holding', 'landlord', 'notice to quit' and 'tenant', see s 87(1).

Severance of land

A1.72

53   Notice to treat in respect of part of agricultural land

(1)   Where an acquiring authority serve notice to treat in respect of any agricultural land on a person (whether in occupation or not) having a greater interest in the land than as tenant for a year or from year to year, and that person has such an interest in other agricultural land comprised in the same agricultural unit as that to which the notice relates, the person on whom the notice is served (hereafter referred to as 'the claimant') may, within the period of two months beginning with the date of service of the notice to treat, serve on the acquiring authority a counter-notice—

    (a)   claiming that the other land is not reasonably capable of being farmed, either by itself or in conjunction with other relevant land, as a separate agricultural unit; and

    (b)   requiring the acquiring authority to purchase his interest in the whole of the other land.

(2)   Where a counter-notice is served under subsection (1) above the claimant shall also, within the period mentioned in that subsection, serve a copy thereof on any other person who has an interest in the land to which the requirement in the counter-notice relates, but failure to comply with this subsection shall not invalidate the counter-notice.

(3)   Subject to subsection (4) below, 'other relevant land' in subsection (1) above means—

    (a)   land comprised in the same agricultural unit as the land to which the notice to treat relates, being land in which the claimant does not have such an interest as is mentioned in that subsection; and

(b) land comprised in any other agricultural unit occupied by him on the date of service of the notice to treat, being land in respect of which he is then entitled to a greater interest than as tenant for a year or from year to year.

(4) Where an acquiring authority have served a notice to treat in respect of any of the other agricultural land mentioned in subsection (1) above or in respect of other relevant land as defined in subsection (3) above [or such a notice is deemed to have been served by virtue of sections 137 to 144 of the Town and Country Planning Act 1990], then, unless and until that notice to treat is withdrawn, this section and section 54 below shall have effect as if that land did not form part of that other agricultural land or did not constitute other relevant land, as the case may be.

(5) This section shall have effect in relation to a case where a notice to treat is deemed to have been served by virtue of any of the provisions of ... [Part III of the Compulsory Purchase (Vesting Declarations) Act 1981] ... (general vesting declarations) as it has effect in relation to a case where a notice to treat is actually served, and section 54 below shall have effect accordingly.

(6) This section is without prejudice to the rights conferred by sections 93 and 94 of the Lands Clauses Consolidation Act 1845 ... or section 8(2) and (3) of the Compulsory Purchase Act 1965 (provisions as to divided land).

NOTES

Initial Commencement

Royal Assent: 23 May 1973: (no specific commencement provision).

Extent

In consequence of the amendment made by the Land Compensation (Scotland) Act 1973, s 81(1), Sch 2, Pt I, to s 89(4), this section does not extend to Scotland.

Amendment

Sub-s (4): words in square brackets inserted by the Planning (Consequential Provisions) Act 1990, s 4, Sch 2, para 29(9)(a).

Sub-s (5): first words omitted repealed by the Planning (Consequential Provisions) Act 1990, ss 3, 4, Sch 1, Part I, Sch 2, para 29(9)(b); words in square brackets substituted by the Compulsory Purchase (Vesting Declarations) Act 1981, s 16(1), Sch 3; final words omitted repealed by the Land Compensation (Scotland) Act 1973, s 81(1), Sch 2, Part I.

Sub-s (6): words omitted repealed by the Land Compensation (Scotland) Act 1973, s 81(1), Sch 2, Part I.

Notes

For a commentary, see para 38.78.

Person. Unless the contrary intention appears this includes a body of persons corporate or unincorporate; see the Interpretation Act 1978, s 5, Sch 1.

Two months beginning with. The use of the words 'beginning with' makes it clear that in computing this period the day from which it runs is to be included; see *Hare v Gocher* [1962] 2 QB 641, [1962] 2 All ER 763, and *Trow v Ind Coope (West Midlands) Ltd* [1967] 2 QB 899, [1967] 2 All ER 900, CA. See also *Dodds v Walker* [1981] 2 All ER 609, [1981] 1 WLR 1027, HL, as to the day of expiry of periods of a month or a specified number of months.

Further provisions. As to the effect of a counter-notice, see s 54. For an analogous procedure relating to notice of entry, see s 55, and s 56.

Definitions. For 'acquiring authority', 'agricultural land' and 'agricultural unit', see s 87(1). Note as to 'other relevant land', sub-s (3) above.

A1.73

54   Effect of counter-notice under section 53

(1) If the acquiring authority do not within the period of two months beginning with the date of service of a counter-notice under section 53 above agree in writing to accept the counter-notice as valid, the claimant or the authority may, within two months after the end of that period, refer it to the Lands Tribunal; and on any such reference the Tribunal shall determine whether the claim in the counter-notice is justified and declare the counter-notice valid or invalid in accordance with its determination of that question.

(2) Where a counter-notice is accepted as, or declared to be, valid under subsection (1) above the acquiring authority shall be deemed—

    (a) to be authorised to acquire compulsorily, under the enactment by virtue of which they are empowered to acquire the land in respect of which the notice to treat was served, the claimant's interest in the land to which the requirement in the counter-notice relates; and

    (b) to have served a notice to treat in respect of that land on the date on which the first-mentioned notice to treat was served.

(3) A claimant may withdraw a counter-notice at any time before the compensation payable in respect of a compulsory acquisition in pursuance of the counter-notice has been determined by the Lands Tribunal or at any time before the end of six weeks beginning with the date on which the compensation is so determined; and where a counter-notice is withdrawn by virtue of this subsection any notice to treat deemed to have been served in consequence thereof shall be deemed to have been withdrawn.

(4) Without prejudice to subsection (3) above, the power conferred by section 31 of the Land Compensation Act 1961 to withdraw a notice to treat shall not be exerciseable in the case of a notice to treat which is deemed to have been served by virtue of this section.

(5) The compensation payable in respect of the acquisition of an interest in land in pursuance of a notice to treat deemed to have been served by virtue of this section shall be assessed on the assumptions mentioned in section 5(2), (3) and (4) above.

(6) Where by virtue of this section the acquiring authority become, or will become, entitled to a lease of any land but not to the interest of the lessor—

    (a) the authority shall offer to surrender the lease to the lessor on such terms as the authority consider reasonable;

    (b) the question of what terms are reasonable may be referred to the Lands Tribunal by the authority or the lessor and, if at the expiration of three months after the date of the offer mentioned in paragraph (a) above, the authority and the lessor have not agreed on that question and that question has not been referred to the Tribunal by the lessor, it shall be so referred by the authority;

    (c) if that question is referred to the Tribunal the lessor shall be deemed to have accepted the surrender of the lease at the expiration of one month after the date of the determination of the Tribunal or on such other date as the Tribunal may direct and to have agreed with the authority on the terms of surrender which the Tribunal has held to be reasonable.

For the purposes of this subsection any terms as to surrender contained in the lease shall be disregarded.

(7) Where the lessor refuses to accept any sum payable to him by virtue of subsection (6) above, or refuses or fails to make out his title to the satisfaction of the

acquiring authority, they may pay into court any sum payable to the lessor by virtue of that subsection; and subsections (2) and (5) of section 9 of the Compulsory Purchase Act 1965 (deposit of compensation in cases of refusal to convey etc) shall apply to that sum with the necessary modifications.

(8) Where an acquiring authority who become entitled to the lease of any land as mentioned in subsection (6) above are a body incorporated by or under any enactment the corporate powers of the authority shall, if they would not otherwise do so, include power to farm that land.

(9) ...

NOTES

Initial Commencement

Royal Assent: 23 May 1973: (no specific commencement provision).

Extent

In consequence of the amendment made by the Land Compensation (Scotland) Act 1973, s 81(1), Sch 2, Pt I, to s 89(4), this section does not extend to Scotland.

Amendment

Sub-s (9): repealed by the Land Compensation (Scotland) Act 1973, s 81(1), Sch 2, Part I.

Notes

For a commentary, see para 38.79.

Two months beginning with. See the note to s 53.

Within two months after. The general rule in cases where an act is to be done within a specified time is that the day from which it runs is not to be counted; see *Goldsmiths' Co v West Metropolitan Rly Co* [1904] 1 KB 1, [1900–3] All ER Rep 667, CA; *Stewart v Chapman* [1951] 2 KB 792, [1951] 2 All ER 613. See also *Dodds v Walker* [1981] 2 All ER 609, [1981] 1 WLR 1027, HL, as to the day of expiry of periods of a month or a specified number of months.

Land Tribunal. See the note to s 3 of this Act (9 Halsbury's Statutes (4th edn, 1994 Reissue) 265).

Application to cases of deemed service. This section applies to cases where notice to treat is deemed to have been served under the Town and Country Planning Act 1971 or the Compulsory Purchase (Vesting Declarations) Act 1981; see s 53(5).

Definitions. For 'acquiring authority' see s 87(1); 'claimant' see s 53(1).

A1.74

55   Notice of entry in respect of part of agricultural holding

(1)   Where an acquiring authority serve notice of entry under section 11(1) of the Compulsory Purchase Act 1965 on the person in occupation of an agricultural holding, being a person having no greater interest therein than as tenant for a year or from year to year, and the notice relates to part only of that holding, the person on whom the notice is served (hereafter referred to as 'the claimant') may, within the period of two months beginning with the date of service of the notice of entry, serve on the acquiring authority a counter-notice—

(a)   claiming that the remainder of the holding is not reasonably capable of being farmed, either by itself or in conjunction with other relevant land, as a separate agricultural unit; and

(b)   electing to treat the notice of entry as a notice relating to the entire holding.

(2) Where a counter-notice is served under subsection (1) above the claimant shall also, within the period mentioned in that subsection, serve a copy thereof on the landlord of the holding, but failure to comply with this subsection shall not invalidate the counter-notice.

(3) Subject to subsection (4) below, 'other relevant land' in subsection (1) above means—

(a) land comprised in the same agricultural unit as the agricultural holding; and
(b) land comprised in any other agricultural unit occupied by the claimant on the date of service of the notice of entry, being land in respect of which he is then entitled to a greater interest than as tenant for a year or from year to year.

(4) Where an acquiring authority have served a notice to treat in respect of land in the agricultural holding other than that to which the notice of entry relates or in respect of other relevant land as defined in subsection (3) above, then, unless and until that notice to treat is withdrawn, this section and section 56 below shall have effect as if that land did not form part of the holding or did not constitute other relevant land, as the case may be.

(5) ...

NOTES

Initial Commencement

Royal Assent: 23 May 1973: (no specific commencement provision).

Extent

In consequence of the amendment made by the Land Compensation (Scotland) Act 1973, s 81(1), Sch 2, Pt I, to s 89(4), this section does not extend to Scotland.

Amendment

Sub-s (5): repealed by the Land Compensation (Scotland) Act 1973, s 81(1), Sch 2, Part I.

Notes

For a commentary, see para 38.81.

Person; two months beginning with. See the notes to s 53.

Counter-notice. As to the effect of a counter-notice, see s 56.

Extension. This section and s 56 are extended, subject to necessary modifications, by the Development of Rural Wales Act 1976, s 5(1), Sch 3, para 31(4).

Definitions. For 'acquiring authority', 'agricultural land' and 'agricultural unit', see s 87(1).

Miscellaneous

A1.75

59   Notice to quit agricultural holding: right to opt for notice of entry compensation

(1) This section has effect where the person in occupation of an agricultural holding, being a person having no greater interest therein than as tenant for a year or from year to year, is served with a notice to quit the holding, and—

(a) the notice is served after an acquiring authority have served notice to treat on the landlord of the holding or, being an authority possessing compulsory purchase powers, have agreed to acquire his interest in the holding; and

(b) either—
  (i) [section 26(1) of the Agricultural Holdings Act 1986] does not apply to the notice by virtue of [Case B in Part I of Schedule 3 to that Act] (land required for non-agricultural use for which planning permission has been granted etc); or
  (ii) the Agricultural Land Tribunal have consented to the operation of the notice and stated in the reasons for their decision that they are satisfied as to the matter mentioned in [section 27(3)(f)] of that Act (land required for non-agricultural use not falling within [the said Case B]

(2) If the person served with the notice to quit elects that this subsection shall apply to the notice and gives up possession of the holding to the acquiring authority on or before the date on which his tenancy terminates in accordance with the notice—

(a) section 20 of the Compulsory Purchase Act 1965 (compensation for tenants from year to year etc) and section 12 of the Agriculture (Miscellaneous Provisions) Act 1968 shall have effect as if the notice to quit had not been served and the acquiring authority had taken possession of the holding in pursuance of a notice of entry under section 11(1) of the said Act of 1965 on the day before that on which the tenancy terminates in accordance with the notice to quit; and

(b) the provisions of the [Agricultural Holdings Act 1986 relating to compensation to a tenancy on the termination of his tenancy] shall not have effect in relation to the termination of the tenancy by reason of the notice to quit.

(3) No election under subsection (2) above shall be made or, if already made, continue to have effect in relation to any land (whether the whole or part of the land to which the notice to quit relates) if, before the expiration of that notice, an acquiring authority take possession of that land in pursuance of an enactment providing for the taking of possession of land compulsorily.

(4) Any election under subsection (2) above shall be made by notice in writing served on the acquiring authority not later than the date on which possession of the holding is given up.

(5) This section shall have effect in relation to a notice to quit part of an agricultural holding as it has effect in relation to a notice to quit an entire holding and references to a holding and the termination of the tenancy shall be construed accordingly.

(6) A person served with a notice to quit part of an agricultural holding shall not be entitled, in relation to that notice, both to make an election under this section and to give a counter-notice under [section 32 of the Agricultural Holdings Act 1986] (tenant's right to cause notice to quit part of holding to operate as notice to quit entire holding).

(7) The reference in subsection (1)(a) above to a notice to treat served by an acquiring authority includes a reference to a notice to treat deemed to have been so served under any of the provisions mentioned in section 53(5) above [and the reference in that subsection to an authority possessing compulsory purchase powers includes a person or body of persons who would be an authority possessing compulsory purchase powers if the landlord's interest were not an interest in Crown land (as defined by section 293 of the Town and Country Planning Act 1990).]

(8) …

NOTES

Initial Commencement

Royal Assent: 23 May 1973: (no specific commencement provision).

A1.76 *Statutes*

Extent

In consequence of the amendment made by the Land Compensation (Scotland) Act 1973, s 81(1), Sch 2, Pt I, to s 89(4), this section does not extend to Scotland.

Amendment

Sub-s (1): words in square brackets substituted, and final amendment continued in force, by the Agricultural Holdings Act 1986, ss 99, 100, Sch 13, para 3, Sch 14, para 55.

Sub-s (2): words in square brackets substituted, and final amendment continued in force, by the Agricultural Holdings Act 1986, ss 99, 100, Sch 13, para 3, Sch 14, para 55.

Sub-s (6): words in square brackets substituted by the Agricultural Holdings Act 1986, ss 99, 100, Sch 13, para 3, Sch 14, para 55.

Sub-s (7): words in square brackets inserted by the Planning and Compensation Act 1991, s 70, Sch 15, para 7.

Sub-s (8): repealed by the Land Compensation (Scotland) Act 1973, s 81(1), Sch 2, Part I.

Notes

Person. See the note to s 53.

Agricultural Land Tribunal. For the establishment, constitution and procedure of Agricultural Land Tribunals, see the Agriculture Act 1947, s 73, Sch 9, paras 13–17.

Elects that this subsection shall apply. Where only a part of a holding is concerned, the election gives the tenant the further right to serve a notice requiring acquisition of the whole holding; see s 61.

Definitions. For 'acquiring authority', 'agricultural holding', 'authority possessing compulsory purchase powers', 'notice to quit', and 'tenant', see s 87(1).

A1.76

61   Notice to quit part of agricultural holding: right to claim notice of entry compensation for remainder of holding

(1)   Where a notice to quit in respect of which a person is entitled to make an election under section 59 above relates to part only of an agricultural holding and that person makes such an election within the period of two months beginning with the date of service of that notice, or, if later, the decision of the Agricultural Land Tribunal, he may also within that period serve a notice on the acquiring authority claiming that the remainder of the holding is not reasonably capable of being farmed, either by itself or in conjunction with other relevant land, as a separate agricultural unit.

(2)   If the acquiring authority do not within the period of two months beginning with the date of service of a notice under subsection (1) above agree in writing to accept the notice as valid, the claimant or the authority may, within two months after the end of that period, refer it to the Lands Tribunal, and on any such reference the Tribunal shall determine whether the claim in the notice is justified and declare the notice valid or invalid in accordance with its determination of that question.

(3)   Where a notice under subsection (1) above is accepted as, or declared to be, valid under subsection (2) above then, if before the end of twelve months after it has been so accepted or declared the claimant has given up to the acquiring authority possession of the part of the holding to which the notice relates, section 20 of the Compulsory Purchase Act 1965 and section 12 of the Agriculture (Miscellaneous Provisions) Act 1968 shall have effect as if the acquiring authority had taken possession of that

1064

part in pursuance of a notice of entry under section 11(1) of the said Act of 1965 on the day before the expiration of the year of the tenancy which is current when the notice is so accepted or declared.

(4) Subsections (2) to (4) of section 55 and subsection (3) of section 56 above shall apply in relation to subsections (1) to (3) above and to a notice under subsection (1) above as they apply in relation to those sections and a counter- notice under subsection (1) of section 55, and shall so apply with the necessary modifications and as if any reference to the notice of entry were a reference to the notice to quit.

(5) Where an election under section 59 above ceases to have effect in relation to any land by virtue of subsection (3) of that section any notice served by virtue of this section shall also cease to have effect in relation thereto.

(6) ...

NOTES

Initial Commencement

Royal Assent: 23 May 1973: (no specific commencement provision).

Extent

In consequence of the amendment made by the Land Compensation (Scotland) Act 1973, s 81(1), Sch 2, Pt I, to s 89(4), this section does not extend to Scotland.

Amendment

Sub-s (6): repealed by the Land Compensation (Scotland) Act 1973, s 81(1), Sch 2, Part I.

Notes

For a commentary, see para 38.63 ff.

Two months beginning with. See the note to s 53.

Decision of the Agricultural Land Tribunal. This refers to a decision under the Agricultural Holdings Act 1986, s 26(1), consenting to the operation of the notice to quit in accordance with s 27(3)(f) of that Act; cf s 59(1)(b).

Writing. See the note to s 15 of this Act (9 Halsbury's Statutes (4th edn, 1994 Reissue) 277).

Land Tribunal. See the note to s 3 of this Act (9 Halsbury's Statutes (4th edn, 1994 Reissue) 265).

Definitions. For 'acquiring authority', 'agricultural holding', 'agricultural unit' and 'notice to quit', see s 87(1).

PART VI: SUPPLEMENTARY PROVISIONS

A1.77

87   General interpretation

(1) In this Act—

    'agriculture', 'agricultural' and 'agricultural land' have the meaning given in section 109 of the Agricultural Act 1947 ... and references to the farming of land include references to the carrying on in relation to the land of any agricultural activities;

    'agricultural holding' has the meaning given in section 1 of the [Agricultural Holdings Act 1986] ... and 'landlord', 'tenant' and 'notice to quit', in relation to an agricultural holding, have the same meaning as in [that Act];

'agricultural unit' has the meaning given in [section 171(1) of the Town and Country Planning Act 1990] ... ;

'acquiring authority' and 'authority possessing compulsory purchase powers' have the same meaning as in the Land Compensation Act 1961 ... ;

['aerodrome' has the same meaning as in the Civil Aviation Act 1982;]

...

'disabled person' means a person who is substantially and permanently handi-capped by illness, injury or congenital infirmity ... ;

'dwelling' means a building or part of a building occupied or (if not occupied) last occupied or intended to be occupied as a private dwelling ... and ... includes any garden, yard, outhouses and appurtenances belonging to or usually enjoyed with that building or part;

...

['housing association' has the same meaning as in the Housing Associations Act 1985 ...;]

'tenancy', ... otherwise than in relation to an agricultural holding, has the same meaning as in the Landlord and Tenant Act 1954.

(2)   In this Act references to the council of a district are, until 1st April 1974, references to the council of a county district or county borough and, thereafter, to the council of a district within the meaning of the Local Government Act 1972; and references to a London borough and the Council of a London borough include references to the City of London and the Common Council.

(3)   ...

(4)   Except where the context otherwise requires, references in this Act to any enactment are references to that enactment as amended, and include references to that enactment as extended or applied, by any other enactment, including this Act.

NOTES

Initial Commencement

Royal Assent: 23 May 1973: (no specific commencement provision).

Extent

In consequence of the amendment made by the Land Compensation (Scotland) Act 1973, s 81(1), Sch 2, Pt I, to s 89(4), this section does not extend to Scotland.

Amendment

Sub-s (1): in defintions "agriculture', 'agricultural' and 'agricultural land" words omitted repealed by the Land Compensation (Scotland) Act 1973, 81(1), Sch 2, Pt I.

Sub-s (1): in definition 'agricultural holding' words 'Agricultural Holdings Act 1986' in square brackets substituted by the Agricultural Holdings Act 1986, ss 99, 100, Sch 13, para 3, Sch 14, para 56.

Sub-s (1): in definition 'agricultural holding' words omitted repealed by the Land Compensation (Scotland) Act 1973, 81(1), Sch 2, Pt I.

Sub-s (1): in definition 'agricultural holding' words 'that Act' in square brackets substituted by the Land Compensation (Scotland) Act 1973, s 81(1), Sch 2, Pt I.

Sub-s (1): in definition 'agricultural unit' words 'section 171(1) of the Town and Country Planning Act 1990' in square brackets substituted by the Planning (Consequential Provisions) Act 1990, s 4, Sch 2, para 29(11).

Sub-s (1): in definition 'agricultural unit' words omitted repealed by the Land Compensation (Scotland) Act 1973, 81(1), Sch 2, Pt I.

Sub-s (1): in definitions "acquiring authority' and 'authority possessing compulsory purchase powers" words omitted repealed by the Land Compensation (Scotland) Act 1973, 81(1), Sch 2, Pt I.

Sub-s (1): definition 'aerodrome' substituted by the Civil Aviation Act 1982, s 109(2), Sch 15, para 12(3).

Sub-s (1): definitions "cottar', 'croft', 'crofter' and 'landlord" (omitted) repealed by the Land Compensation (Scotland) Act 1973, 81(1), Sch 2, Pt I.

Sub-s (1): in definition 'disabled person' words omitted repealed by the Land Compensation (Scotland) Act 1973, 81(1), Sch 2, Pt I.

Sub-s (1): in definition 'dwelling' first words omitted repealed by the Land Compensation (Scotland) Act 1973, 81(1), Sch 2, Pt I.

Sub-s (1): in definition 'dwelling' second words omitted repealed by the Planning and Compulsory Purchase Act 2004, ss 118(2), 120, Sch 7, para 7(1), (4), Sch 9.

Date in force: 31 October 2004 (except in relation to a compulsory purchase order made or made in draft before that date): see SI 2004/2593, art 2(d), (e)(i) and the Planning and Compulsory Purchase Act 2004, Sch 7, para 7(5).

Sub-s (1): definitions "heritable security', 'holding', 'landholder', 'owner', 'road' and 'statutory small tenant" (omitted) repealed by the Land Compensation (Scotland) Act 1973, 81(1), Sch 2, Pt I.

Sub-s (1): definition 'housing association' substituted by the Housing (Consequential Provisions) Act 1985, s 4, Sch 2, para 24.

Sub-s (1): in definition 'housing association' words omitted repealed by SI 1996/2325, art 4(1), Sch 1, Pt I.

Sub-s (1): in definition 'tenancy' words omitted repealed by the Land Compensation (Scotland) Act 1973, 81(1), Sch 2, Pt I.

Sub-s (3): repealed by the Highways Act 1980, s 343 (2), (3), Sch 24, para 23, Sch 25.

Notes

Authority possessing compulsory purchase powers. The term is defined in the Land Compensation Act 1961, s 39. In that Act, as in this, government departments are included; see s 84(2) of this Act and cf s 533 of that Act.

Dwelling. There are numerous cases on the construction of the words 'separate dwelling' in the Rent Acts, and they may be of some assistance in determining whether particular premises are a dwelling within the definition in this section. See *Metropolitan Properties Co (FGC) Ltd v Barder* [1968] 1 All ER 536, [1968] 1 WLR 286; *Marsh Ltd v Cooper* [1969] 2 All ER 498, [1969] 1 WLR 803, and earlier cases cited in those reports.

Agriculture Holdings Act 1986. For the meanings of 'landlord' and 'tenant' see s 96(1), (6) thereof. For provisions as to notices to quit see now the Agricultural Holdings Act 1986.

Land Compensation Act 1961. For the relevant definitions, see s 39 of that Act.

Civil Aviation Act 1982. For the relevant definition, see s 105(1) of that Act.

Landlord and Tenant Act 1954. For the relevant definition, see s 69(1) of that Act.

Local Government Act 1972. As to districts under that Act, see ss 1(3), 20(3) of that Act.

AGRICULTURAL STATISTICS ACT 1979

(1979 C 13)

ARRANGEMENT OF SECTIONS

An Act to consolidate certain enactments relating to agricultural statistics

[22nd March 1979]

A1.78

1   Power to obtain agricultural statistics

(1)   Where it appears to the appropriate Minister expedient so to do for the purpose of obtaining statistical information relating to agriculture, he may serve on any owners or occupiers of land used for agriculture, or of land which he has reason to believe may be so used, notices requiring them to furnish in writing, in such form and manner and to such person as may be specified in the notice, and within such time and with respect to such date or dates or such period or periods as may be so specified, the information referred to in the notice (including, as respects paragraphs (*d*) to (*f*) of this subsection, the information referred to in the notice as to quantities, values, expenditure and receipts) relating to—

(a)   the situation, area and description of relevant land owned or occupied by them, the date of acquisition of the land, and the date at which so much of it as is comprised in any agricultural unit became comprised in that unit, and the rates payable in respect of the land,

[(b)   any person who is an owner or occupier of the land or any part of it and the terms on which, and arrangements under which, the land or any part of it is owned, occupied, managed or farmed by any person;]

(d)   the character and use of different parts of the land, the time at which any use of such parts was begun or will become fully effective, and their produce at any time during the period beginning one year before, and ending one year after, the time at which the information is required to be furnished,

(e)   fixed and other equipment, livestock, and the stocks of agricultural produce and requisites held in respect of the land, and the provision and maintenance of such equipment, livestock and requisites and the provision of agricultural services for the benefit of the land,

(f)   the methods and operations used on the land, the marketing or other disposal of its produce, any payments received under any enactment in respect of such produce, and the provision of agricultural services otherwise than for the benefit of the land,

(g) the number and description of persons employed on the land, or employed by the occupier in disposing of its produce, and the remuneration paid to, and hours worked by, persons so employed or such persons of different descriptions.

(2) For the purpose of obtaining statistical information relating to agriculture, any person authorised by the appropriate Minister in that behalf may, after giving not less than 24 hours notice and on producing if so required evidence of his authority to act for the purposes of this subsection, orally require the owner or occupier of land to furnish to him within a reasonable time, and either orally or in writing as the said owner or occupier may elect, such information, whether or not specified in the notice, as the said person authorised by the appropriate Minister may require, being information which the owner or occupier, as the case may be, could have been required to furnish under subsection (1) above.

(3) References in subsections (1) and (2) above to the owner of land include references to a person exercising, as servant or agent of the owner, functions of estate management in relation to the land, and references in those subsections to the occupier of land include references to a person responsible for the control of the farming of the land as servant or agent of the occupier of the land.

(4) No person shall be required under this section to furnish any balance sheet or profit and loss account, but this subsection shall not prevent the requiring of information by reason only that it is or might be contained as an item in such a balance sheet or account.

(5) ...

NOTES

Derivation

Sub-ss (1)–(4) derived from the Agriculture Act 1947, s 78.

Initial Commencement

Specified date: 22 April 1979: see s 8(2).

Extent

This Act does not extend to Scotland: see s 8(3).

Amendment

Sub-s (1): para (b) substituted for existing paras (b), (c) by the Agriculture (Amendment) Act 1984, s 2.

Sub-s (5): repealed by the Agriculture (Amendment) Act 1984, s 2.

Transfer of Functions

Functions of the appropriate Minister, so far as exercisable in relation to Wales, transferred to the National Assembly for Wales, by the National Assembly for Wales (Transfer of Functions) Order 1999, SI 1999/672, art 2, Sch 1.

A1.79

2 ...

...

NOTES

Amendment

Repealed by the Statute Law (Repeals) Act 2004.

Date in force: 22 July 2004: (no specific commencement provision).

A1.80

3   Restriction on disclosure of information

(1)   Subject to subsection (2) below, no information relating to any particular land or business which has been obtained under section 1 ... above shall be published or otherwise disclosed without the previous consent in writing of the person by whom the information was furnished and every other person who is an owner or the occupier of the land and whose interests may in the opinion of the appropriate Minister be affected by the disclosure.

(2)   Nothing in subsection (1) above shall restrict the disclosure of information—

   (a)   to the Minister in charge of any Government department[, to the Scottish Ministers], to any authority acting under an enactment for regulating the marketing of any agricultural produce, or to any person exercising functions on behalf of any such Minister[, the Scottish Ministers] or authority for the purpose of the exercise of those functions;

   (b)   to an authority having power under any enactment to give permission for the development of land, for the purpose of assisting that authority in the preparation of proposals relating to such development or in considering whether or not to give such permission;

   (c)   if the disclosure is confined to situation, extent, number and kind of livestock, character of land, and name and address of owner and occupier, to any person to whom the appropriate Minister considers that the disclosure is required in the public interest;

   (d)   to any person for the purposes of any criminal proceedings under section 4 below or for the purposes of any report of such proceedings;

   (e)   ...

   (f)   to an institution of the European Communities under section 12 of the European Communities Act 1972,

   [(g)   to the Food Standards Agency for purposes connected with the carrying out of any of its functions,]

or the use of information in any manner which the appropriate Minister thinks necessary or expedient in connection with the maintenance of the supply of food in the United Kingdom.

NOTES

Derivation

This section derived from the Agriculture Act 1947, s 80, the Industrial Training Act 1964, s 2B, and the European Communities Act 1972, s 12.

Initial Commencement

Specified date: 22 April 1979: see s 8(2).

Extent

This Act does not extend to Scotland: see s 8(3).

Amendment

Sub-s (1): words omitted repealed by the Statute Law (Repeals) Act 2004.

Date in force: 22 July 2004: (no specific commencement provision).

Sub-s (2): in para (a) words ', to the Scottish Ministers' in square brackets inserted by SI 1999/1820, art 4, Sch 2, Pt I, para 61(a).

Date in force: 1 July 1999: see SI 1999/1820, art 1(2).

Sub-s (2): in para (a) words ', the Scottish Ministers' in square brackets inserted by SI 1999/1820, art 4, Sch 2, Pt I, para 61(b).

Date in force: 1 July 1999: see SI 1999/1820, art 1(2).

Sub-s (3): para (e) repealed by the Statute Law (Repeals) Act 2004.

Date in force: 22 July 2004: (no specific commencement provision).

Sub-s (2): para (g) inserted by the Food Standards Act 1999, s 40(1), Sch 5, para 5.

Date in force: 1 April 2000: see SI 2000/1066, art 2.

Transfer of Functions

Functions of the appropriate Minister, so far as exercisable in relation to Wales, transferred to the National Assembly for Wales, by the National Assembly for Wales (Transfer of Functions) Order 1999, SI 1999/672, art 2, Sch 1.

A1.81

4   Penalties

(1) Any person who without reasonable excuse fails to furnish information in compliance with a requirement under section 1 ... above shall be liable on summary conviction to a fine not exceeding [level 3 on the standard scale].

(2)   If any person—

  (a)   in purported compliance with a requirement imposed under section 1 ... above knowingly or recklessly furnishes any information which is false in any material particular, or
  (b)   publishes or otherwise discloses any information in contravention of section 3 above,

he shall be liable on summary conviction to imprisonment for a term not exceeding 3 months or to a fine not exceeding the prescribed sum or to both, or on conviction on indictment to imprisonment for a term not exceeding 2 years or to a fine or to both.

NOTES

Derivation

This section derived from the Agriculture Act 1947, s 81.

Initial Commencement

Specified date: 22 April 1979: see s 8(2).

Extent

This Act does not extend to Scotland: see s 8(3).

Amendment

Sub-s (1): words omitted repealed by the Statute Law (Repeals) Act 2004.

Date in force: 22 July 2004: (no specific commencement provision).

Sub-s (1): maximum fine increased and converted to a level on the standard scale by the Criminal Justice Act 1982, ss 37, 38, 46.

Sub-s (2): in para (a) words omitted repealed by the Statute Law (Repeals) Act 2004.

Date in force: 22 July 2004: (no specific commencement provision).

A1.82

5   Service of notices

(1)   Any notice authorised by this Act to be served on any person shall be duly served if it is delivered to him, or left at his proper address or sent to him by post in a registered letter.

(2)   Any such notice authorised to be served on an incorporated company or body shall be duly served if served on the secretary or clerk of the company or body.

(3)   For the purposes of this section and of section 7 of the Interpretation Act 1978, the proper address of any person on whom any such notice is to be served shall, in the case of the secretary or clerk of any incorporated company or body be that of the registered or principal office of the company or body, and in any other case be the last known address of the person in question.

(4)   Where any such notice is to be served on a person as being the person having any interest in land, and it is not practicable after reasonable inquiry to ascertain his name or address, the notice may be served by addressing it to him by the description of the person having that interest in the land (naming it), and delivering the notice to some responsible person on the land or by affixing it, or a copy of it, to some conspicuous object on the land.

(5)   Where any such notice is to be served on any person as being the owner of the land and the land *belongs to an ecclesiastical benefice* [is vested in the incumbent of a benefice of the Church of England] a copy shall be served on the *Church Commissioners* [Diocesan Board of Finance for the diocese in which the land is situated].

(6)   Without prejudice to subsections (1) to (5) above, any notice under this Act to be served on an occupier shall be deemed to be duly served if it is addressed to him by the description of 'the occupier' of the land in question and sent by post to, or delivered to some person on, the land.

NOTES

Derivation

This section derived from the Agriculture Act 1947, ss 78(5), 107.

Initial Commencement

Specified date: 22 April 1979: see s 8(2).

Extent

This Act does not extend to Scotland: see s 8(3).

Amendment

Sub-s (5): words 'belongs to an ecclesiastical benefice' in italics repealed and subsequent words in square brackets substituted by the Church of England (Miscellaneous Provisions) Measure 2006, s 14, Sch 5, para 19.

Date in force: to be appointed: see the Church of England (Miscellaneous Provisions) Measure 2006, s 16(2).

Sub-s (5): words 'Church Commissioners' in italics repealed and subsequent words in square brackets substituted by the Church of England (Miscellaneous Provisions) Measure 2006, s 14, Sch 5, para 19.

Date in force: to be appointed: see the Church of England (Miscellaneous Provisions) Measure 2006, s 16(2).

A1.83

6   Interpretation

(1)   In this Act—

'the appropriate Minister' means, in relation to England, the [Secretary of State] and, in relation to Wales, the Secretary of State;

'land' includes messuages, tenements and hereditaments, houses and buildings of any tenure;

'livestock' includes creatures kept for any purpose;

'owner' means, in relation to land, a person, other than a mortgagee not in possession, who is for the time being entitled to dispose of the fee simple of the land, and includes also a person holding, or entitled to the rents and profits of, the land under a lease or agreement;

'the prescribed sum' means the prescribed sum within the meaning of [section 32 of the Magistrates' Courts Act 1980 (£1,000 or other sum substituted by order under section 143(1) of that Act)]; and

'relevant land' in the case of any owner or occupier of land used for agriculture, means the aggregate of—

(a)   the land owned or occupied by him which is comprised in any agricultural unit; and

(b)   any other land owned or occupied by him which is either—

(i)   used for forestry; or

(ii)   not used for any purpose, but capable of use for agriculture or forestry,

but which, if used as agricultural land by the occupier of that agricultural unit, would be comprised in that unit.

(2)   Section 109 of the Agriculture Act 1947 (interpretation) shall have effect for the purposes of this Act as it has effect for the purposes of that Act except that the definition of 'livestock' shall be omitted from subsection (3).

NOTES

Derivation

Sub-s (1) derived from the Agriculture Act 1947, s 78(1A).

Extent

This Act does not extend to Scotland: see s 8(3).

A1.84 *Statutes*

Amendment

Sub-s (1): in definition 'the appropriate Minister' words 'Secretary of State' in square brackets substituted by SI 2002/794, art 5(1), Sch 1, para 20.

Date in force: 27 March 2002: see SI 2002/794, art 1(2).

Sub-s (1): in definition 'the prescribed sum' words 'section 32 of the Magistrates' Courts Act 1980 (£1,000 or other sum substituted by order under section 143(1) of that Act)' in square brackets substituted by the Magistrates' Courts Act 1980, s 154, Sch 7, para 182.

Transfer of Functions

Functions of the appropriate Minister, so far as exercisable in relation to Wales, transferred to the National Assembly for Wales, by the National Assembly for Wales (Transfer of Functions) Order 1999, SI 1999/672, art 2, Sch 1.

A1.84

7 Amendments and repeals

(1) The enactments specified in Schedule 1 to this Act shall have effect subject to the amendments set out in that Schedule, being amendments consequential on the foregoing provisions of this Act.

(2) The enactments specified in Schedule 2 to this Act are hereby repealed to the extent specified in column 3 of that Schedule.

NOTES

Initial Commencement

Specified date: 22 April 1979: see s 8(2).

Extent

This Act does not extend to Scotland: see s 8(3).

A1.85

8 Citation, etc

(1) This Act may be cited as the Agricultural Statistics Act 1979.

(2) ...

(3) This Act does not extend to Scotland or Northern Ireland.

NOTES

Initial Commencement

Specified date: 22 April 1979: (sub-s (2) stated that this Act would come into force at the expiry of the period of one month beginning on the date on which it was passed).

Extent

This Act does not extend to Scotland: see sub-s (3) above.

Amendment

Sub-s (2): repealed by the Statute Law (Repeals) Act 2004.

Date in force: 22 July 2004: (no specific commencement provision).

SCHEDULE 1

A1.86

...

NOTES

Initial Commencement

Specified date: 22 April 1979: see s 8(2).

Extent

This Act does not extend to Scotland: see s 8(3).

Amendment

Paras 1, 2, 4: amend the Agricultural Marketing Act 1958, s 5(4), the Public Records Act 1958, Sch 2, and the European Communities Act 1972, s 12.

Para 3: repealed by the Agricultural Training Board Act 1982, s 11(1), Sch 2.

SCHEDULE 2
ENACTMENTS REPEALED

Section 7

A1.87

Chapter	Short Title	Extent of Repeal
10 & 11 Geo 6 c 48	Agriculture Act 1947	Sections 78 to 81.
6 & 7 Eliz 2 c 51	Public Records Act 1958	In Schedule 2, the entry relating to section 80 of the Agriculture Act 1947.
1972 c 62	Agriculture (Miscellaneous Provisions) Act 1972	Section 18.
1976 c 55	Agriculture (Miscellaneous Provisions) Act 1976	Section 6. Schedule 2.

NOTES

Initial Commencement

Specified date: 22 April 1979: see s 8(2).

Extent

This Act does not extend to Scotland: see s 8(3).

AGRICULTURAL HOLDINGS ACT 1986

(1986 C 5)

ARRANGEMENT OF SECTIONS

82 Application of section 15 to smallholdings

PART VII: MISCELLANEOUS AND SUPPLEMENTAL
83 Settlement of claims on termination of tenancy
84 Arbitrations
85 Enforcement
86 Power of landlord to obtain charge on holding
87 General provisions as to charges under this Act on holdings
88 Power of limited owners to give consents etc
89 Power of limited owners to apply capital for improvements
90 Estimation of best rent for purposes of Acts and other instruments
91 Power of Minister to vary Schedules 7, 8 and 10
92 Advisory committee on valuation of improvements and tenant-right matters
93 Service of notices
94 Orders and regulations
95 Crown land
96 Interpretation
97 Saving for other rights etc
98 Application of Act to old tenancies etc
99 Transitional provisions and savings
100 Consequential amendments
101 Repeals and revocations
102 Citation, commencement and extent

SCHEDULE 1
Matters for which provision is to be made in written tenancy agreements

SCHEDULE 2
Arbitration of rent: provisions supplementary to section 12

SCHEDULE 3
Cases where consent of tribunal to operation of notice to quit is not required
      Part I: The cases
      Part II: Supplementary provisions applicable to cases A, B, C, D, E and G

SCHEDULE 4
Matters for which provision may be made by order under section 29

SCHEDULE 5
Notice to quit where tenant is a service man

SCHEDULE 6
Eligibility to apply for new tenancy under Part IV of this Act
      Part I: 'Eligible person': supplementary provisions
      Part II: Modifications of Part I of this Schedule in its application to succession on
        retirement

SCHEDULE 7
Long-term improvements begun on or after 1st March 1948 for which compensation is payable
      Part I: Improvements to which consent of landlord required
      Part II: Improvements to which consent of landlord or approval of tribunal required

SCHEDULE 8
Short-term improvements begun on or after 1st March 1948, and other matters, for which
compensation is payable
      Part I: Improvements (to which no consent required)
      Part II: Tenant-right matters

SCHEDULE 9
Compensation to tenant for improvements begun before 1st March 1948
      Part I: Tenant's right to compensation for old improvements
      Part II: Old improvements for which compensation is payable

SCHEDULE 10
Market garden improvements

An Act to consolidate certain enactments relating to agricultural holdings, with amendments to give effect to recommendations of the Law Commission

[18th March 1986]

PART I: INTRODUCTORY

A1.88

1   Principal definitions

(1) In this Act 'agricultural holding' means the aggregate of the land (whether agricultural land or not) comprised in a contract of tenancy which is a contract for an agricultural tenancy, not being a contract under which the land is let to the tenant during his continuance in any office, appointment or employment held under the landlord.

(2) For the purposes of this section, a contract of tenancy relating to any land is a contract for an agricultural tenancy if, having regard to—

    (a)   the terms of the tenancy,
    (b)   the actual or contemplated use of the land at the time of the conclusion of the contract and subsequently, and
    (c)   any other relevant circumstances,

the whole of the land comprised in the contract, subject to such exceptions only as do not substantially affect the character of the tenancy, is let for use as agricultural land.

(3) A change in user of the land concerned subsequent to the conclusion of a contract of tenancy which involves any breach of the terms of the tenancy shall be disregarded for the purpose of determining whether a contract which was not originally a contract for an agricultural tenancy has subsequently become one unless it is effected with the landlord's permission, consent or acquiescence.

(4) In this Act 'agricultural land' means—

    (a)   land used for agriculture which is so used for the purposes of a trade or business, and
    (b)   any other land which, by virtue of a designation under section 109(1) of the Agriculture Act 1947, is agricultural land within the meaning of that Act.

(5) In this Act 'contract of tenancy' means a letting of land, or agreement for letting land, for a term of years or from year to year; and for the purposes of this definition a letting of land, or an agreement for letting land, which, by virtue of subsection (6) of section 149 of the Law of Property Act 1925, takes effect as such a letting of land or

agreement for letting land as is mentioned in that subsection shall be deemed to be a letting of land or, as the case may be, an agreement for letting land, for a term of years.

NOTES

Derivation

Sub-ss (1)–(3) derived from the Agricultural Holdings Act 1948, s 1(1), (1A), (1B), and the Agricultural Holdings Act 1984, s 10(1), Sch 3, para 1(2), (3); sub-s (4) derived from the Agricultural Holdings Act 1948, s 1(2), the Agriculture (Miscellaneous Provisions) Act 1976, s 18(2), and the Agricultural Holdings Act 1984, Sch 1, para 1, Sch 2, para 1(2); sub-s (5) derived from the Agricultural Holdings Act 1948, s 94(1).

Initial Commencement

Specified date: 18 June 1986: see s 102(2).

Extent

This Act does not extend to Scotland.

See Further

See further, in relation to the disapplication of this Act to tenancies beginning on or after 1 September 1995 except in certain specified cases: the Agricultural Tenancies Act 1995, s 4.

See further, as to the exclusion of this Act in relation to leases or tenancies granted to contractors in respect of the running of any removal centre or part of a removal centre: the Immigration and Asylum Act 1999, s 149(3).

Notes

For a commentary, see para 19.3 ff.

Sub-ss (1), (2), (3) contain provisions formerly in the Agricultural Holdings Act 1948, s 1(1), (1A), (1B), respectively, as amended, in the case of sub-s (1) of that section, and as substituted, in the case of sub-ss (1A), (1B) thereof, by the Agricultural Holdings Act 1984, s 10(1), Sch 3, para 1(2), (3). Sub-s (4) contains provisions formerly in s 1(2) of the 1948 Act, as repealed in part by s 10(2) of, and Sch 4 to, the Act, and as applied by the Agriculture (Miscellaneous Provisions) Act 1976, s 18(2) (as amended by s 3(5) of, and Sch 1, para 1(a) to, the 1984 Act), and by Sch 2, para 1(2) to, the 1984 Act. Sub-s (5) contains provisions formerly in the definition of 'contract of tenancy' in s 94(1) of the 1948 Act.

General Note. The decisions of the courts on the meaning of 'agricultural holding' and of the other expressions defined by this section are considered in 1 Halsbury's Law (4th edn, reissue) paras 301–305.

An application for planning permission must be notified to owners (where the applicant is not himself the owner in fee simple or tenant of the whole of the land) and to tenants of agricultural holdings of the land affected; see the Town and Country Planning Act 1990, s 65.

Sub-s (1): Appointment or employment. An arrangement for a farmer to occupy land rent-free retaining profits for one year pending the grant of a tenancy was held not to be an appointment but a tenancy from year to year; see *Verrall v Farnes* [1966] 2 All ER 808, [1966] 1 WLR 1254.

Sub-s (4): Trade or business. Although there is some authority for saying that the expressions 'trade' and 'business' are synonymous (see, in particular, *Grainger & Son v Gough* [1896] AC 325 at 343 per Lord Morris), the balance of authority is to the effect that 'business' is a wider term than 'trade'; see, in particular, *Re A Debtor (No 3 of 1926)* [1927] 1 Ch 97, [1926] All ER Rep 337, CA, and *Re A Debtor (No 490 of 1935)* [1936] Ch 237, CA. In fact it has been said that 'the word "business" means almost anything which is an occupation, as distinguished from a pleasure—anything which is an occupation or duty which requires attention is a business' (*Rolls v Miller* (1884) 27 Ch D 71 at 88, CA per Lindley LJ), and it has also been said that neither the making of a profit nor any commercial activity is essential (*Rael-Brook Ltd v Minister of Housing and Local Government* [1967] 2 QB 65, [1967] 1 All ER 262). Yet the term 'business' has perhaps to be confined to a regularly conducted commercial enterprise; see *IRC v Marine Steam*

Turbine Co Ltd [1920] 1 KB 193 at 202–204; *Re A Debtor (No 3 of 1926)* supra, at 106 and 341, respectively; *Lord Advocate v Glasgow City Corpn* 1958 SLT 2 at 8, 1958 SC 12; *Abernethie v A M & J Kleiman Ltd* [1970] 1 QB 10, [1969] 2 All ER 790, CA; *Customs and Excise Comrs v Royal Exchange Theatre Trust* [1979] 3 All ER 797; and *Customs and Excise Comrs v Lord Fisher* [1981] 2 All ER 147, [1981] STC 238. On the other hand, the expression 'business' is clearly wide enough to include a profession; see *Re Williams' Will Trusts, Chartered Bank of India, Australia and China v Williams* [1953] Ch 138, [1953] 1 All ER 536, and *R v Breeze* [1973] 2 All ER 1141, [1973] 1 WLR 994, CA; and contrast *Stuchbery v General Accident, Fire and Life Assurance Corpn Ltd* [1949] 2 KB 256, [1949] 1 All ER 1026, CA.

Note that the trade or business need not be an agricultural one; see *Rutherford v Maurer* [1962] 1 QB 16, [1961] 2 All ER 775, CA, where the premises were used to graze horses for a riding school.

Land which is let for the purposes of a trade or business may be 'agricultural land' even though it is simultaneously used for another purpose (such as keeping a horse for pleasure) and the fact that there is a period during the term of the letting when the land will be used only for pleasure makes no difference unless either (i) the business purpose is relatively so minor that it can no longer be regarded as the purpose of the letting or (ii) the agreement can be regarded as two distinct agreements, one relating to business use and the other relating to other use; see *Brown v Tiernan* (1992) 65 P & CR 324, [1993] 1 EGLR 11.

Sub-s (5): Contract of tenancy. The definition does not cover a tenancy for successive periods of 364 days (*Land Settlement Association Ltd v Carr* [1944] KB 657, [1944] 2 All ER 126, CA, considered in *Re Land and Premises at Liss, Hants* [1971] Ch 986, [1971] 3 All ER 380); but see s 2 and Sch 12, para 1 which restrict the letting of agricultural land for an interest less than a tenancy from year to year by an agreement made on or after 1 March 1948.

See also the note 'Tenancy' to s 2.

Term of years. A tenancy of agricultural land for a term of more than 12, and less than 24, months is a letting for a 'term of years' within the meaning of sub-s (5) of this section, and as such is an agricultural holding excluded from the protection of the Landlord and Tenant Act 1954, Pt II; see *EWP Ltd v Moore* [1992] QB 460, [1992] 1 All ER 880, CA.

Enfranchisement or extension of long leaseholds. The Leasehold Reform Act 1967, Pt I does not confer on a tenant of a house any right by reference to his occupation of it as his residence if that house is comprised within an agricultural holding within the meaning of this Act; see s 1(3) of the 1967 Act, as amended by the Agricultural Tenancies Act 1995, s 40, Schedule, para 22.

Note also that tenancies of dwelling-houses comprised in agricultural holdings are not protected tenancies under the Rent Act 1977; see s 10 of the 1977 Act, as substituted by the 1995 Act, s 40, Schedule, para 27.

Opencast coal operations. For the effect of opencast planning permission under the Opencast Coal Act 1958, upon an agricultural holding, see s 14 of that Act.

Definitions. For 'agriculture' and 'landlord' see s 96(1); as to 'land used for agriculture', see s 96(5).

Agriculture Act 1947, s 109(1). Note the limit on the powers of the Minister regarding designation in the proviso thereto.

A1.89

2   Restriction on letting agricultural land for less than from year to year

(1)   An agreement to which this section applies shall take effect, with the necessary modifications, as if it were an agreement for the letting of land for a tenancy from year to year unless the agreement was approved by the Minister before it was entered into.

(2)   Subject to subsection (3) below, this section applies to an agreement under which—

   (a)   any land is let to a person for use as agricultural land for an interest less than a tenancy from year to year, or

   (b)   a person is granted a licence to occupy land for use as agricultural land,

if the circumstances are such that if his interest were a tenancy from year to year he would in respect of that land be the tenant of an agricultural holding.

(3)   This section does not apply to an agreement for the letting of land, or the granting of a licence to occupy land—

   (a)   made (whether or not it expressly so provides) in contemplation of the use of the land only for grazing or mowing (or both) during some specified period of the year, or

   (b)   by a person whose interest in the land is less than a tenancy from year to year and has not taken effect as such a tenancy by virtue of this section.

(4)   Any dispute arising as to the operation of this section in relation to any agreement shall be determined by arbitration under this Act.

NOTES

Derivation

This section derived from the Agricultural Holdings Act 1948, s 2, and gives effect to Law Commission Recommendation No 153, Cmnd 9665.

Initial Commencement

Specified date: 18 June 1986: see s 102(2).

Extent

This Act does not extend to Scotland.

See Further

See further, as to the exclusion of this Act in relation to leases or tenancies granted to contractors in respect of the running of any removal centre or part of a removal centre: the Immigration and Asylum Act 1999, s 149(3).

Transfer of Functions

Functions of the Minister, so far as exercisable in relation to Wales, transferred to the National Assembly for Wales, by the National Assembly for Wales (Transfer of Functions) Order 1999, SI 1999/672, art 2, Sch 1.

Notes

For a commentary, see para 20.3 ff.

Sub-ss (1)–(3) contain provisions formerly in the Agricultural Holdings Act 1948, s 2(1) and in the case of sub-s (3) takes account of the first recommendation in the Law Commission's Report on this consolidation (Law Com No 153; Cmnd 9665), as to which, see the note 'Grazing or mowing (or both)' below. Sub-s (4) contains provisions formerly in s 2(2) of the 1948 Act.

General Note. 'Agreement' in sub-ss (1)–(3) above means an agreement enforceable at law, a contract supported by value consideration and capable of being enlarged into a tenancy from year to year, and, notwithstanding sub-s (4) above, a county court has jurisdiction to decide whether a transaction falls within these provisions above (*Goldsack v Shore* [1950] 1 KB 708, [1950] 1 All ER 276, CA), but the court has no general discretion to exclude from the section cases producing surprising results (*Verrall v Farnes* [1966] 2 All ER 808, [1966] 1 WLR 1254). This section will, however, only apply where the 'necessary modifications' are consistent with the terms of the agreement (*Bahamas International Trust Co Ltd v Threadgold* [1974] 3 All ER 881, HL).

Note that this section does not apply to agreements made before 1 March 1948; see Sch 12, para 1.

Agreement; necessary modifications. See the General Note above.

Tenancy. As to the exclusion of agricultural tenancies from the Landlord and Tenant Act 1954, Pt II (relating to security of tenure for business tenants), see s 43(1)(a) of the 1954 Act, as amended by s 100, Sch 14, para 21, and the Agricultural Tenancies Act 1995, s 40, Schedule, para 10(a). As to the effect of opencast coal mining on a tenancy, see the Opencast Coal Act 1958, ss 14(4), 34, Sch 6, paras 24, 25.

A tenant for the purposes of this Act is a protected tenant in relation to provisions for compensation for subsidence damage caused by the coal mining for the purposes of the Coal Mining Subsidence Act 1991, Sch 3; see s 21(3)(a).

An oral arrangement between a father and his son for the latter to farm land and make an annual payment to the former was held to create an agricultural tenancy in *Holder v Holder* [1968] Ch 353, [1968] 1 All ER 665, CA.

Approved by the Minister, etc. The Minister merely has, before any agreement is made, to approve the letting of the particular piece of land which is ultimately the subject of the agreement, and not the terms of the particular agreement; see *Epsom and Ewell Borough Council v C Bell (Tadworth) Ltd* [1983] 2 All ER 59, [1983] 1 WLR 379.

An approval (of licences to be granted by certain government departments) in purported exercise of powers under the Agriculture Act 1947, s 40, after its repeal by the Agricultural Holdings Act 1948, s 98, Sch 8, was held to be a valid approval under s 2(1) of the 1948 Act (as to which, see the derivation note above) in *Finbow v Air Ministry* [1963] 2 All ER 647, [1963] 1 WLR 697.

Interest less than a tenancy from year to year. The Agricultural Holdings Act 1923 (repealed) applied only to tenancies from year to year and larger estates, with the result that its provisions could be excluded by the creation of leases for 364 days or less; see *Land Settlement Association Ltd v Carr* [1944] KB 657, [1944] 2 All ER 126. A letting for three months which the parties expected to be renewed, and which was renewed 21 times, there being no contract for renewal, is for less than a year: *Scene Estates Ltd v Amos* [1957] 2 QB 205, [1957] 2 All ER 325, CA. A seasonal grazing licence, granted for successive years but not specifying the dates of the season, is a licence to occupy land during a 'specified period of the year' and is not protected as a 'tenancy from year to year' (dictum of Denning LJ in *Scene Estates Ltd v Amos* (above) applied in *Watts v Yeend* [1987] 1 All ER 744, [1987] 1 WLR 323, CA). In *Gladstone v Bower* [1960] 2 QB 384, [1960] 3 All ER 353, the Court of Appeal held that a tenancy for eighteen months escaped the Act as it was less than from year to year, even though not for two years or upwards so as to fall within what is now s 3(1), but in *Bernays v Prosser* [1963] 2 QB 592, [1963] 2 All ER 321, CA, a tenancy for one year was distinguished as being for less than from year to year. In *Lower v Sorrell* [1963] 1 QB 959, [1962] 3 All ER 1074, CA, an ineffective notice to quit expiring twelve months after the date of a current notice to quit operated as an offer so as to create a new tenancy from year to year. See also, *Lory v London Borough of Brent* [1971] 1 All ER 1042, [1971] 1 WLR 823, and *Re Land and Premises at Liss, Hants* [1971] Ch 986, [1971] 3 All ER 380.

A tenancy agreement granted for a period of thirteen months and signed a few days before the agreed term was due to expire, creates a tenancy for less than a year, since a grant of land cannot take effect retrospectively to confer an interest before execution of grant: *Keen v Holland* [1984] 1 All ER 75, [1984] 1 WLR 251, CA following *Bradshaw v Pawley* [1979] 3 All ER 273, [1980] 1 WLR 10 and *Hoveringham Group Ltd v Scholey* (1982) unreported.

Licence to occupy. As to the distinction between a lease and a licence, see 27 Halsbury's Laws (4th edn, reissue) paras 6–16. See also, *Harrison-Broadly v Smith* [1964] 1 All ER 867, [1964] 1 WLR 456, CA (sub-s (1) does not apply to a person in occupation in her own right admitting another to occupation on partnership terms) and *Verrall v Farnes,* cited in the note 'Appointment or employment' to s 1.

Grazing or mowing (or both). The insertion of the words 'or both' in this provision gives effect to the first recommendation in the Law Commission's Report on this consolidation (Law Com No 153; Cmnd 9665). Previously the wording of the Agricultural Holdings Act 1948, s 2 (from which the provisions in this section are derived) contained only the wording 'grazing or mowing' which had caused some doubt amongst practitioners as to whether agreements for the use of land for both grazing *and* mowing was within the ambit of the provision. The Law Commission saw no reason why an agreement permitting both grazing and mowing should fall to be treated in any different way from an agreement permitting only one or the other, hence the recommendation, the effect of which is now contained in this section.

Specified period of the year. A grazing and mowing agreement for 364 days was held to be for such a period: *Reid v Dawson* [1955] 1 QB 214, [1954] 3 All ER 498, CA, as were the lettings in *Scene Estates Ltd v Amos* and *Watts v Yeend* cited in the note 'Interest less than a tenancy from year to year' above. See also, *Cox v Husk* (1976) 239 Estates Gazette 123 and *Brown v Tiernan* (1992) 65 P&CR 324, [1993] 1 EGLR 11.

Arbitration. As to arbitration under this Act, see s 84 and Sch 11 as amended by the RRO, SI 2006/2805. Schedule 11 was abolished by the RRO so that as from 19 October 2006, arbitration under this Act is governed by the Arbitration Act 1996.

Definitions. For 'agricultural holding' see s 1(1); for 'agricultural land', see s 1(4); for 'agreement', 'the Minister' and 'tenant', see s 96(1).

A1.90

3   Tenancies for two years or more to continue from year to year unless terminated by notice

(1)   Subject to section 5 below, a tenancy of an agricultural holding for a term of two years or more shall, instead of terminating on the term date, continue (as from that date) as a tenancy from year to year, but otherwise on the terms of the original tenancy so far as applicable, unless—

(a)   not less than one year nor more than two years before the term date a written notice has been given by either party to the other of his intention to terminate the tenancy, or

(b)   section 4 below applies.

(2)   A notice given under subsection (1) above shall be deemed, for the purposes of this Act, to be a notice to quit.

(3)   This section does not apply to a tenancy which, by virtue of subsection (6) of section 149 of the Law of Property Act 1925, takes effect as such a term of years as is mentioned in that subsection.

(4)   In this section 'term date', in relation to a tenancy granted for a term of years, means the date fixed for the expiry of that term.

NOTES

Derivation

Sub-ss (1), (4) derived from the Agricultural Holdings Act 1948, s 3(1), and the Agricultural Holdings Act 1984, s 10(1), Sch 3, para 2(1)(a); sub-ss (2), (3) derived from the Agricultural Holdings Act 1948, s 3(2), (3).

Initial Commencement

Specified date: 18 June 1986: see s 102(2).

Extent

This Act does not extend to Scotland.

See Further

See further, as to the exclusion of this Act in relation to leases or tenancies granted to contractors in respect of the running of any removal centre or part of a removal centre: the Immigration and Asylum Act 1999, s 149(3).

Notes

For a commentary, see para 20.7.

Sub-ss (1), (4) contain provisions formerly in the Agricultural Holdings Act 1948, s 3(1), as amended by the Agricultural Holdings Act 1984, s 10(1), Sch 3, para 2(1)(a). Sub-ss (2), (3) contain provisions formerly in s 3(2), (3) of the 1948 Act.

Tenancy. This section does not apply to a tenancy granted or agreed to be granted before 1 January 1921; see s 65, Sch 12, para 2.

Agricultural holding. For meaning, see s 1(1).

Written. Expressions referring to writing are, unless the contrary intention appears, to be construed as including references to other modes of representing or reproducing words in a visible form; see the Interpretation Act 1978, s 5, Sch 1.

Notice. As to service of notices, see s 93.

Notice to quit. See, generally, as to notices to quit, ss 25 ff.

A1.91

4   Death of tenant before term date

(1)   This section applies where—

    (a)   a tenancy such as is mentioned in subsection (1) of section 3 above is granted on or after 12th September 1984 to any person or persons,

    (b)   the person, or the survivor of the persons, dies before the term date, and

    (c)   no notice effective to terminate the tenancy on the term date has been given under that subsection.

(2)   Where this section applies, the tenancy, instead of continuing as mentioned in section 3(1) above—

    (a)   shall, if the death is one year or more before the term date, terminate on that date, or

    (b)   shall, if the death is at any other time, continue (as from the term date) for a further period of twelve months, but otherwise on the terms of the tenancy so far as applicable, and shall accordingly terminate on the first anniversary of the term date.

(3)   For the purposes of the provisions of this Act with respect to compensation any tenancy terminating in accordance with this section shall be deemed to terminate by reason of a notice to quit given by the landlord of the holding.

(4)   In this section 'term date' has the same meaning as in section 3 above.

NOTES

Derivation

This section derived from the Agricultural Holdings Act 1948, s 3A, and the Agricultural Holdings Act 1984, s 10(1), Sch 3, para 2(2).

Initial Commencement

Specified date: 18 June 1986: see s 102(2).

Extent

This Act does not extend to Scotland.

See Further

See further, as to the exclusion of this Act in relation to leases or tenancies granted to contractors in respect of the running of any removal centre or part of a removal centre: the Immigration and Asylum Act 1999, s 149(3).

Notes

For a commentary, see para 20.8 (b).

Sub-s (1) contains provisions formerly in the Agricultural Holdings Act 1948, s 3A(1), (2), (3), as inserted by the Agricultural Holdings Act 1984, s 10(1), Sch 3, para 2(2). Sub-ss (2), (4) contain provisions formerly in s 3A(2), (3) of the 1948 Act, as so inserted. Sub-s (3) contains provisions formerly in s 3A(4) of the 1948 Act as so inserted.

12 September 1984. This was the date on which the provisions of the Agricultural Holdings Act 1984 which introduced the provisions now contained in this section came into force.

Months. This means calendar months; see the Interpretation Act 1978, s 5, Sch 1.

Provisions of this Act with respect to compensation. See ss 60–78.

Landlord. For meaning, see s 96(1).

A1.92

5   Restriction on agreements excluding effect of section 3

(1)   Except as provided in this section, section 3 above shall have effect notwithstanding any agreement to the contrary.

(2)   Where before the grant of a tenancy of an agricultural holding for a term of not less than two, and not more than five, years—

  (a)   the persons who will be the landlord and the tenant in relation to the tenancy agree that section 3 above shall not apply to the tenancy, and
  (b)   those persons make a joint application in writing to the Minister for his approval of that agreement, and
  (c)   the Minister notifies them of his approval,

section 3 shall not apply to the tenancy if it satisfies the requirements of subsection (3) below.

(2)   A tenancy satisfies the requirements of this subsection if the contract of tenancy is in writing and it, or a statement endorsed upon it, indicates (in whatever terms) that section 3 does not apply to the tenancy.

NOTES

Derivation

This section derived from the Agricultural Holdings Act 1948, ss 3(4), 3B, and the Agricultural Holdings Act 1984, s 10(1), Sch 3, para 2(1)(b), (2).

Initial Commencement

Specified date: 18 June 1986: see s 102(2).

Extent

This Act does not extend to Scotland.

See Further

See further, as to the exclusion of this Act in relation to leases or tenancies granted to contractors in respect of the running of any removal centre or part of a removal centre: the Immigration and Asylum Act 1999, s 149(3).

Transfer of Functions

Functions of the Minister, so far as exercisable in relation to Wales, transferred to the National Assembly for Wales, by the National Assembly for Wales (Transfer of Functions) Order 1999, SI 1999/672, art 2, Sch 1.

Notes

For a commentary, see para 20.15.

Sub-s (1) contains provisions formerly in the Agricultural Holdings Act 1948, s 3(4), as amended by the Agricultural Holdings Act 1984, s 10(1), Sch 3, para 2(1)(b). Sub-s (2) contains provisions formerly in s 3B(1), (2) of the 1948 Act, as inserted by the Agricultural Holdings Act 1984, s 10(1), Sch 3, para 2(2). Sub-s (3) contains provisions formerly in s 3B(3) of the 1948 Act, as so inserted.

Writing. See the note 'Written' to s 3.

Definitions. For 'agricultural holding', see s 1(1); for 'landlord', 'the Minister' and 'tenant', see s 96(1).

PART II: PROVISIONS AFFECTING TENANCY DURING ITS CONTINUANCE

Written tenancy agreements

A1.93

6   Right to written tenancy agreement

(1)   Where in respect of a tenancy of an agricultural holding—

   (a)   there is not in force an agreement in writing embodying all the terms of the tenancy (including any model clauses incorporated in the contract of tenancy by virtue of section 7 below), or
   (b)   such an agreement in writing is in force but the terms of the tenancy do not make provision for one or more of the matters specified in Schedule 1 to this Act,

the landlord or tenant of the holding may, if he has requested the other to enter into an agreement in writing embodying all the terms of the tenancy and containing provision for all of the said matters but no such agreement has been concluded, refer the terms of the tenancy to arbitration under this Act.

(2)   On any such reference the arbitrator in his award—

   (a)   shall specify the existing terms of the tenancy, subject to any variations agreed between the landlord and the tenant,
   (b)   in so far as those terms as so varied neither make provision for, nor make provision inconsistent with, the matters specified in Schedule 1 to this Act, shall make provision for all of the said matters having such effect as may be agreed between the landlord and the tenant or, in default of agreement, as appears to the arbitrator to be reasonable and just between them, and
   (c)   may include any further provisions relating to the tenancy which may be agreed between the landlord and the tenant.

(3) Where it appears to the arbitrator on a reference under this section that, by reason of any provision which he is required to include in his award, it is equitable that the rent of the holding should be varied, he may vary the rent accordingly.

(4) The award of an arbitrator under this section shall have effect as if the terms and provisions specified and made in the award were contained in an agreement in writing entered into by the landlord and the tenant and having effect (by way of variation of the agreement previously in force in respect of the tenancy) as from the making of the award or, if the award so provides, from such later date as may be specified in it.

(5) Where in respect of a tenancy of an agricultural holding—

(a) the terms of the tenancy neither make provision for, nor make provision inconsistent with, the matter specified in paragraph 9 of Schedule 1 to this Act, and

(b) the landlord requests the tenant in writing to enter into such an agreement as is mentioned in subsection (1) above containing provision for all of the matters specified in that Schedule,

the tenant may not without the landlord's consent in writing assign, sub-let or part with possession of the holding or any part of it during the period while the determination of the terms of the tenancy is pending; and any transaction entered into in contravention of this subsection shall be void.

(6) The period mentioned in subsection (5) above is the period beginning with the date of service of the landlord's request on the tenant and ending with the date on which an agreement is concluded in accordance with that request or (as the case may be) with the date on which the award of an arbitrator on a reference under this section relating to the tenancy takes effect.

NOTES

Derivation

Sub-ss (1), (4)–(6) derived from the Agricultural Holdings Act 1948, ss 5(1), (4)–(6), 7(5), and the Agricultural Holdings Act 1984, s 10(1), Sch 3, paras 3(2), (3), 4; sub-ss (2), (3) derived from the Agricultural Holdings Act 1948, ss 5(2), (3), 7(3).

Initial Commencement

Specified date: 18 June 1986: see s 102(2).

Extent

This Act does not extend to Scotland.

See Further

See further, as to the exclusion of this Act in relation to leases or tenancies granted to contractors in respect of the running of any removal centre or part of a removal centre: the Immigration and Asylum Act 1999, s 149(3).

Notes

For a commentary, see para 23.1 ff.

Sub-ss (1), (6) contain provisions formerly in the Agricultural Holdings Act 1948, s 5(1), (5), respectively, as added by the Agricultural Holdings Act 1984, s 10(1), Sch 3, para 3(2), (3). Sub-s (2) contains provisions formerly in s 5(2), (3) of the 1948 Act. Sub-s (3) contains provisions formerly in s 7(3) of the 1948 Act. Sub-s (4) contains provisions formerly in s 7(5) of the 1948 Act, as amended by s 10(1) of, and Sch 3, para 4 to, the 1984 Act. Sub-s (5) contains provisions formerly in s 5(4), (6) of the 1948 Act, as added by s 10(1) of, and Sch 3, para 3(3) to, the 1984 Act.

Writing. Cf the note 'Written' to s 3. As to what may constitute a lease in writing, see *Grieve & Sons v Barr* 1954 SLT 261.

Arbitration. For provisions as to arbitration under this Act, see s 84 and the note to s 2.

Opencast coal operations. See, as to the effect of a compulsory rights order upon the terms of the tenancy, the Opencast Coal Act 1958, s 37, Sch 7, Pt I, paras 4, 7, as amended, in the case of para 4 of that Schedule by s 100, Sch 14, para 33(5).

Transfers of liability for fixed equipment. See s 9 as to transitional arrangements where liability for fixed equipment is transferred by virtue of this section.

Definitions. For 'agricultural holding', see s 1(1); for 'agreed', 'agreement', 'landlord' and 'tenant', see s 96(1).

Fixed equipment

A1.94

7   The model clauses

(1)   The Minister may, after consultation with such bodies of persons as appear to him to represent the interests of landlords and tenants of agricultural holdings, make regulations prescribing terms as to the maintenance, repair and insurance of fixed equipment (in this Act referred to as 'the model clauses').

(2)   Regulations under this section may make provision for any matter arising under them to be determined by arbitration under this Act.

(3)   The model clauses shall be deemed to be incorporated in every contract of tenancy of an agricultural holding except in so far as they would impose on one of the parties to an agreement in writing a liability which under the agreement is imposed on the other.

NOTES

Derivation

Sub-ss (1), (3) derived from the Agricultural Holdings Act 1948, s 6(1); sub-s (2) derived from the Agriculture (Miscellaneous Provisions) Act 1972, s 15(2).

Initial Commencement

Specified date: 18 June 1986: see s 102(2).

Extent

This Act does not extend to Scotland.

See Further

See further, as to the exclusion of this Act in relation to leases or tenancies granted to contractors in respect of the running of any removal centre or part of a removal centre: the Immigration and Asylum Act 1999, s 149(3).

Transfer of Functions

Functions of the Minister, so far as exercisable in relation to Wales, transferred to the National Assembly for Wales, by the National Assembly for Wales (Transfer of Functions) Order 1999, SI 1999/672, art 2, Sch 1.

Subordinate Legislation

Agriculture (Maintenance, Repair and Insurance of Fixed Equipment) (Amendment) Regulations 1988, SI 1988/281 (made under sub-ss (1), (2)).

Notes

For a commentary on 'the Model Clauses', see para 23.8 ff.

Sub-ss (1), (3) contain provisions formerly in the Agricultural Holdings Act 1948, s 6(1). Sub-s (2) contains provisions formerly in the Agriculture (Miscellaneous Provisions) Act 1972, s 15(2).

Consultation. On what constitutes consultation, see, in particular, *Fletcher v Minister of Town and Country Planning* [1947] 2 All ER 496, 111 JP 542; *Rollo v Minister of Town and Country Planning* [1948] 1 All ER 13, [1948] LJR 817, CA; *Re Union of Whippingham and East Cowes Benefices, Derham v Church Comrs for England* [1954] AC 245, [1954] 2 All ER 22, PC; and *Agricultural, Horticultural and Forestry Industry Training Board v Aylesbury Mushrooms Ltd* [1972] 1 All ER 280, [1972] 1 WLR 190.

Arbitration. For provisions as to arbitration under this Act, see s 84 and the note to s 2.

Writing. See the note 'Written' to s 3.

Liability … is imposed on the other. Where the written agreement imposes no liability but is nevertheless in conflict with the regulations, the contractual terms prevail over the statutory terms; *Burden v Hannaford* [1956] 1 QB 142, [1955] 3 All ER 401, CA; *Roper v Prudential Assurance Co Ltd* [1992] 1 EGLR 5, [1992] 09 EG 141.

Opencast coal operations. See the note to s 6.

Transfers of liability for fixed equipment. See s 9 as to transitional arrangements where liability for fixed equipment is transferred by virtue of this section.

Definitions. For 'agricultural holding', see s 1(1); for 'contract of tenancy', see s 1(5); and for 'agreement', 'fixed equipment', 'landlord', 'the Minister', and 'tenant', see s 96(1). Note as to 'the model clauses', sub-s (1) above.

Regulations under this section. The Agriculture (Time-Limit) Regulations 1988, SI 1988/282. The Agriculture (Maintenance, Repair and Insurance of Fixed Equipment) Regulations 1973, SI 1973/1473, as amended by SI 1988/281, which, by virtue of the Interpretation Act 1978, s 17(2)(b) have effect as if made hereunder.

A1.95

8   Arbitration where terms of written agreement are inconsistent with the model clauses

(1) This section applies where an agreement in writing relating to a tenancy of an agricultural holding effects substantial modifications in the operation of regulations under section 7 above.

(2) Where this section applies, then, subject to subsection (6) below, the landlord or tenant of the holding may, if he has requested the other to vary the terms of the tenancy as to the maintenance, repair and insurance of fixed equipment so as to bring them into conformity with the model clauses but no agreement has been reached on the request, refer those terms of the tenancy to arbitration under this Act.

(3) On any reference under this section the arbitrator shall consider whether (disregarding the rent payable for the holding) the terms referred to arbitration are justifiable having regard to the circumstances of the holding and of the landlord and the tenant, and, if he determines that they are not so justifiable, he may by his award vary them in such manner as appears to him reasonable and just between the landlord and tenant.

(4)   Where it appears to the arbitrator on any reference under this section that by reason of any provision included in his award it is equitable that the rent of the holding should be varied, he may vary the rent accordingly.

(5)   The award of an arbitrator under this section shall have effect as if the terms and provisions specified and made in the award were contained in an agreement in writing entered into by the landlord and the tenant and having effect (by way of variation of the agreement previously in force in respect of the tenancy) as from the making of the award or, if the award so provides, from such later date as may be specified in it.

(6)   Where there has been a reference under this section relating to a tenancy, no further such reference relating to that tenancy shall be made before the expiry of three years from the coming into effect of the award of the arbitrator on the previous reference.

NOTES

Derivation

Sub-ss (1)–(4), (6) derived from the Agricultural Holdings Act 1948, ss 6(2), (3), 7(3); sub-s (5) derived from the Agricultural Holdings Act 1948, s 7(5), and the Agricultural Holdings Act 1984, s 10(1), Sch 3, para 4.

Initial Commencement

Specified date: 18 June 1986: see s 102(2).

Extent

This Act does not extend to Scotland.

See Further

See further, as to the exclusion of this Act in relation to leases or tenancies granted to contractors in respect of the running of any removal centre or part of a removal centre: the Immigration and Asylum Act 1999, s 149(3).

Notes

For a commentary, see para 23.21.

Sub-ss (1), (2), (6) contain provisions formerly in the Agricultural Holdings Act 1948, s 6(2). Sub-s (3) contains provisions formerly in s 6(3) of the 1948 Act. Sub-s (4) contains provisions formerly in s 7(3) of the 1948 Act. Sub-s (5) contains provisions formerly in s 7(5) of the 1948 Act, as amended by the Agricultural Holdings Act 1984, s 10(1), Sch 3, para 4.

Sub-s (1): Writing. See the note 'Written' to s 3.

Sub-s (2): Arbitration. As to arbitration under this Act, see s 84 and Sch 11 as amended by the RRO, SI 2006/2805.

Sub-s (6): Three years from, etc. Cf the note 'Two months from, etc' to s 10.

Opencast coal operations. See the note to s 6.

Transfers of liability for fixed equipment. See s 9 as to transitional arrangements where liability for fixed equipment is transferred by virtue of this section.

Definitions. For 'agricultural holding', see s 1(1); for 'the model clauses', see s 7(1); for 'agreement', 'fixed equipment', 'landlord' and 'tenant', see s 96(1).

A1.96

9   **Transitional arrangements where liability in respect of fixed equipment transferred**

(1)   Where by virtue of section 6, 7 or 8 above the liability for the maintenance or repair of any item of fixed equipment is transferred from the tenant to the landlord, the landlord may within the prescribed period beginning with the date on which the transfer takes effect require that there shall be determined by arbitration under this Act and paid by the tenant the amount of any relevant compensation.

(2)   In subsection (1) above 'relevant compensation' means compensation which would have been payable either under subsection (1) of section 71 below or in accordance with subsection (3) of that section, in respect of any previous failure by the tenant to discharge the liability mentioned in subsection (1) above, if the tenant had quitted the holding on the termination of his tenancy at the date on which the transfer takes effect.

(3)   Where by virtue of section 6, 7 or 8 above the liability for the maintenance or repair of any item of fixed equipment is transferred from the landlord to the tenant, any claim by the tenant in respect of any previous failure by the landlord to discharge the said liability shall, if the tenant within the prescribed period beginning with the date on which the transfer takes effect so requires, be determined by arbitration under this Act.

(4)   Where the terms of a tenancy of an agricultural holding as to the maintenance, repair or insurance of fixed equipment (whether established by the operation of regulations under section 7 above or by agreement) are varied by new regulations made under that section, then, if a reference is made under section 6 above within the prescribed period after the coming into operation of the new regulations, the arbitrator shall, for the purposes of subsection (2) of the said section 6, disregard the variation.

NOTES

Derivation

This section derived from the Agricultural Holdings Act 1948, s 7(1), (2), (4).

Initial Commencement

Specified date: 18 June 1986: see s 102(2).

Extent

This Act does not extend to Scotland.

See Further

See further, as to the exclusion of this Act in relation to leases or tenancies granted to contractors in respect of the running of any removal centre or part of a removal centre: the Immigration and Asylum Act 1999, s 149(3).

Subordinate Legislation

Agriculture (Time-Limit) Regulations 1988, SI 1988/282 (made under sub-s (4)).

Notes

For a commentary, see para 23.22.

Sub-s (1), (2) contain provisions formerly in the Agricultural Holdings Act 1948, s 7(1). Sub-ss (3), (4) contain provisions formerly in s 7(2), (4) of that Act, respectively.

Prescribed period. As to 'the prescribed period' in sub-ss (1), (3) above, see, by virtue of the Interpretation Act 1978, s 17(2)(b), the Agriculture (Miscellaneous Time Limits) Regulations 1959, SI 1959/171, reg 2(2), (3).

Arbitration. For provisions as to arbitration under this Act, see s 84 and the note to s 2.

Opencast coal operations. See the note to s 6.

Definitions. For 'agricultural holding', see s 1(1); for 'agreement', 'fixed equipment', 'landlord', 'prescribed', 'tenant' and 'termination', see s 96(1). Note as to 'relevant compensation', sub-s (2) above; and note also as to 'termination', s 74(4).

A1.97

10   Tenant's right to remove fixtures and buildings

(1)   Subject to the provisions of this section—

(a)   any engine, machinery, fencing or other fixture (of whatever description) affixed, whether for the purposes of agriculture or not, to an agricultural holding by the tenant, and

(b)   any building erected by him on the holding,

shall be removable by the tenant at any time during the continuance of the tenancy or before the expiry of two months from its termination, and shall remain his property so long as he may remove it by virtue of this subsection.

(2)   Subsection (1) above shall not apply—

(a)   to a fixture affixed or a building erected in pursuance of some obligation,

(b)   to a fixture affixed or a building erected instead of some fixture or building belonging to the landlord,

(c)   to a building in respect of which the tenant is entitled to compensation under this Act or otherwise, or

(d)   to a fixture affixed or a building erected before 1st January 1884.

(3)   The right conferred by subsection (1) above shall not be exercisable in relation to a fixture or building unless the tenant—

(a)   has paid all rent owing by him and has performed or satisfied all his other obligations to the landlord in respect of the holding, and

(b)   has, at least one month before both the exercise of the right and the termination of the tenancy, given to the landlord notice in writing of his intention to remove the fixture or building.

(4)   If, before the expiry of the notice mentioned in subsection (3) above, the landlord gives to the tenant a counter-notice in writing electing to purchase a fixture or building comprised in the notice, subsection (1) above shall cease to apply to that fixture or building, but the landlord shall be liable to pay to the tenant the fair value of that fixture or building to an incoming tenant of the holding.

(5)   In the removal of a fixture or building by virtue of subsection (1) above, the tenant shall not do any avoidable damage to any other building or other part of the holding, and immediately after the removal shall make good all damage so done that is occasioned by the removal.

(6)   Any dispute between the landlord and the tenant with respect to the amount payable by the landlord under subsection (4) above in respect of any fixture or building shall be determined by arbitration under this Act.

(7)   This section shall apply to a fixture or building acquired by a tenant as it applies to a fixture or building affixed or erected by him.

(8)   This section shall not be taken as prejudicing any right to remove a fixture that subsists otherwise than by virtue of this section.

NOTES

Derivation

Sub-ss (1), (6), (8) derived from the Agricultural Holdings Act 1948, s 13(1), (4A), (4B), and the Agricultural Holdings Act 1984, s 10(1), Sch 3, para 6(2), (3); sub-ss (2)–(5), (7) derived from the Agricultural Holdings Act 1948, s 13(1)–(4), (5).

Initial Commencement

Specified date: 18 June 1986: see s 102(2).

Extent

This Act does not extend to Scotland.

See Further

See further, as to the exclusion of this Act in relation to leases or tenancies granted to contractors in respect of the running of any removal centre or part of a removal centre: the Immigration and Asylum Act 1999, s 149(3).

Notes

For a commentary, see para 23.23 ff.

Sub-s (1) contains provisions formerly in the Agricultural Holdings Act 1948, s 13(1), (4A), as amended in the case of sub-s (1) of that section, and as inserted in the case of sub-s (4A) thereof, by the Agricultural Holdings Act 1984, s 10(1), Sch 3, para 6(2), (3), respectively. Sub-s (2) contains provisions formerly in s 13(1), (5)(b) of the 1948 Act. Sub-ss (3)–(5) contain provisions formerly in s 13(2)–(4), respectively, of the 1948 Act. Sub-ss (6), (8) contain provisions formerly in sub-ss (4B), (4A), respectively, of s 13 of the 1948 Act, as inserted by s 10(1) of, and Sch 3, para 6(3) to the 1984 Act. Sub-s (7) contains provisions formerly in s 13(5)(a) of the 1948 Act.

Sub-s (1): Two months from, etc. See para 42.27 on the computation of time. As a general rule the effect of defining a period in such a manner is to exclude the day on which the event in question occurs; see 45 Halsbury's Laws (4th edn) para 1127. See also *Dodds v Walker* [1981] 2 All ER 609, [1981] 1 WLR 1027, HL, and 45 Halsbury's Laws (4th edn) para 1111, as to the day of expiry of periods of a month or a specified number of months.

Sub-s (2): Subsection (1) above shall not apply, etc. See also Sch 12, para 3 (tenant not entitled to remove, by virtue of sub-s (1) above, fixture or building acquired before 1 January 1901).

Compensation. See, eg, s 64 (tenant's right to compensation for improvements).

1st January 1884. Ie the commencement date of the Agricultural Holdings (England) Act 1883 (repealed).

Sub-s (3): At least one month before, etc. See para 42.27 on the computation of time. The words 'at least' indicate that the period allowed is to be exclusive of the day of service of the notice and that on which the right is exercised or the tenancy is terminated; see *Rightside Properties Ltd v Gray* [1975] Ch 72, [1974] 2 All ER 1169, and the other cases cited in 45 Halsbury's Laws (4th edn) para 1133. See also *Dodds v Walker* [1981] 2 All ER 609, [1981] 1 WLR 1027, HL, and 45 Halsbury's Laws (4th edn) para 1111, as to the day of expiry of periods of a month or a specified number of months.

Notice in writing of his intention. A tenant who removes a fixture without giving notice to the landlord of his intention to remove cannot afterwards claim for expenses or loss suffered through the removal as compensation for disturbance; see *Re Harvey and Mann* (1920) 89 LJKB 687, CA.

See, as to service of notices, s 93; and as to writing, the note 'Written' to s 3.

Sub-s (6): Arbitration. For provisions as to arbitration under this Act, see s 84 and the note to s 2.

Requisitioned land. It is thought that, where possession was taken in the exercise of emergency powers, there must be substituted for the references to the termination of the tenancy, references to the giving up of possession so taken; see the Landlord and Tenant (Requisitioned Land) Act 1942, s 7(2).

Record of fixtures and buildings. A tenant may, during his tenancy, require the making of a record of any fixtures or buildings which he is entitled to remove under this section; see s 22(1).

Contracting-out. The landlord and tenant may contract out of the provisions of this section; see *Mears v Callender* [1901] 2 Ch 388, *Premier Dairies Ltd v Garlick* [1920] 2 Ch 17 but see doubts of this view in *Johnson v Moreton* [1980] AC 37.

Market gardens. See s 79(3) as to the special application of this section with regard to market gardens.

Claims. As to settlement of claims arising on termination of a tenancy, see s 83.

Coal-mining subsidence. For the position of an agricultural tenant where subsidence damage is caused to property which he is entitled to remove, see the Coal Mining (Subsidence) Act 1991, s 21.

Opencast coal operations. Where in consequence of the confirmation of a compulsory rights order for opencast coal operations a loss is incurred in respect of a forced sale of a fixture or building removed in pursuance of this section, compensation is payable in accordance with the Opencast Coal Act 1958, s 27, as amended by s 100, Sch 14, para 29. See also s 29 of that Act. As to market garden fixtures or buildings, see s 28(4) of that Act, as amended by s 100, Sch 14, para 30(3). As to adjustments between landlords and tenants, see s 37 of, and Sch 7, Pt I, para 5 to that Act (as amended, in the case of Sch 7, Pt I, para 5 thereto, by s 100, Sch 14, para 33(6)). For supplementary provisions, see ss 34–36 of, and Sch 6 to, that Act (as amended, in the case of Sch 6 thereto, by (inter alia) s 100, Sch 14, para 32).

Definitions. For 'agricultural holding', see s 1(1); for 'agriculture', 'building', 'landlord', 'tenant' and 'termination', see s 96(1). Note also as to 'termination', s 74(4).

A1.98

11   Provision of fixed equipment necessary to comply with statutory requirements

(1)   Where, on an application by the tenant of an agricultural holding, the Tribunal are satisfied that it is reasonable, having regard to the tenant's responsibilities to farm the holding in accordance with the rules of good husbandry, that he should carry on on the holding an agricultural activity specified in the application to the extent and in the manner so specified and—

(a)   that, unless fixed equipment is provided on the holding, the tenant, in carrying on that activity to that extent and in that manner, will contravene requirements imposed by or under any enactment, or

(b)   that it is reasonable that the tenant should use, for purposes connected with that activity, fixed equipment already provided on the holding, but that, unless that equipment is altered or repaired, the tenant, in using the equipment for those purposes, will contravene such requirements,

the Tribunal may direct the landlord to carry out, within a period specified in the direction, such work for the provision or, as the case may be, the alteration or repair of that fixed equipment as will enable the tenant to comply with the said requirements.

(2)   Where it appears to the Tribunal that an agricultural activity specified in the tenant's application has not been carried on on the holding continuously for a period of at least three years immediately preceding the making of the application the Tribunal shall not direct the landlord to carry out work in connection with that activity unless they are satisfied that the starting of the activity did not or, where the activity

has not yet been started, will not constitute or form part of a substantial alteration of the type of farming carried on on the holding.

(3) The Tribunal shall not direct the landlord to carry out work under this section unless they are satisfied—

(a) that it is reasonable to do so having regard to the landlord's responsibilities to manage the land comprised in the holding in accordance with the rules of good estate management and also to the period for which the holding may be expected to remain a separate holding and to any other material consideration, and

(b) that the landlord has refused to carry out that work on being requested in writing to do so by the tenant or has not agreed to carry it out within a reasonable time after being so requested.

(4) The Tribunal shall not direct the landlord to carry out work under this section if he is under a duty to carry out the work in order to comply with a requirement imposed on him by or under any enactment or if provision is made by the contract of tenancy, or by any other agreement between the landlord and the tenant, for the carrying out of work by one of them.

(5) If the landlord fails to comply with a direction under this section the tenant shall have the same remedies as if the contract of tenancy had contained an undertaking by the landlord to carry out the work required by the direction within the period allowed by the Tribunal.

(6) Notwithstanding any term in the contract of tenancy restricting the carrying out by the tenant of alterations to the holding, the remedies referred to in subsection (5) above shall include the right of the tenant to carry out the work himself and recover the reasonable cost of the work from the landlord.

(7) The Tribunal, on an application by the landlord, may extend or further extend the period specified in a direction under this section if it is shown to their satisfaction that the period so specified, or that period as previously extended under this subsection, as the case may be, will not allow sufficient time both for the completion of preliminary arrangements necessary or desirable in connection with the work required by the direction (including, in appropriate cases, the determination of an application by the landlord for a grant out of money provided by Parliament in respect of that work) and for the carrying out of the said work.

(8) The reference in subsection (6) above to the reasonable cost of work carried out by a tenant shall, where the tenant has received a grant in respect of the work out of money provided by Parliament, be construed as a reference to the reasonable cost reduced by the amount of the grant.

NOTES

Derivation

Sub-ss (1), (3)–(8) derived from the Agriculture Act 1958, s 4(1)–(4), (7); sub-s (2) derived from the Agriculture Act 1958, s 4(1), and the Agricultural Holdings Act 1984, s 10(1), Sch 3, para 30.

Initial Commencement

Specified date: 18 June 1986: see s 102(2).

Extent

This Act does not extend to Scotland.

See Further

See further, as to the exclusion of this Act in relation to leases or tenancies granted to contractors in respect of the running of any removal centre or part of a removal centre: the Immigration and Asylum Act 1999, s 149(3).

Notes

For a commentary, see paras 23.25 to 23.27.

Sub-s (1) contains provisions formerly in the Agriculture Act 1958, s 4(1). Sub-s (2) contains provisions formerly in the proviso to s 4(1) of the 1958 Act, as amended by the Agricultural Holdings Act 1984, s 10(1), Sch 3, para 30. Sub-ss (3), (4) contain provisions formerly in s 4(2) of the 1958 Act. Sub-ss (5), (6) contain provisions formerly in s 4(3) of the 1958 Act. Sub-s (7) contains provisions formerly in s 4(4) of the 1958 Act. Sub-s (8) contains provisions formerly in s 4(7) of the 1958 Act.

Sub-s (1): The Tribunal. Ie the Agricultural Land Tribunal; see s 96(1). See, generally, as to the establishment, constitution and procedure of the Tribunal, the Agriculture Act 1947, s 73, Sch 9, as amended, in the case of s 73 thereof, by s 100, Sch 14, para 18.

Direct the landlord to carry out, etc. As to the increase of rent where the landlord carries out such work, see s 13; and for special provisions as to compensation where the Tribunal have directed the immediate landlord of a sub-tenant to carry out such work, see s 68(2).

Sub-s (2): At least three years ... preceding, etc. Cf the note 'At least one month before, etc' to s 10.

Sub-s (3): Writing. See the note 'Written' to s 3.

Within a reasonable time. Where anything is to be done within a 'reasonable time', the question what is a reasonable time depends on the circumstances of the particular case and is therefore a question of fact; see *Burton v Griffiths* (1843) 11 M & W 817; and see also *Hick v Raymond and Reid* [1893] AC 22 at 29, [1891–4] All ER Rep 491 at 493, HL, per Lord Herschell LC.

Sub-s (4): Requirements imposed on him by or under any enactments. See, eg, the requirements imposed on dairy farmers by the Milk and Dairies (General) Regulations 1959, SI 1959/277, Pt V, as amended by SI 1960/1777, section 85 Water Resources Act 1991 and the Control of Pollution (Silage, Slurry and Agricultural Fuel Oil) Regulations 1991.

Form of application. See, as to the forms of application to be used for the purposes of sub-ss (1), (7) above, the Agricultural Land Tribunals (Rules) Order 1978, SI 1978/259, Sch 1, r 6, Form 5, made under the Agriculture Act 1947, s 73 and as construed in accordance with s 99, Sch 13, para 1.

Crown land. This section is excepted from the application of this Act to Crown land; see s 95.

Definitions. For 'agricultural holding', see s 1(1); for 'contract of tenancy', see s 1(5); for 'agricultural', 'fixed equipment', 'landlord', 'tenant' and 'the Tribunal', see s 96(1). Note as to 'rules of good husbandry' and 'rules of good estate management', s 96(3); and as to 'reasonable cost of work carried out by a tenant', sub-s (8) above.

Variation of rent

A1.99

12   Arbitration of rent

(1)   Subject to the provisions of Schedule 2 to this Act, the landlord or tenant of an agricultural holding may by notice in writing served on the other demand that the rent to be payable in respect of the holding as from the next termination date shall be referred to arbitration under this Act.

(2)   On a reference under this section the arbitrator shall determine what rent should be properly payable in respect of the holding at the [next termination date following

the date of the demand for arbitration and accordingly shall, with effect from that next termination date], increase or reduce the rent previously payable or direct that it shall continue unchanged.

(3)   A demand for arbitration under this section shall cease to be effective for the purposes of this section on the next termination date following the date of the demand unless before the said termination date—

(a)   an arbitrator has been appointed by agreement between the parties, or
(b)   an application has been made to the President of the Royal Institution of Chartered Surveyors for the appointment of an arbitrator by him.

(4)   References in this section (and in Schedule 2 to this Act) in relation to a demand for arbitration with respect to the rent of any holding, to the next termination date following the date of the demand are references to the next day following the date of the demand on which the tenancy of the holding could have been determined by notice to quit given at the date of the demand.

(5)   Schedule 2 to this Act shall have effect for supplementing this section.

NOTES

Derivation

Sub-ss (1)–(4) derived from the Agricultural Holdings Act 1948, ss 8(1), (2), (13), 8A(2), and the Agricultural Holdings Act 1984, ss 1, 8(2).

Initial Commencement

Specified date: 18 June 1986: see s 102(2).

Extent

This Act does not extend to Scotland.

Amendment

Sub-s (2): words from 'next termination date' to 'next termination date' in square brackets substituted by SI 2006/2805, arts 2, 3.

Date in force: 19 October 2006: see SI 2006/2805, art 1(1)(b); for transitional provisions see art 10 thereof.

See Further

See further, in relation to holdings in relation to which a milk quota is registered: the Agriculture Act 1986, s 15.

See further, as to the exclusion of this Act in relation to leases or tenancies granted to contractors in respect of the running of any removal centre or part of a removal centre: the Immigration and Asylum Act 1999, s 149(3).

Notes

For a commentary, see para 25.4 ff.

Sub-ss (1), (2) contain provisions formerly in the Agricultural Holdings Act 1948, s 8(1), (2) respectively, as substituted by the Agricultural Holdings Act 1984, s 1. Sub-s (3) contains provisions formerly in s 8(13) of the 1948 Act, as substituted by s 1 of the 1984 Act, and as affected by s 8(2) of the 1984 Act. Sub-s (4) contains provisions formerly in s 8A(2) of the 1948 Act, as substituted by s 1 of the 1984 Act. Sub-s (5) is a drafting provision.

General Note. The provisions now contained in this section and Sch 2 were introduced by the Agricultural Holdings Act 1984, s 1 (repealed by s 101 and Sch 15), to provide a new formula for assessment of rents for agricultural holdings, replacing the old 'open market' formula with one based on arbitrators' pre-existing practices. The scarcity of tenancies had meant that no true open market existed and this had resulted in the original formula becoming virtually unworkable.

Sub-s (1): Notice. As to service, see s 93.

Writing. See the note 'Written' to s 3.

Arbitration under this Act. For provisions as to arbitration under this Act, see s 84 and the note to s 2.

Sub-s (2): amended by the RRO 2006, SI 2006/2805.

Increase ... the rent. As to the length of notices to quit where the rent is increased, see s 25(3).

Sub-s (3): Demand for arbitration ... shall cease to be effective, etc. Prior to its substitution by the Agricultural Holdings Act 1984, s 1, there was no provision in the Agricultural Holdings Act 1948, s 8, stating when a demand for arbitration should cease to be effective but the matter was considered in *Sclater v Horton* [1954] 2 QB 1, [1954] 1 All ER 712, CA, and *University College, Oxford v Durdy* [1982] Ch 413, [1982] 1 All ER 1108, CA. Those decisions would appear to have been superseded by the provisions now contained in sub-s (3) above.

President of the Royal Institution of Chartered Surveyors. The functions of the Minister with regard to the appointment of arbitrators in the Agricultural Holdings Act 1948 (repealed by s 101, Sch 15, Pt I) were transferred to the President of the Royal Institution of Chartered Surveyors by the Agricultural Holdings Act 1984, s 8 (repealed by s 101, Sch 15, Pt I), hence the reference in this subsection. Note, however, that the reference has effect, in relation to any time before the transfer of functions (ie before 1 January 1986 which, by virtue of the Agricultural Holdings Act 1984 (Commencement) Order 1985, SI 1985/1644, was the date on which s 8 of the 1984 Act came into force), as including a reference to the Minister; see s 99, Sch 13, para 5.

Opencast coal operations. For the effect upon arbitration as to rent of occupation by the National Coal Corporation for opencast working, see the Opencast Coal Act 1958, s 14(6) as amended by the Coal Industry Act 1987. See also s 37 of, and Sch 7, paras 4(5), 7 to, that Act, as amended, in the case of para 4(5) of that Schedule, by s 100, Sch 14, para 33(5)(c).

Milk quotas. See the Agriculture Act 1986, s 15, regarding a reference under this section in respect of land which comprises or is part of a holding in relation to which a quota is registered under the Dairy Produce Quotas Regulations 2005, SI 2005/465.

Definitions. For 'agricultural holding', see s 1(1); for 'landlord' and 'tenant', see s 96(1). Note as to 'next termination date', sub-s (4) above.

A1.100

13   Increases of rent for landlord's improvements

(1)   Where the landlord of an agricultural holding has carried out on the holding any improvement to which this section applies he may by notice in writing served on the tenant within six months from the completion of the improvement increase the rent of the holding as from the completion of the improvement by an amount equal to the increase in the rental value of the holding attributable to the carrying out of the improvement.

(2)   This section applies to—

    (a)   an improvement carried out at the request of, or in agreement with, the tenant,

    (b)   an improvement carried out in compliance with a direction given by the Tribunal under section 11 above,

    (c)   an improvement carried out in pursuance of a notice served by the landlord under section 67(5) below,

    (d)   an improvement carried out in compliance with a direction given by the Minister under powers conferred on him by or under any enactment,

(e)   works executed on the holding for the purpose of complying with the requirements of a notice under section 3 of the Agriculture (Safety, Health and Welfare Provisions) Act 1956 (provision of sanitary conveniences and washing facilities),

(f)   an improvement carried out in compliance with an improvement notice served, or an undertaking accepted, under Part VII of the Housing Act 1985 or Part VIII of the Housing Act 1974.

(3)   No increase of rent shall be made under subsection (1) above in respect of an improvement within paragraph (a), (b) or (f) of subsection (2) above if within six months from its completion the landlord and tenant agree on any increase of rent or other benefit to the landlord in respect of the improvement.

(4)   The increase in rent provided for by subsection (1) above shall be reduced proportionately—

(a)   in the case of an improvement within paragraph (b) of subsection (2) above, where a grant has been made to the landlord in respect of the improvement out of money provided by Parliament,

(b)   in the case of an improvement within any other paragraph of that subsection, where a grant has been made to the landlord in respect of the improvement out of money provided by Parliament or local government funds, and

(c)   in the case of an improvement within paragraph (f) of that subsection, where the tenant has contributed to the cost incurred by his landlord in carrying out the improvement.

(5)   Where, on the failure of a landlord to carry out an improvement specified in such a direction as is referred to in subsection (2)(b) above, the tenant has himself carried out the improvement, the provisions of this section shall apply as if the improvement had been carried out by the landlord and as if any grant made to the tenant in respect of the improvement out of money provided by Parliament had been made to the landlord.

(6)   No increase in rent shall take effect by virtue of subsection (5) above until the tenant has recovered from the landlord the reasonable cost of the improvement reduced by the amount of any grant made to the tenant in respect of the improvement out of money provided by Parliament.

(7)   Any dispute arising between the landlord and the tenant of the holding under this section shall be determined by arbitration under this Act.

(8)   This section applies to an improvement whether or not it is one for the carrying out of which compensation is provided under Part V or VI of this Act.

NOTES

Derivation

Sub-ss (1), (7), (8) derived from the Agricultural Holdings Act 1948, s 9(1), (4); sub-ss (2)–(4) derived from the Agricultural Holdings Act 1948, s 9(1), (2), the Agriculture Act 1958, s 4(5), the Agricultural Holdings Act 1984, s 10(1), Sch 3, para 5(2)(b), (c), (3), and the Housing Act 1985, s 231(1), (2); sub-ss (5), (6) derived from the Agriculture Act 1958, s 4(5), (7).

Initial Commencement

Specified date: 18 June 1986: see s 102(2).

Extent

This Act does not extend to Scotland.

See Further

See further, as to the exclusion of this Act in relation to leases or tenancies granted to contractors in respect of the running of any removal centre or part of a removal centre: the Immigration and Asylum Act 1999, s 149(3).

Transfer of Functions

Functions of the Minister, so far as exercisable in relation to Wales, transferred to the National Assembly for Wales, by the National Assembly for Wales (Transfer of Functions) Order 1999, SI 1999/672, art 2, Sch 1.

Notes

For a commentary, see para 25.48 ff.

Sub-ss (1), (8) contain provisions formerly in the Agricultural Holdings Act 1948, s 9(1). Sub-s (2) contains provisions formerly in s 9(1) of the 1948 Act, as amended by the Agricultural Holdings Act 1984, s 10(1), Sch 3, para 5(2)(b), and as repealed in part by s 10(1), (2) of, and Sch 3, para 5(2)(a), Sch 4 to, the 1984 Act, and as affected by the Agriculture Act 1958, s 4(5), and in the Housing Act 1985, s 231(1). Sub-s (3) contains provisions formerly in s 9(2) of the 1948 Act, as substituted by s 10(1) of, and Sch 3, para 5(3) to, the 1984 Act, and as affected by s 4(5) of the 1958 Act, and by s 231(1) of the 1985 Act. Sub-s (4) contains provisions formerly in s 9(1) of the 1948 Act, as amended by s 10(1) of, and Sch 3, para 5(2)(c) to, the 1984 Act, and as affected by s 4(5) of the 1958 Act, and in s 231(1), (2) of the 1985 Act. Sub-s (5) contains provisions formerly in s 4(5) of the 1958 Act. Sub-s (6) contains provisions formerly in s 4(5), (7) of the 1958 Act. Sub-s (7) contains provisions formerly in s 9(4) of the 1948 Act.

Sub-s (1): Notice. As to service, see s 93.

Writing. See the note 'Written' to s 3.

Within six months from, etc. See para 42.27 on the computation of time. The general rule in cases where an act is to be done within a specified time is that the day from which it runs is not to be counted; see *Goldsmiths' Co v West Metropolitan Rly Co* [1904] 1 KB 1, [1900–3] All ER Rep 667, CA; *Stewart v Chapman* [1951] 2 KB 792, [1951] 2 All ER 613; and the other cases cited in 45 Halsbury's Laws (4th edn) para 1134. See also *Dodds v Walker* [1981] 2 All ER 609, [1981] 1 WLR 1027, HL, and 45 Halsbury's Laws (4th edn) para 1111, as to the day of expiry of periods of a month or a specified number of months.

Sub-s (2): Direction given by the Minister. The Minister was empowered to give directions 'with respect to the cultivation, management or use of land for agricultural purposes' by the Defence (General) Regulations 1939, SR & O 1939/927, reg 62, as amended, until it was revoked in part by SI 1952/2091. Reg 62 has now lapsed.

Sub-s (7): Arbitration under this Act. For provisions as to arbitration under this Act, see s 84 and the note to s 2.

Part V or VI of this Act. Ie ss 60–78 or ss 79–82.

Opencast coal operations. For the application of this section where authorised operations under the Opencast Coal Act 1958 have affected any improvement, see s 14(7) of that Act. See also s 37 of, and Sch 7, paras 3(2), 4(5), (6) to, that Act, as amended by s 100, Sch 14, para 33(4), (5).

Definitions. For 'agricultural holding', see s 1(1); for 'agreement', 'landlord', 'local government funds', 'the Minister', 'tenant' and 'the Tribunal', see s 96(1).

Housing Act 1985, Part VII; Housing Act 1974, Part VIII. The Housing Act 1985, Pt VII (repealed by the Local Government and Housing Act 1989, ss 165, 194, Sch 12, Pt II, subject to a saving in SI 1990/431, Sch 1, para 12) generally replaced the Housing Act 1974, Pt VIII (repealed by the Housing (Consequential Provisions) Act 1985, s 3, Sch 1, Pt I).

Cultivation of land and disposal of produce

A1.101

14   Variation of terms of tenancies as to permanent pasture

(1)   This section applies where a contract for a tenancy of an agricultural holding provides for the maintenance of specified land, or a specified proportion of the holding, as permanent pasture.

(2)   Where this section applies, the landlord or tenant may, by notice in writing served on the other, demand a reference to arbitration under this Act of the question whether it is expedient in order to secure the full and efficient farming of the holding that the area of land required to be maintained as permanent pasture should be reduced.

(3)   On a reference under subsection (2) above the arbitrator may by his award direct that the provisions of the contract of tenancy as to land which is to be maintained as permanent pasture or is to be treated as arable land and as to cropping shall have effect subject to such modifications as may be specified in the direction.

(4)   If, on a reference under subsection (2) above, the arbitrator gives a direction reducing the area of land which under the contract of tenancy is to be maintained as permanent pasture, he may order that the contract of tenancy shall have effect as if it provided that on quitting the holding on the termination of the tenancy the tenant should leave—

(a)   as permanent pasture, or

(b)   as temporary pasture sown with seeds mixture of such kind as may be specified in the order,

such area of land (in addition to the area of land required by the contract of tenancy, as modified by the direction, to be maintained as permanent pasture) as may be so specified.

(5)   The area of land specified in an order made under subsection (4) above shall not exceed the area by which the land required by the contract of tenancy to be maintained as permanent pasture has been reduced by virtue of the direction.

NOTES

Derivation

This section derived from the Agricultural Holdings Act 1948, s 10(1), (2), and the Agriculture Act 1958, s 8(1), Sch 1, Part I, para 6.

Initial Commencement

Specified date: 18 June 1986: see s 102(2).

Extent

This Act does not extend to Scotland.

See Further

See further, as to the exclusion of this Act in relation to leases or tenancies granted to contractors in respect of the running of any removal centre or part of a removal centre: the Immigration and Asylum Act 1999, s 149(3).

Notes

For a commentary, see para 24.8.

Sub-ss (1), (2) contain provisions formerly in the Agricultural Holdings Act 1948, s 10(1), as substituted by the Agriculture Act 1958, s 8, Sch 1, para 6. Sub-s (3) and sub-ss (4), (5) contain provisions formerly in s 10(2)(a) and s 10(2)(b), respectively, of the 1948 Act, as, in both cases, substituted by s 8 of, and Sch 1, para 6 to, the 1958 Act.

Sub-s (2): Notice. As to service, see s 93.

Writing. See the note 'Written' to s 3.

Arbitration under this Act. For provisions as to arbitration under this Act, see s 84 and the note to s 2.

Compensation. No compensation is to be payable to the tenant of an agricultural holding in respect of anything done in pursuance of an order under sub-s (4) above; see s 76(1)(a). See also s 76(1)(b) as to the assessment of compensation to an outgoing tenant where land has been ploughed up under a direction under this section. Where the landlord and tenant agree to any such variation of the tenancy as could be made by direction or order under this section the agreement may provide for the exclusion of compensation in the same manner as under s 76(1); see s 78(3).

Definitions. For 'agricultural holding', see s 1(1); for 'contract of tenancy', see s 1 (5); for 'landlord', 'pasture', 'tenant' and 'termination', see s 96(1). Note also as to 'termination', s 74(4).

A1.102

15   Disposal of produce and cropping

(1)   Subject to the provisions of this section and to section 82 below, the tenant of an agricultural holding shall notwithstanding any custom of the country or the provisions of the contract of tenancy or of any agreement respecting the disposal of crops or the method of cropping of arable land) have, without incurring any penalty, forfeiture or liability, the following rights, namely—

(a)   to dispose of the produce of the holding, other than manure produced on the holding, and

(b)   to practise any system of cropping of the arable land on the holding.

(2)   Subsection (1) above shall not apply—

(a)   in the case of a tenancy from year to year, as respects the year before the tenant quits the holding or any period after he has given or received notice to quit which results in his quitting the holding, or

(b)   in the case of any other tenancy, as respects the year before its termination.

(3)   Subject to any agreement in writing to the contrary, the tenant of an agricultural holding shall not at any time after he has given or received notice to quit the holding sell or remove from the holding any manure or compost or any hay or straw or roots grown in the last year of the tenancy unless the landlord's written consent has been obtained before the sale or removal.

(4)   Before, or as soon as possible after, exercising his rights under subsection (1) above, a tenant shall make suitable and adequate provision—

(a)   in the case of an exercise of the right to dispose of produce, to return to the holding the full equivalent manurial value of all crops sold off or removed from the holding in contravention of the custom, contract or agreement, and

(b)   in the case of an exercise of the right to practise any system of cropping, to protect the holding from injury or deterioration.

(5)   If the tenant of an agricultural holding exercises his rights under subsection (1) above in such manner as to, or to be likely to, injure or deteriorate the holding, the landlord shall have the following remedies, but no other, namely—

(a) the right to obtain, if the case so requires, an injunction to restrain the exercise of those rights in that manner, and

(b) the right in any case, on the tenant's quitting the holding on the termination of the tenancy, to recover damages for any injury to or deterioration of the holding attributable to the exercise by the tenant of those rights.

(6) For the purposes of any proceedings for an injunction brought under paragraph (a) of subsection (5) above, the question whether the tenant is exercising, or has exercised, his rights under subsection (1) above in such a manner as to, or to be likely to, injure or deteriorate his holding shall be determined by arbitration under this Act; and the award of the arbitrator shall, for the purposes of any proceedings brought under subsection (5) (including an arbitration under paragraph (b)) be conclusive proof of the facts stated in the award.

(7) In this section—

'arable land' does not include land in grass which, by the terms of a contract of tenancy, is to be retained in the same condition throughout the tenancy; and

'roots' means the produce of any root crop of a kind normally grown for consumption on the holding.

NOTES

Derivation

Sub-ss (1)–(5), (7) derived from the Agricultural Holdings Act 1948, ss 11(1), (2), (4)(a), (b), (5), 12(1), (2); sub-s (6) derived from the Agricultural Holdings Act 1948, s 11(3), and the Agriculture Act 1958, s 8(1), Sch 1, Part I, para 7.

Initial Commencement

Specified date: 18 June 1986: see s 102(2).

Extent

This Act does not extend to Scotland.

See Further

See further, as to the exclusion of this Act in relation to leases or tenancies granted to contractors in respect of the running of any removal centre or part of a removal centre: the Immigration and Asylum Act 1999, s 149(3).

Notes

For a commentary, see para 24.9.

Sub-ss (1), (4) contain provisions formerly in the Agricultural Holdings Act 1948, s 11(1). Sub-s (2) contains provisions formerly in s 11(4)(a), (b) of the 1948 Act. Sub-s (3) contains provisions formerly in s 12(1) of the 1948 Act. Sub-s (5) contains provisions formerly in s 11(2) of the 1948 Act. Sub-s (6) contains provisions formerly in s 11(3) of the 1948 Act, as amended by the Agriculture Act 1958, s 8(1), Sch 1, Pt I, para 7. Sub-s (7) contains provisions formerly in ss 11(5), 12(2) of the 1948 Act.

Sub-s (3): Writing. See the note 'Written' to s 3.

Shall not ... sell or remove. The combined effect of this provision and s 65 is to pass the property in the crops to the landlord on the tenant's quitting the holding: *Thomas v National Farmers' Union Mutual Insurance Society Ltd* [1961] 1 All ER 363, [1961] 1 WLR 386.

Sub-s (4). For special provisions as to compensation for improvements or matters made or effected for the purposes of this subsection, see s 76(3).

As soon as possible. 'To do a thing "as soon as possible" means to do it within a reasonable time, with an understanding to do it within the shortest possible time': see *King's Old Country Ltd v*

Liquid Carbonic Canadian Corpn Ltd [1942] 2 WR 603 at 606, per Dysart J. See also *Verelst's Administratrix v Motor Union Insurance Co* [1925] 2 KB 137.

Sub-s (5): Likely. 'Likely' has been construed so as to mean a 'reasonable prospect' of something happening: *Dunning v Board of Governors of the United Liverpool Hospitals* [1973] 2 All ER 454 at 460, [1973] 1 WLR 586, CA, per James LJ; overruled on another point by *McIvor v Southern Health and Social Services Board* [1978] 2 All ER 625, [1978] 1 WLR 757, HL, but it has also been said that it is capable of covering a whole range of possibilities from 'it's on the cards' to 'it's more probable than not' (*R v Sheppard* [1981] AC 394, [1980] 3 All ER 899 at 904, HL per Lord Diplock).

Damages. As to settlement of claims, etc, see ss 83 ff.

Sub-s (6): Arbitration under this Act. For provisions as to arbitration under this Act, see s 84 and the note to s 2.

Saving for other rights. The saving for other rights in s 97 does not affect sub-s (5) above.

Smallholdings. Sub-s (1) above does not apply to certain tenancies of land let as a smallholding; see s 82(1). See also s 82(2), (3).

Definitions. For 'agricultural holding', see s 1(1); for 'contract of tenancy', see s 1(5); for 'agreement', 'landlord', 'tenant' and 'termination', see s 96(1). Note as to 'arable land' and 'roots', sub-s (7) above; and see also, as to 'termination', s 74(4).

Distress

A1.103

16   No distress for rent due more than a year previously

(1)   Subject to subsection (2) below, the landlord of an agricultural holding shall not be entitled to distrain for rent which became due in respect of that holding more than one year before the making of the distress.

(2)   Where it appears that, according to the ordinary course of dealing between the landlord and the tenant of the holding, the payment of rent has been deferred until the expiry of a quarter or half-year after the date at which the rent legally became due, the rent shall, for the purposes of subsection (1) above, be deemed to have become due at the expiry of that quarter or half-year and not at the date at which it became legally due.

NOTES

Derivation

This section derived from the Agricultural Holdings Act 1948, s 18.

Initial Commencement

Specified date: 18 June 1986: see s 102(2).

Extent

This Act does not extend to Scotland.

See Further

See further, as to the exclusion of this Act in relation to leases or tenancies granted to contractors in respect of the running of any removal centre or part of a removal centre: the Immigration and Asylum Act 1999, s 149(3).

Notes

For a commentary, see para 26.3.

This section contains provisions formerly in the Agricultural Holdings Act 1948, s 18.

Sub-s (2). This subsection does not limit the common law right to distrain: see *Re Bew, ex p Bull* (1887) 18 QBD 642, DC.

Disputes. See s 19 as to the settlement of disputes as to distress.

Definitions. For 'agricultural holding', see s 1(1); for 'landlord' and 'tenant', see s 96(1).

A1.104

17   Compensation to be set off against rent for purposes of distress

Where the amount of any compensation due to the tenant of an agricultural holding, whether under this Act or under custom or agreement, has been ascertained before the landlord distrains for rent, that amount may be set off against the rent and the landlord shall not be entitled to distrain for more than the balance.

NOTES

Derivation

This section derived from the Agricultural Holdings Act 1948, s 22.

Initial Commencement

Specified date: 18 June 1986: see s 102(2).

Extent

This Act does not extend to Scotland.

See Further

See further, as to the exclusion of this Act in relation to leases or tenancies granted to contractors in respect of the running of any removal centre or part of a removal centre: the Immigration and Asylum Act 1999, s 149(3).

Notes

For a commentary, see para 26.9.

This section contains provisions formerly in the Agricultural Holdings Act 1948, s 22.

Disputes. See s 19 as to the settlement of disputes as to distress.

Definitions. For 'agricultural holding', see s 1(1); for 'agreement', 'landlord' and 'tenant', see s 96(1).

A1.105

18   Restrictions on distraining on property of third party

(1)   Property belonging to a person other than the tenant of an agricultural holding shall not be distrained for rent if—

    (a)   the property is agricultural or other machinery and is on the holding under an agreement with the tenant for its hire or use in the conduct of his business, or

    (b)   the property is livestock and is on the holding solely for breeding purposes.

(2)   Agisted livestock shall not be distrained by the landlord of an agricultural holding for rent where there is other sufficient distress to be found; and if such livestock is distrained by him by reason of other sufficient distress not being found, there shall not be recovered by that distress a sum exceeding the amount of the price agreed to be paid for the feeding, or any part of the price which remains unpaid.

(3)   The owner of the agisted livestock may, at any time before it is sold, redeem it by paying to the distrainer a sum equal to the amount mentioned in subsection (2) above, and payment of that sum to the distrainer shall be in full discharge as against the tenant of any sum of that amount which would otherwise be due from the owner of the livestock to the tenant in respect of the price of feeding.

(4)   Any portion of the agisted livestock shall, so long as it remains on the holding, continue liable to be distrained for the amount for which the whole of the livestock is distrainable.

(5)   In this section 'livestock' includes any animal capable of being distrained; and 'agisted livestock' means livestock belonging to another person which has been taken in by the tenant of an agricultural holding to be fed at a fair price.

NOTES

Derivation

This section derived from the Agricultural Holdings Act 1948, ss 19, 20.

Initial Commencement

Specified date: 18 June 1986: see s 102(2).

Extent

This Act does not extend to Scotland.

See Further

See further, as to the exclusion of this Act in relation to leases or tenancies granted to contractors in respect of the running of any removal centre or part of a removal centre: the Immigration and Asylum Act 1999, s 149(3).

Notes

For a commentary, see para 26.4.

Sub-s (1) contains provisions formerly in the Agricultural Holdings Act 1948, s 20(1). Sub-ss (2)–(4) contain provisions formerly in s 19(1)–(3), respectively, of the 1948 Act. Sub-s (5) contains provisions formerly in ss 19(1), (4), 20(2) of the 1948 Act.

Sub-s (2): Agisted Livestock. At common law agisted stock, except sheep, were liable to distress for the rent of the tenant upon whose land they were. Beasts that gain the land and sheep were exempt by the Statutes of the Exchequer (temp incert), while other distress could be found; the owner of sheep unlawfully distrained could recover the value from the distrainor (*Keen v Priest* (1859) 4 H & N 236). See further 1 Halsbury's Laws (4th edn, reissue) para 334.

Livestock to which this section applies is outside the Law of Distress Amendment Act 1908; see s 4(1) of that Act, as amended by s 100, Sch 14, para 4.

Disputes. See s 19 as to the settlement of disputes as to distress.

Definitions. For 'agricultural holding', see s 1(1); for 'agreement', 'landlord' and 'tenant', see s 96(1). Note as to 'livestock' and 'agisted livestock', sub-s (5) above.

A1.106

19   Settlement of disputes as to distress

(1)   Where a dispute arises—

(a)   in respect of any distress having been levied on an agricultural holding contrary to the provisions of this Act,

(b)   as to the ownership of any livestock distrained or as to the price to be paid for the feeding of that stock, or

(c)   as to any other matter or thing relating to a distress on an agricultural holding,

the dispute may be determined by the county court or on complaint by a magistrates' court, and the court may make an order for restoration of any livestock or things unlawfully distrained, may declare the price agreed to be paid for feeding or may make any other order that justice requires.

(2)   Any person aggrieved by a decision of a magistrates' court under this section may appeal to the Crown Court.

(3)   In this section 'livestock' includes any animal capable of being distrained.

NOTES

Derivation

Sub-ss (1), (3) derived from the Agricultural Holdings Act 1948, s 21(1), (2), (4); sub-s (2) derived from the Agricultural Holdings Act 1948, s 21(3), and the Courts Act 1971, s 56(2), Sch 9, Part I.

Initial Commencement

Specified date: 18 June 1986: see s 102(2).

Extent

This Act does not extend to Scotland.

See Further

See further, as to the exclusion of this Act in relation to leases or tenancies granted to contractors in respect of the running of any removal centre or part of a removal centre: the Immigration and Asylum Act 1999, s 149(3).

Notes

For a commentary, see para 26.11.

Sub-s (1) contains provisions formerly in the Agricultural Holdings Act 1948, s 21(1), (2). Sub-s (2) contains provisions formerly in s 21(3) of the 1948 Act, as amended by the Courts Act 1971, s 56(2), Sch 9, Pt 1. Sub-s (3) contains provisions formerly in s 21(4) of the 1948 Act.

County court. See the note to s 96. Proceedings are commenced by a claim form under CPR Part 8 (reflecting the old originating application procedure under CCR Ord 3, r 4). However, if there are likely to be substantial disputes of fact, it is better to commence proceedings under CPR Part 7.

Magistrates' court. For meaning, see, by virtue of the Interpretation Act 1978, s 5, Sch 1, the Magistrates' Courts Act 1980, s 148.

Crown Court. This is defined by the Interpretation Act 1978, s 5, Sch 1 to mean the Crown Court constituted by the Courts Act 1971, s 4. That section and other provisions of the 1971 Act relating to the Crown Court were repealed by the Supreme Court Act 1981, s 152(4), Sch 7; see now, in particular, ss 8, 45–48 of the 1981 Act.

Definitions. For 'agricultural holding', see s 1(1); for 'county court', see s 96(1). Note as to 'livestock', sub-s(3) above.

Miscellaneous

A1.107

20   Compensation for damage by game

(1)   Where the tenant of an agricultural holding has sustained damage to his crops from any wild animals or birds the right to kill and take which is vested in the landlord or anyone (other than the tenant himself) claiming under the landlord, being animals or birds which the tenant has not permission in writing to kill, he shall, if he complies with the requirements of subsection (2) below, be entitled to compensation from his landlord for the damage.

(2)   The requirements of this subsection are that the tenant shall give his landlord—

(a)   notice in writing within one month after the tenant first became, or ought reasonably to have become, aware of the occurrence of the damage,
(b)   a reasonable opportunity to inspect the damage—
   (i)   in the case of damage to a growing crop, before the crop is begun to be reaped, raised or consumed, and
   (ii)   in the case of damage to a crop which has been reaped or raised, before the crop is begun to be removed from the land, and
(c)   notice in writing of the claim, together with particulars of it, within one month after the expiry of the year in respect of which the claim is made.

(3)   For the purposes of subsection (2) above—

(a)   seed once sown shall be treated as a growing crop whether or not it has germinated, and
(b)   'year' means any period of twelve months ending, in any year, with 29th September or with such other date as may by agreement between the landlord and tenant be substituted for that date.

(4)   The amount of compensation under this section shall, in default or agreement made after the damage has been suffered, be determined by arbitration under this Act.

(5)   Where the right to kill and take the wild animals or birds that did the damage is vested in some person other than the landlord, the landlord shall be entitled to be indemnified by that other person against all claims for compensation under this section; and any question arising under this subsection shall be determined by arbitration under this Act.

NOTES

Derivation

Sub-ss (1)–(3), (5) derived from the Agricultural Holdings Act 1948, s 14(1), (3), and the Agricultural Holdings Act 1984, s 10(1), Sch 3, para 7(2), (3); sub-s (4) derived from the Agricultural Holdings Act 1948, s 14(2).

Initial Commencement

Specified date: 18 June 1986: see s 102(2).

Extent

This Act does not extend to Scotland.

See Further

See further, as to the exclusion of this Act in relation to leases or tenancies granted to contractors in respect of the running of any removal centre or part of a removal centre: the Immigration and Asylum Act 1999, s 149(3).

Notes

For a commentary, see para 24.11.

Sub-ss (1)–(3) contain provisions formerly in the Agricultural Holdings Act 1948, s 14(1), as amended by the Agricultural Holdings Act 1984, s 10(1), Sch 3, para 7(2). Sub-ss (4), (5) contain provisions formerly in s 14(2), (3), respectively, of the 1948 Act, as amended in the case of s 14(3) thereof by s 10(1) of, and Sch 3, para 7(3) to, the 1984 Act.

Sub-s (1): Tenant has not permission … to kill. An occupier of land, however, has the right, as an incident of his occupation, to kill hares and rabbits, and any agreement which purports to divert or alienate this right is void, see the Ground Game Act 1880, ss 1, 3, 8, and 2 Halsbury's Laws (4th edn, reissue) paras 255 ff.

Permission in writing to the tenant to kill any enumerated game excludes compensation for damage caused by that game; see *Ross v Watson* 1943 SC 406.

Writing. See the note 'Written' to s 3.

Sub-s (2): Notice. As to service, see s 93.

Within one month after, etc. Cf the note 'Within six months from, etc' to s 13.

Reasonable opportunity. What is a reasonable opportunity is a question of fact for the arbitrator to decide on the facts of each case: see *Dale v Hatfield Chase Corpn* [1922] 2 KB 282, CA.

Sub-s (3): Months. See the note to s 4.

Sub-s (4): In default of agreement. As to agreements on compensation, see s 78.

Arbitration under this Act. For provisions as to arbitration under this Act, see s 84 and the note to s 2.

Divided holding. As to compensation where the reversionary estate in an agricultural holding is vested in more than one person in several parts, see s 75.

Definitions. For 'agricultural holding', see s 1 (1); for 'agreement', 'landlord' and 'tenant', see s 96(1). Note as to 'growing crop' and 'year', sub-s (3) above.

A1.108

21   Extension of tenancies in lieu of claims to emblements

(1)   Where the tenancy of an agricultural holding held by a tenant at a rackrent determines by the death or cesser of the estate of any landlord entitled for his life, or for any other uncertain interest, instead of claims to emblements the tenant shall continue to hold and occupy the holding until the occupation is determined by a twelve months' notice to quit expiring at the end of a year of the tenancy, and shall then quit upon the terms of his tenancy in the same manner as if the tenancy were then determined by effluxion of time or other lawful means during the continuance of his landlord's estate.

(2)   The succeeding landlord shall be entitled to recover from the tenant, in the same manner as his predecessor could have done, a fair proportion of the rent for the period which may have elapsed from the date of the death or cesser of the estate of his predecessor to the time of the tenant so quitting.

(3)   The succeeding landlord and the tenant respectively shall as between themselves and as against each other be entitled to all the benefits and advantages and be subject to the terms, conditions and restrictions to which the preceding landlord and the tenant respectively would have been entitled and subject if the tenancy had determined in manner aforesaid at the expiry of the said twelve months' notice.

NOTES

Derivation

This section derived from the Agricultural Holdings Act 1948, s 4(1)–(3).

Initial Commencement

Specified date: 18 June 1986: see s 102(2).

Extent

This Act does not extend to Scotland.

See Further

See further, as to the exclusion of this Act in relation to leases or tenancies granted to contractors in respect of the running of any removal centre or part of a removal centre: the Immigration and Asylum Act 1999, s 149(3).

Notes

For a commentary, see para 20.9.

Sub-ss (1)–(3) contain provisions formerly in the Agricultural Holdings Act 1948, s 4(1)–(3), respectively.

Emblements. The right to emblements is the common law right of a tenant to 'reap what he has sown' ie to enter after his tenancy and gather such crops as normally mature within a year: *Graves v Weld* (1833) 5 B & Ad 105. It only applies where a tenant holds for an uncertain interest and his interest determines otherwise than by or in consequence of his own act. The right to emblements is personal property and not an interest in land. See further 1 Halsbury's Laws (4th edn, reissue) para 382.

Months. See the note to s 4.

Benefits. See the note to s 66.

Definitions. For 'agricultural holding', see s 1(1); for 'landlord' and 'tenant', see s 96(1).

A1.109

22   Rights to require certain records to be made

(1)   At any time during the tenancy of an agricultural holding—

    (a)   the landlord or the tenant may require the making of a record of the condition of the fixed equipment on the holding and of the general condition of the holding itself (including any parts not under cultivation), and

    (b)   the tenant may require the making of a record of any fixtures or buildings which, under section 10 above, he is entitled to remove and of existing improvements executed by him or in respect of the execution of which he, with the written consent of the landlord, paid compensation to an outgoing tenant.

(2)   Any such record shall be made by a person appointed, in default of agreement between the landlord and tenant, by the President of the Royal Institution of Chartered Surveyors (referred to in this section as 'the President'); and any person so appointed may, on production of evidence of his appointment, enter the holding at all reasonable times for the purpose of making any such record.

(3)   The cost of making any such record shall, in default of agreement between the landlord and tenant, be borne by them in equal shares.

(4)   No application may be made to the President for a person to be appointed by him under subsection (2) above unless the application is accompanied by such fee as may be prescribed as the fee for such an application.

(5)   Any instrument of appointment purporting to be made by the President by virtue of subsection (2) above and to be signed by or on behalf of the President shall be taken to be such an instrument unless the contrary is shown.

NOTES

Derivation

Sub-ss (1), (2) derived from the Agricultural Holdings Act 1948, s 16(1), (2), and the Agricultural Holdings Act 1984, ss 8(1), (2), 10(1), Sch 3, para 8; sub-s (3) derived from the Agricultural Holdings Act 1948, s 16(3); sub-ss (4), (5) derived from the Agricultural Holdings Act 1984, s 8(3), (4), (5).

Initial Commencement

Specified date: 18 June 1986: see s 102(2).

Extent

This Act does not extend to Scotland.

See Further

See further, as to the exclusion of this Act in relation to leases or tenancies granted to contractors in respect of the running of any removal centre or part of a removal centre: the Immigration and Asylum Act 1999, s 149(3).

Subordinate Legislation

Agricultural Holdings (Fee) Regulations 1996, SI 1996/337 (made under sub-s (4)).

Notes

For a commentary, see para 24.13.

Sub-s (1) contains provisions formerly in the Agricultural Holdings Act 1948, s 16(1), as amended by the Agricultural Holdings Act 1984, s 10(1), Sch 3, para 8(a). Sub-s (2) contains provisions formerly in s 16(2) of the 1948 Act, as affected by s 8(1), (2) of the 1984 Act, and as amended by s 10(1) of, and Sch 3, para 8(b) to, the 1984 Act. Sub-s (3) contains provisions formerly in s 16(3) of the 1948 Act. Sub-s (4) contains provisions formerly in s 8(3), (4) of the 1984 Act. Sub-s (5) contains provisions formerly in s 8(5) of the 1984 Act.

General Note. The making of a record of the condition of a holding under this section is a condition precedent to the recovery of compensation for continuous adoption of special systems of farming under s 70; see sub-s (2)(b).

Sub-s (1): Written. See the note to s 3.

Compensation to an outgoing tenant. See ss 64(4), 69(2) and Sch 9, para 5(2).

Sub-s (2): President of the Royal Institution of Chartered Surveyors. The functions of the Minister with regard to the appointment of a person to make a record of the condition of a holding under the Agricultural Holdings Act 1948, s 16(2) (repealed by s 101, Sch 15 and replaced by sub-s (2) above), were transferred to the President of the Royal Institution of Chartered Surveyors by the Agricultural Holdings Act 1984, s 8(1), (2) (repealed by s 101, Sch 15), hence the reference in this subsection. This section has effect in relation to the appointment of a person in pursuance of an application made before 1 January 1986 (the date on which, by virtue of the Agricultural Holdings Act 1984 (Commencement) Order 1985, SI 1985/1644, s 8 of the 1984 Act came into force) as if for references to the President of the Royal Institution of Chartered Surveyors there were substituted references to the Minister (for meaning, see s 96(1)) and as if sub-ss (4), (5) of this section were omitted; see s 99, Sch 13, para 6.

On production of evidence of his appointment. This does not mean that the right of entry can only be exercised if there is someone to whom the authority can be produced: see *Grove v Eastern Gas Board* [1952] 1 KB 77, [1951] 2 All ER 1051, CA.

At all reasonable times. What is a reasonable time is a question of fact and must necessarily depend on the circumstances of the particular case; see 45 Halsbury's Laws (4th edn) para 1147. The time during which the premises in question are open for business purposes will ordinarily be deemed reasonable (cf *Davies v Winstanley* (1930) 144 LT 433), and presumably an authorised person would not be justified, except in special circumstances, in demanding that premises should be opened at an unusual time such as Sunday afternoon: *Small v Bickley* (1875) 32 LT 726.

Sub-s (4): Such fee as may be prescribed. See the note 'Regulations under this section' below.

Definitions. For 'agricultural holding', see s 1(1): for 'agreement', 'building', 'fixed equipment', 'landlord', 'prescribed' and 'tenant', see s 96(1). Note as to 'the President', sub-s (2) above.

Regulations under this section. The Agricultural Holdings (Fee) Regulations 1996, SI 1996/337 (prescribing a fee of £115).

As to regulations, generally, made under this section, see s 94(1)–(3).

Transitional provisions. See s 99, Sch 13, para 6, and the note 'President of the Royal Institution of Chartered Surveyors' to sub-s (2) above.

A1.110

23   Landlord's power of entry

The landlord of an agricultural holding or any person authorised by him may at all reasonable times enter on the holding for any of the following purposes, namely—

(a) viewing the state of the holding,

(b) fulfilling the landlord's responsibilities to manage the holding in accordance with the rules of good estate management,

(c) providing or improving fixed equipment on the holding otherwise than in fulfilment of those responsibilities.

NOTES

Derivation

This section derived from the Agricultural Holdings Act 1948, s 17.

Initial Commencement

Specified date: 18 June 1986: see s 102(2).

Extent

This Act does not extend to Scotland.

See Further

See further, as to the exclusion of this Act in relation to leases or tenancies granted to contractors in respect of the running of any removal centre or part of a removal centre: the Immigration and Asylum Act 1999, s 149(3).

Notes

For a commentary, see para 24.14.

This section contains provisions formerly in the Agricultural Holdings Act 1948, s 17.

Opencast coal operations. Powers of entry conferred on the landlord where there is a compulsory rights order do not affect rights exercisable under this section; see the Opencast Coal Act 1958, s 37, Sch 7, Pt I, para 6, as amended by s 100, Sch 14, para 33(7), and the Agricultural Tenancies Act 1995, s 40, Schedule, para 20.

Definitions. For 'agricultural holding', see s 1(1); for 'fixed equipment' and 'landlord', see s 96(1). See, as to 'rules of good estate management', s 96(3).

A1.111

24   Restriction of landlord's remedies for breach of contract of tenancy

Notwithstanding any provision in a contract of tenancy of an agricultural holding making the tenant liable to pay a higher rent or other liquidated damages in the event of a breach or non-fulfilment of a term or condition of the contract, the landlord shall not be entitled to recover in consequence of any such breach or non-fulfilment, by distress or otherwise, any sum in excess of the damage actually suffered by him in consequence of the breach or non-fulfilment.

NOTES

Derivation

This section derived from the Agricultural Holdings Act 1948, s 15.

Initial Commencement

Specified date: 18 June 1986: see s 102(2).

Extent

This Act does not extend to Scotland.

See Further

See further, as to the exclusion of this Act in relation to leases or tenancies granted to contractors in respect of the running of any removal centre or part of a removal centre: the Immigration and Asylum Act 1999, s 149(3).

Notes

For a commentary, see para 24.15.

This section contains provisions formerly in the Agricultural Holdings Act 1948, s 15.

Definitions. For 'agricultural holding', see s 1(1); for 'contract of tenancy', see s 1(5); for 'landlord' and 'tenant', see s 96(1).

PART III: NOTICES TO QUIT

Notices to quit whole or part of agricultural holding

A1.112

25   Length of notice to quit

(1)   A notice to quit an agricultural holding or part of an agricultural holding shall (notwithstanding any provision to the contrary in the contract of tenancy of the holding) be invalid if it purports to terminate the tenancy before the expiry of twelve months from the end of the then current year of tenancy.

(2)   Subsection (1) above shall not apply—

(a)   where the tenant is insolvent,

(b)   to a notice given in pursuance of a provision in the contract of tenancy authorising the resumption of possession of the holding or some part of it for some specified purpose other than the use of the land for agriculture,

(c)   to a notice given by a tenant to a sub-tenant,

(d)   where the tenancy is one which, by virtue of subsection (6) of section 149 of the Law of Property Act 1925, has taken effect as such a term of years as is mentioned in that subsection.

(3)   Where on a reference under section 12 above with respect to an agricultural holding the arbitrator determines that the rent payable in respect of the holding shall be increased, a notice to quit the holding given by the tenant at least six months before it purports to take effect shall not be invalid by virtue of subsection (1) above if it purports to terminate the tenancy at the end of the year of the tenancy beginning with the date as from which the increase of rent is effective.

(4)   On an application made to the Tribunal with respect to an agricultural holding under paragraph 9 of Part II of Schedule 3 to this Act, the Tribunal may, if they grant a certificate in accordance with the application—

(a)   specify in the certificate a minimum period of notice for termination of the tenancy (not being a period of less than two months), and

(b)   direct that that period shall apply instead of the period of notice required in accordance with subsection (1) above;

and in any such case a notice to quit the holding which states that the Tribunal have given a direction under this subsection shall not be invalid by virtue of subsection (1) above if the notice given is not less than the minimum notice specified in the certificate.

(5)   A notice to quit within subsection (3) or (4) above shall not be invalid by virtue of any term of the contract of tenancy requiring a longer period of notice to terminate the tenancy, and a notice to quit within subsection (4) above shall not be invalid by reason of its terminating at a date other than the end of a year of the tenancy.

NOTES

Derivation

Sub-s (1) derived from the Agricultural Holdings (Notices to Quit) Act 1977, s 1(1); sub-ss (2)–(5) derived from the Agricultural Holdings (Notices to Quit) Act 1977, s 1(2), (5)–(7), and the Agricultural Holdings Act 1984, ss 5, 10(1), Sch 3, para 36.

Initial Commencement

Specified date: 18 June 1986: see s 102(2).

Extent

This Act does not extend to Scotland.

See Further

See further, as to the exclusion of this Act in relation to leases or tenancies granted to contractors in respect of the running of any removal centre or part of a removal centre: the Immigration and Asylum Act 1999, s 149(3).

Notes

For a commentary, see para 28.12.

Sub-s (1) contains provisions formerly in the Agricultural Holdings (Notices to Quit) Act 1977, s 1(1). Sub-s (2) contains provisions formerly in s 1(2) of the 1977 Act, as amended by the

Agricultural Holdings Act 1984, s 10(1), Sch 3, para 36. Sub-ss (3)–(5) contain provisions formerly in s 1(5)–(7) of the 1977 Act, respectively, as inserted by s 5 of the 1984 Act.

Sub-s (1): Notice to quit. A notice exercising an option to determine a lease before its expiration by effluxion of time is a notice to quit within this section: *Edell v Dulieu* [1924] AC 38. So is a notice to quit given by a tenant to the landlord: *Flather v Hood* (1928) 44 TLR 698.

As to the validity of a notice giving '12 months' notice from this month', see, *Felton v Chester* (1946) 175 LT 103, CA. See also *Elsden v Pick* [1980] 3 All ER 235, [1980] 1 WLR 898, CA, where (although decided under the Agricultural Holdings Act 1948, s 23(1), which this section replaces) it was held that where a notice was given for a period less than 12 months, the landlord and tenant were not precluded from agreeing it should be valid to determine the tenancy.

The notice cannot be given before the commencement of the tenancy: *Lower v Sorrell* [1963] 1 QB 959, [1962] 3 All ER 1074, CA.

As to service of notices, see s 93. A notice to terminate a tenancy under s 3(1) is deemed to be a notice to quit under this Act; see s 3(2).

A notice to quit served by one of several joint owners of a property subject to a periodic tenancy is valid without the concurrence of the others since such a tenancy can only continue at the wish of all the joint owners: *Parsons v Parsons* [1983] 1 WLR 1390, 47 P & CR 494.

For restrictions on operation of notices to quit, see, in particular, ss 26, 28 and Sch 3; as to notice to quit part of a holding, see further ss 31–33; and as to notice to quit where the tenant is a service man, see s 30 and Sch 5.

An agricultural holding or part of an agricultural holding. The latter words are necessitated by s 31. Normally, however, a notice to quit in respect of a part of an agricultural holding is invalid; see the note 'Notice to quit part ... shall not be invalid, etc' to s 31.

12 months. Semble that the notice may expire either on the anniversary of the commencement of the tenancy or on the day before: *Bathavon RDC v Carlisle* [1958] 1 QB 461, [1958] 1 All ER 801 and *Crate v Miller* [1947] KB 946, [1947] 2 All ER 45, CA. Note that the period of twelve months is to be calculated inclusive of the last day of the current year of tenancy and exclusive of the day on which the tenancy is to be terminated: *Schnabel v Allard* [1967] 1 QB 627, [1966] 3 All ER 816, CA. See also, as to 'Months' the note to s 4.

Sub-s (2): Subsection (1) above shall not apply. See also Sch 12, para 4.

Tenant is insolvent. See s 96(2).

Resumption of possession of the holding ... for some specified purpose. Although a contract may provide for less than twelve months' notice for such a purpose, a provision in a contract is void if it authorises notice which is too short to enable the tenant to take advantage of the right to claim increased compensation for disturbance under s 60, or compensation for special system farming under s 70; see *Re Disraeli's Agreement, Cleasby v Park Estate (Hughenden) Ltd* [1939] Ch 382, [1938] 4 All ER 658; *Coates v Diment* [1951] 1 All ER 890. Not less than one month's notice before tenancy termination is required to entitle the tenant to compensation in both those cases; see ss 60(6), 70(2).

It is not necessary that the specified purpose should be that of the landlord: see *Rugby Joint Water Board v Foottit* [1973] AC 202, [1972] 1 All ER 1057, HL.

Sub-s (3): The arbitrator. For provisions as to arbitration under this Act, see s 84 and the note to s 2.

At least six months. It is thought that this period should be reckoned as a period which includes the day on which notice is given and excludes that on which it takes effect. Cf *Schnabel v Allard* [1967] 1 QB 627, [1966] 3 All ER 816, CA. See also the note to s 10.

Definitions. For 'agricultural holding', see s 1(1); for 'contract of tenancy', see s 1(5); for 'agriculture', 'tenant' and 'the Tribunal', see s 96(1). As to 'use of land for agriculture', see s 96(5).

A1.113

26   Restriction on operation of notices to quit

(1)   Where—

    (a)   notice to quit an agricultural holding or part of an agricultural holding is given to the tenant, and

    (b)   not later than one month from the giving of the notice to quit the tenant serves on the landlord a counter-notice in writing requiring that this subsection shall apply to the notice to quit,

then, subject to subsection (2) below, the notice to quit shall not have effect unless, on an application by the landlord, the Tribunal consent to its operation.

(2)   Subsection (1) above shall not apply in any of the Cases set out in Part I of Schedule 3 to this Act; and in this Act 'Case A', 'Case B' (and so on) refer severally to the Cases set out and so named in that Part of that Schedule.

(3)   Part II of that Schedule shall have effect in relation to the Cases there specified.

NOTES

Derivation

Sub-ss (1), (2) derived from the Agricultural Holdings (Notices to Quit) Act 1977, ss 2(1), (2), 12(1).

Initial Commencement

Specified date: 18 June 1986: see s 102(2).

Extent

This Act does not extend to Scotland.

See Further

See further, as to the exclusion of this Act in relation to leases or tenancies granted to contractors in respect of the running of any removal centre or part of a removal centre: the Immigration and Asylum Act 1999, s 149(3).

Notes

For a commentary, see para 30.1 ff.

Sub-s (1) contains provisions formerly in the Agricultural Holdings (Notices to Quit) Act 1977, s 2(1). Sub-s (2) contains provisions formerly in ss 2(2), 12(1) of the 1977 Act. Sub-s (3) is a drafting provision.

Notice to quit. See the note to s 25.

Sub-s (1) does not apply where notice to quit is given to a sub-tenant by a tenant who has himself been given notice to quit and the fact that the tenant has given such notice is stated in the notice given to the sub-tenant; see the Agricultural Holdings (Arbitration on Notices) Order 1987, SI 1987/710, art 16. In *Sherwood v Moody* [1952] 1 All ER 389, 50 LGR 180, the tenant who had been given notice to quit approved under what is now sub-s (1) gave his sub-tenant a notice to quit which did not state that the tenant had been given notice but it was held that the landlord's notice to quit effectively determined both the tenancy and the sub-tenancy.

It is inadvisable to give reasons in a notice intended to be subject to sub-s (1) as this may create the impression that sub-s (2) and the Cases in Sch 3, Pt I are relied upon: *Mills v Edwards* [1971] 1 QB 379, [1971] 1 All ER 922, CA.

An agricultural holding or part of an agricultural holding. See the note to s 25.

One month from, etc. Cf the note 'Two months from, etc' to s 10.

Counter-notice. As to service, see s 93. The document is not to be construed with great strictness but must identify this section: *Mountford v Hodkinson* [1956] 2 All ER 17, [1956] 1 WLR 422, CA. The right to serve a counter-notice may not be excluded by a term of the lease; see *Johnson v Moreton* [1980] AC 37, [1978] 3 All ER 37. Where a notice to quit is given to joint tenants, and a counter-notice is served by one of them without the other's authority, the counter-notice is ineffective: see *Jacobs v Chaudhuri* [1968] 2 QB 470, [1968] 2 All ER 124, *Newman v Keedwell* (1977) 35 P & CR 393, 244 Estates Gazette 469, *Lloyd v Sadler* [1978] QB 774, [1978] 2 All ER 529. Cf also, as to counter-notices where notice to quit is given under Case D (in Sch 3, Pt 1) s 28.

Writing. See the note 'Written' to s 3.

Application by the landlord. For the time limit for applications and the form to be used, see the Agricultural Land Tribunals (Rules) Order 1978, SI 1978/259, Sch 1, r 2, Form 1, as construed in accordance with s 99(1) and Sch 13, para 1(2).

The Tribunal consent, etc. See further s 27.

Sub-s (2). To exclude sub-s (1) a notice to quit need not specify which Case in Sch 3, Pt I, is relied upon or use the precise words of the relevant Case but the notice must nevertheless identify the relevant Case without ambiguity: *Budge v Hicks* [1951] 2 KB 335, [1951] 2 All ER 245, CA. It must also be clear whether the notice purports to rely on any of those Cases or to be an ordinary notice to which a counter-notice may be served: *Cowan v Wrayford* [1953] 2 All ER 1138, [1953] 1 WLR 1340, CA; *Mills v Edwards* [1971] 1 QB 379, [1971] 1 All ER 922, CA. A notice to quit, which does not satisfy the requirements for its operation as a notice not subject to counter-notice and so fails to operate as such a notice, cannot be relied upon on such a failure to operate alternatively as a notice to quit subject to counter-notice unless it is so framed as to make it unmistakably clear to the tenant that it is the landlord's intention that the notice should so operate: *Cowan v Wrayford* [1953] 2 All ER 1138, [1953] 1 WLR 1340, CA; *Mills v Edwards* [1971] 1 QB 379, [1971] 1 All ER 922, CA. See Ch 29 generally.

As to the effect of a fraudulent statement contained in a notice to quit served under this subsection, see *Rous v Mitchell, sub nom Earl of Stradbroke v Mitchell* [1991] 1 All ER 676, (1991) 61 P & CR 314, CA.

Compensation, etc. Compensation for disturbance is not payable under s 60 where the operation of sub-s (1) of this section above in relation to the relevant notice is excluded by virtue of Case C, D, E, F or G in Sch 3, Pt I; see s 61(1). Nor is additional compensation payable where the operation of sub-s (1) above is excluded by virtue of Case A or H in that Schedule; see s 61(2).

Supplementary provisions. See s 29, Sch 4, which inter alia empowers the Lord Chancellor to make orders supplementing the provisions of this section.

Servicemen. As to modifications regarding a notice to quit where the tenant of an agricultural holding is a service man, see s 30, Sch 5.

Definitions. For 'agricultural holding', see s 1(1); for 'landlord', 'tenant' and 'the Tribunal' see s 96(1).

A1.114

27   Tribunal's consent to operation of notice to quit

(1)   Subject to subsection (2) below, the Tribunal shall consent under section 26 above to the operation of a notice to quit an agricultural holding or part of an agricultural holding if, but only if, they are satisfied as to one or more of the matters mentioned in subsection (3) below, being a matter or matters specified by the landlord in his application for their consent.

(2)   Even if they are satisfied as mentioned in subsection (1) above, the Tribunal shall withhold consent under section 26 above to the operation of the notice to quit if in all the circumstances it appears to them that a fair and reasonable landlord would not insist on possession.

(3)   The matters referred to in subsection (1) above are—

(a)   that the carrying out of the purpose for which the landlord proposes to terminate the tenancy is desirable in the interests of good husbandry as respects the land to which the notice relates, treated as a separate unit;

(b)   that the carrying out of the purpose is desirable in the interests of sound management of the estate of which the land to which the notice relates forms part or which that land constitutes;

(c)   that the carrying out of the purpose is desirable for the purposes of agricultural research, education, experiment or demonstration, or for the purposes of the enactments relating to smallholdings;

(d)   that the carrying out of the purpose is desirable for the purposes of the enactments relating to allotments;

(e)   that greater hardship would be caused by withholding than by giving consent to the operation of the notice;

(f)   that the landlord proposes to terminate the tenancy for the purpose of the land's being used for a use, other than for agriculture, not falling within Case B.

(4)   Where the Tribunal consent under section 26 above to the operation of a notice to quit, they may impose such conditions as appear to them requisite for securing that the land to which the notice relates will be used for the purpose for which the landlord proposes to terminate the tenancy.

(5)   Where, on an application by the landlord, the Tribunal are satisfied that, by reason of any change of circumstances or otherwise, any condition imposed under subsection (4) above ought to be varied or revoked, they shall vary or revoke the condition accordingly.

(6)   Where—

(a)   on giving consent under section 26 above to the operation of a notice to quit the Tribunal imposed a condition under subsection (4) above, and

(b)   it is proved on an application to the Tribunal on behalf of the Crown that the landlord has acted in contravention of the condition or has failed within the time allowed by the condition to comply with it,

the Tribunal may by order impose on the landlord a penalty of an amount not exceeding two years' rent of the holding at the rate at which rent was payable immediately before the termination of the tenancy, or, where the notice to quit related to a part only of the holding, of an amount not exceeding the proportion of the said two years' rent which it appears to the Tribunal is attributable to that part.

(7)   The Tribunal may, in proceedings under this section, by order provide for the payment by any party of such sum as the Tribunal consider a reasonable contribution towards costs.

(8)   A penalty imposed under subsection (6) above shall be a debt due to the Crown and shall, when recovered, be paid into the Consolidated Fund.

(9)   An order under subsection (6) or (7) above shall be enforceable in the same manner as a judgment or order of the county court to the like effect.

NOTES

Derivation

This section derived from the Agricultural Holdings (Notices to Quit) Act 1977, ss 3, 6.

Initial Commencement

Specified date: 18 June 1986: see s 102(2).

Extent

This Act does not extend to Scotland.

See Further

See further, as to the exclusion of this Act in relation to leases or tenancies granted to contractors in respect of the running of any removal centre or part of a removal centre: the Immigration and Asylum Act 1999, s 149(3).

Notes

For a commentary, see para 30.4 ff.

Sub-ss (1)–(5) contain provisions formerly in the Agricultural Holdings (Notices to Quit) Act 1977, s 3(1)–(5), respectively. Sub-ss (6), (7), (8), (9) contain provisions formerly in s 6(1), (3), (2), (4), respectively, of the 1977 Act.

Sub-s (1): Notice to quit. See the notes to ss 25, 26.

An agricultural holding or part of an agricultural holding. See the note to s 25.

Sub-s (2). This subsection confers a discretion, but a case for its exercise does not arise unless the Tribunal are satisfied as to one or more of the matters specified in sub-s (3): *Evans v Roper* [1960] 2 All ER 507, [1960] 1 WLR 814.

Sub-s (3)(b). The adverse effect upon the tenant and his farm of the removal of land from the holding is not a factor to be taken into consideration in deciding whether this ground is established, but may well be one of the matters to which the Tribunal will pay regard in considering under sub-s (2) whether a fair and reasonable landlord would insist on possession: *Evans v Roper* [1960] 2 All ER 507, [1960] 1 WLR 814. In order to come within this ground, the purpose must be one which relates to the physical management of the land, and not one which will merely benefit the landlord financially: *National Coal Board v Naylor* [1972] 1 All ER 1153, [1972] 1 WLR 908.

Sub-s (3)(c), (d): Enactments relating to smallholdings; allotments. For the principal enactments relating to smallholdings and allotments, see the Allotments Acts 1922 to 1950, and the Agriculture Act 1970, Pt III.

Sub-s (3)(e): Greater hardship. In assessing hardship the Tribunal are entitled to consider hardship to all who may be affected, and to consider hardship notwithstanding the fact that it may have other contributory causes: *Purser v Bailey* [1967] 2 QB 500, [1967] 2 All ER 189, CA.

Sub-s (3)(f). Use for 'permitted activities' as defined in the Opencast Coal Act 1958, s 1, does not satisfy the requirements of this paragraph; see s 14(5) of the 1958 Act.

Sub-s (4): Condition. A condition requiring the grant to the tenant by the landlord of a new lease of part of the land to which the notice to quit relates is not a condition which the tribunal has power to attach by virtue of this provision: *R v Agricultural Land Tribunal (South-Eastern Area), ex p Boucher* (1952) 159 Estates Gazette 192. Semble that the tenant cannot set up any breach by the landlord of a condition imposed under this subsection as a defence to a summons for possession: *Martin-Smith v Smale* [1954] 1 All ER 237, [1954] 1 WLR 247, CA.

Sub-s (5): Application by the landlord. For the relevant form of application, see the Agricultural Land Tribunals (Rules) Order 1978, SI 1978/259, Sch 1, r 5, Form 4, as construed in accordance with s 99, Sch 13, para 1.

Sub-s (8): Consolidated Fund. Ie the Consolidated Fund of the United Kingdom which was established by the Consolidated Fund Act 1816, s 1.

Sub-s (9): Shall be enforceable in the same manner, etc. In this connection, see, in particular, CCR Ord 44, r 4, (see Civil Procedure 2007 Vol 1 at p 2231) as construed in accordance with s 99, Sch 13, para 1.

Compensation. In connection with sub-s (3) note the provisions of s 61(3)–(5) as to when additional compensation for disturbance under s 60 is not payable.

Applications. This section is applied for the purposes of s 44; see sub-s (2) of that section.

Servicemen. As to modifications regarding a notice to quit where the tenant of an agricultural holding is a service man, see s 30, Sch 5.

Supplementary provisions. See s 29, Sch 4, which inter alia empower the Lord Chancellor to make orders supplementing the provisions of this section.

Definitions. For 'agricultural holding', see s 1(1); for 'contract of tenancy', see s 1(5); for 'Case B', see s 26(2); for 'agriculture', 'landlord', 'termination' and 'the Tribunal', see s 96(1). As to 'interests of good husbandry' and 'interests of sound management', cf s 96(3); and as to 'use of land for agriculture', see s 96(5). Note also as to 'termination', s 74(4).

A1.115

28   Additional restrictions on operation of notice to quit given under Case D

(1)   This section applies where—

   (a)   notice to quit an agricultural holding or part of an agricultural holding is given to the tenant, and

   (b)   the notice includes a statement in accordance with Case D to the effect that it is given by reason of the tenant's failure to comply with a notice to do work.

(2)   If the tenant serves on the landlord a counter-notice in writing in accordance with subsection (3) or (4) below requiring that this subsection shall apply to the notice to quit, the notice to quit shall not have effect (whether as a notice to which section 26(1) above does or does not apply) unless, on an application by the landlord, the Tribunal consent to its operation.

(3)   Subject to subsection (4) below, a counter-notice under subsection (2) above shall be served not later than one month from the giving of the notice to quit.

(4)   Where the tenant not later than one month from the giving of the notice to quit serves on the landlord an effective notice requiring the validity of the reason stated in the notice to quit to be determined by arbitration under this Act—

   (a)   any counter-notice already served under subsection (2) above shall be of no effect, but

   (b)   if the notice to quit would, apart from this subsection, have effect in consequence of the arbitration, the tenant may serve a counter-notice under subsection (2) not later than one month from the date on which the arbitrator's award is delivered to him.

(5)   The Tribunal shall consent under subsection (2) above to the operation of the notice to quit unless it appears to them, having regard—

   (a)   to the extent to which the tenant has failed to comply with the notice to do work,

   (b)   to the consequences of his failure to comply with it in any respect, and

   (c)   to the circumstances surrounding any such failure,

that a fair and reasonable landlord would not insist on possession.

(6)   In this section 'notice to do work' means a notice served on a tenant of an agricultural holding for the purposes of paragraph (b) of Case D, being a notice requiring the doing of any work of repair, maintenance or replacement.

NOTES

Derivation

Sub-ss (1)–(4), (6) derived from the Agricultural Holdings (Notices to Quit) Act 1977, s 4(1)–(3), (5); sub-s (5) derived from the Agricultural Holdings (Notices to Quit) Act 1977, s 4(4), and the Agricultural Holdings Act 1984, s 7.

Initial Commencement

Specified date: 18 June 1986: see s 102(2).

Extent

This Act does not extend to Scotland.

See Further

See further, as to the exclusion of this Act in relation to leases or tenancies granted to contractors in respect of the running of any removal centre or part of a removal centre: the Immigration and Asylum Act 1999, s 149(3).

Notes

For a commentary, see para 31.47.

Sub-ss (1), (3), (6) contain provisions formerly in the Agricultural Holdings (Notices to Quit) Act 1977, s 4(1), (2), (5), respectively. Sub-ss (2), (4) each contain provisions formerly in s 4(4) of the 1977 Act. Sub-s (5) contains provisions formerly in s 4(4) of the 1977 Act, as amended by the Agricultural Holdings Act 1984, s 7.

Sub-s (1): Notice to quit. See the notes to ss 25, 26.

An agricultural holding or part of an agricultural holding. See the note to s 25.

Sub-s (2): Counter-notice. As to service, see s 93. See also, as to the position of counter-notices served under this provision with respect to statutory succession by person nominated by retiring tenant, ss 51(5)(b), 52(3)(b).

Writing. See the note 'Written' to s 3.

Application by the landlord. For the time limit for applications and the form to be used, see the Agricultural Land Tribunals (Rules) Order 1978, SI 1978/259, Sch 1, r 2(2), (3), Form 1, as construed in accordance with s 99(1) and Sch 13, para 1(2).

Sub-s (3): One month from, etc. See the note 'Two months from, etc' to s 10.

Sub-s (4): Arbitration under this Act. For provisions as to arbitration under this Act, see s 84 and the note to s 2.

Supplementary provisions. See s 29, Sch 4, which inter alia empower the Lord Chancellor to make orders supplementing the provisions of this section.

Definitions. For 'agricultural holding', see s 1(1); for 'Case D', see s 26(2); for 'landlord', 'tenant' and 'the Tribunal', see s 96(1).

A1.116

29 Power to make supplementary provision

The Lord Chancellor may by order provide for any of the matters specified in Schedule 4 to this Act.

NOTES

Derivation

This section derived from the Agricultural Holdings (Notices to Quit) Act 1977, s 5(1).

Initial Commencement

Specified date: 18 June 1986: see s 102(2).

Extent

This Act does not extend to Scotland.

See Further

See further, as to the exclusion of this Act in relation to leases or tenancies granted to contractors in respect of the running of any removal centre or part of a removal centre: the Immigration and Asylum Act 1999, s 149(3).

Notes

This section contains provisions formerly in the Agricultural Holdings (Notices to Quit) Act 1977, s 5(1).

Lord Chancellor. Ie the Lord High Chancellor of Great Britain; see the Interpretation Act 1978, s 5, Sch 1.

Servicemen. See the note to Sch 4.

Orders under this section. The Agricultural Holdings (Arbitration on Notices) Order 1987, SI 1987/710.

A1.117

30   Notice to quit where tenant is a service man

Schedule 5 to this Act, which makes provision as to notices to quit in cases where the tenant of an agricultural holding is a service man, shall have effect.

NOTES

Initial Commencement

Specified date: 18 June 1986: see s 102(2).

Extent

This Act does not extend to Scotland.

See Further

See further, as to the exclusion of this Act in relation to leases or tenancies granted to contractors in respect of the running of any removal centre or part of a removal centre: the Immigration and Asylum Act 1999, s 149(3).

Notes

See para 27.9.

Definitions. For 'agricultural holding', see s 1(1); for 'tenant', see s 96(1).

Notices to quit part of agricultural holding

A1.118

31   Notice to quit part of holding valid in certain cases

(1)   A notice to quit part of an agricultural holding held on a tenancy from year to year given by the landlord of the holding shall not be invalid on the ground that it relates to part only of the holding if it is given—

(a)   for the purpose of adjusting the boundaries between agricultural units or amalgamating agricultural units or parts of such units, or

   (b)   with a view to the use of the land to which the notice relates for any of the objects mentioned in subsection (2) below,

and the notice states that it is given for that purpose or with a view to any such use, as the case may be.

(2)   The objects referred to in subsection (1) above are—

   (a)   the erection of cottages or other houses for farm labourers, whether with or without gardens;
   (b)   the provision of gardens for cottages or other houses for farm labourers;
   (c)   the provision of allotments;
   (d)   the letting of land (with or without other land) as a smallholding under Part III of the Agriculture Act 1970;
   (e)   the planting of trees;
   (f)   the opening or working of a deposit of coal, ironstone, limestone, brick-earth or other mineral, or a stone quarry or a clay, sand or gravel pit, or the construction of any works or buildings to be used in connection therewith;
   (g)   the making of a watercourse or reservoir;
   (h)   the making of a road, railway, tramroad, siding, canal or basin, or a wharf, pier, or other work connected therewith.

NOTES

Derivation

Sub-s (1) derived from the Agricultural Holdings (Notices to Quit) Act 1977, s 8(1); sub-s (2) derived from the Agricultural Holdings (Notices to Quit) Act 1977, s 8(2), and the Agricultural Holdings Act 1984, s 10(1), Sch 3, para 39.

Initial Commencement

Specified date: 18 June 1986: see s 102(2).

Extent

This Act does not extend to Scotland.

See Further

See further, as to the exclusion of this Act in relation to leases or tenancies granted to contractors in respect of the running of any removal centre or part of a removal centre: the Immigration and Asylum Act 1999, s 149(3).

Notes

For a commentary, see para 29.4 ff.

Sub-s (1) contains provisions formerly in the Agricultural Holdings (Notices to Quit) Act 1977, s 8(1). Sub-s (2) contains provisions formerly in s 8(2) of that Act, as amended by the Agricultural Holdings Act 1984, s 10(1), Sch 3, para 39.

Notice to quit part ... shall not be invalid, etc. A notice to quit part only of demised premises was bad at common law: see *Re Bebington's Tenancy, Bebington v Wildman* [1921] 1 Ch 559; *Woodward v Earl of Dudley* [1954] Ch 283, [1954] 1 All ER 559. See also s 32, and the notes 'Notice to quit' to ss 25, 26.

Note that the landlord's notice to quit part of the premises must be in writing: cf *R v Shurmer* (1886) 17 QBD 323; *R v Harris* (1918) 82 JP 196.

Resumption of possession, etc. See the Agriculture Act 1986, s 13, Sch 1, para 13.

Supplementary provisions. For the tenant's right to cause a notice to quit rendered valid by this section to operate as respects the entire holding, see s 32. As to reduction of rent where the landlord resumes possession of part of the holding by virtue of sub-s(1) above, see s 33; and as to compensation in such a case, see s 74 (and see also s 63(3)).

Definitions. For 'agricultural holding', see s 1(1); for 'agricultural land', 'landlord' and 'building', see s 96(1).

Agriculture Act 1970, Part III. Ie ss 37–65 of that Act.

A1.119

32   Right to treat notice to quit part of holding as notice to quit entire holding

(1)   Where there is given to the tenant of an agricultural holding a notice to quit part of the holding, being either—

- (a)   such a notice as is rendered valid by section 31 above, or
- (b)   a notice given by a person entitled to a severed part of the reversionary estate in the holding,

subsection (2) below shall apply.

(2)   If—

- (a)   within twenty-eight days after the giving of the notice, or
- (b)   where the operation of the notice depends on any proceedings under this Part of this Act, within twenty-eight days after the time at which it is determined that the notice has effect,

the tenant gives to the landlord or (as the case may be) to the persons severally entitled to the severed parts of the reversion a counter-notice in writing to the effect that he accepts the notice to quit as a notice to quit the entire holding given by the landlord or (as the case may be) those persons, to take effect at the same time as the original notice, the notice to quit shall have effect accordingly.

NOTES

Derivation

This section derived from the Agricultural Holdings (Notices to Quit) Act 1977, s 9.

Initial Commencement

Specified date: 18 June 1986: see s 102(2).

Extent

This Act does not extend to Scotland.

See Further

See further, in relation to a counter-notice: the Land Compensation Act 1973, s 59(6).

See further, as to the exclusion of this Act in relation to leases or tenancies granted to contractors in respect of the running of any removal centre or part of a removal centre: the Immigration and Asylum Act 1999, s 149(3).

Notes

For a commentary, see para 29.7.

This section contains provisions formerly in the Agricultural Holdings (Notices to Quit) Act 1977, s 9.

Notice to quit. See the notes to ss 25, 26.

Twenty-eight days after, etc. See the note 'Two months from, etc' to s 10.

This Part of this Act. Ie Pt III (ss 25–33) of this Act.

Counter-notice. As to service, see s 93; and for the right to compensation for disturbance where a tenancy terminates by virtue of a counter-notice under this section, see s 60.

Writing. See the note 'Written' to s 3.

Notice of entry compensation. A person served with a notice to quit part of an agricultural holding is not entitled to make both an election under the Land Compensation Act 1973, s 59 and to give a counter-notice under this section; see s 59(6) of the 1973 Act, as amended by s 100, Sch 14, para 55(4).

Definitions. For 'agricultural holding', see s 1(1); for 'landlord' and 'tenant', see s 96(1).

A1.120

33   Reduction of rent where notice is given to quit part of holding

(1)   Where the landlord of an agricultural holding resumes possession of part of the holding either—

    (a)   by virtue of section 31(1) above, or

    (b)   in pursuance of a provision in that behalf contained in the contract of tenancy,

the tenant shall be entitled to a reduction of rent proportionate to that part of the holding and in respect of any depreciation of the value to him of the residue of the holding caused by the severance or by the use to be made of the part severed.

(2)   The amount of any reduction of rent under this section shall, in default of agreement made after the landlord resumes possession of the part of the holding concerned, be determined by arbitration under this Act.

(3)   In a case falling within subsection (1)(b) above that falls to be determined by arbitration under this Act the arbitrator, in assessing the amount of the reduction, shall take into consideration any benefit or relief allowed to the tenant under the contract of tenancy in respect of the land possession of which is resumed by the landlord.

NOTES

Derivation

This section derived from the Agricultural Holdings (Notices to Quit) Act 1977, s 10(1), (1A), (2), and the Agricultural Holdings Act 1984, s 10(1), Sch 3, para 40.

Initial Commencement

Specified date: 18 June 1986: see s 102(2).

Extent

This Act does not extend to Scotland.

See Further

See further, as to the exclusion of this Act in relation to leases or tenancies granted to contractors in respect of the running of any removal centre or part of a removal centre: the Immigration and Asylum Act 1999, s 149(3).

Notes

For a commentary, see para 29.8.

Sub-s (1) contains provisions formerly in the Agricultural Holdings (Notices to Quit) Act 1977, s 10(1), as repealed in part by the Agricultural Holdings Act 1984, s 10(1), Sch 3, para 40(a). Sub-ss (2), (3) contain provisions formerly in s 10(1A), (2) of the 1977 Act, respectively, as inserted in the case of sub-s (1A) of that section, and as amended in the case of sub-s (2) thereof, by s 10(1) of, and Sch 3, para 40(b), (c) to, the 1984 Act.

Arbitration under this Act. For provisions as to arbitration under this Act, see s 84 and the note to s 2.

Benefit. Cf the note to s 66.

Definitions. For 'agricultural holding', see s 1(1); for 'contract of tenancy', see s 1(5); for 'landlord' and 'tenant', see s 96(1).

PART IV: SUCCESSION ON DEATH OR RETIREMENT OF TENANT
Tenancies to which Part IV applies

A1.121

34   Tenancies to which Part IV applies

(1)   The provisions of this Part of this Act shall have effect with respect to—

    (a)   any tenancy of an agricultural holding granted before 12th July 1984, and

    (b)   a tenancy granted on or after that date if (but only if)—

        (i)   the tenancy was obtained by virtue of a direction of the Tribunal under section 39 or 53 below,

       (ii)   the tenancy was granted (following a direction under section 39 below) in circumstances within section 45(6) below,

      (iii)   the tenancy was granted by a written contract of tenancy indicating (in whatever terms) that this Part of this Act is to apply in relation to the tenancy, or

      (iv)   the tenancy was granted otherwise than as mentioned in the preceding provisions of this subsection to a person who, immediately before that date, was a tenant of the holding or of any agricultural holding which comprised the whole or a substantial part of the land comprised in the holding.

(2)   In this section 'tenant' does not include an executor, administrator, trustee in bankruptcy or other person deriving title from a tenant by operation of law.

[(3)   Where this Act applies in relation to a tenancy by virtue of section 4(1)(g) of the Agricultural Tenancies Act 1995, the reference in subsection (1)(b)(iv) above to a substantial part of the land comprised in the holding means a substantial part determined by reference to either area or value.]

NOTES

Derivation

Sub-s (1) derived from the Agricultural Holdings Act 1984, s 2, Sch 2, paras 1(1)(a), 10(1)(a); sub-s (2) derived from the Agriculture (Miscellaneous Provisions) Act 1976, s 18(1), and the Agricultural Holdings Act 1984, s 2(3).

Initial Commencement

Specified date: 18 June 1986: see s 102(2).

Extent

This Act does not extend to Scotland.

Amendment

Sub-s (3): inserted by SI 2006/2805, arts 2, 4(1).

Date in force: 19 October 2006: see SI 2006/2805, art 1(1)(b).

See Further

See further, as to the exclusion of this Act in relation to leases or tenancies granted to contractors in respect of the running of any removal centre or part of a removal centre: the Immigration and Asylum Act 1999, s 149(3).

Notes

For a commentary on succession on death, see Chapter 35 and on succession on retirement Chapter 36.

Sub-s (1) contains provisions formerly in the Agricultural Holdings Act 1984, s 2(1), (2), Sch 2, paras 1(1)(a), 10(1)(a). Sub-s (2) contains provisions formerly in the Agriculture (Miscellaneous Provisions) Act 1976, s 18(1), as applied by s 2(3) of the 1984 Act.

General Note. The Agriculture (Miscellaneous Provisions) Act 1976, ss 18–24 (repealed by s 101, Sch 15, Pt I), the provisions of which are now contained, generally, in ss 35 48, introduced a scheme for family succession on the death of a tenant of an agricultural holding (with the possibility of further succession on the death of the first successor). However that scheme was abolished, subject to certain exceptions, in the case of tenancies created on or after 12 July 1984 by the Agricultural Holdings Act 1984, s 2, the effect of which is now preserved by this section. The exceptions, which are now set out in sub-s (1)(b) above, are for tenancies which arise by way of succession to existing tenancies, or which the parties agree shall be subject to succession, or which are granted to a person who immediately before 12 July 1984 was tenant of the same or substantially the same holding.

As to the scheme for succession on the retirement of a tenant, which was introduced by the Agricultural Holdings Act 1984, s 4, Sch 2, and is now replaced by ss 49–58, see the General Note to s 49.

This Part of this Act. Ie Pt IV (ss 34–59) of this Act.

12th July 1984. This was the date on which the Agricultural Holdings Act 1984 (repealed by s 101, Sch 15, Pt I) was passed, ie received the Royal Assent. See, further, the General Note to this section above.

The Tribunal. See the note to s 11.

Written. See the note to s 3.

Definitions. For 'agricultural holding', see s 1(1); for 'contract of tenancy', see s 1(5); and for 'tenant', see s 96(1), but note sub-s (2) above.

Transitional provision. See s 99, Sch 13, para 12.

Succession on death of tenant

A1.122

35   Application of sections 36 to 48

(1)   Sections 36 to 48 below (except sections 40(5), 42 and 45(8) which are of general application) shall apply where—

(a)   an agricultural holding is held under a tenancy which falls within paragraph (a) or (b) of section 34(1) above, and

(b)   the sole (or sole surviving) tenant (within the meaning of that section) dies and is survived by a close relative of his.

(2)   In sections 36 to 48 below (and in Part I of Schedule 6 to this Act)—

'close relative' of a deceased tenant means—

    (a)   the wife[, husband or civil partner] of the deceased;

    (b)   a brother or sister of the deceased;

    (c)   a child of the deceased;

    (d)   any person (not within (b) or (c) above) who, in the case of any marriage [or civil partnership] to which the deceased was at any time a party, was treated by the deceased as a child of the family in relation to that marriage [or civil partnership];

'the date of death' means the date of the death of the deceased;

'the deceased' means the deceased tenant of the holding;

'the holding' (except where the context otherwise requires) means the agricultural holding mentioned in subsection (1) above;

'related holding' means, in relation to the holding, any agricultural holding comprising the whole or a substantial part of the land comprised in the holding;

'the tenancy' means the tenancy of the holding.

[(3)   Where this Act applies in relation to a tenancy by virtue of section 4(1)(g) of the Agricultural Tenancies Act 1995, the reference in subsection (2) above (in the definition of 'related holding') to a substantial part of the land comprised in the holding means a substantial part determined by reference to either area or value.]

NOTES

Derivation

This section derived from the Agriculture (Miscellaneous Provisions) Act 1976, s 18(1), (2), and the Agricultural Holdings Act 1984, ss 2(1), (2), 3, 4, Sch 1, paras 1, 5(1).

Initial Commencement

Specified date: 18 June 1986: see s 102(2).

Extent

This Act does not extend to Scotland.

Amendment

Sub-s (2): in definition 'close relative' in para (a) words ', husband or civil partner' in square brackets substituted by the Civil Partnership Act 2004, s 81, Sch 8, para 36(1), (2).

Date in force: 5 December 2005: see SI 2005/3175, art 2(1), Sch 1.

Sub-s (2): in definition 'close relative' in para (d) words 'or civil partnership' in square brackets in both places they occur inserted by the Civil Partnership Act 2004, s 81, Sch 8, para 36(1), (3).

Date in force: 5 December 2005: see SI 2005/3175, art 2(1), Sch 1.

Sub-s (3): inserted by SI 2006/2805, arts 2, 4(2).

Date in force: 19 October 2006: see SI 2006/2805, art 1(1)(b).

See Further

See further, as to the exclusion of this Act in relation to leases or tenancies granted to contractors in respect of the running of any removal centre or part of a removal centre: the Immigration and Asylum Act 1999, s 149(3).

Notes

For a commentary, see Chapter 35.

Sub-s (1) contains provisions formerly in the Agriculture (Miscellaneous Provisions) Act 1976, s 18(1), as affected by the Agricultural Holdings Act 1984, s 2(1), (2), and as amended by s 4 of, and Sch 1, para 5(1) to, the 1984 Act. Sub-s (2) contains provisions formerly in s 18(1), (2) of the 1976 Act, as amended, in the case of sub-s (2) of that section, by s 3 of, and Sch 1, para 1 to, the 1984 Act. Sub-s (2) was further amended by the Civil Partnerships Act 2004 s 81 and Sch 8. Sub-s (3) – inserted by RRO, SI 2006/2805 arts 2, 4(2).

General Note. See the General Note to s 34.

Close relative. This includes a civil partner. See the Civil Partnerships Act 2004, s 81 and Sch 8 para 36(2), (3).

Child. This includes an adopted child; see the Children Act 1989, s 105 and the Adoption Act 1976, s 39 as amended by the Adoption (Intercountry Aspects) Act 1999, s 4(3).

Child of the family. Cf the definition contained in the Matrimonial Causes Act 1973, s 52.

Definitions. For 'agricultural holding', see s 1(1); for 'tenant', see s 96(1) or s 34(2) (for the purposes of sub-s (1)(b) above). Note as to 'close relative', 'the date of death', 'the deceased', 'the holding', 'related holding' and 'the tenancy', sub-s (2) above.

A1.123

36   Right of any eligible person to apply for new tenancy on death of tenant

(1)   Any eligible person may apply under section 39 below to the Tribunal for a direction entitling him to a tenancy of the holding unless excluded by subsection (2) or section 37 or 38 below.

(2)   Subsection (1) above (and section 41 below) shall not apply if on the date of death the holding was held by the deceased under—

    (a)   a tenancy for a fixed term of years of which more than twenty-seven months remained unexpired, or

    (b)   a tenancy for a fixed term of more than one but less than two years.

(3)   For the purposes of this section and sections 37 to 48 below, 'eligible person' means (subject to the provisions of Part I of Schedule 6 to this Act and without prejudice to section 41 below) any surviving close relative of the deceased in whose case the following conditions are satisfied—

    (a)   in the seven years ending with the date of death his only or principal source of livelihood throughout a continuous period of not less than five years, or two or more discontinuous periods together amounting to not less than five years, derived from his agricultural work on the holding or on an agricultural unit of which the holding forms part, and

    (b)   he is not the occupier of a commercial unit of agricultural land.

(4)   In the case of the deceased's wife the reference in subsection (3)(a) above to the relative's agricultural work shall be read as a reference to agricultural work carried out by either the wife or the deceased (or both of them).

[(4A)   In the case of the deceased's civil partner the reference in subsection (3)(a) above to the relative's agricultural work shall be read as a reference to agricultural work carried out by either the civil partner or the deceased (or both of them).]

(5)   Part I of Schedule 6 to this Act, which supplements subsection (3) above and makes provision with respect to the assessment of the productive capacity of agricultural land for the purposes of paragraph (b) of that subsection, shall have effect.

[(6)   The reference in subsection (3)(a) above to agricultural work carried out by a person on the holding or on an agricultural unit of which the holding forms part includes—

    (a)   agricultural work carried out by him from the holding or an agricultural unit of which the holding forms part, and

(b) other work carried out by him on or from the holding or an agricultural unit of which the holding forms part,

which is of a description approved in writing by the landlord after the commencement of this subsection.]

NOTES

Derivation

Sub-ss (1), (2) derived from the Agriculture (Miscellaneous Provisions) Act 1976, ss 18(1), (4)(d), 20(1); sub-ss (3), (4) derived from the Agriculture (Miscellaneous Provisions) Act 1976, s 18(2), and the Agricultural Holdings Act 1984, s 3(2)(b).

Initial Commencement

Specified date: 18 June 1986: see s 102(2).

Extent

This Act does not extend to Scotland.

Amendment

Sub-s (4A): inserted by the Civil Partnership Act 2004, s 81, Sch 8, para 37.

Date in force: 5 December 2005: see SI 2005/3175, art 2(1), Sch 1.

Sub-s (6): inserted by SI 2006/2805, arts 2, 5(1).

Date in force: 19 October 2006: see SI 2006/2805, art 1(1)(b).

See Further

See further, as to the exclusion of this Act in relation to leases or tenancies granted to contractors in respect of the running of any removal centre or part of a removal centre: the Immigration and Asylum Act 1999, s 149(3).

Notes

For a commentary, see Chapter 35.

Sub-s (1) contains provisions formerly in the Agriculture (Miscellaneous Provisions) Act 1976, ss 18(1), 20(1). Sub-s (2) contains provisions formerly in s 18(4)(d) of the 1976 Act, as repealed in part by the Agricultural Holdings Act 1984, s 10(2), Sch 4. Sub-ss (3), (4) contain provisions formerly in the definition of 'eligible person' in s 18(2) of the 1976 Act, as repealed in part by s 10(2) of, and Sch 4 to, the 1984 Act, and as amended by s 3(2)(b) of the 1984 Act. Sub-s (5) is a drafting provision. Sub-s 6 was inserted by the RRO, SI 2006/2805 and was effective from 19 October 2006.

Sub-s (1): The Tribunal. See the note to s 11.

Sub-s (2): Tenancy for a fixed term of years. See, generally, 27 Halsbury's Laws (4th edn, reissue) paras 205–209.

Months. See the note to s 4.

Sub-s (3): Eligible person. As to application by not fully eligible person to be treated as eligible, see s 41, and *Littlewood v Rolfe* [1981] 2 All ER 51, 258 Estates Gazette 168; *Wilson v Earl Spencer's Settlement Trustees* (1985) 274 Estates Gazette 1254 and *Thomson v Church Commissioners for England* [2006] EWHC 1773 (Admin), [2006] 43 EG 180.

Sub-s 6: Inserted by RRO 2006, SI 2006/2805, art 5. See para 35.31.

Application; exclusion of section. As to the general application of this section, see s 35(1), but note the exclusion of sub-s (1) above regarding statutory succession where two successions have already occurred (s 37), and the other excluded cases contained in s 38. See also, as to the application or exclusion of this section on the death of a retiring tenant, s 57.

Modification of section. This section may be modified by regulations in cases where the person whom a direction (see s 39) entitles to a tenancy dies before the relevant time (defined by s 46(1), (2)); see s 45(8) and the note 'Regulations under this section' thereto.

Definitions. For 'agricultural land', see s 1(4); for 'close relative', 'the date of death', 'the deceased' and 'the holding', see s 35(2); for 'agricultural unit' and 'the Tribunal', see s 96(1); for 'commercial unit of agricultural land', see Sch 6, para 3. Note as to 'eligible person', sub-s (3) above.

A1.124

37   Exclusion of statutory succession where two successions have already occurred

(1)   Section 36(1) above (and section 41 below) shall not apply if on each of the last two occasions when there died a sole (or sole surviving) tenant of the holding or of a related holding there occurred one or other of the following things, namely—

(a)   a tenancy of the holding or of a related holding was obtained by virtue of a direction of the Tribunal under section 39 below, or such a tenancy was granted (following such a direction) in circumstances within section 45(6) below, or

(b)   a tenancy of the holding or of a related holding was granted by the landlord to a person who, being a close relative of the tenant who died on that occasion, was or had become the sole or sole remaining applicant for such a direction.

(2)   If on any occasion prior to the date of death, as a result of an agreement between the landlord and the tenant for the time being of the holding or of a related holding, the holding or a related holding became let—

(a)   under a tenancy granted by the landlord, or

(b)   by virtue of an assignment of the current tenancy,

to a person who, if the said tenant had died immediately before the grant or assignment would have been his close relative, that occasion shall for the purposes of subsection (1) above be deemed to be an occasion such as is mentioned in that subsection on which a tenancy of the holding or a related holding was obtained by virtue of a direction of the Tribunal under section 39 below.

(3)   If any such tenancy was granted as mentioned in subsection (2) above for a term commencing later than the date of the grant, the holding under that tenancy shall for the purposes of that subsection not be taken to have become let under that tenancy until the commencement of the term.

(4)   Subsections (1) and (2) above—

(a)   shall apply whether or not any tenancy granted or obtained (otherwise than by virtue of an assignment) as mentioned in those provisions related to the whole of the land held by the tenant on the occasion of whose death, or with whose agreement, the tenancy was so granted or obtained, as the case may be, and

(b)   shall apply where a joint tenancy is granted by the landlord to persons one of whom is a person such as is mentioned in either of those subsections as they apply where a tenancy is granted by the landlord to any such person alone.

(5)   Subsection (2) above shall apply where a tenancy is assigned to joint tenants one of whom is a person such as is mentioned in that subsection as it applies where a tenancy is assigned to any such person alone.

(6)   Where a tenancy of the holding or of a related holding was obtained by virtue of a direction of the Tribunal under section 53(7) below, that occasion shall for the

purposes of subsection (1) above be deemed to be an occasion such as is mentioned in that subsection on which a tenancy of the holding or a related holding was obtained by virtue of a direction of the Tribunal under section 39 below.

(7) Subsection (2) above shall, in relation to any time before 12th September 1984, have effect with the substitution for the words from 'as a result' to 'grant or assignment' of the words 'the holding or a related holding became let under a new tenancy granted by the landlord, with the agreement of the outgoing tenant, to a person who, if the outgoing tenant had died immediately before the grant'.

(8) Subsections (4) and (5) above shall not apply in relation to any tenancy if—

(a) it was granted before 12th September 1984,
(b) it was obtained by virtue of any direction given in any proceedings arising out of an application made under Part II of the Agriculture (Miscellaneous Provisions) Act 1976 before 12th September 1984, or
(c) it was granted (following such a direction) in circumstances within section 23(6) of the said Act of 1976.

(9) In this section 'tenant' has the same meaning as in section 34 above.

NOTES

Derivation

Sub-ss (1)–(5), (9) derived from the Agriculture (Miscellaneous Provisions) Act 1976, s 18(4)(e), (5), (5A), and the Agricultural Holdings Act 1984, s 3(5), Sch 1, para 2(5), (7); sub-ss (6)–(8) derived from the Agricultural Holdings Act 1984, Sch 2, para 10(1)(b), (2), Sch 5, para 2(2).

Initial Commencement

Specified date: 18 June 1986: see s 102(2).

Extent

This Act does not extend to Scotland.

See Further

See further, as to the exclusion of this Act in relation to leases or tenancies granted to contractors in respect of the running of any removal centre or part of a removal centre: the Immigration and Asylum Act 1999, s 149(3).

Notes

For a commentary, see para 35.14 ff.

Sub-s (1) contains provisions formerly in the Agriculture (Miscellaneous Provisions) Act 1976, s 18(4)(e), as substituted by the Agricultural Holdings Act 1984, s 3(5), Sch 1, para 2(5). Sub-ss (2), (3) contain provisions formerly in s 18(5) of the 1976 Act, as substituted by s 3(5) of, and Sch 1, para 2(7) to, the 1984 Act. Sub-ss (4), (5) contain provisions formerly in s 18(5A) of the 1976 Act, as substituted by s 3(5) of, and Sch 1, para 2(7) to, the 1984 Act. Sub-s (6) contains provisions formerly in Sch 2, para 10(1)(b) to the 1984 Act. Sub-ss (7), (8) contain provisions formerly in Sch 5, para 2(2)(a), (b), respectively, to the 1984 Act. Sub-s (9) contains provisions formerly in s 18(4)(e), (5) of the 1976 Act, as substituted by s 3(5) of, and Sch 1, para 2(5), (7) to, the 1984 Act.

Sub-s (1): The Tribunal. See the note to s 11.

Sub-s (2). As to the construction of this section, and of sub-s (2) in particular, see *Saunders' Trustees v Ralph* (1993) 66 P & CR 335; [1993] 2 EGLR 1.

Sub-s (7): 12th September 1984. This was the commencement date for the relevant provisions of the Agricultural Holdings Act 1984 under s 11(2) of that Act (repealed by s 101, Sch 15, Pt I).

Application; exclusion of section. As to the general application of this section, see s 35(1); and as to the application and modification of this section for the purposes of excluding s 50(1) (right to apply for new tenancy on retirement of tenant), see s 51(1). See also as to the application or exclusion of this section on the death of a retiring tenant, s 57.

Modification of section. This section may be modified by regulations in cases where the person whom a direction (see s 39) entitles to a tenancy dies before the relevant time (defined by s 46(1), (2)); see s 45(8) and the note 'Regulations under this section' thereto.

In addition, sub-s (6) above may be modified by regulations in cases where the nominated successor, being entitled to a tenancy by virtue of a direction under s 53(7), dies before the relevant time (defined in s 55(8)); see s 55(7) and the note 'Regulations under this section' thereto. Cf, also, the note 'Application; exclusion of section' above.

Definitions. For 'close relative', 'the date of death', 'the holding' and 'related holding', see s 35(2); for 'agreement', 'landlord', 'tenant' and 'the Tribunal', see s 96(1) (and see also, as to 'tenant', s 34(2) as applied by sub-s (9) above).

Agriculture (Miscellaneous Provisions) Act 1976, Part II. Ie ss 18–24 of that Act (repealed by s 101, Sch 15, Pt I).

A1.125

38   Other excluded cases

(1)   Section 36(1) above (and section 41 below) shall not apply if on the date of death the tenancy is the subject of a valid notice to quit to which subsection (1) of section 26 above applies, being a notice given before that date in the case of which—

  (a)   the month allowed by that subsection for serving a counter-notice under that subsection expired before that date without such a counter-notice having been served, or

  (b)   the Tribunal consented before that date to its operation.

(2)   Section 36(1) (and section 41) shall not apply if on the date of death the tenancy is the subject of a valid notice to quit given before that date and falling within Case C or F.

(3)   Those sections shall not apply if on the date of death the tenancy is the subject of a valid notice to quit given before that date and falling within Case B, D or E, and

  (a)   the time within which the tenant, could have required any question arising in connection with the notice to be determined by arbitration under this Act expired before that date without such a requirement having been made by the tenant, and the month allowed for serving any counter-notice in respect of the notice expired before that date without any such counter-notice having been served, or

  (b)   questions arising in connection with the notice were referred to arbitration under this Act before that date and were determined before that date in such a way as to uphold the operation of the notice and (where applicable) the month allowed for serving any counter-notice in respect of the notice expired before that date without a counter-notice having been served, or

  (c)   the Tribunal consented before that date to the operation of the notice.

(4)   Those sections shall not apply if the holding consists of land held by a smallholdings authority or the Minister for the purposes of smallholdings within the meaning of Part III of the Agriculture Act 1970 (whether the tenancy was granted before or after the commencement of the said Part III).

(5)   Those sections shall not apply if the tenancy was granted by trustees in whom the land is vested on charitable trusts the sole or principal object of which is the settlement or employment in agriculture of persons who have served in any of Her Majesty's naval, military or air forces.

NOTES

Derivation

Sub-ss (1)–(3) derived from the Agriculture (Miscellaneous Provisions) Act 1976, s 18(4)(a)–(c), the Agricultural Holdings (Notices to Quit) Act 1977, s 13(1), Sch 1, para 7(2)(b)–(d), and the Agricultural Holdings Act 1984, ss 3(5), 10(1), Sch 1, para 2(2), (3), Sch 3, para 34; sub-s (4) derived from the Agriculture (Miscellaneous Provisions) Act 1976, s 18(4)(f), and the Agricultural Holdings Act 1984, s 3(5), Sch 1, para 2(6); sub-s (5) derived from the Agriculture (Miscellaneous Provisions) Act 1976, s 18(4)(g).

Initial Commencement

Specified date: 18 June 1986: see s 102(2).

Extent

This Act does not extend to Scotland.

See Further

See further, as to the exclusion of this Act in relation to leases or tenancies granted to contractors in respect of the running of any removal centre or part of a removal centre: the Immigration and Asylum Act 1999, s 149(3).

Transfer of Functions

Functions of the Minister, so far as exercisable in relation to Wales, transferred to the National Assembly for Wales, by the National Assembly for Wales (Transfer of Functions) Order 1999, SI 1999/672, art 2, Sch 1.

Notes

For a commentary, see para 35.10 ff.

Sub-s (1) contains provisions formerly in the Agriculture (Miscellaneous Provisions) Act 1976, s 18(4)(a), as amended by the Agricultural Holdings (Notices to Quit) Act 1977, s 13(1), Sch 1, para 7(2)(b), and by the Agricultural Holdings Act 1984, s 3(5), Sch 1, para 2(2). Sub-s (2) contains provisions formerly in s 18(4)(b) of the 1976 Act, as amended by s 13(1) of, and Sch 1, para 7(2)(c) to, the 1977 Act, and by s 10(1) of, and Sch 3, para 34 to, the 1984 Act. Sub-s (3) contains provisions formerly in s 18(4)(c) of the 1976 Act, as amended by s 13(1) of, and Sch 1, para 7(2)(d) to, the 1977 Act, and by s 3(5) of, and Sch 1, para 2(3) to, the 1984 Act. Sub-s (4) contains provisions formerly in s 18(4)(f) of the 1976 Act, as amended by s 3(5) of, and Sch 1, para 2(6) to, the 1984 Act. Sub-s (5) contains provisions formerly in s 18(4)(g) of the 1976 Act.

Sub-s (1): The Tribunal. See the note to s 11.

Sub-s (3): Time within which the tenant could have required ... arbitration under this Act. As to arbitration under this Act, see s 84 and the note to s 2. See also the Agricultural Holdings (Arbitration on Notices) Order 1987, SI 1987/710, art 9, which provides that where it is stated in a notice to quit that it is given for one or more of the reasons specified in Case A, B, D or E (as to which, see Sch 3, Pt I), and the tenant wishes to contest any of the reasons so stated, he shall within one month after the service of the notice serve on the landlord notice requiring the question to be determined by arbitration.

Sub-s (4): Smallholdings authority. As to smallholdings authorities, see the Agriculture Act 1970, s 38. See para 35.12.

Whether the tenancy was granted before or after the commencement, etc. The provision, which was originally introduced by the Agricultural Holdings Act 1984, s 3(5), Sch 1, para 2(6) (repealed by s 101, Sch 15, Pt I), negatived the decision in *Saul v Norfolk County Council* [1984] QB 559, [1984] 2 All ER 489, CA, in which it was held that a tenancy granted by a smallholdings authority was not excluded from the statutory succession scheme in those cases where the tenancy had been granted not under the Agriculture Act 1970, Pt III, but under provisions which that Part replaced.

1135

Application; exclusion of section. As to the general application of this section, see s 35(1); and as to the application and modification of this section for the purposes of excluding s 50(1) (right to apply for new tenancy on retirement of tenant), see s 51(1). See also, as to the application or exclusion of this section on the death of a retiring tenant, s 57.

Modification of section. This section may be modified by regulations in cases where the person whom a direction (see s 39) entitles to a tenancy dies before the relevant time (defined by s 46(1), (2)); see s 45(8) and the note 'Regulations under this section' thereto. Cf, also, the note 'Application; exclusion of section' above.

Definitions. For 'the date of death' and 'the tenancy', see s 35(2); for 'Case B' etc, 'Landlord', 'the Minister', 'tenant' and 'the Tribunal', see s 96(1).

Agriculture Act 1970, Part III. Ie ss 37–65 of that Act. The Part came into force on 1 August 1970. As to land held by a smallholdings authority for the purposes of smallholdings, see s 37(2) of the 1970 Act; as to lettings by a smallholdings authority, see, in particular, s 44 of that Act; and as to land held by the Minister for the purposes of smallholdings, see s 54 of that Act.

A1.126

39   Applications for tenancy of holding

(1)   An application under this section by an eligible person to the Tribunal for a direction entitling him to a tenancy of the holding shall be made within the period of three months beginning with the day after the date of death.

(2)   Where only one application is made under this section the Tribunal, if satisfied—

(a)   that the applicant was an eligible person at the date of death, and
(b)   that he has not subsequently ceased to be such a person,

shall determine whether he is in their opinion a suitable person to become the tenant of the holding.

(3)   Where two or more applications are made under this section, then, subject to subsection (4) below, subsection (2) above shall apply to each of the applicants as if he were the only applicant.

(4)   If the applicants under this section include a person validly designated by the deceased in his will as the person he wished to succeed him as tenant of the holding, the Tribunal shall first make a determination under subsection (2) above as regards that person, and shall do so as regards the other applicant or each of the other applicants only if the Tribunal determine that the person so designated is not in their opinion a suitable person to become the tenant of the holding.

(5)   If under the preceding provisions of this section only one applicant is determined by the Tribunal to be in their opinion a suitable person to become the tenant of the holding, the Tribunal shall, subject to subsection (10) and section 44 below, give a direction entitling him to a tenancy of the holding.

(6)   If under the preceding provisions of this section each of two or more applicants is determined by the Tribunal to be in their opinion a suitable person to become the tenant of the holding, the Tribunal—

(a)   shall, subject to subsection (9) below, determine which of those applicants is in their opinion the more or most suitable person to become the tenant of the holding, and
(b)   shall, subject to subsection (10) and section 44 below, give a direction entitling that applicant to a tenancy of the holding.

(7)   Before making a determination under subsection (2) above in the case of any applicant the Tribunal shall afford the landlord an opportunity of stating his views on the suitability of that applicant.

(8) In making a determination under subsection (2) above in the case of a particular applicant, or a determination under subsection (6) above as between two or more applicants, the Tribunal shall have regard to all relevant matters including—

    (a) the extent to which the applicant or each of those applicants has been trained in, or has had practical experience of, agriculture,

    (b) the age, physical health and financial standing of the applicant or each of those applicants, and

    (c) the views (if any) stated by the landlord on the suitability of the applicant or any of those applicants.

(9) Where subsection (6) above would apply apart from this subsection, the Tribunal may, with the consent of the landlord, give instead a direction specifying any two, any three or any four of the applicants within that subsection, and entitling the specified applicants to a joint tenancy of the holding.

(10) Where the person or persons who would, subject to section 44 below, be entitled to a direction under this section entitling him or them to a tenancy or (as the case may be) to a joint tenancy of the holding agree to accept instead a tenancy or joint tenancy of a part of the holding, any direction given by the Tribunal under subsection (5), (6) or (9) above shall relate to that part of the holding only.

NOTES

Derivation

Sub-ss (1), (3), (4), (7)–(9) derived from the Agriculture (Miscellaneous Provisions) Act 1976, ss 18(2), 20(1), (3), (4), (7)–(9); sub-ss (2), (5), (6), (10) derived from the Agriculture (Miscellaneous Provisions) Act 1976, s 20(2), (5), (6), (9A), and the Agricultural Holdings Act 1984, s 3(5), Sch 1, paras 3(3)(a), (b), 4.

Initial Commencement

Specified date: 18 June 1986: see s 102(2).

Extent

This Act does not extend to Scotland.

See Further

See further, as to the exclusion of this Act in relation to leases or tenancies granted to contractors in respect of the running of any removal centre or part of a removal centre: the Immigration and Asylum Act 1999, s 149(3).

Notes

For a commentary, see para 35.15 and 35.86 ff.

Sub-s (1) contains provisions formerly in the Agriculture (Miscellaneous Provisions) Act 1976, ss 18(2), 20(1). Sub-ss (2)–(9), (10) contain provisions formerly in s 20(2)–(9), (9A), respectively, of the 1976 Act, as amended, in the case of sub-s (2) of that section, by the Agricultural Holdings Act 1984, s 3(5), Sch 1, para 4, in the case of sub-ss (5), (6) of that section, by s 3(5) of, and Sch 1, para 3(3)(a) to, the 1984 Act, and as inserted in the case of sub-s (9A) of that section, by s 3(5) of, and Sch 1, para 33(3)(b) to, the 1984 Act.

General Note. Note that this Part of this Act (Pt IV) applies to tenancies obtained, by virtue of a direction of the Tribunal under this section, on or after 12 July 1984, in addition to those granted before that date; see s 34(1).

Sub-s (1): Application ... by an eligible person. See s 41 as to application by a person who is not fully eligible to be treated as eligible. See also, as to when eligible persons may apply under this section, s 36(1); and as to procedure where the deceased held more than one holding, s 42.

Three months beginning with, etc. See para 42.27 on the computation of time. The use of the words 'beginning with' makes it clear that in computing this period the day from which it runs is to be included: see *Hare v Gocher* [1962] 2 QB 641, [1962] 2 All ER 763, and *Trow v Ind Coope (West Midlands) Ltd* [1967] 2 QB 899 at 909, [1967] 2 All ER 900, CA. See also *Dodds v Walker* [1981] 2 All ER 609, [1981] 1 WLR 1027, HL, and 45 Halsbury's Laws (4th edn) para 1111, as to the day of expiry of periods of a month or a specified number of months.

Sub-s (2). Sub-s (2)(a) and (b) make statutory the rule laid down in *Jackson v Hall* [1980] AC 854, [1980] 1 All ER 177, HL, that to satisfy the tests of eligibility for succession the applicant must be an eligible person at the time of the death of the tenant and must continue to be so at the time when the application is heard by the Tribunal.

Sub-s (4): Designated by the deceased in his will. See s 40(1), (2).

Sub-ss (5), (6): Tribunal shall … give a direction, etc. As to the effect of a direction under sub-s (5), (6) and (9) of this section, see s 45 (as read with s 46): as to the terms of the new tenancy, see s 47; and as to arbitration on the terms of the new tenancy, see s 48. See also s 40(3).

Sub-s (9): Tribunal may … give instead a direction. See the note to sub-ss (5), (6) above.

Application; exclusion of section. As to the general application of this section, see s 35(1); and as to the application or exclusion of this section on the death of a retiring tenant, see s 57.

Modification of section. This section may be modified by regulations in cases where the person whom a direction under this section entitles to a tenancy dies before the relevant time (defined by s 46(1), (2)); see s 45(8) and the note 'Regulations under this section' thereto.

Supplementary provisions. See s 40.

Definitions. For 'the date of death' and 'the holding', see s 35(2); for 'eligible person', see s 36(3); for 'will', see s 40(1); for 'agriculture', 'landlord', 'tenant' and 'the Tribunal', see s 96(1).

Rules of procedure. See the note to s 40.

A1.127

40   Provisions supplementary to section 39

(1)   In section 39 above 'will' includes codicil, and for the purposes of that section a person shall be taken to be validly designated by the deceased in his will as the person he wishes to succeed him as tenant of the holding if, but only if, a will of the deceased which is the subject of a grant of probate or administration—

 (a)   contains an effective specific bequest to that person of the deceased's tenancy of the holding, or

 (b)   does not contain an effective specific bequest of that tenancy, but does contain a statement specifically mentioning the holding or the deceased's tenancy of the holding and exclusively designating that person (in whatever words, and whether by name or description) as the person whom the deceased wishes to succeed him as tenant of the holding.

(2)   For the purposes of subsection (1) above a statement which is framed so as to designate as mentioned in paragraph (b) of that subsection different persons in different circumstances shall be taken to satisfy that paragraph if, in the events which have happened, the statement exclusively designates a particular person.

(3)   A direction under section 39 above given in favour of a person by reason of his being a person validly designated by the deceased as mentioned in subsection (4) of that section shall be valid even if the probate or administration by virtue of which he was such a person at the giving of the direction is subsequently revoked or varied.

(4)   For the purposes of this Part of this Act an application under section 39 above which is withdrawn or abandoned shall be treated as if it had never been made.

(5)   Provision shall be made by order under section 73(3) of the Agriculture Act 1947 (procedure of Agricultural Land Tribunals) for requiring any person making an application to the Tribunal under section 39 above or section 41 below to give notice of the application to the landlord of the agricultural holding to which the application relates and to take such steps as the order may require for bringing the application to the notice of other persons interested in the outcome of the application.

NOTES

Derivation

This section derived from the Agriculture (Miscellaneous Provisions) Act 1976, s 20(10)–(14).

Initial Commencement

Specified date: 18 June 1986: see s 102(2).

Extent

This Act does not extend to Scotland.

See Further

See further, as to the exclusion of this Act in relation to leases or tenancies granted to contractors in respect of the running of any removal centre or part of a removal centre: the Immigration and Asylum Act 1999, s 149(3).

Notes

For a commentary, see Ch 35.

Sub-ss (1)–(5) contain provisions formerly in the Agriculture (Miscellaneous Provisions) Act 1976, s 20(10)–(14), respectively.

Sub-s (1): Grant of probate or administration. See, generally, 17(2) Halsbury's Laws (4th edn) re-issue paras 772 ff.

Sub-s (4): This Part of this Act. Ie Pt IV (ss 34–59) of this Act.

Application; exclusion of section. As to the general application of this section, except sub-s (5) above, see s 35(1); and as to the application or exclusion of this section on the death of a retiring tenant, see s 57.

Modification of section. This section may be modified by regulations in cases where the person whom a direction (see s 39) entitles to a tenancy dies before the relevant time (defined by s 46(1), (2)); see s 45(8) and the note 'Regulations under this section' thereto.

Definitions. For 'agricultural holding', see s 1(1); for 'the deceased' and 'the holding' see s 35(2); for 'landlord', 'tenant' and 'the Tribunal', see s 96(1).

Agriculture Act 1947, s 73(3). See the note 'Rules of procedure' below.

Rules of procedure. As to rules of procedure for Agricultural Land Tribunals for the purposes of applications made under this Part of this Act, see, as construed in accordance with s 99, Sch 13, para 1(2), the Agricultural Land Tribunals (Succession to Agricultural Tenancies) Order 1984, SI 1984/1301 (made under the Agriculture Act 1947, s 73(3)). As to applications to the Tribunal under s 39, and s 41, see r 3 in the Schedule to that Order; and as to the provision made for the purposes of sub-s (5) of this section, see r 5 in the Schedule to that Order.

A1.128

41   Application by not fully eligible person to be treated as eligible

(1)   This section applies to any surviving close relative of the deceased who for some part of the seven years ending with the date of death engaged (whether full-time or part-time) in agricultural work on the holding, being a person in whose case—

(a)   the condition specified in paragraph (b) of the definition of 'eligible person' in section 36(3) above is satisfied, and

(b)   the condition specified in paragraph (a) of that definition, though not fully satisfied, is satisfied to a material extent.

(2)   A person to whom this section applies may within the period of three months beginning with the day after the date of death apply to the Tribunal for a determination that he is to be treated as an eligible person for the purposes of sections 36 to 48 of this Act.

(3)   If on an application under this section—

(a)   the Tribunal are satisfied that the applicant is a person to whom this section applies, and

(b)   it appears to the Tribunal that in all the circumstances it would be fair and reasonable for the applicant to be able to apply under section 39 above for a direction entitling him to a tenancy of the holding,

the Tribunal shall determine that he is to be treated as an eligible person for the purposes of sections 36 to 48 of this Act, but shall otherwise dismiss the application.

(4)   In relation to a person in respect of whom the Tribunal have determined as mentioned in subsection (3) above sections 36 to 48 of this Act shall apply as if he were an eligible person.

(5)   A person to whom this section applies may make an application under section 39 above as well as an application under this section; and if the Tribunal determine as mentioned in subsection (3) above in respect of a person who has made an application under that section, the application under that section shall (without prejudice to subsection (4) above) be treated as made by an eligible person.

(6)   Without prejudice to the generality of paragraph (b) of subsection (1) above, cases where the condition mentioned in that paragraph might be less than fully satisfied include cases where the close relative's agricultural work on the holding fell short of providing him with his principal source of livelihood because the holding was too small.

[(7)   The references in subsections (1) and (6) above to agricultural work carried out by a person on the holding include—

(a)   agricultural work carried out by him from the holding, and

(b)   other work carried out by him on or from the holding,

which is of a description approved in writing by the landlord after the commencement of this subsection.]

NOTES

Derivation

This section derived from the Agriculture (Miscellaneous Provisions) Act 1976, ss 18(2), 21.

Initial Commencement

Specified date: 18 June 1986: see s 102(2).

Extent

This Act does not extend to Scotland.

Amendment

Sub-s (7): inserted by SI 2006/2805, arts 2, 5(2).

Date in force: 19 October 2006: see SI 2006/2805, art 1(1)(b).

See Further

See further, as to the exclusion of this Act in relation to leases or tenancies granted to contractors in respect of the running of any removal centre or part of a removal centre: the Immigration and Asylum Act 1999, s 149(3).

Notes

For a commentary, see para 35.51.

This section contains provisions formerly in the Agriculture (Miscellaneous Provisions) Act 1976, s 21, as read with s 18(2) of that Act.

Sub-s (1): Seven years ending with, etc. As a general rule the effect of defining a period in such a manner is to include the day on which the event in question occurs; see 45 Halsbury's Laws (4th edn) para 1127.

Though not fully satisfied. Sub-s (1)(b) should be read in conjunction with sub-s (6) above.

Material extent. This expression is to be widely construed; see *Littlewood v Rolfe* [1981] 2 All ER 51, 258 Estates Gazette 168. See also, *Thomson v Church Commissioners for England* [2006] EWHC 1773 (Admin), [2006] 43 EG 180.

Sub-s (2): Three months beginning with, etc. See the note to s 39.

Application; exclusion of section. As to the general application of this section, see s 35(1); and as to the application or exclusion of this section on the death of a retiring tenant, see s 57.

Modification of section. This section may be modified by regulations in cases where the person whom a direction (see s 39) entitles to a tenancy dies before the relevant time (defined by s 46(1), (2)); see s 45(8) and the note 'Regulations under this section'.

Definitions. For 'close relative', 'the date of death', 'the deceased' and 'the holding', see s 35(2); for 'eligible person', see s 36(3); for 'agricultural' and 'the Tribunal', see s 96(1).

Rules of procedure. See the note to s 40.

A1.129

42   Procedure where deceased held more than one holding

(1)   Subsections (2) and (3) below shall have effect where at the expiry of the period of three months beginning with the day after the date of death of a tenant there are pending before the Tribunal separate applications made under section 39 above by any person, or (as the case may be) by each one of a number of persons, in respect of more than one agricultural holding held by the tenant at that date.

(2)   The applications referred to in subsection (1) above (together with, in each case, any associated application made under section 41 above) shall, subject to and in accordance with the provisions of any such order as is referred to in section 40(5) above, be heard and determined by the Tribunal in such order as may be decided—

   (a)   where the applications were made by one person, by that person,
   (b)   where the applications were made by two or more persons, by agreement between those persons or, in default of agreement, by the chairman of the Tribunal.

(3)   Any decision made by the chairman under subsection (2)(b) above shall be made according to the respective sizes of the holdings concerned so that any application in

respect of any holding which is larger than any other of those holdings shall be heard and determined by the Tribunal before any application in respect of that other holding.

NOTES

Derivation

This section derived from the Agriculture (Miscellaneous Provisions) Act 1976, s 20(15), and the Agricultural Holdings Act 1984, s 3(5), Sch 1, para 5(2).

Initial Commencement

Specified date: 18 June 1986: see s 102(2).

Extent

This Act does not extend to Scotland.

See Further

See further, as to the exclusion of this Act in relation to leases or tenancies granted to contractors in respect of the running of any removal centre or part of a removal centre: the Immigration and Asylum Act 1999, s 149(3).

Notes

For a commentary, see para 35.63.

This section contains provisions formerly in the Agriculture (Miscellaneous Provisions) Act 1976, s 20(15), as added by the Agricultural Holdings Act 1984, s 3(5), Sch 1, para 5(2).

Three months beginning with, etc. See the note to s 39.

Application; exclusion of section. As to the application or exclusion of this section on the death of a retiring tenant, see s 57.

Modification of section. This section may be modified by regulations in cases where the person whom a direction (see s 39) entitles to a tenancy dies before the relevant time (defined by s 46(1), (2)); see s 45(8) and the note 'Regulations under this section'.

Definitions. For 'agricultural holding', see s 1(1); for 'the date of death', see s 35(2); and for 'agreement', 'tenant' and 'the Tribunal', see s 96(1).

Rules of procedure. See the note to s 40.

A1.130

43   Restriction on operation of notice to quit given by reason of death of tenant

(1)   A notice to quit the holding given to the tenant of the holding by reason of the death of the deceased and falling within Case G shall not have effect unless—

(a)   no application to become the tenant of the holding is made (or has already at the time of the notice to quit been made) under section 39 above within the period mentioned in subsection (1) of that section, or

(b)   one or more such applications having been made within that period—

(i)   none of the applicants is determined by the Tribunal to be in their opinion a suitable person to become the tenant of the holding, or

(ii)   the Tribunal consent under section 44 below to the operation of the notice to quit in relation to the whole or part of the holding.

(2)   Where the Tribunal consent under section 44 below to the operation of a notice to quit to which subsection (1) above applies in relation to part only of the holding, the

notice shall have effect accordingly as a notice to quit that part and shall not be invalid by reason that it relates only to part of the holding.

NOTES

Derivation

This section derived from the Agriculture (Miscellaneous Provisions) Act 1976, s 19, the Agricultural Holdings (Notices to Quit) Act 1977, s 13(1), Sch 1, para 7(3), and the Agricultural Holdings Act 1984, ss 3(5), 6(9), Sch 1, para 3(2).

Initial Commencement

Specified date: 18 June 1986: see s 102(2).

Extent

This Act does not extend to Scotland.

See Further

See further, as to the exclusion of this Act in relation to leases or tenancies granted to contractors in respect of the running of any removal centre or part of a removal centre: the Immigration and Asylum Act 1999, s 149(3).

Notes

For a commentary, see para 35.94.

This section contains provisions formerly in the Agriculture (Miscellaneous Provisions) Act 1976, s 19, as amended by the Agricultural Holdings (Notices to Quit) Act 1977, s 13(1), Sch 1, para 7(3), and by the Agricultural Holdings Act 1984, ss 3(5), 6(9), Sch 1, para 3(2).

Part ... of the holding. See s 74 as to compensation where the landlord resumes possession of part of a holding by virtue of sub-s (2) of this section.

Application; exclusion of section. As to the general application of this section, see s 35(1); and as to application or exclusion of this section on the death of a retiring tenant, see s 57.

Modification of section. This section may be modified by regulations in cases where the person whom a direction (see s 39) entitles to a tenancy dies before the relevant time (defined by s 46(1), (2)); see s 45(8) and the note 'Regulations under this section'.

Resumption of possession. See the Agriculture Act 1986, s 13, Sch 1, para 13.

Definitions. For 'the deceased' and 'the holding', see s 35(2); and for 'Case G', 'tenant' and 'the Tribunal', see s 96(1).

A1.131

44   Opportunity for landlord to obtain Tribunal's consent to operation of notice to quit

(1)   Before giving a direction under section 39(5) or (6) above in a case where a notice to quit to which section 43(1) above applies has been given the Tribunal shall afford the landlord an opportunity of applying for their consent under this section to the operation of the notice.

(2)   Subject to subsection (5) below, section 27 above shall apply in relation to an application for, or the giving of, the Tribunal's consent under this section as it applies in relation to an application for, or the giving of, their consent under section 26 above.

(3)   The Tribunal shall not entertain an application for their consent to the operation of a notice to quit to which section 43(1) above applies unless it is made in pursuance of subsection (1) above.

(4) Subject to subsection (5) below, if the Tribunal give their consent on an application made in pursuance of subsection (1) above, they shall dismiss the application or each of the applications made under section 39 above.

(5) Where in any case—

    (a) a notice to quit to which section 43(1) above applies has been given, and

    (b) section 39(10) above applies,

the Tribunal shall give their consent to the operation of the notice to quit in relation to the part of the holding which would, in accordance with section 39(10), be excluded from any direction given by the Tribunal with respect to the holding under section 39; and subsections (2) and (4) above shall not apply.

(6) If on an application made in pursuance of subsection (1) above the Tribunal give their consent to the operation of a notice to quit—

    (a) within the period of three months ending with the date on which the notice purports to terminate the tenancy ('the original operative date'), or

    (b) at any time after that date,

the Tribunal may, on the application of the tenant, direct that the notice shall have effect from a later date ('the new operative date').

(7) The new operative date, in the case of a notice to quit, must be a date not later than the end of the period of three months beginning with—

    (a) the original operative date, or

    (b) the date on which the Tribunal give their consent to the operation of the notice,

whichever last occurs.

NOTES

Derivation

Sub-ss (1), (3) derived from the Agriculture (Miscellaneous Provisions) Act 1976, s 22(1), (3); sub-s (2) derived from the Agriculture (Miscellaneous Provisions) Act 1976, s 22(2), the Agricultural Holdings (Notices to Quit) Act 1977, s 13(1), Sch 1, para 7(4), and the Agricultural Holdings Act 1984, s 3(5), Sch 1, para 3(4)(a); sub-ss (4)–(7) derived from the Agriculture (Miscellaneous Provisions) Act 1976, s 22(4)–(7), and the Agricultural Holdings Act 1984, s 3(5), Sch 1, paras 3(4), 6.

Initial Commencement

Specified date: 18 June 1986: see s 102(2).

Extent

This Act does not extend to Scotland.

See Further

See further, as to the exclusion of this Act in relation to leases or tenancies granted to contractors in respect of the running of any removal centre or part of a removal centre: the Immigration and Asylum Act 1999, s 149(3).

Notes

For a commentary, see para 35.85.

Sub-ss (1)–(7) contain provisions formerly in the Agriculture (Miscellaneous Provisions) Act 1976, s 22(1)–(7), respectively, as amended in the case of sub-s (2) of that section by the Agricultural Holdings (Notices to Quit) Act 1977, s 13(1), Sch 1, para 7(4), and by the Agricultural Holdings

Act 1984, s 3(5), Sch 1, para 3(4)(a); as amended in the case of sub-s (4) thereof by s 3(5) of, and Sch 1, para 3(4)(a) to, the 1984 Act; as added in the case of sub-s (5) thereof by s 3(5) of, and Sch 1, para 3(4)(b) to, the 1984 Act; and as added in the cases of sub-ss (6), (7) thereof by s 3(5) of, and Sch 1, para 6 to, the 1984 Act.

Sub-s (1): The Tribunal. See the note to s 11.

Sub-s (6): Three months ending with, etc. Cf the note 'Seven years ending with, etc' to s 41, and as to 'months', see the note to s 4.

Sub-s (7): Three months beginning with, etc. See the note to s 39.

Application; exclusion of section. As to the general application of this section, see s 35(1); and as to the application or exclusion of this section on the death of a retiring tenant, see s 57.

Modification of section. This section may be modified by regulations in cases where the person whom a direction (see s 39) entitles to a tenancy dies before the relevant time (defined by s 46(1), (2)); see s 45(8) and the note 'Regulations under this section'.

Definitions. For 'landlord', 'tenant' and 'the Tribunal', see s 96(1). Note as to 'the original operative date' and 'the new operative date', sub-s (6) above.

Rules of procedure. See the note to s 40.

A1.132

45   Effect of direction under section 39

(1) A direction by the Tribunal—

  (a) under section 39(5) or (6) above entitling an applicant to a tenancy of the holding, or

  (b) under section 39(9) above entitling two or more applicants to a joint tenancy of the holding,

shall entitle him or them to a tenancy or joint tenancy of the holding as from the relevant time on the terms provided by sections 47 and 48 below; and accordingly such a tenancy or joint tenancy shall be deemed to be at that time granted by the landlord to, and accepted by, the person or persons so entitled.

(2) Where the deceased's tenancy was not derived from the interest held by the landlord at the relevant time, the tenancy or joint tenancy deemed by virtue of subsection (1) above to be granted to, and accepted by, the person or persons so entitled shall be deemed to be granted by the person for the time being entitled to the interest from which the deceased's tenancy was derived, instead of by the landlord, with like effect as if the landlord's interest and any other supervening interest were not subsisting at the relevant time.

(3) The reference in subsection (2) above to a supervening interest is a reference to any interest in the land comprised in the deceased's tenancy, being an interest created subsequently to that tenancy and derived (whether immediately or otherwise) from the interest from which that tenancy was derived and still subsisting at the relevant time.

(4) Subsection (2) above shall not be read as affecting the rights and liabilities of the landlord under this Part of this Act.

(5) Any tenancy of the holding inconsistent with the tenancy to which a direction such as is mentioned in subsection (1) above entitles the person or persons concerned shall, if it would not cease at the relevant time apart from this subsection, cease at that time as if terminated at that time by a valid notice to quit given by the tenant.

(6) If the person or persons whom such a direction entitles to a tenancy or joint tenancy of the holding as from the relevant time becomes or become the tenant or joint

A1.132 *Statutes*

tenants of the holding before that time under a tenancy granted by the landlord to, and accepted by, the person or persons concerned, the direction shall cease to have effect and section 48 below shall not apply.

(7) The rights conferred on any person by such a direction (as distinct from his rights under his tenancy of the holding after he has become the tenant or joint tenant of the holding) shall not be capable of assignment.

(8) The Lord Chancellor may by regulations provide for all or any of the provisions of sections 36 to 48 of this Act (except this subsection) to apply, with such exceptions, additions or other modifications as may be specified in the regulations, in cases where the person or any of the persons whom such a direction entitles to a tenancy or joint tenancy of the holding dies before the relevant time.

NOTES

Derivation

Sub-ss (1), (5)–(8) derived from the Agriculture (Miscellaneous Provisions) Act 1976, s 23(1), (5)–(8); sub-ss (2)–(4) derived from the Agriculture (Miscellaneous Provisions) Act 1976, s 23(1A), and the Agricultural Holdings Act 1984, s 3(1).

Initial Commencement

Specified date: 18 June 1986: see s 102(2).

Extent

This Act does not extend to Scotland.

See Further

See further, as to the exclusion of this Act in relation to leases or tenancies granted to contractors in respect of the running of any removal centre or part of a removal centre: the Immigration and Asylum Act 1999, s 149(3).

Notes

For a commentary, see paras 35.98 and 35.99.

Sub-s (1) contains provisions formerly in the Agriculture (Miscellaneous Provisions) Act 1976, s 23(1). Sub-ss (2)–(4) contain provisions formerly in s 23(1A) of the 1976 Act, as inserted by the Agricultural Holdings Act 1984, s 3(1). Sub-ss (5)–(8) contain provisions formerly in s 23(5)–(8) of the 1976 Act.

General Note. Note that this Part of this Act (Pt IV) applies to tenancies granted (following a direction under s 39) in circumstances within sub-s (6) of this section, on or after 12 July 1984, in addition to those granted before that date; see s 34(1), although note s 37(1)(a).

Sub-s (1): The Tribunal. See the note to s 11.

Sub-s (4): This Part of this Act. Ie Pt IV (ss 34–59) of this Act.

Sub-s (8): Lord Chancellor. See the note to s 29.

Application; exclusion of section. As to the general application of this section (except sub-s (8) above), see s 35(1); and as to the application or exclusion of this section on the death of a retiring tenant, see s 57.

Interpretation of section. See s 46.

Definitions. For 'the deceased', 'the holding' and 'the tenancy', see s 35(2) (and see also, as to 'the holding', s 46(3)); for 'the relevant time', see s 46(1), (2); for 'landlord' and 'the Tribunal', see s 96(1).

1146

Regulations under this section. At the time of going to press no regulations had been made under sub-s (8) above; but, see, by virtue of the Interpretation Act 1978, s 17(2)(b), the Agriculture (Miscellaneous Provisions) Act 1976 (Application of Provisions) Regulations 1977, SI 1977/1215, which have effect as if so made.

As to regulations, generally, under this Act, see s 94.

A1.133

46   Interpretation of section 45

(1)   Subject to subsection (2) below, in sections 45 above and 48 below 'the relevant time'—

    (a)   except where the following paragraph applies, means the end of the twelve months immediately following the end of the year of tenancy in which the deceased died,

    (b)   if a notice to quit the holding was given to the tenant by reason of the death of the deceased, being a notice falling within Case G which, apart from section 43 above, would have terminated the tenancy at a time after the end of those twelve months, means that time.

(2)   Where the Tribunal give a direction under section 39(5), (6) or (9) above in relation to the holding at any time after the beginning of the period of three months ending with the relevant time apart from this subsection ('the original relevant time'), then—

    (a)   if the direction is given within that period, the Tribunal may, on the application of the tenant, specify in the direction, as the relevant time for the purposes of this section and section 48 below, such a time falling within the period of three months immediately following the original relevant time as they think fit,

    (b)   if the direction is given at any time after the original relevant time the Tribunal shall specify in the direction, as the relevant time for those purposes, such a time falling within the period of three months immediately following the date of the giving of the direction as they think fit,

and any time so specified shall be the relevant time for those purposes accordingly.

(3)   Where in accordance with section 39(10) above, the tenancy to which a direction under that section entitles the person or persons concerned is a tenancy of part of the deceased's holding, references in sections 45 above and 48 below to the holding shall be read as references to the whole of the deceased's holding or to the part of that holding to which the direction relates, as the context requires.

NOTES

Derivation

Sub-s (1) derived from the Agriculture (Miscellaneous Provisions) Act 1976, s 23(2), the Agricultural Holdings (Notices to Quit) Act 1977, s 13(1), Sch 1, para 7(5), and the Agricultural Holdings Act 1984, s 3(5), Sch 1, para 7(1); sub-ss (2), (3) derived from the Agriculture (Miscellaneous Provisions) Act 1976, s 23(2A), (9), and the Agricultural Holdings Act 1984, s 3(5), Sch 1, paras 3(5), 7(2).

Initial Commencement

Specified date: 18 June 1986: see s 102(2).

Extent

This Act does not extend to Scotland.

See Further

See further, as to the exclusion of this Act in relation to leases or tenancies granted to contractors in respect of the running of any removal centre or part of a removal centre: the Immigration and Asylum Act 1999, s 149(3).

Notes

For a commentary, see para 35.97.

Sub-s (1) contains provisions formerly in the Agriculture (Miscellaneous Provisions) Act 1976, s 23(2), as amended by the Agricultural Holdings (Notices to Quit) Act 1977, s 13(1), Sch 1, para 7(5), and by the Agricultural Holdings Act 1984, s 3(5), Sch 1, para 7(1). Sub-s (2) contains provisions formerly in s 23(2A) of the 1976 Act, as inserted by s 3(5) of, and Sch 1, para 7(2) to, the 1984 Act. Sub-s (3) contains provisions formerly in s 23(9) of the 1976 Act, as added by s 3(5) of, and Sch 1, para 3(5) to, the 1984 Act.

Sub-s (1). The 'relevant time' for the beginning of a new tenancy, primarily defined in para (a) of this subsection as twelve months from the end of the year of tenancy in which the deceased died, is the normal period of time under s 25 for ending a tenancy on death. The alternative definition in para (b) of this subsection is required because of the possibility that a tenant may die shortly before the term date of his tenancy but the landlord may not serve notice to quit until after the term date; if the notice to quit expires twelve months after the time indicated in para (a) of this subsection the period of the occupancy by the executors would otherwise be cut short.

Months. See the note to s 4.

Sub-s (2): The Tribunal. See the note to s 11.

Three months ending with, etc. Cf the note 'Seven years ending with, etc' to s 41; and as to 'months', see the note to s 4.

Application; exclusion of section. As to the general application of this section, see s 35(1); and as to the application or exclusion of this section on the death of a retiring tenant, see s 57.

Modification of section. This section may be modified by regulations in cases where the person whom a direction (see s 39) entitles to a tenancy dies before the relevant time; see s 45(8) and the note 'Regulations under this section'.

Definitions. For 'the deceased' and 'the holding', see s 35(2); for 'Case G', 'tenant' and 'the Tribunal', see s 96(1). Note as to 'the original relevant time', sub-s (2) above.

A1.134

47   Terms of new tenancy unless varied by arbitration

(1)   Subject to the provisions of this section and section 48 below, the terms of the tenancy or joint tenancy to which a direction under section 39(5), (6) or (9) above entitles the person or persons concerned shall be the same as the terms on which the holding was let immediately before it ceased to be let under the contract of tenancy under which it was let at the date of death.

(2)   If on the date of death the holding was held by the deceased under a tenancy for a fixed term of years, subsection (1) above shall have effect as if the tenancy under which the holding was let at the date of death had before that date become a tenancy from year to year on (with that exception) the terms of the actual tenancy as far as applicable.

(3)   If the terms of the tenancy to which such a direction entitles the person or persons concerned would not, apart from this subsection, include a covenant by the tenant or each of the tenants not to assign, sub-let or part with possession of the holding or any

part of it without the landlord's consent in writing, subsection (1) above shall have effect as if those terms included such a covenant.

NOTES

Derivation

This section derived from the Agriculture (Miscellaneous Provisions) Act 1976, s 23(1), (3), (4).

Initial Commencement

Specified date: 18 June 1986: see s 102(2).

Extent

This Act does not extend to Scotland.

See Further

See further, as to the exclusion of this Act in relation to leases or tenancies granted to contractors in respect of the running of any removal centre or part of a removal centre: the Immigration and Asylum Act 1999, s 149(3).

Notes

For a commentary, see para 35.95 ff.

Sub-ss (1)–(3) contain provisions formerly in the Agriculture (Miscellaneous Provisions) Act 1976, s 23(1), (3), (4), respectively.

Sub-s (2): Tenancy for a fixed term of years; tenancy from year to year. As to tenancies for a term of years, see, generally, 27 Halsbury's Laws (4th edn, reissue) paras 205–209, and as to tenancies from year to year, see ibid paras 178 ff.

Sub-s (3): Covenant ... not to assign, etc. As to covenants against assignment or subletting generally, see 27 Halsbury's Laws (4th edn) paras 363 ff.

Writing. See the note 'Written' to s 3.

Application; exclusion of section. As to the general application of this section, see s 35(1); and as to the application or exclusion of this section on the death of a retiring tenant, see s 57.

Modification of section. This section may be modified by regulations in cases where the person whom a direction (see s 39) entitles to a tenancy dies before the relevant time (defined by s 46(1), (2)); see s 45(8) and the note 'Regulations under this section'.

Definitions. For 'contract of tenancy', see s 1(5); for 'the date of death', 'the holding' and 'the tenancy', see s 35(2); for 'landlord', see s 96(1).

A1.135

48   Arbitration on terms of new tenancy

(1)   Where the Tribunal give a direction such as is mentioned in subsection (1) of section 45 above, the provisions of this section shall apply unless excluded by subsection (6) of that section.

(2)   In the following provisions of this section—

'the landlord' means the landlord of the holding;
'the prescribed period' means the period between the giving of the direction and—
   (a)   the end of the three months immediately following the relevant time, or
   (b)   the end of the three months immediately following the date of the giving
         of the direction,
whichever last occurs;

'the relevant time' has the meaning given by subsection (1) or (as the case may require) subsection (2) of section 46 above;

'the tenant' means the person or persons entitled to a tenancy or joint tenancy of the holding by virtue of the direction;

and references to the holding shall be read in accordance with section 46(3) above.

(3)   At any time within the prescribed period the landlord or the tenant may by notice in writing served on the other demand a reference to arbitration under this Act of one or both of the questions specified in subsection (4) below.

(4)   Those questions (referred to in the following provisions of this section as 'question (a)' and 'question (b)' respectively) are—

(a)   what variations in the terms of the tenancy which the tenant is entitled to or has obtained by virtue of the direction are justifiable having regard to the circumstances of the holding and the length of time since the holding was first let on those terms;

(b)   what rent should be or should have been properly payable in respect of the holding at the relevant time.

(5)   Where question (a) is referred to arbitration under subsection (3) above (with or without question (b)), the arbitrator—

(a)   shall determine what variations, if any, in the terms mentioned in that question are justifiable as there mentioned, and

(b)   without prejudice to the preceding paragraph, shall include in his award such provisions, if any, as are necessary—

(i)   for entitling the landlord to recover from the tenant under those terms a sum equal to so much as is in all the circumstances fair and reasonable of the aggregate amount of the compensation mentioned in subsection (8)(a) below, and

(ii)   for entitling the tenant to recover from the landlord under those terms a sum equal to so much as is in all the circumstances fair and reasonable of the aggregate amount of the compensation mentioned in subsection (8)(b) below,

and shall accordingly, with effect from the relevant time, vary those terms in accordance with his determination or direct that that they are to remain unchanged.

(6)   Where question (a) but not question (b) is referred to arbitration under subsection (3) above and it appears to the arbitrator that by reason of any provision included in his award under subsection (5) above (not being a provision of a kind mentioned in paragraph (b) of that subsection) it is equitable that the rent of the holding should be varied, he may vary the rent accordingly with effect from the relevant time.

(7)   Where question (b) is referred to arbitration under subsection (3) above (with or without question (a)), the arbitrator shall determine what rent should be or should have been properly payable in respect of the holding at the relevant time and accordingly shall, with effect from that time, increase or reduce the rent which would otherwise be or have been payable or direct that it shall remain unchanged.

(8)   The compensation referred to in subsection (5)(b) above is—

(a)   the compensation paid or payable by the landlord, whether under this Act or under agreement or custom, on the termination of the deceased's tenancy of the holding,

(b)   the compensation paid or payable to the landlord, whether under this Act or under agreement, on that termination in respect of any such dilapidation or deterioration of, or damage to, any part of the holding or anything in or on the holding as the tenant is or will be liable to make good under the terms of his tenancy.

(9)   For the purposes of this section the rent properly payable in respect of the holding shall be the rent at which the holding might reasonably be expected to be let by a prudent and willing landlord to a prudent and willing tenant, taking into account all relevant factors, including (in every case) the terms of the tenancy or prospective tenancy (including those relating to rent) and any such other matters as are specifically mentioned in sub-paragraph (1) of paragraph 1 of Schedule 2 to this Act (read with sub-paragraphs (2) and (3) of that paragraph).

(10)   On any reference under subsection (3) above the arbitrator may include in his award such further provisions, if any, relating to the tenancy which the tenant is entitled to or has obtained by virtue of the direction as may be agreed between the landlord and the tenant.

(11)   If the award of an arbitrator under this section is made before the relevant time, section 47(1) above shall have effect subject to, and in accordance with, the award.

(12)   If the award of an arbitrator under this section is made after the relevant time, it shall have effect as if the terms of the award were contained in an agreement in writing entered into by the landlord and the tenant and having effect as from the relevant time.

NOTES

Derivation

Sub-ss (1), (3)–(8), (10)–(12) derived from the Agriculture (Miscellaneous Provisions) Act 1976, s 24(1), (3)–(5), (7), (8); sub-ss (2), (9) derived from the Agriculture (Miscellaneous Provisions) Act 1976, s 24(2), (6), and the Agricultural Holdings Act 1984, ss 3(5), 10(1), Sch 1, paras 3(6), 7(3), Sch 3, para 35.

Initial Commencement

Specified date: 18 June 1986: see s 102(2).

Extent

This Act does not extend to Scotland.

See Further

See further, as to the exclusion of this Act in relation to leases or tenancies granted to contractors in respect of the running of any removal centre or part of a removal centre: the Immigration and Asylum Act 1999, s 149(3).

Notes

For a commentary, see para 35.96 ff.

Sub-ss (1), (2), (8), (9), (10), (12) contain provisions formerly in the Agriculture (Miscellaneous Provisions) Act 1976, s 24(1), (2), (5), (6), (7), (8) respectively, as amended in the case of sub-s (2) of that section by the Agricultural Holdings Act 1984, s 3(5), Sch 1, paras 3(6), 7(3), and as substituted in the case of sub-s (6) of that section by s 10(1) of, and Sch 3, para 35 to, the 1984 Act. Sub-ss (3), (4) contain provisions formerly in s 24(3) of the 1976 Act. Sub-ss (5), (6), (7) contain provisions formerly in s 24(4)(a), (b), (c), respectively, of the 1976 Act. Sub-s (11) contains provisions formerly in s 24(4) (last limb) of the 1976 Act.

Sub-s (1): The Tribunal. See the note to s 11.

Sub-s (2): Months. See the note to s 4.

Sub-s (3): Writing. See the note 'Written' to s 3.

Arbitration under this Act. For provisions as to arbitration under this Act, see s 84 and the note to s 2.

Sub-s (8): Compensation paid ... by the landlord ... under this Act. See, in particular, ss 64–69, Schs 7–9, and also s 70 (compensation for adoption of special system of farming).

Compensation paid ... to the landlord ... under this Act. See ss 71–73.

Application; exclusion of section. As to the general application of this section, see s 35(1); and as to the application or exclusion of this section on the death of a retiring tenant, see s 57 (and see, also, s 56(3)).

Modification of section. This section may be modified by regulations in cases where the person whom a direction (see s 39) entitles to a tenancy dies before the relevant time (defined by s 46(1), (2)); see s 45(8) and the note 'Regulations under this section'.

See, also, as to the modification of sub-ss (8)(a), (11) of this section, in cases where the Tribunal give a direction under s 53(7), s 56(3).

Definitions. For 'the holding' and 'the tenancy', see s 35(2) and see also as to 'the holding', sub-s (2) above and s 46(3); for 'landlord' and 'the Tribunal', see s 96(1). Note as to 'the landlord', 'the prescribed period', 'the relevant time' and 'the tenant', sub-s (2) above; and as to 'question (a)' and 'question (b)', sub-s (4) above.

Succession on retirement of tenant

A1.136

49   **Application of sections 50 to 58**

(1)   Sections 50 to 58 below (except sections 53(11) and 55(7) which are of general application) shall apply where—

  (a)   an agricultural holding is held under a tenancy from year to year, being a tenancy which falls within paragraph (a) or (b) of section 34(1) above, and

  (b)   a notice is given to the landlord by the tenant, or (in the case of a joint tenancy) by all the tenants, of the holding indicating (in whatever terms) that he or they wish a single eligible person named in the notice to succeed him or them as tenant of the holding as from a date specified in the notice, being a date on which the tenancy of the holding could have been determined by notice to quit given at the date of the notice and which falls not less than one year, but not more than two years, after the date of the notice.

(2)   In subsection (1) above 'tenant' has the same meaning as in section 34 above.

(3)   In this section and sections 50 to 58 below (and in Part I of Schedule 6 to this Act as applied by section 50(4))—

  'close relative' of the retiring tenant means—
  (a)   the wife[, husband or civil partner] of the retiring tenant;
  (b)   a brother or sister of the retiring tenant;
  (c)   a child of the retiring tenant;
  (d)   any person (not within (b) or (c) above) who, in the case of any marriage [or civil partnership] to which the retiring tenant has been at any time a party, has been treated by the latter as a child of the family in relation to that marriage [or civil partnership];
  'eligible person' has the meaning given by section 50 below;
  'the holding' means the holding in respect of which the retirement notice is given;
  'the nominated successor' means the eligible person named in the retirement notice;
  'related holding' means, in relation to the holding, any agricultural holding comprising the whole or a substantial part of the land comprised in the holding;

'the retirement date' means the date specified in the retirement notice as the date as from which the proposed succession is to take place;

'the retirement notice' means the notice mentioned in subsection (1) above;

'the retiring tenant' means the tenant by whom the retirement notice was given, or, where it was given by joint tenants (and the context so permits), any one of those tenants, and 'the retiring tenants' accordingly means those tenants;

'the tenancy' means the tenancy of the holding.

[(4) Where this Act applies in relation to a tenancy by virtue of section 4(1)(g) of the Agricultural Tenancies Act 1995, the reference in subsection (3) above (in the definition of 'related holding') to a substantial part of the land comprised in the holding means a substantial part determined by reference to either area or value.]

NOTES

Derivation

This section derived from the Agricultural Holdings Act 1984, Sch 2, paras 1(1), (2), 2(2).

Initial Commencement

Specified date: 18 June 1986: see s 102(2).

Extent

This Act does not extend to Scotland.

Amendment

Sub-s (3): in definition 'close relative' in para (a) words ', husband or civil partner' in square brackets substituted by the Civil Partnership Act 2004, s 81, Sch 8, para 36(1), (2).

Date in force: 5 December 2005: see SI 2005/3175, art 2(1), Sch 1.

Sub-s (3): in definition 'close relative' in para (d) words 'or civil partnership' in square brackets in both places they occur inserted by the Civil Partnership Act 2004, s 81, Sch 8, para 36(1), (3).

Date in force: 5 December 2005: see SI 2005/3175, art 2(1), Sch 1.

Sub-s (4): inserted by SI 2006/2805, arts 2, 4(3).

Date in force: 19 October 2006: see SI 2006/2805, art 1(1)(b).

See Further

See further, as to the exclusion of this Act in relation to leases or tenancies granted to contractors in respect of the running of any removal centre or part of a removal centre: the Immigration and Asylum Act 1999, s 149(3).

Notes

For a commentary, see para 36.2.

Sub-ss (1), (2) contain provisions formerly in the Agricultural Holding Act 1984, Sch 2, para 1(1), (2). Sub-s (3) contains provisions formerly in Sch 2, paras 1(2), 2(2), to the 1984 Act.

General Note. The Agricultural Holdings Act 1984, s 4, Sch 2 (repealed by s 101, Sch 15, Pt I), the provisions of which are now, generally, contained in this section and ss 50–58, implemented certain proposals put forward by the National Farmers' Union and the Country Landowners' Association seeking to facilitate succession when a tenant of an agricultural holding who is over 65 years of age wishes to retire. Under the previously existing law a tenant could pass on his tenancy during his lifetime only if the landlord agreed. This section and ss 50–58 provide that when an existing tenant over the age of 65 whose tenancy falls within ss 34–48 wishes to retire and nominates a close relative as a successor, the Tribunal has discretion to allow succession by that person provided that the applicant satisfies the various requirements as to eligibility and suitability set out in this section and ss 50 ff. A tenant under the age of 65 may also retire in favour of a nominated successor if he is suffering from ill-health to an extent which permanently prevents him from fulfilling his responsibilities to farm in accordance with the rules of good husbandry (see s 51(3)).

Date on which the tenancy … could have been determined by notice to quit, etc. As to the length of notice ordinarily required, see s 25.

Not less than one year, but not more than two years, after etc. Quaere whether the words 'not less than' indicate that one clear year must intervene between the date of the notice and the date on which the tenancy could have been determined by notice to quit given at the date of the notice (*R v Turner* [1910] 1 KB 346; *Re Hector Whaling Ltd* [1936] Ch 208, [1935] All ER Rep 302) or that only one of those dates is to be excluded and not both of them (*Schnabel v Allard* [1967] 1 QB 627, [1966] 3 All ER 816, CA). In calculating the period of two years the date of the notice is not to be counted; see the note 'Two months from, etc' to s 10.

Close relative. See the notes to section 35.

Child; child of the family. See the notes to s 35.

Definitions. For 'agricultural holding', see s 1(1); for 'landlord' and 'tenant', see s 96(1) (but see also, as to 'tenant', s 34(2) as applied by sub-s (2) above). Note as to 'close relative', 'eligible person', 'the holding', 'the nominated successor', 'related holding', 'the retirement date', 'the retirement notice', 'the retiring tenant' and 'the tenancy', sub-s (3) above.

A1.137

50   Right to apply for new tenancy on retirement of tenant

(1)   The eligible person named in the retirement notice may (subject to section 57(2) below) apply under section 53 below to the Tribunal for a direction entitling him to a tenancy of the holding unless excluded by section 51 below.

(2)   For the purposes of sections 49 to 58 of this Act, 'eligible person' means (subject to the provisions of Part I of Schedule 6 to this Act as applied by subsection (4) below) a close relative of the retiring tenant in whose case the following conditions are satisfied—

   (a)   in the last seven years his only or principal source of livelihood throughout a continuous period of not less than five years, or two or more discontinuous periods together amounting to not less than five years, derived from his agricultural work on the holding or on an agricultural unit of which the holding forms part, and
   (b)   he is not the occupier of a commercial unit of agricultural land.

(3)   In the case of the wife of the retiring tenant the reference in subsection (2)(a) above to the relative's agricultural work shall be read as a reference to agricultural work carried out by either the wife or the retiring tenant (or both of them).

[(3A)   In the case of the civil partner of the retiring tenant the reference in subsection (2)(a) above to the relative's agricultural work shall be read as a reference to agricultural work carried out by either the civil partner or the retiring tenant (or both of them).]

(4)   Part I of Schedule 6 to this Act shall apply for the purposes of supplementing subsection (2) above and making provision with respect to the assessment of the productive capacity of agricultural land for the purposes of paragraph (b) of that subsection, but subject to the modifications set out in Part II of that Schedule.

[(5)   The reference in subsection (2)(a) above to agricultural work carried out by a person on the holding or on an agricultural unit of which the holding forms part includes—

(a)   agricultural work carried out by him from the holding or an agricultural unit of which the holding forms part, and

(b)   other work carried out by him on or from the holding or an agricultural unit of which the holding forms part,

which is of a description approved in writing by the landlord after the commencement of this subsection.]

NOTES

Derivation

Sub-ss (1)–(3) derived from the Agricultural Holdings Act 1984, Sch 2, paras 1(1), (2), 5(1).

Initial Commencement

Specified date: 18 June 1986: see s 102(2).

Extent

This Act does not extend to Scotland.

Amendment

Sub-s (3A): inserted by the Civil Partnership Act 2004, s 81, Sch 8, para 38.

Date in force: 5 December 2005: see SI 2005/3175, art 2(1), Sch 1.

Sub-s (5): inserted by SI 2006/2805, arts 2, 5(3).

Date in force: 19 October 2006: see SI 2006/2805, art 1(1)(b).

See Further

See further, as to the exclusion of this Act in relation to leases or tenancies granted to contractors in respect of the running of any removal centre or part of a removal centre: the Immigration and Asylum Act 1999, s 149(3).

Notes

For a commentary, see paras 36.14, 36.20 and 36.24.

Sub-s (1) contains provisions formerly in the Agricultural Holdings Act 1984, Sch 2, paras 1(1), 5(1). Sub-ss (2), (3) contain provisions formerly in Sch 2, para 1(2) to, the 1984 Act. Sub-s (4) is a drafting provision.

The Tribunal. See the note to s 11.

Application; exclusion of section. See s 49(1) as to the general application of this section; and as to those cases excluded from the provisions of sub-s (1) of this section, see s 51.

As to the rights of a nominated successor under this section where a retirement notice is given by joint tenants and one of those tenants subsequently dies, see s 57(5).

Modification of section. This section may be modified by regulations in cases where the nominated successor (being entitled to a tenancy by virtue of a direction under s 53) dies before the relevant time; see s 55(7) and the note 'Regulations under this section'.

Definitions. For 'close relative', 'the holding', 'the retirement notice' and 'the retiring tenant', see s 49(3); for 'agricultural', 'tenant' and 'the Tribunal', see s 96(1). Note as to 'eligible person', sub-s (2) above.

Rules of procedure. See the note to s 53.

A1.138

51   Excluded cases

(1)   Sections 37 and 38 above shall apply for the purpose of excluding the application of section 50(1) above, but subject to the following modifications—

  (a)   references to sections 36(1) and 41 above shall be read as references to section 50(1),
  (b)   references to the holding, a related holding and the tenancy shall be read in accordance with section 49(3) above, and
  (c)   references to the date of death shall be read as references to the date of the giving of the retirement notice.

(2)   Section 50(1) shall not apply if the retiring tenant has at any time given any other notice under section 49(1) above in respect of the holding or a related holding and an application to become the tenant of the holding or a related holding has been duly made by any person under section 53 below in respect of that notice.

(3)   Section 50(1) shall not apply if at the retirement date the retiring tenant will be under sixty-five, unless the retirement notice is given on the grounds that—

  (a)   the retiring tenant or (where the notice is given by joint tenants) each of the retiring tenants is or will at the retirement date be incapable, by reason of bodily or mental infirmity, of conducting the farming of the holding in such a way as to secure the fulfilment of the responsibilities of the tenant to farm in accordance with the rules of good husbandry, and
  (b)   any such incapacity is likely to be permanent,

and that fact is stated in the notice.

(4)   If on the date of the giving of the retirement notice the tenancy is the subject of a valid notice to quit given before that date and including a statement that it is given for any such reason as is referred to in Case B, D or E (not being a notice to quit falling within section 38(3) above as applied by subsection (1) above), section 50(1) shall not apply unless one of the events mentioned in subsection (5) below occurs.

(5)   Those events are as follows—

  (a)   it is determined by arbitration under this Act that the notice to quit is ineffective for the purposes of section 26(2) above on account of the invalidity of any such reason as aforesaid, or
  (b)   where a counter-notice is duly served under section 28(2) above—
     (i)   the Tribunal withhold consent to the operation of the notice to quit, or
     (ii)   the period for making an application to the Tribunal for such consent expires without such an application having been made.

(6)   Where one of the events mentioned in subsection (5) above occurs the relevant period shall for the purposes of sections 53(1) and 54(2) below be the period of one month beginning with the date on which the arbitrator's award is delivered to the tenant, with the date of the Tribunal's decision to withhold consent, or with the expiry of the said period for making an application (as the case may be).

NOTES

Derivation

This section derived from the Agricultural Holdings Act 1984, Sch 2, para 2(1), (3)–(6).

Initial Commencement

Specified date: 18 June 1986: see s 102(2).

Extent

This Act does not extend to Scotland.

See Further

See further, as to the exclusion of this Act in relation to leases or tenancies granted to contractors in respect of the running of any removal centre or part of a removal centre: the Immigration and Asylum Act 1999, s 149(3).

Notes

For a commentary, see paras 36.7 and 36.13.

Sub-s (1), by application, contains provisions formerly in the Agricultural Holdings Act 1984, Sch 2, para 2(1)(a), (b), (c), (f), (g), (4). Sub-s (2) contains provisions formerly in Sch 2, para 2(1)(d) of the 1984 Act. Sub-s (4) contains provisions formerly in Sch 2, para 2(5) to that Act. Sub-ss (5), (6) contain provisions formerly in Sch 2, para 2(6) to that Act.

Sub-s (3): Under sixty-five. A person attains a particular age expressed in years at the commencement of the relevant anniversary of the date of his birth; see the Family Law Reform Act 1969, s 9.

Likely. See the note to s 14.

Sub-s (5): Arbitration under this Act. For provisions as to arbitration under this Act, see s 84 and the note to s 2.

The Tribunal. See the note to s 11.

Period for making an application to the Tribunal for such consent. An application for the Tribunal's consent to the operation of a notice to quit under s 28(2) which is made after service of a counter-notice is to be made within one month of the service of the counter-notice; see the Agricultural Land Tribunals (Rules) Order 1978, SI 1978/259, r 2, Sch 1, r 2(2), as construed in accordance with s 99, Sch 13, para 1.

Sub-s (6): One month beginning with, etc. See the note 'Three months beginning with, etc' to s 39.

Application of section. See s 49(1) as to the general application of this section; and as to the rights of a nominated successor under this section where a retirement notice is given by joint tenants and one of those tenants subsequently dies, see s 57(5).

Modification of section. This section may be modified by regulations in cases where the nominated successor (being entitled to a tenancy by virtue of a direction under s 53) dies before the relevant time; see s 55(7) and the note 'Regulations under this section'.

Definitions. For 'the holding', 'related holding', 'the retirement notice', 'the retiring tenant' and 'the tenancy', see s 49(3); for 'Case B' etc, 'tenant' and 'the Tribunal', see s 96(1). As to 'farm in accordance with the rules of good husbandry', see s 96(3).

A1.139

52   Notices to quit restricting operation of section 53

(1)   If the tenancy becomes the subject of a valid notice to quit given on or after the date of the giving of the retirement notice (but before the Tribunal have begun to hear any application by the nominated successor under section 53 below in respect of the retirement notice) and the notice to quit—

  (a)   falls within Case C and is founded on a certificate granted under paragraph 9 of Part II of Schedule 3 to this Act in accordance with an application made before that date, or

  (b)   falls within Case F,

the retirement notice shall be of no effect and no proceedings, or (as the case may be) no further proceedings, shall be taken under this Part of this Act in respect of it.

(2)   If the tenancy becomes the subject of a valid notice to quit given on or after the date of the giving of the retirement notice (but before the Tribunal have begun to hear any application by the nominated successor under section 53 below in respect of the retirement notice) and the notice to quit—

(a)   includes a statement that it is given for any such reason as is referred to in Case B, or
(b)   includes a statement that it is given for any such reason as is referred to in Case D and is founded on a notice given for the purposes of that Case before that date,

the retirement notice shall be of no effect and no proceedings, or (as the case may be) no further proceedings, shall be taken under this Part of this Act in respect of it unless one of the events mentioned in subsection (3) below occurs.

(3)   Those events are as follows—

(a)   it is determined by arbitration under this Act that the notice to quit is ineffective for the purposes of section 26(2) above on account of the invalidity of any such reason as aforesaid, or
(b)   where a counter-notice is duly served under section 28(2) above—
(i)   the Tribunal withhold consent to the operation of the notice to quit, or
(ii)   the period for making an application to the Tribunal for such consent expires without such an application having been made.

(4)   Where—

(a)   one of the events mentioned in subsection (3) above occurs, and
(b)   the notice to quit was given before the time when the relevant period for the purposes of sections 53(1) and 54(2) would expire apart from this subsection,

that period shall for those purposes expire at the end of the period of one month beginning with the date on which the arbitrator's award is delivered to the tenant, with the date of the Tribunal's decision to withhold consent, or with the expiry of the said period for making an application (as the case may be).

(5)   For the purposes of this Part of this Act an application by the nominated successor under section 53 below which is invalidated by subsection (1) or (2) above shall be treated as if it had never been made.

NOTES

Derivation

This section derived from the Agricultural Holdings Act 1984, Sch 2, para 3.

Initial Commencement

Specified date: 18 June 1986: see s 102(2).

Extent

This Act does not extend to Scotland.

See Further

See further, as to the exclusion of this Act in relation to leases or tenancies granted to contractors in respect of the running of any removal centre or part of a removal centre: the Immigration and Asylum Act 1999, s 149(3).

Notes

For a commentary, see paras 36.8 to 36.10.

Sub-ss (1), (2), (5) contain provisions formerly in the Agricultural Holdings Act 1984, Sch 2, para 3(1), (2), (4) respectively. Sub-ss (3), (4) contain provisions formerly in Sch 2, para 3(3) to that Act.

Sub-s (1): The Tribunal. See the note to s 11.

This Part of this Act. Ie Pt IV (ss 34–59) of this Act.

Sub-s (3): Arbitration under this Act. For provisions as to arbitration under this Act, see s 84 and the note to s 2.

Period for making an application to the Tribunal for such consent. See the note to s 51.

Sub-s (4): One month beginning with, etc. See the note 'Three months beginning with, etc' to s 39.

Application of section. See s 49(1) as to the general application of this section; and as to the rights of a nominated successor under this section where a retirement notice is given by joint tenants and one of those tenants subsequently dies, see s 57(5).

Modification of section. This section may be modified by regulations in cases where the nominated successor (being entitled to a tenancy by virtue of a direction under s 53) dies before the relevant time; see s 55(7) and the note 'Regulations under this section'.

Definitions. For 'the nominated successor', 'the retirement notice' and 'the tenancy', see s 49(3); for 'Case B' etc, 'tenant' and 'the Tribunal', see s 96(1).

A1.140

53   Application for tenancy of holding by nominated successor

(1)   An application under this section by the nominated successor to the Tribunal for a direction entitling him to a tenancy of the holding shall be made within the relevant period.

(2)   In subsection (1) above 'the relevant period' means (subject to sections 51(6) and 52(4) above) the period of one month beginning with the day after the date of the giving of the retirement notice.

(3)   Any such application—

   (a)   must be accompanied by a copy of the retirement notice, and
   (b)   must be signed by both the nominated successor and the retiring tenant or, where the notice was given by joint tenants, by each of the retiring tenants.

(4)   If the retirement notice includes a statement in accordance with section 51(3) above that it is given on the grounds mentioned in that provision, then, before the nominated successor's application is further proceeded with under this section, the Tribunal must be satisfied—

   (a)   that the retiring tenant or (as the case may be) each of the retiring tenants either is or will at the retirement date be incapable, by reason of bodily or mental infirmity, of conducting the farming of the holding in such a way as to secure the fulfilment of the responsibilities of the tenant to farm in accordance with the rules of good husbandry, and
   (b)   that any such incapacity is likely to be permanent.

(5)   If the Tribunal are satisfied—

   (a)   that the nominated successor was an eligible person at the date of the giving of the retirement notice, and
   (b)   that he has not subsequently ceased to be such a person,

the Tribunal shall determine whether he is in their opinion a suitable person to become the tenant of the holding.

(6) Before making a determination under subsection (5) above the Tribunal shall afford the landlord an opportunity of stating his views on the suitability of the nominated successor; and in making any such determination the Tribunal shall have regard to all relevant matters, including—

    (a) the extent to which the nominated successor has been trained in, or has had practical experience of, agriculture,

    (b) his age, physical health and financial standing,

    (c) the views (if any) stated by the landlord on his suitability.

(7) If the nominated successor is determined under that subsection to be in their opinion a suitable person to become the tenant of the holding, the Tribunal shall, subject to subsection (8) below, give a direction entitling him to a tenancy of the holding.

(8) The Tribunal shall not give such a direction if, on an application made by the landlord, it appears to the Tribunal that greater hardship would be caused by giving the direction than by refusing the nominated successor's application under this section.

(9) If the Tribunal dispose of the nominated successor's application otherwise than by the giving of a direction under subsection (7) above the retirement notice shall be of no effect (but without prejudice to section 51(2) above).

(10) For the purposes of this Part of this Act, an application by the nominated successor under this section which is withdrawn or abandoned shall be treated as if it had never been made.

(11) Provision shall be made by order under section 73(3) of the Agriculture Act 1947 (procedure of Agricultural Land Tribunals) for requiring any person making an application to the Tribunal for a direction under this section to give notice of the application to the landlord of the agricultural holding to which the application relates.

NOTES

Derivation

This section derived from the Agricultural Holdings Act 1984, Sch 2, paras 1(2), 5.

Initial Commencement

Specified date: 18 June 1986: see s 102(2).

Extent

This Act does not extend to Scotland.

See Further

See further, as to the exclusion of this Act in relation to leases or tenancies granted to contractors in respect of the running of any removal centre or part of a removal centre: the Immigration and Asylum Act 1999, s 149(3).

Notes

For a commentary, see paras 36.17, 36.26 and 36.27.

Sub-s (1) contains provisions formerly in the Agricultural Holdings Act 1984, Sch 2, para 5(1). Sub-s (2) contains provisions formerly in Sch 2, para 1(2), to the 1984 Act. Sub-ss (3)–(11) contain provisions formerly in Sch 2, para 5(2)–(10), respectively, to that Act.

General Note. Note that this Part of this Act (Pt IV) applies to tenancies obtained, by virtue of a direction of the Tribunal under this section, on or after 12 July 1984, in addition to those granted before that date; see s 34(1).

As to the effect of the death of the retiring tenant on proceedings under this section, see s 57(1), (2).

Sub-s (1): The Tribunal. See the note to s 11.

Sub-s (2): One month beginning with, etc. See the note 'Three months beginning with, etc' to s 39.

Sub-s (7): Tribunal shall ... give a direction. As to the effect of a direction under this subsection, see s 55; and as to the terms of the tenancy to which a direction under this provision relates, see s 56.

Sub-s (10): This Part of this Act. Ie Pt IV (ss 34–59) of this Act.

Application of section. See s 49(1) as to the general application of this section (except sub-s (11) above); and as to the rights of a nominated successor under this section where a retirement notice is given by joint tenants and one of those tenants subsequently dies, see s 57(5). See para 36.24.

See, also, as to notices to quit restricting the operation of this section, s 52.

Modification of section. This section may be modified by regulations in cases where the nominated successor (being entitled to a tenancy by virtue of a direction under this section) dies before the relevant time; see s 55(7) and the note 'Regulations under this section'.

Definitions. For 'agricultural holding', see s 1(1); for 'the holding', 'the nominated successor', 'the retirement date', 'the retirement notice' and 'the retiring tenant', see s 49(3); for 'eligible person', see s 50(2); for 'agriculture', 'landlord', 'tenant' and 'the Tribunal', see s 96(1). As to 'farm in accordance with the rules of good husbandry', see s 96(3). Note as to 'the relevant period', sub-s (2) above.

Agriculture Act 1947, s 73(3). See the note 'Rules of procedure' below.

Rules of procedure. As to rules of procedure for Agricultural Land Tribunals for the purposes of applications made under this Part of this Act, see, as construed in accordance with s 99, Sch 13, para 1(2), the Agricultural Land Tribunals (Succession to Agricultural Tenancies) Order 1984, SI 1984/1301 (made under the Agriculture Act 1947, s 73(3)). As to applications to the Tribunal under this section, generally, see rr 23 ff in the Schedule to that Order.

A1.141

54   Restriction on operation of certain notices to quit

(1)   This section applies to any notice to quit the holding or part of it given to the tenant of the holding (whether before or on or after the date of the giving of the retirement notice), not being a notice to quit falling within any provision of section 38 above (as applied by section 51(1) above) or section 51 or 52 above.

(2)   A notice to quit to which this section applies shall not, if it would otherwise be capable of so having effect, have effect—

   (a)   at any time during the relevant period, or
   (b)   where an application to become the tenant of the holding is made by the nominated successor under section 53 above within that period, at any time before the application has been finally disposed of by the Tribunal or withdrawn or abandoned,

and shall in any event not have effect if any such application is disposed of by the Tribunal by the giving of a direction under section 53(7) above.

(3)   In subsection (2) above 'the relevant period' means (subject to sections 51(6) and 52(4) above) the period of one month beginning with the day after the date of the giving of the retirement notice.

NOTES

Derivation

This section derived from the Agricultural Holdings Act 1984, Sch 2, paras 1(2), 4.

Initial Commencement

Specified date: 18 June 1986: see s 102(2).

Extent

This Act does not extend to Scotland.

See Further

See further, as to the exclusion of this Act in relation to leases or tenancies granted to contractors in respect of the running of any removal centre or part of a removal centre: the Immigration and Asylum Act 1999, s 149(3).

Notes

For a commentary, see para 36.13.

Sub-ss (1), (2) contain provisions formerly in the Agricultural Holdings Act 1984, Sch 2, para 4. Sub-s (3) contains provisions formerly in Sch 2, para 1(2), to that Act.

The Tribunal. See the note to s 11.

One month beginning with, etc. See the note 'Three months beginning with, etc' to s 39.

Application of section. See s 49(1) as to the general application of this section; and as to the rights of a nominated successor under this section where a retirement notice is given by joint tenants and one of those tenants subsequently dies, see s 57(5).

Modification of section. This section may be modified by regulations in cases where the nominated successor (being entitled to a tenancy by virtue of a direction under s 53) dies before the relevant time; see s 55(7) and the note 'Regulations under this section'.

Definitions. For 'the holding', 'the nominated successor' and 'the retirement notice', see s 49(3); for 'tenant' and 'the Tribunal', see s 96(1). Note as to 'the relevant period', sub-s (3) above.

Transitional provisions. See s 99, Sch 13, para 11.

A1.142

55 Effect of direction under section 53

(1) A direction by the Tribunal under section 53(7) above entitling the nominated successor to a tenancy of the holding shall entitle him to a tenancy of the holding as from the relevant time on the terms provided by section 56 below; and accordingly such a tenancy shall be deemed to be at that time granted by the landlord to, and accepted by, the nominated successor.

(2) Where the tenancy of the retiring tenant or (as the case may be) of the retiring tenants was not derived from the interest held by the landlord at the relevant time, the tenancy deemed by virtue of subsection (1) above to be granted to, and accepted by, the nominated successor shall be deemed to be granted by the person for the time being entitled to the interest from which the tenancy of the retiring tenant or tenants was derived, instead of by the landlord, with like effect as if the landlord's interest and any other supervening interest were not subsisting at the relevant time.

(3) The reference in subsection (2) above to a supervening interest is a reference to any interest in the land comprised in the tenancy of the retiring tenant or tenants, being

an interest created subsequently to that tenancy and derived (whether immediately or otherwise) from the interest from which that tenancy was derived and still subsisting at the relevant time.

(4)   Subsection (2) above shall not be read as affecting the rights and liabilities of the landlord under this Part of this Act.

(5)   Any tenancy of the holding inconsistent with the tenancy to which the nominated successor is entitled by virtue of a direction under section 53(7) above shall, if it would not cease at the relevant time apart from this subsection, cease at that time as if terminated at that time by a valid notice to quit given by the tenant.

(6)   The rights conferred on any person by such a direction (as distinct from his rights under his tenancy of the holding after he has become the tenant) shall not be capable of assignment.

(7)   The Lord Chancellor may by regulations provide for all or any of the provisions of sections 37(6) and 50 to 58 of this Act (except this subsection) to apply, with such exceptions, additions or other modifications as may be specified in the regulations, in cases where the nominated successor, being entitled to a tenancy of the holding by virtue of such a direction, dies before the relevant time.

(8)   In this section 'the relevant time' means the retirement date, except that—

  (a)   where such a direction is given within the period of three months ending with the retirement date, the Tribunal may, on the application of the tenant, specify in the direction, as the relevant time for the purposes of this section, such a time falling within the period of three months immediately following the retirement date as they think fit,
  (b)   where such a direction is given at any time after the retirement date, the Tribunal shall specify in the direction, as the relevant time for those purposes, such a time falling within the period of three months immediately following the date of the giving of the direction as they think fit,

and any time so specified shall be the relevant time for those purposes accordingly.

NOTES

Derivation

This section derived from the Agricultural Holdings Act 1984, Sch 2, para 6(1), (2), (4)–(7).

Initial Commencement

Specified date: 18 June 1986: see s 102(2).

Extent

This Act does not extend to Scotland.

See Further

See further, as to the exclusion of this Act in relation to leases or tenancies granted to contractors in respect of the running of any removal centre or part of a removal centre: the Immigration and Asylum Act 1999, s 149(3).

Notes

For a commentary see para 36.37 ff.

Sub-s (1) contains provisions formerly in the Agricultural Holdings Act 1984, Sch 2, para 6(1). Sub-ss (2)–(4) contain provisions formerly in Sch 2, para 6(2), to the 1984 Act. Sub-ss (5)–(8) contain provisions formerly in Sch 2, para 6(4)–(7), respectively, to the 1984 Act.

Sub-s (1): **The Tribunal.** See the note to s 11.

Sub-s (2), (3): **Sub-tenancies and concurrent tenancies.** See para 36.43.

Sub-s (4): **This Part of this Act.** Ie Pt IV (ss 34–59) of this Act.

Sub-s (7): **Lord Chancellor.** See the note to s 29.

Sub-s (8): **Three months ending with, etc.** Cf the note 'Seven years ending with, etc' to s 41, and as to 'Months', see the note to s 4.

Application of section. See s 49(1) as to the general application of this section (except sub-s (7) above); and as to the rights of a nominated successor under this section where a retirement notice is given by joint tenants and one of those tenants subsequently dies, see s 57(5). See para 36.41.

Definitions. For 'the holding', 'the nominated successor', 'the retirement date', 'the retiring tenant' and 'the tenancy', see s 49(3); for 'landlord', 'tenant' and 'the Tribunal', see s 96(1). Note as to 'supervening interest' (in sub-s (2)), sub-s (3) above, and as to 'the relevant time', sub-s (8) above.

Regulations under this section. At the time of going to press no regulations had been made under sub-s (7) above, and none have effect as if so made by virtue of the Interpretation Act 1978, s 17(2)(b).

A1.143

56   Terms of new tenancy

(1)   Subject to subsections (2) and (3) below, the terms of the tenancy to which a direction under section 53(7) above entitles the nominated successor shall be the same as the terms on which the holding was let immediately before it ceased to be let under the contract of tenancy under which it was let at the date of the giving of the retirement notice.

(2)   If the terms of the tenancy to which the nominated successor is entitled as mentioned in subsection (1) above would not, apart from this subsection, include a covenant by the tenant not to assign, sub-let or part with possession of the holding or any part of it without the landlord's consent in writing, subsection (1) above shall have effect as if those terms included that covenant.

(3)   Where the Tribunal give a direction under section 53(7) above, subsections (3) to (12) of section 48 above shall have effect in relation to the tenancy which the nominated successor is entitled to or has obtained by virtue of the direction, but with the substitution—

    (a)   in subsection (8)(a) of a reference to the tenancy of the retiring tenant or (as the case may be) tenants for the reference to the deceased's tenancy,

    (b)   in subsection (11) of a reference to subsection (1) above for the reference to section 47(1).

(4)   In those provisions, as extended by subsection (3) above—

    'the landlord' means the landlord of the holding;

    'the prescribed period' means the period between the giving of the direction and—
        (a)   the end of the three months immediately following the relevant time, or
        (b)   the end of the three months immediately following the date of the giving of the direction,
    whichever last occurs;

    'the relevant time' has the meaning given by section 55(8) above;

    'the tenant' means the nominated successor.

NOTES

Derivation

This section derived from the Agricultural Holdings Act 1984, Sch 2, paras 6(1), (3), 7(1), (2).

Initial Commencement

Specified date: 18 June 1986: see s 102(2).

Extent

This Act does not extend to Scotland.

See Further

See further, as to the exclusion of this Act in relation to leases or tenancies granted to contractors in respect of the running of any removal centre or part of a removal centre: the Immigration and Asylum Act 1999, s 149(3).

Notes

For a commentary, see para 36.37.

Sub-s (1), (2) contain provisions formerly in the Agricultural Holdings Act 1984, Sch 2, para 6(1), (3), respectively. Sub-ss (3), (4) contain provisions formerly in Sch 2, para 7(1), (2), respectively, to the 1984 Act.

Writing. See the note 'Written' to s 3.

The Tribunal. See the note to s 11.

Months. See the note to s 4.

Application of section. See s 49(1) as to the general application of this section; and as to the rights of a nominated successor under this section where a retirement notice is given by joint tenants and one of those tenants subsequently dies, see s 57(5).

Modification of section. This section may be modified by regulations in cases where the nominated successor (being entitled to a tenancy by virtue of a direction under s 53) dies before the relevant time; see s 55(7) and the note 'Regulations under this section' thereto.

Definitions. For 'contract of tenancy', see s 1(5); for 'the deceased' (in sub-s (3)(a)), cf s 35(2); for 'the holding', 'the nominated successor', 'the retirement notice' and 'the tenancy', see s 49(3); for 'landlord', 'tenant' and 'the Tribunal', see s 96(1). Note also the definitions (for the purposes of the provisions extended by this section) contained in sub-s (4) above.

A1.144

57   Effect of death of retiring tenant on succession to the holding

(1)   Subsections (2) to (4) below apply where the retiring tenant, being the sole (or sole surviving) tenant of the holding, dies after giving the retirement notice.

(2)   If the tenant's death occurs at a time when no application by the nominated successor has been made under section 53 above or such an application has not been finally disposed of by the Tribunal, the retirement notice shall be of no effect and no proceedings, or (as the case may be) no further proceedings, shall be taken under section 53 above in respect of it; and accordingly sections 36 to 48 above shall apply on the tenant's death in relation to the holding.

(3)   If the tenant's death occurs at a time when any such application has been so disposed of by the giving of a direction such as is mentioned in subsection (1) of section 55 above, but before the relevant time (within the meaning of that section), that section and section 56 above shall continue to have effect in relation to the holding; and accordingly sections 36 to 48 above shall not apply on the tenant's death in relation to the holding.

(4)   If the tenant's death occurs at a time when any such application has been so disposed of otherwise than by the giving of any such direction, sections 36 to 48 above

shall apply on the tenant's death in relation to the holding, but no application under section 39 (or 41) above may be made on that occasion by the nominated successor in relation to the holding.

(5)   Where the retirement notice was given by joint tenants and one of those tenants, not being the sole surviving tenant of the holding, dies, his death shall not affect any rights of the nominated successor under sections 50 to 56 above.

NOTES

Derivation

This section derived from the Agricultural Holdings Act 1984, Sch 2, para 8.

Initial Commencement

Specified date: 18 June 1986: see s 102(2).

Extent

This Act does not extend to Scotland.

See Further

See further, as to the exclusion of this Act in relation to leases or tenancies granted to contractors in respect of the running of any removal centre or part of a removal centre: the Immigration and Asylum Act 1999, s 149(3).

Notes

For a commentary, see para 36.39.

This section contains provisions formerly in the Agricultural Holdings Act 1984, Sch 2, para 8.

The Tribunal. See the note to s 11.

Application of section. See s 49(1) as to the general application of this section.

Modification of section. This section may be modified by regulations in cases where the nominated successor (being entitled to a tenancy by virtue of a direction under s 53) dies before the relevant time; see s 55(7) and the note 'Regulations under this section'.

Definitions. For 'the holding', 'the nominated successor', 'the retirement notice' and 'the retiring tenant', see s 57(1); for 'tenant' and 'the Tribunal', see s 96(1).

A1.145

58   Effect of direction under section 53 on succession to other holdings

Where—

   (a)   the retiring tenant, being the sole (or sole surviving) tenant of the holding, dies, and
   (b)   the nominated successor is for the time being entitled to a tenancy of the holding by virtue of a direction under section 53(7) above,

then for the purpose of determining whether, in relation to any other agricultural holding held by the retiring tenant at the date of his death, the nominated successor is a person in whose case the condition specified in paragraph (b) of section 36(3) above is satisfied, the nominated successor shall be deemed to be in occupation of the holding.

NOTES

Derivation

This section derived from the Agricultural Holdings Act 1984, Sch 2, para 9.

Initial Commencement

Specified date: 18 June 1986: see s 102(2).

Extent

This Act does not extend to Scotland.

See Further

See further, as to the exclusion of this Act in relation to leases or tenancies granted to contractors in respect of the running of any removal centre or part of a removal centre: the Immigration and Asylum Act 1999, s 149(3).

Notes

For a commentary, see para 36.42.

This section contains provisions formerly in the Agricultural Holdings Act 1984, Sch 2, para 9.

Application of section. See s 49(1) as to the general application of this section.

Modification of section. This section may be modified by regulations in cases where the nominated successor (being entitled to a tenancy by virtue of a direction under s 53) dies before the relevant time; see s 55(7) and the note 'Regulations under this section'.

Definitions. For 'agricultural holding', see s 1(1); for 'the holding', 'the nominated successor' and 'the retiring tenant', see s 49(3); for 'tenant', see s 96(1).

Interpretation

A1.146

59   Interpretation of Part IV

(1)   In sections 36 to 48 above (and in Part I of Schedule 6 to this Act)—

'close relative' of a deceased tenant,
'the date of death',
'the deceased',
'the holding',
'related holding', and
'the tenancy',

have the meanings given by section 35(2) above; and in those sections 'eligible person' has the meaning given by section 36(3) above.

(2)   In sections 49 to 58 above (and in Part I of Schedule 6 to this Act as applied by section 50(4) above)—

'close relative' of the retiring tenant,
'the holding',
'the nominated successor',
'related holding',
'the retirement date',
'the retirement notice',
'the retiring tenant',
'the retiring tenants', and

'the tenancy',

have the meanings given by section 49(3) above; and in those sections 'eligible person' has the meaning given by section 50(2) above.

NOTES

Initial Commencement

Specified date: 18 June 1986: see s 102(2).

Extent

This Act does not extend to Scotland.

See Further

See further, as to the exclusion of this Act in relation to leases or tenancies granted to contractors in respect of the running of any removal centre or part of a removal centre: the Immigration and Asylum Act 1999, s 149(3).

Note

For a commentary, see paras 35.26 ff and 36.19 ff.

This section is a drafting provision.

PART V: COMPENSATION ON TERMINATION OF TENANCY

Compensation to tenant for disturbance

A1.147

60   Right to, and measure of, compensation for disturbance

(1)   This section applies where the tenancy of an agricultural holding terminates by reason—

- (a)   of a notice to quit the holding given by the landlord, or
- (b)   of a counter-notice given by the tenant under section 32 above after the giving to him of such a notice to quit part of the holding as is mentioned in that section,

and the tenant quits the holding in consequence of the notice or counter-notice.

(2)   Subject to section 61 below, where this section applies there shall be payable by the landlord to the tenant by way of compensation for disturbance—

- (a)   a sum computed under subsection (3) below (in this section referred to as 'basic compensation'), and
- (b)   a sum computed under subsection (4) below (in this section referred to as 'additional compensation').

(3)   The amount of basic compensation shall be—

- (a)   an amount equal to one year's rent of the holding at the rate at which rent was payable immediately before the termination of the tenancy, or
- (b)   where the tenant has complied with the requirements of subsection (6) below, a greater amount equal to either the amount of the tenant's actual loss or two years' rent of the holding whichever is the smaller.

(4)   The amount of additional compensation shall be an amount equal to four years' rent of the holding at the rate at which rent was payable immediately before the termination of the tenancy of the holding.

(5)   In subsection (3) above 'the amount of the tenant's actual loss' means the amount of the loss or expense directly attributable to the quitting of the holding which is unavoidably incurred by the tenant upon or in connection with the sale or removal of his household goods, implements of husbandry, fixtures, farm produce or farm stock on or used in connection with the holding, and includes any expenses reasonably incurred by him in the preparation of his claim for basic compensation (not being costs of an arbitration to determine any question arising under this section or section 61 below).

(6)   The requirements of this subsection are—

(a)   that the tenant has not less than one month before the termination of the tenancy given to the landlord notice in writing of his intention to make a claim for an amount under subsection (3)(b) above, and

(b)   that the tenant has, before their sale, given to the landlord a reasonable opportunity of making a valuation of any such goods, implements, fixtures, produce or stock as are mentioned in subsection (5) above.

(7)   Compensation payable under this section shall be in addition to any compensation to which the tenant may be entitled apart from this section.

NOTES

Derivation

Sub-ss (1), (2) derived from the Agricultural Holdings Act 1948, s 34(1), the Agriculture (Miscellaneous Provisions) Act 1968, s 9(1), and the Agricultural Holdings (Notices to Quit) Act 1977, s 13(1), Sch 1, para 1(3)(a); sub-ss (3), (5), (6) derived from the Agricultural Holdings Act 1948, s 34(2); sub-s (4) derived from the Agriculture (Miscellaneous Provisions) Act 1968, s 9(2); sub-s (7) derived from the Agricultural Holdings Act 1948, s 34(5), and the Agriculture (Miscellaneous Provisions) Act 1968, s 9(1).

Initial Commencement

Specified date: 18 June 1986: see s 102(2).

Extent

This Act does not extend to Scotland.

See Further

See further, as to the exclusion of this Act in relation to leases or tenancies granted to contractors in respect of the running of any removal centre or part of a removal centre: the Immigration and Asylum Act 1999, s 149(3).

Notes

For a commentary, see paras 37.8 AND 38.47 ff.

Sub-ss (1), (2) contain provisions formerly in the Agricultural Holdings Act 1948, s 34(1), as amended by the Agricultural Holdings (Notices to Quit) Act 1977, s 13(1), Sch 1, para 1(3)(a), and in the Agriculture (Miscellaneous Provisions) Act 1968, s 9(1). Sub-s (3) contains provisions formerly in s 34(2)(a), (d) of the 1948 Act. Sub-s (4) contains provisions formerly in s 9(2) of the 1968 Act. Sub-s (5) contains provisions formerly in s 34(2) of the 1948 Act. Sub-s (6) contains provisions formerly in s 34(2)(b), (c) of the 1948 Act. Sub-s (7) contains provisions formerly in s 34(5) of the 1948 Act, and in s 9(1) of the 1968 Act.

General Note. This section, together with the other provisions in this Act relating to compensation to a tenant on the termination of his tenancy is excluded in relation to the termination of a tenancy if the person served with the notice to quit elects that the Land Compensation Act 1973, s 59(2), shall apply to the notice and gives up possession of the holding on or before the date on which his tenancy terminates in accordance with the notice; see s 59(2)(b) of the 1973 Act, as amended by s 100, Sch 14, para 55(3).

Sub-s (1): In consequence of the notice. It is a question of fact whether a tenant who holds over for any length of time after receiving a notice and then quits does so in consequence of the notice, but a tenant who disputes the validity of a notice to quit and subsequently quits as a result of a judgment for possession quits 'in consequence of the notice to quit', so as to entitle him to a compensation for disturbance: *Preston v Norfolk County Council* [1947] KB 775, [1947] 2 All ER 124, CA. A tenant who is ejected after service of notice to quit quits in consequence of a notice to quit: *Mills v Rose* (1923) 68 Sol Jo 420, CA. A tenant who quits in consequence of receiving a bad notice is nevertheless entitled to compensation under this section: *Kestell v Langmaid* [1950] 1 KB 233, [1949] 2 All ER 749, CA. As to notices to quit, see also the notes to ss 25 and 26.

Sub-s (2): Compensation. The following provisions are also relevant to compensation for disturbance under this section: s 61 (cases where compensation under this section not payable); s 63 (supplementary provisions); s 74 (termination of tenancy of part of holding); s 75 (compensation where reversionary estate in holding is severed); s 78 (extent to which compensation recoverable under agreements); s 83 (settlement of claims); s 85 (enforcement); s 86 (power of landlord to obtain charging order); and s 87 (general provisions as to charges).

In relation to compensation for disturbance, under sub-s (2)(a) of this section, on amalgamations or adjustments promoted by the Minister or by a Rural Development Board, see the Agriculture Act 1967, ss 29(3)(a), 48(2)(a), as amended by s 100, Sch 14, paras 40, 41(2).

Compensation for disturbance is not subject to capital gains tax: see *Davis (Inspector of Taxes) v Powell* [1977] 1 All ER 471, [1977] 1 WLR 258. See para 38.62.

Sub-s (5): Loss or expense directly attributable. The scope of these words was considered in *Re Evans and Glamorgan County Council* (1912) 76 JP 468; *Barbour v M'Douall* 1914 SC 844, and *Keswick v Wright* 1924 SC 766.

Sale or removal. No compensation can be claimed in respect of a sale or removal that is unlawful as between the tenant and the landlord (eg where fixtures removed without giving the requisite notice to the landlord under s 10(3)(b)): *Re Harvey and Mann* (1920) 89 LJKB 687, CA.

Expenses reasonably incurred. This covers the expense of calling in a surveyor to refute an allegation that the holding was not being cultivated in accordance with the rules of good husbandry: *Re Agricultural Holdings Act 1923, Dunstan v Benney* [1938] 2 KB 1, [1937] 4 All ER 510, CA.

Sub-s (6): Month. Cf the note 'Months' to s 4.

Writing. See the note 'Written' to s 3.

Reasonable opportunity. Cf the note to s 20.

Chequers and Chevening Estates. As to money or property from the Chequers Estate or the Chevening Estate which may be applied in or towards the payment of any compensation in respect of those estates or to raise money on mortgage for that purpose, see the Chequers Estate Act 1917, s 1, Schedule, clauses 6B(b), 8D, as amended by s 100, Sch 14, para 5, and the Chevening Estate Act 1959, s 1, Schedule, clauses 15(i), 23(b), as amended by s 100, Sch 14, para 34. (Note that, in both cases, compensation under sub-s (2)(b) of this section and under s 62 is excluded.)

Definitions. For 'agricultural holding', see s 1(1); for 'landlord' and 'tenant', see s 96(1). Note as to 'basic compensation' and 'additional compensation', sub-s (2) above, and as to 'the amount of the tenant's actual loss' (in sub-s (3)), sub-s (5) above.

A1.148

61   Cases where compensation under section 60 is not payable

(1)   Neither basic compensation nor additional compensation shall be payable under section 60 above where the operation of section 26(1) above in relation to the relevant notice is excluded by virtue of Case C, D, E, F or G.

(2)   Additional compensation shall not be so payable where the operation of section 26(1) above in relation to the relevant notice is excluded by virtue of Case A or H.

(3)   Except as provided by subsection (4) below, additional compensation shall not be payable under section 60 above where—

(a)   the relevant notice contains a statement either that the carrying out of the purpose for which the landlord proposes to terminate the tenancy is desirable on any of the grounds mentioned in paragraphs (a) to (c) of section 27(3) above or that the landlord will suffer hardship unless the notice has effect, and

(b)   if an application for consent in respect of the notice is made to the Tribunal in pursuance of section 26(1) above, the Tribunal consent to its operation and state in the reasons for their decision that they are satisfied as to any of the matters mentioned in paragraphs (a), (b), (c) and (e) of section 27(3).

(4)   Additional compensation shall be payable in a case falling within subsection (3) above where such an application as is mentioned in paragraph (b) of that subsection is made and—

(a)   the reasons given by the Tribunal also include the reason that they are satisfied as to the matter mentioned in paragraph (f) of section 27(3) above, or

(b)   the Tribunal include in their decision a statement under subsection (5) below.

(5)   Where such an application as is mentioned in subsection (3)(b) above is made in respect of the relevant notice and the application specifies the matter mentioned in paragraph (b) of section 27(3) above (but not that mentioned in paragraph (f) of that subsection), the Tribunal shall if they are satisfied as to the matter mentioned in paragraph (b) but would, if it had been specified in the application, have been satisfied also as to the matter mentioned in paragraph (f) include a statement to that effect in their decision.

(6)   In this section—

'basic compensation' and 'additional compensation' have the same meanings as in section 60 above;

'the relevant notice' means the notice to quit the holding or part of the holding, as the case may be, mentioned in section 60(1) above.

NOTES

Derivation

Sub-s (1) derived from the Agricultural Holdings Act 1948, s 34(1), the Agriculture (Miscellaneous Provisions) Act 1968, s 9(1), and the Agricultural Holdings (Notices to Quit) Act 1977, s 13(1), Sch 1, para 1(3)(b); sub-ss (2)–(4) derived from the Agriculture (Miscellaneous Provisions) Act 1968, s 10(1)(b)–(e), (2), (8), the Agricultural Holdings (Notices to Quit) Act 1977, s 13(1), Sch 1, para 5, and the Agricultural Holdings Act 1984, s 10(1), Sch 3, para 32(1), (2); sub-s (5) derived from the Agriculture (Miscellaneous Provisions) Act 1968, s 10(2), and the Agricultural Holdings (Notices to Quit) Act 1977, s 13(1), Sch 1, para 5; sub-s (6) derived from the Agricultural Holdings Act 1948, s 34(1), and the Agriculture (Miscellaneous Provisions) Act 1968, s 10(8).

Initial Commencement

Specified date: 18 June 1986: see s 102(2).

Extent

This Act does not extend to Scotland.

See Further

See further, as to the exclusion of this Act in relation to leases or tenancies granted to contractors in respect of the running of any removal centre or part of a removal centre: the Immigration and Asylum Act 1999, s 149(3).

Notes

For a commentary, see paras 38.48 and 38.55 ff.

Sub-s (1) contains provisions formerly in the Agricultural Holdings Act 1948, s 34(1) (proviso), as repealed in part by the Agriculture Act 1958, s 10(6), Sch 3, and as amended by the Agricultural Holdings (Notices to Quit) Act 1977, s 13(1), Sch 1, para 1(3)(b), and in the Agriculture (Miscellaneous Provisions) Act 1968, s 9(1). Sub-s (2) contains provisions formerly in s 10(1)(d) of the 1968 Act, as amended by s 13(1) of, and Sch 1, para 5(4) to, the 1977 Act, and in s 10(1)(e) of the 1968 Act, as inserted by the Agricultural Holdings Act 1984, s 10(1), Sch 3, para 32(1)(b). Sub-ss (3), (4) contain provisions formerly in s 10(1)(b), (c), (2), (8) of the 1968 Act, as amended in the case of s 10(1)(b), 2, 8 of that Act by s 13(1) of, and Sch 1, Sch 5(3), (6), (7) to the 1977 Act, and as amended in the case of s 10(1)(b), (8) of the 1968 Act by s 10(1) of, and Sch 3, para 32(1)(a), (2) to, the 1984 Act. Sub-s (5) contains provisions formerly in s 10(2) of the 1968 Act, as amended by s 13(1) of, and Sch 1, para 5 to, the 1977 Act. Sub-s (6) contains provisions formerly in s 34(1) of the 1948 Act and in s 10(8) of the 1968 Act.

General Note. See the General Note to s 60.

The Tribunal. See the note to s 11.

Definitions. For 'Case A' etc, 'landlord', 'termination' and 'the Tribunal', see s 96(1). Note as to 'basic compensation', 'additional compensation' and 'the relevant notice', sub-s (6) above; and note also as to 'termination', s 74(4).

A1.149

62   Compensation on termination in pursuance of early resumption clause

(1)   Where—

   (a)   the tenancy of an agricultural holding terminates by reason of a notice to quit the holding given in pursuance of a provision in the contract of tenancy authorising the resumption of possession of the holding for some specified purpose other than the use of the land for agriculture, and

   (b)   the tenant quits the holding in consequence of the notice,

compensation shall be payable by the landlord to the tenant, in addition to any other compensation so payable apart from this section in respect of the holding.

(2)   The amount of compensation payable under this section shall be equal to the value of the additional benefit (if any) which would have accrued to the tenant if the tenancy had, instead of being terminated as provided by the notice, been terminated by it on the expiration of twelve months from the end of the year of tenancy current when the notice was given.

(3)   For the purposes of subsection (2) above, the current year of a tenancy for a term of two years or more is the year beginning with such day in the period of twelve months ending with the date on which the notice is served as corresponds to the day on which the term would expire by the effluxion of time.

NOTES

Derivation

This section derived from the Agriculture (Miscellaneous Provisions) Act 1968, s 15(2), (5).

Initial Commencement

Specified date: 18 June 1986: see s 102(2).

Extent

This Act does not extend to Scotland.

See Further

See further, as to the exclusion of this Act in relation to leases or tenancies granted to contractors in respect of the running of any removal centre or part of a removal centre: the Immigration and Asylum Act 1999, s 149(3).

Notes

For a commentary, see paras 37.12, 38.59 and 40.5.

Sub-ss (1), (2) contain provisions formerly in the Agriculture (Miscellaneous Provisions) Act 1968, s 15(2). Sub-s (3) contains provisions formerly in s 15(5) of the 1968 Act.

General Note. See the note to s 60.

Compensation. The other provisions relating to compensation cited in the note 'Compensation' to s 60 (except s 61 and s 63(1)) are also relevant to compensation under this section.

Twelve months from. See the note 'Two months from, etc' to s 10.

Twelve months ending with, etc. See the note 'Seven years ending with, etc' to s 41; and as to 'months', see the note to s 4.

Definitions. For 'agricultural holding', see s 1(1); for 'contract of tenancy', see s 1(5); for 'landlord', tenant' and 'termination', see s 96(1). Note as to 'use of the land for agriculture', s 96(5); and note also as to 'termination', s 74(4).

A1.150

63   Compensation for disturbance: supplementary provisions

(1)   Where—

    (a)   the tenant of an agricultural holding has sub-let the holding, and

    (b)   the sub-tenancy terminates by operation of law in consequence of the termination of the tenancy by reason of any such notice or counter-notice as is referred to in section 60(1)(a) or (b) above,

section 60 shall apply if the sub-tenant quits the holding in consequence of the termination of the sub-tenancy as mentioned in paragraph (b) above as it applies where a tenant quits a holding in consequence of any such notice or counter-notice.

(2)   Where the tenant of an agricultural holding has sub-let the holding and in consequence of a notice to quit given by his landlord becomes liable to pay compensation under section 60 or 62 above to the sub-tenant, the tenant shall not be debarred from recovering compensation under that section by reason only that, owing to not being in occupation of the holding, on the termination of his tenancy he does not quit the holding.

(3)   Where the tenancy of an agricultural holding terminates by virtue of such a counter-notice as is mentioned in section 60(1)(b) above, and—

    (a)   the part of the holding affected by the notice to quit together with any part of the holding affected by any relevant previous notice rendered valid by section 31 above is less than one-fourth of the original holding, and

    (b)   the holding as proposed to be diminished is reasonably capable of being farmed as a separate holding,

compensation shall not be payable under section 60 above except in respect of the part of the holding to which the notice to quit relates.

(4) In subsection (3) above 'relevant previous notice' means any notice to quit given by the same person who gave the current notice to quit or, where that person is a person entitled to a severed part of the reversionary estate in the holding, by that person or by any other person so entitled.

NOTES

Derivation

Sub-s (1) derived from the Agricultural Holdings Act 1948, s 34(2A), the Agriculture (Miscellaneous Provisions) Act 1968, s 9(1), and the Agricultural Holdings Act 1984, s 10(1), Sch 3, para 9(2); sub-s (2) derived from the Agricultural Holdings Act 1948, s 34(3), and the Agriculture (Miscellaneous Provisions) Act 1968, ss 10(5), 15(4); sub-s (3) derived from the Agricultural Holdings Act 1948, s 34(4), the Agriculture (Miscellaneous Provisions) Act 1968, s 9(1), the Agricultural Holdings (Notices to Quit) Act 1977, s 13(1), Sch 1, para 1(3)(c), and the Agricultural Holdings Act 1984, s 10(1), Sch 3, para 9(3)(a), (b); sub-s (4) derived from the Agricultural Holdings Act 1948, s 34(4), and the Agricultural Holdings Act 1984, s 10(1), Sch 3, para 9(3)(c).

Initial Commencement

Specified date: 18 June 1986: see s 102(2).

Extent

This Act does not extend to Scotland.

See Further

See further, as to the exclusion of this Act in relation to leases or tenancies granted to contractors in respect of the running of any removal centre or part of a removal centre: the Immigration and Asylum Act 1999, s 149(3).

Notes

For a commentary, see paras 38.48 and 38.59.

Sub-s (1) contains provisions formerly in the Agricultural Holdings Act 1948, s 34(2A), as inserted by the Agricultural Holdings Act 1984, s 10(1), Sch 3, para 9(2), and as read with the Agriculture (Miscellaneous Provisions) Act 1968, s 9(1). Sub-s (2) contains provisions formerly in s 34(3) of the 1948 Act, as read with and applied by ss 10(5), 15(4) of the 1968 Act. Sub-s (3) contains provisions formerly in s 34(4) of the 1948 Act, as amended by the Agricultural Holdings (Notices to Quit) Act 1977, s 13(1), Sch 1, para 1(3)(c), and by s 10(1) of, and Sch 3, para 9(3)(a), (b) to, the 1984 Act, as repealed, in part, by the Agriculture (Miscellaneous Provisions) Act 1963, s 18(2), Schedule, Pt I, and as read with s 9(1) of the 1968 Act. Sub-s (4) contains provisions formerly in the last paragraph of s 34(4) of the 1948 Act, as added by s 10(1) of, and Sch 3, para 9(3)(c) to, the 1984 Act.

General Note. See the note to s 60.

In consequence of any such notice. Cf the corresponding note to s 60.

Definitions. For 'agricultural holding', see s 1(1); for 'landlord', 'tenant' and 'termination', see s 96(1). Note as to 'relevant previous notice', sub-s (4) above; and as to 'termination', see also s 74(4).

Compensation to tenant for improvements and tenant-right matters

A1.151

64   Tenant's right to compensation for improvements

(1) The tenant of an agricultural holding shall, subject to the provisions of this Act, be entitled on the termination of the tenancy, on quitting the holding, to obtain from

his landlord compensation for an improvement specified in Schedule 7 or Part I of Schedule 8 to this Act carried out on the holding by the tenant, being an improvement begun on or after 1st March 1948.

(2)   In this Act 'relevant improvement' means an improvement falling within subsection (1) above.

(3)   Subsection (1) above shall have effect as well where the tenant entered into occupation of the holding before 1st March 1948 as where he entered into occupation on or after that date.

(4)   The provisions of Part I of Schedule 9 to this Act shall have effect with respect to the rights of the tenant of an agricultural holding with respect to compensation for improvements specified in Part II of that Schedule carried out on the holding, being improvements begun before 1st March 1948.

NOTES

Derivation

This section derived from the Agricultural Holdings Act 1948, ss 35(1), 46(1), (2), 47(1).

Initial Commencement

Specified date: 18 June 1986: see s 102(2).

Extent

This Act does not extend to Scotland.

See Further

See further, as to the exclusion of this Act in relation to leases or tenancies granted to contractors in respect of the running of any removal centre or part of a removal centre: the Immigration and Asylum Act 1999, s 149(3).

Notes

For a commentary, see paras 37.6 and 38.8 ff.

Sub-s (1) contains provisions formerly in the Agricultural Holdings Act 1948, ss 46(1), 47(1). Sub-s (2) contains provisions derived from s 46(2) of the 1948 Act. Sub-s (3) contains provisions formerly in s 46(1) of that Act. Sub-s (4) contains provisions formerly in s 35(1) of that Act.

General Note. The provisions contained in sub-ss (1)–(3) above and ss 65–69, Schs 7, 8 generally reproduce those provisions relating to compensation for tenants' improvements originally introduced by the Agriculture Act 1947, whilst the provisions of the Agricultural Holdings Act 1923 which applied previous to their repeal and replacement by the 1947 Act, and continue to apply in relation to improvements begun before 1 March 1948, are replaced by Sch 9.

See also the General Note to s 60.

Compensation. The following provisions are also relevant to compensation for improvements under this section: s 66(1)–(3), (5) (measure of compensation); s 67 (long-term improvements: landlord's consent required); s 68 (special cases); s 69 (successive tenancies); s 74 (termination of tenancy of part of holding); s 75 (compensation where reversionary estate in holding is severed); s 76 (restrictions on compensation for things done in compliance with this Act); s 77 (no compensation under custom); s 78 (extent to which compensation recoverable under agreements); ss 79(1), (2), (4), (5), 80, 81 (special provisions as to market gardens); s 83 (settlement of claims); s 85 (enforcement); s 86 (power of landlord to obtain charge on holding); and s 87 (general provisions as to charges).

The right to obtain compensation divests the tenant of his property in crops left on the holding under s 15(3) 'on the termination of the tenancy on quitting the holding': *Thomas v National Farmers' Union Mutual Insurance Society Ltd* [1961] 1 All ER 363, [1961] 1 WLR 386. As to the criteria on which compensation is based, see *Re Duke of Wellington's Parliamentary Estates, King v Wellesley* [1972] Ch 374, [1971] 2 All ER 1140.

1st March 1948. Ie the commencement date of the Agriculture Act 1947, Pt III (repealed). See, further, the General Note to this section above.

Chequers and Chevening Estates. See the note to s 60.

Opencast coal operations. For the position as to compensation for improvements, where a compulsory rights order has been made under the Opencast Coal Act 1958, see ss 24, 25 of that Act, as amended by s 100, Sch 14, paras 26, 27. See, also, the supplementary provisions in ss 34–36 of, and Sch 6 to, that Act, as amended, in the case of Sch 6 to that Act, by s 100, Sch 14, para 32, and the provisions as to adjustments between landlord and tenant in s 37 of, and Sch 7, Pt I, paras 1–3 to, that Act, as amended, in the case of Sch 7, Pt I to that Act, by s 100, Sch 14, para 33.

Modification of section. The tenant of an agricultural holding is not entitled to compensation under sub-s (1) of this section for an improvement which he was required to carry out by the terms of his tenancy where the contract of tenancy was made before 1 January 1921; see Sch 12, para 5.

Definitions. For 'agricultural holding', see s 1(1) note; for 'landlord', 'tenant' and 'termination', see s 96(1). Note as to 'relevant improvement', sub-s (2) above; and as to 'termination', see also s 74(4).

A1.152

65   Tenant's right to compensation for tenant-right matters

(1)   The tenant of an agricultural holding shall, subject to the provisions of this Act, be entitled on the termination of the tenancy, on quitting the holding, to obtain from his landlord compensation for any such matter as is specified in Part II of Schedule 8 to this Act.

(2)   The tenant shall not be entitled to compensation under subsection (1) above for crops or produce grown, seeds sown, cultivations, fallows or acts of husbandry performed, or pasture laid down, in contravention of the terms of a written contract of tenancy unless—

(a)   the growing of the crops or produce, the sowing of the seeds, the performance of the cultivations, fallows or acts of husbandry, or the laying down of the pasture was reasonably necessary in consequence of the giving of a direction under the Agriculture Act 1947, or

(b)   the tenant shows that the term of the contract contravened was inconsistent with the fulfilment of his responsibilities to farm the holding in accordance with the rules of good husbandry.

(3)   Subject to paragraphs 6 and 7 of Schedule 12 to this Act, subsection (1) above shall apply to a tenant on whatever date he entered into occupation of the holding.

NOTES

Derivation

This section derived from the Agricultural Holdings Act 1948, ss 46(1), 47(1).

Initial Commencement

Specified date: 18 June 1986: see s 102(2).

Extent

This Act does not extend to Scotland.

See Further

See further, as to the exclusion of this Act in relation to leases or tenancies granted to contractors in respect of the running of any removal centre or part of a removal centre: the Immigration and Asylum Act 1999, s 149(3).

Notes

For a commentary, see para 38.28 ff.

Sub-s (1) contains provisions formerly in the Agricultural Holdings Act 1948, ss 46(1), 47(1). Sub-s (2) contains provisions formerly in s 47(1)(b) of the 1948 Act. Sub-s (3) contains provisions formerly in s 46(1) of the 1948 Act.

General Note. See the General Notes to ss 60, 64.

Compensation. The following provisions are also relevant to compensation for tenant-right matters under this section: s 66(2), (4) (measure of compensation); s 74 (termination of tenancy of part of holding); s 75 (compensation where reversionary estate in holding is severed); s 76 (restrictions on compensation for things done in compliance with this Act); s 77(1) (no compensation under custom); s 78 (extent to which compensation recoverable under agreements); s 83 (settlement of claims); s 85 (enforcement); s 86 (power of landlord to obtain charge on holding); and s 87 (general provisions as to charges).

Modification of section. As to the modification of this section in cases where the tenant entered into occupation before 1 March 1948, see Sch 12, para 6.

Definitions. For 'agricultural holding', see s 1(1); for 'contract of tenancy', see s 1(5); for 'landlord', 'pasture', 'tenant' and 'termination', see s 96(1). Note as to 'farm ... in accordance with the rules of good husbandry', s 96(3); and as to 'termination', see also s 74(4).

Agriculture Act 1947. See s 95 of that Act as to special directions to secure production.

A1.153

66 Measure of compensation

(1) The amount of any compensation under this Act for a relevant improvement specified in Schedule 7 to this Act shall be an amount equal to the increase attributable to the improvement in the value of the agricultural holding as a holding, having regard to the character and situation of the holding and the average requirements of tenants reasonably skilled in husbandry.

(2) The amount of any compensation under this Act for a relevant improvement specified in Part I of Schedule 8 to this Act, or for any matter falling within Part II of that Schedule, shall be the value of the improvement or matter to an incoming tenant calculated in accordance with such method, if any, as may be prescribed.

(3) Where the landlord and the tenant of an agricultural holding have entered into an agreement in writing whereby any benefit is given or allowed to the tenant in consideration of his carrying out an improvement specified in Part I of Schedule 8 to this Act, the benefit shall be taken into account in assessing compensation under this Act for the improvement.

(4) Nothing in this Act shall prevent the substitution, in the case of matters falling within Part II of Schedule 8 to this Act, for the measure of compensation specified in subsection (2) above, of such measure of compensation, to be calculated according to such method, if any, as may be specified in a written contract of tenancy.

(5) Where a grant out of money provided by Parliament or local government funds has been or will be made to the tenant of an agricultural holding in respect of a relevant improvement, the grant shall be taken into account in assessing compensation under this Act for the improvement.

NOTES

Derivation

Sub-ss (1)–(4) derived from the Agricultural Holdings Act 1948, ss 48, 51; sub-s (5) derived from the Agricultural Holdings Act 1948, s 53, and the Agricultural Holdings Act 1984, s 10(1), Sch 3, para 11.

Initial Commencement

Specified date: 18 June 1986: see s 102(2).

Extent

This Act does not extend to Scotland.

See Further

See further, as to the exclusion of this Act in relation to leases or tenancies granted to contractors in respect of the running of any removal centre or part of a removal centre: the Immigration and Asylum Act 1999, s 149(3).

Notes

For a commentary, see para 38.40 ff.

Sub-s (1) contains provisions formerly in the Agricultural Holdings Act 1948, s 48. Sub-ss (2), (3), (4) contain provisions formerly in s 51(1), (3), (2), respectively, of the 1948 Act. Sub-s (5) contains provisions formerly in s 53 of the 1948 Act, as amended by the Agricultural Holdings Act 1984, s 10(1), Sch 3, para 11.

General Note. See the General Notes to ss 60, 64.

Compensation. Ie compensation under s 64 or s 65. As to consent required for long-term improvement with regard to entitlement for compensation, see s 67 (note sub-s (2) thereof for effect on sub-s (1) of this section). Note that where a person other than the tenant claiming compensation has contributed to the cost of works carried out in compliance with an improvement notice or undertaking under the Housing Act 1985, Pt VII (or the Housing Act 1974, Pt VIII, the provisions of which are now contained in the former Act), compensation assessed under this section is reduced proportionately; see s 68(5)(b).

Writing. See the note 'Written' to s 3.

Benefit. Benefit may be a reduction in rent; see *M'Qater v Ferguson* 1911 SC 640. As to other benefits, see *Earl of Galloway v M'Clelland* 1915 SC 1062 (temporary pasture at commencement of lease held a benefit); *Findlay v Munro* 1917 SC 419 (right to take two white crops not a benefit).

Coal-mining subsidence. As to the position of an agricultural tenant in relation to a damage claim, and the measure of compensation under this section and under Sch 9, Pt I, para 2(1) to this Act, see the Coal Mining Subsidence Act 1991, s 21(1), (3), Sch 3, paras 1(2)(b), 2(4).

Opencast coal operations. As to compensation payable for short-term improvements where a compulsory rights order in respect of opencast coal operations has been made, see the Opencast Coal Act 1958, s 26, Sch 4, Pts I–III, as amended, in the case of s 26 of that Act, by s 100, Sch 14, para 28. See also the note to s 64.

Definitions. For 'agricultural holding', see s 1(1); for 'contract of tenancy', see s 1(5); for 'relevant improvement', see s 64(2); for 'agreement', 'landlord', 'local government funds', 'prescribed' and 'tenant', see s 96(1).

Regulations under this section. At the time of going to press no regulations had been made under sub-s (2) above. See, however, by virtue of the Interpretation Act 1978, s 17(2)(b), the Agriculture (Calculation of Value for Compensation) Regulations 1978, SI 1978/809, as amended by SI 1980/751, SI 1981/822, SI 1983/1475, which have effect as if made thereunder.

Note as to the advisory committee for provisions to be included in regulations made under sub-s (2) above, s 92. As to regulations, generally, see s 94.

A1.154

67   Compensation for long-term improvements: consent required

(1)   The tenant of an agricultural holding shall not be entitled to compensation for a relevant improvement specified in Schedule 7 to this Act unless the landlord has given his consent in writing to the carrying out of the improvement.

(2)   Any such consent may be given by the landlord unconditionally or upon such terms as to compensation or otherwise as may be agreed upon in writing between the landlord and the tenant; and the provisions of section 66(1) above shall have effect subject to the provisions of any such agreement as is made.

(3)   Where, in the case of an improvement specified in Part II of Schedule 7 to this Act, a tenant is aggrieved by the refusal of his landlord to give his consent under subsection (1) above, or is unwilling to agree to any terms subject to which the landlord is prepared to give his consent, the tenant may apply to the Tribunal for approval of the carrying out of the improvement, and the following provisions of this section shall have effect with respect to the application.

(4)   The Tribunal may approve the carrying out of the improvement, either unconditionally or upon such terms, whether as to reduction of the compensation which would be payable if the Tribunal approved unconditionally or as to other matters, as appear to them to be just, or may withhold their approval.

(5)   If the Tribunal grant their approval, the landlord may, within the prescribed period from receiving notification of the Tribunal's decision, serve notice in writing on the Tribunal and the tenant that the landlord proposes himself to carry out the improvement.

(6)   Where the Tribunal grant their approval, then if—

(a)   no notice is duly served by the landlord under subsection (5) above, or

(b)   such a notice is duly served, but on an application made by the tenant the Tribunal determines that the landlord has failed to carry out the improvement within a reasonable time,

the approval of the Tribunal shall have effect for the purposes of subsection (1) above as if it were the consent of the landlord, and any terms subject to which the approval was given shall have effect as if they were contained in an agreement in writing between the landlord and the tenant.

(7)   In subsection (5) above, 'the prescribed period' means the period prescribed by the Lord Chancellor by order.

NOTES

Derivation

Sub-ss (1), (2) derived from the Agricultural Holdings Act 1948, s 49(1), (2); sub-ss (3)–(7) derived from the Agricultural Holdings Act 1948, s 50(1)–(4), and the Agriculture Act 1958, s 8(1), Sch 1, Part I, paras 14, 15.

Initial Commencement

Specified date: 18 June 1986: see s 102(2).

Extent

This Act does not extend to Scotland.

See Further

See further, as to the exclusion of this Act in relation to leases or tenancies granted to contractors in respect of the running of any removal centre or part of a removal centre: the Immigration and Asylum Act 1999, s 149(3).

Notes

For a commentary, see para 38.18 ff.

Sub-s (1) contains provisions formerly in the Agricultural Holdings Act 1948, s 49(1). Sub-s (2) contains provisions formerly in s 49(1), (2) of the 1948 Act. Sub-ss (3)–(6) contain provisions formerly in s 50(1)–(4), respectively, of the 1948 Act, as amended, in each case, by the Agriculture Act 1958, s 8(1), Sch 1, Pt I, para 14(a), and as repealed in part, in the case of sub-ss (1), (2), (4) of that section, by ss 8(1), 10(1) of, and Sch 1, Pt 1, para 14(b), (c), (d), Sch 2, Pt II to, the 1958 Act. Sub-s (7) contains provisions formerly in s 50(3) of the 1948 Act, as amended by s 8(1) of, and Sch 1, Pt I, para 15 to, the 1958 Act.

General Note. See the General Notes to ss 60, 64.

Sub-s (1): Compensation. Ie compensation under s 64. This section does not apply to works (in respect of which compensation is claimed) carried out in compliance with an improvement notice or undertaking under the Housing Act 1985, Pt VII (ss 209–238) (or the Housing Act 1974, Pt VIII, the provisions of which are now contained in the former Act, but see the note to s 13), nor does it apply as respects a claim by an immediate landlord to his superior landlord for work carried out on the application of a sub-tenant under s 11; see s 68(2), (5)(a). As to the application of this section with regard to hill farming, see the special provisions contained in s 68(3).

Consent. As to consent in the lease itself, see *Re Morse and Dixon* (1917) 87 LJKB 1, CA, *Gardner v Beck* [1947] EGD 169. As to consent by limited owners, see s 88.

Writing. See the note 'Written' to s 3.

Sub-s(3): Tribunal. See the note to s 11.

Sub-s (5): Prescribed period. The prescribed period under this subsection is one month from the landlord's receiving notice in writing of the Tribunal's approval of the carrying out of the improvement; see the Agricultural Land Tribunals (Rules) Order 1978, SI 1978/259, r 2, Sch 1, r 7(2), as construed in accordance with s 99, Sch 13, para 1.

Notice. As to service, see s 93.

Sub-s (6): Within a reasonable time. See the note to s 11.

Sub-s (7): Lord Chancellor. See the note to s 29.

Coal-mining subsidence. See the note to s 66.

Forms. As to forms of application to be used for the purposes of sub-ss (3), (6)(b) above, see the Agricultural Land Tribunals (Rules) Order 1978, SI 1978/259, r 2, Sch 1, r 7(1), (3), Forms 6, 7, as construed in accordance with s 99, Sch 13, para 1.

Increase of rent and power of landlord to obtain charge. As to increase of rent for improvements carried out by a landlord in pursuance of a notice served under sub-s (5) above, see s 13. For his power to obtain a charge for the repayment of the cost of an improvement carried out by him in pursuance of such a notice, see s 86.

Opencast coal operations. See the note to s 64.

Definitions. For 'agricultural holding', see s 1(1); for 'relevant improvement', see s 64(2); for 'agreed', 'agreement', 'landlord', 'prescribed', 'tenant' and 'the Tribunal', see s 96(1). Note as to 'the prescribed period', sub-s (7) above.

A1.155

68   Improvements: special cases

(1)   The tenant of an agricultural holding shall not be entitled to compensation for a relevant improvement specified in paragraph 1 of Schedule 8 to this Act unless, not

later than one month before the improvement was begun, he gave notice in writing to the landlord of his intention to carry out the improvement.

(2) Where, on an application of the sub-tenant of an agricultural holding, the Tribunal have directed the immediate landlord of the sub-tenant to carry out work under section 11 above being work which constitutes an improvement specified in Schedule 7 to this Act—

(a) section 67 above shall not apply as respects a claim by the immediate landlord against his superior landlord for compensation in respect of that work, and

(b) if, on the failure of the immediate landlord to comply with the direction of the Tribunal, the sub-tenant has himself carried out the work, sections 64 and 66 above shall have effect for the purposes of a claim for compensation by the immediate landlord against his superior landlord as if the work had been carried out by the immediate landlord and as if any grant made to the sub-tenant in respect of the work out of money provided by Parliament had been made to the immediate landlord.

(3) Where the tenant of an agricultural holding has carried out on the holding an improvement specified in Schedule 7 to this Act in accordance with provision for the making of the improvement and for the tenant's being responsible for doing the work in a hill farming land improvement scheme approved under section 1 of the Hill Farming Act 1946, being provision included in the scheme at the instance or with the consent of the landlord—

(a) the landlord shall be deemed to have consented as mentioned in subsection (1) of section 67 above,

(b) any agreement as to compensation or otherwise made between the landlord and the tenant in relation to the improvement shall have effect as if it had been such an agreement on terms as is mentioned in subsection (2) of that section, and

(c) the provisions of subsections (5) and (6) of that section as to the carrying out of improvements by the landlord shall not apply.

(4) In assessing the amount of any compensation payable under custom or agreement to the tenant of an agricultural holding, if it is shown to the satisfaction of the person assessing the compensation that the cultivations in respect of which the compensation is claimed were wholly or in part the result of or incidental to work in respect of the cost of which an improvement grant has been paid under section 1 of the Hill Farming Act 1946, the amount of the grant shall be taken into account as if it had been a benefit allowed to the tenant in consideration of his executing the cultivations and the compensation shall be reduced to such extent as that person considers appropriate.

(5) Where the tenant of an agricultural holding claims compensation in respect of works carried out in compliance with an improvement notice served, or an undertaking accepted, under Part VII of the Housing Act 1985 or Part VIII of the Housing Act 1974—

(a) section 67 above shall not apply as respects the works, and

(b) if a person other than the tenant has contributed to the cost of carrying out the works, compensation in respect of the works as assessed under section 66 above shall be reduced proportionately.

NOTES

Derivation

Sub-s (1) derived from the Agricultural Holdings Act 1948, s 52; sub-s (2) derived from the Agriculture Act 1958, s 4(6) and gives effect to Law Commission Recommendation No 153,

A1.155 *Statutes*

Cmnd 9665; sub-ss (3), (4) derived from the Hill Farming Act 1946, s 9(2), (4), and the Agricultural Holdings Act 1948, s 95, Sch 7, para 4; sub-s (5) derived from the Housing Act 1985, s 231(3), (4).

Initial Commencement

Specified date: 18 June 1986: see s 102(2).

Extent

This Act does not extend to Scotland.

See Further

See further, as to the exclusion of this Act in relation to leases or tenancies granted to contractors in respect of the running of any removal centre or part of a removal centre: the Immigration and Asylum Act 1999, s 149(3).

Notes

For a commentary, see para 38.23.

Sub-s (1) contains provisions formerly in the Agricultural Holdings Act 1948, s 52. Sub-s (2) contains provisions formerly in the Agriculture Act 1958, s 4(6), taking into account the second recommendation in the Law Commission's Report on this consolidation (Law Com No 153; Cmnd 9665), as to which, see the note 'Grant made to the subtenant, etc below. Sub-ss (3), (4) contain provisions formerly in the Hill Farming Act 1946, s 9(2), (4), as substituted by the Agricultural Holdings Act 1948, s 95, Sch 7, para 4. Sub-s (5) contains provisions formerly in the Housing Act 1985, s 231(3), (4).

General Note. See the General Notes to ss 60, 64.

Sub-s (1): Compensation. Ie compensation under s 64.

Not later than one month before, etc. When an act has to be done not later than a given period before the happening of a certain event, the day on which the event happens is excluded in the calculation of the period; cf *Carapanayoti & Co Ltd v Comptoir Commercial Andre et Cie SA* [1972] 1 Lloyd's Rep 139, CA. See as to 'month' the corresponding note to s 4.

Notice. As to service, see s 93.

Writing. See the note 'Written' to s 3.

Sub-s (2): The Tribunal. See the note to s 11.

Grant made to the sub-tenant, etc. In Sub-s (2)(b) above the words from 'and as if any grant made to the sub-tenant' to the end of that paragraph are added as a consequence of the second recommendation in the Law Commission's Report on this consolidation (Law Com No 153; Cmnd 9665). The effect of this addition is that, where an immediate landlord claims compensation from his superior landlord in respect of work carried out by the sub-tenant, ss 64, 66 are to have effect as if any grant made to the tenant in respect of the work out of money provided by Parliament had been made to the immediate landlord. This removes the anomaly whereby an immediate landlord failing to comply with a direction of the Tribunal under what is now s 11 was only liable to repay the tenant the cost of any work less the amount of any grant received by the tenant out of money provided by Parliament but was still able, on the termination of the tenancy, to claim compensation from the superior landlord without taking any such grant into account (that being the inferred position under the Agriculture Act 1958, s 4(6), as to which, see the derivation note above). The textual addition made in accordance with the Law Commission recommendation brings that provision, now contained in sub-s (2)(b) above, into line with the similar procedure contained in s 13(5) (cf, also, s 66(5)).

Opencast coal operations. See the note to s 64.

Definitions. For 'agricultural holding', see s 1(1); for 'relevant improvement', see s 64(2); for 'agreement', 'landlord', 'tenant' and 'the Tribunal', see s 96(1).

Housing Act 1985, Pt VII; Housing Act 1974, Pt VIII. Pt VIII of the 1974 Act was repealed by the Housing (Consequential Provisions) Act 1985, s 3, Sch 1, and replaced, generally, by Pt VII of the

1985 Act (repealed by the Local Government and Housing Act 1989, ss 165, 194, Sch 12, Pt II, subject to a saving in SI 1990/431, Sch 1, para 12). As to the service of improvement notices, see ss 209 et seq of the 1985 Act, and as to undertakings accepted, see s 211.

A1.156

69   Improvements: successive tenancies

(1)   Where the tenant of an agricultural holding has remained in the holding[, or in any agricultural holding which comprised the whole or a substantial part of the land comprised in the holding,] during two or more tenancies, he shall not be deprived of his right to compensation under this Act in respect of relevant improvements by reason only that the improvements were made during a tenancy other than the one at the termination of which he quits the holding.

[(1A)   Where this Act applies in relation to any tenancy referred to in subsection (1) above by virtue of section 4(1)(g) of the Agricultural Tenancies Act 1995, the reference in that subsection to a substantial part of the land comprised in the holding means a substantial part determined by reference to either area or value.]

(2)   Where, on entering into occupation of an agricultural holding, the tenant—

  (a)   with the consent in writing of his landlord paid to an outgoing tenant any compensation payable by the landlord under or in pursuance of this Act (or the Agricultural Holdings Act 1948 or Part III of the Agriculture Act 1947) in respect of the whole or part of a relevant improvement, or

  (b)   has paid to the landlord the amount of any such compensation payable to an outgoing tenant,

the tenant shall be entitled, on quitting the holding, to claim compensation in respect of the improvement or part in the same manner, if at all, as the outgoing tenant would have been entitled if the outgoing tenant had remained tenant of the holding and quitted it at the time at which the tenant quits it.

(3)   Where, in a case not falling within subsection (2) above, the tenant, on entering into occupation of an agricultural holding, paid to his landlord any amount in respect of the whole or part of a relevant improvement, he shall, subject to any agreement in writing between the landlord and the tenant, be entitled on quitting the holding to claim compensation in respect of the improvement or part in the same manner, if at all, as he would have been entitled if he had been tenant of the holding at the time when the improvement was carried out and the improvement or part had been carried out by him.

NOTES

Derivation

This section derived from the Agricultural Holdings Act 1948, ss 54, 55(1), (2).

Initial Commencement

Specified date: 18 June 1986: see s 102(2).

Extent

This Act does not extend to Scotland.

Amendment

Sub-s (1): words from ', or in any' to 'in the holding,' in square brackets inserted by SI 2006/2805, arts 2, 6(1).

Date in force: 19 October 2006 (except in relation to compensation payable on termination of a tenancy where that tenancy was granted before that date): see SI 2006/2805, arts 1(1)(b), 6(8).

Sub-s (1A): inserted by SI 2006/2805, arts 2, 6(2).

Date in force: 19 October 2006 (except in relation to compensation payable on termination of a tenancy where that tenancy was granted before that date): see SI 2006/2805, arts 1(1)(b), 6(8).

See Further

See further, as to the exclusion of this Act in relation to leases or tenancies granted to contractors in respect of the running of any removal centre or part of a removal centre: the Immigration and Asylum Act 1999, s 149(3).

Notes

For a commentary, see para 40.2 ff.

Sub-s (1) contains provisions formerly in the Agricultural Holdings Act 1948, s 54. Now amended by the RRO, SI 2006/2805 Art 6. Sub-ss (2), (3) contain provisions formerly in s 55(1), (2), respectively, of the 1948 Act.

General Note. See the General Notes to ss 60, 64.

Compensation. Ie compensation under s 64.

Consent. See the note to s 67.

Writing. See the note 'Written' to s 3.

Opencast coal operations. The Opencast Coal Act 1958, s 24(5), as amended by s 100, Sch 14, para 26(5), applies the provisions of this section to the tenant's right to compensation for improvements and other matters where there is a compulsory rights order in force under the 1958 Act. See, also, the note to s 64.

Definitions. For 'agricultural holding', see s 1(1); for 'relevant improvements', see s 64(2); for 'agreement', 'landlord', 'tenant' and 'termination', see s 96(1). Note, also, as to 'termination', s 74(4).

Agricultural Holdings Act 1948. Repealed by s 101, Sch 15, Pt I. For savings, see Sch 13.

Agriculture Act 1947, Pt III. Repealed by the Agricultural Holdings Act 1948, s 98, Sch 8.

Compensation to tenant for adoption of special system of farming

A1.157

70   Compensation for special system of farming

(1)   Where the tenant of an agricultural holding shows that, by the continuous adoption of a system of farming which has been more beneficial to the holding—

(a)   than the system of farming required by the contract of tenancy, or

(b)   in so far as no system of farming is so required, than the system of farming normally practised on comparable agricultural holdings,

the value of the holding as a holding has been increased during the tenancy, having regard to the character and situation of the holding and the average requirements of tenants reasonably skilled in husbandry, the tenant shall be entitled, on quitting the holding on the termination of the tenancy, to obtain from the landlord compensation of an amount equal to the increase.

(2)   Compensation shall not be recoverable under this section unless—

(a)   the tenant has, not later than one month before the termination of the tenancy, given to the landlord notice in writing of his intention to claim compensation under this section, and

(b)   a record has been made under section 22 above of the condition of the fixed equipment on the holding and of the general condition of the holding.

(3)   Compensation shall not be recoverable under this section in respect of any matter arising before the date of the making of the record referred to in subsection (2) above or, if more than one such record has been made, the first of them.

(4)   In assessing the value of an agricultural holding for the purposes of this section due allowance shall be made for any compensation agreed or awarded to be paid to the tenant for an improvement falling within section 64(1) or (4) above or (subject to paragraph 8 of Schedule 12 to this Act) for any such matter as is specified in Part II of Schedule 8 to this Act, being an improvement or matter which has caused, or contributed to, the benefit.

(5)   Nothing in this section shall entitle a tenant to recover for an improvement falling within section 64(1) or (4) above or an improvement to which the provisions of this Act relating to market gardens apply or (subject to the said paragraph 8) for any such matter as is specified in Part II of Schedule 8 to this Act, any compensation which he is not entitled to recover apart from this section.

NOTES

Derivation

Sub-ss (1), (4), (5) derived from the Agricultural Holdings Act 1948, s 56(1)–(3); sub-ss (2), (3) derived from the Agricultural Holdings Act 1948, s 56(1), and the Agricultural Holdings Act 1984, s 10(1), Sch 3, para 12.

Initial Commencement

Specified date: 18 June 1986: see s 102(2).

Extent

This Act does not extend to Scotland.

See Further

See further, as to the exclusion of this Act in relation to leases or tenancies granted to contractors in respect of the running of any removal centre or part of a removal centre: the Immigration and Asylum Act 1999, s 149(3).

Notes

For a commentary, see para 38.87. This is known as 'High Farming'.

Sub-s (1) contains provisions formerly in the Agricultural Holdings Act 1948, s 56(1). Sub-ss (2), (3) contain provisions formerly in s 56(1), proviso, to the 1948 Act, as amended by the Agricultural Holdings Act 1984, s 10(1), Sch 3, para 12. Sub-ss (4), (5) contain provisions formerly in s 56(2), (3), respectively, of the 1948 Act.

General Note. See the General Note to s 60.

Sub-s (1): Compensation. For supplementary provisions as to compensation under this section, see s 74 (termination of tenancy of part of holding); s 75 (compensation where reversionary estate in holding is severed); s 78 (extent to which compensation recoverable under agreements); s 83 (settlement of claims); and s 85 (enforcement).

Sub-s (2): Not later than one month before, etc. See the note to s 68.

Notice. As to service, see s 93.

Writing. See the note 'Written' to s 3.

Record ... made under section 22. This includes a reference to a record made before 12 September 1984 under the Agricultural Holdings Act 1948, s 16 (repealed by s 101, Sch 15, Pt I), as it had effect before that date; see s 99, Sch 13, para 13. See para 24.13.

Sub-s (5): Provisions of this Act relating to market gardens. See ss 79 ff.

Chequers and Chevening Estates. See the note to s 60.

Modification of section. For a modification of sub-ss (4) and (5) above in the case of certain old tenancies, see Sch 12, para 8.

Opencast coal operations. For the position as to compensation for a special system of farming where a compulsory rights order has been made under the Opencast Coal Act 1958, see s 24 of that Act (noting s 25), as amended by s 100, Sch 14, para 26. See, also, the supplementary provisions in ss 34–36 of, and Sch 6 to, that Act, as amended, in the case of Sch 6 to that Act, by s 100, Sch 14, para 32, and the provisions as to adjustments between landlord and tenant in s 37 of, and Sch 7, Pt I, paras 1–3 to, that Act, as amended, in the case of Sch 7, Pt I to that Act, by s 100, Sch 14, para 33.

Requisitioned land. For the application of this section and s 72 in the case of the disclaimer of a holding under the Landlord and Tenant (Requisitioned Land) Act 1942, see s 2(3) of that Act, as read with s 99, Sch 13, paras 1, 2.

Definitions. For 'agricultural holding', see s 1(1); for 'contract of tenancy', see s 1(5); for 'fixed equipment', 'landlord', 'tenant' and 'termination', see s 96(1). Note, also, as to 'termination', s 74(4).

Compensation to landlord for deterioration of holding

A1.158

71 Compensation for deterioration of particular parts of holding

(1) The landlord of an agricultural holding shall be entitled to recover from a tenant of the holding, on the tenant's quitting the holding on the termination of the tenancy, compensation in respect of the dilapidation or deterioration of, or damage to, any part of the holding or anything in or on the holding caused by non-fulfilment by the tenant of his responsibilities to farm in accordance with the rules of good husbandry.

(2) Subject to subsection (5) below, the amount of the compensation payable under subsection (1) above shall be the cost, as at the date of the tenant's quitting the holding, of making good the dilapidation, deterioration or damage.

(3) Notwithstanding anything in this Act, the landlord may, in lieu of claiming compensation under subsection (1) above, claim compensation in respect of matters specified in that subsection under and in accordance with a written contract of tenancy.

(4) Where the landlord claims compensation in accordance with subsection (3) above—

   (a) compensation shall be so claimed only on the tenant's quitting the holding on the termination of the tenancy, and
   (b) compensation shall not be claimed in respect of any one holding both under such a contract as is mentioned in that subsection and under subsection (1) above;

and for the purposes of paragraph (b) above any claim under section 9(1) above shall be disregarded.

(5) The amount of the compensation payable under subsection (1) above, or in accordance with subsection (3) above, shall in no case exceed the amount (if any) by which the value of the landlord's reversion in the holding is diminished owing to the dilapidation, deterioration or damage in question.

NOTES

Derivation

Sub-ss (1), (3), (4) derived from the Agricultural Holdings Act 1948, s 57(1), (3); sub-ss (2), (5) derived from the Agricultural Holdings Act 1948, s 57(2), (4), and the Agricultural Holdings Act 1984, s 10(1), Sch 3, para 13.

Initial Commencement

Specified date: 18 June 1986: see s 102(2).

Extent

This Act does not extend to Scotland.

See Further

See further, as to the exclusion of this Act in relation to leases or tenancies granted to contractors in respect of the running of any removal centre or part of a removal centre: the Immigration and Asylum Act 1999, s 149(3).

Notes

For a commentary, see para 39.3 ff.

Sub-ss (1), (2), (5) contain provisions formerly in the Agricultural Holdings Act 1948, s 57(1), (2), (4), respectively, as amended, in the case of sub-s (2), and as added in the case of sub-s (4) of that section, by the Agricultural Holdings Act 1984, s 10(1), Sch 3, para 13(a), (b), respectively. Sub-ss (3), (4) contain provisions formerly in s 57(3) of the 1948 Act.

Sub-s (1): Compensation. As to the application of this section where there have been successive tenancies, see s 73; and cf s 72 relating to compensation for general deterioration of a holding. For supplementary provision as to compensation under this section, see the enactments cited in the note 'Compensation' to s 70 except s 75.

Non-fulfilment by the tenant of his responsibilities. The arbitrator must take into account the terms of the lease, any other contract between the landlord and the tenant and provisions incorporated in the tenancy by the Agriculture (Maintenance, Repair and Insurance of Fixed Equipment) Regulations 1973, SI 1973/1473, as amended by SI 1988/ 281 (as to which see the note 'Regulations under this section' to s 7) so as not to include in the claim an obligation which the landlord is contractually liable to perform: *Barrow Green Estate Co v Walker's Executors* [1954] 1 All ER 204, [1954] 1 WLR 231, CA. A claim for rehabilitation of fields falls within this section and is not excluded by s 72: *Evans v Jones* [1955] 2 QB 58, [1955] 2 All ER 118, CA.

Sub-s (3): Landlord may ... claim compensation ... under ... a contract of tenancy. A claim for breach of repairing covenants is independent of this section and the jurisdiction of the court is not ousted by s 83 (*Gulliver v Catt* [1952] 2 QB 308, [1952] 1 All ER 929, CA), and a landlord is not precluded by sub-s (4)(a) from suing for forfeiture and damages during the lease (*Kent v Conniff* [1953] 1 QB 361, [1953] 1 All ER 155, CA). Sub-s (4)(b) does not preclude the landlord's claiming in the alternative provided he later abandons one head of claim: *Boyd v Wilton* [1957] 2 QB 277, [1957] 2 All ER 102, CA.

Written. See the note to s 3.

Sub-s (4). See the first note to sub-s (3) above.

Chequers and Chevening Estates. See the note to s 60.

Opencast coal operations. As to deductions from tenant's compensation, in the case of opencast coal operations, of the amount of any compensation recoverable from the tenant by the landlord under this section or s 72, see the Opencast Coal Act 1958, s 25, as amended by s 100, Sch 14, para 27.

Transfer of liability in respect of fixed equipment. As to the payment of compensation in the case of a transfer of the liability for the maintenance or repair of an item of fixed equipment from the tenant to the landlord, see s 9(1).

Definitions. For 'agricultural holding', see s 1(1); for 'contract of tenancy', see s 1(5); for 'landlord', 'tenant' and 'termination', see s 96(1). Note as to 'farm in accordance with the rules of good husbandry', s 96(2). Note, also, as to 'termination', s 74(4).

A1.159

72   Compensation for general deterioration of holding

(1)   This section applies where, on the quitting of an agricultural holding by the tenant on the termination of the tenancy, the landlord shows that the value of the holding generally has been reduced by reason of any such dilapidation, deterioration or damage as is mentioned in section 71(1) above or otherwise by non-fulfilment by the tenant of his responsibilities to farm in accordance with the rules of good husbandry.

(2)   Where this section applies, the landlord shall be entitled to recover from the tenant compensation for the matter in question, in so far as the landlord is not compensated for it under subsection (1), or in accordance with subsection (3), of section 71 above.

(3)   The amount of the compensation payable under this section shall be equal to the decrease attributable to the matter in question in the value of the holding as a holding, having regard to the character and situation of the holding and the average requirements of tenants reasonably skilled in husbandry.

(4)   Compensation shall not be recoverable under this section unless the landlord has, not later than one month before the termination of the tenancy, given notice in writing to the tenant of his intention to claim such compensation.

NOTES

Derivation

This section derived from the Agricultural Holdings Act 1948, s 58.

Initial Commencement

Specified date: 18 June 1986: see s 102(2).

Extent

This Act does not extend to Scotland.

See Further

See further, as to the exclusion of this Act in relation to leases or tenancies granted to contractors in respect of the running of any removal centre or part of a removal centre: the Immigration and Asylum Act 1999, s 149(3).

Notes

For a commentary, see para 39.4 ff.

This section contains provisions formerly in the Agricultural Holdings Act 1948, s 58.

General Note. This section covers, inter alia, the case of a general depreciation of the farm as a whole due to specific failures of the tenant under s 71, but so that the landlord must bring into account anything recovered under that section: *Evans v Jones* [1955] 2 QB 58, [1955] 2 All ER 118, CA.

Non-fulfilment by the tenant of his responsibilities. See the note to s 71.

Compensation. As to the application of this section where there have been successive tenancies, see s 73, and c f s 71 as to compensation for deterioration of particular parts of a holding. For supplementary provisions as to compensation under this section, see the enactments cited in the note 'Compensation' to s 70 except s 75.

Not later than one month before, etc. See the note to s 68.

Notice. As to service, see s 93.

Writing. See the note 'Written' to s 3.

Modification. As to the modification of this section where tenancies are terminated by virtue of the Land Compensation Act 1973, s 56(3)(c), see s 56(4) of that Act, as amended by s 100, Sch 14, para 54(3).

Opencast coal operations. See the note to s 71.

Requisitioned land. See the note to s 70.

Definitions. For 'agricultural holding', see s 1(1); for 'landlord', 'tenant' and 'termination', see s 96(1). Note as to 'farm in accordance with the rules of good husbandry', s 96(2). Note, also, as to 'termination', s 74(4).

A1.160

73   Deterioration of holding: successive tenancies

[(1)]   Where the tenant of an agricultural holding has remained on the holding[, or on any agricultural holding which comprised the whole or a substantial part of the land comprised in the holding,] during two or more tenancies his landlord shall not be deprived of his right to compensation under section 71 or 72 above in respect of any dilapidation, deterioration or damage by reason only that the tenancy during which an act or omission occurred which in whole or in part caused the dilapidation, deterioration or damage was a tenancy other than the tenancy at the termination of which the tenant quits the holding.

[(2)   Where this Act applies in relation to any tenancy referred to in subsection (1) above by virtue of section 4(1)(g) of the Agricultural Tenancies Act 1995, the reference in that subsection to a substantial part of the land comprised in the holding means a substantial part determined by reference to either area or value.]

NOTES

Derivation

This section derived from the Agricultural Holdings Act 1948, s 59.

Initial Commencement

Specified date: 18 June 1986: see s 102(2).

Extent

This Act does not extend to Scotland.

Amendment

Sub-s (1): renumbered as such by SI 2006/2805, arts 2, 6(3).

Date in force: 19 October 2006 (except in relation to compensation payable on termination of a tenancy where that tenancy was granted before that date): see SI 2006/2805, arts 1(1)(b), 6(8).

Sub-s (1): words from ', or on any' to 'in the holding,' in square brackets inserted by SI 2006/2805, arts 2, 6(4).

Date in force: 19 October 2006 (except in relation to compensation payable on termination of a tenancy where that tenancy was granted before that date): see SI 2006/2805, arts 1(1)(b), 6(8).

Sub-s (2): inserted by SI 2006/2805, arts 2, 6(5).

Date in force: 19 October 2006 (except in relation to compensation payable on termination of a tenancy where that tenancy was granted before that date): see SI 2006/2805, arts 1(1)(b), 6(8).

See Further

See further, as to the exclusion of this Act in relation to leases or tenancies granted to contractors in respect of the running of any removal centre or part of a removal centre: the Immigration and Asylum Act 1999, s 149(3).

Notes

For a commentary, see para 40.2 ff.

This section contains provisions formerly in the Agricultural Holdings Act 1948, s 59.

Definitions. For 'agricultural holding', see s 1(1); for 'landlord', 'tenant' and 'termination', see s 96(1). Note, also, as to 'termination', s 74(4).

Supplementary provisions with respect to compensation

A1.161

74 Termination of tenancy of part of holding

(1) Where the landlord of an agricultural holding resumes possession of part of the holding by virtue of section 31 or 43(2) above, the provisions of this Act with respect to compensation shall apply to that part of the holding as if it were a separate holding which the tenant had quitted in consequence of a notice to quit.

(2) Where the landlord of an agricultural holding resumes possession of part of the holding in pursuance of a provision in that behalf contained in the contract of tenancy—

    (a) the provisions of this Act with respect to compensation shall apply to that part of the holding as if it were a separate holding which the tenant had quitted in consequence of a notice to quit, but

    (b) the arbitrator in assessing the amount of compensation payable to the tenant, except the amount of compensation under section 60(2)(b) above, shall take into consideration any benefit or relief allowed to the tenant under the contract of tenancy in respect of the land possession of which is resumed by the landlord.

(3) Where a person entitled to a severed part of the reversionary estate in an agricultural holding resumes possession of part of the holding by virtue of a notice to quit that part given to the tenant by virtue of section 140 of the Law of Property Act 1925 the provisions of this Act with respect to compensation shall apply to that part of the holding as if—

    (a) it were a separate holding which the tenant had quitted in consequence of the notice to quit, and

    (b) the person resuming possession were the landlord of that separate holding.

(4) References in this Act to the termination of the tenancy of, or (as the case may be) of part of, an agricultural holding include references to the resumption of possession of part of an agricultural holding in circumstances within subsection (1), (2) or (3) above.

NOTES

Derivation

Sub-s (1) derived from the Agricultural Holdings Act 1948, s 60(1), the Agriculture (Miscellaneous Provisions) Act 1968, s 9(1), (2), the Agricultural Holdings (Notices to Quit) Act 1977, s 13(1), Sch 1, para 1(5), and the Agricultural Holdings Act 1984, s 10(1), Sch 3, para 14(a); sub-s (2) derived from the Agricultural Holdings Act 1948, s 60(1), and the Agriculture (Miscellaneous Provisions) Act 1968, ss 9(1), (2), 15(2); sub-ss (3), (4) derived from the Agricultural Holdings Act 1948, s 60(2), (3), the Agriculture (Miscellaneous Provisions) Act 1968, ss 9(1A), 17(2), and the Agricultural Holdings Act 1984, s 10(1), Sch 3, paras 14(b), 31, 33.

Initial Commencement

Specified date: 18 June 1986: see s 102(2).

Extent

This Act does not extend to Scotland.

See Further

See further, as to the exclusion of this Act in relation to leases or tenancies granted to contractors in respect of the running of any removal centre or part of a removal centre: the Immigration and Asylum Act 1999, s 149(3).

Notes

See paras 39.20 and 40.6.

Sub-s (1) contains provisions formerly in the Agricultural Holdings Act 1948, s 60(1) (as amended by the Agricultural Holdings (Notices to Quit) Act 1977, s 13(1), Sch 1, para 1(5), and by the Agricultural Holdings Act 1984, s 10(1), Sch 3, para 14(a)), and in the Agriculture (Miscellaneous Provisions) Act 1968, s 9(1), (2). Sub-s (2) contains provisions formerly in s 60(1) of the 1948 Act, as repealed in part by the Agriculture (Miscellaneous Provisions) Act 1963, s 18(2), Schedule, Pt 1, and as read with ss 9(1), (2), 15(2) of the 1968 Act. Sub-s (3) contains provisions formerly in s 60(2) of the 1948 Act, as added by s 10(1) of, and Sch 3, para 14(b) to, the 1984 Act, and as read with s 9(1A) of the 1968 Act, (as inserted by s 10(1) of, and Sch 3, para 31 to, the 1984 Act). Sub-s (4) contains provisions formerly in s 60(3) of the 1948 Act, as added by s 10(1) of, and Sch 3, para 14(b) to, the 1984 Act, and in s 17(2) of the 1968 Act, as amended by s 10(1) of, and Sch 3, para 33 to, the 1984 Act.

Provisions of this Act with respect to compensation. Ie ss 60–73.

Arbitrator. As to the settlement of claims by arbitration on the termination of a tenancy, see s 83 in conjunction with s 84 and the note to s 2.

Benefit. Cf the note to s 66.

Chequers and Chevening Estates. See the note to s 60.

Definitions. For 'agricultural holding', see s 1(1); for 'contract of tenancy', see s 1(5); and for 'landlord' and 'tenant', see s 96(1).

A1.162

75   Compensation where reversionary estate in holding is severed

(1)   Where the reversionary estate in an agricultural holding is for the time being vested in more than one person in several parts, the tenant shall be entitled, on quitting the entire holding, to require that any compensation payable to him under this Act shall be determined as if the reversionary estate were not so severed.

(2) Where subsection (1) above applies, the arbitrator shall, where necessary, apportion the amount awarded between the persons who for the purposes of this Act together constitute the landlord of the holding, and any additional costs of the award caused by the apportionment shall be directed by the arbitrator to be paid by those persons in such proportions as he shall determine.

NOTES

Derivation

This section derived from the Agricultural Holdings Act 1948, s 61, the Agriculture (Miscellaneous Provisions) Act 1968, ss 10(5), 15(4), and the Agricultural Holdings Act 1984, s 10(1), Sch 3, para 15.

Initial Commencement

Specified date: 18 June 1986: see s 102(2).

Extent

This Act does not extend to Scotland.

See Further

See further, as to the exclusion of this Act in relation to leases or tenancies granted to contractors in respect of the running of any removal centre or part of a removal centre: the Immigration and Asylum Act 1999, s 149(3).

Notes

For a commentary, see para 40.8.

This section contains provisions formerly in the Agricultural Holdings Act 1948, s 61 (as amended by the Agricultural Holdings Act 1984, s 10(1), Sch 3, para 15), as read with the Agriculture (Miscellaneous Provisions) Act 1968, ss 10(5), 15(4).

Compensation. Ie compensation under ss 60–70.

Arbitrator. For provisions as to arbitration under this Act, see s 84 and the note to s 2.

Definitions. For 'agricultural holding', see s 1(1); for 'landlord' and 'tenant', see s 96(1).

A1.163

76   Restrictions on compensation for things done in compliance with this Act

(1) Notwithstanding anything in this Act or any custom or agreement—

(a) no compensation shall be payable to the tenant of an agricultural holding in respect of anything done in pursuance of an order under section 14(4) above,

(b) in assessing compensation to an outgoing tenant of an agricultural holding where land has been ploughed up in pursuance of a direction under that section, the value per hectare of any tenant's pasture comprised in the holding shall be taken not to exceed the average value per hectare of the whole of the tenant's pasture comprised in the holding on the termination of the tenancy.

(2) In subsection (1) above 'tenant's pasture' means pasture laid down at the expense of the tenant or paid for by the tenant on entering on the holding.

(3) The tenant of an agricultural holding shall not be entitled to any compensation for a relevant improvement specified in Part I of Schedule 8 to this Act or (subject to

paragraph 8 of Schedule 12 to this Act) for any such matter as is specified in Part II of Schedule 8 if it is an improvement or matter made or effected for the purposes of section 15(4) above.

NOTES

Derivation

Sub-s (1) derived from the Agricultural Holdings Act 1948, s 63(1), the Agriculture Act 1958, s 8(1), Sch 1, Part I, para 16, and SI 1978/447, reg 2(2); sub-ss (2), (3) derived from the Agricultural Holdings Act 1948, s 63(1), (2).

Initial Commencement

Specified date: 18 June 1986: see s 102(2).

Extent

This Act does not extend to Scotland.

See Further

See further, as to the exclusion of this Act in relation to leases or tenancies granted to contractors in respect of the running of any removal centre or part of a removal centre: the Immigration and Asylum Act 1999, s 149(3).

Notes

For a commentary, see para 40.9.

Sub-s (1) contains provisions formerly in the Agricultural Holdings Act 1948, s 63(1), as amended by the Agriculture Act 1958, s 8(1), Sch 1, Pt I, para 16, and by the Agricultural Holdings Act 1948 (Amendment) Regulations 1978, SI 1978/447, reg 2(2). Sub-ss (2), (3) contain provisions formerly in s 63(1), (2) of the 1948 Act, respectively.

Modification of section. For a modification of sub-s (3) above in the case of certain old tenancies, see Sch 12, para 8.

Definitions. For 'agricultural holding', see s 1(1); for 'relevant improvement', see s 64(2); for 'agreement', 'pasture', 'tenant' and 'termination', see s 96(1). Note as to 'tenant's pasture', sub-s (2) above; as to 'termination', see, also, s 74(4).

A1.164

77   No compensation under custom for improvement or tenant-right matter

(1)   A landlord or tenant of an agricultural holding shall not be entitled under custom to any compensation from the other for any improvement, whether or not one in respect of the carrying out of which compensation is provided under this Act, or (subject to paragraph 8 of Schedule 12 to this Act) for any matter specified in Part II of Schedule 8 to this Act or otherwise.

(2)   Subsection (1) above shall not apply to compensation for an improvement of a kind specified in Schedule 7 or Part I of Schedule 8 to this Act begun before 1st March 1948.

NOTES

Derivation

This section derived from the Agricultural Holdings Act 1948, s 64.

Initial Commencement

Specified date: 18 June 1986: see s 102(2).

Extent

This Act does not extend to Scotland.

See Further

See further, as to the exclusion of this Act in relation to leases or tenancies granted to contractors in respect of the running of any removal centre or part of a removal centre: the Immigration and Asylum Act 1999, s 149(3).

Notes

For a commentary, see para 40.10.

This section contains provisions formerly in the Agricultural Holdings Act 1948, s 64.

1st March 1948. Ie the commencement date of the Agriculture Act 1947, Pt III (repealed).

Modification of section. For a modification of sub-s (1) above in the case of certain old tenancies, see Sch 12, para 8.

Definitions. For 'agricultural holding', see s 1(1); for 'landlord' and 'tenant', see s 96(1).

A1.165

78   Extent to which compensation recoverable under agreements

(1)   Save as expressly provided in this Act, in any case for which apart from this section the provisions of this Act provide for compensation, a tenant or landlord shall be entitled to compensation in accordance with those provisions and not otherwise, and shall be so entitled notwithstanding any agreement to the contrary.

(2)   Where the landlord and tenant of an agricultural holding enter into an agreement in writing for any such variation of the terms of the contract of tenancy as could be made by direction or order under section 14 above, the agreement may provide for the exclusion of compensation in the same manner as under section 76(1) above.

(3)   Nothing in the provisions of this Act, apart from this section, shall be construed as disentitling a tenant or landlord to compensation in any case for which the said provisions do not provide for compensation, but (subject to paragraph 8 of Schedule 12 to this Act) a claim for compensation in any such case shall not be enforceable except under an agreement in writing.

NOTES

Derivation

Sub-ss (1), (2) derived from the Agricultural Holdings Act 1948, s 65(1), and the Agriculture (Miscellaneous Provisions) Act 1968, ss 10(4), 15(4); sub-s (3) derived from the Agricultural Holdings Act 1948, s 65(2).

Initial Commencement

Specified date: 18 June 1986: see s 102(2).

Extent

This Act does not extend to Scotland.

See Further

See further, as to the exclusion of this Act in relation to leases or tenancies granted to contractors in respect of the running of any removal centre or part of a removal centre: the Immigration and Asylum Act 1999, s 149(3).

Notes

For a commentary, see para 40.11.

Sub-ss (1), (2) contain provisions formerly in the Agricultural Holdings Act 1948, s 65(1), as read with the Agriculture (Miscellaneous Provisions) Act 1968, ss 10(4), 15(4). Sub-s (3) contains provisions formerly in s 65(2) of the 1948 Act.

Save as expressly provided. See, eg, ss 66(4), 71(3) and s 81(1).

Notwithstanding any agreement to the contrary. A determination clause 'in case required for building or otherwise' of any part without compensation but with proportionate reduction in rent and exercisable without notice to the lessee, was void, as it prevented the lessee from giving notice of claim required under the Agricultural Holdings Act 1923 (*Re Disraeli's Agreement, Cleasby v Park Estate (Hughenden) Ltd* [1939] Ch 382, [1938] 4 All ER 658), and a similar clause was apparently void under the Agricultural Holdings Act 1948 (*Coates v Diment* [1951] 1 All ER 890).

Writing. See the note 'Written' to s 3.

Modification of section. For a modification of sub-s (3) above in the case of certain old tenancies, see Sch 12, para 8.

Definitions. For 'agricultural holding', see s 1(1); for 'agreement', 'landlord' and 'tenant', see s 96(1).

PART VI: MARKET GARDENS AND SMALLHOLDINGS

A1.166

79   Additional rights with respect to improvements for tenants of market gardens

(1)   Subsections (2) to (5) below apply in the case of an agricultural holding in respect of which it is agreed by an agreement in writing that the holding shall be let or treated as a market garden; and where the land to which such agreement relates consists of part of an agricultural holding only, those subsections shall apply as if that part were a separate holding.

(2)   The provisions of this Act shall apply as if improvements of a kind specified in Schedule 10 to this Act begun on or after 1st March 1948 were included amongst the improvements specified in Part I of Schedule 8 to this Act and as if improvements begun before that day consisting of the erection or enlargement of buildings for the purpose of the trade or business of a market gardener were included amongst the improvements specified in Part II of Schedule 9 to this Act.

(3)   In section 10 above—

(a)   subsection (2)(c) shall not exclude that section from applying to any building erected by the tenant on the holding or acquired by him for the purposes of his trade or business as a market gardener, and

(b)   subsection (2)(d) shall not exclude that section from applying to any building acquired by him for those purposes (whenever erected).

(4)   It shall be lawful for the tenant to remove all fruit trees and fruit bushes planted by him on the holding and not permanently set out, but if the tenant does not remove them before the termination of his tenancy they shall remain the property of the landlord and the tenant shall not be entitled to any compensation in respect of them.

(5) The right of an incoming tenant to claim compensation in respect of the whole or part of an improvement which he has purchased may be exercised although his landlord has not consented in writing to the purchase.

NOTES

Derivation

This section derived from the Agricultural Holdings Act 1948, s 67(1), (3), (4), and the Agricultural Holdings Act 1984, s 10(1), Sch 3, paras 16, 27(b).

Initial Commencement

Specified date: 18 June 1986: see s 102(2).

Extent

This Act does not extend to Scotland.

See Further

See further, as to the exclusion of this Act in relation to leases or tenancies granted to contractors in respect of the running of any removal centre or part of a removal centre: the Immigration and Asylum Act 1999, s 149(3).

Notes

For a commentary, see para 38.90 ff.

This section contains provisions formerly in the Agricultural Holdings Act 1948, s 67(1), (3), (4) (as amended in the case of sub-s (1) of that section by the Agricultural Holdings Act 1984, s 10(1), Sch 3, para 16), and in Sch 3, para 27(b) to the 1984 Act.

Sub-s (1): Writing. See the note 'Written' to s 3.

Let or treated as a market garden. A tenancy agreement giving the right to remove fruit bushes etc does not in itself constitute the holding a market garden: *Re Morse and Dixon* (1917) 87 LJKB 1, CA. 'Treated' means treated as between landlord and tenant for the purposes of governing their rights in respect of the holding, rather than 'used' or 'cultivated': *Re Masters and Duveen* [1923] 2 KB 729, CA. See also, *Saunders-Jacob v Yates* [1933] 2 KB 240, CA. The burden of proof as to a holding being a 'market garden' is on the tenant: *Bickerdike v Lucy* [1920] 1 KB 707.

Sub-s (2): 1st March 1948. Ie the commencement date of the Agriculture Act 1947, Pt III (repealed).

Sub-s (4): Compensation. As to agreements on compensation relating to market gardens, see s 81 (and note s 78); and for supplementary provisions as to compensation, see ss 74 ff. See also as to compensation for market garden improvements, the Small Holdings and Allotments Act 1908, s 47 (as amended by s 100, Sch 14, para 1).

Modification of section. See as to the modified application of this section regarding agreements made before 1 January 1896, Sch 12, para 10; and note as to removal of fixtures acquired by a tenant before 1 January 1901, para 3 of that Schedule.

Chequers and Chevening Estates. See the note to s 60.

Opencast coal operations. For the position where agricultural land used as a market garden is comprised in a compulsory rights order under the Opencast Coal Act 1958, see s 28 of (as amended by s 100, Sch 14, para 30), and Sch 4, Pt VI to, that Act. See also, the supplementary provisions in ss 34–36 of, and Sch 6 to, that Act, as amended, in the case of Sch 6 to that Act, by s 100, Sch 14, para 32, and the provisions as to adjustments between landlord and tenant in s 37 of, and Sch 7, Pt I, para 5 to, that Act, as amended, in the case of Sch 7, Pt I, para 5 to, that Act, by s 100, Sch 14, para 33(6).

Definitions. For 'agricultural holding', see s 1(1); for 'agreed', 'agreement', 'building', 'landlord', 'tenant' and 'termination', see s 96(1). Note, also, as to 'termination', s 74(4).

A1.167

80   Power of Tribunal to direct holding to be treated as market garden

(1)   Where the tenant of an agricultural holding desires to make on the holding or any part of it an improvement specified in Schedule 10 to this Act and the landlord refuses, or fails within a reasonable time, to agree in writing that the holding or that part of it, as the case may be, shall be treated as a market garden, the tenant may apply to the Tribunal for a direction under subsection (2) below.

(2)   On such an application, the Tribunal may, after being satisfied that the holding or part is suitable for the purposes of market gardening, direct that subsections (2) to (5) of section 79 above shall, either in respect of all the improvements specified in the said Schedule 10 or in respect of some only of those improvements, apply to the holding or to that part of it; and the said subsections shall apply accordingly as respects any improvements executed after the date on which the direction is given.

(3)   Where a direction is given under subsection (2) above, then, if the tenancy is terminated by notice to quit given by the tenant or by reason of the tenant becoming insolvent, the tenant shall not be entitled to compensation in respect of improvements specified in the direction unless the conditions mentioned in subsection (4) below are satisfied.

(4)   Those conditions are that—

    (a)   the tenant not later than one month after the date on which the notice to quit is given or the date of the insolvency, as the case may be, or such later date as may be agreed, produces to the landlord an offer in writing by a substantial and otherwise suitable person (being an offer which is to hold good for a period of three months from the date on which it is produced)—

        (i)   to accept a tenancy of the holding from the termination of the existing tenancy, and on the terms and conditions of that tenancy so far as applicable, and,

        (ii)   subject as hereinafter provided, to pay to the outgoing tenant all compensation payable under this Act or under the contract of tenancy, and

    (b)   the landlord fails to accept the offer within three months after it has been produced.

(5)   If the landlord accepts any such offer as is mentioned in subsection (4) above, the incoming tenant shall pay to the landlord on demand all sums payable to him by the outgoing tenant on the termination of the tenancy in respect of rent or breach of contract or otherwise in respect of the holding, and any amount so paid may, subject to any agreement between the outgoing tenant and incoming tenant, be deducted by the incoming tenant from any compensation payable by him to the outgoing tenant.

(6)   A direction under subsection (2) above may be given subject to such conditions (if any) for the protection of the landlord as the Tribunal think fit.

(7)   Without prejudice to the generality of subsection (6) above, where a direction relates to part only of an agricultural holding, it may, on the application of the landlord, be given subject to the condition that it shall become operative only in the event of the tenant's consenting to the division of the holding into two parts, of which one shall be that to which the direction relates, to be held at rents settled, in default of agreement, by arbitration under this Act, but otherwise on the same terms and conditions (so far as applicable) as those on which the holding is held.

(8)   A new tenancy created by the acceptance of a tenant in accordance with the provisions of this section on the terms and conditions of the existing tenancy shall be deemed for the purposes of Schedule 2 to this Act not to be a new tenancy.

(9)   For the purposes of subsection (3) above a person has become insolvent if any of the events mentioned in section 96(2)(a) or (b) below has occurred; and the reference in subsection (4) above to the date of the insolvency is a reference to the date of the occurrence of the event in question.

NOTES

Derivation

Sub-ss (1), (2), (6) derived from the Agricultural Holdings Act 1948, s 68(1), (4), and the Agriculture Act 1958, s 8(1), Sch 1, Part I, para 17; sub-ss (3), (4), (9) derived from the Agricultural Holdings Act 1948, s 68(2), (6), and the Agricultural Holdings Act 1984, s 10(1), Sch 3, para 17; sub-ss (5), (7), (8) derived from the Agricultural Holdings Act 1948, s 68(3), (4), (5).

Initial Commencement

Specified date: 18 June 1986: see s 102(2).

Extent

This Act does not extend to Scotland.

See Further

See further, as to the exclusion of this Act in relation to leases or tenancies granted to contractors in respect of the running of any removal centre or part of a removal centre: the Immigration and Asylum Act 1999, s 149(3).

Notes

For a commentary, see para 38.95.

Sub-ss (1), (2) contain provisions formerly in the Agricultural Holdings Act 1948, s 68(1). as amended by the Agriculture Act 1958, s 8(1), Sch 1, Pt I, para 17(a), and as repealed in part by ss 8(1), 10(1) of, and Sch 1, Pt I, para 17(b), Sch 2, Pt II to, the 1958 Act. Sub-ss (3), (4) contain provisions formerly in s 68(2) of the 1948 Act, as amended by the Agricultural Holdings Act 1984, s 10(1), Sch 3, para 17(a). Sub-ss (5), (7), (8) contain provisions formerly in s 68(3), (4), (5), respectively, of the 1948 Act. Sub-s (6) contains provisions formerly in s 68(4) of the 1948 Act, as amended by the Agriculture Act 1958, s 8(1), Sch 1, Pt I, para 17(a). Sub-s (9) contains provisions formerly in s 68(6) of the 1948 Act, as added by s 10(1) of, and Sch 3, para 17(b) to, the 1984 Act.

Sub-s (1): Within a reasonable time; the Tribunal. See the notes to s 11.

Writing. See the note 'Written' to s 3.

Sub-s (3): Compensation. As to agreements on compensation relating to market gardens, see s 81 (and note s 78); and for supplementary provisions as to compensation, see ss 74 ff.

Sub-s (4): Not later than one month after, etc. As a general rule the effect of defining a period in such a manner is to exclude the day on which the event in question occurs; see 45 Halsbury's Laws (4th edn) para 1127. See also, *Dodds v Walker* [1981] 2 All ER 609, [1981] 1 WLR 1027, HL, as to the day of expiry of periods of a month or a specified number of months.

Within three months after, etc. See the note 'Not later than one month after, etc' above.

Sub-s (7): Arbitration under this Act. For provisions as to arbitration under this Act, see s 84 and the note to s 2.

Form. For the form of application to be used for the purposes of this section, see, as construed in accordance with s 99, Sch 13, para 1, the Agricultural Land Tribunals (Rules) Order 1978, SI 1978/259, r 2, Sch 1, r 8, Form 8.

Opencast coal operations. As to compensation payable for market garden improvements where a compulsory rights order in respect of opencast coal operations has been made, see the Opencast

Coal Act 1958, s 28, Sch 4, Pt VI, as amended, in the use of s 28 of that Act, by s 100, Sch 14, para 30. See, also, the supplementary provisions in ss 34–36 of, and Sch 6 to, the 1958 Act.

Definitions. For 'agricultural holding', see s 1(1); for 'agreed', 'agreement', 'landlord', 'tenant', 'termination' and 'the Tribunal', s 96(1). Note as to 'tenant becoming insolvent', by virtue of sub-s (9) above, s 96(2) (and see also s 99 and Sch 13, para 14); and note also as to 'date of insolvency', sub-s (9) above; and see, also, as to 'termination', s 74(4).

A1.168

81 Agreements as to compensation relating to market gardens

(1) Where an agreement in writing secures to the tenant of an agricultural holding, for an improvement for which compensation is payable by virtue of section 79 or section 80 above, fair and reasonable compensation having regard to the circumstances existing when the agreement was made, the compensation so secured shall, as respects that improvement, be substituted for compensation under this Act.

(2) The landlord and tenant of an agricultural holding who have agreed that the holding shall be let or treated as a market garden may by agreement in writing substitute, for the provisions as to compensation which would otherwise be applicable to the holding, the provisions as to compensation known as the 'Evesham custom', and set out in subsections (3) to (5) of section 80 above.

NOTES

Derivation

This section derived from the Agricultural Holdings Act 1948, s 69.

Initial Commencement

Specified date: 18 June 1986: see s 102(2).

Extent

This Act does not extend to Scotland.

See Further

See further, as to the exclusion of this Act in relation to leases or tenancies granted to contractors in respect of the running of any removal centre or part of a removal centre: the Immigration and Asylum Act 1999, s 149(3).

Notes

For a commentary, see para 38.98.

This section contains provisions formerly in the Agricultural Holdings Act 1948, s 69.

Writing. See the note 'Written' to s 3.

Let or treated as a market garden. See the note to s 79.

Definitions. For 'agricultural holding', see s 1(1); for 'agreement', 'landlord' and 'tenant', see s 96(1).

A1.169

82 Application of section 15 to smallholdings

(1) Section 15(1) above shall not apply to a tenancy of land let as a smallholding by a smallholdings authority or by the Minister in pursuance of a scheme, approved by the Minister for the purposes of this section, which—

(a) provides for the farming of such holdings on a co-operative basis,

(b) provides for the disposal of the produce of such holdings, or

(c) provides other centralised services for the use of the tenants of such holdings.

(2) Where it appears to the Minister that the provisions of any scheme approved by him for the purposes of this section are not being satisfactorily carried out, he may, in accordance with subsection (3) below, withdraw his approval to the scheme.

(3) Before withdrawing his approval to a scheme the Minister shall—

(a) serve a notice on the persons responsible for the management of the scheme specifying a date (not being earlier than one month after the service of the notice) and stating that on that date his approval to the scheme will cease to have effect and that, accordingly, section 15(1) will then apply to the tenancies granted in pursuance of the scheme,

(b) give to those persons an opportunity of making representations to him;

and, if the said notice is not withdrawn by the Minister before the said date, section 15(1) shall as from that date apply to the said tenancies.

NOTES

Derivation

Sub-s (1) derived from the Agricultural Holdings Act 1948, s 11(4)(c), the Agriculture (Miscellaneous Provisions) Act 1949, s 10(1), and the Agriculture Act 1970, s 64(2), Sch 4; sub-ss (2), (3) derived from the Agriculture (Miscellaneous Provisions) Act 1949, s 10(2), the Transfer of Functions (Ministry of Food) Order 1955, SI 1955/554, art 3, and the Transfer of Functions (Wales) (No 1) Order 1978, SI 1978/272, art 2(1), Sch 1.

Initial Commencement

Specified date: 18 June 1986: see s 102(2).

Extent

This Act does not extend to Scotland.

See Further

See further, as to the exclusion of this Act in relation to leases or tenancies granted to contractors in respect of the running of any removal centre or part of a removal centre: the Immigration and Asylum Act 1999, s 149(3).

Transfer of Functions

Functions of the Minister, so far as exercisable in relation to Wales, transferred to the National Assembly for Wales, by the National Assembly for Wales (Transfer of Functions) Order 1999, SI 1999/672, art 2, Sch 1.

Notes

For a commentary, see paras 20.19 and 20.20.

Sub-s (1) contains provisions formerly in the Agricultural Holdings Act 1948, s 11(4)(c), as amended by the Agriculture (Miscellaneous Provisions) Act 1949, s 10(1), and by the Agriculture Act 1970, s 64(2), Sch 4. Sub-ss (2), (3) contain provisions formerly in s 10(2) of the 1949 Act.

Land let as a smallholding, etc. As to smallholdings authorities, see the Agriculture Act 1970, s 38, and as to the letting of land as smallholdings, see ss 44 and 54 of that Act.

Serve a notice. See, as to the service of notices, s 93.

One month after, etc. Cf the note 'Not later than one month after, etc' to s 80.

Definitions. For 'the Minister' and 'tenant', see s 96(1).

PART VII: MISCELLANEOUS AND SUPPLEMENTAL

A1.170

83   Settlement of claims on termination of tenancy

(1)   Without prejudice to any other provision of this Act, any claim of whatever nature by the tenant or landlord of an agricultural holding against the other, being a claim which arises—

(a)   under this Act or any custom or agreement, and

(b)   on or out of the termination of the tenancy of the holding or part of it,

shall, subject to the provisions of this section, be determined by arbitration under this Act.

(2)   No such claim as is mentioned in subsection (1) above shall be enforceable unless before the expiry of two months from the termination of the tenancy the claimant has served notice in writing on his landlord or tenant, as the case may be, of his intention to make the claim.

(3)   A notice under subsection (2) above shall specify the nature of the claim; but it shall be sufficient if the notice refers to the statutory provision, custom or term of an agreement under which the claim is made.

(4)   The landlord and tenant may, within the period of eight months from the termination of the tenancy, by agreement in writing settle any such claim as is mentioned in subsection (1) above.

(5)   Where by the expiry of the said period any such claim as is mentioned in subsection (1) above has not been settled, it shall be determined by arbitration under this Act.

(6)   Where a tenant lawfully remains in occupation of part of an agricultural holding after the termination of a tenancy, references in subsections (2) and (4) above to the termination of the tenancy shall, in the case of a claim relating to that part of the holding, be construed as references to the termination of the occupation.

NOTES

Derivation

Sub-ss (1)–(3) derived from the Agricultural Holdings Act 1948, s 70(1), (2), and the Agriculture (Miscellaneous Provisions) Act 1968, ss 10(5), 15(4); sub-ss (4), (5) derived from the Agricultural Holdings Act 1948, s 70(3), (4), and the Agricultural Holdings Act 1984, s 10(1), Sch 3, para 18; sub-s (6) derived from the Agricultural Holdings Act 1948, s 70(5).

Initial Commencement

Specified date: 18 June 1986: see s 102(2).

Extent

This Act does not extend to Scotland.

See Further

See further, as to the exclusion of this Act in relation to leases or tenancies granted to contractors in respect of the running of any removal centre or part of a removal centre: the Immigration and Asylum Act 1999, s 149(3).

1201

Notes

For a commentary, see para 41.1 ff.

Sub-s (1) contains provisions formerly in the Agricultural Holdings Act 1948, s 70(1), as applied by the Agriculture (Miscellaneous Provisions) Act 1968, ss 10(5), 15(4). Sub-ss (2), (3) contain provisions formerly in s 70(2) of the 1948 Act, as applied by ss 10(5), 15(4) of the 1968 Act. Sub-ss (4), (5) contain provisions formerly in s 70(3), (4), respectively, of the 1948 Act, as amended and repealed in part, in both cases, by the Agricultural Holdings Act 1984, s 10, Sch 3, para 18(a), (b), Sch 4. Sub-s (6) contains provisions formerly in s 70(5) of the 1948 Act.

Sub-s (1): Claim ... arises ... on or out of the termination of the tenancy. A claim for damages for breach of covenant, where the tenant is still in possession at the date of the hearing, is not one for compensation under s 71(3), (4), and accordingly is not a claim arising on or out of the termination of the tenancy within the meaning of sub-s (1)(b) of this section: *Gulliver v Catt* [1952] 2 QB 308, [1952] 1 All ER 929, CA. See also, *Kent v Conniff* [1953] 1 QB 361, [1953] 1 All ER 155, CA.

Arbitration under this Act. For provisions as to arbitration under this Act, see s 84 and the note to s 2.

Sub-s (2): Two months from, etc. See the note to s 10.

Has served notice. As to service, see s 93. A notice, signed by the landlord's solicitors, although the name of the landlord's son, who had acted as his father's agent in negotiations with the tenant, was erroneously given as that of the landlord, was nevertheless held to be a good notice: *Frankland v Capstick* [1959] 1 All ER 209, [1959] 1 WLR 205, CA. A notice may be framed in the alternative, leaving the claimant to elect at a later stage which of two mutually inconsistent claims he will pursue: *Boyd v Wilton* [1957] 2 QB 277, [1957] 2 All ER 102, CA.

Writing. See the note 'Written' to s 3.

Sub-s (4): Within ... eight months from, etc. See the note 'Within six months from, etc' to s 13. See *Lady Hallinan v Jones* (1984) 272 EG 1081 and the commentary at para 41.3 ff.

Sub-s (6): Termination of the tenancy, etc. As to the date on which the tenancy terminates if the tenant after vacating the holding has a limited right of entry for a specific purpose, see *Coutts v Barclay-Harvey* 1956 SLT (Sh Ct) 54 (a mere right of access for the purpose of tending and removing a crop is not a continued occupation).

Saving for other rights. The saving for other rights etc in s 97 does not affect sub-s (1) above.

Opencast coal operations. This section is applied, with modifications to sub-s (4), by the Opencast Coal Act 1958, s 24(2), (6), as amended by s 100, Sch 14, para 26 (see, further, the note to s 64, noting s 25(2) of that Act (as amended by s 100, Sch 14, para 27(3)) which excludes sub-s (2) of this section above, and s 37 of, and Sch 7, Pt I, para 1(3) to, that Act).

Definitions. For 'agricultural holding', see s 1(1); for 'agreement', 'landlord', 'tenant' and 'termination', see s 96(1). See, also, as to 'termination', s 74(4).

A1.171

84   Arbitrations

(1)   Any matter which by or by virtue of this Act or regulations made under this Act is required to be determined by arbitration under this Act shall, notwithstanding any agreement (under a contract of tenancy or otherwise) providing for a different method of arbitration, be determined by the arbitration of a single arbitrator ...

[(2)   The arbitrator shall be a person appointed by agreement between the parties or, in default of agreement, a person appointed on the application of either of the parties by the President of the RICS.

(3)   If the arbitrator dies, or is incapable of acting, a new arbitrator may be appointed as if no arbitrator had been appointed.

(4)   No application may be made to the President of the RICS for an arbitrator to be appointed by him under this section unless the application is accompanied by such fee as may be prescribed as the fee for such an application; but once the fee has been paid in connection with any such application no further fee shall be payable in connection with any subsequent application for the appointment by him of a new arbitrator in relation to that arbitration.

(5)   Where by virtue of this Act compensation under an agreement is to be substituted for compensation under this Act for improvements or for any such matters as are specified in Part II of Schedule 8 to this Act, the arbitrator shall award compensation in accordance with the agreement instead of in accordance with this Act.

(6)   In this section 'the RICS' means the Royal Institution of Chartered Surveyors.]

NOTES

Derivation

Sub-s (1) derived from the Agricultural Holdings Act 1948, s 77(1), the Arbitration Act 1950, s 44(3), the Agriculture (Miscellaneous Provisions) Act 1968, ss 10(5), 15(4), the Agriculture (Miscellaneous Provisions) Act 1976, s 24(9), and the Agricultural Holdings Act 1984, s 10(1), Sch 2, para 7(3), Sch 3, para 19(2); sub-ss (2)–(5) derived from the Agricultural Holdings Act 1948, s 77(2)–(4), (6), and the Agricultural Holdings Act 1984, s 10(1), Sch 3, para 19(3).

Initial Commencement

Specified date: 18 June 1986: see s 102(2).

Extent

This Act does not extend to Scotland.

Amendment

Sub-s (1): words omitted repealed by SI 2006/2805, arts 2, 7(1), 18, Sch 2.

Date in force: 19 October 2006: see SI 2006/2805, art 1(1)(b); for transitional provisions see art 10 thereof.

Sub-ss (2)–(6): substituted, for sub-ss (2)–(5) as originally enacted, by SI 2006/2805, arts 2, 7(2).

Date in force: 19 October 2006: see SI 2006/2805, art 1(1)(b); for transitional provisions see art 10 thereof.

See Further

See further, as to the exclusion of this Act in relation to leases or tenancies granted to contractors in respect of the running of any removal centre or part of a removal centre: the Immigration and Asylum Act 1999, s 149(3).

Notes

For a commentary on arbitrations—s 84—see Ch 48. For a commentary on the now repealed Sch 11 see the 8th edition of this book.

Sub-s (1) contains provisions formerly in the Agricultural Holdings Act 1948, s 77(1), as amended by the Agricultural Holdings Act 1984, s 10(1), Sch 3, para 19(2), as applied by the Agriculture (Miscellaneous Provisions) Act 1968, ss 10(5), 15(4), the Agriculture (Miscellaneous Provisions) Act 1976, s 24(9), and by s 4 of, Sch 2, para 7(3) to, the 1984 Act, and as read with the Arbitration Act 1950, s 44(3). Sub-ss (2)–(5) contain provisions formerly in s 77(2) (4), (6), respectively, of the 1948 Act, as substituted by s 10(1) of, and Sch 3, para 19(3) to, the 1984 Act.

In sub-s (1) the words in square brackets are substituted for the preceding words in italics by the Arbitration Act 1996, s 107(1), Sch 3, para 45, as from a day to be appointed.

Sub-s (1): Any matter which by ... this Act, etc. See, with regard to conditions applying to amalgamated agricultural units, the Agriculture Act 1967, Sch 3, para 7(4), as amended by s 100, Sch 14, para 42. For application of this section, see the Agriculture Act 1986, s 13, Sch 1, paras 10(3), 11(5); the Milk (Community Outgoers Scheme) (England and Wales) Regulations 1986, SI 1986/1611, reg 16; and the Milk (Cessation of Production) (England and Wales) Scheme 1987, SI 1987/908, para 16.

Sub-s (2): Lord Chancellor. See the note to s 29.

Opencast coal operations. By the Opencast Coal Act 1958, s 37, Sch 7, para 4(4), as amended by s 100, Sch 14, para 33(5)(b), this section applies to references to arbitration as to variation of tenancies consequent upon a compulsory rights order under that Act (and note as to mortgages, s 37 of, Sch 7, para 7 to, the 1958 Act).

Definitions. For 'contract of tenancy', see s 1(5); for 'agreement', see s 96(1). Note as to 'modifications', sub-s (5) above.

A1.172

85   Enforcement

(1)   Subject to subsection (3) below, where a sum agreed or awarded under this Act to be paid for compensation, costs or otherwise by a landlord or tenant of an agricultural holding is not paid within fourteen days after the time when the payment becomes due, it shall be recoverable, if the county court so orders, as if it were payable under an order of that court.

(2)   Where a sum becomes due to a tenant of an agricultural holding in respect of compensation from the landlord, and the landlord fails to discharge his liability within the period of one month from the date on which the sum becomes due, the tenant shall be entitled to obtain from the Minister an order charging the holding with payment of the amount due.

(3)   Where the landlord of an agricultural holding is entitled to receive the rents and profits of the holding otherwise than for his own benefit (whether as trustee or in any other character)—

    (a) he shall not be under any liability to pay any sum agreed or awarded under this Act to be paid to the tenant or awarded under this Act to be paid by the landlord, and it shall not be recoverable against him personally, but

    (b) if he fails to pay any such sum to the tenant for one month after it becomes due, the tenant shall be entitled to obtain from the Minister an order charging the holding with payment of the sum.

NOTES

Derivation

This section derived from the Agricultural Holdings Act 1948, ss 71, 72, 73, the Agriculture (Miscellaneous Provisions) Act 1968, ss 10(5), 15(4), and gives effect to Law Commission Recommendation No 153, Cmnd 9665.

Initial Commencement

Specified date: 18 June 1986: see s 102(2).

Extent

This Act does not extend to Scotland.

1204

See Further

See further, in relation to charges created pursuant to applications under this section: the Land Charges Act 1972, Sch 2, para 1.

See further, as to the exclusion of this Act in relation to leases or tenancies granted to contractors in respect of the running of any removal centre or part of a removal centre: the Immigration and Asylum Act 1999, s 149(3).

Transfer of Functions

Functions of the Minister, so far as exercisable in relation to Wales, transferred to the National Assembly for Wales, by the National Assembly for Wales (Transfer of Functions) Order 1999, SI 1999/672, art 2, Sch 1.

Notes

For a commentary, see para 42.2 ff.

Sub-ss (1), (2), (3) contain provisions formerly in the Agricultural Holdings Act 1948, ss 71, 72, 73 respectively, as applied, in each case, by the Agriculture (Miscellaneous Provisions) Act 1968, ss 10(5), 15(4), and as affected, in the case of sub-ss (1), (3) of this section above, by the third recommendation in the Law Commission's Report on this consolidation (Law Com No 153; Cmnd 9665), as to which, see the General Note to this section below.

General Note. Sub-ss (1), (3) of this section are modified so as to apply to all sums agreed or awarded under the Act by virtue of the third recommendation in the Law Commission's Report on this consolidation (Law Com No 153; Cmnd 9665). This removes the anomaly whereby the Agricultural Holdings Act 1948, ss 71, 73 were not expressly applied to the recovery of sums payable under the Agriculture (Miscellaneous Provisions) Act 1976, s 24(4)(a)(ii) (as to which, see now s 48(5)), where the parties may have agreed to the payment of such sums without recourse to arbitration.

Within fourteen days after. See the note 'Within six months from, etc' to s 13 and para 42.27 on the computation of time.

Recoverable ... county court. The jurisdiction of the county court is not exclusive; see *Horrell v Lord St John of Bletso* [1928] 2 KB 616 (although doubted in *Jones v Pembrokeshire County Council* [1967] 1 QB 181, [1966] 1 All ER 1027). As to proceedings for enforcement of an award in the county court, see CPR Part 70.5 and the supplemental Practice Direction.

As to 'county court', see the note to s 96.

One month from, etc. Cf the note 'Two months from, etc' to s 10.

Power to obtain charge. See, further, ss 86, 87. Charges under this section and s 86 may be registered as Class A land charges for unregistered land; see the Land Charges Act 1972 s 2(2), Sch 2, para 1(i), as inserted by s 100, Sch 14, para 51(3). For registered land, see the Land Registration Act 2002.

Application. This section and s 86(1), (3), (4) apply to any sum which becomes due to a tenant under the Agriculture Act 1986, Sch 1; see s 13 of, and Sch 1, para 12 to, that Act.

Definitions. For 'agricultural holding', see s 1(1); for 'agreed', 'county court', 'landlord', 'the Minister' and ' tenant', see s 96(1).

A1.173

86   Power of landlord to obtain charge on holding

(1)   Where the landlord of an agricultural holding—

  (a)   has paid to the tenant of the holding an amount due to him under this Act, or under custom or agreement, or otherwise, in respect of compensation for an improvement falling within section 64(1) or (4) above, for any such matter as is specified in Part II of Schedule 8 to this Act or for disturbance, or

(b) has defrayed the cost of the execution by him, in pursuance of a notice served under section 67(5) above, of an improvement specified in Part II of Schedule 7 to this Act,

he shall be entitled to obtain from the Minister an order charging the holding or any part of it with repayment of the amount of the compensation or the amount of the cost, as the case may be.

(2) Where there falls to be determined by arbitration under this Act the amount of compensation for an improvement falling within 64(1) or (4) above or for any such matter as is specified in Part II of Schedule 8 to this Act payment of which entitles the landlord to obtain a charge under subsection (1) above, the arbitrator shall, at the request and cost of the landlord, certify—

(a) the amount of the compensation, and
(b) the term for which the charge may properly be made having regard to the time at which each improvement or matter in respect of which compensation is awarded is to be deemed to be exhausted.

(3) Where the landlord of an agricultural holding is entitled to receive the rents and profits of the holding otherwise than for his own benefit (whether as trustee or in any other character) he shall, either before or after paying to the tenant of the holding any sum agreed or awarded under this Act to be paid to the tenant for compensation or awarded under this Act to be paid by the landlord, be entitled to obtain from the Minister an order charging the holding with repayment of that sum.

(4) The rights conferred by this section on a landlord of an agricultural holding to obtain an order charging land shall not be exercised by trustees for ecclesiastical or charitable purposes except with the approval in writing of the [Charity Commission].

NOTES

Derivation

This section derived from the Agricultural Holdings Act 1948, ss 82(1), (2), 89, and the Agriculture (Miscellaneous Provisions) Act 1968, ss 10(5), 15(4).

Initial Commencement

Specified date: 18 June 1986: see s 102(2).

Extent

This Act does not extend to Scotland.

Amendment

Sub-s (4): words 'Charity Commission' in square brackets substituted by the Charities Act 2006, s 75(1), Sch 8, para 79.

Date in force: 27 February 2007: see SI 2007/309, art 2, Schedule.

See Further

See further, in relation to charges created pursuant to applications under this section: the Land Charges Act 1972, Sch 2, para 1.

See further, as to the exclusion of this Act in relation to leases or tenancies granted to contractors in respect of the running of any removal centre or part of a removal centre: the Immigration and Asylum Act 1999, s 149(3).

Transfer of Functions

Functions of the Minister, so far as exercisable in relation to Wales, transferred to the National Assembly for Wales, by the National Assembly for Wales (Transfer of Functions) Order 1999, SI 1999/672, art 2, Sch 1.

Notes

For a commentary, see para 42.6 ff.

Sub-ss (1), (2) contain provisions formerly in the Agricultural Holdings Act 1948, s 82(1), as applied by the Agriculture (Miscellaneous Provisions) Act 1968, ss 10(5), 15(4). Sub-s (3) contains provisions formerly in s 82(2) of the 1948 Act, as applied by ss 10(5), 15(4) of the 1968 Act. Sub-s (4) contains provisions formerly in s 89 of the 1948 Act, as applied by ss 10(5), 15(4) of the 1968 Act.

Arbitration under this Act. For provisions as to arbitration under this Act, see s 84 and the note to s 2.

The arbitrator. See s 84(1).

Writing. See the note 'Written' to s 3.

Charity Commissioners. Ie the Charity Commissioners for England and Wales referred to in the Charities Act 1993, s 1; see the Interpretation Act 1978, s 5, Sch 1.

Power to obtain charge. For general provisions, see s 87. See also the note to s 85.

Application. See the note to s 85.

Definitions. For 'agricultural holding', see s 1(1); for 'agreement', 'landlord', 'the Minister' and 'tenant', see s 96(1).

A1.174

87 General provisions as to charges under this Act on holdings

(1) An order of the Minister under this Act charging an agricultural holding or any part of an agricultural holding with payment or repayment of a sum shall charge it, in addition, with payment of all costs properly incurred in obtaining the charge.

(2) Any such order shall be made in favour of the person obtaining the charge and of his executors, administrators and assigns, and the order shall make such provision as to the payment of interest and the payment of the sum charged by instalments, and shall contain such directions for giving effect to the charge, as the Minister thinks fit.

(3) In the case of a charge under section 86 above the sum charged shall be a charge on the holding or the part of the holding charged, as the case may be, for the landlord's interest in the holding and for all interests in the holding subsequent to that of the landlord, but so that in any case where the landlord's interest is an interest in a leasehold, the charge shall not extend beyond the interest of the landlord, his executors, administrators and assigns.

(4) In the case of a charge under section 86 above where the landlord is not absolute owner of the holding for his own benefit, no instalment or interest shall be made payable after the time when the improvement in respect of which compensation is paid will, in the opinion of the Minister, have become exhausted.

(5) Notwithstanding anything in any deed, will or other instrument to the contrary, where the estate or interest in an agricultural holding of the landlord is determinable or liable to forfeiture by reason of his creating or suffering any charge on it, that estate or interest shall not be determined or forfeited by reason that the tenant obtains a charge on the holding under section 85(2) above or that the landlord obtains a charge on the holding under section 86 above.

(6) A charge created under section 85 above or section 74 of the Agricultural Holdings Act 1948 shall rank in priority to any other charge, however and whenever created or arising; and charges created under those sections shall, as between themselves, rank in the order of their creation.

(7) Any company now or hereafter incorporated by Parliament, and having power to advance money for the improvement of land, may take an assignment of any charge created under section 85(2) or 86(1) above upon such terms and conditions as may be agreed upon between the company and the person entitled to the charge, and may assign any charge of which they have taken an assignment under this subsection.

(8) Subsection (6) above shall bind the Crown.

NOTES

Derivation

This section derived from the Agricultural Holdings Act 1948, s 83, and the Agriculture (Miscellaneous Provisions) Act 1968, ss 10(5), 15(4).

Initial Commencement

Specified date: 18 June 1986: see s 102(2).

Extent

This Act does not extend to Scotland.

See Further

See further, as to the exclusion of this Act in relation to leases or tenancies granted to contractors in respect of the running of any removal centre or part of a removal centre: the Immigration and Asylum Act 1999, s 149(3).

Transfer of Functions

Functions of the Minister, so far as exercisable in relation to Wales, transferred to the National Assembly for Wales, by the National Assembly for Wales (Transfer of Functions) Order 1999, SI 1999/672, art 2, Sch 1.

Notes

For a commentary, see para 42.6 ff.

This section contains provisions formerly in the Agricultural Holdings Act 1948, s 83, as repealed in part by the Agricultural Holdings Act 1984, s 10, Sch 3, para 20, Sch 4, and as applied by the Agriculture (Miscellaneous Provisions) Act 1968, ss 10(5), 15(4).

Sub-s (5): Obtains a charge on the holding under section 85(2); 86 above. As to registration of those charges, see the note 'Power to obtain charge' to s 85.

Definitions. For 'agricultural holding', see s 1(1); for 'landlord', 'the Minister' and 'tenant', see s 96(1).

Agricultural Holdings Act 1948, s 74. That section was repealed by the Agricultural Holdings Act 1984, s 10(2), Sch 4, as from 12 September 1984. Charges made under that section may be registered as Class A land charges; see the Land Charges Act 1972, s 2(2), Sch 2, para 1(g), as amended by s 100, Sch 14, para 51(2).

A1.175

88   Power of limited owners to give consents etc

The landlord of an agricultural holding, whatever his estate or interest in it, may, for the purposes of this Act, give any consent, make any agreement or do or have done to him any other act which he might give, make, do or have done to him if he were owner in fee simple or, if his interest is an interest in a leasehold, were absolutely entitled to that leasehold.

NOTES

Derivation

This section derived from the Agricultural Holdings Act 1948, s 80, the Agriculture (Miscellaneous Provisions) Act 1968, ss 10(5), 15(4), and gives effect to Law Commission Recommendation No 153, Cmnd 9665.

Initial Commencement

Specified date: 18 June 1986: see s 102(2).

Extent

This Act does not extend to Scotland.

See Further

See further, as to the exclusion of this Act in relation to leases or tenancies granted to contractors in respect of the running of any removal centre or part of a removal centre: the Immigration and Asylum Act 1999, s 149(3).

Notes

For a commentary, see paras 42.8 and 42.9.

This section contains provisions formerly in the Agricultural Holdings Act 1948, s 80, as applied by the Agriculture (Miscellaneous Provisions) Act 1968, ss 10(5), 15(4), and as extended in accordance with the fourth recommendation in the Law Commission's Report on this consolidation (Law Com No 153; Cmnd 9665).

Definitions. For 'agricultural holding', see s 1(1); for 'agreement' and 'landlord', see s 96(1).

A1.176

89   Power of limited owners to apply capital for improvements

(1)   Where under powers conferred by the Settled Land Act 1925 ... capital money is applied in or about the execution of any improvement specified in Schedule 7 to this Act no provision shall be made for requiring the money or any part of it to be replaced out of income, and accordingly any such improvement shall be deemed to be an improvement authorised by Part I of Schedule 3 to the Settled Land Act 1925.

(2)   Where under powers conferred by the Universities and College Estates Act 1925 capital money is applied in payment for any improvement specified in Schedule 7 to this Act no provision shall be made for replacing the money out of income unless the Minister requires such provision to be made under section 26(5) of that Act or, in the case of a university or college to which section 2 of the Universities and College Estates Act 1964 applies, it appears to the university or college to be necessary to make such provision under the said section 26(5) as modified by Schedule 1 to the said Act of 1964.

NOTES

Derivation

Sub-s (1) derived from the Agricultural Holdings Act 1948, s 81(1); sub-s (2) derived from the Agricultural Holdings Act 1948, s 81(2), and the Universities and College Estates Act 1964, s 4(1), Sch 3, Part I.

Initial Commencement

Specified date: 18 June 1986: see s 102(2).

Extent

This Act does not extend to Scotland.

Amendment

Sub-s (1): words omitted repealed by the Trusts of Land and Appointment of Trustees Act 1996, s 25(2), Sch 4; for savings in relation to entailed interests created before the commencement of that Act, and savings consequential upon the abolition of the doctrine of conversion, see s 25(4), (5) thereof.

See Further

See further, as to the exclusion of this Act in relation to leases or tenancies granted to contractors in respect of the running of any removal centre or part of a removal centre: the Immigration and Asylum Act 1999, s 149(3).

Transfer of Functions

Functions of the Minister, so far as exercisable in relation to Wales, transferred to the National Assembly for Wales, by the National Assembly for Wales (Transfer of Functions) Order 1999, SI 1999/672, art 2, Sch 1.

Notes

For a commentary, see para 42.8.

Sub-ss (1), (2) contain provisions formerly in the Agricultural Holdings Act 1948, s 81(1), (2), respectively, as amended, in the case of sub-s (2) of that section, by the Universities and College Estates Act 1964, s 4(1), Sch 3, Pt I.

In sub-s (1) the words in italics are repealed by the Trusts of Land and Appointment of Trustees Act 1996, s 25(2), Sch 4, as from a day to be appointed.

General Note. For cases and a general discussion regarding capital money in connection with agricultural holdings, see 42 Halsbury's Law (4th edn) para 807, note 21 and para 808.

The Minister. The Minister for the purposes of the Universities and Colleges Estates Act 1925 is the Minister of Agriculture, Fisheries and Food; see s 43 of that Act. Cf also s 96(1).

Universities and College Estates Act 1964, s 2, Sch 1. The Minister is now concerned only with Eton and Winchester.

A1.177

90   Estimation of best rent for purposes of Acts and other instruments

In estimating the best rent or reservation in the nature of rent of an agricultural holding for the purposes of any Act of Parliament, deed or other instrument, authorising a lease to be made provided that the best rent, or reservation in the nature of rent, is reserved, it shall not be necessary to take into account against the tenant any increase in the value of the holding arising from any improvements made or paid for by him.

NOTES

Derivation

This section derived from the Agricultural Holdings Act 1948, s 86.

Initial Commencement

Specified date: 18 June 1986: see s 102(2).

Extent

This Act does not extend to Scotland.

See Further

See further, as to the exclusion of this Act in relation to leases or tenancies granted to contractors in respect of the running of any removal centre or part of a removal centre: the Immigration and Asylum Act 1999, s 149(3).

Notes

For a commentary, see para 42.9.

This section contains provisions formerly in the Agricultural Holdings Act 1948, s 86.

Definitions. For 'agricultural holding', see s 1(1); for 'tenant', see s 96(1).

A1.178

91   Power of Minister to vary Schedules 7, 8 and 10

(1)   The Minister may, after consultation with such bodies of persons as appear to him to represent the interests of landlords and tenants of agricultural holdings, by order vary the provisions of Schedules 7, 8 and 10 to this Act.

(2)   An order under this section may make such provision as to the operation of this Act in relation to tenancies current when the order takes effect as appears to the Minister to be just having regard to the variation of the said Schedules effected by the order.

NOTES

Derivation

This section derived from the Agricultural Holdings Act 1948, s 78, and the Housing Act 1985, s 231(2).

Initial Commencement

Specified date: 18 June 1986: see s 102(2).

Extent

This Act does not extend to Scotland.

See Further

See further, as to the exclusion of this Act in relation to leases or tenancies granted to contractors in respect of the running of any removal centre or part of a removal centre: the Immigration and Asylum Act 1999, s 149(3).

Transfer of Functions

Functions of the Minister, so far as exercisable in relation to Wales, transferred to the National Assembly for Wales, by the National Assembly for Wales (Transfer of Functions) Order 1999, SI 1999/672, art 2, Sch 1.

Notes

This section contains provisions formerly in the Agricultural Holdings Act 1948, s 78(1), (2) and in the Housing Act 1985, s 231(2).

Consultation. See the note to s 7.

Appear. See the note 'Thinks fit' to s 87.

Opencast coal operations. For power to make variations in the Opencast Coal Act 1958, Sch 4, Pts I–III, VI, corresponding to those which may be made to Schs 8, 10 to this Act, see ss 26(5), 28(5) of the 1958 Act, as amended by s 100, Sch 14, paras 28(3), 30(4).

Definitions. For 'agricultural holding', see s 1(1); for 'landlord', 'the Minister' and 'tenant', see s 96(1).

Orders under this section. At the time of going to press no orders had been made under this section. Note that the orders made under the Agricultural Holdings Act 1948, s 78 (the provisions of which are now contained in this section; see the derivation note above), are revoked by s 101, Sch 15, Pt II since the amendments made by them are incorporated in this Act.

As to orders, generally, under this Act, see s 94, and note, in particular, with reference to this section, sub-s (4) thereof. Note also that the Minister may revoke or vary the provisions of Sch 12, paras 6–8, so far as they relate to matters specified in Sch 8, Pt II, para 10, as if those provisions were contained in an order made under this section; see Sch 12, para 9.

A1.179

92   Advisory committee on valuation of improvements and tenant-right matters

(1)   The Minister shall appoint a committee to advise him as to the provisions to be included in regulations under section 66(2) above, consisting of such number of persons, having such qualifications, as the Minister thinks expedient, including persons appointed by the Minister as having experience in land agency, farming, estate management and the valuation of tenant-right.

(2)   The Minister may pay to the members of the committee such travelling and other allowances as he may with the consent of the Treasury determine.

NOTES

Derivation

This section derived from the Agricultural Holdings Act 1948, s 79.

Initial Commencement

Specified date: 18 June 1986: see s 102(2).

Extent

This Act does not extend to Scotland.

See Further

See further, as to the exclusion of this Act in relation to leases or tenancies granted to contractors in respect of the running of any removal centre or part of a removal centre: the Immigration and Asylum Act 1999, s 149(3).

Transfer of Functions

Functions of the Minister, so far as exercisable in relation to Wales, transferred to the National Assembly for Wales, by the National Assembly for Wales (Transfer of Functions) Order 1999, SI 1999/672, art 2, Sch 1.

Notes

For a commentary, see para 40.15.

This section contains provisions formerly in the Agricultural Holdings Act 1948, s 79.

The Minister. For meaning, see s 96(1).

Thinks expedient. Cf the note 'Thinks fit' to s 87.

Treasury. Ie the Commissioners of HM Treasury; see the Interpretation Act 1978, s 5, Sch 1.

A1.180

93 Service of notices

(1) Any notice, request, demand or other instrument under this Act shall be duly given to or served on the person to or on whom it is to be given or served if it is delivered to him, or left at his proper address, or sent to him by in a registered letter or by the recorded delivery service.

(2) Any such instrument shall be duly given to or served on an incorporated company or body if it is given or served on the secretary or clerk of the company or body.

(3) Any such instrument to be given to or served on a landlord or tenant shall, where an agent or servant is responsible for the control of the management or farming, as the case may be, of the agricultural holding, be duly given or served if given to or served on that agent or servant.

(4) For the purposes of this section and of section 7 of the Interpretation Act 1978 (service by), the proper address of any person to or on whom any such instrument is to be given or served shall, in the case of the secretary or clerk of an incorporated company or body, be that of the registered or principal office of the company or body, and in any other case be the last known address of the person in question.

(5) Unless or until the tenant of an agricultural holding has received—

(a) notice that the person who before that time was entitled to receive the rents and profits of the holding ('the original landlord') has ceased to be so entitled, and

(b) notice of the name and address of the person who has become entitled to receive the rents and profits,

any notice or other document served upon or delivered to the original landlord by the tenant shall be deemed for the purposes of this Act to have been served upon or delivered to the landlord of the holding.

NOTES

Derivation

Sub-ss (1), (5) derived from the Agricultural Holdings Act 1948, s 92(1), (5), the Agriculture (Miscellaneous Provisions) Act 1968, ss 10(5), 15(4), the Agricultural Holdings (Notices to Quit) Act 1977, s 12(2)(a), the Agricultural Holdings Act 1984, s 10(1), Sch 2, para 1(7), Sch 3, para 21 and give effect to Law Commission Recommendation No 153, Cmnd 9665; sub-ss (2), (3) derived from the Agricultural Holdings Act 1948, s 92(2), (3); sub-s (4) derived from the Agricultural Holdings Act 1948, s 92(4), and the Interpretation Act 1978, s 25(2).

Initial Commencement

Specified date: 18 June 1986: see s 102(2).

Extent

This Act does not extend to Scotland.

See Further

See further, as to the exclusion of this Act in relation to leases or tenancies granted to contractors in respect of the running of any removal centre or part of a removal centre: the Immigration and Asylum Act 1999, s 149(3).

Notes

For a commentary, see para 42.13 ff.

Sub-ss (1), (5) contain provisions formerly in the Agricultural Holdings Act 1948, s 92(1), (5), as applied by the Agriculture (Miscellaneous Provisions) Act 1968, ss 10(5), 15(4) and by the Agricultural Holdings Act 1984, Sch 2, para 1(7), as read with the Agricultural Holdings (Notices to Quit) Act 1977, s 12(2)(a) and as amended, in the case of sub-s (1) of s 92 of the 1948 Act, by s 10(1) of, Sch 3, para 21 to, the 1984 Act. Those subsections also take account of the fifth recommendation in the Law Commission's Report on this consolidation (Law Com No 153; Cmnd 9665), as to which, see the General Note to this section below. Sub-ss (2)–(4) contain provisions formerly in s 92(2) (4), respectively, of the 1948 Act, as construed in accordance with, in the case of sub-s (4) of that section, the Interpretation Act 1978, s 25(2).

General Note. This section makes provision as to the mode of service of notices, etc, under any provision of this Act. However some of the provisions now contained in this consolidation (the Agriculture (Miscellaneous Provisions) Act 1949, s 10(2), and the Agriculture (Miscellaneous Provisions) Act 1976, s 24(3)) did not apply the Agricultural Holdings Act 1948, s 92 (the provisions of which are now contained in this section) to the service of notices under those provisions. The Law Commission in the fifth recommendation in their report on this collection (Law Com No 153; Cmnd 9665) recommended that this provision should apply generally to all notices, etc, under the Act, including those served under the above-mentioned provisions which did not apply to s 92 of the 1948 Act.

Left at his proper address. See *Lord Newborough v Jones* [1975] Ch 90, [1974] 3 All ER 17, CA, where notice was pushed under the tenant's door by the landlord. See also, *Datnow v Jones* [1985] 2 EGLR 1. See para 42.19

Served … on that agent or servant. Where a tenancy had vested in the sole surviving executor of the original tenant, but both he and the landlord's agent erroneously believed the tenancy to be vested in him and his brother as executors for the original tenant's widow, a notice served on the widow's executors was held to be good, they being regarded as agents for the real tenant: *Wilbraham v Colclough* [1952] 1 All ER 979. See para 42.22.

Definitions. For 'agricultural holding', see s 1(1); for 'landlord' and 'tenant', see s 96(1).

A1.181

94   Orders and regulations

(1) Any power to make an order or regulations conferred on the Minister or the Lord Chancellor by any provision of this Act (except section 85 or 86) shall be exercisable by statutory instrument.

(2) Any statutory instrument containing an order or regulations made under any provision of this Act (except section 22(4)[, 84(4)] or 91 …) shall be subject to annulment in pursuance of a resolution of either House of Parliament.

(3) No regulations shall be made under section 22(4) above or [section 84(4) above] unless a draft of the regulations has been laid before and approved by a resolution of each House of Parliament.

(4) An order made under section 91 above shall be of no effect unless approved by a resolution of each House of Parliament.

NOTES

Derivation

Sub-ss (1), (2) derived from the Agricultural Holdings Act 1948, ss 6(4), 50(3), 77(5), 78(1), 94(1), the Agriculture Act 1958, s 8(1), Sch 1, Part I, para 15, the Agriculture (Miscellaneous Provisions) Act 1976, ss 18(3B), 23(8), the Agricultural Holdings (Notices to Quit) Act 1977, ss 5(2), 11(9), and the Agricultural Holdings Act 1984, ss 3(3), 8(4), 10(1), Sch 2, para 6(6), Sch 3, para 19(3); sub-s (3) derived from the Agricultural Holdings Act 1984, s 8(4); sub-s (4) derived from the Agricultural Holdings Act 1948, s 78(3).

Initial Commencement

Specified date: 18 June 1986: see s 102(2).

Extent

This Act does not extend to Scotland.

Amendment

Sub-s (2): words ', 84(4)' in square brackets inserted by SI 2006/2805, arts 2, 7(3)(a).

Date in force: 19 October 2006: see SI 2006/2805, art 1(1)(b); for transitional provisions see art 10 thereof.

Sub-s (2): words omitted repealed by SI 2006/2805, arts 2, 7(3)(b), 18, Sch 2.

Date in force: 19 October 2006: see SI 2006/2805, art 1(1)(b); for transitional provisions see art 10 thereof.

Sub-s (3): words 'section 84(4) above' in square brackets substituted by SI 2006/2805, arts 2, 7(4).

Date in force: 19 October 2006: see SI 2006/2805, art 1(1)(b); for transitional provisions see art 10 thereof.

See Further

See further, as to the exclusion of this Act in relation to leases or tenancies granted to contractors in respect of the running of any removal centre or part of a removal centre: the Immigration and Asylum Act 1999, s 149(3).

Transfer of Functions

Functions of the Minister, so far as exercisable in relation to Wales, transferred to the National Assembly for Wales, by the National Assembly for Wales (Transfer of Functions) Order 1999, SI 1999/672, art 2, Sch 1.

Notes

Sub-ss (1), (2) contain provisions formerly in the Agricultural Holdings Act 1948, ss 6(4), 50(3), 77(5), 78(1), 94(1) (as inserted, in the case of s 50(3) of that Act, by the Agriculture Act 1958, s 8(1), Sch 1, Pt I, para 15, and as substituted, in the case of s 77(5) of the 1948 Act, by the Agricultural Holdings Act 1984, s 10(1), Sch 3, para 19(3)), the Agriculture (Miscellaneous Provisions) Act 1976, ss 18(3B), 23(8) (as inserted, in the case of s 18(3B) of that Act, by s 3(3) of the 1984 Act), the Agricultural Holdings (Notices to Quit) Act 1977, ss 5(2), 11(9) and in s 8(4) of, and Sch 2, para 6(6) to, the 1984 Act. Sub-s (3) contains provisions formerly in s 8(4) of the 1984 Act. Sub-s (4) contains provisions formerly in s 78(3) of the 1948 Act.

The Minister. For meaning, see s 96(1).

Lord Chancellor. See the note to s 29.

Statutory instrument; subject to annulment. For provisions as to statutory instruments generally, see the Statutory Instruments Act 1946; as to statutory instruments which are subject to annulment, see ss 5(1), 7(1) of that Act.

Laid before Parliament. For meaning, see the Laying of Documents before Parliament (Interpretation) Act 1948, s 1(1).

A1.182

95   Crown land

(1)   The provisions of this Act, except section 11 above, shall apply to land belonging to Her Majesty in right of the Crown or the Duchy of Lancaster and to land belonging to the Duchy of Cornwall, subject in either case to such modifications as may be prescribed.

(2)   For the purposes of this Act—

   (a)   as respects land belonging to Her Majesty in right of the Crown, the Crown Estate Commissioners or other the proper officer or body having charge of the land for the time being, or, if there is no such officer or body, such person as Her Majesty may appoint in writing under the Royal Sign Manual, shall represent Her Majesty and shall be deemed to be the landlord,

   (b)   as respects land belonging to Her Majesty in right of the Duchy of Lancaster, the Chancellor of the Duchy shall represent Her Majesty and shall be deemed to be the landlord,

   (c)   as respects land belonging to the Duchy of Cornwall, such person as the Duke of Cornwall or other the possessor for the time being of the Duchy of Cornwall appoints shall represent the Duke of Cornwall or other the possessor aforesaid, and shall be deemed to be the landlord and may do any act or thing which a landlord is authorised or required to do under this Act.

(3)   Without prejudice to subsection (1) above it is hereby declared that the provisions of this Act, except section 11 above, apply to land notwithstanding that the interest of the landlord or tenant is held on behalf of Her Majesty for the purposes of any government department; but those provisions shall, in their application to any land in which an interest is so held, have effect subject to such modifications as may be prescribed.

(4)   Any compensation payable under this Act by the Chancellor of the Duchy of Lancaster for long-term improvements shall, and any compensation so payable under section 60(2)(b) or 62 above may, be raised and paid as an expense incurred in improvement of land belonging to Her Majesty in right of the Duchy within section 25 of the Duchy of Lancaster Act 1817; and any compensation so payable under this Act for short-term improvements and tenant-right matters shall be paid out of the annual revenues of the Duchy.

(5)   Any compensation payable under this Act by the Duke of Cornwall or other the possessor for the time being of the Duchy of Cornwall for long-term improvements shall, and any compensation so payable under section 60(2)(b) or 62 above may, be paid and advances therefor made in the manner and subject to the provisions of section 8 of the Duchy of Cornwall Management Act 1863 with respect to improvements of land mentioned in that section.

(6)   Nothing in subsection (5) above shall be taken as prejudicing the operation of the Duchy of Cornwall Management Act 1982.

(7)   In this section—

   'long-term improvements' means relevant improvements specified in Schedule 7 to this Act, improvements falling within section 64(4) above and improvements specified in Schedule 10 to this Act;

'short-term improvements and tenant-right matters' means relevant improvements specified in Part I of Schedule 8 to this Act and such matters as are specified in Part II of that Schedule.

NOTES

Derivation

Sub-ss (1)–(5), (7) derived from the Agricultural Holdings Act 1948, s 87(1), (2), (4), (5), the Crown Estate Act 1956, s 1(1), (7), the Crown Estate Act 1961, Sch 2, para 4(1), the Agriculture (Miscellaneous Provisions) Act 1968, ss 10(5), 15(4), 17(3), the Agriculture (Miscellaneous Provisions) Act 1976, s 18(8), the Agricultural Holdings (Notices to Quit) Act 1977, s 12(2)(a), and the Agricultural Holdings Act 1984, s 9(3).

Initial Commencement

Specified date: 18 June 1986: see s 102(2).

Extent

This Act does not extend to Scotland.

See Further

See further, as to the exclusion of this Act in relation to leases or tenancies granted to contractors in respect of the running of any removal centre or part of a removal centre: the Immigration and Asylum Act 1999, s 149(3).

Notes

Sub-ss (1)–(3) contain provisions formerly in the Agricultural Holdings Act 1948, s 87(1), (2), as amended, in the case of sub-s (1) of that section, by the Crown Estate Act 1956, s 1(1), (7) (saved by virtue of the Crown Estate Act 1961, s 9, Sch 2, para 4(1)), and as extended by the Agriculture (Miscellaneous Provisions) Act 1968, s 17(3), the Agriculture (Miscellaneous Provisions) Act 1976, s 18(8), the Agricultural Holdings (Notices to Quit) Act 1977, s 12(2)(a), and by the Agricultural Holdings Act 1984, s 9(3). Sub-ss (4), (5), (7) contain provisions formerly in s 87(4), (5) of the 1948 Act, as extended by s 12(2)(a) of the 1977 Act, and as read with ss 10(5), 15(4) of the 1968 Act. Sub-s (6) is a drafting provision.

Sub-s (1): Such modifications as may be prescribed. At the time of going to press no regulations prescribing any modifications had been made for the purposes of this provision and none have effect for those purposes by virtue of the Interpretation Act 1978, s 17(2)(b).

Sub-s (2): Crown Estate Commissioners. Ie the Commissioners referred to in the Crown Estate Act 1961, s 1; see the Interpretation Act 1978, s 5, Sch 1.

Writing. Cf the note 'Written' to s 3.

Definitions. For 'landlord', 'prescribed' and 'tenant', see s 96(1). Note as to 'long-term improvements' and 'short-term improvements and tenant-right matters', sub-s (7) above.

A1.183

96   Interpretation

(1)   In this Act, unless the context otherwise requires—

'agreement' includes an agreement arrived at by means of valuation or otherwise, and 'agreed' has a corresponding meaning;

'agricultural holding' has the meaning given by section 1 above;

'agricultural land' has the meaning given by section 1 above;

'agricultural unit' means land which is an agricultural unit for the purposes of the Agriculture Act 1947;

'agriculture' includes horticulture, fruit growing, seed growing, dairy farming and livestock breeding and keeping, the use of land as grazing land, meadow land, osier land, market gardens and nursery grounds, and the use of land for woodlands where that use is ancillary to the farming of land for other agricultural purposes and 'agricultural' shall be construed accordingly;

'building' includes any part of a building;

'Case A', 'Case B' (and so on) refer severally to the Cases set out and so named in Part I of Schedule 3 to this Act;

'contract of tenancy' has the meaning given by section 1 above;

'county court', in relation to an agricultural holding, means the county court within the district in which the holding or the larger part of the holding is situated;

'fixed equipment' includes any building or structure affixed to land and any works on, in, over or under land, and also includes anything grown on land for a purpose other than use after severance from the land, consumption of the thing grown or of its produce, or amenity, and any reference to fixed equipment on land shall be construed accordingly;

'landlord' means any person for the time being entitled to receive the rents and profits of any land;

'livestock' includes any creature kept for the production of food, wool, skins, or fur or for the purpose of its use in the farming of land or the carrying on in relation to land of any agricultural activity;

'local government funds' means, in relation to any grant in respect of an improvement executed by the landlord or tenant of an agricultural holding, the funds of any body which, under or by virtue of any enactment, has power to make grants in respect of improvements of the description in question within any particular area (whether or not it is a local authority for that area);

'the Minister' means—

    (a) in relation to England, the [Secretary of State], and

    (b) in relation to Wales, the Secretary of State;

'the model clauses' has the meaning given by section 7 above;

'pasture' includes meadow;

'prescribed' means prescribed by the Minister by regulations;

'relevant improvement' has the meaning given by section 64(2) above;

'tenant' means the holder of land under a contract of tenancy, and includes the executors, administrators, assigns, or trustee in bankruptcy of a tenant, or other person deriving title from a tenant;

'termination', in relation to a tenancy, means the cesser of the contract of tenancy by reason of effluxion of time or from any other cause;

'the Tribunal' means an Agricultural Land Tribunal established under Part V of the Agriculture Act 1947.

(2) For the purposes of this Act, a tenant is insolvent if—

    (a) he has been adjudged bankrupt or has made a composition or arrangement with his creditors, or

    (b) where the tenant is a body corporate, a winding-up order has been made with respect to it or a resolution for voluntary winding-up has been passed with respect to it (other than a resolution passed solely for the purposes of its reconstruction or of its amalgamation with another body corporate).

(3) Sections 10 and 11 of the Agriculture Act 1947 (which specify the circumstances in which an owner of agricultural land is deemed for the purposes of that Act to fulfil his responsibilities to manage the land in accordance with the rules of good estate management and an occupier of such land is deemed for those purposes to fulfil his responsibilities to farm it in accordance with the rules of good husbandry) shall apply for the purposes of this Act.

(4)   References in this Act to the farming of land include references to the carrying on in relation to the land of any agricultural activity.

(5)   References in this Act to the use of land for agriculture include, in relation to land forming part of an agricultural unit, references to any use of the land in connection with the farming of the unit.

(6)   The designations of landlord and tenant shall continue to apply to the parties until the conclusion of any proceedings taken under or in pursuance of this Act in respect of compensation.

NOTES

Derivation

Sub-s (1) derived from the Agricultural Holdings Act 1948, s 94(1), the Agriculture Act 1958, s 9(1), the Agriculture (Miscellaneous Provisions) Act 1968, s 17(1), the Agriculture (Miscellaneous Provisions) Act 1976, s 18(2), (7), the Agricultural Holdings (Notices to Quit) Act 1977, ss 2(3) Case H, 12(1), (2)(a), and the Agricultural Holdings Act 1984, ss 3(5) 8(4), 9(2), 10(1), Sch 1, para 1(a), Sch 2, para 1(2), Sch 3, para 23; sub-s (2) derived from the Agricultural Holdings Act 1948, s 68(6), the Agricultural Holdings (Notices to Quit) Act 1977, s 12(1A), the Agricultural Holdings Act 1984, s 10(1), Sch 3, paras 17(b), 42(b), and the Insolvency Act 1985, s 235, Sch 8, paras 9, 30; sub-s (3) derived from the Agricultural Holdings Act 1948, s 94(2), the Agriculture Act 1958, s 4(8), the Agricultural Holdings (Notices to Quit) Act 1977, s 12(2)(a), and the Agricultural Holdings Act 1984, s 9(2); sub-ss (4), (5) derived from the Agricultural Holdings Act 1948, s 94(3), (4); sub-s (6) derived from the Agricultural Holdings Act 1948, s 94(5), and the Agriculture (Miscellaneous Provisions) Act 1968, ss 10(5), 15(4).

Extent

This Act does not extend to Scotland.

Amendment

Sub-s (1): in definition 'the Minister' in para (a) words 'Secretary of State' in square brackets substituted by SI 2002/794, art 5(1), Sch 1, para 27.

Date in force: 27 March 2002: see SI 2002/794, art 1(2).

See Further

See further, as to the exclusion of this Act in relation to leases or tenancies granted to contractors in respect of the running of any removal centre or part of a removal centre: the Immigration and Asylum Act 1999, s 149(3).

Transfer of Functions

Functions of the Minister, so far as exercisable in relation to Wales, transferred to the National Assembly for Wales, by the National Assembly for Wales (Transfer of Functions) Order 1999, SI 1999/672, art 2, Sch 1.

Notes

For a commentary, see para 42.28.

Sub-s (1) contains provisions formerly in the Agricultural Holdings Act 1948, s 94(1) (as amended by the Agricultural Holdings Act 1984, s 10(1), Sch 3, para 23; as applied by the Agriculture Act 1958, s 9(1); and as read with the Agriculture (Miscellaneous Provisions) Act 1968, s 17(1), the Agriculture (Miscellaneous Provisions) Act 1976, s 18(7), the Agricultural Holdings (Notices to Quit) Act 1977, s 12(1), (2)(a), and with s 9(2) of the 1984 Act, s 18(2) (part) of the 1976 Act (as substituted by s 3(5) of, and Sch 1, para 1(a) to, the 1984 Act), and in s 8(4) of, and Sch 2, para 1(2) to, the 1984 Act, or contains drafting provisions. Sub-s (2) contains provisions formerly in s 68(6) of the 1948 Act (as added by s 10(1) of, and Sch 3, para 17(b) to, the 1984 Act, and as amended by the Insolvency Act 1985, s 235, Sch 8, para 9), and in s 12(1A) of the 1977 Act (as inserted by s 10(1) of, and Sch 3, para 42(b) to, the 1984 Act, and as amended by s 235 of, and Sch 8, para 30 to, the 1985 Act). Sub-s (3) contains provisions formerly in s 94(2) of the 1948 Act (as read with s 12(2)(a) of the 1977 Act, and s 9(2) of the 1984 Act), and in s 4(8) of the 1958 Act. Sub-ss (4)–(6) contain provisions formerly in s 94(3)–(5), respectively, of the 1948 Act, as read with, in the case of sub-s (5) of that section, ss 10(5), 15(4) of the 1968 Act.

Sub-s (1): County court. Ie a court held for a district under the County Courts Act 1984; see the Interpretation Act 1978, s 5, Sch 1. As to county court districts, see ss 1, 2 of the 1984 Act.

Landlord. At the termination of the tenancy this is the person then entitled to the rents and profits, having regard to any completed conveyance of reversion: *Bradshaw v Bird* [1920] 3 KB 144, CA, *Dale v Hatfield Chase Corpn* [1922] 2 KB 282, CA; *Tombs v Turvey* (1923) 93 LJKB 785, CA; and *Richards v Pryse* [1927] 2 KB 76, CA. See also, as to estoppel, *Farrow v Orttewell* [1933] Ch 480, CA.

As to who is deemed to be the landlord in the case of Crown land, see s 95(2).

The Secretary of State. For England, see SI 2002/794 art 5(1), Sch 1 para 27. For Wales, the functions of the Minister were transferred to the National Assembly for Wales by the National Assembly for Wales (Transfer of Functions) Order 1999, 1999/672, art 2, Sch 1. [See, further, the introductory note 'Transfer of functions' to this Act.]

Prescribed ... by regulations. As to the making of regulations generally, see s 94.

Tenant. A chargee of the farming stock and other 'agricultural assets' of a tenant is not within this definition: *Ecclesiastical Comrs for England v National Provincial Bank Ltd* [1935] 1 KB 566, CA.

Termination of tenancy. Where different parts were given up at different times, it was held in *Swinburne v Andrews* [1923] 2 KB 483; *Re Arden and Rutter* [1923] 2 KB 865, and *Re Paul, ex p Earl of Portarlington* (1889) 24 QBD 247, that the tenancy determined when the last portion was given up, but in *Black v Clay* [1894] AC 368, and *Morley v Carter* [1898] 1 QB 8, the tenancy was held to have determined in respect of each part as it was given up. For the date of termination where the tenant had to be ejected, see *Cave v Page* (1923) 67 Sol Jo 659, and *Mills v Rose* (1923) 68 Sol Jo 420. Note also s 74(4).

The Tribunal. See the note to s 11.

Sub-s (2). This subsection must be read subject to s 99 and Sch 13, para 14.

Body corporate. For the general law relating to corporations, see 9(2) Halsbury's Laws (4th edn 2006 reissue) paras 1101 ff.

Agriculture Act 1947. As to agricultural units for the purposes of that Act, see s 109(2).

A1.184

97   Saving for other rights etc

Subject to sections 15(5) and 83(1) above in particular, and to any other provision of this Act which otherwise expressly provides, nothing in this Act shall prejudicially affect any power, right or remedy of a landlord, tenant or other person vested in or exercisable by him by virtue of any other Act or law or under any custom of the country or otherwise, in respect of a contract of tenancy or other contract, or of any improvements, deteriorations, waste, emblements, tillages, away-going crops, fixtures, tax, rate, tithe rentcharge, rent or other thing.

NOTES

Derivation

This section derived from the Agricultural Holdings Act 1948, s 101, and the Agriculture (Miscellaneous Provisions) Act 1968, ss 10(5), 15(4).

Initial Commencement

Specified date: 18 June 1986: see s 102(2).

Extent

This Act does not extend to Scotland.

See Further

See further, as to the exclusion of this Act in relation to leases or tenancies granted to contractors in respect of the running of any removal centre or part of a removal centre: the Immigration and Asylum Act 1999, s 149(3).

Notes

For a commentary, see para 42.30.

This section contains provisions formerly in the Agricultural Holdings Act 1948, s 101, as applied by the Agricultural (Miscellaneous Provisions) Act 1968, ss 10(5), 15(4).

Definitions. For 'contract of tenancy', see s 1(5); for 'landlord' and 'tenant', see s 96(1).

A1.185

98   Application of Act to old tenancies etc

(1)   Subject to sections 4 and 34 above, to the provisions of Schedule 12 to this Act and to any other provision to the contrary, this Act applies in relation to tenancies of agricultural holdings whenever created, agreements whenever made and other things whenever done.

(2)   The provisions of this Act shall apply in relation to tenancies of agricultural holdings granted or agreed to be granted, agreements made and things done before the dates specified in paragraphs 1 to 5 and 10 of Schedule 12 to this Act (being dates no later than 1st March 1948) subject to the modifications there specified.

(3)   Paragraphs 6 to 9 of Schedule 12 to this Act, which make provision with respect to compensation for tenant-right matters in relation to tenants of agricultural holdings who entered into occupation before the dates specified in those paragraphs (being dates no later than 31st December 1951), shall have effect.

NOTES

Derivation

Sub-s (1) (in part) derived from the Agricultural Holdings Act 1948, ss 5(1), 6(1), (2), 8A(1), 9(1), 10(1), the Agriculture Act 1958, s 8(1), Sch 1, para 6, and the Agricultural Holdings Act 1984, ss 1, 10(1), Sch 3, para 3(2).

Initial Commencement

Specified date: 18 June 1986: see s 102(2).

Extent

This Act does not extend to Scotland.

See Further

See further, as to the exclusion of this Act in relation to leases or tenancies granted to contractors in respect of the running of any removal centre or part of a removal centre: the Immigration and Asylum Act 1999, s 149(3).

Notes

For a commentary, see para 42.30.

Sub-s (1) (in part) contains provisions formerly in the Agricultural Holdings Act 1948, ss 5(1) (as substituted by the Agricultural Holdings Act 1984, s 10(1), Sch 3, para 3(2)), 6(1), (2), 8A(1) (as substituted by s 1 of the 1984 Act), 9(1), 10(1) (as substituted by the Agriculture Act 1958, s 8, Sch 1, para 6). The remaining provisions in this section are drafting provisions.

1st March 1948. Ie the commencement date of the Agriculture Act 1947, Pt III (repealed).

31st December 1951. Ie the commencement date of the Agricultural Holdings (Variation of Fourth Schedule) Order 1951, SI 1951/2168 (revoked by s 101, Sch 15, Pt II).

Definitions. For 'agricultural holding', see s 1(1); for 'agreement' and 'tenant', see s 96(1).

A1.186

99   Transitional provisions and savings

(1)   Schedule 13 to this Act, which excepts from the operation of this Act certain cases current at the commencement of this Act and contains other transitional provisions and savings, shall have effect.

(2)   The re-enactment in paragraphs 6 to 8 of Schedule 12 to this Act of provisions contained in the Agricultural Holdings Act (Variation of Fourth Schedule) Order 1951 shall be without prejudice to the validity of those provisions; and any question as to the validity of any of those provisions shall be determined as if the re-enacting provisions of this Act were contained in a statutory instrument made under the powers under which the original provision was made.

(3)   Nothing in this Act (except paragraph 8 of Schedule 13) shall be taken as prejudicing the operation of sections 16 and 17 of the Interpretation Act 1978 (which relate to the effect of repeals).

NOTES

Derivation

This section is a drafting provision.

Initial Commencement

Specified date: 18 June 1986: see s 102(2).

Extent

This Act does not extend to Scotland.

See Further

See further, as to the exclusion of this Act in relation to leases or tenancies granted to contractors in respect of the running of any removal centre or part of a removal centre: the Immigration and Asylum Act 1999, s 149(3).

Notes

For a commentary, see para 42.31.

This section is a drafting provision.

Commencement of this Act. This Act came into force on 18 June 1986, in accordance with s 102(2).

Statutory instrument. See the corresponding note to s 94.

Agricultural Holdings (Variation of Fourth Schedule) Order 1951. SI 1951/2168; revoked by s 101, Sch 15, Pt II.

A1.187

100   Consequential amendments

Schedule 14 to this Act shall have effect.

NOTES

Initial Commencement

Specified date: 18 June 1986: see s 102(2).

See Further

See further, as to the exclusion of this Act in relation to leases or tenancies granted to contractors in respect of the running of any removal centre or part of a removal centre: the Immigration and Asylum Act 1999, s 149(3).

Note

This section is a drafting provision.

A1.188

101   Repeals and revocations

(1)   The enactments specified in Part I of Schedule 15 to this Act are hereby repealed to the extent specified in the third column of that Schedule.

(2)   The instruments specified in Part II of Schedule 15 to this Act are hereby revoked to the extent specified in the third column of that Schedule.

NOTES

Initial Commencement

Specified date: 18 June 1986: see s 102(2).

See Further

See further, as to the exclusion of this Act in relation to leases or tenancies granted to contractors in respect of the running of any removal centre or part of a removal centre: the Immigration and Asylum Act 1999, s 149(3).

Note

This section is a drafting provision.

A1.189

102   Citation, commencement and extent

(1)   This Act may be cited as the Agricultural Holdings Act 1986.

(2)   This Act shall come into force at the end of the period of three months beginning with the day on which it is passed.

(3)   Subject to subsection (4) below, this Act extends to England and Wales only.

(4)   Subject to subsection (5) below and to paragraph 26(6) of Schedule 14 to this Act, the amendment or repeal by this Act of an enactment which extends to Scotland or Northern Ireland shall also extend there.

(5)   Subsection (4) above does not apply to the amendment or repeal by this Act of section 9 of the Hill Farming Act 1946, section 48(4) of the Agriculture Act 1967 or an enactment contained in the Agriculture (Miscellaneous Provisions) Act 1968.

NOTES

Initial Commencement

Specified date: 18 June 1986: see sub-s (2) above.

See Further

See further, as to the exclusion of this Act in relation to leases or tenancies granted to contractors in respect of the running of any removal centre or part of a removal centre: the Immigration and Asylum Act 1999, s 149(3).

Notes

This section is a drafting provision.

Three months beginning with, etc. See para 42.27 on the computation of time. 'Months' means calendar months; see the Interpretation Act 1978, s 5, Sch 1. In calculating this period the day (ie 18 March 1986) on which the Act was passed (ie received Royal Assent) is reckoned; see *Hare v Gocher* [1962] 2 QB 641, [1962] 2 All ER 763, and *Trow v Ind Coope (West Midlands) Ltd* [1967] 2 QB 899 at 909, [1967] 2 All ER 900, CA. Accordingly this Act came into force on 18 June 1986.

England; Wales. For meanings, see the Interpretation Act 1978, s 5, Sch 1.

Hill Farming Act 1946, s 9. Repealed by s 101 and Sch 15, Pt I.

Agriculture Act 1967, s 48(4). That subsection is substituted by s 100 and Sch 14, para 41(3).

Agriculture (Miscellaneous Provisions) Act 1968. For repeals in that Act made by this Act, see s 101 and Sch 15, Pt I, and for amendments therein, see s 100 and Sch 14, paras 44–48.

SCHEDULE 1
MATTERS FOR WHICH PROVISION IS TO BE MADE IN WRITTEN TENANCY AGREEMENTS

Section 6

A1.190

1   The names of the parties.

2   Particulars of the holding with sufficient description, by reference to a map or plan, of the fields and other parcels of land comprised in the holding to identify its extent.

3   The term or terms for which the holding or different parts of it is or are agreed to be let.

4   The rent reserved and the dates on which it is payable.

5   The incidence of the liability for rates (including drainage rates).

6   A covenant by the tenant in the event of the destruction by fire of harvested crops grown on the holding for consumption on it to return to the holding the full equivalent manurial value of the crops destroyed, in so far as the return of the value is required for the fulfilment of his responsibilities to farm in accordance with the rules of good husbandry.

7   A covenant by the tenant (except where the interest of the tenant is held for the purposes of a government department or where the tenant has made provision approved by the Minister in lieu of such insurance) to insure against damage by fire all dead stock on the holding and all harvested crops grown on the holding for consumption on it.

8   A power for the landlord to re-enter on the holding in the event of the tenant not performing his obligations under the agreement.

9   A covenant by the tenant not to assign, sub-let or part with possession of the holding or any part of it without the landlord's consent in writing.

NOTES

Derivation

Paras 1–8 derived from the Agricultural Holdings Act 1948, Sch 1, paras 1–5, 8, 9; para 9 derived from the Agricultural Holdings Act 1948, Sch 1, para 10, and the Agriculture (Miscellaneous Provisions) Act 1976, s 17.

Initial Commencement

Specified date: 18 June 1986: see s 102(2).

Extent

This Act does not extend to Scotland.

See Further

See further, as to the exclusion of this Act in relation to leases or tenancies granted to contractors in respect of the running of any removal centre or part of a removal centre: the Immigration and Asylum Act 1999, s 149(3).

Transfer of Functions

Functions of the Minister, so far as exercisable in relation to Wales, transferred to the National Assembly for Wales, by the National Assembly for Wales (Transfer of Functions) Order 1999, SI 1999/672, art 2, Sch 1.

Notes

For a commentary on Sch 1 and s 6, see para 23.1 ff.

Paras 1–5, 8, 9 contain provisions formerly in the Agricultural Holdings Act 1948, Sch 1, paras 1–5, 9, 10, respectively, as added, in the case of para 10 of that Schedule, by the Agriculture (Miscellaneous Provisions) Act 1976, s 17. Paras 6, 7 contain provisions formerly in Sch 1, para 8 to the 1948 Act.

Writing. See the note 'Written' to s 3.

Definitions. For 'landlord', 'the Minister' and 'tenant', see s 96(1). Note as to 'farm in accordance with the rules of good husbandry', s 96(3).

SCHEDULE 2
ARBITRATION OF RENT: PROVISIONS SUPPLEMENTARY TO SECTION 12

Section 12

Amount of rent

A1.191

1   (1) For the purposes of section 12 of this Act, the rent properly payable in respect of a holding shall be the rent at which the holding might reasonably be

expected to be let by a prudent and willing landlord to a prudent and willing tenant, taking into account (subject to sub-paragraph (3) and paragraphs 2 and 3 below) all relevant factors, including (in every case) the terms of the tenancy (including those relating to rent), the character and situation of the holding (including the locality in which it is situated), the productive capacity of the holding and its related earning capacity, and the current level of rents for comparable lettings, as determined in accordance with sub-paragraph (3) below.

(2) In sub-paragraph (1) above, in relation to the holding—

(a) 'productive capacity' means the productive capacity of the holding (taking into account fixed equipment and any other available facilities on the holding) on the assumption that is in the occupation of a competent tenant practising a system of farming suitable to the holding, and

(b) 'related earning capacity' means the extent to which, in the light of that productive capacity, a competent tenant practising such a system of farming could reasonably be expected to profit from farming the holding.

(3) In determining for the purposes of that sub-paragraph the current level of rents for comparable lettings, the arbitrator shall take into account any available evidence with respect to the rents (whether fixed by agreement between the parties or by arbitration under this Act) which are, or (in view of rents currently being tendered) are likely to become, payable in respect of tenancies of comparable agricultural holdings on terms (other than terms fixing the rent payable) similar to those of the tenancy under consideration, but shall disregard—

(a) any element of the rents in question which is due to an appreciable scarcity of comparable holdings available for letting on such terms compared with the number of persons seeking to become tenants of such holdings on such terms,

(b) any element of those rents which is due to the fact that the tenant of, or a person tendering for, any comparable holding is in occupation of other land in the vicinity of that holding that may conveniently be occupied together with that holding, and

(c) any effect on those rents which is due to any allowances or reductions made in consideration of the charging of premiums.

2   (1) On a reference under section 12 of this Act, the arbitrator shall disregard any increase in the rental value of the holding which is due to—

(a) tenant's improvements or fixed equipment other than improvements executed or equipment provided under an obligation imposed on the tenant by the terms of his contract of tenancy, and

(b) landlord's improvements, in so far as the landlord has received or will receive grants out of money provided by Parliament or local government funds in respect of the execution of those improvements.

(2) In this paragraph—

(a) 'tenant's improvements' means any improvements which have been executed on the holding, in so far as they were executed wholly or partly at the expense of the tenant (whether or not that expense has been or will be reimbursed by a grant out of money provided by Parliament or local government funds) without any equivalent allowance or benefit made or given by the landlord in consideration of their execution,

(b) 'tenant's fixed equipment' means fixed equipment provided by the tenant, and

(c) 'landlord's improvements' means improvements executed on the holding by the landlord.

(3) Where the tenant has held a previous tenancy of the holding, then—

(a) in the definition of 'tenant's improvements' in sub-paragraph (2)(a) above, the reference to any such improvements as are there mentioned shall extend to improvements executed during that tenancy, and

(b) in the definition of 'tenant's fixed equipment' in sub-paragraph (2)(b), the reference to such equipment as is there mentioned shall extend to equipment provided during that tenancy,

excluding, however, any improvement or fixed equipment so executed or provided in respect of which the tenant received any compensation on the termination of that (or any other) tenancy.

(4) For the purposes of sub-paragraph (2)(a) above, the continuous adoption by the tenant of a system of farming more beneficial to the holding—

(a) than the system of farming required by the contract of tenancy, or

(b) in so far as no system is so required, than the system of farming normally practised on comparable agricultural holdings,

shall be treated as an improvement executed at his expense.

3   On a reference under section 12 of this Act the arbitrator—

(a) shall disregard any effect on the rent of the fact that the tenant who is a party to the arbitration is in occupation of the holding, and

(b) shall not fix the rent at a lower amount by reason of any dilapidation or deterioration of, or damage to, buildings or land caused or permitted by the tenant.

Frequency of arbitrations under section 12

4   (1) Subject to the following provisions of this Schedule, a demand for arbitration shall not be effective for the purposes of section 12 of this Act if the next termination date following the date of the demand falls earlier than the end of three years from any of the following dates, that is to say—

(a) the commencement of the tenancy, or

(b) the date as from which there took effect a previous increase or reduction of rent (whether made under that section or otherwise), or

(c) the date as from which there took effect a previous direction of an arbitrator under that section that the rent should continue unchanged.

(2) The following shall be disregarded for the purposes of sub-paragraph (1)(b) above—

(a) an increase or reduction of rent under section 6(3) or 8(4) of this Act;

(b) an increase of rent under subsection (1) of section 13 of this Act or such an increase as is referred to in subsection (3) of that section, or any reduction of rent agreed between the landlord and the tenant of the holding in consequence of any change in the fixed equipment provided on the holding by the landlord;

(c) a reduction of rent under section 33 of this Act.

5   (1) This paragraph applies in any case where a tenancy of an agricultural holding ('the new holding') commences under a contract of tenancy between—

(a) a person who immediately before the date of the commencement of the tenancy was entitled to a severed part of the reversionary estate in an agricultural holding ('the original holding') in which the new holding was then comprised, and

(b) the person who immediately before that date was the tenant of the original holding, and where the rent payable in respect of the new holding at the commencement of the tenancy of that holding represents merely the appropriate portion of the rent payable in respect of the original holding immediately before the commencement of that tenancy.

(2)   In any case to which this paragraph applies—

(a)   paragraph (a) of sub-paragraph (1) of paragraph 4 above shall be read as referring to the commencement of the tenancy of the original holding, and

(b)   references to rent in paragraphs (b) and (c) of that sub-paragraph shall be read as references to the rent payable in respect of the original holding,

until the first occasion following the commencement of the tenancy of the new holding on which any such increase or reduction of, or direction with respect to, the rent of the new holding as is mentioned in paragraph (b) or (c) takes effect.

6   Where under an agreement between the landlord and the tenant of the holding (not being an agreement expressed to take effect as a new contract of tenancy between the parties) provision is made for adjustment of the boundaries of the holding or for any other variation of the terms of the tenancy, exclusive of those relating to rent, then, unless the agreement otherwise provides—

(a)   that provision shall for the purposes of sub-paragraph (1) of paragraph 4 above be treated as not operating to terminate the tenancy, and accordingly as not resulting in the commencement of a new contract of tenancy between the parties, and

(b)   any increase or reduction of rent solely attributable to any such adjustment or variation as aforesaid shall be disregarded for the purposes of paragraph (b) of that sub-paragraph.

[7   (1)   This paragraph applies in any case where—

(a)   a tenancy of an agricultural holding ('the new tenancy') is granted to a person who, immediately before the grant of the new tenancy, was the tenant of the holding, or of any agricultural holding which comprised the whole or a substantial part of the land comprised in the holding, under a contract of tenancy ('the previous tenancy'),

(b)   this Act applies in relation to the new tenancy by virtue of section 4(1)(g) of the Agricultural Tenancies Act 1995, and

(c)   the rent payable under the new tenancy is unchanged from that payable under the previous tenancy, disregarding any increase or reduction in rent solely attributable to an adjustment of the boundaries of the holding.

(2)   The reference in sub-paragraph (1) above to a substantial part of the land comprised in the holding means a substantial part determined by reference to either area or value.

(3)   In any case to which this paragraph applies—

(a)   paragraph (a) of sub-paragraph (1) of paragraph 4 above shall be read as referring to the commencement of the previous tenancy, and

(b)   references to rent in paragraphs (b) and (c) of that sub-paragraph shall be read as references to the rent payable under the previous tenancy,

until the first occasion following the commencement of the new tenancy on which any such increase or reduction of, or direction with respect to, the rent payable under the new tenancy as is mentioned in paragraph (b) or (c) takes effect.]

NOTES

Derivation

This Schedule derived from the Agricultural Holdings Act 1948, ss 8(3)–(12), 8A(3)–(5), and the Agricultural Holdings Act 1984, s 1.

Initial Commencement

Specified date: 18 June 1986: see s 102(2).

Extent

This Act does not extend to Scotland.

Amendment

Para 7: inserted by SI 2006/2805, arts 2, 8.

Date in force: 19 October 2006: see SI 2006/2805, art 1(1)(b); for transitional provisions see art 10 thereof.

See Further

See further, as to the exclusion of this Act in relation to leases or tenancies granted to contractors in respect of the running of any removal centre or part of a removal centre: the Immigration and Asylum Act 1999, s 149(3).

Notes

For a commentary, see para 25.4 ff.

Paras 1(1), (2), (3), 2(1) contain provisions formerly in the Agricultural Holdings Act 1948, s 8(3), (4), (5), (6), respectively, as substituted by the Agricultural Holdings Act 1984, s 1. Para 2(2)–(4) contains provisions formerly in s 8A(3)–(5), respectively, of the 1948 Act, as substituted by s 1 of the 1984 Act. Paras 3, 4(1), (2), 5(1), (2), 6 contain provisions formerly in s 8(7), (8), (12), (9), (10), (11), respectively, of the 1948 Act, as substituted by s 1 of the 1984 Act.

General Note. See the General Note to s 12.

Para 1: Arbitration under this Act. For provisions as to arbitration under this Act, see s 84 and the note to s 2.

Shall disregard ... any element ... due to an appreciable scarcity, etc. Para 1(3)(a) may be compared with such provisions as the Rent Act 1977, s 70(2), which provides that for the purposes of the determination of a fair rent under a regulated tenancy of a dwelling-house, it shall be assumed that the number of persons seeking to become tenants of similar dwelling-houses in the locality on the terms of the tenancy is not substantially greater than the number of such dwelling-houses in the locality which are available for letting on such terms; cf also the note to that provision.

Premiums. It is thought that this refers to a premium charged as a condition of the grant of a tenancy.

Para 2: Grants. See, as to the matters relating to agriculture in respect of which grants may be made, the Preliminary Note to title Agriculture in 1 Halsbury's Statutes (4th edn, 1989 reissue) 119, 120.

Benefit. Cf the note to s 66.

Improvement ... in respect of which the tenant received any compensation, etc. As to tenant's right to compensation for improvements see, generally, ss 64 ff.

System of farming more beneficial to the holding, etc. As to tenant's right to compensation on the termination of his tenancy where he has adopted such a system, see s 70.

Para 3: Dilapidation or deterioration ... caused or permitted by the tenant. As to landlord's right to compensation in respect of such matters, see ss 71–73.

Para 4: Next termination date. This is to be construed in accordance with s 12(4).

Three years from, etc. See the note 'Two months from, etc' to s 10.

Change in the fixed equipment. Although a farmhouse is included in the definition 'fixed equipment' for these purposes, the surrender of part of a holding, even where that part consists of a building affixed to the land, is a change in the holding itself and not in the fixed equipment provided by the landlord; see *Mann v Gardner* [1991] 1 EGLR 9, (1990) 61 P & CR 1, CA; *Secretary of State for Defence v Spencer* [2003] 1 WLR 2701.

Para 6: Provision ... for the adjustment of the boundaries of the holding. The surrender of part of a holding where that part consists of a building affixed to the land does not amount to provision for the adjustment of the boundaries of the holding; see *Mann v Gardner* (1990) 61 P & CR 1, CA. See also, *Secretary of State for Defence v Spencer* [2003] 1 WLR 2701. See para 25.12 ff.

Holdings treated as market gardens. It should be noted that a new tenancy created by the acceptance of a tenant in accordance with s 80 (holdings treated as market gardens) on the terms and conditions of the existing tenancy is to be deemed not to be a new tenancy for the purposes of this Schedule; see sub-s (8) of that section.

Para 7: inserted by RRO, SI 2006/2805, arts 2 and 8.

Definitions. For 'agricultural holding', see s 1(1); for 'contract of tenancy', see s 1(5); for 'agreement', 'fixed equipment', 'landlord', 'local government funds' and 'tenant', see s 96(1). Note as to 'productive capacity' and 'related earning capacity', para 1(2) above; as to 'tenant's improvements', 'tenant's fixed equipment' and 'landlord's improvements', para 2(2) above (as read with para 2(3) above); and as to 'the original holding', para 5(1)(a) above.

SCHEDULE 3

CASES WHERE CONSENT OF TRIBUNAL TO OPERATION OF NOTICE TO QUIT IS
NOT REQUIRED

Section 26

PART I: THE CASES

CASE A

A1.192

The holding is let as a smallholding by a smallholdings authority or the Minister in pursuance of Part III of the Agriculture Act 1970 and was so let on or after 12th September 1984, and

    (a)   the tenant has attained the age of sixty-five, and

    (b)   if the result of the notice to quit taking effect would be to deprive the tenant of living accommodation occupied by him under the tenancy, suitable alternative accommodation is available for him, or will be available for him when the notice takes effect, and

    (c)   the instrument under which the tenancy was granted contains an acknowledgment signed by the tenant that the tenancy is subject to the provisions of this Case (or to those of Case I in section 2(3) of the Agricultural Holdings (Notices to Quit) Act 1977),

and it is stated in the notice to quit that it is given by reason of the said matter.

CASE B

[The notice to quit is given on the ground that the land is required for a use, other than for agriculture—

    (a)   for which permission has been granted on an application made under the enactments relating to town and country planning,

   (b)   for which permission under those enactments is granted by a general develop-
         ment order by reason only of the fact that the use is authorised by—
         (i)   a private or local Act,
         (ii) an order approved by both Houses of Parliament, or
         (iii) an order made under section 14 or 16 of the Harbours Act 1964,
   (c)   for which any provision that—
         (i)   is contained in an Act, but
         (ii) does not form part of the enactments relating to town and country
               planning,
   deems permission under those enactments to have been granted,
   (d)   which any such provision deems not to constitute development for the
         purposes of those enactments, or
   (e)   for which permission is not required under the enactments relating to town
         and country planning by reason only of Crown immunity,

and that fact is stated in the notice.]

CASE C

Not more than six months before the giving of the notice to quit, the Tribunal granted
a certificate under paragraph 9 of Part II of this Schedule that the tenant of the holding
was not fulfilling his responsibilities to farm in accordance with the rules of good
husbandry, and that fact is stated in the notice.

CASE D

At the date of the giving of the notice to quit the tenant had failed to comply with a
notice in writing served on him by the landlord, being either—

   (a)   a notice requiring him within two months from the service of the notice to pay
         any rent due in respect of the agricultural holding to which the notice to quit
         relates, or
   (b)   a notice requiring him within a reasonable period specified in the notice to
         remedy any breach by the tenant that was capable of being remedied of any
         term or condition of his tenancy which was not inconsistent with his
         responsibilities to farm in accordance with the rules of good husbandry,

and it is stated in the notice to quit that it is given by reason of the said matter.

CASE E

At the date of the giving of the notice to quit the interest of the landlord in the
agricultural holding had been materially prejudiced by the commission by the tenant of
a breach, which was not capable of being remedied, of any term or condition of the
tenancy that was not inconsistent with the tenant's responsibilities to farm in
accordance with the rules of good husbandry, and it is stated in the notice that it is
given by reason of the said matter.

CASE F

At the date of the giving of the notice to quit the tenant was a person who had become
insolvent, and it is stated in the notice that it is given by reason of the said matter.

CASE G

The notice to quit is given—

   (a)   following the death of a person who immediately before his death was the sole
         (or sole surviving) tenant under the contract of tenancy, and

1231

(b)   not later than the end of the period of three months beginning with the date of any relevant notice,

and it is stated in the notice to quit that it is given by reason of that person's death.

CASE H

The notice to quit is given by the Minister and—

(a)   the Minister certifies in writing that the notice to quit is given in order to enable him to use or dispose of the land for the purpose of effecting any amalgamation (within the meaning of section 26(1) of the Agriculture Act 1967) or the reshaping of any agricultural unit, and

(b)   the instrument under which the tenancy was granted contains an acknowledgement signed by the tenant that the tenancy is subject to the provisions of this Case (or to those of Case H in section 2(3) of the Agricultural Holdings (Notices to Quit) Act 1977 or of section 29 of the Agriculture Act 1967).

NOTES

Derivation

Cases A, C, F, G derived from the Agricultural Holdings (Notices to Quit) Act 1977, s 2(3), Cases I, C, F, G, and the Agricultural Holdings Act 1984, ss 6(3), (5)(a), (6), 10(1), 11(2), Sch 3, para 37; Cases B, D, E, H derived from the Agricultural Holdings (Notices to Quit) Act 1977, s 2(3), Cases B, D, E, H.

Initial Commencement

Specified date: 18 June 1986: see s 102(2).

Extent

This Act does not extend to Scotland.

Amendment

Case B: substituted by the Agricultural Holdings (Amendment) Act 1990, s 1(1), (2).

See Further

See further, as to the exclusion of this Act in relation to leases or tenancies granted to contractors in respect of the running of any removal centre or part of a removal centre: the Immigration and Asylum Act 1999, s 149(3).

Transfer of Functions

Functions of the Minister, so far as exercisable in relation to Wales, transferred to the National Assembly for Wales, by the National Assembly for Wales (Transfer of Functions) Order 1999, SI 1999/672, art 2, Sch 1.

Notes

For a commentary on s 26 and Sch 3 generally, see Ch 30 and Ch 31. Also see para 32.10 in relation to Case B.

Case A contains provisions formerly in the Agricultural Holdings (Notices to Quit) Act 1977, s 2(3). Case I, as added by the Agricultural Holdings Act 1984, s 6(6), and as read with s 11(2) of that Act. Cases C–H contain provisions formerly in s 2(3), Cases C–H, respectively, of the 1977 Act, as amended in the case of Case C in that section, by s 6(3) of the 1984 Act, in the case of Case F, by s 10(1) of. and Sch 3, para 37 to, the 1984 Act, in the case of Case G, by s 6(5)(a) of the 1984 Act, and as repealed in part, in the case of Case H, by s 10(2) of, and Sch 4 to, the 1984 Act.

Case B is substituted, with a saving, by the Agricultural Holdings (Amendment) Act 1990, ss 1(1), (2), 2.

General Note. The Agricultural Holdings (Arbitration on Notices) Order 1987, SI 1987/710, art 9, (as to which, see the note 'Orders under this section' to s 29), requires a tenant contesting a reason specified in Cases A, B, D, E above to refer the question to arbitration (although note art 10 of that order). Accordingly the jurisdiction of the courts is excluded though a point of law can be brought before the county court by special case stated by the arbitrator: *A-G of Duchy of Lancaster v Simcock* [1966] Ch 1, [1965] 2 All ER 32.

As to the effect of a fraudulent statement contained in a notice to quit served under this Part, see *Rous v Mitchell, sub nom Earl of Stradbroke v Mitchell* [1991] 1 All ER 676, [1991] 1 WLR 469, [1991] 1 EGLR 1.

For supplementary provisions applicable to Cases A–E and G in this Part of this Schedule, see Pt II of this Schedule.

Case A: Smallholdings authority. As to these authorities, see the Agriculture Act 1970, s 38. See para 31.18.

12th September 1984. Ie the commencement date of the Agricultural Holdings Act 1984 (repealed by s 101, Sch 15, Pt I).

Attained the age of sixty-five. A person attains a given age expressed in years at the commencement of the relevant anniversary of the date of his birth; see the Family Law Reform Act 1969, s 9.

Notice to quit. Cf the notes to ss 25, 26.

Case I, etc. Ie the statutory antecedent of this Case; see the derivation note above.

Case B: Land is required for a use, other than for agriculture, etc. See para 32.10 ff. The use need not be a use by the landlord (*Rugby Joint Water Board v Foottit* [1973] AC 202, [1972] 1 All ER 1057, HL), but land is not 'required' for another use when the landlord merely has it in mind to sell it for another use if he can find a purchaser (*Jones v Gates* [1954] 1 All ER 158).

As to the assessment of compensation for the compulsory acquisition of land, see the Land Compensation Act 1973, s 48, as amended by s 99, Sch 13, para 53, and by the Agricultural Tenancies Act 1995, s 40, Schedule, para 24; and for the tenant's right to claim compensation from an acquiring authority, see s 59 of that Act, as amended by s 99, Sch 13, para 55.

Permission has been granted ... under the enactments relating to town and country planning. As to applications for planning permission and the determination of them, see the Town and Country Planning Act 1990, ss 62 ff.

Case C: Months. See para 31.21 ff. See the note to s 4.

The Tribunal. See the note to s 11.

Rules of good husbandry. As to the effect of opencast coal operations, see the Opencast Coal Act 1958, s 14(3), as amended by s 99, Sch 14, para 25(3).

Case D. See para 31.27 ff. A tenant does not comply with notice to remedy a breach unless he remedies the breach completely: *Price v Romilly* [1960] 3 All ER 429, [1960] 1 WLR 1360. A notice specifying a number of breaches, some of which the tenant cannot remedy as the landlord has failed in his obligation to supply materials, can nevertheless be relied on by the landlord where the tenant has failed to remedy other breaches (*Shepherd v Lomas* [1963] 2 All ER 902, [1963] 1 WLR 962, CA), but a notice specifying a time for remedying a number of breaches will be invalid if the time specified is insufficient to remedy all of the breaches notwithstanding that it may be a sufficient time to remedy some of them (*Wykes v Davis* [1975] QB 843, [1975] 1 All ER 399, CA). Where a tenant fails to pay his rent within two months after the service of the notice requiring payment, he is not protected by s 26(1) even though he pays the rent before notice to quit is served on him: *Stoneman v Brown* [1973] 2 All ER 225, [1973] 1 WLR 459, CA. A notice to quit may be valid notwithstanding the invalidity of the notice requiring payment of rent, and accordingly if the tenant wishes to contest the reason stated in the notice to quit he must do so in the time limited for this purpose by the Agricultural Holdings (Arbitration on Notices) Order 1987, SI 1987/710, art 9, (as to which, see the General Note above): *Magdalen College, Oxford v Heritage* [1974] 1 All ER 1065, [1974] 1 WLR 441, CA.

The rights given to a landlord under Cases D and E are separate and mutually exclusive: *MacNabb v A and J Anderson* 1955 SC 38 at 43.

Writing. See the note 'Written' to s 3.

Two months from, etc. Cf the note 'Not later than one month after, etc' to s 80. See also para 42.27.

Case E. See *MacNabb v A and J Anderson* 1955 SC 38. See para 31.76 ff.

Case F. See paras 31.88 and 31.89.

Case G: Sole (or sole surviving) tenant. See para 31.90 ff. The reference to the sole (or sole surviving) tenant is required because of the possibility that a joint tenancy may exist. In such a case the interest of a deceased joint tenant will vest in the remaining survivor or survivors until only one is left, and only then will Case G apply.

Three months beginning with, etc. See the note to s 39 and para 42.27.

The return of a rent demand with a cheque drawn on the deceased tenant's wife's account does not constitute notice of the tenant's death for the purposes of this provision: see *Lees v Tatchell* (1990) 60 P & CR 228, [1990] 1 EGLR 10, CA.

Case H. See paras 31.102 and 31.103. By the Agriculture Act 1967, s 48(4), as substituted by s 99, Sch 14, para 41(3), this Case applies in relation to a Rural Development Board (established under s 45 of that Act), as it applies in relation to the Minister.

Forms. See the note to Pt II of this Schedule.

Definitions. For 'agricultural holding', see s 1(1); for 'contract of tenancy', see s 1(5); for 'agricultural unit', 'landlord', 'the Minister', 'tenant' and 'the Tribunal', see s 96(1). As to 'insolvent', see s 96(2); and as to 'farm in accordance with the rules of good husbandry', see s 96(3).

Agricultural Holdings (Notices to Quit) Act 1977. Repealed by s 101, Sch 15, Pt I.

Agriculture Act 1967, ss 26(1), 29. Those provisions are amended by s 99, Sch 14, paras 37, 40, respectively,.

PART II: SUPPLEMENTARY PROVISIONS APPLICABLE TO CASES A, B, C, D, E AND G

Provisions applicable to Case A

1   Paragraphs 2 to 7 below have effect for determining whether, for the purposes of paragraph (b) of Case A, suitable alternative accommodation is or will be available for the tenant.

2   For the purposes of paragraph (b) of Case A, a certificate of the housing authority for the district in which the living accommodation in question is situated, certifying that the authority will provide suitable alternative accommodation for the tenant by a date specified in the certificate, shall be conclusive evidence that suitable alternative accommodation will be available for him by that date.

3   Where no such certificate as is mentioned in paragraph 2 above has been issued, accommodation shall be deemed to be suitable for the purposes of paragraph (b) of Case A if it consists of either—

(a)   premises which are to be let as a separate dwelling such that they will then be let on a protected tenancy (within the meaning of the Rent Act 1977), or

(b)   premises to be let as a separate dwelling on terms which will afford to the tenant security of tenure reasonably equivalent to the security afforded by Part VII of that Act in the case of a protected tenancy, [or

(c)   premises which are to be let as a separate dwelling such that they will then be let on an assured tenancy which is not an assured shorthold tenancy (construing those terms in accordance with Part I of the Housing Act 1988), or

(d) premises to be let as a separate dwelling on terms which will afford to the tenant security of tenure reasonably equivalent to the security afforded by Chapter I of Part I of that Act in the case of an assured tenancy which is not an assured shorthold tenancy]

and the accommodation fulfils the conditions in paragraph 4 below.

[(2) Any reference in sub-paragraph (1) above to an assured tenancy does not include a reference to a tenancy in respect of which possession might be recovered on any of Grounds 1 to 5 in Schedule 2 to the Housing Act 1988.]

4 (1) The accommodation must be reasonably suitable to the needs of the tenant's family as regards proximity to place of work and either—

(a) similar as regards rental and extent to the accommodation afforded by dwelling-houses provided in the neighbourhood by any housing authority for persons whose needs as regards extent are similar to those of the tenant and his family, or

(b) reasonably suitable to the means of the tenant and to the needs of the tenant and his family as regards extent and character.

(2) For the purposes of sub-paragraph (1)(a) above, a certificate of a housing authority stating—

(a) the extent of the accommodation afforded by dwelling-houses provided by the authority to meet the needs of tenants with families of such number as may be specified in the certificate, and

(b) the amount of the rent charged by the authority for dwelling-houses affording accommodation of that extent,

shall be conclusive evidence of the facts so stated.

(3) If any furniture was provided by the landlord for use under the tenancy in question, furniture must be provided for use in the alternative accommodation which is either—

(a) similar to that so provided, or

(b) reasonably suitable to the needs of the tenant and his family.

5 Accommodation shall not be deemed to be suitable to the needs of the tenant and his family if the result of their occupation of the accommodation would be that it would be an overcrowded dwelling-house for the purposes of Part X of the Housing Act 1985.

6 Any document purporting—

(a) to be a certificate of a housing authority named in it issued for the purposes of this Schedule, and

(b) to be signed by the proper officer of the authority,

shall be received in evidence and, unless the contrary is shown, shall be deemed to be such a certificate without further proof.

7 (1) In paragraphs 2, 4 and 6 above 'housing authority', and 'district' in relation to such an authority, mean a local housing authority and their district within the meaning of the Housing Act 1985.

(2) For the purposes of paragraphs 4 and 5 a dwelling-house may be a house or part of a house.

Provisions applicable to Case B

8 (1) For the purposes of Case B no account shall be taken of any permission granted as mentioned in paragraph (a) of that Case if the permission—

(a) ...
(b) relates to the working of coal by opencast operations, and
(c) was granted subject to a restoration condition and to an aftercare condition in which the use specified is use for agriculture or use for forestry.

(2) In this paragraph 'restoration condition' and 'aftercare condition' have the meaning given by [section 336(1) of the Town and Country Planning Act 1990].

[8A (1) For the purposes of Case B—

(a) 'general development order' means an order under section 59 of the Town and Country Planning Act 1990 which is made as a general order, and
(b) 'the enactments relating to town and country planning' means the planning Acts (as defined in section 336(1) of the Town and Country Planning Act 1990) and any enactment amending or replacing any of those Acts.

(2) In relation to any time before the commencement of Part III of the Town and Country Planning Act 1990, sub-paragraph (1) above shall have effect as if—

(a) in paragraph (a), for '59' there were substituted '24' and for '1990' there were substituted '1971', and
(b) in paragraph (b), for the words from 'planning Acts' onwards there were substituted 'repealed enactments (as defined in section 1(1) of the Planning (Consequential Provisions) Act 1990)'.]

Provisions applicable to Case C

9 (1) For the purposes of Case C the landlord of an agricultural holding may apply to the Tribunal for a certificate that the tenant is not fulfilling his responsibilities to farm in accordance with the rules of good husbandry; and the Tribunal, if satisfied that the tenant is not fulfilling his said responsibilities, shall grant such a certificate.

(2) In determining whether to grant a certificate under this paragraph the Tribunal shall disregard any practice adopted by the tenant in pursuance of any provision of the contract of tenancy, or of any other agreement with the landlord, which indicates (in whatever terms) that its object is the furtherance of one or more of the following purposes, namely—

(a) the conservation of flora or fauna or of geological or physiographical features of special interest;
(b) the protection of buildings or other objects of archaeological, architectural or historic interest;
(c) the conservation or enhancement of the natural beauty or amenity of the countryside or the promotion of its enjoyment by the public.

[(3) In determining whether to grant a certificate under this paragraph, the Tribunal shall disregard any practice adopted by the tenant in compliance with any obligation accepted by or imposed on the tenant under [section 94 or 95 of the Water Resources Act 1991].]

Provisions applicable to Case D

10 (1) For the purposes of Case D—

(a) a notice such as that mentioned in paragraph (a) or (b) of that Case must be in the prescribed form,
(b) where such a notice in the prescribed form requires the doing of any work of repair, maintenance or replacement, any further notice requiring the doing of any such work which is served on the tenant less than twelve months after the earlier notice shall be disregarded unless the earlier notice was withdrawn with his agreement in writing,

(c) a period of less than six months shall not be treated as a reasonable period within which to do any such work, and

(d) any provision such as is mentioned in paragraph 9(2) above shall (if it would not otherwise be so regarded) be regarded as a term or condition of the tenancy which is not inconsistent with the tenant's responsibilities to farm in accordance with the rules of good husbandry.

(2) Different forms may be prescribed for the purpose of paragraph (b) of Case D in relation to different circumstances.

[(3) For the purposes of that Case compliance with any obligation accepted by or imposed on the tenant under [section 94 or 95 of the Water Resources Act 1991] shall not be capable of constituting a breach by the tenant of the terms or conditions of his tenancy.]

Provisions applicable to Case E

11 (1) Where—

(a) the landlord is a smallholdings authority, or

(b) the landlord is the Minister and the holding is on land held by him for the purposes of smallholdings,

then, in considering whether the interest of the landlord has been materially prejudiced as mentioned in Case E, regard shall be had to the effect of the breach in question not only on the holding itself but also on the carrying out of the arrangements made by the smallholdings authority or the Minister (as the case may be) for the letting and conduct of smallholdings.

(2) For the purposes of Case E any provision such as is mentioned in paragraph 9(2) above shall (if it would not otherwise be so regarded) be regarded as a term or condition of the tenancy which is not inconsistent with the tenant's responsibilities to farm in accordance with the rules of good husbandry.

[(3) For the purposes of that Case compliance with any obligation accepted by or imposed on the tenant under [section 94 or 95 of the Water Resources Act 1991] shall not be capable of constituting a breach by the tenant of the terms or conditions of his tenancy.]

Provisions applicable to Case G

12 For the purposes of Case G—

(a) 'tenant' does not include an executor, administrator, trustee in bankruptcy or other person deriving title from a tenant by operation of law, and

(b) the reference to the date of any relevant notice shall be construed as a reference—

(i) to the date on which a notice in writing was served on the landlord by or on behalf of an executor or administrator of the tenant's estate informing the landlord of the tenant's death or the date on which the landlord was given notice by virtue of section 40(5) of this Act of any application with respect to the holding under section 39 or 41, or

(ii) where both of those events occur, to the date of whichever of them occurs first.

NOTES

Derivation

Paras 1, 8–12 derived from the Agricultural Holdings (Notices to Quit) Act 1977, s 2(3), Cases D, G, I, (3A)–(6), and the Agricultural Holdings Act 1984, s 6(4), (5)(b), (6)–(8); paras 2–7 derived from the Agricultural Holdings (Notices to Quit) Act 1977, Sch 1A, paras 1–6, the Agricultural Holdings Act 1984, s 10(1), Sch 3, para 43, and the Housing (Consequential Provisions) Act 1985, s 4, Sch 2, para 34.

Initial Commencement

Specified date: 18 June 1986: see s 102(2).

Extent

This Act does not extend to Scotland.

Amendment

Para 3: words in square brackets inserted by the Housing Act 1988, s 140(1), Sch 17, para 69.

Para 8: in sub-para (1) words omitted repealed by the Coal Industry Act 1994, s 67(1), (8), Sch 9, para 35, Sch 11, Part II; in sub-para (2) words in square brackets substituted by the Planning (Consequential Provisions) Act 1990, s 4, Sch 2, para 72.

Para 8A: inserted by the Agricultural Holdings (Amendment) Act 1990, s 1(1), (3).

Paras 9–11: sub-para (3) inserted by the Water Act 1989, s 190(1), Sch 25, para 75, words in square brackets therein substituted by the Water Consolidation (Consequential Provisions) Act 1991, s 2(1), Sch 1, para 43.

See Further

See further, as to the exclusion of this Act in relation to leases or tenancies granted to contractors in respect of the running of any removal centre or part of a removal centre: the Immigration and Asylum Act 1999, s 149(3).

Transfer of Functions

Functions of the Minister, so far as exercisable in relation to Wales, transferred to the National Assembly for Wales, by the National Assembly for Wales (Transfer of Functions) Order 1999, SI 1999/672, art 2, Sch 1.

Subordinate Legislation

Agricultural Holdings (Forms of Notice to Pay Rent or to Remedy) Regulations 1987, SI 1987/711 (made under para 10(1)(a), (2)).

Notes

For a commentary on s 26 and Sch 3 generally, see Ch 30 and Ch 31. Also see para 32.10 in relation to Case B.

Para 1 contains provisions formerly in the Agricultural Holdings (Notices to Quit) Act 1977, s 2(3), Case I, as added by the Agricultural Holdings Act 1984, s 6(6). Paras 2–7 contain provisions formerly in Sch 1A, paras 1–6, respectively, to the 1977 Act, as inserted by s 10(1) of, and Sch 3, para 43 to, the 1984 Act, and as amended, in the case of paras 4, 6 of that Schedule, by the Housing (Consequential Provisions) Act 1985, s 4, Sch 2, para 34. Paras 8, 9(1), 9(2) contain provisions formerly in s 2(3A), (4), (4A), respectively, of the 1977 Act, as inserted, in the case of sub-ss (3A), (4A) of that section by s 6(7), (8), respectively, of the 1984 Act. Para 10(1) contains provisions formerly in s 2(3), Case D, (4B) of the 1977 Act, as amended in the case of Case D in that subsection, by s 6(4) of the 1984 Act, and as inserted, in the case of sub-s (4B) of that section, by s 6(8) of the 1984 Act. Paras 10(2), 11(1), 11(2), 12 contain provisions formerly in s 2(6), (5), (4B), (3) Case G, respectively, of the 1977 Act, as inserted in the case of sub-s (4B) of that section, by s 6(8) of the 1984 Act, and as amended, in the case of Case G in sub-s (3) of that section, by s 6(5)(b) of the 1984 Act.

Para 8(1)(a) was repealed by the Coal Industry Act 1994, s 67(1), (8), Sch 9, para 35, Sch 11, Pt II.

In para 8(2) the words in square brackets were substituted by the Planning (Consequential Provisions) Act 1990, s 4, Sch 2, para 72.

Para 8A was inserted with a saving by the Agricultural Holdings (Amendment) Act 1990, s 1(1), (3), 2.

Paras 9(3), 10(3), 11(3) were inserted by the Water Act 1989, s 190(1), Sch 25, para 75, and the words in square brackets therein were substituted by the Water Consolidation (Consequential Provisions) Act 1991, s 2(1), Sch 1, para 43.

Para 1: Suitable alternative accommodation. Cf the note to the Rent Act 1977, s 98.

Para 2: Conclusive evidence. The tendering of evidence declared by statute to be conclusive precludes evidence to the contrary unless the evidence adduced is inaccurate on the face of it or fraud is shown, but other evidence to the same effect is not made inadmissible; see 17(1) Halsbury's Laws (4th edn) reissue para 578 note 2.

Para 9: Apply to the Tribunal. For the prescribed form of application, see the Agricultural Land Tribunals (Rules) Order 1978, SI 1978/259, Sch 1, r 4, Form 3, as construed in accordance with s 99 and Sch 13, para 1(2). See also the note 'The Tribunal' to s 11.

Amenity. In the words of Scrutton LJ in *Re Ellis and Ruislip-Northwood UDC* [1920] 1 KB 343 at 370, CA, this means 'pleasant circumstances or features, advantages'; and the 'amenity' of land refers to its visual appearance and the pleasure of its enjoyment (*Cartwright v Post Office* [1968] 2 All ER 646 at 648: affd [1969] 1 All ER 421, CA). Modern planning usage, however, has stretched the word to denote personal convenience, so that the convenient arrangement of different but inter-dependent uses of land (e g shopping and housing) or the provision of a service such as a public lavatory is called an amenity. The word may be taken to express that element in the appearance and lay-out of town and country which makes for a comfortable and pleasant life rather than a mere existence; see *Re Parramatta City Council, ex p Tooth & Co Ltd* (1955) 55 SR NSW 282 at 306, 308.

Para 10: Prescribed form. For the prescribed forms of notice, see the Agricultural Holdings (Forms of Notice to Pay Rent or to Remedy) Regulations 1987, SI 1987/711.

Doing ... work. For additional restrictions on the operation of a notice to quit given by reason of the tenant's non-compliance with a notice to do work, see s 26.

Served ... less than twelve months, etc. The days of service of the notices are not to be reckoned; see, in particular, *R v Turner* [1910] 1 KB 346; and *Re Hector Whaling Ltd* [1936] Ch 208.

Earlier notice was withdrawn with his agreement in writing. The relevant date for determining whether an earlier notice to remedy has been withdrawn with the tenant's agreement in writing is the date when the notice to quit was served; furthermore there is no requirement that the agreement should be in any particular form and a letter written on the tenant's behalf may be sufficient: *Mercantile and General Re-Insurance Co Ltd v Groves* [1974] QB 43, [1973] 3 All ER 330, CA.

Para 11: Smallholding authority. See the note to Pt I of this Schedule.

Para 12: Does not include an executor, etc. This excludes the extended definition of 'tenant' in s 96(1) and ensures that a landlord cannot serve an incontestable notice to quit on the death of a sole executor, administrator, etc.

Writing. See the note 'Written' to s 3.

Compensation, etc. See the note to s 26.

Definitions. For 'agricultural holding', see s 1(1); for 'contract of tenancy', see s 1(5); for 'agreement', 'agriculture', 'building', 'landlord', 'the Minister', 'prescribed', 'tenant' and 'the Tribunal', see s 96(1). As to 'farm in accordance with the rules of good husbandry', see s 96(3). Note, for certain of the above provisions, as to 'housing authority', 'district' and 'dwelling-house', para 7 above; as to 'restoration condition' and 'aftercare condition', para 8(2) above; and as to 'tenant' and 'date of any relevant notice', para 12 above.

Rent Act 1977. For meaning of 'protected tenancy', see s 1 of that Act.

Housing Act 1985. For definition of overcrowding in that Act, see s 324 thereof; and as to 'local housing authority' and 'district', see ss 1, 2 of that Act.

SCHEDULE 4
MATTERS FOR WHICH PROVISION MAY BE MADE BY ORDER UNDER SECTION 29

Section 29

A1.193

1   Requiring any question arising under the provisions of section 26(2) of, and Schedule 3 to, this Act to be determined by arbitration under this Act.

2   Limiting the time within which any such arbitration may be required or within which an arbitrator may be appointed by agreement between the parties, or (in default of such agreement) an application may be made under [section 84(2) of] this Act for the appointment of an arbitrator, for the purposes of any such arbitration.

3   Extending the period within which a counter-notice may be given by the tenant under section 26(1) of this Act where any such arbitration is required.

4   Suspending the operation of notices to quit until the expiry of any time fixed in pursuance of paragraph 2 above for the making of any such appointment by agreement or application as is there mentioned or, where any such appointment or application has been duly made, until the termination of any such arbitration.

5   Postponing the date at which a tenancy is to be terminated by a notice to quit which has effect in consequence of any such arbitration or of an application under section 26(1) or 28(2) of this Act or under provisions made by virtue of paragraph 12 below.

6   Excluding the application of section 26(1) of this Act in relation to sub-tenancies in such cases as may be specified in the order.

7   Making such provision as appears to the Lord Chancellor expedient for the purpose of safeguarding the interests of sub-tenants including provision enabling the Tribunal, where the interest of a tenant is terminated by notice to quit, to secure that a sub-tenant will hold from the landlord on the like terms as he held from the tenant.

8   The determination by arbitration under this Act of any question arising under such a notice as is mentioned in paragraph (b) of Case D, being a notice requiring the doing of any work of repair, maintenance or replacement (including the question whether the notice is capable of having effect for the purposes of that Case).

9   Enabling the arbitrator, on an arbitration under this Act relating to such a notice as is mentioned in paragraph 8 above, to modify the notice—

   (a) by deleting any item or part of an item of work specified in the notice as to which, having due regard to the interests of good husbandry as respects the agricultural holding to which the notice relates and of sound management of the estate of which that holding forms part or which that holding constitutes, the arbitrator is satisfied that it is unnecessary or unjustified, or

   (b) by substituting, in the case of any item or part of an item of work so specified, a different method or material for the method or material which the notice would otherwise require to be followed or used where, having regard to the purpose which that item or part is intended to achieve, the arbitrator is satisfied that—

     (i) the last-mentioned method or material would involve undue difficulty or expense,

     (ii) the first-mentioned method or material would be substantially as effective for the purpose, and

     (iii) in all the circumstances the substitution is justified.

10 Enabling the time within which anything is to be done in pursuance of such a notice as is mentioned in paragraph (b) of Case D to be extended or to be treated as having been extended.

11 Enabling a tenancy, in a case where that time is extended, to be terminated either by a notice to quit served less than twelve months before the date on which it is to be terminated, or at a date other than the end of a year of the tenancy, or both by such a notice and at such a date.

12 Securing that, where a subsequent notice to quit is given in accordance with provisions made by virtue of paragraph 11 above in a case where the original notice to quit fell within section 28(1) of this Act, then, if the tenant serves on the landlord a counter-notice in writing within one month after the giving of the subsequent notice to quit (or, if the date specified in that notice for the termination of the tenancy is earlier, before that date), the subsequent notice to quit shall not have effect unless the Tribunal consent to its operation, and applying section 28(5) of this Act as regards the giving of that consent.

13 The recovery by a tenant of the cost of any work which is done by him in compliance with a notice requiring him to do it, but which is found by arbitration under this Act to be work which he was not under an obligation to do.

NOTES

Derivation

This Schedule derived from the Agricultural Holdings (Notices to Quit) Act 1977, s 5(1), and the Agricultural Holdings Act 1984, s 10(1), Sch 3, para 38.

Initial Commencement

Specified date: 18 June 1986: see s 102(2).

Extent

This Act does not extend to Scotland.

Amendment

Para 2: words 'section 84(2) of' in square brackets substituted by SI 2006/2805, arts 2, 7(5).

Date in force: 19 October 2006: see SI 2006/2805, art 1(1)(b); for transitional provisions see art 10 thereof.

See Further

See further, as to the exclusion of this Act in relation to leases or tenancies granted to contractors in respect of the running of any removal centre or part of a removal centre: the Immigration and Asylum Act 1999, s 149(3).

Subordinate Legislation

Agricultural Holdings (Arbitration on Notices) Order 1987, SI 1987/710 (made under paras 1–6, 8–13).

Notes

For a commentary, see Ch 30.

This Schedule contains provisions formerly in the Agricultural Holdings (Notices to Quit) Act 1977, s 5(1), as amended by the Agricultural Holdings Act 1984, s 10(1), Sch 3, para 38.

Para 1: Arbitration under this Act. For provisions as to arbitration under this Act, see s 84 and the note to s 2.

Para 4: Notices to quit. Cf the notes to ss 25, 26.

Para 7: Lord Chancellor. See the note to s 29.

The Tribunal. See the note to s 11.

Para 9: Sound management. As to the meaning of this expression, cf *National Coal Board v Naylor* [1972] 1 All ER 1153, [1972] 1 WLR 908.

Para 11: Served less than twelve months, etc. Under s 25(1) a notice to quit an agricultural holding is normally invalid if it purports to terminate the tenancy before the expiration of twelve months from the end of the then current year of tenancy. See, further, the note 'Notice to quit' to that section.

Para 12: Counter-notice. Cf the note to s 26.

Writing. See the note 'Written' to s 3.

Within one month after, etc. Cf the note 'Within six months from, etc' to s 13.

Servicemen. As to modifications, where the tenant of an agricultural holding is a serviceman, regarding notices to quit, see s 30, Sch 5 (note especially, in connection with paras 1–7 above, para 5 of that Schedule).

Definitions. For 'agricultural holding', see s 1(1); for 'Case D', 'landlord', 'tenant' and 'the Tribunal', see s 96(1). Note as to 'rules of good husbandry', s 96(3).

Orders. See the last note to s 29.

SCHEDULE 5
NOTICE TO QUIT WHERE TENANT IS A SERVICE MAN

Section 30

A1.194

1   In this Schedule—

'the 1951 Act' means the Reserve and Auxiliary Forces (Protection of Civil Interests) Act 1951;

'period of residence protection' in the case of a service man who performs a period of relevant service, other than a short period of training, means the period comprising that period of service and the four months immediately following the date on which it ends;

'relevant service' means service (as defined in section 64(1) of the 1951 Act) of a description specified in Schedule 1 to that Act;

'service man' means a man or woman who performs a period of relevant service;

'short period of training' has the meaning given by section 64(1) of the 1951 Act.

2   (1)   Paragraph 3 below shall have effect where—

(a)   the tenant of an agricultural holding to which this Schedule applies performs a period of relevant service, other than a short period of training, and
(b)   during his period of residence protection there is given to him—
  (i)   notice to quit the holding, or
  (ii)   notice to quit a part of it to which this Schedule applies.

(2)   This Schedule applies to—

(a)   any agricultural holding which comprises such a dwelling-house as is mentioned in section 10 of the Rent Act 1977 [or paragraph 7 of Schedule 1 to the Housing Act 1988], that is to say a dwelling-house occupied by the person responsible for the control (whether as tenant or as servant or agent of the tenant) of the farming of the holding, and

(b) any part of an agricultural holding, being a part which consists of or comprises such a dwelling-house.

3 (1) Section 26(1) of this Act shall apply notwithstanding the existence of any such circumstances as are mentioned in Cases B to G; but where the Tribunal are satisfied that such circumstances exist, then, subject to sub-paragraph (2) below, the Tribunal shall not be required to withhold their consent to the operation of the notice to quit by reason only that they are not satisfied that circumstances exist such as are mentioned in paragraphs (a) to (f) of section 27(3) of this Act.

(2) In determining whether to give or withhold their consent under section 26 of this Act the Tribunal—

(a) if satisfied that circumstances exist such as are mentioned in Cases B to G or in section 27(3) of this Act, shall consider to what extent (if at all) the existence of those circumstances is directly or indirectly attributable to the service man's performing or having performed the period of service in question, and

(b) in any case, shall consider to what extent (if at all) the giving of such consent at a time during the period of protection would cause special hardship in view of circumstances directly or indirectly attributable to the service man's performing or having performed that period of service,

and the Tribunal shall withhold their consent to the operation of the notice to quit unless in all the circumstances they consider it reasonable to give their consent.

4 Where the tenant of an agricultural holding to which this Schedule applies performs a period of relevant service, other than a short period of training, and—

(a) a notice to quit the holding, or a part of it to which this Schedule applies, is given to him before the beginning of his period of residence protection, and

(b) the tenant duly serves a counter-notice under section 26(1) of this Act, and

(c) the Tribunal have not before the beginning of his period of residence protection decided whether to give or withhold consent to the operation of the notice to quit,

paragraph 3(2) above shall (with the necessary modifications) apply in relation to the giving or withholding of consent to the operation of the notice to quit as it applies in relation to the giving or withholding of consent to the operation of a notice to quit given in the circumstances mentioned in paragraph 2(1) above.

5 The Lord Chancellor's power under section 29 of this Act to provide for the matters specified in paragraphs 1 to 7 of Schedule 4 to this Act shall apply in relation to the provisions of sections 26 and 27 of this Act as modified by the preceding provisions of this Schedule as they apply in relation to the provisions of those sections apart from this Schedule.

6 (1) The Lord Chancellor may make regulations—

(a) for enabling a counter-notice under section 26(1) of this Act to be served on behalf of a service man at a time when he is serving abroad, in a case where a notice to quit is given to him as mentioned in paragraph 2(1) above, and

(b) for enabling an act or proceedings consequential upon the service of a counter-notice under section 26(1) to be performed or conducted on behalf of a service man at a time when he is serving abroad, either in such a case as is mentioned in paragraph (a) above or in a case where paragraph 4 above applies in relation to him.

(2) References in sub-paragraph (1) above to a time when a service man is serving abroad are references to a time when he is performing a period of relevant service and is outside the United Kingdom.

(3)   Regulations under this paragraph may contain such incidental and consequential provisions as appear to the Lord Chancellor to be necessary or expedient for the purposes of the regulations.

NOTES

Derivation

Paras 1, 4–6 derived from the Agricultural Holdings (Notices to Quit) Act 1977, s 11(5)–(8), (10); para 2 derived from the Agricultural Holdings (Notices to Quit) Act 1977, s 11(1), (2), and the Interpretation Act 1978, s 17(2)(a); para 3 derived from the Agricultural Holdings (Notices to Quit) Act 1977, s 11(3), (4), and the Agricultural Holdings Act 1984, s 10(1), Sch 3, para 41.

Initial Commencement

Specified date: 18 June 1986: see s 102(2).

Extent

This Act does not extend to Scotland.

Amendment

Para 2: words in square brackets inserted by the Housing Act 1988, s 140, Sch 17, para 70.

See Further

See further, as to the exclusion of this Act in relation to leases or tenancies granted to contractors in respect of the running of any removal centre or part of a removal centre: the Immigration and Asylum Act 1999, s 149(3).

Notes

For a commentary, see para 29.27 ff

Paras 1, 4, 5 contain provisions formerly in the Agricultural Holdings (Notices to Quit) Act 1977, s 11(1), (5), (6), respectively. Paras 2 and 6 contain provisions formerly in s 11(1), (2) and s 11(7), (8), respectively, of the 1977 Act, as read with, in the case of sub-s (2) thereof, the Interpretation Act 1978, s 17(2)(a). Para 3 contains provisions formerly in s 11(3), (4) of the 1977 Act, as amended, in both cases by the Agricultural Holdings Act 1984, s 10(1), Sch 3, para 41.

Para 1: Months. See the note to s 4.

Para 2: Notice to quit. Cf the notes to ss 25, 26.

Para 3: The Tribunal. See the note to s 11.

Directly or indirectly attributable. Aggravation of an already existing inability to pay. caused by performance of the service in question is not enough: see *Tomley v Gower and McAdam* [1939] 4 All ER 460; *Perry v South Metropolitan Gas Co* [1940] 1 All ER 591; *Southern Counties Building Society v Eastwood Priory Ltd* [1947] LJR 1097.

In all the circumstances ... reasonable. Ie the court must take into consideration every circumstance affecting the interests of the landlord or the tenant: see *Williamson v Pallant* [1924] 2 KB 173.

Para 4: Duly serves. See s 93 as to service of notices.

Give or withhold consent. See ss 26–28 as to the relevant powers of the Tribunal.

Para 5: Lord Chancellor. See the note to s 29.

Para 6: United Kingdom. Ie Great Britain and Northern Ireland: see the Interpretation Act 1978, s 5, Sch 1.

Definitions. For 'agricultural holding', see s 1(1); and for 'Case B' etc, 'tenant' and 'the Tribunal', see s 96(1). Note as to 'farming', s 96(4); and note as to 'the 1951 Act', 'period of residence protection', 'relevant service', 'service man' and 'short period of training', para 1 above; and as to 'serving abroad', para 6(2) above.

Orders. See, for the purposes of para 5 above, the Agricultural Holdings (Arbitration on Notices) Order 1987, SI 1987/710, art 17.

Regulations under this Schedule. At the time of going to press no regulations had been made under para 6 above, but see, however, by virtue of the Interpretation Act 1978, s 17(2)(b), the Reserve and Auxiliary Forces (Agricultural Tenants) Regulations 1959, SI 1959/84, which have effect as if made thereunder.

For general provisions as to regulations, see s 94(1), (2).

SCHEDULE 6
ELIGIBILITY TO APPLY FOR NEW TENANCY UNDER PART IV OF THIS ACT

Sections 36, 50

PART I: 'ELIGIBLE PERSON': SUPPLEMENTARY PROVISIONS

Preliminary

A1.195

1   (1)   In this Schedule—

'the livelihood condition' means paragraph (a) of the definition of 'eligible person' in section 36(3)of this Act;
'the occupancy condition' means paragraph (b) of that definition.

(2)   For the purposes of this Schedule a body corporate is controlled by a close relative of the deceased if he or his spouse [or his civil partner], or he and his spouse together [or he and his civil partner together], have the power to secure—

(a)   by means of the holding of shares or the possession of voting power in or in relation to that or any other body corporate, or

(b)   by virtue of any powers conferred by the articles of association or other document regulating that or any other body corporate,

that the affairs of that body corporate are conducted in accordance with his, her or their wishes, respectively.

(3)   Any reference in this Schedule to the spouse of a close relative of the deceased does not apply in relation to any time *when the relative's marriage is the subject of a decree of judicial separation or a decree nisi of divorce or of nullity of marriage.* [when a separation order or a divorce order under the Family Law Act 1996 is in force in relation to the relative's marriage or that marriage is the subject of a decree nisi of nullity.]

[(4)   Any reference in this Schedule to the civil partner of a close relative of the deceased does not apply in relation to any time when the relative's civil partnership is subject to—

(a)   a separation order under Chapter 2 of Part 2 of the Civil Partnership Act 2004, or

(b)   a dissolution order, nullity order or presumption of death order that is a conditional order under that Chapter.]

The livelihood condition

2   For the purposes of the livelihood condition, any period during which a close relative of the deceased was, in the period of seven years mentioned in that condition,

1245

attending a full-time course at a university, college or other [establishment of higher or further education] shall be treated as a period throughout which his only or principal source of livelihood derived from his agricultural work on the holding; but not more than three years in all shall be so treated by virtue of this paragraph.

Commercial unit of agricultural land

3 (1) In the occupancy condition 'commercial unit of agricultural land' means a unit of agricultural land which is capable, when farmed under competent management, of producing a net annual income of an amount not less than the aggregate of the average annual earnings of two full-time, male agricultural workers aged twenty or over.

(2) In so far as any units of production for the time being prescribed by an order under paragraph 4 below are relevant to the assessment of the productive capacity of a unit of agricultural land when farmed as aforesaid, the net annual income which that unit is capable of producing for the purposes of this paragraph shall be ascertained by reference to the provisions of that order.

4 The Minister shall by order—

   (a) prescribe such units of production relating to agricultural land as he considers appropriate, being units framed by reference to any circumstances whatever and designed for the assessment of the productive capacity of such land, and

   (b) for any period of twelve months specified in the order, determine in relation to any unit of production so prescribed the amount which is to be regraded for the purposes of paragraph 3 above as the net annual income from that unit in that period.

Ministerial statements as to net annual income of land

5 (1) For the purposes of any proceedings under sections 36 to 48 of this Act in relation to the holding, the Minister shall—

   (a) at the request of any of the following persons, namely any close relative of the deceased, the landlord or the secretary of the Tribunal, and

   (b) in relation to any relevant land,

determine by reference to the provisions of any order for the time being in force under paragraph 4 above the net annual income which, in his view, the land is capable of producing for the purposes of paragraph 3 above, and shall issue a written statement of his view and the grounds for it to the person making the request.

(2) In sub-paragraph (1) above 'relevant land' means agricultural land which is—

   (a) occupied (or, by virtue of section 58 of this Act or this Part of this Schedule, deemed to be occupied) by any close relative of the deceased (whether he is, where the request is made by such a relative, the person making the request or not), or

   (b) the subject of an application made under section 39 of this Act by any such relative.

(3) Where—

   (a) for the purposes of any proceedings under sections 36 to 48 of this Act the Minister has issued a statement to any person containing a determination under sub-paragraph (1) above made by reference to the provisions of an order under paragraph 4 above, and

   (b) before any hearing by the Tribunal in those proceedings is due to begin it appears to him that any subsequent order under that paragraph has affected any matter on which that determination was based, he shall make a revised determination under sub-paragraph (1) above and shall issue a written statement of his view and the grounds for it to the person in question.

(4)   Any statement issued by the Minister in pursuance of this paragraph shall be evidence of any facts stated in it as facts on which his view is based.

(5)   Any document purporting to be a statement issued by the Minister in pursuance of this paragraph and to be signed for or on behalf of the Minister shall be taken to be such a statement unless the contrary is shown.

Occupation to be disregarded for purposes of occupancy condition

6   (1)   Occupation by a close relative of the deceased of any agricultural land shall be disregarded for the purposes of the occupancy condition if he occupies it only—

(a)   under a tenancy approved by the Minister under subsection (1) of section 2 of this Act or under a tenancy falling within subsection (3)(a) of that section,

(b)   under a tenancy for more than one year but less than two years,

(c)   under a tenancy not falling within paragraph (a) or (b) above and not having effect as a contract of tenancy,

(d)   under a tenancy to which section 3 of this Act does not apply by virtue of section 5 of this Act,

[(dd) under a farm business tenancy, within the meaning of the Agricultural Tenancies Act 1995, for less than five years (including a farm business tenancy which is a periodic tenancy),]

(e)   as a licensee, or

(f)   as an executor, administrator, trustee in bankruptcy or person otherwise deriving title from another person by operation of law.

(2)   Paragraphs (a) to (e) of sub-paragraph (1) above do not apply in the case of a tenancy or licence granted to a close relative of the deceased by his spouse [or civil partner] or by a body corporate controlled by him.

(3)   References in the following provisions of this Schedule to the occupation of land by any person do not include occupation under a tenancy, or in a capacity, falling within paragraphs (a) to (f) of that sub-paragraph.

Joint occupation

7   (1)   Where any agricultural land is jointly occupied by a close relative of the deceased and one or more other persons as—

(a)   beneficial joint tenants,

(b)   tenants in common,

(c)   joint tenants under a tenancy, or

(d)   joint licensees,

the relative shall be treated for the purposes of the occupancy condition as occupying the whole of the land.

(2)   If, however, the Tribunal in proceedings under section 39 of this Act determine on the application of the close relative that his appropriate share of the net annual income which the land is, or was at any time, capable of producing for the purposes of paragraph 3 above is or was then less than the aggregate of the earnings referred to in that paragraph, then, for the purpose of determining whether the occupancy condition is or was then satisfied in his case, the net annual income which the land is, or (as the case may be) was, capable of so producing shall be treated as limited to his appropriate share.

(3)   For the purposes of sub-paragraph (2) above the appropriate share of the close relative shall be ascertained—

    (a)   where he is a beneficial or other joint tenant or a joint licensee, by dividing the net annual income which the land is or was at the time in question capable of producing for the purposes of paragraph 3 above by the total number of joint tenants or joint licensees for the time being,

    (b)   where he is a tenant in common, by dividing the said net annual income in such a way as to attribute to him and to the other tenant or tenants in common shares of the income proportionate to the extent for the time being of their respective undivided shares in the land.

Deemed occupation in case of Tribunal direction

8   (1) Where a close relative of the deceased is, by virtue of a direction of the Tribunal under section 39 of this Act, for the time being entitled (whether or not with any other person) to a tenancy of the whole or part of any agricultural holding held by the deceased at the date of death other than the holding, he shall, for the purposes of the occupancy condition, be deemed to be in occupation of the land comprised in that holding or (as the case may be) in that part of that holding.

(2)   Where by virtue of sub-paragraph (1) above any land is deemed to be occupied by each of two or more close relatives of the deceased as a result of a direction entitling them to a joint tenancy of the land, the provisions of paragraph 7 above shall apply to each of the relatives as if the land were jointly occupied by him and the other relative or relatives as joint tenants under that tenancy.

Occupation by spouse[, civil partner] or controlled company

9   (1) For the purposes of the occupancy condition and of paragraph 7 above, occupation—

    (a)   by the spouse[, or civil partner,] of a close relative of the deceased, or
    (b)   by a body corporate controlled by a close relative of the deceased,

shall be treated as occupation by the relative.

(2)   Where, in accordance with sub-paragraph (1) above, paragraph 7 above applies to a close relative of the deceased in relation to any time by virtue of the [joint occupation of land by—

    (a)   his spouse or civil partner or a body corporate, and
    (b)   any other person or persons,

sub-paragraphs] (2) and (3) of that paragraph shall apply to the relative as if he were the holder of the interest in the land for the time being held by his spouse [or civil partner,] or the body corporate, as the case may be.

Deemed occupation in case of tenancy or licence granted by close relative, spouse[, civil partner] or controlled company

10   (1) Where—

    (a)   any agricultural land is occupied by any person under such a tenancy as is mentioned in paragraphs (a) to (d) of paragraph 6(1) above or as a licensee and,

    (b)   that tenancy or licence was granted by a close relative of the deceased or a connected person (or both), being at the time it was granted a person or persons entitled to occupy the land otherwise than under a tenancy, or in a capacity, falling within paragraphs (a) to (f) of paragraph 6(1),

then, unless sub-paragraph (2) below applies, the close relative shall, for the purposes of the occupancy condition, be deemed to be in occupation of the whole of the land.

(2)   Where the tenancy or licence referred to in sub-paragraph (1) above was granted by the person or persons there referred to and one or more other persons who were at the time it was granted entitled to occupy the land as mentioned in paragraph (b) of that sub-paragraph, sub-paragraphs (2) and (3) of paragraph 7 above shall apply to the close relative as if the land were jointly occupied by him and the said other person or persons as holders of their respective interests for the time being in the land.

(3)   In this paragraph 'connected person', in relation to a close relative of the deceased, means—

(a)   the relative's spouse [or civil partner], or
(b)   a body corporate controlled by the relative;

and for the purposes of sub-paragraph (2) above and the provisions of paragraph 7 there mentioned any interest in the land for the time being held by a connected person by whom the tenancy or licence was granted shall be attributed to the relative.

NOTES

Derivation

This Part derived from the Agriculture (Miscellaneous Provisions) Act 1976, s 18(3), (3A), (3B), (6), (6A), (6B), Sch 3A, paras 1–6, and the Agricultural Holdings Act 1984, ss 3(3), (4), (5), 4, Sch 1, paras 3, 8, Sch 2, paras 1(3)–(6), 9.

Initial Commencement

Specified date: 18 June 1986: see s 102(2).

Extent

This Act does not extend to Scotland.

Amendment

Para 1: in sub-para (2) words 'or his civil partner' and 'or he and his civil partner together' in square brackets inserted by the Civil Partnership Act 2004, s 81, Sch 8, para 39(1), (2).

Date in force: 5 December 2005: see SI 2005/3175, art 2(1), Sch 1.

Para 1: in sub-para (3) words in italics repealed and subsequent words in square brackets substituted by the Family Law Act 1996, s 66(1), Sch 8, para 36, as from a day to be appointed; for savings see s 66(2), Sch 9, para 5 thereto.

Para 1: sub-para (4) inserted by the Civil Partnership Act 2004, s 81, Sch 8, para 39(1), (3).

Date in force: 5 December 2005: see SI 2005/3175, art 2(1), Sch 1.

Para 2: words in square brackets substituted by the Education Reform Act 1988, s 237, Sch 12, para 96.

Para 6: sub-para (1)(dd) inserted by the Agricultural Tenancies Act 1995, s 40, Schedule, para 32.

Para 6: in sub-para (2) words 'or civil partner' in square brackets inserted by the Civil Partnership Act 2004, s 81, Sch 8, para 39(1), (4).

Date in force: 5 December 2005: see SI 2005/3175, art 2(1), Sch 1.

Para 9 heading: words ', civil partner' in square brackets inserted by the Civil Partnership Act 2004, s 81, Sch 8, para 39(1), (8).

Date in force: 5 December 2005: see SI 2005/3175, art 2(1), Sch 1.

Para 9: in sub-para (1)(a) words ', or civil partner,' in square brackets inserted by the Civil Partnership Act 2004, s 81, Sch 8, para 39(1), (5).

Date in force: 5 December 2005: see SI 2005/3175, art 2(1), Sch 1.

Para 9: in sub-para (2) words from 'joint occupation of' to 'sub-paragraphs' in square brackets substituted by the Civil Partnership Act 2004, s 81, Sch 8, para 39(1), (6)(a).

Date in force: 5 December 2005: see SI 2005/3175, art 2(1), Sch 1.

Para 9: in sub-para (2) words 'or civil partner,' in square brackets inserted by the Civil Partnership Act 2004, s 81, Sch 8, para 39(1), (6)(b).

Date in force: 5 December 2005: see SI 2005/3175, art 2(1), Sch 1.

Para 10 heading: words ', civil partner' in square brackets inserted by the Civil Partnership Act 2004, s 81, Sch 8, para 39(1), (8).

Date in force: 5 December 2005: see SI 2005/3175, art 2(1), Sch 1.

Para 10: in sub-para (3)(a) words 'or civil partner' in square brackets inserted by the Civil Partnership Act 2004, s 81, Sch 8, para 39(1), (7).

Date in force: 5 December 2005: see SI 2005/3175, art 2(1), Sch 1.

See Further

See further, as to the exclusion of this Act in relation to leases or tenancies granted to contractors in respect of the running of any removal centre or part of a removal centre: the Immigration and Asylum Act 1999, s 149(3).

Transfer of Functions

Functions of the Minister, so far as exercisable in relation to Wales, transferred to the National Assembly for Wales, by the National Assembly for Wales (Transfer of Functions) Order 1999, SI 1999/672, art 2, Sch 1.

Subordinate Legislation

Agricultural Holdings (Units of Production) (England) Order 2006, SI 2006/2628 (made under para 4).

Agricultural Holdings (Units of Production) (Wales) Order 2006, SI 2006/2796 (made under para 4).

Notes

For a commentary on succession, see Ch 35 (death) and Ch 36 (retirement).

Paras 1, 6, 9, 10 contain provisions formerly in the Agriculture (Miscellaneous Provisions) Act 1976, Sch 3A, paras 1, 2. 5, 6, respectively, as inserted by the Agricultural Holdings Act 1984, s 3(5), Sch 1, para 8, and as applied by s 4 of, and Sch 2, para 1(4)(b) to, that Act. Para 2 contains provisions formerly in s 18(3) of the 1976 Act, and in Sch 2, para 1(3) to the 1984 Act. Paras 3, 4 contain provisions formerly in s 18(3A), (3B), respectively, to the 1976 Act, as inserted by s 3(3) of the 1984 Act, and in Sch 2, para 1(4)(a) to the 1984 Act. Para 5(1) contains provisions formerly in s 18(6) of the 1976 Act. as substituted by s 3(4) of the 1984 Act, and in Sch 2, para 1(5) to the 1984 Act. Para 5(2) contains provisions formerly in s 18(6) of the 1976 Act, as substituted by s 3(4) of the 1984 Act. and as applied by s 18(3C) of, and Sch 3A, para 7 to, the 1976 Act (as inserted by s 3(5) of, and Sch 1, para 8 to, the 1984 Act), and in Sch 2, paras 1(5), 9 to the 1984 Act. Para 5(3) and para 5(4), (5) contain provisions formerly in s 18(6A) and (6B), respectively, of the 1976 Act, as inserted by s 3(4) of the 1984 Act, and as applied by s 4 of, and Sch 2, para 1(6) to, the 1984 Act. Para 7 contains provisions formerly in Sch 3A, para 1(1)–(3) to the 1976 Act, as inserted by s 3(5) of. and Sch 1, para 8 to, the 1984 Act, and as applied by Sch 2, para 1(4)(b) to the 1984 Act. Para 8(1), (2) contains provisions formerly in Sch 3A, paras 3, 4(4), respectively, to the 1976 Act, as inserted by s 3(5) of, and Sch 1, para 8 to, the 1984 Act.

In para 1(3) the words in square brackets are substituted for the preceding words in italics by the Family Law Act 1996, s 66(1), Sch 8, Pt I, para 36, as from a day to be appointed, subject to a saving in s 66(2) of, and Sch 9, para 5 to, the 1996 Act.

The words in square brackets in para 2 were substituted by the Education Reform Act 1988, s 237(1), Sch 12, Pt III, para 96.

Para 6(1)(dd) was inserted by the Agricultual Tenancies Act 1995, s 40, Schedule, para 32.

Para 1: Body corporate. See the note to s 96.

Para 3: Aged twenty or over. Cf the note 'Under sixty-five' to s 51.

Para 4: Months. See the note to s 4.

Para 5: The Tribunal. See the note to s 11.

Written. See the note to s 3.

Para 7: Beneficial joint tenants; tenants in common; joint tenants under a tenancy. As to the different forms of co-ownership, see 39 Halsbury's Laws (4th edn) paras 525 ff.

Joint licensees. As to licences to occupy land, see 27(1) Halsbury's Laws (4th edn, 2006 reissue) paras 6 ff. See para 21.15 ff.

Relative shall be treated ... as occupying the whole of the land. Para 7(1) gives statutory effect to the decision in *Williamson v Thompson* [1980] AC 854, [1980] 1 All ER 177, HL, in which it was held that joint occupation of a commercial unit deprived an applicant of eligibility to apply for a tenancy under what are now ss 35 ff.

Succession on retirement. For modifications of this Part of this Schedule in its application to succession on retirement, see s 50(4) and Pt II of this Schedule.

Rules of procedure. Cf the note to s 40.

Definitions. For 'agricultural holding', see s 1(1); for 'agricultural land', see s 1(4); for 'close relative', 'the date of death', 'the deceased', 'the holding' and 'the tenancy', see s 35(2); for 'agricultural', 'agricultural unit', 'landlord', 'the Minister', 'prescribed' and 'the Tribunal', see s 96(1). Note as to 'the livelihood condition' and 'the occupancy condition', para 1(1) above; as to 'relevant land' (in para 5), para 5(2) above; and as to 'connected person' (in para 10), para 10(3) above.

Order under this Schedule. The current regulations are the Agricultural Holdings (Units of Production) (England) Order 2006, SI 2006/2628. In Wales, order are to be made by the Welsh Assembly Government (following the Government of Wales Act 1998). Currently no orders equivalent to these have been made – for the moment the current regulations applicable to England will also apply to Wales.

For general provisions as to orders, see s 94(1), (2).

PART II: MODIFICATIONS OF PART I OF THIS SCHEDULE IN ITS APPLICATION TO SUCCESSION ON RETIREMENT

11 The modifications of Part I of this Schedule referred to in section 50(4) of this Act are as follows.

12 The reference in paragraph 1(1) to section 36(3) of this Act shall be read as a reference to section 50(2) of this Act.

13 References to a close relative of the deceased shall be read as references to the nominated successor.

14 In paragraph 5—

    (a) references to sections 36 to 48 of this Act shall be read as references to sections 50 to 58 of this Act,

    (b) the reference in sub-paragraph (1) to any close relative of the deceased shall be read as a reference to the nominated successor, and

    (c) for sub-paragraph (2) there shall be substituted—

'(2) In sub-paragraph (1) above 'relevant land' means agricultural land which is occupied (or, by virtue of this Part of this Schedule, is deemed to be occupied) by the nominated successor.'

15 The reference in paragraph 7(2) to section 39 of this Act shall be read as a reference to section 53 of this Act.

16 For paragraph 8 there shall be substituted—

'**8** Where the nominated successor is, by virtue of a direction of the Tribunal under section 53(7) of this Act, for the time being entitled to a tenancy of any agricultural holding held by the retiring tenant other than the holding he shall, for the purposes of the occupancy condition, be deemed to be in occupation of that holding.'

NOTES

Derivation

This Part derived from the Agricultural Holdings Act 1984, Sch 2, para 1(3)–(6).

Initial Commencement

Specified date: 18 June 1986: see s 102(2).

Extent

This Act does not extend to Scotland.

See Further

See further, as to the exclusion of this Act in relation to leases or tenancies granted to contractors in respect of the running of any removal centre or part of a removal centre: the Immigration and Asylum Act 1999, s 149(3).

Notes

For a commentary on succession on retirement, see Ch 36.

This Part of this Schedule contains provisions formerly in the Agricultural Holdings Act 1984, Sch 2, para 1(3)–(6).

The Tribunal. See the note to s 11.

Definitions. For 'agricultural holding', see s 1(1); for 'agricultural land', see s 1(4); for 'the Tribunal', see s 96(1). Cf as to 'close relative' and 'the deceased', s 35(2); and as to 'the nominated successor' and 'the retiring tenant', s 49(3). Note as to 'the occupancy condition', para 1 of this Schedule.

SCHEDULE 7

LONG-TERM IMPROVEMENTS BEGUN ON OR AFTER 1ST MARCH 1948 FOR WHICH COMPENSATION IS PAYABLE

Sections 64, 66 etc

PART I: IMPROVEMENTS TO WHICH CONSENT OF LANDLORD REQUIRED

A1.196

1 Making or planting of osier beds.

2 Making of water meadows.

3 Making of watercress beds.

4 Planting of hops.

5 Planting of orchards or fruit bushes.

6 Warping or weiring of land.

7   Making of gardens.

8   Provision of underground tanks.

NOTES

Derivation

Paras 1–7 derived from the Agricultural Holdings Act 1948, Sch 3, Part I, paras 1–7; para 8 derived from the Agricultural Holdings Act 1948, Sch 3, Part I, para 7A, and the Agricultural Holdings Act 1984, s 10(1), Sch 3, para 25(1)(b).

Initial Commencement

Specified date: 18 June 1986: see s 102(2).

Extent

This Act does not extend to Scotland.

See Further

See further, as to the exclusion of this Act in relation to leases or tenancies granted to contractors in respect of the running of any removal centre or part of a removal centre: the Immigration and Asylum Act 1999, s 149(3).

PART II: IMPROVEMENTS TO WHICH CONSENT OF LANDLORD OR APPROVAL OF TRIBUNAL REQUIRED

9   Erection, alteration or enlargement of buildings, and making or improvement of permanent yards.

10   Carrying out works in compliance with an improvement notice served, or an undertaking accepted, under Part VII of the Housing Act 1985 or Part VIII of the Housing Act 1974.

11   Erection or construction of loading platforms, ramps, hard standings for vehicles or other similar facilities.

12   Construction of silos.

13   Claying of land.

14   Marling of land.

15   Making or improvement of roads or bridges.

16   Making or improvement of water courses, culverts, ponds, wells or reservoirs, or of works for the application of water power for agricultural or domestic purposes or of works for the supply, distribution or use of water for such purposes (including the erection or installation of any structures or equipment which form part of or are to be used for or in connection with operating any such works).

17   Making or removal of permanent fences.

18   Reclaiming of waste land.

19   Making or improvement of embankments or sluices.

20   Erection of wirework for hop gardens.

21   Provision of permanent sheep-dipping accommodation.

22   Removal of bracken, gorse, tree roots, boulders or other like obstructions to cultivation.

23   Land drainage (other than improvements falling within paragraph 1 of Schedule 8 to this Act).

24   Provision or laying-on of electric light or power.

25   Provision of facilities for the storage or disposal of sewage or farm waste.

26   Repairs to fixed equipment, being equipment reasonably required for the proper farming of the holding, other than repairs which the tenant is under an obligation to carry out.

27   The grubbing up of orchards or fruit bushes.

28   Planting trees otherwise than as an orchard and bushes other than fruit bushes.

NOTES

Derivation

Paras 9, 12–15, 17–24, 26 derived from the Agricultural Holdings Act 1948, Sch 3, Part II, paras 8, 9–12, 14–21, 23; para 10 derived from the Housing Act 1985, s 231(2); paras 11, 16, 25, 27, 28 derived from the Agricultural Holdings Act 1948, Sch 3, Part II, paras 8A, 13, 22, 24, 25, and the Agricultural Holdings Act 1984, s 10(1), Sch 3, para 25(2).

Initial Commencement

Specified date: 18 June 1986: see s 102(2).

Extent

This Act does not extend to Scotland.

See Further

See further, as to the exclusion of this Act in relation to leases or tenancies granted to contractors in respect of the running of any removal centre or part of a removal centre: the Immigration and Asylum Act 1999, s 149(3).

Notes

For a commentary, see para 38.17 ff.

Pt I: Paras 1–8 contain provisions formerly in the Agricultural Holdings Act 1948, Sch 3, paras 1–7, 7A, respectively, as repealed in part in the case of para 2 thereof, and as added, in the case of para 7A thereof, by the Agricultural Holdings Act 1984, s 10, Sch 3, para 25(1)(b), Sch 4. Pt II: Paras 9, 12–15, 17–24, 26 contain provisions formerly in Sch 3, paras 8, 9–12, 14–21, 23 to the 1948 Act. Para 10 contains provisions formerly in the Housing Act 1985, s 231(2). Paras 11, 16, 25, 27, 28 contain provisions formerly in Sch 3, paras 8A, 13, 22, 24, 25 to the 1948 Act, as inserted in the case of para 8A, as amended in the case of para 13, as substituted in the case of para 22, and as substituted in the case of paras 24, 25, thereof, by s 10(1) of, and Sch 3, paras 25(2)(a), (b), (c), (d), respectively, to the 1984 Act.

General Note. See the General Note to s 64.

Para 26. S 89(1) does not operate so as to import the words 'other than repairs which the tenant is under an obligation to carry out' into the Settled Land Act 1925, s 73(1)(iv), as amended by s 100, Sch 14, para 11, and accordingly the tenant for life could be reimbursed out of capital for repairs to fixed equipment reasonably required for proper farming without that qualification: *Re Lord Brougham and Vaux's Settled Estates* [1954] Ch 24, [1953] 2 All ER 655.

Opencast coal operations. See the note to s 64.

Definitions. For 'agricultural', 'building', 'fixed equipment' and 'tenant', see s 96(1).

Housing Act 1985, Part VII; Housing Act 1974, Part VIII. The Housing Act 1985, Pt VII (repealed by the Local Government and Housing Act 1989, ss 165, 194, Sch 12, Pt II, subject to a saving in SI 1990/431, Sch 1, para 12) generally replaced the Housing Act 1974, Pt VIII (repealed by the Housing (Consequential Provisions) Act 1985, s 3, Sch 1, Pt I.

SCHEDULE 8
SHORT-TERM IMPROVEMENTS BEGUN ON OR AFTER 1ST MARCH 1948, AND OTHER MATTERS, FOR WHICH COMPENSATION IS PAYABLE

Sections 64, 65 etc

PART I: IMPROVEMENTS (TO WHICH NO CONSENT REQUIRED)

A1.197

1   Mole drainage and works carried out to secure its efficient functioning.

2   Protection of fruit trees against animals.

3   Clay burning.

4   Liming (including chalking) of land.

5   Application to land of purchased manure and fertiliser, whether organic or inorganic.

6   Consumption on the holding of corn (whether produced on the holding or not) or of cake or other feeding stuff not produced on the holding, by horses, cattle, sheep, pigs or poultry.

NOTES

Derivation

Paras 1–3 derived from the Agricultural Holdings Act 1948, Sch 4, Part I, paras 1, 2, 4; paras 4–6 derived from the Agricultural Holdings Act 1948, Sch 4, Part I, paras 5–7, and the Transfer of Functions (Wales) (No 1) Order 1978, SI 1978/742, art 3, Schedule, para 1.

Initial Commencement

Specified date: 18 June 1986: see s 102(2).

Extent

This Act does not extend to Scotland.

See Further

See further, as to the exclusion of this Act in relation to leases or tenancies granted to contractors in respect of the running of any removal centre or part of a removal centre: the Immigration and Asylum Act 1999, s 149(3).

PART II: TENANT-RIGHT MATTERS

7   Growing crops and severed or harvested crops and produce, being in either case crops or produce grown on the holding in the last year of tenancy, but not including crops or produce which the tenant has a right to sell or remove from the holding.

8   Seeds sown and cultivations, fallows and acts of husbandry performed on the holding at the expense of the tenant (including the growing of herbage crops for commercial seed production).

9   Pasture laid down with clover, grass, lucerne, sainfoin or other seeds, being either—

(a) pasture laid down at the expense of the tenant otherwise than in compliance with an obligation imposed on him by an agreement in writing to lay it down to replace temporary pasture comprised in the holding when the tenant entered on the holding which was not paid for by him, or

(b) pasture paid for by the tenant on entering on the holding.

10 (1) Acclimatisation, hefting or settlement of hill sheep on hill land.

(2) In this paragraph—

'hill sheep' means sheep which—
  (a) have been reared and managed on a particular hill or mountain,
  (b) have developed an instinct not to stray from the hill or mountain,
  (c) are able to withstand the climatic conditions typical of the hill or mountain, and
  (d) have developed resistance to diseases which are likely to occur in the area in which the hill or mountain is situated;
'hill land' means any hill or mountain where only hill sheep are likely to thrive throughout the year.

11 (1) In areas of the country where arable crops can be grown in an unbroken series of not less than six years and it is reasonable that they should be grown on the holding or part of it, the residual fertility value of the sod of the excess qualifying leys on the holding, if any.

(2) For the purposes of this paragraph—

(a) the growing of an arable crop includes the growing of clover, grass, lucerne, sainfoin or other seeds grown for a period of less than one year but does not include the laying down of a ley continuously maintained as such for more than one year,

(b) the qualifying leys comprising the excess qualifying leys shall be those indicated to be such by the tenant, and

(c) qualifying leys laid down at the expense of the landlord without reimbursement by the tenant or any previous tenant of the holding or laid down by and at the expense of the tenant pursuant to agreement by him with the landlord for the establishment of a specified area of leys on the holding as a condition of the landlord giving consent to the ploughing or other destruction of permanent pasture or pursuant to a direction given by an arbitrator on a reference under section 14(2) of this Act, shall not be included in the excess qualifying leys.

(3) In this paragraph—

'leys' means land laid down with clover, grass, lucerne, sainfoin or other seeds, but does not include permanent pasture;
'qualifying leys' means—
  (a) leys continuously maintained as such for a period of three or more growing seasons since being laid down excluding, if the leys were undersown or autumn-sown, the calendar year in which the sowing took place, and
  (b) arable land which within the three growing seasons immediately preceding the termination of the tenancy was ley continuously maintained as aforesaid before being destroyed by ploughing or some other means for the production of a tillage crop or crops;
and for the purpose of paragraph (a) above the destruction of a ley (by ploughing or some other means) followed as soon as practicable by re-seeding to a ley without sowing a crop in the interval between such destruction and such re-seeding shall be treated as not constituting a break in the continuity of the maintenance of the ley;

'the excess qualifying leys' means the area of qualifying leys on the holding at the termination of the tenancy which is equal to the area (if any) by which one-third of the aggregate of the areas of leys on the holding on the following dates, namely,

  (a)   at the termination of the tenancy,

  (b)   on the date one year prior to such termination, and

  (c)   on the date two years prior to such termination,

exceeds the accepted proportion at the termination of the tenancy;

'the accepted proportion' means the area which represents the proportion which the total area of the leys on the holding would, taking into account the capability of the holding, be expected to bear to the area of the holding, excluding the permanent pasture on the holding, or, if a greater proportion is provided for by or under the terms of the tenancy, that proportion.

NOTES

Derivation

Paras 7, 9 derived from the Agricultural Holdings Act 1948, Sch 4, Part II, paras 8, 10; para 8 derived from the Agricultural Holdings Act 1948, Sch 4, Part II, para 9, and the Agricultural Holdings Act 1984, s 10(1), Sch 3, para 26; para 10 derived from the Agricultural Holdings Act 1948, Sch 4, Part II, para 11, the Agricultural Holdings Act (Variation of Fourth Schedule) Order 1951, SI 1951/2168, art 3(1), and the Agricultural Holdings Act 1948 (Variation of Fourth Schedule) Order 1985, SI 1985/1947, art 3(2); para 11 derived from the Agricultural Holdings Act 1948, Sch 4, Part II, para 12, the Agricultural Holdings Act 1948 (Variation of Fourth Schedule) Order 1978, SI 1978/742, art 3, Schedule, para 2, and SI 1985/1947, art 3(3).

Initial Commencement

Specified date: 18 June 1986: see s 102(2).

Extent

This Act does not extend to Scotland.

See Further

See further, as to the exclusion of this Act in relation to leases or tenancies granted to contractors in respect of the running of any removal centre or part of a removal centre: the Immigration and Asylum Act 1999, s 149(3).

Notes

For a commentary, see para 38.23 ff.

Pt I: Paras 1, 2, 3, 4, 5, 6 contain provisions formerly in the Agricultural Holdings Act 1948, Sch 4, Pt I, paras 1, 2, 4, 5, 6, 7, respectively, as amended, in the case of paras 5–7 of that Schedule, by the Agricultural Holdings Act 1948 (Variation of Fourth Schedule) Order 1978, SI 1978/742. art 3, Schedule, para 1. Pt II: Paras 7, 9 contain provisions formerly in Sch 4, Pt II, paras 8. 10 to the 1948 Act, as amended by the Agricultural Holdings Act 1984, s 10(1), Sch 3, para 26. Para 10 contains provisions formerly in Sch 4, Pt II, para 11 to the 1948 Act, as added by the Agricultural Holdings Act 1948 (Variation of Fourth Schedule) Order 1951, SI 1951/2168, art 3(1), and as amended by the Agricultural Holdings Act 1948 (Variation of Fourth Schedule) Order 1985, SI 1985/1947, art 3(2). Para 11 contains provisions formerly in Sch 4, Pt II, para 12 to the 1948 Act, as added by SI 1978/742, art 3, Schedule, para 2, and as amended by SI 1985/1947, art 3(3).

General Note. See the General Note to s 64.

Para 7. As to property in the crops left by the tenant and the insurable interest in them, see *Thomas v National Farmers' Union Mutual Insurance Society Ltd* [1961] 1 All ER 363, [1961] 1 WLR 386, CA.

Para 9: Writing. See the note 'Written' to s 3.

Opencast coal operations. See the note to s 66.

Definitions. For 'agreement', 'landlord', 'pasture', 'tenant' and 'termination', see s 96(1). Note as to 'hill sheep' and 'hill land' (in para 10), para 10(2) above; and as to 'leys', 'qualifying leys', 'the excess qualifying leys' and 'the accepted proportion' (in para 11), para 11(3) above.

SCHEDULE 9
COMPENSATION TO TENANT FOR IMPROVEMENTS BEGUN BEFORE 1ST MARCH 1948

Sections 64, 79

PART I: TENANT'S RIGHT TO COMPENSATION FOR OLD IMPROVEMENTS

A1.198

1   (1)   The tenant of an agricultural holding shall, subject to the provisions of this Act, be entitled on the termination of the tenancy, on quitting the holding, to obtain from his landlord compensation for an improvement specified in Part II of this Schedule carried out on the holding by the tenant, being an improvement begun before 1st March 1948.

(2)   Improvements falling within sub-paragraph (1) above are in this Schedule referred to as 'old improvements'.

(3)   The tenant of an agricultural holding shall not be entitled to compensation under this Schedule for an improvement which he was required to carry out by the terms of his tenancy where the contract of tenancy was made before 1st January 1921.

(4)   Nothing in this Schedule shall prejudice the right of a tenant to claim any compensation to which he may be entitled under custom or agreement, or otherwise, in lieu of any compensation provided by this Schedule.

(5)   The tenant of an agricultural holding shall not be entitled to compensation under this Schedule for an old improvement made on land which, at the time when the improvement was begun, was not a holding within the meaning of the Agricultural Holdings Act 1923, as originally enacted, and would not have fallen to be treated as such a holding by virtue of section 33 of that Act.

2   (1)   The amount of any compensation under this Schedule for an old improvement shall be an amount equal to the increase attributable to the improvement in the value of the agricultural holding as a holding, having regard to the character and situation of the holding and the average requirements of tenants reasonably skilled in husbandry.

(2)   In the ascertainment of the amount of the compensation payable under this Schedule to the tenant of an agricultural holding in respect of an old improvement, there shall be taken into account any benefit which the landlord has given or allowed to the tenant in consideration of the tenant's executing the improvement, whether expressly stated in the contract of tenancy to be so given or allowed or not.

3   (1)   Compensation under this Schedule shall not be payable for an old improvement specified in any of paragraphs 1 to 15 of Part II of this Schedule unless, before the execution of the improvement, the landlord consented in writing (whether unconditionally or upon terms as to compensation or otherwise agreed between him and the tenant) to the execution of the improvement.

(2)   Where the consent was given upon agreed terms as to compensation, compensation payable under the agreement shall be substituted for compensation under this Schedule.

4   (1)   Compensation under this Schedule shall not be payable for an old improvement consisting of that specified in paragraph 16 of Part II of this Schedule unless the tenant gave to the landlord, not more than three or less than two months before beginning to execute the improvement, notice in writing under section 3 of the Agricultural Holdings Act 1923 of his intention to execute the improvement and of the manner in which he proposed to execute it, and—

(a)   the landlord and tenant agreed on the terms on which the improvement was to be executed, or

(b)   in a case where no agreement was reached and the tenant did not withdraw the notice, the landlord failed to exercise the right conferred on him by that section to execute the improvement himself within a reasonable time.

(2)   Subsection (1) above shall not have effect if the landlord and tenant agreed, by the contract of tenancy or otherwise, to dispense with notice under the said section 3.

(3)   If the landlord and tenant agreed (whether after notice was given under the said section 3 or by an agreement to dispense with notice under that section) upon terms as to compensation upon which the improvement was to be executed, compensation payable under the agreement shall be substituted for compensation under this Schedule.

5   (1)   Where the tenant of an agricultural holding has remained in the holding[, or in any agricultural holding which comprised the whole or a substantial part of the land comprised in the holding,] during two or more tenancies, he shall not be deprived of his right to compensation under this Schedule in respect of old improvements by reason only that the improvements were made during a tenancy other than the one at the termination of which he quits the holding.

[(1A)   Where this Act applies in relation to any tenancy referred to in sub-paragraph (1) above by virtue of section 4(1)(g) of the Agricultural Tenancies Act 1995, the reference in that sub-paragraph to a substantial part of the land comprised in the holding means a substantial part determined by reference to either area or value.]

(2)   Where, on entering into occupation of an agricultural holding, the tenant, with the consent in writing of his landlord, paid to an outgoing tenant any compensation payable under or in pursuance of this Schedule (or the Agricultural Holdings Act 1948 or the Agricultural Holdings Act 1923) in respect of the whole or part of an old improvement, he shall be entitled, on quitting the holding, to claim compensation for the improvement or part in the same manner, if at all, as the outgoing tenant would have been entitled if the outgoing tenant had remained tenant of the holding and quitted it at the time at which the tenant quits it.

NOTES

Derivation

Paras 1, 3–5 derived from the Agricultural Holdings Act 1948, ss 35(2), 36(1), (2), 38, 39(1), (2), 43(3), 44, 45; para 2 derived from the Agricultural Holdings Act 1948, ss 37, 43(1), and the Agricultural Holdings Act 1984, s 10(1), Sch 3, para 10.

Initial Commencement

Specified date: 18 June 1986: see s 102(2).

Extent

This Act does not extend to Scotland.

Amendment

Para 5: words from ', or in any' to 'in the holding,' in square brackets inserted by SI 2006/2805, arts 2, 6(6).

Date in force: 19 October 2006 (except in relation to compensation payable on termination of a tenancy where that tenancy was granted before that date): see SI 2006/2805, arts 1(1)(b), 6(8).

Para (1A): inserted by SI 2006/2805, arts 2, 6(7).

Date in force: 19 October 2006 (except in relation to compensation payable on termination of a tenancy where that tenancy was granted before that date): see SI 2006/2805, arts 1(1)(b), 6(8).

See Further

See further, as to the exclusion of this Act in relation to leases or tenancies granted to contractors in respect of the running of any removal centre or part of a removal centre: the Immigration and Asylum Act 1999, s 149(3).

Notes

For a commentary, see para 38.3 ff.

Para 1(1), (3) contain provisions formerly in the Agricultural Holdings Act 1948, s 36(1). Para 1(2) contains provisions formerly in s 35(2) of that Act. Para 1(4) contains provisions formerly in s 36(2) of that Act. Para 1(5) contains provisions formerly in s 43(3) of that Act. Para 2(1) contains provisions formerly in s 37 of that Act, as amended by the Agricultural Holdings Act 1984, s 10(1), Sch 3, para 10. Para 2(2) contains provisions formerly in s 43(1)(a) of the 1948 Act. Para 3 contains provisions formerly in s 38 of that Act. Para 4(1), (2) and (3) contain provisions formerly in s 39(1) and (2), respectively, of the 1948 Act. Para 5(1), (2) contain provisions formerly in ss 44, 45, respectively, to the 1948 Act.

General Note. See the General Note to s 64.

Para 1: Compensation. For supplementary provisions as to compensation, see ss 74 ff, 83 ff.

1st March 1948. See the note to s 64, and the General Note to that section.

1st January 1921. Ie the commencement date of the Agriculture Act 1920 (repealed).

Para 2: Benefit. See the note to s 66.

Para 3: Writing. See the note 'Written' to s 3.

Consent. As to consent in the lease itself, see *Re Morse and Dixon* (1917) 87 LJKB 1, CA. As to consent by limited owners, see s 88.

Para 4: Months. See the note to s 4.

Coal-mining subsidence. See the note to s 66.

Definitions. For 'agricultural holding', see s 1(1); for 'contract of tenancy', see s 1(3); for 'agreed', 'agreement', 'landlord', 'tenant' and 'termination', see s 96(1). Note as to 'old improvements', para 1(2) above.

Agricultural Holdings Act 1923. That section was repealed by the Agricultural Holdings Act 1948, s 98, Sch 8. S 57(1) of the 1923 Act, as originally enacted, provided that in that Act, unless the context otherwise required, inter alia—

'Holding' does not include an allotment garden or include any land cultivated as a garden unless it is cultivated wholly or mainly for the purpose of the trade or business of market gardening but, except as aforesaid, means any parcel of land held by a tenant, which is either wholly agricultural or wholly pastoral, or in part agricultural and as to the residue pastoral, or in whole or in part cultivated as a market garden and which is not let to the tenant during his continuance in any office appointment or employment held under the landlord;

'Allotment garden' means an allotment not exceeding forty poles in extent which is wholly or mainly cultivated by the occupier for the production of vegetable or fruit crops for consumption by himself or his family;

'Market garden' means a holding cultivated, wholly or mainly, for the purpose of market gardening.

S 33 extended the compensation provisions to land which was not a holding only because the tenancy included other land which, owing to the nature of the buildings thereon, or the use to which it was put, would not be within the Act if separately let.

Agricultural Holdings Act 1948. Repealed by s 101, Sch 15, Pt I.

PART II: OLD IMPROVEMENTS FOR WHICH COMPENSATION IS PAYABLE

1   Erection, alteration or enlargement of buildings.

2   Formation of silos.

3   Making and planting of osier beds.

4   Making of water meadows or works or irrigation.

5   Making of gardens.

6   Making or improvement of roads or bridges.

7   Making or improvement of watercourses, ponds, wells or reservoirs or of works for the application of water power or for supply of water for agricultural or domestic purposes.

8   Making or removal of permanent fences.

9   Planting of hops.

10   Planting of orchards or fruit bushes.

11   Reclaiming of waste land.

12   Warping or weiring of land.

13   Embankments and sluices against floods.

14   Erection of wirework in hop gardens.

15   Provision of permanent sheep-dipping accommodation.

16   Drainage.

NOTES

Derivation

This Part derived from the Agricultural Holdings Act 1948, Sch 2, Part I, paras 1, 2, 4–11, 13–17, Part II, para 19.

Initial Commencement

Specified date: 18 June 1986: see s 102(2).

Extent

This Act does not extend to Scotland.

See Further

See further, as to the exclusion of this Act in relation to leases or tenancies granted to contractors in respect of the running of any removal centre or part of a removal centre: the Immigration and Asylum Act 1999, s 149(3).

Notes

For a commentary, see para 38.8.

Paras 1–15 contain provisions formerly in the Agricultural Holdings Act 1948, Sch 2, Pt I, paras 1, 2, 4–11, 13–17, respectively. Para 16 contains provisions formerly in Sch 2, Pt II, para 19 to the 1948 Act.

Definitions. For 'agricultural' and 'building', see s 96(1).

SCHEDULE 10
MARKET GARDEN IMPROVEMENTS

Sections 79, 80

A1.199

1   Planting of standard or other fruit trees permanently set out.

2   Planting of fruit bushes permanently set out.

3   Planting of strawberry plants.

4   Planting of asparagus, rhubarb and other vegetable crops which continue productive for two or more years.

5   Erection, alteration or enlargement of buildings for the purpose of the trade or business of a market gardener.

NOTES
Derivation

This Schedule derived from the Agricultural Holdings Act 1948, Sch 5, paras 1–5.

Initial Commencement

Specified date: 18 June 1986: see s 102(2).

Extent

This Act does not extend to Scotland.

See Further

See further, as to the exclusion of this Act in relation to leases or tenancies granted to contractors in respect of the running of any removal centre or part of a removal centre: the Immigration and Asylum Act 1999, s 149(3).

Notes

For a commentary, see para 38.97.

This Schedule contains provisions formerly in the Agricultural Holdings Act 1948, Sch 5.

Buildings. For meaning of 'building' see s 96(1).

Opencast coal operations. See the note to s 79.

SCHEDULE 11
ARBITRATIONS

A1.200

Sections 84 and 94

Appointment and remuneration of arbitrator

1.—   (1)   The arbitrator shall be a person appointed by agreement between the parties or, in default of agreement, a person appointed on the application of either of the parties by the President of the Royal Institution of Chartered Surveyors (referred to in this Schedule as 'the President') from among the members of the panel constituted for the purposes of this paragraph.

(2)   No application may be made to the President for an arbitrator to be appointed by him under this paragraph unless the application is accompanied by such fee as may be prescribed as the fee for such an application; but once the fee has been paid in connection with any such application no further fee shall be payable in connection with any subsequent application for the President to exercise any function exercisable by him in relation to the arbitration by virtue of this Schedule (including an application for the appointment by him in an appropriate case of a new arbitrator).

(3)   Any such appointment by the President shall be made by him as soon as possible after receiving the application; but where the application is referable to a demand for arbitration made under section 12 of this Act any such appointment shall in any event not be made by him earlier than four months before the next termination date following the date of the demand (as defined by subsection (4) of that section).

(4)   A person appointed by the President as arbitrator shall, where the arbitration relates to an agricultural holding in Wales, be a person who possesses a knowledge of Welsh agricultural conditions, and, if either party to the arbitration so requires, a knowledge also of the Welsh language.

(5)   For the purposes of this Schedule there shall be constituted a panel consisting of such number of persons as the Lord Chancellor may determine, to be appointed by him.

[(6)   A member of the panel constituted for the purposes of this Schedule shall vacate his office on the day on which he attains the age of seventy years; but this sub-paragraph is subject to section 26(4) to (6) of the Judicial Pensions and Retirement Act 1993 (power to authorise continuance in office up to the age of seventy-five years).]

2.   If the arbitrator dies, or is incapable of acting, or for seven days after notice from either party requiring him to act fails to act, a new arbitrator may be appointed as if no arbitrator had been appointed.

3.   In relation to an arbitrator who is appointed in place of another arbitrator (whether under paragraph 2 above or otherwise) the reference in section 12(2) of this Act to the date of the reference shall be construed as a reference to the date when the original arbitrator was appointed.

4.   Neither party shall have power to revoke the appointment of the arbitrator without the consent of the other party; and his appointment shall not be revoked by the death of either party.

5.   Every appointment, application, notice, revocation and consent under the foregoing paragraphs must be in writing.

6.   The remuneration of the arbitrator shall be—

    (a)   where he is appointed by agreement between the parties, such amount as may be agreed upon by him and the parties or, in default of agreement, fixed by the registrar of the county court (subject to an appeal to the judge of the court) on an application made by the arbitrator or either of the parties,

    (b)   where he is appointed by the President, such amount as may be agreed upon by the arbitrator and the parties or, in default of agreement, fixed by the President,

and shall be recoverable by the arbitrator as a debt due from either of the parties to the arbitration.

Conduct of proceedings and witnesses

7.   The parties to the arbitration shall, within thirty-five days from the appointment of the arbitrator, deliver to him a statement of their respective cases with all necessary particulars and—

(a)   no amendment or addition to the statement or particulars delivered shall be allowed after the expiry of the said thirty-five days except with the consent of the arbitrator,

(b)   a party to the arbitration shall be confined at the hearing to the matters alleged in the statement and particulars delivered by him and any amendment or addition duly made.

8.   The parties to the arbitration and all persons claiming through them respectively shall, subject to any legal objection, submit to be examined by the arbitrator, on oath or affirmation, in relation to the matters in dispute and shall, subject to any such objection, produce before the arbitrator all samples and documents within their possession or power respectively which may be required or called for, and do all other things which during the proceedings the arbitrator may require.

9.   Witnesses appearing at the arbitration shall, if the arbitrator thinks fit, be examined on oath or affirmation, and the arbitrator shall have power to administer oaths to, or to take the affirmation of, the parties and witnesses appearing.

10.   The provisions of county court rules as to the issuing of witness summonses shall, subject to such modifications as may be prescribed by such rules, apply for the purposes of the arbitration as if it were an action or matter in the county court.

11.—   (1)   Subject to sub-paragraphs (2) and (3) below, any person who—

(a)   having been summoned in pursuance of county court rules as a witness in the arbitration refuses or neglects, without sufficient cause, to appear or to produce any documents required by the summons to be produced, or

(b)   having been so summoned or being present at the arbitration and being required to give evidence, refuses to be sworn or give evidence,

(c)   shall forfeit such fine as the judge of the county court may direct.

(2)   A judge shall not have power under sub-paragraph (1) above to direct that a person shall forfeit a fine of an amount exceeding £10.

(3)   No person summoned in pursuance of county court rules as a witness in the arbitration shall forfeit a fine under this paragraph unless there has been paid or tendered to him at the time of the service of the summons such sum in respect of his expenses (including, in such cases as may be prescribed by county court rules, compensation for loss of time) as may be so prescribed for the purposes of section 55 of the County Courts Act 1984.

(4)   The judge of the county court may at his discretion direct that the whole or any part of any such fine, after deducting costs, shall be applicable towards indemnifying the party injured by the refusal or neglect.

12.—   (1)   Subject to sub-paragraph (2) below, the judge of the county court may, if he thinks fit, upon application on affidavit by either party to the arbitration, issue an order under his hand for bringing up before the arbitrator any person (in this paragraph referred to as a 'prisoner') confined in any place under any sentence or *under committal* [following the transfer of proceedings against him] for trial or otherwise, to be examined as a witness in the arbitration.

(2)   No such order shall be made with respect to a person confined under process in any civil action or matter.

(3)   Subject to sub-paragraph (4) below, the prisoner mentioned in any such order shall be brought before the arbitrator under the same custody, and shall be dealt with in the same manner in all respects, as a prisoner required by a writ of habeas corpus to be brought before the High Court and examined there as a witness.

(4)   The person having the custody of the prisoner shall not be bound to obey the order unless there is tendered to him a reasonable sum for the conveyance and maintenance of a proper officer or officers and of the prisoner in going to, remaining at, and returning from, the place where the arbitration is held.

13.   The High Court may order that a writ of habeas corpus ad testificandum shall issue to bring up a prisoner for examination before the arbitrator, if the prisoner is confined in any prison under process in any civil action or matter.

Award

14.—   (1)   Subject to sub-paragraph (2) below, the arbitrator shall make and sign his award within fifty-six days of his appointment.

(2)   The President may from time to time enlarge the time limited for making the award, whether that time has expired or not.

15.   The arbitrator may if he thinks fit make an interim award for the payment of any sum on account of the sum to be finally awarded.

16.   The arbitrator shall—

(a)   state separately in the award the amounts awarded in respect of the several claims referred to him, and

(b)   on the application of either party, specify the amount awarded in respect of any particular improvements or any particular matter the subject of the award.

17.   Where by virtue of this Act compensation under an agreement is to be substituted for compensation under this Act for improvements or for any such matters as are specified in Part II of Schedule 8 to this Act, the arbitrator shall award compensation in accordance with the agreement instead of in accordance with this Act.

18.   The award shall fix a day not later than one month after the delivery of the award for the payment of the money awarded as compensation, costs or otherwise.

19.   The award shall be final and binding on the parties and the persons claiming under them respectively.

20.   The arbitrator shall have power to correct in the award any clerical mistake or error arising from any accidental slip or omission.

Reasons for award

21.   [Section 10 of the Tribunals and Inquiries Act 1992] (reasons to be given for decisions of tribunals etc) shall apply in relation to the award of an arbitrator appointed under this Schedule by agreement between the parties as it applies in relation to the award of an arbitrator appointed under this Schedule otherwise than by such agreement.

Interest on awards

22.   Any sum directed to be paid by the award shall, unless the award otherwise directs, carry interest as from the date of the award and at the *same rate as a judgment debt* [same rate as that specified in section 17 of the Judgments Act 1838 at the date of the award].

Costs

23. The costs of, and incidental to, the arbitration and award shall be in the discretion of the arbitrator who may direct to and by whom and in what manner the costs, or any part of the costs, are to be paid.

24. On the application of either party, any such costs shall be taxable in the county court according to such of the scales prescribed by county court rules for proceedings in the county court as may be directed by the arbitrator under paragraph 23 above, or, in the absence of any such direction, by the county court.

25.— (1) The arbitrator shall, in awarding costs, take into consideration—

(a) the reasonableness or unreasonableness of the claim of either party, whether in respect of amount or otherwise,

(b) any unreasonable demand for particulars or refusal to supply particulars, and

(c) generally all the circumstances of the case.

(2) The arbitrator may disallow the costs of any witness whom he considers to have been called unnecessarily and any other costs which he considers to have been unnecessarily incurred.

Special case, setting aside award and remission

26. The arbitrator may, at any stage of the proceedings, and shall, upon a direction in that behalf given by the judge of the county court upon an application made by either party, state in the form of a special case for the opinion of the county court any question of law arising in the course of the arbitration and any question as to the jurisdiction of the arbitrator.

27.— (1) Where the arbitrator has misconducted himself, the county court may remove him.

(2) Where the arbitrator has misconducted himself, or an arbitration or award has been improperly procured, or there is an error of law on the face of the award, the county court may set the award aside.

28.— (1) The county court may from time to time remit the award, or any part of the award, to the reconsideration of the arbitrator.

(2) In any case where it appears to the county court that there is an error of law on the face of the award, the court may, instead of exercising its power of remission under subparagraph (1) above, vary the award by substituting for so much of it as is affected by the error such award as the court considers that it would have been proper for the arbitrator to make in the circumstances; and the award shall thereupon have effect as so varied.

(3) Where remission is ordered under that sub-paragraph, the arbitrator shall, unless the order otherwise directs, make and sign his award within thirty days after the date of the order.

(4) If the county court is satisfied that the time limited for making the said award is for any good reason insufficient, the court may extend or further extend that time for such period as it thinks proper.

Miscellaneous

29. Any amount paid, in respect of the remuneration of the arbitrator by either party to the arbitration, in excess of the amount, if any, directed by the award to be paid by him in respect of the costs of the award shall be recoverable from the other party.

30. The provisions of this Schedule relating to the fixing and recovery of the remuneration of an arbitrator and the making and enforcement of an award as to costs, together with any other provision in this Schedule applicable for the purposes of or in connection with those provisions, shall apply where the arbitrator has no jurisdiction to decide the question referred to him as they apply where the arbitrator has jurisdiction to decide that question.

31. For the purposes of this Schedule, an arbitrator appointed by the President shall be taken to have been so appointed at the time when the President executed the instrument of appointment; and in the case of any such arbitrator the periods mentioned in paragraphs 7 and 14 above shall accordingly run from that time.

32. Any instrument of appointment or other document purporting to be made in the exercise of any function exercisable by the President under paragraph 1, 6 or 14 above and to be signed by or on behalf of the President shall be taken to be such an instrument or document unless the contrary is shown.

NOTES

Amendment

Repealed by SI 2006/2805, arts 2, 9(1), 18, Sch 2.

Date in force: 19 October 2006: see SI 2006/2805, art 1(1)(b); for transitional provisions see art 10 thereof.

Notes

For a commentary on arbitration procedures, see Ch 47.

Schedule 11 was abolished by the RRO, SI 2006/2805. For a commentary on Schedule 11 (which applies to arbitrations commenced before 19 October 2006) see the 8th edition of this book at Ch 21.

SCHEDULE 12
MODIFICATIONS APPLICABLE TO OLD TENANCIES AND OTHER SIMILAR CASES

Sections 65, 70, 76, 77, 78, 98

General

A1.201

1 Section 2 of this Act shall not apply to an agreement made before 1st March 1948.

2 Section 3 of this Act shall not apply to a tenancy granted or agreed to be granted before 1st January 1921.

Right to remove fixtures

3 A tenant shall not be entitled by virtue of section 10(1) or 79 of this Act (or the said section 79 as applied by paragraph 10 below) to remove a fixture or building acquired by him before 1st January 1901.

Notices to quit

4 (1) Where a tenancy of an agricultural holding subsists under an agreement entered into before 25th March 1947, section 25(1) of this Act does not apply—

(a) to a notice given by or on behalf of the Secretary of State under the provisions of any agreement of tenancy, where possession of the land is required for naval, military or air force purposes, or

(b) to a notice given by a corporation carrying on a railway, dock, canal, water or other undertaking in respect of land acquired by the corporation for the purposes of their undertaking or by a government department or local authority, where possession of the land is required by the corporation, government department or authority for the purpose (not being the use of the land for agriculture) for which it was acquired by the corporation, department or authority or appropriated under any statutory provision.

(2) In the application of sub-paragraph (1)(b) above to a Board, the reference to land acquired by the corporation for the purposes of their undertaking shall be construed as including a reference to land transferred to that Board by section 31 of the Transport Act 1962 or, in the case of [Transport for London, transferred to the London Transport Executive], by section 16 of the Transport (London) Act 1969, being land—

(a) acquired, for the purpose of an undertaking vested in the British Transport Commission by Part II of the Transport Act 1947, by the body carrying on that undertaking, or

(b) acquired by a body carrying on an undertaking vested in any such undertaking as is mentioned in paragraph (a) above by virtue of an amalgamation or absorption scheme under the Railways Act 1921, being a scheme that came into operation on or after 7th July 1923,

and the reference to the purpose for which the land was acquired or appropriated by the corporation shall be construed accordingly.

(3) In sub-paragraph (2) above 'a Board' means any of the following, namely—

Associated British Ports,
the British Railways Board,
the British Waterways Board, and
[Transport for London].

[(4) Sub-paragraph (2) above shall have effect in relation to a company which is a subsidiary (within the meaning of the Greater London Authority Act 1999) of Transport for London as it has effect in relation to Transport for London, so far as relates to land transferred to the London Transport Executive as there mentioned and subsequently transferred to the company (whether before or after it became a subsidiary of Transport for London).]

(5) Where by a scheme under section 7 of the Transport Act 1968 relevant land has been transferred by the British Railways Board to another body, sub-paragraph (2) above shall (so far as relates to relevant land so transferred) have effect in relation to that body as it has effect in relation to the British Railways Board; and in this sub-paragraph 'relevant land' means land falling within paragraph (a) or (b) of sub-paragraph (2) above and transferred to the British Railways Board as there mentioned.

(6) Where, by virtue of an Act (whether public, general or local) passed, or an instrument having effect under an Act made, after 7th July 1923 and before 30th July 1948, any right of a corporation carrying on a water undertaking or of a local authority to avail itself of the benefit conferred by section 25(2)(b) of the Agricultural Holdings Act 1923 was transferred to some other person, that other person shall have the same right to avail himself of the benefit conferred by sub-paragraph (1)(b) above as the corporation or authority would have had if the Act or instrument by virtue of which the transfer was effected had not been passed or made.

Compensation for improvements

5 The tenant of an agricultural holding shall not be entitled to compensation under section 64(1) of this Act for an improvement which he was required to carry out by the terms of his tenancy where the contract of tenancy was made before 1st January 1921.

Compensation for tenant-right matters

6 (1) Where the tenant of an agricultural holding entered into occupation of the holding before 1st March 1948, section 65(1) of this Act shall not apply to him as regards the matters specified in paragraphs 7 to 10 of Part II of Schedule 8 to this Act, unless, before the termination of the tenancy, he gives notice in writing to the landlord stating that he elects that it is to apply to him as regards those matters.

(2) Where the tenancy terminates by reason of a notice to quit and at any time while the notice to quit is current the landlord gives notice in writing to the tenant requiring him to elect whether section 65(1) of this Act is to apply to him as regards the matters specified in paragraphs 7 to 10 of Part II of Schedule 8 to this Act, the tenant shall not be entitled to give a notice under sub-paragraph (1) above after the expiry of—

    (a)   one month from the giving of the notice under this sub-paragraph, or

    (b)   if the operation of the notice to quit depends upon any proceedings under section 26 or 27 of this Act (including any proceedings under Schedule 3 to this Act), one month from the termination of those proceedings.

7 (1) This paragraph applies where the tenant of an agricultural holding entered into occupation of the holding before 31st December 1951 and immediately before that date subsection (1) of section 47 of the Agricultural Holdings Act 1948 applied to him as regards the matters now specified in paragraphs 7 to 9 of Part II of Schedule 8 to this Act (whether by virtue of his having entered into occupation of the holding on or after 1st March 1948 or by virtue of a notice having been given under paragraph (c) of the proviso to subsection (1) of the said section 47).

(2) Where this paragraph applies, section 65(1) of this Act shall not apply to the tenant as regards the matters specified in paragraph 10 of Part II of Schedule 8 to this Act unless, before the termination of the tenancy, he gives notice in writing to the landlord that it is to apply to him as regards those matters.

(3) Paragraph 6(2) above shall have effect in relation to a notice under this paragraph as if in that provision there were substituted—

    (a)   for the reference to the matters specified in paragraphs 7 to 10 of Part II of Schedule 8 to this Act a reference to the matters specified in paragraph 10 of Part II of that Schedule, and

    (b)   for the reference to a notice under paragraph 6(1) above, a reference to a notice under this paragraph.

8 (1) In a case where, by virtue of paragraph 6 or 7 above, section 65(1) above does not apply to a tenant as regards all or any of the matters specified in paragraphs 7 to 10 of Part II of Schedule 8 to this Act—

    (a)   sections 70(4) and (5) and 76(3) of this Act shall have effect with the omission of references to the excluded matters,

    (b)   section 77(1) of this Act shall not apply to compensation to the tenant for the excluded matters, and

    (c)   section 78(3) of this Act, in so far as it provides that a claim for compensation in a case for which the provisions of this Act do not provide for compensation shall not be enforceable except under an agreement in writing, shall not apply to a claim by a tenant for compensation for the excluded matters.

(2) In this paragraph 'the excluded matters' means, in relation to a case to which this paragraph applies, the matters as regards which section 65(1) does not apply to the tenant.

9 The Minister may revoke or vary the provisions of paragraphs 6 to 8 above so far as they relate to the matters specified in paragraph 10 of Part II of Schedule 8 to this Act as if those provisions were contained in an order made under section 91 of this Act.

Market gardens

10   (1)   Except as provided by this paragraph, subsections (2) to (5) of section 79 of this Act shall not apply unless the agreement in writing mentioned in subsection (1) of that section was made on or after 1st January 1896.

(2)   Where—

(a)   under a contract of tenancy current on 1st January 1896 an agricultural holding was at that date in use or cultivation as a market garden with the knowledge of the landlord, and

(b)   the tenant had then executed on the holding, without having received before the execution a written notice of dissent by the landlord, an improvement of a kind specified in Schedule 10 to this Act (other than one consisting of such an alteration of a building as did not constitute an enlargement of it),

subsections (2) to (5) of section 79 (and section 81) of this Act shall apply in respect of the holding as if it had been agreed in writing after that date that the holding should be let or treated as a market garden.

(3)   The improvements in respect of which compensation is payable under subsections (2) to (5) of section 79 of this Act as applied by this paragraph shall include improvements executed before, as well as improvements executed after, 1st January 1896.

(4)   Where the land used and cultivated as mentioned in sub-paragraph (2) above consists of part of an agricultural holding only, this paragraph shall apply as if that part were a separate holding.

NOTES

Derivation

Paras 1, 2, 5, 10 derived from the Agricultural Holdings Act 1948, ss 2(1), 3(3), 47(1)(a), 67(1)–(3); para 3 derived from the Agricultural Holdings Act 1948, ss 13(5)(a), 67(1)(b), and the Agricultural Holdings Act 1984, s 10(1), Sch 3, para 16; para 4 derived from the Agricultural Holdings (Notices to Quit) Act 1977, s 1(2)(d), (3), (3A), (4), the Transport Act 1981, s 5, and the London Regional Transport Act 1984, s 71(3)(a), Sch 6, para 13; para 6 derived from the Agricultural Holdings Act 1948, s 47(1)(c), (2), and the Agricultural Holdings (Notices to Quit) Act 1977, s 13(1), Sch 1, para 1; para 7 derived from SI 1951/2168, art 4; para 8 derived from the Agricultural Holdings Act 1948, ss 56(4), 63(2), 64, 65(2), and SI 1951/2168, art 4.

Initial Commencement

Specified date: 18 June 1986: see s 102(2).

Extent

This Act does not extend to Scotland.

Amendment

Para 4: in sub-para (2) words 'Transport for London, transferred to the London Transport Executive' in square brackets substituted by SI 2003/1615, art 2, Sch 1, Pt 1, para 13(1), (2).

Date in force: 15 July 2003: see SI 2003/1615, art 1(1).

Para 4: in sub-para (3) words 'Transport for London' in square brackets substituted by SI 2003/1615, art 2, Sch 1, Pt 1, para 13(1), (3).

Date in force: 15 July 2003: see SI 2003/1615, art 1(1).

Para 4: sub-para (4) substituted by SI 2003/1615, art 2, Sch 1, Pt 1, para 13(1), (4).

Date in force: 15 July 2003: see SI 2003/1615, art 1(1).

See Further

See further, as to the exclusion of this Act in relation to leases or tenancies granted to contractors in respect of the running of any removal centre or part of a removal centre: the Immigration and Asylum Act 1999, s 149(3).

Transfer of Functions

See further in relation to the transfer of functions under this Schedule to the National Assembly for Wales, by the National Assembly for Wales (Transfer of Functions) Order 1999, SI 1999/672, art 2, Sch 1.

Notes

Paras 1, 2 contain provisions formerly in the Agricultural Holdings Act 1948, ss 2(1), 3(3), respectively. Para 3 contains provisions formerly in ss 13(5)(a), 67(1)(b) of that Act, as substituted, in the case of s 67(1)(b) of that Act, by the Agricultural Holdings Act 1984, s 10(1), Sch 3, para 16. Para 4 contains provisions formerly in the Agricultural Holdings (Notices to Quit) Act 1977, s 1(2)(d), (3), (3A), (4), as amended, in the case of sub-s (3), and as inserted in the case of sub-s (3A) thereof, by the London Regional Transport Act 1984, s 71(3)(a), Sch 6, Pt I, para 13, and as read with, in the case of sub-s (3) thereof, the Transport Act 1981, s 5. Para 5 contains provisions formerly in s 47(1)(a) of the 1948 Act. Para 6 contains provisions formerly in s 47(1)(c), (2) to the 1948 Act, as amended, in the case of sub-s (2) thereof, by s 13(1) of, and Sch 1, para 1(4) to, the 1977 Act. Para 7 contains provisions formerly in the Agricultural Holdings Act (Variation of Fourth Schedule) Order 1951, SI 1951/2168, art 4. Para 8 contains provisions formerly in ss 56(4), 63(2), 64, 65(2) of the 1948 Act, and in art 4 of the 1951 Order. Para 9 is a drafting provision. Para 10 contains provisions formerly in s 67(1)–(3) of the 1948 Act.

Para 1: 1st March 1948. Ie the commencement date of the Agriculture Act 1947, Pt III (repealed).

Para 2: 1st January 1921. Ie the commencement date of the Agriculture Act 1920 (repealed).

Para 3: 1st January 1901. Ie the commencement date of the Agricultural Holdings Act 1900 (repealed).

Para 4: Secretary of State. Ie one of Her Majesty's Principal Secretaries of State; see the Interpretation Act 1978, s 5, Sch 1. The Secretary of State concerned under para (4)(1)(a) above is the Secretary of State for Defence.

Naval, military or air force purposes. This includes the purposes of a visiting force or headquarters as defined by the Visiting Forces and International Headquarters (Application of Law) Order 1965, SI 1965/1536; see art 12(2) of, and Sch 3 to, that Order, as construed in accordance with s 99 and Sch 13, para 1.

London Regional Transport. Cf the note 'British Transport Commission' below.

British Transport Commission. The British Transport Commission was established under the Transport Act 1947, s 1 (repealed). It was dissolved by the Transport Act 1962, s 80 (repealed), and its assets, functions and staff were distributed among the British Railways Board, the London Transport Board, the British Transport Docks Board and the British Waterways Board, established under s 1 of the 1962 Act.

The London Transport Board was dissolved by the Transport (London) Act 1969, s 39(1) (repealed), and succeeded by the London Transport Executive, established under s 4 of that Act (repealed), which continues to exist but under the name of London Regional Transport, under the London Regional Transport Act 1984, s 1, Sch 1.

The British Transport Docks Board was reconstituted as Associated British Ports by the Transport Act 1981, s 5.

7th July 1923. Ie the commencement date of the Agricultural Holdings Act 1923 (repealed).

Associated British Ports; British Railways Board; British Waterways Board. Cf the note 'British Transport Commission' above.

30th July 1948. Ie the commencement date of the Agricultural Holdings Act 1948 (repealed by s 101, Sch 15, Pt I).

A1.202   *Statutes*

Para 6. This paragraph appears to be excluded from the Opencast Coal Act 1958, s 25(1) (amended by s 100, Sch 14, para 27(2)), relating to deductions from tenant's compensation, by s 25(2) of that Act (as amended by s 100, Sch 14, para 27(3)).

Writing. See the note 'Written' to s 3.

One month from, etc. See the note 'Two months from, etc' to s 10.

Para 7: 31st December 1951. Ie the date on which the Agricultural Holdings Act (Variation of Fourth Schedule) Order 1951, SI 1951/2168 (revoked by s 101, Sch 15, Pt II), came into operation.

Para 10: 1st January 1896. Ie the commencement date of the Market Gardeners' Compensation Act 1895 (repealed).

Saving. As to the validity of the provision re-enacted in paras 6–8 above, see s 99(2).

Definitions. For 'agricultural holding', see s 1(1); for 'contract of tenancy', see s 1(5); for 'agreed', 'agreement', 'landlord', 'the Minister', 'tenant' and 'termination', see s 96(1). Note as to 'a Board' (in para 4(2)) para 4(3) above and as to 'the excluded matters' (in para 8), para 8(2) above. Note, also, as to 'termination', s 74(4).

Transport (London) Act 1969, s 16. That section was repealed by the London Regional Transport Act 1984, s 71(3)(b), Sch 7.

Transport Act 1947, Part II. The provisions of that Part have all been repealed.

Railways Act 1921. Amalgamation and absorption schemes under ss 2, 4 to that Act (repealed) were contained in SR & O 1923/817 (GWR), SR & O 1923/827 (LM & SR), SR & O 1922/1435 (LNER) SR & O 1922/141 (SR) (not printed in annual SR & O volumes, being regarded as local).

London Regional Transport Act 1984. For meaning of 'subsidiary' in that Act, see s 68.

Agricultural Holdings Act 1923, s 25(2)(b). That paragraph corresponded to para 4(1)(b) of this Schedule above and, by the Agriculture Act 1947, s 31(9), ceased to have effect except as to a tenancy entered into before 25 March 1947. The 1923 Act was repealed by the Agricultural Holdings Act 1948, s 98, Sch 8.

Agricultural Holdings Act 1948, s 47(1). That Act is repealed by s 101, Sch 15, Pt I.

SCHEDULE 13
TRANSITIONAL PROVISIONS AND SAVINGS

Section 99

Construction of references to old and new law

A1.202

1 (1) Any reference, whether express or implied, in any enactment, instrument or document (including this Act and any enactment amended by Schedule 14 to this Act), to, or to things done or falling to be done under or for the purposes of, any provision of this Act shall, if and so far as the nature of the reference permits, be construed as including, in relation to the times, circumstances or purposes in relation to which the corresponding provision repealed by this Act has or had effect, a reference to, or as the case may be, to things done or falling to be done under or for the purposes of, that corresponding provision.

(2) Any reference, whether express or implied, in any enactment, instrument or document (including the enactments repealed by this Act and enactments, instruments and documents passed or made after the passing of this Act) to, or to things done or falling to be done under or for the purposes of, any provision repealed by this Act shall, if and so far as the nature of the reference permits, be construed as including, in relation to the times, circumstances or purposes in relation to which the corresponding

1272

provision of this Act has effect, a reference to, or as the case may be, to things done or falling to be done under or for the purposes of, that corresponding provision.

(3) In this paragraph references to any provision repealed by this Act include references to any earlier provision, corresponding to a provision so repealed, which was repealed by the Agricultural Holdings (Notices to Quit) Act 1977, the Agricultural Holdings Act 1948, the Agricultural Holdings Act 1923 or the Agricultural Holdings Act 1908.

2   References, in whatever terms, in any enactment to a holding within the meaning of the Agricultural Holdings Act 1923 shall be construed as references to an agricultural holding within the meaning of this Act.

Continuation of old law for certain pending cases

3   (1)   Nothing in this Act shall apply in relation to—

(a)   a notice to quit an agricultural holding or part of an agricultural holding—
   (i)   given before the commencement of this Act, or
   (ii) in the case of a notice to quit given after that time which includes a statement that it is given by reason of the death of a former tenant, where the date of death was before that time,
(b)   an agricultural holding—
   (i)   the tenancy of which terminated before the commencement of this Act, or
   (ii) the tenant of which quitted the holding before the commencement of this Act or quitted after that time in consequence of a notice to quit falling within paragraph (a) above,
(c)   an arbitration where the arbitrator was appointed under the Agricultural Holdings Act 1948 before the commencement of this Act,
(d)   an application made before the commencement of this Act to the Tribunal under any of the enactments repealed by this Act, or
(e)   an application made after the commencement of this Act to the Tribunal for a direction entitling the applicant to a tenancy of an agricultural holding on the death or retirement of the tenant where the date of death or the date of the giving of the retirement notice was before that time;

and accordingly the enactments repealed or amended by this Act shall in relation to any such notice to quit, agricultural holding, arbitration (including an award made in such an arbitration) or application (including any proceedings arising out of any such application or any direction given in any such proceedings) continue to have effect as if this Act had not been passed.

(2)   This paragraph shall have effect subject to paragraph 1 above and paragraph 11 below.

Periods of time

4   Where a period of time specified in any enactment repealed by this Act is current at the commencement of this Act, this Act shall have effect as if the corresponding provision of this Act had been in force when the period began to run.

Transfer of functions

5   Any reference, whether express or implied, in this Act (or any enactment amended by Schedule 14 to this Act) to, or to anything done by, the Minister, the Tribunal, an arbitrator or the President of the Royal Institution of Chartered Surveyors shall where the relevant function has been transferred to that person be construed, in relation to

any time before the transfer, as including a reference to, or to the corresponding thing done by, the person by whom the function was then exercisable.

6   Section 22 of this Act shall have effect in relation to the appointment of a person in pursuance of an application made before 1st January 1986 under section 16(2) of the Agricultural Holdings Act 1948 as if for references to the President of the Royal Institution of Chartered Surveyors there were substituted references to the Minister and as if subsections (4) and (5) were omitted.

7   ...

Compensation

8   Notwithstanding section 16 of the Interpretation Act 1978, rights to compensation conferred by this Act shall be in lieu of rights to compensation conferred by any enactment repealed by this Act.

Rights to remove fixtures

9   Sections 13 and 67 of the Agricultural Holdings Act 1948 shall continue to have effect (to the exclusion of sections 10 and 79 of this Act) in relation to an agricultural holding in a case where the tenant gave notice under subsection (2)(b) of the said section 13 before 12th September 1984 as the said sections 13 and 67 had effect before that date.

Compensation for damage by game

10   Section 14 of the Agricultural Holdings Act 1948 shall continue to have effect (to the exclusion of section 20 of this Act) in relation to an agricultural holding in a case where a notice was given to the landlord under paragraph (a) of the proviso to subsection (1) of the said section 14 before 12th September 1984 as the said section 14 had effect before that date.

Succession on death or retirement

11   (1)   Where Part IV of this Act has effect in relation to an application under that Part, references in that Part to notices to quit shall include references to notices to quit given before the commencement of this Act and, in particular, section 54 of this Act shall apply (to the exclusion of paragraph 4 of Schedule 2 to the Agricultural Holdings Act 1984) in relation to a notice to quit given before the commencement of this Act as it applies in relation to a notice to quit given after that time.

(2)   Where, by virtue of paragraph 3(1) above, Part II of the Agriculture (Miscellaneous Provisions) Act 1976 or Schedule 2 to the Agricultural Holdings Act 1984 has effect in relation to an application under the said Part II or, as the case may be, under the said Schedule 2, references in the said Part II or the said Schedule 2 to notices to quit shall include references to notices to quit given after the commencement of this Act and, in particular, paragraph 4 of the said Schedule 2 shall apply (to the exclusion of section 54 of this Act) in relation to a notice to quit given after the commencement of this Act as it applies in relation to a notice to quit given before that time.

(3)   This paragraph is without prejudice to the generality of paragraph 1 above.

12   Without prejudice to the generality of section 34(1)(b)(iii) of this Act, a written contract of tenancy which grants the tenancy of an agricultural holding and indicates (in whatever terms) that section 2(1) of the Agricultural Holdings Act 1984 is not to apply in relation to the tenancy shall be taken to be such a contract of tenancy as is mentioned in that section.

Record of condition of holding

13 (1) In section 70(2)(b) of this Act the reference to a record made under section 22 of this Act shall include a reference to a record made before 12th September 1984 under section 16 of the Agricultural Holdings Act 1948 as it had effect before that date.

(2) Sub-paragraph (1) above is without prejudice to the generality of paragraph 1 above.

Insolvency

14 Sections 80(9) and 96(2) of this Act shall have effect—

(a) until the date on which Part III of the Insolvency Act 1985 comes into force, and

(b) on or after that date, in any case in which a petition of bankruptcy was presented, or a receiving order or adjudication in bankruptcy was made, before that date,

as if for paragraph (a) of section 96(2) there were substituted—

'(a) he has become bankrupt or has made a composition or arrangement with his creditors or a receiving order is made against him'.

...

15 ...

Notices to quit

16 Paragraphs 10(1)(d) and 11(2) of Part II of Schedule 3 to this Act shall not apply in relation to any act or omission by a tenant which occurred before 12th September 1984.

NOTES

Derivation

Para 2 derived from the Agricultural Holdings Act 1948, s 96(2); paras 6, 7 (omitted), 9, 10, 13, 15 (omitted), 16 derived from the Agricultural Holdings Act 1984, Sch 5, paras 4(d), 5, 7, 8, 10, 14; para 14 derived from the Insolvency Act 1985, Sch 9, para 11.

Initial Commencement

Specified date: 18 June 1986: see s 102(2).

Extent

This Act does not extend to Scotland.

Amendment

Para 7: repealed by SI 2006/2805, arts 2, 9(2), 18, Sch 2.

Date in force: 19 October 2006: see SI 2006/2805, art 1(1)(b); for transitional provisions see art 10 thereof.

Para 15: repealed by SI 2006/2805, arts 2, 9(2), 18, Sch 2.

Date in force: 19 October 2006: see SI 2006/2805, art 1(1)(b); for transitional provisions see art 10 thereof.

See Further

See further, as to the exclusion of this Act in relation to leases or tenancies granted to contractors in respect of the running of any removal centre or part of a removal centre: the Immigration and Asylum Act 1999, s 149(3).

Notes

Paras 1, 3–5, 8, 11, 12 are new provisions. Para 2 contains provisions formerly in the Agricultural Holdings Act 1948, s 96(2). Paras 6, 7 contain provisions derived from the Agricultural Holdings Act 1984, Sch 5, para 5. Paras 9, 10, 13, 15, 16 contain provisions formerly in Sch 5, paras 7, 8, 10, 14, 4(d), respectively, to the 1984 Act. Para 14 contains provisions derived from the Insolvency Act 1985, Sch 9, para 11. Paras 7 and 15: repealed by the RRO 2006, SI 2006/2805 art 9(2).

Para 3: Commencement of this Act. Ie 18 June 1986; see s 102(2) and the note 'Three months beginning with, etc' thereto. See also para 42.27.

The Tribunal. See the note to s 11.

Para 6: 1st January 1986; President of the Royal Institution of Chartered Surveyors. Cf the note 'President of the Royal Institution of Chartered Surveyors' to s 22.

Paras 9, 10: 12th September 1984. Ie the date on which the amendments made to the Agricultural Holdings Act 1948, ss 13, 14, 67, by the Agricultural Holdings Act 1984, s 10(1), Sch 3, paras 6, 7, 16, came into force. The 1948 and 1984 Acts are repealed by s 101, Sch 15, Pt I.

Para 11: Part IV of this Act. Ie ss 34–59.

Para 13: 12th September 1984. Cf the note to paras 9, 10 above. The Agricultural Holdings Act 1948, s 16, was amended as from that date by the Agricultural Holdings Act 1984, s 10(1), Sch 3, para 8. Paras 7 and 15: repealed by the RRO 2006, SI 2006/2805, art 9(2).

Definitions. For 'agricultural holding', see s 1(1); for 'tenant', 'the Minister' and 'the Tribunal', see s 96(1).

Agricultural Holdings (Notices to Quit) Act 1977. Repealed by s 101, Sch 15, Pt 1.

Agricultural Holdings Act 1948. Sch 6, paras 15, 27, to that Act were repealed by the Agricultural Holdings Act 1948, s 10(2), Sch 4, and the whole Act is repealed by s 101, Sch 15, Pt I.

Agricultural Holdings Act 1923. Repealed by the Agricultural Holdings Act 1948, s 98, Sch 8.

Agricultural Holdings Act 1908. Repealed by the Agricultural Holdings Act 1923, s 58(1), (3), Sch 4.

Agricultural Holdings Act 1984, Sch 2. That Act is repealed by s 101, Sch 15, Pt I.

Agriculture (Miscellaneous Provisions) Act 1976, Part II. Repealed by s 101, Sch 15, Pt I.

Insolvency Act 1985, Part III. Repealed by the Insolvency Act 1986, s 438, Sch 12.

SCHEDULE 14
CONSEQUENTIAL AMENDMENTS

Section 100

A1.203

The Small Holdings and Allotments Act 1908

1.— (1) Section 47 of the Small Holdings and Allotments Act 1908 shall be amended as follows.

(2) In subsection (1) for the words 'section forty-two of the Agricultural Holdings Act 1908' there shall be substituted the words 'subsections (2) to (5) of section 79 of the Agricultural Holdings Act 1986'.

(3) In subsection (2)—

   (a) for the words 'Agricultural Holdings Act 1908', in the first place where they occur, there shall be substituted the words 'Agricultural Holdings Act 1986',

   (b) for the words 'section forty-two of the Agricultural Holdings Act 1908' there shall be substituted the words 'subsections (2) to (5) of section 79 of the Agricultural Holdings Act 1986' and

   (c) for the words 'Part III of the First Schedule to the Agricultural Holdings Act 1908' there shall be substituted the words 'Schedule 8 to the Agricultural Holdings Act 1986'.

(4) In subsection (3) for the words 'Agricultural Holdings Act 1908' there shall be substituted the words 'Agricultural Holdings Act 1986'.

2. In section 58 of that Act for the words 'Agricultural Holdings Act 1908' there shall be substituted the words 'Agricultural Holdings Act 1986'.

3. In paragraph (3) of Part II of Schedule 1 to that Act for the words 'Agricultural Holdings Act 1908' there shall be substituted the words 'Agricultural Holdings Act 1986'.

The Law of Distress Amendment Act 1908

4. In section 4(1) of the Law of Distress Amendment Act 1908 for the words from 'live stock' to 'Act 1908' there shall be substituted the words 'agisted livestock within the meaning of section 18 of the Agricultural Holdings Act 1986 to which that section'.

The Chequers Estate Act 1917

5. In clauses 6B(b) and 8D of the Deed set out in the Schedule to the Chequers Estate Act 1917 for the words 'Agricultural Holdings Act 1948' there shall be substituted the words 'Agricultural Holdings Act 1986, except section 60(2)(b) or 62 of that Act'.

The Land Settlement (Facilities) Act 1919

6. In section 2(3) of the Land Settlement (Facilities Act) 1919 for the words 'Second Schedule of the Agricultural Holdings Act 1908' there shall be substituted the words 'Agricultural Holdings Act 1986'.

7. In section 11(4) of that Act for the words 'Second Schedule to the Agricultural Holdings Act 1908' there shall be substituted the words 'Agricultural Holdings Act 1986'.

8. ...

The Allotments Act 1922

9. In section 3(5) of the Allotments Act 1922—

   (a) for the words 'Agricultural Holdings Act 1908 to 1921' there shall be substituted the words 'Agricultural Holdings Act 1986'.

   (b) for the words 'to which those Acts apply' there shall be substituted the words 'which is an agricultural holding within the meaning of that Act', and

   (c) for the words 'those Acts', in the second and third place where they occur, there shall be substituted the words 'that Act'.

10. In section 11(2) of that Act for the words 'Second Schedule to the Agricultural Holdings Act 1908' there shall be substituted the words 'Agricultural Holdings Act 1986'.

The Settled Land Act 1925

11. In section 73(1) of the Settled Land Act 1925—

(a) for the words 'Agricultural Holdings Act 1923', in both places where they occur, there shall be substituted the words 'Agricultural Holdings Act 1986', and

(b) for the words 'Part I or Part II of the First Schedule' there shall be substituted the words 'Schedule 7'.

12. ...

The Universities and College Estates Act 1925

13. In section 26(1) of the Universities and College Estates Act 1925—

(a) for the words 'Agricultural Holdings Act 1923', in both places where they occur, there shall be substituted the words 'Agricultural Holdings Act 1986', and

(b) for the words 'Part I and Part II of the First Schedule' there shall be substituted the words 'Schedule 7'.

The Landlord and Tenant Act 1927

14. In section 17(1) of the Landlord and Tenant Act 1927 for the words 'Agricultural Holdings Act 1923' there shall be substituted the words 'Agricultural Holdings Act 1986'.

15. In section 19(4) of that Act for the words 'Agricultural Holdings Act 1923' there shall be substituted the words 'Agricultural Holdings Act 1986'.

The Agricultural Credits Act 1928

16. In section 5(7) of the Agricultural Credits Act 1928 for the words 'Agricultural Holdings Act 1923' there shall be substituted the words 'Agricultural Holdings Act 1986, except under section 60(2)(b) or 62,'.

The Leasehold Property (Repairs) Act 1938

17. In section 7(1) of the Leasehold Property (Repairs) Act 1938 for the words 'Agricultural Holdings Act 1948' there shall be substituted the words 'Agricultural Holdings Act 1986'.

The Agriculture Act 1947

18. In section 73(3)(a) of the Agriculture Act 1947 for the words 'Agricultural Holdings Act 1923' there shall be substituted the words 'Agricultural Holdings Act 1986'.

19. In Schedule 2 to that Act—

(a) in paragraph 1 for the words 'any provision of Part III of this Act' there shall be substituted the words 'section 14 of the Agricultural Holdings Act 1986', and

(b) in paragraph 3 for the words 'Part III of this Act' there shall be substituted the words 'the Agricultural Holdings Act 1986' and for the words 'a holding (as defined in the Agricultural Holdings Act 1923)' there shall be substituted the words 'the agricultural holding within the meaning of the Agricultural Holdings Act 1986'.

The Reserve and Auxiliary Forces (Protection of Civil Interests) Act 1951

20. In section 27(1) of the Reserve and Auxiliary Forces (Protection of Civil Interests) Act 1951 for the words 'Agricultural Holdings Act 1948' there shall be substituted the words 'Agricultural Holdings Act 1986'.

The Landlord and Tenant Act 1954

21. In section 43(1)(a) of the Landlord and Tenant Act 1954 for the words from 'the proviso' to 'the said subsection (1)' there shall be substituted the words 'subsection (3) of section 2 of the Agricultural Holdings Act 1986 did not have effect or, in a case where approval was given under subsection (1) of that section'.

22. In section 69(1) of that Act for the Words 'Agricultural Holdings Act 1948' there shall be substituted the words 'Agricultural Holdings Act 1986'.

The Agriculture (Safety, Health and Welfare Provisions) Act 1956

23. In section 24(1) of the Agriculture (Safety, Health and Welfare Provisions) Act 1956 for the words 'Agricultural Holdings Act 1948' there shall be substituted the words 'Agricultural Holdings Act 1986'.

24. ...

The Opencast Coal Act 1958

25. ...

26.— (1) Section 24 of that Act shall be amended as follows.

(2) In subsection (1) for the words 'Act of 1948' there shall be substituted the words 'Act of 1986'.

(3) In subsection (2) for the words 'Act of 1948' there shall be substituted the words 'Act of 1986'.

(4) In subsection (3) for the words 'Act of 1948', in each place where they occur, there shall be substituted the words 'Act of 1986'.

(5) In subsection (5)—

    (a) for the words 'section forty-four or section fifty-four of the Act of 1948' there shall be substituted the words 'section 69(1) of the Act of 1986 or paragraph 5(1) of Part I of Schedule 9 to that Act', and

    (b) for the words 'section forty-five or section fifty-five of the Act of 1948' there shall be substituted the words 'section 69(2) or (3) of the Act of 1986 or paragraph 5(2) of Part I of Schedule 9 to that Act'.

(6) In subsection (6)—

    (a) for the words 'Act of 1948', in both places where they occur, there shall be substituted the words 'Act of 1986', and

    (b) for the words 'section (3) of section seventy' there shall be substituted the words 'section 83(4)';

and that subsection in its application to England and Wales shall continue to have effect with the substitution for each of the words 'four' and 'five' of the word 'eight' made by paragraph 29 of Schedule 3 to the Agricultural Holdings Act 1984.

(7) In subsection (7)—

    (a) for the words 'Act of 1948', in both places where they occur, there shall be substituted the words 'Act of 1986' and

(b) for the words 'section fifty-six' there shall be substituted the words 'section 70'.

(8) In subsection (8) for the words 'Act of 1948' there shall be substituted the words 'Act of 1986'.

(9) In subsection (9) for the words 'the Third Schedule to the Act of 1948' there shall be substituted the words 'Schedule 7 to the Act of 1986'.

(10) After subsection (9) there shall be inserted—

'(9A) In this section the references to the Act of 1986 in subsections (1)(b), (7) and (8) and the second and fourth references to that Act in subsection (3) include references to the Agricultural Holdings Act 1948 (in this Act called the Act of 1948) and the reference to section 70 of the Act of 1986 in subsection (7)(b) includes a reference to section 56 of the Act of 1948'.

(11) (Applies to Scotland only.)

27.— (1) Section 25 of that Act shall be amended as follows.

(2) In subsection (1)—

(a) for the words 'section fifty-seven of the Act of 1948' there shall be substituted the words 'section 71 of the Act of 1986', and

(b) for the words 'section fifty-eight' there shall be substituted the words 'section 72'.

(3) In subsection (2) for the words 'Act of 1948' there shall be substituted the words 'Act of 1986'.

(4) After subsection (2) there shall be inserted—

'(2A) In this section references to the Act of 1986 and to sections 71 and 72 of that Act include respectively references to the Act of 1948 and to sections 57 and 58 of that Act'.

(5) (Applies to Scotland only.)

28.— (1) Section 26 of that Act shall be amended as follows.

(2) In subsection (3) for the words 'Act of 1948' there shall be substituted the words 'Act of 1986'.

(3) In subsection (5) for the words 'section seventy-eight of the Act of 1948, the provisions of the Fourth Schedule' there shall be substituted the words 'section 91 of the Act of 1986, the provisions of Schedule 8'.

(4) After subsection (5) there shall be inserted—

'(5A) The reference in subsection (3) of this section to the 1986 Act includes a reference to the 1948 Act'.

(5) (Applies to Scotland only.)

29.— (1) Section 27 of that Act shall be amended as follows.

(2) In subsection (1)(b) for the words 'section thirteen of the Act of 1948' there shall be substituted the words 'section 10 of the Act of 1986'.

(3) (Applies to Scotland only.)

30.— (1) Section 28 of that Act shall be amended as follows.

(2) In subsection (3)—

  (a) for the words 'section sixty-seven of the Act of 1948' there shall be substituted the words 'subsections (2) to (5) of section 79 of the Act of 1986', and

  (b) for the words 'subsection (1) of section sixty-eight' there shall be substituted the words 'subsection (2) of section 80'.

(3) In subsection (4)—

  (a) for the words 'section thirteen of the Act of 1948' there shall be substituted the words 'section 10 of the Act of 1986', and

  (b) for the words 'paragraph (b) of subsection (1) of section sixty-seven of the Act of 1948' there shall be substituted the words 'subsection (3) of section 79 of the Act of 1986'.

(4) In subsection (5) for the words from 'section seventy-eight' to 'Fifth Schedule' there shall be substituted the words 'section 91 of the Act of 1986 the provisions of Schedule 10'.

(5) (*Applies to Scotland only.*)

31. In section 51(1) of that Act—

  (a) after the definition of 'the Acquisition of Land Act' there shall be inserted— '"the Act of 1986" means the Agricultural Holdings Act 1986;', and

  (b) in the definition of 'agricultural holding' for the words 'Act of 1948' there shall be substituted the words 'Act of 1986'.

32.— (1) Schedule 6 to that Act shall be amended as follows.

(2) In paragraph 20(a) for the words 'made' to 'year' there shall be substituted the words 'falling within section 2(3)(a) of the 1986 Act'.

(3) In paragraph 24—

  (a) for the words from 'by the Minister' to '1948' there shall be substituted the words 'under section 2 of the Act of 1986 or of the Act of 1948 each of, and

  (b) for the words from 'by the said Minister' to 'of the section' there shall be substituted the words 'under that section from the operation of that section'.

(4) In paragraph 25 for the words from 'by the Minister' to 'section two' there shall be substituted the words 'under section 2 of the Act of 1986 or'.

(5) (*Applies to Scotland only.*)

33.— (1) Schedule 7 to that Act shall be amended as follows.

(2) In paragraph 1(2) for the words 'Act of 1948' there shall be substituted the words 'Act of 1986'.

(3) In paragraph 2—

  (a) for the words 'Act of 1948', in each place where they occur, there shall be substituted the words 'Act of 1986', and

  (b) after sub-paragraph (3) there shall be inserted—

'(3A) The references in sub-paragraph (1)(a) of this paragraph to the Act of 1986 include references to the Act of 1948'.

(4) In paragraph 3—

  (a) in sub-paragraph (1) for the words 'Act of 1948' there shall be substituted the words 'Act of 1986', and

  (b) in sub-paragraph (2) for the words 'section nine of the Act of 1948 in so far as the said section nine' there shall be substituted the words 'section 13 of the Act of 1986 in so far as the said section 13'.

(5)   In paragraph 4—

    (a) in sub-paragraph (2) for the words 'Act of 1948' there shall be substituted the words 'Act of 1986',

    (b) in sub-paragraph (4) for the words 'Section seventy-seven of the Act of 1948' there shall be substituted the words 'Section 84 of the Act of 1986' and for the words 'Act of 1948', in the second place where they occur, there shall be substituted the words 'Act of 1986',

    (c) in sub-paragraph (5) for the words 'section eight or section nine of the Act of 1948' there shall be substituted the words 'section 12 or section 13 of the Act of 1986', and

    (d) in sub-paragraph (6) for the words 'section nine of the Act of 1948' there shall be substituted the words 'section 13 of the Act of 1986'.

(6)   In paragraph 5—

    (a) in sub-paragraph (1) for the words 'section thirteen of the Act of 1948' there shall be substituted the words 'section 10 of the Act of 1986'.

    (b) in sub-paragraph (2) for the words 'subsection (2)' there shall be substituted the words 'subsection (3)',

    (c) in sub-paragraph (3) for the words 'subsection (2)' there shall be substituted the words 'subsection (3)' and for the words 'subsection (3)' there shall be substituted the words 'subsection (4)', and

    (d) in sub-paragraph (5) for the words 'section thirteen of the Act of 1948' there shall be substituted the words 'section 10 of the Act of 1986' and for the words 'paragraph (b) of subsection (1) of section sixty-seven' there shall be substituted the words 'subsection (3) of section 79'.

(7)   In paragraph 6(2) for the words 'section seventeen of the Act of 1948' there shall be substituted the words 'section 23 of the Act of 1986'.

(8)   *(Applies to Scotland only.)*

The Chevening Estate Act 1959

34.   In clauses 15(i) and 23(b) of the Trust Instrument set out in the Schedule to the Chevening Estate Act 1959 for the words 'Agricultural Holdings Act 1948' there shall be substituted the words 'Agricultural Holdings Act 1986, except section 60(2)(b) or 62 of that Act,'.

35.   ...

The Agriculture (Miscellaneous Provisions) Act 1963

36.   In subsections (1)(a) and (6)(c) of section 22 of the Agriculture (Miscellaneous Provisions) Act 1963 for the words 'Agricultural Holdings Act 1948' there shall be substituted the words 'Agricultural Holdings Act 1986'.

The Agriculture Act 1967

37.   In section 26(1) of the Agriculture Act 1967 for the words 'Agricultural Holdings Act 1948', in both places where they occur, there shall be substituted the words 'Agricultural Holdings Act 1986'.

38.   In section 27(5B)(a) of that Act for the words 'Agricultural Holdings Act 1948' there shall be substituted the words 'Agricultural Holdings Act 1986'.

39.   In section 28(1)(a) of that Act for the words 'section 34 of the Agricultural Holdings Act 1948' there shall be substituted the words 'section 60(2)(a) of the Agricultural Holdings Act 1986'.

40.   In section 29(3)(a) of that Act for the words 'section 34 of the Agricultural Holdings Act 1948' there shall be substituted the words 'section 60(2)(a) of the Agricultural Holdings Act 1986'.

41.—   (1)   Section 48 of that Act shall be amended as follows.

(2)   In subsection (2)(a) for the words 'section 34 of the Agricultural Holdings Act 1948' there shall be substituted the words 'section 60(2)(a) of the Agricultural Holdings Act 1986'.

(3)   For subsection (4) there shall be substituted—

'(4)   Case H in Part I of Schedule 3 to the Agricultural Holdings Act 1986 shall apply in relation to a Rural Development Board as it applies in relation to the Minister within the meaning of that Act.'

42.   In paragraph 7(4) of Schedule 3 to that Act for the words 'Section 77 of the Agricultural Holdings Act 1948' there shall be substituted the words 'Section 84 of the Agricultural Holdings Act 1986'.

The Leasehold Reform Act 1967

43.   In section 1(3)(b) of the Leasehold Reform Act 1967 for the words 'Agricultural Holdings Act 1948' there shall be substituted the words 'Agricultural Holdings Act 1986'.

The Agriculture (Miscellaneous Provisions) Act 1968

44.   In section 12(1) of the Agriculture (Miscellaneous Provisions) Act 1968, for the words from 'section 9' to the end there shall be substituted the words 'subsection (2)(b) of section 60 of the Agricultural Holdings Act 1986 (additional compensation to tenant for disturbance) shall apply as if the acquiring authority were the landlord of the holding and on the date of the acquisition or taking possession the tenancy of the holding or part of it had terminated, and the tenant had quitted the holding or part of it, in consequence of such a notice or counter-notice as is mentioned in subsection (1) of that section; and section 61 of that Act (exceptions to section 60) shall not apply in such a case'.

45.   In section 13(1) of that Act for the words 'section 2(1) of the principal Act' there shall be substituted the words 'section 2(2) of the Agricultural Holdings Act 1986'.

46.—   (1)   Section 17 of that Act shall be amended as follows.

(2)   In subsection (1) for the words 'principal Act', in the second place where they occur, there shall be substituted the words 'Agricultural Holdings Act 1986'.

(3)   In subsection (3) for the words 'Section 87(1) and (2) of the principal Act' there shall be substituted the words 'Section 95(1), (2) and (3) of the Agricultural Holdings Act 1986'.

47.   In section 42(2) of that Act, as it has effect for the purposes of section 48(6) of the Land Compensation Act 1973, for the words 'section 24 of the principal Act' there shall be substituted the words 'section 26 of the Agricultural Holdings Act 1986' and for the words 'principal Act', in the second place where they occur, there shall be substituted the words 'Agricultural Holdings Act 1986'.

48.—   (1)   Schedule 3 to that Act shall be amended as follows.

(2)   In paragraph 2—

   (a)   for the words 'section 9(2) of this Act' there shall be substituted the words 'section 60(4) of the Agricultural Holdings Act 1986', and

(b) for the words 'section 8 or section 9 of the principal Act' there shall be substituted the words 'section 12 or section 13 of the Agricultural Holdings Act 1986'.

(3) In paragraph 3—

(a) for the words 'section 8 of the principal Act' there shall be substituted the words 'section 12 of the Agricultural Holdings Act 1986', and

(b) for the words 'section 9(2)' there shall be substituted the words 'section 60(4)'.

49. ...

The Town and Country Planning Act 1971

50. In section 27(7) of the Town and Country Planning Act 1971 for the words 'Agricultural Holdings Act 1948' there shall be substituted the words 'Agricultural Holdings Act 1986'.

The Land Charges Act 1972

51.— (1) Schedule 2 to the Land Charges Act 1972 shall be amended as follows.

(2) In paragraph 1(g) for the words from 'Sections' to 'tenant or' there shall be substituted the words 'Section 74 charge in respect of sums due to' and the words from 'Section 82' to 'improvements' shall be omitted.

(3) After paragraph 1(h) there shall be inserted—

'(i)   The Agricultural Holdings
                Act 1986   Section 85 (charges in respect of sums
                                                due to tenant of agricultural holding).
                                                Section 86 (charges in favour of
                                                landlord of agricultural holdings in
                                                respect of compensation for or cost of
                                                certain improvements).'

(4) In paragraph 3 for the words from the beginning to 'Act 1948' there shall be substituted the words 'The reference in paragraph 1(g) above to section 74 of the Agricultural Holdings Act 1948 and the reference in paragraph 1(i) above to section 85 and 86 of the Agricultural Holdings Act 1986'.

The Land Compensation Act 1973

52. In section 34(3)(c) of the Land Compensation Act 1973 for the words 'Agricultural Holdings Act 1948' there shall be substituted the words 'Agricultural Holdings Act 1986'.

53.— (1) Section 48 of that Act shall be amended as follows.

(2) In subsection (2)—

(a) for the words 'Case B in section 2(3) of the Agricultural Holdings (Notices to Quit) Act 1977' there shall be substituted the words 'Case B in Part I of Schedule 3 to the Agricultural Holdings Act 1986',

(b) for the words 'section 3(3)(e)' there shall be substituted the words 'section 27(3)(f)';

and that subsection shall continue to have effect with the substitution of the words 'the said Case B' for the words 'section 24(2)(b)' made by paragraph 6 of Schedule 1 to the Agricultural Holdings (Notices to Quit) Act 1977.

(3) In subsection (3) for the words 'Case B and section 3(3)(e)' there shall be substituted the words 'Case B and section 27(3)(f)'.

(4) After subsection (6) there shall be inserted—

'(6A) In assessing the tenant's compensation no account shall be taken of any benefit which might accrue to the tenant by virtue of section 60(2)(b) of the Agricultural Holdings Act 1986 (additional payments by landlord for disturbance); and in this subsection the reference to the said section 60(2)(b) does not include a reference to it as applied by section 12 of the Agriculture (Miscellaneous Provisions) Act 1968.'

54.— (1) Section 56 of that Act shall be amended as follows.

(2) In subsection (3)(d) for the words 'Agricultural Holdings Act 1948' there shall be substituted the words 'Agricultural Holdings Act 1986'.

(3) In subsection (4) for the words 'section 58 of the Agricultural Holdings Act 1948' there shall be substituted the words 'section 72 of the Agricultural Holdings Act 1986' and for the words 'the proviso' there shall be substituted the words 'subsection (4) of that section'.

55.— (1) Section 59 of that Act shall be amended as follows.

(2) In subsection (1)(b)—

   (a) in paragraph (i) for the words 'subsection (1) of section 2 of the Agricultural Holdings (Notices to Quit) Act 1977' there shall be substituted the words 'section 26(1) of the Agricultural Holdings Act 1986' and for the words 'Case B in subsection (3) of that section' there shall be substituted the words 'Case B in Part I of Schedule 3 to that Act', and

   (b) in paragraph (ii) for the words 'section 3(3)(e)' there shall be substituted the words 'section 27(3)(f)';

and that subsection shall continue to have effect with the substitution of the words 'the said Case B' for the words 'section 24(2)(b)' made by paragraph 6 of Schedule 1 to the Agricultural Holdings (Notices to Quit) Act 1977.

(3) In subsection (2)(b) for the words from 'Agricultural Holdings Act 1948' to 'notice to quit' there shall be substituted the words 'Agricultural Holdings Act 1986 relating to compensation to a tenant on the termination of his tenancy'.

(4) In subsection (6) for the words 'section 9 of the Agricultural Holdings (Notices to Quit) Act 1977' there shall be substituted the words 'section 32 of the Agricultural Holdings Act 1986'.

56. In section 87(1) for the words 'Agricultural Holdings Act 1948' there shall be substituted the words 'Agricultural Holdings Act 1986'.

The Rent (Agriculture) Act 1976

57. In section 9(3) and (4)(c) of the Rent (Agriculture) Act 1976 for the words 'Agricultural Holdings Act 1948' there shall be substituted the words 'Agricultural Holdings Act 1986'.

58. In paragraph 2 of Schedule 2 to that Act for the words 'Agricultural Holdings Act 1948' there shall be substituted the words 'Agricultural Holdings Act 1986'.

The Rent Act 1977

59. In section 10 of the Rent Act 1977 for the words 'Agricultural Holdings Act 1948' there shall be substituted the words 'Agricultural Holdings Act 1986'.

60. In section 137(3) and (4)(c) of that Act for the words 'Agricultural Holdings Act 1948' there shall be substituted the words 'Agricultural Holdings Act 1986'.

The Protection from Eviction Act 1977

61. In section 8(1)(d) of the Protection from Eviction Act 1977 for the words 'Agricultural Holdings Act 1948' there shall be substituted the words 'Agricultural Holdings Act 1986'.

The Cycle Tracks Act 1984

62. In section 3(2) of the Cycle Tracks Act 1984 for the words 'section 1(2) of the Agricultural Holdings Act 1948' there shall be substituted the words 'section 1(4) of the Agricultural Holdings Act 1986'.

The Housing Act 1985

63. In paragraph 8 of Schedule 1 to the Housing Act 1985 for the words 'Agricultural Holdings Act 1948' there shall be substituted the words 'Agricultural Holdings Act 1986'.

The Landlord and Tenant Act 1985

64. In section 14(3) of the Landlord and Tenant Act 1985 for the words 'Agricultural Holdings Act 1948' there shall be substituted the words 'Agricultural Holdings Act 1986'.

< ... >

NOTES

Derivation

This Schedule derived in part from the Agricultural Holdings Act 1948, Sch 7, para 2, and the Agriculture (Miscellaneous Provisions) Act 1968, s 10(3), (8).

Initial Commencement

Specified date: 18 June 1986: see s 102(2).

Amendment

This Schedule contains amendments only.

Repealed in part by the Housing and Planning Act 1986, s 39(4), Sch 12, Part II, the Coal Mining Subsidence Act 1991, s 53(2), Sch 8, the Agricultural Holdings (Scotland) Act 1991, s 88, Sch 13, Part I, the Tribunals and Inquiries Act 1992, s 18(2), Sch 4, Part I, the Statute Law (Repeals) Act 1993 and the Agricultural Tenancies Act 1995, s 31(4).

Repealed in part by the Statute Law (Repeals) Act 2004.

Date in force: 22 July 2004: (no specific commencement provision).

See Further

See further, as to the exclusion of this Act in relation to leases or tenancies granted to contractors in respect of the running of any removal centre or part of a removal centre: the Immigration and Asylum Act 1999, s 149(3).

Notes

This Schedule generally contains consequential amendments only; para 44 contains provisions derived from the Agriculture (Miscellaneous Provisions) Act 1968, s 10(8); para 53(4) contains provisions derived from s 10(3), (8) of the 1968 Act.

Paras 8, 35 were repealed by the SL(R) Act 1993, s 1(1), Sch 1, Pt II.

Para 12 was repealed by the Agricultural Tenancies Act 1995, s 31(4).

Para 24 was repealed by the Coal Mining Subsidence Act 1991, s 53(2), Sch 8.

Para 25 was repealed by the Housing and Planning Act 1986, s 39(4), Sch 12, Pt II.

Para 49 was repealed by the Tribunals and Inquiries Act 1992, s 18(2), Sch 4, Pt I.

Agricultural Holdings (Notices to Quit) Act 1977. That Act is repealed by s 101, Sch 15, Pt I.

Agricultural Holdings Act 1984. That Act is repealed by s 101, Sch 15, Pt I.

SCHEDULE 15
REPEALS AND REVOCATIONS

Section 101

PART I: REPEALS

A1.204

Chapter	Short title	Extent of repeal
9 & 10 Geo 6 c 73	The Hill Farming Act 1946	Section 9.
11 & 12 Geo 6 c 63	The Agricultural Holdings Act 1948	The whole Act.
12 & 13 Geo 6 c 37	The Agriculture (Miscellaneous Provisions) Act 1949	Section 10. In the Schedule, Part II.
6 & 7 Eliz 2 c 71	The Agriculture Act 1958	Section 4. In section 9(1), in the definition of 'agricultural holding' the words from 'as respects England' to '1948 and', the definitions of 'contract of tenancy' and 'fixed equipment' and in the definition of 'landlord and tenant' the words from 'as respects England' to '1948 and'. In Schedule 1, in Part I, paragraphs 6, 7, 14 to 18, 20 and 21. In Schedule 4, paragraphs 5, 9 and 11.
1963 c 11	The Agriculture (Miscellaneous Provisions) Act 1963	In section 20, paragraph (b), the words 'and the period within which the arbitrator is to make his award', the words 'the said paragraph 6 or' and paragraph (ii).
1964 c 51	The Universities and College Estates Act 1964	In Schedule 3, in Part I, the entry relating to the Agricultural Holdings Act 1948.

1968 c 34	The Agriculture (Miscellaneous Provisions) Act 1968	Sections 9 and 10.
		In section 15, subsection (2), in subsection (4) the words from the beginning to 'section and', the words 'subsection (2) or' and the words 'as the case may be' and in subsection (5)(a) the words 'or subsection (2)'. In section 17, in subsection (1) the definition of 'the principal Act' and in subsection (2) the words from 'references to the termination' to 'holding and'.
1970 c 40	The Agriculture Act 1970	In Schedule 4, the entry relating to the Agricultural Holdings Act 1948.
1971 c 23	The Courts Act 1971	In Schedule 9, in Part I, the entry relating to the Agricultural Holdings Act 1948.
1972 c 61	The Land Charges Act 1972	In Schedule 2, in paragraph 1(g), the words from 'Section 82' to 'improvements)'.
1972 c 62	The Agriculture (Miscellaneous Provisions) Act 1972	Section 15.
1976 c 55	The Agriculture (Miscellaneous Provisions) Act 1976	Sections 17 to 24.
		In section 27(5), the words 'and Part II'. In Schedule 3, the entries relating to the Agricultural Holdings Act 1948. Schedule 3A.
1977 c 12	The Agricultural Holdings (Notices to Quit) Act 1977	The whole Act.
1984 c 32	The London Regional Transport Act 1984	In Schedule 6, paragraph 13.
1984 c 41	The Agricultural Holdings Act 1984	The whole Act.
1985 c 65	The Insolvency Act 1985	In Schedule 8, paragraphs 9 and 30.
1985 c 68	The Housing Act 1985	Section 231.
1985 c 71	The Housing (Consequential Provisions) Act 1985	In Schedule 2, paragraph 34.

NOTES

Initial Commencement

Specified date: 18 June 1986: see s 102(2).

See Further

See further, as to the exclusion of this Act in relation to leases or tenancies granted to contractors in respect of the running of any removal centre or part of a removal centre: the Immigration and Asylum Act 1999, s 149(3).

PART II: REVOCATIONS

Number	Title	Extent of Revocation
SI 1951/2168	The Agricultural Holdings Act (Variation of Fourth Schedule) Order 1951	The whole order.
SI 1978/447	The Agricultural Holdings Act 1948 (Amendment) Regulations 1978	The whole instrument.
SI 1978/742	The Agricultural Holdings Act 1948 (Variation of Fourth Schedule) Order 1978	The whole order.
SI 1985/1947	The Agricultural Holdings Act 1948 (Variation of Fourth Schedule) Order 1985	The whole order.

NOTES

Initial Commencement

Specified date: 18 June 1986: see s 102(2).

See Further

See further, as to the exclusion of this Act in relation to leases or tenancies granted to contractors in respect of the running of any removal centre or part of a removal centre: the Immigration and Asylum Act 1999, s 149(3).

AGRICULTURE ACT 1986

(1986 C 49)

ARRANGEMENT OF SECTIONS

1289

SCHEDULE 1
Tenants' compensation for milk quota

An Act to make further provision relating to agriculture and agricultural and other food products, horticulture and the countryside; and for connected matters

[25th July 1986]

Compensation to tenants for milk quotas

A1.205

13   Compensation to outgoing tenants for milk quota

Schedule 1 to this Act shall have effect in connection with the payment to certain agricultural tenants on the termination of their tenancies of compensation in respect of milk quota (within the meaning of that Schedule).

NOTES

Initial Commencement

To be appointed: see s 24(2), (3).

Appointment

Appointment: 25 September 1986: see SI 1986/1484, art 2.

Extent

This section does not extend to Scotland: see s 24(6).

See Further

See further, in relation to the disapplication of this section to a farm business tenancy: the Agricultural Tenancies Act 1995, s 16(3).

Notes

For a commentary, see Ch 49 and Ch 50.

Commencement. See s 24(2), (3) (1 Halsbury's Statutes (4th edn, 1989 reissue) 875.

A1.206

15   Rent arbitrations: milk quotas

(1)   Where there is a reference under section 12 of the Agricultural Holdings Act 1986 (arbitration of rent) in respect of land which comprises or is part of a holding in relation to which quota is registered under the Dairy Produce Quotas Regulations 1986 which was transferred to the tenant by virtue of a transaction the cost of which was borne wholly or partly by him, the arbitrator shall (subject to any agreement between the landlord and tenant to the contrary) disregard—

    (a)   in a case where the land comprises the holding, any increase in the rental value of the land which is due to that quota (or, as the case may be, the corresponding part of that quota); or

(b) in a case where the land is part of the holding, any increase in that value which is due to so much of that quota (or part) as would fall to be apportioned to the land under those Regulations on a change of occupation of the land.

(2)   In determining for the purposes of this section whether quota was transferred to a tenant by virtue of a transaction the cost of which was borne wholly or partly by him—

(a) any payment made by the tenant in consideration for the grant or assignment to him of the tenancy or any previous tenancy of any land comprised in the holding, shall be disregarded;

(b) any person who would be treated under paragraph 2, 3 or 4 of Schedule 1 to this Act as having had quota transferred to him or having paid the whole or part of the cost of any transaction for the purposes of a claim under that Schedule shall be so treated for the purposes of this section; and

(c) any person who would be so treated under paragraph 4 of that Schedule if a sub-tenancy to which his tenancy is subject had terminated, shall be so treated for the purposes of this section.

(3)   In this section—

'quota' and 'holding' have the same meanings as in the Dairy Produce Quotas Regulations 1986;

'tenant' and 'tenancy' have the same meanings as in the Agricultural Holdings Act 1986.

(4)   Section 95 of that Act (Crown land) applies to this section as it applies to the provisions of that Act.

NOTES

Initial Commencement

To be appointed: see s 24(2), (3).

Appointment

Appointment: 25 September 1986: see SI 1986/1484, art 2.

Extent

This section does not extend to Scotland: see s 24(6).

Notes

For a commentary, see Ch 50.

Commencement. See s 24(2), (3) (1 Halsbury's Statutes (4th edn, 1989 reissue) 875).

Agricultural Holdings Act 1986. For the meaning of 'tenant' in that Act, see s 96(1). The expression 'tenancy' is not, it seems, defined for the purposes of that Act generally but cf the definition of 'contract of tenancy' in s 1(5) of the Act.

Dairy Produce Quotas Regulations 1986. SI 1986/470. Those regulations were made under the European Communities Act 1972, s 2(2) and have now been revoked, and superseded by various Dairy Produce Quotas Regulations, those currently in force being the Dairy Produce Quotas Regulations 2005, SI 2005/465.

SCHEDULE 1
TENANTS' COMPENSATION FOR MILK QUOTA

Section 13

PART I: RIGHT TO COMPENSATION

Tenants' rights to compensation

A1.207

1   (1)   Subject to the following provisions of this Schedule, where on the termination of the tenancy of any land the tenant has milk quota registered as his in relation to a holding consisting of or including the land, the tenant shall be entitled, on quitting the land, to obtain from his landlord a payment—

(a)   if the tenant had milk quota allocated to him in relation to land comprised in the holding ('allocated quota'), in respect of so much of the relevant quota as consists of allocated quota; and

(b)   if the tenant had milk quota allocated to him as aforesaid or was in occupation of the land as a tenant on 2nd April 1984 (whether or not under the tenancy which is terminating), in respect of so much of the relevant quota as consists of transferred quota transferred to him by virtue of a transaction the cost of which was borne wholly or partly by him.

(2)   In sub-paragraph (1) above—

'the relevant quota' means—
(a)   in a case where the holding mentioned in sub-paragraph (1) above consists only of the land subject to the tenancy, the milk quota registered in relation to the holding; and
(b)   otherwise, such part of that milk quota as falls to be apportioned to that land on the termination of the tenancy;
'transferred quota' means milk quota transferred to the tenant by virtue of the transfer to him of the whole or part of a holding.

(3)   A tenant shall not be entitled to more than one payment under this paragraph in respect of the same land.

Succession on death or retirement of tenant

2   (1)   This paragraph applies where on the termination of the tenancy of any land after 2nd April 1984 a new tenancy of the land or part of the land has been granted to a different tenant ('the new tenant') and that tenancy—

(a)   was obtained by virtue of a direction under section 39 or 53 of the Agricultural Holdings Act 1986 (direction for grant of tenancy to successor on death or retirement of previous tenant);

(b)   was granted (following a direction under section 39 of that Act) in circumstances within section 45(6) of that Act (new tenancy granted by agreement to persons entitled to tenancy under direction); or

(c)   is such a tenancy as is mentioned in section 37(1)(b) or (2) of that Act (tenancy granted by agreement to close relative).

(2)   Where this paragraph applies—

(a)   any milk quota allocated or transferred to the former tenant (or treated as having been allocated or transferred to him) in respect of the land which is subject to the new tenancy shall be treated as if it had instead been allocated or transferred to the new tenant; and

1292

(b)   in a case where milk quota is treated under paragraph (a) above as having
      been transferred to the new tenant, he shall be treated for the purposes of any
      claim in respect of that quota—
      (i)   as if he had paid so much of the cost of the transaction by virtue of
            which the milk quota was transferred as the former tenant bore (or is
            treated as having borne); and
      (ii) in a case where the former tenant was in occupation of the land on 2nd
            April 1984 (or is treated as having been in occupation of the land on that
            date), as if he had been in occupation of it on that date.

(3)   Sub-paragraph (1) above applies in relation to the grant of a new tenancy before
the date on which the Agricultural Holdings Act 1986 comes into force as if the
references in that sub-paragraph to sections 39, 53 and 45(6) of that Act were
references to section 20 of the Agriculture (Miscellaneous Provisions) Act 1976,
paragraph 5 of Schedule 2 to the Agricultural Holdings Act 1984 and section 23(6) of
the said Act of 1976 respectively.

Assignments

3   Where the tenancy of any land has been assigned after 2nd April 1984 (whether by
deed or by operation of law)—
(a)   any milk quota allocated or transferred to the assignor (or treated as having
      been allocated or transferred to him) in respect of the land shall be treated as
      if it had instead been allocated or transferred to the assignee; and
(b)   in a case where milk quota is treated under paragraph (a) above as having
      been transferred to the assignee, he shall be treated for the purposes of any
      claim in respect of that quota—
      (i)   as if he had paid so much of the cost of the transaction by virtue of
            which the milk quota was transferred as the assignor bore (or is treated
            as having borne); and
      (ii) in a case where the assignor was in occupation of the land on 2nd April
            1984 (or is treated as having been in occupation of the land on that
            date), as if he had been in occupation of it on that date;
and accordingly the assignor shall not be entitled to a payment under paragraph 1
above in respect of that land.

Sub-tenancies

4   Where the sub-tenancy of any land terminates after 2nd April 1984 then, for the
purposes of determining the sub-landlord's entitlement under paragraph 1 above—

(a)   any milk quota allocated or transferred to the sub-tenant (or treated as having
      been allocated or transferred to him) in respect of the land shall be treated as
      if it had instead been allocated or transferred to the sub-landlord;
(b)   in a case where milk quota is treated under paragraph (a) above as having
      been transferred to the sub-landlord, he shall be treated for the purposes of
      any claim in respect of that quota—
      (i)   as if he had paid so much of the cost of the transaction by virtue of
            which the milk quota was transferred as the sub-tenant bore (or is
            treated as having borne); and
      (ii) in a case where the sub-tenant was in occupation of the land on 2nd
            April 1984 (or is treated as having been in occupation of the land on that
            date), as if he had been in occupation of it on that date;
(c)   if the sub-landlord does not occupy the land after the sub-tenancy has ended
      and the sub-tenant has quitted the land, the sub-landlord shall be taken to
      have quitted the land when the sub-tenant quitted it.

NOTES

Initial Commencement

To be appointed: see s 24(2), (3).

Appointment

Appointment: 25 September 1986: see SI 1986/1484, art 2.

Extent

This Schedule does not extend to Scotland: see s 24(6).

See Further

See further, in relation to the disapplication of this Schedule to a farm business tenancy: the Agricultural Tenancies Act 1995, s 16(3).

Notes

For a commentary, see Ch 50, para 50.17 ff.

Commencement. See s 24(2), (3) (1 Halsbury's Statutes (4th edn, 1989 reissue) 875).

Shall be entitled ... to obtain ... a payment, etc. As to the calculation of the amount of the payment to be made under para 1 above, see Pt II of this Schedule.

Application. This Schedule does not apply in relation to a farm business tenancy; see the Agricultural Tenancies Act 1995, s 16(3) (for meaning of 'farm business tenancy', see s 1 of that Act.)

Supplemental provisions. For supplemental provisions relating to compensation under this Part of this Schedule, see Pt III of this Schedule.

Definitions. For "holding', 'landlord', 'sub-landlord', 'milk quota', 'registered', 'tenancy', 'tenant', 'sub-tenant' and 'termination', see para 18(1) in Pt III of this Schedule (and see also as to 'termination', para 13 and as to 'landlord' and 'tenant', para 18(3)). Note as to 'allocated quota', para 1(1)(a) above; as to 'the relevant quota' and 'transferred quota', para 1(2) above; and as to 'the new tenant', para 2(1) above.

Agricultural Holdings Act 1986. That Act came into force on 18 June 1986 by virtue of s 102(2) thereof.

The Agricultural Holdings Act 1986 will not apply to new tenancies beginning on or after 1 September 1995, except in special cases, by virtue of the Agricultural Tenancies Act 1995, s 4.

Agriculture (Miscellaneous Provisions) Act 1976, ss 20, 23(6). Those sections were repealed by the Agricultural Holdings Act 1986, s 101(1), Sch 15, Pt I.

Agricultural Holdings Act 1984, Sch 2, para 5. That Act was repealed by the Agricultural Holdings Act 1986, s 101(1), Sch 15, Pt I.

PART II: AMOUNT OF COMPENSATION PAYABLE

Calculation of payment

5   (1)   The amount of the payment to which the tenant of any land is entitled under paragraph 1 above on the termination of his tenancy shall be determined in accordance with the following provisions of this paragraph.

(2)   The amount of the payment to which the tenant is entitled under paragraph 1 above in respect of allocated quota shall be an amount equal—

    (a)   in a case where the allocated quota exceeds the standard quota for the land, to the value of the sum of—

        (i)   the tenant's fraction of the standard quota, and

        (ii)   the amount of the excess;

(b) in a case where the allocated quota is equal to the standard quota, to the value of the tenant's fraction of the allocated quota; and

(c) in a case where the allocated quota is less than the standard quota, to the value of such proportion of the tenant's fraction of the allocated quota as the allocated quota bears to the standard quota.

(3) The amount of the payment the tenant is entitled to under paragraph 1 above in respect of transferred quota shall be an amount equal—

(a) in a case where the tenant bore the whole of the cost of the transaction by virtue of which the transferred quota was transferred to him, to the value of the transferred quota; and

(b) in a case where the tenant bore only part of that cost, to the value of the corresponding part of the transferred quota.

'Standard quota'

6 (1) Subject to the following provisions of this paragraph the standard quota for any land for the purposes of this Schedule shall be calculated by multiplying the relevant number of hectares by the prescribed quota per hectare; and for the purposes of this paragraph—

(a) 'the relevant number of hectares' means the average number of hectares of the land in question used during the relevant period for the feeding of dairy cows kept on the land or, if different, the average number of hectares of the land which could reasonably be expected to have been so used (having regard to the number of grazing animals other than dairy cows kept on the land during that period); and

(b) 'the prescribed quota per hectare' means such number of litres as the Minister may from time to time by order prescribe for the purposes of this sub-paragraph.

(2) Where by virtue of the quality of the land in question or climatic conditions in the area the amount of milk which could reasonably be expected to have been produced from one hectare of the land during the relevant period ('the reasonable amount') is greater or less than the prescribed average yield per hectare, then sub-paragraph (1) above shall not apply and the standard quota shall be calculated by multiplying the relevant number of hectares by such proportion of the prescribed quota per hectare as the reasonable amount bears to the prescribed average yield per hectare; and the Minister shall by order prescribe the amount of milk to be taken as the average yield per hectare for the purposes of this sub-paragraph.

(3) Where the relevant quota of the land includes milk quota allocated in pursuance of an award of quota made by the Dairy Produce Quota Tribunal for England and Wales[, or by the Secretary of State or the National Assembly for Wales following the appeals procedure,] which has not been allocated in full, the standard quota for the land shall be reduced by the amount by which the milk quota allocated in pursuance of the award falls short of the amount awarded (or, in a case where only part of the milk quota allocated in pursuance of the award is included in the relevant quota, by the corresponding proportion of that shortfall).

[(3A) In sub-paragraph (3) above 'the appeals procedure' means—

(a) in England, the appeals procedure established under the Common Agricultural Policy Non-IACS Support Schemes (Appeals) (England) Regulations 2004 (SI 2004/590); and

(b) in Wales, the appeals procedure established under the Common Agricultural Policy Non-IACS Support Schemes (Appeals) (Wales) Regulations 2004 (SI 2004/685 (W 73)).]

(4) In sub-paragraph (3) above the references to milk quota allocated in pursuance of an award of quota include references to quota allocated by virtue of the amount awarded not originally having been allocated in full.

(5) In this paragraph—

(a) references to land used for the feeding of dairy cows kept on the land do not include land used for growing cereal crops for feeding to dairy cows in the form of loose grain; and

(b) references to dairy cows are to cows kept for milk production (other than uncalved heifers).

(6) An order under this paragraph may make different provision for different cases.

(7) The power to make an order under this paragraph shall be exercisable by statutory instrument and any instrument containing such an order shall be subject to annulment in pursuance of a resolution of either House of Parliament.

'Tenant's fraction'

7 (1) For the purposes of this Schedule 'the tenant's fraction' means the fraction of which—

(a) the numerator is the annual rental value at the end of the relevant period of the tenant's dairy improvements and fixed equipment; and

(b) the denominator is the sum of that value and such part of the rent payable by the tenant in respect of the relevant period as is attributable to the land used in that period for the feeding, accommodation or milking of dairy cows kept on the land.

(2) For the purposes of sub-paragraph (1)(a) above the rental value of the tenant's dairy improvements and fixed equipment shall be taken to be the amount which would fall to be disregarded under paragraph 2(1) of Schedule 2 to the Agricultural Holdings Act 1986 on a reference made in respect of the land in question under section 12 of that Act (arbitration of rent), so far as that amount is attributable to tenant's improvements to, or tenant's fixed equipment on, land used for the feeding, accommodation or milking of dairy cows kept on the land in question.

(3) Where—

(a) the relevant period is less than or greater than 12 months; or

(b) rent was only payable by the tenant in respect of part of the relevant period,

the average rent payable in respect of one month in the relevant period or, as the case may be, in that part shall be determined and the rent referred to in sub-paragraph (1)(b) above shall be taken to be the corresponding annual amount.

(4) For the purposes of sub-paragraph (2) above 'tenant's improvements' and 'tenant's fixed equipment' have the same meanings as in paragraph 2 of Schedule 2 to the 1986 Act, except that—

(a) any allowance made or benefit given by the landlord after the end of the relevant period in consideration of the execution of improvements wholly or partly at the expense of the tenant shall be disregarded for the purposes of sub-paragraph (2)(a) of that paragraph;

(b) any compensation received by the tenant after the end of the relevant period in respect of any improvement or fixed equipment shall be disregarded for the purposes of sub-paragraph (3) of that paragraph; and

(c) where paragraph 2 above applies in respect of any land, improvements or equipment which would be regarded as tenant's improvements or equipment on the termination of the former tenant's tenancy (if he were entitled to a payment under this Schedule in respect of that land) shall be regarded as the new tenant's improvements or equipment.

'Relevant period'

8   In this Schedule 'the relevant period' means—

(a)   the period in relation to which the allocated quota was determined; or

(b)   where it was determined in relation to more than one period, the period in relation to which the majority was determined or, if equal amounts were determined in relation to different periods, the later of those periods.

Valuation of milk quota

9   The value of milk quota to be taken into account for the purposes of paragraph 5 above is the value of the milk quota at the time of the termination of the tenancy in question and in determining that value at that time there shall be taken into account such evidence as is available, including evidence as to the sums being paid for interests in land—

(a)   in cases where milk quota is registered in relation to the land; and

(b)   in cases where no milk quota is so registered.

NOTES

Initial Commencement

To be appointed: see s 24(2), (3).

Appointment

Appointment: 25 September 1986: see SI 1986/1484, art 2.

Extent

This Schedule does not extend to Scotland: see s 24(6).

Amendment

Para 6: in sub-para (3) words ', or by the Secretary of State or the National Assembly for Wales following the appeals procedure,' in square brackets inserted by SI 2007/477, reg 4(1), (2)(a).

Date in force: 6 April 2007: see SI 2007/477, reg 1.

Para 6: sub-para (3A) inserted by SI 2007/477, reg 4(1), (2)(b).

Date in force: 6 April 2007: see SI 2007/477, reg 1.

See Further

See further, in relation to the disapplication of this Schedule to a farm business tenancy: the Agricultural Tenancies Act 1995, s 16(3).

Transfer of Functions

Functions of the Minister, so far as exercisable in relation to Wales, transferred to the National Assembly for Wales, by the National Assembly for Wales (Transfer of Functions) Order 1999, SI 1999/672, art 2, Sch 1.

Subordinate Legislation

Milk Quota (Calculation of Standard Quota) Order 1986, SI 1986/1530 (made under para 6).

Milk Quota (Calculation of Standard Quota) (Amendment) Order 1992, SI 1992/1225 (made under para 6).

Notes

For a commentary, see Ch 50.

Commencement. See s 24(2), (3) and the note 'Orders under this section' thereto (1 Halsbury's Statutes (4th edn, 1989 reissue) 875).

Para 5: Value of the sum of, etc. As to the valuation of milk quota for the purposes of para 5, see para 9 above.

Para 6: Standard quota. As to the determination of the standard quota before the end of a tenancy, see para 10 in Pt III of this Schedule.

Dairy Produce Quota Tribunal for England and Wales. This body is constituted under the Dairy Produce Quotas Regulations 1986, SI 1986/470, reg 37, Sch 18, Pt I.

Statutory instrument; subject to annulment. For provisions as to statutory instruments generally, see the Statutory Instruments Act 1946, and as to statutory instruments which are subject to annulment in pursuance of a resolution of either House of Parliament, see ss 5(1), 7(1) of that Act.

Para 7: Tenant's fraction. As to the determination of the tenant's fraction before the end of a tenancy, see para 10 in Pt III of this Schedule.

Months. This means calendar months; see the Interpretation Act 1978, s 5, Sch 1.

Application; Agricultural Holdings Act 1986. See the notes to Pt I of this Schedule.

Supplemental provisions. See Pt III of this Schedule.

Definitions. For 'allocated quota', see para 1(1)(a) in Pt I of this Schedule; for 'milk quota', 'the Minister', 'registered', 'tenancy', 'tenant', 'termination' and 'transferred quota', see para 18(1) in Pt III of this Schedule (and see also as to 'termination', para 13 and as to 'tenant', para 18(3)). Note as to 'standard quota', para 6 above; as to 'the relevant number of hectares' and 'the prescribed quota per hectare', para 6(1) above; as to 'the reasonable amount', para 6(2) above; as to 'land used for the feeding of dairy cows ...' and 'dairy cows', para 6(5) above; as to 'tenant's fraction', para 7 above; as to 'tenant's improvements' and 'tenant's fixed equipment', para 7(4) above; and as to 'relevant period', para 8 above.

Orders under para 6. The Milk Quota (Calculation of Standard Quota) Order 1986, SI 1986/1530, as amended by SI 1987/626, SI 1988/653, SI 1990/48, SI 1991/1994, SI 1992/1225.

PART III: SUPPLEMENTAL PROVISIONS

Determination of standard quota and tenant's fraction before end of tenancy

10 (1) Where, on the termination of a tenancy of any land, the tenant may be entitled to a payment under paragraph 1 above, the landlord or tenant may at any time before the termination of the tenancy by notice in writing served on the other demand that the determination of the standard quota for the land or the tenant's fraction shall be referred to arbitration.

(2) On a reference under this paragraph the arbitrator shall determine the standard quota for the land or, as the case may be, the tenant's fraction (so far as determinable at the date of the reference).

(3) Section 84 of the Agricultural Holdings Act 1986 (arbitrations) shall apply as if the matters mentioned in this paragraph were required by that Act to be determined by arbitration under that Act.

Settlement of tenant's claim on termination of tenancy

11 (1) Subject to the provisions of this paragraph, any claim arising under paragraph 1 above shall be determined by arbitration under the Agricultural Holdings Act 1986 and no such claim shall be enforceable unless before the expiry of the period of two months from the termination of the tenancy the tenant serves notice in writing on his landlord of his intention to make the claim.

(2) The landlord and tenant may within the period of eight months from the termination of the tenancy by agreement in writing settle the claim but where the claim has not been settled during that period it shall be determined by arbitration under the Agricultural Holdings Act 1986.

(3) In any case where on the termination of the tenancy in question a new tenancy of the land or part of the land may be granted to a different tenant by virtue of a direction under section 39 of the Agricultural Holdings Act 1986 then, as respects any claim in respect of that land or part, references in sub-paragraphs (1) and (2) above to the termination of the tenancy shall be construed as references to the following time, namely—

(a) in a case where no application is made under that section within the period within which such an application may be made, the expiry of that period;

(b) in a case where every such application made within that period is withdrawn, the expiry of that period or the time when the last outstanding application is withdrawn (whichever is the later);

(c) in a case where the Agricultural Land Tribunal refuse every such application for a direction under that section, the time when the last outstanding application is refused; and

(d) in a case where the Tribunal give such a direction, the relevant time for the purposes of section 46 of that Act;

and no notice may be served under sub-paragraph (1) above before that time.

(4) Where a tenant lawfully remains in occupation of part of the land subject to the tenancy after the termination of the tenancy or, in a case where sub-paragraph (3) above applies, after the time substituted for the termination of the tenancy by virtue of that sub-paragraph, the references in sub-paragraphs (1) and (2) above to the termination of the tenancy shall be construed as references to the termination of the occupation.

(5) Section 84 of the Agricultural Holdings Act 1986 (arbitrations) shall apply as if the requirements of this paragraph were requirements of that Act ...

(6) Where—

(a) before the termination of the tenancy of any land the landlord and tenant have agreed in writing the amount of the standard quota for the land or the tenant's fraction or the value of milk quota which is to be used for the purpose of calculating the payment to which the tenant will be entitled under this Schedule on the termination of the tenancy; or

(b) the standard quota or the tenant's fraction has been determined by arbitration in pursuance of paragraph 10 above,

the arbitrator determining the claim under this paragraph shall, subject to sub-paragraph (7) below, award payment in accordance with that agreement or determination.

(7) Where it appears to the arbitrator that any circumstances relevant to the agreement or determination mentioned in sub-paragraph (6) above were materially different at the time of the termination of the tenancy from those at the time the agreement or determination was made, he shall disregard so much of the agreement or determination as appears to him to be affected by the change in circumstances.

Enforcement

12 Section 85 of the Agricultural Holdings Act 1986 (enforcement) and section 86(1), (3) and (4) of that Act (power of landlord to obtain charge on holding) shall apply to any sum which becomes due to a tenant by virtue of this Schedule as they apply to the sums mentioned in those sections.

Termination of tenancy of part of tenanted land

13   References in this Schedule to the termination of a tenancy of land include references to the resumption of possession of part of the land subject to the tenancy—

    (a)   by the landlord by virtue of section 31 or 43(2) of the Agricultural Holdings Act 1986 (notice to quit part);

    (b)   by the landlord in pursuance of a provision in the contract of tenancy; or

    (c)   by a person entitled to a severed part of the reversionary estate in the land by virtue of a notice to quit that part given to the tenant by virtue of section 140 of the Law of Property Act 1925;

and in the case mentioned in paragraph (c) above this Schedule shall apply as if the person resuming possession were the landlord of the land of which he resumes possession.

Severing of reversionary estate

14   (1)   Where the reversionary estate in the land is for the time being vested in more than one person in several parts, the tenant shall be entitled, on quitting all the land, to require that any amount payable to him under this Schedule shall be determined as if the reversionary estate were not so severed.

(2)   Where sub-paragraph (1) above applies, the arbitrator shall, where necessary, apportion the amount awarded between the persons who for the purposes of this Schedule together constitute the landlord of the land, and any additional costs of the award caused by the apportionment shall be paid by those persons in such proportions as the arbitrator may determine.

Powers of limited owners

15   Notwithstanding that a landlord of any land is not the owner in fee simple of the land or, in a case where his interest is an interest in a leasehold, that he is not absolutely entitled to the leasehold, he may for the purposes of this Schedule do anything which he might do if he were such an owner or, as the case may be, were so entitled.

Notices

16   (1)   Any notice under this Schedule shall be duly served on the person on whom it is to be served if it is delivered to him, or left at his proper address, or sent to him by post in a registered letter or by the recorded delivery service.

(2)   Any such notice shall be duly served on an incorporated company or body if it is served on the secretary or clerk of the company or body.

(3)   Any such notice to be served on a landlord or tenant of any land shall, where an agent or servant is responsible for the control of the management or farming, as the case may be, of the land, be duly served if served on that agent or servant.

(4)   For the purposes of this paragraph and of section 7 of the Interpretation Act 1978 (service by post), the proper address of any person on whom any such notice is to be served shall, in the case of the secretary or clerk of an incorporated company or body, be that of the registered or principal office of the company or body, and in any other case be the last known address of the person in question.

(5)   Unless or until the tenant of any land has received—

(a) notice that the person who before that time was entitled to receive the rents and profits of the land ('the original landlord') has ceased to be so entitled; and

(b) notice of the name and address of the person who has become entitled to receive the rents and profits,

any notice served on the original landlord by the tenant shall be deemed for the purposes of this Schedule to have been served on the landlord of the land.

Crown land

17 (1) The provisions of this Schedule shall apply to land which belongs to Her Majesty in right of the Crown or to the Duchy of Lancaster, the Duchy of Cornwall or a Government department or land which is held in trust for Her Majesty for the purposes of a Government department, subject in each case to such modifications as the Minister may by regulations prescribe.

(2) For the purposes of this Schedule—

(a) as respects land belonging to Her Majesty in right of the Crown, the Crown Estate Commissioners or the proper officer or body having charge of the land for the time being, or, if there is no such officer or body, such person as Her Majesty may appoint in writing under the Royal Sign Manual, shall represent Her Majesty and shall be deemed to be the landlord,

(b) as respects land belonging to Her Majesty in right of the Duchy of Lancaster, the Chancellor of the Duchy shall represent Her Majesty and shall be deemed to be the landlord;

(c) as respects land belonging to the Duchy of Cornwall, such person as the Duke of Cornwall or the possessor for the time being of the Duchy of Cornwall appoints shall represent the Duchy and shall be deemed to be the landlord and may do any act or thing which a landlord is authorised or required to do under this Act.

(3) Any sum payable under this Schedule by the Duke of Cornwall (or any other possessor for the time being of the Duchy of Cornwall) may be raised and paid as if it were an expense incurred in permanently improving the possessions of the Duchy as mentioned in section 8 of the Duchy of Cornwall Management Act 1863.

(4) Any sum payable under this Schedule by the Chancellor of the Duchy of Lancaster may—

(a) be raised and paid as if it were an expense incurred in the improvement of land belonging to Her Majesty in right of the Duchy within section 25 of the Duchy of Lancaster Act 1817; or

(b) be paid out of the annual revenues of the Duchy.

(5) The power to make regulations under this paragraph shall be exercisable by statutory instrument and any statutory instrument containing such regulations shall be subject to annulment in pursuance of a resolution of either House of Parliament.

Interpretation

18 (1) In this Schedule—

'allocated quota' has the meaning given in paragraph 1(1) above;
'holding' has the same meaning as in the 1986 Regulations;
'landlord' means any person for the time being entitled to receive the rents and profits of any land and 'sub-landlord' shall be construed accordingly;
'milk quota' means—

(a) in the case of a tenant registered in the direct sales register maintained under the 1986 Regulations, a direct sales quota (within the meaning of the 1986 Regulations); and

(b) in the case of a tenant registered in the wholesale register maintained under those Regulations, a wholesale quota (within the meaning of those Regulations);

'the Minister' means—

(a) in the case of land in England, the [Secretary of State]; and

(b) in the case of land in Wales, the Secretary of State;

'registered', in relation to milk quota, means—

(a) in the case of direct sales quota (within the meaning of the 1986 Regulations) registered in the direct sales register maintained under those Regulations; and

(b) in the case of a wholesale quota (within the meaning of those Regulations) registered in a wholesale register maintained under those Regulations;

'relevant quota' has the meaning given in paragraph 1(2) above;

'standard quota' has the meaning given in paragraph 6 above;

'the 1986 Regulations' means the Dairy Produce Quotas Regulations 1986;

'tenancy' means a tenancy from year to year (including any arrangement which would have effect as if it were such a tenancy by virtue of section 2 of the Agricultural Holdings Act 1986 if it had not been approved by the Minister) or a tenancy to which section 3 of that Act applies (or would apply apart from section 5 of that Act); and 'tenant' and 'sub-tenant' shall be construed accordingly;

'tenant's fraction' has the meaning given in paragraph 7 above;

'termination', in relation to a tenancy, means the cesser of the letting of the land in question or the agreement for letting the land, by reason of effluxion of time or from any other cause;

'transferred quota' has the meaning given in paragraph 1(2) above.

(2) In this Schedule references to land used for the feeding of dairy cows kept on the land and to dairy cows have the same meaning as in paragraph 6 above.

(3) The designations of landlord and tenant shall continue to apply to the parties until the conclusion of any proceedings taken under or in pursuance of this Schedule.

NOTES

Initial Commencement

To be appointed: see s 24(2), (3).

Appointment

Appointment: 25 September 1986: see SI 1986/1484, art 2.

Extent

This Schedule does not extend to Scotland: see s 24(6).

Amendment

Para 11: in sub-para (5) words omitted repealed by SI 2006/2805, art 18, Sch 2.

Date in force: 19 October 2006: see SI 2006/2805, art 1(1)(b).

Para 18: in sub-para (1) in definition 'the Minister' in para (a) words 'Secretary of State' in square brackets substituted by SI 2002/794, art 5(1), Sch 1, para 30.

Date in force: 27 March 2002: see SI 2002/794, art 1(2).

See Further

See further, in relation to the disapplication of this Schedule to a farm business tenancy: the Agricultural Tenancies Act 1995, s 16(3).

Transfer of Functions

Functions of the Minister, so far as exercisable in relation to Wales, transferred to the National Assembly for Wales, by the National Assembly for Wales (Transfer of Functions) Order 1999, SI 1999/672, art 2, Sch 1.

Notes

For a commentary, see Ch 50.

Commencement. See s 24(2), (3) and the note 'Orders under this section' thereto (1 Halsbury's Statutes (4th edn, 1989 reissue) 875).

Para 10: Notice. As to the service of notices, see para 16 above.

Writing. Unless the contrary intention appears this includes other modes of representing or reproducing words in a visible form; see the Interpretation Act 1978, s 5, Sch 1.

Para 11: Months. See the note to Pt II of this Schedule.

Agricultural Land Tribunal. As to the establishment, constitution and procedure of such tribunals, see the Agriculture Act 1947, s 73, Sch 9.

Para 16: Registered or principal office. As to the registered office of a company, see the Companies Act 1985, s 287 as substituted by the Companies Act 1989, ss 136 and 213(2). The 'principal office' is the place where the business of the body corporate is managed and controlled as a whole; see *Garton v Great Western Rly Co* (1858) EB & E 837; *Palmer v Caledonian Rly Co* [1892] 1 QB 823; and *Clokey v London and North-Western Rly Co* [1905] 2 IR 251.

Last known address. Though as a general rule an address which the person concerned is known to have left is not a proper address for service (*White v Weston* [1968] 2 QB 647, [1968] 2 All ER 842, CA), the position is otherwise where the use of the last known address is expressly authorised (*Re Follick, ex p Trustee* (1907) 97 LT 645). However, service at the last known address in England or Wales is not good if a later address abroad is known (*R v Farmer* [1892] 1 QB 637, [1891–4] All ER Rep 921, CA). For other relevant cases, see *Hanrott's Trustees v Evans* (1887) 4 TLR 128; *R v Webb* [1896] 1 QB 487; *Berry v Farrow* [1914] 1 KB 632; *Stylo Shoes Ltd v Prices Tailors Ltd* [1960] Ch 396, [1959] 3 All ER 901; and *McGlynn v Stewart* 1974 SLT 230; *Arundel Corpn v Khokher* [2003] EWCA Civ 1784, [2003] PLSCS 23.

Para 17: Crown Estate Commissioners. Ie the Commissioners referred to in the Crown Estate Act 1961, s 1; see the Interpretation Act 1978, s 5, Sch 1.

Statutory instrument; subject to annulment. For provisions as to statutory instruments generally, see the Statutory Instruments Act 1946, and as to statutory instruments which are subject to annulment in pursuance of a resolution of either House of Parliament, see ss 5(1), 7(1) of that Act.

Para 18: England; Wales. For meanings, see the Interpretation Act 1978, s 5, Sch 1.

Secretary of State. Ie one of Her Majesty's Principal Secretaries of State; see the Interpretation Act 1978, s 5, Sch 1. In relation to land in Wales the functions of the Minister were transferred to the National Assembly of Wales by the National Assembly of Wales (Transfer of Functions) Order 1999, SI 1999/672, art 2, Sch 1.

Application; Agricultural Holdings Act 1986. See the notes to Pt I of this Schedule.

Definitions. For 'standard quota', see para 6 in Pt II of this Schedule; for 'tenant's fraction' see para 7 in that Part. Note as to 'termination of a tenancy', para 13 above; as to 'proper address', para 16(4) above; and as to 'the original landlord', para 16(5)(a) above; and note also the definitions, etc, in para 18 above.

Dairy Produce Quotas Regulations 1986. SI 1986/470. Those regulations were made under the European Communities Act 1972, s 2(2); revoked by SI 1991/2232, reg 36.

Regulations under para 17. At the time of going to press no regulations had been made under para 17(1) above.

AGRICULTURAL HOLDINGS (AMENDMENT) ACT 1990

1990 CHAPTER 15

ARRANGEMENT OF SECTIONS

An Act to amend Case B in Part I of Schedule 3 to the Agricultural Holdings Act 1986; and for connected purposes

[29th June 1990]

A1.208

1   Agricultural Holdings Act 1986 (Amendment)

...

NOTES

Initial Commencement

Specified date: 29 July 1990: see s 3(2).

Extent

This Act does not extend to Scotland: see s 3(3).

Amendment

This section amends the Agricultural Holdings Act 1986, Sch 3.

A1.209

2   Savings

(1) Nothing in this Act shall apply in relation to—

   (a)   a notice to quit an agricultural holding or part of an agricultural holding given before the commencement of this Act, or

   (b)   any application, arbitration or other proceedings which relate to, or arise out of, such a notice.

NOTES

Initial Commencement

Specified date: 29 July 1990: see s 3(2).

Extent

This Act does not extend to Scotland: see s 3(3).

A1.210

3   Citation, commencement and extent

(1)   This Act may be cited as the Agricultural Holdings (Amendment) Act 1990.

(2)   This Act shall come into force at the end of the period of one month beginning with the day on which it is passed.

(3)   This Act extends to England and Wales only.

NOTES

Initial Commencement

Specified date: 29 July 1990: see sub-s (2) above.

Extent

This Act does not extend to Scotland: see sub-s (3) above.

AGRICULTURAL TENANCIES ACT 1995

(1995 C 8)

ARRANGEMENT OF SECTIONS

PART I: GENERAL PROVISIONS

An Act to make further provision with respect to tenancies which include agricultural land.

[9th May 1995]

Northern Ireland. This Act applies to the extent specified by s 41(3), (4).

PART I: GENERAL PROVISIONS

Farm business tenancies

A1.211

1 Meaning of 'farm business tenancy'

(1) A tenancy is a 'farm business tenancy' for the purposes of this Act if—

   (a) it meets the business conditions together with either the agriculture condition or the notice conditions, and

   (b) it is not a tenancy which, by virtue of section 2 of this Act, cannot be a farm business tenancy.

(2) The business conditions are—

   (a) that all or part of the land comprised in the tenancy is farmed for the purposes of a trade or business, and

   (b) that, since the beginning of the tenancy, all or part of the land so comprised has been so farmed.

(3) The agriculture condition is that, having regard to—

   (a) the terms of the tenancy,

   (b) the use of the land comprised in the tenancy,

   (c) the nature of any commercial activities carried on on that land, and

   (d) any other relevant circumstances,

the character of the tenancy is primarily or wholly agricultural.

(4) The notice conditions are—

   (a) that, on or before the relevant day, the landlord and the tenant each gave the other a written notice—

      (i) identifying (by name or otherwise) the land to be comprised in the tenancy or proposed tenancy, and

      (ii) containing a statement to the effect that the person giving the notice intends that the tenancy or proposed tenancy is to be, and remain, a farm business tenancy, and

   (b) that, at the beginning of the tenancy, having regard to the terms of the tenancy and any other relevant circumstances, the character of the tenancy was primarily or wholly agricultural.

(5) In subsection (4) above 'the relevant day' means whichever is the earlier of the following—

   (a) the day on which the parties enter into any instrument creating the tenancy, other than an agreement to enter into a tenancy on a future date, or

   (b) the beginning of the tenancy.

(6) The written notice referred to in subsection (4) above must not be included in any instrument creating the tenancy.

(7) If in any proceedings—

   (a) any question arises as to whether a tenancy was a farm business tenancy at any time, and

   (b) it is proved that all or part of the land comprised in the tenancy was farmed for the purposes of a trade or business at that time,

it shall be presumed, unless the contrary is proved, that all or part of the land so comprised has been so farmed since the beginning of the tenancy.

(8)   Any use of land in breach of the terms of the tenancy, any commercial activities carried on in breach of those terms, and any cessation of such activities in breach of those terms, shall be disregarded in determining whether at any time the tenancy meets the business conditions or the agriculture condition, unless the landlord or his predecessor in title has consented to the breach or the landlord has acquiesced in the breach.

NOTES

Initial Commencement

Specified date: 1 September 1995: see s 41(2).

Extent

This section does not extend to Scotland.

Notes

For a commentary, see para 3.1 ff.

Sub-s (1): Farm business tenancy. This entire Act is devoted to farm business tenancies, but particular attention is drawn to the following provisions; ss 5–7 (termination of farm business tenancies); s 8 (tenant's right to remove fixtures and fittings); Pt II (ss 9–14) (rent review under farm business tenancy); Pt III (ss 15–27) (compensation on termination of farm business tenancies).

A farm business tenancy is a 'statutorily protected tenancy' for the purposes of the Protection from Eviction Act 1977; see s 8(1) of that Act, as amended by s 40, Schedule, para 29(b).

A tenant under a farm business tenancy is a protected tenant for the purposes of the Coal Mining Subsidence Act 1991, Sch 3, (which provides for the protected tenant to be treated, in certain circumstances, as a person liable to make good subsidence damage caused by the withdrawal of support from land in connection with lawful coal-mining operations); see s 21(3) of, Sch 3, para 1(2) to, that Act, as amended by s 40, Schedule, paras 36, 37.

For provision for a situation in which opencast planning permission has been granted subject to a restoration condition and, immediately before that permission is granted, any of the land comprised therein consists of the holding or part of the holding held under a farm business tenancy, see the Opencast Coal Act 1958, s 14(1), as inserted by s 40, Schedule, para 13.

For provision for the payment by an acquiring authority of a reasonable allowance towards removal expenses and loss sustained as a result of the compulsory acquisition or sale by agreement to an authority possessing compulsory purchase powers of land used for the purposes of agriculture (within the meaning of s 38(1)) and is so used by way of a trade or business, or is not so used but is comprised in a farm business tenancy and used for the purposes of a trade or business, see the Agriculture (Miscellaneous Provisions) Act 1963, s 22, as amended (in the case of sub-ss (1), (6)(c) thereof) by s 40, Schedule, para 21. Note that no sum is payable under the Agriculture (Miscellaneous Provisions) Act 1968, s 12(1) (additional payments in consequence of compulsory acquisition, etc of agricultural holdings), in respect of land comprised in a farm business tenancy; see s 12(1A) of that Act, as inserted by s 40, Schedule, para 23.

The following statutory provisions do not apply, or are restricted in their application, in relation to farm business tenancies: the Landlord and Tenant Act 1927, s 19 (provisions as to covenants not to assign, etc, without licence or consent), as amended (in the case of sub-s (4) thereof) by s 40, Schedule, para 6; the Leasehold Property (Repairs) Act 1938 (which controls the enforcement of repairing obligations in most residential and commercial leases), (see s 7(1) of that Act, as amended by s 40, Schedule, para 8, and see also the Landlord and Tenant Act 1954, s 51(1), as amended by s 40, Schedule, para 11); the Reserve and Auxiliary Forces (Protection of Civil Interests) Act 1951, Pt III (protection against insecurity of tenure of business and professional premises), (see s 27 of that Act, as amended by s 40, Schedule, para 9); the Landlord and Tenant Act 1954, Pt II (security of tenure for business, professional and other tenants), (see s 43(1) of that Act, as amended by s 40, Schedule, para 10(b)); the Leasehold Reform Act 1967, Pt I (enfranchisement and extension of long leaseholds), (see s 1(3) of that Act, as amended by s 40, Schedule, para 22); the Rent (Agriculture) Act 1976 (which makes provision as to security of tenure, rents, etc), (see Sch 2, para 2 to that Act, as amended by s 40, Schedule, para 26 (and note also s 9(3), (4) of the 1976 Act, as amended by s 40, Schedule, para 25)); the Rent Act 1977 (protected tenancies), (see s 10(1)(b) of that Act, as substituted by s 40, Schedule, para 27 (and note also s 137(3), (4) of that Act, as amended by s 40, Schedule, para 28)); the Housing Act 1985 (secure tenancies), (see Sch 1, para 8 of that Act, as substituted by s 40, Schedule, para 30); the Landlord and Tenant Act 1985, s 11 (repairing obligations in short leases), (see s 14(3) of that Act, as amended by s 40, Schedule, para 31); the Housing Act 1988 (assured tenancies), (see Sch 1, Pt I, para 7(2), (3) to that Act, as substituted by s 40, Schedule, para 34 and the Commonhold and Leasehold Reform Act 2002 Pt 2 (requirement to notify long leaseholders that rent is due) see s 166(8) of that Act (and note also ss 167, 169, 171 and Sch 2 of that Act).

Sub-s (2): Trade or business. Although there is some authority for saying that the expressions 'trade' and 'business' are synonymous (see, in particular, *Grainger & Son v Gough* [1896] AC 325 at 343 per Lord Morris), the balance of authority is to the effect that 'business' is a wider term than trade; see, in particular, *Re A Debtor (No 3 of 1926)* [1927] 1 Ch 97, [1926] All ER Rep 337, CA, and *Re A Debtor (No 490 of 1935)* [1936] Ch 237, CA. In fact it has been said that the word 'business' means almost anything which is an occupation, as distinguished from a pleasure. Anything which is an occupation or duty which requires attention is a business (*Rolls v Miller* (1884) 27 Ch D 71 at 88, CA per Lindley LJ), and it has also been said that neither the making of a profit nor any commercial activity is essential (*Rael-Brook Ltd v Minister of Housing and Local Government* [1967] 2 QB 65, [1967] 1 All ER 262). But see, *Secretary of State for Transport v Jenkins, Jenkins Spence and Taylor* (1997) 79 P & CR 118. Yet the term business has perhaps to be confined to a regularly conducted commercial enterprise; see *IRC v Marine Steam Turbine Co Ltd* [1920] 1 KB 193 at 202–204; *Re A Debtor (No 3 of 1926)* supra, at 106 and 341, respectively; *Lord Advocate v Glasgow Corpn* 1958 SLT 2 at 8, 1958 SC 12; *Abernethie v A M & J Kleiman Ltd* [1970] 1 QB 10, [1969] 2 All ER 790, CA; *Customs and Excise Comrs v Royal Exchange Theatre Trust* [1979] 3 All ER 797; and *Customs and Excise Comrs v Lord Fisher* [1981] 2 All ER 147, [1981] STC 238. See also *Hickson & Welch Ltd v Cann* (1977) 40 P & CR 218n; *Rutherford v Maurer* [1962] 1 QB 16; *Russell v Booker* (1982) 263 Estates Gazette 513; *Gurton v Parrott* [1991] 1 EGLR 98; *Hawkesbrook Leisure Ltd v The Reece-Jones Partnership* [2003] EWHC 3333 (Ch). See para 3.24.

On the meaning of 'trade', see also 47 Halsbury's Laws (4th edn) para 1 and 4 Words and Phrases (3rd edn) 312–314, and on the meaning of 'business', see also 47 Halsbury's Laws (4th edn) paras 2, 3 and 1 Words and Phrases (3rd edn) 204 ff.

Activities concerning horses requires special mention. Grazing remains an independent agricultural activity, see s 38(1). If the grazing is supporting a trade or business, the business conditions will be satisfied. For further commentary see para 3.25.

Sub-s (3): Regard. This, in the words of Lord Hanworth MR, in *Cohen v West Ham Corpn* [1933] Ch 814 at 833, [1933] All ER Rep 24 at 26, CA, 'is intended to be a loose and indefinite term'.

Sub-s (4): The notice conditions. For provision as to compliance with the notice conditions in cases where a farm business tenancy is surrendered and re-granted under s 3, see sub-s (4) thereof. See para 3.28 ff.

Written. Expressions referring to writing are, unless the contrary intention appears, to be construed as including references to other modes of representing or reproducing words in a visible form; see the Interpretation Act 1978, s 5, Sch 1.

Notice. As to the service of notices required or authorised to be given under this Act, see s 36. See para 17.1 ff.

Person. Unless the contrary intention appears this includes a body of persons corporate or unincorporate; see the Interpretation Act 1978, s 5, Sch 1.

Sub-s (8): Landlord ... has consented, etc. As to the power of a landlord to give consents for the purposes of this Act, see s 32.

Crown land. As to the application of this Act to land in which there subsists or has at any material time subsisted a Crown interest, see s 37.

Definitions. For 'agricultural', 'agriculture' and 'tenancy', see s 38(1); for 'landlord' and 'tenant', see s 38(1), (5); as to the farming of land, see s 38(2); as to the granting of a tenancy, see s 38(3); as to the beginning of a tenancy, see s 38(4).

A1.212

2   Tenancies which cannot be farm business tenancies

(1)   A tenancy cannot be a farm business tenancy for the purposes of this Act if—

   (a)   the tenancy begins before 1st September 1995, or
   (b)   it is a tenancy of an agricultural holding beginning on or after that date with
         respect to which, by virtue of section 4 of this Act, the Agricultural Holdings
         Act 1986 applies.

(2)   In this section 'agricultural holding' has the same meaning as in the Agricultural
Holdings Act 1986.

NOTES

Initial Commencement

Specified date: 1 September 1995: see s 41(2).

Extent

This section does not extend to Scotland.

Notes

For a commentary, see para 3.1 ff.

1st September 1995. Ie the day on which this Act came into force; see s 41(2).

Crown land. As to the application of this Act to land in which there subsists or has at any
material time subsisted a Crown interest, see s 37.

Definitions. For 'farm business tenancy', see s 1; for 'tenancy', see s 38(1); as to the beginning of
a tenancy, see s 38(4). Note as to 'agricultural holding', sub-s (2) above.

Agricultural Holdings Act 1986. For the meaning of 'agricultural holding' in that Act, see AHA
1986, s 1(1). See para 19.2 ff.

A1.213

3   Compliance with notice conditions in cases of surrender and re-grant

(1)   This section applies where—

   (a)   a tenancy ('the new tenancy') is granted to a person who, immediately before
         the grant, was the tenant under a farm business tenancy ('the old tenancy')
         which met the notice conditions specified in section 1(4) of this Act,
   (b)   the condition in subsection (2) below or the condition in subsection (3) below
         is met, and
   (c)   except as respects the matters mentioned in subsections (2) and (3) below and
         matters consequential on them, the terms of the new tenancy are substantially
         the same as the terms of the old tenancy.

(2)   The first condition referred to in subsection (1)(b) above is that the land
comprised in the new tenancy is the same as the land comprised in the old tenancy,
apart from any changes in area which are small in relation to the size of the holding
and do not affect the character of the holding.

(3)   The second condition referred to in subsection (1)(b) above is that the old tenancy
and the new tenancy are both fixed term tenancies, but the term date under the new
tenancy is earlier than the term date under the old tenancy.

(4)   Where this section applies, the new tenancy shall be taken for the purposes of this Act to meet the notice conditions specified in section 1(4) of this Act.

(5)   In subsection (3) above, 'the term date', in relation to a fixed term tenancy, means the date fixed for the expiry of the term.

NOTES

Initial Commencement

Specified date: 1 September 1995: see s 41(2).

Extent

This section does not extend to Scotland.

Notes

For a commentary, see para 3.31.

Crown land. As to the application of this Act to land in which there subsists or has at any material time subsisted a Crown interest, see s 37.

Definitions. For 'farm business tenancy', see s 1; for 'fixed term tenancy', 'holding', and 'tenancy', see s 38(1); for 'tenant', see s 38(1), (5); as to the granting of a tenancy, see s 38(3). Note as to 'the new tenancy' and 'the old tenancy', sub-s (1)(a) above. See para 3.31.

Exclusion of Agricultural Holdings Act 1986

A1.214

4   Agricultural Holdings Act 1986 not to apply in relation to new tenancies except in special cases

(1)   The Agricultural Holdings Act 1986 (in this section referred to as 'the 1986 Act') shall not apply in relation to any tenancy beginning on or after 1st September 1995 (including any agreement to which section 2 of that Act would otherwise apply beginning on or after that date), except [(subject to subsection (2B) below)] any tenancy of an agricultural holding which—

(a)   is granted by a written contract of tenancy entered into before 1st September 1995 and indicating (in whatever terms) that the 1986 Act is to apply in relation to the tenancy,

(b)   is obtained by virtue of a direction of an Agricultural Land Tribunal under section 39 or 53 of the 1986 Act,

(c)   is granted (following a direction under section 39 of that Act) in circumstances falling within section 45(6) of that Act,

(d)   is granted on an agreed succession by a written contract of tenancy indicating (in whatever terms) that Part IV of the 1986 Act is to apply in relation to the tenancy,

(e)   is created by the acceptance of a tenant, in accordance with the provisions as to compensation known as the 'Evesham custom' and set out in subsections (3) to (5) of section 80 of the 1986 Act, on the terms and conditions of the previous tenancy, ...

(f)   is granted to a person who, immediately before the grant of the tenancy, was the tenant of the holding, or of any agricultural holding which comprised the whole or a substantial part of the land comprised in the holding, under a tenancy in relation to which the 1986 Act applied[, and is so granted because an agreement between the parties (not being an agreement expressed to take effect as a new tenancy between the parties) has effect as an implied surrender followed by the grant of the tenancy, or]

A1.214 *Statutes*

[(g) is granted to a person who, immediately before the grant of the tenancy, was the tenant of the holding, or of any agricultural holding which comprised the whole or a substantial part of the land comprised in the holding, under a tenancy in relation to which the 1986 Act applied, and is so granted by a written contract of tenancy indicating (in whatever terms) that the 1986 Act is to apply in relation to the tenancy].

(2) For the purposes of subsection (1)(d) above, a tenancy ('the current tenancy') is granted on an agreed succession if, and only if,—

   (a) the previous tenancy of the holding or a related holding was a tenancy in relation to which Part IV of the 1986 Act applied, ...
   [(b) the current tenancy is granted to a person (alone or jointly with other persons) who, if the tenant under that previous tenancy ('the previous tenant') had died immediately before the grant, would have been his close relative, and
   (c) either of the conditions in subsection (2A) below is satisfied].

[(2A) The conditions referred to in subsection (2)(c) above are—

   (a) the current tenancy is granted to a person (alone or jointly with other persons) who was or had become the sole or sole remaining applicant for a direction of an Agricultural Land Tribunal for a tenancy, and
   (b) the current tenancy—
       (i) is granted as a result of an agreement between the landlord and the previous tenant, and
       (ii) is granted, and begins, before the date of the giving of any retirement notice by the previous tenant, or if no retirement notice is given, before the date of death of the previous tenant.]

[(2B) The 1986 Act shall not apply by virtue of subsection (1)(f) or (g) above in relation to the tenancy of an agricultural holding ('the current holding') where—

   (a) the whole or a substantial part of the land comprised in the current holding was comprised in an agricultural holding ('the previous holding') which was subject to a tenancy granted after the commencement of this subsection in relation to which the 1986 Act applied by virtue of subsection (1)(f) or (g) above;
   (b) the whole or a substantial part of the land comprised in the previous holding was comprised in an agricultural holding ('the original holding') which was at the commencement of this subsection subject to a tenancy in relation to which the 1986 Act applied; and
   (c) the land comprised in the original holding does not, on the date of the grant of the tenancy of the current holding, comprise the whole or a substantial part of the land comprised in the current holding.]

[(2C) The references in subsections (1)(g) and (2B) above to a substantial part of the land comprised in the holding mean a substantial part determined by reference to either area or value.]

(3) In this section—

   (a) 'agricultural holding' and 'contract of tenancy' have the same meaning as in the 1986 Act, ...
   (b) 'close relative' and 'related holding' have the meaning given by section 35(2) of that Act[, and
   (c) 'retirement notice' has the meaning given by section 49(3) of that Act].

NOTES

Initial Commencement

Specified date: 1 September 1995: see s 41(2).

1312

Extent

This section does not extend to Scotland.

Amendment

Sub-s (1): words '(subject to subsection (2B) below)' in square brackets inserted by SI 2006/2805, arts 11, 12(1), (2).

Date in force: 19 October 2006 (except in relation to any tenancy granted before that date): see SI 2006/2805, art 1(1)(b), 12(12).

Sub-s (1): in para (e) word omitted repealed by SI 2006/2805, arts 11, 12(1), (3), 18, Sch 2.

Date in force: 19 October 2006 (except in relation to any tenancy granted before that date): see SI 2006/2805, art 1(1)(b), 12(12).

Sub-s (1): in para (f) words from ', and is so' to 'the tenancy, or' in square brackets substituted by SI 2006/2805, arts 11, 12(1), (4).

Date in force: 19 October 2006 (except in relation to any tenancy granted before that date): see SI 2006/2805, art 1(1)(b), 12(12).

Sub-s (1): para (g) inserted by SI 2006/2805, arts 11, 12(1), (5).

Date in force: 19 October 2006 (except in relation to any tenancy granted before that date): see SI 2006/2805, art 1(1)(b), 12(12).

Sub-s (2): in para (a) word omitted repealed by SI 2006/2805, arts 11, 12(1), (6), 18, Sch 2.

Date in force: 19 October 2006 (except in relation to any tenancy granted before that date): see SI 2006/2805, art 1(1)(b), 12(12).

Sub-s (2): paras (b), (c) substituted, for para (b) as originally enacted, by SI 2006/2805, arts 11, 12(1), (7).

Date in force: 19 October 2006 (except in relation to any tenancy granted before that date): see SI 2006/2805, art 1(1)(b), 12(12).

Sub-s (2A): inserted by SI 2006/2805, arts 11, 12(1), (8).

Date in force: 19 October 2006 (except in relation to any tenancy granted before that date): see SI 2006/2805, art 1(1)(b), 12(12).

Sub-s (2B): inserted by SI 2006/2805, arts 11, 12(1), (9).

Date in force: 19 October 2006 (except in relation to any tenancy granted before that date): see SI 2006/2805, art 1(1)(b), 12(12).

Sub-s (2C): inserted by SI 2006/2805, arts 11, 12(1), (10).

Date in force: 19 October 2006 (except in relation to any tenancy granted before that date): see SI 2006/2805, art 1(1)(b), 12(12).

Sub-s (3): in para (a) word omitted repealed by SI 2006/2805, arts 11, 12(1), (11)(a), 18, Sch 2.

Date in force: 19 October 2006 (except in relation to any tenancy granted before that date): see SI 2006/2805, art 1(1)(b), 12(12).

Sub-s (3): para (c) and word ', and' immediately preceding it inserted by SI 2006/2805, arts 11, 12(1), (11)(b).

Date in force: 19 October 2006 (except in relation to any tenancy granted before that date): see SI 2006/2805, art 1(1)(b), 12(12).

Notes

For a commentary, see para 3.4 ff.

Agricultural Holdings Act 1986 ... shall not apply, etc. The Land Compensation Act 1973, s 48 (compensation in respect of agricultural holdings), does not have effect in relation to a tenancy of an agricultural holding to which, by virtue of this section, the 1986 Act does not apply; see s 48(1A) of the 1973 Act, as inserted by s 40, Schedule, para 24.

For the purposes of the commercial unit test in ss 36(3), 50(2) of the 1986 Act, occupation of agricultural land is to be disregarded if it is occupied only under a farm business tenancy for less than five years (including a farm business tenancy which is a periodic tenancy); see Sch 6, Pt I, paras 1(1), 6(1), Pt II, paras 11–13, to the 1986 Act, as amended (in the case of Sch 6, Pt I, para 6(1)) by s 40, Schedule, para 32.

See *Well Barn Farming Ltd v Backhouse* [2005] EWHC 1520 (Ch) where a rent memorandum purported to vary the existing tenancy by including additional land and the original wording in Ibid subsection (1)(f) was found to apply, thus excluding the provisions of the Act to the tenancy. See para 3.11.

1st September 1995. Ie the day on which this Act was brought into force; see s 41(2).

Written. See the note to s 1.

Agricultural Land Tribunal. As to the establishment, constitution, procedure, etc of Agricultural Land Tribunals, see the Agriculture Act 1947, ss 73, 75, Sch 9. Also see, the Constitutional Reform Act 2005, s 15(1), Sch 4 Pt 1, paras 29, 30.

Crown land. As to the application of this Act to land in which there subsists or has at any material time subsisted a Crown interest, see s 37.

Definitions. For 'tenancy', see s 38(1); for 'tenant', see s 38(1), (5); as to the granting of a tenancy, see s 38(3); as to the beginning of a tenancy, see s 38(4). Note as to 'the 1986 Act' and 'the previous tenancy', sub-s (1) above; as to 'the current tenancy' and 'granted on an agreed succession', sub-s (2) above; and as to 'agricultural holding', 'contract of tenancy', 'close relative', 'related holding' and 'retirement notice' see sub-s (3) above.

Agricultural Holdings Act 1986. As to the tenancies in relation to which Pt IV of that Act applies, see AHA 1986, s 34 (as amended by the Regulatory Reform (Agricultural Tenancies) (England and Wales) Order 2006. SI 2006/2805 arts 2, 4(1). For the meaning of 'agricultural holding' and 'contract of tenancy' in that Act, see AHA 1986, s 96(1).

For a commentary on the exceptions within s 4, see para 3.4 ff.

Termination of the tenancy

A1.215

5   Tenancies for more than two years to continue from year to year unless terminated by notice

(1)   A farm business tenancy for a term of more than two years shall, instead of terminating on the term date, continue (as from that date) as a tenancy from year to year, but otherwise on the terms of the original tenancy so far as applicable, unless at least twelve months ... before the term date a written notice has been given by either party to the other of his intention to terminate the tenancy.

(2)   In subsection (1) above 'the term date', in relation to a fixed term tenancy, means the date fixed for the expiry of the term.

(3)   For the purposes of section 140 of the Law of Property Act 1925 (apportionment of conditions on severance of reversion), a notice under subsection (1) above shall be taken to be a notice to quit.

(4)   This section has effect notwithstanding any agreement to the contrary.

NOTES

Initial Commencement

Specified date: 1 September 1995: see s 41(2).

Extent

This section does not extend to Scotland.

Amendment

Sub-s (1): words omitted repealed by SI 2006/2805, arts 11, 13, 18, Sch 2.

Date in force: 19 October 2006: see SI 2006/2805, art 1(1)(b).

Notes

For a commentary, see para 12.3 ff.

The notice may now be served twenty four months or more before the term date.

Term of more than two years. Where a farm business tenancy is a tenancy for a term of more than two years, any notice to quit the holding or part of the holding given in pursuance of any provision of the tenancy is, notwithstanding any provision to the contrary in the tenancy, invalid unless it is in writing and is given at least twelve months before the date on which it is to take effect; see s 7(1).

Continue ... as a tenancy from year to year. As to tenancies from year to year, see 27(1) Halsbury's Laws (4th edn reissue) paras 178 ff. For provision as to the quitting of a tenancy from year to year, see s 6.

At least twelve months before, etc. The words 'at least' indicate that the period allowed is to be exclusive of the day of service of the notice and that on which the right is to be exercised or the tenancy is terminated; see *Rightside Properties Ltd v Gray* [1975] Ch 72, [1974] 2 All ER 1169, and the other cases cited in 45 Halsbury's Laws (4th edn) para 1133. See also, *Dodds v Walker* [1981] 2 All ER 609, [1981] 1 WLR 1027, HL; *E J Riley Investments Ltd v Eurostile Holdings Ltd* [1985] 3 All ER 181, [1985] 1 WLR 1139, CA, *Country and Metropolitan Homes Surrey Ltd v Topclaim Ltd* [1996] Ch 307, [1997] 1 All ER 254, *Chief Constable of Merseyside v Reynolds* [2004] EWHC 2862 (Admin), (2004) Times, 27 November and 45 Halsbury's Laws (4th edn) para 1111, as to the day of expiry of periods of a month or a specified number of months. See Ch 17 and para 42.27.

Written. See the note to s 1.

Notice. See further s 7. As to the service of notices required or authorised to be given under this Act, see s 36.

Terminate the tenancy. As to compensation on the termination of a farm business tenancy, see Pt III (ss 15–27) of this Act.

Crown land. As to the application of this Act to land in which there subsists or has at any material time subsisted a Crown interest, see s 37.

Definitions. For 'farm business tenancy', see s 1; for 'fixed term tenancy' and 'tenancy', and as to the termination of a tenancy, see s 38(1).

A1.216

6 Length of notice to quit

(1) Where a farm business tenancy is a tenancy from year to year, a notice to quit the holding or part of the holding shall (notwithstanding any provision to the contrary in the tenancy) be invalid unless—

   (a) it is in writing,

   (b) it is to take effect at the end of a year of the tenancy, and

   (c) it is given at least twelve months ... before the date on which it is to take effect.

(2) Where, by virtue of section 5(1) of this Act, a farm business tenancy for a term of more than two years is to continue (as from the term date) as a tenancy from year to

year, a notice to quit which complies with subsection (1) above and which is to take effect on the first anniversary of the term date shall not be invalid merely because it is given before the term date; and in this subsection 'the term date' has the meaning given by section 5(2) of this Act.

(3) Subsection (1) above does not apply in relation to a counter-notice given by the tenant by virtue of subsection (2) of section 140 of the Law of Property Act 1925 (apportionment of conditions on severance of reversion).

NOTES

Initial Commencement

Specified date: 1 September 1995: see s 41(2).

Extent

This section does not extend to Scotland.

Amendment

Sub-s (1): in para (c) words omitted repealed by SI 2006/2805, arts 11, 13, 18, Sch 2.

Date in force: 19 October 2006: see SI 2006/2805, art 1(1)(b).

Notes

For a commentary, see para 12.11 ff.

The notice may now be served twenty four months or more before the term date. See para 12.11.

Tenancy from year to year. As to tenancies from year to year, see 27(1) Halsbury's Laws (4th edn reissue) paras 178 ff.

Notice to quit. As to the service of notices required or authorised to be given under this Act, see s 36.

In writing. See the note 'Written' to s 1.

At least twelve months before, etc. See the note to s 5.

Crown land. As to the application of this Act to land in which there subsists or has at any material time subsisted a Crown interest, see s 37.

Definitions. For 'farm business tenancy', see s 1; for 'holding' and 'tenancy', see s 38(1).

A1.217

7   Notice required for exercise of option to terminate tenancy or resume possession of part

(1) Where a farm business tenancy is a tenancy for a term of more than two years, any notice to quit the holding or part of the holding given in pursuance of any provision of the tenancy shall (notwithstanding any provision to the contrary in the tenancy) be invalid unless it is in writing and is given at least twelve months ... before the date on which it is to take effect.

(2) Subsection (1) above does not apply in relation to a counter-notice given by the tenant by virtue of subsection (2) of section 140 of the Law of Property Act 1925 (apportionment of conditions on severance of reversion).

(3) Subsection (1) above does not apply to a tenancy which, by virtue of subsection (6) of section 149 of the Law of Property Act 1925 (lease for life or lives or for a

term determinable with life or lives or on the marriage of[, or formation of a civil partnership by,] the lessee), takes effect as such a term of years as is mentioned in that subsection.

NOTES

Initial Commencement

Specified date: 1 September 1995: see s 41(2).

Extent

This section does not extend to Scotland.

Amendment

Sub-s (1): words omitted repealed by SI 2006/2805, arts 11, 13, 18, Sch 2.

Date in force: 19 October 2006: see SI 2006/2805, art 1(1)(b).

Sub-s (3): words ', or formation of a civil partnership by,' in square brackets inserted by the Civil Partnership Act 2004, s 81, Sch 8, para 49.

Date in force: 5 December 2005: see SI 2005/3175, art 2(1), Sch 1.

Notes

For a commentary, see para 12.7 ff.

The notice may now be served twenty-four months or more before the term date.

Tenancy for a term of more than two years. For the meaning of 'tenancy', see s 38(1). As to the continuation as a tenancy from year to year of a tenancy for a term of more than two years unless terminated by notice, see s 5(1).

Notice to quit. As to the service of notices required or authorised to be given under this Act, see s 36.

In writing. See the note 'Written' to s 1.

At least twelve months before, etc. See the note to s 5.

Crown land. As to the application of this Act to land in which there subsists or has at any material time subsisted a Crown interest, see s 37.

Definitions. For 'farm business tenancy', see s 1; for 'holding' and 'tenancy', see s 38(1).

Tenant's right to remove fixtures and buildings

A1.218

8   Tenant's right to remove fixtures and buildings

(1) Subject to the provisions of this section—

(a) any fixture (of whatever description) affixed, whether for the purposes of agriculture or not, to the holding by the tenant under a farm business tenancy, and

(b) any building erected by him on the holding,

may be removed by the tenant at any time during the continuance of the tenancy or at any time after the termination of the tenancy when he remains in possession as tenant (whether or not under a new tenancy), and shall remain his property so long as he may remove it by virtue of this subsection.

(2) Subsection (1) above shall not apply—

(a)   to a fixture affixed or a building erected in pursuance of some obligation,

(b)   to a fixture affixed or a building erected instead of some fixture or building belonging to the landlord,

(c)   to a fixture or building in respect of which the tenant has obtained compensation under section 16 of this Act or otherwise, or

(d)   to a fixture or building in respect of which the landlord has given his consent under section 17 of this Act on condition that the tenant agrees not to remove it and which the tenant has agreed not to remove.

(3)   In the removal of a fixture or building by virtue of subsection (1) above, the tenant shall not do any avoidable damage to the holding.

(4)   Immediately after removing a fixture or building by virtue of subsection (1) above, the tenant shall make good all damage to the holding that is occasioned by the removal.

(5)   This section applies to a fixture or building acquired by a tenant as it applies to a fixture or building affixed or erected by him.

(6)   Except as provided by subsection (2)(d) above, this section has effect notwithstanding any agreement or custom to the contrary.

(7)   No right to remove fixtures that subsists otherwise than by virtue of this section shall be exercisable by the tenant under a farm business tenancy.

NOTES

Initial Commencement

Specified date: 1 September 1995: see s 41(2).

Extent

This section does not extend to Scotland.

Notes

For a commentary, see Ch 15.

Sub-s (1): Fixture. As to the determination of what are fixtures, and their ownership, etc, see 27(1) Halsbury's Laws (4th edn reissue) col 143 ff. See also, the Court of Appeal decision in *TSB Bank plc v Botham* [1996] EGCS 149.

Sub-s (2): Fixture affixed or building erected instead of some fixture or building belonging to the landlord. Sub-s (2)(b) above follows the existing rule that where a tenant substitutes a non-agricultural trade fixture for one belonging to a landlord, that fixture cannot be removed by the tenant as of right (see the Agricultural Holdings Act 1986, s 10(2)(b)). As to compensation for tenant's improvements, see Pt III (ss 15–27) of this Act.

Landlord has given his consent. As to the power of a landlord to give consents for the purposes of this Act, see s 32.

Sub-s (4): Make good all damage. To 'make good' damage done to property means to restore the property to the condition in which it was immediately before the damage, and not that pecuniary compensation be paid; see *Wells v Ody* (1836) 5 LJ Ex 199; *Crofts v Haldane* (1867) LR 2 QB 194.

Crown land. As to the application of this Act to land in which there subsists or has at any material time subsisted a Crown interest, see s 37.

Definitions. For 'farm business tenancy', see s 1; for 'agriculture', 'building', 'holding', 'tenancy' and 'termination', see s 38(1); for 'landlord' and 'tenant', see s 38(1), (5).

PART II: RENT REVIEW UNDER FARM BUSINESS TENANCY

A1.219

9 Application of Part II

This Part of this Act applies in relation to a farm business tenancy (notwithstanding any agreement to the contrary) unless the tenancy is created by an instrument which—

(a) expressly states that the rent is not to be reviewed during the tenancy, ...

(b) provides that the rent is to be varied, at a specified time or times during the tenancy—

    (i) by or to a specified amount, or

    (ii) in accordance with a specified formula which does not preclude a reduction and which does not require or permit the exercise by any person of any judgment or discretion in relation to the determination of the rent of the holding,

but otherwise is to remain fixed[, or

(c) does not contain any provision which precludes a reduction in the rent during the tenancy, and—

    (i) expressly states that this Part of this Act does not apply, or

    (ii) makes provision for the reference of rent reviews to an independent expert whose decision is final].

NOTES

Initial Commencement

Specified date: 1 September 1995: see s 41(2).

Extent

This section does not extend to Scotland.

Amendment

In para (a) word omitted repealed by SI 2006/2805, arts 11, 14(1)(a), 18, Sch 2.

Date in force: 19 October 2006: see SI 2006/2805, art 1(1)(b); for effect see art 14(3).

Para (c) and word '; or' immediately preceding it inserted by SI 2006/2805, arts 11, 14(1)(b).

Date in force: 19 October 2006: see SI 2006/2805, art 1(1)(b); for effect see art 14(3).

Notes

For a commentary, see para 9.6 ff.

This Part of this Act. Ie Pt II (ss 9–14).

Crown land. As to the application of this Act to land in which there subsists or has at any material time subsisted a Crown interest, see s 37.

Definitions. For 'farm business tenancy', see s 1; for 'holding' and 'tenancy', see s 38(1).

A1.220

10 Notice requiring statutory rent review

(1) The landlord or tenant under a farm business tenancy in relation to which this Part of this Act applies may by notice in writing given to the other (in this Part of this

Act referred to as a 'statutory review notice') require that the rent to be payable in respect of the holding as from the review date shall be referred to arbitration in accordance with this Act.

(2)   In this Part of this Act 'the review date', in relation to a statutory review notice, means a date which—

    (a)   is specified in the notice, and
    (b)   complies with subsections (3) to (6) below.

(3)   The review date must be at least twelve months but less than twenty-four months after the day on which the statutory review notice is given.

(4)   If the parties have agreed in writing that the rent is to be, or may be, varied as from a specified date or dates, or at specified intervals, the review date must be a date as from which the rent could be varied under the agreement.

(5)   If the parties have agreed in writing that the review date for the purposes of this Part of this Act is to be a specified date or dates, the review date must be that date or one of those dates.

(6)   If the parties have not agreed as mentioned in subsection (4) or (5) above, the review date—

    (a)   must be an anniversary of the beginning of the tenancy or, where the landlord and the tenant have agreed in writing that the review date for the purposes of this Act is to be some other day of the year, that day of the year, and
    (b)   must not fall before the end of the period of three years beginning with the latest of any of the following dates—
       (i)   the beginning of the tenancy,
      (ii)   any date as from which there took effect a previous direction of an arbitrator as to the amount of the rent,
     (iii)   any date as from which there took effect a previous determination as to the amount of the rent made, otherwise than as arbitrator, by a person appointed under an agreement between the landlord and the tenant, and
     (iv)   any date as from which there took effect a previous agreement in writing between the landlord and the tenant, entered into since the grant of the tenancy, as to the amount of the rent.

NOTES

Initial Commencement

Specified date: 1 September 1995: see s 41(2).

Extent

This section does not extend to Scotland.

Notes

Sub-s (1): Farm business tenancy in relation to which this Part of this Act applies. As to farm business tenancies, see s 1; as to the farm business tenancies to which this Part (ie Pt II (ss 9–14)) of this Act applies, see s 9.

Notice. As to the service of notices required or authorised to be given under this Act, see s 36.

In writing. See the note 'Written' to s 1.

Statutory review notice. As to the determination of the rent properly payable in respect of a holding on any reference made in pursuance of a statutory review notice, see s 13.

S 28(1)–(3), which make provision for disputes between landlords and tenants to be resolved by reference to arbitration, do not apply in relation to the determination of rent in pursuance of a statutory review notice; see s 28(5)(a).

Shall be referred to arbitration in accordance with this Act. As to the appointment of an arbitrator, see s 12, and for general provisions applying to arbitrations under this Act, see s 30.

The provisions of the Arbitration Act 1996 apply to an arbitration under this section: see para 44.2.

Sub-s (2): The review date. S 11 makes provision for the determination of the rent review date where a new farm business tenancy of a severed part of a reversion arises.

Sub-s (3): At least twelve months before, etc. The words 'at least' indicate that the period allowed is to be exclusive of the day on which the notice is given and the review date; see *Rightside Properties Ltd v Gray* [1975] Ch 72, [1974] 2 All ER 1169, and the other cases cited in 45 Halsbury's Laws (4th edn) para 1133. See also *Dodds v Walker* [1981] 2 All ER 609, [1981] 1 WLR 1027, HL; *E J Riley Investments Ltd v Eurostile Holdings Ltd* [1985] 3 All ER 181, [1985] 1 WLR 1139, CA, *Country and Metropolitan Homes Surrey Ltd v Topclaim Ltd* [1996] Ch 307, [1997] 1 All ER 254, *Chief Constable of Merseyside v Reynolds* [2004] EWHC 2862 (Admin), (2004) Times, 27 November and 45 Halsbury's Laws (4th edn) para 1111, as to the day of expiry of periods of a month or a specified number of months.

Sub-s (6): Three years beginning with, etc. The use of the words 'beginning with' makes it clear that in computing this period the day from which it runs is to be included; see *Hare v Gocher* [1962] 2 QB 641, [1962] 2 All ER 763, *Trow v Ind Coope (West Midlands) Ltd* [1967] 2 QB 899 at 909, [1967] 2 All ER 900, CA and *Zoan v Rouamba* [2000] 2 All ER 620, [2000] 1 WLR 1509, CA.

Crown land. As to the application of this Act to land in which there subsists or has at any material time subsisted a Crown interest, see s 37.

Definitions. For 'farm business tenancy', see s 1; for 'holding' and 'tenancy', see s 38(1); for 'landlord' and 'tenant', see s 38(1), (5); as to a grant of a tenancy, see s 38(3); as to the beginning of a tenancy, see s 38(4). Note as to 'statutory review notice', sub-s (1) above; and as to 'the review date', sub-s (2) above.

A1.221

11   Review date where new tenancy of severed part of reversion

(1)   This section applies in any case where a farm business tenancy ('the new tenancy') arises between—

    (a)   a person who immediately before the date of the beginning of the tenancy was entitled to a severed part of the reversionary estate in the land comprised in a farm business tenancy ('the original tenancy') in which the land to which the new tenancy relates was then comprised, and

    (b)   the person who immediately before that date was the tenant under the original tenancy,

and the rent payable under the new tenancy at its beginning represents merely the appropriate portion of the rent payable under the original tenancy immediately before the beginning of the new tenancy.

(2)   In any case where this section applies—

    (a)   references to the beginning of the tenancy in subsection (6) of section 10 of this Act shall be taken to be references to the beginning of the original tenancy, and

    (b)   references to rent in that subsection shall be taken to be references to the rent payable under the original tenancy, until the first occasion following the beginning of the new tenancy on which any such direction, determination or agreement with respect to the rent of the new holding as is mentioned in that subsection takes effect.

NOTES

Initial Commencement

Specified date: 1 September 1995: see s 41(2).

Extent

This section does not extend to Scotland.

Notes

For a commentary, see para 9.23.

Person. See the note to s 1.

Crown land. As to the application of this Act to land in which there subsists or has at any material time subsisted a Crown interest, see s 37.

Definitions. For 'farm business tenancy', see s 1; for 'holding' and 'tenancy', see s 38(1); for 'tenant', see s 38(1), (5); as to the beginning of a tenancy, see s 38(4). Note as to 'the new tenancy' and 'the original tenancy', sub-s (1) above.

A1.222

12   Appointment of arbitrator

Where a statutory review notice has been given in relation to a farm business tenancy, but—

(a) no arbitrator has been appointed under an agreement made since the notice was given, and

(b) no person has been appointed under such an agreement to determine the question of the rent (otherwise than as arbitrator) on a basis agreed by the parties,

either party may, at any time during the period of six months ending with the review date, apply to the President of the Royal Institution of Chartered Surveyors (in this Act referred to as 'the RICS') for the appointment of an arbitrator by him.

NOTES

Initial Commencement

Specified date: 1 September 1995: see s 41(2).

Extent

This section does not extend to Scotland.

Notes

For a commentary, see para 9.26.

Statutory review notice has been given. For the meaning of 'statutory review notice', see s 10(1). As to the service of notices required or authorised to be given under this Act, see s 36.

Person. See the note to s 1.

1322

Six months ending with, etc. As a general rule the effect of defining a period in such a manner is to include the day on which the event in question occurs; see 45 Halsbury's Laws (4th edn) para 1127.

Appointment of an arbitrator. As to the determination by an arbitrator of the rent properly payable in respect of a holding on any reference made in pursuance of a statutory review notice, see s 13. For general provisions applying to arbitrations under this Act, see s 30.

Crown land. As to the application of this Act to land in which there subsists or has at any material time subsisted a Crown interest, see s 37.

Definitions. For 'farm business tenancy', see s 1; for 'statutory review notice', see s 10(1); for 'the review date', see s 10(2).

A1.223

13   Amount of rent

(1)   On any reference made in pursuance of a statutory review notice, the arbitrator shall determine the rent properly payable in respect of the holding at the review date and accordingly shall, with effect from that date, increase or reduce the rent previously payable or direct that it shall continue unchanged.

(2)   For the purposes of subsection (1) above, the rent properly payable in respect of a holding is the rent at which the holding might reasonably be expected to be let on the open market by a willing landlord to a willing tenant, taking into account (subject to subsections (3) and (4) below) all relevant factors, including (in every case) the terms of the tenancy (including those which are relevant for the purposes of section 10(4) to (6) of this Act, but not those [which (apart from this section) preclude a reduction in the rent during the tenancy)].

(3)   The arbitrator shall disregard any increase in the rental value of the holding which is due to tenant's improvements other than—

   (a)   any tenant's improvement provided under an obligation which was imposed on the tenant by the terms of his tenancy or any previous tenancy and which arose on or before the beginning of the tenancy in question,
   (b)   any tenant's improvement to the extent that any allowance or benefit has been made or given by the landlord in consideration of its provision, and
   (c)   any tenant's improvement to the extent that the tenant has received any compensation from the landlord in respect of it.

(4)   The arbitrator—

   (a)   shall disregard any effect on the rent of the fact that the tenant who is a party to the arbitration is in occupation of the holding, and
   (b)   shall not fix the rent at a lower amount by reason of any dilapidation or deterioration of, or damage to, buildings or land caused or permitted by the tenant.

(5)   In this section 'tenant's improvement', and references to the provision of such an improvement, have the meaning given by section 15 of this Act.

NOTES

Initial Commencement

Specified date: 1 September 1995: see s 41(2).

Extent

This section does not extend to Scotland.

Amendment

Sub-s (2): words from 'which (apart from' to 'during the tenancy)' in square brackets substituted by SI 2006/2805, arts 11, 15.

Date in force: 19 October 2006: see SI 2006/2805, art 1(1)(b).

Notes

For a commentary, see para 9.16 ff.

Sub-s (1): The arbitrator. As to appointment, see s 12, and for general provisions applying to arbitrations under this Act, see s 30. The provisions of the Arbitration Act 1996 apply to an arbitration under this section.

Sub-s (2): Rent properly payable, etc. As to the determination under sub-ss (1), (2) above of the rent properly payable where opencast planning permission has been granted subject to a restoration condition and, immediately before that permission is granted, any of the land comprised therein consists of the holding or part of the holding held under a farm business tenancy, see the Opencast Coal Act 1958, s 14B(4), as inserted by s 40, Schedule, para 14.

Let on the open market. 'A value, ascertained by reference to an amount obtainable in an open market, shows an intention to include every possible purchaser. The market is to be the open market, as distinguished from an offer to a limited class only, such as the members of the family'; see *IRC v Clay, IRC v Buchanan* [1914] 3 KB 466 at 475, CA, per Swinfen Eady J (decided under the Finance (1909–10) Act 1910, s 25 (repealed), where the words in question related to sale in the open market). See also *Sterling Land Office Developments v Lloyds Bank plc* [1984] 2 EGLR 135.

Sub-s (3): Tenant's improvements. For meaning, see, by virtue of sub-s (5) above, s 15. For provision as to compensation for tenant's improvements, see Pt III (ss 15–27) of this Act.

Crown land. As to the application of this Act to land in which there subsists or has at any material time subsisted a Crown interest, see s 37.

Definitions. For 'statutory review notice', see s 10(1); for 'the review date', see s 10(2); for 'tenant's improvement', and as to the provision of such an improvement, see, by virtue of sub-s (5) above, s 15; for 'building', 'holding' and 'tenancy', see s 38(1); for 'landlord' and 'tenant', see s 38(1), (5); as to the beginning of a tenancy, see s 38(4). Note as to 'tenant's improvement', sub-s (5) above.

A1.224

14   Interpretation of Part II

In this Part of this Act, unless the context otherwise requires—

'the review date', in relation to a statutory review notice, has the meaning given by
    section 10(2) of this Act;
'statutory review notice' has the meaning given by section 10(1) of this Act.

NOTES

Initial Commencement

Specified date: 1 September 1995: see s 41(2).

Extent

This section does not extend to Scotland.

Notes

For a commentary, see Ch 16.

This Part of this Act. Ie Pt II (ss 9–14).

Crown land. As to the application of this Act to land in which there subsists or has at any material time subsisted a Crown interest, see s 37.

A1.225

15   Meaning of 'tenant's improvement'

For the purposes of this Part of this Act a 'tenant's improvement', in relation to any farm business tenancy, means—

 (a)   any physical improvement which is made on the holding by the tenant by his own effort or wholly or partly at his own expense, or

 (b)   any intangible advantage which—

 (i)   is obtained for the holding by the tenant by his own effort or wholly or partly at his own expense, and

 (ii)   becomes attached to the holding,

and references to the provision of a tenant's improvement are references to the making by the tenant of any physical improvement falling within paragraph (a) above or the obtaining by the tenant of any intangible advantage falling within paragraph (b) above.

NOTES

Initial Commencement

Specified date: 1 September 1995: see s 41(2).

Extent

This section does not extend to Scotland.

Notes

This Part of this Act. Ie Pt III (ss 15–27).

Tenant's improvement. In estimating the best rent or reservation in the nature of rent of land comprised in a farm business tenancy for the purposes of a 'relevant instrument' (as defined), it is not necessary to take into account against the tenant any increase in the value of that land arising from any tenant's improvements; see s 34.

Compensation. As to rights to compensation in respect of tenant's improvements, see s 16.

Crown land. As to the application of this Act to land in which there subsists or has at any material time subsisted a Crown interest, see s 37.

Definitions. For 'farm business tenancy', see s 1; for 'holding', see s 38(1); for 'tenant', see s 38(1), (5).

A1.226

16   Tenant's right to compensation for tenant's improvement

(1)   The tenant under a farm business tenancy shall, subject to the provisions of this Part of this Act, be entitled on the termination of the tenancy, on quitting the holding, to obtain from his landlord compensation in respect of any tenant's improvement.

(2)   A tenant shall not be entitled to compensation under this section in respect of—

 (a)   any physical improvement which is removed from the holding, or

 (b)   any intangible advantage which does not remain attached to the holding.

(3)   Section 13 of, and Schedule 1 to, the Agriculture Act 1986 (compensation to outgoing tenants for milk quota) shall not apply in relation to a farm business tenancy.

NOTES

Initial Commencement

Specified date: 1 September 1995: see s 41(2).

Extent

This section does not extend to Scotland.

Notes

For a commentary, see para 16.2 ff.

Tenant ... shall ... be entitled ... to obtain ... compensation in respect of any tenant's improvement. For the meaning of 'tenant', see s 38(1), (5); for the meaning of 'tenant's improvement', see s 15. See further ss 17–19 (conditions of eligibility for compensation for tenant's improvements, including planning permission, and references to arbitration of refusal or failure to give consent for improvements or of conditions attached to consent); ss 20–22 (amount of compensation for tenant's improvements and settlement of claims for compensation); and ss 23–27 (supplementary provisions with respect to compensation, extent to which compensation is recoverable under agreements, and interpretation).

For the application of statutory powers under the Settled Land Act 1925, ss 71, 73, and the Universities and College Estates Act 1925, s 26, authorising the raising or application of capital money for the purpose of paying compensation under this section, and for the power of a landlord who is a tenant for life or in a fiduciary position to require to be paid out of capital money held on the same trusts as the settled land sums he is liable to pay in compensation under this section, see s 33(1)(b), (2)–(4). For provision as to the payment of compensation under this section by the Chancellor of the Duchy of Lancaster and in connection with land belonging to the Duchy of Cornwall, see s 37(5)–(7).

The right of a tenant under s 8 to remove fixtures affixed to, or buildings erected on, the holding by the tenant does not apply to a fixture or building in respect of which the tenant has obtained compensation under this section (or otherwise); see s 8(2)(c).

S 28(1)–(3), which make provision for disputes between landlords and tenants to be resolved by reference to arbitration, do not apply in relation to any claim for compensation under this Part of this Act; see s 28(5)(c).

A tenant's right to compensation under this section is an agricultural asset for the purposes of the Agricultural Credits Act 1928, Pt I; see s 5(7) of that Act, as amended by s 40, Schedule, para 7.

As to a tenant's right to compensation under this section in relation to land comprised in a compulsory rights order made under the Opencast Coal Act 1958, s 4, where that land was held, immediately before the date on which the rights conferred by the order are to become exercisable, under a farm business tenancy, see s 25A of the 1958 Act, as inserted by s 40, Schedule, para 16, and Sch 7, Pt I, paras 1A, 2, 2A, 3A, 4 to that Act, as inserted or amended by s 40, Schedule, para 20(1), (2), (4), (5).

The following provisions allowing for the payment of compensation for tenant's improvements do not apply to holdings, land etc let under farm business tenancies: the Small Holdings and Allotments Act 1908, s 47, as amended by s 40, Schedule, para 1; the Allotments Act 1922, ss 1–5, (see ss 3, 6(1) of that Act, as amended (in the case of ss 3(7), 6(1) thereof) by s 40, Schedule, paras 3, 4); the Landlord and Tenant Act 1927, Pt I, (see s 17(1) of that Act, as amended by s 40, Schedule, para 5); the Opencast Coal Act 1958, ss 26, 28, (see ss 26(1), 28(1) of that Act, as amended by s 40, Schedule, paras 17(1), (2), 18(1), (2)).

This Part of this Act. Ie Pt III (ss 15–27).

Crown land. As to the application of this Act to land in which there subsists or has at any material time subsisted a Crown interest, see s 37 (in particular, sub-ss (5)–(7)).

Definitions. For 'farm business tenancy', see s 1; for 'tenant's improvement', see s 15; for 'holding', 'tenancy' and 'termination', see s 38(1); for 'landlord' and 'tenant', see s 38(1), (5).

Conditions of eligibility

A1.227

17   Consent of landlord as condition of compensation for tenant's improvement

(1)   A tenant shall not be entitled to compensation under section 16 of this Act in respect of any tenant's improvement unless the landlord has given his consent in writing to the provision of the tenant's improvement.

(2)   Any such consent may be given in the instrument creating the tenancy or elsewhere.

(3)   Any such consent may be given either unconditionally or on condition that the tenant agrees to a specified variation in the terms of the tenancy.

(4)   The variation referred to in subsection (3) above must be related to the tenant's improvement in question.

(5)   This section does not apply in any case where the tenant's improvement consists of planning permission.

NOTES

Initial Commencement

Specified date: 1 September 1995: see s 41(2).

Extent

This section does not extend to Scotland.

Notes

For a commentary, see para 16.13 ff.

Sub-s (1): Landlord has given his consent. As to the power of a landlord to give consents for the purposes of this Act, see s 32.

For the power of a tenant who is aggrieved by his landlord's refusal to give his consent under sub-s (1) above, by his landlord's failure to give such consent within two months of a written request by the tenant for that consent, or by any variation in the terms of the tenancy required by his landlord as a condition of giving such consent, to demand that the question be referred to arbitration, see s 19(1); and see further as to such arbitration the remaining provisions of that section.

In writing. See the note 'Written' to s 1.

Sub-s (3): Consent may be given … on condition, etc. An arbitrator, in approving a proposed tenant's improvement following a reference to arbitration under s 19(1), may not vary any condition required by the landlord under sub-s (3) above; see s 19(6).

The right of a tenant under s 8 to remove fixtures affixed to, or buildings erected on, the holding by the tenant does not apply to a fixture or building in respect of which a landlord has given his consent under this section on condition that the tenant agrees not to remove it and which the tenant has agreed not to remove; see s 8(2)(d).

Crown land. As to the application of this Act to land in which there subsists or has at any material time subsisted a Crown interest, see s 37.

Definitions. For 'tenant's improvement', see s 15; for 'planning permission', see s 27; for 'tenancy', see s 38(1); for 'landlord' and 'tenant', see s 38(1), (5).

A1.228

18   Conditions in relation to compensation for planning permission

(1)   A tenant shall not be entitled to compensation under section 16 of this Act in respect of a tenant's improvement which consists of planning permission unless—

    (a)   the landlord has given his consent in writing to the making of the application for planning permission,

    (b)   that consent is expressed to be given for the purpose—

        (i)   of enabling a specified physical improvement falling within paragraph (a) of section 15 of this Act lawfully to be provided by the tenant, or

        (ii)   of enabling the tenant lawfully to effect a specified change of use, and

    (c)   on the termination of the tenancy, the specified physical improvement has not been completed or the specified change of use has not been effected.

(2)   Any such consent may be given either unconditionally or on condition that the tenant agrees to a specified variation in the terms of the tenancy.

(3)   The variation referred to in subsection (2) above must be related to the physical improvement or change of use in question.

NOTES

Initial Commencement

Specified date: 1 September 1995: see s 41(2).

Extent

This section does not extend to Scotland.

Notes

Landlord has given his consent. As to the power of a landlord to give consents for the purposes of this Act, see s 32.

In writing. See the note 'Written' to s 1, and cf the second paragraph of the corresponding note to s 17.

Consent may be given ... on condition, etc. Cf the first paragraph of the corresponding note to s 17.

Crown land. As to the application of this Act to land in which there subsists or has at any material time subsisted a Crown interest, see s 37.

Definitions. For 'tenant's improvement', see s 15; for 'planning permission', see s 27; for 'tenancy' and 'termination', see s 38(1); for 'landlord' and 'tenant', see s 38(1), (5).

A1.229

19   Reference to arbitration of refusal or failure to give consent or of condition attached to consent

(1)   Where, in relation to any tenant's improvement, the tenant under a farm business tenancy is aggrieved by—

    (a)   the refusal of his landlord to give his consent under section 17(1) of this Act,

    (b)   the failure of his landlord to give such consent within two months of a written request by the tenant for such consent, or

    (c)   any variation in the terms of the tenancy required by the landlord as a condition of giving such consent, the tenant may by notice in writing given to the landlord demand that the question shall be referred to arbitration under this section; but this subsection has effect subject to subsections (2) and (3) below.

(2)   No notice under subsection (1) above may be given in relation to any tenant's improvement which the tenant has already provided or begun to provide, unless that improvement is a routine improvement.

(3)   No notice under subsection (1) above may be given—

   (a)   in a case falling within paragraph (a) or (c) of that subsection, after the end of the period of two months beginning with the day on which notice of the refusal or variation referred to in that paragraph was given to the tenant, or

   (b)   in a case falling within paragraph (b) of that subsection, after the end of the period of four months beginning with the day on which the written request referred to in that paragraph was given to the landlord.

(4)   Where the tenant has given notice under subsection (1) above but no arbitrator has been appointed under an agreement made since the notice was given, the tenant or the landlord may apply to the President of the RICS, subject to subsection (9) below, for the appointment of an arbitrator by him.

(5)   The arbitrator shall consider whether, having regard to the terms of the tenancy and any other relevant circumstances (including the circumstances of the tenant and the landlord), it is reasonable for the tenant to provide the tenant's improvement.

(6)   Subject to subsection (9) below, the arbitrator may unconditionally approve the provision of the tenant's improvement or may withhold his approval, but may not give his approval subject to any condition or vary any condition required by the landlord under section 17(3) of this Act.

(7)   If the arbitrator gives his approval, that approval shall have effect for the purposes of this Part of this Act and for the purposes of the terms of the farm business tenancy as if it were the consent of the landlord.

(8)   In a case falling within subsection (1)(c) above, the withholding by the arbitrator of his approval shall not affect the validity of the landlord's consent or of the condition subject to which it was given.

(9)   Where, at any time after giving a notice under subsection (1) above in relation to any tenant's improvement which is not a routine improvement, the tenant begins to provide the improvement—

   (a)   no application may be made under subsection (4) above after that time,
   (b)   where such an application has been made but no arbitrator has been appointed before that time, the application shall be ineffective, and
   (c)   no award may be made by virtue of subsection (6) above after that time except as to the costs of the reference and award in a case where the arbitrator was appointed before that time.

(10)   For the purposes of this section—

   'fixed equipment' includes any building or structure affixed to land and any works constructed on, in, over or under land, and also includes anything grown on land for a purpose other than use after severance from the land, consumption of the thing grown or its produce, or amenity;
   'routine improvement', in relation to a farm business tenancy, means any tenant's improvement which—
      (a)   is a physical improvement made in the normal course of farming the holding or any part of the holding, and

   (b)   does not consist of fixed equipment or an improvement to fixed
         equipment,

but does not include any improvement whose provision is prohibited by the terms
of the tenancy.

NOTES

Initial Commencement

Specified date: 1 September 1995: see s 41(2).

Extent

This section does not extend to Scotland.

Notes

For a commentary, see para 16.20.

Sub-s (1): Within two months of, etc. The general rule in cases where an act is to be done within
a specified time is that the day from which it runs is not to be counted; see *Goldsmiths' Co v West
Metropolitan Rly Co* [1904] 1 KB 1, [1900–3] All ER Rep 667, CA; *Stewart v Chapman* [1951]
2 KB 792, [1951] 2 All ER 613; and the other cases cited in 45 Halsbury's Laws (4th edn)
para 1134. A requirement that something be done within a specified period means that the full
amount of that period up to midnight on the last day is available; see *Manorlike Ltd v Le Vitas
Travel Agency and Consultancy Services Ltd* [1986] 1 All ER 573, 278 Estates Gazette 412, CA.
See also *Dodds v Walker* [1981] 2 All ER 609, [1981] 1 WLR 1027, HL; *E J Riley
Investments Ltd v Eurostile Holdings Ltd* [1985] 3 All ER 181, [1985] 1 WLR 1139, CA,
Country and Metropolitan Homes Surrey Ltd v Topclaim Ltd [1996] Ch 307, [1997] 1 All ER
254, *Chief Constable of Merseyside v Reynolds* [2004] EWHC 2862 (Admin), (2004) Times,
27 November and 45 Halsbury's Laws (4th edn) para 1111, as to the day of expiry of periods of
a month or a specified number of months. Also see paras 17.13 and 42.27.

Written; in writing. See the note 'Written' to s 1.

Notice. As to the service of notices required or authorised to be given under this Act, see s 36.

Question shall be referred to arbitration. For general provisions applying to arbitrations under
this Act, see s 30. The provisions of the Arbitration Act 1996 apply to an arbitration under this
section.

For the application of statutory powers under the Settled Land Act 1925, s 73, and the
Universities and College Estates Act 1925, s 26, authorising the application of capital money for
the purpose of paying the costs, charges and expenses incurred by a landlord on a reference to
arbitration under this section, see s 33(1)(c).

S 28(1)–(3), which make provision for disputes between landlords and tenants to be resolved by
reference to arbitration, do not apply to any case falling within sub-s (1) above; see s 28(5)(b).

Sub-s (3): Two (four) months beginning with, etc. The use of the words 'beginning with' makes it
clear that in computing this period the day from which it runs is to be included; see *Hare v
Gocher* [1962] 2 QB 641, [1962] 2 All ER 763, and *Trow v Ind Coope (West Midlands) Ltd*
[1967] 2 QB 899 at 909, [1967] 2 All ER 900, CA and *Zoan v Rouamba* [2000] 2 All ER 620,
[2000] 1 WLR 1509, CA. See also *Dodds v Walker* [1981] 2 All ER 609, [1981] 1 WLR
1027, HL; *E J Riley Investments Ltd v Eurostile Holdings Ltd* [1985] 3 All ER 181, [1985]
1 WLR 1139, CA, *Country and Metropolitan Homes Surrey Ltd v Topclaim Ltd* [1996] Ch 307,
[1997] 1 All ER 254, *Chief Constable of Merseyside v Reynolds* [2004] EWHC 2862 (Admin),
(2004) Times, 27 November and 45 Halsbury's Laws (4th edn) para 1111, as to the day of expiry
of periods of a month or a specified number of months. Also see paras 17.13 and 42.27.

Sub-s (5): Regard. See the note to s 1.

Sub-s (7): This Part of this Act. Ie Pt III (ss 15–27).

Crown land. As to the application of this Act to land in which there subsists or has at any
material time subsisted a Crown interest, see s 37.

Definitions. For 'farm business tenancy', see s 1; for 'tenant's improvement', see s 15; for 'building', 'holding', 'the RICS' and 'tenancy', see s 38(1); as to 'farming', see s 38(2); for 'landlord' and 'tenant', see s 38(1), (5). Note as to 'fixed equipment' and 'routine improvement', sub-s (10) above.

Amount of compensation

A1.230

20   Amount of compensation for tenant's improvement not consisting of planning permission

(1)   [Subject to subsection (4A) below,] the amount of compensation payable to the tenant under section 16 of this Act in respect of any tenant's improvement shall be an amount equal to the increase attributable to the improvement in the value of the holding at the termination of the tenancy as land comprised in a tenancy.

(2)   Where the landlord and the tenant have entered into an agreement in writing whereby any benefit is given or allowed to the tenant in consideration of the provision of a tenant's improvement, the amount of compensation otherwise payable in respect of that improvement shall be reduced by the proportion which the value of the benefit bears to the amount of the total cost of providing the improvement.

(3)   Where a grant has been or will be made to the tenant out of public money in respect of a tenant's improvement, the amount of compensation otherwise payable in respect of that improvement shall be reduced by the proportion which the amount of the grant bears to the amount of the total cost of providing the improvement.

(4)   Where a physical improvement which has been completed or a change of use which has been effected is authorised by any planning permission granted on an application made by the tenant, section 18 of this Act does not prevent any value attributable to the fact that the physical improvement or change of use is so authorised from being taken into account under this section in determining the amount of compensation payable in respect of the physical improvement or in respect of any intangible advantage obtained as a result of the change of use.

[(4A)   Where the landlord and the tenant have agreed in writing, after the commencement of this subsection, to limit the amount of compensation payable under section 16 of this Act in respect of any tenant's improvement, that amount shall be the lesser of—

(a)   the amount determined in accordance with subsections (1) to (4) above, and
(b)   the compensation limit.

(4B)   In subsection (4A) above, 'the compensation limit' means—

(a)   an amount agreed by the parties in writing, or
(b)   where the parties are unable to agree on an amount, an amount equal to the cost to the tenant of making the improvement.]

(5)   This section does not apply where the tenant's improvement consists of planning permission.

NOTES

Initial Commencement

Specified date: 1 September 1995: see s 41(2).

Extent

This section does not extend to Scotland.

Amendment

Sub-s (1): words 'Subject to subsection (4A) below,' in square brackets inserted by SI 2006/2805, arts 11, 16(1).

Date in force: 19 October 2006: see SI 2006/2805, art 1(1)(b).

Sub-ss (4A), (4B): inserted by SI 2006/2805, arts 11, 16(2).

Date in force: 19 October 2006: see SI 2006/2805, art 1(1)(b).

Notes

For a commentary, see para 16.23 ff.

Sub-s (1): Amount of compensation payable. As to the settlement of claims for compensation, see s 22; for supplementary provisions with respect to compensation, see ss 23–26 (in particular, s 24(2), (4)).

Sub-s (2): In writing. See the note 'Written' to s 1.

Crown land. As to the application of this Act to land in which there subsists or has at any material time subsisted a Crown interest, see s 37.

Definitions. For 'tenant's improvement', see s 15; for 'planning permission', see s 27; for 'holding', 'tenancy' and 'termination', see s 38(1); for 'landlord' and 'tenant', see s 38(1), (5).

A1.231

21   Amount of compensation for planning permission

(1)   The amount of compensation payable to the tenant under section 16 of this Act in respect of a tenant's improvement which consists of planning permission shall be an amount equal to the increase attributable to the fact that the relevant development is authorised by the planning permission in the value of the holding at the termination of the tenancy as land comprised in a tenancy.

(2)   In subsection (1) above, 'the relevant development' means the physical improvement or change of use specified in the landlord's consent under section 18 of this Act in accordance with subsection (1)(b) of that section.

(3)   Where the landlord and the tenant have entered into an agreement in writing whereby any benefit is given or allowed to the tenant in consideration of the obtaining of planning permission by the tenant, the amount of compensation otherwise payable in respect of that permission shall be reduced by the proportion which the value of the benefit bears to the amount of the total cost of obtaining the permission.

NOTES

Initial Commencement

Specified date: 1 September 1995: see s 41(2).

Extent

This section does not extend to Scotland.

Notes

For a commentary, see para 16.29.

Amount of compensation payable. As to the settlement of claims for compensation, see s 22; for supplementary provisions with respect to compensation, see ss 23–26 (in particular, s 24(3), (4)). The ability for the landlord and tenant to limit the amount of compensation payable in respect of a tenant's improvement under s 20 is specifically excluded in the case of tenant's improvements consisting of planning permission, see s 20(5).

In writing. See the note 'Written' to s 1.

Crown land. As to the application of this Act to land in which there subsists or has at any material time subsisted a Crown interest, see s 37.

Definitions. For 'tenant's improvement', see s 15; for 'planning permission', see s 27; for 'holding', 'tenancy' and 'termination', see s 38(1); for 'landlord' and 'tenant', see s 38(1), (5).

A1.232

22   Settlement of claims for compensation

(1)   Any claim by the tenant under a farm business tenancy for compensation under section 16 of this Act shall, subject to the provisions of this section, be determined by arbitration under this section.

(2)   No such claim for compensation shall be enforceable unless before the end of the period of two months beginning with the date of the termination of the tenancy the tenant has given notice in writing to his landlord of his intention to make the claim and of the nature of the claim.

(3)   Where—

    (a)   the landlord and the tenant have not settled the claim by agreement in writing, and

    (b)   no arbitrator has been appointed under an agreement made since the notice under subsection (2) above was given,

either party may, after the end of the period of four months beginning with the date of the termination of the tenancy, apply to the President of the RICS for the appointment of an arbitrator by him.

(4)   Where—

    (a)   an application under subsection (3) above relates wholly or partly to compensation in respect of a routine improvement (within the meaning of section 19 of this Act) which the tenant has provided or has begun to provide, and

    (b)   that application is made at the same time as an application under section 19(4) of this Act relating to the provision of that improvement,

the President of the RICS shall appoint the same arbitrator on both applications and, if both applications are made by the same person, only one fee shall be payable by virtue of section 30(2) of this Act in respect of them.

(5)   Where a tenant lawfully remains in occupation of part of the holding after the termination of a farm business tenancy, references in subsections (2) and (3) above to the termination of the tenancy shall, in the case of a claim relating to that part of the holding, be construed as references to the termination of the occupation.

NOTES

Initial Commencement

Specified date: 1 September 1995: see s 41(2).

Extent

This section does not extend to Scotland.

Notes

For a commentary, see para 16.30.

Claim ... for compensation. As to a tenant's entitlement to recover the compensation provided for by this section, see further s 26.

Be determined by arbitration under this section. For general provisions applying to arbitrations under this Act, see s 30. The provisions of the Arbitration Act 1996 apply to an arbitration under this section.

For the application of statutory powers under the Settled Land Act 1925, s 73, and the Universities and College Estates Act 1925, s 26, authorising the raising or application of capital money for the purpose of paying the costs, charges and expenses incurred by a landlord on a reference to arbitration under this section, see s 33(1)(c).

Two (four) months beginning with, etc. See the note to s 19.

Notice. As to the service of notices required or authorised to be given under this Act, see s 36.

In writing. See the note 'Written' to s 1.

Person. See the note to s 1.

Crown land. As to the application of this Act to land in which there subsists or has at any material time subsisted a Crown interest, see s 37.

Definitions. For 'farm business tenancy', see s 1; for 'holding', 'the RICS', 'tenancy' and 'termination', see s 38(1); for 'landlord' and 'tenant', see s 38(1), (5).

Supplementary provisions with respect to compensation

A1.233

23 Successive tenancies

(1) Where the tenant under a farm business tenancy has remained in the holding during two or more such tenancies, he shall not be deprived of his right to compensation under section 16 of this Act by reason only that any tenant's improvement was provided during a tenancy other than the one at the termination of which he quits the holding.

(2) The landlord and tenant under a farm business tenancy may agree that the tenant is to be entitled to compensation under section 16 of this Act on the termination of the tenancy even though at that termination the tenant remains in the holding under a new tenancy.

(3) Where the landlord and the tenant have agreed as mentioned in subsection (2) above in relation to any tenancy ('the earlier tenancy'), the tenant shall not be entitled to compensation at the end of any subsequent tenancy in respect of any tenant's improvement provided during the earlier tenancy in relation to the land comprised in the earlier tenancy.

NOTES

Initial Commencement

Specified date: 1 September 1995: see s 41(2).

Extent

This section does not extend to Scotland.

Notes

For a commentary, see para 16.12.

Shall not be deprived of his right to compensation. As to a tenant's entitlement to recover the compensation provided for by this section, see further s 26.

Crown land. As to the application of this Act to land in which there subsists or has at any material time subsisted a Crown interest, see s 37.

Definitions. For 'farm business tenancy', see s 1; for 'tenant's improvement', see s 15; for 'holding', 'tenancy' and 'termination', see s 38(1); for 'landlord' and 'tenant', see s 38(1), (5). Note as to 'the earlier tenancy', sub-s (3) above.

A1.234

24   Resumption of possession of part of holding

(1) Where—

    (a)   the landlord under a farm business tenancy resumes possession of part of the holding in pursuance of any provision of the tenancy, or

    (b)   a person entitled to a severed part of the reversionary estate in a holding held under a farm business tenancy resumes possession of part of the holding by virtue of a notice to quit that part given to the tenant by virtue of section 140 of the Law of Property Act 1925,

the provisions of this Part of this Act shall, subject to subsections (2) and (3) below, apply to that part of the holding (in this section referred to as 'the relevant part') as if it were a separate holding which the tenant had quitted in consequence of a notice to quit and, in a case falling within paragraph (b) above, as if the person resuming possession were the landlord of that separate holding.

(2) The amount of compensation payable to the tenant under section 16 of this Act in respect of any tenant's improvement provided for the relevant part by the tenant and not consisting of planning permission shall, subject to section 20(2) to [(4A)] of this Act, be an amount equal to the increase attributable to the tenant's improvement in the value of the original holding on the termination date as land comprised in a tenancy.

(3) The amount of compensation payable to the tenant under section 16 of this Act in respect of any tenant's improvement which consists of planning permission relating to the relevant part shall, subject to section 21(3) of this Act, be an amount equal to the increase attributable to the fact that the relevant development is authorised by the planning permission in the value of the original holding on the termination date as land comprised in a tenancy.

(4) In a case falling within paragraph (a) or (b) of subsection (1) above, sections 20 and 21 of this Act shall apply [(subject to subsection (4A) below)] on the termination of the tenancy, in relation to the land then comprised in the tenancy, as if the reference in subsection (1) of each of those sections to the holding were a reference to the original holding.

[(4A)   Where—

    (a)   the landlord and the tenant have agreed in writing, after the commencement of this subsection, to limit the amount of compensation payable under section 16 of this Act in respect of any tenant's improvement not consisting of planning permission,

    (b)   that improvement is provided for both the relevant part and the land comprised in the tenancy after the termination date,

    (c)   the case falls within paragraph (a) or (b) of subsection (1) above,

    (d)   the tenant has already received compensation in respect of the improvement, determined in accordance with subsection (2) above, and

    (e)   further compensation in respect of the improvement is payable under section 16 of this Act on termination of the tenancy, the compensation limit referred to in section 20(4A) of this Act shall, for the purposes of determining that further compensation, be reduced by an amount equal to the amount of compensation already received by the tenant in respect of the improvement.]

(5) In subsections (2) to [(4A)] above—

'the original holding' means the land comprised in the farm business tenancy—
    (a) on the date when the landlord gave his consent under section 17 or 18 of this Act in relation to the tenant's improvement, or
    (b) where approval in relation to the tenant's improvement was given by an arbitrator, on the date on which that approval was given,
'the relevant development', in relation to any tenant's improvement which consists of planning permission, has the meaning given by section 21(2) of this Act, and
'the termination date' means the date on which possession of the relevant part was resumed.

NOTES

Initial Commencement

Specified date: 1 September 1995: see s 41(2).

Extent

This section does not extend to Scotland.

Amendment

Sub-s (2): reference to '(4A)' in square brackets substituted by SI 2006/2805, arts 11, 17(1).

Date in force: 19 October 2006: see SI 2006/2805, art 1(1)(b).

Sub-s (4): words '(subject to subsection (4A) below)' in square brackets inserted by SI 2006/2805, arts 11, 17(2).

Date in force: 19 October 2006: see SI 2006/2805, art 1(1)(b).

Sub-s (4A): inserted by SI 2006/2805, arts 11, 17(3).

Date in force: 19 October 2006: see SI 2006/2805, art 1(1)(b).

Sub-s (5): reference to '(4A)' in square brackets substituted by SI 2006/2805, arts 11, 17(4).

Date in force: 19 October 2006: see SI 2006/2805, art 1(1)(b).

Notes

For a commentary, see paras 16.34 and 16.35.

Sub-s (1): This Part of this Act. Ie Pt III (ss 15–27).

Sub-s (2): Compensation payable. As to a tenant's entitlement to recover the compensation provided for by this section, see further s 26.

Sub-s (5): Approval in relation to the tenant's improvement was given by an arbitrator. Ie under s 19(6).

Crown land. As to the application of this Act to land in which there subsists or has at any material time subsisted a Crown interest, see s 37.

Definitions. For 'farm business tenancy', see s 1; for 'tenant's improvement', see s 15; for 'planning permission', see s 27; for 'holding', 'tenancy' and 'termination', see s 38(1); for 'landlord' and 'tenant', see s 38(1), (5). Note as to 'the relevant part', sub-s (1) above; and as to 'the original holding', 'the relevant development' and 'the termination date' in sub-ss (2)–[(4A)] above, sub-s (5) above.

A1.235

25   Compensation where reversionary estate in holding is severed

(1)   Where the reversionary estate in the holding comprised in a farm business tenancy is for the time being vested in more than one person in several parts, the tenant shall be entitled, on quitting the entire holding, to require that any compensation payable to him under section 16 of this Act shall be determined as if the reversionary estate were not so severed.

(2)   Where subsection (1) applies, the arbitrator shall, where necessary, apportion the amount awarded between the persons who for the purposes of this Part of this Act together constitute the landlord of the holding, and any additional costs of the award caused by the apportionment shall be directed by the arbitrator to be paid by those persons in such proportions as he shall determine.

NOTES

Initial Commencement

Specified date: 1 September 1995: see s 41(2).

Extent

This section does not extend to Scotland.

Notes

For a commentary, see para 16.36.

Person. See the note to s 1.

Compensation payable. As to a tenant's entitlement to recover the compensation provided for by this section, see further s 26.

The arbitrator shall, etc. For general provisions applying to arbitrations under this Act, see s 30.

This Part of this Act. Ie Pt III (ss 15–27).

Crown land. As to the application of this Act to land in which there subsists or has at any material time subsisted a Crown interest, see s 37.

Definitions. For 'farm business tenancy', see s 1; for 'holding', see s 38(1); for 'landlord' and 'tenant', see s 38(1), (5).

A1.236

26   Extent to which compensation recoverable under agreements

(1)   In any case for which apart from this section the provisions of this Part of this Act provide for compensation, a tenant shall be entitled to compensation in accordance with those provisions and not otherwise, and shall be so entitled notwithstanding any agreement to the contrary.

(2)   Nothing in the provisions of this Part of this Act, apart from this section, shall be construed as disentitling a tenant to compensation in any case for which those provisions do not provide for compensation.

NOTES

Initial Commencement

Specified date: 1 September 1995: see s 41(2).

Extent

This section does not extend to Scotland.

Notes

For a commentary, see para 16.32.

This Part of this Act. Ie Pt III (ss 15–27).

Tenant. For meaning, see s 38(1), (5).

Crown land. As to the application of this Act to land in which there subsists or has at any material time subsisted a Crown interest, see s 37.

A1.237

27   Interpretation of Part III

In this Part of this Act, unless the context otherwise requires—

'planning permission' has the meaning given by section 336(1) of the Town and
    Country Planning Act 1990;
'tenant's improvement', and references to the provision of such an improvement,
    have the meaning given by section 15 of this Act.

NOTES

Initial Commencement

Specified date: 1 September 1995: see s 41(2).

Extent

This section does not extend to Scotland.

Notes

This Part of this Act. Ie Pt III (ss 15–27).

Unless the context otherwise requires. There is authority for saying that, before it could be held that the context otherwise requires, it would have to be shown not only that the application of the definition leads to a result which Parliament cannot be supposed to have intended but also that, if the definition is excluded, the result will be a more reasonable result which Parliament can be supposed to have intended, and that, where the context requires that part of a definition should not apply, this does not necessarily prevent the application of the rest of that definition; see *London Corpn v Cusack-Smith* [1955] AC 337 at 362, [1955] 1 All ER 302 at 316, HL, per Lord Reid and *McAuley Catholic High School v CC* [2003] EWHC 3045 (Admin), [2004] 2 All ER 436.

Crown land. As to the application of this Act to land in which there subsists or has at any material time subsisted a Crown interest, see s 37.

PART IV: MISCELLANEOUS AND SUPPLEMENTAL

Resolution of disputes

A1.238

28   Resolution of disputes

(1)   Subject to subsections (4) and (5) below and to section 29 of this Act, any dispute between the landlord and the tenant under a farm business tenancy, being a dispute

concerning their rights and obligations under this Act, under the terms of the tenancy or under any custom, shall be determined by arbitration.

(2)   Where such a dispute has arisen, the landlord or the tenant may give notice in writing to the other specifying the dispute and stating that, unless before the end of the period of two months beginning with the day on which the notice is given the parties have appointed an arbitrator by agreement, he proposes to apply to the President of the RICS for the appointment of an arbitrator by him.

(3)   Where a notice has been given under subsection (2) above, but no arbitrator has been appointed by agreement, either party may, after the end of the period of two months referred to in that subsection, apply to the President of the RICS for the appointment of an arbitrator by him.

(4)   ...

(5)   Subsections (1) to (3) above do not apply in relation to—

    (a)   the determination of rent in pursuance of a statutory review notice (as defined in section 10(1) of this Act),

    (b)   any case falling within section 19(1) of this Act, ...

    (c)   any claim for compensation under Part III of this Act[, or

    (d)   any dispute relating to rent review, in any case where Part II of this Act is excluded by virtue of section 9(c)(ii) of this Act].

NOTES

Initial Commencement

Specified date: 1 September 1995: see s 41(2).

Extent

This section does not extend to Scotland.

Amendment

Sub-s (4): repealed by the Arbitration Act 1996, s 107(2), Sch 4.

Sub-s (5): in para (a) word omitted repealed by SI 2006/2805, arts 11, 14(2)(a), 18, Sch 2.

Date in force: 19 October 2006: see SI 2006/2805, art 1(1)(b); for effect see art 14(3).

Sub-s (5): para (d) and word ', or' immediately preceding it inserted by SI 2006/2805, arts 11, 14(2)(b).

Date in force: 19 October 2006: see SI 2006/2805, art 1(1)(b); for effect see art 14(3).

Notes

For a commentary, see para 47.3.

Sub-s (1): Shall be determined by arbitration. For general provisions as to arbitrations under this Act, see s 30. The provisions of the Arbitration Act 1996 apply to an arbitration under this section. See para 44.1.

As to the reference to arbitration of the question whether any of the terms or conditions of a farm business tenancy should be varied in consequence of a change in the state of the land resulting from the occupation or use of the land in the exercise of rights conferred by a compulsory rights order made under the Opencast Coal Act 1958, s 4, see Sch 7, Pt I, para 4A to that Act, as inserted by s 40, Schedule, para 20(1), (7). See also, in relation to mortgages, Pt I, para 7A to the 1958 Act, as inserted by s 40, Schedule, para 20(1), (11).

Sub-s (2): Notice. As to the service of notices required or authorised to be given under this Act, see s 36.

In writing. See the note 'Written' to s 1.

Two months beginning with, etc. See the note 'Two (four) months beginning with, etc' to s 19.

Sub-s (5): Part III of this Act. Ie ss 15–27.

Crown land. As to the application of this Act to land in which there subsists or has at any material time subsisted a Crown interest, see s 37.

Definitions. For 'farm business tenancy', see s 1; for 'the RICS' and 'tenancy', see s 38(1); for 'landlord' and 'tenant', see s 38(1), (5).

A1.239

29   Cases where right to refer claim to arbitration under section 28 does not apply

(1)   Section 28 of this Act does not apply in relation to any dispute if—

  (a)   the tenancy is created by an instrument which includes provision for disputes to be resolved by any person other than—
    (i)   the landlord or the tenant, or
    (ii)   a third party appointed by either of them without the consent or concurrence of the other, and
  (b)   either of the following has occurred—
    (i)   the landlord and the tenant have jointly referred the dispute to the third party under the provision, or
    (ii)   the landlord or the tenant has referred the dispute to the third party under the provision and notified the other in writing of the making of the reference, the period of four weeks beginning with the date on which the other was so notified has expired and the other has not given a notice under section 28(2) of this Act in relation to the dispute before the end of that period.

(2)   For the purposes of subsection (1) above, a term of the tenancy does not provide for disputes to be 'resolved' by any person unless that person (whether or not acting as arbitrator) is enabled under the terms of the tenancy to give a decision which is binding in law on both parties.

NOTES

Initial Commencement

Specified date: 1 September 1995: see s 41(2).

Extent

This section does not extend to Scotland.

Notes

For a commentary, see para 47.4.

Person. See the note to s 1.

Notified. As to the service of notices required or authorised to be given under this Act, see s 36.

In writing. See the note 'Written' to s 1.

Four weeks beginning with, etc. See the note 'Three years beginning with, etc' to s 10.

Crown land. As to the application of this Act to land in which there subsists or has at any material time subsisted a Crown interest, see s 37.

Definitions. For 'tenancy', see s 38(1); for 'landlord' and 'tenant', see s 38(1), (5). Note as to 'resolved', sub-s (2) above.

A1.240

30   General provisions applying to arbitrations under Act

(1)   Any matter which is required to be determined by arbitration under this Act shall be determined by the arbitration of a sole arbitrator.

(2)   Any application under this Act to the President of the RICS for the appointment of an arbitrator by him must be made in writing and must be accompanied by such reasonable fee as the President may determine in respect of the costs of making the appointment.

(3)   Where an arbitrator appointed for the purposes of this Act dies or is incapable of acting and no new arbitrator has been appointed by agreement, either party may apply to the President of the RICS for the appointment of a new arbitrator by him.

NOTES

Initial Commencement

Specified date: 1 September 1995: see s 41(2).

Extent

This section does not extend to Scotland.

Notes

For a commentary, see para 47.5.

Arbitration under this Act. For the matters which may be required to be determined by arbitration under this Act, see ss 10(1), 19(1), 22(1), 28(1). The provisions of the Arbitration Act 1996 apply to arbitrations under this Act. See para 44.1.

The RICS. Ie the Royal Institution of Chartered Surveyors; see s 38(1).

In writing. See the note 'Written' to s 1.

Incapable of acting. The arbitrator is only incapable of acting if the disability is serious enough to put him out of action altogether in acting in the arbitration; see *Succula Ltd and Pomona Shipping Co Ltd v Harland and Wolff Ltd* [1980] 2 Lloyd's Rep 381 at 388.

Crown land. As to the application of this Act to land in which there subsists or has at any material time subsisted a Crown interest, see s 37.

Miscellaneous

A1.241

31   Mortgages of agricultural land

(1)   Section 99 of the Law of Property Act 1925 (leasing powers of mortgagor and mortgagee in possession) shall be amended in accordance with subsections (2) and (3) below.

(2)   At the beginning of subsection (13), there shall be inserted 'Subject to subsection (13A) below,'.

(3)   After that subsection, there shall be inserted—

'(13A)   Subsection (13) of this section—

(a)   shall not enable the application of any provision of this section to be excluded or restricted in relation to any mortgage of agricultural land made after 1st March 1948 but before 1st September 1995, and

1341

(b)   shall not enable the power to grant a lease of an agricultural holding to which, by virtue of section 4 of the Agricultural Tenancies Act 1995, the Agricultural Holdings Act 1986 will apply, to be excluded or restricted in relation to any mortgage of agricultural land made on or after 1st September 1995.

(13B)   In subsection (13A) of this section—

'agricultural holding' has the same meaning as in the Agricultural Holdings Act 1986; and

'agricultural land' has the same meaning as in the Agriculture Act 1947.'

(4)   Paragraph 12 of Schedule 14 to the Agricultural Holdings Act 1986 (which excludes the application of subsection (13) of section 99 of the Law of Property Act 1925 in relation to a mortgage of agricultural land and is superseded by the amendments made by subsections (1) to (3) above) shall cease to have effect.

NOTES

Initial Commencement

Specified date: 1 September 1995: see s 41(2).

Extent

This section does not extend to Scotland.

Amendment

This section amends the Law of Property Act 1925, s 99(13), and inserts s 99(13A), (13B), and repeals the Agricultural Holdings Act 1986, Sch 14, para 12.

Notes

For a commentary, see para 17.18 ff and Ch 43.

1st March 1948. The Agricultural Holdings Act 1986, Sch 14, para 12, was originally enacted as the Agriculture Act 1947, Sch 7, para 24. This was consolidated in the Agricultural Holdings Act 1948, Sch 7, para 2, and then in Sch 14, para 12 to the 1986 Act. Sch 7, para 24 to the 1947 Act was stated to apply in relation to mortgages made after the commencement of Part III of this Act which, by virtue of the Agriculture Act 1947 (Commencement) (No 1) Order 1948, SI 1948/342, was 1 March 1948; hence the consolidating provisions were expressed as applying from that date. The date appears in the amendments made by sub-ss (2), (3) above in order to continue the exclusion of the restrictions on leasing agricultural land that previously benefited from that exclusion.

1 September 1995. Ie the commencement date of this Act; see s 41(2). This date appears in the amendments made by sub-ss (2), (3) above in order to continue the exclusion of the restrictions on leasing agricultural land that previously benefited from that exclusion and to ensure that the amendments made by this section do not operate retrospectively.

Definitions. For 'lease' and 'mortgage', see the Law of Property Act 1925, s 205(1).

Agricultural Holdings Act 1986. For the meaning of 'agricultural holding' in that Act, see s 96(1) thereof.

Agriculture Act 1947. For the meaning of 'agricultural land' in that Act, see s 109(1).

A1.242

32   Power of limited owners to give consents etc

The landlord under a farm business tenancy, whatever his estate or interest in the holding, may, for the purposes of this Act, give any consent, make any agreement or do or have done to him any other act which he might give, make, do or have done to him if he were owner in fee simple or, if his interest is an interest in a leasehold, were absolutely entitled to that leasehold.

NOTES

Initial Commencement

Specified date: 1 September 1995: see s 41(2).

Extent

This section does not extend to Scotland.

Notes

For a commentary, see para 17.14.

Consent. See for instance *Aubergine Enterprises Ltd v Lakewood International Ltd* [2001] 39 EG 141.

Crown land. As to the application of this Act to land in which there subsists or has at any material time subsisted a Crown interest, see s 37.

Definitions. For 'farm business tenancy', see s 1; for 'holding', see s 38(1); for 'landlord', see s 38(1), (5).

A1.243

33   Power to apply and raise capital money

(1) The purposes authorised by section 73 of the Settled Land Act 1925 ... or section 26 of the Universities and College Estates Act 1925 for the application of capital money shall include—

    (a)   the payment of expenses incurred by a landlord under a farm business tenancy in, or in connection with, the making of any physical improvement on the holding,

    (b)   the payment of compensation under section 16 of this Act, and

    (c)   the payment of the costs, charges and expenses incurred by him on a reference to arbitration under section 19 or 22 of this Act.

(2) The purposes authorised by section 71 of the Settled Land Act 1925 ... as purposes for which money may be raised by mortgage shall include the payment of compensation under section 16 of this Act.

(3) Where the landlord under a farm business tenancy—

    (a)   is a tenant for life or in a fiduciary position, and

    (b)   is liable to pay compensation under section 16 of this Act,

he may require the sum payable as compensation and any costs, charges and expenses incurred by him in connection with the tenant's claim under that section to be paid out of any capital money held on the same trusts as the settled land.

(4) In subsection (3) above—

'capital money' includes any personal estate held on the same trusts as the land; ...
...

NOTES

Initial Commencement

Specified date: 1 September 1995: see s 41(2).

Extent

This section does not extend to Scotland.

Amendment

Sub-ss (1), (2), (4): words omitted repealed by the Trusts of Land and Appointment of Trustees Act 1996, s 25(2), Sch 4; for savings in relation to entailed interests created before the commencement of that Act, and savings consequential upon the abolition of the doctrine of conversion, see s 25(4), (5) thereof.

Notes

For a commentary, see para 17.14.

Crown land. As to the application of this Act to land in which there subsists or has at any material time subsisted a Crown interest, see s 37.

Definitions. For 'farm business tenancy', see s 1; for 'holding', see s 38(1); for 'landlord' and 'tenant', see s 38(1), (5).

A1.244

34 Estimation of best rent for purposes of Acts and other instruments

(1) In estimating the best rent or reservation in the nature of rent of land comprised in a farm business tenancy for the purposes of a relevant instrument, it shall not be necessary to take into account against the tenant any increase in the value of that land arising from any tenant's improvements.

(2) In subsection (1) above—

'a relevant instrument' means any Act of Parliament, deed or other instrument which authorises a lease to be made on the condition that the best rent or reservation in the nature of rent is reserved;

'tenant's improvement' has the meaning given by section 15 of this Act.

NOTES

Initial Commencement

Specified date: 1 September 1995: see s 41(2).

Extent

This section does not extend to Scotland.

Notes

For a commentary, see para 17.16.

Crown land. As to the application of this Act to land in which there subsists or has at any material time subsisted a Crown interest, see s 37.

Definitions. For 'farm business tenancy', see s 1; for 'tenant', see s 38(1), (5).

A1.245

35 Preparation of documents etc by valuers and surveyors

(1) Section 22 of the Solicitors Act 1974 (unqualified person not to prepare certain instruments) shall be amended as follows.

(2) In subsection (2), after paragraph (ab) there shall be inserted—

'(ac) any accredited person drawing or preparing any instrument—
  (i) which creates, or which he believes on reasonable grounds will create, a farm business tenancy (within the meaning of the Agricultural Tenancies Act 1995), or
  (ii) which relates to an existing tenancy which is, or which he believes on reasonable grounds to be, such a tenancy;'.

(3) In subsection (3A), immediately before the definition of 'registered trade mark agent' there shall be inserted—

"accredited person' means any person who is—
  (a) a Full Member of the Central Association of Agricultural Valuers,
  (b) an Associate or Fellow of the Incorporated Society of Valuers and Auctioneers, or
  (c) an Associate or Fellow of the Royal Institution of Chartered Surveyors;'.

NOTES

Initial Commencement

Specified date: 1 September 1995: see s 41(2).

Amendment

This section amends the Solicitors Act 1974, s 22(2), (3A).

Notes

For a commentary, see para 3.36.

Believes on reasonable grounds. It is submitted that these words require not only that the person in question has reasonable grounds for believing but also that he does actually believe; see *R v Banks* [1916] 2 KB 621, [1916–17] All ER Rep 356, and *R v Harrison* [1938] 3 All ER 134, 159 LT 95; and see also *Nakkuda All v Jayaratne* [1951] AC 66, PC.

The existence of the reasonable grounds and of the belief founded on them is ultimately a question of fact to be tried on evidence and the grounds on which the person acted must be sufficient to induce in a reasonable person the required belief; see in particular, *McArdle v Egan* (1933) 150 LT 412, [1933] All ER Rep 611, CA; *Nakkuda Ali v Javaratne* above; *Registrar of Restrictive Trading Agreements v W H Smith & Son Ltd* [1969] 3 All ER 1065 at 1070, [1969] 1 WLR 1460 at 1468, CA, per Lord Denning MR, and *R v IRC, ex p Rossminster Ltd* [1980] AC 952, [1980] 1 All ER 80 at 84, 92, 103, 104, HL.

Farm business tenancy. For meaning, see s 1.

Crown land. As to the application of this Act to land in which there subsists or has at any material time subsisted a Crown interest, see s 37.

Supplemental

A1.246

36 Service of notices

(1) This section applies to any notice or other document required or authorised to be given under this Act.

(2)   A notice or other document to which this section applies is duly given to a person if—

(a)   it is delivered to him,
(b)   it is left at his proper address, or
(c)   it is given to him in a manner authorised by a written agreement made, at any time before the giving of the notice, between him and the person giving the notice.

(3)   A notice or other document to which this section applies is not duly given to a person if its text is transmitted to him by facsimile or other electronic means otherwise than by virtue of subsection (2)(c) above.

(4)   Where a notice or other document to which this section applies is to be given to a body corporate, the notice or document is duly given if it is given to the secretary or clerk of that body.

(5)   Where—

(a)   a notice or other document to which this section applies is to be given to a landlord under a farm business tenancy and an agent or servant of his is responsible for the control of the management of the holding, or
(b)   such a document is to be given to a tenant under a farm business tenancy and an agent or servant of his is responsible for the carrying on of a business on the holding,

the notice or document is duly given if it is given to that agent or servant.

(6)   For the purposes of this section, the proper address of any person to whom a notice or other document to which this section applies is to be given is—

(a)   in the case of the secretary or clerk of a body corporate, the registered or principal office of that body, and
(b)   in any other case, the last known address of the person in question.

(7)   Unless or until the tenant under a farm business tenancy has received—

(a)   notice that the person who before that time was entitled to receive the rents and profits of the holding ('the original landlord') has ceased to be so entitled, and
(b)   notice of the name and address of the person who has become entitled to receive the rents and profits,

any notice or other document given to the original landlord by the tenant shall be deemed for the purposes of this Act to have been given to the landlord under the tenancy.

NOTES

Initial Commencement

Specified date: 1 September 1995: see s 41(2).

Extent

This section does not extend to Scotland.

Notes

For a commentary, see para 17.1 ff.

Sub-s (1): Document. A letter may come within this description; see *Carlish v East Ham Corpn and Edwards* [1948] 2 KB 380, [1948] 2 All ER 550, and *Lewisham Borough and Town Clerk v Roberts* [1949] 2 KB 608, [1949] 1 All ER 815.

Sub-s (2): Person. See the note to s 1.

Left at his proper address. If a notice is served in this way it must be left in a manner which a reasonable person, minded to bring the document to the attention of the person to whom it is addressed, would adopt; see *Lord Newborough v Jones* [1975] Ch 90, [1974] 3 All ER 17, CA.

Written. See the note to s 1.

Sub-s (4): Body corporate. For the general law relating to corporations, see 9 Halsbury's Laws (4th edn) paras 1201 ff.

Sub-s (5): Agent or servant. An agent is a person who has authority, express or implied, to act on behalf of another, called the 'principal', and who consents so to act (*Pole v Leask* (1863) 33 LJ Ch 155 at 161). See, further, 1(2) Halsbury's Laws (4th edn reissue) para 1 and 16 Halsbury's Laws (4th edn reissue) paras 1 ff. Whether one person is the servant (or employee) of another is a question of fact (*Brady v Giles* (1835) 1 Mood & R 494; *Jones v Scullard* [1898] 2 QB 565), but, in general, a servant (or employee) is a person who is subject to the commands of his master (or employer) not only as to what work he is to do but also as to the manner in which it is to be done (*Yewens v Noakes* (1880) 6 QBD 530 at 532, CA, per Bramwell LJ; *Simmons v Heath Laundry Co* [1910] 1 KB 543 at 552, CA per Buckley LJ).

Carrying on of a business. The words 'carrying on of a business' denote something of a permanent character, not merely an isolated transaction and a business is carried on only where there is some degree of management or control; see *Brown v London and North-Western Rly Co* (1863) 32 LJQB 318, [1861–73] All ER Rep 487; *Graham v Lewis* (1888) 22 QBD 1, CA; and *Cain v Butler* [1916] 1 KB 759 at 762; but contrast *Cornelius v Phillips* [1918] AC 199, [1916–17] All ER Rep 685, HL. See also *Kirkwood v Gadd* [1910] AC 422 at 423, [1908–10] All ER Rep 768 at 771, HL; *Newman v Oughton* [1911] 1 KB 792; *Transport and General Credit Corpn Ltd v Morgan* [1939] Ch 531, [1939] 2 All ER 17; *Re Brauch (a debtor), ex p Britannic Securities and Investments Ltd* [1978] Ch 316, [1978] 1 All ER 1004, CA; and *Re Sarflax Ltd* [1979] Ch 592, [1979] 1 All ER 529. On the meaning of 'business', see 47 Halsbury's Laws (4th edn) paras 2, 3, and 1 Words and Phrases (3rd edn) 204 ff, and the note 'Trade or business' to s 1.

Sub-s (6): Registered or principal office. As to the registered office of a company, see the Companies Act 2006 Pt 6 (to come into force on a day to be appointed – see s 1300(2)), s 1295 and Sch 16 of the 2006 Act repeals the Companies Act 1985, s 287, as from a day to be appointed. The 'principal office' is the place where the business of the body corporate is managed and controlled as a whole; see *Garton v Great Western Rly Co* (1858) EB & E 837; *Palmer v Caledonian Rly Co* [1892] 1 QB 823; and *Clokey v London and North-Western Rly Co* [1905] 2 IR 251.

Last known address. Though as a general rule an address which the person concerned is known to have left is not a proper address for service (*White v Weston* [1968] 2 QB 647, [1968] 2 All ER 842, CA and *Adram v Adam* [2004] EWCA Civ 1601, [2005] 1 All ER 741), the position is otherwise where the use of the last known address is expressly authorised (*Re Follick, ex p Trustee* (1907) 97 LT 645). However, service at the last known address in England or Wales is not good if a later address abroad is known (*R v Farmer* [1892] 1 QB 637, [1891–4] All ER Rep 921, CA). For other relevant cases, see *Hanrott's Trustees v Evans* (1887) 4 TLR 128; *R v Webb* [1896] 1 QB 487; *Berry v Farrow* [1914] 1 KB 632; *Stylo Shoes Ltd v Prices Tailors Ltd* [1960] Ch 396, [1959] 3 All ER 901; *McGlynn v Stewart* 1974 SLT 230 and *Arundel Corpn v Khokher* [2003] EWCA Civ 1784, 148 Sol Jo LB 25.

Sub-s (7): Deemed. The primary function of the word 'deem' is to bring in something which would otherwise be excluded; see *IRC v Barclays Bank Ltd* [1961] AC 509 at 523, [1960] 2 All ER 817 at 820, HL per Viscount Simonds. For other relevant cases, see 2 Words and Phrases (2nd edn) 27, 28, and *Public Trustee v IRC* [1960] AC 398, [1960] 1 All ER 1 at 510, HL per Lord Radcliffe. See also *WX Investments Ltd v Begg (Fraser, Part 20 defendant)* [2002] EWHC 925 (Ch), [2002] 1 WLR 2849 and *CA Webber (Transport) Ltd v Railtrack plc* [2003] EWCA Civ 1167, [2004] 3 All ER 202. See para 42.16.

Crown land. As to the application of this Act to land in which there subsists or has at any material time subsisted a Crown interest, see s 37.

Definitions. For 'farm business tenancy', see s 1; for 'holding' and 'tenancy', see s 38(1); for 'landlord' and 'tenant', see s 38(1), (5). Note as to the proper address of a person, sub-s (6) above, and as to 'the original landlord', sub-s (7) above.

A1.247

37   Crown land

(1)   This Act shall apply in relation to land in which there subsists, or has at any material time subsisted, a Crown interest as it applies in relation to land in which no such interest subsists or has ever subsisted.

(2)   For the purposes of this Act—

   (a)   where an interest belongs to Her Majesty in right of the Crown and forms part of the Crown Estate, the Crown Estate Commissioners shall be treated as the owner of the interest,

   (b)   where an interest belongs to Her Majesty in right of the Crown and does not form part of the Crown Estate, the government department having the management of the land or, if there is no such department, such person as Her Majesty may appoint in writing under the Royal Sign Manual shall be treated as the owner of the interest,

   (c)   where an interest belongs to Her Majesty in right of the Duchy of Lancaster, the Chancellor of the Duchy shall be treated as the owner of the interest,

   (d)   where an interest belongs to a government department or is held in trust for Her Majesty for the purposes of a government department, that department shall be treated as the owner of the interest, and

   (e)   where an interest belongs to the Duchy of Cornwall, such person as the Duke of Cornwall or the possessor for the time being of the Duchy of Cornwall appoints shall be treated as the owner of the interest and, in the case where the interest is that of landlord, may do any act or thing which a landlord is authorised or required to do under this Act.

(3)   If any question arises as to who is to be treated as the owner of a Crown interest, that question shall be referred to the Treasury, whose decision shall be final.

(4)   In subsections (1) and (3) above 'Crown interest' means an interest which belongs to Her Majesty in right of the Crown or of the Duchy of Lancaster or to the Duchy of Cornwall, or to a government department, or which is held in trust for Her Majesty for the purposes of a government department.

(5)   Any compensation payable under section 16 of this Act by the Chancellor of the Duchy of Lancaster may be raised and paid under section 25 of the Duchy of Lancaster Act 1817 (application of monies) as an expense incurred in improvement of land belonging to Her Majesty in right of the Duchy.

(6)   In the case of land belonging to the Duchy of Cornwall, the purposes authorised by section 8 of the Duchy of Cornwall Management Act 1863 (application of monies) for the advancement of parts of such gross sums as are there mentioned shall include the payment of compensation under section 16 of this Act.

(7)   Nothing in subsection (6) above shall be taken as prejudicing the operation of the Duchy of Cornwall Management Act 1982.

NOTES

Initial Commencement

Specified date: 1 September 1995: see s 41(2).

Extent

This section does not extend to Scotland.

Notes

For a commentary, see para 17.17.

Sub-s (2): Crown Estate, and the Crown Estate Commissioners. For the property which is known as the 'Crown Estate', see the Crown Estate Act 1961, s 1(1). The Crown Estate Commissioners are the Commissioners referred to in that section; see the Interpretation Act 1978, s 5, Sch 1.

Person. See the note to s 1.

In writing. See the note 'Written' to s 1.

Duchy of Lancaster; Chancellor of the Duchy. As to the Duchy of Lancaster and the Chancellor of the Duchy, see 8 Halsbury's Laws (4th edn) paras 1523–1559.

Duchy of Cornwall; Duke of Cornwall. As to the Duchy of Cornwall and the Duke of Cornwall, see 8 Halsbury's Laws (4th edn) paras 1560–1612.

Do any act or thing which a landlord is authorised or required to do under this Act. See also, in this regard, s 32.

Sub-s (3): Treasury. Ie the Commissioners of HM Treasury; see the Interpretation Act 1978, s 5, Sch 1.

Definitions. For 'landlord', see s 38(1), (5). Note as to 'Crown interest' in sub-ss (1), (3) above, sub-s (4) above.

A1.248

38   Interpretation

(1)   In this Act, unless the context otherwise requires—

'agriculture' includes horticulture, fruit growing, seed growing, dairy farming and livestock breeding and keeping, the use of land as grazing land, meadow land, osier land, market gardens and nursery grounds, and the use of land for woodlands where that use is ancillary to the farming of land for other agricultural purposes, and 'agricultural' shall be construed accordingly;

'building' includes any part of a building;

'fixed term tenancy' means any tenancy other than a periodic tenancy;

'holding', in relation to a farm business tenancy, means the aggregate of the land comprised in the tenancy;

'landlord' includes any person from time to time deriving title from the original landlord;

'livestock' includes any creature kept for the production of food, wool, skins or fur or for the purpose of its use in the farming of land;

'the RICS' means the Royal Institution of Chartered Surveyors;

'tenancy' means any tenancy other than a tenancy at will, and includes a sub-tenancy and an agreement for a tenancy or sub-tenancy;

'tenant' includes a sub-tenant and any person deriving title from the original tenant or sub-tenant;

'termination', in relation to a tenancy, means the cesser of the tenancy by reason of effluxion of time or from any other cause.

(2)   References in this Act to the farming of land include references to the carrying on in relation to land of any agricultural activity.

(3)   A tenancy granted pursuant to a contract shall be taken for the purposes of this Act to have been granted when the contract was entered into.

(4)   For the purposes of this Act a tenancy begins on the day on which, under the terms of the tenancy, the tenant is entitled to possession under that tenancy; and references in this Act to the beginning of the tenancy are references to that day.

(5) The designations of landlord and tenant shall continue to apply until the conclusion of any proceedings taken under this Act in respect of compensation.

NOTES

Initial Commencement

Specified date: 1 September 1995: see s 41(2).

Extent

This section does not extend to Scotland.

Notes

Sub-s (1): Unless the context otherwise requires. See the note to s 27.

Building. It is thought that this expression must be given its ordinary meaning, which, in the words of Byles J in *Stevens v Gourley* (1859) 7 CBNS 99 at 112, is 'a structure of considerable size and intended to be permanent or at least to endure for a considerable time'. Perhaps there must also be added, in accordance with the view expressed by Lord Esher MR in *Moir v Williams* [1892] 1 QB 264 at 270, that the structure must be covered by a roof. It is submitted, however, that contrary to that view, the structure need not consist of bricks and stone-work. In fact a wooden structure of considerable size was held to be a building in *Stevens v Gourley* above, and in any case the presence of bricks and stone-work seems to be irrelevant in the light of modern technology. Nevertheless, it would seem that a structure cannot be regarded as a building unless it can be said to form part of the realty and change the physical character of the land; see *Cheshire County Council v Woodward* [1962] 2 QB 126, [1962] 1 All ER 517. See also *Holding & Barnes plc v Hill House Hammond Ltd* [2001] EWCA Civ 1334, [2002] 2 P & CR 11 where, in construing a landlord's repairing covenant the word 'building' was deemed to mean the demised property. See also the cases cited in 1 Words and Phrases (3rd edn) 196 ff.

Farm business tenancy. For meaning, see s 1.

Livestock. See *Field v Bryant* [2003] EWCA Civ 1957, [2004] PLSCS 22, where a user covenant in a farm business tenancy requiring the tenant to use the holding for 'permanent pasture for livestock only' was to be read against the material background of facts known to the parties at the time the terms of the tenancy were agreed. In that context, they were found to allow the tenant to continue to carry on his milk and dairy business from the holding. Also see, *Cook v Horne* [2006] PLSCS 18 where the claimant's fish were held not to be 'kept for the production of food' as this was not the predominant purpose for which they were kept.

Person. See the note to s 1.

Sub-s (2): Carrying on … any agricultural activity. Cf the note 'Carrying on of a business' to s 36.

Sub-s (4): Crown land. As to the application of this Act to land in which there subsists or has at any material time subsisted a Crown interest, see s 37.

A1.249

39 Index of defined expressions

In this Act the expressions listed below are defined by or otherwise fall to be construed in accordance with the provisions indicated—

agriculture, agricultural	section 38(1)
begins, beginning (in relation to a tenancy)	section 38(4)
building	section 38(1)
farm business tenancy	section 1
farming (of land)	section 38(2)
fixed term tenancy	section 38(1)
grant (of a tenancy)	section 38(3)

holding (in relation to a farm business tenancy)	section 38(1)
landlord	section 38(1) and (5)
livestock	section 38(1)
planning permission (in Part III)	section 27
provision (of a tenant's improvement) (in Part III)	section 15
the review date (in Part II)	section 10(2)
the RICS	section 38(1)
statutory review notice (in Part II)	section 10(1)
tenancy	section 38(1)
tenant	section 38(1) and (5)
tenant's improvement (in Part III)	section 15
termination (of a tenancy)	section 38(1).

NOTES

Initial Commencement

Specified date: 1 September 1995: see s 41(2).

Extent

This section does not extend to Scotland.

A1.250

40   Consequential amendments

The Schedule to this Act (which contains consequential amendments) shall have effect.

NOTES

Initial Commencement

Specified date: 1 September 1995: see s 41(2).

A1.251

41   Short title, commencement and extent

(1)   This Act may be cited as the Agricultural Tenancies Act 1995.

(2)   This Act shall come into force on 1st September 1995.

(3)   Subject to subsection (4) below, this Act extends to England and Wales only.

(4)   The amendment by a provision of the Schedule to this Act of an enactment which extends to Scotland or Northern Ireland also extends there, except that paragraph 9 of the Schedule does not extend to Northern Ireland.

NOTES

Initial Commencement

Specified date: 1 September 1995: see sub-s (2) above.

Note

England; Wales. For meanings, see the Interpretation Act 1978, s 5, Sch 1.

SCHEDULE
CONSEQUENTIAL AMENDMENTS

Section 40

The Small Holdings and Allotments Act 1908 (c 36)

A1.252

1   (1)   Section 47 of the Small Holdings and Allotments Act 1908 (compensation for improvements) shall be amended as follows.

(2)   In subsection (1), after 'to any tenant' there shall be inserted 'otherwise than under a farm business tenancy'.

(3)   In subsection (2), after 'small holdings or allotments' there shall be inserted 'otherwise than under a farm business tenancy'.

(4)   In subsection (3), after 'if there shall be inserted 'he is not a tenant under a farm business tenancy and'.

(5)   In subsection (4), after 'allotment' there shall be inserted 'who is not a tenant under a farm business tenancy'.

(6)   After that subsection, there shall be inserted—

'(5)   In this section, farm business tenancy has the same meaning as in the Agricultural Tenancies Act 1995.'

The Law of Distress Amendment Act 1908 (c 53)

2   In section 4(1) of the Law of Distress Amendment Act 1908 (exclusion of certain goods), for 'to which that section applies' there shall be substituted 'on land comprised in a tenancy to which that Act applies'.

The Allotments Act 1922 (c 51)

3   In section 3(7) of the Allotments Act 1922 (provision as to cottage holdings and certain allotments), after 'landlord' there shall be inserted 'otherwise than under a farm business tenancy (within the meaning of the Agricultural Tenancies Act 1995)'.

4   In section 6(1) of that Act (assessment and recovery of compensation), after 'contract of tenancy' there shall be inserted '(not being a farm business tenancy within the meaning of the Agricultural Tenancies Act 1995)'.

The Landlord and Tenant Act 1927 (c 36)

5   In section 17(1) of the Landlord and Tenant Act 1927 (holdings to which Part I applies), for the words from 'not being' to the end there is substituted—

'not being—
(a) agricultural holdings within the meaning of the Agricultural Holdings Act 1986 held under leases in relation to which that Act applies, or
(b) holdings held under farm business tenancies within the meaning of the Agricultural Tenancies Act 1995.'

6   In section 19(4) of that Act (provisions as to covenants not to assign etc without licence or consent), after 'the Agricultural Holdings Act 1986' there shall be inserted 'which are leases in relation to which that Act applies, or to farm business tenancies within the meaning of the Agricultural Tenancies Act 1995'.

The Agricultural Credits Act 1928 (c 43)

7   In section 5(7) of the Agricultural Credits Act 1928 (agricultural charges on farming stock and assets) in the definition of 'other agricultural assets', after 'otherwise' there shall be inserted 'a tenant's right to compensation under section 16 of the Agricultural Tenancies Act 1995,'.

The Leasehold Property (Repairs) Act 1938 (c 34)

8   In section 7(1) of the Leasehold Property (Repairs) Act 1938 (interpretation), at the end there shall be added 'which is a lease in relation to which that Act applies and not being a farm business tenancy within the meaning of the Agricultural Tenancies Act 1995'.

The Reserve and Auxiliary Forces (Protection of Civil Interests) Act 1951 (c 65)

9   (1)   Section 27 of the Reserve and Auxiliary Forces (Protection of Civil Interests) Act 1951 (renewal of tenancy expiring during period of service or within two months thereafter) shall be amended as follows.

(2)   In subsection (1), for the words from 'are an agricultural holding' onwards there shall be substituted—

'(a)   are an agricultural holding (within the meaning of the Agricultural Holdings Act 1986) held under a tenancy in relation to which that Act applies,
(b)   are a holding (other than a holding excepted from this provision) held under a farm business tenancy, or
(c)   consist of or comprise premises (other than premises excepted from this provision) licensed for the sale of intoxicating liquor for consumption on the premises.'

(3)   In subsection (5), after paragraph (b) there shall be inserted—

'(bb) the expressions farm business tenancy and holding, in relation to such a tenancy, have the same meaning as in the Agricultural Tenancies Act 1995;'.

(4)   After that subsection, there shall be inserted—

'(5A) In paragraph (b) of the proviso to subsection (1) of this section the reference to a holding excepted from the provision is a reference to a holding held under a farm business tenancy in which there is comprised a dwelling-house occupied by the person responsible for the control (whether as tenant or servant or agent of the tenant) of the management of the holding.'

(5)   In subsection (6), for the words from the beginning to 'liquor' there shall be substituted 'In paragraph (c) of the proviso to subsection (1) of this section, the reference to premises excepted from the provision'.

The Landlord and Tenant Act 1954 (c 56)

10   In section 43(1) of the Landlord and Tenant Act 1954 (tenancies excluded from Part II)—

(a)   in paragraph (a), for the words from 'or a tenancy' to '1986' there shall be substituted 'which is a tenancy in relation to which the Agricultural Holdings Act 1986 applies or a tenancy which would be a tenancy of an agricultural holding in relation to which that Act applied if subsection (3) of section 2 of that Act', and
(b)   after that paragraph there shall be inserted—
'(aa) to a farm business tenancy;'.

11 In section 51(1) of that Act (extension of Leasehold Property (Repairs) Act 1938), for paragraph (c) there shall be substituted—

'(c) that the tenancy is neither a tenancy of an agricultural holding in relation to which the Agricultural Holdings Act 1986 applies nor a farm business tenancy.'

12 In section 69(1) of that Act (interpretation), after the definition of 'development corporation' there shall be inserted—

"farm business tenancy' has the same meaning as in the Agricultural Tenancies Act 1995;'.

The Opencast Coal Act 1958 (c 69)

13 (1) Section 14 of the Opencast Coal Act 1958 (provisions as to agricultural tenancies in England and Wales) shall be amended as follows.

(2) In subsection (1)(b), for 'or part of an agricultural holding' there shall be substituted 'held under a tenancy in relation to which the Agricultural Holdings Act 1986 (in this Act referred to as 'the Act of 1986') applies or part of such an agricultural holding'.

(3) In subsection (2), for the words from 'Agricultural' to 'of 1986')' there shall be substituted 'Act of 1986'.

14 After section 14A of that Act, there shall be inserted—

'14B   Provisions as to farm business tenancies

(1) Without prejudice to the provisions of Part III of this Act as to matters arising between landlords and tenants in consequence of compulsory rights orders, the provisions of this section shall have effect where—

(a) opencast planning permission has been granted subject to a restoration condition, and

(b) immediately before that permission is granted, any of the land comprised therein consists of the holding or part of the holding held under a farm business tenancy,

whether any of that land is comprised in a compulsory rights order or not.

(2) For the purposes of section 1 of the Agricultural Tenancies Act 1995 (in this Act referred to as 'the Act of 1995'), the land shall be taken, while it is occupied or used for the permitted activities, to be used for the purposes for which it was used immediately before it was occupied or used for the permitted activities.

(3) For the purposes of the Act of 1995, nothing done or omitted by the tenant or by the landlord under the tenancy by way of permitting any of the land in respect of which opencast planning permission has been granted to be occupied for the purpose of carrying on any of the permitted activities, or by way of facilitating the use of any of that land for that purpose, shall be taken to be a breach of any term or condition of the tenancy, either on the part of the tenant or on the part of the landlord.

(4) In determining under subsections (1) and (2) of section 13 of the Act of 1995 the rent which should be properly payable for the holding, in respect of any period for which the person with the benefit of the opencast planning permission is in occupation of the holding, or of any part thereof, for the purpose of carrying on any of the permitted activities, the arbitrator shall disregard any increase or diminution in the rental value of the holding in so far as that increase or diminution is attributable to the occupation of the holding, or of that part of the holding, by that person for the purpose of carrying on any of the permitted activities.

(5)   In this section 'holding', in relation to a farm business tenancy, has the same meaning as in the Act of 1995.

(6)   (*Applies to Scotland only.*)'

15   (1)   Section 24 of that Act (tenant's right to compensation for improvements and other matters) shall be amended as follows.

(2)   In subsection (1)(a), after 'holding' there shall be inserted 'held under a tenancy in relation to which the Act of 1986 applies'.

(3)   (*Applies to Scotland only.*)

16   After section 25 of that Act, there shall be inserted—

'25A   **Tenant's right to compensation for improvements etc: farm business tenancies**

(1)   The provisions of this section shall have effect where—

(a)   any part of the land comprised in a compulsory rights order is held, immediately before the date of entry, under a farm business tenancy;

(b)   there have been provided in relation to the land which is both so comprised and so held ('the tenant's land') tenant's improvements in respect of which, immediately before that date, the tenant had a prospective right to compensation under section 16 of the Act of 1995 on quitting the holding on the termination of the tenancy;

(c)   at the end of the period of occupation, the tenant's land has lost the benefit of any such improvement; and

(d)   immediately after the end of that period, the tenant's land is comprised in the same tenancy as immediately before the date of entry, or is comprised in a subsequent farm business tenancy at the end of which the tenant is not deprived, by virtue of section 23(3) of that Act, of his right to compensation under section 16 of that Act in respect of any tenant's improvement provided during the earlier tenancy in relation to the tenant's land.

(2)   For the purposes of subsection (1) of this section, subsection (2) of section 22 of the Act of 1995 (which requires notice to be given of the intention to make a claim) shall be disregarded.

(3)   Subject to subsection (4) of this section, Part III of the Act of 1995 shall apply as if—

(a)   the tenant's land were in the state in which it was immediately before the date of entry, and

(b)   the tenancy under which that land is held at the end of the period of occupation had terminated immediately after the end of that period and the tenant had then quitted the holding.

(4)   Where the tenant's land has lost the benefit of some tenant's improvements but has not lost the benefit of all of them, Part III of the Act of 1995 shall apply as mentioned in subsection (3) above, but as if the improvements of which the tenant's land has not lost the benefit had not been tenant's improvements.

(5)   For the purposes of subsections (1) and (4) of this section, the tenant's land shall be taken to have lost the benefit of a tenant's improvement if the benefit of that improvement has been lost (wholly or in part) without being replaced by another improvement of comparable benefit to the land.

(6)   In this section 'holding', in relation to a farm business tenancy, 'tenant's improvement', 'termination', in relation to a tenancy, and references to the provision of a tenant's improvement have the same meaning as in the Act of 1995.

(7) (*Applies to Scotland only.*)'

17 (1) Section 26 of that Act (compensation for short-term improvements and related matters) shall be amended as follows.

(2) In subsection (1), after 'agricultural land' there shall be inserted 'and was not comprised in a farm business tenancy'.

(3) (*Applies to Scotland only.*)

18 (1) Section 28 of that Act (special provision as to market gardens) shall be amended as follows.

(2) In subsection (1), after 'market garden' there shall be inserted 'and was not comprised in a farm business tenancy'.

(3) (*Applies to Scotland only.*)

19 In section 51 of that Act (interpretation) in subsection (1)—

    (a) after the definition of 'the Act of 1986' there shall be inserted—
        "the Act of 1995' means the Agricultural Tenancies Act 1995;'
    and

    (b) after the definition of 'emergency powers' there shall be inserted—
        "farm business tenancy' has the same meaning as in the Act of 1995;'.

20 (1) Schedule 7 to that Act (adjustments between landlords and tenants and in respect of mortgages and mining leases and orders) shall be amended as follows.

(2) After paragraph 1, there shall be inserted—

'1A (1) The provisions of this paragraph shall have effect where—

    (a) paragraphs (a) and (b) of subsection (1) of section 25A of this Act apply, and
    (b) the farm business tenancy at the end of which the tenant could have claimed compensation for tenant's improvements terminates on or after the date of entry, but before the end of the period of occupation, without being succeeded by another such subsequent tenancy.

(2) In the circumstances specified in sub-paragraph (1) of this paragraph, the provisions of Part III of the Act of 1995—

    (a) shall apply, in relation to the tenancy mentioned in that sub-paragraph, as if, at the termination of that tenancy, the land in question were in the state in which it was immediately before the date of entry, and
    (b) if the tenant under that tenancy quitted the holding before the termination of his tenancy, shall so apply as if he had quitted the holding on the termination of his tenancy.

(3) In sub-paragraph (2) of this paragraph, 'holding', in relation to a farm business tenancy, and 'termination', in relation to a tenancy, have the same meaning as in the Act of 1995.'

(3) In paragraph 2, in sub-paragraph (1), after 'agricultural holding' there shall be inserted 'held under a tenancy in relation to which the Act of 1986 applies'.

(4) After that paragraph there shall be inserted—

'2A (1) The provisions of this paragraph shall have effect where land comprised in a farm business tenancy is comprised in a compulsory rights order (whether any other land is comprised in the holding, or comprised in the order, or not), and—

    (a) before the date of entry there had been provided in relation to the land in question tenant's improvements (in this paragraph referred to as 'the former tenant's improvements') in respect of which, immediately before that date, the tenant had a prospective right to compensation under section 16 of the Act of 1995 on quitting the holding on the termination of the tenancy, and

(b) at the end of the period of occupation the circumstances are such that Part III of that Act would have applied as mentioned in subsections (3) and (4) of section 25A of this Act, but for the fact that the benefit of the former tenant's improvements has been replaced, on the restoration of the land, by other improvements (in this paragraph referred to as 'the new improvements') of comparable benefit to the land.

(2) In the circumstances specified in sub-paragraph (1) of this paragraph, Part III of the Act of 1995 shall have effect in relation to the new improvements as if those improvements were tenant's improvements.

(3) Subsections (2) and (6) of section 25A of this Act shall apply for the purposes of this paragraph as they apply for the purposes of that section.'

(5) After paragraph 3 there shall be inserted—

'**3A** Where by virtue of section 25A of this Act a tenant is entitled to compensation for tenant's improvements as mentioned in that section and—

(a) after the end of the period of occupation expenses are incurred in replacing the benefit of the tenant's improvements by other improvements of comparable benefit to the land, and

(b) the person incurring those expenses (whether he is the landlord or not) is entitled to compensation in respect of those expenses under section 22 of this Act,

section 13 of the Act of 1995 shall apply as if the works in respect of which those expenses are incurred were not tenant's improvements, if apart from this paragraph they would constitute such improvements.'

(6) At the end of paragraph 4, there shall be added—

'(7) In this paragraph 'agricultural holding' does not include an agricultural holding held under a farm business tenancy.'

(7) After that paragraph there shall be inserted—

'**4A** (1) The provisions of this paragraph shall apply where—

(a) immediately before the operative date of a compulsory rights order, any of the land comprised in the order is subject to a farm business tenancy, and

(b) that tenancy continues until after the end of the period of occupation.

(2) The landlord or tenant under the tenancy may, by notice in writing served on his tenant or landlord, demand a reference to arbitration of the question whether any of the terms and conditions of the tenancy (including any term or condition relating to rent) should be varied in consequence of any change in the state of the land resulting from the occupation or use of the land in the exercise of rights conferred by the order; and subsection (3) of section 28 of the Act of 1995 shall apply in relation to a notice under this sub-paragraph as it applies in relation to a notice under subsection (2) of that section.

(3) On a reference by virtue of this paragraph, the arbitrator shall determine what variations (if any) should be made in the terms and conditions of the tenancy, and the date (not being earlier than the end of the period of occupation) from which any such variations are to take effect or to be treated as having taken effect; and as from that date the tenancy shall have effect, or, as the case may be, shall be treated as having had effect, subject to any variations determined by the arbitrator under this paragraph.

(4)   The provisions of this paragraph shall not affect any right of the landlord or the tenant, or the jurisdiction of the arbitrator, under Part II of the Act of 1995; but where—

(a)   there is a reference by virtue of this paragraph and a reference under Part II of that Act in respect of the same tenancy, and

(b)   it appears to the arbitrator that the reference under Part II of that Act relates wholly or mainly to the consequences of the occupation or use of the land in the exercise of rights conferred by the order,

he may direct that proceedings on the two references shall be taken concurrently.'

(8)   In paragraph 5(1), after 'agricultural holding' there shall be inserted 'held under a tenancy in relation to which the Act of 1986 applies'.

(9)   In paragraph 6—

(a)   in sub-paragraph (1), for 'an agricultural holding' there shall be substituted

'—

(a)   an agricultural holding held under a tenancy in relation to which the Act of 1986 applies, or

(b)   a holding under a farm business tenancy,'

; and

(b)   after sub-paragraph (2) there shall be added—

'(2A)   In sub-paragraph (1) of this paragraph, 'holding', in relation to a farm business tenancy, has the same meaning as in the Act of 1995.'

(10)   In paragraph 7—

after 'The provisions of there shall be inserted 'sub-paragraphs (1) to (6) of';
for 'that paragraph' there shall be substituted 'those sub-paragraphs'; and
after 'subject to a mortgage' there shall be inserted 'but not comprised in a farm business tenancy'.

(11)   After that paragraph there shall be inserted—

'7A   The provisions of paragraph 4A of this Schedule shall apply in relation to mortgages of land comprised in farm business tenancies as they apply in relation to such tenancies, as if any reference in that paragraph to such a tenancy were a reference to such a mortgage, and any reference to a landlord or to a tenant were a reference to a mortgagee or to a mortgagor, as the case may be.'

(12)   In paragraph 12(1)(a), for the words from 'did' to 'holding' there shall be substituted 'was not comprised in a tenancy in relation to which the Act of 1986 applies or in a farm business tenancy'.

(13)   In paragraph 13, after 'or to a tenancy' there shall be inserted '(other than a reference to a tenancy in relation to which the Act of 1986 applies or a farm business tenancy)'.

(14)   (*Applies to Scotland only.*)

The Agriculture (Miscellaneous Provisions) Act 1963 (c 11)

21   (1)   Section 22 of the Agriculture (Miscellaneous Provisions) Act 1963 (allowances to persons displaced from agricultural land) shall be amended as follows.

(2)   In subsection (1), for paragraph (a) there shall be substituted—

'(a)   the land—

    (i) is used for the purposes of agriculture (within the meaning of the Agricultural Tenancies Act 1995) and is so used by way of a trade or business, or

    (ii) is not so used but is comprised in a farm business tenancy (within the meaning of the Agricultural Tenancies Act 1995) and used for the purposes of a trade or business,'.

(3) In subsection (6)(c), for 'the Agricultural Holdings Act 1986' there shall be substituted ', the Agricultural Tenancies Act 1995'.

The Leasehold Reform Act 1967 (c 88)

22 In section 1(3) of the Leasehold Reform Act 1967 (tenants entitled to enfranchisement or extension), for paragraph (b) there shall be substituted—

'(b) it is comprised in—

    (i) an agricultural holding within the meaning of the Agricultural Holdings Act 1986 held under a tenancy in relation to which that Act applies, or

    (ii) the holding held under a farm business tenancy within the meaning of the Agricultural Tenancies Act 1995.'

The Agriculture (Miscellaneous Provisions) Act 1968 (c 34)

23 In section 12 of the Agriculture (Miscellaneous Provisions) Act 1968 (additional payments in consequence of compulsory acquisition etc of agricultural holdings), after subsection (1) there shall be inserted—

'(1A) No sum shall be payable by virtue of subsection (1) of this section in respect of any land comprised in a farm business tenancy within the meaning of the Agricultural Tenancies Act 1995.'

The Land Compensation Act 1973 (c 26)

24 In section 48 of the Land Compensation Act 1973 (compensation in respect of agricultural holdings) at the beginning of subsection (1) there shall be inserted 'Subject to subsection (1A) below' and after subsection (1) there shall be inserted—

'(1A) This section does not have effect where the tenancy of the agricultural holding is a tenancy to which, by virtue of section 4 of the Agricultural Tenancies Act 1995, the Agricultural Holdings Act 1986 does not apply.'

The Rent (Agriculture) Act 1976 (c 80)

25 (1) Section 9 of the Rent (Agriculture) Act 1976 (effect of determination of superior tenancy, etc) shall be amended as follows.

(2) In subsection (3), after 'the Agricultural Holdings Act 1986' there shall be inserted 'held under a tenancy in relation to which that Act applies and land comprised in a farm business tenancy within the meaning of the Agricultural Tenancies Act 1995'.

(3) In subsection (4), for the words from 'or' at the end of paragraph (b) onwards there shall be substituted—

'(c) a tenancy of an agricultural holding within the meaning of the Agricultural Holdings Act 1986 which is a tenancy in relation to which that Act applies; or

(d) a farm business tenancy within the meaning of the Agricultural Tenancies Act 1995.'

26 In Schedule 2 to that Act (meaning of 'relevant licence' and 'relevant tenancy'), in paragraph 2 for the words from 'and a tenancy' to the end there shall be substituted ', a tenancy of an agricultural holding within the meaning of the Agricultural Holdings

Act 1986 which is a tenancy in relation to which that Act applies, and a farm business tenancy within the meaning of the Agricultural Tenancies Act 1995'.

The Rent Act 1977 (c 42)

27   For section 10 of the Rent Act 1977 there shall be substituted—

'**10   Agricultural holdings etc**

(1)   A tenancy is not a protected tenancy if—

    (a)   the dwelling-house is comprised in an agricultural holding and is occupied by the person responsible for the control (whether as tenant or as servant or agent of the tenant) of the farming of the holding, or

    (b)   the dwelling-house is comprised in the holding held under a farm business tenancy and is occupied by the person responsible for the control (whether as tenant or as servant or agent of the tenant) of the management of the holding.

(2)   In subsection (1) above—

'agricultural holding' means any agricultural holding within the meaning of the Agricultural Holdings Act 1986 held under a tenancy in relation to which that Act applies, and

'farm business tenancy', and 'holding' in relation to such a tenancy, have the same meaning as in the Agricultural Tenancies Act 1995.'

28   (1)   Section 137 of that Act (effect on sub-tenancy of determination of superior tenancy) shall be amended as follows.

(2)   In subsection (3), after 'the Agricultural Holdings Act 1986' there shall be inserted 'held under a tenancy to which that Act applies and land comprised in a farm business tenancy within the meaning of the Agricultural Tenancies Act 1995'.

(3)   In subsection (4), in paragraph (c), for the words from 'applies' onwards there shall be substituted—

'applies—

    (i)   a tenancy of an agricultural holding within the meaning of the Agricultural Holdings Act 1986 which is a tenancy in relation to which that Act applies, or

    (ii)   a farm business tenancy within the meaning of the Agricultural Tenancies Act 1995.'

The Protection from Eviction Act 1977 (c 43)

29   In section 8(1) of the Protection from Eviction Act 1977 (interpretation)—

    (a)   in paragraph (d), after 'Agricultural Holdings Act 1986' there shall be inserted 'which is a tenancy in relation to which that Act applies', and

    (b)   at the end there shall be added—

        '(g)   a farm business tenancy within the meaning of the Agricultural Tenancies Act 1995.'

The Housing Act 1985 (c 68)

30   In Schedule I to the Housing Act 1985 (tenancies which are not secure tenancies), for paragraph 8 there shall be substituted—

'*Agricultural holdings etc*

8   (1)   A tenancy is not a secure tenancy if—

(a) the dwelling-house is comprised in an agricultural holding and is occupied by the person responsible for the control (whether as tenant or as servant or agent of the tenant) of the farming of the holding, or

(b) the dwelling-house is comprised in the holding held under a farm business tenancy and is occupied by the person responsible for the control (whether as tenant or as servant or agent of the tenant) of the management of the holding.

(2) In sub-paragraph (1) above—

'agricultural holding' means any agricultural holding within the meaning of the Agricultural Holdings Act 1986 held under a tenancy in relation to which that Act applies, and
'farm business tenancy', and 'holding' in relation to such a tenancy, have the same meaning as in the Agricultural Tenancies Act 1995.'

The Landlord and Tenant Act 1985 (c 70)

31 In section 14(3) of the Landlord and Tenant Act 1985 (leases to which section 11 does not apply), at the end there shall be added 'and in relation to which that Act applies or to a farm business tenancy within the meaning of the Agricultural Tenancies Act 1995'.

The Agricultural Holdings Act 1986 (c 5)

32 In Schedule 6 to the Agricultural Holdings Act 1986 (eligibility to apply for a new tenancy under Part IV of that Act), in paragraph 6 (occupation to be disregarded for purposes of occupancy condition), in sub-paragraph (1) after paragraph (d) there shall be inserted—

'(dd) under a farm business tenancy, within the meaning of the Agricultural Tenancies Act 1995, for less than five years (including a farm business tenancy which is a periodic tenancy),'.

The Housing Act 1988 (c 50)

33 ...

34 In Schedule 1 to that Act (tenancies which cannot be assured tenancies), for paragraph 7 there shall be substituted—

'Tenancies of agricultural holdings etc

7 (1) A tenancy under which the dwelling-house—

(a) is comprised in an agricultural holding, and
(b) is occupied by the person responsible for the control (whether as tenant or as servant or agent of the tenant) of the farming of the holding.

(2) A tenancy under which the dwelling-house—

(a) is comprised in the holding held under a farm business tenancy, and
(b) is occupied by the person responsible for the control (whether as tenant or as servant or agent of the tenant) of the management of the holding.

(3) In this paragraph—

'agricultural holding' means any agricultural holding within the meaning of the Agricultural Holdings Act 1986 held under a tenancy in relation to which that Act applies, and
'farm business tenancy' and 'holding', in relation to such a tenancy, have the same meaning as in the 'Agricultural Tenancies Act 1995.'

The Town and Country Planning Act 1990 (c 8)

35 (1) Section 65 of the Town and Country Planning Act 1990 (notice etc of applications for planning permissions) shall be amended as follows.

(2) In subsection (2), for 'a tenant of any agricultural holding any part of which is comprised in that land' there shall be substituted 'an agricultural tenant of that land'.

(3) In subsection (8), for the definition of 'agricultural holding' there shall be substituted—

'agricultural tenant', in relation to any land, means any person who—
   (a) is the tenant, under a tenancy in relation to which the Agricultural Holdings Act 1986 applies, of an agricultural holding within the meaning of that Act any part of which is comprised in that land; or
   (b) is the tenant, under a farm business tenancy (within the meaning of the Agricultural Tenancies Act 1995), of land any part of which is comprised in that land;'.

The Coal Mining Subsidence Act 1991 (c 45)

36 In section 21 of the Coal Mining Subsidence Act 1991 (property belonging to protected tenants) in subsection (3), after paragraph (a) there shall be inserted—

'(aa) a tenant under a farm business tenancy within the meaning of the Agricultural Tenancies Act 1995;'.

37 In Schedule 3 to that Act (property belonging to protected tenants) in paragraph 1(2), after paragraph (b) there shall be inserted—

'(bb) section 20 of the Agricultural Tenancies Act 1995;'.

NOTES

Initial Commencement

Specified date: 1 September 1995: see s 41(2).

Amendment

This Schedule contains amendments only.

Para 33 is repealed by the Housing Act 1996, s 227, Sch 19, Part IX, para 1.

Notes

Para 2: Tenancy to which that Act applies. As to the tenancies to which the Agricultural Holdings Act 1986 applies, see s 98.

Paras 5, 6, 8: Leases in relation to which that Act applies. Cf the last foregoing note.

Paras 9, 10, 11, 12, 15, 20, 22, 25, 31, 34, 35: Tenancy in relation to which the Agricultural Holdings Act 1986 (that Act) applies. As to the tenancies to which the Agricultural Holdings Act 1986 applies, see s 98.

Para 9: Premises. The term 'premises', though originally possessing a very limited meaning, ie the parts of a deed which precede the habendum, is widely used in the popular sense as including land, houses, buildings, etc; see, eg, *Metropolitan Water Board v Paine* [1907] 1 KB 285; *Whitley v Stumbles* [1930] AC 544, HL; *Bracey v Read* [1963] Ch 88, [1962] 3 All ER 472; *Maunsell v Olins* [1975] AC 373, [1975] 1 All ER 16, HL and *Spring House (Freehold) Ltd v Mount Cook Land Ltd* [2001] EWCA Civ 1833, [2002] 2 All ER 822. In general 'premises' would seem to have been construed as meaning a whole property in either one occupation or one ownership according to the context in which it is used; see, eg, *Cadbury Bros Ltd v Sinclair* [1934] 2 KB 389 at 393 (revsd on other grounds (1933) 103 LJKB 29, [1933] All ER Rep 218, CA).

Dwelling house. It is clear that, in the words of Lord Atkinson in *Lewin v End* [1906] AC 299 at 304, HL, 'a house in which people actually live or which is physically capable of being used for human habitation' is a dwelling-house. Yet there is authority for saying that the necessity of making small alterations to restore a house formerly used as a dwelling-house to its former use does not prevent it from being a dwelling-house; see *Lewin v End* above. There is also authority for saying that a house may be a dwelling-house although the larger part of it is for the time being used for non-residential purposes; see *Lewin v Newnes Ltd* (1904) 90 LT 160. See also *Patel v Pirabakaran* [2006] EWCA Civ 685, [2006] 4 All ER 506. On the other hand, business premises are not to be regarded as a dwelling-house by reason only of their being used for having meals there or being used for sleeping there at night; cf *Macmillan & Co Ltd v Rees* [1946] 1 All ER 675, CA; and see also *Lewin v End* above at 302, per Lord Loreburn LC (caretaker).

Cooking facilities were not an essential attribute of a 'dwelling'house'; the concept of 'dwelling-house' described a place where someone dwelt, lived or resided: see *Uratemp Ventures Ltd v Collins* [2001] UKHL 43, [2002] 1 AC 301.

The expression 'dwelling-house' includes not only a house which is dwelt in, but also a house which is constructed or adapted for dwelling in, although it may at the relevant time be vacant or even not fit and ready for occupation: see *Re 1–4 White Row Cottages, Bewerley* [1991] Ch 441, [1991] 4 All ER 50.

It seems that 'dwelling-house' should not be construed so as to connote only that part of a building in which the occupant dwells and that it therefore includes such parts as a cellar: see *Grigsby v Melville* [1973] 3 All ER 455 at 462, [1974] 1 WLR 80, CA, per Stamp LJ.

A dwelling-house may comprise several buildings not physically joined together and it is a matter of degree in every case whether a separate building forms part of the dwelling-house in question: see *Batey (Inspector of Taxes) v Wakefield* [1982] 1 All ER 61, [1981] STC 521, CA. See also, *Martin v David Wilson Homes Ltd* [2004] EWCA Civ 1027, [2004] 3 EGLR 77.

A caravan jacked up and resting on bricks and connected to the electricity and water supplies has been held to be a dwelling-house: see *Makins v Elson (Inspector of Taxes)* [1977] 1 All ER 572, [1977] 1 WLR 221.

See further, on the meaning of 'dwelling-house', 2 Words and Phrases (3rd edn) 128–130.

Servant or agent. See the note 'Agent or servant' to s 36.

Para 14: S 14B(1): Part III of this Act. Ie the Opencast Coal Act 1958, Pt III (ss 37–53 and Schs 7–9), as amended by paras 19, 20 above.

Compulsory rights orders. See the Opencast Coal Act 1958, s 4.

Para 16: S 25A(3): Part III of the Act of 1995. Ie Pt III (ss 15–27) of this Act; see the Opencast Coal Act 1958, 14B(2), as inserted by para 14 above.

Para 20: Sch 7, para 1A(2): Part III of the Act of 1995. Ie Pt III (ss 15–27) of this Act; see the Opencast Coal Act 1958, 14B(2), as inserted by para 14 above.

Sch 7, para 3A(b): Person. See the note to s 1.

Sch 7, Para 4A: Notice. As to the service, etc, of notices under the Opencast Coal Act 1958, see s 47(1) thereof, Sch 9.

In writing. See the note 'Written' to s 1.

Part II of the Act of 1995. Ie Pt II (ss 9–14) of this Act; see the Opencast Coal Act 1958, 14B(2), as inserted by para 14 above.

Wholly or mainly. The word 'mainly' probably means 'more than half; cf *Fawcett Properties Ltd v Buckingham County Council* [1961] AC 636 at 669, [1960] 3 All ER 503 at 512, HL per Lord Morton of Henryton. See also as to the meaning of 'wholly or mainly' (or 'exclusively or mainly'), *Re Hatschek's Patents, ex p Zerenner* [1909] 2 Ch 68; *Miller v Ottilie (Owners)* [1944] KB 188, [1944] 1 All ER 277; *Franklin v Gramophone Co Ltd* [1948] 1 KB 542 at 555, [1948] 1 All ER 353 at 358, CA per Somervell LJ; and *Berthelemy v Neale* [1952] 1 All ER 437, 96 Sol Jo 165, CA.

Para 21: Trade or business. See the note to s 1.

Para 27: Dwelling house. This expression is not defined for the purposes of the Rent Act 1977, beyond the provision in s 1 that this may be a house or part of a house. See also the corresponding note above.

Paras 27, 30, 34: Servant or agent. See the note 'Agent or servant' to s 36.

Paras 27, 30, 34: Farming of the holding. 'Farming' is not defined in the Rent Act 1977, the Housing Act 1985, or the Housing Act 1988, Sch 1, as amended, respectively, by paras 27, 30, 34 above, but cf, for the purposes of those provisions as so amended, the definition contained in the Agricultural Holdings Act 1986, s 96(4), (references to farming include references to the carrying on in relation to the land of any agricultural activity).

Definitions. In the Landlord and Tenant Act 1954, for 'farm business tenancy' and 'tenancy', see s 69(1) of that Act, as amended (definition 'farm business tenancy' inserted) by para 12 above.

In the Opencast Coal Act 1958, for 'compulsory rights order' and 'operative date', see s 4 of that Act; for 'date of entry' and 'period of occupation', see s 5 thereof; for 'the Act of 1986', 'the Act of 1995', 'agricultural holding', 'farm business tenancy', 'land', 'mortgage', 'mortgagee', 'mortgagor', 'opencast planning permission', 'permitted activities', 'restoration' and 'tenancy', see s 51(1) thereof, as amended (definitions 'the Act of 1995' and 'farm business tenancy' inserted) by para 19 above; as to the person with the benefit of opencast planning permission, see s 51(1A); as to the 'state' in which land was, see s 51(4). Note also the definitions, etc in ss 14B(2), (5), 25A(1)(b), (6) of, Sch 7, paras 2A(1), 4(7) to, that Act, as inserted by paras 14, 16, 20(1), (4), (6) above.

In the Land Compensation Act 1973, for 'agricultural holding' and 'tenancy', see s 87(1).

In the Rent Act 1977, for 'protected tenancy', see s 1; for 'tenancy', see s 152(1).

In the Housing Act 1985, for 'secure tenancy', see s 79; for 'dwelling-house', see s 112; for 'tenancy' and 'tenant', see s 621.

In the Housing Act 1988, for 'tenancy', see ss 1(2)(a), 45(1); for 'dwelling-house', see s 45(1).

In the Town and Country Planning Act 1990, for 'land', see s 336(1).

Agricultural Holdings Act 1986. For the meaning of 'agricultural holding' in that Act, see s 1(1). As to the tenancies to which that Act applies, see s 98.

Town and Country Planning Act 1990, s 65. Substituted by the Planning and Compensation Act 1991, s 16(1).

ARBITRATION ACT 1996

(1996 C 23)

ARRANGEMENT OF SECTIONS

An Act to restate and improve the law relating to arbitration pursuant to an arbitration agreement; to make other provision relating to arbitration and arbitration awards; and for connected purposes

[17th June 1996]

PART I: ARBITRATION PURSUANT TO AN ARBITRATION AGREEMENT

Introductory

A1.253

1   General principles

The provisions of this Part are founded on the following principles, and shall be construed accordingly—

(a)   the object of arbitration is to obtain the fair resolution of disputes by an impartial tribunal without unnecessary delay or expense;

(b)   the parties should be free to agree how their disputes are resolved, subject only to such safeguards as are necessary in the public interest;

(c)   in matters governed by this Part the court should not intervene except as provided by this Part.

NOTES

Initial Commencement

To be appointed: see s 109(1).

Appointment

Appointment: 31 January 1997: see SI 1996/3146, art 3; for transitional provisions see art 4, Sch 2 thereto.

Extent

This section does not extend to Scotland: see s 108(1).

A1.254

2   Scope of application of provisions

(1)   The provisions of this Part apply where the seat of the arbitration is in England and Wales or Northern Ireland.

(2)   The following sections apply even if the seat of the arbitration is outside England and Wales or Northern Ireland or no seat has been designated or determined—

   (a)   sections 9 to 11 (stay of legal proceedings, &c), and
   (b)   section 66 (enforcement of arbitral awards).

(3)   The powers conferred by the following sections apply even if the seat of the arbitration is outside England and Wales or Northern Ireland or no seat has been designated or determined—

   (a)   section 43 (securing the attendance of witnesses), and
   (b)   section 44 (court powers exercisable in support of arbitral proceedings);

but the court may refuse to exercise any such power if, in the opinion of the court, the fact that the seat of the arbitration is outside England and Wales or Northern Ireland, or that when designated or determined the seat is likely to be outside England and Wales or Northern Ireland, makes it inappropriate to do so.

(4)   The court may exercise a power conferred by any provision of this Part not mentioned in subsection (2) or (3) for the purpose of supporting the arbitral process where—

   (a)   no seat of the arbitration has been designated or determined, and
   (b)   by reason of a connection with England and Wales or Northern Ireland the court is satisfied that it is appropriate to do so.

(5)   Section 7 (separability of arbitration agreement) and section 8 (death of a party) apply where the law applicable to the arbitration agreement is the law of England and Wales or Northern Ireland even if the seat of the arbitration is outside England and Wales or Northern Ireland or has not been designated or determined.

NOTES

Initial Commencement

To be appointed: see s 109(1).

Appointment

Appointment: 31 January 1997: see SI 1996/3146, art 3; for transitional provisions see art 4, Sch 2 thereto.

Extent

This section does not extend to Scotland: see s 108(1).

A1.255

3   The seat of the arbitration

In this Part 'the seat of the arbitration' means the juridical seat of the arbitration designated—

(a)   by the parties to the arbitration agreement, or
(b)   by any arbitral or other institution or person vested by the parties with powers in that regard, or
(c)   by the arbitral tribunal if so authorised by the parties,

or determined, in the absence of any such designation, having regard to the parties' agreement and all the relevant circumstances.

NOTES

Initial Commencement

To be appointed: see s 109(1).

Appointment

Appointment: 31 January 1997: see SI 1996/3146, art 3; for transitional provisions see art 4, Sch 2 thereto.

Extent

This section does not extend to Scotland: see s 108(1).

A1.256

4   Mandatory and non-mandatory provisions

(1)   The mandatory provisions of this Part are listed in Schedule 1 and have effect notwithstanding any agreement to the contrary.

(2)   The other provisions of this Part (the 'non-mandatory provisions') allow the parties to make their own arrangements by agreement but provide rules which apply in the absence of such agreement.

(3)   The parties may make such arrangements by agreeing to the application of institutional rules or providing any other means by which a matter may be decided.

(4)   It is immaterial whether or not the law applicable to the parties' agreement is the law of England and Wales or, as the case may be, Northern Ireland.

(5)   The choice of a law other than the law of England and Wales or Northern Ireland as the applicable law in respect of a matter provided for by a non-mandatory provision of this Part is equivalent to an agreement making provision about that matter.

   For this purpose an applicable law determined in accordance with the parties' agreement, or which is objectively determined in the absence of any express or implied choice, shall be treated as chosen by the parties.

NOTES

Initial Commencement

To be appointed: see s 109(1).

Appointment

Appointment: 31 January 1997: see SI 1996/3146, art 3; for transitional provisions see art 4, Sch 2 thereto.

Extent

This section does not extend to Scotland: see s 108(1).

A1.257

5   Agreements to be in writing

(1)   The provisions of this Part apply only where the arbitration agreement is in writing, and any other agreement between the parties as to any matter is effective for the purposes of this Part only if in writing.

The expressions 'agreement', 'agree' and 'agreed' shall be construed accordingly.

(2)   There is an agreement in writing—

   (a)   if the agreement is made in writing (whether or not it is signed by the parties),
   (b)   if the agreement is made by exchange of communications in writing, or
   (c)   if the agreement is evidenced in writing.

(3)   Where parties agree otherwise than in writing by reference to terms which are in writing, they make an agreement in writing.

(4)   An agreement is evidenced in writing if an agreement made otherwise than in writing is recorded by one of the parties, or by a third party, with the authority of the parties to the agreement.

(5)   An exchange of written submissions in arbitral or legal proceedings in which the existence of an agreement otherwise than in writing is alleged by one party against another party and not denied by the other party in his response constitutes as between those parties an agreement in writing to the effect alleged.

(6)   References in this Part to anything being written or in writing include its being recorded by any means.

NOTES

Initial Commencement

To be appointed: see s 109(1).

Appointment

Appointment: 31 January 1997: see SI 1996/3146, art 3; for transitional provisions see art 4, Sch 2 thereto.

Extent

This section does not extend to Scotland: see s 108(1).

The arbitration agreement

A1.258

6   Definition of arbitration agreement

(1)   In this Part an 'arbitration agreement' means an agreement to submit to arbitration present or future disputes (whether they are contractual or not).

(2)   The reference in an agreement to a written form of arbitration clause or to a document containing an arbitration clause constitutes an arbitration agreement if the reference is such as to make that clause part of the agreement.

NOTES

Initial Commencement

To be appointed: see s 109(1).

Appointment

Appointment: 31 January 1997: see SI 1996/3146, art 3; for transitional provisions see art 4, Sch 2 thereto.

Extent

This section does not extend to Scotland: see s 108(1).

A1.259

7   Separability of arbitration agreement

Unless otherwise agreed by the parties, an arbitration agreement which forms or was intended to form part of another agreement (whether or not in writing) shall not be regarded as invalid, non-existent or ineffective because that other agreement is invalid, or did not come into existence or has become ineffective, and it shall for that purpose be treated as a distinct agreement.

NOTES

Initial Commencement

To be appointed: see s 109(1).

Appointment

Appointment: 31 January 1997: see SI 1996/3146, art 3; for transitional provisions see art 4, Sch 2 thereto.

Extent

This section does not extend to Scotland: see s 108(1).

A1.260

8   Whether agreement discharged by death of a party

(1)   Unless otherwise agreed by the parties, an arbitration agreement is not discharged by the death of a party and may be enforced by or against the personal representatives of that party.

(2)   Subsection (1) does not affect the operation of any enactment or rule of law by virtue of which a substantive right or obligation is extinguished by death.

NOTES

Initial Commencement

To be appointed: see s 109(1).

Appointment

Appointment: 31 January 1997: see SI 1996/3146, art 3; for transitional provisions see art 4, Sch 2 thereto.

Extent

This section does not extend to Scotland: see s 108(1).

Stay of legal proceedings

A1.261

9   Stay of legal proceedings

(1)   A party to an arbitration agreement against whom legal proceedings are brought (whether by way of claim or counterclaim) in respect of a matter which under the agreement is to be referred to arbitration may (upon notice to the other parties to the proceedings) apply to the court in which the proceedings have been brought to stay the proceedings so far as they concern that matter.

(2)   An application may be made notwithstanding that the matter is to be referred to arbitration only after the exhaustion of other dispute resolution procedures.

(3)   An application may not be made by a person before taking the appropriate procedural step (if any) to acknowledge the legal proceedings against him or after he has taken any step in those proceedings to answer the substantive claim.

(4)   On an application under this section the court shall grant a stay unless satisfied that the arbitration agreement is null and void, inoperative, or incapable of being performed.

(5)   If the court refuses to stay the legal proceedings, any provision that an award is a condition precedent to the bringing of legal proceedings in respect of any matter is of no effect in relation to those proceedings.

NOTES

Initial Commencement

To be appointed: see s 109(1).

Appointment

Appointment: 31 January 1997: see SI 1996/3146, art 3; for transitional provisions see art 4, Sch 2 thereto.

Extent

This section does not extend to Scotland: see s 108(1).

A1.262

10   Reference of interpleader issue to arbitration

(1)   Where in legal proceedings relief by way of interpleader is granted and any issue between the claimants is one in respect of which there is an arbitration agreement between them, the court granting the relief shall direct that the issue be determined in accordance with the agreement unless the circumstances are such that proceedings brought by a claimant in respect of the matter would not be stayed.

(2)   Where subsection (1) applies but the court does not direct that the issue be determined in accordance with the arbitration agreement, any provision that an award is a condition precedent to the bringing of legal proceedings in respect of any matter shall not affect the determination of that issue by the court.

NOTES

Initial Commencement

To be appointed: see s 109(1).

Appointment

Appointment: 31 January 1997: see SI 1996/3146, art 3; for transitional provisions see art 4, Sch 2 thereto.

Extent

This section does not extend to Scotland: see s 108(1).

A1.263

11   **Retention of security where Admiralty proceedings stayed**

(1)   Where Admiralty proceedings are stayed on the ground that the dispute in question should be submitted to arbitration, the court granting the stay may, if in those proceedings property has been arrested or bail or other security has been given to prevent or obtain release from arrest—

    (a)   order that the property arrested be retained as security for the satisfaction of any award given in the arbitration in respect of that dispute, or

    (b)   order that the stay of those proceedings be conditional on the provision of equivalent security for the satisfaction of any such award.

(2)   Subject to any provision made by rules of court and to any necessary modifications, the same law and practice shall apply in relation to property retained in pursuance of an order as would apply if it were held for the purposes of proceedings in the court making the order.

NOTES

Initial Commencement

To be appointed: see s 109(1).

Appointment

Appointment: 31 January 1997: see SI 1996/3146, art 3; for transitional provisions see art 4, Sch 2 thereto.

Extent

This section does not extend to Scotland: see s 108(1).

Commencement of arbitral proceedings

A1.264

12   **Power of court to extend time for beginning arbitral proceedings, &c**

(1)   Where an arbitration agreement to refer future disputes to arbitration provides that a claim shall be barred, or the claimant's right extinguished, unless the claimant takes within a time fixed by the agreement some step—

    (a)   to begin arbitral proceedings, or

    (b)   to begin other dispute resolution procedures which must be exhausted before arbitral proceedings can be begun,

the court may by order extend the time for taking that step.

(2)   Any party to the arbitration agreement may apply for such an order (upon notice to the other parties), but only after a claim has arisen and after exhausting any available arbitral process for obtaining an extension of time.

(3)   The court shall make an order only if satisfied—

    (a)   that the circumstances are such as were outside the reasonable contemplation of the parties when they agreed the provision in question, and that it would be just to extend the time, or

    (b)   that the conduct of one party makes it unjust to hold the other party to the strict terms of the provision in question.

(4)   The court may extend the time for such period and on such terms as it thinks fit, and may do so whether or not the time previously fixed (by agreement or by a previous order) has expired.

(5)   An order under this section does not affect the operation of the Limitation Acts (see section 13).

(6)   The leave of the court is required for any appeal from a decision of the court under this section.

NOTES

Initial Commencement

To be appointed: see s 109(1).

Appointment

Appointment: 31 January 1997: see SI 1996/3146, art 3; for transitional provisions see art 4, Sch 2 thereto.

Extent

This section does not extend to Scotland: see s 108(1).

A1.265

13   Application of Limitation Acts

(1)   The Limitation Acts apply to arbitral proceedings as they apply to legal proceedings.

(2)   The court may order that in computing the time prescribed by the Limitation Acts for the commencement of proceedings (including arbitral proceedings) in respect of a dispute which was the subject matter—

    (a)   of an award which the court orders to be set aside or declares to be of no effect, or

    (b)   of the affected part of an award which the court orders to be set aside in part, or declares to be in part of no effect,

the period between the commencement of the arbitration and the date of the order referred to in paragraph (a) or (b) shall be excluded.

(3)   In determining for the purposes of the Limitation Acts when a cause of action accrued, any provision that an award is a condition precedent to the bringing of legal proceedings in respect of a matter to which an arbitration agreement applies shall be disregarded.

(4)   In this Part 'the Limitation Acts' means—

    (a)   in England and Wales, the Limitation Act 1980, the Foreign Limitation Periods Act 1984 and any other enactment (whenever passed) relating to the limitation of actions;

(b)   in Northern Ireland, the Limitation (Northern Ireland) Order 1989, the Foreign Limitation Periods (Northern Ireland) Order 1985 and any other enactment (whenever passed) relating to the limitation of actions.

NOTES

Initial Commencement

To be appointed: see s 109(1).

Appointment

Appointment: 31 January 1997: see SI 1996/3146, art 3; for transitional provisions see art 4, Sch 2 thereto.

Extent

This section does not extend to Scotland: see s 108(1).

A1.266

14   Commencement of arbitral proceedings

(1)   The parties are free to agree when arbitral proceedings are to be regarded as commenced for the purposes of this Part and for the purposes of the Limitation Acts.

(2)   If there is no such agreement the following provisions apply.

(3)   Where the arbitrator is named or designated in the arbitration agreement, arbitral proceedings are commenced in respect of a matter when one party serves on the other party or parties a notice in writing requiring him or them to submit that matter to the person so named or designated.

(4)   Where the arbitrator or arbitrators are to be appointed by the parties, arbitral proceedings are commenced in respect of a matter when one party serves on the other party or parties notice in writing requiring him or them to appoint an arbitrator or to agree to the appointment of an arbitrator in respect of that matter.

(5)   Where the arbitrator or arbitrators are to be appointed by a person other than a party to the proceedings, arbitral proceedings are commenced in respect of a matter when one party gives notice in writing to that person requesting him to make the appointment in respect of that matter.

NOTES

Initial Commencement

To be appointed: see s 109(1).

Appointment

Appointment: 31 January 1997: see SI 1996/3146, art 3; for transitional provisions see art 4, Sch 2 thereto.

Extent

This section does not extend to Scotland: see s 108(1).

The arbitral tribunal

A1.267

15   The arbitral tribunal

(1)   The parties are free to agree on the number of arbitrators to form the tribunal and whether there is to be a chairman or umpire.

(2)   Unless otherwise agreed by the parties, an agreement that the number of arbitrators shall be two or any other even number shall be understood as requiring the appointment of an additional arbitrator as chairman of the tribunal.

(3)   If there is no agreement as to the number of arbitrators, the tribunal shall consist of a sole arbitrator.

NOTES

Initial Commencement

To be appointed: see s 109(1).

Appointment

Appointment: 31 January 1997: see SI 1996/3146, art 3; for transitional provisions see art 4, Sch 2 thereto.

Extent

This section does not extend to Scotland: see s 108(1).

A1.268

16   Procedure for appointment of arbitrators

(1)   The parties are free to agree on the procedure for appointing the arbitrator or arbitrators, including the procedure for appointing any chairman or umpire.

(2)   If or to the extent that there is no such agreement, the following provisions apply.

(3)   If the tribunal is to consist of a sole arbitrator, the parties shall jointly appoint the arbitrator not later than 28 days after service of a request in writing by either party to do so.

(4)   If the tribunal is to consist of two arbitrators, each party shall appoint one arbitrator not later than 14 days after service of a request in writing by either party to do so.

(5)   If the tribunal is to consist of three arbitrators—

    (a)   each party shall appoint one arbitrator not later than 14 days after service of a request in writing by either party to do so, and

    (b)   the two so appointed shall forthwith appoint a third arbitrator as the chairman of the tribunal.

(6)   If the tribunal is to consist of two arbitrators and an umpire—

    (a)   each party shall appoint one arbitrator not later than 14 days after service of a request in writing by either party to do so, and

    (b)   the two so appointed may appoint an umpire at any time after they themselves are appointed and shall do so before any substantive hearing or forthwith if they cannot agree on a matter relating to the arbitration.

(7)   In any other case (in particular, if there are more than two parties) section 18 applies as in the case of a failure of the agreed appointment procedure.

NOTES

Initial Commencement

To be appointed: see s 109(1).

Appointment

Appointment: 31 January 1997: see SI 1996/3146, art 3; for transitional provisions see art 4, Sch 2 thereto.

Extent

This section does not extend to Scotland: see s 108(1).

A1.269

17   Power in case of default to appoint sole arbitrator

(1)   Unless the parties otherwise agree, where each of two parties to an arbitration agreement is to appoint an arbitrator and one party ('the party in default') refuses to do so, or fails to do so within the time specified, the other party, having duly appointed his arbitrator, may give notice in writing to the party in default that he proposes to appoint his arbitrator to act as sole arbitrator.

(2)   If the party in default does not within 7 clear days of that notice being given—

    (a)   make the required appointment, and
    (b)   notify the other party that he has done so,

the other party may appoint his arbitrator as sole arbitrator whose award shall be binding on both parties as if he had been so appointed by agreement.

(3)   Where a sole arbitrator has been appointed under subsection (2), the party in default may (upon notice to the appointing party) apply to the court which may set aside the appointment.

(4)   The leave of the court is required for any appeal from a decision of the court under this section.

NOTES

Initial Commencement

To be appointed: see s 109(1).

Appointment

Appointment: 31 January 1997: see SI 1996/3146, art 3; for transitional provisions see art 4, Sch 2 thereto.

Extent

This section does not extend to Scotland: see s 108(1).

A1.270

18 Failure of appointment procedure

(1) The parties are free to agree what is to happen in the event of a failure of the procedure for the appointment of the arbitral tribunal.

There is no failure if an appointment is duly made under section 17 (power in case of default to appoint sole arbitrator), unless that appointment is set aside.

(2) If or to the extent that there is no such agreement any party to the arbitration agreement may (upon notice to the other parties) apply to the court to exercise its powers under this section.

(3) Those powers are—

    (a)   to give directions as to the making of any necessary appointments;

    (b)   to direct that the tribunal shall be constituted by such appointments (or any one or more of them) as have been made;

    (c)   to revoke any appointments already made;

    (d)   to make any necessary appointments itself.

(4) An appointment made by the court under this section has effect as if made with the agreement of the parties.

(5) The leave of the court is required for any appeal from a decision of the court under this section.

NOTES

Initial Commencement

To be appointed: see s 109(1).

Appointment

Appointment: 31 January 1997: see SI 1996/3146, art 3; for transitional provisions see art 4, Sch 2 thereto.

Extent

This section does not extend to Scotland: see s 108(1).

A1.271

19 Court to have regard to agreed qualifications

In deciding whether to exercise, and in considering how to exercise, any of its powers under section 16 (procedure for appointment of arbitrators) or section 18 (failure of appointment procedure), the court shall have due regard to any agreement of the parties as to the qualifications required of the arbitrators.

NOTES

Initial Commencement

To be appointed: see s 109(1).

Appointment

Appointment: 31 January 1997: see SI 1996/3146, art 3; for transitional provisions see art 4, Sch 2 thereto.

Extent

This section does not extend to Scotland: see s 108(1).

A1.272

20   Chairman

(1)   Where the parties have agreed that there is to be a chairman, they are free to agree what the functions of the chairman are to be in relation to the making of decisions, orders and awards.

(2)   If or to the extent that there is no such agreement, the following provisions apply.

(3)   Decisions, orders and awards shall be made by all or a majority of the arbitrators (including the chairman).

(4)   The view of the chairman shall prevail in relation to a decision, order or award in respect of which there is neither unanimity nor a majority under subsection (3).

NOTES

Initial Commencement

To be appointed: see s 109(1).

Appointment

Appointment: 31 January 1997: see SI 1996/3146, art 3; for transitional provisions see art 4, Sch 2 thereto.

Extent

This section does not extend to Scotland: see s 108(1).

A1.273

21   Umpire

(1)   Where the parties have agreed that there is to be an umpire, they are free to agree what the functions of the umpire are to be, and in particular—

    (a)   whether he is to attend the proceedings, and
    (b)   when he is to replace the other arbitrators as the tribunal with power to make decisions, orders and awards.

(2)   If or to the extent that there is no such agreement, the following provisions apply.

(3)   The umpire shall attend the proceedings and be supplied with the same documents and other materials as are supplied to the other arbitrators.

(4)   Decisions, orders and awards shall be made by the other arbitrators unless and until they cannot agree on a matter relating to the arbitration.
In that event they shall forthwith give notice in writing to the parties and the umpire, whereupon the umpire shall replace them as the tribunal with power to make decisions, orders and awards as if he were sole arbitrator.

(5)   If the arbitrators cannot agree but fail to give notice of that fact, or if any of them fails to join in the giving of notice, any party to the arbitral proceedings may (upon notice to the other parties and to the tribunal) apply to the court which may order that the umpire shall replace the other arbitrators as the tribunal with power to make decisions, orders and awards as if he were sole arbitrator.

(6)   The leave of the court is required for any appeal from a decision of the court under this section.

NOTES

Initial Commencement

To be appointed: see s 109(1).

Appointment

Appointment: 31 January 1997: see SI 1996/3146, art 3; for transitional provisions see art 4, Sch 2 thereto.

Extent

This section does not extend to Scotland: see s 108(1).

A1.274

22   Decision-making where no chairman or umpire

(1)   Where the parties agree that there shall be two or more arbitrators with no chairman or umpire, the parties are free to agree how the tribunal is to make decisions, orders and awards.

(2)   If there is no such agreement, decisions, orders and awards shall be made by all or a majority of the arbitrators.

NOTES

Initial Commencement

To be appointed: see s 109(1).

Appointment

Appointment: 31 January 1997: see SI 1996/3146, art 3; for transitional provisions see art 4, Sch 2 thereto.

Extent

This section does not extend to Scotland: see s 108(1).

A1.275

23   Revocation of arbitrator's authority

(1)   The parties are free to agree in what circumstances the authority of an arbitrator may be revoked.

(2)   If or to the extent that there is no such agreement the following provisions apply.

(3)   The authority of an arbitrator may not be revoked except—

    (a)   by the parties acting jointly, or
    (b)   by an arbitral or other institution or person vested by the parties with powers in that regard.

(4)   Revocation of the authority of an arbitrator by the parties acting jointly must be agreed in writing unless the parties also agree (whether or not in writing) to terminate the arbitration agreement.

(5)   Nothing in this section affects the power of the court—

(a)   to revoke an appointment under section 18 (powers exercisable in case of failure of appointment procedure), or
(b)   to remove an arbitrator on the grounds specified in section 24.

NOTES

Initial Commencement

To be appointed: see s 109(1).

Appointment

Appointment: 31 January 1997: see SI 1996/3146, art 3; for transitional provisions see art 4, Sch 2 thereto.

Extent

This section does not extend to Scotland: see s 108(1).

A1.276

24   Power of court to remove arbitrator

(1)   A party to arbitral proceedings may (upon notice to the other parties, to the arbitrator concerned and to any other arbitrator) apply to the court to remove an arbitrator on any of the following grounds—

(a)   that circumstances exist that give rise to justifiable doubts as to his impartiality;
(b)   that he does not possess the qualifications required by the arbitration agreement;
(c)   that he is physically or mentally incapable of conducting the proceedings or there are justifiable doubts as to his capacity to do so;
(d)   that he has refused or failed—
(i)   properly to conduct the proceedings, or
(ii)   to use all reasonable despatch in conducting the proceedings or making an award,

and that substantial injustice has been or will be caused to the applicant.

(2)   If there is an arbitral or other institution or person vested by the parties with power to remove an arbitrator, the court shall not exercise its power of removal unless satisfied that the applicant has first exhausted any available recourse to that institution or person.

(3)   The arbitral tribunal may continue the arbitral proceedings and make an award while an application to the court under this section is pending.

(4)   Where the court removes an arbitrator, it may make such order as it thinks fit with respect to his entitlement (if any) to fees or expenses, or the repayment of any fees or expenses already paid.

(5)   The arbitrator concerned is entitled to appear and be heard by the court before it makes any order under this section.

(6)   The leave of the court is required for any appeal from a decision of the court under this section.

NOTES

Initial Commencement

To be appointed: see s 109(1).

Appointment

Appointment: 31 January 1997: see SI 1996/3146, art 3; for transitional provisions see art 4, Sch 2 thereto.

Extent

This section does not extend to Scotland: see s 108(1).

See Further

See further, in relation to the application of this section, with modifications, for the purposes of arbitrations conducted in accordance with the Scheme: the ACAS Arbitration Scheme (Great Britain) Order 2004, SI 2004/753, art 4, Schedule, para 52EW.

A1.277

25   Resignation of arbitrator

(1)   The parties are free to agree with an arbitrator as to the consequences of his resignation as regards—

    (a)   his entitlement (if any) to fees or expenses, and
    (b)   any liability thereby incurred by him.

(2)   If or to the extent that there is no such agreement the following provisions apply.

(3)   An arbitrator who resigns his appointment may (upon notice to the parties) apply to the court—

    (a)   to grant him relief from any liability thereby incurred by him, and
    (b)   to make such order as it thinks fit with respect to his entitlement (if any) to fees or expenses or the repayment of any fees or expenses already paid.

(4)   If the court is satisfied that in all the circumstances it was reasonable for the arbitrator to resign, it may grant such relief as is mentioned in subsection (3)(a) on such terms as it thinks fit.

(5)   The leave of the court is required for any appeal from a decision of the court under this section.

NOTES

Initial Commencement

To be appointed: see s 109(1).

Appointment

Appointment: 31 January 1997: see SI 1996/3146, art 3; for transitional provisions see art 4, Sch 2 thereto.

Extent

This section does not extend to Scotland: see s 108(1).

A1.278

26   Death of arbitrator or person appointing him

(1)   The authority of an arbitrator is personal and ceases on his death.

(2)   Unless otherwise agreed by the parties, the death of the person by whom an arbitrator was appointed does not revoke the arbitrator's authority.

NOTES

Initial Commencement

To be appointed: see s 109(1).

Appointment

Appointment: 31 January 1997: see SI 1996/3146, art 3; for transitional provisions see art 4, Sch 2 thereto.

Extent

This section does not extend to Scotland: see s 108(1).

A1.279

27   Filling of vacancy, &c

(1)   Where an arbitrator ceases to hold office, the parties are free to agree—

  (a)   whether and if so how the vacancy is to be filled,
  (b)   whether and if so to what extent the previous proceedings should stand, and
  (c)   what effect (if any) his ceasing to hold office has on any appointment made by him (alone or jointly).

(2)   If or to the extent that there is no such agreement, the following provisions apply.

(3)   The provisions of sections 16 (procedure for appointment of arbitrators) and 18 (failure of appointment procedure) apply in relation to the filling of the vacancy as in relation to an original appointment.

(4)   The tribunal (when reconstituted) shall determine whether and if so to what extent the previous proceedings should stand.
   This does not affect any right of a party to challenge those proceedings on any ground which had arisen before the arbitrator ceased to hold office.

(5)   His ceasing to hold office does not affect any appointment by him (alone or jointly) of another arbitrator, in particular any appointment of a chairman or umpire.

NOTES

Initial Commencement

To be appointed: see s 109(1).

Appointment

Appointment: 31 January 1997: see SI 1996/3146, art 3; for transitional provisions see art 4, Sch 2 thereto.

Extent

This section does not extend to Scotland: see s 108(1).

A1.280

28   Joint and several liability of parties to arbitrators for fees and expenses

(1)   The parties are jointly and severally liable to pay to the arbitrators such reasonable fees and expenses (if any) as are appropriate in the circumstances.

(2)   Any party may apply to the court (upon notice to the other parties and to the arbitrators) which may order that the amount of the arbitrators' fees and expenses shall be considered and adjusted by such means and upon such terms as it may direct.

(3)   If the application is made after any amount has been paid to the arbitrators by way of fees or expenses, the court may order the repayment of such amount (if any) as is shown to be excessive, but shall not do so unless it is shown that it is reasonable in the circumstances to order repayment.

(4)   The above provisions have effect subject to any order of the court under section 24(4) or 25(3)(b) (order as to entitlement to fees or expenses in case of removal or resignation of arbitrator).

(5)   Nothing in this section affects any liability of a party to any other party to pay all or any of the costs of the arbitration (see sections 59 to 65) or any contractual right of an arbitrator to payment of his fees and expenses.

(6)   In this section references to arbitrators include an arbitrator who has ceased to act and an umpire who has not replaced the other arbitrators.

NOTES

Initial Commencement

To be appointed: see s 109(1).

Appointment

Appointment: 31 January 1997: see SI 1996/3146, art 3; for transitional provisions see art 4, Sch 2 thereto.

Extent

This section does not extend to Scotland: see s 108(1).

A1.281

29   Immunity of arbitrator

(1)   An arbitrator is not liable for anything done or omitted in the discharge or purported discharge of his functions as arbitrator unless the act or omission is shown to have been in bad faith.

(2)   Subsection (1) applies to an employee or agent of an arbitrator as it applies to the arbitrator himself.

(3)   This section does not affect any liability incurred by an arbitrator by reason of his resigning (but see section 25).

NOTES

Initial Commencement

To be appointed: see s 109(1).

Appointment

Appointment: 31 January 1997: see SI 1996/3146, art 3; for transitional provisions see art 4, Sch 2 thereto.

Extent

This section does not extend to Scotland: see s 108(1).

Jurisdiction of the arbitral tribunal

A1.282

30   Competence of tribunal to rule on its own jurisdiction

(1)   Unless otherwise agreed by the parties, the arbitral tribunal may rule on its own substantive jurisdiction, that is, as to—

   (a)   whether there is a valid arbitration agreement,

   (b)   whether the tribunal is properly constituted, and

   (c)   what matters have been submitted to arbitration in accordance with the arbitration agreement.

(2)   Any such ruling may be challenged by any available arbitral process of appeal or review or in accordance with the provisions of this Part.

NOTES

Initial Commencement

To be appointed: see s 109(1).

Appointment

Appointment: 31 January 1997: see SI 1996/3146, art 3; for transitional provisions see art 4, Sch 2 thereto.

Extent

This section does not extend to Scotland: see s 108(1).

A1.283

31   Objection to substantive jurisdiction of tribunal

(1)   An objection that the arbitral tribunal lacks substantive jurisdiction at the outset of the proceedings must be raised by a party not later than the time he takes the first step in the proceedings to contest the merits of any matter in relation to which he challenges the tribunal's jurisdiction.

A party is not precluded from raising such an objection by the fact that he has appointed or participated in the appointment of an arbitrator.

(2)   Any objection during the course of the arbitral proceedings that the arbitral tribunal is exceeding its substantive jurisdiction must be made as soon as possible after the matter alleged to be beyond its jurisdiction is raised.

(3)   The arbitral tribunal may admit an objection later than the time specified in subsection (1) or (2) if it considers the delay justified.

(4)   Where an objection is duly taken to the tribunal's substantive jurisdiction and the tribunal has power to rule on its own jurisdiction, it may—

(a) rule on the matter in an award as to jurisdiction, or

(b) deal with the objection in its award on the merits.

If the parties agree which of these courses the tribunal should take, the tribunal shall proceed accordingly.

(5) The tribunal may in any case, and shall if the parties so agree, stay proceedings whilst an application is made to the court under section 32 (determination of preliminary point of jurisdiction).

NOTES

Initial Commencement

To be appointed: see s 109(1).

Appointment

Appointment: 31 January 1997: see SI 1996/3146, art 3; for transitional provisions see art 4, Sch 2 thereto.

Extent

This section does not extend to Scotland: see s 108(1).

A1.284

32   Determination of preliminary point of jurisdiction

(1) The court may, on the application of a party to arbitral proceedings (upon notice to the other parties), determine any question as to the substantive jurisdiction of the tribunal.

A party may lose the right to object (see section 73).

(2) An application under this section shall not be considered unless—

(a) it is made with the agreement in writing of all the other parties to the proceedings, or

(b) it is made with the permission of the tribunal and the court is satisfied—

(i) that the determination of the question is likely to produce substantial savings in costs,

(ii) that the application was made without delay, and

(iii) that there is good reason why the matter should be decided by the court.

(3) An application under this section, unless made with the agreement of all the other parties to the proceedings, shall state the grounds on which it is said that the matter should be decided by the court.

(4) Unless otherwise agreed by the parties, the arbitral tribunal may continue the arbitral proceedings and make an award while an application to the court under this section is pending.

(5) Unless the court gives leave, no appeal lies from a decision of the court whether the conditions specified in subsection (2) are met.

(6) The decision of the court on the question of jurisdiction shall be treated as a judgment of the court for the purposes of an appeal.

But no appeal lies without the leave of the court which shall not be given unless the court considers that the question involves a point of law which is one of general importance or is one which for some other special reason should be considered by the Court of Appeal.

NOTES

Initial Commencement

To be appointed: see s 109(1).

Appointment

Appointment: 31 January 1997: see SI 1996/3146, art 3; for transitional provisions see art 4, Sch 2 thereto.

Extent

This section does not extend to Scotland: see s 108(1).

The arbitral proceedings

A1.285

33   General duty of the tribunal

(1)   The tribunal shall—

   (a)   act fairly and impartially as between the parties, giving each party a reasonable opportunity of putting his case and dealing with that of his opponent, and
   (b)   adopt procedures suitable to the circumstances of the particular case, avoiding unnecessary delay or expense, so as to provide a fair means for the resolution of the matters falling to be determined.

(2)   The tribunal shall comply with that general duty in conducting the arbitral proceedings, in its decisions on matters of procedure and evidence and in the exercise of all other powers conferred on it.

NOTES

Initial Commencement

To be appointed: see s 109(1).

Appointment

Appointment: 31 January 1997: see SI 1996/3146, art 3; for transitional provisions see art 4, Sch 2 thereto.

Extent

This section does not extend to Scotland: see s 108(1).

A1.286

34   Procedural and evidential matters

(1)   It shall be for the tribunal to decide all procedural and evidential matters, subject to the right of the parties to agree any matter.

(2)   Procedural and evidential matters include—

   (a)   when and where any part of the proceedings is to be held;
   (b)   the language or languages to be used in the proceedings and whether translations of any relevant documents are to be supplied;

(c) whether any and if so what form of written statements of claim and defence are to be used, when these should be supplied and the extent to which such statements can be later amended;

(d) whether any and if so which documents or classes of documents should be disclosed between and produced by the parties and at what stage;

(e) whether any and if so what questions should be put to and answered by the respective parties and when and in what form this should be done;

(f) whether to apply strict rules of evidence (or any other rules) as to the admissibility, relevance or weight of any material (oral, written or other) sought to be tendered on any matters of fact or opinion, and the time, manner and form in which such material should be exchanged and presented;

(g) whether and to what extent the tribunal should itself take the initiative in ascertaining the facts and the law;

(h) whether and to what extent there should be oral or written evidence or submissions.

(3) The tribunal may fix the time within which any directions given by it are to be complied with, and may if it thinks fit extend the time so fixed (whether or not it has expired).

NOTES

Initial Commencement

To be appointed: see s 109(1).

Appointment

Appointment: 31 January 1997: see SI 1996/3146, art 3; for transitional provisions see art 4, Sch 2 thereto.

Extent

This section does not extend to Scotland: see s 108(1).

A1.287

35   Consolidation of proceedings and concurrent hearings

(1) The parties are free to agree—

(a) that the arbitral proceedings shall be consolidated with other arbitral proceedings, or

(b) that concurrent hearings shall be held,

on such terms as may be agreed.

(2) Unless the parties agree to confer such power on the tribunal, the tribunal has no power to order consolidation of proceedings or concurrent hearings.

NOTES

Initial Commencement

To be appointed: see s 109(1).

Appointment

Appointment: 31 January 1997: see SI 1996/3146, art 3; for transitional provisions see art 4, Sch 2 thereto.

Extent

This section does not extend to Scotland: see s 108(1).

A1.288

36   Legal or other representation

Unless otherwise agreed by the parties, a party to arbitral proceedings may be represented in the proceedings by a lawyer or other person chosen by him.

NOTES

Initial Commencement

To be appointed: see s 109(1).

Appointment

Appointment: 31 January 1997: see SI 1996/3146, art 3; for transitional provisions see art 4, Sch 2 thereto.

Extent

This section does not extend to Scotland: see s 108(1).

A1.289

37   Power to appoint experts, legal advisers or assessors

(1)   Unless otherwise agreed by the parties—

    (a)   the tribunal may—
        (i)   appoint experts or legal advisers to report to it and the parties, or
        (ii)   appoint assessors to assist it on technical matters,
    and may allow any such expert, legal adviser or assessor to attend the proceedings; and
    (b)   the parties shall be given a reasonable opportunity to comment on any information, opinion or advice offered by any such person.

(2)   The fees and expenses of an expert, legal adviser or assessor appointed by the tribunal for which the arbitrators are liable are expenses of the arbitrators for the purposes of this Part.

NOTES

Initial Commencement

To be appointed: see s 109(1).

Appointment

Appointment: 31 January 1997: see SI 1996/3146, art 3; for transitional provisions see art 4, Sch 2 thereto.

Extent

This section does not extend to Scotland: see s 108(1).

A1.290

38   General powers exercisable by the tribunal

(1)   The parties are free to agree on the powers exercisable by the arbitral tribunal for the purposes of and in relation to the proceedings.

(2)   Unless otherwise agreed by the parties the tribunal has the following powers.

(3)   The tribunal may order a claimant to provide security for the costs of the arbitration.
This power shall not be exercised on the ground that the claimant is—

   (a)   an individual ordinarily resident outside the United Kingdom, or
   (b)   a corporation or association incorporated or formed under the law of a country outside the United Kingdom, or whose central management and control is exercised outside the United Kingdom.

(4)   The tribunal may give directions in relation to any property which is the subject of the proceedings or as to which any question arises in the proceedings, and which is owned by or is in the possession of a party to the proceedings—

   (a)   for the inspection, photographing, preservation, custody or detention of the property by the tribunal, an expert or a party, or
   (b)   ordering that samples be taken from, or any observation be made of or experiment conducted upon, the property.

(5)   The tribunal may direct that a party or witness shall be examined on oath or affirmation, and may for that purpose administer any necessary oath or take any necessary affirmation.

(6)   The tribunal may give directions to a party for the preservation for the purposes of the proceedings of any evidence in his custody or control.

NOTES

Initial Commencement

To be appointed: see s 109(1).

Appointment

Appointment: 31 January 1997: see SI 1996/3146, art 3; for transitional provisions see art 4, Sch 2 thereto.

Extent

This section does not extend to Scotland: see s 108(1).

A1.291

39   Power to make provisional awards

(1)   The parties are free to agree that the tribunal shall have power to order on a provisional basis any relief which it would have power to grant in a final award.

(2)   This includes, for instance, making—

   (a)   a provisional order for the payment of money or the disposition of property as between the parties, or
   (b)   an order to make an interim payment on account of the costs of the arbitration.

(3) Any such order shall be subject to the tribunal's final adjudication; and the tribunal's final award, on the merits or as to costs, shall take account of any such order.

(4) Unless the parties agree to confer such power on the tribunal, the tribunal has no such power.

This does not affect its powers under section 47 (awards on different issues, &c).

NOTES

Initial Commencement

To be appointed: see s 109(1).

Appointment

Appointment: 31 January 1997: see SI 1996/3146, art 3; for transitional provisions see art 4, Sch 2 thereto.

Extent

This section does not extend to Scotland: see s 108(1).

A1.292

40   General duty of parties

(1) The parties shall do all things necessary for the proper and expeditious conduct of the arbitral proceedings.

(2) This includes—

(a) complying without delay with any determination of the tribunal as to procedural or evidential matters, or with any order or directions of the tribunal, and

(b) where appropriate, taking without delay any necessary steps to obtain a decision of the court on a preliminary question of jurisdiction or law (see sections 32 and 45).

NOTES

Initial Commencement

To be appointed: see s 109(1).

Appointment

Appointment: 31 January 1997: see SI 1996/3146, art 3; for transitional provisions see art 4, Sch 2 thereto.

Extent

This section does not extend to Scotland: see s 108(1).

A1.293

41   Powers of tribunal in case of party's default

(1) The parties are free to agree on the powers of the tribunal in case of a party's failure to do something necessary for the proper and expeditious conduct of the arbitration.

(2) Unless otherwise agreed by the parties, the following provisions apply.

(3) If the tribunal is satisfied that there has been inordinate and inexcusable delay on the part of the claimant in pursuing his claim and that the delay—

 (a) gives rise, or is likely to give rise, to a substantial risk that it is not possible to have a fair resolution of the issues in that claim, or
 (b) has caused, or is likely to cause, serious prejudice to the respondent,

the tribunal may make an award dismissing the claim.

(4) If without showing sufficient cause a party—

 (a) fails to attend or be represented at an oral hearing of which due notice was given, or
 (b) where matters are to be dealt with in writing, fails after due notice to submit written evidence or make written submissions,

the tribunal may continue the proceedings in the absence of that party or, as the case may be, without any written evidence or submissions on his behalf, and may make an award on the basis of the evidence before it.

(5) If without showing sufficient cause a party fails to comply with any order or directions of the tribunal, the tribunal may make a peremptory order to the same effect, prescribing such time for compliance with it as the tribunal considers appropriate.

(6) If a claimant fails to comply with a peremptory order of the tribunal to provide security for costs, the tribunal may make an award dismissing his claim.

(7) If a party fails to comply with any other kind of peremptory order, then, without prejudice to section 42 (enforcement by court of tribunal's peremptory orders), the tribunal may do any of the following—

 (a) direct that the party in default shall not be entitled to rely upon any allegation or material which was the subject matter of the order;
 (b) draw such adverse inferences from the act of non-compliance as the circumstances justify;
 (c) proceed to an award on the basis of such materials as have been properly provided to it;
 (d) make such order as it thinks fit as to the payment of costs of the arbitration incurred in consequence of the non-compliance.

NOTES

Initial Commencement

To be appointed: see s 109(1).

Appointment

Appointment: 31 January 1997: see SI 1996/3146, art 3; for transitional provisions see art 4, Sch 2 thereto.

Extent

This section does not extend to Scotland: see s 108(1).

Powers of court in relation to arbitral proceedings

A1.294

42 Enforcement of peremptory orders of tribunal

(1) Unless otherwise agreed by the parties, the court may make an order requiring a party to comply with a peremptory order made by the tribunal.

(2) An application for an order under this section may be made—

    (a) by the tribunal (upon notice to the parties),

    (b) by a party to the arbitral proceedings with the permission of the tribunal (and upon notice to the other parties), or

    (c) where the parties have agreed that the powers of the court under this section shall be available.

(3) The court shall not act unless it is satisfied that the applicant has exhausted any available arbitral process in respect of failure to comply with the tribunal's order.

(4) No order shall be made under this section unless the court is satisfied that the person to whom the tribunal's order was directed has failed to comply with it within the time prescribed in the order or, if no time was prescribed, within a reasonable time.

(5) The leave of the court is required for any appeal from a decision of the court under this section.

NOTES

Initial Commencement

To be appointed: see s 109(1).

Appointment

Appointment: 31 January 1997: see SI 1996/3146, art 3; for transitional provisions see art 4, Sch 2 thereto.

Extent

This section does not extend to Scotland: see s 108(1).

A1.295

43   Securing the attendance of witnesses

(1) A party to arbitral proceedings may use the same court procedures as are available in relation to legal proceedings to secure the attendance before the tribunal of a witness in order to give oral testimony or to produce documents or other material evidence.

(2) This may only be done with the permission of the tribunal or the agreement of the other parties.

(3) The court procedures may only be used if—

    (a) the witness is in the United Kingdom, and

    (b) the arbitral proceedings are being conducted in England and Wales or, as the case may be, Northern Ireland.

(4) A person shall not be compelled by virtue of this section to produce any document or other material evidence which he could not be compelled to produce in legal proceedings.

NOTES

Initial Commencement

To be appointed: see s 109(1).

Appointment

Appointment: 31 January 1997: see SI 1996/3146, art 3; for transitional provisions see art 4, Sch 2 thereto.

Extent

This section does not extend to Scotland: see s 108(1).

A1.296

44   Court powers exercisable in support of arbitral proceedings

(1)   Unless otherwise agreed by the parties, the court has for the purposes of and in relation to arbitral proceedings the same power of making orders about the matters listed below as it has for the purposes of and in relation to legal proceedings.

(2)   Those matters are—

  (a)   the taking of the evidence of witnesses;
  (b)   the preservation of evidence;
  (c)   making orders relating to property which is the subject of the proceedings or as to which any question arises in the proceedings—
    (i)   for the inspection, photographing, preservation, custody or detention of the property, or
    (ii)   ordering that samples be taken from, or any observation be made of or experiment conducted upon, the property;
  and for that purpose authorising any person to enter any premises in the possession or control of a party to the arbitration;
  (d)   the sale of any goods the subject of the proceedings;
  (e)   the granting of an interim injunction or the appointment of a receiver.

(3)   If the case is one of urgency, the court may, on the application of a party or proposed party to the arbitral proceedings, make such orders as it thinks necessary for the purpose of preserving evidence or assets.

(4)   If the case is not one of urgency, the court shall act only on the application of a party to the arbitral proceedings (upon notice to the other parties and to the tribunal) made with the permission of the tribunal or the agreement in writing of the other parties.

(5)   In any case the court shall act only if or to the extent that the arbitral tribunal, and any arbitral or other institution or person vested by the parties with power in that regard, has no power or is unable for the time being to act effectively.

(6)   If the court so orders, an order made by it under this section shall cease to have effect in whole or in part on the order of the tribunal or of any such arbitral or other institution or person having power to act in relation to the subject-matter of the order.

(7)   The leave of the court is required for any appeal from a decision of the court under this section.

NOTES

Initial Commencement

To be appointed: see s 109(1).

Appointment

Appointment: 31 January 1997: see SI 1996/3146, art 3; for transitional provisions see art 4, Sch 2 thereto.

Extent

This section does not extend to Scotland: see s 108(1).

A1.297

45   Determination of preliminary point of law

(1)   Unless otherwise agreed by the parties, the court may on the application of a party to arbitral proceedings (upon notice to the other parties) determine any question of law arising in the course of the proceedings which the court is satisfied substantially affects the rights of one or more of the parties.

An agreement to dispense with reasons for the tribunal's award shall be considered an agreement to exclude the court's jurisdiction under this section.

(2)   An application under this section shall not be considered unless—

- (a)   it is made with the agreement of all the other parties to the proceedings, or
- (b)   it is made with the permission of the tribunal and the court is satisfied—
  - (i)   that the determination of the question is likely to produce substantial savings in costs, and
  - (ii)   that the application was made without delay.

(3)   The application shall identify the question of law to be determined and, unless made with the agreement of all the other parties to the proceedings, shall state the grounds on which it is said that the question should be decided by the court.

(4)   Unless otherwise agreed by the parties, the arbitral tribunal may continue the arbitral proceedings and make an award while an application to the court under this section is pending.

(5)   Unless the court gives leave, no appeal lies from a decision of the court whether the conditions specified in subsection (2) are met.

(6)   The decision of the court on the question of law shall be treated as a judgment of the court for the purposes of an appeal.

But no appeal lies without the leave of the court which shall not be given unless the court considers that the question is one of general importance, or is one which for some other special reason should be considered by the Court of Appeal.

NOTES

Initial Commencement

To be appointed: see s 109(1).

Appointment

Appointment: 31 January 1997: see SI 1996/3146, art 3; for transitional provisions see art 4, Sch 2 thereto.

Extent

This section does not extend to Scotland: see s 108(1).

See Further

See further, in relation to the application of this section, with modifications, for the purposes of arbitrations conducted in accordance with the Scheme: the ACAS Arbitration Scheme (Great Britain) Order 2004, SI 2004/753, art 4, Schedule, para 110EW.

The award

A1.298

46   Rules applicable to substance of dispute

(1) The arbitral tribunal shall decide the dispute—

    (a) in accordance with the law chosen by the parties as applicable to the substance of the dispute, or

    (b) if the parties so agree, in accordance with such other considerations as are agreed by them or determined by the tribunal.

(2) For this purpose the choice of the laws of a country shall be understood to refer to the substantive laws of that country and not its conflict of laws rules.

(3) If or to the extent that there is no such choice or agreement, the tribunal shall apply the law determined by the conflict of laws rules which it considers applicable.

NOTES

Initial Commencement

To be appointed: see s 109(1).

Appointment

Appointment: 31 January 1997: see SI 1996/3146, art 3; for transitional provisions see art 4, Sch 2 thereto.

Extent

This section does not extend to Scotland: see s 108(1).

See Further

Sub-s (1)(b): see further, in relation to the application of this sub-s, with modifications, for the purposes of arbitrations conducted in accordance with the Scheme: the ACAS Arbitration Scheme (Great Britain) Order 2004, SI 2004/753, art 5.

A1.299

47   Awards on different issues, &c

(1) Unless otherwise agreed by the parties, the tribunal may make more than one award at different times on different aspects of the matters to be determined.

(2) The tribunal may, in particular, make an award relating—

    (a) to an issue affecting the whole claim, or

    (b) to a part only of the claims or cross-claims submitted to it for decision.

(3) If the tribunal does so, it shall specify in its award the issue, or the claim or part of a claim, which is the subject matter of the award.

NOTES

Initial Commencement

To be appointed: see s 109(1).

Appointment

Appointment: 31 January 1997: see SI 1996/3146, art 3; for transitional provisions see art 4, Sch 2 thereto.

Extent

This section does not extend to Scotland: see s 108(1).

A1.300

48   Remedies

(1)   The parties are free to agree on the powers exercisable by the arbitral tribunal as regards remedies.

(2)   Unless otherwise agreed by the parties, the tribunal has the following powers.

(3)   The tribunal may make a declaration as to any matter to be determined in the proceedings.

(4)   The tribunal may order the payment of a sum of money, in any currency.

(5)   The tribunal has the same powers as the court—

    (a)   to order a party to do or refrain from doing anything;
    (b)   to order specific performance of a contract (other than a contract relating to land);
    (c)   to order the rectification, setting aside or cancellation of a deed or other document.

NOTES

Initial Commencement

To be appointed: see s 109(1).

Appointment

Appointment: 31 January 1997: see SI 1996/3146, art 3; for transitional provisions see art 4, Sch 2 thereto.

Extent

This section does not extend to Scotland: see s 108(1).

A1.301

49   Interest

(1)   The parties are free to agree on the powers of the tribunal as regards the award of interest.

(2)   Unless otherwise agreed by the parties the following provisions apply.

(3)   The tribunal may award simple or compound interest from such dates, at such rates and with such rests as it considers meets the justice of the case—

    (a)   on the whole or part of any amount awarded by the tribunal, in respect of any period up to the date of the award;
    (b)   on the whole or part of any amount claimed in the arbitration and outstanding at the commencement of the arbitral proceedings but paid before the award was made, in respect of any period up to the date of payment.

(4)   The tribunal may award simple or compound interest from the date of the award (or any later date) until payment, at such rates and with such rests as it considers meets the justice of the case, on the outstanding amount of any award (including any award of interest under subsection (3) and any award as to costs).

(5)   References in this section to an amount awarded by the tribunal include an amount payable in consequence of a declaratory award by the tribunal.

(6)   The above provisions do not affect any other power of the tribunal to award interest.

NOTES

Initial Commencement

To be appointed: see s 109(1).

Appointment

Appointment: 31 January 1997: see SI 1996/3146, art 3; for transitional provisions see art 4, Sch 2 thereto.

Extent

This section does not extend to Scotland: see s 108(1).

A1.302

50   Extension of time for making award

(1)   Where the time for making an award is limited by or in pursuance of the arbitration agreement, then, unless otherwise agreed by the parties, the court may in accordance with the following provisions by order extend that time.

(2)   An application for an order under this section may be made—

  (a)   by the tribunal (upon notice to the parties), or
  (b)   by any party to the proceedings (upon notice to the tribunal and the other parties),

but only after exhausting any available arbitral process for obtaining an extension of time.

(3)   The court shall only make an order if satisfied that a substantial injustice would otherwise be done.

(4)   The court may extend the time for such period and on such terms as it thinks fit, and may do so whether or not the time previously fixed (by or under the agreement or by a previous order) has expired.

(5)   The leave of the court is required for any appeal from a decision of the court under this section.

NOTES

Initial Commencement

To be appointed: see s 109(1).

Appointment

Appointment: 31 January 1997: see SI 1996/3146, art 3; for transitional provisions see art 4, Sch 2 thereto.

Extent

This section does not extend to Scotland: see s 108(1).

A1.303

51   Settlement

(1) If during arbitral proceedings the parties settle the dispute, the following provisions apply unless otherwise agreed by the parties.

(2) The tribunal shall terminate the substantive proceedings and, if so requested by the parties and not objected to by the tribunal, shall record the settlement in the form of an agreed award.

(3) An agreed award shall state that it is an award of the tribunal and shall have the same status and effect as any other award on the merits of the case.

(4) The following provisions of this Part relating to awards (sections 52 to 58) apply to an agreed award.

(5) Unless the parties have also settled the matter of the payment of the costs of the arbitration, the provisions of this Part relating to costs (sections 59 to 65) continue to apply.

NOTES

Initial Commencement

To be appointed: see s 109(1).

Appointment

Appointment: 31 January 1997: see SI 1996/3146, art 3; for transitional provisions see art 4, Sch 2 thereto.

Extent

This section does not extend to Scotland: see s 108(1).

A1.304

52   Form of award

(1) The parties are free to agree on the form of an award.

(2) If or to the extent that there is no such agreement, the following provisions apply.

(3) The award shall be in writing signed by all the arbitrators or all those assenting to the award.

(4) The award shall contain the reasons for the award unless it is an agreed award or the parties have agreed to dispense with reasons.

(5) The award shall state the seat of the arbitration and the date when the award is made.

NOTES

Initial Commencement

To be appointed: see s 109(1).

Appointment

Appointment: 31 January 1997: see SI 1996/3146, art 3; for transitional provisions see art 4, Sch 2 thereto.

Extent

This section does not extend to Scotland: see s 108(1).

A1.305

53   Place where award treated as made

Unless otherwise agreed by the parties, where the seat of the arbitration is in England and Wales or Northern Ireland, any award in the proceedings shall be treated as made there, regardless of where it was signed, despatched or delivered to any of the parties.

NOTES

Initial Commencement

To be appointed: see s 109(1).

Appointment

Appointment: 31 January 1997: see SI 1996/3146, art 3; for transitional provisions see art 4, Sch 2 thereto.

Extent

This section does not extend to Scotland: see s 108(1).

A1.306

54   Date of award

(1)   Unless otherwise agreed by the parties, the tribunal may decide what is to be taken to be the date on which the award was made.

(2)   In the absence of any such decision, the date of the award shall be taken to be the date on which it is signed by the arbitrator or, where more than one arbitrator signs the award, by the last of them.

NOTES

Initial Commencement

To be appointed: see s 109(1).

Appointment

Appointment: 31 January 1997: see SI 1996/3146, art 3; for transitional provisions see art 4, Sch 2 thereto.

Extent

This section does not extend to Scotland: see s 108(1).

A1.307

55   Notification of award

(1)   The parties are free to agree on the requirements as to notification of the award to the parties.

(2)   If there is no such agreement, the award shall be notified to the parties by service on them of copies of the award, which shall be done without delay after the award is made.

(3)   Nothing in this section affects section 56 (power to withhold award in case of non-payment).

NOTES

Initial Commencement

To be appointed: see s 109(1).

Appointment

Appointment: 31 January 1997: see SI 1996/3146, art 3; for transitional provisions see art 4, Sch 2 thereto.

Extent

This section does not extend to Scotland: see s 108(1).

A1.308

56   Power to withhold award in case of non-payment

(1)   The tribunal may refuse to deliver an award to the parties except upon full payment of the fees and expenses of the arbitrators.

(2)   If the tribunal refuses on that ground to deliver an award, a party to the arbitral proceedings may (upon notice to the other parties and the tribunal) apply to the court, which may order that—

   (a)   the tribunal shall deliver the award on the payment into court by the applicant of the fees and expenses demanded, or such lesser amount as the court may specify,

   (b)   the amount of the fees and expenses properly payable shall be determined by such means and upon such terms as the court may direct, and

   (c)   out of the money paid into court there shall be paid out such fees and expenses as may be found to be properly payable and the balance of the money (if any) shall be paid out to the applicant.

(3)   For this purpose the amount of fees and expenses properly payable is the amount the applicant is liable to pay under section 28 or any agreement relating to the payment of the arbitrators.

(4)   No application to the court may be made where there is any available arbitral process for appeal or review of the amount of the fees or expenses demanded.

(5)   References in this section to arbitrators include an arbitrator who has ceased to act and an umpire who has not replaced the other arbitrators.

(6)   The above provisions of this section also apply in relation to any arbitral or other institution or person vested by the parties with powers in relation to the delivery of the tribunal's award.

As they so apply, the references to the fees and expenses of the arbitrators shall be construed as including the fees and expenses of that institution or person.

(7)   The leave of the court is required for any appeal from a decision of the court under this section.

(8)   Nothing in this section shall be construed as excluding an application under section 28 where payment has been made to the arbitrators in order to obtain the award.

NOTES

Initial Commencement

To be appointed: see s 109(1).

Appointment

Appointment: 31 January 1997: see SI 1996/3146, art 3; for transitional provisions see art 4, Sch 2 thereto.

Extent

This section does not extend to Scotland: see s 108(1).

A1.309

57   Correction of award or additional award

(1)   The parties are free to agree on the powers of the tribunal to correct an award or make an additional award.

(2)   If or to the extent there is no such agreement, the following provisions apply.

(3)   The tribunal may on its own initiative or on the application of a party—

   (a)   correct an award so as to remove any clerical mistake or error arising from an accidental slip or omission or clarify or remove any ambiguity in the award, or

   (b)   make an additional award in respect of any claim (including a claim for interest or costs) which was presented to the tribunal but was not dealt with in the award.

These powers shall not be exercised without first affording the other parties a reasonable opportunity to make representations to the tribunal.

(4)   Any application for the exercise of those powers must be made within 28 days of the date of the award or such longer period as the parties may agree.

(5)   Any correction of an award shall be made within 28 days of the date the application was received by the tribunal or, where the correction is made by the tribunal on its own initiative, within 28 days of the date of the award or, in either case, such longer period as the parties may agree.

(6)   Any additional award shall be made within 56 days of the date of the original award or such longer period as the parties may agree.

(7)   Any correction of an award shall form part of the award.

NOTES

Initial Commencement

To be appointed: see s 109(1).

Appointment

Appointment: 31 January 1997: see SI 1996/3146, art 3; for transitional provisions see art 4, Sch 2 thereto.

Extent

This section does not extend to Scotland: see s 108(1).

A1.310

58   Effect of award

(1)   Unless otherwise agreed by the parties, an award made by the tribunal pursuant to an arbitration agreement is final and binding both on the parties and on any persons claiming through or under them.

(2)   This does not affect the right of a person to challenge the award by any available arbitral process of appeal or review or in accordance with the provisions of this Part.

NOTES

Initial Commencement

To be appointed: see s 109(1).

Appointment

Appointment: 31 January 1997: see SI 1996/3146, art 3; for transitional provisions see art 4, Sch 2 thereto.

Extent

This section does not extend to Scotland: see s 108(1).

Costs of the arbitration

A1.311

59   Costs of the arbitration

(1)   References in this Part to the costs of the arbitration are to—

    (a)   the arbitrators' fees and expenses,
    (b)   the fees and expenses of any arbitral institution concerned, and
    (c)   the legal or other costs of the parties.

(2)   Any such reference includes the costs of or incidental to any proceedings to determine the amount of the recoverable costs of the arbitration (see section 63).

NOTES

Initial Commencement

To be appointed: see s 109(1).

Appointment

Appointment: 31 January 1997: see SI 1996/3146, art 3; for transitional provisions see art 4, Sch 2 thereto.

A1.312   *Statutes*

Extent

This section does not extend to Scotland: see s 108(1).

A1.312

60   Agreement to pay costs in any event

An agreement which has the effect that a party is to pay the whole or part of the costs of the arbitration in any event is only valid if made after the dispute in question has arisen.

NOTES

Initial Commencement

To be appointed: see s 109(1).

Appointment

Appointment: 31 January 1997: see SI 1996/3146, art 3; for transitional provisions see art 4, Sch 2 thereto.

Extent

This section does not extend to Scotland: see s 108(1).

A1.313

61   Award of costs

(1)   The tribunal may make an award allocating the costs of the arbitration as between the parties, subject to any agreement of the parties.

(2)   Unless the parties otherwise agree, the tribunal shall award costs on the general principle that costs should follow the event except where it appears to the tribunal that in the circumstances this is not appropriate in relation to the whole or part of the costs.

NOTES

Initial Commencement

To be appointed: see s 109(1).

Appointment

Appointment: 31 January 1997: see SI 1996/3146, art 3; for transitional provisions see art 4, Sch 2 thereto.

Extent

This section does not extend to Scotland: see s 108(1).

A1.314

62   Effect of agreement or award about costs

Unless the parties otherwise agree, any obligation under an agreement between them as to how the costs of the arbitration are to be borne, or under an award allocating the costs of the arbitration, extends only to such costs as are recoverable.

1404

NOTES

Initial Commencement

To be appointed: see s 109(1).

Appointment

Appointment: 31 January 1997: see SI 1996/3146, art 3; for transitional provisions see art 4, Sch 2 thereto.

Extent

This section does not extend to Scotland: see s 108(1).

A1.315

63   The recoverable costs of the arbitration

(1)   The parties are free to agree what costs of the arbitration are recoverable.

(2)   If or to the extent there is no such agreement, the following provisions apply.

(3)   The tribunal may determine by award the recoverable costs of the arbitration on such basis as it thinks fit.
If it does so, it shall specify—

    (a)   the basis on which it has acted, and

    (b)   the items of recoverable costs and the amount referable to each.

(4)   If the tribunal does not determine the recoverable costs of the arbitration, any party to the arbitral proceedings may apply to the court (upon notice to the other parties) which may—

    (a)   determine the recoverable costs of the arbitration on such basis as it thinks fit, or

    (b)   order that they shall be determined by such means and upon such terms as it may specify.

(5)   Unless the tribunal or the court determines otherwise—

    (a)   the recoverable costs of the arbitration shall be determined on the basis that there shall be allowed a reasonable amount in respect of all costs reasonably incurred, and

    (b)   any doubt as to whether costs were reasonably incurred or were reasonable in amount shall be resolved in favour of the paying party.

(6)   The above provisions have effect subject to section 64 (recoverable fees and expenses of arbitrators).

(7)   Nothing in this section affects any right of the arbitrators, any expert, legal adviser or assessor appointed by the tribunal, or any arbitral institution, to payment of their fees and expenses.

NOTES

Initial Commencement

To be appointed: see s 109(1).

Appointment

Appointment: 31 January 1997: see SI 1996/3146, art 3; for transitional provisions see art 4, Sch 2 thereto.

Extent

This section does not extend to Scotland: see s 108(1).

A1.316

64   Recoverable fees and expenses of arbitrators

(1)   Unless otherwise agreed by the parties, the recoverable costs of the arbitration shall include in respect of the fees and expenses of the arbitrators only such reasonable fees and expenses as are appropriate in the circumstances.

(2)   If there is any question as to what reasonable fees and expenses are appropriate in the circumstances, and the matter is not already before the court on an application under section 63(4), the court may on the application of any party (upon notice to the other parties)—

    (a)   determine the matter, or
    (b)   order that it be determined by such means and upon such terms as the court may specify.

(3)   Subsection (1) has effect subject to any order of the court under section 24(4) or 25(3)(b) (order as to entitlement to fees or expenses in case of removal or resignation of arbitrator).

(4)   Nothing in this section affects any right of the arbitrator to payment of his fees and expenses.

NOTES

Initial Commencement

To be appointed: see s 109(1).

Appointment

Appointment: 31 January 1997: see SI 1996/3146, art 3; for transitional provisions see art 4, Sch 2 thereto.

Extent

This section does not extend to Scotland: see s 108(1).

A1.317

65   Power to limit recoverable costs

(1)   Unless otherwise agreed by the parties, the tribunal may direct that the recoverable costs of the arbitration, or of any part of the arbitral proceedings, shall be limited to a specified amount.

(2)   Any direction may be made or varied at any stage, but this must be done sufficiently in advance of the incurring of costs to which it relates, or the taking of any steps in the proceedings which may be affected by it, for the limit to be taken into account.

NOTES

Initial Commencement

To be appointed: see s 109(1).

Appointment

Appointment: 31 January 1997: see SI 1996/3146, art 3; for transitional provisions see art 4, Sch 2 thereto.

Extent

This section does not extend to Scotland: see s 108(1).

Powers of the court in relation to award

A1.318

66   Enforcement of the award

(1)   An award made by the tribunal pursuant to an arbitration agreement may, by leave of the court, be enforced in the same manner as a judgment or order of the court to the same effect.

(2)   Where leave is so given, judgment may be entered in terms of the award.

(3)   Leave to enforce an award shall not be given where, or to the extent that, the person against whom it is sought to be enforced shows that the tribunal lacked substantive jurisdiction to make the award.
  The right to raise such an objection may have been lost (see section 73).

(4)   Nothing in this section affects the recognition or enforcement of an award under any other enactment or rule of law, in particular under Part II of the Arbitration Act 1950 (enforcement of awards under Geneva Convention) or the provisions of Part III of this Act relating to the recognition and enforcement of awards under the New York Convention or by an action on the award.

NOTES

Initial Commencement

To be appointed: see s 109(1).

Appointment

Appointment: 31 January 1997: see SI 1996/3146, art 3; for transitional provisions see art 4, Sch 2 thereto.

Extent

This section does not extend to Scotland: see s 108(1).

See Further

See further, in relation to the application of this section, with modifications, for the purposes of arbitrations conducted in accordance with the Scheme: the ACAS Arbitration Scheme (Great Britain) Order 2004, SI 2004/753, art 4, Schedule, para 183EW.

A1.319

67   Challenging the award: substantive jurisdiction

(1)   A party to arbitral proceedings may (upon notice to the other parties and to the tribunal) apply to the court—

  (a)   challenging any award of the arbitral tribunal as to its substantive jurisdiction; or

   (b)   for an order declaring an award made by the tribunal on the merits to be of no effect, in whole or in part, because the tribunal did not have substantive jurisdiction.

A party may lose the right to object (see section 73) and the right to apply is subject to the restrictions in section 70(2) and (3).

(2)   The arbitral tribunal may continue the arbitral proceedings and make a further award while an application to the court under this section is pending in relation to an award as to jurisdiction.

(3)   On an application under this section challenging an award of the arbitral tribunal as to its substantive jurisdiction, the court may by order—

   (a)   confirm the award,
   (b)   vary the award, or
   (c)   set aside the award in whole or in part.

(4)   The leave of the court is required for any appeal from a decision of the court under this section.

NOTES

Initial Commencement

To be appointed: see s 109(1).

Appointment

Appointment: 31 January 1997: see SI 1996/3146, art 3; for transitional provisions see art 4, Sch 2 thereto.

Extent

This section does not extend to Scotland: see s 108(1).

See Further

See further, in relation to the application of this section, with modifications, for the purposes of arbitrations conducted in accordance with the Scheme: the ACAS Arbitration Scheme (Great Britain) Order 2004, SI 2004/753, art 4, Schedule, para 187EW.

A1.320

68   Challenging the award: serious irregularity

(1)   A party to arbitral proceedings may (upon notice to the other parties and to the tribunal) apply to the court challenging an award in the proceedings on the ground of serious irregularity affecting the tribunal, the proceedings or the award.

   A party may lose the right to object (see section 73) and the right to apply is subject to the restrictions in section 70(2) and (3).

(2)   Serious irregularity means an irregularity of one or more of the following kinds which the court considers has caused or will cause substantial injustice to the applicant—

   (a)   failure by the tribunal to comply with section 33 (general duty of tribunal);
   (b)   the tribunal exceeding its powers (otherwise than by exceeding its substantive jurisdiction: see section 67);
   (c)   failure by the tribunal to conduct the proceedings in accordance with the procedure agreed by the parties;
   (d)   failure by the tribunal to deal with all the issues that were put to it;

(e) any arbitral or other institution or person vested by the parties with powers in relation to the proceedings or the award exceeding its powers;

(f) uncertainty or ambiguity as to the effect of the award;

(g) the award being obtained by fraud or the award or the way in which it was procured being contrary to public policy;

(h) failure to comply with the requirements as to the form of the award; or

(i) any irregularity in the conduct of the proceedings or in the award which is admitted by the tribunal or by any arbitral or other institution or person vested by the parties with powers in relation to the proceedings or the award.

(3) If there is shown to be serious irregularity affecting the tribunal, the proceedings or the award, the court may—

(a) remit the award to the tribunal, in whole or in part, for reconsideration,

(b) set the award aside in whole or in part, or

(c) declare the award to be of no effect, in whole or in part.

The court shall not exercise its power to set aside or to declare an award to be of no effect, in whole or in part, unless it is satisfied that it would be inappropriate to remit the matters in question to the tribunal for reconsideration.

(4) The leave of the court is required for any appeal from a decision of the court under this section.

NOTES

Initial Commencement

To be appointed: see s 109(1).

Appointment

Appointment: 31 January 1997: see SI 1996/3146, art 3; for transitional provisions see art 4, Sch 2 thereto.

Extent

This section does not extend to Scotland: see s 108(1).

See Further

See further, in relation to the application of this section, with modifications, for the purposes of arbitrations conducted in accordance with the Scheme: the ACAS Arbitration Scheme (Great Britain) Order 2004, SI 2004/753, art 4, Schedule, para 194EW.

A1.321

69   Appeal on point of law

(1) Unless otherwise agreed by the parties, a party to arbitral proceedings may (upon notice to the other parties and to the tribunal) appeal to the court on a question of law arising out of an award made in the proceedings.

An agreement to dispense with reasons for the tribunal's award shall be considered an agreement to exclude the court's jurisdiction under this section.

(2) An appeal shall not be brought under this section except—

(a) with the agreement of all the other parties to the proceedings, or

(b) with the leave of the court.

The right to appeal is also subject to the restrictions in section 70(2) and (3).

(3) Leave to appeal shall be given only if the court is satisfied—

(a) that the determination of the question will substantially affect the rights of one or more of the parties,
(b) that the question is one which the tribunal was asked to determine,
(c) that, on the basis of the findings of fact in the award—
    (i) the decision of the tribunal on the question is obviously wrong, or
    (ii) the question is one of general public importance and the decision of the tribunal is at least open to serious doubt, and
(d) that, despite the agreement of the parties to resolve the matter by arbitration, it is just and proper in all the circumstances for the court to determine the question.

(4) An application for leave to appeal under this section shall identify the question of law to be determined and state the grounds on which it is alleged that leave to appeal should be granted.

(5) The court shall determine an application for leave to appeal under this section without a hearing unless it appears to the court that a hearing is required.

(6) The leave of the court is required for any appeal from a decision of the court under this section to grant or refuse leave to appeal.

(7) On an appeal under this section the court may by order—

(a) confirm the award,
(b) vary the award,
(c) remit the award to the tribunal, in whole or in part, for reconsideration in the light of the court's determination, or
(d) set aside the award in whole or in part.

The court shall not exercise its power to set aside an award, in whole or in part, unless it is satisfied that it would be inappropriate to remit the matters in question to the tribunal for reconsideration.

(8) The decision of the court on an appeal under this section shall be treated as a judgment of the court for the purposes of a further appeal.

But no such appeal lies without the leave of the court which shall not be given unless the court considers that the question is one of general importance or is one which for some other special reason should be considered by the Court of Appeal.

NOTES

Initial Commencement

To be appointed: see s 109(1).

Appointment

Appointment: 31 January 1997: see SI 1996/3146, art 3; for transitional provisions see art 4, Sch 2 thereto.

Extent

This section does not extend to Scotland: see s 108(1).

See Further

See further, in relation to the application of this section, with modifications, for the purposes of arbitrations conducted in accordance with the Scheme: the ACAS Arbitration Scheme (Great Britain) Order 2004, SI 2004/753, art 4, Schedule, para 200EW.

A1.322

70   **Challenge or appeal: supplementary provisions**

(1)   The following provisions apply to an application or appeal under section 67, 68 or 69.

(2)   An application or appeal may not be brought if the applicant or appellant has not first exhausted—

- (a)   any available arbitral process of appeal or review, and
- (b)   any available recourse under section 57 (correction of award or additional award).

(3)   Any application or appeal must be brought within 28 days of the date of the award or, if there has been any arbitral process of appeal or review, of the date when the applicant or appellant was notified of the result of that process.

(4)   If on an application or appeal it appears to the court that the award—

- (a)   does not contain the tribunal's reasons, or
- (b)   does not set out the tribunal's reasons in sufficient detail to enable the court properly to consider the application or appeal,

the court may order the tribunal to state the reasons for its award in sufficient detail for that purpose.

(5)   Where the court makes an order under subsection (4), it may make such further order as it thinks fit with respect to any additional costs of the arbitration resulting from its order.

(6)   The court may order the applicant or appellant to provide security for the costs of the application or appeal, and may direct that the application or appeal be dismissed if the order is not complied with.

    The power to order security for costs shall not be exercised on the ground that the applicant or appellant is—

- (a)   an individual ordinarily resident outside the United Kingdom, or
- (b)   a corporation or association incorporated or formed under the law of a country outside the United Kingdom, or whose central management and control is exercised outside the United Kingdom.

(7)   The court may order that any money payable under the award shall be brought into court or otherwise secured pending the determination of the application or appeal, and may direct that the application or appeal be dismissed if the order is not complied with.

(8)   The court may grant leave to appeal subject to conditions to the same or similar effect as an order under subsection (6) or (7).

    This does not affect the general discretion of the court to grant leave subject to conditions.

NOTES

Initial Commencement

To be appointed: see s 109(1).

Appointment

Appointment: 31 January 1997: see SI 1996/3146, art 3; for transitional provisions see art 4, Sch 2 thereto.

Extent

This section does not extend to Scotland: see s 108(1).

See Further

See further, in relation to the application of this section, with modifications, for the purposes of arbitrations conducted in accordance with the Scheme: the ACAS Arbitration Scheme (Great Britain) Order 2004, SI 2004/753, art 4, Schedule, para 205EW.

A1.323

71   Challenge or appeal: effect of order of court

(1) The following provisions have effect where the court makes an order under section 67, 68 or 69 with respect to an award.

(2) Where the award is varied, the variation has effect as part of the tribunal's award.

(3) Where the award is remitted to the tribunal, in whole or in part, for reconsideration, the tribunal shall make a fresh award in respect of the matters remitted within three months of the date of the order for remission or such longer or shorter period as the court may direct.

(4) Where the award is set aside or declared to be of no effect, in whole or in part, the court may also order that any provision that an award is a condition precedent to the bringing of legal proceedings in respect of a matter to which the arbitration agreement applies, is of no effect as regards the subject matter of the award or, as the case may be, the relevant part of the award.

NOTES

Initial Commencement

To be appointed: see s 109(1).

Appointment

Appointment: 31 January 1997: see SI 1996/3146, art 3; for transitional provisions see art 4, Sch 2 thereto.

Extent

This section does not extend to Scotland: see s 108(1).

See Further

See further, in relation to the application of this section, with modifications, for the purposes of arbitrations conducted in accordance with the Scheme: the ACAS Arbitration Scheme (Great Britain) Order 2004, SI 2004/753, art 4, Schedule, para 212EW.

Miscellaneous

A1.324

72   Saving for rights of person who takes no part in proceedings

(1) A person alleged to be a party to arbitral proceedings but who takes no part in the proceedings may question—

    (a) whether there is a valid arbitration agreement,

    (b) whether the tribunal is properly constituted, or

    (c)   what matters have been submitted to arbitration in accordance with the arbitration agreement,

by proceedings in the court for a declaration or injunction or other appropriate relief.

(2)   He also has the same right as a party to the arbitral proceedings to challenge an award—

    (a)   by an application under section 67 on the ground of lack of substantive jurisdiction in relation to him, or
    (b)   by an application under section 68 on the ground of serious irregularity (within the meaning of that section) affecting him;

and section 70(2) (duty to exhaust arbitral procedures) does not apply in his case.

NOTES

Initial Commencement

To be appointed: see s 109(1).

Appointment

Appointment: 31 January 1997: see SI 1996/3146, art 3; for transitional provisions see art 4, Sch 2 thereto.

Extent

This section does not extend to Scotland: see s 108(1).

A1.325

73   Loss of right to object

(1)   If a party to arbitral proceedings takes part, or continues to take part, in the proceedings without making, either forthwith or within such time as is allowed by the arbitration agreement or the tribunal or by any provision of this Part, any objection—

    (a)   that the tribunal lacks substantive jurisdiction,
    (b)   that the proceedings have been improperly conducted,
    (c)   that there has been a failure to comply with the arbitration agreement or with any provision of this Part, or
    (d)   that there has been any other irregularity affecting the tribunal or the proceedings,

he may not raise that objection later, before the tribunal or the court, unless he shows that, at the time he took part or continued to take part in the proceedings, he did not know and could not with reasonable diligence have discovered the grounds for the objection.

(2)   Where the arbitral tribunal rules that it has substantive jurisdiction and a party to arbitral proceedings who could have questioned that ruling—

    (a)   by any available arbitral process of appeal or review, or
    (b)   by challenging the award,

does not do so, or does not do so within the time allowed by the arbitration agreement or any provision of this Part, he may not object later to the tribunal's substantive jurisdiction on any ground which was the subject of that ruling.

NOTES

Initial Commencement

To be appointed: see s 109(1).

Appointment

Appointment: 31 January 1997: see SI 1996/3146, art 3; for transitional provisions see art 4, Sch 2 thereto.

Extent

This section does not extend to Scotland: see s 108(1).

A1.326

74   Immunity of arbitral institutions, &c

(1)   An arbitral or other institution or person designated or requested by the parties to appoint or nominate an arbitrator is not liable for anything done or omitted in the discharge or purported discharge of that function unless the act or omission is shown to have been in bad faith.

(2)   An arbitral or other institution or person by whom an arbitrator is appointed or nominated is not liable, by reason of having appointed or nominated him, for anything done or omitted by the arbitrator (or his employees or agents) in the discharge or purported discharge of his functions as arbitrator.

(3)   The above provisions apply to an employee or agent of an arbitral or other institution or person as they apply to the institution or person himself.

NOTES

Initial Commencement

To be appointed: see s 109(1).

Appointment

Appointment: 31 January 1997: see SI 1996/3146, art 3; for transitional provisions see art 4, Sch 2 thereto.

Extent

This section does not extend to Scotland: see s 108(1).

A1.327

75   Charge to secure payment of solicitors' costs

The powers of the court to make declarations and orders under section 73 of the Solicitors Act 1974 or Article 71H of the Solicitors (Northern Ireland) Order 1976 (power to charge property recovered in the proceedings with the payment of solicitors' costs) may be exercised in relation to arbitral proceedings as if those proceedings were proceedings in the court.

NOTES

Initial Commencement

To be appointed: see s 109(1).

Appointment

Appointment: 31 January 1997: see SI 1996/3146, art 3; for transitional provisions see art 4, Sch 2 thereto.

Extent

This section does not extend to Scotland: see s 108(1).

Supplementary

A1.328

76   Service of notices, &c

(1)   The parties are free to agree on the manner of service of any notice or other document required or authorised to be given or served in pursuance of the arbitration agreement or for the purposes of the arbitral proceedings.

(2)   If or to the extent that there is no such agreement the following provisions apply.

(3)   A notice or other document may be served on a person by any effective means.

(4)   If a notice or other document is addressed, pre-paid and delivered by post—

   (a)   to the addressee's last known principal residence or, if he is or has been carrying on a trade, profession or business, his last known principal business address, or

   (b)   where the addressee is a body corporate, to the body's registered or principal office,

it shall be treated as effectively served.

(5)   This section does not apply to the service of documents for the purposes of legal proceedings, for which provision is made by rules of court.

(6)   References in this Part to a notice or other document include any form of communication in writing and references to giving or serving a notice or other document shall be construed accordingly.

NOTES

Initial Commencement

To be appointed: see s 109(1).

Appointment

Appointment: 31 January 1997: see SI 1996/3146, art 3; for transitional provisions see art 4, Sch 2 thereto.

Extent

This section does not extend to Scotland: see s 108(1).

A1.329

77   Powers of court in relation to service of documents

(1)   This section applies where service of a document on a person in the manner agreed by the parties, or in accordance with provisions of section 76 having effect in default of agreement, is not reasonably practicable.

(2)   Unless otherwise agreed by the parties, the court may make such order as it thinks fit—

   (a)   for service in such manner as the court may direct, or
   (b)   dispensing with service of the document.

(3)   Any party to the arbitration agreement may apply for an order, but only after exhausting any available arbitral process for resolving the matter.

(4)   The leave of the court is required for any appeal from a decision of the court under this section.

NOTES

Initial Commencement

To be appointed: see s 109(1).

Appointment

Appointment: 31 January 1997: see SI 1996/3146, art 3; for transitional provisions see art 4, Sch 2 thereto.

Extent

This section does not extend to Scotland: see s 108(1).

See Further

See further, in relation to the application of this section, with modifications, for the purposes of arbitrations conducted in accordance with the Scheme: the ACAS Arbitration Scheme (Great Britain) Order 2004, SI 2004/753, art 4, Schedule, para 223EW.

A1.330

78   Reckoning periods of time

(1)   The parties are free to agree on the method of reckoning periods of time for the purposes of any provision agreed by them or any provision of this Part having effect in default of such agreement.

(2)   If or to the extent there is no such agreement, periods of time shall be reckoned in accordance with the following provisions.

(3)   Where the act is required to be done within a specified period after or from a specified date, the period begins immediately after that date.

(4)   Where the act is required to be done a specified number of clear days after a specified date, at least that number of days must intervene between the day on which the act is done and that date.

(5)   Where the period is a period of seven days or less which would include a Saturday, Sunday or a public holiday in the place where anything which has to be done within the period falls to be done, that day shall be excluded.
   In relation to England and Wales or Northern Ireland, a 'public holiday' means Christmas Day, Good Friday or a day which under the Banking and Financial Dealings Act 1971 is a bank holiday.

NOTES

Initial Commencement

To be appointed: see s 109(1).

Appointment

Appointment: 31 January 1997: see SI 1996/3146, art 3; for transitional provisions see art 4, Sch 2 thereto.

Extent

This section does not extend to Scotland: see s 108(1).

See Further

See further, in relation to the application of this section, with modifications, for the purposes of arbitrations conducted in accordance with the Scheme: the ACAS Arbitration Scheme (Great Britain) Order 2004, SI 2004/753, art 4, Schedule, para 224EW.

A1.331

79 Power of court to extend time limits relating to arbitral proceedings

(1) Unless the parties otherwise agree, the court may by order extend any time limit agreed by them in relation to any matter relating to the arbitral proceedings or specified in any provision of this Part having effect in default of such agreement.

This section does not apply to a time limit to which section 12 applies (power of court to extend time for beginning arbitral proceedings, &c).

(2) An application for an order may be made—

    (a) by any party to the arbitral proceedings (upon notice to the other parties and to the tribunal), or

    (b) by the arbitral tribunal (upon notice to the parties).

(3) The court shall not exercise its power to extend a time limit unless it is satisfied—

    (a) that any available recourse to the tribunal, or to any arbitral or other institution or person vested by the parties with power in that regard, has first been exhausted, and

    (b) that a substantial injustice would otherwise be done.

(4) The court's power under this section may be exercised whether or not the time has already expired.

(5) An order under this section may be made on such terms as the court thinks fit.

(6) The leave of the court is required for any appeal from a decision of the court under this section.

NOTES

Initial Commencement

To be appointed: see s 109(1).

Appointment

Appointment: 31 January 1997: see SI 1996/3146, art 3; for transitional provisions see art 4, Sch 2 thereto.

Extent

This section does not extend to Scotland: see s 108(1).

A1.332

80 Notice and other requirements in connection with legal proceedings

(1) References in this Part to an application, appeal or other step in relation to legal proceedings being taken 'upon notice' to the other parties to the arbitral proceedings, or to the tribunal, are to such notice of the originating process as is required by rules of court and do not impose any separate requirement.

(2) Rules of court shall be made—

    (a) requiring such notice to be given as indicated by any provision of this Part, and

    (b) as to the manner, form and content of any such notice.

(3) Subject to any provision made by rules of court, a requirement to give notice to the tribunal of legal proceedings shall be construed—

    (a) if there is more than one arbitrator, as a requirement to give notice to each of them; and

    (b) if the tribunal is not fully constituted, as a requirement to give notice to any arbitrator who has been appointed.

(4) References in this Part to making an application or appeal to the court within a specified period are to the issue within that period of the appropriate originating process in accordance with rules of court.

(5) Where any provision of this Part requires an application or appeal to be made to the court within a specified time, the rules of court relating to the reckoning of periods, the extending or abridging of periods, and the consequences of not taking a step within the period prescribed by the rules, apply in relation to that requirement.

(6) Provision may be made by rules of court amending the provisions of this Part—

    (a) with respect to the time within which any application or appeal to the court must be made,

    (b) so as to keep any provision made by this Part in relation to arbitral proceedings in step with the corresponding provision of rules of court applying in relation to proceedings in the court, or

    (c) so as to keep any provision made by this Part in relation to legal proceedings in step with the corresponding provision of rules of court applying generally in relation to proceedings in the court.

(7) Nothing in this section affects the generality of the power to make rules of court.

NOTES

Initial Commencement

To be appointed: see s 109(1).

Appointment

Appointment: 31 January 1997: see SI 1996/3146, art 3; for transitional provisions see art 4, Sch 2 thereto.

Extent

This section does not extend to Scotland: see s 108(1).

See Further

See further, in relation to the application of this section, with modifications, for the purposes of arbitrations conducted in accordance with the Scheme: the ACAS Arbitration Scheme (Great Britain) Order 2004, SI 2004/753, art 4, Schedule, para 217EW.

A1.333

81   Saving for certain matters governed by common law

(1)   Nothing in this Part shall be construed as excluding the operation of any rule of law consistent with the provisions of this Part, in particular, any rule of law as to—

    (a)   matters which are not capable of settlement by arbitration;
    (b)   the effect of an oral arbitration agreement; or
    (c)   the refusal of recognition or enforcement of an arbitral award on grounds of public policy.

(2)   Nothing in this Act shall be construed as reviving any jurisdiction of the court to set aside or remit an award on the ground of errors of fact or law on the face of the award.

NOTES

Initial Commencement

To be appointed: see s 109(1).

Appointment

Appointment: 31 January 1997: see SI 1996/3146, art 3; for transitional provisions see art 4, Sch 2 thereto.

Extent

This section does not extend to Scotland: see s 108(1).

See Further

See further, in relation to the application of this section, with modifications, for the purposes of arbitrations conducted in accordance with the Scheme: the ACAS Arbitration Scheme (Great Britain) Order 2004, SI 2004/753, art 4, Schedule, para 209EW.

A1.334

82   Minor definitions

(1)   In this Part—

    'arbitrator', unless the context otherwise requires, includes an umpire;
    'available arbitral process', in relation to any matter, includes any process of appeal to or review by an arbitral or other institution or person vested by the parties with powers in relation to that matter;
    'claimant', unless the context otherwise requires, includes a counterclaimant, and related expressions shall be construed accordingly;
    'dispute' includes any difference;
    'enactment' includes an enactment contained in Northern Ireland legislation;
    'legal proceedings' means civil proceedings in the High Court or a county court;
    'peremptory order' means an order made under section 41(5) or made in exercise of any corresponding power conferred by the parties;

'premises' includes land, buildings, moveable structures, vehicles, vessels, aircraft and hovercraft;

'question of law' means—

(a) for a court in England and Wales, a question of the law of England and Wales, and

(b) for a court in Northern Ireland, a question of the law of Northern Ireland;

'substantive jurisdiction', in relation to an arbitral tribunal, refers to the matters specified in section 30(1)(a) to (c), and references to the tribunal exceeding its substantive jurisdiction shall be construed accordingly.

(2) References in this Part to a party to an arbitration agreement include any person claiming under or through a party to the agreement.

NOTES

Initial Commencement

To be appointed: see s 109(1).

Appointment

Appointment: 31 January 1997: see SI 1996/3146, art 3; for transitional provisions see art 4, Sch 2 thereto.

Extent

This section does not extend to Scotland: see s 108(1).

Modification

The Northern Ireland Act 1998 makes new provision for the government of Northern Ireland for the purpose of implementing the Belfast Agreement (the agreement reached at multi-party talks on Northern Ireland and set out in Command Paper 3883). As a consequence of that Act, any reference in this section to the Parliament of Northern Ireland or the Assembly established under the Northern Ireland Assembly Act 1973, s 1, certain office-holders and Ministers, and any legislative act and certain financial dealings thereof, shall, for the period specified, be construed in accordance with Sch 12, paras 1–11 to the 1998 Act.

A1.335

83 Index of defined expressions: Part I

In this Part the expressions listed below are defined or otherwise explained by the provisions indicated—

agreement, agree and agreed	section 5(1)
agreement in writing	section 5(2) to (5)
arbitration agreement	sections 6 and 5(1)
arbitrator	section 82(1)
available arbitral process	section 82(1)
claimant	section 82(1)
commencement (in relation to arbitral proceedings)	section 14
costs of the arbitration	section 59
the court	section 105
dispute	section 82(1)
enactment	section 82(1)
legal proceedings	section 82(1)

Limitation Acts	section 13(4)
notice (or other document)	section 76(6)
party–	
– in relation to an arbitration agreement	section 82(2)
– where section 106(2) or (3) applies	section 106(4)
peremptory order	section 82(1) (and see section 41(5))
premises	section 82(1)
question of law	section 82(1)
recoverable costs	sections 63 and 64
seat of the arbitration	section 3
serve and service (of notice or other document)	section 76(6)
substantive jurisdiction (in relation to an arbitral tribunal)	section 82(1) (and see section 30(1)(a) to(c))
upon notice (to the parties or the tribunal)	section 80
written and in writing	section 5(6)

NOTES

Initial Commencement

To be appointed: see s 109(1).

Appointment

Appointment: 31 January 1997: see SI 1996/3146, art 3; for transitional provisions see art 4, Sch 2 thereto.

Extent

This section does not extend to Scotland: see s 108(1).

A1.336

84   Transitional provisions

(1)   The provisions of this Part do not apply to arbitral proceedings commenced before the date on which this Part comes into force.

(2)   They apply to arbitral proceedings commenced on or after that date under an arbitration agreement whenever made.

(3)   The above provisions have effect subject to any transitional provision made by an order under section 109(2) (power to include transitional provisions in commencement order).

NOTES

Initial Commencement

To be appointed: see s 109(1).

Appointment

Appointment: 31 January 1997: see SI 1996/3146, art 3; for transitional provisions see art 4, Sch 2 thereto.

Extent

This section does not extend to Scotland: see s 108(1).

PART II: OTHER PROVISIONS RELATING TO ARBITRATION

Domestic arbitration agreements

A1.337

85   Modification of Part I in relation to domestic arbitration agreement

(1)   In the case of a domestic arbitration agreement the provisions of Part I are modified in accordance with the following sections.

(2)   For this purpose a 'domestic arbitration agreement' means an arbitration agreement to which none of the parties is—

    (a)   an individual who is a national of, or habitually resident in, a state other than the United Kingdom, or

    (b)   a body corporate which is incorporated in, or whose central control and management is exercised in, a state other than the United Kingdom,

and under which the seat of the arbitration (if the seat has been designated or determined) is in the United Kingdom.

(3)   In subsection (2) 'arbitration agreement' and 'seat of the arbitration' have the same meaning as in Part I (see sections 3, 5(1) and 6).

NOTES

Initial Commencement

To be appointed: see s 109(1).

Extent

This section does not extend to Scotland: see s 108(1).

A1.338

86   Staying of legal proceedings

(1)   In section 9 (stay of legal proceedings), subsection (4) (stay unless the arbitration agreement is null and void, inoperative, or incapable of being performed) does not apply to a domestic arbitration agreement.

(2)   On an application under that section in relation to a domestic arbitration agreement the court shall grant a stay unless satisfied—

    (a)   that the arbitration agreement is null and void, inoperative, or incapable of being performed, or

    (b)   that there are other sufficient grounds for not requiring the parties to abide by the arbitration agreement.

(3)   The court may treat as a sufficient ground under subsection (2)(b) the fact that the applicant is or was at any material time not ready and willing to do all things necessary for the proper conduct of the arbitration or of any other dispute resolution procedures required to be exhausted before resorting to arbitration.

(4)   For the purposes of this section the question whether an arbitration agreement is a domestic arbitration agreement shall be determined by reference to the facts at the time the legal proceedings are commenced.

NOTES

Initial Commencement

To be appointed: see s 109(1).

Extent

This section does not extend to Scotland: see s 108(1).

A1.339

87   Effectiveness of agreement to exclude court's jurisdiction

(1)   In the case of a domestic arbitration agreement any agreement to exclude the jurisdiction of the court under—

   (a)   section 45 (determination of preliminary point of law), or
   (b)   section 69 (challenging the award: appeal on point of law),

is not effective unless entered into after the commencement of the arbitral proceedings in which the question arises or the award is made.

(2)   For this purpose the commencement of the arbitral proceedings has the same meaning as in Part I (see section 14).

(3)   For the purposes of this section the question whether an arbitration agreement is a domestic arbitration agreement shall be determined by reference to the facts at the time the agreement is entered into.

NOTES

Initial Commencement

To be appointed: see s 109(1).

Extent

This section does not extend to Scotland: see s 108(1).

A1.340

88   Power to repeal or amend sections 85 to 87

(1)   The Secretary of State may by order repeal or amend the provisions of sections 85 to 87.

(2)   An order under this section may contain such supplementary, incidental and transitional provisions as appear to the Secretary of State to be appropriate.

(3)   An order under this section shall be made by statutory instrument and no such order shall be made unless a draft of it has been laid before and approved by a resolution of each House of Parliament.

NOTES

Initial Commencement

To be appointed: see s 109(1).

Appointment

Appointment: 31 January 1997: see SI 1996/3146, art 3; for transitional provisions see art 4, Sch 2 thereto.

Extent

This section does not extend to Scotland: see s 108(1).

Consumer arbitration agreements

A1.341

89   Application of unfair terms regulations to consumer arbitration agreements

(1)   The following sections extend the application of the Unfair Terms in Consumer Contracts Regulations 1994 in relation to a term which constitutes an arbitration agreement.
    For this purpose 'arbitration agreement' means an agreement to submit to arbitration present or future disputes or differences (whether or not contractual).

(2)   In those sections 'the Regulations' means those regulations and includes any regulations amending or replacing those regulations.

(3)   Those sections apply whatever the law applicable to the arbitration agreement.

NOTES
Initial Commencement

To be appointed: see s 109(1).

Appointment

Appointment: 31 January 1997: see SI 1996/3146, art 3; for transitional provisions see art 4, Sch 2 thereto.

A1.342

90   Regulations apply where consumer is a legal person

The Regulations apply where the consumer is a legal person as they apply where the consumer is a natural person.

NOTES
Initial Commencement

To be appointed: see s 109(1).

Appointment

Appointment: 31 January 1997: see SI 1996/3146, art 3; for transitional provisions see art 4, Sch 2 thereto.

A1.343

91   Arbitration agreement unfair where modest amount sought

(1)   A term which constitutes an arbitration agreement is unfair for the purposes of the Regulations so far as it relates to a claim for a pecuniary remedy which does not exceed the amount specified by order for the purposes of this section.

(2)   Orders under this section may make different provision for different cases and for different purposes.

(3)   The power to make orders under this section is exercisable—

   (a)   for England and Wales, by the Secretary of State with the concurrence of the Lord Chancellor,
   (b)   for Scotland, by the Secretary of State ..., and
   (c)   for Northern Ireland, by the Department of Economic Development for Northern Ireland with the concurrence of the Lord Chancellor.

(4)   Any such order for England and Wales or Scotland shall be made by statutory instrument which shall be subject to annulment in pursuance of a resolution of either House of Parliament.

(5)   Any such order for Northern Ireland shall be a statutory rule for the purposes of the Statutory Rules (Northern Ireland) Order 1979 and shall be subject to negative resolution, within the meaning of section 41(6) of the Interpretation Act (Northern Ireland) 1954.

NOTES

Initial Commencement

To be appointed: see s 109(1).

Appointment

Appointment (for the purposes of making orders): 17 December 1996: see SI 1996/3146, art 2, Sch 1.

Appointment (for remaining purposes): 31 January 1997: see SI 1996/3146, art 3; for transitional provisions see art 4, Sch 2 thereto.

Amendment

Sub-s (3): in para (b) words omitted repealed by SI 1999/678, art 6.

Date in force: 19 May 1999: see SI 1999/678, art 1.

Miscellaneous

Amount specified under sub-s (1) above, for the purposes of Northern Ireland , is £3,000: see the Unfair Arbitration Agreements (Specified Amount) Order (Northern Ireland) 1996, SR 1996/598.

Subordinate Legislation

Unfair Arbitration Agreements (Specified Amount) Order 1999, SI 1999/2167 (made under sub-ss (1), (3)(a), (b)).

Small claims arbitration in the county court

A1.344

92   Exclusion of Part I in relation to small claims arbitration in the county court

Nothing in Part I of this Act applies to arbitration under section 64 of the County Courts Act 1984.

NOTES

Initial Commencement

To be appointed: see s 109(1).

Appointment

Appointment: 31 January 1997: see SI 1996/3146, art 3; for transitional provisions see art 4, Sch 2 thereto.

Extent

This section does not extend to Scotland: see s 108(1).

Appointment of judges as arbitrators

A1.345

93   Appointment of judges as arbitrators

(1)   A judge of the Commercial Court or an official referee may, if in all the circumstances he thinks fit, accept appointment as a sole arbitrator or as umpire by or by virtue of an arbitration agreement.

(2)   A judge of the Commercial Court shall not do so unless the Lord Chief Justice has informed him that, having regard to the state of business in the High Court and the Crown Court, he can be made available.

(3)   An official referee shall not do so unless the Lord Chief Justice has informed him that, having regard to the state of official referees' business, he can be made available.

(4)   The fees payable for the services of a judge of the Commercial Court or official referee as arbitrator or umpire shall be taken in the High Court.

(5)   In this section—

'arbitration agreement' has the same meaning as in Part I; and
'official referee' means a person nominated under section 68(1)(a) of the *Supreme Court Act 1981* [Senior Courts Act 1981] to deal with official referees' business.

(6)   The provisions of Part I of this Act apply to arbitration before a person appointed under this section with the modifications specified in Schedule 2.

NOTES

Initial Commencement

To be appointed: see s 109(1).

Appointment

Appointment: 31 January 1997: see SI 1996/3146, art 3; for transitional provisions see art 4, Sch 2 thereto.

Extent

This section does not extend to Scotland: see s 108(1).

Amendment

Sub-s (5): in definition 'official referee' words 'Supreme Court Act 1981' in italics repealed and subsequent words in square brackets substituted by the Constitutional Reform Act 2005, s 59(5), Sch 11, Pt 1, para 1(2).

Date in force: to be appointed: see the Constitutional Reform Act 2005, s 148(1).

Statutory arbitrations

A1.346

94   Application of Part I to statutory arbitrations

(1)   The provisions of Part I apply to every arbitration under an enactment (a 'statutory arbitration'), whether the enactment was passed or made before or after the commencement of this Act, subject to the adaptations and exclusions specified in sections 95 to 98.

(2)   The provisions of Part I do not apply to a statutory arbitration if or to the extent that their application—

   (a)   is inconsistent with the provisions of the enactment concerned, with any rules or procedure authorised or recognised by it, or

   (b)   is excluded by any other enactment.

(3)   In this section and the following provisions of this Part 'enactment'—

   (a)   in England and Wales, includes an enactment contained in subordinate legislation within the meaning of the Interpretation Act 1978;

   (b)   in Northern Ireland, means a statutory provision within the meaning of section 1(f) of the Interpretation Act (Northern Ireland) 1954.

NOTES

Initial Commencement

To be appointed: see s 109(1).

Appointment

Appointment: 31 January 1997: see SI 1996/3146, art 3; for transitional provisions see art 4, Sch 2 thereto.

Extent

This section does not extend to Scotland: see s 108(1).

A1.347

95   General adaptation of provisions in relation to statutory arbitrations

(1)   The provisions of Part I apply to a statutory arbitration—

   (a)   as if the arbitration were pursuant to an arbitration agreement and as if the enactment were that agreement, and

   (b)   as if the persons by and against whom a claim subject to arbitration in pursuance of the enactment may be or has been made were parties to that agreement.

(2)   Every statutory arbitration shall be taken to have its seat in England and Wales or, as the case may be, in Northern Ireland.

NOTES

Initial Commencement

To be appointed: see s 109(1).

A1.348 *Statutes*

Appointment

Appointment: 31 January 1997: see SI 1996/3146, art 3; for transitional provisions see art 4, Sch 2 thereto.

Extent

This section does not extend to Scotland: see s 108(1).

A1.348

96   Specific adaptations of provisions in relation to statutory arbitrations

(1)   The following provisions of Part I apply to a statutory arbitration with the following adaptations.

(2)   In section 30(1) (competence of tribunal to rule on its own jurisdiction), the reference in paragraph (a) to whether there is a valid arbitration agreement shall be construed as a reference to whether the enactment applies to the dispute or difference in question.

(3)   Section 35 (consolidation of proceedings and concurrent hearings) applies only so as to authorise the consolidation of proceedings, or concurrent hearings in proceedings, under the same enactment.

(4)   Section 46 (rules applicable to substance of dispute) applies with the omission of subsection (1)(b) (determination in accordance with considerations agreed by parties).

NOTES

Initial Commencement

To be appointed: see s 109(1).

Appointment

Appointment: 31 January 1997: see SI 1996/3146, art 3; for transitional provisions see art 4, Sch 2 thereto.

Extent

This section does not extend to Scotland: see s 108(1).

A1.349

97   Provisions excluded from applying to statutory arbitrations

The following provisions of Part I do not apply in relation to a statutory arbitration—

   (a)   section 8 (whether agreement discharged by death of a party);
   (b)   section 12 (power of court to extend agreed time limits);
   (c)   sections 9(5), 10(2) and 71(4) (restrictions on effect of provision that award condition precedent to right to bring legal proceedings).

NOTES

Initial Commencement

To be appointed: see s 109(1).

Appointment

Appointment: 31 January 1997: see SI 1996/3146, art 3; for transitional provisions see art 4, Sch 2 thereto.

Extent

This section does not extend to Scotland: see s 108(1).

A1.350

98   Power to make further provision by regulations

(1) The Secretary of State may make provision by regulations for adapting or excluding any provision of Part I in relation to statutory arbitrations in general or statutory arbitrations of any particular description.

(2) The power is exercisable whether the enactment concerned is passed or made before or after the commencement of this Act.

(3) Regulations under this section shall be made by statutory instrument which shall be subject to annulment in pursuance of a resolution of either House of Parliament.

NOTES

Initial Commencement

To be appointed: see s 109(1).

Appointment

Appointment: 31 January 1997: see SI 1996/3146, art 3; for transitional provisions see art 4, Sch 2 thereto.

Extent

This section does not extend to Scotland: see s 108(1).

PART III: RECOGNITION AND ENFORCEMENT OF CERTAIN FOREIGN AWARDS

Enforcement of Geneva Convention awards

A1.351

99   Continuation of Part II of the Arbitration Act 1950

Part II of the Arbitration Act 1950 (enforcement of certain foreign awards) continues to apply in relation to foreign awards within the meaning of that Part which are not also New York Convention awards.

NOTES

Initial Commencement

To be appointed: see s 109(1).

Appointment

Appointment: 31 January 1997: see SI 1996/3146, art 3; for transitional provisions see art 4, Sch 2 thereto.

Extent

This section does not extend to Scotland: see s 108(1).

Recognition and enforcement of New York Convention awards

A1.352

100   New York Convention awards

(1)   In this Part a 'New York Convention award' means an award made, in pursuance of an arbitration agreement, in the territory of a state (other than the United Kingdom) which is a party to the New York Convention.

(2)   For the purposes of subsection (1) and of the provisions of this Part relating to such awards—

(a)   'arbitration agreement' means an arbitration agreement in writing, and

(b)   an award shall be treated as made at the seat of the arbitration, regardless of where it was signed, despatched or delivered to any of the parties.

In this subsection 'agreement in writing' and 'seat of the arbitration' have the same meaning as in Part I.

(3)   If Her Majesty by Order in Council declares that a state specified in the Order is a party to the New York Convention, or is a party in respect of any territory so specified, the Order shall, while in force, be conclusive evidence of that fact.

(4)   In this section 'the New York Convention' means the Convention on the Recognition and Enforcement of Foreign Arbitral Awards adopted by the United Nations Conference on International Commercial Arbitration on 10th June 1958.

NOTES

Initial Commencement

To be appointed: see s 109(1).

Appointment

Appointment: 31 January 1997: see SI 1996/3146, art 3; for transitional provisions see art 4, Sch 2 thereto.

Extent

This section does not extend to Scotland: see s 108(1).

Subordinate Legislation

Arbitration (Foreign Awards) Order 1984, SI 1984/1168 (has effect as if made under sub-s (3)).

Arbitration (Foreign Awards) Order 1989, SI 1989/1348 (has effect as if made under sub-s (3)).

Arbitration (Foreign Awards) Order 1993, SI 1993/1256 (has effect as if made under sub-s (3)).

A1.353

101   Recognition and enforcement of awards

(1)   A New York Convention award shall be recognised as binding on the persons as between whom it was made, and may accordingly be relied on by those persons by way of defence, set-off or otherwise in any legal proceedings in England and Wales or Northern Ireland.

(2)   A New York Convention award may, by leave of the court, be enforced in the same manner as a judgment or order of the court to the same effect.

As to the meaning of 'the court' see section 105.

(3)   Where leave is so given, judgment may be entered in terms of the award.

NOTES

Initial Commencement

To be appointed: see s 109(1).

Appointment

Appointment: 31 January 1997: see SI 1996/3146, art 3; for transitional provisions see art 4, Sch 2 thereto.

Extent

This section does not extend to Scotland: see s 108(1).

A1.354

102   Evidence to be produced by party seeking recognition or enforcement

(1)   A party seeking the recognition or enforcement of a New York Convention award must produce—

  (a)   the duly authenticated original award or a duly certified copy of it, and
  (b)   the original arbitration agreement or a duly certified copy of it.

(2)   If the award or agreement is in a foreign language, the party must also produce a translation of it certified by an official or sworn translator or by a diplomatic or consular agent.

NOTES

Initial Commencement

To be appointed: see s 109(1).

Appointment

Appointment: 31 January 1997: see SI 1996/3146, art 3; for transitional provisions see art 4, Sch 2 thereto.

Extent

This section does not extend to Scotland: see s 108(1).

A1.355

103   Refusal of recognition or enforcement

(1)   Recognition or enforcement of a New York Convention award shall not be refused except in the following cases.

(2)   Recognition or enforcement of the award may be refused if the person against whom it is invoked proves—

  (a)   that a party to the arbitration agreement was (under the law applicable to him) under some incapacity;

(b) that the arbitration agreement was not valid under the law to which the parties subjected it or, failing any indication thereon, under the law of the country where the award was made;

(c) that he was not given proper notice of the appointment of the arbitrator or of the arbitration proceedings or was otherwise unable to present his case;

(d) that the award deals with a difference not contemplated by or not falling within the terms of the submission to arbitration or contains decisions on matters beyond the scope of the submission to arbitration (but see subsection (4));

(e) that the composition of the arbitral tribunal or the arbitral procedure was not in accordance with the agreement of the parties or, failing such agreement, with the law of the country in which the arbitration took place;

(f) that the award has not yet become binding on the parties, or has been set aside or suspended by a competent authority of the country in which, or under the law of which, it was made.

(3)   Recognition or enforcement of the award may also be refused if the award is in respect of a matter which is not capable of settlement by arbitration, or if it would be contrary to public policy to recognise or enforce the award.

(4)   An award which contains decisions on matters not submitted to arbitration may be recognised or enforced to the extent that it contains decisions on matters submitted to arbitration which can be separated from those on matters not so submitted.

(5)   Where an application for the setting aside or suspension of the award has been made to such a competent authority as is mentioned in subsection (2)(f), the court before which the award is sought to be relied upon may, if it considers it proper, adjourn the decision on the recognition or enforcement of the award.

It may also on the application of the party claiming recognition or enforcement of the award order the other party to give suitable security.

NOTES

Initial Commencement

To be appointed: see s 109(1).

Appointment

Appointment: 31 January 1997: see SI 1996/3146, art 3; for transitional provisions see art 4, Sch 2 thereto.

Extent

This section does not extend to Scotland: see s 108(1).

A1.356

104   Saving for other bases of recognition or enforcement

Nothing in the preceding provisions of this Part affects any right to rely upon or enforce a New York Convention award at common law or under section 66.

NOTES

Initial Commencement

To be appointed: see s 109(1).

Appointment

Appointment: 31 January 1997: see SI 1996/3146, art 3; for transitional provisions see art 4, Sch 2 thereto.

Extent

This section does not extend to Scotland: see s 108(1).

PART IV: GENERAL PROVISIONS

A1.357

105   Meaning of 'the court': jurisdiction of High Court and county court

(1)   In this Act 'the court' means the High Court or a county court, subject to the following provisions.

(2)   The Lord Chancellor may by order make provision—

    (a)   allocating proceedings under this Act to the High Court or to county courts; or

    (b)   specifying proceedings under this Act which may be commenced or taken only in the High Court or in a county court.

(3)   The Lord Chancellor may by order make provision requiring proceedings of any specified description under this Act in relation to which a county court has jurisdiction to be commenced or taken in one or more specified county courts.

Any jurisdiction so exercisable by a specified county court is exercisable throughout England and Wales or, as the case may be, Northern Ireland.

[(3A)   The Lord Chancellor must consult the Lord Chief Justice of England and Wales or the Lord Chief Justice of Northern Ireland (as the case may be) before making an order under this section.

(3B)   The Lord Chief Justice of England and Wales may nominate a judicial office holder (as defined in section 109(4) of the Constitutional Reform Act 2005) to exercise his functions under this section.

(3C)   The Lord Chief Justice of Northern Ireland may nominate any of the following to exercise his functions under this section—

    (a)   the holder of one of the offices listed in Schedule 1 to the Justice (Northern Ireland) Act 2002;

    (b)   a Lord Justice of Appeal (as defined in section 88 of that Act).]

(4)   An order under this section—

    (a)   may differentiate between categories of proceedings by reference to such criteria as the Lord Chancellor sees fit to specify, and

    (b)   may make such incidental or transitional provision as the Lord Chancellor considers necessary or expedient.

(5)   An order under this section for England and Wales shall be made by statutory instrument which shall be subject to annulment in pursuance of a resolution of either House of Parliament.

(6)   An order under this section for Northern Ireland shall be a statutory rule for the purposes of the Statutory Rules (Northern Ireland) Order 1979 which shall be subject to annulment in pursuance of a resolution of either House of Parliament in like manner as a statutory instrument and section 5 of the Statutory Instruments Act 1946 shall apply accordingly.

A1.358   *Statutes*

NOTES

Initial Commencement

To be appointed: see s 109(1).

Appointment

Appointment: 17 December 1996: see SI 1996/3146, art 2, Sch 1.

Extent

This section does not extend to Scotland: see s 108(1).

Amendment

Sub-ss (3A)–(3C): inserted by the Constitutional Reform Act 2005, s 15(1), Sch 4, Pt 1, para 250.

Date in force: 3 April 2006: see SI 2006/1014, art 2(a), Sch 1, paras 10, 11(v).

Subordinate Legislation

High Court and County Courts (Allocation of Arbitration Proceedings) Order 1996, SI 1996/3215.

High Court and County Courts (Allocation of Arbitration Proceedings) Order 1996, SI 1996/3215.

High Court and County Courts (Allocation of Arbitration Proceedings) (Amendment) Order 1999, SI 1999/1010 (made under sub-s (3)).

A1.358

106   Crown application

(1)   Part I of this Act applies to any arbitration agreement to which Her Majesty, either in right of the Crown or of the Duchy of Lancaster or otherwise, or the Duke of Cornwall, is a party.

(2)   Where Her Majesty is party to an arbitration agreement otherwise than in right of the Crown, Her Majesty shall be represented for the purposes of any arbitral proceedings—

    (a)   where the agreement was entered into by Her Majesty in right of the Duchy of Lancaster, by the Chancellor of the Duchy or such person as he may appoint, and

    (b)   in any other case, by such person as Her Majesty may appoint in writing under the Royal Sign Manual.

(3)   Where the Duke of Cornwall is party to an arbitration agreement, he shall be represented for the purposes of any arbitral proceedings by such person as he may appoint.

(4)   References in Part I to a party or the parties to the arbitration agreement or to arbitral proceedings shall be construed, where subsection (2) or (3) applies, as references to the person representing Her Majesty or the Duke of Cornwall.

NOTES

Initial Commencement

To be appointed: see s 109(1).

Appointment

Appointment: 31 January 1997: see SI 1996/3146, art 3; for transitional provisions see art 4, Sch 2 thereto.

Extent

This section does not extend to Scotland: see s 108(1).

A1.359

107   Consequential amendments and repeals

(1)   The enactments specified in Schedule 3 are amended in accordance with that Schedule, the amendments being consequential on the provisions of this Act.

(2)   The enactments specified in Schedule 4 are repealed to the extent specified.

NOTES

Initial Commencement

To be appointed: see s 109(1).

Appointment

Appointment (for certain purposes): 17 December 1996: see SI 1996/3146, art 2, Sch 1.

Appointment (for remaining purposes): 31 January 1997: see SI 1996/3146, art 3; for transitional provisions see art 4, Sch 2 thereto.

A1.360

108   Extent

(1)   The provisions of this Act extend to England and Wales and, except as mentioned below, to Northern Ireland.

(2)   The following provisions of Part II do not extend to Northern Ireland—

section 92 (exclusion of Part I in relation to small claims arbitration in the county court), and
section 93 and Schedule 2 (appointment of judges as arbitrators).

(3)   Sections 89, 90 and 91 (consumer arbitration agreements) extend to Scotland and the provisions of Schedules 3 and 4 (consequential amendments and repeals) extend to Scotland so far as they relate to enactments which so extend, subject as follows.

(4)   The repeal of the Arbitration Act 1975 extends only to England and Wales and Northern Ireland.

NOTES

Initial Commencement

To be appointed: see s 109(1).

Appointment

Appointment: 17 December 1996: see SI 1996/3146, art 2, Sch 1.

A1.361

109 Commencement

(1) The provisions of this Act come into force on such day as the Secretary of State may appoint by order made by statutory instrument, and different days may be appointed for different purposes.

(2) An order under subsection (1) may contain such transitional provisions as appear to the Secretary of State to be appropriate.

NOTES

Initial Commencement

To be appointed: see sub-s (1) above.

Appointment

Appointment: 17 December 1996: see SI 1996/3146, art 2, Sch 1.

Subordinate Legislation

Arbitration Act 1996 (Commencement No 1) Order 1996, SI 1996/3146.

A1.362

110 Short title

This Act may be cited as the Arbitration Act 1996.

NOTES

Initial Commencement

To be appointed: see s 109(1).

Appointment

Appointment: 17 December 1996: see SI 1996/3146, art 2, Sch 1.

SCHEDULE 1
MANDATORY PROVISIONS OF PART I

Section 4(1)

A1.363

sections 9 to 11 (stay of legal proceedings);

section 12 (power of court to extend agreed time limits);

section 13 (application of Limitation Acts);

section 24 (power of court to remove arbitrator);

section 26(1) (effect of death of arbitrator);

section 28 (liability of parties for fees and expenses of arbitrators);

section 29 (immunity of arbitrator);

section 31 (objection to substantive jurisdiction of tribunal);

section 32 (determination of preliminary point of jurisdiction);

section 33 (general duty of tribunal);

section 37(2) (items to be treated as expenses of arbitrators);

section 40 (general duty of parties);

section 43 (securing the attendance of witnesses);

section 56 (power to withhold award in case of non-payment);

section 60 (effectiveness of agreement for payment of costs in any event);

section 66 (enforcement of award);

sections 67 and 68 (challenging the award: substantive jurisdiction and serious irregularity), and sections 70 and 71 (supplementary provisions; effect of order of court) so far as relating to those sections;

section 72 (saving for rights of person who takes no part in proceedings);

section 73 (loss of right to object);

section 74 (immunity of arbitral institutions, &c);

section 75 (charge to secure payment of solicitors' costs).

NOTES

Initial Commencement

To be appointed: see s 109(1).

Appointment

Appointment: 31 January 1997: see SI 1996/3146, art 3; for transitional provisions see art 4, Sch 2 thereto.

Extent

This section does not extend to Scotland: see s 108(1).

SCHEDULE 2
MODIFICATIONS OF PART I IN RELATION TO JUDGE-ARBITRATORS

Section 93(6)

Introductory

A1.364

1   In this Schedule 'judge-arbitrator' means a judge of the Commercial Court or official referee appointed as arbitrator or umpire under section 93.

General

2   (1)   Subject to the following provisions of this Schedule, references in Part I to the court shall be construed in relation to a judge-arbitrator, or in relation to the appointment of a judge-arbitrator, as references to the Court of Appeal.

(2)   The references in sections 32(6), 45(6) and 69(8) to the Court of Appeal shall in such a case be construed as references to the *House of Lords* [Supreme Court].

1437

Arbitrator's fees

3 (1) The power of the court in section 28(2) to order consideration and adjustment of the liability of a party for the fees of an arbitrator may be exercised by a judge-arbitrator.

(2) Any such exercise of the power is subject to the powers of the Court of Appeal under sections 24(4) and 25(3)(b) (directions as to entitlement to fees or expenses in case of removal or resignation).

Exercise of court powers in support of arbitration

4 (1) Where the arbitral tribunal consists of or includes a judge-arbitrator the powers of the court under sections 42 to 44 (enforcement of peremptory orders, summoning witnesses, and other court powers) are exercisable by the High Court and also by the judge-arbitrator himself.

(2) Anything done by a judge-arbitrator in the exercise of those powers shall be regarded as done by him in his capacity as judge of the High Court and have effect as if done by that court.
  Nothing in this sub-paragraph prejudices any power vested in him as arbitrator or umpire.

Extension of time for making award

5 (1) The power conferred by section 50 (extension of time for making award) is exercisable by the judge-arbitrator himself.

(2) Any appeal from a decision of a judge-arbitrator under that section lies to the Court of Appeal with the leave of that court.

Withholding award in case of non-payment

6 (1) The provisions of paragraph 7 apply in place of the provisions of section 56 (power to withhold award in the case of non-payment) in relation to the withholding of an award for non-payment of the fees and expenses of a judge-arbitrator.

(2) This does not affect the application of section 56 in relation to the delivery of such an award by an arbitral or other institution or person vested by the parties with powers in relation to the delivery of the award.

7 (1) A judge-arbitrator may refuse to deliver an award except upon payment of the fees and expenses mentioned in section 56(1).

(2) The judge-arbitrator may, on an application by a party to the arbitral proceedings, order that if he pays into the High Court the fees and expenses demanded, or such lesser amount as the judge-arbitrator may specify—

    (a) the award shall be delivered,
    (b) the amount of the fees and expenses properly payable shall be determined by such means and upon such terms as he may direct, and
    (c) out of the money paid into court there shall be paid out such fees and expenses as may be found to be properly payable and the balance of the money (if any) shall be paid out to the applicant.

(3) For this purpose the amount of fees and expenses properly payable is the amount the applicant is liable to pay under section 28 or any agreement relating to the payment of the arbitrator.

(4) No application to the judge-arbitrator under this paragraph may be made where there is any available arbitral process for appeal or review of the amount of the fees or expenses demanded.

(5)   Any appeal from a decision of a judge-arbitrator under this paragraph lies to the Court of Appeal with the leave of that court.

(6)   Where a party to arbitral proceedings appeals under sub-paragraph (5), an arbitrator is entitled to appear and be heard.

Correction of award or additional award

8   Subsections (4) to (6) of section 57 (correction of award or additional award: time limit for application or exercise of power) do not apply to a judge-arbitrator.

Costs

9   Where the arbitral tribunal consists of or includes a judge-arbitrator the powers of the court under section 63(4) (determination of recoverable costs) shall be exercised by the High Court.

10   (1)   The power of the court under section 64 to determine an arbitrator's reasonable fees and expenses may be exercised by a judge-arbitrator.

(2)   Any such exercise of the power is subject to the powers of the Court of Appeal under sections 24(4) and 25(3)(b) (directions as to entitlement to fees or expenses in case of removal or resignation).

Enforcement of award

11   The leave of the court required by section 66 (enforcement of award) may in the case of an award of a judge-arbitrator be given by the judge-arbitrator himself.

Solicitors' costs

12   The powers of the court to make declarations and orders under the provisions applied by section 75 (power to charge property recovered in arbitral proceedings with the payment of solicitors' costs) may be exercised by the judge-arbitrator.

Powers of court in relation to service of documents

13   (1)   The power of the court under section 77(2) (powers of court in relation to service of documents) is exercisable by the judge-arbitrator.

(2)   Any appeal from a decision of a judge-arbitrator under that section lies to the Court of Appeal with the leave of that court.

Powers of court to extend time limits relating to arbitral proceedings

14   (1)   The power conferred by section 79 (power of court to extend time limits relating to arbitral proceedings) is exercisable by the judge-arbitrator himself.

(2)   Any appeal from a decision of a judge-arbitrator under that section lies to the Court of Appeal with the leave of that court.

NOTES

Initial Commencement

To be appointed: see s 109(1).

Appointment

Appointment: 31 January 1997: see SI 1996/3146, art 3; for transitional provisions see art 4, Sch 2 thereto.

A1.365   *Statutes*

Extent

This section does not extend to Scotland: see s 108(1).

Amendment

Para 2: in sub-para (2) words 'House of Lords' in italics repealed and subsequent words in square brackets substituted by the Constitutional Reform Act 2005, s 40(4), Sch 9, Pt 1, para 60.

Date in force: to be appointed: see the Constitutional Reform Act 2005, s 148(1).

SCHEDULE 3
CONSEQUENTIAL AMENDMENTS

Section 107(1)

A1.365

< . . . >

NOTES

Initial Commencement

To be appointed: see s 109(1).

Appointment

Appointment (in part, in relation to the provision made by county court rules): 17 December 1996: see SI 1996/3146, art 2, Sch 1.

Appointment (remainder): 31 January 1997: see SI 1996/3146, art 3; for transitional provisions see art 4, Sch 2 thereto.

Amendment

This Schedule contains amendments only.

Repealed in part by the Industrial Tribunals (Northern Ireland) Order 1996, SI 1996/1921, art 28, Sch 3.

Repealed in part by the Housing Act 1996, s 227, Sch 19, Part III.

Repealed in part by the Education Act 1996, s 582(2), Sch 38, Pt I.

Repealed in part by the Social Security (Northern Ireland) Order 1998, SI 1998/1506, art 78(2), Sch 7.

Date in force: to be appointed: see the Social Security (Northern Ireland) Order 1998, SI 1998/1506, art 1(2).

Repealed in part by the Social Security Act 1998, s 86(2), Sch 8.

Date in force (for certain purposes): 29 November 1999: see SI 1999/3178, art 2(1), Sch 1.

Date in force (for remaining purposes): to be appointed: see the Social Security Act 1998, s 87(2).

Repealed in part by the Care Standards Act 2000, s 117(2), Sch 6.

Date in force (in relation to England): 1 April 2002: see SI 2001/4150, art 3(3)(c)(xi); for transitional provisions see SI 2001/4150, arts 3(2), 4(1)–(3), (5) and SI 2002/1493, art 4 (as amended by SI 2002/1493, art 6).

Date in force (in relation to Wales): 1 April 2002: see SI 2002/920, art 3(3)(g); for transitional provisions see arts 2, 3(2), (4), (6)–(10), Sch 1 thereto.

Repealed in part by SI 2003/431, art 50(2), Sch 5.

1440

Date in force: 1 April 2005: see the Health and Personal Social Services (Quality, Improvement and Regulation) (2003 Order) (Commencement No 3 & Transitional Provisions) Order (Northern Ireland) 2005, SR 2005/44, art 3, Sch 1.

Repealed in part by the Fair Employment and Treatment (Northern Ireland) Order 1998, SI 1998/3162, art 105(4), Sch 5.

Date in force: 1 March 1999: see the Fair Employment and Treatment (1998 Order) (Commencement No 1) Order (Northern Ireland) 1999, SR 1999/81, art 3(1).

Repealed in part by the Communications Act 2003, s 406(7), Sch 19(1).

Date in force (for the purpose only of enabling the networks and services functions and the spectrum functions to be carried out by the Director General of Telecommunications and the Secretary of State respectively, during the transitional period (as provided for by the Communications Act 2003, s 408(6)): 25 July 2003–29 December 2003: see SI 2003/1900, arts 2(1), 3(1), Sch 1 and the Communications Act 2003, ss 406(6), 408, Sch 18, para 2.

Date in force (for the purpose of conferring the networks and services functions and the spectrum functions on OFCOM): 29 December 2003: by virtue of SI 2003/3142, art 3(2).

Repealed in part by the Statute Law (Repeals) Act 2004.

Date in force: 22 July 2004: (no specific commencement provision).

Repealed in part by the International Organisations Act 2005, ss 1(2), 9, Schedule.

Date in force: 11 July 2005 (except in relation to any written contract entered into by or on behalf of the Commonwealth Secretariat before that date): see SI 2005/1870, art 2 and the International Organisations Act 2005, s 1(3).

Repealed in part by SI 2006/2805, art 18, Sch 2.

Date in force: 19 October 2006: see SI 2006/2805, art 1(1)(b).

SCHEDULE 4
REPEALS

Section 107(2)

A1.366

Chapter	Short title	Extent of repeal
1892 c 43	Military Lands Act 1892.	In section 21(b), the words 'under the Arbitration Act 1889'.
1922 c 51	Allotments Act 1922.	In section 21(3), the words 'under the Arbitration Act 1889'.
1937 c 8 (NI)	Arbitration Act (Northern Ireland) 1937.	The whole Act.
1949 c 54	Wireless Telegraphy Act 1949.	In Schedule 2, paragraph 3(3).
1949 c 97	National Parks and Access to the Countryside Act 1949.	In section 18(4), the words from 'Without prejudice' to 'England or Wales'.
1950 c 27	Arbitration Act 1950.	Part I. Section 42(3).
1958 c 47	Agricultural Marketing Act 1958.	Section 53(8).
1962 c 46	Transport Act 1962.	In Schedule 11, Part II, paragraph 7.

1964 c 14	Plant Varieties and Seeds Act 1964.	In section 10(4) the words from 'or in section 9' to 'three arbitrators)'. Section 39(3)(b)(i).
1964 c 29 (NI)	Lands Tribunal and Compensation Act (Northern Ireland) 1964.	In section 9(3) the words from 'so, however, that' to the end.
1965 c 12	Industrial and Provident Societies Act 1965.	In section 60(8)(b), the words 'by virtue of section 12 of the said Act of 1950'.
1965 c 37	Carriage of Goods by Road Act 1965.	Section 7(2)(b).
1965 c 13 (NI)	New Towns Act (Northern Ireland) 1965.	In section 27(2), the words from 'under and in accordance with' to the end.
1969 c 24 (NI)	Industrial and Provident Societies Act (Northern Ireland) 1969.	In section 69(7)–
		(a) in the opening words, the words from 'and without prejudice' to '1937'; (b) in paragraph (b), the words 'the registrar or' and 'registrar or'.
1970 c 31	Administration of Justice Act 1970.	Section 4. Schedule 3.
1973 c 41	Fair Trading Act 1973.	Section 33(2)(d).
1973 NI 1	Drainage (Northern Ireland) Order 1973.	In Article 15(4), the words from 'under and in accordance' to the end. Article 40(4). In Schedule 7, in paragraph 9(2), the words from 'under and in accordance' to the end.
1974 c 47	Solicitors Act 1974.	In section 87(1), in the definition of 'contentious business', the words 'appointed under the Arbitration Act 1950'.
1975 c 3	Arbitration Act 1975.	The whole Act.
1975 c 74	Petroleum and Submarine Pipe-Lines Act 1975.	In Part II of Schedule 2–
		(a) in model clause 40(2), the words 'in accordance with the Arbitration Act 1950'; (b) in model clause 40(2B), the words 'in accordance with the Arbitration Act (Northern Ireland) 1937'.

		In Part II of Schedule 3, in model clause 38(2), the words 'in accordance with the Arbitration Act 1950'.
1976 NI 12	Solicitors (Northern Ireland) Order 1976.	In Article 3(2), in the entry 'contentious business', the words 'appointed under the Arbitration Act (Northern Ireland) 1937'. Article 71H(3).
1977 c 37	Patents Act 1977.	In section 52(4) the words 'section 21 of the Arbitration Act 1950 or, as the case may be, section 22 of the Arbitration Act (Northern Ireland) 1937 (statement of cases by arbitrators); but'. Section 131(e).
1977 c 38	Administration of Justice Act 1977.	Section 17(2).
1978 c 23	Judicature (Northern Ireland) Act 1978.	In section 35(2), paragraph (g)(v). In Schedule 5, the amendment to the Arbitration Act 1950.
1979 c 42	Arbitration Act 1979.	The whole Act.
1980 c 58	Limitation Act 1980.	Section 34.
1980 NI 3	County Courts (Northern Ireland) Order 1980.	Article 31(3).
1981 c 54	Supreme Court Act 1981.	Section 148.
1982 c 27	Civil Jurisdiction and Judgments Act 1982.	Section 25(3)(c) and (5). In section 26– (a) in subsection (1), the words 'to arbitration or'; (b) in subsection (1)(a)(i), the words 'arbitration or'; (c) in subsection (2), the words 'arbitration or'.
1982 c 53	Administration of Justice Act 1982.	Section 15(6). In Schedule 1, Part IV.
1984 c 5	Merchant Shipping Act 1984.	Section 4(8).
1984 c 12	Telecommunications Act 1984.	Schedule 2, paragraph 13(8).
1984 c 16	Foreign Limitation Periods Act 1984.	Section 5.
1984 c 28	County Courts Act 1984.	In Schedule 2, paragraph 70.
1985 c 61	Administration of Justice Act 1985.	Section 58. In Schedule 9, paragraph 15.

1985 c 68	Housing Act 1985.	In Schedule 18, in paragraph 6(2) the words from 'and the Arbitration Act 1950' to the end.
1985 NI 12	Credit Unions (Northern Ireland) Order 1985.	In Article 72(7)–
		(a) in the opening words, the words from 'and without prejudice' to '1937';
		(b) in sub-paragraph (b), the words 'the registrar or' and 'registrar or'.
1986 c 45	Insolvency Act 1986.	In Schedule 14, the entry relating to the Arbitration Act 1950.
1988 c 8	Multilateral Investment Guarantee Agency Act 1988.	Section 8(3).
1988 c 21	Consumer Arbitration Agreements Act 1988.	The whole Act.
1989 NI 11	Limitation (Northern Ireland) Order 1989.	Article 72.
		In Schedule 3, paragraph 1.
1989 NI 19	Insolvency (Northern Ireland) Order 1989.	In Part II of Schedule 9, paragraph 66.
1990 c 41	Courts and Legal Services Act 1990.	Sections 99 and 101 to 103.
1991 NI 7	Food Safety (Northern Ireland) Order 1991.	In Articles 8(8) and 11(10), the words from 'and the provisions' to the end.
1992 c 40	Friendly Societies Act 1992.	In Schedule 16, paragraph 30(1).
1995 c 8	Agricultural Tenancies Act 1995.	Section 28(4).
1995 c 21	Merchant Shipping Act 1995.	Section 96(10).
		Section 264(9).
1995 c 42	Private International Law (Miscellaneous Provisions) Act 1995.	Section 3.

NOTES

Initial Commencement

To be appointed: see s 109(1).

Appointment

Appointment (in part, in relation to the provision made by county court rules): 17 December 1996: see SI 1996/3146, art 2, Sch 1.

Appointment (remainder): 31 January 1997: see SI 1996/3146, art 3; for transitional provisions see art 4, Sch 2 thereto.

PLANNING AND COMPULSORY PURCHASE ACT 2004

(2004 C 5)

ARRANGEMENT OF SECTIONS

1448

SCHEDULE 9
Repeals

An Act to make provision relating to spatial development and town and country planning; and the compulsory acquisition of land.

[13th May 2004]

PART 1: REGIONAL FUNCTIONS

Spatial strategy

A1.367

1   Regional Spatial Strategy

(1)   For each region there is to be a regional spatial strategy (in this Part referred to as the 'RSS').

(2)   The RSS must set out the Secretary of State's policies (however expressed) in relation to the development and use of land within the region.

(3)   In subsection (2) the references to a region include references to any area within a region which includes the area or part of the area of more than one local planning authority.

(4)   If to any extent a policy set out in the RSS conflicts with any other statement or information in the RSS the conflict must be resolved in favour of the policy.

(5)   With effect from the appointed day the RSS for a region is so much of the regional planning guidance relating to the region as the Secretary of State prescribes.

(6)   The appointed day is the day appointed for the commencement of this section.

NOTES

Initial Commencement

To be appointed: see s 121(1).

Appointment

Appointment (for the purpose of making, or making provision by means of, subordinate legislation): 6 August 2004: see SI 2004/2097, art 2.

Appointment (for remaining purposes): 28 September 2004: see SI 2004/2202, art 2(a).

Extent

This section does not extend to Scotland: see s 124(1).

Subordinate Legislation

Town and Country Planning (Initial Regional Spatial Strategy) (England) Regulations 2004, SI 2004/2206 (made under sub-s (5)).

Planning bodies

A1.368

2   Regional planning bodies

(1)   The Secretary of State may give a direction recognising a body to which subsection (2) applies as the regional planning body for a region (in this Part referred to as the 'RPB').

(2)   This subsection applies to a body (whether or not incorporated) which satisfies such criteria as are prescribed.

(3)   The Secretary of State must not give a direction under subsection (1) in relation to a body unless not less than 60% of the persons who are members of the body fall within subsection (4).

(4)   A person falls within this subsection if he is a member of any of the following councils or authorities and any part of the area of the council or authority (as the case may be) falls within the region to which the direction (if given) will relate—

    (a)   a district council;
    (b)   a county council;
    (c)   a metropolitan district council;
    (d)   a National Park authority;
    (e)   the Broads authority.

(5)   The Secretary of State may give a direction withdrawing recognition of a body.

(6)   Subsection (7) applies if the Secretary of State—

    (a)   does not give a direction under subsection (1) recognising a body, or
    (b)   gives a direction under subsection (5) withdrawing recognition of a body and does not give a direction under subsection (1) recognising any other body.

(7)   In such a case the Secretary of State may exercise such of the functions of the RPB as he thinks appropriate.

(8)   A change in the membership of a body which is not incorporated does not (by itself) affect the validity of the recognition of the body.

NOTES

Initial Commencement

To be appointed: see s 121(1).

Appointment

Appointment (for the purpose of making, or making provision by means of, subordinate legislation): 6 August 2004: see SI 2004/2097, art 2.

Appointment (for remaining purposes): 28 September 2004: see SI 2004/2202, art 2(a).

Extent

This section does not extend to Scotland: see s 124(1).

Subordinate Legislation

Town and Country Planning (Regional Planning) (England) Regulations 2004, SI 2004/2203 (made under sub-s (2)).

A1.369

3   RPB: general functions

(1)   The RPB must keep under review the RSS.

(2)   The RPB must keep under review the matters which may be expected to affect—

(a)   development in its region or any part of the region;
(b)   the planning of that development.

(3)   The RPB must—

(a)   monitor the implementation of the RSS throughout the region;
(b)   consider whether the implementation is achieving the purposes of the RSS.

(4)   The RPB must for each year prepare a report on the implementation of the RSS in the region.

(5)   The report—

(a)   must be in respect of such period of 12 months as is prescribed;
(b)   must be in such form and contain such information as is prescribed;
(c)   must be submitted to the Secretary of State on such date as is prescribed.

(6)   The RPB must give advice to any other body or person if it thinks that to do so will help to achieve implementation of the RSS.

NOTES

Initial Commencement

To be appointed: see s 121(1).

Appointment

Appointment (for the purpose of making, or making provision by means of, subordinate legislation): 6 August 2004: see SI 2004/2097, art 2.

Appointment (for remaining purposes): 28 September 2004: see SI 2004/2202, art 2(a).

Extent

This section does not extend to Scotland: see s 124(1).

Subordinate Legislation

Town and Country Planning (Regional Planning) (England) Regulations 2004, SI 2004/2203 (made under sub-s (5)).

A1.370

4   Assistance from certain local authorities

(1)   For the purpose of the exercise of its functions under sections 3(1) and (3)(a) and 5(1) the RPB must seek the advice of each authority in its region which is an authority falling within subsection (4).

(2)   The authority must give the RPB advice as to the exercise of the function to the extent that the exercise of the function is capable of affecting (directly or indirectly) the exercise by the authority of any function it has.

(3)   The advice mentioned in subsection (1) includes advice relating to the inclusion in the RSS of specific policies relating to any part of the region.

(4)   Each of the following authorities fall within this subsection if their area or any part of their area is in the RPB's region—

(a)   a county council;
(b)   a metropolitan district council;
(c)   a district council for an area for which there is no county council;
(d)   a National Park authority.

(5)   The RPB may make arrangements with an authority falling within subsection (4) or with any district council the whole or part of whose area is in the region for the discharge by the authority or council of a function of the RPB.

(6)   The RPB may reimburse an authority or council which exercises functions by virtue of such arrangements for any expenditure incurred by the authority or council in doing so.

(7)   Subsection (5) does not apply to a function of the RPB under section 5(8).

(8)   Any arrangements made for the purposes of subsection (5) must be taken to be arrangements between local authorities for the purposes of section 101 of the Local Government Act 1972 (c 70).

(9)   Nothing in this section affects any power which a body which is recognised as an RPB has apart from this section.

NOTES

Initial Commencement

To be appointed: see s 121(1).

Appointment

Appointment: 28 September 2004: see SI 2004/2202, art 2(a).

Extent

This section does not extend to Scotland: see s 124(1).

RSS revision

A1.371

5   RSS: revision

(1)   The RPB must prepare a draft revision of the RSS—

(a)   when it appears to it necessary or expedient to do so;
(b)   at such time as is prescribed;
(c)   if it is directed to do so under section 10(1).

(2)   But the RPB must give notice to the Secretary of State of its intention to prepare a draft revision under subsection (1)(a).

(3)   In preparing a draft revision the RPB must have regard to—

(a)   national policies and advice contained in guidance issued by the Secretary of State;
(b)   the RSS for each adjoining region;
(c)   the spatial development strategy if any part of its region adjoins Greater London;
(d)   the Wales Spatial Plan if any part of its region adjoins Wales;
(e)   the resources likely to be available for implementation of the RSS;

(f)   the desirability of making different provision in relation to different parts of the region;

(g)   such other matters as are prescribed.

(4)   In preparing a draft revision the RPB must also—

(a)   carry out an appraisal of the sustainability of the proposals in the draft, and

(b)   prepare a report of the findings of the appraisal.

(5)   If the RPB decides to make different provision for different parts of the region the detailed proposals for such different provision must first be made by an authority which falls within section 4(4).

(6)   But if the RPB and the authority agree, the detailed proposals may first be made—

(a)   by a district council which is not such an authority, or

(b)   by the RPB.

(7)   The Secretary of State may by regulations make provision as to—

(a)   the subject matter of a draft revision prepared in pursuance of subsection (1)(b);

(b)   any further documents which must be prepared by the RPB in connection with the preparation of a draft revision;

(c)   the form and content of any draft, report or other document prepared under this section.

(8)   When the RPB has prepared a draft revision, the report to be prepared under subsection (4)(b) and any other document to be prepared in pursuance of subsection (7)(b) it must—

(a)   publish the draft revision, report and other document;

(b)   submit them to the Secretary of State.

(9)   But the RPB may withdraw a draft revision at any time before it submits the draft to the Secretary of State under subsection (8)(b).

NOTES

Initial Commencement

To be appointed: see s 121(1).

Appointment

Appointment (for the purpose of making, or making provision by means of, subordinate legislation): 6 August 2004: see SI 2004/2097, art 2.

Appointment (for remaining purposes): 28 September 2004: see SI 2004/2202, art 2(a).

Extent

This section does not extend to Scotland: see s 124(1).

Subordinate Legislation

Town and Country Planning (Regional Planning) (England) Regulations 2004, SI 2004/2203 (made under sub-ss (3)(g), (7)(b), (c)).

A1.372

6   RSS: community involvement

(1)   For the purposes of the exercise of its functions under section 5, the RPB must prepare and publish a statement of its policies as to the involvement of persons who appear to the RPB to have an interest in the exercise of those functions.

(2)   The RPB must keep the policies under review and from time to time must—

   (a)   revise the statement;
   (b)   publish the revised statement.

(3)   The RPB must comply with the statement or revised statement (as the case may be) in the exercise of its functions under section 5.

(4)   The documents mentioned in section 5(7)(b) and (c) include the statement and revised statement.

NOTES

Initial Commencement

To be appointed: see s 121(1).

Appointment

Appointment: 28 September 2004: see SI 2004/2202, art 2(a).

Extent

This section does not extend to Scotland: see s 124(1).

A1.373

7   RSS: Secretary of State's functions

(1)   This section applies when the Secretary of State receives a draft revision of the RSS.

(2)   Any person may make representations on the draft.

(3)   The Secretary of State may arrange for an examination in public to be held into the draft.

(4)   In deciding whether an examination in public is held the Secretary of State must have regard to—

   (a)   the extent of the revisions proposed by the draft;
   (b)   the extent and nature of the consultation on the draft before it was published;
   (c)   the level of interest shown in the draft;
   (d)   such other matters as he thinks appropriate.

NOTES

Initial Commencement

To be appointed: see s 121(1).

Appointment

Appointment: 28 September 2004: see SI 2004/2202, art 2(a).

Extent

This section does not extend to Scotland: see s 124(1).

A1.374

8   RSS: examination in public

(1)   This section applies if the Secretary of State decides that an examination in public is to be held of a draft revision of the RSS.

(2)   The examination must be held before a person appointed by the Secretary of State.

(3)   No person has a right to be heard at an examination in public.

(4)   The Secretary of State may, after consultation with the Lord Chancellor, make regulations with respect to the procedure to be followed at an examination in public.

(5)   The person appointed under subsection (2) must make a report of the examination to the Secretary of State.

(6)   The Secretary of State may by regulations make provision as to the procedure to be followed in connection with the recommendations of the person appointed under subsection (2).

(7)   An examination in public—

 (a)   is a statutory inquiry for the purposes of section 1(1)(c) of the Tribunals and Inquiries Act 1992 (c 53) (report on administrative procedures);
 (b)   is not a statutory inquiry for any other purpose of that Act.

NOTES

Initial Commencement

To be appointed: see s 121(1).

Appointment

Appointment (for the purpose of making, or making provision by means of, subordinate legislation): 6 August 2004: see SI 2004/2097, art 2.

Appointment (for remaining purposes): 28 September 2004: see SI 2004/2202, art 2(a).

Extent

This section does not extend to Scotland: see s 124(1).

A1.375

9   RSS: further procedure

(1)   If no examination in public is held the Secretary of State must consider any representations made on the draft revision of the RSS under section 7(2).

(2)   If an examination in public is held the Secretary of State must consider—

 (a)   the report of the person appointed to hold the examination;
 (b)   any representations which are not considered by the person appointed to hold the examination.

(3)   If after proceeding under subsection (1) or (2) the Secretary of State proposes to make any changes to the draft he must publish—

(a)   the changes he proposes to make;

(b)   his reasons for doing so.

(4)   Any person may make representations on the proposed changes.

(5)   The Secretary of State must consider any such representations.

(6)   The Secretary of State must then publish—

(a)   the revision of the RSS incorporating such changes as he thinks fit;

(b)   his reasons for making the changes.

(7)   But the Secretary of State may withdraw a draft revision of an RSS at any time before he publishes the revision of the RSS under subsection (6).

NOTES

Initial Commencement

To be appointed: see s 121(1).

Appointment

Appointment: 28 September 2004: see SI 2004/2202, art 2(a).

Extent

This section does not extend to Scotland: see s 124(1).

A1.376

10   Secretary of State: additional powers

(1)   If the Secretary of State thinks it is necessary or expedient to do so he may direct an RPB to prepare a draft revision of the RSS.

(2)   Such a direction may require the RPB to prepare the draft revision—

(a)   in relation to such aspects of the RSS as are specified;

(b)   in accordance with such timetable as is specified.

(3)   The Secretary of State may prepare a draft revision of the RSS if the RPB fails to comply with—

(a)   a direction under subsection (1),

(b)   section 5(1)(b), or

(c)   regulations under section 5(7) or 11.

(4)   If the Secretary of State prepares a draft revision under subsection (3)—

(a)   section 7 applies as it does if the Secretary of State receives a draft revision from the RPB, and

(b)   sections 8 and 9 apply.

(5)   If the Secretary of State thinks it necessary or expedient to do so he may at any time revoke—

(a)   an RSS;

(b)   such parts of an RSS as he thinks appropriate.

(6)   The Secretary of State may by regulations make provision as to the procedure to be followed for the purposes of subsection (3).

(7)   Subsection (8) applies if—

(a) any step has been taken in connection with the preparation of any part of regional planning guidance, and

(b) the Secretary of State thinks that the step corresponds to a step which must be taken under this Part in connection with the preparation and publication of a revision of the RSS.

(8) The Secretary of State may by order provide for the part of the regional planning guidance to have effect as a revision of the RSS.

NOTES

Initial Commencement

To be appointed: see s 121(1).

Appointment

Appointment (for the purpose of making, or making provision by means of, subordinate legislation): 6 August 2004: see SI 2004/2097, art 2.

Appointment (for remaining purposes): 28 September 2004: see SI 2004/2202, art 2(a).

Extent

This section does not extend to Scotland: see s 124(1).

Subordinate Legislation

Town and Country Planning (Regional Planning Guidance as Revision of Regional Spatial Strategy) Order 2004, SI 2004/2208 (made under sub-s (8)).

Supplementary

A1.377

11   Regulations

(1) The Secretary of State may by regulations make provision in connection with the exercise by any person of functions under this Part.

(2) The regulations may in particular make provision as to—

(a) the procedure to be followed for the purposes of section 5;

(b) the procedure to be followed by the RPB in connection with its functions under section 6;

(c) requirements about the giving of notice and publicity;

(d) requirements about inspection by the public of a draft revision or any other document;

(e) the nature and extent of consultation with and participation by the public in anything done under this Part;

(f) the making of representations about any matter to be included in an RSS;

(g) consideration of any such representations;

(h) the remuneration and allowances payable to a person appointed to carry out an examination in public under section 8;

(i) the determination of the time at which anything must be done for the purposes of this Part;

(j) the manner of publication of any draft, report or other document published under this Part;

(k) monitoring the exercise by RPBs of their functions under this Part;

(l) the making of reasonable charges for the provision of copies of documents required by or under this Part.

A1.378 *Statutes*

NOTES

Initial Commencement

To be appointed: see s 121(1).

Appointment

Appointment (for the purpose of making, or making provision by means of, subordinate legislation): 6 August 2004: see SI 2004/2097, art 2.

Appointment (for remaining purposes): 28 September 2004: see SI 2004/2202, art 2(a).

Extent

This section does not extend to Scotland: see s 124(1).

Subordinate Legislation

Town and Country Planning (Regional Planning) (England) Regulations 2004, SI 2004/2203.

Town and Country Planning (Regional Spatial Strategies) (Examinations in Public) (Remuneration and Allowances) (England) (Revocation) Regulations 2006, SI 2006/3320 (made under sub-s (2)(h)).

A1.378

12 Supplementary

(1) A region is a region (except London) specified in Schedule 1 to the Regional Development Agencies Act 1998 (c 45).

(2) But the Secretary of State may by order direct that if the area of a National Park falls within more than one region it is treated as falling wholly within such region as is specified in the order.

(3) Regional planning guidance for a region is a document issued by the Secretary of State setting out his policies (however expressed) in relation to the development and use of land within the region.

(4) The Secretary of State is the Secretary of State for the time being having general responsibility for policy in relation to the development and use of land.

(5) Subsection (4) does not apply for the purposes of section 5(3)(a).

(6) References to a revision or draft revision of an RSS include references to a revision or draft revision—

    (a) of any part of an RSS;

    (b) of the RSS as it relates to any part of a region.

(7) This section has effect for the purposes of this Part.

NOTES

Initial Commencement

To be appointed: see s 121(1).

Appointment

Appointment (for the purpose of making, or making provision by means of, subordinate legislation): 6 August 2004: see SI 2004/2097, art 2.

Appointment (for remaining purposes): 28 September 2004: see SI 2004/2202, art 2(a).

Extent

This section does not extend to Scotland: see s 124(1).

Subordinate Legislation

Town and Country Planning (Regions) (National Parks) (England) Order 2004, SI 2004/2207 (made under sub-s (2)).

PART 2: LOCAL DEVELOPMENT

Survey

A1.379

13   Survey of area

(1)   The local planning authority must keep under review the matters which may be expected to affect the development of their area or the planning of its development.

(2)   These matters include—

(a)   the principal physical, economic, social and environmental characteristics of the area of the authority;
(b)   the principal purposes for which land is used in the area;
(c)   the size, composition and distribution of the population of the area;
(d)   the communications, transport system and traffic of the area;
(e)   any other considerations which may be expected to affect those matters;
(f)   such other matters as may be prescribed or as the Secretary of State (in a particular case) may direct.

(3)   The matters also include—

(a)   any changes which the authority think may occur in relation to any other matter;
(b)   the effect such changes are likely to have on the development of the authority's area or on the planning of such development.

(4)   The local planning authority may also keep under review and examine the matters mentioned in subsections (2) and (3) in relation to any neighbouring area to the extent that those matters may be expected to affect the area of the authority.

(5)   In exercising a function under subsection (4) a local planning authority must consult with the local planning authority for the neighbouring area in question.

(6)   If a neighbouring area is in Wales references to the local planning authority for that area must be construed in accordance with Part 6.

NOTES

Initial Commencement

To be appointed: see s 121(1).

Appointment

Appointment (for the purpose of making, or making provision by means of, subordinate legislation): 6 August 2004: see SI 2004/2097, art 2.

Appointment (for remaining purposes): 28 September 2004: see SI 2004/2202, art 2(b); for transitional provisions see SI 2004/2205, reg 6.

Extent

This section does not extend to Scotland: see s 124(1).

Subordinate Legislation

Town and Country Planning (Local Development) (England) Regulations 2004, SI 2004/2204 (made under sub-s (2)(f)).

A1.380

14   Survey of area: county councils

(1)   A county council in respect of so much of their area for which there is a district council must keep under review the matters which may be expected to affect development of that area or the planning of its development in so far as the development relates to a county matter.

(2)   Subsections (2) to (6) of section 13 apply for the purposes of subsection (1) as they apply for the purposes of that section; and references to the local planning authority must be construed as references to the county council.

(3)   The Secretary of State may by regulations require or (in a particular case) may direct a county council to keep under review in relation to so much of their area as is mentioned in subsection (1) such of the matters mentioned in section 13(1) to (4) as he prescribes or directs (as the case may be).

(4)   For the purposes of subsection (3)—

    (a)   it is immaterial whether any development relates to a county matter;

    (b)   if a matter which is prescribed or in respect of which the Secretary of State gives a direction falls within section 13(4) the county council must consult the local planning authority for the area in question.

(5)   The county council must make available the results of their review under subsection (3) to such persons as the Secretary of State prescribes or directs (as the case may be).

(6)   References to a county matter must be construed in accordance with paragraph 1 of Schedule 1 to the principal Act (ignoring sub-paragraph (1)(i)).

NOTES

Initial Commencement

To be appointed: see s 121(1).

Appointment

Appointment (for the purpose of making, or making provision by means of, subordinate legislation): 6 August 2004: see SI 2004/2097, art 2.

Appointment (for remaining purposes): 28 September 2004: see SI 2004/2202, art 2(b); for transitional provisions see SI 2004/2205, reg 6.

Extent

This section does not extend to Scotland: see s 124(1).

Subordinate Legislation

Town and Country Planning (Local Development) (England) Regulations 2004, SI 2004/2204 (made under sub-ss (3), (5)).

Development schemes

A1.381

15   Local development scheme

(1)   The local planning authority must prepare and maintain a scheme to be known as their local development scheme.

(2)   The scheme must specify—

    (a)   the documents which are to be local development documents;
    (b)   the subject matter and geographical area to which each document is to relate;
    (c)   which documents are to be development plan documents;
    (d)   which documents (if any) are to be prepared jointly with one or more other local planning authorities;
    (e)   any matter or area in respect of which the authority have agreed (or propose to agree) to the constitution of a joint committee under section 29;
    (f)   the timetable for the preparation and revision of the documents;
    (g)   such other matters as are prescribed.

(3)   The local planning authority must—

    (a)   prepare the scheme in accordance with such other requirements as are prescribed;
    (b)   submit the scheme to the Secretary of State at such time as is prescribed or as the Secretary of State (in a particular case) directs;
    (c)   at that time send a copy of the scheme to the RPB or (if the authority are a London borough) to the Mayor of London.

(4)   The Secretary of State may direct the local planning authority to make such amendments to the scheme as he thinks appropriate.

(5)   Such a direction must contain the Secretary of State's reasons for giving it.

(6)   The local planning authority must comply with a direction given under subsection (4).

(7)   The Secretary of State may make regulations as to the following matters—

    (a)   publicity about the scheme;
    (b)   making the scheme available for inspection by the public;
    (c)   requirements to be met for the purpose of bringing the scheme into effect.

(8)   The local planning authority must revise their local development scheme—

    (a)   at such time as they consider appropriate;
    (b)   when directed to do so by the Secretary of State.

(9)   Subsections (2) to (7) apply to the revision of a scheme as they apply to the preparation of the scheme.

NOTES

Initial Commencement

To be appointed: see s 121(1).

Appointment

Appointment (for the purpose of making, or making provision by means of, subordinate legislation): 6 August 2004: see SI 2004/2097, art 2.

Appointment (for remaining purposes): 28 September 2004: see SI 2004/2202, art 2(b); for transitional provisions see SI 2004/2205, reg 6.

Extent

This section does not extend to Scotland: see s 124(1).

Subordinate Legislation

Town and Country Planning (Local Development) (England) Regulations 2004, SI 2004/2204 (made under sub-ss (2)(g), (3), (7)).

A1.382

16   Minerals and waste development scheme

(1)   A county council in respect of any part of their area for which there is a district council must prepare and maintain a scheme to be known as their minerals and waste development scheme.

(2)   Section 15 (ignoring subsections (1) and (2)(e)) applies in relation to a minerals and waste development scheme as it applies in relation to a local development scheme.

(3)   This Part applies to a minerals and waste development scheme as it applies to a local development scheme and for that purpose—

   (a)   references to a local development scheme include references to a minerals and waste development scheme;
   (b)   references to a local planning authority include references to a county council.

(4)   But subsection (3) does not apply to—

   (a)   section 17(3);
   (b)   section 24(1)(b), (4) and (7);
   (c)   the references in section 24(5) to subsection (4) and the Mayor;
   (d)   sections 29 to 31.

NOTES

Initial Commencement

To be appointed: see s 121(1).

Appointment

Appointment (for the purpose of making, or making provision by means of, subordinate legislation): 6 August 2004: see SI 2004/2097, art 2.

Appointment (for remaining purposes): 28 September 2004: see SI 2004/2202, art 2(b); for transitional provisions see SI 2004/2205, reg 6.

Extent

This section does not extend to Scotland: see s 124(1).

Documents

A1.383

17   Local development documents

(1)   Documents which must be specified in the local development scheme as local development documents are—

(a)   documents of such descriptions as are prescribed;

(b)   the local planning authority's statement of community involvement.

(2)   The local planning authority may also specify in the scheme such other documents as they think are appropriate.

(3)   The local development documents must (taken as a whole) set out the authority's policies (however expressed) relating to the development and use of land in their area.

(4)   In the case of the documents which are included in a minerals and waste development scheme they must also (taken as a whole) set out the authority's policies (however expressed) in relation to development which is a county matter within the meaning of paragraph 1 of Schedule 1 to the principal Act (ignoring sub-paragraph (1)(i)).

(5)   If to any extent a policy set out in a local development document conflicts with any other statement or information in the document the conflict must be resolved in favour of the policy.

(6)   The authority must keep under review their local development documents having regard to the results of any review carried out under section 13 or 14.

(7)   Regulations under this section may prescribe—

(a)   which descriptions of local development documents are development plan documents;

(b)   the form and content of the local development documents;

(c)   the time at which any step in the preparation of any such document must be taken.

(8)   A document is a local development document only in so far as it or any part of it—

(a)   is adopted by resolution of the local planning authority as a local development document;

(b)   is approved by the Secretary of State under section 21 or 27.

NOTES

Initial Commencement

To be appointed: see s 121(1).

Appointment

Appointment (for the purpose of making, or making provision by means of, subordinate legislation): 6 August 2004: see SI 2004/2097, art 2.

Appointment (for remaining purposes): 28 September 2004: see SI 2004/2202, art 2(b); for transitional provisions see SI 2004/2205, reg 6.

Extent

This section does not extend to Scotland: see s 124(1).

Subordinate Legislation

Town and Country Planning (Local Development) (England) Regulations 2004, SI 2004/2204 (made under sub-ss (1)(a), (7)).

A1.384

18   Statement of community involvement

(1)   The local planning authority must prepare a statement of community involvement.

(2)   The statement of community involvement is a statement of the authority's policy as to the involvement in the exercise of the authority's functions under sections 19, 26 and 28 of this Act and Part 3 of the principal Act of persons who appear to the authority to have an interest in matters relating to development in their area.

(3)   For the purposes of sections 19(2) and 24 the statement of community involvement is not a local development document.

(4)   Section 20 applies to the statement of community involvement as if it were a development plan document.

(5)   But in section 20(5)(a)—

  (a)   the reference to section 19 must be construed as if it does not include a reference to subsection (2) of that section;
  (b)   the reference to section 24(1) must be ignored.

(6)   In the following provisions of this Part references to a development plan document include references to the statement of community involvement—

  (a)   section 22;
  (b)   section 23(2) to (5).

NOTES

Initial Commencement

To be appointed: see s 121(1).

Appointment

Appointment: 28 September 2004: see SI 2004/2202, art 2(b); for transitional provisions see SI 2004/2205, reg 6.

Extent

This section does not extend to Scotland: see s 124(1).

A1.385

19   Preparation of local development documents

(1)   Local development documents must be prepared in accordance with the local development scheme.

(2)   In preparing a local development document the local planning authority must have regard to—

  (a)   national policies and advice contained in guidance issued by the Secretary of State;
  (b)   the RSS for the region in which the area of the authority is situated, if the area is outside Greater London;
  (c)   the spatial development strategy if the authority are a London borough or if any part of the authority's area adjoins Greater London;
  (d)   the RSS for any region which adjoins the area of the authority;
  (e)   the Wales Spatial Plan if any part of the authority's area adjoins Wales;

(f)   the community strategy prepared by the authority;

(g)   the community strategy for any other authority whose area comprises any part of the area of the local planning authority;

(h)   any other local development document which has been adopted by the authority;

(i)   the resources likely to be available for implementing the proposals in the document;

(j)   such other matters as the Secretary of State prescribes.

(3)   In preparing the other local development documents the authority must also comply with their statement of community involvement.

(4)   But subsection (3) does not apply at any time before the authority have adopted their statement of community involvement.

(5)   The local planning authority must also—

(a)   carry out an appraisal of the sustainability of the proposals in each document;

(b)   prepare a report of the findings of the appraisal.

(6)   The Secretary of State may by regulations make provision—

(a)   as to any further documents which must be prepared by the authority in connection with the preparation of a local development document;

(b)   as to the form and content of such documents.

(7)   The community strategy is the strategy prepared by an authority under section 4 of the Local Government Act 2000 (c 22).

NOTES

Initial Commencement

To be appointed: see s 121(1).

Appointment

Appointment (for the purpose of making, or making provision by means of, subordinate legislation): 6 August 2004: see SI 2004/2097, art 2.

Appointment (for remaining purposes): 28 September 2004: see SI 2004/2202, art 2(b); for transitional provisions see SI 2004/2205, reg 6.

Extent

This section does not extend to Scotland: see s 124(1).

Subordinate Legislation

Town and Country Planning (Local Development) (England) Regulations 2004, SI 2004/2204 (made under sub-s (2)(j)).

A1.386

20   Independent examination

(1)   The local planning authority must submit every development plan document to the Secretary of State for independent examination.

(2)   But the authority must not submit such a document unless—

(a)   they have complied with any relevant requirements contained in regulations under this Part, and

(b)   they think the document is ready for independent examination.

(3) The authority must also send to the Secretary of State (in addition to the development plan document) such other documents (or copies of documents) and such information as is prescribed.

(4) The examination must be carried out by a person appointed by the Secretary of State.

(5) The purpose of an independent examination is to determine in respect of the development plan document—

    (a) whether it satisfies the requirements of sections 19 and 24(1), regulations under section 17(7) and any regulations under section 36 relating to the preparation of development plan documents;

    (b) whether it is sound.

(6) Any person who makes representations seeking to change a development plan document must (if he so requests) be given the opportunity to appear before and be heard by the person carrying out the examination.

(7) The person appointed to carry out the examination must—

    (a) make recommendations;

    (b) give reasons for the recommendations.

(8) The local planning authority must publish the recommendations and the reasons.

NOTES

Initial Commencement

To be appointed: see s 121(1).

Appointment

Appointment (for the purpose of making, or making provision by means of, subordinate legislation): 6 August 2004: see SI 2004/2097, art 2.

Appointment (for remaining purposes): 28 September 2004: see SI 2004/2202, art 2(b); for transitional provisions see SI 2004/2205, reg 6.

Extent

This section does not extend to Scotland: see s 124(1).

Subordinate Legislation

Town and Country Planning (Local Development) (England) Regulations 2004, SI 2004/2204 (made under sub-s (3)).

A1.387

21   Intervention by Secretary of State

(1) If the Secretary of State thinks that a local development document is unsatisfactory—

    (a) he may at any time before the document is adopted under section 23 direct the local planning authority to modify the document in accordance with the direction;

    (b) if he gives such a direction he must state his reasons for doing so.

(2) The authority—

    (a) must comply with the direction;

    (b)   must not adopt the document unless the Secretary of State gives notice that he is satisfied that they have complied with the direction.

(3)   But subsection (2) does not apply if the Secretary of State withdraws the direction.

(4)   At any time before a development plan document is adopted by a local planning authority the Secretary of State may direct that the document (or any part of it) is submitted to him for his approval.

(5)   The following paragraphs apply if the Secretary of State gives a direction under subsection (4)—

    (a)   the authority must not take any step in connection with the adoption of the document until the Secretary of State gives his decision;
    (b)   if the direction is given before the authority have submitted the document under section 20(1) the Secretary of State must hold an independent examination and section 20(4) to (7) applies accordingly;
    (c)   if the direction is given after the authority have submitted the document but before the person appointed to carry out the examination has made his recommendations he must make his recommendations to the Secretary of State;
    (d)   the document has no effect unless it or (if the direction relates to only part of a document) the part has been approved by the Secretary of State.

(6)   The Secretary of State must publish the recommendations made to him by virtue of subsection (5)(b) or (c) and the reasons of the person making the recommendations.

(7)   In considering a document or part of a document submitted under subsection (4) the Secretary of State may take account of any matter which he thinks is relevant.

(8)   It is immaterial whether any such matter was taken account of by the authority.

(9)   In relation to a document or part of a document submitted to him under subsection (4) the Secretary of State—

    (a)   may approve, approve subject to specified modifications or reject the document or part;
    (b)   must give reasons for his decision under paragraph (a).

(10)   In the exercise of any function under this section the Secretary of State must have regard to the local development scheme.

NOTES

Initial Commencement

To be appointed: see s 121(1).

Appointment

Appointment (for the purpose of making, or making provision by means of, subordinate legislation): 6 August 2004: see SI 2004/2097, art 2.

Appointment (for remaining purposes): 28 September 2004: see SI 2004/2202, art 2(b); for transitional provisions see SI 2004/2205, reg 6.

Extent

This section does not extend to Scotland: see s 124(1).

A1.388

22   Withdrawal of local development documents

(1)   A local planning authority may at any time before a local development document is adopted under section 23 withdraw the document.

(2)   But subsection (1) does not apply to a development plan document at any time after the document has been submitted for independent examination under section 20 unless—

  (a)   the person carrying out the examination recommends that the document is withdrawn and that recommendation is not overruled by a direction given by the Secretary of State, or

  (b)   the Secretary of State directs that the document must be withdrawn.

NOTES

Initial Commencement

To be appointed: see s 121(1).

Appointment

Appointment (for the purpose of making, or making provision by means of, subordinate legislation): 6 August 2004: see SI 2004/2097, art 2.

Appointment (for remaining purposes): 28 September 2004: see SI 2004/2202, art 2(b); for transitional provisions see SI 2004/2205, reg 6.

Extent

This section does not extend to Scotland: see s 124(1).

A1.389

23   Adoption of local development documents

(1)   The local planning authority may adopt a local development document (other than a development plan document) either as originally prepared or as modified to take account of—

  (a)   any representations made in relation to the document;
  (b)   any other matter they think is relevant.

(2)   The authority may adopt a development plan document as originally prepared if the person appointed to carry out the independent examination of the document recommends that the document as originally prepared is adopted.

(3)   The authority may adopt a development plan document with modifications if the person appointed to carry out the independent examination of the document recommends the modifications.

(4)   The authority must not adopt a development plan document unless they do so in accordance with subsection (2) or (3).

(5)   A document is adopted for the purposes of this section if it is adopted by resolution of the authority.

1468

NOTES

Initial Commencement

To be appointed: see s 121(1).

Appointment

Appointment: 28 September 2004: see SI 2004/2202, art 2(b); for transitional provisions see SI 2004/2205, reg 6.

Extent

This section does not extend to Scotland: see s 124(1).

A1.390

24   Conformity with regional strategy

(1)   The local development documents must be in general conformity with—

    (a)   the RSS (if the area of the local planning authority is in a region other than London);

    (b)   the spatial development strategy (if the local planning authority are a London borough).

(2)   A local planning authority whose area is in a region other than London—

    (a)   must request the opinion in writing of the RPB as to the general conformity of a development plan document with the RSS;

    (b)   may request the opinion in writing of the RPB as to the general conformity of any other local development document with the RSS.

(3)   Not later than the end of the period prescribed for the purposes of this section the RPB must send its opinion to—

    (a)   the Secretary of State;

    (b)   the local planning authority.

(4)   A local planning authority which are a London borough—

    (a)   must request the opinion in writing of the Mayor of London as to the general conformity of a development plan document with the spatial development strategy;

    (b)   may request the opinion in writing of the Mayor as to the general conformity of any other local development document with the spatial development strategy.

(5)   Whether or not the local planning authority make a request mentioned in subsection (2) or (4) the RPB or the Mayor (as the case may be) may give an opinion as to the general conformity of a local development document with the RSS or the spatial development strategy (as the case may be).

(6)   If in the opinion of the RPB a document is not in general conformity with the RSS the RPB must be taken to have made representations seeking a change to the document.

(7)   If in the opinion of the Mayor a document is not in general conformity with the spatial development strategy the Mayor must be taken to have made representations seeking a change to the document.

(8)   But the Secretary of State may in any case direct that subsection (6) must be ignored.

(9)   If at any time no body is recognised as the RPB under section 2 the functions of the RPB under this section must be exercised by the Secretary of State and subsections (3)(a), (6) and (8) of this section must be ignored.

NOTES

Initial Commencement

To be appointed: see s 121(1).

Appointment

Appointment (for the purpose of making, or making provision by means of, subordinate legislation): 6 August 2004: see SI 2004/2097, art 2.

Appointment (for remaining purposes): 28 September 2004: see SI 2004/2202, art 2(b); for transitional provisions see SI 2004/2205, reg 6.

Extent

This section does not extend to Scotland: see s 124(1).

Subordinate Legislation

Town and Country Planning (Local Development) (England) Regulations 2004, SI 2004/2204 (made under sub-s (3)).

A1.391

25   Revocation of local development documents

The Secretary of State—

    (a)   may at any time revoke a local development document at the request of the local planning authority;

    (b)   may prescribe descriptions of local development document which may be revoked by the authority themselves.

NOTES

Initial Commencement

To be appointed: see s 121(1).

Appointment

Appointment (for the purpose of making, or making provision by means of, subordinate legislation): 6 August 2004: see SI 2004/2097, art 2.

Appointment (for remaining purposes): 28 September 2004: see SI 2004/2202, art 2(b); for transitional provisions see SI 2004/2205, reg 6.

Extent

This section does not extend to Scotland: see s 124(1).

A1.392

26   Revision of local development documents

(1)   The local planning authority may at any time prepare a revision of a local development document.

1470

(2)   The authority must prepare a revision of a local development document—

(a)   if the Secretary of State directs them to do so, and
(b)   in accordance with such timetable as he directs.

(3)   This Part applies to the revision of a local development document as it applies to the preparation of the document.

(4)   Subsection (5) applies if any part of the area of the local planning authority is an area to which an enterprise zone scheme relates.

(5)   As soon as practicable after the occurrence of a relevant event—

(a)   the authority must review every local development document in the light of the enterprise zone scheme;
(b)   if they think that any modifications of the document are required in consequence of the scheme they must prepare a revised document containing the modifications.

(6)   The following are relevant events—

(a)   the making of an order under paragraph 5 of Schedule 32 to the Local Government, Planning and Land Act 1980 (c 65) (designation of enterprise zone);
(b)   the giving of notification under paragraph 11(1) of that Schedule (approval of modification of enterprise zone scheme).

(7)   References to an enterprise zone and an enterprise zone scheme must be construed in accordance with that Act.

NOTES

Initial Commencement

To be appointed: see s 121(1).

Appointment

Appointment (for the purpose of making, or making provision by means of, subordinate legislation): 6 August 2004: see SI 2004/2097, art 2.

Appointment (for remaining purposes): 28 September 2004: see SI 2004/2202, art 2(b); for transitional provisions see SI 2004/2205, reg 6.

Extent

This section does not extend to Scotland: see s 124(1).

A1.393

27   Secretary of State's default power

(1)   This section applies if the Secretary of State thinks that a local planning authority are failing or omitting to do anything it is necessary for them to do in connection with the preparation, revision or adoption of a development plan document.

(2)   The Secretary of State must hold an independent examination and section 20(4) to (7) applies accordingly.

(3)   The Secretary of State must publish the recommendations and reasons of the person appointed to hold the examination.

(4)   The Secretary of State may—

(a) prepare or revise (as the case may be) the document, and

(b) approve the document as a local development document.

(5) The Secretary of State must give reasons for anything he does in pursuance of subsection (4).

(6) The authority must reimburse the Secretary of State for any expenditure he incurs in connection with anything—

(a) which is done by him under subsection (4), and

(b) which the authority failed or omitted to do as mentioned in subsection (1).

NOTES

Initial Commencement

To be appointed: see s 121(1).

Appointment

Appointment: 28 September 2004: see SI 2004/2202, art 2(b); for transitional provisions see SI 2004/2205, reg 6.

Extent

This section does not extend to Scotland: see s 124(1).

A1.394

28   Joint local development documents

(1) Two or more local planning authorities may agree to prepare one or more joint local development documents.

(2) This Part applies for the purposes of any step which may be or is required to be taken in relation to a joint local development document as it applies for the purposes of any step which may be or is required to be taken in relation to a local development document.

(3) For the purposes of subsection (2) anything which must be done by or in relation to a local planning authority in connection with a local development document must be done by or in relation to each of the authorities mentioned in subsection (1) in connection with a joint local development document.

(4) Any requirement of this Part in relation to the RSS is a requirement in relation to the RSS for the region in which each authority mentioned in subsection (1) is situated.

(5) If the authorities mentioned in subsection (1) include one or more London boroughs the requirements of this Part in relation to the spatial development strategy also apply.

(6) Subsections (7) to (9) apply if a local planning authority withdraw from an agreement mentioned in subsection (1).

(7) Any step taken in relation to the document must be treated as a step taken by—

(a) an authority which were a party to the agreement for the purposes of any corresponding document prepared by them;

(b) two or more other authorities who were parties to the agreement for the purposes of any corresponding joint local development document.

(8) Any independent examination of a local development document to which the agreement relates must be suspended.

(9) If before the end of the period prescribed for the purposes of this subsection an authority which were a party to the agreement request the Secretary of State to do so he may direct that—

(a) the examination is resumed in relation to the corresponding document;
(b) any step taken for the purposes of the suspended examination has effect for the purposes of the resumed examination.

(10) A joint local development document is a local development document prepared jointly by two or more local planning authorities.

(11) The Secretary of State may by regulations make provision as to what is a corresponding document.

NOTES

Initial Commencement

To be appointed: see s 121(1).

Appointment

Appointment (for the purpose of making, or making provision by means of, subordinate legislation): 6 August 2004: see SI 2004/2097, art 2.

Appointment (for remaining purposes): 28 September 2004: see SI 2004/2202, art 2(b); for transitional provisions see SI 2004/2205, reg 6.

Extent

This section does not extend to Scotland: see s 124(1).

Subordinate Legislation

Town and Country Planning (Local Development) (England) Regulations 2004, SI 2004/2204 (made under sub-ss (9), (11)).

Joint committees

A1.395

29   Joint committees

(1) This section applies if one or more local planning authorities agree with one or more county councils in relation to any area of such a council for which there is also a district council to establish a joint committee to be, for the purposes of this Part, the local planning authority—

(a) for the area specified in the agreement;
(b) in respect of such matters as are so specified.

(2) The Secretary of State may by order constitute a joint committee to be the local planning authority—

(a) for the area;
(b) in respect of those matters.

(3) Such an order—

(a) must specify the authority or authorities and county council or councils (the constituent authorities) which are to constitute the joint committee;
(b) may make provision as to such other matters as the Secretary of State thinks are necessary or expedient to facilitate the exercise by the joint committee of its functions.

(4) Provision under subsection (3)(b)—

(a) may include provision corresponding to provisions relating to joint committees in Part 6 of the Local Government Act 1972 (c 70);

(b) may apply (with or without modifications) such enactments relating to local authorities as the Secretary of State thinks appropriate.

(5) If an order under this section is annulled in pursuance of a resolution of either House of Parliament—

(a) with effect from the date of the resolution the joint committee ceases to be the local planning authority as mentioned in subsection (2);

(b) anything which the joint committee (as the local planning authority) was required to do for the purposes of this Part must be done for their area by each local planning authority which were a constituent authority of the joint committee;

(c) each of those local planning authorities must revise their local development scheme accordingly.

(6) Nothing in this section or section 30 confers on a local planning authority constituted by virtue of an order under this section any function in relation to section 13 or 14.

(7) The policies adopted by the joint committee in the exercise of its functions under this Part must be taken for the purposes of the planning Acts to be the policies of each of the constituent authorities which are a local planning authority.

(8) Subsection (9) applies to any function—

(a) which is conferred on a local planning authority (within the meaning of the principal Act) under or by virtue of the planning Acts, and

(b) which relates to the authority's local development scheme or local development documents.

(9) If the authority is a constituent authority of a joint committee references to the authority's local development scheme or local development documents must be construed as including references to the scheme or documents of the joint committee.

(10) For the purposes of subsection (4) a local authority is any of the following—

(a) a county council;

(b) a district council;

(c) a London borough council.

NOTES

Initial Commencement

To be appointed: see s 121(1).

Appointment

Appointment (for the purpose of making, or making provision by means of, subordinate legislation): 6 August 2004: see SI 2004/2097, art 2.

Appointment (for remaining purposes): 28 September 2004: see SI 2004/2202, art 2(b); for transitional provisions see SI 2004/2205, reg 6.

Extent

This section does not extend to Scotland: see s 124(1).

A1.396

30   Joint committees: additional functions

(1)   This section applies if the constituent authorities to a joint committee agree that the joint committee is to be, for the purposes of this Part, the local planning authority for any area or matter which is not the subject of—

(a)   an order under section 29, or

(b)   an earlier agreement under this section.

(2)   Each of the constituent authorities and the joint committee must revise their local development scheme in accordance with the agreement.

(3)   With effect from the date when the last such revision takes effect the joint committee is, for the purposes of this Part, the local planning authority for the area or matter mentioned in subsection (1).

NOTES

Initial Commencement

To be appointed: see s 121(1).

Appointment

Appointment: 28 September 2004: see SI 2004/2202, art 2(b); for transitional provisions see SI 2004/2205, reg 6.

Extent

This section does not extend to Scotland: see s 124(1).

A1.397

31   Dissolution of joint committee

(1)   This section applies if a constituent authority requests the Secretary of State to revoke an order constituting a joint committee as the local planning authority for any area or in respect of any matter.

(2)   The Secretary of State may revoke the order.

(3)   Any step taken by the joint committee in relation to a local development scheme or a local development document must be treated for the purposes of any corresponding scheme or document as a step taken by a successor authority.

(4)   A successor authority is—

(a)   a local planning authority which were a constituent authority of the joint committee;

(b)   a joint committee constituted by order under section 29 for an area which does not include an area which was not part of the area of the joint committee mentioned in subsection (1).

(5)   If the revocation takes effect at any time when an independent examination is being carried out in relation to a local development document the examination must be suspended.

(6)   But if before the end of the period prescribed for the purposes of this subsection a successor authority falling within subsection (4)(a) requests the Secretary of State to do so he may direct that—

(a) the examination is resumed in relation to the corresponding document;
(b) any step taken for the purposes of the suspended examination has effect for the purposes of the resumed examination.

(7) The Secretary of State may by regulations make provision as to what is a corresponding scheme or document.

NOTES

Initial Commencement

To be appointed: see s 121(1).

Appointment

Appointment (for the purpose of making, or making provision by means of, subordinate legislation): 6 August 2004: see SI 2004/2097, art 2.

Appointment (for remaining purposes): 28 September 2004: see SI 2004/2202, art 2(b); for transitional provisions see SI 2004/2205, reg 6.

Extent

This section does not extend to Scotland: see s 124(1).

Subordinate Legislation

Town and Country Planning (Local Development) (England) Regulations 2004, SI 2004/2204 (made under sub-ss (6), (7)).

Miscellaneous

A1.398

32   Exclusion of certain representations

(1) This section applies to any representation or objection in respect of anything which is done or is proposed to be done in pursuance of—

(a) an order or scheme under section 10, 14, 16, 18, 106(1) or (3) or 108(1) of the Highways Act 1980 (c 66);
(b) an order or scheme under section 7, 9, 11, 13 or 20 of the Highways Act 1959 (c 25), section 3 of the Highways (Miscellaneous Provisions) Act 1961 (c 63) or section 1 or 10 of the Highways Act 1971 (c 41) (which provisions were replaced by the provisions mentioned in paragraph (a));
(c) an order under section 1 of the New Towns Act 1981 (c 64).

(2) If the Secretary of State or a local planning authority thinks that a representation made in relation to a local development document is in substance a representation or objection to which this section applies he or they (as the case may be) may disregard it.

NOTES

Initial Commencement

To be appointed: see s 121(1).

Appointment

Appointment: 28 September 2004: see SI 2004/2202, art 2(b); for transitional provisions see SI 2004/2205, reg 6.

Extent

This section does not extend to Scotland: see s 124(1).

A1.399

33   Urban development corporations

The Secretary of State may direct that this Part does not apply to the area of an urban development corporation.

NOTES

Initial Commencement

To be appointed: see s 121(1).

Appointment

Appointment: 28 September 2004: see SI 2004/2202, art 2(b); for transitional provisions see SI 2004/2205, reg 6.

Extent

This section does not extend to Scotland: see s 124(1).

See Further

See further, in relation to the application of this section, with modifications, in respect of the Olympic Delivery Authority as it applies in relation to an urban development corporation: the London Olympic Games and Paralympic Games Act 2006, s 5.

A1.400

34   Guidance

In the exercise of any function conferred under or by virtue of this Part the local planning authority must have regard to any guidance issued by the Secretary of State.

NOTES

Initial Commencement

To be appointed: see s 121(1).

Appointment

Appointment: 28 September 2004: see SI 2004/2202, art 2(b); for transitional provisions see SI 2004/2205, reg 6.

Extent

This section does not extend to Scotland: see s 124(1).

A1.401

35   Annual monitoring report

(1) Every local planning authority must make an annual report to the Secretary of State.

(2)   The annual report must contain such information as is prescribed as to—

    (a)   the implementation of the local development scheme;

    (b)   the extent to which the policies set out in the local development documents are being achieved.

(3)   The annual report must—

    (a)   be in respect of such period of 12 months as is prescribed;

    (b)   be made at such time as is prescribed;

    (c)   be in such form as is prescribed;

    (d)   contain such other matter as is prescribed.

NOTES

Initial Commencement

To be appointed: see s 121(1).

Appointment

Appointment (for the purpose of making, or making provision by means of, subordinate legislation): 6 August 2004: see SI 2004/2097, art 2.

Appointment (for remaining purposes): 28 September 2004: see SI 2004/2202, art 2(b); for transitional provisions see SI 2004/2205, reg 6.

Extent

This section does not extend to Scotland: see s 124(1).

Subordinate Legislation

Town and Country Planning (Local Development) (England) Regulations 2004, SI 2004/2204 (made under sub-ss (2), (3)).

General

A1.402

36   Regulations

(1)   The Secretary of State may by regulations make provision in connection with the exercise by any person of functions under this Part.

(2)   The regulations may in particular make provision as to—

    (a)   the procedure to be followed by the local planning authority in carrying out the appraisal under section 19;

    (b)   the procedure to be followed in the preparation of local development documents;

    (c)   requirements about the giving of notice and publicity;

    (d)   requirements about inspection by the public of a local development document or any other document;

    (e)   the nature and extent of consultation with and participation by the public in anything done under this Part;

    (f)   the making of representations about any matter to be included in a local development document;

    (g)   consideration of any such representations;

    (h)   the remuneration and allowances payable to a person appointed to carry out an independent examination under section 20;

(i)   the determination of the time at which anything must be done for the purposes of this Part;

(j)   the manner of publication of any draft, report or other document published under this Part;

(k)   monitoring the exercise by local planning authorities of their functions under this Part;

(l)   the making of reasonable charges for the provision of copies of documents required by or under this Part.

NOTES

Initial Commencement

To be appointed: see s 121(1).

Appointment

Appointment: 6 August 2004: see SI 2004/2097, art 2.

Extent

This section does not extend to Scotland: see s 124(1).

Subordinate Legislation

Town and Country Planning (Local Development) (England) Regulations 2004, SI 2004/2204.

A1.403

37   Interpretation

(1)   Local development scheme must be construed in accordance with section 15.

(2)   Local development document must be construed in accordance with section 17.

(3)   A development plan document is a document which—

(a)   is a local development document, and
(b)   forms part of the development plan.

(4)   Local planning authorities are—

(a)   district councils;
(b)   London borough councils;
(c)   metropolitan district councils;
(d)   county councils in relation to any area in England for which there is no district council;
(e)   the Broads Authority.

(5)   A National Park authority is the local planning authority for the whole of its area and subsection (4) must be construed subject to that.

(6)   RSS and RPB must be construed in accordance with Part 1.

(7)   This section applies for the purposes of this Part.

NOTES

Initial Commencement

To be appointed: see s 121(1).

Appointment

Appointment: 28 September 2004: see SI 2004/2202, art 2(b); for transitional provisions see SI 2004/2205, reg 6.

Extent

This section does not extend to Scotland: see s 124(1).

See Further

See further, in relation to the New Forest National Park Authority: the New Forest National Park Authority (Establishment) Order 2005, SI 2005/421, art 17, Sch 4, para 12.

PART 3: DEVELOPMENT

Development plan

A1.404

38   Development plan

(1)   A reference to the development plan in any enactment mentioned in subsection (7) must be construed in accordance with subsections (2) to (5).

(2)   For the purposes of any area in Greater London the development plan is—

    (a)   the spatial development strategy, and
    (b)   the development plan documents (taken as a whole) which have been adopted or approved in relation to that area.

(3)   For the purposes of any other area in England the development plan is—

    (a)   the regional spatial strategy for the region in which the area is situated, and
    (b)   the development plan documents (taken as a whole) which have been adopted or approved in relation to that area.

(4)   For the purposes of any area in Wales the development plan is the local development plan adopted or approved in relation to that area.

(5)   If to any extent a policy contained in a development plan for an area conflicts with another policy in the development plan the conflict must be resolved in favour of the policy which is contained in the last document to be adopted, approved or published (as the case may be).

(6)   If regard is to be had to the development plan for the purpose of any determination to be made under the planning Acts the determination must be made in accordance with the plan unless material considerations indicate otherwise.

(7)   The enactments are—

    (a)   this Act;
    (b)   the planning Acts;
    (c)   any other enactment relating to town and country planning;
    (d)   the Land Compensation Act 1961 (c 33);
    (e)   the Highways Act 1980 (c 66).

(8)   In subsection (5) references to a development plan include a development plan for the purposes of paragraph 1 of Schedule 8.

NOTES

Initial Commencement

To be appointed: see s 121(1), (2)(a).

Appointment

Appointment (in relation to England): 28 September 2004: see SI 2004/2202, art 2(c).

Appointment (in relation to Wales): 15 October 2005: see SI 2005/2847, art 2(a); for transitional provisions see art 3(1), (2) thereof.

Extent

This section does not extend to Scotland: see s 124(1).

Sustainable development

A1.405

39   Sustainable development

(1)   This section applies to any person who or body which exercises any function—

(a)   under Part 1 in relation to a regional spatial strategy;
(b)   under Part 2 in relation to local development documents;
(c)   under Part 6 in relation to the Wales Spatial Plan or a local development plan.

(2)   The person or body must exercise the function with the objective of contributing to the achievement of sustainable development.

(3)   For the purposes of subsection (2) the person or body must have regard to national policies and advice contained in guidance issued by—

(a)   the Secretary of State for the purposes of subsection (1)(a) and (b);
(b)   the National Assembly for Wales for the purposes of subsection (1)(c).

NOTES

Initial Commencement

To be appointed: see s 121(1), (2)(a).

Appointment

Appointment (in relation to England): 28 September 2004: see SI 2004/2202, art 2(d).

Appointment (in relation to Wales): 15 October 2005: see SI 2005/2847, art 2(b).

Extent

This section does not extend to Scotland: see s 124(1).

PART 4: DEVELOPMENT CONTROL

Local development orders

A1.406

40   Local development orders

(1)   In the principal Act after section 61 (supplementary provision about development orders) there are inserted the following sections—

'Local development orders

61A   Local development orders

(1)   A local planning authority may by order (a local development order) make provision to implement policies—

  (a)   in one or more development plan documents (within the meaning of Part 2 of the Planning and Compulsory Purchase Act 2004);
  (b)   in a local development plan (within the meaning of Part 6 of that Act).

(2)   A local development order may grant planning permission—

  (a)   for development specified in the order;
  (b)   for development of any class so specified.

(3)   A local development order may relate to—

  (a)   all land in the area of the relevant authority;
  (b)   any part of that land;
  (c)   a site specified in the order.

(4)   A local development order may make different provision for different descriptions of land.

(5)   But a development order may specify any area or class of development in respect of which a local development order must not be made.

(6)   A local planning authority may revoke a local development order at any time.

(7)   Schedule 4A makes provision in connection with local development orders.

61B   Intervention by Secretary of State or National Assembly

(1)   At any time before a local development order is adopted by a local planning authority the appropriate authority may direct that the order (or any part of it) is submitted to it for its approval.

(2)   If the appropriate authority gives a direction under subsection (1)—

  (a)   the authority must not take any step in connection with the adoption of the order until the appropriate authority gives its decision;
  (b)   the order has no effect unless it (or, if the direction relates to only part of an order, the part) has been approved by the appropriate authority.

(3)   In considering an order or part of an order submitted under subsection (1) the appropriate authority may take account of any matter which it thinks is relevant.

(4)   It is immaterial whether any such matter was taken account of by the local planning authority.

(5)   The appropriate authority—

  (a)   may approve or reject an order or part of an order submitted to it under subsection (1);
  (b)   must give reasons for its decision under paragraph (a).

(6)   If the appropriate authority thinks that a local development order is unsatisfactory—

  (a)   it may at any time before the order is adopted by the local planning authority direct them to modify it in accordance with the direction;
  (b)   if it gives such a direction it must state its reasons for doing so.

(7)   The local planning authority—

    (a)   must comply with the direction;

    (b)   must not adopt the order unless the appropriate authority gives notice that it is satisfied that they have complied with the direction.

(8)   The appropriate authority—

    (a)   may at any time by order revoke a local development order if it thinks it is expedient to do so;

    (b)   must, if it revokes a local development order, state its reasons for doing so.

(9)   Subsections (3) to (6) of section 100 apply to an order under subsection (8) above as they apply to an order under subsection (1) of that section and for that purpose references to the Secretary of State must be construed as references to the appropriate authority.

(10)   The appropriate authority is—

    (a)   the Secretary of State in relation to England;

    (b)   the National Assembly for Wales in relation to Wales.

61C   Permission granted by local development order

(1)   Planning permission granted by a local development order may be granted—

    (a)   unconditionally, or

    (b)   subject to such conditions or limitations as are specified in the order.

(2)   If the permission is granted for development of a specified description the order may enable the local planning authority to direct that the permission does not apply in relation to—

    (a)   development in a particular area, or

    (b)   any particular development.'

(2)   In each of the following provisions of the principal Act in each place where it occurs after 'development order' there is inserted 'or a local development order'—

    (a)   section 56(5)(a) (definition of material development);

    (b)   section 57(3) (extent of permission granted by development order);

    (c)   section 58(1)(a) (grant of planning permission by development order);

    (d)   section 77(1) (certain applications to be referred to the Secretary of State);

    (e)   section 78(1)(c) (right of appeal in relation to certain planning decisions);

    (f)   section 88(9) (grant of planning permission in enterprise zone);

    (g)   section 91(4)(a) (no limit to duration of planning permission granted by development order);

    (h)   section 108 (compensation for refusal of planning permission formerly granted by development order);

    (i)   section 109(6) (apportionment of compensation for depreciation);

    (j)   section 253(2)(c) (cases in which certain procedures may be carried out in anticipation of planning permission);

    (k)   section 264(5)(b) (land treated not as operational land);

    (l)   section 279(1)(a)(i) (compensation for certain decisions and orders).

(3)   Section 333 of the principal Act (regulations and orders) is amended as follows—

    (a)   in subsection (4) after '55(2)(f),' there is inserted '61A(5)';

    (b)   in subsection (5)(b) after '28,' there is inserted '61A(5) (unless it is made by the National Assembly for Wales),'.

(4)   Schedule 1 further amends the principal Act.

NOTES

Initial Commencement

To be appointed: see s 121(1), (2)(b).

Appointment

Appointment (for the purpose of making, or making provision by means of, subordinate legislation): 6 August 2004: see SI 2004/2097, art 2.

Appointment (in relation to England for remaining purposes): 10 May 2006: see SI 2006/1061, art 2(a).

Extent

This section does not extend to Scotland: see s 124(1).

Revision of development orders

A1.407

41   Effect of revision or revocation of development order on incomplete development

In the principal Act after section 61C (planning permission granted by local development orders) (inserted by section 40 of this Act) there is inserted the following section—

'61D   Effect of revision or revocation of development order on incomplete development

(1)   A development order or local development order may include provision permitting the completion of development if—

    (a)   planning permission is granted by the order in respect of the development, and

    (b)   the planning permission is withdrawn at a time after the development is started but before it is completed.

(2)   Planning permission granted by a development order is withdrawn—

    (a)   if the order is revoked;

    (b)   if the order is amended so that it ceases to grant planning permission in respect of the development or materially changes any condition or limitation to which the grant of permission is subject;

    (c)   by the issue of a direction under powers conferred by the order.

(3)   Planning permission granted by a local development order is withdrawn—

    (a)   if the order is revoked under section 61A(6) or 61B(8);

    (b)   if the order is revised in pursuance of paragraph 2 of Schedule 4A so that it ceases to grant planning permission in respect of the development or materially changes any condition or limitation to which the grant of permission is subject;

    (c)   by the issue of a direction under powers conferred by the order.

(4)   The power under this section to include provision in a development order or a local development order may be exercised differently for different purposes.'

NOTES

Initial Commencement

To be appointed: see s 121(1), (2)(b).

Appointment

Appointment (for the purpose of making, or making provision by means of, subordinate legislation): 6 August 2004: see SI 2004/2097, art 2.

Appointment (in relation to England for remaining purposes): 10 May 2006: see SI 2006/1061, art 2(a).

Extent

This section does not extend to Scotland: see s 124(1).

Applications

A1.408

42   Applications for planning permission and certain consents

(1)   In the principal Act for section 62 (form and content of applications for planning permission) there is substituted the following section—

'62   Applications for planning permission

(1)   A development order may make provision as to applications for planning permission made to a local planning authority.

(2)   Provision referred to in subsection (1) includes provision as to—

  (a)   the form and manner in which the application must be made;
  (b)   particulars of such matters as are to be included in the application;
  (c)   documents or other materials as are to accompany the application.

(3)   The local planning authority may require that an application for planning permission must include—

  (a)   such particulars as they think necessary;
  (b)   such evidence in support of anything in or relating to the application as they think necessary.

(4)   But a requirement under subsection (3) must not be inconsistent with provision made under subsection (1).

(5)   A development order must require that an application for planning permission of such description as is specified in the order must be accompanied by such of the following as is so specified—

  (a)   a statement about the design principles and concepts that have been applied to the development;
  (b)   a statement about how issues relating to access to the development have been dealt with.

(6)   The form and content of a statement mentioned in subsection (5) is such as is required by the development order.'

(2)   In section 73 of the principal Act (determination of applications to develop land without compliance with conditions previously attached) subsection (3) is omitted.

(3)   In section 198 of that Act (tree preservation orders) after subsection (7) there is inserted—

'(8)   In relation to an application for consent under a tree preservation order the appropriate authority may by regulations make provision as to—

  (a)   the form and manner in which the application must be made;

(b)   particulars of such matters as are to be included in the application;

(c)   the documents or other materials as are to accompany the application.

(9)   The appropriate authority is—

(a)   the Secretary of State in relation to England;

(b)   the National Assembly for Wales in relation to Wales,

and in the case of regulations made by the National Assembly for Wales section 333(3) must be ignored.'

(4)   In section 220 of that Act (regulations controlling display of advertisements) after subsection (2) there is inserted the following subsection—

'(2A)   The regulations may also make provision as to—

(a)   the form and manner in which an application for consent must be made;

(b)   particulars of such matters as are to be included in the application;

(c)   any documents or other materials which must accompany the application.'

(5)   In the principal Act before section 328 (settled land and land of universities and colleges) there is inserted the following section—

'327A   Applications: compliance with requirements

(1)   This section applies to any application in respect of which this Act or any provision made under it imposes a requirement as to—

(a)   the form or manner in which the application must be made;

(b)   the form or content of any document or other matter which accompanies the application.

(2)   The local planning authority must not entertain such an application if it fails to comply with the requirement.'

(6)   In section 10(2) of the listed buildings Act (applications for listed buildings consent) the words from 'shall be made' to 'require and' are omitted.

(7)   In section 10(3) of that Act for paragraph (a) there are substituted the following paragraphs—

'(a)   the form and manner in which such applications are to be made;

(aa)   particulars of such matters as are to be included in such applications;

(ab)   the documents or other materials as are to accompany such applications;'.

(8)   In section 10 of that Act after subsection (3) there are inserted the following subsections—

'(4)   The regulations must require that an application for listed building consent of such description as is prescribed must be accompanied by such of the following as is prescribed—

(a)   a statement about the design principles and concepts that have been applied to the works;

(b)   a statement about how issues relating to access to the building have been dealt with.

(5)   The form and content of a statement mentioned in subsection (4) is such as is prescribed.'

(9)   In section 89(1) of that Act (application of certain provisions of the principal Act) after the entry relating to section 323 there is inserted—

'section 327A (compliance with requirements relating to applications),'.

NOTES

Initial Commencement

To be appointed: see s 121(1), (2)(b).

Appointment

Appointment (for the purpose of making, or making provision by means of, subordinate legislation): 6 August 2004: see SI 2004/2097, art 2.

Sub-ss (1), (5)–(9): Appointment (in relation to England for remaining purposes): 10 August 2006: see SI 2006/1061, art 3(a); for savings see art 4 thereof.

Sub-ss (1), (5)–(9): Appointment (in relation to Wales for remaining purposes): 30 June 2007: see SI 2007/1369, art 2(a); for savings see art 3 thereof.

Extent

This section does not extend to Scotland: see s 124(1).

A1.409

43   Power to decline to determine applications

(1)   For section 70A of the principal Act (power of local planning authority to decline to determine application) there are substituted the following sections—

'70A   Power to decline to determine subsequent application

(1)   A local planning authority may decline to determine a relevant application if—

(a)   any of the conditions in subsections (2) to (4) is satisfied, and
(b)   the authority think there has been no significant change in the relevant considerations since the relevant event.

(2)   The condition is that in the period of two years ending with the date on which the application mentioned in subsection (1) is received the Secretary of State has refused a similar application referred to him under section 76A or 77.

(3)   The condition is that in that period the Secretary of State has dismissed an appeal—

(a)   against the refusal of a similar application, or
(b)   under section 78(2) in respect of a similar application.

(4)   The condition is that—

(a)   in that period the local planning authority have refused more than one similar application, and
(b)   there has been no appeal to the Secretary of State against any such refusal.

(5)   A relevant application is—

(a)   an application for planning permission for the development of any land;
(b)   an application for approval in pursuance of section 60(2).

(6)   The relevant considerations are—

(a)   the development plan so far as material to the application;
(b)   any other material considerations.

(7)   The relevant event is—

(a)   for the purposes of subsections (2) and (4) the refusal of the similar application;

(b)   for the purposes of subsection (3) the dismissal of the appeal.

(8)   An application for planning permission is similar to another application if (and only if) the local planning authority think that the development and the land to which the applications relate are the same or substantially the same.

70B   Power to decline to determine overlapping application

(1)   A local planning authority may decline to determine an application for planning permission for the development of any land which is made at a time when any of the conditions in subsections (2) to (4) applies in relation to a similar application.

(2)   The condition is that a similar application is under consideration by the local planning authority and the determination period for that application has not expired.

(3)   The condition is that a similar application is under consideration by the Secretary of State in pursuance of section 76A or 77 or on an appeal under section 78 and the Secretary of State has not issued his decision.

(4)   The condition is that a similar application—

  (a)   has been granted by the local planning authority,
  (b)   has been refused by them, or
  (c)   has not been determined by them within the determination period,

and the time within which an appeal could be made to the Secretary of State under section 78 has not expired.

(5)   An application for planning permission is similar to another application if (and only if) the local planning authority think that the development and the land to which the applications relate are the same or substantially the same.

(6)   The determination period is—

  (a)   the period prescribed by the development order for the determination of the application, or
  (b)   such longer period as the applicant and the authority have agreed for the determination of the application.'

(2)   In section 78(2)(aa) of that Act after '70A' there is inserted 'or 70B'.

(3)   After section 81 of the listed buildings Act (authorities with functions under the Act) there are inserted the following sections—

'Power to decline to determine application

81A   Power to decline to determine subsequent application

(1)   A local planning authority may decline to determine an application for a relevant consent if—

  (a)   one or more of the conditions in subsections (2) to (4) is satisfied, and
  (b)   the authority think there has been no significant change in any material considerations since the relevant event.

(2)   The condition is that in the period of two years ending with the date on which the application mentioned in subsection (1) is received the Secretary of State has refused a similar application referred to him under section 12.

(3)   The condition is that in that period the Secretary of State has dismissed an appeal—

  (a)   against the refusal of a similar application, or
  (b)   under section 20(2) in respect of a similar application.

(4)   The condition is that—

(a)   in that period the local planning authority have refused more than one similar application, and

(b)   there has been no appeal to the Secretary of State against any such refusal.

(5)   Relevant consent is—

(a)   listed building consent, or
(b)   conservation area consent.

(6)   The relevant event is—

(a)   for the purposes of subsections (2) and (4) the refusal of the similar application;

(b)   for the purposes of subsection (3) the dismissal of the appeal.

(7)   An application for relevant consent is similar to another application if (and only if) the local planning authority think that the building and works to which the applications relate are the same or substantially the same.

(8)   For the purposes of an application for conservation area consent a reference to a provision of this Act is a reference to that provision as excepted or modified by regulations under section 74.

81B   Power to decline to determine overlapping application

(1)   A local planning authority may decline to determine an application for a relevant consent which is made at a time when any of the conditions in subsections (2) to (4) applies in relation to a similar application.

(2)   The condition is that a similar application is under consideration by the local planning authority and the determination period for that application has not expired.

(3)   The condition is that a similar application is under consideration by the Secretary of State in pursuance of section 12 or on an appeal under section 20 and the Secretary of State has not issued his decision.

(4)   The condition is that a similar application—

(a)   has been granted by the local planning authority,
(b)   has been refused by them, or
(c)   has not been determined by them within the determination period,

and the time within which an appeal could be made to the Secretary of State under section 20 has not expired.

(5)   Relevant consent is—

(a)   listed building consent, or
(b)   conservation area consent.

(6)   An application for relevant consent is similar to another application if (and only if) the local planning authority think that the building and works to which the applications relate are the same or substantially the same.

(7)   The determination period is—

(a)   the period prescribed for the determination of the application, or
(b)   such longer period as the applicant and the authority have agreed for the determination of the application.

(8)   For the purposes of an application for conservation area consent a reference to a provision of this Act is a reference to that provision as excepted or modified by regulations under section 74.'

(4) Section 20(2) of that Act (appeals) is amended as follows—

    (a)   for 'neither' there is substituted 'done none of the following';

    (b)   after paragraph (a) for 'nor' there is substituted—

'(aa) given notice to the applicant that they have exercised their power under section 81A or 81B to decline to determine the application;'.

(5) This section has effect only in relation to applications made under the principal Act or the listed buildings Act which are received by the local planning authority after this section comes into force.

NOTES

Initial Commencement

To be appointed: see s 121(1), (2)(b).

Appointment

Appointment (in relation to England for certain purposes): 24 August 2005: see SI 2005/2081, art 2(a).

Extent

This section does not extend to Scotland: see s 124(1).

Major infrastructure projects

A1.410

44   **Major infrastructure projects**

In the principal Act the following sections are inserted before section 77 (Reference of applications to the Secretary of State)—

'76A   **Major infrastructure projects**

(1) This section applies to—

    (a)   an application for planning permission;

    (b)   an application for the approval of a local planning authority required under a development order,

if the Secretary of State thinks that the development to which the application relates is of national or regional importance.

(2) The Secretary of State may direct that the application must be referred to him instead of being dealt with by the local planning authority.

(3) If the Secretary of State gives a direction under subsection (2) he may also direct that any application—

    (a)   under or for the purposes of the planning Acts, and

    (b)   which he thinks is connected with the application mentioned in subsection (1),

must also be referred to him instead of being dealt with by the local planning authority.

(4) If the Secretary of State gives a direction under this section—

    (a)   the application must be referred to him;

    (b)   he must appoint an inspector to consider the application.

(5) If the Secretary of State gives a direction under subsection (2) the applicant must prepare an economic impact report which must—

(a) be in such form and contain such matter as is prescribed by development order;

(b) be submitted to the Secretary of State in accordance with such provision as is so prescribed.

(6) For the purposes of subsection (5) the Secretary of State may, by development order, prescribe such requirements as to publicity and notice as he thinks appropriate.

(7) A direction under this section or section 76B may be varied or revoked by a subsequent direction.

(8) The decision of the Secretary of State on any application referred to him under this section is final.

(9) Regional relates to a region listed in Schedule 1 to the Regional Development Agencies Act 1998 (c 45).

(10) The following provisions of this Act apply (with any necessary modifications) to an application referred to the Secretary of State under this section as they apply to an application which falls to be determined by a local planning authority—

(a) section 70;
(b) section 72(1) and (5);
(c) section 73;
(d) section 73A.

(11) A development order may apply (with or without modifications) any requirements imposed by the order by virtue of section 65 or 71 to an application referred to the Secretary of State under this section.

(12) This section does not apply to an application which relates to the development of land in Wales.

76B   Major infrastructure projects: inspectors

(1) This section applies if the Secretary of State appoints an inspector under section 76A(4)(b) (the lead inspector).

(2) The Secretary of State may direct the lead inspector—

(a) to consider such matters relating to the application as are prescribed;
(b) to make recommendations to the Secretary of State on those matters.

(3) After considering any recommendations of the lead inspector the Secretary of State may—

(a) appoint such number of additional inspectors as he thinks appropriate;
(b) direct that each of the additional inspectors must consider such matters relating to the application as the lead inspector decides.

(4) An additional inspector must—

(a) comply with such directions as to procedural matters as the lead inspector gives;
(b) report to the lead inspector on the matters he is appointed to consider.

(5) A copy of directions given as mentioned in subsection (4)(a) must be given to—

(a) the person who made the application;
(b) the local planning authority;
(c) any other person who requests it.

(6) If the Secretary of State does not act under subsection (3) he must direct the lead inspector to consider the application on his own.

(7) In every case the lead inspector must report to the Secretary of State on—

    (a) his consideration of the application;

    (b) the consideration of the additional inspectors (if any) of the matters mentioned in subsection (3)(b).

(8) The function of the lead inspector in pursuance of subsection (2)—

    (a) may be exercised from time to time;

    (b) includes making recommendations as to the number of additional inspectors required from time to time.

(9) The power of the Secretary of State under subsection (3) to appoint an additional inspector includes power to revoke such an appointment.'

NOTES

Initial Commencement

To be appointed: see s 121(1).

Appointment

Appointment (for the purpose of making, or making provision by means of, subordinate legislation): 6 August 2004: see SI 2004/2097, art 2.

Appointment (in relation to England for remaining purposes): 24 August 2005: see SI 2005/2081, art 2(b); for savings see art 4(1) thereof.

Extent

This section does not extend to Scotland: see s 124(1).

Simplified planning zones

A1.411

45   Simplified planning zones

(1) In section 83 of the principal Act (making simplified planning zone schemes) subsection (1) is omitted.

(2) Before section 83(2) of that Act there are inserted the following subsections—

'(1A) This section applies if—

    (a) the regional spatial strategy for the region in which the area of a local planning authority in England is situated identifies the need for a simplified planning zone in that area (or any part of it);

    (b) the criteria prescribed by the National Assembly for Wales for the need for a simplified planning zone are satisfied in relation to the area (or any part of the area) of a local planning authority in Wales.

(1B) The local planning authority must consider the question for which part or parts of their area a simplified planning zone scheme is desirable.

(1C) The local planning authority must keep under review the question mentioned in subsection (1B).'

(3) For section 83(2) of that Act there are substituted the following subsections—

'(2) A local planning authority must make a simplified planning zone scheme for all or any part of their area—

(a) if as a result of the consideration mentioned in subsection (1B) or the review mentioned in subsection (1C) they decide that it is desirable to do so;

(b) if they are directed to do so by the Secretary of State or the National Assembly for Wales (as the case may be).

(2A) A local planning authority may at any time—

(a) alter a scheme adopted by them;

(b) with the consent of the Secretary of State alter a scheme made or altered by him under paragraph 12 of Schedule 7 or approved by him under paragraph 11 of that Schedule;

(c) with the consent of the National Assembly for Wales alter a scheme made or altered by it under paragraph 12 of Schedule 7 or approved by it under paragraph 11 of that Schedule.

(2B) A simplified planning zone scheme for an area in England must be in conformity with the regional spatial strategy.'

(4) In section 83 of that Act after subsection (3) there is inserted the following subsection—

'(4) In this section and in Schedule 7—

(a) a reference to the regional spatial strategy must be construed in relation to any area in Greater London as a reference to the spatial development strategy;

(b) a reference to a region must be construed in relation to such an area as a reference to Greater London.'

(5) In section 85(1) of that Act (duration of simplified planning zone scheme) for the words from 'period' to the end there is substituted 'specified period'.

(6) After section 85(1) of that Act there is inserted the following subsection—

'(1A) The specified period is the period not exceeding 10 years—

(a) beginning with the date when the scheme is adopted or approved, and

(b) which is specified in the scheme.'

(7) In Schedule 7 of that Act in paragraph 2 (notification of proposal to make scheme) for 'decide under section 83(2) to make or' there is substituted 'are required under section 83(2) to make or decide under section 83(2A) to'.

(8) In Schedule 7 of that Act paragraphs 3 and 4 are omitted.

(9) In Schedule 7 of that Act in paragraph 12 (default powers of Secretary of State) for sub-paragraph (1) there are substituted the following sub-paragraphs—

'(1) This paragraph applies if each of the following conditions is satisfied.

(1A) The first condition is that—

(a) the regional spatial strategy for the region in which the area of a local planning authority is situated identifies the need for a simplified planning zone in any part of their area, or

(b) the criteria prescribed by the National Assembly for Wales for the need for a simplified planning zone are satisfied in relation to the area of a local planning authority in Wales.

(1B) The second condition is that the Secretary of State or the National Assembly for Wales (as the case may be) is satisfied after holding a local inquiry or other hearing that the authority are not taking within a reasonable period the steps required by this Schedule for the adoption of proposals for the making or alteration of a scheme.

(1C) The Secretary of State or the National Assembly for Wales (as the case may be) may make or alter the scheme.'

NOTES

Initial Commencement

To be appointed: see s 121(1), (2)(b).

Extent

This section does not extend to Scotland: see s 124(1).

Planning contribution

A1.412

46   Planning contribution

(1)   The Secretary of State may, by regulations, make provision for the making of a planning contribution in relation to the development or use of land in the area of a local planning authority.

(2)   The contribution may be made—

    (a)   by the prescribed means,
    (b)   by compliance with the relevant requirements, or
    (c)   by a combination of such means and compliance.

(3)   The regulations may require the local planning authority to include in a development plan document (or in such other document as is prescribed)—

    (a)   a statement of the developments or uses or descriptions of development or use in relation to which they will consider accepting a planning contribution;
    (b)   a statement of the matters relating to development or use in relation to which they will not consider accepting a contribution by the prescribed means;
    (c)   the purposes to which receipts from payments made in respect of contributions are (in whole or in part) to be put;
    (d)   the criteria by reference to which the value of a contribution made by the prescribed means is to be determined.

(4)   The regulations may make provision as to circumstances in which—

    (a)   except in the case of a contribution to which subsection (3)(b) applies, the person making the contribution (the contributor) must state the form in which he will make the contribution;
    (b)   the contribution may not be made by compliance with the relevant requirements if it is made by the prescribed means;
    (c)   the contribution may not be made by the prescribed means if it is made by compliance with the relevant requirements;
    (d)   a contribution must not be made.

(5)   The prescribed means are—

    (a)   the payment of a sum the amount and terms of payment of which are determined in accordance with criteria published by the local planning authority for the purposes of subsection (3)(d),
    (b)   the provision of a benefit in kind the value of which is so determined, or
    (c)   a combination of such payment and provision.

(6)   The relevant requirements are such requirements relating to the development or use as are—

(a)   prescribed for the purposes of this section, and
(b)   included as part of the terms of the contribution,

and may include a requirement to make a payment of a sum.

(7)   Development plan document must be construed in accordance with section 37(3).

NOTES

Initial Commencement

To be appointed: see s 121(1), (2)(b).

Appointment

Appointment (for the purpose of making, or making provision by means of, subordinate legislation): 6 August 2004: see SI 2004/2097, art 2.

Extent

This section does not extend to Scotland: see s 124(1).

A1.413

47   Planning contribution: regulations

(1)   This section applies for the purpose of regulations made under section 46.

(2)   Maximum and minimum amounts may be prescribed in relation to a payment falling within section 46(5)(a).

(3)   Provision may be made to enable periodic adjustment of the criteria mentioned in section 46(3)(d).

(4)   The local planning authority may be required to publish an annual report containing such information in relation to the planning contribution as is prescribed.

(5)   If a document is prescribed for the purposes of section 46(3) the regulations may prescribe—

(a)   the procedure for its preparation and the time at which it must be published;
(b)   the circumstances in which and the procedure by which the Secretary of State may take steps in relation to the preparation of the document.

(6)   Provision may be made for the enforcement by the local planning authority of the terms of a planning contribution including provision—

(a)   for a person obstructing the taking of such steps as are prescribed to be guilty of an offence punishable by a fine not exceeding level 3 on the standard scale;
(b)   for a person deriving title to the land from the contributor to be bound by the terms of the contribution;
(c)   for a condition to be attached to any planning permission relating to the land requiring the contribution to be made before any development is started;
(d)   for the enforcement of a planning contribution in respect of land which is Crown land within the meaning of section 293(1) of the principal Act.

(7)   The regulations may—

(a)   require the local planning authority to apply receipts from planning contributions made by the prescribed means only to purposes mentioned in section 46(3)(c);
(b)   make provision for setting out in writing the terms of the planning contribution;

    (c)   make provision in relation to the modification or discharge of a planning contribution.

(8) The regulations may—

    (a)   make different provision in relation to the areas of different local planning authorities or different descriptions of local planning authority;

    (b)   exclude their application (in whole or in part) in relation to the area of one or more local planning authorities or descriptions of local planning authority.

NOTES

Initial Commencement

To be appointed: see s 121(1), (2)(b).

Appointment

Appointment (for the purpose of making, or making provision by means of, subordinate legislation): 6 August 2004: see SI 2004/2097, art 2.

Extent

This section does not extend to Scotland: see s 124(1).

A1.414

48   Planning contribution: Wales

In relation to land in Wales, sections 46 and 47 apply subject to the following modifications—

    (a)   references to the Secretary of State must be construed as references to the National Assembly for Wales;

    (b)   the reference to a development plan document must be construed as a reference to a local development plan (within the meaning of section 62).

NOTES

Initial Commencement

To be appointed: see s 121(1), (2)(b).

Appointment

Appointment (for the purpose of making, or making provision by means of, subordinate legislation): 6 August 2004: see SI 2004/2097, art 2.

Miscellaneous

A1.415

49   Development to include certain internal operations

(1) In the principal Act in section 55 (meaning of development) after subsection (2) there are inserted the following subsections—

'(2A) The Secretary of State may in a development order specify any circumstances or description of circumstances in which subsection (2) does not apply to operations mentioned in paragraph (a) of that subsection which have the effect of increasing the gross floor space of the building by such amount or percentage amount as is so specified.

(2B) The development order may make different provision for different purposes.'

(2) This subsection applies if—

(a) section 55(2) of the principal Act is disapplied in respect of any operations by virtue of a development order under section 55(2A) of that Act,

(b) at the date the development order comes into force a certificate under section 192 of the principal Act (certificate of lawfulness of proposed use or development) is in force in respect of the operations, and

(c) before that date no such operations have been begun.

(3) If subsection (2) applies the certificate under section 192 of the principal Act is of no effect.

(4) A development order made for the purposes of section 55(2A) of the principal Act does not affect any operations begun before it is made.

NOTES

Initial Commencement

To be appointed: see s 121(1), (2)(b).

Appointment

Appointment (for the purpose of making, or making provision by means of, subordinate legislation): 6 August 2004: see SI 2004/2097, art 2.

Appointment (in relation to England for remaining purposes): 10 May 2006: see SI 2006/1061, art 2(b).

Extent

This section does not extend to Scotland: see s 124(1).

A1.416

50   Appeal made: functions of local planning authority

(1) In the principal Act after section 78 (right to appeal) there is inserted the following section—

'78A   Appeal made: functions of local planning authorities

(1) This section applies if a person who has made an application mentioned in section 78(1)(a) appeals to the Secretary of State under section 78(2).

(2) At any time before the end of the additional period the local planning authority may give the notice referred to in section 78(2).

(3) If the local planning authority give notice as mentioned in subsection (2) that their decision is to refuse the application—

(a) the appeal must be treated as an appeal under section 78(1) against the refusal;

(b) the Secretary of State must give the person making the appeal an opportunity to revise the grounds of the appeal;

(c) the Secretary of State must give such a person an opportunity to change any option the person has chosen relating to the procedure for the appeal.

(4) If the local planning authority give notice as mentioned in subsection (2) that their decision is to grant the application subject to conditions the Secretary of State must give the person making the appeal the opportunity—

(a) to proceed with the appeal as an appeal under section 78(1) against the grant of the application subject to conditions;
(b) to revise the grounds of the appeal;
(c) to change any option the person has chosen relating to the procedure for the appeal.

(5) The Secretary of State must not issue his decision on the appeal before the end of the additional period.

(6) The additional period is the period prescribed by development order for the purposes of this section and which starts on the day on which the person appeals under section 78(2).'

(2) In the listed buildings Act after section 20 (right to appeal) there is inserted the following section—

'20A   Appeal made: functions of local planning authorities

(1) This section applies if a person who has made an application mentioned in section 20(1)(a) appeals to the Secretary of State under section 20(2).

(2) At any time before the end of the additional period the local planning authority may give the notice referred to in section 20(2).

(3) If the local planning authority give notice as mentioned in subsection (2) that their decision is to refuse the application—

(a) the appeal must be treated as an appeal under section 20(1) against the refusal;
(b) the Secretary of State must give the person making the appeal an opportunity to revise the grounds of the appeal;
(c) the Secretary of State must give such a person an opportunity to change any option the person has chosen relating to the procedure for the appeal.

(4) If the local planning authority give notice as mentioned in subsection (2) that their decision is to grant the application subject to conditions the Secretary of State must give the person making the appeal the opportunity—

(a) to proceed with the appeal as an appeal under section 20(1) against the grant of the application subject to conditions;
(b) to revise the grounds of the appeal;
(c) to change any option the person has chosen relating to the procedure for the appeal.

(5) The Secretary of State must not issue his decision on the appeal before the end of the additional period.

(6) The additional period is the period prescribed for the purposes of this section and which starts on the day on which the person appeals under section 20(2).'

(3) This section has effect only in relation to relevant applications which are received by the local planning authority after the commencement of this section.

(4) The following are relevant applications—

(a) an application mentioned in section 78(1)(a) of the principal Act;
(b) an application mentioned in section 20(1)(a) of the listed buildings Act;
(c) an application mentioned in section 20(1)(a) of the listed buildings Act as given effect by section 74(3) of that Act (application of certain provisions to the control of demolition in conservation areas).

NOTES

Initial Commencement

To be appointed: see s 121(1), (2)(b).

Appointment

Appointment (for the purpose of making, or making provision by means of, subordinate legislation): 6 August 2004: see SI 2004/2097, art 2.

Extent

This section does not extend to Scotland: see s 124(1).

A1.417

51   Duration of permission and consent

(1)   Section 91 of the principal Act (limit on duration of planning permission) is amended as follows—

   (a)   in subsections (1)(a) and (3) for the words 'five years' there is substituted 'three years';
   (b)   after subsection (3) there are inserted the following subsections—

'(3A)   Subsection (3B) applies if any proceedings are begun to challenge the validity of a grant of planning permission or of a deemed grant of planning permission.

(3B)   The period before the end of which the development to which the planning permission relates is required to be begun in pursuance of subsection (1) or (3) must be taken to be extended by one year.

(3C)   Nothing in this section prevents the development being begun from the time the permission is granted or deemed to be granted.'

(2)   In section 92 of that Act (outline planning permission)—

   (a)   in subsection (2)(b) sub-paragraph (i) is omitted;
   (b)   in subsection (2)(b) in sub-paragraph (ii) the words 'if later' are omitted;
   (c)   in subsection (4) 'five years' is omitted.

(3)   In section 73 of the principal Act (applications to develop land without compliance with existing conditions) after subsection (4) there is inserted the following subsection—

'(5)   Planning permission must not be granted under this section to the extent that it has effect to change a condition subject to which a previous planning permission was granted by extending the time within which—

   (a)   a development must be started;
   (b)   an application for approval of reserved matters (within the meaning of section 92) must be made.'

(4)   Section 18 of the listed buildings Act (limit of duration of listed buildings consent) is amended as follows—

   (a)   in subsections (1)(a) and (2) for the words 'five years' there is substituted 'three years';
   (b)   after subsection (2) there are inserted the following subsections—

'(2A)   Subsection (2B) applies if any proceedings are begun to challenge the validity of a grant of listed building consent or of a deemed grant of listed building consent.

1499

(2B)   The period before the end of which the works to which the consent relates are required to be begun in pursuance of subsection (1) or (2) must be taken to be extended by one year.

(2C)   Nothing in this section prevents the works being begun from the time the consent is granted.'

(5)   In section 19 of that Act (variation or discharge of conditions) after subsection (4) there is inserted the following subsection—

'(5)   But a variation or discharge of conditions under this section must not—

    (a)   vary a condition subject to which a consent was granted by extending the time within which the works must be started;

    (b)   discharge such a condition.'

(6)   This section has effect only in relation to applications made under the principal Act or the listed buildings Act which are received by the local planning authority after the commencement of the section.

NOTES

Initial Commencement

To be appointed: see s 121(1), (2)(b).

Appointment

Appointment (in relation to England): 24 August 2005: see SI 2005/2081, art 2(c); for savings see art 4(2) thereof.

Extent

This section does not extend to Scotland: see s 124(1).

A1.418

52   **Temporary stop notice**

After section 171D of the principal Act (penalties for non-compliance with planning contravention notice) there are inserted the following sections—

'Temporary stop notices

171E   **Temporary stop notice**

(1)   This section applies if the local planning authority think—

    (a)   that there has been a breach of planning control in relation to any land, and

    (b)   that it is expedient that the activity (or any part of the activity) which amounts to the breach is stopped immediately.

(2)   The authority may issue a temporary stop notice.

(3)   The notice must be in writing and must—

    (a)   specify the activity which the authority think amounts to the breach;

    (b)   prohibit the carrying on of the activity (or of so much of the activity as is specified in the notice);

    (c)   set out the authority's reasons for issuing the notice.

(4)   A temporary stop notice may be served on any of the following—

    (a)   the person who the authority think is carrying on the activity;

   (b)   a person who the authority think is an occupier of the land;
   (c)   a person who the authority think has an interest in the land.

(5)   The authority must display on the land—

   (a)   a copy of the notice;
   (b)   a statement of the effect of the notice and of section 171G.

(6)   A temporary stop notice has effect from the time a copy of it is first displayed in pursuance of subsection (5).

(7)   A temporary stop notice ceases to have effect—

   (a)   at the end of the period of 28 days starting on the day the copy notice is so displayed,
   (b)   at the end of such shorter period starting on that day as is specified in the notice, or
   (c)   if it is withdrawn by the local planning authority.

171F   **Temporary stop notice: restrictions**

(1)   A temporary stop notice does not prohibit—

   (a)   the use of a building as a dwelling house;
   (b)   the carrying out of an activity of such description or in such circumstances as is prescribed.

(2)   A temporary stop notice does not prohibit the carrying out of any activity which has been carried out (whether or not continuously) for a period of four years ending with the day on which the copy of the notice is first displayed as mentioned in section 171E(6).

(3)   Subsection (2) does not prevent a temporary stop notice prohibiting—

   (a)   activity consisting of or incidental to building, engineering, mining or other operations, or
   (b)   the deposit of refuse or waste materials.

(4)   For the purposes of subsection (2) any period during which the activity is authorised by planning permission must be ignored.

(5)   A second or subsequent temporary stop notice must not be issued in respect of the same activity unless the local planning authority has first taken some other enforcement action in relation to the breach of planning control which is constituted by the activity.

(6)   In subsection (5) enforcement action includes obtaining the grant of an injunction under section 187B.

171G   **Temporary stop notice: offences**

(1)   A person commits an offence if he contravenes a temporary stop notice—

   (a)   which has been served on him, or
   (b)   a copy of which has been displayed in accordance with section 171E(5).

(2)   Contravention of a temporary stop notice includes causing or permitting the contravention of the notice.

(3)   An offence under this section may be charged by reference to a day or a longer period of time.

(4)   A person may be convicted of more than one such offence in relation to the same temporary stop notice by reference to different days or periods of time.

(5)   A person does not commit an offence under this section if he proves—

(a)   that the temporary stop notice was not served on him, and
(b)   that he did not know, and could not reasonably have been expected to know, of its existence.

(6)   A person convicted of an offence under this section is liable—

(a)   on summary conviction, to a fine not exceeding £20,000;
(b)   on conviction on indictment, to a fine.

(7)   In determining the amount of the fine the court must have regard in particular to any financial benefit which has accrued or has appeared to accrue to the person convicted in consequence of the offence.

171H   Temporary stop notice: compensation

(1)   This section applies if and only if a temporary stop notice is issued and at least one of the following paragraphs applies—

(a)   the activity which is specified in the notice is authorised by planning permission or a development order or local development order;
(b)   a certificate in respect of the activity is issued under section 191 or granted under that section by virtue of section 195;
(c)   the authority withdraws the notice.

(2)   Subsection (1)(a) does not apply if the planning permission is granted on or after the date on which a copy of the notice is first displayed as mentioned in section 171E(6).

(3)   Subsection (1)(c) does not apply if the notice is withdrawn following the grant of planning permission as mentioned in subsection (2).

(4)   A person who at the time the notice is served has an interest in the land to which the notice relates is entitled to be compensated by the local planning authority in respect of any loss or damage directly attributable to the prohibition effected by the notice.

(5)   Subsections (3) to (7) of section 186 apply to compensation payable under this section as they apply to compensation payable under that section; and for that purpose references in those subsections to a stop notice must be taken to be references to a temporary stop notice.'

NOTES

Initial Commencement

To be appointed: see s 121(1), (2)(b).

Appointment

Appointment (for the purpose of making, or making provision by means of, subordinate legislation): 6 August 2004: see SI 2004/2097, art 2.

Appointment (in relation to England for remaining purposes): 7 March 2005: see SI 2005/204, art 2.

Extent

This section does not extend to Scotland: see s 124(1).

A1.419

53   Fees and charges

(1)   Section 303 (fees for planning applications, etc) of the principal Act is amended as follows.

(2)   The following subsections are substituted for subsections (1) and (2)—

'(1)   The appropriate authority may by regulations make provision for the payment of a charge or fee to a local planning authority in respect of—

    (a)   the performance by the local planning authority of any function they have;
    (b)   anything done by them which is calculated to facilitate or is conducive or incidental to the performance of any such function.

(2)   The regulations may prescribe—

    (a)   the person by whom the charge or fee is payable;
    (b)   provision as to the calculation of the charge or fee (including the person by whom it is to be calculated);
    (c)   circumstances in which no charge or fee is to be paid;
    (d)   circumstances in which a charge or fee is to be transferred from one local planning authority to another.

(2A)   The appropriate authority is—

    (a)   the Secretary of State in relation to England;
    (b)   the National Assembly for Wales in relation to Wales,

and in the case of regulations made by the National Assembly for Wales section 333(3) must be ignored.'

(3)   In subsection (4) after the first 'prescribed' there is inserted 'charge or'.

(4)   After subsection (5) there are inserted the following subsections—

'(5A)   If the local planning authority calculate the amount of fees or charges in pursuance of provision made by regulations under subsection (1) the authority must secure that, taking one financial year with another, the income from the fees or charges does not exceed the cost of the performance of the function or doing of the thing (as the case may be).

(5B)   A financial year is the period of 12 months beginning with 1 April.'

(5)   Subsection (6) is omitted.

NOTES

Initial Commencement

To be appointed: see s 121(1), (2)(b).

Appointment

Appointment (for the purpose of making, or making provision by means of, subordinate legislation): 6 August 2004: see SI 2004/2097, art 2.

Sub-ss (1)–(4): Appointment (in relation to England for remaining purposes): 7 March 2005: see SI 2005/204, art 2.

Appointment (in relation to Wales for remaining purposes): 1 April 2006: see SI 2006/931, art 2.

Sub-s (5): Appointment (in relation to England for remaining purposes): 28 September 2004: by virtue of SI 2004/2202, arts 2(k), 3(d), Sch 1, Pt 1.

Extent

This section does not extend to Scotland: see s 124(1).

A1.420

54   Duty to respond to consultation

(1)   This section applies to a prescribed requirement to consult any person or body (the consultee) which exercises functions for the purposes of any enactment.

(2)   A prescribed requirement to consult is a requirement—

    (a)   with which the appropriate authority or a local planning authority must comply before granting any permission, approval or consent under or by virtue of the planning Acts;

    (b)   which is prescribed for the purposes of this subsection.

(3)   At any time before an application is made for any permission, approval or consent mentioned in subsection (2) any person may in relation to a proposed development consult the consultee on any matter in respect of which the appropriate authority is or the local planning authority are required to consult the consultee.

(4)   The consultee must give a substantive response to any consultation mentioned in subsection (2) or by virtue of subsection (3) before the end of—

    (a)   the period prescribed for the purposes of this subsection, or

    (b)   such other period as is agreed in writing between the consultee and the appropriate authority or the local planning authority (as the case may be).

(5)   The appropriate authority may also prescribe—

    (a)   the procedure to be followed for the purposes of this section;

    (b)   the information to be provided to the consultee for the purposes of the consultation;

    (c)   the requirements of a substantive response.

(6)   Anything prescribed for the purposes of subsections (1) to (5) must be prescribed by development order.

(7)   A development order may—

    (a)   require consultees to give the appropriate authority a report as to their compliance with subsection (4);

    (b)   prescribe the form and content of the report;

    (c)   prescribe the times at which the report is to be made.

(8)   The appropriate authority is—

    (a)   the Secretary of State in relation to England;

    (b)   the National Assembly for Wales in relation to Wales.

NOTES

Initial Commencement

To be appointed: see s 121(1), (2)(b).

Appointment

Appointment (for the purpose of making, or making provision by means of, subordinate legislation): 6 August 2004: see SI 2004/2097, art 2.

Appointment (in relation to England for remaining purposes): 24 August 2005: see SI 2005/2081, art 2(d)(i); for savings see art 4(3) thereof.

Extent

This section does not extend to Scotland: see s 124(1).

Subordinate Legislation

Town and Country Planning (General Development Procedure) (Amendment) (England) Order 2005, SI 2005/2087.

A1.421

55   Time in which Secretary of State to take decisions

(1)   Schedule 2 contains provisions about the time in which the Secretary of State must take certain decisions.

(2)   But Schedule 2 does not apply in relation to any decision taken in the exercise of a function in relation to Wales if the function is exercisable in relation to Wales by the National Assembly for Wales by virtue of an order under section 22 of the Government of Wales Act 1998 (c 38).

NOTES

Initial Commencement

To be appointed: see s 121(1).

Appointment

Appointment (in relation to England): 1 April 2005: see SI 2005/204, art 3; for savings see art 4 thereof.

Extent

This section does not extend to Scotland: see s 124(1).

PART 5: CORRECTION OF ERRORS

A1.422

56   Correction of errors in decisions

(1)   This section applies if the Secretary of State or an inspector issues a decision document which contains a correctable error.

(2)   The Secretary of State or the inspector (as the case may be) may correct the error—

   (a)   if he is requested to do so in writing by any person;
   (b)   if he sends a statement in writing to the applicant which explains the error and states that he is considering making the correction.

(3)   But the Secretary of State or inspector must not correct the error unless—

   (a)   not later than the end of the relevant period he receives a request mentioned in subsection (2)(a) or sends a statement mentioned in subsection (2)(b),
   (b)   he informs the local planning authority of that fact, and
   (c)   he obtains the appropriate consent.

1505

(4) The relevant period—

  (a) is the period within which an application or appeal may be made to the High Court in respect of the decision recorded in the decision document;

  (b) does not include any time by which such a period may be extended by the High Court.

(5) It is immaterial whether any such application or appeal is made.

(6) The appropriate consent is—

  (a) the consent in writing of the applicant;

  (b) if the applicant is not the owner of the land in respect of which the decision was made, the consent in writing of both the applicant and the owner.

(7) But consent is not appropriate consent if it is given subject to a condition.

NOTES

Initial Commencement

To be appointed: see s 121(1), (2)(c).

Appointment

Appointment: 28 September 2004: see SI 2004/2202, art 3(a).

Extent

This section does not extend to Scotland: see s 124(1).

A1.423

57   Correction notice

(1) If paragraph (a) or (b) of section 56(2) applies the Secretary of State or the inspector must as soon as practicable after making any correction or deciding not to make any correction issue a notice in writing (a correction notice) which—

  (a) specifies the correction of the error, or

  (b) gives notice of his decision not to correct such an error.

(2) The Secretary of State or the inspector (as the case may be) must give the correction notice to—

  (a) the applicant;

  (b) if the applicant is not the owner of the land in respect of which the original decision was made, the owner;

  (c) the local planning authority for the area in which the land in respect of which the decision was made is situated;

  (d) if the correction was requested by any other person, that person.

(3) The Secretary of State may by order specify any other person or description of persons to whom the correction notice must be given.

NOTES

Initial Commencement

To be appointed: see s 121(1), (2)(c).

Appointment

Appointment (for the purpose of making, or making provision by means of, subordinate legislation): 6 August 2004: see SI 2004/2097, art 2.

Appointment (for remaining purposes): 1 September 2004: see SI 2004/2202, art 3(a).

Extent

This section does not extend to Scotland: see s 124(1).

A1.424

58   Effect of correction

(1)   If a correction is made in pursuance of section 56—

    (a)   the original decision is taken not to have been made;
    (b)   the decision is taken for all purposes to have been made on the date the correction notice is issued.

(2)   If a correction is not made—

    (a)   the original decision continues to have full force and effect;
    (b)   nothing in this Part affects anything done in pursuance of or in respect of the decision.

(3)   Section 288 of the principal Act (proceedings for questioning the validity of certain decisions) applies to the correction notice as if it were an action on the part of the Secretary of State to which that section applies, if the decision document in respect of which the correction notice is given records a decision mentioned in—

    (a)   paragraph (a) of section 59(4) below, or
    (b)   paragraph (b) of that section, if it is a decision mentioned in section 177 of the principal Act (grant or modification of planning permission on appeal against enforcement notice).

(4)   Section 289 of the principal Act (appeals to the High Court relating to enforcement notices and notices under section 207 of that Act) applies to the correction notice as if it were a decision of the Secretary of State mentioned in—

    (a)   subsection (1) of that section, if the decision document in respect of which the correction notice is given records a decision mentioned in paragraph (b) of section 59(4) below (not being a decision mentioned in section 177 of the principal Act), or
    (b)   subsection (2) of that section, if the decision document in respect of which the correction notice is given records a decision mentioned in paragraph (c) of section 59(4) below.

(5)   Section 63 of the listed buildings Act (proceedings for questioning the validity of certain decisions) applies to the correction notice as if it were a decision of the Secretary of State to which that section applies, if the decision document in respect of which the correction notice is given records a decision mentioned in any of paragraphs (d) to (f) of section 59(4) below.

(6)   Section 22 of the hazardous substances Act (proceedings for questioning the validity of certain decisions) applies to the correction notice as if it were a decision of the Secretary of State under section 20 or 21 of that Act, if the decision document in respect of which the correction notice is given records a decision mentioned in paragraph (g) of section 59(4) below.

(7) If the decision document in respect of which the correction notice is given records a decision mentioned in paragraph (h) of section 59(4) the Secretary of State must by order make provision for questioning the validity of the notice which corresponds to the provisions of the planning Acts mentioned in subsections (3) to (6) above.

(8) Except to the extent provided for by virtue of this section a correction notice must not be questioned in any legal proceedings.

NOTES

Initial Commencement

To be appointed: see s 121(1), (2)(c).

Appointment

Appointment: 28 September 2004: see SI 2004/2202, art 3(a).

Extent

This section does not extend to Scotland: see s 124(1).

A1.425

59   Supplementary

(1) This section applies for the purposes of this Part.

(2) An inspector is a person appointed under any of the planning Acts to determine appeals instead of the Secretary of State.

(3) In the case of a decision document issued by an inspector any other inspector may act under this Part.

(4) A decision document is a document which records any of the following decisions—

(a) a decision of any description which constitutes action on the part of the Secretary of State under section 284(3) of the principal Act (decisions which are not to be questioned in legal proceedings);

(b) a decision in proceedings on an appeal under Part 7 of that Act (enforcement notices);

(c) a decision in proceedings on an appeal under section 208 of that Act (appeals against enforcement notices relating to trees);

(d) a decision mentioned in section 62(2) of the listed buildings Act (decisions which are not to be questioned in legal proceedings);

(e) a decision on an appeal under section 39 of that Act (appeals against listed building enforcement notices);

(f) a decision relating to conservation area consent within the meaning of section 74(1) of that Act (consent required for demolition of certain buildings);

(g) a decision under section 20 or 21 of the hazardous substances Act (certain applications referred to and appeals determined by the Secretary of State);

(h) a decision under any of the planning Acts which is of a description specified by the Secretary of State by order.

(5) A correctable error is an error—

(a) which is contained in any part of the decision document which records the decision, but

(b) which is not part of any reasons given for the decision.

(6) The applicant is—

(a) in the case of a decision made on an application under any of the planning Acts, the person who made the application;

(b) in the case of a decision made on an appeal under any of those Acts, the appellant.

(7) The owner in relation to land is a person who—

(a) is the estate owner in respect of the fee simple;

(b) is entitled to a tenancy granted or extended for a term of years simple of which not less than seven years remain unexpired;

(c) is entitled to an interest in any mineral prescribed by a development order, in the case of such applications under the principal Act as are so prescribed.

(8) Error includes omission.

(9) For the purposes of the exercise of any function under this Part in relation to Wales references to the Secretary of State must be construed as references to the National Assembly for Wales.

NOTES

Initial Commencement

To be appointed: see s 121(1), (2)(c).

Appointment

Appointment (for the purpose of making, or making provision by means of, subordinate legislation): 6 August 2004: see SI 2004/2097, art 2.

Appointment (for remaining purposes): 1 September 2004: see SI 2004/2202, art 3(a).

Extent

This section does not extend to Scotland: see s 124(1).

PART 6: WALES

Spatial plan

A1.426

60   Wales Spatial Plan

(1) There must be a spatial plan for Wales to be known as the 'Wales Spatial Plan'.

(2) The Wales Spatial Plan must set out such of the policies (however expressed) of the [Welsh Ministers] as [they think] appropriate in relation to the development and use of land in Wales.

(3) The [Welsh Ministers] must—

(a) prepare and publish the Plan;

(b) keep under review the Plan;

(c) consider from time to time whether it should be revised.

(4) If the [Welsh Ministers revise the Plan, they must publish (as they consider appropriate)]—

(a) the whole Plan as revised, or

(b) the revised parts.

(5)   The [Welsh Ministers] must consult such persons or bodies as [they consider] appropriate in preparing or revising the Plan.

[(6)   The Welsh Ministers may not publish the Plan as revised or the revised parts of the Plan unless the Plan or the revised parts have been laid before, and approved by a resolution of, the National Assembly for Wales.]

(7)   …

NOTES

Initial Commencement

To be appointed: see s 121(5).

Appointment

Appointment: 14 July 2004: see SI 2004/1814, art 2; for transitional provision in relation to any step taken by the National Assembly for the preparation of the Wales Spatial plan before that date see art 3 thereof.

Amendment

Sub-s (2): words 'Welsh Ministers' in square brackets substituted by the Government of Wales Act 2006, s 160(1), Sch 10, para 66(1), (2)(a).

Date in force: this amendment came into force on 25 May 2007 being the date on which the initial period ended (following the appointment of the First Minister): see the Government of Wales Act 2006, ss 46, 161(4), (5).

Sub-s (2): words 'they think' in square brackets substituted by the Government of Wales Act 2006, s 160(1), Sch 10, para 66(1), (2)(b).

Date in force: this amendment came into force on 25 May 2007 being the date on which the initial period ended (following the appointment of the First Minister): see the Government of Wales Act 2006, ss 46, 161(4), (5).

Sub-s (3): words 'Welsh Ministers' in square brackets substituted by the Government of Wales Act 2006, s 160(1), Sch 10, para 66(1), (3).

Date in force: this amendment came into force on 25 May 2007 being the date on which the initial period ended (following the appointment of the First Minister): see the Government of Wales Act 2006, ss 46, 161(4), (5).

Sub-s (4): words 'Welsh Ministers revise the Plan, they must publish (as they consider appropriate)' in square brackets substituted by the Government of Wales Act 2006, s 160(1), Sch 10, para 66(1), (4).

Date in force: this amendment came into force on 25 May 2007 being the date on which the initial period ended (following the appointment of the First Minister): see the Government of Wales Act 2006, ss 46, 161(4), (5).

Sub-s (5): words 'Welsh Ministers' in square brackets substituted by the Government of Wales Act 2006, s 160(1), Sch 10, para 66(1), (5)(a).

Date in force: this amendment came into force on 25 May 2007 being the date on which the initial period ended (following the appointment of the First Minister): see the Government of Wales Act 2006, ss 46, 161(4), (5).

Sub-s (5): words 'they consider' in square brackets substituted by the Government of Wales Act 2006, s 160(1), Sch 10, para 66(1), (5)(b).

Date in force: this amendment came into force on 25 May 2007 being the date on which the initial period ended (following the appointment of the First Minister): see the Government of Wales Act 2006, ss 46, 161(4), (5).

Sub-s (6): substituted by the Government of Wales Act 2006, s 160(1), Sch 10, para 66(1), (6).

Date in force: this amendment came into force on 25 May 2007 being the date on which the initial period ended (following the appointment of the First Minister): see the Government of Wales Act 2006, ss 46, 161(4), (5).

Sub-s (7): repealed by the Government of Wales Act 2006, ss 160(1), 163, Sch 10, para 66(1), (7), Sch 12.

Date in force: this repeal came into force on 25 May 2007 being the date on which the initial period ended (following the appointment of the First Minister): see the Government of Wales Act 2006, ss 46, 161(4), (5).

Survey

A1.427

61   Survey

(1)   The local planning authority must keep under review the matters which may be expected to affect the development of their area or the planning of its development.

(2)   These matters include—

   (a)   the principal physical, economic, social and environmental characteristics of the area of the authority;
   (b)   the principal purposes for which land is used in the area;
   (c)   the size, composition and distribution of the population of the area;
   (d)   the communications, transport system and traffic of the area;
   (e)   any other considerations which may be expected to affect those matters;
   (f)   such other matters as may be prescribed or as the Assembly in a particular case may direct.

(3)   These matters also include—

   (a)   any changes which the authority think may occur in relation to any other matter;
   (b)   the effect such changes are likely to have on the development of the authority's area or on the planning of such development.

(4)   The local planning authority may also keep under review and examine the matters mentioned in subsections (2) and (3) in relation to any neighbouring area to the extent that those matters may be expected to affect the area of the authority.

(5)   In exercising a function under subsection (4) a local planning authority must consult the local planning authority for the neighbouring area in question.

(6)   If a neighbouring area is in England references to the local planning authority for that area must be construed in accordance with Part 2.

NOTES

Initial Commencement

To be appointed: see s 121(5).

Appointment

Appointment (for the purpose of making regulations): 5 October 2005: see SI 2005/2722, art 2(1)(a).

Appointment (for remaining purposes): 15 October 2005: see SI 2005/2722, art 2(1)(a).

Plans

A1.428

62   Local development plan

(1)   The local planning authority must prepare a plan for their area to be known as a local development plan.

(2)   The plan must set out—

    (a)   the authority's objectives in relation to the development and use of land in their area;

    (b)   their general policies for the implementation of those objectives.

(3)   The plan may also set out specific policies in relation to any part of the area of the authority.

(4)   Regulations under this section may prescribe the form and content of the plan.

(5)   In preparing a local development plan the authority must have regard to—

    (a)   current national policies;

    (b)   the Wales Spatial Plan;

    (c)   the RSS for any region which adjoins the area of the authority;

    (d)   the community strategy prepared by the authority;

    (e)   the community strategy for any other authority whose area comprises any part of the area of the local planning authority;

    (f)   the resources likely to be available for implementing the plan;

    (g)   such other matters as the Assembly prescribes.

(6)   The authority must also—

    (a)   carry out an appraisal of the sustainability of the plan;

    (b)   prepare a report of the findings of the appraisal.

(7)   The community strategy is the strategy prepared by an authority under section 4 of the Local Government Act 2000 (c 22).

(8)   A plan is a local development plan only in so far as it—

    (a)   is adopted by resolution of the local planning authority as a local development plan;

    (b)   is approved by the Assembly under section 65 or 71.

NOTES

Initial Commencement

To be appointed: see s 121(5).

Appointment

Sub-ss (1)–(3), (5)(a)–(f), (6)–(8): Appointment: 30 April 2005: see SI 2005/1229, art 2(a).

Sub-ss (4), (5)(g): Appointment: 1 August 2004: see SI 2004/1813, art 2(a).

Subordinate Legislation

Town and Country Planning (Local Development Plan) (Wales) Regulations 2005, SI 2005/2839 (made under sub-s (4)).

A1.429

63   Preparation requirements

(1) A local development plan must be prepared in accordance with—

(a)   the local planning authority's community involvement scheme;

(b)   the timetable for the preparation and adoption of the authority's local development plan.

(2) The authority's community involvement scheme is a statement of the authority's policy as to the involvement in the exercise of the authority's functions under this Part of the persons to which subsection (3) applies.

(3) The persons mentioned in subsection (2)—

(a)   must include such persons as the Assembly prescribes;

(b)   may include such other persons as appear to the authority to have an interest in matters relating to development in the area of the authority.

(4) The authority and the Assembly must attempt to agree the terms of the documents mentioned in paragraphs (a) and (b) of subsection (1).

(5) But to the extent that the Assembly and the authority cannot agree the terms the Assembly may direct that the documents must be in the terms specified in the direction.

(6) The authority must comply with the direction.

(7) The Assembly may prescribe—

(a)   the procedure in respect of the preparation of the documents mentioned in paragraphs (a) and (b) of subsection (1);

(b)   the form and content of the documents;

(c)   the time at which any step in the preparation of the documents must be taken;

(d)   publicity about the documents;

(e)   making the documents available for inspection by the public;

(f)   circumstances in which the requirements of the documents need not be complied with.

NOTES

Initial Commencement

To be appointed: see s 121(5).

Appointment

Sub-ss (1), (2), (3)(b), (4)–(7): Appointment: 30 April 2005: see SI 2005/1229, art 2(b).

Sub-ss (3)(a), (7): Appointment: 1 August 2004: see SI 2004/1813, art 2(b).

Subordinate Legislation

Town and Country Planning (Local Development Plan) (Wales) Regulations 2005, SI 2005/2839 (made under sub-ss (3)(a), (7)).

A1.430

64   Independent examination

(1) The local planning authority must submit their local development plan to the Assembly for independent examination.

(2) But the authority must not submit a plan unless—

    (a)   they have complied with any relevant requirements contained in regulations under this Part, and

    (b)   they think the plan is ready for independent examination.

(3)   The authority must also send to the Assembly (in addition to the local development plan) such other documents (or copies of documents) and such information as is prescribed.

(4)   The examination must be carried out by a person appointed by the Assembly.

(5)   The purpose of the independent examination is to determine in respect of a local development plan—

    (a)   whether it satisfies the requirements of sections 62 and 63 and of regulations under section 77;

    (b)   whether it is sound.

(6)   Any person who makes representations seeking to change a local development plan must (if he so requests) be given the opportunity to appear before and be heard by the person carrying out the examination.

(7)   The person appointed to carry out the examination must—

    (a)   make recommendations;

    (b)   give reasons for the recommendations.

(8)   The local planning authority must publish the recommendations and the reasons.

NOTES

Initial Commencement

To be appointed: see s 121(5).

Appointment

Appointment (for the purpose of making regulations): 5 October 2005: see SI 2005/2722, art 2(1)(b).

Appointment (for remaining purposes): 15 October 2005: see SI 2005/2722, art 2(1)(b).

Subordinate Legislation

Town and Country Planning (Local Development Plan) (Wales) Regulations 2005, SI 2005/2839 (made under sub-s (3)).

A1.431

65   Intervention by Assembly

(1)   If the Assembly thinks that a local development plan is unsatisfactory—

    (a)   it may at any time before the plan is adopted by the local planning authority direct them to modify the plan in accordance with the direction;

    (b)   if it gives such a direction it must state its reasons for doing so.

(2)   The authority—

    (a)   must comply with the direction;

    (b)   must not adopt the plan unless the Assembly gives notice that it is satisfied that they have complied with the direction.

(3)   But subsection (2) does not apply if the Assembly withdraws the direction.

(4)   At any time before a local development plan is adopted by a local planning authority the Assembly may direct that the plan is submitted to it for its approval.

(5)   The following paragraphs apply if the Assembly gives a direction under subsection (4)—

  (a)   the authority must not take any step in connection with the adoption of the plan until the Assembly gives its decision;
  (b)   if the direction is given before the authority have submitted the plan under section 64(1) the Assembly must hold an independent examination and section 64(4) to (7) applies accordingly;
  (c)   if the direction is given after the authority have submitted the plan the person appointed to carry out the examination must make his recommendations to the Assembly;
  (d)   the plan has no effect unless it has been approved by the Assembly.

(6)   The Assembly must publish the recommendations made to it by virtue of subsection (5)(b) or (c) and the reasons of the person making the recommendations.

(7)   In considering a plan submitted under subsection (4) the Assembly may take account of any matter which it thinks is relevant.

(8)   It is immaterial whether any such matter was taken account of by the authority.

(9)   The Assembly—

  (a)   may approve, approve subject to specified modifications or reject a plan submitted to it under subsection (4);
  (b)   must give reasons for its decision under paragraph (a).

(10)   In the exercise of any function under this section the Assembly must have regard to the documents mentioned in paragraphs (a) and (b) of section 63(1).

NOTES

Initial Commencement

To be appointed: see s 121(5).

Appointment

Appointment (for the purpose of making regulations): 5 October 2005: see SI 2005/2722, art 2(1)(c).

Appointment (for remaining purposes): 15 October 2005: see SI 2005/2722, art 2(1)(c).

A1.432

66   Withdrawal of local development plan

(1)   A local planning authority may at any time before a local development plan is adopted under section 67 withdraw the plan.

(2)   But subsection (1) does not apply to a local development plan at any time after the plan has been submitted for independent examination under section 64 unless—

  (a)   the person carrying out the examination recommends that the plan is withdrawn and that recommendation is not overruled by a direction given by the Assembly, or
  (b)   the Assembly directs that the plan must be withdrawn.

NOTES

Initial Commencement

To be appointed: see s 121(5).

Appointment

Appointment (for the purpose of making regulations): 5 October 2005: see SI 2005/2722, art 2(1)(d).

Appointment (for remaining purposes): 15 October 2005: see SI 2005/2722, art 2(1)(d).

A1.433

67   Adoption of local development plan

(1)   The local planning authority may adopt a local development plan as originally prepared if the person appointed to carry out the independent examination of the plan recommends that the plan as originally prepared is adopted.

(2)   The authority may adopt a local development plan with modifications if the person appointed to carry out the independent examination of the plan recommends the modifications.

(3)   A plan is adopted for the purposes of this section if it is adopted by resolution of the authority.

(4)   But the authority must not adopt a local development plan if the Assembly directs them not to do so.

NOTES

Initial Commencement

To be appointed: see s 121(5).

Appointment

Appointment (for the purpose of making regulations): 5 October 2005: see SI 2005/2722, art 2(1)(e).

Appointment (for remaining purposes): 15 October 2005: see SI 2005/2722, art 2(1)(e).

A1.434

68   Revocation of local development plan

The Assembly may at any time revoke a local development plan at the request of the local planning authority.

NOTES

Initial Commencement

To be appointed: see s 121(5).

Appointment

Appointment (for the purpose of making regulations): 5 October 2005: see SI 2005/2722, art 2(1)(f).

Appointment (for remaining purposes): 15 October 2005: see SI 2005/2722, art 2(1)(f).

A1.435

69   Review of local development plan

(1)   A local planning authority must carry out a review of their local development plan at such times as the Assembly prescribes.

(2)   The authority must report to the Assembly on the findings of their review.

(3)   A review must—

    (a)   be in such form as is prescribed;
    (b)   be published in accordance with such requirements as are prescribed.

NOTES

Initial Commencement

To be appointed: see s 121(5).

Appointment

Appointment (for the purpose of making regulations): 5 October 2005: see SI 2005/2722, art 2(1)(g).

Appointment (for remaining purposes): 15 October 2005: see SI 2005/2722, art 2(1)(g).

Subordinate Legislation

Town and Country Planning (Local Development Plan) (Wales) Regulations 2005, SI 2005/2839.

A1.436

70   Revision of local development plan

(1)   The local planning authority may at any time prepare a revision of a local development plan.

(2)   The authority must prepare a revision of a local development plan—

    (a)   if the Assembly directs them to do so;
    (b)   if, following a review under section 69, they think that the plan should be revised.

(3)   This Part applies to the revision of a local development plan as it applies to the preparation of the plan.

NOTES

Initial Commencement

To be appointed: see s 121(5).

Appointment

Appointment (for the purpose of making regulations): 5 October 2005: see SI 2005/2722, art 2(1)(h).

Appointment (for remaining purposes): 15 October 2005: see SI 2005/2722, art 2(1)(h).

A1.437

71   Assembly's default power

(1)   This section applies if the Assembly thinks that a local planning authority are failing or omitting to do anything it is necessary for them to do in connection with the preparation, revision or adoption of a local development plan.

(2)   The Assembly must hold an independent examination and section 64(4) to (7) applies accordingly.

(3)   The Assembly must publish the recommendations and reasons of the person appointed to hold the examination.

(4)   The Assembly may—

    (a)   prepare or revise (as the case may be) the plan, and
    (b)   approve the plan as a local development plan.

(5)   The Assembly must give reasons for anything it does in pursuance of subsection (4).

(6)   The authority must reimburse the Assembly for any expenditure it incurs in connection with anything—

    (a)   which is done by it under subsection (4), and
    (b)   which the authority failed or omitted to do as mentioned in subsection (1).

NOTES

Initial Commencement

To be appointed: see s 121(5).

Appointment

Appointment (for the purpose of making regulations): 5 October 2005: see SI 2005/2722, art 2(1)(i).

Appointment (for remaining purposes): 15 October 2005: see SI 2005/2722, art 2(1)(i).

A1.438

72   Joint local development plans

(1)   Two or more local planning authorities may agree to prepare a joint local development plan.

(2)   This Part applies for the purposes of the preparation, revision, adoption, withdrawal and revocation of a joint local development plan as it applies for the purposes of the preparation, revision, adoption, withdrawal and revocation of a local development plan.

(3)   For the purposes of subsection (2) anything which must be done by or in relation to a local planning authority in connection with a local development plan must be done by or in relation to each of the authorities mentioned in subsection (1) in connection with a joint local development plan.

(4)   Subsections (5) to (7) apply if a local planning authority withdraw from an agreement mentioned in subsection (1).

(5)   Any step taken in relation to the plan must be treated as a step taken by—

(a) an authority which was a party to the agreement for the purposes of any corresponding plan prepared by them;

(b) two or more other authorities who were parties to the agreement for the purposes of any corresponding joint local development plan.

(6) Any independent examination of a local development plan to which the agreement relates must be suspended.

(7) If before the end of the period prescribed for the purposes of this subsection an authority which was a party to the agreement requests the Assembly to do so it may direct that—

(a) the examination is resumed in relation to the corresponding plan;

(b) any step taken for the purposes of the suspended examination has effect for the purposes of the resumed examination.

(8) A joint local development plan is a local development plan prepared jointly by two or more local planning authorities.

NOTES

Initial Commencement

To be appointed: see s 121(5).

Appointment

Appointment: 30 April 2005: see SI 2005/1229, art 2(c).

Subordinate Legislation

Town and Country Planning (Local Development Plan) (Wales) Regulations 2005, SI 2005/2839 (made under sub-s (7)).

Miscellaneous

A1.439

73   Exclusion of certain representations

(1) This section applies to any representation or objection in respect of anything which is done or is proposed to be done in pursuance of—

(a) an order or scheme under section 10, 14, 16, 18, 106(1) or (3) or 108(1) of the Highways Act 1980 (c 66);

(b) an order or scheme under section 7, 9, 11, 13 or 20 of the Highways Act 1959 (c 25), section 3 of the Highways (Miscellaneous Provisions) Act 1961 (c 63) or section 1 or 10 of the Highways Act 1971 (c 41) (which provisions were replaced by the provisions mentioned in paragraph (a));

(c) an order under section 1 of the New Towns Act 1981 (c 64).

(2) If the Assembly or a local planning authority thinks that a representation made in relation to a local development plan is in substance a representation or objection to which this section applies it or they (as the case may be) may disregard it.

NOTES

Initial Commencement

To be appointed: see s 121(5).

Appointment

Appointment: 30 April 2005: see SI 2005/1229, art 2(d).

A1.440

74   Urban development corporations

The Assembly may direct that this Part (except section 60) does not apply to the area of an urban development corporation.

NOTES

Initial Commencement

To be appointed: see s 121(5).

Appointment

Appointment (for the purpose of making regulations): 5 October 2005: see SI 2005/2722, art 2(1)(j).

Appointment (for remaining purposes): 15 October 2005: see SI 2005/2722, art 2(1)(j).

A1.441

75   Guidance

In the exercise of any function conferred under or by virtue of this Part the local planning authority must have regard to any guidance issued by the Assembly.

NOTES

Initial Commencement

To be appointed: see s 121(5).

Appointment

Appointment: 1 August 2004: see SI 2004/1813, art 2(c).

A1.442

76   Annual monitoring report

(1) Every local planning authority must make an annual report to the Assembly.

(2) The annual report must contain such information as is prescribed as to the extent to which the objectives set out in the local development plan are being achieved.

(3) The annual report must—

    (a) be made at such time as is prescribed;
    (b) be in such form as is prescribed;
    (c) contain such other matter as is prescribed.

NOTES

Initial Commencement

To be appointed: see s 121(5).

Appointment

Sub-s (1): Appointment (for the purpose of making regulations): 5 October 2005: see SI 2005/2722, art 2(1)(k).

Sub-s (1): Appointment (for remaining purposes): 15 October 2005: see SI 2005/2722, art 2(1)(k).

Sub-ss (2), (3): Appointment (for the purpose of empowering the National Assembly to make regulations): 1 August 2004: see SI 2004/1813, art 2(d).

Subordinate Legislation

Town and Country Planning (Local Development Plan) (Wales) Regulations 2005, SI 2005/2839 (made under sub-ss (2), (3)).

General

A1.443

77   Regulations

(1)   The Assembly may by regulations make provision in connection with the exercise of functions conferred by this Part on any person.

(2)   The regulations may in particular make provision as to—

- (a)   the procedure to be followed by the local planning authority in carrying out the appraisal under section 62(6);
- (b)   the procedure to be followed in the preparation of local development plans;
- (c)   requirements about the giving of notice and publicity;
- (d)   requirements about inspection by the public of a plan or any other document;
- (e)   the nature and extent of consultation with and participation by the public in anything done under this Part;
- (f)   the making of representations about any matter to be included in a local development plan;
- (g)   consideration of any such representations;
- (h)   the remuneration and allowances payable to the person appointed to carry out an independent examination under section 64;
- (i)   the time at which anything must be done for the purposes of this Part;
- (j)   the manner of publication of any draft, report or other document published under this Part;
- (k)   monitoring the exercise by local planning authorities of their functions under this Part.

NOTES

Initial Commencement

To be appointed: see s 121(5).

Appointment

Appointment: 1 August 2004: see SI 2004/1813, art 2(e).

A1.444

78   Interpretation

(1)   Local development plan must be construed in accordance with section 62.

(2)   Local planning authorities are—

(a)   county councils in Wales;
(b)   county borough councils.

(3)   A National Park authority is the local planning authority for the whole of its area and subsection (2) must be construed subject to that.

(4)   The Assembly is the National Assembly for Wales.

(5)   RSS must be construed in accordance with Part 1.

(6)   This section applies for the purposes of this Part.

NOTES

Initial Commencement

To be appointed: see s 121(5).

Appointment

Appointment: 1 August 2004: see SI 2004/1813, art 2(f).

PART 7: CROWN APPLICATION OF PLANNING ACTS

CHAPTER 1: ENGLAND AND WALES

Crown application

A1.445

79   Crown application of planning Acts

(1)   In Part 13 of the principal Act before section 293 (preliminary definitions for Part 13) there is inserted the following section—

'292A   Application to the Crown

(1)   This Act binds the Crown.

(2)   But subsection (1) is subject to express provision made by this Part.'

(2)   In the listed buildings Act after section 82 there is inserted the following section—

'82A   Application to the Crown

(1)   This Act (except the provisions specified in subsection (2)) binds the Crown.

(2)   These are the provisions—

(a)   section 9;
(b)   section 11(6);
(c)   section 21(7);
(d)   section 42(1), (5) and (6);
(e)   section 43;
(f)   section 44A;
(g)   section 54;
(h)   section 55;
(i)   section 59;
(j)   section 88A.

(3)   But subsection (2)(a) does not have effect to prohibit the doing of anything by or on behalf of the Crown which falls within the circumstances described in section 9(3)(a) to (d) and the doing of that thing does not contravene section 7.'

(3)   In the hazardous substances Act after section 30 there are inserted the following sections—

'30A   Application to the Crown

(1)   This Act (except the provisions specified in subsection (2)) binds the Crown.

(2)   The provisions are—

- (a)   section 8(6);
- (b)   section 23;
- (c)   section 26AA;
- (d)   section 36A;
- (e)   section 36B(2).'

30B   Crown application: transitional

(1)   This section applies if at any time during the establishment period a hazardous substance was present on, over or under Crown land.

(2)   The appropriate authority must make a claim in the prescribed form before the end of the transitional period.

(3)   The claim must contain the prescribed information as to—

- (a)   the presence of the substance during the establishment period;
- (b)   how and where the substance was kept and used.

(4)   Unless subsection (5) or (7) applies, the hazardous substances authority is deemed to have granted the hazardous substances consent claimed in pursuance of subsection (2).

(5)   This subsection applies if the hazardous substances authority think that a claim does not comply with subsection (3).

(6)   If subsection (5) applies, the hazardous substances authority must, before the end of the period of two weeks starting with the date they received the claim—

- (a)   notify the claimant that they think the claim is invalid;
- (b)   give their reasons.

(7)   This subsection applies if at no time during the establishment period was the aggregate quantity of the substance equal to or greater than the controlled quantity.

(8)   Hazardous substances consent which is deemed to be granted under this section is subject—

- (a)   to the condition that the maximum aggregate quantity of the substance that may be present for the purposes of this subsection at any one time must not exceed the established quantity;
- (b)   to such other conditions (if any) as are prescribed for the purposes of this section and are applicable in the case of the consent.

(9)   A substance is present for the purposes of subsection (8)(a) if—

- (a)   it is on, over or under land to which the claim for consent relates,
- (b)   it is on, over or under other land which is within 500 metres of it and is controlled by the Crown, or
- (c)   it is in or on a structure controlled by the Crown any part of which is within 500 metres of it,

and in calculating whether the established quantity is exceeded a quantity of a substance which falls within more than one of paragraphs (a) to (c) must be counted only once.

(10) The establishment period is the period of 12 months ending on the day before the date of commencement of section 79(3) of the Planning and Compulsory Purchase Act 2004.

(11) The transitional period is the period of six months starting on the date of commencement of that section.

(12) The established quantity in relation to any land is the maximum quantity which was present on, over or under the land at any one time within the establishment period.'

(4) Schedule 3 amends the planning Acts in relation to the application of those Acts to the Crown.

NOTES

Initial Commencement

To be appointed: see s 121(1), (2)(d), (g).

Appointment

Appointment (for the purpose of making, or making provision by means of, subordinate legislation): 6 August 2004: see SI 2004/2097, art 2.

Appointment (for remaining purposes): 7 June 2006: see SI 2006/1281, art 2(a).

National security

A1.446

80   Special provision relating to national security

(1) In section 321 of the principal Act (planning inquiries to be held in public subject to certain exceptions) after subsection (4) there are inserted the following subsections—

'(5) If the Secretary of State is considering giving a direction under subsection (3) the Attorney General may appoint a person to represent the interests of any person who will be prevented from hearing or inspecting any evidence at a local inquiry if the direction is given.

(6) If before the Secretary of State gives a direction under subsection (3) no person is appointed under subsection (5), the Attorney General may at any time appoint a person as mentioned in subsection (5) for the purposes of the inquiry.

(7) The Lord Chancellor may by rules make provision—

    (a)   as to the procedure to be followed by the Secretary of State before he gives a direction under subsection (3) in a case where a person has been appointed under subsection (5);

    (b)   as to the functions of a person appointed under subsection (5) or (6).

(8) Rules made under subsection (7) must be contained in a statutory instrument subject to annulment in pursuance of a resolution of either House of Parliament.

(9) If a person is appointed under subsection (5) or (6) (the appointed representative) the Secretary of State may direct any person who he thinks is interested in the inquiry in relation to a matter mentioned in subsection (4) (the responsible person) to pay the fees and expenses of the appointed representative.

(10) If the appointed representative and the responsible person are unable to agree the amount of the fees and expenses, the amount must be determined by the Secretary of State.

(11) The Secretary of State must cause the amount agreed between the appointed representative and the responsible person or determined by him to be certified.

(12) An amount so certified is recoverable from the responsible person as a civil debt.'

(2) After section 321 of the principal Act (planning inquiries to be held in public subject to certain exceptions) there is inserted the following section—

'**321A**   **Appointed representative: no inquiry**

(1) This section applies if—

    (a) a person is appointed under subsection (5) or (6) of section 321, but

    (b) no inquiry is held as mentioned in subsection (1) of that section.

(2) Subsections (9) to (12) of section 321 apply in respect of the fees and expenses of the person appointed as if the inquiry had been held.

(3) For the purposes of subsection (2) the responsible person is the person to whom the Secretary of State thinks he would have given a direction under section 321(9) if an inquiry had been held.

(4) This section does not affect section 322A.'

(3) In Schedule 3 to the listed buildings Act (determination of certain appeals by person appointed by the Secretary of State) after paragraph 6 there is inserted the following paragraph—

'**6A**   (1) If the Secretary of State is considering giving a direction under paragraph 6(6) the Attorney General may appoint a person to represent the interests of any person who will be prevented from hearing or inspecting any evidence at a local inquiry if the direction is given.

(2) If before the Secretary of State gives a direction under paragraph 6(6) no person is appointed under sub-paragraph (1), the Attorney General may at any time appoint a person as mentioned in sub-paragraph (1) for the purposes of the inquiry.

(3) The Lord Chancellor may by rules make provision—

    (a) as to the procedure to be followed by the Secretary of State before he gives a direction under paragraph 6(6) in a case where a person has been appointed under sub-paragraph (1);

    (b) as to the functions of a person appointed under sub-paragraph (1) or (2).

(4) If a person is appointed under sub-paragraph (1) or (2) (the appointed representative) the Secretary of State may direct any person who he thinks is interested in the inquiry in relation to a matter mentioned in paragraph 6(7) (the responsible person) to pay the fees and expenses of the appointed representative.

(5) If the appointed representative and the responsible person are unable to agree the amount of the fees and expenses, the amount must be determined by the Secretary of State.

(6) The Secretary of State must cause the amount agreed between the appointed representative and the responsible person or determined by him to be certified.

(7) An amount so certified is recoverable from the responsible person as a civil debt.

(8) Rules made under sub-paragraph (3) must be contained in a statutory instrument subject to annulment in pursuance of a resolution of either House of Parliament.

(9) Sub-paragraph (10) applies if—

    (a) a person is appointed under sub-paragraph (1) or (2), but

(b) no inquiry is held as mentioned in paragraph 6(1).

(10) Sub-paragraphs (4) to (7) above apply in respect of the fees and expenses of the person appointed as if the inquiry had been held.

(11) For the purposes of sub-paragraph (10) the responsible person is the person to whom the Secretary of State thinks he would have given a direction under sub-paragraph (4) if an inquiry had been held.

(12) Sub-paragraphs (9) to (11) do not affect paragraph 6(8).'

(4) In the Schedule to the hazardous substances Act (determination of certain appeals by person appointed by the Secretary of State) after paragraph 6 there is inserted the following paragraph—

'6A (1) If the Secretary of State is considering giving a direction under paragraph 6(6) the Attorney General may appoint a person to represent the interests of any person who will be prevented from hearing or inspecting any evidence at a local inquiry if the direction is given.

(2) If before the Secretary of State gives a direction under paragraph 6(6) no person is appointed under sub-paragraph (1), the Attorney General may at any time appoint a person as mentioned in sub-paragraph (1) for the purposes of the inquiry.

(3) The Lord Chancellor may by rules make provision—

 (a) as to the procedure to be followed by the Secretary of State before he gives a direction under paragraph 6(6) in a case where a person has been appointed under sub-paragraph (1);
 (b) as to the functions of a person appointed under sub-paragraph (1) or (2).

(4) If a person is appointed under sub-paragraph (1) or (2) (the appointed representative) the Secretary of State may direct any person who he thinks is interested in the inquiry in relation to a matter mentioned in paragraph 6(7) (the responsible person) to pay the fees and expenses of the appointed representative.

(5) If the appointed representative and the responsible person are unable to agree the amount of the fees and expenses, the amount must be determined by the Secretary of State.

(6) The Secretary of State must cause the amount agreed between the appointed representative and the responsible person or determined by him to be certified.

(7) An amount so certified is recoverable from the responsible person as a civil debt.

(8) Rules made under sub-paragraph (3) must be contained in a statutory instrument subject to annulment in pursuance of a resolution of either House of Parliament.

(9) Sub-paragraph (10) applies if—

 (a) a person is appointed under sub-paragraph (1) or (2), but
 (b) no inquiry is held as mentioned in paragraph 6(1).

(10) Sub-paragraphs (4) to (7) above apply in respect of the fees and expenses of the person appointed as if the inquiry had been held.

(11) For the purposes of sub-paragraph (10) the responsible person is the person to whom the Secretary of State thinks he would have given a direction under sub-paragraph (4) if an inquiry had been held.

(12) Sub-paragraphs (9) to (11) do not affect paragraph 6(8).'

NOTES

Initial Commencement

To be appointed: see s 121(1), (2)(d).

Appointment

Appointment (for the purpose of making, or making provision by means of, subordinate legislation): 6 August 2004: see SI 2004/2097, art 2.

Appointment (for remaining purposes): 7 June 2006: see SI 2006/1281, art 2(a).

A1.447

81   Special provision relating to national security: Wales

(1)   After section 321A of the principal Act (inserted by section 80 above) there is inserted the following section—

'**321B   Special provision in relation to planning inquiries: Wales**

(1)   This section applies if the matter in respect of which a local inquiry to which section 321 applies is to be held relates to Wales.

(2)   The references in section 321(5) and (6) to the Attorney General must be read as references to the Counsel General to the National Assembly for Wales.

(3)   The Assembly may by regulations make provision as mentioned in section 321(7) in connection with a local inquiry to which this section applies.

(4)   If the Assembly acts under subsection (3) rules made by the Lord Chancellor under section 321(7) do not have effect in relation to the inquiry.

(5)   The Counsel General to the National Assembly for Wales is the person appointed by the Assembly to be its chief legal adviser (whether or not he is known by that title).

(6)   Section 333(3) does not apply to regulations made under subsection (4).'

(2)   In Schedule 3 to the listed buildings Act (determination of certain appeals by person appointed by the Secretary of State), after paragraph 7 there is inserted the following paragraph—

'Local inquiries: Wales

8   (1)   This paragraph applies in relation to a local inquiry held in pursuance of this Schedule if the matter in respect of which the inquiry is to be held relates to Wales.

(2)   The references in paragraph 6A(1) and (2) to the Attorney General must be read as references to the Counsel General to the National Assembly for Wales.

(3)   The Assembly may by regulations make provision as mentioned in paragraph 6A(3) in connection with a local inquiry to which this section applies.

(4)   If the Assembly acts under sub-paragraph (3) rules made by the Lord Chancellor under paragraph 6A(3) do not have effect in relation to the inquiry.

(5)   The Counsel General to the National Assembly for Wales is the person appointed by the Assembly to be its chief legal adviser (whether or not he is known by that title).

(6)   Section 93(3) does not apply to regulations made under this paragraph.'

(3)   In the Schedule to the hazardous substances Act, after paragraph 7 there is inserted the following paragraph—

'*Local inquiries: Wales*

8   (1) This paragraph applies in relation to a local inquiry held in pursuance of this Schedule if the matter in respect of which the inquiry is to be held relates to Wales.

(2)   The references in paragraph 6A(1) and (2) to the Attorney General must be read as references to the Counsel General to the National Assembly for Wales.

(3)   The Assembly may by regulations make provision as mentioned in paragraph 6A(3) in connection with a local inquiry to which this section applies.

(4)   If the Assembly acts under sub-paragraph (3) rules made by the Lord Chancellor under paragraph 6A(3) do not have effect in relation to the inquiry.

(5)   The Counsel General to the National Assembly for Wales is the person appointed by the Assembly to be its chief legal adviser (whether or not he is known by that title).

(6)   Section 40(3) does not apply to regulations made under this paragraph.'

NOTES

Initial Commencement

To be appointed: see s 121(1), (2)(d).

Appointment

Appointment (for the purpose of making, or making provision by means of, subordinate legislation): 6 August 2004: see SI 2004/2097, art 2.

Appointment (for remaining purposes): 7 June 2006: see SI 2006/1281, art 2(a).

Urgent development and works

A1.448

82   Urgent Crown development

(1)   Before section 294 of the principal Act (special enforcement notices in relation to development on Crown land) there is inserted the following section—

'293A   Urgent Crown development: application

(1)   This section applies to a development if the appropriate authority certifies—

(a)   that the development is of national importance, and

(b)   that it is necessary that the development is carried out as a matter of urgency.

(2)   The appropriate authority may, instead of making an application for planning permission to the local planning authority in accordance with Part 3, make an application for planning permission to the Secretary of State under this section.

(3)   If the appropriate authority proposes to make the application to the Secretary of State it must publish in one or more newspapers circulating in the locality of the proposed development a notice—

(a)   describing the proposed development, and

(b)   stating that the authority proposes to make the application to the Secretary of State.

(4)   For the purposes of an application under this section the appropriate authority must provide to the Secretary of State—

(a)   any matter required to be provided by an applicant for planning permission in pursuance of regulations made under section 71A;

    (b) a statement of the authority's grounds for making the application.

(5) If the appropriate authority makes an application under this section subsections (6) to (9) below apply.

(6) The Secretary of State may require the authority to provide him with such further information as he thinks necessary to enable him to determine the application.

(7) As soon as practicable after he is provided with any document or other matter in pursuance of subsection (4) or (6) the Secretary of State must make a copy of the document or other matter available for inspection by the public in the locality of the proposed development.

(8) The Secretary of State must in accordance with such requirements as are contained in a development order publish notice of the application and of the fact that such documents and other material are available for inspection.

(9) The Secretary of State must consult—

    (a) the local planning authority for the area to which the proposed development relates, and

    (b) such other persons as are specified or described in a development order,

about the application.

(10) Subsection (7) does not apply to the extent that the document or other matter is subject to a direction under section 321(3) (matters related to national security).

(11) Subsections (4) to (7) of section 77 apply to an application under this section as they apply to an application in respect of which a direction under section 77 has effect.'

(2) In section 284 of the principal Act (validity of certain matters) in subsection (3) at the end there is inserted the following paragraph—

    '(i) any decision on an application for planning permission under section 293A.'

NOTES

Initial Commencement

To be appointed: see s 121(1), (2)(d).

Appointment

Appointment (for the purpose of making, or making provision by means of, subordinate legislation): 6 August 2004: see SI 2004/2097, art 2.

Appointment (for remaining purposes): 7 June 2006: see SI 2006/1281, art 2(a).

A1.449

83   Urgent works relating to Crown land

(1) After section 82A of the listed buildings Act (inserted by section 79(2)) there is inserted the following section—

'82B   Urgent works relating to Crown land: application

(1) This section applies to any works proposed to be executed in connection with any building which is on Crown land if the appropriate authority certifies—

    (a) that the works are of national importance, and

    (b) that it is necessary that the works are carried out as a matter of urgency.

(2)   The appropriate authority may, instead of making an application for consent to the local planning authority in accordance with this Act, make an application for consent to the Secretary of State under this section.

(3)   If the appropriate authority proposes to make the application to the Secretary of State it must publish in one or more newspapers circulating in the locality of the building a notice—

(a)   describing the proposed works, and

(b)   stating that the authority proposes to make the application to the Secretary of State.

(4)   For the purposes of an application under this section the appropriate authority must provide to the Secretary of State a statement of the authority's grounds for making the application.

(5)   If the appropriate authority makes an application under this section subsections (6) to (9) below apply.

(6)   The Secretary of State may require the authority to provide him with such further information as he thinks necessary to enable him to determine the application.

(7)   As soon as practicable after he is provided with any document or other matter in pursuance of subsection (4) or (6) the Secretary of State must make a copy of the document or other matter available for inspection by the public in the locality of the proposed development.

(8)   The Secretary of State must in accordance with such requirements as may be prescribed publish notice of the application and of the fact that such documents and other material are available for inspection.

(9)   The Secretary of State must consult—

(a)   the local planning authority for the area to which the proposed development relates, and

(b)   such other persons as may be prescribed,

about the application.

(10)   Subsection (7) does not apply to the extent that the document or other matter is subject to a direction under paragraph 6(6) of Schedule 3 (matters related to national security).

(11)   Subsections (4) and (5) of section 12 apply to an application under this section as they apply to an application in respect of which a direction under section 12 has effect.'

(2)   In section 62 of the listed buildings Act (validity of certain matters) in subsection (2) at the end there is inserted the following paragraph—

'(d)   any decision on an application for listed building consent under section 82B.'

NOTES

Initial Commencement

To be appointed: see s 121(1), (2)(d).

Appointment

Appointment (for the purpose of making, or making provision by means of, subordinate legislation): 6 August 2004: see SI 2004/2097, art 2.

Appointment (for remaining purposes): 7 June 2006: see SI 2006/1281, art 2(a).

Enforcement

A1.450

84 Enforcement in relation to Crown land

(1) Section 296 of the principal Act (exercise of powers in relation to Crown land) is omitted.

(2) After section 296 there are inserted the following sections—

'296A Enforcement in relation to the Crown

(1) No act or omission done or suffered by or on behalf of the Crown constitutes an offence under this Act.

(2) A local planning authority must not take any step for the purposes of enforcement in relation to Crown land unless it has the consent of the appropriate authority.

(3) The appropriate authority may give consent under subsection (2) subject to such conditions as it thinks appropriate.

(4) A step taken for the purposes of enforcement is anything done in connection with the enforcement of anything required to be done or prohibited by or under this Act.

(5) A step taken for the purposes of enforcement includes—

    (a) entering land;
    (b) bringing proceedings;
    (c) the making of an application.

(6) A step taken for the purposes of enforcement does not include—

    (a) service of a notice;
    (b) the making of an order (other than by a court).

296B References to an interest in land

(1) Subsection (2) applies to the extent that an interest in land is a Crown interest or a Duchy interest.

(2) Anything which requires or is permitted to be done by or in relation to the owner of the interest in land must be done by or in relation to the appropriate authority.

(3) An interest in land includes an interest only as occupier of the land.'

(3) After section 82C of the listed buildings Act (inserted by Schedule 3) there are inserted the following sections—

'82D Enforcement in relation to the Crown

(1) No act or omission done or suffered by or on behalf of the Crown constitutes an offence under this Act.

(2) A local planning authority must not take any step for the purposes of enforcement in relation to Crown land unless it has the consent of the appropriate authority.

(3) The appropriate authority may give consent under subsection (2) subject to such conditions as it thinks appropriate.

(4) A step taken for the purposes of enforcement is anything done in connection with the enforcement of anything required to be done or prohibited by or under this Act.

(5) A step taken for the purposes of enforcement includes—

    (a)   entering land;
    (b)   bringing proceedings;
    (c)   the making of an application.

(6)   A step taken for the purposes of enforcement does not include—

    (a)   service of a notice;
    (b)   the making of an order (other than by a court).

82E   References to an interest in land

(1)   Subsection (2) applies to the extent that an interest in land is a Crown interest or a Duchy interest.

(2)   Anything which requires or is permitted to be done by or in relation to the owner of the interest in land must be done by or in relation to the appropriate authority.

(3)   An interest in land includes an interest only as occupier of the land.'

(4)   After section 30B of the hazardous substances Act (inserted by section 79(3)) there are inserted the following sections—

'30C   Enforcement in relation to the Crown

(1)   No act or omission done or suffered by or on behalf of the Crown constitutes an offence under this Act.

(2)   A local planning authority must not take any step for the purposes of enforcement in relation to Crown land unless it has the consent of the appropriate authority.

(3)   The appropriate authority may give consent under subsection (2) subject to such conditions as it thinks appropriate.

(4)   A step taken for the purposes of enforcement is anything done in connection with the enforcement of anything required to be done or prohibited by or under this Act.

(5)   A step taken for the purposes of enforcement includes—

    (a)   entering land;
    (b)   bringing proceedings;
    (c)   the making of an application.

(6)   A step taken for the purposes of enforcement does not include—

    (a)   service of a notice;
    (b)   the making of an order (other than by a court).

30D   References to an interest in land

(1)   Subsection (2) applies to the extent that an interest in land is a Crown interest or a Duchy interest.

(2)   Anything which requires or is permitted to be done by or in relation to the owner of the interest in land must be done by or in relation to the appropriate authority.

(3)   An interest in land includes an interest only as occupier of the land.'

NOTES

Initial Commencement

To be appointed: see s 121(1), (2)(d).

Appointment

Appointment: 7 June 2006: see SI 2006/1281, art 2(a).

A1.451

85   Tree preservation orders: Forestry Commissioners

For section 200 of the principal Act (Orders affecting land where Forestry Commissioners interested) there is substituted the following section—

'200   Tree preservation orders: Forestry Commissioners

(1)   A tree preservation order does not have effect in respect of anything done—

   (a)   by or on behalf of the Forestry Commissioners on land placed at their disposal in pursuance of the Forestry Act 1967 or otherwise under their management or supervision;

   (b)   by or on behalf of any other person in accordance with a relevant plan which is for the time being in force.

(2)   A relevant plan is a plan of operations or other working plan approved by the Forestry Commissioners under—

   (a)   a forestry dedication covenant within the meaning of section 5 of the Forestry Act 1967, or

   (b)   conditions of a grant or loan made under section 1 of the Forestry Act 1979.

(3)   A reference to a provision of the Forestry Act 1967 or the Forestry Act 1979 includes a reference to a corresponding provision replaced by that provision or any earlier corresponding provision.'

NOTES

Initial Commencement

To be appointed: see s 121(1), (2)(d).

Appointment

Appointment: 7 June 2006: see SI 2006/1281, art 2(a).

A1.452

86   Trees in conservation areas: acts of Crown

After section 211(4) of the principal Act (preservation of trees in conservation areas) there are inserted the following subsections—

'(5)   An emanation of the Crown must not, in relation to a tree to which this section applies, do an act mentioned in subsection (1) above unless—

   (a)   the first condition is satisfied, and

   (b)   either the second or third condition is satisfied.

(6)   The first condition is that the emanation serves notice of an intention to do the act (with sufficient particulars to identify the tree) on the local planning authority in whose area the tree is situated.

(7)   The second condition is that the act is done with the consent of the authority.

(8)   The third condition is that the act is done—

   (a)   after the end of the period of six weeks starting with the date of the notice, and

(b) before the end of the period of two years starting with that date.'

NOTES

Initial Commencement

To be appointed: see s 121(1), (2)(d).

Appointment

Appointment: 7 June 2006: see SI 2006/1281, art 2(a).

Miscellaneous

A1.453

87   Old mining permissions

(1) Subsection (2) applies if—

(a) an old mining permission relates to land which is Crown land, and
(b) the permission has not been registered in pursuance of Schedule 2 to the Planning and Compensation Act 1991.

(2) Section 22 of and Schedule 2 to that Act apply to the old mining permission subject to the following modifications—

(a) in section 22(3) for 'May 1, 1991' there is substituted 'the date of commencement of section 87(2) of the Planning and Compulsory Purchase Act 2004';
(b) in paragraph 1(3) of Schedule 2 for 'the day on which this Schedule comes into force' there is substituted 'the date of commencement of section 87(2) of the Planning and Compulsory Purchase Act 2004'.

(3) Old mining permission must be construed in accordance with section 22 of the Planning and Compensation Act 1991.

(4) Crown land must be construed in accordance with Part 13 of the principal Act.

NOTES

Initial Commencement

To be appointed: see s 121(1), (2)(d).

Appointment

Appointment: 7 June 2006: see SI 2006/1281, art 2(a).

A1.454

88   Subordinate legislation

(1) The Secretary of State may by order provide that relevant subordinate legislation applies to the Crown.

(2) The order may modify such subordinate legislation to the extent that the Secretary of State thinks appropriate for the purposes of its application to the Crown.

(3) Relevant subordinate legislation is an instrument which—

(a) is made under or (wholly or in part) for the purposes of any of the planning Acts,
(b) is made before the commencement of section 79 of this Act, and

(c)   is specified in the order.

NOTES

Initial Commencement

To be appointed: see s 121(1), (2)(d).

Appointment

Appointment: 6 August 2004: see SI 2004/2097, art 2.

Subordinate Legislation

Town and Country Planning (Application of Subordinate Legislation to the Crown) Order 2006, SI 2006/1282.

A1.455

89   Crown application: transitional

Schedule 4 (which makes transitional provisions in consequence of the application to the Crown of the planning Acts) has effect.

NOTES

Initial Commencement

To be appointed: see s 121(1), (2)(d), (g).

Appointment

Appointment: 7 June 2006: see SI 2006/1281, art 2(a).

CHAPTER 2: SCOTLAND

Crown application

A1.456

90   Crown application of Scottish planning Acts

(1)   In Part 12 of the Town and Country Planning (Scotland) Act 1997, before section 242 (preliminary definitions for Part 12) there is inserted the following section—

'241A   Application to the Crown

(1)   This Act binds the Crown.

(2)   But subsection (1) is subject to express provision made by this Part.'

(2)   In the Planning (Listed Buildings and Conservation Areas) (Scotland) Act 1997, after section 73 (application of Act to land and works of planning authorities) there is inserted the following section—

'73A   Application to the Crown

(1)   This Act (except the provisions specified in subsection (2)) binds the Crown.

(2)   These are the provisions—

(a)   section 8,

    (b)   section 10(3),
    (c)   section 19(7),
    (d)   section 38(1) and (8),
    (e)   section 39,
    (f)   section 49,
    (g)   section 50,
    (h)   section 53,
    (i)   section 77.

(3)   But subsection (2)(a) does not have effect to prohibit the doing of anything by or on behalf of the Crown which falls within the circumstances described in section 8(3)(a) to (d) and the doing of that thing does not contravene section 6.'

(3)   In the Planning (Hazardous Substances) (Scotland) Act 1997, after section 30 (application of Act to planning authorities) there is inserted the following section—

'**30A**   **Application to the Crown**

(1)   This Act (except the provisions specified in subsection (2)) binds the Crown.

(2)   The provisions are—

    (a)   section 6(3),
    (b)   section 21,
    (c)   section 25,
    (d)   section 34,
    (e)   section 35(2).'

(4)   Schedule 5 amends the Scottish planning Acts in relation to the application of those Acts to the Crown.

NOTES

Initial Commencement

To be appointed: see s 121(4)(a).

Appointment

Appointment: 12 June 2006: see SSI 2006/268, art 3(a); for transitional provisions see SSI 2006/269, arts 2–4.

National security

A1.457

91   **Special provision for certain circumstances where disclosure of information as to national security may occur: Scotland**

(1)   In the Town and Country Planning (Scotland) Act 1997 (c 8), there is inserted after section 265 (local inquiries) the following section—

'**265A**   **Planning inquiries to be held in public subject to certain exceptions**

(1)   This section applies in relation to the holding of inquiries under section 265(1), paragraph 6 of Schedule 4, paragraph 5 of Schedule 6 or paragraph 8 of Schedule 7.

(2)   Subject to subsection (3), at any such inquiry oral evidence shall be heard in public and documentary evidence shall be open to public inspection.

(3)   If the Secretary of State is, or after consultation with the Secretary of State the Scottish Ministers are, satisfied in the case of any such inquiry—

(a) that giving evidence of a particular description or, as the case may be, making it available for inspection would be likely to result in the disclosure of information as to any of the matters mentioned in subsection (4), and

(b) that the public disclosure of that information would be contrary to the national interest,

he or as the case may be they may direct that evidence of the description indicated in the direction shall only be heard or, as the case may be, open to inspection at that inquiry by such persons, or persons of such descriptions, as may be specified in the direction.

(4) The matters referred to in subsection (3)(a) are—

(a) national security, and

(b) the measures taken, or to be taken, to ensure the security of any premises or property.

(5) The Lord Advocate may appoint a person to represent the interests of any person who—

(a) if a direction is given under subsection (3), will be prevented from hearing or inspecting any evidence at any such inquiry; or

(b) is so prevented by such a direction given before any appointment is made by virtue of paragraph (a).

(6) By rules—

(a) the Secretary of State may make provision as to the procedure to be followed by him before he gives a direction under subsection (3) in a case where a person has been appointed under subsection (5) and as to the functions of a person appointed under subsection (5),

(b) the Scottish Ministers may make provision as to the procedure to be followed by them before they give such a direction in such a case and as to such functions.

(7) If a person (the representative) is appointed—

(a) under paragraph (a) of subsection (5) and either no direction in relation to the evidence in question has been given under subsection (3) or any such direction so given has been given by the Secretary of State, the Secretary of State may direct any person who he thinks,

(b) under paragraph (a) of subsection (5) and such a direction has been given under subsection (3) by the Scottish Ministers, the Scottish Ministers may direct any person who they think,

(c) under paragraph (b) of subsection (5) and the direction referred to in that paragraph was given by the Secretary of State, the Secretary of State may direct any person who he thinks,

(d) under paragraph (b) of that subsection and the direction so referred to was given by the Scottish Ministers, the Scottish Ministers may direct any person who they think,

is interested in the inquiry, or prospective inquiry, in relation to a matter mentioned in subsection (4) (the responsible person) to pay remuneration or allowances to, and to reimburse any expenses incurred by, the representative.

(8) If the representative and the responsible person are unable to agree an amount payable by virtue of—

(a) paragraph (a) or (c) of subsection (7), the amount must be determined by the Secretary of State,

(b) paragraph (b) or (d) of that subsection, the amount must be determined by the Scottish Ministers.

(9) The Secretary of State must cause an amount payable by virtue of paragraph (a) or (c) of subsection (7) (whether determined under subsection (8) or agreed between the representative and the responsible person) to be certified.

(10) The Scottish Ministers must cause an amount payable by virtue of paragraph (b) or (d) of subsection (7) (whether so determined or so agreed) to be certified.

(11) An amount certified under subsection (9) or (10) is recoverable from the responsible person as a debt.

(12) Subsections (7) to (11) apply even if the inquiry does not take place.

(13) The power to make rules under—

(a) paragraph (a) of subsection (6) must be exercised by statutory instrument subject to annulment in pursuance of a resolution of either House of Parliament,
(b) paragraph (b) of that subsection must be exercised by statutory instrument subject to annulment in pursuance of a resolution of the Scottish Parliament.'

(2) In Schedule 3 to the Planning (Listed Buildings and Conservation Areas) (Scotland) Act 1997 (determination of certain appeals by person appointed by the Scottish Ministers), in paragraph 6, after sub-paragraph (6) there is inserted the following sub-paragraph—

'(7) Subsections (2) to (13) of section 265A of the principal Act apply to the holding of an inquiry under this paragraph as they apply to the holding of an inquiry under section 265 of that Act.'

(3) In the Schedule to the Planning (Hazardous Substances) (Scotland) Act 1997 (determination of certain appeals by person appointed by Scottish Ministers), in paragraph 6, after sub-paragraph (6) there is inserted the following sub-paragraph—

'(7) Subsections (2) to (13) of section 265A of the principal Act apply to the holding of an inquiry under this paragraph as they apply to the holding of an inquiry under section 265 of that Act.'

NOTES

Initial Commencement

To be appointed: see s 121(1), (3).

Appointment

Appointment (for the purpose of making, or making provision by means of, subordinate legislation): 6 August 2004: see SI 2004/2097, art 2.

Appointment (for remaining purposes): 7 June 2006: see SI 2006/1281, art 4.

Urgent development and works

A1.458

92 Urgent Crown development: Scotland

(1) In the Town and Country Planning (Scotland) Act 1997 (c 8), before section 243 (control of development on Crown land: special enforcement notices) there is inserted the following section—

'242A   Urgent Crown development: application

(1)   This section applies to a development if the appropriate authority certifies—

(a)   that the development is of national importance, and
(b)   that it is necessary that the development is carried out as a matter of urgency.

(2)   The appropriate authority may, instead of making an application for planning permission to the planning authority in accordance with Part 3, make an application for planning permission to the Scottish Ministers under this section.

(3)   If the appropriate authority proposes to make the application to the Scottish Ministers, it must publish in one or more newspapers circulating in the locality of the proposed development a notice—

(a)   describing the proposed development, and
(b)   stating that the authority proposes to make the application to the Scottish Ministers.

(4)   For the purposes of an application under this section the appropriate authority must provide to the Scottish Ministers—

(a)   any matter required to be provided by an applicant for planning permission in pursuance of regulations made under section 40,
(b)   a statement of the authority's grounds for making the application.

(5)   If the appropriate authority makes an application under this section subsections (6) to (11) below apply.

(6)   The Scottish Ministers may require the authority to provide them with such further information as they think necessary to enable them to determine the application.

(7)   As soon as practicable after they are provided with any document or other matter in pursuance of subsection (4) or (6) the Scottish Ministers must make a copy of the document or other matter available for inspection by the public in the locality of the proposed development.

(8)   The Scottish Ministers must in accordance with such requirements as they may specify in a development order publish notice of the application and of the fact that such documents and other material are available for inspection.

(9)   The Scottish Ministers must consult—

(a)   the planning authority, and
(b)   such other persons as may be so specified,

about the application.

(10)   Subsection (7) above does not apply to the extent that the document or other matter is subject to any direction given under section 265A(3) of this Act.

(11)   Subsections (4) to (7) of section 46 apply to an application under this section as they apply to an application in respect of which a direction under section 46 has effect.'

(2)   In section 237 of that Act, (validity of certain matters) in subsection (3) at the end there is added the following paragraph—

'(i)   any decision on an application for planning permission under section 242A.'

NOTES

Initial Commencement

To be appointed: see s 121(4)(a).

Appointment

Sub-s (1): Appointment (for the purpose of enabling provision to be made by development order): 20 March 2006: see SSI 2006/101, art 2, Schedule.

Sub-s (1): Appointment (for remaining purposes): 11 May 2006: see SSI 2006/243, art 3.

Sub-s (2): Appointment: 11 May 2006: see SSI 2006/243, art 3.

A1.459

93   Urgent works relating to Crown land: Scotland

(1)   In the Planning (Listed Buildings and Conservation Areas) (Scotland) Act 1997 (c 9), after section 73A (inserted by section 90(2)) there is inserted the following section—

'73B   Urgent works relating to Crown land: application

(1)   This section applies to any works proposed to be executed in connection with any building which is on Crown land if the appropriate authority certifies—

    (a)   that the works are of national importance, and

    (b)   that it is necessary that the works are carried out as a matter of urgency.

(2)   The appropriate authority may, instead of making an application for consent to the planning authority in accordance with this Act, make an application for consent to the Scottish Ministers under this section.

(3)   If the appropriate authority proposes to make the application to the Scottish Ministers it must publish in one or more newspapers circulating in the locality of the building a notice—

    (a)   describing the proposed works, and

    (b)   stating that the authority proposes to make the application to the Scottish Ministers.

(4)   For the purposes of an application under this section the appropriate authority must provide to the Scottish Ministers a statement of the authority's grounds for making the application.

(5)   If the appropriate authority makes an application under this section subsections (6) to (11) below apply.

(6)   The Scottish Ministers may require the authority to provide them with such further information as they think necessary to enable them to determine the application.

(7)   As soon as practicable after they are provided with any document or other matter in pursuance of subsection (4) or (6) the Scottish Ministers must make a copy of the document or other matter available for inspection by the public in the locality of the proposed development.

(8)   The Scottish Ministers must in accordance with such requirements as may be prescribed publish notice of the application and of the fact that such documents and other material are available for inspection.

(9)   Subsection (7) above does not apply to the extent that the document or other matter is subject to any direction given under section 265A(3) of the principal Act.

(10)   The Scottish Ministers must consult—

    (a)   the planning authority, and

    (b)   such other persons as may be prescribed,

about the application.

(11)   Subsections (4) and (5) of section 11 apply to an application under this section as they apply to an application in respect of which a direction under section 11 has effect.'

(2)   In section 57 of that Act (validity of certain matters), in subsection (2) at the end there is added the following paragraph—

'(d)   any decision on an application for listed building consent under section 73B.'

NOTES

Initial Commencement

To be appointed: see s 121(4)(a).

Appointment

Sub-s (1): Appointment (for the purpose of making regulations): 20 March 2006: see SSI 2006/101, art 2, Schedule.

Sub-s (1): Appointment (for remaining purposes): 11 May 2006: see SSI 2006/243, art 3.

Sub-s (2): Appointment: 11 May 2006: see SSI 2006/243, art 3.

Enforcement

A1.460

94   Enforcement in relation to Crown land: Scotland

(1)   In the Town and Country Planning (Scotland) Act 1997 (c 8), section 245 (exercise of powers in relation to Crown land) is omitted.

(2)   After section 245 there is inserted the following section—

'245A   Enforcement in relation to the Crown

(1)   No act or omission done or suffered by or on behalf of the Crown constitutes an offence under this Act; but the Court of Session may, on the application of a public authority or office-holder responsible for the enforcement of anything required to be done, or prohibited, by or under this Act, declare unlawful any act or omission so done or suffered.

(2)   A planning authority must not take any step for the purposes of enforcement in relation to Crown land unless it has the consent of the appropriate authority.

(3)   The appropriate authority may give consent under subsection (2) subject to such conditions as it thinks appropriate.

(4)   A step taken for the purposes of enforcement is anything done in connection with the enforcement of anything required to be done or prohibited by or under this Act.

(5)   A step taken for the purposes of enforcement includes—

(a)   entering land,
(b)   initiating proceedings,
(c)   the making of an application.

(6)   A step taken for the purposes of enforcement does not include—

(a)   service of a notice,
(b)   the making of an order (other than a court order).'

(3) In the Town and Country Planning (Scotland) Act 1997 (c 8), after section 245A (inserted by subsection (2) above) there is inserted the following section—

'245B   References to an interest in land

(1) Subsection (2) applies to the extent that an interest in land is a Crown interest.

(2) Anything which requires or is permitted to be done by or in relation to the owner of the interest in land must be done by or in relation to the appropriate authority.

(3) An interest in land includes an interest only as occupier of the land.'

(4) In the Planning (Listed Buildings and Conservation Areas) (Scotland) Act 1997 (c 9) after section 73C (inserted by Schedule 5) there are inserted the following sections—

'73D   Enforcement in relation to the Crown

(1) No act or omission done or suffered by or on behalf of the Crown constitutes an offence under this Act; but the Court of Session may on the application of a public authority or office-holder responsible for the enforcement of anything required to be done, or prohibited, by or under this Act, declare unlawful any act or omission so done or suffered.

(2) A planning authority must not take any step for the purposes of enforcement in relation to Crown land unless it has the consent of the appropriate authority.

(3) The appropriate authority may give consent under subsection (2) subject to such conditions as it thinks appropriate.

(4) A step taken for the purposes of enforcement is anything done in connection with the enforcement of anything required to be done or prohibited by or under this Act.

(5) A step taken for the purposes of enforcement includes—

    (a)   entering land,
    (b)   initiating proceedings,
    (c)   the making of an application.

(6) A step taken for the purposes of enforcement does not include—

    (a)   service of a notice,
    (b)   the making of an order (other than a court order).

73E   Reference to an interest in land

(1) Subsection (2) applies to the extent that an interest in land is a Crown interest.

(2) Anything which requires or is permitted to be done by or in relation to the owner of the interest in land must be done by or in relation to the appropriate authority.

(3) An interest in land includes an interest only as occupier of the land.'

(5) In the Planning (Hazardous Substances) (Scotland) Act 1997, after section 30A (inserted by section 90(3)) there are inserted the following sections—

'30B   Enforcement in relation to the Crown

(1) No act or omission done or suffered by or on behalf of the Crown constitutes an offence under this Act; but the Court of Session may, on the application of a public authority or office-holder responsible for the enforcement of anything required to be done, or prohibited, by or under this Act, declare unlawful any act or omission so done or suffered.

(2)   A planning authority must not take any step for the purposes of enforcement in relation to Crown land unless it has the consent of the appropriate authority.

(3)   The appropriate authority may give consent under subsection (2) subject to such conditions as it thinks appropriate.

(4)   A step taken for the purposes of enforcement is anything done in connection with the enforcement of anything required to be done or prohibited by or under this Act.

(5)   A step taken for the purposes of enforcement includes—

(a)   entering land,
(b)   initiating proceedings,
(c)   the making of an application.

(6)   A step taken for the purposes of enforcement does not include—

(a)   service of a notice,
(b)   the making of an order (other than a court order).

30C   Reference to an interest in land

(1)   Subsection (2) applies to the extent that an interest in land is a Crown interest.

(2)   Anything which requires or is permitted to be done by or in relation to the owner of the interest in land must be done by or in relation to the appropriate authority.

(3)   An interest in land includes an interest only as occupier of the land.'

NOTES

Initial Commencement

To be appointed: see s 121(4)(a).

Appointment

Sub-ss (1)–(3), (5): Appointment: 12 June 2006: see SSI 2006/268, art 3(b).

Sub-s (4): Appointment: 11 May 2006: see SSI 2006/243, art 3.

Trees

A1.461

95   Tree preservation orders: Scotland

For section 162 of the Town and Country Planning (Scotland) Act 1997 (Orders affecting land where Forestry Commissioners interested) there is substituted the following section—

'162   Tree preservation: Forestry Commissioners

(1)   A tree preservation order does not have effect in respect of anything done—

(a)   by or on behalf of the Forestry Commissioners on land placed at their disposal in pursuance of the Forestry Act 1967 or otherwise under their management or supervision;
(b)   by or on behalf of any other person in accordance with a relevant plan which is for the time being in force.

(2)   A relevant plan is a plan of operations or other working plan approved by the Forestry Commissioners under—

   (a) a forestry dedication agreement within the meaning of section 5 of the Forestry Act 1967, or

   (b) conditions of a grant or loan made under section 1 of the Forestry Act 1979.

(3) A reference to a provision of the Forestry Act 1967 or the Forestry Act 1979 includes a reference to a corresponding provision replaced by that provision or any earlier corresponding provision.'

NOTES

Initial Commencement

To be appointed: see s 121(4)(a).

Appointment

Appointment: 12 June 2006: see SSI 2006/268, art 3(b).

A1.462

96   **Trees in conservation areas in Scotland: acts of Crown**

In the Town and Country Planning (Scotland) Act 1997 (c 8), after section 172(4) (preservation of trees in conservation areas) there are inserted the following subsections—

'(5) An emanation of the Crown must not, in relation to a tree to which this section applies, do an act mentioned in subsection (1) above unless—

   (a) the first condition is satisfied, and

   (b) either the second or third condition is satisfied.

(6) The first condition is that the emanation serves notice of an intention to do the act (with sufficient particulars to identify the tree) on the planning authority in whose area the tree is situated.

(7) The second condition is that the act is done with the consent of the authority.

(8) The third condition is that the act is done—

   (a) after the end of the period of six weeks starting with the date of the notice, and

   (b) before the end of the period of two years starting with that date.'

NOTES

Initial Commencement

To be appointed: see s 121(4)(a).

Appointment

Appointment: 12 June 2006: see SSI 2006/268, art 3(b).

Miscellaneous

A1.463

97   **Old mining permissions: Scotland**

(1) Subsection (2) applies if—

   (a) an old mining permission relates to land which is Crown land, and

(b) the permission has not been registered in pursuance of Part 2 of Schedule 8 to the Town and Country Planning (Scotland) Act 1997.

(2) Paragraph 10 of that Schedule and that Part apply to the old mining permission subject to the following modifications—

(a) in sub-paragraph (3) of that paragraph, for '16th May 1991' there is substituted 'the date of commencement of section 97(2) of the Planning and Compulsory Purchase Act 2004',

(b) in paragraph 13(3) of that Part, for '24 January 1992' there is substituted 'the date of commencement of section 97(2) of the Planning and Compulsory Purchase Act 2004'.

(3) 'Old mining permission' must be construed in accordance with paragraph 10 and Part 2 of that Schedule.

(4) 'Crown land' must be construed in accordance with Part 12 of the Town and Country Planning (Scotland) Act 1997.

NOTES

Initial Commencement

To be appointed: see s 121(4)(a).

Appointment

Appointment: 12 June 2006: see SSI 2006/268, art 3(b).

A1.464

98   Subordinate legislation: Scotland

(1) The Scottish Ministers may by order provide that relevant subordinate legislation applies to the Crown.

(2) The order may modify such subordinate legislation to the extent that the Scottish Ministers think appropriate for the purposes of its application to the Crown.

(3) Relevant subordinate legislation is an instrument which—

(a) is made under or (wholly or in part) for the purposes of any of the Scottish planning Acts,

(b) is made before the commencement of section 90 of this Act, and

(c) is specified in the order.

(4) In subsection (3), 'instrument' includes an instrument made under an Act of the Scottish Parliament.

NOTES

Initial Commencement

To be appointed: see s 121(4)(a).

Appointment

Appointment: 20 March 2006: see SSI 2006/101, art 2, Schedule.

PART 8: COMPULSORY PURCHASE

Acquisition of land for development

A1.465

99   Compulsory acquisition of land for development etc

(1)   Section 226 of the principal Act (compulsory acquisition of land for development and other planning purposes) is amended as follows.

(2)   In subsection (1)—

   (a)   the first 'which' is omitted;
   (b)   for paragraph (a) there is substituted the following paragraph—
   '(a)   if the authority think that the acquisition will facilitate the carrying out of development, re-development or improvement on or in relation to the land,';
   (c)   in paragraph (b) at the beginning there is inserted 'which'.

(3)   After subsection (1) there is inserted the following subsection—

'(1A)   But a local authority must not exercise the power under paragraph (a) of subsection (1) unless they think that the development, re-development or improvement is likely to contribute to the achievement of any one or more of the following objects—

   (a)   the promotion or improvement of the economic well-being of their area;
   (b)   the promotion or improvement of the social well-being of their area;
   (c)   the promotion or improvement of the environmental well-being of their area.'

(4)   Subsection (2) is omitted.

(5)   Nothing in this section affects a compulsory purchase order made before the commencement of this section.

NOTES

Initial Commencement

To be appointed: see s 121(1), (2)(e).

Appointment

Appointment: 31 October 2004: see SI 2004/2593, art 2(a).

Extent

This section does not extend to Scotland: see s 124(1).

Authorisation of compulsory acquisition

A1.466

100   Procedure for authorisation by authority other than a Minister

(1)   The Acquisition of Land Act 1981 (c 67) (the '1981 Act') is amended as follows.

(2)   In section 6 (service of documents), in subsection (4)—

   (a)   after 'lessee' in each place there is inserted ', tenant';
   (b)   after "lessee' there is inserted ', 'tenant".

(3)   In section 7 (interpretation), after subsection (2) there is added—

'(3)   But an instrument containing regulations made for the purposes of section 13A or paragraph 4A of Schedule 1 is subject to annulment in pursuance of a resolution of either House of Parliament.'

(4)   In section 11 (notices in newspapers), after subsection (2) there is added—

'(3)   In addition, the acquiring authority shall affix a notice in the prescribed form to a conspicuous object or objects on or near the land comprised in the order.

(4)   The notice under subsection (3) must—

    (a)   be addressed to persons occupying or having an interest in the land, and

    (b)   set out each of the matters mentioned in subsection (2) (but reading the reference there to first publication of the notice as a reference to the day when the notice under subsection (3) is first affixed).'

(5)   In section 12 (notices to owners, lessees and occupiers)—

    (a)   in subsection (1), for the words from 'owner' to 'order' (where it first appears) there is substituted 'qualifying person';

    (b)   for subsection (2) there is substituted—

'(2)   A person is a qualifying person, in relation to land comprised in an order, if—

    (a)   he is an owner, lessee, tenant (whatever the tenancy period) or occupier of the land, or

    (b)   he falls within subsection (2A).

(2A)   A person falls within this subsection if he is—

    (a)   a person to whom the acquiring authority would, if proceeding under section 5(1) of the Compulsory Purchase Act 1965, be required to give a notice to treat, or

    (b)   a person the acquiring authority thinks is likely to be entitled to make a relevant claim if the order is confirmed and the compulsory purchase takes place, so far as he is known to the acquiring authority after making diligent inquiry.

(2B)   A relevant claim is a claim for compensation under section 10 of the Compulsory Purchase Act 1965 (compensation for injurious affection).'

(6)   For section 13 (confirmation of compulsory purchase order) there are substituted the following sections—

'13   Confirmation of order: no objections

(1)   The confirming authority may confirm a compulsory purchase order with or without modifications if it is satisfied—

    (a)   that the notice requirements have been complied with, and

    (b)   that one of the conditions in subsection (2) is satisfied.

(2)   The conditions are—

    (a)   no relevant objection is made;

    (b)   every relevant objection made is either withdrawn or disregarded.

(3)   The confirming authority may require every person who makes a relevant objection to state the grounds of the objection in writing.

(4)   If the confirming authority is satisfied that an objection relates exclusively to matters which can be dealt with by the tribunal by whom the compensation is to be assessed it may disregard the objection.

(5) The notice requirements are the requirements under sections 11 and 12 to publish, affix and serve notices in connection with the compulsory purchase order.

(6) A relevant objection is an objection by a person who is a qualifying person for the purposes of section 12(2), but if such a person qualifies only by virtue of section 12(2A)(b) and the confirming authority thinks that he is not likely to be entitled to make a relevant claim his objection is not a relevant objection.

(7) Disregarded means disregarded under subsection (4) or under any other power to disregard a relevant objection contained in the enactment providing for the compulsory purchase.

13A   Confirmation of order: remaining objections

(1) This section applies to the confirmation of a compulsory purchase order if a relevant objection is made which is neither—

    (a) withdrawn, nor
    (b) disregarded,

(a remaining objection).

(2) The confirming authority may proceed under the written representations procedure—

    (a) if the order is not subject to special parliamentary procedure,
    (b) in the case of an order to which section 16 applies, if a certificate has been given under subsection (2) of that section, and
    (c) if every person who has made a remaining objection consents in the prescribed manner.

(3) If subsection (2) does not apply or if the confirming authority decides not to proceed under that subsection, it must either—

    (a) cause a public local inquiry to be held, or
    (b) give every person who has made a remaining objection an opportunity of appearing before and being heard by a person appointed by the confirming authority for the purpose.

(4) If a person who has made a remaining objection takes the opportunity to appear before a person appointed under subsection (3)(b) the confirming authority must give the acquiring authority and any other person it thinks appropriate the opportunity to be heard at the same time.

(5) The confirming authority may confirm the order with or without modifications if it has considered the objection and either—

    (a) it has followed the written representations procedure, or
    (b) in a case which falls within subsection (3), if an inquiry was held or a person was appointed under subsection (3)(b), it has considered the report of the person who held the inquiry or who was so appointed.

(6) The written representations procedure is such procedure as is prescribed for the purposes of this section including provision affording an opportunity to—

    (a) every person who has made a remaining objection,
    (b) the acquiring authority, and
    (c) any other person the confirming authority thinks appropriate,

to make written representations as to whether the order should be confirmed.

(7) Relevant objection and disregarded must be construed in accordance with section 13.

13B   **Written representations procedure: supplementary**

(1)   This section applies where the confirming authority decides under section 13A to follow the written representations procedure.

(2)   The confirming authority may make orders as to the costs of the parties to the written representations procedure, and as to which party must pay the costs.

(3)   An order under subsection (2) may be made a rule of the High Court on the application of any party named in the order.

(4)   The costs incurred by the confirming authority in connection with the written representations procedure must be paid by the acquiring authority, if the confirming authority so directs.

(5)   The confirming authority may certify the amount of its costs, and any amount so certified and directed to be paid by the acquiring authority is recoverable summarily by the confirming authority as a civil debt.

(6)   Section 42(2) of the Housing and Planning Act 1986 (recovery of Minister's costs in connection with inquiries) applies to the written representations procedure as if the procedure is an inquiry specified in section 42(1) of that Act.

(7)   Regulations under section 13A(6) may make provision as to the giving of reasons for decisions taken in cases where the written representations procedure is followed.

13C   **Confirmation in stages**

(1)   The confirming authority may confirm an order (with or without modifications) so far as it relates to part of the land comprised in the order (the 'relevant part') if each of the conditions in subsection (2) is met.

(2)   The conditions are—
   (a)   the confirming authority is satisfied that the order ought to be confirmed so far as it relates to the relevant part but has not for the time being determined whether the order ought to be confirmed so far as it relates to the remaining part;
   (b)   the confirming authority is satisfied that the notice requirements have been complied with.

(3)   If there is a remaining objection in respect of the order, the confirming authority may only act under subsection (1) after complying with section 13A(2) or (3) (as the case may be).

(4)   But it may act under subsection (1) without complying with those provisions if it is satisfied that all remaining objections relate solely to the remaining part of the land.

(5)   If the confirming authority acts under subsection (1)—
   (a)   it must give a direction postponing consideration of the order, so far as it relates to the remaining part, until such time as may be specified by or under the direction;
   (b)   the order so far as it relates to each part of the land must be treated as a separate order.

(6)   The notices to be published, affixed and served under section 15 must include a statement as to the effect of the direction given under subsection (5)(a).

(7)   Notice requirements must be construed in accordance with section 13.

(8)   Remaining objection must be construed in accordance with section 13A.'

(7)   For section 15 there is substituted—

'15   Notices after confirmation of order

(1)   After the order has been confirmed, the acquiring authority must—

    (a)   serve a confirmation notice and a copy of the order as confirmed on each person on whom a notice was required to be served under section 12, and

    (b)   affix a confirmation notice to a conspicuous object or objects on or near the land comprised in the order.

(2)   The notice under subsection (1)(b) must—

    (a)   be addressed to persons occupying or having an interest in the land;

    (b)   so far as practicable, be kept in place by the acquiring authority until the expiry of a period of six weeks beginning with the date when the order becomes operative.

(3)   The acquiring authority must also publish a confirmation notice in one or more local newspapers circulating in the locality in which the land comprised in the order is situated.

(4)   A confirmation notice is a notice—

    (a)   describing the land;

    (b)   stating that the order has been confirmed;

    (c)   (except in the case of a notice under subsection (1)(a)) naming a place where a copy of the order as confirmed and of the map referred to there may be inspected at all reasonable hours;

    (d)   that a person aggrieved by the order may apply to the High Court as mentioned in section 23.

(5)   A confirmation notice must be in the prescribed form.'

(8)   The amendments made by this section do not apply to orders of which notice under section 11 of the 1981 Act has been published before commencement of this section.

NOTES

Initial Commencement

To be appointed: see s 121(1), (2)(e).

Appointment

Appointment (for the purpose of making, or making provision by means of, subordinate legislation): 6 August 2004: see SI 2004/2097, art 2.

Appointment (for remaining purposes): 31 October 2004: see SI 2004/2593, art 2(a).

Extent

This section does not extend to Scotland: see s 124(1).

A1.467

101   Procedure for authorisation by a Minister

(1)   Schedule 1 to the Acquisition of Land Act 1981 (c 67) (the '1981 Act') is amended as follows.

(2)   In paragraph 2 (notices in newspapers), after sub-paragraph (2) there is added—

'(3)   In addition, the Minister shall affix a notice in the prescribed form to a conspicuous object or objects on or near the land comprised in the draft order.

(4)   The notice under sub-paragraph (3) must—

    (a)   be addressed to persons occupying or having an interest in the land, and

    (b)   set out each of the matters mentioned in sub-paragraph (2) (but reading the reference there to first publication of the notice as a reference to the day when the notice under sub-paragraph (3) is first affixed).'

(3)   In paragraph 3 (notices to owners, lessees and occupiers)—

    (a)   in sub-paragraph (1), for the words from 'owner' to 'order' (where it first appears) there is substituted 'qualifying person';

    (b)   for sub-paragraph (2) there is substituted—

'(2)   A person is a qualifying person, in relation to land comprised in a draft order, if—

    (a)   he is an owner, lessee, tenant (whatever the tenancy period) or occupier of any such land, or

    (b)   he falls within sub-paragraph (2A).

(2A)   A person falls within this sub-paragraph if he is—

    (a)   a person to whom the Minister would, if proceeding under section 5(1) of the Compulsory Purchase Act 1965, be required to give a notice to treat, or

    (b)   a person the Minister thinks is likely to be entitled to make a relevant claim if the order is made and the compulsory purchase takes place, so far as he is known to the Minister after making diligent inquiry.

(2B)   A relevant claim is a claim for compensation under section 10 of the Compulsory Purchase Act 1965 (compensation for injurious affection).'

(4)   For paragraph 4 there are substituted the following paragraphs—

'4   (1)   The Minister may make a compulsory purchase order with or without modifications if he is satisfied—

    (a)   that the notice requirements have been complied with, and

    (b)   that one of the conditions in sub-paragraph (2) is satisfied.

(2)   The conditions are—

    (a)   no relevant objection is made;

    (b)   every relevant objection made is either withdrawn or disregarded.

(3)   The appropriate authority may require every person who makes a relevant objection to state the grounds of the objection in writing.

(4)   If the appropriate authority is satisfied that an objection relates exclusively to matters which can be dealt with by the tribunal by whom the compensation is to be assessed it may disregard the objection.

(5)   The notice requirements are the requirements under paragraphs 2 and 3 to publish, affix and serve notices in connection with the compulsory purchase order.

(6)   A relevant objection is an objection by a person who is a qualifying person for the purposes of paragraph 3(2), but if such a person qualifies only by virtue of paragraph 3(2A)(b) and the Minister thinks that he is not likely to be entitled to make a relevant claim his objection is not a relevant objection.

(7)   Disregarded means disregarded under sub-paragraph (4) or under any other power to disregard a relevant objection contained in the enactment providing for the compulsory purchase.

(8)   The appropriate authority is—

(a) in the case of an order proposed to be made in the exercise of highway land acquisition powers, the Minister and the planning Minister acting jointly,

(b) in any other case, the Minister.

(9) Highway land acquisition powers must be construed in accordance with the Highways Act 1980.

(10) The planning Minister is the Secretary of State for the time being having general responsibility in planning matters.

4A (1) This paragraph applies to the making of a compulsory purchase order if a relevant objection is made which is neither—

(a) withdrawn, nor

(b) disregarded,

(a remaining objection).

(2) The appropriate authority may proceed under the written representations procedure—

(a) if the order is not subject to special parliamentary procedure;

(b) in the case of an order to which section 16 applies, if a certificate has been given under subsection (2) of that section, and

(c) if every person who has made a remaining objection consents in the prescribed manner.

(3) If sub-paragraph (2) does not apply or if the appropriate authority decides not to proceed under that sub-paragraph, it must either—

(a) cause a public local inquiry to be held, or

(b) give every person who has made a remaining objection an opportunity of appearing before and being heard by a person appointed by the appropriate authority for the purpose.

(4) If a person who has made a remaining objection takes the opportunity to appear before a person appointed under sub-paragraph (3)(b) the appropriate authority must give any other person it thinks appropriate the opportunity to be heard at the same time.

(5) The Minister may make the order with or without modifications if—

(a) the appropriate authority has considered the objection, and

(b) one of the conditions in sub-paragraph (6) is satisfied.

(6) The conditions are—

(a) the appropriate authority has followed the written representations procedure;

(b) in a case which falls within sub-paragraph (3), if an inquiry was held or a person was appointed under sub-paragraph (3)(b), the appropriate authority has considered the report of the person who held the inquiry or who was so appointed.

(7) The written representations procedure is such procedure as is prescribed for the purposes of this paragraph including provision affording an opportunity to—

(a) every person who has made a remaining objection, and

(b) any other person the appropriate authority thinks appropriate,

to make written representations as to whether the order should be made.

(8) Regulations under sub-paragraph (7) may make provision as to the giving of reasons for decisions taken in cases where the written representations procedure is followed.

(9) Expressions used in this paragraph and in paragraph 4 must be construed in accordance with paragraph 4.

4B (1) The Minister may make an order (with or without modifications) so far as it relates to part of the land comprised in the draft order (the 'relevant part') if each of the conditions in sub-paragraph (2) is met.

(2) The conditions are—

    (a) the Minister or, if there is a remaining objection in respect of the order, the appropriate authority is satisfied that the order ought to be made so far as it relates to the relevant part but has not for the time being determined whether the order ought to be made so far as it relates to the remaining part;

    (b) the Minister is satisfied that the notice requirements have been complied with.

(3) If there is a remaining objection in respect of the order, the Minister may only act under sub-paragraph (1) after the appropriate authority has complied with paragraph 4A(2) or (3) (as the case may be).

(4) But he may act under sub-paragraph (1) without the appropriate authority having complied with those provisions if he is satisfied that all remaining objections relate solely to the remaining part of the land.

(5) If the Minister acts under sub-paragraph (1)—

    (a) he must give a direction postponing consideration of the order, so far as it relates to the remaining part, until such time as may be specified by or under the direction;

    (b) the order so far as it relates to each part of the land must be treated as a separate order.

(6) The notices to be published, affixed and served under paragraph 6 must include a statement as to the effect of the direction given under sub-paragraph (5)(a).

(7) Expressions used in this paragraph and in paragraph 4 or 4A must be construed in accordance with paragraph 4 or 4A (as the case may be).'

(5) For paragraph 6 there is substituted—

'**6** (1) After the order has been made, the Minister must—

    (a) serve a making notice, and a copy of the order as made, on each person on whom a notice was required to be served under paragraph 3, and

    (b) affix a making notice to a conspicuous object or objects on or near the land comprised in the order.

(2) The notice under sub-paragraph (1)(b) must—

    (a) be addressed to persons occupying or having an interest in the land;

    (b) so far as practicable, be kept in place by the acquiring authority until the expiry of a period of six weeks beginning with the date when the order becomes operative.

(3) The Minister must also publish a making notice in one or more local newspapers circulating in the locality in which the land comprised in the order is situated.

(4) A making notice is a notice—

    (a) describing the land;

    (b) stating that the order has been made;

    (c) (except in the case of a notice under sub-paragraph (1)(a)) naming a place where a copy of the order as made and of the map referred to there may be inspected at all reasonable hours;

(d) that a person aggrieved by the order may apply to the High Court as mentioned in section 23.

(5) A making notice must be in the prescribed form.'

(6) The amendments made by this section do not apply to orders of which notice under paragraph 2 of Schedule 1 to the 1981 Act has been published before commencement of this section.

NOTES

Initial Commencement

To be appointed: see s 121(1), (2)(e).

Appointment

Appointment (for the purpose of making, or making provision by means of, subordinate legislation): 6 August 2004: see SI 2004/2097, art 2.

Appointment (for remaining purposes): 31 October 2004: see SI 2004/2593, art 2(a).

Extent

This section does not extend to Scotland: see s 124(1).

A1.468

102   Confirmation by acquiring authority

(1) The Acquisition of Land Act 1981 (c 67) (the '1981 Act') is amended as follows.

(2) After section 14 there is inserted—

'**14A   Confirmation by acquiring authority**

(1) The power to confirm an order may be exercised by the acquiring authority (instead of the confirming authority) if—

(a) the confirming authority has notified the acquiring authority to that effect, and
(b) the notice has not been revoked.

(2) But this section does not apply to an order in respect of land—

(a) falling within section 16(1) or paragraph 3(1) of Schedule 3, or
(b) forming part of a common, open space or fuel or field garden allotment for the purposes of section 19.

(3) The confirming authority may give notice under subsection (1) if it is satisfied—

(a) that the notice requirements have been complied with,
(b) that no objection has been made in relation to the proposed confirmation or that all objections have been withdrawn, and
(c) that the order is capable of being confirmed without modification.

(4) An objection is an objection made by any person (whether or not a person mentioned in section 12(2)), including an objection which is disregarded.

(5) The power to confirm an order under subsection (1) does not include any power—

(a) to confirm the order with modifications, or
(b) to confirm only a part of the order.

(6)   The acquiring authority must notify the confirming authority as soon as reasonably practicable after it has determined whether or not to confirm the order.

(7)   The confirming authority may revoke a notice given by it under subsection (1).

(8)   But a notice may not be revoked if the determination has already been made and notified by the acquiring authority under subsection (6).

(9)   An order confirmed by the acquiring authority under subsection (1) is to have the same effect as if it were confirmed by the confirming authority.

(10)   Notices under this section must be in writing.

(11)   Notice requirements and disregarded must be construed in accordance with section 13.'

(3)   The amendments made by this section do not apply to orders of which notice has been published under section 11 of the 1981 Act before commencement of this section.

NOTES

Initial Commencement

To be appointed: see s 121(1), (2)(e).

Appointment

Appointment: 31 October 2004: see SI 2004/2593, art 2(a).

Extent

This section does not extend to Scotland: see s 124(1).

Valuation date

A1.469

103   Assessment of compensation: valuation date

(1)   The Land Compensation Act 1961 (c 33) is amended as follows.

(2)   After section 5 there is inserted—

'5A   Relevant valuation date

(1)   If the value of land is to be assessed in accordance with rule (2) in section 5, the valuation must be made as at the relevant valuation date.

(2)   No adjustment is to be made to the valuation in respect of anything which happens after the relevant valuation date.

(3)   If the land is the subject of a notice to treat, the relevant valuation date is the earlier of—

   (a)   the date when the acquiring authority enters on and takes possession of the land, and
   (b)   the date when the assessment is made.

(4)   If the land is the subject of a general vesting declaration, the relevant valuation date is the earlier of—

   (a)   the vesting date, and
   (b)   the date when the assessment is made,

and 'general vesting declaration' and 'vesting date' have the meanings given in section 2 of the Compulsory Purchase (Vesting Declarations) Act 1981.

(5) If the acquiring authority enters on and takes possession of part of the land—

(a) specified in a notice of entry, or

(b) in respect of which a payment into court has been made,

the authority is deemed, for the purposes of subsection (3)(a), to have entered on and taken possession of the whole of that land on that date.

(6) Subsection (5) also applies for the purposes of calculating interest under the following enactments—

(a) section 11(1) of the Compulsory Purchase Act 1965;

(b) paragraph 3 of Schedule 3 to that Act;

(c) section 85 of the Lands Clauses Consolidation Act 1845;

(d) section 52A of the Land Compensation Act 1973,

and references there to the date or time of entry are to be construed accordingly.

(7) An assessment by the Lands Tribunal is treated as being made on the date certified by the Tribunal as—

(a) the last hearing date before it makes its determination, or

(b) in a case to be determined without an oral hearing, the last date for making written submissions before it makes its determination.

(8) Nothing in this section affects—

(a) any express provision in any other enactment which requires the valuation of land subject to compulsory acquisition to be made at a particular date;

(b) the valuation of land for purposes other than the compulsory acquisition of that land (even if the valuation is to be made in accordance with the rules in section 5).

(9) In this section—

(a) a notice of entry is a notice under section 11(1) of the Compulsory Purchase Act 1965;

(b) a payment into court is a payment into court under Schedule 3 to that Act or under section 85 of the Lands Clauses Consolidation Act 1845.'

NOTES

Initial Commencement

To be appointed: see s 121(1), (2)(e).

Appointment

Appointment: 31 October 2004: see SI 2004/2593, art 2(a).

Extent

This section does not extend to Scotland: see s 124(1).

Advance payments

A1.470

104 Compensation: advance payments to mortgagees

(1) The Land Compensation Act 1973 is amended as follows.

(2) In section 52 (right to advance payment of compensation)—

(a)   after subsection (1) there are inserted the following subsections—

'(1A)   If the acquiring authority have taken possession of part of the land—

(a)   specified in a notice of entry, or
(b)   in respect of which a payment into court has been made,

the compensation mentioned in subsection (1) is the compensation payable for the compulsory acquisition of the interest in the whole of the land.

(1B)   Notice of entry and payment into court must be construed in accordance with section 5A of the Land Compensation Act 1961.',

(b)   for subsection (6) there is substituted the following subsection—

'(6)   If the land is subject to a mortgage sections 52ZA and 52ZB apply.'

(3)   After section 52 of that Act there are inserted the following sections—

'52ZA   Advance payments: land subject to mortgage

(1)   This section applies if—

(a)   an acquiring authority take possession of land,
(b)   a request is made in accordance with section 52(2) for an advance payment, and
(c)   the land is subject to a mortgage the principal of which does not exceed 90% of the relevant amount.

(2)   The advance payment made to the claimant must be reduced by the amount the acquiring authority think will be required by them to secure the release of the interest of the mortgagee (or all the mortgagees if there is more than one).

(3)   The acquiring authority must pay to the mortgagee the amount the acquiring authority think will be required by them to secure the release of the mortgagee's interest, if—

(a)   the claimant so requests, and
(b)   the mortgagee consents to the making of the payment.

(4)   If there is more than one mortgagee—

(a)   subsection (3) applies to each mortgagee individually, but
(b)   payment must not be made to a mortgagee before the interest of each mortgagee whose interest has priority to his interest is released.

(5)   The amount of the advance payment made to the claimant under section 52 and the amount of the payments made to mortgagees under this section must not in aggregate exceed 90% of the relevant amount.

(6)   Subsection (7) applies if—

(a)   the acquiring authority estimated the compensation,
(b)   it appears to the acquiring authority that their estimate was too low and they revise the estimate, and
(c)   a request is made by the claimant in accordance with section 52(2).

(7)   The provisions of subsections (2) to (5) must be re-applied on the basis of the revised estimate.

52ZB   Advance payments: land subject to mortgage exceeding 90% threshold

(1)   This section applies if—

(a)   an acquiring authority take possession of land,

    (b)   a request is made in accordance with section 52(2) for an advance payment, and

    (c)   the land is subject to a mortgage the principal of which exceeds 90% of the relevant amount.

(2)   No advance payment is to be made to the claimant.

(3)   But the acquiring authority must pay to the mortgagee the amount found under subsection (4), if—

    (a)   the claimant so requests, and

    (b)   the mortgagee consents to the making of the payment.

(4)   The amount is whichever is the lesser of—

    (a)   90% of the value of the land;

    (b)   the principal of the mortgagee's mortgage.

(5)   The value of the land is the value—

    (a)   agreed by the claimant and the acquiring authority, or (failing such agreement)

    (b)   estimated by the acquiring authority.

(6)   For the purposes of subsection (5) the value of the land is to be calculated in accordance with rule 2 of section 5 of the Land Compensation Act 1961 (market value), whether or not compensation is or is likely to be assessed in due course in accordance with rule 5 of that section (equivalent re-instatement).

(7)   If there is more than one mortgagee, payment must not be made to a mortgagee until the interest of each mortgagee whose interest has priority to his interest is released.

(8)   But the total payments under subsection (3) must not in any event exceed 90% of the value of the land.

(9)   Subsection (10) applies if—

    (a)   the acquiring authority estimated the compensation,

    (b)   it appears to the acquiring authority that their estimate was too low and they revise the estimate,

    (c)   the condition in section 52ZA(1)(b) would have been satisfied if the revised estimate had been used instead of their estimate, and

    (d)   a request is made by the claimant in accordance with section 52(2).

(10)   The provisions of section 52ZA(2) to (5) must be applied on the basis of the revised estimate.

(11)   If—

    (a)   the acquiring authority estimated the value of the land,

    (b)   it appears to the acquiring authority that their estimate was too low and they revise the estimate, and

    (c)   a request is made by the claimant in writing,

any balance found to be due to a mortgagee on the basis of the revised estimate is payable in accordance with this section.

52ZC   Land subject to mortgage: supplementary

(1)   This section applies for the purposes of sections 52ZA and 52ZB.

(2)   The claimant must provide the acquiring authority with such information as they may require to enable them to give effect to those sections.

(3)   A request under section 52ZA(3) or 52ZB(3) must be made in writing and must be accompanied by the written consent of the mortgagee.

(4)   Subsections (4) and (8) to (9) of section 52 apply to a payment which may be or is made under section 52ZA or 52ZB as they apply to a payment which may be or is made under section 52.

(5)   The relevant amount is the amount of the compensation agreed or estimated as mentioned in section 52(3).

(6)   If the land is subject to more than one mortgage, the reference in sections 52ZA(1)(c) and 52ZB(1)(c) to the principal is to the aggregate of the principals of all of the mortgagees.

(7)   A payment made to a mortgagee under section 52ZA or 52ZB—

   (a)   must be applied by the mortgagee in or towards the discharge of the principal, interest and costs and any other money due under the mortgage;
   (b)   must be taken to be a payment on account of compensation and treated for the purposes of section 52(10) as if it were an advance payment made under section 52;
   (c)   must be taken, with effect from the date of the payment, to reduce by the amount of the payment the amount in respect of which interest accrues for the purposes of section 11(1) of the Compulsory Purchase Act 1965, any bond under Schedule 3 to that Act or section 85 of the Lands Clauses Compensation Act 1845;
   (d)   must be taken into account for the purposes of determining any payments (or payments into court) which may be made for the purposes of sections 14 to 16 of the Compulsory Purchase Act 1965.

(8)   If the amount, or aggregate amount, of any payments under—

   (a)   sections 52 and 52ZA, or
   (b)   section 52ZB,

on the basis of the acquiring authority's estimate of the compensation exceed the compensation as finally determined or agreed, the excess must be repaid by the claimant.

(9)   No payment must be made to a mortgagee—

   (a)   if any of the circumstances mentioned in subsection (10) applies, or
   (b)   if the compulsory acquisition is only of a right over land.

(10)   The circumstances are—

   (a)   payment has been made under section 14(2) of the Compulsory Purchase Act 1965;
   (b)   a notice under section 14(3) of that Act has been given;
   (c)   there is an agreement under section 15(1) or 16(1) of that Act or the matter has been referred to the Lands Tribunal under that section.

(11)   The claimant in relation to settled land for the purposes of the Settled Land Act 1925 is the persons entitled to give a discharge for capital money.'

(4)   In section 52A (right to interest where advance payment made) for subsection (2) there is substituted—

'(2)   If the authority make a payment under section 52(1) to any person on account of the compensation—

    (a)   they must at the same time make a payment to that person of accrued interest, for the period beginning with the date of entry, on the amount of the compensation agreed or estimated under section 52(3) (the total amount), and

    (b)   the difference between the paid amount and the total amount is an unpaid balance for the purposes of this section.

(2A)   The paid amount is—

    (a)   the amount of the payment under section 52(1), or

    (b)   if the land is subject to a mortgage, the aggregate of that amount and the amount of any payment made under section 52ZA(3).'

NOTES

Initial Commencement

To be appointed: see s 121(1), (2)(e).

Appointment

Appointment: 31 October 2004: see SI 2004/2593, art 2(a).

Extent

This section does not extend to Scotland: see s 124(1).

Information

A1.471

105   Power to require information

(1)   The Acquisition of Land Act 1981 (c 67) is amended as follows.

(2)   After section 5 (local inquiries) there is inserted—

'5A   Power to require information

(1)   This section applies to information about land in relation to which an acquiring authority is entitled to exercise a power of compulsory purchase.

(2)   The acquiring authority may serve a notice on a person mentioned in subsection (4) requiring him to give to the authority in writing the following information—

    (a)   the name and address of any person he believes to be an owner, lessee, tenant (whatever the tenancy period) or occupier of the land;

    (b)   the name and address of any person he believes to have an interest in the land.

(3)   The power in subsection (2) is exercisable for the purpose of enabling the acquiring authority to acquire the land.

(4)   The persons are—

    (a)   the occupier of the land;

    (b)   any person who has an interest in the land either as freeholder, mortgagee or lessee;

    (c)   any person who directly or indirectly receives rent for the land;

    (d)   any person who, in pursuance of an agreement between himself and a person interested in the land, is authorised to manage the land or to arrange for the letting of it.

(5)   The notice must specify the period within which the information must be given to the acquiring authority (being a period of not less than 14 days beginning with the day on which the notice is served).

(6)   The notice must also specify or describe—

    (a)   the land,

    (b)   the compulsory purchase power, and

    (c)   the enactment which confers the power.

(7)   The notice must be in writing.

(8)   Section 6(4) does not apply to notices to be served under this section.

5B   Offences relating to information

(1)   A person commits an offence if he fails without reasonable excuse to comply with a notice served on him under section 5A.

(2)   A person commits an offence if, in response to a notice served on him under section 5A—

    (a)   he gives information which is false in a material particular, and

    (b)   when he does so, he knows or ought reasonably to know that the information is false.

(3)   If an offence under this section committed by a body corporate is proved to have been committed with the consent or connivance of, or to be attributable to any neglect on the part of—

    (a)   a director, manager, secretary or other similar officer of the body corporate, or

    (b)   a person purporting to act in any such capacity,

he, as well as the body corporate, is guilty of that offence and liable to be proceeded against accordingly.

(4)   The reference in subsection (3) to a director must be construed in accordance with section 331(2) of the Town and Country Planning Act 1990.

(5)   A person guilty of an offence under this section is liable on summary conviction to a fine not exceeding level 5 on the standard scale.'

NOTES

Initial Commencement

To be appointed: see s 121(1), (2)(e).

Appointment

Appointment: 31 October 2004: see SI 2004/2593, art 2(a).

Extent

This section does not extend to Scotland: see s 124(1).

Loss payments

A1.472

106   Basic loss payment

(1)   After section 33 of the Land Compensation Act 1973 (c 26) (home loss payments for certain caravan dwellers) there is inserted the following section—

'*Other loss payments*

33A   **Basic loss payment**

(1)   This section applies to a person—

    (a)   if he has a qualifying interest in land,

    (b)   if the interest is acquired compulsorily, and

    (c)   to the extent that he is not entitled to a home loss payment in respect of any part of the interest.

(2)   A person to whom this section applies is entitled to payment of whichever is the lower of the following amounts—

    (a)   7.5% of the value of his interest;

    (b)   £75,000.

(3)   A payment under this section must be made by the acquiring authority.

(4)   An interest in land is a qualifying interest if it is a freehold interest or an interest as tenant and (in either case) it subsists for a period of not less than one year ending with whichever is the earliest of—

    (a)   the date on which the acquiring authority takes possession of the land under section 11 of the Compulsory Purchase Act 1965 (entry to take possession of land);

    (b)   the date on which the acquiring authority enters the land if it proceeds under Schedule 3 to that Act;

    (c)   the vesting date (within the meaning of the Compulsory Purchase (Vesting Declarations) Act 1981) if a declaration is made under section 4 of that Act (general vesting declaration);

    (d)   the date on which compensation is agreed between the person and the acquiring authority;

    (e)   the date on which the amount of compensation is determined by the Lands Tribunal.

(5)   The compulsory acquisition of an interest in land includes acquisition of the interest in consequence of the service of—

    (a)   a purchase notice under section 137 of the Town and Country Planning Act 1990 (right to require purchase of certain interests);

    (b)   a notice under section 150 of that Act (purchase of blighted land).

(6)   The value of an interest is its value for the purpose of deciding the amount of compensation payable in respect of the acquisition; but this is subject to subsections (7) and (8).

(7)   If an interest consists partly of a dwelling in respect of which the person is entitled to a home loss payment the value of the interest is the value of the whole interest less the value of so much of the interest as is represented by the dwelling.

(8)   If rule (5) of section 5 of the Land Compensation Act 1961 (equivalent reinstatement) applies for the purpose of assessing the amount of compensation the value of the interest is nil.'

(2)   Section 33A of the Land Compensation Act 1973 (c 26) (as inserted by subsection (1) above) does not apply in relation to a pre-commencement acquisition of an interest in land.

(3)   A pre-commencement acquisition of an interest in land is any of the following—

    (a)   acquisition by means of a compulsory purchase order if the order is made or made in draft before the commencement of this section;

    (b)   acquisition by means of an order made under section 1 or 3 of the Transport and Works Act 1992 (c 42) (orders relating to certain transport works) if the application for the order was made to the Secretary of State before the commencement of this section;

    (c)   acquisition by means of an order under section 1 or 3 of that Act if the order is made in pursuance of section 7 of that Act (orders made without application) and the order is made in draft before the commencement of this section;

    (d)   acquisition by means of a power contained in an enactment (including a private or local Act) to acquire compulsorily specified land or a specified interest in land if the Bill providing for the power is introduced into Parliament before the commencement of this section.

NOTES

Initial Commencement

To be appointed: see s 121(1), (2)(e).

Appointment

Appointment: 31 October 2004: see SI 2004/2593, art 2(a).

Extent

This section does not extend to Scotland: see s 124(1).

A1.473

107   Occupier's loss payment

(1)   After section 33A of the Land Compensation Act 1973 (inserted by section 106 of this Act) there are inserted the following sections—

'33B   Occupier's loss payment: agricultural land

(1)   This section applies to a person if—

    (a)   he has a qualifying interest in land for the purposes of section 33A,

    (b)   the land is agricultural land,

    (c)   the interest is acquired compulsorily, and

    (d)   he occupied the land for the period specified in section 33A(4).

(2)   A person to whom this section applies is entitled to a payment of whichever is the greatest of the following amounts—

    (a)   2.5% of the value of his interest;

    (b)   the land amount;

    (c)   the buildings amount.

(3)   But the maximum amount which may be paid to a person under this section in respect of an interest in land is £25,000.

(4)   A payment under this section must be made by the acquiring authority.

(5)   The value of an interest is its value for the purpose of deciding the amount of compensation payable in respect of the acquisition; but this is subject to subsections (6) and (7).

(6)   If an interest consists partly of a dwelling in respect of which the person is entitled to a home loss payment the value of the interest is the value of the whole interest less the value of so much of the interest as is represented by the dwelling.

(7) If rule (5) of section 5 of the Land Compensation Act 1961 (equivalent reinstatement) applies for the purpose of assessing the amount of compensation the value of the interest is nil.

(8) The land amount is the greater of £300 and the amount found in accordance with the following Table—

Area of the land	Amount per hectare
Not exceeding 100 hectares	£100 per hectare or part of a hectare
Exceeding 100 hectares	(a) £100 per hectare for the first 100 hectares;
	(b) £50 per hectare for the next 300 hectares or part of a hectare.

(9) The buildings amount is £25 per square metre (or part of a square metre) of the gross floor space of any buildings on the land.

(10) The gross floor space must be measured externally.

33C   Occupier's loss payment: other land

(1) This section applies to a person if—

(a) he has a qualifying interest in land for the purposes of section 33A,
(b) the land is not agricultural land,
(c) the interest is acquired compulsorily, and
(d) he occupied the land for the period specified in section 33A(4).

(2) A person to whom this section applies is entitled to a payment of whichever is the greatest of the following amounts—

(a) 2.5% of the value of his interest;
(b) the land amount;
(c) the buildings amount.

(3) But the maximum amount which may be paid to a person under this section in respect of an interest in land is £25,000.

(4) A payment under this section must be made by the acquiring authority.

(5) The value of an interest is its value for the purpose of deciding the amount of compensation payable in respect of the acquisition; but this is subject to subsections (6) and (7).

(6) If an interest consists partly of a dwelling in respect of which the person is entitled to a home loss payment the value of the interest is the value of the whole interest less the value of so much of the interest as is represented by the dwelling.

(7) If rule (5) of section 5 of the Land Compensation Act 1961 (equivalent reinstatement) applies for the purpose of assessing the amount of compensation the value of the interest is nil.

(8) The land amount is the greater of—

(a) £2,500;
(b) £2.50 per square metre (or part of a square metre) of the area of the land.

(9) But if only part of land in which a person has an interest is acquired, for the figure specified in subsection (8)(a) there is substituted £300.

(10) The buildings amount is £25 per square metre (or part of a square metre) of the gross floor space of any buildings on the land.

(11) The gross floor space must be measured externally.'

(2)   Sections 33B and 33C of the Land Compensation Act 1973 (c 26) (as inserted by subsection (1) above) do not apply in relation to a pre-commencement acquisition of an interest in land.

(3)   A pre-commencement acquisition of an interest in land is any of the following—

(a)   acquisition by means of a compulsory purchase order if the order is made or made in draft before the commencement of this section;

(b)   acquisition by means of an order made under section 1 or 3 of the Transport and Works Act 1992 (c 42) (orders relating to certain transport works) if the application for the order was made to the Secretary of State before the commencement of this section;

(c)   acquisition by means of an order under section 1 or 3 of that Act if the order is made in pursuance of section 7 of that Act (orders made without application) and the order is made in draft before the commencement of this section;

(d)   acquisition by means of a power contained in an enactment (including a private or local Act) to acquire compulsorily specified land or a specified interest in land if the Bill providing for the power is introduced into Parliament before the commencement of this section.

NOTES

Initial Commencement

To be appointed: see s 121(1), (2)(e).

Appointment

Appointment: 31 October 2004: see SI 2004/2593, art 2(a).

Extent

This section does not extend to Scotland: see s 124(1).

A1.474

108   Loss payments: exclusions

(1)   After section 33C of the Land Compensation Act 1973 (inserted by section 107 of this Act) there is inserted the following section—

'33D   Loss payments: exclusions

(1)   This section applies to a person if—

(a)   he is a person to whom section 33A, 33B or 33C applies,

(b)   a notice falling within subsection (4) has been served on him in relation to the land mentioned in that section,

(c)   at the relevant time the notice has effect or is operative, and

(d)   he has failed to comply with any requirement of the notice.

(2)   This section also applies to a person if—

(a)   he is a person to whom section 33A, 33B or 33C applies,

(b)   a copy of an order falling within subsection (5) has been served on him in relation to the land mentioned in that section, and

(c)   the order has not been quashed on appeal.

(3)   No payment may be made under section 33A, 33B or 33C to a person to whom this section applies.

(4) These are the notices—

  (a) notice under section 215 of the Town and Country Planning Act 1990 (power to require proper maintenance of land);
  (b) notice under section 189 of the Housing Act 1985 (requirement to repair dwelling etc unfit for human habitation);
  (c) notice under section 190 of that Act (requirement to repair dwelling etc in state of disrepair);
  (d) notice under section 48 of the Planning (Listed Buildings and Conservation Areas) Act 1990 (repairs notice prior to compulsory notice of acquisition of listed building).

(5) These are the orders—

  (a) an order under section 264 of the Housing Act 1985 (closure of dwelling etc unfit for human habitation);
  (b) an order under section 265 of that Act (demolition of dwelling etc unfit for human habitation).

(6) The relevant time is the time at which the compulsory purchase order in relation to the person's interest in the land—

  (a) is confirmed, in the case of an order falling within section 2(2) of the Acquisition of Land Act 1981 (procedure for authorisation);
  (b) is made, in the case of an order falling within section 2(3) of that Act.

(7) The Secretary of State may by regulations amend subsections (4) and (5).'

(2) Section 33D of the Land Compensation Act 1973 (c 26) (as inserted by subsection (1) above) does not apply in relation to a notice or order specified in subsection (4) or (5) of that section if the notice or copy of the order was served on a person to whom that section applies before the commencement of this section.

NOTES

Initial Commencement

To be appointed: see s 121(1), (2)(e).

Appointment

Appointment: 31 October 2004: see SI 2004/2593, art 2(a).

Extent

This section does not extend to Scotland: see s 124(1).

A1.475

109   Loss payments: supplementary

After section 33D of the Land Compensation Act 1973 (inserted by section 108 of this Act) there are inserted the following sections—

'33E   Claims

(1) This section applies for the purposes of sections 33A to 33C

(2) A claim for payment must be made in writing to the acquiring authority.

(3) The claim must give such particulars as the authority may reasonably require for the purpose of deciding—

(a)   whether a payment is to be made;

(b)   the amount of any such payment.

(4)   For the purposes of the Limitation Act 1980 a person's right of action to recover a payment must be taken to have accrued—

(a)   in the case of a claim under section 33A on the last day of the period specified in subsection (4) of that section;

(b)   in the case of a claim under section 33B or 33C on the date of his displacement from the land.

33F   Insolvency

(1)   This section applies if a person is entitled to a payment under section 33A, 33B or 33C but before a claim is made under section 33E insolvency proceedings are started in relation to the person.

(2)   Any of the following may make a claim instead of the person mentioned in subsection (1)—

(a)   a receiver, trustee in bankruptcy or the official receiver in the case of an individual;

(b)   an administrator, administrative receiver, liquidator or provisional liquidator or the official receiver in the case of a company or a partnership.

(3)   Insolvency proceedings are—

(a)   proceedings in bankruptcy;

(b)   proceedings under the Insolvency Act 1986 for the winding up of a company or an unregistered company (including voluntary winding up of a company under Part 4 of that Act);

(c)   proceedings for the winding up of a partnership.

33G   Death

(1)   This section applies if a person is entitled to a payment under section 33A, 33B or 33C but before a claim is made under section 33E the person dies (the deceased).

(2)   A claim may be made by a person who—

(a)   occupied the land for a period of not less than one year ending with the date on which the deceased is displaced from the land, and

(b)   is entitled to benefit on the death of the deceased by virtue of a ground mentioned in subsection (3).

(3)   The grounds are—

(a)   a testamentary disposition;

(b)   the law of intestate succession;

(c)   the right of survivorship between joint tenants.

33H   Agricultural land: dual entitlement

(1)   This section applies if a person is entitled in respect of the same interest in agricultural land to a payment both—

(a)   under section 33B of this Act, and

(b)   by virtue of section 12(1) of the Agriculture (Miscellaneous Provisions) Act 1968 (additional payments in consequence of compulsory acquisition of agricultural holding).

(2)   Payment may be made in respect of only one entitlement.

(3) If the person makes a claim under both provisions he must be paid in respect of the entitlement which produces the greater amount.

33I Payment

(1) Any dispute as to the amount of a payment to be made under section 33A, 33B or 33C must be determined by the Lands Tribunal.

(2) The acquiring authority must make any payment required by section 33A not later than whichever is the latest of the following dates—

    (a) the last day of the period specified in section 33A(4);

    (b) the last day of the period of three months beginning with the day the claim is made;

    (c) the day on which the amount of the payment is determined.

(3) The authority must make any payment required by section 33B or 33C not later than whichever is the latest of the following dates—

    (a) the date the person is displaced from the land;

    (b) the last day of the period of three months beginning with the day the claim is made;

    (c) the day on which the amount of the payment is determined.

(4) If paragraph (c) of subsection (2) or (3) applies the authority may at any time make a payment in advance to the person entitled to a payment (the claimant).

(5) If when the value of the interest is agreed or determined the amount of a payment made under subsection (4) differs from the payment required by section 33A, 33B or 33C—

    (a) the amount by which the advance payment exceeds the payment required must be repaid by the claimant to the authority;

    (b) the amount by which the payment required exceeds the advance payment must be paid by the authority to the claimant.

(6) The acquiring authority must pay interest on the amount required to be paid at the rate prescribed by regulations under section 32 of the Land Compensation Act 1961.

(7) Interest accrues from the date specified in paragraph (a) of subsection (2) or (3) (as the case may be).

(8) The authority may, at the request of the person entitled to the payment, make a payment on account of the interest mentioned in subsection (6).

33J Acquisition by agreement

(1) This section applies if—

    (a) an interest in land which is a qualifying interest for the purpose of section 33A is acquired by agreement by an authority which has power to acquire the interest compulsorily, and

    (b) the interest is acquired from a person who would be entitled to a payment under section 33A, 33B or 33C if the interest is acquired compulsorily.

(2) The authority may make a payment to the person of an amount equal to the amount they would be required to pay if the interest is acquired compulsorily.

33K Regulations

(1) This section applies for the purposes of sections 33A to 33I.

(2)   The Secretary of State may by regulations substitute for any amount or percentage figure specified in these sections such other amount or percentage figure (as the case may be) as he thinks fit.

(3)   Except as provided in the following provisions of this section, a power to make regulations must be exercised by statutory instrument subject to annulment in pursuance of a resolution of either House of Parliament.

(4)   This subsection applies to regulations under subsection (2) which substitute—

    (a)   a percentage figure, or

    (b)   an amount, in a case where the change in value condition is not satisfied.

(5)   A statutory instrument containing regulations to which subsection (4) applies must not be made unless a draft of the regulations has been laid before and approved by resolution of each House of Parliament.

(6)   The change in value condition is satisfied if the Secretary of State thinks that in the case of the substitution of an amount it is expedient to make the substitution in consequence of changes in the value of money or land.

(7)   Regulations under subsection (2) may make different provision for different purposes.'

NOTES

Initial Commencement

To be appointed: see s 121(1), (2)(e).

Appointment

Appointment: 31 October 2004: see SI 2004/2593, art 2(a).

Extent

This section does not extend to Scotland: see s 124(1).

Corresponding amendments of other enactments

A1.476

110   Corresponding amendments of other enactments

(1)   This section applies to any enactment passed or made before or in the same session as the passing of this Act (other than an enactment amended by this Part) which makes provision—

    (a)   in connection with the compulsory acquisition of an interest in land,

    (b)   creating a power which permits the interference with or affectation of any right in relation to land, or

    (c)   for the payment of any sum in connection with the acquisition, interference or affectation.

(2)   The Secretary of State may by order amend an enactment to which this section applies for the purpose of making provision which—

    (a)   corresponds to provision made by this Part, or

    (b)   applies any such provision or corresponding provision.

A1.477 *Statutes*

NOTES

Initial Commencement

To be appointed: see s 121(1), (2)(e).

Appointment

Appointment: 31 October 2004: see SI 2004/2593, art 2(a).

Extent

This section does not extend to Scotland: see s 124(1).

PART 9: MISCELLANEOUS AND GENERAL

Crown

A1.477

111   Crown

(1)   This Act (except Part 8) binds the Crown.

(2)   The amendment of an enactment by or by virtue of Part 8 applies to the Crown to the extent that the enactment amended so applies.

NOTES

Initial Commencement

To be appointed: see s 121(1).

Appointment

Sub-s (1): Appointment: 7 June 2006: see SI 2006/1281, art 3.

Sub-s (2): Appointment: 31 October 2004: see SI 2004/2593, art 2(b).

Parliament

A1.478

112   Parliament

The planning Acts and this Act have effect despite any rule of law relating to Parliament or the law and practice of Parliament.

NOTES

Initial Commencement

To be appointed: see s 121(1).

Appointment

Appointment: 7 June 2006: see SI 2006/1281, art 2(b).

Extent

This section does not extend to Scotland: see s 124(1).

A1.479

113　　Validity of strategies, plans and documents

(1)　This section applies to—

(a)　a revision of the regional spatial strategy;
(b)　the Wales Spatial Plan;
(c)　a development plan document;
(d)　a local development plan;
(e)　a revision of a document mentioned in paragraph (b), (c) or (d);
(f)　the Mayor of London's spatial development strategy;
(g)　an alteration or replacement of the spatial development strategy,

and anything falling within paragraphs (a) to (g) is referred to in this section as a relevant document.

(2)　A relevant document must not be questioned in any legal proceedings except in so far as is provided by the following provisions of this section.

(3)　A person aggrieved by a relevant document may make an application to the High Court on the ground that—

(a)　the document is not within the appropriate power;
(b)　a procedural requirement has not been complied with.

(4)　But the application must be made not later than the end of the period of six weeks starting with the relevant date.

(5)　The High Court may make an interim order suspending the operation of the relevant document—

(a)　wholly or in part;
(b)　generally or as it affects the property of the applicant.

(6)　Subsection (7) applies if the High Court is satisfied—

(a)　that a relevant document is to any extent outside the appropriate power;
(b)　that the interests of the applicant have been substantially prejudiced by a failure to comply with a procedural requirement.

(7)　The High Court may quash the relevant document—

(a)　wholly or in part;
(b)　generally or as it affects the property of the applicant.

(8)　An interim order has effect until the proceedings are finally determined.

(9)　The appropriate power is—

(a)　Part 1 of this Act in the case of a revision of the regional spatial strategy;
(b)　section 60 above in the case of the Wales Spatial Plan or any revision of it;
(c)　Part 2 of this Act in the case of a development plan document or any revision of it;
(d)　sections 62 to 78 above in the case of a local development plan or any revision of it;
(e)　sections 334 to 343 of the Greater London Authority Act 1999 (c 29) in the case of the spatial development strategy or any alteration or replacement of it.

(10)　A procedural requirement is a requirement under the appropriate power or contained in regulations or an order made under that power which relates to the adoption, publication or approval of a relevant document.

(11) References to the relevant date must be construed as follows—

   (a) for the purposes of a revision of the regional spatial strategy, the date when the Secretary of State publishes the revised strategy under section 9(6) above;

   (b) for the purposes of the Wales Spatial Plan (or a revision of it), the date when it is approved by the National Assembly for Wales;

   (c) for the purposes of a development plan document (or a revision of it), the date when it is adopted by the local planning authority or approved by the Secretary of State (as the case may be);

   (d) for the purposes of a local development plan (or a revision of it), the date when it is adopted by a local planning authority in Wales or approved by the National Assembly for Wales (as the case may be);

   (e) for the purposes of the spatial development strategy (or an alteration or replacement of it), the date when the Mayor of London publishes it.

NOTES

Initial Commencement

To be appointed: see s 121(1), (2)(f).

Appointment

Appointment (in relation to England): 28 September 2004: see SI 2004/2202, art 2(e).

Appointment (in relation to Wales): 15 October 2005: see SI 2005/2847, art 2(c).

Extent

This section does not extend to Scotland: see s 124(1).

A1.480

114   Examinations

An examination of any document or plan for the purposes of Part 2 or Part 6 of this Act is a statutory inquiry within the meaning of the Tribunals and Inquiries Act 1992 (c 53).

NOTES

Initial Commencement

To be appointed: see s 121(1), (2)(f).

Appointment

Appointment (in relation to England in so far as relating to Part 2): 28 September 2004: see SI 2004/2202, art 2(f).

Appointment (in relation to Wales): 15 October 2005: see SI 2005/2847, art 2(d).

Extent

This section does not extend to Scotland: see s 124(1).

A1.481

115   Grants for advice and assistance

In the principal Act after section 304 (grants for research and education) there is inserted the following section—

'304A   Grants for advice and assistance

(1)   The appropriate authority may make grants for the purpose of assisting any person to provide advice and assistance in connection with any matter which is related to—

    (a)   the planning Acts;
    (b)   the Planning and Compulsory Purchase Act 2004;
    (c)   the enactments mentioned in subsection (2).

(2)   The enactments are enactments which relate to planning contained in the following Acts—

    (a)   the Planning and Compensation Act 1991;
    (b)   the Transport and Works Act 1992;
    (c)   the Environment Act 1995.

(3)   The appropriate authority may make a grant subject to such terms and conditions as it thinks appropriate.

(4)   Person includes a body whether or not incorporated.

(5)   The appropriate authority is—

    (a)   the Secretary of State in relation to England;
    (b)   the National Assembly for Wales in relation to Wales.'

NOTES

Initial Commencement

Royal Assent: 13 May 2004: see s 121(1).

Extent

This section does not extend to Scotland: see s 124(1).

A1.482

116   Isles of Scilly

(1)   This Act applies to the Isles of Scilly subject to such exceptions, adaptations and modifications as the Secretary of State may by order direct.

(2)   An order may in particular provide for—

    (a)   the Council of the Isles of Scilly to enter into arrangements in pursuance of section 4;
    (b)   the exercise by the Council of the Isles of Scilly of any function exercisable by a local planning authority under Part 2.

(3)   But an order must not be made under this section unless the Secretary of State has consulted the Council of the Isles of Scilly.

NOTES

Initial Commencement

To be appointed: see s 121(1).

Appointment

Appointment (for the purpose of making, or making provision by means of, subordinate legislation): 6 August 2004: see SI 2004/2097, art 2.

Appointment (for remaining purposes): 24 August 2005: see SI 2005/2081, art 3.

Subordinate Legislation

Town and Country Planning (Isles of Scilly) Order 2005, SI 2005/2085.

A1.483

117   Interpretation

(1)   Expressions used in this Act and in the principal Act have the same meaning in this Act as in that Act.

(2)   Expressions used in this Act and in the listed buildings Act have the same meaning in this Act as in that Act.

(3)   Expressions used in this Act and in the hazardous substances Act have the same meaning in this Act as in that Act.

(4)   The planning Acts are—

 (a)   the principal Act;
 (b)   the listed buildings Act;
 (c)   the hazardous substances Act;
 (d)   the Planning (Consequential Provisions) Act 1990 (c 11).

(5)   The principal Act is the Town and Country Planning Act 1990 (c 8).

(6)   The listed buildings Act is the Planning (Listed Buildings and Conservation Areas) Act 1990 (c 9).

(7)   The hazardous substances Act is the Planning (Hazardous Substances) Act 1990 (c 10).

(8)   The Scottish planning Acts are—

 (a)   the Town and Country Planning (Scotland) Act 1997 (c 8);
 (b)   the Planning (Listed Buildings and Conservation Areas) (Scotland) Act 1997 (c 9);
 (c)   the Planning (Hazardous Substances) (Scotland) Act 1997 (c 10); and
 (d)   the Planning (Consequential Provisions) (Scotland) Act 1997 (c 11).

NOTES

Initial Commencement

To be appointed: see s 121(1), (2)(f), (4)(c).

Appointment

Sub-ss (1)–(7): Appointment (for the purpose of making, or making provision by means of, subordinate legislation): 6 August 2004: see SI 2004/2097, art 2.

Sub-ss (1)–(7): Appointment (for remaining purposes): 28 September 2004: see SI 2004/2202, art 3(b).

Sub-s (8): Appointment: 12 June 2006: see SSI 2006/268, art 3(c).

General

A1.484

118   Amendments

(1)   Schedule 6 contains amendments of the planning Acts.

(2)   Schedule 7 contains amendments of other enactments.

(3)   A reference in Schedule 1 to the National Assembly for Wales (Transfer of Functions) Order 1999 to an enactment amended by this Act must be taken to be a reference to the enactment as so amended.

(4)   But subsection (3) does not affect such an enactment to the extent that the amendment makes express provision in connection with the exercise of a function in relation to Wales.

NOTES

Initial Commencement

Sub-s (2): Specified date (for certain purposes): 13 July 2004: see s 121(6).

Sub-ss (1), (3), (4): To be appointed: see s 121(1), (2)(f), (g).

Sub-s (2): To be appointed (for remaining purposes): see s 121(1), (2)(f), (g), (4)(d).

Appointment

Sub-ss (1), (3), (4): Appointment (for the purpose of making, or making provision by means of, subordinate legislation): 6 August 2004: see SI 2004/2097, art 2.

Sub-ss (1), (3), (4): Appointment (for remaining purposes): 28 September 2004: see SI 2004/2202, arts 2(h), 3(c); for transitional provisions and savings see art 4, Sch 2 thereto.

Sub-s (2): Appointment (for certain purposes): 6 August 2004: see SI 2004/2097, art 2.

Sub-s (2): Appointment (for certain purposes): 28 September 2004: see SI 2004/2202, art 3(c); for transitional provisions and savings see art 4, Sch 2 thereto.

Sub-s (2): Appointment (in relation to Scotland for certain purposes): 12 June 2006: see SSI 2006/268, art 3(d).

A1.485

119   Transitionals

(1)   Schedule 8 contains transitional provisions relating to Parts 1 and 2.

(2)   The Scottish Ministers may by order make such transitional provision for Scotland, corresponding to the provisions of Schedule 4 and to section 30B of the hazardous substances Act (inserted by section 79(3)), as they consider necessary or expedient.

NOTES

Initial Commencement

To be appointed: see s 121(1), (4)(e).

Appointment

Sub-s (1): Appointment (for the purpose of making, or making provision by means of, subordinate legislation): 6 August 2004: see SI 2004/2097, art 2.

Sub-s (1): Appointment (in relation to England for remaining purposes): 28 September 2004: see SI 2004/2202, art 2(g).

Sub-s (2): Appointment: 20 March 2006: see SSI 2006/101, art 2, Schedule.

Subordinate Legislation

Planning and Compulsory Purchase Act 2004 (Transitional Provisions) (Scotland) Order 2006, SSI 2006/269 (made under sub-s (2)).

A1.486

120   Repeals
Schedule 9 contains repeals.

NOTES

Initial Commencement

To be appointed: see s 121(1), (2)(f), (g), (4)(f).

Appointment

Appointment (for certain purposes): 6 August 2004: see SI 2004/2097, art 2.

Appointment (for certain purposes): 28 September 2004: see SI 2004/2202, art 3(d).

Appointment (in relation to England for certain purposes): 10 August 2006: by virtue of SI 2006/1061, art 3.

Appointment (for certain purposes): 7 June 2006: by virtue of SI 2006/1281, art 2(f).

Appointment (in relation to Scotland for certain purposes): 12 June 2006: see SSI 2006/268, art 3(e).

A1.487

121   Commencement

(1)   The preceding provisions of this Act (except section 115 and the provisions specified in subsections (4), (5) and (6)) come into force on such day as the Secretary of State may by order appoint.

(2)   But the Secretary of State must not make an order which relates to any of the following provisions unless he first consults the National Assembly for Wales—

  (a)   Part 3;
  (b)   Part 4, except sections 44 and 55;
  (c)   Part 5;
  (d)   in Part 7, Chapter 1;
  (e)   Part 8;
  (f)   in this Part sections 113, 114, 117, 118 and 120;
  (g)   Schedules 3, 4, 6, 7 and 9.

(3)   And the Secretary of State must not make an order which relates to section 91 unless he first consults and has the agreement of the Scottish Ministers.

(4)   The following provisions come into force on such day as the Scottish Ministers may by order appoint—

  (a)   sections 90 and 92 to 98;
  (b)   Schedule 5;

(c)   section 117(8);
(d)   in so far as relating to the Town and Country Planning (Scotland) Act 1997, section 118(2) and Schedule 7;
(e)   section 119(2); and
(f)   in so far as relating to that Act, to the Planning (Listed Buildings and Conservation Areas) (Scotland) Act 1997 or to the Planning (Hazardous Substances) (Scotland) Act 1997, section 120 and Schedule 9.

(5)   Part 6 comes into force in accordance with provision made by the National Assembly for Wales by order.

(6)   In Schedule 7, paragraph 10(7) comes into force at the end of the period of two months starting on the day this Act is passed.

NOTES

Initial Commencement

Royal Assent: 13 May 2004: (no specific commencement provision).

Subordinate Legislation

Planning and Compulsory Purchase Act 2004 (Commencement No 2) (Wales) Order 2004, SI 2004/1813 (made under sub-s (5)).

Planning and Compulsory Purchase Act 2004 (Commencement No 1 and Transitional Provision) (Wales) Order 2004, SI 2004/1814 (made under sub-s (5)).

Planning and Compulsory Purchase Act 2004 (Commencement No 1) Order 2004, SI 2004/2097 (made under sub-ss (1)–(3)).

Planning and Compulsory Purchase Act 2004 (Commencement No 2, Transitional Provisions and Savings) Order 2004, SI 2004/2202.

Planning and Compulsory Purchase Act 2004 (Commencement No 3) Order 2004, SI 2004/2593 (made under sub-ss (1), (2)).

Planning and Compulsory Purchase Act 2004 (Commencement No 4 and Savings) Order 2005, SI 2005/204 (made under sub-ss (1), (2)).

Planning and Compulsory Purchase Act 2004 (Commencement No 3 and Consequential and Transitional Provisions) (Wales) Order 2005, SI 2005/1229 (made under sub-s (5)).

Planning and Compulsory Purchase Act 2004 (Commencement No 5 and Savings) Order 2005, SI 2005/2081 (made under sub-ss (1), (2)).

Planning and Compulsory Purchase Act 2004 (Commencement No 4 and Consequential, Transitional and Savings Provisions) (Wales) Order 2005, SI 2005/2722 (made under sub-s (5)).

Planning and Compulsory Purchase Act 2004 (Commencement No 6, Transitional Provisions and Savings) Order 2005, SI 2005/2847 (made under sub-ss (1), (2)).

Planning and Compulsory Purchase Act 2004 (Commencement No 4 and Consequential, Transitional and Savings Provisions) (Wales) (Amendment) Order 2006, SI 2006/842 (made under sub-s (5)).

Planning and Compulsory Purchase Act 2004 (Commencement No 7) Order 2006, SI 2006/931 (made under sub-ss (1), (2)).

Planning and Compulsory Purchase Act 2004 (Commencement No 8 and Saving) Order 2006, SI 2006/1061.

Planning and Compulsory Purchase Act 2004 (Commencement No 9 and Consequential Provisions) Order 2006, SI 2006/1281.

Planning and Compulsory Purchase Act 2004 (Commencement No 4 and Consequential, Transitional and Savings Provisions) (Wales) (Amendment No 2) Order 2006, SI 2006/1700 (made under sub-s (5)).

Planning and Compulsory Purchase Act 2004 (Commencement No 4 and Consequential, Transitional and Savings Provisions) (Wales) (Amendment No 3) Order 2006, SI 2006/3119 (made under sub-s (5)).

Planning and Compulsory Purchase Act 2004 (Commencement No 4 and Consequential, Transitional and Savings Provisions) (Wales) (Amendment No 1) Order 2007, SI 2007/546 (made under sub-s (5)).

Planning and Compulsory Purchase Act 2004 (Commencement No 4 and Consequential, Transitional and Savings Provisions) (Wales) (Amendment No 2) Order 2007, SI 2007/1023 (made under sub-s (5)).

Planning and Compulsory Purchase Act 2004 (Commencement No 10 and Saving) Order 2007, SI 2007/1369.

Planning and Compulsory Purchase Act 2004 (Commencement No 1) (Scotland) Order 2006, SSI 2006/101 (made under sub-s (4)).

Planning and Compulsory Purchase Act 2004 (Commencement No 2 and Consequential Provisions) (Scotland) Order 2006, SSI 2006/243 (made under sub-s (4)).

Planning and Compulsory Purchase Act 2004 (Commencement No 3) (Scotland) Order 2006, SSI 2006/268 (made under sub-s (4)).

A1.488

122   Regulations and orders

(1)   A power to prescribe is (unless express provision is made to the contrary) a power to prescribe by regulations exercisable—

    (a)   by the Secretary of State in relation to England;
    (b)   by the National Assembly for Wales in relation to Wales.

(2)   References in this section to subordinate legislation are to any order or regulations under this Act.

(3)   Subordinate legislation—

    (a)   may make different provision for different purposes;
    (b)   may include such supplementary, incidental, consequential, saving or transitional provisions (including provision amending, repealing or revoking enactments) as the person making the subordinate legislation thinks necessary or expedient.

(4)   A power to make subordinate legislation must be exercised by statutory instrument.

(5)   A statutory instrument is subject to annulment in pursuance of a resolution of either House of Parliament unless it contains—

    (a)   regulations made by the Secretary of State under section 46;
    (b)   an order under section 98, 116(1) or 119(2);
    (c)   an order under section 110(2);
    (d)   an order under section 121(1) to which subsection (8) applies;
    (e)   an order under section 121(4);
    (f)   provision amending or repealing an enactment contained in an Act;
    (g)   subordinate legislation made by the National Assembly for Wales.

(6)   A statutory instrument mentioned in subsection (5)(a), (c) or (f) must not be made unless a draft of the instrument has been laid before and approved by resolution of each House of Parliament.

(7)   A statutory instrument containing an order under section 98 or 119(2) is subject to annulment in pursuance of a resolution of the Scottish Parliament.

(8)   This subsection applies to an order which does not contain provision amending or repealing an enactment contained in an Act.

(9)   A statutory instrument containing an order under section 121(4), if it includes provision amending or repealing an enactment contained in an Act, must not be made unless a draft of the instrument has been laid before and approved by resolution of the Scottish Parliament.

(10)   In subsection (3), 'enactment' includes an enactment comprised in, or in an instrument made under, an Act of the Scottish Parliament and in subsections (8) and (9), 'Act' includes such an Act and 'enactment' includes an enactment comprised in such an Act.

NOTES

Initial Commencement

Royal Assent: 13 May 2004: (no specific commencement provision).

Subordinate Legislation

Planning and Compulsory Purchase Act 2004 (Commencement No 9 and Consequential Provisions) Order 2006, SI 2006/1281.

Planning and Compulsory Purchase Act 2004 (Commencement No 4 and Consequential, Transitional and Savings Provisions) (Wales) (Amendment No 3) Order 2006, SI 2006/3119 (made under sub-s (3)).

Planning and Compulsory Purchase Act 2004 (Commencement No 4 and Consequential, Transitional and Savings Provisions) (Wales) (Amendment No 1) Order 2007, SI 2007/546 (made under sub-s (3)).

Planning and Compulsory Purchase Act 2004 (Commencement No 4 and Consequential, Transitional and Savings Provisions) (Wales) (Amendment No 2) Order 2007, SI 2007/1023 (made under sub-s (3)).

Planning and Compulsory Purchase Act 2004 (Commencement No 10 and Saving) Order 2007, SI 2007/1369.

Planning and Compulsory Purchase Act 2004 (Corresponding Amendments) Order 2007, SI 2007/1519 (made under sub-s (6)).

Town and Country Planning (Application of Subordinate Legislation to the Crown) (Scotland) Order 2006, SI 2006/270 (made under sub-s (3)).

Town and Country Planning (Application of Subordinate Legislation to the Crown) (Inquiries Procedure) (Scotland) Order 2006, SSI 2006/339 (made under sub-s (3)).

Town and Country Planning (Application of Subordinate Legislation to the Crown) (Scotland) Amendment Order 2007, SSI 2007/221 (made under sub-s (3)).

A1.489

123   Finance

(1)   There is to be paid out of money provided by Parliament—

   (a)   any expenses of the Secretary of State in making grants in connection with the provision of advice and assistance in relation to the planning Acts;
   (b)   any increase attributable to this Act in the sums payable out of money so provided under any other enactment.

(2)   There is to be paid into the Consolidated Fund any increase attributable to this Act in the sums so payable under any other enactment.

NOTES

Initial Commencement

Royal Assent: 13 May 2004: (no specific commencement provision).

Extent

This section does not extend to Scotland: see s 124(1).

A1.490

124   Extent

(1)   Except as otherwise provided in this section, this Act extends to England and Wales only.

(2)   Sections 111(1), 118(2), 120 to 122, this section and section 125 extend also to Scotland.

(3)   Sections 90 to 98, 117(8) and 119(2) extend to Scotland only.

(4)   The extent of any amendment, repeal or revocation made by this Act is the same as that of the enactment amended, repealed or revoked.

NOTES

Initial Commencement

Royal Assent: 13 May 2004: (no specific commencement provision).

A1.491

125   Short Title

This Act may be cited as the Planning and Compulsory Purchase Act 2004.

NOTES

Initial Commencement

Royal Assent: 13 May 2004: (no specific commencement provision).

SCHEDULE 1
LOCAL DEVELOPMENT ORDERS: PROCEDURE

Section 40

A1.492

In the principal Act after Schedule 4 (special provision as to land use in 1948) there is inserted the following Schedule—

'SCHEDULE 4A
LOCAL DEVELOPMENT ORDERS: PROCEDURE

Preparation

1 (1) A local development order must be prepared in accordance with such procedure as is prescribed by a development order.

(2) A development order may include provision as to—

    (a) the preparation, submission, approval, adoption, revision, revocation and withdrawal of a local development order;

    (b) notice, publicity, and inspection by the public;

    (c) consultation with and consideration of views of such persons and for such purposes as are prescribed;

    (d) the making and consideration of representations.

(3) Regulations under this paragraph may include provision as to the matters relating to a local development order to be included in the report to be made by a local planning authority under section 35 or 76 of the Planning and Compulsory Purchase Act 2004.

Revision

2 (1) The local planning authority may at any time prepare a revision of a local development order.

(2) An authority in England must prepare a revision of a local development order—

    (a) if the Secretary of State directs them to do so, and

    (b) in accordance with such timetable as he directs.

(3) An authority in Wales must prepare a revision of a local development order—

    (a) if the National Assembly for Wales directs them to do so, and

    (b) in accordance with such timetable as it directs.

(4) If a development plan document mentioned in section 61A(1) is revised under section 26 of the Planning and Compulsory Purchase Act 2004 (revision of local planning documents) or revoked under section 25 of that Act (revocation by Secretary of State) a local development order made to implement the policies in the document must be revised accordingly.

(5) If a local development plan mentioned in section 61A(1) is revised under section 70 of the Planning and Compulsory Purchase Act 2004 (revision of local development plan) or revoked under section 68 of that Act (revocation by National Assembly for Wales) a local development order made to implement the policies in the plan must be revised accordingly.

(6) This Schedule applies to the revision of a local development order as it applies to the preparation of the order.

Order to be adopted

3 A local development order is of no effect unless it is adopted by resolution of the local planning authority.

Annual report

4 (1) The report made under section 35 of the Planning and Compulsory Purchase Act 2004 must include a report as to the extent to which the local development order is achieving its purposes.

(2) The Secretary of State may prescribe the form and content of the report as it relates to the local development order.

5 (1) The report made under section 76 of the Planning and Compulsory Purchase Act 2004 must include a report as to the extent to which the local development order is achieving its purposes.

(2) The National Assembly for Wales may prescribe the form and content of the report as it relates to the local development order.'

NOTES

Initial Commencement

To be appointed: see s 121(1), (2)(b).

Appointment

Appointment (for the purpose of making, or making provision by means of, subordinate legislation): 6 August 2004: see SI 2004/2097, art 2.

Appointment (in relation to England for remaining purposes): 10 May 2006: see SI 2006/1061, art 2(c).

Extent

This Schedule does not extend to Scotland: see s 124(1).

SCHEDULE 2'
TIMETABLE FOR DECISIONS

Section 55

Decisions

A1.493

1 This Schedule applies to any decision which must be taken by the Secretary of State under—

(a) section 77 of the principal Act (reference of applications to Secretary of State);
(b) section 78 of the principal Act (right to appeal against planning decisions).

2 (1) This Schedule also applies to a decision not mentioned in paragraph 1 if each of the following two conditions applies.

(2) The first condition is that the Secretary of State thinks the decision is connected with a decision mentioned in paragraph 1.

(3) The second condition is that—

(a) the Secretary of State is required by virtue of any enactment to take the decision, or
(b) (in any case to which paragraph (a) does not apply) the Secretary of State by virtue of a power under any enactment directs that the decision must be referred to him.

3 But the Secretary of State may by order specify decisions or descriptions of decisions to which a timetable is not to apply.

Timetable

4 (1) The Secretary of State must make one or more timetables for the purposes of decisions to which this Schedule applies.

(2)   A timetable may make different provision for different decisions or different descriptions of decision.

(3)   A timetable—

    (a)   has effect from such time as the Secretary of State determines;
    (b)   must set out the time within which the decision must be taken;
    (c)   may set out the time within which any other step to be taken for the purposes of the decision must be taken.

(4)   A timetable made under this paragraph must be published in such form and manner as the Secretary of State thinks appropriate.

Notice

5   (1)   The Secretary of State must notify the following persons as soon as practicable of the published timetable which applies to a decision—

    (a)   the applicant or appellant (as the case may be) in relation to the decision;
    (b)   the local planning authority for the area to which the decision relates;
    (c)   any other person who requests such notification.

(2)   But the Secretary of State may direct that the timetable is subject to such variation as he specifies in the notice under sub-paragraph (1).

(3)   If the Secretary of State acts under sub-paragraph (2) the notice under sub-paragraph (1) must also specify the reasons for the variation.

(4)   The timetable notified under this paragraph is the applicable timetable.

Variation

6   (1)   This paragraph applies if before the time at which any step must be taken in accordance with the applicable timetable the Secretary of State thinks that there are circumstances which are likely to prevent the taking of the step at that time.

(2)   The Secretary of State may vary the applicable timetable accordingly.

(3)   If the Secretary of State varies the applicable timetable under sub-paragraph (2) he must notify the persons mentioned in paragraph 5(1) of the variation and the reason for it.

Written reasons

7   If the Secretary of State fails to take any step in accordance with the applicable timetable (or that timetable as varied under paragraph 6) he must give written reasons to the persons mentioned in paragraph 5(1).

Annual report

8   (1)   The Secretary of State must lay before Parliament a report in respect of each year which—

    (a)   reviews his performance under the provisions of this Schedule;
    (b)   explains any failure to comply with a timetable.

(2)   The report must be published in such form and manner as the Secretary of State thinks appropriate.

NOTES

Initial Commencement

To be appointed: see s 121(1).

Appointment

Paras 1, 2, 4–8: Appointment (in relation to England): 1 April 2005: see SI 2005/204, art 3; for savings see art 4 thereof.

Para 3: Appointment: 6 August 2004: see SI 2004/2097, art 2.

Extent

This Schedule does not extend to Scotland: see s 124(1).

Subordinate Legislation

Town and Country Planning (Timetable for Decisions) (England) Order 2005, SI 2005/205 (made under para 3).

SCHEDULE 3
CROWN APPLICATION

Section 79

Purchase notices

A1.494

1   After section 137 of the principal Act (circumstances in which a purchase notice may be served) there is inserted the following section—

'**137A   Purchase notices: Crown land**

(1)   A purchase notice may be served in respect of Crown land only as mentioned in this section.

(2)   The owner of a private interest in Crown land must not serve a purchase notice unless—

    (a)   he first offers to dispose of his interest to the appropriate authority on equivalent terms, and
    (b)   the offer is refused by the appropriate authority.

(3)   The appropriate authority may serve a purchase notice in relation to the following land—

    (a)   land belonging to Her Majesty in right of Her private estates;
    (b)   land belonging to Her Majesty in right of the Duchy of Lancaster;
    (c)   land belonging to the Duchy of Cornwall;
    (d)   land which forms part of the Crown Estate.

(4)   An offer is made on equivalent terms if the price payable for the interest is equal to (and, in default of agreement, determined in the same manner as) the compensation which would be payable in respect of it if it were acquired in pursuance of a purchase notice.

(5)   Expressions used in this section and in Part 13 must be construed in accordance with that Part.'

2   After section 32 of the listed buildings Act (circumstances in which a purchase notice may be served) there is inserted the following section—

'**32A   Purchase notices: Crown land**

(1)   A listed building purchase notice may be served in respect of Crown land only as mentioned in this section.

(2) The owner of a private interest in Crown land must not serve a listed building purchase notice unless—

  (a) he first offers to dispose of his interest to the appropriate authority on equivalent terms, and
  (b) the offer is refused by the appropriate authority.

(3) The appropriate authority may serve a listed building purchase notice in relation to the following land—

  (a) land belonging to Her Majesty in right of Her private estates;
  (b) land belonging to Her Majesty in right of the Duchy of Lancaster;
  (c) land belonging to the Duchy of Cornwall;
  (d) land which forms part of the Crown Estate.

(4) An offer is made on equivalent terms if the price payable for the interest is equal to (and, in default of agreement, determined in the same manner as) the compensation which would be payable in respect of it if it were acquired in pursuance of a listed building purchase notice.'

Compulsory acquisition

3 (1) Section 226 of the principal Act (compulsory acquisition of land for development and other planning purposes) is amended as follows.

(2) After subsection (2) there is inserted the following subsection—

'(2A) The Secretary of State must not authorise the acquisition of any interest in Crown land unless—

  (a) it is an interest which is for the time being held otherwise than by or on behalf of the Crown, and
  (b) the appropriate authority consents to the acquisition.'

(3) After subsection (8) there is inserted the following subsection—

'(9) Crown land must be construed in accordance with Part 13.'

4 (1) Section 228 of the principal Act (compulsory acquisition of land by the Secretary of State) is amended as follows.

(2) After subsection (1) there is inserted the following subsection—

'(1A) But subsection (1) does not permit the acquisition of any interest in Crown land unless—

  (a) it is an interest which is for the time being held otherwise than by or on behalf of the Crown, and
  (b) the appropriate authority consents to the acquisition.'

(3) After subsection (7) there is inserted the following subsection—

'(8) Crown land must be construed in accordance with Part 13.'

5 (1) Section 47 of the listed buildings Act (compulsory acquisition of listed building in need of repair) is amended as follows.

(2) After subsection (6) there is inserted the following subsection—

'(6A) This section does not permit the acquisition of any interest in Crown land unless—

  (a) it is an interest which is for the time being held otherwise than by or on behalf of the Crown, and

(b) the appropriate authority (within the meaning of section 82C) consents to the acquisition.'

Definitions

6   (1)   Section 293 of the principal Act (preliminary definitions) is amended as follows.

(2)   In subsection (1) for the definition of 'Crown interest' there is substituted the following definition—

"Crown interest' means any of the following—
  (a)   an interest belonging to Her Majesty in right of the Crown or in right of Her private estates;
  (b)   an interest belonging to a government department or held in trust for Her Majesty for the purposes of a government department;
  (c)   such other interest as the Secretary of State specifies by order;'.

(3)   In subsection (2) after paragraph (b) there is inserted the following paragraph—

'(ba) in relation to land belonging to Her Majesty in right of Her private estates means a person appointed by Her Majesty in writing under the Royal Sign Manual or, if no such appointment is made, the Secretary of State;'.

(4)   In subsection (2) after paragraph (e) there are inserted the following paragraphs—

'(f)   in relation to Westminster Hall and the Chapel of St Mary Undercroft, means the Lord Great Chamberlain and the Speakers of the House of Lords and the House of Commons acting jointly;
  (g)   in relation to Her Majesty's Robing Room in the Palace of Westminster, the adjoining staircase and ante-room and the Royal Gallery, means the Lord Great Chamberlain.'

(5)   After subsection (2) there is inserted the following subsection—

'(2A)   For the purposes of an application for planning permission made by or on behalf of the Crown in respect of land which does not belong to the Crown or in respect of which it has no interest a reference to the appropriate authority must be construed as a reference to the person who makes the application.'

(6)   After subsection (3) there are inserted the following subsections—

'(3A)   References to Her Majesty's private estates must be construed in accordance with section 1 of the Crown Private Estates Act 1862.

(3B)   In subsection (2A) the Crown includes—

  (a)   the Duchy of Lancaster;
  (b)   the Duchy of Cornwall;
  (c)   a person who is an appropriate authority by virtue of subsection (2)(f) and (g).'

(7)   After subsection (4) there are inserted the following subsections—

'(5)   An order made for the purposes of paragraph (c) of the definition of Crown interest in subsection (1) must be made by statutory instrument.

(6)   But no such order may be made unless a draft of it has been laid before and approved by resolution of each House of Parliament.'

7   In the listed buildings Act after section 82B (inserted by section 83(1)) there is inserted the following section—

'**82C**   **Expressions relating to the Crown**

(1) In this Act, expressions relating to the Crown must be construed in accordance with this section.

(2) Crown land is land in which there is a Crown interest or a Duchy interest.

(3) A Crown interest is any of the following—

    (a)   an interest belonging to Her Majesty in right of the Crown or in right of Her private estates;

    (b)   an interest belonging to a government department or held in trust for Her Majesty for the purposes of a government department;

    (c)   such other interest as the Secretary of State specifies by order.

(4) A Duchy interest is—

    (a)   an interest belonging to Her Majesty in right of the Duchy of Lancaster, or

    (b)   an interest belonging to the Duchy of Cornwall.

(5) A private interest is an interest which is neither a Crown interest nor a Duchy interest.

(6) The appropriate authority in relation to any land is—

    (a)   in the case of land belonging to Her Majesty in right of the Crown and forming part of the Crown Estate, the Crown Estate Commissioners;

    (b)   in relation to any other land belonging to Her Majesty in right of the Crown, the government department having the management of the land;

    (c)   in relation to land belonging to Her Majesty in right of Her private estates, a person appointed by Her Majesty in writing under the Royal Sign Manual or, if no such appointment is made, the Secretary of State;

    (d)   in relation to land belonging to Her Majesty in right of the Duchy of Lancaster, the Chancellor of the Duchy;

    (e)   in relation to land belonging to the Duchy of Cornwall, such person as the Duke of Cornwall, or the possessor for the time being of the Duchy, appoints;

    (f)   in the case of land belonging to a government department or held in trust for Her Majesty for the purposes of a government department, the department;

    (g)   in relation to Westminster Hall and the Chapel of St Mary Undercroft, the Lord Great Chamberlain and the Speakers of the House of Lords and the House of Commons acting jointly;

    (h)   in relation to Her Majesty's Robing Room in the Palace of Westminster, the adjoining staircase and ante-room and the Royal Gallery, the Lord Great Chamberlain.

(7) If any question arises as to what authority is the appropriate authority in relation to any land it must be referred to the Treasury, whose decision is final.

(8) For the purposes of an application for listed building consent made by or on behalf of the Crown in respect of land which does not belong to the Crown or in respect of which it has no interest a reference to the appropriate authority must be construed as a reference to the person who makes the application.

(9) For the purposes of subsection (8) the Crown includes—

    (a)   the Duchy of Lancaster;

    (b)   the Duchy of Cornwall;

    (c)   a person who is an appropriate authority by virtue of subsection (6)(g) and (h).

(10) The reference to Her Majesty's private estates must be construed in accordance with section 1 of the Crown Private Estates Act 1862.

1587

(11)   An order made for the purposes of paragraph (c) of subsection (3) must be made by statutory instrument.

(12)   But no such order may be made unless a draft of it has been laid before and approved by resolution of each House of Parliament.'

8   (1)   Section 31 of the hazardous substances Act (exercise of powers in relation to Crown land) is amended as follows.

(2)   Subsections (1) and (2) are omitted.

(3)   In subsection (3) for the definition of 'Crown interest' there is substituted the following definition—

"Crown interest' means any of the following—
   (a)   an interest belonging to Her Majesty in right of the Crown or in right of Her private estates;
   (b)   an interest belonging to a government department or held in trust for Her Majesty for the purposes of a government department;
   (c)   such other interest as the Secretary of State specifies by order;'.

(4)   In subsection (5) after paragraph (a) there is inserted the following paragraph—

'(aa) in relation to land belonging to Her Majesty in right of Her private estates means a person appointed by Her Majesty in writing under the Royal Sign Manual or, if no such appointment is made, the Secretary of State;'.

(5)   In subsection (5) after paragraph (d) there are inserted the following paragraphs—

'(e)   in relation to Westminster Hall and the Chapel of St Mary Undercroft, means the Lord Great Chamberlain and the Speakers of the House of Lords and the House of Commons acting jointly;
   (f)   in relation to Her Majesty's Robing Room in the Palace of Westminster, the adjoining staircase and ante-room and the Royal Gallery, means the Lord Great Chamberlain.'

(6)   After subsection (6) there are inserted the following subsections—

'(7)   References to Her Majesty's private estates must be construed in accordance with section 1 of the Crown Private Estates Act 1862.

(8)   An order made for the purposes of paragraph (c) of the definition of Crown interest in subsection (3) must be made by statutory instrument.

(9)   But no such order may be made unless a draft of it has been laid before and approved by resolution of each House of Parliament.'

Special enforcement notices

9   (1)   Sections 294 and 295 of the principal Act (control of development on Crown land: special enforcement notices) are omitted.

(2)   But the repeal of sections 294 and 295 does not affect their operation in relation to development carried out before the commencement of this paragraph.

Applications for planning permission, etc

10   (1)   After section 298 of the principal Act (supplementary provision as to Crown and Duchy interests) there is inserted the following section—

'298A   Applications for planning permission by Crown**

(1)   This section applies to an application for planning permission or for a certificate under section 192 made by or on behalf of the Crown.

(2) The Secretary of State may by regulations modify or exclude any statutory provision relating to the making and determination of such applications.

(3) A statutory provision is a provision contained in or having effect under any enactment.'

(2) Section 299 of the principal Act is omitted.

(3) The repeal of section 299 of the principal Act does not does not affect any requirement made in pursuance of regulations made under subsection (5)(b) of that section.

11 After section 82E of the listed buildings Act (inserted by section 84) there is inserted the following section—

'82F Applications for listed building or conservation area consent by Crown

(1) This section applies to an application for listed building consent or conservation area consent made by or on behalf of the Crown.

(2) The Secretary of State may by regulations modify or exclude any statutory provision relating to the making and determination of such applications.

(3) A statutory provision is a provision contained in or having effect under any enactment.'

12 (1) After section 31 of the hazardous substances Act (exercise of powers in relation to Crown land) there is inserted the following section—

'31A Applications for hazardous substances consent by Crown

(1) This section applies to an application for hazardous substances consent made by or on behalf of the Crown.

(2) The Secretary of State may by regulations modify or exclude any statutory provision relating to the making and determination of such applications.

(3) A statutory provision is a provision contained in or having effect under any enactment.'

(2) Section 32 of the hazardous substances Act is omitted.

Rights of entry

13 After section 325 of the principal Act (supplementary provisions as to rights of entry) there is inserted the following section—

'325A Rights of entry: Crown land

(1) Section 324 applies to Crown land subject to the following modifications.

(2) A person must not enter Crown land unless he has the relevant permission.

(3) Relevant permission is the permission of—

  (a) a person appearing to the person seeking entry to the land to be entitled to give it, or
  (b) the appropriate authority.

(4) In subsection (8) the words 'Subject to section 325' must be ignored.

(5) Section 325 does not apply to anything done by virtue of this section.

(6) 'Appropriate authority' must be construed in accordance with section 293(2).'

14   After section 88B of the listed buildings Act (rights of entry: supplementary provisions) there is inserted the following section—

'88C   Rights of entry: Crown land

(1)   Section 88 applies to Crown land subject to the following modifications.

(2)   A person must not enter Crown land unless he has the relevant permission.

(3)   Relevant permission is the permission of—

    (a)   a person appearing to the person seeking entry to the land to be entitled to give it, or

    (b)   the appropriate authority.

(4)   In subsection (6) the words 'Subject to section 88B(8)' must be ignored.

(5)   Section 88B does not apply to anything done by virtue of this section.

(6)   'Appropriate authority' must be construed in accordance with section 82C(6).'

15   After section 36B of the hazardous substances Act (rights of entry: supplementary provisions) there is inserted the following section—

'36C   Rights of entry: Crown land

(1)   Section 36 applies to Crown land subject to the following modifications.

(2)   A person must not enter Crown land unless he has the relevant permission.

(3)   Relevant permission is the permission of—

    (a)   a person appearing to the person seeking entry to the land to be entitled to give it, or

    (b)   the appropriate authority.

(4)   Section 36B does not apply to anything done by virtue of this section.

(5)   'Appropriate authority' must be construed in accordance with section 31(5).'

Service of notices

16   After section 329 of the principal Act (service of notices) there is inserted the following section—

'329A   Service of notices on the Crown

(1)   Any notice or other document required under this Act to be served on the Crown must be served on the appropriate authority.

(2)   Section 329 does not apply for the purposes of the service of such a notice or document.

(3)   'Appropriate authority' must be construed in accordance with section 293(2).'

Information as to interests in land

17   After section 330 of the principal Act (power to require information as to interests in land) there is inserted the following section—

'330A   Information as to interests in Crown land

(1)   This section applies to an interest in Crown land which is not a private interest.

(2)   Section 330 does not apply to an interest to which this section applies.

(3) For a purpose mentioned in section 330(1) the Secretary of State may request the appropriate authority to give him such information as to the matters mentioned in section 330(2) as he specifies in the request.

(4) The appropriate authority must comply with a request under subsection (3) except to the extent—

    (a) that the matter is not within the knowledge of the authority, or

    (b) that to do so will disclose information as to any of the matters mentioned in section 321(4).

(5) Expressions used in this section and in Part 13 must be construed in accordance with that Part.'

Listed buildings and conservation areas

18 (1) Sections 83 and 84 of the listed buildings Act (provisions relating to Crown land) are omitted.

(2) The repeal of section 84 of the listed buildings Act does not affect any requirement made in pursuance of regulations made under subsection (4)(b) of that section.

19 (1) Section 89(1) of the listed buildings Act (application of certain general provisions of principal Act) is amended as follows.

(2) After the entry relating to section 329 there is inserted—

'section 329A(1) and (2) (service of notices on the Crown)'.

(3) After the entry relating to section 330 there is inserted—

'section 330A(1) to (4) (information as to interests in Crown land)'.

Hazardous substances

20 In section 17 of the hazardous substances Act (revocation of consent on change of control of land) after subsection (2) there is inserted the following subsection—

'(3) This section does not apply if the control of land changes from one emanation of the Crown to another.'

21 (1) Section 37(2) of the hazardous substances Act (application of certain general provisions of the principal Act) is amended as follows.

(2) After the entry relating to section 329 there is inserted—

'section 329A(1) and (2) (service of notices on the Crown)'.

(3) After the entry relating to section 330 there is inserted—

'section 330A(1) to (4) (information as to interests in Crown land)'.

Miscellaneous

22 Section 293(4) of the principal Act (certain persons treated as having an interest in Crown land) is omitted.

23 Section 297 of the principal Act (agreements relating to Crown land) is omitted.

24 (1) Section 298 of the principal Act (supplementary provisions as to Crown and Duchy interests) is amended as follows.

(2) Subsections (1) and (2) are omitted.

(3) In subsection (3) after 'in which there is' there is inserted 'a Crown interest or'.

25 Section 299A of the principal Act (Crown planning obligations) is omitted.

26 (1) Section 300 of the principal Act (tree preservation orders in anticipation of disposal of Crown land) is omitted.

(2) But the repeal of section 300 does not affect its operation in relation to a tree preservation order made by virtue of that section before the commencement of this paragraph.

27 (1) Section 301 of the principal Act (requirement of planning permission for continuance of use instituted by the Crown) is omitted.

(2) But the repeal of section 301 does not affect its operation in relation to an agreement made as mentioned in subsection (1) of that section before the commencement of this paragraph.

NOTES

Initial Commencement

To be appointed: see s 121(1), (2)(d), (g).

Appointment

Paras 1–5, 9, 13–27: Appointment: 7 June 2006: see SI 2006/1281, art 2(c).

Paras 6–8, 10–12: Appointment (for the purpose of making, or making provision by means of, subordinate legislation): 6 August 2004: see SI 2004/2097, art 2.

Paras 6–8, 10–12: Appointment (for remaining purposes): 7 June 2006: see SI 2006/1281, art 2(c).

Extent

This Schedule does not extend to Scotland: see s 124(1).

SCHEDULE 4
TRANSITIONAL PROVISIONS: CROWN APPLICATION

Section 89

PART 1: THE PRINCIPAL ACT

Introduction

A1.495

1 This Part applies to a development if—

    (a) it is a development for which before the relevant date no planning permission is required,

    (b) it is not a development or of a description of development for which planning permission is granted by virtue of a development order, and

    (c) before the relevant date proposed development notice had been given to the local planning authority.

2 In this Part—

    (a) the relevant date is the date of commencement of section 79(1);

    (b) proposed development notice is notice of a proposal for development given by the developer in pursuance of arrangements made by the Secretary of State in relation to development by or on behalf of the Crown;

    (c) the developer is the Crown or a person acting on behalf of the Crown.

Acceptable development

3 (1) This paragraph applies if before the relevant date in pursuance of the arrangements either the local planning authority have or the Secretary of State has given notice to the developer that they or he (as the case may be) find the proposed development acceptable.

(2) The notice must be treated as if it is planning permission granted under Part 3 of the principal Act.

(3) If the notice is subject to conditions the conditions have effect as if they are conditions attached to the planning permission.

4 (1) This paragraph applies if before the relevant date the local planning authority have in pursuance of the arrangements kept a register of proposed development notices.

(2) The register must be treated as if it is part of the register kept by them in pursuance of section 69 of the principal Act.

Referred proposals

5 (1) This paragraph applies if—

   (a) before the relevant date the local planning authority have notified the developer in pursuance of the arrangements that they do not find the development acceptable, and

   (b) the matter has been referred to but not decided by the Secretary of State.

(2) This paragraph also applies if—

   (a) before the relevant date the local planning authority have notified the developer in pursuance of the arrangements that they find the development acceptable subject to conditions, and

   (b) the matter has been referred to but not decided by the Secretary of State.

(3) The Secretary of State must deal with the proposal as if it is an appeal by an applicant for planning permission under section 78 of the principal Act.

Pending proposals

6 (1) This paragraph applies if before the relevant date—

   (a) proposed development notice has been given, but

   (b) the local planning authority have not given notice to the developer as mentioned in paragraph 3 or 5.

(2) The principal Act applies as if the proposal is an application for planning permission duly made under Part 3 of that Act.

NOTES

Initial Commencement

To be appointed: see s 121(1), (2)(d), (g).

Appointment

Appointment: 7 June 2006: see SI 2006/1281, art 2(d).

Extent

This Schedule does not extend to Scotland: see s 124(1).

PART 2: THE LISTED BUILDINGS ACT

Introduction

7   This Part applies to works if—

(a)   they are works for which before the relevant date no listed building consent is required, and

(b)   before the relevant date proposed works notice had been given to the local planning authority.

8   In this Part—

(a)   the relevant date is the date of commencement of section 79(1);

(b)   proposed works notice is notice of a proposal for works given by the person proposing to carry out the works (the developer) in pursuance of arrangements made by the Secretary of State in relation to development by or on behalf of the Crown;

(c)   the developer is the Crown or a person acting on behalf of the Crown.

Acceptable works

9   (1)   This paragraph applies if before the relevant date in pursuance of the arrangements either the local planning authority have or the Secretary of State has given notice to the developer that they or he (as the case may be) find the proposed works acceptable.

(2)   The notice must be treated as if it is listed building consent granted under the listed buildings Act.

(3)   If the notice is subject to conditions the conditions have effect as if they are conditions attached to the consent.

10   (1)   This paragraph applies if before the relevant date the local planning authority have in pursuance of the arrangements kept a register of proposed works notices.

(2)   The register must be treated as if it is part of the register kept by them in pursuance of the listed buildings Act.

Referred proposals

11   (1)   This paragraph applies if—

(a)   before the relevant date the local planning authority have notified the developer in pursuance of the arrangements that they do not find the works acceptable, and

(b)   the matter has been referred to but not decided by the Secretary of State.

(2)   This paragraph also applies if—

(a)   before the relevant date the local planning authority have notified the developer in pursuance of the arrangements that they find the works acceptable subject to conditions, and

(b)   the matter has been referred to but not decided by the Secretary of State.

(3)   The Secretary of State must deal with the proposal as if it is an appeal by an applicant for listed building consent under section 20 of the listed buildings Act.

Pending proposals

12   (1)   This paragraph applies if before the relevant date—

(a)   proposed works notice has been given, but

(b)   the local planning authority have not given notice to the developer as mentioned in paragraph 9 or 11.

(2)   The listed buildings Act applies as if the proposal is an application for listed building consent duly made under that Act.

NOTES

Initial Commencement

To be appointed: see s 121(1), (2)(d), (g).

Appointment

Appointment: 7 June 2006: see SI 2006/1281, art 2(d).

Extent

This Schedule does not extend to Scotland: see s 124(1).

SCHEDULE 5
CROWN APPLICATION: SCOTLAND

Section 90

Purchase notices

A1.496

1   In the Town and Country Planning (Scotland) Act 1997 (c 8) (referred to in this Schedule as the 'principal Scottish Act'), there is inserted after section 88 (circumstances in which purchase notices may be served) the following section—

'**88A   Purchase notices: Crown land**

(1)   A purchase notice may be served in respect of Crown land only as mentioned in this section.

(2)   The owner of a private interest in Crown land must not serve a purchase notice unless—

(a)   he first offers to dispose of his interest to the appropriate authority on equivalent terms, and

(b)   the offer is refused by the appropriate authority.

(3)   The appropriate authority may serve a purchase notice in relation to the following land—

(a)   land belonging to Her Majesty in right of her private estates,

(b)   land which forms part of the Crown Estate.

(4)   An offer is made on equivalent terms if the price payable for the interest is equal to (and, in default of agreement, determined in the same manner as) the compensation which would be payable in respect of it if it were acquired in pursuance of a purchase notice.

(5)   Expressions used in this section and in Part 12 (Crown Land) must be construed in accordance with that Part.'

2   In the Planning (Listed Buildings and Conservation Areas) (Scotland) Act 1997 (c 9) (referred to in this Schedule as the 'Scottish listed buildings Act'), after section 28 (circumstances in which purchase notices may be served) there is inserted the following section—

'28A   Purchase notices: Crown land

(1)   A listed building purchase notice may be served in respect of Crown land only as mentioned in this section.

(2)   The owner of a private interest in Crown land must not serve a listed building purchase notice unless—

   (a)   he first offers to dispose of his interest to the appropriate authority on equivalent terms, and
   (b)   the offer is refused by the appropriate authority.

(3)   The appropriate authority may serve a listed building purchase notice in relation to the following land—

   (a)   land belonging to Her Majesty in right of her private estates,
   (b)   land which forms part of the Crown Estate.

(4)   An offer is made on equivalent terms if the price payable for the interest is equal to (and, in default of agreement, determined in the same manner as) the compensation which would be payable in respect of it if it were acquired in pursuance of a listed building purchase notice.'

Compulsory acquisition

3   (1)   In the principal Scottish Act, section 189 (compulsory acquisition of land for development and other planning purposes) is amended as follows.

(2)   After subsection (2) there is inserted the following subsection—

'(2A)   The Scottish Ministers must not authorise the acquisition of any interest in Crown land unless—

   (a)   it is an interest which is for the time being held otherwise than by or on behalf of the Crown, and
   (b)   the appropriate authority consents to the acquisition.'

(3)   After subsection (8) there is inserted the following subsection—

'(9)   Crown land must be construed in accordance with Part 12.'

4   (1)   Section 190 of that Act (compulsory acquisition of land by Secretary of State for the Environment) is amended as follows.

(2)   After subsection (1) there is inserted the following subsection—

'(1A)   But subsection (1) does not permit the acquisition of any interest in Crown land unless—

   (a)   it is an interest which is for the time being held otherwise than by or on behalf of the Crown, and
   (b)   the appropriate authority consents to the acquisition.'

(3)   After subsection (7) there is added the following subsection—

'(8)   Crown land must be construed in accordance with Part 12.'

5   (1)   In the Scottish listed buildings Act, section 42 (compulsory acquisition of listed building in need of repair) is amended as follows.

(2) After subsection (6) there is inserted the following subsection—

'(6A) This section does not permit the acquisition of any interest in Crown land unless—

   (a) it is an interest which is for the time being held otherwise than by or on behalf of the Crown, and
   (b) the appropriate authority consents to the acquisition.'

Definitions

6   (1) In the principal Scottish Act, section 242 (preliminary definitions) is amended as follows.

(2) In subsection (1) for the definition of 'Crown interest' there is substituted the following definition—

   "Crown interest' means any of the following—
      (a) an interest belonging to Her Majesty in right of the Crown or in right of Her private estates,
      (b) an interest belonging to a government department or held in trust for Her Majesty for the purposes of a government department,
      (c) such other interest as the Scottish Ministers specify by order;'.

(3) In subsection (2) after paragraph (b) there is inserted the following paragraph—

   '(ba) in relation to land belonging to Her Majesty in right of Her private estates means a person appointed by Her Majesty in writing under the Royal Sign Manual or, if no such appointment is made, the Scottish Ministers;'.

(4) After subsection (2) there is inserted the following subsection—

'(2A) For the purposes of an application for planning permission made by or on behalf of the Crown in respect of land which does not belong to the Crown or in respect of which the Crown has no interest, a reference to the appropriate authority must be construed as a reference to the person who makes the application.'

(5) After subsection (3) there is inserted the following subsection—

'(3A) References to Her Majesty's private estates must be construed in accordance with section 1 of the Crown Private Estates Act 1862 (c 37).'

(6) After subsection (4) there are inserted the following subsections—

'(5) An order made for the purposes of paragraph (c) of the definition of Crown interest in subsection (1) must be made by statutory instrument.

(6) But no such order may be made unless a draft of it has been laid before and approved by resolution of the Scottish Parliament.'

7   In the Scottish listed buildings Act, after section 73B (inserted by section 93(1)), there is inserted the following section—

'**73C   Expressions relating to the Crown**

(1) Expressions relating to the Crown must be construed in accordance with this section.

(2) Crown land is land in which there is a Crown interest.

(3) A Crown interest is any of the following—

   (a) an interest belonging to Her Majesty in right of the Crown or in right of Her private estates,

    (b)   an interest belonging to a government department or held in trust for Her Majesty for the purposes of a government department,

    (c)   such other interest as the Scottish Ministers specify by order.

(4)   A private interest is an interest which is not a Crown interest.

(5)   The appropriate authority in relation to any land is—

    (a)   in the case of land belonging to Her Majesty in right of the Crown and forming part of the Crown Estate, the Crown Estate Commissioners,

    (b)   in relation to any other land belonging to Her Majesty in right of the Crown, the government department having the management of the land,

    (c)   in relation to land belonging to Her Majesty in right of Her private estates, a person appointed by Her Majesty in writing under the Royal Sign Manual or, if no such appointment is made, the Scottish Ministers,

    (d)   in the case of land belonging to a government department or held in trust for Her Majesty for the purposes of a government department, the department.

(6)   If any question arises as to what authority is the appropriate authority in relation to any land it must be referred to the Scottish Ministers, whose decision is final.

(7)   For the purpose of an application for listed building consent made by or on behalf of the Crown in respect of land which does not belong to the Crown or in respect of which the Crown has no interest, a reference to the appropriate authority must be construed as a reference to the person who makes the application.

(8)   The reference to Her Majesty's private estates must be construed in accordance with section 1 of the Crown Private Estates Act 1862 (c 37).

(9)   An order made for the purposes of paragraph (c) of subsection (3) must be made by statutory instrument.

(10)   But no such order may be made unless a draft of it has been laid before and approved by resolution of the Scottish Parliament.

(11)   This section applies for the purposes of this Act.'

8   (1)   In the Planning (Hazardous Substances) (Scotland) Act 1997 (c 10) (referred to in this Schedule as the 'Scottish hazardous substances Act'), section 31 (exercise of powers in relation to Crown land) is amended as follows.

(2)   Subsections (1) and (2) are omitted.

(3)   In subsection (3) for the definition of 'Crown interest' there is substituted the following definition—

    "Crown interest' means any of the following—

        (a)   an interest belonging to Her Majesty in right of the Crown or in right of Her private estates,

        (b)   an interest belonging to a government department or held in trust for Her Majesty for the purposes of a government department,

        (c)   such other interest as the Scottish Ministers specify by order.'

(4)   In subsection (5) after paragraph (b) there is inserted the following paragraph—

    '(ba) in relation to land belonging to Her Majesty in right of Her private estates means a person appointed by Her Majesty in writing under the Royal Sign Manual or, if no such appointment is made, the Scottish Ministers,'.

(5)   After subsection (6) there are inserted the following subsections—

'(7)   References to Her Majesty's private estates must be construed in accordance with section 1 of the Crown Private Estates Act 1862 (c 37).

(8) An order made for the purposes of paragraph (c) of the definition of Crown interest in subsection (3) must be made by statutory instrument.

(9) But no such order may be made unless a draft of it has been laid before and approved by resolution of the Scottish Parliament.'

Special enforcement notices

9 (1) Sections 243 and 244 of the principal Scottish Act (control of development on Crown land: special enforcement notices) are omitted.

(2) But the repeal of sections 243 and 244 does not affect their operation in relation to development carried out before the commencement of this paragraph.

Applications for planning permission, etc

10 (1) In the principal Scottish Act, after section 247 (supplementary provision as to Crown interest) there is inserted the following section—

'247A   Applications for planning permission by Crown

(1) This section applies to an application for planning permission or for a certificate under section 151 made by or on behalf of the Crown.

(2) The Scottish Ministers may by regulations modify or exclude any statutory provision relating to the making and determination of such applications.

(3) A statutory provision is a provision contained in or having effect under any enactment (including any enactment comprised in, or in an instrument made under, an Act of the Scottish Parliament).'

(2) Section 248 (application for planning permission etc in anticipation of disposal of Crown land) is omitted.

(3) The repeal of that section does not affect any requirement made in pursuance of regulations made under subsection (5)(b) of that section.

11 After section 73E of the Scottish listed buildings Act (inserted by section 94(4)) there is inserted the following section—

'73F   Applications for listed building or conservation area consent by Crown

(1) This section applies to an application for—

(a) listed building consent, or
(b) conservation area consent,

made by or on behalf of the Crown.

(2) The Scottish Ministers may by regulations modify or exclude any statutory provision relating to the making and determination of such applications.

(3) A statutory provision is a provision contained in or having effect under any enactment (including any enactment comprised in, or in an instrument made under, an Act of the Scottish Parliament).'

12 In the Scottish hazardous substances Act, section 32 (application for hazardous substances consent in anticipation of disposal of Crown land) is omitted.

13 Before section 33 of that Act there is inserted—

'32A **Applications for hazardous substances consent by Crown**

(1) This section applies to an application for hazardous substances consent made by or on behalf of the Crown.

(2) The Scottish Ministers may by regulations modify or exclude any statutory provision relating to the making and determination of such applications.

(3) A statutory provision is a provision contained in or having effect under any enactment (including any enactment comprised in, or in an instrument made under, an Act of the Scottish Parliament).'

Rights of entry

14 After section 270 of the principal Scottish Act (supplementary provisions as to rights of entry) there is inserted the following section—

'270A **Rights of entry: Crown land**

(1) Section 269 applies to Crown land subject to the following modifications.

(2) A person must not enter Crown land unless he has the relevant permission.

(3) Relevant permission is the permission of—

  (a) a person appearing to the person seeking entry to the land to be entitled to give it, or
  (b) the appropriate authority.

(4) In subsection (6) the words 'Subject to section 270' must be ignored.

(5) Section 270 does not apply to anything done by virtue of this section.

(6) 'Appropriate authority' must be construed in accordance with section 242.'

15 After section 78 of the Scottish listed buildings Act (rights of entry: supplementary provisions) there is inserted the following section—

'78A **Rights of entry: Crown land**

(1) Section 76 applies to Crown land subject to the following modifications.

(2) A person must not enter Crown land unless he has the relevant permission.

(3) Relevant permission is the permission of—

  (a) a person appearing to the person seeking entry to the land to be entitled to give it, or
  (b) the appropriate authority.

(4) In subsection (6) the words 'and 78' must be ignored.

(5) Section 78 does not apply to anything done by virtue of this section.

(6) 'Appropriate authority' must be construed in accordance with section 73C'

16 After section 35 of the Scottish hazardous substances Act (rights of entry: supplementary provisions) there is inserted the following section—

'35A **Rights of entry: Crown land**

(1) Section 33 applies to Crown land subject to the following modifications.

(2) A person must not enter Crown land unless he has the relevant permission.

(3) Relevant permission is the permission of—

(a) a person appearing to the person seeking entry to the land to be entitled to give it, or

(b) the appropriate authority.

(4) In subsection (5), the words 'and 35' must be ignored.

(5) Section 35 does not apply to anything done by virtue of this section.

(6) 'Appropriate authority' must be construed in accordance with section 31(5).'

Service of notices

17 After section 271 of the principal Scottish Act (service of notices) there is inserted the following section—

'271A   Service of notices on the Crown

(1) Any notice or other document required under this Act to be served on the Crown must be served on the appropriate authority.

(2) Section 271 does not apply for the purposes of the service of such a notice or document.

(3) 'Appropriate authority' must be construed in accordance with section 242.'

Information as to interests in land

18 In the principal Scottish Act, after section 272 (power to require information as to interests in land) there is inserted the following section—

'272A   Information as to interests in Crown land

(1) This section applies to an interest in Crown land which is not a private interest.

(2) Section 272 does not apply to an interest to which this section applies.

(3) For a purpose mentioned in section 272(1) the Scottish Ministers may request the appropriate authority to give them such information as to the matters mentioned in section 272(2) as they specify in the request.

(4) The appropriate authority must comply with a request under subsection (3) except to the extent—

(a) that the matter is not within the knowledge of the authority, or

(b) that to do so will disclose information as to any of the matters mentioned in section 265A(4).

(5) Expressions used in this section and in Part 12 (Crown Land) must be construed in accordance with that Part.'

Listed buildings and conservation areas

19 (1) In the Scottish listed buildings Act, sections 74 and 75 (provisions relating to Crown land) are omitted.

(2) The repeal of section 75 does not affect any requirement made in pursuance of regulations made under subsection (4)(b) of that section.

20 (1) In the Scottish listed buildings Act, section 79 (application of certain general provisions of the principal Scottish Act) is amended as follows.

(2) In subsection (1)—

(a) after the entry relating to section 265 there is inserted—

'section 265A (planning inquiries to be held in public subject to certain exceptions),',
(b)   after the entry relating to section 271 there is inserted—
'section 271A(1) and (2) (service of notices on the Crown),', and
(c)   after the entry relating to section 272 there is inserted—
'section 272A(1) to (4) (information as to interests in Crown land),'.

(3)   After subsection (2) there is inserted the following subsection—

'(3)   In the application of section 265A of the principal Act for the purposes of this
Act, the provisions mentioned in subsection (1) of the section shall be construed as
including any inquiry held by virtue of this section.'

Hazardous substances

21   In the Scottish hazardous substances Act, in section 15 (revocation of consent on
change of control of land) after subsection (2) there is inserted the following
subsection—

'(3)   This section does not apply if the control of the land changes from one
emanation of the Crown to another.'

22   (1)   In the Scottish hazardous substances Act, section 36 (application of certain
general provisions of the principal Scottish Act) is amended as follows—

(a)   after the entry relating to section 265 there is inserted—
'section 265A (planning inquiries to be held in public subject to certain exceptions),',
(b)   after the entry relating to section 271 there is inserted—
'section 271A(1) to (2) (service of notices on the Crown),', and
(c)   after the entry relating to section 272 there is inserted—
'section 272A(1) to (4) (information as to interests in Crown land),'.

(2)   The existing provision as so amended becomes subsection (1), and after that
subsection there is added—

'(2)   In the application of section 265A of the principal Act for the purposes of this
Act, the provisions mentioned in subsection (1) of the section shall be construed as
including any inquiry held by virtue of this section.'

Miscellaneous

23   Sections 242(4) (certain persons treated as having an interest in Crown land) and
246 (agreements relating to Crown land) of the principal Scottish Act are omitted.

24   In the principal Scottish Act, for section 247 (supplementary provisions as to
Crown interest) there is substituted the following section—

'247   Supplementary provisions as to Crown interest

Where, in accordance with an agreement under section 246, the approval of a planning
authority is required in respect of any development of land in which there is a Crown
interest, sections 78 to 82 have effect in relation to the withholding of that approval, or
the giving of it subject to conditions, as if it were a refusal of planning permission, or,
as the case may be, a grant of planning permission subject to conditions.'

25   (1)   In the principal Scottish Act, section 249 (tree preservation orders in
anticipation of disposal of Crown land) is omitted.

(2)   But the repeal of section 249 does not affect its operation in relation to a tree
preservation order made by virtue of that section before the commencement of this
paragraph.

26   (1)   In the principal Scottish Act, section 250 (requirement of planning permission for continuance of use instituted by the Crown) is omitted.

(2)   But the repeal of section 250 does not affect its operation in relation to an agreement made as mentioned in subsection (1) of that section before the commencement of this paragraph.

NOTES

Initial Commencement

To be appointed: see s 121(4)(a), (b).

Appointment

Paras 1–5, 9, 12, 14–26: Appointment: 12 June 2006: see SSI 2006/268, art 3(f).

Paras 6–8, 10, 11, 13: Appointment (for the purposes of enabling rules, regulations, development order or other order to be made): 20 March 2006: see SSI 2006/101, art 2, Schedule.

Paras 6–8, 10, 11, 13: Appointment (for remaining purposes): 12 June 2006: see SSI 2006/268, art 3(f).

SCHEDULE 6
AMENDMENTS OF THE PLANNING ACTS

Section 118

Town and Country Planning Act 1990 (c 8)

A1.497

1   The Town and Country Planning Act 1990 is amended as follows.

2   In section 55(2)(b) (meaning of development) the word 'local' is omitted.

3   For section 69 there is substituted the following section—

'69   Register of applications etc

(1)   The local planning authority must keep a register containing such information as is prescribed as to—

    (a)   applications for planning permission;

    (b)   requests for statements of development principles (within the meaning of section 61E);

    (c)   local development orders;

    (d)   simplified planning zone schemes.

(2)   The register must contain—

    (a)   information as to the manner in which applications mentioned in subsection (1)(a) and requests mentioned in subsection (1)(b) have been dealt with;

    (b)   such information as is prescribed with respect to any local development order or simplified planning zone scheme in relation to the authority's area.

(3)   A development order may require the register to be kept in two or more parts.

(4)   Each part must contain such information as is prescribed relating to the matters mentioned in subsection (1)(a) and (b).

(5)   A development order may also make provision—

    (a)   for a specified part of the register to contain copies of applications or requests and of any other documents or material submitted with them;

   (b) for the entry relating to an application or request (and everything relating to it) to be removed from that part of the register when the application (including any appeal arising out of it) or the request (as the case may be) has been finally disposed of.

(6) Provision made under subsection (5)(b) does not prevent the inclusion of a different entry relating to the application or request in another part of the register.

(7) The register must be kept in such manner as is prescribed.

(8) The register must be kept available for inspection by the public at all reasonable hours.

(9) Anything prescribed under this section must be prescribed by development order.'

4 Section 76 (Duty to draw attention to certain provisions for benefit of disabled) is omitted.

5 Sections 106 to 106B (planning obligations) are omitted.

6 In section 108 (compensation for refusal of planning permission formerly granted by development order) after subsection (3) there is inserted the following subsection—

'(3A) This section does not apply if—

   (a) development authorised by planning permission granted by a development order or local development order is started before the permission is withdrawn, and
   (b) the order includes provision in pursuance of section 61D permitting the development to be completed after the permission is withdrawn.'

7 (1) In section 245 (modification of incorporated enactments), subsections (2) and (3) are omitted.

(2) The amendments made by sub-paragraph (1) do not apply to compulsory purchase orders of which notice under section 11 of or, as the case may be, paragraph 2 of Schedule 1 to the Acquisition of Land Act 1981 (c 67) is published before commencement of this paragraph.

8 In section 284(1) (restriction on challenge to validity of certain documents), paragraph (a) is omitted.

9 (1) Section 287 (procedure for questioning the validity of certain matters) is amended as follows.

(2) For subsections (1) to (3) there are substituted the following subsections—

'(1) This section applies to—

   (a) a simplified planning zone scheme or an alteration of such a scheme;
   (b) an order under section 247, 248, 249, 251, 257, 258 or 277,

and anything falling within paragraphs (a) and (b) is referred to in this section as a relevant document.

(2) A person aggrieved by a relevant document may make an application to the High Court on the ground that—

   (a) it is not within the appropriate power, or
   (b) a procedural requirement has not been complied with.

(3) The High Court may make an interim order suspending the operation of the relevant document—

   (a) wholly or in part;
   (b) generally or as it affects the property of the applicant.

(3A) Subsection (3B) applies if the High Court is satisfied—

   (a) that a relevant document is to any extent outside the appropriate power;
   (b) that the interests of the applicant have been substantially prejudiced by a failure to comply with a procedural requirement.

(3B) The High Court may quash the relevant document—

   (a) wholly or in part;
   (b) generally or as it affects the property of the applicant.

(3C) An interim order has effect until the proceedings are finally determined.

(3D) The appropriate power is—

   (a) in the case of a simplified planning zone scheme or an alteration of the scheme, Part III;
   (b) in the case of an order under section 247, 248, 249, 251, 257, 258 or 277, the section under which the order is made.'

(3) In subsection (5)—

   (a) paragraph (a) is omitted;
   (b) in each of paragraphs (b) to (e) the words 'by virtue of subsection (3)' are omitted.

(4) Subsection (6) is omitted.

10 (1) Section 296 (exercise of powers in relation to Crown land) is amended as follows.

(2) In subsection (1) for paragraph (a) there is substituted the following paragraph—

   '(a) a document, plan or strategy specified in subsection (1A) may include proposals relating to the use of Crown land;'.

(3) After subsection (1) there is inserted the following subsection—

'(1A) These are the documents, plans and strategies—

   (a) the regional spatial strategy (or a revision of it) within the meaning of Part 1 of the Planning and Compulsory Purchase Act 2004;
   (b) a local development document (or a revision of it) adopted or approved under Part 2 of that Act;
   (c) a local development plan (or a revision of it) adopted or approved under Part 6 of that Act;
   (d) the Mayor of London's spatial development strategy (or any alteration or replacement of it) published in pursuance of section 337 of the Greater London Authority Act 1999.'

11 (1) Section 303A (recovery of costs of certain inquiries) is amended as follows.

(2) For subsection (1) there are substituted the following subsections—

'(1) This section applies if the appropriate authority appoints a person to carry out or hold a qualifying procedure.

(1A) A qualifying procedure is—

   (a) an independent examination under section 20 or 64 of the Planning and Compulsory Purchase Act 2004;
   (b) a local inquiry or other hearing under paragraph 8(1)(a) of Schedule 7;
   (c) the consideration of objections under paragraph 8(1)(b) of that Schedule.

(1B) The appropriate authority is—

(a) the Secretary of State if the local planning authority causing the procedure to be carried out or held is in England;

(b) the National Assembly for Wales if the local planning authority causing the procedure to be carried out or held is in Wales.'

(3) In each of subsections (2) to (6) and (10)(a) in each place where it occurs—

(a) for 'Secretary of State' there is substituted 'appropriate authority';

(b) for 'him' there is substituted 'it';

(c) for 'he' there is substituted 'it'.

(4) In each of subsections (2), (4), (5) and (6) in each place where it occurs for 'inquiry' there is substituted 'procedure'.

(5) In subsection (5) each of the following is omitted—

(a) 'or appointed as one of the persons who are to hold it';

(b) ' (in addition to what may be recovered by virtue of the appointment of any other person)';

(c) in paragraph (c), '(or, in a case where that person is appointed as one of the persons who are to hold the qualifying inquiry, an appropriate proportion of any costs attributable to the appointment of an assessor to assist those persons)'.

(6) Subsections (7) to (9) are omitted.

(7) Before subsection (10) there is inserted the following subsection—

'(9A) References to a local planning authority causing a qualifying inquiry to be held include references to a requirement under the Planning and Compulsory Purchase Act 2004 on the authority to submit a plan to the appropriate authority for independent examination.'

12 In section 306(2) (local authorities and statutory undertakers may contribute to certain costs of local planning authorities) for paragraph (a) there are substituted the following paragraphs—

'(a) any expenses incurred by a local planning authority for the purposes of carrying out a review under section 13 or 61 of the Planning and Compulsory Purchase Act 2004 (duty of local planning authority to keep under review certain matters affecting development);

(ab) any expenses incurred by a county council for the purposes of carrying out a review under section 14 of that Act (duty of county council to keep under review certain matters affecting development);'

13 In section 324(1) (rights of entry) for paragraph (a) there is substituted the following paragraph—

'(a) the preparation, revision, adoption or approval of a local development document under Part 2 of the Planning and Compulsory Purchase Act 2004 or a local development plan under Part 6 of that Act;'

14 (1) Section 333 (provision about regulations and orders) is amended as follows.

(2) After subsection (2) there is inserted the following subsection—

'(2A) Regulations may make different provision for different purposes.'

15 In section 336(1) (interpretation) for the definition of development plan there is substituted—

"development plan' must be construed in accordance with section 38 of the Planning and Compulsory Purchase Act 2004;'.

16   (1)   Schedule 1 (distribution of functions of local planning authorities) is amended as follows.

(2)   Paragraph 2 is omitted.

(3)   In paragraph 3(7) the words 'but paragraph 4 shall apply to such applications instead' are omitted.

(4)   For paragraph 7 there is substituted the following paragraph—

'**7**   (1)   A local planning authority must not determine an application for planning permission to which the consultation requirements apply unless it complies with sub-paragraph (7).

(2)   The consultation requirements are—

    (a)   consultation with the RPB for the region in which the authority's area is situated if the development is one to which sub-paragraph (3) applies;

    (b)   consultation by a district planning authority with the county planning authority for their area if the development is one to which sub-paragraph (4) applies.

(3)   This sub-paragraph applies to—

    (a)   a development which would by reason of its scale or nature or the location of the land be of major importance for the implementation of the RSS or a relevant regional policy, or

    (b)   a development of a description in relation to which the RPB has given notice in writing to the local planning authority that it wishes to be consulted.

(4)   This sub-paragraph applies to—

    (a)   a development which would materially conflict with or prejudice the implementation of a relevant county policy,

    (b)   a development in an area in relation to which the county planning authority have given notice in writing to the district planning authority that development is likely to affect or be affected by the winning and working of minerals, other than coal,

    (c)   a development of land in respect of which the county planning authority have given notice in writing to the district planning authority that they propose to carry out development,

    (d)   a development which would prejudice a proposed development mentioned in paragraph (c) in respect of which notice has been given as so mentioned,

    (e)   a development of land in relation to which the county planning authority have given notice in writing to the district planning authority that it is proposed to use the land for waste disposal, or

    (f)   a development which would prejudice a proposed use mentioned in paragraph (e) in respect of which notice has been given as so mentioned.

(5)   The consultation requirements do not apply—

    (a)   in respect of a development to which sub-paragraph (3) applies if the RPB gives a direction authorising the determination of the application without compliance with the requirements;

    (b)   in respect of a development to which sub-paragraph (4) applies if the county planning authority gives a direction authorising the determination of the application without compliance with the requirements.

(6)   A direction under sub-paragraph (5) may be given in respect of a particular application or a description of application.

(7)   If the consultation requirements apply the local planning authority—

(a) must give notice to the RPB or county planning authority (as the case may be) (the consulted body) that they propose to consider the application,

(b) must send a copy of the application to the consulted body, and

(c) must not determine the application until the end of such period as is prescribed by development order beginning with the date of the giving of notice under paragraph (a).

(8) Sub-paragraph (7)(c) does not apply if before the end of the period mentioned in that sub-paragraph—

(a) the local planning authority have received representations concerning the application from the consulted body, or

(b) the consulted body gives notice that it does not intend to make representations.

(9) A relevant regional policy is—

(a) a policy contained in a draft revision of the RSS which has been submitted to the Secretary of State in pursuance of section 5(8) of the 2004 Act, or

(b) a policy contained in a structure plan which has effect by virtue of paragraph 1 of Schedule 8 to the 2004 Act.

(10) A relevant county policy is—

(a) a policy contained in a local development document which has been prepared in accordance with a minerals and waste scheme and submitted to the Secretary of State in pursuance of section 20(1) of the 2004 Act or adopted by the county planning authority in pursuance of section 23 of that Act, or

(b) a policy contained in a structure plan which has effect by virtue of paragraph 1 of Schedule 8 to the 2004 Act.

(11) RPB and RSS must be construed in accordance with Part 1 of the 2004 Act.

(12) The 2004 Act is the Planning and Compulsory Purchase Act 2004.'

17 In Schedule 2 (transitional provisions relating to development plans) Parts 1, 2 and 3 are omitted.

18 (1) Schedule 13 (blighted land) is amended as follows.

(2) Paragraphs 1 to 4 are omitted.

(3) The following paragraph is inserted as paragraph 1A—

'1A Land which is identified for the purposes of relevant public functions by a development plan document for the area in which the land is situated.

Notes

(1) Relevant public functions are—

(a) the functions of a government department, local authority, National Park authority or statutory undertakers;

(b) the establishment or running by a public telecommunications operator of a telecommunication system.

(2) For the purposes of this paragraph a development plan document is—

(a) a development plan document which is adopted or approved for the purposes of Part 2 of the Planning and Compulsory Purchase Act 2004 (in this paragraph, the 2004 Act);

(b) a revision of such a document in pursuance of section 26 of the 2004 Act which is adopted or approved for the purposes of Part 2 of the 2004 Act;

(c) a development plan document which has been submitted to the Secretary of State for independent examination under section 20(1) of the 2004 Act;

(d) a revision of a development plan document in pursuance of section 26 of the 2004 Act if the document has been submitted to the Secretary of State for independent examination under section 20(1) of that Act.

(3) But Note (2)(c) and (d) does not apply if the document is withdrawn under section 22 of the 2004 Act at any time after it has been submitted for independent examination.

(4) In Note (2)(c) and (d) the submission of a development plan document to the Secretary of State for independent examination is to be taken to include the holding of an independent examination by the Secretary of State under section 21 or section 27 of the 2004 Act.'

(4) In paragraph 5 for 'any such functions as are mentioned in paragraph 1(a)(i) or (ii)' there is substituted 'relevant public functions (within the meaning of paragraph 1A)'.

(5) In paragraph 6 for 'any such functions as are mentioned in paragraph 5' there is substituted 'relevant public functions (within the meaning of paragraph 1A)'.

(6) In paragraph 13, for 'paragraphs 1, 2, 3 and 4' there is substituted 'paragraph 1A'.

Planning (Listed Buildings and Conservation Areas) Act 1990 (c 9)

19 The Planning (Listed Buildings and Conservation Areas) Act 1990 is amended as follows.

20 In section 10(3) (regulations relating to applications for listed building consent)—

(a) for paragraph (b) and the word 'and' following it there is substituted the following paragraph—
'(b) requirements as to publicity in relation to such applications;';
(b) after paragraph (c) there are inserted the following paragraphs—
'(d) requirements as to consultation in relation to such applications;
(e) prohibiting the determination of such applications during such period as is prescribed;
(f) requirements on the local planning authority to take account of responses from persons consulted.'

21 In section 23(2) (matters to which regard is to be had by local planning authority in exercising function of revoking or modifying consent) for 'the development plan and to any other' there is substituted 'any'.

22 In section 26(2) (matters to which regard is to be had by the Secretary of State in exercising function of revoking or modifying consent) for 'the development plan and to any other' there is substituted 'any'.

23 In section 67 (publicity for applications affecting the setting of listed buildings) for subsections (1) to (7) there is substituted the following subsection—

'(1) The Secretary of State may prescribe requirements as to publicity for applications for planning permission in cases where the local planning authority think that the development of land would affect the setting of a listed building.'

24 In section 73 (publicity for applications affecting conservation areas) for subsection (1) there is substituted the following subsection—

'(1) The Secretary of State may prescribe requirements as to publicity for applications for planning permission in cases where the local planning authority think that the development of land would affect the character or appearance of a conservation area.'

25 In section 91(2) (interpretation) "development plan" is omitted.

26 In section 93 (provision about regulations and orders) after subsection (6) there are inserted the following subsections—

'(6A) Regulations and orders may make different provision for different purposes.

(6B) The powers to make regulations under sections 10(3)(b), 67(1) and 73(1) must be taken to be powers mentioned in section 100(2) of the Local Government Act 2003 (powers exercisable in relation to descriptions of certain local authorities which fall into particular categories for the purposes of section 99 of that Act).'

Planning (Hazardous Substances) Act 1990 (c 10)

27 In section 40 of the Planning (Hazardous Substances) Act 1990 (provision about regulations) after subsection (3) there is inserted the following subsection—

'(4) Regulations may make different provision for different purposes.'

NOTES

Initial Commencement

To be appointed: see s 121(1), (2)(f), (g).

Appointment

Paras 1, 3, 14, 16, 19, 20, 23, 24, 26, 27: Appointment (for the purpose of making, or making provision by means of, subordinate legislation): 6 August 2004: see SI 2004/2097, art 2.

Paras 1, 16(1), (2), 19: Appointment (in relation to England for remaining purposes): 28 September 2004: see SI 2004/2202, art 2(h); for transitional provisions and savings see art 4, Sch 2 thereto.

Paras 1, 19: Appointment (in relation to Wales for remaining purposes): 15 October 2005: see SI 2005/2847, art 2(4); for savings see art 3(3), Sch 2 thereto.

Para 2: Appointment: 7 June 2006: see SI 2006/1281, art 2(e).

Para 4: Appointment (in relation to England): 10 August 2006: by virtue of SI 2006/1061, art 3(b).

Para 7: Appointment: 31 October 2004: see SI 2004/2593, art 2(c).

Paras 8–13, 15, 17, 18, 21, 22: Appointment (in relation to England): 28 September 2004: see SI 2004/2202, art 2(h); for transitional provisions and savings see art 4, Sch 2 thereto.

Paras 8–13, 15, 17, 18, 21, 22: Appointment (in relation to Wales): 15 October 2005: see SI 2005/2847, art 2(e); for savings see art 3(3), Sch 2 thereto.

Para 16(4): Appointment (in relation to England for remaining purposes): 24 August 2005: see SI 2005/2081, art 2(d)(ii); for savings see art 4(4) thereof.

Paras 20, 23, 24, 26: Appointment (for remaining purposes): 28 September 2004: see SI 2004/2202, art 3(c), (e).

Para 25: Appointment (in relation to England): 28 September 2004: see SI 2004/2202, arts 2(h), 3(c), (d), (f), Sch 1, Pt 2

Para 25: Appointment (in relation to Wales): 15 October 2005: see SI 2005/2847, art 2(e).

Extent

This Schedule does not extend to Scotland: see s 124(1).

SCHEDULE 7
AMENDMENTS OF OTHER ENACTMENTS

Section 118

Gas Act 1965 (c 36)

A1.498

1 In paragraph 7(2) of Schedule 3 of the Gas Act 1965 after 'development order' there is inserted 'or local development order'.

Finance Act 1969 (c 32)

2 In section 58(4) of the Finance Act 1969 (disclosure of information for statistical purposes), in the Table in the entry relating to local planning authorities—

(a) in the first column for 'the Town and Country Planning Act 1990' there is substituted 'Part 2 or 6 of the Planning and Compulsory Purchase Act 2004';
(b) In the second column for 'Part II of the Town and Country Planning Act 1990' there is substituted 'Part 2 or 6 of the Planning and Compulsory Purchase Act 2004'.

Leasehold Reform Act 1967 (c 88)

3 In section 28(6)(a) of the Leasehold Reform Act 1967 (development for certain public purposes) for 'Town and Country Planning Act 1990' there is substituted 'Planning and Compulsory Purchase Act 2004'.

Agriculture (Miscellaneous Provisions) Act 1968 (c 34)

4 In section 12 of the Agriculture (Miscellaneous Provisions) Act 1968 after subsection (3) there is inserted the following subsection—

'(4) If a person is entitled in respect of the same interest in land to a payment both—

(a) by virtue of subsection (1), and
(b) under section 33B of the Land Compensation Act 1973 (additional loss payment for agricultural land),

section 33H of that Act (only one payment to be made if a person has dual entitlement) applies.'

Countryside Act 1968 (c 41)

5 (1) Paragraph 3 of Schedule 2 to the Countryside Act 1968 is amended as follows.

(2) In sub-paragraph (2), after 'published' there is inserted ', affixed'.

(3) In sub-paragraph (4)(a), after 'published' there is inserted ', affixed'.

(4) The amendments made by this paragraph do not apply to compulsory purchase orders of which notice under section 11 of the Acquisition of Land Act 1981 (c 67) is published before commencement of this paragraph.

Greater London Council (General Powers) Act 1969 (c lii)

6 In section 13 of the Greater London Council (General Powers) Act 1969 (exercise of powers relating to walkways), in the proviso for the words from 'any local plan' to 'Schedule 1 to that Act)' there is substituted 'a local development document (within the meaning of Part 2 of the Planning and Compulsory Purchase Act 2004)'.

Land Compensation Act 1973 (c 26)

7   (1)   The Land Compensation Act 1973 is amended as follows.

(2)   In section 29 (home loss payments) after subsection (3A) there is inserted the following subsection—

'(3B)   For the purposes of this section a person must not be treated as displaced from a dwelling in consequence only of the compulsory acquisition of part of a garden or yard or of an outhouse or appurtenance belonging to or usually enjoyed with the building which is occupied or is intended to be occupied as the dwelling.'

(3)   Sections 34 to 36 are omitted.

(4)   In section 87(1) (general interpretation) in the definition of 'dwelling' '(except in section 29)' is omitted.

(5)   But the amendments made by this paragraph do not have effect in relation to a compulsory purchase order made or made in draft before the commencement of this paragraph.

Greater London Council (General Powers) Act 1973 (c xxx)

8   In section 24(4) of the Greater London Council (General Powers) Act 1973 (definitions for the purpose or provision relating to parking place agreements)—

    (a)   in the definition of appropriate provision for 'the Greater London' there is substituted 'their';

    (b)   in the second place where it occurs 'Greater London development plan' is omitted.

Welsh Development Agency Act 1975 (c 70)

9   (1)   Schedule 4 to the Welsh Development Agency Act 1975 is amended as follows.

(2)   Paragraph 2 is omitted.

(3)   In paragraph 3, in sub-paragraph (1)(c), for 'section 13 of that Act to objections made by an owner, lessee or occupier' there is substituted 'sections 13 and 13A of that Act to relevant objections'.

(4)   The amendments made by this paragraph do not apply to compulsory purchase orders of which notice under section 11 of the Acquisition of Land Act 1981 (c 67) is published before commencement of this paragraph.

Local Government, Planning and Land Act 1980 (c 65)

10   (1)   The Local Government, Planning and Land Act 1980 is amended as follows.

(2)   In section 142 (acquisition by corporation), in subsection (2A), '(subject to section 144(2))' is omitted.

(3)   In section 143 (acquisition by local highway authority), in subsection (3A), '(subject to section 144(2))' is omitted.

(4)   In section 144, in subsection (2), 'the 1981 Act and' is omitted.

(5)   In Schedule 28, in paragraph 1, 'The 1981 Act and' and the words from 'and in paragraph 2' to the end are omitted.

(6) The amendments made by this paragraph do not apply to compulsory purchase orders of which notice under section 11 of or, as the case may be, paragraph 2 of Schedule 1 to the Acquisition of Land Act 1981 is published before commencement of this paragraph.

(7) In Schedule 26 (Urban Development Corporations), after paragraph 14 there are inserted the following paragraphs—

'Delegation of planning functions

14A (1) This paragraph applies in relation to any function conferred on the corporation by virtue of an order under section 149 above.

(2) The corporation may appoint committees and such committees may appoint sub-committees.

(3) Anything which is authorised or required to be done by the corporation—

(a) may be done by any member of the corporation or of its staff who is authorised for the purpose either generally or specifically;
(b) may be done by a committee or sub-committee which is so authorised.

(4) The corporation may—

(a) determine the quorum of a committee or sub-committee;
(b) make such arrangements as it thinks appropriate relating to the meetings and procedure of a committee or sub-committee.

(5) Anything done for the purposes of sub-paragraph (4) is subject to directions given by the Secretary of State.

(6) The validity of anything done by a committee or sub-committee is not affected by—

(a) any vacancy among its members;
(b) any defect in the appointment of any of its members.

(7) This paragraph does not extend to Scotland.

14B (1) This paragraph has effect in relation to the membership of committees and sub-committees appointed under paragraph 14A.

(2) A committee may consist of—

(a) such members of the corporation as it appoints;
(b) such other persons as the corporation (with the consent of the Secretary of State) appoints.

(3) A sub-committee of a committee may consist of—

(a) such members of the committee as it appoints;
(b) such persons who are members of another committee of the corporation (whether or not they are members of the corporation) as the committee appoints;
(c) such other persons as the corporation (with the consent of the Secretary of State) appoints.

(4) The membership of a committee or sub-committee—

(a) must always include at least one person who is a member of the corporation;
(b) must not include any person who is a member of the staff of the corporation.'

Highways Act 1980 (c 66)

11 (1) The Highways Act 1980 is amended as follows.

(2)   In section 232(8) after '1990' there is inserted 'and Parts 2 and 6 of the Planning and Compulsory Purchase Act 2004'.

(3)   In section 232(9) for the definition of development plan there is substituted—

"development plan' must be construed in accordance with section 38 of the Planning and Compulsory Purchase Act 2004;
'local authority' has the same meaning as in the Town and Country Planning Act 1990.'

(4)   Section 259 (power to confirm, etc, compulsory purchase order in part) is omitted.

(5)   The amendment made by sub-paragraph (4) does not apply to a compulsory purchase order of which notice under section 11 of or, as the case may be, paragraph 2 of Schedule 1 to the Acquisition of Land Act 1981 is published before the commencement of that sub-paragraph.

Acquisition of Land Act 1981 (c 67)

12   In section 29(5) of the Acquisition of Land Act 1981 for the words 'any reference to any owner, lessee or occupier' there are substituted the words 'the reference to a qualifying person for the purposes of section 12(2)'.

Housing Act 1985 (c 68)

13   (1)   In section 578A of the Housing Act 1985 (modification of compulsory purchase order in case of acquisition of land for clearance), in subsection (2), for 'section 13' there is substituted 'sections 13 to 13C'.

(2)   The amendment made by sub-paragraph (1) does not apply to compulsory purchase orders of which notice under section 11 of the Acquisition of Land Act 1981 is published before commencement of this paragraph.

Education Reform Act 1988 (c 40)

14   (1)   The Education Reform Act 1988 is amended as follows.

(2)   In section 190 (wrongful contracts or disposals), in subsection (6) for the words from 'references' to the end there is substituted 'the reference in section 12 of that Act to an owner of the land included reference to the London Residuary Body'.

(3)   In section 201 (wrongful disposals), in subsection (6), for the words from 'references' to the end there is substituted 'the reference in section 12 of that Act to an owner of the land included reference to the local education authority concerned'.

(4)   The amendments made by this paragraph do not apply to compulsory purchase orders of which notice under section 11 of the Acquisition of Land Act 1981 (c 67) is published before commencement of this paragraph.

Housing Act 1988 (c 50)

15   (1)   Paragraph 2 of Schedule 10 to the Housing Act 1988 (modifications of Acquisition of Land Act 1981) is omitted.

(2)   The amendment made by sub-paragraph (1) does not apply to compulsory purchase orders of which notice under section 11 of or, as the case may be, paragraph 2 of Schedule 1 to the Acquisition of Land Act 1981 is published before commencement of this paragraph.

Planning and Compensation Act 1991 (c 34)

16   In Schedule 4 to the Planning and Compensation Act 1991 Part 3 is omitted.

Local Government Act 1992 (c 19)

17   In section 14(5) of the Local Government Act 1992 (structural changes which may be recommended by the Electoral Commission), paragraph (d) is omitted.

Leasehold Reform, Housing and Urban Development Act 1993 (c 28)

18   (1)   Schedule 20 to the Leasehold Reform, Housing and Urban Development Act 1993 (modification of Acquisition of Land Act 1981) is amended as follows.

(2)   In paragraph 1, for 'modifications specified in paragraphs 2 and' there is substituted 'modification specified in paragraph'.

(3)   Paragraph 2 is omitted.

(4)   The amendments made by this paragraph do not apply to compulsory purchase orders of which notice under section 11 of or, as the case may be, paragraph 2 of Schedule 1 to the Acquisition of Land Act 1981 (c 67) is published before commencement of this paragraph.

Environment Act 1995 (c 25)

19   (1)   The Environment Act 1995 is amended as follows.

(2)   In section 67 (which makes provision for a National Park authority to be the local planning authority) subsections (2) to (4) are omitted.

(3)   In Schedule 14 (periodic review of mineral planning permissions) in paragraph 2(1), in the definition of 'first review date', for 'paragraph 5' there is substituted 'paragraphs 3A and 5'.

(4)   In Schedule 14 after paragraph 3 there is inserted the following paragraph—

'**3A**   (1)   The Secretary of State may by order specify a first review date different from the first review date found in pursuance of paragraph 3(1) or (2).

(2)   Sub-paragraph (3) applies if no first review date is found in pursuance of paragraph 3(1) or (2).

(3)   The Secretary of State may by order specify a first review date.

(4)   An order under sub-paragraph (3) may make different provision for different cases or different classes of case.

(5)   An order under this paragraph must be made by statutory instrument subject to annulment in pursuance of a resolution of either House of Parliament.'

Town and Country Planning (Scotland) Act 1997 (c 8)

20   (1)   The Town and Country Planning (Scotland) Act 1997 is amended as follows.

(2)   In section 26(2)(b) (meaning of 'development'), for 'local roads authority' there is substituted 'roads authority (as defined by section 151(1) of the Roads (Scotland) Act 1984)'.

(3)   In section 275 (regulations and orders), after subsection (2) there is inserted—

'(2A)   Regulations may make different provision for different purposes.'

(4)   In Schedule 10 (periodic review of mineral planning permissions)—

(a) in paragraph 2(1), in the definition of 'first review date', for 'paragraph 5' there is substituted 'paragraphs 3A and 5'; and

(b) after paragraph 3, there is inserted the following paragraph—

'3A   (1)   The Scottish Ministers may by order specify a first review date different from the first review date found in pursuance of paragraph 3(1) or (2).

(2)   Sub-paragraph (3) applies if no first review date is found in pursuance of paragraph 3(1) or (2).

(3)   The Scottish Ministers may by order specify a first review date.

(4)   An order under sub-paragraph (3) may make different provision for different cases or different classes of case.

(5)   An order under this paragraph must be made by statutory instrument subject to annulment in pursuance of a resolution of the Scottish Parliament.'

Regional Development Agencies Act 1998 (c 45)

21   (1)   Paragraph 1 of Schedule 5 to the Regional Development Agencies Act 1998 (modifications of Acquisition of Land Act 1981) is omitted.

(2)   The amendment made by sub-paragraph (1) does not apply to compulsory purchase orders of which notice has been published under section 11 of or, as the case may be, paragraph 2 of Schedule 1 to the Acquisition of Land Act 1981 (c 67) before commencement of this paragraph.

Greater London Authority Act 1999 (c 29)

22   (1)   The Greater London Authority Act 1999 is amended as follows.

(2)   In section 337 (publication)—

(a) for 'relevant regional planning guidance' there is substituted 'the regional spatial strategy for a region which adjoins Greater London';

(b) subsection (10) is omitted.

(3)   In section 342(1) (matters to which Mayor is to have regard) for paragraph (a) there is substituted the following—

'(a)   the regional spatial strategy for a region which adjoins Greater London;'.

(4)   In section 346(b) (Mayor to monitor plans) for 'unitary development plan' there is substituted 'local development documents (within the meaning of Part 2 of the Planning and Compulsory Purchase Act 2004)'.

Countryside and Rights of Way Act 2000 (c 37)

23   In section 86(4) of the Countryside and Rights of Way Act 2000—

(a) 'II,' is omitted;

(b) at the end there is inserted 'or under Part 2 or 6 of the Planning and Compulsory Purchase Act 2004'.

NOTES

Initial Commencement

Para 10(7): Specified date: 13 July 2004: see s 121(6).

Paras 1–9, 10(1)–(6), 11–23: To be appointed: see s 121(1), (2)(f), (g), (4)(d).

Appointment

Paras 2, 3, 6, 8, 11(1)–(3), 16, 17, 22, 23: Appointment (in relation to England): 28 September 2004: see SI 2004/2202, art 2(i); for transitional provisions and savings see art 4, Sch 2 thereto.

Paras 2, 3, 11(1)–(3), 16, 17, 23: Appointment (in relation to Wales): 15 October 2005: see SI 2005/2847, art 2(f).

Paras 4, 5, 7, 9, 10(1)–(6), 11(4), (5), 12–15, 18, 21: Appointment: 31 October 2004: see SI 2004/2593, art 2(d).

Para 19: Appointment (for the purpose of making, or making provision by means of, subordinate legislation): 6 August 2004: see SI 2004/2097, art 2.

Para 19(2): Appointment (in relation to England for remaining purposes): 28 September 2004: see SI 2004/2202, art 2(i).

Para 19(2): Appointment (in relation to Wales for remaining purposes): 15 October 2005: see SI 2005/2847, art 2(f).

Para 20: Appointment: 12 June 2006: see SSI 2006/268, art 3(d).

SCHEDULE 8
TRANSITIONAL PROVISIONS: PARTS 1 AND 2

Section 119

Development plan

A1.499

1   (1) During the transitional period a reference in an enactment mentioned in section 38(7) above to the development plan for an area in England is a reference to—

   (a) the RSS for the region in which the area is situated or the spatial development strategy for an area in Greater London, and

   (b) the development plan for the area for the purposes of section 27 or 54 of the principal Act.

(2) The transitional period is the period starting with the commencement of section 38 and ending on whichever is the earlier of—

   (a) the end of the period of three years;

   (b) the day when in relation to an old policy, a new policy which expressly replaces it is published, adopted or approved.

(3) But the Secretary of State may direct that for the purposes of such policies as are specified in the direction sub-paragraph (2)(a) does not apply.

(4) An old policy is a policy which (immediately before the commencement of section 38) forms part of a development plan for the purposes of section 27 or 54 of the principal Act.

(5) A new policy is a policy which is contained in—

   (a) a revision of an RSS;

   (b) an alteration or replacement of the spatial development strategy;

   (c) a development plan document.

(6) But—

   (a) an old policy contained in a structure plan is replaced only by a new policy contained in a revision to an RSS;

   (b) an old policy contained in a waste local plan or a minerals local plan is replaced in relation to any area of a county council for which there is a district council only by a new policy contained in a development plan document which is prepared in accordance with a minerals and waste development scheme.

(7)   A new policy is published if it is contained in—

(a)   a revision of an RSS published by the Secretary of State under section 9(6);

(b)   an alteration or replacement of the Mayor of London's spatial development strategy published in pursuance of section 337 of the Greater London Authority Act 1999 (c 29).

(8)   A new policy is adopted or approved if it is contained in a development plan document which is adopted or approved for the purposes of Part 2.

(9)   A minerals and waste development scheme is a scheme prepared in accordance with section 16.

(10)   The development plan mentioned in sub-paragraph (1)(b) does not include a street authorisation map which continued to be treated as having been adopted as a local plan by virtue of paragraph 4 of Part 3 of Schedule 2 to the principal Act.

Structure plans

2   (1)   This paragraph applies to proposals for the alteration or replacement of a structure plan for the area of a local planning authority.

(2)   If before the commencement of Part 1 of this Act the authority have complied with section 33(2) of the principal Act (making copies of proposals and the explanatory memorandum available for inspection) the provisions of Chapter 2 of Part 2 of the principal Act continue to have effect in relation to the proposals.

(3)   In any other case—

(a)   the authority must take no further step in relation to the proposals;

(b)   the proposals have no effect.

(4)   If the proposals are adopted or approved by virtue of sub-paragraph (2) above, paragraph 1 of this Schedule applies to the policies contained in the proposals as if—

(a)   they were policies contained in a development plan within the meaning of section 54 of the principal Act;

(b)   the date of commencement of section 38 is the date when the proposals are adopted or approved (as the case may be).

Unitary development plan

3   (1)   This paragraph applies to proposals for the alteration or replacement of a unitary development plan for the area of a local planning authority.

(2)   If before the relevant date the authority have not complied with section 13(2) of the principal Act (making copies of the proposals available for inspection)—

(a)   they must take no further step in relation to the proposals;

(b)   the proposals have no effect.

(3)   In any other case paragraph 4 or 5 below applies.

4   (1)   This paragraph applies if—

(a)   before the relevant date the local planning authority is not required to cause an inquiry or other hearing to be held by virtue of section 16(1) of the principal Act (inquiry must be held if objections made), or

(b)   before the commencement of Part 2 of this Act a person is appointed under that section to hold an inquiry or other hearing.

(2) If this paragraph applies the provisions of Chapter 1 of Part 2 of the principal Act continue to have effect in relation to the proposals.

(3) The relevant date is whichever is the later of—

    (a) the end of any period prescribed by regulations under section 26 of the principal Act for the making of objections to the proposals;

    (b) the commencement of Part 2 of this Act.

5 (1) If paragraph 4 does not apply the provisions of Chapter 1 of Part 2 of the principal Act continue to have effect in relation to the proposals subject to the modifications in sub-paragraphs (2) to (5) below.

(2) If before the commencement of Part 2 of this Act the local planning authority have not published revised proposals in pursuance of regulations under section 26 of the principal Act—

    (a) any provision of the regulations relating to publication of revised proposals must be ignored,

    (b) the authority must comply again with section 13(2) of the principal Act.

(3) If before the commencement of Part 2 of this Act the local planning authority have published revised proposals in pursuance of regulations under section 26 of the principal Act the authority must comply again with section 13(2) of that Act.

(4) Any provision of regulations under section 26 of the principal Act which permits the local planning authority to modify proposals after an inquiry or other hearing has been held under section 16 of that Act must be ignored.

(5) If such an inquiry or other hearing is held the authority must adopt the proposals in accordance with the recommendations of the person appointed to hold the inquiry or other hearing.

6 If proposals are adopted or approved in pursuance of paragraph 4 or 5 above paragraph 1 of this Schedule applies to the policies contained in the proposals as if—

    (a) they were policies contained in a development plan for the purposes of section 27 of the principal Act;

    (b) the date of commencement of section 38 is the date when the proposals are adopted or approved.

7 (1) This paragraph applies if at the date of commencement of Part 1 a local planning authority have not prepared a unitary development plan in pursuance of section 12 of the principal Act.

(2) References in paragraphs 3 to 6 to proposals for the alteration or replacement of a plan must be construed as references to the plan.

Local plan

8 (1) This paragraph applies to proposals for the alteration or replacement of a local plan for the area of a local planning authority.

(2) If before the commencement of Part 2 of this Act the authority have not complied with section 40(2) of the principal Act (making copies of the proposals available for inspection)—

    (a) they must take no further step in relation to the proposals;

    (b) the proposals have no effect.

(3) In any other case paragraph 9 or 10 below applies.

9 (1) This paragraph applies if—

(a) before the relevant date the local planning authority is not required to cause an inquiry or other hearing to be held by virtue of section 42(1) of the principal Act (inquiry must be held if objections made), or

(b) before the commencement of Part 2 of this Act a person is appointed under that section to hold an inquiry or other hearing.

(2)   If this paragraph applies the provisions of Chapter 2 of Part 2 of the principal Act continue to have effect in relation to the proposals.

(3)   The relevant date is whichever is the later of—

(a) the end of any period prescribed by regulations under section 53 of the principal Act for the making of objections to the proposals;

(b) the commencement of Part 2 of this Act.

10   (1)   If paragraph 9 does not apply the provisions of Chapter 2 of Part 2 of the principal Act continue to have effect in relation to the proposals subject to the modifications in sub-paragraphs (2) to (5) below.

(2)   If before the commencement of Part 2 of this Act the local planning authority have not published revised proposals in pursuance of regulations under section 53 of the principal Act—

(a) any provision of the regulations relating to publication of revised proposals must be ignored,

(b) the authority must comply again with section 40(2) of the principal Act.

(3)   If before the commencement of Part 2 of this Act the local planning authority have published revised proposals in pursuance of regulations under section 53 of the principal Act the authority must comply again with section 40(2) of that Act.

(4)   Any provision of regulations under section 53 of the principal Act which permits the local planning authority to modify proposals after an inquiry or other hearing has been held under section 42 of that Act must be ignored.

(5)   If such an inquiry or other hearing is held the authority must adopt the proposals in accordance with the recommendations of the person appointed to hold the inquiry or other hearing.

11   (1)   This paragraph applies if the Secretary of State thinks—

(a) that the conformity requirement is likely to give rise to inconsistency between the proposals and relevant policies or guidance, and

(b) that it is necessary or expedient to avoid such inconsistency.

(2)   The Secretary of State may direct that to the extent specified in the direction the conformity requirement must be ignored.

(3)   The Secretary of State must give reasons for the direction.

(4)   The conformity requirement is—

(a) the requirement under section 36(4) of the principal Act that the local plan is to be in general conformity with the structure plan;

(b) the prohibition under section 43(3) of the principal Act on the adoption of proposals for a local plan or for its alteration or replacement which do not conform generally with the structure plan.

(5)   Relevant policies and guidance are—

(a) national policies;

(b) advice contained in guidance;

(c) policies in the RSS.

12 If proposals are adopted or approved in pursuance of paragraphs 9 to 11 above paragraph 1 of this Schedule applies to the policies contained in the proposals as if—

(a) they were policies contained in a development plan for the purposes of section 54 of the principal Act;

(b) the date of commencement of section 38 is the date when the proposals are adopted or approved.

13 (1) This paragraph applies if at the date of commencement of Part 1 a local planning authority have not prepared a local plan in pursuance of section 36 of the principal Act.

(2) References in paragraphs 8 to 12 to proposals for the alteration or replacement of a plan must be construed as references to the plan.

Minerals and waste local plans

14 Paragraphs 8 to 13 above apply to a minerals local plan and a waste local plan as they apply to a local plan and references in those paragraphs to a local planning authority must be construed as including references to a mineral planning authority and an authority who are entitled to prepare a waste local plan.

Schemes

15 (1) This paragraph applies to—

(a) the local development scheme which a local planning authority are required to prepare and maintain under section 15 of this Act;

(b) the minerals and waste development scheme which a county council are required to prepare and maintain for any part of their area for which there is a district council.

(2) During the transitional period the local planning authority or county council (as the case may be) must include in the scheme as a development plan document—

(a) any plan or document which relates to an old policy (for the purposes of paragraph 1 above) which has not been replaced by a new policy;

(b) any proposals adopted or approved by virtue of paragraphs 3 to 12 above.

Savings

16 (1) The repeal by this Act of paragraphs 1 to 4 of Schedule 13 to the principal Act does not affect anything which is required or permitted to be done for the purposes of Chapter 2 of Part 6 of the principal Act during any time when a plan mentioned in any of those paragraphs continues to form part of the development plan by virtue of—

(a) paragraph 1 of this Schedule, or

(b) that paragraph as applied by any other provision of this Schedule.

(2) References to a plan mentioned in any of paragraphs 1 to 4 include any proposal for the alteration or replacement of the plan.

(3) The development plan is the development plan for the purposes of section 27 or 54 of the principal Act.

Regulations and orders

17 (1) The Secretary of State may by regulations make provision for giving full effect to this Schedule.

(2) The regulations may, in particular—

(a) make such provision as he thinks is necessary in consequence of this Schedule;

   (b)   make provision to supplement any modifications of the principal Act required by this Schedule.

(3)   The Secretary of State may by order make such provision as he thinks is necessary in consequence of anything done under or by virtue of this Schedule.

(4)   Provision under sub-paragraph (3) includes provisions corresponding to that which could be made by order under Schedule 2 of the principal Act.

18   The Secretary of State may by regulations make provision—

   (a)   for treating anything done or purported to have been done for the purposes of Part 2 before the commencement of that Part as having been done after that commencement;

   (b)   for disregarding any requirement of section 19 in respect of anything done or purported to have been done for the purposes of any other provision of Part 2.

19

Interpretation

(1)   References to section 27 of the principal Act must be construed subject to section 28(3)(a) and (c) of that Act.

(2)   RSS must be construed in accordance with Part 1 of this Act.

(3)   Development plan document must be construed in accordance with Part 2 of this Act.

NOTES

Initial Commencement

To be appointed: see s 121(1), (4)(e).

Appointment

Paras 1–3, 5–8, 10–16, 19: Appointment (in relation to England): 28 September 2004: see SI 2004/2202, art 2(g), (j).

Paras 4, 9: Appointment (for the purpose of making, or making provision by means of, subordinate legislation): 6 August 2004: see SI 2004/2097, art 2.

Paras 4, 9: Appointment (in relation to England for remaining purposes): 28 September 2004: see SI 2004/2202, art 2(g), (j).

Paras 17, 18: Appointment: 6 August 2004: see SI 2004/2097, art 2.

Extent

This Schedule does not extend to Scotland: see s 124(1).

Subordinate Legislation

Town and Country Planning (Transitional Arrangements) (England) Regulations 2004, SI 2004/2205 (made under paras 17(1), (2), 18).

Section 120

A1.500

Short title and chapter	Extent of repeal
Land Compensation Act 1973 (c 26)	Sections 34 to 36.
	In section 87(1), in the definition of 'dwelling', '(except in section 29)'.
Greater London Council (General Powers) Act 1973 (c xxx)	In section 24(4), the second 'Greater London development plan'.
Welsh Development Agency Act 1975 (c 70)	In Schedule 4, paragraph 2.
Local Government, Planning and Land Act 1980 (c 65)	In section 142(2A), '(subject to section 144(2))'.
	In section 143(3A), '(subject to section 144(2))'.
	In section 144(2), 'the 1981Act and'.
	In Schedule 28, in paragraph 1, 'The 1981 Act and' and the words from 'and in paragraph 2' to the end.
Highways Act 1980 (c 66)	Section 259.
Housing Act 1988 (c 50)	In Schedule 10, paragraph 2.
Town and Country Planning Act 1990 (c 8)	Part 2.
	In section 55(2)(b), the word 'local'.
	Section 73(3).
	Section 76.
	Section 83(1).
	Sections 106 to 106B.
	In section 220(3), the expression '62'.
	In section 226, in subsection (1) the first 'which' and subsection (2).
	Section 245(2) and (3).
	In section 284(1), paragraph (a).
	In section 287, in subsection (5), paragraph (a) and in each of paragraphs (b) to (e) the words 'by virtue of subsection (3)' and subsection (6).
	Section 293(4).
	Sections 294 to 297.
	Section 298(1) and (2).
	Sections 299 to 301.
	Section 303(6).

	In section 303A, in subsection (5) the words 'or appointed as one of the persons who are to hold it', the words '(in addition to what may be recovered by virtue of the appointment of any other person)' and in paragraph (c) the words '(or, in a case where that person is appointed as one of the persons who are to hold the qualifying inquiry, an appropriate proportion of any costs attributable to the appointment of an assessor to assist those persons)' and subsections (7) to (9).
	In Schedule 1, paragraph 2, in paragraph 3(7) the words 'but paragraph 4 shall apply to such applications instead'.
	In Schedule 2, Parts 1, 2 and 3.
	In Schedule 7, paragraphs 3 and 4.
	In Schedule 13, paragraphs 1 to 4.
Planning (Listed Buildings and Conservation Areas) Act 1990 (c 9)	In section 10, in subsection (2) the words 'shall be made in such form as the authority may require and' and in subsection (3) the word 'and' after paragraph (b).
	Section 67(2) to (7).
	Sections 83 and 84.
	In section 91(2), "development plan".
	In section 92(2)(a), '83, 84,'.
Planning (Hazardous Substances) Act 1990 (c 10)	Section 31(1) and (2).
	Section 32.
Planning and Compensation Act 1991 (c 34)	Section 17(1).
	In Schedule 4, Part 3.
	In Schedule 18, Part 2 in the entry relating to the Land Compensation Act 1973, 'section 36(6) (farm loss payment),'.
Local Government Act 1992 (c 19)	In section 14(5), paragraph (d).
Leasehold Reform, Housing and Urban Development Act 1993 (c 28)	In Schedule 20, paragraph 2.
Environment Act 1995 (c 25)	In section 67, subsections (2) to (4).
Town and Country Planning (Scotland) Act 1997 (c 8)	Section 242(4).
	Sections 243 to 250.
Planning (Listed Buildings and Conservation Areas) (Scotland) Act 1997 (c 9)	Sections 74 and 75.
Planning (Hazardous Substances) (Scotland) Act 1997 (c 10)	Section 31(1) and (2).
	Section 32.

Regional Development Agencies Act 1998 (c 45)	In Schedule 5, paragraph 1.
Countryside and Rights of Way Act 2000 (c 37)	In section 86(4), 'II,'.

Note: The repeal of sections 34 to 36 of the Land Compensation Act 1973 does not have effect in relation to a compulsory purchase order made or made in draft before the commencement of paragraph 7(3) of Schedule 7.

NOTES

Initial Commencement

To be appointed: see s 121(1), (2)(f), (g), (4)(f).

Appointment

Appointment (in part for certain purposes): 6 August 2004: see SI 2004/2097, art 2.

Appointment (in relation to England in part): 28 September 2004: see SI 2004/2202, arts 2(k), 3(d), Sch 1, Pt 1; for transitional provisions and savings see art 4, Sch 2 thereto.

Appointment (in part for certain purposes): 28 September 2004: see SI 2004/2202, art 3(d), (f), Sch 1, Pt 2.

Appointment (in part): 31 October 2004: see SI 2004/2593, art 2(e).

Appointment (in relation to Wales in part): 30 April 2005 (except in relation to certain specified local authorities and their areas): see SI 2005/1229, arts 2, 3, 4(b).

Appointment (in relation to Wales in part): 15 October 2005: see SI 2005/2847, art 2(g), Sch 1; for savings see art 3(3), Sch 2 thereto.

Appointment (in relation to Wales in part): 1 April 2006: by virtue of SI 2006/931, art 2.

Appointment (in relation to England in part): 10 August 2006: see SI 2006/1061, art 3(b).

Appointment (in relation to England and Wales in part): 7 June 2006: see SI 2006/1281, art 2(f).

Appointment (in relation to Scotland in part): 12 June 2006: see SSI 2006/268, art 3(e).

Appointment (in relation to Wales in part): 30 June 2007: see SI 2007/1369, art 2(b); for savings see art 3 thereof.

Part 2

STATUTORY INSTRUMENTS

Contents

Part 2

STATUTORY INSTRUMENTS

AGRICULTURE (MAINTENANCE, REPAIR AND INSURANCE OF FIXED EQUIPMENT) REGULATIONS 1948

SI 1948/184

In pursuance of subsection (i) of section thirty-seven of the Agriculture Act, 1947 (hereinafter called 'the said Act'), and of all other powers enabling him in that behalf, the Minister of Agriculture and Fisheries (hereinafter called 'the Minister'), after consultation with such bodies of persons as appear to him to represent the interests of landlords and tenants of holdings, hereby makes the following regulations:—

A1.501

1   The provisions set forth in the Schedule hereto relating to the maintenance, repair and insurance of fixed equipment, shall be deemed to be incorporated in every contract of tenancy of a holding, whether made before or after the commencement of Part III of the said Act, except in so far as they would impose on one of the parties to an agreement in writing a liability which under the agreement is imposed on the other:

Provided that where the interest of the landlord is held for the purposes of a Government department, or a person representing His Majesty or the Duke of Cornwall under sections forty-three to forty-five of the Agricultural Holdings Act, 1923, is deemed to be the landlord, or where the landlord has made provision approved by the Minister for defraying the cost of any such works of repair or replacement as are referred to in paragraph 2 of the Schedule hereto, the provisions of the said paragraph 2 requiring the landlord to insure against loss or damage by fire shall not apply.

A1.502

2   The Interpretation Act, 1889, shall apply to the interpretation of these regulations as it applies to the interpretation of an Act of Parliament.

A1.503

3

(1)   These regulations may be cited as the Agriculture (Maintenance, Repair and Insurance of Fixed Equipment) Regulations, 1948, and apply to England and Wales.

(2)   These regulations shall come into operation on the first day of March, 1948.

1629

SCHEDULE

MAINTENANCE, REPAIR AND INSURANCE OF THE FIXED EQUIPMENT OF A HOLDING

Part I Rights and Liabilities of the Landlord

A1.504

1   (1)   To execute all repairs and replacements to the undermentioned parts of the farmhouse, cottages and farm buildings, namely:—main walls and exterior walls, including walls of open and covered yards and garden walls (whether constructed of brick, stone, timber or other material) but excluding the interior covering of exterior walls save where such interior covering is affected by structural defect of the wall; roofs, including eaves-guttering and downpipes (tenant supplying straw and reed for thatching); and floors, doors and windows (excepting glass, locks and fastenings); provided that in the case of repairs and replacements to floor-boards, doors, windows, eaves-guttering and downpipes, the landlord may recover one half of the reasonable cost thereof from the tenant.

(2)   To execute all repairs and replacements to the water mains, the sewage disposal systems (excepting the cleaning thereof and excepting the drains) and to the structure of reservoirs or pump houses of a water supply system.

2   To keep the farmhouse, cottages and farm buildings insured to their full value against loss or damage by fire and to execute all works of repair or replacement to the farmhouse, cottages and farm buildings necessary to make good damage by fire, being damage not due to the wilful act or negligence of the tenant.

3   As often as may be necessary in order to prevent deterioration, and in any case at intervals of not more than five years, properly to paint with at least two coats of a suitable quality or properly and adequately to gas-tar or creosote all outside wood and ironwork (including the inside of all external doors and windows which open outward) of the farmhouse, cottages and farm buildings which have been previously painted, gas-tarred or creosoted, or which it is necessary so to paint, gas-tar or creosote: provided that in respect of doors, windows, eaves-guttering and downpipes the landlord may recover one half of the reasonable cost of such work from the tenant, subject nevertheless to the provisions of sub-paragraph (2) of paragraph 12 hereof.

4   (1)   The landlord shall be under no liability to execute repairs or replacements or to insure buildings or fixtures which are the property of the tenant, or to execute repairs or replacements rendered necessary by the wilful act or negligence of the tenant, or any members of his household or his employees.

(2)   If the tenant fails to execute repairs for which he is liable under paragraphs 5, 6 and 7 hereof within one month of receiving from the landlord a written request specifying the necessary repairs and calling on him to execute them, the landlord may enter and execute such repairs and recover the reasonable cost from the tenant forthwith.

Part II Rights and Liabilities of the Tenant

Except in so far as such liabilities fall to be undertaken by the landlord under Part I hereof:

5   To repair and to keep and leave clean and in good tenantable repair, order and condition, the farmhouse, cottages and farm buildings together with all fixtures and fittings, drains, sewers, water supplies, pumps, fences, live and dead hedges, gates, field walls, posts, stiles, bridges, culverts, ponds, water courses, ditches, roads and yards in and upon the holding, or which during the tenancy may be erected or provided thereon, and to keep clean and in good working order all roof valleys, eaves-guttering

and downpipes, gulleys and grease-traps; and also to use carefully so as to protect from wilful, reckless or negligent damage all items for the repair of which the landlord is responsible under paragraph 1 hereof, and also to report in writing immediately to the landlord any damage, however caused, to items for the repair of which the landlord is responsible.

6 To replace or repair and, upon replacement or repair, adequately to paint, gas-tar or creosote as may be proper, all items of fixed equipment, and to do any work, where such replacement, repair or work is rendered necessary by the wilful act or negligence of the tenant or any members of his household or his employees.

7 As often as may be necessary, and in any case at intervals of not more than seven years, properly to clean, colour, whiten, paper and paint with materials of suitable quality the inside of the farmhouse, cottages, and buildings which have been previously so treated, and in each year of the tenancy to limewash the inside of all farm buildings which previously have been limewashed.

8 Notwithstanding the general liability of the landlord for repairs and replacements, to renew all broken or cracked tiles or slates and replace all slipped tiles or slates from time to time as the damage occurs, but so that the cost shall not exceed five pounds in any one year of the tenancy.

9 To cut out and lay a proper proportion of the hedges in each year of the tenancy so as to maintain them in good and sound condition.

10 To dig out, scour and cleanse all ponds, water courses, ditches and grips, as may be necessary to maintain them at sufficient width and depth, and to keep clear from obstruction all field drains and their outlets.

11 To provide free of charge suitable straw or reed for the repair or renewal of thatch.

12 (1) If the last year of the tenancy is not a year in which such cleaning, colouring, whitening, papering and painting as is mentioned in paragraph 7 hereof is due to be carried out, the tenant shall then pay to the landlord at the end of such last year one-seventh part of the estimated reasonable cost thereof in respect of each year'that has elapsed since such last cleaning, colouring, whitening, papering and painting as aforesaid; and in such a case, the landlord shall pay to the tenant at the time of the next subsequent occasion that such work is carried out, the reasonable cost thereof less one-seventh part in respect of each year that has elapsed since the commencement of the tenancy.

(2) If the last year of the tenancy is not a year in which the landlord is liable, under paragraph 3 hereof, to paint, gas-tar or creosote the doors, windows, eaves-guttering and downpipes of buildings, the tenant shall then pay to the landlord at the end of such last year one-tenth part of the estimated reasonable cost thereof in respect of each year that has elapsed since such last painting, gas-tarring or creosoting as aforesaid; and in such a case, the landlord shall be entitled to recover from the tenant at the time of the next subsequent occasion that such work is carried out, one-tenth part only of the reasonable cost thereof in respect of each year that has elapsed since the commence-ment of the tenancy.

(3) In the assessment of any compensation payable by an outgoing tenant in respect of dilapidations, any accrued liability under the two preceding sub-paragraphs shaft be taken into account.

13 If the landlord fails to execute repairs which are his liability within three months of receiving from the tenant a written request specifying the necessary repairs and calling on him to execute them, the tenant may execute such repairs and, except to the

extent to which under the terms of Part I hereof the tenant is liable to bear the cost, recover the reasonable cost from the landlord forthwith.

Part III General Proviso

14   Nothing contained in Part I or Part II hereof shall create any liability on the part of either landlord or tenant:

(1)   to maintain, repair or insure any item of fixed equipment which is obsolete, and which the landlord and the tenant agree in writing that neither party shall be liable to maintain, repair or insure;

(2)   to execute any work if and so far as the execution of such work is rendered impossible (except at prohibitive or unreasonable expense) by reason of subsidence of any land or by the blocking of outfalls which are not under the control of either the landlord or the tenant.

RESERVE AND AUXILIARY FORCES (AGRICULTURAL TENANTS) REGULATIONS 1959

SI 1959/84

Authority: Agricultural Holdings Act 1986, s 30, Sch 5, para 6

NOTES

Continuation

Authority: following the consolidation of the original enabling power, these Regulations have effect as if made under the Agricultural Holdings Act 1986, s 30, Sch 5, para 6.

A1.505

1

These Regulations, which may be cited as the Reserve and Auxiliary Forces (Agricultural Tenants) Regulations 1959, shall come into operation on the 26th day of January, 1959.

A1.506

2

The Reserve and Auxiliary Forces (Protection of Civil Interests) (Agricultural Tenants' Representation) Regulations 1951, are hereby revoked, so however that any direction given under those Regulations shall have effect as if it had been given under these Regulations.

A1.507

3

In these Regulations, unless the context otherwise requires—

'1948 Act' means the Agricultural Holdings Act 1948, as amended;

'1951 Act' means the Reserve and Auxiliary Forces (Protection of Civil Interests) Act 1951, as amended;

'chairman' means the chairman of an Agricultural Land Tribunal established under section 73 of the Agriculture Act 1947, for the area in which the holding which is the subject of a notice to quit or of proceedings to which these Regulations apply is wholly or in the greater part situate, or a person nominated under paragraph 16 (1)(a) or appointed under paragraph 16A of the Ninth Schedule to that Act to act as chairman in that area, and 'secretary' means the secretary of that tribunal.

A1.508

4

The Interpretation Act 1889, shall apply to the interpretation of these Regulations as it applies to the interpretation of an Act of Parliament.

A1.509

5

Where the chairman is satisfied on an application by any person that—

(a) a notice to quit has been given to a service man as mentioned in subsection (1) of section 21 of the 1951 Act,

(b) the service man is serving abroad,

(c) the applicant is a fit person to serve a counter-notice under subsection (1) of section 24 of the 1948 Act on the service man's behalf but is not duly authorised to do so, and

(d) the application is made in good faith in the interests of the service man, the chairman may direct that the applicant be deemed to be duly authorised to serve the counter-notice on the service man's behalf.

A1.510

6

Where a counter-notice under subsection (1) of section 24 of the 1948 Act has been served—

(a) in a case where a notice to quit has been given to a service man as mentioned in subsection (1) of section 21 of the 1951 Act, or

(b) in a case where subsection (5) of the said section 21 applies in relation to a service man,

and it appears to the chairman that—

(i) it is necessary for any act or proceedings consequential upon the service of the counter-notice to be performed or conducted by the service man;

(ii) the service man is serving abroad, and

(iii) no person has been duly authorised to perform the act or conduct the proceedings on the service man's behalf,

the chairman may, whether on an application by any person or otherwise, direct that some fit person who is willing to perform the act or conduct the proceedings shall be deemed to be authorised for that purpose and to take all such steps as may be necessary or incidental thereto.

A1.511

7

(1)   An application to the chairman for a direction under these Regulations shall be made in writing and delivered or sent to the secretary.

(2)   The chairman may, for the purpose of deciding whether to give the direction, require the applicant to furnish such testimonial or other evidence in support of his application as the chairman may think fit.

AGRICULTURE (MISCELLANEOUS TIME-LIMITS) REGULATIONS 1959

SI 1959/171

Authority: Agricultural Holdings Act 1986, ss 9(1), (3), 94, 96(1)

NOTES

Continuation

Authority: following the consolidation of the original enabling power, these Regulations have effect as if made under the Agricultural Holdings Act 1986, ss 9(1), (3), 94, 96(1).

A1.512

1

(1)   These regulations may be cited as the Agriculture (Miscellaneous Time-Limits) Regulations 1959 and shall come into operation on the 4th day of February, 1959.

(2)   ...

(3)   In these regulations the expression 'the Act' means the Agricultural Holdings Act 1948.

(4)   The Interpretation Act 1889 shall apply to the interpretation of these Regulations as it applies to the interpretation of an Act of Parliament.

NOTES

Amendment

Para (2): revokes SI 1948/188.

A1.513

2

(1) ...

(2)   The time within which a landlord may, pursuant to sub-section (1) of section 7 of the Act, require that there shall be determined by arbitration and paid by the tenant the amount of any compensation referred to in the said sub-section, shall be one month from the date on which there takes effect by virtue of section 5 or section 6 of the Act any transfer from the tenant to the landlord of liability for the maintenance or repair of any item of fixed equipment.

(3)   The time within which a tenant may, pursuant to sub-section (2) of section 7 of the Act, require that any claim in respect of a previous failure by the landlord to discharge a liability for the maintenance or repair of any item of fixed equipment shall be determined by arbitration, shall be one month from the date on which there takes effect by virtue of section 5 or section 6 of the Act any transfer from the landlord to the tenant of the said liability for the maintenance or repair of any item of fixed equipment.

NOTES

Amendment

Para (1): spent on the repeal of the Agricultural Holdings Act 1948, s 30.

AGRICULTURE (MAINTENANCE, REPAIR AND INSURANCE OF FIXED EQUIPMENT) REGULATIONS 1973

SI 1973/1473

Authority: Agricultural Holdings Act 1986, s 7

NOTES

Continuation

Authority: changed as a result of the consolidation of certain enactments relating to agricultural holdings in the Agricultural Holdings Act 1986.

A1.514

Citation and commencement

1

These regulations may be cited as the Agriculture (Maintenance, Repair and Insurance of Fixed Equipment) Regulations 1973, and shall come into operation on 29th September 1974.

A1.515

Interpretation

2

The Interpretation Act 1889 shall apply for the interpretation of these regulations as it applies for the interpretation of an Act of Parliament and as if these regulations and the regulations hereby revoked were Acts of Parliament.

A1.516

Incorporation of provisions in tenancy agreements

3

The provisions set forth in the Schedule hereto relating to the maintenance, repair and insurance of fixed equipment shall be deemed to be incorporated in every contract of tenancy of an agricultural holding, whether made before or after the commencement of the Agricultural Holdings Act 1948, except in so far as they would impose on one of the parties to an agreement in writing a liability which under the agreement is imposed on the other:

Provided that where the interest of the landlord is held for the purposes of a Government department, or where a person representing Her Majesty or the Duke of Cornwall under section 87 of the Agricultural Holdings Act 1948 is deemed to be the landlord, or where the landlord has made provision approved by the Minister for defraying the cost of any such works of repair or replacement as are referred to in sub-paragraph (1)(*b*) of paragraph 2 of the Schedule hereto, the provision of sub-paragraph (1)(*a*) of the said paragraph 2 requiring the landlord to insure against loss or damage by fire shall not apply.

SCHEDULE

MAINTENANCE REPAIR AND INSURANCE OF THE FIXED EQUIPMENT OF A HOLDING

Regulation 3

PART I: RIGHTS AND LIABILITIES OF THE LANDLORD

A1.517

1 (1) To execute all repairs and replacements to the under-mentioned parts of the farmhouse, cottages and farm buildings, namely:- roofs, including chimney stacks, chimney pots, eaves-guttering and downpipes, main walls and exterior walls, howsoever constructed, including walls and fences of open and covered yards and garden walls, together with any interior repair or decoration made necessary as a result of structural defect to such roofs or walls, floors, floor joists, ceiling joists and timbers, exterior and interior staircases and fixed ladders (including banisters or handrails) of the farmhouse and cottages, and doors, windows and skylights, including the frames of such doors, windows and skylights (but excepting glass or glass substitute, sashcords, locks and fastenings): provided that in the case of repairs and replacements to floor-boards, interior staircases and fixed ladders (including banisters or handrails), doors and windows and opening skylights (including frames), eaves-guttering and downpipes, the landlord may recover one-half of the reasonable cost thereof from the tenant.

(2) To execute all repairs and replacements to underground water supply pipes wells, bore-holes and reservoirs and all underground installations connected therewith and to sewage disposal systems, including septic tanks, filtering media and cesspools (but excluding covers and tops).

(3) Except as provided by paragraph 8, to replace anything mentioned in paragraph 5(1) which has worn out or otherwise become incapable of further repair unless the tenant is himself liable to replace it under paragraph 6.

2 (1)

(a) To keep the farmhouse, cottages and farm buildings insured to their full value against loss or damage by fire; and

(b) as often as the farmhouse, cottages and farm buildings or any, or any part, of them shall be destroyed or damaged by fire, to execute all works of repair or replacement thereto necessary to make good damage by fire and to cause all money received in respect of such destruction or damage by virtue of such insurance to be laid out in the execution of such works.

(2) The proviso to paragraph 1(1) shall not apply to works falling within sub-paragraph (1)(*b*) of this paragraph.

3 (1) As often as may be necessary in order to prevent deterioration, and in any case at intervals of not more than five years, properly to paint with at least two coats of a suitable quality or properly and adequately to gas-tar, creosote or otherwise effectively treat with a preservative material all outside wood and ironwork of the farmhouse, cottages and farm buildings, the inside wood and ironwork of all external outward opening doors and windows of farm buildings (but not of the farmhouse or cottages), and the interior structural steelwork of open-sided farm buildings which have been previously painted, gas-tarred, creosoted or otherwise treated with preservative material or which it is necessary in order to prevent deterioration of the same so to paint, gas-tar, creosote or treat with preservative material: provided that in respect of doors, windows, eaves-guttering and downpipes the landlord may recover one-half of the reasonable cost of such work from the tenant, but if any such work to any of those items is completed before the commencement of the fifth year of the tenancy the sum which the landlord may so recover from the tenant shall be restricted to an amount equal to the aggregate of one-tenth part of such reasonable cost in respect of each year that has elapsed between the commencement of the tenancy and the completion of such work.

(2) In the last foregoing sub-paragraph "open-sided" means having the whole or the greater part of at least one side or end permanently open, apart from roof supports, if any.

4 (1) The landlord shall be under no liability—

(a) to execute repairs or replacements or to insure buildings or fixtures which are the property of the tenant, or

(b) subject to paragraph 2(1)(*b*), to execute repairs or replacements rendered necessary by the wilful act or the negligence of the tenant or any members of his household or his employees.

(2) If the tenant does not start work on the repairs or replacements for which he is liable under paragraphs 5, 6, 7 and 8 within two months, or if he fails to complete them within three months of receiving from the landlord a written notice (not being a notice to remedy breach of tenancy agreement by doing work of repair, maintenance or replacement in a form prescribed under section 19(1) and (3) of the Agriculture (Miscellaneous Provisions) Act 1963) specifying the necessary repairs or replacements and calling on him to execute them the landlord may enter and execute such repairs or replacements and recover the reasonable cost from the tenant forthwith.

(3)

(a) If the tenant wishes to contest his liability to execute any repairs or replacements specified in a notice served upon him by the landlord under the last foregoing sub-paragraph he shall within one month serve a counter-notice in writing upon the landlord specifying the grounds on which and the items of repair or replacement in respect of which he denies liability and requiring the question of liability in respect thereof to be determined by arbitration under the Act.

(b) Upon service of the counter-notice on the landlord, the operation of the notice (including the running of time thereunder) shall be suspended, in so far as it relates to the items specified in the counter-notice, until the termination of an arbitration determining the question of liability in respect of those items.

(c) In this sub-paragraph, "termination", in relation to an arbitration, means the date on which the arbitrator's award is delivered to the tenant.

PART II: RIGHTS AND LIABILITIES OF THE TENANT

Except in so far as such liabilities fall to be undertaken by the landlord under Part I hereof:

5 (1) To repair and to keep and leave clean and in good tenantable repair, order and condition the farmhouse, cottages and farm buildings together with all fixtures and fittings, boilers, ranges and grates, drains, sewers, gulleys, grease-traps, manholes and inspection chambers, electrical supply systems and fittings, water supply systems and fittings in so far as they are situated above ground, including pipes, tanks, cisterns, sanitary fittings, drinking troughs and pumping equipment, hydraulic rams (whether situated above or below ground), fences, hedges, field walls, stiles, gates and posts, cattle grids, bridges, culverts, ponds, watercourses, sluices, ditches, roads and yards in and upon the holding, or which during the tenancy may be erected or provided thereon.

(2) To repair or replace all removable covers to manholes, to inspection chambers and to sewage disposal systems.

(3) To keep clean and in good working order all roof valleys, eves-guttering and downpipes, wells, septic tanks, cesspools and sewage disposal systems.

(4) To use carefully so as to protect from wilful, reckless or negligent damage all items for the repair or replacement of which the landlord is responsible under paragraph 1; and also to report in writing immediately to the landlord any damage, however caused, to items for the repair or replacement of which the landlord is responsible.

6 Subject to paragraph 2(1)(b)—

(1) to replace or repair and, upon replacement or repair, adequately to paint, gas-tar, creosote or otherwise treat with effective preservative material as may be proper, all items of fixed equipment, and to do any work, where such replacement, repair or work is rendered necessary by the wilful act or negligence of the tenant or any members of his household or his employees; and

(2) to replace anything mentioned in paragraph 5(1) which has worn out or otherwise become incapable of repair if its condition has been brought about by or is substantially due to the tenant's failure to repair it.

7 As often as may be necessary, and in any case at intervals of not more than seven years, properly to clean, colour, whiten, paper, paint, limewash or otherwise treat with materials of suitable quality the inside of the farmhouse, cottages and farm buildings, including the interior of outward opening doors and windows of the farmhouse and cottages, which have been previously so treated and in the last year of the tenancy to limewash the inside of all buildings which previously have been limewashed.

[8 (1) Notwithstanding the general liability of the landlord for repairs and replacements, to renew all broken or cracked tiles or slates and to replace all slipped tiles or slates from time to time as the damage occurs, but so that the cost shall not exceed £100 in any one year of the tenancy.

(2) This paragraph shall not have effect so as to render a tenant liable for the cost of any renewals or replacement of tiles in excess of £25 which have been carried out by the landlord prior to 24th March 1988.]

9 To cut, trim or lay a proper proportion of the hedges in each year of the tenancy so as to maintain them in good and sound condition.

10 To dig out, scour and cleanse all ponds, watercourses, ditches and grips, as may be necessary to maintain them at sufficient width and depth, and to keep clear from obstruction all field drains and their outlets.

11 (1) If the last year of the tenancy is not a year in which such cleaning, colouring, whitening, papering, painting, limewashing or other treatment as is mentioned in paragraph 7 is due to be carried out, the tenant shall pay to the landlord at the end of such last year either the estimated reasonable cost thereof or a sum equal to the aggregate of one-seventh part of that cost in respect of each year that has elapsed since such last cleaning, colouring, whitening, papering, painting, limewashing or other treatment as aforesaid, was completed, whichever is the less.

(2) If the last year of the tenancy is not a year in which the landlord is liable, under paragraph 3, to paint, gas-tar, creosote or otherwise treat the doors, windows, eaves-guttering and downpipes of buildings, the tenant shall pay to the landlord at the end of such last year either one-half of the estimated reasonable cost thereof or a sum equal to the aggregate of one-tenth part of that cost in respect of each year that has elapsed since such last painting, gas-tarring, creosoting or other treatment as aforesaid, was completed, whichever is the less.

(3) In the assessment of any compensation payable by the tenant on the termination of the tenancy in respect of dilapidation, any accrued liability under the two preceding sub-paragraphs shall be taken into account.

[12 (1) If the landlord fails to execute repairs other than repairs to an underground waterpipe which are his liability within three months of receiving from the tenant a written notice specifying the necessary repairs and calling on him to execute them, the tenant may execute such repairs and, except to the extent to which under the terms of Part I hereof the tenant is liable to bear the cost, recover (subject to the landlord's rights to require arbitration under sub-paragraph (5) below) the reasonable cost from the landlord forthwith.

(2) If the landlord fails to execute any repairs which are his liability to an underground waterpipe within one week of receiving from the tenant a written notice specifying the necessary repairs and calling on him to execute them, the tenant may execute such repaids and, except to the extent to which under the terms of Part I hereof the tenant is liable to bear the cost, recover (subject to the landlord's rights to require arbitration under sub-paragraph (5) below) the reasonable cost from the landlord upon the expiry of a period of one month from the execution of the repairs.

(3) Subject to sub-paragraph (4) below, if the landlord fails to execute any replacements which are his liability within three months of receiving from the tenant a written notice specifying the necessary replacements and calling on him to execute them, the tenant may execute such replacements and, except to the extent to which under the terms of Part I hereof the tenant is liable to bear the cost, recover (subject to the landlord's rights to require arbitration under sub-paragraph (5) below) the reasonable cost from the landlord forthwith.

(4) The tenant shall not be entitled to recover, in respect of the aggregate of the replacements executed by him after being specified in a notice given in pursuance of sub-paragraph (3) above, in any year of the tenancy any sum in excess of whichever of the following sums is hereinafter specified in relation to the replacements so executed, that is to say—

(a) in relation to replacements executed in any year of the tenancy terminating on or before 24th March 1988, a sum equal to the rent of the holding for that year or £500, whichever is the smaller, or

(b) in relation to replacements executed in any year of the tenancy terminating after 24th March 1988, a sum equal to the rent of the holding for that year or £2,000, whichever is the smaller.

(5)

(a) If the landlord wishes to contest his liability to execute any repairs or replacements specified in a notice served upon him by the tenant under sub-paragraph (1), (2) or (3) above he shall within one month of the service of that notice serve a counter-notice in writing upon the tenant specifying the grounds on which and the items of repair or replacement in respect of which he denies liability and requiring the question of liability in respect thereof to be determined under the Act.

(b) Upon service of a counter-notice on the tenant which relates to a notice served on the landlord under sub-paragraph (1) or (3) above, the operation of the notice so served upon sub-paragraph (1) or (3) (including the running of time thereunder) shall be suspended, in so far as it relates to the items specified in the counter-notice, until the termination of an arbitration determining the question of liability in respect of those items.

(c) Upon service of a counter-notice on the tenant which relates to a notice served on the landlord under sub-paragraph (2) above, the tenant's right under that sub-paragraph to recover the reasonable cost of the repairs specified in the counter-notice shall not arise unless the question of liability to execute those repairs is first determined by arbitration in favour of the tenant, and shall thereupon arise from the termination of the arbitration.

(d) In this sub-paragraph "termination" in relation to an arbitration means the date on which the arbitrator's award is delivered to the landlord.]

NOTES

Amendment

Paras 8, 12: substituted by SI 1988/281, reg 2.

PART III: GENERAL PROVISIONS

13 (1) If at any time and from time to time the landlord or the tenant shall be of opinion that any item of fixed equipment is, or before the same was damaged or destroyed by fire was, redundant to the farming of the holding, the landlord or the tenant may by giving two months' notice in writing to the other of them require that the question whether such item of fixed equipment is, or before such damage or destruction was, so redundant shall be determined, in default of agreement, by arbitration under the Act, and if the arbitrator shall award that the said item of fixed equipment is, or before such damage or destruction by fire was, redundant to the farming of the holding then, as from the date of such award, paragraph 14(1) shall apply to that item and both the landlord and the tenant shall be relieved from all liability in respect of any antecedent breach of any obligation to maintain, repair or replace the item of fixed equipment so awarded to be redundant and the landlord shall be entitled to demolish and remove such item of fixed equipment and to enter upon the holding for those purposes.

(2) In any arbitration to which sub-paragraph (1) of this paragraph applies, no item of fixed equipment shall be determined to be, or to have been before damage or destruction by fire, as the case may be, redundant to the farming of the holding, unless the arbitrator shall be satisfied that the repair or replacement of such item is or, as the case may be, was, not reasonably required having regard to—

(a)
   (i) the landlord's responsibilities to manage the holding in accordance with the rules of good estate management; and
   (ii) the period for which the holding may reasonably be expected to remain a separate holding; and

(b) the character and situation of the holding and the average requirements of a tenant reasonably skilled in husbandry.

14 Nothing contained in Part I or Part II hereof shall create any liability on the part of either landlord or tenant:

(1) to maintain, repair, replace or insure any item of fixed equipment which the landlord and the tenant agree in writing to be obsolete or redundant to the farming of the holding or which in the event of any dispute between them as to whether it is, or before the same was damaged or destroyed by fire was, redundant to the farming of the holding, shall be awarded to be so redundant by an arbitrator in an arbitration as mentioned in paragraph 13; or

(2) to execute any work if and so far as the execution of such work is rendered impossible (except at prohibitive or unreasonable expense) by reason of subsidence of any land or the blocking of outfalls which are not under the control of either the landlord or the tenant.

15 If any claim, question or difference shall arise between the landlord and the tenant under the foregoing provisions hereof, not being a matter which, otherwise than under the provisions of this paragraph, is required by or by virtue of the Act or section 19 of the Agriculture (Miscellaneous Provisions) Act 1963 (notice to remedy breach of tenancy agreement) or regulations or orders made thereunder or the foregoing provisions hereof to be determined by arbitration under the Act, such claim, question or difference shall be determined, in default of agreement, by arbitration under the Act.

Interpretation

16 (1) In this Schedule, unless the context otherwise requires, "the Act" means the Agricultural Holdings Act 1948 as amended by any other enactment.

(2) Any reference in this Schedule to a numbered paragraph is a reference to the paragraph bearing that number in this Schedule.

AGRICULTURE (MISCELLANEOUS PROVISIONS) ACT 1976 (APPLICATION OF PROVISIONS) REGULATIONS 1977

SI 1977/1215

Authority: Agricultural Holdings Act 1986, ss 45(8), 94

NOTES

Continuation

Authority: following the consolidation of the original enabling powers, these Regulations have effect as if made under the Agricultural Holdings Act 1986, ss 45(8), 94.

A1.518

1 Citation, commencement and interpretation

(1) These Regulations may be cited as the Agriculture (Miscellaneous Provisions) Act 1976 (Application of Provisions) Regulations 1977 and shall come into operation on 23rd August 1977.

(2) In these Regulations 'the Act' means the Agriculture (Miscellaneous Provisions) Act 1976.

(3) The Interpretation Act 1889 shall apply to the interpretation of these Regulations as it applies to the interpretation of an Act of Parliament.

A1.519

2 Application of the Act in cases of death before succession

(1) Where a person entitled to a joint tenancy of an agricultural holding by virtue of a direction under section 20(9) of the Act dies before the relevant time (as defined in section 23(2) of the Act) without having become the tenant or a joint tenant of that holding, that direction shall from the date of his death cease to have effect in relation to that person if he is survived by any other person jointly entitled under the direction; but the direction shall continue to have effect (subject to the provisions of the Act) in relation to the other person or persons as if the dead person had not been named therein; and the provisions of Part II of the Act, so far as relevant, shall apply accordingly.

(2) Where—

    (a) a person entitled to a tenancy of an agricultural holding by virtue of a direction under section 20(5) or (6) of the Act; or

    (b) the sole survivor of two or more persons entitled to a joint tenancy of an agricultural holding by virtue of a direction under section 20(9) of the Act

dies before the relevant time (as defined in section 23(2) of the Act) without having become the tenant or joint tenant of that holding, the provisions of Part II of the Act, except section 23(8), shall apply in accordance with the provisions of the Schedule to these Regulations subject to the exceptions, additions and modifications set out therein.

(3) Where two or more persons who are jointly entitled to a tenancy of the holding by virtue of a direction under section 20(9) of the Act have died in circumstances

rendering it uncertain which of them survived the other, such deaths shall for the purposes of these Regulations be presumed to have occurred in order of seniority, and accordingly the younger shall be deemed to have survived the elder.

SCHEDULE
APPLICATION OF PART II OF THE ACT

Article 2

A1.520

1   Sections 16 and 17 shall not apply.

2   Section 18 shall apply—

(a)   with the addition of the following subsection after subsection (1):—

'(1A)   In subsection (1) and in the definition of 'the deceased' in sub-section (2), the expression 'tenant' includes a person who is—

(i)   entitled to a tenancy of an agricultural holding by virtue of a direction by the Tribunal under section 20(5) or (6) of this Act; or

(ii)   the sole survivor of two or more persons entitled to a joint tenancy of an agricultural holding by virtue of such a direction under section 20(9) of this Act,

and who dies before the time at which, had he survived, he would have been deemed to have been granted and to have accepted that tenancy or joint tenancy';

(b)   with the addition in subsection (4) of the words '(except section 19A)' after the words 'this Part of this Act';

(c)   as if the reference in subsection (4)(e) to subsection (1) included a reference to subsection (1A);

(d)   with the exception of subsection (5).

3   Section 19 shall not apply, but instead the following section shall be added:—

'19A   (1)   Where at the date of death of the deceased the holding is the subject of a relevant notice to quit, the operation of that notice shall, subject to subsection (2) below and notwithstanding any provision of this Act having effect prior to the death of the deceased, take effect at the date specified in the notice for the termination of the tenancy to which it relates:

Provided that where, in the case of a relevant notice to quit, there remains at the date of death of the deceased a period of less than twelve months before the date specified in the notice for the termination of the tenancy of the holding, the operation of the notice shall be postponed for a period of twelve months.

(2)   A relevant notice to quit shall not have effect unless either—

(a)   no application to become the tenant of the holding is made under section 20 of this Act within the relevant period; or

(b)   one or more such applications having been made within that period, either—
(i)   none of the applicants is determined by the Tribunal to be in their opinion a suitable person to become the tenant of the holding; or
(ii)   the Tribunal consent under section 22 of this Act to the operation of the notice to quit.

(3)   In this section 'relevant notice to quit' means a notice to quit the holding falling within section 24(2)(g) of the 1948 Act.'.

4   Sections 20 and 21 shall apply.

5   Section 22 shall apply as if the references to section 19 of the Act were references to section 19A.

6   Section 23 shall apply:—

  (a)   as if, in subsection (1), for the words 'the date of death', there were substituted the words 'the date when the original tenant died';
  (b)   as if for subsection (2) there were substituted the following subsection:—

'(2A)   In this and the following section 'the relevant time' means the end of the twelve months immediately following the end of the year of tenancy in which the deceased died.';

  (c)   as if, in subsection (3), for the words 'on the date of death the holding was held by the deceased' there were substituted the words 'immediately before the death of the original tenant he held the holding';
  (d)   as if the following subsection were added:—

'(9)   In this and the next following section 'the original tenant' means the tenant of the holding to whose tenancy the deceased would have succeeded, had he survived, by virtue of the provisions of this Part of this Act.'.

7   Section 24 shall apply as if in subsection (5)(a) for the word 'deceased's' there were substituted the words 'the original tenant's'.

AGRICULTURAL LAND TRIBUNALS (RULES) ORDER 1978

SI 1978/259

Authority: Agriculture Act 1947, s 73(3), (4); Agriculture (Miscellaneous Provisions) Act 1954, s 6(4), (6); Agricultural Holdings Act 1986, s 67(5), (7)

NOTES

Continuation

Authority: following the consolidation of the Agricultural Holdings Act 1948, this Order, to the extent that it had effect thereunder, has effect as if made under the Agricultural Holdings Act 1986, s 67(5), (7).

A1.521

1   Citation, commencement and interpretation

(1)   This Order may be cited as the Agricultural Land Tribunals (Rules) Order 1978 and shall come into operation on 7th April 1978.

(2)   The Interpretation Act 1889 shall apply to the interpretation of this Order as it applies to the interpretation of an Act of Parliament.

A1.522

2   Rules of procedure

The Rules set out in Schedule 1 to this Order shall apply for the purposes of proceedings before Agricultural Land Tribunals other than proceedings arising from any application made under Part II of the Agriculture (Miscellaneous Provisions) Act 1976 [or under Schedule 2 to the Agricultural Holdings Act 1984].

NOTES

Amendment

Words in square brackets inserted by SI 1984/1301, art 3.

A1.523

4   Revocation of orders

(1)   The Agricultural Land Tribunals and Notices to Quit Order 1959,

the Agricultural Land Tribunals (Amendment) Order 1959,
the Agricultural Land Tribunals (Amendment) Order 1961, and
the Agricultural Land Tribunals (Amendment) Order 1974

are hereby revoked except to such extent as may be necessary for the disposal of an application pending at the commencement of this Order.

(2)   The Agriculture (Procedure of Agricultural Land Tribunals) Order 1954 (which was revoked with a saving in 1959) shall continue to have effect for the purpose of references to an Agricultural Land Tribunal under section 86 of the Agriculture Act 1947.

SCHEDULE 1
RULES OF PROCEDURE FOR AGRICULTURAL LAND TRIBUNALS

Article 2

PRELIMINARY

A1.524

1   Citation and interpretation

(1)   These Rules may be cited as the Agricultural Land Tribunals Rules 1978.

(2)   In these Rules, unless the context otherwise requires—

'the 1948 Act' means the Agricultural Holdings Act 1948;
'the 1977 Act' means the Agricultural Holdings (Notices to Quit) Act 1977;
'chairman' means the chairman of the tribunal or a person nominated under
    paragraph 16(1)(a) or appointed under paragraph 16A of the Ninth Schedule to
    the Agriculture Act 1947 to act as chairman;
'drainage case' means proceedings on an application under section 40 or 41 of the
    Land Drainage Act 1976;
'secretary' means the secretary of the tribunal;
'tribunal' means the Agricultural Land Tribunal for the area in which the
    agricultural holding which is the subject of an application, or the greater part of
    that holding, is situate.

(3)   A form referred to by number means the form so numbered in the Appendix to these Rules, or a form substantially to the like effect, with such variations as the circumstances may require.

(4)   Any reference in these Rules to any rule or enactment shall, unless the context otherwise requires, be construed as a reference to that rule or enactment as amended, extended or applied by any other rule or enactment.

(5)   Expressions defined in or used for the purposes of the 1977 Act have the same meaning in these Rules.

FORM OF APPLICATION

2   Consent to operation of notice to quit

(1)   An application for the tribunal's consent to the operation of a notice to quit under section 2(1) of the 1977 Act which is made by the landlord before the giving of the said notice shall be made not more than twelve months and not less than three months before the commencement of the period at the expiration of which the notice to quit is intended to have effect.

(2)   An application for the tribunal's consent to the operation of a notice to quit under section 2(1) or 4(2) or (3) of the 1977 Act which is made by the landlord after service upon him by the tenant of a counter-notice shall be made within one month of the service of the counter-notice.

(3)   An application under this rule shall be made in form 1.

3   Postponement of operation of notice to quit

An application under Article 12(1) of the Agricultural Holdings (Arbitration on Notices) Order 1978 to postpone the termination of a tenancy shall, unless made at the hearing of the proceedings before the tribunal on an application under the 1977 Act, be made in form 2.

4   Certificate of bad husbandry (Case C)

An application under section 2(4) of the 1977 Act shall be made in form 3.

5   Variation or revocation of conditions

An application under section 3(5) of the 1977 Act shall be made in form 4.

6   Directions relating to fixed equipment

(1)   An application under section 4(1) of the Agriculture Act 1958 for a direction for the provision, alteration or repair of fixed equipment shall be made in form 5.

(2)   An application under section 4(4) of the Agriculture Act 1958 for the extension of the period specified in a direction under section 4(1) shall be made in writing and shall state the grounds of the application.

7   Approval of long-term improvements

(1)   An application under section 50(1) of the 1948 Act for the tribunal's approval of the carrying out of a long-term improvement shall be made in form 6.

(2)   The time within which a landlord may serve a notice under section 50(3) of the 1948 Act that he proposes himself to carry out an improvement shall be one month from the date on which he receives notice in writing of the tribunal's approval of the carrying out of the improvement.

(3)   An application under section 50(4)(b) of the 1948 Act for a determination that the landlord has failed to carry out an improvement within a reasonable time shall be made in form 7.

8   Treating agricultural holding as market garden

An application under section 68 of the 1948 Act for a direction that an agricultural holding shall be treated as a market garden shall be made in form 8.

9   Restrictions on burning of heather or grass

An application under section 21 of the Hill Farming Act 1946 for a direction shall be made in form 9.

10   Section 20(5) of the Mineral Workings Act 1951

(1)   An application under section 21(2)(b) of the Agriculture Act 1947 as it applies for the purposes of section 20(5) of the Mineral Workings Act 1951 for a determination that some person should be treated as owner of the land other than the person who would be so treated apart from the determination shall be made in form 10.

(2)   Any person who is specified in an application under paragraph (1) as being affected by the determination shall be a party to the proceedings on the application for the purposes of these Rules.

11   Applications under Land Drainage Act 1976

(1)   An application under section 40 or 41 of the Land Drainage Act 1976 for an order requiring the carrying out of work for putting a ditch in proper order or authorising the applicant to carry out drainage work on land shall be made in form 11.

(2)   Without prejudice to rule 12(1), on any application under section 40 of the Land Drainage Act 1976, the occupier of any land which may be entered in pursuance of the order shall be a party to the application.

(3)   Without prejudice to rule 12(1), on any application under section 41 of the Land Drainage Act 1976, the owner of any land on which it is proposed that any work should be carried out and the occupier of any land which may be entered in pursuance of the order shall be parties to the application.

(4)   Where, on the hearing of an application under section 40, the applicant states that he desires also to apply under section 41 for an order authorising him to carry out the same or substantially the same work as that referred to in his application, the tribunal may, if they think fit, deal with the application as if it had been made under section 41 as well as under section 40.

PARTIES ETC

12   Persons affected to be parties

(1)   Without prejudice to rule 10(2), any person against whom any relief is sought on an application under rules 2 to 11 (or on an application by the Crown under section 6 of the 1977 Act) shall be a party to the proceedings on that application.

(2)   Any authority having power to enforce the statutory requirement specified in an application under rule 6(1) shall be entitled to be heard on the proceedings on an application under that paragraph, and shall be treated as a party thereto except for the purposes of rule 15.

1647

13   Sub-tenancies

(1)   Where an application is made to the tribunal in respect of an agricultural holding the whole or any part of which has been sublet, every landlord, tenant and sub-tenant of that holding shall be a party to the proceedings on that application.

(2)   Paragraph (1) shall not apply in a drainage case.

14   Joinder of parties

If it appears to the chairman or to the tribunal, whether on the application of a party or otherwise, that it is desirable to join any person as a party to the proceedings, the chairman or the tribunal, as the case may be, may order such person to be joined and may give such consequential directions as may be just, including directions as to the service of documents on any person so joined and as to the time within which he may reply to the application.

FORM OF REPLY

15   Reply

(1)   Any party who intends to oppose the whole or any part of an application to the tribunal shall, within one month of a copy of the application being served on him under rule 17 (or, in a drainage case, within the time allowed by rule 21(5)), reply thereto in the form appended to the copy of the application served on him.

(2)   Where no reply is received by the secretary within the time allowed by paragraph (1), the tribunal may decide to make an order in the terms of the application without a formal hearing.

(3)   Paragraph (1) does not apply to an application under rule 5 or to an application by the Crown under section 6 of the 1977 Act, and paragraph (2) does not apply in a drainage case.

GENERAL PROVISIONS AS TO APPLICATIONS AND REPLIES

16   Application, reply and supporting documents

(1)   Every application and reply shall be signed by the party making it or by some person authorised to do so on his behalf, and shall be delivered or sent in duplicate to the secretary.

(2)   Every application shall be accompanied by two copies of a map of the land which is the subject of the application on a scale of 6' to one mile or 1/10,000 or larger.

(3)   Where a party intends to give evidence about any land which is not shown on the map referred to in paragraph (2), his application or reply shall be accompanied by two copies of a map of that land on a scale of 6' to one mile or 1/10,000 or larger.

(4)   Every application and reply shall be accompanied by two copies of any plan or other document which the party making the application or reply intends to adduce in support of his case.

(5)   Where there are more than two parties to proceedings, the party making an application or reply, as the case may be, shall deliver or send to the secretary one additional copy thereof, and of any map, plan or other document accompanying the application or reply, for service on each additional party.

(6)   The chairman may, on such terms as he thinks fit, dispense with any map, plan or other document required to be furnished by any party under this rule where it appears to him that the map, plan or other document, or a copy thereof, is already in the

possession of the tribunal or of some other party to the proceedings, or that to require it to be furnished would be unreasonable on the ground of expense or otherwise.

(7)   A request for the chairman's direction under this rule shall be made in writing and shall be delivered or sent to the secretary on or before the delivery of the application or reply of the party making the request.

17   Service of documents by secretary

On receiving from any party an application, reply or other document referred to in rule 16, the secretary shall forthwith serve one copy thereof on every other party to the proceedings.

18   Withdrawal of application or reply

(1)   A party may withdraw his application or reply by giving notice in writing to the secretary at any time before the hearing and on receipt of such a notice the secretary shall forthwith notify all other parties.

(2)   Where a reply is withdrawn the tribunal may, except in a drainage case, decide to make an order in the terms of the application without a formal hearing.

(3)   If, on the withdrawal of an application or reply, it appears to the chairman that the case is a proper one for the award of costs under the power conferred by section 5 of the Agriculture (Miscellaneous Provisions) Act 1954, he shall cause the tribunal to be convened for the purpose of determining whether costs should be awarded, and the secretary shall give to all parties not less than seven days' notice of the date, time and place appointed for that purpose.

PREPARATION FOR HEARING

19   Interlocutory applications

Unless the chairman otherwise orders, an application for directions on any matter which the chairman has power to determine under these Rules shall be made in writing stating the grounds of the application and shall be delivered or sent to the secretary together with a sufficient number of copies for service on the other party or parties.

20   Disclosure of documents

(1)   A party shall furnish to the secretary on his request any document or other information which the tribunal may require and which it is in the power of that party to furnish, and shall afford to all other parties an opportunity to inspect such document or a copy of such document, and to take copies thereof.

(2)   Nothing in paragraph (1) shall require the furnishing of any information which it would be contrary to the public interest to disclose.

21   Minister's report in drainage cases

(1)   On receipt of an application in a drainage case, the tribunal shall call on the Minister of Agriculture, Fisheries and Food to provide a report on the matters to which the application relates, and for that purpose the tribunal may authorise any officer of the Minister to enter and inspect any land specified by the tribunal.

(2)   A report made under paragraph (1) may recommend that no order or that an order in the terms set out in the report be made by the tribunal.

(3)   On receipt of the report the secretary shall serve a copy thereof on every party.

(4) Within one month of a copy of the report being served on him the applicant shall serve a notice on the tribunal in form 12 stating whether or not he agrees with the facts stated and the recommendations made in the report; and rules 16(1) and (5) and 17 shall apply to the notice as if it were an application.

(5) The time within which a party is required by rule 15 to reply to the application shall, in a drainage case, run from the date of the service on him of the notice under paragraph (4).

(6) A report under this rule shall be *prima facie* evidence of the facts set out therein, but the maker of the report shall, unless the tribunal otherwise direct, attend any formal hearing of the application for the purpose of being examined and cross-examined on the contents of the report.

22   Summary determination in drainage cases

Where, in a drainage case,—

- (a) the report received under rule 21—
    - (i) recommends that an order be made and
    - (ii) in the case of an application under section 40 of the Land Drainage Act 1976 names a party to the application as the person whom it recommends should be required to carry out any work; and
- (b) the applicant has notified the tribunal of his acceptance of the recommendation, and
- (c) every other party has either—
    - (i) notified the tribunal of his acceptance of the recommendation, or
    - (ii) failed to reply to the application within the time allowed by rule 21(5), or
    - (iii) withdrawn his reply,

the tribunal may decide to make an order on the application substantially in the terms of the recommendation without a formal hearing.

23   Notice of hearing

(1) As soon as practicable after receipt of the reply or, as the case may be, after the time for replying has expired, the chairman shall fix a date, time and place for the hearing of the application.

(2) Where rule 15(1) does not apply, the chairman shall fix a date, time and place for the hearing as soon as practicable after receipt of the application.

(3) The chairman may alter the date, time or place fixed for any hearing if it appears to him necessary or desirable to do so to avoid hardship to the parties or for other good cause.

(4) The secretary shall send to every party notice in form 13 of the date, time and place of any hearing which, except with the consent of the parties, shall not be earlier than fourteen days after the date on which the notice is sent.

THE HEARING

24   Tribunal to sit in public

The tribunal shall sit in public unless it appears to them that there are exceptional reasons which make it desirable that the hearing or some part of it should take place in private:

Provided that where a hearing or part of a hearing takes place in private, a member of the Council on Tribunals in his capacity as such shall be entitled to attend.

25   Right of audience

Any party may appear and be heard in person or by counsel or solicitor or by a representative appointed in writing.

26   Procedure at hearing

(1)   At the hearing the party making the application shall begin and other parties shall be heard in such order as the tribunal may determine.

(2)   Subject to the provisions of these Rules and to any direction given by the chairman, the procedure at the hearing shall be such as the tribunal may direct.

(3)   The tribunal may adjourn the hearing from time to time if for any reason it appears to them necessary or desirable to do so.

27   Default of appearance

If a party fails to appear at the time fixed for the hearing, the tribunal, if they are satisfied that the party has been afforded an adequate opportunity of attending, may—

- (a)   where the party failing to appear is the applicant, dismiss the application, or
- (b)   in any other case, proceed to determine the application in the absence of that party.

EVIDENCE

28   Evidence

(1)   The tribunal may admit evidence notwithstanding that it would not be admissible in a court of law.

(2)   Evidence before the tribunal may be given—

- (a)   orally, on oath or on affirmation or otherwise,
- (b)   by affidavit, if the parties consent, or
- (c)   by means of written statements produced by the maker when giving evidence or, if the tribunal consent, by another witness.

(3)   At any stage of the proceedings the tribunal may, of their own motion or on the application of any party, order the personal attendance of a deponent or of the maker of any written statement for examination and cross-examination, or admit any map, plan or other document in evidence.

29   Witnesses

(1)   The tribunal shall give each party an opportunity to call witnesses and to cross-examine any witness called by or on behalf of any other party and to re-examine his own witnesses after cross-examination, and a party may, if he so desires, give evidence as a witness on his own behalf.

(2)   The tribunal may call a witness who may, after giving evidence, be cross-examined by any party.

(3)   The tribunal may require any witness to give evidence on oath or affirmation.

(4)   The provisions of the County Court Rules 1936 as to the issuing of witness summonses shall apply for the purposes of any proceedings before the tribunal as they apply for the purposes of an arbitration under the 1948 Act.

30

Inspection of land (1) The tribunal may enter on and inspect an agricultural holding owned or occupied by any party (whether the holding is the subject of the proceedings or not) and inspect any fixed or other equipment, produce or livestock thereon.

(2) Notice of the tribunal's intention to inspect a holding shall be given by the secretary to all parties and to any other occupier of the holding and, unless given orally at the hearing, shall be given in writing at least twenty-four hours before the intended entry.

(3) The parties, their representatives and expert witnesses and any other occupier of the holding may attend the inspection.

THE DECISION

31 Decision of the tribunal

(1) The decision of the tribunal, which in the event of disagreement between the members shall be the decision of the majority, shall be given in writing, together with a statement of the tribunal's reasons for their decision.

(2) The chairman may correct any clerical mistake in the written record of the tribunal's decision.

(3) The secretary shall send to each party a copy of the tribunal's decision and reasons.

(4) The secretary may supply a further copy of the tribunal's decision and reasons or any part thereof to any party who appears reasonably to require it.

(5) A copy issued under paragraph (3) or (4) shall be certified by the secretary as a true copy and shall be *prima facie* evidence of the matters contained therein.

32 Variation of order in drainage cases

Any order made following a decision of the tribunal in a drainage case may be varied whether as to the time within which any work is to be carried out or otherwise and on an application to vary the order which shall be made in form 14 the chairman may give all such directions as may be just.

REFERENCE TO HIGH COURT

33 Request under section 6 of Agriculture (Miscellaneous Provisions) Act 1954

(1) A request for the reference to the High Court of a question of law arising in the course of proceedings before the tribunal shall, unless made at the hearing, be made in writing to the secretary not later than fourteen days from the date on which a copy of the tribunal's decision was sent to the party making the request and shall be accompanied by as many copies of the request as there are other parties; and the secretary shall thereupon serve a copy of the request on every such party.

(2) If the tribunal refuse the request, the secretary shall, not later than fourteen days from the date of his receipt of the request, notify all parties of the refusal; and if the party making the request, being aggrieved by the refusal, intends to apply for an order directing the tribunal to refer the question of law to the High Court, he shall, within seven days after receiving notice of the refusal, serve on the secretary notice in writing of the intended application accompanied by as many copies of the notice as there are other parties; and the secretary shall thereupon serve a copy of the notice on every such party.

(3)   A case stated on a question of law for the decision of the High Court shall set out the question of law and the facts found by the tribunal and shall be signed by the chairman and sent to the party who requested the reference within two months after the date of the request or, as the case may be, within two months after the making of an order by the High Court directing the reference.

34   Modification of tribunal's decision following High Court proceedings

(1)   The powers of the tribunal under section 6(5) of the Agriculture (Miscellaneous Provisions) Act 1954 may be exercised by the chairman in any case where he does not consider it necessary to convene the tribunal for that purpose; but if it appears to the chairman that there should be a further hearing before the tribunal, he shall fix a date, time and place for the hearing.

(2)   Where a further hearing consequent on the reference to the High Court cannot conveniently take place before the tribunal as originally constituted, the chairman shall cause a fresh tribunal to be constituted for that purpose.

SUPPLEMENTAL

35   Mode of service

(1)   Every application, reply or other document required or authorised by these Rules to be served on any person shall be deemed to have been duly served if it is delivered to him or left at his proper address, or sent to him by post in a registered letter or by recorded delivery.

(2)   Any such document required or authorised to be given to, or served on, an incorporated company or body shall be duly given or served if given to or served on the secretary or clerk of the company or body.

(3)   The proper address of any person to or on whom any such document is to be given or served shall, in the case of a secretary or clerk of any incorporated company or body, be that of the registered or principal office of the company or body and, in any other case, be the last known address of the person in question.

(4)   Where any such document is to be given to, or served on, any person as being the owner of land and the land belongs to an ecclesiastical benefice, a copy thereof shall be served on the Church Commissioners.

36   Substituted service

If any person on whom any document is required to be served for the purpose of these Rules cannot be found, or has died and has no known personal representative, or is out of the United Kingdom, or if for any other reason service on him cannot be readily effected, the chairman may dispense with service on such person or may make an order for substituted service on such other person or in such other form (whether by advertisement in a newspaper or otherwise) as the chairman may think fit.

37   Extension of time

The time appointed by or under these Rules for doing any act or taking any step in connection with any proceedings may be extended by the chairman on such terms and conditions, if any, as appear to him just.

38   Failure to comply with rules

Any failure on the part of any person to comply with the provisions of these Rules shall not render the proceedings, or anything done in pursuance thereof, invalid unless the chairman or the tribunal so direct.

NOTES

Transfer of Functions

Functions of the Minister of Agriculture, Fisheries and Food referred to in r 21 above, so far as exercisable in relation to Wales, transferred to the National Assembly for Wales, by the National Assembly for Wales (Transfer of Functions) Order 1999, SI 1999/672, art 2, Sch 1.

APPENDIX

FORM 1

rule 2(3)

Ref No

To be inserted by the Secretary.

AGRICULTURAL LAND TRIBUNAL

Application for Consent to Operation of Notice to Quit

To the Secretary of the Agricultural Land Tribunal for the .... Area.

1 I, ... *block capitals*)

of .... (*address*),

hereby apply under—

    *(a) Section 2(1),
    *(b) Section 4(2),
    *(c) Section 4(3),

of the Agricultural Holdings (Notices to Quit) Act 1977 for the consent of the Tribunal to the operation of a notice to quit which I *propose to give/have given to my tenant,

.... (*block capitals*)

of .... (*address*)

2 *(a) I propose to serve the notice before the .... day of .... , 19 ....

*(b) The notice was served on the .... day of .... , 19 .... , and a counter-notice was served by the tenant on the .... day of .... 19 ....

3 The holding in respect of which the notice *will be/has been given is known as .... and consists of:—

  (a) .... hectares of arable land (including temporary grass) (Ordnance Survey Field Nos ....);
  (b) .... hectares of permanent pasture (Ordnance Survey Field Nos ....);
  (c) .... hectares of rough grazing (Ordnance Survey Field Nos ....);
  (d) .... hectares of other land (including orchards) (Ordnance Survey Field Nos ....);

Total .... hectares.   ANNUAL RENT £ ....

4 The holding includes the following buildings (*give a general description*):—

**5 I apply for the Tribunal's consent to the operation of the notice to quit on the following ground(s) provided in paragraph(s) .... of section 3(3) of the Agricultural Holdings (Notices to Quit) Act 1977(1). (*This paragraph is relevant to an application under section 2(1) of the Act, in which case it is important to refer to footnote (1). In other cases the paragraph should be struck out.*)

6   The main facts on which I will base my case are (*give a brief outline*):—(2)

7   If I obtain possession of the land I intend:—

*(a) to farm it myself;
*(b) to let it to another tenant (*state name and address if known*).

8   I/The future tenant*(3) at present farm(s) other land consisting of:—

(a)   .... hectares of arable land (including temporary grass) (Ordnance Survey Field Nos ....);
(b)   .... hectares of permanent pasture (Ordnance Survey Field Nos ....);
(c)   .... hectares of rough grazing (Ordnance Survey Field Nos ....);
(d)   .... hectares of other land (including orchards) (Ordnance Survey Field Nos ....);

Total .... hectares.

9   I attach the following documents which I intend to produce in support of my case:—

(a)   two (4) copies of a 6' to one mile or 1/20,000(5) map of the holding described in paragraph 3 above (and of the other land referred to in paragraph 8)**(6);
(b)   two (4) copies of (7):—

Date ....   Signed(8) ....

*Strike out whichever is inapplicable.

**Strike out if inapplicable.

(1)   The applicant must state on which paragraph or paragraphs of the subsection he intends to rely. The five paragraphs, as amended, are as follows:

(a)   that the carrying out of the purpose for which the landlord proposes to terminate the tenancy is desirable in the interests of good husbandry as respects the land to which the notice relates, treated as a separate unit; or
(b)   that the carrying out thereof is desirable in the interests of sound management of the estate of which the land to which the notice relates forms part or which that land constitutes (*see footnote (6) below*); or
(c)   that the carrying out thereof is desirable for the purposes of agricultural research, education, experiment or demonstration, or for the purposes of the enactments relating to small-holdings or allotments; or
(d)   that greater hardship would be caused by withholding than by giving consent to the operation of the notice; or
(e)   that the landlord proposes to terminate the tenancy for the purpose of the land's being used for a use, other than for agriculture, not falling within Case B (i.e. in section 2(3) of the Agricultural Holdings (Notices to Quit) Act 1977).

(2)   Where the tenant is a serviceman within the meaning of section 11 of the Agricultural Holdings (Notices to Quit) Act 1977, and the notice to quit is given for one or more of the reasons specified in Case B, D or E, the reasons for the giving of the notice must be stated and, if any question arising out of them has been determined by arbitration, the determination should also be stated.

(3)   Paragraph 8 need not be completed if the name of the future tenant is unknown. Where land is described, a map should be provided (*footnote (6) below*).

(4)   Two copies of the application and of any map and document must be sent to the Secretary, and if there are more than two parties (*e.g.* if the holding or part of it is

sub-let), an additional copy of the application, etc., must be supplied for, and the Secretary must be informed of the name and address of, each additional party.

(5) A larger scale map may be used if preferred. Ordnance Survey Field Numbers must be marked on the map.

(6) Where it is intended to give evidence about any land other than that which is the subject of the notice to quit, it must be shown either on the map produced or on a separate map of a scale of 6' to one mile or 1/10,000 or larger.

(7) Mention any other document which is attached to this application.

(8) If signed by any person other than the applicant himself, he should state in what capacity or by what authority he signs.

FORM 1R

Ref No

To be inserted by the Secretary.

AGRICULTURAL LAND TRIBUNAL

Reply to Application for Consent to Operation of Notice to Quit

To the Secretary of the Agricultural Land Tribunal for the .... Area.

I, ... *(block capitals)*

of .... *(address)*,

tenant(1) of .... *(name or description of holding)*, having received a copy of the application (bearing the above reference number) for the Tribunal's consent to the operation of a notice to quit, reply as follows:

1   The facts stated in the first four paragraphs of the application are correct except that:—

2   In addition to the land which is the subject of the application, I farm the following land(2):—

which includes the following buildings (*give a general description*):—

3   My main reasons for resisting the application are:—

4   My landlord is not acting fairly and reasonably because(3):—

5   I attach copies of the following relevant documents(4):—

Date ....   Signed(5) ....

(1)

    (a) If this form is completed by a sub-tenant, he should state whether he is sub-tenant of the whole or part of the holding; if of part, he should describe the part with reference to paragraphs 3 and 4 of the application and should state Ordnance Survey Field Numbers.

    (b) If this form is completed by a superior landlord, he should omit paragraph 2.

(2)

    (a) If you farm other land as part of the same unit with that which is the subject of the application, give a description, stating the area (in hectares) which is arable (including temporary grass), pasture (including rough grazing) and other land (including orchards) and giving the Ordnance Survey Field Numbers. If the land is farmed separately, give a general description, stating area, kind of farming and approximate distance from the holding in question.

(b) If the other land is not shown on the map produced by the landlord, you should produce a map of it of a scale of 6' to one mile or 1/10,000 (or larger) and giving the Ordnance Survey Field Numbers. If the land is not farmed as part of the same unit, or for any other good reason, you may, before or at the time of sending your reply, apply to the Secretary of the Tribunal in writing for the Chairman to dispense with the map.

(3) The Tribunal will not give consent if, in all the circumstances, it appears to them that a fair and reasonable landlord would not insist on possession. If you have any special reasons for saying your landlord is acting unfairly or unreasonably which do not appear under paragraph 3, you should state them under paragraph 4.

(4)

(a) Two copies of the reply and of any document which you wish to submit to the Tribunal must be sent to the Secretary, and, if there are more than two parties (*e.g.*, if holding or part of it is sublet), an additional copy of each must be supplied for each additional party.

(b) If you disagree with any map or plan attached to the application, your reply should be accompanied by two copies of a 6' to one mile or 1/10,000 (or larger) map showing what you consider to be the true position and marking the Ordnance Survey Field Numbers.

(5) If signed by any person other than the tenant himself, he should state in what capacity or by what authority he signs.

FORM 2

rule 3

Ref No

To be inserted by the Secretary.

AGRICULTURAL LAND TRIBUNAL

Application to Postpone Operation of Notice to Quit

To the Secretary of the Agricultural Land Tribunal for the .... Area.

1   I, ... (*block capitals*)

of .... (*address*),

hereby apply under Article 12(1) of the Agricultural Holdings (Arbitration on Notices) Order 1978 for the Tribunal to postpone the operation of the Notice to Quit served on me by my landlord:—

.... (*block capitals*)

of .... (*address*),

in respect of .... [*name or description of holding*].

2   The Tribunal consented on the .... day of .... 19 .... to the operation of the said notice on the application of my landlord bearing reference number ....

3   If its operation is not postponed the Notice will expire on the .... day of .... 19 ...

4   My main reasons for this application are:—

5   I attach two(1) copies of a 6' to one mile or 1/10,000(2) map of the land which was the subject of the notice to quit(3) and of the following documents which I intend to produce in support of my case:—

Date ....   Signed(4) ....

(1)   Two copies of the application and any map or document must be sent to the Secretary, and if there are more than two parties (*e.g.*, if the land is held under a sub-tenancy) an additional copy of the application etc., must be supplied for, and the Secretary must be informed of the name and address of, each additional party. A written notice is required (by Article 12(2) of the 1978 Order referred to above) to be given at the same time to the landlord.

(2)   A larger scale map may be used if preferred. Ordnance Survey Field Numbers must be marked on the map.

(3)   The Chairman of the Tribunal has power in all cases to dispense with maps, etc. A request for a direction on this subject should be made in writing before or at the time of sending the application.

(4)   If signed by any person other than the applicant himself, he should state in what capacity or by what authority he signs.

FORM 2R

Ref No

To be inserted by the Secretary.

AGRICULTURAL LAND TRIBUNAL

Reply to Application to Postpone Operation of Notice to Quit

To the Secretary of the Agricultural Land Tribunal for the .... Area.

I, ... (*block capitals*)

of .... (*address*),

landlord of .... (*name or description of holding*),

having received a copy of the application (bearing the above reference number) for the Tribunal to postpone the operation of the notice to quit the above named holding, reply as follows:—

1   The facts stated in the first three paragraphs of the application are correct except that:—

2
   *(a) I request that there should be no postponement.
   *(b) I would agree to postponement up to the .... day of .... ,
      19 ....

3   My main reasons for resisting the application are:—

4   I attach copies of the following relevant documents(1):—

Date ....   Signed(2) ....

* Strike out whichever is inapplicable.

(1)

(a) Two copies of the reply and of any document which you wish to submit to the Tribunal must be sent to the Secretary, and, if there are more than two parties (*e.g.*, if the land is sub-let), an additional copy of each must be supplied for each additional party.

(b) If you disagree with any map or plan attached to the application, your reply should be accompanied by two copies of a 6' to one mile or 1/10,000 (or larger) map showing what you consider to be the true position and marking the Ordnance Survey Field Numbers.

(2) If signed by any person other than the landlord himself, he should state in what capacity or by what authority he signs.

FORM 3

rule 4

Ref No

To be inserted by the Secretary.

AGRICULTURAL LAND TRIBUNAL

Application for Certificate of Bad Husbandry

To the Secretary of the Agricultural Land Tribunal for the .... Area.

1   I, ... (*block capitals*)

of .... (*address*),

hereby apply under section 2(4) of the Agricultural Holdings (Notices to Quit) Act 1977 for a certificate that my tenant, ... (*block capitals*)

of .... (*address*)

is not fulfilling his responsibility to farm .... (*name or description of holding*) in accordance with the rules of good husbandry.

2   The land consists of:—

(a)   .... hectares of arable land (including temporary grass) (Ordnance Survey Field Nos ....);

(b)   .... hectares of permanent pasture (Ordnance Survey Field Nos ....)

(c)   .... hectares of rough grazing (Ordnance Survey Field Nos ....);

(d)   .... hectares of other land (including orchards) (Ordnance Survey Field Nos ....);

Total .... hectares.

3   The holding includes the following buildings (*give a general description*):—

4   If a certificate of bad husbandry is granted I propose to serve a notice to quit.

5   The main grounds on which I allege bad husbandry are:—

6   I attach the following documents which I intend to produce in support of my case:—

(a)   two(1) copies of a 6' to one mile or 1/10,000(2) map of the holding described in paragraph 3 above;

(b)   two(1) copies of(3):—

Date ....   Signed(4) ....

1659

(1)   Two copies of the application and of any map and document must be sent to the Secretary, and if there are more than two parties (*e.g.*, if the holding or part of it is sub-let), an additional copy of the application, etc., must be supplied for, and the Secretary must be informed of the name and address of, each additional party.

(2)   A larger scale map may be used if preferred. Ordnance Survey Field Numbers must be marked on the map.

(3)   Mention any other document which is attached to this application.

(4)   If signed by any person other than the applicant himself, he should state in what capacity or by what authority he signs.

FORM 3R

Ref No

To be inserted by the Secretary.

AGRICULTURAL LAND TRIBUNAL

Reply to Application for Certificate of Bad Husbandry

To the Secretary of the Agricultural Land Tribunal for the .... Area.

I, ... (*block capitals*)

of .... (*address*),

tenant(1) of .... (*name or description of holding*),

having received a copy of the application (bearing the above reference number) for the Tribunal's certificate of bad husbandry, reply as follows:

1   The facts stated in the first three paragraphs of the application are correct except that:—

2   My main reasons for resisting the application are:—

3   I attach copies of the following relevant documents(2)

Date .... Signed(3) ....

(1)   If this form is completed by a sub-tenant, he should state whether he is sub-tenant of the whole or part of the holding; if of part, he should describe the part with reference to paragraph 2 and 3 of the application and should state Ordnance Survey Field Numbers.

(2)

    (a)   Two copies of the reply and of any document which you wish to submit to the Tribunal must be sent to the Secretary, and, if there are more than two parties (*e.g.*, if holding or part of it is sub-let), an additional copy of each must be supplied for each additional party.

    (b)   If you disagree with any map or plan attached to the application, your reply should be accompanied by two copies of a 6' to one mile or 1/10,000 (or larger) map showing what you consider to be the true position and marking the Ordnance Survey Field Numbers.

(3)   If signed by any person other than the tenant himself, he should state in what capacity or by what authority he signs.

FORM 4

rule 5

Ref No

To be inserted by the Secretary.

AGRICULTURAL LAND TRIBUNAL

Application for Variation or Revocation of Condition Imposed by the Tribunal

To the Secretary of the Agricultural Land Tribunal for the .... Area.

1   I, ... (*block capitals*)

of .... (*address*),

hereby apply under section 3(5) of the Agricultural Holdings (Notices to Quit) Act 1977 for the Tribunal to vary or revoke the condition imposed by them under section 3(4) thereof on granting my application bearing the reference number ....

2

    *(a) I wish the Tribunal to revoke the condition.

    *(b) I wish the Tribunal to revoke the condition; but if they are unwilling to do so, I request them to make the following variation:—

    *(c) I do not wish the Tribunal to revoke the condition, but only to make the following variation:—

3   The main reasons for my application are:—

4   I attach two(1) copies of a 6' to one mile or 1/10,000(2) map of the holding which was the subject of the notice to quit(3) and of the following documents which I intend to produce is support of my case(4):—

Date ....   Signed(5) ....

* Strike out whichever is inapplicable.

(1)   Two copies of the application and of any map and document must be sent to the Secretary.

(2)   A larger scale map may be used if preferred. Ordnance Survey Field Number must be marked on the map.

(3)   The Chairman of the Tribunal has power in all cases to dispense with maps, etc. (*e.g.*, if they are already in the possession of the Tribunal). A request for a direction on this subject should be made in writing before or at the time of sending the application.

(4)   Mention any other document which is attached to the application.

(5)   If signed by any person other than the applicant himself, he should state in what capacity or by what authority he signs.

FORM 5

rule 6(1)

Ref No

To be inserted by the Secretary.

AGRICULTURAL LAND TRIBUNAL

Application for Direction to Provide Fixed Equipment

To the Secretary of the Agricultural Land Tribunal for the .... Area.

1 I, ... (*block capitals*)

of .... (*address*),

tenant of .... (*name or description of holding*),

hereby apply under section 4 of the Agriculture Act 1958 for the Tribunal to direct my landlord .... (*block capitals*) of .... (*address*)

to carry out the following work on the said holding:—

2

    (a)   On the .... day of .... , 19 .... , I requested my landlord in writing to carry out the said work and he *refused on the .... day of .... , 19 .... ,has had reasonable time to agree but has not done so.

    (b)   No term in my contract of tenancy or in any other agreement binds me or my landlord to carry out the said work.

    (c)   My landlord is not bound by any enactment to carry out the said work.

3 The holding consists of:—

    (a)   .... hectares of arable land (including temporary grass) (Ordnance Survey Field Nos ....);

    (b)   .... hectares of permanent pasture (Ordnance Survey Field Nos ....);

    (c)   .... hectares of rough grazing (Ordnance Survey Field Nos ....);

    (d)   .... hectares of other land (including orchards) (Ordnance Survey Field Nos ....).

Total .... hectares.

4 The holding includes the following buildings:—

5 The type of farming carried on the holding is(1):—

6 I wish to carry on the following agricultural activity on the said holding to the extent and in the manner specified, *viz.*:—

7 If I were to do so without the said work being carried out, I should contravene the following statutory requirements in the following respects:—

8 I attach the following documents which I intend to produce in support of my case:—

    (a)   two(2) copies of a 6' to one mile or 1/10,000(3) map of the holding described in paragraph 3 above,

    (b)   two(2) copies of the following plan:—

    (c)   two(2) copies of my contract of tenancy and any other document(4):—

Date ....   Signed(5) ....

* Strike out whichever is inapplicable.

(1) Under section 4(1) of the Agriculture Act 1958 the Tribunal cannot direct a landlord to carry out work in connection with an agricultural activity specified in the tenant's application where the activity has not been carried on the holding for a period of at least three years immediately preceding the making of the application unless they

are satisfied that the starting of the activity did not or, where it has not yet been started, will not constitute or form part of a substantial alteration of the type of farming carried on the holding.

(2) Two copies of the application and of any map and document must be sent to the Secretary, and if there are more than two parties (*e.g.*, if the land is held under a sub-tenancy), an additional copy of the contract of tenancy and of the application, etc., must be supplied for, and the Secretary must be informed of the name and address of, each additional party.

(3) A larger scale map may be used if preferred. Ordnance Survey Field Numbers must be marked on the map.

(4) Mention any other document which is attached to this application. The Chairman of the Tribunal has power in all cases to dispense with maps or other documents (*e.g.*, where the landlord already has a copy of the contract of tenancy). A request for a direction on this subject should be made in writing before or at the time of sending the application.

(5) If signed by any person other than the applicant himself, he should state in what capacity or by what authority he signs.

FORM 5R

Ref No

To be inserted by the Secretary.

AGRICULTURAL LAND TRIBUNAL

Reply to Application for Direction to Provide Fixed Equipment

To the Secretary of the Agricultural Land Tribunal for the .... Area.

I, ... (*block capitals*)

of .... (*address*),

landlord(1) of .... (*name or description of holding*),

having received a copy of the application (bearing the above reference number) for the Tribunal's direction to me to carry out certain work on the said holding, reply as follows:—

1 With regard to paragraph 2(a) of the application, I—

*(a) agree that the request was made and refused;
*(b) agree that the request was made, but
    *(i) deny that it was refused,
    *(ii) say that I have not yet had reasonable time to agree to it;
*(c) deny that the request was made.

2 The other facts stated in the first four paragraphs of the application are correct, except that:—

3 My main reasons for resisting the application are:—

*(a) that the carrying on of the activity specified in paragraph 6 of the application to the extent and in the manner specified therein—
    *(i) will not involve the contravention of any statutory requirement even if the said work is not carried out;
    *(ii) would be unreasonable having regard to the tenant's responsibilities to farm the holding in accordance with the rules of good husbandry;

*(b) that the activity specified in paragraph 6 of the application has not been carried on on the holding for a period of at least three years immediately preceding the making of the application and that the starting of the activity *constitutes/forms part of a substantial alteration of the type of farming carried on on the holding;

*(c) that the direction asked for would be unreasonable having regard to—

*(i) my responsibilities to manage the land comprised in the holding in accordance with the rules of good estate management;

*(ii) the period for which the holding may be expected to remain a separate holding;

*(iii) (*any other reasons*).

4   I attach copies of the following relevant documents(2):—

Date .... Signed(3) ....

* Strike out whichever is inapplicable.

(1)   If this form is completed by a superior landlord he should omit paragraph 1.

(2)

(a)   Two copies of the reply and of any document which you wish to submit to the Tribunal must be sent to the Secretary, and, if there are more than two parties (*e.g.*, if the holding is sublet), an additional copy of each must be supplied for each additional party.

(b)   If you disagree with any map or plan attached to the application, your reply should be accompanied by two copies of a 6' to one mile or 1/10,000 (or larger) map showing what you consider to be the true position and marking the Ordnance Survey Field Numbers.

(3)   If signed by any person other than the landlord himself, he should state in what capacity or by what authority he signs.

FORM 6

rule 7(1)

Ref No

To be inserted by the Secretary.

AGRICULTURAL LAND TRIBUNAL

Application for Approval of Long–Term Improvement

To the Secretary of the Agricultural Land Tribunal for the .... Area.

1   I, ... (*block capitals*)

of .... (*address*),

tenant of .... (*name or description of holding*),

hereby apply for the Tribunal's approval under section 50 of the Agricultural Holdings Act 1948 (as amended by the Agriculture Act 1958) of the carrying out of the following improvement(s) on the said holding:—

2   My landlord is .... (*block capitals*)

of .... (*address*).

3   The holding consists of:—

(a) .... hectares of arable land (including temporary grass) (Ordnance Survey Field Nos ....);

(b) .... hectares of permanent pasture (Ordnance Survey Field Nos ....);

(c) .... hectares of rough grazing (Ordnance Survey Field Nos ....);

(d) .... hectares of other land (including orchards) (Ordnance Survey Field Nos ....).

Total .... hectares.

4   The holding includes the following buildings:— (*give a general description*)

5   I requested my landlord on the .... day of .... , 19 .... , to consent in writing to the carrying out of the said improvement(s), but he—

*(a) refuses to give his consent.

*(b) will only consent subject to the following terms to which I am unwilling to agree:—(*state the terms and your reason for not agreeing*)

6   My main reasons for wishing for the improvements to be carried out are:—

7   I attach the following documents which I intend to produce in support of my case:—

(a) two(1) copies of a 6' to one mile or 1/10,000(2) map of the holding described in paragraph 4 above;

(b) two(1) copies of the following plan:—

(c) two(1) copies of (3):—

Date ....   Signed(4) ....

* Strike out whichever is inapplicable.

(1)   Two copies of the application and of any map and document must be sent to the Secretary, and if there are more than two parties (*e.g.*, if the holding is held under a sub-tenancy), an additional copy of the application, etc., must be supplied for, and the Secretary must be informed of the name and address of, each additional party.

(2)   A larger scale map may be used if preferred. Ordnance Survey Field Numbers must be marked on the map.

(3)   Mention any other document which is attached to this application.

(4)   If signed by any person other than the applicant himself, he should state in what capacity or by what authority he signs.

FORM 6R

Ref No

To be inserted by the Secretary.

AGRICULTURAL LAND TRIBUNAL

Reply to Application for Approval of Long–Term Improvement

To the Secretary of the Agricultural Land Tribunal for the .... Area.

I, ... (*block capitals*)

of .... (*address*),

landlord of .... (*name or description of holding*),

1665

having received a copy of the application (bearing the above reference number) for the Tribunal's approval under section 50 of the Agricultural Holdings Act 1948 (as amended) of the carrying out on the said holding of the improvement(s) specified therein, reply as follows:

1   The facts stated in the first four paragraphs of the application are correct except that:—

2

*(a) I deny that the request referred to in paragraph 5 of the application was made.
*(b) I do not wish the improvements to be carried out because:—
*(c) I agree the improvements being carried out subject to the following terms:—
   (*state terms and any special reasons*)

3   My main reasons for resisting the application are:—

4   I attach copies of the following relevant documents(1):—

Date ....   Signed(2) ....

* Strike out whichever is inapplicable.

(1)

   (a) Two copies of the reply and of any document which you wish to submit to the Tribunal should be sent to the Secretary, and, if there are more than two parties (*e.g..*, if the holding is sub-let), an additional copy of each must be supplied for each additional party.

   (b) If you disagree with any map or plan attached to the application your reply should be accompanied by two copies of a 6' to one mile or 1/10,000 (or larger) map or plan showing what you consider to be the true position and marking the Ordnance Survey Field Numbers.

(2)   If signed by any person other than the landlord himself, he should state in what capacity or by what authority he signs.

FORM 7

rule 7(3)

Ref. No

To be inserted by the Secretary.

AGRICULTURAL LAND TRIBUNAL

Application for Determination that Landlord has Failed to carry out Improvement within a Reasonable Time

To the Secretary of the Agricultural Land Tribunal for the .... Area.

1   I, ... (*block capitals*)

of .... (*address*),

tenant of .... (*name or description of holding*),

hereby apply to the Tribunal in pursuance of section 50(4)(b) of the Agricultural Holdings Act 1948 (as amended by the Agriculture Act 1958) to determine that my landlord: .... (*block capitals*)

of .... (*address*)

has failed within a reasonable time to carry out the following improvements to the said holding:—

2   The said improvement was approved by the Tribunal on my application bearing reference number ....

3   The Tribunal's decision was dated .... day of .... , 19 .... , and my landlord notified me of his proposal to carry out the said improvement himself on the .... day of .... , 19 .... ,

4   My landlord has failed to carry out the said improvements:—(*if he has done any part of them, give particulars*)

5   My main reasons for saying that the delay is unreasonable are:—

6   I attach two(1) copies each of—

    (a) a 6' to one mile or 1/10,000(2) map of the holding(3);
    (b) the following plan showing the intended improvement(s):—
    (c) the following other documents(4):—

Date ....   Signed(5) ....

(1)   Two copies of the application and of any map and document must be sent to the Secretary, and if there are more than two parties (*e.g.*, if the holding is held under a sub-tenancy), an additional copy of the application, etc., must be supplied for, and the Secretary must be informed of the name and address of, each additional party.

(2)   A larger scale map may be used if preferred. Ordnance Survey Field Numbers must be marked on the map.

(3)   The Chairman of the Tribunal has power in all cases to dispense with maps, etc. (*e.g.*, if they are already in the possession of the Tribunal or the other parties). A request for a direction on this subject should be made in writing before or at the time of sending the application.

(4)   Mention any other documents which are attached to the application.

(5)   If signed by any person other than the applicant himself, he should state in what capacity or by what authority he signs.

FORM 7R

Ref No

To be inserted by the Secretary.

AGRICULTURAL LAND TRIBUNAL

Reply to Application for Determination that Landlord has Failed to carry out Improvement within a Reasonable Time

To the Secretary of the Agricultural Land Tribunal for the .... Area.

I, ... (*block capitals*)

of .... (*address*),

landlord of .... (*name or description of holding*),

having received a copy of the application (bearing the above reference number) for the Tribunal's determination that I have failed within a reasonable time to carry out on the said holding the improvements(s) specified therein, reply as follows:—

1   The facts stated in the first three paragraphs of the application are correct except that:—

2 My main reasons for resisting the application are:—

*(a) I have adequately carried out the said improvement(s);

*(b) I intend to carry out the said improvement(s) but have not yet had reasonable time to do so for the following reasons:— (*give particulars*)

*(c) (*any other reasons*)

3 I attach copies of the following relevant documents(1):—

Date .... Signed(2) ....

* Strike out whichever is inapplicable.

(1)

(a) Two copies of the reply and of any document which you wish to submit to the Tribunal must be sent to the Secretary, and, if there are more than two parties (*e.g.*, if the holding is sub-let) an additional copy of each must be supplied for each additional party.

(b) If you disagree with any map or plan attached to the application your reply should be accompanied by two copies of a 6' to one mile to 1/10,000 (or larger) map or plan showing what you consider to be the true position and marking the Ordnance Survey Field Numbers.

(2) If signed by any person other than the landlord himself he should state in what capacity or by what authority he signs.

FORM 8

rule 8

Ref No

To be inserted by the Secretary.

AGRICULTURAL LAND TRIBUNAL

Application for Direction to Treat an Agricultural Holding as a Market Garden

To the Secretary of the Agricultural Land Tribunal for the .... Area.

1 I, ... (*block capitals*)

of .... (*address*),

tenant of .... (*name or description of holding*),

hereby apply to the Tribunal to direct under section 68 of the Agricultural Holdings Act 1948 (as amended by the Agriculture Act 1958) that *the said holding/the part of the said holding specified in paragraph 6 below shall be treated as a market garden so that section 67 of the said Act shall apply.

2 My landlord is .... (*block capitals*)

of .... (*address*).

3 I requested him on the .... day of .... 19 .... , to agree in writing to the (part of the) holding being so treated, but he *refused on the .... day of .... 19 .... , /has had reasonable time but has failed to do so.

4 The holding consists of:—

(a) .... hectares of arable land (including temporary grass) (Ordnance Survey Field Nos ....);

(b) .... hectares of permanent pasture (Ordnance Survey Field Nos ....);

(c) .... hectares of rough grazing (Ordnance Survey Field Nos ....);

(d) .... hectares of other land (including orchards) (Ordnance Survey Field Nos ....);

Total .... hectares.

5 The holding includes the following buildings:—(*give a general description*)

6 I wish to make the following improvements:—

Ordnance Survey Field Nos .... Improvements

7 For the following main reasons I request the Tribunal to direct that the *holding/part of the holding described in paragraph 6 above be treated as a market garden:—

8 I attach the following documents which I intend to produce in support of my case:—

(a) two(1) copies of a 6' to one mile or 1/10,000(2) map of the holding described in paragraph 4 above;

(b) two(1) copies of the following plan:—

(c) two(1) copies of(3):—

Date ....   Signed(4) ....

* Strike out whichever is inapplicable.

(1) Two copies of the application and of any map and document must be sent to the Secretary, and if there are more than two parties (*e.g.*, if the holding is held under a sub-tenancy), an additional copy of the application, etc., must be supplied for, and the Secretary must be informed of the name and address of, each additional party.

(2) A larger scale map may be used if preferred. Ordnance Survey Field Numbers must be marked on the map.

(3) Mention any other document which is attached to this application.

(4) If signed by any person other than the applicant himself, he should state in what capacity or by what authority he signs.

FORM 8R

Ref No

To be inserted by the Secretary.

AGRICULTURAL LAND TRIBUNAL

Reply to Application for Direction to Treat an Agricultural Holding as a Market Garden

To the Secretary of the Agricultural Land Tribunal for the .... Area.

I, ... (*block capitals*)

of .... (*address*),

landlord(1) of .... (*name or description of holding*),

having received a copy of the application (bearing the above reference number) for the Tribunal's direction under section 68 of the Agricultural Holdings Act 1948 (as amended) that the said holding or part thereof should be treated as a market garden in respect of the improvement(s) specified therein, reply as follows):—

1   With regard to paragraph 3 of the application, I—

   *(a) agree that the request was made and refused;
   *(b) agree that the request was made, but say that
        *(i) I did agree to it in writing on the .... day of .... 19 ....
        *(ii) I have not yet had reasonable time to agree to it;
   (c)   deny that the request was made.

2   The other facts stated in the application are correct except that:—

3   My main reasons for resisting the application are:—

   (a)   the land is unsuitable for market gardening for the following reasons:—
   (b)   (*any other reasons*)

4   (1)   If the Tribunal decide to give the direction applied for, I request them to limit its effect to the following improvement(s):—

(2)   My main reasons for this would be:—

5   I attach copies of the following relevant documents(2):—

Date ....   Signed(3) ....

* Strike out whichever is inapplicable.

(1)   If this form is completed by a superior landlord, he should omit paragraph 1.

(2)

   (a)   Two copies of the reply and of any document you wish to submit to the Tribunal must be sent to the Secretary, and, if there are more than two parties (*e.g.*, if the holding is sub-let), an additional copy of each must be supplied for each additional party.
   (b)   If you disagree with any map or plan attached to the application your reply should be accompanied by two copies of a 6' to one mile or 1/10,000 (or larger) map or plan showing what you consider to be the true position and marking the Ordnance Survey Field Numbers.

(3)   If signed by any person other than the landlord himself he should state in what capacity or by what authority he signs.

FORM 9

rule 9

Ref No

To be inserted by the Secretary.

AGRICULTURAL LAND TRIBUNAL

Application for Direction to Avoid or Relax Covenant against the Burning of Heather or Grass

To the Secretary of the Agricultural Land Tribunal for the .... Area.

1   I, ... (*block capitals*)

of .... (*address*),

tenant of .... (*name or description of holding*), hereby apply under section 21 of the Hill Farming Act 1946 (as amended by the Agriculture Act 1958) for the Tribunal's direction that the covenants, conditions or agreements contained in my lease and specified in paragraph 3 below be avoided or relaxed.

2   My landlord is .... (*block capitals*)

of .... (*address*).

3   The *covenant(s)/condition(s)/agreement(s) to which I refer is (are) numbered .... in my lease and I ask the Tribunal to direct that it (they) be—

   *(a) avoided completely;
   *(b) relaxed in the following way:—
      *(i) permanently;
      *(ii) for the following period:—

4   The holding consists of:—

   (a)   .... hectares of arable land (including temporary grass) (Ordnance Survey Field Nos ....);
   (b)   .... hectares of permanent pasture (Ordnance Survey Field Nos ....);
   (c)   .... hectares of rough grazing (Ordnance Survey Field Nos ....);
   (d)   .... hectares of other land (including orchards) (Ordnance Survey field Nos ....);

Total .... hectares.

5   The *covenant(s)/condition(s)/agreement(s) mentioned in paragraph 3 above is (are) *impeding/preventing the proper use of the land for agricultural purposes in the following way:—

and I wish it (them) to be *avoided/relaxed so as to allow me to burn .... hectares of *heather/grass.

6   I attach:—

   (a)   two(1) copies of my lease(2);
   (b)   two(1) copies of a 6' to one mile or 1/10,000(3) map of the land described in paragraph 4 above;
   (c)   two(1) copies each of the following other documents(4):—

Date ....   Signed(5) ....

* Strike out whichever is inapplicable.

(1)   Two copies of the application and of any map and document must be sent to the Secretary, and if there are more than two parties (*e.g.*, if the land is held under a sub-tenancy), an additional copy of the application, etc., must be supplied for, and the Secretary must be informed of the name and address of, each additional party.

(2)   The Chairman of the Tribunal has power in all cases to dispense with maps or other documents (*e.g.*, where the landlord already has a copy of the lease). A request for a direction on this subject should be made in writing before or at the time of sending the application.

(3)   A larger scale map may be used if preferred. Ordnance Survey Field Numbers must be marked on the map.

(4)   Mention any other document which is attached to this application.

(5) If signed by any person other than the applicant himself, he should state in what capacity or by what authority he signs.

FORM 9R

Ref No

To be inserted by the Secretary.

AGRICULTURAL LAND TRIBUNAL

Reply to Application for Direction to Avoid or Relax Covenant against the Burning of Heather or Grass

To the Secretary of the Agricultural Land Tribunal for the .... Area.

I, ... (*block capitals*)

of .... (*address*),

landlord of .... (*name or description of holding*),

having received a copy of the application (bearing the above reference number) for the Tribunal's direction that certain covenants, conditions or agreements in the applicant's lease should be avoided or relaxed, reply as follows:—

1 The facts contained in the first four paragraphs of the application are correct except that:—

2

*(a) I do not wish any covenant, condition or agreement to be avoided or relaxed in any way.

*(b) I would agree to the following * covenant(s)/condition(s)/agreement(s) being avoided/relaxed as follows:—

3 For the following main reasons I do not agree that the * covenant(s)/condition(s)/agreement(s) is (are) impeding or preventing the proper use of the land for agricultural purposes or that (except as agreed in paragraph (2)(b) above) it would be expedient to relax or avoid it (them):—

4 I attach copies of the following relevant documents(1):—

Date ....   Signed(2) ....

* Strike out whichever is inapplicable.

(1)

(a) Two copies of the reply and of any document which you wish to submit to the Tribunal must be sent to the Secretary, and, if there are more than two parties (*e.g.*, if the holding is sub-let), an additional copy of each must be supplied for each additional party.

(b) If you disagree with any map or plan attached to the application, your reply should be accompanied by two copies of a 6' to one mile or 1/10,000 (or larger) map showing what you consider to be the true position and marking the Ordnance Survey Field Numbers.

(2) If signed by any person other than the landlord himself, he should state in what capacity or by what authority he signs.

FORM 10

rule 10(1)

Ref No

To be inserted by the Secretary.

AGRICULTURAL LAND TRIBUNAL

Application for Determination that a Person be Treated as Owner of Land

To the Secretary of the Agricultural Land Tribunal for the .... Area.

1   I, ... (*block capitals*)

of .... (*address*),

hereby apply to the Tribunal to determine under section 21 of the Agriculture Act 1947 that—

   *(a) .... (*block capitals*)
   of .... (*address*)
   *(b) I

be treated for the purposes of section 20 of the Mineral Workings Act 1951 as the owner of the land known as:— .... (*name or description*).

2   My own interest in the land is:—

3   The following person(s) would be affected by the granting of this application(1):—

4   The land consists of:—

   (a)   .... hectares of arable land (including temporary grass) (Ordnance Survey Field Nos ....);

   (b)   .... hectares of permanent pasture (Ordnance Survey Field Nos .... ;

   (c)   .... hectares of rough grazing (Ordnance Survey Field Nos ....);

   (d)   .... hectares of other land (including orchards) (Ordnance Survey Field Nos ....);

Total .... hectares.

5   The land includes the following buildings:—(*give a general description*)

6   The Minister of Agriculture, Fisheries and Food proposes to make the following arrangements for the purpose of taking the following special steps (as referred to in the said section 20):—(*describe briefly*)

7   My main reasons for this application are:—

8   I attach the following documents which I intend to produce in support of my case:—

   (a)   two(2) copies of a 6' to one mile or 1/10,000(3) map of the land described in paragraph 4 above;

   (b)   two(2) copies of(4):—

Date ....   Signed(5) ....

*Strike out whichever is inapplicable.

(1)   State name and address of any person mentioned and whether he is owner or occupier or what other interest he has in the land.

(2) Two copies of the application and of any map and document must be sent to the Secretary, and if there is more than one party named in paragraph 3, an additional copy of the application, etc., must be supplied for each additional party.

(3) A larger scale map may be used if preferred. Ordnance Survey Field Numbers must be marked on the map.

(4) Mention any other document which is attached to the application.

(5) If signed by any person other than the applicant himself, he should state in what capacity or by what authority he signs.

FORM 10R

Ref No

To be inserted by the Secretary.

AGRICULTURAL LAND TRIBUNAL

Reply to Application for Determination that a Person be Treated as Owner of Land

To the Secretary of the Agricultural Land Tribunal for the .... Area.

I, ... (*block capitals*)

of .... (*address*),

having received a copy of the application (bearing the above reference number), reply as follows:—

1 The facts stated in the first five paragraphs of the application are correct except that:—

2 My main reasons for resisting the application are:

3 I attach copies of the following relevant documents(1)—

Date .... Signed(2) ....

(1)

    (a) Two copies of the reply and of any document which you wish to submit to the Tribunal must be sent to the Secretary, and, if there are more than two parties, an additional copy of each must be supplied for each additional party.

    (b) If you disagree with any map or plan attached to the application, your reply should be accompanied by two copies of a 6' to one mile or 1/10,000 (or larger) map showing what you consider to be the true position and marking the Ordnance Survey Field Numbers.

(2) If signed by any person other than the party himself, he should state in what capacity or by what authority he signs.

FORM 11

rule 11(1)

Ref No

To be inserted by the Secretary.

AGRICULTURAL LAND TRIBUNAL

Application Under Land Drainage Act 1976

To the Secretary of the Agricultural Land Tribunal for the .... Area.

1 I, ... (*block capitals*)

of .... (*address*),

hereby apply to the Tribunal for an order under section 40 of the Land Drainage Act 1976 requiring .... (*state name(s) of person(s) against whom order is sought*)(1) to carry out the work mentioned in paragraph 6 on the ground that (the land mentioned in paragraph 3, of which I am the ** owner/occupier, is being injured) (*or* the improvement of the drainage of the land mentioned in paragraph 3, of which I am the ** owner/occupier, is being prevented) by the condition of the ditch mentioned in paragraph 4.

* To be used for application under s 40.

** Strike out whichever is inapplicable.

**(In the event of the Tribunal deciding not to make such an order I hereby apply in the alternative under section 41 of the said Act for an order authorising me to carry out the said work.)

**Strike out if inapplicable.

OR

*(1 I, ... (*block capitals*)

of .... (*address*),

hereby apply to the Tribunal under section 41 of the Land Drainage Act 1976 for an order authorising me to carry out the work mentioned in paragraph 6 on the ground that the drainage of the land mentioned in paragraph 3, of which I am the ** owner/occupier, requires the carrying out of such work.)

*To be used for application under s 41.

**Strike out whichever is inapplicable.

*(2 I ask that the said order should authorise me (*or* the person required to carry out the said work) to enter on the land mentioned in paragraph 4 (and paragraph 7) so far as may be necessary for the carrying out of the said work.)

*To be used for application under s 40 or s 41: strike out if no such authority is asked for.

3 I am the *owner/occupier of (*describe the land affected by application and give Ordnance Survey Field Numbers*).

*Strike out whichever is inapplicable.

*4 Injury to my said land is being caused (and/or the improvement of the drainage of my said land is being prevented) by the condition of the under-mentioned ditch (*specify ditch, stating land through which it passes and if possible the Ordnance Survey Field Numbers of that land*).

*To be used for application under s 40.

OR

*(4   The drainage of my said land requires:—

*(a) the carrying out of work in connection with the under-mentioned ditch:
*(b) and/or the replacement or construction of the under-mentioned ditch:
*(c) and/or the alteration or removal of drainage work in connection with the under-mentioned ditch:

(*specify ditch, stating land through which it passes and if possible the Ordnance Survey Field Numbers of that land*)   ....)

*to be used for application under s 41.

**Strike out whichever is inapplicable.

5   The condition of the said ditch and its effect on my land is as follows (and/or the construction of the said ditch is required for the following reason):

6   The work which is required to be carried out is as follows:—

*(7   For the purpose of carrying out the said work it will be necessary to enter the under-mentioned land in addition to that mentioned in paragraph 4 (*described land, stating Ordnance Survey Field Numbers if possible*).

*Strike out if inapplicable.

8   This application affects the interests of the following persons:(2)

(a)   .... (*block capitals*)

of .... (*address*)

who is the *owner/occupier of (the following part of) the land mentioned in paragraph 4 (*or* 7) of this application (*or as the case may be*)(3)

(b)   .... (*block capitals*)

of .... (*address*)

who is the * owner/occupier of (the following part of) the land mentioned in paragraph 4 (*or* 7) of this application (*or as the case may be*).(3)

* Strike out whichever is inapplicable.

* (9   To the best of my information and belief the following persons in addition to those named in paragraph 8 have rights in or over the said ditch and the land through which it passes:

(a)   .... (*block capitals*)

of .... (*address*)

who is ....

(b)   .... (*block capitals*)

of .... (*address*)

who is ....)

* Strike out if inapplicable.

10   I attach the following documents which I intend to produce in support of my case:—

(a)   two(4) copies of a 6' to one mile or 1/10,000(5) map of the land described in paragraphs 3 and 4 (and 7) above;
(b)   two(4) copies of(6):—

Date .... Signed(7) ....

(1) Section 40 enables an order to be made against the owner or occupier of land through which the ditch passes or which abuts on the ditch or against any person who, although not such an owner or occupier, has a right to carry out the work specified in the order.

(2) State the names of all persons who are to be parties to the proceedings. These must include any person against whom an order is applied for under section 40 as well as the name of the occupier of any land on which entry may be necessary for carrying out work under section 40 or 41 and, in the case of an application under section 41, the name of the owner of any land on which it is proposed that any work should be carried out. If more than two persons are named, continue on separate sheet.

(3) State whether owner or occupier of the land or persons having a right to carry out the proposed work on the ditch mentioned in paragraph 4.

(4) Two copies of the application and of any map and document must be sent to the Secretary, and if there are more than two parties, an additional copy of the application, etc., must be supplied for each additional party.

(5) A larger scale map may be used if preferred. Ordnance Survey Field Numbers must be marked on the map where required.

(6) Mention any other document which is attached to this application.

(7) If signed by any person other than the applicant himself, he should state in what capacity or by what authority he signs.

FORM 11R

Ref No

To be inserted by the Secretary.

AGRICULTURAL LAND TRIBUNAL

Reply to Application Under Land Drainage Act 1976

To the Secretary of the Agricultural Land Tribunal for the .... Area.

I, ... (*block capitals*)

of .... (*address*),

having received a copy of the application (bearing the above reference number) and of the report provided by the Minister of Agriculture, Fisheries and Food for the purpose thereof and of the applicant's notice in Form 12 reply as follows:—

1 The facts stated in the said application and in the said report are correct except that:—

2
  *(a) I agree to an order being made
    *(i) in the terms of the recommendation in the report; or
    *(ii) in the terms asked for in the application [*if different from those recommended in the report*]; or
    *(iii) in the terms stated in the applicant's notice.
  *(b) I resist the application

*Strike out whichever is inapplicable.

1677

3   * My main reasons for resisting the application are:—

*Strike out if inapplicable.

4   I attach copies of the following relevant documents(1):—

Date .... Signed(2) ....

(1)

(a) Two copies of the reply and of any document which you wish to submit to the Tribunal must be sent to the Secretary, and, if there are more than two parties, an additional copy of each must be supplied for each additional party.

(b) If you disagree with any map or plan attached to the application or if, in your reply, you mention any land not shown thereon, your reply should be accompanied by two copies of a 6' to one mile or 1/10,000 (or larger) map showing what you consider to be the true position or showing the other land mentioned in your reply, as the case may be, and marking the Ordnance Survey Field Numbers.

(2)   If signed by any person other than the party himself, he should state in what capacity or by what authority he signs.

FORM 12

rule 21(4)

Ref No

To be inserted by the Secretary.

AGRICULTURAL LAND TRIBUNAL

Land Drainage Act 1976
Notice by Applicant under Rule 21(4) of the Agricultural Land Tribunals Rules 1978

To the Secretary of the Agricultural Land Tribunal for the .... Area.

I, ... (*block capitals*)

of .... (*address*),

having applied to the Tribunal on the .... day of .... 19 .... (under reference number ....) for an order under section 40 (and/or section 41)* of the Land Drainage Act 1976, and having received a copy of the report provided by the Minister of Agriculture, Fisheries and Food for the purpose of my application, state as follows:

*Strike out whichever is inapplicable.

1   I accept the facts stated in the report with the exception of:

2

*(a) I accept the recommendation made in the report and hereby request the Tribunal to make an order on my application in the terms of the recommendation.

*(b) I do not accept the recommendation made in the report and I request the Tribunal to make an order on my application in the terms asked for therein (*or* in the following modified terms).

* Strike out whichever is inapplicable.

3   I attach the following documents which I intend to produce in support of my case:—(1)

Date .... Signed(2) ....

(1) Two copies of this notice must be sent to the Secretary together with two copies of any map or document which you wish to submit to the Tribunal and which has not already been submitted with the application. If there are more than two parties, an additional copy of the notice, etc., must be supplied for each additional party.

(2) If signed by any person other than the applicant himself, he should state in what capacity or by what authority he signs.

FORM 13

rule 23(4)

Ref No

To be inserted by the Secretary.

AGRICULTURAL LAND TRIBUNAL

Notice of Hearing

Land at: ....

Applicant/s: ....

Respondent/s: ....

TAKE NOTICE that the HEARING of the APPLICATION in respect of the above named Holding will be held on .... at .... commencing at ....

Dated .... 19 .... Signed ....
                    (Secretary of the Tribunal)

NOTE TO PARTIES

You may find of assistance the following note of rules of evidence and procedure, which apply to this hearing and which are contained in the Agricultural Land Tribunals Rules 1978.

1 Rules of Evidence

    (a) Any evidence may be admitted by the tribunal, including evidence that would not be admissible in a court of law.

    (b) Evidence before the tribunal may be given—
        (i) orally, on oath or on affirmation or otherwise,
        (ii) by affidavit, if the parties consent, or
        (iii) by means of written statements produced by the maker when giving evidence or, if the tribunal consent, by another witness.

If evidence is tendered in the form of a written statement, four copies of the statement should be available at the hearing for the tribunal and two copies for the other parties.

    (c) At any stage of the proceedings the tribunal may, of their own motion or on the application of any party, order the personal attendance of the maker of any written statement for examination and cross-examination.

    (d) The secretary may require a party to give to the tribunal documents or other information, and to afford to all other parties an opportunity to inspect such documents, or copies of them, and to take copies of them.

If the parties intend to produce documents at the hearing, they should if possible agree them beforehand, list them in order and put them into one agreed bundle. Four copies of this bundle should be available if possible for the use of the tribunal.

(e) The tribunal may, after giving notice to all parties and to any other occupier of the land, enter and inspect any agricultural holding owned or occupied by any party, whether the holding is the subject of the proceedings or not, and may inspect any fixed or other equipment, produce or livestock thereon.

2 Procedure at the Hearing

(a) The tribunal sit in public unless exceptional circumstances make it desirable that the hearing, or some part of it, should take place in private.

(b) A party may appear and be heard in person or by counsel or solicitor or by a representative appointed in writing.

(c) The party making the application will begin and the other parties will be heard in such order as the tribunal may determine.

3 Witnesses

(a) Each party will be given an opportunity to call and cross-examine witnesses, and a party may if he wishes give evidence as a witness on his own behalf.

(b) The tribunal may call witnesses, who may after giving evidence be cross-examined by any party.

(c) The provisions of the County Court Rules 1936, as amended, as to the issue of witness summonses (Order 20, rule 8) apply for the purposes of any proceedings before the tribunal. Under these Rules, a party desiring a person to be summoned as a witness must apply to the [district judge] by filling in the prescribed form in the county court office.

4 Default of Appearance

If a party fails to appear at the time fixed for the hearing, the tribunal may—

(i) dismiss the application where the party failing to appear is the applicant, or

(ii) proceed in any other case to determine the application in the party's absence, if satisfied that the party failing to appear has been afforded an adequate opportunity of attending.

FORM 14

rule 32

Ref No

To be inserted by the Secretary.

AGRICULTURAL LAND TRIBUNAL

Application for Variation of Order made under Land Drainage Act 1976

To the Secretary of the Agricultural Land Tribunal for the .... Area.

1 I, ... (*block capitals*)

of .... (*address*),

hereby apply to the Tribunal to vary its order dated the .... day of .... 19 ....

2 The order was made on *(my application) (the application of .... (*block capitals*)

of .... (*address*))

bearing the reference number ....

* Strike out whichever is inapplicable.

3 The variation for which I apply is:—

4 My main reasons for making this application are:—

5 I attach copies of the following documents which I intend to produce in support of my case(1):—

Date .... Signed(2) ....

(1) Two copies of this application and of any document which you wish to submit to the Tribunal must be sent to the Secretary, and, if there are more than two parties, an additional copy of each must be supplied for each additional party.

(2) If signed by any person other than the applicant himself, he should state in what capacity or by what authority he signs.

NOTES

Amendment

Form 13: in para 3(c) words 'district judge' in square brackets substituted by the Courts and Legal Services Act 1990, s 74(1)(a), (3).

Date in force: 1 January 1991: see SI 1990/2484, art 2, Schedule.

See Further

See further, in relation to references to orders made under the Land Drainage Act 1976: the Water Consolidation (Consequential Provisions) Act 1991, Sch 2, para 15(2).

AGRICULTURE (CALCULATION OF VALUE FOR COMPENSATION) REGULATIONS 1978

SI 1978/809

Authority: Agricultural Holdings Act 1986, s 66(2)

NOTES

Continuation

Authority: following the consolidation of the original enabling power, these Regulations have effect as if made under the Agricultural Holdings Act 1986, s 66(2).

A1.525

1 Citation and commencement

These regulations may be cited as the Agriculture (Calculation of Value for Compensation) Regulations 1978, and shall come into operation on 1st July 1978.

A1.526

2 Interpretation

(1) In these regulations, unless the context otherwise requires,—

'the Act' means the Agricultural Holdings Act 1948;

'roots' means the produce of any root crop of a kind normally grown for consumption on the holding;

'tenant' means the outgoing tenant;

'year' means a period of twelve consecutive calendar months.

(2)   The Interpretation Act 1889 applies for the interpretation of these regulations as it applies for the interpretation of an Act of Parliament and as if these regulations and the regulations hereby revoked were Acts of Parliament.

(3)   Any reference in these regulations to any enactment shall be construed as a reference to that enactment as amended, varied or extended under that enactment or by or under any other enactment.

A1.527

3   Compensation for improvements and other matters

Subject to subsections (2) and (3) of section 51 of the Act and to regulation 4 below, the compensation for any improvement or other matter specified in a numbered paragraph of the Fourth Schedule to the Act shall, where the tenancy of the tenant claiming such compensation terminates on or after the coming into operation of these regulations, be calculated in accordance with the paragraph so numbered in Schedule 1 to these regulations.

A1.528

4   Reduction of compensation

(1)   Where any work in relation to an improvement or other matter has not been carried out in the most efficient and economical manner practicable in the circumstances, or any improvement or other matter has been adversely affected by—

   (a)   any breach by the tenant of the rules of good husbandry, or
   (b)   any other act or omission of the tenant, whether intentional or negligent,

and the compensation for that improvement or other matter calculated pursuant to regulation 3 above exceeds the actual value to an incoming tenant, the compensation shall be reduced so as not to exceed such actual value, but no reduction shall be made for any adverse effects of seasonal conditions which the tenant could not reasonably have been expected to guard against or mitigate.

(2)   Where—

   (a)   any hay, fodder crops, straw, roots, manure or compost are destroyed by fire or otherwise or, after the giving of a notice to quit by the tenant or the landlord and without the landlord's written consent, are sold by the tenant or removed by him from the holding, and
   (b)   but for the destruction, sale or removal, compensation would have been payable to the tenant under paragraph 8 of the Fourth Schedule to the Act in respect of the produce destroyed, sold or removed,

the compensation which would otherwise be payable to the tenant under these regulations shall be reduced by an amount equal to the reasonable cost to an incoming tenant of replacing on the holding produce similar in all respects to that which has been destroyed, sold or removed, less the value of the replaced produce itself, calculated under these regulations as if it had been on the holding when the tenant quitted at the termination of the tenancy.

(3)   Paragraphs 8 to 10 of Part II of Schedule 1 to these regulations do not apply to crops or produce grown, seeds sown, cultivations, fallows or acts of husbandry performed or pasture laid down in contravention of the terms of a written contract of tenancy unless either—

   (a)   the tenant shows that the terms contravened were inconsistent with the fulfilment of the tenant's responsibilities to farm the holding in accordance with the rules of good husbandry, or

   (b)   the contravention was reasonably necessary in consequence of the giving of a direction by the Minister under the Agriculture Act 1947 or by the Secretary of State for Wales under that Act as read with the Transfer of Functions (Wales) (No. 1) Order 1978.

A1.529

5   Revocations

The instruments mentioned in Schedule 2 to these regulations are hereby revoked, but without prejudice to their application in relation to tenancies terminating before the coming into operation of these regulations.

SCHEDULE 1

Regulation 3

PART I

A1.530

1   Mole drainage and works carried out to secure the efficient functioning thereof

(1)

   (a)   Where the moles discharge into a piped main drain, the value shall (subject to sub-paragraph (2) below) be the reasonable cost of the work less one-sixth for each year since the work was completed;

   (b)   Where the moles discharge direct into an open ditch (whether the outfalls are piped or not), the value shall (subject to sub-paragraph (2) below) be the reasonable cost of the work less one-third for each year since the work was completed.

(2)   If the value of any work, calculated in accordance with sub-paragraph (1) above, exceeds the actual value to an incoming tenant, in any case where—

   (a)   plans on a suitable scale, made at the time when the work was done, and showing the position of all moles, mains and outfalls, are not made available to the landlord; or

   (b)   moles were not drawn at a proper depth, having regard to the nature of the soil and subsoil; or

   (c)   any ditches into which the outfalls discharge have not been maintained clean, free from obstruction and at a proper depth since the work was done; or

   (d)   deep cultivation or other work interfering with the efficient functioning of the drains has been done on the land since the drainage work was completed; or

   (e)   the land is not of consistently suitable slope or soil texture for mole drainage to be effective; or

   (f)   the drainage scheme was not a proper one, having regard to all the conditions, or was not efficiently carried out; or

1683

(g) for any other reason, the drainage system does not function efficiently,

the value so calculated shall be reduced so as not to exceed such actual value.

2   Protection of fruit trees against animals

The value shall be the reasonable cost of the protection, whether around each tree or around the perimeter of the orchard or both, reduced where necessary according to—

  (a)   the existing condition of the protection;
  (b)   the existing condition of the fruit trees;
  (c)   the further period for which protection is likely to be necessary.

3   —

4   Clay burning

The value shall be the reasonable cost of the work, less one-quarter for each growing season since the work was completed.

[5   Liming (including chalking) of land

(1)   Subject to sub-paragraph (2), the value shall be, for a period of one year following the application of lime to the land, the reasonable cost of the lime so applied and shall thereafter reduce by equal annual depreciation of such an amount that, at the end of a period of years calculated from the date of such application in accordance with Table 1 by reference to mean annual excess winter rainfall in respect of the land and to type of land and rate of application to the land (subsequent to the application of lime) of nitrogenous fertiliser, the value shall be nil.

(2)   For the purposes of sub-paragraph (1), the cost shall not be regarded as reasonable to the extent that it exceeds the higher of—

  (a)   the cost (calculated as at the time when lime was applied to the land) of the quantity of ground limestone or chalk (whichever is the cheaper) which would have been used in the application to the land of calcium oxide at a rate of 7.5 tonnes per hectare, and
  (b)   the cost (calculated as at the time when lime was applied to the land) of lime recommended for application to the land in scientific advice relating to the condition of the soil.

(3)   In this paragraph and Table 1—

  'cost' includes the cost of delivery and application;
  'lime' includes chalk;
  'mean annual excess winter rainfall' means the mean annual amount of rain falling between the date in autumn when the soil reaches field capacity and the end of March in the following year, less the amount of evapotranspiration from the soil during that period, as is indicated by the data on such rainfall in relation to different areas of England and Wales produced by the Meteorological Office for the period commencing with the winter of 1940–1941 and finishing with the winter of 1969–1970 and contained in Ministry of Agriculture, Fisheries and Food Technical Bulletins 34 ('Climate and Drainage') and 35 ('The Agricultural Climate of England and Wales'), both published in 1976 by Her Majesty's Stationery Office, and the map 'Mean Annual Excess Winter Rainfall' published in 1979 by the Ministry of Agriculture, Fisheries and Food.]

6   Application to land of purchased manure and fertiliser, whether organic or inorganic

A Purchased fertilisers containing nitrogen, phosphate or potash:
  IFertilisers other than bulky organic manures:

1684

(1) Where no crop has been taken from the land since the fertiliser was applied, the value shall be the reasonable cost of the fertiliser as applied to the land (including the cost of delivery and application).

(2) Where one crop or more has been taken from the land since the fertiliser was applied, the value shall be,—

    (a) for nitrogen contained in the fertiliser, nil;

    (b) subject as provided below, for each Unit of phosphoric acid (as P2O5) contained in the fertiliser, the amount calculated in accordance with Table 2 below: Provided that—

       (i) where a phosphatic fertiliser contains less than one-tenth of its total phosphoric acid content in an insoluble form, as indicated by the solubility test appropriate to that fertiliser, its total phosphoric acid content shall be treated as soluble;

      (ii) where a phosphatic fertiliser other than a fertiliser specified and applied as described in items 2(a), 2(b)(i) or 3(a) in Table 2 contains more than one-tenth of its total phosphoric acid content in an insoluble form, the value shall be restricted to and determined only for each Unit of phosphoric acid in soluble form in that fertiliser;

      (iii) for the purpose of this sub-paragraph, permanent grassland shall be taken to mean grassland which at the termination of the tenancy has been established for five or more years;

      (iv) in the case of land situated in an area in which rapid fixation of phosphate occurs, the foregoing provisions of this sub-paragraph shall not apply and the value for each Unit of phosphoric acid contained in fertiliser applied to that land shall be the residual value (if any) determined in accordance with scientific evidence and by reference to the reasonable cost of the fertiliser as applied to the land (including the cost of delivery and application);

    (c) for each Unit of potash (K2O) contained in the fertiliser, the amount calculated in accordance with Table 3 below: Provided that—

       (i) where a vegetable crop has been produced from the land following the application of the fertiliser and the majority of the stem and leaf was removed, the value shall be nil, but where the said majority was left on the land, the value shall be calculated in accordance with item 1 in Table 3, and where an intermediate proportion of stem and leaf was removed, the value shall be calculated in accordance with such proportion;

      (ii) in the case of land comprised in holdings which are entirely or mainly horticultural holdings, the value shall be calculated in accordance with item 1 in Table 3.

(3) For the purposes of sub-paragraph (2) above, a Unit of nutrient (phosphoric acid (as P2O5) or, as the case may be, potash (K2O)) is the amount of nutrient contained in one per cent of a tonne of fertiliser calculated on the basis of the percentage content of the nutrient in the fertiliser as stated in the relevant statutory statement given in relation to the fertiliser under section 68 of the Agriculture Act 1970.

IIBulky organic manures brought on to the holding:

Subject to sub-paragraphs (3) and (4) below, the values of bulky organic manures brought on and applied to the holding shall be in accordance with the provisions of sub-paragraphs (1) and (2) below:—

(1) Farmyard manure:

    (a) Where no payment was made for the manure and—

       (i) no crop has been taken from the land since the manure was applied, the value shall be the cost of delivery and application;

      (ii) one crop or more has been taken from the land since the manure was applied, the value shall be, after the first growing season, one-half, and after the second growing season, one-quarter, of the cost of delivery and application, and thereafter, nil;

  (b) Where payment was made for the manure and—

      (i) no crop has been taken from the land since the manure was applied, the value shall be the cost of the manure as applied to the land (including the cost of delivery and application);

      (ii) one crop or more has been taken from the land since the manure was applied, the value shall be, after the first growing season, one-half, and after the second growing season, one-quarter, of the said cost, and thereafter, nil:

Provided that the value of any type of manure specified in Table 4 below shall not exceed the value specified in relation to that type in the appropriate circumstances set out in that Table.

(2) Slurry:

Where manure is brought on and applied to the land in the form of slurry, the value shall be the reasonable cost of cartage (if any) and application.

(3) No compensation shall be payable under sub-paragraph (1) or (2) above in respect of the excess (if any) of the rates of application set out in the second column below in relation to the type of bulky organic manure specified in the first column below:—

Bulky Organic Manure

Type applied (1)	Application per hectare per annum (2)
Cattle, horse or pig manure	50 tonnes
Deep litter poultry manure	18 tonnes
Broiler poultry manure	12.5 tonnes

(4) No value shall be given to, and no compensation shall be payable in respect of, any purchased manure applied to land during the last year of the tenancy after the last crop was removed from that land unless such application was made at the written request, or with the written consent, of the landlord.

B Magnesium and copper:

(1)

  (a)

      (i) Subject to sub-paragraph (b) of this paragraph, where magnesium (in whatever chemical compound form) has been applied to land following and in accordance with scientific advice, the value of the magnesium so applied shall be taken to be the amount (if any) by which the net cost (including the cost of delivery and application) of the quantity of calcined magnesite required to provide the same quantity of magnesium as was actually applied (such net cost being calculated by reference to average prices and costs prevailing at the time of the purchase, delivery and application respectively, of the magnesium) exceeds the net cost (including, and calculated, as aforesaid) of the quantity of calcined magnesite which would provide 60 kilogrammes of magnesium per hectare.

      (ii) After the first, second and third growing seasons following application of the magnesium, the value calculated in accordance with sub-paragraph (a)(i) above shall be reduced to three-quarters, one-half and one-quarter, respectively, and to nil thereafter.

  (b) Sub-paragraph (a) above shall not apply to magnesium applied to land in the form of a magnesian fertiliser specified in Group 5 of Section A of Schedule 1 to the Fertilisers Regulations 1977.

(2)

(a) Subject to sub-paragraph (b) below, where copper (in whatever chemical compound form) has been applied to land following and in accordance with scientific advice, the value of the copper so applied shall be taken to be the amount (if any) by which the net cost (including the cost of delivery and application) of the quantity of hydrated copper sulphate required to provide the same quantity of copper as was actually applied (such net cost being calculated by reference to average prices and costs prevailing at the time of the purchase, delivery and application, respectively, of the copper) exceeds the net cost (including, and calculated, as aforesaid) of the quantity of hydrated copper sulphate which would provide six kilogrammes of copper per hectare;

(b) The value of copper applied calculated in accordance with sub-paragraph (a) above shall be reduced by one-eighth for each year following application of the copper.

7   Consumption on the holding of corn (whether produced on the holding or not) or of cake or other feeding stuffs not produced on the holding by horses, cattle, sheep, pigs or poultry

(1) The values per tonne of feeding stuff consumed on the holding set out in Tables 5(a), and (b) in Part I of this Schedule shall apply in all cases where feeding stuffs are fed to the animals and poultry specified in those Tables in buildings or open yards and the open slurry is stored under average conditions.

(2) Where the conditions of storage of the open slurry are other than average, for closed slurry or farm yard manure or where the feeding stuffs are fed directly on the land the values set out in the said Tables 5(a) and (b) shall be adjusted in accordance with Table 6 set out below.

(3) For the purpose of sub-paragraph (2) above and the said Table 6, the expression 'closed slurry' means slurry stored under slats or in a covered container.]

[TABLE 1
DEPRECIATION OF VALUE OF LIME

Mean annual excess winter rainfall (millimetres)	Where the land comprises permanent pasture or long-term leys with more than 250 kilogrammes per hectare of nitrogen applied annually, or arable or mixed ley and arable land	Where the land comprises permanent pasture or long-term leys with up to 250 kilogrammes per hectare or nitrogen applied annually
	Value of lime to be depreciated over:—	Value of lime to be depreciated over:—
Less than 250	8 years	9 years
250 to 500	6 years	7 years
More than 500	4 years	5 years]

[TABLE 2
UNIT VALUE OF PHOSPHORIC ACID (AS P2O5) IN ONE PER CENT OF A TONNE OF FERTILISER

Nature of Fertiliser	After		
	One	Two	Three
	Growing Seasons		
	p	p	p

1 Organic forms and inorganic forms (including basic slag) but excluding rock phosphates and calcined aluminium calcium phosphate	158	79	39
2 Soft ground rock phosphates (1) applied in—			
(a) areas with a mean annual excess winter rainfall (2) of 450 mm or more	158	79	39
(b) areas with a mean annual excess winter rainfall (2) of less than 450 mm			
(i) Permanent grassland	158	79	39
(ii) Other crops	nil	nil	nil
3 Other ground rock phosphates applied in—			
(a) areas with a mean annual excess winter rainfall (2) of 450 mm or more	39	39	39
(b) areas with a means annual excess winter rainfall (2) of less than 450 mm	nil	nil	nil
4 Calcined aluminium calcium phosphate	The value, if any, shall be such as may be determined in accordance with scientific evidence		

NOTES:

(1) 'Soft' ground rock phosphates in this Table means the material of that name described in Group 2 in Section A of Schedule 1 to the Fertilisers Regulations 1977.

(2) 'Mean annual excess winter rainfall' in this Table has the same meaning as in paragraph 5(3).]

[TABLE 3
UNIT VALUE OF POTASH (K2O) IN ONE PER CENT OF A TONNE

	After		
Type of crops to which fertiliser is applied	One	Two	Three
		Growing Seasons	
	p	p	p
1 Applied to arable crops (except forage crops) and all root crops where tops are left on the land, except potatoes (see also 4 below)	92	46	nil
2 Applied to leys, permanent grassland or forage crops which are grazed or the product cut and fed on the holding	94	47	nil
3 Applied to leys and permanent grassland the product of which is cut and removed from the holding	nil	nil	nil
4 Applied to roots (including potatoes) and forage crops which are removed from the holding]	nil	nil	nil

[TABLE 4
VALUE PER TONNE OF PURCHASED FARMYARD

Type of manure	No crop off	After one growing season	After two growing seasons	After three growing seasons
	p	p	p	p
Cattle (farmyard manure)	735	368	184	nil
Horse (stable manure)	800	400	200	nil

Pig (farmyard manure)	770	385	193	nil
Poultry (deep litter)	1380	690	345	nil
Poultry (broiler manure)	1625	813	406	nil]

[TABLE 5(A)]
UNEXHAUSTED MANURIAL VALUES OF FEEDING STUFFS PER TONNE: CATTLE, SHEEP AND PIGS—OPEN SLURRY

Feeding Stuff	No crop off	After one growing season	
		of arable crops (except forage crops) or of leys, permanent grass-land or forage crops grazed or the product cut and fed on the holding or of root crops the tops of which are left on the land	of leys, permanent grassland, roots or forage crops where the product is removed from the holding
p	p	p	p
1 Grass hay	395	197	53
2 Clover hay	470	235	78
3 Dried grass	523	262	88
4 Dried lucerne	532	266	92
5 Straw	133	66	26
6 Mangels	63	31	8
7 Swedes	47	23	8
8 Turnips	47	23	8
9 Potatoes	89	44	13
10 Sugar beet pulp (dried-molasses)	309	155	40
11 Sugar beet pulp (wet-double pressed 18% DM)	62	31	8
12 Brewers grains (wet)	67	34	33
13 Field beans	407	204	139
14. Field peas	310	155	103
15 Barley	204	102	67
16 Wheat	185	92	70
17 Oats	190	95	71
18 Maize	145	72	52
19 Rice meal	203	101	80
20 Middlings/Bran	411	205	148
21 Cassava (Manioc)	70	33	21
22 Hominy chop	277	139	97
23 Locust beans	137	68	32
24 Citrus pulp	158	79	40
25 Fish meal	1422	711	642
26 Soya bean meal	615	308	184
27 Decorticated cotton cake	685	342	267
28 Undecorticated cotton cake	563	281	206
29 Linseed cake/meal	524	262	180

1689

30 Palm kernel cake/meal	265	133	107
31 Coconut cake/meal	521	261	135
32 Decorticated groundnut cake	502	251	173
33 Rapeseed cake/meal	607	303	222
34 Meat meal	1325	663	628
35 Meat and bone meal	1711	855	768
36 Dried skimmed milk	601	300	196
37 Skimmed milk (liquid)	59	29	19
38 Liquid whey	29	14	7
39 Liquid urea	452	226	70
40 Urea	1014	507	507
41 Compounded cake: for each 1% CP	20	10	8

After two growing seasons

1 Grass hay	395	84	12
2 Clover hay	470	96	18
3 Dried grass	523	106	20
4 Dried lucerne	532	106	19
5 Straw	133	25	5
6 Mangels	63	14	3
7 Swedes	47	10	2
8 Turnips	47	10	2
9 Potatoes	89	19	3
10 Sugar beet pulp (dried-molasses)	309	61	4
11 Sugar beet pulp (wet-double pressed 18% DM)	62	12	1
12 Brewers grains (wet)	67	10	9
13 Field beans	407	69	37
14 Field peas	310	51	25
15 Barley	204	37	20
16 Wheat	185	33	22
17 Oats	190	32	21
18 Maize	145	25	15
19 Rice meal	203	37	26
20 Middlings/Bran	411	80	52
21 Cassava (Manioc)	70	14	7
22 Hominy chop	277	53	32
23 Locust beans	137	25	7
24 Citrus pulp	158	27	8
25 Fish meal	1422	287	252
26 Soya bean meal	615	105	43
27 Decorticated cotton cake	685	123	85
28 Undecorticated cotton cake	563	108	70
29 Linseed cake/meal	524	93	52
30 Palm kernel cake/meal	265	45	32
31 Coconut cake/meal	521	103	41
32 Decorticated groundnut cake	502	76	37
33 Rapeseed cake/meal	607	108	67
34 Meat meal	1325	276	259

35 Meat and bone meal	1711	368	324
36 Dried skimmed milk	601	117	65
37 Skimmed milk (liquid)	59	11	6
38 Liquid whey	29	6	3
39 Liquid urea	452	81	3
40 Urea	1014	0	0
41 Compounded cake: for each 1% CP	20	4	3]

[TABLE 5(B)

UNEXHAUSTED MANUAL VALUES OF FEEDING STUFFS PER TONNE: CATTLE, POULTRY—OPEN SLURRY

Feeding Stuff	No crop off	After one growing season of arable crops (except forage crops) or of leys, permanent grass-land or forage crops grazed or the product cut and fed on the holding or of root crops the tops of which are left on the land	of leys, permanent grassland, roots or forage crops where the product is removed from the holding
	p	p	p
1 Dried grass	493	213	39
2 Field beans	371	138	74
3 Field peas	284	102	50
4 Barley	189	75	40
5 Wheat	171	66	44
6 Oats	173	65	41
7 Maize	133	51	30
8 Rice meal	188	73	52
9 Middlings/Bran	384	161	104
10 Cassava (Manioc)	65	28	13
11 Fish meal	1360	574	505
12 Soya bean meal	570	210	87
13 Decorticated cotton cake	637	246	171
14 Undecorticated cotton cake	526	216	141
15 Linseed cake/meal	486	186	104
16 Palm Kernel cake/meal	245	89	63
17 Decorticated groundnut	456	152	74
18 Rapeseed cake/meal	561	215	134
19 Meat meal	1280	552	518
20 Meat and bone meal	1643	735	648
21 Compounded cake: for each 1% CP	19	8	5
After two growing seasons			
1 Dried grass	493	106	20
2 Field beans	371	69	37
3 Field peas	284	51	25
4 Barley	189	37	20

5 Wheat	171	33	22
6 Oats	173	32	21
7 Maize	133	25	15
8 Rice Meal	188	37	26
9 Middlings/Bran	384	80	52
10 Cassava (Manioc)	65	14	7
11 Fish meal	136	287	252
12 Soya bean meal	570	105	43
13 Decorticated cotton cake	637	123	85
14 Undecorticated cotton cake	526	108	70
15 Linseed cake/meal	486	93	52
16 Palm Kernel cake/meal	245	45	32
17 Decorticated groundnut cake	456	76	37
18 Rapeseed cake/meal	1280	276	259
19 Meat and bone meal	1643	368	324
20 Meat and bone meal	1643	368	324
21 Compound cake: for each 1% CP	19	4	3]

[TABLE 6

ADJUSTMENTS FOR PREPARATION AND STORAGE OF EFFLUENT

Method of preparation and storage	Adjustment to open slurry (average conditions) tables
Closed slurry under average conditions	Add 20 per cent
Closed slurry under ideal conditions	Add 30 per cent
Farmyard manure under average conditions	Add 40 per cent
Farmyard manure under ideal conditions	Add 50 per cent
Slurry under adverse conditions	Subtract up to 50 per cent depending on conditions
Farmyard manure under adverse conditions	Add up to 30 per cent depending on conditions
Feedingstuffs fed directly on the land	Add 35 per cent]

NOTES

Amendment

Para 5: substituted by SI 1981/822, reg 3, Schedule, Part I.

Para 7: substituted by SI 1983/1475, reg 3, Schedule, Part I.

Table 1: substituted by SI 1981/822, reg 3, Schedule, Part II.

Table 2: substituted by SI 1983/1475, reg 3, Schedule, Part II.

Table 3: substituted by SI 1983/1475, reg 3, Schedule, Part II.

Table 4: substituted by SI 1983/1475, reg 3, Schedule, Part II.

Table 5a: substituted by SI 1983/1475, reg 3, Schedule, Part II.

Table 5b: substituted by SI 1983/1475, reg 3, Schedule, Part II.

Table 6: substituted by SI 1983/1475, reg 3, Schedule, Part II.

PART II

8 *Growing crops and severed or harvested crops and produce, being in either case crops or produce grown on the holding in the last year of the tenancy, but not including crops or produce which the tenant has a right to sell or remove from the holding.*

(1) Growing crops:—

(a) The value of growing crops, except root and green crops of a kind normally grown on a holding held under an autumn tenancy, shall be the reasonable cost of seeds sown, and cultivations, fallows and acts of husbandry performed, calculated in accordance with the provisions of paragraph 9 below;

(b) The value of growing root and green crops of a kind normally grown on a holding held under an autumn tenancy shall be the average market value on the holding of good quality crops, less the manurial value thereof calculated in accordance with [Tables 5(a) and (b)] above on the basis of 'no crop off ':

Provided that if the value so calculated exceeds the actual value to an incoming tenant in any case where—

(i) the crops are of inferior quality, or

(ii) the quantity of any kind of crops exceeds the quantity reasonably required for the system of farming practised on the holding,

the value so calculated shall be reduced so as not to exceed such actual value;

(c) In the case of—

(i) autumn-sown crops where the land was held under a spring tenancy, and

(ii) grass and clover seeds sown on land held under a spring or autumn tenancy from which no crop has been taken before termination of the tenancy,

the value shall be increased by an additional amount representing the enhancement of the value to an incoming tenant of the growing crop, but such additional amount shall not in any case exceed the rental value, at the termination of the tenancy, of the land sown to the crop, such rental value to be calculated by reference to the same matters and criteria as are by section 8 of the Act required to be taken into consideration or applied for the determination of the rent of a holding pursuant to that enactment:

Provided that if the area of any such crop exceeds the area of such crop which would normally be grown on the holding, having regard to the character and type of the holding and the terms of the tenancy (hereinafter referred to as 'the normal area') the foregoing provisions of this sub-paragraph shall apply only to the normal area of such crop.

(2) For the purposes of sub-paragraph (1) above 'spring tenancy' means a yearly tenancy the last yearly term of which commenced between 1st January and 30th June inclusive, and 'autumn tenancy' means a yearly tenancy the last yearly term of which commenced between 1st September and 31st December inclusive.

(3) Severed or harvested crops and produce:—

The value shall be the market value for consumption by agricultural livestock on the holding of hay, fodder crops, straw, roots and other crops or produce of good quality less the manurial value thereof calculated in accordance with Tables 5(a)–(j) above on the basis of 'no crop off ': Provided that if the value so calculated exceeds the actual value to an incoming tenant in any case where—

(a) the crops or produce are of inferior quality; or

(b) the quantity of any kind of crops or produce exceeds the quantity reasonably required for the system of farming practised on the holding; or

(c) the crops or produce are not left in convenient or proper places on the farm; or

(d) any hay or straw is not properly stacked and thatched or otherwise protected, the value so calculated shall be reduced so as not to exceed such actual value.

9 *Seeds sown and cultivations, fallows and acts of husbandry performed on the holding at the expense of the tenant*

(1) The value shall be the reasonable cost of seeds sown and of cultivations, fallows and acts of husbandry performed, taking into account—

(a) normal current costs, having regard to the current agricultural wage, the cost of horse and tractor operations, the size and shape of the fields, and other relevant conditions;

(b) reasonable costs of hired tractor cultivations;

(c) increased costs over normal tractor rates, where owing to the size of the farm or fields, the shape of the fields, or to other special circumstances, it was reasonable to use horse labour;

but leaving out of account any expenditure incurred by the tenant up to and including the removal from the land of the last preceding crop and any rent paid by the tenant.

(2) For the purposes of sub-paragraph (1) above, the reasonable cost shall not be regarded as reduced merely because more than one operation was carried out by the tenant at the same time.

(3) Nothing in sub-paragraph (1) above shall be taken to limit the operation of this paragraph to any particular method of sowing nor to cultivations, fallows or acts of husbandry performed in any particular way.

10 *Pasture laid down with clover, grass, lucerne, sainfoin or other seeds, being either—*

(a) *pasture laid down at the expense of the tenant otherwise than in compliance with an obligation imposed on him by an agreement in writing to lay it down to replace temporary pasture comprised in the holding when the tenant entered thereon which was not paid for by him; or*

(b) *pasture paid for by the tenant on entering on the holding.*

(1) Where no crop has been removed either by mowing or by grazing, the value shall be the reasonable cost of seeds sown, and cultivations, fallows and acts of husbandry performed, calculated in accordance with paragraph 9 above, but also taking into account any expenditure incurred solely for the benefit of the pasture before the removal of any crop in or with which the pasture was sown.

(2) Where one crop or more has been removed either by mowing or by grazing, the value shall be the face value of the pasture, taking into account—

(a) present condition;

(b) management since sowing;

(c) situation on the holding;

(d) fencing;

(e) water supply;

(f) any other circumstances appearing to be relevant.

11 *Acclimatisation, hefting or settlement of hill sheep on hill land*

(1) The value of hill sheep on hill land shall include such amount (if any) as represents the value attributable to the acclimatisation, hefting or settlement of the sheep on such land, but the said amount shall not [[exceed a sum of eight pounds per sheep plus ten per cent of the market value of each sheep].

(2)   Any amount which may be included in the value of hill sheep under the provisions of the last foregoing sub-paragraph shall be apportioned and separately shown by the person carrying out the valuation as being attributable to the value of acclimatisation, hefting or settlement of such sheep.

12   *Residual sod fertility value in certain districts*

(1)   In this paragraph—

['arable crop' does not include a ley of more than one years duration;]

'leys' means land laid down with clover, grass, lucerne, sainfoin or other seeds, but does not include permanent pasture;

'continuously maintained leys' means leys continuously maintained as such for a period of three or more growing seasons since being laid down excluding, if the leys were undersown or autumn-sown, the calendar year in which the sowing took place; and, for the purpose of this definition, the destruction of a ley (by ploughing or some other means) followed as soon as practicable by re-seeding to a ley without sowing a crop in the interval between such destruction and such re-seeding shall be treated as not constituting a break in the continuity of the maintenance of the ley;

'former leys' means arable land which within the three growing seasons immediately preceding the termination of the tenancy was ley which was continuously maintained ley before being destroyed by ploughing or some other means for the production of a tillage crop or crops;

'qualifying leys' means continuously maintained leys and former leys or either of them;

'the excess qualifying leys' means, subject as provided below, the area of qualifying leys on the holding at the termination of the tenancy which is equal to the area (if any) by which one-third of the aggregate of the areas of leys on the holding on the following dates, namely,—

(a)   at the termination of the tenancy,

(b)   on the date one year prior to such termination, and

(c)   on the date two years prior to such termination

exceeds the accepted proportion at the termination of the tenancy: Provided that for the purpose of this definition qualifying leys laid down at the expense of the landlord without reimbursement by the tenant or any previous tenant of the holding or laid down by and at the expense of the tenant pursuant to agreement by him with the landlord for the establishment of a specified area of leys on the holding as a condition of the landlord giving consent to the ploughing or other destruction of permanent pasture or pursuant to a direction given by an arbitrator on a reference under section 10(1) of the Act shall not be included in the area of qualifying leys on the holding at the termination of the tenancy;

['the accepted proportion' means the area which represents the proportion which the total area of the leys on the holding would, taking into account the capability of the holding, be expected to bear to the area of the holding, excluding the permanent pasture thereon, or, if a greater proportion is provided for by or under the terms of the tenancy, that proportion.]

(2)   [In areas of the country where arable crops can be grown in an unbroken series of not less than six years, and it is reasonable that they should be grown on the holding or part thereof, the residual fertility value of the sod of the excess qualifying leys shall be calculated (subject to sub-paragraph (3) below) as follows:—]

(a)   in respect of continuously maintained leys, [£24 per hectare] if any herbage has been cut and removed in the last growing season before the termination of the tenancy and [£40 per hectare] if the sward was, during such last growing season, grazed only;

1695

(b)   [in respect of continuously maintained leys, the values specified in sub-paragraph (a) above shall be increased by £8 per hectare for each additional growing season over three growing seasons for which the leys have been established, but such increase shall not exceed a total of £48 per hectare if any herbage was cut and removed during the last growing season before the termination of the tenancy and shall not exceed £64 per hectare if the herbage was, during such last growing season, grazed only;]

(c)   [in respect of any former ley where the first crop which has been sown in the last growing season before the termination of the tenancy has not been removed from the ground, the value shall be the value specified in sub-paragraphs (a) and (b) above according to the period for which the ley had been established before it was ploughed or otherwise destroyed and to whether the herbage was cut and removed, or grazed only, in the last growing season before the ley was ploughed or otherwise destroyed;]

(d)   in respect of any former ley to which sub-paragraph (c) above does not apply,—

   (i)

      (aa)   if only one arable crop was removed from the land following ploughing or other destruction of the ley, the value shall be two-thirds of the value specified in sub-paragraphs (a) and (b), and

      (bb)   if only two arable crops were removed from the land following ploughing or other destruction of the ley, the value shall be one-third of the value specified in sub-paragraphs (a) and (b),

      according, in each case, to the period for which the ley had been established before it was ploughed or otherwise destroyed and to whether the herbage was cut and removed, or grazed only, in the last growing season before the ley was ploughed or otherwise destroyed; and

   (ii)   if more than two arable crops were removed from the land following ploughing or other destruction of the ley, the value shall be nil.

(3)   Where the tenant is entitled to compensation in respect of a ley both under sub-paragraph (2) of paragraph 10 above and under sub-paragraph (2)(a) and, if applicable, sub-paragraph (2)(b) of this paragraph, the aggregate of the respective values per hectare thereunder, taken together, shall not exceed £148 per hectare.

NOTES

Amendment

Paras 8, 11: amended by SI 1983/1475, reg 3.

Para 12: fourth and fifth amendments made by SI 1980/751, reg 3; other amendments made by SI 1983/1475, reg 3.

AGRICULTURE (CALCULATION OF VALUE FOR COMPENSATION) (AMENDMENT) REGULATIONS 1980

SI 1980/751

The Minister of Agriculture, Fisheries and Food, in relation to England, and the Secretary of State for Wales, in relation to Wales, with the advice of the committees respectively appointed by them under the provisions of section 79 of the Agricultural Holdings Act 1948 and in exercise of the powers conferred by section 51(1) of the Agricultural Holdings Act 1948, and now vested in them, and of all other powers enabling them in that behalf, hereby make the following regulations:—

NOTES

Continuation

Authority: following the consolidation of the Agricultural Holdings Act 1948, s 51, these Regulations have effect as if made under the Agricultural Holdings Act 1986, s 66(2).

A1.531

1   Citation, commencement and interpretation

(1)   These regulations may be cited as the Agriculture (Calculation of Value for Compensation) (Amendment) Regulations 1980 and shall come into operation on 1st July 1980.

(2)   In these regulations 'the principal regulations' means the Agriculture (Calculation of Value for Compensation) Regulations 1978.

NOTES

Initial Commencement

Specified date: 1 July 1980: see para (1) above.

A1.532

2   Application

These regulations shall apply in relation to the calculation of the value of improvements and other matters in any case where the tenancy of the outgoing tenant claiming compensation for such improvements and other matters by virtue of the provisions of the Agricultural Holdings Act 1948 terminates on or after the day on which these regulations shall come into operation.

NOTES

Initial Commencement

Specified date: 1 July 1980: see reg 1(1).

A1.533

3   Amendment of principal regulations

(1)   Part I of Schedule 1 to the principal regulations shall be amended so that for Tables 2, 3, 4, 5(a), 5(b), 5(c), 5(d), 5(e), 5(f), 5(g), 5(h) and 5(j) set out therein there

shall be substituted respectively Tables 2, 3, 4, 5(a), 5(b), 5(c), 5(d), 5(e), 5(f), 5(g), 5(h) and 5(j) set out in the Schedule to these regulations.

(2)   Part II of Schedule 1 to the principal regulations shall be amended as follows:—

(a)   in paragraph 11(1), for 'four pounds per sheep' there shall be substituted 'eight pounds per sheep';

(b)   in paragraph 12(2)(a)—
    (i)   for '£18 per hectare' there shall be substituted '£24 per hectare';
    (ii)   for '£30 per hectare' there shall be substituted '£40 per hectare';

(c)   in paragraph 12(2)(b)—
    (i)   for '£6 per hectare' there shall be substituted '£8 per hectare';
    (ii)   for '£36 per hectare' there shall be substituted '£48 per hectare';
    (iii)   for '£48 per hectare' there shall be substituted '£64 per hectare';

(d)   in paragraph 12(3), for '£148 per hectare' there shall be substituted '£164 per hectare'.

NOTES

Initial Commencement

Specified date: 1 July 1980: see reg 1(1).

SCHEDULE

Regulation 3

A1.534

< ... >

NOTES

Initial Commencement

Specified date: 1 July 1980: see reg 1(1).

Amendment

This Schedule is now spent

AGRICULTURE (CALCULATION OF VALUE FOR COMPENSATION) (AMENDMENT) REGULATIONS 1981

SI 1981/822

The Minister of Agriculture, Fisheries and Food, in relation to England, and the Secretary of State for Wales, in relation to Wales, with the advice of the committees respectively appointed by them under the provisions of section 79 of the Agricultural Holdings Act 1948 and in exercise of the powers conferred by section 51(1) of the Agricultural Holdings Act 1948, and now vested in them, and of all other powers enabling them in that behalf, hereby make the following regulations:—

NOTES

Continuation

Authority: following the consolidation of the Agricultural Holdings Act 1948, s 51, these Regulations have effect as if made under the Agricultural Holdings Act 1986, s 66(2).

A1.535

1   Citation, commencement and interpretation

(1)   These regulations may be cited as the Agriculture (Calculation of Value for Compensation) (Amendment) Regulations 1981 and shall come into operation on 6th July 1981.

(2)   In these regulations 'the principal regulations' means the Agriculture (Calculation of Value for Compensation) Regulations 1978, and the principal regulations, the Agriculture (Calculation of Value for Compensation) (Amendment) Regulations 1980 and these regulations may together be cited as the Agriculture (Calculation of Value for Compensation) Regulations 1978 to 1981.

NOTES

Initial Commencement

Specified date: 6 July 1981: see para (1) above.

A1.536

2   Application

These regulations shall apply in relation to the calculation of the value of improvements and other matters in any case where the tenancy of the out-going tenant claiming compensation for such improvements and other matters by virtue of the provisions of the Agricultural Holdings Act 1948 terminates on or after the day on which these regulations shall come into operation.

NOTES

Initial Commencement

Specified date: 6 July 1981: see reg 1(1).

A1.537

3   Amendment of principal regulations

(1)   Part I of Schedule 1 to the principal regulations shall be amended so that—

   (a)   for paragraph 5 there shall be substituted the paragraph set out in Part I of the Schedule to these regulations, and

   (b)   for Tables 1, 2, 3, 4, 5(a), 5(b), 5(c), 5(d), 5(e), 5(f), 5(g), 5(h) and 5(j) set out therein there shall be substituted respectively Tables 1, 2, 3, 4, 5(a), 5(b), 5(c), 5(d), 5(e), 5(f), 5(g), 5(h) and 5(j) set out in Part II of the Schedule to these regulations.

(2)   Part II of Schedule 1 to the principal regulations shall be amended so that, in paragraph 11(1), for 'eight pounds per sheep' there shall be substituted 'ten pounds per sheep'.

NOTES

Initial Commencement

Specified date: 6 July 1981: see reg 1(1).

SCHEDULE

Regulation 3

PART I

Paragraph to be substituted for paragraph 5 of Part I of Schedule 1 to the principal regulations

A1.538

Liming (including chalking) of land

5   (1)   Subject to sub-paragraph (2), the value shall be, for a period of one year following the application of lime to the land, the reasonable cost of the lime so applied and shall thereafter reduce by equal annual depreciation of such an amount that, at the end of a period of years calculated from the date of such application in accordance with Table 1 by reference to mean annual excess winter rainfall in respect of the land and to type of land and rate of application to the land (subsequent to the application of lime) of nitrogenous fertiliser, the value shall be nil.

(2)   For the purposes of sub-paragraph (1), the cost shall not be regarded as reasonable to the extent that it exceeds the higher of—

   (a)   the cost (calculated as at the time when lime was applied to the land) of the quantity of ground limestone or chalk (whichever is the cheaper) which would have been used in the application to the land of calcium oxide at a rate of 7.5 tonnes per hectare, and

   (b)   the cost (calculated as at the time when lime was applied to the land) of lime recommended for application to the land in scientific advice relating to the condition of the soil.

(3)   In this paragraph and Table 1—

   'cost' includes the cost of delivery and application;
   'lime' includes chalk;

1700

'mean annual excess winter rainfall' means the mean annual amount of rain falling between the date in autumn when the soil reaches field capacity and the end of March in the following year, less the amount of evapotranspiration from the soil during that period, as is indicated by the data on such rainfall in relation to different areas of England and Wales produced by the Meteorological Office for the period commencing with the winter of 1940–1941 and finishing with the winter of 1969–1970 and contained in Ministry of Agriculture, Fisheries and Food Technical Bulletins 34 ('Climate and Drainage') and 35 ('The Agricultural Climate of England and Wales'), both published in 1976 by Her Majesty's Stationery Office, and the map 'Mean Annual Excess Winter Rainfall' published in 1979 by the Ministry of Agriculture, Fisheries and Food.

NOTES

Initial Commencement

Specified date: 6 July 1981: see reg 1(1).

PART II

< ... >

NOTES

Initial Commencement

Specified date: 6 July 1981: see reg 1(1).

Amendment

This Part is now spent.

AGRICULTURAL LAND TRIBUNALS (AREAS) ORDER 1982

SI 1982/97

Authority: Agriculture Act 1947, s 73

A1.539

1

This Order may be cited as the Agricultural Land Tribunals (Areas) Order 1982 and shall come into operation on 2nd March 1982.

A1.540

2

(1) For the purposes of section 73 of the Agriculture Act 1947 there shall be eight areas as specified in column 1 of the Schedule to this Order.

(2)   Each area shall comprise the counties and the London Boroughs which are set out in respect of it in column 2 of the said Schedule.

(3)   For the purposes of the preceding paragraph and of the said Schedule the Isles of Scilly shall be treated as if they were a county.

3

Any proceedings which on the coming into operation of this Order are pending before an Agricultural Land Tribunal may thereafter be continued before the Agricultural Land Tribunal for the area in which the whole or the greater part of the agricultural holding to which the proceedings relate is situate, and that tribunal shall have power to hear and determine them.

SCHEDULE

Article 2

A1.541

Column 1 Areas	Column 2 Counties and London Boroughs
Northern	Cleveland Cumbria Durham Northumberland Tyne and Wear
Yorkshire and Humberside	Humberside North Yorkshire South Yorkshire West Yorkshire
Eastern	Bedfordshire Cambridgeshire Essex Hertfordshire Lincolnshire Norfolk Northamptonshire Suffolk London Boroughs north of the river Thames except Richmond upon Thames
Midlands	Derbyshire Herefordshire and Worcestershire Leicestershire Nottinghamshire Warwickshire West Midlands
Western	Cheshire Greater Manchester Lancashire Merseyside

	Shropshire
	Staffordshire
South Western	Avon
	Cornwall
	Devon
	Dorset
	Gloucestershire
	Somerset
	Wiltshire
	Isles of Scilly
South Eastern	Berkshire
	Buckinghamshire
	East Sussex
	Hampshire
	Isle of Wight
	Kent
	Oxfordshire
	Surrey
	West Sussex
	London Boroughs south of the river Thames including Richmond upon Thames
Welsh	Clwyd
	Dyfed
	Gwent
	Gwynedd
	Mid Glamorgan
	Powys
	South Glamorgan
	West Glamorgan

AGRICULTURE (CALCULATION OF VALUE FOR COMPENSATION) (AMENDMENT) REGULATIONS 1983

SI 1983/1475

Authority: Agricultural Holdings Act 1986, s 66(2)

NOTES

Continuation

Authority: following the consolidation of the original enabling power, these Regulations have effect as if made under the Agricultural Holdings Act 1986, s 66(2).

A1.542

1   Title, commencement and interpretation

(1)   These regulations may be cited as the Agriculture (Calculation of Value for Compensation) (Amendment) Regulations 1983 and shall come into operation on 14th November 1983.

(2)   In these regulations 'the principal regulations' means the Agriculture (Calculation of Value for Compensation) Regulations 1978, and the principal regulations, the Agriculture (Calculation of Value for Compensation) (Amendment) Regulations 1980, the Agriculture (Calculation of Value for Compensation) (Amendment) Regulations 1981 and these regulations may together be cited as the Agriculture (Calculation of Value for Compensation) Regulations 1978 to 1983.

A1.543

2   Application

These regulations shall apply in relation to the calculation of the value of improvements and other matters specified in a numbered paragraph of the Fourth Schedule to the Agricultural Holdings Act 1948 in any case where the tenancy of the outgoing tenant claiming compensation for such improvements and other matters by virtue of the provisions of that Act terminates on or after the day on which these regulations come into operation.

A1.544

3   Amendment of principal regulations

...

NOTES

Amendment

This regulation amends SI 1978/809, Sch 1.

SCHEDULE

Regulation 3

A1.545

...

NOTES

Amendment

This Schedule amends SI 1978/809, Sch 1.

AGRICULTURAL LAND TRIBUNALS (SUCCESSION TO AGRICULTURAL TENANCIES) ORDER 1984

SI 1984/1301

Authority: Agriculture Act 1947, ss 73(3), (4), 108(3)

A1.546

1   Citation and commencement

This Order may be cited as the Agricultural Land Tribunals (Succession to Agricultural Tenancies) Order 1984 and shall come into operation on 12th September 1984.

A1.547

2   Rules of procedure

The rules set out in the Schedule to this Order shall apply to any proceedings before Agricultural Land Tribunals arising from any application made after the commencement of this Order under Part II of the Agriculture (Miscellaneous Provisions) Act 1976 or under Schedule 2 to the Agricultural Holdings Act 1984.

A1.548

3   Variation of the Agricultural Land Tribunals (Rules) Order 1978

...

NOTES

Amendment

This article amends SI 1978/259, art 2.

A1.549

4   Revocation

The Agricultural Land Tribunals (Succession to Agricultural Tenancies) Order 1976 is hereby revoked except to such extent as may be necessary for the disposal of an application pending at the commencement of this Order.

SCHEDULE

RULES OF PROCEDURE FOR AGRICULTURAL LAND TRIBUNALS UNDER PART II OF THE AGRICULTURAL (MISCELLANEOUS PROVISIONS) ACT 1976 AND SCHEDULE 2 TO THE AGRICULTURAL HOLDINGS ACT 1984

Article 2

PART I: PRELIMINARY

A1.550

1   Citation and interpretation

(1) These rules may be cited as the Agricultural Land Tribunals (Succession) Rules 1984.

(2) In these rules 'the principal rules' means the Agricultural Land Tribunals Rules 1978 and expressions defined in the principal rules have the same meaning in these rules.

(3) Unless the context otherwise requires, any reference in these rules—

(a) to a numbered rule shall be construed as a reference to the rule bearing that number in these rules; or

(b) to a numbered form shall be construed as a reference to the form bearing that number in the Appendix to these rules, or a form substantially to the like effect with such variations as the circumstances may require.

PART II: APPLICATION FOR SUCCESSION ON DEATH OF TENANT UNDER PART II OF THE AGRICULTURE (MISCELLANEOUS PROVISIONS) ACT 1976

2   Interpretation of Part II

(1) In this Part of these rules, unless the context otherwise requires—

'the 1976 Act' means the Agriculture (Miscellaneous Provisions) Act 1976;
'applicant' means a person who has made an application under rule 3(1);
'designated applicant' means an applicant who has been validly designated by the deceased in his will in accordance with section 20(10) of the 1976 Act;
'holding' means a holding in respect of which an application under rule 3(1) is made;
'landlord' means the landlord of the holding;
'the relevant period' means the period of three months beginning with day after the date of death.

(2) Other expressions defined for the purposes of, or of any provision in, sections 18 to 23 of the 1976 Act (notably in sections 18(1), (2) and (7), 20(10), 22(6) and 23(2) have the same meaning in this Part of these rules.

Forms of Application and Reply

3   Application by eligible person wishing to be treated as eligible person

(1) An application to the tribunal under section 21 of the 1976 Act for a direction entitling the applicant to a tenancy of an agricultural holding shall be made in Form 1.

(2) An application to the tribunal under section 2 of the 1976 Act for a determination that the applicant is to be treated as an eligible person shall be made in Form 1 and if the applicant also makes an application under section 20 of that Act, both applications shall be made at the same time and in the same Form.

(3) An application made under this rule shall not be entertained by the tribunal if it is not made within the relevant period.

4   Landlord's application for consent to operation of notice to quit

(1) An application by the landlord under section 22 of the 1976 Act for the tribunal's consent to the operation of a notice to quit shall be in Form 2 and, subject to paragraphs (3) and (4), may be made at any time after the landlord receives notice of an application under rule 3(1).

(2) Where the landlord bases his application under section 22 of the 1976 Act on the ground of hardship to a person or persons other than himself, he shall give particulars in his application of that person or those persons and of the hardship on which he relies.

(3) Where, at the expiry of the relevant period, only one application under rule 3(1) in respect of the holding is pending, any application by the landlord shall be made within four months after a copy of the application under rule 3(1) is served on him.

(4) Where, at the expiry of the relevant period, more than one application under rule 3(1) in respect of the holding is pending, any application by the landlord shall be made—

    (a)   within four months after a copy of the first application under rule 3(1) is served on him, or

    (b)   within one month after the date on which the number of applications under rule 3(1) which are pending is reduced to one or within one month after such earlier date as the tribunal may direct,

whichever of those periods expires last.

(5) The secretary shall forthwith inform the landlord of the start of any period of four months under paragraph (3) or paragraph (4) and any period of one month under paragraph (4).

5   Notice of application

(1) An applicant shall at the time of making his application serve notice of the application in Form 3 on the landlord and on any person who, to the knowledge of the applicant, has made or may be able to make an application under rule 3(1), and shall inform the tribunal in his application of the name and address of every person to be notified by him.

(2) The applicant shall also inform the tribunal in his application of the name and address of—

    (a)   the personal representatives of the deceased, or, if a grant of probate or of letters of administration has not been made, any person who appears to be responsible for the management of the holding on behalf of the deceased's estate;

    (b)   any other person who to the knowledge of the applicant may be interested in the outcome of the application,

and in each case shall give the tribunal an indication of the nature of that person's interest in the outcome of the application.

6   Landlord's reply

A landlord who intends to oppose the whole or any part of an application under rule 3(1) shall, within one month after a copy of the application has been served on him, reply thereto in Form 1R (which is the form appended to the copy of the application served on him).

7   Applicant's reply to landlord's application

An applicant who intends to oppose an application to the tribunal under rule 4 shall, within one month after a copy of the application has been served on him, reply thereto in Form 2R (which is the form appended to the copy of the application served on him).

8   Applicant's reply to other applications under rule 3(1)

(1) An applicant who intends to oppose any application under rule 3(1) by any other person shall, within one month after the expiry of the relevant period, reply to that application in Form 4.

(2) Any request by two, three or four applicants for the consent of the landlord to a direction entitling them to a joint tenancy of the holding under section 20(9) of the 1976 Act may be made in the reply of each of them under this rule.

Parties etc

9   Applications to be heard together, and parties

Subject to the following provision of these rules, all applications under rule 3(1) or (2) in respect of any particular holding which are made within the relevant period, and any applications in respect thereof by the landlord, shall be heard and determined together as if each of them other than the first had been made by a party in the course of the proceedings on the first of them to be made, and, accordingly, there shall be parties to the proceedings on each application by an applicant—

(a)   that applicant,
(b)   the landlord, and
(c)   any other applicant whose application was made within the relevant period and is still pending.

General Provisions as to Applications and Replies

10   Service of documents by secretary

(1) As soon as possible after receiving from any person any document under rule 3, 4, 6, 7 or 8 the secretary shall serve one copy thereof on every other person who, in accordance with rule 9, is a party to the proceedings on that application.

(2) As soon as possible after any fresh application under rule 3(1) is made in respect of a holding, the secretary shall serve on the fresh applicant one copy of every document which has not already been served on him but which would have been served on him had he been a party from the outset to the proceedings.

(3) As soon as possible after the expiry of the relevant period, the secretary shall serve on all those persons whose names and addresses were supplied under rule 5(2) by an applicant notice of the existence of the proceedings in respect of the holding and of the names and addresses of the parties thereto, and shall inform each of those persons that, if he so requests in writing, a copy of the eventual decision of the tribunal will be sent to him by the secretary.

11   Application of principal rules relating to applications and replies

(1) Rules 16 (except for paragraph (5)) and 18 (except for paragraph (2)) of the principal rules shall apply to applications and replies under this Part of these rules.

(2) Rule 15(2) of the principal rules shall apply in the case of an application by the landlord under this Part of these rules.

(3) Rule 18(2) of the principal rules shall apply to a reply under rule 7 of these rules if the relevant period has expired and, following the withdrawal of the reply, there is no other outstanding reply to the application by the landlord.

Hearings

12   Date and place of hearing

As soon as practicable the chairman shall fix a date, time and place for the hearing of all applications made in the proceedings under this Part of these rules.

13   Duty to adjourn part of hearing

(1)   Where on the date of the hearing the landlord has not made an application under rule 4(3) but the time allowed for him to do so has not expired, the tribunal shall not proceed to give a direction under section 20 of the 1976 Act except with the consent of the landlord.

(2)   Where on the date of the hearing the time allowed for a reply under rule 7 has not expired, or has not started to run, the tribunal shall not proceed to hear the application of the landlord except with the consent of every applicant who has not yet replied thereto.

(3)   Where under this rule consent is required but is not given the tribunal shall adjourn the proceedings and the chairman shall give such directions as he thinks fit for the further hearing of the proceedings.

14   Application of principal rules relating to preparation for hearing and to hearing

Rules 19, 20, 23(3) and (4), 24, 25, 26(2) and (3) and 27 of the principal rules shall apply with the necessary modifications to applications under this Part of these rules.

Further provisions relating to hearings

15   Sanctions for failure to reply

(1)   If no reply to an application under rule 3(1) is received from the landlord by the secretary within the time allowed by rule 6, then, subject to section 20(7) of the 1976 Act, the landlord shall not be entitled to dispute any matter alleged in that application, but this paragraph does not affect any right of the landlord to rely upon his own application under rule 4.

(2)   Where pursuant to rule 15(2) or 18(2) of the principal rules (as applied by rule 11(2) and (3) of these rules), the tribunal decide to make an order in the terms of the application by the landlord without a formal hearing, any application under rule 3(1) in respect of the holding shall be dismissed.

(3)   If no reply to an application under rule 3(1) is received from an applicant by the secretary within the time allowed by rule 8(1), the applicant who has not replied shall not be entitled to dispute any matter alleged in the application, but this paragraph does not affect the right of that applicant to claim before the tribunal that he is more suitable than the other applicant.

Further provisions relating to hearings

16   Procedure at hearing in case of sole applicant

Where on the date of the hearing only one application under rule 3(1) is pending before the tribunal, the applicant shall begin, and the order of proceedings shall be the same as in civil proceedings in the High Court as if the application were an action begun by writ and as if any application by the landlord were a counterclaim.

17   Procedure at hearing in case of multiple accidents where designation is claimed

(1)   Where any applicant under rule 3(1) claims to be a designated applicant the tribunal shall first hear him as to the validity of his claim to be a designated applicant (and if more than one applicant so claims, the tribunal shall hear them on those

respective claims in the order determined by the tribunal), and shall then afford any other applicant (including any applicant who himself so claims) an opportunity to reply to that claim.

(2) The tribunal shall thereupon determine the validity of each claim to be a designated applicant.

(3) If the tribunal determine that an applicant under rule 3(1) is a designated applicant, they shall then hear that person's application as if he were the only applicant.

(4) If under paragraph (3) the tribunal determine that the designated applicant is a suitable person to become the tenant of the holding, they—

(a) shall, subject to rule 13, hear any application by the landlord.
(b) shall, subject to rule 13, hear any application by the landlord.

(5) If under paragraph (3) the tribunal determine that the designated applicant is not a suitable person to become the tenant of the holding, they—

(a) shall dismiss his application, and
(b) shall, unless there is any remaining issue to be determined under paragraph (2) above, hear the remaining applications under rule 3(1) in accordance with rules 13 and 16 (or, in the case of two or more such applications, under rule 18) as if no applicant had claimed to be a designated applicant.

(6) If under paragraphs (1) and (2) the tribunal determine that there is no designated applicant, rule 18 shall apply.

18   Procedure at hearing is ease of multiple applicants where designation is not claimed

(1) Where the tribunal have to hear more than one application under rule 3(1) and no applicant claims or has been determined to be a designated applicant, then, subject to any direction by the chairman, the tribunal shall—

(a) dispose of the various matters before them in the following order, that is to say—
    (i) any determination as to eligibility under section 21(3) of the 1976 Act;
    (ii) any remaining issue as to eligibility under section 20(3) of the 1976 Act;
    (iii) any determination as to suitability under section 20(3) of the 1976 Act;
    (iv) any question of exercising the discretion conferred by section 20(9) of the 1976 Act;
    (v) any determination as to relative suitability under section 20(6) of the 1976 Act;
    (vi) any question arising under section 20(9A) of the 1976 Act;
    (vii) subject to rule 13, any question arising on an application by the landlord under section 22 of the 1976 Act, and
(b) hear the person who is in the position of applicant in respect of any of the matters referred to in subparagraph (a) above and then the other parties in such order as the tribunal may determine, and, for the purpose of this subparagraph, any request for the landlord's consent made under rule 8(2) or at the hearing shall be treated as if it were an application.

(2) Where, under paragraph (1)(a)(iii), two or more applicants are determined to be suitable persons to become the tenant of the holding, then—

(a) the tribunal shall ask the landlord if he will consent to the giving of a direction in accordance with section 20(9) of the 1976 Act specifying any two, any three, or any four of the suitable applicants and entitling them to a joint tenancy of the holding, and if the landlord then consents the tribunal may (after hearing such of the suitable applicants as wish to be heard) give a direction specifying the applicants in respect of whom the landlord's consent is given, and entitling them to a joint tenancy of the holding;

(b) the tribunal may give the landlord an opportunity to consent within such time as they may allow, and may regard his consent as refused if not given within that time.

(3) Where the tribunal dispose of any matter under paragraph (1)(a)(i),(ii),(iii),(v) or (vii) in such a way that any particular application can no longer succeed, that application shall be dismissed.

19   Further provisions relating to notice to quit

Where the proceedings are adjourned under rule 13(1) and the landlord then fails to make an application under rule 4 within the time allowed by that rule, the tribunal may, without a formal hearing, give a direction under section 20(5) or 20(6) of the 1976 Act (as the case may be) entitling the suitable applicant to a tenancy of the holding.

20   Application of principal rules relating to evidence, decisions, etc

(1) Rules 28 to 31 and 33 to 38 of the principal rules shall apply with the necessary modifications to proceedings under this Part of these rules as they apply to other proceedings before the tribunal.

(2) For the purposes of rules 31, 33 and 34 of the principal rules, any dismissal of an application under these rules shall be a decision, and all such decisions, and the reasons for them, may be given in a single document at the conclusion of the proceedings unless the chairman otherwise decides.

21   Postponement of operation of notice to quit or direction

(1) Where the tribunal give their consent to the operation of a notice to quit under section 22 of the 1976 Act within the period of three months ending with the original operative date or at any time after that date, any application by the tenant under subsection (6) of that section for the notice to have effect from a later date shall be made in writing to the secretary before the hearing or verbally at the hearing.

(2) Where the tribunal give a direction under section 20(5), (6) or (9) of the 1976 Act within the period of three months ending with the relevant time apart from section 23 (2A) of that Act, any application by the tenant under that subsection for the direction to have effect from a later time shall be made in writing to the secretary before the hearing or verbally at the hearing.

PART III: APPLICATION FOR SUCCESSION BY PERSON NOMINATED BY RETIRING TENANT UNDER SCHEDULE 2 TO THE AGRICULTURAL HOLDINGS ACT 1984

22   Interpretation of Part III

(1) In this Part of these rules 'the 1984 Act' means the Agricultural Holdings Act 1984.

(2) Expressions defined for the purposes of, or of any provision in, paragraphs 1 to 6 of Schedule 2 to the 1984 Act (notably in paragraphs 1 (1) and (2) and 6(7), have the same meaning in this Part of these rules.

Form of Application and Reply

23   Application by nominated successor

(1)   An application by the nominated successor to the tribunal under paragraph 5(1) of Schedule 2 to the 1984 Act for a direction entitling him to a tenancy of an agricultural holding shall be made in Form 5.

(2)   An application made under this rule shall not be entertained by the tribunal if it is not made within the relevant period.

24   Notice of application

The nominated successor shall at the time of making his application serve notice of the application in Form 6 on the landlord.

25   Landlord's reply

A landlord who intends to oppose the whole or any part of an application under rule 23(1) shall, within one month after a copy of the application has been served on him, reply thereto in Form 5R (which is the form appended on the copy of the application served on him).

Parties

26   Parties

There shall be parties to the proceedings on an application by the nominated successor—

  (a)   the nominated successor,
  (b)   the landlord, and
  (c)   the retiring tenant or (in the case of a joint tenancy) all the retiring tenants.

General Provisions As To Applications And Replies

27   Service of documents by secretary

As soon as possible after receiving from any person any document under rule 23 or 25 the secretary shall serve one copy thereof on every other person who, in accordance with rule 26, is a party to the proceedings on that application.

28   Application of principal rules relating to applications and replies under this Part of these rules.

Rules 16 (except for paragraph (5)) and 18 (except for paragraph (2)) of the principal rules shall apply to applications and replies under this Part of these rules.

Hearings

29   Date and place of hearing

As soon as practicable the chairman shall fix a date, time and place for the hearing of an application made under this Part of these rules.

30   Application of principal rules relating to preparation for hearing and to hearing

Rules 19, 20, 23(3) and (4), 24, 25, 26(2) and (3) and 27 of the principal rules shall apply with the necessary modifications to applications under this Part of these rules.

Further Provisions Relating To Hearings:

31   Sanctions for failure to reply

If no reply to an application under rule 23(1) is received from the landlord by the secretary within the time allowed by rule 25, then, subject to paragraph 5(5) of Schedule 2 to the 1984 Act, the landlord shall not be entitled to dispute any matter alleged in that application.

32   Procedure at hearing

(1)   Subject to paragraph (2), at the hearing the nominated successor shall begin and the other parties shall be heard in such order as the tribunal may determine.

(2)   Where the retirement notice to which the nominated successor's application relates includes a statement in accordance with paragraph 2(3) of Schedule 2 to the 1984 Act that the notice is given on the grounds mentioned in that provision, the tribunal shall first consider whether the conditions specified in paragraph 5(3)(*a*) and (*b*) of that Schedule are satisfied and, if the tribunal determine that those conditions are not satisfied, they shall dismiss the nominated successor's application.

33   Application of principal rules relating to evidence, decisions etc.

(1)   Rules 28 to 31 and 33 to 38 of the principal rules shall apply with the necessary modifications to proceedings under this Part of these rules as they apply to other proceedings before the tribunal.

(2)   For the purposes of rules 31, 33 and 34 of the principal rules, any dismissal of an application under these rules shall be a decision, and all such decisions, and the reasons for them, may be given in a single document at the conclusion of the proceedings unless the chairman otherwise decides.

34   Postponement of operation of direction

Where the tribunal give a direction under paragraph 5(6) of Schedule 2 to the 1984 Act within the period of three months ending with the retirement date, any application by the tenant under paragraph 6(7) of that Schedule for the direction to have effect from a later time shall be made in writing to the secretary before the hearing or verbally at the hearing.

APPENDIX: FORMS

Rule 1(3)(b)

FORM 1 (SUCCESSION ON DEATH)

Rule 3(1) and (2)

Ref. No. To be inserted by the secretary.

AGRICULTURAL LAND TRIBUNAL

APPLICATION FOR DIRECTION GIVING ENTITLEMENT TO TENANCY OF AGRICULTURAL HOLDING

APPLICATION FOR DETERMINATION THAT APPLICANT BE TREATED AS AN ELIGIBLE PERSON

[In completing this form it is important to refer to the notes]

Part A: To be completed by all applicants

To the secretary of the Agricultural Land Tribunal

for the .... Area.

1. I, ... (block capitals)

.... (address)

hereby apply under section 20(1) of the Agriculture (Miscellaneous Provisions) Act 1976 for a direction entitling me to a tenancy of the holding specified in paragraph 2 below.

2. The holding in respect of which the application is made as known as

.... and consists of:—

    (a)   hectares of arable land (including temporary grass)
           (Ordnance Survey Field Nos ....)
    (b)   hectares of permanent pasture
           (Ordnance Survey Field Nos ....)
    (c)   hectares of rough grazing
           (Ordnance Survey Field Nos ....)
    (d)   hectares of other land (including orchards)
           (Ordnance Survey Field Nos ....)

TOTAL .... hectares .... ANNUAL RENT £ ......

3. The current year of the tenancy of the holding expires on

4. The holding includes the following buildings [give a general description]:—

**5. The holding forms part of a larger agricultural unit known as and consisting of [give a general description]:—

6. The application arises on the death of .... formerly the tenant of the holding referred to in paragraph 2, who died on (1)

His/her tenancy was—

    *(a) granted before 12th July 1984.
    *(b) obtained on or after 12th July 1984 by virtue of a direction of the Agricultural Land Tribunal under section 20 of the 1976 Act.
    *(c) granted on or after 12th July 1984 following a direction of the Agricultural Land Tribunal under section 20 of the 1976 Act but commenced before the relevant time for the purposes of section 23 of that Act.
    *(d) granted on or after 12th July 1984 by a written contract of tenancy indicating that the succession provisions in Part II of the 1976 Act should apply.
    *(e) granted on or after 12th July 1984 to a person who, immediately before that date, was a tenant of the holding or of any agricultural holding which comprised the whole or a substantial part of the land comprised in the holding.

7. The landlord of the holding is .... of .... (address).

**8. I am the sole person validly designated by the deceased tenant of the holding in his will as the person he wished to succeed him as tenant of the holding. A copy of the relevant part of the will in which I am designated is attached [attach a copy of or extract from the will marking the relevant passage)(2).

9

    **(a)I am the *wife/*husband/*brother/*sister/*child of the deceased tenant (3).

**(b)I was treated by the deceased tenant as a child of the family in relation to his marriage to .... (4)

on .... (give date of marriage).

**10

(a) During the seven years ending with the date of death of the deceased tenant my only or my principal source of livelihood was derived from—

    *(i) my agricultural work on the holding, or on an agricultural unit of which the holding forms a part;

    *(ii) his/his and my agricultural work on the holding, or on an agricultural unit of which the holding forms a part;

during the following period(s) and in the following manner (give details of the way livelihood derived from agricultural work on the holding)(5):—

*(b) During the period(s) specified in paragraph 10(a) I had the following source(s) of livelihood other than those derived from the holding or from an agricultural unit of which the holding forms a part (give details of other sources of livelihood):—

*(c) During the period(s) specified in paragraph 10(a) I had no other source of livelihood.

**11. During the seven years ending with the date of death of the deceased tenant I attended a full-time course at .... (name of university, college or other establishment of further education) during the following period(s) (give details of time spent at university, etc.)(5), (6):—

During this period/these periods I studied the following subjects and obtained the following qualifications (give details of subjects studied and any qualifications obtained):—

**12

(a) The following agricultural land is occupied by me, my spouse or a company under my control, the control of my spouse or our joint control as owner-occupier/tenant/licensee, whether alone or jointly with other (give particulars of any land occupied, including area and any land occupied jointly with others):—

**(b)The following agricultural land is occupied by a person under a licence or such a (7) tenancy as is mentioned in paragraph 2(1)(a) to (d) of Schedule 3A to the 1976 Act (8) granted by *me and/or *my spouse and/or *a company controlled by me and/or my spouse **together with one or more other persons, being at the time it was granted a person or persons entitled to occupy the land otherwise than under a tenancy, or in a capacity, falling within paragraph 2(1)(a) to (f) of that Schedule(8) (give particulars of any land occupied, including area):—

**(c)I apply under paragraph 4(2) of Schedule 3A to the 1976 Act for the net annual income from the following agricultural land which is—

    *(i) jointly occupied;

    *(ii) deemed by virtue of paragraph 6(2) of that Schedule to be jointly occupied;

by me and one or more other persons (not being only my spouse or a company under my control, the control of my spouse or our joint control) to be treated as limited to my appropriate share of that net annual income (give particulars of any land in joint occupation or deemed joint occupation)(9):—

13. I was born on

14. I claim to be a suitable person to receive the tenancy of this holding because (10):—

Part B: To be completed if you think that you may not fully satisfy the requirements of paragraph 10(a)

15. Further to the application set out in the preceding paragraphs of this Form, I, ... (block capitals) of the above address also apply under section 21(2) of the 1976 Act for a determination that I am to be treated as an eligible person for the purposes of Part II of that Act(11).

16

(a)   During the seven years ending with the date of death of the deceased tenant my livelihood was derived from—

  *(i) my agricultural work on the holding referred to in paragraph 2, or on an agricultural unit of which the holding forms a part;
  *(ii) his/his and my agricultural work on the holding referred to in paragraph 2, or on an agricultural unit of which the holding forms a part;

to a material extent during the following period(s) and in the following manner (give details of the extent to which livelihood was derived from agricultural work on the holding)(12):—

**(b)   During the period(s) specified in paragraph 16(a) I had no other source of livelihood.

**17. During the seven years ending with the date of death of the deceased tenant I attended a full-time course at .... (name of university, college or other establishment of further education) during the following period(s) (give details of time spent at university, etc.)(6):—

During this period/these periods I studied the following subjects and obtained the following qualifications (give details of subjects studied and any qualifications obtained):—

**18. I claim that, because of the following circumstances, it is fair and reasonable for me to be able to apply under section 20 of the 1976 Act for a direction entitling me to a tenancy of the holding referred to in paragraph 2(13):—

Part C: To be completed by all applicants

19. I attach the following documents which I intend to produce in support of my case:—

  (a)   two(14) copies of a 6' to one mile or 1/10,000(15) map of the holding described in paragraph 2 above (and of the other land referred to in paragraph 5);
  (b)   two(14) copies of (16):—

20. The persons whom I shall notify of this application/these applications are (17):—

  (a)   the landlord of the holding whose name and address are:—
  (b)   ....
  (c)   ....
  (d)   ....

21

(a)   The following is/are the personal representative(s) of the deceased tenant or (if there are no personal representatives) the person or persons responsible for the management of the holding on behalf of the deceased's estate(18):—

Name(s) ....

Address(es) ....

....

....

(b)   The following person(s) is/are or my be interested in the outcome of this application(18):—

Name(s) ....

Address(es) ....

....

....

Nature of interest ....

Date .... Signed(19) ....

*Strike out whichever is inapplicable.

**Strike out if inapplicable.

Notes:

(1)   Formal proof of the date of death will be required at the hearing.

(2)   This paragraph should be completed only if the applicant received a specific bequest of the deceased's tenancy under his will or is specifically named in the will as the person whom the deceased tenant wished to succeed him as tenant of the holding. It will be necessary for a grant of probate or administration to be obtained from the Family Division of the High Court in respect of the will before the tribunal can hear any claim to be a designated applicant. Where an applicant establishes that he is so designated under the deceased tenant's will, no other application will be considered unless the tribunal determine that the designated applicant is not an eligible person or is not a suitable person to become the tenant of the holding.

(3)   Formal proof of the relationship to the deceased, e.g., by production of marriage or birth certificates, may be required at the hearing. Adopted children should complete this sub-paragraph, and not paragraph 9(b) following.

(4)   Paragraph 9(b) may apply where the applicant was the step-child or foster child or the deceased or was otherwise treated by him as his child. An outline should be given of the circumstances relied on as establishing that the applicant was treated by the deceased as his child in relation to the marriage. Production of the relevant marriage certificate and any relevant birth certificate may be required at the hearing.

(5)   To qualify under paragraph 10(a)(i) the applicant should have derived his only or principal source of livelihood from his agricultural work on the holding (or on a larger unit of which the holding forms part) during a total of five years of the seven years ending with the death of the deceased tenant. Paragraph 10(a)(ii) is available only to a widow of the deceased tenant. The total of five years may be made up of one continuous period, or one or more separate periods. A period of full-time education at a university etc., may, in the circumstances set out in note (6), count towards the five-year period of earning a livelihood from the holding, and reference should be made to paragraph 11 and note(6) in deciding whether the requirements of this paragraph can be satisfied. An applicant who cannot satisfy the requirements of paragraph 10(a) fully but who believes he can satisfy them to a material extent should not complete paragraphs 10 and 11 but should complete instead paragraph 15, together with paragraphs 16, 17 (if relevant) and 18 in Part B of the Form. The Notes to those paragraphs should also be consulted. Where an applicant is in any doubt as to whether or not he can satisfy the requirements of paragraph 10 fully, he is advised to complete paragraphs 10 and 11 (if relevant) and Part B of the Form.

(6)   Any period or periods (up to an aggregate total of three years) during the seven years ending with the date of death of the deceased tenant during which the applicant was attending a full-time course at a university, college or other establishment of further education will be treated as a period throughout which his only or principal source of livelihood was derived from his agricultural work on the holding. Any subject may have been studied.

(7)   Land occupied by the applicant's spouse or by a company controlled by that person or jointly by that person and the applicant should not be included in paragraph 12 where either of the parties has obtained a decree of judicial separation or a decree nisi of divorce or of nullity of marriage and in each case that decree remains unrescinded. In addition, land should not be included in paragraph 12 if it is occupied by the applicant, his spouse or a controlled company—

   (a)   under a tenancy approved under section 2(1) of the Agricultural Holdings Act 1948 or under such a tenancy relating to the use of land for grazing or mowing as is referred to in the proviso to that provision;
   (b)   under a tenancy for more than one year but less than two years;
   (c)   under a tenancy not falling within (a) or (b) above and not having effect as a contract of tenancy;
   (d)   under a tenancy to which section 3 of the 1948 Act does not apply by virtue of section 3B of that Act;
   (e)   as a licensee; or
   (f)   as an executor, administrator, trustee in bankruptcy or person otherwise deriving title from another person by operation of law.

However, where the applicant occupies land in accordance with (a) to (e) above under a licence or tenancy granted to him by his spouse or by a body corporate controlled by him, that land should be included in paragraph 12.

(8)   Paragraph 2(1)(a) to (f) of Schedule 3A to the Agriculture (Miscellaneous Provisions) Act 1976 is set out in note (7).

(9)   If the applicant occupies land jointly with one or more other persons (not being only his spouse or a company under the control of the applicant or his spouse or under their joint control), or if the applicant is deemed to occupy land jointly with one or more such persons, he may in either case complete the application set out in paragraph 12(c) of the Form for the net annual income which the land is or was capable of producing to be treated as limited to his appropriate share.

(10)   All matters relied on as supporting the claim to be a suitable person to become the tenant of the holding should be summarised. These should include details of the applicant's training and practical experience of agriculture, physical health, financial standing and any educational qualifications not already listed in paragraph 11 or 17.

(11)   This paragraph should be completed (together with paragraphs 16, 17 (if relevant) and 18) in any case where the applicant, while otherwise meeting the conditions contained in paragraphs (a) and (c) of the definition of 'eligible person' in section 18(2) of the 1976 Act cannot fully satisfy the conditions as to deriving his principal or main source of livelihood from the holding contained in paragraph (b) of that subsection. (It is also necessary for the application set out in paragraph 1 of the Form to be completed in addition to completing this paragraph.) An applicant who fully satisfies the requirements of paragraph 10(a) need not complete this paragraph or paragraphs 16, 17 and 18.

(12)   The applicant should state to what extent he has derived his livelihood from his agricultural work on the holding (or on a larger unit of which the holding forms part) during a total of five years of the seven years ending with the death of the deceased tenant. Paragraph 16(a)(ii) applies only to a widow of the deceased tenant. The total of

five years may be made up of one continuous period, or one or more separate periods. A period of full-time education at a university, etc., may in certain circumstances count in relation to the five year period as a period in which a livelihood was derived from agricultural work on the holding, and paragraph 17 should also be completed where relevant.

(13) A summary should be given of matters relied on as establishing that it is fair and reasonable that the applicant should be entitled to apply under section 20 of the 1976 Act for a tenancy of the holding, though not fully satisfying the conditions specified in paragraph (b) of the definition of 'eligible person' in section 18(2) of that Act. The length of time the applicant has lived on the holding, details of work done by him on the holding (apart from those already given in paragraph 16) and any special circumstances which have prevented him from qualifying in full as an eligible person under paragraph (b) of the definition of 'eligible person' should be given. (Note (5) describes the requirements needed to qualify fully under paragraph (b) of the definition.)

(14) By virtue of rule 11(1) of the Agricultural Land Tribunals (Succession) Rules 1984 two copies of the application and of any map and document must be sent to the secretary.

(15) A larger scale map may be used if preferred. Ordnance Survey Field Numbers must be marked on the map.

(16) Mention any other document which is attached to this application.

(17) The applicant is required to send to the landlord of the holding, and to every other person who to his knowledge has made or may be able to make an application for a tenancy of the holding, notice of this application in Form 3 (Succession on Death) which is set out in the Appendix to the Agricultural Land Tribunals (Succession) Rules 1984. The applicant should enter the name and address of the landlord at (a) and the names and addresses of appropriate other persons (if any) respectively at (b), (c) and (d), etc.

(18) This information is required by rule 5(2) of those Rules.

(19) If signed by any person other than the applicant himself, he should state in what capacity or by what authority he signs.

FORM 1R
(SUCCESSION ON DEATH)

Rule 6

Ref. No. To be inserted by the secretary.

AGRICULTURAL LAND TRIBUNAL

REPLY TO APPLICATION FOR DIRECTION GIVING ENTITLEMENT TO TENANCY OF
AGRICULTURAL HOLDING

REPLY TO APPLICATION FOR DETERMINATION THAT APPLICANT BE TREATED AS AN
ELIGIBLE PERSON

To the secretary of the Agricultural Land Tribunal

for the .... Area.

I, ... (block capitals)

of .... (address)

landlord of .... (name or description of holding) having received a copy of the application bearing the above reference number reply as follows:—

1. The facts stated in paragraphs 1, 2, 4 and 7 of the application are, to the best of any knowledge, information and belief, correct **except that:—

**2. I dispute the claim of the applicant to be an eligible person (1) on the following grounds:—

**3. I dispute the claim of the applicant to be treated as an eligible person (2) on the following grounds:—

4. I have the following comments on the suitability of the applicant to become the tenant of the above holding:—

5. I attach two copies of the following relevant documents(3):—

6. I consider the application to be invalid by reason of(>4>):—

Date .... Signed(5) ....

**Strike out if inapplicable.

TAKE NOTICE THAT IF YOU DO NOT REPLY IN THIS FORM WITHIN ONE MONTH OF THE DATE OF SERVICE ON YOU OF THE ATTACHED APPLICA-TION, THEN, SUBJECT TO SECTION 20(7) OF THE AGRICULTURE (MISCEL-LANEOUS PROVISIONS) ACT 1976, YOU WILL NOT BE ENTITLED AT THE HEARING OF THE APPLICATION TO DISPUTE ANY MATTER ALLEGED IN IT.

Notes:

(1) The paragraphs of the application which (where completed) will be relevant to the applicant's claim to be an eligible person are paragraphs 9, 10, 11 and 12.

(2) The paragraphs of the application which (where completed) will be relevant to the applicant's claim to be treated as an eligible person are paragraphs 15, 16, 17 and 18.

(3) By virtue of rule 11(1) of the Agricultural Land Tribunals (Succession) Rules 1984 two copies of this reply and of any document which you wish to submit to the tribunal must be sent to the secretary. If you disagree with any map or plan attached to the application, your reply should be accompanied by two copies of a 6' to one mile or 1/10,000 (or larger) map showing what you consider to be the true position and marking the Ordnance Survey Field Numbers.

(4) If you consider that, for any reason, the applicant is not legally entitled to make his application, you should state succinctly the grounds on which you rely.

(5) If signed by any person other than the landlord himself, he should state in what capacity or by what authority he signs.

FORM 2 (SUCCESSION ON DEATH)

Rule 4(1)

Ref. No. To be inserted by the secretary.

AGRICULTURAL LAND TRIBUNAL

APPLICATION FOR CONSENT TO OPERATION OF NOTICE TO QUIT

To the secretary of the Agricultural Land Tribunal

for the .... Area.

1. I, ... (block capitals)

of .... (address)

hereby apply under section 22(1) of the Agriculture (Miscellaneous Provisions) Act 1976 for the consent of the tribunal to the operation of a notice to quit which I gave to

.... and ....

being the personal representative(s) of .... (block capitals)

deceased, formerly of .... (address).

I was officially notified of his/her death by .... on ....

2. The notice to quit was served on (insert date) .... in respect of the holding known as ....

3. An application (bearing reference number ....) to the tribunal under Part II of the 1976 Act or a tenancy of this holding was made on ....

Full particulars of the holding are set out in that application **(as amended in reply to that application dated ....).

4. I apply for the tribunal's consent to the operation of the notice to quit in the event of an applicant under the application referred to in paragraph 3, or any other such applicant, being determined by the tribunal to be a suitable person to become the tenant of the holding.

5. The grounds upon which I make this application are those provided by paragraphs(s) ... . of section 3(3) of the Agricultural Holdings (Notices to Quit) Act 1977 as read with section 22(2) of the 1976 Act, as amended. (It is important to refer to note(1).)

6. The main facts on which I will base my case are:—

7. If I obtain possession of the land I intend:—

   *(a) to farm it myself.
   *(b) to let it to another tenant (state name and address if known).
   *(c) (state any other intention)

**8. The future tenant referred to in paragraph 7(b)(2) at present farms other land consisting of:—

   (a) hectares of arable land (including temporary grass)
       (Ordnance Survey Field Nos ....)
   (b) hectares of permanent pasture
       (Ordnance Survey Field Nos ....)
   (c) hectares of rough grazing
       (Ordnance Survey Field Nos ....)
   (d) hectares of other land (including orchards)
       (Ordnance Survey Field Nos ....)

TOTAL .... hectares.

9. I attach the following documents which I intend to produce in support of my case:—

   (a) two copies(3) of a 6' to one mile or 1/10,000(4) map of the land described in paragraph 8(5) above;
   (b) two copies(3) of(6):—

Date .... Signed(7) ....

*Strike out whichever is inapplicable

**Strike out if inapplicable.

Notes:

(1)   The applicant must state on which paragraph or paragraphs of the subsection he intends to rely. The five paragraphs state as follows:—

   (a)   that the carrying out of the purpose for which the landlord proposes to terminate the tenancy is desirable in the interests of good husbandry as respects the land to which the notice relates, treated as a separate unit;

   (b)   that the carrying out thereof is desirable in the interests of sound management of the estate of which the land to which the notice relates forms part or which that land constitutes (see note (5) below);

   (c)   that the carrying out thereof is desirable for the purposes of agricultural research, education, experiment or demonstration, or for the purposes of the enactments relating to smallholdings or allotments;

   (d)   that greater hardship would be caused by withholding than by giving consent to the operation of the notice;

   (e)   that the landlord proposes to terminate the tenancy for the purpose of the land's being used for a use, other than for agriculture, not falling within Case B in section 2(3) of the Agricultural Holdings (Notices to Quit) Act 1977.

If, under paragraph (d) above, the applicant intends to rely on hardship to a person or persons other than himself, he should set out in paragraph 6 the name of every person who will be so affected, and the relationship of that person to himself, and should state the nature of the hardship on which he relies.

(2)   Paragraph 8 need not be completed if the name of the future tenant is unknown. Where land is described, a map should be provided (see note (5) below).

(3)   By virtue of rule 11(1) of the Agricultural Land Tribunals (Succession) Rules 1984 two copies of the application and of any map and document must be sent to the secretary.

(4)   A larger scale map may be used if preferred. Ordnance Survey Field Numbers must be marked on the map.

(5)   Where it is intended to give evidence about any land other than that which is the subject of the notice to quit, it must be shown either on the map produced or on a separate map of a scale of 6' to one mile or 1/10,000 (or larger).

(6)   Mention any other document which is attached to this application.

(7)   If signed by any person other than the applicant himself, he should state in what capacity or by what authority he signs.

FORM 2R (SUCCESSION ON DEATH)

Rule 7

Ref. No. To be inserted by the secretary.

AGRICULTURAL LAND TRIBUNAL

REPLY TO APPLICATION FOR CONSENT TO OPERATION OF NOTICE TO QUIT

To the secretary of the Agricultural Land Tribunal

for the .... Area.

I, ... (block capitals)

of .... (address) having applied to the tribunal on .... for a direction entitling me to a tenancy of .... and having received a copy of the application (bearing the above reference number) for the tribunal's consent to the operation of a notice to quit, reply as follows:—

1. The facts stated in the first three paragraphs of the application are correct **except that:—

2. My main reasons for resisting the application are:—

**3. The landlord is not acting fairly and reasonably because(1):—

4. I attach copies of the following relevant documents(2):—

Date .... Signed(3) ....

TAKE NOTICE THAT IF YOU DO NOT REPLY IN THIS FORM WITHIN ONE MONTH OF THE DATE OF SERVICE ON YOU OF THE ATTACHED APPLICATION BY THE LANDLORD OF THE HOLDING FOR THE TRIBUNAL'S CONSENT TO THE OPERATION OF THE LANDLORD'S NOTICE TO QUIT, THE TRIBUNAL MAY GIVE THAT CONSENT SUMMARILY AND SUMMARILY DISMISS YOUR OWN APPLICATION TO BE GRANTED A TENANCY OF THE HOLDING, WITHOUT HEARING YOUR CASE.

**Strike out if inapplicable.

Notes:

(1)   The tribunal must withhold consent if, in all the circumstances, it appears that a fair and reasonable landlord would not insist on possession. If you have any special reasons for saying the landlord is acting unfairly or unreasonably which do not appear under paragraph 2, you should state them under paragraph 3.

(2)   By virtue of rule 11(1) of the Agricultural Land Tribunals (Succession) Rules 1984 two copies of the reply and of any document which you wish to submit to the tribunal must be sent to the secretary.

If you disagree with any map or plan attached to the application, your reply should be accompanied by two copies of a 6' to one mile or 1/10,000 (or larger) map showing what you consider to be the true position and marking the Ordnance Survey Field Numbers.

(3)   If signed by any person other than the applicant himself, he should state in what capacity or by what authority he signs.

FORM 3 (SUCCESSION ON DEATH)

Rule 5(1)

Ref. No. To be inserted by the secretary.

AGRICULTURAL LAND TRIBUNAL

NOTICE OF APPLICATION FOR ENTITLEMENT TO TENANCY UNDER PART II OF THE AGRICULTURE (MISCELLANEOUS PROVISIONS) ACT 1976

To: .... (name)

of: .... (address)

I, ... (block capitals)

of .... (address)

hereby give you notice that I applied on .... (date of application) under Part II of the above-named Act for a direction entitling me to a tenancy of the agricultural holding known as ....

(address or brief description of holding) in succession to

(name of deceased tenant of the holding) who died on

Dated .... Signed ....

A copy of the full application will in due course be sent to the landlord and any other applicants by the secretary to the tribunal.

FORM 4 (SUCCESSION ON DEATH)

Rule 8

Ref. No. To be inserted by the secretary.

AGRICULTURAL LAND TRIBUNAL

To the secretary of the Agricultural Land Tribunal

for the .... Area.

I, ... (block capitals)

of .... (address)

having received a copy of the application of ....

(hereinafter called 'the applicant') bearing the above reference number, reply as follows:—

1. The facts stated in the first seven paragraphs of the application are correct **except that:—

2. *I accept the applicant's claim to be a designated applicant, as stated in paragraph 8 of the application.

OR

*I dispute the applicant's claim to be designated applicant, as stated in paragraph 8 of the application, on the following grounds:—

3. I do not dispute any of the matters stated in paragraphs 9—13, 16 and 17 of the application **except that:—

4. I claim to be a more suitable person than the applicant to be granted a tenancy of the holding; and I base this claim on the following grounds:—

**5. The applicant and I **(and ....) have agreed to request the landlord's consent to a direction entitling us to a joint tenancy of the holding.

Date .... Signed ....

**Strike out if inapplicable

*Strike out whichever is inapplicable.

FORM 5
(SUCCESSION ON RETIREMENT)

Rule 23(1)

Ref. No. To be inserted by the secretary.

AGRICULTURAL LAND TRIBUNAL

APPLICATION FOR DIRECTION GIVING ENTITLEMENT TO TENANCY OF
AGRICULTURAL HOLDING

[In completing this form it is important to refer to the notes]

To the secretary of the Agricultural Land Tribunal

for the .... Area.

1. I, ... (block capitals)

of .... (address)

hereby apply under paragraph 5(1) of Schedule 2 to the Agricultural Holdings
Act 1984 for a direction entitling me to a tenancy of the holding specified in
paragraph 2 below.

2. The holding in respect of which the application is made is known as
.... and consists of:—

   (a)   hectares of arable land (including temporary grass)
         (Ordnance Survey Field Nos ....)
   (b)   hectares of permanent pasture
         (Ordnance Survey Field Nos ....)
   (c)   hectares of rough grazing
         (Ordnance Survey Field Nos ....)
   (d)   hectares of other land (including orchards)
         (Ordnance Survey Field Nos ....)

TOTAL .... hectares .... ANNUAL RENT £ ......

3. The current year of the tenancy of the holding expires on ....

4. The holding includes the following buildings (give a general description):—

**5. The holding forms part of a larger agricultural unit known as and consisting of
(give general description):—

6. The landlord of the holding is ....

of .... (address)

The tenant(s) of the holding is/are ....

of .... (address(es)).

7. This application arises as a result of a retirement notice given by the tenant(s) to the
landlord on ....

8. I am the nominated successor.

9

**(a)   I am the *wife/*husband/*brother/*sister/*child of the tenant (where there is
more than one tenant, specify which)(1).

**(b)   I am treated by the tenant (where there is more than one tenant, specify which)
as a child of the family in relation to his marriage to .... (2)on
.... (give date of marriage).

10

(a)   During the seven years ending with the date on which the tenant(s) gave the
retirement notice to the landlord my only or principal source of livelihood was derived
from—

*(i) my agricultural work on the holding, or on an agricultural unit of which the holding forms a part;

*(ii) the tenant's/the tenant's and my (where there is more than one tenant, specify which) agricultural work on the holding, or on an agricultural unit of which the holding forms a part;

during the following period(s) and in the following manner (give details of the way livelihood derived from agricultural work on the holding)(3):—

*(b) During the period(s) specified in paragraph 10(a) I had the following source(s) of livelihood other than those derived from the holding or from an agricultural unit of which the holding forms a part (give details of other sources of livelihood):—

*(c) During the period(s) specified in paragraph 10(a) I had no other source of livelihood.

**11. During the seven years ending with the date on which the tenant(s) gave the retirement notice to the landlord I attended a full-time course at .... (name of university, college or other establishment of further education) during the following period(s) (give details of time spent at university, etc.)(4):—

During this period/these periods I studied the following subjects and obtained the following qualifications (give details of subjects studied and any qualifications obtained):—

**12

(a) The following agricultural land is occupied by me, my spouse or a company under my control, the control of my spouse or our joint control as owner-occupier/tenant/ licensee, whether alone or jointly with other (give particulars of any land occupied, including area and any land occupied jointly with others)(5):—

(b) The following agricultural land is occupied by a person under a licence or such a tenancy as is mentioned in paragraph 2(1)(a) to (d) of Schedule 3A to the Agriculture (Miscellaneous Provisions) Act 1976(6) granted by *me and/or *my spouse and/or *a company controlled by me and/or my spouse together with one or more other persons, being at the time it was granted a person or persons entitled to occupy the land otherwise than under a tenancy, or in a capacity, falling within paragraph 2(1)(a) to (f) of that Schedule(6) (give particulars of any land occupied including area):—

**(c) I apply under paragraph 4(2) of Schedule 3A to the 1976 Act, as applied by paragraph 1(4)(b) of Schedule 2 to the 1984 Act, for the net annual income from the following agricultural land which is—

*(i) jointly occupied;

*(ii) deemed by virtue of paragraph 6(2) of the said Schedule 3A, as applied by the said paragraph 1(4)(b), to be jointly occupied;

by me and one or more other persons (not being only my spouse or a company under may control, the control of my spouse or our joint control) to be treated as limited to my appropriate share of that net annual income (give particulars of any land in joint occupation or deemed joint occupation)(7):—

13. I was born on ....

14. I claim to be a suitable person to receive the tenancy of this holding because (8):—

15. I attach the following documents which I intend to produce in support of my case:—

(a) two(9) copies of a 6' to one mile or 1/10,000(10) map of the holding described in paragraph 2 above (and of the other land referred to in paragraph 5);

(b) two(9) copies of the retirement notice;

(c) two(9) copies of(11):—

16. I shall notify the landlord of this application(12).

Date .... Signed(13) ....

Signature of retiring tenant(s) ....

....

....

....

*Strike out whichever is inapplicable.

**Strike out if inapplicable.

Notes

(1) Formal proof of the relationship to the tenant, e.g., by production of marriage or birth certificates, may be required at the hearing. Adopted children should complete this sub-paragraph, and not paragraph 9(b) following.

(2) Paragraph 9(b) may apply where the applicant is the step-child or foster child of the tenant or is otherwise treated by him as his child. An outline should be given of the circumstances relied on as establishing that the applicant is treated by the tenant as his child in relation to the marriage. Production of the relevant marriage certificate and any relevant birth certificate may be required at the hearing.

(3) To qualify under paragraph 10(a)(i) the applicant should have derived his only or principal source of livelihood from his agricultural work on the holding (or on a larger unit of which the holding forms part) during a total of five years of the seven years ending with the date on which the tenant(s) gave the landlord the retirement notice. Paragraph 10(a)(ii) is available only to a tenant's wife. The total of five years may be made up of one continuous period, or one or more separate periods. A period of full-time education at a university etc., may, in the circumstances set out in note (4), count towards the five-year period of earning a livelihood from the holding, and reference should be made to paragraph 11 and note (4) in deciding whether the requirements of this paragraph can be satisfied.

(4) Any period or periods (up to an aggregate total of three years) during the seven years ending with the date on which the tenant(s) gave the retirement notice to the landlord during which the applicant was attending a full-time course at a university, college or other establishment of further education will be treated as a period throughout which his only or principal source of livelihood was derived from his agricultural work on the holding. Any subject may have been studied.

(5) Land occupied by the applicant's spouse or by a company controlled by that person or jointly by that person and the applicant should not be included in paragraph 12 where either of the parties has obtained a decree of judicial separation or a decree nisi of divorce or of nullity of marriage and in each case that decree remains unrescinded. In addition, land should not be included in paragraph 12 if it is occupied by the applicant, his spouse or a controlled company—

(a) under a tenancy approved under section 2(1) of the Agricultural Holdings Act 1948 or under such a tenancy relating to the use of land for grazing or mowing as is referred to in the proviso to that provision;

(b) under a tenancy for more than one year but less than two years;

(c) under a tenancy not falling within (a) or (b) above and not having effect as a contract of tenancy;

(d) under a tenancy to which section 3 of the 1948 Act does not apply by virtue of section 3B of that Act;

(e)   as a licensee; or

(f)   as an executor, administrator, trustee in bankruptcy or person otherwise deriving title from another person by operation of law.

However, where the applicant occupies land in accordance with (a) to (e) above under a licence or tenancy granted to him by his spouse or by a body corporate controlled by him, that land should be included in paragraph 12.

(6)   Paragraph 2(1)(a) to (f) of Schedule 3A to the Agriculture (Miscellaneous Provisions) Act 1976 is set out in note(5).

(7)   If the applicant occupies land jointly with one or more other persons (not being only his spouse or a company under the control of the applicant or his spouse or under their joint control), or if the applicant is deemed to occupy land jointly with one or more such persons, he may in either case complete the application set out in paragraph 12(c) of the Form for the net annual income which the land is or was capable of producing to be treated as limited to his appropriate share.

(8)   All matters relied on as supporting the claim to be a suitable person to become the tenant of the holding should be summarised. These should include details of the applicant's training and practical experience of agriculture, physical health, financial standing and any educational qualifications not already listed in paragraph 11.

(9)   By virtue of rule 28 of the Agricultural Land Tribunals (Succession) Rules 1984 two copies of the application and of any map and document must be sent to the secretary.

(10)   A larger scale map may be used if preferred. Ordnance Survey Field Numbers must be marked on the map.

(11)   Mention any other document which is attached to this application.

(12)   The applicant is required to send to the landlord of the holding notice of this application in Form 6 (Succession on Retirement) which is set out in the Appendix to the Agricultural Land Tribunals (Succession) Rules 1984.

(13)   If signed by any person other than the applicant himself, he should state in what capacity or by what authority he signs.

FORM 5R (SUCCESSION ON RETIREMENT)

Rule 25

Ref. No. To be inserted by the secretary.

AGRICULTURAL LAND TRIBUNAL

REPLY TO APPLICATION FOR DIRECTION GIVING ENTITLEMENT TO TENANCY OF AGRICULTURAL HOLDING

To the secretary of the Agricultural Land Tribunal

for the .... Area.

1. I, ... (block capitals)

of .... (address)

landlord of .... (name or description of holding)

having received a copy of the application bearing the above reference number reply as follows:—

1. The facts stated in paragraphs 1, 2, 4, 6 and 7 of the application are, to the best of my knowledge, information and belief, correct **except that:—

**2. I dispute the claim of the applicant to be an eligible person(1) on the following grounds:—

3. I have the following comments on the suitability of the applicant to become the tenant of the above holding:—

**4. I claim that greater hardship would be caused by the tribunal giving the direction sought by the applicant than by refusing his application and my reasons for this claim are:—

**5. The tenancy is the subject of a notice to quit Case *B/*C/*D/*E/*F served on .... (date).

**(For Case C only) The notice to quit is founded on a certificate granted in accordance with an application made on .... (date).

**(For Case D only) The notice to quit is founded on a notice given for the purposes of that Case on .... (date).

6. I attach two copies of the following relevant documents(2):—

7. I consider the application to be invalid by reason of(3):—

Date .... Signed(4) ....

*Strike out whichever is inapplicable.

**Strike out if inapplicable.

TAKE NOTICE THAT IF YOU DO NOT REPLY IN THIS FORM WITHIN ONE MONTH OF THE DATE OF SERVICE ON YOU OF THE ATTACHED APPLICATION, THEN, SUBJECT TO PARAGRAPH 5(5) OF SCHEDULE 2 TO THE AGRICULTURAL HOLDINGS ACT 1984, YOU WILL NOT BE ENTITLED AT THE HEARING OF THE APPLICATION TO DISPUTE ANY MATTER ALLEGED IN IT.

Notes:

(1)   The paragraphs of the application which (where completed) will be relevant to the applicant's claim to be an eligible person are paragraphs 9, 10, 11 and 12.

(2)   By virtue of rule 28 of the Agricultural Land Tribunals (Succession) Rules 1984 two copies of this reply and of any document which you wish to submit to the tribunal must be sent to the secretary. If you disagree with any map or plan attached to the application, your reply should be accompanied by two copies of a 6' to one mile or 1/10,000 (or larger) map showing what you consider to be the true position and marking the Ordnance Survey Field Numbers.

(3)   If you consider that, for any reason, the applicant is not legally entitled to make his application, you should state succinctly the grounds on which you rely.

(4)   If signed by any person other than the landlord himself, he should state in what capacity or by what authority he signs.

FORM 6 (SUCCESSION ON RETIREMENT)

Rule 24

Ref. No. To be inserted by the secretary.

AGRICULTURAL LAND TRIBUNAL

NOTICE OF APPLICATION FOR ENTITLEMENT TO TENANCY UNDER SCHEDULE 2 TO THE AGRICULTURAL HOLDINGS ACT 1984

To: .... (name)

of .... (address)

I, ... (block capitals)

of .... (address)

hereby give you notice that I applied on .... (date of application)

under Schedule 2 to the above-named Act for a direction entitling me to a tenancy of the agricultural holding known as .... (address or brief description of holding) in succession to .... (name of present tenant(s) of the holding) who served on you his/their retirement notice on ....

Dated .... Signed ....

A copy of the full application will in due course be sent to you by the secretary to the tribunal.

AGRICULTURAL HOLDINGS (ARBITRATION ON NOTICES) ORDER 1987

SI 1987/710

Authority: Agricultural Holdings Act 1986, s 29, Sch 4, paras 1–6, 8–13, Sch 5, para 5

PART I: PRELIMINARY

A1.551

1 Citation and commencement

This Order may be cited as the Agricultural Holdings (Arbitration on Notices) Order 1987 and shall come into force on 12th May 1987.

A1.552

2 Interpretation

(1) In this Order, unless the context otherwise requires—

'the 1986 Act' means the Agricultural Holdings Act 1986;
'notice to remedy' means a notice served on the tenant of an agricultural holding for the purposes of Case D requiring him to remedy a breach of a term or condition of his tenancy;
'notice to do work' means a notice to remedy which requires the doing of any work of repair, maintenance or replacement;
'termination', in relation to an arbitration, means the date on which the arbitrator's award is delivered to the tenant.

(2) Any reference in this Order to a numbered article shall be construed as a reference to the article bearing that number in this Order.

PART II: NOTICES TO DO WORK

Notices requiring arbitration

A1.553

3 Notice where arbitration is available at the notice to remedy stage only

(1) Where a tenant on whom a notice to do work has been served wishes to have determined by arbitration under the 1986 Act any of the following questions, namely—

(a) his liability under the terms or conditions of his tenancy to any of the work specified in the notice,

(b) the deletion from the notice of any item or part of an item of work on the ground that it is unnecessary or unjustified, or

(c) the substitution, in the case of any item or part of an item of work, of a different method or material for the method or material which the notice would otherwise required to be followed or used,

he shall do so by service of a notice requiring the question or questions to be determined by arbitration under the 1986 Act.

(2) A notice under paragraph (1) above shall be in writing, and shall be served on the landlord within one month after the service on the tenant of the notice to do work.

(3) A notice under paragraph (1) above shall specify, as the case may be—

(a) any items in respect of which the tenant denies liability,

(b) any items or parts of items which the tenant claims to be unnecessary or unjustified, and

(c) any method or material in respect of which the tenant desires a substitution to be made.

A1.554

4 Notice on other questions or in other cases

(1) Where the tenant on whom a notice to do work has been served wishes to have determined by arbitration under the 1986 Act in addition to a question specified in article 3(1) any other question arising under that notice which is not a question so specified, he shall do so by serving on the landlord within one month after the service of the notice to do work a notice in writing requiring the question to be so determined.

(2) Where the tenant on whom a notice to do work has been served does not wish any question specified in article 3(1) to be determined by arbitration under the 1986 Act but wishes to have determined by such arbitration any other question arising under that notice, he shall do so—

(a) by serving on the landlord within one month after the service of the notice to do work a notice in writing requiring the question to be so determined, or

(b) by serving a notice in accordance with article 9.

(3) Nothing in this article shall preclude a tenant who has required arbitration under this article and who has been found liable to comply with a notice to do work or with any part of it from subsequently requiring arbitration under article 9 on the ground that, in consequence of anything happening before the expiration of the time for doing

the work as extended by the arbitrator in pursuance of article 6(2), if would have been unreasonable to require the tenant to do the work within that time.

Powers of arbitrator

A1.555

5   Power to modify notice

In addition to any powers otherwise available to him, an arbitrator may—

(a) in relation to any question specified in article 3(1)(b), modify, a notice to do work by deleting any item or part of an item of work specified in the notice as to which, having due regard to the interests of good husbandry as respects the agricultural holding to which the notice relates and of sound management of the estate of which that holding forms part or which that holding constitutes, the arbitrator is satisfied that it is unnecessary or unjustified, and

(b) in relation to a question specified in article 3(1)(c) modify a notice to do work by substituting, in the case of any item or part of an item of work specified in the notice, a different method or material for the method or material which the notice would otherwise require to be followed or used where, having regard to the purpose which that item or part is intended to achieve, the arbitrator is satisfied that—

(i) the last-mentioned method or material would involve undue difficulty or expense,

(ii) the first-mentioned method or material would be substantially as effective for that purpose, and

(iii) in all the circumstances the substitution is justified.

Supplementary

A1.556

6   Extension of time for doing work

(1) Where a tenant requires any question to be determined by arbitration under article 3 or 4, the time specified for doing the work which is the subject of the arbitration shall be extended until the termination of the arbitration.

(2) Where the arbitrator finds that the tenant is liable to comply with a notice to do work or with any part of it, he shall extend the time for doing that work by such further period as he thinks fit.

A1.557

7   Date of termination of tenancy on failure to do work

(1) Where the time specified for doing any work is extended under article 6(2), the arbitrator may, either of his own motion or on the application of the landlord made not later than fourteen days after the termination of the arbitration, specify a date for the termination of the tenancy by notice to quit in the event of the tenant's failure to do the work within the extended time.

(2) A date specified under paragraph (1) above shall not be earlier than—

(a) the date on which the tenancy could have been terminated by notice to quit served on the expiration of the time originally specified in the notice to do work, or

(b)   six months after the expiration of the extended time,

whichever is the later.

(3)   Where the landlord applies to the arbitrator under paragraph (1) above, he shall at the same time give written notice of the application to the tenant (except where the application is made at the arbitration) and the tenant shall be entitled to be heard on the application.

(4)   A notice to quit on a date specified under paragraph (1) above shall be served on the tenant within one month after the expiration of the extended time, and shall (subject to any right to contest its effectiveness available to the tenant) be valid notwithstanding that it is served less than twelve months before the date on which the tenancy is to be terminated or that that date is not the end of a year of the tenancy.

A1.558

8   Recovery of cost of work

Where, on an arbitration relating to whole or in part to the question specified in article 3(1)(a), it appears to the arbitrator that the tenant has done work required by a notice to do work which he was under no obligation to do, the arbitrator shall determine the reasonable cost of such work, which shall be recoverable from the landlord by the tenant in accordance with section 85(1) of the 1986 Act.

PART III: NOTICES TO QUIT

Arbitration concerning notices to quit

A1.559

9   Notice requiring arbitration

Where it is stated in a notice to quit an agricultural holding or part thereof that the notice is given for one or more of the reasons specified in Case A, B, D or E and the tenant wishes to contest any question arising under the provisions of section 26(2) of, and Schedule 3 to, the 1986 Act relating to any of the reasons so stated, he shall within one month after the service of the notice serve on the landlord notice in writing requiring the question to be determined by arbitration under the 1986 Act.

A1.560

10   Appointment of arbitrator

A notice under article 9 requiring arbitration under the 1986 Act shall cease to be effective three months after the date of the service of that notice unless before the expiry of those three months—

(a)   an arbitrator has been appointed by agreement between the parties, or
(b)   (in default of such agreement) an application has been made by the tenant or the landlord under [section 84(2) of] that Act for the appointment of an arbitrator,

for the purposes of that arbitration.

NOTES

Amendment

In para (b) words 'section 84(2) of' in square brackets substituted by SI 2006/2805, art 18, Sch 1, Pt 2, para 2.

Date in force: 19 October 2006: see SI 2006/2805, art 1(1)(b).

A1.561

11   Service of counter-notice

Where—

(1)   an arbitration is required under article 9 in respect of a notice to quit which is capable of taking effect either as notice to quit to which section 26(2) of the 1986 Act applies or in the alternative as a notice to quit to which section 26(1) of that Act applies, and

(2)   in consequence of the arbitration that notice takes effect as a notice to quit to which section 26(1) applies,

the time within which a counter-notice may be served by the tenant on the landlord under section 26(1) of the 1986 Act shall be one month from the termination of the arbitration.

Postponement of operation of notice to quit

A1.562

12   During arbitration

Where a tenant requires a question arising out of a notice to quit to be determined by arbitration under article 9, the operation of the notice shall be suspended until—

   (a)   the expiry of the time fixed in article 10 for appointing an arbitrator by agreement or for making an application under [section 84(2) of] the 1986 act, or

   (b)   where any such appointment or application has been duly made, the termination of the arbitration.

NOTES

Amendment

In para (a) words 'section 84(2) of' in square brackets substituted by SI 2006/2805, art 18, Sch 1, Pt 2, para 2.

Date in force: 19 October 2006: see SI 2006/2805, art 1(1)(b).

A1.563

13   After arbitration or proceedings

(1)   Where—

   (a)   a notice to quit has effect in consequence of an arbitration under article 9, or the Tribunal have consented to the operation of the notice under section 26(1) or 28(2) of the 1986 Act or article 15(5), and

(b) the notice would, but for the provisions of this article, come into operation on or within six months fatter the termination of the arbitration, or the giving of the consent,

the arbitrator or the Tribunal may, either of his or their own motion or on the application of the tenant made not later than fourteen days after the termination of the arbitration or the giving of the consent, postpone the termination of the tenancy for a period not exceeding twelve months.

(2) Where the tenant applies to the arbitrator or the Tribunal under paragraph (1) above, he shall at the same time give written notice of the application to the landlord (except where the application is made at the arbitration or at the hearing before the Tribunal) and the landlord shall be entitled to be heard on the application.

Extension of time under notice to remedy after notice to quit

A1.564

14   Extension by arbitrator

Where—

(a) notice to quit is stated to be given by reason of the tenant's failure to remedy a breach of any term or condition of his tenancy—
   (i) within the time specified in a notice to remedy, or
   (ii) within that time as extended by the landlord, or in pursuance of article 6 or of this article, and
(b) it appears to the arbitrator on an arbitration under article 9 that, notwithstanding that the time originally specified or extended was reasonable, it would, in consequence of anything happening before the expiration of that time, have been unreasonable to require the tenant to remedy the breach within that time,

the arbitrator may treat the time as having been extended, or further extended, and may make his award as if the time had not expired; and where the breach has not been remedied at the date of the award, the arbitrator may extend the time by such period as he considers reasonable, having regard to the length of time which has elapsed since the service of the notice to remedy.

A1.565

15   Termination of tenancy following extension

(1) Where the time specified for doing any work is extended under article 14, the arbitrator may, either of his own motion or on the application of the landlord made not later than fourteen days after the termination of the arbitration, specify a date for the termination of the tenancy by a subsequent notice to quit in the event of the tenant's failure to do the work within the extended time.

(2) A date specified under paragraph (1) above shall not be earlier than—

(a) the date on which the tenancy could have been terminated by the original notice to quit (that is, the notice which was the subject of the arbitration), or
(b) six months after the expiration of the extended time,

whichever is the later.

(3)   Where the landlord applies to the arbitrator under paragraph (1) above, he shall at the same time give written notice of the application to the tenant (except where the application is made at the arbitration) and the tenant shall be entitled to be heard on the application.

(4)   A notice to quit on a date specified under paragraph (1) above shall be served on the tenant within one month after the expiration of the extended time, and, subject to paragraph (5) below, shall be valid notwithstanding it is served less than twelve months before the date on which the tenancy is to be terminated or that that date is not the end of a year of the tenancy.

(5)   Where a subsequent notice to quit is given in accordance with paragraph (1) above in a case where the original notice to quit included a statement in accordance with Case D to the effect that it was given by reason of the tenant's failure to comply with a notice to do work, then, if the tenant serves on the landlord a counter-notice in writing within one month after the giving of the subsequent notice to quit (or, if the date specified in that notice for the termination of the tenancy is earlier, before that date), the subsequent notice to quit shall not have effect unless the Tribunal consent to its operation.

(6)   On an application made for the consent of the Tribunal under paragraph (5) above on the part of the landlord, the Tribunal shall consent to the operation of the notice to quit unless it appears to them, having regard—

(a)   to the extent to which the tenant has failed to comply with the notice to do work,
(b)   to the consequences of his failure to comply with it in any respect, and
(c)   to the circumstances surrounding any such failure,

that a fair and reasonable landlord would not insist on possession.

Supplementary

A1.566

16   Notice to sub-tenants

(1)   Section 26(1) of the 1986 Act shall not apply where notice to quit an agricultural holding or part thereof is given to a sub-tenant by a tenant who has himself been given notice to quit that holding or part thereof and the fact that the tenant has been given such notice is stated in the notice given to the sub-tenant.

(2)   Such a notice given to a sub-tenant shall have effect only if the notice to quit given to the tenant by the landlord itself has effect.

(3)   Where a tenant accepts notice to quit part of a holding as notice to quit the whole under section 32 of the 1986 Act, then, for the purpose of this article, the notice given by him shall be deemed to be a notice to quit the entire holding.

A1.567

17   Service men

(1)   In any case to which, notwithstanding the existence of any such circumstances as are mentioned in Cases B to G, section 26(1) of the 1986 Act applies by virtue of the modification of that section by paragraph 3 of Schedule 5 to that Act, paragraphs (2) to (4) below shall have effect.

(2)   Where, on an application by the landlord for the consent of the Tribunal to the operation of a notice to quit, it appears to the Tribunal that the notice to quit was

given for one or more of the reasons specified in Case B, D or E, and that it is expedient that any question arising under the provisions of section 26(2) of, and Schedule 3 to, the 1986 Act relating to any of the reasons so stated should be determined by arbitration between the landlord and tenant under that Act before the Tribunal consider whether to grant or withhold consent to the operation of the notice to quit, they may require that the question be determined accordingly.

(3)   Article 9 shall apply with the addition of the following words—

'so, however, that the tenant's failure to serve such a notice shall not affect his right to contest the question in proceedings before the Tribunal consequent upon the service of a counter-notice under section 26(1) of the 1986 Act or in any arbitration by which the Tribunal may require any such question to be determined'.

(4)   Article 11 shall not apply, but where a tenant requires a question to be determined by arbitration in pursuance of article 9, the time within which a counter-notice under section 26(1) of the 1986 Act may be served by the tenant on the landlord under that subsection shall be one month from the termination of the arbitration.

PART IV: REVOCATION

A1.568

18   Revocation

The Agricultural Holdings (Arbitration on Notices) Order 1978 and the Agricultural Holdings (Arbitration on Notices) (Variation) Order 1984 are hereby revoked, but without prejudice to their application in relation to notices to do work and notices to quit which have been served before the commencement of this Order, and to any proceedings relating to or consequent upon any such notices.

AGRICULTURAL HOLDINGS (FORMS OF NOTICE TO PAY RENT OR TO REMEDY) REGULATIONS 1987

SI 1987/711

Authority: Agricultural Holdings Act 1986, Sch 3, Part II, para 10(1)(a), (2)

A1.569

1   Citation and commencement

These Regulations may be cited as the Agricultural Holdings (Forms of Notice to Pay Rent or to Remedy) Regulations 1987 and shall come into force on 12th May 1987.

A1.570

2   Interpretation

(1)   In these Regulations—

'the 1986 Act' means the Agricultural Holdings Act 1986;

'notice to pay rent' means a notice served on the tenant of an agricultural holding for the purposes of Case D requiring him to pay rent due;

'notice to remedy' means a notice served on the tenant of an agricultural holding for the purposes of Case D requiring him to remedy a breach of a term or condition of his tenancy.

(2)   A form referred to by number in these Regulations means the form so numbered in the Schedule to these Regulations or a form substantially to the same effect.

A1.571

3   Form of notice to pay rent

A notice to pay rent shall be in Form 1.

A1.572

4   Forms of notice to remedy

A notice to remedy which requires the doing of any work of repair, maintenance or replacement shall be in Form 2 and any other notice to remedy shall be in Form 3.

A1.573

5   Revocation

The Agricultural Holdings (Forms of Notice to Pay Rent or to Remedy) Regulations 1984 are hereby revoked, but without prejudice to their application in relation to any notice served before the coming into operation of these Regulations.

SCHEDULE

Regulations 2(2), 3, 4

A1.574

FORM 1

AGRICULTURAL HOLDINGS ACT 1986

Schedule 3, Part I, Case D

Notice to tenant to pay rent due

Re: the holding known as ... ...

To ... ...

(Name and address of tenant)

IMPORTANT-FAILURE TO COMPLY WITH THIS NOTICE MAY BE RELIED ON AS REASON FOR A NOTICE TO QUIT UNDER CASE D. IF YOU WANT YOUR TENANCY TO CONTINUE YOU MUST ACT QUICKLY. READ THE NOTICE AND ALL THE NOTES CAREFULLY. IF YOU ARE IN ANY DOUBT ABOUT THE ACTION YOU SHOULD TAKE, GET ADVICE IMMEDIATELY, e.g. FROM A SOLICITOR, SURVEYOR OR CITIZENS ADVICE BUREAU.

1 I hereby give you notice that I require you to pay within two months from the date of service of this Notice* the rent due in respect of the above holding as set out below:

*Note: This Notice may not be served before the rent is due.

Particulars of rent not paid

Date when due   Amount due

2 This Notice is given in accordance with Case D in Part I of Schedule 3 to the Agricultural Holdings Act 1986, and failure to comply with it within the period specified above may be relied on as a reason for a notice to quit under Case D.

3 Your attention is drawn to the Notes following the signature to this Notice.

Signed ... ... Date ... ...

(If signed by any person other than the landlord of the holding, state in what capacity or by what authority the signature is affixed.)

      Address ... ...

      ... ...

      ... ...

      ... ...

Notes

1 You cannot at this stage refer to arbitration either your liability to comply with this Notice to pay rent or any other question as to the validity of the Notice. You will, however, be entitled to do so later if a notice to quit is served on you on the ground that you have failed to comply with this Notice to pay rent. That is the *only* opportunity you will have to challenge this Notice.

2 At that stage under article 9 of the Agricultural Holdings (Arbitration on Notices) Order 1987 (SI 1987/710) you have one month after the service of the notice to quit within which you can serve on your landlord a notice in writing requiring the question to be determined by arbitration under the Agricultural Holdings Act 1986 (c. 5).

3 You will then have three months from the date of service of that notice in which to appoint an arbitrator by agreement or (in default of such agreement) to make an application under paragraph 1 of Schedule 11 to that Act for the appointment of an arbitrator. If this is not done by you or your landlord your notice requiring arbitration ceases to be effective (see article 10 of that Order).

FORM 2

AGRICULTURAL HOLDINGS ACT 1986

Schedule 3, Part I, Case D

Notice to tenant to remedy breach of tenancy by doing work of repair, maintenance or replacement

Re: the holding known as ... ...

To ... ...

(Name and address of tenant)

IMPORTANT-FAILURE TO COMPLY WITH THIS NOTICE MAY BE RELIED ON AS REASON FOR A NOTICE TO QUIT UNDER CASE D. IF YOU WANT YOUR TENANCY TO CONTINUE YOU MUST ACT QUICKLY. READ THE NOTICE AND ALL THE NOTES CAREFULLY. IF YOU ARE IN ANY DOUBT ABOUT THE

ACTION YOU SHOULD TAKE, GET ADVICE IMMEDIATELY, e.g. FROM A SOLICITOR, SURVEYOR OR CITIZENS ADVICE BUREAU.

1   I hereby give you notice that I require you to remedy within ... .. months* from the date of service of this Notice the breaches, set out below, of the terms or conditions of your tenancy, being breaches which are capable of being remedied of terms or conditions which are not inconsistent with your responsibilities to farm the holding in accordance with the rules of good husbandry.

*Note: This period must be a reasonable period for the tenant to remedy the breaches and must in any event be not less than six months.

2   This Notice requires the doing of the work of repair, maintenance or replacement specified below.

Particulars of breaches of terms or conditions of tenancy

Term or condition of tenancy   Particulars of breach and work required to
                                      remedy it

3   This Notice is given in accordance with Case D in Part I of Schedule 3 to the Agricultural Holdings Act 1986, and failure to comply with it within the period specified above may be relied on as a reason for a notice to quit under Case D.

4   Your attention is drawn to the Notes following the signature to this Notice.

Signed ... ... Date ... ...

(If signed by any person other than the landlord of the holding, state in what capacity or by what authority the signature is affixed.)

          Address ... ...

          ... ...

Notes

In these Notes 'the Order' means the Agricultural Holdings (Arbitration on Notices) Order 1987 (S.I. 1987/710).

What to do if you wish—

(a)   *to contest your liability to do the work, required by this notice to remedy (Question (a)); or*

(b)   *to request the deletion from this Notice to remedy of any item or part of an item of work on the ground that it is unnecessary or unjustified (Question (b)); or*

(c)   *to request the substitution in the case of any item or part of an item of a different method or material for the method or material for the method which this Notice to remedy would otherwise require to be followed or used (Question (c)).*

1   Questions (a), (b) and (c) mentioned in the heading to these Notes can be referred to arbitration under article 3(1) of the Order. To do so you *must* serve a notice in writing upon your landlord *within one month* of the service upon you of this Notice to remedy. The notice you serve upon your landlord should specify—

(a)   if you are referring Question (a), the items for which you deny liability,

(b)   if you are referring Question (b), the items you wish to be deleted,

(c)   if you are referring Question (c), the different methods or materials you wish to be substituted,

and in each case should require the matter to be determined by arbitration under the Agricultural Holdings Act 1986 (c. 5). You will not be able to refer Question (a), (b) or (*c*) to arbitration later, on receipt of a notice to quit. This action does not prevent you settling the matter in writing by agreement with your landlord.

2   Carrying out the work

If you refer any of these Questions (*a*), (*b*) and (*c*) to arbitration, you are not obliged to carry out the work which is the subject of the reference to arbitration unless and until the arbitrator decides that you are liable to do it; but you *must* carry out any work which you are not referring to arbitration.

3   If you are referring Question (*a*) to arbitrtion you may if you wish carry out any of the work which is the subject of that reference to arbitration without waiting for the arbitrator's award. If you do this and the arbitrator finds that you have carried out any such work which you were under no obligation to do, he will determine at the time he makes his award the reasonable cost of any such work which you have done and you will be entitled to recover this from your landlord (see article 8 of the Order). This provision does *not* apply in the case of work referred to arbitration under Question (*b*) or Question (*c*).

4   What to do if you wish to contest any other question arising under this Notice to remedy

If you wish to contest any other question arising under this Notice other than Question (*a*), (*b*) or (*c*), such as whether the time specified in the Notice to do work is a reasonable period in which to carry out the work, you should refer the question to arbitration in either of the following ways, according to whether or not you are also at the same time referring Question (*a*), (*b*) or (*c*) to arbitration—

(a)   If you are referring Question (*a*), (*b*) or (*c*) to arbitration, then you *must* also refer to arbitration at the same time any other questions relevant to this Notice which you may wish to dispute.

To do this, you should include in the Notice to your landlord referred to in Note 1 above a statement of the other questions which you require to be determined by arbitration under the Agricultural Holdings Act 1986 (see article 4(1) of the Order).

(b)   If you are not referring Question (*a*), (*b*) or (*c*) to arbitration, but wish to contest some other question arising under this Notice to remedy, you may refer that question to arbitration either now, on receipt of this Notice, or later, if you get a notice to quit.

To refer the question to arbitration now, you should serve on your landlord *within one month* after the service of this Notice to remedy a notice in writing setting out what it is you require to be determined by arbitration under the Agricultural Holdings Act 1986 (see article 4(2)(*a*) of the Order).

Alternatively, you have one month after the service of the notice to quit within which you can serve on your landlord a notice in writing requiring the question to be determined by arbitration under the 1986 Act (see article 9 of the Order). You will then have three months from the date of service of service of that notice in which to appoint an arbitrator by agreement or (in default of such agreement) to make an application under paragraph 1 of Schedule 11 to that Act for the appointment of an arbitrator. If this is not done by you or your landlord your notice requiring arbitration ceases to be effective (see article 10 of the Order).

5   Warning

Notes 1 to 4 above outline the *only* opportunities you have to challenge this Notice to remedy.

6

Extensions of time allowed for complying with this Notice to remedy   If you refer to arbitration now any question arising from this Notice to remedy, the time allowed for complying with the Notice will be extended until the termination of the arbitration. If the arbitrator decides that you are liable to do any of the work specified in this Notice to remedy, he will extend the time in which the work is to be done by such period as he thinks fit (see article 6(2) of the Order)

7   Warning as to the effect which any extension of the time allowed for complying with this Notice to remedy may have upon a subsequent notice to quit

If your time for doing the work is extended as mentioned in note 6 above, the arbitrator can specify a date for the termination of your tenancy should you fail to complete the work you are liable to do within the extended time. Then, if you did fail to complete that work within the extended time, your landlord could serve a notice to quit upon you expiring on the date which the arbitrator had specified, and the notice would be valid even though that date might be less than twelve months after the next term date, and might not expire on a term date. The arbitrator cannot, however, specify a termination date which is less than six months after the expiry of the extended time to do the work. Nor can he specify a date which is earlier than would have been possible if you had not required arbitration on this Notice to remedy and had failed to do the work (see article 7 of the Order).

FORM 3

AGRICULTURAL HOLDINGS ACT 1986

Schedule 3, Part I, Case D

Notice to tenant to remedy breach of tenancy (not being a notice requiring the doing of any work of repair, maintenance or replacement)

Re: the holding known as ... ...

To ... ...

(Name and address of tenant)

IMPORTANT-FAILURE TO COMPLY WITH THIS NOTICE MAY BE RELIED ON AS REASON FOR A NOTICE TO QUIT UNDER CASE D. IF YOU WANT YOUR TENANCY TO CONTINUE YOU MUST ACT QUICKLY. READ THE NOTICE AND ALL THE NOTES CAREFULLY. IF YOU ARE IN ANY DOUBT ABOUT THE ACTION YOU SHOULD TAKE, GET ADVICE IMMEDIATELY, e.g. FROM A SOLICITOR, SURVEYOR OR CITIZENS ADVICE BUREAU.

1   I hereby give you notice that I require you to remedy within ... .. months* from the date of service of this Notice the breaches, set out below, of the terms or conditions of your tenancy, being breaches which are capable of being remedied of terms or conditions which are not inconsistent with your responsibilities to farm the holding in accordance with the rules of good husbandry.

Particulars of breaches of terms or conditions of tenancy

Term or condition of tenancy	Particulars of breach

2   This Notice is given in accordance with Case D in Part I of Schedule 3 to the Agricultural Holdings Act 1986 and failure to comply with it within the period specified may be relied on as a reason for a notice to quit under Case D.

3   Your attention is drawn to the Notes following the signature to this Notice.

Signed ... ... Date ... ...

(If signed by any person other than the landlord of the holding, state in what capacity or by what authority the signature is affixed)   .

        Address ... ...
        ... ...

Notes

1   You cannot at this stage refer to arbitration either your liability to comply with this Notice to remedy or any other question as to the validity of the Notice. You will, however, be entitled to do so later if a notice to quit is served on you on the ground that you have failed to comply with this Notice to remedy. That is the *only* opportunity you will have to challenge this Notice.

2   At that stage under article 9 of the Agricultural Holdings (Arbitration on Notices) Order 1987 (S.I. 1987/710), you have one month after the service of the notice to quit within which you can serve on your landlord a notice in writing requiring the question to be determined by arbitration under the Agricultural Holdings Act 1986 (c.5).

3   You will then have three months from the date of service of that notice in which to appoint an arbitrator by agreement or (in default of such agreement) to make an application under paragraph 1 of Schedule 11 to that Act for the appointment of an arbitrator. If this is not done by you or your landlord your notice requiring arbitration ceases to be effective (see article 10 of that Order).

AGRICULTURE (TIME-LIMIT) REGULATIONS 1988

SI 1988/282

Authority: Agricultural Holdings Act 1986, s 9(4)

A1.575

1   Citation and commencement

These Regulations may be cited as the Agriculture (Time–Limit) Regulations 1988, and shall come into force on 24th March 1988.

A1.576

2   Time limit

The prescribed period after the coming into force of the Agriculture (Maintenance, Repair and Insurance of Fixed Equipment) (Amendment) Regulations 1988 (which vary the model terms of a tenancy of an agricultural holding as to maintenance, repair and insurance established by the operation of regulations under section 7 of the Agricultural Holdings Act 1986) within which an arbitrator shall for the purposes of specifying the terms of a tenancy of an agricultural holding pursuant to section 6(2) of that Act disregard the variation effected by the said Agriculture (Maintenance, Repair and Insurance of Fixed Equipment) (Amendment) Regulations 1988 shall be three months from the date of the coming into force of those Regulations.

MILK QUOTA (CALCULATION OF STANDARD QUOTA) (AMENDMENT) ORDER 1992

SI 1992/1225

The Minister of Agriculture, Fisheries and Food, in the case of land in England, and the Secretary of State, in the case of land in Wales, in exercise of the powers conferred on them by paragraph 6 of Schedule 1 to the Agriculture Act 1986, and of all other powers enabling them in that behalf, hereby make the following Order

A1.577

1   Title and commencement

This Order may be cited as the Milk Quota (Calculation of Standard Quota) (Amendment) Order 1992 and shall come into force on 19th June 1992.

A1.578

2   Amendment of principal Order

(1)   The Milk Quota (Calculation of Standard Quota) Order 1986 is hereby amended in accordance with the following provisions of this article.

(2)   ...

(3)   For the Schedule there shall be substituted the provisions contained in the Schedule to this Order.

NOTES

Amendment

Para (2): substitutes SI 1986/1530 , art 2.

SCHEDULE

Article 2

A1.579

...

NOTES

Amendment

This Schedule substitutes SI 1986/1530, Schedule.

PUBLIC TRUSTEE (NOTICES AFFECTING LAND) (TITLE ON DEATH) REGULATIONS 1995

SI 1995/1330

The Lord Chancellor, in exercise of the powers conferred on him by section 19 of the Law of Property (Miscellaneous Provisions) Act 1994, hereby makes the following Regulations

A1.579A

1   Citation and commencement

These Regulations may be cited as the Public Trustee (Notices Affecting Land) (Title on Death) Regulations 1995 and shall come into force on 1st July 1995.

A1.579B

2   Interpretation

In these Regulations—

(a)   'the Act' means the Law of Property (Miscellaneous Provisions) Act 1994;
(b)   a form referred to by number means the form so numbered in the Schedule to these Regulations.

A1.579C

3   Keeping and recording of documents served under section 18 of the Act

(1)   The Public Trustee shall keep a register on which he shall record the details set out in paragraph (2) in respect of every document which is—

(a)   served on him under section 18 of the Act, and
(b)   is accompanied by an application to register in Form NL(1).

(2)   The details referred to in paragraph (1) are—

(a)   the name of the deceased person;
(b)   a description of the land to which the document relates; and
(c)   the date on which the entry on the register was made.

(3)   The Public Trustee shall file every document in respect of which a registration is made against the name of the deceased person in respect of whom the document is served.

A1.579D

4   Search of the register

(1)   A person shall be entitled to request the Public Trustee to search the register against the name of a deceased person by sending to him an application to search in Form NL(2).

(2)   On receipt of such a request the Public Trustee shall cause a search to be made in the register against the name of the deceased person in the exact form provided to him by the applicant.

(3) The Public Trustee shall notify the applicant of the result of the search, and in the event that it reveals an entry on the register, shall send to him a copy of the document whose service on the Public Trustee caused the registration to be made.

SCHEDULE

Regulation 2

A1.579E

FORM NL(1)

[THE PUBLIC TRUSTEE]

...

APPLICATION FOR REGISTRATION OF NOTICE AFFECTING LAND

PUBLIC TRUSTEE (NOTICES AFFECTING LAND) (TITLE ON DEATH) REGULATIONS 1995

For explanatory notes see overleaf.	For official use only		
Please type or complete in **BLOCK CAPITALS**			
To:			
	Date of Registra-tion		
	Registration No	I .... of .... *(enter name and address of person or firm making application)* apply for registration against the name of the deceased person referred to below of the attached Notice in respect of the land described.	The fee of £............. accompanies this application. (*Cheques should be made payable to the Public Trust Office*) Signed .... Date .... Telephone No .... Refer-ence ....

Enter name of deceased Forename(s) .... Surname .... Date of Notice .... Description of Notice (see explanatory notes)...........	Enter details of land to which Notice realates. (See expanatory notes)...........	

EXPLANATORY NOTES

1. The fee payable is prescribed by the current Public Trustee Fees Order. Please ensure that such fee accompanies your application.

2. A practice note explaining the procedure for the keeping of a Register of Notices served under section 18 of the Law of Property (Miscellaneous Provisions) Act 1994 is available from the Public Trust Office free of charge.

3. Separate applications should be made per property except where more than one property is included in the same title.

4. The entry on the register will be made in the name of the deceased person and will record the details of the land to which the document relates and the date of registration.

5. The date and description of Notice are requested for office purposes only and will not be entered on the register. Examples of a description of Notice are: Notice to Quit or Notice of Exercise of Option.

6. Please ensure that the Notice to be registered accompanies your application.

7. Acknowledgment of your application will be sent to you indicating the date of registration.

FORM NL(2)

[THE PUBLIC TRUSTEE]

...

APPLICATION FOR SEARCH OF REGISTER OF NOTICES AFFECTING LAND

PUBLIC TRUSTEE (NOTICES AFFECTING LAND) (TITLE ON DEATH) REGULATIONS 1995

For explanatory notes see overleaf.	**For official use only**	
Please type or complete in **BLOCK CAPITALS**		

To:		Number of Notices registered Notices registered dated	I .... of .... (*enter name and address of person or firm making application*) apply for a search of the Register kept by the Public Trustee of Notices affecting Land against the name of the deceased referred to below.	The fee of £............. accompanies this application. (*Cheques should be made payable to the Public Trust Office*) Signed .... Date .... Telephone No .... Reference ....
Enter name of deceased and date of death Fore-name(s) .... Surname .... Date of death	Enter address of any property(ies) owned by the deceased (see explanatory notes) if known			
OFFI-CIAL STAMP	**Public Trust Office Certificate of Search Form NL(2) result** The search applied for has been made with the following result: Name searched	Reference *Enter above the name and address or DX number of the person to whom the Certificate of Search is to be sent*		No Notice has been registered. Notice(s) dated .... has/have been registered and a copy(ies) is/are enclosed.

EXPLANATORY NOTES

1. The fee payable is prescribed by the current Public Trustee Fees Order. Please ensure that such fee accompanies your application.

2. A practice note explaining the procedure for the keeping of a Register of Notices served under section 18 of the Law of Property (Miscellaneous Provisions) Act 1994 is available from the Public Trust Office free of charge.

3. The search will be made against the name of the deceased person in the exact form provided by the applicant. If it is required to search a variation of the name, a separate search form should be completed and a separate fee paid.

4. The details of the property are requested for office purposes only. Searches will be made where no property details are given.

5. The Registter of Notices kept by the Public Trustee only records Notices served on the Public Trustee on or after 1 July 1995. Enquiries should be made of the Treasury Solicitor in respect of Notices served (on the President of the Family Division) prior to that date.

NOTES

Amendment

Form NL(1): in the heading words 'The Public Trustee' in square brackets substituted by SI 2001/3902, reg 3(1)(a).

Date in force: 1 January 2002: see SI 2001/3902, reg 1(1); for transitional provisions see reg 2(1), (2) thereof.

Form NL(1): in the heading words omitted revoked by SI 2001/3902, reg 3(1)(a).

Date in force: 1 January 2002: see SI 2001/3902, reg 1(1); for transitional provisions see reg 2(1), (2) thereof.

Form NL(1): amended by SI 2001/3902, reg 3(1)(b), (c).

Date in force: 1 January 2002: see SI 2001/3902, reg 1(1); for transitional provisions see reg 2(1), (2) thereof.

Form NL(2): in the heading words 'The Public Trustee' in square brackets substituted by SI 2001/3902, reg 3(2)(a).

Date in force: 1 January 2002: see SI 2001/3902, reg 1(1); for transitional provisions see reg 2(1), (3) thereof.

Form NL(2): in the heading words omitted revoked by SI 2001/3902, reg 3(2)(a).

Date in force: 1 January 2002: see SI 2001/3902, reg 1(1); for transitional provisions see reg 2(1), (3) thereof.

Form NL(2): amended by SI 2001/3902, reg 3(2)(b)–(d).

Date in force: 1 January 2002: see SI 2001/3902, reg 1(1); for transitional provisions see reg 2(1), (3) thereof.

AGRICULTURAL HOLDINGS (FEE) REGULATIONS 1996

SI 1996/337

The Minister of Agriculture, Fisheries and Food in relation to England and the Secretary of State in relation to Wales, in exercise of the powers conferred on them by sections 22(4) and 96(1) of and paragraph 1(2) of Schedule 11 to the Agricultural Holdings Act 1986, and of all other powers enabling them in that behalf, and both Houses of Parliament having approved a draft of the Regulations, hereby make the following Regulations

A1.580

1   Title and commencement

These Regulations may be cited as the Agricultural Holdings (Fee) Regulations 1996 and shall come into force on 1st March 1996.

A1.581

2   Prescribed fee

The fee for an application to the President of the Royal Institution of Chartered Surveyors—

(a)   for a person to be appointed by him under section 22(2) of the Agricultural Holdings Act 1986, or

(b)   for an arbitrator to be appointed by him under [section 84(2) of] that Act

is hereby increased from £70 to £115.

NOTES

Amendment

In para (b) words 'section 84(2) of' in square brackets substituted by SI 2006/2805, art 18, Sch 1, Pt 2, para 3.

Date in force: 19 October 2006: see SI 2006/2805, art 1(1)(b).

A1.582

3   Revocation

…

NOTES

Amendment

This regulation revokes SI 1985/1967.

NATIONAL ASSEMBLY FOR WALES (TRANSFER OF FUNCTIONS) ORDER 1999

SI 1999/672

Whereas the draft of this Order has been laid before, and approved by a resolution of, each House of Parliament:

Now, therefore, Her Majesty, in pursuance of sections 22, 24(1), 42(4), 44(5), 96(7), 144(6), 146(4), 147(3), 151(2) and 155(2) of, and paragraphs 1 to 4, 6(3), 7, 8 and 9 of Schedule 3 to, the Government of Wales Act 1998, is pleased, by and with the advice of Her Privy Council, to order, and it is hereby ordered, as follows—

NOTES

Continuation

Following the repeal of the Government of Wales Act 1998, ss 22, 155(2), this Order has effect as if made under the Government of Wales Act 2006, ss 58, 158(3), by virtue of Sch 11, para 26(1), (3) thereto.

A1.583

Citation, commencement and interpretation

1

(1) This Order may be cited as the National Assembly for Wales (Transfer of Functions) Order 1999.

(2) This Order shall come into force on 1st July 1999 immediately after the coming into force of section 53 of the Scotland Act 1998 but, if that section does not come into force on 1st July 1999, this Order shall come into force on that date.

(3) In this Order—

'the 1965 transfer order' means the Secretary of State for Wales and Minister of Land and Natural Resources Order 1965;
'the 1969 transfer order' means the Transfer of Functions (Wales) Order 1969;
'the 1978 transfer order' means the Transfer of Functions (Wales) (No 1) Order 1978;
'the Act' means the Government of Wales Act 1998;
'the Assembly' means the National Assembly for Wales;
'the catchment areas of the rivers Dee, Wye and Severn' means the areas delineated by a continuous red line on the map published by the Environment Agency (but not part of this Order) on 10th February 1999 and marked 'Map indicating the catchment areas of the rivers Dee, Wye and Severn for the purposes of the National Assembly for Wales (Transfer of Functions) Order 1999—map reference EAW/TFO.1(1–7)'.

NOTES

Initial Commencement

Specified date: 1 July 1999: see para (2) above.

A1.584

Transfer of functions

2

Schedule 1 to this Order shall have effect as follows—

(a) except as provided in sub-paragraphs (b)–(f), all functions of a Minister of the Crown under the enactments specified in Schedule 1 are, so far as exercisable in relation to Wales, transferred to the Assembly;

(b) where so directed in Schedule 1 functions exercisable by a Minister of the Crown shall, so far as exercisable in relation to Wales, be exercisable by the Assembly concurrently with the Minister;

(c) it is directed that (except in the case of functions which are exercisable by the Assembly 'jointly' with a Minister of the Crown) functions under any of the enactments specified in Schedule 1 which are exercisable by a Minister of the Crown in relation to a cross-border body but which, by their nature, are not functions which can be specifically exercised in relation to Wales, shall be exercisable by the Assembly in relation to that body concurrently with the Minister of the Crown;

(d) where so indicated in Schedule 1, functions of a Minister of the Crown under the enactments specified therein are transferred to the Assembly in relation to Wales (or such part of Wales as may be specified) together with such English border area as is specified;

(e) Schedule 1 does not transfer any power under which provisions of an Act of Parliament may be brought into force by order made by a Minister of the Crown;

(f) Schedule 1 does not transfer any functions of the Lord Chancellor or the Attorney General;

(g) functions of the Comptroller and Auditor General shall, as indicated in Schedule 1, be transferred to, or become functions also of, the Auditor General for Wales;

(h) all other provisions contained in Schedule 1 in relation to the enactments specified therein shall have effect.

NOTES

Initial Commencement

Specified date: 1 July 1999: see art 1(2).

A1.585

3

Any reference in this Order to a function of a Minister of the Crown under an enactment includes a reference to any functions of that Minister which are included in any scheme, regulations, rules, order, bye-laws or other instrument having effect under or in relation to that enactment, and the power to confer functions on that Minister by any such scheme, regulations, rules, order, bye-laws or other instrument shall have effect as a power to confer such functions on the Assembly.

NOTES

Initial Commencement

Specified date: 1 July 1999: see art 1(2).

A1.586

4

(1)   This article applies where—

- (a)   any function under an enactment is expressly required to be exercised by two or more Ministers of the Crown acting 'jointly', and
- (b)   any transfer in respect thereof in this Order does not transfer to the Assembly the functions of all such Ministers of the Crown.

(2)   Where this article applies, section 42 of the Act shall not have effect to allow the function to be exercised by the Assembly otherwise than in accordance with the joint action requirement.

NOTES

Initial Commencement

Specified date: 1 July 1999: see art 1(2).

A1.587

Minister of the Crown functions exercisable with Assembly agreement or consultation

5

(1)   Subject to paragraph (2) of this article, it is directed that functions exercisable by a Minister of the Crown under the enactments specified in Schedule 2 to this Order shall, so far as they are exercisable in relation to Wales and as specified in the said Schedule, be exercisable by the Minister only with the agreement of, or after consultation with, the Assembly.

(2)   In respect of the enactments referred to in paragraph 4(1)(a) and (b) of Schedule 3 to the Act, paragraph (1) of this article shall have effect not in respect of functions exercisable in relation to Wales but in respect of functions exercisable in relation to 'Welsh controlled waters' as defined in paragraph 4(2) of the said Schedule 3.

NOTES

Initial Commencement

Specified date: 1 July 1999: see art 1(2).

A1.588

The sea adjacent to Wales

6

For the purposes of the definition of 'Wales' in the Act the boundary between those parts of the sea within the Severn and Dee Estuaries which are to be treated as adjacent to Wales and those which are not shall be, in each case, a line drawn between the co-ordinates set out in Schedule 3 to this Order.

NOTES

Initial Commencement

Specified date: 1 July 1999: see art 1(2).

A1.589

Transfer of property

7

The provisions of section 23(1) of the Act shall not apply to—

(a) the premises comprising Gwydyr House, Whitehall, London and the furnishings and equipment contained therein, or to any rights or liabilities relating thereto,

(b) any documentary or electronic records.

NOTES

Initial Commencement

Specified date: 1 July 1999: see art 1(2).

SCHEDULE 1
ENACTMENTS CONFERRING FUNCTIONS TRANSFERRED BY ARTICLE 2

Article 2

Public General Acts

A1.590

School Sites Act 1841 (c 38)

Inclosure Act 1845 (c 118) except section 12.

Inclosure Act 1846 (c 70)

Inclosure Act 1847 (c 111)

Inclosure Act 1848 (c 99)

Inclosure Act 1849 (c 83)

Inclosure Act 1852 (c 79)

Burial Act 1853 (c 134)

Inclosure Act 1854 (c 97)

Literary and Scientific Institutions Act 1854 (c 112) section 6.

Burial Act 1855 (c 128)

Inclosure Act 1857 (c 31)

Burial Act 1857 (c 81) except section 25.

Burial Act 1859 (c 1)

Inclosure Act 1859 (c 43)

Improvement of Land Act 1864 (c 114) in respect of the functions transferred to the Secretary of State by the 1978 transfer order.

Inclosure, &c Expenses Act 1868 (c 89) except so far as it applies in relation to any other of the Tithe Acts 1836 to 1951.

Limited Owners Residences Act 1870 (c 56)

Public Health Act 1875 (c 55) except section 327.

Commons Act 1876 (c 56)

Commons (Expenses) Act 1878 (c 56)

Commonable Rights Compensation Act 1882 (c 15)

Places of Worship Sites Amendment Act 1882 (c 21)

Corn Returns Act 1882 (c 37) in respect of the functions exercisable by the Secretary of State by the 1978 transfer order and in respect of the functions exercisable by the Secretary of State under section 5 as substituted by the Deregulation (Corn Returns Act 1882) Order 1996 (SI 1996/848).

Local Government Act 1888 (c 41)

Local Government Act 1894 (c 73)

District Councils (Water Supply Facilities) Act 1897 (c 44)

Commons Act 1899 (c 30)

Improvement of Land Act 1899 (c 46)

Open Spaces Act 1906 (c 25)

Public Health Acts Amendment Act 1907 (c 53) except sections 12 and 94(4).

Finance Act 1908 (c 16)

Small Holdings and Allotments Act 1908 (c 36)

Commons Act 1908 (c 44)

Welsh Church Act 1914 (c 91) sections 19 and 24.

Local Government (Emergency Provisions) Act 1916 (c 12)

...

Ministry of Transport Act 1919 (c 50) No functions under this Act are transferred but it is directed that the functions under sections 17 and 20 shall be exercisable by the Assembly concurrently with the Secretary of State. The function under section 17 shall be exercisable by the Assembly free from the requirement for Treasury approval.

Land Settlement (Facilities) Act 1919 (c 59) except the function of the 'Local Government Board' under paragraph 10 of the First Schedule.

Ferries (Acquisition by Local Authorities) Act 1919 (c 75) except section 3.

Corn Sales Act 1921 (c 35)

Allotments Act 1922 (c 51) except section 1(4).

Agricultural Credits Act 1923 (c 34)

Law of Property Act 1925 (c 20) sections 193 and 194.

Allotments Act 1925 (c 61)

Public Health Act 1925 (c 71) section 6.

Small Holdings and Allotments Act 1926 (c 52)

Landlord and Tenant Act 1927 (c 36) section 20.

Local Government Act 1929 (c 17)

Agricultural Land (Utilisation) Act 1931 (c 41)

Destructive Imported Animals Act 1932 (c 12) except that the functions under sections 1, 2 and 10, so far as they relate to the importation of the types of animals to which this Act relates, are transferred to the Assembly so far as they have been transferred to the Secretary of State by the 1969 transfer order.

Children and Young Persons Act 1933 (c 12) except sections 53, 58, 79 to 81 and the Fourth Schedule.

Public Health Act 1936 (c 49) except the Treasury function under section 341(3).

Diseases of Fish Act 1937 (c 33) It is directed that the functions under this Act shall be exercisable by the Assembly concurrently with any Minister of the Crown by whom they are exercisable. The functions under this Act shall be exercisable by the Assembly free from the requirements for Treasury consent.

Public Health (Drainage of Trade Premises) Act 1937 (c 40)

Physical Training and Recreation Act 1937 (c 46)

Statutory Orders (Special Procedure) Act 1945 (c 18) section 7(3).

Welsh Church (Burial Grounds) Act 1945 (c 27)

Requisitioned Land and War Works Act 1945 (c 43) section 52.

Agriculture (Artificial Insemination) Act 1946 (c 29) in respect of the functions transferred to the Secretary of State by the 1978 transfer order.

The Assembly may only incur expenses under section 1 to such amount as may be sanctioned by the Treasury.

Hill Farming Act 1946 (c 73) except section 32(4).

In section 32(2), the functions of 'the appropriate Minister' in relation to the Advisory Committee for England, Wales and Northern Ireland are transferred to the Assembly so far as they have been transferred to the Secretary of State by the 1969 transfer order.

Section 35 shall have effect as if the expression 'the Ministers or either of them' included reference to the Assembly.

Section 32(4) shall be amended by omitting the words 'by him'.

Polish Resettlement Act 1947 (c 19) sections 4 and 6.

Industrial Organisation and Development Act 1947 (c 40) The functions of 'the Minister of Agriculture, Fisheries and Food' except that Minister's functions under—

    (a)   section 7(4) so far as it relates to a development council exercising functions in relation to England and Wales or in relation to Great Britain; and

    (b)   The Apple and Pear Research Council Order 1989 (SI 1989/2277).

It is directed that the function of the 'Board of Trade' under section 11 shall be exercisable by the Assembly concurrently with the Board of Trade. The function under section 11 shall be exercisable by the Assembly free from the requirement for Treasury approval.

The functions of the Comptroller and Auditor General in section 9(4) are, in relation to financial years beginning in and after 1999, transferred to the Auditor General for Wales in respect of an account of sums recovered under an order made by the Assembly alone under section 9 and of the disposal of those sums by the Assembly, and in relation thereto section 9(4) shall have effect so that for the requirement to lay before Parliament the documents referred to therein, there shall be substituted a requirement for the Auditor General for Wales to lay those documents before the Assembly.

Fire Services Act 1947 (c 41) section 3(5).

Agriculture Act 1947 (c 48) except section 105.

The function under section 75 is transferred only so far as it relates to a reference to an Agricultural Land Tribunal under section 86.

It is directed that the functions under section 83 shall be exercisable by the Assembly concurrently with any Minister of the Crown by whom they are exercisable.

The functions under section 88 are transferred only to the extent that they are functions of 'the Minister'.

Section 92 shall have effect as if the reference to 'the Minister' included a reference to the Assembly.

National Assistance Act 1948 (c 29)

Agricultural Wages Act 1948 (c 47) except—

(a) the requirement under section 13 for 'the Minister' to submit an annual report to Parliament of his proceedings under this Act; and

(b) the functions of the Secretary of State under section 15A.

The functions of 'the Minister' under sections 13 (as it applies in relation to the Agricultural Wages Board), 16 and Schedule 1 are transferred to the Assembly so far as they have been transferred to the Secretary of State under the 1978 transfer order.

The reference to the Minister of Agriculture, Fisheries and Food in section 3A(4) shall be construed as including a reference to the Assembly.

Prevention of Damage by Pests Act 1949 (c 55) All functions are transferred, save that to the extent that this Act provides for the carrying out of research (as referred to in section 27(1)(c) and in article 8(b) of the 1978 transfer order) by either the Minister of Agriculture, Fisheries and Food or the Secretary of State, it is directed that that function shall be exercisable by the Assembly concurrently with those Ministers of the Crown.

Docking and Nicking of Horses Act 1949 (c 70)

Coast Protection Act 1949 (c 74) except—

(a) any function conferred on a Minister of the Crown other than 'the Minister' by sections 2, 5(4), 8(4), 46 and Schedules 1 and 2;

(b) any function conferred on a Minister of the Crown other than 'the Minister' or 'the Minister of Agriculture, Fisheries and Food' by section 17;

(c) section 18(2) and Part II; and

(d) the Treasury function under section 32(5).

National Parks and Access to the Countryside Act 1949 (c 97) except—

(a) sections 9(2), 65(3), 72, 78(1) and paragraph 4 of the First Schedule;

(b) so far as they relate to a route of which a part but not the whole is in Wales, the functions under sections 51 to 55 which were transferred to the 'Minister of Land and Natural Resources' by article 6 of the 1965 transfer order;

(c) the regulation-making function under section 63(1); and

(d) the Treasury function under section 101(11).

Allotments Act 1950 (c 31)

Sea Fish Industry Act 1951 (c 30) in respect of the functions transferred to the Secretary of State by the 1978 transfer order.

Cremation Act 1952 (c 31)

Town Development Act 1952 (c 54)

Local Government (Miscellaneous Provisions) Act 1953 (c 26) except section 8(3).

Dogs (Protection of Livestock) Act 1953 (c 28)

...

Historic Buildings and Ancient Monuments Act 1953 (c 49)

Agriculture (Miscellaneous Provisions) Act 1954 (c 39)

Protection of Animals (Anaesthetics) Act 1954 (c 46)

Landlord and Tenant Act 1954 (c 56) except that in relation to sections 57(1) to (6) and 58 it is directed that the certification function shall be exercisable by the Assembly concurrently with any Minister of the Crown by whom it is exercisable.

Pests Act 1954 (c 68)

Fisheries Act 1955 (c 7)

Parish Councils Act 1957 (c 42)

Agriculture Act 1957 (c 57) except section 32.

The functions of 'the Ministers' under section 6 are transferred so far as they have been transferred to the Secretary of State for Wales by the 1978 transfer order.

Disabled Persons (Employment) Act 1958 (c 33)

Agricultural Marketing Act 1958 (c 47) in respect of functions vested in the Secretary of State for Wales by the 1969 transfer order and the 1978 transfer order.

Article 2(c) of this Order shall not have effect in relation to functions under this Act.

The Treasury consultation requirement under section 28 shall continue in effect.

Opencast Coal Act 1958 (c 69) except the functions of the Treasury under sections 35(8) and 44(4).

The function of 'the appropriate Minister' under section 39(6) is only transferred so far as it relates to—

(a)   internal drainage boards; and
(b)   water and sewerage undertakers and the Environment Agency (which are treated as statutory undertakers for these purposes by virtue of paragraph 1(1) and (2)(viii) of Schedule 25 to the Water Act 1989 (c 15) (as amended by the Environment Act 1995 (Consequential Amendments) Regulations 1996 (SI 1996/593)).

Town and Country Planning Act 1959 (c 53) in respect of the functions transferred to the Secretary of State by the 1965 transfer order.

Weeds Act 1959 (c 54)

Mental Health Act 1959 (c 72)

Road Traffic Act 1960 (c 16) No functions under this Act are transferred but it is directed that the functions under sections 248 and 249 shall be exercisable by the Assembly concurrently with any Minister of the Crown by whom they are exercisable.

Caravan Sites and Control of Development Act 1960 (c 62) except the Treasury function under paragraph 6 of the Second Schedule.

Public Bodies (Admission to Meetings) Act 1960 (c 67)

Land Compensation Act 1961 (c 33)

Public Health Act 1961 (c 64) except functions of a Minister of the Crown exercisable as 'appropriate authority' under section 45 and Schedule 4 in respect of buildings of the following descriptions in the Table in Schedule 4—

(a) a building owned by railway, canal, dock, harbour or inland navigation undertakers;
(b) a building owned by electricity or gas undertakers;
(c) a building forming part of an aerodrome;
(d) a building owned by the Post Office;
(e) a building owned by British Telecommunications.

Local Government (Records) Act 1962 (c 56)

Pipe-Lines Act 1962 (c 58) section 15.

Towyn Trewan Common Act 1963 (c 4) except section 5.

Local Authorities (Land) Act 1963 (c 29)

Public Lavatories (Turnstiles) Act 1963 (c 32)

Children and Young Persons Act 1963 (c 37)

Local Government (Financial Provisions) Act 1963 (c 46)

Plant Varieties and Seeds Act 1964 (c 14) in respect of the functions transferred to the Secretary of State by the 1978 transfer order.

Licensing Act 1964 (c 26) sections 108 to 110, 115, 116, 118 to 121 and Schedules 10 and 11.

Agriculture and Horticulture Act 1964 (c 28) except the function of any Minister of the Crown other than the Secretary of State for Wales.

Harbours Act 1964 (c 40) sections [14,] 15, 15A, 16, 30, 31, 60 and Schedule 3 so far as they relate to fishery harbours.

…

Public Libraries and Museums Act 1964 (c 75)

Science and Technology Act 1965 (c 4) No functions under this Act are transferred but it is directed that the functions of a Minister of the Crown under section 5, except so far as relating to Research Councils, shall be exercisable by the Assembly concurrently with the Secretary of State. The functions under section 5 shall be exercisable by the Assembly free from the requirement for Treasury consent.

Cereals Marketing Act 1965 (c 14) section 16, and Schedules 1 and 3. The remaining functions under this Act are transferred to the extent that they have been transferred to the Secretary of State for Wales by the 1969 transfer order and the 1978 transfer order.

The Treasury approval requirements under sections 1(6), 21(2) and paragraph 10(2) of Schedule 1 shall continue in effect.

Finance Act 1965 (c 25) section 92.

Commons Registration Act 1965 (c 64)

Mines (Working Facilities and Support) Act 1966 (c 4) section 7(8).

Sea Fisheries Regulation Act 1966 (c 38) in respect of the functions transferred to the Secretary of State by the 1978 transfer order.

Local Government Act 1966 (c 42) except the functions of 'The Treasury' under Part II of Schedule 3.

Education Act 1967 (c 3)

Plant Health Act 1967 (c 8) The Treasury consent requirements under sections 4 and 4A shall continue in effect.

Forestry Act 1967 (c 10) except—

(a)   section 33(5);
(b)   section 38(4) so far as it relates to the Home Grown Timber Advisory Committee;
(c)   section 41(4A) and (6);
(d)   the Treasury function under section 42(3)(b);
(e)   sections 44 and 45 and paragraphs 2(2), 6(1) and 12 of Schedule 1.

The functions under paragraphs 6(2), 9(1) and 10(1) of Schedule 1 are transferred so far as they are exercisable by the Secretary of State.

The function under paragraph 7(2) of Schedule 1 is transferred only so far as it relates to a committee for Wales appointed under section 2(3).

The requirement for the approval of 'the Treasury' under paragraphs 6(2), 9(1) and 10(1) of Schedule 1 shall continue in effect.

Agriculture Act 1967 (c 22) section 65. Except so far as this entry provides otherwise, the remaining functions under this Act are transferred to the extent that they have been transferred to the Secretary of State by the 1969 transfer order and the 1978 transfer order.

The requirement for consultation with the 'Secretary of State for Trade' under section 9(11) and the Treasury approval requirements under sections 15(1), 19, 53 and Part II of Schedule 5 shall continue in effect.

It is directed that the notification functions of 'the appropriate Minister' under section 54(3) and of 'the Ministers' under sections 20(2) and 60(3) shall be exercisable by the Assembly concurrently with any Minister of the Crown by whom they are exercisable.

Section 19(1) and (4) shall have effect so that in addition to the requirement to lay before each House of Parliament the documents referred to therein, there shall be a requirement for those documents to be laid before the Assembly.

Slaughter of Poultry Act 1967 (c 24) It is directed that the function under section 4 shall be exercisable by the Assembly concurrently with the Minister of Agriculture, Fisheries and Food.

Civic Amenities Act 1967 (c 69)

Sea Fisheries (Shellfish) Act 1967 (c 83)

Sea Fish (Conservation) Act 1967 (c 84) except the functions of the 'Board of Trade' under section 8.

It is directed that the functions under sections 4, 4A and 15(3) shall be exercisable by the Assembly concurrently with any Minister of the Crown by whom they are exercisable. The functions under sections 4 and 4A shall be exercisable by the Assembly free from the requirement for Treasury consent.

Abortion Act 1967 (c 87)

Leasehold Reform Act 1967 (c 88)

Trade Descriptions Act 1968 (c 29) in respect of the function of the Minister of Agriculture, Fisheries and Food under section 38(2).

Agriculture (Miscellaneous Provisions) Act 1968 (c 34) Part I and section 46.

Countryside Act 1968 (c 41) except the Treasury function under section 47(4).

Health Services and Public Health Act 1968 (c 46)

Caravan Sites Act 1968 (c 52)

Medicines Act 1968 (c 67) section 108. In subsection (1) of section 132, the definition of 'enforcement authority' shall have effect as if the reference to the Minister included a reference to the Assembly.

Sea Fisheries Act 1968 (c 77) It is directed that the functions under section 5 (so far as they relate to the identification and marking of fishing boats) and the functions of 'the appropriate Minister' under section 7 shall be exercisable by the Assembly concurrently with any Minister of the Crown by whom they are exercisable.

Transport Act 1968 (c 78) section 56.

It is directed that the functions of 'the Minister' under section 57 shall be exercisable by the Assembly concurrently with that Minister. The functions under section 57 shall be exercisable by the Assembly free from the requirement for Treasury approval.

Local Government Grants (Social Need) Act 1969 (c 2) It is directed that the functions under this Act shall be exercisable by the Assembly concurrently with the Secretary of State. The functions under this Act shall be exercisable by the Assembly free from the requirement for Treasury consent.

Mines and Quarries (Tips) Act 1969 (c 10) except Part I.

Development of Tourism Act 1969 (c 51) ...

...

The Treasury approval requirements under section 6(1) and (2) shall continue in effect.

...

The functions of the Comptroller and Auditor General in section 6(3) and (4) are, in relation to statements of account prepared by the Wales Tourist Board for financial years beginning in and after 1999, transferred to the Auditor General for Wales and in relation thereto section 6(4) shall have effect so that for the requirement to lay before Parliament the documents referred to therein, there shall be substituted a requirement for the Auditor General for Wales to lay those documents before the Assembly.

Section 17(4) (including that provision as applied by section 18(2)) shall have effect so that reference to the Assembly shall be substituted for the reference to the Secretary of State for Wales.

Children and Young Persons Act 1969 (c 54) except sections 7, 19, 23(12), 30, 46, 65 and Schedule 3.

Sea Fish Industry Act 1970 (c 11)

Parish Councils and Burial Authorities (Miscellaneous Provisions) Act 1970 (c 29)

Conservation of Seals Act 1970 (c 30) except section 1(2).

Local Authorities (Goods and Services) Act 1970 (c 39)

Agriculture Act 1970 (c 40) except section 53. The Treasury approval requirement under section 78(10) shall continue in effect.

Local Authority Social Services Act 1970 (c 42)

Chronically Sick and Disabled Persons Act 1970 (c 44) except sections 9, 13(2) and 28.

Radiological Protection Act 1970 (c 46) in respect of the functions of 'the Health Ministers' exercisable by the Secretary of State for Wales.

It is directed that the function under paragraph 13(5) of Schedule 1 shall be exercisable by the Assembly concurrently with the Secretary of State.

The Treasury approval requirements under section 3 shall continue in effect.

Misuse of Drugs Act 1971 (c 38) section 1.

Defective Premises Act 1972 (c 35)

Agriculture (Miscellaneous Provisions) Act 1972 (c 62) in respect of the functions transferred to the Secretary of State by the 1978 transfer order.

Poisons Act 1972 (c 66) except section 1(2).

It is directed that the function of the Secretary of State in appointing additional members to the Poisons Board under paragraphs 2 and 3 of Schedule 1 and the function of the Secretary of State under paragraph 4 of that Schedule shall be exercisable by the Assembly concurrently with the Secretary of State.

European Communities Act 1972 (c 68) in respect of the functions transferred to the Secretary of State by the 1978 transfer order.

Local Government Act 1972 (c 70) except sections 58 (so far as it relates to the making of an order in relation to police areas), 103 (so far as it applies to joint committees of police authorities by virtue of section 107), 119(3), 244(2), 259, 260, paragraph 37 of Schedule 12 and paragraphs 3, 5(2) and (3) and 6 of Schedule 13.

It is directed that the functions of the Secretary of State under section 236(11) and paragraph 25 of Schedule 14 shall be exercisable by the Assembly concurrently with the Secretary of State.

In section 121(1) the reference to 'the Minister concerned with that purpose' shall, in relation to any purpose in respect of which the Assembly is concerned, have effect as if it were a reference to the Assembly; and following references in section 121 to 'Minister' or 'Ministers' shall be construed accordingly.

Section 128(1) shall have effect as if the reference to 'the Minister' included a reference to the Assembly; and following references in that section to 'Minister' shall be construed accordingly.

Section 141(2) shall, in relation to any matter with which the Assembly is concerned, have effect, as if the reference to 'the appropriate Minister' were a reference to the Assembly.

Section 238 shall have effect as if after 'the Secretary of State' there were inserted 'or, as the case may be, the National Assembly for Wales'.

Section 240 shall have effect as if references to 'the Secretary of State' included reference to the Assembly.

Section 250 shall have effect as if references to 'Minister' or 'Secretary of State' included reference to the Assembly.

In paragraph 8 of Schedule 8 for 'Parliament' there shall be substituted 'the National Assembly for Wales'.

Land Compensation Act 1973 (c 26)

National Health Service Reorganisation Act 1973 (c 32)

Protection of Wrecks Act 1973 (c 33) except section 2.

Employment and Training Act 1973 (c 50) except sections 2, 4, 5 and 11, in respect of which it is directed that the Ministerial functions contained therein shall be exercisable by the Assembly concurrently with any Ministers of the Crown by whom they are exercisable, save that the functions exercisable by the Assembly under section 2 shall not include the function of making arrangements for the principal purpose of helping all those (as distinct from a particular section of the population of Wales) without work to find employment and to help employers to fill vacancies, or any function ancillary to that function.

The functions under sections 2, 5(3) and 11(1) shall be exercisable by the Assembly free from the requirement for Treasury approval and the function under section 5(2)(b) shall be exercisable by the Assembly free from the requirement for the approval of the 'Minister for the Civil Service'.

Slaughterhouses Act 1974 (c 3) except in relation to the functions under Part I which were retained as functions of the Minister of Agriculture, Fisheries and Food by virtue of article 4(1) of the 1978 transfer order.

Horticulture (Special Payments) Act 1974 (c 5)

Local Government Act 1974 (c 7) except—

(a) section 9 so far as it relates to the Countryside Commission;
(b) section 23;
(c) the function of the Secretary of State in discharging a notice under section 32(3) so far as the notice relates to a police authority or to any other body (other than a regional flood defence committee) exercising functions in England and Wales;
(d) the function of the Secretary of State under section 35(3) and (4) so far as it relates to the removal or relaxation of any control conferred by or under any enactment on a body other than the Assembly; and
(e) paragraph 3(1) of Schedule 4 so far as it relates to 'Local Commissioners' (but not 'officers') and paragraph 3(2) of that Schedule.

It is directed that the function of a Minister of the Crown of giving notice (other than a notice of discharge) under section 32(3) shall be exercisable by the Assembly concurrently with any Minister of the Crown by whom it is exercisable.

The requirement for the approval of 'the Minister for the Civil Service' under paragraph 3(1) of Schedule 4 shall continue in effect.

Control of Pollution Act 1974 (c 40) except section 102(2).

Reservoirs Act 1975 (c 23) [except section 12A(4).]

Mobile Homes Act 1975 (c 49)

Salmon and Freshwater Fisheries Act 1975 (c 51) except—

(a) the functions of 'the Minister' under section 37A; and
(b) section 38.

Sex Discrimination Act 1975 (c 65) sections 25, 66(5), 67(6), 78 and Schedule 2.

Welsh Development Agency Act 1975 (c 70) except ... the functions of 'the appropriate Minister' under paragraphs 11 and 12 of Schedule 4.

...

The Treasury approval requirements under paragraph 3(2) and (3) of Schedule 3 shall continue in effect so far as they relate to borrowing in currencies other than sterling.

The functions of the Comptroller and Auditor General in paragraphs 4(3) and 8(3) to (5) of Schedule 3 are, in relation to financial or, as the case may be, accounting years beginning in and after 1999, transferred to the Auditor General for Wales and in relation thereto paragraph 4(3) and 8(4) of Schedule 3 shall have effect so that for the requirement to lay before Parliament the documents referred to therein, there shall be substituted a requirement for the Auditor General for Wales to lay those documents before the Assembly.

Adoption Act 1976 (c 36) sections 3 to 5, 8, ..., 28, 51A, 57A, 58A and 65A.

Agriculture (Miscellaneous Provisions) Act 1976 (c 55)

Local Government (Miscellaneous Provisions) Act 1976 (c 57) except section 30(3).

Race Relations Act 1976 (c 74) sections 19(2), 19A(3), 57(5) and 58(6).

It is directed that the certification function under section 69 shall be exercisable by the Assembly concurrently with any Minister of the Crown by whom it is exercisable.

The references in section 41 to a Minister of the Crown shall be construed as including reference to the Assembly.

Development of Rural Wales Act 1976 (c 75) section 26.

Rent (Agriculture) Act 1976 (c 80)

Fishery Limits Act 1976 (c 86)

Rentcharges Act 1977 (c 30)

Rent Act 1977 (c 42)

Protection from Eviction Act 1977 (c 43)

...

Refuse Disposal (Amenity) Act 1978 (c 3)

Inner Urban Areas Act 1978 (c 50) except section 2(5).

Agricultural Statistics Act 1979 (c 13)

Forestry Act 1979 (c 21)

Ancient Monuments and Archaeological Areas Act 1979 (c 46) except the Treasury function under section 50.

Bees Act 1980 (c 12) except the functions of any Minister of the Crown other than the Secretary of State for Wales.

National Heritage Act 1980 (c 17) sections 9 (except the function of the Secretary of State as a recipient of property transferred to him pursuant to a direction made under subsection (2) and except subsection (6)), 16 and 16A.

Any sums received by the Assembly under section 3 shall be treated as if they were sums received by the Assembly within the meaning of section 84(5) of the Government of Wales Act 1998 (c 38) and section 3A(5) shall be construed accordingly.

In section 9(2), the reference to the Secretary of State, where it occurs for the second time, shall be construed as including a reference to the Assembly.

Education Act 1980 (c 20)

Import of Live Fish (England and Wales) Act 1980 (c 27) It is directed that the functions under sections 1 and 3(2) shall be exercisable by the Assembly concurrently with any Minister of the Crown by whom they are exercisable. The functions under section 1 shall be exercisable by the Assembly free from the requirement for Treasury consent.

Industry Act 1980 (c 33) section 2.

Housing Act 1980 (c 51)

Health Services Act 1980 (c 53)

Local Government, Planning and Land Act 1980 (c 65) except—

(a) section 95(4) so far as it applies to land other than Crown land held by the Assembly;
(b) section 99(6)(b);
(c) the Treasury functions under section 170(4) and paragraphs 4(4) and 9(4) of Schedule 31;
(d) the functions of 'the appropriate Minister' under Schedule 28 and the function of the Secretary of State under paragraph 8(1) of Schedule 31.

The Treasury approval requirements under paragraphs 4(1)(b) and (2)(b), 6 and 7 of Schedule 31 and the Treasury consent requirements under paragraphs 3, 10(3) and (4) of Schedule 31 and paragraphs 5(3)(b) and 15(4)(b) of Schedule 32 shall continue in effect.

The requirement for consultation with the Treasury under paragraph 7(1) of Schedule 31 shall continue in effect.

The functions of the Comptroller and Auditor General in paragraph 9(1) and (2) of Schedule 31 are, in relation to statement of account prepared for financial years beginning in and after 1999, transferred to the Auditor General for Wales and in relation thereto paragraph 9(3) of that Schedule shall have effect so that for the requirement to lay before Parliament the documents referred to therein, there shall be substituted a requirement for the Auditor General for Wales to lay those documents before the Assembly.

Highways Act 1980 (c 66) except—

(a) the Treasury function under section 327(4);
(b) functions exercisable by the Secretary of State in pursuance of section 329(5); and
(c) functions exercisable by the Secretary of State in relation to that part of the M4 Motorway in Wales which comprises 'the New Toll Plaza area' and 'the New Bridge', as defined in section 39(1) of the Severn Bridges Act 1992 (c 3).

Animal Health Act 1981 (c 22) in respect of—

(a) the functions exercisable by 'the appropriate Minister'; and
(b) the functions of 'the Ministers' so far as exercisable by the Secretary of State for Wales.

Fisheries Act 1981 (c 29) in respect of—

(a) the functions of 'the Ministers' in Part I and Schedules 1, 2 and 3 so far as exercisable by the Secretary of State concerned with the sea fish industry in Wales; and
(b) Parts II to IV.

The Treasury approval requirements under Part II shall continue in effect.

Zoo Licensing Act 1981 (c 37)

New Towns Act 1981 (c 64) except the Treasury functions under sections 69(1) and 78(3)(a).

The Treasury approval requirements under sections 59, 66 and 67 and the Treasury consent requirement under Schedule 9 shall continue in effect.

The functions of the Comptroller and Auditor General in section 69 are, in relation to financial years beginning in and after 1999, transferred to the Auditor General for Wales and in relation thereto section 69(2) shall have effect so that for the requirement to lay before Parliament the documents referred to therein, there shall be substituted a requirement for the Auditor General for Wales to lay those documents before the Assembly.

Orders confirmed by the Assembly shall be subject to special parliamentary procedure to the extent provided for under paragraph 12(b) of Schedule 4.

Compulsory Purchase (Vesting Declarations) Act 1981 (c 66)

Acquisition of Land Act 1981 (c 67) except sections 8(4) and 32(6A).

The regulation-making function provided for in section 7(2) is only transferred so far as it is exercisable in relation to such orders as fall to be made or confirmed by the Assembly.

The functions of the Secretary of State as 'the appropriate Minister' (in pursuance of the definition in section 8(3)) are only transferred so far as they relate to water and sewerage undertakers (treated as statutory undertakers for the purposes of this Act by virtue of Schedule 25 to the Water Act 1989) except under section 16 where those functions are also transferred in relation to the bodies and trusts referred to in section 16(3). It is directed that, in relation to water and sewerage undertakers, these functions shall, in relation to land situated in the catchment areas of the rivers Dee, Wye and Severn be exercisable by the Assembly concurrently with the Secretary of State.

Orders made or confirmed by the Assembly shall be subject to special parliamentary procedure as provided for in section 18 and paragraph 5 of Schedule 3.

Wildlife and Countryside Act 1981 (c 69) It is directed that the functions under sections 2(6), 16, 29(1) and (2) and paragraph 13(3) of Schedule 13 shall be exercisable by the Assembly concurrently with any Minister of the Crown by whom they are exercisable.

Agricultural Training Board Act 1982 (c 9) except section 7A(2) and the functions of 'the Ministers' other than those exercisable by the Minister concerned with agriculture in Wales so far as they relate to the Agricultural Training Board.

Section 8(4) shall have effect so that in addition to the requirement for that Board to lay a report before Parliament, there shall be a requirement for that report to be laid before the Assembly.

Local Government (Miscellaneous Provisions) Act 1982 (c 30)

Industrial Development Act 1982 (c 52) No functions under this Act are transferred but it is directed that—

(a) the functions of the Secretary of State under this Act shall, with the exception of the functions under sections 1, 8(5) and (7), 10, 15 and 16, be exercisable by the Assembly concurrently with the Secretary of State; and

(b) the functions of a Minister of the Crown under section 13 shall be exercisable by the Assembly concurrently with any Minister of the Crown by whom they are exercisable.

The functions under sections 5, 7, 8 (except subsections (5) and (7)) and 13 shall be exercisable by the Assembly free from the requirements for Treasury consent and the functions under section 12 shall be exercisable by the Assembly free from the requirements for Treasury approval.

Section 15 shall have effect so that reports prepared by the Secretary of State in compliance therewith shall include, in addition to the information required in relation to the Secretary of State's exercise of functions under this Act, all such information in relation to the exercise by the Assembly of such functions, and the Assembly shall ensure that all necessary information is supplied to the Secretary of State for this purpose.

Agricultural Marketing Act 1983 (c 3) The functions exercisable by the Secretary of State for Wales under sections 1, 5, 6(3)(b) and (4) and paragraph 4(4) of Schedule 1.

It is directed that the functions under sections 6(3)(a), 7(2) and paragraph 4(3) of Schedule 1 shall be exercisable by the Assembly concurrently with any Minister of the Crown by whom they are exercisable. The function under section 7(2) shall be exercisable by the Assembly free from the requirement for Treasury consent.

Pig Industry Levy Act 1983 (c 4) in respect of the functions of 'the Ministers' so far as exercisable by the Secretary of State for Wales.

Conwy Tunnel (Supplementary Powers) Act 1983 (c 7)

British Fishing Boats Act 1983 (c 8) so far as exercisable by the Secretary of State concerned with the sea fishing industry in Wales.

[**Mental Health Act 1983** (c 20) except sections 41, 42, 45A(10) and (11), 45B to 51, 53, 71, 73 to 75, 80A, 81A, 82A, 83A, 84, 85A, 86, and Schedule 2.

Functions under sections 80, 81 and 83 are transferred except in relation to a patient who is subject to one or more of the following, namely:

(a) a restriction order;
(b) a hospital direction;
(c) a limitation direction; or
(d) a restriction direction,

made under sections 41, 45A or, as the case may be, 49.

In section 19(3) and in paragraph (a) in the definition of 'the managers' in section 145(1), references to a hospital vested in the Secretary of State for the purposes of his functions under the National Health Service Act 1977 shall have effect as if they included a reference to a hospital vested in the Assembly for purposes of its functions under that Act.

Section 23(4) and (5) shall not apply to the exercise by the Assembly of the powers conferred by that section.

Section 24(3) shall have effect as if it applied to an application by the Assembly as well as to an application by the Secretary of State.

Sections 54(1) and 117(2A)(a) shall have effect as if references to a registered medical practitioner approved for the purposes of section 12 by the Secretary of State (including references to be construed as such) included a reference to such a practitioner approved by the Assembly.

Section 139(4) shall have effect as if after the words 'the Secretary of State' there were inserted 'the National Assembly for Wales'.

Section 142(1) shall have effect as if the reference to a government department included a reference to the Assembly.

The Treasury approval requirements under sections 119(1), 120(6) and 121(6) shall continue in effect so far as they relate to pensions.]

Diseases of Fish Act 1983 (c 30)

Mobile Homes Act 1983 (c 34)

Litter Act 1983 (c 35)

Education (Fees and Awards) Act 1983 (c 40) except section 1.

Health and Social Services and Social Security Adjudications Act 1983 (c 41) except Schedule 8.

It is directed that the functions of the Secretary of State under Schedule 3 shall be exercisable by the Assembly concurrently with the Secretary of State.

Public Health (Control of Disease) Act 1984 (c 22) except section 28 and the Treasury function under section 73(4).

Registered Homes Act 1984 (c 24) except sections 43 to 45.

Road Traffic Regulation Act 1984 (c 27) except—

(a) section 17(2) and (3) with respect to special roads generally;
(b) sections 20, 21 and 23;
(c) section 25 (other than subsection (4) together with the other provisions of section 25 so far as relating thereto);
(d) section 28;
(e) section 64 other than so far as it confers the power to—
   (i) prescribe a variant of any sign of a type prescribed by 'the Ministers' and carrying words in English, being a variant identical with a sign of that type except for the substitution or addition of words in Welsh (and any increase in size needed to accommodate the substituted or added words); and
   (ii) authorise signs not otherwise prescribed;
(f) section 65 so far as it relates to the giving of general directions;
(g) section 81;
(h) section 85(2) so far as it relates to the giving of general directions;
(i) sections 86, 88, 95 to 97, 99 to 106, 130 to 132, 136 to 140, 141A and Schedule 6.

It is directed that the function under section 128 shall be exercisable by the Assembly concurrently with the Secretary of State.

Food Act 1984 (c 30) except—

(a) the functions of 'the appropriate Minister' under section 68 other than so far as they are exercisable by the Secretary of State for Wales;
(b) section 68(5);
(c) the functions of 'the Ministers' under section 69 other than so far as they are exercisable by the Secretary of State for Wales; and
(d) section 110.

It is directed that the functions of 'the appropriate Minister' under section 69A shall be exercisable by the Assembly concurrently with that Minister.

Section 68(5) shall have effect so that in addition to the requirement to lay before Parliament the documents referred to therein, there shall be a requirement for those documents to be laid before the Assembly.

Cycle Tracks Act 1984 (c 38) section 3.

Animal Health and Welfare Act 1984 (c 40)

Health and Social Security Act 1984 (c 48) section 10.

[**Building Act 1984 (c 55)** except—

(a) sections 1, 2, 3(1), 5(1), 6, 8(2), (3) and (6), 9(1), 11 to 13, 14, and 16(9);
(b) section 16(10) so far as it relates to the function of prescribing fees;
(c) sections 17 and 19(7);
(d) section 20(5) so far as it relates to the function of prescribing the time and manner of appeals;
(e) sections 20(10), 35, 38(1), 43(3), 44, 47 to 49, 50 (except subsection (2)), 51 to 58, 92, 120 and Schedules 1 and 4; and
(f) the Treasury function under section 87(4).

The Treasury approval requirement under section 87(3) shall continue in effect.]

Milk (Cessation of Production) Act 1985 (c 4)

New Towns and Urban Development Corporations Act 1985 (c 5)

Hospital Complaints Procedure Act 1985 (c 42) sections 1 and 1A.

Further Education Act 1985 (c 47)

Food and Environment Protection Act 1985 (c 48) except—

(a) functions under Part II so far as exercisable in relation to matters concerning or arising from the exploration for, or production of, petroleum;

(b) the functions of the Minister of Agriculture, Fisheries and Food under sections 16 and 18 and paragraphs 1 to 3 of Schedule 5.

It is directed that the functions under sections 1(1), 3(1) and (2), 13, 14(2) and (3), 17 and paragraphs 4 to 6 of Schedule 5 shall be exercisable by the Assembly concurrently with any Minister of the Crown by whom they are exercisable.

The Treasury consent requirements under sections 8(9), 16(2) and 18(4) shall continue in effect.

Transport Act 1985 (c 67) section 19(7), and Parts IV and V (except sections 110 and 111).

Housing Act 1985 (c 68) except section 5(1)(b).

The Treasury consent requirement under paragraph 4(4) of Schedule 6A shall continue in effect.

Housing Associations Act 1985 (c 69) except the Treasury function under section 1(1)(b).

The Treasury consent requirement under section 76(2) and the Treasury approval requirement under section 92(6) (so far as it applies to section 92(3)) shall continue in effect.

Landlord and Tenant Act 1985 (c 70)

Agricultural Holdings Act 1986 (c 5) except paragraph 4(1)(a) of Schedule 12.

Local Government Act 1986 (c 10)

Horticultural Produce Act 1986 (c 20)

Health Service Joint Consultative Committees (Access to Information) Act 1986 (c 24)

Disabled Persons (Services, Consultation and Representation) Act 1986 (c 33) sections 1, 2, 5, 7 and 11.

Education Act 1986 (c 40)

Agriculture Act 1986 (c 49) except the functions of the Minister of Agriculture, Fisheries and Food under sections 6 and 9.

Education (No 2) Act 1986 (c 61)

Salmon Act 1986 (c 62)

Local Government Finance Act 1987 (c 6)

Reverter of Sites Act 1987 (c 15)

Landlord and Tenant Act 1987 (c 31)

Aids (Control) Act 1987 (c 33)

Access to Personal Files Act 1987 (c 37)

Income and Corporation Taxes Act 1988 (c 1) sections 79, 84, 488 and 489.

Local Government Act 1988 (c 9)

Farm Land and Rural Development Act 1988 (c 16)

Employment Act 1988 (c 19) except sections 26 and 29(3).

Environment and Safety Information Act 1988 (c 30) in respect of—

(a) 'the responsible authority' function under section 2(2)(d) in relation to any individual employed and authorised by the Assembly; and
(b) 'the appropriate Minister' function under section 4 in relation to any notice served by the Assembly.

[Education Reform Act 1988 (c 40) except sections 197, 199, 209, 226 and Schedules 8 and 11.
It is directed that the functions under section 218(6) and, so far as it relates thereto, (6ZA) shall be exercisable by the Assembly concurrently with the Secretary of State.]

Local Government Finance Act 1988 (c 41) except the function of the Minister of Agriculture, Fisheries and Food under section 118 and the Treasury function under paragraph 1(2) of Schedule 8.

It is directed that the functions of the Secretary of State under section 88B, so far as they relate to police authorities, shall be exercisable by the Assembly concurrently with the Secretary of State. The functions under section 88B shall be exercisable by the Assembly free from the requirements for Treasury consent.

The functions of the Comptroller and Auditor General in paragraph 1 of Schedule 8 are, so far as they relate to the non-domestic rating account for Wales for financial years beginning in and after 1999, transferred to the Auditor General for Wales and in relation thereto paragraph 1(3) shall have effect so that for the requirement to lay before each House of Parliament the documents referred to therein, there shall be substituted a requirement for the Auditor General for Wales to lay those documents before the Assembly.

Notwithstanding section 45(3) of the Government of Wales Act 1998, any reference to the approval of a report by the House of Commons shall, in relation to a report laid before the Assembly, be construed as a reference to the publication of the report by the Assembly.

Health and Medicines Act 1988 (c 49) sections 7, 8, 17(1)(d) and 23.

Housing Act 1988 (c 50) except the Treasury function under paragraph 3(2) of Schedule 9.

The Treasury approval requirements under paragraphs 2, 4, 6 and 7 of Schedule 8 and the Treasury consent requirement under paragraph 10 of that Schedule shall continue in effect.

Road Traffic Act 1988 (c 52) in respect of—

(a) sections 13(2), 13A, 27(6) and 31(2);
(b) section 36(5) so far as exercisable by the Secretary of State for Wales but only to the extent that functions are exercisable by the Assembly under section 64 of the Road Traffic Regulation Act 1984 (c 27); and
(c) section 159.

It is directed that the functions under sections 39(1) and 40 shall be exercisable by the Assembly concurrently with the Secretary of State. The functions under sections 39(1) and 40 shall be exercisable by the Assembly free from the requirement for Treasury approval.

1770

Road Traffic Offenders Act 1988 (c 53) sections 34A, 34B (except subsection (9)) and 34C.

Official Secrets Act 1989 (c 6) in respect of the power to prescribe persons or classes of member or employee for the purposes of paragraphs (f) and (g) of section 12(1) so far as exercisable in respect of bodies or offices in relation to which the Assembly exercises functions, and in respect of the power of certification under section 12(2)(b) so far as exercisable in respect of agreements or arrangements entered into by the Assembly.

It is directed that where the power to prescribe persons or classes of member or employee for the purposes of paragraphs (f) and (g) of section 12(1) is exercisable in respect of bodies or offices in relation to which both the Assembly and a Minister of the Crown exercise functions, that prescribing function shall be exercisable by the Assembly concurrently with the Secretary of State.

Control of Pollution (Amendment) Act 1989 (c 14)

Employment Act 1989 (c 38) sections 2, 5, 6, 8 and 28.

Children Act 1989 (c 41)

Local Government and Housing Act 1989 (c 42) except sections 43(2), 53(1) and 54(1) so far as they relate to a fire authority or police authority, and except section 43(3).

The Treasury consent requirements under sections 43(2), (5) and (6) and 46(6) shall continue in effect.

It is directed that the function of a Minister of the Crown under section 54(1) shall be exercisable by the Assembly concurrently with any Minister of the Crown by whom it is exercisable except so far as it relates to a National Park authority.

...

[**Town and Country Planning Act 1990 (c 8)** except—

(a) section 90(2);
(b) the functions of the Ministers of the Crown other than the Secretary of State for Wales under sections 90(1), 101 and Schedule 8, 170(12), 238(1)(a), 239(1)(a), 241(1)(a), 263(3) and (4), 266, 268, 279(5) and (6), 305, 325(9) and 336(3);
(c) the functions of the Secretary of State for Trade and Industry under section 272(5) and (6); and
(d) the Treasury functions under sections 293(3) and 336(2).

The requirement to consult the Lord Chancellor under section 20(5) shall continue in effect.

The functions of the Secretary of State as 'the appropriate Minister' (in pursuance of the definition in section 265) are only transferred so far as they relate to water and sewerage undertakers.

It is directed that the functions under sections 304 and 321 shall be exercisable by the Assembly concurrently with the Secretary of State. The functions under section 304 shall be exercisable by the Assembly free from the requirement for Treasury consent.

The Treasury approval requirement under section 297(3) shall continue in effect.

The functions under sections 238, 239 and 241 shall apply to land vested in the Assembly under section 23 of the Government of Wales Act 1998 or otherwise which was acquired by a Minister of the Crown or other government department before it was so vested, as it applies to land acquired by the Assembly.

Paragraph 8(2)(b) of Schedule 6 shall have effect as if the references to the Welsh Office were references to the Assembly and in relation thereto the reference to the Parliamentary Commissioner Act 1967 (c 13) shall have effect as if it were a reference to Schedule 9 to the Government of Wales Act 1998.]

Planning (Listed Buildings and Conservation Areas) Act 1990 (c 9) except the Treasury function under section 83(8).

It is directed that the function under paragraph 6(6) of Schedule 3 shall be exercisable by the Assembly concurrently with the Secretary of State.

Paragraph 7(2)(b) of Schedule 3 shall have effect as if the references to the Welsh Office were references to the Assembly and in relation thereto the reference to the Parliamentary Commissioner Act 1967 (c 13) shall have effect as if it were a reference to Schedule 9 to the Government of Wales Act 1998.

Planning (Hazardous Substances) Act 1990 (c 10) except sections 12(2) and 31(6).

In respect of section 36B the function of the 'appropriate Minister' is transferred only to the extent of its operation in cases where the Environment Agency and water and sewerage undertakers are deemed to be the statutory undertakers.

It is directed that the functions under sections 31(2), 38(1) and paragraph 6(6) of the Schedule shall be exercisable by the Assembly concurrently with any Minister of the Crown by whom they are exercisable.

The function under section 38(1) shall be exercisable by the Assembly free from the requirement for Treasury consent.

Paragraph 7(2)(b) of the Schedule shall have effect as if the references to the Welsh Office were references to the Assembly and in relation thereto the reference to the Parliamentary Commissioner Act 1967 (c 13) shall have effect as if it were a reference to Schedule 9 to the Government of Wales Act 1998.

Food Safety Act 1990 (c 16) except section 54(4).

It is directed that the function under section 47 of paying remuneration and allowances shall be exercisable by the Assembly concurrently with the Minister of Agriculture, Fisheries and Food. The function under section 47 shall be exercisable by the Assembly free from the requirement for Treasury approval.

...

Access to Health Records Act 1990 (c 23)

Social Security Act 1990 (c 27) No functions under this Act are transferred but it is directed that the functions under section 15 shall be exercisable by the Assembly concurrently with the Secretary of State. The functions under section 15 shall be exercisable by the Assembly free from the requirement for Treasury consent.

Environmental Protection Act 1990 (c 43) except—

  (a) the functions under section 140 and Schedule 12 relating to the importation into and the landing and unloading in the United Kingdom of any specified substance or article;
  (b) sections 141, 153, 156 [(other than as it applies to Part 2 of the Act)] and Schedule 7;
  (c) the functions of the Minister of Agriculture, Fisheries and Food under Part VI;
  (d) ...

It is directed that the functions of the Secretary of State under sections 4(8A), 20(6) so far as relating to section 21, 21, 65, 71, 78S, 123(1) and 159(4) shall be exercisable by the Assembly concurrently with the Secretary of State.

The functions of the Secretary of State under Part VII are transferred so far as relating to the Countryside Council for Wales.

It is directed that the functions of the Secretary of State under section 153, so far as they conduce to the protection, improvement or better understanding of the environment of, or any part of, Wales, shall be exercisable by the Assembly concurrently with the Secretary of State. Article 2(c) of this Order shall not have effect in relation to the exercise by the Assembly of its functions under section 153.

Sections 132(1)(c) and 133(2)(b) shall have effect so that reference to 'the Secretary of State or any other Minister' includes a reference to the Assembly.

The Treasury approval requirements under sections 8(2), 113 and paragraph 21(1) of Schedule 6 shall continue in effect.

The functions of the Comptroller and Auditor General in paragraph 21 of Schedule 6 are, in relation to statements of account prepared by the Countryside Council for Wales for financial years beginning in and after 1999, transferred to the Auditor General for Wales and in relation thereto paragraph 21(3) of Schedule 6 shall have effect so that for the requirement to lay before each House of Parliament the documents referred to therein, there shall be substituted a requirement for the Auditor General for Wales to lay those documents before the Assembly.

Caldey Island Act 1990 (c 44) No functions under this Act are transferred but it is directed that the function under section 4(3) shall be exercisable by the Assembly concurrently with the Secretary of State.

Caravans (Standard Community Charge and Rating) Act 1991 (c 2)

New Roads and Street Works Act 1991 (c 22) except section 167(3).

Agriculture and Forestry (Financial Provisions) Act 1991 (c 33) sections 2 and 3.

The Treasury approval requirement under section 2(1) shall continue in effect.

Planning and Compensation Act 1991 (c 34)

Smoke Detectors Act 1991 (c 37)

Road Traffic Act 1991 (c 40) sections 31(6), 43 and Schedule 3.

Deer Act 1991 (c 54) sections 2 and 7 except that in relation to section 7(5)(b) only the function of the Secretary of State as 'agriculture Minister' is transferred to the Assembly.

[**Water Industry Act 1991 (c 56)** except sections 1, [2A,] 14, 15, [16A, 17 to 17D, 17F to 17K, 17N to 17P, 17R, 22A to 22F], 24(2)(d), 27(3), [27A, 27B, 27E, 27G, 27I to 27K, 29, 29A,] 32 to 35, [38B, 66B, 66F to 66L, 86(1A), 87B, 88A, 89,] 92, [95B,] 152(2), [192A, 192B,] 193(3), [195A,] 206(3)(e) and Schedules 1[, 1A, 3A] and 4 [and except functions under such other sections or Schedules as are expressly stated in the succeeding paragraphs to be so excepted (but only to the extent stated)].

Functions under sections ...5, 6 to 13, ...24 (except 24(2)(d)), 26, [37, 38, 39, [47(2)(g),] 51A], [53(2)(c), 55(4),] 65, [66A(6),] ...74, ...[94, 95, 96,] 101A, 103, 104, [105A to 105C,] 143(3A), (7) and (8), 143A, 144A, 144B, 149, 150A, 153, 154, 156, [158,] 182, 195, [198 to 200]... and Schedule 5 are transferred to the Assembly, in relation to any water or sewerage undertaker whose area is wholly or mainly in Wales [(but not in relation to any licensed water suppliers)].

...

[Functions under sections 2, 18 to 22, 68 to 70, 93A and 201 to 203 are transferred to the Assembly in relation to—

(a) any water or sewerage undertaker whose area is wholly or mainly in Wales;
(b) any licensed water supplier so far as relating to licensed activities using the supply system of any such water undertaker; and

(c) in the case of functions under section 70, any other person who is a relevant person (as defined in that section) in relation to any such undertaker or licensed water supplier.]

Functions under section 67 are transferred to the Assembly as follows—

[(a) for the making of regulations concerning water supplied using the supply system of a water undertaker, the function is transferred in relation to the supply system of any water undertaker whose area is wholly or mainly in Wales;

(b) for the making of regulations concerning water supplied other than using the supply system of a water undertaker, the function is transferred in relation to Wales].

Functions under sections 3, [86 (except subsection (1A))], 213 to 215 and paragraph 11(3)(b) of Schedule 6 shall be exercisable by the Assembly to the same extent as the powers, duties and other provisions to which those sections apply are exercisable by the Assembly.

[In respect of the functions under sections 37A to 37D, 39B and 39C it is provided as follows—

(a) functions under those provisions so far as relating to matters concerning the construction or enlargement of reservoirs are transferred to the Assembly in relation to Wales;

(b) functions under those provisions so far as relating to matters other than the construction or enlargement of reservoirs are transferred to the Assembly in relation to any water undertaker whose area is wholly or mainly in Wales; and

(c) the functions of the Assembly referred to in paragraph (b) above so far as they are exercisable in relation to England shall be exercisable only after consultation with the Secretary of State.]

In respect of the functions under sections 155, 167, 169(4) and (5) and Schedule 11 it is provided as follows—

(a) functions under these provisions so far as relating to matters concerning the construction or enlargement of reservoirs are transferred to the Assembly in relation to Wales;

(b) functions under these provisions so far as relating to matters other than the construction or enlargement of reservoirs are transferred to the Assembly in relation to such parts of Wales as are outside the catchment areas of the rivers Dee, Wye and Severn;

(c) it is directed that functions under these provisions so far as relating to matters other than the construction or enlargement of reservoirs shall, in relation to such parts of Wales as are within the catchment areas of the rivers Dee, Wye and Severn, be exercisable by the Assembly concurrently with the Secretary of State.

[In respect of the functions under section 208 it is provided as follows—

(a) the functions under that section of giving directions for the purpose of mitigating the effects of any civil emergency and the function (in the case of sub-paragraphs (i) and (ii) below) of enforcing such directions are transferred to the Assembly—

  (i) in relation to any water or sewerage undertaker whose area is wholly or mainly in Wales;

  (ii) in relation to any licensed water supplier so far as relating to licensed activities using the supply system of any such water undertaker; and

  (iii) in relation to the Consumer Council for Water so far as relating to its functions in connection with any such water undertaker; and

(b)   it is directed that the other functions under that section shall be exercisable by the Assembly concurrently with the Secretary of State in relation to the bodies and so far as mentioned in paragraph (a)(i) to (iii) above.]

It is directed that functions under sections 19(4), 20(9), 27(4), 207 and 221(4) shall be exercisable by the Assembly concurrently with the Ministers of the Crown by whom they are exercisable.

It is directed that the functions under section 152(1) shall be exercisable by the Assembly concurrently with the Secretary of State in relation to any water or sewerage undertaker whose area is wholly or mainly in Wales [or (so far as relating to licensed activities using the supply system of any such water undertaker) any licensed water supplier] and it shall be so exercisable free from the Treasury approval requirement under section 152(2).

Article 2(c) of this Order shall not have effect in relation to those functions which, under the above provisions, are transferred to the Assembly in relation to any water or sewerage undertaker whose area is wholly or mainly in Wales] [or any licensed water supplier using the supply system of any such water undertaker].

Water Resources Act 1991 (c 57) except—

(a)   section 82 so far as exercisable in relation to those parts of Wales which are within the catchment areas of the rivers Dee, Wye and Severn;
(b)   section 102 and paragraph 2(2) of Schedule 25;
(c)   any function of the Minister of Agriculture, Fisheries and Food as 'the relevant Minister' under sections 108, 140 and 141, or paragraph 7(a) of Schedule 26;
[(d)   any function which is expressly referred to in this Act as a function of the Secretary of State for Transport].

In respect of the functions of a Minister of the Crown under sections 20(3)[, 20B(3)] and 75(5)(c) it is provided as follows—

(a)   functions under these provisions so far as relating to matters concerning the construction or enlargement of reservoirs are transferred to the Assembly in relation to Wales;
(b)   functions under these provisions so far as relating to matters other than the construction or enlargement of reservoirs are transferred to the Assembly in relation to those parts of Wales which are outside the catchment areas of the rivers Dee, Wye and Severn;
(c)   it is directed that the functions under these provisions so far as relating to matters other than the construction or enlargement of reservoirs shall, in relation to those parts of Wales which are within the catchment areas of the rivers Dee, Wye and Severn, be exercisable by the Assembly concurrently with the Secretary of State.

Functions under section 92 are transferred to the Assembly only in relation to those parts of Wales which are outside the catchment areas of the rivers Dee, Wye and Severn and in relation to those parts of Wales which are within those catchment areas it is directed that the functions under section 92 shall be exercisable by the Assembly concurrently with the Secretary of State.

The functions under section 207 of giving directions for the purpose of mitigating the effects of any civil emergency are transferred to the Assembly and it is directed that the other functions under that section shall be exercisable by the Assembly concurrently with the Secretary of State.

It is directed that the functions under sections 191A and 222(4) shall be exercisable by the Assembly concurrently with the Secretary of State.

Paragraph 6 of Schedule 3 to the Government of Wales Act 1998 shall apply to the functions of the Secretary of State under the following provisions to the extent that they are transferred to the Assembly by this Order:

sections 21, 22 and Schedule 5,

[section 27A and (so far as it relates to section 27A) Schedule 6,]

section 33 and Schedule 6,

[section 33A,]

sections 41 and 42,

section 43 except in relation to the power to prescribe matters as referred to therein,

section 44,

[section 51(1C) to 51(1F),]

section 52 except in relation to the power to prescribe matters as referred to in subsection (4),

sections 53(4) and 54,

section 55 except the power to prescribe matters as referred to in subsection (4),

section 56,

section 71 so far as it applies to section 33,

section 73 and Schedule 8,

section 74,

section 75 except subsection (5)(c),

sections 76, 78 and 83,

section 88 and Schedule 10,

section 90B,

section 91 except subsection (2K),

section 93 and Schedule 11,

sections 154, 157, 158(2), 168, 171(4) and (5), and Schedule 19 except, in all cases, in respect of any functions relating to matters concerning the construction or enlargement of reservoirs,

section 161A(12),

section 161C (except the power to make regulations)[, but not including section 161C as applied by section 25B].

The Treasury consent requirement under paragraph 7 of Schedule 12 shall continue in effect.

Statutory Water Companies Act 1991 (c 58)

Land Drainage Act 1991 (c 59) except section 31, and except the functions of the Minister of Agriculture, Fisheries and Food under sections 1 to 7, 9, 10, 19, 33, 34, 38, 39, 47, 51, 52, 55, 57, 58, 61A, 61B, 61D, 62(1), 63, 66 and 69, and Schedules 1 and 2, paragraph 8 of Schedule 3 (so far as relating to matters concerning orders under sections 3 to 5) and Schedule 5.

The Secretary of State consent requirements under section 35(3) shall continue in effect.

In the case of any order proposed to be made under section 61E which relates only to Wales, the requirement to consult the Countryside Commission, [English Nature] and the Historic Buildings and Monuments Commission for England shall not have effect.

Water Consolidation (Consequential Provisions) Act 1991 (c 60)

Dangerous Dogs Act 1991 (c 65) except section 1.

Further and Higher Education Act 1992 (c 13) except sections 1(7), 62(8) and paragraph 7(6) and (7) of Schedule 1.

The Treasury approval requirement under paragraph 5(4) of Schedule 1 and the Treasury consent requirement under paragraph 7(4) of that Schedule shall continue in effect so far as they relate to pensions.

The Treasury approval requirements under paragraph 16(2) of Schedule 1 shall continue in effect and reference to the Assembly shall be substituted for the reference therein to Parliament.

The functions of the Comptroller and Auditor General in paragraph 16 of Schedule 1 are, in relation to statements of accounts of the Further Education Funding Council for Wales and the Higher Education Funding Council for Wales for financial years beginning in and after 1999, transferred to the Auditor General for Wales and in relation thereto paragraph 16(3) shall have effect so that for the requirement to lay before each House of Parliament the documents referred to therein, there shall be substituted a requirement for the Auditor General for Wales to lay those documents before the Assembly.

Local Government Finance Act 1992 (c 14) except section 13(9), paragraph 5(1) of Schedule 3 and paragraph 6 of Schedule 4.

The power to make regulations under section 1(3) is transferred to the Assembly except as regards a dwelling part only of which falls within the area of a Welsh billing authority.

It is directed that the functions under paragraphs 14 and 15 of Schedule 2 shall be exercisable by the Assembly concurrently with the Secretary of State.

The functions of the Secretary of State under Chapter V of Part I shall be transferred only in respect of financial years beginning in and after 2000. Notwithstanding section 45(3) of the Government of Wales Act 1998, any reference to the approval of a report by the House of Commons shall be construed as a reference to the publication of the report by the Assembly.

Local Government Act 1992 (c 19)

Tourism (Overseas Promotion) (Wales) Act 1992 (c 26) subject to the modification that the requirement in section 1(2) for consultation with the British Tourist Authority shall cease to have effect.

Sea Fisheries (Wildlife Conservation) Act 1992 (c 36)

Transport and Works Act 1992 (c 42) except—

(a) the order-making function under sections 1 and 3 where any order made thereunder would have effect both in Wales and England;

(b) section 25(4), Part II and section 60;

(c) the order, rule and regulation-making powers conferred by sections 2, 4, 6(2) to (6), 7(1)(a) and (4), 8, 10 and 15; and

(d) the functions vested in a 'Minister of the Crown' under section 9(4) and (5).

It is directed that the functions of 'the Secretary of State' under section 9 shall be exercisable by the Assembly concurrently with the Secretary of State.

Orders made by the Assembly shall be subject to special parliamentary procedure to such extent as is provided for by the references under section 12, to section 18 of, and paragraph 5 of Schedule 3 to, the Acquisition of Land Act 1981.

Section 23(10) shall have effect as if the references to the Welsh Office were references to the Assembly and in relation thereto the reference to the Parliamentary Commissioner Act 1967 (c 13) shall have effect as if it were a reference to Schedule 9 to the Government of Wales Act 1998.

Museums and Galleries Act 1992 (c 44) sections 6(6) and 9 so far as they relate to the Court of Governors of the National Library of Wales and the Council of the National Museum of Wales.

The Treasury consent requirement under section 9(5) shall continue in effect.

The functions of the Comptroller and Auditor General in section 9(7) and (8) are, in relation to statements of account prepared by the above-named bodies for financial years beginning in and after 1999, transferred to the Auditor General for Wales and in relation thereto section 9(8) shall have effect so that for the requirement to lay before Parliament the documents referred to therein, there shall be substituted a requirement for the Auditor General for Wales to lay those documents before the Assembly.

Protection of Badgers Act 1992 (c 51)

Clean Air Act 1993 (c 11) except sections 30 to 32, 36(6) and 48.

It is directed that the function under section 46(1) shall be exercisable by the Assembly concurrently with any Minister of the Crown by whom it is exercisable.

Radioactive Substances Act 1993 (c 12) except sections 1(5), 8(6), 11(1), 15 and 25.

It is directed that the functions of the Secretary of State under sections 25 and 39 shall be exercisable by the Assembly concurrently with the Secretary of State.

Leasehold Reform, Housing and Urban Development Act 1993 (c 28)

Agriculture Act 1993 (c 37) except the functions of the Minister of Agriculture, Fisheries and Food.

Welsh Language Act 1993 (c 38) except any function of the Treasury.

It is directed that the functions under sections 25 and 26 shall be exercisable by the Assembly concurrently with any Minister of the Crown by whom they are exercisable.

The Treasury approval requirement under paragraph 12(2) of Schedule 1 shall continue in effect.

The functions of the Comptroller and Auditor General in paragraph 12(3) and (4) of Schedule 1 are transferred to the Auditor General for Wales in relation to accounting years beginning in and after 1999 and in relation thereto paragraph 12(4) shall have effect so that for the requirement to lay before each House of Parliament the documents referred to therein, there shall be substituted a requirement for the Auditor General for Wales to lay those documents before the Assembly.

Paragraph 6(3) of Schedule 1 shall have effect only to allow attendance at meetings of the Board of a person appointed by the Assembly.

National Lottery etc Act 1993 (c 39) in respect of—

    (a)   sections 25C (except subsection (3)(b)), 26(1) and (5) and 27 so far as they relate to the Arts Council of Wales and the Sports Council for Wales;

    (b)   section 43B(1) so far as it relates to initiatives of the New Opportunities Fund that apply only in respect to Wales or any part of Wales and section 43C(4) and (5) so far as it relates thereto;

(c) paragraphs 2(1) and (2) and 7(1) and (2) of Schedule 3A so far as they relate to a joint scheme in which the only participating bodies are the Arts Council of Wales and the Sports Council for Wales.

It is directed that the functions under the following provisions shall be exercisable by the Assembly concurrently with the Secretary of State—

(a) section 26(1) so far as it relates to the National Lottery Charities Board and the New Opportunities Fund but excluding any power to give a direction to such bodies as to the allocation of resources to Wales (or any part of Wales) or between Wales (or any part of Wales) and any other part of the United Kingdom or as to conditions that apply to the whole of the United Kingdom;

(b) section 26(2) but excluding any power to give a direction to the National Heritage Memorial Fund as to the allocation of resources to Wales (or any part of Wales) or between Wales (or any part of Wales) and any other part of the United Kingdom or as to conditions that apply to the whole of the United Kingdom;

(c) section 26(5) so far as it relates to the concurrently exercisable functions specified in paragraphs (a) and (b) above;

(d) section 43C(1) but excluding any power of direction as to the allocation of resources to Wales (or any part of Wales) or between Wales (or any part of Wales) and any other part of the United Kingdom or as to conditions that apply to the whole of the United Kingdom;

(e) section 43C(2) so far as it relates to the concurrently exercisable function specified in the preceding paragraph (d).

The requirements in the following provisions for documents to be laid before Parliament shall have effect so as to require those documents additionally to be laid before the Assembly—

(a) sections 14(3) and 34(3) so far as they require the Secretary of State to lay before Parliament copies of reports by or relating to the Arts Council of Wales, the Sports Council for Wales, the National Lotteries Charities Board, the National Heritage Memorial Fund and the New Opportunities Fund;

(b) section 35(5) so far as it requires the Comptroller and Auditor General to lay before Parliament copies of the statement of accounts of the Arts Council of Wales and the Sports Council for Wales and of his reports thereon;

(c) section 25C(6)(b) so far as it requires the Secretary of State to lay before Parliament a copy of the document containing the strategic plan of the National Lottery Charities Board, the National Heritage Memorial Fund or the New Opportunities Fund.

The requirement under section 25C(3)(a) that a strategic plan of a distributing body must contain a statement of any direction given to that body by the Secretary of State under section 26(1) or 43C(1) shall, in relation to such plan of the Arts Council of Wales, the Sports Council for Wales, the National Lotteries Charity Board and the New Opportunities Fund, have effect so that any such strategic plan must also include a statement of any such direction given by the Assembly and section 25C(4) shall be construed accordingly.

Section 60(6) of the 1993 Act shall have effect as if the reference to the Secretary of State included a reference to the Assembly.

Noise and Statutory Nuisance Act 1993 (c 40)

Cardiff Bay Barrage Act 1993 (c 42) except paragraphs 2(2), 7, 8(1) and 9 of Schedule 2 and paragraphs 2, 3 and 7 of Schedule 6.

Railways Act 1993 (c 43) sections 139 and 140.

Local Government (Wales) Act 1994 (c 19) sections 17, 25, 38, 54(6), 57(7), 58, 60(4) and Part III of Schedule 5.

Coal Industry Act 1994 (c 21) sections 53 and 54.

Education Act 1994 (c 30) except—

(a)   sections 2, 3(2), 17 and Schedule 1; and
(b)   functions relating to the Teacher Training Agency other than so far as functions are conferred by section 1(3).

Criminal Justice and Public Order Act 1994 (c 33) section 80.

Home Energy Conservation Act 1995 (c 10)

Carers (Recognition and Services) Act 1995 (c 12)

Activity Centres (Young Persons' Safety) Act 1995 (c 15)

Health Authorities Act 1995 (c 17)

Environment Act 1995 (c 25) except—

(a)   section 1(2)(a) and (3);
(b)   section 41 and section 42 other than subsection (10);
(c)   sections 45(4), 48(5) and 52(3);
(d)   the function of laying copy accounts and reports before each House of Parliament under section 46(3);
(e)   the function of the Treasury under section 49(5);
[(f)   functions exercisable by the Secretary of State in pursuance of sub-paragraph (bb) of the definition of 'the relevant Minister' in paragraph 1(5) of Schedule 4;
(g)   the function of the Secretary of State under section 16A(5)(a)].

Functions under the following provisions are transferred not in relation to Wales but in the manner indicated, and article 2(c) of this Order shall not have effect in relation thereto—

(a)   the function under section 1(2)(b) is transferred to the Assembly to the extent that it may make such appointments as will ensure that there is at all times one member of the Agency appointed by it, and under Schedule 1 only functions vested in 'the appropriate Minister' are transferred to the Assembly; and only to the extent that such functions relate to any member appointed by the Assembly;
(b)   functions under section 12 and Schedule 3 are transferred to the Assembly in relation to such region as is determined under section 12(6) and the committee which is established for that region;
(c)   functions under section 13 are transferred to the Assembly in relation to such region as is determined under subsection (5) and the committee which is established for that region and such local advisory committees, and their respective areas of responsibility, as are established within that region;
(d)   the functions under sections 15 and 16 which are transferred to the Assembly are only the functions of the Secretary of State but those functions are transferred to the full extent that they are exercisable by the Secretary of State;
(e)   functions under sections 17 and 18 are transferred to the Assembly in relation to the regional flood defence committee for an area the whole or the greater part of which is in Wales;
[(ea) functions under section 18A are transferred to the Assembly in relation to the local flood defence scheme for a district which is in the area of a regional flood defence committee the whole or the greater part of which is in Wales;]

(f) the functions under Schedule 4 which are transferred to the Assembly are only the functions of the Secretary of State except that there are also transferred to the Assembly functions exercisable by the Minister of Agriculture, Fisheries and Food in pursuance of sub-paragraph (a) of the definition of 'the relevant Minister' in paragraph 1(5) in relation to the alteration of the boundaries of an area the whole of which is in Wales;

(g) functions under Schedule 5 are transferred to the Assembly in relation to any regional flood defence committee for an area wholly or mainly in Wales and in relation to any local flood defence committee for a district within the area of that regional flood defence committee.

It is directed that the function under section 48(2) and (4) shall be exercisable by the Assembly concurrently with any other Minister of the Crown by whom it is exercisable but subject to the limitation that the Assembly shall not have power to consent to any borrowing which would cause the aggregate amount outstanding in respect of the principal of sums borrowed by the Environment Agency in pursuance of consent given by the Assembly under subsection (2) to exceed £10 million.

It is directed that the functions under sections 37(2) and (4), 38, 44, 46(1), 47, 48(3), 49 (except the function of the Treasury under subsection (5)), 50, 51, 52(2) and (4), 53(1)(b), 113 and 115(5) shall be exercisable by the Assembly concurrently with any other Minister of the Crown by whom they are exercisable. The function under section 47 shall be exercisable by the Assembly free from the requirement for Treasury approval.

In respect of section 40 it is provided as follows—

(a) it is directed that the functions under this section shall be exercisable by the Assembly concurrently with any Minister of the Crown by whom they are exercisable;

(b) this direction is made, not in relation to Wales, but in relation to the Environment Agency as a cross-border body;

(c) to the extent specified in paragraph (d) below, functions under section 40 shall be exercisable by the Assembly only with the agreement of the Secretary of State or the Minister of Agriculture, Fisheries and Food;

(d) the requirement for the Assembly to exercise functions only with the agreement of the Secretary of State or the Minister of Agriculture, Fisheries and Food applies where such exercise would have any effect in England or, additionally, being an exercise of the functions in relation to water resources management, water supply, rivers or other watercourses, control of pollution of water resources, sewerage or land drainage, it would have any effect in those parts of Wales which are within the catchment areas of the rivers Dee, Wye and Severn.

The requirement under section 9(3) for consultation with the Countryside Commission, [English Nature], the Historic Buildings and Monuments Commission for England and the Sports Council shall not apply to the Assembly.

In section 42 references to the Secretary of State in the context of functions carried out under or in consequence of the Radioactive Substances Act 1993 shall include the Assembly to the extent that those functions are functions of the Assembly.

The requirements under sections 46(3) and 52(1) for the Environment Agency to send copy accounts and reports to 'the appropriate Ministers' shall have effect to require the Agency additionally to send those documents to the Assembly.

The functions of the Comptroller and Auditor General under sections 46(4) and 49(3) and (4) shall become functions also of the Auditor General for Wales so far as they relate to any of the Welsh functions of the Environment Agency or to any funding provided to that Agency by the Assembly and in relation thereto section 46(4) shall have effect as if—

(a) paragraph (b) thereof empowered the Auditor General for Wales to report to the Assembly the result of any inspection carried out by him under paragraph (a) thereof; and

(b) it empowered the Auditor General for Wales to carry out an examination under section 145 of the Government of Wales Act 1998 in relation to the Environment Agency's Welsh functions or to any funding provided to that Agency by the Assembly as if that Agency were to that extent a body specified in Schedule 17 to that Act.

The Treasury consent requirement under section 45(2) and the Treasury approval requirements under sections 44(1) and 49(1) and (2) shall continue in effect.

Gas Act 1995 (c 45) paragraph 12 of Schedule 5.

Town and Country Planning (Costs of Inquiries etc) Act 1995 (c 49)

National Health Service (Residual Liabilities) Act 1996 (c 15)

Dogs (Fouling of Land) Act 1996 (c 20)

Community Care (Direct Payments) Act 1996 (c 30)

Noise Act 1996 (c 37)

Party Wall etc Act 1996 (c 40)

Asylum and Immigration Act 1996 (c 49) section 9.

Nursery Education and Grant-maintained Schools Act 1996 (c 50)

Housing Act 1996 (c 52) except Part IV and sections 186, 187 and 221(5).

It is directed that the functions under section 185 shall be exercisable by the Assembly concurrently with the Secretary of State. Article 3 of this Order shall not have effect in relation to regulations made under this provision.

Housing Grants, Construction and Regeneration Act 1996 (c 53)

Education Act 1996 (c 56) except—

(a) sections 333(5) and (6), 334(2), 335 and 336;

(b) the regulation-making functions under sections 492 to 494;

(c) sections 492(5), 494(4) and 495 so far as they relate to a dispute to which only one party is in Wales; and

(d) paragraph 5 of Schedule 34.

School Inspections Act 1996 (c 57) except section 4(4) and paragraphs 1, 2(3) and 3 of Schedule 1.

Section 5(6) shall have effect as if the reference to 'government policy' was a reference to policy adopted or formulated by the Assembly.

In paragraphs 1 and 2(3) of Schedule 1, the references to the Treasury shall have effect as references to the Assembly.

The Treasury approval requirement under paragraph 4(3) of Schedule 5 shall continue in effect so far as it relates to pensions.

[Nurses, Midwives and Health Visitors Act 1997 (c 24) sections 5, 6(1)(e) and 17 so far as they relate to the Welsh National Board for Nursing, Midwifery and Health Visiting ('the Board').

The functions under section 18 are transferred (so far as they relate to the Board) in relation to financial years beginning in and after 1999 except that in respect of section 18(6) they are transferred in relation to annual reports of the Board for years commencing on 1st April 1999 and after.

The Treasury consent requirement under section 5(5), so far as it relates to pensions, and the Treasury approval requirement under section 18(1)(b), shall continue in effect.

The functions of the Comptroller and Auditor General in section 18(2), (4), (5) and (7) are, in relation to statements of account prepared by the Board for financial years beginning in and after 1999, transferred to the Auditor General for Wales.]

Education Act 1997 (c 44) except sections 21, 26, Schedule 4 and paragraph 10(2) of Schedule 5.

The functions of the Secretary of State under section 36 are transferred so far as relating to the Qualifications, Curriculum and Assessment Authority for Wales.

The Treasury approval requirement under paragraph 17(2) of Schedule 5 shall continue in effect.

The functions of the Comptroller and Auditor General in paragraph 17 of Schedule 5 are, in relation to statements of accounts for financial years beginning in and after 1999, transferred to the Auditor General for Wales and in relation thereto paragraph 17(3) shall have effect so that for the requirement to lay before each House of Parliament the documents referred to therein, there shall be substituted a requirement for the Auditor General for Wales to lay those documents before the Assembly.

National Health Service (Primary Care) Act 1997 (c 46)

Road Traffic Reduction Act 1997 (c 54)

National Health Service (Private Finance) Act 1997 (c 56)

Education (Schools) Act 1997 (c 59)

Local Government (Contracts) Act 1997 (c 65)

Plant Varieties Act 1997 (c 66) except the functions of 'the Ministers' so far as exercisable by a Minister of the Crown other than the Secretary of State for Wales under sections 2, 11, 18, 27 to 29, Schedule 1 and paragraphs 7, 14 and 15 of Schedule 3.

Audit Commission Act 1998 (c 18) except sections 1, 4, 38, 39, 40(2), 50 and paragraphs 4 to 14 of Schedule 1.

It is directed that the functions of the Secretary of State under section 29(1) shall be exercisable by the Assembly concurrently with the Secretary of State.

Section 32(1) and (2) shall, in relation to a police authority established for a police area in Wales, have effect as if the references to 'the Secretary of State' included reference to the Assembly.

The function of the Comptroller and Auditor General under section 33(5) and (6)(c) shall, in relation to a health service body in Wales specified in Part II of Schedule 17 to the Government of Wales Act 1998, be exercisable also by the Auditor General for Wales.

Section 34(2) to (6) shall, in relation to reports prepared under section 34(1) on the provision of services in Wales or the financial management of a body exercising functions in Wales, have effect as if references to the Comptroller and Auditor General included a reference to the Auditor General for Wales but so that the provision under section 34(5) for laying a report before the House of Commons were, in relation to the Auditor General for Wales, a provision for laying a report before the Assembly.

Section 49(1)(c) shall have effect as if the reference to 'the Secretary of State' included a reference to the Assembly and as if the reference to 'the Comptroller and Auditor General' included a reference to the Auditor General for Wales.

Paragraphs 11(4) and 14(2) of Schedule 1, so far as they provide for the laying of documents before Parliament, shall have effect as if they also provided for the laying of such documents before the Assembly.

Road Traffic Reduction (National Targets) Act 1998 (c 24)

...

Teaching and Higher Education Act 1998 (c 30) in respect of the functions under—

  (a) Part I;
  (b) section 25 so far as it relates to the power to make discretionary awards under the Education Act 1962 (c 12);
  (c) section 26;
  (d) section 28(1)(e) so far as it relates to sections 22 and 26; and
  (e) Part IV.

School Standards and Framework Act 1998 (c 31) except sections 81, 136, 137 and 144.

Government of Wales Act 1998 (c 38) sections 3(4), 36(5) and paragraph 17(9) of Schedule 9, together with Part VII so far as relating thereto.

National Minimum Wage Act 1998 (c 39) in respect of—

  (a) the function of the 'relevant authority' under section 16 so far as exercisable by the Secretary of State for Wales; and
  (b) the function of the Secretary of State under section 47.

[In the Health Act 1999—

  (a) ...
  (b) section 63, so far as it relates to any of the provisions which, by virtue of section 66(2), may be brought into force by the Assembly.]

[Countryside and Rights of Way Act 2000 (c 37) Schedule 11.]

Local and Private Acts

National Trust Act 1937 (c lvii) sections 7 and 12.

Towyn Trewan Common Act 1950 (c xli) except sections 4(2) and 5(3)(b).

Pembrokeshire County Council Act 1965 (c xxxvi) except sections 28, 32 to 34, 71 and 72.

National Trust Act 1971 (c vi) except section 22.

Anglesey Marine Terminal Act 1972 (c li) except sections 19, 20(6), 32, 47(1), 55, 57, 58 and 60.

It is directed that the power under section 64(1) for a Minister of the Crown to hold inquiries shall be exercisable by the Assembly concurrently with any Minister of the Crown by whom it is exercisable.

Glamorgan County Council Act 1973 (c i) It is directed that the power under section 163 for a Minister of the Crown to hold inquiries shall be exercisable by the Assembly concurrently with any Minister of the Crown by whom it is exercisable.

Coity Wallia Commons Act 1976 (c xxix)

Clwyd County Council Act 1985 (c xliv)

Mid Glamorgan County Council Act 1987 (c vii) It is directed that the power under section 45 for a Minister of the Crown to hold inquiries shall be exercisable by the Assembly concurrently with any Minister of the Crown by whom it is exercisable.

West Glamorgan Act 1987 (c viii) It is directed that the power under section 75 for a Minister of the Crown to hold inquiries shall be exercisable by the Assembly concurrently with any Minister of the Crown by whom it is exercisable.

Dyfed Act 1987 (c xxiv) except sections 48 and 52.

It is directed that the power under section 68 for a Minister of the Crown to hold inquiries shall be exercisable by the Assembly concurrently with any Minister of the Crown by whom it is exercisable.

Statutory Instruments

The Intervention Functions (Delegation) Regulations 1972 (SI 1972/1679)

The Tourism (Sleeping Accommodation Price Display) Order 1977 (SI 1977/1877) Article 7.

The Agricultural Land Tribunals (Rules) Order 1978 (SI 1978/259) Rule 21 of Schedule 1.

The Agriculture and Horticulture Development Regulations 1980 (SI 1980/1298)

The Farm and Horticulture Development Regulations 1981 (SI 1981/1707) except the function of the Minister of Agriculture, Fisheries and Food under regulation 4.

The Building (Approved Inspectors etc) Regulations 1985 (SI 1985/1066) Regulation 19.

The Agriculture Improvement Regulations 1985 (SI 1985/1266)

The Horticultural Development Council Order 1986 (SI 1986/1110) in respect of the functions exercisable by the Secretary of State.

The Ionising Radiation (Protection of Persons Undergoing Medical Examination or Treatment) Regulations 1988 (SI 1988/778) Regulation 11(2) so far as it applies to regulation 4.

The Town and Country Planning (Assessment of Environmental Effects) Regulations 1988 (SI 1988/1199)

The Land Drainage Improvement Works (Assessment of Environmental Effects) Regulations 1988 (SI 1988/1217)

The Farm and Conservation Grant Regulations 1989 (SI 1989/219)

The Air Quality Standards Regulations 1989 (SI 1989/317)

...

The Farm and Conservation Grant Regulations 1991 (SI 1991/1630)

The Sheep Annual Premium Regulations 1992 (SI 1992/2677)

The Environmental Information Regulations 1992 (SI 1992/3240)

The Integrated Administration and Control System Regulations 1993 (SI 1993/1317)

The Suckler Cow Premium Regulations 1993 (SI 1993/1441)

The Ozone Monitoring and Information Regulations 1994 (SI 1994/440)

The Waste Management Licensing Regulations 1994 (SI 1994/1056)

1785

The Traffic Signs Regulations and General Directions 1994 (SI 1994/1519) Direction 49.

The Organic Farming (Aid) Regulations 1994 (SI 1994/1721)

The Countryside Access Regulations 1994 (SI 1994/2349)

The Conservation (Natural Habitats, & c) Regulations 1994 (SI 1994/2716) except the functions of the Secretary of State under regulations 71 to 78.

The Hill Livestock (Compensatory Allowances) Regulations 1994 (SI 1994/2740)

The Habitat (Broadleaved Woodland) (Wales) Regulations 1994 (SI 1994/3099)

The Habitat (Water Fringe) (Wales) Regulations 1994 (SI 1994/3100)

The Habitat (Coastal Belt) (Wales) Regulations 1994 (SI 1994/3101)

The Habitat (Species-Rich Grassland) (Wales) Regulations 1994 (SI 1994/3102)

The Bovine Animals (Records, Identification and Movement) Order 1995 (SI 1995/12)

The Milk Development Council Order 1995 (SI 1995/356) in respect of the functions exercisable by the Secretary of State for Wales.

The Agricultural Processing and Marketing Grant Regulations 1995 (SI 1995/362)

The Town and Country Planning (Environmental Assessment and Permitted Development) Regulations 1995 (SI 1995/417)

The Welfare of Animals (Slaughter or Killing) Regulations 1995 (SI 1995/731) in respect of—

(a)   the functions of 'the Minister'; and
(b)   the functions of 'the Ministers' so far as exercisable by the Secretary of State for Wales.

The Moorland (Livestock Extensification) (Wales) Regulations 1995 (SI 1995/1159)

The Eggs (Marketing Standards) Regulations 1995 (SI 1995/1544)

The Town and Country Planning (Environmental Assessment and Unauthorised Development) Regulations 1995 (SI 1995/2258)

The Rural Development Grants (Agriculture) (Wales) Regulations 1996 (SI 1996/529)

The Common Agricultural Policy (Wine) Regulations 1996(SI 1996/696) except the function of the Minister of Agriculture, Fisheries and Food under regulation 3(2).

The Protection of Water Against Agricultural Nitrate Pollution (England and Wales) Regulations 1996 (SI 1996/888) except the functions of the Minister of Agriculture, Fisheries and Food.

The Special Waste Regulations 1996 (SI 1996/972)

The Welfare Food Regulations 1996 (SI 1996/1434) except regulations 6, 8, 12, 13(4) and 15.

The Hill Livestock (Compensatory Allowances) Regulations 1996 (SI 1996/1500)

The Arable Area Payments Regulations 1996 (SI 1996/3142)

The Potato Industry Development Council Order 1997 (SI 1997/266) in respect of the functions exercisable by the Secretary of State for Wales.

The Dairy Produce Quotas Regulations 1997 (SI 1997/733) in respect of the functions exercisable by the Secretary of State for Wales.

The Sheep Annual Premium and Suckler Cow Premium Quotas Regulations 1997 (SI 1997/2644)

The Cattle Identification Regulations 1998 (SI 1998/871) except the functions of the Minister of Agriculture, Fisheries and Food.

The Action Programme for Nitrate Vulnerable Zones (England and Wales) Regulations 1998 (SI 1998/1202)

The Town and Country Planning (Environmental Impact Assessment) (England and Wales) Regulations 1999 (SI 1999/293)

NOTES

Initial Commencement

Specified date: 1 July 1999: see art 1(2).

Amendment

Entry relating to the 'Ministry of Health Act 1919' revoked by SI 2006/1407, art 3, Sch 2.

Date in force: this revocation came into force on 1 March 2007, immediately before the National Health Service Act 2006 came into force: see the National Health Service Act 2006, s 277(1) and SI 2006/1407, art 1(1).

Entry relating to the 'Post Office Act 1953 (c 36)' (omitted) revoked by SI 2001/1149, art 3(2), Sch 2.

Date in force: 26 March 2001: see SI 2001/1149, art 1(2).

In entry relating to the 'Harbours Act 1964 (c 40)' reference to '14,' in square brackets inserted by SI 2000/253, art 4, Sch 3, para (a).

Date in force: 16 February 2000: see SI 2000/253, art 1(2).

In entry relating to the 'Harbours Act 1964 (c 40)' words omitted revoked by SI 2000/253, art 4, Sch 3, para (a).

Date in force: 16 February 2000: see SI 2000/253, art 1(2).

In entry relating to the 'Development of Tourism Act 1969 (c 51)' words omitted revoked by SI 2005/3225, art 6(2), Sch 2, Pt 2, para 3(a)–(c).

Date in force: 1 April 2006: see SI 2005/3225, arts 1(2), 6(2); for transitional provisions see art 3 thereof.

In entry relating to the 'Development of Tourism Act 1969 (c 51)' words from 'The Treasury approval' to 'continue in effect.' and words from 'The functions of' to 'before the Assembly.' in italics revoked by SI 2005/3225, arts 3, 6(2), Sch 2, Pt 2, para 3(d), except for the purposes of the statement of account for the financial year 2005 to 2006.

Date in force: 1 April 2006: see SI 2005/3225, arts 1(2), 6(2).

In entry relating to the 'Reservoirs Act 1975 (c 23)' words 'except section 12A(4).' in square brackets inserted by the Water Act 2003, s 100(1).

Date in force: 1 October 2004: see SI 2004/2528, art 2(s)(i).

In entry relating to the 'Welsh Development Agency Act 1975 (c 70)' words omitted revoked by SI 2005/3226, art 7(1)(b), Sch 2, Pt 1, para 3(a), (b).

Date in force: 1 April 2006: see SI 2005/3226, arts 1(2), 7(1)(b); for transitional provisions see art 3 thereof.

In entry relating to the 'Welsh Development Agency Act 1975 (c 70)' words from 'The functions of ' to 'before the Assembly.' in italics revoked by SI 2005/3226, arts 3, 7(1)(b), Sch 2, Pt 1, para 3(c), except for the purposes of the statement of account for the financial year 2005 to 2006.

Date in force: 1 April 2006: see SI 2005/3226, arts 1(2), 7(1)(b).

In entry relating to the 'Adoption Act 1976' reference omitted revoked by the Adoption and Children Act 2002, s 145(3).

Date in force: 7 November 2002: (no specific commencement provision).

Entry relating to the 'National Health Act 1977 (c 49)' (omitted) revoked by the National Health Service (Consequential Provisions) Act 2006, s 6, Sch 4.

Date in force: 1 March 2007: see the National Health Service (Consequential Provisions) Act 2006, s 8(2).

Entry relating to the 'Mental Health Act 1983 (c 20)' substituted by SI 2000/253, art 4, Sch 3, para (b).

Date in force: 16 February 2000: see SI 2000/253, art 1(2).

Entry relating to the 'Building Act 1984 (c 55)' substituted by SI 2000/253, art 4, Sch 3, para (c).

Date in force: 16 February 2000: see SI 2000/253, art 1(2).

Entry relating to the 'Education Reform Act 1988 (c 40)' substituted by SI 2000/1829, art 2.

Date in force: 1 August 2000: see SI 2000/1829, art 1(1).

Entry relating to the 'Local Government and Housing Act 1989, s 80' (omitted) revoked by the Local Government Act 2003, s 127(1), (2), Sch 7, para 79, Sch 8, Pt 2.

Date in force: 27 November 2003 (only for the purpose of and in relation to financial years beginning on or after 1 April 2004): see SI 2003/3034, art 2, Sch 1, Pt I.

Entry relating to the 'Town and Country Planning Act 1990 (c 8)' substituted by SI 2000/253, art 4, Sch 3, para (d).

Date in force: 16 February 2000: see SI 2000/253, art 1(2).

Entry relating to the 'National Health Service and Community Care Act 1990 (c 19)' (omitted) revoked by the National Health Service (Consequential Provisions) Act 2006, s 6, Sch 4.

Date in force: 1 March 2007: see the National Health Service (Consequential Provisions) Act 2006, s 8(2).

In entry relating to the 'Environmental Protection Act 1990 (c 43)' in para (b) words '(other than it applies to Part 2 of the Act)' in square brackets inserted by SI 2006/3334, art 2, Schedule, para (a).

Date in force: 15 December 2006: see SI 2006/3334, art 1(2).

In entry relating to the 'Environmental Protection Act 1990 (c 43)' para (d) revoked by the Natural Environment and Rural Communities Act 2006, s 105(2), Sch 12.

Date in force: 1 October 2006: see SI 2006/2541, art 2.

Entry relating to the 'Water Industry Act 1991 (c 56)' substituted by SI 2000/253, art 4, Sch 3, para (e).

Date in force: 16 February 2000: see SI 2000/253, art 1(2).

In entry relating to the 'Water Industry Act 1991 (c 56)' reference to '2A,' in square brackets inserted by the Water Act 2003, s 100(2)(a)(i).

Date in force: 1 April 2005: see SI 2005/968, art 2(l)(i), (iii), (iv); for transitional provisions see art 4(1), Sch 2, para 3 thereto.

In entry relating to the 'Water Industry Act 1991 (c 56)' words from '16A, 17 to 17D' to '22A to 22F' in square brackets substituted by the Water Act 2003, s 100(2)(a)(ii).

Date in force (for certain purposes): 1 April 2004: see SI 2004/641, art 3(x)(i); for transitional provisions see art 6, Sch 3, para 7 thereto.

Date in force (for certain purposes): 1 October 2004: see SI 2004/2528, art 2(s)(ii).

Date in force (for certain purposes): 1 April 2005: see SI 2005/968, art 2(l)(i), (iii), (iv); for transitional provisions see art 4(1), Sch 2, para 3 thereto.

Date in force (for certain purposes): 1 August 2005: see SI 2005/968, art 3(c); for transitional provisions see art 4(1), Sch 2, para 3 thereto.

Date in force (for remaining purposes): 1 December 2005: see SI 2005/2714, art 3(b); for transitional provisions see art 5(1), Schedule, paras 7, 8 thereto.

In entry relating to the 'Water Industry Act 1991 (c 56)' words '27A, 27B, 27E, 27G, 27I to 27K, 29, 29A,' in square brackets inserted by the Water Act 2003, s 100(2)(a)(iii).

Date in force (for certain purposes): 1 August 2005: see SI 2005/968, art 3(c); for transitional provisions see art 4(1), Sch 2, para 3 thereto.

Date in force (for certain purposes): 1 October 2005: see SI 2005/2714, art 2(k)(i), (iii), (iv); for transitional provisions see art 5(1), Schedule, paras 7, 8 thereto.

Date in force (for remaining purposes): 1 April 2006: see SI 2005/2714, art 4(e); for transitional provisions see art 5(1), Schedule, paras 7, 8 thereto.

In entry relating to the 'Water Industry Act 1991 (c 56)' words '38B, 66B, 66F to 66L, 86(1A), 87B, 88A, 89,' in square brackets inserted by the Water Act 2003, s 100(2)(a)(iv).

Date in force (for certain purposes): 1 April 2004: see SI 2004/641, art 3(x)(i); for transitional provisions see art 6, Sch 3, para 7 thereto.

Date in force (for certain purposes): 1 April 2005: see SI 2005/968, art 2(l)(i), (iii), (iv); for transitional provisions see art 4(1), Sch 2, para 3 thereto.

Date in force (for certain purposes): 1 October 2005: see SI 2005/2714, art 2(k)(i), (iii), (iv); for transitional provisions see art 5(1), Schedule, paras 7, 8 thereto.

Date in force (for certain purposes): 1 December 2005: see SI 2005/2714, art 3(b); for transitional provisions see art 5(1), Schedule, paras 7, 8 thereto.

Date in force (for remaining purposes): 1 April 2006: see SI 2005/2714, art 4(e); for transitional provisions see art 5(1), Schedule, paras 7, 8 thereto.

In entry relating to the 'Water Industry Act 1991 (c 56)' reference to '95B,' in square brackets inserted by the Water Act 2003, s 100(2)(a)(v).

Date in force: 1 October 2005: see SI 2005/2714, art 2(k)(i), (iii), (iv); for transitional provisions see art 5(1), Schedule, paras 7, 8 thereto.

In entry relating to the 'Water Industry Act 1991 (c 56)' references to '192A, 192B,' in square brackets inserted by the Water Act 2003, s 100(2)(a)(vi).

Date in force: 1 October 2004: see SI 2004/2528, art 2(s)(ii).

In entry relating to the 'Water Industry Act 1991 (c 56)' reference to '195A,' in square brackets inserted by the Water Act 2003, s 100(2)(a)(vii).

Date in force: 1 April 2005: see SI 2005/968, art 2(l)(i), (iii), (iv); for transitional provisions see art 4(1), Sch 2, para 3 thereto.

In entry relating to the 'Water Industry Act 1991 (c 56)' references to ', 1A, 3A' in square brackets inserted by the Water Act 2003, s 100(2)(a)(viii).

Date in force (for certain purposes): 1 October 2005: see SI 2005/2714, art 2(k)(i), (iii), (iv); for transitional provisions see art 5(1), Schedule, paras 7, 8 thereto.

Date in force (for remaining purposes): 1 April 2006: see SI 2005/2714, art 4(e); for transitional provisions see art 5(1), Schedule, paras 7, 8 thereto.

In entry relating to the 'Water Industry Act 1991 (c 56)' words from 'and except functions' to 'the extent stated)' in square brackets inserted by the Water Act 2003, s 100(2)(a)(ix).

Date in force (for certain purposes): 1 April 2004: see SI 2004/641, art 3(x)(i); for transitional provisions see art 6, Sch 3, para 7 thereto.

Date in force (for certain purposes): 1 October 2004: see SI 2004/2528, art 2(s)(ii).

Date in force (for certain purposes): 1 April 2005: see SI 2005/968, art 2(l)(i), (iii), (iv); for transitional provisions see art 4(1), Sch 2, para 3 thereto.

Date in force (for certain purposes): 1 August 2005: see SI 2005/968, art 3(c); for transitional provisions see art 4(1), Sch 2, para 3 thereto.

Date in force (for certain purposes): 1 October 2005: see SI 2005/2714, art 2(k)(i), (iii), (iv); for transitional provisions see art 5(1), Schedule, paras 7, 8 thereto.

Date in force (for certain purposes): 1 December 2005: see SI 2005/2714, art 3(b); for transitional provisions see art 5(1), Schedule, paras 7, 8 thereto.

Date in force (for remaining purposes): 1 April 2006: see SI 2005/2714, art 4(e); for transitional provisions see art 5(1), Schedule, paras 7, 8 thereto.

In entry relating to the 'Water Industry Act 1991 (c 56)' first reference omitted revoked by the Water Act 2003, ss 100(2)(b)(i), 101(2), Sch 9, Pt 3.

Date in force (for certain purposes): 1 April 2005: see SI 2005/968, art 2(l)(i), (iii), (iv), (n)(v); for transitional provisions see art 4(1), Sch 2, para 3 thereto.

Date in force (for remaining purposes): 1 December 2005: see SI 2005/2714, art 3(b), (d); for savings see art 5(1), Schedule, paras 7, 8 thereto.

In entry relating to the 'Water Industry Act 1991 (c 56)' second words omitted revoked by the Water Act 2003, ss 100(2)(b)(ii), 101(2), Sch 9, Pt 3.

Date in force (for certain purposes): 1 October 2004: see SI 2004/2528, art 2(s)(ii).

Date in force (for remaining purposes): 1 December 2005: see SI 2005/2714, art 3(b), (d); for savings see art 5(1), Schedule, paras 7, 8 thereto.

In entry relating to the 'Water Industry Act 1991 (c 56)' reference to '37, 38, 39, 51A' in square brackets substituted by the Water Act 2003, s 100(2)(b)(iii).

Date in force (for certain purposes): 28 May 2004: see SI 2004/641, art 4(c); for transitional provisions see art 6, Sch 3, para 7 thereto.

Date in force (for certain purposes): 1 April 2005: see SI 2005/968, art 2(l); for transitional provisions see art 4(1), Sch 2, paras 3, 4 thereto.

Date in force (for remaining purposes): 1 April 2007: see SI 2007/1021, art 2(c).

In entry relating to the 'Water Industry Act 1991 (c 56)' reference to '47(2)(g),' in square brackets inserted by SI 2006/3334, art 2, Schedule, para (b)(i).

Date in force: 15 December 2006: see SI 2006/3334, art 1(2).

In entry relating to the 'Water Industry Act 1991 (c 56)' reference to '53(2)(c), 55(4),' in square brackets inserted by SI 2006/3334, art 2, Schedule, para (b)(ii).

Date in force: 15 December 2006: see SI 2006/3334, art 1(2).

In entry relating to the 'Water Industry Act 1991 (c 56)' reference to '66A(6),' in square brackets inserted by SI 2006/3334, art 2, Schedule, para (b)(iii).

Date in force: 15 December 2006: see SI 2006/3334, art 1(2).

In entry relating to the 'Water Industry Act 1991 (c 56)' third words omitted revoked by the Water Act 2003, ss 100(2)(b)(iv), 101(2), Sch 9, Pt 3.

Date in force (for certain purposes): 1 April 2004: see SI 2004/641, art 3(x)(i), (z)(vii); for transitional provisions see art 6, Sch 3, para 7 thereto.

Date in force (for certain purposes): 1 October 2004: see SI 2004/2528, art 2(s)(ii).

Date in force (for remaining purposes): 1 December 2005: see SI 2005/2714, art 3(b), (d); for savings see art 5(1), Schedule, para 7 thereto.

In entry relating to the 'Water Industry Act 1991 (c 56)' fourth reference omitted revoked by the Water Act 2003, ss 100(2)(b)(v), 101(2), Sch 9, Pt 3.

Date in force: 1 December 2005: see SI 2005/2714, art 3(b), (d); for savings see art 5(1), Schedule, para 7 thereto.

In entry relating to the 'Water Industry Act 1991 (c 56)' reference to '94, 95, 96,' in square brackets substituted by the Water Act 2003, s 100(2)(b)(vi).

Date in force (for certain purposes): 1 April 2005: see SI 2005/968, art 2(l)(i), (iii), (iv); for transitional provisions see art 4(1), Sch 2, para 3 thereto.

Date in force (for certain purposes): 1 October 2005: see SI 2005/2714, art 2(k)(i), (iii), (iv); for transitional provisions see art 5(1), Schedule, paras 7, 8 thereto.

Date in force (for remaining purposes): 1 April 2007: see SI 2007/1021, art 2(c).

In entry relating to the 'Water Industry Act 1991 (c 56)' words '105A to 105C,' in square brackets inserted by the Water Act 2003, s 100(2)(b)(vii).

Date in force: 1 April 2007: see SI 2007/1021, art 2(c).

In entry relating to the 'Water Industry Act 1991 (c 56)' reference to '158,' in square brackets inserted by SI 2004/3044, art 4, Sch 2.

Date in force: 18 November 2004: see SI 2004/3044, art 1(2).

In entry relating to the 'Water Industry Act 1991 (c 56)' words '198 to 200' in square brackets substituted by the Water Act 2003, s 100(2)(b)(viii).

Date in force (for certain purposes): 1 April 2004: see SI 2004/641, art 3(x)(i); for transitional provisions see art 6, Sch 3, para 7 thereto.

Date in force (for remaining purposes): 1 December 2005: see SI 2005/2714, art 3(b); for transitional provisions see art 5(1), Schedule, para 7 thereto.

In entry relating to the 'Water Industry Act 1991 (c 56)' fifth reference omitted revoked by the Water Act 2003, ss 100(2)(b)(ix), 101(2), Sch 9, Pt 3.

Date in force: 1 December 2005: see SI 2005/2714, art 3(b), (d); for savings see art 5(1), Schedule, paras 7, 8 thereto.

In entry relating to the 'Water Industry Act 1991 (c 56)' words '(but not in relation to any licensed water suppliers)' in square brackets inserted by the Water Act 2003, s 100(2)(b)(x).

Date in force (for certain purposes): 1 April 2004: see SI 2004/641, art 3(x)(i); for transitional provisions see art 6, Sch 3, para 7 thereto.

Date in force (for certain purposes): 1 October 2004: see SI 2004/2528, art 2(s)(ii).

Date in force (for certain purposes): 1 April 2005: see SI 2005/968, art 2(l)(i), (iii), (iv); for transitional provisions see art 4(1), Sch 2, para 3 thereto.

Date in force (for certain purposes): 1 October 2005: see SI 2005/2714, art 2(k)(i), (iii), (iv); for transitional provisions see art 5(1), Schedule, paras 7, 8 thereto.

Date in force (for certain purposes): 1 December 2005: see SI 2005/2714, art 3(b); for transitional provisions see art 5(1), Schedule, paras 7, 8 thereto.

Date in force (for remaining purposes): 1 April 2007: see SI 2007/1021, art 2(c).

In entry relating to the 'Water Industry Act 1991 (c 56)' sixth words omitted revoked by the Water Act 2003, ss 100(2)(c), 101(2), Sch 9, Pt 3.

Date in force: 1 October 2005: see SI 2005/2714, art 2(m)(v).

In entry relating to the 'Water Industry Act 1991 (c 56)' words from 'Functions under sections 2' to 'licensed water supplier.' in square brackets inserted by the Water Act 2003, s 100(2)(d).

Date in force (for certain purposes): 1 April 2004: see SI 2004/641, art 3(x)(i); for transitional provisions see art 6, Sch 3, para 7 thereto.

Date in force (for certain purposes): 1 October 2004: see SI 2004/2528, art 2(s)(ii).

Date in force (for certain purposes): 1 April 2005: see SI 2005/968, art 2(l)(i), (iii), (iv); for transitional provisions see art 4(1), Sch 2, para 3 thereto.

Date in force (for remaining purposes): 1 December 2005: see SI 2005/2714, art 3(b); for transitional provisions see art 5(1), Schedule, paras 7, 8 thereto.

In entry relating to the 'Water Industry Act 1991 (c 56)' in the paragraph relating to functions under section 67, paras (a), (b) substituted by the Water Act 2003, s 100(2)(e).

Date in force (for certain purposes): 1 April 2004: see SI 2004/641, art 3(x)(i); for transitional provisions see art 6, Sch 3, para 7 thereto.

Date in force (for certain purposes): 1 December 2005: see SI 2005/2714, art 3(b); for transitional provisions see art 5(1), Schedule, para 7 thereto.

Date in force (for remaining purposes): 1 April 2007: see SI 2007/1021, art 2(c).

In entry relating to the 'Water Industry Act 1991 (c 56)' words '86 (except subsection (1A))' in square brackets substituted by the Water Act 2003, s 100(2)(f).

Date in force (for certain purposes): 1 April 2004: see SI 2004/641, art 3(x)(i); for transitional provisions see art 6, Sch 3, para 7 thereto.

Date in force (for remaining purposes): 1 April 2007: see SI 2007/1021, art 2(c).

In entry relating to the 'Water Industry Act 1991 (c 56)' words from 'In respect of' to 'Secretary of State.' in square brackets inserted by the Water Act 2003, s 100(2)(g).

Date in force (for certain purposes): 1 October 2004: see SI 2004/2528, art 2(s)(ii).

Date in force (for certain purposes): 1 October 2005: see SI 2005/2714, art 2(k)(i), (iii), (iv); for transitional provisions see art 5(1), Schedule, paras 7, 8 thereto.

Date in force (for certain purposes): 1 April 2006: see SI 2006/984, art 2(r)(ii), (iv); for transitional provisions and savings see art 3(1), Schedule, para 9 thereto.

Date in force (for remaining purposes): 1 April 2007: see SI 2007/1021, art 2(c).

In entry relating to the 'Water Industry Act 1991 (c 56)' words from 'In respect of the functions' to 'paragraph (a)(i) to (iii) above.' in square brackets substituted by the Water Act 2003, s 100(2)(i).

Date in force (for certain purposes): 1 April 2004: see SI 2004/641, art 3(x)(i); for transitional provisions see art 6, Sch 3, para 7 thereto.

Date in force (for certain purposes): 1 December 2005: see SI 2005/2714, art 3(b); for transitional provisions see art 5(1), Schedule, para 7 thereto.

Date in force (for remaining purposes): 1 April 2007: see SI 2007/1021, art 2(c).

In entry relating to the 'Water Industry Act 1991 (c 56)' words from 'or (so far' to 'licensed water supplier' in square brackets inserted by the Water Act 2003, s 100(2)(h).

Date in force: 1 December 2005: see SI 2005/2714, art 3(b); for transitional provisions see art 5(1), Schedule, para 7 thereto.

In entry relating to the 'Water Industry Act 1991 (c 56)' words 'or any licensed water supplier using the supply system of any such water undertaker' in square brackets inserted by the Water Act 2003, s 100(2)(j).

Date in force (for certain purposes): 1 April 2004: see SI 2004/641, art 3(x)(i); for transitional provisions see art 6, Sch 3, para 7 thereto.

Date in force (for certain purposes): 1 August 2005: see SI 2005/968, art 3(c); for transitional provisions see art 4(1), Sch 2, para 3 thereto.

Date in force (for certain purposes): 1 December 2005: see SI 2005/2714, art 3(b); for transitional provisions see art 5(1), Schedule, paras 7, 8 thereto.

Date in force (for remaining purposes): 1 April 2007: see SI 2007/1021, art 2(c).

In entry relating to the 'Water Resources Act 1991 (c 57)' para (d) substituted by SI 2002/2626, art 20, Sch 2, para 23.

Date in force: 25 November 2002: see SI 2002/2626, art 1(2).

In entry relating to the 'Water Resources Act 1991 (c 57)' reference to ', 20B(3)' in square brackets inserted by the Water Act 2003, s 100(4)(a).

Date in force: 1 October 2004: see SI 2004/2528, art 2(s)(iv).

In entry relating to the 'Water Resources Act 1991 (c 57)' words 'section 27A and (so far as it relates to section 27A) Schedule 6,' in square brackets inserted by the Water Act 2003, s 100(4)(b)(i).

Date in force: 1 April 2004: see SI 2004/641, art 3(x)(ii).

In entry relating to the 'Water Resources Act 1991 (c 57)' words 'section 33A,' in square brackets inserted by the Water Act 2003, s 100(4)(b)(ii).

Date in force: 1 April 2004: see SI 2004/641, art 3(x)(ii).

In entry relating to the 'Water Resources Act 1991 (c 57)' words 'section 51(1C) to 51(1F),' in square brackets inserted by the Water Act 2003, s 100(4)(b)(iii).

Date in force: 1 April 2006: see SI 2006/984, art 2(r)(iii)–(v); for transitional provisions and savings see art 3(1), Schedule, para 9 thereto.

In entry relating to the 'Water Resources Act 1991 (c 57)' words ', but not including section 161C as applied by section 25B' in square brackets inserted by the Water Act 2003, s 100(4)(b).

Date in force: to be appointed: see the Water Act 2003, s 105(3), (5).

In entry relating to the 'Land Drainage Act 1991 (c 59)' words 'English Nature' in square brackets substituted by virtue of the Countryside and Rights of Way Act 2000, s 73(2).

Date in force: 30 January 2001: see the Countryside and Rights of Way Act 2000, s 103(2).

In entry relating to the 'Environment Act 1995 (c 25)' paras (f), (g) inserted by the Water Act 2003, s 100(5)(a).

Date in force: 1 April 2004: see SI 2004/641, art 3(x)(iii).

In entry relating to the 'Environment Act 1995 (c 25)' in the paragraph relating to the list of functions which are transferred not in relation to Wales, para (ea) inserted by the Water Act 2003, s 100(5)(b).

Date in force: 1 April 2004: see SI 2004/641, art 3(x)(iii).

In entry relating to the 'Environment Act 1995 (c 25)' words 'English Nature' in square brackets substituted by virtue of the Countryside and Rights of Way Act 2000, s 73(2).

Date in force: 30 January 2001: see the Countryside and Rights of Way Act 2000, s 103(2).

Entry relating to the 'Nurses, Midwives and Health Visitors Act 1997 (c 24)' substituted by SI 2000/253, art 4, Sch 3, para (f).

Date in force: 16 February 2000: see SI 2000/253, art 1(2).

Entry relating to the 'Data Protection Act 1998 (c 29)' (omitted) revoked by SI 2000/253, art 4, Sch 3, para (g).

Date in force: 16 February 2000: see SI 2000/253, art 1(2).

Entry relating to the 'Health Act 1999' inserted by the Health Act 1999, s 66(4), (5)(c); this amendment has effect as if made under an Order in Council under s 22 of the Government of Wales Act 1998.

Date in force: 30 June 1999: see the Health Act 1999, s 67(4)(a).

In entry relating to the 'Health Act 1999' para (a) revoked by the National Health Service (Consequential Provisions) Act 2006, s 6, Sch 4.

Date in force: 1 March 2007: see the National Health Service (Consequential Provisions) Act 2006, s 8(2).

Entry relating to the 'Countryside and Rights of Way Act 2000 (c 37)' inserted by the Countryside and Rights of Way Act 2000, s 99(2).

Date in force: 30 January 2001: see SI 2001/203, art 2.

Entry relating to 'The Clinical Standards Advisory Group Regulations 1991 (SI 1991/578)' (omitted) revoked by virtue of the Health Act 1999, s 25.

Date in force: 1 November 1999: see SI 1999/2793, art 2(1)(c).

See Further

Reference to the National Health Service Act 1977 shall be treated as a reference to that Act, as amended by the Health and Social Care Act 2001, excluding those amendments made by s 27 thereof: see the Health and Social Care Act 2001, s 68(1), (2).

Reference to the Children Act 1989 shall be treated as a reference to that Act, as amended by the Carers and Disabled Children Act 2000, s 7 but only in so far as relating to the insertion of s 17B of that Act: see the Health and Social Care Act 2001, s 67(1), Sch 5, Pt 2, para 16.

Reference to the Housing Act 1985 shall be treated as a reference to that Act, as amended by the Regulatory Reform (Housing Management Agreements) Order 2003: see the Regulatory Reform (Housing Management Agreements) Order 2003, SI 2003/940, art 3.

References to the Housing Act 1985, the Housing Act 1988 and the Housing Act 1996 shall be treated as references to those Acts, as amended by the Anti-social Behaviour Act 2003: see the Anti-Social Behavious Act 2003, s 17.

Reference to the Noise Act 1996 shall be treated as a reference to that Act, as amended by the Anti-social Behaviour Act 2003: see the Anti-Social Behaviour Act 2003, s 42(7).

Reference to the Environmental Protection Act 1990 shall be treated as a reference to that Act, as amended by the Anti-social Behaviour Act 2003: see the Anti-Social Behaviour Act 2003, ss 55(10), 56(2).

Reference to the Wildlife and Countryside Act 1981 shall be treated as a reference to that Act, as amended by the Wildlife and Countryside Act 1981 (England and Wales) (Amendment) Regulations 2004, SI 2004/1487 and the Wildlife and Countryside Act 1981 (Amendment) (Wales) Regulations 2004: see the Wildlife and Countryside Act 1981 (Amendment) (Wales) Regulations 2004, SI 2004/1733, reg 3(2).

References to the Radiological Protection Act 1970, the Local Government Act 1972 and the National Health Service and Community Care Act 1990 shall be treated as references to those Acts, as amended by the Health Protection Agency Act 2004: see the Health Protection Agency Act 2004, s 11(3).

References to the Town and Country Planning Act 1990, the Planning (Listed Buildings and Conservation Areas) Act 1990 and the Environment Act 1995 shall be treated as references to those Acts, as amended by the Town and Country Planning (Electronic Communications) (Wales) (No 1) Order 2004: see the Town and Country Planning (Electronic Communications) (Wales) (No 1) Order 2004, SI 2004/3156, art 14.

References to the Ministry of Transport Act 1919, the Agricultural Marketing Act 1958, the Mental Health Act 1959, the National Health Service Act 1977, the Mental Health Act 1983, the Road Traffic Regulation Act 1984, the Road Traffic Act 1988, the Children Act 1989, the Further and Higher Education Act 1992 and the Education Act 1996 shall be treated as references to those Acts, as amended by the Inquiries Act 2005: see the Inquiries Act 2005, s 48(2).

References to the National Health Service Act 1977, the National Health Service and Community Care Act 1990, the National Health Service (Primary Care) Act 1997, the Health Act 1999, the Health and Social Services and Social Security Adjudications Act 1983, the Health Authorities Act 1995, the Health and Social Security Act 1984 and the Health and Medicines Act 1998 shall be treated as references to those Acts, as amended by the National Health Service (Pre-consolidation Amendments) Order 2006 (excluding the amendment made by Sch 1, Pt 1, para 15): see the National Health Service (Pre-consolidation Amendments) Order 2006, SI 2006/1407, art 5.

Reference to the Cattle Identification Regulations 1998 shall be treated as a reference to those Regulations, as amended by the Cattle Identification (Amendment) Regulations 2006, SI 2006/1538, reg 8.

Reference to the Eggs (Marketing Standards) Regulations 1995 shall be treated as a reference to those Regulations, as amended by the Eggs (Marketing Standards) (Amendment) (England and Wales) Regulations 2006, SI 2006/1540, reg 3.

Reference to the Highways Act 1980 shall be treated as a reference to that Act, as amended by the Highways (Environmental Impact Assessment) Regulations 2007: see the Highways (Environmental Impact Assessment) Regulations 2007, reg 6.

SCHEDULE 2

ENACTMENTS SUBJECT TO CONSTRAINT ON MINISTERIAL EXERCISE

Article 5

A1.591

Copyright Act 1911 c 46

...

Forestry Act 1967 c 10

The function of 'the Treasury' under paragraph 6(1) of Schedule 1 shall be exercisable only after consultation with the Assembly.

Sex Discrimination Act 1975 c 65

The function of the Secretary of State under section 53(1) of making appointments to the Equal Opportunities Commission shall be exercisable only with the agreement of the Assembly so far as necessary to ensure that there is at all times one Commissioner who has been appointed with the agreement of the Assembly.

Race Relations Act 1976 c 74

The function of the Secretary of State under section 43(1) of making appointments to the Commission for Racial Equality shall be exercisable only with the agreement of the Assembly so far as necessary to ensure that there is at all times one Commissioner who has been appointed with the agreement of the Assembly.

Local Government, Planning and Land Act 1980 c 65

The function of the Secretary of State under paragraph 8(1) of Schedule 31 shall be exercisable only with the agreement of the Assembly.

Industrial Development Act 1982 c 52

The functions of the Secretary of State under section 8(5) and (7) shall be exercisable only after consultation with the Assembly.

The functions of the Secretary of State under section 15, so far as a report required to be made under this section relates to functions of the Assembly under this Act, shall be exercisable only with the agreement of the Assembly.

Mental Health Act 1983 c 20

The function of the Lord Chancellor under paragraph 1(b) and (c) of Schedule 2 shall be exercisable only after consultation with the Assembly.

Registered Homes Act 1984 c 23

The functions of the Secretary of State under sections 43 and 45 shall be exercisable only with the agreement of the Assembly.

The functions of the Secretary of State under section 44 shall be exercisable only after consultation with the Assembly.

Road Traffic Regulation Act 1984 c 27

The functions of 'the Ministers' under section 81(2) shall be exercisable only after consultation with the Assembly.

Food and Environment Protection Act 1985 c 48

To the extent that functions exercisable under sections 8 and 10(1) relate to the abandonment of an 'offshore installation' as defined in section 44 of the Petroleum Act 1988 (c 17), such functions shall be exercisable by a Minister of the Crown only after consultation with the Assembly.

Environmental Protection Act 1990 c 43

The function of the Secretary of State under paragraph 7(3) of Schedule 7 shall be exercisable only after consultation with the Assembly.

[Water Industry Act 1991 c 56

The functions of the Secretary of State under sections 37A to 37D, 39B and 39C so far as relating to matters other than the construction or enlargement of reservoirs shall be exercisable only after consultation with the Assembly.]

Water Resources Act 1991 c 57

The function of the Secretary of State under section 82 shall be exercisable only with the agreement of the Assembly.

Further and Higher Education Act 1992 c 13

The function of the Secretary of State under sections 1(7), 62(8) and 82 shall be exercisable only after consultation with the Assembly.

Local Government Finance Act 1992 c 14

The function of the Secretary of State under section 1(3) shall, as regards a dwelling part only of which falls within the area of a Welsh billing authority, be exercisable only with the agreement of the Assembly.

Transport and Works Act 1992 c 42

The order, rule and regulation-making functions of the Secretary of State under sections 1, 3, 6, 7(4), 8, 10 and 15 shall be exercisable only with the agreement of the Assembly.

National Lottery etc Act 1993 c 39

The functions specified in paragraphs (a), (b) and (d) of the entry in relation to this Act in Schedule 1 which are to be exercisable by the Assembly concurrently with the Secretary of State, shall, to the extent that they are so exercisable by the Secretary of State, be exercisable by him only after consultation with the Assembly.

The functions under the following provisions shall be exercisable by the Secretary of State only with the agreement of the Assembly—

(a) sections 26(3) and (3A), 29(1) and (3)(b) and 35(3) so far as they relate to the Arts Council of Wales and the Sports Council for Wales;
(b) paragraphs 2(1) and (2) and 7(1) and (2) of Schedule 3A so far as they relate to a joint scheme (other than one in which the only participating bodies are the Arts Council of Wales and the Sports Council for Wales) the area of which includes all or any part of Wales;
(c) paragraph 1(1) of Schedule 5 so far as necessary to ensure that there is at all times one member of the National Lottery Charities Board who has been appointed with agreement of the Assembly;
(d) paragraph 1 of Schedule 6A so far as it relates to the appointment, as a member of the New Opportunities Fund, of a person who appears to the Secretary of State to be suited to make the interests of Wales his special care.

Education Act 1994 c 30

The function of the Secretary of State under section 3(2) shall be exercisable only with the agreement of the Assembly.

Environment Act 1995 c 25

The functions of the Secretary of State under sections 41 and 42 so far as relating to the making of regulations and the approval of charging schemes shall be exercisable only after consultation with the Assembly.

Education Act 1996 c 56

The functions of the Secretary of State under sections 333(5) and (6), 334(2), 335 and 336 shall be exercisable only with the agreement of the Assembly.

The regulation-making functions of the Secretary of State under sections 492 to 494 shall be exercisable only after consultation with the Assembly.

The functions of the Secretary of State under sections 492(5), 494(4) and 495, so far as they relate to a dispute to which only one party is in Wales, shall be exercisable only after consultation with the Assembly.

Nurses, Midwives and Health Visitors Act 1997 c 24

The function of the Secretary of State under section 19(5), so far as it relates to rules affecting the Board together with one or more other Boards, shall be exercisable only after consultation with the Assembly.

Petroleum Act 1998 c 17

The functions of the Secretary of State under sections 32(1) and (2), 33(1), 34(1), and (7), 35(1), 37(1) and 39(1) shall be exercisable only after consultation with the Assembly.

Audit Commission Act 1998 c 18

The functions of the Secretary of State under section 1(2) and under paragraph 4(4) of Schedule 1 shall be exercisable only with the agreement of the Assembly so far as necessary to ensure that, at all material times, one of the persons appointed as a member of the Commission shall have been appointed with the agreement of the Assembly.

The functions of the Secretary of State under section 1(3) and under paragraphs 7(1) and 11(1) of Schedule 1 shall be exercisable only after consultation with the Assembly.

[Health Act 1999 (c 8)

...]

NOTES

Initial Commencement

Specified date: 1 July 1999: see art 1(2).

Amendment

Entry relating to the 'Copyright Act 1911 c 46' (omitted) revoked by the Legal Deposit Libraries Act 2003, s 15(1), Schedule.

Date in force: 1 February 2004: see SI 2004/130, art 2.

Entry relating to the 'Water Industry Act 1991 c 56' inserted by the Water Act 2003, s 100(3).

Date in force (for certain purposes): 1 October 2004: see SI 2004/2528, art 2(s)(iii).

Date in force (for certain purposes): 1 October 2005: see SI 2005/2714, art 2(k)(ii)–(iv); for transitional provisions see art 5(1), Schedule, paras 7, 8 thereto.

Date in force (for remaining purposes): 1 April 2007: see SI 2007/1021, art 2(c).

Entry relating to the 'Health Act 1999 (c 8)' (omitted) inserted by the Health Act 1999, s 66(4), (6); this amendment has effect as if made under an Order in Council under s 22 of the Government of Wales Act 1998.

Date in force: 30 June 1999: see the Health Act 1999, s 67(4)(a).

Entry relating to the 'Health Act 1999 (c 8)' (omitted) revoked by the Health and Social Care (Community Health and Standards) Act 2003, s 196, Sch 14, Pt 2.

Date in force: 1 April 2004: see SI 2004/759, art 13(1), (2)(h).

See Further

Reference to the Environment Act 1995 shall be treated as a reference to that Act, as amended by the Town and Country Planning (Electronic Communications) (Wales) (No 1) Order 2004: see the Town and Country Planning (Electronic Communications) (Wales) (No 1) Order 2004, SI 2004/3156, art 14.

SCHEDULE 3
THE SEA ADJACENT TO WALES

Article 6

The Severn Estuary

A1.592

Point No	Latitude				Longitude			
1	51	34	09	N	02	42	33	W
2	51	33	51	N	02	42	27	W
3	51	32	30	N	02	42	52	W
4	51	31	33	N	02	47	04	W
5	51	27	19	N	02	59	28	W
6	51	25	30	N	03	01	33	W
7	51	21	29	N	03	06	13	W
8	51	21	24	N	03	06	51	W
9	51	20	58	N	03	11	02	W
10	51	17	43	N	03	14	31	W
11	51	17	09	N	03	18	18	W
12	51	19	17	N	03	38	46	W
13	51	23	49	N	03	57	30	W
14	51	21	38	N	04	26	30	W
15	51	24	16	N	04	37	03	W

The Dee Estuary

Point No	Latitude				Longitude			
1	53	20	17	N	03	12	56	W
2	53	20	20	N	03	13	23	W
3	53	21	04	N	03	14	41	W
4	53	24	13	N	03	17	44	W
5	53	25	30	N	03	21	17	W
6	53	27	07	N	03	24	30	W
7	53	31	34	N	03	31	52	W
8	53	33	18	N	03	34	09	W

All positions Ordnance Survey of Great Britain 1936 datum.

NOTES

Initial Commencement

Specified date: 1 July 1999: see art 1(2).

MINISTRY OF AGRICULTURE, FISHERIES AND FOOD (DISSOLUTION) ORDER 2002

SI 2002/794

Whereas copies of the draft of this Order have been laid before Parliament in pursuance of section 5(1) of the Ministers of the Crown Act 1975, and each House has presented an Address to Her Majesty praying that the Order be made:

Now, therefore, Her Majesty, in pursuance of section 1 of the Ministers of the Crown Act 1975, is pleased, by and with the advice of Her Privy Council, to order, and it is hereby ordered, as follows:

A1.593

1   Citation, commencement and interpretation

(1) This Order may be cited as the Ministry of Agriculture, Fisheries and Food (Dissolution) Order 2002.

(2) This Order shall come into force on the day after the day on which it is made.

(3) Any provision of this Order for the transfer of functions of the Minister of Agriculture, Fisheries and Food acting alone to the Secretary of State or a named Secretary of State (however described) shall be construed, in relation to any of those functions so far as they are already exercisable concurrently with the Minister of Agriculture, Fisheries and Food by the Secretary of State acting alone or (as the case may be) the named Secretary of State acting alone, as providing that the functions shall cease to be exercisable by the Minister of Agriculture, Fisheries and Food; and references in this Order to functions transferred or to a transfer by the Order shall be construed accordingly.

(4) In determining for the purposes of this Order whether a share of a joint function is held by the Secretary of State or a named Secretary of State (however described), any transfer under the Transfer of Functions (Wales) Order 1969 or the Transfer of Functions (Wales) (No 1) Order 1978 which was expressed to be a transfer to the Secretary of State, or to the Secretary of State and another person jointly, shall, irrespective of any supplementary provision in the Order, be treated as a transfer to, or (as the case may be) including a transfer to, the Secretary of State (and not a named Secretary of State).

(5) In this Order, unless the context otherwise requires, any reference to a function of, or exercisable by, a Minister or Ministers shall, in the case of a function which is exercisable by the Minister or Ministers jointly with another person or is otherwise shared by the Minister or Ministers with another person, be construed as a reference to the share of the Minister or Ministers in that function.

(6) In this Order any description in article 2(3) or (4)(c) or article 3(4), (6), (9)(c) or (10)(c) of a function to be transferred does not, so far as it refers to a function of, or

exercisable by, the Secretary of State, include a reference to a function of, or exercisable by, a named Secretary of State (however described); and article 6(6), (7) and (8) do not apply in relation to a transfer to a named Secretary of State and the other references in article 6(7) and (8) to the Secretary of State also do not include references to a named Secretary of State.

(7)   In this Order 'instrument', without prejudice to the generality of that expression, includes in particular Royal Charters, Orders in Council, Letters Patent, judgments, decrees, orders, rules, regulations, schemes, bye-laws, awards, contracts and other agreements, memoranda and articles of association, warrants, certificates and other documents.

(8)   In this Order—

    'the transferor' means—

        (a)   in relation to anything transferred by article 2(3), (4)(c) or (d) or (5) or article 3(4), (5), (6), (7), (8), (9)(c), (10)(c) or (11), the Minister of Agriculture, Fisheries and Food and the Minister or Ministers concerned, or any of them;

        (b)   in relation to anything transferred by article 2(4)(b), 3(9)(b) or (10)(b) or 4(2), the Minister concerned; and

        (c)   in any other case, the Minister of Agriculture, Fisheries and Food; and

    'the transferee' means—

        (a)   in relation to anything transferred by article 2(5) or 3(4) or (11)(a) or (c), the Secretary of State for Environment, Food and Rural Affairs and the Minister or Ministers concerned, or (as the case may be) the Secretary of State for Environment, Food and Rural Affairs or the Minister or Ministers concerned;

        (b)   in relation to anything transferred by article 3(3), each Secretary of State having responsibility for any matters connected with the regulation of veterinary products;

        (c)   in relation to anything transferred by article 4(2), the Secretary of State to whom the transferred function is entrusted on the coming into force of this Order; and

        (d)   in any other case, the Secretary of State or (as the case may be) the Secretary of State for Environment, Food and Rural Affairs.

NOTES

Initial Commencement

Specified date: 27 March 2002: see para (2) above.

A1.594

2   Dissolution of Ministry and general transfer of functions

(1)   The Ministry of Agriculture, Fisheries and Food is hereby dissolved.

(2)   Subject as follows, the functions of the Minister of Agriculture, Fisheries and Food are hereby transferred to the Secretary of State.

(3)   Any function which is exercisable by the Minister of Agriculture, Fisheries and Food and the Secretary of State acting jointly is hereby transferred to the Secretary of State.

(4)   Any function of—

    (a)   the Minister of Agriculture, Fisheries and Food;

    (b)   a named Secretary of State (however described);

    (c)   the Minister of Agriculture, Fisheries and Food and the Secretary of State acting jointly; or

    (d)   the Minister of Agriculture, Fisheries and Food and one or more named Secretaries of State (however described) acting jointly;

under any scheme, regulations, Order in Council, order, bye-laws or similar instrument made (or having effect as if made) in the exercise of, or in relation to, any function which is transferred (whether wholly or partly) by paragraph (3) is, so far as is consistent with the transfer effected by that paragraph, hereby transferred to the Secretary of State.

(5) Subject to paragraphs (3) and (4), any function which is exercisable by the Minister of Agriculture, Fisheries and Food and one or more named Secretaries of State (however described) acting jointly is hereby transferred to the Secretary of State for Environment, Food and Rural Affairs and the one or more named Secretaries of State acting jointly.

(6) Any function of the Minister of Agriculture, Fisheries and Food under any scheme, regulations, Order in Council, order, bye-laws or similar instrument made (or having effect as if made) in the exercise of, or in relation to, any function which is transferred (whether wholly or partly) by paragraph (5) is, so far as is consistent with the transfer effected by that paragraph, hereby transferred to the Secretary of State for Environment, Food and Rural Affairs.

(7) Paragraphs (2) to (6) do not apply so far as article 3 does apply.

NOTES

Initial Commencement

Specified date: 27 March 2002: see art 1(2).

A1.595

3   Specific transfers of functions

(1) Subject to paragraphs (4) and (7), any function of the Minister of Agriculture, Fisheries and Food—

    (a)   under the New Forest Act 1949, the New Forest Act 1964 or the New Forest Act 1970;

    (b)   under section 19 of the Veterinary Surgeons Act 1966;

    (c)   under the Medicines Act 1968 or the Medicines Act 1971 (other than any function of laying a copy of a report under section 5(2) of the Act of 1968 and any function under section 108 of that Act);

    (d)   under paragraph 3 of Schedule 1 to the Poisons Act 1972;

    (e)   under section 51 of the Fair Trading Act 1973 or any related provision of that Act;

    (f)   as 'the Minister' under section 7 of the Agricultural Marketing Act 1983; or

    (g)   which is exercisable by virtue of section 265(3)(a) or (4) of the Town and Country Planning Act 1990;

is hereby transferred to the Secretary of State for Environment, Food and Rural Affairs.

(2) Any function of the Minister of Agriculture, Fisheries and Food under any scheme, regulations, Order in Council, order, bye-laws or similar instrument made (or having effect as if made) in the exercise of, or in relation to, any function which is transferred (whether wholly or partly) by paragraph (1) is, so far as is consistent with the transfer effected by that paragraph, hereby transferred to the Secretary of State for Environment, Food and Rural Affairs.

(3) Any function of the Minister of Agriculture, Fisheries and Food under section 29 of the Food Standards Act 1999 is hereby transferred to each Secretary of State having responsibility for any matters connected with the regulation of veterinary products.

(4) Any function under the New Forest Act 1949, the New Forest Act 1964 or the New Forest Act 1970 which is exercisable by the Minister of Agriculture, Fisheries and Food and the Secretary of State acting jointly is hereby transferred to the Secretary of State for Environment, Food and Rural Affairs and the Secretary of State for Transport, Local Government and the Regions acting jointly.

(5) Any function under Schedule 1 to the Forestry Act 1967 which is exercisable by the Minister of Agriculture, Fisheries and Food and the Secretary of State for Wales acting jointly is hereby transferred to the Secretary of State.

(6) Any function under section 2, 3 or 5 of the Agriculture (Miscellaneous Provisions) Act 1968 which is exercisable by the Minister of Agriculture, Fisheries and Food, the Secretary of State and the Secretary of State for Wales acting jointly is hereby transferred to the Secretary of State.

(7) Any function under the Medicines Act 1968 or the Medicines Act 1971 which is exercisable, by the Minister of Agriculture, Fisheries and Food and the Secretary of State concerned with health in England acting jointly, by virtue of the definition of 'the Ministers' in section 1(1) of the Act of 1968 (including any function so exercisable by virtue of the definition of 'the appropriate Ministers' in section 1(2) of that Act) is hereby transferred to the Secretary of State.

(8) Any function under the Dairy Produce Quotas Regulations 1997 which is exercisable by—

   (a)   the Minister of Agriculture, Fisheries and Food and the Secretary of State for Wales acting jointly; or
   (b)   the Minister of Agriculture, Fisheries and Food, the Secretary of State for Wales and the Secretary of State for Scotland acting jointly;

is hereby transferred to the Secretary of State.

(9) Any function of—

   (a)   the Minister of Agriculture, Fisheries and Food;
   (b)   a named Secretary of State (however described); or
   (c)   the Minister of Agriculture, Fisheries and Food and the Secretary of State for Wales, the Secretary of State for Scotland or the Secretary of State, or more than one of them, acting jointly;

under any scheme, regulations, Order in Council, order, bye-laws or similar instrument made (or having effect as if made) in the exercise of, or in relation to, any function which is transferred (whether wholly or partly) by paragraph (5), (6) or (8) is, so far as is consistent with the transfer effected by that paragraph, hereby transferred to the Secretary of State.

(10) Any function of—

   (a)   the Minister of Agriculture, Fisheries and Food;
   (b)   a named Secretary of State (however described); or
   (c)   the Minister of Agriculture, Fisheries and Food and the Secretary of State concerned with health in England acting jointly or the Minister of Agriculture, Fisheries and Food and the Secretary of State acting jointly;

under any scheme, regulations, Order in Council, order, bye-laws or similar instrument made (or having effect as if made) in the exercise of, or in relation to, any function which is transferred (whether wholly or partly) by paragraph (7) is, so far as is consistent with the transfer effected by that paragraph, hereby transferred to the Secretary of State.

(11) Any function of making regulations under section 2(2) of the European Communities Act 1972 which is exercisable by the Minister of Agriculture, Fisheries and Food and one or more Secretaries of State acting jointly is hereby transferred—

(a) in a case where the Secretary of State for Environment, Food and Rural Affairs is not the Secretary of State concerned or one of the Secretaries of State concerned, to the Secretary of State for Environment, Food and Rural Affairs and the Secretary of State, or (as the case may be) Secretaries of State, concerned acting jointly;

(b) in a case where the Secretary of State for Environment, Food and Rural Affairs is the Secretary of State concerned, to the Secretary of State; and

(c) in a case where the Secretary of State for Environment, Food and Rural Affairs is one of the Secretaries of State concerned, to those Secretaries of State acting jointly.

NOTES

Initial Commencement

Specified date: 27 March 2002: see art 1(2).

A1.596

4   Transfer of property, rights and liabilities

(1) Subject to paragraphs (2) to (5), all property, rights and liabilities to which the Minister of Agriculture, Fisheries and Food is entitled or subject immediately before the coming into force of this Order are hereby transferred to the Secretary of State for Environment, Food and Rural Affairs.

(2) Subject to paragraphs (3) and (5), all property, rights and liabilities to which the Minister of Agriculture, Fisheries and Food or a Secretary of State is entitled or subject immediately before the coming into force of this Order in connection with any functions transferred by article 2(3) or (4) or article 3(5), (6), (7), (8), (9) or (10) of this Order are hereby transferred to the Secretary of State to whom the transferred function is entrusted on the coming into force of this Order.

(3) Paragraphs (1) and (2) do not apply in relation to—

(a) any property outside the United Kingdom which is not capable of transfer by this Order; and

(b) rights and liabilities of the Minister of Agriculture, Fisheries and Food or a Secretary of State in relation to any such property.

(4) The person from time to time holding office as Secretary of State for Environment, Food and Rural Affairs shall by virtue of that office be Minister of Agriculture, Fisheries and Food so long as any property, rights or liabilities of the kind mentioned in paragraph (3) remain vested in that Minister.

(5) Paragraph (2) does not operate so as to transfer property, rights or liabilities to which a Secretary of State is entitled or subject immediately before the coming into force of this Order in connection with a function if that Secretary of State is the Secretary of State to whom the function is entrusted on the coming into force of this Order.

NOTES

Initial Commencement

Specified date: 27 March 2002: see art 1(2).

A1.597

5   Specific modifications of enactments and instruments

(1)   The amendments specified in Schedule 1 (consequential amendments) shall have effect.

(2)   The repeals and revocations specified in Schedule 2 shall have effect.

(3)   Any amendment made by virtue of paragraph (1) to a reference to the Minister of Agriculture and Fisheries or his department which has effect as a reference to the Minister of Agriculture, Fisheries and Food or his department by virtue of article 3(3) of the Transfer of Functions (Ministry of Food) Order 1955 shall not apply to the reference to the Minister of Agriculture and Fisheries or his department so far as it continues to have effect in relation to matters past at the coming into force of the Order of 1955.

(4)   Sections 6(2) and 7 of the Board of Agriculture Act 1889 and section 1(2) of the Ministry of Agriculture and Fisheries Act 1919 shall continue to apply on and after the coming into force of this Order in relation to the Secretary of State for Environment, Food and Rural Affairs in his capacity as Minister of Agriculture, Fisheries and Food.

(5)   In their continued application by virtue of paragraph (4), sections 6(2) and 7 of the Act of 1889 and section 1(2) of the Act of 1919 shall have effect as they had effect immediately before the coming into force of this Order except that—

   (a)   section 6(2) of the Act of 1889 shall have effect, in relation to the authentica-
         tion of the official seal, as if it provided for the official seal to be authenticated
         by the signature of the Secretary of State for Environment, Food and Rural
         Affairs in his capacity as Minister of Agriculture, Fisheries and Food or of
         some person authorised by him to act on his behalf;

   (b)   section 7(1) of that Act shall have effect as if the reference to every document
         purporting to be signed by a secretary or any person authorised by the
         President of the Board to act on behalf of the secretary were a reference to
         every document purporting to be signed by any person authorised by the
         Secretary of State for Environment, Food and Rural Affairs in his capacity as
         Minister of Agriculture, Fisheries and Food to act on his behalf; and

   (c)   section 1(2) of the Act of 1919 shall have effect as if the reference to the
         Ministry of Agriculture and Fisheries were a reference to the Department for
         Environment, Food and Rural Affairs.

(6)   The repeal of section 7 of the Act of 1889 (and of any enactments amending that section) shall not apply in relation to documents sealed or signed, or (as the case may be) certificates signed, before the coming into force of this Order.

NOTES

Initial Commencement

Specified date: 27 March 2002: see art 1(2).

A1.598

6   Other supplementary provisions

(1)   This Order shall not affect the validity of anything done (or having effect as if done) by or in relation to the transferor before the coming into force of this Order.

(2)   Anything (including any legal proceedings) which, at the coming into force of this Order, is in the process of being done by or in relation to the transferor may, so far as it relates to anything transferred by this Order, be continued by or in relation to the transferee.

(3)   Anything done (or having effect as if done) by or in relation to the transferor for the purposes of or in connection with anything transferred by this Order shall, if in force at the coming into force of this Order, have effect as if done by or in relation to the transferee in so far as that is required for continuing its effect after the coming into force of this Order.

(4)   Subject to paragraphs (5) to (13), any enactment or instrument passed or made before the coming into force of this Order shall have effect, so far as may be necessary for the purposes of or in consequence of any transfer effected by this Order or the dissolution of the Ministry of Agriculture, Fisheries and Food, as if any references (including references which are to be construed as such references) to the transferor or his department or officers were references to the transferee or his department or officers, as the context may require.

(5)   Any enactment or instrument passed or made before the coming into force of this Order shall have effect, so far as may be necessary for the purposes of or in consequence of a function ceasing to be exercisable by the Minister of Agriculture, Fisheries and Food by virtue of article 2 or 3 as read with article 1(3), as if any references (including references which are to be construed as such references) to the Minister of Agriculture, Fisheries and Food or his department or officers were omitted.

(6)   Any enactment or instrument passed or made before the coming into force of this Order shall have effect, so far as may be necessary for the purposes of or in consequence of any transfer effected by this Order from the Minister of Agriculture, Fisheries and Food to the Secretary of State of a share of a function which is exercisable by the Minister of Agriculture, Fisheries and Food acting alone concurrently with (whether with or without others) a named Secretary of State (however described) acting alone, as if any references (including references which are to be construed as such references) to the Minister of Agriculture, Fisheries and Food and the named Secretary of State, or either of them, or their departments or officers were references to the Secretary of State or his department or officers, as the context may require.

(7)   Any enactment or instrument passed or made before the coming into force of this Order shall have effect, so far as may be necessary for the purposes of or in consequence of any transfer effected by this Order from the Minister of Agriculture, Fisheries and Food to the Secretary of State of, or in connection with, any function or share of a function which is exercisable only with the agreement of, or after consulting with, the Secretary of State acting alone as if any requirement for the agreement of, or (as the case may be) for consultation with, the Secretary of State in connection with the exercise of the function were omitted.

(8)   Any enactment or instrument passed or made before the coming into force of this Order shall have effect, so far as may be necessary for the purposes of or in consequence of any transfer effected by this Order from the Minister of Agriculture, Fisheries and Food acting alone to the Secretary of State of, or in connection with, any function of deciding whether to agree with, or of being consulted by, the Secretary of State (whether acting alone or jointly) as if any such function were omitted.

(9) Documents or forms printed or duplicated for use in connection with any function of the Minister of Agriculture, Fisheries and Food may, subject to paragraph (10), be used in connection with that function on and after the coming into force of this Order notwithstanding that they contain, or are to be construed as containing, references to the Minister of Agriculture, Fisheries and Food, the Ministry of Agriculture, Fisheries and Food or any officer of either of them.

(10) For the purposes of the use of any such documents or forms on or after the coming into force of this Order, those references shall be construed in accordance with paragraphs (4) to (8).

(11) Paragraphs (4) to (8) are subject to any specific amendment, repeal or revocation made by this Order but any such amendment, repeal or revocation is without prejudice to the operation of those paragraphs in relation to anything not specifically dealt with by that amendment, repeal or revocation.

(12) Section 5(1) of the Government Resources and Accounts Act 2000 shall apply, in relation to the Department for Environment, Food and Rural Affairs and resource accounts in its name, as if the resources acquired, held, disposed of or used by the Ministry of Agriculture, Fisheries and Food during the relevant financial year and before its dissolution had been acquired, held, disposed of or (as the case may be) used by the Department for Environment, Food and Rural Affairs.

(13) In paragraph (12) 'relevant financial year' means the year ending with 31st March 2002.

NOTES

Initial Commencement

Specified date: 27 March 2002: see art 1(2).

SCHEDULE 1
CONSEQUENTIAL AMENDMENTS

Article 5(1)

Law of Property Act 1922 (c 16)

A1.599

1   In the following provisions of Schedule 15 to the Law of Property Act 1922 for the word 'Minister', in each place where it appears, there shall be substituted 'Secretary of State'—

    (a)   paragraph 6(2);
    (b)   paragraph 10(2);
    (c)   paragraph 12(2), (3), (5) and (6); and
    (d)   paragraph 16.

Settled Land Act 1925 (c 18)

2   In section 84(3) of the Settled Land Act 1925 for the word 'Minister' there shall be substituted 'Secretary of State'.

3   (1)   Section 88 of that Act shall be amended as follows.

(2)   In subsection (1) for the word 'Minister', in both places where it appears, there shall be substituted 'Secretary of State'.

(3)   In subsection (3) for the word 'Minister', in both places where it appears, there shall be substituted 'Secretary of State'.

(4)   In subsection (4) for the word 'Minister' there shall be substituted 'Secretary of State'.

4   (1)   Section 115 of that Act shall be amended as follows.

(2)   In subsection (1) for the word 'Minister' there shall be substituted 'Secretary of State'.

(3)   In subsection (2) for the word 'Minister' there shall be substituted 'Secretary of State'.

(4)   In subsection (3) for the word 'Minister', in both places where it appears, there shall be substituted 'Secretary of State'.

5   (1)   Section 116(1) of that Act shall be amended as follows.

(2)   For the word 'Minister', in the first place where it appears, there shall be substituted 'Secretary of State'.

(3)   For the words 'Minister of Agriculture and Fisheries' there shall be substituted 'Secretary of State'.

Land Registration Act 1925 (c 21)

6   In section 144(1) of the Land Registration Act 1925 for the words 'Minister of Agriculture and Fisheries' there shall be substituted 'Secretary of State'.

New Forest Act 1949 (c 69)

7   In section 1(c) of the New Forest Act 1949 for the words 'Minister of Agriculture and Fisheries' there shall be substituted 'Secretary of State for Environment, Food and Rural Affairs'.

8   (1)   Section 16 of that Act shall be amended as follows.

(2)   In subsection (4) for the words 'said Ministers' there shall be substituted 'Minister and the Secretary of State for Transport, Local Government and the Regions'.

(3)   In subsection (7) for the words 'said Ministers' there shall be substituted 'Minister and the Secretary of State for Transport, Local Government and the Regions'.

(4)   In subsection (9)(b), for the words 'said Ministers' there shall be substituted 'Minister and the Secretary of State for Transport, Local Government and the Regions'.

9   (1)   Section 17 of that Act shall be amended as follows.

(2)   In subsection (3)(a) for the words 'Minister of Transport' there shall be substituted 'Secretary of State for Transport, Local Government and the Regions'.

(3)   In subsection (5) for the words 'Minister of Transport' there shall be substituted 'Secretary of State for Transport, Local Government and the Regions'.

Public Records Act 1958 (c 51)

10   In Schedule 1 to the Public Records Act 1958, in Part 1 of the Table at the end of paragraph 3, for the words 'Ministry of Agriculture, Fisheries and Food' there shall be substituted 'Department for Environment, Food and Rural Affairs'.

New Forest Act 1964 (c 83)

11   In section 3(2) of the New Forest Act 1964 for the words 'Minister of Agriculture, Fisheries and Food' there shall be substituted 'Secretary of State for Environment, Food and Rural Affairs'.

12 In section 4(3) of that Act for the words 'Minister of Transport' there shall be substituted 'Secretary of State for Transport, Local Government and the Regions'.

Forestry Act 1967 (c 10)

13 In section 49(1) of the Forestry Act 1967, in the definition of 'the Minister'—

(a) for the words 'Schedules 1 and 3' there shall be substituted 'Schedule 1'; and
(b) for the words 'Minister of Agriculture, Fisheries and Food' there shall be substituted 'Secretary of State'.

Parliamentary Commissioner Act 1967 (c 13)

14 In Schedule 2 to the Parliamentary Commissioner Act 1967, at the appropriate place, there shall be inserted 'Department for Environment, Food and Rural Affairs'.

Medicines Act 1968 (c 67)

15 (1) Section 1(1) of the Medicines Act 1968 shall be amended as follows.

(2) In the definition of 'the Agriculture Ministers', for the words 'Minister of Agriculture, Fisheries and Food' there shall be substituted 'Secretary of State for Environment, Food and Rural Affairs'.

(3) In the definition of 'the Ministers'—

(a) after the words 'all the Ministers' there shall be inserted 'for Northern Ireland'; and
(b) after the word 'subsection' there shall be inserted 'and the Secretary of State'.

16 (1) Section 5 of that Act shall be amended as follows.

(2) In subsection (2) after the word 'Ministers', where it appears for the second time, there shall be inserted 'specified in paragraphs (a) and (b) of section 1(1) of this Act'.

(3) In subsection (3) after the word 'Ministers' there shall be inserted 'specified in paragraphs (a) and (b) of section 1(1) of this Act'.

New Forest Act 1970 (c 21)

17 (1) Section 2 of the New Forest Act 1970 shall be amended as follows.

(2) In subsection (1) for the words 'Minister of Agriculture, Fisheries and Food' there shall be substituted 'Secretary of State for Environment, Food and Rural Affairs'.

(3) In subsection (3) for the words 'Minister of Transport' there shall be substituted 'Secretary of State for Transport, Local Government and the Regions'.

Poisons Act 1972 (c 66)

18 In paragraph 3 of Schedule 1 to the Poisons Act 1972 for the words 'Minister of Agriculture, Fisheries and Food' there shall be substituted 'Secretary of State for Environment, Food and Rural Affairs'.

Land Drainage Act 1976 (c 70)

19 In paragraph 1(2) of Schedule 5 to the Land Drainage Act 1976 for the word 'Minister' there shall be substituted 'Secretary of State'.

Agricultural Statistics Act 1979 (c 13)

20   In section 6(1) of the Agricultural Statistics Act 1979, in the definition of 'the appropriate Minister', for the words 'Minister of Agriculture, Fisheries and Food' there shall be substituted 'Secretary of State'.

Diseases of Fish Act 1983 (c 30)

21   In section 7(8) of the Diseases of Fish Act 1983, in the definition of 'the Minister', in paragraph (a), for the words 'Minister of Agriculture, Fisheries and Food' there shall be substituted 'Secretary of State'.

National Heritage Act 1983 (c 47)

22   (1)   Section 24 of the National Heritage Act 1983 shall be amended as follows.

(2)   In subsection (6) for the words 'Minister of Agriculture, Fisheries and Food' there shall be substituted 'Secretary of State'.

(3)   In subsections (7) and (8) for the words 'that Minister's consent' there shall, in each case, be substituted 'the consent of the Secretary of State'.

23   In section 25(1) of that Act for the words 'Minister of Agriculture, Fisheries and Food' there shall be substituted 'Secretary of State'.

24   (1)   Section 29 of that Act shall be amended as follows.

(2)   In subsection (1) for the words 'Minister of Agriculture, Fisheries and Food' there shall be substituted 'Secretary of State'.

(3)   In subsection (2) for the word 'Minister' there shall be substituted 'Secretary of State'.

25   (1)   Part IV of Schedule 1 to that Act shall be amended as follows.

(2)   In paragraph 33, in sub-paragraph (2), for the words from 'Minister of' to the end of the sub-paragraph there shall be substituted 'Secretary of State'.

(3)   In the following provisions for the word 'Minister', in each place where it appears, there shall be substituted 'Secretary of State'—

> (a)   paragraph 33(3), (4) and (6);
> (b)   paragraph 34(1) and (6);
> (c)   paragraph 37;
> (d)   paragraph 39(4), (5) and (6); and
> (e)   paragraph 40(1), (3), (4) and (6).

Mineral Workings Act 1985 (c 12)

26   In section 9 of the Mineral Workings Act 1985, in the definition of 'the Minister', for the words 'Minister of Agriculture, Fisheries and Food' there shall be substituted 'Secretary of State'.

Agricultural Holdings Act 1986 (c 5)

27   In section 96(1) of the Agricultural Holdings Act 1986, in the definition of 'the Minister', in paragraph (a), for the words 'Minister of Agriculture, Fisheries and Food' there shall be substituted 'Secretary of State'.

Agriculture Act 1986 (c 49)

28   In section 17(2) of the Agriculture Act 1986, in the definition of 'the Minister', for the words 'Minister of Agriculture, Fisheries and Food' there shall be substituted 'Secretary of State'.

29   In section 18(11) of that Act, in the definition of 'the Minister', for the words 'Minister of Agriculture, Fisheries and Food' there shall be substituted 'Secretary of State'.

30   In paragraph 18(1) of Schedule 1 to that Act, in the definition of 'the Minister', for the words 'Minister of Agriculture, Fisheries and Food' there shall be substituted 'Secretary of State'.

Income and Corporation Taxes Act 1988 (c 1)

31   In section 486(12) of the Income and Corporation Taxes Act 1988, in the definition of 'the Minister', for the words 'Minister of Agriculture, Fisheries and Food' there shall be substituted 'Secretary of State'.

Farm Land and Rural Development Act 1988 (c 16)

32   In section 1(5) of the Farm Land and Rural Development Act 1988, in the definition of 'the appropriate Minister', in paragraph (a), for the words 'Minister of Agriculture, Fisheries and Food' there shall be substituted 'Secretary of State'.

Scotch Whisky Act 1988 (c 22)

33   The definition of 'the Ministers' in section 3(1) of the Scotch Whisky Act 1988 shall, so far as it applies in relation to England and Wales, have effect as if for the reference to the Minister of Agriculture, Fisheries and Food and the Secretary of State acting jointly there were substituted a reference to the Secretary of State.

Deer Act 1991 (c 54)

34   In section 7(7)(a) of the Deer Act 1991 for the words 'Minister of Agriculture, Fisheries and Food' there shall be substituted 'Secretary of State'.

Protection of Badgers Act 1992 (c 51)

35   In section 10(5)(a) of the Protection of Badgers Act 1992 for the words 'Minister of Agriculture, Fisheries and Food' there shall be substituted 'Secretary of State'.

Merchant Shipping Act 1995 (c 21)

36   In section 15(6)(a) of the Merchant Shipping Act 1995 for the word 'General,' there shall be substituted 'General or'.

Employment Rights Act 1996 (c 18)

37   In section 35(3)(b) of the Employment Rights Act 1996 for the words 'Minister of Agriculture, Fisheries and Food' there shall be substituted 'Secretary of State'.

Food Standards Act 1999 (c 28)

38   In section 29(4) of the Food Standards Act 1999 for the words 'the Minister of Agriculture, Fisheries and Food' there shall be substituted 'each Secretary of State having responsibility for any matters connected with the regulation of veterinary products'.

Regulation of Investigatory Powers Act 2000 (c 23)

39 In Part 1 of Schedule 1 to the Regulation of Investigatory Powers Act 2000 there shall be inserted at the appropriate place 'The Department for Environment, Food and Rural Affairs'.

Fur Farming (Prohibition) Act 2000 (c 33)

40 In section 5(1) of the Fur Farming (Prohibition) Act 2000 for the words 'Minister of Agriculture, Fisheries and Food' there shall be substituted 'Secretary of State'.

41 In section 6(a) of that Act for the words 'Minister of Agriculture, Fisheries and Food' there shall be substituted 'Secretary of State'.

42 In section 7(2) of that Act for the words 'Minister of Agriculture, Fisheries and Food' there shall be substituted 'Secretary of State'.

Countryside and Rights of Way Act 2000 (c 37)

43 (1) Section 29 of the Countryside and Rights of Way Act 2000 shall be amended as follows.

(2) In subsection (2)(a) for the words 'appropriate Minister' there shall be substituted 'Secretary of State'.

(3) In subsection (3) for the words 'appropriate Minister', in both places where they appear, there shall be substituted 'Secretary of State'.

44 (1) Section 30 of that Act shall be amended as follows.

(2) In subsection (3)(a) for the words 'appropriate Minister' there shall be substituted 'Secretary of State'.

(3) In subsection (4) for the words 'appropriate Minister', in both places where they appear, there shall be substituted 'Secretary of State'.

Protection of Animals (Amendment) Act 2000 (c 40)

45 In section 1(3)(e) of the Protection of Animals (Amendment) Act 2000 for the words 'Minister of Agriculture, Fisheries and Food' there shall be substituted 'Secretary of State'.

Sea Fishing (Enforcement of Community Satellite Monitoring Measures) Order 2000 (SI 2000/181)

46 In article 4(3) of the Sea Fishing (Enforcement of Community Satellite Monitoring Measures) Order 2000 for the words 'Minister of Agriculture, Fisheries and Food' there shall be substituted 'Secretary of State for Environment, Food and Rural Affairs'.

Sea Fishing (Enforcement of Community Conservation Measures) Order 2000 (SI 2000/1081)

47 In article 9(1)(a) of the Sea Fishing (Enforcement of Community Conservation Measures) Order 2000 for the words 'Minister of Agriculture, Fisheries and Food' there shall be substituted 'Secretary of State for Environment, Food and Rural Affairs'.

Regulation of Investigatory Powers (Prescription of Offices, Ranks and Positions) Order 2000 (SI 2000/2417)

48 In Part 1 of the Schedule to the Regulation of Investigatory Powers (Prescription of Offices, Ranks and Positions) Order 2000—

A1.600   *Statutory Instruments*

(a) for the words in the first column 'Ministry of Agriculture, Fisheries and Food' there shall be substituted 'Department for Environment, Food and Rural Affairs'; and

(b) for the words in the second column 'MAFF Investigation Branch' there shall be substituted 'DEFRA Investigation Branch'.

NOTES

Initial Commencement

Specified date: 27 March 2002: see art 1(2).

SCHEDULE 2
REPEALS AND REVOCATIONS

Article 5(2)

A1.600

Chapter	Short title	Extent of repeal or revocation
52 & 53 Vict c 30	The Board of Agriculture Act 1889	Section 5(1) and (2). Sections 6 to 8.
3 Edw 7 c 31	The Board of Agriculture and Fisheries Act 1903	Section 2(2).
9 Edw 7 c 15	The Board of Agriculture and Fisheries Act 1909	Section 1(1).
9 & 10 Geo 5 c 91	The Ministry of Agriculture and Fisheries Act 1919	In section 1, in subsection (1), the words from the beginning to 'pleasure', and subsection (2).
12 & 13 Geo 5 c 16	The Law of Property Act 1922	Section 188(31).
15 & 16 Geo 5 c 18	The Settled Land Act 1925	Section 117(1)(xvi).
9 & 10 Eliz 2 c 6	The Ministers of the Crown (Parliamentary Secretaries) Act 1960	In Schedule 1, the entries relating to the Board of Agriculture Act 1889 and the Board of Agriculture and Fisheries Act 1909.
1967 c 10	The Forestry Act 1967	Section 15(8). Section 19(4). In section 49(1), in the definition of 'the Minister', the words 'sections 15(8) and 19(4), and'. In Schedule 3, paragraph 4.
1967 c 13	The Parliamentary Commissioner Act 1967	In Schedule 2, the entry relating to the Ministry of Agriculture, Fisheries and Food.
1968 c 67	The Medicines Act 1968	In section 1(1), in the definition of 'the Ministers', the word 'all' where it appears for the first time. In section 5(2), the words 'and the Minister of Agriculture, Fisheries and Food' and the word 'jointly'.

1974 c 37	The Health and Safety at Work etc Act 1974	In section 15(1), the words from ', the Minister' to 'jointly'. In section 43(6), the words from ', the Minister' to 'jointly'. In section 49(4), the words from ', the Minister' to 'jointly'. In section 52(3), the words from ', the Minister' to 'jointly'. In section 80(4), the words from ', the Minister' to 'jointly'.
1975 c 24	The House of Commons Disqualification Act 1975	In Schedule 2, the words 'Minister of Agriculture, Fisheries and Food'.
1975 c 27	The Ministerial and other Salaries Act 1975	In Part 1 of Schedule 1, the entry relating to the Minister of Agriculture, Fisheries and Food.
1981 c 22	The Animal Health Act 1981	In section 86(2), the words from 'the Ministry' to '1919, and'.
1981 c 69	The Wildlife and Countryside Act 1981	Section 52(5).
1986 c 49	The Agriculture Act 1986	In section 18(2)(a), the words 'the Secretary of State,'.
1988 c 22	The Scotch Whisky Act 1988	In section 3(1), in the definition of 'the Ministers', the words from 'except' to 'not act'.
1990 c 8	The Town and Country Planning Act 1990	Section 15(3). Section 18(3). Section 43(6). Section 44(3).
1990 c 16	The Food Safety Act 1990	In section 6, in subsection (3), the words ', the Minister of Agriculture, Fisheries and Food' and, in subsection (4)(a), the words ', the Minister of Agriculture, Fisheries and Food,'.
1991 c 56	The Water Industry Act 1991	In section 3(1), paragraph (b). In section 5(2), the words 'and the Minister of Agriculture, Fisheries and Food' and 'each'. In section 207(2), the words ', the Minister of Agriculture, Fisheries and Food'.
1995 c 21	The Merchant Shipping Act 1995	In section 15, in subsection (6)(a), the words 'or the Minister' and, in subsection (7), paragraph (a) and the word 'and' at the end of that paragraph.

1999 c 28	The Food Standards Act 1999	In section 29, in subsection (1), the words 'The Minister of Agriculture, Fisheries and Food, and' and, in subsection (3), the words 'The Minister or'. In section 30(8)(a), the words 'and the Minister of Agriculture, Fisheries and Food, acting jointly'.
SI 1999/1820	The Scotland Act 1998 (Consequential Modifications) (No 2) Order 1999	In Schedule 2, paragraph 90.
2000 c 23	The Regulation of Investigatory Powers Act 2000	In Part 1 of Schedule 1, the entry relating to the Ministry of Agriculture, Fisheries and Food.
2000 c 37	The Countryside and Rights of Way Act 2000	In section 29, in subsection (4), the words from 'but' to the end of the subsection and, in subsection (5), the definition of 'the appropriate Minister'. In section 30, in subsection (5), the words from 'but' to the end of the subsection, and subsection (6).

NOTES

Initial Commencement

Specified date: 27 March 2002: see art 1(2).

DAIRY PRODUCE QUOTAS REGULATIONS 2005

SI 2005/465

The Secretary of State is a Minister designated for the purposes of section 2(2) of the European Communities Act 1972 in relation to the common agricultural policy of the European Community:

In accordance with section 56(1) of the Finance Act 1973, the Treasury consents to the making of these Regulations:

The Secretary of State makes these Regulations in exercise of the powers conferred by section 2(2) of the European Communities Act 1972 and by section 56(1) of the Finance Act 1973:

PART 1: PRELIMINARY

A1.601

1   Citation and commencement

These Regulations may be cited as the Dairy Produce Quotas Regulations 2005 and shall come into force on 31st March 2005.

NOTES

Initial Commencement

Specified date: 31 March 2005: see above.

A1.602

2   Interpretation

(1)   In these Regulations, unless the context otherwise requires—

'the Commission Regulation' means Commission Regulation (EC) No 595/2004 laying down detailed rules for applying Council Regulation (EC) No 1788/2003 establishing a levy in the milk and milk products sector[, as amended by Commission Regulation (EC) No 1468/2006 (OJ No L274, 5.10.2006, p 6)];
...

'the Community legislation' means the Council Regulation [and the Commission Regulation];

'competent authority' has the meaning given by regulation 2 of the General Provisions Regulations;

'consent or sole interest notice' means a notice, in relation to a holding, which states that—

(a)   the person providing the notice is the occupier of that holding and that no other person has an interest in that holding or part of that holding; or

(b)   every person having an interest in that holding or any part of it, the value of which interest might be reduced by the apportionment or prospective apportionment to which the notice relates, agrees to that apportionment or prospective apportionment;

'converted quota' means quota converted by the Secretary of State following an application made under regulation 21;

'the Council Regulation' means Council Regulation (EC) No 1788/2003 establishing a levy in the milk and milk products sector[, as amended by Council Regulation (EC) No 1406/2006 (OJ No L265, 26.9.2006, p 8)];

'cow' includes a heifer that has calved;

'dairy enterprise' means an area stated by the occupier of that area to be run as a self-contained dairy produce business;

'dairy produce' means produce, expressed in kilograms or litres (one kilogram being 0.971 litres), in respect of which levy is payable;

'delivery' has the same meaning as in Article 5(f) of the Council Regulation, and 'deliver' shall be construed accordingly;

'direct sale' has the same meaning as in Article 5(g) of the Council Regulation;

'direct sales quota' means the quantity of dairy produce which may be sold or transferred free of charge by direct sale by a producer in a quota year without that producer being liable to pay levy;

'direct sales quota holder' means a person in whose name direct sales quota is registered pursuant to regulation 4;

'direct seller' means a producer who produces milk and treats that milk or processes it into milk products on his holding and subsequently sells or transfers free of charge that milk or those milk products without their having been further treated or processed by a different undertaking which treats or processes milk or milk products;

'electronic communication' has the same meaning as in section 15 of the Electronic Communications Act 2000;

'the General Provisions Regulations' means the Dairy Produce Quotas (General Provisions) Regulations 2002;

'holding' has the same meaning as in Article 5(d) of the Council Regulation;

'interest' includes a licence to occupy land and the interest of a mortgagee and a trustee, but does not include the interest of a beneficiary under a trust or settlement;

'levy' means the levy payable under the Community legislation and these Regulations to the Secretary of State;

'milk' has the same meaning as in Article 5(a) of the Council Regulation;

'national reserve' has the meaning given it by regulation 2 of the General Provisions Regulations;

'occupier', in relation to land, includes the person entitled to grant occupation of that land to another, and, during the currency of an interest mentioned in regulation 16(1), the person entitled to grant occupation when that interest terminates, and 'occupation' shall be construed accordingly;

'producer' has the same meaning as in Article 5(c) of the Council Regulation;

'prospective apportionment', in relation to quota in respect of a holding, means an apportionment of quota between the persons with an interest in the holding for the purposes of ascertaining the quota referable to a part of that holding in the event of a transfer of that part;

'purchaser' means a purchaser within the meaning of Article 5(e) of the Council Regulation and, other than in regulation 5(1) to (4) and regulation 31(7), approved by the Secretary of State pursuant to regulation 5 and Article 23 of the Commission Regulation;

'purchaser quota' means the quantity of milk which may be delivered to a purchaser during a quota year without any liability for levy arising;

'quota' means direct sales quota or wholesale quota, as the case may be;

'quota holder', in relation to quota, means the person in whose name the quota is registered;

'quota year' means any of the periods of 12 months referred to in Article 1(1) of the Council Regulation (which concerns the introduction of the levy);

'registered wholesale quota' means wholesale quota registered pursuant to regulation 4(3) and (4);

'relevant competent authority' has the meaning given by regulation 3 of the General Provisions Regulations;

'relevant person' means a producer, a purchaser, any employee or agent of a producer or of a purchaser, any milk haulier, any person undertaking butterfat testing for purchasers in a laboratory, a processor of milk or milk products, or any other person involved in the buying, selling or supply of milk or milk products obtained directly from a producer or purchaser, but does not include a consumer of milk or milk products;

'Scottish Islands area' means either—

    (a) the islands of Orkney except for the island of Stronsay; or

    (b) the islands of Jura, Gigha, Arran, Bute, Great Cumbrae and Little Cumbrae, the Kintyre peninsula south of Tarbert and the areas of land within the Argyll and Bute District comprising those parts of the parishes of Dunoon and Kilmun and Inverchaolain shown bounded by a red line on a map marked 'Map referred to in sub-paragraph (b) of the definition of Scottish Islands area in regulation 2(1) of the Dairy Produce Quotas Regulations 2005', dated 31st January 2005, signed on behalf of the Secretary of State and deposited at the offices of the Department for Environment, Food and Rural Affairs at Nobel House, 17 Smith Square, London SW1P 3JR;

'the Secretary of State' means the Secretary of State for Environment, Food and Rural Affairs;

'transferee' means—

    (a) where quota is transferred with a holding or part of a holding, a person who replaces another as occupier of that holding or part of a holding; and

(b) in any other case, the person to whom quota is transferred;
'transferor' means—

(a) where quota is transferred with a holding or part of a holding, a person who is replaced by another occupier of that holding or part of a holding; and

(b) in any other case, the person from whom quota is transferred;

'unused quota' means quota remaining unused after any direct sales or deliveries have been taken into account, following such adjustment (if any) as is required by Article 10(1) of the Commission Regulation (which concerns the fat content of milk), and 'used quota' shall be construed accordingly;

'wholesale producer' means a producer who delivers milk to a purchaser;

'wholesale quota' means the quantity of milk which may be delivered to a purchaser by a producer in a quota year without that producer being liable to pay levy;

'wholesale quota holder' means a person in whose name wholesale quota is registered pursuant to regulation 4; and

'working day' means any day other than a Saturday, a Sunday, Christmas Day, Good Friday or a day which is a bank holiday under the Banking and Financial Dealings Act 1971.

(2) In these Regulations any reference to anything done in writing or produced in written form includes a reference to an electronic communication which has been recorded and is capable of being subsequently reproduced.

(3) Other expressions which are used—

(a) in these Regulations; and
(b) in the Community legislation,

shall have the same meaning as in the Community legislation and cognate expressions shall be construed accordingly.

NOTES

Initial Commencement

Specified date: 31 March 2005: see reg 1.

Amendment

Para (1): in definition 'Commission Regulation' words ', as amended by Commission Regulation (EC) No 1468/2006 (OJ No L274, 5.10.2006, p 6)' in square brackets inserted by SI 2007/106, reg 2(1), (2)(a).

Date in force: 31 March 2007: see SI 2007/106, reg 1.

Para (1): definition 'Commission Regulation 1756/93' (omitted) revoked by SI 2007/106, reg 2(1), (2)(b).

Date in force: 31 March 2007: see SI 2007/106, reg 1.

Para (1): in definition 'the Community legislation' words 'and the Commission Regulation' in square brackets substituted by SI 2007/106, reg 2(1), (2)(c).

Date in force: 31 March 2007: see SI 2007/106, reg 1.

Para (1): in definition 'the Council Regulation' words from ', as amended by' to '(OJ No L265, 26.9.2006, p 8)' in square brackets inserted by SI 2007/106, reg 2(1), (2)(d).

Date in force: 31 March 2007: see SI 2007/106, reg 1.

A1.603

3   Application

Except as otherwise provided, these Regulations apply to relevant persons in respect of whom the Secretary of State is the relevant competent authority.

NOTES

Initial Commencement

Specified date: 31 March 2005: see reg 1.

PART 2: REGISTRATION OF QUOTA

A1.604

4   Registers and notices to be maintained and prepared by the Secretary of State

(1)   The Secretary of State must—

  (a)   maintain a direct sales register; and
  (b)   send to each direct seller a copy of the entry in the direct sales register relating to him.

(2)   The direct sales register must contain an entry in respect of each direct seller setting out in particular—

  (a)   his name;
  (b)   his trading address;
  (c)   a reference number which serves to identify him;
  (d)   the direct sales quota available to him for the quota year; and
  (e)   the details of his direct sales.

(3)   The Secretary of State must—

  (a)   maintain a wholesale register;
  (b)   send to each wholesale producer a copy of the entry in the wholesale register relating to him; and
  (c)   send to each purchaser named in the list referred to in paragraph (4)(e) a copy of that part of the entry relating to his purchaser quota.

(4)   The wholesale register must contain an entry in respect of each wholesale producer setting out in particular—

  (a)   his name;
  (b)   his trading address;
  (c)   a reference number which serves to identify him;
  (d)   the wholesale quota available to him for the quota year; and
  (e)   a list of the name and address of each purchaser whose purchaser quota will be calculated to take into account all or part of that wholesale producer's total wholesale quota, and of the wholesale quota registered with each purchaser, showing the representative fat content base of that quota calculated in accordance with Article 7 of the Commission Regulation.

(5)   The Secretary of State must—

  (a)   maintain a register of purchasers; and
  (b)   send to each purchaser a copy of the purchaser entry relating to him.

(6)   The register of purchasers must contain an entry in respect of each purchaser setting out in particular—

1818

(a)   his name; and
(b)   his purchaser quota.

(7)   For the purposes of paragraphs (1) to (4), where the holding of a quota holder comprises more than one dairy enterprise, that quota holder may, after submitting to the Secretary of State a consent or sole interest notice in respect of that holding, agree with the Secretary of State the partition of the quota available to that quota holder relating to that holding between separate direct sales register entries or separate wholesale register entries, as the case may be.

(8)   The Secretary of State—

(a)   may make such enquiries as she reasonably considers necessary for the purposes of ensuring the accuracy of the registers which she is required to maintain under this regulation;
(b)   must amend the registers—
  (i)   to record any allocation or adjustments made under or by virtue of these Regulations, or
  (ii)   to make any correction or amendment which she reasonably considers to be necessary; and
(c)   must notify any person affected by any correction or amendment made by her.

(9)   Notwithstanding that a person is no longer a producer, he must—

(a)   remain registered pursuant to this regulation; and
(b)   for the purposes of this regulation and regulations, 6, 7(a) and 33(1), continue to be regarded as a producer,

until the start of the quota year following the year in which the quota available to him has been transferred or until the quota has been withdrawn under Article 15 of the Council Regulation.

(10)   The obligation under paragraphs (1)(b), (3)(b) and (c) and (5)(b) is an obligation to send a copy of—

(a)   an entry; or
(b)   part of an entry,

as the case may be, as it has effect on 1st April in each year.

NOTES

Initial Commencement

Specified date: 31 March 2005: see reg 1.

A1.605

5   Approval of purchasers

(1)   For the purposes of Article 23 of the Commission Regulation (which concerns the approval of purchasers), a purchaser must make an application to the Secretary of State for approval in such form as the Secretary of State may reasonably require.

(2)   An application under paragraph (1) must state the purchaser's trading address, or, if there is more than one such address, each such address and his principal trading address.

(3)   For the purposes of Article 23(2) of the Commission Regulation (which permits member States to lay down stricter rules on the approval of purchasers), the Secretary of State may only approve a purchaser if the purchaser has complied with the requirements of paragraph (4).

(4) The requirements referred to in paragraph (3) are that the purchaser—

(a) has given an undertaking to the Secretary of State to comply with the provisions of these Regulations and the Community legislation;

(b) has not materially contravened the provisions of any scheme for support in the agricultural sector derived from legislation; and

(c) either—

(i) by submitting to the Secretary of State such information as she may reasonably require, has demonstrated to the reasonable satisfaction of the Secretary of State that he has a sound financial basis upon which to operate, or

(ii) if the Secretary of State considers that the purchaser has not been trading long enough for that to be so demonstrated, has provided such security as the Secretary of State may reasonably require.

(5) Each purchaser must inform the Secretary of State of—

(a) any change in his trading address, or, where there is more than one such address, any change in any such trading address, any additional trading address and any change in his principal trading address; and

(b) any factor or change in circumstances which the Secretary of State might reasonably consider materially to affect any matter that was relevant to her consideration of his application for approval, or which affects his ability to comply with the undertaking referred to in paragraph (4)(a).

(6) Each purchaser must—

(a) confirm to each producer supplying him that he is approved pursuant to Article 23 of the Commission Regulation and this regulation and provide details of the approval if requested; and

(b) notify each producer supplying him if the approval is withdrawn.

NOTES

Initial Commencement

Specified date: 31 March 2005: see reg 1.

A1.606

6   Obligations of producers and purchasers with respect to registration and deliveries

(1) Every—

(a) direct seller; and
(b) wholesale producer,

must register his quota with the Secretary of State.

(2) Each purchaser must maintain, in respect of all wholesale producers whose register entries include that purchaser's name on the list referred to in regulation 4(4)(e)—

(a) a register corresponding to that maintained by the Secretary of State under regulation 4(3) in respect of that part of his purchaser quota attributable to each of those producers;

(b) a register of particulars of deliveries from each of those producers to that purchaser; and

(c)   the information required by paragraphs 2 to 4 of Article 24 of the Commission Regulation (which concerns the records required in connection with levy assessment).

(3)   Each person who holds registered wholesale quota, including any producer who has temporarily ceased or who intends temporarily to cease making deliveries, must register his quota with a purchaser.

(4)   A wholesale producer may supply milk only to a purchaser.

(5)   Each purchaser must maintain a system approved by the Secretary of State for—

(a)   sampling the milk of each wholesale producer whose register entries include the purchaser's name on the list referred to in regulation 4(4)(e); and
(b)   determining its fat content.

(6)   Each purchaser must amend the register referred to in paragraph (2)(a) on each occasion when he is notified by the Secretary of State that the equivalent register maintained by the Secretary of State has been amended in relation to wholesale producers registered in that purchaser's register.

NOTES

Initial Commencement

Specified date: 31 March 2005: see reg 1.

A1.607

7   Inspection of entries in the Secretary of State's registers

If a request—

(a)   is made in respect of a register entry referred to in regulation 4(2) or (4) by any person who—
 [(i)   is the quota holder identified in that entry, or
  (ii) gives the Secretary of State a statement in writing that he has an interest in the holding of the quota holder identified in that entry; or]
(b)   is made by a purchaser in respect of an entry in the register referred to in regulation 4(6) relating to himself,

the Secretary of State may, on payment of a reasonable charge, supply to the person making the request a copy of the register entry.

NOTES

Initial Commencement

Specified date: 31 March 2005: see reg 1.

Amendment

In para (a) sub-paras (i), (ii) substituted, for sub-paras (i)–(iii) as originally enacted, by SI 2007/106, reg 2(1), (3).

Date in force: 31 March 2007: see SI 2007/106, reg 1.

A1.608

8   Registers as evidence

In any proceedings, any entry in a register which the Secretary of State is required by these Regulations to maintain is evidence of the matters stated in it.

NOTES

Initial Commencement

Specified date: 31 March 2005: see reg 1.

PART 3: TRANSFERS OF QUOTA

A1.609

9   Transfer of quota with transfer of land: general

(1)   Subject to regulations 14 and 16, this regulation applies for the purposes of Article 17 of the Council Regulation (which concerns the transfer of quota with a holding when the holding is sold, leased, transferred by inheritance or subjected to other cases of transfer involving comparable legal effects for producers) in respect of a transfer of a holding or part of a holding.

(2)   The transferee of the holding or the part of the holding must submit to the Secretary of State—

(a)   a notice of transfer in such form; and
(b)   such other information relating to the transfer,

as the Secretary of State may reasonably require.

(3)   The notice of transfer must reach the Secretary of State [no later than 31st March in the quota year in which the transfer takes place].

(4)   The information referred to in paragraph (2)(b) must reach the Secretary of State within such time as the Secretary of State may reasonably require.

(5)   The notice of transfer must include—

(a)   statements from the transferor and transferee specifying the amounts of used and unused quota transferred;
(b)   in the case of a transfer of part of a holding—
   (i)   statements from the transferor and transferee to the effect that they have agreed that the quota is to be apportioned taking account of the areas used for milk production as specified in the notice of transfer or that no such apportionment has been agreed, and
   (ii)   where such an apportionment has been agreed, a consent or sole interest notice, provided by the transferor in respect of the holding; and
(c)   in the case of a transfer of the whole of a holding, a consent or sole interest notice, provided by the transferor in respect of the holding.

NOTES

Initial Commencement

Specified date: 31 March 2005: see reg 1.

Amendment

Para (3): words 'no later than 31st March in the quota year in which the transfer takes place' in square brackets substituted by SI 2007/106, reg 2(1), (4).

Date in force: 31 March 2007: see SI 2007/106, reg 1.

A1.610

10   Transfer of part of holding

(1)   Subject to regulations 14 and 16, this regulation applies where there is a transfer of part of a holding.

(2)   Subject to regulations 11(4) and (5) and 12, where a notice of transfer has been duly submitted in accordance with regulation 9, an apportionment of the quota relating to the holding must—

(a)   be made in accordance with the agreed apportionment set out in that notice; or

(b)   if there is no such agreement, be determined by arbitration in accordance with Schedule 1.

(3)   Subject to paragraph (4) and regulations 11(4) and (5) and 12, any dairy produce which has been—

(a)   the subject of a direct sale; or

(b)   delivered,

from the holding during the quota year in which the change of occupation takes place and prior to the transfer of the part of the holding is treated for the purposes of any levy calculation as if it was sold, transferred free of charge or delivered, as the case may be, from each part of the holding in proportion to the apportionment under paragraph (2).

(4)   Paragraph (3) does not apply if the parties agree otherwise and submit to the Secretary of State a notice of that agreement.

(5)   A notice referred to in paragraph (4) must be submitted—

(a)   in such form as the Secretary of State may reasonably require; and

(b)   at the same time as the submission of the notice of transfer in accordance with regulation 9.

NOTES

Initial Commencement

Specified date: 31 March 2005: see reg 1.

A1.611

11   Prospective apportionment of quota

(1)   Where the occupier of a holding requires a prospective apportionment of quota relating to that holding, he must apply for such an apportionment to the Secretary of State in such form as the Secretary of State may reasonably require, requesting either—

(a)   that a prospective apportionment of quota relating to the holding be made taking account of areas used for milk production as set out in the application; or

(b)   that a prospective apportionment of quota be determined by arbitration in accordance with Schedule 1.

(2)   A request for a prospective apportionment may be withdrawn by a notice in writing given to the Secretary of State by the person who made the request.

(3)   If the occupier of a holding—

(a) requests that a prospective apportionment be made in accordance with paragraph (1)(a); or

(b) gives notice of the withdrawal of such a request in accordance with paragraph (2),

the request or notice must be accompanied by a consent or sole interest notice in respect of the holding.

(4) Subject to paragraph (6), where there is a change of occupation of part of a holding and within the period of six months ending with the date of that change of occupation—

(a) the occupier of the holding—

(i) has requested a prospective apportionment of quota in respect of that part of the holding, and

(ii) has duly submitted a notice of transfer in accordance with regulation 9, indicating that an apportionment of quota has been agreed; or

(b) a prospective apportionment of quota relating to that part of that holding has been or is in the process of being determined by arbitration under Schedule 1,

paragraph (5) applies.

(5) The apportionment of quota must be carried out in accordance with—

(a) the prospective apportionment of quota relating to that part of that holding made or determined following a request under paragraph (1) unless the request for that prospective apportionment was withdrawn before the change of occupation to which it relates takes place; or

(b) if no such prospective apportionment has been made or determined, but one is in the process of being made or determined, the prospective apportionment of quota relating to that part of that holding which is in the process of being made or determined under paragraph (1); or

(c) in any other case, regulation 10(2).

(6) Paragraph (4) does not apply to a change of occupation to which regulation 16(1) applies.

NOTES

Initial Commencement

Specified date: 31 March 2005: see reg 1.

A1.612

12   Cases where apportionment of quota by arbitration is required

(1) This regulation applies where—

(a) there is a transfer of part of a holding; and

(b) the Secretary of State has reasonable grounds for believing that the areas used for milk production on the holding—

(i) are not as specified in a notice duly submitted pursuant to regulation 9 or an application duly submitted pursuant to regulation 11(1)(a), or

(ii) in a case where no such notice or no such application have been duly submitted, were not fully taken into account by the parties at the time of apportionment.

(2) The Secretary of State may give notice that she has reasonable grounds for believing the matters referred to in paragraph (1)(b)—

    (a)   to the person who submitted the notice or application referred to in paragraph (1)(b)(i); or,

    (b)   in the case where neither was submitted, to the quota holder of the holding in question.

(3)   Where the Secretary of State gives a notice under paragraph (2), the apportionment or prospective apportionment of the quota concerned is to be determined by arbitration in accordance with Schedule 1.

NOTES

Initial Commencement

Specified date: 31 March 2005: see reg 1.

A1.613

13   Transfer of quota without transfer of land

(1)   This regulation is subject to regulation 16(2) and (3).

(2)   This regulation applies where the competent authorities in England, Wales, Scotland and Northern Ireland have jointly determined, in accordance with paragraphs (1)(e) and (2) of Article 18 of the Council Regulation, that within each United Kingdom quota region transfer of quota without transfer of the corresponding land is authorised.

(3)   A transferee of quota for whom the Secretary of State is the relevant competent authority must submit to her a notice of any such transfer within the general quota region in such form as the Secretary of State may reasonably require.

(4)   The notice must reach the Secretary of State no later than 31st March in the quota year in which the transfer takes place and must include—

    (a)   statements by the transferor and transferee that they have agreed to the transfer of quota, stating the amounts of used and unused quota transferred;

    (b)   a consent or sole interest notice given by the transferor in respect of the holding from which the quota is to be transferred; and

    (c)   a statement by the transferee that he is a producer.

(5)   Where the Secretary of State has received a notice pursuant to paragraph (3), she may require the transferor or transferee to produce such other information relating to the transfer, and within such time, as the Secretary of State may reasonably require.

(6)   In this regulation—

    (a)   'general quota region' means the United Kingdom other than the Scottish Islands area; and

    (b)   'United Kingdom quota region' means a Scottish Islands area or the general quota region.

NOTES

Initial Commencement

Specified date: 31 March 2005: see reg 1.

A1.614

14   Retention of quota at the end of a tenancy

(1)   This regulation has effect as respects tenancies ending after 31st March 2005.

(2)   Where—

(a)   a tenant of any land in a holding has quota registered as available to him;

(b)   the quota is so registered by virtue of a transfer referred to in regulation 13 the cost of which was not borne by the tenant's landlord;

(c)   the tenancy of the land in question expires without any possibility of renewal on similar terms;

(d)   the tenant and his landlord have not agreed that, after the expiry of the tenancy, the quota should no longer be available to the tenant; and

(e)   the tenant continues to be a producer after the expiry of the tenancy in relation to—

(i)   another holding, or

(ii)   another part of the holding of which the land formed part,

the tenant may submit a notice to the Secretary of State that the quota is to be available to him by virtue of his occupation of that other holding or that other part of the holding of which the land formed part.

(3)   A notice submitted pursuant to paragraph (2) must—

(a)   be in such form as the Secretary of State may reasonably require;

(b)   reach the Secretary of State no later than 31st March in the quota year in which the tenancy expires; and

(c)   include a statement by the tenant—

(i)   that he and his landlord have not agreed that, after the expiry of the tenancy, the quota should be registered in relation to the holding which then comprises or, as the case may be, includes, the land, stating the amounts of used and unused quota involved, and

(ii)   that he continues to be a producer.

(4)   Where a tenant submits a notice pursuant to this regulation, he shall not be entitled to receive compensation under paragraph 1 of Schedule 1 to the Agriculture Act 1986 on the termination of the tenancy in question.

NOTES

Initial Commencement

Specified date: 31 March 2005: see reg 1.

A1.615

15   Temporary transfer of quota

(1)   Subject to regulation 16(2), for the purposes of Article 16 of the Council Regulation (which concerns the temporary transfer of quota), a producer may agree with another producer to make a temporary transfer to that other producer of any unused quota which is registered under regulation 4 as permanently held by the producer if other quota (whether or not unused) remains so registered.

(2)   Quota may only be temporarily transferred pursuant to paragraph (1) for such period as shall end on the 31st March in the quota year in which the transfer takes place.

(3) The Secretary of State may require a reasonable charge to be paid for the registration of any temporary transfer of quota if, before the quota year in which the transfer takes place, she has announced that she intends to make such a charge in respect of such transfers in that year in such a manner as she considers likely to come to the attention of producers.

(4) Where there is an agreement to make a temporary transfer pursuant to paragraph (1), the transferee must submit to the Secretary of State notice of the agreement, together with any charge payable under paragraph (3), so that the notice and any charge reach her no later than 31st March in the quota year in which the transfer takes place.

(5) A notice referred to in paragraph (4) must be in such form as the Secretary of State may reasonably require.

NOTES

Initial Commencement

Specified date: 31 March 2005: see reg 1.

A1.616

16 Restrictions on transfer of quota

(1) No person may transfer quota on the grant or termination of—

   (a) a licence to occupy land; or
   (b) a tenancy of any land under which a holding, or part of a holding, is occupied for a period of less than ten months.

(2) No person may transfer quota if the transfer would result in an increase or reduction in the total wholesale quota or the total direct sales quota available for use by dairy enterprises located within a Scottish Islands area.

(3) No person may transfer[, as unused,] quota that is necessary to cover—

   (a) deliveries, after an adjustment for fat content; and
   (b) direct sales,

made by him before the date of the transfer.

NOTES

Initial Commencement

Specified date: 31 March 2005: see reg 1.

Amendment

Para (3): words ', as unused,' in square brackets inserted by SI 2006/120, regs 2, 3.

Date in force: 31 March 2006: see SI 2006/120, reg 1.

A1.617

17 Consequences of failure duly to submit a transfer notice

(1) This regulation applies if a notice of transfer is not duly submitted in accordance with regulation 9 or 13.

(2) Any unused quota transferred is not to be treated as a part of the transferee's quota entitlement for the relevant quota year, but is to be treated as if it remained unused quota and available where appropriate for reallocation by the Secretary of State in that quota year in accordance with regulation 27 or 30.

(3) The transfer of quota has effect only from the beginning of the quota year in which the notice of transfer is received.

(4) The amount of quota, if any, which has been reallocated to the transferee under regulations 27 or 30 for the relevant quota year (or any subsequent year) shall not be varied to take the transfer into account until the quota year in which the transfer notice is received.

(5) In this regulation 'relevant quota year' means—

    (a) in the case of a notice that should have been submitted in accordance with regulation 9, the quota year in which the transfer of the holding or the part of the holding takes effect; and

    (b) in the case of a notice that should have been submitted in accordance with regulation 13, the quota year in which the transfer of quota takes effect.

NOTES

Initial Commencement

Specified date: 31 March 2005: see reg 1.

PART 4: ALLOCATIONS AND ADJUSTMENTS OF QUOTA

A1.618

18   Allocation from national reserve

The Secretary of State may make allocations from the national reserve in accordance with the Community legislation.

NOTES

Initial Commencement

Specified date: 31 March 2005: see reg 1.

A1.619

19   Temporary reallocation of quota

(1) This regulation applies where a producer has quota registered as his in relation to a holding which—

    (a) at any time during a quota year is in whole or in part subject to a notice served, or declaration made, under an order made pursuant to section 17(1) of the Animal Health Act 1981 prohibiting or regulating the movement of dairy cows; or

    (b) is situated wholly or partly within an area which at any time during a quota year has been designated by an order made pursuant to section 1 of the Food and Environment Protection Act 1985.

(2) For the purposes of the reallocation of quota referred to in Article 10(3) of the Council Regulation and subject to paragraph (10), the Secretary of State may award to a producer a temporary reallocation of an amount of any surplus quota in accordance with the provisions of paragraphs (3) to (5).

(3)   An award may only be made for a quota year in which the notice, declaration or order referred to in paragraph (1) has effect or remains in force.

(4)   The amount of any such award is the lower of—

    (a)   the amount equal to 16 litres per qualifying cow per qualifying day in the quota year referred to in paragraph (3); and

    (b)   the amount by which the producer's production exceeds his quota entitlement in that quota year.

(5)   An award to a producer under this regulation is not available in respect of a quota year during which the producer—

    (a)   transfers unused quota pursuant to regulation 9 or 13;

    (b)   makes a temporary transfer of quota pursuant to regulation 15; or

    (c)   purchases cows or in-calf heifers for dairy purposes,

unless the Secretary of State is satisfied that the agreement to transfer, temporarily to transfer or to purchase, was entered into before the service of the notice or the making of the declaration referred to in paragraph (1)(a) or, as the case may be, the coming into force of the order referred to in paragraph (1)(b).

(6)   If a producer requires an award of a temporary reallocation of quota under this regulation, he must submit to the Secretary of State an application in such form as the Secretary of State may reasonably require.

(7)   An application referred to in paragraph (6) must reach the Secretary of State no later than 30th April following the end of the quota year in which the holding, or part of the holding, in question, was—

    (a)   subject to a relevant notice or a relevant declaration; or

    (b)   situated in an area designated by a relevant order.

(8)   If the Secretary of State awards to a producer a temporary reallocation of an amount of any surplus quota in accordance with this regulation, the Secretary of State must notify each purchaser to whom the producer makes deliveries of that reallocation.

(9)   The Secretary of State can make an award of a temporary reallocation of quota only from the aggregate of the amounts of quota referred to in regulation 27(3)(a) and 30(9)(a) once the aggregate has been determined under those regulations.

(10)   An eligible heifer which is a qualifying cow for the purposes of a quota year shall not be a qualifying cow for the purposes of any subsequent quota year.

(11)   In this regulation—

    (a)   'eligible heifer' means a qualifying heifer which calves for the first time on a relevant calving day;

    (b)   'qualifying cow', for the purposes of a quota year, means an eligible heifer which calves for the first time at a time when the number of eligible heifers exceeds the replacement number, whether or not the time of such calving falls during that quota year;

    (c)   'qualifying heifer' means a heifer which either—

      (i)   at the date of service of a relevant notice or the making of a relevant declaration, was on land subject to that notice or, as the case may be, that declaration; or

      (ii)   at the date of the coming into force of a relevant order, was on land subject to that order;

    (d)   'qualifying day', in relation to any qualifying cow, means the day on which it calves and each later day or part of a later day during which the relevant notice, the relevant declaration or the relevant order in question has effect or, as the case may be, remains in force;

(e) 'relevant declaration' means a declaration referred to in paragraph (1)(a);

(f) 'relevant notice' means a notice referred to in paragraph (1)(a);

(g) 'relevant order' means an order referred to in paragraph (1)(b).

(12) In this regulation, 'relevant calving day', in relation to a qualifying heifer, means a day which falls—

(a) in a case where the relevant notice, the relevant declaration or the relevant order in question has effect or is in force for a period which expires at or before the end of the quota year during which it is served or, as the case may be, made, within the period of twelve months ending with the date on which that notice, declaration or order ceases to have effect or, as the case may be, to be in force; and

(b) in any other case, within the quota year during which the relevant notice, the relevant declaration or the relevant order is served or made or at any later time when the relevant notice, the relevant declaration or the relevant order has effect or is in force.

(13) In this regulation, 'replacement number' means the nearest whole number to 20% of the total number of dairy cows on land—

(a) in a case where the land is subject to a relevant notice or a relevant declaration, as at the date of service of that notice or declaration; or

(b) in a case where the land is subject to a relevant order, as at the date of the coming into force of that order,

and where 20% of the total number is half way between two whole numbers, the nearest even whole number is deemed to be the nearest one.

NOTES

Initial Commencement

Specified date: 31 March 2005: see reg 1.

A1.620

20   Special allocation of quota

(1) This regulation applies if by reason of a mistake made by the Secretary of State—

(a) a person has not been allocated any quota; or

(b) has been allocated a smaller quantity of quota than he would have been allocated if the mistake had not been made.

(2) The Secretary of State may allocate to that person from the national reserve such quota as will compensate, in whole or in part, for that mistake.

NOTES

Initial Commencement

Specified date: 31 March 2005: see reg 1.

A1.621

21   Conversion of quota: general

(1) For the purposes of—

(a) the provisions of Article 6(2) and (5) of the Council Regulation (which concern changes from direct sales to delivery and vice versa); and

(b) Article 11(2) of the Council Regulation (which concerns replacements of purchasers and changes of purchasers by producers),

a producer may apply to convert direct sales quota to wholesale quota or wholesale quota to direct sales quota either temporarily or permanently.

(2) If a producer wishes to convert quota in any quota year, he must submit to the Secretary of State an application in such form as the Secretary of State may reasonably require—

(a) stating—

(i) the amount (if any) of that producer's direct sales quota, wholesale quota, direct sales and deliveries for the quota year in which the application is made,

(ii) the amount of unused quota which he holds at the time of the application, and

(iii) the amount which he wishes the Secretary of State to convert; and

(b) including such other information as the Secretary of State may reasonably require in order to assess whether the requirements of Article 6(2) and (5) of the Council Regulation and Article 7 of the Commission Regulation (which concerns representative fat content) are met.

(3) The application must reach the Secretary of State—

(a) in the case of a permanent conversion of quota, not later than 31st December in the quota year in which the conversion is intended to take effect; and

(b) in the case of a temporary conversion of quota, not later than 14th May in the year following the end of the quota year in which that temporary conversion is intended to take effect.

NOTES

Initial Commencement

Specified date: 31 March 2005: see reg 1.

A1.622

22   Conversion of quota: restriction on transfers of converted quota in conversion year

(1) This regulation does not apply to permanently converted quota which is transferred with a holding pursuant to Article 17 of the Council Regulation.

(2) Subject to paragraphs (3) and (6), where a producer has permanently converted quota in any quota year, he must not transfer later in that quota year quota of the type to which he has converted, whether temporarily or otherwise.

(3) Where a producer who has permanently converted quota in any quota year applies to the Secretary of State for a release from the restriction in paragraph (2), the Secretary of State, being satisfied as to the matters set out in paragraph (5), may release that producer from that restriction.

(4) A release from the restriction in paragraph (2) shall be to the extent necessary to allow the transfer of the amount of quota that the Secretary of State considers has remained unused in the particular case.

(5) The matters referred to in paragraph (3) are—

(a) that, as regards the producer, exceptional circumstances have resulted in a significant fall in milk production or a significant failure to achieve a planned increase in milk production; and

(b) those circumstances could not have been foreseen or avoided by the producer at the time of his permanent conversion of quota.

(6) The restriction in paragraph (2) does not apply if—

(a) in a case where the permanent conversion is from direct sales quota to wholesale quota, the producer temporarily converted direct sales quota to wholesale quota in the immediately preceding quota year; or

(b) in a case where the permanent conversion is from wholesale quota to direct sales quota, the producer temporarily converted wholesale quota to direct sales quota in the immediately preceding quota year.

(7) The following are examples of circumstances which are to be taken to be exceptional for the purposes of paragraph (5)—

(a) the death of the producer or his inability to conduct his business for a prolonged period as a result of the onset of ill-health, injury or disability;

(b) a natural disaster seriously affecting the holding;

(c) the accidental destruction of buildings used for the purposes of milk production;

(d) an outbreak of illness or disease seriously affecting the dairy herd;

(e) the serving of a notice or the making of a declaration under an order made pursuant to section 17(1) of the Animal Health Act 1981 or the making of an order pursuant to section 1 of the Food and Environment Protection Act 1985;

(f) the loss of a significant proportion of the forage area as a result of the compulsory purchase of the holding or a part of the holding; and

(g) where the transferee is a tenant, the serving of a notice to quit coming within any case specified in Part I of Schedule 3 to the Agricultural Holdings Act 1986.

NOTES

Initial Commencement

Specified date: 31 March 2005: see reg 1.

A1.623

23   Adjustment of purchaser quota

(1) Where a quota holder's wholesale quota is increased or reduced in accordance with the Community legislation or these Regulations, the purchaser quota of any purchaser to whom that wholesale quota is applicable is correspondingly increased or reduced.

(2) As regards a transaction to which Article 11(2) of the Council Regulation applies (which concerns replacements of purchasers and changes of purchasers by producers), a purchaser whose purchaser quota has been increased by virtue of such a transaction must submit to the Secretary of State an application for his purchaser quota to be increased by the specified amount.

(3) An application referred to in paragraph (2) must include—

(a) a statement setting out the particulars of the transaction; and

(b) a declaration made and signed by the producer that the purchaser whose purchaser quota is to decrease has been notified of the particulars set out in the application referred to in paragraph (2).

(4) The application referred to in paragraph (2)—

(a) must [be sent to the Secretary of State on or before] 14th May in the quota year immediately following that in which the transaction took place; and

(b) must be made in such form as the Secretary of State may reasonably require.

(5) The specified amount must not include the remaining registered wholesale quota except so far as the increase registered in pursuance of paragraph (8) includes that quota.

(6) The remaining registered wholesale quota shall remain available to the original purchaser.

(7) If insufficient quota is registered with the original purchaser to cover deliveries made by the producer before the date of change of purchaser, any additional quota obtained by a producer is to be allocated to the original purchaser until all deliveries to the original purchaser made by the producer before that date are covered after any adjustment for butterfat content in accordance with Article 10(1) of the Commission Regulation.

(8) At the beginning of the quota year immediately following the quota year in which the increase referred to in paragraph (2) took place, the purchaser quota of the purchaser with whom the producer is newly registered is to be increased by such part of the remaining registered wholesale quota of the producer as is included in the specified amount.

(9) If the amount of quota necessary to cover the deliveries made to an original purchaser is affected by—

(a) a transfer of quota to the producer under these Regulations; or

(b) an adjustment for butterfat content in accordance with Article 10(1) of the Commission Regulation,

then, subject to paragraph (10), the Secretary of State must make such adjustments in the purchaser quota of the original purchaser, and of the purchaser with whom the producer is newly registered, as are required to ensure that sufficient quota is registered with the original purchaser to cover deliveries made.

(10) The Secretary of State must make an adjustment pursuant to paragraph (9) after the end of the quota year in question.

(11) Where a producer has quota registered with two or more purchasers, the producer may apply to the Secretary of State temporarily to change the quota registered between them, except so far as the quota registered with each of them is necessary to cover the deliveries made by him before the date of the transfer after any adjustment for butterfat content in accordance with Article 10(1) of the Commission Regulation.

(12) A producer who makes an application to the Secretary of State pursuant to paragraph (11) must submit with his application—

(a) a statement setting out particulars of the quota to be temporarily re-registered; and

(b) a declaration made and signed by the producer that the purchaser whose purchaser quota is to decrease has been notified of the particulars set out in the statement.

(13) The statement and declaration referred to in paragraph (12)—

(a) must be in such form as the Secretary of State may reasonably require; and

(b) must reach the Secretary of State no later than 15th June in the quota year immediately following the quota year for which the temporary re-registration is requested.

(14) In this regulation—

(a) 'remaining registered wholesale quota' means the amount of quota necessary to cover the deliveries made by a producer before the date of the change of purchaser (adjusted in accordance with Article 10(1) of the Commission Regulation); and

(b) 'specified amount' means an amount equivalent to so much of a producer's registered wholesale quota as is specified by that producer.

NOTES

Initial Commencement

Specified date: 31 March 2005: see reg 1.

Amendment

Para (4): in sub-para (a) words 'be sent to the Secretary of State on or before' in square brackets substituted by SI 2006/120, regs 2, 4.

Date in force: 31 March 2006: see SI 2006/120, reg 1.

A1.624

24   Restriction on use of quota in Scottish Islands Area

(1) Quota registered under regulation 4 to quota holders within a Scottish Islands area may be used by producers and purchasers only against direct sales or deliveries of milk produced within that Scottish Islands area.

(2) If a quota holder has a part of his dairy enterprise outside a Scottish Islands area, he is treated for the purposes of this regulation as a quota holder within a Scottish Islands area if he has 50% or more of his dairy enterprise within that area.

(3) Paragraph (1) does not apply to the reallocation of quota undertaken in accordance with regulations 27 and 30.

NOTES

Initial Commencement

Specified date: 31 March 2005: see reg 1.

PART 5: THE LEVY

A1.625

25   Determination whether reduction in downward butterfat adjustment is required in relation to deliveries

(1) After the end of each quota year, the Secretary of State must make a determination of—

(a) the total volume of deliveries to purchasers; and

(b) the total volume of such deliveries after an adjustment for butterfat content in accordance with Article 10(1) of the Commission Regulation.

(2)   The determination under paragraph (1) must be made by reference to the summaries purchasers are required to submit to the Secretary of State for the purposes of Article 8(2) of the Commission Regulation.

(3)   If for any quota year a purchaser has not submitted the summaries so required or is unable to provide such proof of the volume of milk delivered to him in that year as the Secretary of State may reasonably require for the purposes of these Regulations, the Secretary of State must for the purposes of paragraph (1)—

(a)   make her own determination of that volume of milk based on all the information available to her for the purposes of calculating any levy payable on deliveries made to that purchaser; and

(b)   inform the purchaser of her determination.

(4)   If the volume referred to in paragraph (1)(a) exceeds that referred to in paragraph (1)(b), the Secretary of State must calculate the proportionate reduction required to be made in all downward butterfat adjustments that have previously been made in order to increase the volume referred to in paragraph (1)(b) so that it equals the volume referred to in paragraph (1)(a).

(5)   If paragraph (4) applies, the Secretary of State must—

(a)   notify all purchasers that any downward butterfat adjustments made by them in the deliveries to them are reduced; and

(b)   specify the reduction.

(6)   If the volume referred to in paragraph (1)(b) equals or exceeds that referred to in paragraph (1)(a), the Secretary of State must notify all purchasers that no such reduction need be made.

(7)   In this regulation, 'downward butterfat adjustment', in relation to deliveries to a purchaser, means an adjustment of the volume of the deliveries for butterfat content that results in that volume being reduced for the purposes of the levy calculation in accordance with Article 10(2) of the Council Regulation.

NOTES

Initial Commencement

Specified date: 31 March 2005: see reg 1.

A1.626

26   Determination whether levy on deliveries is payable

(1)   Where the total amount of the wholesale quota of producers, including converted quota, together with the total amount of wholesale quota in the national reserve exceeds whichever is the higher of—

(a)   the total volume of deliveries referred to in regulation 25(1)(a); or

(b)   the total volume of deliveries referred to in regulation 25(1)(b),

the Secretary of State must determine that no levy is payable on deliveries.

(2)   The Secretary of State must notify all purchasers of a determination made under paragraph (1).

(3)   Where the total amount of the wholesale quota of producers, including converted quota, together with the total amount of wholesale quota in the national reserve is less than whichever is the higher of—

(a)   the total volume of deliveries referred to in regulation 25(1)(a); or

(b)   the total volume of deliveries referred to in regulation 25(1)(b),

the Secretary of State must notify all purchasers that levy is payable on the higher volume of deliveries.

NOTES

Initial Commencement

Specified date: 31 March 2005: see reg 1.

A1.627

27   Reallocation of producers' quota

(1)   This regulation applies for the purposes of Article 10(3) of the Council Regulation (which concerns the calculation of levy on deliveries).

(2)   After the end of each quota year, the Secretary of State must determine for each producer the amount, if any, of unused quota available to that producer, taking into account any adjustment required under regulation 25(4) and the amount of any converted quota.

(3)   If the Secretary of State determines, pursuant to paragraph (2), that a producer has unused quota, she must—

(a)   add the total amount of unused quota to the national reserve;

(b)   subject to paragraph (4), make an award of any temporary reallocation of quota in accordance with regulation 19; and

(c)   having made such an award, reallocate any remaining amount of unused quota to any producers whose deliveries are in excess of their quotas in proportion to their respective quotas.

(4)   The amount of an award made under paragraph (3)(b) shall be reduced proportionately if there is insufficient quota after the Secretary of State has complied with paragraph (3)(a) to make a full award to all producers who are eligible to receive a temporary allocation of quota under regulation 19.

(5)   Subject to paragraph (6), if the total amount of unused quota available for reallocation to a producer under paragraph (3)(c) is not required by that producer to cover his butterfat-adjusted deliveries, the Secretary of State must reallocate the amount of unused quota not required amongst all producers whose butterfat-adjusted deliveries are in excess of their quota in proportion to their respective quotas.

(6)   No producer may receive any unused quota under paragraph (5) in excess of the amount of quota required by him to cover the amount by which his butterfat-adjusted deliveries exceed his quota.

(7)   In this regulation, 'butterfat-adjusted deliveries' means deliveries adjusted for butterfat content in accordance with Article 10(1) of the Commission Regulation.

NOTES

Initial Commencement

Specified date: 31 March 2005: see reg 1.

A1.628

28 Determination of liability for levy on deliveries

(1)   This regulation applies for the purposes of Article 10(3) of the Council Regulation (which concerns the calculation of levy on deliveries).

(2)   After the end of each quota year, the Secretary of State must—

    (a)   ascertain which producers have made deliveries which exceed the quota allocated to them after taking into account any adjustments made under regulations 25 and 27; then

    (b)   establish the total amount of the levy payable by each such producer at the rate of levy set in Article 2 of the Council Regulation; and then

    (c)   establish the total amount of levy payable by each purchaser on deliveries made to that purchaser.

NOTES

Initial Commencement

Specified date: 31 March 2005: see reg 1.

A1.629

29 Notification of levy liability

After the end of each quota year, the Secretary of State must—

    (a)   notify each purchaser of the total amount of levy payable on deliveries made to that purchaser; and

    (b)   give details to that purchaser of the amount of levy attributable to each producer who has made deliveries to that purchaser.

NOTES

Initial Commencement

Specified date: 31 March 2005: see reg 1.

A1.630

30 Determination of liability for levy on direct sales

(1)   This regulation applies for the purposes of Article 12 of the Council Regulation (which concerns the calculation of levy on direct sales).

(2)   After the end of each quota year, the Secretary of State must make a determination of the total quantity of dairy produce sold or transferred free of charge by direct sellers in the quota year in question.

(3)   A determination under paragraph (2) must be made by reference to the declarations direct sellers are required to submit to the Secretary of State in accordance with Article 11(2) of the Commission Regulation.

(4)   If for any quota year a direct seller has not submitted to the Secretary of State a declaration in accordance with that Article or is unable to provide such proof of the quantities of dairy produce sold or transferred free of charge by him in that year as the Secretary of State may reasonably require for the purposes of these Regulations, the Secretary of State must for the purposes of paragraph (2)—

    (a)   make her own determination of such quantities based on all the information available to her for the purposes of calculating any levy payable by that direct seller, and

    (b)   inform the direct seller of her determination.

(5) Where, in respect of a quota year—

    (a)   the total amount of direct sales quota of direct sales quota holders, including any converted quota; and

    (b)   the total amount of direct sales quota in the national reserve,

together exceed the total quantity determined by the Secretary of State under paragraph (2), the Secretary of State must determine that no levy in respect of direct sales is payable.

(6) The Secretary of State must notify all direct sales quota holders of her determination made under paragraph (5).

(7) Where, in respect of a quota year—

    (a)   the total amount of direct sales quota of direct sales quota holders, including any converted quota; and

    (b)   the total amount of direct sales quota in the national reserve,

together are less than the total quantity determined by the Secretary of State under paragraph (2), the Secretary of State must notify all direct sellers that levy is payable.

(8) After the end of each quota year, the Secretary of State must determine in respect of each direct sales quota holder the amount of any unused direct sales quota available to that direct sales quota holder in the quota year in question, taking into account any converted quota.

(9) If the Secretary of State determines under paragraph (8) that a direct sales quota holder has unused direct sales quota, she must—

    (a)   add that unused quota to the national reserve; and

    (b)   subject to paragraph (10), make such awards of temporary reallocation of quota under regulation 19 as she considers it appropriate to make.

(10) If, after the Secretary of State has complied with paragraph (9)(a), there is insufficient direct sales quota to make a full award under regulation 19 to each direct sales quota holder who is eligible to receive such an award, the amount of each award under paragraph (9)(b) shall be reduced proportionately.

(11) In respect of the quota year in question, the Secretary of State must then establish—

    (a)   the amount by which the total quantity referred to in paragraph (2) exceeds the total of—
        (i)   the direct sales quota of all direct sales quota holders, including converted quota, and
        (ii) the direct sales quota in the national reserve;

    (b)   the total amount of levy payable by direct sales quota holders by multiplying the amount determined under sub-paragraph (a) by the rate of levy set in Article 2 of the Council Regulation; and

    (c)   the amount by which the total quantity referred to in paragraph (2) exceeds all the direct sales quota of the direct sales quota holders whose direct sales are greater than their quota.

(12) The Secretary of State must establish the rate of levy per litre to be paid by each direct sales quota holder by dividing the amount determined in accordance with paragraph (11)(b) by the amount determined in accordance with paragraph (11)(c).

(13) The Secretary of State must—

(a) ascertain which direct sales quota holders have sold or transferred free of charge dairy produce in excess of the quota available to them including any converted quota and any quota temporarily reallocated by an award under paragraph (9)(b);

(b) establish the total amount of levy payable by each such direct sales quota holder at the rate of levy established in accordance with paragraph (12); and

(c) notify each direct sales quota holder of the total amount of levy payable by him.

(14) If a direct seller fails to submit to the Secretary of State in accordance with Article 11(2) of the Commission Regulation a declaration of the total quantity of dairy produce sold or transferred free of charge by him in a quota year, the rate of levy per litre to be paid by that direct seller on the quantity not notified or determined under paragraph (4) is the rate set in Article 2 of the Commission Regulation.

NOTES

Initial Commencement

Specified date: 31 March 2005: see reg 1.

A1.631

31   Payment and recovery of levy

(1) In respect of the collection of levy, the Secretary of State is the competent authority for the purposes of the Community legislation.

(2) For the purposes of—

(a) Article 11(1) of the Council Regulation (which concerns payment of levy by purchasers in respect of deliveries);

(b) Article 12(4) of the Council Regulation (which concerns payment of levy by direct sellers);

(c) Article 8 of the Commission Regulation (which concerns statements by purchasers of deliveries by producers); and

(d) Article 11 of the Commission Regulation (which concerns declarations of direct sales by producers),

the levy and penalties referred to in those provisions must be paid to the Secretary of State.

(3) Paragraph (4) applies for the purposes of Article 11(3) of the Council Regulation (which concerns deduction of levy liability) where a producer making deliveries to a purchaser exceeds his wholesale quota.

(4) Following any adjustment of the quantity delivered in accordance with Article 10(1) of the Commission Regulation, the purchaser may immediately deduct from the sums owed to the producer in respect of the deliveries an amount corresponding to the amount of levy that would otherwise be payable by him in respect of the excess.

(5) Where any part of the levy remains unpaid after [30th September] in any year, the Secretary of State may recover the amount of the levy outstanding at that date together with interest in respect of each day after that date until that amount is recovered—

(a) from the direct seller or, as the case may be, the purchaser; or

(b) from the producer, in a case within paragraph (4) where—

(i) the purchaser has not paid the levy, and

(ii) the producer has not paid the purchaser the levy either directly or by deduction and the purchaser is not taking steps to recover it from him.

(6) Interest under paragraph (5) is payable at the rate of one percentage point above the sterling three month London interbank offered rate.

(7) If—

    (a) a purchaser has not been approved pursuant to regulation 5; or

    (b) a purchaser has had his approval withdrawn by the Secretary of State pursuant to Article 23(3) of the Commission Regulation,

subject to paragraph (8), the Secretary of State may require any levy payable by the purchaser that has not been paid by him to be paid in such proportions as she may reasonably require by any producers whose deliveries to that purchaser have given rise to the liability for levy.

(8) Paragraph (7) does not apply in respect of a producer who has paid the purchaser in question, either directly or by deduction, the levy payable by that producer.

NOTES

Initial Commencement

Specified date: 31 March 2005: see reg 1.

Amendment

Para (5): words '30th September' in square brackets substituted by SI 2007/106, reg 2(1), (5).

Date in force: 31 March 2007: see SI 2007/106, reg 1.

A1.632

32   Prevention of avoidance of levy

(1) Subject to paragraphs (2) and (3), if—

    (a) a producer ('A') makes sales or deliveries of milk or milk products in any quota year from milk produced by any cows; and

    (b) later in the same quota year another producer ('B') makes sales or deliveries of milk or milk products from milk produced by any or all of the same cows,

B is deemed for the purposes of these Regulations to have made those sales or deliveries as agent of A.

(2) Paragraph (1) does not apply if—

    (a) an agreement has been entered into by A for the sale or lease of the cows in question to B;

    (b) the cows are kept on B's holding; and

    (c) after the making of the agreement—

        (i) B is actively involved in the management of the herd which the cows mentioned in paragraph (1)(b) comprise and production from it, and

        (ii) A has no further involvement in that management and production.

(3) Paragraph (1) does not apply if—

    (a) B has inherited the cows in question from A; and

    (b) the cows are kept on B's holding.

NOTES

Initial Commencement

Specified date: 31 March 2005: see reg 1.

PART 6: INFORMATION AND RECORDS

A1.633

33 Information

(1) Every relevant person must provide such information to the Secretary of State as the Secretary of State may reasonably require to perform her functions under these Regulations and the Community legislation.

(2) Each purchaser must provide the Secretary of State with such information as she may reasonably require relating to deliveries made or to be made to the purchaser by such person or persons as the Secretary of State may identify for the purpose of monitoring deliveries in relation to the total national reference quantity for the United Kingdom referred to in Article 1(3) and Annex I of the Council Regulation.

(3) The information referred to in paragraph (2) must be provided—

  (a) for such periods; and
  (b) in such form,

as the Secretary of State may reasonably require.

(4) The information referred to in paragraph (2) must be submitted so as to reach the Secretary of State before the expiry of the period of three working days beginning with the end of the period to which the information relates or within seven working days beginning with the date of notification of the requirement, whichever is the later.

(5) Each purchaser must [send to the Secretary of State] a list of those quota holders registered with that purchaser at 31st March in each quota year (whether they have been so registered for the whole or part of that quota year) who—

  (a) hold quota in respect of that quota year that has not been acquired by temporary transfer for that quota year; and
  (b) have not made deliveries to that purchaser during that quota year,

[on or before] 14th May following the end of that quota year.

(6) The Secretary of State must provide each purchaser with a copy of such information as the purchaser may reasonably require for the purposes of—

  (a) that purchaser's registration obligations under regulation 6; and
  (b) Article 8 of the Commission Regulation (which concerns the submission of summaries of producers' statements of deliveries or declarations that no deliveries have been received).

NOTES

Initial Commencement

Specified date: 31 March 2005: see reg 1.

Amendment

Para (5): words 'send to the Secretary of State' in square brackets substituted by SI 2006/120, regs 2, 5(a).

Date in force: 31 March 2006: see SI 2006/120, reg 1.

Para (5): words 'on or before' in square brackets substituted by SI 2006/120, regs 2, 5(b).

Date in force: 31 March 2006: see SI 2006/120, reg 1.

A1.634

34 Keeping and retention of records

(1) For the purposes of Article 17 of the Commission Regulation (which requires member States to take all necessary measures to ensure that the levy is correctly charged), a relevant person must comply with the requirements of paragraph (2) in addition to meeting any relevant requirement of paragraphs 2 to 6 of Article 24 of the Commission Regulation (which concerns record keeping obligations of purchasers and producers).

(2) The requirements referred to in paragraph (1) are—

(a) to keep and retain such records; and
(b) to comply with sub-paragraph (a) for such periods,

as are specified in Schedule 2.

(3) Paragraph (1) is without prejudice to regulation 3 of the Common Agricultural Policy (Protection of Community Arrangements) Regulations 1992.

NOTES

Initial Commencement

Specified date: 31 March 2005: see reg 1.

A1.635

35 Annual declarations and summaries

(1) If—

(a) a producer in whose name any direct sales quota is registered pursuant to regulation 4 fails to [send] to the Secretary of State any declaration which he is required to [send] by Article 11(2) of the Commission Regulation ... on or before 14th May in any year; or
(b) a purchaser fails to [send] any summary which he is required to [send] to her by Article 8(2) of the Commission Regulation ... on or before 14th May in any year,

the Secretary of State may recover a reasonable charge from that producer or that purchaser, as the case may be, in respect of any visit to any premises which she reasonably considers an authorised officer should make in order to obtain the declaration or summary in question.

(2) If the Secretary of State sends to a purchaser a revised version of a summary [sent] by him in accordance with Article 8(2) of the Commission Regulation, the purchaser must submit either—

(a) confirmation that the revised version is agreed; or
(b) amendments to the revised version,

so that such confirmation or amendments, as the case may be, reach the Secretary of State before the expiry of the period of ten working days beginning with the date on which the revised version was sent to the purchaser.

(3)   In this regulation, 'authorised officer' means a person (whether or not an officer of the Secretary of State) who is authorised by the Secretary of State, either generally or specifically, to act in matters arising under these Regulations and the Community legislation.

NOTES

Initial Commencement

Specified date: 31 March 2005: see reg 1.

Amendment

Para (1): in sub-para (a) word 'send' in square brackets in both places it occurs substituted by SI 2006/120, regs 2, 6(a)(i).

Date in force: 31 March 2006: see SI 2006/120, reg 1.

Para (1): in sub-para (a) words omitted revoked by SI 2006/120, regs 2, 6(a)(ii).

Date in force: 31 March 2006: see SI 2006/120, reg 1.

Para (1): in sub-para (b) word 'send' in square brackets in both places it occurs substituted by SI 2006/120, regs 2, 6(b)(i).

Date in force: 31 March 2006: see SI 2006/120, reg 1.

Para (1): in sub-para (b) words omitted revoked by SI 2006/120, regs 2, 6(b)(ii).

Date in force: 31 March 2006: see SI 2006/120, reg 1.

Para (2): word 'sent' in square brackets substituted by SI 2006/120, regs 2, 6(c).

Date in force: 31 March 2006: see SI 2006/120, reg 1.

PART 7: PENALTIES AND MISCELLANEOUS PROVISIONS

A1.636

36   Administrative penalties

(1)   Subject to the provisions of Article 23(4) of the Commission Regulation (which authorises member States not to impose penalties in certain circumstances) and paragraph (5), purchasers are subject to the administrative penalties specified in paragraphs [(2A) and (3)].

(2)   ...

[(2A)Where a purchaser—

    (a)   sends to the Secretary of State a summary of producers' statements required to be submitted under Article 8(2) of the Commission Regulation, which is inaccurate; and

    (b)   by doing so causes an overstatement or an understatement by him, of deliveries made to him,

he is liable to pay to the Secretary of State a penalty equivalent to the theoretical amount of levy that would be due on 0.5% of the quantity by volume of milk which comprises the overstatement or understatement.]

(3)   Where a purchaser fails to maintain accurate and updated records pursuant to Article 24(2) of the Commission Regulation and regulation 34, he is liable to pay to the Secretary of State a penalty equivalent to the theoretical amount of the levy that would be due on 0.5% of the quantity by volume of milk concerned.

(4) For the purposes of the third sub-paragraph of Article 11(3) of the Commission Regulation (which requires member States to impose proportionate penalties where producers submit incorrect declarations), and subject to the provisions of Article 11(5) of that Regulation (which authorises member States not to impose penalties in certain circumstances) and to paragraph (5), where a direct seller submits an annual declaration which overstates or understates the volume of direct sales for the quota year covered by that declaration, he is liable to pay to the Secretary of State—

(a) in the case of an overstatement, a penalty equivalent to the theoretical amount of levy that would be due on 0.5% of the quantity by volume of the milk which comprises the overstatement;

(b) in the case of an understatement, a penalty equivalent to the theoretical amount of levy that would be due on 0.5% of the quantity by volume of the milk which comprises the understatement,

except in any case where, for the quota year covered by the declaration, he is liable to pay to the Secretary of State levy which exceeds that amount.

(5) Notwithstanding anything in [paragraphs (2A), (3), (4) and (6A)], the penalties referred to in those paragraphs—

(a) in the case of purchasers and direct sellers, are not to be less than £60;

(b) in the case of purchasers, are not to exceed £60,000; and

(c) in the case of direct sellers, are not to exceed £600.

[(6) Subject to Article 8(5) of the Commission Regulation, if a purchaser fails to submit a summary required to be submitted under Article 8(2) of the Commission Regulation, by the end of the period specified in Article 8(4), he is liable to pay to the Secretary of State a penalty equivalent to the theoretical amount of levy that would be due on 0.01% of the quantity by volume of milk covered by that declaration for each day of the period of the delay in the submission reaching the Secretary of State.]

[(6A) Subject to paragraphs (5) and (7), where a purchaser fails to provide or submit to the Secretary of State—

(a) an application, statement or declaration concerning the adjustment of purchaser quota in accordance with regulation 23(2) to (4);

(b) information in accordance with regulation 33(2) to (4); or

(c) a confirmation or amendments relating to a revised version of a summary in accordance with regulation 35(2),

he is liable to pay to the Secretary of State a penalty equivalent to the theoretical amount of levy that would be due on 0.01% of the quantity by volume of milk covered by that application, statement, declaration or revised version, or that information, for each day of the period of delay in the submission reaching the Secretary of State.]

(7) A purchaser is not liable to pay a penalty under paragraph [(6A)] if, in the opinion of the Secretary of State, the failure—

(a) was neither deliberate nor the result of serious negligence;

(b) is negligible in terms of the functioning of the scheme or the effectiveness of the checks; or

(c) is attributable to force majeure.

NOTES

Initial Commencement

Specified date: 31 March 2005: see reg 1.

Amendment

Para (1): words '(2A) and (3)' in square brackets substituted by SI 2007/106, reg 2(1), (6)(a).

Date in force: 31 March 2007: see SI 2007/106, reg 1.

Para (2): revoked by SI 2007/106, reg 2(1), (6)(b).

Date in force: 31 March 2007: see SI 2007/106, reg 1.

Para (2A): inserted by SI 2006/120, regs 2, 7(b).

Date in force: 31 March 2006: see SI 2006/120, reg 1.

Para (5): words 'paragraphs (2A), (3), (4) and (6A)' in square brackets substituted by SI 2007/106, reg 2(1), (6)(c).

Date in force: 31 March 2007: see SI 2007/106, reg 1.

Para (6): substituted by SI 2007/106, reg 2(1), (6)(d).

Date in force: 31 March 2007: see SI 2007/106, reg 1.

Para (6A): inserted by SI 2007/106, reg 2(1), (6)(e).

Date in force: 31 March 2007: see SI 2007/106, reg 1.

Para (7): reference to '(6A)' in square brackets substituted by SI 2007/106, reg 2(1), (7).

Date in force: 31 March 2007: see SI 2007/106, reg 1.

A1.637

37   Withholding or recovery of compensation

(1)   Where—

   (a)   a producer has submitted an application for compensation in accordance with the Community compensation scheme; and
   (b)   it appears to the Secretary of State that the producer has—
      (i)   made a false or misleading statement in his application, or
      (ii)   failed to comply with any of the requirements of the scheme,

the Secretary of State may withhold, or recover on demand from that producer, the whole or any part of the compensation payable or paid to him.

(2)   In this regulation, 'Community compensation scheme' means the scheme instituted by Council Regulation (EC) No 2330/98 providing for an offer of compensation to certain producers of milk and milk products temporarily restricted in carrying out their trade and Commission Regulation (EC) No 2647/98 laying down detailed rules for the application of Council Regulation (EC) No 2330/98.

NOTES

Initial Commencement

Specified date: 31 March 2005: see reg 1.

A1.638

38   Confiscation of quota

(1)   In pursuance of Article 15 of the Council Regulation (which relates to the confiscation and restoration of quota in cases of inactivity), the Secretary of State must notify a quota holder that his quota has been taken into the national reserve if it

appears from information available to the Secretary of State that he has made no deliveries or direct sales during the previous quota year.

(2) ...

(3) Any quota withdrawn pursuant to Article 15 of the Council Regulation must be placed in the national reserve with effect from 1st April following the quota year for which information became available to the Secretary of State indicating to her that no deliveries or no direct sales, as the case may be, were made.

(4) A wholesale quota holder or direct sales quota holder who receives a notification of confiscation under paragraph (1) or, as the case may be, paragraph (2) must notify any person with an interest in the land comprised in the holding in question of the contents of that notification before the expiry of the period of 28 days beginning with the day on which he received it.

NOTES

Initial Commencement

Specified date: 31 March 2005: see reg 1.

Amendment

Para (2): revoked by SI 2007/106, reg 2(1), (8).

Date in force: 31 March 2007: see SI 2007/106, reg 1.

A1.639

39   Restoration of quota

(1) Subject to the second sub-paragraph of Article 15(1) of the Council Regulation (which specifies the time limit for quota restoration), a person whose quota has been taken into the national reserve may request the Secretary of State to restore to him the quota in respect of the holding from which it was confiscated or in respect of part of that holding if he is a producer.

(2) Subject to paragraph (3), a request under paragraph (1)—

    (a)   must reach the Secretary of State—
        (i) no later than the end of the quota year to which it relates, or
        (ii) in the case of confiscation of quota notified [under article 11(4) of the Commission Regulation], no later than the end of the quota year before the quota year in which the quota is to be restored; and
    (b)   in a case falling within sub-paragraph (a)(ii), must include the declaration which the person making the request failed to submit under Article 11 of the Commission Regulation.

(3) Where—

    (a)   there is a change of occupation of all or part of the holding in respect of which quota has been taken into the national reserve; and
    (b)   the new occupier is a producer,

the new occupier may submit a request to the Secretary of State to restore to him the quota relating to that holding or part holding before the expiry of the time limit for quota restoration specified by the second sub-paragraph of Article 15(1) of the Council Regulation.

(4) A request for restoration of quota to part of a holding made under paragraph (1) or (3) must include—

(a) a statement of the agreed apportionment of quota taking account of the areas used for milk production, signed by every person with an interest in the land comprised in the holding; or

(b) a statement requesting apportionment of the quota in accordance with an arbitration under paragraphs 1(5), 3(2), 4 and 6 to 34 of Schedule 1.

(5) Where quota is restored to part of a holding in accordance with a request made under paragraph (1) or (3), the amount of quota to be restored to that part must be determined in accordance with the apportionment referred to in paragraph (4)(a) or (b).

NOTES

Initial Commencement

Specified date: 31 March 2005: see reg 1.

Amendment

Para (2): in sub-para (a)(ii) words 'under article 11(4) of the Commission Regulation' in square brackets substituted by SI 2007/106, reg 2(1), (9).

Date in force: 31 March 2007: see SI 2007/106, reg 1.

A1.640

40   Offences and criminal penalties

(1) A person is guilty of an offence if—

(a) being a relevant person, he fails without reasonable excuse to comply with a requirement imposed on him by or under these Regulations or the Community legislation; or

(b) in connection with these Regulations or the Community legislation, he—
   (i) makes or causes to be made a statement, or uses or causes to be used a document, which he knows to be false in a material particular, or
   (ii) recklessly makes or causes to be made a statement, or recklessly uses or causes to be used a document, which is false in a material particular; or

(c) disposes of quota which he knows or might reasonably be expected to know is incorrectly registered in his name.

(2) A person guilty of an offence under paragraph (1) is liable—

(a) on summary conviction, to a fine not exceeding the statutory maximum, or to imprisonment for a term not exceeding three months, or to both; or

(b) on conviction on indictment, to a fine, or to imprisonment for a term not exceeding two years, or to both.

(3) The Secretary of State may, following any conviction under paragraph (1)(b) against which there is no subsisting right of appeal or further appeal, by notice served on the person whose quota that conviction relates withdraw from him such quota as may reasonably be regarded by the Secretary of State as obtained by him by reason of the falsehood upon which the conviction was founded.

(4) A notice served under paragraph (3) may not be served after the expiry of the period of twelve months beginning with the first day on which the notice may be served.

(5) Where an offence under this regulation which has been committed by a body corporate is proved to have been committed with the consent or connivance of, or to be attributable to any neglect on the part of, any director, manager, secretary or similar

officer of the body corporate, or any person who was purporting to act in any such capacity, he as well as the body corporate is deemed to be guilty of that offence and is liable to be proceeded against and punished accordingly.

(6)   Where the affairs of a body corporate are managed by its members, the provisions of paragraphs (1) and (2) apply in relation to the acts and defaults of a member in connection with his functions of management as if he were a director of the body corporate.

(7)   In this regulation 'requirement' does not include any restriction or obligation in or under regulations 11(1) and (3), 14(3), 16, 19(6) and (7), 21(2) and (3), 22(2), 23(12) and (13) and 39(2) and (4).

NOTES

Initial Commencement

Specified date: 31 March 2005: see reg 1.

A1.641

41   Revocations and amendments

(1)   The Dairy Produce Quotas Regulations 2002 and the Dairy Produce Quotas (Amendment) Regulations 2004 are revoked.

(2)   In article 8(3)(b) of the Milk Development Council Order 1995, for the words 'the Dairy Produce Quotas Regulations 2002' there are substituted 'the Dairy Produce Quotas Regulations 2005'.

NOTES

Initial Commencement

Specified date: 31 March 2005: see reg 1.

SCHEDULE 1
APPORTIONMENT AND PROSPECTIVE APPORTIONMENT BY ARBITRATION

Regulations 10(2) 11, 12(3) and 39(4)

Appointment and remuneration of arbitrator

A1.642

1   (1)   Subject to sub-paragraph (2), in any case where an apportionment is to be carried out by arbitration, an arbitrator must be appointed by agreement between the transferor and transferee, and the transferee must give notice of the appointment of the arbitrator to the Secretary of State.

(2)   The transferor or the transferee may at any time make an application to the President of the Royal Institution of Chartered Surveyors (referred to in this Schedule as 'the President') for the appointment of an arbitrator ..., and the person who makes such an application to the President must give notice of that fact to the Secretary of State.

(3)   If an arbitrator has not been appointed by agreement between the transferor and the transferee and no application has been made to the President under sub-paragraph (2), the Secretary of State may make an application to the President for the appointment of an arbitrator.

(4) Where the Secretary of State gives a notice pursuant to regulation 12(2), she must make an application to the President for the appointment of an arbitrator and the Secretary of State must be a party to the arbitration.

(5) Where an apportionment under regulation 39(4)(b) is to be carried out by arbitration, the producer must either appoint an arbitrator by agreement with all persons with an interest in the holding or make an application to the President for the appointment of an arbitrator ...

2 (1) In any case where a prospective apportionment is to be made by arbitration, an arbitrator must be appointed—

  (a) where regulation 11(1)(b) or (4)(b) applies, by agreement between the occupier of the relevant holding and any other interested party, or, in default, by the President on an application by the occupier; and
  (b) where regulation 12(3) applies, by the President.

(2) Where sub-paragraph (1)(a) applies, the occupier must give notice to the Secretary of State of the appointment of the arbitrator pursuant to the agreement, or of the application to the President for the appointment of an arbitrator.

3 (1) An arbitrator appointed in accordance with paragraph 1(1) to (4) or 2 must conduct the arbitration in accordance with this Schedule and must base his award on findings made by him as to areas used for milk production in the last five-year period during which production took place before the change of occupation, or, in the case of a prospective apportionment, in the last five- year period during which production took place before the appointment of the arbitrator.

(2) An arbitrator appointed in accordance with paragraph 1(5) must conduct the arbitration in accordance with this Schedule and must base his award on findings made by him as to the areas used for milk production in the last five-year period during which production took place before the appointment of the arbitrator.

(3) An arbitrator appointed under any paragraph of this Schedule must base his award on findings made by him in accordance with the law in force at the time the event giving rise to an application for arbitration took place.

4 (1) No application may be made to the President for an arbitrator to be appointed by him under this Schedule unless the application is accompanied by the appropriate fee for such an application; but once the fee has been paid in connection with any such application no further fee is payable in connection with any subsequent application for the President to exercise any function exercisable by him in relation to the arbitration by virtue of this Schedule (including an application for the appointment by him in an appropriate case of a new arbitrator).

(2) In sub-paragraph (1), the 'appropriate fee' means such reasonable fee as the President may direct having regard to, and in no case exceeding, such fee as is for the time being prescribed under [section 84(4) of] the Agricultural Holdings Act 1986.

5 Where the Secretary of State makes an application to the President under paragraph 1(3) or (4), the fee payable to the President in respect of that application referred to in paragraph 4 is recoverable by the Secretary of State as a debt due from the other parties to the arbitration jointly or severally.

6 Any appointment of an arbitrator by the President must be made by him as soon as possible after receiving the application.

7 ...

8 If the arbitrator dies, or is incapable of acting, or for seven days after notice from any party requiring him to act fails to act, a new arbitrator may be appointed as if no arbitrator had been appointed.

9   No party to the arbitration may revoke the appointment of the arbitrator without the consent of any other party, and his appointment is not revoked by the death of any party.

10   Every appointment, application, notice, revocation and consent under paragraph 1, 2, 8 or 9 must be in writing.

11   (1)   The remuneration of the arbitrator—

   (a)   in a case where he is appointed by agreement between the parties, is such amount as may be agreed upon by him and the parties or, in default of agreement, fixed by the registrar of the county court (subject to an appeal to the judge of the court) on an application made by the arbitrator or any party;

   (b)   in a case where he is appointed by the President, is such amount as may be agreed upon by the arbitrator and the parties or, in default of agreement, fixed by the President.

(2)   The remuneration of the arbitrator is recoverable by the arbitrator as a debt due from the parties to the arbitration, jointly or severally.

Conduct of proceedings and witnesses

12   (1)   Subject to sub-paragraph (2), in any arbitration to which this Schedule applies, the arbitrator may join as a party to the arbitration any person having an interest in the holding, whether or not such person has applied to become a party to the arbitration, provided that such person consents to be so joined.

(2)   Where an apportionment pursuant to a request in a statement under regulation 39(4)(b) is to be carried out by arbitration, any person with an interest in the holding who has refused to sign such a statement as is referred to in regulation 39(4)(a) must be a party to the arbitration.

13   Within 35 days of the appointment of the arbitrator, or within such further period as the arbitrator may determine, the parties to the arbitration must deliver to him a statement of their respective cases with all necessary particulars and—

   (a)   no amendment or addition to the statement or particulars delivered is allowed after the expiry of the 35 days, or such further period as the arbitrator may determine, except with the consent of the arbitrator; and

   (b)   a party to the arbitration is confined at the hearing to the matters alleged in the statement and particulars delivered by him and any amendment or addition duly made.

14   The parties to the arbitration and all persons claiming through them must, subject to any legal objection, submit to being examined by the arbitrator, on oath or affirmation, in relation to the matters in dispute and must, subject to any such objection, produce before the arbitrator all samples and documents within their possession or power which may be required or called for, and do such other things as the arbitrator reasonably may require for the purposes of the arbitration.

15   Any person having an interest in the holding to which the arbitration relates is entitled to make representations to the arbitrator.

16   Witnesses appearing at the arbitration must, if the arbitrator thinks fit, be examined on oath or affirmation, and the arbitrator may administer oaths to, or take the affirmation of, the parties and witnesses appearing.

17   The provisions of county court rules as to the issuing of witness summonses apply, subject to such modifications as may be prescribed by such rules, for the purposes of the arbitration as if it were an action or matter in the county court.

18   (1)   Subject to sub-paragraphs (2) and (3), any person who—

(a) having been summoned in pursuance of county court rules as a witness in the arbitration refuses or neglects, without sufficient cause, to appear or to produce any documents required by the summons to be produced; or

(b) having been so summoned or being present at the arbitration and being required to give evidence, refuses to be sworn or give evidence,

forfeits such fine as the judge of the county court may direct.

(2) A judge may not direct under sub-paragraph (1) that a person forfeits a fine of an amount exceeding £400.

(3) No person summoned in pursuance of county court rules as a witness in the arbitration forfeits a fine under this paragraph unless there has been paid or tendered to him at the time of the service of the summons such reasonable sum in respect of his expenses as the arbitrator may direct (including, in appropriate cases, compensation for loss of time), having regard to such sums payable in such cases as may be prescribed for the purposes of section 55 of the County Courts Act 1984.

(4) The judge of the county court may at his discretion direct that the whole or any part of any such fine, after deducting costs, is applicable towards indemnifying a party injured by the refusal or neglect.

19 (1) Subject to sub-paragraph (2), upon application by any party to the arbitration, the judge of the county court may, if he thinks fit, issue an order under his hand for bringing before the arbitrator any person (in this paragraph referred to as 'the prisoner') confined in any place under any sentence or under committal for trial or otherwise, to be examined as a witness in the arbitration.

(2) No such order may be made with respect to a person confined under process in any civil action or matter.

(3) Subject to sub-paragraph (4), the prisoner mentioned in any such order must be brought before the arbitrator under the same custody, and dealt with in the same manner in all respects, as a prisoner required by a writ of habeas corpus to be brought before the High Court and examined there as a witness.

(4) The person having the custody of the prisoner is not bound to obey the order unless there is tendered to him a reasonable sum for the conveyance and maintenance of a proper officer or officers and of the prisoner in going to, remaining at, and returning from, the place where the arbitration is held.

20 The High Court may order that a writ of habeas corpus ad testificandum must issue to bring a prisoner for examination before the arbitrator, if that prisoner is confined in any prison under process in any civil action or matter.

Award

21 (1) Subject to sub-paragraph (2), the arbitrator must make and sign his award within 56 days of his appointment.

(2) The President may from time to time extend the time limited for making the award, whether that time has expired or not.

(3) The arbitrator must notify the terms of his award to the Secretary of State within eight days of delivery of that award.

(4) The award must fix a date not later than one month after the delivery of the award for the payment of any costs awarded under paragraph 25.

22 The award is final and binding on the parties and any persons claiming under them.

23 The arbitrator may correct any clerical mistake or error in the award arising from any accidental slip or omission.

Reasons for award

24 Where the arbitrator is requested by any party to the arbitration, on or before the making of the award, to make a statement, either written or oral, of the reasons for the award, the arbitrator must furnish such a statement.

Costs

25 The costs of and incidental to the arbitration and award are in the discretion of the arbitrator who may direct to and by whom and in what manner the costs, or any part of the costs, are to be paid. The costs for the purposes of this paragraph include any fee paid to the President in respect of the appointment of an arbitrator and any sum paid to the Secretary of State pursuant to paragraph 5.

26 On the application of any party, any such costs are taxable in the county court according to such of the scales prescribed by county court rules for proceedings in the county court as may be directed by the arbitrator under paragraph 25 or, in the absence of any such direction, by the county court.

27 (1) The arbitrator must, in awarding costs, take into consideration—

    (a) the reasonableness or unreasonableness of the claim of any party, whether in respect of the amount or otherwise;

    (b) any unreasonable demand for particulars or refusal to provide particulars; and

    (c) generally all the circumstances of the case.

(2) The arbitrator may disallow any costs which he considers to have been unnecessarily incurred, including the costs of any witness whom he considers to have been called unnecessarily.

Special case, setting aside award and remission

28 The arbitrator—

    (a) may state at any stage of the proceedings; and

    (b) must state, upon a direction in that behalf given by the judge of the county court following an application made by any party,

any question of law arising in the course of the arbitration and any question as to the jurisdiction of the arbitrator in the form of a special case for the opinion of the county court.

29 (1) Where the arbitrator has misconducted himself, the county court may remove him.

(2) Where—

    (a) the arbitrator has misconducted himself; or

    (b) an arbitration or award has been improperly procured; or

    (c) there is an error of law on the face of the award,

the county court may set the award aside.

30 (1) The county court may from time to time remit the award, or any part of the award, to the arbitrator for reconsideration.

(2) Paragraph (3) applies in any case where it appears to the county court that there is an error of law on the face of the award.

(3)   Instead of exercising its power of remission under sub-paragraph (1), the court may vary the award by substituting for so much of it as is affected by the error such award as the court considers that it would have been proper for the arbitrator to make in the circumstances.

(4)   An award varied pursuant to paragraph (3) has effect as so varied.

(5)   Where remission is ordered under sub-paragraph (1), the arbitrator must, unless the order otherwise directs, make and sign his award within 30 days of the date of the order.

(6)   If the county court is satisfied that the time for making the award is for any good reason insufficient, the court may extend or further extend that time for such period as it thinks proper.

Miscellaneous

31   Any amount paid, in respect of the remuneration of the arbitrator by any party to the arbitration in excess of the amount, if any, directed by the award to be paid by him in respect of the costs of the award, is recoverable from the other party or jointly from the other parties.

32   For the purposes of this Schedule, an arbitrator appointed by the President must be taken to have been so appointed at the time when the President executed the instrument of appointment, in accordance with the law in force at the time of such execution and in the case of any such arbitrator the periods mentioned in paragraphs 13 and 21 accordingly run from that time.

33   Any instrument of appointment or other document purporting to be made in the exercise of any function exercisable by the President under paragraph 1, 2, 6, 11 or 21 and to be signed by or on behalf of the President is to be taken to be such an instrument or document unless the contrary is shown.

34   The Arbitration Act 1996 does not apply to an arbitration determined in accordance with this Schedule.

NOTES

Initial Commencement

Specified date: 31 March 2005: see reg 1.

Amendment

Para 1: in sub-para (2) words omitted revoked by SI 2006/2805, art 18, Sch 3.

Date in force: 19 October 2006: see SI 2006/2805, art 1(1)(b).

Para 1: in sub-para (5) words omitted revoked by SI 2006/2805, art 18, Sch 3.

Date in force: 19 October 2006: see SI 2006/2805, art 1(1)(b).

Para 4: in sub-para (2) words 'section 84(4) of' in square brackets substituted by SI 2006/2805, art 18, Sch 1, Pt 2, para 4.

Date in force: 19 October 2006: see SI 2006/2805, art 1(1)(b).

Para 7: revoked by SI 2006/2805, art 18, Sch 3.

Date in force: 19 October 2006: see SI 2006/2805, art 1(1)(b).

SCHEDULE 2
KEEPING AND RETENTION OF RECORDS

Regulation 34(2)

Records to be kept by purchasers

A1.643

1   In respect of each quota year, a purchaser must keep, and retain for the relevant period, records comprising—

(a)   details of each producer making deliveries to him, including—
(i)   that producer's name and address,
(ii)   the wholesale quota available to that producer at the beginning and end of each quota year,
(iii)   the representative fat content (butterfat base) of the milk delivered by that producer, and
(iv)   the total quota available for all the producers who make deliveries to the purchaser and the weighted butterfat of that quota;

(b)   details, in terms of each delivery and each month, of the quantities of milk which each producer has delivered to him;

(c)   details of the cumulative total of the quantities delivered to him each month by all producers;

(d)   details of the average fat content of each producer's deliveries per month;

(e)   details of the weighted average fat content of the cumulative total referred to in sub-paragraph (c);

(f)   a list of purchasers and other undertakings which supply treated or processed milk or milk products to him;

(g)   details, in terms of each such purchaser or undertaking and each month, of the quantities supplied to him by that purchaser or undertaking;

(h)   details of the use to which milk and milk products collected from him has been put;

(i)   records of individual deliveries and supplies and accompanying collection documents identifying each delivery or supply by producer, purchaser or other undertaking; and

(j)   all books, registers, accounts, correspondence, commercial data, vouchers and supporting documents relating to his business activities.

Records to be kept by producers

2   (1)   In respect of each quota year, a direct seller must keep, and retain for the relevant period, records comprising—

(a)   details of the quota held by him, including any permanent and temporary transfers of quota if appropriate;

(b)   his herd records (comprising number and breed of cows and calved heifers in dairy herd with details of number of cows in milk and number of cows dry);

(c)   daily records of milk produced;

(d)   invoices of any feed purchased;

(e)   details recorded as a result of his participation in the National Milk Recording Scheme or other similar recording scheme;

(f)   details of quantities of milk processed, methods of processing and quantities and type of milk products produced;

(g)   details of quantities of whole milk used in the production of milk products (with conversion rates applied);

(h) [if he holds 4,855 or more litres of direct sales quota,] details of quantities and types of milk and milk products which are produced and used on his holding for stock feeding and human consumption;

(i) [if he holds 4,855 or more litres of direct sales quota,] details of quantities and types of milk and milk products which are disposed of (other than under paragraph (h)) or wasted on the holding;

(j) without prejudice to paragraph (i), details of any milk or milk products which—

  (i) were transported from his holding to be destroyed elsewhere for sanitary purposes pursuant to a decision of the Secretary of State or the Secretary of State for Health,

  (ii) were so destroyed, and

  (iii) as a consequence, are to be excluded from the levy calculation,

including information about the reason why such destruction was necessary and details of where, when and how such destruction occurred;

(k) details of quantities and types of milk and milk products sold directly to the consumer or transferred free of charge from his holding (including milk and milk products sold on his holding);

(l) details of quantities and types of milk and milk products purchased, exchanged or otherwise received by him, and records relating to their disposal; and

(m) details of stocks of milk and milk products held by him on a monthly basis.

(2) Where a direct seller also delivers milk or milk products to a purchaser, he must, in respect of each quota year, also keep, and retain for the relevant period, records comprising—

(a) details of quantities and types of milk and milk products delivered by him and the name and address of any purchaser involved;

(b) the payment slips issued in respect of any such purchaser; and

(c) where there is a discrepancy between a purchaser's payment slip and the relevant tanker receipt, that tanker receipt.

3 A wholesale quota holder who makes deliveries to a purchaser must, in respect of each quota year, keep, and retain for the relevant period, records, comprising—

(a) details of the quota held by him, showing permanent and temporary transfers of quota if appropriate;

(b) his herd records (comprising number and breed of cows and calved heifers in dairy herd with details of number of cows in milk and number of cows dry);

(c) daily records of milk produced;

(d) invoices of any feed purchased;

(e) details of quantities of milk delivered by him, and the name and address of the purchaser involved;

(f) the payment slips issued in respect of any such purchaser;

(g) where there is a discrepancy between a purchaser's payment slip and the relevant tanker receipt, that tanker receipt;

(h) details recorded as a result of his participation in the National Milk Recording Scheme or other similar recording scheme;

(i) details of quantities of milk produced and used on his holding for stock feeding and human consumption;

(j) details of quantities of milk which are disposed of (other than under sub-paragraph (i)) or wasted on the holding;

(k) without prejudice to sub-paragraph (j), details of any milk which—

  (i) was transported from his holding to be destroyed elsewhere for sanitary purposes pursuant to a decision of the Secretary of State or the Secretary of State for Health,

(ii) was so destroyed, and

(iii) as a consequence, is to be excluded from the levy calculation,

including information about the reason why such destruction was necessary and details of where, when and how such destruction occurred;

(l)   details of quantities and types of milk and milk products transferred free of charge from his holding;

(m) details of quantities of milk purchased, swapped or otherwise received, and records relating to its disposal; and

(n) details of stocks of milk produced on his holding.

Records to be kept by any person undertaking butterfat testing in a laboratory

4   Any person undertaking butterfat testing for a purchaser in a laboratory must keep, and retain for the relevant period, records comprising details of all samples of milk analysed, showing—

(a) the time and date the sample was taken on the holding;

(b) the time and date of his receipt of the sample;

(c) the time and date of the analysis;

(d) the identity of the purchaser concerned;

(e) the identity of the producer concerned (by name or reference number);

(f) the butterfat content of each sample recorded to two decimal places;

(g) the method of analysis used; and

(h) the results of any repeat analyses undertaken.

Records to be kept by hauliers

5   Any haulier collecting milk or milk products on behalf of a purchaser must keep, and retain for the relevant period, records comprising details of all quantities of milk or milk products so collected, showing—

(a) the time and date of collection from each producer;

(b) the time and date of sampling of the milk or milk products of each producer;

(c) the identity of the producer concerned;

(d) the volume of milk collected (including a copy of the tanker receipt in the cases referred to in paragraphs 2(2)(c) and 3(g));

(e) the identity of the purchaser concerned;

(f) the volume of milk delivered, and the name and address of each reception site;

(g) the sources of all the milk carried on each tanker; and

(h) details of any malfunction in any equipment used by him.

Records to be kept by processors

6   Any processor in receipt of milk or milk products for processing or treating must keep, and retain for the relevant period, records comprising details of all quantities of milk or milk products received, showing—

(a) the time and date of their delivery;

(b) their volume or weight per delivery (including copies of tanker receipts and weighbridge tickets in the cases referred to in paragraphs 2(2)(c) and 3(g));

(c) the name and address of the haulier concerned;

(d) the name and address of their vendor or donor;

(e) the quantities of milk processed, types of processing undertaken, and quantities and types of milk products produced;

(f) the quantities of milk used in the production of milk products (if not ascertainable from the information provided under sub-paragraph (e));

(g)   the calculated stocks of milk and milk products held by that processor at the end of each month and details of actual stocks physically held as at 31st March each year; and

(h)   the quantities of milk or milk products sold or otherwise disposed of, with the date of supply or disposal, and the names and addresses of the buyers or recipients concerned.

Records to be kept by persons buying, selling or supplying milk or milk products obtained directly from a producer or purchaser

7   Any person who in the course of a business buys, sells or supplies milk or milk products obtained directly from a producer or purchaser must keep, and retain for the relevant period, records comprising details of all quantities of milk or milk products received, showing—

(a)   the time and date of their receipt;

(b)   their volume or weight per delivery (including copies of tanker receipts or invoices in the cases referred to in paragraphs 2(2)(c) and 3(g));

(c)   the name and address of the haulier concerned;

(d)   the name and address of their vendor or donor;

(e)   the quantities of milk or milk products sold or supplied, with the date of sale or supply, and the names and addresses of the buyers or recipients concerned other than the consumers of such milk or milk products; and

(f)   the quantities of milk or milk products returned to the producer or purchaser unsold or unused, and the date of that return.

8   In this Schedule, in relation to any records—

'the relevant period' means the remainder of the year of record and a period of at least three years thereafter; and

'the remainder of the year of record' means, following the making of the records, the remainder of the year in which they were made.

NOTES

Initial Commencement

Specified date: 31 March 2005: see reg 1.

Amendment

Para 2: in sub-para (1)(h) words 'if he holds 4,855 or more litres of direct sales quota,' in square brackets inserted by SI 2007/106, reg 2(1), (10).

Date in force: 31 March 2007: see SI 2007/106, reg 1.

Para 2: in sub-para (1)(i) words 'if he holds 4,855 or more litres of direct sales quota,' in square brackets inserted by SI 2007/106, reg 2(1), (10).

Date in force: 31 March 2007: see SI 2007/106, reg 1.

DAIRY PRODUCE QUOTAS (GENERAL PROVISIONS) (AMENDMENT) REGULATIONS 2005

SI 2005/466

The Secretary of State is a Minister designated for the purposes of section 2(2) of the European Communities Act 1972 in relation to the common agricultural policy of the European Community:

The Secretary of State makes these Regulations in exercise of the powers conferred by section 2(2) of the European Communities Act 1972:

A1.644

1   Citation and commencement

These Regulations may be cited as the Dairy Produce Quotas (General Provisions) (Amendment) Regulations 2005 and shall come into force on 31st March 2005.

NOTES

Initial Commencement

Specified date: 31 March 2005: see above.

A1.645

2   Amendment of the Dairy Produce Quotas (General Provisions) Regulations 2002

Regulation 2 of the Dairy Produce Quotas (General Provisions) Regulations 2002 is amended as follows—

(a)   for the definition of 'the Commission Regulation', there is substituted—
"the Commission Regulation' means Commission Regulation (EC) No 595/2004 laying down detailed rules for applying Council Regulation (EC) No 1788/2003 establishing a levy in the milk and milk products sector;';

(b)   the definitions of 'Commission Regulation 2562/93' and 'Council Regulation 2055/93' are omitted;

(c)   for the definition of 'the Community legislation', there is substituted—
"the Community legislation' means the Council Regulation, the Commission Regulation, and Commission Regulation 1756/93;';

(d)   for the definition of 'the Council Regulation', there is substituted—
"the Council Regulation' means Council Regulation (EC) No 1788/2003 establishing a levy in the milk and milk products sector;';

(e)   in the definition of 'delivery', for the words 'Article 9(g)' there are substituted 'Article 5(f)';

(f)   for the definition of 'direct sale', there is substituted—
"direct sale' has the same meaning as in Article 5(g) of the Council Regulation;';

(g)   for the definition of 'direct sales quota', there is substituted—
"direct sales quota' means the quantity of dairy produce which may be sold or transferred free of charge by direct sale by a producer in a quota year without that producer being liable to pay levy;';

(h)   for the definition of direct seller, there is substituted—

"direct seller' means a producer who produces milk and treats that milk or processes it into milk products on his holding and subsequently sells or transfers free of charge that milk or those milk products without their having been further treated or processed by a different undertaking which treats or processes milk or milk products;';

(i) in the definition of 'holding', for the words 'Article 9(d)' there are substituted 'Article 5(d)';

(j) in the definition of 'national reserve', for all the words after 'in accordance with' there are substituted 'Article 14 of the Council Regulation';

(k) in the definition of 'producer', for the words 'Article 9(c)' there are substituted 'Article 5(c)';

(l) in the definition of 'purchaser', for the words 'Article 9(e)' there are substituted 'Article 5(e)';

(m) in the definition of 'quota year', for the words 'Article 1' there are substituted 'Article 1(1)';

(n) at the end of the definition of 'relevant person', there are added the words ', but does not include a consumer of milk or milk products';

(o) the definition of 'wholesale delivery' is omitted; and

(p) for the definition of 'wholesale quota', there is substituted—

"wholesale quota' means the quantity of milk which may be delivered to a purchaser by a producer in a quota year without that producer being liable to pay levy;'.

NOTES

Initial Commencement

Specified date: 31 March 2005: see reg 1.

DAIRY PRODUCE QUOTAS (WALES) REGULATIONS 2005

SI 2005/537 (W 47)

The National Assembly for Wales, being designated for the purposes of section 2(2) of the European Communities Act 1972 in relation to the common agricultural policy of the European Community, in exercise of powers conferred on it by virtue of the said section 2(2), hereby makes the following Regulations:—

PART 1: PRELIMINARY

A1.646

1 Citation and commencement

These Regulations may be cited as the Dairy Produce Quotas (Wales) Regulations 2005 and shall come into force on 31 March 2005.

NOTES

Initial Commencement

Specified date: 31 March 2005: see above.

A1.647

2   **Interpretation**

(1)   In these Regulations, unless the context otherwise requires—

'the Commission Regulation' (*'Rheoliad y Comisiwn'*) means Commission Regulation (EC) No 595/2004 laying down detailed rules for applying Council Regulation (EC) No 1788/2003 establishing a levy in the milk and milk products sector[, as last amended by Commission Regulation (EC) No 1468/2006 (OJ No L274, 5.10.2006, p 6)];
...
'the Community legislation' (*'deddfwriaeth y Gymuned'*) means the Council Regulation [and the Commission Regulation];

'competent authority' (*'awdurdod cymwys'*) has the meaning given by regulation 2 of the General Provisions Regulations;

'consent or sole interest notice' (*'hysbysiad cydsyniad neu hysbysiad unig fuddiant'*) means a notice, in relation to a holding, which states that—
   (a)   the person providing the notice is the occupier of that holding and that no other person has an interest in that holding or part of that holding; or
   (b)   every person having an interest in that holding or any part of it, the value of which interest might be reduced by the apportionment or prospective apportionment to which the notice relates, agrees to that apportionment or prospective apportionment;

'converted quota' (*'cwota addasedig'*) means quota converted by the National Assembly following an application made under regulation 21;

'the Council Regulation' (*'Rheoliad y Cyngor'*) means Council Regulation (EC) No 1788/2003 establishing a levy in the milk and milk products sector[, as last amended by Council Regulation (EC) No 1406/2006 (OJ No L265, 26.9.2006, p 8)];

'cow' (*'buwch'*) includes a heifer that has calved;

'dairy enterprise' (*'menter laeth'*) means an area stated by the occupier of that area to be run as a self-contained dairy produce business;

'dairy produce' (*'cynnyrch llaeth'*) means produce, expressed in kilograms or litres (one kilogram being 0.971 litres), in respect of which levy is payable;

'delivery' (*'danfon'*) has the same meaning as in Article 5(f) of the Council Regulation, and 'deliver' shall be construed accordingly;

'direct sale' (*'gwerthiant uniongyrchol'*) has the same meaning as in Article 5(g) of the Council Regulation;

'direct sales quota' (*'cwota gwerthiannau uniongyrchol'*) means the quantity of dairy produce which may be sold or transferred free of charge by direct sale by a producer in a quota year without that producer being liable to pay levy;

'direct sales quota holder' (*'deiliad cwota gwerthiannau uniongyrchol'*) means a person in whose name direct sales quota is registered pursuant to regulation 4;

'direct seller' (*'gwerthwr uniongyrchol'*) means a producer who produces milk and treats that milk or processes it into milk products on his holding and subsequently sells or transfers free of charge that milk or those milk products without their having been further treated or processed by a different undertaking which treats or processes milk or milk products;

'electronic communication' (*'cyfathrebu uniongyrchol'*) has the same meaning as in section 15 of the Electronic Communications Act 2000;

'the General Provisions Regulations' (*'y Rheoliadau Darpariaethau Cyffredinol'*) means the Dairy Produce Quotas (General Provisions) Regulations 2002;

'holding' (*'daliad'*) has the same meaning as in Article 5(d) of the Council Regulation;

'interest' (*'buddiant'*) includes a licence to occupy land and the interest of a mortgagee and a trustee, but does not include the interest of a beneficiary under a trust or settlement;

'levy' (*'ardoll'*) means the levy payable under the Community legislation and these Regulations to the National Assembly;

'milk' (*'llaeth'*) has the same meaning as in Article 5(a) of the Council Regulation;

'the National Assembly' (*'y Cynulliad Cenedlaethol'*) means the National Assembly for Wales;

'national reserve' (*'cronfa genedlaethol'*) has the meaning given it by regulation 2 of the General Provisions Regulations;

'occupier' (*'deiliad'*), in relation to land, includes the person entitled to grant occupation of that land to another, and, during the currency of an interest mentioned in regulation 16(1), the person entitled to grant occupation when that interest terminates, and 'occupation' shall be construed accordingly;

'producer' (*'cynhyrchwr'*) has the same meaning as in Article 5(c) of the Council Regulation;

'prospective apportionment' (*'dosraniad rhagolygol'*), in relation to quota in respect of a holding, means an apportionment of quota between the persons with an interest in the holding for the purposes of ascertaining the quota referable to a part of that holding in the event of a transfer of that part;

'purchaser' (*'prynwr'*) means a purchaser within the meaning of Article 5(e) of the Council Regulation and, other than in regulation 5(1) to (4) and regulation 31(7), approved by the National Assembly pursuant to regulation 5 and Article 23 of the Commission Regulation;

'purchaser quota' (*'cwota prynwr'*) means the quantity of milk which may be delivered to a purchaser during a quota year without any liability for levy arising;

'quota' (*'cwota'*) means direct sales quota or wholesale quota, as the case may be;

'quota holder' (*'deiliad cwota'*), in relation to quota, means the person in whose name the quota is registered;

'quota year' (*'blwyddyn gwota'*) means any of the periods of 12 months referred to in Article 1(1) of the Council Regulation (which concerns the introduction of the levy);

'registered wholesale quota' (*'cwota cyfanwerthol cofrestredig'*) means wholesale quota registered pursuant to regulation 4(3) and (4);

'relevant competent authority' (*'awdurdod cymwys perthnasol'*) has the meaning given by regulation 3 of the General Provisions Regulations;

'relevant person' (*'person perthnasol'*) means a producer, a purchaser, any employee or agent of a producer or of a purchaser, any milk haulier, any person undertaking butterfat testing for purchasers in a laboratory, a processor of milk or milk products, or any other person involved in the buying, selling or supply of milk or milk products obtained directly from a producer or purchaser, but does not include a consumer of milk or milk products;

'Scottish Islands area' (*'ardal Ynysoedd yr Alban'*) means either—

(a) the islands of Orkney except for the island of Stronsay; or

(b) the islands of Jura, Gigha, Arran, Bute, Great Cumbrae and Little Cumbrae, the Kintyre peninsula south of Tarbert and the areas of land within the Argyll and Bute District comprising those parts of the parishes of Dunoon and Kilmun and Inverchaolain shown bounded by a red line on a map marked 'Map referred to in sub-paragraph (b) of the definition of Scottish Islands area in regulation 2(1) of the Dairy Produce Quotas (Wales) Regulations 2005', dated 31 January 2005, signed on behalf of the National Assembly and deposited at its offices at Cathays Park, Cardiff CF10 3NQ;

'transferee' (*'trosglwyddai'*) means—

  (a) where quota is transferred with a holding or part of a holding, a person who replaces another as occupier of that holding or part of a holding; and

  (b) in any other case, the person to whom quota is transferred;

'transferor' ('*trosglwyddwr*') means

  (a) where quota is transferred with a holding or part of a holding, a person who is replaced by another occupier of that holding or part of a holding; and

  (b) in any other case, the person from whom quota is transferred;

'unused quota' ('*cwota nas defnyddiwyd*') means quota remaining unused after any direct sales or deliveries have been taken into account, following such adjustment (if any) as is required by Article 10(1) of the Commission Regulation (which concerns the fat content of milk), and 'used quota' shall be construed accordingly;

'wholesale producer' ('*cynhyrchwr cyfanwerthol*') means a producer who delivers milk to a purchaser;

'wholesale quota' ('*cwota cyfanwerethol*') means the quantity of milk which may be delivered to a purchaser by a producer in a quota year without that producer being liable to pay levy;

'wholesale quota holder' ('*deiliad cwota cyfanwerthol*') means a person in whose name wholesale quota is registered pursuant to regulation 4; and

'working day' ('*diwrnod gwaith*') means any day other than a Saturday, a Sunday, Christmas Day, Good Friday or a day which is a bank holiday under the Banking and Financial Dealings Act 1971.

(2) In these Regulations any reference to anything done in writing or produced in written form includes a reference to an electronic communication which has been recorded and is capable of being subsequently reproduced.

(3) Other expressions which are used—

  (a) in these Regulations; and
  (b) in the Community legislation,

shall have the same meaning as in the Community legislation and cognate expressions shall be construed accordingly.

NOTES

Initial Commencement

Specified date: 31 March 2005: see reg 1.

Amendment

Para (1): in definition 'the Commission Regulation' words ', as last amended by Commission Regulation (EC) No 1468/2006 (OJ No L274, 5.10.2006, p 6)' in square brackets inserted by SI 2007/844, reg 2(1), (2)(a).

Date in force: 31 March 2007: see SI 2007/844, reg 1.

Para (1): definition 'Commission Regulation 1756/93' (omitted) revoked by SI 2007/844, reg 2(1), (2)(b).

Date in force: 31 March 2007: see SI 2007/844, reg 1.

Para (1): in definition 'the Community legislation' words 'and the Commission Regulation' in square brackets substituted by SI 2007/844, reg 2(1), (2)(c).

Date in force: 31 March 2007: see SI 2007/844, reg 1.

Para (1): in definition 'the Council Regulation' words ', as last amended by Council Regulation (EC) No 1406/2006 (OJ No L265, 26.9.2006, p 8)' in square brackets inserted by SI 2007/844, reg 2(1), (2)(d).

Date in force: 31 March 2007: see SI 2007/844, reg 1.

A1.648

3 Application

Except as otherwise provided, these Regulations apply to relevant persons in respect of whom the National Assembly is the relevant competent authority.

NOTES

Initial Commencement

Specified date: 31 March 2005: see reg 1.

PART 2: REGISTRATION OF QUOTA

A1.649

4 Registers and notices to be maintained and prepared by the National Assembly

(1) The National Assembly must—

  (a) maintain a direct sales register; and
  (b) send to each direct seller a copy of the entry in the direct sales register relating to him or her.

(2) The direct sales register must contain an entry in respect of each direct seller setting out in particular—

  (a) his or her name;
  (b) his or her trading address;
  (c) a reference number which serves to identify him or her;
  (d) the direct sales quota available to him or her for the quota year; and
  (e) the details of his or her direct sales.

(3) The National Assembly must—

  (a) maintain a wholesale register;
  (b) send to each wholesale producer a copy of the entry in the wholesale register relating to him or her; and
  (c) send to each purchaser named in the list referred to in paragraph (4)(e) a copy of that part of the entry relating to his or her purchaser quota.

(4) The wholesale register must contain an entry in respect of each wholesale producer setting out in particular—

  (a) his or her name;
  (b) his or her trading address;
  (c) a reference number which serves to identify him or her;
  (d) the wholesale quota available to him or her for the quota year; and
  (e) a list of the name and address of each purchaser whose purchaser quota will be calculated to take into account all or part of that wholesale producer's total wholesale quota, and of the wholesale quota registered with each purchaser, showing the representative fat content base of that quota calculated in accordance with Article 7 of the Commission Regulation.

(5) The National Assembly must—

(a)   maintain a register of purchasers; and

(b)   send to each purchaser a copy of the purchaser entry relating to him or her.

(6)   The register of purchasers must contain an entry in respect of each purchaser setting out in particular—

(a)   his or her name; and

(b)   his or her purchaser quota.

(7)   For the purposes of paragraphs (1) to (4), where the holding of a quota holder comprises more than one dairy enterprise, that quota holder may, after submitting to the National Assembly a consent or sole interest notice in respect of that holding, agree with the National Assembly the partition of the quota available to that quota holder relating to that holding between separate direct sales register entries or separate wholesale register entries, as the case may be.

(8)   The National Assembly—

(a)   may make such enquiries as it reasonably considers necessary for the purposes of ensuring the accuracy of the registers which it is required to maintain under this regulation;

(b)   must amend the registers—

(i)   to record any allocation or adjustments made under or by virtue of these Regulations, or

(ii)   to make any correction or amendment which it reasonably considers to be necessary; and

(c)   must notify any person affected by any correction or amendment made by it.

(9)   Notwithstanding that a person is no longer a producer, he or she must—

(a)   remain registered pursuant to this regulation; and

(b)   for the purposes of this regulation and regulations, 6, 7(a) and 33(1), continue to be regarded as a producer,

until the start of the quota year following the year in which the quota available to him or her has been transferred or until the quota has been withdrawn under Article 15 of the Council Regulation.

(10)   The obligation under paragraphs (1)(b), (3)(b) and (c) and (5)(b) is an obligation to send a copy of—

(a)   an entry; or

(b)   part of an entry,

as the case may be, as it has effect on 1 April in each year.

NOTES

Initial Commencement

Specified date: 31 March 2005: see reg 1.

A1.650

5   Approval of purchasers

(1)   For the purposes of Article 23 of the Commission Regulation (which concerns the approval of purchasers), a purchaser must make an application to the National Assembly for approval in such form as the National Assembly may reasonably require.

(2)   An application under paragraph (1) must state the purchaser's trading address, or, if there is more than one such address, each such address and his or her principal trading address.

(3)   For the purposes of Article 23(2) of the Commission Regulation (which permits Member States to lay down stricter rules on the approval of purchasers), the National Assembly may only approve a purchaser if the purchaser has complied with the requirements of paragraph (4).

(4)   The requirements referred to in paragraph (3) are that the purchaser—

   (a)   has given an undertaking to the National Assembly to comply with the provisions of these Regulations and the Community legislation;

   (b)   has not materially contravened the provisions of any scheme for support in the agricultural sector derived from legislation; and

   (c)   either—

      (i)   by submitting to the National Assembly such information as it may reasonably require, has demonstrated to the reasonable satisfaction of the National Assembly that he or she has a sound financial basis upon which to operate, or

     (ii)   if the National Assembly considers that the purchaser has not been trading long enough for that to be so demonstrated, has provided such security as the National Assembly may reasonably require.

(5)   Each purchaser must inform the National Assembly of—

   (a)   any change in his or her trading address, or, where there is more than one such address, any change in any such trading address, any additional trading address and any change in his or her principal trading address; and

   (b)   any factor or change in circumstances which the National Assembly might reasonably consider materially to affect any matter that was relevant to its consideration of his or her application for approval, or which affects his or her ability to comply with the undertaking referred to in paragraph (4)(a).

(6)   Each purchaser must—

   (a)   confirm to each producer supplying him or her that he or she is approved pursuant to this regulation and provide details of the approval if requested; and

   (b)   notify each producer supplying him or her if the approval is withdrawn.

NOTES

Initial Commencement

Specified date: 31 March 2005: see reg 1.

A1.651

6   Obligations of producers and purchasers with respect to registration and deliveries

(1)   Every—

   (a)   direct seller; and

   (b)   wholesale producer,

must register his or her quota with the National Assembly.

(2) Each purchaser must maintain, in respect of all wholesale producers whose register entries include that purchaser's name on the list referred to in regulation 4(4)(e)—

(a)   a register corresponding to that maintained by the National Assembly under regulation 4(3) in respect of that part of his or her purchaser quota attributable to each of those producers;
(b)   a register of particulars of deliveries from each of those producers to that purchaser; and
(c)   the information required by paragraphs 2 to 4 of Article 24 of the Commission Regulation (which concerns the records required in connection with levy assessment).

(3) Each person who holds registered wholesale quota, including any producer who has temporarily ceased or who intends temporarily to cease making deliveries, must register his or her quota with a purchaser.

(4) A wholesale producer may supply milk only to a purchaser.

(5) Each purchaser must maintain a system approved by the National Assembly for—

(a)   sampling the milk of each wholesale producer whose register entries include the purchaser's name on the list referred to in regulation 4(4)(e); and
(b)   determining its fat content.

(6) Each purchaser must amend the register referred to in paragraph (2)(a) on each occasion when he or she is notified by the National Assembly that the equivalent register maintained by the National Assembly has been amended in relation to wholesale producers registered in that purchaser's register.

NOTES

Initial Commencement

Specified date: 31 March 2005: see reg 1.

A1.652

7   Inspection of entries in the National Assembly's registers

If a request—

(a)   is made in respect of a register entry referred to in regulation 4(2) or (4) by any person who—
   [(i)   is the quota holder identified in that entry, or
   (ii)   gives the National Assembly a statement in writing that he or she has an interest in the holding of the quota holder identified in that entry; or]
(b)   is made by a purchaser in respect of an entry in the register referred to in regulation 4(6) relating to himself or herself,

the National Assembly may, on payment of a reasonable charge, supply to the person making the request a copy of the register entry.

NOTES

Initial Commencement

Specified date: 31 March 2005: see reg 1.

Amendment

Para (a)(i), (ii) substituted, for para (a)(i)–(iii) as originally enacted, by SI 2007/844, reg 2(1), (3).

Date in force: 31 March 2007: see SI 2007/844, reg 1.

A1.653

8   Registers as evidence

In any proceedings, any entry in a register which the National Assembly is required by these Regulations to maintain is evidence of the matters stated in it.

NOTES

Initial Commencement

Specified date: 31 March 2005: see reg 1.

PART 3: TRANSFERS OF QUOTA

A1.654

9   Transfer of quota with transfer of land: general

(1)   Subject to regulations 14 and 16, this regulation applies for the purposes of Article 17 of the Council Regulation (which concerns the transfer of quota with a holding when the holding is sold, leased, transferred by inheritance or subjected to other cases of transfer involving comparable legal effects for producers) in respect of a transfer of a holding or part of a holding.

(2)   The transferee of the holding or the part of the holding must submit to the National Assembly—

   (a)   a notice of transfer in such form; and
   (b)   such other information relating to the transfer,

as the National Assembly may reasonably require.

(3)   The notice of transfer must reach the National Assembly [no later than 31 March in the quota year in which the transfer takes place].

(4)   The information referred to in paragraph (2)(b) must reach the National Assembly within such time as the National Assembly may reasonably require.

(5)   The notice of transfer must include—

   (a)   statements from the transferor and transferee specifying the amounts of used and unused quota transferred;
   (b)   in the case of a transfer of part of a holding—
      (i)   statements from the transferor and transferee to the effect that they have agreed that the quota is to be apportioned taking account of the areas used for milk production as specified in the notice of transfer or that no such apportionment has been agreed, and
      (ii)   where such an apportionment has been agreed, a consent or sole interest notice, provided by the transferor in respect of the holding; and
   (c)   in the case of a transfer of the whole of a holding, a consent or sole interest notice, provided by the transferor in respect of the holding.

NOTES

Initial Commencement
Specified date: 31 March 2005: see reg 1.

Amendment
Para (3): words 'no later than 31 March in the quota year in which the transfer takes place' in square brackets substituted by SI 2007/844, reg 2(1), (4).

Date in force: 31 March 2007: see SI 2007/844, reg 1.

A1.655

10   Transfer of part of holding

(1)   Subject to regulations 14 and 16, this regulation applies where there is a transfer of part of a holding.

(2)   Subject to regulations 11(4) and (5) and 12, where a notice of transfer has been duly submitted in accordance with regulation 9, an apportionment of the quota relating to the holding must—

   (a)   be made in accordance with the agreed apportionment set out in that notice; or

   (b)   if there is no such agreement, be determined by arbitration in accordance with Schedule 1.

(3)   Subject to paragraph (4) and regulations 11(4) and (5) and 12, any dairy produce which has been—

   (a)   the subject of a direct sale; or

   (b)   delivered

from the holding during the quota year in which the change of occupation takes place and prior to the transfer of the part of the holding is treated for the purposes of any levy calculation as if it was sold, transferred free of charge or delivered, as the case may be, from each part of the holding in proportion to the apportionment under paragraph (2).

(4)   Paragraph (3) does not apply if the parties agree otherwise and submit to the National Assembly a notice of that agreement.

(5)   A notice referred to in paragraph (4) must be submitted—

   (a)   in such form as the National Assembly may reasonably require; and

   (b)   at the same time as the submission of the notice of transfer in accordance with regulation 9.

NOTES

Initial Commencement
Specified date: 31 March 2005: see reg 1.

A1.656

11   Prospective apportionment of quota

(1)   Where the occupier of a holding requires a prospective apportionment of quota relating to that holding, he or she must apply for such an apportionment to the National Assembly in such form as the National Assembly may reasonably require, requesting either—

(a) that a prospective apportionment of quota relating to the holding be made taking account of areas used for milk production as set out in the application; or

(b) that a prospective apportionment of quota be determined by arbitration in accordance with Schedule 1.

(2) A request for a prospective apportionment may be withdrawn by a notice in writing given to the National Assembly by the person who made the request.

(3) If the occupier of a holding—

(a) requests that a prospective apportionment be made in accordance with paragraph (1)(a); or

(b) gives notice of the withdrawal of such a request in accordance with paragraph (2),

the request or notice must be accompanied by a consent or sole interest notice in respect of the holding.

(4) Subject to paragraph (6), where there is a change of occupation of part of a holding and within the period of six months ending with the date of that change of occupation—

(a) the occupier of the holding—

(i) has requested a prospective apportionment of quota in respect of that part of the holding, and

(ii) has duly submitted a notice of transfer in accordance with regulation 9, indicating that an apportionment of quota has been agreed; or

(b) a prospective apportionment of quota relating to that part of that holding has been or is in the process of being determined by arbitration under Schedule 1,

paragraph (5) applies.

(5) The apportionment of quota must be carried out in accordance with—

(a) the prospective apportionment of quota relating to that part of that holding made or determined following a request under paragraph (1) unless the request for that prospective apportionment was withdrawn before the change of occupation to which it relates takes place; or

(b) if no such prospective apportionment has been made or determined, but one is in the process of being made or determined, the prospective apportionment of quota relating to that part of that holding which is in the process of being made or determined under paragraph (1); or

(c) in any other case, regulation 10(2).

(6) Paragraph (4) does not apply to a change of occupation to which regulation 16(1) applies.

NOTES

Initial Commencement

Specified date: 31 March 2005: see reg 1.

A1.657

12   Cases where apportionment of quota by arbitration is required

(1) This regulation applies where—

(a) there is a transfer of part of a holding; and

  (b) the National Assembly has reasonable grounds for believing that the areas used for milk production on the holding—

     (i) are not as specified in a notice duly submitted pursuant to regulation 9 or an application duly submitted pursuant to regulation 11(1)(a), or

     (ii) in a case where no such notice or no such application have been duly submitted, were not fully taken into account by the parties at the time of apportionment.

(2) The National Assembly may give notice that it has reasonable grounds for believing the matters referred to in paragraph (1)(b)—

  (a) to the person who submitted the notice or application referred to in paragraph (1)(b)(i); or,

  (b) in the case where neither was submitted, to the quota holder of the holding in question.

(3) Where the National Assembly gives a notice under paragraph (2), the apportionment or prospective apportionment of the quota concerned is to be determined by arbitration in accordance with Schedule 1.

NOTES

Initial Commencement

Specified date: 31 March 2005: see reg 1.

A1.658

13   Transfer of quota without transfer of land

(1) This regulation is subject to regulation 16(2) and (3).

(2) This regulation applies where the competent authorities in England, Wales, Scotland and Northern Ireland have jointly determined, in accordance with paragraphs (1)(e) and (2) of Article 18 of the Council Regulation, that within each United Kingdom quota region transfer of quota without transfer of the corresponding land is authorised.

(3) A transferee of quota for whom the National Assembly is the relevant competent authority must submit to it a notice of any such transfer within the general quota region in such form as the National Assembly may reasonably require.

(4) The notice must reach the National Assembly no later than 31 March in the quota year in which the transfer takes place and must include—

  (a) statements by the transferor and transferee that they have agreed to the transfer of quota, stating the amounts of used and unused quota transferred;

  (b) a consent or sole interest notice given by the transferor in respect of the holding from which the quota is to be transferred; and

  (c) a statement by the transferee that he or she is a producer.

(5) Where the National Assembly has received a notice pursuant to paragraph (3), it may require the transferor or transferee to produce such other information relating to the transfer, and within such time, as the National Assembly may reasonably require.

(6) In this regulation—

  (a) 'general quota region' means the United Kingdom other than the Scottish Islands areas; and

  (b) 'United Kingdom quota region' means a Scottish Islands area or the general quota region.

NOTES

Initial Commencement

Specified date: 31 March 2005: see reg 1.

A1.659

14   Retention of quota at the end of a tenancy

(1)   This regulation has effect as respects tenancies ending after 31 March 2005.

(2)   Where—

   (a)   a tenant of any land in a holding has quota registered as available to him or her;

   (b)   the quota is so registered by virtue of a transfer referred to in regulation 13 the cost of which was not borne by the tenant's landlord;

   (c)   the tenancy of the land in question expires without any possibility of renewal on similar terms;

   (d)   the tenant and his or her landlord have not agreed that, after the expiry of the tenancy, the quota should no longer be available to the tenant; and

   (e)   the tenant continues to be a producer after the expiry of the tenancy in relation to—

      (i)   another holding, or

      (ii)   another part of the holding of which the land formed part,

the tenant may submit a notice to the National Assembly that the quota is to be available to him or her by virtue of his or her occupation of that other holding or that other part of the holding of which the land formed part.

(3)   A notice submitted pursuant to paragraph (2) must—

   (a)   be in such form as the National Assembly may reasonably require;

   (b)   reach the National Assembly no later than 31 March in the quota year in which the tenancy expires; and

   (c)   include a statement by the tenant—

      (i)   that he or she and his or her landlord have not agreed that, after the expiry of the tenancy, the quota should be registered in relation to the holding which then comprises or, as the case may be, includes, the land, stating the amounts of used and unused quota involved, and

      (ii)   that he or she continues to be a producer.

(4)   Where a tenant submits a notice pursuant to this regulation, he or she shall not be entitled to receive compensation under paragraph 1 of Schedule 1 to the Agriculture Act 1986 on the termination of the tenancy in question.

NOTES

Initial Commencement

Specified date: 31 March 2005: see reg 1.

A1.660

15   Temporary transfer of quota

(1)   Subject to regulation 16(2), for the purposes of Article 16 of the Council Regulation (which concerns the temporary transfer of quota), a producer may agree with another producer to make a temporary transfer to that other producer of any

unused quota which is registered under regulation 4 as permanently held by the producer if other quota (whether or not unused) remains so registered.

(2)   Quota may only be temporarily transferred pursuant to paragraph (1) for such period as shall end on the 31 March in the quota year in which the transfer takes place.

(3)   The National Assembly may require a reasonable charge to be paid for the registration of any temporary transfer of quota if before the quota year in which the transfer takes place it has announced that it intends to make such a charge in respect of such transfers in that year in such a manner as it considers likely to come to the attention of producers.

(4)   Where there is an agreement to make a temporary transfer pursuant to paragraph (1), the transferee must submit to the National Assembly notice of the agreement, together with any charge payable under paragraph (3), so that the notice and any charge reach it no later than 31 March in the quota year in which the transfer takes place.

(5)   A notice referred to in paragraph (4) must be in such form as the National Assembly may reasonably require.

NOTES

Initial Commencement

Specified date: 31 March 2005: see reg 1.

A1.661

16   Restrictions on transfer of quota

(1)   No person may transfer quota on the grant or termination of—

   (a)   a licence to occupy land; or
   (b)   a tenancy of any land under which a holding, or part of a holding, is occupied for a period of less than ten months.

(2)   No person may transfer quota if the transfer would result in an increase or reduction in the total wholesale quota or the total direct sales quota available for use by dairy enterprises located within a Scottish Islands area.

(3)   No person may transfer[, as unused,] quota that is necessary to cover—

   (a)   deliveries, after an adjustment for fat content; and
   (b)   direct sales,

made by him or her before the date of the transfer.

NOTES

Initial Commencement

Specified date: 31 March 2005: see reg 1.

Amendment

Para (3): words ', as unused,' in square brackets inserted by SI 2006/762, regs 2, 3.

Date in force: 31 March 2006: see SI 2006/762, reg 1.

A1.662

17   Consequences of failure to duly submit a transfer notice

(1)   This regulation applies if a notice of transfer is not duly submitted in accordance with regulation 9 or 13.

(2)   Any unused quota transferred is not to be treated as a part of the transferee's quota entitlement for the relevant quota year, but is to be treated as if it remained unused quota and available where appropriate for reallocation by the National Assembly in that quota year in accordance with regulation 27 or 30.

(3)   The transfer of quota has effect only from the beginning of the quota year in which the notice of transfer is received.

(4)   The amount of quota, if any, which has been reallocated to the transferee under regulations 27 or 30 for the relevant quota year (or any subsequent year) shall not be varied to take the transfer into account until the quota year in which the transfer notice is received.

(5)   In this regulation 'relevant quota year' means—

  (a)   in the case of a notice that should have been submitted in accordance with regulation 9, the quota year in which the transfer of the holding or the part of the holding takes effect; and

  (b)   in the case of a notice that should have been submitted in accordance with regulation 13, the quota year in which the transfer of quota takes effect.

NOTES

Initial Commencement

Specified date: 31 March 2005: see reg 1.

PART 4: ALLOCATIONS AND ADJUSTMENTS OF QUOTA

A1.663

18   Allocation from national reserve

The National Assembly may make allocations from the national reserve in accordance with the Community legislation.

NOTES

Initial Commencement

Specified date: 31 March 2005: see reg 1.

A1.664

19   Temporary reallocation of quota

(1)   This regulation applies where a producer has quota registered as his or hers in relation to a holding which—

  (a)   at any time during a quota year is in whole or in part subject to a notice served, or declaration made, under an order made pursuant to section 17(1) of the Animal Health Act 1981 prohibiting or regulating the movement of dairy cows; or

1873

(b) is situated wholly or partly within an area which at any time during a quota year has been designated by an order made pursuant to section 1 of the Food and Environment Protection Act 1985.

(2) For the purposes of the reallocation of quota referred to in Article 10(3) of the Council Regulation and subject to paragraph (10), the National Assembly may award to a producer a temporary reallocation of an amount of any surplus quota in accordance with the provisions of paragraphs (3) to (5).

(3) An award may only be made for a quota year in which the notice, declaration or order referred to in paragraph (1) has effect or remains in force.

(4) The amount of any such award is the lower of—

(a) the amount equal to 16 litres per qualifying cow per qualifying day in the quota year referred to in paragraph (3); and
(b) the amount by which the producer's production exceeds his or her quota entitlement in that quota year.

(5) An award to a producer under this regulation is not available in respect of a quota year during which the producer—

(a) transfers unused quota pursuant to regulation 9 or 13;
(b) makes a temporary transfer of quota pursuant to regulation 15; or
(c) purchases cows or in-calf heifers for dairy purposes,

unless the National Assembly is satisfied that the agreement to transfer, temporarily to transfer or to purchase, was entered into before the service of the notice or the making of the declaration referred to in paragraph (1)(a) or, as the case may be, the coming into force of the order referred to in paragraph (1)(b).

(6) If a producer requires an award of a temporary reallocation of quota under this regulation, he or she must submit to the National Assembly an application in such form as the National Assembly may reasonably require.

(7) An application referred to in paragraph (6) must reach the National Assembly no later than 30 April following the end of the quota year in which the holding, or part of the holding, in question, was—

(a) subject to a relevant notice or a relevant declaration; or
(b) situated in an area designated by a relevant order.

(8) If the National Assembly awards to a producer a temporary reallocation of an amount of any surplus quota in accordance with this regulation, the National Assembly must notify each purchaser to whom the producer makes deliveries of that reallocation.

(9) The National Assembly can make an award of a temporary reallocation of quota only from the aggregate of the amounts of quota referred to in regulation 27(3)(a) and 30(9)(a) once the aggregate has been determined under those regulations.

(10) An eligible heifer which is a qualifying cow for the purposes of a quota year shall not be a qualifying cow for the purposes of any subsequent quota year.

(11) In this regulation—

(a) 'eligible heifer' means a qualifying heifer which calves for the first time on a relevant calving day;
(b) 'qualifying cow', for the purposes of a quota year, means an eligible heifer which calves for the first time at a time when the number of eligible heifers exceeds the replacement number, whether or not the time of such calving falls during that quota year;
(c) 'qualifying heifer' means a heifer which either—

    (i) at the date of service of a relevant notice or the making of a relevant declaration, was on land subject to that notice or, as the case may be, that declaration; or

    (ii) at the date of the coming into force of a relevant order, was on land subject to that order;

  (d) 'qualifying day', in relation to any qualifying cow, means the day on which it calves and each later day or part of a later day during which the relevant notice, the relevant declaration or the relevant order in question has effect or, as the case may be, remains in force;

  (e) 'relevant declaration' means a declaration referred to in paragraph (1)(a);

  (f) 'relevant notice' means a notice referred to in paragraph (1)(a);

  (g) 'relevant order' means an order referred to in paragraph (1)(b).

(12)   In this regulation, 'relevant calving day', in relation to a qualifying heifer, means a day which falls—

  (a) in a case where the relevant notice, the relevant declaration or the relevant order in question has effect or is in force for a period which expires at or before the end of the quota year during which it is served or, as the case may be, made, within the period of twelve months ending with the date on which that notice, declaration or order ceases to have effect or, as the case may be, to be in force; and

  (b) in any other case, within the quota year during which the relevant notice, the relevant declaration or the relevant order is served or made or at any later time when the relevant notice, the relevant declaration or the relevant order has effect or is in force.

(13)   In this regulation, 'replacement number' means the nearest whole number to 20% of the total number of dairy cows on land—

  (a) in a case where the land is subject to a relevant notice or a relevant declaration, as at the date of service of that notice or declaration; or

  (b) in a case where the land is subject to a relevant order, as at the date of the coming into force of that order,

and where 20% of the total number is half way between two whole numbers, the nearest even whole number is deemed to be the nearest one.

NOTES

Initial Commencement

Specified date: 31 March 2005: see reg 1.

A1.665

20   Special allocation of quota

(1) This regulation applies if by reason of a mistake made by the National Assembly—

  (a) a person has not been allocated any quota; or

  (b) has been allocated a smaller quantity of quota than he or she would have been allocated if the mistake had not been made.

(2) The National Assembly may allocate to that person from the national reserve such quota as will compensate, in whole or in part, for that mistake.

NOTES

Initial Commencement

Specified date: 31 March 2005: see reg 1.

A1.666

21   Conversion of quota: general

(1) For the purposes of—

(a) the provisions of Article 6(2) and (5) of the Council Regulation (which concern changes from direct sales to delivery and vice versa); and

(b) Article 11(2) of the Council Regulation (which concerns replacements of purchasers and changes of purchasers by producers),

a producer may apply to convert direct sales quota to wholesale quota or wholesale quota to direct sales quota either temporarily or permanently.

(2) If a producer wishes to convert quota in any quota year, he or she must submit to the National Assembly an application in such form as the National Assembly may reasonably require—

(a) stating—

(i) the amount (if any) of that producer's direct sales quota, wholesale quota, direct sales and deliveries for the quota year in which the application is made,

(ii) the amount of unused quota which he or she holds at the time of the application, and

(iii) the amount which he or she wishes the National Assembly to convert; and

(b) including such other information as the National Assembly may reasonably require in order to assess whether the requirements of Article 6(2) and (5) of the Council Regulation and Article 7 of the Commission Regulation (which concerns representative fat content) are met.

(3) The application must reach the National Assembly—

(a) in the case of a permanent conversion of quota, not later than 31 December in the quota year in which the conversion is intended to take effect; and

(b) in the case of a temporary conversion of quota, not later than 14 May in the year following the end of the quota year in which that temporary conversion is intended to take effect.

NOTES

Initial Commencement

Specified date: 31 March 2005: see reg 1.

A1.667

22   Conversion of quota: restriction on transfers of converted quota in conversion year

(1) This regulation does not apply to permanently converted quota which is transferred with a holding pursuant to Article 17 of the Council Regulation.

(2)   Subject to paragraphs (3) and (6), where a producer has permanently converted quota in any quota year, he or she must not transfer later in that quota year quota of the type to which he or she has converted, whether temporarily or otherwise.

(3)   Where a producer who has permanently converted quota in any quota year applies to the National Assembly for a release from the restriction in paragraph (2), the National Assembly, being satisfied as to the matters set out in paragraph (5), may release that producer from that restriction.

(4)   A release from the restriction in paragraph (2) shall be to the extent necessary to allow the transfer of the amount of quota that the National Assembly considers has remained unused in the particular case.

(5)   The matters referred to in paragraph (3) are—

(a)   that, as regards the producer, exceptional circumstances have resulted in a significant fall in milk production or a significant failure to achieve a planned increase in milk production; and

(b)   those circumstances could not have been foreseen or avoided by the producer at the time of his or her permanent conversion of quota.

(6)   The restriction in paragraph (2) does not apply if—

(a)   in a case where the permanent conversion is from direct sales quota to wholesale quota, the producer temporarily converted direct sales quota to wholesale quota in the immediately preceding quota year; or

(b)   in a case where the permanent conversion is from wholesale quota to direct sales quota, the producer temporarily converted wholesale quota to direct sales quota in the immediately preceding quota year.

(7)   The following are examples of circumstances which are to be taken to be exceptional for the purposes of paragraph (5)—

(a)   the death of the producer or his or her inability to conduct his or her business for a prolonged period as a result of the onset of ill-health, injury or disability;

(b)   a natural disaster seriously affecting the holding;

(c)   the accidental destruction of buildings used for the purposes of milk production;

(d)   an outbreak of illness or disease seriously affecting the dairy herd;

(e)   the serving of a notice or the making of a declaration under an order made pursuant to section 17(1) of the Animal Health Act 1981 or the making of an order pursuant to section 1 of the Food and Environment Protection Act 1985;

(f)   the loss of a significant proportion of the forage area as a result of the compulsory purchase of the holding or a part of the holding; and

(g)   where the transferee is a tenant, the serving of a notice to quit coming within any case specified in Part I of Schedule 3 to the Agricultural Holdings Act 1986.

NOTES

Initial Commencement

Specified date: 31 March 2005: see reg 1.

A1.668

23   Adjustment of purchaser quota

(1)   Where a quota holder's wholesale quota is increased or reduced in accordance with the Community legislation or these Regulations, the purchaser quota of any purchaser to whom that wholesale quota is applicable is correspondingly increased or reduced.

(2)   As regards a transaction to which Article 11(2) of the Council Regulation applies (which concerns replacements of purchasers and changes of purchasers by producers), a purchaser whose purchaser quota has been increased by virtue of such a transaction must submit to the National Assembly an application for his or her purchaser quota to be increased by the specified amount.

(3)   An application referred to in paragraph (2) must include—

   (a)   a statement setting out the particulars of the transaction; and
   (b)   a declaration made and signed by the producer that the purchaser whose purchaser quota is to decrease has been notified of the particulars set out in the application referred to in paragraph (2).

(4)   The application referred to in paragraph (2)—

   (a)   must [be sent to the National Assembly on or before] 14 May in the quota year immediately following that in which the transaction took place; and
   (b)   must be made in such form as the National Assembly may reasonably require.

(5)   The specified amount must not include the remaining registered wholesale quota except so far as the increase registered in pursuance of paragraph (8) includes that quota.

(6)   The remaining registered wholesale quota shall remain available to the original purchaser.

(7)   If insufficient quota is registered with the original purchaser to cover deliveries made by the producer before the date of change of purchaser, any additional quota obtained by a producer is to be allocated to the original purchaser until all deliveries to the original purchaser made by the producer before that date are covered after any adjustment for butterfat content in accordance with Article 10(1) of the Commission Regulation.

(8)   At the beginning of the quota year immediately following the quota year in which the increase referred to in paragraph (2) took place, the purchaser quota of the purchaser with whom the producer is newly registered is to be increased by such part of the remaining registered wholesale quota of the producer as is included in the specified amount.

(9)   If the amount of quota necessary to cover the deliveries made to an original purchaser is affected by—

   (a)   a transfer of quota to the producer under these Regulations; or
   (b)   an adjustment for butterfat content in accordance with Article 10(1) of the Commission Regulation,

then, subject to paragraph (10), the National Assembly must make such adjustments in the purchaser quota of the original purchaser, and of the purchaser with whom the producer is newly registered, as are required to ensure that sufficient quota is registered with the original purchaser to cover deliveries made.

(10)   The National Assembly must make an adjustment pursuant to paragraph (9) after the end of the quota year in question.

(11)   Where a producer has quota registered with two or more purchasers, the producer may apply to the National Assembly temporarily to change the quota registered between them, except so far as the quota registered with each of them is necessary to cover the deliveries made by him or her before the date of the transfer after any adjustment for butterfat content in accordance with Article 10(1) of the Commission Regulation.

(12) A producer who makes an application to the National Assembly pursuant to paragraph (11) must submit with his or her application—

    (a)   a statement setting out particulars of the quota to be temporarily reregistered; and

    (b)   a declaration made and signed by the producer that the purchaser whose purchaser quota is to decrease has been notified of the particulars set out in the statement.

(13) The statement and declaration referred to in paragraph (12)—

    (a)   must be in such form as the National Assembly may reasonably require; and

    (b)   must reach the National Assembly no later than 15 June in the quota year immediately following the quota year for which the temporary re-registration is requested.

(14) In this regulation—

    (a)   'remaining registered wholesale quota' means the amount of quota necessary to cover the deliveries made by a producer before the date of the change of purchaser (adjusted in accordance with Article 10(1) of the Commission Regulation); and

    (b)   'specified amount' means an amount equivalent to so much of a producer's registered wholesale quota as is specified by that producer.

NOTES

Initial Commencement

Specified date: 31 March 2005: see reg 1.

Amendment

Para (4): in sub-para (a) words 'be sent to the National Assembly on or before' in square brackets substituted by SI 2006/762, regs 2, 4.

Date in force: 31 March 2006: see SI 2006/762, reg 1.

A1.669

24   Restriction on use of quota in Scottish Islands Area

(1) Quota registered under regulation 4 to quota holders within a Scottish Islands area may be used by producers and purchasers only against direct sales or deliveries of milk produced within that Scottish Islands area.

(2) If a quota holder has a part of his or her dairy enterprise outside a Scottish Islands area, he or she is treated for the purposes of this regulation as a quota holder within a Scottish Islands area if he or she has 50% or more of his or her dairy enterprise within that area.

(3) Paragraph (1) does not apply to the reallocation of quota undertaken in accordance with regulations 27 and 30.

NOTES

Initial Commencement

Specified date: 31 March 2005: see reg 1.

PART 5: THE LEVY

A1.670

25   Determination whether reduction in downward butterfat adjustment is required in relation to deliveries

(1)   After the end of each quota year, the National Assembly must make a determination of—

   (a) the total volume of deliveries to purchasers; and
   (b) the total volume of such deliveries after an adjustment for butterfat content in accordance with Article 10(1) of the Commission Regulation.

(2)   The determination under paragraph (1) must be made by reference to the summaries purchasers are required to submit to the National Assembly for the purposes of Article 8(2) of the Commission Regulations.

(3)   If for any quota year a purchaser has not submitted the summaries so required or is unable to provide such proof of the volume of milk delivered to him or her in that year as the National Assembly may reasonably require for the purposes of these Regulations, the National Assembly must for the purposes of paragraph (1)—

   (a) make its own determination of that volume of milk based on all the information available to it for the purposes of calculating any levy payable on deliveries made to that purchaser; and
   (b) inform the purchaser of its determination.

(4)   If the volume referred to in paragraph (1)(a) exceeds that referred to in paragraph (1)(b), the National Assembly must calculate the proportionate reduction required to be made in all downward butterfat adjustments that have previously been made in order to increase the volume referred to in paragraph (1)(b) so that it equals the volume referred to in paragraph (1)(a).

(5)   If paragraph (4) applies, the National Assembly must—

   (a) notify all purchasers that any downward butterfat adjustments made by them in the deliveries to them are reduced; and
   (b) specify the reduction.

(6)   If the volume referred to in paragraph (1)(b) equals or exceeds that referred to in paragraph (1)(a), the National Assembly must notify all purchasers that no such reduction need be made.

(7)   In this regulation, 'downward butterfat adjustment', in relation to deliveries to a purchaser, means an adjustment of the volume of the deliveries for butterfat content that results in that volume being reduced for the purposes of the levy calculation in accordance with Article 10(2) of the Council Regulation.

NOTES

Initial Commencement

Specified date: 31 March 2005: see reg 1.

A1.671

26   Determination whether levy on deliveries is payable

(1)   Where the total amount of the wholesale quota of producers, including converted quota, together with the total amount of wholesale quota in the national reserve exceeds whichever is the higher of—

(a) the total volume of deliveries referred to in regulation 25(1)(a); or

(b) the total volume of deliveries referred to in regulation 25(1)(b),

the National Assembly must determine that no levy is payable on deliveries.

(2) The National Assembly must notify all purchasers of a determination made under paragraph (1).

(3) Where the total amount of the wholesale quota of producers, including converted quota, together with the total amount of wholesale quota in the national reserve is less than whichever is the higher of—

(a) the total volume of deliveries referred to in regulation 25(1)(a); or

(b) the total volume of deliveries referred to in regulation 25(1)(b),

the National Assembly must notify all purchasers that levy is payable on the higher volume of deliveries.

NOTES

Initial Commencement

Specified date: 31 March 2005: see reg 1.

A1.672

27   Reallocation of producers' quota

(1) This regulation applies for the purposes of Article 10(3) of the Council Regulation (which concerns the calculation of levy on deliveries).

(2) After the end of each quota year, the National Assembly must determine for each producer the amount, if any, of unused quota available to that producer, taking into account any adjustment required under regulation 25(4) and the amount of any converted quota.

(3) If the National Assembly determines pursuant to paragraph (2) that a producer has unused quota, it must—

(a) add the total amount of unused quota to the national reserve;

(b) subject to paragraph (4), make an award of any temporary reallocation of quota in accordance with regulation 19; and

(c) having made such an award, reallocate any remaining amount of unused quota to any producers whose deliveries are in excess of their quotas in proportion to their respective quotas.

(4) The amount of an award made under paragraph (3)(b) shall be reduced proportionately if there is insufficient quota after the National Assembly has complied with paragraph (3)(a) to make a full award to all producers who are eligible to receive a temporary allocation of quota under regulation 19.

(5) Subject to paragraph (6), if the total amount of unused quota available for reallocation to a producer under paragraph (3)(c) is not required by that producer to cover his or her butterfat adjusted deliveries, the National Assembly must reallocate the amount of unused quota not required amongst all producers whose butterfat adjusted deliveries are in excess of their quota in proportion to their respective quotas.

(6) No producer may receive any unused quota under paragraph (5) in excess of the amount of quota required by him or her to cover the amount by which his or her butterfat adjusted deliveries exceed his or her quota.

(7) In this regulation, 'butterfat adjusted deliveries' means deliveries adjusted for butterfat content in accordance with Article 10(1) of the Commission Regulation.

NOTES

Initial Commencement

Specified date: 31 March 2005: see reg 1.

A1.673

28 Determination of liability for levy on deliveries

(1) This regulation applies for the purposes of Article 10(3) of the Council Regulation (which concerns the calculation of levy on deliveries).

(2) After the end of each quota year, the National Assembly must—

    (a) ascertain which producers have made deliveries which exceed the quota allocated to them after taking into account any adjustments made under regulations 25 and 27; then

    (b) establish the total amount of the levy payable by each such producer at the rate of levy set in Article 2 of the Council Regulation; and then

    (c) establish the total amount of levy payable by each purchaser on deliveries made to that purchaser.

NOTES

Initial Commencement

Specified date: 31 March 2005: see reg 1.

A1.674

29 Notification of levy liability

After the end of each quota year, the National Assembly must—

    (a) notify each purchaser of the total amount of levy payable on deliveries made to that purchaser; and

    (b) give details to that purchaser of the amount of levy attributable to each producer who has made deliveries to that purchaser.

NOTES

Initial Commencement

Specified date: 31 March 2005: see reg 1.

A1.675

30 Determination of liability for levy on direct sales

(1) This regulation applies for the purposes of Article 12 of the Council Regulation (which concerns the calculation of levy on direct sales).

(2) After the end of each quota year, the National Assembly must make a determination of the total quantity of dairy produce sold or transferred free of charge by direct sellers in the quota year in question.

(3) A determination under paragraph (2) must be made by reference to the declarations direct sellers are required to submit to the National Assembly in accordance with Article 11(2) of the Commission Regulation.

(4) If for any quota year a direct seller has not submitted to the National Assembly a declaration in accordance with that Article or is unable to provide such proof of the quantities of dairy produce sold or transferred free of charge by him or her in that year as the National Assembly may reasonably require for the purposes of these Regulations, the National Assembly must for the purposes of paragraph (2)—

   (a)   make its own determination of such quantities based on all the information available to it for the purposes of calculating any levy payable by that direct seller, and

   (b)   inform the direct seller of its determination.

(5) Where, in respect of a quota year—

   (a)   the total amount of direct sales quota of direct sales quota holders, including any converted quota; and

   (b)   the total amount of direct sales quota in the national reserve,

together exceed the total quantity determined by the National Assembly under paragraph (2), the National Assembly must determine that no levy in respect of direct sales is payable.

(6) The National Assembly must notify all direct sales quota holders of its determination made under paragraph (5).

(7) Where, in respect of a quota year—

   (a)   the total amount of direct sales quota of direct sales quota holders, including any converted quota; and

   (b)   the total amount of direct sales quota in the national reserve,

together are less than the total quantity determined by the National Assembly under paragraph (2), the National Assembly must notify all direct sellers that levy is payable.

(8) After the end of each quota year, the National Assembly must determine in respect of each direct sales quota holder the amount of any unused direct sales quota available to that direct sales quota holder in the quota year in question, taking into account any converted quota.

(9) If the National Assembly determines under paragraph (8) that a direct sales quota holder has unused direct sales quota, it must—

   (a)   add that unused quota to the national reserve; and

   (b)   subject to paragraph (10), make such awards of temporary reallocation of quota under regulation 19 as it considers it appropriate to make.

(10) If, after the National Assembly has complied with paragraph (9)(a), there is insufficient direct sales quota to make a full award under regulation 19 to each direct sales quota holder who is eligible to receive such an award, the amount of each award under paragraph (9)(b) shall be reduced proportionately.

(11) In respect of the quota year in question, the National Assembly must then establish—

   (a)   the amount by which the total quantity referred to in paragraph (2) exceeds the total of—

      (i)   the direct sales quota of all direct sales quota holders, including converted quota, and

      (ii)   the direct sales quota in the national reserve;

(b)   the total amount of levy payable by direct sales quota holders by multiplying the amount determined under sub-paragraph (a) by the rate of levy set in Article 2 of the Council Regulation; and

(c)   the amount by which the total quantity referred to in paragraph (2) exceeds all the direct sales quota of the direct sales quota holders whose direct sales are greater than their quota.

(12)   The National Assembly must establish the rate of levy per litre to be paid by each direct sales quota holder by dividing the amount determined in accordance with paragraph (11)(b) by the amount determined in accordance with paragraph (11)(c).

(13)   The National Assembly must—

(a)   ascertain which direct sales quota holders have sold or transferred free of charge dairy produce in excess of the quota available to them including any converted quota and any quota temporarily reallocated by an award under paragraph (9)(b);

(b)   establish the total amount of levy payable by each such direct sales quota holder at the rate of levy established in accordance with paragraph (12); and

(c)   notify each direct sales quota holder of the total amount of levy payable by him or her.

(14)   If a direct seller fails to submit to the National Assembly in accordance with Article 11(2) of the Commission Regulation a declaration of the total quantity of dairy produce sold or transferred free of charge by him or her in a quota year, the rate of levy per litre to be paid by that direct seller on the quantity not notified or determined under paragraph (4) is the rate set in Article 2 of the Commission Regulation.

NOTES

Initial Commencement

Specified date: 31 March 2005: see reg 1.

A1.676

31   Payment and recovery of levy

(1)   In respect of the collection of levy, the National Assembly is the competent authority for the purposes of the Community legislation.

(2)   For the purposes of—

(a)   Article 11(1) of the Council Regulation (which concerns payment of levy by purchasers in respect of deliveries);

(b)   Article 12(4) of the Council Regulation (which concerns payment of levy by direct sellers);

(c)   Article 8 of the Commission Regulation (which concerns statements by purchasers of deliveries by producers); and

(d)   Article 11 of the Commission Regulation (which concerns declarations of direct sales by producers);

the levy and penalties referred to in those provisions must be paid to the National Assembly.

(3)   Paragraph (4) applies for the purposes of Article 11(3) of the Council Regulation (which concerns deduction of levy liability) where a producer making deliveries to a purchaser exceeds his or her wholesale quota .

(4)   Following any adjustment of the quantity delivered in accordance with Article 10(1) of the Commission Regulation, the purchaser may immediately deduct from

the sums owed to the producer in respect of the deliveries an amount corresponding to the amount of levy that would otherwise be payable by him or her in respect of the excess.

(5)   Where any part of the levy remains unpaid after [30 September] in any year, the National Assembly may recover the amount of the levy outstanding at that date together with interest in respect of each day after that date until that amount is recovered—

(a)   from the direct seller or, as the case may be, the purchaser; or

(b)   from the producer, in a case within paragraph (4) where—

    (i)   the purchaser has not paid the levy, and

    (ii) the producer has not paid the purchaser the levy either directly or by deduction and the purchaser is not taking steps to recover it from him or her.

(6)   Interest under paragraph (5) is payable at the rate of one percentage point above the sterling three month London interbank offered rate.

(7)   If—

(a)   a purchaser has not been approved pursuant to regulation 5; or

(b)   a purchaser has had his or her approval withdrawn by the National Assembly pursuant to Article 23(3) of the Commission Regulation,

subject to paragraph (8), the National Assembly may require any levy payable by the purchaser that has not been paid by him or her to be paid in such proportions as it may reasonably require by any producers whose deliveries to that purchaser have given rise to the liability for levy.

(8)   Paragraph (7) does not apply in respect of a producer who has paid the purchaser in question either directly or by deduction the levy payable by that producer.

NOTES

Initial Commencement

Specified date: 31 March 2005: see reg 1.

Amendment

Para (5): words '30 September' in square brackets substituted by SI 2007/844, reg 2(1), (5).

Date in force: 31 March 2007: see SI 2007/844, reg 1.

A1.677

32   Prevention of avoidance of levy

(1)   Subject to paragraphs (2) and (3), if—

(a)   a producer ('A') makes sales or deliveries of milk or milk products in any quota year from milk produced by any cows; and

(b)   later in the same quota year another producer ('B') makes sales or deliveries of milk or milk products from milk produced by any or all of the same cows,

B is deemed for the purposes of these Regulations to have made those sales or deliveries as agent for A.

(2)   Paragraph (1) does not apply if—

(a)   an agreement has been entered into by A for the sale or lease of the cows in question to B;

    (b)   the cows are kept on B's holding; and
    (c)   after the making of the agreement—
        (i) B is actively involved in the management of the herd which the cows
            mentioned in paragraph (1)(b) comprise and production from it, and
       (ii) A has no further involvement in that management and production.

(3) Paragraph (1) does not apply if—

    (a)   B has inherited the cows in question from A; and
    (b)   the cows are kept on B's holding.

NOTES

Initial Commencement

Specified date: 31 March 2005: see reg 1.

PART 6: INFORMATION AND RECORDS

A1.678

33   Information

(1) Every relevant person must provide such information to the National Assembly as the National Assembly may reasonably require to perform its functions under these Regulations and the Community legislation.

(2) Each purchaser must provide the National Assembly with such information as it may reasonably require relating to deliveries made or to be made to the purchaser by such person or persons as the National Assembly may identify for the purpose of monitoring deliveries in relation to the total national reference quantity for the United Kingdom referred to in Article 1(3) and Annex I of the Council Regulation.

(3) The information referred to in paragraph (2) must be provided—

    (a)   for such periods; and
    (b)   in such form,

as the National Assembly may reasonably require.

(4) The information referred to in paragraph (2) must be submitted so as to reach the National Assembly before the expiry of the period of three working days beginning with the end of the period to which the information relates or within seven working days beginning with the date of notification of the requirement, whichever is the later.

(5) Each purchaser must [send to the National Assembly] a list of those quota holders registered with that purchaser at 31 March in each quota year (whether they have been so registered for the whole or part of that quota year) who—

    (a)   hold quota in respect of that quota year that has not been acquired by temporary transfer for that quota year, and
    (b)   have not made deliveries to that purchaser during that quota year; ...

[on or before] 14 May following the end of that quota year.

(6) The National Assembly must provide each purchaser with a copy of such information as the purchaser may reasonably require for the purposes of—

    (a)   that purchaser's registration obligations under regulation 6; and
    (b)   Article 8 of the Commission Regulation (which concerns the submission of summaries of producers' statements of deliveries or declarations that no deliveries have been received).

NOTES

Initial Commencement

Specified date: 31 March 2005: see reg 1.

Amendment

Para (5): words 'send to the National Assembly' in square brackets substituted by SI 2006/762, regs 2, 5(a).

Date in force: 31 March 2006: see SI 2006/762, reg 1.

Para (5): in para (b) word omitted revoked by virtue of SI 2006/762, regs 2, 5(b).

Date in force: 31 March 2006: see SI 2006/762, reg 1.

Para (5): words 'on or before' in square brackets substituted by SI 2006/762, regs 2, 5(b).

Date in force: 31 March 2006: see SI 2006/762, reg 1.

A1.679

34 Keeping and retention of records

(1) For the purposes of Article 17 of the Commission Regulation (which requires Member States to take all necessary measures to ensure that the levy is correctly charged), a relevant person must comply with the requirements of paragraph (2) in addition to meeting any relevant requirement of paragraphs 2 to 6 of Article 24 of the Commission Regulation (which concerns record keeping obligations of purchasers and producers).

(2) The requirements referred to in paragraph (1) are—

    (a)   to keep and retain such records; and
    (b)   to comply with sub-paragraph (a) for such periods,

as are specified in Schedule 2.

(3) Paragraph (1) is without prejudice to regulation 3 of the Common Agricultural Policy (Protection of Community Arrangements) Regulations 1992.

NOTES

Initial Commencement

Specified date: 31 March 2005: see reg 1.

A1.680

35 Annual declarations and summaries

(1) If—

    (a)   a producer in whose name any direct sales quota is registered pursuant to regulation 4 fails to [send] to the National Assembly any declaration which he or she is required to [send] by Article 11(2) of the Commission Regulation ... on or before 14 May in any year; or
    (b)   a purchaser fails to [send] any summary which he or she is required to [send] to it by Article 8(2) of the Commission Regulation ... on or before 14 May in any year,

the National Assembly may recover a reasonable charge from that producer or that purchaser, as the case may be, in respect of any visit to any premises which it reasonably considers an authorised officer should make in order to obtain the declaration or summary in question.

(2) If the National Assembly sends to a purchaser a revised version of a summary [sent] by him or her in accordance with Article 8(2) of the Commission Regulation, the purchaser must submit either—

(a) confirmation that the revised version is agreed; or

(b) amendments to the revised version,

so that such confirmation or amendments, as the case may be, reach the National Assembly before the expiry of the period of ten working days beginning with the date on which the revised version was sent to the purchaser.

(3) In this regulation, 'authorised officer' means a person (whether or not an officer of the National Assembly) who is authorised by the National Assembly, either generally or specifically, to act in matters arising under these Regulations and the Community legislation.

NOTES

Initial Commencement

Specified date: 31 March 2005: see reg 1.

Amendment

Para (1): in sub-para (a) word 'send' in square brackets in both places it occurs substituted by SI 2006/762, regs 2, 6(a)(i).

Date in force: 31 March 2006: see SI 2006/762, reg 1.

Para (1): in sub-para (a) words omitted revoked by SI 2006/762, regs 2, 6(a)(ii).

Date in force: 31 March 2006: see SI 2006/762, reg 1.

Para (1): in sub-para (b) word 'send' in square brackets in both places it occurs substituted by SI 2006/762, regs 2, 6(b)(i).

Date in force: 31 March 2006: see SI 2006/762, reg 1.

Para (1): in sub-para (b) words omitted revoked by SI 2006/762, regs 2, 6(b)(ii).

Date in force: 31 March 2006: see SI 2006/762, reg 1.

Para (2): word 'sent' in square brackets substituted by SI 2006/762, regs 2, 6(c).

Date in force: 31 March 2006: see SI 2006/762, reg 1.

PART 7: PENALTIES AND MISCELLANEOUS PROVISIONS

A1.681

36 Administrative penalties

(1) Subject to the provisions of Article 23(4) of the Commission Regulation (which authorises member States not to impose penalties in certain circumstances) and paragraph (5), purchasers are subject to the administrative penalties specified in paragraphs [(2A) and (3)].

(2) ...

[(2A) Where a purchaser—

(a) sends to the National Assembly a summary of producers' statements required to be submitted under Article 8(2) of the Commission Regulation, which is inaccurate; and

(b) by doing so causes an overstatement or an understatement by him or her, of deliveries made to him or her,

he or she is liable to pay to the National Assembly a penalty equivalent to the theoretical amount of levy that would be due on 0.5% of the quantity by volume of milk which comprises the overstatement or understatement.]

(3) Where a purchaser fails to maintain accurate and updated records pursuant to Article 24(2) of the Commission Regulation and regulation 34, he or she is liable to pay to the National Assembly a penalty equivalent to the theoretical amount of the levy that would be due on 0.5% of the quantity by volume of milk concerned.

(4) For the purposes of the third sub-paragraph of Article 11(3) of the Commission Regulation (which requires Member States to impose proportionate penalties where producers submit incorrect declarations), and subject to the provisions of Article 11(5) of that Regulation (which authorises member States not to impose penalties in certain circumstances) and to paragraph (5), where a direct seller submits an annual declaration which overstates or understates the volume of direct sales for the quota year covered by that declaration, he or she is liable to pay to the National Assembly—

(a) in the case of an overstatement, a penalty equivalent to the theoretical amount of levy that would be due on 0.5% of the quantity by volume of the milk which comprises the overstatement;

(b) in the case of an understatement, a penalty equivalent to the theoretical amount of levy that would be due on 0.5% of the quantity by volume of the milk which comprises the understatement,

except in any case where, for the quota year covered by the declaration, he or she is liable to pay to the National Assembly levy which exceeds that amount.

(5) Notwithstanding anything in [paragraphs (2A), (3), (4) and (6A)], the penalties referred to in those paragraphs—

(a) in the case of purchasers and direct sellers, are not to be less than £60;

(b) in the case of purchasers, are not to exceed £60,000; and

(c) in the case of direct sellers, are not to exceed £600.

[(6) Subject to Article 8(5) of the Commission Regulation, if a purchaser fails to submit a summary required to be submitted under Article 8(2) of the Commission Regulation, by the end of the period specified in Article 8(4), he or she is liable to pay to the National Assembly a penalty equivalent to the theoretical amount of levy that would be due on 0.01% of the quantity by volume of milk covered by that declaration for each day of the period of the delay in the submission reaching the National Assembly.]

[(6A) Subject to paragraphs (5) and (7), where a purchaser fails to provide or submit to the National Assembly—

(a) an application, statement or declaration concerning the adjustment of purchaser quota in accordance with regulation 23(2) to (4);

(b) information in accordance with regulation 33(2) to (4); or

(c) a confirmation or amendments relating to a revised version of a summary in accordance with regulation 35(2),

he or she is liable to pay to the National Assembly a penalty equivalent to the theoretical amount of levy that would be due on 0.01% of the quantity by volume of milk covered by that application, statement, declaration or revised version, or that information, for each day of the period of delay in the submission reaching the National Assembly.]

(7)   A purchaser is not liable to pay a penalty under paragraph [(6A)] if, in the opinion of the National Assembly, the failure—

(a)   was neither deliberate nor the result of serious negligence;
(b)   is negligible in terms of the functioning of the scheme or the effectiveness of the checks; or
(c)   is attributable to force majeure.

NOTES

Initial Commencement

Specified date: 31 March 2005: see reg 1.

Amendment

Para (1): words '(2A) and (3)' in square brackets substituted by SI 2007/844, reg 2(1), (6)(a).

Date in force: 31 March 2007: see SI 2007/844, reg 1.

Para (2): revoked by SI 2007/844, reg 2(1), (6)(b).

Date in force: 31 March 2007: see SI 2007/844, reg 1.

Para (2A): inserted by SI 2006/762, regs 2, 7(b).

Date in force: 31 March 2006: see SI 2006/762, reg 1.

Para (5): words 'paragraphs (2A), (3), (4) and (6A)' in square brackets substituted by SI 2007/844, reg 2(1), (6)(c).

Date in force: 31 March 2007: see SI 2007/844, reg 1.

Para (6): substituted by SI 2007/844, reg 2(1), (6)(d).

Date in force: 31 March 2007: see SI 2007/844, reg 1.

Para (6A): inserted by SI 2007/844, reg 2(1), (6)(e).

Date in force: 31 March 2007: see SI 2007/844, reg 1.

Para (7): reference to '(6A)' in square brackets substituted by SI 2007/844, reg 2(1), (7).

Date in force: 31 March 2007: see SI 2007/844, reg 1.

A1.682

37   Withholding or recovery of compensation

(1)   Where—

(a)   a producer has submitted an application for compensation in accordance with the Community compensation scheme; and
(b)   it appears to the National Assembly that the producer has—
   (i)   made a false or misleading statement in his or her application, or
   (ii)   failed to comply with any of the requirements of the scheme,

the National Assembly may withhold or recover on demand from that producer the whole or any part of the compensation payable or paid to him or her.

(2)   In this regulation, 'Community compensation scheme' means the scheme instituted by Council Regulation (EC) No 2330/98 providing for an offer of compensation to certain producers of milk and milk products temporarily restricted in carrying out

their trade and Commission Regulation (EC) No 2647/98 laying down detailed rules for the application of Council Regulation (EC) No 2330/98.

NOTES

Initial Commencement

Specified date: 31 March 2005: see reg 1.

A1.683

38 Confiscation of quota

(1) In pursuance of Article 15 of the Council Regulation (which relates to the confiscation and restoration of quota in cases of inactivity), the National Assembly must notify a quota holder that his or her quota has been taken into the national reserve if it appears from information available to the National Assembly that he or she has made no deliveries or direct sales during the previous quota year.

(2) ...

(3) Any quota withdrawn pursuant to Article 15 of the Council Regulation must be placed in the national reserve with effect from 1 April following the quota year for which information became available to the National Assembly indicating to it that no deliveries or no direct sales, as the case may be, were made.

(4) A wholesale quota holder or direct sales quota holder who receives a notification of confiscation under paragraph (1) or, as the case may be, paragraph (2) must notify any person with an interest in the land comprised in the holding in question of the contents of that notification before the expiry of the period of 28 days beginning with the day on which he or she received it.

NOTES

Initial Commencement

Specified date: 31 March 2005: see reg 1.

Amendment

Para (2): revoked by SI 2007/844, reg 2(1), (8).

Date in force: 31 March 2007: see SI 2007/844, reg 1.

A1.684

39 Restoration of quota

(1) Subject to the second sub-paragraph of Article 15(1) of the Council Regulation (which specifies the time limit for quota restoration), a person whose quota has been taken into the national reserve may request the National Assembly to restore to him or her the quota in respect of the holding from which it was confiscated or in respect of part of that holding if he or she is a producer.

(2) Subject to paragraph (3), a request under paragraph (1)—

    (a) must reach the National Assembly—
        (i) no later than the end of the quota year to which it relates, or
        (ii) in the case of confiscation of quota notified [under article 11(4) of the Commission Regulation], no later than the end of the quota year before the quota year in which the quota is to be restored; and

(b) in a case falling within sub-paragraph (a)(ii), must include the declaration which the person making the request failed to submit under Article 11 of the Commission Regulation.

(3) Where—

(a) there is a change of occupation of all or part of the holding in respect of which quota has been taken into the national reserve; and

(b) the new occupier is a producer,

the new occupier may submit a request to the National Assembly to restore to him or her the quota relating to that holding or part holding before the expiry of the time limit for quota restoration specified by the second sub-paragraph of Article 15(1) of the Council Regulation.

(4) A request for restoration of quota to part of a holding made under paragraph (1) or (3) must include—

(a) a statement of the agreed apportionment of quota taking account of the areas used for milk production, signed by every person with an interest in the land comprised in the holding; or

(b) a statement requesting apportionment of the quota in accordance with an arbitration under paragraphs 1(5), 3(2), 4 and 6 to 34 of Schedule 1.

(5) Where quota is restored to part of a holding in accordance with a request made under paragraph (1) or (3), the amount of quota to be restored to that part must be determined in accordance with the apportionment referred to in paragraph (4)(a) or (b).

NOTES

Initial Commencement

Specified date: 31 March 2005: see reg 1.

Amendment

Para (2): in sub-para (a)(ii) words 'under article 11(4) of the Commission Regulation' in square brackets substituted by SI 2007/844, reg 2(1), (9).

Date in force: 31 March 2007: see SI 2007/844, reg 1.

A1.685

40   Offences and criminal penalties

(1) A person is guilty of an offence if—

(a) being a relevant person, he or she fails without reasonable excuse to comply with a requirement imposed on him or her by or under these Regulations or the Community legislation; or

(b) in connection with these Regulations or the Community legislation, he or she—

(i) makes or causes to be made a statement, or uses or causes to be used a document, which he or she knows to be false in a material particular, or

(ii) recklessly makes or causes to be made a statement, or recklessly uses or causes to be used a document, which is false in a material particular; or

(c) disposes of quota which he or she knows or might reasonably be expected to know is incorrectly registered in his or her name.

(2) A person guilty of an offence under paragraph (1) is liable—

(a)   on summary conviction, to a fine not exceeding the statutory maximum, or to imprisonment for a term not exceeding three months; or to both, or

(b)   on conviction on indictment, to a fine, or to imprisonment for a term not exceeding two years, or to both.

(3)   The National Assembly may, following any conviction under paragraph (1)(b) against which there is no subsisting right of appeal or further appeal, by notice served on the person whose quota that conviction relates to, withdraw from him or her such quota as may reasonably be regarded by the National Assembly as obtained by him or her by reason of the falsehood upon which the conviction was founded.

(4)   A notice served under paragraph (3) may not be served after the expiry of the period of twelve months beginning with the first day on which the notice may be served.

(5)   Where an offence under this regulation which has been committed by a body corporate is proved to have been committed with the consent or connivance of, or to be attributable to any neglect on the part of, any director, manager, secretary or similar officer of the body corporate, or any person who was purporting to act in any such capacity, he or she as well as the body corporate is deemed to be guilty of that offence and is liable to be proceeded against and punished accordingly.

(6)   Where the affairs of a body corporate are managed by its members, the provisions of paragraphs (1) and (2) apply in relation to the acts and defaults of a member in connection with his or her functions of management as if he or she were a director of the body corporate.

(7)   In this regulation 'requirement' does not include any restriction or obligation in or under regulations 11(1) and (3), 14(3), 16, 19(6) and (7), 21(2) and (3), 22(2), 23(12) and (13) and 39(2) and (4).

NOTES

Initial Commencement

Specified date: 31 March 2005: see reg 1.

A1.686

41   Revocations and amendments

(1)   The Dairy Produce Quotas (Wales) Regulations 2002, are revoked.

(2)   In article 8(3)(b) of the Milk Development Council Order 1995, for the words 'the Dairy Produce Quotas (Wales) Regulations 2002' there are substituted 'the Dairy Produce Quotas (Wales) Regulations 2005'.

NOTES

Initial Commencement

Specified date: 31 March 2005: see reg 1.

SCHEDULE 1

APPORTIONMENT AND PROSPECTIVE APPORTIONMENT BY ARBITRATION

Regulations 10(2) 11, 12(3) and 39(4)

Appointment and remuneration of arbitrator

A1.687

1   (1)   Subject to paragraph (2), in any case where an apportionment is to be carried out by arbitration, an arbitrator must be appointed by agreement between the transferor and transferee, and the transferee must give notice of the appointment of the arbitrator to the National Assembly.

(2)   The transferor or the transferee may at any time make an application to the President of the Royal Institution of Chartered Surveyors (referred to in this Schedule as 'the President') for the appointment of an arbitrator ..., and the person who makes such an application to the President must give notice of that fact to the National Assembly.

(3)   If an arbitrator has not been appointed by agreement between the transferor and the transferee and no application has been made to the President under sub-paragraph (2), the National Assembly may make an application to the President for the appointment of an arbitrator.

(4)   Where the National Assembly gives a notice pursuant to regulation 12(2), it must make an application to the President for the appointment of an arbitrator and the National Assembly must be a party to the arbitration.

(5)   Where an apportionment under regulation 39(4)(b) is to be carried out by arbitration, the producer must either appoint an arbitrator by agreement with all persons with an interest in the holding or make an application to the President for the appointment of an arbitrator ...

2   (1)   In any case where a prospective apportionment is to be made by arbitration, an arbitrator must be appointed—

   (a)   where regulation 11(1)(b) or (4)(b) applies, by agreement between the occupier of the relevant holding and any other interested party, or, in default, by the President on an application by the occupier; and
   (b)   where regulation 12(3) applies, by the President.

(2)   Where sub-paragraph (1)(a) applies, the occupier must give notice to the National Assembly of the appointment of the arbitrator pursuant to the agreement, or of the application to the President for the appointment of an arbitrator.

3   (1)   An arbitrator appointed in accordance with paragraph 1(1) to (4) or 2 must conduct the arbitration in accordance with this Schedule and must base his or her award on findings made by him or her as to areas used for milk production in the last five year period during which production took place before the change of occupation, or, in the case of a prospective apportionment, in the last five year period during which production took place before the appointment of the arbitrator.

(2)   An arbitrator appointed in accordance with paragraph 1(5) must conduct the arbitration in accordance with this Schedule and must base his or her award on findings made by him or her as to the areas used for milk production in the last five-year period during which production took place before the appointment of the arbitrator.

(3)   An arbitrator appointed under any paragraph of this Schedule must base his or her award on findings made by him or her in accordance with the law in force at the time the event giving rise to an application for arbitration took place.

4   (1)   No application may be made to the President for an arbitrator to be appointed by him or her under this Schedule unless the application is accompanied by the appropriate fee for such an application; but once the fee has been paid in connection with any such application no further fee is payable in connection with any subsequent application for the President to exercise any function exercisable by him or her in relation to the arbitration by virtue of this Schedule (including an application for the appointment by him or her in an appropriate case of a new arbitrator).

(2)   In sub-paragraph (1), the 'appropriate fee' means such reasonable fee as the President may direct having regard to, and in no case exceeding, such fee as is for the time being prescribed under [section 84(4) of] the Agricultural Holdings Act 1986.

5   Where the National Assembly makes an application to the President under paragraph 1(3) or (4), the fee payable to the President in respect of that application referred to in paragraph 4 is recoverable by the National Assembly as a debt due from the other parties to the arbitration jointly or severally.

6   Any appointment of an arbitrator by the President must be made by him or her as soon as possible after receiving the application.

7   ...

8   If the arbitrator dies, or is incapable of acting, or for seven days after notice from any party requiring him or her to act fails to act, a new arbitrator may be appointed as if no arbitrator had been appointed.

9   No party to the arbitration may revoke the appointment of the arbitrator without the consent of any other party, and his or her appointment is not revoked by the death of any party.

10   Every appointment, application, notice, revocation and consent under paragraph 1, 2, 8 or 9 must be in writing.

11   (1)   The remuneration of the arbitrator—

  (a)   in a case where he or she is appointed by agreement between the parties, is such amount as may be agreed upon by him or her and the parties or, in default of agreement, fixed by the District Judge of the county court (subject to an appeal to the Judge of the court) on an application made by the arbitrator or any party;

  (b)   in a case where he or she is appointed by the President, is such amount as may be agreed upon by the arbitrator and the parties or, in default of agreement, fixed by the President.

(2)   The remuneration of the arbitrator is recoverable by the arbitrator as a debt due from the parties to the arbitration, jointly or severally.

Conduct of proceedings and witnesses

12   (1)   Subject to sub-paragraph (2), in any arbitration to which this Schedule applies, the arbitrator may join as a party to the arbitration any person having an interest in the holding, whether or not such person has applied to become a party to the arbitration, provided that such person consents to be so joined.

(2)   Where an apportionment pursuant to a request in a statement under regulation 39(4)(b) is to be carried out by arbitration, any person with an interest in the holding who has refused to sign such a statement as is referred to in regulation 39(4)(a) must be a party to the arbitration.

13   Within 35 days of the appointment of the arbitrator, or within such further period as the arbitrator may determine, the parties to the arbitration must deliver to him or her a statement of their respective cases with all necessary particulars and—

  (a)   no amendment or addition to the statement or particulars delivered is allowed after the expiry of the 35 days, or such further period as the arbitrator may determine, except with the consent of the arbitrator; and

  (b)   a party to the arbitration is confined at the hearing to the matters alleged in the statement and particulars delivered by him or her and any amendment or addition duly made.

14   The parties to the arbitration and all persons claiming through them must, subject to any legal objection, submit to being examined by the arbitrator, on oath or affirmation, in relation to the matters in dispute and must, subject to any such objection, produce before the arbitrator all samples and documents within their possession or power which may be required or called for, and do such other things as the arbitrator reasonably may require for the purposes of the arbitration.

15   Any person having an interest in the holding to which the arbitration relates is entitled to make representations to the arbitrator.

16   Witnesses appearing at the arbitration must, if the arbitrator thinks fit, be examined on oath or affirmation, and the arbitrator may administer oaths to, or to take the affirmation of, the parties and witnesses appearing.

17   The provisions of county court rules as to the issuing of witness summonses apply, subject to such modifications as may be prescribed by such rules, for the purposes of the arbitration as if it were an action or matter in the county court.

18   (1)   Subject to sub-paragraphs (2) and (3), any person who—

  (a)   having been summoned in pursuance of county court rules as a witness in the arbitration refuses or neglects, without sufficient cause, to appear or to produce any documents required by the summons to be produced; or
  (b)   having been so summoned or being present at the arbitration and being required to give evidence, refuses to be sworn or give evidence,

forfeits such fine as the judge of the county court may direct.

(2)   A judge may not direct under sub-paragraph (1) that a person forfeits a fine of an amount exceeding £400.

(3)   No person summoned in pursuance of county court rules as a witness in the arbitration forfeits a fine under this paragraph unless there has been paid or tendered to him or her at the time of the service of the summons such reasonable sum in respect of his or her expenses as the arbitrator may direct (including, in appropriate cases, compensation for loss of time), having regard to such sums payable in such cases as may be prescribed for the purposes of section 55 of the County Courts Act 1984.

(4)   The judge of the county court may at his or her discretion direct that the whole or any part of any such fine, after deducting costs, is applicable towards indemnifying a party injured by the refusal or neglect.

19   (1)   Subject to sub-paragraph (2), upon application by any party to the arbitration, the judge of the county court may, if he or she thinks fit, issue an order under his or her hand for bringing before the arbitrator any person (in this paragraph referred to as 'the prisoner') confined in any place under any sentence or under committal for trial or otherwise, to be examined as a witness in the arbitration.

(2)   No such order may be made with respect to a person confined under process in any civil action or matter.

(3)   Subject to sub-paragraph (4), the prisoner mentioned in any such order must be brought before the arbitrator under the same custody, and dealt with in the same manner in all respects, as a prisoner required by a writ of habeas corpus to be brought before the High Court and examined there as a witness.

(4)   The person having the custody of the prisoner is not bound to obey the order unless there is tendered to him or her a reasonable sum for the conveyance and maintenance of a proper officer or officers and of the prisoner in going to, remaining at, and returning from, the place where the arbitration is held.

20   The High Court may order that a writ of habeas corpus ad testificandum must issue to bring a prisoner for examination before the arbitrator, if that prisoner is confined in any prison under process in any civil action or matter.

Award

21 (1) Subject to sub-paragraph (2), the arbitrator must make and sign his or her award within 56 days of his or her appointment.

(2) The President may from time to time extend the time limit for making the award, whether that time has expired or not.

(3) The arbitrator must notify the terms of his or her award to the National Assembly within eight days of delivery of that award.

(4) The award must fix a date not later than one month after the delivery of the award for the payment of any costs awarded under paragraph 25.

22 The award is final and binding on the parties and any persons claiming under them.

23 The arbitrator may correct any clerical mistake or error in the award arising from any accidental slip or omission.

Reasons for award

24 Where the arbitrator is requested by any party to the arbitration, on or before the making of the award, to make a statement, either written or oral, of the reasons for the award, the arbitrator must furnish such a statement.

Costs

25 The costs of and incidental to the arbitration and award are in the discretion of the arbitrator who may direct to and by whom and in what manner the costs, or any part of the costs, are to be paid. The costs for the purposes of this paragraph include any fee paid to the President in respect of the appointment of an arbitrator and any sum paid to the National Assembly pursuant to paragraph 5.

26 On the application of any party, any such costs are taxable in the county court according to such of the scales prescribed by county court rules for proceedings in the county court as may be directed by the arbitrator under paragraph 25 or, in the absence of any such direction, by the county court.

27 (1) The arbitrator must, in awarding costs, take into consideration—

    (a) the reasonableness or unreasonableness of the claim of any party, whether in respect of the amount or otherwise;

    (b) any unreasonable demand for particulars or refusal to provide particulars; and

    (c) generally all the circumstances of the case.

(2) The arbitrator may disallow any costs which he or she considers to have been unnecessarily incurred, including the costs of any witness whom he or she considers to have been called unnecessarily.

Special case, setting aside award and remission

28 The arbitrator—

    (a) may state at any stage of the proceedings; and

    (b) must state, upon a direction in that behalf given by the judge of the county court following an application made by any party,

any question of law arising in the course of the arbitration and any question as to the jurisdiction of the arbitrator in the form of a special case for the opinion of the county court.

29 (1) Where the arbitrator has misconducted himself or herself, the county court may remove him or her.

(2) Where—

(a)   the arbitrator has misconducted himself or herself; or

(b)   an arbitration or award has been improperly procured; or

(c)   there is an error of law on the face of the award,

the county court may set the award aside.

30   (1)   The county court may from time to time remit the award, or any part of the award, to the arbitrator for reconsideration.

(2)   Paragraph (3) applies in any case where it appears to the county court that there is an error of law on the face of the award.

(3)   Instead of exercising its power of remission under sub-paragraph (1), the court may vary the award by substituting for so much of it as is affected by the error such award as the court considers that it would have been proper for the arbitrator to make in the circumstances.

(4)   An award varied pursuant to paragraph (3) has effect as so varied.

(5)   Where remission is ordered under sub-paragraph (1), the arbitrator must, unless the order otherwise directs, make and sign his or her award within 30 days of the date of the order.

(6)   If the county court is satisfied that the time for making the award is for any good reason insufficient, the court may extend or further extend that time for such period as it thinks proper.

Miscellaneous

31   Any amount paid, in respect of the remuneration of the arbitrator by any party to the arbitration in excess of the amount, if any, directed by the award to be paid by him or her in respect of the costs of the award, is recoverable from the other party or jointly from the other parties.

32   For the purposes of this Schedule, an arbitrator appointed by the President must be taken to have been so appointed at the time when the President executed the instrument of appointment, in accordance with the law in force at the time of such execution and in the case of any such arbitrator the periods mentioned in paragraphs 13 and 21 accordingly run from that time.

33   Any instrument of appointment or other document purporting to be made in the exercise of any function exercisable by the President under paragraph 1, 2, 6, 11 or 21 and to be signed by or on behalf of the President is to be taken to be such an instrument or document unless the contrary is shown.

34   The Arbitration Act 1996 does not apply to an arbitration determined in accordance with this Schedule.

NOTES

Initial Commencement

Specified date: 31 March 2005: see reg 1.

Amendment

Para 1: in para (2) words omitted revoked by SI 2006/2805, art 18, Sch 3.

Date in force: 19 October 2006: see SI 2006/2805, art 1(1)(b).

Para 1: in sub-para (5) words omitted revoked by SI 2006/2805, art 18, Sch 3.

Date in force: 19 October 2006: see SI 2006/2805, art 1(1)(b).

Para 4: in sub-para (2) words 'section 84(4) of' in square brackets substituted by SI 2006/2805, art 18, Sch 1, Pt 2, para 5.

Date in force: 19 October 2006: see SI 2006/2805, art 1(1)(b).

Para 7: revoked by SI 2006/2805, art 18, Sch 3.

Date in force: 19 October 2006: see SI 2006/2805, art 1(1)(b).

SCHEDULE 2
KEEPING AND RETENTION OF RECORDS

Regulation 34(2)

A1.688

Records to be kept by purchasers

1 In respect of each quota year, a purchaser must keep, and retain for the relevant period, records comprising—

(a) details of each producer making deliveries to him or her, including—
  (i) that producer's name and address,
  (ii) the wholesale quota available to that producer at the beginning and end of each quota year, and
  (iii) the representative fat content (butterfat base) of the milk delivered by that producer, and
  (iv) the total quota available for all the producers who make deliveries to the purchaser and the weighted butterfat of that quota;

(b) details, in terms of each delivery and each month, of the quantities of milk which each producer has delivered to him or her;

(c) details of the cumulative total of the quantities delivered to him or her each month by all producers;

(d) details of the average fat content of each producer's deliveries per month;

(e) details of the weighted average fat content of the cumulative total referred to in sub-paragraph (c),

(f) a list of purchasers and other undertakings which supply treated or processed milk or milk products to him or her;

(g) details, in terms of each such purchaser or undertaking and each month, of the quantities supplied to him or her by that purchaser or undertaking;

(h) details of the use to which milk and milk products collected from him or her has been put;

(i) records of individual deliveries and supplies and accompanying collection documents identifying each delivery or supply by producer, purchaser or other undertaking; and

(j) all books, registers, accounts, correspondence, commercial data, vouchers and supporting documents relating to his or her business activities.

Records to be kept by producers

2 (1) In respect of each quota year, a direct seller must keep, and retain for the relevant period, records comprising—

(a) details of the quota held by him or her, including any permanent and temporary transfers of quota if appropriate;

(b) his or her herd records (comprising number and breed of cows and calved heifers in dairy herd with details of number of cows in milk and number of cows dry);

(c) daily records of milk produced;

(d) invoices of any feed purchased;

(e) details recorded as a result of his or her participation in the National Milk Recording Scheme or other similar recording scheme;

(f)   details of quantities of milk processed, methods of processing and quantities and type of milk products produced;

(g)   details of quantities of whole milk used in the production of milk products (with conversion rates applied);

(h)   [if he or she holds 4,855 or more litres of direct sales quota,] details of quantities and types of milk and milk products which are produced and used on his or her holding for stock feeding and human consumption;

(i)   [if he or she holds 4,855 or more litres of direct sales quota,] details of quantities and types of milk and milk products which are disposed of (other than under paragraph (h)) or wasted on the holding;

(j)   without prejudice to paragraph (i), details of any milk or milk products which—

   (i)   were transported from his or her holding to be destroyed elsewhere for sanitary purposes pursuant to a decision of the National Assembly,

   (ii)   were so destroyed, and

   (iii)   as a consequence, are to be excluded from the levy calculation,

including information about the reason why such destruction was necessary and details of where, when and how such destruction occurred;

(k)   details of quantities and types of milk and milk products sold directly to the consumer or transferred free of charge from his or her holding (including milk and milk products sold on his or her holding);

(l)   details of quantities and types of milk and milk products purchased, exchanged or otherwise received by him or her, and records relating to their disposal; and

(m)   details of stocks of milk and milk products held by him or her on a monthly basis.

(2)   Where a direct seller also delivers milk or milk products to a purchaser, he or she must, in respect of each quota year, also keep, and retain for the relevant period, records comprising—

(a)   details of quantities and types of milk and milk products delivered by him or her and the name and address of any purchaser involved;

(b)   the payment slips issued in respect of any such purchaser; and

(c)   where there is a discrepancy between a purchaser's payment slip and the relevant tanker receipt, that tanker receipt.

3   A wholesale quota holder who makes deliveries to a purchaser must, in respect of each quota year, keep, and retain for the relevant period, records, comprising—

(a)   details of the quota held by him or her, showing permanent and temporary transfers of quota if appropriate;

(b)   his or her herd records (comprising number and breed of cows and calved heifers in dairy herd with details of number of cows in milk and number of cows dry);

(c)   daily records of milk produced;

(d)   invoices of any feed purchased;

(e)   details of quantities of milk delivered by him or her, and the name and address of the purchaser involved;

(f)   the payment slips issued in respect of any such purchaser;

(g)   where there is a discrepancy between a purchaser's payment slip and the relevant tanker receipt, that tanker receipt;

(h)   details recorded as a result of his or her participation in the National Milk Recording Scheme or other similar recording scheme;

(i)   details of quantities of milk produced and used on his or her holding for stock feeding and human consumption;

(j)   details of quantities of milk which are disposed of (other than under sub-paragraph (i)) or wasted on the holding;

(k) without prejudice to sub-paragraph (j), details of any milk which—

    (i) was transported from his or her holding to be destroyed elsewhere for sanitary purposes pursuant to a decision of the National Assembly,

    (ii) was so destroyed, and

    (iii) as a consequence, is to be excluded from the levy calculation,

including information about the reason why such destruction was necessary and details of where, when and how such destruction occurred;

(l) details of quantities and types of milk and milk products transferred free of charge from his or her holding;

(m) details of quantities of milk purchased, swapped or otherwise received, and records relating to its disposal; and

(n) details of stocks of milk produced on his or her holding.

Records to be kept by any person undertaking butterfat testing in a laboratory

4   Any person undertaking butterfat testing for a purchaser in a laboratory must keep, and retain for the relevant period, records comprising details of all samples of milk analysed, showing—

(a) the time and date the sample was taken on the holding;

(b) the time and date of his or her receipt of the sample;

(c) the time and date of the analysis;

(d) the identity of the purchaser concerned;

(e) the identity of the producer concerned (by name or reference number);

(f) the butterfat content of each sample recorded to two decimal places;

(g) the method of analysis used; and

(h) the results of any repeat analyses undertaken.

Records to be kept by hauliers

5   Any haulier collecting milk or milk products on behalf of a purchaser must keep, and retain for the relevant period, records comprising details of all quantities of milk or milk products so collected, showing—

(a) the time and date of collection from each producer;

(b) the time and date of sampling of the milk or milk products of each producer;

(c) the identity of the producer concerned;

(d) the volume of milk collected (including a copy of the tanker receipt in the cases referred to in paragraphs 2(2)(c) and 3(g));

(e) the identity of the purchaser concerned,

(f) the volume of milk delivered, and the name and address of each reception site;

(g) the sources of all the milk carried on each tanker; and

(h) details of any malfunction in any equipment used by him or her.

Records to be kept by processors

6   Any processor in receipt of milk or milk products for processing or treating must keep, and retain for the relevant period, records comprising details of all quantities of milk or milk products received, showing—

(a) the time and date of their delivery;

(b) their volume or weight per delivery (including copies of tanker receipts and weighbridge tickets in the cases referred to in paragraphs 2(2)(c) and 3(g));

(c) the name and address of the haulier concerned;

(d) the name and address of their vendor or donor;

(e) the quantities of milk processed, types of processing undertaken, and quantities and types of milk products produced;

(f) the quantities of milk used in the production of milk products (if not ascertainable from the information provided under sub-paragraph (e));

(g) the calculated stocks of milk and milk products held by that processor at the end of each month and details of actual stocks physically held as at 31 March each year; and

(h) the quantities of milk or milk products sold or otherwise disposed of, with the date of supply or disposal, and the names and addresses of the buyers or recipients concerned.

Records to be kept by persons buying, selling or supplying milk or milk products obtained directly from a producer or purchaser

7 Any person who in the course of a business buys, sells or supplies milk or milk products obtained directly from a producer or purchaser must keep, and retain for the relevant period, records comprising details of all quantities of milk or milk products received, showing—

(a) the time and date of their receipt;

(b) their volume or weight per delivery (including copies of tanker receipts or invoices in the cases referred to in paragraphs 2(2)(c) and 3(g));

(c) the name and address of the haulier concerned;

(d) the name and address of their vendor or donor;

(e) the quantities of milk or milk products sold or supplied, with the date of sale or supply, and the names and addresses of the buyers or recipients concerned other than the consumers of such milk or milk products; and

(f) the quantities of milk or milk products returned to the producer or purchaser unsold or unused, and the date of that return.

8 In this Schedule, in relation to any records—

'the relevant period' means the remainder of the year of record and a period of at least three years thereafter; and

'the remainder of the year of record' means, following the making of the records, the remainder of the year in which they were made.

NOTES

Initial Commencement

Specified date: 31 March 2005: see reg 1.

Amendment

Para 2: in sub-para (1)(h), (i) words 'if he or she holds 4,855 or more litres of direct sales quota,' in square brackets inserted by SI 2007/844, reg 2(1), (10).

Date in force: 31 March 2007: see SI 2007/844, reg 1.

DAIRY PRODUCE QUOTAS (AMENDMENT) REGULATIONS 2006

SI 2006/120

The Secretary of State has been designated for the purposes of section 2(2) of the European Communities Act 1972 in relation to the common agricultural policy of the European Community.

She makes the following Regulations under the powers conferred by that section.

A1.689

Title and commencement

1

These Regulations may be cited as the Dairy Produce Quotas (Amendment) Regulations 2006 and come into force on 31st March 2006.

NOTES

Initial Commencement

Specified date: 31 March 2006: see above.

A1.690

Amendment of the Dairy Produce Quotas Regulations 2005

2

The Dairy Produce Quotas Regulations 2005 are amended as follows.

NOTES

Initial Commencement

Specified date: 31 March 2006: see reg 1.

A1.691

3

In regulation 16(3), before the word 'quota' insert ', as unused,'.

NOTES

Initial Commencement

Specified date: 31 March 2006: see reg 1.

A1.692

4

In regulation 23(4)(a), for 'reach the Secretary of State no later than' substitute 'be sent to the Secretary of State on or before'.

NOTES

Initial Commencement

Specified date: 31 March 2006: see reg 1.

A1.693

5

In regulation 33(5)—

(a)   for 'provide the Secretary of State with' substitute 'send to the Secretary of State';

(b)   for 'and ensure that the list reaches her no later than' substitute 'on or before'.

NOTES

Initial Commencement

Specified date: 31 March 2006: see reg 1.

A1.694.

6

In regulation 35—

(a)   in paragraph (1)(a)—
    (i)   for 'submit' (wherever occurring) substitute 'send';
    (ii) omit 'so that the declaration reaches her';

(b)   in paragraph (1)(b)—
    (i)   for 'submit' (wherever occurring) substitute 'send';
    (ii) omit 'so that the summary reaches her';

(c)   in paragraph (2), for 'submitted' substitute 'sent'.

NOTES

Initial Commencement

Specified date: 31 March 2006: see reg 1.

A1.695

7

In regulation 36—

(a)   in paragraph (1), for 'and (3)' substitute 'to (3)';

(b)   after paragraph (2), insert—

'(2A)   Where a purchaser—

(a)   sends to the Secretary of State a summary of producers' statements required to be submitted under Article 8(2) of the Commission Regulation, which is inaccurate; and

(b)   by doing so causes an overstatement or an understatement by him, of deliveries made to him, he is liable to pay to the Secretary of State a penalty equivalent to the theoretical amount of levy that would be due on 0.5% of the quantity by volume of milk which comprises the overstatement or understatement.';

    (c) in paragraph (6)—
        (i) after 'liable to pay to the Secretary of State' insert ', if she serves notice,';
       (ii) at the end add 'starting on the thirtieth day after service of the notice'.

NOTES

Initial Commencement

Specified date: 31 March 2006: see reg 1.

AGRICULTURAL HOLDINGS (UNITS OF PRODUCTION) (ENGLAND) ORDER 2006

SI 2006/2628

The Secretary of State, in exercise of the powers conferred by paragraph 4 of Schedule 6 to the Agricultural Holdings Act 1986, and now vested in him, makes the following Order:

A1.696

1   Title, commencement and interpretation

(1) This Order may be cited as the Agricultural Holdings (Units of Production) (England) Order 2006 and comes into force on 7th November 2006.

(2) In this Order—

'Council Regulation 1782/2003' means Council Regulation (EC) No 1782/2003 establishing common rules for direct support schemes under the common agricultural policy and establishing certain direct support schemes for farmers and amending certain regulations, as last amended by Commission Regulation (EC) No 1156/2006;

'disadvantaged land' (except in the expression 'severely disadvantaged land') means any area of land shown coloured blue on the England LFA maps;

'eligible hectare' has the same meaning as in Article 44(2) of Council Regulation 1782/2003;

'the England LFA maps' means the three volumes of maps numbered 1 to 3, each volume being marked 'Volume of maps of less-favoured farming areas in England', dated 20th May 1991, signed and sealed by the Minister of Agriculture, Fisheries and Food and deposited at the offices of the Department for Environment, Food and Rural Affairs, Ergon House, Horseferry Road, London SW1P 2AL;

'moorland' means all the land that is—
    (a) severely disadvantaged land, and
    (b) shown coloured pink in the three volumes of maps entitled 'Moorland Map of England 2006' each volume being marked with the number of the volume, dated 13th February 2006, signed on behalf of the Secretary of State for Environment, Food and Rural Affairs and deposited at the

offices of the Department for Environment, Food and Rural Affairs, Ergon House, Horseferry Road, London SW1P 2AL;

'severely disadvantaged land' means any area of land shown coloured pink on the England LFA maps.

NOTES

Initial Commencement

Specified date: 7 November 2006: see para (1) above.

A1.697

2   Assessment of productive capacity of land

(1)   Paragraphs (2) and (3) of this article have effect for the purpose of the assessment of the productive capacity of a unit of agricultural land situated in England, in order to determine whether that unit is a commercial unit of agricultural land within the meaning of paragraph 3(1) of Schedule 6 to the Agricultural Holdings Act 1986.

(2)   Where the land in question is capable, when farmed under competent management, of being used to produce any livestock, farm arable crop, outdoor horticultural crop or fruit as is mentioned in any of the entries 1 to 3 in column 1 of the Schedule to this Order, then—

   (a)   the unit of production prescribed in relation to that use of the land shall be the unit in the entry in column 2 of that Schedule opposite to that entry; and

   (b)   the amount determined, for the period of 12 months beginning with 7th November 2006, as the net annual income from that unit of production in that period shall be the amount in the entry in column 3 of that Schedule opposite to that entry as read with any relevant note to that Schedule.

(3)   Where land capable, when farmed under competent management, of producing a net annual income is in receipt of hill farm allowance, or was set aside from production in 2005, or was an eligible hectare in 2005, as is mentioned in entries 4, 5 and 6 respectively in column 1 of the Schedule to this Order, then—

   (a)   the unit of production prescribed in relation to that use of the land shall be the unit in the entry in column 2 of that Schedule opposite to that entry; and

   (b)   the amount determined, for the period of 12 months beginning with 7th November 2006, as the net annual income from that unit of production in that period shall be the amount in the entry in column 3 of that Schedule opposite to that entry.

NOTES

Initial Commencement

Specified date: 7 November 2006: see art 1(1).

A1.698

3   Revocation

The Agricultural Holdings (Units of Production) (England) Order 2005 is revoked.

NOTES

Initial Commencement

Specified date: 7 November 2006: see art 1(1).

SCHEDULE
PRESCRIBED UNITS OF PRODUCTION AND DETERMINATION OF NET ANNUAL INCOME

Article 2

A1.699

Column 1 *Farming use*		Column 2 *Unit of production*	Column 3 *Net annual income from unit of production (£)*
1 Livestock			
Dairy cows (other than Channel Islands breeds)		cow	302
Beef breeding cows:			
	On less favoured area land under the Hill Farm Allowance Regulations 2006	cow	–138
	On other land	cow	–59
Beef fattening cattle (semi-intensive)		head	–57(1)
Dairy replacements		head	80(2)
Ewes:			
	On less favoured area land under the Hill Farm Allowance Regulations 2006	ewe	8
	On other land	ewe	19
Store lambs (including ewe lambs sold as shearlings)		head	2
Pigs:			
	Sows and gilts in pig	sow or gilt	160
	Porker	head	3
	Cutter	head	5.50
	Bacon	head	8.20
Poultry:			
	Laying hens	bird	2
	Broilers	bird	0.24
	Point-of-lay pullets	bird	0.45
Christmas Turkeys		bird	4.50
2 Farm arable crops			
Barley		hectare	24
Beans		hectare	54.18(3)
Herbage seed		hectare	230
Oilseed rape		hectare	22
Peas:			
	Dried	hectare	14.18(3)

1907

		Vining	hectare	350
Potatoes:				
		First early	hectare	1800
		Maincrop (including seed)	hectare	1500
Sugar Beet			hectare	250
Wheat			hectare	35

3 Outdoor horticultural crops and fruit

Root vegetables and onions	hectare	2500
Brassicas	hectare	1750
Fresh peas and beans	hectare	1100
Orchard fruit	hectare	1300
Soft fruit	hectare	3600

4 Forage Land

| Eligible forage area as defined in regulation 2(1) of the Hill Farm Allowance Regulations 2006 | hectare | The amount of hill farm allowance required to be paid under regulations 3 and 7 of the Hill Farm Allowance Regulations 2006 |

5 Set-aside

Land which was, in 2005, set-aside from production under Article 54(3) of Council Regulation 1782/2003		
Severely disadvantaged land, excluding moorland:	hectare	−19.91
Disadvantaged land	hectare	−16.77
All other land	hectare	−120.77

6 Eligible hectares

Land which was, in 2005, an eligible hectare for the purposes of Council Regulation 1782/2003, except land which was set-aside from production under Article 54(3) of that Regulation:

| Moorland | hectare | −9.85 |

Severely disadvantaged land, excluding moorland	hectare	128.40
Disadvantaged land	hectare	169.43
All other land	hectare	65.63

NOTES TO THE SCHEDULE

1 This is the figure for animals which would be kept for 12 months. In the case of animals kept for less than 12 months a pro-rata adjustment of this figure is to be made.

2 This is the figure for animals (irrespective of age) which would be kept for 12 months. In the case of animals kept for less than 12 months a pro-rata adjustment of this figure is to be made.

3 This figure includes the protein crop premium provided for in Article 76 of Council Regulation 1782/2003.

NOTES

Initial Commencement

Specified date: 7 November 2006: see art 1(1).

AGRICULTURAL HOLDINGS (UNITS OF PRODUCTION) (WALES) ORDER 2006

SI 2006/2796 (W 235)

In exercise of the powers conferred by paragraph 4 of Schedule 6 to the Agricultural Holdings Act 1986, which are now vested in it, the National Assembly for Wales makes the following Order:—

A1.700

1 Title, commencement and interpretation

(1) The title of this Order is the Agricultural Holdings (Units of Production) (Wales) Order 2006 and it comes into force on 27 October 2006.

(2) This Order applies in relation to Wales.

(3) Any reference in this Order to 'Schedule 1' or 'Schedule 2' is a reference to the appropriate Schedule attached to this Order.

(4) In this Order:

  (a) 'Council Regulation 1251/99' ('*Rheoliad y Cyngor 1251/99*') means Council Regulation (EC) No 1251/1999 establishing a support system for producers of certain arable crops as last amended by Council Regulation (EC) No 1782/2003;

  (b) 'Council Regulation 1254/99' ('*Rheoliad y Cyngor 1254/99*') means Council Regulation (EC) No 1254/1999 on the common organisation of the market in beef and veal as amended by Council Regulation (EC) No 1455/2001; Council Regulation (EC) No 1512/2001; Council Regulation (EC) No 2345/2001; the Act concerning the conditions of accession of the Czech Republic, the Republic of Estonia, the Republic of Cyprus, the Republic of Latvia, the Republic of Lithuania, the Republic of Hungary, the Republic of Malta, the Republic of Poland, the Republic of Slovenia and the Slovak Republic and the adjustments to the Treaties on which the European Union is founded; Council Regulation (EC) No 806/2003 and the amendments made by Council Regulation (EC) No 1782/2003 to Article 10(1) and Annexes 1 and 2 of Council Regulation 1254/99;

(c) 'Council Regulation 2529/01' ('*Rheoliad y Cyngor 2529/01*') means Council Regulation (EC) No 2529/2001 on the common organisation of the market in sheepmeat and goatmeat as amended by the Act concerning the conditions of accession of the Czech Republic, the Republic of Estonia, the Republic of Cyprus, the Republic of Latvia, the Republic of Lithuania, the Republic of Hungary, the Republic of Malta, the Republic of Poland, the Republic of Slovenia and the Slovak Republic and the adjustments to the Treaties on which the European Union is founded;

(d) 'marketing year' ('*blwyddyn farchnata*') is to be construed in accordance with Council Regulation 1251/1999.

NOTES

Initial Commencement

Specified date: 27 October 2006: see para (1) above.

A1.701

2   Assessment of productive capacity of land

(1)   This article has effect for the purpose of the assessment of the productive capacity of a unit of agricultural land situated in Wales, in order to determine whether that unit is a commercial unit of agricultural land within the meaning of paragraph 3(1) of Schedule 6 to the Agricultural Holdings Act 1986.

(2)   For the period of 12 months beginning with 12 September 2004, where the land in question is capable, when farmed under competent management, of being used to produce any livestock, crop, fruit or miscellaneous product, as is mentioned in any of the entries 1 to 6 in column 1 of Schedule 1, then—

(a) the unit of production prescribed in relation to that use of the land is the unit specified in column 2 of Schedule 1 opposite to that entry, and

(b) the amount determined as the net annual income from that unit of production in that period is the amount specified in column 3 of Schedule 1 opposite to that entry as read with any relevant Note to Schedule 1.

(3)   For the period of 12 months beginning with 12 September 2004, where land capable, when farmed under competent management, of producing a net annual income is the subject of Tir Mynydd payments or is designated as set aside land, as is mentioned in entries 7 and 8 in column 1 of Schedule 1, then—

(a) the unit of production prescribed in relation to that use of the land is the unit specified in column 2 of Schedule 1 opposite to that entry, and

(b) the amount determined as the net annual income from that unit of production in that period is the amount in the entry in column 3 of Schedule 1 opposite to that entry.

(4)   For the period of 12 months beginning with 12 September 2005, where the land in question is capable, when farmed under competent management, of being used to produce any livestock, crop, fruit or miscellaneous product, as is mentioned in any of the entries 1 to 6 in column 1 of Schedule 2, then—

(a)   the unit of production prescribed in relation to that use of the land is the unit specified in column 2 of Schedule 2 opposite to that entry, and

(b)   the amount determined as the net annual income from that unit of production in that period is the amount specified in column 3 of Schedule 2 opposite to that entry as read with any relevant Note to Schedule 2.

(5)   For the period of 12 months beginning with 12 September 2005, where land capable, when farmed under competent management, of producing a net annual income is the subject of Tir Mynydd payments or was in the marketing year 2004/2005 designated as set aside land, as is mentioned in entries 7 and 8 in column 1 of Schedule 2, then—

(a)   the unit of production prescribed in relation to that use of the land is the unit specified in column 2 of Schedule 2 opposite to that entry, and

(b)   the amount determined as the net annual income from that unit of production in that period is the amount in the entry in column 3 of Schedule 2 opposite to that entry.

NOTES

Initial Commencement

Specified date: 27 October 2006: see art 1(1).

A1.702

3   Revocation

The Agricultural Holdings (Units of Production) (Wales) Order 2004 is hereby revoked.

NOTES

Initial Commencement

Specified date: 27 October 2006: see art 1(1).

SCHEDULE 1
PRESCRIBED UNITS OF PRODUCTION AND DETERMINATION OF NET ANNUAL INCOME

Articles 1(3), 2(2) and 2(3)

A1.703

Column 1 Farming use	Column 2 Unit of production	Column 3 Net annual income from unit of production (£)
1 Livestock		
Dairy cows (other than Channel Islands breeds)	cow	260
Beef breeding cows:		

On land which is 'eligible land' for the purposes of the Tir Mynydd (Wales) Regulations 2001	cow	31 (1)
On other land	cow	80 (1)
Beef fattening cattle (semi-intensive)	head	63 (2)
Dairy replacements	head	45 (3)
Ewes:		
On land which is 'eligible land' for the purposes of the Tir Mynydd (Wales) Regulations 2001	ewe	14 (4)
On other land	ewe	21 (5)
Store lambs (including ewe lambs sold as shearlings)	head	1.05
Pigs:		
Sows and gilts in pig	sow or gilt	95
Porker	head	1.90
Cutter	head	3.50
Bacon	head	5.50
Poultry:		
Laying hens	bird	1.25
Broilers	bird	0.15
Point-of-lay pullets	bird	0.30
Christmas turkeys	bird	3.00

2 Farm arable crops

Barley	hectare	199 (6)
Beans	hectare	175 (7)
Herbage seed	hectare	120
Oats	hectare	131 (8)
Oilseed rape	hectare	188 (9)
Peas:		
Dried	hectare	201 (10)
Vining	hectare	175
Potatoes:		
First early	hectare	900
Maincrop (including seed)	hectare	780
Sugar Beet	hectare	270
Wheat	hectare	266 (11)

3 Outdoor horticultural crops

Broad beans	hectare	575
Brussels sprouts	hectare	1600
Cabbage, savoys and sprouting broccoli	hectare	2000
Carrots	hectare	3100
Cauliflower and winter broccoli	hectare	1000
Celery	hectare	8000
Leeks	hectare	3600

Lettuce		hectare	4150
Onions:			
	Dry bulb	hectare	1305
	Salad	hectare	3800
Parsnips		hectare	3250
Rhubarb (natural)		hectare	6900
Turnips and swedes		hectare	1500
4 Orchard fruit			
Apples:			
	Cider	hectare	380
	Cooking	hectare	1250
	Dessert	hectare	1400
Cherries		hectare	900
Pears		hectare	1000
Plums		hectare	1250
5 Soft fruit			
Blackcurrants		hectare	850
Raspberries		hectare	3100
Strawberries		hectare	4200
6 Miscellaneous			
Hops		hectare	1700
7 Forage Land			
On land which is 'eligible land' for the purposes of the Tir Mynydd (Wales) Regulations 2001		hectare	The amount of the Tir Mynydd payment required to be paid under Regulation 2A of the Tir Mynydd (Wales) Regulations 2001
8 Set-aside			
Land which is set-aside under Article 2(3) of Council Regulation 1251/99, except where such land is used (in accordance with Article 6(3) of Council Regulation 1251/99) for the provision of materials for the manufacture within the Community of products not primarily intended for human or animal consumption		hectare	37

NOTES TO SCHEDULE 1

(1)   Deduct £135 from the figure in column 3 in the case of animals for which the net annual income during the period 12 September 2004 to 31 December 2004 inclusive did not include a sum in respect of the premium for maintaining suckler cows (suckler cow premium) provided for in Article 6 of Council Regulation 1254/99 on the common organisation of the market in beef and veal.

Add £27 to the figure in column 3 in the case of animals for which the net annual income during the period 12 September 2004 to 31 December 2004 inclusive included a sum in respect of the lower rate of extensification premium provided for in Article 13 of Council Regulation 1254/99.

Add £54 to the figure in column 3 in the case of animals for which the net annual income during the period 12 September 2004 to 31 December 2004 inclusive included a sum in respect of the higher rate of extensification premium provided for in Article 13 of Council Regulation 1254/99.

(2)   This is the figure for animals which would be kept for 12 months.

Deduct £115 in the case of animals which are kept for 12 months and for which the net annual income during the period 12 September 2004 to 31 December 2004 inclusive did not include a sum in respect of the special premium for holding male bovine animals (beef special premium) provided for in Article 4 of Council Regulation 1254/99.

Add £27 to the figure in column 3 in the case of animals which are kept for 12 months and for which the net annual income during the period 12 September 2004 to 31 December 2004 inclusive included a sum in respect of the lower rate of extensification premium.

Add £54 to the figure in column 3 in the case of animals which would be kept for that period and for which the net annual income during the period 12 September 2004 to 31 December 2004 inclusive included a sum in respect of the higher rate of extensification premium.

In the case of animals which are kept for less than 12 months and for which the net annual income during the period 12 September 2004 to 31 December 2004 inclusive did not include a sum in respect of beef special premium, the net annual income is to be calculated by deducting £115 from the figure in column 3 and then making a pro rata adjustment of the resulting figure.

In the case of animals which are kept for less than 12 months and for which the net annual income during the period 12 September 2004 to 31 December 2004 inclusive included a sum in respect of beef special premium, the net annual income is to be calculated by first deducting £115 from the figure in column 3, then making a pro rata adjustment of the resulting figure, then adding to that figure the sum of £115 and (where the net annual income during the period 12 September 2004 to 31 December 2004 inclusive included a sum in respect of extensification premium) the sum of £27 (where the said extensification premium was paid at the lower rate) or £54 (where the said extensification premium was paid at the higher rate).

(3)   This indicates the figure for animals (irrespective of age) which would be kept for 12 months. In the case of animals which are kept for less than 12 months a pro rata adjustment of this figure is to be made.

(4)   Deduct £19 from the figure in column 3 in the case of animals for which the net annual income during the period 12 September 2004 to 31 December 2004 inclusive did not include a sum in respect of the premium for offsetting income loss sustained by sheep meat producers (sheep annual premium) provided for in Articles 4 and 5 of Council Regulation 2529/01 on the common organisation of the market in sheepmeat and goatmeat.

(5)   Deduct £15 from the figure in column 3 in the case of animals for which the net annual income during the period 12 September 2004 to 31 December 2004 inclusive did not include a sum in respect of sheep annual premium.

(6)   Deduct £238 from the figure in column 3 in the case of land for which the net annual income during the period 12 September 2004 to 30 June 2005 inclusive did not

include a sum in respect of the compensatory payment for which producers of arable crops may apply (area payment) provided for in Article 2 of Council Regulation 1251/99.

(7)   Deduct £274 from the figure in column 3 in the case of land for which the net annual income during the period 12 September 2004 to 30 June 2005 inclusive did not include a sum in respect of area payment.

(8)   Deduct £238 from the figure in column 3 in the case of land for which the net annual income during the period 12 September 2004 to 30 June 2005 inclusive did not include a sum in respect of area payment.

(9)   Deduct £238 from the figure in column 3 in the case of land for which the net annual income during the period 12 September 2004 to 30 June 2005 inclusive did not include a sum in respect of area payment.

(10)   Deduct £274 from the figure in column 3 in the case of land for which the net annual income during the period 12 September 2004 to 30 June 2005 inclusive did not include a sum in respect of area payment.

(11)   Deduct £238 from the figure in column 3 in the case of land for which the net annual income during the period 12 September 2004 to 30 June 2005 inclusive did not include a sum in respect of area payment.

NOTES

Initial Commencement

Specified date: 27 October 2006: see art 1(1).

SCHEDULE 2
PRESCRIBED UNITS OF PRODUCTION AND DETERMINATION OF NET ANNUAL INCOME

Articles 1(3), 2(4) and 2(5)

A1.704

Column 1 Farming use		Column 2 Unit of produc- tion	Column 3 Net annual income from unit of production (£)
1 Livestock			
Dairy cows (other than Channel Islands breeds):		cow	260
Beef breeding cows:			
	On land which is 'eligible land' for the purposes of the Tir Mynydd (Wales) Regulations 2001	cow	31 **(1)**
	On other land	cow	80 **(1)**
Beef fattening cattle (semi-intensive)		head	63 **(2)**
Dairy replacements		head	45 **(3)**
Ewes:			

1915

	On land which is 'eligible land' for the purposes of the Tir Mynydd (Wales) Regulations 2001	ewe	14 (4)
	On other land	ewe	21 (5)
Store lambs (including ewe lambs sold as shearlings)		head	1.05

Pigs:

	Sows and gilts in pig	sow or gilt	95
	Porker	head	1.90
	Cutter	head	3.50
	Bacon	head	5.50

Poultry:

	Laying hens	bird	1.25
	Broilers	bird	0.15
	Point-of-lay pullets	bird	0.30
Christmas turkeys		bird	3.00

2 Farm arable crops

Barley	hectare	199
Beans	hectare	175
Herbage seed	hectare	120
Oats	hectare	131
Oilseed rape	hectare	188

Peas:

	Dried	hectare	201 (10)
	Vining	hectare	175

Potatoes:

	First early	hectare	900
	Maincrop (including seed)	hectare	780
Sugar Beet		hectare	270
Wheat		hectare	266 (11)

3 Outdoor horticultural crops

Broad beans	hectare	575
Brussels sprouts	hectare	1600
Cabbage, savoys and sprouting broccoli	hectare	2000
Carrots	hectare	3100
Cauliflower and winter broccoli	hectare	1000
Celery	hectare	8000
Leeks	hectare	3600
Lettuce	hectare	4150

Onions:

	Dry bulb	hectare	1305
	Salad	hectare	3800
Parsnips		hectare	3250
Rhubarb (natural)		hectare	6900
Turnips and swedes		hectare	1500

4 Orchard fruit

Apples:

	Cider	hectare	380

	Cooking	hectare	1250
	Dessert	hectare	1400
Cherries		hectare	900
Pears		hectare	1000
Plums		hectare	1250
5 Soft fruit			
Blackcurrants		hectare	850
Raspberries		hectare	3100
Strawberries		hectare	4200
6 Miscellaneous			
Hops		hectare	1700
7 Forage Land			
On land which is 'eligible land' for the purposes of the Tir Mynydd (Wales) Regulations 2001		hectare	The amount of the Tir Mynydd payment required to be paid under Regulation 2A of the Tir Mynydd (Wales) Regulations 2001
8 Set-aside			
Land which was, in the marketing year 2004/2005, set-aside under Article 2(3) of Council Regulation 1251/99, except where such land was used (in accordance with Article 6(3) of Council Regulation 1251/99) for the provision of materials for the manufacture within the Community of products not primarily intended for human or animal consumption		hectare	37

NOTES TO SCHEDULE 2

(1) Deduct £135 from the figure in column 3 in the case of animals for which the net annual income would not include a sum in respect of the premium for maintaining suckler cows (suckler cow premium) provided for in Article 6 of Council Regulation 1254/99 if that premium were still available and the conditions for receiving it were the same as for the calendar year 2004.

Add £27 to the figure in column 3 in the case of animals for which the net annual income would include a sum in respect of the lower rate of extensification premium provided for in Article 13 of Council Regulation 1254/99 if that premium were still available and the conditions for receiving it were the same as for the calendar year 2004.

Add £54 to the figure in column 3 in the case of animals for which the net annual income would include a sum in respect of the higher rate of extensification premium

1917

provided for in Article 13 of Council Regulation 1254/99 if that premium were still available and the conditions for receiving it were the same as for the calendar year 2004.

(2)   This is the figure for animals which would be kept for 12 months.

Deduct £115 in the case of animals which are kept for 12 months and for which the net annual income would not include a sum in respect of the special premium for holding male bovine animals (beef special premium) provided for in Article 4 of Council Regulation 1254/99 if that premium were still available and the conditions for receiving it were the same as for the calendar year 2004.

Add £27 to the figure in column 3 in the case of animals which are kept for 12 months and for which the net annual income would include a sum in respect of the lower rate of extensification premium if that premium were still available and the conditions for receiving it were the same as for the calendar year 2004.

Add £54 to the figure in column 3 in the case of animals which would be kept for that period and for which the net annual income would include a sum in respect of the higher rate of extensification premium if that premium were still available and the conditions for receiving it were the same as for the calendar year 2004.

In the case of animals which—

 (1) are kept for less than 12 months, and
 (2) for which the net annual income would not include a sum in respect of beef special premium if that premium were still available and the conditions for receiving it were the same as for the calendar year 2004,

the net annual income is to be calculated by deducting £115 from the figure in column 3 and then making a pro rata adjustment of the resulting figure.

In the case of animals which—

 (1)   are kept for less than 12 months, and
 (2)   for which the net annual income would include a sum in respect of beef special premium if that premium were still available and the conditions for receiving it were the same as for the calendar year 2004,

the net annual income is to be calculated by first deducting £115 from the figure in column 3, then making a pro rata adjustment of the resulting figure, then adding to that figure the sum of £115 and (where the net annual income would include a sum in respect of extensification premium if that premium were still available and the conditions for receiving it were the same as for the calendar year 2004) the sum of £27 (when the extensification premium would be paid at the lower rate) or £54 (when the extensification premium would be paid at the higher rate).

(3)   This indicates the figure for animals (irrespective of age) which would be kept for 12 months. In the case of animals which are kept for less than 12 months a pro rata adjustment of this figure is to be made.

(4)   Deduct £19 from this figure in the case of animals for which the net annual income would not include a sum in respect of the premium for offsetting income loss sustained by sheep meat producers (sheep annual premium) provided for in Articles 4 and 5 of Council Regulation 2529/01 if that premium were still available and the conditions for receiving it were the same as for the calendar year 2004.

(5)   Deduct £15 from the figure in column 3 in the case of animals for which the net annual income would not include a sum in respect of sheep annual premium if that premium were still available and the conditions for receiving it were the same as for the calendar year 2004.

(6) Deduct £238 from the figure in column 3 in the case of land for which the net annual income would not include a sum in respect of the compensatory payment for which producers of arable crops may apply (area payment) provided for in Article 2 of Council Regulation 1251/99 if that payment were still available and the conditions for receiving it were the same as for the marketing year 2004/2005.

(7) Deduct £274 from the figure in column 3 in the case of land for which the net annual income would not include a sum in respect of area payment if that payment were still available and the conditions for receiving it were the same as for the marketing year 2004/2005.

(8) Deduct £238 from the figure in column 3 in the case of land for which the net annual income would not include a sum in respect of area payment if that payment were still available and the conditions for receiving it were the same as for the marketing year 2004/2005.

(9) Deduct £238 from the figure in column 3 in the case of land for which the net annual income would not include a sum in respect of area payment if that payment were still available and the conditions for receiving it were the same as for the marketing year 2004/2005.

(10) Deduct £274 from the figure in column 3 in the case of land for which the net annual income would not include a sum in respect of area payment if that payment were still available and the conditions for receiving it were the same as for the marketing year 2004/2005.

(11) Deduct £238 from the figure in column 3 in the case of land for which the net annual income would not include a sum in respect of area payment if that payment were still available and the conditions for receiving it were the same as for the marketing year 2004/2005.

NOTES

Initial Commencement

Specified date: 27 October 2006: see art 1(1).

REGULATORY REFORM (AGRICULTURAL TENANCIES) (ENGLAND AND WALES) ORDER 2006

SI 2006/2805

The Secretary of State has—

(1)consulted, in accordance with section 5(1) of the Regulatory Reform Act 2001, such organisations as appear to him to be representative of interests substantially affected by his proposals for this Order, the National Assembly for Wales, and such other persons as he considered appropriate;

(2)following that consultation, considered it appropriate to vary part of his proposals, and undertaken such further consultation with respect to the variations as appeared to him to be appropriate;

(3)following those consultations, considered it appropriate to proceed with the making of this Order;

(4)laid a document containing his proposals before Parliament, in accordance with section 6 of the Regulatory Reform Act 2001, and the period for Parliamentary consideration under section 8 of the Act has expired;

(5)had regard to the representations made during that period and in particular to the 6th Report of the Regulatory Reform Committee of the House of Commons and the 21st Report of the Delegated Powers and Regulatory Reform Committee of the House of Lords;

(6)laid a draft of this Order before Parliament with a statement giving details of those representations and of the changes he has made to his proposals in the light of them;

(7)reached the opinion that this Order does not remove any necessary protection, or prevent any person from continuing to exercise any right or freedom which he might reasonably expect to continue to exercise;

(8)as this Order creates burdens affecting persons, reached the opinion that—

(a) the provisions of this Order, taken as a whole, strike a fair balance between the public interest and the interests of the persons affected by the burdens being created, and

(b) the extent to which this Order removes or reduces one or more burdens, or has other beneficial effects for persons affected by the burdens imposed by the existing law, makes it desirable for this Order to be made.

The draft of this Order has been approved by resolution of each House of Parliament.

Accordingly, the Secretary of State makes the following Order, in exercise of the powers conferred by section 1 of the Regulatory Reform Act 2001:

A1.705

1   Citation, extent and commencement

(1) This Order—

(a) may be cited as the Regulatory Reform (Agricultural Tenancies) (England and Wales) Order 2006,

(b) comes into force on the day after the day on which it is made, and

(c) subject to paragraph (2), extends to England and Wales only.

(2) The amendment, repeal or revocation by a provision of Schedule 1, 2 or 3 to this Order of an enactment which extends to Scotland or Northern Ireland also extends there.

NOTES

Initial Commencement

Specified date: 19 October 2006: see para (1)(b) above.

Extent

This article does not extend to Scotland: see para (1)(c) above.

A1.706

2   Amendments to the Agricultural Holdings Act 1986

Articles 3 to 9 amend the Agricultural Holdings Act 1986.

NOTES

Initial Commencement

Specified date: 19 October 2006: see art 1(1)(b).

Extent

This article does not extend to Scotland: see art 1(1)(c).

A1.707

3   Arbitration of rent

In section 12, in subsection (2), for the words from 'date of the reference' to 'arbitration' there shall be substituted 'next termination date following the date of the demand for arbitration and accordingly shall, with effect from that next termination date'.

NOTES

Initial Commencement

Specified date: 19 October 2006: see art 1(1)(b).

Extent

This article does not extend to Scotland: see art 1(1)(c).

A1.708

4   Meaning of 'substantial part'

(1)   In section 34, after subsection (2) there shall be inserted—

'(3)   (3) Where this Act applies in relation to a tenancy by virtue of section 4(1)(g) of the Agricultural Tenancies Act 1995, the reference in subsection (1)(b)(iv) above to a substantial part of the land comprised in the holding means a substantial part determined by reference to either area or value.'.

(2)   In section 35, after subsection (2) there shall be inserted—

'(3)   Where this Act applies in relation to a tenancy by virtue of section 4(1)(g) of the Agricultural Tenancies Act 1995, the reference in subsection (2) above (in the definition of 'related holding') to a substantial part of the land comprised in the holding means a substantial part determined by reference to either area or value.'.

(3)   In section 49, after subsection (3) there shall be inserted—

'(4)   Where this Act applies in relation to a tenancy by virtue of section 4(1)(g) of the Agricultural Tenancies Act 1995, the reference in subsection (3) above (in the definition of 'related holding') to a substantial part of the land comprised in the holding means a substantial part determined by reference to either area or value.'.

NOTES

Initial Commencement

Specified date: 19 October 2006: see art 1(1)(b).

Extent

This article does not extend to Scotland: see art 1(1)(c).

A1.709

5   Succession on retirement or death of tenant—meaning of 'eligible person'

(1)   In section 36, after subsection (5) there shall be inserted—

'(6)   The reference in subsection (3)(a) above to agricultural work carried out by a person on the holding or on an agricultural unit of which the holding forms part includes—

(a)   agricultural work carried out by him from the holding or an agricultural unit of which the holding forms part, and

(b)   other work carried out by him on or from the holding or an agricultural unit of which the holding forms part,

which is of a description approved in writing by the landlord after the commencement of this subsection.' .

(2)   In section 41, after subsection (6) there shall be inserted—

'(7)   The references in subsections (1) and (6) above to agricultural work carried out by a person on the holding include—

(a)   agricultural work carried out by him from the holding, and

(b)   other work carried out by him on or from the holding,

which is of a description approved in writing by the landlord after the commencement of this subsection.'.

(3)   In section 50, after subsection (4) there shall be inserted—

'(5)   The reference in subsection (2)(a) above to agricultural work carried out by a person on the holding or on an agricultural unit of which the holding forms part includes—

(a)   agricultural work carried out by him from the holding or an agricultural unit of which the holding forms part, and

(b)   other work carried out by him on or from the holding or an agricultural unit of which the holding forms part,

which is of a description approved in writing by the landlord after the commencement of this subsection.'.

NOTES

Initial Commencement

Specified date: 19 October 2006: see art 1(1)(b).

Extent

This article does not extend to Scotland: see art 1(1)(c).

A1.710

6   Compensation on termination of tenancy

(1)   In section 69, in subsection (1), after 'in the holding' there shall be inserted ', or in any agricultural holding which comprised the whole or a substantial part of the land comprised in the holding,'.

(2)   In that section, after subsection (1) there shall be inserted—

'(1A) Where this Act applies in relation to any tenancy referred to in subsection (1) above by virtue of section 4(1)(g) of the Agricultural Tenancies Act 1995, the reference in that subsection to a substantial part of the land comprised in the holding means a substantial part determined by reference to either area or value.'.

(3) In section 73, the existing provision shall be renumbered as subsection (1).

(4) In that section, in subsection (1) (as renumbered by paragraph (3) above), after 'on the holding' there shall be inserted ', or on any agricultural holding which comprised the whole or a substantial part of the land comprised in the holding,'.

(5) In that section, at the end there shall be inserted—

'(2) Where this Act applies in relation to any tenancy referred to in subsection (1) above by virtue of section 4(1)(g) of the Agricultural Tenancies Act 1995, the reference in that subsection to a substantial part of the land comprised in the holding means a substantial part determined by reference to either area or value.'.

(6) In paragraph 5 of Schedule 9, in sub-paragraph (1), after 'in the holding' there shall be inserted ', or in any agricultural holding which comprised the whole or a substantial part of the land comprised in the holding,'.

(7) In that paragraph, after sub-paragraph (1) there shall be inserted—

'(1A) Where this Act applies in relation to any tenancy referred to in sub-paragraph (1) above by virtue of section 4(1)(g) of the Agricultural Tenancies Act 1995, the reference in that sub-paragraph to a substantial part of the land comprised in the holding means a substantial part determined by reference to either area or value.'.

(8) The amendments made by this article do not apply in relation to compensation payable on termination of a tenancy where that tenancy was granted before this article comes into force.

NOTES

Initial Commencement

Specified date: 19 October 2006: see art 1(1)(b).

Extent

This article does not extend to Scotland: see art 1(1)(c).

A1.711

7   Arbitrations

(1) In section 84, in subsection (1), the words from 'in accordance with' to the end of the subsection shall be omitted.

(2) In that section, for subsections (2) to (5) there shall be substituted—

'(2) The arbitrator shall be a person appointed by agreement between the parties or, in default of agreement, a person appointed on the application of either of the parties by the President of the RICS.

(3) If the arbitrator dies, or is incapable of acting, a new arbitrator may be appointed as if no arbitrator had been appointed.

(4) No application may be made to the President of the RICS for an arbitrator to be appointed by him under this section unless the application is accompanied by such fee as may be prescribed as the fee for such an application; but once the fee has been paid

in connection with any such application no further fee shall be payable in connection with any subsequent application for the appointment by him of a new arbitrator in relation to that arbitration.

(5) Where by virtue of this Act compensation under an agreement is to be substituted for compensation under this Act for improvements or for any such matters as are specified in Part II of Schedule 8 to this Act, the arbitrator shall award compensation in accordance with the agreement instead of in accordance with this Act.

(6) In this section 'the RICS' means the Royal Institution of Chartered Surveyors.'.

(3) In section 94, in subsection (2)—

(a) after the words 'section 22(4)' there shall be inserted ', 84(4)', and
(b) the words 'or paragraph 1(2) of Schedule 11' shall be omitted.

(4) In that section, in subsection (3), for the words 'paragraph 1(2) of Schedule 11 to this Act' there shall be substituted 'section 84(4) above'.

(5) In paragraph 2 of Schedule 4, for 'paragraph 1 of Schedule 11 to' there shall be substituted 'section 84(2) of'.

NOTES

Initial Commencement

Specified date: 19 October 2006: see art 1(1)(b).

Extent

This article does not extend to Scotland: see art 1(1)(c).

A1.712

8   Frequency of arbitrations under section 12

In Schedule 2, after paragraph 6 there shall be inserted—

'7   (1)   This paragraph applies in any case where—

(a) a tenancy of an agricultural holding ('the new tenancy') is granted to a person who, immediately before the grant of the new tenancy, was the tenant of the holding, or of any agricultural holding which comprised the whole or a substantial part of the land comprised in the holding, under a contract of tenancy ('the previous tenancy'),
(b) this Act applies in relation to the new tenancy by virtue of section 4(1)(g) of the Agricultural Tenancies Act 1995, and
(c) the rent payable under the new tenancy is unchanged from that payable under the previous tenancy, disregarding any increase or reduction in rent solely attributable to an adjustment of the boundaries of the holding.

(2) The reference in sub-paragraph (1) above to a substantial part of the land comprised in the holding means a substantial part determined by reference to either area or value.

(3) In any case to which this paragraph applies—

(a) paragraph (a) of sub-paragraph (1) of paragraph 4 above shall be read as referring to the commencement of the previous tenancy, and
(b) references to rent in paragraphs (b) and (c) of that sub-paragraph shall be read as references to the rent payable under the previous tenancy,

until the first occasion following the commencement of the new tenancy on which any such increase or reduction of, or direction with respect to, the rent payable under the new tenancy as is mentioned in paragraph (b) or (c) takes effect.'.

NOTES

Initial Commencement

Specified date: 19 October 2006: see art 1(1)(b).

Extent

This article does not extend to Scotland: see art 1(1)(c).

A1.713

9   Repeal of arbitration provisions

(1)   Schedule 11 is repealed.

(2)   Paragraphs 7 and 15 of Schedule 13 are repealed.

NOTES

Initial Commencement

Specified date: 19 October 2006: see art 1(1)(b).

Extent

This article does not extend to Scotland: see art 1(1)(c).

A1.714

10   Transitional provision for arbitration

(1)   Nothing in this Order affects an arbitration under the Agricultural Holdings Act 1986 or the Agricultural Holdings Act 1948 which commences before this Order comes into force.

(2)   For the purposes of paragraph (1) an arbitration commences when an arbitrator is appointed.

NOTES

Initial Commencement

Specified date: 19 October 2006: see art 1(1)(b).

Extent

This article does not extend to Scotland: see art 1(1)(c).

A1.715

11   Amendments to the Agricultural Tenancies Act 1995

Articles 12 to 17 amend the Agricultural Tenancies Act 1995.

NOTES

Initial Commencement

Specified date: 19 October 2006: see art 1(1)(b).

Extent

This article does not extend to Scotland: see art 1(1)(c).

A1.716

12   Exclusion of the Agricultural Holdings Act 1986

(1)   Section 4 is amended as follows.

(2)   In subsection (1), after 'except', there shall be inserted ' (subject to subsection (2B) below)'.

(3)   In that subsection, in paragraph (e), at the end, 'or' shall be omitted.

(4)   In that subsection, in paragraph (f), for the words '('the previous tenancy')' to the end, there shall be substituted—

'', and is so granted because an agreement between the parties (not being an agreement expressed to take effect as a new tenancy between the parties) has effect as an implied surrender followed by the grant of the tenancy, or'.

(5)   In that subsection, at the end there shall be inserted—

'(g)   is granted to a person who, immediately before the grant of the tenancy, was the tenant of the holding, or of any agricultural holding which comprised the whole or a substantial part of the land comprised in the holding, under a tenancy in relation to which the 1986 Act applied, and is so granted by a written contract of tenancy indicating (in whatever terms) that the 1986 Act is to apply in relation to the tenancy.'.

(6)   In subsection (2), at the end of paragraph (a), 'and' shall be omitted.

(7)   In that subsection, for paragraph (b) there shall be substituted—

'(b)   the current tenancy is granted to a person (alone or jointly with other persons) who, if the tenant under that previous tenancy ('the previous tenant') had died immediately before the grant, would have been his close relative, and

(c)   either of the conditions in subsection (2A) below is satisfied.'.

(8)   After that subsection there shall be inserted—

'(2A)   The conditions referred to in subsection (2)(c) above are—

(a)   the current tenancy is granted to a person (alone or jointly with other persons) who was or had become the sole or sole remaining applicant for a direction of an Agricultural Land Tribunal for a tenancy, and

(b)   the current tenancy—

   (i)   is granted as a result of an agreement between the landlord and the previous tenant, and

   (ii)   is granted, and begins, before the date of the giving of any retirement notice by the previous tenant, or if no retirement notice is given, before the date of death of the previous tenant.'.

(9)   After subsection (2A) there shall be inserted—

'(2B)   The 1986 Act shall not apply by virtue of subsection (1)(f) or (g) above in relation to the tenancy of an agricultural holding ('the current holding') where—

   (a) the whole or a substantial part of the land comprised in the current holding was comprised in an agricultural holding ('the previous holding') which was subject to a tenancy granted after the commencement of this subsection in relation to which the 1986 Act applied by virtue of subsection (1)(f) or (g) above;

   (b) the whole or a substantial part of the land comprised in the previous holding was comprised in an agricultural holding ('the original holding') which was at the commencement of this subsection subject to a tenancy in relation to which the 1986 Act applied; and

   (c) the land comprised in the original holding does not, on the date of the grant of the tenancy of the current holding, comprise the whole or a substantial part of the land comprised in the current holding.'.

(10)   After subsection (2B) there shall be inserted—

'(2C)   The references in subsections (1)(g) and (2B) above to a substantial part of the land comprised in the holding mean a substantial part determined by reference to either area or value.'.

(11)   In subsection (3)—

   (a) at the end of paragraph (a), 'and' shall be omitted;

   (b) at the end of paragraph (b), there shall be inserted—

', and

   (c) 'retirement notice' has the meaning given by section 49(3) of that Act.'.

(12)   The amendments made by this article shall not apply in relation to any tenancy granted before this article comes into force.

NOTES

Initial Commencement

Specified date: 19 October 2006: see art 1(1)(b).

Extent

This article does not extend to Scotland: see art 1(1)(c).

A1.717

13   Notice to terminate the tenancy

In sections 5(1), 6(1)(c) and 7(1) the words 'but less than twenty-four months' shall be omitted.

NOTES

Initial Commencement

Specified date: 19 October 2006: see art 1(1)(b).

Extent

This article does not extend to Scotland: see art 1(1)(c).

A1.718

14   Application of Part II of the Agricultural Tenancies Act 1995

(1)   In section 9—

(a)   at the end of paragraph (a), 'or' shall be omitted;

(b)   at the end of paragraph (b), there shall be inserted—

', or

(c)   does not contain any provision which precludes a reduction in the rent during the tenancy, and—

   (i)   expressly states that this Part of this Act does not apply, or

   (ii)   makes provision for the reference of rent reviews to an independent expert whose decision is final.'.

(2)   In section 28(5)—

(a)   at the end of paragraph (b), 'or' shall be omitted;

(b)   at the end of paragraph (c), there shall be inserted—

', or

(d)   any dispute relating to rent review, in any case where Part II of this Act is excluded by virtue of section 9(c)(ii) of this Act.'.

(3)   The amendments made by this article shall not apply where the provision in the instrument creating the tenancy referred to in section 9(c)(i) or (ii), as inserted by paragraph (1) above, is made before this article comes into force.

NOTES

Initial Commencement

Specified date: 19 October 2006: see art 1(1)(b).

Extent

This article does not extend to Scotland: see art 1(1)(c).

A1.719

15   Factors to be taken into account on rent review

In section 13(2) for the words 'relating to the criteria by reference to which any new rent is to be determined)' there shall be substituted 'which (apart from this section) preclude a reduction in the rent during the tenancy)'.

NOTES

Initial Commencement

Specified date: 19 October 2006: see art 1(1)(b).

Extent

This article does not extend to Scotland: see art 1(1)(c).

A1.720

16   Agreement to limit tenant's compensation

(1)   In section 20(1), at the beginning there shall be inserted 'Subject to subsection (4A) below,'.

(2)   After section 20(4) there shall be inserted—

'(4A)   Where the landlord and the tenant have agreed in writing, after the commencement of this subsection, to limit the amount of compensation payable under section 16 of this Act in respect of any tenant's improvement, that amount shall be the lesser of—

    (a) the amount determined in accordance with subsections (1) to (4) above, and

    (b) the compensation limit.

(4B) In subsection (4A) above, 'the compensation limit' means—

    (a) an amount agreed by the parties in writing, or

    (b) where the parties are unable to agree on an amount, an amount equal to the cost to the tenant of making the improvement.'.

NOTES

Initial Commencement

Specified date: 19 October 2006: see art 1(1)(b).

Extent

This article does not extend to Scotland: see art 1(1)(c).

A1.721

17   Application of agreed limit on resumption of possession of part of holding

(1) In section 24(2), for ' (4)' there shall be substituted ' (4A)'.

(2) In section 24(4), after 'shall apply', there shall be inserted ' (subject to subsection (4A) below)'.

(3) After section 24(4) there shall be inserted—

'(4A) Where—

    (a) the landlord and the tenant have agreed in writing, after the commencement of this subsection, to limit the amount of compensation payable under section 16 of this Act in respect of any tenant's improvement not consisting of planning permission,

    (b) that improvement is provided for both the relevant part and the land comprised in the tenancy after the termination date,

    (c) the case falls within paragraph (a) or (b) of subsection (1) above,

    (d) the tenant has already received compensation in respect of the improvement, determined in accordance with subsection (2) above, and

    (e) further compensation in respect of the improvement is payable under section 16 of this Act on termination of the tenancy,

the compensation limit referred to in section 20(4A) of this Act shall, for the purposes of determining that further compensation, be reduced by an amount equal to the amount of compensation already received by the tenant in respect of the improvement.'.

(4) In section 24(5), for ' (4)' there shall be substituted ' (4A)'.

NOTES

Initial Commencement

Specified date: 19 October 2006: see art 1(1)(b).

Extent

This article does not extend to Scotland: see art 1(1)(c).

A1.722

18   Consequential amendments, repeals and revocations

Schedule 1 (which contains consequential amendments), Schedule 2 (which contains repeals) and Schedule 3 (which contains revocations) shall have effect.

NOTES

Initial Commencement

Specified date: 19 October 2006: see art 1(1)(b).

SCHEDULE 1
CONSEQUENTIAL AMENDMENTS

Article 18

PART 1: AMENDMENTS OF PRIMARY LEGISLATION

A1.723

Tribunals and Inquiries Act 1992

1   In Schedule 1 to the Tribunals and Inquiries Act 1992, in the column headed 'Tribunal and statutory authority', in sub-paragraph (b) of paragraph 1, for 'Schedule 11 to' there shall be substituted 'section 84 of'.

NOTES

Initial Commencement

Specified date: 19 October 2006: see art 1(1)(b).

PART 2: AMENDMENTS OF SUBORDINATE LEGISLATION

Agricultural Holdings (Arbitration on Notices) Order 1987

2   In Articles 10(b) and 12(a) of the Agricultural Holdings (Arbitration on Notices) Order 1987, for the words 'paragraph 1 of Schedule 11 to' there shall be substituted 'section 84(2) of'.

Agricultural Holdings (Fee) Regulations 1996

3   In regulation 2(b) of the Agricultural Holdings (Fee) Regulations 1996, for the words 'paragraph 1(1) of Schedule 11 to' there shall be substituted 'section 84(2) of'.

Dairy Produce Quotas Regulations 2005

4   In paragraph 4(2) of Schedule 1 to the Dairy Produce Quotas Regulations 2005, for the words 'paragraph 1(2) of Schedule 11 to' there shall be substituted 'section 84(4) of'.

Dairy Produce Quotas (Wales) Regulations 2005

5   In paragraph 4(2) of Schedule 1 to the Dairy Produce Quotas (Wales) Regulations 2005, for the words 'paragraph 1(2) of Schedule 11 to' there shall be substituted 'section 84(4) of'.

NOTES

Initial Commencement

Specified date: 19 October 2006: see art 1(1)(b).

Article 18

A1.724

SCHEDULE 2
REPEALS

Title	Reference	Extent of repeal
Agricultural Holdings Act 1986	c 5	In section 84, in subsection (1), the words from 'in accordance with' to the end of the subsection. In section 94, in subsection (2), the words 'or paragraph 1(2) of Schedule 11'. Schedule 11. In Schedule 13, paragraphs 7 and 15.
Agriculture Act 1986	c 49	In Schedule 1, in paragraph 11(5), the words from 'but paragraph 18' to 'three months'.
Tribunals and Inquiries Act 1992	c 53	In Schedule 3, paragraph 18.
Judicial Pensions and Retirement Act 1993	c 8	In Schedule 5, the words 'Arbitrator appointed under paragraph 1(5) of Schedule 11 to the Agricultural Holdings Act 1986'. In Schedule 6, paragraph 45. In Schedule 7, paragraph 5(5), head (xxi) (arbitrator appointed under paragraph 1(5) of Schedule 11 to the Agricultural Holdings Act 1986).
Agricultural Tenancies Act 1995	c 8	In section 4, in subsection (1)(e), at the end, the word 'or'. In that section, in subsection (2)(a), at the end, the word 'and'. In that section, in subsection (3)(a), at the end, the word 'and'. In section 5, in subsection (1), the words 'but less than twenty-four months'. In section 6, in subsection (1)(c), the words 'but less than twenty-four months'. In section 7, in subsection (1), the words 'but less than twenty-four months'. In section 9, in paragraph (a), at the end, the word 'or'.

		In section 28, in subsection (5)(b), at the end, the word 'or'.
Private International Law (Miscellaneous Provisions) Act 1995	c 42	Section 4(2).
Arbitration Act 1996	c 23	In Schedule 3, paragraph 45.
Constitutional Reform Act 2005	c 4	In Schedule 7, paragraph 4, part A, the words 'Agricultural Holdings Act 1986 (c 5) Schedule 11, paragraph 1(5)'. In Part 3 of Schedule 14, in the column headed 'Office', the words 'Member of panel constituted for the purpose of Schedule 11', and in the column headed 'Enactment', the words 'Paragraph 1(5) of Schedule 11 to the Agricultural Holdings Act 1986 (c 5)'.

NOTES

Initial Commencement

Specified date: 19 October 2006: see art 1(1)(b).

SCHEDULE 3
REVOCATIONS

Article 18

A1.725

Title	Reference	Extent of revocation
Milk (Community Outgoers Scheme) (England and Wales) Regulations 1986	SI 1986/1611	In regulation 16, in paragraph (1), the words 'Subject to paragraphs (2) to (5),'. In that regulation, paragraphs (2) to (5).
Milk (Cessation of Production) (England and Wales) Scheme 1987	SI 1987/908	In paragraph 16, in sub-paragraph (1), the words 'Subject to sub-paragraphs (2) to (5),'. In that paragraph, sub-paragraphs (2) to (5).
Agricultural Holdings (Form of Award in Arbitration Proceedings) Order 1990	SI 1990/1472	The whole Order.
Civil Procedure Rules 1998	SI 1998/3132	In CCR Order 44, rules 1 to 3.

Dairy Produce Quotas Regulations 2005	SI 2005/465	In Schedule 1, in paragraph 1(2), the words 'from amongst the members of the panel referred to in paragraph 7'. In that Schedule, in paragraph 1(5), the words 'from amongst the members of the panel referred to in paragraph 7'. In that Schedule, paragraph 7.
Dairy Produce Quotas (Wales) Regulations 2005	SI 2005/537	In Schedule 1, in paragraph 1(2), the words 'from amongst the members of the panel referred to in paragraph 7'. In that Schedule, in paragraph 1(5), the words 'from amongst the members of the panel referred to in paragraph 7'. In that Schedule, paragraph 7.

NOTES

Initial Commencement

Specified date: 19 October 2006: see art 1(1)(b).

DAIRY PRODUCE QUOTAS (AMENDMENT) REGULATIONS 2007

SI 2007/106

The Secretary of State has been designated for the purposes of section 2(2) of the European Communities Act 1972 in relation to the common agricultural policy of the European Community.

He makes the following Regulations under the powers conferred by that section.

A1.726

1   Title and commencement

These Regulations may be cited as the Dairy Produce Quotas (Amendment) Regulations 2007 and come into force on 31st March 2007.

NOTES

Initial Commencement

Specified date: 31 March 2007: see above.

A1.727

2   Amendment of the Dairy Produce Quotas Regulations 2005

(1)   The Dairy Produce Quotas Regulations 2005 are amended as follows.

(2)   In regulation 2(1)—

(a)   at the end of the definition of 'the Commission Regulation' add ', as amended by Commission Regulation (EC) No 1468/2006 (OJ No L274, 5.10.2006, p 6)';

(b)   omit the definition of 'Commission Regulation 1756/93';

(c)   in the definition of 'the Community legislation', for ', the Commission Regulation and Commission Regulation 1756/93' substitute 'and the Commission Regulation';

(d)   at the end of the definition of 'the Council Regulation' add ', as amended by Council Regulation (EC) No 1406/2006 (OJ No L265, 26.9.2006, p 8)'.

(3)   In regulation 7(a), for sub-paragraphs (i) to (iii) substitute—

'(i)   is the quota holder identified in that entry, or

(ii)   gives the Secretary of State a statement in writing that he has an interest in the holding of the quota holder identified in that entry; or'.

(4)   In regulation 9(3), for the words after 'Secretary of State' to the end of the paragraph substitute 'no later than 31st March in the quota year in which the transfer takes place.'.

(5)   In regulation 31(5), for '1st September' substitute '30th September'.

(6)   In regulation 36—

(a)   in paragraph (1), for '(2) to (3)' substitute '(2A) and (3)';

(b)   omit paragraph (2);

(c)   in paragraph (5), for 'paragraphs (2) to (4)' substitute 'paragraphs (2A), (3), (4) and (6A)';

(d)   for paragraph (6), substitute—

'(6)   Subject to Article 8(5) of the Commission Regulation, if a purchaser fails to submit a summary required to be submitted under Article 8(2) of the Commission Regulation, by the end of the period specified in Article 8(4), he is liable to pay to the Secretary of State a penalty equivalent to the theoretical amount of levy that would be due on 0.01% of the quantity by volume of milk covered by that declaration for each day of the period of the delay in the submission reaching the Secretary of State.';

(e)   after paragraph (6) insert—

'(6A)   Subject to paragraphs (5) and (7), where a purchaser fails to provide or submit to the Secretary of State—

(a)   an application, statement or declaration concerning the adjustment of purchaser quota in accordance with regulation 23(2) to (4);

(b)   information in accordance with regulation 33(2) to (4); or

(c)   a confirmation or amendments relating to a revised version of a summary in accordance with regulation 35(2),

he is liable to pay to the Secretary of State a penalty equivalent to the theoretical amount of levy that would be due on 0.01% of the quantity by volume of milk covered by that application, statement, declaration or revised version, or that information, for each day of the period of delay in the submission reaching the Secretary of State.'.

(7)   In paragraph 7, for '(6)' substitute '(6A)'.

(8)   In regulation 38, omit paragraph (2).

(9)   In regulation 39(2)(a)(ii), for 'by virtue of regulation 38(2)' substitute 'under article 11(4) of the Commission Regulation'.

(10)   In paragraph 2(1) of Schedule 2, at the beginning of both sub-paragraph (h) and (i) insert 'if he holds 4,855 or more litres of direct sales quota,'.

NOTES

Initial Commencement

Specified date: 31 March 2007: see reg 1.

Part 3

EUROPEAN UNION LEGISLATION

Contents

Part 3

EUROPEAN UNION LEGISLATION

COUNCIL REGULATION (EC) NO 1782/2003

((EC) NO 1782/2003)

OF 29 SEPTEMBER 2003

establishing common rules for direct support schemes under the common agricultural policy and establishing certain support schemes for farmers and amending Regulations (EEC) No 2019/93, (EC) No 1452/2001, (EC) No 1453/2001, (EC) No 1454/2001, (EC) 1868/94, (EC) No 1251/1999, (EC) No 1254/1999, (EC) No 1673/2000, (EEC) No 2358/71 and (EC) No 2529/2001

[TEXT UP TO DATE UNTIL MAY 2007 ONLY]

CONTENTS

1939

TITLE IV OTHER AID SCHEMES
Chapter 1 Specific quality premium for durum wheat
Chapter 2 Protein crop premium
Chapter 3 Crop specific payment for rice
Chapter 4 Area payment for nuts
Chapter 5 Aid for energy crops
Chapter 6 Aid for starch potato
Chapter 7 Dairy premium and additional payments
Chapter 8 Specific regional aid for arable crops
Chapter 9 Seed aid
Chapter 10 Arable crops area payment
Chapter 11 Sheep and goat premiums
Chapter 12 Beef and veal payments
Chapter 13 Grain legumes aid

TITLE V TRANSITIONAL AND FINAL RULES

ANNEX I List of support schemes fulfilling the criteria set out in Article 1

ANNEX II National ceilings referred to in Article 12(2)

ANNEX III Statutory management requirements referred to in Articles 3 and 4

ANNEX IV Good agricultural and environmental condition referred to in Article 5

ANNEX V Compatible support schemes referred to in Article 26

ANNEX VI List of direct payments in relation to the single payment referred to in Article 33

ANNEX VII Calculation of the reference amount referred to in Article 37

ANNEX VIII National ceilings referred to in Article 41

ANNEX IX List of arable crops referred to in Article 66

ANNEX X Traditional production zones for durum wheat as referred to in Article 74

ANNEX XI List of seed species referred to in Article 99

A1.728

THE COUNCIL OF THE EUROPEAN UNION,

Having regard to the Treaty establishing the European Community, and in particular Articles 36, 37 and 299(2) thereof,
Having regard to the proposal from the Commission,
Having regard to the Opinion of the European Parliament[1],
Having regard to the Opinion of the European Economic and Social Committee[2],
Having regard to the Opinion of the Committee of the Regions[3],
Whereas:

(1) Common conditions should be established for direct payments under the various income support schemes in the framework of the common agricultural policy.

(2) The full payment of direct aid should be linked to compliance with rules relating to agricultural land, agricultural production and activity. Those rules should serve to incorporate in the common market organisations basic standards for the environment, food safety, animal health and welfare and good agricultural and environmental condition. If those basic standards are not met, Member States should withdraw direct aid in whole or in part on the basis of criteria which are proportionate, objective and graduated. Such withdrawal should be without prejudice to sanctions laid down now or in the future under other provisions of Community or national law.

(3) In order to avoid the abandonment of agricultural land and ensure that it is maintained in good agricultural and environmental condition, standards should be established which may or may not have a basis in provisions of the Member States. It is therefore appropriate to establish a Community framework within which Member States may adopt standards taking account of the specific characteristics of the areas concerned, including soil and climatic conditions and existing farming systems (land use, crop rotation, farming practices) and farm structures.

(4) Since permanent pasture has a positive environmental effect, it is appropriate to adopt measures to encourage the maintenance of existing permanent pasture to avoid a massive conversion into arable land.

(5) In order to achieve a better balance between policy tools designed to promote sustainable agriculture and those designed to promote rural development, a system of progressive reduction of direct payments should be introduced on a compulsory Community-wide basis for the years 2005 to 2012. All direct payments, beyond certain amounts, should be reduced by a certain percentage each year. The savings made should be used to finance measures under the rural development and allocated between Member States according to objective criteria to be defined. However, it is appropriate to establish that a certain percentage of the amounts should remain in the Member States where they have been generated. Until 2005, Member States may continue to apply the current modulation on an optional basis under Council Regulation (EC) No 1259/1999 of 17 May 1999 establishing common rules for direct support schemes under the common agricultural policy[4].

(6) With a view to ensure that the amounts for the financing of the common agricultural policy (subheading 1a) respect the annual ceilings set in the financial perspectives, it is appropriate to provide for a financial mechanism to adjust, where necessary, the direct payments. An adjustment of direct support should be fixed when the forecasts indicate that the subheading 1a, with a security margin of EUR 300 million, is exceeded in a given budget year.

(7) In view of the structure adjustments resulting from the abolition of rye intervention, it is appropriate to provide for transitional measures for certain rye production regions financed with part of the amounts generated by modulation.

(8) In order to help farmers to meet the standards of modern, high-quality agriculture, it is necessary that Member States establish a comprehensive system offering advice to commercial farms. The farm advisory system should help farmers to become more aware of material flows and on-farm processes relating to the environment, food safety, animal health and welfare without in any way affecting their obligation and responsibility to respect those standards.

(9) In order to facilitate the introduction of the farm advisory system, it should be provided for a time-period for Member States to set-up the system. Entry into the system should be on a voluntary basis for farmers with a priority for those who receive more than a certain amount per year in direct payments. Due to its nature of affording advice to farmers, it is appropriate for the information obtained in the course of the advisory activity to be treated as confidential, except in case of serious infringements of Community or national law.

(10) Member States must, in accordance with Article 8 of Council Regulation (EC) No 1258/1999 of 17 May 1999 on the financing of the common agricultural policy[5], take the measures necessary to satisfy themselves that transactions financed by the 'Guarantee' Section of the European Agricultural Guidance and Guarantee Fund (EAGGF) are actually carried out and are executed correctly, and prevent and deal with irregularities.

(11) In order to improve the effectiveness and usefulness of the administration and control mechanisms, it is necessary to adapt the system established by Council Regulation (EEC) No 3508/92 of 27 November 1992 establishing an integrated administration and control system for certain Community aid schemes[6] with a view to including the single payment scheme, the support schemes for durum wheat, protein crops, energy crops, rice, potato starch, nuts, milk, seed, grain legumes and

specific regional aids as well as controls on the application of the rules on cross compliance, modulation and the farm advisory system. Provision should be made for the possibility of including, at a later stage, other aid schemes.

(12) For the sake of effective control and to prevent the submission of multiple aid applications to different paying agencies within one Member State, each Member State should set up a single system to record the identity of farmers submitting aid applications subject to the integrated system.

(13) The various components of the integrated system are aimed at a more effective administration and control. Therefore, in the case of Community schemes not covered by this Regulation, the Member States should be authorised to avail themselves of the system, on condition they do not in any way act contrary to the provisions concerned.

(14) Given the complexity of the system and the large number of aid applications to be processed, it is essential to use the appropriate technical resources and administration and control methods. As a result, the integrated system should comprise, in each Member State, a computerised data base, an identification system for agricultural parcels, aid applications from farmers, a harmonised control system and, in the single payment scheme, a system for the identification and recording of payment entitlements.

(15) To enable the data collected to be processed and used for the verification of aid applications, it is necessary to set up high-performance computerised data bases which make it possible in particular to carry out cross-checks.

(16) The identification of agricultural parcels is a key element in the correct application of schemes linked to surface area. Experience has shown that the existing methods have certain deficiencies. Therefore, provision should be made for an identification system to be set up, where necessary, with the aid of remote sensing.

(17) For the sake of simplification, Member States should be authorised to make provision for the submission of a single application for several aid schemes and to replace the annual application by a permanent application subject only to annual confirmation.

(18) Member States should be enabled to use amounts which become available as a result of payment reductions under modulation for certain additional measures in the framework of rural development support provided for under Council Regulation (EC) No 1257/1999 of 17 May 1999 on support for rural development from the European Agricultural Guidance and Guarantee Fund (EAGGF)[7].

(19) Since the amounts which will become available as a result of cross compliance are not foreseeable sufficiently far ahead to be used for additional measures in the framework of rural development support, those amounts should be credited to the EAGGF 'Guarantee' Section, except for a certain percentage which should be retained by the Member States.

(20) Payments provided for under Community support schemes should be made by the competent national authorities to beneficiaries in full, subject to any reductions provided for in this Regulation, and within prescribed periods.

(21) The support schemes under the common agricultural policy provide for direct income support in particular with a view to ensuring a fair standard of living for the agricultural community. This objective is closely related to the maintenance of rural areas. In order to avoid misallocations of Community funds, no support payments should be made to farmers who have artificially created the conditions required to obtain such payments.

(22) Common support schemes have to be adapted to developments, if necessary within short time limits. Beneficiaries cannot, therefore, rely on support conditions remaining unchanged and should be prepared for a possible review of schemes in the light of market developments.

(23) In view of the significant budgetary implications of direct payment support and in order to better appraise their impact, Community schemes should be subject to a proper evaluation.

(24) Enhancing the competitiveness of Community agriculture and promoting food quality and environment standards necessarily entail a drop in institutional prices for agricultural products and an increase in the costs of production for agricultural holdings in the Community. To achieve those aims and promote more market-oriented and sustainable agriculture, it is necessary to complete the shift from production support to producer support by introducing a system of decoupled income support for each farm. While decoupling will leave the actual amounts paid to farmers unchanged, it will significantly increase the effectiveness of the income aid. It is, therefore, appropriate to make the single farm payment conditional upon cross-compliance with environmental, food safety, animal health and welfare, as well as the maintenance of the farm in good agricultural and environmental condition.

(25) Such a system should combine a number of existing direct payments received by a farmer from various schemes in a single payment, determined on the basis of previous entitlements, within a reference period, adjusted to take into account the full implementation of measures introduced in the framework of Agenda 2000 and of the changes to the amounts of aid made by this Regulation.

(26) Since the benefits in terms of administrative simplification will increase if many sectors are included the scheme should, in a first stage, cover all products included in the arable crops regime as well as grain legumes, seeds, beef and sheep. The revised payments for rice and durum wheat as well as the payment in the milk sector once the reform is fully implemented, should also be integrated into the scheme. Payments for starch potatoes and dried fodder should also be included in the scheme, while separate payments for the processing industry should be maintained.

(27) Specific measures should be laid down for hemp, to ensure that illegal crops cannot be hidden among the crops eligible for the single payment, thereby adversely affecting the common market organisation for hemp. Provision should therefore be made for area payments to be granted only for areas sown to varieties of hemp offering certain guarantees with regard to the psychotropic substance content. The references to the specific measures provided for by Council Regulation (EC) No 1673/2000 of 27 July 2000 on the common organisation of the markets in flax and hemp grown for fibre[8] should be adapted accordingly.

(28) In order to leave farmers free to choose what to produce on their land, including products which are still under coupled support, thus increasing market orientation, the single payment should not be conditional on production of any specific product. However, in order to avoid distortions of competition some products should be excluded from production on eligible land.

(29) In order to establish the amount to which a farmer should be entitled under the new scheme, it is appropriate to refer to the amounts granted to him during a reference period. To take account of specific situations, a national reserve should be established. That reserve may also be used to facilitate the participation of new farmers in the scheme. The single payment should be established at farm level.

(30) The overall amount to which a farm is entitled should be split into parts (payment entitlements) and linked to a certain number of eligible hectares to be defined, in order to facilitate transfer of the premium rights. To avoid speculative transfers leading to the accumulation of payment entitlements without a corresponding agricultural basis, in granting aid, it is appropriate to provide for a link between entitlements and a certain number of eligible hectares, as well as the possibility of limiting the transfer of entitlements within a region. Specific provisions should be laid down for aid not directly linked to an area taking into account the peculiar situation of sheep and goat rearing.

(31) To ensure that the total level of support and entitlements do not exceed current budgetary constraints at Community or national level and, where applicable, at regional level, it is appropriate to provide for national ceilings calculated as the sum of all funds granted in each Member State for the payment of aids under the relevant support schemes, during the reference period and taking into account later adjustments. Proportional reductions should be applicable if the ceiling is overshot.

(32) In order to maintain the supply control benefits of set-aside, while reinforcing its environmental benefits under the new system of support, the set-aside conditions for arable land should be maintained.

(33) In order to allow flexibility to respond to specific situations, Member States should have the option to define a certain balance between individual payment entitlements and regional or national averages and between existing payments and the single payment. A specific derogation to the prohibition on cultivating fruits and vegetables including table potatoes should be provided for avoiding that in case of regionalisation this does not lead to a disruption of the production whilst minimizing any effect on distortion of competition. Moreover, in order to take into account its agricultural specific conditions, it is appropriate to provide for the possibility for a Member State to ask for a transitional period to implement the single payment scheme while continuing to respect the budgetary ceilings fixed for the single payment scheme. In case of severe distortions of competition during the transitional period and in order to ensure the respect of the Community international obligations, it is appropriate that the Commission can take the necessary measures to cope with such situations.

(34) In case of optional or transitional implementation, in order to protect the legitimate expectations of farmers, it is appropriate to fix a date before which Member States have to take their decision to apply the single payment scheme. Moreover, to ensure the continuation of the current regimes, certain conditions for entitlement to aid should be established, leaving to the Commission the powers to lay down the implementing rules.

(35) In order to maintain the role of durum wheat production in traditional production area while strengthening the granting of the aid to durum wheat respecting certain minimum quality requirements, it is appropriate to reduce, over a transitional period, the current specific supplement for durum wheat in traditional areas and to abolish the special aid in established areas. Only cultivation which produces durum wheat suitable for use in the manufacture of semolina and pasta products should be eligible for that aid.

(36) In order to strengthen the role of protein-rich crops and to provide an incentive to increase the production of these crops, it is appropriate to provide for a supplementary payment for farmers producing these crops. To ensure a correct application of the new scheme, certain conditions for entitlement to aid should be established. A maximum guaranteed area should be prescribed and proportional reductions applied if the maximum guaranteed area is exceeded.

(37) In order to maintain the role of rice production in traditional production areas, it is appropriate to provide for a supplementary payment for rice producers. To ensure a correct application of the new scheme, certain conditions for entitlement to aid should be established. National base areas should be established and reductions applied if the areas are exceeded.

(38) New support arrangements for nuts should be established to avoid the potential disappearance of nut production in traditional areas and the subsequent negative environmental, rural, social and economic consequences. To ensure a correct application of the new arrangements, certain conditions for entitlement to aid should be established, including a minimum tree density and plot size. In order to cater for specific needs, Member States should be entitled to provide additional aid.

(39) To avoid budgetary overshoot, a maximum guaranteed area should be prescribed and proportional reductions applied if the maximum guaranteed area is exceeded, concentrated in Member States which overshoot their area. To ensure balanced application throughout the Community, this area should be allocated in proportion to areas of nut production in Member States. The Member States should be responsible for allocating the areas within their territory. Areas subject to improvement plans should not be eligible for aid under the new scheme until the plan has expired.

(40) In order to capitalise on the success of improvement plans in regrouping supply, Member States may make entitlement to Community aid and national aid conditional on membership of producer organisations. To avoid disruption, a smooth transition must be ensured to the new scheme.

(41) Currently, support for energy crops consists of the possibility to grow industrial crops on set-aside land. Energy crops account for the largest amount of non-food production on set-aside land. Specific aid for energy crops with the objective of increasing carbon dioxide substitution should be established. A maximum guaranteed area should be prescribed and proportional reductions applied if the maximum guaranteed area is exceeded. The arrangements should be reviewed after a prescribed period taking into account the implementation of the Community biofuels initiative.

(42) In order to maintain starch production in traditional areas of production and to recognise the role of potato production in the agronomic cycle, it is appropriate to provide for a supplementary payment for potato starch producers. Moreover, in so far as the payment system for starch potato producers is to be partially included in the single payment scheme, Council Regulation (EC) No 1868/94 of 27 July 1994 establishing a quota system in relation to the production of potato starch[9] should be amended.

(43) The inclusion of arable crops, beef and sheep extends the single payment scheme to premiums which are paid in the outermost regions and Aegean islands, in order to achieve further simplification and to avoid leaving in place a legal and administrative framework for a limited number of farmers in those areas. However, in order to maintain the role of certain type of production in these regions of the Community, it is appropriate to provide that Member States may decide that they need not include those payments in the single payment scheme. The same possibility should apply to the supplementary payments in certain regions of Sweden and Finland as well as to seed aid. In this cases, the continuation of the current regimes requires that certain conditions for entitlement to aid shall be established, leaving to the Commission the powers to lay down the implementing rules.

(44) In order to facilitate the transition between the current regimes for arable crops payments and livestock premiums and the new single payment scheme, it is appropriate to provide for some adaptations to the current direct payments in those sectors.

(45) Agricultural activity in the Azores is highly dependent on milk production. It thus is advisable to renew and extend the measures taken in Article 23 of Regulation (EC) No 1453/2001 of 28 June 2001 introducing specific measures for certain agricultural products for the Azores and Madeira[10] and to derogate for a period of six marketing years in total beginning in 1999/2000 from certain provisions of the common market organisation for milk and milk products as regard of limitation of production in order to take account of the level of development of and the conditions for local production. Over the period of its application, this measure should enable the sector in the Azores to continue being restructured without interfering with the milk market and without appreciably affecting the sound working of the levy scheme at Portuguese or Community level.

(46) The application of the single farm payment scheme will de facto imply that the conversion programme of land currently under arable crops to extensive

livestock farming in Portugal laid down in Regulation (EC) No 1017/94[11] becomes without object. Regulation (EC) No L 1017/94 should therefore be repealed by the entry into force of the single payment scheme.

(47) As a result of the aforementioned changes and new provisions, Council Regulations (EEC) No 3508/92, (EC) No 1577/96 of 30 July 1996 introducing a specific measure in respect of certain grain legumes[12] and (EC) No 1251/1999 of 17 May 1999 establishing a support system for producers of certain arable crops[13] should be repealed. Regulation (EC) No 1259/1999 should also be repealed, except some provisions which provide for specific temporary and optional regimes.

(48) The specific provisions concerning direct payments in Council Regulations (EEC) No 2358/71 of 26 October 1971 on the common organisation of the market in seeds[14], No 2019/93 of 19 July 1993 introducing specific measures for the smaller Aegean islands concerning certain agricultural products[15], (EC) No 1254/1999 of 17 May 1999 on the common organisation of the market in beef and veal[16], (EC) No 1452/2001 of 28 June 2001 introducing specific measures for certain agricultural products for the French overseas departments[17], (EC) No 1454/2001 of 28 June 2001 introducing specific measures for certain agricultural products for the Canary Islands[18] and (EC) No 2529/2001 of 19 December 2001 on the common organisation of the market in sheepmeat and goatmeat[19] have effectively lost their substance and should therefore be deleted.

(49) At the time of entry into force of this regulation, the Community consists of 15 Member States. Taking into account the fact that, according to the Treaty of Accession of 2003, the accession of the new Member States is to take place on 1 May 2004, this Regulation should be adapted, by the date of accession, according to the procedures provided for by that Treaty, in order to make it applicable to the new Member States.

(50) The measures necessary for the implementation of this Regulation should be adopted in accordance with Council Decision 1999/468/EC of 28 June 1999 laying down the procedures for the exercise of implementing powers conferred on the Commission[20],

---

[1]   Opinion delivered on 5 June 2003 (not yet published in the Official Journal).
[2]   OJ 2003 C 208/64.
[3]   Opinion delivered on 2 July 2003 (not yet published in the Official Journal).
[4]   OJ 1999 L 160/113. Regulation as amended by Regulation (EC) No 1244/2001 (OJ 2001 L 173/1).
[5]   OJ 1999 L 160/103.
[6]   OJ 1992 L 355/1. Regulation as last amended by Commission Regulation (EC) No 495/2001 (OJ 2001 L 72/6).
[7]   OJ 1999 L 160/80.
[8]   OJ 2000 L 193/16. Regulation as amended by Commission Regulation (EC) No 651/2002 (OJ 2002 L 101/3).
[9]   OJ 2002 L 197/4. Regulation as last amended by Regulation (EC) No 962/2002 (OJ 2002 L 149/1).
[10] OJ 2001 L 198/26.
[11] OJ 1994 L 112/2. Regulation as last amended by Regulation (EC) No 2582/2001 (OJ 2001 L 345/5).
[12] OJ 1996 L 206/4. Regulation as last amended by Regulation (EC) No 811/2000 (OJ 2000 L 100/1).
[13] OJ 1999 L 160/1. Regulation as last amended by Regulation (EC) No 1038/2001 (OJ 2001 L 145/16).
[14] OJ 2002 L 246/1. Regulation as last amended by Regulation (EC) No 154/2002 (OJ 2002 L 25/18).
[15] OJ 1993 L 184/1 (OJ 2002 L 68/4). Regulation as last amended by Regulation (EC) No 442/2002.
[16] OJ 1999 L 160/21. Regulation as last amended by Regulation (EC) No 806/2003 (OJ 2003 L 122/1).
[17] OJ 2001 L 198/11.

18 OJ 2001 L 198/45. Regulation as last amended by Commission Regulation (EC) No 1922/2002 (OJ 2002 L 293/11).
19 OJ 2001 L 341/3.
20 OJ 1999 L 184/23.

HAS ADOPTED THIS REGULATION:

TITLE I
SCOPE AND DEFINITIONS

A1.729

Article 1   Scope

This Regulation establishes:

— common rules on direct payments under income support schemes in the framework of the common agricultural policy which are financed by the 'Guarantee' Section of the European Agricultural Guidance and Guarantee Fund (EAGGF), except those provided for under Regulation (EC) No 1257/1999;

— an income support for farmers (hereinafter referred to as the 'single payment scheme');

[— a transitional simplified income support for farmers in the new Member States (hereinafter referred to as the 'single area payment scheme');]

[— support schemes for farmers producing durum wheat, protein crops, rice, nuts, energy crops, starch potatoes, milk, seeds, arable crops, sheep meat and goat meat, beef and veal, grain legumes, cotton, tobacco, hops, as well as for farmers maintaining olive groves.]

NOTES

Amendment

Third entry: words in square brackets inserted by Council Decision 2004/281 Adapting the Act of Accession for the 10 new member states in 2004. This is not an official amendment to Regulation 1782/2003 according to EUR-LEX.

Date in force: 1 May 2004.

Fourth entry: words in square brackets substituted by Council Regulation 864/2004.

Date in force: 1 May 2004 and applicable from 1 January 2006 except for provisos contained in Regulation 864/2004 (see EU Official Journal version).

A1.730

Article 2   Definitions

For the purposes of this Regulation, the following definitions shall apply:

(a) 'farmer' means a natural or legal person, or a group of natural or legal persons, whatever legal status is granted to the group and its members by national law, whose holding is situated within Community territory, as referred to in Article 299 of the Treaty, and who exercises an agricultural activity,

(b) 'holding' means all the production units managed by a farmer situated within the territory of the same Member State,

(c) 'agricultural activity' means the production, rearing or growing of agricultural products including harvesting, milking, breeding animals and keeping animals for farming purposes, or maintaining the land in good agricultural and environmental condition as established under Article 5,

- (d) 'direct payment' means a payment granted directly to farmers under an income support scheme listed in Annex I,
- (e) 'payments in a given calendar year' or 'payments in the reference period' means the payments granted or to be granted in respect of the year/years concerned, including all payments in respect of other periods starting in that calendar year/years,
- (f) 'agricultural products' means the products listed in Annex I of the Treaty, including cotton, but with the exception of fishery products.
- [(g) 'new Member States' means Bulgaria, the Czech Republic, Estonia, Cyprus, Latvia, Lithuania, Hungary, Malta, Poland, Romania, Slovenia and Slovakia.]

NOTES

Amendment

Para (g): inserted by the Act of Accession 2005.

Date in force: 1 January 2005 and applicable from 1 January 2007.

TITLE II
GENERAL PROVISIONS

CHAPTER 1
CROSS COMPLIANCE

A1.731

Article 3   Main requirements

1.   A farmer receiving direct payments shall respect the statutory management requirements referred to in Annex III, according to the timetable fixed in that Annex, and the good agricultural and environmental condition established under Article 5.

2.   The competent national authority shall provide the farmer with the list of statutory management requirements and good agricultural and environmental condition to be respected.

A1.732

Article 4   Statutory management requirements

1.   The statutory management requirements referred to in Annex III shall be established by Community legislation in the following areas:

— public, animal and plant health,
— environment,
— animal welfare.

2.   The acts referred to in Annex III shall apply within the framework of this Regulation in the version as amended from time to time and, in case of Directives, as implemented by the Member States.

A1.733

Article 5   Good agricultural and environmental condition

1.   Member States shall ensure that all agricultural land, especially land which is no longer used for production purposes, is maintained in good agricultural and environmental condition. Member States shall define, at national or regional level, minimum

requirements for good agricultural and environmental condition on the basis of the framework set up in Annex IV, taking into account the specific characteristics of the areas concerned, including soil and climatic condition, existing farming systems, land use, crop rotation, farming practices, and farm structures. This is without prejudice to the standards governing good agricultural practices as applied in the context of Council Regulation (EC) No 1257/1999 and to agri-environment measures applied above the reference level of good agricultural practices.

2. Member States shall ensure that land which was under permanent pasture at the date provided for the area aid applications for 2003 is maintained under permanent pasture. [The new Member States shall ensure that land which was under permanent pasture on 1 May 2004 is maintained under permanent pasture.]

[However, Bulgaria and Romania shall esnure that land which was under permanent pasture on 1 January 2007 is maintained under permanent pasture.]

However a Member State may, in duly justified circumstances, derogate from the first subparagraph, provided that it takes action to prevent any significant decrease in its total permanent pasture area.

The first subparagraph shall not apply to land under permanent pasture to be afforested, if such afforestation is compatible with the environment and with the exclusion of plantations of Christmas trees and fast growing species cultivated in the short term.

NOTES

Amendment

Para 2: first paragraph: words in square brackets inserted by Council Regulation 583/2004.

Date in force: 1 May 2004.

Para 2: second paragraph: inserted by the Act of Accession 2005.

Date in force: 1 January 2005 and applicable from 1 January 2007.

A1.734

Article 6   Reduction or exclusion from payments

1. Where the statutory management requirements or good agricultural and environmental condition are not complied with, as a result of an action or omission directly attributable to the individual farmer, the total amount of direct payments to be granted in the calendar year in which the non-compliance occurs, and after application of Articles 10 and 11, shall be reduced or cancelled in accordance with the detailed rules laid down under Article 7.

2. The reductions or exclusions referred to in paragraph 1 shall only apply if the non-compliance relates to:

    (a) an agricultural activity, or

    (b) an agricultural land of the holding, including the parcels on set aside.

A1.735

Article 7   Detailed rules for reduction or exclusion

1. Detailed rules for the reductions and exclusions referred to in Article 6 shall be laid down in accordance with the procedure referred to in Article 144(2). In this context,

account shall be taken of the severity, extent, permanence and repetition of the non-compliance found as well as of the criteria set out in paragraphs 2, 3 and 4 of this Article.

2. In case of negligence, the percentage of reduction shall not exceed 5% and, in case of repeated non-compliance, 15%.

3. In case of intentional non-compliance, the percentage of reduction shall not in principle be less than 20% and may go as far as total exclusion from one or several aid schemes and apply for one or more calendar years.

4. In any case, the total amount of reductions and exclusions for one calendar year shall not be more than the total amount referred to in Article 6(1).

A1.736

Article 8   Review

By 31 December 2007 at the latest, the Commission shall submit a report on the application of the system of cross compliance accompanied, if necessary, by appropriate proposals notably with the view of amending the list of statutory management requirements set out in Annex III.

A1.737

Article 9   Amounts resulting from cross compliance

The amount resulting from the application of this Chapter shall be credited to the EAGGF 'Guarantee' Section. Member State may retain 25% of those amounts.

CHAPTER 2
MODULATION AND FINANCIAL DISCIPLINE

A1.738

Article 10   Modulation

1. All the amounts of direct payments to be granted in a given calendar year to a farmer in a given Member State shall be reduced for each year until 2012 by the following percentages:

— 2005: 3%,
— 2006: 4%,
— 2007: 5%,
— 2008: 5%,
— 2009: 5%,
— 2010: 5%,
— 2011: 5%,
— 2012: 5%.

2. The amounts resulting from application of the reductions provided for in paragraph 1, after deducting the total amounts referred to in Annex II, shall be available as additional Community support for measures under rural development programming financed under the EAGGF 'Guarantee' Section according to Regulation (EC) No 1257/1999.

3. The amount corresponding to one percentage point shall be allocated to the Member State where the corresponding amounts have been generated. The remaining

amounts shall be allocated to the Member States concerned in accordance with the procedure referred to in Article 144(2) on the basis of the following criteria:

— agricultural area,
— agricultural employment,
— gross domestic product (GDP) per capita in purchasing power.

However, any Member State shall receive at least 80% of the total amounts which the modulation has generated in that Member State.

4. By way of derogation from the second subparagraph of paragraph 3, if in a Member State the proportion of rye as part of its total cereal production exceeded 5% on average during the period 2000–2002 and its proportion of the total Community production of rye exceeded 50% during the same period, at least 90% of the amounts which the modulation generated in the Member State concerned shall be reallocated to that Member State, until 2013 included.

In such a case, without prejudice to the possibility provided for by Article 69, at least 10% of the amount allocated to the Member State concerned shall be available for measures referred to in paragraph 2 of this Article in rye producing regions.

For the purpose of this paragraph, 'cereals' mean the cereals referred to in Annex IX.

5. Paragraph 1 shall not apply to direct payments granted to farmers in the French overseas departments, in the Azores and Madeira, in the Canary and Aegean islands.

TITLE III
SINGLE PAYMENT SCHEME

CHAPTER 1
GENERAL PROVISIONS

A1.739

Article 33   Eligibility

1. Farmers shall have access to the single payment scheme if:

   [(a) they have been granted a payment in the reference period referred to in Article 38 under at least one of the support schemes referred to in Annex VI or, in the case of olive oil, in the marketing years referred to in the second subparagraph of Article 37(1), or, in the case of sugar beet, cane and chicory, if they have benefited from market support in the representative period referred to in point K of Annex VII, or, in the case of bananas, if they have benefited from compensation for loss of income in the representative period referred to in point L of Annex VII], or
   (b) they have received the holding or part of the holding, by way of actual or anticipated inheritance, by a farmer who met the conditions referred to in point (a), or
   (c) they have received a payment entitlement from the national reserve or by transfer.

2. In case the farmer who has been granted a direct payment in the reference period changes his legal status or denomination in that period or not later than 31 December of the year preceding the year of application of the single payment scheme, he shall have access to the single payment scheme under the same conditions as the farmer originally managing the holding.

3. In case of mergers during the reference period or not later than 31 December of the year preceding the year of application of the single payment scheme, the farmer

managing the new holding shall have access to the single payment scheme under the same conditions as the farmers managing the original holdings.

In case of scissions during the reference period or not later than 31 December of the year preceding the year of application of the single payment scheme, the farmers managing the holdings shall have access, pro rata, to the single payment scheme under the same conditions as the farmer managing the original holding.

NOTES

Amendment

Para 1(a): substituted by Council Regulation 2013/2006.

Date in force: 1 January 2007.

A1.740

Article 34   Application

1. The first year of application of the single payment scheme, the competent authority of the Member State shall send an application form to the farmers referred to in Article 33(1)(a) indicating:

- (a) the amount referred to in Chapter 2 (hereinafter referred to as the 'reference amount');
- (b) the number of hectares referred to in Article 43;
- (c) the number and value of payment entitlements as defined in Chapter 3.

2. Farmers shall apply to the single payment scheme by a date, to be fixed by Member States, but not later than 15 May.

However, the Commission, in accordance with the procedure referred to in Article 144(2), may allow the date of 15 May to be postponed in certain zones where exceptional climatic conditions render the normal dates inapplicable.

3. Except in case of force majeure and exceptional circumstances within the meaning of Article 40(4), no entitlements shall be allocated to farmers referred to in Article 33(1)(a) and (b) and to those who receive payment entitlements from the national reserve, if they do not apply to the single payment scheme by 15 May of the first year of application of the single payment scheme.

The amounts corresponding to those entitlements not allocated shall revert to the national reserve referred to in Article 42 and shall be available for reallocation by a date to be fixed by the Member State but not later than 15 August of the first year of application of the single payment scheme.

A1.741

Article 35   Double claims

[1. The area corresponding to the number of eligible hectares as defined in Article 44(2) in respect of which a single payment application is submitted may be the subject of an application for any other direct payment as well as for any other aid not covered by this Regulation, save as otherwise provided.

2. Farmers who have participated in the tobacco quota buy-back scheme according to Regulation (EEC) No 2075/92 shall be entitled to either the single payment or the quota buy-back price. However, where the quota buy-back price is higher than the amount calculated for tobacco to be included in the reference amount, the farmer shall still be entitled, in addition to the single payment, to a part of the buy-back price

corresponding to the difference between the price amount and the amount calculated in accordance with point I of Annex VII to this Regulation.]

NOTES

Amendment

Paras 1 and 2: substituted by Council Regulation 864/2004.

Date in force: 1 May 2004 and applicable from 1 January 2006 except for provisos contained in Regulation 864/2004 (see EU Official Journal version).

A1.742

Article 36   Payment

1. Aid under the single payment scheme shall be paid in respect of payment entitlements as defined in Chapter 3, accompanied by an equal number of eligible hectares as defined in Article 44(2).

2. Member States may decide to combine payments under the single payment scheme with payments under any other support scheme.

CHAPTER 2
ESTABLISHMENT OF THE AMOUNT

A1.743

Article 37   Calculation of the reference amount

1. The reference amount shall be the three-year average of the total amounts of payments, which a farmer was granted under the support schemes referred to in Annex VI, calculated and adjusted according to Annex VII, in each calendar year of the reference period referred to in Article 38.

[However, for olive oil the reference amount shall be the four-year average of the total amounts of payments which a farmer was granted under the olive oil support scheme referred to in Annex VI, calculated and adjusted according to Annex VII, during the marketing years 1999/2000, 2000/2001, 2001/2002 and 2002/2003.]

[For sugar beet, cane and chicory used for the production of sugar or inulin syrup the reference amount shall be calculated and adjusted in accordance with point K of Annex VII.]

[For bananas the reference amount shall be calculated and adjusted in accordance with point L of Annex VII.]

2. By way of derogation from paragraph 1, when a farmer commences an agricultural activity in the reference period, the average shall be based on the payments he was granted in the calendar year or years during which he exercised the agricultural activity.

NOTES

Amendment

Para 1: second para: inserted by Council Regulation 864/2004.

Date in force: 1 May 2004 and applicable from 1 January 2006 except for provisos contained in Regulation 864/2004 (see EU Official Journal version).

Para 1:third para: inserted by Council Regulation 319/2006.

Date in force: 3 March 2006 and applicable from 1 January 2006.

Para 1:fourth para: inserted by Council Regulation 2013/2006.

Date in force: 1 January 2007.

A1.744

Article 38   Reference period

The reference period shall comprise the calendar years 2000, 2001 and 2002.

A1.745

Article 39   Application of modulation and cross-compliance laid down under Regulation (EC) No 1259/1999

In case of application of Articles 3 and 4 of Regulation (EC) No 1259/1999 during the reference period, the amounts referred to in Annex VII shall be those that would have been granted before application of the said Articles.

A1.746

Article 40   Hardship cases

1.   By way of derogation from Article 37, a farmer whose production was adversely affected during the reference period by a case of force majeure or exceptional circumstances occurring before or during that reference period shall be entitled to request that the reference amount be calculated on the basis of the calendar year or years in the reference period not affected by the case of force majeure or exceptional circumstances.

[2.   If the whole reference period was affected by the case of force majeure or exceptional circumstances, the Member State shall calculate the reference amount on the basis of the 1997 to 1999 period or, in case of sugar beet, cane and chicory on the basis of the closest marketing year prior to the representative period chosen in accordance with point K of Annex VII, or, in case of bananas on the basis of the closest marketing year prior to the representative period chosen in accordance with point L of Annex VII. In this case, paragraph 1 shall apply mutatis mutandis.]

3.   A case of force majeure or exceptional circumstances, with relevant evidence to the satisfaction of the competent authority, shall be notified by the farmer concerned in writing to the authority within a deadline to be fixed by each Member State.

4.   Force majeure or exceptional circumstances shall be recognised by the competent authority in cases such as, for example:

(a)   the death of the farmer;
(b)   long-term professional incapacity of the farmer;
(c)   a severe natural disaster gravely affecting the holding's agricultural land;
(d)   the accidental destruction of livestock buildings on the holding;
(e)   an epizootic affecting part or all of the farmer's livestock.

[5.   Paragraphs 1, 2 and 3 of this Article shall apply, mutatis mutandis, to farmers who, during the reference period, were under agri-environmental commitments in accordance with Regulations (EEC) No 2078/92* and (EC) No 1257/1999, to hop farmers who, during the same period, were under a grubbing-up commitment in accordance with Regulation (EC) No 1098/98**, as well as to tobacco farmers who have participated in the quota buy-back programme in accordance with Regulation (EEC) No 2075/92.

Council Regulation (EC) No 1782/2003 **A1.747**

In the case where the measures referred to in the first subparagraph covered both the reference period and the period referred to in paragraph 2, Member States shall establish, according to objective criteria and in such a way as to ensure equal treatment between farmers and to avoid market and competition distortions, a reference amount in accordance with the detailed rules to be laid down by the Commission in accordance with the procedure referred to in Article 144(2).

* OJ 1992 L 215/85.
** OJ 1998 L 157/7.]

NOTES

Amendment

Para 2: substituted by Council Regulation 2013/2006.

Date in force: 1 January 2007.

Para 5: substituted by Council Regulation 864/2004.

Date in force: 1 May 2004 and applicable from 1 January 2006 except for provisos contained in Regulation 864/2004 (see EU Official Journal version).

A1.747

Article 41   Ceiling

1.   For each Member State, the sum of the reference amounts shall not be higher than the national ceiling referred to in Annex VIII.

[In the case of chicory and taking into account the latest data made available to it by the Member States until 31 March 2006, the Commission may, in accordance with the procedure referred to in Article 144(2), reallocate the national amounts set out in point K(2) of Annex VII and adapt the national ceilings set out in Annex VIII accordingly without changing the global amounts or the ceilings respectively.

1a.   Where some of the quantities of the quota sugar or the quota inulin syrup were produced in a Member State on the basis of sugar beet, cane or chicory grown in another Member State during any of the marketing years 2000/2001, 2001/2002, 2002/2003, 2003/2004, 2004/2005 or 2005/2006, the ceilings set out in point K of Annex VII and the national ceilings set out in Annexes VIII and VIIIa of the Member States concerned shall be adapted by transferring the amounts corresponding to the relevant quantities from the national ceilings of the Member State where the relevant sugar or inulin syrup was produced to those of the Member State where the relevant quantities of sugar beet, cane or chicory were grown.

The Member States concerned shall inform the Commission by 31 March 2006 of the quantities concerned.

The transfer shall be decided by the Commission in accordance with the procedure referred to in Article 144(2).]

2.   Where necessary, a Member State shall proceed to a linear percentage reduction of the reference amounts in order to ensure respect of its ceiling.

NOTES

Amendment

Para 1: words in square brackets inserted by Council Regulation 319/2006.

Date in force: 3 March 2006 and applicable from 1 January 2006.

Para 1a: inserted by Council Regulation 319/2006.

1955

Date in force: 3 March 2006 and applicable from 1 January 2006.

A1.748

Article 42   National reserve

1.   Member States shall, after any possible reduction under Article 41(2), proceed to a linear percentage reduction of the reference amounts in order to constitute a national reserve. This reduction shall not be higher than 3%.

2.   The national reserve shall further include the difference between the ceiling referred to in Annex VIII and the sum of the reference amounts to be granted to farmers under the single payment scheme, before the reduction referred to in paragraph 1 second sentence.

3.   Member States may use the national reserve to grant, in priority, reference amounts to farmers who commence their agricultural activity after 31 December 2002, or in 2002 but without receiving any direct payment in that year, according to objective criteria and in such a way as to ensure equal treatment between farmers and to avoid market and competition distortions.

4.   Member States shall use the national reserve for the purpose of establishing, according to objective criteria and in such a way as to ensure equal treatment between farmers and to avoid market and competition distortions, reference amounts for farmers finding themselves in a special situation, to be defined by the Commission in accordance with the procedure referred to in Article 144(2).

5.   Member States may use the national reserve for the purpose of establishing, according to objective criteria and in such a way as to ensure equal treatment between farmers and to avoid market and competition distortions, reference amounts for farmers in areas subject to restructuring and/or development programs relating to one or the other form of public intervention in order to avoid abandoning of land and/or in order to compensate specific disadvantages for farmers in those areas.

6.   In application of paragraphs 3 to 5 Member States may increase the unit value, within the limit of the regional average of the value of entitlements, and/or the number of entitlements allocated to farmers.

7.   Member States shall proceed to linear reductions of the entitlements in case their national reserve is not sufficient to cover the cases referred to in paragraphs 3 and 4.

[8.   Except in the case of a transfer by actual or anticipated inheritance and of mergers and scissions, and by way of derogation from Article 46, the entitlements established using the national reserve shall not be transferred for a period of five years starting from their allocation. In the case of a merger or scission, the farmer(s) managing the new holding(s) shall keep the entitlements which were originally allocated from the national reserve until the remaining part of the five-year period.]

By way of derogation from Article 45(1), any entitlement which has not been used during each year of the five year period shall revert immediately to the national reserve.

9.   By way of derogation from Articles 33 and 43, in case of sale or lease for six or more years of the holding or part of it or premium rights in the reference period or not later than [15 May 2004], part of the entitlements to be allocated to the seller or the lessor may revert to the national reserve under conditions to be defined by the Commission, in accordance with the procedure referred to in Article 144(2).

NOTES

Amendment

Para 8: substituted by Council Regulation 2012/2006.

Date in force: 1 January 2007 and applicable from 1 January 2007.

Para 9: words in square brackets substituted by Council Regulation 864/2004.

Date in force: 1 May 2004 and applicable from 1 January 2006 except for provisos contained in Regulation 864/2004 (see EU Official Journal version).

CHAPTER 3
PAYMENT ENTITLEMENTS

Section 1
Payment entitlements based on areas

A1.749

Article 43 Determination of the payment entitlements

1. Without prejudice to Article 48, a farmer shall receive a payment entitlement per hectare which is calculated by dividing the reference amount by the three-year average number of all hectares which in the reference period gave right to direct payments listed in Annex VI.

The total number of payment entitlements shall be equal to the above mentioned average number of hectares.

However, in the case referred to in Article 37(2), the total number of payment entitlements shall be equal to the average number of hectares of the same period used for the establishment of the reference amounts and Article 42(6) shall apply to these payment entitlements.

2. The number of hectares referred to in paragraph 1 shall further include:

[(a) in case of potato starch, dried fodder, seed, olive groves, and tobacco aids listed in Annex VII, the number of hectares whose production has been granted the aid in the reference period, as calculated in points B, D, F, H, I of Annex VII, in case of sugar beet, cane and chicory, the number of hectares as calculated in accordance with point 4 of point K of that Annex and in the case of bananas, the number of hectares as calculated in accordance with point L of that Annex;]

(b) all forage area in the reference period.

3. For the purpose of paragraph 2(b) of this Article, 'forage area' shall mean the area of the holding that was available throughout the calendar year, in accordance with Article 5 of Commission Regulation (EC) No 2419/2001[1], for rearing animals including areas in shared use and areas which were subject to mixed cultivation. The forage area shall not include:

— buildings, woods, ponds, paths,
— areas used for other crops eligible for Community aid or for permanent crops or horticultural crops,
— areas qualifying for the support system laid down for the producers of certain arable crops, used for the aid scheme for dried fodder or subject to a national or Community set-aside scheme.

4. The payment entitlements per hectare shall not be modified save as otherwise provided.

¹ Commission Regulation (EC) No 2419/2001 of 11 December 2001 laying down detailed rules for applying the integrated administration and control system for certain Community aid schemes established by Council Regulation (EEC) No 3508/92 (OJ 2001 L 327/11). Regulation as amended by Commission Regulation (EC) No 2550/2001 (OJ 2001 L 341/105).

NOTES

Amendment

Para 2(a): substituted by Council Regulation 2013/2006.

Date in force: 1 January 2007.

A1.750

Article 44   Use of payment entitlements

1.   Any payment entitlement accompanied by an eligible hectare shall give right to the payment of the amount fixed by the payment entitlement.

2.   'Eligible hectare' shall mean any agricultural area of the holding taken up by arable land and permanent pasture except areas under permanent crops, forests or used for non agricultural activities.

['Eligible hectare' shall also mean areas planted with hope or being under a temporary resting obligation [or planted with bananas], or areas under olive trees.]

3.   The farmer shall declare the parcels corresponding to the eligible hectare accompanying any payment entitlement. Except in case of force majeure or exceptional circumstances, these parcels shall be at the farmer's disposal for a period of at least 10-months, starting from a date to be fixed by the Member State, but not earlier than 1 September of the calendar year preceding the year of lodging the application for participation in the single payment scheme.

4.   Member States may, in duly justified circumstances, authorise the farmer to modify his declaration on condition that he respects the number of hectares corresponding to his payment entitlements and the conditions for granting the single payment for the area concerned.

NOTES

Amendment

Para 2: second para: substituted by Council Regulation 2012/2006.

Date in force: 1 January 2007 and applicable from 1 January 2007.

Para 2: second para: words 'or planted with bananas' in square brackets inserted by Council Regulation 2013/2006.

Date in force: 1 January 2007.

A1.751

Article 45   Unused payment entitlements

1.   Any payment entitlement which has not been used for a period of 3 years shall be allocated to the national reserve.

2.   However, unused payment entitlements shall not revert to the national reserve in case of force majeure and exceptional circumstances within the meaning of Article 40(4).

A1.752

Article 46 Transfer of payment entitlements

1. Payment entitlements may only be transferred to another farmer established within the same Member State except in case of transfer by actual or anticipated inheritance.

However, even in the case of actual or anticipated inheritance, payment entitlements may only be used in the Member State where the payment entitlements were established.

A Member State may decide that payment entitlements may only be transferred or used within one and the same region.

2. Payment entitlements may be transferred by sale or any other definitive transfer with or without land. In contrast, lease or similar types of transactions shall be allowed only if the payment entitlements transferred are accompanied by the transfer of an equivalent number of eligible hectares.

Except in case of force majeure or exceptional circumstances as referred to in Article 40(4), a farmer may transfer his payment entitlements without land only after he has used, within the meaning of Article 44, at least 80% of his payment entitlements during at least one calendar year or, after he has given up voluntarily to the national reserve all the payment entitlements he has not used in the first year of application of the single payment scheme.

3. In case of sale of payment entitlements, with or without land, Member States may, acting in compliance with the general principle of Community law, decide that part of the payment entitlements sold revert to the national reserve or that their unit value is reduced in favour of the national reserve, according to criteria to be fixed by the Commission in accordance with the procedure referred to in Article 144(2).

Section 2
Payment entitlements subject to special conditions

A1.753

Article 47 Payments giving right to payment entitlements subject to special conditions

1. By way of derogation from Articles 43 and 44, the following amounts resulting from payments granted in the reference period shall be included in the reference amount under the conditions provided for in Article 48 and point C of Annex VII:

(a) the deseasonalisation premium provided for in Article 5 of Regulation (EC) No 1254/1999;

(b) the slaughter premium provided for in Article 11 of Regulation (EC) No 1254/1999;

(c) the special premium for male bovine animals and the suckler cow premium, where the farmer was exempted from the stocking rate requirement pursuant to Article 12(1) of Regulation (EC) No 1254/1999, provided that the farmer did not apply for the extensification payment provided for in Article 13 of that Regulation;

(d) additional payments provided for in Article 14 of Regulation (EC) No 1254/1999 where paid in addition to aid provided for under (a), (b) and (c) of this paragraph;

(e) the aids provided for under the sheep and goats aid scheme:

— in the calendar years 2000 and 2001, in Article 5 of Regulation (EC) No 2467/98 and in Article 1 of Regulation (EEC) No 1323/90[1],

— in the calendar year 2002, in Articles 4, 5 and 11(1) and in the first, second and fourth indent of Article 11(2) of Regulation (EC) No 2529/2001.

2. Starting from 2007 and by way of derogation from Articles 33, 43 and 44, the amounts resulting from dairy premium and additional payments, provided for in Articles 95 and 96 and to be granted in 2007 shall be included in the single payment scheme under the conditions provided for in Articles 48 to 50.

¹ OJ 1990 L 132/17. Regulation repealed by Regulation (EC) No 2529/2001 (OJ 2001 L 341/3).

A1.754

Article 48   Determination of the payment entitlements subject to special conditions

When farmer was granted payments referred to in Article 47, but had no hectares as referred to in Article 43 in the reference period, or the entitlement per hectare results in an amount higher than EUR 5000, the farmer shall have right, respectively, to a payment entitlement:

(a) equal to the reference amount corresponding to the direct payments he was granted in the three-year average period;

(b) for each EUR 5000 or fraction of the reference amount corresponding to the direct payments he was granted in the three-year average period.

A1.755

Article 49   Conditions

1. Save as otherwise provided for in this section, the other provisions of this Title shall apply to the payment entitlements subject to special conditions.

2. By way of derogation from Articles 36(1) and 44(1), a farmer who has such payment entitlements for which he did not have hectares in the reference period, shall be authorised by the Member State to derogate from the obligation to provide a number of eligible hectares equivalent to the number of entitlements on the condition he maintains at least 50% of the agricultural activity exercised in the reference period expressed in livestock units (LU).

In case of a transfer of the payment entitlements, the transferee may benefit from this derogation only if all the payment entitlements subject to the derogation are transferred.

3. The payment entitlements determined according to Article 48 shall not be modified.

A1.756

Article 50   Dairy premium and additional payments

1. Without prejudice to Article 48 and by way of derogation from Articles 37 and 43, a farmer shall receive a supplementary amount per entitlement resulting by dividing the amounts to be granted under Articles 95 and 96 by the number of entitlements he owns in 2007 except set-aside entitlements.

The unit value of each payment entitlement he owns in 2007 shall be increased by this supplementary amount.

2. In cases where he does not own any entitlement, Articles 48 and 49 shall apply mutatis mutandis. In this case, for the purpose of applying Article 48, the term 'hectares' shall mean the eligible hectares the farmer owns in 2007.

CHAPTER 4
LAND USE UNDER THE SINGLE PAYMENT SCHEME

Section 1
Use of the land

A1.757

Article 51   Agricultural use of the land

[Farmers may use the parcels declared accordance with Article 44(3) for any agricultural activity except for:

   [(a) permanent crops, apart from olive trees or hops] [or bananas];
   (b) the production of the products referred to in Article 1(2) of Regulation (EC) No 2200/96* and in Article 1(2) of Regulation (EC) No 2201/96**.

   However, Member States may decide to allow secondary crops to be cultivated on the eligible hectares during a period of maximum three months starting each year on 15 August; however, at the request of a Member State, this date is modified in accordance with the procedure laid down in Article 144(2) for regions where cereals are normally harvested earlier for climatic reasons;
   (c) potatoes other than those intended for the manufacture of potato starch for which aid is granted under Article 93.

*   OJ 1996 L 297/1.
** OJ 1996 L 297/29.]

NOTES

Amendment

Art 51: substituted by Council Regulation 864/2004.

Date in force: 1 May 2004 and applicable from 1 January 2006 except for provisos contained in Regulation 864/2004 (see EU Official Journal version).

Para (a): words 'permanent crops, apart from olive trees or hops' in first set of square brackets inserted by Council Regulation 2012/2006.

Date in force: 1 January 2007.

Para (a): words 'or bananas' in second set of square brackets inserted by Council Regulation 2013/2006.

Date in force: 1 January 2007.

A1.758

Article 52   Production of hemp

[1. In case of production of hemp, the varieties used shall have a tetrahydrocannabinol content not exceeding 0,2%. Member States shall establish a system for verifying the tetrahydrocannabinol content of the crops grown on at least 30% of the areas on hemp. However, if a Member State introduces a system of prior approval for such cultivation, the minimum shall be 20%.

1961

2. In accordance with the procedure referred to in Article 144(2), the granting of payments shall be made subject to the use of certified seeds of certain varieties.]

NOTES

Amendment

Art 52: substituted by Council Regulation 953/2006.

Date in force: 6 July 2006 and applicable from 1 January 2007.

Section 2
Set-aside entitlements

A1.759

Article 53   Determination of the set-aside entitlements

1. By way of derogation from Articles 37 and 43 of this Regulation, where in the reference period a farmer was subject to the obligation to set aside part of the land of his holding pursuant to Article 6(1) of Regulation (EC) No 1251/1999, the three-year average amount corresponding to the compulsory set-aside payment calculated and adjusted according to Annex VII and the three-year average number of compulsory set-aside hectares shall not be included in the determination of the entitlements referred to in Article 43 of this Regulation.

2. In the case referred to in paragraph 1, the farmer shall receive an entitlement per hectare (hereinafter referred to as 'set-aside entitlement') which is calculated by dividing the three-year set-aside average amount by the three-year average number of hectares set-aside, as referred to in paragraph 1.

The total number of set-aside entitlements shall be equal to the average number of compulsory set-aside hectares.

A1.760

Article 54   Use of set-aside entitlements

1. Any set-aside entitlement accompanied by a hectare eligible for set-aside entitlement shall give right to the payment of the amount fixed by the set-aside entitlement.

2. By way of derogation from Article 44(2), 'hectare eligible for set-aside entitlement' shall mean any agricultural area of the holding taken up by arable land, except areas which at the date provided for the area aid applications for 2003 were under permanent crops, forests or used for non agricultural activities or under permanent pasture. [For the new Member States, the reference to the date provided for the area aid applications for 2003 shall be construed as a reference to 30 June 2003.]

[However, for Bulgaria and Romania, the date provided for the area aid applications shall be 30 June 2005.]

However, the following areas may be counted as being set aside, as a result of an application made after 28 June 1995:

— areas set aside pursuant to Articles 22 to 24 of Regulation (EC) No 1257/1999, which are neither put to any agricultural use nor used for any lucrative purposes other than those accepted for other land set aside under this Regulation, or
— areas afforested pursuant to Article 31 of Regulation (EC) No 1257/1999.

3. Farmers shall set aside from production the hectares eligible for set-aside entitlements.

4. Set aside areas shall not be less than 0,1 ha in size and 10 metres wide. For duly justified environmental reasons, Member States may accept areas at least 5 metres wide and 0,05 ha in size.

5. Member States may, on terms to be determined in accordance with the procedure referred to in Article 144(2), derogate from first subparagraph of paragraph 2 of this Article, provided that they take action to prevent any significant increase in the total agricultural area eligible to set-aside entitlements.

6. By way of derogation from Articles 36(1) and 44(1), set-aside entitlements shall be claimed before any other entitlement.

7. The set aside obligation shall continue to apply in respect of the set-aside entitlements which are transferred.

NOTES

Amendment

Para 2: Words in first set of square brackets inserted by Council Regulation 583/2004.

Date in force: 1 May 2004.

Para 2: Words in second set of square brackets inserted by the Act of Accession 2005.

Date in force: 1 January 2005 and applicable from 1 January 2007.

A1.761

Article 55   Exemption from set-aside

A farmer shall not be subject to the obligation referred to in Article 54 if:

   (a)   his entire holding is managed for the totality of its production in compliance
         with the obligations laid down in Council Regulation (EEC) No 2092/91 of
         24 June 1991 on organic production of agricultural products and indications
         referring thereto on agricultural products and foodstuffs[1];
   (b)   the land set-aside is used for the provision of materials for the manufacture
         within the Community of products not primarily intended for human or
         animal consumption, provided that effective control systems are applied.

[1]   OJ 1999 L 198/1. Regulation as last amended by Commission Regulation (EC)
      No 806/2003 (OJ 2003 L 122/1).

A1.762

Article 56   Use of the set aside land

1. The land set aside shall be maintained in good agricultural and environmental condition as established under Article 5.

Without prejudice to Article 55, it shall not be used for agricultural purposes and shall not produce any crop for commercial purposes.

2. It may be subject to rotation.

3. If the quantity of by-products for feed or food uses likely to be made available as a result of the cultivation of oilseeds on land set-aside under Article 55(b), will, on the basis of the forecast quantities covered by contracts made with farmers, exceed 1 million tonnes annually expressed in soya bean meal equivalents, in order to limit such quantity to 1 million tonnes, the amount of the forecast quantity under each contract, which may be used of feed or food uses, shall be reduced.

[4.   Member States shall be authorised to pay national aid up to 50% of the costs associated with establishing permanent crops intended for bio-mass production on set-aside land.]

NOTES

Amendment

Para 4: substituted by Council Regulation 2012/2006.

Date in force: 1 January 2007 and applicable from 1 January 2007.

A1.763

Article 57   Application of other provisions

Save as otherwise provided for in this section, the other provisions of this Title shall apply to the set-aside entitlements.

CHAPTER 5
REGIONAL AND OPTIONAL IMPLEMENTATION

Section 1
Regional implementation

A1.764

Article 58   Regional allocation of the ceiling referred to in Article 41

1.   A Member State may decide, by 1 August 2004 at the latest, to apply the single payment scheme provided for in Chapters 1 to 4 at regional level under the conditions laid down in this Section.

2.   Member States shall define the regions according to objective criteria.

Member States with less than three million eligible hectares may be considered as one single region.

3.   The Member State shall subdivide the ceiling referred to in Article 41 between the regions according to objective criteria.

A1.765

Article 59   Regionalisation of the single payment scheme

1.   In duly justified cases and according to objective criteria the Member State may divide the total amount of the regional ceiling established under Article 58 or part of it between all the farmers whose holdings are located in the region concerned, including those who do not meet the eligibility criterion referred to in Article 33.

2.   In this case of division of the total amount of the regional ceiling, farmers shall receive entitlements, whose unit value is calculated by dividing the regional ceiling established under Article 58 by the number of eligible hectares, within the meaning of Article 44(2), established at regional level.

3.   In case of partial division of the total amount of the regional ceiling, farmers shall receive entitlements whose unit value is calculated by dividing the corresponding part of the regional ceiling established under Article 58 by the number of eligible hectares, within the meaning of Article 44(2), established at regional level.

In case the farmer is also entitled to receive entitlements calculated on the remaining part of the regional ceiling, the regional unit value of each of his entitlements, except for set-aside entitlements, shall be increased by an amount corresponding to the reference amount divided by the number his entitlements established in accordance with paragraph 4.

Articles 48 and 49 shall apply mutatis mutandis.

4. The number of entitlements per farmer shall be equal to the number of hectares he declares in accordance with Article 44(2) the first year of application of the single payment scheme, except in case of force majeure or exceptional circumstances within the meaning of Article 40(4).

A1.766

Article 60 Use of the land

[1. Where a Member State makes use of the option provided for in Article 59, farmers may, by way of derogation from Article 51(b) and (c) and in accordance with this Article, also use the parcels declared in accordance with Article 44(3) for the production of products referred to in Article 1(2) of Regulation (EC) No 2200/96 or in Article 1(2) of Regulation (EC) No 2201/96 and of potatoes other than those intended for the manufacture of potato starch for which aid is granted under Article 93 of this Regulation, except crops referred to in Article 51(a).]

2. The Member State shall establish the number of hectares that may be used according to paragraph 1 of this Article by subdividing, according to objective criteria, the average of the number of hectares that were used for the production of the products referred to in paragraph 1 at national level during the three-year period 2000–2002 amongst the regions defined pursuant to Article 58(2). The average number of hectares at national level and the number of hectares at regional level shall be fixed by the Commission in accordance with the procedure referred to in Article 144(2) on the basis of the data communicated by the Member State.

3. Within the limit established according to paragraph 2 for the region concerned, a farmer shall be allowed to make use of the option referred to in paragraph 1:

   (a) within the limit of the number of hectares that he used for the production of the products referred to in paragraph 1 in 2003;
   (b) in case of application, mutatis mutandis, of Articles 40 and 42(4), within the limit of a number of hectares to be established according to objective criteria and in such a way as to ensure equal treatment between farmers and to avoid market and competition distortions.

4. Within the limit of the number of hectares that remain available after application of paragraph 3, farmers shall be allowed to produce the products referred to in paragraph 1 on a number of hectares other than the number of hectares falling under paragraph 3 within the limit of a number of hectares used for the production of the products referred to in paragraph 1 in 2004 and/or 2005, whereby priority shall be given to the farmers who produced the products already in 2004 within the limit of the number of hectares used in 2004.

In case of application of Article 71, 2004 and 2005 shall be replaced by, respectively, the year previous to the year of application of the single payment scheme and the year of application itself.

5. In order to establish the individual limits referred to in paragraphs 3 and 4, the Members State shall use the farmer's individual data, where available, or any other evidence at its satisfaction provided by the farmer.

6.   The number of hectares for which the authorisation has been established according to paragraphs 3 and 4 of this Article, shall in no case exceed the number of eligible hectares as defined in Article 44(2) declared in the first year of application of the single payment scheme.

7.   The authorisation shall be used, within the region concerned, with the corresponding payment entitlement.

8.   By at the latest 2007, the Commission shall submit a report to the Council, accompanied, if necessary, by appropriate proposals, on the possible consequences, in terms of market and structural developments, of the implementation by Member States of this Article.

NOTES

Amendment

Para 1: substituted by Council Regulation 2012/2006.

Date in force: 1 January 2007 and applicable from 1 January 2007.

A1.767

Article 61   Grassland

In case of application of Article 59, Member States may also, according to objective criteria, fix, within the regional ceiling or part of it, different per unit values of entitlements to be allocated to farmers referred to in Article 59(1), for hectares under grassland at the date provided for the area aid applications for 2003 and for any other eligible hectare or alternatively for hectares under permanent pasture at the date provided for the area aid applications for 2003 and for any other eligible hectare.

A1.768

Article 62   Dairy premium and additional payments

By way of derogation from Article 47(2), Member State may decide that the amounts resulting from dairy premiums and additional payments, provided for in Articles 95 and 96, shall be included, in part or in full, in the single payment scheme starting from 2005. Entitlements established under this paragraph shall be modified accordingly.

The reference amount for those payments shall be equal to the amounts to be granted according to Articles 95 and 96 calculated on the basis of the individual reference quantity for milk available on the holding on 31 March of the year of inclusion, in part or in full, of those payments in the single payment scheme.

Articles 48 to 50 shall apply mutatis mutandis.

A1.769

Article 63   Conditions for the entitlements established under this section

1.   In case of application of Article 59, entitlements established under this section may only be transferred or used within the same region or between regions where the entitlements per hectare are the same.

2.   In case of application of Article 59, by way of derogation from Article 53, any farmer in the region concerned shall receive set-aside entitlements.

The number of set-aside entitlements is established by multiplying a farmer's eligible land within the meaning of Article 54(2) declared in the first year of application of the single payment scheme with a set-aside rate.

The set aside rate is calculated by multiplying the basic rate of compulsory set-aside of 10% by the proportion, in the region concerned, between the land for which arable crops area payments referred to in Annex VI have been granted in the reference period and the eligible land within the meaning of Article 54(2) in the reference period.

The value of the set-aside entitlements shall be the regional value for payment entitlements as established according to Article 59(2) or, as the case may be, Article 59(3) first subparagraph.

Those farmers shall not receive set-aside entitlements who declare less than a number of hectares within the meaning of Article 54(2) which would be needed to produce a number of tonnes equal to 92 tonnes of cereals as defined in Annex IX on the basis of the yields determined according to the regionalisation plan applicable in the region concerned in the year before the year of application of the single payment scheme divided by the proportion referred to in the third subparagraph of paragraph 2 of this Article.

3. By way of derogation from Articles 43(4) and 49(3), Member States may also decide, by 1 August 2004 at the latest, and acting in compliance with the general principle of Community law, that entitlements established under this section shall be subject to progressive modifications according to pre-established steps and objective criteria.

[However, with regard to the inclusion of the sugar beet, cane and chicory payments component in the single payment scheme, Members States may decide by 30 April 2006, to apply the derogation provided for in the first subparagraph.]

4. Save as otherwise provided for in this Section, the other provisions of this Title shall apply.

NOTES

Amendment

Para 3: words in square brackets inserted by Council Regulation 319/2006.

Date in force: 3 March 2006 and applicable from 1 January 2006.

TITLE IV
OTHER AID SCHEMES

CHAPTER 2
PROTEIN CROP PREMIUM

A1.770

Article 76   Scope

An aid shall be granted to farmers producing protein crops under the conditions laid down in this Chapter.

Protein crops shall include:

— peas falling within CN code 0713 10,
— field beans falling within CN code 0713 50,
— sweet lupins falling within CN code ex 1209 29 50.

A1.771

Article 77   Amount and eligibility

The aid shall be EUR 55,57 per hectare of protein crops harvested after the stage of lactic ripeness.

However, crops grown on areas which are fully sown and which are cultivated in accordance with local standards, but which do not attain the stage of lactic ripeness as a result of exceptional weather conditions recognised by the Member State concerned, shall remain eligible for aid provided that the areas in question are not used for any other purpose up to this growing stage.

A1.772

Article 78   Area

[1.   A maximum guaranteed area of 1 648 000 ha for which the aid may be granted is hereby established.]

2.   Where the area for which aid is claimed exceeds the maximum guaranteed area, the area per farmer for which aid is claimed shall be reduced proportionally in that year in accordance with the procedure referred to in Article 144(2).

NOTES

Amendment

Para 1: substituted by the Act of Accession 2005.

Date in force: 1 January 2005 and applicable from 1 January 2007.

CHAPTER 5
AID FOR ENERGY CROPS

A1.773

Article 88   Aid

An aid of EUR 45 per hectare per year shall be granted for areas sown under energy crops used under the conditions laid down in this Chapter.

Energy crops shall mean crops supplied essentially for the production of the following energy products:

— products considered biofuels listed in Article 2, point 2 of Directive 2003/30/EC of the European Parliament and of the Council of 8 May 2003 on the promotion of the use of biofuels or other renewable fuels for transport[1],
— electric and thermal energy produced from biomass.

[Articles 143a and 143c shall not apply to the aid for energy crops in the Community as constituted on 1 January 2007.]

[1]   OJ 2003 L 123/42.

NOTES

Amendment

Words in square brackets inserted by Council Regulation 2012/2006.

Date in force: 1 January 2007 and applicable from 1 January 2007.

A1.774

Article 89   Areas

[1.   A maximum guaranteed area of 2 000 000 ha for which the aid may be granted is hereby established.]

2.   Where the area for which aid is claimed exceeds the maximum guaranteed area, the area per farmer for which aid is claimed shall be reduced proportionately in that year in accordance with the procedure referred to in Article 144(2).

NOTES

Amendment

Para 1: substituted by Council Regulation 2012/2006.

Date in force: 1 January 2007 and applicable from 1 January 2007.

A1.775

Article 90   Conditions for eligibility

[The aid shall be granted only in respect of areas whose production is covered by a contract between the farmer and the processing industry or by a contract between the farmer and the collector, except in case of processing undertaken by the farmer himself/herself on the holding.]

[Areas which have been subject to an application for energy crops scheme may not be counted as being set aside for the purposes of the set-aside requirement indicated in Article 6(1) of Regulation (EC) No 1251/1999 and in Articles 54(2), 63(2), 71j and 107(1) of this Regulation.]

NOTES

Amendment

First para: substituted by Council Regulation 2012/2006.

Date in force: 3 March 2006 and applicable from 1 January 2006.

Second para: substituted by Council Regulation 583/2004.

Date in force: 1 May 2004.

A1.776

[Article 90a   National aid

Member States shall be authorised to pay national aid up to 50% of the costs associated with establishing permanent crops for the areas which have been subject to an application for the aid for energy crops.]

NOTES

Amendment

Article 90a: inserted by Council Regulation 2012/2006.

Date in force: 1 January 2007 and applicable from 1 January 2007.

A1.777

Article 91   Review of the list of energy crops

Products may be added or removed to Article 88 in accordance with the procedure referred to in Article 144(2).

A1.778

Article 92   Review of energy crops scheme

By 31 December 2006, the Commission shall submit a report to the Council on the implementation of the scheme, accompanied, where appropriate, by proposals taking into account the implementation of the EU biofuels initiative.

CHAPTER 7
DAIRY PREMIUM AND ADDITIONAL PAYMENT

A1.779

Article 95   Dairy premium

1. From 2004 to 2007, milk producers shall qualify for a dairy premium. It shall be granted per calendar year, per holding and per tonne of individual reference quantity eligible for premium and available on the holding.

2. Without prejudice to paragraph 3 and to reductions resulting from the application of paragraph 4, the individual reference quantity for milk available on the holding on 31 March of the calendar year concerned, expressed in tonnes, shall be multiplied by:

— EUR 8,15/t for the calendar year 2004,
— EUR 16,31/t for the calendar year 2005,
— EUR 24,49/t for the calendar years 2006 and 2007, and

in case of application of Article 70, for the following calendar years.

3. Individual reference quantities which have been the subject of temporary transfers in accordance with Article 6 of Council Regulation (EEC) No 3950/92 of 28 December 1992 establishing an additional levy in the milk and milk products sector[1] or Article 16 of Council Regulation (EC) No 1788/2003 of 29 September 2003 establishing a levy in the milk and milk products sector[2] on 31 March of the calendar year concerned shall be deemed to be available on the holding of the transferee for that calendar year.

4. For the purpose of applying paragraph 2, where, on 31 March of a calendar year, the sum of all individual reference quantities in a Member State exceeds the sum of the corresponding total quantities of that Member State set out in Annex I of Regulation (EEC) No 3950/92, for the 12-month period 1999/2000, the Member State concerned shall, on the basis of objective criteria, take the necessary steps to reduce accordingly the total amount of individual reference quantities eligible for premium on its territory.

[However, for Germany and Austria the ceiling fixed on the basis of the reference quantities for the 12-month period of 1999/2000, shall be, respectively, 27 863 827, 288 and 2 750 389, 712 tonnes.]

[For Bulgaria and Romania the total quantities referred to in the first subparagraph are set out in table (f) of Annex I of Council Regulation (EC) No 1788/2003 and reviewed in accordance with Article 6(1) sixth subparagraph of Council Regulation (EC) No 1788/2003.

For Bulgaria and Romania the 12-month period referred to in the first subparagraph shall be that of 2006/2007.]

1   OJ 1992 L 405/1. Regulation as last amended by Commission Regulation (EC) No 572/2003 (OJ 2003 L 82/20).
2   See page 123 of this Official Journal.

NOTES

Amendment

Para 4: second para: inserted by Council Regulation 2217/2004.

Date in force: 23 December 2004 and applicable from 1 January 2005.

Para 4: third and fourth paras: inserted by the Act of Accession.

Date in force: 1 January 2005 and applicable from 1 January 2007.

A1.780

Article 96   Additional payments

1.   From 2004 to 2007, Member States shall, on a yearly basis, make additional payments to producers in their territory totalling the global amounts per year set out in paragraph 2. Such payments shall be made according to objective criteria and in such a way as to ensure equal treatment between producers and to avoid market and competition distortions. Moreover, such payments shall not be linked to fluctuations of market prices.

Premium supplements shall only be granted as a supplementary amount per premium amount as set out in Article 95(2).

2.   Additional payments: global amounts expressed in EUR million:

	2004	2005	2006 and 2007[1]
Belgium	12,12	24,30	36,45
Denmark	16,31	32,70	49,05
[*Germany	101,99	204,52	306,78]
Greece	2,31	4,63	6,94
Spain	20,38	40,86	61,29
France	88,70	177,89	266,84
Ireland	19,20	38,50	57,76
Italy	36,34	72,89	109,33
Luxembourg	0,98	1,97	2,96
Netherlands	40,53	81,29	121,93
[*Austria	10,06	20,19	30,28]
Portugal	6,85	13,74	20,62
Finland	8,81	17,66	26,49
Sweden	12,09	24,24	36,37
United Kingdom	53,40	107,09	160,64

1   And, in case of applications of Article 70, for the following calendar years.

NOTES

Amendment

Entries for Germany and Austria: substituted by Council Regulation 2217/2004.

Date in force: 23 December 2004 and applicable from 1 January 2005.

A1.781

Article 97   Definitions

For the purpose of this Chapter, the definitions of 'producer' laid down in Article 5 of Regulation (EC) No 1788/2003 shall apply.

Done at Brussels, 29 September 2003.

For the Council

The President

G. ALEMANNO

ANNEX I

LIST OF SUPPORT SCHEMES FULFILLING THE CRITERIA SET OUT IN ARTICLE 1

A1.782

Sector	Legal base	Notes
Single payment	Title III of this Regulation	Decoupled payment (see Annex VI) (*)
Single area payment	Title IVa, Article 143b of this Regulation	Decoupled payment replacing all the direct payments listed in this Annex
Durum wheat	Title IV, Chapter 1 of this Regulation	Area payment (quality premium)
Protein crop	Title IV, Chapter 2 of this Regulation	Area payment
Rice	Title IV, Chapter 3 of this Regulation	Area payment
Nuts	Title IV, Chapter 4 of this Regulation	Area payment
Energy crops	Title IV, Chapter 5 of this Regulation	Area payment
Starch potatoes	Title IV, Chapter 6 of this Regulation	Production aid
Milk and milk products	Title IV, Chapter 7 of this Regulation	Dairy premium and additional payment
Arable crops in Finland and in certain regions of Sweden	Title IV, Chapter 8 of this Regulation (**) (*****)	Special regional aid for arable crops

Seeds	Title IV, Chapter 9 of this Regulation (**) (*****)	Production aid
Arable crops	Title IV, Chapter 10 of this Regulation (***) (*****)	Area payment, include set-aside payments, grass silage payments, supplementary amounts (**) and durum wheat supplement and special aid
Sheepmeat and goatmeat	Title IV, Chapter 11 of this Regulation (***) (*****)	Ewe and she-goat premium, supplementary premium and certain additional payments
Beef and veal	Title IV, Chapter 12 of this Regulation (*****)	Special premium (***), deseasonalisation premium, suckler cow premium (including when paid for heifers and including the additional national suckler cow premium when part-financed) (***), slaughter premium (***), extensification payment, additional payments
Grain legumes	Title IV, Chapter 13 of this Regulation (*****)	Area payment
Specific types of farming and quality production	Article 69 of this Regulation (****)	
Dried fodder	Article 71(2) second paragraph of this Regulation (*****)	
Small farmers' scheme	Article 2a Regulation (EC) No 1259/1999	Transitional area aid for farmers receiving less than EUR 1 250
[Olive oil	Title IV, Chapter 10b, of this Regulation	Area aid
	Article 48a(11) of Commission Regulation (EC) No 795/2004 (OJ L 141, 30.4.2004, p. 1)	For Malta and Slovenia in 2006]
Silkworms	Article 1 Regulation (EEC) No 845/72	Aid to encourage rearing
Bananas	*Article 12 Regulation (EEC) No 404/93*	*Production oil*
[Dried grapes	Article 7(1) Regulation (EC) No 2201/96	Area payment

Tobacco	Title IV, Chapter 10c, of this Regulation	Production oil
[Hops	Title IV, Chapter 10d, of this Regulation (***) (*****)	Area aid
	Article 48a(12) of Regulation (EC) No 795/2004	For Slovenia in 2006]
Posei	Title III of Council Regulation (EC) No 247/2006 (******)	Direct payments within the meaning of Article 2, under measures established in the programmes
Aegean Islands	*Article 6 (**) (*****), 8, 11 and 12 Regulation (EEC) No 2019/93*	*Sectors: beef and veal; potatoes; olives; honey*
Cotton	Title IV, Chapter 10a, of this Regulation	Area payment]

(*) Starting from 1 January 2005 or later in the case of application of Article 71. For 2004, or later on in the case of application of Article 71, the direct payments listed in Annex VI are included in Annex I except for dried fodder.
(**) In case of application of Article 70.
(***) In case of application of Articles 66, 67, 68 or 68a.
(****) In case of application of Article 69.
(*****) In case of application of Article 71.
(******) OJ 2006 L 42/1.

NOTES
Amendment

Entry for 'Olive oil' substituted by Council Regulation 2012/2006.

Date in force: 1 January 2007 and applicable from 1 January 2006.

Entry for 'Bananas' revoked by Council Regulation 2013/2006.

Date in force: 1 January 2007.

Entries for 'Dried grapes' to 'Cotton' inclusive inserted by Council Regulation 247/2006.

Date in force: 15 February 2006 and applicable from 14 April 2006 at the latest.

Entry for 'Hops' substituted by Council Regulation 2012/2006.

Date in force: 1 January 2007 and applicable from 1 January 2006.

Entry for 'Aegean Islands' revoked by Council Regulation 1405/2006.

Date in force: 3 October 2006 and applicable from 1 January 2007.

ANNEX III
STATUTORY MANAGEMENT REQUIREMENTS REFERRED TO IN ARTICLES 3 AND 4

A1.783

A. APPLICABLE FROM 1.1.2005

ENVIRONMENT

1	Council Directive 79/409/EC of 2 April 1979 on the conservation of wild birds (OJ L 103, 25.4.1979, p. 1)	Articles 3, 4(1), (2), (4), 5, 7 and 8
2	Council Directive 80/68/EEC of 17 December 1979 on the protection of groundwater against pollution caused by certain dangerous substances (OJ L 20, 26.1.1980, p. 43)	Articles 4 and 5
3	Council Directive 86/278/EEC of 12 June 1986 on the protection of the environment, and in particular of the soil, when sewage sludge is used in agriculture (OJ L 181, 4.7.1986, p. 6)	Article 3
4	Council Directive 91/676/EEC of 12 December 1991 concerning the protection of waters against pollution caused by nitrates from agricultural sources (OJ L 375, 31.12.1991, p. 1)	Articles 4 and 5
5	Council Directive 92/43/EEC of 21 May 1992 on the conservation of natural habitats and of wild flora and fauna (OJ L 206, 22.7.1992, p. 7)	Articles 6, 13, 15 and 22(b)

PUBLIC AND ANIMAL HEALTH

Identification and registration of animals

6	Council Directive 92/102/EEC of 27 November 1992 on identification and registration of animals (OJ L 355, 5.12.1992, p. 32)	Articles 3, 4 and 5
7	Commission Regulation (EC) No 2629/97 of 29 December 1997 laying down detailed rules for the implementation of Council Regulation (EC) No 820/97 as regards eartags, holding registers and passports in the framework of the system for the identificaiton and registration of bovine animals (OJ L 354, 30.12.1997, p. 19)	Articles 6 and 8
8	Regulation (EC) No 1760/2000 of the European Parliament and of the Council of 17 July 2000 establishing a system for the identification and registration of bovine animals and regarding the labelling of beef and beef products and repealing Council Regulation (EC) No 820/97 (OJ L 204, 11.8.2000, p. 1)	Articles 4 and 7

[8a	Council Regulation (EC) No 21/2004 of 17 December 2003 establishing a system for the identification and registration of ovine and caprine animals and amending Regulation (EC) No 1782/2003 and Directives 92/102/EEC and 64/432/EEC (OJ L 5, 9.1.2004, p. 8)	Articles 3, 4 and 5]

NOTES

Amendment

Entry 8a: inserted by Council Regulation 21/2004.

Date in force: 29 January 2004 and applicable from 9 July 2005.

Modification

Entry 8a: For Bulgaria and Romania the reference to 2005 should be read as a reference to the first year of application of the Single Payment Scheme: see the Act of Accession 2005.

Date in force: 1 January 2005 and applicable from 1 January 2007.

B. APPLICABLE FROM 1.1.2006

PUBLIC, ANIMAL AND PLANT HEALTH

9	Council Directive 91/414/EEC of 15 July 1991 concerning the placing of plant protection products on the market (OJ L 230, 19.8.1991, p. 1)	Article 3
10	Council Directive 96/22/EC of 29 April 1996 concerning the prohibition on the use in stockfarming of certain substances having a hormonal or thyrostatic action and of beta-agonists, and repealing Directives 81/602/EEC, 88/146/EEC and 88/299/EEC (OJ L 125, 23.5.1996, p. 3)	Articles 3, 4, 5 and 7
11	Regulation (EC) No 178/2002 of the European Parliament and of the Council of 28 January 2002 laying down the general principles and requirements of food law, establishing the European Food Safety Authority and laying down procedures in matters of food safety (OJ L 31, 1.2.2002, p. 1)	Articles 14, 15, 17(1), 18, 19 and 20
12	Regulation (EC) No 999/2001 of the European Parliament and of the Council of 22 May 2001 laying down rules for the prevention, control and eradication of certain transmissible spongiform encephalopathies (OJ L 147, 31.5.2001, p. 1)	Articles 7, 11, 12, 13 and 15
13	Council Directive 85/511/EEC of 18 November 1985 introducing Communing measures for the control of foot-and-mouth disease (OJ L 315, 26.11.1985, p. 11)	Article 3

14	Council Directive 92/119/EEC of 17 December 1992 introducing general Community measures for the control of certain animal diseases and specific measures relating to swine vesicular disease (OJ L 62, 15.3.1993, p. 69)	Article 3
15	Council Directive 2000/75/EC of 20 November 2000 laying down specific provisions for the control and eradication of bluetongue (OJ L 327, 22.12.2000, p. 74)	Article 3

NOTES

Modification

For Bulgaria and Romania the reference to 2006 should be read as a reference to the second year of application of the Single Payment Scheme: see the Act of Accession 2005.

Date in force: 1 January 2005 and applicable from 1 January 2007.

C. APPLICABLE FROM 1.1.2007

ANIMAL WELFARE

16	Council Directive 91/629/EEC of 19 November 1991 laying down minimum standards for the protection of calves (OJ L 340, 11.12.1991, p. 28)	Articles 3 and 4
17	Council Directive 91/630/EEC of 19 November 1991 laying down minimum standards for the protection of pigs (OJ L 340, 11.12.1991, p. 33)	Articles 3 and 4(1)
18	Council Directive 98/58/EC of 20 July 1998 concerning the protection of animals kept for farming purposes (OJ L 221, 8.8.1998, p. 23)	Article 4

NOTES

Modification

For Bulgaria and Romania the reference to 2007 should be read as a reference to the third year of application of the Single Payment Scheme: see the Act of Accession 2005.

Date in force: 1 January 2005 and applicable from 1 January 2007.

ANNEX IV

GOOD AGRICULTURAL AND ENVIRONMENTAL CONDITION REFERRED TO IN ARTICLE 5

A1.784

Issue	*Standards*

Soil erosion: Protect soil through appropriate measures	– Minimum soil cover – Minimum land management reflecting site-specific conditions – Retain terraces
Soil organic matter: Maintain soil organic matter levels through appropriate practices Soil structure: Maintain soil structure through appropriate measures	– Standards for crop rotations where applicable – Arable stubble management – Appropriate machinery use
Mimimum level of maintenance: Ensure a minimum level of maintenance and avoid the deterioration of habitats	– Minimum livestock stocking rates or/and appropriate regimes – Protection of permanent pasture [– Retention of landscape features, including, where appropriate, the prohibition of the grubbing up of olive trees – Avoiding the encroachment of unwanted vegetation on agricultural land – Maintenance of olive groves in good vegetative condition]

NOTES

Amendment

Entry in square brackets: substituted by Council Regulation 864/2004.

Date in force: 1 May 2004 and applicable from 1 January 2006 except for provisos contained in Regulation 864/2004 (see Official Journal version).

ANNEX VI

LIST OF DIRECT PAYMENTS IN RELATION TO THE SINGE PAYMENT REFERRED TO IN ARTICLE 33

A1.785

Sector	Legal base	Notes
Arable crops	Articles 2, 4 and 5 Regulation (EC) No 1251/1999	Area payment, including set-aside payments, grass silage payments, supplementary amounts (*), durum wheat supplement and special aid
Potato starch	Article 8(2) Regulation (EEC) No 1766/92	Payment for farmers producing potatoes for the manufacture of potato starch
Grain legumes	Article 1 Regulation (EC) No 1577/96	Area payment

Rice	Article 6 Regulation (EC) No 3072/95	Area payment
Seeds (*)	Article 3 Regulation (EEC) No 2358/71	Production aid
Beef and veal	Articles 4, 5, 6, 10, 11, 13 and 14 Regulation (EC) No 1254/1999	Special premium, deseasonalisation premium, suckler cow premium (including when paid for heifers and including the additional national suckler cow premium when part-financed), slaughter premium, extensification payment, additional payments
Milk and milk products	Title IV, Chapter 7 of this Regulation	Dairy premium and additional payments (**)
[Sheepmeat and goatmeat	Article 5 Regulation (EC) No 2467/98 Article 1 Regulation (EEC) No 1323/90 Articles 4, 5 and 11(1) and (2), first, second and fourth indents Regulation (EC) No 2529/2001	Ewe and she-goat premium, supplementary premium and certain additional payments
Aegean Islands (*)	*Articles 6(2) and (3)* *Regulation (EEC)* *No 2019/93*	*Sectors: beef and veal*
Dried fodder	Article 3 Regulation IEC) No 603/95	Payment for processed products (as applied according to Annex VII point D of the Regulation)
Cotton	Paragraph 3 of Protocol No 4 on cotton annexed to the Act of Accession of Greece	Support in the form of payment for unginned cotton
Olive oil	Article 5 of Regulation No 136/66/EEC	Production aid
Tobacco	Article 3 of Regulation (EEC) No 2075/92	Production aid
Hops	Article 12 of Regulation (EEC) No 1696/71	Area payment
	Article 2 of Regulation (EC) No 1098/98	Aid for temporary resting]

[Sugar beet, cane and chicory used for the production of sugar or insulin syrup	Regulation (EC) No 1260/2001	Market support to sugar beet or cane growers and producers of chicory used for the production of sugar or insulin syrup]
[Bananas	Article 12 of Regulation (EEC) No 404/93	Compensation for loss of income]

(*) Except in case of application of Article 70.
(**)Starting from 2007, except in case of application of Article 62.

NOTES

Amendment

Entries for 'Sheepmeat and goatmeat' to 'Hops' inclusive inserted by Council Regulation 247/2006.

Date in force: 15 February 2006 and applicable from 14 April 2006 at the latest.

Entry for 'Aegean Islands' revoked by Council Regulation 1405/2006.

Date in force: 3 October 2006 and applicable from 1 January 2007.

Entry for 'Sugar beet, cane and chicory used for the production of sugar or insulin syrup' inserted by Council Regulation 319/2006.

Date in force: 3 March 2006 and applicable from 1 January 2006.

Entry for 'Bananas' inserted by Council Regulation 2013/2006.

Date in force: 1 January 2007.

A1.786

Amendments to Council Regulation (EC) 1782/2003

Regulation	Into Force	Effective From
Commission Regulation (EC) 552/2007, OJ 2007 L 131/10	30 May 2007	
Council Regulation (EC) 2013/2006, OJ 2006 L 384/13	1 Jan 2007	
Council Regulation (EC) 2012/2006, OJ 2006 L 384/8	1 Jan 2007	1 Jan 2007 (with some Article exceptions)
Council Regulation (EC) 2011/2006, OJ 2006 L 384/1	1 Jan 2007	
Council Regulation (EC) 1405/2006, OJ 2006 L 265/1	3 Oct 2006	1 January 2007

Commission Regulation (EC) 1156/2006, OJ 2006 L 208/3	5 Aug 2006	
Council Regulation (EC) 953/2006, OJ 2006 L 175/1	6 July 2006	1 January 2007
Council Regulation (EC) 319/2006, OJ 2006 L 58/32	3 March 2006	1 January 2006
Council Regulation (EC) 247/2006, OJ 2006 L 42/1	15 Feb 2006	14 April 2006 at the latest
Commission Regulation (EC) 2183/2005, OJ 2005 L 347/56	30 Dec 2005	1 January 2006
Commission Regulation (EC) 118/2005, OJ 2004 L 24/15	3 Feb 2005	
Act of Accession 2005	1 Jan 2005	1 January 2007
Council Regulation (EC) 2217/2004, OJ 2004 L 375/1	23 Dec 2004	1 January 2005
Council Regulation (EC) 864/2004, OJ 2004 L 161/48	1 May 2004	1 January 2006 (except for Article 1, (7a), (14), (14a), (16) and 18(a) as well as (23) as regards Annexes VIII and VIIIa which shall apply as from the date of entry into force of this Regulation; (b) Article 1(1) as regards the insertion of hops, (7), (9) as regards hops, (10), (11), (11a), (11b), (12), (13) as regards hops, (15) as regards Chapter 10d , (19) as regards point (e), (20) as regards 4b, (23) as regards annexes I, VI and VII for the parts concerning hops which shall apply as from 1 January 2005.
Council Regulation (EC) 583/2004, OJ 2004 L 91/1	1 May 2004	

| Council Regulation (EC) 21/2004, OJ 2004 L 5/8 | 29 Jan 2004 | 9 July 2005 |

COUNCIL REGULATION (EC) NO 1788/2003

((EC) NO 1788/2003)

OF 29 SEPTEMBER 2003

establishing a levy in the milk and milk products sector

[TEXT UP TO DATE UNTIL MAY 2007 ONLY]

A1.787

THE COUNCIL OF THE EUROPEAN UNION,
Having regard to the Treaty establishing the European Community, and in particular Article 37 thereof,
Having regard to the proposal from the Commission,
Having regard to the opinion of the European Parliament[1],
Whereas:
(1) Council Regulation (EEC) No 856/84 of 31 March 1984 amending Regulation (EEC) No 804/68 on the common organisation of the market in milk and milk products[2] introduced an additional levy scheme in that sector from 2 April 1984. The scheme has been extended several times, in particular by Council Regulation (EEC) No 3950/92 of 28 December 1992 establishing an additional levy in the milk and milk products sector[3] and most recently, until 31 March 2008, by Council Regulation (EC) No 1256/1999 of 17 May 1999 amending Regulation (EEC) No 3950/92 establishing an additional levy in the milk and milk products sector[4].
(2) In order both to benefit from the lessons learned and to simplify and clarify the scheme, Regulation (EEC) No 3950/92 should be repealed and the rules governing the extended scheme should be reorganised and clarified.
(3) The main purpose of the scheme is to reduce the imbalance between supply and demand on the milk and milk products market and the resulting structural surpluses, thereby achieving better market equilibrium. It should therefore continue to be applied for seven further consecutive twelve-month periods starting on 1 April 2008. Those periods are to be added to the periods already provided for in Regulation (EEC) No 3950/92.
(4) The method adopted in 1984, which consists of applying a levy to quantities of milk collected or sold for direct consumption above a certain guarantee threshold, should be maintained. This guarantee threshold is fixed for each Member State as a guaranteed total quantity for a reference milk-fat content.
(5) The levy should be set at a dissuasive level and be payable by the Member States as soon as the national reference quantity is exceeded. The Member State should then divide the burden of payment among the producers who have contributed to the overrun. The latter must be liable vis-à-vis the Member State for payment of their contribution to the levy due for the mere fact of having overrun their available quantity.

(6) Member States shall pay to the EAGGF, Guarantee Section, the levy corresponding to the overrun of their national reference amount, reduced by a flat-rate amount of 1 % in order to take account of cases of bankruptcy or the definitive inability of certain producers to make their contribution to the payment of the levy due.

(7) Member States should be allowed a certain amount of time to allocate the levy to be paid among producers and to pay it to the EAGGF Guarantee Section. If they are unable to meet the time limit set, it should be ensured that the amounts due are available in the EAGGF Guarantee Section, by deducting them from the monthly refunds made to Member States. This involves derogating from the procedure laid down in Article 14 of Council Regulation (EC) No 2040/2000 of 26 September 2000 on budgetary discipline[5].

(8) Regulation (EEC) No 3950/92 provided for a distinction between deliveries and direct sales. Experience has shown that administration should be simplified by restricting deliveries to whole milk and excluding all other milk products. Consequently, direct sales must henceforth include sales and direct transfers of milk to consumers, as well as all sales and transfers of other milk products.

(9) For each individual reference quantity for deliveries there should be a matching representative fat rate established with reference to existing and modifiable rates in accordance with rules to be defined. Rules should be laid down to ensure that the difference between the weighted average of the individual representative fat contents and the relevant national reference fat content remains minimal.

(10) A simplified procedure should be laid down to divide the individual reference quantities between deliveries and direct sales, with an obligation to provide the Commission with the necessary information to make that allocation and to calculate the levy. This allocation should be based on the reference quantities held by producers for the twelve-month period commencing on 1 April 2003. The sum of the quantities allocated to the producers by the Member States may not exceed the national reference quantities. The national reference quantities are to be established for the eleven periods from 1 April 2004 and to take account of the different components of the previous scheme.

(11) It is necessary to determine the way the fat content of milk is to be taken into account when drawing up the definitive statement of quantities delivered. It should be stressed that under no circumstances may individual downward corrections of the fat content of delivered milk or the separation of milk into its different components result in a deduction from the levy payment of any quantity in excess of the guaranteed total quantity in a Member State. In view of the negligible quantities concerned, there is no need to take account of fat content for direct sales.

(12) In order to ensure that the scheme runs effectively, the contribution to the levy due from the producers should be collected by the purchasers, who are in the best position to carry out the necessary transactions and who should therefore be given the means to ensure that they can collect this contribution. Conversely, any amount collected which exceeds the levy due by the Member State should be used to finance national restructuring programmes and/or reimbursed to certain categories of producers or those in an exceptional situation. However, where it is found that no levy is due by the Member State, any advances collected should be reimbursed.

(13) Experience has shown that implementing this scheme presupposes the existence of a national reserve enabling, on the basis of objective criteria, producers to obtain extra quantities or new producers to start up, and replenished with any quantities which, for whatever reason, are not or no longer allocated individually. In order to enable the Member State to respond to specific situations, determined by objective criteria, it should be authorised to make allocations to the national reserve by across-the-board reductions in all reference quantities or by deductions from definitive transfers of these quantities.

(14) In order to ensure that administration of the scheme remains sufficiently flexible, the Member States should be authorised to reallocate unused reference quantities at the end of a period, either nationally or among purchasers.

(15) The under-use of reference quantities by producers can prevent milk production from developing properly. In order to avoid such problems, Member States should be able to decide that, in cases of inactivity or substantial under-use over a significant period of time, unused reference quantities are to revert to the national reserve to be re-allocated to other producers. However, provision must be made for cases where producers who are temporarily unable to produce wish to resume production.

(16) The temporary transfer of parts of individual reference quantities in Member States which have authorised this has proved to enhance the effectiveness of the scheme. However, this mechanism should not be implemented where it might run counter to structural trends and adjustments, nor should any resulting administrative difficulties be underrated, nor should former producers who have given up production be allowed to keep their quota beyond the time strictly needed for it to be transferred to an active producer.

(17) When the scheme was introduced in 1984, the principle was established that when a farm is sold, leased or transferred by inheritance, the corresponding reference quantity is transferred to the purchaser, tenant or heir together with the relevant land. It would not be appropriate to alter this original decision. However, national provisions to safeguard the legitimate interests of the parties should be implemented in all cases of transfer where the parties are not in agreement.

(18) In order to continue the restructuring of milk production and improve the environment, some exceptions should be made to the principle that reference quantities are tied to farms, and the Member States should be authorised to keep open the option to implement national or regional restructuring programmes. Member States should also be entitled to organise the transfer of reference quantities in other ways than through individual transactions between producers.

(19) In line with the various types of transfer of reference quantities and using objective criteria, Member States should be authorised to place part of the transferred quantities in the national reserve.

(20) Experience with the additional levy scheme has shown that the transfer of reference quantities through legal constructions such as leases which do not necessarily lead to a permanent allocation of the reference quantities concerned to the transferee, can be an additional cost factor for milk production hampering the improvement of production structures. In order to strengthen the regulatory effect of the reference quantities on the market for milk and milk products, the Member States should be authorised to allocate reference quantities which have been transferred through leases or comparable legal means to the national reserve for re-distribution on the basis of objective criteria to active producers, in particular to those who have used them before. Member States should also have the right to organise the transfer of reference quantities by means other than by individual transactions between producers.

(21) In order to avoid increasing the cost of means of production or causing unequal treatment, it should be stressed that all public financial assistance during acquisition or transfer of quotas is prohibited.

(22) The main purpose of the levy provided for in this Regulation is to regularise and stabilise the market in milk products. The revenue accruing from this levy should therefore be used to finance expenditure in the milk sector.

(23) The measures needed to implement this Regulation should be taken pursuant to Council Decision 1999/468/EC of 28 June 1999 laying down the procedures for the exercise of implementing powers conferred on the Commission (1),

---

[1]   Opinion delivered on 5 June 2003 (not yet published in the Official Journal).

2   OJ 1984 L 90/10.
3   OJ 1992 L 405/1. Regulation as last amended by Regulation (EC) No 2028/2002 (OJ 2002 L 313/3).
4   OJ 1999 L 160/73.
5   OJ 2000 L 244/27.
6   OJ 1999 L 184/23.

HAS ADOPTED THIS REGULATION:

CHAPTER 1
GENERAL PROVISIONS

A1.788

Article 1   Scope

1   For 11 consecutive periods of twelve months commencing on 1 April 2004 (hereinafter referred to as 'twelve-month periods'), a levy is hereby introduced (hereinafter referred to as 'the levy') on quantities of cow's milk and other milk products marketed during the twelve-month period concerned in excess of the national reference quantities fixed in Annex I.

2   These quantities shall be divided between producers in accordance with Article 6, distinguishing between deliveries and direct sales as defined in Article 5. Any overrun of the national reference quantity and the resulting levy shall be determined nationally in each Member State, in accordance with Chapter 3 and making a distinction between deliveries and direct sales.

3   The national reference quantities in Annex I shall be fixed without prejudice to possible review in the light of the general market situation and particular conditions existing in certain Member States.

[4.   For Bulgaria and Romania a special restructuring reserve shall be established as set out in table (g) of Annex I. This reserve shall be released as from 1 April 2009 to the extent that the on-farm consumption of milk and milk products in each of these countries has decreased since 2002. The decision on releasing the reserve and its distribution to the deliveries and direct sales quota shall be taken by the Commission in accordance with the procedure referred to in Article 23(2) on the basis of an assessment of a report to be submitted by Bulgaria and Romania to the Commission by 31 December 2008. This report shall detail the results and trends of the actual restructuring process in the country's dairy sector and, in particular the shift from production for on-farm consumption to production for the market.

5.   For Bulgaria, the Czech Republic, Estonia, Cyprus, Latvia, Lithuania, Hungary, Malta, Poland, Romania, Slovenia and Slovakia the national reference quantities shall include all cow's milk or milk equivalent delivered to a purchaser or sold directly, as defined under Article 5 of this Regulation, irrespective of whether it is produced or marketed under a transitional measure applicable in these countries.

6.   For Bulgaria and Romania the levy shall apply from 1 April 2007.]

NOTES

Amendment

Paras 4–6: inserted by the Act of Accession 2005.

Date in force: 1 January 2007.

A1.789

Article 2   Levy

The levy shall be set, per 100 kilograms of milk, at EUR 33.27 for the 2004/2005 period, EUR 30.91 for 2005/2006, EUR 28.54 for 2006/2007 and EUR 27.83 for the period 2007/2008 and thereafter.

A1.790

Article 3   Payment of the levy

[1.   Member States shall be liable to the Community for the levy resulting from overruns of the national reference quantity fixed in Annex I, determined nationally and separately for deliveries and direct sales, and between 16 October and 30 November following the twelve-month period concerned, shall pay it, within the limit of 99% of the amount due, into the European Agricultural Guidance and Guarantee Fund (EAGGF).]

2   If the levy provided for in paragraph 1 has not been paid before the due date and after consultation of the Committee of the European Agricultural Guidance and Guarantee Fund, the Commission shall deduct a sum equivalent to the unpaid levy from the monthly advances on the provision for expenditure effected by the Member State concerned within the meaning of Article 5(1) and Article 7(2) of Council Regulation (EC) No 1258/1999 of 17 May 1999 on the financing of the common agricultural policy[1]. Before taking its decision, the Commission shall warn the Member State concerned, which shall make its position known within one week. The provisions of Article 14 of Regulation (EC) No 2040/2000 shall not apply.

3   The Commission shall determine the arrangements for implementation of this Article in accordance with the procedure laid down in Article 23(2).

[1]   OJ 1999 L 160/103.

NOTES

Amendment

Para 1: substituted by Council Regulation 1406/2006.

Date in force: 3 October 2006 and applicable from 1 September 2006.

A1.791

Article 4   Contribution of producers to the levy due

The levy shall be entirely allocated, in accordance with the provisions of Articles 10 and 12, among the producers who have contributed to each of the overruns of the national reference quantities referred to in Article 1(2).

Without prejudice to Article 10(3) and Article 12(1), producers shall be liable vis-à-vis the Member State for payment of their contribution to the levy due, calculated in accordance with the provisions of Chapter 3, for the mere fact of having overrun their available reference quantities.

A1.792

Article 5   Definitions

For the purposes of this Regulation:

(a) 'milk' shall mean the produce of the milking of one or more cows;

(b) 'other milk products' means any milk product other than milk, in particular skimmed milk, cream, butter, yoghurt and cheese; when relevant, these shall be converted into 'milk equivalents' by applying coefficients to be fixed in accordance with the procedure provided for in Article 23(2);

(c) 'producer' means farmers as defined in Article 2(a) of Regulation (EC) No 1782/2003 establishing common rules for direct support schemes under the common agricultural policy and support schemes for producers of certain crops[1], with a holding located within the geographical territory of a Member State, who produce and market milk or who are preparing to do so in the very near future;

(d) 'holding' means holdings as defined in Article 2(b) of Regulation (EC) No 1782/2003;

(e) 'purchaser' means undertakings or groups which buy milk from producers:
— to subject it to collecting, packing, storing, chilling and processing, including under contract,
— to sell it to one or more undertakings treating or processing milk or other milk products.
However, any group of purchasers in the same geographical area which carries out the administrative and accounting operations necessary for the payment of the levy on behalf of its members shall be regarded as a purchaser. For the purposes of the first sentence of this subparagraph, Greece shall be considered a single geographical area and it may deem an official body to be a group of purchasers as referred to above;

(f) 'delivery' means any delivery of milk, not including any other milk products, by a producer to a purchaser, whether the transport is carried out by the producer, a purchaser, an undertaking processing or treating such products or a third party;

(g) 'direct sale' means any sale or transfer of milk by a producer directly to consumers, as well as any sale or transfer of other milk products by a producer. The Commission may, in accordance with the procedure referred to in Article 23(2) and while respecting the definition of 'delivery' given in (f) of this Article, adjust the definition of 'direct sale' in order to ensure, in particular, that no quantity of milk or other marketed milk products is excluded from the levy arrangements;

(h) 'marketing' means deliveries of milk or direct sales of milk or other milk products;

(i) 'national reference quantity' means the reference quantity fixed in Annex I for each Member State;

(j) 'individual reference quantity' means a producer's reference quantity at 1 April of any twelve-month period;

(k) 'available reference quantity' means the reference quantity available to producers on 31 March of the twelve-month period for which the levy is calculated, taking account of all transfers, sales, conversions and temporary re-allocations provided for in this Regulation which have taken place during that twelve-month period.

[1]   See page 1 of this Official Journal.

CHAPTER 2
ALLOCATION OF REFERENCE QUANTITIES

A1.793

Article 6   Individual reference quantities

1   Before 1 June 2004 the Member States shall establish the producers' individual reference quantities on the basis of the individual reference quantity or quantities

allocated in accordance with Article 4 of Regulation (EEC) No 3950/92 during the twelve-month period beginning on 1 April 2003.

[For Bulgaria, the Czech Republic, Estonia, Cyprus, Latvia, Lithuania, Hungary, Malta, Poland, Romania, Slovenia and Slovakia the basis for the individual reference quantities referred to is set out in table (f) of Annex I.

In the case of Bulgaria, the Czech Republic, Estonia, Cyprus, Latvia, Lithuania, Hungary, Malta, Poland, Romania, Slovenia and Slovakia the twelve month period for the establishment of the individual reference quantities shall commence on: 1 April 2001 for Hungary, 1 April 2002 for Malta and Lithuania, 1 April 2003 for the Czech Republic, Cyprus, Estonia, Latvia and Slovakia, 1 April 2004 for Poland and Slovenia and 1 April 2006 for Bulgaria and Romania.]

[For Poland the distribution of the total quantity between deliveries and direct sales shall be reviewed on the basis of its actual 2003 figures on deliveries and direct sales and, if necessary, adjusted by the Commission in accordance with the procedure referred to in Article 23(2) of Regulation (EC) No 1788/2003.]

[For Bulgaria and Romania the distribution of the total quantity between deliveries and direct sales as set out in table (f) of Annex I shall be reviewed on the basis of its actual 2006 figures on deliveries and direct sales and, if necessary, adjusted by the Commission in accordance with the procedure referred to in Article 23(2).]

2   Producers may have either one or two individual reference quantities, one for deliveries and the other for sales. A producer's quantities may be converted from one reference quantity to the other only by the competent authority of the Member State, at the duly justified request of the producer.

3   Where a producer has two reference quantities, his contribution to any levy due shall be calculated separately for each one.

4   The part of the Finnish national reference quantity allocated to the deliveries referred to in Article 1 may be increased in accordance with the procedure laid down in Article 23(2) to compensate Finnish SLOM producers up to 200 000 tonnes. This reserve, to be allocated in accordance with Community legislation, must be used exclusively on behalf of producers whose right to take up production again has been affected as a result of accession.

5   Individual reference quantities shall be modified, where appropriate, for each of the twelve-month periods concerned, so that, for each Member State, the sum of the individual reference quantities for the deliveries and that for the direct sales does not exceed the corresponding part of the national reference quantity adapted in accordance with Article 8, taking account of any reductions made for allocation to the national reserve as provided for in Article 14.

NOTES

Amendment

Para 1: 2nd and 3rd paras inserted by the Act of Accession 2005.

Date in force: 1 January 2007.

Para 1: 4th para inserted by Council Decision 2004/281.

Date in force: 1 May 2004.

Para 1: 5th para inserted by the Act of Accession 2005.

Date in force: 1 January 2007.

A1.794

Article 7   Allocation of quantities from the national reserve

The Member States shall adopt rules allowing for allocation to producers of all or part of the quantities from the national reserve provided for in Article 14 on the basis of objective criteria to be notified to the Commission.

CHAPTER 3
CALCULATION OF THE LEVY

A1.795

Article 8   Management of reference quantities

1   In accordance with the procedure provided for in Article 23(2), the Commission shall adapt, for each Member State and for each period, before the end of that period, the division between 'deliveries' and 'direct sales' of national reference quantities, in the light of the conversions requested by producers, between individual reference quantities for deliveries and for sales.

[For the 2005/2006 period, in accordance with the same procedure, and for the Czech Republic, Estonia, Cyprus, Latvia, Lithuania, Hungary, Poland, Slovenia and Slovakia, the Commission may also adapt the division between 'deliveries' and 'direct sales' of the national reference quantities after the end of that period at the request of the Member State concerned. This request shall be submitted to the Commission before 10 October 2006. The Commission shall subsequently adapt the division as soon as possible.]

2   Member States shall each year forward to the Commission, by dates and according to rules to be fixed in accordance with the procedure provided for in Article 23(2), the information necessary to:

(a)   make the adaptation referred to in paragraph 1;
(b)   calculate the levy to be paid by them.

NOTES

Amendment

Para 1: 2nd para inserted by Council Regulation 1406/2006.

Date in force: 3 October 2006.

A1.796

Article 9   Fat content

1   Each producer shall be assigned a reference fat content, to be applied to the individual reference quantity or quantities allocated to that producer.

2   For the reference quantities allocated to producers on 31 March 2004 in accordance with Article 6(1), the content referred to in paragraph 1 of this Article shall be the same as the reference fat content of that quantity at that date.

[For Bulgaria, the Czech Republic, Estonia, Cyprus, Latvia, Lithuania, Hungary, Poland, Romania, Slovenia and Slovakia, the reference fat content referred to in paragraph 1 shall be the same as the reference fat content of the quantities allocated to producers on the following dates: 31 March 2002 for Hungary, 31 March 2003 for Lithuania, 31 March 2004 for the Czech Republic, Cyprus, Estonia, Latvia and Slovakia, 31 March 2005 for Poland and Slovenia and 31 March 2007 for Bulgaria and Romania.]

3   That content shall be altered during the conversion referred to in Article 6(2) and where reference quantities are acquired or transferred, under the rules to be laid down in accordance with the procedure referred to in Article 23(2).

4   For new producers having an individual reference quantity for the total deliveries from the national reserve, the fat content shall be fixed in accordance with the rules referred to in Article 23(2).

5   The individual reference fat content referred to in paragraph 1 shall be adjusted, where appropriate, upon the entry into force of this Regulation and thereafter, at the beginning of each twelve-month period as necessary, so that, for each Member State, the weighted average of the individual representative fat contents does not exceed by more than 0.1 gram per kg the reference fat content set in Annex II.

[For Romania the reference fat content set in Annex II shall be reviewed on the basis of the figures for the full year 2004 and, if necessary, adjusted by the Commission in accordance with the procedure referred to in Article 23(2).]

NOTES

Amendment

Para 2: 2nd para substituted by the Act of Accession 2005.

Date in force: 1 January 2007.

Para 5: 2nd para inserted by the Act of Accession 2005.

Date in force: 1 January 2007.

A1.797

Article 10   Levy on deliveries

1   In order to draw up the definitive levy statement, the quantities delivered by each producer shall be increased or reduced to reflect any difference between the real fat content and the reference fat content, using coefficients and on terms to be laid down in accordance with Article 23(2).

2   Where, at national level, the sum of deliveries adjusted in accordance with paragraph 1 is less than the deliveries actually made, the levy shall be calculated on the basis of the latter. In such cases, each downward adjustment shall be proportionately reduced so as to bring the sum of adjusted deliveries into line with the deliveries actually made.

Where the sum of the deliveries adjusted in accordance with paragraph 1 is greater than the deliveries actually made, the levy shall be calculated on the basis of the former.

3   Each producer's contribution to payment of the levy shall be established by decision of the Member State, after any unused part of the national reference quantity allocated to deliveries has or has not been re-allocated, in proportion to the individual reference quantities of each producer or according to objective criteria to be set by the Member States:

  (a) either at national level on the basis of the amount by which each producer's reference quantity has been exceeded,
  (b) or firstly at the level of the purchaser and thereafter at national level where appropriate.

A1.798

Article 11   Role of purchasers

1   Purchasers shall be responsible for collecting from producers contributions due from the latter by virtue of the levy and shall pay to the competent body of the Member State, before a date and following a procedure to be laid down in accordance with Article 23(2), the amount of these contributions deducted from the price of the milk paid to the producers responsible for the overrun or, failing this, collected by any other appropriate means.

2   Where a purchaser fully or partially replaces one or more other purchasers, the individual reference quantities available to the producers shall be taken into account for the remainder of the twelve-month period in progress, after deduction of quantities already delivered and account being taken of their fat content. The same provisions shall apply where a producer transfers from one purchaser to another.

3   Where, during the reference period, quantities delivered by a producer exceed that producer's available reference quantity, the relevant Member State may decide that the purchaser shall deduct part of the price of the milk in any delivery by the producer concerned in excess of the reference quantity, by way of an advance on the producer's contribution, in accordance with detailed rules laid down by the Member State. The Member State may make specific arrangements to enable purchasers to deduct this advance where producers deliver to several purchasers.

A1.799

Article 12   Levy on direct sales

1   In the case of direct sales, each producer's contribution to payment of the levy shall be established by decision of the Member State, after any unused part of the national reference quantity allocated to direct sales has or has not been re-allocated, at the appropriate territorial level or at national level.

2   Member States shall establish the basis of calculation of the producer's contribution to the levy due on the total quantity of milk sold, transferred or used to manufacture the milk products sold or transferred by applying criteria fixed in accordance with the procedure laid down in Article 23(2).

3   No correction linked to fat content shall be taken into account for the purpose of drawing up the definitive levy statement.

4   How and when the levy must be paid to the Member State's competent body shall be determined in accordance with the procedure laid down in Article 23(2).

CHAPTER 4
ADMINISTERING THE LEVY

A1.800

Article 13   Amounts paid in excess or unpaid

1   Where, in the case of deliveries or direct sales, the levy is found to be payable and the contribution collected from producers is greater than that levy, the Member State may:

    (a)   use partially or totally the excess to finance the measures referred to in Article 18(1)(a), and/or

    (b)   redistribute it partially or totally to producers who fall within priority categories established by the Member State on the basis of objective criteria and within the period to be laid down in accordance with the procedure laid down in Article 23(2) or who are affected by an exceptional situation resulting from a national rule unconnected with the present scheme.

2 Where it is established that no levy is payable, any advances collected by purchasers or the Member State shall be reimbursed no later than the end of the following twelve-month period.

3 Where a purchaser does not meet the obligation to collect the producers' contribution to the levy in accordance with Article 11, the Member State may collect unpaid amounts directly from the producer, without prejudice to any penalties it may impose upon the defaulting purchaser.

4 Where a producer or a purchaser fails to comply with the time limit for payment, interest on arrears to be fixed in accordance with the procedure laid down in Article 23(2) shall be paid to the Member State.

A1.801

Article 14 National reserve

1 Each Member State shall set up a national reserve as part of the quantities fixed in Annex I, in particular with a view to making the allocations provided for in Article 7. The national reserve shall be replenished, as appropriate, by taking back some quantities as provided for in Article 15, retaining part of transfers as provided for in Article 19, or by making an across-the-board reduction in all individual reference quantities. The quantities in question shall retain their original purpose, ie deliveries or direct sales.

2 Any additional reference quantity allocated to a Member State shall automatically be placed in the national reserve and divided into deliveries and direct sales according to foreseeable needs.

3 The quantities placed in the national reserve shall not have a reference fat content.

A1.802

Article 15 Cases of inactivity

1 When a natural or legal person holding individual reference quantities no longer meets the conditions referred to in Article 5(c) during a twelve-month period, these quantities shall revert to the national reserve no later than 1 April of the following calendar year, except where he once again becomes a producer as defined in Article 5(c) no later than that date.

Where the person or entity concerned once again becomes a producer no later than the end of the second twelve-month period following withdrawal, all or part of the individual reference quantity which had been withdrawn from that person or entity shall revert to him or it no later than 1 April following the date of application.

2 Where producers do not market a quantity equal to at least 70 % of their individual reference quantity during at least one twelve-month period, Member States may decide whether and on what conditions all or part of the unused reference quantity shall revert to the national reserve.

Member States may determine on what conditions a reference quantity shall be re-allocated to the producer concerned should he resume marketing.

3   However, paragraphs 1 and 2 shall not apply in cases of force majeure and in duly justified cases temporarily affecting the production capacity of the producers concerned and recognised by the competent authority.

A1.803

Article 16   Temporary transfers

1   By the end of each twelve-month period, Member States shall authorise, for the period concerned, any temporary transfers of part of individual reference quantities which the producers who are entitled thereto do not intend to use.

Member States may regulate transfer operations according to the categories of producers or milk production structures concerned, may limit them to the level of the purchaser or within regions, authorise complete transfers in the cases provided for in Article 15(3) and determine to what extent the transferor can repeat transfer operations.

2   Any Member State may decide not to implement paragraph 1 on the basis of one or both of the following criteria:

(a)   the need to facilitate structural changes and adjustments,

(b)   overriding administrative needs.

A1.804

Article 17   Transfers of reference quantities together with land

1   The individual reference quantities shall be transferred with the holding to the producers taking it over when it is sold, leased, transferred by actual or anticipated inheritance or any other means involving comparable legal effects for the producers, in accordance with detailed rules to be determined by the Member States, taking account of the areas used for dairy production or other objective criteria and, where applicable, of any agreement between the parties. The part of the reference quantity which, where applicable, has not been transferred with the holding shall be added to the national reserve.

2   Where reference quantities have been or are transferred in accordance with paragraph 1 by means of rural leases or by other means involving comparable legal effects, Member States may decide, on the basis of objective criteria and with the aim of ensuring that reference quantities are solely attributed to producers, that the reference quantity shall not be transferred with the holding.

3   Where land is transferred to the public authorities and/or for use in the public interest, or where the transfer is carried out for non-agricultural purposes, Member States shall ensure that the necessary measures are taken to protect the legitimate interests of the parties, and in particular that producers giving up such land are in a position to continue milk production if they so wish.

4   Where there is no agreement between the parties, in the case of tenancies due to expire without any possibility of renewal on similar terms, or in situations involving comparable legal effects, the individual reference quantities in question shall be transferred in whole or in part to the producer taking them over, in accordance with provisions adopted or to be adopted by the Member States, taking account of the legitimate interests of the parties.

A1.805

Article 18   Special transfer measures

1   With a view to successfully restructuring milk production or improving the environment, Member States may, in accordance with detailed rules which they shall lay down taking account of the legitimate interests of the parties concerned:

   (a)   grant compensation in one or more annual instalments to producers who undertake to abandon permanently all or part of their milk production and place the individual reference quantities thus released in the national reserve;

   (b)   determine on the basis of objective criteria the conditions on which producers may obtain, in return for payment, at the beginning of a twelve-month period, the re-allocation by the competent authority or a body designated by that authority of individual reference quantities released definitively at the end of the preceding twelve-month period by other producers in return for compensation in one or more annual instalments equal to the abovementioned payment;

   (c)   centralise and supervise transfers of reference quantities without land;

   (d)   provide, in the case of land transferred with a view to improving the environment, for the individual reference quantity concerned to be allocated to a producer giving up the land but wishing to continue milk production;

   (e)   determine, on the basis of objective criteria, the regions or collection areas within which the permanent transfer of reference quantities without transfer of the corresponding land is authorised, with the aim of improving the structure of milk production;

   (f)   authorise, upon application by a producer to the competent authority or a body designated by that authority, the definitive transfer of reference quantities without transfer of the corresponding land, or vice versa, with the aim of improving the structure of milk production at the level of the holding or to allow for extensification of production.

2   The provisions of paragraph 1 may be implemented at national level, at the appropriate territorial level or in specified collection areas.

A1.806

Article 19   Retaining part of transfers

1   In the case of transfers as referred to in Articles 17 and 18 Member States may, on the basis of objective criteria, retain part of the individual reference quantity for their national reserve.

2   Where reference quantities have been or are transferred in accordance with Articles 17 and 18 with or without the corresponding land by means of rural leases or by other means involving comparable legal effects, Member States may decide, on the basis of objective criteria and with the aim of ensuring that reference quantities are solely attributed to producers, whether and under which conditions all or part of the transferred reference quantity shall revert to the national reserve.

A1.807

Article 20   Aid for the acquisition of reference quantities

No financial assistance linked directly to the acquisition of quotas may be granted by any public authority for the sale, transfer or allocation of reference quantities under this Regulation.

A1.808

Article 21   Approval

Purchaser status shall be subject to prior approval by the Member State in accordance with criteria to be laid down in accordance with Article 23(2).

Conditions to be fulfilled and information to be provided by producers in the case of direct sales shall be fixed in accordance with the procedure in Article 23(2).

CHAPTER 5
TRANSITIONAL AND FINAL PROVISIONS

A1.809

Article 22   Application of the levy

The levy shall be considered as intervention to stabilise agricultural markets and shall be applied to financing expenditure in the milk sector.

A1.810

Article 23   Management Committee

1   The Commission shall be assisted by the Management Committee for Milk and Milk Products set up by Article 41 of Council Regulation (EC) No 1255/1999 of 17 May 1999 on the common organisation of the market in milk and milk products[1], hereinafter referred to as 'Committee'.

2   Where reference is made to this paragraph, Articles 4 and 7 of Decision 1999/468/EC shall apply.

The period provided for in Article 4(3) of Decision 1999/468/EC shall be one month.

3   The Committee shall adopt its Rules of Procedure.

[1]   OJ 1999 L 160/48.

A1.811

Article 24   Implementation measures

The measures necessary for implementation of this Regulation shall be adopted in accordance with the procedure laid down in Article 23(2).

A1.812

Article 25   Repeal

Regulation (EEC) No 3950/92 is hereby repealed as from 1 April 2004.

References to the repealed Regulation shall be construed as references to this Regulation and should be read in accordance with the correlation table in Annex III.

A1.813

Article 26   Transitional measures

Any transitional measures necessary to facilitate the implementation of the changes to the scheme provided for in this Regulation shall be adopted in accordance with the procedure laid down in Article 23(2).

A1.814

Article 27   Entry into force

This Regulation shall enter into force on the third day following its publication in the Official Journal of the European Union.

It shall apply from 1 April 2004, with the exception of Articles 6 and 24, which shall apply from the date of entry into force of this Regulation.

This Regulation shall be binding in its entirety and directly applicable in all Member States.

Done at Brussels, 29 September 2003.

For the Council

The President

G. ALEMANNO

ANNEX I
REFERENCE QUANTITIES

A1.815

[(A) PERIOD 2004/2005

For the Czech Republic, Estonia, Cyprus, Latvia, Lithuania, Hungary, Malta, Poland, Slovenia and Slovakia the national reference quantities referred to in Article 1(1) are applicable from 1 May 2004 to 31 March 2005.

Member State	Quantities, tonnes
Belgium	3 310 431,000
Czech Republic	2 682 143,000
Denmark	4 455 348,000
Germany	27 864 816,000
Estonia	624 483,000
Greece	820 513,000
Spain	6 116 950,000
France	24 235 798,000
Ireland	5 395 764,000
Italy	10 530 060,000
Cyprus	145 200,000
Latvia	695 395,000
Lithuania	1 646 939,000
Luxembourg	269 049,000
Hungary	1 947 280,000
Malta	48 698,000
Netherlands	11 074 692,000
Austria	2 749 401,000
Poland	8 964 017,000
Portugal	1 870 461,000
Slovenia	560 424,000
Slovakia	1 013 316,000
Finland	2 407 003,324
Sweden	3 303 000,000
United Kingdom	14 609 747,000]

NOTES

Amendment

Substituted by Council Decision 2004/281.

Date in force: 1 May 2004.

[(B) PERIOD 2005/2006

Member State	Quantities, tonnes
Belgium	3 310 431,000
Czech Republic	2 682 143,000
Denmark	4 455 348,000
Germany	27 864 816,000
Estonia	624 483,000
Greece	820 513,000
Spain	6 116 950,000
France	24 235 798,000
Ireland	5 395 764,000
Italy	10 530 060,000
Cyprus	145 200,000
Latvia	695 395,000
Lithuania	1 646 939,000
Luxembourg	269 049,000
Hungary	1 947 280,000
Malta	48 698,000
Netherlands	11 074 692,000
Austria	2 749 401,000
Poland	8 964 017,000
Portugal *	1 920 461,000
Slovenia	560 424,000
Slovakia	1 013 316,000
Finland	2 407 003,324
Sweden	3 303 000,000
United Kingdom	14 609 747,000

* Special increase of 50 000 tonnes for exclusive allocation to producers in the Azores.]

NOTES

Amendment

Substituted by Council Decision 2004/281.

Date in force: 1 May 2004.

[(C) PERIOD 2006/2007

Member State	Quantities, tonnes
Belgium	3 326 983,000
Czech Republic	2 682 143,000
Denmark	4 477 624,000
Germany	28 004 140,000
Estonia	624 483,000
Greece	820 513,000
Spain	6 116 950,000
France	24 356 977,000
Ireland	5 395 764,000

Italy	10 530 060,000
Cyprus	145 200,000
Latvia	695 395,000
Lithuania	1 646 939,000
Luxembourg	270 394,000
Hungary	1 947 280,000
Malta	48 698,000
Netherlands	11 130 066,000
Austria	2 763 148,000
Poland	8 964 017,000
Portugal	1 929 824,000
Slovenia	560 424,000
Slovakia	1 013 316,000
Finland	2 419 025,324
Sweden	3 319 515,000
United Kingdom	14 682 697,000]

NOTES

Amendment

Substituted by Council Decision 2004/281.

Date in force: 1 May 2004.

[(D) PERIOD 2007/2008

Member State	*Quantities, tonnes*
Belgium	3 343 535,000
Bulgaria	979 000,000
Czech Republic	2 682 143,000
Denmark	4 499 900,000
Germany	28 143 464,000
Estonia	624 483,000
Greece	820 513,000
Spain	6 116 950,000
France	24 478 156,000
Ireland	5 395 764,000
Italy	10 530 060,000
Cyprus	145 200,000
Latvia	695 395,000
Lithuania	1 646 939,000
Luxembourg	271 739,000
Hungary	1 947 280,000
Malta	48 698,000
Netherlands	11 185 440,000
Austria	2 776 895,000
Poland	8 964 017,000
Portugal	1 939 187,000
Romania	3 057 000,000
Slovenia	560 424,000
Slovakia	1 013 316,000
Finland	2 431 047,324
Sweden	3 336 030,000
United Kingdom	14 755 647,000]

NOTES

Amendment

Substituted by the Act of Accession 2005.

Date in force: 1 January 2007.

[(E) PERIODS 2008/2009 TO 2014/2015

Member State	Quantities, tonnes
Belgium	3 360 087,000
Bulgaria	979 000,000
Czech Republic	2 682 143,000
Denmark	4 522 176,000
Germany	28 282 788,000
Estonia	624 483,000
Greece	820 513,000
Spain	6 116 950,000
France	24 599 335,000
Ireland	5 395 764,000
Italy	10 530 060,000
Cyprus	145 200,000
Latvia	695 395,000
Lithuania	1 646 939,000
Luxembourg	273 084,000
Hungary	1 947 280,000
Malta	48 698,000
Netherlands	11 240 814,000
Austria	2 790 642,000
Poland	8 964 017,000
Portugal	1 948 550,000
Romania	3 057 000,000
Slovenia	560 424,000
Slovakia	1 013 316,000
Finland	2 443 069,324
Sweden	3 352 545,000
United Kingdom	14 828 597,000]

NOTES

Amendment

Substituted by the Act of Accession 2005.

Date in force: 1 January 2007.

[(F) REFERENCE QUANTITIES FOR DELIVERIES AND DIRECT SALES REFERRED TO IN THE SECOND SUBPARAGRAPH OF ARTICLE 6(1)

Member State	Reference quantities for deliveries, tonnes	Reference quantities for direct sales, tonnes
Bulgaria	722 000	257 000
Czech Republic	2 613 239	68 904
Estonia	537 188	87 365
Cyprus	141 337	3 863
Latvia	468 943	226 452
Lithuania	1 256 440	390 499

Hungary	1 782 650	164 630
Malta	48 698	–
Poland	8 500 000	464 017
Romania	1 093 000	1 964 000
Slovenia	467 063	93 361
Slovakia	990 810	22 506]

NOTES

Amendment

Inserted by the Act of Accession 2005.

Date in force: 1 January 2007.

[(G) SPECIAL RESTRUCTURING RESERVE QUANTITIES REFERRED TO IN ARTICLE 1(4)

Member State	*Special restructuring reserve quantities, tonnes*
Bulgaria	39 180
Czech Republic	55 788
Estonia	21 885
Latvia	33 253
Lithuania	57 900
Hungary	42 780
Poland	416 126
Romania	188 400
Slovenia	16 214
Slovakia	27 472]

NOTES

Amendment

Inserted by the Act of Accession 2005.

Date in force: 1 January 2007.

ANNEX II
REFERENCE FAT CONTENT

A1.816

Member State	*Reference fat content (g/kg)*
Belgium	36.91
[Bulgaria	39.10
Czech Republic	42.10]
Denmark	43.68
Germany	40.11
[Estonia	43.10]
Greece	36.10
Spain	36.37
France	39.48
Ireland	35.81
Italy	36.88
[Cyprus	34.60
Latvia	40.70

Lithuania	39.90]
Luxembourg	39.17
[Hungary	38.50]
Netherlands	42.36
Austria	40.30
[Poland	39.00]
Portugal	37.30
[Romania	[38.50]
Slovenia	41.30
Slovakia	37.10]
Finland	43.40
Sweden	43.40
United Kingdom	39.70

NOTES

Amendment

Entries for Bulgaria, Czech Republic, Estonia, Cyprus, Latvia, Lithuania, Hungary, Poland, Romania, Slovenia and Slovakia: inserted by the Act of Accession 2005.

Date in force: 1 January 2007.

In entry for Romania: number in square brackets substituted by Commission Regulation 336/2007.

Date in force: 1 April 2007.

ANNEX III
CORRELATION TABLE

A1.817

Present Regulation		*Regulation (EEC) 3950/92*
Article 1	(1)	Article 1, first subparagraph
	(2)	—
	(3)	Article 3(2)
Article 2		Article 1, second subparagraph
Article 3		—
Article 4		Article 2(1), first subparagraph
Article 5		Article 9
Article 6	(1), (2) and (3)	—
	(4)	Article 3(2)
	(5)	Article 4(2)
Article 7		—
Article 8		—
Article 9		—
Article 10	(1) and (2)	—
	(3)	Article 2(1), second subparagraph
Article 11	(1)	Article 2(2), first subparagraph
	(2)	Article 2(2), second subparagraph
	(3)	Article 2(2), third subparagraph
Article 12	(1)	Article 2(1)
	(2) and (3)	—
	(4)	Article 2(3)
Article 13	(1)	Article 2(4)
	(2), (3), (4)	—

Article 14	(1)	Article 5, first subparagraph
	(2) and (3)	—
Article 15		Article 5, second and third subparagraphs
Article 16		Article 6
Article 17	(1)	Article 7(1)
	(2)	Article 8a (b)
	(3) and (4)	Article 7(1), third subparagraph and (3)
Article 18		Article 8
Article 19	(1)	Article 7(1), second subparagraph
	(2)	Article 8a (a)
Article 20		—
Article 21		—
Article 22		Article 10
Article 23	(1)	Article 11, first subparagraph
	(2) and (3)	—
Article 24		Article 11, first subparagraph
Article 25		Article 12
Annex I		Annex
Annex II		—
Annex III		—

A1.818

Amendments to Council Regulation (EC) 1788/2003

Regulation	Into Force	Effective From
Commission Regulation (EC) 336/2007, OJ 2007 L 88/43	1 April 2007	1 April 2007
Council Regulation (EC) 1406/2006, OJ 2006 L 265/8	3 Oct 2006	Art 1(1) 1 Sept 2006
Act of Accession 2005	1 Jan 2005	
Council Regulation (EC) 2217/2004, OJ 2004 L 375/1	23 Dec 2004	1 April 2004
Council Decision 2004/281, OJ 2004 L 93/1	1 May 2004	

Appendix II
FORMS AND PRECEDENTS

Part 1

FARM BUSINESS TENANCIES UNDER THE AGRICULTURAL TENANCIES ACT 1995

Contents

Part 1

FARM BUSINESS TENANCIES UNDER THE AGRICULTURAL TENANCIES ACT 1995

A: THE NOTICE CONDITIONS

A2.1

A1   Notice to landlord or tenant of farm business tenancy[1]

AGRICULTURAL TENANCIES ACT 1995 NOTICE PURSUANT TO SECTION 1(4)

To: (*name of tenant or landlord*) of (*address*)

Re: The Holding known as (*identify the holding*)[2]

I, (*name of landlord or tenant*) of (*address*), GIVE YOU NOTICE pursuant to the Agricultural Tenancies Act 1995 Section 1(4) that I intend that the tenancy of the Holding referred to above which we are proposing to enter into is to be and remain a farm business tenancy within the meaning of the Agricultural Tenancies Act 1995 and that the character of the tenancy will at its beginning be primarily or wholly agricultural.

(*signature of landlord or tenant*)

Dated: (*insert date*)

---

[1]   As to the notice conditions see the Agricultural Tenancies Act 1995 (ATA 1995), s 1(4) and see para 3.28 ff. As to service, see ATA 1995, s 36 and para 17.1.
[2]   The land to be comprised in the tenancy must be identified by name or otherwise: see ibid, s 1(4)(a)(i). It is advisable to identify the land in the same way as will be used in the tenancy agreement.

B: RENT REVIEW

A2.2

B1   **Farm business tenancy – statutory rent review notice[1]**

AGRICULTURAL TENANCIES ACT 1995 NOTICE PURSUANT TO SECTION 10

To: (*name of tenant or landlord*) of (*address*)

Re: The Holding known as (*identify the holding*)

I, (*name of landlord or tenant*) of (*address*), GIVE YOU NOTICE pursuant to the Agricultural Tenancies Act 1995 Section 10 that I require the rent payable in respect of the Holding referred to above, as from the first date (after the end of 12 months from the date of service on you of this notice) on which the rent could be reviewed under the Agricultural Tenancies Act 1995 Section 10,[2] to be referred to arbitration in accordance with that Act.

(*signature of landlord or tenant*)

Dated: (*insert date*)

1 As to rent review options in relation to farm business tenancies, see para 9.6. As to service, see the ATA 1995, s 36 and para 17.1.
2 As to the rent review date to be specified in the statutory review notice, see para 9.22.

A2.3

B2   **Farm business tenancy – agreement as to rent[1]**

AGRICULTURAL TENANCIES ACT 1995

Re: The Holding known as (*identify the holding*)

WE, (*name of landlord*) of (*address*) and (*name of tenant*) of (*address*) the Landlord and Tenant of the Holding referred to above, agree that with effect from (*insert date*) the rent payable in respect of the Holding pursuant to the terms of the Agreement between us dated (*insert date*) will be (*insert amount*) per year.

(*signatures of landlord and tenant*)

Dated: (*insert date*)

1 As to rent review options in relation to farm business tenancies, see para 9.6, and as to the statutory rent review procedure under the ATA 1995, see para A1.219 and Ch 9. As to service, see ATA 1995, s 36 and para 17.1.

C: TERMINATION OF FARM BUSINESS TENANCIES

A2.4

C1   Notice to terminate fixed term farm business tenancy of more than two years[1]

AGRICULTURAL TENANCIES ACT 1995 NOTICE PURSUANT TO SECTION 5

To: (*name of tenant or landlord*) of (*address*)

Re: The Holding known as (*identify the holding*)

I, (*name of landlord or tenant*) of (*address*), as [Landlord or Tenant] GIVE YOU NOTICE to terminate the tenancy of the Holding referred to above pursuant to the Agricultural Tenancies Act 1995 Section 5 on the expiry of the term granted by a [Lease or Tenancy Agreement] dated the (*insert date*) and made between (*insert details of parties*) or on the first date on which the tenancy can lawfully be terminated, being at least twelve months after service of this notice.

(*signature of landlord or tenant*)

Dated: (*insert date*)

[1]   As to termination of a fixed term farm business tenancy if more than two years see the ATA 1995, s 5 and see para 12.3. Fixed-term tenancies of a term of two years or less are not governed by the Act and will come to an end by effluxion of time on the expiry of the term. As to service, see ATA 1995, s 36 and para 17.1.

A2.5

C2   Notice to terminate a farm business tenancy for a term of more than two years in exercise of a provision contained in the lease or tenancy agreement[1]

AGRICULTURAL TENANCIES ACT 1995 NOTICE PURSUANT TO SECTION 7

To: (*name of tenant or landlord*) of (*address*)

Re: The Holding known as (*identify the holding*)

I, (*name of landlord or tenant*) of (*address*), as [Landlord or Tenant] GIVE YOU NOTICE pursuant to clause (*number*) of a [Lease or Tenancy Agreement] of the Holding referred to above dated the (*insert date*) and made between (*insert details of parties*) to terminate the tenancy on (*insert date*) or (if later) on the first date on which the tenancy can be terminated pursuant to the said clause, being at least twelve months after service of this notice.

(signature of landlord or tenant)

Dated: (*insert date*)

1   As to termination of a farm business tenancy for a term of more than two years in pursuance of a provision of the tenancy agreement see the ATA 1995, s 7. As to service, see ATA 1995, s 36 and para 17.1.

A2.6

C3   Landlord's notice to terminate periodic farm business tenancy[1]

AGRICULTURAL TENANCIES ACT 1995

To: (*name of tenant*) of (*address*)

Re: The Holding known as (*identify the holding*)

I, (*name of landlord*) of (*address*), GIVE YOU NOTICE TO QUIT and deliver up to me possession of the Holding referred to above which you hold of me as tenant on (*insert date of expiry of current period of tenancy*) or at the expiry of [12 months] from the end of the now current [year] of the tenancy.

(signature of landlord)

Dated: (*insert date*)

1   Twelve months' written notice, taking effect at the end of the year of the tenancy is required to terminate an annual periodic farm business tenancy: see the ATA 1995, s 6. As to service, see ATA 1995, s 36 and para 17.1. The common law rules as to notice periods apply to other periodic farm business tenancies: see Ch 17.

A2.7

C4   Tenant's notice to terminate periodic farm business tenancy[1]

AGRICULTURAL TENANCIES ACT 1995

To: (*name of landlord*) of (*address*)

Re: The Holding known as (*identify the holding*)

I, (*name of tenant*) of (*address*), GIVE YOU NOTICE that I shall quit and deliver up to you possession of the Holding referred to above which I hold of you as tenant on (*insert date of expiry of current period of tenancy*) or at the expiry of [12 months] from the end of the now current [year] of the tenancy.

(*signature of tenant*)

Dated: (*insert date*)

1   Twelve months' written notice, taking effect at the end of the year of the tenancy is required to terminate an annual periodic farm business tenancy: see the ATA 1995, s 6. As to service, see ATA 1995, s 36 and para 17.1. The common law rules as to notice periods apply to other periodic farm business tenancies: see Ch 17.

D: IMPROVEMENTS

A2.8

D1   Farm business tenancy – tenant's request for consent to improvements[1]

AGRICULTURAL TENANCIES ACT 1995

To: (*name of landlord*) of (*address*)

Re: The Holding known as (*identify the holding*)

I, (*name of tenant*) of (*address*), Tenant of the Holding referred to above request your written consent to the provision by me of the improvement[s] specified in the schedule below.

SCHEDULE

(*insert full details of proposed improvements*)

(*signature of tenant*)

Dated: (*insert date*)

1   Landlord's written consent is a condition for compensation entitlement for tenant's improvements which are physical improvements or intangible advantages, see the ATA 1995, s 17 and Ch 16. As to routine improvements, see para 16.5. As to service, see ATA 1995, s 36 and para 17.1.

A2.9

D2   Farm business tenancy – landlord's consent to tenant's improvements (other than planning permission)[1]

AGRICULTURAL TENANCIES ACT 1995

To: (*name of tenant*) of (*address*)

Re: The Holding known as (*identify the holding*)

I, *(name of landlord)* of *(address)* Landlord of the Holding referred to above, consent to the provision by you of the improvement[s] specified in schedule 1 below

1   on condition[2] that you agree to the terms specified in schedule 2 below related to [that improvement *or* those improvements] such terms to be incorporated in a memorandum to be annexed to both parts of the [Lease *or* Tenancy Agreement] pursuant to which you occupy the Holding prior to the commencement of such improvement.

2   on the basis of the compensation limit for such improvement[s] of £*(insert amount)* which we have agreed between us.[3]

SCHEDULE 1

(insert full details of proposed improvements)

SCHEDULE 2

(set out terms as to eg location, materials, user etc)

(signature of landlord)

Dated: *(insert date)*

[1]   As to tenant's improvements, see Ch 16. For consent in relation to an application for planning permission, see Form D4 (at para A2.11).

[2]   A landlord's consent may be given either unconditionally or on condition that the tenant agrees to a specified variation in the terms of the tenancy, see the ATA 1995, s 17 and para 16.13 ff.

[3]   The ATA 1995, s 20(4A), as amended, permits the parties, since 19 October 2006 to agree an upper limit on the amount of compensation payable in respect of an improvement, see para 16.1.

A2.10

D3   Farm business tenancy – landlord's consent allowing tenant to make an application for planning permission[1]

AGRICULTURAL TENANCIES ACT 1995

To: *(name of tenant)* of *(address)*

Re: The Holding known as *(identify the holding)*

I, *(name of landlord)* of *(address)* Landlord of the Holding referred to above, consent to the making by you of the application for planning permission specified in schedule 1 below for the purpose of enabling [a physical improvement on the Holding by you by your own effort or wholly or partly at your expense or you lawfully to effect a change of use][2] comprising *(insert details)* on condition that you agree to the terms specified in schedule 2 below related to that [physical improvement or change of use] such terms to be incorporated in a memorandum to be annexed to both parts of the [Lease or Tenancy Agreement] pursuant to which you occupy the Holding prior to your making the said application.

SCHEDULE 1

(insert details of planning application and of any other relevant documentation)

SCHEDULE 2

(set out any terms to be included)

(signature of landlord)

Dated: *(insert date)*

1   As to a landlord's consent to the making of an application for planning permission, see the
    ATA 1995, s 18 and para 16.13 ff.
2   See ATA 1995, ss 15(a), 18(1)(b).

A2.11

D4   Farm business tenancy – tenant's notice demanding that question of consent to improvements be referred to arbitration[1]

AGRICULTURAL TENANCIES ACT 1995 NOTICE PURSUANT TO SECTION 19

To: *(name of landlord)* of *(address)*

Re: The Holding known as *(identify the holding)*

I, *(name of tenant)* of *(address)*, GIVE YOU NOTICE that I am aggrieved by

[your refusal to give written consent[2] to my proposed improvement to the Holding comprising *(insert details)* or

your failure to give written consent to my proposed improvement to the Holding comprising *(insert details)* within two months of my written request[3] or

your requiring that as a condition of your giving written consent to my proposed improvement to the Holding comprising *(insert details)* I agree to the variation in the terms of the tenancy[4] related to that improvement set out in your approval *(identify variations required by landlord)*]

AND I DEMAND that the question be referred to arbitration under the Agricultural Tenancies Act 1995 Section 19.

(signature of tenant)

Dated: *(insert date)*

1   ATA 1995, s 19 sets out the procedures for making a reference to arbitration in any of the
    three circumstances described in this notice. As to service, see ATA 1995, s 36 and para
    17.1.
2   See ATA 1995, s 19(1)(a). As to the time limit for the service of such notice, see ATA 1995,
    s 19(3)(a).

3   See ATA 1995, s 19(1)(b). As to the time limit for the service of such notice, see ATA 1995, s 19(3)(b).
4   See ATA 1995, s 19(1)(c). As to the time limit for the service of such notice, see ATA 1995, s 19(3)(a).

A2.12

D5   **Farm business tenancy – tenant's notice of intention to claim compensation for improvements[1]**

AGRICULTURAL TENANCIES ACT 1995 NOTICE PURSUANT TO SECTIONS 16 AND 22

To: (*name of landlord*) of (*address*)

Re: The Holding known as (*identify the holding*)

I, (*name of tenant*) of (*address*), GIVE YOU NOTICE that I intend to claim compensation under the Agricultural Tenancies Act 1995 Section 16 in respect of the improvements for which [you gave consent in writing or approval was given by (*insert name of arbitrator*) as arbitrator] on (*insert date*). Details of the improvements and the nature of the claim are set out in the schedule below.

SCHEDULE

(*insert full details of the improvements and the nature of the claim*)

(*signature of tenant*)

Dated: (*insert date*)

1   A tenant's claim for compensation for a tenant's improvement under the ATA 1995, s 16 is only enforceable if before the end of the period of two months beginning with the date of termination of the tenancy the tenant has given notice in writing to his landlord of his intention to make the claim and of the nature of the claim: see ATA 1995, s 22(2) and para 16.30. As to service, see ATA 1995, s 36 and para 17.1.

E: MISCELLANEOUS

A2.13

This section contains the precedents for an arbitration under the Agricultural Tenancies Act 1995. Practitioners are also referred to Forms AA4 (at para A3.5) and AA5 (at para A3.6) of the Agricultural Holdings Act 1986, precedents which relate to an application to the RICS for the appointment of an arbitrator in rent disputes and all non-rent disputes. Following the commencement of the Regulatory Reform (Agricultural Tenancies) (England and Wales) Order 2006, SI 2006/2805, the RICS amended the application forms, producing two forms to be used in all cases, regardless of whether the dispute relates to one statute or the other. The two forms, DRS3 and DRS4, have not been repeated in this section of the precedents.

A2.14

E1 Notice to tenant of change of landlord

AGRICULTURAL TENANCIES ACT 1995 NOTICE PURSUANT TO SECTION 36(7)

To: (*name of tenant*) of (*address*)

Re: The Holding known as (*identify the holding*)

I, (*name of original or new landlord*) of (*address*), GIVE YOU NOTICE pursuant to the Agricultural Tenancies Act 1995 Section 36(7) that with effect from (*date*) the Landlord of the Holding described above who is entitled to receive the rent from the Holding will be (*name of new landlord*) of (*address*).

(*signature of original or new landlord*)

Dated: (*insert date*)

A2.15

E2 Notice of intention to apply for the appointment of an arbitrator in relation to a dispute (other than a dispute governed by particular statutory provisions as to rent, improvements or compensation)

AGRICULTURAL TENANCIES ACT 1995 NOTICE PURSUANT TO SECTION 28(2)

To: (*name of tenant or landlord*) of (*address*)

Re: The Holding known as (*identify the holding*)

I, (*name of landlord or tenant*) of (*address*), GIVE YOU NOTICE that, unless before the end of the period of 2 months beginning with the day on which this notice is given to you we have appointed an arbitrator by agreement, I propose to apply to the President of the Royal Institution of Chartered Surveyors for the appointment of an arbitrator by him in respect of the dispute specified below.

NATURE OF THE DISPUTE

(*specify the dispute and give details*)

(*signature of or on behalf of landlord or tenant*)

Dated: (*insert date*)

E3   **Agreement to appoint an arbitrator to determine claims, questions or differences between landlord and tenant in relation to rent, improvements, compensation or other disputes**

AGRICULTURAL TENANCIES ACT 1995

Re: The Holding described in the Particulars set out in Part II of this agreement

PART I

The Landlord and the Tenant (named in the Particulars set out in Part II below) having failed to resolve the claims, questions or differences set out in Part II below, agree to the appointment of an arbitrator to determine such issues in dispute.

(*name*) of (*name and address of firm*) has agreed to act as arbitrator [by a letter dated (*date*)].

IT IS AGREED that (*name of agreed arbitrator*) will be appointed as at the date of this agreement to act as arbitrator in respect of the issues set out in Part II below.

(*signatures of or on behalf of landlord and tenant*)

Dated: (*insert date*)

PART II

Particulars	Details
1 Name and address of the Holding	Holding: Parish: County:
2 Name and address of Landlord	
3 Name and address of Landlord's agents (if any)	
4 Name and address of Landlord's solicitors (if any)	
5 Name and address of Tenant	
6 Name and address of Tenant's agents (if any)	
7 Name and address of Tenant's solicitors (if any)	
8 Approximate area of Holding	

Particulars	Details
9 Description of Holding	(*eg mixed, arable, dairy, market garden*)
10 State the provision of the Agricultural Tenancies Act 1995 (or otherwise) in respect of which the arbitration is required	
11 Nature of the dispute	
12 Conflicts of interest	(*state the names of any persons who should not be considered for appointment/nomination*)

Part 2

AGRICULTURAL HOLDINGS UNDER THE AGRICULTURAL HOLDINGS ACT 1986

GENERAL NOTES

A2.17

(a) Some forms included in the contents lists to Divisions I to IV in Part 2 are shown as official forms. These are forms prescribed by statutory instruments, and reprinted here by consent of HM Stationery Office. Most of the prescribed forms were prescribed under legislation such as the Agricultural Holdings Act 1986 (AHA 1986). The Agricultural Land Tribunal (Rules) Order 1978, SI 1978/259 and the Agricultural Land Tribunal (Succession to Agricultural Tenancies) Order 1984, SI 1984/1301 incorporate land tribunal prescribed forms and refer, in many instances, to enactments that have subsequently been repealed. A new Order, the Land Tribunal (Rules) Order 2007 is proposed, with the intention of updating and consolidating the 1978 and 1984 Orders. It is a continuing source of considerable irritation to practitioners that prescribed forms, particularly in respect of applications to the Agricultural Land Tribunal and replies, have not been revised following statutory changes in the law[1]. As a result, statutory forms which are long out of date are required to be used which renders them more unintelligible to the recipient than they need to be. They sometimes give rise to disputes as to the validity of the forms used and add to the costs of litigation. However, until such time as new forms are prescribed it is presumptuous as well as strictly incorrect to amend and notionally improve the statutorily prescribed forms by bringing them up to date. However, where the current relevant statutory authorities and sections are inserted in substitution for the repealed provisions, such forms, being 'substantially to the like effect'[2] as those statutorily prescribed, will be valid and effective for their purposes.

(b) All other forms not shown as official forms have been included to help busy practitioners and are entirely *unofficial*.

(c) Such *unofficial forms* (like the book itself) are copyright reserved and may not be reproduced for sale without the permission of the author or the publishers of this book.

(d) In practice it may be found convenient for the forms to be signed by solicitors or valuers or other authorised agents for the party concerned.

Many of the forms have been drafted for signature by an authorised agent, while others may be suitably adapted for the purpose. Except in the limited types of agency stated in s 93 of the AHA 1986, express authority to an agent will be required[3]. Service of notices on an agent for a recipient party who is not duly authorised to accept service on behalf of the party concerned will not constitute good service.

(e)　As to manner of signature by an agent for a party on whose behalf a notice etc is given, any method indicating the agency will suffice, but the following method is suggested:

Type in the name of the Principal –

	say <u>A.B. Smith</u>	
		(Landlord) or (Tenant)
(*Address*)	of	....
		X.Y.C.
	By	....
		(*Handwritten signature of signing agent*)
		[His] [Her] [Solicitor(s) & Agent(s)]
		or [*Valuer(s) & Agent(s)*][4]
		or [Duly Authorised Agent(s)]
		of and whose address for service of all
		Notices, etc
		on the above-named Landlord's/Tenant's
		behalf
		under the said Act is
		....
	(*Address of*	....
	Agent)	....

(f)　If a notice has to be given in a prescribed form itself required the notice to be signed by the party giving it or his duly authorised agent's signature of the covering letter will be sufficient compliance with the prescribed form[5]. There is no general requirement that notices have to be signed or dated, although it is a convenient and normal practice.

(g)　Special care is required for service of notices to quit on death of a tenant (Case G)[6], notices to remedy and notices to pay[7] and notices subject to statutory time limits[8].

[1]　As a general rule subordinate legislation ceases to be in force on the repeal of the enactment under which it was made (but see Interpretation Act 1978, s 17(2)(b) which prevents subordinate legislation lapsing where the repeal and re-enactment is without modifications).

[2]　The courts have tended to interpret 'substantially to the same effect' strictly: see *Manel v Memon* [2000] 33 EG 74, [2000] 2 EGLR 40.

[3]　See *Lodgepower Ltd v Taylor and others* [2004] EWCA Civ 1367, [2005] 1 EGLR 1, where it was held that service on an erstwhile agent of the original but not deceased landlord was not valid service under the AHA 1986, s 93(5).

[4]　This is permissible. See *Frankland v Capstick* [1959] 1 All ER 209, [1959] 1 WLR 205; see also *Galinski v McHugh* [1989] 1 EGLR 109, but note *Pickard v Bishop* (1975) 31 P & CR 108 – failure correctly to identify the party on whose behalf the notice is given will render a penal notice invalid. Strict rules of construction apply particularly to notices to remedy and notices to pay. A retirement notice and application for succession on

retirement must be signed by the retiring tenant and prospective successor (in the latter case). An agent's signature is not sufficient, see *White v de Pelet*, South Western Agricultural Land Tribunal, 1995.

5   *Stidolph v American School in London Educational Trust Ltd* (1969) 211 Estates Gazette 925.

6   As to which, see para 31.90 ff.

7   As to which, see para 31.27 ff.

8   These are nearly all subject to express, inflexible time limits. See *R v Agricultural Land Tribunal (Wales), ex p Hughes* (1980) 255 Estates Gazette 703.

Part 2

AGRICULTURAL HOLDINGS UNDER THE AGRICULTURAL HOLDINGS ACT 1986

Contents

N.B. Arbitration under the 1986 Act is dealt with in Appendix III of this book.

More detailed tables of contents will be found at the start of each Division. For ease of reference, the numbers used on the forms correspond with the numbers used in the eighth edition of this book.

Division I

MATTERS ARISING DURING TENANCY

A2.17A Note: All the forms listed in Division I are unofficial forms which may, therefore, be freely adapted as circumstances require. The number ascribed to each form is *unofficial*.

All relate to matters arising during the currency of the tenancy, excluding notices which carry the sanction of notice to quit for non-compliance, e g notices to pay or notices to remedy which are listed in Division III.

Division I

MATTERS ARISING DURING TENANCY

Contents

Division I

MATTERS ARISING DURING TENANCY

A2.18

AH36   Request by landlord or tenant to enter into written tenancy agreement

AGRICULTURAL HOLDINGS ACT 1986

To (*landlord or tenant*) of (*address*) (*date*)
(*description of holding*)

BACKGROUND: [it is your contention that *or* there is uncertainty whether][1] there is [no *or* any] agreement in writing between us which embodies all the terms of the tenancy of the above holding

NOW I (*landlord or tenant*) of (*address*) request you in accordance with the Agricultural Holdings Act 1986 section 6(1)[2] to enter into a written agreement embodying all the terms of the tenancy[3] and containing provision for all the matters specified in Schedule 1 to that Act[4]

(*signature of landlord or tenant*)

Notes

[1]   The alternative may be used where eg there may be a tenancy agreement but such agreement has been mislaid. As to written terms, see para 23.1 ff.
[2]   Ie the Agricultural Holdings 1986, s 6(1) (see para A1.93). This Form should not be used where there is already a written agreement which does not make provision for all the matters specified in AHA 1986, Sch 1: see Form AH37.
[3]   Any terms established after the execution of the written agreement by the operations of regulations pursuant to AHA 1986, s 7 are deemed to be incorporated in the written agreement except in so far as they would impose on one of the parties to a written agreement a liability which, under the agreement, is imposed on the other: AHA 1986, s 7(3).
[4]   AHA 1986, s 6(1)(b), Sch 1 establishes terms to be included in the written agreement but see also note 3 above and para 23.2.

AH37 Request by landlord or tenant to supplement existing written tenancy agreement to provide for certain matters in the Agricultural Holdings Act 1986 Schedule 1[1]

AGRICULTURAL HOLDINGS ACT 1986

To (*landlord or tenant*) of (*address*) (*date*)
(*description of holding*)

BACKGROUND: the tenancy agreement in respect of the above holding made the ...
... day of ... . contains no provision for the following matters specified in the
Agricultural Holdings Act 1986 Schedule 1[2] (*specify relevant matters*)

NOW I (*landlord or tenant*) of (*address*) request you in accordance with section 6(1) of
that Act to enter into an agreement supplemental to the tenancy agreement containing
provision for such matters

(signature of landlord or tenant)

Notes

[1]   This Form should be used when there is a written agreement in existence which does not
     provide for all the matters specified in the AHA 1986, Sch 1 (see para A1.190). Where
     there is no written agreement or there is uncertainty as to whether one exists, Form AH36
     should be used. As to the situation where the terms of the tenancy neither make provision
     for nor make provision inconsistent with AHA 1986, Sch 1 para 9 and the landlord serves
     a request under AHA 1986, s 6(1), see AHA 1986, s 6(5). As to written terms, see para
     23.1.
[2]   Any prescribed terms relating to the maintenance, repair and insurance of fixed equipment
     specified by the Agriculture (Maintenance, Repair and Insurance of Fixed Equipment)
     Regulations 1973, SI 1973/1473 (as amended by SI 1988/281) are and any subsequent
     regulations will be deemed to be incorporated in the agreement except in so far as they
     would impose on one of the parties a liability which under the agreement is imposed on the
     other: AHA 1986, s 7(3). Where the written agreement contains terms which are
     inconsistent with the prescribed provisions, either party may refer the matter to arbitration
     provided that a notice requesting the variation of the terms has been served and no
     agreement has been reached: AHA 1986, s 8(1), (2). As to fixed equipment generally, see
     Ch 23.

A2.20

AH38 Reference to arbitration by landlord or tenant on failure to enter into a written agreement[1]

AGRICULTURAL HOLDINGS ACT 1986

To (*landlord or tenant*) of (*address*) (*date*)
(*description of holding*)

BACKGROUND: following my request to you dated the ... ... day of ... . to enter into [a written agreement embodying all the terms of the tenancy between us in accordance with the Agricultural Holdings Act 1986, Schedule 1 *or* an agreement supplemental to the tenancy agreement between us made the ... ... day of ... . in respect of the above holding containing provision for certain matters specified in the Agricultural Holdings Act 1986, Schedule 1 but not provided for in the tenancy agreement] no [supplemental] agreement has been concluded.

NOW I (*landlord or tenant*) of (*address*) give you notice under section 6 of that Act that I require that the terms of the tenancy shall be referred to arbitration under that Act

(*signature of landlord or tenant*)

Notes

1   This reference must be preceded by a request to enter into a written agreement (see Form AH36) or a request requiring the variation of the terms of a written agreement (see Form AH37), following which no agreement has been reached between the parties: AHA 1986, s 6(1) (see para A1.93). This notice may be sent with a letter giving the names of suggested arbitrators. If there is a written tenancy agreement, any relevant arbitration clause must be borne in mind, particularly the method of appointing arbitrators. As to written terms, see para 23.1 ff.

The arbitration will be governed by the Arbitration Act 1996 for those arbitrations occurring after the coming into force of the Regulatory Reform (Agricultural Tenancies) (England and Wales) Order 2006, SI 2006/2805 on 19 October 2006. See also, AHA 1986, s 84, as amended by SI 2006/2805, art 7.

A2.21

AH39   Request by landlord or tenant to vary terms of tenancy agreement to comply with prescribed regulations relating to maintenance etc of fixed equipment[1]

AGRICULTURAL HOLDINGS ACT 1986

To (*landlord or tenant*) of (*address*) (*date*)
(*description of holding*)

BACKGROUND: the tenancy agreement between us made the ... ... day of ... . in respect of the above holding effects substantial modifications in the operation of the regulations prescribed by the [Secretary of State for the Environment Food and Rural Affairs *or* Secretary of State for Wales][2] under the Agricultural Holdings Act 1986 section 7(1) relating to the maintenance repair and insurance of fixed equipment

NOW I (*landlord or tenant*) of (*address*) request you to vary the tenancy agreement so that it complies with the provisions of those regulations[3]

(*signature of landlord or tenant*)

2033

Notes

1   This Form is for use where the tenancy agreement contains provisions which are inconsistent with any regulations made pursuant to the AHA 1986, s 7(1) (see para A1.94). If no agreement is reached between the parties, the party requiring the variation may refer the matter to arbitration: AHA 1986, s 8(1), (2). As to the form of reference, see Form AH40. As to fixed equipment, see Ch 23.

2   The regulations are prescribed in England by the Secretary of State for the Environment Food and Rural Affairs: see the AHA 1986, ss 7(1) and 96. Functions of the Minister, so far as exercisable in relation to Wales, transferred to the National Assembly for Wales under the National Assembly for Wales (Transfer of Functions) Order 1999, SI 1999/672, art 2, Sch 1.

3   The prescribed regulations currently in force are the Agriculture (Maintenance, Repair and Insurance of Fixed Equipment) Regulations 1973, SI 1973/1473, as amended by SI 1988/281.

A2.22

AH40 Reference to arbitration by landlord or tenant on failure to agree the variation of terms of existing agreement to comply with prescribed regulations relating to fixed equipment[1]

AGRICULTURAL HOLDINGS ACT 1986

To (*landlord or tenant*) of (*address*) (*date*)
(*description of holding*)

BACKGROUND: no agreement has been reached between us following my request to you dated the ... ... day of ... . to vary the tenancy agreement between us made the ... ... day of ... . in respect of the above holding so that it complies with the provisions of the prescribed regulations relating to maintenance repair and insurance of fixed equipment

NOW I (*landlord or tenant*) of (*address*) give you notice under the Agricultural Holdings Act 1986 Sections 8(1) and 8(2) that I refer to arbitration under that Act the terms of the tenancy between us with respect to the maintenance, repair and insurance of fixed equipment

(*signature of landlord or tenant*)

Notes

1   This Form is for use where the party requiring arbitration has requested the other party to vary the terms of the tenancy agreement so that they comply with the provisions of the prescribed regulations and no agreement has been reached between the parties: as to the form of request see Form AH39 and notes 1, 3. If the arbitrator varies any terms and he considers it appropriate, he may vary the rent payable: AHA 1986, s 8(4) (see para A1.95). As to specifying particular arbitrators etc see Form AH38 note 1. Where there has been a reference to arbitration under AHA 1986 s 8, no further such reference relating to that tenancy may be made for 3 years from the coming into effect of the award of the arbitrator on the previous reference: AHA 1986, s 8(6). As to fixed equipment see Ch 23.

A2.23

AH41 Request by tenant to landlord to provide, alter or repair fixed equipment[1]

AGRICULTURAL HOLDINGS ACT 1986

To (*landlord*) of (*address*) (*date*)
(*description of holding*)

Pursuant to the provisions of the Agricultural Holdings Act 1986 section 11 I (*tenant*) of (*address*) request you to provide *or* alter *or* repair the fixed equipment particulars of which are set out in the schedule below

SCHEDULE

(*particulars of proposed work in sufficient detail to enable landlord to know what is required*)

(*signature of tenant*)

Notes

[1]   The Agricultural Land Tribunal will not direct the landlord to carry out the work under the AHA 1986, s 11 (see para A1.98) unless, inter alia, the tenant has served the landlord with a request in writing and the landlord has either refused to do the work in question or has not agreed to do it within a reasonable time: AHA 1986, s 11(3)(b). As to fixed equipment, see Ch 23.

A2.24

AH42 Requirement by tenant for arbitration of claim by tenant against landlord on transfer of liability for maintenance or repair of fixed equipment[1]

AGRICULTURAL HOLDINGS ACT 1986

To (*landlord*) of (*address*) (*date*)
(*description of holding*)

BACKGROUND: by virtue of the Agricultural Holdings Act 1986 section [6 *or* 7 *or* 8] liability for the maintenance or repair of the item[s] of fixed equipment mentioned in the schedule below has been transferred with effect from the ... ... day of ... . from you to me under the [agreement between us *or* award of (*arbitrator*) made the ... ... day of ... .]

NOW I (*tenant*) of (*address*) require that my claim in respect of your previous failure to discharge such liability is referred to and determined by arbitration under that Act

SCHEDULE

(item(s) of fixed equipment liability for which is transferred)

(signature of tenant)

Notes

1   This reference must be made within the prescribed time limit: AHA 1986, s 9(3). The time limit is one month from the date on which the transfer of liability takes effect: Agriculture (Miscellaneous Time-Limits) Regulations 1959, SI 1959/171, reg 2(3). As to fixed equipment, see Ch 23.

A2.25

AH43   Requirement by landlord for arbitration as to amount of compensation payable by tenant on transfer of liability for maintenance or repair of fixed equipment[1]

AGRICULTURAL HOLDINGS ACT 1986

To *(tenant)* of *(address)* *(date)*
(description of holding)

BACKGROUND: by virtue of the Agricultural Holdings Act 1986 section [6 *or* 7 *or* 8] liability for the maintenance or repair of the item[s] of fixed equipment mentioned in the schedule below has been transferred with effect from the …. . day of … … . . from you to me under the [agreement between us *or* award of *(arbitrator)* made the …
… day of … … . .]

NOW I *(landlord)* of *(address)* require under section 9(1) of that Act that there shall be determined by arbitration under that Act and paid by you to me the amount of compensation due from you[2] in respect of your liability up to the date of transfer as above in accordance with the provisions of sections 9(1) and 9(2) of that Act

SCHEDULE

(item(s) of fixed equipment liability for which is transferred)

(signature of landlord)

Notes

1   This reference to arbitration must be made within the prescribed time limit: AHA 1986, s 9(1). The time limit is one month from the date on which the transfer of liability takes effect: Agriculture (Miscellaneous Time-Limits) Regulations 1959, SI 1959/171, reg 2(2). As to fixed equipment, Ch 23.
2   Ie the compensation which would have been payable either under AHA 1986, s 71(1) or s 71(3) in respect of any previous failure by the tenant to discharge his liability in accordance with AHA 1986, s 9(1) if he had quitted the holding on the termination of his tenancy at the date on which the transfer takes effect: AHA 1986, s 9(2).

A2.26

AH44 Notice by landlord to tenant requesting and specifying repairs to be effected by tenant[1]

AGRICULTURAL HOLDINGS ACT 1986

To (*tenant*) of (*address*) (*date*)
(*description of holding*)

TAKE NOTICE that:

1   I (*landlord*) of (*address*) request you pursuant to the regulations made under the Agricultural Holdings Act 1986 for the maintenance repair and insurance of fixed equipment[2] to execute the repair[s] for which you are liable as specified in those regulations and set out in the schedule below, and

2   I require you to execute such repair[s], and

3   if you fail to carry out any such repair[s] within 3 months from the date of service of this notice I shall exercise my right under the regulations to enter and execute such repair[s] and recover the reasonable cost of such repair[s] incurred by me from you immediately

SCHEDULE

(*item(s) of repair for which tenant is liable and necessary repair*)

(*signature of landlord*)

Notes

1   This notice is not a notice to remedy a breach of any term or condition of the tenancy failure to comply with which would entitle the landlord to serve a notice to quit under the AHA 1986, s 26(2), Sch 3, Pt I, Case D (see para A1.110). If this notice is not complied with, the landlord may do the work himself and recover the reasonable cost incurred by him from the tenant: Agriculture (Maintenance, Repair and Insurance of Fixed Equipment) Regulations 1973, SI 1973/1473, reg 3, Sch para 4(2). If the tenant wishes to dispute his liability, he should serve a counter-notice within one month on the landlord specifying the grounds on which and the times of which he denies liability: SI 1973/1473, reg 3, Sch para 4(3)(a): see para 23.17. As to the form of counter-notice, see Form AH45.

2   These regulations are prescribed by the Secretary of State for the Environment Food and Rural Affairs (see Form AH39 note 2) under the AHA 1986, s 7(1) and in Wales by the Welsh Assembly (pursuant to the National Assembly for Wales (Transfer of Functions) Order 1999, SI 1999/672). The current regulations are the Agriculture (Maintenance, Repair and Insurance of Fixed Equipment) Regulations 1973, SI 1973/1473, as amended by SI 1988/281. This notice applies only to repairs for which the tenant is liable under SI 1973/1473, reg 3, Sch paras 5–8: SI 1973/1473, reg 3, Sch para 4(2). The tenancy agreement may have imposed the liability for some of these items on the landlord in which case the tenancy agreement prevails, unless the terms of the tenancy agreement have been varied by an arbitrator under the AHA 1986, ss 7 or 8.

A2.27

AH45   Counter-notice by tenant requiring question of liability to execute repairs or replacements to be determined by arbitration[1]

AGRICULTURAL HOLDINGS ACT 1986

To (*landlord*) of (*address*) (*date*)
(*description of holding*)

BACKGROUND: I have received from you notice dated the ... ... day of ... . specifying repairs or replacements and requiring me to execute such repairs or replacements.

TAKE NOTICE that:

1   I (*tenant*) of (*address*) wish to contest my liability to execute such of those items of repair or replacement as are set out in the schedule below on the grounds set out in such schedule, and

2   that I require the question of my liability to execute such items of repair or replacement to be determined by arbitration under the provisions of the Agricultural Holdings Act 1986[2]

SCHEDULE

(*items of repair or replacement in respect of which and the grounds on which the tenant denies liability*)

(*signature of tenant*)

Notes

[1]   This counter-notice must be served within one month of the tenant's receipt of the landlord's notice (see Form AH44), specifying the grounds on which and the items of repair or replacement in respect of which he denies liability and require the question of liability to be determined by arbitration: see Form AH44 note 1. On service of this counter-notice on the landlord, the operation of the landlord's notice (including the running of time under it) is suspended until the date on which the arbitrator's award is delivered to the tenant: Agriculture (Maintenance, Repair and Insurance of Fixed Equipment) Regulations 1973, SI 1973/1473, reg 3, Sch paras 4(3)(b), 4(3)(c).

[2]   Ie the AHA 1986, ss 7(2), 8(1), 8(2) (see para A1.94–A1.95).

A2.28

AH46 Notice by tenant requesting and specifying repairs to be effected by landlord[1]

AGRICULTURAL HOLDINGS ACT 1986

To (*landlord*) of (address) (*date*)
(*description of holding*)

TAKE NOTICE that:

1   I (*tenant*) of (*address*) request you pursuant to the regulations made under the Agricultural Holdings Act 1986 for the maintenance repair and insurance of fixed equipment to execute the repairs or replacements for which you are liable as [specified in the regulations and[2] *or* set out] in the schedule below, and

2   that I require you to execute such repairs or replacements and

3   if you fail to carry out any such repairs or replacements within 3 months from the date of service of this notice I shall exercise my right under the above regulations to execute any such repairs or replacements and recover the reasonable cost incurred by me from you immediately except to the extent if any to which I am liable to bear the cost under the terms of the above regulations[3]

SCHEDULE

(*items of repair or replacement and necessary work for which landlord is liable*)

(*signature of tenant*)

Notes

[1]   Ie under the AHA 1986, s 7: see para 23.4.
[2]   This Form may be used where eg the landlord's liability for repairs or replacements arises from the tenancy agreement and not from the regulations in which case the words 'specified in the regulations and' should be deleted. The regulations currently in force are the Agriculture (Maintenance, Repair and Insurance of Fixed Equipment) Regulations 1973, SI 1973/1473, as amended by SI 1988/281.
[3]   If the landlord fails to execute the specified repairs within 3 months from his receipt of the notice, the tenant may execute them himself and recover the reasonable cost incurred (subject to SI 1973/1473, reg 3, Sch Pt I) from the landlord immediately: SI 1973/1473, reg 3, Sch para 12(1), (2), as substituted by SI 1988/281.If the landlord fails to execute any replacements which are his liability within 3 months of receipt of the notice, the tenant may execute any replacements which are his liability within 3 months of receipt of the notice, the tenant may execute the replacements himself and recover the reasonable cost incurred (subject to SI 1973/1473, reg 3, Sch Pt I) from the landlord except that the tenant may not recover in any one year of the tenancy terminating after 24 March 1988 any sum in excess of either a sum equal to the rent of the holding for that year or £2000 whichever is the smaller: SI 1973/1473, reg 3, Sch para 12(3), (4) (as substituted). If the landlord wishes to contest liability, he should serve a counter-notice: SI 1973/1473, reg 3, Sch para 12(5)(a) (as substituted): see para 23.13 ff. For a form of counter-notice, see Form AH47.

A2.29

AH47   Counter-notice by landlord requesting question of liability for repairs or replacements to be determined by arbitration[1]

AGRICULTURAL HOLDINGS ACT 1986

To (*tenant*) of (*address*) (*date*)
(*description of holding*)

BACKGROUND: I have received from you notice[2] dated the ... ... day of ... ...
. . specifying repairs and replacements and requiring me to execute such repairs and
replacements.

TAKE NOTICE that I (*landlord*) of (*address*) wish to contest my liability to execute
such of those items of repair and replacement as are set out in the schedule below on
the grounds set out in such schedule and that I require the question of my liability to
execute such items of repair and replacement to be determined by arbitration[3] under
the provisions of the Agricultural Holdings Act 1986

SCHEDULE

(*items of repair and replacement in respect of which landlord denies liability and
grounds for denial of liability*)

(*signature of landlord*)

Notes

1   Ie under the Agriculture (Maintenance, Repair and Insurance of Fixed Equipment)
    Regulations 1973, SI 1973/1473, reg 3, Sch para 12(5)(a) as substituted by SI 1988/281.
    The provisions relating to the tenant's counter-notice apply also to this notice: see Form
    AH45 note 1.
2   See Form AH46.
3   For arbitrations occurring after the coming into force of the Regulatory Reform (Agricul-
    tural Tenancies) (England and Wales) Order 2006, SI 2006/2805 on 19 October 2006 the
    arbitration will be governed by the Arbitration Act 1996. See also the AHA 1986, s 84, as
    amended by SI 2006/2805, art 7 in respect of the appointment of the arbitrator: see para
    47.19.

A2.30

AH48 Notice by landlord or tenant requiring question of whether an item of fixed equipment is or was redundant to the farming of the holding to be determined by arbitration[1]

AGRICULTURAL HOLDINGS ACT 1986

To (*landlord or tenant*) of (*address*) (*date*)
(*description of holding*)

BACKGROUND: I am of the opinion that the item of fixed equipment described in the
schedule below [is *or* was before it was [damaged *or* destroyed] by fire on the ... ... day
of ... .]redundant to the farming of the holding.

TAKE NOTICE that I (*landlord or tenant*) of (*address*) require the question of whether
such item of fixed equipment [is *or* was before it was [damaged or destroyed] by fire]
redundant to the farming of the holding to be agreed between us in writing within 2
months of the date of service on you of this notice and that if no agreement is reached
between us I require the question to be determined by arbitration under the provisions
of the Agricultural Holdings Act 1986

SCHEDULE

(*item of fixed equipment considered to be redundant*)

(*signature of landlord or tenant*)

Notes

1   Ie under the Agriculture (Maintenance, Repair and Insurance of Fixed Equipment) Regulations 1973, SI 1973/1473, reg 3, Sch para 13. As to fixed equipment, see Ch 23.

A2.31

AH49   Agreement that certain fixed equipment is obsolete or redundant[1]

AGRICULTURAL HOLDINGS ACT 1986

(*description of holding*) (*date*)

WE (*landlord*) of (*address*) and (*tenant*) of (*address*) landlord and tenant respectively of the above holding agree that the item[s] of fixed equipment specified in the schedule below [is *or* are] [obsolete *or* redundant] and that neither of us is to be liable to maintain repair or insure [it *or* them]

SCHEDULE

(*fixed equipment considered to be obsolete or redundant*)

(*signature of landlord and tenant*)

Notes

1   Ie under the Agriculture (Maintenance, Repair and Insurance of Fixed Equipment) Regulations 1973, SI 1973/1473, reg 3, Sch para 14(1). In default of agreement as to whether or not equipment is redundant, either party may require arbitration under SI 1973/1473, reg 3, Sch para 13(1) (see Form AH48): SI 1973/1473, reg 3, Sch para 14(1). As to fixed equipment, see Ch 23.

A2.32

AH50   Demand by landlord or tenant for arbitration of rent payable[1]

AGRICULTURAL HOLDINGS ACT 1986

To (*landlord or tenant*) of (*address*) (*date*)
(*description of holding*)

TAKE NOTICE that pursuant to the Agricultural Holdings Act 1986 section 12 I (*landlord or tenant*) of (*address*) demand that the rent to be payable in respect of the above holding as from the next termination date as defined in that Act[2] shall be referred to arbitration.[3]

This notice is given without prejudice to any other notice or act in connection with the tenancy which has been or may after the date of this notice be given or done by me or on behalf of me or any other interested party

(*signature of landlord or tenant*)

Notes

1   Any demand for reference to arbitration as to rent must be made by a notice in writing: AHA 1986, s 12(1): see para 25.7 ff.
2   Ie the next day following the date of the demand on which the tenancy of the holding could have been determined by notice to quit given at the date of the demand: AHA 1986, s 12(4).
3   For a form of appointment of an arbitrator by agreement, see Form AA2. As to a form of application to the President of the Royal Institution of Chartered Surveyors for the appointment of an arbitrator, see Form AA4.

A2.33

AH51   Memorandum for indorsement on tenancy agreement to provide for increase in rent when agreed between parties instead of under an arbitration[1]

MEMORANDUM

(*description of holding*)

In consideration of [the within-named landlord] of the above holding undertaking not to refer to arbitration under the Agricultural Holdings Act 1986 section 12[2] the question of rent to be payable for the above holding in respect of the period prior to the ..... day of ... .[3] [the within-named tenant] of the above holding agrees that:

1   The rent payable in respect of the above holding (including all existing increases in respect of improvements or otherwise) shall as from the ..... day of ... . be £... (... pounds) which shall be payable in the same way as the present rent of the above holding

[2   The proviso for re-entry contained in the within-written tenancy agreement relating to the above holding shall be exercisable in respect of non-payment of the increased rent or any part of it]; and

3   In consideration of the premises all the terms and conditions of the within-written tenancy agreement varied as above shall remain in full force and effect

AS WITNESS our hands the ..... day of ... .

(*signature of landlord and tenant*)

Notes

1   For a form of demand for arbitration as to rent, see Form AH50.
2   Ie the AHA 1986, s 12: see para 27.7 ff.
3   This date must be such that the next termination date following this date is at least 3 years from the date on which the increase is stated to take effect in the memorandum. If it is not, there is no consideration passing from the landlord to the tenant as the landlord cannot in any event serve an effective demand for arbitration if the next termination date following the demand falls earlier than 3 years from, inter alia, the date of the previous increase in rent ie the date specified in the memorandum on which the increase is to take effect: see AHA 1986, Sch 2 para 4(1). As to 'termination date', see AHA 1986, ss 12(4), 25.

A2.34

AH52   Notice by landlord requiring increase of rent on completion of improvements[1]

AGRICULTURAL HOLDINGS ACT 1986

To (*tenant*) of (*address*) (*date*)
(*description of holding*)

TAKE NOTICE that I (*landlord*) of (*address*) require under the Agricultural Holdings Act 1986 section 13 that the rent of the above holding shall be increased from the ... ... day of ... . being the date of completion of the improvement[s] specified in the schedule below by an amount equal to the increase in the rental value of the above holding attributable to the carrying out of the improvement[s] namely the sum of £... (... pounds) per year

Section 13(7) of that Act provides that where the parties do not agree on the amount of the proposed increase of rent the dispute shall be determined by arbitration under that Act[2]

SCHEDULE

(*short description of improvement(s) and date when each was completed*)

(*signature of landlord*)

Notes

1   A rent increase may be claimed in respect of an improvement carried out by the landlord, even though he may also be entitled to compensation for the same, provided the improvement is within the AHA 1986, s 13(2) (see para 25.48 ff): AHA 1986, s 13(1), (8). The notice must be served within 6 months of the completion of the improvement: AHA 1986, s 13(1).
2   For a form of appointment of an arbitrator by agreement, see Form AA2.

A2.35

AH53 **Memorandum for indorsement on tenancy agreement to provide for increase in rent in respect of improvements under the Agricultural Holdings Act 1986 section 13 when agreed between parties instead of under arbitration[1]**

MEMORANDUM

(description of holding)

In consideration of [the within-named landlord] having carried out in agreement with [the within-named tenant] on the above holding the improvement[s] specified in the schedule below it has been agreed between them that:

1   The rent payable in respect of the above holding shall with effect from the day of ... .[2] be increased to £... (... pounds) per year;

2   This increase of rent shall operate by virtue of the Agricultural Holdings Act 1986 section 13;

3   The proviso for re-entry contained in the within-written tenancy agreement shall be exercisable in respect of non-payment of the increase rent or any part of it; and

4   In consideration of the premises all the terms and conditions of the within-written tenancy agreement varied as above shall remain in full force and effect

AS WITNESS our hands the ... . . day of ... .

SCHEDULE

(improvement(s) carried out by landlord)

(signature of landlord and tenant)

Notes

[1]   As to improvements in respect of which a landlord may recover increased rent see Form AH52 note 1.
[2]   Ie the date when the improvements were completed.

A2.36

AH54 Demand by landlord or tenant for arbitration as to variation of terms of tenancy relating to permanent pasture[1]

AGRICULTURAL HOLDINGS ACT 1986

To *(landlord or tenant)* of *(address)* *(date)*
(description of holding)

BACKGROUND: under the contract for tenancy in respect of the above holding between us made the ... ... day of ... ... provision is made for the maintenance of [specified land *or* a specified proportion of the above holding] as permanent pasture

NOW I (*landlord or tenant*) of (*address*) give you notice under the Agricultural Holdings Act 1986 section 14[2] that I demand a reference to arbitration under that Act of the question whether it is expedient in order to secure the full and efficient farming of the above holding that the area of land required to be maintained as permanent pasture should be reduced

(*signature of landlord or tenant*)

Notes

[1] This notice may be accompanied by a letter specifying suggested arbitrators. If there is a written tenancy agreement in existence, any relevant arbitration clause must be kept in mind particularly any specified method of appointing an arbitrator. The arbitration will be governed by the Arbitration Act 1996 for those arbitrations occurring after the coming into force of the Regulatory Reform (Agricultural Tenancies) (England and Wales) Order 2006, SI 2006/2805 on 19 October 2006. See also the AHA 1986, s 84 as amended by SI 2006/2805, art 7 in respect of the appointment of the arbitrator: see para 47.19.

[2] Ie the AHA 1986, s 14: see para 24.8.

A2.37

AH55   Notice by tenant to landlord of intention to remove fixtures or buildings[1]

AGRICULTURAL HOLDINGS ACT 1986

To (*landlord*) of (*address*) (*date*)
(*description of holding*)

I (*tenant*) of (*address*) give you notice under the Agricultural Holdings Act 1986 section 10 that I intend to exercise my rights under that Section to remove the [fixture[s] [and] building[s] specified in the schedule below

SCHEDULE

(*fixtures and/or buildings which tenant intends to remove*)

(*signature of tenant*)

Notes

[1] This notice must be served at least one month before the exercise of the right and the termination of the tenancy and the tenant must have paid all rent owed by him and performed or satisfied all his other obligations to the landlord in respect of the holding: AHA 1986, s 10(3) (see para 23.24). Subject to the provisions of AHA 1986, s 10(2) and to any counter-notice served by the landlord under AHA 1986, s 10(4) (as to counter-notice, see Form AH56), the fixtures and buildings specified in this notice remain the tenant's property and are removable by him at any time during the continuance of the tenancy or before the expiry of two months from its termination: AHA 1986, s 10(1). As to the tenant's right to remove fixtures or buildings, see para 23.23.

A2.38

AH56   Counter-notice by landlord electing to purchase fixtures and buildings comprised in tenant's notice[1]

AGRICULTURAL HOLDINGS ACT 1986

To (*tenant*) of (*address*) (*date*)
(*description of holding*)

With reference to your notice to me dated the ... ... day of ... . under the Agricultural Holdings Act 1986 section 10 of your intention to remove the [fixture[s] and] building[s]] specified in your notice I (*landlord*) of (*address*) give you counter-notice under section 10(4) of that Act that I elect to purchase at the fair value to an incoming tenant the [fixture[s] and] building[s]] specified in your notice and described in the schedule below

SCHEDULE

(*fixtures and/or buildings specified in tenant's notice which landlord intends to purchase*)

(*signature of landlord*)

Notes

[1]   This counter-notice must be given before the expiration of the tenant's notice: AHA 1986, s 10(4) (see para 23.24). As to the tenant's notice, see Form AH55.

A2.39

AH57   Notice of change of landlord[1]

AGRICULTURAL HOLDINGS ACT 1986

To (*tenant*) of (*holding*) (*date*)
(*description of holding*)

TAKE NOTICE pursuant to the Agricultural Holdings Act 1986 that:

1   as from the ... . . day of ... . I (*original landlord*) of (*address*) cease[d] to be entitled to receive the rents and profits of the above holding;

2   as from that date the person[s] who [is *or* are] given below [is *or* are] entitled to receive the rents and profits of the above holding [is *or* are] (*new landlord*) of (*address*) ('the New Landlord')

3   accordingly all notices or other documents required to be served on the landlord with regard to the above holding should as from the date [mentioned above *or* of this notice] be served on [him *or* them]; and

4   the rent due from you for the period up to the ..... day of ... . should be paid to the New Landlord

(*signature of original landlord*)[2]

Notes

[1]   Unless or until the tenant receives notice of the change of landlord, he is entitled to serve or deliver any notice or other document on the original landlord: AHA 1986, s 93(5) (see para 42.25).

[2]   It is desirable that this notice should be given by the original landlord, but there may be cases where it has to be given by the new landlord; if so, it may be suitably amended.

Division II

TERMINATION OF TENANCY

A2.39A Forms AH60 to AH62 are statutorily prescribed forms which *must* be used without modification or 'improvement' by the draftsman. Although in general a form substantially to the like effect will suffice, draftsmen are recommended not in fact to alter or vary the prescribed form in any particular and also to ensure that the statutorily prescribed notes which comprise part of the form are reproduced as well as the form itself.

Division II

TERMINATION OF TENANCY

Contents

Division II
TERMINATION OF TENANCY

A: PRELIMINARY NOTICES: NOTICE TO PAY AND NOTICE TO REMEDY

A2.40

AH58   Notice to tenant to pay rent[1]

SCHEDULE   Regulations 2(2), 3 and 4

FORM 1
AGRICULTURAL HOLDINGS ACT 1986

Schedule 3, Part 1, Case D

Notice to tenant to pay rent due

Re: the holding known as ....

To ....

(Name and address of tenant)

> IMPORTANT—FAILURE TO COMPLY
> WITH THIS NOTICE MAY BE RELIED
> ON AS REASON FOR A NOTICE TO
> QUIT UNDER CASE D. IF YOU WANT
> YOUR TENANCY TO CONTINUE YOU
> MUST ACT QUICKLY. READ THE
> NOTICE AND ALL THE NOTES
> CAREFULLY. IF YOU ARE IN ANY
> DOUBT ABOUT THE ACTION YOU
> SHOULD TAKE, GET ADVICE
> IMMEDIATELY, eg FROM A SOLICITOR,
> SURVEYOR OR CITIZENS ADVICE
> BUREAU.

1   I hereby give you notice that I require you to pay within two months from the date of service of this Notice* the rent due in respect of the above holding as set out below:

*   Note: This Notice may not be served before the rent is due.

PARTICULARS OF RENT NOT PAID

Date when due   *Amount due*

....

2   This Notice is given in accordance with Case D in Part I of Schedule 3 to the Agricultural Holdings Act 1986, and failure to comply with it within the period specified above may be relied on as a reason for a notice to quit under Case D.

3   Your attention is drawn to the Notes following the signature to this Notice.

Signed ....

Date ....

(If signed by any person other than the landlord of the holding, state in what capacity or by what authority the signature is affixed.)

Address ....
... .
... .
....

NOTES

1   You cannot at this stage refer to arbitration either your liability to comply with this Notice to pay rent or any other question as to the validity of the Notice. You will, however, be entitled to do so later if a notice to quit is served on you on the ground that you have failed to comply with this Notice to pay rent. That is the *only* opportunity you will have to challenge this Notice.

2   At this stage under article 9 of the Agricultural Holdings (Arbitration on Notices) Order 1987 (SI 1987/710) you have one month after the service of the notice to quit within which you can serve on your landlord a notice in writing requiring the question to be determined by arbitration under the Agricultural Holdings Act 1986 (c 5).

3   You will then have three months from the date of service of that notice in which to appoint an arbitrator by agreement or (in default of such agreement) to make an application under paragraph 1 of Schedule 11 to that Act for the appointment of an arbitrator. If this is not done by you or your landlord your notice requiring arbitration ceases to be effective (see article 10 of that Order).

Notes (not part of the prescribed form)

¹   This Form is form 1 in the Agricultural Holdings (Forms of Notice to Pay Rent or to Remedy) Regulations 1987, SI 1987/711, Schedule. The notice must be in the prescribed form or one substantially to the same effect: SI 1987/711, regs 2, 3. The form as reproduced here follows the precise wording of the prescribed form, but not the exact layout and design. It is recommended that the prescribed form is not altered or varied in any way. This Form may be used under the AHA 1986, Sch 3 Pt I, Case D (see para 31.27) by virtue of the Interpretation Act 1978, s 17(2)(a), (b) (41 Halsbury's Statutes (4th Edn)

STATUTES) and the AHA 1986, s 99, Sch 13 para 1(2). The provisions of the Agricultural Holdings (Notices to Quit) Act 1977, s 2(3), Case D have been repealed and re-enacted in the AHA 1986, Sch 3 Pt I, Case D.

2   The first set of notes above are part of the prescribed form and must be included with the notice served on the tenant.

A2.41

AH59   Notice to tenant to remedy breach of tenancy agreement by doing work of repair, maintenance or replacement[1]

FORM 2
AGRICULTURAL HOLDINGS ACT 1986

Schedule 3, Part 1, Case D

Notice to tenant to remedy breach of tenancy by doing work of repair, maintenance or replacement

Re: the holding known as ....

To ....

(Name and address of tenant)

> **IMPORTANT—FAILURE TO COMPLY WITH THIS NOTICE MAY BE RELIED ON AS REASON FOR A NOTICE TO QUIT UNDER CASE D. IF YOU WANT YOUR TENANCY TO CONTINUE YOU MUST ACT QUICKLY. READ THE NOTICE AND ALL THE NOTES CAREFULLY. IF YOU ARE IN ANY DOUBT ABOUT THE ACTION YOU SHOULD TAKE, GET ADVICE IMMEDIATELY, eg FROM A SOLICITOR, SURVEYOR OR CITIZENS ADVICE BUREAU.**

1   I hereby give you notice that I require you to remedy within ... ... months* from the date of service of this Notice the breaches, set out below, of the terms or conditions of your tenancy, being breaches which are capable of being remedied of terms or conditions which are not inconsistent with your responsibilities to farm the holding in accordance with the rules of good husbandry.

*   Note: This period must be a reasonable period for the tenant to remedy the breaches and must in any event be not less than six months: see para 31.51.

2   This Notice requires the doing of work of repair, maintenance or replacement specified below.

PARTICULARS OF BREACHES OF TERMS OR CONDITIONS OF TENANCY

Term or condition of tenancy	Particulars of breach and work required to remedy it
....	....
....	....

3 This Notice is given in accordance with Case D in Part I of Schedule 3 to the Agricultural Holdings Act 1986, and failure to comply with it within the period specified above may be relied on as a reason for a notice to quit under Case D.

4 Your attention is drawn to the Notes following the signature to this Notice.

Signed ....

Date ....

(If signed by any person other than the landlord of the holding, state in what capacity or by what authority the signature is affixed.)

Address ....
....
....
....

NOTES

In these Notes 'the Order' means the Agricultural Holdings (Arbitration on Notices) Order 1987 (SI 1987/710)

What to do if you wish –

(a) to contest your liability to do the work, or any part of the work, required by this notice to remedy (Question (a)); or

(b) to request the deletion from this Notice to remedy of any item or part of an item of work on the ground that it is unnecessary or unjustified (Question (b)); or

(c) to request the substitution in the case of any item or part of an item of work of a different method or material for the method or material which this Notice to remedy would otherwise require to be followed or used (Question (c)).

1 Questions (a), (b) and (c) mentioned in the heading to these Notes can be referred to arbitration under article 3(1) of the Order. To do so you *must* serve a notice in writing upon your landlord *within one month* of the service upon you of this Notice to remedy. The notice you serve upon your landlord should specify

(a) if you are referring Question (a), the items for which you deny liability,

(b) if you are referring Question (b), the items you wish to be deleted,

(c) if you are referring Question (c), the different methods or materials you wish to be substituted,

and in each case should require the matter to be determined by arbitration under the Agricultural Holdings Act 1986 (c 5). You will not be able to refer Question (a), (b) or (c) to arbitration later, on receipt of a notice to quit. This action does not prevent your settling the matter in writing by agreement with your landlord.

Carrying on the work

2   If you refer to any of these Questions (a), (b) and (c) to arbitration, you are not obliged to carry out the work which is the subject of the reference to arbitration unless and until the arbitrator decides that you are liable to do it; but you *must* carry out any work which you are not referring to arbitration.

3   If you are referring Question (a) to arbitration you may if you wish carry out any of the work which is the subject of that reference to arbitration without waiting for the arbitrator's award. If you do this and the arbitrator finds that you have carried out any such work which you were under no obligation to do, he will determine at the time he makes his award the reasonable cost of any such work which you have done and you will be entitled to recover this from your landlord (see article 8 of the Order). This provision does *not* apply in the case of work referred to arbitration under Question (b) or Question (c).

What to do if you wish to contest any other question arising under this Notice to remedy

4   If you wish to contest any other question arising under this Notice other than Question (a), (b) or (c), such as whether the time specified in the Notice to do work is a reasonable period in which to carry out the work, you should refer the question to arbitration in either of the following ways, according to whether or not you are also at the same time referring Question (a), (b) or (c) to arbitration—

    (a)   If you are referring Question (a), (b) or (c) to arbitration, then you *must* also refer to arbitration at the same time any other questions relevant to this Notice which you may wish to dispute.

        To do this, you should include in the Notice to your landlord referred to in Note 1 above a statement of the other questions which you require to be determined by arbitration under the Agricultural Holdings Act 1986 (see article 4(1) of the Order).

    (b)   If you are not referring Questions (a), (b) or (c) to arbitration but wish to contest some other question arising under this Notice to remedy, you may refer that question to arbitration either now, on receipt of this Notice, or later, if you get a notice to quit.

        To refer the question to arbitration now, you should serve on your landlord *within one month* after the service of this Notice to remedy a notice in writing setting out what it is you require to be determined by arbitration under the Agricultural Holdings Act 1986 (see article 4(2)(a) of the Order).

        Alternatively, you have one month after the service of the notice to quit within which you can serve on your landlord a notice in writing requiring the question to be determined by arbitration under the 1986 Act (see article 9 of the Order). You will then have three months from the date of service of that notice in which to appoint an arbitrator by agreement or (in default of such agreement) to make an application under paragraph 1 of Schedule 11 to that Act for the appointment of an arbitrator. If this is not done by you or your landlord your notice requiring arbitration ceases to be effective (see article 10 of the Order).

Warning

5   Notes 1 to 4 above outline the *only* opportunities you have to challenge this Notice to remedy.

Extensions of time allowed for complying with this Notice to remedy

6   If you refer to arbitration now any question arising from this Notice to remedy, the time allowed for complying with the Notice will be extended until the

termination of the arbitration. If the arbitrator decides that you are liable to do any of the work specified in this Notice to remedy, he will extend the time in which the work is to be done by such period as he thinks fit (see article 6(2) of the Order).

Warning as to the effect which any extension of the time allowed for complying with this notice to remedy may have upon a subsequent notice to quit

7   If your time for doing the work is extended as mentioned in note 6 above, the arbitrator can specify a date for the termination of your tenancy should you fail to complete the work you are liable to do within the extended time. Then, if you did fail to complete that work within the extended time, your landlord could serve a notice to quit upon you expiring on the date which the arbitrator had specified, and the notice would be valid even though that date might be less than twelve months after the next term date, and might not expire on a term date. The arbitrator cannot, however, specify a termination date which is less than six months after the expiry of the extended time to do the work. Nor can he specify a date which is earlier than would have been possible if you had not required arbitration on this Notice to remedy and had failed to do the work (see article 7 of the Order).

Notes (not part of the prescribed form)

¹   This Form is form 2 in the Agricultural Holdings (Forms of Notice to Pay Rent or to Remedy) Regulations 1987, SI 1987/711, Sch. The notice must be in the prescribed form: or one substantially to the same effect: SI 1987/711, regs 2, 4. The form, as reproduced here, follows the precise wording of the prescribed form, but not the exact layout and design. It is recommended that the prescribed form is not altered or varied in any way. This Form may be used under the AHA 1986, Sch 3, Pt I, Case D (see para 31.27) by virtue of the Interpretation Act 1978, s 17(2)(a), (b) [(41 Halsbury's Statutes (4th Edn) STATUTES)] and the AHA 1986, s 99, Sch 13 para 1(2). The provisions of the Agricultural Holdings (Notices to Quit) Act 1977, s 2(3), Case D have been repealed and re-enacted in the AHA 1986, Sch 3 Pt I, Case D.
²   The statutory notes must be included with the notice to remedy served on the tenant. These notes should not be included.

A2.42

AH60   Notice to tenant to remedy breach of tenancy agreement (not being a notice requiring the doing of any work of repair, maintenance or replacement)¹

FORM 3
AGRICULTURAL HOLDINGS ACT 1986

Schedule 3, Part 1, Case D

Notice to tenant to remedy breach of tenancy (not being a notice requiring the doing of any work of repair, maintenance or replacement)

Re: the holding known as ....

To ....

(Name and address of tenant)

> **IMPORTANT—FAILURE TO COMPLY WITH THIS NOTICE MAY BE RELIED ON AS REASON FOR A NOTICE TO QUIT UNDER CASE D. IF YOU WANT YOUR TENANCY TO CONTINUE YOU MUST ACT QUICKLY. READ THE NOTICE AND ALL THE NOTES CAREFULLY. IF YOU ARE IN ANY DOUBT ABOUT THE ACTION YOU SHOULD TAKE, GET ADVICE IMMEDIATELY, eg FROM A SOLICITOR, SURVEYOR OR CITIZENS ADVICE BUREAU.**

1   I hereby give you notice that I require you to remedy within ... ... months from the date of service of this Notice the breaches, set out below, of the terms or conditions of your tenancy, being breaches which are capable of being remedied of terms or conditions which are not inconsistent with your responsibilities to farm the holding in accordance with the rules of good husbandry.

Particulars of breaches of terms or conditions of tenancy

Term or condition of tenancy   *Particulars of breach*

....

....

2   This Notice is given in accordance with Case D in Part I of Schedule 3 to the Agricultural Holdings Act 1986, and failure to comply with it within the period specified may be relied on as a reason for a notice to quit under Case D.

3   Your attention is drawn to the Notes following the signature to this Notice.

Signed ....

Date ....

(If signed by any person other than the landlord of the holding, state in what capacity or by what authority the signature is affixed.)

Address ....

....

....

....

NOTES

1   You cannot at this stage refer to arbitration either your liability to comply with this Notice to remedy or any other question as to the validity of the Notice. You will, however, be entitled to do so later if a notice to quit is served on you on the ground that you have failed to comply with this Notice to remedy. That is the *only* opportunity you will have to challenge this Notice.

2   At that stage under article 9 of the Agricultural Holdings (Arbitration on Notices) Order 1987 (SI 1987/710), you have one month after the service of the

notice to quit within which you can serve on your landlord a notice in writing requiring the question to be determined by arbitration under the Agricultural Holdings Act 1986 (c 5).

3   You will then have three months from the date of service of that notice in which to appoint an arbitrator by agreement or (in default of such agreement) to make an application under paragraph 1 of Schedule II to that Act for the appointment of an arbitrator. If this is not done by you or your landlord your notice requiring arbitration ceases to be effective (see article 10 of that Order).

Notes (not part of the prescribed form)

1   This Form is Form 3 in the Agricultural Holdings (Forms of Notice to Pay Rent or to Remedy) Regulations 1987, SI 1987/711, Sch. The notice must be in the prescribed form or one substantially to the same effect: SI 1987/711, reg 3. The Form, as reproduced here, follows the precise wording of the prescribed form, but not the exact layout and design. It is recommended that the prescribed form is not altered or varied in any way. The Notes above which appear at the end of all three prescribed forms – Forms 1, 2 and 3 – form part of the forms which *must* be reproduced and served on the tenant as part of the form. Failure to reproduce the forms in their entirety will invalidate the forms served.

2   This note should not be included in the notice served.

B: NOTICES TO QUIT

A2.43

AH61 Notice to determine lease or tenancy of two years or more at end of term[1]

AGRICULTURAL HOLDINGS ACT 1986

To (*landlord or tenant*) of (*address*) (*date*)
(*description of holding*)

I (*landlord or tenant*) of (*address*) your [landlord *or* tenant] of the above holding give you notice that it is my intention to determine [your *or* my] tenancy of ALL THAT holding and premises known as (*description of holding*) which [you *or* I] hold as tenant under a[n] [agreement for] lease made the .... day of .... between (1) myself and (2) yourself on the .... day of .... being the date fixed for the expiration of the term granted by the [agreement for] lease and I [require you *or* intend] to quit and deliver up possession of the above holding accordingly

[The reason I intend to determine your tenancy is : *specify*]

(*signature of landlord or tenant*)

Notes

1   This notice must be served not less than one nor more than 2 years before the date fixed for the expiry of the term: AHA 1986, s 3(1)(a) (see para 20.7). If the reason the landlord wishes to determine the tenancy is one of those referred to in AHA 1986, s 27(3)(a)–(c), he should state the reason specifically in the notice as this precludes the tenant from recovering 'additional' compensation (AHA 1986, s 60(2)) for disturbance: AHA 1986, s 61(3)(a). If the landlord wishes to rely on any of the cases referred to in AHA 1986,

Sch 3, Pt I, he should specifically refer to the relevant case in this notice because this precludes the tenant from issuing a counter-notice: AHA 1986, s 26(2). As to notices to quit, see Ch 28.

A2.44

AH62   Notice to quit given by landlord without any special reason stated[1]

AGRICULTURAL HOLDINGS ACT 1986

To (*tenant*) of (*address*) (*date*)
(*description of holding*)

[I *or* We] [(*name of agents*) of (*address*) as agents for and on behalf of] (*landlord*) of (*address*) give you notice to quit and deliver up possession of ALL THAT holding and premises known as (*description of holding*) which you hold of [me *or* him] as tenant [on the .... day of .... or at the expiration of the year of your tenancy which shall expire after the end of 12 months from the date of service of this notice][2]

(*signature of* (*agents of*) *landlord*)

Notes

[1]   As to the advisability of the inclusion of the landlord's reasons for serving the notice see Form AH61 note 1 ante. As to counter-notice by the tenant see Form AH72. As to notices to quit and counter-notices, see Chs 28 and 30.

[2]   A notice to quit an agricultural holding is invalid if it purports to determine the tenancy before the expiry of 12 months from the end of the then current year of the tenancy: AHA 1986, s 25(1) (see para 28.12). See the exceptions in AHA 1986, s 25(2). As to service, see AHA 1986, s 93: see para 42.13 ff.

A2.45

AH63 Notice to quit given by landlord with indorsement of special reason[s] where none of the grounds in the Agricultural Holdings Act 1986 Schedule 3 Part I applies[1]

AGRICULTURAL HOLDINGS ACT 1986

To (*tenant*) of (*address*) (*date*)
(*description of holding*)

[I *or* We] [(*name of agents*) of (*address*) as agents for and on behalf of] (*landlord*) of (*address*) give you notice to quit[2] and deliver up possession of ALL THAT holding and premises known as (*description of holding*) which you hold of [me *or* him] as tenant [on the .... day of .... or at the expiration of the year of your tenancy which shall expire next after the end of 12 months from the date of service[3] of this notice] This notice is given on and for the following ground[s] and reason[s]:

1   The carrying out of the purpose for which [your landlord *or* I] propose[s] to determine the tenancy is desirable:

     1.1   in the interests of good husbandry with regard to the above holding treated as a separate unit; *and/or*

     1.2   in the interests of sound management of the above holding [or the estate of which the above holding forms part]; *and/or*

     1.3   for the purposes of [agricultural research education experiment or demonstration *or* the enactments relating to smallholdings]; *and/or*

     1.4   for the purposes of the enactments relating to allotments; *and/or*

2   [Your landlord *or* I] will suffer hardship unless this notice has effect

(signature of (agents of) landlord)

Notes

1   If any of the grounds referred to in the AHA 1986, s 26, Sch 3, Pt I (as amended) applies, this Form should not be used: see Form AH67. The tenant will be entitled to basic and additional compensation for disturbance (AHA 1986, s 60) unless this is excluded or restricted by the AHA 1986, s 61. As to the advisability of indorsing the reason for the notice see Form AH61 note 1. As to notices to quit, see Ch 28.
2   See Form AH62 note 2.
3   As to service, see the AHA 1986, s 93: see para 42.13 ff.

A2.46

AH64   Notice to quit by tenant[1]

AGRICULTURAL HOLDINGS ACT 1986

To (*landlord*) of (*address*) (*date*)
(*description of holding*)

[I *or* We] [(*name of agents*) of (*address*) as agents for and on behalf of] (*tenant*) of (*address*) give you notice of [my *or* his] intention to quit and deliver up possession of ALL THAT holding and premises known as (*description of holding*) which [I *or* he] hold[s] as tenant from you [on the .... day of .... or at the expiration of the year of the tenancy which shall expire next after the end of 12 months from the date of service[2] of this notice]

(signature of (agents of) tenant)

Notes

1   See Form AH62 note 2. A tenant will, by giving notice to quit to his landlord, destroy any underlease he has created: see *Pennell v Payne* [1995] QB 192, [1995] 2 All ER 592, [1995] 2 WLR 261, CA, *Barrett and others v Morgan* [2000] 1 All ER 481 and *PW & Co v Milton Gate Investments Ltd* [2003] EWHC 1994 (Ch), [2004] Ch 142 (see para 29.17 ff).
2   As to service, see the AHA 1986, s 93: see para 42.13 ff.

A2.47

AH65 Notice to quit by landlord pursuant to a provision in the contract of tenancy for non-agricultural purpose¹

AGRICULTURAL HOLDINGS ACT 1986

To (*tenant*) of (*address*) (*date*)
(*description of holding*)

[I *or* We] [(*name of agents*) of (*address*) as agents for and on behalf of] (*landlord*) of (*address*) give you notice to quit and deliver up possession of [ALL THAT holding and premises known as (*description of holding*) or OS No[s] .... [and ....]forming part of the holding and premises known as (*description of holding*) which you hold of [me *or* him] as tenant on the .... day of .... ²

The landlord requires these premises for the purpose of a non-agricultural use namely (*specify use*) and this notice is given pursuant to clause .... of your contract of tenancy³

(*signature of* (*agents of*) *landlord*)

Notes

¹   A notice to quit an agricultural holding which purports to determine the tenancy before the expiry of 12 months from the end of the then current year of the tenancy is not invalid if given pursuant to a provision in the contract of tenancy authorising the resumption of possession of the whole or part for some specified non-agricultural use: AHA 1986, s 25(2)(*b*) (see para 32.9). As to service, see AHA 1986, s 93: see para 42.13 ff. As to notices to quit, see Ch 28.

²   In practice, more than one month's notice should be given to enable the tenant to take advantage of the right to increased basic compensation for disturbance: see AHA 1986, s 60(3), (6)(a). If the clause provides for resumption of possession on one month's notice or less, the whole clause is void: *Re Disraeli's Agreement, Cleasby v Park Estate (Hughenden) Ltd* [1939] Ch 382, [1938] 4 All ER 658; *Coates v Diment* [1951] 1 All ER 890; *Parry v Million Pigs Ltd* (1980) 260 Estates Gazette 281.

³   If the requirements of the AHA 1986, s 26(2), Sch 3 Pt I, Case B as substituted by the AH(A)A 1990 (AH(A)A 1990), s 1(1), (2) are satisfied, this ground should also be given as the tenant may otherwise give counter-notice invoking the jurisdiction of the Agricultural Land Tribunal: see para 32.13 ff.

A2.48

AH66   Notice to quit given by tenant to subtenant¹

AGRICULTURAL HOLDINGS ACT 1986

To (*subtenant*) of (*address*) .... (*date*)
(*description of holding*)

[I *or* We] [(*name of agents*) of (*address*) as agents for and on behalf of] (*tenant*) give you notice to quit and deliver up possession of ALL THAT holding and premises known as (*description of holding*) which you hold of [me *or* him] as tenant on the .... day of .... and [I *or* We] further give you notice that [I *or* he] [have *or* has] been given notice to quit the above holding and premises by (*landlord*) of whom [I *or* he] hold[s] as tenant[2]

(signature of (agents of) tenant)

Notes

[1] A notice to quit an agricultural holding given by a tenant to his subtenant is not invalid even though it purports to determine the tenancy before the expiry of 12 months from the end of the then current year of the tenancy: AHA 1986, s 25(2)(c) (see para 30.10). As to service of the notice see AHA 1986, s 93: see para 42.13 ff. As to notices to quit and sub-tenancies, see Ch 28 and para 29.17 ff.

[2] AHA 1986, s 26(1) which provides for a counter-notice requiring consent of the tribunal to a notice to quit does not apply where the tenant's notice states that he has received notice to quit from his landlord: Agricultural Holdings (Arbitration on Notices) Order 1987, SI 1987/710, art 16. The tenant's notice to quit to his sub-tenant has effect only if the notice to quit given to the tenant by the landlord itself has effect: SI 1987/710, art 16(2). Where under the AHA 1986, s 32 the tenant accepts notice to quit part of a holding as notice to quit the whole, the notice to quit given by the tenant to his subtenant is deemed to be a notice to quit the whole for the purposes of the Agricultural Holdings (Arbitration on Notices) Order 1987, art 16: SI 1987/710, art 16(3): see para 29.1 ff.

A2.49

AH67   Notice to quit given by landlord for one of the special cases to be stated in the notice under the Agricultural Holdings Act 1986 Schedule 3 Part I[1]

AGRICULTURAL HOLDINGS ACT 1986

To (*tenant*) of (*address*) (*date*)
(*description of holding*)

[I *or* We] [(*name of agents*) of (*address*) as agents for and on behalf of] (*landlord*) of (*address*) give you notice to quit and deliver up possession of ALL THAT holding and premises known as (*description of holding*) which you hold of [me *or* us *or* him] as tenant [on the .... day of .... *or* at the expiration of the year of your tenancy which shall expire next after the end of 12 months from the date of service[2] of this notice]

This notice is given on and for the following ground[s] and reason[s] and pursuant to the appropriate paragraph[s] set out in the Agricultural Holdings Act 1986 Schedule 3 Part I:

[Case A   The holding is let as a smallholding by [a smallholding authority *or* the Minister] in pursuance of the Agriculture Act 1970 Part III and was so let on the .... day of .... [3] and you have attained the age of 65 [and suitable alternative accommodation is available for you *or* will be available for you when this notice takes effect[4]]] and the instrument under which the tenancy was granted contains an acknowledgment signed by you that the tenancy is subject to the provisions of [this Case *or* the Agricultural Holdings (Notices to Quit) Act 1977 Section 2(3) Case I]] [5]

[Case B   The land which is the subject of this notice is required for a use other than for agriculture [*state the use in question*].]

for which permission has been granted on an application made under the enactments relating to town and country planning[6]

or

for which permission under the enactments relating to town and country planning is granted by a general development order by reason only of the fact that the use is authorised by (i) a private or local Act or (ii) an order approved by both Houses of Parliament or (iii) an order made under sections 14 or 16 of the Harbours Act 1964[7]

or

for which a provision that (i) is contained in any Act but (ii) does not form part of the enactments relating to town and country planning deems permission under those enactments to have been granted[8]

or

which the provisions referred to in Case B(c) of Schedule 3 of the Agricultural Holdings Act 1986 deem not to constitute development for the purposes of the enactments relating to town and country planning[9]

or

for which permission is not required under the enactments relating to town and country planning by reason only of Crown immunity

[Case C   The Agricultural Land Tribunal certified not more than 6 months before the giving of this notice that under the Agricultural Holdings Act 1986 Schedule 3 Part II paragraph 9 it was satisfied in relation to the holding that you were not fulfilling your responsibilities to farm in accordance with the rules of good husbandry][11]

[Case D   At the date of the giving of this notice you have failed to comply with a written notice[12] dated the .... day of .... served on you by your landlord which required you [within 2 months of service of the notice to pay rent due in respect of the holding *or* within the reasonable period specified in the notice to remedy the breach[es] by you capable of being remedied of the terms and conditions of your tenancy not inconsistent with your responsibilities to farm in accordance with the rules of good husbandry]] [5]

[Case E   At the date of the giving of this notice the interest of your landlord in the holding has been materially prejudiced by your commission of a breach incapable of remedy of [a *or* the] term[s] or condition[s] of your tenancy not inconsistent with your responsibilities to farm in accordance with the rules of good husbandry in that (*specify breach*)] [5]

[Case F   At the date of the giving of this notice you have become insolvent]
[Case H][13]

(signature of (agents of) landlord)

Notes

¹ The cases where the ALT's consent to the operation of the notice to quit is not required are set out in the AHA 1986, s 26(2), Sch 3, Pt I as amended by the AH(A)A 1990 (see Ch 31). No compensation for disturbance is payable where Cases C to G are relied on (as to Case G see Form 68) and no additional compensation is payable where Cases A or H are relied on: AHA 1986, s 61(1), (2).

² As to service of the notice, see AHA 1986, s 93: see para 42.13 ff.

³ This date must be on or after 12 September 1984: AHA 1986, Sch 3 Pt I, Case A.

⁴ The words in square brackets are relevant only if the result of the notice to quit taking effect will be to deprive the tenant of living accommodation occupied by him under the tenancy: see AHA 1986, s 26(2), Sch 3 Pt 1, Case A(b).

⁵ A tenant in receipt of a notice to quit which relies on Cases A, B (as substituted by the AH(A)A 1990, s 1(2)), D or E who wishes to dispute the reason or reasons stated must require arbitration within one month of service of the notice: Agricultural Holdings (Arbitration on Notices) Order 1987, SI 1987/710, art 9.

⁶ See the AHA 1986, Sch 3 Pt I, Case B(a) as substituted by the AH(A)A 1990 s 1(1), (2): See para 32.13 ff.

⁷ See the AHA 1986, Sch 3 Pt I Case B(b) as substituted by the AH(A)A 1990, s 1(1), (2): see para 32.13 ff.

⁸ Ie where the non-agricultural use is one for which any provision contained in an Act, but not forming part of the enactments relating to town and country planning (as defined) deems permission under those enactments to have been granted: see the AHA 1986, Sch 3 Pt I, Case B(c) as substituted by the AH(A)A 1990, s 1(1), (2). See para 32.13 ff.

⁹ AHA 1986, Sch 3 Pt I, Case B(d) as substituted by the AH(A)A 1990, s 1(1), (2): see para 32.13 ff.

¹⁰ AHA 1986, Sch 3 Pt I, Case B(e) as substituted by the AH(A)A 1990, s 1(1), (2): see para 32.13 ff.

¹¹ AHA 1986, Sch 3 Pt I, Case C: see para 31.21 ff.

¹² See Forms AH58–AH60.

¹³ The AHA 1986 s 26(2), Sch 3 Pt I, Case H applies to notices given by the Minister (as defined by AHA 1986, s 96) to enable him to use or dispose of the land for the purpose of effecting an amalgamation or the reshaping of an agricultural unit. No suggested wording can, therefore, be provided. Note that functions of the Minister, so far as exercisable in relation to Wales, transferred to the National Assembly for Wales, by the National Assembly for Wales (Transfer of Functions) Order 1999, SI 1999/672, art 2, Sch 1.

A2.50

AH68 Notice to quit given to the personal representatives of the tenant¹

CASE G:
AGRICULTURAL HOLDINGS ACT 1986

Re the Holding known as (*date*)

To: The Personal Representatives of the late (*name of tenant*)

of (*address*) and sent to the Public Trustee, PO Box 3010, London WC2A 1AX.²

As solicitors and agents for and on behalf of your landlord, (*name of landlord*) of (*address*) we (*name of firm*) of (*address*) hereby give you NOTICE TO QUIT and deliver up to him/her/me possession of ALL THAT holding and premises known as (*description of holding*) which was held of him/her/me by the late (*name of late tenant*) as Tenant thereof until his/her death on or about the .... day of 20

... . and now held by you as Personal Representatives, on the .... day of .... 20 .... or at the expiration of the year of the said tenancy which shall expire next after the end of twelve months from the date of service[3] of this Notice.

PLEASE TAKE NOTICE that this Notice to Quit is given in pursuance of the provisions of section 26 and Schedule 3, Part I, Case G of the Agricultural Holdings Act 1986:

(a)   Following the death of a person who immediately before his death was the sole (or sole surviving) tenant under the contract of tenancy;

(b)   Not later than the end of the period of three months beginning with the date of the relevant notice[4] within the meaning of the said section 26 of the said Act of 1986; and

(c)   By reason of the said death.

(signature of landlord's solicitors)

Notes

[1]   Ie the sole or sole surviving tenant: AHA 1986, Sch 3 Pt I, Case G (see para 31.90 ff). As to the meaning of 'tenant' see also AHA 1986, Sch 3 Pt II para 12(a). As to compensation, see Form AH67 note 1.

[2]   If there are no personal representatives, notice to quit should be served on the Public Trustee (formerly the President of the Family Division). Note that the notice served on the Public Trustee should be addressed in the manner described to accord with the Public Trustee requirements. If notice to quit is also being served on the persons believed to be the administrators, executors or persons in control of the farming then the notice should be separately addressed. This Form should be accompanied by Form NL(1) (see Form AH69) as prescribed by the Public Trustee (Notices Affecting Land) (Title on Death) Regulations 1995, SI 1995/1330, a cheque for the prescribed fee currently £40 payable to the Public Trustee and a letter setting out the facts and indicating that the notice is sent by virtue of the Administration of Estates Act 1925, s 9 (as substituted by the Law of Property (Miscellaneous Provisions) Act 1994, s 14(1)). As to service, when it is not known whether there are personal representatives, see para 31.96.

[3]   As to service, see AHA 1986, s 93: see para 42.13 ff.

[4]   The date of any relevant notice is the date on which a written notice was served on the landlord by or on behalf of the tenant's personal representatives informing the landlord of the tenant's death or the date on which the landlord was given notice under AHA 1986, s 39 or AHA 1986, s 41 ie an application for a tenancy of the holding on the tenant's death or, where both occur, the earlier date: AHA 1986, s 26(2), Sch 3 para 12(b).

A2.51

AH69

FORM NL (1)

PUBLIC TRUST OFFICE

AN EXECUTIVE AGENCY

Application for Registration of Notice Affecting Land

PUBLIC TRUSTEE (NOTICES AFFECTING LAND) (TITLE ON DEATH) REGULATIONS 1995

For explanatory notes see overleaf.
Please type or complete in BLOCK CAPITALS

For official use only

To: The Public Trustee
       PO Box 3010
       London WC2A 1AX

Date of Registration
....

Registration No.
....

I
....
of
....
....
....
....
....

(enter name and address of person or firm making application) apply for registration against the name of the deceased person referred to below of the attached Notice in respect of the land described.

The fee of £
....................................accompanies this application. (*Cheques should be made payable to the Public Trust Office*)
Signed
....
Date
....
Telephone No.
....
Reference
....

Enter name of deceased
Forename(s)
....
Surname
....
....

Enter details of land to which Notice relates. (See explanatory notes).
....
....
....
....
....

2070

Date of Notice ....

....

Description of Notice (*see explanatory* ....
notes). ....

....

....

....

....

....

....

....

....

....

Explanatory Notes

1   The fee payable is prescribed by the current Public Trustee Fees Order. Please ensure that such fee accompanies your application.

2   A practice note explaining the procedure for the keeping of a Register of Notices served under section 18 of the Law of Property (Miscellaneous Provisions) Act 1994 is available from the Public Trust Office fee of charge.

3   Separate applications should be made per property except where more than one property is included in the same title.

4   The entry on the Register will be made in the name of the deceased person and will record the details of the land to which the document relates and the date of registration.

5   The date and description of Notice are requested for office purposes only and will not be entered on the Register. Examples of a description of Notice are: Notice to Quit or Notice of Exercise of Option.

6   Please ensure that the Notice to be registered accompanies your application.

7   Acknowledgement of your application will be sent to you indicating the date of registration.

A2.52

AH70   Notice to quit given by landlord of part of the holding[1]

AGRICULTURAL HOLDINGS ACT 1986

To (*tenant*) of (*address*) (*date*)
(*description of holding*)

[I *or* We][1] (*name of agents*) of (*address*) as agents for and on behalf of] (*landlord*) of (*address*) give you notice pursuant to the provisions of the Agricultural Holdings Act 1986 section 31 to quit[2] and deliver up possession of fields numbered .... on sheet .... of the (*date*) Edition of the Ordnance Survey Map [together with their buildings premises and appurtenances] forming part of ALL THAT holding and premises known as (*description of holding*) which you hold of [me *or* him] as tenant [on the .... day of .... *or* at the expiration of the year of your tenancy which shall expire next after the end of 12 months from the date of service³ of this notice]

This notice is given [for the purpose of [adjusting the boundaries between the agricultural units *or* amalgamating [part of] agricultural units] *or* with a view to the use of the land for (*specify user*)⁴]

(*signature of (agents of) landlord*)

Notes

¹   This notice is given under the AHA 1986, s 31(1) (see para 29.1 ff) which enables a notice to quit part of an agricultural holding to be given on certain grounds. As to compensation for disturbance on termination of a tenancy of part of a holding, see AHA 1986, s 73. Where the tenant serves an effective counter-notice under AHA 1986, s 32 (see Form AH74) to the effect that he treats the notice to quit part as a notice to quit the entire holding, the compensation provisions in AHA 1986, s 60 apply: AHA 1986, s 60(1)(b). As to notices to quit, see Ch 28.

²   The notice to quit part will be invalid if it purports to determine the tenancy before the expiry of 12 months from the end of the current year of the tenancy, even if the contract of tenancy provides otherwise (AHA 1986, s 25(1)) unless either the reason stated under AHA 1986, s 31 is one of the non-agricultural reasons eg the opening of a quarry and the contract of tenancy authorises the resumption of possession for that purpose (AHA 1986, s 25(2)(b)) or one of the other exceptions contained in AHA 1986, s 25(2) applies. In the former case Form AH65 would be appropriate.

³   As to service, see AHA 1986, s 93: see para 42.13 ff.

⁴   The permitted objects are set out in AHA 1986, s 31(2).

C: COUNTER-NOTICES/DEMANDS FOR ARBITRATION

A2.53

AH71   Counter-notice by tenant following notice to remedy under the Agricultural Holdings Act 1986 Schedule 3 Part I Case D being a notice to do work¹

AGRICULTURAL HOLDINGS ACT 1986 SCHEDULE 3 PART I CASE D

To (*landlord*) of (*address*) (*date*)
(*description of holding*)

[I (*tenant*) of (*address*) give you notice¹ that:

[1]   I wish to contest my liability under the terms and conditions of my tenancy to do the work specified in the notice to do work dated the .... day of .... which you have given to me in respect of the following item[s]:

(*set out contested item(s) exactly as in landlord's notice*)

[2]   The ground[s] on which I deny liability to do the above work [is *or* are]:

(*set out grounds*)²]

[3]   I [also] wish to contest the following [further] matter[s] arising under the notice to *or* do work dated the .... day of .... which you have given me on the following ground[s]:

(*set out contested item(s) and the ground(s)[2] relied on*)

[4]   I require that the above matters shall be determined by arbitration under the provisions of that Act

[5]   This notice is not to be taken as any admission on my part as to the validity of the notice to remedy and it is given without prejudice to any matters arising in respect of that notice

(*signature of tenant or duly authorised agent*)

Notes

[1]   This notice is given under the Agricultural Holdings (Arbitration on Notices) Order 1987, SI 1987/710, arts 3, 4. It must be served not later than one month from the giving of the notice to quit: SI 1987/710, arts 3(2), 4(1). As to service, see the AHA 1986, s 93: see para 42.13 ff. As to arbitration generally, see Ch 47.
[2]   The tenant is not required to give his grounds but it may be desirable to do so to assist the resolution of the dispute.

A2.54

AH72   Counter-notice by tenant under the Agricultural Holdings Act 1986 section 26(1)[1]

AGRICULTURAL HOLDINGS ACT 1986

To (*landlord*) of (*address*) (*date*)
(*description of holding*)

Pursuant to the Agricultural Holdings Act 1986 [I *or* we] [(*name of agents*) of (*address*) as agents for and on behalf of] (*tenant*) of (*address*) give you notice that [I *or* he] require[s] that section 26(1) of that Act shall apply to your notice to quit in respect of the above holding served on [me *or* him] and dated the .... day of ....

This notice is not to be taken as any admission on [my *or* his] part as to the validity of your notice to quit and is given without prejudice to any matters arising in respect of that notice

(*signature of (agents of) tenant*)

Notes

[1]   This counter-notice (see para 30.2 ff) must be served not later than one month from the giving of the notice to quit: AHA 1986, s 26(1)(b). As to service of the counter-notice, see AHA 1986, s 93: see para 42.13 ff.

A2.55

AH73   Counter-notice by tenant enlarging notice to quit part to notice to quit entire holding[1]

AGRICULTURAL HOLDINGS ACT 1986

To (*landlord*) of (*address*) (*date*)
(*description of holding*)

Pursuant to the Agricultural Holdings Act 1986 section 32 [I *or* we] [(*name of agents*) of (*address*) as agents for and on behalf of] (*tenant*) of (*address*) give you counter-notice that [I *or* he] accept[s] your notice to quit part of the above holding served on [me *or* him] and dated the .... day of .... as notice to quit the entire holding to take effect at the same time as the original notice to quit

(*signature of (agents of tenant*)

Notes

[1]   This counter-notice is given under the AHA 1986, s 32 (see para 29.7) and must be served within 28 days after the giving of the notice to quit: AHA 1986, s 32(2). If the operation of the notice to quit depends on any proceedings under AHA 1986, Pt III (ss 25–33) eg proceedings before the tribunal following a tenant's counter-notice under AHA 1986, s 26(1) (see Form AH72), the 28 days run from the date at which it is determined that the notice has effect: AHA 1986, s 32(2)(b). As to compensation, see Form AH70 note 1. As to service, see AHA 1986, s 93: see para 42.13 ff.

A2.56

AH74   Notice by tenant requiring reference to arbitration of questions (other than as to liability to do work) arising from certain reasons stated in notice to quit[1]

AGRICULTURAL HOLDINGS ACT 1986

Schedule 3 Part I Case[s] [A or B or D or E]

To (*landlord*) of (*address*) (*date*)
(*description of holding*)

I (*tenant*) of (*address*) give you notice that I wish to contest all matters arising out of the reason[s] stated in the notice to quit the above holding dated the .... day of .... which you have served on me and that I require all questions so arising to be determined by arbitration under the Agricultural Holdings Act 1986

This notice is not to be taken as any admission on my part as to the validity of the notice to quit and it is given without prejudice to any matters arising in respect of that notice

.... (*signature of tenant*)

Notes

¹ This notice must be given within one month after the service of the notice to quit: Agricultural Holdings (Arbitration on Notices) Order 1987, SI 1987/710, art 9. As to service see the AHA 1986, s 93 (see para 42.13 ff). If the tenant wishes to contest his liability to do work required of him by a notice to do work, he should use Form AH71. Having served his notice contesting the reasons stated in the notice to quit, the tenant must within 3 months either agree with the landlord on the appointment of an arbitrator or apply for the appointment of an arbitrator under AHA 1986, s 84(2) (as amended by the Regulatory Reform (Agricultural Tenancies) (England and Wales) Order 2006, SI 2006/2805, art 7, otherwise the notice ceases to be effective: SI 1987/710, art 10. As to arbitration generally, see Ch 47.

A2.57

AH75 Counternotice by tenant under the Agricultural Holdings Act 1986, section 28 following Case D (notice to do work) notice to quit¹

AGRICULTURAL HOLDINGS ACT 1986

To (*landlord*) of (*address*) (*date*)
(*description of holding*)

Pursuant to the Agricultural Holdings Act 1986, section 28, [I]/[we] (*name of agents*) of (*address*) as agents for and on behalf of (*tenant*) of (*address*) give you notice that [I]/[he] require(s) that section 28(2) of that Act shall apply to your notice to quit in respect of the holding served on [me]/[him] and dated the .... day of .... 20 ....

This notice is not to be taken as any admission on [my]/[his] part as to the validity of your notice to quit and is given without prejudice to any matters arising in respect of that notice.

(*signature of tenant or duly authorised agent*)

Notes

¹ This counternotice must be served not later than one month from the giving of the notice to quit: AHA 1986, s 28(2): see para 30.2. As to service of the counternotice, see AHA 1986, s 93: see para 42.13 ff. Section 28 counternotices are only appropriate following the giving by the landlord of a notice to quit pursuant to Case D including a statement 'to the effect that it is given by reason of the tenant's failure to comply with a notice to do work'. In such circumstances the tenant has an option. If he disputes whether he has been guilty of not complying with a notice to remedy, or he otherwise wishes to put in issue the validity of the reasons stated in the notice to quit, then he must give a demand for arbitration. If, in the alternative, he acknowledges that he has not complied with the notice to quit but contends that a fair and reasonable landlord would not insist upon possession, then he

should give the counternotice above referred to. The landlord will then have to refer the matter to the Agricultural Land Tribunal to determine whether the tribunal shall consent to the notice to quit: see AHA 1986, s 28(5).

See also, *William Smith (Wakefield) Ltd v Parisride Ltd* [2005] EWHC 462 (Admin), [2005] 2 EGLR 22 where the simultaneous service of a counter-notice, and a tenant's notice referring the notice to quit to arbitration under AHA 1986, s 28 did not render the counter-notice invalid, and the Tribunal were entitled to determine, in the substantive issue, that a fair and reasonable landlord would not insist upon possession.

This form of counter-notice may also be used where, following arbitration as to the reason(s) stated in the notice to quit, the notice to quit is effective and the tenant wishes to question the landlord's fairness or reasonableness: see AHA 1986, s 28(4)(b). The tenant must then serve the counter-notice not later than one month from the date on which the arbitrator's award is delivered to him.

Division III

IMPROVEMENTS AND COMPENSATION CLAIMS

Contents

Division III

IMPROVEMENTS AND COMPENSATION CLAIMS

A2.58

AH76 Application by tenant for written consent to long-term improvements[1]

AGRICULTURAL HOLDINGS ACT 1986

To (*landlord*) of (*address*) (*date*)
(*description of holding*)

I (*tenant*) of (*address*) give you notice that I desire to carry out on the above holding improvements specified in the Agricultural Holdings Act 1986 Schedule 7 short particulars of which are given below and as required by section 67 of that Act I request you to give your written consent to the carrying out of those improvements [unconditionally *or* on such terms as to compensation or otherwise as may be agreed in writing between us].[2]

(*details of proposed improvements*)

(signature of tenant)

Notes
1. As to long-term improvements, see para 38.17 ff.
2. The alternatives in square brackets follow the wording of the AHA 1986, s 67(2). If any particular conditions are suggested by the tenant, they may be incorporated in this notice. As to service, see AHA 1986, s 93: see para 42.13 ff.

A2.59

AH77 Consent by landlord to long-term improvements[1]

AGRICULTURAL HOLDINGS ACT 1986

To (*tenant*) of (*address*) (*date*)
(*description of holding*)

Pursuant to the Agricultural Holdings Act 1986 section 67(1) I (*landlord*) of (*address*) give you [notice that I am prepared to give] my consent to the carrying out by you on the above holding of the improvements specified in the schedule below being improvements to which you requested my written consent by notice dated the .... day of .... [on the terms specified in the schedule below]²

SCHEDULE

(*details of improvements* (*and conditions*))

(*signature of landlord*)

Notes

¹   As to long-term improvements, see para 38.17 ff.
²   If the landlord is prepared to consent on terms, such terms should be set out in the schedule. Since any terms have to be agreed in writing between the landlord and the tenant (AHA 1986, s 67(2): see para 38.18), the best course is to have a written agreement between the parties duly signed. No doubt, however, a written acceptance of the landlord's terms by the tenant would suffice. As to service, see AHA 1986, s 93: see para 42.13 ff.

A2.60

AH78   Notice by landlord to the Agricultural Land Tribunal and tenant that he proposes to carry out approved improvements¹

AGRICULTURAL HOLDINGS ACT 1986

To the Secretary of the .... Agricultural Land Tribunal .... (*date*) and (*tenant*) of (*address*)
(*description of holding*)

BACKGROUND: the Agricultural Land Tribunal has given its approval to the carrying out of the improvements² specified in the schedule below

NOW I (*landlord*) of (*address*) give you notice in accordance with the Agricultural Holdings Act 1986 section 67(5) that I propose myself to carry out the improvements specified in the schedule below

SCHEDULE

(*details of improvements*)

(*signature of landlord*)

Notes

¹   This notice must be served within the prescribed period: AHA 1986, s 67(5) (see para 38.21). The prescribed period is one month from the date on which the landlord receives written notice of the tribunal's approval of the carrying out of the improvements: Agricultural Land Tribunals (Rules) Order 1978, SI 1978/259, art 2, Sch 1, r 7(2). This notice must be served on the tribunal and the tenant: AHA 1986, s 67(5). As to service, see AHA 1986, s 93: see para 42.13 ff. If the landlord fails to carry out the improvements

within a reasonable time, the tenant may apply to the tribunal to determine that the landlord has so failed; and if such a determination is made, the tribunal's previous approval has effect as if it were the landlord's consent to the improvement: AHA 1986, s 67(6)(b).

² See para 38.19.

A2.61

AH79   Notice by tenant to carry out mole drainage[1]

AGRICULTURAL HOLDINGS ACT 1986

To (*landlord*) of (*address*) (*date*)
(*description of holding*)

I (*tenant*) of (*address*) give you notice as required by the Agricultural Holdings Act 1986 section 68(1) that after the expiry of one month from the date of service of this notice I intend to carry out on the above holding the improvement short particulars of which are specified in the schedule below

SCHEDULE

(*details of mole drainage and/or works necessary to secure the efficient functioning of the* (*existing*) *mole drainage system including OS numbers of field(s) affected*)

(signature of tenant)

Notes

¹   For the tenant to qualify for compensation in respect of the improvement this notice must be served not later than one month before the improvement is begun: AHA 1986, s 68(1) (see para 38.23). As to service, see AHA 1986, s 93: see para 42.13 ff.

A2.62

AH80   Notice by tenant of intention to claim compensation for continuous adoption of special system of farming[1]

AGRICULTURAL HOLDINGS ACT 1986

To (*landlord*) of (*address*) (*date*)
(*description of holding*)

I (*tenant*) of (*address*) give you notice of my intention on quitting the above holding on the termination of my tenancy to claim compensation under the Agricultural Holdings Act 1986 section 70(1) for the continuous adoption of a special system of farming as mentioned in section 70(1) of that Act

(signature of tenant)

2081

Notes

[1] This notice must be given not later than one month before the termination of the tenancy: AHA 1986, s 70(2)(a) (see para 38.87). It is also a condition precedent to any such claim that a record of the condition of fixed equipment on the holding and of the general condition of the holding has been made under AHA 1986, s 22 (see para 24.13): AHA 1986, s 70(2)(b): see para 38.88. As to service, see AHA 1986, s 93: see para 42.13 ff.

A2.63

AH81 Notice by tenant of intention to claim more than one year's rent as compensation for disturbance and giving an opportunity to value stock etc[1]

AGRICULTURAL HOLDINGS ACT 1986

To (*landlord*) of (*address*) (*date*)
(*description of holding*)

I (tenant) of (address) give you notice that on quitting the above holding pursuant to your notice to quit served on me and dated the .... day of .... [and my counter-notice under the Agricultural Holdings Act 1986 section 32 served on you and dated the .... day of ....]I intend to claim under section 60 of that Act a greater amount than one year's rent of the above holding as compensation for disturbance and that you are at liberty to make a valuation of my household goods implements of husbandry fixtures farm produce or farm stock prior to their sale.

(signature of tenant)

Notes

[1] See para 38.47 ff. This notice of intention must be given not less than one month before the termination of the tenancy (AHA 1986, s 60(6)(a): see para 38.58) and must be followed by notice of intention specifying the nature of the claim under AHA 1986, s 83(2), (3) (see Form AH83). Loss or expense exceeding one year's rent must be strictly proved. As to service, see AHA 1986, s 93: see para 42.13 ff.

A2.64

AH82   Notice by landlord of intention to claim compensation for general deterioration of holding[1]

AGRICULTURAL HOLDINGS ACT 1986

To (*tenant*) of (*address*) (*date*)
(*description of holding*)

I (*landlord*) of (*address*) give you notice of my intention on your quitting the above holding on the termination of your tenancy to claim compensation under the Agricultural Holdings Act 1986 section 72 for the general deterioration as mentioned in section 72 of that Act

(*signature of landlord*)

Notes

¹   See paras 39.4 and 39.12 ff. This notice must be given not later than one month before the termination of the tenancy: AHA 1986, s 72(4) (see para 39.14). As to service, see AHA 1986, s 93: see para 42.13 ff.

A2.65

AH83   Notice by landlord or tenant of intention to make claim against the other on termination of tenancy specifying nature of claim¹

AGRICULTURAL HOLDINGS ACT 1986

Re the Holding known as .... (*date*)

To (*landlord or tenant*) of (*address*)

I HEREBY GIVE YOU NOTICE pursuant to s 83 of the above Act of my intention to make against you certain claims arising out of the termination of the tenancy of the above holding or part thereof, the nature of which claims is set out in the Schedule hereto.

SCHEDULE

Nature of Claim	Statutory provision, Custom or term of agreement under which the claim is made
Examples for tenant's claims:	
COMPENSATION FOR DISTURBANCE	Section 60 of the above Act
One year's rent	
COMPENSATION FOR DISTURBANCE	
Exceeding one year's rent, viz:	
Loss on sale of Implements	
Loss on sale of Stock	
Expenses of removal of household goods, etc	Sections 60 to 63 of the above Act
Expenses of sale	
Valuer's fee	
(or as the case may be)	
Total	
COMPENSATION FOR IMPROVEMENTS	Sections 64 to 79 and Sch 9 to the above Act

Nature of Claim	Statutory provision, Custom or term of agreement under which the claim is made
Compensation for Old Improvements, viz	Tenancy agreement clauses .... and/or custom
Compensation for Old Improvements .... Compensation for New Improvements viz	Sections 64 to 69, Sch 7 and Sch 8, Part I of the above Act.
COMPENSATION FOR TENANT-RIGHT	Section 65 and Sch 8, Part II of the above Act.
Compensation for tenant-right matters, viz	Tenancy agreement clauses .... and/or custom
Compensation for tenant-right matters, viz	
MILK QUOTA Compensation for milk quota to include transferred quota, excess quota and tenant's fraction.	Agriculture Act 1986—Section 13 and Sch 1.
GENERAL Failure to repair roof to barn	Tenancy agreement clause
EXAMPLES FOR LANDLORD'S CLAIMS Dilapidations	Tenancy agreement clauses ....
or Dilapidations	Section 71(1) of above Act.
General deterioration of holding	Section 72
Failure to give possession of cottage	Tenancy agreement clause

(signature of landlord or tenant)[2]

Notes

[1]   As to claims for compensation, see Chs 37 to 39. Claims between the landlord and the tenant of an agricultural holding arising out of the termination of the tenancy must (subject to the statutory provisions) be determined by arbitration under the AHA 1986: AHA 1986, s 83(1). See also, AHA 1986, s 84, as amended by the Regulatory Reform (Agricultural Tenancies) (England and Wales) Order 2006, SI 2006/2805, art 7: see para 41.1 ff Notice in writing of intention to make a claim must be served on the other party before the expiry of 2 months from termination: AHA 1986, s 83(2). The parties may, within 8 months from the termination of the tenancy, settle the claim by agreement in writing (AHA 1986, s 83(4)) but, if they fail to do so within that period, the claim must be determined by arbitration (see AHA 1986, s 84): AHA 1986, s 83(5). The arbitration will be governed by the Arbitration Act 1996 for those arbitrations occurring after the coming into force of the Regulatory Reform (Agricultural Tenancies) (England and Wales) Order 2006, SI 2006/2805 on 19 October 2006.

[2]   The notice of intention must specify the nature of the claim and it is sufficient for this purpose to refer to the statutory provision, custom or term of the agreement under which the claim is made: AHA 1986, s 83(3). It will be convenient to state some particulars in the notice as well as referring specifically to the relevant section of the AHA 1986 or the custom or the term of the tenancy agreement under which the claim is made. It is safer to give too much rather than too little information in the notice about the claim intended.

A2.66

AH84 Notice by tenant who entered before 1 March 1948 electing for compensation for certain tenant-right matters[1]

AGRICULTURAL HOLDINGS ACT 1986

To (*landlord*) of (*address*) (*date*)
(*description of holding*)

I (*tenant*) of (*address*) give you notice pursuant to the Agricultural Holdings Act 1986 Schedule 12 paragraph 6(1) that I elect that section 65(1) of that Act shall apply to me as regards compensation for matters specified in Schedule 8 Part II paragraphs 7 to 10 to that Act on the termination of my tenancy of the above holding

(*signature of tenant*)

Notes

[1] See para 38.35. This notice may be given at any time before the termination of the tenancy by a tenant who entered into occupation before 1 March 1948: AHA 1986, Sch 12 para 6(1) (see para 38.36). If the landlord has, while a notice is current, given the tenant a notice requiring him to elect whether AHA 1986, s 65(1) is to apply to him as regards tenant-right matters (see Form AH85), then this notice of election must be given either within one month of the landlord's notice or within one month of the termination proceedings as to the operation of the notice to quit: AHA 1986, Sch 12 para 6(2). If the tenant does not wish to elect for the new basis, there is no need for him to serve a notice electing against it. If it is desired to serve such a notice in reply to the landlord's notice under AHA 1986, Sch 12 para 6(2), insert 'not' between 'shall' and 'apply' in this Form. As to service, see AHA 1986, s 93: see para 42.13 ff.

A2.67

AH85 Notice by landlord requiring tenant to elect whether he will require compensation for certain tenant-right matters[1]

AGRICULTURAL HOLDINGS ACT 1986

To (*tenant*) of (*address*) (*date*)
(description of holding)

I (*landlord*) of (*address*) give you notice pursuant to the Agricultural Holdings Act 1986 Schedule 12 paragraph 6(2) that I require you to elect whether section 65(1) of that Act is to apply to you as regards compensation for matters specified in Schedule 8 Part II paragraphs 7 to 10 to that Act on the termination of your tenancy of the above holding

(*signature of landlord*)

Notes

1 See para 38.38. This notice may be served at any time during the currency of a notice to quit: AHA 1986, Sch 12, para 6(2) (see para 38.38). If the tenant does not wish to elect for the new basis, he need not serve a notice electing against it. For the tenant's notice of election for the new basis see Form AH84. As to service, see AHA 1986, s 93: see para 42.13 ff.

A2.68

AH86 Agreement between landlord and outgoing and incoming tenants as to compensation for improvements[1]

THIS AGREEMENT is made the .... day of .... BETWEEN (1) EF (*incoming tenant*) of (*address*) ('the New Tenant') (2) CD (*outgoing tenant*) of (*address*) ('the Outgoing Tenant') and (3) AB (*landlord*) of (*address*) ('the Landlord')

BACKGROUND

(1) Old and new leases

The Outgoing Tenant holds the holding known as (*description of holding*) ('the Holding') containing approximately .... [acres *or* hectares] as tenant to the Landlord under [lease for a term of .... years *or* tenancy from year to year] which will expire on the .... day of .... and the Landlord has agreed to [grant a lease of *or* let] the Holding to the New Tenant [for a term of .... years *or* from year to year] from the .... day of ....

(2) Claims by Outgoing Tenant

The Outgoing Tenant claims to be entitled under the [Agricultural Holdings Act 1986 *or* lease mentioned above] to payment of compensation in respect of the outlay and improvements specified in the schedule below and the amount payable to him in respect of such claim has [been agreed at £ .... (................ pounds) *or* not yet been ascertained][2]

NOW IT IS AGREED as follows:

1 Agreement for payment by New Tenant

The New Tenant will immediately after taking possession of the Holding [or as soon afterwards as compensation shall have been ascertained under the provisions of the Agricultural Holdings Act 1986] pay to the Outgoing Tenant the amount payable to him as compensation in respect of all matters specified in the schedule below and will at all times keep the Landlord indemnified against the same and all relative actions proceedings (including valuations and arbitration) claims demands and expenses[3]

2 Release of landlord

In consideration of the provisions of clause 1 above the Outgoing Tenant accepts the liability imposed in consequence on the New Tenant in full satisfaction of the liability of the Landlord and releases the Landlord from all liability to make compensation to him in respect of all or any of the matters specified in the schedule below under the Agricultural Holdings Act 1986 or otherwise

AS WITNESS etc

SCHEDULE

(*particulars of outgoing tenant's claim*)

(*signature of all parties*)

Notes

1　As to claims for compensation see Chs 37 to 39.
2　It is strongly recommended that the amount of compensation should be ascertained beforehand and inserted in the agreement.
3　In so far as the AHA 1986, ss 60–70 (see Ch 38) entitle the tenant to obtain compensation from his landlord, and that, notwithstanding any agreement to the contrary, it may perhaps be doubted whether a release of the landlord by the outgoing tenant is valid, it is submitted that the object of the statutory provisions is to ensure that compensation under the AHA 1986 is paid and that an agreement as to the method of payment is valid. It is further considered that a release of the landlord by the outgoing tenant in consideration of an agreement for payment by the income tenant is valid. It is prudent for the landlord to take an indemnity from the incoming tenant.

A2.69

AH87　Consent by landlord to payment of compensation for old or new improvements by incoming tenant to outgoing tenant[1]

AGRICULTURAL HOLDINGS ACT 1986

To (*incoming tenant*) of (*address*) .... (*date*)
(*description of holding*)

I (*landlord*) of (*address*) consent to the payment by you to (*outgoing tenant*) of (*address*) the outgoing tenant of the above holding of which I am the landlord of the compensation payable by me under (*statutory provision(s) under which compensation is payable*) in respect of the [old *or* old and new *or* new] improvements executed by him and specified in the schedule below

SCHEDULE

(*improvements paid for wholly or in part by incoming tenant*)

(*signature of landlord*)

Notes

1　As to compensation for improvements, see Ch 38. This written consent must be obtained before payment in order to entitle the incoming tenant, on quitting the holding, to claim compensation in respect of the whole or part of an improvement for which he has paid: AHA 1986, s 69(2) (see para 38.26).

A2.70

AH88   Notice by tenant of occurrence of damage by game[1]

AGRICULTURAL HOLDINGS ACT 1986

To (*landlord*) of (*address*) (*date*)
(*description of holding*)

I (*tenant*) of (*address*) give you notice pursuant to the Agricultural Holdings Act 1986 section 20 that damage has occurred to my crops through game as follows:

1   Damage to growing crops in fields numbered ....
2   Damage to crops reaped or raised in fields numbered ....

You are at liberty to inspect the damage and I will give you any reasonable facilities for so doing on hearing from you within the next .... days after your receipt of this notice[2]

(*signature of tenant*)

Notes

[1]   See para 24.11 ff. This notice must be given within one month after the tenant first became or ought reasonably to have become aware of the occurrence of the damage: AHA 1986, s 20(2)(a) (see para 24.11 ff). The notice must be followed by a notice in writing of the claim together with the particulars of it within one month after the expiry of the year in respect of which the claim is made: AHA 1986, s 20(2)(c). See Form AH89.
[2]   A reasonable opportunity must be given to the landlord to inspect the damage. In the case of damage to a growing crop, such opportunity must be given before the crop is begun to be reaped, raised or consumed and in the case of a crop reaped or raised, it must be before the crop is begun to be removed from the land: AHA 1986, s 20(2)(b)(i), (ii).

A2.71

AH89   Notice by tenant of claim for damage by game and particulars of such damage under the Agricultural Holdings Act 1986 section 20[1]

AGRICULTURAL HOLDINGS ACT 1986

To (*landlord*) of (*address*) (*date*)
(*description of holding*)

I (*tenant*) of (*address*) give you notice pursuant to the Agricultural Holdings Act 1986 section 20(2)(c) of my claim for damage by game to my crops on the above holding during the year[2] to the .... day of .... The details of my claim are as follows:

1   Damage to growing crops in fields numbered ... ...   £ ... .

2   Damage to crops reaped or raised in fields numbered ......   £ ... .

         TOTAL   £ ... .

(signature of tenant)

Notes

1   See para 24.11 ff. This notice must be given within one month after the expiry of the year (see note 2 infra) in respect of which the claim is made: AHA 1986, s 20(2)(c) (see para 24.11 ff).

2   'Year' means any period of 12 months ending in any year with 29 September or with such other date as may, by agreement, between the landlord and the tenant be substituted for that date: AHA 1986, s 20(3)(b).

A2.72

AH90 Request by landlord or tenant for making of record of condition of holding or by tenant of improvements, fixtures or buildings under the Agricultural Holdings Act 1986 section 22[1]

AGRICULTURAL HOLDINGS ACT 1986

To *(landlord)* of *(address)* *(date)*
(description of holding)

I *(landlord or tenant)* of *(address)* give you notice pursuant to the Agricultural Holdings Act 1986 section 22 that I require the making of a record[2] of the [condition of the buildings fences gates roads drains and ditches on and cultivation of the above holding *or* existing improvements executed by me *or* existing improvements for which with your written consent I paid compensation to the outgoing tenant *or* fixtures *or* buildings which pursuant to section 10 of the Act I am entitled to remove]

(signature of landlord or tenant)

Notes

1   These requests may be made at any time during the currency of the tenancy: AHA 1986, s 22(1) (see para 24.13).

2   Such record must be made by a person appointed in default of agreement between the landlord and the tenant by the President of the Royal Institution of Chartered Surveyors and any person so appointed may, on production of evidence of his appointment, enter the holding at all reasonable times for the purpose of making any such record: AHA 1986, s 22(2): see para 24.13.

AH90 Request by landlord or tenant for making of record of condition of holding or by tenant of improvements, fixtures or buildings under the Agricultural Holdings Act 1986 section 22

Division IV

AGRICULTURAL LAND TRIBUNALS

A2.73 Most of the forms in this Division (with the exception of the retirement notice, the 'appeal applications' and the arbitration demands) are statutorily prescribed which *must* be used without modification or 'improvement' by the draftsman. Although in general a form substantially to the like effect will suffice, draftsmen are recommended not, in fact, to alter or vary the prescribed form in any particular and also to ensure that the statutorily prescribed notes which comprise part of the form are reproduced as well as the form itself.

Many secretaries of Agricultural Land Tribunals have themselves made amendments by deleting references to repealed statutes and substituting the equivalent provision in the Agricultural Holdings Act 1986 (AHA 1986). This is, strictly speaking, incorrect and inappropriate, though such forms if used will almost certainly be found to be valid as being substantially to the like effect as the prescribed form, see *Morris v Patel* [1986] 281 Estates Gazette 419. Technically, the more correct procedure to adopt is to use the prescribed form without amendment.

Note that new rules are expected which will have new forms: see para 46.20.

Division IV

AGRICULTURAL LAND TRIBUNALS

Contents

AH35 Notice to the Agricultural Land Tribunal of intention to apply to the High Court for order directing the Tribunal to refer question of law to the High Court   2160

Agriculture (Miscellaneous Provisions) Act 1954, section 6
and the Agricultural Land Tribunals and Notices to Quit
Order, 1959 (SI 1959/81)

Notes

*   The forms as statutorily prescribed, or a form 'substantially to the like effect', *must* be used – see Agricultural Land Tribunals (Rules) Order 1978, SI 1978/259 (at para A1.521). The number ascribed to each form in this book is unofficial and for the purposes of this text only.

AGRICULTURAL LAND TRIBUNALS

A: GENERAL

A2.74

AH1

Form 1[1]
rule 2(3)

Ref. No.
To be inserted
by the Secretary

Agricultural Land Tribunal[2]

APPLICATION FOR CONSENT TO OPERATION OF NOTICE TO QUIT[3]

To the Secretary of the Agricultural Land Tribunal
for the .... Area.

1.   I, ... [*block capitals*] of .... [*address*],
hereby apply under—

*(a)   Section 2(1)[4],

*(b)   Section 4(2)[5],

*(c)   Section 4(3)[5],

of the Agricultural Holdings (Notices to Quit) Act 1977 for the consent of the Tribunal to the operation of a notice to quit which I *propose to give/have given have given to my tenant, ... [*block capitals*] of .... [*address*]

2.

(a)   I propose to serve the notice before the .... day of .... , 20 ... .

(b)   The notice was served on the .... day of .... , 20 .... ,
and a counter-notice was served by the tenant on the .... day of
.... 20 .... .

3.   The holding in respect of which the notice *will be/has been given is known as
.... and consists of:

(a)   ....   hectares of arable land (including temporary grass)
(Ordnance Survey Field Nos ....);

(b)   ....   hectares of permanent pasture
(Ordnance Survey Field Nos ....);

(c)   ....   hectares of rough grazing
(Ordnance Survey Field Nos ....);

(d)   ....   hectares of other land (including orchards)
(Ordnance Survey Field Nos ....);

Total   ....   hec-   ANNUAL
tares.   RENT £

4.   The holding includes the following buildings [*give a general description*]:—

†5.   I apply for the Tribunal's consent to the operation of the notice to quit on the
following ground(s) provided in paragraphs(s) .... of section 3(3)[5] of
the Agricultural Holdings (Notices to Quit) Act 1977([1]).

[*This paragraph is relevant to an application under section 2(1) of the Act, in which
case it is important to refer to footnote* ([1]). *In other cases the paragraph should be
struck out.*]

6.   The main facts on which I will base my case are (*give a brief outline*):—([2])

7.   If I obtain possession of the land I intend:—

*(a)   to farm it myself;

*(b)   to let it to another tenant (*state name and address if known*).

8.   I/The future tenant ([3]) at present farm(s) other land consisting of:—

(a)   ....   hectares of arable land (including temporary grass)
(Ordnance Survey Field Nos);

(b)   ....   hectares of permanent pasture
(Ordnance Survey Field Nos);

(c)   ....   hectares of rough grazing
(Ordnance Survey Field Nos);

(d)   ....   hectares of other land (including orchards)
(Ordnance Survey Field Nos);

Total   ....   hectares.

9.   I attach the following documents which I intend to produce in support of my
case:—

(a)   two ([4]) copies of a 6" to one mile or 1/10,000([5]) map of the holding
described in paragraph 3 above (and of the other land referred to in
paragraph 8)†([6]):

(b)   two ([4]) copies of ([7]):—

Date ....

Signed ([8]) ....

*   Strike out whichever is inapplicable.
†   Strike out if inapplicable.

(^{1}) The applicant must state on which paragraph or paragraphs of the subsection he intends to rely. The five paragraphs, as amended, are as follows:

  (a) that the carrying out of the purpose for which the landlord^6 proposes to terminate the tenancy is desirable in the interests of good husbandry as respects the land to which the notice relates, treated as a separate unit; or

  (b) that the carrying out thereof is desirable in the interests of sound management of the estate of which the land to which the notice relates forms part or which that land constitutes (*see footnote* (^{6}) *below*); or

  (c) that the carrying out thereof is desirable for the purposes of agricultural research, education, experiment or demonstration, or for the purposes of the enactments relating to small-holdings or allotments;^{7} or

  (d) that greater hardship would be caused by withholding than by giving consent to the operation of the notice; or

  (e) that the landlord proposes to terminate the tenancy for the purpose of the land's being used for a use, other than for agriculture,^{8} not falling within Case B (ie in section 2(3) of the Agricultural Holdings (Notices to Quit) Act 1977).

(^{2}) Where the tenant^9 is a serviceman within the meaning of section 11 of the Agricultural Holdings (Notices to Quit) Act 1977,^{10} and the notice to quit is given for one or more of the reasons specified in Case B, D or E, the reasons for the giving of the notice must be stated and, if any question arising out of them has been determined by arbitration, the determination should also be stated.

(^{3}) Paragraph 8 need not be completed if the name of the future tenant is unknown. Where land is described, a map should be provided^{1}1 (*footnote* (^{6}) *below*).

(^{4}) Two copies of the application and of any map and document must be sent to the Secretary,^{12} and if there are more than two parties (eg if the holding or part of it is sub-let), an additional copy of the application, etc, must be supplied for, and the Secretary must be informed of the name and address of, each additional party.^{13}

(^{5}) A larger scale map may be used if preferred. Ordnance Survey Field Numbers must be marked on the map.

(^{6}) Where it is intended to give evidence about any land other than that which is the subject of the notice to quit, it must be shown either on the map produced or on a separate map of a scale of 6" to one mile or 1/10,000 or larger.^{14}

(^{7}) Mention any other document which is attached to this application.

(^{8}) If signed by any person other than the applicant himself, he should state in what capacity or by what authority he signs.

Notes (not part of the prescribed form)

1 This form is Form 1 in the Appendix to the Agricultural Land Tribunals Rules 1978 contained in the Agricultural Land Tribunals (Rules) Order 1978, SI 1978/259, Sch 1, r 2. Although in general a form substantially to the like effect will suffice it is recommended that the prescribed form is used without alteration or variation in any particular, including reproduction of the statutorily prescribed notes which comprise part of the form. As reproduced, this Form follows the precise wording of the prescribed form, but not the exact layout and design. The Form as reproduced here refers to repealed enactments while the footnotes refer to the current equivalent provisions. ALTs have updated legislative references in some forms and are circulating them for use. A request may therefore be made to the relevant ALT for their version of the relevant form. An application for the tribunal's consent to the operation of a notice to quit under the AHA 1986, s 26(1) which is made by the landlord before the giving of the notice must be made not more than 12 nor less than 3 months before the commencement of the period at the expiration of which the notice to quit is intended to have effect: Agricultural Land Tribunals Rules 1978, SI 1978/259, r 2(1). An application for the tribunal's consent to the operation of a notice to quit under the AHA 1986, s 26(1), s 28(2), (3) or s 28(2), (4) (formerly the Agricultural Holdings (Notices to Quit) Act 1977, ss 2(1), 4(2), 4(3) (repealed) respectively) which is made by the landlord after service upon him by the tenant of a counter-notice must be made within one month of the service of the counter-notice: Agricultural Land Tribunals Rules 1978, r 2(2). An application under SI 1978/259, r 2 must be made in Form 1: r 2(3). As to notices to quit, see Ch 28.

2 As to Agricultural Land Tribunals generally, see Ch 46. See the Agricultural Land Tribunals (Rules) Order 1978, Sch 1 for the rules of procedure for Agricultural Land Tribunals ('the ALT'), which are to be cited as the Agricultural Land Tribunals Rules 1978 (see the Agricultural Land Tribunals Rules 1978, r 1(1)). See also the 2003 Council on Tribunals 'Model Rules of Procedure for Tribunals'. A new Order, the Agricultural Land Tribunal

(Rules) Order 2007, is proposed with the intention of consolidating and updating the current Agricultural Land Tribunals Rules 1978 (as amended by the Agricultural Land Tribunal (Succession to Agricultural Tenancies) Order 1984, SI 1984/1301 for England and Wales. It is intended that the new Order will bring the procedure of the ALTs into line with current best practice for Tribunals, update legislative references and ensure equal and consistent procedures across all Tribunals for England and Wales. Necessary changes to ensure compliance with the Human Rights Act 1998 are also to be taken into account. The proposed new Order does not prescribe statutory forms for applications and replies to applications to the ALT. Specified forms are intended to continue to be made available from the ALT for those who wish to use them, but they are no longer intended to form part of the statutory order. The current Agricultural Land Tribunal Rules 1978 as amended by the Agricultural Land Tribunals (Succession to Agricultural Tenancies) Order 1984, SI 1984/1301 are intended to continue to apply in only limited transitional circumstances such as when an application has been made before the commencement of the new Order. Since the Agricultural Land Tribunal (Rules) Order 2007 has not as yet come into operation references are to the current Agricultural Land Tribunal Rules 1978, SI 1978/259, as amended by SI 1984/1301.

3   As to notices to quit in relation to agricultural holdings, see Ch 28.

4   Where notice to quit an agricultural holding or part of an agricultural holding is given to the tenant and not later than one month from the giving of the notice the tenant serves on the landlord a counter-notice in writing requiring that the AHA 1986, s 26(1) is to apply to the notice then, subject to certain exceptions, the notice to quit will not have effect unless the tribunal consents to its operation: AHA 1986, s 26(1), (2). As to the exceptions, see AHA 1986, s 26(2), Sch 3, Pt I as amended by the Agricultural Holdings (Amendment) Act 1990, s 1(2).

5   The ALT must consent to the operation of a notice to quit an agricultural holding or part of an agricultural holding if, but only if, it is satisfied as to one or more of the matters mentioned in AHA 1986, s 27(3) and specified by the landlord in his application for its consent: AHA 1986, s 27(1). Even if the ALT is so satisfied, it must withhold consent under AHA 1986, s 26 if in all the circumstances it appears to it that a fair and reasonable landlord would not insist on possession: AHA 1986, s 27(2).

6   As to the meaning of 'landlord', see AHA 1986, s 96.

7   For the principal enactments relating to smallholdings and allotments, see the Allotments Acts 1908 to 1950 and the Agriculture Act 1970, Pt III (ss 37–65) (2 Halsbury's Statutes (4th Edn) ALLOTMENTS AND SMALLHOLDINGS).

8   As to the meaning of 'agriculture', see the AHA 1986, s 96.

9   As to the meaning of 'tenant' and 'contract of tenancy', see AHA 1986, s 96.

10 'Serviceman' means a man or woman who performs a period of relevant service: AHA 1986, s 30, Sch 5, para 1. 'Relevant service' means service (as defined in the Reserve and Auxiliary Forces (Protection of Civil Interests) Act 1951, s 64(1)) of a description specified in Sch 1 to that Act: AHA 1986, s 30, Sch 5, para 1. The Reserve and Auxiliary Forces (Protection of Civil Interests) Act 1951, s 64(1) and Sch 1 are amended by the Statute Law (Repeals) Act 1977, s 1(1), Sch 1, Part I (see 3 Halsbury's Statutes (4th Edn) ARMED FORCES). The Reserve and Auxiliary Forces (Protection of Civil Interests) Act 1951, Sch 1 is further amended by the Armed Forces Act 1981, s 28(2), Sch 4, Part I and the Reserve Forces (Safeguard of Employment) Act 1985, s 21, Sch 4. As to the special provisions relating to servicemen, see para 29.27 ff.

11 SI 1978/259, r 16(2).

12 SI 1978/259, r 16(1), (2), (4).

13 SI 1978/259, r 16(5).

14 SI 1978/259, r 16(3).

A2.75

AH2

Form 1R[1]
rule 2(3)

Ref. No.
To be inserted

Forms: *Agricultural Holdings under AHA 1986* **A2.75**

by the Secretary

Agricultural Land Tribunal

REPLY TO APPLICATION FOR CONSENT TO OPERATION OF NOTICE TO QUIT[2]

To the Secretary of the Agricultural Land Tribunal
for the .... Area.

1.   I .... [*block capitals*] of .... [*address*], tenant ([1])
.... [*name or description of holding*], having received a
copy of the application[3] (bearing the above reference number) for the Tribunal's
consent to the operation of a notice to quit, reply as follows:

    1.   The facts stated in the first four paragraphs of the application are
        correct except that:—

    2.   In addition to the land which is the subject of the application, I farm the
        following land ([2]) which includes the following buildings [*give a general
        description*]:—

    3.   My main reasons for resisting the application are:—

    4.   My landlord is not acting fairly and reasonably because ([3]):—

    5.   I attach copies of the following relevant documents([4]):—

Date ....

Signed ([5]) ....

([1])(a) If this form is completed by a sub-tenant,[4] he should state whether he is sub-tenant of the whole or part of the holding; if of part, he should describe the part with reference to paragraphs 3 and 4 of the application and should state Ordnance Survey Field Numbers.
(b) If this form is completed by a superior landlord, he should omit paragraph 2.
([2])(a) If you farm other land as part of the same unit with that which is the subject of the application, give a description, stating the area (in hectares) which is arable (including temporary grass), pasture (including rough grazing) and other land (including orchards) and giving the Ordnance Survey Field Numbers. If the land is farmed separately, give a general description, stating area, kind of farming and approximate distance from the holding in question.
(b) If the other land is not shown on the map produced by the landlord, you should produce a map of it of a scale of 6" to one mile or 1/10,000 (or larger) and giving the Ordnance Survey Field Numbers. If the land is not farmed as part of the same unit, or for any other good reason, you may, before or at the time of sending your reply, apply to the Secretary of the Tribunal in writing for the Chairman to dispense with the map.
([3]) The Tribunal will not give consent if, in all the circumstances, it appears to them that a fair and reasonable landlord would not insist on possession.[5] If you have any special reasons for saying your landlord is acting unfairly or unreasonably which do not appear under paragraph 3, you should state them under paragraph 4.
([4])(a) Two copies of the reply and of any document which you wish to submit to the Tribunal must be sent to the Secretary, and, if there are more than two parties (eg, if holding or part of it is sublet), an additional copy of each must be supplied for each additional party.
(b) If you disagree with any map or plan attached to the application, your reply should be accompanied by two copies of a 6" to one mile or 1/10,000 (or larger) map showing what you consider to be the true position and marking the Ordnance Survey Field Numbers.
([5]) If signed by any person other than the tenant himself, he should state in what capacity or by what authority he signs.[6]

Notes (**not part of the prescribed form**)
1   This form is Form 1R in the Appendix to the Agricultural Land Tribunals Rules 1978
     contained in the Agricultural Land Tribunals (Rules) Order 1978, SI 1978/259, Sch 1, r 2.
     Although in general a form substantially to the like effect will suffice it is recommended that
     the prescribed form is used without alteration or variation in any particular, including
     reproduction of the statutorily prescribed notes which comprise part of the form. As
     reproduced, this Form follows the precise wording of the prescribed form, but not the exact
     layout and design. The Form as reproduced here refers to repealed enactments while the
     footnotes refer to the current equivalent provisions. ALTs have updated legislative references
     in some forms and are circulating them for use. A request may therefore be made to the
     relevant ALT for their version of the relevant form. As to proposals for a new Tribunals Rules
     Order, see Form AH1 note 2 and para 46.20. As to notices to quit, see Ch 28.
2   Any party who intends to oppose the whole or any part of an application to the tribunal
     must, within one month of a copy of the application being served on him, reply to it in the
     form appended to the copy of the application served on him: see the Agricultural Land
     Tribunals Rules, r 15(1). Where no reply is received by the secretary to the ALT within the
     time allowed by SI 1978/259, r 15(1), the ALT may decide to make an order in the terms of
     the application without a formal hearing: SI 1978/259, r 15(2).
3   For the application, see Form AH1.
4   Where an application is made to the tribunal in respect of an agricultural holding the whole
     or any part of which has been sublet, every landlord, tenant and subtenant of that holding
     must be a party to the proceedings on that applicant: Agricultural Land Tribunals Rules 1978,
     r 13(1).
5   See Form AH1 note 6.
6   For the provisions relating to the reply and supporting documents, see the Agricultural Land
     Tribunals Rules 1978, SI 1978/259, r 16.

A2.76

AH3

Form 2[1]
rule 3

Ref. No.
To be inserted
by the Secretary

Agricultural Land Tribunal

APPLICATION TO POSTPONE OPERATION OF NOTICE TO QUIT[2]

To the Secretary of the Agricultural Land Tribunal
for the .... Area.

1.   I, ... *block capitals]*
      of .... [*address*],
      hereby apply under Article 12(1)[3] of the Agricultural Holdings (Arbitration on
      Notices) Order 1978 for the Tribunal to postpone the operation of the Notice
      to Quit served on me by my landlord:—
      .... [*block capitals*]
      of .... [*address*]
      in respect of: ....
      .... [*name or description of holding*].

2.   The Tribunal consented on the .... day of .... 20 .... , to the

operation of the said notice on the application[4] of my landlord bearing reference number
....

3.   If its operation is not postponed the Notice will expire on the .... day of
.... 20 ....

4.   My main reasons for this application are—:

5.   I attach two ([1]) copies of a 6" to one mile or 1/10,000([2]) map of the land which was the subject of the notice to quit([3]) and of the following documents which I intend to produce in support of my case:—

Date ....

Signed([4]) ....

([1])   Two copies of the application and any map or document must be sent to the Secretary, and if there are more than two parties (eg, if the land is held under a sub-tenancy) an additional copy of the application etc, must be supplied for, and the Secretary must be informed of the name and address of, each additional party. A written notice is required (by Article 12(2) of the 1978 Order referred to above) to be given at the same time to the landlord.
([2])   A larger scape map may be used if preferred. Ordnance Survey Field Numbers must be marked on the map.
([3])   The Chairman of the Tribunal has power in all cases to dispense with maps, etc. A request for a direction on this subject should be made in writing before or at the time of sending the application.[5]
([4])   If signed by any person other than the applicant himself, he should state in what capacity or by what authority he signs.

Notes (not part of the prescribed form)
[1]   This form is Form 1R in the Appendix to the Agricultural Land Tribunals Rules 1978 contained in the Agricultural Land Tribunals (Rules) Order 1978, SI 1978/259, Sch 1, r 2. Although in general a form substantially to the like effect will suffice it is recommended that the prescribed form is used without alteration or variation in any particular, including reproduction of the statutorily prescribed notes which comprise part of the form. As reproduced, this Form follows the precise wording of the prescribed form, but not the exact layout and design. The Form as reproduced here refers to repealed enactments while the footnotes refer to the current equivalent provisions. ALTs have updated legislative references in some forms and are circulating them for use. A request may be made to the relevant ALT for their version of the relevant form. As to proposals for a new Tribunal Rules Order, see Form AH1 note 2 and para 46.20. As to notices to quit, see Ch 28.
[2]   An application under the Agricultural Holdings (Arbitration on Notices) Order 1987, SI 1987/710, art 13 to postpone the termination of a tenancy must, unless made at the hearing of the proceedings before the ALT on an application under the AHA 1986 (see para A1.88), be made in Form 2: Agricultural Land Tribunals Rules 1978, rr 1(2), (3).
[3]   Where the Agricultural Land Tribunal has consented to the operation of a notice to quit under the AHA 1986 and the notice would, but for the provisions of the Agricultural Holdings (Arbitration on Notices) Order 1987, SI 1987/710, art 13, come into operation on or within 6 months after the giving of the consent, the ALT may, on the application of the tenant made not later than 14 days after the giving of the consent, postpone the termination of the tenancy for a period not exceeding 12 months: SI 1987/710, art 13(1).
[4]   See Form AH1.
[5]   Agricultural Land Tribunals Rules 1978, r 16(6), (7). As to general provisions relating to applications and supporting documents, see SI 1978/259, r 16.

A2.77

AH4

Form 2R[1]

Ref. No.
To be inserted
by the Secretary

Agricultural Land Tribunal

REPLY TO APPLICATION TO POSTPONE OPERATION OF NOTICE TO QUIT

To the Secretary of the Agricultural Land Tribunal
for the .... Area.

1.   I, ... [*block capitals*]
      of .... [*address*],
      landlord of .... [*name or description of holding*],
      having received a copy of the application[2] (bearing the above reference number)
      for the Tribunal to postpone the operation of the notice to quit the above
      named holding, reply as follows:—

    1.   The facts stated in the first three paragraphs of the application are
              correct except that:—

    2.

    *(a)   I request that there should be no postponement.

    *(b)   I would agree to postponement up to the .... day of
              .... , 20 .

    3.   My main reasons for resisting the application are:—

    4.   I attach copies of the following relevant documents([1]):—

Date ....

Signed([2]) ....

*   Strike out whichever is inapplicable.
([1])(a) Two copies of the reply and of any document which you wish to submit to the Tribunal
must be sent to the Secretary, and, if there are more than two parties (eg, if the land is sub-let),
an additional copy of each must be supplied for each additional party.
(b) If you disagree with any map or plan attached to the application, your reply should be
    accompanied by two copies of a 6" to one mile or 1/10,000 (or larger) map showing what
    you consider to be the true position and marking the Ordnance Survey Field Numbers.
([2]) If signed by any person other than the landlord himself, he should state in what capacity or
    by what authority he signs.[3]

Notes (not part of the prescribed form)
[1]   This form is Form 2R in the Appendix to the Agricultural Land Tribunals Rules 1978,
      contained in the Agricultural Land Tribunals (Rules) Order 1978, SI 1978/259, Sch 1, r 2.
      Although in general a form substantially to the like effect will suffice it is recommended that
      the prescribed form is used without alteration or variation in any particular, including
      reproduction of the statutorily prescribed notes which comprise part of the form. As

reproduced, this Form follows the precise wording of the prescribed form, but not the exact layout and design. The Form as reproduced here refers to repealed enactments while the footnotes refer to the current equivalent provisions. Some ALTs have updated legislative references in some forms and are circulating them for use. A request may therefore be made to the relevant ALT for their version of the relevant form. As to proposals for a new Tribunal Rules Order, see Form AH1 note 2 and para 46.20. As to replies to applications, see Form AH2 note 2. As to notices to quit, see Ch 28.

2   For the application, see Form AH3.
3   For the provisions relating to replies and supporting documents, see the Agricultural Land Tribunals Rules 1978, SI 1978/259, r 16.

A2.78

AH5

Form 3[1]
rule 4

Ref. No.
To be inserted
by the Secretary

Agricultural Land Tribunal

APPLICATION FOR CERTIFICATE OF BAD HUSBANDRY[2]

To the Secretary of the Agricultural Land Tribunal
for the .... Area.

1.   I, ... [*block capitals*] of .... [*address*], hereby apply under section 2(4) of the Agricultural Holdings (Notices to Quit) Act 1977[2] for a certificate that my tenant, ... [*block capitals*] of .... [*address*] is not fulfilling his responsibility to farm .... [*name or description of holding*] in accordance with the rules of good husbandry.

2.   The land consists of:—

(a)	hectares of arable land (including temporary grass) (Ordnance Survey Field Nos ....);
(b)	hectares of permanent pasture (Ordnance Survey Field Nos ....);
(c)	hectares of rough grazing (Ordnance Survey Field Nos ....);
(d)	hectares of other land (including orchards) (Ordnance Survey Field Nos ....);

Total .... hectares.

3.   The holding includes the following buildings [*give a general description*]:—

4.   If a certificate of bad husbandry is granted I propose to serve a notice to quit.[3]

5.   The main grounds on which I allege bad husbandry are:—

6.   I attach the following documents which I intend to produce in support of my case:—

(a)   two (¹) copies of a 6" to one mile or 1/10,000(²) map of the holding described in paragraph 3 above;

(b)   two (¹) copies of (³):—

Date ....

Signed(⁴) ....

(¹) Two copies of the application and of any map and document must be sent to the Secretary, and if there are more than two parties (eg, if the holding or part of it is sub-let), an additional copy of the application, etc, must be supplied for, and the Secretary must be informed of the name and address of, each additional party.
(²) A larger scale map may be used if preferred. Ordnance Survey Field Numbers must be marked on the map.
(³) Mention any other document which is attached to this application.
(⁴) If signed by any person other than the applicant himself, he should state in what capacity or by what authority he signs.⁴

Notes (not part of the prescribed form)

1   This form is Form 3 in the Appendix to the Agricultural Land Tribunals Rules 1978 contained in the Agricultural Land Tribunals (Rules) Order 1978, SI 1978/259, Sch 1, r 2. Although in general a form substantially to the like effect will suffice it is recommended that the prescribed form is used without alteration or variation in any particular, including reproduction of the statutorily prescribed notes which comprise part of the form. As reproduced, this Form follows the precise wording of the prescribed form, but not the exact layout and design. The Form as reproduced here refers to repealed enactments while the footnotes refer to the current equivalent provisions. ALTs have updated legislative references in some forms and are circulating them for use. A request may therefore be made to the relevant ALT for their version of the relevant form. As to proposals for a new Tribunal Rules Order see Form AH 1 note 2 and para 46.20. An application under the AHA 1986, s 26(3), Sch 3 Pt II para 9(1) (see para A1.113) (formerly the Agricultural Holdings) (Notice to Quit) Act 1977, s 2(4) (repealed) must be made in Form 3: Agricultural Land Tribunals Rules 1978, r 4.

2   For the purposes of the AHA 1986, s 26(2), Sch 3, Pt I, Case C (formerly the Agricultural Holdings (Notices to Quit) Act 1977, s 2(3), Case C (repealed)) the landlord of an agricultural holding may apply to the ALT for a certificate that the tenant is not fulfilling his responsibilities to farm in accordance with the rules of good husbandry; and the ALT, if satisfied that the tenant is not fulfilling his responsibilities, must grant a certificate: AHA 1986, Sch 3 Pt II para 9(1). As to the 'rules of good husbandry', see the Agriculture Act 1947, s 11 as applied by the AHA 1986, s 96(3): see para 24.4 ff. In determining whether to grant a certificate under AHA 1986, Sch 3 Pt II para 9(1) the tribunal must disregard any practice adopted by the tenant in pursuance of any provision of the contract of tenancy, or of any other agreement with the landlord, which indicates that its object is the furtherance of one or more of certain purposes to do with conservation and the protection of historic buildings etc: AHA 1986, Sch 3 Pt II para 9(2).

3   The consent of the ALT to the operation of a notice to quit an agricultural holding is not necessary in any of the Cases set out in AHA 1986, Sch 3 Pt I: AHA 1986, s 26(1), (2). The situation in Case C is that not more than 6 months before the giving of the notice to quit, the ALT granted a certificate under AHA 1986, Sch 3 Pt II para 9(1) that the tenant of the holding was not fulfilling his responsibilities to farm in accordance with the rules of good husbandry and that fact is stated in the notice: AHA 1986, s 26(2), Sch 3 Pt I, Case C. See para 31.21 ff.

4   For the general provisions relating to applications and supporting documents see the Agricultural Land Tribunals Rules 1978, SI 1978/259, r 16.

A2.79

AH6

Form 3R[1]

Ref. No.
To be inserted
by the Secretary

Agricultural Land Tribunal

REPLY TO APPLICATION FOR CERTIFICATE OF BAD HUSBANDRY

To the Secretary of the Agricultural Land Tribunal
for the .... Area.

1.   I, ... [*block capitals*] of .... *address*], tenant ([1]) of
.... [*name or description of holding*], having received a copy of
the application[2] (bearing the above reference number) for the Tribunal's
certificate of bad husbandry, reply as follows:

1.   The facts stated in the first three paragraphs of the application are correct
except that:—

2.   My main reasons for resisting the application are:—

3.   I attach copies of the following relevant documents ([2])

Date ....

Signed ....

([1]) If this form is completed by a sub-tenant, he should state whether he is sub-tenant of the
whole or part of the holding; if of part, he should describe the part with reference to
paragraph 2 and 3 of the application and should state Ordnance Survey Field Numbers.
([2])(a) Two copies of the reply and of any document which you wish to submit to the Tribunal
must be sent to the Secretary, and, if there are more than two parties (eg, if holding or part of
it is sub-let), an additional copy of each must be supplied for each additional party.
(b) If you disagree with any map or plan attached to the application, your reply should be
accompanied by two copies of a 6" to one mile or 1/10,000 (or larger) map showing what
you consider to be the true position and marking the Ordnance Survey Field Numbers.
(c) If signed by any person other than the tenant himself, he should state in what capacity or
by what authority he signs.[3]

Notes (not part of the prescribed form)
[1]   This form is Form 3R in the Appendix to the Agricultural Land Tribunals Rules 1978
contained in the Agricultural Land Tribunals (Rules) Order 1978, SI 1978/259, Sch 1, r 2.
Although in general a form substantially to the like effect will suffice it is recommended that
the prescribed form is used without alteration or variation in any particular, including
reproduction of the statutorily prescribed notes which comprise part of the form. As
reproduced, this Form follows the precise wording of the prescribed form, but not the exact
layout and design. The Form as reproduced here refers to repealed enactments while the
footnotes refer to the current equivalent provisions. ALTs have updated legislative references
in some forms and are circulating them for use. A request may therefore be made to the
relevant ALT for their version of the relevant form. As to proposals for a new Tribunal Rules
Order, see Form AH1 note 2 and para 46.20. As to replies to applications, see Form AH2
note 2.

²   For the application see Form AH5.
³   For the provisions relating to replies and supporting documents, see the Agricultural Land
   Tribunals Rules, SI 1978/259, r 16.

A2.80

AH7

Form 4¹
rule 5

Ref. No.
To be inserted
by the Secretary

Agricultural Land Tribunal

APPLICATION FOR VARIATION OR REVOCATION OF CONDITION IMPOSED BY
THE TRIBUNAL

To the Secretary of the Agricultural Land Tribunal
for the .... Area.

1.   I, ... [*block capitals*]
        of .... [*address*],
        hereby apply under section 3(5) of the Agricultural Holdings (Notices to Quit)
        Act 1977 for the Tribunal to vary or revoke the conditions imposed by them
        under section 3(4) thereof on granting my application bearing the reference
        number ....

2.

        *(a)   I wish the Tribunal to revoke the condition.

        *(b)   I wish the Tribunal to revoke the condition; but if they are unwilling to
               do so, I request them to make the following variation:—

        *(c)   I do not wish the Tribunal to revoke the condition, but only to make the
               following variation:—

3.   The main reasons for my application are:—

4.   I attach two (¹) copies of a 6" to one mile or 1/10,000(²) map of the holding
        which was the subject of the notice to quit(³) and of the following documents
        which I intend to produce in support of my case (⁴):—

Date ....

Signed(⁵) ....

*(a)Strike out whichever is inapplicable.
(¹) Two copies of the application and of any map and document must be sent to the Secretary.
(²) A larger scale map may be used if preferred. Ordnance Survey Field Numbers must be
   marked on the map.
(³) The Chairman of the Tribunal has power in all cases to dispense with maps, etc (eg, if they
   are already in the possession of the Tribunal). A request for a direction on this subject
   should be made in writing before or at the time of sending the application.

(⁴) Mention any other document which is attached to the application.
(⁵) If signed by any person other than the applicant himself, he should state in what capacity or by what authority he signs.²

Notes (not part of the prescribed form)
¹ This form is Form 4 in the Appendix to the Agricultural Land Tribunals Rules 1978 contained in the Agricultural Land Tribunals (Rules) Order 1978, SI 1978/259, Sch 1, r 2. Although in general a form substantially to the like effect will suffice it is recommended that the prescribed form is used without alteration or variation in any particular, including reproduction of the statutorily prescribed notes which comprise part of the form. As reproduced, this Form follows the precise wording of the prescribed form, but not the exact layout and design. The Form as reproduced here refers to repealed enactments while the footnotes refer to the current equivalent provisions. ALTs have updated legislative references in some forms and are circulating them for use. A request may therefore be made to the relevant ALT for their version of the relevant form. As to proposals for a new Tribunal Rules Order see Form AH1 note 2. Where the ALT consents under the AHA 1986, s 26 (see para A1.113) to the operation of a notice to quit, it may impose such conditions as appear to it requisite for securing that the land to which the notice relates will be used for the purpose for which the landlord proposes to terminate the tenancy: AHA 1986, s 27(4). As to the penalty for breach of such conditions, see AHA 1986, s 27(6), (8), (9). Where, on an application by the landlord, the ALT is satisfied that, by reason of any change of circumstances or otherwise, any condition imposed under AHA 1986, s 27(4) ought to be varied or revoked, it must vary or revoke the condition accordingly: AHA 1986, s 27(5). An application under AHA 1986, s 27(5) (formerly the Agricultural Holdings (Notice to Quit) Act 1977, s 3(5) (repealed)) must be made in Form 4: Agricultural Land Tribunals Rules 197,8 r 5.
² As to general provisions relating to applications and supporting documents, see SI 1978/259, r 16. The provisions relating to replies under r 15(1) do not apply in the case of an application under r 5: SI 1978/259, r 15(3).

A2.81

AH8

Form 5¹
rule 6(1)

Ref. No.
To be inserted
by the Secretary

Agricultural Land Tribunal

APPLICATION FOR DIRECTION TO PROVIDE FIXED EQUIPMENT

To the Secretary of the Agricultural Land Tribunal
for the .... Area.

1. I, ... [*block capitals*] of .... [*address*], tenant³
    of .... [*name or description of holding*],
    hereby apply under Section 4 of the Agriculture Act 1958 for the Tribunal to
    direct my landlord⁴ [*block capitals*]
    Of [*address*]
    to carry out the following work on the said holding:—

2.

(a)   On the .... day of .... 20 ,
I requested my landlord in writing to carry out the said work and he
*refused on the .... day of .... , 20 , /has had reason-
able time to agree but has not done so.[5]

(b)   No term in my contract of tenancy or in any other agreement binds me
or my landlord to carry out the said work.

(c)   My landlord is not bound by any enactment to carry out the said work.

3.   The holding consists of:—

(a) ....   hectares of arable land (including temporary grass)
(Ordnance Survey Field Nos ....);

(b) ....   hectares of permanent pasture
(Ordnance Survey Field Nos ....);

(c) ....   hectares of rough grazing
(Ordnance Survey Field Nos ....);

(d) ....   hectares of other land (including orchards)
(Ordnance Survey Field Nos ....);

Total ....   hectares.

4.   The holding includes the following buildings:—

5.   The type of farming carried on on the holding is ([2]):—

6.   I wish to carry on the following agricultural activity on the said holding to the
extent and in the manner specified, *viz*:—

7.   If I were to do so without the said work being carried out, I should contravene
the following statutory requirements[6] in the following respects:—

8.   I attach the following documents which I intend to produce in support of my
case:e:

(a)   two ([3]) copies of a 6" to one mile or 1/10,000([4]) map of the holding
described in paragraph 3 above,

(b)   two ([3]) copies of the following plan:—

(c)   two ([3]) copies of my contract of tenancy and any other document ([5]):—

Date ....

Signed([6]) ....

*   Strike out whichever is inapplicable.
([1])   Under section 4(1) of the Agriculture Act 1958 the Tribunal cannot direct a landlord to
carry out work in connection with an agricultural activity specified in the tenant's
application where the activity has not been carried on on the holding for a period of at
least three years immediately preceding the making of the application unless they are
satisfied that the starting of the activity did not or, where it has not yet been started, will
not constitute or form part of a substantial alteration of the type of farming carried on on
the holding.[7]
([2])   Two copies of the application and of any map and document must be sent to the Secretary,
and if there are more than two parties (eg, if the land is held under a sub-tenancy) for the
Secretary must be informed of the name and address of, each additional party.
([3])   A larger scale map may be used if preferred. Ordnance Survey Field Numbers must be
marked on the map.
([4])   Mention any other document which is attached to this application. The Chairman of the
Tribunal has power in all cases to dispense with maps or other documents (eg, where the
landlord already has a copy of the contract of tenancy). A request for a direction on this
subject should be made in writing before or at the time of sending the application.

(^{5}) If signed by any person other than the applicant himself, he should state in what capacity or by what authority he signs.[8]

Notes (not part of the prescribed form)

[1]   As to the requirements of the AHA 1986, s 11, see para 23.27 ff.

[2]   This form is Form 5 in the Appendix to the Agricultural Land Tribunals Rules 1978 contained in the Agricultural Land Tribunals (Rules) Order 1978, SI 1978/259, Sch 1, r 2. Although in general a form substantially to the like effect will suffice it is recommended that the prescribed form is used without alteration or variation in any particular, including reproduction of the statutorily prescribed notes which comprise part of the form. As reproduced, this Form follows the precise wording of the prescribed form, but not the exact layout and design. The Form as reproduced here refers to repealed enactments while the footnotes refer to the current equivalent provisions. ALTs have updated legislative references in some forms and are circulating them for use. A request may therefore be made to the relevant ALT for their version of the relevant form. As to proposals for a new Tribunal Rules Order, see Form AH1 note 2 and para 46.20. An application under the AHA 1986, s 11(1) (see para A1.98) (formerly the Agriculture Act 1958, s 4(1) (repealed)) for a direction for the provision, alteration or repair of fixed equipment must be made in Form 5: Agricultural Land Tribunals Rules 1978, r 6(1). As to fixed equipment, see Ch 23.

[3]   As to the meaning of 'tenant', see the AHA 1986, s 96.

[4]   As to the meaning of 'landlord', see AHA 1986, s 96.

[5]   AHA 1986, s 11(3).

[6]   Any authority having power to enforce the statutory requirement specified in an application under the Agricultural Land Tribunals Rules 1978, r 6(1) is entitled to be heard on the proceedings on the application, and must be treated as a party to it except for the purposes of SI 1978/259, r 15 (replies): r 12(2).

[7]   AHA 1986, s 11(2).

[8]   As to general provisions relating to applications and supporting documents, see the Agricultural Land Tribunals Rules 1978, r 16.

A2.82

AH9

Form 5R[1]

Ref. No.
To be inserted
by the Secretary

Agricultural Land Tribunal

REPLY TO APPLICATION FOR DIRECTION TO PROVIDE FIXED EQUIPMENT

To the Secretary of the Agricultural Land Tribunal
for the .... Area.

1.   I .... [*block capitals*]
of .... [*address*],
landlord(^{1}) of .... [*name or description of holding*],
having received a copy of the application[2] (bearing the above reference number) for the Tribunal's direction to me to carry out certain work on the said holding, reply as follows:—

1.   With regard to paragraph 2(a) of the application, I—

     *(a)   agree that the request was made and refused;

*(b)   agree that the request was made, but

(i)   deny that it was refused,

(ii)   say that I have not yet had reasonable time to agree to it;

*(c)   deny that the request was made.

2.   The other facts stated in the first four paragraphs of the application are correct, except that:—

3.   My main reasons for resisting the application are:—

*(a)   that the carrying on of the activity specified in paragraph 6 of the application to the extent and in the manner specified therein—

(i)   will not involve the contravention of any statutory requirement even if the said work is not carried out;

(ii)   would be unreasonable having regard to the tenant's responsibilities to farm the holding in accordance with the rules of good husbandry,[3]

*(b)   that the activity specified in paragraph 6 of the application has not been carried on on the holding for a period of at least three years immediately preceding the making of the application and that the starting of the activity *constitutes/forms part of a substantial alteration of the type of farming carried on on the holding;

*(c)   that the direction asked for would be unreasonable having regard to—

(i)   my responsibilities to manage the land comprised in the holding in accordance with the rules of good estate management;[4]

(ii)   the period for which the holding may be expected to remain a separate holding;

(iii)   [*any other reasons*].

4.   I attach copies of the following relevant documents([2]):—

Date ....

Signed([3]) ....

*   Strike out whichever is inapplicable.

([1])   If this form is completed by a superior landlord he should omit paragraph 1.

([2])(a)   Two copies of the reply and of any document which you wish to submit to the Tribunal must be sent to the Secretary, and, if there are more than two parties (eg, if the holding is sublet), an additional copy of each must be supplied for each additional party.

(b)   If you disagree with any map or plan attached to the application, your reply should be accompanied by two copies of a 6" to one mile or 1/10,000 (or larger) map showing what you consider to be the true position and marking the Ordnance Survey Field Numbers.

([3])   If signed by any person other than the landlord himself, he should state in what capacity or by what authority he signs.[5]

Notes (not part of the prescribed form)

[1]   This form is Form 5R in the Appendix to the Agricultural Land Tribunals Rules 1978 contained in the Agricultural Land Tribunals (Rules) Order 1978, SI 1978/259, Sch 1, r 2. Although in general a form substantially to the like effect will suffice it is recommended that the prescribed form is used without alteration or variation in any particular, including reproduction of the statutorily prescribed notes which comprise part of the form. As reproduced, this Form follows the precise wording of the prescribed form, but not the exact layout and design. The Form as reproduced here refers to repealed enactments while the footnotes refer to the current equivalent provisions. ALTs have updated legislative references in some forms and are circulating them for use. A request may therefore be made to the

relevant ALT for their version of the relevant form. As to proposals for a new Tribunal Rules Order, see Form AH1 note 2 and para 46.20. A landlord may, alternatively, apply under the AHA 1986, s 11(7) for an extension of the period specified in a direction under AHA 1986 s 11(1), and such application must be in writing and state the grounds for the application: see the Agricultural Land Tribunals Rules 1978, r 6(2): see para 23.27 ff. As to fixed equipment, see Ch 23.

2   See Form AH8.
3   As to the 'rules of good husbandry', see the Agriculture Act 1947, s 11, as applied by the AHA 1986, s 96(3).
4   As to the 'rules of good estate management', see the Agriculture Act 1947, s 10 applied by the AHA 1986, s 96(3): see para 24.4 ff.
5   As to the general provisions relating to replies and supporting documents, see the Agricultural Land Tribunals Rules 1978, r 16.

A2.83

AH10

Form 6[1]
rule 7(1)

Ref. No.
To be inserted
by the Secretary

Agricultural Land Tribunal

APPLICATION FOR APPROVAL OF LONG-TERM IMPROVEMENT

To the Secretary of the Agricultural Land Tribunal for the Area.

1.   I, ... [*block capitals*]
     of .... [*address*],
     tenant of .... [*name or description of holding*],
     hereby apply for the Tribunal's approval under section 50[2] of the Agricultural Holdings Act 1948 (as amended by the Agriculture Act 1958) of the carrying out of the following improvement(s) on the said holding:—

2.   My landlord[3] is .... [*block capitals*]
     of .... [*address*]

3.   The holding consists of:

(a) ....   hectares of arable land (including temporary grass)
                         (Ordnance Survey Field Nos ....);

(b) ....   hectares of permanent pasture
                         (Ordnance Survey Field Nos ....);

(c) ....   hectares of rough grazing
                         (Ordnance Survey Field Nos ....);

(d) ....   hectares of other land (including orchards)
                         (Ordnance Survey Field Nos ....);

Total ....   hectares.

4.   The holding includes the following buildings:— [*give a general description*]

2115

5.   I requested my landlord on the .... day of .... 20 , to consent in writing to the carrying out of the said improvement(s), but he—

　　　*(a)   refuses to give his consent.

　　　*(b)   will only consent subject to the following terms to which I am unwilling to agree:— [*state the terms and your reason for not agreeing*]

6.   My main reasons for wishing for the improvements to be carried out are:—

7.   I attach the following documents which I intend to produce in support of my case:—

　　　(a)   two (^{1}) copies of a 6" to one mile or 1/10,000(^{2}) map of the holding described in paragraph 4 above;

　　　(b)   two (^{1}) copies of the following plan:—

　　　(c)   two (^{1}) copies of (^{2}):—

Date ....

　　　　　　　　　　　　　　　　　　　　　Signed(^{4}) ....

* Strike out whichever is inapplicable.
(^{1}) Two copies of the application and of any map and document must be sent to the Secretary, and if there are more than two parties (eg, if the holding is held under a sub-tenancy), an additional copy of the application, etc, must be supplied for, and the Secretary must be informed of the name and address of, each additional party.
(^{2}) A larger scale map may be used if preferred. Ordnance Survey Field Numbers must be marked on the map.
(^{3}) Mention any other document which is attached to this application.
(^{4}) If signed by any person other than the applicant himself, he should state in what capacity or by what authority he signs.^{4}

Notes (not part of the prescribed form)
1   This form is Form 6 in the Appendix to the Agricultural Land Tribunals Rules 1978 contained in the Agricultural Land Tribunals (Rules) Order 1978, SI 1978/259, Sch 1, r 2. Although in general a form substantially to the like effect will suffice it is recommended that the prescribed form is used without alteration or variation in any particular, including reproduction of the statutorily prescribed notes which comprise part of the form. As reproduced, this Form follows the precise wording of the prescribed form, but not the exact layout and design. The Form as reproduced here refers to repealed enactments while the footnotes refer to the current equivalent provisions. ALTs have updated legislative references in some forms and are circulating them for use. A request may therefore be made to the relevant ALT for their version of the relevant form. As to proposals for a new Tribunal Rules Order, see Form AH1 note 2 and para 46.20.
2   Where, in the case of an improvement specified in the AHA 1986, Sch 7 Pt II (see para A1.196), the tenant is aggrieved by the refusal of his landlord to give his consent to the carrying out of the improvement, or is unwilling to agree to any terms subject to which the landlord is prepared to give his consent, the tenant may apply to the ALT for approval of the carrying out of the improvement: AHA 1986, s 67(3). An application under AHA 1986, s 67(3) (formerly the Agricultural Holdings Act 1948, s 50(1) (repealed)) must be made in Form 6: Agricultural Land Tribunals Rules 1978, r 7(1).
3   For the meaning of 'landlord', see Form AH8 note 4.
4   As to the general provisions relating to applications and supporting documents, see the Agricultural Land Tribunal Rules 1978, r 16.

A2.84

AH11

Form 6R¹

Ref. No.
To be inserted
by the Secretary

Agricultural Land Tribunal

REPLY TO APPLICATION FOR APPROVAL OF LONG-TERM IMPROVEMENT

To the Secretary of the Agricultural Land Tribunal
for the .... Area.

1.   I, ... [block capitals]
     of .... [address],
     landlord of .... [name or description of holding],
     having received a copy of the application² (bearing the above reference number)
     for the Tribunal's approval under section 50 of the Agricultural Holdings
     Act 1948 (as amended)³ of the carrying out on the said holding of the
     improvement(s) specified therein, reply as follows:

1.   The facts stated in the first four paragraphs of the application are correct except
     that:—

2.

     *(a)   I deny that the request referred to in paragraph 5 of the application was
            made.

     *(b)   I do not wish the improvements to be carried out because:—

     *(c)   I agree the improvements being carried out subject to the following
            terms:— [state terms and any special reasons]

3.   My main reasons for resisting the application are:—

4.   I attach copies of the following relevant documents(¹):—

Date ....

Signed(²) ....

* Strike out whichever is inapplicable.
(¹)(a) Two copies of the reply and of any document which you wish to submit to the Tribunal
should be sent to the Secretary, and, if there are more than two parties (eg, if the holding is
sub-let), an additional copy of each must be supplied for each additional party.
(b) If you disagree with any map or plan attached to the application your reply should be
     accompanied by two copies of a 6" to one mile or 1/10,000 (or larger) map or plan
     showing what you consider to be the true position and marking the Ordnance Survey Field
     Numbers.
(²) If signed by any person other than the landlord himself, he should state in what capacity or
     by what authority he signs.⁴

2117

Notes (not part of the prescribed form)

1   This form is Form 6R in the Appendix to the Agricultural Land Tribunals Rules 1978 contained in the Agricultural Land Tribunals (Rules) Order 1978, SI 1978/259, Sch 1, r 2. Although in general a form substantially to the like effect will suffice it is recommended that the prescribed form is used without alteration or variation in any particular, including reproduction of the statutorily prescribed notes which comprise part of the form. As reproduced, this Form follows the precise wording of the prescribed form, but not the exact layout and design. The Form as reproduced here refers to repealed enactments while the footnotes refer to the current equivalent provisions. ALTs have updated legislative references in some forms and are circulating them for use. A request may therefore be made to the relevant ALT for their version of the relevant form. As to proposals for a new Tribunal Rules Order, see Form AH1 note 2 and para 46.20. See also Form AH12 and notes. The provisions of the Agricultural Holdings Act 1948, s 50 (as amended) were repealed and re-enacted in the AHA 1986, s 67 (see para A1.154).
   If despite the reply made by the landlord to the application by the tenant for approval of long term improvements, the ALT grants the tenant's application, the landlord may, if he wishes, carry out the improvements himself. In that event the landlord must, before undertaking the improvements, give notice within the prescribed period under the AHA 1986, s 67(5) and he must serve notice in writing on the ALT and the tenant that the landlord proposes himself to carry out the improvements. The period now prescribed by the SI 1978/259, r 7(2) is one month.

2   See Form AH10.

3   See Form AH10 note 2.

4   For the general provisions relating to replies and supporting documents see the Agricultural Land Tribunals Rules 1978, r 16.

A2.85

AH12

Form 7[1]
rule 7(3)

Ref. No.
To be inserted
by the Secretary

Agricultural Land Tribunal

APPLICATION FOR DETERMINATION THAT LANDLORD HAS FAILED TO CARRY OUT
IMPROVEMENT WITHIN A REASONABLE TIME

To the Secretary of the Agricultural Land Tribunal
for the .... Area.

1.   I .... [*block capitals*]
   of .... [*address*],
   tenant[2]
   [*name or description of holding*],
   hereby apply to the Tribunal in pursuance of section 50(4)(b) of the Agricultural Holdings Act 1948 (as amended by the Agriculture Act 1958)[3] to determine that my landlord[4] .... [*block capitals*]
   of .... [*address*]
   has failed within a reasonable time to carry out the following improvements to the said holding:—

2.   The said improvement was approved by the Tribunal on my application bearing reference number ....

3.   The Tribunal's decision was dated .... day of .... , 20 , and my landlord notified me of his proposal to carry out the said improvement himself on the .... day of .... , 20

4.   My landlord has failed to carry out the said improvements:— *[if he has done any part of them, give particulars]*

5.   My main reasons for saying that the delay is unreasonable are:—

6.   I attach two (^{1}) copies each of —

       (a)   a 6" to one mile or 1/10,000(^{2}) map of the holding(^{3});

       (b)   the following plan showing the intended improvements(s):—

       (c)   the following other documents(^{4}):—

Date ....

Signed(^{5}) ....

(^{1}) Two copies of the application and of any map and document must be sent to the Secretary, and if there are more than two parties (eg, if the holding is held under a sub-tenancy), an additional copy of the application, etc, must be supplied for, and the Secretary must be informed of the name and address of, each additional party.

(^{2}) A larger scale map may be used if preferred. Ordnance Survey Field Numbers must be marked on the map.

(^{3}) The Chairman of the Tribunal has power in all cases to dispense with maps, etc. (eg, if they are already in the possession of the Tribunal or the other parties). A request for a direction on this subject should be made in writing before or at the time of sending the application.

(^{4}) Mention any other documents which are attached to the application.

(^{5}) If signed by any person other than the applicant himself, he should state in what capacity or by what authority he signs.^{6}

Notes (not part of the prescribed form)

1   This form is Form 7 in the Appendix to the Agricultural Land Tribunals Rules 1978 contained in the Agricultural Land Tribunals (Rules) Order 1978, SI 1978/259, Sch 1, r 2. Although in general a form substantially to the like effect will suffice it is recommended that the prescribed form is used without alteration or variation in any particular, including reproduction of the statutorily prescribed notes which comprise part of the form. As reproduced, this Form follows the precise wording of the prescribed form, but not the exact layout and design. The Form as reproduced here refers to repealed enactments while the footnotes refer to the current equivalent provisions. ALTs have updated legislative references in some forms and are circulating them for use. A request may therefore be made to the relevant ALT for their version of the relevant form. As to proposals for a new Tribunal Rules Order, see Form AH1 note 2 and para 46.20. If the ALT grants its approval to the carrying out of an improvement on an application by a tenant under the AHA 1986, s 67(3) (see para A1.154) the landlord may, within the prescribed period from receiving notification of the ALT's decision serve notice in writing on the ALT and the tenant that the landlord proposes himself to carry out the improvement: AHA 1986, s 67(5). The 'prescribed period' means the period prescribed by the Minister (as defined by AHA 1986, s 96) by regulations: AHA 1986, s 96. The time within which a landlord may serve a notice is one month from the date on which he receives notice in writing of the ALT's approval of the carrying out of the improvement: see the Agricultural Land Tribunals Rules 1978, r 7(2).

2   For the meaning of 'tenant', see Form AH8 note 2.

3   Where the ALT grants its approval to the carrying out of an improvement, then if a notice is duly served by the landlord under the AHA 1986, s 67(5), but on an application in that behalf made by the tenant under AHA 1986, s 67(6)(b) (formerly the Agricultural Holdings Act 1948, s 50(4)(b) (repealed)) the tribunal determines that the landlord has failed to carry out the improvement within a reasonable time, the approval of the tribunal has effect for the

purposes of compensation for the new improvement under the AHA 1986, s 67(1) as if it were the consent of the landlord, and any terms subject to which the approval was given shall have effect as if they were contained in an agreement in writing between the landlord and the tenant: AHA 1986, s 67(6). As to compensation for long-term new improvements see para 38.14 ff. An application under AHA 1986, s 67(6)(b) for a determination that the landlord has failed to carry out an improvement within a reasonable time shall be made in Form 7: see the Agricultural Land Tribunals Rules 1978, r 7(3).

4   For the general provisions relating to applications and supporting documents, see Agricultural Land Tribunals Rules 1978, SI 1978/259, r 16.

A2.86

AH13

Form 7R[1]

Ref. No.
To be inserted
by the Secretary

Agricultural Land Tribunal

REPLY TO APPLICATION FOR DETERMINATION THAT LANDLORD HAS FAILED TO CARRY
OUT IMPROVEMENT WITHIN A REASONABLE TIME

To the Secretary of the Agricultural Land Tribunal
for the .... Area.

1.   I, ... [*block capitals*]
      of .... [*address*],
      landlord of .... [*name or description of holding*],
      having received a copy of the application[2] (bearing the above reference number) for the Tribunal's determination that I have failed within a reasonable time to carry out on the said holding the improvement(s) specified there, reply as follows:—

1.   The facts stated in the first three paragraphs of the application are correct except that:—

2.   My main reasons for resisting the application are:—

      *(a)   I have adequately carried out the said improvement(s);

      *(b)   I intend to carry out the said improvement(s) but have not yet had reasonable time to do so for the following reasons:—

      [*give particulars*]

      *(c)   [*any other reasons*]

3.   I attach copies of the following relevant documents([1]):—

Date ....

Signed([2]) ....

*   Strike out whichever is inapplicable.

2120

(^{1})(a) Two copies of the reply and of any document which you wish to submit to the Tribunal must be sent to the Secretary, and, if there are more than two parties (eg, if the holding is sub-let) an additional copy of each must be supplied for each additional party.

(b) If you disagree with any map or plan attached to the application your reply should be accompanied by two copies of a 6" to one mile or 1/10,000 (or larger) map or plan showing what you consider to be the true position and marking the Ordnance Survey Field Numbers.

(^{2}) If signed by any person other than the landlord himself he should state in what capacity or by what authority he signs.^{3}

Notes (not part of the prescribed form)
^{1} This form is Form 7R in the Appendix to the Agricultural Land Tribunals Rules 1978 contained in the Agricultural Land Tribunals (Rules) Order 1978, SI 1978/259, Sch 1, r 2. Although in general a form substantially to the like effect will suffice it is recommended that the prescribed form is used without alteration or variation in any particular, including reproduction of the statutorily prescribed notes which comprise part of the form. As reproduced, this Form follows the precise wording of the prescribed form, but not the exact layout and design. The Form as reproduced here refers to repealed enactments while the footnotes refer to the current equivalent provisions. ALTs have updated legislative references in some forms and are circulating them for use. A request may therefore be made to the relevant ALT for their version of the relevant form. As to proposals for a new Tribunal Rules Order, see Form AH1 note 2 and para 46.20.
^{2} See Form AH12.
^{3} For the general provisions relating to replies and supporting documents see the Agricultural Land Tribunals Rules 1978, SI 1978/259, r 16.

A2.87

AH14

Form 8^1
rule 8

Ref. No.
To be inserted
by the Secretary

Agricultural Land Tribunal

APPLICATION FOR DIRECTION TO TREAT AN AGRICULTURAL HOLDING AS A
MARKET GARDEN

To the Secretary of the Agricultural Land Tribunal
for the .... Area.

1.   I, ... [*block capitals*]
      of .... [*address*],
      tenant^2 of
      .... [*name or description of holding*],
      hereby apply to the Tribunal to direct under section 68 of the Agricultural Holdings Act 1948 (as amended by the Agriculture Act 1958) that * the said holding /* the part of the said holding specified in paragraph 6 below shall be treated as a market garden so that section 67 of the said Act shall apply^3.

2.   My landlord^4 is .... [*block capitals*]
      of .... [*address*]

3.   I requested him on the .... day of 20   , to agree in writing to the (part of the) holding being so treated, but he * refused on the .... day of .... , 20   . / * has had reasonable time but has failed to do so.

4.   The holding consists of:—

(a) ....   hectares of arable land (including temporary grass)
                                         (Ordnance Survey Field Nos ....);
(b) ....   hectares of permanent pasture
                                         (Ordnance Survey Field Nos ....);
(c) ....   hectares of rough grazing
                                         (Ordnance Survey Field Nos ....);
(d) ....   hectares of other land (including orchards)
                                         (Ordnance Survey Field Nos ....);
Total ....   hectares.

5.   The holding includes the following buildings:— [*give a general description*]

6.   I wish to make the following improvements:—

Ordnance Survey Field Nos.   Improve-
                                                    ments

7.   For the following main reasons I request the Tribunal to direct that the *holding/ *part of the holding described in paragraph 6 above be treated as a market garden:—

8.   I attach the following documents which I intend to produce in support of my case:—

(a)   two (^{1}) copies of a 6" to one mile or 1/10,000(^{2}) map of the holding described in paragraph 4 above;

(b)   two (^{1}) copies of the following plan:—

(c)   two (^{1}) copies of(^{3}):—

Date ....

Signed(^{4}) ....

*   Strike out whichever is inapplicable.
(^{1})   Two copies of the application and of any map and document must be sent to the Secretary, and if there are more than two parties (eg, if the holding is held under a sub-tenancy), an additional copy of the application, etc, must be supplied for, and the Secretary must be informed of the name and address of, each additional party.
(^{2})   A larger scale map may be used if preferred. Ordnance Survey Field Numbers must be marked on the map.
(^{3})   Mention any other document which is attached to this application.
(^{4})   If signed by any person other than the applicant himself, he should state in what capacity or by what authority he signs.

Notes (not part of the prescribed form)
1   Generally, see para 38.90 ff. This form is Form 8 in the Appendix to the Agricultural Land Tribunals Rules 1978 contained in the Agricultural Land Tribunals (Rules) Order 1978, SI 1978/259, Sch 1, r 2. Although in general a form substantially to the like effect will suffice it is recommended that the prescribed form is used without alteration or variation in any particular, including reproduction of the statutorily prescribed notes which comprise part of the form. As reproduced, this Form follows the precise wording of the prescribed form, but not the exact layout and design. The Form as reproduced here refers to repealed enactments

while the footnotes refer to the current equivalent provisions. ALTs have updated legislative references in some forms and are circulating them for use. A request may therefore be made to the relevant ALT for their version of the relevant form. As to proposals for a new Tribunal Rules Order, see Form AH1 note 2 and para 46.20.

An application under the AHA 1986, s 80 (see para A1.167) (formerly the Agricultural Holdings Act 1948, s 68 (repealed)) for a direction that an agricultural holding should be treated as a market garden must be made in Form 8: Agricultural Land Tribunals Rules 1978, r 8.

²   For the meaning of 'tenant', see Form AH12.

³   In the case of an agricultural holding in respect of which, or in respect of part of which, it is agreed in writing that the holding is to be let or treated as a market garden, all statutory provisions as to compensation for improvements apply to that holding or part of a holding: AHA 1986, s 79(1), (2); see para 38.90 ff.

Where a tenant desires to make on his holding, or part of it, any of the improvements applicable to market gardens and the landlord refuses or fails within a reasonable time to agree in writing that the holding, or that part, shall be treated as a market garden, the ALT may, on the application of the tenant and after being satisfied that the holding, or part of it, is suitable for market gardening, direct that the provisions as to compensation under AHA 1986, s 79 shall, in respect of all or some only of those improvements, apply to the holding or to that part: see AHA 1986, s 80(1), (2). As to the ALT's power to make such a direction, subject to conditions for the protection of the landlord see AHA 1986, s 80(6), (7); see also para 38.95.

⁴   As to the meaning of 'landlord', see Form AH8 note 4.

⁵   For the general provisions relating to applications and supporting documents, see the Agricultural Land Tribunals Rules 1978, SI 1978/259, r 16.

A2.88

AH15

Form 8R¹

Ref. No.
To be inserted
by the Secretary

Agricultural Land Tribunal

REPLY TO APPLICATION FOR DIRECTION TO TREAT AN AGRICULTURAL HOLDING AS A
MARKET GARDEN

To the Secretary of the Agricultural Land Tribunal
for the .... Area.

1.   I .... [*block capitals*]
       of .... [*address*],
       landlord(¹) of .... [*name or description of holding*],
       having received a copy of the application² (bearing the above reference number) for the Tribunal's direction under section 68 of the Agricultural Holdings Act 1948 (as amended)³ that the said holding or part thereof should be treated as a market garden in respect of the improvement(s) specified therein, reply as follows—:

1.   With regard to paragraph 3 of the application, I—

       *(a)   agree that the request was made and refused;

*(b)   agree that the request was made, but say that

*(i)   I did agree to it in writing on the .... day of 20

*(ii)   I have not yet had reasonable time to agree to it;

*(c)   deny that the request was made.

2.   The other facts stated in the application are correct except that:—

3.   My main reasons for resisting the applications are:—

*(a)   the land is unsuitable for market gardening for the following reasons:—

*(b)   [*any other reasons*]

4.

(1)   If the Tribunal decide to give the direction applied for, I request them to limit its effect to the following improvement(s):

(2)   My main reasons for this would be:—

5.   I attach copies of the following relevant documents(^{2}):—

Date ....

Signed(^{3}) ....

*   Strike out whichever is inapplicable.

(^{1}) If this form is completed by a superior landlord, he should omit paragraph 1.

(^{2})(a) Two copies of the reply and of any document you wish to submit to the Tribunal must be sent to the Secretary, and, if there are more than two parties (eg, if the holding is sub-let), an additional copy of each must be supplied for each additional party.

(b) If you disagree with any map or plan attached to the application your reply should be accompanied by two copies of a 6" to one mile or 1/10,000 (or larger) map or plan showing what you consider to be the true position and marking the Ordnance Survey Field Numbers.

(^{3}) If signed by any person other than the landlord himself he should state in what capacity or by what authority he signs.[4]

Notes (not part of the prescribed form)

[1]   This form is Form 8R in the Appendix to the Agricultural Land Tribunals Rules 1978 contained in the Agricultural Land Tribunals (Rules) Order 1978, SI 1978/259, Sch 1, r 2. Although in general a form substantially to the like effect will suffice it is recommended that the prescribed form is used without alteration or variation in any particular, including reproduction of the statutorily prescribed notes which comprise part of the form. As reproduced, this Form follows the precise wording of the prescribed form, but not the exact layout and design. The Form as reproduced here refers to repealed enactments while the footnotes refer to the current equivalent provisions. ALTs have updated legislative references in some forms and are circulating them for use. A request may therefore be made to the relevant ALT for their version of the relevant form. As to proposals for a new Tribunal Rules Order see Form AH1 note 2 and para 46.20. The Agricultural Holdings Act 1948, s 68 was repealed and re-enacted in the AHA 1986, s 80: see para 38.90 ff.

[2]   See Form AH14.

[3]   See Form AH14 note.

[4]   For the general provisions relating to replies and supporting documents, see the Agricultural Land Tribunals Rules 1978, SI 1978/259, r 16.

A2.89

AH16

Form 9[1]
rule 9

Ref. No.
To be inserted
by the Secretary

Agricultural Land Tribunal

APPLICATION FOR DIRECTION TO AVOID OR RELAX COVENANT AGAINST THE BURNING
OF HEATHER OR GRASS

To the Secretary of the Agricultural Land
Tribunal the .... Area.

1.   I, ... [*block capitals*]
of .... [*address*],
tenant[2] of .... [*name or description of holding*], hereby apply under
section 21 of the Hill Farming Act 1946 (as amended by the Agriculture
Act 1958)[3] for the Tribunal's direction that the covenants, conditions or
agreements contained in my lease[4] and specified in paragraph 3 below be
avoided or relaxed.

2.   My landlord[5] is .... [*block capitals*]
of .... [*address*]

3.   The covenant(s)/condition(s)/agreement(s) to which I refer is (are) numbered
.... in my lease and I ask the Tribunal to direct that it (they) be—

    *(a)   avoided completely;

    *(b)   relaxed in the following way:—

    *(i)   permanently;

    *(ii)   for the following period:—

4.   The holding consists of:—

  (a) ....   hectares of arable land (including temporary
                   grass)
                   (Ordnance Survey Field Nos ....);
  (b) ....   hectares of permanent pasture
                   (Ordnance Survey Field Nos ....);
  (c) ....   hectares of rough grazing
                   (Ordnance Survey Field Nos ....);
  (d) ....   hectares of other land (including orchards)
                   (Ordnance Survey Field Nos ....);
Total ....   hectares.

5.   The covenant(s)/condition(s)/agreement(s) mentioned in paragraph 3 above is
(are) *impeding/preventing the proper use of the land for agricultural purposes

2125

in the following way:—

and I wish it (them) to be *avoided/relaxed so as to allow me to burn .... hectares of *heather/grass.

6.   I attach:—

    (a)   two ([1]) copies of my lease ([2]);

    (b)   two ([1]) copies of a 6" to one mile or 1/10,000([3]) map of the land described in paragraph 4 above;

    (c)   two ([1]) copies each of the following other documents ([4]):—

Date ....

Signed([5]) ....

* Strike out whichever is inapplicable.
([1]) Two copies of the application and of any map and document must be sent to the Secretary, and if there are more than two parties (eg, if the land is held under a sub-tenancy), an additional copy of the application, etc, must be supplied for, and the Secretary must be informed of the name and address of, each additional party.
([2]) The Chairman of the Tribunal has power in all cases to dispense with maps or other documents (eg, where the landlord already has a copy of the lease). A request for a direction on this subject should be made in writing before or at the time of sending the application.
([3]) A larger scale map may be used if preferred. Ordnance Survey Field Numbers must be marked on the map.
([4]) Mention any other document which is attached to this application.
([5]) If signed by any person other than the applicant himself, he should state in what capacity or by what authority he signs.[6]

Notes (not part of the prescribed form)
[1]   This form is Form 9 in the Appendix to the Agricultural Land Tribunals Rules 1978 contained in the Agricultural Land Tribunals (Rules) Order 1978, SI 1978/259, Sch 1, r 2. Although in general a form substantially to the like effect will suffice it is recommended that the prescribed form is used without alteration or variation in any particular, including reproduction of the statutorily prescribed notes which comprise part of the form. As reproduced, this Form follows the precise wording of the prescribed form, but not the exact layout and design. The Form as reproduced here refers to repealed enactments while the footnotes refer to the current equivalent provisions. ALTs have updated legislative references in some forms and are circulating them for use. A request may therefore be made to the relevant ALT for their version of the relevant form. As to proposals for a new Tribunal Rules Order, see Form AH1 note 2 and para 46.20.

    Where a lease of land contains a covenant, condition or agreement under which the burning of heather or grass by the tenant is prohibited or restricted, the ALT, on an application by the tenant, may, if it appears to it that the covenant, condition or agreement is preventing or impending the proper use for agricultural purposes of the land comprised in the lease or any of that land and that it is expedient in all the circumstances so to do, give such directions for avoiding or relaxing the covenant, condition or agreement as it thinks fit: Hill Farming Act 1946 (HFA 1946), s 21(1) as substituted by the Agriculture Act 1958, s 8(1), Sch 1, Pt I, para 1 (1 Halsbury's Statutes (4th Edn) AGRICULTURE). For the current statutory conditions and limitations on the burning of plant tissue and agricultural works see the Environmental Protection Act 1990, s 33(1)(a), (b) and the Waste Management Licensing Regulations 1994, SI 1994/1056, Sch 3 para 30(1), as amended by the Waste Management (England and Wales) Regulations 2006, SI 2006/937, regs 6(1), 9(c)(i), (ii). An application under the HFA 1946, s 21(1) as substituted (see supra) shall be made in Form 9: Agricultural Land Tribunals Rules 1978, r 9.
[2]   As to the meaning of 'tenant', see the Landlord and Tenant Act 1927 (LTA 1927), s 25(1), by virtue of the HFA 1946, s 21(3).
[3]   See note 1.
[4]   As to the meaning of 'lease', see the LTA 1927, s 25(1), by virtue of the HFA 1946, s 21(3).

5   As to the meaning of 'landlord', see the LTA 1927, s 25(1), by virtue of the HFA 1946, s 21(3).
6   For the general provisions relating to applications and supporting documents, see the Agricultural Land Tribunals Rules 1978, SI 1978/259, r 16.

A2.90

AH17

Form 9R¹

Ref. No.
To be inserted
by the Secretary

Agricultural Land Tribunal

REPLY TO APPLICATION FOR DIRECTION TO AVOID OR RELAX COVENANT AGAINST
THE BURNING OF HEATHER OR GRASS

To the Secretary of the Agricultural Land Tribunal
for the .... Area.

1.   I, ... [*block capitals*] of .... [*address*], landlord of .... [*name or description of holding*], having received a copy of the application² (bearing the above reference number) for the Tribunal's direction that certain covenants, conditions or agreements in the applicant's lease should be avoided or relaxed, reply as follows:—

1.   The facts contained in the first four paragraphs of the application are correct except that:—

2.

*(a)   I do not wish any covenant, condition or agreement to be avoided or relaxed in any way.

*(b)   I would agree to the following covenant(s)/conditions(s)/ avoided agreement(s) being *avoided/relaxed as follows:—

3.   For the following main reasons I do not agree that the covenant(s)/condition(s) /agreement(s) is (are) impending or preventing the proper use of the land for agricultural purposes or that (except as agreed in paragraph (2)(b) above) it would be expedient to relax or avoid it (them):—

4.   I attach copies of the following relevant documents(1):—

Date ....

Signed(²) ....

*   Strike out whichever is inapplicable
(¹)(a) Two copies of the reply and of any document which you wish to submit to the Tribunal must be sent to the Secretary, and, if there are more than two parties (eg, if the holding is sub-let), an additional copy of each must be supplied for each additional party.

(b) If you disagree with any map or plan attached to the application, your reply should be accompanied by two copies of a 6" to one mile or 1/10,000 (or larger) map showing what you consider to be the true position and marking the Ordnance Survey Field Numbers.

(²) If signed by any person other than the landlord himself, he should state in what capacity or by what authority he signs.³

Notes (not part of the prescribed form)
1   This form is Form 9R in the Appendix to the Agricultural Land Tribunals Rules 1978 contained in the Agricultural Land Tribunals (Rules) Order 1978, SI 1978/259, Sch 1, r 2. Although in general a form substantially to the like effect will suffice it is recommended that the prescribed form is used without alteration or variation in any particular, including reproduction of the statutorily prescribed notes which comprise part of the form. As reproduced, this Form follows the precise wording of the prescribed form, but not the exact layout and design. The Form as reproduced here refers to repealed enactments while the footnotes refer to the current equivalent provisions. ALTs have updated legislative references in some forms and are circulating them for use. A request may therefore be made to the relevant ALT for their version of the relevant form. As to proposals for a new Tribunal Rules Order see Form AH1 note 2 and para 46.20.
2   See Form AH16.
3   For the general provisions relating to replies and supporting documents, see the Agricultural Land Tribunals Rules 1978, SI 1978/259, r 16.

A2.91

AH18

Form 11¹

<table>
<tr><td></td><td>Ref. No.</td></tr>
<tr><td></td><td>To be inserted</td></tr>
<tr><td></td><td>by the Secretary</td></tr>
</table>

Agricultural Land Tribunal

APPLICATION UNDER LAND DRAINAGE ACT 1976

To the Secretary of the Agricultural Land Tribunal
for the .... Area.

I, ... [*block capitals*] of .... [*address*], hereby apply to the Tribunal for an order under section 40 of the Land Drainage Act 1976 requiring
.... [*state name(s) of person(s) against whom order is sought*] (¹) to carry out the work mentioned in paragraph 6 on the ground that [the land² mentioned in paragraph 3, of which I am the †owner/occupier, is being prevented] by the condition of the ditch³ mentioned in paragraph 4.

*   To be used for application under s 40.⁴
†   Strike out whichever is inapplicable.

* [In the event of the Tribunal deciding not to make such an order I hereby apply in the alternative under section 41 of the said Act for an order authorising me to carry out the said work.]

*   Strike out if inapplicable.

OR

* [1.   I, ... [*block capitals*] of .... [*address*], hereby apply to the Tribunal under section 41 of the Land Drainage Act 1976 for an order authorising me to carry out the work mentioned in paragraph 6 on the ground that the drainage of the land mentioned in paragraph 3, of which I am the †owner/occupier, requires the carrying out of such work.]

*   To be used for application under s 41.
†   Strike out whichever is inapplicable.

*[2.   I ask that the said order should authorise me [*or* the person required to carry out the said work] to enter on the land mentioned in paragraph 4 [and paragraph 7] so far as may be necessary for the carrying out of the said work.]

*   To be used for application under s 40 or s 41; strike out if no such authority is asked for.

3.   I am the *owner/occupier of [describe the land affected by application and give Ordnance Survey Field Numbers].

*   Strike out whichever is inapplicable.

*4.   Injury to my said land is being caused [and/or the improvement of the drainage of my said land is being prevented] by the condition of the undermentioned ditch [*specify ditch, stating land through which it passes and if possible the Ordnance Survey Field Numbers of that land*].

*   To be used for application under s 40.

OR

*[4.   The drainage of my said land requires:—

    †(a)   the carrying out of work in connection with the under-mentioned ditch:

    †(b)   and/or the replacement or construction of the under-mentioned ditch:

    †(c)   and/or the alteration or removal of drainage work in connection with the under-mentioned ditch:

[*specify ditch, stating land through which it passes and if possible the Ordnance Survey Field Numbers of that land*].

*   To be used for application under s 41.
†   Strike out whichever is inapplicable.

5.   The condition of the said ditch and its effect on my land is as follows [and/or the construction of the said ditch is required for the following reason]:

6.   The work which is required to be carried out is as follows:—

*[7.   For the purpose of carrying out the said work it will be necessary to enter the under-mentioned land in addition to that mentioned in paragraph 4 [*describe land, stating Ordnance Survey Field Numbers if possible*].

*   Strike out if inapplicable.

8.   This application affects the interests of the following persons:(²)

    (a)   .... [*block capitals*] of ... . [*address*] who is the *owner/occupier of [the following part of] the land mentioned in paragraph 4 [*or* 7] of this application [*or as the case may be*] (³)

    (b)   .... [*block capitals*] of .... [*address*] who is the *owner/occupier of [the

2129

following part of] the land mentioned in paragraph 4 [*or* 7] of this application [*or as the case may be*].(^{3})

* Strike out whichever is inapplicable.

*[9. To the best of my information and belief the following persons in addition to those named in paragraph 8 have rights in or over the said ditch and the land through which it passes:

(a) ... . [*block capitals*] of .... [*address*] who is ....

(b) .... [*block capitals*] of .... [*address*] who is ....

* Strike out if inapplicable.

10. I attach the following documents which I intend to produce in support of my case:—

(a) two(^{4}) copies of a 6" to one mile or 1/10,000(^{5}) map of the land described in paragraphs 3 and 4 [and 7] above;

(b) two(^{4}) copies of (^{6}):—

Date ....

Signed(^{7}) ....

(^{1}) Section 40 enables an order to be made against the owner or occupier of land through which the ditch passes or which abuts on the ditch or against any person who, although not such an owner or occupier, has a right to carry out the work specified in the order.^{5}

(^{2}) State the names of all persons who are to be parties to the proceedings. These must include any person against whom an order is applied for under section 40 as well as the name of the occupier of any land on which entry may be necessary for carrying out work under section 40 or 41 and, in the case of an application under section 41, the name of the owner of any land on which it is proposed that any work should be carried out.^{6} If more than two persons are named, continue on separate sheet.

(^{3}) State whether owner or occupier of the land or persons having a right to carry out the proposed work on the ditch mentioned in paragraph 4.

(^{4}) Two copies of the application and of any map and document must be sent to the Secretary, and if there are more than two parties, an additional copy of the application, etc, must be supplied for each additional party.

(^{5}) A larger scale map may be used if preferred. Ordnance Survey Field Numbers must be marked on the map where required.

(^{6}) Mention any other document which is attached to this application.

(^{7}) If signed by any person other than the applicant himself, he should state in what capacity or by what authority he signs.^{7}

Notes (not part of the prescribed form)

1   This form is Form 11 in the Appendix to the Agricultural Land Tribunals Rules 1978 contained in the Agricultural Land Tribunals (Rules) Order 1978, SI 1978/259, Sch 1, r 2. Although in general a form substantially to the like effect will suffice it is recommended that the prescribed form is used without alteration or variation in any particular, including reproduction of the statutorily prescribed notes which comprise part of the form. As reproduced, this Form follows the precise wording of the prescribed form, but not the exact layout and design. The Form as reproduced here refers to repealed enactments while the footnotes refer to the current equivalent provisions. ALTs have updated legislative references in some forms and are circulating them for use. A request may therefore be made to the relevant ALT for their version of the relevant form. As to proposals for a new Tribunal Rules Order see Form AH1 note 2 and para 46.20.

An application under the Land Drainage Act 1991, ss 28 or 30, formerly the Land Drainage Act 1976, s 40 or 41 (repealed) (22 Halsbury's Statutes (4th Edn) LAND DRAINAGE) for an order requiring the carrying out of work for putting a ditch in proper order or authorising the applicant to carry out drainage work on land must be made in Form 11: Agricultural Land Tribunals Rules 1978, r 11(1). See further 1 Halsbury's Laws (4th Edn) para 1238–1241.

2   'Land' includes water and any interests in land or water and any easement or right in, to, or over land or water: Land Drainage Act 1991, s 72(1).

3   'Drainage' includes defence against water (including sea water), irrigation, other than spray irrigation, warping and the carrying on, for any purpose, of any other practice which involves management of the level of water in a watercourse: see AHA 1986, s 72(1) as amended by the Environment Act 1995, s 100(2), Sch 22.

4   In AHA 1986, ss 28 and 30 'ditch' includes a culverted and a piped ditch but does not include a watercourse vested in or under the control of a drainage body: AHA 1986, ss 28(5), 30(4). For the meanings of 'watercourse' and 'drainage body' see AHA, 1986 s 72(1) as amended by the Environment Act 1995, ss 120, Sch 22, Sch 24.

5   Where, on the hearing of an application under AHA 1986, s 28, the applicant states that he desires also to apply under AHA 1986, s 30 for an order authorising him to carry out the same or substantially the same work as that referred to in his application, the tribunal may, if it thinks fit, deal with the application as if it had been made under AHA 1986, s 30 as well as under AHA 1986, s 28: Agricultural Land Tribunals Rules 1978, r 11(4).

6   Land Drainage Act 1991, s 28(2).

7   SI 1978/259, rr 11(2), 12(1), 13.

8   For the general provisions relating to applications and supporting documents, see SI 1978/259, r 16.

A2.92

AH19

Form 11R[1]

Ref. No.
To be inserted
by the Secretary

Agricultural Land Tribunal

REPLY TO APPLICATION UNDER LAND DRAINAGE ACT 1976

To the Secretary of the Agricultural Land Tribunal
for the .... Area.

I, ... [*block capitals*] of ... . [*address*], having received a copy of the application[2] (bearing the above reference number) and of the report[3] provided by the Minister of Agriculture, Fisheries and Food for the purpose thereof and of the applicant's notice in Form 12[4] reply[5] as follows:—

1.   The facts stated in the said application and in the said report are correct except that:—

*2.

(a)   I agree to an order being made

*(i)   in the terms of the recommendation in the report;6 or

*(ii)   in the terms asked for in the application [if different from those recommended in the report]; or

*(iii)   I resist the application

*(b)   I resist the application

*   Strike out whichever is inapplicable.

3.   * My main reasons for resisting the application are:—

*   Strike out if inapplicable.

4.   I attach copies of the following relevant documents(¹):—

Date ....

Signed(²) ....

(¹)(a) Two copies of the reply and of any document which you wish to submit to the Tribunal
must be sent to the Secretary, and, if there are more than two parties, an additional copy of
each must be supplied for each additional party.
(b) If you disagree with any map or plan attached to the application or if, in your reply, you
mention any land not shown thereon, your reply should be accompanied by two copies of
a 6" to one mile or a 1/10,000 (or larger) map showing what you consider to be the true
position or showing the other land mentioned in your reply, as the case may be, and
marking the Ordnance Survey Field Numbers.
(²) If signed by any person other than the party himself, he should state in what capacity or by
what authority he signs[7].

Notes (not part of the prescribed form)
1   This form is Form 11R in the Appendix to the Agricultural Land Tribunals Rules 1978
contained in the Agricultural Land Tribunals (Rules) Order 1978, SI 1978/259, Sch 1, r 2.
Although in general a form substantially to the like effect will suffice it is recommended that
the prescribed form is used without alteration or variation in any particular, including
reproduction of the statutorily prescribed notes which comprise part of the form. As
reproduced, this Form follows the precise wording of the prescribed form, but not the exact
layout and design. The Form as reproduced here refers to repealed enactments while the
footnotes refer to the current equivalent provisions. ALTs have updated legislative references
in some forms and are circulating them for use. A request may therefore be made to the
relevant ALT for their version of the relevant form. As to proposals for a new Tribunal Rules
Order, see Form AH1 note 2 and para 46.20.
2   See Form AH18.
3   On receipt of an application in a drainage case, the ALT must call on the Secretary of State for
Environment Food and Rural Affairs and (in relation to Wales) the Secretary of State for
Wales to provide a report on the matters to which the application relates, and for the purpose
the tribunal may authorise any officer of the Secretary of State to enter and inspect any land
specified by the tribunal: Agricultural Land Tribunals Rules 1978, r 21(1) as amended by the
National Assembly for Wales (Transfer of Functions) Order 1999, SI 1999/672, art 2, Sch 1
and the Ministry of Agriculture Fisheries and Food (Dissolution) Order 2002, SI 2002/794.
'Drainage case' means proceedings on an application under the Land Drainage Act 1991, s 28
or s 30 (22 Halsbury's Statutes (4th Edn) LAND DRAINAGE): Agricultural Land Tribunals
Rules 1978, r 1(2).
4   The applicant's notice must state whether or not he agrees with the facts stated and the
recommendations made in the report: SI 1978/259, r 21(4); see further Form AH202 note 4.
5   The time within which a party is required by SI 1978/259, r 15 to reply to the application
will, in a drainage case, run from the date of the service on him of the notice under
SI 1978/259, r 21(4): SI 1978/259, rr 15(1), 21(5).
6   A report made under SI 1978/259, r 21(1) may recommend that no order or that an order in
the terms set out in the report be made by the ALT: SI 1978/259, r 21(2).
7   For the general provisions relating to replies and supporting documents, see SI 1978/259,
r 16.

A2.93

AH20

Form 12[1]
Rule 21(4)

Ref. No.
To be inserted
by the Secretary

Agricultural Land Tribunal

LAND DRAINAGE ACT 1976
NOTICE BY APPLICANT UNDER RULE 21(4) OF THE AGRICULTURAL LAND TRIBUNALS
RULES 1978

To the Secretary of the Agricultural Land Tribunal
for the .... Area.

I, ... [block capitals] of .... [address],
having applied[2] to the Tribunal on the .... day of .... 20 (under
reference number ....) for an order under section 40 [and/or section 41]* of
the Land Drainage Act 1976, and having received a copy of the report[3] provided by the
Minister of Agriculture, Fisheries and Food for the purposes of my application,[4] state
as follows:

*   Strike out whichever is inapplicable.

1.   I accept the facts stated in the report with the exception of:

2.

   *(a)   I accept the recommendation made in the report and hereby request the
            Tribunal to make an order on my application in the terms of the
            recommendation.

   *(b)   I do not accept the recommendation made in the report and I request the
            Tribunal to make an order on my application in the terms asked for
            therein [or in the following modified terms]

*   Strike out whichever is inapplicable.

3.   I attach the following documents which I intend to produce in support of my
      case:—([1])

Date ....

Signed([2]) ....

([1]) Two copies of this notice must be sent to the Secretary together with two copies of any
    map or document which you wish to submit to the Tribunal and which has not already
    been submitted with the application. If there are more than two parties, an additional copy
    of the notice, etc, must be supplied for each additional party.
([2]) If signed by any person other than the applicant himself, he should state in what capacity
    or by what authority he signs.

2133

Notes (not part of the prescribed form)

1   This form is Form 12 in the Appendix to the Agricultural Land Tribunals Rules 1978 contained in the Agricultural Land Tribunals (Rules) Order 1978, SI 1978/259, Sch 1, r 2. Although in general a form substantially to the like effect will suffice it is recommended that the prescribed form is used without alteration or variation in any particular, including reproduction of the statutorily prescribed notes which comprise part of the form. As reproduced, this Form follows the precise wording of the prescribed form, but not the exact layout and design. The Form as reproduced here refers to repealed enactments while the footnotes refer to the current equivalent provisions. ALTs have updated legislative references in some forms and are circulating them for use. A request may therefore be made to the relevant ALT for their version of the relevant form. As to proposals for a new Tribunal Rules Order, see Form AH1 note 2 and para 46.20.

2   See Form AH18.

3   See Form AH19 note 3.

4   Within one month of a copy of the report being served on him the applicant must serve a notice on the ALT in Form 12 stating whether or not he agrees with the facts stated and the recommendations made in the report; and the Agricultural Land Tribunals Rules 1978, rr 16(1), (5), 17 will apply to the notice as if it were an application: r 21(4).

A2.94

AH21

Form 13[1]

Rule 23(4)

Agricultural Land Tribunal

NOTICE OF HEARING

Land at:

Applicant/s:

Respondent/s:

TAKE NOTICE that the HEARING of the APPLICATION in respect of the above named Holding will be held on at commencing at

Dated .... 20 .

Signed ....

(Secretary of the Tribunal)

Note to parties

You may find of assistance the following note of rules of evidence and procedure, which apply to this hearing and which are contained in the Agricultural Land Tribunals Rules 1978.

1.   *Rules of Evidence*

(a)   Any evidence may be admitted by the tribunal, including evidence that would not be admissible in a court of law.

(b)   Evidence before the tribunal may be given—

(i)   orally, on oath or on affirmation or otherwise,

(ii)   by affidavit, if the parties consent, or

(iii)   by means of written statements produced by the maker when giving evidence or, if the tribunal consent, by another witness.

If evidence is tendered in the form of a written statement, four copies of the statement should be available at the hearing for the tribunal and two copies for the other parties.

(c)   At any stage of the proceedings the tribunal may, of their own motion or on the application of any party, order the personal attendance of the maker of any written statement for examination and cross-examination.[2]

(d)   The secretary may require a party to give to the tribunal documents or other information, and to afford to all other parties an opportunity to inspect such documents, or copies of them, and to take copies of them.[3]

If the parties intend to produce documents at the hearing, they should if possible agree them beforehand, list them in order and put them into one agreed bundle. Four copies of this bundle should be available if possible for the use of the tribunal.

(e)   The tribunal may, after giving notice to all parties and to any other occupier of the land, enter and inspect any agricultural holding owned or occupied by any party, whether the holding is the subject of the proceedings or not, and may inspect any fixed or other equipment, produce or livestock thereon.[4]

2.   *Procedure at the Hearing*

(a)   The tribunal sit in public unless exceptional circumstances make it desirable that the hearing, or some part of it, should take place in private.[5]

(b)   A party may appear and be heard in person or by counsel or solicitor or by a representative appointed in writing.[6]

(c)   The party making the application will begin and the other parties will be heard in such order as the tribunal may determine.[7]

3.   *Witnesses*

(a)   Each party will be given an opportunity to call and cross-examine witnesses, and a party may if he wishes give evidence as a witness on his own behalf.

(b)   The tribunal may call witnesses, who may after giving evidence be cross-examined by any party.[8]

(c)   The provisions of the County Court Rules 1936, as amended, as to the issue of witness summonses (Order 20, rule 8)[9] apply for the purposes of any proceedings before the tribunal.[10] Under these Rules, a party desiring a person to be summoned as a witness must apply to the county court registrar by filling in the prescribed form in the county court office.

4.   *Default of Appearance*

If a party fails to appear at the time fixed for the hearing, the tribunal may—

    (i)   dismiss the application where the party failing to appear is the applicant, or

    (ii)   proceed in any other case to determine the application in the party's absence, if satisfied that the party failing to appear has been afforded an adequate opportunity of attending.[11]

Notes (not part of the prescribed form)

[1]   This form is Form 13 in the Appendix to the Agricultural Land Tribunals Rules 1978 contained in the Agricultural Land Tribunals (Rules) Order 1978, SI 1978/259, Sch 1, r 2. Although in general a form substantially to the like effect will suffice it is recommended that the prescribed form is used without alteration or variation in any particular, including reproduction of the statutorily prescribed notes which comprise part of the form. As reproduced, this Form follows the precise wording of the prescribed form, but not the exact layout and design. The Form as reproduced here refers to repealed enactments while the footnotes refer to the current equivalent provisions. ALTs have updated legislative references in some forms and are circulating them for use. A request may therefore be made to the relevant ALT for their version of the relevant form. As to proposals for a new Tribunal Rules Order, see Form AH1 note 2 and para 46.20.

The secretary of the ALT must send to every party notice in Form 13 of the date, time and place of any hearing which, except with the consent of the parties, shall not be earlier than 14 days after the date on which the notice is sent: Agricultural Land Tribunals Rules 1978, r 23(4).

[2]   SI 1978/259, r 28.
[3]   SI 1978/259, r 20(1).
[4]   SI 1978/259, r 30.
[5]   SI 1978/259, r 24.
[6]   SI 1978/259, r 25.
[7]   SI 1978/259, r 26(1).
[8]   SI 1978/259, r 29(1), (2).
[9]   See now the Civil Procedure Rules 1998, SI 1998/3132, Part 34.
[10] SI 1978/259, r 29(4).
[11] SI 1978/259, r 27.

A2.95

AH22

Form 14[1]
Rule 32

Ref. No.
To be inserted
by the Secretary

Agricultural Land Tribunal

APPLICATION FOR VARIATION OF ORDER MADE UNDER LAND DRAINAGE ACT 1976

To the Secretary of the Agricultural Land Tribunal
for the .... Area.

1. I, ... [*block capitals*] of ... . [*address*], hereby apply to the Tribunal to vary its order² dated the .... , day of .... 20 .

2. The order was made on *[my application]³ [the application of .... [*block capitals*] of .... [*address*]] bearing the reference number ....

*   Strike out whichever is inapplicable.

3. The variation for which I apply is:—

4. My main reasons for making this application are:—

5. I attach copies of the following documents which I intend to produce in support of my case(¹):—

Date ....

Signed(²) ....:......

(¹) Two copies of this application and of any document which you wish to submit to the Tribunal must be sent to the Secretary, and, if there are more than two parties, an additional copy of each must be supplied for each additional party.

(²) If signed by any person other than the applicant himself, he should state in what capacity or by what authority he signs.⁴

Notes (not part of the prescribed form)

¹   This form is Form 14 in the Appendix to the Agricultural Land Tribunals Rules 1978 contained in the Agricultural Land Tribunals (Rules) Order 1978, SI 1978/259, Sch 1, r 2. Although in general a form substantially to the like effect will suffice it is recommended that the prescribed form is used without alteration or variation in any particular, including reproduction of the statutorily prescribed notes which comprise part of the form. As reproduced, this Form follows the precise wording of the prescribed form, but not the exact layout and design. The Form as reproduced here refers to repealed enactments while the footnotes refer to the current equivalent provisions. ALTs have updated legislative references in some forms and are circulating them for use. A request may therefore be made to the relevant ALT for their version of the relevant form. As to proposals for a new Tribunal Rules Order, see Form AH1 note 2 and para 46.20.

²   Any order made following a decision of the ALT in a drainage case may be varied whether as to the time within which any work is to be carried out or otherwise and on an application to vary the order which must be made in Form 14, the chairman may give all such directions as may be just: Agricultural Land Tribunals Rules 1978, r 32. For the meaning of 'drainage case', see Form AH18 note 3.

³   For a form of application in a drainage case see Form AH18.

⁴   For the general provisions relating to applications and supporting documents, see the Agricultural Land Tribunals Rules 1978, SI 1978/259, r 16.

B: SUCCESSION TO TENANCIES ON DEATH OF TENANT

A2.96

AH23

Form 1 (Succession on Death)¹
Rule 3(1 and (2))

Ref. No.
To be inserted

by the Secretary

Agricultural Land Tribunal

APPLICATION FOR DIRECTION GIVING ENTITLEMENT TO TENANCY OF AGRICULTURAL
HOLDING
APPLICATION FOR DETERMINATION THAT APPLICANT BE TREATED AS AN
ELIGIBLE PERSON[2]

[In completing this form it is important to refer to the notes]

Part A—To be completed by all applicants

To the Secretary of the Agricultural Land Tribunal
for the .... Area.

1. I, ... [*block capitals*] of
    .... [*address*], hereby apply under section 20(1) of
    the Agriculture (Miscellaneous Provisions) Act 1976 for a direction entitling me
    to a tenancy of the holding specified in paragraph 2 below.

2. The holding in respect of which the application is made is known as
    .... and consists of:—

    (a) ....   hectares of arable land (including temporary
                                       grass)
                                       (Ordnance Survey Field Nos ....);

    (b) ....   hectares of permanent pastures
                                       (Ordnance Survey Field Nos ....);

    (c) ....   hectares of rough grazing
                                       (Ordnance Survey Field Nos ....);

    (d) ....   hectares of other land (including orchards)
                                       (Ordnance Survey Field Nos ....);

    Total ....   hectares   Annual
                                       Rent £

3. The current year of the tenancy of the holding expires on

4. The holding includes the following buildings [*give a general description*]:—

†5. The holding forms part of a larger agricultural unit known as and consisting of
    [*give a general description*]:—

6. The application arises on the death of .... formerly the tenant of the
    holding referred to in paragraph 2, who died on ([1]) His/her tenancy was—

    *(a) granted before 12th July 1984.

    *(b) obtained on or after 12th July 1984 by virtue of a direction of the
    Agricultural Land Tribunal under section 20 of the 1976 Act.

    *(c) granted on or after 12th July 1984 following a direction of the
    Agricultural Land Tribunal under section 20 of the 1976 Act but
    commenced before the relevant time for the purposes of section 23 of
    that Act.

*(d)   granted on or after 12th July 1984 by a written contract of tenancy indicating that the succession provisions in Part II of the 1976 Act should apply.

*(e)   granted on or after 12th July 1984 to a person who, immediately before that date, was a tenant of the holding or of any agricultural holding which comprised the whole or a substantial part of the land comprised in the holding.

7.   The landlord of the holding is .... of .... [*address*].

†8.   I am the sole person validly designated by the deceased tenant of the holding in his will as the person he wished to succeed him as tenant of the holding. A copy of the relevant part of the will in which I am designated is attached [*attach a copy of or extract from the will marking the relevant passage*] (²).

9.

†(a)   I am the *wife/*husband/*brother/*sister/*child of the deceased tenant(³).

(b)   I was treated by the deceased tenant as a child of the family in relation to his marriage to .... (⁴) on .... [*give date of marriage*].

†10.

(a)   During the seven years ending with the date of death of the deceased tenant my only or my principal source of livelihood was derived from—

*(i)   my agricultural work on the holding, or on an agricultural unit of which the holding forms a part;

*(ii)   his/his and my agricultural work on the holding, or on an agricultural unit of which the holding forms a part;

during the following period(s) and in the following manner [give details of the way livelihood derived from agricultural work on the holding] (⁵):—

*(b)   During the period(s) specified in paragraph 10(a) I had the following source(s) of livelihood other than those derived from the holding or from an agricultural unit of which the holding forms a part [give details of other sources of livelihood]:

*(c)   During the period(s) specified in paragraph 10(a) I had no other source of livelihood.

†11.   During the seven years ending with the date of death of the deceased tenant I attended a full-time course at .... [*name of university, college or other establishment of further education*] during the following period(s) [*give details of time spent at university, etc*] (⁵),(⁶):—

During this period/these periods I studied the following subjects and obtained the following qualifications [*give details of subjects studied and any qualifications obtained*]:—

12.

(a)   The following agricultural land is occupied by me, my spouse or a company under my control, the control of my spouse or our joint control as owner-occupier/tenant/licensee, whether alone or jointly with others [*give particulars of any land occupied, including area and any land occupied jointly with others*]:—

(b)   The following agricultural land is occupied by a person under a licence or such a tenancy([7]) as is mentioned in paragraph 2(1)(a) to (d) of Schedule 3A to the 1976 Act ([8]) granted by me and/or my spouse and/or *a company controlled by me and/or my spouse together with one or more other persons, being at the time it was granted a person or persons entitled to occupy the land otherwise than under a tenancy, or in a capacity, falling within paragraph 2(1)(a) to (f) of that Schedule([8]) [*give particulars of any land occupied, including area*]:—

†(c)   I apply under paragraph 4(2) of Schedule 3A to the 1976 Act for the net annual income from the following agricultural land which is—

*(i)   jointly occupied;

*(ii)   deemed by virtue of paragraph 6(2) of that Schedule to be jointly occupied by me and one or more other persons (not being only my spouse or a company under my control, the control of my spouse or our joint control) to be treated as limited to my appropriate share of that net annual income [*give particulars of any land in joint occupation or deemed joint occupation*] ([9]):—

13.   I was born on ....

14.   I claim to be a suitable person to receive the tenancy of this holding because([10]):—

Part B—To be completed if you think that you may not fully satisfy the requirements of paragraph 10(a)

15.   Further to the application set out in the preceding paragraphs of this Form,

I, ... [*block capitals*] of the above address also apply under section 21(2) of the 1976 Act for a determination that I am to be treated as an eligible person for the purposes of Part II of that Act ([11]).

16.

(a)   During the seven years ending with the date of death of the deceased tenant my livelihood was derived from—

*(i)   my agricultural work on the holding referred to in paragraph 2, or on an agricultural unit of which the holding forms a part;

*(ii)   his/his and my agricultural work on the holding referred to in paragraph 2, or on an agricultural unit of which the holding forms a part;

to a material extent during the following period(s) and in the following manner [*give details of the extent to which livelihood was derived from agricultural work on the holding*] ([12]):—

(b)   During the period(s) specified in paragraph 16(a) I had the following source(s) of livelihood other than those derived from the holding or from an agricultural unit of which the holding forms a part [*give details of other sources of livelihood*]:—

†(c)   During the period(s) specified in paragraph 16(a) I had no other source of livelihood.

†17.   During the seven years ending with the date of death of the deceased tenant I attended a full-time course at

[name of university, college or other establishment of further education] during the following period(s) [*give details of time spent at university, etc*] ([6]):—

During this period/these periods I studied the following subjects and obtained the following qualifications [give details of subjects studied and any qualifications obtained]:—

†18.　I claim that, because of the following circumstances, it is fair and reasonable for me to be able to apply under section of 20 of the 1976 Act for a direction entitling me to a tenancy of the holding referred to in paragraph 2([13]):—

Part C—To be completed by all applicants

19.　I attach the following documents which I intend to produce in support of my case:—

(a)　two([14]) copies of a 6" to one mile or 1/10,000([15]) map of the holding described in paragraph 2 above (and of the other land referred to in paragraph 5);

(b)　two([14]) copies of ([16]):—

20.　The persons whom I shall notify of this application/these applications are([17]):—

(a)　the landlord of the holding whose name and address are:

(b)　....................

(c)　....................

(d)　....................

21.

(a)　The following is/are the personal representative(s) of the deceased tenant or [*if there are no personal representatives*] the person or persons responsible for the management of the holding on behalf of the deceased's estate([18]):—

Name(s) ....

Address(es) ....

... .;

... .

(b)　The following person(s) is/are or may be interested in the outcome of this application([18]):—

Name(s) ....

Address(es) ....

... .

....

Nature of interest ....

Date ....

Signed([19]) ....

*　Strike out whichever is inapplicable.
†　Strike out if inapplicable.
([1])　Formal proof of the date of death will be required at the hearing.
([2])　This paragraph should be completed only if the applicant received a specific bequest of the deceased's tenancy under his will or is specifically named in the will as the person whom the deceased tenant wished to succeed him as tenant of the holding. It will be necessary for a grant of probate or administration to be obtained from the Family Division of the High Court in respect of the will before the tribunal can hear any claim to be a designated

applicant. Where an applicant establishes that he is so designated under the deceased tenant's will, no other application will be considered unless the tribunal determine that the designated applicant is not an eligible person or is not a suitable person to become the tenant of the holding.

(³) Formal proof of the relationship to the deceased, eg, by production of marriage or birth certificates, may be required at the hearing. Adopted children should complete this sub-paragraph, and not paragraph 9(b) following.

(⁴) Paragraph 9(b) may apply where the applicant was the step-child or foster child of the deceased or was otherwise treated by him as his child. An outline should be given of the circumstances relied on as establishing that the applicant was treated by the deceased as his child in relation to the marriage. Production of the relevant marriage certificate and any relevant birth certificate may be required at the hearing.

(⁵) To qualify under paragraph 10(a)(i) the applicant should have derived his only or principal source of livelihood from his agricultural work on the holding (or on a larger unit of which the holding forms part) during a total of five years of the seven years ending with the death of the deceased tenant. Paragraph 10(a)(ii) is available only to a widow of the deceased tenant. The total of five years may be made up of one continuous period, or one or more separate periods. A period of full-time education at a university etc, may, in the circumstances set out in note (⁶), count towards the five-year period of earning a livelihood from the holding, and reference should be made to paragraph 11 and note (⁶) in deciding whether the requirements of this paragraph can be satisfied. An applicant who cannot satisfy the requirements of paragraph 10(a) fully but who believes he can satisfy them to a material extent should not complete paragraphs 10 and 11 but should complete instead paragraph 15, together with paragraphs 16, 17 (if relevant) and 18 in Part B of the Form. The Notes to those paragraphs should also be consulted. Where an applicant is in any doubt as to whether or not he can satisfy the requirements of paragraph 10 fully, he is advised to complete paragraphs 10 and 11 (if relevant) and Part B of the Form.

(⁶) Any period or periods (up to an aggregate total of three years) during the seven years ending with the date of death of the deceased tenant during which the applicant was attending a full-time course at a university, college or other establishment of further education will be treated as a period throughout which his only or principal source of livelihood was derived from his agricultural work on the holding. Any subject may have been studied.

(⁷) Land occupied by the applicant's spouse or by a company controlled by that person or jointly by that person and the applicant should not be included in paragraph 12 where either of the parties has obtained a decree of judicial separation or a decree nisi of divorce or of nullity of marriage and in each case that decree remains unrescinded. In addition, land should not be included in paragraph 12 if it is occupied by the applicant, his spouse or a controlled company—

(a) under a tenancy approved under section2(1) of the Agricultural Holdings Act 1948 or under such a tenancy relating to the use of land for grazing or mowing as is referred to in the proviso to that provision;

(b) under a tenancy for more than one year but less than two years;

(c) under a tenancy not falling within (a) or (b) above and not having effect as a contract of tenancy;

(d) under a tenancy to which section 3 of the 1948 Act does not apply by virtue of section 3B of that Act;

(e) as a licensee; or

(f) as an executor, administrator, trustee in bankruptcy or person otherwise deriving title from another person by operation of law.

However, where the applicant occupies land in accordance with (a) to (e) above under a licence or tenancy granted to him by his spouse or by a body corporate controlled by him, that land should be included in paragraph 12.

(⁸) Paragraph 2(1)(a) to (f) of Schedule 3A to the Agriculture (Miscellaneous Provisions) Act 1976 is set out in note (⁷).

(⁹) If the applicant occupies land jointly with one or more other persons (not being only his spouse or a company under the control of the applicant or his spouse or under their joint control), or if the applicant is deemed to occupy land jointly with one or more such persons, he may in either case complete the application set out in paragraph 12(c) of the Form for the net annual income which the land is or was capable of producing to be treated as limited to his appropriate share.

(^{10}) All matters relied on as supporting the claim to be a suitable person to become the tenant of the holding should be summarised. These should include details of the applicant's training and practical experience of agriculture, physical health, financial standing and any educational qualifications not already listed in paragraph 11 or 17.

(^{11}) This paragraph should be completed (together with paragraphs 16, 17 (if relevant) and 18) in any case where the applicant, while otherwise meeting the conditions contained in the definition of 'eligible person' in section 18(2) of the 1976 Act cannot fully satisfy the conditions as to deriving his principal or main source of livelihood from the holding contained in paragraph (b) of that subsection. (It is also necessary for the application set out in paragraph 1 of the Form to be completed in addition to completing this paragraph.) An applicant who fully satisfies the requirements of paragraph 10(a) need not complete this paragraph or paragraphs 16, 17 and 18.

(^{12}) The applicant should state to what extent he has derived his livelihood from his agricultural work on the holding (or on a larger unit of which the holding forms part) during a total of five years of the seven years ending with the death of the deceased tenant. Paragraph 16(a)(ii) applies only to a widow of the deceased tenant. The total of five years may be made up of one continuous period, or one or more separate periods. A period of full-time education at a university, etc, may in certain circumstances count in relation to the five year period as a period in which a livelihood was derived from agricultural work on the holding, and paragraph 17 should also be completed where relevant.

(^{13}) A summary should be given of matters relied on as establishing that it is fair and reasonable that the applicant should be entitled to apply under section 20 of the 1976 Act for a tenancy of the holding, though not fully satisfying the conditions specified in paragraph (b) of the definition of 'eligible person' in section 18(2) of that Act. The length of time the applicant has lived on the holding, details of work done by him on the holding (apart from those already given in paragraph 16) and any special circumstances which have prevented him from qualifying in full as an eligible person under paragraph (a) of the definition of 'eligible person' should be given. (Note (^{5}) describes the requirements needed to qualify fully under paragraph (a) of the definition.)

(^{14}) By virtue of rule 11(1) of the Agricultural Land Tribunals (Succession) Rules 1984 two copies of the application and of any map and document must be sent to the secretary.

(^{15}) A larger scale map may be used if preferred. Ordnance Survey Field Numbers must be marked on the map.

(^{16}) Mention any other document which is attached to this application.

(^{17}) The applicant is required to send to the landlord of the holding, and to every other person who to his knowledge has made or may be able to make an application for a tenancy of the holding, notice of this application in Form 3 (Succession on Death) which is set out in the Appendix to the Agricultural Land Tribunals (Succession) Rules 1984. The applicant should enter the name and address of the landlord at (a) and the names and addresses of appropriate other persons (if any) respectively at (b), (c) and (d), etc.

(^{18}) This information is required by rule 5(2) of those Rules.

(^{19}) If signed by any person other than the applicant himself, he should state in what capacity or by what authority he signs.

Notes (not part of the prescribed form)

1 This form is Form 1 in the Appendix to the Agricultural Land Tribunals (Succession) Rules 1984, contained in the Agricultural Land Tribunals (Succession to Agricultural Tenancies) Order 1984, SI 1984/1301, Sch, r 3(1), (2). Although in general a form substantially to the like effect will suffice it is recommended that the prescribed form is used without alteration or variation in any particular, including reproduction of the statutorily prescribed notes which comprise part of the form. As reproduced, this Form follows the precise wording of the prescribed form, but not the exact layout and design. The Form as reproduced here refers to repealed enactments while the footnotes refer to the current equivalent provisions. ALTs have updated legislative references in some forms and are circulating them for use. A request may therefore be made to the relevant ALT for their version of the relevant form. As to proposals for a new Tribunal Rules Order, see Form AH1 note 2 and para 46.20.

2 Generally, see Ch 35 and para 35.51 ff as to an applicant being treated as eligible. Any eligible person may within 3 months from the date of death apply to the Agricultural Land Tribunal for a direction entitling him to a tenancy of an agricultural holding after the death of a sole (or sole surviving) tenant: AHA 1986, ss 35, 36(1), 39(1) (see para A1.122, A1.123 and A1.126) (formerly the Agriculture (Miscellaneous Provisions) Act 1976, s 20 (repealed)).

As to the meaning of 'eligible person' and agricultural work carried out by a person on the holding, see the AHA 1986, s 36 as amended by the Regulatory Reform (Agricultural Tenancies) (England and Wales) Order 2006, SI 2006/2805, art 5(1).

An application under the AHA 1986, s 39 or s 41 or under both provisions must be made in Form 1: Agricultural Land Tribunals (Succession) Rules 1984, r 3(1), (2) and, where application is made under both provisions, it must be made at the same time and in the same form: r 3(2).

As to the right of any surviving close relative of a deceased tenant who for some part of the 7 years ending with the date of death engaged whether full-time or part-time in agricultural work upon the holding to apply for a direction to the ALT, see the AHA 1986, s 41 as amended by SI 2006/2805, arts 2, 5(2).

A2.97

AH24

Form 1R (Succession on Death)[1]
Rule 6

Ref. No.
To be inserted
by the Secretary

Agricultural Land Tribunal

REPLY TO APPLICATION FOR DIRECTION GIVING ENTITLEMENT TO TENANCY OF
AGRICULTURAL HOLDING[2]
REPLY TO APPLICATION FOR DETERMINATION THAT APPLICANT BE TREATED AS AN
ELIGIBLE PERSON[2]

To the Secretary of the Agricultural Land Tribunal
for the .... Area.

1.   I, ... [*block capitals*] of ... . [*address*], landlord
        of .... [*name or description of holding*] having received a
        copy of the application bearing the above reference number reply as follows:—

1.   The facts stated in paragraphs 1, 2, 4 and 7 of the application are, to the best of
        my knowledge, information and belief, correct except that:—

†2.   I dispute the claim of the applicant to be an eligible person[1] on the following
        grounds:—

3.   I dispute the claim of the applicant to be treated as an eligible person[2] on the
        following grounds:—

4.   I have the following comments on the suitability of the applicant to become
        tenant of the above holding:—

5.   I atttach two copies of the following releant documents[3]:—

6.   I consider the application to be invalid by reason of (4):—

Date ....

Signed([5]) ....

†   Strike out if inapplicable.

TAKE NOTICE THAT IF YOU DO NOT REPLY IN THIS FORM WITHIN ONE MONTH OF THE DATE OF SERVICE ON YOU OF THE ATTACHED APPLICA-TION, THEN, SUBJECT TO SECTION 20(7) OF THE AGRICULTURE (MISCEL-LANEOUS PROVISIONS) ACT 1976, YOU WILL NOT BE ENTITLED AT THE HEARING OF THE APPLICATION TO DISPUTE ANY MATTER ALLEGED IN IT.

(¹) The paragraphs of the application which (where completed) will be relevant to the applicant's claim to be an eligible person are paragraphs 9, 10, 11 and 12.

(²) The paragraphs of the application which (where completed) will be relevant to the applicant's claim to be treated as an eligible person are paragraphs 15, 16, 17 and 18.

(³) By virtue of rule 11(1) of the Agricultural Land Tribunals (Succession) Rules 1984 two copies of this reply and of any document which you wish to submit to the tribunal must be sent to the secretary. If you disagree with any map or plan attached to the application, your reply should be accompanied by two copies of a 6" to one mile or 1/10,000 (or larger) map showing what you consider to be the true position and marking the Ordnance Survey Field Numbers.

(⁴) If you consider that, for any reason, the applicant is not legally entitled to make his application, you should state succinctly the grounds on which you rely.

(⁵) If signed by any person other than the landlord himself, he should state in what capacity or by what authority he signs.

Notes (not part of the prescribed form)

1 This form is Form 1R in the Appendix to the Agricultural Land Tribunals (Succession) Rules 1984 contained in the Agricultural Land Tribunals (Succession to Agricultural Tenancies) Order 1984, SI 1984/1301, Sch, r 6. Although in general a form substantially to the like effect will suffice it is recommended that the prescribed form is used without alteration or variation in any particular, including reproduction of the statutorily prescribed notes which comprise part of the form. As reproduced, this Form follows the precise wording of the prescribed form, but not the exact layout and design. The Form as reproduced here refers to repealed enactments while the footnotes refer to the current equivalent provisions. ALTs have updated legislative references in some forms and are circulating them for use. A request may therefore be made to the relevant ALT for their version of the relevant form. As to proposals for a new Tribunal Rules Order, see Form AH1 note 2 and para 46.20.

2 Generally, see Ch 35 and para 35.51 ff as to an applicant being treated as eligible. A landlord of the relevant holding who intends to oppose the whole or any part of an application under the Agricultural Land Tribunals (Succession) Rules 1984, r 3(1) (see Form AH23) must, within one month after a copy of the application has been served on him, reply to it in Form 1R: SI 1984/1301, r 6. Before making a determination as to whether an applicant is in its opinion a suitable person, the tribunal must afford the landlord an opportunity of stating his views on the suitability of the applicant: AHA 1986, ss 39(2), (7) (see para A1.126).

A2.98

AH25

Form 2 (Succession on Death)¹
Rule 4(1)

> Ref. No.
> To be inserted
> by the Secretary

Agricultural Land Tribunal

APPLICATION FOR CONSENT TO OPERATION OF NOTICE TO QUIT

To the Secretary of the Agricultural Land Tribunal
for the .... Area.

1.   I, ... [*block capitals*] of ... . [*address*], hereby apply under section 22(1) of the Agriculture (Miscellaneous Provisions) Act 1976 for the consent of the tribunal to the operation of a notice to quit which I gave to .... and .... being the personal representative(s) of .... [*block capitals*] deceased, formerly of .... [*address*] I was officially notified of his/her death by .... on

2.   The notice to quit was served on [*insert date*] in respect of the holding known as

3.   An application (bearing reference number ....) to the tribunal under Part II of the 1976 Act for a tenancy of this holding was made on .... particulars of the holding are set out in that application †(as amended in my reply to that application dated ....).

4.   I apply for the tribunal's consent to the operation of the notice to quit in the event of an applicant under the application referred to in paragraph 3, or any other such applicant, being determined by the tribunal to be a suitable person to become the tenant of the holding.

5.   The grounds upon which I make this application are those provided in paragraph(s) of section 3(3) of the Agricultural Holdings (Notices to Quit) Act 1977 as read with section 22(2) of the 1976 Act, as amended. [*It is important to refer to note* (¹).]

6.   The main facts on which I will base my case are:—

7.   If I obtain possession of the land I intend:—

    *(a)   to farm it myself.

    *(b)   to let it to another tenant [*state name and address if known*].

    *(c)   [*state any other intention*]

†8.   The future tenant referred to in paragraph 7(b)(²) at present farms other land consisting of:—

    (a) ....   hectares of arable land (including temporary grass) (Ordnance Survey Field Nos ....);
    (b) ....   hectares of permanent pasture (Ordnance Survey Field Nos ....);
    (c) ....   hectares of rough grazing (Ordnance Survey Field Nos ....);
    (d) ....   hectares of other land (including orchards) (Ordnance Survey Field Nos ....);
    Total ....   hectares.

9.   I attach the following documents which I intend to produce in support of my case:—

    (a)   two copies(³) of a 6" to one mile or 1/10,000(⁴) map of the land described in paragraph 8(⁵) above;

    (b)   two copies(³) of (⁶):—

Date ....

                                        Signed(⁷) ....

*   Strike out whichever is inapplicable.
†   Strike out if inapplicable.

(^{1}) The applicant must state on which paragraph or paragraphs of the subsection he intends to rely. The five paragraphs state as follows:—

(a) that the carrying out of the purpose for which the landlord proposes to terminate the tenancy is desirable in the interests of good husbandry as respects the land to which the notice relates, treated as a separate unit;

(b) that the carrying out thereof is desirable in the interests of sound management of the estate of which the land to which the notice relates forms part or which that land constitutes (see note (^{5}) below);

(c) that the carrying out thereof is desirable for the purposes of agricultural research, education, experiment or demonstration, or for the purposes of the enactments relating to smallholdings or allotments;

(d) that greater hardship would be caused by withholding than by giving consent to the operation of the notice;

(e) that the landlord proposes to terminate the tenancy for the purpose of the land's being used for a use, other than for agriculture, not falling within Case B in section 2(3) of the Agricultural Holdings (Notices to Quit) Act 1977.

If, under paragraph (d) above, the applicant intends to rely on hardship to a person or persons other than himself, he should set out in paragraph 6 the name of every person who will be so affected, and the relationship of that person to himself, and should state the nature of the hardship on which he relies.

(^{2}) Paragraph 8 need not be completed if the name of the future tenant is unknown. Where land is described, a map should be provided (see note (^{5}) below).

(^{3}) By virtue of rule 11(1) of the Agricultural Land Tribunals (Succession)Rules 1984 two coies of the application and of any map and document must be sent to the secretary.

(^{4}) A larger scale map may be used if preferred. Ordnance Survey Field Numbers must be marked on the map.

(^{5}) Where it is intended to give evidence about any land other than that which is the subject of the notice to quit, it must be shown either on the map produced or on a separate map of a scale of 6" to one mile or 1/10,000 (or larger).

(^{6}) Mention any other document which is attached to this application.

(^{7}) If signed by any person other than the applicant himself, he should state in what capacity or by what authority he signs.

Notes (not part of the prescribed form)

1   This form is Form 2 in the Appendix to the Agricultural Land Tribunals (Succession) Rules 1984 contained in the Agricultural Land Tribunals (Succession to Agricultural Tenancies) Order 1984, SI 1984/1301, Sch, r 4(1). Although in general a form substantially to the like effect will suffice it is recommended that the prescribed form is used without alteration or variation in any particular, including reproduction of the statutorily prescribed notes which comprise part of the form. As reproduced, this Form follows the precise wording of the prescribed form, but not the exact layout and design. The Form as reproduced here refers to repealed enactments while the footnotes refer to the current equivalent provisions. ALTs have updated legislative references in some forms and are circulating them for use. A request may therefore be made to the relevant ALT for their version of the relevant form. As to proposals for a new Tribunal Rules Order, see Form AH1 note 2 and para 46.20.

2   An application by a landlord of an agricultural holding under the AHA 1986, s 44 (see para A1.131) (formerly the Agriculture (Miscellaneous Provisions) Act 1976, s 22 (repealed)) for the consent of the Agricultural Land Tribunal to the operation of a notice to quit must be in Form 2 Agricultural Land Tribunals (Succession) Rules 1984, r 4(1). Subject to r 4(3), (4) the application may be made at any time after the landlord receives notice of an application under SI 1984/1301, r 3(1).

A2.99

AH26

Form 2R (Succession on Death)^1
Rule 7(1)   Ref. No.

To be inserted
by the Secretary

Agricultural Land Tribunal

REPLY TO APPLICATION FOR CONSENT TO OPERATION OF NOTICE TO QUIT[2]

To the Secretary of the Agricultural Land Tribunal
for the .... Area.

I, ... [*block capitals*] of .... [*address*], having applied
to the tribunal on .... for a direction entitling me to a tenancy of
.... and having received a copy of the application (bearing the above
reference number) for the tribunal's consent to the operation of a notice to quit, reply
as follows:—

1.   The facts stated in the first three paragraphs of the application are correct
†except that:—

2.   My main reasons for resisting the application are:—

†3.   The landlord is not acting fairly and reasonably because([1]):—

4.   I attach copies of the following relevant documents([2]):—

Date ....

Signed([3]) ....

TAKE NOTICE THAT IF YOU DO NOT REPLY IN THIS FORM WITHIN ONE
MONTH OF THE DATE OF SERVICE ON YOU OF THE ATTACHED APPLICA-
TION BY THE LANDLORD OF THE HOLDING FOR THE TRIBUNAL'S CON-
SENT TO THE OPERATION OF THE LANDLORD'S NOTICE TO QUIT, THE
TRIBUNAL MAY GIVE THAT CONSENT SUMMARILY AND SUMMARILY DIS-
MISS YOUR OWN APPLICATION TO BE GRANTED A TENANCY OF THE
HOLDING, WITHOUT HEARING YOUR CASE.

†   Strike out if inapplicable.
([1])   The tribunal must withhold consent if, in all the circumstances, it appears that a fair and
reasonable landlord would not insist on possession. If you have any special reasons for
saying the landlord is acting unfairly or unreasonably which do not apply under
paragraph 2, you should state them under paragraph 3.
([2])   By virtue of rule 11(1) of the Agricultural Land Tribunals (Succession) Rules 1984 two
copies of the reply and of any document which you wish to submit to the tribunal must be
sent to the secretary.
If you disagree with any map or plan attached to the application, your reply should be
accompanied by two copies of a 6" to one mile or 1/10,000 (or larger) map showing what you
consider to be the true position and marking the Ordnance Survey Field Numbers.
([3])   If signed by any person other than the applicant himself, he should state in what capacity
or by what authority he signs.

Notes (not part of the prescribed form)
1   This form is Form 2R in the Appendix to the Agricultural Land Tribunals Rules (Succession)
Rules 1984 contained in the Agricultural Land Tribunals (Succession to Agricultural
Tenancies) Order 1984, SI 1984/1301, Sch, r 7. Although in general a form substantially to
the like effect will suffice it is recommended that the prescribed form is used without
alteration or variation in any particular, including reproduction of the statutorily prescribed
notes which comprise part of the form. As reproduced, this Form follows the precise wording

of the prescribed form, but not the exact layout and design. The Form as reproduced here refers to repealed enactments while the footnotes refer to the current equivalent provisions. ALTs have updated legislative references in some forms and are circulating them for use. A request may therefore be made to the relevant ALT for their version of the relevant form. As to proposals for a new Tribunal Rules Order, see Form AH1 note 2 and para 46.20.

2   An applicant who intends to oppose an application to the ALT for consent to the operation of a notice to quit must within one month after a copy of the application has been served on him reply to it in Form 2R: the Agricultural Land Tribunals (Succession) Rules 1984, r 7.

A2.100

AH27

Form 3 (Succession on Death)[1]
Rule 5(1)

Ref. No.
To be inserted
by the Secretary

Agricultural Land Tribunal

NOTICE OF APPLICATION FOR ENTITLEMENT TO TENANCY UNDER PART II OF THE AGRICULTURE (MISCELLANEOUS PROVISIONS) ACT 1976[2]

To .... [*name*] of .... [*address*]

I, ... [*block capitals*] of ... . [*address*], hereby give you notice that I applied on .... [*date of application*] under Part II of the above-named Act for a direction entitling me to a tenancy of the agricultural holding known as

[*address or brief description of holding*] in succession to ....

[*name of deceased tenant of the holding*] who died on ....

Dated ....

Signed ....

A copy of the full application will in due course be sent to the landlord and any other applicants by the secretary to the tribunal.

Notes (not part of the prescribed form)

1   This form is Form 3 in the Appendix to the Agricultural Land Tribunals (Succession) Rules 1984, contained in the Agricultural Land Tribunals (Succession to Agricultural Tenancies) Order 1984, SI 1984/1301, Sch, r 5(1). Although in general a form substantially to the like effect will suffice it is recommended that the prescribed form is used without alteration or variation in any particular, including reproduction of the statutorily prescribed notes which comprise part of the form. As reproduced, this Form follows the precise wording of the prescribed form, but not the exact layout and design. The Form as reproduced here refers to repealed enactments while the footnotes refer to the current equivalent provisions. ALTs have updated legislative references in some forms and are

circulating them for use. A request may therefore be made to the relevant ALT for their version of the relevant form. As to proposals for a new Tribunal Rules Order see Form AH1 note 2 and para 46.20.

2   An applicant under the Agricultural Land Tribunals (Succession) Rules 1984, r 3(1) (see Form AH23) must at the time of making his application serve notice of the application in Form 3 on the landlord and on any person who, to the applicant's knowledge, has made or may be able to make an application under SI 1984/1301, r 3(1) and must inform the ALT in his application of the name and address of the person to be notified by him: r 5(1).

A2.101

AH28

Form 4 (Succession on Death)[1]
Rule 8

Ref. No.
To be inserted
by the Secretary

Agricultural Land Tribunal

REPLY TO APPLICATION FOR DIRECTION GIVING ENTITLEMENT TO TENANCY OF AGRICULTURAL HOLDING[2]

To the Secretary of the Agricultural Land Tribunal
for the .... Area.

I, ... [*block capitals*] of .... [*address*], having received a copy of the application of (hereinafter called 'the applicant') bearing the above reference number, reply as follows:—

1.   The facts stated in the first seven paragraphs of the application are correct except that:—

2.   *I accept the applicant's claim to be a designated applicant, as stated in paragraph 8 of the application.

OR

*I dispute the applicant's claim to be a designated applicant, as stated in paragraph 8 of the application, on the following grounds:—

3.   I do not dispute any of the matters stated in paragraphs 9–13, 16, and 17 of the application except that:—

4.   I claim to be a more suitable person than the applicant to be granted a tenancy of the holding; and I base this claim on the following grounds:—

†5. The applicant and I †(and) .... have agreed to request the landlord's consent to a direction entitling us to a joint tenancy of the holding.

Date ....

Signed ....

†   Strike out if inapplicable.

2150

* Strike out whichever is inapplicable.

Notes (not part of the prescribed form)
1 This form is Form 4 in the Appendix to the Agricultural Land Tribunals (Succession) Rules 1984, contained in the Agricultural Land Tribunals (Succession to Agricultural Tenancies) Order 1984, SI 1984/1301, Sch, r 8. Although in general a form substantially to the like effect will suffice it is recommended that the prescribed form is used without alteration or variation in any particular, including reproduction of the statutorily prescribed notes which comprise part of the form. As reproduced, this Form follows the precise wording of the prescribed form, but not the exact layout and design. The Form as reproduced here refers to repealed enactments while the footnotes refer to the current equivalent provisions. ALTs have updated legislative references in some forms and are circulating them for use. A request may therefore be made to the relevant ALT for their version of the relevant form. As to proposals for a new Tribunal Rules Order, see Form AH1 note 2 and para 46.20.
2 An applicant under the Agricultural Land Tribunals (Succession) Rules 1984, SI 1984/1301, r 3(1) who intends to oppose an application under r 3(1) by any other person must within one month after the expiry of the relevant period reply to that application in Form 4: r 8(1). The 'relevant period' means the period of 3 months beginning with the date after the date of death: r 2(1).

C: SUCCESSION TO TENANCIES ON RETIREMENT OF TENANT

A2.102

AH29   Retirement notice under Agricultural Holdings Act 1986 section 49 on the grounds of age or incapacity[1]

AGRICULTURAL HOLDINGS ACT 1986

To *(landlord)* of *(address)* .... *(date)*
(description of holding ....

TAKE NOTICE that [I *(tenant)* or we *(joint tenants)*] of *(address(es))* being the [tenant or joint tenants] of the above holding nominate *(successor)*[2] of *(address)* to succeed to the tenancy of the above holding on the .... day of 20   [or on the next date on which the tenancy of the above holding could have been determined by notice to quit given on the date of this notice and which falls not less than one year and not more than 2 years after the date of this notice under the provisions of the Agricultural Holdings Act 1986 section 49(1)(b)][3]

[This notice is given on the grounds specified in section 51(3) of that Act namely that [I am *or* we are *or* [I *or* we] will be] at the .... day of 20   incapable by reason of [bodily *or* mental] infirmity of conducting the farming of the above holding in such a way as to secure the fulfilment of the tenant's responsibilities to farm in accordance with the rules of good husbandry and the incapacity is likely to be permanent][4]

(signature of tenant(s))

Notes (this is not a statutorily prescribed form)

1. Generally, see Ch 36. A tenant wishing to retire may nominate by notice a single eligible person named in the notice to be his successor as from a date specified in the notice: AHA 1986, s 49(1)(b) (see para A1.136). For forms relating to succession on retirement, see Forms AH30–AH32.

2. The person nominated to succeed to the tenancy must be an eligible person ie a person who (1) is a close relative of the retiring tenant (2) has derived his sole or principal source of livelihood throughout a period of at least 5 years in the last 7 years from his agricultural work on the holding or agricultural unit of which the holding forms part and (3) is not the occupier of a commercial unit of agricultural land: AHA 1986, s 50(2).

3. The retirement date must be a date on which the tenancy of the holding could have been determined by notice to quit given at the time of the retirement notice and it must fall not less than one nor more than 2 years after the date of the retirement notice: AHA 1986, s 49(1)(b). It is suggested that the words in square brackets are included to avoid the notice being rendered void if the date selected is found to be the incorrect term date.

4. Normally a tenant cannot give a retirement notice to take effect before the tenant attains the age of 65: AHA 1986, s 51(3). In exceptional circumstances which are specified in this paragraph, a younger tenant or tenants can give an appropriate notice: AHA 1986, s 51(3)(a), (b). However, the tenant or tenants will have to have the necessary mental capacity to be able to understand and appreciate the notice given and it will be comparatively rare for a tenant, therefore, to suffer from sufficient mental, as opposed to physical infirmity, to be unable to conduct the farming business but nevertheless be of sufficient mental capacity to be able to give the appropriate form of notice.

A2.103

AH30

Form 5 (Succession on Retirement)[1]
Rule 23(1)

> Ref. No.
> To be inserted
> by the Secretary

Agricultural Land Tribunal

APPLICATION FOR DIRECTION GIVING ENTITLEMENT TO TENANCY OF AGRICULTURAL HOLDING[2]

[In completing this form it is important to refer to the notes]

To the Secretary of the Agricultural Land Tribunal
for the .... Area.

1. I, ... [*block capitals*] of .... [*address*], hereby apply under paragraph 5(1) of Schedule 2 to the Agricultural Holdings Act 1984 for a direction entitling me to a tenancy of the holding specified in paragraph 2 below.

2. The holding in respect of which the application is made is known as and .... consists of:—

    (a) ....   hectares of arable land (including temporary grass)
                              (Ordnance Survey Field Nos ....);

(b) .... hectares of permanent pasture
(Ordnance Survey Field Nos ....);

(c) .... hectares of rough grazing
(Ordnance Survey Field Nos ....);

(d) .... hectares of other land (including orchards)
(Ordnance Survey Field Nos ....);

Total .... hectares   ANNUAL RENT £

3.   The current year of the tenancy of the holding expires on ....

4.   The holding includes the following buildings [*give a general description*]:—

†5.   The holding forms part of a larger agricultural unit known as and consisting of [*give a general description*]:—

6.   The landlord of the holding is .... of .... [*address*]
The tenant(s) of the holding is/are .... of .... [*address(es)*].

7.   This application arises as a result of a retirement notice given by the tenant(s) to the landlord on ....

8.   I am the nominated successor.

9.

†(a)   I am the *wife/*husband/*brother/*sister/*child of the tenant [*where there is more than one tenant, specify which*] (¹).

(b)   I am treated by the tenant [*where there is more than one tenant, specify which*] as a child of the family in relation to his marriage to .... (²) on .... [*give date of marriage*].

10.

(a)   During the seven years ending with the date on which the tenant(s) gave the retirement notice to the landlord my only or principal source of livelihood was derived from—

*(i)   my agricultural work on the holding, or on an agricultural unit of which the holding forms a part;

*(ii)   the tenant's/the tenant's and my [*where there is more than one tenant, specify which*] agricultural work on the holding, or on an agricultural unit of which the holding forms a part;

during the following period(s) and in the following manner [give details of the way livelihood derived from agricultural work on the holding] (³):—

*(b)   During the period(s) specified in paragraph 10(a) I had the following source(s) of livelihood other than those derived from the holding or from an agricultural unit of which the holding forms a part [*give details of other sources of livelihood*]:—

*(c)   During the period(s) specified in paragraph 10(a) I had no other source of livelihood.

11.   During the seven years ending with the date on which the tenant(s) gave the retirement notice to the landlord I attended a full-time course at .... [*name of university, college or other establishment of further education*] during the following period(s) [give details of time spent at university, etc] (⁴):—

2153

During this period/these periods I studied the following subjects and obtained the following qualifications [*give details of subjects studied and any qualifications obtained*]:—

12.

(a) The following agricultural land is occupied by me, my spouse or a company under my control, the control of my spouse or our joint control as owner-occupier/tenant/licensee, whether alone or jointly with others [*give particulars of any land occupied, including area and any land occupied jointly with others*] (⁵):—

†(b) The following agricultural land is occupied by a person under a licence or such a tenancy as is mentioned in paragraph 2(1)(a) to (d) of Schedule 3A to the Agriculture (Miscellaneous Provisions) Act 1976(⁶) granted by *me and/or *my spouse and/or *a company controlled by me and/or my spouse together with one or more other persons, being at the time it was granted a person or persons entitled to occupy the land otherwise than under a tenancy, or in a capacity, falling within paragraph 2(1)(a) to (f) of that Schedule(⁶) [*give particulars of any land occupied including area*]:—

†(c) I apply under paragraph 4(2) of Schedule 3A to the 1976 Act, as applied by paragraph 1(4)(b) of Schedule 2 to the 1984 Act, for the net annual income from the following agricultural land which is—

*(i) jointly occupied;

*(ii) deemed by virtue of paragraph 6(2) of the said Schedule 3A, as applied by the said paragraph 1(4)(b), to be jointly occupied;

by me and one or more other persons (not being only my spouse or a company under my control, the control of my spouse or our joint control) to be treated as limited to my appropriate share of that net annual income [*give particulars of any land in joint occupation or deemed joint occupation*] (⁷):—

13. I was born on ....

14. I claim to be a suitable person to receive the tenancy of this holding because(⁸):—

15. I attach the following documents which I intend to produce in support of my case:—

(a) two(⁹) copies of a 6" to one mile or 1/10,000(¹⁰) map of the holding described in paragraph 2 above (and of the other land referred to in paragraph 5);

(b) two(⁹) copies of the retirement notice;

(c) two(⁹) copies of (¹¹):—

16. I shall notify the landlord of this application(¹²).

Date ....

Signed(¹³) ....

Signature of retiring tenant(s) ....

....

....

....

* Strike out whichever is inapplicable.
† Strike out if inapplicable.

(^{1}) Formal proof of the relationship to the tenant, eg, by production of marriage or birth certificates, may be required at the hearing. Adopted children should complete this sub-paragraph, and not paragraph 9(b) following.

(^{2}) Paragraph 9(b) may apply where the applicant is the step-child or foster child of the tenant or is otherwise treated by him as his child. An outline should be given of the circumstances relied on as establishing that the applicant is treated by the tenant as his child in relation to the marriage. Production of the relevant marriage certificate and any relevant birth certificate may be required at the hearing.

(^{3}) To qualify under paragraph 10(a)(i) the applicant should have derived his only or principal source of livelihood from his agricultural work on the holding (or on a larger unit of which the holding forms part) during a total of five years of the seven years ending with the date on which the tenant(s) gave the landlord the retirement notice. Paragraph 10(a)(ii) is available only to a tenant's wife. The total of five years may be made up of one continuous period, or one or more separate periods. A period of full-time education at a university etc, may, in the circumstances set out in note (^{4}), count towards the five-year period of earning a livelihood from the holding, and reference should be made to paragraph 11 and note (^{4}) in deciding whether the requirements of this paragraph can be satisfied.

(^{4}) Any period or periods (up to an aggregate total of three years) during the seven years ending with the date on which the tenant(s) gave the retirement notice to the landlord during which the applicant was attending a full-time course at a university, college or other establishment of further education will be treated as a period throughout which his only or principal source of livelihood was derived from his agricultural work on the holding. Any subject may have been studied.

(^{5}) Land occupied by the applicant's spouse or by a company controlled by that person or jointly by that person and the applicant should not be included in paragraph 12 where either of the parties has obtained a decree of judicial separation or a decree nisi of divorce or of nullity of marriage and in each case that decree remains unrescinded. In addition, land should not be included in paragraph 12 if it is occupied by the applicant, his spouse or a controlled company—

(a) under a tenancy approved under section 2(1) of the Agricultural Holdings Act 1948 or under such a tenancy relating to the use of land for grazing or mowing as is referred to in the proviso to that provision;

(b) under a tenancy for more than one year but less than two years;

(c) under a tenancy not falling within (a) or (b) above and not having effect as a contract of tenancy;

(d) under a tenancy to which section 3 of the 1948 Act does not apply by virtue of section 3B of that Act;

(e) as a licensee; or

(f) as an executor, administrator, trustee in bankruptcy or person otherwise deriving title from another person by operation of law.

However, where the applicant occupies land in accordance with (a) to (e) above under a licence or tenancy granted to him by his spouse or by abody controlled by him, that land should be included in paragraph 12.

(^{6}) Paragraph 2(1)(a) to (f) of Schedule 3A to the Agriculture (Miscellaneous Provisions) Act 1976 is set out in note(^{5}).

(^{7}) If the applicant occupies land jointly with one or more other persons (not being only his spouse or a company under the control of the applicant or his spouse or under their joint control), or if the applicant is deemed to occupy land jointly with one or more such persons, he may in either case complete the application set out in paragraph 12(c) of the Form for the net annual income which the land is or was capable of producing to be treated as limited to his appropriate share.

(^{8}) All matters relied on as supporting the claim to be a suitable person to become the tenant of the holding should be summarised. These should include details of the applicant's training and practical experience of agriculture, physical health, financial standing and any educational qualifications not already listed in paragraph 11.

(^{9}) By virtue of rule 28 of the Agricultural Land Tribunals (Succession) Rules 1984 two copies of the application and of any map and document must be sent to the secretary.

(^{10}) A larger scale map may be used if preferred. Ordnance Survey Field Numbers must be marked on the map.

(^{11}) Mention any other document which is attached to this application.

(^{12}) The applicant is required to send to the landlord of the holding notice of this application in Form 6 (Succession on Retirement) which is set out in the Appendix to the Agricultural Land Tribunals (Succession) Rules 1984.

(^{13}) If signed by any person other than the applicant himself, he should state in what capacity or by what authority he signs.

Notes (not part of the prescribed form)

1   This form is Form 5 in the Appendix to the Agricultural Land Tribunals (Succession) Rules 1984, contained in the Agricultural Land Tribunals (Succession to Agricultural Tenancies) Order 1984, SI 1984/1301, Sch, r 23(1). Although in general a form substantially to the like effect will suffice it is recommended that the prescribed form is used without alteration or variation in any particular, including reproduction of the statutorily prescribed notes which comprise part of the form. As reproduced, this Form follows the precise wording of the prescribed form, but not the exact layout and design. The Form as reproduced here refers to repealed enactments while the footnotes refer to the current equivalent provisions. ALTs have updated legislative references in some forms and are circulating them for use. A request may therefore be made to the relevant ALT for their version of the relevant form. As to proposals for a new Tribunal Rules Order, see Form AH1 note 2 and para 46.20.

2   An application by the nominated successor to the tribunal under the AHA 1986, s 53(1) (see para A1.140) (formerly the Agricultural Holdings Act 1984, Sch 2, para 5(1) (repealed)) for a direction entitling him to a tenancy of an agricultural holding must be made in Form 5: Agricultural Land Tribunals (Succession) Rules 1984, r 23(1). For the definition of 'eligible person' for the purposes of the AHA 1986, ss 49(3), 50(2) and 53, as amended by the Civil Partnership Act 2004, s 81, Sch 8 para 36(1)(2). For the meaning of agricultural work carried out by a person on the holding, see the AHA 1986, s 50 as amended by the Regulatory Reform (Agricultural Tenancies) (England and Wales) Order 2006, SI 2006/2805, art 5(1): see para 35.42

A2.104

AH31

Form 5R (Succession on Retirement)^1
Rule 25

Ref. No.
To be inserted
by the Secretary

Agricultural Land Tribunal

REPLY TO APPLICATION FOR DIRECTION GIVING ENTITLEMENT TO TENANCY OF AGRICULTURAL HOLDING^2

To the Secretary of the Agricultural Land Tribunal
for the .... Area.

I .... [*block capitals*] of ... . [*address*], landlord of .... [*name or description of holding*] having received a copy of the application bearing the above reference number reply as follows:—

1.   The facts stated in paragraphs 1, 2, 4, 6 and 7 of the application are, to the best of my knowledge, information and belief, correct †except that:—

†2.   I dispute the claim of the applicant to be an eligible person(^{1}) on the following grounds:—

3.   I have the following comments on the suitability of the applicant to become the tenant of the above holding:—

†4.   I claim that greater hardship would be caused by the tribunal giving the direction sought by the applicant than by refusing his application and my reasons for this claim are:—

†5.   The tenancy is the subject of a notice to quit Case *B/*C/*D/*E/*F served on .... [*date*].

†[*For Case C only*] The notice to quit is founded on a certificate granted in accordance with an application made on .... [*date*].

†[*For Case D only*] The notice to quit is founded on a notice given for the purposes of that Case on .... [*date*].

6.   I attach two copies of the following relevant documents(²):—

7.   I consider the application to be invalid by reason of(³):—

Date ....

                                                        Signed(⁴) ....

*   Strike out whichever is inapplicable.
†   Strike out if inapplicable.

TAKE NOTICE THAT IF YOU DO NOT REPLY IN THIS FORM WITHIN ONE MONTH OF THE DATE OF SERVICE ON YOU OF THE ATTACHED APPLICATION, THEN, SUBJECT TO PARAGRAPH 5(5) OF SCHEDULE 2³ TO THE AGRICULTURAL HOLDINGS ACT 1984, YOU WILL NOT BE ENTITLED AT THE HEARING OF THE APPLICATION TO DISPUTE ANY MATTER ALLEGED IN IT.

(¹)   The paragraphs of the application which (where completed) will be relevant to the applicant's claim to be an eligible person are paragraphs 9, 10, 11 and 12.
(²)   By virtue of rule 28 of the Agricultural Land Tribunals (Succession) Rules 1984 two copies of this reply and of any document which you wish to submit to the tribunal must be sent to the secretary. If you disagree with any map or plan attached to the application, your reply should be accompanied by two copies of a 6" to one mile or 1/10,000 (or larger) map showing what you consider to be the true position and marking the Ordnance Survey Field Numbers.
(³)   If you consider that, for any reason, the applicant is not legally entitled to make his application, you should state succinctly the grounds on which you rely.
(⁴)   If signed by any person other than the landlord himself, he should state in what capacity or by what authority he signs.

Notes (not part of the prescribed form)
¹   This form is Form 5R in the Appendix to the Agricultural Land Tribunals (Succession) Rules 1984, contained in the Agricultural Land Tribunals (Succession to Agricultural Tenancies) Order 1984, SI 1984/1301, Sch, r 25. Although in general a form substantially to the like effect will suffice it is recommended that the prescribed form is used without alteration or variation in any particular, including reproduction of the statutorily prescribed notes which comprise part of the form. As reproduced, this Form follows the precise wording of the prescribed form, but not the exact layout and design. The Form as reproduced here refers to repealed enactments while the footnotes refer to the current equivalent provisions. ALTs have updated legislative references in some forms and are circulating them for use. A request may therefore be made to the relevant ALT for their version of the relevant form. As to proposals for a new Tribunal Rules Order, see Form AH1 note 2 and para 46.20.

2 A landlord who intends to oppose the whole or any part of an application (see Form AH30) under the Agricultural Land Tribunals (Succession) Rules 1984 must within one month after a copy of the application has been served on him reply in Form 5R: SI 1984/1301, r 25.

3 AHA 1986, s 53 (formerly the Agricultural Holdings Act 1984, Sch 2 para 5(5) (repealed)).

A2.105

AH32

Form 6 (Succession on Retirement)[1]
Rule 24

Ref. No.
To be inserted
by the Secretary

Agricultural Land Tribunal

NOTICE OF APPLICATION FOR ENTITLEMENT TO TENANCY UNDER SCHEDULE 2 TO
THE AGRICULTURAL HOLDINGS ACT 1984[2]

To: .... [*name*] of ... . [*address*]

I .... [*block capitals*] of ... . [*address*] hereby give you notice that I applied on .... [*date of application*] under Schedule 2 to the above-named Act for a direction entitling me to a tenancy of the agricultural holding known as .... [*address or brief description of holding*] in succession to .... [*name of present tenant(s) of the holding*] .... who served on you his/their retirement notice on ....

Date ....

Signed ....

A copy of the full application will in due course be sent to you by the secretary to the tribunal.

Notes (not part of the prescribed form)

1 This form is Form 6 in the Appendix to the Agricultural Land Tribunals (Succession) Rules 1984, contained in the Agricultural Land Tribunals (Succession to Agricultural Tenancies) Order 1984, SI 1984/1301, Sch, r 24. Although in general a form substantially to the like effect will suffice it is recommended that the prescribed form is used without alteration or variation in any particular, including reproduction of the statutorily prescribed notes which comprise part of the form. As reproduced, this Form follows the precise wording of the prescribed form, but not the exact layout and design. The Form as reproduced here refers to repealed enactments while the footnotes refer to the current equivalent provisions. ALTs have updated legislative references in some forms and are circulating them for use. A request may therefore be made to the relevant ALT for their version of the relevant form. As to proposals for a new Tribunal Rules Order, see Form AH1 note 2 and para 46.20.

² The nominated successor must at the time of making his application under the Agricultural
Land Tribunals (Succession) Rules 1984, r 23(1) (see Form AH30) serve notice of the
application in Form 6 on the landlord: SI 1984/1301, r 24. The provisions of the
Agricultural Holdings Act 1984, Sch 2 were repealed and re-enacted in the AHA 1986,
ss 49–58 (see para A1.136 to A1.145).

A2.106

AH33 Demand by landlord or tenant for arbitration following direction by the Agricultural Land Tribunal for grant of new tenancy for variation in terms and conditions of new tenancy and/or rent

AGRICULTURAL HOLDINGS ACT 1986

To (*landlord*) of (*address*) (*date*) ....
(*description of holding*) ....

WHEREAS the Agricultural Land Tribunal on the .... day of .... gave
a direction entitling [me *or* you] to a tenancy of the above holding TAKE NOTICE that
I (*landlord or tenant*) of (*address*) demand a reference to arbitration pursuant to
section 48 of the above Act [and section 56(3)] ¹ of the following question(s):—

(a) What variation in the terms of the tenancy to which the tenant is entitled or as
obtained by virtue of the direction above referred to are justifiable having
regard to the circumstances of the holding and the length of time since the
holding was first let on those terms and/or

(b) What rent should be or should have been properly payable in respect of the
holding at the relevant time.

(*signature of landlord or tenant*)

Notes (this is not a prescribed form)

¹ Section 48 of the AHA 1986 provides for arbitration as to the rent or terms of the new
tenancy following a direction for succession on the death of the tenant. Section 56 of the
AHA 1986 is the appropriate section dealing with the equivalent arbitration provisions
following a direction on retirement. Section 56(3) merely incorporates referentially the
provisions of s 48: see para 35.95 ff and 36.38.

D: APPEALS

A2.107

AH34 Request to the Agricultural Land Tribunal for reference of question of law to the High Court¹

AGRICULTURE (MISCELLANEOUS PROVISIONS) ACT 1954

Ref ...

To the Secretary of the .... Agricultural Land Tribunal .... (*date*)
(*description of holding*)

BACKGROUND: I have received a copy of the tribunal's decision with regard to the above holding sent to me on the .... day of .... under the above reference.

NOW I (*landlord or tenant*) of (*address*) request the tribunal pursuant to the Agriculture (Miscellaneous Provisions) Act 1954 section 6 to refer to the High Court the following question[s] of law:

(*set out in exact terms the question(s) of law to be referred to the High Court*)

(*signature of landlord or tenant*)

Notes (this is not a prescribed form)

1   A request for the reference to the High Court of a question of law arising in the course of proceedings before the ALT must, unless made at the time of the hearing, be made in writing to the secretary not later than 14 days from the date on which a copy of the tribunal's decision was sent to the party making the request and must be accompanied by as many copies of the request as there are other parties: Agricultural Land Tribunals (Rules) Order 1978, SI 1978/259, r 33(1). As to the procedure to be adopted if the request is refused see Form AH35 note 1. As to proposals for a new Tribunal Rules Order, see Form AH1 note 2 and para 46.20.

A2.108

AH35   Notice to the Agricultural Land Tribunal of intention to apply to the High Court for order directing the Tribunal to refer question of law to the High Court

AGRICULTURE (MISCELLANEOUS PROVISIONS) ACT 1954

Ref ...

To the Secretary of the .... Agricultural Land Tribunal .... (*date*)
(*description of holding*)

BACKGROUND: I have received from you the notification dated the .... day of .... of the Tribunal's refusal of my request dated the .... day of ....

NOW I (*landlord or tenant*) of (*address*) give you notice pursuant to the Agriculture (Miscellaneous Provisions) Act 1954 section 6 and the regulations made under that Act that I intend to apply to the High Court for an order directing the Tribunal to refer to the High Court the question[s] of law set out in my request:

(*set out in exact terms the question(s) of law set out in my request*)

(*signature of landlord or tenant*)

Notes (this is not a prescribed form)

1   If the tribunal refuses the request for the reference to the High Court of a question of law (see Form AH36), the secretary must not later than 14 days from the date of receipt of the request notify all parties of the refusal and, if the party making the request, being aggrieved by the refusal, intends to apply to the High Court for an order directing the tribunal to refer the question of law to the High Court, he must within 7 days after receiving notice of refusal serve on the secretary notice in writing of the intended application with as many copies as there are other parties: Agricultural Land Tribunals (Rules) Order 1978, SI 1978/259, r 33(2). For proposals for a new Tribunal Rules Order, see Form AH 1 note 2 and para 46.20.

Appendix III
ARBITRATION

Appendix III

ARBITRATION

Contents

ARBITRATION

A3.1 Following the introduction of the Regulatory Reform (Agricultural Tenancies) (England and Wales) Order 2006, SI 2006/2805, the Royal Institution of Chartered Surveyors have amended the application forms for a request for the appointment of an arbitrator. There are two forms; the first for use in all rent review cases (Form DRS3) and the second for the appointment of an arbitrator or independent expert in all agricultural non-rent disputes (Form DRS4). Practitioners should use these forms for applications under the Agricultural Holdings Act 1986 (AHA 1986) and the Agricultural Tenancies Act 1995 (ATA 1995). Copies are available from the RICS website or by post from RICS Dispute Resolution Services, Surveyor Court, Westwood Way, Coventry, CV4 8JE.

A3.2

AA1   Appointment of valuer and agent[1]

AGRICULTURE ACT 1947

ARBITRATION ACT 1996

AGRICULTURAL HOLDINGS ACT 1986

(description of holding)

I *(landlord or tenant)* of *(address)* appoint *(valuer)* of *(address etc)* as my valuer and agent to ascertain determine and agree on my behalf all matters and questions arising as between landlord and tenant in respect of the above holding whether arising under the above Acts or otherwise with full power and authority in case of disagreement to refer any such matters or questions to arbitration under any of the above Acts and for such purposes to nominate and appoint or to concur in the nomination and appointment of a single arbitrator any person he may think fit and in default of agreement to apply to the President of the Royal Institution of Chartered Surveyors to appoint a single arbitrator or to take the necessary steps to obtain the appointment of an arbitrator by the court or otherwise where necessary as the case may be in accordance with the appropriate provisions of the above Acts or any of them or any statutory modification or re-enactment of them for the time being in force or otherwise as the case may be

I undertake to confirm and allow any act agreement matter or thing done made suffered or allowed by him in any such matters or questions

I further authorise him to sign on my behalf and serve on the appropriate persons and to accept service on my behalf of all notices claims or other documents requisite for any of the above purposes[2]

AS WITNESS my hand the .... day of ....

(signature of landlord or tenant)

Notes

[1]   The Arbitration Act 1996, save where it is inconsistent with the AHA 1986, applies to all arbitrations under the AHA 1986 commenced after 19 October 2006. As to the arbitration generally, see Ch 47.

[2]   Before risking service of any notices or particulars etc on an agent for the party to be served, it should first be ascertained that such agent is duly authorised to accept service. If appointed in the terms of this Form, he would be so authorised, unless and until the appointment has been validly revoked.

A3.3

AA2   Appointment of arbitrator by agreement[1]

AGRICULTURAL HOLDINGS ACT 1986

(*description of holding*)

WE (*valuer*) of (*address etc*) valuer and agent for (*landlord*) the landlord of the above holding and (*valuer*) of (*address etc*) valuer and agent for (*tenant*) the tenant of the above holding appoint (*arbitrator*) of (*address etc*) as sole arbitrator under the Agricultural Holdings Act 1986 [to determine in accordance with the provisions of that Act the rent to be paid for the above holding as from the next ensuing date at which the tenancy could have been determined by notice to quit given by the [landlord or tenant] or for the purpose of settling and determining in accordance with the provisions of that Act all claims questions and differences between the landlord and the tenant of the above holding [as set out in the schedule below or arising under that Act or any previous Act concerning agricultural holdings or any custom or agreement and on or out of the termination of the tenancy of the above holding or any part of it]]

AS WITNESS our hands the .... day of ....

[Schedule
Short particulars of claims, questions and differences

Claims by tenant	*Claims by landlord*
To be a tenant of the above holding from year to year by virtue of section 2 of the above Act[2]	That the tenant is not a tenant from year to year of above land under Section 2 of the above Act
For a written tenancy agreement	For a written tenancy agreement
For a tenancy agreement providing for all matters in the First Schedule to the above Act	For a tenancy agreement providing for all matters in the First Schedule to the above Act
For a variation of terms of the tenancy agreement with respect to maintenance repair and insurance of fixed equipment	For variation of terms of the tenancy agreement with respect to maintenance repair and insurance of fixed equipment
For compensation on transfer of liability for maintenance or repair of fixed equipment	For compensation on transfer of liability for maintenance or repair of fixed equipment
For variation of terms of the tenancy agreement as to permanent pasture	For increase of rent for certain improvements
For compensation for damage by game	Dilapidations
	Deterioration or damage
To determine the extent of the tenant's liability to do the work specified in the landlord's notice to do work dated the .... day of .... pursuant to the above Act orders and regulations	General deterioration in value of holding

To determine the extent of the tenant's
liability to do the work specified in the
landlord's notice to do work dated the
.... day of .... pursuant
to the above Act orders and regulations
To determine all questions arising on the
landlord's notice to do work dated the
.... day of .... pursuant
to the above Act orders and regulations
To determine all questions arising out of
the reasons stated in the notice to quit
dated the .... day of
.... and served on the tenant by
the landlord pursuant to the above Act
orders and regulations
For reduction in rent following notice to
quit part of holding
For compensation for improvements
For tenant-right compensation
Continuous adoption of special system
of farming
Disturbance compensation]

(*signature of both valuers*)

Notes

1. See the AHA 1986, s 84 (see para 47.13 ff). This Form is for use with regard to matters specifically referred to arbitration by various provisions of the AHA 1986 and also for use in the usual arbitration at the end of the tenancy for claims covered by AHA 1986, s 83. Where there is any doubt whether some particular matter is referred to arbitration under the AHA 1986, Form AA3 below (see para A3.4) may be used. As to arbitration generally, see Ch 47.

2   See the AHA 1986, s 2(4). A dispute as to whether an agreement relating to agricultural land involves the formation of an agricultural holding is not compulsorily referable to arbitration: *Goldsack v Shore* [1950] 1 KB 708, [1950] 1 All ER 276, CA. A dispute as to how the AHA 1986, s 2 should be operated must be referred to arbitration.

A3.4

AA3   **Appointment of arbitrator by agreement – alternative form for use to determine all questions including those not specifically referrable under the Agricultural Holdings Act 1986[1]**

AGRICULTURE ACT 1947

ARBITRATION ACT 1996

AGRICULTURAL HOLDINGS ACT 1986

(*description of holding*)

WE (*valuer*) of (*address etc*) valuer and agent for (*landlord*) (*address*) the landlord of the above holding and (*valuer*) of (*address etc*) valuer and agent for (*tenant*) of (*address*) the tenant of the above holding appoint (*arbitrator*) of (*address etc*) as sole arbitrator under the above Acts or any of them to settle and determine all claims questions and differences arising between the landlord and the tenant of the above holding under the above Acts or any of them or any custom or agreement concerning the matters specified in the schedule below[2]

[We further agree that no objection shall be raised to the issue by the arbitrator of one award determining all matters so referred to him which shall be final and binding on the landlord and the tenant and the persons claiming under them respectively in accordance with the above provisions[3]]

We undertake and agree to sign any further submissions appointments or other documents and do any other acts or things which may be required by the arbitrator in his opinion to empower him legally and effectively to hear settle and determine the above matters or any of them

AS WITNESS our hands the .... day of ....

Schedule
(general headings sufficient to cover required types of claim)

(*signature of both valuers*)

Notes

1   The Arbitration Act 1996 applies, save where it is inconsistent with the AHA 1986 to any matter that is required to be determined by arbitration in accordance with the AHA 1986 provided the arbitration commenced after 19 October 2006 (see para 47.13): AHA 1986, s 84(1). As to arbitration generally, see Ch 47.

2   See Form AA3.

³ If a single award is made, it is advisable to make it clear that it is made under the AHA 1986 and the Arbitration Act 1996 and to set out clearly exactly what is awarded under each Act. Alternatively, two separate awards could be made.

A3.5

AA4 Application for the appointment of an arbitrator (for use in all rent review cases)¹

REQUEST FOR THE APPOINTMENT OF AN ARBITRATOR

AGRICULTURAL HOLDINGS ACT 1986 & AGRICULTURAL TENANCIES ACT 1995

(This application form to be used for all agricultural rent review cases. Please see accompanying explanatory notes)

THE HOLDING

Name & Address of the Holding including postcode	
Parish	
County	
Description of Holding	
Approx area	Hectares

REVIEW DETAILS – Please complete the appropriate box according to which Act you are applying under.

Agricultural Holdings Act 1986

Date of Demand	
Demand made by	Landlord/Tenant (Delete as appropriate)
Please state the next termination date following the date of demand	

2171

A3.5 *Forms: Arbitration*

Date of commencement of tenancy	
Date of last review	

Agricultural Tenancies Act 1995

Date of Review	
Date of Trigger Notice (if applicable)	

PARTIES

Landlord

Name	
Address	
Town/City	
Postcode	

Tenant

Name	
Address	
Town/City	
Post Code	

Landlord's Representative (if any)

Name and Reference (if any)	
Company	
Address	
Town/City	
Post Code	
Telephone	

2172

Email		Fax	

Tenant's Representative (*if any*)

Name and Reference (if any)	
Company	
Address	
Town/City	
Post Code	
Telephone	
Email		Fax	

Application submitted by:

Name			
Company			
Acting for	Landlord	Tenant	(Delete as appropriate)
Dated			

FEES

I enclose cheque for £115 payable to RICS Business Services Ltd. (There is no VAT payable.)

RICS Dispute Resolution Services	T +44 (0) 020 7334 3806
Surveyor Court, Westwood Way	F +44 (0) 020 7334 3802
COVENTRY, CV4 8JE	E drs@rics.org

Notes

1 This is Form DRS3 available from the RICS Dispute Resolution Service and incorporates changes introduced by the Regulatory Reform (Agricultural Tenancies) (England and Wales) Order 2006. The RICS have produced one form to be used in rent reviews under the AHA 1986 and the ATA 1995. Explanatory notes to the Form DRS3 are also available from the RICS.

2173

AA5

REQUEST FOR THE APPOINTMENT OF AN ARBITRATOR OR
INDEPENDENT EXPERT TO DETERMINE CLAIMS, QUESTIONS, OR
DIFFERENCES BETWEEN THE LANDLORD AND TENANT OF A HOLDING
IN ALL AGRICULTURAL NON-RENT DISPUTES

**AGRICULTURAL HOLDINGS ACT 1986 & AGRICULTURAL TENANCIES
ACT 1995**

*(This application form to be used for all agricultural cases **except** rent review cases.
Please see accompanying explanatory notes – applications are processed on the basis
that these notes have been read and accepted by the applicant.)*

THE HOLDING

Name & Address of the Holding including postcode	
Parish	
County	
Description of Holding	
Approx area	Hectares

DISPUTE DETAILS

Please state below whether you are applying under the Agricultural Holdings Act 1986 or Agricultural Tenancies Act 1995.	
AHA 1986 OR ATA 1995?	
Arbitrator or Independent Expert	
State the provision of the relevant Act or Statutory Instrument in respect of which determination is required and where appropriate give the particulars listed in Part B in the explanatory notes which accompany this form.	

PARTIES

Landlord

Name	
Address	
Town/City	
Postcode	

Tenant

Name	
Address	
Town/City	
Post Code	

Landlord's Representative (*if any*)

Name and Reference (if any)		
Company		
Address		
Town/City		
Post Code		
Telephone		
Email		Fax	

Tenant's Representative (*if any*)

Name and Reference (if any)	
Company	
Address	

Town/City			
Post Code			
Telephone			
Email		Fax	

Application submitted by:

Name			
Company			
Acting for	Landlord	Tenant	(Delete as appropriate)
Dated			

FEES

I enclose cheque for £115 payable to RICS. (There is no VAT payable.)

RICS Dispute Resolution Services	T +44 (0) 020 7334 3806
Surveyor Court, Westwood Way	F +44 (0) 020 7334 3802
COVENTRY, CV4 8JE	E drs@rics.org

Explanatory Notes

These notes are to be read in conjunction with the application form (DRS4) for the appointment of an arbitrator or independent expert in relation to a non-rent dispute on an agricultural holding. The application form and notes are only intended for use in those cases where specific provision is made under the relevant Act or Statutory Instrument. Contractual disputes arising from contracts for sale or partnership agreements etc are not covered. Application for this type of dispute should be made on our standard application form for commercial non-rent disputes.

These notes are for information only. They are not intended as a full statement of the law and cannot override statutory requirements; it must be for applicants to ensure that they have complied with all necessary formalities.

GENERAL

This application form is for use in all non-rent cases under the Agricultural Holdings Act 1986, Agricultural Tenancies Act 1995, and any other statutes referred to in these notes. This form should be used where the parties have been unable to agree an arbitrator or independent expert and wish the President of RICS to appoint under the Act(s). A copy of your application form will be sent to the non-applicant party.

To constitute a valid application, the application form must be accompanied by the appropriate fee.

2176

The duty of RICS when appointing an arbitrator is reasonably straightforward. We receive a request and select a surveyor from our panel of agricultural arbitrators. After checking to ensure the selected surveyor is suitably qualified and impartial, an appointment is confirmed by, or on behalf of, the President. The parties are then notified.

The application form contains 3 sections, designed to elicit information about the agricultural holding, nature of dispute and the parties.

If more than one holding is to be referred to arbitration, a fee is payable (and a separate form must be submitted) in respect of each holding.

Both the Agricultural Holdings Act 1986 and the Agricultural Tenancies Act 1995 provide for various conditions (including strict time limits) to be satisfied before the President can appoint. The President will not be responsible for checking that these conditions have been satisfied, it is the responsibility of the parties to do so.

Where the request for an arbitrator is in respect of Cases A, B, D or E Notice to Quit, the application, accompanied by the fee, must be received by RICS before the expiry of 3 months after the date of the service of the notice under Article 9 of the Agricultural Holdings (Arbitration on Notices) Order 1987.

Please note, following the Regulatory Reform (Agricultural Tenancies) (England and Wales) Order 2006, all arbitrations are now regulated by the Arbitration Act 1996. (This does not apply to an application under the Dairy Product Quotas Regulations 2005).

(A) INFORMATION ABOUT THE HOLDING

We need to understand the nature and location of the holding. This aids the selection of someone who is appropriately qualified and experienced.

You must provide the full address of the holding, particularly details of the parish it is in. We also require a description of the holding (for example, if it is arable, dairy, market garden), along with an approximate indication of the size of the holding in hectares.

(B) DISPUTE DETAILS

Please state whether the application is made under the Agricultural Holdings Act 1986, Agricultural Tenancies Act 1995 or other statute referred to below.

The majority of applications we receive are for the appointment of an arbitrator. The Agricultural Tenancies Act 1995 does envisage that the parties can agree to an independent expert determining their dispute. It is important to state whether the appointment is for an arbitrator or independent expert.

Agricultural Holdings Act 1986 disputes

Section   **Details Required**

Section 6 (securing written tenancy agreements)	The date of service of the request to the landlord or tenant from the tenant or landlord seeking to enter into a written agreement, or to provide in the existing agreement for any matter specified in the First Schedule to the 1986 Act that is not included in the existing agreement.
Section 8(1) & (2) (terms of tenancy relating to maintenance, repair and insurance of fixed equipment)	The date of service of the landlord's or tenant's request to bring the existing tenancy agreement into conformity with regulations made under Section 7(1) of the 1986 Act prescribing terms as the maintenance, repair and insurance of fixed equipment. The current regulations are The Agricultural (Maintenance, Repair and Insurance of Fixed Equipment) Regulations 1973 SI No 1473 as amended.
Section 9(1) (compensation on transfer of liability for maintenance or repair of fixed equipment from tenant to landlord)	(a) The date on which the liability for the maintenance or repair of any item of fixed equipment was transferred (by virtue of Sections 6, 7 or 8 of the 1986 Act). (b) The date of service of the landlord's demand for the matter to be determined by arbitration (this must be within one month from the date when the transfer takes effect as laid down in the Agriculture (Miscellaneous Time-Limits) Regulations 1959: SI No 171 Regulation 2(2).
Section 9(3) (compensation to the tenant for the landlord's failure to comply with existing terms on transfer of liability for maintenance or repair of fixed equipment from landlord to tenant)	(a) The date on which the liability for the maintenance or repair of any item of fixed equipment was transferred (by virtue of Section 6, 7 or 8 of the 1986 Act). (b) The date of service of the tenant's demand for the matter to be determined by arbitration (this must be within one month from the date when the transfer takes effect as laid down in the Agriculture (Miscellaneous Time-Limits) Regulations 1959: SI No 171 Regulation 2(3)).
Section 10 (tenant's right to remove fixtures and buildings)	(a) The date the tenancy terminated (if applicable). (b) The date of service of the notice by the tenant on the landlord of his intention to remove fixtures or buildings (notice must have been served at least one month before the right is exercised and the tenancy is terminated). (c) The date of service of the landlord's counter-notice electing to purchase the fixtures or buildings. (Counter-notice must have been served before the expiry of the tenant's notice above).
Section 13 (increase of rent for landlord's improvements)	(a) The date of completion of the improvement. (b) The date of service of the landlord's notice requiring the rent to be increased (notice must have been served within six months from the completion of the improvement).
Section 14 (terms of tenancy as to area of permanent pasture)	The date of service of the notice by the landlord or tenant on his tenant or landlord demanding arbitration on the question whether the area of land required to be maintained as permanent pasture should be reduced.

Section 15
(claims under s15(6) for injury or deterioration of holding as a result of the tenant's exercising rights under s15(1))

State whether or not the arbitration is required for the purposes of any proceedings for an injunction to restrain the exercise of the tenant's rights under Section 15(5) of the 1986 Act.

Section 20
(tenant's right to compensation for damage by wild animals or birds)

(a) The date of service of the tenant's notice to the landlord before the expiration of one month after the tenant first became or ought reasonably to have become aware of the damage.
(b) The date of service of the claim given to the landlord within one month after the expiration of the year in respect of which the claim is made.
(c) The date which is the end of the year for the purposes of question (b) above. (Unless the landlord or tenant agree on a different date, 29 September will be taken as the year-ending date).

Section 33
(reduction of rent following resumption of possession of part of holding by landlord)

The date the landlord resumed possession of part of the holding.

Section 48(3) & (4)
(succession on death – rent and/or terms of new tenancy, please specify)

(a) The annual term date of the tenancy.
(b) The date the tenant died.
(c) The ALT which gave the direction under Section 39 of the 1986 Act.
(d) The date of the direction.
(e) The date of service of the notice to quit (if applicable).
(f) The date of service of the demand for arbitration by the landlord or the tenant.
(g) If the ALT extended the relevant time under Section 46(2) of the 1986 Act, give the extended date.

Section 56(1) & (3)
(succession on retirement – rent and/or terms of new tenancy, please specify)

(a) The annual term date of the tenancy.
(b) The date of service of the retirement notice under Section 49(1)(b).
(c) The ALT which gave the direction under Section 53(7).
(d) The date of the direction.
(e) The retirement date.
(f) If the ALT extended the relevant time under Section 55(8) give the extended date.
(g) The date of service of the demand for arbitration by the landlord or tenant.

A3.6   Forms: Arbitration

Section 83
(settlement of claims on termination of the tenancy)

(a) The date of the termination of the tenancy.
(b) The date of service of the notice(s) by the landlord/tenant on the tenant/landlord of his/their intention to make a claim. (For the claim to be enforceable, the landlord/tenant must, before the expiry of 2 months from the termination of the tenancy, have served notice in writing on his tenant/landlord of his intention to make the claim.)
(c) In the case of a claim for disturbance under Section 60 of the 1986 Act:
i) the date of service of the notice to quit;
ii) the date of service of the tenant's counter-notice under section 32 of the 1986 Act (if applicable);
iii) the date of service of the tenant's notice, on the landlord, before the termination of the tenancy stating his intention to make a claim greater than that stated in Section 60(3)(a) of the 1986 Act (if applicable).

The Agriculture (Maintenance, Repair and Insurance of Fixed Equipment Regulations 1973, SI 1973/1473

Schedule	Details Required
Para 4(3)(a) (rights and liabilities of the landlord with respect to repairs and replacements)	(a) The date of service of the landlord's notice under paragraph 4(2) of the Schedule to the 1973 Regulations calling on the tenant to execute necessary repairs or replacements. (b) The date of service of the tenant's counter-notice denying liability and requiring arbitration. (This must be served within one month of service of the landlord's notice).
Paragraph 12(3)(a) (rights and liabilities of the tenant with respect to repairs and replacements)	(a) The date of service of the tenant's notice under paragraph 12(1) and/or 12(2) calling on the landlord to execute the necessary repairs and/or replacements. (b) The date of service of the landlord's counter-notice denying liability and requiring arbitration.
Paragraph 13 (redundant fixed equipment)	The date of service of the notice by the landlord or tenant requiring arbitration on the question whether any item of fixed equipment is redundant to the farming of the holding.
Paragraph 15 (other matters)	If any claim, question or differences shall arise between the landlord and the tenant under the foregoing provisions hereof, not being a matter which, otherwise than under the provisions of the paragraph, is required by or by virtue of the Act or regulations or orders made thereunder or the foregoing provisions hereof to be determined by arbitration under the Act, such claim, question or difference shall be determined, in default of agreement, by arbitration under the Act.

The Agriculture Holding (Arbitration Notices) Order 1987, SI 1987/710, as varied

Article	Details Required
3 & 4 (notices served on the tenant to remedy breach of tenancy agreement by doing work or repair maintenance or replacement)	(a) The date Form 2 of the Agricultural Holdings (Forms of Notices to Pay Rent or to Remedy) Regulations 1984 was served on the tenant. (b) The date of service of the tenant's notice requiring arbitration (must be within one month of (a) above). (c) State whether the demand for arbitration requires matters to be determined in respect of Article 3 only, Article 4 only or both Articles 3 & 4 of the Agricultural Holdings (Arbitration on Notices) Order 1987.
9 (notices to quit served on the tenant under s26 & schedule 3: Part 1 of the Agricultural Holdings Act 1986, Cases A, B, D or E)	(a) The date of service of the notice to quit. (b) State the case under which the notice to quit was given (A, B, D or E). (c) The date of the tenant's notice requiring arbitration (must be within one month of the service of the notice to quit).

Agriculture Act 1986 (Milk Quotas)

Schedule	Details Required
Schedule 1, paragraph 10 (determination of standard quota and tenant's fraction before end of tenancy)	(a) The termination date of the tenancy. (b) The date of service of the notice by the landlord or tenant demanding the determination by arbitration of the standard quota for the land or the tenant's fraction (the notice must be served before the termination of the tenancy).
Schedule 1, paragraph 11 (settlement of tenant's claim on termination of tenancy)	(a) The termination of the tenancy as defined in paragraph 11. (b) The date of service of the tenant's notice to the landlord of his intention to make a claim. (This must be before the expiry of two months from the termination of the tenancy as defined in paragraph 11).

Agricultural Tenancies Act 1995

Section	Details Required

Section 19(4) (refusal or failure of landlord to give consent or imposition of condition attached to consent in relation to tenant's improvement)	(a) Date of tenant's notice demanding that the question shall be referred to arbitration. (b) Details of the improvement or proposed improvement. (c) The matter in respect of which the tenant is aggrieved.
Section 22(3) (compensation for tenant's improvement)	(a) Date of termination of the tenancy. (b) Date of the tenant's notice of intention to make a claim. (c) Details of the claim. (d) Has an application been made under section 19(4)? (e) If so, who made that application? **Please note:** If an application is made under section 22(3) involving routine improvements at the same time as an application under s19(4) then the President shall appoint the same arbitrator on both applications. If both applications are made by the same person only one application fee is payable.
Section 28(3) (disputes between the landlord and tenant concerning their rights and obligations under the Act, under the terms of the tenancy or under any custom)	(a) Date of notice specifying the dispute. (b) Details of the dispute.

(C) INFORMATION ABOUT THE PARTIES

RICS owes you a duty of care, and must take reasonable steps to ensure the appointed arbitrator is free from conflicts of interest.

It is therefore necessary for us to have details of the landlord and tenant. Please inform us if there are any associated or subsidiary companies connected with either party which the arbitrator should check for potential conflict of interest. This can be submitted on a separate sheet of paper if necessary.

The parties' professional representatives must be stated and, unless you notify us to the contrary, we will forward all relevant correspondence to them. Normally communications from RICS are sent by fax or email. It is therefore essential that you give us valid fax numbers and/or email addresses to which any notices can be sent. Giving these numbers and addresses will be taken as authorisation for RICS to use them for all purposes of the arbitration. If email or fax details are not supplied, we will communicate by post.

A copy of the application form will be passed on to one or more prospective appointees. The independent third party will use the information to make a judgment as to whether they are suitably qualified and can take on the appointment. It is important that we are informed of any person connected with the application in order that the third party can carry out a full check for potential conflict of interest. The proposed appointee will disclose any involvements to the President prior to appointment. (See PAG/S(99)1 which sets out the President's policy on conflicts of interest. This document can be found on our website at www.rics.org/drs).

SUPPLEMENTAL

RICS charges a fee of £115.00 for administering an appointment. There is no VAT payable on agricultural applications. Cheques should be made payable to RICS. Payment may also be made by BACS Transfer or Credit/Debit card (Please contact Dispute Resolution Services for more details).

The fee is non-refundable whether or not the President makes the appointment (e g if the matter is settled by agreement).

Please ensure you denote whether you are applying as, or on behalf of, the landlord or tenant and you have read the conditions outlined in these explanatory notes.

Your application will be processed on the basis that appointments are often made on behalf of the President of RICS by one of his duly appointed agents.

A3.7

AA6   Statement of landlord's or tenant's case for arbitration[1]

IN THE MATTER OF THE AGRICULTURAL HOLDINGS ACT 1986
AND
IN THE MATTER OF AN ARBITRATION

BETWEEN   AB   *(landlord)*
                         and
                        CD   *(tenant)*

[1   The tenant became tenant to the landlord of the holding known as (*description of holding*) containing .... [acres *or* hectares] from the .... day of .... on a yearly tenancy under a written tenancy agreement made the .... day of ....

2   The tenancy was determined by notice to quit given by the landlord expiring on the .... day of .... [to which the consent of the Agricultural Land Tribunal has been obtained by the landlord][2]

3   The tenant claims £ .... (.................. pounds) being the amount of one year's rent as compensation for disturbance and other amounts for improvements and fixtures and usual tenant-right matters set out in the particulars below

4   The tenant disputes the landlord's claim of £ .... (.................. pounds) for dilapidations to the farmhouse and buildings on the ground that the same is excessive

5   The tenant disputes the landlord's claims to compensation for general deterioration of the above holding

Particulars of tenant's claim

1 Compensation for disturbance

One year's rent[3]   £ ...

2 Improvements

2.1.1   Old improvements begun before 1 March 1948[4].
      2.1:   Formation of silos in OS .... (landlord's consent in   £ ....
             writing dated the .... day of ....)[5]
      2.1:2 Drainage is OS .... (written notice given to   £ ....
             landlord by letter dated the .... day of
             ....)[6] ....
2.2   New improvements begun after 1 March 1948[7]:
      2.2:1 Mole drainage in OS .... (written notice given to   £ ....
             landlord by letter dated the .... day of
             ....)[8] ....
      2.2:2 Consumption on the holding of feeding stuffs ....   £ ....

3 Fixtures

Fowlhouse in OS .... for which the landlord has given notice to   £ ....
purchase[9] ....

4 Tenant-right matters

[4.1   Under statutory provisions[10]
      4.1:1 Pasture laid down with clover in OS ....   £ ....
      4.1:2 Settlement of hill sheep on OS .... (written notice of   £ ....]
      election given to landlord by letter dated the .... day of
      ....)[11]
[4.2   Under tenancy agreement[12] made the .... day of   £ . ...]
      .... clause .... at consuming price ....
[4.3   Under custom[13]
      4.3:1 OS .... tillages and cultivations for winter wheat   £ ....
      4.3:2 OS .... summer fallow   £ . ...]
or

1   The tenant became tenant to the landlord of the holding known as (*description of holding*) containing .... [acres *or* hectares] from the .... day of .... under a tenancy agreement for .... years which expired on the .... day of .... since when the tenant has remained as tenant from year to year

2   The tenancy was determined by notice to quit expiring on the .... day o .... given by the landlord under the Agricultural Holdings Act 1986 section 26 Schedule 3 Part I Case B. The reason stated in the notice to quit was referred to arbitration and by his award made the .... day of .... the arbitrator (*name of arbitrator*) of (*address etc*) determined that the landlord had established the reason stated

3   The landlord claims £.................. (.................. pounds) under the [provisions of the tenancy agreement for dilapidations to the farmhouse buildings and other fixed equipment *or* Agricultural Holdings Act 1986 section 71(1) for dilapidation or deterioration of or damage to the holding][14] set out in the [particulars

below *or* schedule annexed and marked 'AB 1'] and a further sum of £
.... (................. pounds) for compensation for general deterioration of
the holding under the Agricultural Holdings Act 1986 section 72.

4   The landlord disputes the tenant's claim for compensation for disturbance
       above the amount of one year's rent on the ground that the expenses in respect
       of which the claim is made were not directly attributable to the tenant's quitting
       the holding

5   The landlord disputes the tenant's claim for compensation for [old [and] *or*
       new] improvements on the ground that the written consent of the landlord
       where necessary was not obtained and in any event that the amounts claimed
       are excessive

Particulars of dilapidations

(*itemised particulars with price against each item*)]

Dated the .... day of ....

(*signature and address for service of landlord or tenant*)

Notes

1   If the arbitration commenced after 19 October 2006, there is no obligation under the AHA
       1986 or the Arbitration Act 1996 to prepare statements of case. The arbitrator is free to
       decide, in the absence of any agreement by the parties, whether statements of case are
       required and if so, by what date. The arbitrator has a discretion to allow further statements
       of case. As to arbitration generally, see Ch 47.
2   AHA 1986, s 26(1).
3   AHA 1986, s 60(2)(a).
4   AHA 1986, s 64(4), Sch 9, Pts I (paras 1–5), II (paras 1–16).
5   AHA 1986, s 64(4), Sch 9, Pt I, para 3(1)
6   AHA 1986, s 64(4), Sch 9, Pt I, para 4.
7   AHA 1986, s 64(1), Schs 7, 8, Pt I (paras 1–6).
8   AHA 1986, s 68(1).
9   AHA 1986, s 10(4).
10   See AHA 1986, s 65(1), Sch 8, Pt II (paras 7–11). See also AHA 1986, s 65(3), Sch 12
       para 6 regarding a tenant who entered occupation of a holding before 1 March 1948 and
       his right to elect as to whether the statutory provisions laid down by AHA 1986, s 65(1),
       Sch 8 Pt II paras 7–10 should be applicable to his claim and AHA 1986, s 65(3), Sch 12
       para 7 giving a similar right of election to a tenant who entered occupation of a holding
       before 31 December 1951 in respect of whether AHA 1986, s 65(1), Sch 8 Pt II para 10
       should be applicable to his claim. Subject to AHA 1986, s 65(3), Sch 12 paras 6, 7, the
       statutory provisions laid down by s 65(1) shall apply to all tenants on whatever date they
       entered occupation of the holding: s 65(3).
11   See AHA 1986, s 65(3), Sch 12 para 7 and note 10.
12   This clause would be applicable if the tenant had not exercised his right of election (see
       note 10) or if compensation is to be measured in accordance with the tenancy agreement:
       AHA 1986, s 66(4).
13   This clause would be applicable if the tenant had not exercised his right of election (see
       note 10); in no other circumstances is a landlord or tenant entitled under custom to
       compensation for tenant-right matters: AHA 1986, s 77(1), Sch 12 para 8.
14   The landlord must choose whether to claim under the terms of the tenancy agreement (see
       the AHA 1986, s 71(3)) or under the statutory provisions (see the AHA 1986, s 71(1), (4)
       (b)).

AA7   **Form of award**[1]

Arbitrator: [name and
                                                                     address]
Date of appointment:
Time for making award extended to:
Present landlord: [name and
                                                                     address]
Present tenant: [name and
                                                                     address]
Rent payable prior to arbitration:

AWARD OF THE ARBITRATOR

The claims or questions set out in the Schedule to this award have been referred to
arbitration and, having considered the evidence and the submissions of the parties, I,
the arbitrator, award as follows:

1   The landlord is to pay to the tenant in respect of the claims set out in Column
         1 of Part I of the Schedule the sum(s) set out in Column 2 thereof.

2   The tenant is to pay to the landlord in respect of the claims set out in Column
         1 of Part II of the Schedule the sum(s) set out in Column 2 thereof.

3   As from (the next day on which the tenancy could have been brought to an end
         by notice to quit given at the date of the notice demanding arbitration under
         section 12 of the Act) the rent previously payable [is [increased] [reduced] to £
         ] [continues unchanged at £] being the rent properly payable in respect of the
         holding at the date of the reference to arbitration.

4   The notice to quit referred to in Part IV of the Schedule shall [not] have effect.
         [I postpone the termination of the tenancy until].

5   My award in respect of the claims set out in Column 1 of Part V of the Schedule
         is set out in Column 2 thereof.

6   The landlord must pay to the tenant the sum(s) awarded by me to the tenant on
         the day after delivery of this award, and the tenant must pay to the landlord the
         sum(s) awarded by me to the landlord on the same day.

7   The costs of and incidental to the arbitration and the award shall be dealt with
         as follows:

         (a)   My costs of the award amounting to £ must be paid by the [landlord]
                 [tenant] [landlord and the tenant in the following proportions]:

         (b)   As respects the costs of and incidental to this arbitration [each party
                 must bear his own costs] [the landlord must pay [% of] the costs of the
                 tenant] [the tenant must pay [% of] the costs of the landlord] [to be
                 assessed by the Court] [according to Scale [   ] as prescribed by the
                 Civil Procedure Rules] [[the landlord] [the tenant] must pay £ to the
                 [tenant] [landlord] on account of his costs]:

         (c)   All costs ordered by me to be paid shall be paid on the day after delivery
                 of this award.

Signed by the arbitrator in the presence of:[2]

2186

Date:³
This award was delivered to the [landlord] [tenant] on
[date].⁴

Part I

Column 1   *Column 2*
Claims made by the landlord   *Sum(s) awarded*

Part II

Column 1   *Column 2*
Claims made by the tenant   *Sum(s) awarded*

Part III

Rent

Part IV

Question(s) arising out of a notice to quit

Part V

Column 1   *Column 2*
Other claims   *Award*

APPENDIX
STATEMENT OF REASONS FOR AWARD⁵

Notes

1   There is no prescribed form of award. The arbitrator may make more than one award at different times on different issues: see the Arbitration Act 1996, s 47(1). The Arbitration Act 1996 does not place any restriction upon the time for making an award. The parties can impose a time limit if they wish. If there is no agreement on the form of the award the Arbitration Act 1996 provides that the Award must be in writing: see the Arbitration Act 1996, s 52(2), (3).
2   The award must be signed by the arbitrator or if it is made by consent by all those assenting to it: see the Arbitration Act 1996, s 52(2), (3).
3   Unless otherwise agreed by the parties the arbitrator may decide the date of the award. In the absence of any such decision the date of the award shall be taken as the date on which it is signed by the arbitrator: see the Arbitration Act 1996, s 52(2), (3).
4   The parties are free to agree the requirements as to the notification of the award to the parties. If there is no such agreement the award shall be notified by service on them of copies which shall be done without delay after the award is made. The arbitrator has the power to withhold the award in the event of non-payment of his fees: see the Arbitration Act 1996, s 55.
5   The award must contain the reasons for the award unless it is an agreed award or the parties have agreed to dispense with reasons: see the Arbitration Act 1996, s 52(4). The award must state the seat of the arbitration: see the Arbitration Act 1996, s 52(5).

Index

Index

Index

Landlord's dilapidations
compensation, and,   38.89
Landlord's improvements
notice by landlord to the
Agricultural Land Tribunal
and tenant that he proposes to
carry out approved
improvements   A2.60
rent review, and,   25.41
Landowner
lettings to himself and partners,   19.36, 19.37
Leasehold covenants, standard,   24.16–24.26
alienation,   24.18, 24.19
conservation,   24.23
farmhouse residence,   24.20
forfeiture,   24.26
good husbandry,   24.22
quota protection,   24.25
repair,   24.24
short notice,   24.17
user,   24.21
Licence
at will,   19.23
Limited owners,
farm business tenancies,   17.14, 17.15
powers of,   42.8, 42.9
Liquidated damages
penal rents, and,   24.15

Maintenance
fixed equipment, of,   23.4
Maintenance obligations,   23.5–23.20
contractual obligations,   23.5
model clauses,   23.6–23.8
obsolete and redundant buildings,   23.19
rights and liabilities of landlord,   23.9–23.15
rights and liabilities of tenant,   23.16–23.18
Manure
prohibition of removal after notice
to terminate tenancy,   24.10
Market gardens,   18.11, 20.21, 38.90–38.101
agreement that holding shall be let
or treated as,   38.94
compensation, and,   38.96
amount of,   38.101
contracting out,   38.98, 40.11, 40.12
definition,   38.91
direction by Agricultural Land
Tribunal,   38.95
Evesham Custom,   38.99, 38.100
provisions as to compensation,   38.96
qualifications for compensation,   38.92

Market gardens—*contd*
quitting, compensation as to,   37.15A
tenancy in existence on 1 January
1896,   38.93
Marriage value
rent review, and,   25.32
Mid-term Review of Common
Agricultural Policy,   52.1–52.33
European Community legislation.
See EUROPEAN
COMMUNITY
LEGISLATION
implementation in England and
Wales,   52.16–52.23
cross-compliance,   52.19
dairy premium,   52.18
minimum size of holding,   52.23
regional implementation,   52.17
set-aside,   52.20
unlocking payment entitlements,
detailed rules,   52.21
voluntary modulation,   52.22
landlord and tenant issues,   52.24–52.33
occupation of the land,   52.25
quota protection clauses,   52.29, 52.30
rent review,   52.31
succession,   52.33
termination of tenancies,   52.28
transfer,   52.32
use of land/user clauses,   52.26, 52.27
Milk quota,   1.18, 25.22–25.27, 49.1–49.32
arbitral process, background to,   49.13–49.15
arbitral code,   49.15
assessment of compensation,   50.6
excess over standard quota,   50.8–50.11
'normal case',   50.8, 50.9
special situations,   50.10, 50.11
tenant's fraction,   50.12–50.15
calculating,   50.13
denominator,   50.14
numerator,   50.13
statutory scheme,   50.6
transferred quota,   50.7
comparables,   25.30
compensation, and
arbitration, and,   50.23
assignments, and,   50.18
Crown land,   50.26
enforcement,   50.24
procedural matters,   50.17–50.26
service of notices,   50.25
settlement of tenant's claims on
termination,   50.22
severance of reversionary estate,   50.21

2200

Index